ATLANTIC OCEAN

Equator

ST. KITTS & NEVIS
ANTIGUA & BARBUDA
GUADELOUPE (Fr.)
DOMINICA
MARTINIQUE (Fr.)
BARBADOS
ST. LUCIA
ST. VINCENT
GRENADA
TRINIDAD &
TOBAGO

Cayenne

FR. GUIANA

SURINAM

GUYANA

AMAPÁ

Belém

RIO GRANDE
DO NORTE
CEARÁ
PARAÍBA
PERNAMBUCO
ALAGOAS
SERGIPE

Recife

Caracas
Ciudad
Bolívar

VENEZUELA

Maracaibo

RORAIMA

MARANHÃO
PIAUÍ

Salvador

Manaus

PARÁ

TOCANTINS

BAHIA

Bogotá

COLOMBIA

Cali

BRAZIL

AMAZONAS

MATO GROSSO

Brasília

GOIÁS

MINAS GERAIS

ESPÍRITO
SANTO
RIO DE
JANEIRO

Rio de Janeiro

Quito

ECUADOR

aquil

RONDÔNIA

ACRE

MATO GROSSO
DO SUL

São Paulo

SÃO PAULO

Cajamarca

PERU

BOLIVIA

Cochabamba

PARANÁ

SANTA CATARINA

Cuzco

Sucre

PARAGUAY

MISIONES

Asunción

Pôrto Alegre

Ayacucho

La Paz

FORMOSA
CHACO

RIO GRANDE
DO SUL

Lima

Potosí

Arequipa

JUJUY

CORRIENTES

SALTA
TUCUMÁN

SANTIAGO
DEL
ESTERO

ENTRE
SANTA FÉ RÍOS

URUGUAY

Antofagasta

CATAMARCA

Rosario

Montevideo

Córdoba

LA RIOJA
SAN JUAN

CÓRDOBA

Buenos Aires

SAN LUIS

BUENOS AIRES

MENDOZA

ARGENTINA

Santiago

Bahía Blanca

Valparaíso

LA PAMPA

NEUQUÉN

CHILE

RÍO NEGRO

CHUBUT

SANTA
CRUZ

TIERRA
DEL
FUEGO

N

Encyclopedia of

LATIN AMERICAN

LITERATURE

Encyclopedia of

LATIN AMERICAN

LITERATURE

VERITY SMITH

Editor

LONDON • CHICAGO

FITZROY DEARBORN PUBLISHERS
70 East Walton Street
Chicago, Illinois 60611
USA

or

11 Rathbone Place
London W1P 1DE
England

British Library Cataloguing in Publication Data
Encyclopedia of Latin American literature
   1. Latin American literature – Encyclopedias   2. Latin
   American literature – History and criticism – Encyclopedias
I. Smith, Verity
860'.03

ISBN 1–884964–18–4

Library of Congress Cataloging in Publication Data is available.

First published in the USA and UK 1997

Typeset by Florencetype Ltd, Stoodleigh, Devon, UK
Printed by Braun-Brumfield, Inc., Ann Arbor, Michigan

Cover illustration: *Mate en la vereda* by Héctor Balsadúa. Private Collection

The encyclopedia is dedicated to its contributors in the Americas, Europe, the Near East and the Antipodes. It is also dedicated to the memory of one particular contributor, Sally Harvey, who at the time of her sad, untimely death in March of 1995, was professor of Spanish at the University of Auckland.

VERITY SMITH

CONTENTS

La bibliografía enumeraba cuatro volúmenes que no
hemos encontrado hasta ahora, aunque el tercero – Silas Haslam:
Hystory of the Land Called Uqbar, 1874 – figura en los
catálogos de librería de Bernard Quaritch.
Jorge Luis Borges, "Tlön, Uqbar, Orbis Tertius"

EDITOR'S NOTE

The *Encyclopedia of Latin American Literature* contains entries on writers, works and topics relating to the literature of Latin America, including survey articles on all the continent's individual countries. The selection of entries was made by the editor in consultation with the Advisers (listed on page xiii).

The encyclopedia is quite large but consists of only one volume. Therefore the criteria used are of the utmost importance since there is very little room for mistakes. In undertaking this truly daunting task any editor who is also a Latin Americanist is forcefully reminded of Borges's parable about cartographers and their successive maps of the same empire which grew and grew until the final version was the same size as the empire itself. It is not possible to provide a faithful synopsis of anything and certainly not of anything as vast, protean and contentious as the "literature" of an entire continent. Nevertheless since those who are new to the field must start somewhere, the task has to be undertaken, and in doing so the following points have been taken into account.

The first point an editor must note is the work of others in the same or related fields since there is now a proliferation of works of reference in English, Spanish and Portuguese on the literature and (increasingly) the culture of Latin America. Granted that this particular volume will not be sitting alone on a shelf, in constructing it the editor has had to bear in mind what has already been done, with a view to filling perceived gaps, noting new trends while avoiding fashionable ephemera, incorporating new areas of academic interest and reviving an interest in older ones, which for one reason or another have been neglected. And chiefly it is the past that has been neglected in the case of this continent, partly owing to a veritable fixation by publishers, critics and readers alike with the works of authors of the so-called Boom. Consequently this encyclopedia participates in the task of re-igniting an interest in the literature of the continent's past and also in stimulating interest in that of some of the smaller countries of the region such as Ecuador and Bolivia. Other points that have been taken into consideration are 1) the increasing importance of writing by Hispanic minorities in the US, and 2) the literature of the Francophone Caribbean since, not before time, scholars are ignoring the diversity of language in the literary production of the Caribbean in order to explore those common features that are the legacy of European colonialism; also 3) the encyclopedia seeks, though this is now no novelty – even in the relatively staid world of works of reference – to give prominence to the work of women writers, of the past as well as contemporary ones. It should be remembered, however, in both this and other contexts, that this work is not a dictionary of writers, so the women authors included form a selection. Comprehensiveness lies beyond the scope of this volume, and to find it readers must consult more specialized works.

The entry for each writer consists of a signed critical overview of the writer's literary work written by an expert in the field; a brief biographical sketch of the subject; a select list of the writer's primary works in chronological order and grouped by genre where applicable; an annotated list of further reading; and, in some cases one or more essays on individual literary works, followed by a note of editions, translations and further reading. The list of selected works includes separately published books, including translations into English. Under the heading Compilations and Anthologies we have listed the most recent collection of the complete works; only those collections that have some editorial authority are cited; on-going editions are indicated by a dash after the date of publication. Dates refer to the first publication in book form unless indicated otherwise; we have attempted to list the actual year of publication, sometimes different from the date given on the title page. Reprints of works, including facsimile editions are generally not listed unless a revision of a text or a change of title is involved. Titles are always in *italic*. The first mention of a title in the text is followed by an English translation in parenthesis. In cases where there are no published translations a literal translation is provided within square brackets. Topic entries include a signed critical essay and an annotated list of further reading.

The book concludes with a Title Index to the Selected Works, which contains titles in the original language and English translation, and a General Index.

It is to be hoped that since all the entries are in alphabetical order, readers will have no difficulty in finding the items of interest to them. An Alphabetical List of Entries is provided on page xv, followed by an Alphabetical List of Works (with relevant page numbers) on page xix. It should be noted that in the case of compound surnames in Spanish America, the rule is that they are entered under the first element. Thus Mario Vargas Llosa appears under **Vargas Llosa**. The rule is different in the case of Brazilian surnames which are generally entered under the last component. So João Ubaldo Ribeiro appears under **Ribeiro**. However, readers should be(a)ware of exceptions: Joaquim Maria Machado de Assis is known as Machado de Assis and therefore appears under **Machado de Assis** and not **Assis**. (Cross-references of names are provided in the body of the book.) A further point to bear in mind is that the surveys of the literature of the various countries in the region do not include either dramatists or the literature of the Colonial period in Latin America. These have separate, long entries.

A word should be said also about the entries on individual writers. Where a writer's output is prolific and there is no separate entry on a given text or texts by the writer, the entry may deal selectively rather than comprehensively with his or her production, focusing on a few major works. The idea is that the entry should consist of more than a string of titles and predictable phrases about every text the author every produced. In this way, the criteria used in this encyclopedia may seem to differ from that adopted in similar works: the emphasis here is placed squarely on quality rather than on comprehensiveness, since the latter, in any event, is impossible to achieve in a single volume. However, each author entry is accompanied by a list of publications by and about him or her and this is where readers will find information about lesser-known works.

Another point which, alas, must be made is that any editor of a work of reference learns very quickly that this type of book is either a transmitter or a veritable breeding ground of misinformation. I concur completely with the opinion expressed by David William Foster, at once the most productive and the most learned bibliographer in the field of Latin American literature, when he makes this statement in the introduction to one of his research guides:

Any residual errors are the combined responsibility of the compiler and *the lamentably long-lived tradition in Hispanic bibliography of incomplete, confusing and inaccurate references.* (my italics)

Foster adds, "I hope, however, that this compilation represents a step toward the sort of bibliographic control the several national literatures so clearly deserve." I echo Foster's hope, but readers should be aware that the epigraph from Borges that heads this encyclopedia serves as a warning and not as a decoration.

Finally, this encyclopedia has been assembled in a relatively brief period of time, something that it would not have been possible to achieve without the goodwill, enthusiasm, intelligence, learning and punctuality of all its contributors. It follows that there is one guaranteed zone of truth in this book and that is the sentiments behind the dedication.

Acknowledgments

Properly to acknowledge all the help I have received in putting together this encyclopedia would require a second volume of some four hundred entries. No project of this kind can be completed successfully without the academic freemasonry that turns it into a truly collaborative venture. Nevertheless, an attempt must be made in a few words. So I shall start with the Advisers, most of whom are also contributors but, then, they deserve to be thanked (at least) twice. My thanks also to scholars in the US who work in the Colonial period: Raquel Chang-Rodríguez, Margarita Zamora, Georgina Sabat de Rivers and Stacey Schlau. To Roberto Reis who helped with Brazil; to Maryse Condé for her assistance with the Francophone Caribbean; to Angela Dellepiane for hers with Argentina, and to Marjorie Agosín for her benevolent support of this project. Gratitude should also be expressed to those university departments on both sides of the Atlantic which have made a sizeable contribution to this project: to David Foster and Emil Volek at Arizona State University, together with several junior members of staff in the same department; to staff and research students at King's College, London, and to several members of staff at the University of Wisconsin (at both Madison and Eau Claire). My gratitude to Jim Higgins at Liverpool for allowing me to treat him as an encyclopedia of Peruvian literature (which, of course, he is) and also to my friend and former colleague at QMW, Omar García, for feeding me long, helpful lists of potential contributors. Jenny Shubow at Birkbeck (University of London), revised the information sections of the entry on Eduardo Galeano with the learned fastidiousness that editors dream about. Also within London University, my thanks, as ever, to the library staff at both the Institute of Latin American Studies and at the University of London Library for their unfailing efficiency and pleasantness. In this context, I am particularly indebted to Christine Anderson at ULL for her considerable help with "Melvyl." Fortunate, indeed, is the editor of an encyclopedia of Latin American literature who has the resources of the University of London Library (virtually) on her doorstep. I would also like to express my gratitude to the two imported proof-readers, Marina Michalski, who checked the articles on Brazil, and Anthony Edkins who read everything. My particular thanks to him for his thoroughness and constructive suggestions.

Within "the company," thanks are owed to Daniel Kirkpatrick, both for guiding my first steps and for fostering such a pleasant atmosphere in the workplace. However, at the London office of Fitzroy Dearborn, my particular thanks must go to Lesley Henderson, for her balanced judgment and sound sense, her skilful defusing of my (alas, several) temper tantrums and, above all, for her Pinocchio sense of humour. No encyclopedia can be assembled without its makers being possessed of a strong sense of the absurd. "Paris," an idea she liked, is dedicated (sotto voce) to her.

VERITY SMITH
Honorary Research Fellow, Queen Mary and
Westfield College (University of London)

ADVISERS

Roy C. Boland
David Brookshaw
Catherine Davies
David William Foster
Stephen M. Hart
Peter T. Johnson
John King

Gerald Martin
Nélida Piñón
William Rowe
Vivian Schelling
Donald L. Shaw
Edwin Williamson
Jason Wilson

CONTRIBUTORS

Christopher Abel
Rolena Adorno
Marjorie Agosín
Severino J. Albuquerque
José B. Alvarez IV
Carmen S. Alverio
Fanny D. Arango-Ramos
Elia J. Armacanqui-Tipacti
Emilio de Armas
Melvin S. Arrington, Jr
Teresa R. Arrington
Pamela Bacarisse
Daniel Balderston
Heloisa Gonçalves Barbosa
Maurice Biriotti
Roy C. Boland
Steven Boldy
Paul W. Borgeson, Jr
Catherine Boyle
Sara Brandellero
Ana María Brenes-García
David Brookshaw
Nick Caistor
Mireya Camurati
Claudio Canaparo
Marie-Magdeleine Chirol
Francesca Colecchia
Jaime Concha
Linda Craig

Dermot Curley
Teresinha V. Zimbrão Da Silva
Mary L. Daniel
Catherine Davies
Lloyd Hughes Davies
Greg Dawes
Elena De Costa
Sabine Dedenbach-Salazar Sáenz
Francesca Denegri
Mark Dinneen
Peter G. Earle
Anthony Edkins
Jo Evans
Jorge Febles
Salvador C. Fernández
Nuala Finnegan
Evelyn Fishburn
Denise Ganderton
Ana García Chichester
Magdalena García Pinto
Dick Gerdes
Lourdes Gil
Nora Glickman
Cedomil Goic
Janet N. Gold
Miguel Gomes
Gilberto Gómez Ocampo
Mike Gonzalez
Carl Good

Catherine Grant
Leland Guyer
David T. Haberly
Michael Handelsman
Regina Harrison
Stephen M. Hart
Sally Harvey
James Higgins
Jerry Hoeg
Léon-François Hoffmann
Edward Waters Hood
Elizabeth Horan
Psiche Hughes
Julie Greer Johnson
Anny Brooksbank Jones
Paul Jordan
Bella Jozef
William H. Katra
William P. Keeth
Ron Keightley
Lucille Kerr
John King
John Myles Kinsella
Tracy K. Lewis
Naomi Lindstrom
Maria Manuel Lisboa
Luiza Lobo
Darrell B. Lockhart
Melissa A. Lockhart
María Begoña de Luis
Magdalena Maíz-Peña
Jorge Marbán
Kathleen N. March
Ismael P. Márquez
Gerald Martin
Mario Martín
Pablo A. Martínez
Luis Martul Tobío
Juan Antonio Masoliver
George R. McMurray
Frank McQuade
Teresa Méndez-Faith
Yolanda Molina Gavilán
Marie Murphy
Patricia Murray
Wilson Neate
María L. Negrín
Pat Noble
R.J. Oakley
Patricia Anne Odber de Baubeta
Beverley Ormerod
José Miguel Oviedo
Adriana Silvina Pagano

J. Agustín Pastén B.
Brigida Pastor
Luis H. Peña
John Perivolaris
Charles A. Perrone
Laura Podalsky
Luis Rebaza-Soraluz
Roberto Reis
Keith J. Richards
Nicole Roberts
Christine A.F. Robinson
Angela I. Robledo
Linda M. Rodríguez
William Rowe
Patricia Rubio
Jorge Ruffinelli
Georgina Sabat de Rivers
Nélida Salvador
Gustavo San Román
George D. Schade
Vivian Schelling
Nina M. Scott
Renée Scott
Jacobo Sefamí
Juan Antonio Serna
Deborah A. Shaw
Donald L. Shaw
Jenny Shubow
K.M. Sibbald
Amelia Simpson
Robert L. Sims
Sam L. Slick
Ian Isidore Smart
Verity Smith
Myrna Solotorevsky
Marie-Agnès Sourieau
William Spindler Li
Peter Standish
Ilan Stavans
Benjamín Torres Cabellero
Abril Trigo
Maarten Van Delden
Nelson H. Vieira
Emil Volek
C. Michael Waag
John Walker
Helene Carol Weldt-Basson
Steven F. White
Jason Wilson
David Wood
Andrea Yannuzzi
Regina Zilberman

ALPHABETICAL LIST OF ENTRIES

ALPHABETICAL
LIST OF WORKS

GENERAL
READING LIST

Literature of the Colonial Period

Cevallos-Candau, Francisco J., Jeffrey A. Cole, Nina M. Scott and Nicómedes Suárez Arauz (editors), *Coded Encounters: Writing, Gender and Ethnicity in Colonial Latin America*, Amherst: University of Massachusetts Press, 1994

Chang-Rodríguez, Raquel, *Violencia y subversión en la prosa colonial hispanoamericana, siglos XVI y XVII*, Madrid: José Porrúa Turanzas, 1982

Chang-Rodríguez, Raquel and Gabriella de Beer (editors), *La historia en la literatura iberoamericana: memorias del XXVI Congreso del Instituto Internacional de Literatura Iberoamericana*, Hanover, New Hampshire: Ediciones del Norte, 1989

Johnson, Julie Greer, *Women in Colonial Spanish American Literature: Literary Images*, Westport, Connecticut: Greenwood Press, 1983

_____ *The Book in the Americas: The Role of Books and Printing in the Development of Culture and Society in Colonial Latin America*, Providence, Rhode Island: John Carter Brown Library, 1988

_____ *Satire in Colonial Spanish America: Turning the New World Upside Down*, Austin: University of Texas Press, 1993

Promis Ojeda, José, *The Identity of Hispanoamerica: an Interpretation of Colonial Literature*, translated by Alita Kelley and Alec E. Kelley, Tucson, Arizona: University of Arizona Press, 1991

19th and 20th Centuries

Beverley, John, *Against Literature*, Minneapolis: University of Minnesota Press, 1993

Bloom, Harold (editor), *Modern Latin American Fiction*, New York: Chelsea House, 1990

Borinsky, Alicia, *Theoretical Fables: the Pedagogical Dream in Contemporary Latin American Fiction*, Philadelphia: University of Pennsylvania Press, 1994 [Largely devoted to 20th century Argentine and Chilean prose writers]

Brushwood, John S., *Genteel Barbarism: Experiments in Analysis of Nineteenth-Century Spanish-American Novels*, Lincoln, Nebraska: University of Nebraska Press, 1981

Fernández Moreno, César, Julio Ortega and Ivan Schulman (editors), *Latin America in Its Literature*, Mexico City: Siglo XXI, 1972; translated by Mary G. Berg, New York: Holmes and Meier, 1980 [The quality of contributions remains outstanding]

Foster, David William and Virginia Ramos Foster (editors), *Alternate Voices in the Contemporary Latin American Narrative*, Columbia: University of Missouri Press, 1985

González Echevarría, Roberto, *The Voice of the Masters: Writing and Authority in Modern Latin American Literature*, Austin: University of Texas Press, 1985

_____ *Myth and Archive: a Theory of Latin American Narrative*, Cambridge and New York: Cambridge University Press, 1990

_____ *Celestina's Brood: Continuities of the Baroque in Spanish and Latin American Literatures*, Durham, North Carolina: Duke University Press, 1993

Graham-Yooll, Andrew, *After the Despots: Latin American Views and Interviews*; edited by Norman Thomas di Giovanni, London: Bloomsbury, 1991

Kadir, Djelal, *Questing Fictions: Latin America's Family Romance*, Minneapolis: University of Minnesota Press, 1986

Kerr, Lucille, *Reclaiming the Author: Figures and Fictions from Spanish America*, Durham, North Carolina: Duke University Press, 1991

Losada, Alejandro, *La literatura en la sociedad de América Latina: Perú y el Río de la Plata 1837–1880*, Frankfurt: Vervuert Verlag, 1983

Ludmer, Josefina (editor), *Las culturas de fin de siglo en América Latina*, Rosario, Argentina: B. Viterbo, 1994

Martin, Gerald, *Journeys through the Labyrinth. Latin American Fiction in the Twentieth Century*, London and New York: Verso, 1989

McGuirk, Bernard and Mark Millington (editors), *Inequality and Difference in Hispanic and Latin American Cultures. Critical Theoretical Approaches*, Lampeter, Wales: Edwin Mellen Press, 1995

McMurray, George R., *Spanish American Writing Since 1941. A Critical Survey*, New York: Ungar, 1987

Millington, Mark and Paul Julian Smith (editors), *New Hispanisms: Literature, Culture, Theory*, Ottawa: Dovehouse Editions, 1994

Picon Garfield, Evelyn and Ivan Schulman, *"Las entrañas del vacío:" ensayos sobre la modernidad hispanoamericana*, Mexico City: Cuadernos Americanos, 1984

Ortega, Julio, *Poetics of Change: the New Spanish-American Narrative*, translated by Galen D. Greaser, Austin: University of Texas Press, 1984

Oviedo, José Miguel, *Historia de la literatura hispanoamericana*, vol. 1, *De los orígenes a la emancipación*, Madrid: Alianza, 1995

Rama, Ángel, *Transculturación narrativa en América Latina*, Mexico City: Siglo XXI, 1982

_____ *La ciudad letrada*, Hanover, New Hampshire: Ediciones del Norte, 1984

_____ *La novela en América Latina: panoramas 1920–1980*, Bogotá: Instituto Colombiano de Cultura, 1982

Ramos, Julio, *Desencuentros de la modernidad en América Latina: literatura y política en el siglo XIX*, Mexico City: Fondo de Cultura Económica, 1989

Rodríguez Monegal, Emir, *Narradores de esta América*, Caracas: Monte Ávila, 1969

Rowe, William and Vivian Schelling, *Memory and Modernity: Popular Culture in Latin America*, London and New York: Verso, 1991

Sommer, Doris, *Foundational Fictions: the National Romances of Latin America*, Berkeley: University of California Press, 1991

Shaw, Donald L., *Nueva narrativa hispanoamericana*, 2nd edition, Madrid: Cátedra, 1983

Yurkievich, Saúl, *Fundadores de la nueva poesía latinoamericana: Vallejo, Huidobro, Borges, Girondo, Neruda, Paz, Lezama Lima*, Barcelona: Ariel, 1984

_____ *Identidad cultural de Iberoamérica en su literatura*, Madrid: Alhambra, 1986

Zea, Leopoldo (editor), *Fuentes de la cultura latinoamericana*, 3 vols, Mexico City: Fondo de Cultura Económica, 1993 [Important selection of essays by men of ideas. In the 3 volumes there is only one essay by a woman]

Bibliographies and Works of Reference

Balderston, Daniel (editor), *The Latin American Short Story: an Annotated Guide to Anthologies and Criticism*, New York: Greenwood Press, 1992

Brower, Keith H., *Contemporary Latin American Fiction. An Annotated Bibliography*, Pasadena, California: Salem Press, 1989 [Useful because it includes Brazilian writers and provides criticism on individual texts]

Coutinho, Afrânio and José Galante de Sousa (general editors), *Enciclopédia de literatura brasileira*, 2 vols, Rio de Janiero: Ministério da Educação, 1990

Foster, David William (editor), *Handbook of Latin American Literature*, New York: Garland, 2nd edition, 1992

Gullón, Ricardo (editor), *Diccionario de literatura española e hispanoamericana*, 2 vols, Madrid: Alianza, 1993 [Entries generally very sketchy and information not necessarily reliable; selection of Spanish American topics extremely limited, but author coverage is comprehensive and, as generally applies to works of this type on "Latin America" published in Spain, authors from the Phillipines are included]

Sefamí, Jacobo (editor), *Contemporary Spanish American Poets: a Bibliography of Primary and Secondary Sources*, Westport, Connecticut: Greenwood Press, 1992

Solé, Carlos A. (editor-in-chief), *Latin American Writers*, 3 vols, New York: Scribner, 1989

Standish, Peter (editor), *Dictionary of Twentieth-Century Culture*, 2 vols, Detroit: Gale Research, 1996 [vol.1, *Hispanic Culture of Mexico Central America and the Caribbean*; vol.2, *Hispanic Culture of South America*]

Stern, Irwin (editor-in-chief), *Dictionary of Brazilian Literature*, Westport, Connecticut: Greenwood Press, 1988

Encyclopedia of

LATIN AMERICAN

LITERATURE

A

Soledad Acosta de Samper 1833–1913

Colombian prose writer

Once obscure and long neglected, Soledad Acosta de Samper has come into her own as the most important woman writer of the 19th century in Colombia and an influential force in Spanish American letters. Her early travels caused her to question the status of women in her native country and her work constitutes a courageous yet subtle and non-confrontational advocacy of women's issues. It is pioneering work in Spanish American feminism.

Women writers in Colombia were not uncommon, but it was unusual for a woman to publish, and to publish as profusely as did Acosta was indeed rare. Using a variety of pseudonyms she published novels, dramas, history, essays and translations. Between 1878 and 1881 she founded newspapers and magazines in Lima and Bogotá such as *La Mujer* [Woman], which was written, edited and published by women – truly a woman's enterprise. The astounding number of publications places her among the most prolific Colombian writers of the 19th century as well as making her the one who contributed most to the visibility of women as artists in their own right in Latin America. Unlike many of her contemporaries who were taken up with the then popular theories of social progress and Utopian constructs, Acosta in her fiction depicts the everyday reality of ordinary women and posits principles of change for women centered on the idea of education as a liberating force. Many of her works have stood the test of time but others are seriously marred by their heavy didacticism, while some are flawed because of their often hasty serial publication.

In her first published volume, a collection of novellas entitled *Novelas y cuadros de la vida sur-americana*, 1869 [Novellas and Sketches of Life in South America] each story describes problems that affect women such as illness, solitude and injustice. This volume carried a foreword by her husband, the noted politician and writer, José María Samper. In this foreword Samper endorses the moral posture and the literary qualities of his wife's work. Whatever value Samper's endorsement may have had at the time, Acosta was to be taken to task for including it because his support suggests women's dependency on male approval of their literary efforts.

Soledad Acosta's novels fall within the representational mimetic style of the 19th century. There is, at the same time, a clear attempt to draw her characters' inner worlds and especially to develop the consciousness of the female characters. This is clear in her first full-length novel *Dolores: cuadros de la vida de una mujer* [Dolores: the Story of a Leper], originally published in 1867 and reprinted two years later as the the most important component of *Novelas y cuadros*. The title is a play on words; it is both the heroine's name and a correlative of her sorrows and sufferings. Dolores (the name signifies pain), believing herself an orphan, learns that her father is not dead but suffers from leprosy and has been in hiding for years. Shortly before his death he returns and briefly meets his daughter. The meeting is fatal for Dolores. She realizes that she too has the disease and therefore must cancel her marriage plans. The novel traces the fragmentation of her conscience which arises from the vicissitudes of her now woeful life. Dolores withdraws from the world but not from her inner struggle wherein she simultaneously asserts and denies her essence as a woman. Stylistically, the fragmentation of her essential "I" is captured by a chaotic use of verbal tenses and by a wild blizzard of exclamation marks. Apart from the world, Dolores seeks salvation through her writing. Her diary, which serves as an epilogue to the novel, becomes a testimony of her search for a female identity. Alone, Dolores resists the ravages to her body and the social alienation brought by her disease. She resists by writing. That is, the creative act of writing brings salvation, for it allows Dolores to develop as a woman and thereby to gain a measure of victory over death and the limits it imposes.

A second novel of Acosta's developing feminism is *Teresa la limeña, pájinas de la vida de una peruana*, 1869 [Teresa of Lima: Pages from a Peruvian Woman's Life]. The novel is a reaction to the contention that love had become an emotion "good only to fill the pages of a novel" and that "marriage is a form of business, good or bad, but still business." The novel's circular structure enhances the sense that a woman's lot is unrewarding and repetitive. Acosta's view is that romantic values of the heart have become alien in a world of acute mercantilism where women are little more that chattel to be bought and sold. In *Teresa la limeña*, Acosta denounces marriage as a commercial transaction that victimizes women and she condemns calculating fathers who give their daughters in marriage only to cement business transactions. Teresa, a motherless child, discovers that she is to be sent to a convent for a good education so that her ambitious father will be able to make a good match for her. In the convent she meets Lucila and the two girls are taken with notions of romantic idealism. Both young women see their ideals crushed when their fiancés abandon them to marry richer women who can save them from bankruptcy. Out of the convent Teresa learns to take charge of her own life in spite of the regulations imposed by a patriarchal society. Married, and widowed, Teresa leaves for Europe where she meets her convent friend Lucila again. Teresa begins to shed the social controls around her, while Lucila, trapped by her past and influenced by her time in the convent, remains totally dependent on others until her premature death. Teresa's father, who is in fear of losing the inheritance from her dead husband, orchestrates a new exile for Teresa, this time in Chile. But Teresa is fatally ill. She retreats from society to live alone in a house by the sea and there resolves to leave a written memory of her life.

For the protagonist, writing is a way to revive happier days. It provides the path to self-knowledge and creates a kind of symbolic liberation from crass reality. Here, as in the case of *Dolores*, writing – that is recovering the past by reminiscing – is seen as the ultimate form of transcendence. It is noteworthy that neither Dolores nor Teresa has children – maternity not being important to them as women. But *Teresa la limeña* suggests alternative life choices for Latin American women in the example of the frail dying woman who asserts herself in the face of overwhelming social conventions. Feminine stereotypes are subverted and literature emerges as the realm that allows women to find self-fulfillment. In both novels, establishing one's own autonomy is the important requisite for women writers who aspire to success as creators of literature in Latin America.

Acosta further developed this concept in her now famous essay "Aptitudes de la mujer para ejercer todas las profesiones," 1893 [On the Ability of Women to Practice All Professions], which she read in Spain on the fourth centenary of the discovery of America. On that occasion she called for society to include women as equals in all spheres, especially the professions.

El corazón de la mujer (1869) [A Woman's Heart], also included in *Novelas y cuadros*, presents the stories of half a dozen women of different ages whose common ground is suffering: "A woman's heart has four ages: in childhood, it grows and suffers; in adolescence, it dreams and suffers; in youth, it loves and suffers; in old age, it understands and suffers." *Una holandesa en América*, 1888 [A Dutch Woman in America] ostensibly a *novela de costumbres* interspersed with descriptions of events of Colombian history, is also important for its projection of the world of women and its progressive awareness of their condition. A travel narrative, it deviates from standard models in that the hero is a woman, Lucía, whose travels give her an awareness of things that are bigger than she, through which she finds a sense of the transcendent. The protagonist returns to her native Colombia after having grown up in the Netherlands. This Europe-to-America transition becomes crucial to her development as a woman as she confronts new realities that clash with the romantic

fantasies of her youth. This literal discovery of a new world – America – is also the discovery of the self. Her idealism is tested. Meeting her father and brothers is a disappointment which demonstrates the insufficiency of romantic feelings in the real world. As she searches for an organizing principle to end her confusion she embraces Catholicism and, having decided to remain single, she enters a convent. Conversely, her friend Mercedes marries happily, and – in sharp contrast to Acosta's other novels – the narrator indicates that marriage can be an important stabilizing factor in the lives of women. All ends well in the novel. Lucía establishes harmony in what was a chaotic world; she regenerates her family and becomes an agent of change and civilization. Her status as a woman is now of great importance in the lives of those around her.

Acosta's work is seen today as a milestone in women's writing in Latin America, and her contribution to the formation of a national literature in Colombia is being re-evaluated. Her fiction focuses on the role of women in society and issues of nationhood. It deals with women's themes such as family, marriage and the domestic world, but it goes beyond to question the dominance of patriarchal values and the limitations they impose on women, rejecting the notion that being a wife was the only way for a woman to achieve self-realization. Instead, she sought alternatives for women such as their incorporation in the economy as equals, an idea that in retrospect can be seen as a radical position in spite of the subtlety of its formulation. It was not until the second half of the 20th century that other Colombian writers acquired an interest in women's issues. The renewed interest in the work of Soledad Acosta, together with the re-issue of her work, will lead to a reassessment of one of Colombia's major writers.

GILBERTO GÓMEZ OCAMPO

See also entries on Juana Manuela Gorriti, Clorinda Matto de Turner, Women's Writing: 19th Century

Biography

Born in Bogotá, Colombia, 5 May 1833, the daughter of General Joaquín Acosta and his English wife, Caroline Kemble. Parents moved to Halifax, Nova Scotia, in 1835 and shortly after to Paris where Soledad attended school. She returned to Bogotá and married the writer José María Samper in 1855. Moved to Europe in 1857 where couple stayed until 1862. On returning to Colombia, after a brief period in Lima, they both wrote regularly for the press. Acosta de Samper founded several magazines for women and the family, among them *La Mujer* [Woman] and *La Familia* [The Family]. Her husband died in 1888 whereupon she moved to Paris with her mother and daughters in 1890. Represented Colombia at the Congress of Americanists that took place in Huelva in 1892 to mark the fourth centenary of the conquest of America. Also published fiction in French and translated works of literature from English. Died 17 March 1913.

Selected Works

Dolores: cuadros de la vida de una mujer, in *El mensajero* (1867)
Teresa la limeña: pájinas de la vida de una peruana, in *La Prensa* (1868)
Novelas y cuadros de la vida sur-americana, Ghent: Vanderhaeghen, 1869 [Includes *Dolores* and *El corazón de la mujer*]
Biografías de hombres ilustres o notables, Bogotá: Imprenta de La Luz, 1883

Los piratas en Cartagena, Bogotá: Imprenta de La Luz, 1886
[Has been reprinted several times this century, most recently in 1972]

Episodios novelescos de la historia patria, Bogotá: Imprenta de La Luz, 1887

Una holandesa en América, Curaçao: A. Bethencourt e Hijos, 1888

La mujer en la sociedad moderna, Paris: Garnier, 1895

Hidalgos de Zamora, Bogotá: Imprenta de La Luz, 1898

Un hidalgo conquistador, Bogotá: Imprenta de la Luz, 1907

Further Reading

A comprehensive primary bibliography by Daniel Samper Ortega is included in the volume *Soledad Acosta de Samper: una nueva lectura*, edited with an introduction by Montserrat Ordóñez, Bogotá: Fondo Cultural Cafetero, 1988. Samper Ortega's bibliography is most helpful because much of Acosta de Samper's work appeared in a range of magazines and a selection in book form is yet to appear.

Gómez Ocampo, Gilberto, *Entre "María" y "La vorágine." La literatura colombiana finisecular (1886–1903)*, Bogotá: Fondo Cultural Cafetero, 1988

Martín Adán 1908–1985

Peruvian poet

Martín Adán, the pseudonym of Rafael de la Fuente y Benavides, began to publish his first poems in literary reviews during the late 1920s and the early 1930s. These early poems such as "Navidad," [Nativity] "Gira" [Revolve] and "Sol" [Sun] are clearly influenced by the Spanish avant-garde, more specifically by *ultraísmo*. They illustrate the poet's tendency to emphasize the images for their own sake, for engaging in an ingenious game of words, and reveal a deliberately cosmopolitan attitude. At this stage of his poetic career there is also a vacillation between traditional forms and the experimental range of the avant-garde. This latter direction is most evident in a short novel entitled *La casa de cartón*, 1928 (*The Cardboard House*), which explores the problematic relationship between the artistic self and a growing sense of national and cosmopolitan identity. This is a novel about a young man, his awakenings to the joys and traumas of love, and his observations of the society around him. However, the referential dimension of the work is frequently diminished and is overshadowed by the play of verbal images as the reader's attention is directed less towards the events narrated and more to the level of language which thrusts itself to the fore. Hence, it concentrates on the aesthetic or poetic pattern rather than on the social dimension typical of the regionalist novels of this period.

In common with poets such as Jorge Eduardo Eielson and Emilio Adolfo Westphalen, Adán's verses tend to be inward-looking and the themes of language and poetry itself play an important part in his work. The attempts to yoke together both transcendental experience and poetry is expressed in a series of conceptual balances and oppositions which appear throughout one of his most important collections *Travesía de extramares*, 1950 [Voyage Beyond the Oceans]. His adherence to the strictures of traditional verse forms and the use of epigraphs from classical Latin as well as from Spanish, French and Italian writers also implies that he is locating himself firmly within a European cultural tradition. Primary features of this poetry are paradox, conceptual complexity, and the use of archaisms and rare words taken from dictionaries. The principal attribute of these unusual, obsolete, or technical words is their focus inwards towards the poet's own emotional state. A recurring symbol is that of the rose which is vitally important in these sonnets as well as in *La rosa de la espinela*, 1939 [The Rose of the Espinela], a collection of *décimas* or *espinelas*, a Spanish verse form consisting of ten octosyllabic lines. This symbol establishes both a sense of a perfect aesthetic beauty and a sublime manifestation of human spirituality. The use of suspension points, exclamation marks, and ellipses reflects the primary aim of calling into question the relation between language and silence, presence and absence, as he struggles to comprehend the emotional state in which he finds himself and the uncertainty of his ability to communicate it.

The next phase of his writing undergoes a reassessment as he moves away from the traditional verse forms and the earlier mobilization of a more portentous vocabulary. Thus *Escrito a ciegas*, 1961 [Written Blindly] represents the poet's first attempts to express himself in free verse and seems to correspond to a more urgent need to inject a more personal note into his poetry. The poetic voice which emerges here is that of a tortured individual who puts everything into question as he attempts to explain the relationship between his poetry and life on a more general level. As the title itself suggests, he advances very tentatively to some sort of definition of himself and his role as poet. The contradictions which emerge are articulated through an admixture of the mundane and the sublime, the conceptually abstract and the very basic and concrete details of his environment.

The other long, rambling poems of this same period are *La mano desasida (Canto a Macchu Picchu)* 1964 [The Hand Let Go (Song to Macchu Picchu)] and *La piedra absoluta*, 1966 [The Absolute Stone] in which he contrasts the duality of Machu Picchu with the duality and illusory nature of poetry and (by extension) of life itself. There is an internal dialogue carried on throughout these poems which is emphasized through the complex interrelation of pronouns and verb forms. These correspond to the manner in which the poet perceives various aspects of the self. Pablo Neruda begins his "Alturas de Macchu Picchu," (*The Heights of Macchu Picchu*) with a physical approach, an encounter with a physical object and recognizes that through place he can be in contact with these human lives, with history, and with life itself. Adán refuses to construct any sense of the real physical Machu Picchu but rather addresses the self in terms of the "recondite, high stone." There is a continual undermining of any sense of epistemological certainty, a splintering or fragmentation of the self, which all contribute to the undecidability of the text.

In the final stage of Adán's writing there is a return to the sonnet form with the publication of *Mi Darío*, 1967 [My Darío] and *Diario de poeta*, 1975 [Diary of a Poet]. The opaqueness and density of the earlier sonnets gives way to much greater transparency of language and more simple, direct statements about himself. An effect of directness is achieved by the use of a vocabulary which stresses the more humble, often squalid details of everyday life. The relationship between poetry, the poet, and external reality are especially prominent as he continues to probe the limits of a particular technical form. A continual use of suspension points, a plethora of exclamations, and a frequently rhetorical tone permeate the collection. A familiar pattern consists of drifting thoughts punctuated by silences which brings out the discursive nature of some sonnets whilst yet others are more conversational, often more urgent, tense, and even violent. This all draws attention to the writing process itself and how this is inextricably bound up with the poet's inner world, his "volume of agony."

While earlier critical attention had focussed on anecdotes about the poet himself, more recent studies suggest serious efforts to come to terms with one of the most difficult and yet most important writers in Peruvian literature of the 20th century.

JOHN MYLES KINSELLA

Biography

Born Rafael de la Fuente y Benavides in Barranco, Lima, Peru, 27 October 1908. Attended the Deutsche Schule in Lima, 1916–24: Emilio Adolfo Westphalen and Xavier Abril were fellow pupils at the school; National University of San Marcos, Lima. Completed doctoral thesis *De lo barroco en el Perú*, 1938 [Concerning the Baroque in Peru]. Worked in legal department of the Agricultural Bank for some years. Embarked on a critical/biographical dictionary of Peruvian letters, but never got beyond the 16th century because he was so scrupulous. Entered a private clinic because of grave psychological problem. Appointed member of the Peruvian Academy of the Language while still in the clinic. Awarded José Santos Chocano National Prize for Poetry in 1947 and National Prize for Literature in 1974. Died on 29 January 1985.

Selected Works

Poetry

La rosa de la espinela, Lima: Cuadernos de Cocodrilo, 1939
Travesía de extramares, Lima: Dirección de Educación Artística y Extensión Cultural del Ministerio de Educación Pública, 1950
Escrito a ciegas, Lima: Mejía Baca, 1961
La mano desasida (Canto a Macchu Picchu), Lima: Mejía Baca, 1964
La piedra absoluta, Lima: Mejía Baca, 1966
Diario de poeta, Lima: Inti-Sol, 1975

Novel

La casa de cartón, Lima: Talleres de Impresiones y Encuadernaciones, 1928; as *The Cardboard House*, translated by Katherine Silver, St Paul, Minnesota: Graywolf Press, 1990

Other Writings

De lo barroco en el Perú, Lima: Universidad de San Marcos, 1968

Compilations and Anthologies

Obra poética, edited by Ricardo Silva-Santisteban, Lima: Edubanco, 1980
Obras en prosa, edited by Ricardo Silva-Santisteban, Lima: Edubanco, 1982

Further Reading

Bendezú, Edmundo, *La poética de Martín Adán*, Lima: Villanueva, 1969
Greene, Roland, "Measuring Space, Becoming Space," in *Post-Petrarchism: Origins and Innovations of the Western Lyric Sequence*, Princeton, New Jersey: Princeton University Press, 1991 [Chapter on Adán and Neruda]
Higgins, James, *The Poet in Peru*, Liverpool: Liverpool Monographs in Hispanic Studies, 1982 [Devotes one chapter to the poetry of Adán]
Kinsella, John Myles, "The Theme of Poetry in Martín Adán's *Travesía de extramares*," *Bulletin of Hispanic Studies*, vol. 64 (1987)
———— *Lo trágico y su consuelo: un estudio de la obra de Martín Adán*, Lima: Mosca Azul, 1989
Lauer, Mirko, *Los exilios interiores: una introducción a Martín Adán*, Lima: Hueso Húmero, 1983
Loayza, Luis, "Martín Adán en *La Casa de cartón*," *Proceso*, Lima (1964)
Ortega, Julio, *Figuración de la persona*, Barcelona: Edhasa, 1970 [short section on Adán]

Bibliographies

Weller, Hubert P., *Bibliografía analítica y anotada de y sobre Martín Adán*, Lima: Instituto Nacional de Cultura, 1975

Jorge Enrique Adoum 1926–

Ecuadorian poet, novelist, dramatist and critic

Jorge Enrique Adoum is a Marxist intellectual and a committed revolutionary writer. His extensive literary production and his constant experimentation in various genres – poetry, narrative, essay and theater – place him among the Latin American literary avant-garde and establish him as a fundamental landmark in contemporary Ecuadorian letters.

Adoum's work focuses on the literary amalgamation of the central motifs of his creation: Marxist and socialist ideology, its relationship with Ecuadorian and Latin American history from prehistoric times to the present, and an obsessive search for a new, original and raging language to convey the frustrations, conflicts and hopes of both Latin American people and society subordinated internally to the alienating pressures of an unjust social system and externally to the manipulation of capitalism and North American neocolonialism.

Culturally speaking, Adoum's works illustrate a dual unity of political criticism and sociological aesthetics. Adoum is essentially a poet whose dialectical conception of poetry and the social genesis of the literary work are quite obvious in his first period, since *Ecuador amargo*, 1949 [Bitter Ecuador], *Relato del extranjero*, 1953 [Foreigner's Story], up to the substantial contribution to the Spanish American epic of the 20th century, the tetralogy *Los cuadernos de la tierra* [The Notebooks of the Earth], published in a single volume in 1963. In a second and mature period, the problems of denunciation and commitment become more subtle and their development more artistic, carefully avoiding the danger of falling into political propaganda and pamphleteering. Here the poet's obsession becomes a struggle between words and world, language and popular languages, individual and society as presented in *Yo me fui con tu nombre por la tierra*, 1964 [I Went Away with Your Name Around the World], *Curriculum mortis* of 1968, *Informe personal sobre la situación* 1973 [Personal Report on the Situation] and *Prepoemas en postespañol*, 1979 [Prepoems in Post-Spanish]. This last work in particular is an unexpected and challenging *tour de force* in verbal and non-verbal experimentation because it combines philosophical and political reflections with linguistic economy and an aggressive style employing surprising neologisms, morphological disintegration, and unpredictable metaphors. A third period in the evolution towards a unique language, style, and aesthetically committed literature had a curious turn. Adoum, the poet in revolt, explored other territories, theater and novel, in an attempt to find new boundaries and channels of communication. Adoum's theater belongs to popular and documentary drama. On the one hand, *El sol bajo las patas de los caballos*, 1972 (*The Sun Trampled beneath the Horses' Hooves*) is a devastating attack on all forms of conquest, oppression, and colonization; on the other, *La subida a los infiernos*, 1976 [Ascent to Hell], is a satirical and grotesque plea against the shady business dealings of the bourgeoisie as it tramples upon religious beliefs and the human rights of the people.

Adoum's successful incursion into narrative is a surprising case: a major poet becomes an influential novelist. His novel

Entre Marx y una mujer desnuda: texto con personajes, 1976 [Between Marx and a Naked Woman: Text with Characters], winner of that year's Xavier Villaurrutia prize for fiction, has come to be seen as the best and most complex "new novel" ever written in Ecuador. It is a work that relies on both the author's literary theory – explicitly stated and developed in the fiction – and the narrative praxis of that theory. It is not only a text conveying cultural and political criticism but also a moving poetic and experimental novel whose content and structure surpasses by far the pioneering complexities of Cortázar's *Rayuela*, 1963 (*Hopscotch*). The structural labyrinth of concentric circles allows Adoum to create an open novel whose interpretive possibilities are numerous. Even though the plot itself seems to be straightforward – a writer writes a book about a writer who is thinking of writing another book on another writer – the novel embodies, at complementary levels, all the obsessive themes Adoum has written about since 1944. Even more, the novel is the synthesis of the poetical, artistic and ideological themes of his writings, summarizing the complex evolution and powerful stylistic expression which shape Adoum's aesthetics of violence, an effective artistic answer to the problems of underdevelopment and to the daily realities, in Ecuador and Latin America, of institutionalized violence, exploitation, cruelty, injustice, and death.

Thus Marxist ideology, aesthetics of violence and continental history may well summarize Adoum's painful but nevertheless fruitful relationships with politics, and literature. These major themes reappear constantly in his later writings, which are an attempt to find "el realismo de la otra realidad" (the realism of the other reality) and "lo real espantoso" (the frightening experience) of Latin America, as described by Adoum himself in many of his essays. However it must be emphasized that Adoum – well distanced by the 1970s from any trace of Socialist Realism as practiced by many members of the Ecuadorian "Generation of 1930" – thought as follows: art is not a magical door that opens up to reality but rather constitutes an autonomous reality; neither a photograph nor a symbol of nature or society but, rather, a re-presentation of reality, parallel to some philosophical and even scientific forms of representation in a continuous exchange of meanings. His position has always been against "el sectarismo del realismo" (the sectarianism of realism). Therefore, those reading Adoum should consider that, as stated by Terry Eagleton in *Literary Theory: an Introduction* (1983), "You simply have to argue about politics. It is not a question of debating whether 'literature' should be related to 'history' or not: it is a question of different readings of history itself."

Adoum's career of over fifty years profiles a writer who has found, through political and artistic commitment, a key path to explore the past and future of his people. It is true that Adoum considers literature to be a weapon in the revolutionary struggle. However, he has also maintained that such a weapon, in order to be politically useful, must be artistically created. This position is the result of key experiences throughout his career: the early discovery of the writers of the Group of

Guayaquil; his work as Pablo Neruda's personal secretary in Chile and their longlasting friendship; the progressive and critical discovery of Vallejo, Rimbaud, Mallarmé, Apollinaire, Whitman, Cavafy, Pessoa, Joyce, Kafka, Mishima, Tanizaki, Kawabata; the close ties with the Cuban Revolution; and his personal voluntary exile of nearly twenty-five years in Europe, sixteen of which he spent in Paris working for UNESCO; his active participation, in Paris, in political and literary discussions with a group of Latin American writers and artists with whom he would maintain a long and mutually influential friendship: Alejo Carpentier, Julio Cortázar, Juan Rulfo, Eduardo Galeano, Gabriel García Márquez, Juan Gelman, Augusto Monterroso, René Depestre, Roberto Matta, Wilfredo Lam, Antonio Seguí, Edouard Glissant, and Antonio Saura, among others.

All Adoum's works develop a general theme according to which Latin America is a subjugated, invaded, and raped continent. Predominating in these works are a dissatisfaction with the status quo, a corrosive doubt, and a defiant and combative attitude: that of historical optimism against geographical pessimism, in so far as violence is the result of negation of our own history. This reality frustrates the self-realization of Adoumian characters, narrators, and lyrical voices, torn between their individual inability to transform social reality, and the alienating pressures of physical and ideological mechanisms of power and manipulation of society.

In his poetic works Adoum assumes a collective rather than an individual lyrical voice. The writer witnesses the pervasive situation that needs to be deconstructed politically and artistically with the systematic innovation of language and expression. Thus official violence at the thematic level is met with formal, structural, and stylistic violence at the linguistic level. For instance, in 3,742 verses, Los cuadernos de la tierra deals with both prehistorical and historical forms of violence up to the 18th century in what is now Ecuador. With this work, Adoum ends his obsessive return to the past in search of identity and moves on to the 20th century, still plagued by violence and repression. Henceforth, Adoum's poetry may be considered field reports by a war correspondent of society, in so far as his Latin American leitmotifs explore social, political, and economic fluctuations, the pressures of imperialism and neocolonialism, the proliferation of dictatorships both civilian and military, the despair of the lower classes, and the abuses of power. It is impossible to separate in Adoum's extensive production art from politics or history, creative freedom from political freedom, theory from praxis. Everywhere in his poetical praxis, metaphors associated with death, suffering, and alienation are overwhelming; all of them challenge us one way or the other to face ourselves in somebody else's mirror, to think and talk about personal and collective memories, to explore the past in order to understand the future. This piercing irony combined with caustic humor, the fluctuations between geographical pessimism and historical optimism, and a vigorous solidarity with the downtrodden are trademarks of Adoum's style. It allows the poet to convey a plurality of meanings in his fight against all forms of social, political, linguistic and grammatical status quo. Thus, as stated in key poems like "Epitafio del extranjero vivo" [Epitaph of the Foreigner Alive], "Lo insólito cotidiano" [The Everyday Unusual], "Casi como Dios" [Almost Like God], "Pasadología" [Past-ology], and

"Surrealismo al aire libre" [Outdoor Surrealism], language breaks down as it goes beyond the limits of its own referentiality, creating and destroying meanings that end up in the vicious circle of life and death.

PABLO A. MARTÍNEZ

Biography

Born in Ambato, Ecuador, 1926. Studied for an arts degree at the University of Santiago de Chile. Private secretary to Pablo Neruda for about two years. Taught literature in Ecuador; head of the publishing department of the Casa de la Cultura Ecuatoriana; also headed section of National Culture at the Ministry of Education, 1961–63. In 1963 travelled to Egypt, India and Japan as part of UNESCO's East/West cultural programme; lived in China from 1964 to 1966. Worked for French state radio up to 1968. From 1969 to 1986 he worked for the United Nations in Geneva and for UNESCO in Paris. Returned to Ecuador in 1987. Recipient of the following awards: Ecuadorian National Prize for Poetry, 1952 for the first two volumes of Los cuadernos de la tierra; Casa de las Américas Prize, 1960 (the first year it was awarded) for Dios trajo la sombra; the Mexican Xavier Villaurrutia Prize, 1976 for Entre Marx y una mujer desnuda; the Ecuadorian Eugenio Espejo National Prize for Culture, 1989.

Selected Works

Poetry

Ecuador amargo, Quito: Casa de la Cultura Ecuatoriana, 1949
Carta para Alejandra, Quito: La Andariega, 1952
Los cuadernos de la tierra:
  I. Los orígenes, Quito: Casa de la Cultura Ecuatoriana, 1952
  II. El enemigo y la mañana, Quito: Casa de la Cultura Ecuatoriana, 1952
  III. Dios trajo la sombra, Quito: Casa de la Cultura Ecuatoriana, 1959
  IV. Eldorado y las ocupaciones nocturnas, Quito: Casa de la Cultura Ecuatoriana, 1961
Notas del hijo pródigo, Quito: Rumiñahui, 1953
Relato del extranjero: poesía, Quito: Ediciones del Ateneo Ecuatoriano, 1955
Yo me fui con tu nombre por la tierra, Quito: n.p., 1964 [clandestine edition]
Informe personal sobre la situación, Madrid: Aguaribay, 1973
Los 37 poemas de Mao Tsetung, Buenos Aires: Schapire, 1974
El amor desenterrado y otros poemas, Quito: El Conejo, 1993

Novels

Entre Marx y una mujer desnuda: texto con personajes, Mexico City: Siglo XXI, 1976; revised edition, 1978
Ciudad sin ángel, Mexico City: Siglo XXI, 1995

Plays

Jorge Enrique Adoum: teatro, Quito: Casa de la Cultura Ecuatoriana, 1981 [Contains El sol bajo las patas de los caballos and La subida a los infiernos. The former appeared first in Conjunto (Havana) on 14 December 1972. An English version, The Sun Trampled beneath the Horses' Hooves, by Arthur McMurray and Roberto Márquez, was published in The Massachusetts Review, vol. 15/1–2 (Winter–Spring 1974)]

Essays

Poesía del siglo XX, Quito: Casa de la Cultura Ecuatoriana, 1957
La gran literatura ecuatoriana del 30, Quito: El Conejo, 1984
Sin ambages (textos y contextos), Quito: Planeta-Letraviva, 1989
Guayasamín: el hombre, la obra, la crítica, Nuremberg: D.A.Verlag Das Andere, 1996

Compilations and Anthologies

Los cuadernos de la Tierra, Quito: Casa de la Cultura Ecuatoriana, 1963 [one-volume edition]

No son todos los que están: poemas, 1949–1979, Barcelona: Seix Barral, 1979

El tiempo y las palabras (poemas 1949–1989), with an introduction by Vladimiro Rivas I., Quito: Libresa, Colección Antares, 1992

Further Reading

Calderón Chico, Carlos, *Jorge Enrique Adoum: entrevista en dos tiempos*, Quito: Editorial Universitaria, 1988

Donoso Pareja, Miguel, "Adoum y sus texto con personajes," in *Nuevo realismo ecuatoriano. La novela después del 30*, Quito: El Conejo, 1984

Hamilton, Carlos, "Jorge Enrique Adoum," in *Nuevo lenguaje poético (de Silva a Neruda)*, Bogotá: Publicaciones del Instituto Caro y Cuervo, 1965

Martínez Arévalo, Pablo, *Jorge Enrique Adoum: ideología, estética e historia (1944–1990)*, Kentucky: University of Kentucky, U.M.I., 1990

Rodríguez Ortíz, Oscar, "Jorge Enrique Adoum: por ambas partes (A propósito de *Entre Marx y una mujer desnuda*)," in *Sobre narradores y héroes (A propósito de Arenas, Scorza y Adoum)*, Caracas: Monte Ávila, 1981

Sacoto, Antonio, "*Entre Marx y una mujer desnuda*," in *14 novelas claves de la literatura ecuatoriana*, Cuenca, Ecuador: Publicaciones del Departamento de Difusión Cultural de la Universidad de Cuenca, 1990

Yurkievich, Saúl, "De lo lúcido a lo lúdico," in *La confabulación con la palabra*, Madrid: Taurus, 1978

Entre Marx y una mujer desnuda: texto con personajes

Novel by Jorge Enrique Adoum

Entre Marx y una mujer desnuda is the most important, complex, and radically experimental new novel ever written in Ecuador and a representative example of the new Latin American novel. Its socialist ideology and its original, angry language highlight the powerful stylistic expression of Adoum's aesthetics of violence. It conveys the conflicts and hopes of both Latin American people and society, subordinated to an unjust social system and to North American neocolonialism. The novel includes a literary theory of its own that challenges the reader systematically. The triple narrative structure of concentric circles and the wide variety of topics and styles deal with the contemporary tension between sociability and individualism, and the dismemberment of the writer, torn between political commitment and literary experimentation.

The novel is organized on three levels: textuality (the different narrative strata), intertextuality (the relationships between Adoum's works and those of other writers), and visualization (first, through visual and textual devices; second, through images and symbols: Marx, a set of wheelchairs, a naked woman, the Centaur Joaco, the Man of Punín). These strategies develop key theoretical premises: the necessity of genre transformation, the shock value of art, the inevitable creation of new languages, the unavoidable destruction of the text, the freedom in fragmentation, and the consumption of aesthetics. We confront a text based on its own negation, that could be read in any order or even be left unfinished in order "poner a trabajar al lector acostumbrado a siglos de pereza" (to force the reader, accustomed to centuries of laziness, to work).

In the panorama of the new Ecuadorian novel, *Entre Marx y una mujer desnuda* stands out as one of the best. Adoum's disintegrating aesthetics of violence combines linguistic renovation, situational parody, and corrosive irony. Its labyrinthine structure of concentric circles implies a critique of the politics, art and culture of Latin America and a devastating inquiry into society. However, Adoum's text is also a historical novel, a political essay, a revolutionary manifesto, a prose poem, an autobiographical confession. It presents a period that begins in 1930 with the North American imposition of the dictator José Ubico in Guatemala and ends in 1973, with the assassination of Salvador Allende and the North American installation of the fascist dictatorship of Pinochet, in Chile. It also presents the idiosyncrasy, culture, and history of Ecuador vis-à-vis the sociopolitical reality of Latin America. In the process of writing his fiction, Adoum eliminates the strait-jacket of the plot and proposes instead the rejection of reality. He attacks the idealism underpinning Socialist Realism, the tyranny of the plot line, uni-dimensional characterization, literary determinism. Most importantly, Adoum includes himself in the work as a character insisting on artistic commitment. And because the self-questioning of the reader is the cathartic process that sets in motion this text, each reader becomes a character. The outcome is the aesthetic configuration of an original and violent "new novel" corresponding to the daily violence that goes unpunished all over Latin America and frustrates the self-realization of women and men. As a result, the characters, a motley assortment of divided, alienated beings, are trapped in the morass of an imposed ideology and a culture of violence. As a response, the novel (re)presents the underdevelopment of culture and the culture of underdevelopment in order to attack capitalism by using the fragmentation of the structure and language. Therefore, the title bespeaks crucial dualities – politics and ethics, Marxism and psychoanalysis, society and eroticism – which resolve themselves dialectically in a cultural and literary critique of capitalistic ideology. This criticism runs throughout the novel pointing out literary, social, and historical problems. Thus as cultural critique, it is a defiant and coherent text whose critical strategies reproduce themselves in the chaotic fictional world created and narrated in thirty-two long segments. Adoum disrupts the traditional codes of reading and narrative discourse by renovating language and technique, content and form, and transforming the reader into a consumer and producer of the text. However, textual power stems from the mythic/visual symbols generated by the leitmotifs in the narration: the naked woman, the Man of Punín, and the Centaur Joaco.

In this textual geography, Adoum's characters live in an alienated world. The first narrative circle embraces the remaining ones. There we find the "Autor," Jorge Enrique Adoum, in the process of writing *Entre Marx y una mujer desnuda*, and submerged in painful self-questioning. In the second circle, we find another writer, the "Narrador," about whom the "Autor" of the first circle is writing his novel. This "Narrador" also writes another book about his problematic relationship with his lover Rosana, wife of landowner Fabián Golmés, el Cretino. Through the pretense of this love story he fictionalizes the contradictions and limitations of the bourgeoisie and internalizes his own isolation and conflicts.

Galo Gálvez, alias Joaco, a fictionalization of the Ecuadorian writer Joaquín Gallegos Lara, is the protagonist of the third and densest circle, consisting of the autobiography of the "Narrador" of the second circle. It focuses on Galo Gálvez, protagonist of the novel that the "Narrador" writes. Here we face a *roman à clef* that forces the reader to participate, for it interprets reality instead of imitating it. The complexity of Adoum's narrative theory is also built upon the use of paraphrases and quotations, whose proliferation make the novel into a totalizing cultural and dialogical project.

Galo Gálvez is a progressive leftist intellectual who along with the "Autor/Adoum" shares the main role in the third narrative circle. Despite being paraplegic, he is the most dynamic and active character. A contemporary centaur and symbol of the frustrations and hopes of Latin American people, he traverses all circles of the novel. His model, as we learn in the Prologue, was the paraplegic writer Joaquín Gallegos Lara, a member of the circle of writers known as the Group of Guayaquil. Gálvez, like the "Autor," is a stoic, an ironic intellectual, a challenger of the religious, military, and civil power, who always acts in solidarity with the people. His companion, Falcón de Aláquez, a popular character, lends him his legs and transports him everywhere on his shoulders. They form a metaphorical and mythological unit, the centaur Joaco/Gálvez/Falcón, a contemporary political allegory of the revolution.

The character called "Autor," a figure for Jorge Enrique Adoum, is a type of demiurge. He has freedom of movement in the narrative circles. His devastating sociocultural criticism runs constantly throughout the novel. As a censor, a self-critic, the "Autor" transcends the cultural world of the novel and gives it a continental and universal dimension. With him we travel through the prehistory of violence, the conflictive origins of the mother country, and the contradictions and injustices of contemporary reality: from the Man of Punín through to the Man of Santiago. His language forms a poetic, demythologizing, and sarcastic discourse. He is the most polemical and honest character, the synthesis of Adoum/Gálvez/Gallegos Lara.

The "Narrador," another main character, is also an intellectual and a writer torn between his vocation and his sentimental conflicts. His vicissitudes show him as suffering the traumas, betrayals and "claudicaciones" (imperfections) which occur in the false and bourgeois world in which he lives. He is the protagonist of his own fiction and failure, something which is reflected in the characters he creates while narrating his autobiography in the third narrative circle.

In Adoum, aesthetic counterviolence aspires to the change implicit in the social dialectics and ideology that support the text. On one hand, Adoum destroys and demythologizes the history and culture of Ecuador; on the other, he places us at the core of Latin American reality, attacking violently North American imperialism and the instruments of its penetration. Through its thematic dispersion, *Entre Marx y una mujer desnuda* is reminiscent of Jorge Luis Borges's "aleph." In the continuous reading process each element comes out uninterruptedly in the reader's mind by way of an analogical organization. Thus the narrative contents are presented by symbols (the naked woman, the Man of Punín, the centaur Joaco, Los Esdrújulos), by metaphors (of love, adolescence, friendship, politics, repression, sexuality, literature, the legal system), by anaphorical images (the father's skull, the revolution, past, history, daily life, motherland). Adoum dramatizes the historical present by interspersing the leitmotif of the unending aggressions of North American imperialism. This chain of violent aggressions from the outside conditions the internal violence of the countries of Latin America and determines the alienation and frustration of Adoumian characters. The only way out of this oppressive situation is revolutionary change and armed struggle to which the novel only alludes but whose ideology it demands constantly.

The strategies of Adoum's world are defiant, suggestive and complex. This "text with characters" invites intense debate and reflection and, once read, proves difficult, even impossible, to forget. As a fundamental novel of our time, Adoum's text is a potent legacy. Ultimately, this quasi-jigsaw puzzle novel is a deliberately elusive text, an impassioned testimony, a thoughtful document of individual and collective memory, a scream of frustration and rage.

PABLO A. MARTÍNEZ

Editions
First edition: *Entre Marx y una mujer desnuda: texto con personajes*, Mexico City: Siglo XXI, 1976

Further Reading
Hidalgo, Laura, "'Entre Marx y una mujer desnuda: texto con personajes,' de Jorge Enrique Adoum," *Revista Iberoamericana* 144–45 (1988)

Navas, Griselda, *Perspectivas críticas de una novela de Adoum*, Caracas: Tipografía Navas, 1981

Waag, C. Michael, "Frustration and Rage in Jorge Enrique Adoum's 'Entre Marx y una mujer desnuda,'" *Perspectives on Contemporary Literature*, vol. 10 (1984)

African-American Literature

Central and South America

The recent far-reaching developments in the field of Afrocentric studies have altered radically and irrevocably not just the entire range of "Afro"- disciplines, but the so-called "Western" academy itself. Cheikh Anta Diop's challenge in *The African Origin of Civilization: Myth or Reality* (1975) is not mere academic speculation. There is an entire school of brilliant scholars and a rapidly expanding corpus of works that support his position. It is clear that the so-called "Moors" who gave definitive shape to Hispanicity were Africans plain and simple, as African as those ancients from the Nile Valley who first created a great human civilization, as African as the citizens of present-day Senegal, Nigeria, Kenya, etc. Furthermore, according to Ivan Van Sertima's compellingly argued study of 1976, *They Came before Columbus*, Africans were a decisive shaping force in the development of high civilization in the Americas from as early as the 8th century BC. For practical purposes and as is also the case in the entry on African-Caribbean Literature, a new working definition of African-American Literature" is called for. It must be one with which every scholar can live, no matter her/his ideological orientation. It is simply that literature, emanating from Central and South America, in which the problematic African heritage is given overt focus. This literature will not, however, be viewed through the traditional Eurocentric prism.

Henry Louis Gates, Jr in *The Signifying Monkey: a Theory of African-American Literary Criticism* (1988) established parameters that are valid for the entire continent. The "Signifying Monkey" is a manifestation of Legba, the Yoruba Trickster "god," *Orisha*, or *Loa*, the symbol of literariness, a West African version of Thoth of ancient Egypt, after whom, the Greco-Romans fashioned their Hermes and Mercury. In the Americas created by the 1492 process, the quest for liberation has to be close to the core of any African literary symbol. And certainly all over the Americas Tricksters like Brother Rabbit, Brother Anancy (the Spider), Brother Tortoise, and, of course, the Signifying Monkey himself have been an integral part of the people's struggle. In this context the *pícaro* of Peninsular literature can be considered a legitimate Trickster. Shango the great warrior, "god" of thunder, another "Orisha" from the Yoruba pantheon, has also been intimately connected with the liberation movement. The freedom fighter *par excellence* in the Americas has been the *cimarrón* (runaway slave) and the struggle itself can be labeled a *cimarronaje*. In a *sui generis* African Central and South American literary theory, then, such figures as the *cimarrón*, Legba, the *pícaro*, and Shango would play a central role.

Careful analysis reveals that Latin American fiction writers of the 20th century who can be deemed to be representative of those who have made an aesthetic issue of the Black presence have either consciously or unconsciously fashioned their protagonists on the picaresque model. Furthermore, in doing so it can be argued that they were guided by a cultural reflex that dates back to the dawn of human civilization, in Africa. In 1942 the Ecuadorian Adalberto Ortiz gave the world the first widely-read Latin American novel, *Juyungo*, with an uncompromisingly black protagonist, Ascensión Lastre. Lastre is in many respects a classic *pícaro*. He enters upon the scene as a young child cast adrift in a sea of adversity, and has to learn to swim immediately lest he drown. Like the original Peninsular *pícaro*, Lazarillo de Tormes, at an early age he leaves what little shelter his "home" provides. Tutored by his own "smarts" and a series of contacts with others who served as his "masters" in a more or less formal way, he seeks to negotiate the perils of existence as a black man in a white man's world.

The same picaresque paradigm is adopted by the Colombian Arnoldo Palacios in the development of his principal character, Irra, of the novel *Las estrellas son negras* [The Stars are Black]. (Richard L. Jackson, who has encyclopedic knowledge in these matters, gives 1949 as the date for this novel although the only edition extant was published in 1971). The young male confronts the desperate circumstances of poverty, hunger, and above all a pervasive racism. Although he realizes that the only road to liberation is that of a bold *cimarronaje*, he balks at employing what Frantz Fanon calls the "cleansing force" of armed revolt. An existential *pícaro*, he opts for a most precarious liberation that the reader must deduce for her/himself to be either death by drowning or a life of complete abandonment to illusion. However, it might well be argued that Irra's final solution, structurally parallels that of Lazarillo: it is an accommodation to the prevailing and ineluctable adversity.

The Venezuelan Ramón Díaz Sánchez authored in 1950 a novel about a rural Black community, *Cumboto*. The first-person narrator, the anti-hero Natividad, expressly rejects the picaresque option: "Más de una vez había pensado en huir, emanciparme y forjarme mi propia vida. Pero no lo hice ... la idea de partir sin rumbo, sin una brújula que orientase mis pasos me aterraba. ¡Me sentía tan débil e incapaz!" (On more than one occasion I had thought about running away, emancipating myself and forging my own life. But I didn't do it ... the thought of taking off without any direction, without a compass to guide my steps, terrified me. I felt so weak and inept).

José Antonio Pastrana is the protagonist of the Ecuadorian Nelson Estupiñán Bass's 1966 novel, *El último río* [Pastrana's Last River]. The burly black man takes charge of his life lifting himself from the ranks of the oppressed to those of the oppressor. His metamorphosis is achieved through trickery. He is not a classic *pícaro*, however. He becomes far too powerful for that. Indeed, he is a *cimarrón* gone awry becoming worse than the slavemaster himself. Natividad presented an example of refusal to use the Trickster/*pícaro* access to *cimarronaje*. Lastre and Irra followed a path that is closer to that of the original Lazarillo. Whereas Estupiñán appears not to have relied on the Trickster/*pícaro* paradigm in the development of his Pastrana, the theme of *cimarronaje* seems to have been expressly evoked.

It is in *Chango, el gran putas* [Shango the Baddest SOB], the 1983 magnum opus by the Colombian Manuel Zapata Olivella, that the reader finds the clearest expression of the central relationship between the Trickster/*pícaro* and liberation (*cimarronaje*). The title appears to reduce Shango, god of thunder, mighty warrior and liberator of his people to a mere trickster, albeit the "baddest" of them (*el gran putas*). Zapata means no irreverence. On the contrary, he displays the profoundest respect for traditional Yoruba theology, for he understands that Legba, the Trickster "god," is as important a figure as Shango. In the novel it is only through Legba's instrumentality that Shango can become "*el gran putas*," who foretells and realizes the final liberation of his people.

The Costa Rican Quince Duncan born in 1940 is considered to be one of his country's greatest authors. He comes from that nation's "West Indian" province, Limón, and he traces his ancestry to West Africa via the island of Jamaica. The thrust to liberation is the fundamental motor of his fictive universe, and so the central protagonist is a liberator (*cimarrón*), like Shango. Duncan does not highlight the role played by Legba, rather the medium through which spiritual forces effect their inspiration is the *samamfo* (a concept explained below). His hero is more warrior than Trickster, and he is a fully New World Orisha, one, in fact, "made in the West Indies." For Duncan has crafted a "god" called *Cuminá* from the tradition of African-Christian Jamaicans. In all but one of his novels the main character is a messianic African-ancestored young man fully committed to the struggle for liberation.

The concept of the *samamfo* has evolved over the development of Duncan's fictional universe, a sure indicator of its fundamental importance. The definition proffered in the glossary of *Kimbo*, a later novel, that was finished in 1982 but reworked until 1985 to be finally published in 1990, is, then, the most appropriate: "Espíritu y herencia de los Ancestros. En el samamfo están los valores y tradiciones del pueblo. Es la memoria colectiva de la raza-cultura que pasa de generación a generación y que se actualiza en los ritos religioso-seculares del pueblo, en sus luchas, en sus experiencias. Los ancestros nunca han abandonado a sus herederos." (The spirit and inheritance of the Ancestors. It is in the *samamfo* that the values and traditions of the people reside. It is the collective memory of the race-culture that passes from generation to generation and that is actualized in the religious/secular rites of the people, in their struggles, in their experiences. The Ancestors have never abandoned their heirs). The *samamfo* is but one of the four central tropes that constitute the neo-African core of Duncan's creativity. The others are the *cimarrón*, the river, and laughter. Duncan might be considered the leader of a school of Central American writers who by building on all of the rich potential of their full cultural heritage have created one of the most vibrant literatures in the Americas.

The others are his fellow Costa Rican Eulalia Bernard and the Panamanians Gerardo Maloney, Melvin Brown and Carlos Guillermo Wilson.

The Dialectical Theory of Identification inspired by Frantz Fanon and developed by Amilcar Cabral (this theory is explained in the entry on African-Caribbean literature) offers the most complete analytical framework for the material presented above. The representative works chosen for discussion in the present entry belong to the "Radicalization" phase. It is important, however, not to disparage in anyway the work of those who labored over the years when the night of racist oppression was darkest. In those days the relatively few men-of-words (and they were, in fact, mostly "men") who might have had some interest in evoking the African heritage could barely emerge from the slumber of "Capitulation" to attain some measure of "Revitalization." It is equally important, however, to recognize and support the contributions of the writers who have evolved to the "Radicalization" phase, for without vigilance there is real danger of regressing to the dark night of "Capitulation."

IAN ISIDORE SMART

Further Reading

Captain-Hidalgo, Yvonne, *The Culture of Fiction in the Works of Manuel Zapata Olivella*, Columbia: University of Missouri Press, 1993

Gates, Jr, Henry Louis, *The Signifying Monkey: a Theory of African-American Literary Criticism*, Oxford and New York: Oxford University Press, 1988

Gordon, Donald K., *Lo jamaicano y lo universal en la obra del costarricense Quince Duncan*, San José: Editorial Costa Rica, 1989

Jackson, Richard L., *Black Writers in Latin America*, Albuquerque: University of New Mexico Press, 1979

Lewis, Marvin A., *Treading the Ebony Path: Ideology and Violence in Contemporary Afro-Colombian Prose Fiction*, Columbia: University of Missouri Press, 1987

_____ *Afro-Argentine Discourse: Another Dimension of the Black Diaspora*, Columbia: University of Missouri Press, 1995

Prescott, Laurence E., *Candelario Obeso y la iniciación de la poesía negra en Colombia*, Bogotá: Caro y Cuervo, 1985

Richards, Henry J., *La jornada novelística de Nelson Estupiñán Bass: búsqueda de la perfección*, Quito: El Conejo, 1989

Smart, Ian Isidore, *Central American Writers of West Indian Origin: a New Hispanic Literature*, Washington, DC: Three Continents Press, 1984

_____ "Quince Duncan," in *Dictionary of Literary Biography: Modern Latin-American Fiction Writers*, vol. 145, edited by William Luis and Ann González, Detroit: Gale Research, 1994

African-Brazilian Literature

The term "African-Brazilian Literature" does not describe a literary movement as such, but rather a thematic tendency within modern Brazilian literature, sometimes also known in the 1920s as "Literatura Negra," a term which is currently used to describe the literary expression of the black movement in Brazil. In discussing African-Brazilian literature, it is therefore important to be aware that it has two strands to it, one evoking the literary consciousness of a minority group, the other associated with a major movement of cultural nationalism, Modernism, which was to affect the course of mainstream Brazilian literature from the 1920s onwards.

Black literary aspirations began to find expression in the first black newspapers, which appeared in São Paulo, from 1915. By the 1930s, the black voice was being heard through newspapers such as *Clarim d'Alvorada* [Dawn Clarion] and *Voz da Raça* [Voice of the Race], which sought to inculcate middle-class values into their readership, in order to better prepare blacks for integration. Literary values were correspondingly conservative, usually taking the form of the Parnassian sonnet. The main poetic voice of the black movement in São Paulo was Lino Guedes who, in books such as *Canto do cisne preto*, 1927 [Song of the Black Swan], *Urucungo* (1936) and *Negro preto cor da noite*, 1938 [Jet Black Man Colour of Night], managed to reconcile erudite models, such as the sonnet, with popular themes and humour.

More or less at the same time, but within the mainstream of Brazilian literary life, the Modernist Movement was born in São Paulo in 1922. The Modernists belonged to the social elite, and sought to blend Amerindian and African-Brazilian folk motifs into a new expression of national identity. While this movement of cultural nationalism, whose main representatives were Oswald de Andrade, Mário de Andrade and Raul Bopp, exalted the mestizo character of Brazilian culture, it also generated a sentiment of regional consciousness in the Northeast of the country, where the influence of African culture was particularly marked. Its principal instigator was the Pernambuco sociologist Gilberto Freyre, author of the *Manifesto regionalista* (1926), and of the later classic of social history, *Casa grande e senzala*, 1933 (*The Masters and the Slaves*), in which he analysed in considerable detail and from a very positive viewpoint, the contribution of the black slave to the social and cultural life of the plantation belt during the colonial period. Freyre also organised the first African-Brazilian Congress in Recife, in 1934. In literature, Jorge Amado's novel *Jubiabá* (1935), was the first in a long line of novels by this author to focus on black life in Bahia, and to exploit "macumba" (African-Brazilian religious ritual) and slave folk history to underpin its social message. In the same year, José Lins do Rego published his novel, *O moleque Ricardo* [Richard the Street Kid], which detailed the experiences of a young black migrant from the plantation, in the city of Recife. In poetry, Jorge de Lima, in *Poemas negros*, 1947 [Black Poems] and Solano Trindade, in *Poemas de uma vida simples*, 1944 [Poems of a Simple Life], reflected in their work an African-Brazilian aesthetic: the cultivation of black rhythms and vocabulary, in a free verse form exalting the vitality of black culture and displaying an awareness of the social injustices to which blacks were subjected. As in Cuba, this strand of African-Brazilian literature implied, for some writers, a political militancy. Amado and Trindade joined the Brazilian Communist Party after 1945, both having explored in their work, the revolutionary possibilities of black culture, while at the same time identifying the black struggle as part of the universal struggle of the proletariat.

In the Brazil of the 1930s and 1940s, African-Brazilian literature was therefore not limited to black authors. Indeed, most authors were white and middle class. The black press occasionally included, with some pride, news of the activities of mestizo intellectuals such as Mário de Andrade, and from time to time published a "black" poem by a white author, such as Cecília Meireles. The only writer who co-existed with both the world of black militancy and the artistic and literary elite, was the black poet and theatre director, Solano Trindade.

Since the 1950s, the two strands of African-Brazilian literature have continued to exist in apparent ignorance of each other. On the one hand, Jorge Amado has become the country's most widely-known exponent in fiction of African-Brazilian culture. Contemporary classics such as *Gabriela, cravo e canela*, 1958 (*Gabriela, Clove and Cinnamon*), and *Dona Flor e seus dois maridos*, 1966 (*Dona Flor and Her Two Husbands*), both exploit to its fullest potential the rich vein of Bahian culture, frequently resorting to African-Brazilian magic for the resolution of their plots. *Tenda dos milagres*, 1969 (*Tent of Miracles*), however, is Amado's main testimony to the struggle for black culture to be accepted nationally, and to the fight against racism, incorporating both the social and cultural themes visible in his earlier novels.

At the same time, an African-Brazilian literature has accompanied the fortunes of the black social and cultural movements, which have surfaced with some regularity, mainly in São Paulo, since the 1950s. Abdias do Nascimento, black polemicist, heavily influenced by the black experience in the United States, where he resided for many years, was instrumental in attempts to create a black theatre in the years after the war, which would more closely reflect the lives and aspirations of blacks in Brazil, as well as provide an outlet for black actors.

During the 1960s, a number of black poets were influenced by the *Négritude* aesthetic of the Francophone African poet and statesman, Léopold Senghor. Oswaldo Camargo's *Um homem tenta ser anjo*, 1959 [A Man Attempts to Be an Angel], and Eduardo de Oliveira's *Gestas líricas da negritude*, 1967 [Lyric Epics of Négritude], both focus on the inner experience of being black in a world which denies any value to the African contribution to the country. A poetry of rejection and exile seeks to rekindle the link with a distant and elusive mother continent. Camargo's later collection of short stories, *O carro do êxito*, 1972 [The Gravy Train], focuses, with sometimes gently ironic humour, upon the contradictions of the black movements in São Paulo, in their struggle to express a black identity.

In the 1970s and 1980s the link with Mother Africa was revived with the emergence of Angola and Mozambique as independent Portuguese-speaking nations, whose revolutionary literatures coincided with the dynamization of the black movement in Brazil in the wake of the political opening of the late 1970s, and the centenary of Abolition in 1988. Poets in São Paulo, such as Cuti, in Rio, such as Ele Semog, Antônio Vieira, from Bahia, and Oliveira Silveira, from Pôrto Alegre, not to mention black women poets like Miriam Alves and Lourdes Teodoro, have redefined African-Brazilian literature in terms of their individual, regional, or socio-cultural predicament. What is apparent is that while established white writers, like Jorge Amado, continue to base their novels within an unchanging African-Brazilian setting, African-Brazilian literature as such, owes its evolution to the small but growing number of black writers in Brazil.

DAVID BROOKSHAW

Further Reading

Bernd, Zilá, *Introdução à literatura negra*, São Paulo: Brasiliense, 1988

Brookshaw, David, *Race and Color in Brazilian Literature*, Metuchen, New Jersey: Scarecrow Press, 1986

Marotti, Giorgio, *Black Characters in the Brazilian Novel*, translated by Mario O. Marotti and Harry Lawton, Los Angeles: University of California, Center for Afro-American Studies, 1987

African-Caribbean Literature

With the recent intensification in the quest for clarity on the part of numerous scholars of African ancestry, especially those based in the United States, some of the traditional terminology employed in our academy has been shown to be inadequate. Since the term "African Caribbean" assumes that "Caribbean" plain and simple is not necessarily "African," it needs to be replaced, for the assumption is incorrect. On the other hand, however, because white supremacist ideology has taken firm root from the time of the so-called Enlightenment at least, there are many well-meaning scholars of all races who have absolutely no quarrel with the fundamentally flawed assumption. Indeed, it may well be the case that the majority of Caribbean artists and intellectuals, even at the present time – the dawn of the second half of the millennium ushered in by Columbus – still labor under an essentially white supremacist approach.

What, then, is "African-Caribbean" literature? It is simply that literature, emanating from the Caribbean, in which the problematic African heritage is given overt focus. Cowed by white supremacy, writers from the region opted not to touch the Africa thing. This was and is especially the case for those who were most vulnerable, the ones whose external indicators of ethnicity linked them inextricably to Africa. To raise the question of Africa even indirectly was to court disaster, from physical death (see the case of Plácido discussed below) to economic and/or social death, as is more likely to be the case today. In these circumstances any writer from the region, no matter her/his ethnicity or even motivation, who overtly and with artistic consciousness focuses on any aspect of the African heritage, can be deemed to be working within the pale of "African-Caribbean literature."

Frantz Fanon viewed the colonial world as an essentially polarized, "Manichean" universe. Amilcar Cabral developed this insight into the Dialectical Theory of Identification. It would be impossible to understand the evolution of literature in the Caribbean without these analytical tools. From the very beginning of brutal European presence in the region there had been two worlds, two cultures, two literatures, one scribal, the other oral, one proper to the dominant minority, the other emanating from the oppressed majority.

The letters and chronicles of the few literate among the marauding multitudes coming from Europe after 1492 constitute the first works of this New World literature. The Colombian man-of-words Manuel Zapata Olivella, *Las claves mágicas de América: Raza, clase y cultura*, 1989 [The Secrets to Understanding America: Race, Class, and Culture] proclaims: "America is a product that was 'made in the Caribbean.'" Understandably it is this region, the very model after which every society in the Americas was fashioned, that has nurtured some of the best known Spanish American writers: Andrés Bello, José Martí, Rubén Darío, and Gabriel García Márquez.

So successful was the genocide initiated by Columbus that within one generation the new barbaric society had to meet its critical manpower needs with captive African labor. These Africans degraded to the utmost and unconscionably separated from a literary heritage that dated back to the third millennium BC had to content themselves with a merely oral literary practice. Afrocentric scholars continue to uncover the indisputable organic connection between the post-1492 Africans who came to America as cargo in the infamous slave ships and their ancestors who gave humankind the gift of civilization itself. The language of this oral literature was and still is Creole, a blend of a general West African syntax with a specific European lexicon. In the case of the Spanish Caribbean this lexicon would clearly be Spanish. Some of the few written samples of this literature can be found in Rosa E. Valdés Cruz's *La poesía negroide en América* (1970).

Literature written in Spanish emanating from the privileged domains of the ruling minority was consciously derivative, a slavish imitation of the Old World models. Such was the literature of Bello, Darío, Martí, etc. Completely separated in the apartheid conditions of the "Manichean" colonial universe the new Caribbean natives, the transplanted Africans, graced their existence with the fervent practice of the literary arts, albeit exclusively oral. Their literary expression was also consciously rooted in the secular tradition of their Original World. Their imitation was, ironically, not slavish, for they did not enjoy the luxury of adjudication by the experts back home. True, the African artistic community in the Caribbean of colonial times was constantly invigorated by new entrants fresh from the source. The traffic was one way, however. There was no possibility of feedback from the literary elders resident in the Yoruba nation, or the Igbo nation, or the Ashante nation, etc.

Africans, the new Caribbean natives, then, created the most vibrant regional literature. This vibrancy could only inform the written literature of the region when the "Manichean" gap between native and colonizer, between "orature" and literature was closed. The "orature" was consciously African. And African-Caribbean literature is by the definition articulated for this essay a literary expression that consciously evokes some aspect of the African heritage. It follows, then, that unless and until the scribal literary expression of the dominant minority was touched in some way by the vibrant oral literary tradition it could not be Caribbean.

Gabriel de la Concepción Valdés, who wrote under the pseudonym Plácido, was an almost white Cuban Romantic poet born in 1809. There is little in his work to distinguish him from his Spanish (European) contemporaries and predecessors who were the main luminaries of Romanticism and pre-Romanticism: Manuel José Quintana, José Espronceda, José Zorilla and Francisco Martínez de la Rosa. There was in Plácido's work no overt evocation of the "real" African cultural heritage. His Africans were "Moors," straight from the pages of Eurocentric Spanish literature. The criminally repressive Cuban government of the time, however, saw some glimmer of reference in his work to the plight of the hundreds of thousands of real Africans who lived in Cuba. Poor Plácido, the Eurocentric Romantic poet, was executed in 1844 for alleged complicity in a slave uprising. In terms of Cabral's Dialectical Theory of Identification, Plácido did not advance beyond the first phase, that of "Capitulation." At this stage, in the words of Frantz Fanon, "the colonized artist's writings correspond point by point with those of his opposite numbers in the mother country. His inspiration is European and we can easily link up these works with definite trends in the literature of the mother country."

Scholars have given some attention to the Spanish American equivalent of the slave narrative and the anti-slavery novel. Lorna V. Williams has contributed significantly to our appreciation of this literature with *The Representation of Slavery in Cuban Fiction*, and Edward J. Mullen's *The Life and Poems of a Cuban Slave: Juan Francisco Manzano 1797–1854* is a useful tool for research on the topic. All of this literature by our broad definition is African-Caribbean, but, in the final analysis it belongs to the "Capitulation" phase. It was absolutely contemporaneous with a vibrant oral literature created by Africans who were slaves for the most part.

In the 1920s when an effete Europe sought renewal in things African; when Picasso and his school turned to and even plagiarized traditional West African principles of composition, when white folks went, as Nicolás Guillén put it, to Harlem and Havana to look for jazz and *son*, a white-skinned Puerto Rican by the name of Luis Palés Matos began to write a so-called *poesía negrista* (focusing on Blacks). The female poetic personae were earthy, sensual, but stereotypically erotic. In his insensitive haste to recreate the spirit of the oral literature and its rhythmic use of repeated strange, non-Spanish words, Palés Matos and his followers (who were many, and almost all white) simply invented mumbo-jumbo sounds. The Cuban Alejo Carpentier is the most important of Palés Matos's aesthetic progeny, but there were many others: Ramón Guirao, José Z. Tallet, and Emilio Ballagas being the best known. The literary expression of this "Afro-Antillean" school might be deemed to pertain to the second phase of Identification, the "Revitalization" phase.

Nicolás Guillén (see separate entry) took the African-Antillean movement to its fullest potential. His art and that of other African-ancestored Cuban contemporaries, notably Marcelino Arozarena and Regino Pedroso, attained the third phase, "Radicalization." This, according to Cabral, is "the fighting phase [when] the native . . . turns himself into an awakener of the people; hence comes a fighting literature, a revolutionary literature." The Fanonian model was, however, in Cuba preempted by the Marxist-Leninist revolutionary process in which race consciousness is subsumed under the class struggle. Essentially Guillén and Cuba returned to a version of Afro-Antillean "Revitalization." Official Cuban culture is locked into this phase, and so even a singularly gifted poet like Nancy Morejón, who is of pronounced African ancestry, tends to eschew any vibrant race consciousness.

In his study *Narciso descubre su trasero: el negro en la cultura puertorriqueña*, the Puerto Rican scholar Isabelo Zenón Cruz has brilliantly demonstrated that the cultural establishment of his native land still slumbers in "Capitulation." The same is true for the Dominican Republic. Indeed, it is in Panama and Costa Rica where the blossoms of Guillen's art have evolved into real fruit. (Although these two coun-tries are culturally Caribbean, they are geographically part of Central America and will be so considered for the purposes of this Encyclopedia). Fanon has argued compellingly that "Radicalization" is the sole route to liberation and hence artistic fullness. There is no reason to question the validity of his theory.

IAN ISIDORE SMART

Further Reading

Fanon, Frantz, *Les Damnés de la terre*, Paris: Maspero, 1961; as *The Wretched of the Earth*, translated by Constance Farrington, New York: Grove Press, 1965; Harmondsworth: Penguin, 1967

Fernández Robaina, Tomás, *El negro en Cuba 1902–1958*, Havana: Ciencias Sociales, 1994

____ *Hablen paleros y santeros*, Havana: Ciencias Sociales, 1994

Kutzinski, Vera M., *Sugar's Secrets: Race and the Erotics of Cuban Nationalism*, Charlottesville: University of Virginia Press, 1993 [Principally on Cuban literature and graphics of the 19th and 20th centuries from a feminist perspective. Chapters on Plácido, Villaverde, Morúa Delgado and Guillén]

Mullen, Edward J., *The Life and Poems of a Cuban Slave: Juan Francisco Manzano 1797–1854*, Hamden, Connecticut: Archon, 1981

Valdés Cruz, Rosa, *La poesía negroide en América*, New York: Las Américas, 1970

Williams, Lorna V., *The Representation of Slavery in Cuban Fiction*, Columbia: University of Missouri Press, 1994

Wilson, Leslie N., *La poesía afroantillana*, Miami: Universal, 1979

Zapata Olivella, Manuel, *Las claves mágicas de América: raza, clase y cultura*, Bogotá: Plaza y Janés, 1989

Zenón Cruz, Isabelo, *Narciso descubre su trasero: el negro en la cultura puertorriqueña*, 2 vols, Humacao, Puerto Rico: Furidi, 1974–75

Demetrio Aguilera Malta 1909–1981

Ecuadorian prose writer

Demetrio Aguilera Malta brings to his production vast and varied experiences accumulated over the course of his long life. At one point he was a businessman in Guayaquil; at another he reported events of the Spanish Civil War from besieged Madrid; he held diplomatic posts in several Latin American countries and for a period during his youth he lived with the descendants of African and Native Americans on a remote island in the Gulf of Guayaquil. Aguilera Malta began to write and publish before he left high school and his works eventually included poetry, drama, short stories, novels, essays, screenplays and literary criticism. His plays and short stories are to be found in numerous anthologies published in various countries, four of his novels have been translated into several languages and the amount of critical attention his works have received surpasses that of any other Ecuadorian writer save Jorge Icaza, author of *Huasipungo*, 1934 (*The Villagers*). Among the claims of the extensive critical literature on Aguilera Malta is that he is one of the first practitioners of the magical realist mode in Latin American fiction.

Aguilera Malta first gained recognition in 1930 along with two other young writers from Ecuador's coast, Enrique Gil Gilbert (1912–70), and Joaquín Gallegos Lara (1911–47). The three published a collection of short stories, *Los que se van: cuentos del cholo i del montuvio* [Those Who Go Away: Stories of the Cholo and the Montuvio]. The volume's twenty-four stories of similar style scandalized Ecuador, while they drew accolades from the international literary community. Quasi-ethnic peoples of native American and African origin, *montuvios*, from the mountains, and coastal *cholos* are the protagonists of telluric incidents that often emphasize the brutal, the violent, and the crude, sometimes to the point of exaggeration. The language of the dialogue imitates coastal, Ecuadorian Spanish, and metaphors reflect the ambience and psychology of the characters. Most innovative at the time of writing is an objective narrative voice which refuses to patronize or denigrate the characters but simply implies that they are as they are. Downtrodden though they may be, the denizens of the Ecuadorian coast retain a vitality which inspires admiration. The volume marked the opening of Ecuador's Social Realist period and its three authors, together with José de la Cuadra (1903–41) and Alfredo Pareja Diezcanseco (1908–93), came to be known as the Grupo de Guayaquil.

Aguilera Malta wrote about a dozen plays. Recently returned from the Spanish Civil War, he staged his first, *España leal*, 1938 [Loyal Spain], which was his effort to heighten awareness of the conflict and garner support for the Republican cause. It was followed by *Lázaro*, 1941 [Lazarus], the tragedy of an inspired school teacher who, for lack of funding for public education, is forced to abandon his calling and to waste his time and talent on petty economic pursuits. Significantly Aguilera Malta wrote the play to raise money for a Guayaquil high school. A job as a reporter in Panama and the Canal Zone heightened his awareness of racial prejudice against Blacks. *Dientes blancos*, 1956 [White Teeth], denounces racially motivated discrimination, a theme he took up again in *Infierno negro*, 1967 [Black Hell]. In his monographic study of Aguilera Malta's dramatic works, Gerardo Luzuriaga demonstrates that Aguilera Malta's plays can be grouped into three stages which move progressively toward and culminate in the expressionistic theatrical mode of *Infierno negro*. Aguilera Malta's most anthologized play, *El tigre*, 1956 [The Jaguar], deals with a hapless peon obsessed with being devoured by a jaguar. It is developed from an incident in Aguilera Malta's second novel and will be mentioned below.

Aguilera Malta is best known for his thirteen novels, which fall into four categories. The most important works of his career are two early narratives about people of the Ecuadorian coast, *Don Goyo*, 1933 and *La isla virgen*, 1942 [The Virgin Island]. They were followed by a group of three novels written in response to specific political situations and events, the Spanish Civil War, the US occupation of the Panama Canal Zone, and the Cuban Revolution. The third category comprises three biographical-historical novels about Manuela Sáenz, Vasco Núñez de Balboa, and Francisco de Orellana. The last consists of five novels written in the 1970s that are influenced by the Latin American New Novel: *Siete lunas y siete serpientes*, 1970 (*Seven Serpents and Seven Moons*); *El secuestro del general*, 1973 (*Babelandia*); *Jaguar*, 1977 [The Jaguar]; *Réquiem para el diablo*, 1978 [Requiem for the Devil]; and *Una pelota, un sueño y diez centavos*, 1988 [A Soccer Ball, a Dream, and Ten Cents]. The last novel was left unfinished and published posthumously.

Consistent with his experience, Aguilera Malta's literary works vary widely in style, subject and theme. The last five are stylistically sophisticated and structurally complex. His first two novels are simple, but they retain greater narrative power and historical importance.

Don Goyo constitutes one of the earliest manifestations of the magical realist mode in Latin American fiction. The non-Western world view manifest in the action and attitude of the characters in *Don Goyo* sets it apart from earlier works, especially others set in the tropical forest. Don Goyo Quimí is the one hundred and fifty-year-old patriarch of an island community in the mouth of the Guayas river. He lives in communion with the tropical forest and is a spiritual extension of it; he is the guardian of an ancient tropical forest culture, and his mission is to preserve the traditional way of life of the island people. Despite his near mythical status in the community, however, he fails to fend off the economic tentacles and cultural influences that emanate from the developed Western world through the Ecuadorian port city of Guayaquil. His death symbolizes the extinction of a tropical forest culture and it is magically marked by the simultaneous fall of the greatest mangrove tree on the island. Reality in the novel is viewed from a native American rather than from a Western perspective. For Don Goyo and the inhabitants of the island the magical incidents portrayed are not miraculous but real and even mundane. Don Goyo's relationship with nature is symbiotic, not adversarial as it is in Western culture.

The distinct world views presented in *Don Goyo* are brought more sharply into focus in Aguilera Malta's second novel, *La isla virgen*. Again, the action transpires on an island in the Guayas Estuary, but now the comparison of Western and the non-Western cosmovisions is emphasized by dual protagonists who represent contrasting attitudes toward the insular, tropical habitat. Guayamabe, like Don Goyo, is a knowledgeable native of the islands; Don Nestor is the white owner of the island property who has recently taken refuge there, the last of his land holdings, after suffering financial collapse in Guayaquil. At first Nestor presumptuously ignores Guayamabe's advice and pursues schemes to exploit the Island. In time, however, he comes to recognize that he is dependent on Guayamabe for the cultural keys to adapt and live on the island, while in the process Guayamabe assumes the role of Nestor's guru in a surprisingly egalitarian relationship between European and native American.

The episode from *La isla virgen* that is the basis for the play *El tigre* takes place in a remote area of the island tropical forest, Guayamabe tries to rescue a peon, Aguayo, who is pursued over the course of several days by a jaguar. Aguayo is not from the area and is overwhelmed by the alien ambiance. His generalized fear crystalizes in an obsession with being devoured by the jaguar, and the jaguar, magically attracted by Aguayo's fear and disorientation, tenaciously stalks his victim. The fascinating episode was dramatized as *El tigre* and developed into a novel *Jaguar*.

Of the five novels written in the 1970s *Siete lunas y siete serpientes* is the most widely read. It is a parable about contemporary Latin America, cast in the archetypical framework of apocalyptic struggle, and set in a mythical town, Santorontón, similar to many towns on the Ecuadorian coast. The social, economic, political, and cultural problems that wrack Latin America are played out in microcosm by characters such as a stern but socially committed priest, a homicidal colonel,

a partially burned, talking crucifix and a black shaman. The work's sophisticated treatment of issues and its broad focus on Latin America create a distance that sets it apart from *Don Goyo* with its simple, intimate portrayal of life on a mangrove-laden island off the Ecuadorian coast. It is an irony of literary history that while Aguilera Malta's last five novels are influenced by the technical innovations and success of the writers of the Boom in Latin American fiction, *Don Goyo*, with its magical vision of reality, was a corner-stone for what would eventually become the Latin American New Novel.

C. MICHAEL WAAG

Biography

Born in Guayaquil, Ecuador, 24 May 1909. Attended Colegio Rocafuerte, Guayaquil. Founder member of the Ecuadorian Socialist Party, 1926. Studied law for two years at University of Guayaquil. Spent five years living on an island in the Gulf of Guayaquil with the local inhabitants, of American Indian and African descent. Impact of this experience evident in his creative writing. In 1930s earned his living partly from journalism. Moved to Panama in 1932; editor of the review *Hoy*. Awarded studentship at University of Salamanca, 1936, but unable to take it up because of outbreak of Spanish Civil War. Joined Spanish Republican forces and worked as journalist. Returned to Ecuador in 1937 and appointed Under Secretary at Ministry of Education. Visiting Professor at universities in Guatemala, Mexico, Brazil and United States, 1939–43. Later cultural attaché in Argentina, Brazil, Chile, Mexico and Uruguay. Invested all his money in a film, *La cadena infinita* [The Infinite Chain], which was a commercial failure. Returned to Ecuador where he made a film about the Salasaca Indians. Also made internationally acclaimed documentary film on the Rio de Janeiro carnival. Established publishing house in Quito to produce very cheap paperbacks, but this venture failed. Died in Mexico City, 29 December 1981.

Selected Works

Poetry
Primavera interior, in collaboration with Jorge Pérez Concha, Guayaquil, Ecuador: Imprenta de la Sociedad Filantrópica del Guayas, 1927
El libro de los mangleros, Guayaquil, Ecuador: n.p., 1929

Short Fiction
Los que se van: cuentos del cholo i del montuvio, in collaboration with Joaquín Gallegos Lara and Enrique Gil Gilbert, Guayaquil: Zea y Paladines, 1930
Hechos y leyendas de nuestra América: relatos hispánicos, Mexico City: Talleres Gráficos de la Nación, 1975

Novels
Don Goyo, Madrid: Cenit 1933; as *Don Goyo*, translated by John S. Brushwood and Carolyn Brushwood, Clifton, New Jersey: Humana Press, 1980
C. Z. (Canal Zone): los yanquis en Panamá, Santiago de Chile: Ercilla, 1935
Madrid: reportaje novelado de una retaguardia heróica, Barcelona: Orion, 1936
La isla virgen, Guayaquil, Ecuador: Vera y Compañía, 1942
Una cruz en la Sierra Maestra, Buenos Aires: Sophos, 1960
El Quijote de El Dorado: Orellana y el Río de las Amazonas, Madrid: Ediciones Guadarrama, 1964
La caballeresa del sol: el gran amor de Bolívar, Madrid: Ediciones Guadarrama, 1964; as *Manuela; la caballeresa del sol*, translated

by Willis Knapp Jones, Carbondale: Southern Illinois University Press, 1967

Un nuevo mar para el rey: Balboa, Anayansi y el Océano Pacífico, Madrid: Ediciones Guadarrama, 1965

Siete lunas y siete serpientes, Mexico City: Fondo de Cultura Económica, 1970; as *Seven Serpents and Seven Moons*, translated by Gregory Rabassa, Austin: University of Texas Press, 1979

El secuestro del general, Mexico City: Joaquín Mortiz, 1973; as *Babelandia*, translated by Peter G. Earle, Clifton, New Jersey: Humana Press, 1985

Jaguar, Mexico City: Grijalbo, 1977

Réquiem para el diablo, Mexico City: Joaquín Mortiz, 1978

Una pelota, un sueño y diez centavos, Mexico City: Joaquín Mortiz, 1988

Plays

España leal: tragedia en un prólogo y tres actos, el último dividido en tres cuadros, Quito: Ministerio de Educación, 1938

"Lázaro: caricaturas; tres escenas y un prólogo," *Revista del Colegio Nacional Vicente Rocafuerte* 2 (October 1941)

"Amor y vino," in collaboration with Willis Knapp Jones, *Revista de la Casa de la Cultura Ecuatoriana*, vol. 2/3 (1946)

Sangre azul, in collaboration with Willis Knapp Jones, Washington, DC: Pan American Union, 1948; as *Blue Blood*, translated by the author and Willis Knapp Jones, Washington, DC: Pan American Union, 1948

Dos comedias fáciles, Boston: Houghton Mifflin, 1950 [Includes *Sangre azul* and *El pirata fantasma*]

"No bastan los átomos" y "Dientes blancos," Quito: Casa de la Cultura Ecuatoriana, 1955

Dientes blancos, Quito: Casa de la Cultura Ecuatoriana, 1956; as "White Teeth: a Play in One Act," translated by Robert Losada Jr, *Odyssey Review* 3 (March 1963)

El tigre: pieza en un acto dividido en tres cuadros, Quito: Casa de la Cultura Ecuatoriana, 1956

Infierno negro: pieza en dos actos, Xalapa, Mexico: Universidad Veracruzana, 1967; as "Black Hell," translated by Elizabeth Lowe, *Modern International Drama* 10 (Spring 1977)

"Una mujer para cada acto," in collaboration with Velia Márquez in *Tres comedias*, Mexico City: Finisterre, 1970

Compilations and Anthologies

Trilogía ecuatoriana, teatro breve, Mexico City: Andrea, 1959

Teatro completo, Mexico City: Finisterre, 1970

Further Reading

Allen, Richard F., "La obra literaria de Demetrio Aguilera Malta," *Mundo Nuevo* 41 (1969)

Carter, Boyd G., "La novelística de Aguilera Malta: enfoques y pareceres," *Chasqui* 3 (May 1974)

Díez, Luis A., "The Apocalyptic Tropics of Aguilera Malta," *Latin American Literary Review* 10 (Spring–Summer 1982)

Fama, Anthony, "Entrevista con Demetrio Aguilera Malta," *Chasqui* 7 (May 1978)

____ *Realismo mágico en la narrativa de Aguilera Malta*, Madrid: Playor, 1978

Fama, Michael H., "*El secuestro del general, El pueblo soy yo* y 'La desmitificación del caudillo,'" *Revista Interamericana* 10 (Summer 1980)

Heise, Karl H., *El grupo de Guayaquil: arte y técnica de sus novelas sociales*, Madrid: Playor, 1975

Koldewyn, Phillip, "Protesta guerrillera y mitología: novela nueva de Aguilera Malta," *Nueva Narrativa Hispanoamericana* 5 (1975)

Luzuriaga, Gerardo A., "Aguilera Malta se incorpora a la nueva narrativa," *Nueva Narrativa Hispanoamericana* 1 (1971)

____ *Del realismo al expresionismo: el teatro de Aguilera Malta*, Madrid: Ediciones Plaza Mayor, 1971

Siemens, William L., "The Antichrist-Figure in Three Latin American Novels," in *The Power of Myth in Literature and Film*, edited by Victor Carrabino, Tallahassee: University Press of Florida, 1980

Waag, C. Michael, "Sátira política a través de la historia mitificada: *El secuestro del general* de Demetrio Aguilera Malta," *Revista Iberoamericana* 55 (1988)

____ "Absurdity, Hyperbole and the Grotesque in Demetrio Aguilera Malta's Last Novel, *Requiem para el diablo*," *SECOLAS Annals* 20 (March 1989)

Bibliographies

de Andrea, Pedro Frank, "Demetrio Aguilera Malta: bibliografía," *Boletín de la Comunidad Latinoamericana de Escritores* 5 (September 1969)

José Agustín 1944–

Mexican prose writer and dramatist

José Agustín is one of the Mexican writers credited with creating the type of novel known as *la Onda* (New Wave or "Hip" writing), a form of literary expression that appeared in Mexico in the mid-1960s and continued up to the 1970s. *La Onda* established a new generation of Mexican authors characterized by rebellion against the status quo, an interest in rock and roll, jazz and street language, together with the influence of Sartrean Existentialism, and of European art movies, particularly by directors such as Fellini and Visconti.

Agustín's first novel, *La tumba*, 1964 [The Tomb], is concerned with the lack of communication among parents and children, the overthrow of bourgeois values, and the disintegration of the nuclear family in contemporary urban society. The novel provides a negative vision of Mexican society through the eyes of an adolescent who could not care less about his life: "Porque no voy a ningún lado. Porque odio la vida" (Because I'm not going anywhere. Because I hate life). Agustín utilizes the speech of adolescents to criticize on the one hand, the upper middle class, and on the other, to provide a prophetic vision of events that will occur in Mexico four years later (the 1968 Tlatelolco massacre of students). If in 1964 adolescents in Mexico were hostile to the political system because of its corruption, conservative values and outdated traditions, they would exploit in 1968 the radical politics that united university-based adolescents in the Western world who were intent on transforming their societies. Thus *La tumba* gives voice to a young generation of Latin American adolescents who were seeking control over their own lives, access to freedom and power, and participation in the social, political, educational, and economic aspects of Third World countries. At the same time, Agustín is not averse to satirizing the anti-Establishment posturing of his own contemporaries and his early novels are not to be viewed simply as Mexico's answer to James Dean in the field of letters.

La tumba shares with *Ciudades desiertas*, 1982 [Deserted Cities], the transgression of women in society, the quest for individual identity and the demystification of male chauvinism. The novel critiques machismo and foregrounds women's feelings and beliefs together with their struggle for both power and the satisfaction of their sexual needs. The female character in this novel leaves everything behind: her home, her husband, her country, her work, and her academic career. Her quest involves a transgression of the status quo and the search for her own space.

In spite of the power that the female character wields in the specific contexts of family and class, she still wishes to achieve control over her husband through gender struggle. Agustín once more breaks with the gender hierarchy on two levels: by providing the feminine discourse with independence and power; and by demystifying the concept of the Mexican macho, something which is achieved by creating a male character who happens to be understanding and nice: "Jamás hiciste de comer ¿no? nunca quisiste tener un hijo" (You never cooked a meal right? You never wanted to have a child). Agustín uses the masculine discourse to make the feminine voice aware of her search: "Que huir de mí en realidad significa huir de ti" (That in fact by running away from me you are running away from yourself). *Ciudades desiertas* is the voice of a new generation of women in society, who wish not only to achieve a better position in the patriarchal structures, but also to obtain the freedom that will allow them to satisfy all their needs as human beings. The novel also represents an example of young Latin American couples who truly believe that communication and mutual respect will help to make the necessary transformation in their societies that are ruled by a male-dominated power structure.

Dos horas de sol, 1994 [Two Hours of Sun] shares with *La tumba* and *Ciudades desiertas* the search for identity, the use of humor, of popular speech, and of double meanings. In this work Agustín utilizes a journalistic report as a device to denounce the discrimination against minority groups (women, and the economically unprivileged), the controversies of The Free Trade Agreement among Mexico, Canada and the US (NAFTA), the denial of popular culture, the consequences of modernity, the corruption of Mexico's Institutionalized Revolutionary Party (P.R.I), the silence of subalterns, the games of power and the ecological problem.

In *Dos horas de sol*, Acapulco represents the various strata of contemporary Mexican society and therefore the report is a mere excuse to provide the reader with a guided tour of an unjust society. The bad weather and the forecast of a hurricane clearly point to the country's ailing economy, with the hurricane destroying the illusions of prosperity fostered by politicians.

Even though a feminine presence is established here through two American women, the gender struggle is overwhelmed by the masculine discourse that develops into a stronger bid for power. Agustín emphasizes authority over the petty bourgeoisie and the poor: "Para que notara quien era la autoridad, Tranquilo le indicó al Nigromante que no nada más grabara la conversación sino que también tomase notas" (Tranquilo, in order to show his friend who the boss was, asked him not only to record the interview, but also to take notes). The isolation (from Mexico City to Acapulco) and existentialist crisis function as a means of discovering personal identity and space: "Es mi vida la que se está yendo, fue lo único que pude pensar" (It's my life that is ebbing away, that was all I could think of). *Dos horas de sol* is the voice of the masculine intellectual who rebels against oppression, questions the paradigms of obedience and power, and the avowed plans to preserve the natural resources of the nation.

In *La tumba*, *Ciudades desiertas* and *Dos horas de sol*, Agustín is revealed as an author who is committed to speak out for subaltern groups in Mexico, largely marginalized and ignored by those in authority.

JUAN ANTONIO SERNA

Biography

Born José Agustín Ramírez Gómez in Huatla, a small town in the state of Oaxaca, Mexico, 19 August 1944. Spent most of his childhood and adolescence in Acapulco, a city whose atmosphere made a considerable impact on him. Worked there in a travel agency and as a hotel clerk. Attended the prestigious Simón Bolivar school in Mexico City, a place that he detested. Family settled in the Navarte district of Mexico City in 1955. At the age of sixteen married Margarita Dalton, political radical and sister of the poet Roque Dalton. Couple eloped to Cuba and participated in the literacy campaign of 1960–61. Later (in 1963) married, divorced and remarried Margarita Bermúdez. His works were best-sellers in the mid-1960s, but he could not handle the attendant publicity. Developed serious interest in film and adapted works by José Revueltas, Malcolm Lowry and Gabriel García Márquez. After the break up of his second marriage he turned to the study of psychoanalysis and to experimenting with drugs. Arrested on a drugs charge and spent seven months in Lecumberri prison. After his release he remarried Margarita Bermúdez and they had three sons, Andrés (1972), Jesús (1973) and Agustín (1975). Wrote a novel and a play (*Círculo vicioso*) based on his prison experiences: the authorities did not grant permission to have the play performed. Visiting Professor at universities in Irvine, Denver and New Mexico. Awarded the Juan Ruiz de Alarcón Prize, 1974, for *Círculo vicioso*; Colina Prize, 1982, for *Ciudades desiertas*.

Selected Works

Novels

La tumba, Mexico City: Mester, 1964
De perfil, Mexico City: Joaquín Mortiz, 1966
La nueva música clásica, Mexico City: Cuadernos de la Juventud, 1968
Abolición de la propiedad, Mexico City: Joaquín Mortiz, 1969
Se está haciendo tarde, Mexico City: Joaquín Mortiz, 1973
Círculo vicioso, Mexico City: Joaquín Mortiz, 1974
La mirada en el centro, Mexico City: Joaquín Mortiz, 1977
Ciudades desiertas, Mexico City: Edivisión, 1982
Confrontaciones, Mexico City: UNAM, 1984

Furor matutino, Mexico City: Diana, 1985
Ahí viene la plaga, Mexico City: Diana, 1985
El rock de la cárcel, Mexico City: Editores Mexicanos Unidos, 1985
Cerca del fuego, Mexico City: Plaza y Janés, 1986
No hay censura, Mexico City: Primera Narrativa Hispánica, 1988
Tragicomedia mexicana 1: La vida en México de 1940 a 1970, Mexico City: Planeta, 1990
No pases esta puerta, Mexico City: Joaquín Mortiz, 1992
Tragicomedia mexicana 2: La vida en México de 1970 a 1988, Mexico City: Planeta, 1992
La miel derramada, Mexico City: Planeta, 1992
Dos horas de sol, Mexico City: Seix Barral, 1994

Short Fiction
Inventando que sueño, Mexico City: Joaquín Mortiz, 1968
El rey se acerca a su templo, Mexico City: Grijalbo, 1978

Further Reading
Carter, June C. D. and Donald L. Schmidt, *José Agustín: Onda and Beyond*, Columbia: University of Missouri Press, 1986 [Contains valuable contributions by Juan Bruce-Novoa, John S. Brushwood, John Kirk, George R. McMurray and others, including Agustín himself]
Duncan, J. Ann, *Voices, Visions, and a New Reality: Mexican Fiction since 1970*, Pittsburgh: University of Pittsburgh Press, 1986

García Núñez, Fernando, "Notas sobre la frontera norte en la novela mexicana," *Cuadernos Americanos*, vol. 2/4 (1988)
Hadley, Scott, "José Agustín y el lenguaje coloquial literario: una entrevista," *Chasqui*, vol. 17/4 (1988)
Herz, Theda, "Artistic Iconoclasm in México: Countertexts of Arreola, Agustín, Avilés and Hiriart," *Chasqui*, vol. 18/1 (1989)
Jiménez, Antonio, "Las nuevas ondas de José Agustín: una entrevista," *Mester*, vol. 22/1 (1993)
Prado, Marcial, "Audacias lingüísticas en *De perfil* de José Agustín," *Selecta 8* (1987)
Rojas, Mario, "José Agustín y el 'rock' como poética," in *Spanish American Literature and Popular Culture*, edited by Rose S. Minc, Gaithersburg, Maryland: Hispamérica, 1981
Schaffer, Susan, "The Drug Experience in José Agustín's Fiction," *Mosaic*, vol. 19/4 (1986)
_____"The Process of Individuation in José Agustín's *Cerca del fuego*," *Mester*, vol. 21/1 (1992)
Steele, Cynthia, "Patriarchy and Apocalypse in *Cerca del fuego*, by José Agustín," *Studies in Twentieth Century Literature*, vol. 14/1 (1990)

Interviews
Teichmann, Reinhard, *De la onda en adelante: conversaciones con 21 novelistas mexicanos*, Mexico City: Posada, 1987
Torres, Francisco Vicente, *Esta narrativa mexicana: ensayos y entrevistas*, Mexico City: Leega, 1991

Delmira Agustini 1886–1914

Uruguayan poet

"Of all the women who today write poetry, none has moved me more than Delmira Agustini," wrote Rubén Darío in 1912. More than eighty years after her tragic and premature death at the age of twenty eight, killed, perhaps, by her former husband who afterwards shot himself, Agustini's poetry still "moves" all who read it. Agustini's life and work are still shrouded in mystery. How could a young woman with little formal education (she was educated mostly at home) write such accomplished poems? How could such a woman – overprotected and smothered in the bosom of a traditional, upper-middle-class family – dare to write and publish some of the most erotic feminine poems of her time?

The central topic of Agustini's poetry is love, and the desire to satisfy her spiritual and erotic needs; one recurring motif is the female subject lying in her bed, waiting for the visit of her nocturnal lover. In Agustini's poems the delights of the body acquired independent value. Further, they became an art, spiritualized in powerful images, sprouting up when least expected like "gigantic mushrooms."

Agustini wrote at a time when the *Modernismo* introduced by Darío had outmoded the Romantic movement; she carried the sensuality and eroticism expressed in some of Darío's poems to new limits. The poems in *El libro blanco*, 1907 [The White Book], may still be considered Romantic. They express

feelings of love in a sentimental and exalted manner, although the influence of the *modernistas* such as Rubén Darío, Julio Herrera y Reissig, and Leopoldo Lugones can be recognized particularly in the images: the ivory tower, swans, statues, irises, precious stones, mythological flowers and animals, mysterious castles and even more mysterious princesses.

Although at this point Agustini had not yet perfected her poetic style, her preoccupation with language and form appealing directly to the senses and emotions is evident. For example, the first two lines of the sonnet "El intruso" [The Intruder] illustrate the emotions and suffering of her tortured and captive soul: "Amor, la noche estaba trágica y sollozante / cuando tu llave de oro entró en mi cerradura" (Love, the night was tragic and sobbing / When your gold key sang in my lock).

From her second collection, *Cantos de la mañana*, 1910 [Morning Songs], to the posthumous *Los astros del abismo*, 1924 [The Stars of the Abyss], Agustini's poems became more passionate and sexually explicit; they also showed an increasing fixation with suffering, the passage of time and death. A reading of Agustini's poems play a dual role; while they project feeling of love and wonder, they also elicit sensations of anguish; there are passionate odes that turn themselves into funereal songs. Two lines from "El rosario de Eros" [The

Rosary of Eros] depict these themes: "Los lechos negros logran la más fuerte / Rosa de amor; arraigan en la muerte." (Black beds bear the strongest / rose of love, they are rooted in death).

Agustini wrote during a period of profound historical, social, and cultural change in Uruguay. Intellectual and social life was characterized by openness to diverse positions and currents. Nevertheless, this turn-of-the-century openness did not necessarily mean more sexual freedom for women. It is not surprising, then, that Agustini's poems were met with both admiration and astonishment in Montevideo's intellectual community. Instead of rebuffing or admonishing the unusual eroticism in Agustini's work, her male contemporaries referred to her as a "child prodigy," even though she was twenty when she published her first collection.

Agustini's poems expressed for the first time, and without modesty, woman's desire for complete union (and parity) with man. Whether she intended to or not, she forged the path which would be followed by Alfonsina Storni of Argentina, Gabriela Mistral of Chile, her compatriot, Juana de Ibarbourou, and others who use sexual imagery to express their most intimate desires as women.

RENÉE SCOTT

Biography

Born in Montevideo, Uruguay, 24 October 1886. Daughter of members of the bourgeoisie. Protected by mother's possessive love. Poetry developed from a distraction into a passion, but although well read she never had a library. Thus it is said that her poetry is not heavily influenced by the work of others. Using, perhaps not without irony, the pseudonym "Joujou" (a French word for toy), she wrote about women intellectuals and artists of her time. Agustini developed something of a split personality: female intellectual and young lady. Married a horse trader, Enrique Job Reyes, 14 August 1913, but left her husband six weeks later and began divorce proceedings. However, the couple continued to meet in rooms furnished according to Delmira's taste and their unusual, tormented relationship ended only when both died a violent death together. It is not known whether their death, on 6 July 1914, was the result of a suicide pact or whether Enrique Reyes first shot his wife and then himself.

Selected Works

Poetry

El libro blanco, Montevideo: O.M. Bertani, 1907 [With a prologue and illustrations]
Cantos de la mañana, Montevideo: O.M. Bertani, 1910
Los cálices vacíos, Montevideo: O.M. Bertani, 1913
Los astros del abismo, Montevideo: M. García, 1924
El rosario de Eros, Montevideo: M. García, 1924

Compilations and Anthologies

Poesías completas, prologue by A. Zum Felde, Buenos Aires: Losada, 1944
Poesías completas, edited by Magdalena García Pinto, Madrid: Cátedra, 1993

Further Reading

The "tabloid" circumstances of Agustini's death have tended to distract attention from her literary production and little serious criticism was produced before the 1980s.

García Pinto, Magdalena, "Eros in Reflection: the Poetry of Delmira Agustini," *Review* 48 (Spring 1994) [Includes several of Agustini's poems in translation]
Kirkpatrick, Gwen, "The Limits of Modernismo: Delmira Agustini and Julio Herrera y Reissig," *Romance Quarterly*, vol. 36/3 (August 1989)
Koch, Dolores, "Delmira, Alfonsina, Juana y Gabriela," *Revista Iberoamericana* 132–33 (July–December 1985)
Loynaz, Dulce María, "Delmira Agustini," in her *Ensayos literarios*, Salamanca: Ediciones Universidad de Salamanca, 1993 [Dulce María Loynaz had an extremely high opinion of Agustini's poetry, and says in this well-informed article that she would have liked to have written a study of her work]
Medina Vidal, Jorge, *et al.*, *Delmira Agustini: seis ensayos críticos*, Montevideo: Ciencias, 1982
Molloy, Sylvia, "Dos lecturas del cisne: Rubén Darío y Delmira Agustini," in *La sartén por el mango*, edited by Patricia Elena González and Eliana Ortega, Río Piedras, Puerto Rico: Huracán, 1985
Perricone, Catherine, "A Bibliographic Approach to the Study of Latin American Women Poets: Delmira Agustini," *Hispania*, vol. 71/2 (May 1988)
Rodríguez Monegal, Emir, *Sexo y poesía en el 900 uruguayo*, Montevideo: Alfa, 1969
Silva, Clara, *Genio y figura de Delmira Agustini*, Buenos Aires: Editorial Universitaria, 1968
Vitale, Ida, "Los cien años de Delmira Agustini," *Vuelta*, Mexico City, no. 2 (September 1986)

Íntima

Poem from *El Libro blanco* by Delmira Agustini

As in most of Agustini's poems, the subject of "Íntima" is love. The poetic voice addresses an ideal lover who will liberate her from a world in which she feels imprisoned. The poem is too long to be quoted in its entirety here:

> ¡Ah! tú sabrás mi amor, mas viajamos lejos
> a través de la noche florecida;
> Acá lo humano asusta, acá se oye,
> se ve, se siente sin cesar la vida.

> [Ah! You will know my love, but we travel far, / Across the flowering night; / Here what is human frightens, here life / Is endlessly heard, seen, felt].

The tone of the poem is pessimistic. The speaker in the poem feels alone, misunderstood, and yearns to satisfy her spiritual and carnal desires, something she realizes is impossible.

The poem contains erotically-charged images, uncommon at the time they were written:

> Vamos más lejos en la noche, vamos
> donde ni un eco repercuta en mí,
> como una flor nocturna allá en la sombra
> Yo abriré dulcemente para tí.

> [Let us go further into the night, let us go / where not even an echo rebounds within me, / Like a nocturnal flower over there in the shadows / I will sweetly open for you].

The spirit of the poem is still Romantic, although *modernista* undertones surface with the images of the ivory tower, the cross, icy tombs and Olympus. There is an evident search for musical forms in which to express ideas and states of mind. Also present are two constant themes in her poetry: tragic destiny and erotic desire.

Otra estirpe

Poem from Los cálices vacíos by Delmira Agustini

Here, the speaker in the poem no longer addresses a flesh and blood lover, but rather Eros, God of Love, to whom she offers *Los cálices vacíos*, recognizing that only a supreme force would be able to satisfy her most intimate yearnings and be worthy of her surrender.

Feminine sexuality is expressed openly in this poem. Eros is presented as a human being to whom the poet wishes to make love in order to satisfy her unlimited desire. The language and the images surge naturally throughout the poem to express an intense and pathetic eroticism. The poem is quoted in its entirety:

Eros, yo quiero guiarte, Padre ciego . . .
Pido a tus manos todopoderosas,
¡su cuerpo excelso derramado en fuego
Sobre mi cuerpo desmayado en rosas!
La eléctrica corola que hoy despliego
Brinda el nectario de un jardín de Esposas;
para sus buitres en mi carne entrego
Todo un enjambre de palomas rosas!

Da a las dos sierpes de su abrazo, crueles,
Mi gran tallo febril . . . Absintio, mieles,
Viérteme de sus venas, de su boca . . .
¡Así tendida soy un surco ardiente,
Donde puede nutrirse la simiente,
De otra Estirpe sublimamente loca!

[Eros, I wish to guide you, Blind father / I ask for your all-powerful hands, / His sublime body overflowing on fire / upon my body swooning among the roses! // The electric corola that I spread out today / Offers all the nectar of a Brides' garden; / to its vultures I deliver with my flesh / An entire swarm of rose-coloured doves! // Give my great febrile stem to the cruel embrace of the two serpents . . . / Absinthe, honey, / Pour me out of his veins, his mouth . . . / Thus spread out I am a furrow on fire / Where the seed of sublimely mad new beings may be nourished!]

The erotic tension in the poem is constructed on opposite elements: fire/rose, vultures/doves, and as in other Agustini's poems sexual desire is associated with death, as the final stanza makes clear.

Los cálices vacíos contains twelve poems, and each one, by virtue of images charged with mystery and beauty, is a small literary gem, the manifestations of a gifted woman whose extraordinary voluptuousness is sublimated in poetry.

RENÉE SCOTT

poems translated by Renée Scott and Verity Smith

Editions
First editions: *El libro blanco*, Montevideo: O.M. Bertani, 1907
Los cálices vacíos, Montevideo: O.M. Bertani, 1913

Claribel Alegría 1924 –

Salvadorean prose writer, poet and literary translator

The work of Claribel Alegría is finally attracting the critical attention it deserves after decades of relative obscurity. She is now being acknowledged as one of Central America's foremost poetic voices. Much of this belated attention is the result of the formidable task undertaken by her translators (Darwin Flakoll, Amanda Hopkinson and Carolyn Forché among others) in bringing her work to the attention of an international English-speaking public. Alegría's work encompasses a considerable range of genres, incorporating poetry, novels, novellas and short stories. Like many other women writers in Latin America, she has also published for children and displays a keen interest in literary translation. In collaboration with her husband, Darwin Flakoll, Claribel Alegría has translated (either into or from Spanish) the work of a range of writers, including Salman Rushdie, Robert Graves and Miguel Ángel Asturias.

There is an undoubted political resonance in Alegría's work, articulated directly, but also ironically and allegorically in many of her poems and stories. Forceful too is the prevailing presence of women in Alegría's work and her commitment to invest the voiceless with the power of the word. There is a palpable sense of solidarity throughout her work, though perhaps it is in her later prose works like *Album familiar*, 1982 (*Family Album*) and *No me agarran viva*, 1983 (*They Won't Take Me Alive*) that this becomes more evident. Much of Alegría's work is realist narrative, with straightforward plot lines invested with multiple layers of symbolic meaning. *Luisa en el país de la realidad*, 1987 (*Luisa in Realityland*), deviates most obviously from this path with its unusual structure of poems, vignettes and short stories.

Such a range of literary output renders any critical analysis challenging and, up to the mid-1990s, only one book – a collection of essays on her work – has been published (1994). It is rather useful for the purpose of analysis to employ her own terminology which she has devised to compartmentalise her work. She labels one strand of her work "crisis journalism;" her direct response to the political situation in Central America, which finds its best expression in her testimonial work. The second strand is better defined as literary poetics or the more lyrical subjective strand, and this one is manifested eloquently by her many collections of poetry.

Alegría is probably best known as a poet, and she has published fifteen collections of poetry since 1948. Her early poetry is lyrical, sensuous and introverted but the recurring motifs of her work – suffering, silence and death are all present in these collections; *Anillo de silencio* [Ring of Silence], *Vigilias* [Vigils], *Acuario* [Aquarium], and *Huésped de mi tiempo* [Guest of My Time]. The call at the end of one of her first poems "Aquí estoy" (Here I Am) for an island without protective walls, where all voices can be heard, is one which reverberates throughout her poetic career: "Y llévame a una isla sin murallas / donde lleguen a mí todas las voces." (And take me to an island without stout walls / where every voice may reach me.)

Alegría isolates the Cuban Revolution of 1959 as a turning-point in her literary trajectory and one which made her work overtly political. She has always distanced herself from any categorisation as a political poet saying: "I consider my poetry love poems to my people." She defines Central America, however, as her major obsession , which she cannot help but confront in her poetry.

There are many notable influences on Alegría's poetry, mainly Juan Ramón Jiménez with whom she studied in Washington, DC while pursuing a degree course in the Arts. Emily Dickinson is another poet to whom Alegría is much indebted, to the extent that she has even suggested that she could be accused of plagiarism. This influence is perhaps most noticeable in the 1978 collection *Sobrevivo* [I Survive] which won a Casa de las Américas prize, confirming Alegría as a poet of international stature.

Archbishop Romero's assassination in San Salvador (1980) proved to be another decisive moment in Alegría's career and the ensuing decade saw her interest in politics receive vivid expression in her work. The yearning to articulate the pain of her own exile from El Salvador (she returned only in 1991 and has chosen to live in Nicaragua and Mallorca since 1982) is fervently evoked in her poem "Mallorca – mi paraíso" [Majorca – My Paradise] in which she details the phantoms that crowd her thoughts and restrict her attempts to gain peace of mind. The 1980s saw a more sustained interest in fiction but she returned to what she terms her "pasión" in 1987 with the publication of *Luisa en el país de la realidad*, (translated as *Luisa in Realityland* and published, interestingly, before the Spanish version). *Luisa en el país de la realidad* is a series of anecdotes, poems and vignettes that interweave to create a fragmented picture of its young protagonist Luisa. The autobiographical tone of the book is unmistakeable, a tone that permeates many other prose works by Alegría, for example

El detén, 1977 [The Detainee] and *Cenizas de Izalco*, 1966 (*Ashes of Izalco*). *Luisa en el país de la realidad* is a complex portrait of female identity and is in many ways Alegría's most mature work. The feminist concerns of her work are forcefully present but are couched in humorous and ironic terms, as in Luisa's prayer at First Communion: "Niñito Jesús," dijo Luisa en voz baja, "Yo no me quiero casar, no me gusta como son los hombres con las mujeres, pero quiero tener un hijo, niñito Jesús. La Chaba dice que sólo las mujeres casadas pueden tener hijos, por eso yo te pido con toda mi alma que me case y que cuando tenga el niño mi marido se muera. La hostia se le acabó de deshacer en la boca y Luisa levantó la mirada. Una sonrisa beatífica la iluminaba el rostro." ("Dear Little Jesus," Luisa said under her breath, "I don't want to be married; I don't like the way men treat women, but I do want to have a baby, Dear Jesus, and Chabe says that only married women can have babies. So that's why I ask you with all my heart to let me get married, and as soon as I have my baby, to let my husband die." The host dissolved in her mouth, and Luisa lifted her gaze, a beatific smile illuminating her features.)

Much of her other poetry is of the testimonial kind or the related "letras de emergencia" (emergency letters), in which the terror and the threat of successive political regimes in El Salvador are elegantly expressed, but indirectly and often ironically. Revealing examples of this are the poems "Pequeña patria" [Little Homeland] and "Mis adioses" [My Goodbyes] from the collection *Aprendizaje*, 1970 [Apprenticeship]. Alegría has definitively returned again to poetry and has been writing a long autobiographical poem entitled "Umbrales" [Thresholds], published in 1996.

Alegría's earliest attempt at prose (with the exception of a book of children's stories published in 1958) was a joint project with her husband Darwin Flakoll. The very successful *Cenizas de Izalco* details the events of the 1932 massacre (La Matanza) that took place when government troops brutally slaughtered over 30,000 peasants after a peaceful uprising. Alegría testified personally to these events and remained traumatized for many years afterwards by the tragic scenes witnessed in the aftermath of the uprising. *Cenizas de Izalco*, in common with her poetry, does not deal with the terror directly, but recounts the story of illicit love between the protagonist's mother, Carmen, and her North American lover, Frank. The affair is recalled by his diaries, found many years after Carmen's death, and read now by her daughter. Impeccably crafted, the diaries are a painful reconstruction of Carmen's life and a cathartic method of release for the protagonist who is trying to come to terms with her mother's death. They also bear eloquent testimony to the massacre; the violence erupts in the final section and has a catatonic effect that is savage and compelling. The book is a remarkable narrative skein that aims to excavate and recover El Salvador's past. Ironically, *Cenizas de Izalco* has been a secondary school textbook in El Salvador since 1977, benefitting from some more progressive tendencies within the Ministry of Education. It successfully passed the government's official censors due possibly to its subtle and often muted critical treatment of the political regime.

This joint project was the first of many undertaken with Darwin Flakoll and efforts to recreate parts of her country's history were realized again in 1983 with the publication of *No me agarran viva*. This project was the first of two experiments with the testimonial form of the novel. *No me agarran viva* is a deftly constructed collage of interviews, observations and historical background that recounts the story of one of the *guerrilleras* during the struggle of the FMLN (Farabundo Martí Liberation Front). It is a powerful and sensitive portrait of Eugenia as revolutionary, leader, mother and political visionary. The English translation of *No me agarran viva* in 1987 ensured a greater reading public for Alegría and secured her reputation as a writer with major political concerns. The experiment with *testimonio* was repeated in 1984 with *Para romper el silencio* [To Break the Silence]. In this novel Alegría reconstructs a series of interviews with Salvadorean prisoners. The concern with the voiceless and the silenced of El Salvador's society is again articulated.

Alegría continues to write, publishing *On the Front Line* (an anthology of *guerilla* poetry with Darwin Flakoll) in 1990 and has recently devoted much time to literary translation (a translation of thirty Irish poems is forthcoming). She continues to travel extensively in a bid to communicate part of her Central American heritage to a wider public. In her poetry, prose, translations and other work she has left a resounding legacy that poignantly captures the intersection of her private self with that of the social and historical dimension of her people.

NUALA FINNEGAN

Biography

Born in Estelí, Nicaragua, 12 May 1924, but grew up in El Salvador and considers herself Salvadorean. Family forced into political exile in El Salvador, 1925. Attended José Ingenieros school, El Salvador, 1929; finishing school, Hammond, Louisiana, 1943; won scholarship and spent summer term at Loyola University, New Orleans, 1944; George Washington University, Washington, DC, received B.A.in 1948. Married Darwin J. Flakoll in 1947; three daughters and one son. First poetry collection published, 1948. Moved to Mexico, 1951 and to Santiago de Chile, 1953 where she and her husband worked on an anthology of Latin American writers; returned to the United States, 1956. Accompanied her husband on diplomatic posting to Argentina, 1960, and the couple lived in Paris, 1962, Palma Nova, Mallorca, 1966, Deyá, Mallorca, 1968. Travelled to Nicaragua in 1979 after the Sandinistas had taken power. Following the assassination of Archbishop Romero, Alegría denounced the government atrocities in Nicaragua and as a result became a political exile from El Salvador. Returned to Nicaragua in 1983. Awarded the Casa de las Américas Prize, 1978, for *Sobrevivo*.

Selected Works

Poetry

Anillo de silencio, Mexico City: Botas, 1948
Suite de amor, angustia y soledad, San Rafael, Mendoza: Brigadas Líricas, 1951
Vigilias, Mexico City: Poesía de América, 1953
Acuario, Santiago de Chile: Editorial Universitaria, 1955
Huésped de mi tiempo, Buenos Aires: Américalee, 1961
Vía única, Montevideo: Alfa, 1965
Aprendizaje, San Salvador: Editorial Universitaria, 1970
Pagaré a cobrar y otros poemas, Barcelona: Ocnos, 1973
Sobrevivo, Havana: Casa de las Américas, 1978
La mujer del rio Sumpul, Colombia: Museo Rayo, 1987; as *Woman of the River*, translated by Darwin J. Flakoll, Pittsburgh: University of Pittsburgh Press, 1989 [bilingual edition]

Y este poema-río, Managua: Nueva Nicaragua, 1988
Fuga de canto grande, in collaboration with Darwin J. Flakoll, San Salvador: UCA, 1992; as *Fugues*, translated by Darwin J. Flakoll, Willimantic, Connecticut: Curbstone Press, 1993 [bilingual edition]
Variaciones en clave de mí, Madrid: Libertarias/Prodhufi, 1993

Novels and Short Fiction

Cenizas de Izalco, in collaboration with Darwin J. Flakoll, Barcelona: Seix Barral, 1966; as *Ashes of Izalco*, translated by Darwin J. Flakoll, Willimantic, Connecticut: Curbstone Press, 1989
El detén, Barcelona: Lumen, 1977
Album familiar, San José, Costa Rica: Universitaria Centroamericana, 1982; augmented edition, Barcelona: Lumen, 1986; as *Family Album: Three Novellas*, translated by Amanda Hopkinson, London: Women's Press, 1990; Willimantic, Connecticut: Curbstone Press, 1991
Pueblo de Dios y de mandinga, Mexico City: Era, 1985
Despierta mi bien, despierta, San Salvador: UCA, 1986

Testimonial and Other Writings

Tres cuentos, San Salvador: Ministry of Culture, 1958 [for children]
Nicaragua: la revolución sandinista: una crónica política, 1855–1979, in collaboration with Darwin J. Flakoll, Mexico City: Era, 1982 [testimonial]
No me agarran viva: la mujer salvadoreña en lucha, Mexico City: Era, 1983; as *They Won't Take Me Alive: Salvadoran Women in Struggle for National Liberation*, translated by Amanda Hopkinson, London: Women's Press, 1987 [testimonial]
Para romper el silencio, Mexico City: Era, 1984 [testimonial]
Luisa en el país de la realidad, Mexico City: Universidad Autónoma de Zacatecas, 1987; as *Luisa in Realityland*, translated by Darwin J. Flakoll, Willimantic, Connecticut: Curbstone Press, 1987 [mixed genre]
Somoza, expediente cerrado, la historia de un ajusticiamiento, in collaboration with Darwin J. Flakoll, Managua: Latino Editores, 1993

Compilations and Anthologies

Suma y sigue, Madrid: Visor, 1981
Flowers from the Volcano, translated by Carolyn Forché, Pittsburgh: University of Pittsburgh Press, and London: Feffer and Simons, 1982 [bilingual edition]
Petit Pays, Paris: Femmes, 1983
Poesía viva, London: El Salvador Solidarity Campaign, 1984 [bilingual edition]
Lovers and Comrades: Womens' Resistance Poetry from Central America, translated by Amanda Hopkinson, London: Women's Press, 1989

Further Reading

Acevedo, Ramón Luis, *Los senderos del volcán: narrativa centroamericana contemporánea*, Guatemala City: Editorial Universitaria, 1991 [Contains an essay on *Cenizas de Izalco*]
Arenal, Electra, "Two Poets of the Sandinista Struggle," *Feminist Studies*, vol. 7/1 (1981) [Discussion of *Sobrevivo* and *Línea de fuego* by Gioconda Belli]
Beverley, John and Marc Zimmerman, *Literature and Politics in the Central American Revolutions*, Austin: University of Texas Press, 1990 [Alegría is discussed in the chapter on Salvadorean revolutionary poetry]
Boschetto-Sandoval, Sandra M. and Marcia Phillips McGowan, *Claribel Alegría and Central American Literature: Critical Essays*, Athens: Ohio University Center for European Studies, 1994

Coronel Utrecho, José, *Líneas para un boceto de Claribel Alegría*, Managua: Nueva Nicaragua, 1989

Rojas, Mario A., "Some Central American Writers of Liberation," in *Culture, Human Rights and Peace in Central America*, edited by George F. McLean, *et al.*, Lanham, Maryland: University Press of America, 1989

Sternbach, Nancy Saporta, " Claribel Alegría: Nicaragua, El Salvador," in *Escritoras de Hispanoamérica: una guía bio-bibliográfica*, edited by Diane E. Marting, Mexico City: Siglo XXI, 1990

____ "Remembering the Dead: Latin American Women's 'Testimonial' Discourse," *Latin American Perspectives*, vol. 18/3 (Summer 1991) [On *No me agarran viva* and *Flowers from the Volcano*]

Yúdice, George, "Letras de emergencia: Claribel Alegría," *Revista Iberoamericana*, vol. 51/132–33 (July–December 1985)

Zamora, Daisy, *La mujer nicaragüense en la poesía*, Managua: Nueva Nicaragua, 1992

Zimmerman, Marc, *El Salvador at War: a Collage Epic*, Minneapolis: Marxist Education Press, 1988

Zoreda, Margaret Lee, "La función pública-política del escritor: Hannah Arendt y Claribel Alegría," *Iztapalapa*, vol. 10/21 (1990)

Interviews

Forché, Carolyn, "Interview with Claribel Alegría," *Index on Censorship*, vol. 13/2 (1984)

Graham-Yool, Andrew, "Claribel Alegía: the Smile Amid the Sadness," in *After the Despots: Latin American Views and Interviews*, London: Bloomsbury, 1991

José de Alencar 1829–1877

Brazilian novelist

José de Alencar was not the first Brazilian novelist, but he did establish the genre as central to the nation's literature. This was a more considerable accomplishment than it might appear today, when we take for granted the utility of prose fiction as a vehicle for communicating both emotions and ideas. In the 1850s, however, when Alencar began experimenting with the novel, Brazilian intellectuals generally viewed the novel with a combination of disdain and trepidation. The novel, in their eyes, was a very recent European invention, far inferior in literary quality and potential to poetry and didactic prose. It was seen as very much a popular genre, designed to appeal to the poorly-educated and unsophisticated. Moreover, the novel's popularity among unsophisticated readers – a group defined, at this point, as including all of the nation's very small number of female readers – made it appear particularly dangerous to the traditional values and social stability of Brazil. Such readers might not be able to distinguish between reality and fiction, and might come to believe that the social patterns reflected in contemporary European fiction – for example, the idea that true romantic love could overcome parental opposition and disparities of social class – could or should apply within the far more rigid and hierarchical context of Brazilian society, a society in which virtually all upper-class marriages were arranged.

Near the end of his life, Alencar claimed to have begun his career as a novelist with a master plan to produce a series of texts, a tapestry of all of Brazilian life and history from before the arrival of the Portuguese in 1500 to the second half of the 19th century; those texts would refine or initiate a set of sub-genres of the novel – the indianist novel, the Brazilian historical novel, the regionalist novel, and the novel of urban life. The end result, as he very accurately described it, was the creation of an independent national literature in prose. He appears to have believed, moreover, that this goal was a natural extension of his family's important role in the nation's political independence during the 1820s.

In fact, however, there was no master plan; Alencar became a novelist almost by chance, and the fundamental changes he brought to the genre in Brazil were in large measure the result of circumstance and of his efforts to respond to the special challenges the novel confronted within the context of Brazilian society. In 1856, Alencar published a series of pseudonymous letters attacking the form and conception of an indianist epic by one of the founders of Brazilian romanticism, Domingos José Gonçalves de Magalhães (1811–82); these letters make it clear that Alencar, while unhappy with this particular text, still believed that epic poetry was the only genre suitable for the expression of national history and national pride. At the same time, eager to boost the circulation of the newspaper he edited in Rio de Janeiro, Alencar began serializing his first novel, *Cinco minutos* [Five Minutes]. This sentimental novel of mystery and passion was well-received by his readers, and he began a second serialization, *A viuvinha* [The Widow], early in 1857.

As Alencar wrote *A viuvinha*, however, he quite suddenly came to an important realization: Brazilian fiction was not necessarily limited to contemporary settings. He stopped the serialization of *A viuvinha* and began publishing *O guarani* [The Guarani Indian], the first indianist novel. *O guarani*'s 17th-century setting, Alencar discovered, allowed him to finesse the central problem of earlier Brazilian novels: the need to combine realistic descriptions of contemporary urban environments familiar to his readers with imported plot structures which were inherently unrealistic within the context of Brazilian society. Novels set in the national past or in the distant and unknown interior of Brazil could ignore reality or, more precisely, could create their own reality – and that created reality could be utilized to construct both a mythic national history and a national identity.

This concept of the novel as national mythology can be seen in *O guarani* and in Alencar's historical novels about the colonial past, but is clearest in his 1865 masterpiece, *Iracema* (*Iracema, the Honey-Lips, a Legend of Brazil*), the most overtly mythical of all 19th-century novels of the Americas. This charming and deeply poetic tale of the beautiful Indian maiden Iracema and her Portuguese lover Martim Soares Moreno, set on the coast of Ceará in the early 16th century, remains the most popular of all Brazilian novels. At a deeper level, the relationship between Iracema, the "virgin of the forests" whose name is an anagram of "America," and Martim, "the warrior of the sea," is a national Genesis; Iracema dies at the novel's end, symbolizing the inevitable destruction of the Indian world, but she first gives birth to their son Moacir, whose name means "child of pain." Moacir, the fusion of the Indian and Portuguese pasts, the product of both the forests and the sea, is the first Brazilian.

Alencar and his readers viewed his regionalist novels – descriptions of the landscapes and customs of specific regions of the nation – as equally important in establishing a national identity. Alencar largely invented the regionalist sub-genre in his *O gaúcho* [The Gaucho] of 1870. It is one mark of the novelist's enduring influence that subsequent writers, intimately familiar with the areas Alencar described in his regionalist fiction but which he, in most cases, had never actually visited, have frequently felt compelled to reproduce his quite inaccurate descriptions of those regions.

At the same time, Alencar continued to produce a few novels of contemporary Brazilian urban life. These texts have long been overshadowed by his indianist and regionalist fiction, but have recently attracted considerable attention. It is increasingly clear that these works, beginning with *Lucíola*, 1862 [Lucíola], Alencar's novel of prostitution, represent a conscious effort to move away from the tradition of the sentimental novel in Brazil, a tradition best represented by the texts of Joaquim Manuel de Macedo (1820–82) and by Alencar's own *Cinco minutos* and *A viuvinha*. These later urban novels, first, introduce a level of detail, in their descriptions of the artifacts of contemporary life, which is comparable to that of European and North American Realism; equally a part of the Realist tradition is Alencar's evident belief in the novelist's ability to represent the totality of reality through such detail, and to link both social class and individual personality to the artifacts which surround his characters. Second, these novels reflect an attempt to move away from earlier attempts to adapt European plots, to the Brazilian context; rather, Alencar is endeavoring, not always successfully, to utilize the specific social patterns of Brazilian society as integral components of the plot structure. And, finally, Alencar departs dramatically from the norm of the 19th-century Brazilian novel in his creation of strong and relatively independent female characters at the very center of his texts, a departure that can be seen in *Iracema* as well as in these urban novels. Alencar believed very strongly in the need to educate Brazilian women of all classes, something very close to heresy at the time, not just because he wanted to increase the market for fiction but because he held the very modern conviction that women were the key agents of social change and modernization. Traces of this conviction can be seen even in his earliest novels, but it is fully and remarkably developed in the best and most interesting of his urban texts, the overtly feminist *Senhora* (*Senhora: Profile of a Woman*) of 1875. It is one of the ironies of Alencar's career that his efforts, in these later urban novels, to move the Brazilian novel towards Realism in both detail and plot and to encourage the modernization of Brazilian society were negated, a few years after the publication of *Senhora*, by the appearance of Naturalist novelists like Aluísio Azevedo, whose primary message was the danger of social change in general and, in particular, of female challenges to patriarchy.

DAVID T. HABERLY

Biography

Born José Mariniano de Alencar in Ceará, Brazil, 1 May 1829. Son of a prominent liberal politician (of the same name). Moved to Rio de Janeiro with family in 1838. Read law at São Paulo Law School, and later at Recife Law School, Pernambuco. Worked in law office, Rio de Janeiro, 1850. From 1853 began to contribute to newspapers in Rio de Janeiro (also published under the pseudonym "Ig"). Conservative deputy, Ceará, 1860; minister of justice, Imperial Cabinet, 1868–70 (resigned, and abandoned political career after conflict with the emperor). Intensely interested in Brazilian national literature, language of the aboriginal Indians, and interior regions of Brazil. Died in Rio de Janeiro, 12 December 1877.

Selected Works

Novels

Cinco minutos, Rio de Janeiro: *Diário do Rio de Janeiro*, 1856
A viuvinha, Rio de Janeiro: *Diário do Rio de Janeiro*, 1857
O guarani, Rio de Janeiro: *Diário do Rio de Janeiro*, 1857
As minas de prata, 1 vol., Rio de Janeiro: Biblioteca Brasileira, 1862; complete work, 6 vols, Rio de Janeiro: Garnier, 1865–66
Lucíola: um perfil de mulher, Rio de Janeiro: Biblioteca Brasileira, 1862
Diva: perfil de mulher, Rio de Janeiro: Biblioteca Brasileira, 1864
Iracema: lenda do Ceará, Rio de Janeiro: Viana, 1865; as *Iracema, the Honey-Lips, a Legend of Brazil*, translated by Sir Richard and Lady Isabel Burton, London: Bickers and Son, 1886; New York: H. Fertig, 1976; centennial edition, Rio de Janeiro: Instituto Nacional do Livro, 1965; critical edition, edited by Manuel Cavalcanti Proença, Rio de Janeiro: José Olympio, 1965
O gaúcho, 2 vols, Rio de Janeiro: Garnier, 1870
A pata da gazila, Rio de Janeiro: Garnier, 1870
O tronco do ipê, 2 vols, Rio de Janeiro: Garnier, 1871
Til, 4 vols, Rio de Janeiro: Garnier, 1872
Sonhos d'ouro, Rio de Janeiro: Garnier, 1872
Alfarrábios: crônicas dos tempos coloniaes
  1. *O Garatuja*, Rio de Janeiro: Garnier, 1873
  2. *O ermitão da Glória* and *A alma do Lazaro*, Rio de Janeiro: Garnier, 1873
A guerra dos Mascates, 2 vols, Rio de Janeiro: Garnier, 1873–74
Ubirajara: lenda tupi, Rio de Janeiro: Garnier, 1874; as *Ubirajara: a Legend of the Tupi Indians*, translated by J.T.W. Sadler, London: Ronald Massey, 1922
O sertanejo, 2 vols, Rio de Janeiro: Garnier, 1875
Encarnação, Rio de Janeiro: Garnier, 1875
Senhora, 2 vols, Rio de Janeiro: Garnier, 1875; as *Senhora: Profile of a Woman*, translated by Catarina Feldmann Edinger, Austin: University of Texas Press, 1994
O que tinha de ser, Rio de Janeiro: Garnier, 1912

Plays

O demônio familiar, Rio de Janeiro: Soares e Irmão, 1857
A noite de S. João, Rio de Janeiro: Soares e Irmão, 1857
O Rio de Janeiro, Rio de Janeiro: Soares e Irmão, 1857
As asas de um anjo, Rio de Janeiro: Soares e Irmão, 1860
Mãe, Rio de Janeiro: Ginasio Dramático, 1862
A expiação, Rio de Janeiro: Garnier, 1867
O Jesuíta, Rio de Janeiro: Garnier, 1867; as *The Jesuit*, translated
   by Edgardo R. de Britto, in *Poet Lore* 30 (1919)

Other Writings

O marquês de Caxias: biografia, Rio de Janeiro: Garnier, 1867

Compilations and Anthologies

Obra completa, 4 vols, Rio de Janeiro: Aguilar, 1959
Teatro completo, 2 vols, Rio de Janeiro: Ministerio de Educação e
   Cultura, 1977

Further Reading

The listings below include both some standard critical studies and
biographies, together with samples of recent criticism which has
focused on comparative studies of indianism in the New World and
on feminist readings of the novels.

Ao correr da pena, São Paulo, 1874 [weekly chronicles published
   by the *Correio Mercantil* and *Diário do Rio de Janeiro*,
   1854–55]
Faria, João Roberto Gomes, "José de Alencar: a polêmica em torno
   da adaptação teatral de *O guarani*," *Letras*, Curitiba, Brasil, 31
   (1972)
Freyre, Gilberto, *José de Alencar*, Rio de Janeiro: Ministério da
   Educação e Cultura, 1952
Girão, Raimundo, "Ecologia de um poema," *Cla*, Fortaleza, Brazil,
   vol. 17/21 (1963)

___ *Botânica cearense na obra de Alencar e caminhos de
   "Iracema,"* Fortaleza, Brazil: Imprensa Universitária da
   Universidade Federal do Ceará, 1976
Magalhães, Jr, Raimundo, *José de Alencar e a sua época*, São Paulo:
   Civilização Brasileira, 1971
Marco, Valéria de, *O império da cortesã: Luciola, um perfil de
   Alencar*, São Paulo: M. Fontes, 1986
___ *A perda das ilusões: o romance histórico de José de Alencar*,
   Campinas, São Paulo: Unicamp, 1993
Martins, Cláudio, *Cem anos depois*, Fortaleza, Brazil: Imprensa
   Universitária da Universidade Federal do Ceará, 1977 [Includes
   essays by Joaryvar Macedo, Manuel Cavalcanti Proença,
   Raimundo de Menezes, Fran Martins, and Sanzio de Azevedo]
Menezes, Raimundo de, *José de Alencar: literato e político*, São
   Paulo: Martins, 1965
Pontieri, Regina Lúcia, *A voragem do olhar*, São Paulo: Perspectiva,
   1988
Proença, Manuel Cavalcanti, *José de Alencar na literatura brasileira*,
   Rio de Janeiro: Civilização Brasileira, 1966
Schwarz, Roberto, *A sereia e o desconfiado: ensaios críticos*, Rio de
   Janeiro: Civilização Brasileira, 1965; 2nd edition, 1981
___ *Ao vencedor as batatas: forma literária e processo social nos
   inícios do romance brasileiro*, São Paulo: Duas Cidades, 1977
Sommer, Doris, *Foundational Fictions: the National Romances of
   Latin America*, Berkeley: University of California Press, 1991
   [Chapter 5 is on *O guaraní* and *Iracema*]
Viana Filho, Luís, *A vida de José de Alencar*, Rio de Janeiro: José
   Olympio, 1979
Wasserman, Renata R. Mautner, *Exotic Nations: Literature and
   Cultural Identity in the United States and Brazil, 1830–1930*,
   Ithaca, New York: Cornell University Press, 1994
Wolff, Maria Tai, "*Luciola*: Critical Frames," *Bulletin of Hispanic
   Studies*, vol. 65/1 (1988)
Zilberman, Regina, "Natureza e mulher: uma visão do Brasil no
   romance romântico," *Modern Language Studies*, vol. 19/2
   (1989)

Jacques-Stéphen Alexis 1922–1961(?)

Haitian novelist

Jacques-Stéphen Alexis's place in the history of Haitian letters
should remain secure for several reasons. Along with his
contemporaries Jacques Roumain and René Depestre, he was
one of the first Haitian writers to attain an international reputation: his works, recently published in popular collections by
Gallimard, have remained in print for over thirty years and
have been widely translated; further, they were seminal in indicating the directions that Haitian fiction was going to take;
Alexis is also one of the very few of Haiti's writers to have
authored theoretical reflexions on the nation's literature; finally,
his death during the tyranny of François Duvalier added his
name to the martyrology of writers who gave their lives in the
cause of human dignity.

Alexis's often quoted theoretical texts, especially "Du réalisme merveilleux des Haïtiens," 1956 [On the Haitians'
Marvellous Realism] and "Débat autour des conditions d'un

roman national chez les peuples noirs: où va le roman?" 1957
[Debate on the Conditions of a National Novel produced by
Black Peoples: Where is the Novel Heading To?], actually did
little more than elaborate upon the ideas regarding literary
matters that his mentor Jean Price-Mars had outlined in the
1920s and 1930s in *Ainsi parla l'Oncle*, 1928 (*So Spoke
the Uncle*) and other works. Both essayists stressed the definition and cultivation of national authenticity (as opposed to
the imitation of Parisian models) and the adoption of popular
(as opposed to aristocratic and middle-class) culture as a source
of inspiration. They encouraged the judicious inclusion of
Creole expressions in French texts, but never proposed the
abandonment of French or the creation of a literature in the
vernacular; neither man, for that matter, ever wrote in Creole.
However, while Price-Mars, the "Father of *Négritude*," saw
the aesthetic celebration of what was national and popular as

a form of collective therapy for the treatment of the class, color and cultural divisions which afflicted the Black Republic, Alexis saw them rather as an integral part and an important factor in the political struggle for the dictatorship of the proletariat and the subsequent advent of a classless society.

At the risk of over simplification, each of Alexis's novels can be characterized by its principal theme. *Compère Général Soleil* [Comrade General Sun] is a proletarian novel with a Marxist perspective; it recounts the life of Hilarion, an illiterate petty thief, whose social conscience is awakened and developed in prison by his cell mate, the political prisoner Pierre Roumel (a transparent incarnation of Jacques Roumain). *Les Arbres musiciens* [The Music-Making Trees] can be considered as a peasant novel in so far as the action takes place in the lovingly evoked countryside. Peasant everyday life is described at length, and the struggle betweeen a benevolent and a malevolent voodoo priest for the leadership of the rural community forms an important secondary plot. *L'Espace d'un cillement* [In the Space of a Blink] stresses Alexis's preoccupation with Caribbean brotherhood: his main protagonist is La Niña (The Girl), a Cuban prostitute working in a Port-au-Prince dive, and her redemption by a half-Haitian, half-Cuban ship's mechanic. The stories included in the collection *Romancero aux étoiles* [Romancero with Stars] are further variations on these themes, as well as French adaptations of Creole traditional folk-tales, and a celebration of Anacaona, the Arawak queen traitorously put to death by the Conquistadors, whom Haitians have always considered their first national heroine.

Haitian history is a preoccupation Alexis shares with most of his fellow Haitian writers. In *Compère Général Soleil*, for example, he evokes the 1937 "Dominican Vespers," as the massacre by Trujillo's thugs of several thousand Haitians who had settled on the other side of the border with the Dominican Republic came to be known. The central plot of *Les Arbres musiciens* concerns the forced dispossession of peasants in 1941 by the American owners of SHADA (in English: Haitian-American society for the Development of Agriculture) and their Haitian upper-class allies. On a more mundane plane, *Chronique d'un faux-amour* [Chronicle of an Untrue Love], the interior monologue of a high society young woman who has been turned into a zombi, is based on a supposedly historic occurrence.

For evident reasons, most critics – and nearly all Haitian critics – have focussed their studies on the political convictions for which Alexis sacrificed his life, and which are manifest, sometimes in heavily didactic fashion, throughout his fiction. Yet, while Alexis never composed poetry, his obvious delight in linguistic effects may very well constitute his most lasting contribution to Haitian letters. He has frequent recourse to the technical vocabularies of seamanship, music, cooking, liturgy, medicine, flora and fauna and, of course, vodùn, not to mention English and Spanish words. Enumeration and repetition, as well as the proliferation of a great variety of metaphors, characterize his *sui generis* stylistic eloquence.

In *L'Espace d'un cillement* as well as in some of the *Romancero* stories, Alexis's erotic descriptions are quite detailed and uninhibited. Some critics, who would have preferred a more allusive treatment, have accused Alexis of salaciousness, arguing that his tropical sensuality is in fact the expression of a traditional male chauvinist ideology.

Be that as it may, most of Alexis's novels (as the critic Boadas has correctly observed) are characterized by the ambiguity, or even the absence of closure, both in individual chapters and in the whole work. The frequent use of suspension points is significant: it allows readers to supply their own conclusion and can also suggest the possibility of eventual further developments of the plot. This happens in six of the nine stories which make up the *Romancero*; in the same way, at the conclusion of *Compère Général Soleil*, Hilarion dies on the Dominican-Haitian border, which his wife Claire-Heureuse will cross to return home and take up his struggle. On the last page of *L'Espace d'un cillement*, while La Niña has disappeared, "El Caucho believes that he will find her, he believes it with all his heart . . . Perhaps. . . ¡ *Quién sabe !*" (. . . Who knows!). In the last paragraph of *Les Arbres musiciens*: " With his arm around her shoulder, Gonaïbo leads Harmonise away. Life is beginning."

With his last published work, Jacques-Stéphen Alexis was well on the way to achieving a sustained tone, a metaphorical baroque no longer in danger of veering off into rococo excess. Just when his talent was reaching its full maturity, the writer's voice was silenced by the dictatorship; thus was one more disaster inflicted upon the country he had so lovingly celebrated.

LÉON-FRANÇOIS HOFFMANN

Biography

Born in Gonaïves, Haiti, 22 April 1922. His father, Stéphen Alexis, wrote a biography of Toussaint Louverture and the novel, *Le Nègre masqué*. Educated at Collège Stanislas, Paris; Collège Saint-Louis de Gonzague, Port-au-Prince. Studied medicine in Port-au-Prince and neurology in Paris. Joined the Haitian Communist Party in 1938. Co-founder, with René Depestre and other young intellectuals, of the important journal *La Ruche* and leader of the student strikes which forced President Lescot to resign in 1946. While in Paris, joined the French Communist Party and became a friend of Louis Aragon, Léopold Senghor and Aimé Césaire, as well as of Latin American writers, Nicolás Guillén, Pablo Neruda and Jorge Amado, among others. In 1959 he traveled to Moscow to attend the 30th Conference of the Union of Soviet Writers. On his way back he visited China, where he was received by Mao Tse Tung. With four comrades, he sailed from Cuba in April, 1961 in order to organize an uprising against the Duvalier dictatorship. On their landing on the north coast of Haiti, the five men were betrayed to the authorities by local peasants. It is almost certain that Alexis was taken to Port-au-Prince and savagely tortured before being executed. The regime never acknowledged his death, and his remains have never been located.

Selected Works

Novels
Compère Général Soleil, Paris: Gallimard, 1955
Les Arbres musiciens, Paris: Gallimard, 1957
L'Espace d'un cillement, Paris: Gallimard, 1959

Short Fiction
"La Belle amour humaine," *Europe*, Paris, 501 (January 1957)
Romancero aux étoiles, Paris: Gallimard, 1960

Other Writings

"Du Réalisme merveilleux des Haïtiens," *Présence Africaine*, Paris, 8–10 (June–November 1956)

"Débat autour des conditions d'un roman national chez les peuples noirs: où va le roman?" *Présence Africaine*, Paris, 13 (April–May 1957)

"Florilège du romanesque haïtien," *Étincelles*, Montréal, 8–9 (May–June 1984) [dated January 1959]

Further Reading

Boadas, Aura Marina, *Lo barroco en la obra de Jacques Stéphen Alexis*, Caracas: Fundación CELARG, 1990

Dash, J. Michael, *Jacques-Stéphen Alexis*, Toronto: Black Images, 1975 [An excellent, short (60 pages), comprehensive essay, which stresses Alexis's ideology and his contributions to the Peasant Novel and to Marvellous Realism]

Depestre, René, "Parler de Jacques-Stéphen Alexis," in *Pour la Révolution, pour la poésie*, Québec: Léméac, 1974; reprinted in *Bonjour et adieu à la négritude*, Paris: Robert Laffont, 1980 [Personal reminiscences from a long-time friend and political companion, from whom Alexis broke off shortly before his death because of tactical disagreements]

Allende, Isabel

See Best-Sellers

José Américo de Almeida 1887–1980

Brazilian prose writer and politician

Following his graduation in law from the Recife Law School in 1908, José Américo de Almeida pursued a political career that saw him fulfil several important posts in regional and national government, but which would also impose considerable restrictions on his literary activities. He wrote three novels, and only the first, *A bagaçeira* (*Trash*), published in 1928, has received serious attention from scholars. Almeida's reputation as a novelist rests almost entirely on this one work. Whilst recognising its clear limitations, most critics agree to its historical significance, arguing that it initiated a new phase in the development of Brazilian fiction, for through its approach and thematic content, it established the pattern for the series of regionalist social novels produced in the Brazilian northeast throughout the 1930s by such authors as Jorge Amado, José Lins do Rego and Graciliano Ramos.

Regionalism has been a major force in defining the historical development of literature in the northeast of Brazil, and it provided the vital stimulus for Almeida's work. Whilst working as a young man for the state government of Paraíba, he wrote a series of essays studying the social and economic conditions of the state, entitled *A Paraíba e seus problemas* [Paraiba and its Problems], published in 1922, and he later participated in the Northeast Regionalist Movement. This was launched in Recife in 1926 by Gilberto Freyre, with the objective of promoting the cultural traditions of the region through a series of educational and artistic activities. Almeida's subsequent novels were undoubtedly influenced by the ideas and aims of that movement. All of them are characterised by a strong inclination for the sociological study of local life and a broadly realist treatment of such northeast themes as the drought, life on the plantations and rural migration.

The heightened interest in regional issues in the northeast in the late 1920s, and the more general concern with social problems, provided a receptive environment for the publication of *A bagaçeira*, and four editions of the work were printed within a year of its publication. Almeida's knowledge of regional problems enabled him to debate a wide range of issues in the novel, which he used as a vehicle to denounce the poverty and injustice suffered by the majority of the inhabitants of the rural northeast. In many ways, Almeida continued the work of the earlier generation of Naturalist novelists of the northeast, who, turning away from Romanticism, sought to present a more realistic interpretation of regional life and environment through rigorous observation and description. The most significant difference was that whereas the Naturalist novelists, imbued with determinist philosophy, tended to highlight biological and environmental factors as explanations for the backwardness, poverty and suffering of the region, Almeida emphasised instead problems of social organization. However, his social criticism must not be overestimated, for it was by no means radical. *A bagaçeira* does not penetrate to the fundamental socio-economic mechanisms underlying such conditions. That limitation diminishes the potential dramatic tension of the thematic material, where a family of drought victims, *retirantes*, flees from the misery of the backlands and seek refuge on the sugar estate of a wealthy landowner, only to suffer even greater degradation once immersed in the dehumanizing life of the plantation. The adverse social conditions of the region's rural life are attributed to society's negligence and disorganization, which is particularly exposed in the face of a natural disaster such as drought. All this blunts the sensibility of those in a position of power. The fundamental structures and processes of that society remain unquestioned. It falls to Lúcio, the landowner's progressive, university-educated son, to condemn society's shortcomings, and seek his own personal solution by taking over the plantation on the death of his father and initiating a series of reforms and technical innovations, which happily combine improved efficiency with the advancement of the welfare of the workers.

On the new model plantation, Lúcio not only improves the material conditions of the labourers, but also offers incentives to encourage them to take an active interest in the production process, and thereby break out of their previous state of inertia and apathy. It was this view of an enlightened, benevolent capitalism that orientated Almeida's own liberal, reformist politics, first as an active supporter of the Revolution of 1930, then as a minister in the Vargas government that resulted, and finally as a candidate for the presidency in 1938. The result of this approach towards social criticism in *A bagaçeira* can be seen in the tendency towards the picturesque, complemented by a very florid, lyrical prose style, and a somewhat sentimental treatment of the characters, who are generally presented as hapless, passive victims of the vicissitudes of the natural and social environment, a tendency that reduces the sense of conflict and tension. Almeida's treatment of the rural poor is essentially paternalistic, a tendency shared by many of the northeastern social novelists who emerged during the same era. The peasants and plantation workers in *A bagaçeira* are presented as stoic and fatalistic, devoid of the necessary initiative to alter their situation in any significant way. It is up to the more progressive and charitable members of the dominant classes, represented by Lúcio, to undertake the reforms needed to relieve their plight.

Significantly however, Almeida draws a distinction between the courageous and independent backlanders, or *sertanejos*, and the plantation workers who have been dehumanized by the work and conditions of the plantation. The backlanders are idealised, so that their own conditions of poverty and exploitation are covered by an abstract, bucolic vision of a haven, potentially self-sufficient if it were not for the periodic drought, where humans can live freely and independently, according to a strict code of honour. The contrast between the purity and dignity of the *sertanejos* and the degraded lives of the sugar workers is epitomized in the figure of Soledad, the *sertaneja* who arrives at the plantation innocent and dignified, only to be corrupted by the depravity of plantation life. This Utopian, pastoral vision, constructing a mythical realm uncontaminated by humans, is a legacy of Romanticism that recurs frequently in Brazilian regionalist fiction. Almeida's eulogy of the traditional cultural values of the backlands, threatened perhaps, but surviving still, clearly reveals the influence of the regionalist thought of the time, with its sense of nostalgic longing for a past era.

The demands of public office fully occupied the latter part of his life, but Almeida continued his interest in regional social issues in his last two novels, *O boqueirão*, 1935 [The Gully] and *Coiteiros*, 1935 [Bandits' Refuge] and his project of critical examination of northeast social structures and social relations was taken up by other, more talented regionalist writers who followed.

MARK DINNEEN

See also entries on Jorge Amado, Rachel de Queiroz

Biography

Born on a sugar mill owned by his parents at Areia in the state of Paraíba, Brazil, 10 January 1887. Spent childhood there. Father died when he was twelve and an uncle sent him to a seminary in 1901. Left the seminary in 1904 to study law at Recife University. Became interested in politics while still a student and published controversial articles in newspapers. Acquired important post in state administration by nepotism in 1911. Published his first work, *Poetas da abolição* in 1921. Appointed Secretary of the Interior in Paraíba state in 1928. Stood as deputy for national assembly in 1928 and won. Appointed minister of Communications in 1931; ambassador to the Vatican, 1934; senator for the state of Paraíba, 1935. Stood for the presidency in 1937, but was not elected. Governor of his state, 1951; retired from politics in 1956. Named Intellectual of the Year in 1977 by the Brazilian Union of Writers. Died on 10 March 1980.

Selected Works

Novels
A bagaçeira, Rio de Janeiro: n.p., 1928; as *Trash*, translated by R.L. Scott-Buccleuch, London: Peter Owen, 1978
O boqueirão, Rio de Janeiro: José Olympio, 1935
Coiteiros, São Paulo: Companhia Editora Nacional, 1935

Other Writings
A Paraíba e seus problemas, n.p., 1922
Ocasos de sangue, Rio de Janeiro: José Olympio, 1954 [memoirs]

Compilations and Anthologies
Tres novelas de José Américo de Almeida, Rio de Janeiro: Leitura, 1971 [Contains *O boqueirão*, *Coiteiros* and *Reflexões de uma cabra*]

Further Reading

Américo de Almeida's importance as a politician seems to have cast a shadow over his creative writing. Such interest as has been shown to date in the latter focuses exclusively on *A bagaçeira*.

Ellison, Fred P., "Soledade-Persephone: a Cyclical Myth in *A bagaçeira*," in *Woman as Myth and Metaphor in Latin American Literature*, edited by Naomi Lindstrom and Carmelo Virgillo, Missouri: University of Columbia Press, 1985
Pereira, José Carlos Seabra, "Programas de gêneros e sintagmântica narrativa: sobre *A bagaçeira* como romance de formação," *Revista Brasileira de Língua e Literatura*, Rio de Janeiro, vol. 3/7 (1981)

Ignacio Manuel Altamirano 1834–1893

Mexican prose writer

Ignacio Manuel Altamirano was one of the most sophisticated Mexican intellectuals in the second half of the 19th century. Altamirano was the ideological founding father of Mexican culture, appearing at an unstable and chaotic time in the construction of the new Mexican state. His life's work is part of Mexico's most turbulent times when new republican institutions and political tolerance had to be learned; competing liberal and conservative ideologies provoked endless civil wars; and foreign interventions were cyclical catastrophes. Altamirano represents a turning-point in Mexican intellectual history at a moment when the nation oscillated between enthusiasm and despair. Altamirano became the spiritual guide of the 1867 second Romantic generation, assumed the leadership of the most influential of literary societies, the *Liceo Hidalgo*, and founded the prestigious literary weekly, *El Renacimiento* [The Renaissance] which published the finest examples of Mexican writing of 1869. He explored various genres, poetry, costumbrist articles (feature articles on manners and customs), essays on cultural criticism and literary theory, short stories, and novels.

Altamirano felt that his mission was to contribute morally and aesthetically to the cultural development of Mexico and mainly he addressed the middle classes recently provided with access to education, who could be influenced about the value and richness of their native land. His best-known prose works are *Clemencia*, 1869 [Clemency], "La navidad en las montañas," 1871 (*Christmas in the Mountains*), and *El Zarco*, 1901 (*El Zarco: the Bandit*). *Clemencia* is a sentimental novel set in and around Guadalajara, dealing with a tragic romance during the French invasion (1864–67). The four main characters, Fernando, Enrique, Clemencia and Isabel are almost geometrically contrasted through their physical appeareance (blond/dark) moral character (frivolous/spiritual), social intentions (opportunistic/loyal), and their political and military participation (collaborationists/nationalists). "La navidad en las montañas" portrays the life of an army captain seeking asylum in a small town after being exiled from his state. As narrator the captain recounts his childhood, and how a priest on his way to the Christmas Eve festivities helped him to overcome his isolation in exile. The author uses the dual point of view provided by the captain and the priest to reconcile opposing political ideologies. In his narration, Altamirano includes history, religion, politics, manners and customs, allegorizing the reconciliation of political factions during the Guerra de la Reforma (Mexican Civil War). *El Zarco* is a historical novel based on the criminal deeds carried out by el Zarco and his bandits, "los plateados" (the Silver Army) in the town of Yautepec. The story is about Nicolás, a blacksmith who is in love with an upper-middle-class woman named Manuela, but she does not return his love because, instead, she loves the bandit, El Zarco. Manuela elopes with El Zarco, thereby making her mother ill. Her goddaughter Pilar, an orphan girl, loves Nicolás deeply, and with time they fall in love and get married. On the way home, a band of highwaymen plan to kill him. A rural guard saves Nicolás and his

bride, but kills El Zarco, and subsequently Manuela dies from grief. The novel thus seeks to promote the moral victory of the heroic characters in the face of societal disarray. Many characters are historical figures such as Benito Juárez, the rural guard (*vigilante*) Martín Sánchez, El Zarco, and some of the bandits. The situation he described included expressions of the social disorder of the times, such as abuses committed by both the military and civil authorities. He incorporates realism in the description of unpleasant scenes, the swearing and cursing of the bandits, their obscene songs, and their grotesque drunkenness. In general terms, one can say that his creative works centered on the representation of diverse national types, and the suffering of unrequited love.

Altamirano's works focus on the concept of Nation through the experience of critical historical moments such as foreign interventions or civil wars. The Nation for Altamirano is the sum of legends, customs, habits, pious sentiments, love and prudent filial relationships. These convey harmony in the home, family, and society, thus reflecting his conceptualization of what a Nation should be. His feature articles on Mexican culture and civilization in *El Renacimiento* are indispensable to understand the Mexican history of the time. His *Paisajes y leyendas* [Landscapes and Legends] describes Holy Week in his hometown, his pride in his birthplace of Tixtla, and the sacred dances of the native population. In his essays and feature articles on manners and customs he passionately defended a nationalistic literary agenda, and a nationalistic culture that could express the originality and conciousness of the emerging national identity. In *Revistas Literarias de México*, 1868 [Mexican Literary Journals], Altamirano states that writers are the most important creators of symbols of the Nation; their commitment to the formation of national identity should be unequivocal. He calls upon the writers to give themselves to the task of documenting the Nation, its traditions, its books, its habits and costumes, its psychological traits, and its landscape. For him, to write means literally to name, to originate, and to build a mirror that reflects an imaginary and emotional repertoire in which the people can recognize themselves. Altamirano's literary agenda brings to the fore patriotism, religion and language, advocating an organic cultural expression which could give coherence to the Mexican experience of the time.

The fundamental concepts in Altamirano's intellectual discourse are culture and national literature. His literary and cultural nationalism can be understood since national affirmation was the only way to avoid the complete disintegration of an already fragmented nation. Altamirano's nationalistic agenda is a culmination of the Mexican liberal movement, its decades of struggle and political adjustment, and the desire to participate in Western civilization without surrendering national identity. What he demanded was a decolonizing process: to be part of the Universal culture, to use their repertoire of artistic models, while insisting on the right to use Mexican themes, landscape, language, history, and tradition. The literary nationalism that Altamirano advocated has a double function, arguing the need for internal political cohesiveness of the Nation as well as the defense against imperialism. Altamirano's works reflect his desire for national unity as part of the political agenda of the emerging middle class liberalism. This class should strive to transform the country, to construct an enduring Mexican image and character, to understand its past and to remake history in order to achieve economic and political progress. He sought to compress his vision of Mexico, one of monumental proportions, into a single book. Thus most of his novels are a synthesis of the country, of its past, its present, its future.

Mexican nationalism in the 19th century demanded a writer able to develop a cultural consciousness to consolidate a historical destiny. The political situation demanded that literature reaffirm an educational system organized around a cult of symbols and heroes. The heroes were to be part of that educational, aesthetic and political agenda: their sacrifice and their genius had to be imitated. The Nation that Altamirano imagined was vital in the formation of a Mexican consciousness because it gave meaning and purpose to those aware of their place in history. For him culture is the fertile soil where the seeds of nationalism are to be planted; culture should be the frame of reference to oppose the chaos and anarchy of the times. The liberal cultural discourse incarnated in Altamirano's quest for a nationalistic literature and culture as a symbolic force, established a repertoire of themes, mental and affective attitudes, heroes and legends, to be passed on to a later generation. All his writings aimed to build a common feeling of belonging to a singular historical destiny named Mexico. His attemps to create the symbolic profile of the national character, the construction of national symbols, and their elaboration in the expression of the national experience, synthesized in a dramatic way the baptism of a modern Nation.

LUIS H. PEÑA

Biography
Born in the village of Tixtla, Mexico, 13 November 1834, of Amerindian parents. Father became mayor of village. Able to attend primary school with children of European parents and thus learned Spanish. A scholarship for Indian children enabled him to study at the Literary Institute in Toluca, followed by law at the Colegio de Letrán. Fought against the Conservatives in the Reform War (Guerra de la Reforma). Congressman. Supported Benito Juárez in his struggle against the emperor Maximilian. Fought in several battles, including Querétaro. Held rank of colonel at end of war. Opposed Juárez's policies during latter's presidency because Altamirano demanded a closer adherence to Liberal Party ideology. Contributed to several newspapers and journals including *El Correo de México* (1867), *El Renacimiento* (1869) and *El Federalista* (1871). Died in 1893 when on a consular mission to Europe.

Selected Works

Novels
Clemencia, Mexico City: El Renacimiento, 1869
"La Navidad en las montañas," in *Album de Navidad*, Mexico City: Ignacio Escalante, 1871; as *Christmas in the Mountains*, edited and translated by Harvey L. Johnson, Gainesville: University Presses of Florida, 1961
El Zarco, episodios de la vida mexicana en 1861–1863, Barcelona: J. Ballesca, 1901; as *El Zarco: the Bandit*, translated by Mary Alt, London: Folio Society, 1957

Poetry
Rimas, Mexico City: Imprenta de F. Díaz de León y S. White, 1871

Compilations and Anthologies
Obras literarias completas, edited by Salvador Reyes Nevares, Mexico City: Oasis, 1959

Other Writings
Paisajes y leyendas, tradiciones y costumbres de México, Mexico City: Imprenta Española, 1884; reprinted, Mexico City: Antigua Librería Robredo, 1949
Biografía de Ignacio Ramírez, Mexico City: Oficina de Tipografía de la Secretaría de Fomento, 1889
Aires de México (Prosas), Mexico City: UNAM, 1940
La literatura nacional, edited by José Luis Martínez, 3 vols, Mexico City: Porrúa, 1949

Further Reading
Batis's study is indispensable. Brushwood's book is valuable in terms of structural development, concepts, and an identification with Mexican reality in Altamirano's works. However, to date the most important contribution to Altamirano studies is that made by José Luis Martínez. Altamirano's notion of cultural nationalism is very well explained by Carlos Monsiváis and Nicole Girón.

Batis, Huberto, *Índices de "El Renacimiento." Semanario Literario Mexicano (1869)*, Mexico City: Centro de Estudios Literarios, 1963
Brushwood, John S., *The Romantic Novel in Mexico*, Columbia: University of Missouri Press, 1954
Girón, Nicole, "La idea de la 'cultura nacional' en el siglo XIX: Altamirano y Ramírez," in *En torno a la cultura nacional*, edited by Carlos Monsiváis, *et al.*, Mexico City: Fondo de Cultura Económica/SEP, 1982
Martínez, José Luis, *La expresión nacional (Letras mexicanas del siglo XIX)*, Mexico City: Editorial Universitaria, 1955
_____ *La emancipación literaria de México*, Mexico City: Antigua Librería Robredo, 1955
Monsiváis, Carlos, "La nación de unos cuantos y las esperanzas románticas. Notas sobre la historia del término cultura nacional en México," in *En torno a la cultura nacional*, Mexico City: Fondo de Cultura Económica/SEP, 1982

Alves, Antônio de Castro

See Castro Alves

Jorge Amado 1912–

Brazilian novelist

Jorge Amado is without doubt the best-known and most widely read Brazilian novelist of the 20th century. He is also a prolific writer, who, having published his first novel at the age of nineteen, has now produced over thirty literary works. Several of those have been best-sellers, and none of his compatriots has achieved such wide acclaim abroad. However, his work has generated much controversy among critics, some of whom argue that the effort to produce commercially successful novels has resulted in a form of literary populism, in which regional exoticism and intense sentimentalism have come to prevail over the critical exploration of society which orientated his early writing.

He established his career in the 1930s, with the development of his so-called "proletarian novel," dealing essentially with the development of political consciousness among the poorest sectors of his native state of Bahia: rural in the case of *Cacau*, 1933 [Cocoa], and urban in *Suor*, 1934 [Sweat]. In these novels, Amado, armed with a simplified breakdown of Soviet Union ideology of the time, employs a very stark, simple documentary style in order to convey the misery and exploitation of the working poor and their struggle to free themselves from those circumstances. In its compilation of snippets of descriptive detail, this realist style succeeds in providing some earthy images of the squalid living conditions of the poor, but there are also signs of the sentimentality and romanticism that would become prevalent in Amado's later works. *Cacau*, for example, ends with the hero, a young plantation worker who gradually develops his sense of solidarity with his fellow-workers, finally renouncing the opportunity of marrying the landowner's daughter and becoming a landowner himself, and setting off to join the class-struggle in Rio. Amado attempts to avoid the sense of fatalism detectable in other Social Realist novelists of the Brazilian northeast, and lend a more optimistic note to the class-struggle in his country. Yet by reducing his social criticism to a framework of dogmatic formulas he tends to dissipate the potential power of the content of this early work.

Escaping from those restrictions enabled Amado to write what is considered by many to be his most powerful novel, *Terras do sem fim*, 1942 (*The Violent Land*), documenting the struggle that developed between rival planters in the south of Bahia in an effort to secure for themselves a privileged position in the increasingly prosperous cocoa trade. That environment is the centre of attention, rather than individual characters. Cocoa is shown to determine the life of everybody in the region, and they are all dehumanized by the values and conflicts it generates.

Of all the Social Realist novelists who emerged in the northeast of Brazil in the 1930s, the so-called "Generation of 1930," it is Amado who has made the greatest use of popular cultural expressions in his work. Popular songs are occasionally incorporated into *Terras do sem fim* to give the struggle taking place an epic, legendary quality, and to emphasize the suffering of the exploited workers, who express their anguish through song, and their hopes for an alternative existence. Amado had already developed the use of regional popular culture in earlier works. *Jubiabá*, 1935, for example, examines the African-Brazilian culture of Bahia, and continues the theme of development of political consciousness among the working class. Again, however, the tension generated by the political content tends to be diluted by the sentimental way in which the lives of the poor are narrated. In addition, the popular cultural expressions are described in such a way that the attempt to demonstrate the creativity and rebelliousness of the poor often results in exoticism. Other novels of the period, namely *Mar morto*, 1936 (*Sea of Death*) and *Capitães da areia*, 1937 (*Captains of the Sands*), follow a similar pattern, with colourful stories idealizing the struggle of the poor developed from popular materials.

An active member of the Communist Party, Amado went into exile when the Party was outlawed in 1947. The award of the Stalin Prize for literature three years later confirmed his standing in the Eastern bloc countries, but Amado then began a new phase of his literary career, which would see him obtain equal acclaim in the West, with the publication of his most commercially successful novels. *Gabriela, cravo e canela*, 1958 (*Gabriela, Clove and Cinnamon*), *Os velhos marinheiros*, 1961 (*Home is the Sailor*) and *Dona Flor e seus dois maridos*, 1967 (*Dona Flor and Her Two Husbands*) are representative of this phase, dominated by colourful tales and anecdotes of regional life, without any of the ideological orientation of his earlier writing. Instead of overt political protest these works centre on criticism, frequently conveyed through satire, of the petty and hollow world of the bourgeoisie, against which his protagonists rebel and seek fulfilment in an alternative lifestyle, with alternative values. They are novels which focus on the desires of the individual rather than on collective struggle. As a result, Amado creates some of his most colourful and distinctive characters, though it is doubtless true that the liberal measures of picturesque description, sex and humour which characterize these works considerably helped to widen their appeal both at home and abroad. Indeed, *Dona Flor e seus dois maridos*, made into one of the most successful films in the history of the Brazilian cinema, in 1976, has been heralded as a comic masterpiece by some critics. It is far removed from his early political novels.

The greater individualization of characters in these more light-hearted stories gave Amado the opportunity to develop his penchant for strong, exuberant female protagonists, determined to assert their independence, such as Gabriela, Flor and Tereza, from *Tereza Batista, cansada de guerra*, 1972 (*Tereza Batista, Home from the Wars*), a prostitute whose battle to overcome hardship and adversity comes to symbolize the courage and unbreakable resolution of the people. If, on the one hand these characters broke from the more passive and meek representations of women commonly found in earlier Brazilian fiction, on the other some feminist critics argued that one stereotype had simply taken the place of another, and that Amado's bold and voluptuous females essentially served to satisfy male fantasy.

However, perhaps the most striking feature of Amado's novels of the 1970s is the more direct use they make of northeast popular culture. Through such works Amado aimed to express once more his solidarity with the struggle of the poor and oppressed by highlighting the strength, defiance and creativity embodied in their various forms of cultural expression. Recreating popular forms that recount the experience of the poor, Amado argued, permitted him to analyze that experience from the inside, rather than observing and documenting it from afar and making his own condemnations, as in his first political novels. All the resulting works, however, undoubtedly convey Amado's own idealised vision of a pure and gallant people heroically battling against adverse social conditions. In the romanticized atmosphere created in such novels, the creativity of the people is ingenuously, and at times sentimentally, extolled. In *Tenda dos milagres*, 1969 (*Tent of Miracles*), for example, Amado, with vivid description of popular music, dance and ritual, attempts to trace the struggle of the people of Bahia through the life of the main character, Pedro Arcanjo, who begins composing popular poetry, and then writes erudite literature, but always uses his literary skills and intellectual abilities to defend the rights of the poor. He becomes a popular hero, and the result is a romantic view of the writer at one with the people, sharing their vision of the world and serving their interests. *Tereza Batista, cansada de guerra*, already mentioned, goes even further, for its structure, tone and characterization are all drawn directly from the traditional popular poetry of the Brazilian northeast (*literatura de cordel*). Again, popular material is adapted to convey Amado's personal vision of Bahian society and culture.

Amado's success lies in the ability he has persistently shown to combine the required ingredients in his work so as to continue producing novels of popular appeal throughout a literary career of over sixty years. His more recent work has not provided his readers with anything new, but essentially repeats the tried and tested formula that brought success throughout the 1960s and 1970s. *Tocaia grande* (*Showdown*), a novel published in 1984, is another re-examination of Brazilian history, with the familiar Bahian characters and world

of voodoo ritual encountered in previous novels. Film and television adaptations of his work have helped to widen his appeal, and his novels have now been translated into many different languages, enhancing his international popularity. However, the production of such marketable novels has undoubtedly compromised the quality and value of his writing.

MARK DINNEEN

See also the Brazilian sections of the following entries: Film, Popular Culture, Regionalism

Biography

Born in Ferradas, Itabuna, Bahia, Brazil, 10 August 1912. Attended the Jesuit Colégio Antônio Vieira, Salvador, 1923–26; entered the Ginásio Ipiranga, Salvador, 1926; studied law at the Federal University, Rio de Janeiro from 1931 to 1935 and received a diploma in law. Reporter with *Diário da Bahia*, 1927, and contributor to *A Luva, Samba, Meridiano, A Semana, O Momento, O Jornal, Diário de Notícias, A Gazeta de Notícias*, and *O Correio do Povo*, 1927–30. Moved to Rio de Janeiro in 1930. Married Matilde Garcia Roas in 1933 (separated 1944), one daughter. Editor for *Revista Rio*, 1933; worked for the publishing company José Olympio from 1934; editor for *A Manhã*, the publication of the opposition Aliança Nacional Libertadora [National Freedom Alliance]; co-editor, Centro de Cultura Moderna's *Movimento*, 1934–35; imprisoned for suspected involvement in coup attempt, 1935, and his books banned, 1938–43. Travelled to Mexico and the US in 1937. Editor, *Dom Casmurro*, 1938–39, and contributor to *Diretrizes*, 1939. Lived mainly in Argentina, 1941–42; returned to Brazil, 1942, and was re-arrested and confined to the Bahia region; contributor to "Diário da Guerra" column for *O Imparcial*, from 1943; delegate at the first Brazilian Writers' Congress, 1945; editor, *Hoje*, São Paulo, 1945. After the fall of Getúlio Vargas's regime (1930–45) elected Communist deputy for the São Paulo region, 1945, until the Party was again declared illegal in 1947. Went into exile in Paris, 1947–49, in Scandinavia and Eastern Europe, 1949–50, and in Prague, 1950–51. Travelled to China and Mongolia in 1952. Vice-President of the Brazilian union, 1954. Founder, *Para Todos*, Rio de Janeiro, and its editor from 1956 to 1958. Co-organizer, first Festival of Brazilian Writing, 1960. Travelled to Cuba and Mexico in 1962; settled in Salvador in 1963. Writer-in-Residence at Pennsylvania State University, 1971. Recipient of numerous awards including the Graça Aranha Foundation Prize, 1936; Stalin Peace Prize, 1951; National Literary Prize, 1958; Gulbenkian Prize (Portugal), 1971; Italian Latin-American Institute Prize, 1976; Neruda Prize, 1989. Member of the Brazilian Academy, since 1961; corresponding member, East German Academy of Science and Letters. Commander, Légion d'Honneur, 1984.

Selected Works

Novels

O país do carnaval, Rio de Janeiro: Schmidt, 1931

Cacau, Rio de Janeiro: Ariel, 1933

Suor, Rio de Janeiro: Ariel, 1934

Jubiabá, Rio de Janeiro: José Olympio, 1935; as *Jubiabá*, translated by Margaret A. Neves, New York: Avon, 1984

Mar morto, Rio de Janeiro: José Olympio, 1936; as *Sea of Death*, translated by Gregory Rabassa, New York: Avon, 1984

Capitães da areia, Rio de Janeiro: José Olympio, 1937; as *Captains of the Sands*, translated by Gregory Rabassa, New York: Avon, 1988

Terras do sem fim, São Paulo: Martins, 1943; as *The Violent Land*, translated by Samuel Putnam, New York: Knopf, 1945; revised edition, London: Collins Harvill, 1989

São Jorge dos Ilhéus, São Paulo: Martins, 1944; as *Golden Harvest*, translated by Clifford E. Landers, New York: Avon, 1992
Seara vermelha, São Paulo: Martins, 1946
Gabriela, cravo e canela, São Paulo: Martins, 1959; as *Gabriela, Clove and Cinnamon*, translated by James L. Taylor and William Grossman, New York: Knopf and London: Souvenir Press, 1962
Os velhos marinheiros: duas histórias do cais da bahia, São Paulo: Martins, 1961; as *Home is the Sailor*, translated by Harriet de Onís, New York: Knopf, and London: Chatto and Windus, 1964
Os pastores da noite, São Paulo: Martins, 1964; as *Shepherds of the Night*, translated by Harriet de Onís, New York: Knopf, 1966; London: Collins Harvill, 1989
Dona Flor e seus dois maridos, São Paulo: Martins, 1966; as *Dona Flor and Her Two Husbands*, translated by Harriet de Onís, New York: Knopf, 1969; London: Weidenfeld and Nicolson, 1970
Tenda dos milagres, São Paulo: Martins, 1969; as *Tent of Miracles*, translated by Barbara Shelby, New York: Knopf, 1971; London: Collins Harvill, 1989
Tereza Batista, cansada de guerra, São Paulo: Martins, 1972; as *Tereza Batista, Home from the Wars*, translated by Barbara Shelby, New York: Knopf, 1975; London: Souvenir Press, 1982
Tieta do agreste, pastora de cabras, Rio de Janeiro: Record, 1977; as *Tieta, the Goat Girl*, translated by Barbara Shelby Merello, New York: Knopf, 1979; London: Souvenir Press, 1981
Farda, fardão, camisola de dormir, Rio de Janeiro: Record, 1979; as *Pen, Sword, Camisole: a Fable to Kindle a Hope*, translated by Helen Lane, Boston: Godine, 1985
Tocaia grande: a face obscura, Rio de Janeiro: Record, 1984; as *Showdown*, translated by Gregory Rabassa, New York and London: Bantam, 1988
O sumiço da santa, Rio de Janeiro: Record, 1988; as *The War of the Saints*, translated by Gregory Rabassa, New York: Bantam, 1993; London: Serpent's Tail, 1994

Poetry
A estrada do mar, Estância: Tipografia Popular, 1938

Other Writings
ABC de Castro Alves, São Paulo: Martins, 1941 [biography]
Bahia de todos os santos; guia das ruas e dos mistérios de cidade do Salvador, São Paulo: Martins, 1945 [travel writing]
O mundo da paz, Rio de Janeiro: Vitória, 1951 [travel writing]
O gato malhado e a Andorinha Sinhá, Rio de Janeiro: Record, 1976; as *The Swallow and the Tomcat: a Love Story*, translated by Barbara Shelby Merello, New York: Delacorte Press, 1982 [for children]

Further Reading
Almeida, Alfredo Wagner Berno de, *Jorge Amado: política e literatura: um estudo sobre a trajetória intelectual de Jorge Amado*, Rio de Janeiro: Campus, 1979
Batista, Juarez da Gama, *O barroco e o maravilhoso no romance de Jorge Amado*, João Pessoa: Tipografia Chaves, 1973
Brookshaw, David, *Race and Color in Brazilian Literature*, Metuchen, New Jersey: Scarecrow Press, 1986
Chamberlain, Bobby J., *Jorge Amado*, Boston: Twayne, 1990
Costa, Lígia Militz da, *O condicionamento telúrico-ideológico do desejo em "Terras do sem fim" de Jorge Amado*, Pôrto Alegre, Brazil: Movimento-Instituto Estadual do Libro, 1976
Curran, Mark J., *Jorge Amado e a literatura de cordel*, Salvador: Fundação Cultural do Estado da Bahia, 1981
Paes, José Paulo, *De "Cacau" a "Gabriela": um percurso pastoral*, Salvador, Brazil: Fundação Casa de Jorge Amado, 1991
Patai, Daphne, *Myth and Ideology in Contemporary Brazilian Fiction*, Rutherford, New Jersey: Fairleigh Dickinson University Press, 1983
Rabassa, Gregory, *O negro na ficção brasileira: meio século de história literária*, Rio de Janeiro: Tempo Brasileiro, 1965
Rubim, Rosane and Maried Carneiro (editors), *Jorge Amado, oitenta anos de vida e obra: subsídios para pesquisa*, Salvador, Brazil: Fundação Casa de Jorge Amado, 1992
Silverman, Malcolm N., "Allegory in Two Works of Jorge Amado," *Romance Notes*, vol. 13/1 (1971)
Tavares, Paulo, *O baiano Jorge Amado e sua obra*, Rio de Janeiro: Record, 1980
Vincent, Jon S., "Jorge Amado, Jorge Desperado," *Luso-Brazilian Review*, vol. 15 (1978)

America

The Invention of America

When Columbus espied land on 12 October 1492, he announced to his travelling companions the "discovery" of a new world. What he found, of course, was not an empty space, but a place unknown to *Europe*. The inhabitants of the Caribbean islands met him and his crews with curiosity but without excess of suspicion; as Columbus himself noted in his first accounts with a degree of puzzlement, "they were so liberal with what they possessed that it would not be believed by those who had not seen it." The compelling search for gold led the new colonisers to torture and murder many of those original inhabitants. Yet Columbus was impressed, albeit briefly, by their egalitarian societies, their lack of property laws, their readiness to share what they had among themselves and even with strangers. His accounts of their ways of living, sketchy though they were, provided an important source of a multiple – and contradictory – mythical America. Peter Martyr reported Columbus's words: "the land among these people is as common as sun or water, and that 'mine or thine,' the seeds of all mischief, have no place with them".

These first impressions of the "new world" reinforced the medieval vision of a community of perfect order and moral construction such as Sir Thomas More idealized in his *Utopia* (1516). In fact the myths of perfect places had long been circulating – from the Land of Cockaigne, through the *Travels* of

Sir John Mandeville to the land of Prester John. So at first sight the island communities did seem to confirm an *anticipated* utopia. For here was an actual society without property or hierarchy. The problem was that while it displayed the qualities of good order, it was disturbingly free of hierarchy. The Reformation continued to see order and authority as indivisible. Subsequent attacks on these communities, like Hobbes's description of their life as "nasty, brutish and short," focused on the perils of a moral and social order without a designated authority – in a word, anarchy – with a tendency towards an excess of personal and sexual freedom. But for much of the 16th century, and repeatedly after that, those who yearned for a world without exploitation or inequality would find here a validation of their vision – and condemn its destruction. It was a reassurance of continuity at a time of change and upheaval.

The "discovery" of America itself was a factor in that instability. The paintings of Hieronymous Bosch showed clearly a world so corrupt and hypocritical (*Garden of Earthly Delights*) that it was inexorably rushing towards its own destruction. One corner of that famous painting shows a perfect world of beings naked and innocent amid a lush and protective nature. And this corresponded quite closely to what the colonisers had found in the Caribbean, according to their rather sketchy reports, upon which the European mind enthusiastically elaborated. The paradox, however, was that the driving force behind colonization and conquest was the search for gold and silver. For Spain, in particular, the discovery of sources of precious metal was a matter of urgency. A latecomer to the race for control of world trade and possession of overseas colonies, Spain was at a disadvantage compared to Portugal. If the newly unified kingdom of Castile was to survive, it must find a route to the spice routes of the East – or an alternative source of wealth. Internally, the crown faced resistance and discontent as the currents of Reformation flowed through the Iberian Peninsula. The ideas of Erasmus, with their humanist emphasis on religion as a code of ethics, focused public debate on the venality of the feudal classes and the sham nature of much religious observance. Furthermore, a restive merchant class (the *comuneros*) was balking at the impositions of the Crown.

In making sense of this "new world," then, Europe faced a challenge to many of its assumptions about itself, its authority and its place at the centre of a universal (Catholic) system. Two contradictory imperatives struggled for the dominant voice in explaining this monumental event – this "Discovery" of a new world. On the one hand, there was the demand that his event be used to demonstrate the moral authority of the Old World, its unimpeachable sense of *justice*. On the other, the impulse for Columbus's exploration was less humane. Columbus's own journals show a fixation with gold, and the tempting rewards offered to him by Queen Isabella of Spain were all conditional upon him returning with gold aplenty. That it why his journals make so many exaggerated claims – and why his desperation to win the glittering prizes led him to treat the indigenous populations of the Caribbean with such bestial cruelty.

The paradox was made manifest in the "Requerimiento," a complex legal undertaking to be given by all recently invaded peoples to their conquerors that they accepted the justice of Spanish imperial dominion. Any reluctance to swear the oath, or indeed any failure to comprehend it, was deemed to be wilful rejection of the precepts of universal justice, and thus a legitimation of war against the errant subject peoples.

Those who followed Columbus saw, as he never did (though he retired a very wealthy man), the true quantities of precious metal that the Conquest of America put at Spain's disposal. Spain's "golden century" of culture, as well as the Emperor Charles V's expansion into Europe floated on a sea of American gold – a treasure that also ensured the allegiance to absolutism of an unproductive aristocracy. It was also the certainty of that gold supply that gave Charles the confidence to take on and to crush the rebellious merchant classes in 1521. While the rest of Europe was experiencing the beginnings of a mercantile revolution, Spain was progressively immured in a recalcitrant feudal absolutism.

The mining of gold and silver required that the new colonial rulers of Latin America had at their disposal a large and passive labour force. This relationship of exploitation, however, was difficult to reconcile with the evangelical purposes which legitimated Conquest. The Laws of the Indies of 1512 (and the later ones of 1546 and 1571) enshrined the elevated objectives of protection and education of the Indians and the winning of their souls. Yet those purposes sat ill with the insatiable appetite for gold and silver of Charles's European armies and the unproductive Spanish land-owning class which relied on American wealth. In the debates that arose in an effort to reconcile the irreconcilable, the figure of Bartolomé de Las Casas, Dominican friar, later Bishop of Chiapas, and Defender of the Indians, occupied a central place for most of the 16th century. He was instrumental in framing all the laws regarding the Indies, and was an indomitable fighter for the rights of Indians whose protection was a moral obligation upon the colonial authorities.

Later, in 1548, Las Casas was to debate these matters with Archbishop Sepúlveda, who insisted that the original inhabitants of America were "barbarians", whose lack of understanding of concepts of law and morality made any war against them "just" in a sense derived from Aristotle. Las Casas, by contrast, insisted that the Conquest of America was justified as an act of evangelization only – and that the relation between Spain and America must be that of Father and Protector of his children.

There were those, like Father Montesinos (in 1511), who asked: "By what right and by what justice do you hold the Indians in such cruel and horrible bondage? Aren't they dying, or rather aren't you killing them to get gold every day? Aren't you obliged to love them as yourselves?" But their voices soon fell silent. America was about to be invented, and it would form part of the history of Spain – and provide the justification for Conquest and its depredations. The key to this new invention was the replacement of that Innocent America born of the first encounter with a Barbarous America inimical to Civilization.

The discovery of the Aztec empire (in 1519) and of the Incas (in 1532) posed difficult questions. These were complex and structured societies; indeed (as Inca Garcilaso de la Vega would comment later in his description of Inca society, the *Comentarios reales* of 1609) they may have experienced a very similar intellectual and social development to Spain itself, having themselves reached a concept of an Omnipotent Deity and a Moral law. How was it possible for such societies to have emerged in parallel with Europe; and how could Europe's Universal Catholic Church and its powerful Spanish representatives lay claim to Divine Will if such they were?

Later it became very clear that the American empires of Anáhuac and Tahuantinsuyu were in a sense authoritarian societies bound by the cement of state religion. If they fell to Spain's advances it was due in major part to a combination of Spanish technological superiority and the internal rifts that weakened each empire at this crucial time. But that is not how the history was told. Instead, America was invented for a second time – this time as a cruel and godless barbarism prone to human sacrifice on a massive scale. Thus all war against it was "just" and the fundamentally material dynamic of conquest skilfully relegated to a subordinate role. The laws of the Indies, especially their most liberal version of 1542–43, were thus more notable in their omission than their commission – as the suppressed chronicles of Felipe Guaman Poma de Ayala would later show.

There now occurred a curious process whereby Spain became the engine of the emergence of a "modern" mercantile economy fuelled by American gold (whatever disputes may still remain to be resolved about the exact degree of inflation it encouraged). By dint of its conquest and control of America, Spain also became the heartland of absolutism in Europe, its grand purpose the restoration of a feudal empire. The impact of America on Spain, indeed on Europe in general, was to create a crisis in Europe's idea of its centrality in world history – Europe at the centre of the world just as planet earth lay at the heart of the solar system in the orchestration of the spheres. It responded, in J.H. Elliott's words, by "bringing down the mental shutters" and reinventing a Renaissance Europe at grips with barbarism. And the medieval myths resurfaced again and again as travellers continued to search for the Golden Man (El Dorado), the Seven Cities of Cíbola, and the Amazons.

In the greater purposes of Conquest and Exploitation, the other America, Utopian America, was largely – but not entirely – forgotten. At the outer edges of empire, the missions set out to recreate the ordered moral community envisaged in the commentaries upon the first discoveries, in Paraguay, in California, on the island of Janitzio in Mexico. In his reflections at the century's end, the great French essayist Montaigne noted how little credit civilization had brought upon itself by its conduct of the Conquest of America. "I do not find that there is anything barbarous or wild in this nation, excepting

that everyone gives the denomination barbarism to what is not the custom of this country. There the people are wild, just as we call fruits wild which nature produces of itself . . . whereas in truth we ought to call those wild whose natures we have changed by our artifice and diverted from the common order . . ." It was this America that was rediscovered by Rousseau and the Enlightenment, and even, to some extent, by the ecological movements of the 20th century. The Inca and Aztec empires have been seen, in recent years, as contradictory sources of an alternative history – both absolutist empires and sources of ideas and structures of common ownership and shared responsibility.

In some ways, then, the invention of America is not a moment but a continuous activity in which this act of Conquest, what Gómara called "the greatest event in the world since the Creation," is assessed and reassessed by those who have need to rewrite their history, to understand the laws and dynamics that move their own world, and to find evidence there of all that humanity is capable of – for good and for ill.

MIKE GONZALEZ

See also entries on Caliban, Civilization and Barbarism, Magical Realism

Further Reading

Brandon, William, *New Worlds for Old: Reports from the New World and Their Effect on the Development of Social Thought in Europe, 1500–1800*, Athens: Ohio University Press, 1986 [A wonderful account of the impact of discovery on European thought]

Elliott, J.H., *The Old World and the New 1492–1650*, Cambridge: Cambridge University Press, 1970; reprinted Cambridge: Canto, 1994

O'Gorman, Edmundo, *La invención de América; el universalismo de la cultura de Occidente*, Mexico City: Fondo de Cultura Económica, 1950; as *The Invention of America; an Inquiry into the Historical Nature of the New World and the Meaning of Its History*, Bloomington: Indiana University Press, 1961

Said, Edward, *Orientalism: Western Conceptions of the Orient*, New York: Pantheon, and London: Routledge and Kegan Paul, 1978 [Said studies here another classic example of Europe's "invention" of a part of the world]

Sale, Kirkpatrick, *The Conquest of Paradise: Christopher Columbus and the Columbian Legacy*, New York: Knopf, 1990; London: Hodder and Stoughton, 1991 [A passionate and well-written account of the Conquest from an environmental perspective]

Américo de Almeida, José

See Almeida

Enrique Amorim 1900–1960

Uruguayan prose writer and poet

Enrique Amorim was many things at once: dandy, novelist, poet, wealthy man, traveller, film maker, landowner, writer of detective stories, Communist Party intellectual (from 1947). His complex and contradictory personality made him one of the most dynamic and interesting men of his time, friend of famous European figures because of his frequent trips, especially to Paris. Amorim started his literary career in 1920 with a book of poems, *Veinte años* [At Twenty], which made him part of the avant-garde movement. He nevertheless had a rather ambiguous association with cultural movements, switching back and forth from the avant-garde to Realism as often as he wished.

Only one of Amorim's short stories, "Las Quitanderas" [The Travelling Whores] can be considered "realist." His short novel *Tangarupá* (1925) was also classed as "rural" literature but had a flavour of the aesthetic. The following year, *Horizontes y bocacalles* [Horizons and Street Corners] compared countryside and city, the two settings in which the rest of his work would be set, without settling for one of them. Six years later, he developed the theme of "the travelling whores" in his novel *La carreta*, 1932 [The Wagon], and explored a new aspect of novels of the Uruguyan countryside: sexuality. *La carreta* tells the story of a group of ambulant whores who travelled the pampas selling love. Amorim said: "In *La carreta* I have examined from one particular angle the sexual mores of people living in northern Uruguay, on the frontier with Brazil. It is a region where women are notable by their absence, and this particular shortage is no doubt what roused in me the painful bitter image of the travelling whore."

In 1934, the novelist's eye probed deeper and alighted deliberately on a historical figure, the gaucho, who had disappeared by then in real life (although not from literature) to be replaced by the "paisano," the rural labourer. The result was the novel *El paisano Aguilar* [Aguilar the Countryman]. Amorim wanted to refute Ricardo Güiraldes's portrait of the mythical gaucho in *Don Segundo Sombra*. He wanted to show instead the "real" gaucho, without make-up or "literature." As Borges said: "Enrique Amorim works in the present. His novels show the Uruguayan countryside as it is now. He doesn't write to serve a myth or to deny it. He, like all true novelists, is interested in people, things, motives, and not generic symbols." Nevertheless, Amorim described a "type" through one particular character, something he would do again in *El caballo y su sombra* (*The Horse and His Shadow*). In *El paisano Aguilar* he emphasized the idiosyncrasies of the typical countryman whom modern life had transformed from nomadic (gaucho) to settled (*paisano*). While the gaucho was still seen as a rebel, the *paisano* personified patience, calm, peace, and mediocrity.

In *El caballo y su sombra*, Amorim provided a clear portrayal of the two poles of the social equation. On the one side, the landowner Nicolás Azara, who represented the ranch-owning bourgeoisie. And on the other, the immigrants herded together in their camps, with no land to cultivate, overcrowded and despised by the *criollos*. The novel's sympathies lie with the immigrant but it offers no real life answers to the social and economic divisions. Criticism of the *latifundistas*, for example, does not stem from ownership of the land itself but from the inefficient use of the land. For Amorim, the evil was not that some owned land and others did not, but that the former did not comply with their paternalistic duties: creating schools, building roads, allowing mobility of labour, and even giving up part (the uncultivated part) of his land. The principle of property was not questioned.

Realism, nourished by a growing social concern, continued in books like *La victoria no viene sola*, 1952 [Victory Does not Come by Itself], a failed exercise in "socialist realism" and *Nueve lunas sobre Neuquén*, 1946 [Nine Moons over Neuquen], which dealt with Fascists in post-war Argentina. The former, although flawed, is interesting for the description of the forces that were operating during that period and which, basically, is anecdote transferred to text. As Stalin said "Victory doesn't come by itself, you have to organize it". Behind this slogan is a whole plan of action. Two characters of different social background and position – a worker and a lawyer – represent the struggle of the proletariat and its fellow traveller, liberalism, to change the structure of an unjust world. Although the characters are comrades, the author sees them quite differently. The lawyer makes his classmates sign petitions and declarations of support for the workers, while the worker takes more direct action like helping a colony of immigrants occupy a *latifundio*. They work towards the same end in two different ways, since these are the means of struggle traditionally conceived and carried out by their respective social classes. This demonstrates both Amorim's militancy and, at the same time, its limitations. He belonged to the bourgeoisie and sympathized with the proletariat.

Apart from a few subsequent minor novels, Amorim finished his productive period with three of his best novels towards the end of the 1950s: *Corral abierto* [Open Corral], *Los montaraces* [The Backwoods Men], *La desembocadura* [The River Mouth]. They demonstrate a combination of narrative skill and freedom of fantasy. In *Corral abierto*, Amorim selected Montevideo and a town in the interior of Uruguay as a backdrop, and dealt with contemporary themes: juvenile delinquence, life in children's hostels, and also the famous "rats' towns" – the rings of shanty towns round the big cities. *Los montaraces*, penetrating the "Goddess Fantasy" he talks about in *La desembocadura*, invented a world of nature, inspired by the problems and characters created by Horacio Quiroga in the province of Misiones. His hero reaches "the accursed island," protected from curious eyes by legends of fear and death. His deed acts as a cathartic example for a group of men – forest wardens and lumberjacks – who through courage and desperation throw off both their wall of superstition and their exploitation by the lumber company. Finally, in *La desembocadura*, Amorim attempted a summary of his world, looking back over the years since the turn of the century. Despite covering barely a hundred pages, it spans the different periods described in his novels, and makes direct allusions to them. The book has a particular structure which demonstrates what has been the central feature of Amorim's work. It recreates almost a century of history, from the invasion of Indian land (the infamous "conquest of the desert"), to the war with the English in the River Plate, passing through world revolutions, influences on daily life in the modern cities, and social changes in the countryside.

These three works are the pinnacle of Amorim's intellectual development. From concern for society, he passed to concern for humanity with its principle of responsibility. His total commitment to a political and ideological line was not exclusively due to belonging to a body of ideas but rather to an awareness of the futility of solitary literary output and the need to join forces to fight for man's freedom. This is where the Amorim of 1930 differs from the Amorim of 1940 and the Amorim of 1950, although, as the whole body of his work demonstrates, he followed the normal path of a man wanting to participate actively in the world around him.

JORGE RUFFINELLI

translated by Ann Wright

Biography

Born in Salto, a provincial town in northern Uruguay, 25 July 1900. First-born of seven brothers. His mother, Doña Candelaria, was something of a feminist and had thwarted literary aspirations. She wrote for the local press and saw in Enrique the extension of her literary self. His secondary education was completed in Buenos Aires. Studied law at the University of La Plata, but dropped out. Published collection of poems, *Veinte años* [At Twenty], in 1920. Associated with the politically radical "Boedo" group of writers. Their publishing house, *Claridad*, brought out his short novel, *Tangarupá* (1925). Married Esther Haedo in 1928. Represented Argentina at PEN Club congress in 1931. Mother died in 1935, the year in which his only child, Liliana, was born. Although he loved the good life when he was young and travelled frequently to Europe, he joined the Communist Party in 1947. Forced to leave Argentina in 1950 because of his politics. Returned to Salto. Developed heart condition but continued to write prolifically until his death. Died in Buenos Aires, 28 July 1960.

Selected Works

Novels

Las quitanderas, Buenos Aires: Latina, 1924
La carreta: novela de quitanderas y vagabundos, Buenos Aires: Claridad, 1932
El paisano Aguilar, Montevideo: Amigos del Libro Ríoplatense, 1934
La edad despareja, Buenos Aires: Claridad, 1938
El caballo y su sombra, Buenos Aires: Club del Libro A.L.A, 1941; as *The Horse and His Shadow*, translated by Richard L. O'Connell and James Graham Luján, New York: Scribner, 1943
La luna se hizo con agua, Buenos Aires: Claridad, 1944
El asesino desvelado, Buenos Aires: Emecé, 1945
Nueve lunas sobre Neuquén, Buenos Aires: Lautaro, 1946
La victoria no viene sola, Montevideo: Bolsa de los Libros, 1952
Feria de farsantes, Buenos Aires: Futuro, 1952

Todo puede suceder, Montevideo: Vir, 1955
Corral abierto, Buenos Aires: Losada, 1956
Los montaraces, Buenos Aires: Goyanarte, 1957
La desembocadura, Buenos Aires: Losada, 1958
Eva Burgos, Montevideo: Alfa, 1960

Short Fiction

Amorim, Montevideo: Editorial Pegaso, 1923
Tangarupá, Buenos Aires: Claridad, 1925 [novella]
Horizontes y bocacalles, Buenos Aires: El Inca, 1926
Tráfico: Buenos Aires; cuentos y notas, Buenos Aires: Latina, 1927; as *Buenos Aires y sus aspectos*, Buenos Aires: Galerna, 1967
La trampa del pajonal: cuentos y novelas, Buenos Aires: L.J. Rosso, 1928
Del uno al seis, Montevideo: Impresora Uruguaya, 1932
Presentación de Buenos Aires, Buenos Aires: Triángulo, 1936
La plaza de las carretas, Buenos Aires: Viau, 1937
Cuentos de amor, Santiago de Chile: Eralle, 1938; as *Historias de amor*, Santiago de Chile: Eralle, 1938
Después del temporal, Buenos Aires: Quetzal, 1953
Temas de amor, Buenos Aires: Instituto Amigos del Libro Argentino, 1960
Los pájaros y los hombres, Montevideo: Galería Libertad, 1960
Prostibulario, with others, Buenos Aires: Merlín, 1967
Miel para la luna, y otros relatos, Paysandú, Uruguay: Cerno, 1969

Poetry

Veinte años, versos, Buenos Aires: Imprenta Mercatali, 1920
Un sobre con versos, privately printed, 1925
Visitas al cielo, Buenos Aires: Manuel Gleizer, 1929
Cinco poemas uruguayos, Salto, Uruguay: Magall, 1935
Dos poemas, Salto, Uruguay: Ediciones Populares, 1940
Cuaderno salteño, Montevideo: Impresora Uruguaya, 1942
Primero de mayo, Montevideo: Adelante, 1949
Quiero, Montevideo: Impresora Uruguaya, 1954
Sonetos del amor en octubre, Buenos Aires: Botella al Mar, 1954
Mi patria: poemas, Montevideo: Ediciones Papel de Poesía, 1960

Other Writings

Juan Carlos Castagnino, Buenos Aires: Losada, 1945 [monograph]
La segunda sangre, Pausa en la selva, Yo voy más lejos, Buenos Aires: Conducta, 1950 [plays]
Don Juan 38: pasatiempo en tres actos, Montevideo: Ediciones del Autor, 1959 [play]
El Quiroga que yo conocí, Montevideo: Arca, 1983 [biography of Horacio Quiroga]

Further Reading

Ainsa, Fernando (editor), *La carreta*, Madrid: UNESCO, Colección Archivos, 1988 [Critical edition; contains a range of articles on this novel by important scholars]
Buranelli, Álvaro Miranda and Carlos Nodar Freire, *Enrique Amorim: enfoques críticos*, Montevideo: Editores Asociados, 1990 [Includes contributions by Mario Benedetti, Ángel Rama and Emir Rodríguez Monegal]
Garet, Leonardo, *La pasión creadora de Enrique Amorim*, Montevideo: Editorial Asociados, 1990
Mose, K.E.A., *Enrique Amorim: the Passion of a Uruguayan*, Madrid: Playor, 1973

Carlos Drummond de Andrade 1902–1987

Brazilian poet

Carlos Drummond de Andrade was born in 1902, in Itabira do Mato Dentro, Minas Gerais, about three hundred miles from Rio de Janeiro. He is widely considered to be his country's foremost poet, and there have been a number of translations of his work into English. In his poetry there is a tension between a deep sense of introspection and a desire to reach some form of dialogue with the world. He expresses this in a range of often conflicting tones of voice as he moves through a wide span of themes. These include the multifold dimensions of love, his awareness of the social and political problems of the modern age, and poetry and language themselves.

This latter concern and the crisis which surrounds it in the Brazil of the 1920s is apparent in his very first writings. In his first collection of poetry, *Alguma poesia*, 1930 [Some Poetry], a significant manifestation of this crisis is to be found in his little masterpiece "No meio do caminho" where the poet's attention is obsessively focussed on the memory of a stone in the middle of the road. He cannot seem to translate this basic experience into discursive language, and it just goes round and round in his mind. Inert and unyielding, the stone is both external to him and yet it transfuses his inner world as all physical activity is reduced to the operation of his "fatigued retinas" and the repetition of the almost meaningless statement – "in the middle of the road there was a stone." This poem encapsulates the crisis facing the poet as he moves away from the fading conventional literary forms towards Modernism and its new challenges. This whole problem of literary expression is indeed the subject of a series of articles written by Drummond during this period.

On the other hand, the poet is able to cultivate an ironic and natural response to the contradictions of poetry and of the world. One of the important stylistic devices that shape his poetry is the assembling of refined and banal imagery, elevated and prosaic experience with shifting and ironic points of view. It is undoubtedly the case that these profound internal dissonances and reassessments subvert of all that constitutes conventional poetry and call into question the relation between the poet and the world. There is a homology between the contradictions and paradoxes of the poem and the human condition as he takes us through assorted changes of direction in his suppositions.

One of the most pervasive themes is that of love as he shifts back and forth, frequently sabotaging the feeling from inside. Features of such poems include a chaotic enumeration in the listing of words for humorous effect, quirky and contradictory points of view, and a tentative sense of groping his way through the syntax. In "Aurora" he makes the claim that love is a wonderful thing and then immediately subverts this with the parenthetical inclusion of "(love and other products)." In "Necrológio dos desiludidos do amor" a mocking tone is emphasized in relation to those disillusioned in love with their "stomachs full of poetry." Irony is present in the way perspectives are inverted and matters of intense human interiority are flaunted and treated in a manner which

appears to diminish and devitalize them. However, this use of irony empathetically draws the reader towards the acceptance of a tone of voice which is not normally associated with the love experience.

The same contrasts, the continual references to the ambiguous and discordant nature of poetry become particularly prominent as the poet struggles to come to terms with what is also a very personal matter. Poetry and expression are frequently contrasted with conflicting images of silence as in "Secreto" or "Poema patético" in *Brejo das almas*, 1934 [Morass of Souls]. The long poem "Procura da poesia" [The Search for Poetry] from the collection *A rosa do povo*, 1945 [The Rose of the People] introduces a whole gamut of contradictory precepts. It is difficult to locate the identity of the speaker in this poem, a strategy which further subverts the reader's grasp of the speech situation. "Nosso tempo" [Our Time] is another long poem from this collection which this time addresses the problem of alienation in modern society, a condition characterized by "a time of splintering, /a time of split men." The poet reacts against this but finds in his efforts to resist that the words "have lost their meaning." In the final climactic lines of the poem, he poses the controversial question of the poet's social effectiveness, a liberation based on words and symbols. The poet has been powerless to withstand the historic forces which are responsible for the current state of affairs and the promise of future help is summed up in the final image of the "worm."

Another integral component of his poetry is the attempt to recreate his childhood world in the state of Minas Gerais. However, whilst poems such as "Viagem na família" [Journey with the Family] and "Retrato de família" [Family Portrait] do of course incorporate the theme of the family and of Itabira, there is also present the depressing reality of the present and the challenge of what this past really represents to him now. Yet again in "Nos áureos tempos" [Our Golden Times], childhood is linked with a utopian quest for a reconstituted world as he painfully recognizes that such a reconstruction is no more than a distant ideal. In this way, Drummond takes the world of family and childhood beyond their narrower periphery and in the direction of issues of more universal import. He explores the intricate network of family and self, imagination and reality, the utopian aspirations blocked by the diminished spaces and debased values of a world of surplus accumulation characterized by "gardens of sickness" and "stores of tears."

Drummond's poetry moves through successive stages from the earlier Modernist collections of *Alguma poesia* and *Brejo das almas* to the social and political notes of *Sentimento do mundo*, 1940 [Feeling about the World] and *A rosa do povo*, and the broader sweeps of *Claro enigma*, 1951 [Clear Enigma]. However, throughout his work there is a strong current that encompasses the dialectical admixture of contraries and his engagement with his own personal and national origins. There is a struggle to mediate between the "big world" and the "little heart" and, furthermore, to reconcile to some degree the conflictual nature of existence. This carries over from one collection to another and forms a complex web of continuity which transcends the changes and transitions of his work.

JOHN MYLES KINSELLA

Biography

Born in Itabira do Mato Dentro, Minas Gerais, Brazil, 31 October 1902. Educated at Arnaldo College, Belo Horizonte, 1910–13; obliged to return home because of poor health, where he was educated privately. Attended Jesuit Anchieta College, Nova Friburgo, 1916–18 (expelled); studied pharmacy from 1923 to 1924 and qualified the following year but never practised. Married Dolores Dutra de Morais in 1925 and had a son who died in infancy and one daughter. Took up a career in journalism in Belo Horizonte and Rio de Janeiro, 1920–22. Co-founding editor of the magazine, *A Revista*, 1925: closed after three issues. Teacher of geography and Portuguese in Itabira, 1926. Worked on the newspapers *Diário de Minas*, 1926–29, and *Minas Gerais*, 1929, both in Belo Horizonte. Civil servant from 1928, served as chief secretary to minister of education in Rio de Janeiro, 1934–45 (resigned). Co-editor of *Tribuna Popular*, an organ of the Brazilian Communist Party, 1945. Director of the history section of the Office of the National Historical and Artistic Heritage, 1945–62. Visited Buenos Aires in 1950 and 1953. Contributor to several newspapers and journals, including *Correio de Manhã* and *Jornal do Brasil*, 1963–84. Awarded Brasília Prize for Literature (refused), 1975 and the National Walmap Prize for Literature, 1975. Died 17 August 1987.

Selected Works

Poetry

Alguma poesia, Belo Horizonte, Brazil: Pindorama, 1930
Brejo das almas, Belo Horizonte, Brazil: Os Amigos da Poesia, 1934
Sentimento do mundo, Rio de Janeiro: Pongetti, 1940
A rosa do povo, Rio de Janeiro: José Olympio, 1945
Poesía até agora, Rio de Janeiro: José Olympio, 1948 [Includes previous collections and *Novos poemas*]
Claro enigma, Rio de Janeiro: José Olympio, 1951
Viola de bolso, Rio de Janeiro: Serviço de documentação do MEC, 1952
Fazendeiro do ar e poesía até agora, Rio de Janeiro: José Olympio, 1953 [Includes previous collections and *Fazendeiro do ar*]
Poemas, Rio de Janeiro: José Olympio, 1959 [Includes previous collections and *A vida passada a limpo*]
Lição de coisas, Rio de Janeiro: José Olympio, 1962
Versiprosa, Rio de Janeiro: José Olympio, 1967
Boitempo e A falta que ama, Rio de Janeiro: José Olympio, 1969
Reunião, Rio de Janeiro: José Olympio, 1969 [Includes collections published between 1930 and 1962, except *Viola de bolso*]
Menino antigo, Rio de Janeiro: José Olympio, 1973
As impurezas do branco, Rio de Janeiro: José Olympio, 1974
Amor, amores, Rio de Janeiro: Record, 1975
Discursos de primavera e algumas sombras, Rio de Janeiro: José Olympio, 1977; augmented 2nd edition, 1978
Esquecer para lembrar, Rio de Janeiro: José Olympio, 1979
A paixão medida, Rio de Janeiro: José Olympio, 1980
Nova reunião, Rio de Janeiro: José Olympio, 1983
Corpo, Rio de Janeiro: Record, 1984
Amar se aprende amando, Rio de Janeiro: Record, 1985
Poesia errante: derrames líricos (e outros, nem tanto, ou nada), Rio de Janeiro: Record, 1988

Other Writings

De notícias e não notícias faz-se a crônica, histórias, diálogos, divagações, Rio de Janeiro: José Olympio, 1974
Os dias lindos: crônicas, Rio de Janeiro: José Olympio, 1977
Moça deitada na grama, Rio de Janeiro: Record, 1987
Auto-retrato e outras crônicas, edited by Fernando Py, Rio de Janeiro: Record, 1989

Anthologies in Translation

An Anthology of Twentieth-Century Brazilian Poetry, translated by Elizabeth Bishop and Emanuel Brasil, Middletown, Connecticut: Wesleyan University Press, 1972
Souvenir of the Ancient World, translated by Mark Strand, New York: Antaeus Editions, 1976
The Minus Sign: a Selection from the Poetic Anthology, translated by Virgínia de Araújo, Manchester: Carcanet, 1981
Travelling in the Family: Selected Poems, translated by Thomas Colchie and Mark Strand, New York: Random House, 1986

Further Reading

Brasil, Assis, *Carlos Drummond de Andrade*, Rio de Janeiro: Livros do Mundo Inteiro, 1971
Brayner, Sônia (editor), *Carlos Drummond de Andrade: fortuna crítica*, Rio de Janeiro: Civilização Brasileira, 1977
Cândido, Antônio, "Inquietudes na poesia de Drummond," in *Vários escritos*, São Paulo: Martins, 1967
Coelho, Joaquim-Francisco Mártires, *Terra e família na poesia de Carlos Drummond de Andrade*, Belém do Pará: Universidade Federal do Pará, 1973
Fonseca, José Eduardo da, *O telurismo na literatura brasileira e na obra de Carlos Drummond de Andrade*, Belo Horizonte, Brazil: Seção de Publicações do Departamento de Letras Vernáculas da Faculdade de Letras da Universidade de Minas Gerais, 1970
Gledson, John, *Poesia e poética de Carlos Drummond de Andrade*, São Paulo: Duas Cidades, 1981
Gonzalez, Mike and David Treece, *The Gathering of Voices: the Twentieth-Century Poetry of Latin America*, London and New York: Verso, 1992 [Book on Latin American poetry which contains detailed discussion of Drummond's work]
Houaiss, Antônio, *Drummond: mais seis poetas e um problema*, Rio de Janeiro: Imago, 1976
Kinsella, John Myles, "Colliding Discourses: a Reading of Drummond's *Brejo das almas*," *Brasil/Brazil* 8 (1992)
____ *Diálogo de conflito: a poesia de Carlos Drummond de Andrade*, Rio Grande do Norte, Brazil: Universidade Federal do Rio Grande do Norte, and Maine: University of Southern Maine, 1994–95
Lima, Luís Costa, "O princípio-corrosão na poesia de Carlos Drummond" in *Lira e antilira: Mário, Drummond, Cabral*, Rio de Janeiro: Civilização Brasileira, 1968
Merquior, José Guilherme, *Verso e universo em Drummond*, Rio de Janeiro: José Olympio, 1975
Sant'Anna, Affonso Romano de, *Drummond*, Rio de Janeiro: Lia, 1972
Simon, Iumna Maria, *Drummond: uma poética do risco*, São Paulo: Ática, 1978
Sternberg, Ricardo da Silveira Lobo, *The Unquiet Self: Self and Society in the Poetry of Carlos Drummond de Andrade*, Valencia: Albatros/Hispanófila, 1986
Teles, Gilberto Mendonço, *Drummond: a estilística da repetição*, Rio de Janeiro: José Olympio, 1970
Williams, Frederick G., *Carlos Drummond de Andrade and His Generation*, Santa Barbara: University of California, 1986

A rosa do povo

Collection of poems by Carlos Drummond de Andrade

A rosa do povo, published in 1945, consists of the poems written during the years of World War II. Critics are unanimous in declaring this to be an outstanding collection by Drummond de Andrade. The poems of A rosa do povo reveal the spirit of a mature writer, one who acknowledges straightforwardly his own responsibility both as a craftsman of language and as a member of society. In his 1945 book, Drummond indicates that he is still pursuing the objectives he had devised in Sentimento do mundo, 1940 [Feeling about the World] and which are defined in the final verses of the poem "Mãos dadas" [Holding Hands]: "O tempo é a minha matéria, o tempo presente, os homens presentes, / a vida presente" (Time is my matter, present time, present men, / present life). The problem of time, of our human inability to comprehend fully and accept its position within the inexorable flowing of the hours is one of the main themes of A rosa do povo. However, besides the metaphysical approach, Drummond deals with time in its present dimension and adopts a critical posture towards the world around him, with its social injustices and the everyday struggle of men and women in 20th-century society.

The two opening poems of A rosa do povo, "Consideração do poema" [Considering the Poem] and "Procura da poesia" [The Search for Poetry], draw attention to the question of poetic composition and its role within human existence. They reveal the two leading concerns in Drummond's poetry: to take part in a programme of social reform and to explore the full potential of language, in the pursuit of verbal art. "Consideração do poema" illustrates Drummond's commitment to social matters, his rejection of traditional notions of poetic excellence, in favour of the Brazilian Modernists' aspiration to create a type of poetry congenial to life in the modern age. As he announces his aversion to uncontrolled sentimentality, "Poeta do finito e da matéria, / cantor sem piedade, sim, sem frágeis lágrimas" (Poet of the finite and of matter, / poet without pity, yes, without easy tears), Drummond ends his first poem by summarising his commitment in some of the most important verses in the book: "Tal uma lâmina, / o povo, meu poema, te atravessa." (Just like a blade, / the people, my poem, cuts through you). The confident tone of the first poem does not match that of the exordial verses of the following, "Procura da poesia." Here Drummond appears more interested in admonishing than in asserting: "Não faças versos sobre acontecimentos. / Não há criação nem morte perante a poesia." (Do not write verses on events. / There is no creation or death before poetry). What may seem openly supportive of the cult of beauty is in fact the declaration of the poet's other primary task: to dive into the mysteries of language and the secret forces of words to unveil the poetry they hold.

In the third poem in the book, "A flor e a náusea" [The Flower and Nausea], Drummond leads the reader to the greyness of modern urban life. The focus is on the poet's critical posture towards the contemporary world, with which he identifies himself in extremely negative terms when he says:

"O tempo pobre, o poeta pobre / fundem-se no mesmo impasse." (Poor time, and the poor poet / are cast as one in the same impasse). The poet declares his failure as a magician of language and feels part of the world's inadequacy, with its tedium and lack of justice. But as the poet observes the world around him and despairs of hope, a flower makes its appearance and restores his confidence in the future. The flower without a name, which seems to be a sign of the rose of the people, can overturn the status quo: "É feia. Mas é uma flor. Furou o asfalto, o tédio, o nojo e o ódio." (It is ugly. But it is a flower. It pierced the asphalt, the boredom, the nausea and the hatred).

"Nosso tempo" [Our Time], is a long poem divided in eight parts that also touches upon the theme of industrial society. Drummond focuses on the alienation of men and women, the mechanisation of life and the process of reification it suffers under the capitalist system, and in part V of the poem creates what is one of the most dramatic pictures of daily existence in the big city. The subject here is the hurried lunch hour in town and the opulent classes of society are portrayed by grotesque imagery of fragmented bodies, such as mouths avidly sucking up the soup or arms mechanically engaged in the act of eating. Drummond also depicts the plight of those who are excluded by the system: "Os subterrâneos da fome choram caldo de sopa, / olhos líquidos de cão através do vidro devoram teu osso." (The underground of hunger pleads for some broth, / a dog's watery eyes devour your bone through the window).

Drummond's political thought at the time of writing comes through clearly in A rosa do povo. Several poems in the book are in praise of communism, such as "Carta a Stalingrado" [Letter to Stalingrad] and "Telegrama de Moscou" [Telegram from Moscow]. The horrors of war constitute an important theme in the book, and the poem "Visão de 1944" [Vision of 1944] expresses the poet's anguish as he witnesses the destruction of the world and the debasement of the human race.

But apart from events of world repercussion, Drummond finds inspiration in the daily life of ordinary people in urban and rural surroundings. Drummond exploits popular idioms and colloquialisms to create a realistic picture of his time. "Caso do vestido" [The Dress Episode] is a narrative poem with a distinct dramatic character which tells a story of marital infidelity and the suffering of a woman, whose love for her husband leads her to sacrifice her self-respect and to intercede before the "other" woman in order to help her partner in his escapade. The poem revolves around the conversation of the wife and her daughters, who insist on knowing the full details of the story, which results in a true sociological account of the condition of women in Brazil's patriarchal society. The popular mood of the composition is emphasised by the metre Drummond chose to employ, which is that of the popular ballads of Brazil, known as romances. "Morte do leiteiro" [The Milkman's Death] also centres on the struggle of everyday life. The poem creates an intensely dramatic atmosphere as it focuses on one of the many anonymous victims of urban violence. "O mito" [The Myth] is a poem on unrequited love and a further example of Drummond's ability to extract his material from contemporary society. Traditional lyricism is rejected since the author refuses to apply a "poetic" name to his muse, identifying her instead as fulana, the feminine form of a Brazilian colloquialism for "so-and-so."

Reminiscence of the past also represents an important theme within the book. The memory of Itabira, the poet's birthplace, and the motif of *ubi sunt* are ever recurring in Drummond's work. His father's stern figure stands out among the other characters of time revisited, and with him Drummond brings to light the ruthless world of the all-powerful landowners of Brazil. Drummond's preoccupation with the question of time includes his reflection on the inexorable fate of all human beings. Death is in the foreground in "Os últimos dias" [The Final Days], in which the poet expresses his anguish over the approach of death and his hope that he will have the necessary strength to confront the truth. At the end of the poem Drummond refers explicitly to himself, in these terms: "E a matéria se veja acabar: adeus, composição/ que um dia se chamou Carlos Drummond de Andrade." (May matter come to an end: farewell, composition / which was once called Carlos Drummond de Andrade). The ambiguity perceived within the word "composition," which is suggested in these verses – that of a piece of poetic creation as well as of a physical and material reality – is an indication of Drummond's views on art as an integral part of the world with which it should be strongly engaged. This is undoubtedly one of the key ideas expressed in *A rosa do povo*. The homage to Mário de Andrade, in the book's penultimate poem, is proof of Drummond's recognition of the power of art within the boundaries of his country. Charlie Chaplin, celebrated in the closing poem, embodies the universal power of communication that art is endowed with, in all its forms, and its capacity to unite people from different worlds.

SARA BRANDELLERO

Editions
First edition: *A rosa do povo*, Rio de Janeiro: José Olympio, 1945

Further Reading
Campos, Maria do Carmo, "*A rosa do povo*: memória e mutilação," *Minas Gerais, Suplemento Literário*, vol. 22/1104 (20 August 1988)

Mário de Andrade 1893–1945

Brazilian prose writer and poet

It is common in many critical writings on Mário de Andrade to introduce the discussion of his work by referring to a well-known poem of his entitled "Eu sou trezentos" [I am Three Hundred]. In this poem Mário, as he is informally known in the Brazilian literary world, expresses his painful sense of being torn between many identities, in particular between Europe and Brazil. And indeed, this is a fruitful way of approaching his work since it is the extraordinary manifoldness of his preoccupations which is the hallmark of his life's work, dedicated not only to the writing of poetry and novels but also to the renewal of Brazilian culture and its emancipation from the legacy of colonialism and dependence on Europe.

Mário de Andrade was one of the leaders of the Brazilian Modernist movement of the 1920s, and his work spanned an intense involvement with the aesthetic preoccupations of the avant-garde, exploration of the role of the intellectual in an undeveloped country, research into popular culture, and practical endeavours to promote the growth of a national and democratised culture. However, in order to understand how Mário's concerns – his three hundred selves as it were – were related to each other and to his literary work it is necessary to contextualize them within the Modernist movement.

In the 1920s Brazil was undergoing a process of industrialisation which, it seemed, was enabling the country to break with its dependence on the export of primary products, a legacy inherited from the colonial period. At a cultural level, a parallel attempt to renew elite culture in accordance with the social and economic modernisation of Brazil was being formulated by the Modernist movement. This was reflected in the Modernists' use of the revolutionary aesthetic theories of the European avant-garde. The aspiration to modernity however also contained a strong nationalist element expressed in the Modernists' attack on the subservient attitude towards European culture, which characterised the conservative cultural establishment of the period, in particular the Parnassian school of poetry with its predilection for themes from Classical antiquity. Brazilian Modernism was thus characterised by two interrelated tendencies: first, aesthetic experimentation as a way of creating new forms and significations, and second, the search for a national identity through the use of popular culture and analysis of the role of the intellectual and art in the development of an autonomous national culture.

Mário de Andrade's life and work could be seen as a synthesis of these two tendencies within the Modernist movement. Several of Mário's early writings are considered seminal in that in many ways they defined the character of the early "heroic" period of Modernism. In " Mestres do passado," 1921 [Past Masters], Mário fiercely attacks the narrow formalism of Parnassianism while in *A escrava que não é Isaura*, 1923 [The Slave Who is not Isaura] and in the "Prefácio interessantíssimo" [Riveting Preface], introducing *Paulicéia desvairada*, 1922 (*Hallucinated City*), a collage-like poetic evocation of São Paulo, he sets out the precepts and objectives which characterised the Modernist movement.

He champions the use of free verse, experimentalism, non-representational art, the incorporation of spoken Portuguese into literature and the importance of the unconscious as a source of lyrical inspiration. Of particular interest in these early writings, in addition to their value as documents of Brazilian Modernism, is Mário's conception of his role as an artist working in the context of an undeveloped society marked by the colonial legacy. The aesthetics of the avant-garde, in their attack on artistic convention, enabled the subjective truth of the artist, imprisoned in the alienating language of established elite culture, to be recovered. This act of liberation was at the same time a means through which inherited European traditions were to be remade or discarded in the search for forms which were expressive and representative of Brazil. What this commitment to cultural "brazilianisation" (*abrasileiramento*), as it was defined, entailed is set out in numerous letters to Mário's friends, in critical articles on Brazilian music and musicians, and it is exemplified in his poetic and literary work. In Mário's collected letters to the poets Manuel Bandeira and Carlos Drummond de Andrade he emphasizes that while artists from cultures with secure and established traditions could afford to be solely preoccupied with aesthetic perfection, the contemporary period of national construction and self-definition demanded that he devote himself to writing what Mário defined as "circumstantial literature" (*literatura de circunstância*), that is, literary and critical work which advanced the growth of an autonomous national culture.

With this purpose in mind Mário developed some extremely interesting ideas on the relationship between language, national identity and popular culture. In order to develop a national literary culture, he argued, it was necessary to draw on popular sources, however not in a populist or arbitrary manner, thus giving the work of art a superficially folkloristic flavour, but through systematic research into the popular use of language and the compositional principles of popular music and poetry. Only this immersion in local traditions would enable Brazil to produce independent and original contributions to the Western culture of which it was after all part. Mário's nationalism was thus not isolationist or xenophobic; it was conceived primarily as a cultural practice through which the discrepancy between "Brazilian reality" and artistic forms uncritically adopted from other, European contexts might be transcended. Several works produced in the 1920s illustrate what this entailed in terms of his own literary and artistic output.

Mário's sense of his own identity was intimately connected with his conception of Brazilian identity; both were riven contradictions and dualities. In *Paulicéia desvairada*, for example, it is symbolised in the image of an Indian playing a European instrument; "Sou um tupi tangendo um alaúde!" (I am a Tupi Indian strumming a lute!) he exclaims. To this feeling of inner fragmentation and ambiguity, he counterposes the possibility of human solidarity in a spiritually unified Brazil. Thus, in "O poeta come amendoim," 1926 [The Peanut-eating Poet], he elaborates on the sensual and intimate nature of this spiritual fusion: "Brasil . . . / Mastigado na gostosura quente do amendoim . . . / falado numa língua curumim / De palavras incertas num remeleixo melancólico / . . . Brasil que eu sou porque é minha expressão muito engraçada / Porque é meu sentimento pachorrento / Porque é meu jeito de

ganhar dinheiro, de comer e de dormir. (Brazil . . . / chewed in the warm deliciousness of peanuts / spoken in a child-like tongue / of vague words in a melancholic sweet swinging gait / . . . Brazil, that is me because it is my funny expression / because it is my unhurried feeling / because it is my way of earning a living, of eating and sleeping.) It is however in the novel *Macunaíma, o herói sem nehum caráter*, 1928 (*Macunaíma*), that the many facets of Mário's preoccupations with national identity and the relationship between high and popular culture are articulated in their full complexity and richness.

Macunaíma is a mercurial trickster figure, discovered by Mário in his readings of the work of a German anthropologist on the Venezuelan Indians. He is depicted as having no character, an idea which Mário uses as a metaphor for Brazil. A mythical tribal Indian from the Amazon, Macunaíma is given a magical amulet by his lover, Ci, the Empress of the Amazon which unwittingly lands in the hands of a wealthy cannibalist/giant/industrialist in São Paulo. In order to retrieve it, Macunaíma must visit São Paulo, but his encounter with "civilisation" in the modern city leads him to betray his Amazonic origin and his eventual return to the tropical forest is marked by death and defeat. Anarchic and proficient in the use of magic to attain his ends, Macunaíma is like Brazil: multiple and full of possibility. However, his melancholy end is also a commentary on the dire consequences of not being grounded in a solid identity, of being "characterless." In its surreal construction and incorporation of elements from popular culture, this novel exemplifies perhaps most clearly the synthesis between avant-garde techniques and "the national" which the Modernists advocated.

In the late 1920s and 1930s Mário's concern with literary nationalism is broadened to include ethnographic studies of popular culture, carried out during two journeys to the Amazon and the northeast of Brazil, as well as practical experiments in cultural politics. This is accompanied by a gradual commitment to socialism, a critique of civilisation and a re-articulation of his views on the role of art, which in the context of the rise of fascism in Europe and the dictatorial state of Brazil in 1937, become increasingly critical of those who claim that art should exist only for its own sake.

Mário's journeys to the north of Brazil, informed by his readings of Freud and Keyserling, and on Surrealism and the anthropological work of Frazer, Levy-Brühl and Tyler, documented in his witty travel journals "O turista aprendiz," 1929 [An Apprentice in Tourism], led Mário to elaborate an interesting theory, first set out in "A divina preguiça," 1918 [Divine Idleness], on the importance of idleness and the principle of Being in the development of a genuine Brazilian identity. Macunaíma and the Amazon typify this quality of Being and Macunaíma's defeat after his encounter with "civilisation" encapsulates Mário's critical stance towards the instrumental rationality of Western civilisation and his growing ambivalence towards Modernity.

The 1930s was a period of political radicalisation, in which the Modernists split into right and left-wing tendencies. As a supporter of the liberal Democratic Party, Mário wrote copiously for its daily paper, the *Diário Nacional* on the relationship between art and politics. Brought together in the volume *Taxi e crônicas no Diário Nacional* [Taxi and Chronicles in the National Daily], these writings prefigure his activities as director of the Municipal Department of Culture in São Paulo in the mid 1930s.

Overviews of Mário's work rarely discuss his achievements in the Department of Culture in any great depth. They are however an important testimony of his conviction that culture, understood as a process of the spiritual growth of a people, was equally essential to the development of Brazil as economic growth. The overall aim of the Department of Culture was to disseminate both high and popular culture. This included the promotion of drama, cinema and music, research and archival work, the creation of a Museum of Ethnography and Folklore and of several music and book libraries.

Among his late essays the collections *O baile das quatro artes* [The Ball of the Four Arts] and *Aspectos da literatura brasileira* [Aspects of Brazilian Literature] contain some of his most interesting reflections on art and society; in a re-creation of Plato's Symposium, *O banquete* [The Banquet], they are placed in the mouths of several characters seated around a sumptuous dinner-table. At a different level, Mário's anguish about the state of the world is expressed in two major poetic works *Costela do grão cão*, 1937 [Great Hell Hound of October] and *Carro da miséria*, 1943 [Wagon of Misery]. "Meditação sobre o Tietê" [Meditation on the Tietê], written shortly before his death in 1945, could perhaps be considered his most poetically dense reflection on the human condition and the power of art to act as a humanising force.

VIVIAN SCHELLING

Biography

Born in São Paulo, Brazil, 9 October 1893. Attended the Escola de Nossa Senhora do Carmo from 1905 to 1909, the Álvares Penteado Commercial School in 1910 and studied piano at the Musical and Dramatic Conservatory, 1911–17, all in São Paulo. During the 1920s he was a member of avant-garde artistic circles: co-organizer of the Modern Art Week at the Teatro Municipal, São Paulo in 1922. Professor of the History of Music and Aesthetics, São Paulo Conservatory, 1925. From 1928 Andrade wrote the "Taxi" column for *Diário Nacional*. Worked for the Ministry of Educations's schools' music reform programme in 1930. With Paulo Duarte he co-founded and became the director of the Municipal Department of Culture, 1934–37. During this period he founded the Municipal Library, the Department of National Heritage, the journal *Revista do Arquivo Municipal de São Paulo* and São Paulo's Ethnography and Folklore Society (of which he became the first president). In 1937 he moved to Rio de Janeiro and in the following year became the director of the Federal University Institute of Arts. He held the Chair of Philosophy and History of Art, and headed the *Enciclopédia brasileira* project for the National Book Institute in 1939. In 1941, under commission from the Department of National Heritage, Andrade made anthropological research trips to northern Brazil. Co-founder of the Brazilian Society of Writers in 1942. Died in São Paulo, 25 February 1945.

Selected Works

Poetry

Há uma gota de sangue em cada poema, São Paulo: Pocai, 1917 [Published under the pseudonym Mário Sobral]
Paulicéia desvairada, São Paulo: Mayença, 1926; as *Hallucinated City*, edited and translated by Jack E. Tomlins, Nashville:
Vanderbilt University Press, 1968 [bilingual edition]
Clã do jaboti, São Paulo: Eugênio Cupolo, 1927
Remate de males, São Paulo: Eugênio Cupolo, 1930
Lira paulistana, São Paulo: Martins, 1946

Novels

Amar, verbo intransitivo, São Paulo, Antônio Tisi, 1927; as *Fräulein*, translated by Margaret Richardson Hollingsworth, New York: Macaulay, 1933
Macunaíma, São Paulo: Eugênio Cupolo;1928; as *Macunaíma*, translated by Edward Arthur Goodland, New York: Random House and London: Quartet, 1984
Belazart, São Paulo: Pitatininga, 1934

Short Fiction

Primeiro andar, São Paulo: Antônio Tisi, 1926
Contos novos, São Paulo: Martins, 1947 [Includes "Nelson," "Frederico Paciência," "Artás da catedral de Ruão," "O ladrão," "Primeiro de maio," and "O Peru de natal;" the last of these as "The Christmas Turkey," translated by Richard B. Brenneman, *Latin American Literary Review*, vol. 7/14 (1979)]

Essays

A escrava que não é Isaura, São Paulo: Lealdade, 1925
O movimento modernista, Rio de Janeiro: Casa do Estudante, 1942
Aspectos da literatura brasileira, Rio de Janeiro: America-Edit, 1943
O baile das quarto artes, São Paulo: Martins, 1943
Os filhos da Candinha, São Paulo: Martins, 1943

Other Writings

Compêndio da história da música, São Paulo: Chiarato, 1929; revised edition as *Pequena história da música*, São Paulo: Martins, 1942
Danças dramáticas do Brasil, 3 vols, São Paulo: Martins, 1959
Taxi e crônicas no Diário Nacional, São Paulo: Duas Cidades, 1976
O banquete, São Paulo: Duas Cidades, 1977

Compilations and Anthologies

Obras completas, 20 vols, São Paul: Martins, 1972 –
Poesias completas, edited by Diléa Zanotto Manfio, São Paulo: Martins, 1987

Further Reading

Albuquerque, Severino J., "Construction and Destruction: *Macunaíma*," *Hispania* (March 1987)
Ancona Lopez, Tele, *Mário de Andrade: ramais e caminhos*, São Paulo: Duas Cidades, 1972
Dassin, Joan, *Política e poesia em Mário de Andrade*, São Paulo: Duas Cidades, 1978
Johnson, Randal, "Macunaíma as Brazilian Hero," *Latin American Literary Review* (1978)
Lafetá, João Luiz, *Figuração da intimidade: imagens na poesia de Mário de Andrade*, São Paulo: Martins, 1986
Mello e Souza, Gilda de, *O tupi e o alaúde*, São Paulo: Duas Cidades, 1979
Proença, Manuel Cavalcanti, *Roteiro de Macunaíma*, Rio de Janeiro: Civilização Brasileira, 1978
Rosenfeld, Anatol, "Mário e o cabotinismo," in *Texto / Contexto*, São Paulo: Perspectiva, 1976
Schelling, Vivian, *A presença do povo na cultura brasileira: ensaio sobre o pensamento de Mário de Andrade e Paulo Freire*, Campinas, Brazil: Unicamp, 1991
Schwarz, Roberto, "O psicologismo na poética de Mário de Andrade," in *A sereia e o desconfiado*, Rio de Janeiro: Civilização Brasileira, 1965

Oswald de Andrade 1890–1954

Brazilian poet and prose writer

One of the most expressive writers of the first moment of Brazilian Modernism, both in the field of poetry and prose, Oswald de Andrade was also the author of two of the principal manifestos of the movement: "Poesia pau-brasil" [Brazil-Wood Poetry] and "Antropófago" [Cannibal]. The "Manifesto da poesia pau-brasil," which would be later rescued and deepened by "Antropófago," was conceived in Paris on the occasion of one of his recurrent trips to Europe. Oswald then kept in fruitful contact with representatives of the European avant-garde, allowing himself to be influenced, among all the "isms" that abounded, especially by Futurism and Primitivism (generally one can say that the former proposed to experiment with language from elements related to modern civilization, while the latter used exactly the elements repressed by it). This influence can be felt throughout his works and is evident in this first manifesto, where the writer defined the programme for his literature, i.e., a satire on the previous literary style and the class that sponsored it (of which he was the prodigal son): the "erudite" and "graduate" Brazil of the coffee aristocracy became bourgeoisie in the big cities.

He would immediately exemplify his poetry with the publication of *Pau-brasil* and *Primeiro caderno do aluno de poesia Oswald de Andrade* [The Poetry Apprentice Oswald de Andrade's First Notebook]. Both works consist of poems that are extremely short, anti-metric, anti-rhetoric, where the colloquial intervenes all the time, immediately revealing the "futurist" preoccupation with maximum conciseness in addition to the "primitivist" quest for expression free of literary prejudice, above all, the prejudice against the spontaneity of the spoken language that in his writings appears "with the millionfold contribution of all mistakes". Oswald was most successful in extracting poetry from what was previously considered apoetic. Another means invoked by him to fight the seriousness, grandiloquence, and "scholarliness" until then predominant in Brazilian literature was humour, especially parody, e.g., the poem made of fragments of the historic first letter informing Portugal of the newly found land, or the ones made of "anthological" poems such as Goncalves Dias's "Canção do Exílio"[Exile's Song].

Oswald aimed at freeing himself from the prejudice of the "erudite" and "graduate" Brazil by incorporating the primitive purity of the indigenous in *Pau brasil*, and of the child in *Primeiro caderno*, only then the poetic experience would be rediscovered: "A poesia pau-brasil. Ágil e cândida. Como uma criança" [Brazil-Wood Poetry. Agile and pure. Like a child]. To this primitivism corresponded an equivalent futurism in that this "agile" and "pure" poetry, in its economy and simplicity, dismantled the complex logical structure of the language, substituting for the old order the modern ideas of discontinuity, fragmentation, simultaneity and juxtaposition of "words in freedom." Hence the curious coexistence between the primitivism of the "pure" intuition of the child and the indian, and the modernity of the spirit of conciseness animated by the pragmatism inherent in the civilization of technique and speed.

The translation of his poetry into prose produced two (equally dismantling) novels – or inventions, as he preferred to call them: *Memórias sentimentais de João Miramar* (*The Sentimental Memoirs of John Seaborne*) and *Serafim Ponte Grande* (*Serafim grosse Pointe*). Deeply influenced, as a reader of the futurists, by the technique of cinematographic montage, Oswald inaugurated in Brazilian literature, with the publication of *Miramar*, what became known as the "aesthetics of the fragmented." Just as the rapid collage of many stills produces a film, his novel would be created from the montage of diverse text fragments, more precisely 163 fleeting chapters, displayed in blocks in a non-sequential way, juxtaposed with telegraphic conciseness, the only common axis being the character João Miramar. So in 1924 the linearity of the novel was ruptured in Brazil, through *Miramar* in which the traditional order was subverted in favour of a revolutionary one marked by the discontinuous rhythms of modern life. With *Serafim Ponte Grande*, published almost a decade later, Oswald further developed the modern technique of producing a novel by the montage of fragments, their rapid collage without supporting comparisons suggesting at the same time the primitivism of seeing with "free eyes." This time he also mixed styles, such as narrative in the first and third person and also narrative in the form of a diary. Thus, as predicted in the manifesto, his prose would be "agile" and "pure," like a child.

In the 1930s Oswald ventured into making theatre concerning social issues, *O homen e o cavalo* [The Man and the Horse], *O rei da vela* [The Candle Baron], plays that would later be acknowledged as the beginning of modern Brazilian theatre. He returned to poetry in the 1940s, and even though by then he had reached a happy combination of experimental and politically engaged literature, mainly with "Cântico dos cânticos para flauta e violão" [The Chant of Chants for Flute and Guitar] and "O escaravelho de ouro" [The Golden Beetle], the image of him that remains as the most remarkable is the one framed by the constant anarchic Primitivism of his first creations.

Teresinha V. Zimbrão da Silva

Biography

Born in São Paulo, Brazil, 11 January 1890, the only child of prosperous parents. Took up study of law, 1909. Founded the weekly *O Pirralho*, 1911; made his first trip to Europe in 1912 where he became aware of avant-garde movements. Married in 1917 and again in 1926. Second wife was the painter Tarsila do Amaral (divorced in 1930). Relationship with Patricia Galvão by whom he had a son, Rudá. Third marriage to Maria Antonieta D'Alkimin. Two children, Paulo Marcos and Antonieta Marília. Travelled to Europe and Orient in 1926. *Manifesto antropófago* published in 1928. Joined Communist Party in 1931; resigned in 1945. Stood as candidate for the PRT (Workers Revolutionary Party) in federal elections of 1950. Died on 22 October 1954.

Selected Works

Novels

A trilogia do exílio, 3 vols, 1917–21: *Alma, A estrela de absinto, A escada*; in 1 volume, as *Os condenados*, Pôrto Alegre, Brazil: Globo, 1941

Memórias sentimentais de João Miramar, São Paulo: Livraria Editora Independência, 1924; as *The Sentimental Memoirs of John Seaborne*, translated by Ralph Niebuhr and Albert Bork, Austin, Texas: Nefertiti Head Press, 1979

Serafim Ponte Grande, Rio de Janeiro: Ariel, 1933; as *Seraphim Grosse Pointe*, translated by Albert Bork and Kenneth D. Jackson, Austin, Texas: New Latin Quarter Editions, 1979

Marco zero, Rio de Janeiro: José Olympio, 1943

Um homem sem profissão: sob as ordens de mamãe, Rio de Janeiro: José Olympio, 1953

Plays

Teatro: A morta; O rei da vela, Rio de Janeiro: José Olympio, 1937

Other Writings

Ponta de lança, São Paulo: Martins, n.d.

Primeiro caderno do aluno de poesia Oswald de Andrade, São Paulo: privately printed, 1927

Compilations and Anthologies

Obras completas, 24 vols, Rio de Janeiro: Civilização Brasileira, 1972– ; 2nd edition, São Paulo: Globo, 1990–

Further Reading

Only after the publication of the monograph by Haroldo de Campos was critical interest awakened in Oswald de Andrade's works.

Brito, Mário da Silva, *As metamorfoses de Oswald de Andrade*, São Paulo: Conselho Estadual de Cultura, Comissão de Literatura, 1972

Campos, Haroldo de, *Oswald de Andrade*, Rio de Janeiro: Agir, 1967

Cândido, Antônio, "Oswald viajante," in his *Vários escritos*, São Paulo: Duas Cidades, 1970

Chalmers, Vera, *3 linhas e 4 verdades – o jornalismo de Oswald de Andrade*, São Paulo: Duas Cidades, 1976

Gonzalez, Mike and David Treece, *The Gathering of Voices: the Twentieth Century Poetry of Latin America*, London and New York: Verso, 1992 [chapter 3 is on Brazilian Modernism]

Helena, Lúcia, *Totens e tabus da modernidade brasileira: símbolo e alegoria na obra de Oswald de Andrade*, Rio de Janeiro: Tempo Brasileiro, 1985

Jackson, Kenneth D., *A prosa vanguardista na literatura brasileira: Oswald de Andrade*, São Paulo: Perspectiva, 1978

Schwartz, Jorge, *Oswald de Andrade*, São Paulo: Abril Educação, 1980

Manifesto antropófago

Manifesto by Oswald de Andrade

Published in 1928, the "Manifesto antropófago" consolidated the cultural and poetic vision of Modernist writer Oswald de Andrade, which is here made explicit through praising the "evil" wild man, the cannibal devourer of the white European.

Oswald thus abandoned the submissive image of "the noble savage" – defined by an idealization of the wild – in favour of an immaculate perspective of the opposite, to be admired in its difference, i.e., not in spite of, but because of cannibalism. Whereupon this stifled root – a taboo of the Brazilian national identity – was daringly proclaimed a legitimate expression of culture (totem). And so immediately one of the main principles of the manifesto came of age: "A transformação permanente do Tabu em totem" (The permanent transformation of the taboo into totem). The principle had important consequences for Brazilian literature since it entailed proclaiming that the country's barbarism – taboo because until then it was a cause for embarrassment (or at best romantic idealization) when compared to the civilized metropolis, the mirror in which the colony was always contemplating itself – should therefore be seen as a source of inspiration, and not any more as a hindrance in the production of culture. And a most original source of inspiration since it represented the native element in all its rusticity, radically modifying the foreign model.

So, if on the one hand it is true that the poetic and cultural vision of Oswald de Andrade was inspired by European Primitivism (in the sense that the latter proposed experimentation with language from elements repressed by modern society), on the other hand it is no less true that this primitivism underwent a radical modification when it was itself "digested" by the cannibalism of the "Brasil Caraíba." Hence it was primarily cannibalism, persistent instinct: "Nunca fomos catequisados" (We have never been catechized) inherited from the indigenous, intended as the major source of inspiration for the Cannibal movement. The movement, in the spirit of the metaphor after which it was named, then proposed the critical devouring of the European contribution – to the point of transforming the latter into some other product, with its own characteristics – instead of the previous passive acceptance predominant in the country's literary media. In other words, just like the cannibal who critically devoured his enemies, thus incorporating the Other, though only to obtain his "essence" necessary for the renewal of his or her forces; in the same way, Brazilian literature in order to obtain what it needed – originality – should in its turn critically devour foreign models: "Antropofagia. Absorção do inimigo sacro. Para transformá-lo em totem" (Cannibalism. Absorption of the sacred enemy to transform it into totem). In brief, in this process of incorporation the foreign models in contact with the "native enzymes" during "digestion" would be radically modified, to the point of being transformed into something original.

Oswald symbolically dates his "Manifesto antropófago" from the day the indigenous people devoured Dom Pedro Sardinha, the first bishop in Brazil: "Ano 374 da Deglutição do Bispo Sardinha" (Year 374 after the Swallowing of Bishop Sardinha). This event could be claimed to be the first of the most expressive ones that have been taking place in the country in a cannibalistic process of assimilation of European culture: the cannibals were in their own way assimilating the supposed religious virtues (totem) of the missionary enemy (taboo), sent from Europe to catechize them. More than three hundred years later, one could add to that one another major event, the original Oswaldian ingestion of European Primitivism, and the further ingestion of Shakespeare who, after being critically "digested" by the Brazilian became: "Tupi or not Tupi, that is the question".

The Cannibalist movement was one of the most important aspects of Brazilian Modernism, contributing to the definitive liberation of Brazilian literature from historic and ethnic repression. In addition, from the 1920s, it created a daring programme of literary autonomy that today is considered to be one of the most coherent ever.

TERESINHA V. ZIMBRÃO DA SILVA

See also entries on Caliban, Civilization and Barbarism

Editions

First edition: *Antropofagia* in *Obras completas*, vol. 6, Rio de Janeiro: Civilização Braileira, 1978

Further Reading

Campos, Haroldo de, *Oswald de Andrade*, Rio de Janeiro: Agir, 1967

—— "Da razão antropofágica: a Europa sob o signo da devoração" in *Colóquio/Letras* 62 (July 1981)

Gonzalez, Mike and David Treece, *The Gathering of Voices: the Twentieth Century Poetry of Latin America*, London and New York: Verso, 1992

Johnson, Randal, "Tupy or not Tupy: Cannibalism and Nationalism in Contemporary Brazilian Literature and Culture," in *Modern Latin American Fiction: a Survey*, edited by John King, London: Faber and Faber, 1987 [Chapter 3 has section on this manifesto]

Nunes, Benedito, "Antropofagia ao alcance de todos," in *Do Pau-Brasil à antropofagia e às utopias: manifestos, teses de concursos e ensaios, Obras completas*, vol. 6, Rio de Janeiro: Civilização Brasileira, 1978

José Pereira da Graça Aranha 1868–1931

Brazilian prose writer

This lawyer-diplomat-judge from the northern Brazilian state of Maranhão became, almost in spite of himself, one of Brazil's best known turn-of-the-century fiction writers. His literary output is small in quantity, consisting of a half-dozen works; one of these, however – the novel *Canaã* (originally published as *Chanaãn*), 1902 (*Canaan*), based on a legal case over which he had presided – served to guarantee his fame as a writer thoroughly imbued with a heightened sense of national consciousness, great aesthetic appreciation, and an awareness of the problems of his place and time in history.

A precocious graduate of the College of Law of Recife, and disciple of Professor Tobias Barreto in particular, Graça Aranha combined an illustrious career of public service with continuous personal dedication to the creation of aesthetic beauty and the stimulation of cultural and political movements or tendencies which he perceived to be imaginative or constructive in a broad or global sense. It was the latter commitment which inspired his enthusiastic support of, and participation in, the "Semana de Arte Moderna," a multimedia inaugural manifestation of the nascent Brazilian Modernist movement in 1922.

Graça Aranha burst on the Brazilian literary scene in 1902 with his best fictional work, *Canaã*, a thesis novel dealing with German immigration to the central coastal area of Brazil during the decade of the 1890s. Though the novel espouses no fixed philosophical system, it is in large part a dialogue between two German immigrants of widely divergent persuasions and life experiences: Lentz, a Prussian racist convinced that Brazil needs strong Aryan blood to set it on a positive future course, and Milkau, an idealistic altruist dedicated to racial harmony and miscegenation. The lengthy rhetorical dialogues, or "position statements," are interspersed among narrative segments depicting the relations of the new immigrants, older groups of Germanic *colonos*, and the Portuguese-speaking mixed-race rural population, along with vividly drawn descriptions of the natural environment of the state of Espírito Santo. In the midst of this lyric prose flow (described by some anthological histories as "symbolist") falls a pathologically naturalistic episode in which a single mother of Germanic descent, expelled from home because of her pregnancy and rejected by all the other families of the immigrant colony, gives birth in the open country to a child who is almost immediately devoured by a rampaging herd of wild pigs. Justice is quick to condemn and sentence young Maria Perutz to jail, but eventually Milkau manages to liberate her and flees with her in search of an elusive Edenic future as the novel ends. "Canaã," the work's title, denotes diverse and contradictory things to the several principal actors of this dramatic novel, which in spite of its unevenness of style communicates a lasting and thought-provoking impression of a Brazil seeking its 20th-century destiny in a pluralistic world fraught with ethnic strife.

While serving as a diplomat in western Europe, Graça Aranha composed and staged (in Paris) the play *Malazarte* (1911), in which the Brazilian folkloric figure of the same name appears, along with the symbolic character Dionísia, opposite a realistic family in the throes of economic straits. Reality and fantasy intermix in Graça Aranha's only full-fledged stage play, which privileges a philosophically pantheistic view of nature as an ideally atemporal and lyric refuge for those burdened by life.

The author's 1930 novel, *A viagem maravilhosa* [The Marvelous Journey], focuses on love and revolutionary activity as the two essential pillars of life for a modern couple (Filipe and Teresa), with love winning out as the ultimate solution for all ills. As a fictional work it lacks the impact of *Canaã*.

Graça Aranha's most noteworthy non-fictional prose work is his 1921 philosophical essay, *A estética da vida* [The Aesthetics of Life]. Although it espouses no systematic body of beliefs, the book is relevant to the cultural ferment operating in western Europe and the Americas (especially Brazil) in the post-World War I period and about to explode in the advent of Modernism. Starting with an intuitive, anti-scientific view of the universe, this essay attempts to fuse the individual and the cosmic into an infinite, integrated and creative whole. Four paths to such an integration are discerned by Graça Aranha: art, philosophy, religion and love, with feeling rather than thinking serving as the best human method of achievement of the goal of transcendental happiness. Such is the author's definition of what he calls the "Metafísica brasileira." Graça Aranha's eclectic predisposition to all that might be considered culturally creative led to his involvement in the organization and coordination of the "Semana de Arte Moderna" soon after the publication of *A estética da vida*. He was a "cultural cannibal" several years before Oswald de Andrade coined the term in 1928, and in 1924 hotly defended the young Modernist writers, musicians, and artists in a speech ("O espírito moderno") before the Academia Brasileira de Letras, of which he had been a member since its founding in 1896. In the face of incomprehension and outright hostility from the majority in the traditional Academia, he severed relations with the prestigious entity and threw in his lot with the "Young Turks," for whom he served as moral support and galvanizing force.

Graça Aranha was a fairly prolific public speaker and author of newspaper articles. As editor of the works of others, he published in 1923 an annotated edition of the *Correspondência de Machado de Assis e Joaquim Nabuco* [Correspondence between Machado de Assis and Joaquim Nabuco]. Though not an original philosophical mind, he was successful in synthesizing currents of contemporary thought and communicating them in essay form and through the dialogues of his rather abstract fictional characters. His literary/cultural role in turn-of-the-century Brazil may be described as that of catalyst and "antenna" of the contradictory voices of tradition and innovation in multiple facets of national life.

MARY L. DANIEL

Biography

Born in Maranhão State, Brazil, 21 June 1868. Studied law at the University of Recife. Awarded degree, 1886. Entered diplomatic corps and worked in several countries of northern Europe. Among the founding members of the Brazilian Academy of Letters, 1896; resigned 1924. Returned to Brazil on permanent basis, 1921. Supported Brazilian *Modernismo*. Died in 1931.

Selected Works

Novels

Canaã [originally published as *Chanaān*], Rio de Janeiro: Garnier, 1902; as *Canaan*, translated by Mariano Joaquín Lorente, Boston: Four Seas Company, and London: Allen and Unwin, 1921
A viagem maravilhosa, Rio de Janeiro and Paris: Garnier, 1929

Play

Malazarte, Rio de Janeiro: F. Briquiet, 1911

Other Writings

A estética da vida, Rio de Janeiro and Paris: Garnier, 1921
O meu próprio romance, São Paulo: Companhia Editora Nacional, 1931 [autobiography]

Compilations and Anthologies

Obra completa, edited by Afrânio Coutinho, Rio de Janeiro: Instituto Nacional do Livro, 1969
Trechos escolhidos, selected by Renato Almeida, Rio de Janeiro: Livraria AGIR, 1970

Further Reading

Aiex, Anoar, "Graça Aranha and Brazilian Modernism," in *Tradition and Renewal: Essays on Twentieth-Century Latin American Literature and Culture*, edited by Merlin H. Forster, Urbana: University of Illinois Press, 1975
Lins, Augusto Emilio Estellita, *Variações estéticas do "Canaã,"* Rio de Janeiro: Editoria Lidador, 1981
Pacheco, Armando Correia, *Graça Aranha – La obra y el hombre (Escritores de América)* Washington, DC: n.p., 1951
Valério, Américo, *Graça Aranha*, Rio de Janeiro: n.p., 1932

Reinaldo Arenas 1943–1990

Cuban prose writer, poet and dramatist

The relationship between this Cuban writer's life and work is almost symbiotic. As a son abandoned by a father he never knew, as a homosexual rejected by a repressive society, as an intellectual who criticized repression in all its forms, Reinaldo Arenas's work is a cry for freedom which reaches across the frontiers of his island and takes on a universal dimension. His writing if often called the literature of exile, but it also has all the characteristics of postmodernity.

Arenas is noted for his re-writing: time and time again he had to remake stolen, confiscated, or lost novels. He devoted a large part of his life to writing what he called a pentagony, a series of five novels which recount the life of Cuba from the point of view of an almost always marginal character who dies and is reborn in the next novel to tell of some new horror. The novels are based on the historical and political cycle of Cuba over the last forty years, and begin with the publication in 1967 of *Celestino antes del alba* (*Singing from the Well*). In this novel, the narrator is a country boy who, now dead, tells of a childhood of domestic violence, wives abandoned by their husbands, children without fathers. Celestino comes back to life in *El palacio de las blanquísimas mofetas* (*The Palace of the White Skunks*). The narrator, an adolescent, also dead, tells of life under the Batista dictatorship. *Otra vez el mar* (*Farewell to the Sea*) denounces the tyranny and repression of the revolutionary regime which followed Batista to power in 1959. *El color del verano* [The Color of Summer] takes place at the end of the 20th century. It is a cruel carnavalesque parody in which the island sinks into the sea, destroyed by a people incapable of governing her. This novel also rewrites Arenas's own life story in that some chapters are a fictional version of events recounted in his autobiography. *El asalto* (*The Assault*) is Orwellian in tone in that it deals with the decomposition of a being who, under a terrible dictatorship loses his humanity and becomes, in turn, just another represser. This novel brings together all the Arenian themes and sources of anger. In a kind of catharsis, the author through his main character manages to destroy his mother who is in turn the great dictator, the origin and symbol of all repression. *El mundo alucinante* (*Hallucinations*) is based on the memoirs of the Mexican Friar Servando Teresa de Mier (1765–1827). It has a double historical plot and raises the issue of the human being's need of liberty. The entire narrative, which involves a continual switch from character to author, develops from a sentence in the prologue, presented as a letter: "The most useful thing was to discover that you and I are the same person." This sentence prefigures the novel since the fictionalized version of Fray Servando's life is mixed up with an account of the author's own life. They share repression, marginalization, prison, constant flight and exile. Aside from the autobiographical element common to all Arenas's works, *El mundo alucinante* also resembles other fictions by this author through the themes of homosexuality, eroticism, violence, death, the sea (which he loved) as a recurrent symbol, and the play of doubles. To some extent the friar's exile anticipates that of the author: "Viene de una isla salvaje a tratar con salvajes descono-

cidos. Se inicia en el destierro. Debo ser más piadoso" (He comes from a savage island to deal with unknown savages. He is learning about exile. I must be more compassionate).

Unfortunately, at the time of writing *El mundo alucinante* the writer was totally ostracized in his own country, where by this time (early 1970s) he was not allowed to publish. This, however, did not stop him writing. *Arturo, la estrella más brillante* (*Arthur the Brightest Star*) and *Que Eva trine*, 1971 [Let Eva Fume], together with *La vieja Rosa* (*Old Rosa*) written a few years earlier, form the first cycle of his short novels. The three are part of this total all-encompassing work he wanted to write.

When Arenas finally managed to escape to the United States in 1980, he recomposed and published his unpublished works. His novels written in exile began dealing with new themes. The verbal violence, suicide, death and despair, and the cruel parody of the pentagony cycle and some other short novels and stories, were abandoned. The work he wrote abroad suggests that Arenas's untimely death interrupted a possible new cycle. It shows a less brutal type of humour and a glimmer of hope. *El portero* (*The Doorman*) and *Viaje a La Habana* [Journey to Havana] demonstrate this. The more mature reflective writer abandons the structure of a closed circle, which we saw in the pentagony, and leaves the reader to recreate the ending. The end is not determined at the beginning. Arenas takes the anguish of all human life and suggests possible relief, a certain salvation, which in *El portero* seems to be the door that the hero seeks tirelessly. This door represents another dimension, perhaps spiritual, which the characters, like the author, seem to welcome.

Arenas's poetry is to a large extent part of this total work he was trying to write. It is in his poetry that art demonstrates the power to make human beings transcend their own limitations, because as he says in *El color del verano*, poetry envelops him in "el éxtasis de la belleza" (the ecstasy of beauty). *Leprosorio* [The Leper Colony] combines the themes found in most of his other work. This long poem unearths fifty years of continual slavery and pain under different oppressive systems. Like the French philosopher, Michel Foucault, Reinaldo Arenas mentioned on various occasions the possibility of transcendence through words, through creation. In the work which closes the cycle of his life, his highly coloured autobiography *Antes que anochezca* (*Before Night Falls*), he affirms, talking about José Lezama Lima: "la ratificación de la labor creadora, del amor a la palabra, de la lucha por la imagen completa contra todos los que se oponían a ella" (the creative urge, the love of words, the struggle for imagination against those who oppose it). The very title of this book draws to a close Arenas's literary cycle: from the initial dawn of his first novel, he moves on to the night of his autobiography which presages his own end. *Necesidad de libertad* [Need for Freedom], a collection of his essays, repeatedly affirms transcendence through art. He states that "la verdadera patria de un autor es la hoja en blanco" (the writer's real country is the blank page). Both these books are indispensable if we are to understand the fusion of life and art in this Cuban artist, to understand his recurring themes and symbols, and above all understand the heartrending anguish of each one of the exiles that produces his literature.

MARÍA L. NEGRÍN

translated by Ann Wright

Biography
Born in the province of Holguín, Cuba, 16 July 1943. His formal education was sketchy and he was largely self-taught. Researcher at José Martí National Library in Havana, 1963–68. Befriended by Eliseo Diego, Cintio Vitier and other intellectuals who worked at the José Martí National Library in 1960s. Repaid them by running them down in his autobiography. Editor of *La Gaceta de Cuba*, 1968–74. Deeply rebellious by nature, it was inevitable that he would clash with an authoritarian government. Had manuscripts confiscated and was denied access to employment. From 1974 to 1976 he was in prison in El Morro, Havana. Left Cuba during the Mariel exodus in 1980. Professor of Cuban literature, University of Florida, 1980; Professor of literature, Cornell University, 1985. Awarded the French prize for the best foreign novel in 1969 for *El mundo alucinante*. In the United States he was awarded Cintas (1982) and Guggenheim grants (1983). Terminally ill with AIDS, he committed suicide in New York, 7 December 1990.

Selected Works

Novels
Celestino antes del alba, Havana: Unión, 1967; as *Singing from the Well*, translated by Andrew Hurley, New York: Viking, 1987
El mundo alucinante, Mexico City: Diógenes, 1969; as *Hallucinations: Being an Account of the Life and Adventures of Friar Servando Teresa de Mier*, translated by Gordon Brotherston, New York: Harper and Row, and London: Jonathan Cape, 1971; as *The Ill-Fated Peregrinations of Fray Servando*, translated by Andrew Hurley, New York: Avon, 1987
El palacio de las blanquísimas mofetas, Caracas: Monte Ávila, 1980; as *The Palace of the White Skunks*, translated by Andrew Hurley, New York: Viking, 1990
Otra vez el mar, Barcelona: Arcos Vergara, 1982; as *Farewell to the Sea*, translated by Andrew Hurley, New York: Viking, 1986
Cantando en el pozo, Barcelona: Arcos Vergara, 1982
La loma del Ángel, Málaga: DADOR, 1987; as *Graveyard of the Angels*, translated by Alfred MacAdam, New York: Avon, 1987 [Based on the novel *Cecilia Valdés* by the 19th-century Cuban writer Cirilo Villaverde]
El portero, Málaga: Quinto Centenario, 1989; as *The Doorman*, translated by Dolores Koch, New York: Grove Weidenfeld, 1991
Viaje a La Habana (novela en tres viajes), Madrid: Mondadori, 1990
El asalto, Miami: Universal, 1991; as *The Assault*, translated by Andrew Hurley, New York and London: Viking, 1994
El color del verano, Miami: Universal, 1991
Adiós a mamá (de La Habana a Nueva York), Barcelona: Altera, 1995

Novellas and Short Fiction
La vieja Rosa, Caracas: Librería Cruz del Sur, 1980; as *Old Rosa: a Novel in Two Stories*, translated by Andrew Hurley and Ann Tashi Slater, New York: Grove Press, 1989 [This volume contains also a translation of *Arturo, la estrella más brillante*]

Termina el desfile, Barcelona: Seix Barral, 1981
Arturo, la estrella más brillante, Barcelona: Montesinos, 1984

Play
Persecución: cinco piezas de teatro experimental, Miami: Universal, 1986

Poetry
Leprosorio, trilogía poética, Madrid: Betania, 1989

Mixed Genre and Non-Fiction
El central, Barcelona: Seix Barral, 1981; as *El central: a Cuban Sugar Mill*, translated by Anthony Kerrigan, New York: Avon, 1984 [A very powerful work that combines prose and poetry]
Homenaje a Ángel Cuadra, Miami: Solar, 1981 [Cuadra is a Cuban poet who spent many years in prison after Castro came to power]
Necesidad de libertad, Mexico City: Kosmos, 1986 [essays]
Voluntad de vivir manifestándose, Madrid: Betania, 1989
Un plebiscito a Fidel Castro, Madrid: Betania, 1990
Antes que anochezca, Barcelona: Seix Barral, 1992; as *Before Night Falls*, translated by Dolores Koch, London: Viking, 1993

Further Reading
Diego, Eliseo, "Sobre *Celestino antes del alba*," *Casa de las Américas* 45 (1967)
Ette, Otmar (editor), *La escritura de la memoria*, Frankfurt: Vervuert Verlag, 1992
Hernández-Miyares, Julio and Perla Rozencvaig (editors), *Reinaldo Arenas: alucinaciones, fantasías y realidad*, Glenview, Illinois: Scott Foresman Montesinos, 1990
Lugo Nazario, Félix, *La alucinación y los recursos literarios en las novelas de Reinaldo Arenas*, Miami: Universal, 1995
Ortega, Julio, "The Dazzling World of Fray Servando," in *Modern Latin American Fiction*, edited by Harold Bloom, New York: Chelsea House, 1990
Rodríguez Ortiz, Oscar, *Sobre narradores y héroes: a propósito de Arenas, Scorza y Adoum*, Caracas: Monte Ávila, 1980
Sánchez, Reinaldo (editor), *Reinaldo Arenas: recuerdo y presencia*, Miami: Universal, 1994
Solotorevsky, Myrna, *La relación mundo-escritura en textos de Reinaldo Arenas, Juan José Saer y Juan Carlos Martínez*, Gaithersburg, Maryland: Hispamérica, 1993
Soto, Francisco, *Conversación con Reinaldo Arenas*, Madrid: Betania, 1990
_____ *Reinaldo Arenas: the "Pentagonía,"* Gainesville: University Presses of Florida, 1994
Tomás, Lourdes, *Fray Servando alucinado*, Miami: Iberian Studies Institute, University of Miami, 1994
Valero, Roberto, *El desamparado humor de Reinaldo Arenas*, Miami: Iberian Studies Institute, University of Miami, 1991
Volek, Emil, "La carnavalización y la alegoría en *El mundo alucinante* de Reinaldo Arenas," *Revista Iberoamericana* 130–31 (1985)

Arturo, la estrella más brillante

Novella by Reinaldo Arenas

This text by Arenas presents the relationship between the depicted world and writing, the deception of writing being the attitude which imposes itself on this depicted world. The work opens by making writing evident, through the following quote:

"He visto un lugar remotísimo habitado por elefantes regios" (I have seen a most remote place inhabited by regal elephants) and the nature of writing is immediately explained: "había escrito hacía unos años" (He had written a few years ago).

Right from the beginning, the novella introduces a skeptical perspective on language, negating a relationship – previously postulated by the protagonist – between writing and salvation: "cuando aún pensaba que un grupo de signos, que la cadencia de unas imágenes adecuadamente descritas, que las palabras, podrían salvarlo ..." (when he still thought that a group of signs, the cadence of some adequately described images, the words, could save him ...).

Analeptically, that is to say, by moving backwards in time, the text focuses on the moment in which the act of writing begins, as though this act were the only means the character has of defending himself from an oppressive and hostile world: "esa misma noche decidió que para salvarse tenía que comenzar a escribir inmediatamente, e inmediatamente comenzó (that same night he decided that in order to save himself he had to begin writing immediately, and he began at once).

Writing is conceived as a testimony and an instrument of rebellion: "porque él se iba a rebelar, dando testimonio de todo el horror, comunicándole a alguien, a muchos, al mundo, o aunque fuese a una sola persona que aún conservara incorruptible su capacidad de pensar, la realidad; y las libretas traídas por Rosa se fueron saturando de una letra mínima, veloz, casi ilegible, había que darse prisa, había que seguir rápido, y tomando precauciones" (because he was going to rebel, attesting to all the horror, communicating to someone, to many people, to the world, even to one single person whose capacity to think still remains incorruptible: reality; and the notebooks brought by Rosa were becoming glutted with a tiny, rapid, almost illegible script; he had to hurry, he had to act quickly and take precautions).

In this text, the author and the reader are configured merely as the means by which what happens in the work takes place: "y tuvo casi terror al pensar que también él podría ser un instrumento, un simple artefacto, y que la gran melodía, la gran creación, la obra, surgía, surgiría, estaba allí, inexorable, y que sencillamente lo utilizaba, como pudo haber utilizado a cualquier otro, como utilizaba también a sus intérpretes" (and he was almost seized by terror at the thought that he, too, could be an instrument, a mere artefact, and that the grand melody, the grand creation, the work, was issuing forth, would issue forth, was there, relentless, and that it was simply using him, just as it could have used anyone else, just as it was also using its interpreters).

Arthur's mistrust of language is a consequence of the character becoming aware of his physical perfection and its ephemeral nature: "fue por entonces cuando por primera vez comenzó a temerle a la muerte y a dudar de la eficacia de las palabras" (it was then for the first time that he began to fear death and to entertain doubts about the effectiveness of words).

Arthur will substitute the act of writing for a mere unfolding of images, which cannot do without – unbeknownst to the character – language or writing as a model. The lack of distinction between writing and images is shown by the text itself, in repeating the images "jacintos, turquesas, ónix, ópalos, calcedonias, jades" (hyacinths, turquoises, onyxes, opals, chal-

cedonies, jades), which correspond to the words previously written by Arthur – "jacintos, turquesas, ónix, ópalos, calcedonias, jades"(hyacinths, turquoises, onyxes, opals, chalcedonies, jades). The images emphasize the "impression of reality," which is so necessary to the character.

The construction to which Arthur devotes himself and which will culminate in the "*magnum opus*" is certainly an analogon of the act of writing. The state of creation, according to Arthur, corresponds to an aerial situation of ascension and weightlessness, related to the title, *Arturo, la estrella más brillante*, and to the dedication: "A Nelson, en el aire" (To Nelson, in the Air):

era como si de pronto lo estuviesen levantando, lo alzasen, flotase (otra vez, otra vez), y en ese espacio sin atmósfera, él ascendía, ascendía, ascendía

[it was as though they were suddenly raising him, lifting him up and he was floating (again and again); and in this atmosphere-less space he ascended – up and up and up]

In the Notes at the very end of the text, Arenas states: "Pienso en ese momento en que, granada en mano, sobrevolando la isla con sus campos de trabajo y sus cárceles, Nelson se sintió libre, en el aire." (I think of that moment when, with the grenade in his hand, while flying over the island with its labor camps and prisons, Nelson felt free, in the air). The references to Nelson are specularly related to a poem titled "Si te llamaras Nelson" [If You Were Called Nelson] in which are found motifs that persist in Arenas's work: clandestine writing, transport to a forced labor camp, denunciation by one's best friend, the sight of one's own brothers taking aim to kill. (It should be noted that Nelson Rodríguez Leyva was the name of a friend of Arenas who died in an attempt to escape from Cuba by plane).

The plot justifies the protagonist's skepticism – a skepticism which turns out to be valid not only with regard to writing but also with regard to its analogon, the imaginative creation: the "real" world is fatally imposed onto the construction effected by the character: "fue entonces cuando la gran música, el canto coral de los ángeles, se apagó y Arturo se vio corriendo hacia una tropa de soldados que, arma al pecho avanzaban también hacia él" (it was then when the great music, the choral chant of the angels, was extinguished and Arthur saw himself running toward a band of soldiers who, their weapons held chest high, were also advancing towards him). Starting with the title and the dedication and continuing until the end of the text, a fatal movement has been sketched – from ascension to descent, from air to earth.

The dominant actor in the imposition of the "real" world which will affect the protagonist, is his mother, her dominance being psychologically understandable given Arthur's homosexuality; in his view, his mother, "enfurecida y vestida de militar" (furious and dressed like a soldier) appears at the head of a band of soldiers which will liquidate him.

The mother's dominance can also be estimated from the text's title: the protagonist feels repugnance for the coincidence rightly discovered in *Astronomía para las damas* (Astronomy for Ladies), between his name and that of a star "que su madre llamaba el lucero de la tarde, o por otro nombre parecido" (which his mother called the evening star, or by some similar name). It is interesting to note that "la estrella vespertina" (the evening star) is another name for Venus, the goddess of Love. In Arthur's view, his mother points to this star threateningly as a contrast to his hand on his penis; his mother's gesture is imposed while "Arturo, la estrella más brillante" becomes the title of the novella, but the character's hand remains fixed on his penis, his sexual problems unresolved.

As a supreme annihilation of his creation, the addressee of Arthur's creation, who is also the culmination of that same creation, he, the god, his god – in a repeated inversion in Arenas's works – has joined the contingent of his adversaries:

y entre los anónimos y sonrientes soldados de rostros impenetrables vio también al divino muchacho para quien había construido aquel castillo, radiante dentro del uniforme ceñido, también enarbolando el arma y apun-tándole . . .

[and among the anonymous and smiling soldiers with impenetrable faces he also saw the divine boy for whom he had constructed that castle, radiant in his tight-fitting uniform, who was also raising his weapon and aiming it at him . . .]

Arturo, la estrella más brillante is a prolongation of a plot found in another work by Arenas: *La vieja Rosa (Old Rosa)*; the latter work ends with the protagonist being consumed by fire and our novel analeptically depicts – through an evocation by Arthur – his mother's funeral and Arthur's ultimate fate, from the moment Old Rosa discovers he is a homosexual. A knowledge of *La vieja Rosa* is necessary to understand completely what is simply alluded to in *Arturo, la estrella más brillante*, e.g., the following phrases from the latter text: "la única persona que lo había querido hasta el punto de haberle dado muerte de no haber sido por un error de cálculo y el mal estado del arma" (the only person who had loved him to the point of killing him had it not been for an error of judgement and the disrepair of the weapon) recall a scene from *La vieja Rosa*, in which his mother surprises Arthur in an embrace with another boy: "Con gran precisión se llevó el arma hasta la altura de los hombros e hizo fuego. La primera descarga resonó en el cuarto cerrado, pasó por sobre los muchachos y fue a dar en la radio que saltó en pedazos." (With great precision, she raised the weapon to shoulder height and fired. The first shot resounded in the closed room, went over the boys' heads and hit the radio, smashing it to bits).

This novella includes a work: "la gran obra" (the *magnum opus*), "la gran melodía," "la gran creación" (the great melody, the great creation), "la gran construcción" (the great construction), which Arthur performs; thus, a *mise en abyme* is configured (a specular presence of a microtext within a macrotext).

The work thus constructed depicts a world which maintains an antithetical relationship to that which is represented in the novella; this antithesis corresponds to the terms "paradise-hell." On the linguistic level, both texts coincide – which is understandable because most of the text is referred to by a narrator from the protagonist's perspective (free indirect style) and in this way, the narrator's language and Arthur's writing, which is also presented by the said narrator by means of a free indirect style, become homogeneous.

A free indirect style does not appear in the text for those instances in which what is referred to escapes Arthur's notice, e.g., the moment in which the order to pursue and capture him is granted or the one in which his belongings are listed. Worthy of note, however, is the fact that the mood infusing the discourse is always uniform, one of exaltation starting at the beginning of the text, resulting from the existence, for Arthur, of the desired lover.

The entire text and Arthur's "construction" are delivered in an overflowing torrent of language, which imposes on the reading a veritable struggle for breath to adjust to a rhythm which proceeds uninterrupted from the first line to the last of the text, from the construction (the writing and its prolongation) until the destruction by Arthur of his own work ("se lanzó hacia el horizonte, destruyendo arbolarios, kioskos y parasoles, invernaderos, camafeos, aljives y hasta el solitario pluviómetro sobre el cual el desconcertado lofororo, que allí se había posado, miraba avanzar la tropa . . . (he hurtled towards the horizon, destroying herbariums, stands and parasols, hot-houses, cameos, cisterns and even the solitary rain gauge on top of which the baffled lophophore, which had perched there, watched the troops advance . . .); this destruction coincides – as is to be expected – with the conclusion of the text. The homogeneous mood of exaltation contributes to this effect of un-interrupted writing-reading, which expends itself only with the final term; the intensification of the poetic function – noticeable at the given moment – creates a lyrical effect.

The world thus depicted appears to constitute very clear-cut categories: [he] (the desired lover), ellos [they] (homosexuals confined like him in a labor camp), los otros [the others] (the guards), los demás [the rest]; the language, employing the sign of three leader dots, transports us clearly away from present reality (A) to past sequences (B) and to imaginary constructions (C), thus creating in the following moment, the configuration B // A // C:

pero aún entonces, quedaban los árboles, algún refugio, los demás, y, luego, estar solo, disfrutar de la soledad, aunque ya supiera, aunque ya supiera . . . / el soldado, como siempre, culminó con un resoplido, y como siempre, retirando el cuerpo le dijo espera, no salgas hasta que yo no haya entrado en el campamento . . . / parques, tenía que haber parques, parques inmensos y sombreados replegándose hasta el horizonte

[but even then, there remained the trees, some shelter, the rest, and then, to be alone, to enjoy the solitude, even though he already knew, even though he already knew . . . / the soldier, as always, climaxed with a snort, and, as always, withdrawing, he said to him: 'Stay; don't go out until I have entered the encampment . . . / parks, there had to be parks, huge shady parks stretching back to the horizon]

The textual plot is easily constructible once one focuses on certain moments of flashback or analepsis, which assists in the text's intelligibility despite the persistent gush of language, thus establishing a successful balance between the depicted world and writing.

MYRNA SOLOTOREVSKY

Editions
First edition: *Arturo, la estrella más brillante*, Barcelona:
  Montesinos, 1984
Translation: *Old Rosa: a Novel in Two Stories*, by Andrew Hurley
  and Ann Tashi Slater, New York: Grove Press, 1989 [Contains *La
  vieja Rosa* and *Arturo . . .*]

Note: To date there are no specific studies on *Arturo, la estrella
más brillante*, thus readers should consult the Further Reading
section at the end of the general entry on Arenas.

Rafael Arévalo Martínez 1884–1975

Guatemalan poet and prose writer

The so-called Generation of 1920, which includes Miguel
Ángel Asturias and Luis Cardoza y Aragón, is generally considered the outstanding group of writers and intellectuals to
have emerged in Guatemala this century. The most important
of their predecessors, though perhaps the least threatening,
was Rafael Arévalo Martínez, whose early story, "El hombre
que parecía un caballo," 1914 [The Man Who Looked Like a
Horse], has become a classic point of reference in the development of Latin American fiction and for many critics one of
the distant precursors of the linguistically sophisticated Boom
of the 1960s, fully half a century later. Earlier than other
frequently mentioned precursors – Felisberto Hernández of
Uruguay or Macedonio Fernández of Argentina, for example
– Arévalo invented a literary mode, which to some seems to
anticipate the magical realism of his compatriot Asturias, and
to others the fantastical "fictions" of Jorge Luis Borges. (Like
Borges, Arévalo became director of his country's national
library, 1926–45).

Arévalo was a physically slight, shy and hopelessly myopic
character, a poet as well as a novelist and short-story writer.
None of his later works was ever as successful as that famous
early story – inspired, it seems, by Arevalo's repressed desire
for the legendary homosexual poet from Colombia, Porfirio
Barba-Jacob (el señor de Aretal in the story), who made several
extended visits to Guatemala. Arévalo never acknowledged –
indeed, he denied – this submerged motivation, but his story
speaks, one might say, for him and remains a fascinating and
indeed arousing study in ambivalence with a magical radiance
all of its own. His novella *Las noches en el Palacio de la
Nunciatura*, 1927 [Nights in the Nunciature Palace] returns to
the subject of Barba-Jacob, but to less stirring effect. His early
stories appeared in *El hombre que parecía un caballo y otros
cuentos*, a title used later until the end of his life as an umbrella
to incorporate new stories as they appeared, and *in El señor
Monitot* [Mr Monitot].

Two early novels, *Una vida* [A Life] and *Manuel Aldano*,
were largely autobiographical works tracing his difficult childhood and painful adolescence, when he had to work at a series
of menial occupations in stores and offices. There are parallels with the experience of Britain's H.G. Wells, except that
Arévalo was unable to develop Wells's aggressive self-confidence; but he did follow him in one respect, for Arévalo later
produced works of fantasy which were very close to science
fiction, with novels like *El mundo de los maharachías* [The
World of the Maharachías] and *Viaje a Ipanda* [Journey to
Ipanda].

Whilst never actively political in any way, Arévalo's work
did deal occasionally with political issues. *La oficina de la paz
de Orolandia* [The Office for Peace in Goldland] has a Candide
character called Felix Buendía, who innocently discovers the
imperialist cynicism of the North Americans, the corrupt
passivity of the Central Americans and the farcical nature of
Pan-Americanism. In 1945 he published *¡Ecce Pericles!* [Behold
Pericles!], a history of the dictatorship of Estrada Cabrera
(1898–1920) full of the same bitter indignation which would
characterize Miguel Ángel Asturias's *El señor Presidente*,
published the following year.

Arévalo presents the curious picture of a writer who lived
an immensely long life, became the grand old man of
Guatemalan letters and yet never again wrote anything
remotely as interesting as that strange early story composed in
a rapture sixty years before his death. *Hondura* [Depth] is
another semi-autobiographical novel about his youth and
about student life during the Estrada Cabrera era. In addition
Arévalo continued to write simple lyrical poems until the end
of his days, but these belied the attractions of the best of his
stories: in them the central themes were the contradiction
between the essential simplicity and the endless mystery of life,
the question of doubles and doubling of every kind, and the
equivocal relations between the sexes and between gender and
sexuality. More interesting as a precursor than as an
outstanding creator, Arévalo's work nevertheless undoubtedly
deserves attention in its own right.

GERALD MARTIN

Biography
Born in Guatemala City, 24 July 1884, to middle class parents.
Father a lawyer. Married Evangelina Andrade Díaz in 1911; seven
children. Bank-teller, teacher, journalist. Founding editor of *Juan
Chapín*, 1913–15; editor of *Centro América*, 1915–20. Director of
the National Library of Guatemala, 1926–45; delegate, Pan-
American Union, Washington, DC, 1945–46. Recipient: Great Cross
of Rubén Darío (Nicaragua), and Order of the Quetzal (Guatemala),
both in 1958. Died in Guatemala City, 12 June 1975.

Selected Works

Novels and Novellas

Una vida, Guatemala City: Electra, 1914
Manuel Aldano, Guatemala City: Gutenberg, 1922
La oficina de la paz de Orolandia: novela del imperialismo yanqui, Guatemala City: Sánchez y de Guise, 1925
Las noches en el Palacio de la Nunciatura, Guatemala City: Sánchez y de Guise, 1927
El mundo de los maharachías, Guatemala City: Muñoz Plaza, 1939
Viaje a Ipanda, Guatemala City: Centro Editorial, 1939 [Sequel to *El mundo de los maharachías*]
Hondura, Guatemala City: Centro Editorial, 1947
El embajador de Torlania, Guatemala City: Landívar, 1960

Short Fiction

El hombre que parecía un caballo, Quezaltenango, Guatemala City: Arte Nuevo, 1915
El hombre que parecía un caballo; El ángel, Guatemala City: Ayestas, 1920
El señor Monitot, Guatemala City: Sánchez y de Guise, 1922
La signatura de la esfinge, Guatemala City: Electra, G.M. Stabler, 1933
Cratilo y los otros cuentos, Guatemala City: Universidad de San Carlos de Guatemala, 1968
Cuatro contactos con lo sobrenatural y otros relatos, Guatemala City: Landívar, 1971

Poetry

Los atormentados, Guatemala City: Unión Tipográfica, 1914
Las rosas de Engaddi, Guatemala City: Sánchez y de Guise, 1923
Llama, Guatemala City: Renacimiento, 1934
Por un caminito así, Guatemala City: Unión Tipográfica, 1947
Poemas, 1901–1959, Guatemala City: Landívar, 1958
Poemas, Guatemala City: Nacional, 1965

Other Writings

Los duques de Endor: drama en tres actos y en verso, Guatemala City: Centro, 1940
Influencia de España en la formación de la nacionalidad centroamericana, Guatemala City: Nacional, 1943
Nietzsche el conquistador: la doctrina que engendró la segunda guerra mundial, Guatemala City: Sánchez y de Guise, 1943
¡Ecce Pericles!, Guatemala City: Nacional, 1945 [biography]
Concepción del cosmos, Guatemala City: Landívar, 1954; revised edition, 1956
El hijo pródigo: drama en tres actos y en verso, Guatemala City: Tipografía Nacional, 1956
Narración sumaria de mi vida, Guatemala City: Landívar, 1968

Compilations and Anthologies

Selección poética, Guatemala City: José de Pineda Ibarra, 1944
El hombre que parecía un caballo, y otros cuentos, Guatemala City: Universitaria, 1951
Obras escogidas, Guatemala City: Universitaria, 1959 [poetry and prose]
Cuentos y poesías, edited by Carlos García Prada, Madrid: Iberoamericana, 1961

Further Reading

Carrera, Mario Alberto, *Las ocho novelas de Rafael Arévalo Martínez*, Guatemala City: Ediciones de la Casa de la Cultura Flavio Herrera de la Universidad de San Carlos, 1975
Foster, David William, *Gay and Lesbian Themes in Latin American Writing*, Austin: University of Texas Press, 1991 [Contains analysis of "El hombre que parecía un caballo"]
Homenaje del Instituto Guatemalteco-americano al cumplirse cincuenta años de vida literaria de este gran escritor guatemalteco, Guatemala City, 1959
Liano, Dante, *Rafael Arévalo Martínez, fuentes europeas, lengua y estilo*, Rome: Bulzoni, 1992

Argentina

19th-Century Prose and Poetry

The movement for independence from Spain, the subsequent period of fierce civil wars, the dictatorship of Buenos Aires strongman, Juan Manuel de Rosas, and then the trying struggle for supremacy between Buenos Aires and the Confederacy of internal provinces, constitute the historical backdrop for Argentine literature during the greater part of the 19th century. The country's literature provides a testimony of this period of social turbulence and change.

Buenos Aires's urban society, having experienced rapid demographic and commercial growth since the middle decades of the 18th century, possessed a predominantly aristocratic spirit, and emulated the cultural and literary forms of European centers. It was here that the struggle for independence from Spain found its center. In 1813, the poem, "Marcha patriótica" by Vicente López y Planes (1785–1856) was officially sanc-

tioned as the Argentine national anthem. This poem and others of the period were heavily influenced by the European Enlightenment, with the Neoclassical predication of patriotic themes and with pastoral treatment of the American republic's natural beauty. An early anthology, *La lira argentina*, 1824 [The Argentine Lyre] collected the most notable of this poetic production, headed by the names of Esteban de Luca (1786–1824), Cayetano Rodríguez (1761–1823), Juan Crisóstomo Lafinur (1797–1824), and Juan Cruz Varela (1794–1839).

In contrast to the new urban center, the provincial society of the interior provinces, constituted by *caudillos* (individuals wielding economic, social, and political power) leading an essentially populist rural population, valued the forms and structures prevalent during the colonial past, and honored the region's distinctly rural art forms. The unsettled regions of the north, in addition to the area of the humid pampas inland from Buenos Aires, with their plentiful cattle and wide expanses of open ranges, gave rise to the voluntarily, marginalized society of gauchos (stemming from "orphan" in Quechua, the River Plate cowboys). While the more organized and better educated society of Argentina's north continued singing the religious, chivalresque, and burlesque ballads that had direct links with the oral tradition of the Spanish peninsula, the gaucho's expression featured narrative ballads that exaggerated the power and ferocity of brave and clever heroes. Itinerant gaucho poets, comparable to medieval bards or minstrel singers, endlessly traveled from region to region, singing or reciting verses accompanied by the primitive music of the guitar or the more primitive *vihuela* at cattle round-ups or in rural stores cum bars termed *pulperías*. Especially popular was the *cielito* (creole tune), with intentionally archaic language and monotonous beat, through which gaucho poets chronicled customs, history, and biography, and shared their misery over abuses of urban authority. These folk poets also possessed a repertoire of intensely lyrical poems highlighting a colorful rural imagery, that were recited in octosyllabic lines variously combined into stanzas of five, eight, or ten lines. However, the most original of the gaucho poet's craft was the *payada*, or improvised duels in verse which, according to the wildly romanticized version, often concluded in combat with knives. A *payada* could be a monologue, but it was best when two versatile singers pitted against each other, would improvise verses in *cifra* or *milonga* forms in counterpoint fashion. Today, scant written traces survive of this orally transmitted poetry.

With the advent of the independence struggle less than a decade into the new century, there emerged a new literary practice that took its inspiration from the oral tradition of the gaucho: the gauchesque. The first important protagonist of this essentially cultured, urban stylization of gaucho literature, was Bartolomé Hidalgo (1788–1822), a soldier-poet serving the populist revolutionary movement originating in the Banda Oriental (literally the "East Bank," or today's Uruguay), who composed and then distributed one-page broadsides of patriotic verses using the gaucho idiom. Hidalgo's intention was to have his poems circulate, first in written form, then orally, in order to "teach by entertaining," with the desired results of instilling in the illiterate popular classes a sense of patriotism and integrating them into the emancipation cause against Spain. But his well-crafted, witty verses also attracted an urban readership that was entertained by exotic gaucho protagonists with their heavy rural dialect.

Most exceptional was Hidalgo's treatment of the Río de la Plata gaucho, which went hand in hand with his fervid support for the struggles of Uruguay-born leader, José Gervasio Artigas, whom he served as a soldier against the English in 1811. Hidalgo's *cielitos*, written in the gaucho idiom between 1812 and 1814, during the siege of Montevideo, were regarded highly for their faithful rendering of the uneducated soldiers' love of freedom and justice, their antipathy towards the English and Spanish, and their wry humor. While modern readers may find these early verses often dry and overly didactic, the three "Diálogos" [Dialogues] written in Buenos Aires between 1821 and 1822, are considered among the best of the gauchesque

genre. Their genuinely popular flavor and the playful portraits of customs, sentiments and social types account for the immense acclaim that they enjoyed in Hidalgo's day. Later gauchesque poets would find a worthy model in his mistrust, typical of the creole population, toward the "cultured" minorities of the metropolis, the rhymed dialogue between two rural protagonists, and his example of representing the perplexed gaucho's first contact with the modern city.

Most gauchesque poets following Hidalgo continued with the practice of placing their art at the service of politics. After 1829, Juan Gualberto Godoy (1793–1864) circulated his compositions of "gauchi-political poetry" that were flavored by his militant opposition to Rosas. For the next thirty years the inspired poetry of Hilario Ascasubi (1807–71) dominated the literary scene: his most famous gauchesque poems, *Paulino Lucero* (1839–51) and *Aniceto el Gallo* (1854), although literary masterpieces in their own right, also served in that poet's objective of promoting progressive values and discrediting the principles of federalism (that is the political system based on regional separatism and *caudillo* personalism) among the gaucho masses.

The region's first poetry of overtly Romantic orientation was *Los consuelos*, 1834 [Consolations] by Esteban Echeverría (1805–51), who had recently returned from nearly a decade of study in Paris. Under the influence of Byron, Goethe, Chateaubriand, and Ausias March, his "lugubrious tone" and the "fleeting melodies" of his poetic lyre consoled the sad or suffering reader. In the critical note accompanying this collection, he implicitly embraced the ideals of his country's independence movement by calling for the creation of a national literature based on the country's unique customs, predominant ideas, and social types. In 1837, he published *Rimas* [Rhymes], which contained, among other pieces, "La cautiva" [The Captive] and several important essays on literary theory. This long narrative poem, perhaps the best that he would write during his short but intense career, passionately depicted the country's wild natural setting as a backdrop for the drama of the Europeanized Brian and his virginal companion, María, in their near tragic confrontation with uncivilized Amerindian hordes. Future president, Bartolomé Mitre, at the age of sixteen, wrote in the Montevidean press that this exemplary model of national literature would inspire a "literary revolution."

Indeed, this poem was conceived in large part out of Echeverría's awareness of the need to direct the energies of the country's writers and thinkers to the urgent task of constructing an independent, national culture that would better respond to the needs of their society, already two decades after gaining independence from Spain. Present-day literary historians associate this poem and similar writings with the Romantic movement. In truth, Echeverría and the young men of 1837 were attracted to European Romanticism's rebellion against Neoclassical norms, which they compared to their own struggle against the decrepit colonial (Hispanic) legacy and on behalf of liberal orientations more conducive to progress. In apparent contradiction, their mission received its primary inspiration from the advanced thought emanating primarily from France, while it simultaneously aimed toward the foundation of an original, local culture and literature. Yet, for them literary and cultural renovation were merely the means for a far wider transformation in economics, politics, and customs. Primarily for that reason they rejected for themselves the label of Romantics, and initially embraced instead the name of "socialistas" (no relationship to the socialism of later decades), which they borrowed from their primary influence for liberal renovation, Claude Henri de Rouvroy, comte de Saint-Simon.

A most important milestone in the region's cultural history was the foundation of the short-lived *Salón Literario* (Literary Salon) that met in the bookstore owned by Marcos Sastre (1808–87) during the early months of 1837. While Sastre and the other two founders, Juan Bautista Alberdi (1810–84), and Juan María Gutiérrez (1809–78) articulated a moral and peda-gogical function for the group's young membership, the Salon was quickly perceived as a focus of opposition to the growing authoritarianism of the Rosas regime. This was especially so in light of Echeverría's two addresses to that group, which discussed the region's political economy and did not stop short of criticizing the Rosas government.

In June 1838, months after the Salon's forced closure, Echeverría called a secret meeting of some of its more militant youths in order to form what would later be known as the Asociación de Mayo (May Association). It was modeled on similar groups of that period in France and Italy and had as its goal the formation of a tight cadre of individuals who would dedicate themselves to the social, cultural, and intellectual renovation of the country. Within months, most of its members would be driven into exile in neighboring Chile and Uruguay, and their activities would expand to include the organization of a military invasion against the Rosas tyranny.

The manifesto of the Association was the *Creencia*, 1838 [Creed], authored by Echeverría with key paragraphs written by Alberdi. This document was later revised and preceded by a long introduction, *Ojeada retrospectiva sobre el movimiento intelectual en el Río de la Plata desde el año 37* [A Brief Retrospective Consideration of Intellectual Activity in the Río de la Plata since 1837] and then renamed *Dogma socialista*, 1846 [Socialist Dogma]. Several of the symbolic words reveal Echeverría's primarily moral and spiritual orientation for the young militants: Association, Progress, Fraternity, Equality, Liberty, Honor and Sacrifice, Compatibility of Principles, etc. This "utopian socialist" emphasis reflected Echeverría's varied readings of works by Giuseppe Mazzini, Félicité de Lamennais, Charles Fourier, Charles Augustin Sainte-Beuve and Pierre Leroux. However, the second half of the document addressed specifically Argentine imperatives: re-embrace the social, polit-ical, and cultural goals articulated by the leaders of the country's independence movement, reject the retrograde influ-ences of the colonial regime, promote democratic institutions and cultivate a national, American culture. The document's heavy, dramatic language and quasi-"religious" tone were modeled on creeds of similar secret societies that were then organizing in Europe's revolutionary circles – and they would reappear in documents by the transcendentalist followers of Ralph Waldo Emerson in the United States. For these reasons, contemporary readers often overlook the *Dogma*'s importance in calling to action the idealistic youth of the country and unifying them under a common banner in the struggles that awaited them.

The young exiles' passionate opposition to Rosas inspired the most creative and original of writings that they were to produce. The first of these widely-read propagandistic works was *Rosas y sus opositores*, 1843 [Rosas and his Detractors] by José Rivera Indarte (1814?–45), that enumerated the crimes committed by the *porteño* (port, that is Buenos Aires) dictator in the first fourteen years of his government, and ended with a long pseudo-philosophical essay that called for his assas-sination. *La gloria del tirano Rosas*, 1847 [The Glory of the Tyrant Rosas] by Félix Frías (1816–81), also featured the abuses of the Rosas regime. This work anticipated the fertile ideas of Alberdi and Sarmiento in promoting an influx of North European immigrants whose superior culture (as they saw it) would displace that of the country's Spanish descen-dants, gaucho half-breeds, and Amerindians. Two other ideas strenuously argued by Frías were the danger to society of revolutionary change and the indispensable role of religious instruction in educating citizens for a responsible role in demo-cratic societies.

Many readers at the time had theorized about the desirability of a national literature in the form of poetry, drama, and the novel, but they hardly knew how to respond when they first confronted *Civilización y barbarie. La vida de Juan Facundo Quiroga*, 1846 (*Life in the Argentine Republic in the Days of the Tyrants, or Civilization and Barbarism*), by Domingo Faustino Sarmiento (1811–88), the work that posterity has unanimously recognized as the "foundation book" for not only Argentina's literary and cultural tradition, but also Latin America's Romantic canon. The work, composed in a "rapture of lyricism" during a few intense weeks and published in instal-ments in Santiago de Chile's daily newspaper, *El Progreso*, has confounded readers with its juxtaposition of imaginative and socio-scientific discourses. The work unites three highly contrasting sections. The first, which was inspired by socio-logical or ethnographic theory rendered through the idiosyn-cratic beliefs of the author, attempted to account for the present state of Argentine society as it existed after twenty years of devastating civil skirmishes. Within these pages Sarmiento did not fail to include memorable *costumbrista* passages (sketches of local customs) that portrayed in a Romantic fashion char-acter types of the Argentine pampas: the pathfinder, the cattle hand, the gaucho outlaw, and the gaucho singer.

The work's second section, which was Sarmiento's subjec-tive incursion into biography and romantically rendered history, recreated the events surrounding the life and exploits of the Promethean *caudillo* from the province of La Rioja, Juan Facundo Quiroga, whose assassination had sent the whole country into turmoil eleven years earlier. Sarmiento's own origins in the neighboring province of San Juan gave him access to first-hand data that provided a semblance of authenticity to his historical and literary portrait. However, his skewed selec-tion and presentation of that data largely followed from his political objective of attacking Facundo – and by extension, Rosas. The third section, which was excluded entirely from later editions, analyzed Rosas's tyrannical practices and denounced the dictator's ideas and record in power.

The conceptual axis of the entire work, which has wielded enormous influence over subsequent writers and students of Argentine society, is the dichotomy between civilization and barbarism. His arguments in that work in favor of civilization (that is, Buenos Aires, the city, liberal ideals, and European influences), and his corresponding condemnation of barbarism (that is, the gaucho, the *caudillo*, and many aspects of rural life), anticipated Sarmiento's emerging political agenda that largely favored Buenos Aires at the expense of the country's interior provinces.

Among the several polemics on literature and language that involved members of the 1837 generation, the most important took place between 1841 and 1842 in several daily and weekly newspapers of Santiago and Valparaíso, Chile. The ambitious Argentine youths, imbued with the latest Romantic ideas of the century, pitted their militant perspectives against the more conservative tendencies of Santiago's cultural elite, headed by Andrés Bello (1781–1865), a native of present-day Venezuela and the continent's most distinguished legal expert, literary scholar, and philosopher. In frank contrast to Bello's ideas of a decorous language and normative literature, Sarmiento argued that a writing practice based on spontaneity and emotion most effectively promoted social and material progress.

The exiled militants, weighed down by the imperatives and privations of exile, found in journalism their most effective means for organizing a resistance to the hated Rosas regime. Superior to the sometimes tendentious propaganda of their companions in exile, were excellent essays analyzing national and regional affairs. Most outstanding was the writing by Sarmiento in Santiago de Chile's *El Progreso*, and Florencio Varela (1807–48) in Montevideo's *El Comercio del Plata*.

Echeverría, with deteriorating health, could not take an active part in the military or propagandistic struggle against Rosas, but instead lent his creative energies to literary and pedagogical pursuits. Before his early death in 1851 he concluded several long narrative poems that contemporary readers appraise more for historical than literary merits, among them *La guitarra* [The Guitar] and *Insurección del sur de la Provincia de Buenos Aires* [Insurrection of the South of the Province of Buenos Aires]. An essay, *Manual de enseñanza moral*, 1846 [Manual for Moral Instruction] advocated the fortification of traditional moral values among the youth as a prerequisite for the spread of practices related to liberty and democracy.

Echeverría perceived himself primarily as a poet and a thinker, yet the short story, *El matadero* (*The Slaughter House*), published posthumously in 1871, has done most to immortalize his name in the canon of Argentine and Hispanic American literature. The style of this Romantic classic combines crude realism, political satire, and vivid chiaroscuro symbolism. The story features the brutal lower-class society frequenting the outskirts of Buenos Aires, where cattle were slaughtered for local meat consumption. The central event is the chance arrival of the rain-muddied slaughterhouse grounds of a proud, refined gentlemen. His taunting and then humiliation at the hands of the unsavory lower-class mob was intended as an allegory of how Rosas's barbarism had put asunder the vestiges of refinement and civilization. Socio-political readings have highlighted the author's affective pact with the latter, as well as the story's innuendos against people of color or of lower-class extraction. Although it is undeniable that Echeverría disdained the behavior of the brutish masses obedient to the Rosas regime, it is also true that no other individual of his generation demonstrated as high a degree of confidence in the popular classes and the role they would play in a modern Argentina.

Essays written during the exile period had already won Alberdi the distinction of the clearest and most profound thinker of his generation. With the fall of Rosas, no individual was better qualified than him to guide the provincial representatives in formulating a new constitution for the future governance of the country. Such was the origin of *Bases y puntos de partida para la organización política de la República Argentina*, 1852 [Bases and Points of Departure for the Political Organization of the Argentine Republic] known more simply as *Bases*. The work's primary thesis was the need for an original constitution that addressed the reality, beliefs, and past history of the inhabitants of the country. More important, however, was Alberdi's reiteration of the need for the framers of the constitution to provide the legal means for attracting an immigrant population, encouraging capital investments, and fomenting free trade practices to increase the material wealth of all. Noteworthy was Alberdi's catch-phrase, "Gobernar es poblar" [To Govern is to Populate], which summarized his generation's push to increase North European immigration in the region – and their implicit disdain for the indigenous, gaucho, and Hispanic descendants of the region. The work as a whole was Alberdi's means for promoting a conservative brand of progress that would not endanger the country's painfully achieved stability and order.

For Sarmiento, as for Alberdi, writing came as naturally as public service, the two great passions in his life. *Viajes por Europa, Africa y América* [Journeys through Europe, Africa and the United States] contains Sarmiento's penetrating observations of customs and practices observed during a two-year visit to Europe and the United States. Noteworthy was his light but fascinating style; his buoyant descriptions of progressive and democratic practices in North America make this – along with the next work to be considered – the most "utopian" of his entire written output. This trip had been commissioned by the Chilean government with the express purpose of observing and studying the systems of public education then existing in those lands. Much of these conclusions and observations were published separately in *De la educación común*, 1849 [About Public Education], the first of many studies he would publish in the next two decades to promote the free and universal schooling for the masses of the continent. He was a precursor in his promotion of education for women, especially to prepare them as school teachers. However, he was less than optimistic about the receptivity of the continent's Amerindians and the "barbaric" gauchos for learning progressive ideas and practices.

General José María Paz and other public figures published important memoirs of their participation in the historical events of their time, but it is Sarmiento's autobiographical work that has proven most memorable. *Recuerdos de provincia*, 1850 [Memoirs of Provincial Life] demonstrated Sarmiento's considerable talents as historian and *costumbrista* writer – although the work also betrays his political objective of projecting a favorable public image that would be advantageous for future political ambitions. The work, a hymn of veneration for the progressive patriarchal society that existed in San Juan during Sarmiento's youth, revealed the provincial core of the author's increasingly accentuated cosmopolitanism. He traces his lineage to the oldest families of the region and describes in personal terms the region's social and political turmoil that had been unleashed by the independence struggle. Sarmiento, usually demonstrating in idea and act an unbridled egotism and confidence in his own advanced ideas, here uncharacteristically demonstrates humility and deference to respected opinion. The work provides an explanation for the conservative character and thought of this man who was emerging as protagonist in the region's struggle on behalf of liberal institutions and an open-ended progress.

During the exile years, José Mármol (1818–71) earned the distinction of being the most versatile writer of his generation. To his credit are the patriotic poem, "Al 25 de mayo" [To the 25th of May] and *Cantos del peregrino* [Pilgrim's Songs], the latter being one of the finest Romantic poems in the Hispanic American canon; plays *El poeta*, 1842 [The Poet] and *El cruzado*, 1851 [The Crusader]; and political essays such as "Asesinato del S. Dr D. Florencio Varela, Redactor del *Comercio del Plata*," 1849 [Assassination of Dr Don Florencio Varela, editor of *Comercio del Plata*] and "Manuela Rosas" (1850); and the regular flow of articles that were published in the most reputable organs of the Montevidean press: *El Nacional*, *Muera Rosas*, *El Conservador* and especially, *El Comercio del Plata* (respectively: The National, Death to Rosas, The Conservative and Commerce of the River Plate).

Several writers attempted the novel, but none with the success of Mármol in *Amalia* (1855). Juana Manuela Gorriti (1818–92) and Juana Manso (1819–75) published, respectively, *La quena*, 1845 [The Indian Flute] and *Los misterios del Plata*, 1846 [The Mysteries of the River Plate Region], historical novels of romantic inspiration; also of note was *Soledad*, 1847 [Solitude] by Bartolomé Mitre (1821–1906), of sentimental theme. More successful was Vicente Fidel López (1815–1903), in whose novel, *La novia del hereje*, 1846 [The Heretic's Bride] the action takes place within Peru's colonial society; the novel, for López, was, above all, a pedagogical instrument that served the objective of fomenting strong family and affective values which would, in their turn, provide a foundation for the individual's participation in public life in the coming democratic age.

All these other efforts are dwarfed by Mármol's achievement in *Amalia*, a work that is only rivaled by Sarmiento's *Facundo* in its sociological, historical, and ideological value in interpreting Argentine politics and society. The novel provides literary portraits of individuals active in the Rosas regime, and explains key aspects of the regime in several lengthy essayistic passages. The action revolves around a pair of young lovers with political ideals that pit them against the Rosas tyranny. When their clandestine activities are discovered, they attempt to flee to exile in Montevideo, but are discovered and then executed. This melodramatic tragedy, with the Argentine political scene reduced to the Romantic opposition between spirit and body, Good and Evil, civilization and barbarism, was a tool in Mármol's ideological campaign to discredit Rosas, the federalist creed, and the league of barbarous *caudillos* exercising power across the interior. The novel did not fail to indicate a path out of the social and political chaos: it certified Mármol's generational cohorts as those most indicated for leading the nation toward regeneration in the post-Rosas period.

A result of Rosas losing power in 1852 was the outbreak of long repressed regional passions, and a new cycle of conflict that would last another thirty years. The country's foremost writers were divided in their loyalties: of the 1837 generation, Alberdi and Gutiérrez initially supported the Confederation uniting the provinces of the interior, while Sarmiento, Mármol, and others placed their intellectual and writing talents at the service of Buenos Aires. José Hernández (1834–86), the most talented of a new generation of writer/militants, first gained national attention as the author of a series of articles that passionately denounced the brutal slaying of the beloved *caudillo* patriarch of the Province of La Rioja, Ángel "El Chacho" Peñaloza. These articles, immensely popular across the country's interior provinces, were immediately united in the form of a short book, *Vida del Chacho*, 1872 [Life of the "Chacho"]. Because of the fierce repression unleashed by Buenos Aires armies across that interior in the previous months, the book was received enthusiastically by readers in the interior who quickly canonized it in their elevation of Peñaloza to the status of martyr for the fallen federalist cause.

Sarmiento, temporarily discredited in Argentina for his complicity in El Chacho's death, eloquently defended his actions in the biographical-political essay, *El Chacho: último caudillo de la montonera de los llanos*, 1866 [The Chacho: Last Caudillo of the Plains' Gaucho Soldiers]. The work was vintage Sarmiento in its presentation of biographical, ethnographic, and sociological information, as well as correspondence and historical documents, as a means of substantiating his politicized thesis that the *caudillo* protagonist represented the most retrograde of tendencies. In re-elaborating the civilization versus barbarism thesis that reduced his protagonist to a single dimension, he revealed the Romantic, literary quality of his thought.

Alberdi was to leave an indelible mark on the conscience of his compatriots in a related area: his anti-war sentiment, that flowered into the most eloquent statement of Argentine pacifism of all times: *El crimen de la guerra*, 1870 [The Crime of War]. Although the work remained unpublished in his own lifetime, it is this Alberdian work that, after *Bases*, has seen the greatest number of reprintings and has been circulated most widely.

Of an entirely different character was Alberdi's historico-philosophical fictional work, *Peregrinación de Luz del Día o viajes y aventuras de la verdad en el Nuevo Mundo*, 1874 [Pilgrimage of Light of Day, or Trips and Adventures of Truth in the New World]. Here, the thin facade of allegory hardly masked Alberdi's primary objective of debunking his political enemies through caricature and satire. The identity of Sarmiento and Mitre was barely hidden – Alberdi's two nemeses – in fictional garb, and his condemnation of Buenos Aires's corrupt and oligarchical Liberal Party. Slightly less crude was Alberdi's *Grandes y pequeños hombres del Plata* [Great and Small Men of the Plate Region], which first appeared posthumously in *Escritos póstumos* (1895–1901) and then under separate title in 1912. The overriding objective of this work, as in *Luz del día*, was to lambast both Mitre and Sarmiento and to denounce the ruling class that was cementing its power throughout the country.

Gauchesque poetry continued to be practiced through the end of the century. Most worthy of mention during this later period is Estanislao del Campo (1834–80), whose *Fausto*, 1866 [Faust] further popularized the genre, but this time among primarily an urban reading public. This poem mines humor in depicting how one "country bumpkin" gaucho translates to an even more unsophisticated companion his recent experiences in the large city. The climax to his misadventures was when he stumbled into one of Buenos Aires's finest highbrow theaters and witnessed a production of Goethe's *Faust*. The poem, as such, expertly exploits multiple possibilities of literary translation and creative mis-interpretation. For the public of the 1860s, when the city more and more dominated the social, political, and cultural life of the entire country, the poem was generally interpreted as a criticism of the inadequate cultural baggage of the unprogressive rural sector. Yet the debunking was two-edged: transparent also is the author's portrayal of an urban culture caught up in the pretension of its own importance and flaunting imported cultural norms.

The culmination of the gauchesque was José Hernández's long narrative poem, *El gaucho Martín Fierro* (1872, continued in *La vuelta de Martín Fierro*, 1879), the first part of which was born of anger and political passion. After the defeat of the federalist uprising led by his friend and cohort, Ricardo López Jordán, Hernández's suffering found an outlet in his poetic defense of the traditional rural society and its gaucho population that were threatened by an encroaching modernity. The second part was a poetic gesture intended to mend fences with the liberal regime that was now in the ascendant throughout the country. Seen in its entirety, this poem combines two artistically similar, but ideologically dissimilar parts. Nevertheless, it succeeded like no previous literary work in straddling Argentina's traditional and cultured literary traditions and in appealing to both the unschooled or semi-literate rural society and an educated, urban reading public. The poem masterfully reproduced the archaic variant of the Spanish spoken in the Buenos Aires countryside several decades earlier, without exaggerating that dialect's deformative characteristics. Its superb verses build upon the themes and forms of the region's fertile oral tradition, and steer clear of theatricalized, picturesque descriptions that marred most other literary incursions by educated poets into the gaucho world. The poem's reception by the region's rural population was instantaneous and fervid, and its popularity continues unchallenged even today. But three decades would have to pass after its publication before the educated groups of the region's cities would, first belatedly then enthusiastically, embrace this work as the highest expression of Argentine – and more broadly Río de la Plata – society.

Ricardo V. Gutiérrez (1838–96), Carlos Guido y Spano (1827–1918), and Olegario V. Andrade (1839–82) constitute the nucleus of Argentina's "second Romantic generation," a label which hardly suggests the polemical nature of their literary and political initiation. During the 1860s and 1870s the mission fell to them of recording the tragic struggles of federalist militants across Argentina's interior provinces as they beat a steady retreat before the advance of Buenos Aires's armies. Theirs was the task of combatting the official histories emanating from Buenos Aires with their own, sometimes lyrical, testimonies of federalism's final tragic days.

This group's primary contribution was in the field of poetry. Gutiérrez's early poem, "La fiebre salvaje," 1860 [The Savage Fever], modeled after the exalted Romantic verses of Byron, united a series of lyrical laments over the unfortunate destiny

of a suffering hero. Of historical resonance was "La victoria," a poem inspired by his painful participation as a doctor in the tragic Triple Alliance War with Paraguay (1866–70). The poem, which laments the war's destruction and terrible cost in human lives, reveals the pacifist orientation of Gutiérrez, whose tender, humanitarian feelings clashed violently with the horrors he witnessed.

The war with Paraguay also left an indelible mark on the sensitivies of Guido y Spano. His essay, *El gobierno y la alianza*, 1866 [The Government and the Alliance] was a strong indictment of the Mitre administration's dishonorable maneuverings that contributed to igniting the destructive conflict. In the poem "Nenia," one of the most memorable of the period, he offered a funeral lament over the death and destruction of Paraguay by the armies of Argentina and Brazil. A decade later, however, Guido would shelve his anti-*porteño* militancy. His *Autobiografía*, 1879 [Autobiography] revealed a newly positive assessment of national reality that announced the voluntary forgetfulness of the bitter past. Having made peace with the new coalition of social and political forces that now predominated, his poetic trajectory in works like *Ráfagas*, 1879 [Gusts of Wind] focused on domestic or civic themes, sometimes with deep emotion, that totally avoided political issues. These were the celebratory verses that subsequently earned him recognition as the country's poet laureate.

A similar ideological trajectory was that of Andrade, whose poetic initiation was also in response to the tragic social and political turmoil of his youth. An early poem, "Canto a Paysandú" [Song for Paysandú], which lamented the tragic destruction of that Uruguayan city by Brazilian forces – the act that helped to ignite the Paraguayan War – communicated his strong identification with the federalist cause and opposition to Mitre's liberal politics. However, by the 1870s, Andrade's politics yielded to moderation, and his poetry now exhalted national values and sang the hymn of liberty. His patriotic poetry henceforth spoke to an optimism for Argentina's "Promethean race" and the brilliant future awaiting his country in the coming positivist age. Official recognition soon followed: he was called "Poet of the the New Democracy" for his Romantic exaltation of collective values and profound faith in the young nation with its doors open to the future.

1880 marks the year when the *porteño* brand of liberalism reigned supreme and the country initiated a period of dramatic progress whose benefits were shared by all classes to some degree. The political and material successes of the regime were reflected in the country's literature, which communicated a new and wide-spread optimism. A young generation of writers – those of 1880 – now dominated the literary scene. These, in contrast to the previous generation, had received the best education that their elitist circle was able to offer. Thus they accepted without question the prevailing liberal values, supported the law and order of the newly hegemonic state, and mythified the life and rigors of the countryside. These writers, who were at the same time leading participants in the most important social and political events of their time, produced a literature typified by brief sketches and a conversational tone that were first published in newspapers and only later collected in book form.

Heading the list of 1880 writers was Lucio Victorio Mansilla (1831–1913), whose *Una excursión a los indios ranqueles*, 1870 [An Excursion to the Ranquel Indian Nation] combines personal memoir and ethnology in its unsurpassed considerations of indigenous culture and its relationship to white, urban society. Mansilla, a nephew of the dictator Rosas, had already distinguished himself in a military career on the frontier, and was to play an important role in the future politics of the country. The predominance of the author's personal commentary and its "personalization" of an important aspect of Argentine political history account for the work's "novelistic" nature. Early European settlers in the region found only impoverished, nomadic groups of native American people, in contrast to the more developed civilizations of Peru and Mexico. Since colonial days, relations between the whites and the Indians were characterized by continual conflict. The country's literature, with few exceptions, records an image of the Indians as a cruel, barbaric people. Mansilla's work is important because it stands almost alone in projecting a humanistic vision of a place for the Indian in the modern culture that was evolving. This optimism was short-lived, however, since only a few years later the future president, Julio A. Roca, would lead a military expedition into the unsettled regions of the country that culminated with the massive destruction of Indian lives and livelihood, and the abrupt closure to a century of frontier conflict.

The only important publication of Miguel Cané (1852–1905) was *Juvenilia* (1884), a minor classic of autobiographical literature. In anecdotal fashion, Cané records the intimate experiences of his cadre of privileged students during their years of internship in the Colegio Nacional. In doing so, he presents a most memorable microscopic view of the disputes dividing the Argentine society of the time.

Outside the 1880 group was Eduardo Gutiérrez (1851–89), whose serial novel, *Juan Moreira* (1879–80), was to eternalize the literary figure of the honorable gaucho rebel who is able to outwit his more "civilized" antagonists. The popularization of this literary folk hero through sequels written, performed, or sung by many imitators, testifies to the continuing attraction of rural themes and the enduring importance of the urban-rural conflict in the nation's consciousness.

Gutiérrez, by transforming *Juan Moreira* into the mimodramatic production of 1884, initiated what was to become a theatrical revolution. Until about 1870 dramatic activity sporadically manifested itself in the country's larger cities, but primarily with translated works or those written about "universal" themes by national writers. However, the burgeoning urban public – swollen by European immigrants and migrants from rural areas – now enjoyed peace accompanying the end to the country's long civil struggles. The new public, without class distinction, found aesthetic enjoyment in scenes of legendary gaucho heroes and outlaws. This would culminate with itinerant "drama criollo" (creole theater) of the Podestá family, whose talented actors and impresario-producers would mesmerize audiences all over the region. Before the end of the century, the dramas of Abdón Arósteguy, Vicente Pérez Petit – and then the immensely popular *Calandria* (1896), by Martiniano Leguizamón (1858–1935), would follow.

If the literature of the 1880s reflected optimism in the country's present and future, that of the 1890s revealed greater pessimism – especially after the 1890 stock market crash and an aborted coup. *La bolsa*, 1891 [The Stock Market] by Julián Martel (real name, José Miró, 1867–96) communicated cynicism over the country's boom-bust prosperity gained through indebtedness to European financial interests, in which wealth was measured by one's conspicuous consumption and not by productive capacity. Implicit was the condemnation of past immigration policies, which had resulted in the passing of control to a new group of Argentines, represented in the novel by Dr Glow. This figure is an intelligent Jewish lawyer who progressively becomes sucked into the immoral practices of the commercial world. The novel's rather fanciful solution for contemporary ills seems to be the return to less complicated times, when the country's institutions had been managed by more down-to-earth Argentines of Spanish descent.

Sin rumbo, 1885 [Aimless] by Eugenio Cambaceres (1843–89), is the nadir of this literary descent into despair. In keeping with the Naturalist school of Émile Zola, the author sets out to depict the degrading aspects of character and scene in a supposed "scientific" attempt to understand society's ills in general. In the novel, a rootless young Argentine protagonist grows to despise the routine aspects of ranch living that he had experienced as a child and that make possible his sumptuous lifestyle in the capital city. Like other members of the country's ruling class, his excessive refinement breeds contempt, and perversion, and leads to exploitation of others. Displaying at times a lucid understanding of the psychological, social, and moral malaise afflicting him, nevertheless he is unable to muster the will necessary to return to a more stable universe.

WILLIAM H. KATRA

See also entries on Eugenio Cambaceres, Caudillismo and Dictatorship, Esteban Echeverría, José Hernández and *Martín Fierro*, José Mármol, Nationalism

20th-Century Prose and Poetry

Latin American countries have similar forms of literary expression, stemming originally from their Hispanic roots and, from the 19th century onwards, a common acceptance of cultural models – especially those of French origin. Nevertheless, each region has particular characteristics which have been accentuated over the years. Specific to Argentine literature is the importance of the city as a theme, due to its being a predominantly urban society. Buenos Aires, which developed differently from its surrounding rural environment, manifested increasingly strong ties with Europe and subsequently absorbed influences from the United States.

Another characteristic is the absence of autochthonous literature, since the indigenous people of the Southern Cone did not have an advanced culture. Nor are influences from the rest of Hispanic America particularly strong. In fact, the opposite is the case: Argentine publishers sold books throughout the continent; magazines and newspapers with (literary) supplements were read in the most diverse places. Add to this the prestige of Buenos Aires, a cosmospolitan city, always open to the newest trends.

The early decades of the 20th century saw important changes in the country's social structure. A large middle class was formed, sustained by continuous waves of immigration which improved both the economy and the level of intellectual attainment. Far removed from the solitary artistic activity and extreme individualism of the Romantic period, the writer began to see himself as part of a profession and established contact with his fellow writers through artistic and literary institutions which identified with the current aesthetic trends.

Realism persisted in the early years of the 20th century. Unlike the writers of the 1880s – characterized as fragmentary – certain novelists of this period attempted to paint a vast panorama of contemporary society. A certain analytical zeal took over and in its better Argentine exponents – Carlos María Ocantos, Francisco Sicardi, Robert J. Payró, Manuel Gálvez and Hugo Wast – this went beyond mere *costumbrista* attention to detail, to capture something that was authentically Argentine.

Applying the rules of European Realism to the Argentine environment, these writers managed to capture its own specific circumstances. In an organic and organized way, they undertook to explain current situations through a reconstruction of the past. This meant focusing on several different areas of the surrounding environment – urban, suburban, rural – and adopting linguistic modes which reflected regional forms of speech. The organization of the story remained traditional; linear development, descriptive devices, and moral conclusions, turned out to be almost always – in the novels of Payró, for instance – the most effective way of representing daily life.

The *modernista* movement developed simultaneously, as a vehicle for a new expressive impulse, and a continual generational polemic began with Realism and subsequently with the avant-garde. The presence of Rubén Darío in Buenos Aires (1897) and the circulation of his work deeply influenced the development of Argentine poetry at the turn of the century. It is worth remembering that when Leopoldo Lugones published his first books and became the foremost exponent of *Modernismo* in the River Plate area, there were still echoes of Romantic poetry in the work of Olegario Victor Andrade, Rafael Obligado and Almafuerte (pseudonym of Pedro Bonifacio Palacios). Lugones's vigorous personality brought criticism as well as admiration, but many followed his rigorous style and verbal preciousness. His multifarious activities as poet, story-teller and essayist opened up new perspectives for writers of the time. The quality of his prose in *La guerra gaucha*, 1905 [The Gaucho War] and his collection of stories of the fantastic are only equalled by the work of Enrique Larreta who, in *La gloria de don Ramiro*, 1908 (*The Glory of Don Ramiro*) produced an exemplar of the Modernist novel. The cosmopolitanism and aestheticism characteristic of this genre, not widely cultivated in Argentine literature, were succesfully displayed in Larreta's recreation of the Spain of Phillip II.

The centenary celebrations of Argentine Independence heralded a decade of transition in which there were no major aesthetic changes nor outstanding literary figures. It was a period reaffirming the Realism which had dominated the novel and short story since the beginning of the century. While the major writers, Payró, Ocantos, and Wast, continued in their same style, others revived a *costumbrismo* rooted in local life. The novels of Manuel Gálvez, *La maestra normal*, 1914 [The Training School Teacher], *El mal metafísico*, 1916 [The Metaphysical Ill] – are set in the city; those of Benito Lynch in the province of Buenos Aires; Horacio Quiroga's short stories in the jungle of Misiones. Meanwhile, the status of literature itself received a boost. In 1913 a Department of Argentine Literature was created in the University of Buenos Aires under Ricardo Rojas. Ambitious collections dedicated to disseminating the work of Argentine writers were planned. Among them was *La cultura argentina* [Argentine Culture], edited by José Ingenieros. In 1919, Manuel Gálvez edited the anthology *Los mejores cuentos argentinos* [The Best Argentine Short Stories], with a prologue stressing the importance, not as yet recognized, of that narrative form. Now, such collections provide excellent examples of the canon prevailing at the time.

There was an expansion of literary journals, formed around small groups of writers. *Nosotros* [Ourselves] founded in 1907 by Alfredo Bianchi and Roberto F. Giusti, was notable for its range of views and the quality of its contributors over several decades. First seen in its pages were works of the post-*modernista* group: Rafael A. Arrieta, Arturo Capdevila, Alfredo R. Bufano, Carlos Obligado and Arturo Marasso, among others, characterized, despite the diversity of themes, by a refinement of expression and formal cohesion.

Although they had markedly different features, other writers can also be linked with this group: Enrique Banchs, undisputed master of verse culminating in *La urna*, 1911 [The Urn] his stylised lyrical work; Baldomero Fernández Moreno, founder of *sencillismo* (emphasis on simplicity), projected an emotive and ironic view of daily life harking back to Evaristo Carriego; and the early work of Alfonsina Storni. Storni, however, transcended the limits of this trend both through the bitter mocking tone, which added an edge to her writing, and her intellectual treatment of social problems.

The 1920s announced a period of innovation in Argentine literature; its iconoclasm coincided with that of other European and Latin America countries (Brazil is a case in point). This process of transformation developed during the declining years of *Modernismo* and when Realism was still a respectable option. Isolated works like *Lunario sentimental*, 1909 [Sentimental Lunar Calendar] by Leopoldo Lugones or *El cencerro de cristal*, 1915 [The Crystal Cowbell] by Ricardo Güiraldes were clear forerunners of an unprecedented break with tradition.

During the avant-garde period, Jorge Luis Borges stood out as the principal theorist and diseminator of *ultraísmo*. Borges came back to Buenos Aires in 1921 after a stay in Europe where he was in contact with all the main postwar literary movements. Shortly afterwards he and a group of fellow writers founded a highly experimental wall magazine, *Prisma* [Prism] and the journal *Proa* [Prow]) which despite their brief existence succeeded in establishing their innovatory aims. They sought a different vision, ridding language of conventional formulae, extracting from it its most lucid power of suggestion. These were *ultraísmo*'s guiding principles and the movement confronted head on the Realism still in vogue at the time. The *ultraísts* also attacked Spanish American *Modernismo*, criticising a rhetoric which until then had seemed synonymous with literature. Its innovations influenced poetry more than prose. Poets rejected anecdote and rhyme, concentrated on liberating metaphor, combined the sublime and the ordinary, mixed prose and verse. They composed short, almost rhythmless poems and preferred descriptive fragments to the set pattern of verse.

These innovations increased with the appearance of *Martín Fierro*, a journal which brought other poets into the original group. The Manifesto, written by Oliverio Girondo, stated "the need to define and explore a new sensibility which is able to open up unexpected horizons and discover new means and forms of expression." Although this statement of intent was not fully realized, they did find different thematic approaches and achieved greater technical freedom. Fantasy opened up completely new perspectives for them.

Girondo's *Veinte poemas para ser leídos en el tranvía* [Twenty Poems to be Read in the Tram], Borges's *Luna de enfrente* [Moon Opposite], González Lanuza's *Prismas* [Prisms], Marechal's *Días como flechas* [Days Like Arrows] and Ricardo Molinari's *Fábula del pez* [Fable of the Fish], in rapid succession consolidated the heralded anti-formalism and use of metaphor. Córdova Iturburu, González Tuñón, Norah Lange and, a little later, Petit de Murat, intensified the search for new themes and rhythm effects and deepened the split between traditional and experimental approaches to literature.

Contrasting with the bold slogans of this group – which called itself Florida – was the Boedo group, more interested in political statements than stylistic definitions. In the footsteps of French Naturalism and Russian Realism, these writers expounded their own particular historical and ideological interpretation in their novels and short stories. Leónidas Barletta, Roberto Mariani, Elías Castelnuovo, Aristóbulo Echegaray were renowned both for the quality of their prose and militant defence of the 1917 Russian Revolution in the pages of their journals *Los Pensadores* [Men of Ideas] and *Claridad* [Clarity].

In 1926, two important novels appeared: *Don Segundo Sombra* by Ricardo Güiraldes and *El juguete rabioso* [The Rabid Toy] by Roberto Arlt. Both initiated, in different ways, the break with traditional Realism and the intertwining of planes of narrative which, decades later, would characterize the postmodern novel. There were contrasting tendencies in both these writers which adapted the prevailing techniques to their own personal, creative needs.

During this period, Macedonio Fernández's humorous reflective tales, which so influenced Borges and other members of the Martín Fierro group, heralded the fragmentation and discontinuity of experimental writing which exploded in the 1960s throughout Latin America. This role of precursor separated, and to a large extent, isolated him from the regional *costumbrismo* still in vogue at the time.

The disappearance of the journal *Martín Fierro* at the end of 1927 marked the end of a stage of cultural activity, begun in 1920, which was concerned with spreading avantgarde aesthetics. From then on the members of the Florida group started to disperse and channelled their energies in diverse directions, only occasionally coming together in certain publishing projects or some other late resurgence which fizzled out.

More or less the same applied to the members of the Boedo group, which gradually lost its fighting spirit despite the prolonged life of *Claridad* and some later publications. They directed their concerns towards political activity so that by around 1930 we can consider this important innovative movement at an end. It was a movement which produced a profound change in the perspective of the artistic-literary concepts of the time.

As the critic Luis Emilio Soto pointed out in an appreciation of this period written in 1938, it was not easy to evaluate the real achievements of the aesthetic transformation brought about by the Martín Fierro group. "One day," he wrote, "someone will chronicle the intellectual movement which began in 1920. Among other phenomena which we don't yet fully appreciate, it will show how Argentine writers discovered the virtues of apprenticeship, how the nobility of the profession was established by imposing obligations, how writers acquired a new awareness of their social function as they exchanged a sense of the international for the universal."

This new professional attitude adopted by Argentine writers, a sign of maturity and self-critical responsibility towards their own work, was demonstrated most clearly by the wide variety of programmes and projects undertaken by the literary reviews. Although many of them initially continued the polarity of the Florida and Boedo groups, they gradually outlined wider criteria which no longer conformed to generational splits or ideological battles, but sought to improve the status of creativity over and above incidental controversies.

The polemical tensions of the avant-garde gave way to a decade of transition in which a few belated echoes still resounded while isolated ideas cropped up in response to disparate impulses. The founding of *Sur* [South] in 1931 by Victoria Ocampo and the reappearance of *Nosotros*, were two notable events in the evolution of Argentine literature, important because of their eclecticism and enthusiasm for the most up-to-date cultural output.

Sur was noted for its prestigious contributors and its spirit of innovation which helped to disseminate the latest literary ideas and introduced a new wave of young writers. This was the so-called Generation of 1940. Foremost among them were Juan Rodolfo Wilcock, Vicente Barbieri, César Rosales, León Benaros and Alfonso Sola González, who at this stage expressed in *Sur* early signs of their poetic concerns. Both the literary output and the process of transformation between modernity and the postmodern era are to be found in the pages of this journal.

When the first issue of this publication appeared, Argentine politics and society were going through a period of acute turmoil. After the fall of Yrigoyen (1930), the right wing had imposed a very narrow framework of reference into which *Sur* burst, as a bold unexpected attempt to gain access to a less rigid intellectual dimension. The journal continually reiterated its desire to identify with Latin American reality, but relating it to the fundamentals of European culture. It maintained this stance throughout its existence.

Political events like the Spanish Civil War and World War II influenced the journal's activities. Its emphasis on disseminating aspects of art, science and sociology gradually changed the physiognomy of the journal. Issues devoted to criticism, the essay, poetry and fiction, meant that it published all the major intellectuals of the day. Jorge Luis Borges, Eduardo González Lanuza, Oliverio Girondo, Ricardo Molinari, Guillermo de Torre, all exponents of the avant-garde, figured among its most prolific contributors. Joining them later were Eduardo Mallea, Silvina Ocampo, Ernesto Sábato, Ezequiel Martínez Estrada, Adolfo Bioy Casares and Manuel Mujica Láinez, who marked out incontrovertible aesthetic routes from then on.

In contrast to previous stages where we can clearly see Realism confronting the distortion of reality expressed by the new currents, both these approaches fused in the literature which emerged after 1930. The novella and the short story, genres skilfully employed by numerous writers like Lugones, Quiroga, Güiraldes, Mariani and Cancela, were now the most obvious conduits of the referential change which introduced the fantastic into post- avant-garde Argentine literature. Macedonio Fernández and Oliverio Girondo had experimented with very similar forms before. Borges would become a past master of this form of literary creation. From 1935 onwards, *Historia universal de la infamia* (*A Universal History of Infamy*) and "El jardín de senderos que se bifurcan" (included in *Ficciones*), demonstrated a total sustained dedication to the literature of the fantastic. Cohesion of expression, skilled handling of writing techniques, and above all a powerful imagination which allowed him to combine the most absurd circumstances with absolute normality, made Borges's narrative style unmistakable.

At the same time Borges also tackled other areas. The singular critical wit of *Inquisiciones* [Inquisitions], *Discusión* [Discussion] and *Historia de la eternidad* [History of Eternity] made Borges one of the most remarkable essayists of the time. His work already showed the aesthetic and philosophical concerns which were to become the keys to his writing. Controversial articles were often merely a pretext for asking himself fundamental questions which attempted to define the relationship between beings and things.

Others essays which sought to establish national identity and the way in which telluric conditions effected it, stemmed from sociological concerns, like Ezequiel Martínez Estrada's *Radiografía de la pampa* (*X-Ray of the Pampa*) and *La cabeza de Goliat* [Goliath's Head], or from philosophical or even metaphysical approaches in the case of Raúl Scalabrini Ortiz, Carlos Alberto Erro or Bernardo Canal Feijóo. Subsequently, Argentina's political evolution would come under the intensely critical gaze of Juan José Sebreli, Julio Mafud, Ismael Viñas, and the rigorous pithy approach of Héctor A. Murena.

The destruction of the rigid divide between truth and fiction was accentuated throughout this period and literature became testimonial, incorporating historical evaluation and biography in its discourse. This was certainly the case with the novels of Eduardo Mallea: *La bahía de silencio* (*The Bay of Silence*), *Todo verdor perecerá* (*All Green Shall Perish*), *Fiesta en noviembre* (*Fiesta in November*), *La torre* [The Tower]. Many of his characters' concerns, expressed in clear, refined prose, reflected the basic premises in his essays.

The work of Ernesto Sábato, from *Sobre héroes y tumbas* (*On Heroes and Tombs*) to *Abaddón, el exterminador* (*The Angel of Darkness*), also employed a fusion of the reflective and the imaginary and stemmed from his meditations in *Uno y el universo* [One and the Universe] and *Hombres y engranajes*

[Men and Gears]. The same thing occurred in Leopoldo Marechal's *Adán Buenosayres*: the multifaceted plot made up of constant textual interlacing paradoxically allowed him to reconstruct the avant-garde scene in which he was an active participant. For his part, Manuel Mujica Láinez's brilliant evocation of the past in *Aquí vivieron* [They Lived Here], *Misterioso Buenos Aires* [Mysterious Buenos Aires] and *Bomarzo* (*Bomarzo, a Novel*), succeeded in combining artistic and historical erudition with stylistic elegance.

The use of the fantastic reached extraordinary heights during this decade, beginning with the original exponents of the genre: Adolfo Bioy Casares in *La invención de Morel* (*The Invention of Morel*), *El sueño de los héroes* (*The Dream of the Hero*) and *Diario de la guerra del cerdo* (*Diary of the War of the Pig*); and Silvina Ocampo in several collections of short stories such as *La furia* (included in *Leopoldina's Dream*) and *Autobiografía de Irene* (also in *Leopoldina's Dream*), the latter being a work of singular construction. In 1940, in collaboration with Jorge Luis Borges, they brought out the *Antología de la literatura fantástica* (*The Book of Fantasy*), which systematically displayed the diverse forms of this kind of narrative.

Julio Cortázar, who began his literary career with a collection of poems, devoted himself exclusively to prose writing from 1950. His short stories and tales, *Bestiario* (Bestiary, in *End of the Game and Other Stories*), *Las armas secretas* (*Secret Weapons*, also in *End of the Game . . .*), *Historias de cronopios y de famas* (*Cronopios and Famas*), transfigure ordinary every day things into magical distortions where fate acts as an unpredictable element. His close attention to form and constant experimentation with technique reached a peak in 1963 with *Rayuela* (*Hopscotch*), one of the most important novels of the time and one which would become a model for later generations.

After World War II, publishing output in Argentina increased with a large number of writers producing many different types of literature. The influence of French Existentialism was seen in certain writers – Antonio Di Benedetto, Abelardo Arias, Jorge Masciángoli, Mario A. Lancelotti – where an obsessive intellectual atmosphere prevailed. Other writers such as Manuel Peyrou, María Angélica Bosco, and Marco Denevi, skilfully cultivated the detective story.

At the beginning of the 1960s, women entered the literary arena in greater numbers and with unusual intensity and rigour. The questioning of inherited values and the norms of behaviour which the patriarchal society had taught them became a constant theme in the novels of Beatriz Guido, Silvina Bullrich, Marta Lynch, Griselda Gambaro, Jorgelina Loubet, María Esther de Miguel and Elvira Orphée.

The critical rigour which the journal *Contorno*, 1953–59 [Outline] imposed on literary circles for several years meant that that generation of writers had to re-evaluate attitudes and criteria of expression. David Viñas, Haroldo Conti, Rodolfo Walsh, Daniel Moyano and Germán Rozenmacher state clearly their intention to confront the country's political problems, especially from 1966 onwards. This was a foretaste of the reaction which was to come after 1970 with the crisis of Peronism and the military coup of 1976.

From 1976 until 1983, Argentine intellectuals fled to other countries, some for ideological reasons, others to improve their financial situation. In exile, they assumed the task of keeping alive cultural continuity during those years. Cases in point are Antonio Di Benedetto, David Viñas, Daniel Moyano, Manuel Puig, Juan José Saer and Carlos Soriano. Despite the emotional break imposed by exile, they were able to express the trauma of that era with greater freedom. Each used his own particular criteria and was conditioned by his chosen form of expression and the circumstances under which he left Argentina.

The authors who stayed in Argentina writing subversive literature reflected on historical or symbolic themes which masked the truth of their discourse. These hidden meanings are most interestingly expressed in *Respiración artificial*, 1980 (*Artificial Respiration*) by Ricardo Piglia, *En el corazón de junio*, 1983 [In the Heart of June] by Luis Gusman, *Nada que perder*, 1982 [Nothing to Lose] and *La vida entera*, 1981 [The Whole of Life] by Juan Carlos Martini.

In addition to this combative attitude which modified the Argentine novel thematically, there was a change in form which sometimes resorted to intertextuality, parody and historical reconstruction through memoirs, letters and documents. The narrative style initiated by Manuel Puig in the 1960s found adherents in this decade, especially the juxtaposition of elite culture and mass culture seen in his novels *La traición de Rita Hayworth*, 1968 (*Betrayed by Rita Hayworth*) and *Boquitas pintadas*, 1969 (*Heartbreak Tango*).

Other writers, like Enrique Medina in *Las tumbas* [The Tombs] and *Las muecas del miedo* [Grimaces of Fear], Jorge Asís in *Flores robadas en los jardines de Quilmes* [Flowers Stolen from Gardens in Quilmes], Geno Díaz in *Kermesse*, Carlos Dámaso Martínez in *Hay cenizas en el viento* [There Are Ashes in the Wind], were increasingly preoccupied with the themes of death, persecution and fear. This discourse of evasion, otherness and concealment generated forms of resistance which characterized this literary period and which continue in different forms of expression to this day.

Around 1960, Argentine poetry developed new trends which resulted from a new aesthetics. The new generation of poets needed to identify with their own age and consciously assumed the responsibility of being the protagonists in a world going through a period of rapid change. The aestheticism which characterized Argentine verse until the mid-20th century would be replaced by numerous individual manifestations which contributed to diversifying the complex panorama of poetry at the time.

What prompted these new approaches most directly could be the desire to get closer to the earth, something which was felt by writers in the 1940s. This idea, only partially achieved by the elegiac intimate lyricism of the Neoromantics, would be expressed in the work of this generation's Neopopulist group, involved in social problems and themes specific to the world around them.

The avant-garde forms which surfaced around 1950 finally channelled their rejection of form into a hermetic style, coded in the techniques of verbal automatism which did not always achieve the all-encompassing vision or the ambitious plan to transform the world so often reiterated in their journal *Poesía de Buenos Aires* [Buenos Aires Poetry]. Apart from a few isolated exceptions such as Rodolfo Alonso and Raúl Gustavo Aguirre, an escapist attitude, provoked by instability, disorientation and personal tragedy, prevailed at this time.

The work of Alberto Girri, governed from his very first books by intellectual rigour and analysis, proved an important experience within this lyrical search to affirm one's identity. Exponents of this investigative approach, which sought to demonstrate their contact with things through purgative, often conversational, language, were H.A. Murena, Betina Edelberg, Juan L. Ortiz, Amelia Biagioni and Roberto Juarroz. They sought to decipher problems and examine the human condition from their own particular vision of the cosmos.

Towards the end of the 1960s, the confrontation with society and historical events intensified and diversified. External influences combined with local circumstances to change fundamentally contemporary literature. The influence of Existentialism, a strong gravitational pull in those days, forced poets to identify with their age in more important ways than through exclusively aesthetic approaches.

The dialogue that was initiated turned into a polemical search and a strong commitment to reality. The poems of Joaquín O. Gianuzzi, Elizabeth Azcona de Cranwell, Alfredo Veiravé, María Elena Walsh and, in a very personal way, Alejandra Pizarnik, were totally devoted to the task of meshing with their own time and space. With a Neoromantic past behind them, Olga Orozco, Enrique Molina, Manuel J. Castilla, César Fernández Moreno and other avant-garde poets like Juan José Ceselli, Edgar Bayley or Francisco Madariaga, now tackled the complex experiences of modern humankind more incisively.

After 1970, the country's progressive political disintegration – starting with the military coups of 1966 and 1976 – resulted in the younger generation's disenchantment with both the historical past and the social present. The lyrical discourse masked critical positions which could not be openly expressed. Protest was sometimes translated into parody or a symbolic representation of persecution and authoritarianism. Juan Gelman, Máximo Simpson, Alberto Szpunberg, Susana Thénon and Rubén Vela are all examples of this questioning, intensely dramatic attitude to the reality of their time.

The persistence of this anti-formal and testimonial position – made up of emphatic adhesions and rejections – typifies the work of Argentine poets in recent years, combining very diverse aesthetic and ideological perspectives. Since 1984, literary workshops, colloquia, and poetry readings have brought together very personal voices: Leonidas Lamborghini, Diana Bellesi, Daniel Freidemberg, Arturo Carrera, Tamara Kamenszain and Dolores Etchecopar. *Diario de Poesía* [Poetry Daily] and *El último reino* [Last Kingdom] keep alive a combative, rebellious attitude which justifies the presence of this genre in Argentine literature.

NÉLIDA SALVADOR

translated by Ann Wright

Further Reading

General

Foster, David William, *Violence in Argentine Literature: Cultural Responses to Tyranny*, Columbia: University of Missouri Press, 1995

Onega, Gladys S., *La inmigración en la literatura argentina: 1880–1910*, Santa Fe, Argentina: Universidad Nacional de Litoral, 1965; Buenos Aires: Centro Editor de América Latina, 1982

Viñas, David, *Literatura argentina y realidad política. De Sarmiento a Cortázar*, Buenos Aires: Siglo XX, 1971

Viñas, David and Eva Tabakián (general editors), *Historia social de la literatura argentina*, vol. 7, Buenos Aires: Contrapunto, 1989

19th Century

Fishburn, Evelyn, *The Portrayal of Immigration in Nineteenth Century Argentine Fiction (1845–1902)*, Berlin: Collloquium Verlag, 1981

Foster, David William, *The Argentine Generation of 1880: Ideology and Cultural Texts*, Columbia: University of Missouri Press, 1990

Katra, William H., *The Argentine Generation of 1837: Echeverría, Sarmiento, Alberdi, Mitre. An ideological Interpretation*, Rutherford, New Jersey: Fairleigh Dickinson University Press, 1996

Losada, Alejandro, *La literatura en la sociedad de América Latina: Perú y el Río de la Plata, 1837–1880*, Frankfurt: Vervuert Verlag, 1983

Ludmer, Josefina, *El género gauchesco: un tratado sobre la patria*, Buenos Aires: Sudamericana, 1988

Masiello, Francine, *Between Civilization and Barbarism: Women, Nation and Literary Culture in Modern Argentina*, Lincoln: University of Nebraska Press, 1992

Meyer-Minneman, Klaus, *La novela hispanoamericana del "fin de siècle,"* Mexico City: Fondo de Cultura Económica, 1991 [Chapter 5 is on Naturalism in the River Plate]

Pagés Larraya, Antonio, *Nace la novela argentina (1880–1900)*, Buenos Aires: Academia Argentina de Letras, 1994

20th Century

Balderston, Daniel, *et al.*, *Ficción y política. La narrativa argentina durante el proceso militar*, Buenos Aires: Alianza, 1987

Barletta, Leónidas, *Boedo y Florida: una versión distinta*, Buenos Aires: Ediciones Metrópolis, 1987

Borello, Rodolfo A., *El peronismo (1943–1955) en la narrativa argentina*, Ottawa: Dovehouse Editions, 1991

Colás, Santiago, *Postmodernity in Latin America: the Argentine Paradigm*, Durham, North Carolina: Duke University Press, 1994

Dellepiane, Ángela B., "La novela argentina desde 1950 a 1965," *Revista Iberoamericana* 66 (1968)

Jitrik, Noé, *Las armas y las razones. Ensayos sobre el peronismo, el exilio y la literatura, 1975–80*, Buenos Aires: Sudamericana, 1984

Katra, William H., *"Contorno": Literary Engagement in Post-Peronist Argentina*, Madison, New Jersey: Fairleigh Dickinson University Press, 1986

Kohurt, Karl and Andrea Pagni (editors), *Literatura argentina hoy: de la dictadura a la democracia*, Frankfurt: Vervuert Verlag, 1989; 2nd edition, 1993

Leland, Christopher Towne, *The Last Happy Men: the Generation of 1922, Fiction and the Argentine Reality*, Syracuse, New York: Syracuse University Press, 1986

Lewis, Colin M. and Nissa Torrents (editors), *Argentina in the Crisis Years (1983–1990): from Alfonsín to Menem*, London: Institute of Latin American Studies, 1993 [Contains three essays on culture]

Lindstrom, Naomi, *Literary Expressionism in Argentina: the Presentation of Incoherence*, Tempe, Arizona: Center for Latin American Studies, Arizona State University, 1977

Masiello, Francine, *Lenguaje e ideología. Las escuelas aregentinas de vanguardia*, Buenos Aires: Hachette, 1986

Salvador, Nélida, *La nueva poesía argentina: estudio y antología*, Buenos Aires: Columba, 1969

Salvador, Nélida (editor), *Lírica argentina posterior a 1950*, Buenos Aires: Instituto de Literatura Argentina "Ricardo Rojas," Facultad de Filosofía y Letras, Universidad de Buenos Aires, 1988

Sarlo, Beatriz, *El imperio de los sentimientos: narraciones de circulación periódica en la Argentina (1917–1927)*, Buenos Aires: Catálogos Editora, 1985

____ *Una modernidad periférica: Buenos Aires 1920 y 1930*, Buenos Aires: Nueva Visión, 1988

Sosnowski, Saúl (editor), *Represión y reconstrucción de una cultura: el caso argentino*, Buenos Aires: Eudeba, 1988

Ulla, Noemí, *Identidad rioplatense, 1930: la escritura coloquial: Borges, Arlt, Hernández, Onetti*, Buenos Aires: Torres Agüero, 1990

Bibliographies

Foster, David William, *Argentine Literature: a Research Guide*, 2nd edition, New York: Garland, 1982

Salvador, Nélida, *et al.*, *Novela argentina del siglo XX. Bibliografía crítica*, Buenos Aires: Centro de Investigaciones Bibliotecnológicas, Universidad de Buenos Aires, 1994

Special Issues of Journals

Revista Iberoamericana 142 and 143 (1988)

Katra, William H. (guest editor), "Argentine Writing in the Eighties," *The Literary Review*, vol. 32/4 (1989)

José María Arguedas 1911–1969

Peruvian prose writer and ethnographer

The political upheaval of the first two decades of the 20th century in Latin America, and particularly in Peru, promoted an intense movement on behalf of indigenous populations, a campaign that intended to vindicate native culture as well as to improve the social status of the Indian. The early fictional expressions of indigenism (as this social and intellectual project is usually called) were limited to a crude realism denouncing the oppression of the Indian, portrayed primarily as the victim of institutionalized injustice in contrast to the idealized and exotic image of the "noble savage" projected by European Romanticism. Such is the case of works like the Peruvian Clorinda Matto de Turner's *Aves sin nido*, 1889 (*Birds without a Nest*), the Ecuadorian Jorge Icaza's *Huasipungo*, 1934 (*The Villagers*), the Bolivian Alcides Arguedas's *Raza de bronce*, 1919 [Race of Bronze], and the Mexican Gregorio López y Fuentes's *El indio*, 1935 (*They That Reap*). The publication in 1941 of *Yawar fiesta* (*Yawar Fiesta*) by José María Arguedas signified the end of indigenism and the emergence of neoindigenism. Neoindigenism, an ideological and esthetic position adopted by Arguedas, goes beyond the exaltation of Andean culture; it proposes an internal view of indigenous values with the purpose of legitimizing and preserving their intrinsic features. The hallmark of Arguedas's fiction is his intimate knowledge of the Indian mind and his thorough identification with autochthonous cultures. Arguedas's works of fiction include *Agua* [Water], *Yawar fiesta*, *Diamantes y pedernales*, [Diamonds and Quartz], *Los ríos profundos* (*Deep Rivers*); his account of life in a Lima prison, *El Sexto*, *La agonía de "Rasu Ñiti"* [The Agony of Rasu Ñiti], and *Todas las sangres* [Everyone's Blood]. Lastly, there is the novel that was published posthumously, *El zorro de arriba y el zorro de abajo* [The Fox from the Mountains and the Fox from the Coast].

Born in an Andean community of a white father and an Indian mother, Arguedas spent his youth among Indians and learned Quechua as his first language. His training in anthropology allowed him to study Quechua folklore and to publish translations of Quechua poetry as well as essays on Andean myths, legends, customs and traditions. In his fiction he took up the task of correcting the distorted image of the Indian as portrayed previously in indigenist literature, a movement whose expressions had essentially revolved around themes centered predominantly on the conflict between Western civilization and indigenous culture. Arguedas moves beyond this limited vision and uses his fiction to explore vast social processes that include not only Indians and whites, but also mestizos, and the very complex ethnic, political and economic relationships among these groups, as in the case of *Agua* and *Yawar fiesta*. Also in *Yawar fiesta*, and later in *Los ríos profundos*, Arguedas examines regional cultural conflicts between Andean and coastal communities. In his two last major novels, *Todas las sangres* and *El zorro de arriba y el zorro de abajo*, Arguedas deals with the encroachment of multinational companies on incipient Third World economies, and also with the subject of massive migrations from the Andes to industrial urban centers.

One of Arguedas's major artistic accomplishments was the creation of a special language that would express Indian attitudes and intimate feelings without resorting to linguistic distortions, a technique that had been the norm in more traditional indigenist literature. From the very beginning of his literary career, Arguedas faced the enormous task of writing for Spanish-speaking readers about the affective relationships of peoples whose native language is Quechua. The core of the problem was how to capture the subjectivity of the Andean Indian, but also, how to represent in correct written Spanish the nuances of Quechua orality. His first attempts, as in *Agua* and *Yawar fiesta*, were not entirely successful as they still relied on structural changes that rendered the language artificial. It was only with *Los ríos profundos* that Arguedas was able to weave basic structures of Quechua speech syntax within the framework of Spanish, thus creating a language that more authentically reflected not only Indian sensibilities but their magical-religious concept of the universe.

Arguedas's place in literary history goes beyond his immense contribution to indigenism, and its variant neoindigenism, considered as ideologies and as esthetic movements. The undisputed quality of his works puts him solidly in the top rank of Latin American writers, and at the same level as the more visible writers of the so-called Boom of Spanish American fiction, such as his compatriot Mario Vargas Llosa, or the Colombian Nobel Laureate Gabriel García Márquez. Indigenism, contrary to statements claiming its demise, still continues to flourish in the works of a new generation of writers dedicated to the preservation of José María Arguedas's legacy.

ISMAEL P. MÁRQUEZ

Biography

Born in Andahuaylas, Apurímac region, Peru, 18 January 1911. Mother died in his childhood and father remarried. Stepmother treated him cruelly, insisting that he sleep with the servants in the kitchen. In this way grew up with close knowledge (and love) of the Quechua people, their language and culture. Lived in San Juan de Lucanas, 1917–24. Attended Colegio Miguel Grau de los Padres Mercedarios, Abancay, 1924–25; Colegio San Luis Gonzaga, Ica, 1926–27; Colegio Santa Isabel, Huancayo, 1928–30; Colegio de Mercedarios, Lima, 1929–30; studied literature and anthropology at San Marcos University, Lima, 1931–32 (university closed by authorities, 1932), 1935–37, 1947–50, degree 1957, doctorate 1963. Worked for the Peruvian postal service, Lima, 1932–37; co-founder and co-editor, *Palabra*, 1936; imprisoned for involvement in demonstrations against the insurrection led by Franco in Spain, 1937–38; teacher of Spanish and geography, Colegio Nacional Mateo Pumacahua, Sicuani, 1939, and continued as secondary school teacher until 1946. Married Celia Bustamante in 1939 (divorced 1966); lived in Mexico, 1940–42; returned to Lima, 1942, and worked with government commission for education reforms; teacher, 1942–47, Colegio Alfonso Ugarte and Colegio Guadalupe, both Lima, and the Instituto Pedagógico, Varones, 1950–53. Suffered nervous breakdown in 1943, which caused him to dry up as a creative writer for many years. Curator-general, 1947–50, then director, 1950–53, Ministry of Education Department of Folklore and Fine Art, Lima; travelled to Chile, 1951; director, Museum of Peruvian Culture Institute of Ethnological Studies, 1953; travelled to Spain, 1957–58; professor of Quechua and ethnic studies, San Marcos University, 1958–63, and later lectured at the Agrarian University, 1962–66; director, Institute of Contemporary Arts, Lima, 1961; director, Casa de la Cultura, 1963–64; director, Museum of the Republic (Museum of National History), Lima, 1964–66; founder, *Cultura y Pueblo*, 1964. Visited the United States, 1965; attempted suicide by overdose of barbiturates, 1966; married Sybila Arredondo in 1967; visited Cuba, 1968. Awarded the Javier Prado Prize in 1958; Ricardo Palma Prize, 1959 and 1962; William Faulkner Foundation certificate of merit, 1963; Garcilaso de la Vega Prize, 1968. Committed suicide 2 December 1969, as the result of feeling that he had nothing more to contribute to his country.

Selected Works

Novels and Short Fiction
Agua, Lima: Talleres de la CIP, 1935
Runa yu pay, Lima: Comisión Central del Censo, 1939 [novel]
Yawar fiesta, Lima: Talleres de la CIP, 1941; revised and corrected edition, 1958; as *Yawar Fiesta*, translated by Frances Horning Barraclough, Austin: University of Texas Press, and London: Quartet, 1985
Diamantes y pedernales, Lima: Mejía Baca, 1954 [Contains "Diamantes y pedernales," "Orovilca," and the stories of *Agua*]
Los ríos profundos, Buenos Aires: Losada, 1958; as *Deep Rivers*, translated by Frances Horning Barraclough, Austin: University of Texas Press, 1978
El Sexto, Lima: Mejía Baca, 1961
La agonía de "Rasu-Ñiti," Lima: Talleres Gráficos Ícaro, 1962
Todas las sangres, Buenos Aires: Losada, 1964
El zorro de arriba y el zorro de abajo (unfinished), Buenos Aires: Losada, 1971; critical edition, edited by Eve Marie Fell, Madrid: Archivos, 1990 [Contains articles on this novel by leading specialists on the work of Arguedas]

Other Writings (including works on Quechua culture)
Canto kechwa, Lima: Club del Libro Peruano, 1938; translated in *The Singing Mountaineers*, 1957 [songs in Spanish and Quechua]
Canciones y cuentos del pueblo quechua, in collaboration with Jorge A. Lira, Lima: Huascarán, 1949; translated in *The Singing Mountaineers*, 1957
Mesa redonda sobre el monolingüismo quechua y aymara y la educación en el Perú, Lima: Casa de la Cultura del Perú, 1966
Dioses y hombres de Huarochirí, Lima: Museo Nacional de Historia e Instituto de Estudios Peruanos, 1966; 2nd edition, Mexico City: Siglo XXI, 1975
Las comunidades de España y del Perú, Lima: Universidad Mayor de San Marcos, 1968
Temblar Katatay y otros poemas, Lima: Instituto Nacional de Cultura, 1972 [Spanish and Quechua]
Formación de una cultura nacional indoamericana, edited by Ángel Rama, Mexico City: Siglo XXI, 1975
Señores e indios: acerca de la cultura quechua, edited by Ángel Rama, Buenos Aires: Era, 1976 [essays and lectures]
Temblar/El sueño del pongo, Havana: Casa de las Américas, 1980 [bilingual edition]

Compilations and Anthologies
Amor mundo y otros cuentos, Montevideo: Arca, 1967; augmented 2nd edition, 1972 [Contains "La agonía de Rasu-Ñiti" and the stories of *Agua*]
Amor mundo y todos los cuentos, Lima: Francisco Moncloa, 1967
Páginas escogidas, edited by Emilio Adolfo Westphalen, Lima: Universo, 1972
Relatos completos, edited by Jorge Lafforgue, Buenos Aires: Losada, 1975; revised edition, 1977

Obras completas, edited by Sybilia Arrendondo de Arguedas, 5 vols, Lima: Horizonte, 1983

Translations
The Singing Mountaineers: Songs and Tales of the Quechua People, edited and translated by Ruth Stephan, Austin: University of Texas Press, and Edinburgh: Nelson, 1957

Further Reading
Castro Klarén, Sara, *El mundo mágico de José María Arguedas*, Lima: Instituto de Estudios Peruanos, 1973
Columbus, Claudette Kemper, *Mythological Consciousness and the Future: José María Arguedas*, New York: Peter Lang, 1986
Cornejo Polar, Antonio, *Los universos narrativos de José María Arguedas*, Buenos Aires: Losada, 1973
Fell, Eve Marie (editor), *El zorro de arriba y el zorro de abajo*, Madrid: Archivos, 1990 [Critical edition with essays by Cornejo Polar, Martin Lienhard, William Rowe and others]
Harrison, Regina, "José María Arguedas: el substrato quechua," *Revista Iberoamericana* 49 (January–March 1983)
Larco, Juan (editor), *Recopilación de textos sobre José María Arguedas*, Havana: Casa de las Américas, 1976
Lienhard, Martin, *Cultura popular andina y forma novelesca: zorros y danzantes en la última novela de Arguedas*, Lima: Tarea, 1981; revised edition, Lima: Horizonte, 1990
Rama, Ángel, *Transculturación narrativa en América Latina*, Mexico City: Siglo XXI, 1982
Rowe, William, *Mito e ideología en la obra de José María Arguedas*, Lima: Instituto Nacional de Cultura, 1979

Bibliographies
Rowe, William, "Bibliografía sobre José María Arguedas," *Revista Peruana de Cultura* 13–14 (December 1970)

Special Issues of Journals
Revista Iberoamericana 122 (January–March 1983)

Los ríos profundos

Novel by José María Arguedas

Los ríos profundos, without doubt José María Arguedas's most popular novel, is also generally considered his masterpiece. By far the most genuine representation of Andean culture in Peruvian indigenist fiction, this novel is not only rich in its portrayal of Quechua folklore, music and language, but in the careful treatment of the Indian magical-religious vision of the world. Arguedas's linguistic innovations in this novel are a critical element in the representation of a more authentic and convincing image of the Indian. Rather than resorting to the stylistic experiments found in his early works, techniques that relied on structural distortions which rendered the language artificial, Arguedas succeeds in creating a new language that skilfully incorporates Quechua syntax and oral qualities into a carefully crafted, correct Spanish.

Narrated in the first person by a mature, well-educated man, the novel is a recollection of the predicaments of the fourteen-year-old boy Ernesto as he struggles to cope with life in a religious boarding school in the Andean town of Abancay where he had been left by his father, an itinerant lawyer. Generally viewed as autobiographical because of the similarities with

Arguedas's own upbringing, the novel consists of a series of episodes in which Ernesto, who has been brought up in an Indian rural community, suddenly finds himself in the alien and hostile environment of the school. There he meets with rampart violence and oppression, an endemic condition resulting from ethnic, cultural and racial differences. Ernesto's life with the Indians before he was brought to Abancay had been full of wonderful nurturing experiences, in close contact with nature, immersed in myths and legends, and in an intimate, spiritual relationship with the universe. In sharp and painful contrast, his life at the boarding school was dominated by violence, sexual debasement and repression, psychological and physical abuse, all promoted and condoned by the school's director and staff.

The closed universe of the school is in itself a microcosm reflecting the same values of the society to which it belongs. The town of Abancay is totally surrounded by large haciendas or estates, where the landowners are all-powerful and un-disputed masters over the lives and destinies of every living creature. Overwhelmed by this suffocating and dehumanizing environment, Ernesto seeks refuge in the *chicherías* (taverns) where he can mingle with Indians and mestizos, but where he can also listen to *huaynos*, Andean songs which bring him spiritual solace and mitigate his nostalgia for a paradise lost. In his quest for a closer communion with nature, Ernesto appeals to the supernatural powers of the *zumbayllu*, a spinning top that can conjure up magical experiences and visions of the idyllic world for which he yearns.

The violence that permeates the novel is a direct reflection of the oppressive structures and feudal nature of the society it depicts. It is essentially a violence that emerges from socioeconomic, cultural and religious domination, a condition that, from the point of view of the subject classes, implies the total collapse of the world's natural order. Constantly exacerbated by a powerful landowning class supported by civil, military and ecclesiatic authorities, this violation results in a subversive reaction of unforeseen magnitude and consequences against the established social order. Ernesto, who at first has been a passive witness to the rapidly unfolding events, is caught up in the euphoria and determination of the insurgents and participates enthusiastically in the ensuing riots. The first of such incidents is the revolt of the *chicheras* (waitresses in the tavern) against the landowners to protest the rationing of salt to the peasants. Led by the charismatic doña Felipa, the women defy the authorities, confront the town's priest, break into the government warehouses and distribute the salt among the poor. The reprisal by the army is swift and brutal; doña Felipa is hunted down by the troops but manages to escape in an episode of epic proportions that transforms her into a mythical figure in the eyes of Ernesto and of her followers. The second subversive event is the uprising of the *colonos* (peasants belonging to the *haciendas*), who flee to Abancay from the plague that has erupted among them, demanding that a special mass be said on their behalf to eradicate the evil spirit that is destroying them. The revolt is successful and forces the authorities to accede to their demands. The novel brings to a head not only the conflict between two different social orders, but between two diverging views of the world. Ernesto's identification with the poor and the downtrodden is more than an expression of his social conscience, it represents his total embrace of Quechua cultural values with full confidence in its virtues and powers. The victory of the *colonos* reaffirms and vindicates his faith, and helps him resolve his conflictive feelings of identity.

There is throughout this novel an underlying ideological component that closely reflects Arguedas's well-known sociopolitical inclinations. The sudden turn half-way through the novel from the narration of Ernesto's vicissitudes in the boarding school to the account of the momentous events of the revolts of the *chicheras* and the *colonos* would at first seem like a break in the book's unity. Taken as a whole, however, the novel offers a comprehensive view of Arguedas's vision of the Indian and its role in Peruvian society. Arguedas's literary and ideological projects go hand in hand in portraying Andean culture as a self-sufficient alternate to Occidental culture. Furthermore, Arguedas uses the Spanish language, and the novel itself, a genre totally identified with European cultural values, to subvert from the inside the hegemony of the dominant social classes. If, in the novel there appears to be a disproportion between the awesome power of the *colonos* and the apparently modest results of their challenge to the established order, the implication remains that, properly channeled, this power could be used to bring about social and political change of unprecedented magnitude. Arguedas himself would claim several years after the publication of the novel that the episode of the revolt by the *colonos* had been the prelude to the bloody uprisings of the Andean *campesinos* that brought to an end the feudal system of land ownership in Peru, a traumatic episode that permanently changed the nature of Peruvian society as a whole.

Whether in fact *Los ríos profundos* was instrumental in the social changes brought about by the peasants' armed struggle is highly debatable. What is certain is that Arguedas's novel remains as one of the greatest works of Peruvian literature, representing the standard against which all future indigenist fiction would have to be measured.

ISMAEL P. MÁRQUEZ

Editions

First edition: *Los ríos profundos*, Buenos Aires: Losada, 1958
Critical edition: edited by William Rowe, Oxford: Pergamon Press, 1973
Translation: *Deep Rivers*, by Frances Horning Barraclough, Austin: University of Texas Press, 1978

Further Reading

Dorfman, Ariel, *Imaginación y violencia en América*, Santiago de Chile: Editorial Universitaria, 1970 [Contains chapter on *Los ríos profundos* and Vargas Llosa's *La ciudad y los perros*]
Larco, Juan (editor), *Recopilación de textos sobre José María Arguedas*, Havana: Casa de las Américas, 1976 [Contains several worthwhile articles on this novel]
Ortega, Julio, *Texto comunicación y cultura en "Los ríos profundos,"* Lima: OCEDEP, 1982
Vargas Llosa, Mario, "*Los ríos profundos*: ensoñación y magia," in *Nueva novela latinoamericana*, vol. 1, edited by Jorge Lafforgue, Buenos Aires: Paidós, 1969

Manlio Argueta 1935–

Salvadorean prose writer and poet

Although also an accomplished poet of social and political commitment, Manlio Argueta has made his mark primarily as a novelist, earning the Casa de las Américas prize in 1977 for *Caperucita en la zona roja* [Little Red Riding Hood in the Red Zone]. In general terms Argueta has evolved from being the sophisticated, occasionally self-indulgent spokesman of the dissident intellectual elite of urban San Salvador, to the mature, disciplined craftsman of testimonial fiction recording the collective voice of El Salvador's forgotten people: its long-suffering peasantry.

Begun originally as a poem, Argueta's first novel, *El valle de las hamacas*, 1970 [The Valley of the Hammocks], sets the tone for his subsequent fiction, which ranges from passages of lyrical beauty and simplicity, on the one hand, to passages of grotesque coprology or baffling complexity, on the other. His first novel betrays the keenness for experimentation of a raw talent striving to find an original voice amidst the polyphony of the Latin American Boom. Divided into three parts, *El valle de las hamacas* (the indigenous name for the site of earthquake-prone San Salvador), moves back and forth between past, present and future and switches, sometimes disconcertingly so, from first- to third-person narrative, with the occasional foray into second person singular or plural. The novel could well be described as a Salvadorean *nouveau roman*, with its quick-fire sequence of flashbacks, interior monologues, speeches, radio transcripts, police reports, prose poems and contrapuntal chronicles of the conquest by both conqueror and conquered. In the midst of such formal pyrotechnics, the reader runs the risk of losing track of the novel's basic plot: the ill-fated search by a group of inexperienced guerrillas for a Sandinista cache in a remote area of Central America.

The name of the god-forsaken valley where the wretched storehouse of arms is hidden – "El Encanto," meaning "the Charm" or "the Spell" – is an ironic reference to the legendary "El Dorado," Argueta's point being that everything in post-conquest El Salvador and Central America, even its legends and heroes, are more ignominious than in the rest of Latin America. Infusing the milieu of would-be student conspirators and guerrillas with a spirit of Sartrean nausea and bad faith, Argueta succeeds in depicting El Salvador during the regime of Colonel Lemus in the mid-1950s as the "arsehole of the world" governed by "a little shit who thinks he is God."

Caperucita en la zona roja (1977), is, on the surface, Argueta's most cryptic and challenging novel. Set principally in the urban jungle of San Salvador, this time in the 1970s during the regime of the simian Colonel Molina, Argueta mockingly subverts the story of Little Red Riding Hood, transposing it to the suburb of El Bosque (The Woods), where two anguished characters (Al and Horm) live out their existential frustrations and sexual fantasies. Once again Argueta indulges his penchant for technical experimentation, but with a sense of fun absent from his first novel. Al's delirious monologues and his passionate dialogues with Horm tell a melodramatic tale reminiscent of a Mexican *bolero*, while parodies of political speeches and sermons, a blasphemous rendition of the national anthem, a farcical cuckolding scene, fables, wordplay and particularly humorous usage of Salvadorean sayings help turn the novel into a burlesque vision of love and politics in El Salvador.

Simultaneously, however, another story is told; that of the sordid betrayal and execution of Al, a poet-revolutionary, by his fellow-guerrillas. For all his hypochondria, maudlin sentimentality, intellectual arrogance and chauvinism, Al is committed to the ideal of a "cerebral" revolution infused with the "beautiful" and "honest" spirit of poetry. His dream is to liberate his country from a fascist regime that quashes spiritual life, tortures dissidents and massacres students. As the creative reader strives to reconstruct this novelistic jigsaw puzzle, s/he cannot help but recall an early description of Al as a "pobrecito poeta" (a dud little poet), an intertextual clue that, among a series of others, helps to identify Al as none other than Roque Dalton, El Salvador's tragic left-wing literary and political icon and the writer of the celebrated mock-biography *¡Pobrecito poeta que era yo!* [What a Dud Poet I Was!]. Indeed, the very collage technique employed by Argueta in his novel may be seen as a teasing emulation of the poetic technique favoured by Dalton in *Las historias prohibidas del Pulgarcito*, 1974 [The Forbidden Stories of Tom Thumb]. Ultimately, therefore, Argueta's novel may be read as a homage to his illustrious comrade, a revolutionary poet and poet-revolutionary, a complex, flawed but good human being with a sense of fun and a love of life whose flame was prematurely extinguished by murderers who betrayed everything he stood for.

In his third novel, *Un día en la vida*, 1980 (*One Day of Life*), Argueta leaves the urban milieu of San Salvador and turns to the forgotten rural provinces of his perpetually convulsed republic. Most significantly, for the first time he allows his text to speak consistently and simply in the voice(s) of the marginalized *campesinos* (peasants), the subaltern community in a country despoiled since independence by an oligarchical network of "fourteen families" and their military and imperialistic allies. In this short novel, Argueta utilises an alternating sequence of interior monologues and first-person testimonies to convey the nightmarish violence that has racked El Salvador since the Great Slaughter of 1932, when "dogs used to eat corpses." The country's bloody history is compressed into one day in the life of Lupe Fuentes, a peasant woman haunted by the memory of how her son had his head "chopped off" with a machete and how her husband was reduced to a bruised "piece of meat" before he was fed to the worms and vultures. Both men in her life were peasant leaders involved in a peaceful struggle to obtain better prices for their eggs, chickens and pigs, and the right to health care, to food and to schooling for their children. As far as the shocked, bewildered but stoic Lupe can tell, the National Guard killed them for the crime of possessing a conscience.

Interestingly, for the first time Argueta leaves an imprint, however subtle, of "magical realism" in the pages of this novel, as the peasants' ancestral gods fill the sky with bloody wounds in angry response to the bloodbath in the countryside below. Ghosts and gremlins materialise before Lupe's eyes and a mixture of pagan and Catholic superstition shapes her vision of life. In this case, however, the spirit of magic is overwhelmed by the sheer horror of human reality as conveyed by such images of children eaten from within by worms that have been expelled through their noses and mouths, and a naked priest lying on a road with a stick up his anus. Published just as the civil war of the 1980s was about to flare, *Un día en la vida* can now be interpreted as a lugubrious prophesy of the orgy of violence that was soon to descend upon the country.

In *Cuzcatlán: donde bate la mar del sur*, 1986 (*Cuzcatlán: Where the Southern Sea Beats*), Argueta applies pervious devices and motifs to narrate a syncopated history of Cuzcatlán, the indigenous name for El Salvador. A bus trip to San Salvador by Beatriz Martínez (alias Lucía, a guerrilla) comprises the frame within which four generations of the Martínez clan provide their personal testimonies. By adroit exploitation of his preferred technique of yoking together a variety of styles, voices and registers (flashbacks, interior monologues, prose poems, dramatic dialogue, proverbs, songs, repetition of the same episode from different points of view and even instances of telepathic communication) Argueta manages to impart to his narrative a ritualistic tone reminiscent of that of tribal storytellers. The stories told by the various characters throb with the wisdom, poetry, physical courage and spiritual strength of the *náhuatls*, the pre-Columbian inhabitants of Cuzcatlán, whose "flying princes" were shot down by the crossbows and arquebuses of the conquering Spaniards.

Probably no other writer, apart from Salarrué in *Cuentos de barro*, 1933 [Clay Stories], has succeeded in humanising the Salvadorean peasant so movingly and persuasively as Argueta in this novel. Particularly impressive is his representation of the female members of the Martínez dynasty, with Beatriz/Lucía, in her function as the "collective voice of her race," eulogising them as "the centre of the household, the sun round which revolved the twin planets of poverty and hope." In the midst of the devastations wrought upon the countryside by political massacres and volcanic eruptions, the indomitable spirit of the Salvadoran woman is symbolised by the "metate," the volcanic stone utilized since time immemorial to grind the corn to make the tortilla, the peasants' principal sustenance to fend off rickets, diarrhoea or starvation. The antithetical symbol to the *metate* is the helicopter, a dark, foreboding agent of evil sent by a foreign power to scorch the earth in order to destroy the peasant's spirit, for maize is a sacred crop which refuses to grow when burnt. Through this dramatic juxtaposition of symbols – the natural against the artificial, the autochthonous against the foreign, primordial lava against the military-industrial complex – Argueta pointedly denounces North American imperialism in Central America.

Scenes of military butchery and passages plumbing the psychology of paternalism and racism in El Salvador stay in the reader's mind as the novel moves towards its dramatic dénouement. Ultimately, however, it is Beatriz/Lucía's female voice of compassion and reconciliation that prevails, as she forgives the murderous blood-relative who has been poisoned

against his own kind by the *gringos*. Published six years before the peace accords of 1992, *Cuzcatlán* finishes on a message of hope that anticipates Manlio Argueta's own clarion call in July 1993 for "la necesaria cultura por la paz" (the necessary culture for peace). It is with considerable expectation that readers await his next novel, *Milagro de la paz* [The Miracle of Peace].

ROY C. BOLAND

See also entry on Roque Dalton

Biography

Born in San Miguel, El Salvador, 24 November 1935. Studied law briefly. Member of group of angry young writers known as Círculo Universitario de Escritores. Director of University of El Salvador's publishing house until the storming of the university by the military in 1972. Suffered imprisonment and was in exile for over twenty years in Costa Rica, where he taught Central American literature and established the Salvadorean-Costa Rican Cultural Centre. In the mid 1990s resides in San Salvador, where he is director of the University of El Salvador's bookshop. Recipient of many literary awards, including the Casa de las Américas Prize, 1977, for *Caperucita en la zona roja*, and the University of Central America Editores Prize in 1980.

Selected Works

Novels
El valle de las hamacas, Buenos Aires: Sudamericana, 1970
Caperucita en la zona roja, Havana: Casa de las Américas, 1977
Un día en la vida, San Salvador: University of Central America, 1980; as *One Day of Life*, translated by Bill Brow, London: Chatto and Windus, 1984; New York: Aventura, 1985
Cuzcatlán: donde bate la mar del sur, Tegucigalpa, Honduras: Guaymuras, 1986; as *Cuzcatlán: Where the Southern Sea Beats*, translated by Clark Hansen, London: Chatto and Windus, and New York: Random House, 1987

Poetry
Poemas, San Salvador: n.p., 1967
De aquí en adelante, San Salvador: Editorial Universitaria de El Salvador, 1967
En el costado de la luz, San Salvador: Editorial Universitaria de El Salvador, 1968
Las bellas armas reales, Costa Rica: EDUCA, 1979
El Salvador, with photographs by Adam Kufeld, New York: Norton, 1990

Further Reading

For a writer of Manlio Argueta's achievement and reputation, there is very little critical commentary or analysis worthy of note on his work. This may be attributed to the fact that he comes from a very small country not generally given prominence in courses on Latin American literature taught in the North. Histories of modern Latin American literature (e.g., Fernando Alegría's *Nueva historia de la novela hispanoamericana*, Hanover, New Hampshire: Ediciones del Norte, 1986) tend to concentrate on his best known novel, *Un día en la vida*, and pay lip-service to his poetry and other novels. The best interview is by Greg Price in *Latin America. The Writer's Journey* (London: Hamish Hamilton, 1990). The MLA Bibliography has reference to a few articles on *Cuzcatlán: donde bate la mar del sur*. Other articles are listed below.

López, Silvia L., "Argueta, Dalton y la crítica de la historia," in *Cambios estéticos y nuevos proyectos culturales en Centroamérica*, edited by Amelia Mondragón, Washington, DC: Literal, 1994 [This volume includes also an essay by Nicasio Urbina, "Novela y testimonio en la narrativa de Manlio Argueta: el contrato autorial"]

Martínez, J., "Manlio Argueta," *Hispamérica*, vol. 15/42 (December 1985)

Rodríguez, Hernández R., "Nueva novela 'histórica' hispanoamericana: *La insurección* y *Un día en la vida*," *Texto Crítico* 13 (1987)

Interviews

Martínez, Zulma Nelly, *Hispamérica*, vol. 15/42 (December 1985)

Price, Greg, *Latin America. The Writer's Journey*, London: Hamish Hamilton, 1990

Roberto Arlt 1900–1942

Argentine prose writer, journalist and dramatist

A first-generation Argentine, and native of Buenos Aires, Roberto Arlt was virtually an autodidact, acquiring most of his education in the libraries of religious and political organisations. While he certainly knew well the members of the Boedo group, a loose association of left-wing writers, he belonged to no established social group or party, and in his writing principally sought to articulate the little person's struggle to survive in the expanding, alienating metropolis of the 1920s and 1930s. He consistently denounced exploitation, particularly under capitalism, and pointed out the ways in which the petit bourgeois, especially, collaborated in their own exploitation. In 1932 he was involved in a bitter dispute with the Communist Party, which he had considered joining, but then rejected as authoritarian.

Best known of Arlt's prolific and varied journalism are the sketches about Buenos Aires life and issues of the day, which appeared from 1928 in the newspaper, *El Mundo*. In 1933 Arlt published a selection of these as the *Aguafuertes porteñas* [Buenos Aires Sketches], and many more have been collected posthumously.

However, it is Arlt's novels that have generated most critical interest. Arlt's political independence, his contempt for what passed for good taste, for verisimilitude and generic continuity – as well as some eccentricities of orthography and syntax – have traditionally caused his long fiction to be recognised more for its destruction of the essentially Realist models employed by contemporary Argentine novelists, whether elitist or popular, than for its constructive achievements.

In his first major fiction work, *El juguete rabioso* [The Rabid Toy], Arlt for the first time engages with problems of identity, and survival in the city, and uses extensively the colloquial language of Buenos Aires (*lunfardo*). The frustrated progress of his impoverished urban protagonist, Silvio, seems to be a riposte to the journey towards integration of Fabio, the rural protagonist of the patrician Ricardo Güiraldes's *Don Segundo Sombra*. (Both novels were published in 1926, and both were completed while Arlt was working with Güiraldes).

The most discussed of Arlt's long fiction is the double novel *Los siete locos* (The Seven Madmen), and *Los lanzallamas* [The Flamethrowers], published respectively in 1929 and 1931.

Here, alienation and fragmentation are most intensely expressed, through stark and bizarre inner states, and through the absurd, melodramatic events of the life of the protagonist, Erdosain. The novel opens with Erdosain, a lowly salesman, caught defrauding his employer. From this, two narrative branches develop. In the emotional sphere, Erdosain's wife, Elsa, leaves him, eventually to be replaced by a teenage girl, purchased from her mother, whom subsequently Erdosain gratuitously murders, before committing suicide. Secondly, Erdosain's quest for money to repay his employer leads him to a group of bizarre conspirators, led by the Astrologer, who plan to take over the state, and instal a tyranny based on a new religion. Arlt uses the obviously fictional, melodramatic framework and caricatured characters to present numerous observations (but no analysis) about the life of Buenos Aires's less affluent inhabitants, and about the dreams (riches, Hollywood films, mass ideologies, novels with happy endings) which sustain them. Techniques which prevent the novel being read passively as the image of a coherent reality, encourage the reader to question and assemble meaning. The individuality of the already marginal, caricatured figures is further dismantled through the use of shared turns of phrase, or similar dreams. The clearest example is that of Erdosain, and Elsa's cousin Barsut, in which the two can be seen as alternative versions of the same character. A second important case is the partial merging of Erdosain and the narrator, which calls into question the assumed relationship between narrator, character and reader. The novel is criss-crossed by a surreal network of identical or slowly- evolving images and phrases, and by repeated events, in which the reader may discover/create thematic patterns of association. There are also experiments with the imaging of the experience of time and space: boundaries between wakefulness and dream, sanity and madness, present, past and future become uncertain, while diverse elements, such as geometrical and other mechanical imagery from the modern city, film scenes, memories, contribute to a mental labyrinth.

El amor brujo [Love the Magician], published in 1932, is very different. Set shortly before the 1930 military coup, in the city centre, the suburb of Tigre, and in the train that links the two, it is a naturalistic account of an affair between a young music student, Irene, and a married engineer, Balder. In it are juxtaposed the individual cynicism of the characters, the mechanical inevitability of their behaviour as members of their social groups, and the dreams and myths in which individuals and society wrap sexuality. Like Erdosain, Balder is an alienated figure (he has a failed marriage and an unsatisfying career) and a dreamer, but unlike Erdosain he is an educated figure who analyses and denounces a clearly identifiable society. As well as using a protagonist who controls the narrative (here the chronicler figure is simply a disguise), Arlt also introduces direct presentation of modern elements like flashing neon signs, whose immediacy collapses the distinction between perception and thought. Although *El amor brujo* has found little favour with readers and critics, the Uruguayan novelist Juan Carlos Onetti was influenced by Arlt's work at this period.

Aguafuertes españolas [Spanish Sketches], the fruit of Arlt's time as correspondent for *El Mundo* in Spain just before the outbreak of the Civil War, and published in 1936, continues from *El amor brujo*, and reflects on the novel cycle. The sketches are set in Spain and North Africa, but make surprisingly few allusions to the political situation; rather, they explore the imaginary nature of the Spain seen from Argentina – the Spain to which the characters of *El amor brujo* nostalgically looked. (There is even a scene in which some Sacro Monte gypsies perform a song from Falla's ballet of the same name). A striking feature is the grouping of the sketches into a journey structure which shows many similarities of incident – and divergence of conclusions drawn – to the *Viajes por Europa, Africa y América* [Journeys through Europe, Africa and the United States] of the 19th-century Argentine educator and statesman, Domingo Faustino Sarmiento. It is as if Arlt the authorised journalist, reporting the "reality" of Spain, partially emulates his prestigious predecessor, while the novelist undermines his cultural authority.

Arlt's plays, most of which were written for Leónidas Barletta's *Teatro del Pueblo*, and which date from 1932 onwards, generally intensify elements from his fiction: interiors were already described as if they were stage sets, and many characters voluntarily or involuntarily played artificial roles. A third feature from the novels, dramatised dialogues between real and imaginary characters, occurs extensively in the early *Trescientos millones* [Three Hundred Million], and *El fabricante de fantasmas* [The Creator of Phantoms]. The most accomplished drama is *Saverio el cruel* [Saverio the Cruel], a tragic farce about a demented butter salesman whose alter ego is a pantomime colonel. Here Arlt combines elements from contemporary Buenos Aires with implicit and explicit references to *Don Quixote,* in an ambiguous exploration of individual and social insanity. In later plays Arlt continues to use the exaggerated, the insane and the absurd, although usually ambiguity is replaced by clearer messages, often about militarism or commercial exploitation. A similar tendency towards direct statement is observed in Arlt's late journalism, and can be attributed, at least in part, to a change in priorities occasioned by World War II.

His finest short stories date from around 1930 and were collected, in 1933, in *El jorobadito* [The Hunchbacked Dwarf]. They are generally caricatured but plausible accounts of episodes from the city, such as a bridegroom's flight to Uruguay

on the night before the wedding: ("Noche terrible") [A Terrible Night]; or the comic competitive behaviour of two married couples: ("Pequeños propietarios") [Small Property-owners]. Later stories are set in more exotic locations, and rely for their effect on artificial elements such as mysterious psychological and natural phenomena, and unexpected endings.

PAUL JORDAN

See also entry on Ricardo Piglia

Biography

Born in Buenos Aires, Argentina, 7 April 1900. His father was Prussian and his mother from the South Tyrol. Arlt's first language was German. He had little formal education and worked at a variety of menial jobs including docker, factory worker and travelling salesman. Moved to Córdoba in 1920 returning to Buenos Aires four years later. Married Carmen Antinucci in 1922, who died of tuberculosis in 1940; one daughter. Wrote for numerous newspapers and journals including *El Mundo, Martín Fierro,* and *Claridad.* Worked as secretary to Ricardo Güiraldes. Travelled to Uruguay and Brazil in 1930. His first play, *Trescientos millones* was produced in Buenos Aires in 1932. Visited Spain and Morocco in 1935, and Chile and Uruguay in 1941. Married Elizabeth Mary Shine in 1940. Died in Buenos Aires of a heart attack on 26 July 1942.

Selected Works

Novels and Short Fiction
El juguete rabioso, Buenos Aires: Latina, 1926
Los siete locos, Buenos Aires: Latina, 1929; as *The Seven Madmen,* translated by Naomi Lindstrom, Boston: Godine, 1984
Los lanzallamas, Buenos Aires: Claridad, 1931
El amor brujo, Buenos Aires: Victoria, 1932
El jorobadito, Buenos Aires: Anaconda, 1933
El criador de gorilas, Santiago de Chile: Zig-Zag, 1941

Plays
Trescientos millones, Buenos Aires: Victoria, 1932
El fabricante de fantasmas, Buenos Aires: Futuro, 1950
Saverio el cruel, Buenos Aires: Futuro, 1950
El desierto entra en la ciudad, Buenos Aires: Futuro, 1950
La isla desierta, Buenos Aires: Eudeba, 1965

Journalism
Aguafuertes porteñas, Buenos Aires: Victoria, 1933
Aguafuertes españolas, Buenos Aires: Rosso, 1936
Nuevas aguafuertes porteñas, Buenos Aires: Hachette, 1960
Cronicón de sí mismo: el idioma de los argentinos, Buenos Aires: Edicom, 1969
Entre crotos y sabihondos, Buenos Aires: Edicom, 1969
Las muchachas de Buenos Aires, Buenos Aires: Edicom, 1969
El traje del fantasma, Buenos Aires: Edicom, 1969

Compilations and Anthologies
Novelas completas y cuentos, edited by Mirta Arlt, 3 vols, Buenos Aires: Fabril, 1963
Teatro completo, edited by Mirta Arlt, 2 vols, Buenos Aires: Schapire, 1968
Obra completa, 3 vols, Buenos Aires: Planeta Argentina and Carlos Lohlé, 1991
  1. *El juguete rabioso, Los siete locos, Los lanzallamas* and *Las ciencias ocultas en Buenos Aires*
  2. *El amor brujo, El jorobadito, Dos relatos, Aguafuertes porteñas*

3. *El criador de gorilas, Aguafuertes españolas,* and the plays –
   Prueba de amor, Trescientos millones, Saverio el cruel,
   El fabricante de fantasmas, La isla desierta, África, La fiesta
   del hierro, El desierto entra en la ciudad, La juerga de los
   polichinelas, Un hombre sensible

Further Reading

Amícola, José, *Astrología y fascismo en la obra de Arlt,* Buenos Aires: Weimar, 1984

Arlt, Mirta, *Prólogos a la obra de mi padre,* Buenos Aires: Torres Agüero, 1985

Arlt, Mirta and Omar Borré, *Para leer a Robert Arlt,* Buenos Aires: Torres Agüero, 1985

Castagnino, Raúl H., *El teatro de Roberto Arlt,* La Plata: Universidad Nacional de La Plata, 1970

Corral, Rose, *El obsesivo circular de la ficción, asedios a "Los Siete locos" y "Los Lanzallamas" de Roberto Arlt,* Mexico City: Colegio de México, 1992

Flint, Jack M., *The Prose Works of Roberto Arlt: a Thematic Approach,* Durham, England: University of Durham, 1985

Giordano, Jaime, "El espacio en la narrativa de Roberto Arlt," *Nueva Narrativa Hispanoamericana,* vol. 2/2 (1972)

Gnutzmann, Rita, *Roberto Arlt o, el arte del calidoscopio,* Vitoria, Spain: Universidad del País Vasco, 1984 [useful bibliography]

González Lanuza, Eduardo, *Roberto Arlt,* Buenos Aires: Centro Editor de América Latina, 1981

Gostautas, Stasys, *Buenos Aires y Arlt,* Madrid: Insula, 1977

Guerrero, Diana, *Roberto Arlt: el habitante solitario,* Buenos Aires: Catálogos Granica, 1972 [useful bibliography]

Hayes, Aden W., *Roberto Arlt: la estragia de su ficción,* London: Támesis, 1981

Jarkowski, Aníbal, "*El amor brujo*: la novela 'mala' de Arlt," in *Yrigoyen entre Borges y Arlt,* edited by Graciela Montaldo, Buenos Aires: Cuntrapunto, 1989

Larra, Raúl, *Roberto Arlt; el torturado,* Buenos Aires: Alpe, 1951

Lindstrom, Naomi, "Arlt's Exposition of the Myth of Women," in *Woman as Myth and Metaphor in Latin American Literature,* edited by Lindstrom and Carmelo Virgillo, Columbia: University of Missouri Press, 1985

Maldavsky, David, *La crisis en la narrativa de Roberto Arlt,* Buenos Aires: Escuela, 1968

Masotta, Oscar, *Sexo y traición en Roberto Arlt,* Buenos Aires: Jorge Álvarez, 1982

Núñez, Ángel, *La obra narrativa de Roberto Arlt,* Buenos Aires: Nova, 1968

Pastor, Beatriz, *Roberto Arlt y la rebelión alienada,* Gaithersburg, Maryland: Hispamérica, 1980

Piglia, Ricardo, "Roberto Arlt: una crítica de la economía literaria," *Los Libros* 29 (March–April 1973)

Rivera, Jorge B., *Borges y Arlt, literatura y periodismo,* Buenos Aires: Universidad de Buenos Aires, 1992

Rodríguez, Raimundo, *Divagiones en torno del misterio de un autor,* Buenos Aires: Nuevo Meridión, 1987

Viñas, David, *De Sarmiento a Cortázar: literatura argentina y realidad política,* Buenos Aires: Siglo XX, 1971 [Includes material on Arlt]

Zubieta, Ana María, *El discurso narrativo arltiano, intertextualidad, grotesco y utopía,* Buenos Aires: Hachette, 1987

El juguete rabioso (novel) and Aguafuertes porteñas (sketches)

By Roberto Arlt

Roberto Arlt published his first novel, *El juguete rabioso,* in 1926 while he was working as a journalist, and the selection of articles titled *Aguafuertes porteñas* are inspired by his work. Most of them were published in the newspaper *El Mundo* in Buenos Aires around 1930 and a selection first appeared in book form in 1933. The treatment of time in these two works by Roberto Arlt is not only chronological but also thematic.

Aguafuertes porteñas consists of around 100 articles giving views on daily life in Buenos Aires and, on more than one occasion, commenting on the work of the writer and the journalist. A wide variety of issues are dealt with: customs, social types, events in the city, political opinions, etc. *Aguafuertes porteñas* constitutes without doubt a snapshot of Buenos Aires in 1930. However, the value of these texts lies not only in the sensitivity and intuition with which Arlt successfully captures the spirit of the era but also in the style in which they were written.

Lunfardo was the term applied at that time to the sociolect which the working class and marginalized sectors of Buenos Aires spoke: the language of the street. And it is in just this slang – with a few concessions to more classical and less colloquial words – that Arlt wrote *Aguafuertes.* In this sense, *Aguafuertes porteñas* constitutes a landmark in Argentine literature because these sketches were daily speech turned into writing, that is a colloquial or "street" form of the language brought into a medium with a massive readership: the newspaper. And from then on the language was legitimized as a means of daily communication. Arlt gave this colloquial language of Buenos Aires, seen by many as the language of the underclass, rights of citizenship. Through its format (each article was about 800 words long) as well as its content and style (Buenos Aires life told in an understandable and purified *lunfardo*) *Aguafuertes* has become a model in the history of Argentine journalism.

El juguete rabioso, Arlt's first and also his most intuitive novel, tells the story of Silvio Astier, a hot-headed and conceited young man of humble origins who has to face up to earning his living at a young age. He is pushed on above all by his mother who represents both the moral aspect of the story and the reality of it. Her reality is one of poverty and a social situation difficult to alter by means of work.

Initiation – a theme taken from the picaresque genre that Arlt was to use with frequency in his work – comes about when Silvio starts to work in various different jobs where he is badly treated and underpaid and thus becomes increasingly resentful. Arlt, through the figure of Silvio Astier, achieves two simultaneous narrative goals. On the one hand he describes the life of a social sector of Buenos Aires: humble people and petty proprietors, their taste and behaviour. On the other hand, he narrates the psychological and material struggles of the characters in their social context.

Throughout the novel these two aspects lead to a common theme: the fatality of poverty is accompanied by the fatality of all the feelings and desires of the characters. The condition of this fatality – as Oscar Masotta has correctly observed – is resolved through the theme of betrayal. Through various actions – leaving the school of aviation, to pick one example among many – Silvio Astier betrays his sister and mother since, to continue with the example, they had both pinned all their material hopes and social aspirations on Silvio's possible future as an aeroplane mechanic. Through the denunciation of Rengo, Silvio Astier betrays his best friend and himself. And it is this last betrayal that defines the whole novel.

Silvio Astier's self-betrayal comes about principally in two ways. Firstly, in order to denounce Rengo (the Limping Man) who belongs to the same social class as he and is poor and unhappy, Silvio has to collude with a character of a wealthy class, different from his own. This character, the owner of the house they had both planned to rob, seems to confirm their class difference by never ceasing to treat Silvio as a young product of the misery and poverty of Buenos Aires. This social distance – essential to understand the vileness of Astier's action – can be observed in the story not only when the architect Arsenio Vitri offers Silvio money for having denounced his friend (deep down Vitri himself disapproves of this betrayal) but also when he offers to find Silvio a "good job" through his own social contacts. This is, to give it a label, the "social betrayal" of Silvio Astier.

Silvio Astier's self-betrayal has another side. It is this that Oscar Masotta has dealt with: he focuses on the apathy and sterility into which Astier's existence is plunged towards the end of the novel as a consequence of his unfortunate social initiation. It is through the betrayal, and the stigma that the betrayal of his best friend constitutes (denouncing him to Vitri) that Silvio Astier finds his "salvation." The inevitable derision that follows the betrayal is the only way Silvio Astier can take a step forward to overcome the apathy into which he has sunk. And it is when his attempted suicide fails that the psycho-logical route of this betrayal – as the only means of escape – gathers significance.

Finally, the very title of the novel, *El juguete rabioso*, brilliantly defines the two sides of Silvio Astier. On the one hand he is a young man who, owing to his poverty and with terrible consequences, has to face up to "earning his living" at a very young age. This is how his own mother refers to the act of going out to work and bringing home money. On the other hand he is a young man who, after a failed attempt at suicide, chooses betrayal and derision as a means of social survival. In a way, Silvio Astier is a child who hangs on to his childhood toys – the fatality of the time and social circumstance chance assigned to him – but turns them into dangerous sentimental machines.

The thematic similarity of these two works that was mentioned at the beginning of this article lies in their defining of Arlt's favourite motif and an ongoing controversy of his time: the language of the Argentines. In this sense and in the words of Arlt, *Aguafuertes porteñas* expresses the language of the Argentines described in its social and collective context, while *El juguete rabioso* expresses an intimate psychological language of the people of Buenos Aires. It is as if Arlt in these two works (and later in *Los siete locos* which reached a wider readership) has handed us one work which is at the same time specific, personal and social, and which speaks of an era, a time and a place which we can call "Buenos Aires, around 1930."

CLAUDIO CANAPARO

translated by Jo Glen

Editions
First Editions: *El juguete rabioso*, Buenos Aires: Latina, 1926
Aguafuertes porteñas, Buenos Aires: Victoria, 1933

Further Reading
Scroggins, Daniel C., *Las aguafuertes de Roberto Arlt*, Buenos Aires: Ediciones Culturales Argentinas, 1981

Juan José Arreola 1918–

Mexican prose writer

In the late 1940s, seemingly from nowhere, the work of Juan José Arreola burst onto the Mexican literary scene. The stories collected in *Varia invención*, 1949 [Varied Inventions], innovative, entertaining, displaying a considerable narrative skill, mark an important moment in the development of Mexican fiction. An instant hit with a Mexican readership accustomed mainly to European texts, these stories enjoyed a brief period of fame and have certainly had a great influence. Their success, however, was soon overshadowed by that of Arreola's more sombre and laconic contemporary, Juan Rulfo.

Arreola's literary output is confined to a few collections of short pieces and a novel, and his list of publications tailed off in the 1960s and 1970s. Increasingly obsessed with the musicality and rhythm of the spoken word, most of his later work has consisted of public speaking and television appearances. In a sense most of the literary work of his maturity can be said to be his spoken output. His prodigious memory, engaging wit and tendency towards frank, personal confession have made him a highly popular performer, but also a self-avowed figure of fun. Perhaps for this reason, his work, always honourably mentioned in surveys of Mexican literature, has not received the critical attention and acclaim it deserves.

Arreola's written output is something of an oddity. For one thing, among Mexican writers he stands out as one of the very few who place a high premium on humour. His prose style – precious, lapidary, rhythmical – is characterised by a subtle and assured mastery of the minutiae of irony. It is suffused with contradictions: ostentatiously erudite, and yet demonstrating an autodidact's anxiety of literary influence; pyrotechnic in its verbal sophistication, and yet betraying a predilection for the unpretentiousness of rural simplicity; self-consciously striving for the so-called universality of the European literary canon, and yet resolutely Mexican in its themes, its images and its most immediate preoccupations.

Arreola's reputation, rightly, rests on his short prose pieces, particularly the texts contained in *Confabulario*, 1952 (*Confabulario and Other Inventions*), later updated in various editions with selections of the best of other volumes too. Profoundly influenced by European writers such as Claudel, Schwob and Papini, Arreola's interests are strictly humanist in these texts. As one of the last surviving heirs of the tradition of Mexican scholars and writers which includes the Ateneo de la Juventud (especially Reyes and Torri) and, more specifically, the Contemporáneos of the 1930s, Arreola maintains a principled adherence to the aesthetics of language, shunning direct political references or nationalist bandwagons. The result is a literary output which often seems at odds with the technocratic realities of late 20th-century Mexico. Some of the stories: "En verdad os digo," "Anuncio," "Baby HP" (I'm Telling You the Truth, Announcement and Baby HP) indeed take on the technological innovation of the contemporary world with wry sarcasm, mocking both the project of modernity and the glibness and corruption of its linguistic abuses. Others, such as "El discípulo" (The Disciple), offer profound philosophical insights into the nature of aesthetics.

Many of Arreola's most famous stories have a timeless and inscrutable quality, recalling the angst-ridden emptiness of the work of Franz Kafka, Arreola's greatest literary hero. Narratives such as "El guardagujas" (The Switchman) and "El prodigioso miligramo" (The Prodigious Milligram) are complex, ambitious fables, which reward careful reading with their rich ironies and barely perceptible inconsistencies. Critics who have attempted to unravel them have often struggled to ascribe definitive meanings to these texts. But the texts seem destined to elude them, their slipperiness belied by the apparent lucidity of their prose and the deceptively child-like simplicity of their narrative strategies.

This interest in the vast intricacies made possible by the written word has led to Arreola's being dubbed the Mexican Borges, a comparison which is as misleading as it is understandable. The affinity for writing in Arreola may be reminiscent of the impossible labyrinthine libraries of Borges, but in the mocking tones at which the Mexican excels, the arid precision of scholarship is savagely debunked in stories such as "De balística" (About Ballistics).

Above all, however, Arreola's texts are far more involved with the weaknesses and vagaries of the human spirit than those of his more rigorous, more intellectual Argentine counterpart. In particular this is manifested in a discussion of the relationship between the sexes that runs through his work, drawing on the vitriolic misogyny of Otto Weininger on the one hand and studies on matriarchal culture by J.J. Bachofen on the other. Hovering between these two erudite poles, many of his texts are clever satires on the nature and frailty of human sexuality, denouncing both femininity and *machismo* in outstanding examples of biting observation. Often accused of sexism, these stories deserve to be read again in the light of contemporary criticism's more sophisticated attitude towards the deconstructive qualities of irony.

Arreola's two later collections of texts, *Bestiario*, 1958 [Bestiary] and *Palindroma*, 1964 [Palindrome], confirmed his profound interest in the possibilities and the incongruities of language. The texts in *Bestiario* are short, considered pieces which play with and confound traditional notions of metaphor, developing a dense, enigmatic linguistic texture suspended between the spirituality of poetic discourse and the sharp profanities of satirical prose. In *Palindroma*, there is a mixture of texts: an absurdist play, a couple of problematic narratives reminiscent of his earlier style and some short pieces which deal with the relationship between words and meaning.

Even more important than the themes developed by Arreola is the contribution he has made to Mexican prose style. Writing for him is akin to the artisan's labour of meticulous creation, and his generosity in passing on his experience and skill to younger writers is almost legendary. Two related ingredients make up Arreola's distinctive voice: the first is an almost religious reverence for the rhythm of spoken language. Arreola trained as an actor and wrote two plays, each of which is redolent with subtle, almost musical, ironies in the details of its prose. Much of the humour generated by Arreola's stories lies in the disparity between the pompous construction of the rhetoric and the bathos provided by the sense – often rude, hypocritical or simply foolish – of what his characters and narrators have to say. The second ingredient is his belief in the power of the written word to manifest something beyond the contingencies of everyday experience. Although Arreola has published no verse, some of his prose has been anthologised in collections of poetry. He is the author of astonishing short pieces, reminiscent of Baudelaire's prose poems.

Arreola's only novel, *La feria*, 1963 (*The Fair*), has not been taken up as a key text in the Latin American novelistic Boom. This is regrettable, as it is certainly worthy of more consideration and attention. Its subject is Arreola's rural home in Jalisco, and it develops its narrative through a fragmentary series of documents, diaries and dialogues spanning several generations. The wit of his shorter pieces is there in abundance, as is a fond but devastating critique of Mexican rural attitudes; the novel's main innovation lies in its contrapuntal technique.

Since Arreola stopped writing, two collections of epigrammatic quotations from his spoken output have appeared: *La palabra educación*, 1973 [The Word Education] and *Inventario*, 1976 [Inventory]. At worst, these pieces are bland and sententious, but at best they combine the enigmatic wit of his finest written work with the freshness and intimacy of conversation.

Arreola will be remembered both as a brilliant prose stylist and as a champion of young writers.

MAURICE BIRIOTTI

Biography

Born in Ciudad Guzmán, Jalisco, Mexico, 12 September 1918. Studied drama at the Instituto de Bellas Artes in Mexico City, 1939 and on a French government scholarship, in Paris: returned to Mexico City because of poor health. Teacher in Ciudad Guzmán, from 1941.Worked on a newspaper in Guadalajara, 1943–45; co-editor, with Juan Rulfo, *Pan* and *Eos* magazines, 1940s; proofreader and translator, Fondo de Cultura Económica publishing house, Mexico City, 1946; director of creative writing workshop, Universidad Nacional Autónoma de México (UNAM), Mexico City, 1958, host of television program; founding member and actor, Poesía en Voz Alta group. Awarded the Institute of Fine Arts Drama Festival Prize, and El Colegio de México Fellowship, late 1940s; Xavier Villaurrutia Prize, 1963.

Selected Works

Short Fiction

Gunther Stapenhorst: viñetas de Isidoro Ocampo. Mexico City: n.p., 1946
Varia invención, Mexico City: Fondo de Cultura Económica, 1949; augmented edition, Mexico City: Joaquín Mortiz, 1971
Cinco cuentos, Mexico City: Los Presentes, 1951
Confabulario, Mexico City: Fondo de Cultura Económica, 1952; revised edition, published with *Varia invención*, as *Confabulario y Varia invención: 1951–1955*, Fondo de Cultura Económica, 1955; published with *Bestiario* and *Punta de plata*, as *Confabulario total, 1941–1961*, Fondo de Cultura Económica, 1962; as *Confabulario and Other Inventions*, translated by George D. Schade, Austin: University of Texas Press, 1964; revised edition, as *Confabulario definitivo*, Madrid: Cátedra, 1986

Bestiario, Mexico City: UNAM, 1958; published with *Confabulario* and *Punta de plata*, as *Confabulario total, 1941–1961*, Mexico City: Fondo de Cultura Económica, 1962; revised edition, Mexico City: Joaquín Mortiz, 1981
Punta de plata, Mexico City: n.p., 1958; published with *Confabulario* and *Bestiario*, as *Confabulario total, 1941–61*, Mexico City: Fondo de Cultura Económica, 1962
Cuentos, Havana: Casa de las Américas, 1969
Antología de Juan José Arreola, edited by Jorge Arturo Ojeda, Mexico City: Oasis, 1969
Palindroma (includes play), Mexico City: Joaquín Mortiz, 1971
Mujeres, animales, y fantasías mecánicas, Barcelona: Tusquets, 1972
Confabulario antológico, Madrid: Círculo de Lectores, 1973
Mi confabulario, Mexico City: Promexa, 1979
Confabulario personal, Barcelona: Bruguera, 1980
Imagen y obra escogida, Mexico City: UNAM, 1984
Estas páginas mías, Mexico City: Fondo de Cultura Económica, 1985

Novel

La feria, Mexico City: Joaquín Mortiz, 1963; as *The Fair*, translated by John Upton, Austin: University of Texas Press, 1977

Play

La hora de todos: juguete cómico en un acto, Mexico City: Los Presentes, 1954

Other Writings

La palabra educación, edited by Jorge Arturo Ojeola, Mexico City: Secretaría de Educación Pública, 1973
Y ahora, la mujer, edited by Jorge Arturo Ojeola, Mexico City: Utopía, 1975
Inventario, Mexico City: Grijalbo, 1976
Ramón López Velarde: una lectura parcial, Mexico City: Cultural Bancen, 1988
El arte de Nicolás Moreno, in collaboration with Carlos Pellicer and Elisa García Barragán, Mexico City: Banco Nacional de Obras y Servicios Públicos, 1990

Further Reading

Acker, Bertie, *El cuento mexicano contemporáneo, Rulfo, Arreola y Fuentes, temas y cosmovisión*, Madrid: Playor, 1984
Barrenechea, Ana María, "Elaboración de la 'circumstancia mexicana' en tres cuentos de Arreola," *Textos hispanoamericanos: de Sarmiento a Sarduy*, Caracas (1978)
Burt, John R., "This is No Way to Run a Railroad: Arreola's Allegorical Railroad and a Possible Source," *Hispania*, vol. 71 (1988)
Castellanos, Rosario, "Tendencias de la narrativa mexicana contemporánea," in her *El mar y sus pescaditos*, Mexico City: Secretaría de Educación Pública, 1975
Cheever, Leonard A., "The Little Girl and the Cat: 'Kafkaesque' Elements in Arreola's 'The Switchman,'" *American Hispanist* 34–35 (1979)
D'Lugo, Carol Clark, "Arreola's *La feria*: the Author and the Reader in the Text," *Hispanófila*, vol. 97 (1989)
Gilgen, Read G., "Absurdist Techniques in the Short Stories of Juan José Arreola," *Journal of Spanish Studies: 20th Century*, vol. 8 (1980)
Herz, Theda Mary, "Continuity in Evolution: Juan José Arreola as Dramatist," *Latin American Theatre Review*, vol. 8/2 (1975)
Heusinkveld, Paula, "Juan José Arreola: Allegorist in an Age of Uncertainty," *Chasqui*, vol. 13/2–3 (1984)
Lagmanovich, David, "Estructura y efecto en 'La migala' de Juan José Arreola," *Cuadernos Hispanoamericanos* 320–21 (1977)

Leal, Luis, "The New Mexican Short Story," *Studies in Short Fiction*, vol. 8/1 (1971)

McMurray, George R., "Albert Camus's Concept of the Absurd and Juan José Arreola's 'The Switchman,'" *Latin American Literary Review*, vol. 6/11 (1977)

Menton, Seymour, "Juan José Arreola and the Twentieth-Century Short Story," *Hispania*, vol. 42/3 (1959)

Tomanek, Thomas J., "The Estranged Man: Kafka's Influence on Arreola," in *Revue des Langues Vivantes* 37 (1971)

Washburn, Yulan M., "An Ancient Mold for Contemporary Casting: the Beast Book of Juan José Arreola," *Hispania*, vol. 56 (1973)

____ *Juan José Arreola*, Boston: Twayne, 1983

Assis, Joaquim Maria Machado de

See Machado de Assis

Miguel Ángel Asturias 1899–1974

Guatemalan novelist

From first to last, the works of Miguel Ángel Asturias manifest his deep and abiding interest in the beliefs and worldview of the indigenous peoples of Central America. His early *Leyendas de Guatemala* [Legends of Guatemala] retell traditional myths and folk-tales, and the first drafts of *El Señor Presidente* (*The President*) at times adopt points of view and narrative modes akin to those of the pre-Columbian myths with which he was becoming increasingly familiar through his studies. From *Hombres de maíz* (*Men of Maize*) through to the end of the Banana Trilogy this style is adapted to express socio-economic and political themes. *El alhajadito* (*The Bejeweled Boy*) inaugurates the final period, in which the mythopoeic element and fantasy again dominate Asturias's work, as he strives to fashion new legends and tales in the traditional manner.

Like many others of his generation, Asturias was living in Paris when Surrealism was at its height, artistically and politically, and its impact was strong, though its concerns with the unconscious led towards Jung's work on myth rather than Freudian analysis of human personality. Few of Asturias's characters have much psychological depth; their inner conflicts tend to be externalised and played out at the archetypal level, in reenactments of mythical events. At the same time, an animistic treatment of the environment creates a powerful interplay between people and the natural world. Insofar as Jung and Asturias, from their different perspectives, develop similar interpretations of myth, Asturias may be said to be Jungian, though the expression of myth in his fiction is distinctly local. In his vision of a magical world in which humans have their animal counterpart (*nahual*) and in which a supernatural dimension is part and parcel of everyday life, the animals and plants are distinctly Central American and the people are engaged in activities typical of the region.

Asturias's early work is generally held to introduce magical realism (*realismo mágico*) as a literary mode. While most of the tales in *Leyendas de Guatemala* are conventional in form, in "Cuculcán" Asturias presents the myth as a sequence of stylised balletic/dramatic scenes, written in lyrical prose, in which birds and animals mingle with archetypal human figures. Gaspar Ilóm's vision of his world opens *Hombres de maíz*, as landscape and natural phenomena are described in terms of their mythical correlates; his defence of tradition, his betrayal and his death themselves pass into legend and are seen to determine and explain the fate of his enemies, as the corn-people attempt to defend their land and way of life against newcomers who seek to grow maize for profit by methods which destroy the land. The second half of the novel introduces new characters, from a later generation, coming into contact with these figures from the past as they in turn achieve legendary status; the maintenance of ancestral traditions is revealed as vital for the survival of Guatemalan culture. Though less immediately evident in *El Señor Presidente*, animistic elements surface occasionally in the characters' streams of consciousness. Thus the dance of Tohil, a Mayan god who demanded human sacrifice, glimpsed as Cara de Ángel is sent on the mission which ends in his death, is a powerful sign of the President's evil nature and purposes. In *Mulata de tal* (*Mulatta*), the major novel of the final period, an equivalent of the Faust legend provides the framework for the story of a battle for control of Yumí between his wife Catalina and Mulata, a moon-spirit.

Yumí and Catalina become adepts in sorcery and for a time come into conflict with a Church which has itself absorbed traditional, non-Christian elements.

The revolutionary aspect of Surrealism also finds a place in Asturias's fiction, most specifically in the final novel of the Banana Trilogy, *Los ojos de los enterrados* (*The Eyes of the Interred*), which ends with the collapse of the regime after a general strike. The exploitation of small Central American nations by US interests controlling plantation economies dominates the first two novels of the trilogy. *Viento fuerte* (*Strong Wind*) relates the setting up of the Pacific coast plantations and the installation of necessary infrastructure, leading to struggles between local growers and the foreign enterprise (a fictional representation of the United Fruit Company). The creation of a growers' cooperative under the direction of Lester Mead merely provokes Chicago to exert greater pressure. *El papa verde* (*The Green Pope*) tells how Geo Maker Thompson built up the company's operations on the Atlantic side, ruthlessly seizing land and burning villages. Many years later, when the members of the cooperative inherit Lester Mead's fortune, they transfer their allegiance to the company, won over by their new wealth; in return, Maker Thompson uses them and their holding to win control of the company through its Guatemalan operation. The intervention of the United States against the Arbenz government in 1954 provided the setting for Asturias's next work of fiction, *Week-end en Guatemala*, a collection of short stories on aspects of the operation: bungling on the ground, propaganda designed to win support in the United States, anti-communist witch-hunts, a sense of betrayal among some Americanised Guatemalans. Writing this work held up completion of *Los ojos de los enterrados*, by far the longest of Asturias's novels, set principally in the years immediately before Arbenz assumed power. The central action concerns the efforts of Octavio Sansur to build support among plantation workers for a general strike planned by industrial and transport workers. The younger generation of the original cooperative members is now thoroughly americanised, but Juambo, Geo Maker Thompson's former driver, is torn between loyalty to his master and respect for his father's bones, i.e. between the material benefits of a foreign culture and the spiritual power of native tradition. In another subplot Sansur's relationship with the schoolmistress Milena Tabay connects the workers' movements to intellectual dissent: Milena was active in developing education for workers, and schoolteachers eventually join the strike. In the end, both peasant/worker cooperatives and labour unionism are faced with formidable obstacles, erected by external forces, in the struggle to achieve a just society. Taken as a whole, these works present powerful criticism of the degree and manner of US control of the Guatemalan economy and of US political intervention in Guatemalan affairs.

The novel on which Asturias's reputation was founded was completed in 1933, though not published until 1946. The society of *El Señor Presidente* is one where evil has triumphed and corruption has spread downwards from its ruler, a creature lacking self-control and activated by cruelty, spite and malice. Justice is a mockery, with a corrupt judiciary and venial police using torture as normal practice; every member of society is prepared to inform against his or her neighbours. Army officers spend their time plotting or in brothels. Love is

a tool of destruction, and the word "madre" (mother) can provoke a man to murder. At the other end of Asturias's career, *Viernes de Dolores* [Good Friday] shows how popular customs and a student prank, when enlisted in the cause of political protest, however justified, come into conflict with family loyalties and damages relationships. Worse still, corruption in the police and the bureaucracy convert an accident and a few careless words into sufficient cause for the arrest, torture and execution of the innocent, repeating, nearly forty years later, many elements of *El Señor Presidente*.

Asturias's unsubtle presentation of political corruption and foreign economic exploitation is lifted out of the rut by his use of myth. A deeper appreciation of all of his fiction, especially *Hombres de maíz* and *Mulata de tal*, can be achieved through a knowledge of the themes and modes of thought of Central American mythology, dominant in Asturias's mind from his earliest writings, and most of the advances in recent criticism have followed that path.

RON KEIGHTLEY

Biography

Born in Guatemala City, 19 October 1899. Family moved to Salamá fearing government persecution, 1903; returned to Guatemala City in 1908. Attended schools in Guatemala City; gave up studying medicine in 1917 and studied law at San Carlos University, Guatemala City, 1917–23; helped found the People's University [Universidad Popular] of Guatemala, 1922, and the Association of University Students; studied anthropology under Georges Raymond at the Sorbonne, Paris, 1923–28. Founder of *Tiempos Nuevos*, 1923; travelled to England in the same year and was based in Paris, 1923–32; travelled through Europe and the Middle East in the 1920s. Returned to Guatemala in 1933, and worked as radio broadcaster (co-creator, "Diario del aire" series, 1937) and journalist, 1933–42. Served as a deputy at the Guatemalan National Congress, 1942. Held a number of diplomatic posts, 1945–54: cultural attaché, Mexico City, 1945–47, and Buenos Aires, 1947–53, minister-counsellor, Buenos Aires, 1951–52, Guatemalan ambassador, Paris, 1952–53, and San Salvador (El Salvador), 1953–54. Separated from his wife, Clemencia Amado, 1946–47; married Blanca de Mora y Aruaho in 1950. Exiled for his support of the left-wing leader Jacobo Árbenz Guzmán, 1954, and moved to Argentina. Journalist on *El Nacional* (Venezuela), 1954–62; cultural exchange programme member, Columanum, Italy, 1962; Guatemalan ambassador in Paris, 1966–70. Spent his final years in Madrid. Recipient of numerous awards including the Sylla Monsegur Prize for translation, 1932; William Faulkner Foundation Latin American Award, 1962; International Lenin Peace Prize, 1966; and the Nobel Prize for Literature, 1967. Died in Madrid, 9 June 1974.

Selected Works

Novels and Short Fiction

Leyendas de Guatemala, Madrid: Oriental, 1930; augmented edition, 1948; as *Leyendas*, 1960

El Señor Presidente, Mexico City: Costa-Amic, 1946; as *The President*, translated by Frances Partridge, London: Gollancz, 1963; retitled as *El Señor Presidente*, New York: Atheneum, 1964

Hombres de maíz, Buenos Aires: Losada, 1949; as *Men of Maize*, translated by Gerald Martin, New York: Delacorte Press, 1974; London: Verso, 1988

Viento fuerte, Buenos Aires: Losada, 1949; as *The Cyclone*, translated by Darwin Flakoll and Claribel Alegría, London: Peter Owen, 1967; as *Strong Wind*, translated by Gregory Rabassa, New York: Delacorte Press, 1969

El papa verde, Buenos Aires: Losada, 1954; as *The Green Pope*, translated by Gregory Rabassa, New York: Delacorte Press, and London: Jonathan Cape, 1971

Week-end en Guatemala, Buenos Aires: Goyanarte, 1956 [short fiction]

Los ojos de los enterrados, Buenos Aires: Losada, 1960; as *The Eyes of the Interred*, translated by Gregory Rabassa, New York: Delacorte Press, 1973; London: Jonathan Cape, 1974

El alhajadito, Buenos Aires: Goynarte, 1961; as *The Bejeweled Boy*, translated by Martin Shuttleworth, New York: Doubleday, 1971 [novella]

Mulata de tal, Buenos Aires: Losada, 1963; as *Mulatta*, translated by Gregory Rabassa, New York: Delacorte Press, 1967; retitled as *The Mulatta and Mister Fly*, London: Peter Owen, 1967

El espejo de Lida Sal, Mexico City: Siglo XXI, 1967

Maladrón: epopeya de los Andes verdes, Buenos Aires: Losada, 1969

Novelas y cuentos de juventud, edited by Claude Couffon, Paris: Centre de Recherches de L'Institut d'Études Hispaniques, 1971

Viernes de Dolores, Buenos Aires: Losada, 1972

Poetry

Rayito de estrella, Paris: n.p., 1925

Emulo lipolidón, Guatemala City: Tipografía América, 1935

Sonetos, Guatemala City: Tipografía América, 1937

Alclasán: fantomina, Guatemala City: Tipografía América, 1939

Anoche, 10 de marzo de 1543, Guatemala City: Talleres Tipográficos de Cordón, 1943

Poesía: sien de alondra, Buenos Aires: Argos, 1949; complete edition, 1954

Ejercicios poéticos en forma de soneto sobre temas de Horacio, Buenos Aires: Botella al Mar, 1951

Alto es el sur, La Plata: Talleres Gráficos Moreno, 1952

Bolívar, San Salvador: Ministerio de Cultura, 1955

Nombre custodio, e Imagen pasajera, Havana: Úcar, 1959

Clarivigilia primaveral, Buenos Aires: Losada, 1965

Sonetos de Italia, Milan: Instituto Editoriale Cisalpino, 1965

Tres de cuatro soles, edited by Dorita Nouhaud, Mexico City: Fondo de Cultura Económica, 1977 [prose poem]

Plays

Soluna: comedia prodigiosa en dos jornados y un final, Buenos Aires: Losagne, 1955

La audiencia de los confines: crónica en tres andanzas, Buenos Aires: Ariadna, 1957

Teatro: Chantaje; Dique seco; Soluna; La audiencia de los confines, Buenos Aires: Losada, 1964

Juárez, Mexico City: Comisión Nacional para la conmemoración del centenario del Fallecimiento de don Benito Juárez, 1972

Other Writings

Sociología guatemalteca: el problema social del indio, Guatemala City: Sánchez y de Guise, 1923; as *Guatemalan Sociology: the Social Problem of the Indian*, translated by Maureen Ahern, Tempe: Arizona State University, Centre for Latin American Studies, 1977

La arquitectura de la vida nueva, Guatemala City: Goubaud, 1928 [essays and lectures]

Carta aérea a mis amigos de América, Buenos Aires: Francisco A. Colombo, 1952

Rumania, su nueva imagen, Xalapa, Mexico: Universidad Veracruzana, 1964

Juan Girador, Paris: Centre de Recherches de l'Institut d'Études Hispaniques, 1964

Torotumbo; La audiencia de los confines; Mensajes indios, Barcelona: Plaza y Janés, 1967

Latinoamérica y otros ensayos, Madrid: Guadiana de Publicaciones, 1968

Comiendo en Hungría, with Pablo Neruda, Barcelona: Lumen, 1969; as *Sentimental Journey around the Hungarian Cuisine*, translated by Barna Balogh, 1969 [verse and illustrations]

El novelista en la universidad, Santander: Universidad Internacional Menéndez Pelayo, 1971

América, fábula de fábulas y otros ensayos, Caracas: Monte Ávila, 1972

Mi mejor obra, Mexico City: Novaro, 1973; as *Lo mejor de mi obra*, Barcelona: Novaro, 1974

Sinceridades, edited by Epaminondas Quintana, Guatemala City: Académica Centroamericana, 1980 [essays]

Actos de fe en Guatemala, photographs by Sara Facio and María Cristina Orive, Buenos Aires: La Azotea, 1980

El hombre que lo tenía todo, todo, todo, illustrated by Jacqueline Duheme, Barcelona: Bruguera, 1981

Compilations and Anthologies

Obras escogidas, 3 vols, Madrid: Aguilar, 1955

Obras escogidas, 2 vols, Madrid: Aguilar, 1964

Obras completas, introduction by José María Souviron, 3 vols, Madrid: Aguilar, 1968

Antología, edited by Pablo Palomina, Mexico City: Costa-Amic, 1968

Tres obras, edited by Giuseppe Bellini, Caracas: Biblioteca Ayacucho, 1977 [Contains *Leyendas de Guatemala*; *El Alhajadito*; *El Señor Presidente*]

Edición crítica de las obras completas, 24 vols, Madrid: Fondo de Cultura Económica, 1977 –

Viajes, ensayos y fantasías, edited by Richard J. Callan, Buenos Aires: Losada, 1981

París 1922–1923: Periodismo y creación literaria, edited by Amos Segala, Madrid: CSIC, 1988 [journalism]

Cartas de amor, with Blanca de Mora y Araujo, edited by Felipe Mellizo, Madrid: Cultura Hispánica, 1989

Further Reading

Andrea, Pedro F. de, *Miguel Ángel Asturias. Anticipo bibliográfico*, Mexico City: Libros de México, 1969

Asturias, Miguel Ángel, *Hombres de maíz*, edited by Gerald Martin, Madrid: Archivos/CSIC, 1992 [critical edition]

Bellini, Giuseppe, *De tiranos, héroes y brujos: estudios sobre la obra de Miguel Ángel Asturias*, Rome: Bulzoni, 1982

Callan, Richard J., *Miguel Ángel Asturias*, New York: Twayne, 1970

Cardoza y Aragón, Luis, *Miguel Ángel Asturias: casi novela*, Mexico City: Era, 1991

Castelpoggi, Atilio Jorge, *Miguel Ángel Asturias*, Buenos Aires: La Mandrágora, 1961

Giacoman, Helmy F. (editor), *Homenaje a Miguel Ángel Asturias: variaciones interpretativas en torno a su obra*, New York: Las Américas, 1971

Hill, Eladia León, *Miguel Ángel Asturias. Lo ancestral en su obra literaria*, New York: Eliseo Torres, 1972

Leal, Luis, *Myth and Social Realism in Miguel Ángel Asturias*, Urbana: University of Illinois Press, 1968

Miñonis, Juan José, "Discurso mítico en *Leyendas de Guatemala*," *Escritura*, vol. 13/25–26 (1988)

Olivero, Juan, *El Miguel Ángel Asturias que yo conocí: relato anecdótico*, Guatemala City: Cultural Centroamericana, 1980

Pilón, Marta, *Miguel Ángel Asturias: semblanza para el estudio de su vida y obra*, Guatemala City: Cultural Centroamericana, 1968

Prieto, René, *Miguel Ángel Asturias's Archaeology of Return*, Cambridge: Cambridge University Press, 1990

Rodríguez, Teresita, *La problemática de la identidad en "El Señor Presidente" de Miguel Ángel Asturias*, Amsterdam: Rodopi, 1989

Royano Gutiérrez, Lourdes, *Las novelas de Miguel Ángel Asturias desde la teoría de la recepción*, Valladolid: Universidad de Valladolid, 1993

Sáenz, Jimena, *Genio y figura de Miguel Ángel Asturias*, Buenos Aires: Editorial Universitaria, 1974

Terry, Edward D. (editor), *Artists and Writers in the Evolution of Latin America*, University: University of Alabama, 1969

Verdugo, Iber, *El carácter de la literatura hispanoamericana y la novelística de Miguel Ángel Asturias*, Guatemala City: Editorial Universitaria, 1968

Bibliographies

Moore, Richard E., *Miguel Ángel Asturias: a Checklist of Works and Criticism*, New York: American Institute for Marxist Studies, 1979

Interviews

López Álvarez, Luis, *Conversaciones con Miguel Ángel Asturias*: Magisterio Español, 1974

El Señor Presidente

Novel by Miguel Ángel Asturias

El Señor Presidente (*The President*) published in 1946 – though written between 1922 and 1933 – is a landmark text since it is both Latin America's most notable dictator novel and the first to exploit the literary potentialities of Surrealism. These factors are not unconnected since the force of the narrative derives largely from Asturias's innovative use of dream imagery, his emphasis on the irrational, his frequent appeal to the senses (particularly the auditory) and his often incantatory style. The bounds of normality quickly recede as the reader is plunged into the physical and psychological horrors of human life under dictatorship.

Although the figure of the dictator stands behind the gruesome episodes of torture and assassination, the novel's chief concern is not with one individual but rather with the reality of his barbarous rule. It is set in the unnamed capital of an unnamed state and begins with the description of a group of beggars preparing to settle down for the night on the Cathedral steps. One of them, the half-crazed and mother-fixated Pelele is provoked by the President's henchman, Colonel Parrales Sonriente, whom the idiot kills. The dictator uses this incident to eliminate two unreliable supporters and suspected enemies, General Canales and the lawyer, Carvajal, who are accused of the killing: in Latin America both the "honourable soldier," sometimes, and the intellectual, more commonly, have long been associated with resistance to tyranny. The beggars are tortured into acting as false witnesses against them; the one who insists on telling the truth, *El Mosco*, is put to death – as is Carvajal following a stage-managed trial. The fate of the General, however, relates to the main plot and so his elimination is delayed: the President's favourite, Miguel Cara de Ángel, is ordered to fake an escape for him so that he can be shot under the "ley de fuga" (that is, supposedly when attempting to escape); but the General contrives a genuine escape while Cara de Ángel concentrates on abducting his daughter, Camila. He subsequently falls in love with her and his marriage – to the daughter of the President's enemy – inevitably marks his fall from grace. General Canales dies of heart failure on reading a false newspaper report that the President had attended his daughter's wedding and given the bride away. The President's will is served with more systematic brutality in the case of Cara de Ángel: told he is being assigned to a government position in Washington, he is in fact arrested following a train journey to the coast. Tortured and imprisoned, the cause of his eventual demise recalls the circumstances of Canales's: a false report that Camila had become the President's mistress.

This is a historical novel inspired by a specific set of political circumstances: Estrada Cabrera's dictatorship in Guatemala (1898–1920) which impinged directly on Asturias's family. Estrada Cabrera's torture of a political adversary, Manuel Paz, included deceiving the latter into believing that his innocent wife had been unfaithful to him – an episode clearly reworked in *El Señor Presidente*.

Despite these clear links with the Guatemalan context, however, the novel's import extends to the entire Hispanic world and beyond to suggest the essential mechanics of a police state wherever it be found. Chapter 23 consists of spies' reports addressed to the President while the image of invisible threads linking each leaf of the trees in his monstruous forest (chapter 6) suggests the frightening capabilities of modern surveillance techniques.

Asturias seems on occasion to revel in the explicitly negative and debased: human degeneracy, for example, ranges from the enmity which characterizes relations among the beggars – described as "animales con moquillo" (diseased animals) – who would favour dogs above their fellow sufferers (chapter 1) to the children who delight in the sufferings of the puppets at don Benjamín's Punch and Judy show (chapter 10). Neither is the reader spared sordid physical details, for example, the disgusting conditions attending Carvajal's imprisonment (chapter 29) and especially Cara de Ángel's (chapter 41). Prospects of change appear to be stifled by a pervasive sense of futility. Images of thwarted progress recur: Carvajal's wife, for example, desperate to intercede with the President on her husband's behalf, feels that her carriage is going round in circles (chapter 31). Hope is constantly frustrated – the expectant Camila is spurned by her uncle, Juan Canales; premonitions of entrapment extinguish any glimmerings of happiness and freedom (Cara de Ángel and Camila cannot avoid the President's country-house party despite their awareness of danger, chapter 25). Explicit too is the allusion to economic injustice whereby some people (including the president's friends) have what they do not need while others go without basic necessities (chapter 3). The regime is said to be dependent on "oro norteamericano" (North American gold) and the President is anxious to retain US support (chapters 33 and 37). That the merciless Judge Advocate is a devout Catholic suggests Church complicity with the regime as does the ominous sound of the church bells, representing an incantation to evil, in the opening lines; on the other hand, the sacristan's imprisonment for the inadvertent removal of a notice relating to the President's mother indicates the paranoid excesses of a government which respects no authority other than its own.

In many of these instances the realities of dictatorship are conveyed with documentary plainness. But Asturias's portrait would not be nearly as powerful had his dependence on realist procedures been total. The President obviously represents political corruption but his presentation as an evil deity who is worshipped in terms that mockingly echo religious ritual (chapter 14) elevates him to a mythical plane. This status is confirmed through his implicit association with Tohil, the Maya deity of fire and water, seen in a vision by Cara de Ángel. Tohil's favours were obtained only in exchange for human sacrifice. Here Asturias returns us to the pre-Hispanic tradition of a people for whom the spilling of blood was regarded as the spring which renewed life. The President is an inverted image of both the Christian and Mayan deities since he is the source only of death. Though his mythical aura may appear to remove him from concrete reality, it is well to remember that his real life model, Estrada Cabrera, himself achieved mythical status.

The novel is marked by its abrupt changes of style and viewpoint which recall the techniques of cinema. At the end of chapter 7, Vásquez's boisterous laughter becomes an ominous silence prior to his killing of Pelele; sudden changes of perspective disorientate the reader as the narrative shifts from Pelele's point of view to that of Vásquez's accomplice, Rodas, finally jumping to the Archbishop's view of the episode which closes the chapter. The tempo accelerates at the beginning of chapter 8 with the focus on the killers' dash through the narrow streets switching to the streets themselves which – personified now – rush hither and thither in a frantic search for details of the horrific event. Then the mood and rhythm lighten with the shift to the puppeteer, Don Benjamín, and his wife who introduce a note of comedy. But the overwhelming impression left by the novel – that of pervasive evil transcending normal boundaries – is reinforced by the surreal dream sequences in which logic is overshadowed by unreason. Pelele's nightmare (chapter 3), which springs from his physical and mental suffering, is described in terms of grotesque configuration and uncontrollable movement:

> Las uñas aceradas de la fiebre le aserraban la frente. Disociación de ideas. Elasticidad del mundo en los espejos. Desproporción fantástica. Huracán delirante. Fuga vertiginosa, horizontal, vertical, oblicua, recién nacida y muerta en espiral . . .

> [The steel finger-nails of fever were clawing at his forehead. Disassociation of ideas. A fluctuating world seen in a mirror. Fantastic disproportion. Hurricane of delirium. Vertiginous flight, horizontal, vertical, oblique, newly-born and dead in a spiral . . .]

Chapter 38 describes Cara de Ángel's journey to the coast: the insistent and accelerating rhythm of the prose suggests both the train's movement and Cara de Ángel's state of mind. The succession of images is also notable for its cinematic immediacy and flow:

> Uno tras otro, uno tras otro, uno tras otro . . . La casa perseguía al árbol, el árbol a la cerca, la cerca al puente, el puente al camino, el camino al río . . .

> [One behind the other, one behind the other, one behind the other. The house chased the tree, the tree chased the fence, the fence the bridge, the bridge the road, the road the river . . .]

The rhythm assumes a more noticeably ominous quality when Cara de Ángel himself returns to focus and lapses into a somniferous though restless state of mind in which he experiences:

> la sensación confusa de ir en el tren, de no ir en el tren, de irse quedando atrás del tren, cada vez más atrás del tren, más atrás del tren, más atrás del tren, más atrás del tren, cada vez más atrás, cada vez más atrás, más y más cada vez, cada vez cada vez, cada ver cada vez, cada ver cada vez, cada ver cada vez, cada ver cada ver cada ver cada ver . . .

> [a confused feeling of being in the train, of not being in the train, of lagging behind the train, further behind the train, further behind, still further behind, still further behind, further, further, further, further . . .]

The sinister import of the word play in the original (cadáver = body) is unmistakable. Stylistic techniques such as onomatopeia, simile and repetition, together with a discontinuous structure give the text its Surrealistic and nightmarish atmosphere.

The discussion thus far may suggest that the gloom of the novel is unbroken. But there are several moments of relief, one being the narrative of Camila's childhood and, in particular, the inspirational effect of her first visit to the seaside. The cinematic flux of her experience in chapter 12 – "La inmensidad en movimiento. Ella en movimiento. Todo lo que en ella estaba inmóvil, en movimiento . . ." (Immensity in motion. Herself in motion. Everything in her that was by nature still was in motion) – suggests the fluid quality of the novel whose everchanging form itself suggests the transcience of an apparently static dictatorship.

Relief from general gloom is also provided by frequent touches of humour: thus on the Day of National Celebrations, just after the President has left the balcony to the acclaim of the adoring crowd, panic spreads when what appears to be a series of explosions is heard and the President disappears. The noise turns out to have been produced by a military drummer (and drum) falling down a flight of steps. This episode belongs to the slapstick humour of the silent movie era and serves to indicate a tangible though less obvious aspect of this barbarous dictatorship, namely its comic and ridiculous side.

The novel by no means excludes the positive elements of human existence which are shown to survive even under conditions of dictatorship. Asturias maintains a play of *sombra* (darkness) and *luz* (light) with human generosity and goodness never being totally extinguished by evil. Thus the woodcutter takes pity on Pelele when he flees from the police (chapter 4) and when he is finally gunned down by police on the Cathedral steps, the Archbishop who has observed the scene gives him absolution (chapter 7). Neither is the future entirely bleak: following the disappearance of her husband (Cara de Ángel), Camila has her baby to console her and, on a broader level, the vision of the puppeteer, Don Benjamín, of the city in ruins may be seen positively since Estrada Cabrera's regime was undermined as the result of a disastrous earthquake which demolished Guatemala City on Christmas Day, 1917; a brief reference to a newspaper article on the battle between the French and German armies at Verdun (chapter 32) suggests that the action of the novel takes place in 1916 or thereabouts. The implication seems to be that the President's days are numbered. The novel closes to the sound of bells, which recalls the opening; but now they strike a more cheerful note and the initial incantation to evil seems far removed from the peaceful evening prayer recited by the mother of the newly released student.

Despite its lighter and more positive moments, however, *El Señor Presidente* is open to charges of over-explicitness, of wearisome emphasis on human depravity which, of course, diminish rather than enhance the novel's impact: understatement, a technique used to great effect by other writers – such as García Márquez in *El coronel no tiene quien le escriba* (*No One Writes to the Colonel*) – would undoubtedly have given Asturias's message greater force.

The novel has also been seen as ideologically suspect: while it can be read in general as a critique of Positivism – whose Latin American adherents frequently subordinated political freedom to the pursuit of material wealth – Asturias seems at times to subscribe to Positivist class and racial prejudices. The masses are depicted in the main as hopelessly passive, mere puppets manipulated at will by the President; the treatment of the Indian can also appear dubious – following his visit to Cara de Ángel's house (chapter 10), General Canales's military bearing "se licuó en carrerita de indio que va al mercado a vender una gallina" (degenerated into the scuttling run of an Indian going to market to sell a hen). It is not perhaps insignificant that opponents of the regime – Cara de Ángel, General Canales, the lawyer Carvajal and the student – are drawn from the upper classes. A more serious *literary* objection is that Cara de Ángel's "redemption" and the sentimental aspect of his relationship with Camila detract from the force of the novel's opening episodes (particularly Pelele's flight) and compounds a subsequent note of anti-climax. It is important to remember however that Cara de Ángel, though a reformed character, is motivated by a basically selfish love for Camila and settles for

personal salvation (as it seemed) rather than engage in more meaningful collective opposition.

The plainly documentary aspects of this novel are obvious and their rawness occasionally appears obtrusive. But *El Señor Presidente* is redeemed as a *literary* text by the universality of its appeal, its highly original style and telling deployment of Surrealist techniques which both challenge passive "consumption" by the reader and also sweep him along in their compulsive ebb and flow. It is such qualities which confirm Asturias's status as the major precursor of the new Latin American novel of the 1950s and 1960s.

LLOYD HUGHES DAVIES

Editions
First edition: *El Señor Presidente*, Mexico City: Costa-Amic, 1946
Critical edition: *Miguel Ángel Asturias: El Señor Presidente*, Paris: Klincksieck, 1978
Translation: *The President*, by Frances Partridge, Harmondsworth: Penguin, 1972

Further Reading
Giacoman, Helmy F. (editor), *Homenaje a Miguel Ángel Asturias: variaciones interpretativas en torno a su obra*, New York: Las Américas, 1971 [See in particular the articles by Carlos Navarro]
Harss, Luis, *Los nuestros*, Buenos Aires: Sudamericana, 1968 [Critical comments are supplemented by Asturias's own remarks on his major literary preoccupations]
Himelblau, Jack, "*El señor Presidente*: Antecedents, Sources and Reality," *Hispanic Review*, vol. 41 (1973)
Langowski, Gerald J., *El surrealismo en la ficción hispanoamericana*, Madrid: Gredos, 1982
Martin, Gerald, "Miguel Ángel Asturias: *El señor Presidente*," in *Landmarks in Modern Latin American Fiction*, edited by Philip Swanson, London and New York: Routledge, 1990
Rodríguez Monegal, Emir, "Los dos Asturias," *Revista Iberoamericana*, vol. 35/67 (1969)

Autobiography

Autobiographical writing is an account of a person's life written by the subject, marked or dealing with his/her own experiences or life history. An account of a life is to be distinguished from the memoir – in which the emphasis is not so much on the author's developing self, but on the people s/he has known and the events s/he has witnessed. It must also be distinguished from the private diary or journal, which is a day-to-day record of the events in a person's life, written for private use and pleasure and often with little or no thought of publication.

Autobiography is not a literary genre in the traditional sense, since autobiographical writings, particularly in Latin America, demonstrate a protean character, and are devoid of a definitive set of coherent principles and rules, save the unwritten creed of writing in retrospect about the author's own life.

Autobiographical writing has a long history, all forms having in common the authors' need to give to the world their version of the events and personalities involved in their life. The autobiographical genre in Latin America, however, presents unique canonical problems of classification due to the rise of subgenres (testimonial and documentary narratives) in recent years. A growing interest in Latin American writing has contributed in the past twenty years to the discovery and expansion of a corpus that had remained, until then, in obscurity. While first-person narratives abound in Colonial literature (Cabeza de Vaca's *Naufragios* [Shipwrecks] and Garcilaso de la Vega's *Comentarios reales* [Royal Commentaries] are but two prime examples), such texts are only tangentially autobiographical, since the narration of self is more a means to achieve a public goal than to reveal the personal self. Scholars have routinely characterized contemporary Latin American fiction as predominantly a social testimonial. But social struggles invariably give rise to new forms of literature. While the documentary imperative will never quite disappear from Spanish American self-writing, it will continue to take on more varied and more subtle literary forms. Indeed, a strong testimonial stance informs much of autobiographical writing in Spanish America today, with the autobiographers seeing themselves as witnesses to collective memory. The phenomenon of a collective subject of the testimonial is hardly the result of a personal style on the part of the writer who testifies. The tradition assumes that the autobiographer is continuous with his community, as opposed to assuming the radical individualism that we associate with, say, some European writers of the genre. After all, the testimonial is not usually produced by great writers, and often not by writers at all – in many instances. This is so, in part, due to the illiteracy or low-literacy levels of the testimonial's often peasant informant, who conveys orally his/her story to a journalist or sociologist, who, in their turn, organize the narrative in written form. For this reason, it has always been seen as a kind of writing from the margins and, by many critics, may not even be considered as autobiography at all due to the conditions which govern its production and the unwritten rules which give it shape, making it a genre in itself in their view. So it is that Spanish American autobiographies are fascinating hybrids, often involving several discourses and purposes at once. They aspire to the aforementioned documentary status while unabashedly exalting the self as they dwell on personal experience while purporting to be exercises in historiography.

Yet, in the early period of Spanish American letters, a more personal note predominated in the prolific production of autobiographical narratives. Domingo Faustino Sarmiento's *Facundo* (*Life in the Argentine Republic in the Days of the Tyrants*) about the Rosas dictatorship in Argentina, creates, as Sylvia Molloy notes, intimacy and complicity with the Argentine ideal reader, as a result of excluding others. In fact, Sarmiento himself dedicates his *Recuerdos de provincia*, 1850 [*Memoirs of Provincial Life*] "to my compatriots only" – those who will truly understand him and give him being. In this work, Sarmiento's account of his youth written while in exile in Chile, a gentle, romantic nostalgia for times past is apparent. But the aim of the work was chiefly polemical. Sarmiento's attacks on the dictator Rosas had caused his name to be reviled in official Argentine circles, and *Recuerdos* was composed as a defense of himself, his ancestry, and his active life; "a patriot's desire to preserve the esteem of his fellow citizens," as he said.

Many recent novels have a subtext that reveals this interplay between autobiographical documentation and social narrative, and, as such, may be considered to be as politically motivated as Sarmiento's writings. The narrating "I" often takes the form of an oppressor, most often a dictator, (Paraguay's Augusto Roa Bastos's *Yo el Supremo* (*I the Supreme*); Guatemala's Miguel Ángel Asturias's *El Señor Presidente* (*The President*)) or an individual who represents the interests of a jeopardized social group (Cuba's Edmundo Desnoes's *Memorias del subdesarrollo* (*Memories of Underdevelopment*), or a marginalized group of the population as in Miguel Barnet's *Biografía de un cimarrón* (*Autobiography of a Runaway Slave*), in order to portray sociohistorical events of a specific

period. In other instances the author/narrator himself recreates a particular experience through personal testimonial accounts for the purpose of denunciation of a political figure or system (Hernán Valdés's *Tejas Verdes*, subtitled *Diario de un campo de concentración en Chile* (*Diary of a Concentration Camp in Chile*) and the personal testimony of the Chilean Jacobo Timerman, *Preso sin nombre, celda sin número* (*Prisoner without a Name, Cell without a Number*). Although such works have the life of the first-person narrator as an organizing point of reference, the narrative deliberately relates the author to historically "real" individuals.

Sociopolitical continuity links Latin American novels from their origins in the late Renaissance chronicles of the Conquest, together with a testimonial quality which is one of the dominant strands of contemporary writing in the continent. Such autobiographical accounts may often fictionalize and allegorize recognizable individuals and events in Latin American society and politics. By using strategies of narrative discourse reminiscent of mainstream contemporary novels, the writer of autobiographical narratives underscores the continuity between imaginative literature and documentary history in Latin American culture. Such is the case of Gabriel García Márquez in many of his works, particularly *Cien años de soledad* (*One Hundred Years of Solitude*).

It will be clear by now that representativeness and identity are closely linked in Spanish American self-writing. This tension between consolidation and individuation is most keenly mirrored in particular post-1960s testimonials by Latin American women. Arguably the social tradition of Latin American autobiography had anticipated the 1992 Nobel Peace Prize winner, Rigoberta Menchú's book, *Me llamo Rigoberta Menchú y así me nació la conciencia* (*I, Rogoberta Menchí an Indian Woman in Guatemala*) and the Bolivian Domitila Barrios de Chungara's *¡Si me permiten hablar! Testimonio de Domitila, una mujer de las minas de Bolivia* (*Let Me Speak! Testimony of Domitila, a Woman of the Bolivian Mines*). Such works are examples of non-fictional Bildungsromans or testimonials in which the autobiographical voice of each text, during the course of the life-telling narration, identifies with a cultural group outside of which the text would be misread. Yet, despite its current popularity as a recognized literary form, the testimonial almost always raises issues about genre which remain irresolvable due to its protean nature. In the volume *Testimonio y literatura* (1986), edited by René Jara and Hernán Vidal, seventeen essays represent the testimonial as sharing significant territory with autobiography, ethnography, biography, history, fiction, oral literature, documentary, journalism, and even photo-journalism. Despite problems of generic classification of the interesting variations that testimonial narration presents, it is undeniably an autobiographical life history narration in a first-person voice that stresses development and continuity.

First-person accounts of various types, travelogues, *testimonios* (testimonials or eye-witness accounts), diaries, autobiographies, and other hybrid modes of self-representation from the 19th century onward reflect on individual and national identity, thus demonstrating the complexity of forms to which the autobiography may be ascribed. Such texts not only inform us about the autobiographical voice's life, but, in addition, may also provide us with equally significant information about the community, traditional practices, armed political struggles, and strategic decisions in the life of the author and his people. The testimonial constructs a collective self. And, unlike the private and even lonely moment of autobiographical writing, the testimonial "subgenre" and its basis in orality (testimonies) becomes a series of public events. As a consequence, the testimonial "I" in such narratives neither presumes nor even invites us to identity with it. In the very convention of autobiographical form, there is implicit an ideology of individualism that, as John Beverley asserts in an article of 1989, is "built on the notion of a coherent, self-evident, self-conscious, commanding subject that appropriates literature precisely as a means of 'self-expression' and that in turn constructs textually for the reader the liberal imagery of a unique, 'free,' autonomous ego as the natural form of being and public achievement."

A broad definition of the genre encompasses all these forms of autobiographical narration. In Philippe Lejeune's *On Autobiography*, the critic, while recognizing autobiography to be a complex and unstable literary category, historically speaking, proposes the following working definition of the genre: "we shall define autobiography as the retrospective prose narrative that someone writes concerning his own existence, where the focus is his individual life, in particular the story of his personality." It might be noted that Latin American critics have begun to confront the fact that when elite criteria are applied to some works, all too often they are attempting to make them fit canons and categories of dominant Western models, which, inevitably, do not apply wholly to literary works of underdeveloped countries.

ELENA DE COSTA

Further Reading

Bruss, Elizabeth W., *Autobiographical Acts. The Changing Situation of a Literary Genre*, Baltimore: Johns Hopkins University Press, 1976

Eakin, Paul John, *Fictions in Autobiography: Studies in the Art of Self-Invention*, Princeton, New Jersey: Princeton University Press, 1988

_____ *Touching the World: Reference in Autobiography*, Princeton, New Jersey: Princeton University Press, 1992

Egan, Susanna, *Patterns of Experience in Autobiography*, Chapel Hill: University of North Carolina Press, 1984

Elbaz, Robert, *The Changing Nature of the Self: a Critical Study of the Autobiographic Discourse*, Iowa City: University of Iowa Press, 1987; London: Croom Helm, 1988

Feal, Rosemary Geisdorfer, *Novel Lives: the Fictional Autobiographies of Guillermo Cabrera Infante and Mario Vargas Llosa*, Chapel Hill: University of North Carolina Press, 1986

Molloy, Sylvia, *At Face Value: Autobiographical Writing in Spanish America*, Cambridge and New York: Cambridge University Press, 1991

Avant-Garde

The avant-garde movements in Latin America sprang up throughout the continent in the 1920s as manifestations of rebellion against 19th-century literary and artistic tradition, with the intention of breaking away, of antagonizing, and of creating and promoting innovative artistic concepts that defied and revised the very tradition in which these artists and writers had learned their craft. "*Martinfierrismo*", *atalayismo*, *diepalismo*, *euforismo*, *integralismo*, *avancismo*, *estridentismo*, *auguralismo*, *creacionismo*, *runrunismo*, *ultraísmo* are some of the names of these manifestations. Art was conceived as an unmediated expression of the genius and singularity of its creator: "*el poeta es un pequeño dios*" (the poet is a small god). The avant-garde was an attempt to free art from having to respond to needs other than those of artistic creation and expression. These movements advocated stripping poetic language of ornamental devices, confessional tones or any other linguistic or conceptual debris that intercepted the innovative spirit of renewal that sustained these various and somewhat ephemeral movements. Emphasis was on the power of newly created imagery; to create from scratch was the main thrust: "*la primera condición del poeta es crear, la segunda crear, y la tercera, crear*" (it is in the poet's nature, firstly, secondly and thirdly to create), proclaimed the Chilean vanguardist poet Vicente Huidobro in his essay "El creacionismo" of 1925, one of his influential manifestos.

The avant-garde groups were also connected to social and political antagonism against the political trends of the time, between World War I and World War II, and in many instances, against the racist appeal on both sides of the Atlantic. Thus, it should be viewed as an international movement that reached Eastern and Western Europe, the United States and Latin America.

The merging of the arts was of great interest to these artists, many of whom practised painting, visual or Cubist poetry, pure poetry, even embroidered poetry. Among these artists and writers were some of the most important innovators of poetic language in 20th-century Latin American literature, the framers of vanguard and Surrealist conceptions of art that were to have a major impact on most writers of the continent during the decades that followed, both in Spanish and Portuguese.

The various manifestations of the avant-garde evolved throughout the subcontinent during the first thirty years of the 20th century, and their impact on cultural and literary production was most strongly felt in Argentina, Chile, Peru, Cuba and Mexico.

In Buenos Aires, vanguard movements had strong links with European cultural forms such as the music of trains presented by Honegger in the Colón Theatre. Also the prestigious Witcomb Gallery in fashionable Florida Street sponsored an exhibition of early Cubist painting. Cosmopolitanism and the exuberance of the *belle époque* and Art Deco contributed to the embellishment of downtown areas of the city of Buenos Aires sponsored by the then President Marcelo T. de Alvear, following the architectural planning of the remodelling of Paris under Haussmann. The project intended to make of Buenos Aires the cosmopolis envisioned by the dominant political class well represented by Alvear himself.

The two most representative artistic groups that championed opposing philosophies or aesthetics in this city were those of Boedo and of Florida: they positioned themselves in a struggle for the power to control cultural forms and the signs governing society.

In Chile the movement was initiated by two young poets who were to become major cultural figures in Latin American literary history: Vicente Huidobro (1895–1948) and Pablo Neruda (1904–73). Huidobro wrote manifestos that circulated inside and outside of Chile; they had considerable impact in the Hispanic literary world. Huidobro's major books of poems are *El espejo de agua*, 1916 [The Mirror of Water], the Cubist poems written in French, *Horizon carré*, 1917 [Square Horizon], *Poemas árticos*, 1918 (*Arctic Poems*), and a major poetic text, the long poem *Altazor* (1931) in seven cantos. Pablo Neruda, less flamboyant at first, soon emerged as the other innovative voice with one of the most, if not the most, popular collection of poems written in the subcontinent, *Veinte poemas de amor y una canción desesperada*, 1924 (*Twenty Love Poems and a Song of Despair*). The youth of Latin America learned these poems by heart and in the 1960s they were incorporated into folk music. This collection of poems sold the largest number of copies ever in the continent. The second book of poems is more vanguardist and hermetic, *Tentativa del hombre infinito*, 1926 [Attempt of the Infinite Man]. Of Neruda's major works, his most important vanguardist poetic contribution are the hermetic poems of *Residencia en la tierra*, 1933–35 (*Residence on Earth*).

In Mexico, the vanguard movement was best represented by poets gathered around two different groups: the *estridentismo* movement and the group known as Contemporáneos, the latter constituted by Gorostiza, Carlos Pellicer, Roberto Owen, Salvador Novo, Xavier Villaurrutia and Ortiz de Montellano.

In Cuba *Revista de Avance* (1927–30) gave vanguard artists a successful outlet to publish their work and to voice their concern. In Peru, *Amauta* (1928–30), a magazine founded by the influential thinker José Carlos Mariátegui, attempted to synthesize Marxist theory as a tool for analyzing Peru's reality. The most prominent figure of Peruvian letters is César Vallejo, who developed an uncommonly original system of poetic expression with no predecessors or followers. The first work contains the remarkable and hermetic poems of *Los heraldos negros*, 1919 [The Black Heralds]. His most innovative poetic language is displayed in the still enigmatic poems of *Trilce* (1922).

In Puerto Rico, Luis Palés Matos, Ildefonso Pereda Valdés and Ramón Guirao are the creators of the vanguard poems that integrated their vision of *Négritude* with these movements, an important contribution that incorporates African-Hispanic literary works into Latin American literature.

MAGDALENA GARCÍA PINTO

Further Reading

Córdova Iturburu, Cayetano, *La revolución martínfierrista*, Buenos Aires: Ediciones Culturales Argentinas, 1962

Jackson, K. David (editor), *Transformations of Literary Language in Latin American Literature: from Machado de Assis to the Vanguards*, Austin, Texas: Abaporu Press, 1987

Masiello, Francine, *Lenguaje e ideología. Las escuelas argentinas de vanguardia*, Buenos Aires: Hachette, 1986

Osorio, Nelson, "Para una caracterización histórica del vanguardismo literario hispanoamericano," *Revista Iberoamericana* 114-15 (January–June 1981)

Osorio, Nelson (editor), *Manifiestos, proclamas y polémica de la vanguardia literaria*, Caracas: Biblioteca Ayacucho, 1988

Prieto, Adolfo, *Antología de Boedo y Florida*, Buenos Aires: Galerna, 1967

Teles, Gilberto Mendonça, *Vanguarda européia e Modernismo brasileiro*, Rio de Janeiro: Vozes, 1972 [A collection of European and Brazilian manifestos, each preceded by an introductory note]

Torre, Guillermo de, *Historia de las literaturas de vanguardia*, Madrid: Guadarrama, 1965, 3rd edition, 1974

Unruh, Vicky, *Latin American Vanguards: the Art of Contentious Encounters*, Berkeley: University of California Press, 1994

Videla de Rivero, Gloria, *Direcciones del vanguardismo hispanoamericano. Estudios sobre poesía de vanguardia en la década del veinte*, Mendoza, Argentina: Universidad Nacional de Cuyo, 1990; Pittsburgh: Instituto Internacional de Literatura Iberoamericana, 1994

Bibliographies

Forster, Merlin H. and K. David Jackson, *Vanguardism in Latin American Literature: an Annotated Bibliographical Guide*, Westport, Connecticut: Greenwood Press, 1990

Special Issues of Journals

Revista Iberoamericana 106–07 (January–June 1979) [A special issue on "Vicente Huidobro y la vanguardia," with René De Costa as guest editor]

Aymara Literature

The following Aymara song, quoted by Felipe Guaman Poma de Ayala at the beginning of the 17th century, acts as a fitting introduction to this subject:

el haylli aymarana dize aci
moyoristi tomani mama
tumiriste aruini mama
todos canta a este tono,
luego dize el hombre
chuna
rresponde la muger
oy-uayta-oy
chucho
oy canto-oy

[The Aymara haylli is like this / the one who turns round and round / is the one who has the circle, my lady / the one who makes the circle is the one has the word there, my lady / They all sing in this tone / afterwards the man says / girl / the woman replies / oh flower oh / closeness / oh cantuta flower oh]

The Aymara language is spoken in southern Peru, northwest Bolivia, and northern Chile, with most of the speakers living on the shores of Lake Titicaca and in the Bolivian *departamentos* or administrative districts of La Paz and Potosí. Aymara shares many words with Quechua because both languages have been in close geographical contact for many centuries; and although typologically they are very similar, a genetic relationship has not been proved conclusively. There are more than two million Aymara speakers today living in the Andean countries, and about a third of the Bolivian population are considered Aymara, a term which does not only imply the language, but also a culture different from mestizo and criollo culture. Traditionally, the Aymara population has been related to a high altitude herding and peasant economy, but with a strong migratory movement to the cities, La Paz in particular has become a stronghold of Aymara speaking people.

The Andean peoples did not have writing systems in pre-European times, but there were other forms of artistic expression, such as the designs on pottery and textiles. Moreover, there is clear evidence, from historical sources as well as from contemporary traditions, that the Aymara used music, dance and verbal art as oral tradition long before the European invasion, although there are obviously no direct and untouched traces left of such an original Aymara literary tradition. In this context mention should be made of the quipu, knotted cords representing a complex counting system as mnemotechnical device, also used in the memorization of oral traditions.

As in other Amerindian languages, the oldest known testimonials of their literature date back to the 16th century and were written by Europeans in their zeal to Christianise the indigenous American cultures. By 1584 the Third Lima Council had published a voluminous book containing the Christian doctrine (*Doctrina Christiana*) and a collection of sermons, translated from Spanish into Aymara (and Quechua), probably with the help of native speakers. Of course, this kind of literature is not the original expression of the people themselves,

and the contents are not those of Aymara culture. Rather, these texts reflect the immediate attempt to colonise Andean language and thought by re-interpreting indigenous concepts of, for example, the sacred, providing them with new, additional Christian meanings. The missionary efforts of the colonial church also produced dictionaries and grammars of Aymara which codified the language in European terms and served for centuries as the basis for teaching Aymara (Bertonio 1603, 1612). During the centuries which followed different editions and versions of Christian religious didactic texts were published. The only Aymara texts written at the beginning of the 17th century with a cultural content which actually referred to Aymara life are the ones written down, or "quoted" by the native Quechua speaker Guaman Poma de Ayala in his chronicle. As Xavier Albó and Félix Layme have noted, owing to Guaman's competence in Aymara the texts are not easily understandable. Until well into the 18th century all known texts were written by non-Aymara speakers or bilinguals dominant in Spanish, resulting in a form of Aymara which has been called missionary or *patrón* Aymara. A remarkable collection of texts of that period is an anonymous phrase book, the first one entirely secular in character, which deals with different topics, such as writing a letter or buying and selling animals, written in Aymara and Spanish, with each language showing influence of the other.

In the period of independence, the leaders of the new American states became aware of the importance of the support by the indigenous population for their cause, and this resulted in the translation of some political documents into Aymara, e.g., on tribute or the declaration of independence.

It is only in the 20th century, with anthropologists and linguisticians becoming interested in Aymara culture and language, that texts have been published which were narrated by Aymara native speakers and written down, "transcribed" by the researchers. They are mainly stories (*cuentos*) which deal with Aymara cultural values in a symbolic way, and they reflect a complex and often artistically elaborate language.

Recently, texts containing cultural information began to be collected; these include material on matrimonial rites and agricultural cultivation as well as ritual texts. Members of the Workshop of Andean Oral History (THOA) are developing new methods of historical research and gathering testimonials by native speakers in their own language.

An altogether different genre of Aymara literature consists of numerous collections of poetry, written directly in Aymara by native speakers or translated from Spanish into Aymara. The latter display the characteristics of modern Spanish language lyrics and are yet another example of translation, whereas the former are often characterised by their authors' participation in two worlds: the modern, westernised world, and the more traditional Andean one.

Just as written poetry has become a means of artistic expression for Andean authors themselves, methods for the analysis of Aymara art are now not only being developed by European and US anthropologists and linguists, but also by Aymara researchers who analyse Aymara traditional literature according to culture-internal criteria and discover more and more about an Aymara way of producing and classifying literature. Parallel semantic structures, often binary or triple expressions, as well as juxtapositions and repetitions such as recurrent expressions of lexical, semantic and syntactic type, are means of structuring a text. An important stylistic device is the interlacing of topics: in song performances verses are sung alternatingly ("topic braiding"); in prose texts a topic can be introduced by a single word or expression – seemingly "out of context" – which is taken up again much later ("interlaced sentences"). In Aymara, the speaker or narrator has to mark grammatically his/her source of knowledge so that a story can have a rather complex structure of different levels of reported speech and an elaborate intercalation of narrative and dialogue, which may give the impression of several voices present in the text. Stories are narrated as cycles and in a certain order within those cycles; for example, the first stories to be told will deal with big animals, moving on to those about smaller animals. Aymara speakers compare the learning of story-telling and story-telling itself to the rhythm of spinning; and stories are seen as moving downwards in that they are handed down from a knowledgeable person to a learner.

In addition to this rich literary production, modern media have produced a quantity of radio editorials, novels and dramas as well as films.

Thus the last 400 documented years of Aymara literature have seen a shift from an initially European and mission dominated literature to a literature created by those members of the national states Peru, Bolivia and Chile who consider themselves Aymara and who wish to express themselves artistically or to contribute to setting down the history, documentation and analysis of their own cultural traditions. With an increasing number of projects on bilingual education, in which framework oral literature is also being edited, more individuals will be able to guarantee the future of the Aymara language and its literature in both traditional and modern forms. To round off this introduction to the subject, here is an Aymara poem with accompanying Spanish and English versions:

Aynachajjaru

Qhitiraqui inti jalanta chhakaypacha
llamt'ataro samanaruw tucusi
kotapampas yatituwa
acjan sarnakascäwsin jan acanquirjamaw uñjasta
Yatitpachasa nän cancañajajj
janiw nampïquiti
Pachpa Marcajan jaya jakëtwa
uqhampachasa janiwa pä chuymanïcti
janiw / janiw / janiw
jawirijja asir asa siqhasica punniniwa apunacan
arupajja wiñayataquiw
iyaw sañaquiscaniwa

Latitud Sur

Alguien borra el horizonte
todo se desvanece al tocarlo
El altiplano adivina
que estando aquí no estoy
Aunque reconozca
mi persona no está conmigo
Extranjero en mi propio Continente
mas nunca aculturado

Jamás / jamás / jamás
el río dejará de ser serpiente
eterna la cosmogonía
el mito realidad

(Poem in Aymara and Spanish by Felipe Guaman Poma de Ayala)

Downwards

Somebody must be causing the west to disappear
when touched it evaporates
and the altiplano prophesies to me
that living here I am as if not being here
Although I know of my being
I am not with myself
In my own Country I am from far away
thus ever am I not of two hearts
never / never / never
the river being like a serpent will flow in a line
the forefathers' words forever
will be accepted

(English versions of Aymara poems by Sabine Dedenbach-Salazar Sáenz)

Sabine Dedenbach-Salazar Sáenz

See also entries on Felipe Guaman Poma de Ayala, Mayan Literature, Náhuatl Literature, Quechua Literature

Further Reading

Albó, Xavier (editor), *Raíces de América: el mundo aymara*, Madrid: Alianza, 1988 [This collection of essays on all important aspects of Aymara culture is a valuable introduction. It also contains brief Aymara texts of different genres]

Albó, Xavier and Félix Layme, *Literatura aymara. Antología. 1. Prosa*, La Paz: CIPCA/Hisbol/JAYMA, 1992 [In this anthology, the editors have assembled Aymara texts which include, chronologically and thematically ordered samples of all periods and different topics and genres]

____ "Los textos aymaras de Waman Puma," in *Religions des Andes et langues indigènes: Équateur – Pérou - Bolivie avant et après la conquête espagnole*, edited by Pierre Duviols, Centre Aixois de Recherches Latino-Àmericaines (CARLAM), (Actes du Colloque III d'Études Andines), Publications de l'Université de Provence, 1993

Arnold, Denise and Juan de Dios Yapita, "'Fox Talk': Addressing the Wild Beasts in the Southern Andes," *Latin American Indian Literatures Journal*, McKeesport, Pennsylvania, vol. 8/1 (1992)

Ayala, José Luis, *Jake aru*, Lima: El Pez de Oro, 1980 [bilingual Spanish/Aymara edition]

Bertonio, Ludovico, *Arte y grammatica muy copiosa de la lengua aymara*, Rome: Luigi Zannetti, 1603

____ *Vocabulario de la lengua aymara*, Juli, Chucuyto: Francisco del Canto, 1612

Briggs, Lucy, "Missionary, patrón, and radio Aymara," in *The Aymara Language in its Social and Cultural Context*, edited by Martha J. Hardman, Gainesville, Florida: University of Florida Social Sciences Monograph, Number 67, 1981

____ "El k 'arik' ari en dos textos de lengua aymara: análisis morfosintáctico y del discurso," in *Andean Oral Traditions: Discourse and Literature/Tradiciones Orales Andinas: Discurso y Literatura*, edited by Margot Beyersdorff and Sabine Dedenbach-Salazar Sáenz, Bonn: Holos, 1994

Briggs, Lucy (editor), *Latin American Indian Literatures Journal*, vol. 8/1, McKeesport, Pennsylvania (1992) [This volume dedicated to Aymara language and literature contains two analyses of oral traditions in their cultural context (Arnold/Yapita in English, Yapita in Spanish), an Aymara poem (Vásquez), and a good overview of the state of research in Aymara literature (Briggs) as well as several book reviews]

____ *Vocabolario para saber hablar, y prununciar la Castellana compuesta á la Ydioma Aymarà. A Colonial Bilingual Text in Spanish and Aymara*, Institute of Amerindian Studies Occasional Papers no. 26, University of St Andrews, Scotland, 1995

Doctrina Christiana y catecismo para instrvccion de indios . . . Tercero Cathecismo, Lima, 1584–85

Hardman, Martha, Juana Vázquez, Juan de Dios Yapita, *et al.*, *Aymara. Compendio de estructura fonológica y gramatical*, Instituto de Lengua y Cultura Aymara, La Paz: Gramma Impresión, 1988 [This grammar provides a comprehensive analysis of modern La Paz Aymara language structure]

Huanca L., Tomás, *El yatiri en la comunidad aymara*, La Paz: Ediciones CADA, 1989

____ *Jilirinaksan arsüwipa – Testimonios de nuestros mayores*, La Paz: Taller de Historia Oral Andina, 1991

Johannessen Lino, Elizabeth, *Ofrenda de agradecimiento a la tierra*, La Paz: Editorial Acuario, 1981

LaBarre, Weston, "Aymara folktales," *International Journal of American Linguistics*, vol. 16/1 (1950)

López, Luis Enrique and Domingo Sayritupac Asqui, *Wiñay pacha. Aymar arut Qullasuyun kwiñtunakapa*, Instituto de Estudios Aymara, Chucuito/Puno, 1985 [bilingual edition]

Aluísio Azevedo 1857–1913

Brazilian novelist

Aluísio Azevedo is generally described by critics and literary historians as Brazil's most important Naturalist novelist. This reputation, however, is based upon only four of the eleven novels Azevedo produced during the sixteen years of his life (1879–95) that he devoted to fiction. Only those four – *O mulato* (*Mulatto*) of 1881; *Casa de pensão*, 1884 [Boarding-House]; *O homem*, 1887 [The Man], and *O cortiço* (*A Brazilian Tenement*) of 1890 – attempt to follow the stylistic and thematic precepts of French Naturalism and its leading exponent, Émile Zola. The other seven novels are, in general, pedestrian romantic pot-boilers, with titles like *O mistério da Tijuca* [The Mystery of Tijuca], or *A mortalha de Alzira* [Alzira's Shroud], many of which first appeared serialized in newspapers. Nor is there any clear progression in Azevedo's literary career; he simultaneously produced both Naturalist and Romantic texts, and *A mortalha de Alzira*, a simply ludicrous novel, appeared four years after *O cortiço* – Azevedo's masterpiece and one of the greatest novels of 19th-century Brazilian literature.

These anomalies are significant for understanding Azevedo's view of literature in general and of the Naturalist novel in particular. Azevedo occasionally claimed that destiny had forced him to become a writer, but it is clear that he was always extremely conscious of the economic and social benefits literary success could bring. One of the ironies of Azevedo's career is that his Naturalist novels frequently attack capitalism, commerce, and even the profit motive itself, but he argued with his publishers over contractual details and aggressively pushed the sales of his novels – even putting up advertising posters himself. When he was thirty-eight years old, Azevedo obtained a position in Brazil's diplomatic service, and gave up writing fiction for good; he later told a friend that "the only books that count are checkbooks."

Azevedo's determination to use fiction to earn money and gain a government job helps to explain his simultaneous production of both Naturalist and Romantic novels. He recognized the fact that two quite separate audiences for fiction had developed by the last years of the Brazilian Empire: a small but influential group of sophisticated, highly-educated upper-class readers, largely male, who were aware of the latest trends in European literature; and a much larger group of readers, primarily composed of upper-class women and less educated men, who were not interested in literary innovation but simply enjoyed traditional and highly melodramatic tales of romance and mystery. Azevedo managed to satisfy these two audiences from the very beginning of his literary career. His first novel, *Uma lágrima de mulher*, 1879 [A Woman's Tear], was, as its title suggests, a romantic tear-jerker; his second, *O mulato* (written in 1880 and published in 1881), was one of the first Brazilian Naturalist novels to appear, and was unquestionably the most influential of those early texts.

Azevedo's leap from full-blown Romanticism to something very close to standard French Naturalism is symbolic of the whole development of Brazilian fiction in the second half of the 19th century. The novel in Brazil similarly moved directly from Romanticism to Naturalism – almost entirely skipping Realism, the central movement in European fiction after Flaubert. While some Brazilian Naturalists trumpeted their movement as a revolution against Romanticism, in practice it is evident that their novels endeavored to reformulate Romanticism through a surface texture of detailed observation and references to what the Naturalists viewed as science; beneath that surface texture, the Naturalists, like their predecessors, sought to use literature to communicate universal truths rather than simply to describe reality. But while the truths of Brazilian Romanticism were generally positive –

national pride and optimism about the future, the inherent goodness of most of humanity, the saving power of true love – those of Naturalism were darkly pessimistic: social change is painfully difficult, and its consequences are invariably negative; most individuals, their behavior totally determined by genetics and by their environment, are deeply flawed; sexual desire the engine that drives human existence. These ideas, moreover, were communicated through plot structures, relying heavily upon mystery and melodrama, which were virtually indistinguishable from those of the Brazilian Romantic novel.

Azevedo and other Brazilian Naturalists claimed to be disciples of Zola, and their works contain both stylistic and thematic elements which support that claim: the use of scientific language to establish the validity of the narrative; detailed descriptions of the artifacts and routines of daily life at various social and economic levels; the frank portrayal of sexuality; the creation of characters largely devoid of complexity or ambiguity because they are defined in terms of social or biological pathologies (avarice, hysteria, nymphomania, homosexuality, and so on), pathologies which determine their actions; a strongly anti-clerical and anti-capitalist stance; the focus on enclosed physical spaces (the small provincial city of São Luís do Maranhão in *O mulato*, the urban slum in *O cortiço*) within which, as in Zola's theoretical model of the laboratory test tube, the assorted pathologies of the characters interact.

None the less, the Naturalism of Azevedo and his contemporaries departed from their European models in significant ways. Because the audience for their fiction was overwhelmingly male, the sexual content of their novels went far beyond anything found in Zola. Nothing comparable to the most extreme examples of Brazilian Naturalism, Júlio Ribeiro's *A carne*, 1888 [Flesh] or Adolfo Caminha's 1895 novel of interracial homosexuality *Bom crioulo* (*The Black Man and the Cabin Boy*), could have been published and marketed in England or the United States before the middle of the 20th century. Even the 1926 English translation of Azevedo's much tamer *O cortiço* had to be extensively cut before publication.

There are, however, other even more fundamental differences between Brazilian and European Naturalism. Zola and his French followers described the human suffering and degradation caused by an unjust social and economic system in order to create support among bourgeois readers for fundamental changes in that system. In Brazil, Naturalism flourished at a time of enormous changes in Brazilian society – the abolition of African slavery in 1888, the end of the Empire and the proclamation of the Republic in 1889, the rise of European-style capitalism, and the start of large-scale European immigration. Azevedo, like the other members of the Brazilian movement, used fiction as a means to explore and to warn against what he viewed as the potentially destructive consequences of these changes for the traditional structures of Brazilian society, structures dominated by the elite male readers for whom he wrote. The great dangers, for Azevedo, included potential competition from educated and ambitious mulattos, the upward mobility of European immigrants whose prosperity, the result of their domination of commerce and capital, threatened an agriculture-based economy and aristocracy, and the challenge to patriarchal society posed by the education of women and by any free expression of female sexuality. In Azevedo's Naturalist novels, something approaching order is restored at the end of the text – but that order is fragile, artificial, and very often ironic, reflecting his own deep pessimism about the future of traditional Brazilian society.

DAVID T. HABERLY

Biography

Born Aluísio Tancredo Gonçalves de Azevedo in the northeastern coastal city of São Luís in the province of Maranhão, Brazil, 14 April 1857. His brother Artur, with whom Aluísio would sometimes collaborate, became a leading playwright of the day. Neither brother was successful at school and they both began to work as warehouse clerks when they reached the age of thirteen. Aluísio went to Rio in 1876 but returned to Maranhão on his father's death in 1878 and began a career in journalism. Earned a reputation as a radical with anti-Establishment and anti-clerical ideas. Returned to Rio in 1881 and led a comfortable life in café society. Appointed to Brasil's consular service in 1895 at which point he gave up writing for good. Travelled widely. Died of a heart attack in Buenos Aires, 21 January 1913.

Selected Works

Novels

Uma lágrima de mulher, São Luís do Maranhão: Tipografia do Frias, 1879
O mulato, in *O País*, (São Luís do Maranhão), 1881; as *Mulatto*, translated by Murray Graeme MacNicoll, Rutherford, New Jersey: Fairleigh Dickinson University Press, 1990
O mistério da Tijuca, in *Folha Nova* (Rio de Janeiro), 1883 [retitled as *Girândola de amores* in all subsequent editions]
Casa de pensão, Rio de Janeiro: Militar de Santos e Companhia, 1884
Filomena Borges, in *Gazeta de Notícias* (Rio de Janeiro), 1884
Memórias de um condenado, Ouro Preto: Liberal Mineiro, 1886 [retitled as *A Condessa Vésper*, Rio de Janeiro, 1901]
O homem, Rio de Janeiro: Afonso de Castro e Silva, 1887
O cortiço, Rio de Janeiro: Garnier, 1890; as *A Brazilian Tenement*, translated by Harry W. Brown, New York: R. M. McBride, 1926; reprinted, New York: H. Fertig, 1976
O coruja, Rio de Janeiro: Montalverne, 1890
Demônios, São Paulo: Teixeim e Irmãos, 1893 [novella]
A mortalha de Alzira, Rio de Janeiro: Fauchon, 1894
Livro de uma sogra, Rio de Janeiro: Magalhães e Companhia, 1895
Pegadas, Rio de Janeiro: Garnier Livreiro, 1897 [novella]

Compilations and Anthologies

Obras completas, edited by Nogueira da Silva, 12 vols, Rio de Janeiro: Briguiet e Companhia, 1937–44; São Paulo: Martins, 1959–65

Further Reading

Brayner, Sônia, *A metáfora do corpo no romance naturalista*, Rio de Janeiro: Civilização Brasileira, 1973
_____ *Labirinto do espaço romanesco*, Rio de Janeiro: Civilização Brasileira, 1979
Loos, Dorothy Scott, *The Naturalistic Novel of Brazil*, New York: Hispanic Institute, 1963
MacNicoll, Murray Graeme, "*O mulato* and Maranhão: the Socio-Historical Context," *Luso-Brazilian Review*, vol. 12/2 (1975)
Marotti, Giorgio, *Black Characters in the Brazilian Novel*, translated by Maria O. Marotti and Henry Lawton, Los Angeles: Center for Afro-American Studies of the University of California, 1987

Mérian, Jean-Yves, *Aluísio Azevedo, vida e obra*, Rio de Janeiro: Espaço e Tempo, 1988 [The most complete biography of Azevedo]

Patai, Daphne and Murray Graeme MacNicoll, introduction to *Mulatto*, translated by MacNicoll, Rutherford, New Jersey: Fairleigh Dickinson University Press, 1990

Sales, Herberto (editor), *Para conhecer melhor Aluísio Azevedo*, Rio de Janeiro: Civilização Brasileira, 1973

Sedycias, João, *The Naturalistic Novel of the New World: a Comparative Study of Stephen Crane, Aluísio de Azevedo and Federico Gamboa*, Lanham, Maryland: University Press of America, 1993

Mariano Azuela 1873–1952

Mexican prose writer, dramatist and critic

Known primarily for his novels, Mariano Azuela was a medical doctor and an officer in Pancho Villa's army during the Mexican Revolution (1910–20). His early novels, written in the naturalistic vein before the Revolution, reflect the influence of Zola. The best of these is *Mala yerba* (*Marcela*), which exposes the corruption of wealthy *hacendados* (landowners) and the judicial system. Marcela, the protagonist, is a peasant girl whose lover is murdered by Julián Andrade, the local *hacendado*, because he himself desires her. Marcela, too, dies in the end, victimized by both Andrade and her oppressive environment. Perhaps Azuela's most popular novel after *Los de abajo* (*The Underdogs*), *Mala yerba* not only attacks social injustice, but also describes scenes of country life such as horse races and bull fights. In his dialogues Azuela displays a sharp ear for rural speech patterns, which he observed as a youth on the haciendas of his native state of Jalisco.

The next cycle of Azuela's novels depicts the Revolution, initiating the type of fiction that would predominate in Mexico until approximately 1945. The most widely acclaimed of these works is *Los de abajo*, but others include *Andrés Pérez, maderista* [Andrés Pérez, Supporter of Madero]; *Los caciques* (*The Bosses*); *Las moscas* (*The Flies*); and *Las tribulaciones de una familia decente* (*The Trials of a Respectable Family*). The first Mexican novel of the Revolution, *Andrés Pérez, maderista* portrays a youth who, at the outbreak of the Revolution, pretends to support Francisco Madero, but who ultimately betrays the revolutionary leader as well as his best friend. *Los caciques* takes place during Madero's presidency (1911–13), its principal theme being the exploitation by unscrupulous *caciques* (political bosses), a major cause of the civil conflict. In this novel Don Juanito, an honest but naive businessman, is robbed of his livelihood by the *caciques*, while Rodríguez, an outspoken, idealistic store clerk, pays with his life for critizing them. *Las moscas* consists of a series of brief scenes on a train carrying followers of Pancho Villa to northern Mexico after his defeat by General Obregón at Celaya. Without a true protagonist, this novel has as its central theme the reactions of individuals to the danger and confusion wrought by the Revolution. Other unifying aspects of the work are its flashes of humor and its mordant satire of human weaknesses that surface under stress.

Las tribulaciones de una familia decente is Azuela's most important novel of the Revolution after *Los de abajo*. In this bitter, humorless saga, the author portrays the Vázquez Prados, an upper-middle-class family from Zacatecas that seeks refuge in Mexico City during a time of social and political turmoil (1916–17). Here in the capital, however, the family is again engulfed by the Revolution and forced to adapt to a dog-eat-dog environment in which corrupt opportunists are awarded political plums and soldiers are permitted to roam the streets robbing and terrorizing civilians. Azuela strongly condemns the regime of President Venustiano Carranza, known in the novel as "el Primer Jefe" (the Number-One Boss). The most memorable characters include Procopio Vázquez, the family patriarch, who loses his fortune and ultimately comes to terms with his situation when he finds work as an office employee, a fate he could never have accepted in Zacatecas; Agustinita, Procopio's proud and less adaptable wife; and Pascual, their unscrupulous son-in-law, who robs them of their wealth and cavorts with venal government officials. Although two of the themes (the betrayal of the Revolution and the virtue of honest work) are set forth perhaps too explicitly, this remains one of Azuela's three or four most successful endeavors.

Between 1918 and 1923 Azuela did not publish any novels, in part because he felt discouraged over the lack of attention accorded him by critics and readers. (*Los de abajo*, which had been published in El Paso, Texas in 1916, was not acclaimed in Mexico City as a major achievement until 1924.) So, in an effort to elicit recognition, he resorted to the use of avant-garde techniques in his next three novels, the most successful of which is *La luciérnaga* (*The Firefly*). In this novel, which shares the same theme as *Las tribulaciones de una familia decente* (the problems experienced by a provincial middle-class family in adjusting to life in Mexico City), chronological time is disrupted and, instead of an omniscient or first-person narrator, interior monologues convey much of the plot.

A psychological as well as a social-protest novel, *La luciérnaga* portrays three major characters: Dionisio, his wife Conchita (La Luciérnaga), and his brother José María. Dionisio decides to move his family from Cieneguilla to Mexico City, where he plans to invest Conchita's inheritance and make a better life for all of them. However, once in the capital he soon loses their fortune to unscrupulous, would-be business partners and succumbs to alcoholism. Meanwhile, his daughter is killed, his son dies of tuberculosis, and his miserly brother, who has remained in Cieneguilla to die, also of tuberculosis, refuses to save him from financial ruin. Conchita returns to Cieneguilla but, in the final pages, reappears in Mexico City to rescue her bedridden husband from physical, moral, and spiritual degradation.

Some critics have proclaimed *La luciérnaga* Azuela's best work, primarily because of his adept manipulation of stylistic and structural techniques that were seldom seen in Mexican fiction before 1932. Thus, presented from within by means of their unarticulated thoughts, Dionisio, José María, and Conchita emerge as vivid, well-rounded characters whose tragic fate elicits the reader's interest and sympathy. The temporal and spatial shifts from the capital to the family's home town, moreover, inject dynamic momentum and challenge the reader to reorganize events in chronological order. Finally, the eponymous Firefly (Conchita) symbolizes the ideal Mexican wife, whose virtues sparkle silently in the blackness of adversity.

Although during the last twenty years of his life Azuela published eight novels (plus two posthumously), none of these is ranked among his best. The majority deal with political issues and, in their technique, mark a return to Naturalism. Perhaps the most notable is *Nueva burguesía* [New Bourgeoisie], consisting of a series of cinemagraphic close-ups of the new middle-class that seized political and economic power after the Revolution. Reminiscent of *Las moscas* in its technique and in its lack of a true protagonist, this novel attacks once again the failure to enact the reforms promised by Mexico's revolutionary leaders.

As the initiator of the novel of the Mexican Revolution, Azuela set his nation's literature on an entirely new course. He broke with European models and Spanish American *Modernismo* in order to forge a different type of fiction, one dealing with real social issues from the point of view of the common man. Thus his heroes are either the exploited and downtrodden or those of the upper classes who, as a result of the Revolution, come to realize the value of hard work and social justice. In his better novels, instead of the verbose style of the Naturalists (who influenced him most in his early years), Azuela used a terse, elliptical prose designed to profile a nation in the throes of dramatic change. Also new in his works is the adroit recording of colloquial Mexican Spanish, especially in the dialogues between illiterate peasants. Major themes running throughout his *oeuvre* are the betrayal of the Revolution and the corrupting influence of city life. An unyielding idealist, Azuela never declared a truce in his attacks on Mexico's *nouveaux riches*. He has been overshadowed in recent years by younger, more experimental writers, but he remains a beacon of both Mexican and Spanish American fiction.

GEORGE R. McMURRAY

Biography

Born in Lagos de Moreno in the state of Jalisco, Mexico, 1 January 1873, of middle-class parents. After completing his secondary education he was sent in 1887 to Guadalajara to study for the priesthood. Left seminary in 1889. In 1892 he registered in the School of Medicine at the University of Guadalajara; awarded degree in 1899. Returned to Lagos de Moreno to practice medicine there but unable to re-adjust to small town life. Married Carmen Rivera in 1900; ten children. Witnessed action described in *Los de abajo (The Underdogs)* when working as a surgeon in the army of Pancho Villa. After the latter's División del Norte was routed, Azuela took refuge in El Paso, Texas, where he completed and published *Los de abajo* in 1915. By 1916 he was in Mexico City, practising medicine among the poorest members of the community. Honours rained on him in later life: awarded the Premio de Letras by the Ateneo Nacional de Ciencias y Artes in 1940. Became member of the Seminario de Cultura Mexicana and of the Academia de la Lengua in 1942. Assisted in foundation of the Colegio Nacional in 1943, and became one of its founding members. Died in Mexico City, 1 March 1952.

Selected Works

Novels and Novellas

María Luisa, Lagos de Moreno, Jalisco: Imprenta López Arce, 1907

Los fracasados, Mexico City: Tipografía y Litografía de Müller Hermanos, 1908

Mala yerba, Guadalajara: Talleres de *La Gaceta de Guadalajara*, 1909; as *Marcela; a Mexican Love Story*, translated by Anita Brenner, New York: Farrar and Rinehart, 1932

Andrés Pérez, maderista, Mexico City: Imprenta de Blanco y Botas, 1911

Sin amor, Mexico City: Tipografía y Litografía de Müller Hermanos, 1912

Los de abajo, El Paso, Texas: Imprenta de *El Paso del Norte*, 1916 [Serialized in this newspaper in 1915]; as *The Underdogs*, translated by Frederick H. Fornoff, Pittsburgh: University of Pittsburgh Press, 1992

Los caciques, Mexico City: Ediciones de *El Universal*, Editoral de la Compañía Periodística Nacional, 1917; as *The Bosses*, translated by Lesley Byrd Simpson, in *Two Novels of Mexico: The Flies. The Bosses*, Berkeley: University of California Press, 1956

Las moscas, Mexico City: Carranza e Hijos, 1918; as *The Flies*, translated by Lesley Byrd Simpson, in *Two Novels of Mexico: The Flies. The Bosses*, Berkeley: University of California Press, 1956

Domitilo quiere ser diputado, Mexico City: Tipografía A. Carranza e Hijos, 1918

Las tribulaciones de una familia decente, Tampico: Biblioteca de *El Mundo*, 1918; as *The Trials of a Respectable Family*, in *Three Novels*, 1979

La malhora, Mexico City: Rosendo Terrazas, 1923

La luciérnaga, Madrid and Barcelona: Espasa Calpe, 1932; as *The Firefly*, in *Three Novels*, 1979

El camarada Pantoja, Mexico City: Botas, 1937

San Gabriel de Valdivias, comunidad indígena, Santiago de Chile: Ercilla, 1938

Regina Landa, Mexico City: Botas, 1939

Avanzada, Mexico City: Botas, 1940

El desquite, Mexico City: Botas, 1941 [First published in *La novela semanal*, 1925]

Nueva burguesía, Buenos Aires: Club del Libro, 1941

La marchanta, Mexico City: Ediciones del Seminario de Cultura Mexicana, 1944

La mujer domada, Mexico City: El Colegio Nacional, 1946

Sendas perdidas, Mexico City: Botas, 1949 [Limited edition of 200 copies]

La maldición, Mexico City: Fondo de Cultura Económica, 1955

Esa sangre, Mexico City: Fondo de Cultura Económica, 1956

Compilations and Anthologies

Obras completas, 3 vols, Mexico City: Fondo de Cultura Económica, 1958–60

Translations

Two Novels of the Mexican Revolution [Includes *The Trials of a Respectable Family* and *The Underdogs*], translated by Frances Kellam Hendricks and Beatrice Berler, San Antonio, Texas: Trinity University Press, 1963; revised and augmented edition as *Three Novels: The Trials of a Respectable Family; The Underdogs; The Firefly*, 1979

Further Reading

A cursory look at the bibliography on Azuela reveals that the majority of the studies deal with *Los de abajo* and were published before 1975. Thus, the criticism of Azuela's work is mostly traditional, treating themes, stylistic devices, and structure.

Dulsey, Bernard M., "The Mexican Revolution as Mirrored in the Novels of Mariano Azuela," *Modern Language Journal*, vol. 35 (1951)

Herbst, Gerhard R., *Mexican Society as Seen by Mariano Azuela*, New York: Abra, 1977

Langford, Walter M., "Mariano Azuela: a Break with the Past," in his *The Mexican Novel Comes of Age*, Notre Dame, Indiana: Notre Dame University Press, 1971

Leal, Luis, *Mariano Azuela*, New York: Twayne, 1971

Ruffinelli, Jorge, *Literatura e ideología: el primer Mariano Azuela (1896–1918)*, Mexico City: Premiá Editor, 1982

Wood, Cecil G., "Nuevas técnicas novelísticas en *La luciérnaga* de Mariano Azuela," *Revista Canadiense de Estudios Hispánicos*, vol. 1 (1977)

Los de abajo

Novel by Mariano Azuela

A classic in Spanish American literature, *Los de abajo* was written while its author, Mariano Azuela, was serving as a medical officer in Pancho Villa's army in northern Mexico. After Villa was defeated by Álvaro Obregón in the battle of Celaya in April 1915, Azuela crossed the border into El Paso, Texas, where he published his recently completed manuscript as a weekly serial in the local newspaper, *El Paso del Norte*. In this novel Azuela strove to capture the passions and the immediacy of the cataclysmic events he had just witnessed.

Los de abajo dramatizes the second phase of the Mexican Revolution, that is, the time frame between the assassination of Francisco Madero by Victoriano Huerta in February 1913 and the above-mentioned battle of Celaya. Divided into three parts, the novel first introduces Demetrio Macías, an illiterate peasant who leads a ragtag band of revolutionaries against federal troops, defeating them in a series of skirmishes and then joining Pánfilo Natera's division. Part I also introduces the opportunist Luis Cervantes, an educated youth who becomes Demetrio's secretary (Demetrio soon attains the rank of colonel) and contrasts sharply with the rustic men under Demetrio's command. Part I ends with Demetrio's heroic exploits during the battle of Zacatecas, which signals the triumph of the Revolution, but this section also concludes with the death of Captain Alberto Solís, the only true idealist of the novel. Thus, whereas Part I dramatizes the enthusiasm and idealism of the Revolution, Part II depicts the looting and brutality of the conflict, in addition to its division into factions interested solely in seizing power.

Two characters best typifying the bestiality of Part II are Margarito (Blondie), who tortures a federalist soldier before hacking him to death with a saber, and La Pintada, a camp-follower who out of jealousy stabs Camila after the latter confesses her affection for Demetrio. Animal imagery in this part also conveys the dehumanizing influence of the war: "They [Demetrio and La Pintada] stared at each other face to face like two strange dogs smelling one another with suspicion." The final pages of Part II describe the chaotic atmosphere of Aguascalientes (October–November 1914), where attempts to unify the various revolutionary factions fail. Part III represents the disillusion and defeat of Demetrio's men in Juchipila Canyon, the location of their first triumphant encounter with the federal troops.

The novel's carefully planned structure is demonstrated by its symmetrical design, Part I consisting of twenty-one chapters, Part II of fourteen, and Part III of seven. Another important aspect of *Los de abajo* is its epic characteristics. The plot dramatizes not only events of historic and national transcendence, but also heroic exploits reminiscent of the *Iliad* (especially Demetrio's role in the battle of Zacatecas and the scene immediately thereafter). Like the *Poem of the Cid*, Azuela's novel is divided into three parts, and the *Song of Roland* comes to mind when Demetrio blows a horn to summon his men. At least two episodes of *Los de abajo* evoke the *Divine Comedy*: when a luxury edition of Dante's masterpiece is destroyed by looters, suggesting Mexico's metaphoric descent into Hell; and when, in the final lines, Demetrio's ascent to Heaven is implied: "At the foot of a hollow, sumptuous and huge as the portico of an old cathedral, Demetrio Macías, his eyes leveled in an eternal glance, continues to point the barrel of his gun." This final image of Demetrio also suggests that the spirit of the Revolution survives despite the death of its hero.

Although, as seen below, Azuela had serious doubts about Mexico's future after the Revolution, his literary techniques do indeed capture the essence of the upheaval that was transforming his native land as he was creating his masterwork. Perhaps the most basic aspect of his novel is its dynamic, headlong pace, an impression conveyed by its terse, elliptical style. Thus, one-sided dialogues generate forward momentum by obliging the reader to fill in the retorts; similarly, the temporal and spatial gaps between chapters must be closed by a participating reader in order to sustain the narrative thread. Azuela's use of dialogue and fragmentary action to portray character is enhanced, moreover, by colloquial discourse and brief metaphoric descriptions of superficial reality reflecting the unsophisticated peasant mentality of his characters – rather than lengthy description and detailed, analytical narration. In its form, then, *Los de abajo* emerges as a truly "revolutionary" novel for its time.

Several critics have emphasized the ambiguity of Azuela's attitude toward the Revolution. Thus, although the author served on the side of the revolutionary forces and does indeed portray Demetrio as an epic hero who dies fighting for the oppressed, he clearly abhors the barbarism he witnessed and the greed and opportunism of his compatriots. Two embodiments of these attitudes are Cervantes and Solís. The former deserts the federal army and joins the rebels solely to be on the winning side and then absconds with his loot to El Paso, where he launches a successful business career. On the other hand, Captain Solís, the disillusioned idealist and probably the author's mouthpiece, expresses to Cervantes his loss of faith in the Revolution and its deterministic effect on those who participate in it:

> Yo pensé una pradera florida al remate de un camino ... Y me encontré un pantano ... La revolución es el huracán, y el hombre que se entrega a ella no es ya el hombre, es la miserable hoja seca arrebatada por el vendaval ...

> [I hoped to find a meadow at the end of the road, I found a swamp ... the revolution is like a hurricane: if you're in it, you're not a man ... you're a leaf, a dead leaf, blown by the wind]

At a later point, shortly before he is killed, Solís looks toward the future, and says:

> Hay que esperar un poco ... a que la psicología de nuestra raza resplandezca diáfana ... ¡robar, matar! ... ¡Qué chasco, amigo mío, si los que venimos a ofrecer nuestra ... vida por derribar a un miserable asesino, resultásemos los obreros de un enorme pedestal ... de la misma especie! ... ¡Lástima de sangre!

> [We must wait until the psychology of our race ... shines clear and luminous ... Robbery! Murder! What a colossal failure we would make of it, friend, if we, who offer our ... lives to crush a wretched tyrant [Huerta],

became the builders of a monstrous edifice ... of exactly the same sort ... Vain bloodshed!]

Innovative in its literary form, *Los de abajo* broke with the long, naturalistic novels and family sagas that had captivated audiences since the 19th century. It is a masterpiece for its unity of theme (the Mexican Revolution) and epic design reflecting the three phases of a nation's tragic struggle for justice. Despite its episodic nature, it is a carefully structured work of art, modern both in its camera-eye technique and in its conceptual ambiguity.

GEORGE R. MCMURRAY

Editions
First publication: serialized in newspaper *El Paso del Norte*, El Paso, Texas (October–December 1915). First edition in book form: Imprenta de "El Paso del Norte," El Paso, Texas, 1916
Critical edition: edited by Jorge Ruffinelli, Madrid: Archivos, 1988
Translation: *The Underdogs*, by Frederick H. Fornoff, Pittsburgh: University of Pittsburgh Press, 1992 [A scholarly edition with articles by Carlos Fuentes, Seymour Menton and Jorge Ruffinelli. There are earlier translations]

Further Reading
Early criticism of *The Underdogs* generally considered it an episodic work lacking a clearly defined, unified structure. Recent critics, however, have discerned its epic characteristics and structural unity.

Robe, Stanley L., *Azuela and the Mexican Underdogs*, Berkeley: University of California Press, 1979 [Provides detailed picture of the two years of political upheaval, 1914 and 1915, in which this novel is set]
Sommers, Joseph, "The Underdogs (Los de abajo)," in his *After the Storm: Landmarks of the Modern Mexican Novel*, Albuquerque: University of New Mexico Press, 1968

B

Emilio Ballagas 1908–1954

Cuban poet

Emilio Ballagas's first book of poems, *Júbilo y fuga* [Joy and Flight], appeared in 1931. This collection placed him amongst the foremost practitioners of the so called "pure" poetry, and thus a member of an innovative movement with other outstanding exponents in Cuba. These included Mariano Brull and Eugenio Florit and the movement's theoretical bases were formulated by the Frenchman Henri Brémond. With *Cuaderno de poesía negra*, 1934 [Black Poetry Notebook] he ventured successfully into African-Cuban poetry, a sub-genre whose principal literary figure was Nicolás Guillén. Ballagas's African-Cuban poetry is restricted, in essence, to a markedly folkloric expression, though it contains social nuances. His poetic career is made up of three stages. *Júbilo y fuga* and *Cuaderno de poesía negra* correspond to the first stage, and represent, respectively, the cultured and popular aspects of "pure" poetry in Cuba. In these two initial books, the poet is essentially a voice that is trying out for the first time the joy of singing the delights of the world, with an almost childlike sensibility still innocent of passion and sexual couplings. This joy, which in his first book points towards a sensuality that the critics have called "Adam-like," that is to say, innocent of the biblical notions of blame and punishment, turns into a real sense of pleasure in Ballagas's African-Cuban poetry. The poet, through the vocabulary and rhythms of Cuban urban folklore, where the presence of the African tradition of nationality is strong, produces some texts where the verbal recreation broadens the repercussions of his poetic voice considerably. However, his Black poetry is no more than a pleasant parenthesis in Ballagas's *oeuvre*, that achieves its first great moment of maturity in the shape of two poems in a markedly Neoromantic style: "Elegía sin nombre" [Elegy without a Name], and "Nocturno y elegía" [Nocturne and Elegy], both of which were incorporated into his book *Sabor eterno*, 1939 [Eternal Taste]. These poems constitute two of the most exceptional love poems in 20th-century Cuban poetry. *Sabor eterno* expresses, in relation to the previous stage, the moments of the fall and contrition within Ballagas's poetry. The earlier innocent enjoyment of the senses has been transformed in *Sabor eterno* into knowledge, suffering, and solitude, which are reached through the experiences of love and the loss of love. The verse becomes broader and freer, and the expression carries images where the empty space and the growing presence of the night create an atmosphere that is apt for the dissolution of sensuality into loneliness. Because of its confessional style, where the "I" surrenders itself through obfuscating metaphors that constitute any given number of ways to stimulate the reader to unveil the poet's message, making him his accomplice as well as the ultimate addressee of his voice, *Sabor eterno* can be placed in the line that – within the Spanish language poetry of the time – Pablo Neruda and Xavier Villaurrutia represented in Latin America, and Luis Cernuda and Vicente Aleixandre in Spain.

From the publication of this book, Ballagas's poetry enters a phase of withdrawal, both in formal and in spiritual terms, represented by the expression of religious feeling through traditional forms: the *décima* (ten line octosyllabic verse form); the *lira* (five line stanza); and the sonnet. With *Nuestra señora del mar*, 1943 [Our Lady of the Sea], inspired by the Marian name of the Virgen de la Caridad del Cobre, who is greatly revered in Cuba, Ballagas once again approaches the Island's popular traditions, on this occasion the religious ones. The "Adam-like" sensitivity reverts here to the outlook of the child that returns to its mother's lap seeking protection, and is expressed through the use of stanzas – modelled on those of the great religious poets of the Spanish language: San Juan de la Cruz and Fray Luis de León – whose construction takes Ballagas towards a Neoclassicism where the intimate and the confessional are subdued, without losing their voice totally. This third stage of his production culminates in his collection of sonnets *Cielo en rehenes* [Sky in Hostages], which offers a mature expressive tone, characterized by the balance between pain and serenity, between the sensual and the spiritual. Stylistically, the collection's best sonnets display, in like manner, a balance between the Neoclassical and the Baroque. Ballagas also excelled as a lucid and impassioned essayist, a genre in which he produced a series of texts – many of them delivered as lectures – in which he undertook an enterprise of aesthetic exploration running parallel to the innovative strain in his poetic works. Emilio Ballagas had an unmistakable voice and he achieved a thematic and stylistic richness which make him, together with the exceptional quality of some of his texts, one of the principal figures of 20th-century Cuban poetry.

EMILIO DE ARMAS

translated by Luis González Fernández

Biography
Born in Camagüey, Cuba, 7 November 1908. Finished secondary education in 1926. Obtained the title of Doctor of Pedagogy, 1933, and appointed to Chair of Literature and Grammar at teacher's training college in Santa Clara. Editor of *Elegía sin nombre* in the 1930s. Travelled to France, Portugal and the United States, 1937–38. Travelled to New York in 1946; actively involved with New York Institute for the Education of the Blind. Renewed friendship with Antonia López Villaverde, whom he married in 1947. Son, Manolo Francisco, born in 1948. Awarded National Prize for Poetry, 1951. Died in Havana, 11 September 1954.

Selected Works

Poetry
Júbilo y fuga, Havana: n.p, 1931
Cuaderno de poesía negra, Havana: Santa Clara, 1934

Elegía sin nombre, Havana: Úcar García, 1936
Nocturno y elegía, Havana: n.p., 1938
Sabor eterno, Havana: Úcar García, 1939
Nuestra señora del mar, Havana: Entrega de Fray Junípero, 1943

Anthologies and Compilations
Antología de la poesía negra hispanoamerica, Madrid: Aguilar, 1935
Mapa de la poesía negra americana, Buenos Aires: Pleamar, 1946
Obra poética, with an introduction by Cintio Vitier, Havana: Úcar García, 1955 [includes *Cielo en rehenes*]
Órbita de Emilio Ballagas, Santa Clara, Cuba: Universidad Central de las Villas, 1958

Further Reading
Pallas, Rosa, *La poesía de Emilio Ballagas*, Madrid: Playor, 1973
Piñera, Virgilio, "Ballagas en persona," *Ciclón*, Havana, vol. 1/5 (September 1955) [Bold for its time in that it engages with the poet's homosexuality]
Pryor Rice, Argyll, *Emilio Ballagas: poeta o poesía*, Mexico City: Andrea, 1966
Vitier, Cintio, *Lo cubano en la poesía*, Santa Clara: Universidad Central de las Villas, 1958; Havana: Instituto del Libro, 1970 [Chapter on Brull, Ballagas and Florit]

Manuel Bandeira 1886–1968

Brazilian poet and literary translator

Although recognised as one of the outstanding and most respected figures of the Brazilian Modernist Movement, Manuel Bandeira passed through several different literary phases during his long writing career. The range of styles and forms found in his collected work is considerable, but he is doubtless best known for simple, lyrical poems, characterised by tenderness and melancholy, which seek to express everyday experience and emotions.

Bandeira published his first volume of poetry, *A cinza das horas* [The Hours' Ash], in 1917. The fifty poems all show the influence of Parnassianism in the formal discipline employed, and Symbolism in the thematic content, but in poems such as "Paisagem noturna" [Nocturnal Landscape] and "Renúncia" [Surrender] there are also indications of the gentle sadness and intimacy that would characterise so much of his work. There is a strong sense of suffering and vulnerability in many of these verses, related in part to Bandeira's personal experience of serious ill health, which plagued him all his life and deeply marked his vision of the world.

Form was a major concern for Bandeira during these early years of poetic creation, and each subsequent published volume records the increasing effort he made to free himself from the formal dictates of traditional verse, which he regarded as restrictive and oppressive. In *Carnaval* (1919), many of the poems conform to traditional formal patterns, but the

collection also includes "Os sapos" [The Toads], a poem which satirizes the narrow conservatism of the Parnassian School. It was an early statement of rebellion as Bandeira searched for a freer form of expression, and moved towards Modernism. Although he did not fully integrate himself into the movement until much later, "Os sapos" was recited at the opening night of the Modern Art Week in São Paulo which inaugurated it in 1922. A further step in that direction was signalled in *O ritmo dissoluto*, 1924 [The Dissolute Rhythm], which Bandeira himself described as a work of transition. Some of the poems reveal a greater degree of freedom of form and rhythm, but not all are convincing. In some, Bandeira is still unable to find adequate forms of expression for his sentiments, and tends towards the melodramatic or the sentimental.

The activities of the Modernists in the 1920s, during the so called "heroic phase" of the movement, provided vital stimulus for Bandeira's development as a writer, for through them he discovered new ways to continue the renovation of his poetry. Irony, humour and colloquial speech now become the key characteristics of his work, and are clearly in evidence in *Libertinagem*, published in 1930. This volume signalled his full adherence to Modernism, and contains some of his most memorable poems. Among them is "Poética," which, in its strident rejection of the consecrated conventions of traditional verse, summarizes the spirit of rebellion of early Modernism.

Another is "Vou-me embora pra Pasárgada" [I'm Off to Pasárgada], which envisages a mythical, ideal realm where the poet can enjoy the health and true happiness so far denied him. Humour and playfulness are used to combat the anguish and adversity which had previously produced a tone of despondency in many of his poems. Bandeira became an influential figure among Modernist circles in Rio de Janeiro, where he lived most of his life, but he never completely severed his ties with his native Pernambuco, in northeast Brazil, recollections of which are scattered through his poetry. The most notable example in *Libertinagem* is "Evocação do Recife," [Evoking Recife] which, in recalling with a mixture of gentle humour and sadness the city of his early childhood, evokes an era now past, but which has marked his life forever. This poem, more than any other in the collection, exemplifies Bandeira's concern to make the everyday and the commonplace a central part of his poetry, recalling street sellers, gossiping neighbours, children games, and colloquial speech patterns. For Bandeira, the language of the streets gives vitality to the poet's work, freeing it from the web of formal, linguistic conventions. Few other contemporary Brazilian poets have so successfully incorporated popular, oral speech into their work, and in doing so Bandeira made a vital contribution to the Modernist objective of broadening literary language.

For many critics, *Libertinagem* signified Bandeira's maturity as a poet, bringing together all the individual traits that would distinguish the rest of his work, but he continued to experiment with technique in the years that followed, introducing metrical innovations and seeking to extend the possibilities of free verse. Dividing lines between poetry and prose are blurred in some of the poems collected in *Estrela da manhã*, 1936 [Morning Star]. Bandeira believed strongly that poetry should be a constant exploration of different forms of expression, and his subsequent volumes of verse contain a variety of styles and structures. *Estrela da tarde* [Evening Star], for example, a collection published in 1960, contains many examples of traditional verse forms, but also some experiments in concrete poetry. Inevitably, not all attempts were successful, but Bandeira was always attentive to matters of form – a legacy of the early Parnassian influence – and his experimentation was carefully considered and measured. Discipline and caution characterized his approach to writing.

From the 1930s onwards, he also explored new themes, such as the African-Brazilian popular culture that had already attracted a number of other Modernist poets, but he returned to themes of universal concern to produce some of his most moving poems. Of those themes, the contemplation of death, a haunting obsession, is perhaps the most notable, and can be traced through all his work, where his response gradually moves from the restlessness and anguish found in some of his early poems, such as "Delírio" (in *A cinza das horas*), to spiritual peace through the acceptance of the inevitable in later works, like "A morte absoluta" from *Lira dos cinqüent'anos*, 1940 [The Lyre at Fifty] and "Preparação para a morte" [Preparing for Death] from *Estrela da tarde*. Overcoming his own anguish enabled Bandeira to express more solidarity and compassion with others in their suffering, evident in some of the poems of *Estrela da tarde*, for example, where his characteristic warmth and sensitivity is expressed in simple, accessible verses, colloquial in style, which had become the hallmark of his work. Bandeira dedicated himself uncompromisingly to literature, producing a significant body of critical studies and translations of works written in French and English, but it was his ability to explore basic human emotions and to express his personality sincerely and intimately through clear and concise verse that made him one of Brazil's outstanding poets of the 20th century.

MARK DINNEEN

Biography

Born in Recife, Brazil, 19 April 1886. Early years peripatetic, but by 1896 family had settled in Rio de Janeiro where he studied at the Ginásio Nacional, a conservative school that emphasized the Classics. Entered São Paulo Polytechnic to study architecture and engineering, 1903. Tuberculosis diagnosed, 1904. Travelled to Switzerland, 1913, and spent several months at a sanatorium in Davos. There he read German poets in the original. Returned to Brazil after outbreak of World War I. Between 1916–22 he lost both parents and two siblings. Formed friendship with Mário de Andrade (see separate entry). Professor of Spanish American literature at University of Rio, 1943. This experience made him aware of how little contact there was between Brazilian and Spanish American writers. From this time, concentrated more on translation (translated Schiller, Shakespeare and Sor Juana Inés de la Cruz into Portuguese) and editorial work. Elected to the Brazilian Academy of Letters, 1946. Died in Rio de Janeiro, 13 October 1968.

Selected Works

Poetry
A cinza das horas, Rio de Janeiro: Tipografia do *Jornal do Comércio*, 1917
Carnaval, Rio de Janeiro: Tipografia do *Jornal do Comércio*, 1919
Poesias, Rio de Janeiro: Tipografia da Revista de Língua Portuguesa, 1924 [Contains *A cinza das horas*, *Carnaval*, and *O ritmo dissoluto*]
Libertinagem, Rio de Janeiro: Irmãos Pongetti, 1930
Estrela da manhã, Rio de Janeiro: Tipografia do Ministério da Educação e Saúde, 1936
Lira dos cinqüent'anos, Rio de Janeiro: Companhia Carioca de Artes Gráficas, 1940
Belo belo, Rio de Janeiro: Casa do Estudante do Brasil, 1948
Mafuá do Malungo, Barcelona: privately printed, 1948
Opus 10, Niterói: Edições Hipocampo, 1952
Estrela da tarde, Salvador: Editora Dinamene, 1960

Prose Writings
Crônicas da província do Brasil, Rio de Janeiro: Civilização Brasileira, 1937
Guia de Ouro Preto, Rio de Janeiro: Ministério da Educação e Saúde, 1938
Noções de história das literaturas, São Paulo: Editora Nacional, 1940; as *A Brief History of Brazilian Literature*, translated by Ralph Edward Dimmick, Washington, DC: Pan American Union, 1958
Literatura hispano-americana, Rio de Janeiro: Irmãos Pongetti, 1949
Gonçalves Dias (Esboço biográfico), Rio de Janeiro: Irmãos Pongetti, 1952
Itinerário de Passárgada, Rio de Janeiro: Livraria São José, 1954
De poetas e de poesia, Rio de Janeiro: Ministerio da Educação e Cultura, 1954
Versificação em língua portuguesa, Rio de Janeiro: Delta, 1956
Flauta de papel, Rio de Janeiro: Edições de Arte, 1957
Andorinha, Andorinha, Rio de Janeiro: José Olympio, 1966

Os reis vagabundos e mais 50 crônicas, Rio de Janeiro: Editora do
Autor, 1966
Colóquio unilateralmente sentimental, Rio de Janeiro: Record,
1968

Compilations and Anthologies
Poesia e prosa, Rio de Janeiro: Aguilar, 1958
Estrela da vida inteira: poesias reunidas, Rio de Janeiro: José
Olympio, 1965
Meus poemas preferidos, Rio de Janeiro: Edições de Ouro,
1966
Poesia completa e prosa, Rio de Janeiro: Aguilar, 1967

Anthologies in Translation
Recife, translated by Eddie Flintoff, Bradford, England: Rivelin
Grapheme Press, 1984

This Earth, That Sky: Poems by Manuel Bandeira, translated by
Candace Slater, Berkeley: University of California Press, 1988

Further Reading
Arriquicci, Jr, David, *Humildade, paixão e morte. A poesia de
Manuel Bandeira*, Rio de Janeiro: José Olympio, 1990
Athayde, Tristão de, *Manuel Bandeira: poesia*, Rio de Janeiro:
Livraria Agir Editora, 1970
Homenagen a Manuel Bandeira, Rio de Janeiro: Tipografia do
Jornal do Comércio, 1936
Jozef, Bella, "Manuel Bandeira," in *Poetas do Modernismo 2*, edited
by Leodegário A. Azevedo Filho, Rio de Janeiro: Ministério da
Educação e Cultura, Instituto Nacional do Livro, 1972
Pontiero, Giovanni, *Manuel Bandeira: visão geral de sua obra*, Rio
de Janeiro: José Olympio, 1986
Rosenbaum, Yudith, *Manuel Bandeira: uma poesia da ausência*, São
Paulo: Imago, 1993

Miguel Barnet 1940–

Cuban ethnographer, poet and prose writer

Ethnographer and poet Miguel Barnet also became known as
a prose writer after the appearance of his first two novels:
Biografía de un cimarrón (*The Autobiography of a Runaway
Slave*) in 1966, followed by *Canción de Rachel* (*Rachel's Song*)
in 1969. These narratives placed Barnet's literature at the forefront of testimonial writing in Latin America, a literary tradition that had its roots in the chronicles of the conquest. In
particular, Columbus's and Bartolomé de Las Casas's writings
offered the earliest commentary on the newly "discovered"
continent. Although of great epistemological value to this
period of history, these accounts contributed greatly to the
mythification of America because they were marked by authorial distortion and exaggeration. From as early as these first
Spanish-language discourses, therefore, testimonial literature
revealed itself as a fictionalization of everyday life in the
Americas.

It is not coincidental that contemporary Latin American
testimonial narrative first reappeared in earnest around the
1960s in Cuba. Factors such as a tradition of historical writing,
and the emphasis that the Cuban Revolution of 1959 placed
in the functional nature of literature contributed to the resurgence of the genre. Toward the end of the next decade, in
contrast to earlier testimonials, these narratives no longer
focused on the heroes of important historical events but on
the everyday person. It is within this testimonial tradition,
whose intention is the vindication of marginal human beings,
voices without history, that we must place the work of Miguel
Barnet.

Barnet has spoken at length in *La fuente viva*, 1983 [The
Living Source] about the relationship testimonial narrative
establishes between the *producer* of the text (author) and the
narrator or historical witness, who is presented to the reader

as the *real author*. The symbiosis reflects the ambivalence
between reality and fiction, or more specifically in the testimonial novel, between historical memory and fiction. The
question that comes back time and again regarding Barnet's
testimonial novel is whether the testimony of a witness trying
to recall an event quite removed from the present time could
be considered "factual." If memory is not only subjected to
the distortions of time but also corrupted by the perceptions
the present effects upon the past, in what way, if any, is the
contemporary testimonial novel more accurate in its portrayal
of life than the colonial literary tradition that preceded it? In
Biografía the narrative voice belongs to Esteban Montejo, a
runaway slave Barnet had interviewed in preparation for the
book. Much has been written regarding Montejo's assumed
authorial role as opposed to Barnet's so-called "editorializing"
of the memoirs (this reached an absurd extreme when the book
actually appeared in English under Montejo's name as author).
As Roberto González Echevarría aptly puts it, the relationship
between Montejo and Barnet is no more or no less complex
than that of any author in relation to his character. While the
reader may be asked to believe that the "real" voice in the
memoirs is that of the old slave (or the synthesis of voices that
make up the voices of Rachel) there can be little doubt that
there is another voice in the text besides Montejo's.

Biografía and *Canción de Rachel* were followed by two other
novels also within the testimonial tradition: *Gallego*, 1981
[Man from Galicia], a novel which examines, through the experiences of Manuel Ruiz, the painful immigration of many
northern Spaniards to Cuba in the early part of the 20th
century, and their difficult adaptation to their adoptive land;
and *La vida real*, 1986 [Real Life], whose main character Julián
Mesa, recalls with nostalgia his childhood in a poor and rural

sugar-mill town, his subsequent escape to Havana, and then his final emigration to the United States, in the 1950s, in the hope of a better life. Aside from a unity of authorial intention and of structure (all the novels are supposedly based on interviews by the author and/or research on the period), there is also a nostalgia for the past which serves to give coherence to the narrative voices.

In *La vida real*, Barnet tried to "fill in the gaps of Cuban historiography," by recording the memories of a Cuban exile living in New York City. By choosing as his narrator and "author" a poor hillbilly from the provinces, a mulatto as well as a political sympathizer of the Cuban Revolution, Barnet once again chose to portray the liminal voice of the underdog, otherwise ignored by official, historical accounts. As narrator and "creator" of the story, Julián Mesa recalls his childhood and youth in Cuba, a country that treated him as an exile already, as a marginal being. During the time of Julián's actual physical exile in the United States, although his narrative voice is still predominant, Barnet's authorial voice overtakes the narrative's intention. By making certain dialogical associations between this text and the literature of Cuban exile of the past (and by extension of the present), Barnet manipulates the narrative in order to convey the notion that Cuban identity is to be found inside as well as outside its borders. There comes a point in the narrative, in which Julián's testimony of *real life* and Barnet's *fictionalization* of it (linguistically and thematically) are fused, rendering the difference and distance between *author* and *producer* practically meaningless. What remains, however, is the question of *reality*. Indeed, in the end, it falls on the reader to determine to what extent is the narrator *real*, and where if at all the lines of demarcation between life and fiction are actually to be found.

Barnet may have closed this cycle of historical novels with his most recent *Oficio de ángel*, 1989 [An Angel's Craft]. Of a markedly different style from the others, *Oficio* explores the adolescence of a young man in Havana just prior to the Revolution of 1959. Unlike the testimonial novels, the narrator in *Oficio* is not a marginal being, nor is he presented to the reader as a subject of study. Notably absent from this narrative is the customary "foreword" by the author-interviewer as well as the confidential and conversational tone adopted by the narrators of the previous novels.

ANA GARCÍA CHICHESTER

See also entry on Testimonial Writing

Biography

Born in Havana, Cuba, 28 January 1940, into a middle-class family. Educated at US schools in Havana. Student at School of Advertising at the start of the Cuban Revolution. Enrolled in seminar on ethnology in 1960 and, in 1961, began working as professor of folklore at the School of Art Instructors; continued there until 1966. Gained research experience at Institute of Ethnology and Folklore of Academy of Science where Fernando Ortiz (see separate entry) worked at that time. Latter's interdisciplinary approach helped to nourish Barnet's testimonial narrative. Barnet worked also at the Editorial Nacional, run in the early 1960s by Alejo Carpentier. He was a member at this time of the "El Puente" (The Bridge) group of poets, who took their name from a private publishing house of the same name which operated between 1960 and 1965.

They published his second volume, *Isla de güijes* [Goblin Island]. But El Puente, another of whose leading members was Nancy Morejón, fell foul of the cultural police because it was thought that this group gave more importance to aesthetic than to ideological matters. As from 1968 life grew harsher for a "liberal" like Barnet, and he was silenced during the so-called "grey years" of the 1970s. But he, like others of his generation, began to thrive again as from the early 1980s, and was placed in charge of foreign affairs at the UNEAC (Union of Artists and Writers) in the mid-1980s when Lisandro Otero took over the presidency from Nicolás Guillén. Barnet also received a Guggenheim award to research his testimonial novel, *La vida real* [Real Life] and spent nine months in the US. Some of his works have been made into operas or films. Recipient of the Cuban Premio de la Crítica in 1984 and 1988; National Prize for Literature in 1994; holder of the Alejo Carpentier medal. Member of National Assembly.

Selected Works

Testimonial Writing and Novels

Biografía de un cimarrón, Havana: Instituto de Etnología y Folklore, 1966; as *The Autobiography of a Runaway Slave*, translated by Jocasta Innes, New York: Pantheon, 1968; critical edition with an introduction and bibliographical essay by Alistair Hennessy, London: Macmillan, 1993
Canción de Rachel, Havana: Instituto del Libro, 1969; as *Rachel's Song: a Novel*, translated by W. Nick Hill, Willimantic, Connnecticut: Curbstone Press, 1991
Gallego, Madrid: Alfaguara, 1981
La vida real, Havana: Letras Cubanas, 1986
Oficio de ángel, Havana: Letras Cubanas, 1989

Poetry

La piedra fina y el pavorreal, Havana: Unión, 1963
Isla de güijes, Havana: El Puente, 1964
La sagrada familia, Havana: Casa de las Américas, 1967
Orikis y otros poemas, Havana: Letras Cubanas, 1980
Carta de noche, Havana: Unión, 1982
Viendo mi vida pasar, Havana: Letras Cubanas, 1987 [anthology]

Other Writings

Akeké y la jutía, Havana: Unión, 1978 [Fables for children, belonging to popular tradition]
La fuente viva, Havana: Letras Cubanas, 1983 [essays on literature]
Claves por Rita Montaner, Matanzas: Cuba, 1987
Autógrafos cubanos, Havana: Unión, 1990 [Short pieces on contemporary Cuban writers and popular entertainers]

Further Reading

Fernández Guerra, Ángel Luis, "Edipo y Cayo Graco (Para leer a Miguel Barnet)," *Casa de las Américas* 30 (1990) [On Barnet's poetry, and its influence on his narrative production]
García Chichester, Ana, "La intención unificadora en *La vida real* de Miguel Barnet," in *Critical Essays in Honor of María A. Salgado*, Newark, New Jersey: Cuesta, 1994
González Echevarría, Roberto, *The Voice of the Masters: Writing and Authority in Modern Latin American Literature*, Austin: University of Texas Press, 1985 [chapter on *Biografía*]
Luis, William, *Literary Bondage: Slavery in Cuban Narrative*, Austin: University of Texas Press, 1990 [Contains an excellent discussion of *Biografía*]
Perus, Françoise, review article of *La vida real*, *Revista Casa de las Américas* 165 (1988)
Riccio, Alessandra, "Lo testimonial y la novela testimonio," *Revista Iberoamericana* 152–53 (July–December 1990)
Sklodowska, Elzbieta, "Miguel Barnet y la novela-testimonio," *Revista Iberoamericana* 152–53 (July–December 1990)

Afonso Henriques de Lima Barreto 1881–1922

Brazilian prose writer

It has become a commonplace to state that Lima Barreto was a marginalized figure in his own lifetime and forgotten thereafter, so that only in recent times has his importance been grudgingly recognized. Neither of these assertions is true, while the second in no way would have depended upon the first in any case. Lima Barreto's first published novel was *Recordações do escrivão Isaías Caminha*, 1909 [Memoirs of the Registrar Isaías Caminha]. The fact that Lima Barreto's name was already known in literary circles is borne out by the following anecdote. Earlier that same year, one of Brazil's most eminent literary critics, Gonzaga Duque, having heard rumours that the young civil servant and occasional journalist was preparing a novel for publication, wrote to him enquiring whether or not this novel was *Gonzaga de Sá. Vida e morte de M.J. Gonzaga de Sá*, 1919 [Life and Death of Gonzaga de Sá]. The latter work was not published for another ten years, but when it finally was, it obtained second place "with honourable mention" in a Brazilian Book of the Year contest and glowing reviews. With hindsight, the other principal assertion concerning Lima Barreto remains at least partially correct: that his importance lies in his contribution towards the forming of a bridge between the age of Machado de Assis, the age of classic Realism in Brazil, and that of the Brazilian Modernist Movement that burst upon an unsuspecting Brazilian public in 1922.

Lima Barreto undoubtedly occupies a preeminent position in the period that is customarily dubbed *pré-modernista* (pre-Modernist) – the *belle époque*, World War I, and its immediate aftermath. *Recordações* [Recollections] is certainly a revolt against the serene and polished language and style of Machado de Assis, whom Lima Barreto affected to disdain but secretly admired. Lima's Balzacian story of provincial lost illusions in the capital, with its mordant satire of the world of journalism and letters, is certainly a protest novel. In one sense, the book is a thinly veiled autobiography in its endeavour to treat the colour question in Brazil. The first-person narrator and protagonist is, like Lima, a young mulatto, failed student and apprentice journalist, who feels victimized and disdained by society because of his colour and lack of powerful friends; but this theme (the importance of which has been persistently overestimated by generations of critics) fades swiftly in the opening chapters after which Lima Barreto can give voice to his far more transcendent and profound preoccupation with the destiny of literature itself, the written word, as a force to move hearts and provoke awareness of the human condition in all its aspects. Rarely has the frightening power of the press to influence and manipulate the masses been more tellingly depicted in a work of prose fiction.

Vida e morte de M.J. Gonzaga de Sá, written coterminously with *Recordações*, presents the other face of the same drama. The young mulatto narrator, one Augusto Machado, sets out to write the biography of his friend and mentor, Gonzaga de Sá, an aristocratic white civil servant who traces his lineage back to the very founder of Rio de Janeiro, Estácio de Sá, commander of the Portuguese forces that drove the French

invaders from Guanabara Bay in 1557–59. The narrative begins with a description of Gonzaga's death on the hillside above Rio and then retraces the crucial meetings between the sceptical old man and his young disciple, to whom he communicates before he dies his contempt for the Republic that arrived by *coup-d'état* in 1889, and his love for old, colonial Rio that in the early years of the 20th century was being systematically destroyed before Lima Barreto's eyes. *Vida e morte* is a strange amalgam of revolutionary polemic and nostalgic regret for the passing of an era. The novel is the quintessence of Lima Barreto's complex and tragic vision of misery, poverty and death in a crumbling and alienating city.

To the themes of his first two works he adds treachery and man's inhumanity to man in his best-known novel, *Triste fim de Policarpo Quaresma*, 1915 (*The Patriot*). Set during the chaotic aftermath of the fall of the Brazilian Monarchy in 1889, it tells of the vain endeavours and shattered dreams of the naive patriot, Policarpo Quaresma, who loses his life in the civil war of 1891–95 when he protests to the dictator, Marshal Floriano, against the arbitrary execution of rebel prisoners. Again, intelligence and idealism are defeated by stupidity, egotism and greed. *Numa e a Ninfa*, 1915 [Numa and the Nymph], like *Triste fim*, a third-person narrative, transposes into a contemporary Brazilian setting Plutarch's famous story: the Brazilian Numa is the archetypal, faceless, and mediocre politician manipulated by the Nymph (his intelligent wife Edgarda), and by her lover. Superficially, the novel is just one more cruel satire of political corruption in the Brazilian *belle époque*, but on a deeper level it reminds us of Lima Barreto's overarching mission: a meditation on the destiny of the written word and human intelligence.

This meditation is sustained in his last years in the unfinished *Cemitério dos vivos* [The Cemetery of the Living], inspired by Dostoevsky's *House of the Dead*, and in the posthumous novella, *Clara dos Anjos*, 1948 [Clara of the Angels]. This last is the completion of a project that Lima Barreto had on the stocks as early as 1904: a story of the sexual exploitation of a mulatta girl by white Brazilian society. The completed narrative shows us again how Lima had evolved as a novelist and commentator by the year of his death. While he never lost his sense of persecution on account of the colour of his skin, he exhibited again and again his compassion for and understanding of the whole of Brazil. His two most arresting protagonists, Gonzaga de Sá and Policarpo Quaresma, are both white; and in *Clara dos Anjos*, the plight of the poor and the forgotten of whatever race, creed or colour in the slums of Rio, is illuminated with deep pathos and humanity.

Admirer of the great European Realists though he was, especially of Tolstoy and Dostoevsky, Lima Barreto, like Machado de Assis before him, was no slavish imitator. He broke with the poise and solemnity of the previous generation, and with his more corrosive irony and an acute ear for the language of the street, pointed the way towards the Brazilian Modernist and post-Modernist fiction, poetry, and theatre of the mid-20th century. Like Machado de Assis, whose mantle he inherited whether he knew it or not, he achieved an acute analysis of Brazilian social and political history and was able to transmute this awareness into a series of short and longer fiction that now can be seen to contain telling metaphors and metonymies of early 20th-century Brazil. The isolation of Gonzaga's house on the heights of Santa Teresa above the city of Rio de Janeiro and Quaresma's smallholding in which he tries and fails to create the rural paradise that he is convinced is Brazil's destiny, are metaphors that point us toward the disaster that Lima Barreto felt Brazilian republicanism had visited upon his countrymen. So is the library conserved by Fausto Carregal in memory of his father, a distinguished chemist, even though he finally admits to himself that neither he nor any of his family will ever read the erudite works it contains; and so, in a fit of despair, he douses the books with paraffin and sets them ablaze. In another short story, whose black humour and interpenetration of fantasy and reality anticipate magical realism, a mysterious alchemist convinces the entire population of a village that gold can be obtained from human bones. A gold fever of Californian intensity grips the villagers who proceed to sack the local cemetery, killing one another in their struggle to obtain the precious ingredients with which they hope to solve all their problems. "A Biblioteca" [The Library] and "A Nova Califórnia" (The New California) are two of the most moving stories that Lima Barreto wrote. His achievement in the short-story form is as uneven as in that of the novel; yet at his best he expresses as powerfully as any writer the New World has produced the tribulations and the problems of Latin America at the dawn of the 20th century.

R.J. OAKLEY

Biography
Born in Rio de Janeiro, Brazil, 1881. A mestizo of modest background, Lima Barreto spent his childhood on the Ilha do Governador, an island near his native Rio de Janeiro. Attended the prestigious Colégio Pedro II but was later unable to finish a course in engineering owing to lack of funds. Became a civil servant in Ministry of War. Looked after his father after latter lost his reason. Various pressures caused him to lead a dissipated life with the result that he died prematurely, in 1922.

Selected Works

Novels
Recordações do escrivão Isaías Caminha, Lisbon: n.p., 1909
Triste fim de Policarpo Quaresma, Rio de Janeiro: n.p., 1915; as The Patriot, translated by Robert Scott-Buccleuch, London: Collings, 1978
Numa e a Ninfa, Rio de Janeiro: Oficinas de A Noite, 1915
Vida e morte de M.J. Gonzaga de Sá, São Paulo: Revista do Brasil, 1919
Clara dos Anjos, Rio de Janeiro: Mérito, 1948

Short Fiction
Histórias e sonhos, Rio de Janeiro: Gianlorenzo Schettino, 1920

Journalism (crônicas)
Bagatelas, Rio de Janeiro: Empresa de Romances Populares, 1923
Feiras e mafuás, Rio de Janeiro: Mérito, 1953
Marginália, Rio de Janeiro: Mérito, 1953

Other Writings
Os Bruzundagas, Rio de Janeiro: n.p., 1922 [humour]
Diário íntimo, São Paulo: Mérito, 1953 [memoirs]
A correspondência entre Monteiro Lobato e Lima Barreto, edited by Edgard Cavalheiro, Rio de Janeiro: Ministério da Educação e Cultura, 1955
Impressões de leitura, São Paulo: n.p., 1956
Um longo sonho do futuro; diários, cartas, entrevistas e confissões dispersas, Rio de Janeiro: Graphia, 1993

Compilations and Anthologies
Obra completa de Lima Barreto, general editor, Francisco de Assis Barbosa, São Paulo: Editora Brasiliense, 1956; 2nd edition, 1959–61

Further Reading
Aiex, Anoar, As idéias socio-literárias de Lima Barreto, São Paulo: Vertice, 1990
Barbosa, Francisco de Assis, Aldebara ou A vida de Lima Barreto (1881–1922), Rio de Janeiro: José Olympio, 1952
Coutinho, Carlos Nelson, "O significado de Lima Barreto na literatura brasileira," in Realismo e anti-realismo na literatura brasileira, Rio de Janeiro: Paz e Terra, 1974
Fantinati, Carlos Erivany, O profeta e o escrivão: estudo sobre Lima Barreto, Assis-São Paulo: ILPHA-HUCITEC, 1978
Kinnear, J.C., "The 'Sad End' of Lima Barreto's Policarpo Quaresma," Bulletin of Hispanic Studies, vol. 51 (1974)
Lins, Osman, Lima Barreto e o espaço romanesco, São Paulo: Ática, 1976
Marquês dos Santos, Afonso Carlos (editor), O Rio de Janeiro de Lima Barreto, Rio de Janeiro: Rioarte, 1983
Oakley, R.J., "Vida e morte de M.J. Gonzaga de Sá: a Carlyleian View of Brazilian History," Bulletin of Hispanic Studies, vol. 63 (1986)
Prado, Antonio Arnoni, Lima Barreto: o crítico e a crise, São Paulo: "Leituras" Martins Fontes, 2nd edition, 1989
Santiago, Silviano, "Uma ferroada no peito de pé: dupla leitura de Triste fim de Policarpo Quaresma," Revista Iberoamericana, vol. 50 (1984)
Sevcenko, Nicolau, Literatura como missão: tensões sociais e criação cultural na Primeira República, São Paulo: Editora Brasiliense, 1983

Bibliographies
Nunes, Maria Luisa (editor), Lima Barreto, Bibliography and Translations, Boston: G.K. Hall, 1979 [bibliographic information is scant]

Rafael Barrett 1876–1910

Paraguayan journalist

It is in fact problematical to define Rafael Barrett's nationality, since he was born in Spain and wrote for audiences in a number of South American and European countries. No nation, however, has more claim to Barrett's work than Paraguay, of which he wrote in *El dolor paraguayo* [Paraguay's Pain]: "I do not feel the terror. I will speak. Nor should you lament that it is a foreigner who says these things. I am no foreigner . . . Truth and justice are not foreign in any corner of the world ('Bajo el terror,' [Under Terror])." Though he resided in Paraguay for only five years, it was there that Barrett's notions of social and economic justice took definitive shape as word and deed. It was there that *El dolor paraguayo* and *Lo que son los yerbales* [What the *Mate* Estates Are] flowed from his pen even as his activism on behalf of workers led to repeated episodes with the authorities.

To say this is not to diminish Barrett's work elsewhere. Indeed, his clashes with the Paraguayan government led ironically to deeper involvements outside the country: he was deported for several months to Uruguay, where he found new readers for his stunning blend of passion and erudition. Wherever he went, in or out of Paraguay, Barrett showered the public with a remarkably diverse literary output. International affairs, the arts, religion, education, mathematics, science, the environment: all were subjects about which he wrote with eloquence and authority. Though his favorite genre was the short editorial essay, he also produced short stories, philosophical dialogues, lectures, and fantasies.

Beset by financial difficulties and terminally ill with tuberculosis – he died tragically in his mid-thirties – Barrett wrote with the conceptual consistency of one who has had little time to contradict himself. Indeed, it may be said that his poor health and hard times imposed on him an intellectual coherence rare in persons of such varied interests. Said he of his illness, "I have loved the unfortunate ever since I became one of them" ("La última primavera" [Final Springtime] in *Cuentos breves* [Brief Stories]). The philosophical basis of Barrett's writing was the late 19th-century anarchism of the likes of Tolstoy and Anatole France, an intellectual anarchism which eschewed dynamite for the pen and sought to dismantle repressive structures through the free and egalitarian exchange of ideas. From this single concept flowed the vast and eddied stream of Barrett's inquisitiveness, and the totality of his scorn for governmental, economic and religious authorities. Barrett disdained politics, including the democratic kind, and dreamt of a society in which the organizing institution was not government but the family. He thundered against the abuse of women and children, and his pleas for "family values" were a rare point of contact between him and his right-wing contemporaries. His notion of family differed sharply from theirs, however, in that he was, by the standards of his day, a feminist. In "El problema sexual" [The Sexual Problem], a speech to a group of Paraguayan workers, presumably all men, he called for the treatment of women as equal partners, for "where women are not respected and not loved, there can be no country, no liberty, no vigor, no movement."

Implicit throughout Barrett's work is the notion that values, not laws, are what creates good or evil in a society. The *yerba mate* workers, he wrote, would suffer even without the legal underpinning of oppression in Paraguay, because their bosses carried evil in their hearts (*Lo que son los yerbales*). Education is a farce where it fails to teach the love of justice ("Instrucción primaria" [Primary Education] in *El dolor paraguayo*), and Catholicism is a venal travesty of pristine Christian teaching ("El materialismo católico" [Catholic Materialism] in *Mirando vivir* [Watching Life]). Christ was something of an anarchist whose values are absent from the ecclesiastical shell that bears his name (*El terror argentino* [Argentine Terror]). Genuine wealth, which is to say well-being, arises not from money or property, but from a value system, a belief in fairness, in freedom, in work, in service, and in the imagination.

Barrett's loyalty to this set of ideas was nearly complete, but the instances where he does depart from it are worth mentioning. One notes, for example, a certain ambivalence in the matter of race. Barrett denounced lynchings in the United States ("Lynch" in *Moralidades actuales* [Current Moralities]) and cheered for black boxer Jack Johnson, yet we wonder what he means when he says that Johnson showed the possibility of black dominance over whites "in certain circumstances" ("Johnson" in *Mirando vivir*). Likewise the paucity of indigenous subjects in his writing about Paraguay seems curious in a country where Guarani is the majority language and monolingual Spanish speakers are a tiny minority. Not unrelated to this cultural "blind spot" is Barrett's problematical attitude toward nature. At times his anarchist's dream of unfettered human creativity seems at odds with his laments against environmental destruction, and he fails to articulate a meaningful ecological difference between anarchistic innovation and capitalistic "progress."

It is, of course, a mistake to measure Barrett solely by the standards of a later time. Surely, by the yardstick of his own day he was an enlightened voice in these and many other matters. Whatever his inconsistencies on the subject of race, for instance, few of his contemporaries in journalism would have said as he did in "Johnson," "Black, white? . . . What does it matter? It's all an illusion of hatred." Barrett's renown as a purveyor of ideas, however, owes as much to his dazzling prose as to the ideas themselves. He imbibed the major writing styles of his day without sacrificing his own independence as a crafter of language. His short stories bear elements of Spanish American *Modernismo*, yet fall somehow outside the orbit of this movement. And his expository prose – the vast majority of his output – never overdoes its debt to French Naturalists and American muckrakers. Barrett was an original whose vast lexicon and rhetorical repertoire astound readers even today. Though his prose swings between ironic detachment and lofty accusation, it is probably in the latter vein that he is best remembered. "I have seen," wrote Barrett in *El dolor paraguayo*, "que los peones 'robustos' no pasan dos semanas sin . . . diarrea o . . . fiebre. Pobre carne, herida hasta en el sexo, pobre carne morena y marchita . . . He visto los . . . pies de las madres, pies agrietados y . . . heroicos, buscar el sustento a lo largo de las sendas del cansancio . . . Y he visto a los niños . . . arrugados, que no ríen ni lloran, las larvas del silencio." ("robust" peasants who cannot go two weeks without . . . diarrhoea or fever. Poor flesh, wounded even in its genitals, poor dark desiccated flesh . . . I have seen the cracked . . . heroic feet of mothers seeking food along paths of exhaustion . . . And I have seen . . . shriveled children who neither cry nor laugh, larvae of silence) ("Lo que he visto" [What I Have Seen]). Lush with parallelisms, potent adjectives, haunting metaphors and many other devices, Barrett's style has had the variety and vigor to withstand the unpredictable evolution of 20th-century tastes. More than a journalist, Barrett was a prophet who understood the power of language to project thought through time and whose articulation of the world's ills remains contemporary today. Whether or not they agree with his prescriptions, generations of readers after Rafael Barrett's death are sure to find his concerns uncannily like their own.

TRACY K. LEWIS

Biography
Born in Torrelavega, near Santander, Spain, in 1876, the son of an English father and a Spanish mother. Studied mathematics, as well as humanities, in France and Spain. Left Europe for Buenos Aires, 1903, worked as a journalist. Moved to Asunción (the capital of Paraguay) in 1904, where he worked for government engineering agency till 1906, and gave science classes at the Instituto Paraguayo. Journalist with *Los Sucesos* and *La Tarde*, 1905. Married a Paraguayan, Francisca López Maiz, April 1906. Worked, briefly, for British railways in Paraguay. Left this due to battle with tuberculosis. Wrote for *El País*, 1908. Founded short-lived opposition weekly *El Germinal*, 1908. Lectured to workers' groups, 1908, arrested and deported to Brazil and Uruguay. Returned to Paraguay early 1909, wrote for *El Nacional*. Wrote for *La Razón* in Uruguay and other newspapers of the region, 1909–10. Very ill, left Paraguay in September 1910. Died of tuberculosis in France, 17 December 1910.

Selected Works

Journalism and Essays
El dolor paraguayo, Buenos Aires: "La Protesta," 1909
Lo que son los yerbales, Montevideo: Talleres Gráficos "El Arte," 1910
Moralidades actuales, Montevideo: O.M. Bertani, 1910
Mirando vivir, Montevideo: O.M. Bertani, 1912
Al margen: críticas literarias y científicas, Montevideo: O.M. Bertani, 1912
Artículos diversos, San José, Costa Rica: Alsina, 1913
Ideas y críticas, Montevideo: O.M. Bertani, 1915
El terror argentino, Buenos Aires: Proyección, 1971

Compilations and Anthologies
Cuentos breves, Montevideo: O.M. Bertani, 1910
Diálogos, conversaciones y otros escritos, Montevideo: C. García, 1918
Cartas inocentes, Obras completas, Buenos Aires: Américalee, 1954
Conferencias, Obras completas, Buenos Aires: Américalee, 1954
Obras completas, Buenos Aires: Américalee, 1954 [Includes short story "El proprietario (cuento inocente)"]

Cartas íntimas, edited by Francisca López Maiz de Barrett, Montevideo: Biblioteca Artigas, 1967
Obras completas, Montevideo: Ediciones Populares para América Latina, 1988

Further Reading
Díaz-Pérez, Viriato, "Rafael Barrett, el periodista genial," in his *Ensayos II: notas, una conferencia sobre Rafael Barrett*, Palma de Mallorca, Spain: Luis Ripoll, 1988
Forteza, J.R., *Rafael Barrett: su obra, su prédica, su moral*, Buenos Aires: Editorial Atlas, 1927
Maeztu, Ramiro de and Emilio Frugoni, *Lo que son los yerbales paraguayos: semblanzas de Barrett*, Montevideo: C. García, 1926
Marcos, Juan Manuel, "Un perfil sumergido del discurso barrettiano," *Río de la Plata: Culturas*, Creteil, France, 3 (1986)
Massuh, Víctor, *En torno a Rafael Barrett*, Tucumán, Argentina: Editorial La Raza, 1943
Mendonça de Spinzi, Lucy, "Rafael Barrett," in *Primer simposio internacional de estudios latinoamericanos*, Asunción: IDIAL, 1989
Meneses, Carlos, "Barrett: personaje quijotesco," *Cuadernos Hispanoamericanos*, Madrid, 462 (December 1988)
Muñoz, Vladimiro, "Cartas a Peyrot," *Hispamérica*, vol. 11/32 (August 1982)
Roa Bastos, Augusto, *Rafael Barrett y la realidad paraguaya a comienzos del siglo*, Stockholm: Instituto de Estudios Latinoamericanos de Estocolmo, 1981
Silva, Lincoln, "Los caminos de Arenguay," *Plural*, Mexico City, vol. 12/1 (133) (October 1982)

Lo que son los yerbales

Essay by Rafael Barrett

Though it is difficult to define Rafael Barrett's literary career in terms of nationality, style and content, no such problem exists with respect to the powerful essay *Lo que son los yerbales*, Barrett's unambiguous blast against worker exploitation in the production of *yerba mate* tea. Despite Barrett's European upbringing and international literary production, Paraguayan intellectuals rightly regard *Lo que son los yerbales* as part of their own national literary heritage.

First published in June, 1908 as a series of articles for the Paraguayan newspaper *El Diario*, *Lo que son los yerbales* is considered by some to be one of Barrett's crowning achievements. Certainly it has become a classic of Latin American editorial journalism. If the ideal of the genre is to render an accurate account of a specific, remediable circumstance, thereby stimulating public discourse, then Barrett's essay must be judged a resounding success.

Barrett's effort emerged indirectly from his admiration for the muckraking fiction of Zola and other naturalistic writers, as well as from his sympathy for anarchist movements on both sides of the Atlantic and his hatred for imperialist economics. Undoubtedly he saw the *yerba mate* industry as part of a global pattern. He was wise, however, to leave this theoretical framework unstated in *Lo que son los yerbales* and to concentrate instead on the concrete situation unfolding in the Alto Paraná region. In the decades prior to the article's publication, powerful interests in Argentina, Brazil and Paraguay had consolidated their hold on *yerba mate* production in a large area of the upper Paraná basin, employing great numbers of Paraguayan *campesinos* in a condition of virtual slavery. *Lo que son los yerbales* details the deceptions employed in recruiting workers, the physical and economic methods of perpetuating their bondage, and the appalling conditions under which they labored. Here in the classic tradition of crusading journalism one reads of governmental collusion with the *mate* industry, of the cruel fraud of the *anticipo* tendered new workers "up front" to begin the process of indebtedness, of negligible wages and exorbitant prices at company stores to continue that process, of malnutrition and sleeping in the proximity of snakes, of beatings for failure to meet the day's harvest quota, of the hopelessness of escape through miles of forest, of eventual death in the service of the company.

The degree of Barrett's first-hand experience with the *yerba mate* industry is a matter of debate. Certainly, however, he was a well-known figure among the workers of other industries, and his participation in the labor unrest of June and July 1908 coincides with the publication of *Lo que son los yerbales*. Few would accuse this author of dilettantism, and fewer still have questioned the overall factual accuracy of his charges. At the interpretive level, of course, there is much more room for argument. One may wonder, for instance, at the wisdom of Barrett's rhetoric against the forest itself, as if the snakes and vines were deliberate accomplices in the crimes he describes. And one may question his apparent optimism that his article would help provoke a solution to the problem: "Yo acuso de . . . homicidas a los administradores de la Industrial Paraguaya y de las demás empresas yerbales. Yo maldigo su dinero manchado en sangre, y yo les anuncio que no deshonrarán mucho tiempo más este desgraciado país." (I denounce as . . . murderers the management of Industrial Paraguaya and the other *yerba* companies. I curse their money stained in blood. And I warn them that they shall not dishonor this wretched nation very much longer).

Lo que son los yerbales is a work of journalism, and it naturally sparks debate on these and other matters of "content."

One should not forget, however, that it is also a piece of literary art, as remarkable for its style as for its ideas. Indeed, without his singular expressiveness, it is doubtful that Barrett's article would enjoy the reputation that it does. *Lo que son los yerbales* is a masterpiece of the propagandist's art: sheer passion given the flesh of language. The detached, ironic voice of some of Barrett's other writings is here discarded in favor of undisguised anger. Irony becomes sharp sarcasm and open accusation, replete with all the devices of the skilled polemicist: rhetorical questions ("Oh flesh shaken by lash . . . and jackboot . . . dark, somber flesh, what is there within you?"), parallelisms ("I denounce . . . I curse . . . I warn . . . ."), surprising adjective-noun pairs ("opulent scum"), and unusual metaphors ("Paraguay has always been the great provisioner of flesh that sweats gold"). These and many other mechanisms are the stuff of Barrett's eloquence, and a substantial reason why we remember him today.

Directly or indirectly, *Lo que son los yerbales* has had an undeniable impact on subsequent literature. Much, for example, of Augusto Roa Bastos's *Hijo de hombre* (*Son of Man*) reads like a fictionalization of Barrett's article, and one can only speculate on the degree to which Roa Bastos conceived his novel on the basis of the earlier piece. Likewise we may wonder at Barrett's influence on José Eustasio Rivera's *La vorágine* (*The Vortex*) and other fictional outcries against worker exploitation in the South American interior. Whether or not Roa Bastos and others had Barrett consciously in mind, there is no doubt that the author of *Lo que son los yerbales* helped create the atmosphere of protest in which they produced their work.

TRACY K. LEWIS

See also entries on José Eustasio Rivera, Augusto Roa Bastos

Note: See the main entry on Rafael Barret (above) for items of Further Reading.

Eduardo Barrios 1884–1963

Chilean prose writer and dramatist

During the last few years of his life, which coincided with the birth of the Boom novel in Latin America, and certainly in the post-Boom criticism of today, little attention has been paid to the works of so-called traditional novelists like Eduardo Barrios and Manuel Gálvez who in their time commanded the front pages of literary periodicals. Barrios, a prize-winning novelist in Chile, was something of an exception, in a sense, throughout the first half of the 20th century. While everyone around him was composing regional novels of the land, indigenous works of social protest, and historical works of revolutionary themes and motives, Barrios was producing novels written in the mould of what might be termed European philosophical fiction, following in the footsteps of his Romantic/Realist masters like Balzac, Flaubert, Galdós, even at times the naturalistic Zola – with the pessimistic ideas of Schopenhauer and Nietzsche also playing a part. Barrios, however, was never to forget the lessons about art which he learned from his *modernista* mentors.

As a product of his age, Barrios early gained a deserved reputation as a psychological novelist, for the penetrating studies of the human mind which characterised the work of his first trilogy, *El niño que enloqueció de amor*, 1915 [The Boy Who Went Mad with Love], *Un perdido*, 1918 [A Lost Soul] and *El hermano asno*, 1922 (*Brother Asno*). This important aspect of Barrios's work has been well documented by scholars like Ned Davison and Vázquez-Bigi in the 1950s and 1960s. There is no doubt that Barrios was a shrewd analytical writer (in the school of Stendhal and Paul Bourget) who dissected the mysteries of the soul of the abnormal types who people his novels, as their titles indicate – *locos, feos, perdidos, pobres diablos* and the like. Clearly, though, literature is based on more than defective genes, the class struggle, and the law of evolution. Important as these psychological elements may be in Barrios's work, like the few creole and social components also visible in his fiction, they do not constitute the most important level of his novels. In fact, they serve only as a pretext, as a background, for Barrios's main concern, which is metaphysical, i.e., the human condition.

It is not a coincidence that the aforementioned Gálvez, a kindred spirit, should capture the essence of Barrios's work in the prologue to *Un perdido*: "Yo creo que lo esencial en un novelista es su visión de la vida" (I think that the essential thing in a novelist is his view of life). In other words, beneath the surface of the apparent themes of Barrios – sexual repression (*El hermano asno*), excessive sentimentalism (*Un perdido*), childish abnormality and madness (*El niño que enloqueció de amor*), one finds a concern which transcends regional frontiers and chronological barriers. These texts reveal Barrios's view of life and his changing perspective towards the metaphysical problems which manifest themselves in all his novels, from the first trilogy to the later works.

Although *Del natural*, 1907 [Drawn from Nature], his first published work, is poorly written, it is important because it contains in the story "Tirana Ley" [The Tyrannical Law] the seeds of his future works: the role of emotion and its function in the never-ending struggle between the heart and the brain; plus a *modernista* concern for art, and the metaphysical role of art in the struggle for life. In addition, one should mention the characterisation of his protagonist and his (Spanish) "Generation of 98" affinities with the *abúlico/fuerte* (weak/strong) contrast, the essence of Barrios's future novels and the key to his metaphysical view of life. But *Del natural* was only a beautiful promise, and his mature work really begins with *El niño que enloqueció del amor*, which takes up the tone and the atmosphere of "Tirana ley," that is, the tyrannical law of love. Rooted in the Romantic theme of love leading to madness, this short novel is a tragic study of a sensitive child whose weakness and sentimentality are not alleviated by Art. Like the protagonist of "Tirana ley." The basic theme and the constant in all of Barrios's work is the importance of emotion, especially as a motivating force which can, however, lead to tragedy: "La emoción es la esencia virtual de las cosas." (Emotion is the virtual essence of things). "La emoción es el alma." (Emotion is the soul). With penetrating analysis and linguistic skill, Barrios in *El niño . . .* produced a small masterpiece. But these are only techniques, and, as Sartre states, fictional techniques refer back to the writer's metaphysics. It is the critics' task to define the latter before evaluating the former. There is no doubt that Barrios in *El niño . . .* is already beginning to formulate a tragic view of life which was intensified in *Un perdido*, written very much in the Naturalist mode.

The protagonist, Luis Bernales, is a much more developed portrait of the type created in *El niño . . .*, a timid, sentimental boy tied to his mother's apron-strings. With the death of beloved family members, his experiences in a military college confirm the deterministic doctrines of his friend Blanco. Faced with the harshness of life, he takes refuge in the arms of prostitutes, in drugs and alcohol, and in a world of dreams and illusions. Without the complementary qualities of energy, action and will-power, and without the support of either religion or art, he follows the path of *el niño*, convinced of the absurdity and hostility of life. Barrios's message, under the strong influence of Naturalism, is that life is tragic, especially for poor lost souls like Luis who follow their instincts in their search for emotional fulfilment. If *Un perdido* is less satisfactory aesthetically, it is more by excess than by default, since Barrios seems intent on hammering home the pessimistic view of life, seen in the works of Schopenhauer, Luis's favourite reading.

With the publication of *El hermano asno*, Barrios reached the peak of his first period, both from the psychological and aesthetic points of view. Artistically superior to the earlier works, *El hermano asno* is linked to them metaphysically, since emotion torments both protagonists, Fray Lázaro and Fray Rufino. With shrewd analysis and skilful development of the character of both monks, Barrios achieves a subtle and ironic reversal of their roles. Nevertheless, *El hermano asno* is still a tragedy in that the three main characters are indelibly marked, injustice seems to prevail, while an indifferent God looks on.

El hermano asno confirms the constant theory of Barrios that emotion without discipline leads to tragedy, and that religion *can* be a valuable formative force in life. Although *Un perdido* was aesthetically unsatisfactory, if philosophically powerful, there is no doubt that *El hermano asno* was Barrios's literary masterpiece. Always the conscious artist in a search (characteristic of his time) for a simple, transparent, diaphanous, musical style – "I would like to write without words," he once stated – Barrios was to achieve that ideal *completely* only once in his literary career, in *El hermano asno*. In the autobiographical essay "También algo de mí," 1923 [Also Something of Me], he sought to articulate his concerns on the theory of art and his work, as well as the religious role of art which can help to give meaning to life. In *El hermano asno*, Barrios was to produce that perfect fusion of content and form, that unique correspondence of effect and vehicle, which he was never able to emulate again completely, although some of the later novels achieve a high standard in parts. Yet he was never able again to match the sustained beauty, spirituality, and poetic simplicity of style which characterises *El hermano asno*.

After a quiet period of twenty years, devoted to politics, journalism and agricultural pursuits, Barrios broke his silence with the publication of *Tamarugal*, 1944 [Tamarugo Grove], an inferior novel of Chilean mining life. As always, the main theme is the role of emotion in the life of the three main characters. But now with two decades of experience and maturity, Barrios appears to be formulating a new philosophy of life, more balanced, less pessimistic, and less conducive to tragedy. Still searching for the elusive complementary qualities of strength, energy, and will-power to counterbalance the still desirable tenderness and religious sentiment, Barrios reveals a compromise through the composite portraits of his three main characters, who incarnate all the human qualities necessary for *one* whole fictional creation.

Four years later *Gran señor y rajadiablos* [Great Lord and Hell-raiser] appeared, at first glance a *criollista* novel, but more linked to the first trilogy than it appears, since it represents a further shift in sensiblity on the part of Barrios. The key to the novel lies in the figure of the hero, Valverde, who manages to embody a certain balance in his character, thus preserving two opposite attitudes in his make-up without contradicting his psychological authenticity. After the faltering steps of *Tamarugal*, Barrios succeeds in incorporating in the protagonist the complementary and disciplinary qualities which his previous sentimental heroes lacked. The balance suggested by the title becomes more explicit in the prologue where Valverde is portrayed as "duro y tierno, serio y tarambana, democrático y feudal, rajadiablos ... pero gran señor" (Hard and tender, serious and wild, democratic and feudal, a hell-raiser ... but a great Lord).

Two years after the publication of this apparently anachronistic and atypical novel of the land, Barrios takes up the theme again in *Los hombres del hombre*, 1950 [The Man within Man], a more analytical and psychological novel (in the spirit of the first trilogy), which underscores and completes the change in attitude and the metaphysical point of view expressed in *Gran señor* ... By means of the two main characters, who are kindred spirits: an anguished, analytical father and a sensitive, artistic son, Barrios points to the link with the first trilogy and the evolution of his fictional creations in the second trilogy. The son, Charlie, makes the connection with Valverde and the early *perdidos*. Although sentimental and imaginative, Charlie is psychologically stable in the face of life's problems. With the spiritual support of his father, and his capacity for self-evaluation, his imagination and sensibility are counterbalanced by his energy, action and will-power. Emotion, as always, is the key: "Sigue al instinto ... yo me guío por mi ternura ... vivimos de nuestras emociones ..." (Follow your instincts ... I am guided by my heart ... we live by our emotions), but not without discipline. In his last novel, as in his first, Barrios does not abandon his belief in the role of emotion, nor his tragic view of life, but he does provide possible means of combating the hostility of the world, and so prevents the realisation of the tragic potential inherent in the character of his sensitive protagonists.

Although the driving force behind Barrios's view of life was essentially Romantic, he never forgot the lessons of his *modernista* masters. Of course, *Los hombres del hombre* cannot match the overall artistic beauty of *El hermano asno*, but its poetic and sensorial prose captures the mood and tone of its refined protagonists. Here at the end of his creative career Barrios was looking for a way of making existence tolerable. This view of life becomes progressively clearer as one studies the novels from beginning to end. As a whole, they constitute a true expression of Barrios's philosophy and present his metaphysical perspective, in aesthetic terms – no mean achievement for the underrated Chilean master.

JOHN WALKER

Biography

Born in Valparaíso, Chile, 25 October 1884; only child. After father's death in 1889, mother returned to Lima where Barrios was brought up in the home of his maternal grandparents. Mother and son returned to Santiago de Chile in 1899, and in 1900 he entered the city's military academy. Discharged from academy in 1902, and abandoned the idea of a military career. Attempted a rubber-gathering expedition in the eastern Andes, 1903, but this failed. Office job in nitrate company in northern Chile, 1904–08. Travelled to Buenos Aires, 1908, and subsequently to Rio de Janeiro and to Ecuador. On returning to Chile in 1909, obtained post as pro-Rector of the University of Santiago. Married Deifiria Passe; two children, Raúl and Roberto. Marriage later dissolved. First play, *Mercaderes en el templo* [Merchants in the Temple] staged, 1911. Worked as shorthand reporter in Chilean Congress, 1912. Began publishing in magazines *Pluma y Lápiz* [Pen and Pencil] and *La Mañana* [The Morning], 1912, and literary criticism for the weekly journal *Zig-Zag*, 1914. Married Carmen Rivadeneira in 1920; three children. Minister of Education, 1927–28. General Supervisor of Libraries, Archives and Museums, 1927–31. Resigned in 1931, bought country property and entered cattle business. Contributed regularly to two Santiago newspapers, *El Mercurio* [Mercury] and *Las Últimas Noticias* [The Latest News]. In 1953 he took up his earlier post as General Supervisor of Libraries, Archives and Museums. Became member of the Chilean Academy of the Language and was again appointed Minister of Education, 1953. Retired from active life in 1959. Awarded Chilean National Prize for Literature, 1946, and the Atenea Prize of the University of Concepción, 1949. Died on 13 September 1963.

Selected Works

Novels

El niño que enloqueció de amor, Santiago de Chile: n.p., 1915
Un perdido, Santiago de Chile: Editorial Chilena, 1918
El hermano asno, Santiago de Chile: Nascimento, 1922; as *Brother Asno*, translated by Edmundo García Girón, New York: Las Américas, 1969
Tamarugal, Santiago de Chile: Nascimento, 1944
Gran señor y rajadiablos, Buenos Aires: Espasa Calpe, 1948
Los hombres del hombre, Santiago de Chile: Nascimento, 1950

Short Fiction

Del natural, Iquique, Chile: n.p., 1907
Páginas de un pobre diablo, Santiago de Chile: Nascimento, 1923
Y la vida sigue, Buenos Aires: Tor, 1925

Compilations and Anthologies

Teatro escogido, Santiago de Chile: Zig-Zag, 1947
Obras completas, 2 vols, introduction by Milton Russel, Santiago de Chile: Zig-Zag, 1962

Further Reading

Barrios has not been well served by the critics over the last three decades and more. Apart from the sterling work of Ned J. Davison in the late 1950s and early 1960s, and Ángel Manuel Vázquez-Bigi in the 1960s (unpublished dissertation and several articles), both on the psychological values/truth in Barrios's work, there has been little else of value, aside from Joel Hancock's work (unpublished dissertation and a few articles) on *Los hombres del hombre* (compositional modes and sensorial prose).

Davison, Ned J., *Sobre Eduardo Barrios y otros: estudios y crónicas*, Albuquerque, New Mexico: Foreign Books, 1966
_____ *Eduardo Barrios*, New York: Twayne, 1970
Lozada, Alfredo, *Estudios críticos*, Buenos Aires: El Cid Editor, 1978 [Chapter on *El hermano asno*]
Martínez Dacosta, Silvia, *Dos ensayos literarios: sobre Eduardo Barrios y José Donoso*, Miami: Universal, 1976
_____ *Los personajes en la obra de Eduardo Barrios*, New York: Senda Nueva de Ediciones, 1988
Morínigo, Mariano, *Eduardo Barrios, novelista*, Tucumán: Universidad Nacional de Tucumán, 1971
Walker, John, *Metaphysics and Aesthetics in the Works of Eduardo Barrios*, London: Támesis, 1983

Carlos Germán Belli 1927–

Peruvian poet

Carlos Germán Belli is one of three or four candidates for Peru's leading contemporary poet, along with Alejandro Romualdo, Javier Sologuren and perhaps Antonio Cisneros. What has attracted most attention about Belli's work is his unique fusion of seeming disparate elements into a poetic style quite his own, which crosses space and time to connect the Spanish Golden Age (especially the Baroque) with the most contemporary and topical aspects of life in dreary Lima, itself portrayed as the polar opposite of the *locus amoenus* of pastoral poetry: *locus horribilis,* it has been called. The evolution of his body of work has moved from the more immediate and specific, often loosely autobiographical portrayal of dispossession and the unrelenting tedium of anonymous and under-rewarded labor, in which the "I" is also middle-class (at times even under-class) Everyman, to an increasingly mystical portrayal of love and art as possible vehicles of transcendence. With this thematic shift, his language has moved away from its typical uses of parody and satire to portray disenchantment and frustration, to a more lyrical and dense imagery, allusive no longer to today's Lima but to that longed-for time and place where, just possibly, the Absolute may finally be glimpsed. Belli's poetry, then, moves from the ironic to the open expression of faith: from hopeless despair of change ever coming to his country or his own life, to the recurrent assurance that liberation can indeed happen, even if it takes the miracle of divine intervention.

Belli is also notable for his creation of an extensive and highly characteristic series of images and symbols, at times personal in their origins (allusions to family members and jobs he has held, for example). Reading Belli without sufficient context in both his own poetry and the Hispanic literary and cultural tradition can render initially difficult this web of unique signifiers. Let us take first some of Belli's personal symbols: what or who, for example, are Alfonso-Anfriso, Fisco, or the "Cybernetic Goddess" (*Hada Cibernética*; the English rendering is the specific preference of the poet himself, to stress her supernatural nature)? Creations of the poet himself, unique to his work and decipherable only by the clues to be found in it. Fisco, as further reading uncovers, is the harsh and impersonal supervisor, a personification of the political, legal and economic system which keeps the anonymous worker under its thumb: all the forces and sources of oppression of daily life in a society still suffering from neocolonial and pseudo-feudal remnants. Alfonso – Belli's brother, born with severe physical handicaps, rendered most frequently as "Anfriso" – is one of several Bellian images of the person whose fate is fore-ordained to be far less than what life seems to promise. Similar to Alfonso-Anfriso are the one-armed, cross-eyed, or otherwise physically deformed characters, with all of whom Belli often identifies: their exterior disabilities reflect his own interior, more spiritual, ones. The Cybernetic Goddess, until the emergence of the Lady (Señora, or "Filis") who becomes its later incarnation, is the uplifting power of technology (the computer, quite specifically) to free this oppressed line-worker from menial and stultifying daily routine, meaningful to him only as a way to earn a living: and this, by the narrowest of margins. As over time the Cybernetic Goddess evolves into the Lady, such escape becomes increasingly divine in nature and more identified with Art (the Muse) and Love. While Belli is assuredly not a Marxist, Fisco can be read as confirmation of the enslavement of the middle class, as Marx perceived it: the Goddess/Lady/Muse, then, is a way out, not through social revolution but a revolution of the quality of life through liberation from the empty motions of every day.

Along with his own personal symbolic system, Belli also makes frequent use of the tropes typical of the Spanish Golden Age (Renaissance through Baroque, with a strong Italian influence). Some of these include many of his ways of representing the issue of conflict versus fulfilment (more on which later), such as the "sublunar" (the earthly and hence lowly, in contrast with the celestial); plants or animals seeking their Other (mate, support, destiny); the four directions, or material elements (earth, air, fire and water) and their three manifestations (animal, vegetable and mineral); symbols of class divisions: the *amos* and *dueños* [bosses or owners], who gluttonously devour mountains of fine delights ("bolos alimenticios") while the poetic speaker must beg for crumbs.

Belli, then, rather contrary to the general tendency in recent Spanish American literature to write in ways increasingly more accessible to non-academic readers (Rosario Castellanos, Nicanor Parra, Ernesto Cardenal), elaborates a language quite as challenging and complex as the system of sometimes-private symbols he uses, which are often rather obscure to the reader lacking a relatively solid grounding in the Hispanic (and even Italian) literary heritage. He is in large measure a "poet's poet": a term which should not be taken as disparagement, for the same may be said about many of the Hispanic world's greatest writers: Góngora, Quevedo, Calderón or Sor Juana Inés de la Cruz, during the Golden Age, or Carpentier, Cortázar and Borges more recently). This very tension between intellectual elitism and populism is another and striking characteristic of Belli's style (although in his more recent neo-mystical verse the populist aspect is played down). One notable instance of this daring con-fusion is "Menú," which suggests that the ingredients of a humble stew, once eaten, ask the enduring questions of philosophers: "de dónde vienen / por qué están allí / hacia dónde van" (from where do they come, why are they there / where will they go). Aside from the doubly scatological implications of the unstated answer, the poem pokes fun at Rubén Darío's famous poem of metaphysical frustration "Lo fatal."

Belli's verse is complex and rich: a literary tour through both the Golden Age and our own, be it of lead or leftovers. This complexity should be taken as part of what he offers his reader, just as Baroque art exalts the reader (or hearer or viewer) precisely through this quality. One issue may be seen as a useful clue in reading him, for it marks all his poetry, and under it are subsumed all his more specific tropes: conflict and fulfilment. Belli questions whether the divisions and fragmentations he finds everywhere and in all times must really be permanent; whether there cannot be some way to transcend them; whether we cannot, as individuals and as societies, become more than

we have thus far been. If we cannot, the world is ridiculous, perhaps a game the gods play to laugh at us but in which we must participate because there is no other. But if we can, perhaps we can finally find fulfillment and joy, in an elusive "Pedazo de Edén" [Piece of Eden]; and possibly "Los talleres del tiempo" [Time's Workshop] will at last produce, as Belli has in his poetry, a jewel of great value.

PAUL W. BORGESON, JR

Biography

Born in Lima, Peru, 15 September 1927. Spent part of his childhood in Amsterdam. Attended Colegio Italiano, Lima. Doctorate on poet Carlos Oquendo de Amat from the University of San Marcos, Lima, where he is a professor; also literary translator. Worked for over twenty years for the Peruvian Senate, transcribing official documents. Recipient of Guggenheim awards in 1969 and 1977. Member of the Peruvian Academy of the Language. Has participated in International Writers' Program at University of Iowa and attended poetry festivals in Toronto, New Delhi and Florence. Recipient of National Poetry Prize, 1962, and the Civic Medal of the Municipality of Lima, 1986.

Selected Works

Poetry
Poemas, Lima: privately printed, 1958 [Limited edition of 200 copies]
Dentro & fuera, Lima: Ediciones de la Escuela Normal de Bellas Artes / La Rama Florida, 1960 [Limited edition of 300 copies]
¡Oh, Hada Cibernética!, Lima: El Timonel, 1961
El pie sobre el cuello, Lima: La Rama Florida, 1964
Por el monte abajo: Poemas, Lima: La Rama Florida, 1966
Sextinas y otros poemas, Santiago de Chile: Editorial Universitaria, 1970
En alabanza del bolo alimenticio, Mexico City: Premiá Editora, 1979
Canciones y otros poemas, Mexico City: Premiá Editora, 1979
Más que señora humana, Lima: Ediciones del Tapir, 1986; re-titled *Bajo el sol de la medianoche rojo*, Mexico City: Premiá, 1990
El buen mudar, Madrid: Ediciones del Tapir, 1986 [prose and verse]
En el restante tiempo terrenal, Madrid: Editorial Perla, 1988

Compilations and Anthologies
Antología crítica, edited by John Garganigo, Hanover, New Hampshire: Ediciones del Norte, 1988
Antología personal, Lima: CONCYTEC, 1988 [Includes articles by Enrique Lihn, Mario Vargas Llosa and Roberto Paoli; an interview with Marithelma Costa and Adelaida López; a page of autobiography and bibliography]
Los talleres del tiempo: verso escogido, edited with a prologue by Paul W. Borgeson, Jr, Madrid: Visor, 1992

Further Reading
Cánepa, Mario A., *Lenguaje en conflicto: la poesía de Carlos Germán Belli*, Madrid: Orígenes, 1987
Cornejo Polar, Jorge, *La poesía de Carlos Germán Belli. Una aproximación*, Lima: Universidad de San Marcos, 1994
Higgins, James, *Hitos de la poesía peruana siglo XX*, Lima: Milla Batres, 1993 [Section on Belli's poetry in chapter 3]
Hill, W. Nick, *Tradición y modernidad en la poesía de Carlos Germán Belli*, Madrid: Pliegos, 1985
Lihn, Enrique, "En alabanza de Carlos Germán Belli," *Inti* 18–19 (1983–84)

Ortega, Julio, "La poesía de Carlos Germán Belli," in his *Figuración de la persona*, Madrid: Edhasa, 1971

Solorguren, Javier, *Tres poetas, tres obras: Belli, Delgado, Salazar Bondy*, Lima: Instituto Raúl Porras Barrenechea, 1969

Interviews

Garganigo, John F., "Entrevista con Carlos Germán Belli: Lima, 15 de mayo de 1983," *Revista de Estudios Hispánicos*, vol. 20/2 (1986)

En Bética no bella

Poem from ¡*Oh, Hada Cibernética!* by Carlos Germán Belli

Ya calo, crudos zagales desta Bética
no bella, mi materia, y me doy cuenta
que de abolladuras ornado estoy
por faenas que me habéis señalado
tan sólo a mí y a nadie más ¿por qué?;
mas del corzo la priesa privativa
ante el venablo, yo no podré haber,
o que el seso se me huya de sus arcas
por el cerúleo claustro, pues entonces
ni un olmo habría donde granjear
la sombra para Filis, o a mis vástagos,
o a Anfriso tullido, hermano mío;
pero no cejaré, no, aunque no escriba
ni copule ni baile en esta Bética
                no bella, en donde tantos años vivo

[I now descry, coarse shepherds of this Betis / unlovely, my substance, and become aware / that I am adorned with bruises / acquired in tasks you have assigned me, / only to me and to none other: Why?; / but the speed of the stag / fleeing the lance I can n'er possess, / nor will my brain flee its box / for the cerulean cloister, for then / there would be no elmtree under which to gather / shade for Filis, nor my offspring, / nor my brother, crippled Anfriso; / but no, I shall not yield, though I not write, / copulate nor dance in this Betis / unlovely, wherein so long I dwell]

These blank hendcasyllables well typify the poet's style, themes and overall esthetic stance, and thus offer an appropriate introduction to Belli's poetry. We may begin by observing some characteristic aspects of Belli's use of poetic language, most obviously perhaps the use of now-archaic vocabulary and syntax: "calo" (descry), "zagales," "desta" ("de esta" in contemporary Spanish), the use of "venablo" for lance, "cejar," "haber" (to have) for the expected "tener," etc. The imagery is also allusive to the pastoral poetry associated with Renaissance and Baroque Spain and imitated, of course, in the early Spanish American colony: the use of shepherds; Betis (Andalusia, image of the rustic *locus ameonus* of idyllic pasturelands in many Spanish poets of the time); the elm (symbol of reliable solidity and loyalty), the cerulean cloister (heaven/s) and the "brainbox." Since the context of this poem is not 17th-century Andalusia but the Lima of Belli's day, we

then have a tension of time and place: the idealized Andalusia of the 17th century serves as a bitterly ironic reflection of the repugnance the poet feels toward his 20th-century life in Lima. Lima, then, is "anti-Betis," as Belli's critics have called it; the figure of the poet, encumbered with ridiculous, tedious and thankless jobs, is an "anti-shepherd," having neither natural beauty, innocent shepherdesses nor the music of his flute to fill his free time, for he has none of these. All the bucolic imagery serves only to name that which the poet does *not* enjoy, that for which he longs but of whose acquisition he has no real hope, since he lacks the ability to flee like a stag and cannot take the escape of death because he is obligated by family responsibilities ("Filis," his lover-wife, and his brother "Anfriso," a figuration of Belli's real brother Alfonso).

Just as the language of the lovely conflicts with the dull and soul-killing reality of the poet's life, his aspirations – love (couple), pleasure (dance), art (writing) – conflict with social and economic reality. Hence this poem contains a double irony: just as the poets of the Renaissance were certainly not "shepherds" (they were increasingly citified as the knight-errant evolved into the gentleman of the court), so that the pastoral tradition in Spain was an inverted parody and rejection of life in the metropolis, Belli doubly criticizes life in Lima. Just as Andalusia seemed Arcadian to the sophisticated Madrid court, so this setting appears doubly preferable to Belli's Lima. (Note that Lima's "shepherds" are described as coarse, rather than the expected "gentle" or "sweet"). It is not only not the bucolic image of Betis, it is not even the Renaissance court of Madrid. His rejection and repugnance, then, are redoubled; and even this seemingly-escapist art provides no real compensation, for it is never, and cannot be, an adequate compensation for his multiple frustrations and alienation since it must always fall short of the perfection he seeks – and it can never really change his life, inextricably shackled by the material.

The closure of "Betis Unlovely" marks this poem as one of a smallish group of poems of resistance (Belli is often more pessimistic and resigned). In this sense one may call it "anti-heroic" or "anti-epic." While the voice is fully cognizant that he is trapped, in this piece he does not give up, although the temptation to do so, in the form of suicide, does present itself. Yet the determination to persist is not really heroic, since the motivation comes not from within himself but from outside, in the form of those dependent on him. He is a reluctant and hence unheroic victim because such sacrifice is imposed, as the definitive slamming shut of the trap of modern life.

Belli, as in this poem, is rarely rebellious and never revolutionary. Most often, his poetic figure is a pseudo-Christological metaphor for meaningless suffering, endless isolation and tedium, an on-going sacrifice which lacks the apocalyptic promise of true ritual or metaphysical escape or compensation alike. He is one of many oppressed by a socio-economic structure lacking any cosmic meaning, functioning to create pain with no hope of release nor meaning to it. Thus the final words, "I live," become themselves ironic, and cypher the bitter irony underlying the entire conception and explicit content of this, and many other, Belli poems.

A last observation should be made, to contextualize properly Belli's unique fusion of times, places, motifs and themes. There is one partial compensation to life, even though it it less than fully satisfying and at times even discarded by Belli: that of treating the creation of art itself as a serious game. Indeed, the laborious creation of such complex verses – he cultivates with particular success and pleasure such demanding verseforms as the sestina – suggests that both poet and reader may, even when convinced that life is merely an affirmation of the absurd, find a measure of compensation in the cyphering and decyphering of a highly-coded and conventionalized art form, which itself becomes a meeting-ground for both. Neither he, in the game of writing, nor we, in ours of reading – the ludic attitude of much Baroque art should be remembered here – are likely to change our lives, he tells us: but perhaps, as in the narratives of García Márquez (whose existential attitude is comparable), we can at least have some fun together while

we're around. And, if we are lucky, we may with Belli give voice to our place and time, and our community with our others.

PAUL W. BORGESON, JR

Poem translated by Paul W. Borgeson, Jr

Editions
First edition: *¡Oh, Hada Cibernética!*, Lima: El Timonel, 1961

Further Reading
Lasarte, Francisco, "Pastoral and Counter-Pastoral: the Dynamics of Belli's Poetic Despair," *Modern Language Notes* 94 (1979)

Gioconda Belli 1948–

Nicaraguan poet and novelist

One of the fruits of the Revolution in Nicaragua was the emergence of several fine women poets, among them Gioconda Belli. During the decade of insurrection preceding the Sandinista triumph in 1979, Belli wrote award-winning feminist and revolutionary poetry. Although she dedicated herself to writing poetry for nearly two decades – she published five collections between 1974 and 1991 – in the late 1980s – Belli turned her poetic sensibility to the novel. Since then, she has published two successful novels and is presently completing a third one. Belli's unusual success as a poet and transition to novelist can best be understood within the context of recent political events in Nicaragua.

Thematically, Belli's poetry shares many characteristics with the works of other contemporary Nicaraguan female poets. According to the poet Daisy Zamora, in the introduction to her anthology *La mujer nicaragüense en la poesía*, 1992 [The Nicaraguan Woman in Poetry], these poets exalt the human body, celebrate sensuality and sexuality, and glorify social protest and revolution. Zamora also calls attention to the testimonial nature of many of the poems by Nicaraguan women poets, specifically, the use of the first person.

The poems of Belli's first collection, *Sobre la grama*, 1974 [On the Grass], explore the marvels of the female body, maternity, and sexual desire. In poems such as "Menstruación" [Menstruation], "Maternidad II" [Maternity II] and "Parto" [Childbirth], the poet celebrates the nature of her womanhood. Through her intimist approach, Belli reveals the extraordinary aspects of the ordinary. She addresses the revolutionary struggle in her second book, *Línea de fuego*, 1978 [Line of Fire], which she dedicated to her friends of the Sandinista National Liberation Front. In poems like "Hasta que seamos libres" [Until We Are Free], "Seremos nuevos" [We Shall Be New], and "Amo a los hombres y les canto" [I Love Men and Sing of Them], she praises and idealizes the revolutionary struggle and announces the advent of a new country of free men and women. Her third and fourth books of poetry,

Truenos y arco iris, 1982 [Thunder and Rainbow], and *De la costilla de Eva*, 1986 (*From Eve's Rib*), consist of poems written after the triumph of the Revolution during the period of national reconstruction and the Contra War. Although Belli continues to write intimist poems, she focuses here on the tasks of protecting the Revolution and constructing a new society. Her fifth book of poetry, *El ojo de la mujer*, 1991 [Woman's Eye], is an anthology of her previous books and other poems written between 1976 and 1991. José Coronel Urtecho, one of Nicaragua's finest poets of this century, praised Belli's poetry with the following words: "Those who read this book of poems by Gioconda Belli and do not achieve an immediate knowledge, the direct experience of what poetry is, should give up all hope – *lasciate ogni speranza* – of ever knowing it."

Since the late 1980s, Belli has dedicated herself almost exclusively to the novel and has written little poetry. Her transition from poet to novelist is somewhat of an anomaly in Nicaragua, a country which since the time of Rubén Darío has produced many fine poets. Although Nicaragua has been known principally as "a land of poets," many novels have been written by Nicaraguans. However, as a genre the novel has been undervalued and has received little critical attention. In addition, Nicaragua has had few women novelists. At present, Gioconda Belli, Rosario Aguilar, and Mónica Zalaquett are the country's only female novelists. Therefore, Belli's commitment to the novel is an important development in contemporary Nicaraguan literature.

Belli's novels contain many of the themes she exploited earlier in her poetry. Her first novel, *La mujer habitada*, 1988 (*The Inhabited Woman*), deals with the incorporation of a bourgeois professional woman, an architect, into the revolutionary movement in the 1970s. Belli presents a contemporary female protagonist involved in a struggle for political and sexual liberation, one that for the author is rooted deeply in Central American history. Belli also employs a parallel story of a Mayan woman's struggle against the Spanish conquest to demonstrate the continuities of the political struggle in Central America and the limitations imposed by two distinct societies on women's participation in the defense of their cultures. This novel contains many autobiographical elements and shares some characteristics with the testimonial literature produced in Nicaragua after the Revolution. Translations of *La mujer habitada* have appeared in English and several European languages, and the German edition has been a best-seller.

In Belli's second novel, *Sofía de los presagios*, 1990 [Sofía of the Prophecies], the political struggle as theme is secondary to women's liberation. Through the life of Sofía, a gypsy girl who is separated from her parents at an early age and is raised by an elderly couple in Diría, Nicaragua, Belli explores the dynamics of sexual oppression in Nicaraguan society. Sofía feels she is trapped in circular time, reliving the experiences of her mother's life. She experiences both sides of sexual power struggles. At first she is a victim in sexual relations, but then she uses her sexual power to victimize men. In the end, she is liberated from this power struggle through her love for her daughter.

Belli's emphasis on feminist themes in her novels is reminiscent of her early poetry of the 1970s, before political events in Nicaragua came to dominate her texts. Her political commitment to *Sandinismo* was almost absolute. During the early 1980s, Belli, like many Nicaraguan writers, believed that literature had to serve the Revolution. She, like them, is currently reevaluating the relationship of literature to society. It is not surprising that both Feminist and Marxist critics encounter what they perceive as contradictions in many of the views presented in Belli's poetry. Greg Dawes, for example, states in *Aesthetics and Revolution: Nicaraguan Poetry, 1979–1990*: "Feminism's engagement with revolution, is not, however, without contradictions in Belli's poetry. They include the "militarization" of some of her erotic verses, as well as an awkward attitude toward reproduction." It could be argued, however, that these contradictions, which may be the result of her individual subjective experience, give Belli's poetry its power.

Without question, part of Belli's literary success in the 1980s was tied to political events in Nicaragua. Although she has demonstrated considerable talent as a poet and novelist, her work has been promoted for political motives, inside Nicaragua as well as in Europe and the United States, by groups and individuals sympathetic to the Sandinista cause. While it is possible that the demise of the revolutionary government and subsequent internal conflicts within the Sandinista National Liberation Front might diminish the amount of attention Belli's works receive in the future from certain quarters, she has unquestionably produced original, powerful texts that have enriched Nicaraguan literature and are worthy of admiration and study.

EDWARD WATERS HOOD

Biography

Born in 1948. The daughter of wealthy parents, she was educated in the US and Europe. Married at the age of eighteen, making what her parents perceived as "a good match." Had two children and worked in an advertising agency in Managua. Began to publish poetry in *La Prensa Literaria* in 1970. Became involved with the FSLN (Sandinista Front for the Liberation of Nicaragua) and this led to the breakdown of her marriage and to her being forced into exile. Worked on behalf of the Sandinistas in Mexico and Costa Rica and visited Europe to raise funds for them. After the fall of the dictator Anastasio Somoza in 1979, she returned to Nicaragua and worked in communications for the Ministry of Propaganda. Has lived in Los Angeles since the mid-1990s. Awarded the Mariano Fiallos Gil Prize of the National Autonomous University of Nicaragua, 1972 and the Casa de las Américas Prize for Poetry, 1978.

Selected Works

Poetry
Sobre la grama, Managua: INDESA, 1974
Línea de fuego, Havana: Casa de las Américas, 1978
Truenos y arco iris, Managua: Nueva Nicaragua, 1982
De la costilla de Eva, Managua: Nueva Nicaragua, 1986; as *From Eve's Rib*, translated by Stephen F. White, Willimantic, Connecticut: Curbstone Press, 1989

Anthologies of Poetry
Amor insurrecto, Managua: Nueva Nicaragua, 1984
Poesía reunida, Mexico City: Diana, 1989
El ojo de la mujer, Managua: Nueva Nicaragua, 1991

Novels
La mujer habitada, México City: Diana, 1988; as *The Inhabited Woman*, translated by Kathleen N. March, Willimantic, Connecticut: Curbstone Press, 1994
Sofía de los presagios, Managua: Vanguardia, 1990

Further Reading

Beverley, John and Marc Zimmerman, *Literature and Politics in the Central American Revolutions*, Austin: University of Texas Press, 1990 [Chapter 4, "Nicaraguan Poetry of the Insurrection and Reconstruction," provides some treatment of Belli's poetry]

Cabrera, Vicente, "La intertextualidad subversiva en *La mujer habitada* de Gioconda Belli," *Monographic Review / Revista Monográfica*, vol. 8 (1992)

Dawes, Greg, *Aesthetics and Revolution: Nicaraguan Poetry, 1979–1990*, Minneapolis: University of Minnesota Press, 1993 [Dawes dedicates a section, "Gioconda Belli: Eros and Revolution," to Belli's poetry]

March, Kathleen N., "Gioconda Belli: the Erotic Politics of the Great Mother," *Monographic Review / Revista Monográfica*, vol. 6 (1990)

____ "Engendering the Political Novel: Gioconda Belli's *La mujer habitada*," in *Women Writers in Twentieth Century Spain and Spanish America*, edited by Catherine Davies, Lampeter, Wales: Edwin Mellen Press, 1993

Moyano, Pilar, "La transformación de la mujer y la nación en la poesía comprometida de Gioconda Belli," *Revista Canadiense de Estudios Hispánicos*, vol. 17/2 (Winter 1993)

Murray, Patricia, "A Place for Eve in the Revolution," in *Knives and Angels: Women Writers in Latin America*, edited by Susan Bassnett, London: Zed Books, 1990

Richards, Timothy, "Resistance and Liberation: the Mythic Voice and Textual Authority in Belli's *La mujer habitada*," in *Critical Essays on the Literatures of Spain and Spanish-America*, edited by Luis T. González-Del-Valle and Julio Baena, Boulder, Colorado: Society of Spanish and Spanish-American Studies, 1991

Rodríguez, Ileana, *House/Garden/Nation: Space, Gender, and Ethnicity in Post-Colonial Latin American Literatures by Women*, translated by Rodríguez and Robert Carr, Durham, North Carolina: Duke University Press, 1994 [Chapter 6 is on Belli's fiction]

Interviews

Hood, Edward Waters, with Cecilia Ojeda, "Entrevista con Gioconda Belli," *Chasqui*, vol. 23/2 (November 1994)

Randall, Margaret (editor), *Risking a Somersault in the Air: Conversations with Nicaraguan Writers*, Willimantic, Connecticut: Curbstone Press, 1984 [Includes interview with Belli]

Andrés Bello 1781–1865

Venezuelan writer, statesman and man of ideas

The life and career of Andrés Bello present us with numerous aspects worthy of consideration. He was a man of science, a thinker, politician, legal consultant, philosopher, grammarian, legislator, historian, journalist, and translator. Critics have been unanimous in according him the most prestigious epithets: "prince of South American humanists," "wise," among others. An interesting biographical fact is that he was Simón Bolívar's teacher and that he guided the latter towards the disciplines of geography and literature. He was very enthusiastic about learning languages and he cultivated the natural sciences.

While he was in his own country he wrote a few poems, a summary of the *Historia de Venezuela* and some other texts which subsequently were lost. When he moved to London in 1810, his writing acquired a different character. His sensitivity was refined in exile, where he mastered Spanish more thoroughly. That is when he completed his training and did important journalistic work. He published the two *silvas* (the title refers to a particular poetic form) and erudite essays on literary subjects, which circulated among critics and writers.

In 1823, jointly with Juan García del Río and Luis López Méndez he edited the journal *Biblioteca Americana* or *Miscelánea de Literatura, Artes y Ciencias*, whose existence was short-lived. In the first volume, consisting of 472 pages, there began to appear the works of this vastly knowledgeable writer on a wide variety of subjects; at once the humanist of profound erudition and the writer and poet with a clear and brilliant style. It was in this journal that he published his *Alocución a la poesía* [Address to Poetry], with a geographical and historical theme, containing a light descriptive passage, which acts as a link to introduce the longest part of the work. In the first fragment, which extends to verse 447, he inserts praise of the outstanding South American peoples and heroes from the Wars of Independence (songs addressed to Bolívar, Paez, Miranda, and others) in different regions of South America. The poem is a South American profession of faith, written on the basis of classical and Spanish reminiscences, with a poetic and social intention.

In 1826 he published another journal, *El Repertorio Americano*. In its first 320-page edition, we find another essay on pages seven to eighteen, also in *silva* form, which opens the section entitled "Humanidades y Artes liberales." Under the general heading of "Silvas americanas," the following title appears: *Silva I. La agricultura de la zona tórrida* [Silva I. The Agriculture of the Torrid Zone]. This other *silva*, a more powerful and coherent work than the previous one, is Virgilian by its title but the fragment is only partly georgic. It consists of expressive stanzas with which he describes the natural beauties of the torrid region of South America. In this way his work is almost epic, as well as geographical and historical, descriptive and moral.

Bello was not a prolific poet. He worked hard on his stanzas refining them carefully, deleting mannerisms which would reduce their delicacy. In musical stanzas of great suppleness he blends philosophy, science, and poetry and the grandeur of the luscious nature of the tropics, loaded with "local colour," the attractiveness of the South American world, the charms of the countryside, to which the poet recommends a return. After the War of Independence, facing a time of reconstruction, he depicts the wondrous nature of peace. He exhorts South Americans to forget heroism in favour of dignifying work on the land, the source of prosperity.

Those two *silvas* laid the foundations of and immortalized his fame as a descriptive poet. They contain passages where he allows the pain and sadness of exile, when memories of his native land overwhelmed him with grief, to be discerned. There are passages of elegiac quality but full of gentle fortitude. He never achieved his intention of writing a long poem – *América* – perhaps because he felt that, although so popular in earlier centuries, well into the 19th century, the time for great epic poetry had long passed.

In spite of his objectivity and a certain tone with a didactic tendency, in the descriptive and narrative passages all the stanzas come over tinted with a purely subjective lyricism. This characteristic makes the *silvas* truly original, although echoes of famous poems resound in them. In Bello, the poet and critic follow a parallel path, beginning in his youth and continuing until the end of his life. His works on the literary origins of the Middle Ages are outstanding (such as his research on the *Poema del Cid*) and among the foremost in the Spanish language. His artistic theory is based on "the innate feeling of the beauty that is in man": art is a means of reaching that beauty.

With regard to the set of philological works, with the analytical school of the 18th century the *Análisis ideológico de los tiempos de la conjugación castellana* [An Ideological Analysis of the Tenses in Castilian Conjugation] is considered the most original and profound of his linguistic studies.

Principios del derecho de gentes, 1832 [People's Rights] consolidated his authority and prestige both within his own country and abroad. In this book he displays his anxiety about the balance and fortune of "the recently emancipated countries" and drew up wise rules of conduct which they should adopt in order to gain the respect of the imperialist powers. The *Gramática de la lengua castellana*, 1847 [Grammar of the Castilian Tongue] brought him well-deserved fame and is considered the most important of his scientific works.

The corruption of the language worried Bello, as well as excessive neologisms, which would convert Spanish into dialects characteristic of each part of the Continent. He believed the preservation of the unity and purity of the language was the most powerful fraternal bond among Spanish Americans. That is why he used to say that his *Gramática* "was destined for the use of Americans." It was Bolívar's ideal of the unity of the hemisphere which Bello took from the political to the spiritual sphere; he also freed Spanish grammar from the obligation to respect Latin grammar. The source of linguistic correctness is popular usage: "the true and only architect of languages."

Among his translations, Victor Hugo's "La oración por todos" [A Prayer for All] is worthy of mention, considered by many critics as being better than the original.

A descriptive poet *par excellence* of the Hispanic literary canon, an uncompromising poet, his work, of a manifold character, can be considered as a poetic declaration of independence, proclaiming that the time had come for Latin Americans to free themselves from subjection to Iberian literature. Classical by education, steeped in a secure culture, he opposed dogmatism and the imitative approach with flexibility and a generous spirit. A characteristic of his work is balance: he blended innovation with tradition, Classicism and Romanticism, his imagination curbed by a sense of restraint. He longed to achieve beauty, without conventionalities, accepting Romanticism as long as it did not alter universal artistic principles.

BELLA JOZEF

translated by Patricia James

Biography
Born in Caracas, Venezuela, 29 November 1781. Parents belonged to petty bourgeoisie. Privately educated until he entered the Royal and Pontifical University of Caracas. Graduated in 1800 and became officer of the Spanish Crown; also found time for journalism, becoming the editor of the first Caracas newspaper, *La Gaceta de Caracas*, in 1808. In 1810 sent to London as Secretary of a diplomatic mission intent on securing Britain's neutrality in the War of Independence against Spain. Unbeknown to Bello, his exile was to be permanent. Endured real poverty in London where, in 1821, he also lost his first wife, Ann Boyland whom he had married in 1814. Lived in London from 1810 to 1829. Appointed Secretary to Chilean Legation in 1822 and later (1824) to Colombian Chargé d'Affaires. In that year he married Isabel Antonia Dunn. Founding editor of the *Biblioteca Americana* (1823) and of the *Repertorio Americano*, 1826–27, both published in London. Appointed member of Venezuelan National Academy in 1826. Straitened circumstances obliged him in 1829 to settle in Chile where he had been offered the position of Senior Official in the Ministry of Finance. From 1830, he held a post in the Ministry of Foreign Affairs. Edited *El Araucano*, 1830–53. Senator of the Chilean Republic, 1837–55; rector of the University of Chile from 1843. Honorary member of the Royal Spanish Academy, 1851. Criticized for serving an oligarchical regime. Endured much personal suffering; outlived eight of his children. Died on 15 October 1865.

Selected Works
El calendario manual y guía universal de forasteros en Venezuela para el año 1810, Caracas: n.p., 1810
Principios del derecho de gentes, Santiago de Chile, n.p., 1832
Principios de ortología y métrica de la lengua castellana, Santiago de Chile: Opinión, 1835
El incendio de la Compañía: canto elegíaco, Santiago de Chile: n.p., 1841
Análisis ideológico de los tiempos de la conjugación castellana, Valparaíso, Chile: Rivadeneyra, 1841
Compendio de gramática castellana escrita para el uso de las escuelas primarias, Santiago de Chile: Morales, 1841
Instituciones de derecho romano, Santiago de Chile: Crepúsculo, 1843
Proyecto de Código civil (1841–1845), Santiago de Chile: n.p., 1846

Gramática de la lengua castellana destinada al uso de los americanos, Santiago de Chile: Cuervo, 1847
Discurso pronunciado . . . en la instalación de la Universidad de Chile el día 17 de septiembre de 1843, Santiago de Chile: Imprenta de la Sociedad, 1848
Cosmografía, o descripción del universo conforme a los últimos descubrimientos, Santiago de Chile: Opinión, 1848
Compendio de historia de la literatura, Santiago de Chile: Chilena, 1850
Filosofía del entendimiento, Santiago de Chile: Ramírez, 1881; as *Philosophy of the Understanding*, translated by O. Carlos Stoetzer, Washington, DC: General Secretariat, Organisation of American States, 1984
Gramática castellana, Santiago de Chile: Dirección General de Prisiones, 1937

Compilations and Anthologies
Colección de poesías originales por Andrés Bello, Caracas: Torres Caicedo, 1870
Obras completas, 15 vols, Santiago de Chile: Consejo de Instrucción Pública, 1881–93
Obras completas, 26 vols, Caracas: La Casa de Bello, 1981–86

Translations
The Odes of Bello, Olmedo and Heredia, with an introduction by Elijah Clarence Hills, New York and London: Putnam, 1920
A Georgic of the Tropics, translated by Barbara D. Huntley and Pilar Liria, Washington, DC: King Lindsays, 1981
Anthology of Andrés Bello, edited by Pedro Grases, translated by Barbara D. Huntley and Pilar Liria, Washington, DC: General Secretariat, Organisation of American States, 1981

Further Reading
Álvarez, O., *Labor periodística de Andrés Bello*, Caracas: Casa de Bello, 1981
Amunátegui (Aldunate), Miguel Luis, *Vida de Don Andés Bello*, Santiago de Chile: Ramírez, 1882
Balbín de Unquera, Antonio, *Andrés Bello: su época y sus obras*, Madrid: Imprenta de los hijos de M.G. Hernández, 1910
Brewer-Carías, Allan R., *La concepción del estado en la obra de Andrés Bello*, Madrid: Instituto de Estudios de Administración Local, 1983
Caldera, Rafael, *Andrés Bello: Philosopher, Poet, Philologist, Educator, Legislator, Statesman*, translated by John Street, London: Allen and Unwin, 1977
Cussen, Antonio, *Poetry and Politics in the Spanish American Revolution: Bello, Bolívar and the Classical Tradition*, Cambridge and New York: Cambridge University Press, 1991
Fernández, David, *Los antepasados de Bello*, Caracas: La Casa de Bello, 1978
Fernández Larraín, Sergio, *Cartas a Bello en Londres, 1810–1829*, Santiago de Chile: Andrés Bello, 1968
Grases, Pedro, *Los retratos de Bello: notas históricas sobre las representaciones en vida del humanista*, Caracas: Publicaciones del Banco Central de Venezuela, 2nd edition, 1980
Isaza Calderón, Baltasar, *La doctrina gramatical de Bello*, 2nd edition, Madrid: *Añejos del Boletín de la Real Academia Española* 15 (1967)
Loynaz, Dulce María, "Andrés Bello: misionero de la poesía Hispanoamericana," in her *Ensayos literarios*, Salamanca: Ediciones Universidad, 1993
Lynch, John (editor), *Andrés Bello: the London Years*, Richmond, Surrey: Richmond Publications, 1982
Rodríguez Monegal, Emir, *El otro Andrés Bello*, Caracas: Monte Ávila, 1969

Mario Benedetti 1920–

Uruguayan prose writer, dramatist
and poet

Mario Benedetti has cultivated all the literary genres, being the author of novels, short stories, poems, plays, newspaper articles, essays, humorous writing and lyrics for songs. And in all of them he has developed an outlook and critical perspective which at the beginning of his career was centered on Uruguay and Uruguayan problems, but at a later stage shifted into the international arena. His support of the Cuban Revolution has been unwavering and he spent several years of his life in the island. The United States has always been a target for both analysis and criticism (the latter as much on account of the government's foreign policy as for its history of racism, individualism and consumerism as ways of life).

Benedetti's literary career may be divided into two phases: the first begins around 1945 with the poetry collection *La víspera indeleble* [The Indelible Eve] and expands into narrative with the novel *Quién de nosotros*, 1953 [Who Among Us], the short stories of *Montevideanos*, 1959 [People of Montevideo], the essay *El país de la cola de paja*, 1960 [The Straw-tailed Country], and the novel *Gracias por el fuego*, 1965 [Thanks for the Light]. The prevailing feature of these works is criticism of society and morality. The second phase results from his becoming politicized, and it is apparent in his work. *Gracias por el fuego* began to earn him an international reputation because the action is set in New York, but its preoccupations are almost entirely Uruguayan. Shortly after, the radical changes that took place in Latin America in the 1960s, and above all, the intellectual ferment and militancy of the Left (the Cuban Revolution, the attacks on US imperialism and the search for a "new" Guevara-type man) had a powerful influence on Benedetti's writing and in it he combined a moral judgment – which is ever present in his works – with a more sophisticated political outlook.

Benedetti's essays of the 1970s and 1980s were collected in book form: *Terremoto y después*, 1973 [Earthquake and After]; *El desexilio y otras conjeturas*, 1984 [Unexile and Other Conjectures] which are a kind of mirror of the itinerant life and problems that beset the author. Many of them are excellent examples of cultural journalism.

The theme of his novel in verse, *El cumpleaños de Juan Ángel*, 1971 [Juan Ángel's Birthday] is the armed struggle in Uruguay, that is, the clandestine guerrilla war. At that time Benedetti was one of the leaders of the 26 of May Movement, a political group whose ideology was close to that of the Tupamaro guerrillas. Later, the dictatorship of 1973 and the military governments proscribed not only the "26 May" but all independent political activity in Uruguay, driving many into exile. In this new period (1973–85) Benedetti lived first in Cuba and later in Spain (where, in the mid 1990s he still spends periods of time), and the theme of exile also found expression in his work.

Pessimism and optimism are key terms in Benedetti's work. Up to *Gracias por el fuego*, Benedetti belonged in the ranks of the "pessimists," as the author himself pointed out on several occasions, because he lived in a country without

a "future," sworn to the mediocre dreams of individualism. By then Benedetti was a very popular writer, as a poet (*Poemas de la oficina*), as a writer of narrative (*Montevideanos*), as an essayist (*El país de la cola de paja*) or humour (*Mejor es Meneallo* [The More Said, the Better]), as though his readers were searching for mirrors in which to see their reflection.

These writings focused on "average citizens," middle-of-the-roaders, absorbed by their petty, selfish aspirations, in a crass social atmosphere in which the only possible modes of behaviour are hypocrisy or betrayal (of a friend; of one's spouse). Benedetti helped to create the figure of this "national type" within the "social imaginary." Thus the love triangle of *Quién de nosotros*, the parricide and betrayal of one's country in *Gracias por el fuego*, the small-scale, personal tragedy of the office worker in *La tregua* (*The Truce*) come as no surprise. The last of these is considered his finest novel – and probably is. It fuses social and individual points of view without one affecting adversely the other. And he fashions credible characters with whom readers may identify. Beginning with a cliché (a man of retirement age begins an affair with a much younger colleague), it turns into a sensitive and intelligent story and a melancholy reflection on the elusive nature of happiness.

Martín Santomé, the central character of *La tregua*, is a man defeated by the social structure. For Kafka, bureaucracy was a labyrinth or a spider's web that created anguish; for Benedetti – a perceptive reader of Kafka – bureaucracy is the moderate tragedy of mediocrity. It is most curious that the novel ends with a question. *Quién de nosotros* ended with a metaphysical question, an anxious search for the hidden God (Who judges whom?), but the final question of *La tregua* refers in a desolate way to the petty bourgeois without a future: "Desde mañana y hasta el día de mi muerte, el tiempo estará a mis órdenes. Después de tanta espera, esto es el ocio. ¿Qué haré con él?" (As from tomorrow and until I die, time will take orders from me. After so much waiting, here is leisure. What am I to do with it?)

Very different is *Gracias por el fuego*. The narrow focus of *La tregua* has been replaced by a socio-political perspective. The author passes judgment on his country in all his texts; here, though, this becomes a theme. Through three generations of a family (grandson, son, father), he tells the story of an old newspaper boss, corrupt and venal, his cowardly sons and a cautiously rebellious grandson. The most dramatic aspects concern the old man's son, Ramón Budiño, who has a love-hate relationship with his father, and decides to kill him as a way of saving the country, or the multiple victims of this "terrible father." *La tregua* was chamber work; *Gracias por el fuego* is an attempt at a symphony, a reflexion on the collectivity – the amorality of the country.

During Benedetti's "pessimistic" phase there were more questions than answers. The former could be personal, metaphysical, made painful by uncertainty. Slowly they would make way for questions charged with indignation, appropriate to a lucid witness, a conscious citizen, an engaged writer: "¿Es que este país no tiene fondo? (Can't one strike bottom in this country?).

In *El cumpleaños de Juan Ángel* Benedetti sought to bring these sombre reflections to a close so as to give way to a brighter, clearer and more hopeful vision. And this change applied also to the literary "form." Thus one of the novel's most original features is that it is written in verse. Blank verse – within the aesthetics of conversational poetry – but not stripped of rhythm; on the contrary, *El cumpleaños de Juan Ángel* has an undeniable, pleasurable, successfully realized rhythm. This work is the correlate of its author's restlessness, an expression of his desire for personal, political and aesthetic change. And it is the key moment of a transformation which from the beginning involved overcoming pessimism. Even in troubled times, Benedetti was able to detect and to ally himself with the preoccupations of progressive elements in Latin America and to pin the few hopes of the Latin American on political activism. It is for these reasons that *El cumpleaños de Juan Ángel* is so central and fundamental to his evolution: during the 1960s, the grey Uruguay of the *Poemas de la oficina* and *Montevideanos* gave way to the Robin Hood epic of the Tupamaros who fought against the rich and were liked by the people.

For some years that guerrilla movement was genuinely popular and was represented in the social imaginary as behaviour that was intrepid, courageous and (at last) fit for a country which until then appeared defeated by a spirit of corruption, decadence and red tape. The Tupamaros were the reply that Edmundo Budiño searched for ironically in *Gracias por el fuego*. They became the only ones determined to combat Power and, if possible, to destroy it, to ensure that a tranquil death would not reach them in old age in their beds. The novel recounts and sings about the country's history through its collective character. It is dedicated to Raúl Sendic, the Tupamaro leader whom Benedetti had known from his youth. Thus *El cumpleaños* is a magnificent, undoubtedly original *tour de force* in which the frontiers dividing poetry from prose are broken down; the various ages of the character are "liberated" in the course of a single day; Uruguay's dramatic history is recreated without having recourse to any documentary elements; and, above all, the language itself, through its stylistic figures, creates an atmosphere of uncertainty, action and passion. A novel/poem, its theme is revolution and love, denunciation in the face of repression, joy in heroism, and the story of how Benedetti, like many other Uruguayans of the period, grasped a problem (a nettle) and, having done so, experienced and lived it.

The dictatorship of 1973 and its consequences: internal repression, imprisonment and death, the exodus of Uruguayans on a massive scale, challenged the "optimism" that Benedetti supported. Or, rather, they turned it into historical optimism, in a conviction that the steps taken backwards by a regime or a country in the socio-political spheres, no longer signified that the country was condemned. They are obstacles in a historical unfolding which will of necessity end in freedom. This historical vision, which Benedetti struggled to make his own, remained a feature of his production during the years of exile. What he did was to make a theme of his own exile, giving it a place in the imaginary and a category in social, political and aesthetic reflexion.

As from 1973 Benedetti published several books of narrative and poetry which express the theme of exile. Among them are *Poemas de otros*, 1974 [Poems by Others], *Con y sin nostalgia*, 1977 [With and without Nostalgia], *Cotidianas*, 1979 [Everydays], *Vientos de exilio*, 1983 [Winds of Exile] and *Geografías*, 1984 [Geographies]. *Pedro y el capitán*, 1979 [Peter and the Captain] is an extremely representative play about the denunciation of repression; at the same time it is an attempt to analyze dialectically and ethically the relationship between torturer and tortured. In narrative, without a doubt *Primavera con una esquina rota*, 1982 [Spring with a Chipped Corner] and *Recuerdos olvidados*, 1988 [Forgotten Memories] are two of the texts that best illustrate his "new" optimism. An optimism which, basically, rests on a modern historical confidence (more than the "postmodern" kind) and on the idea that reason and justice will prevail. *Primavera*, like *El cumpleaños* before it, is an innovative novel in formal terms: it gives an account of several lives along parallel and converging narrative lines. The imprisoned, exiled and repressed all figure here, encapsulated in their monologues, letters and dialogues. In following these personal histories, Benedetti was looking for a greater social resonance while, at the same time, as the title indicates, embedding the ideology of hope in the verbal and cultural codes. The word spring (*primavera*) alone, which serves for a character as a tacit source of optimism and gaiety, is the symbolic season of rebirth.

Seldom has Benedetti been more autobiographical than in this novel. The same applies to *Despistes y franquezas*, 1989 [Frank and Off the Point], but this time he acknowledges it openly: "De antiguo aspiré secretamente a escribir . . . mi personal libro-entrevero, ya que siempre consideré ese atajo como un signo de libertad creadora y, también, del derecho a seguir el derrotero de la imaginación y no siempre el de las estructuras rigurosas y prefijadas." (From a long way back I secretly aspired to write . . . my personal bran-tub-book, since I always viewed this shortcut as a mark of creative freedom and, in addition, of the duty to follow the leadings of the imagination and not always those of certain rigorous and established structures.) However, *La borra del café* [Coffee Dregs] was to be Benedetti's most autobiographical text and the novel that combines stylistic maturity with the narrative freshness of the early books.

Fifty years after his literary beginnings, Mario Benedetti has demonstrated various things, without setting out to do so, as befits an authentic writer: fidelity to a nucleus of moral principles has made his personal and literary world one of great integrity in Uruguayan and, more generally, Latin American literature; a considerable gift of literary expression which has enabled him – quite legitimately – to seduce innumerable readers in a range of countries (he is the author of sixty books, and has sold over a million and a half copies). In addition, he has been admirably true to himself; barbed with critics who frequently have written unfavourable reviews; endowed with a sense of history which, finally, allowed him to see that beneath the debris of national corruption, another young and bold country, and a continent imbued with hope, were worth uncovering, so as to be told and narrated. Benedetti has devoted the best of his energy to this task in the last few decades. He is a unique example of hopelessness turned into hope, seeing this as the best instrument to turn the latter into a reality.

JORGE RUFFINELLI

translated by Verity Smith

Biography

Born in Paso de los Toros in the interior of Uruguay, 14 September 1920. Family moved to Montevideo in 1924. Attended the German School in Montevideo, 1928–34. From 1938–41 spent most of his time in Buenos Aires. Married Luz López Alegre. Editor of the literary journal *Marginalia*, Montevideo, 1948–49. Staff writer for *Número* (1949–55), an important literary journal of the period. Between 1954–60 was three times editor of the weekly *Marcha* (see under Journals). Travelled to the United States in 1959 after being awarded the Montevideo Municipal Prize for *Montevideanos*. *El país de la cola de paja* (1960) proved very controversial and became a best-seller. Travelled to Cuba in 1966 to act as juror for Casa de las Américas awards. In the period 1966–67 worked in Paris as broadcaster and translator. From 1968–71 member of the executive board of Casa de las Américas. Founder and head of their Centro de Investigaciones Literarias. In April 1971 he was one of the founders of the "26 de mayo" movement which later became part of a coalition of the Left, the Frente Amplio (Broad Front). Went into exile after military coup of 1973. Spent time in Argentina, Peru and Cuba before settling in Madrid. His work almost completely republished in Mexico and thus acquired an international audience. After Uruguay's return to democracy (1985) began to divide his time between Uruguay and Spain.

Selected Works

Poetry and Narrative
Out of respect for the cultivated hybridity of some of the texts listed below, no attempt has been made to separate poetry from narrative fiction.

La víspera indeleble, Montevideo: Prometeo, 1945
Esta mañana, Montevideo: Prometeo, 1949
Sólo mientras tanto, Montevideo: Número, 1950
El último viaje y otros cuentos, Montevideo: Número, 1951
Quién de nosotros, Montevideo; Número, 1953
Ustedes, por ejemplo, Montevideo; Número, 1953
Poemas de la oficina, Montevideo: Número, 1956
Montevideanos, Montevideo: Alfa, 1959
La tregua, Montevideo: Alfa, 1960; as *The Truce*, translated by Benjamin Graham, New York: Harper and Row, 1969
Poemas del hoy por hoy, Montevideo: Alfa, 1961
Gracias por el fuego, Montevideo: Alfa, 1965
Contra los puentes levadizos, Montevideo: Alfa, 1966
A ras del sueño, Montevideo: Alfa, 1967
La muerte y otras sorpresas, Mexico City: Siglo XXI, 1968
El cumpleaños de Juan Ángel, Mexico City: Siglo XXI, 1971
Hasta aquí, Buenos Aires: Cuadernos de la Línea, 1974
Poemas de otros, Madrid: Visor, 1974
Letras de emergencia, Buenos Aires: Alfa, 1974
La casa y el ladrillo, Mexico City: Siglo XXI, 1976
Con y sin nostalgia, Mexico City: Siglo XXI, 1977
Cotidianas, Mexico City: Siglo XXI, 1979
Primavera con una esquina rota, Madrid: Alfaguara, 1982
Vientos de exilio, Madrid: Visor, 1983
Geografías, Madrid: Alfaguara, 1984
Preguntas al azar, Buenos Aires: Nueva Imagen, 1986
Yesterday y mañana, Montevideo: Arca, 1987
Recuerdos olvidados, Montevideo: Trilce, 1988

Despistes y franquezas, Montevideo: Arca/Nueva Imagen, 1989
Las soledades de Babel, Madrid: Visor, 1991
La borra del café, Montevideo: Arca, 1992
Canciones del más acá, Montevideo: Cal y Canto, 1993

Plays
El reportaje, Montevideo: Marcha, 1958
Ida y vuelta, Buenos Aires: Talía, 1963
Pedro y el capitán, Mexico City: Nueva Imagen, 1979

Essays and Testimonial Writing
Marcel Proust y otros ensayos, Montevideo: Número, 1951
El país de la cola de paja, Montevideo: Asir, 1960
Mejor es Meneallo, Montevideo: Alfa, 1961
Literatura uruguaya del siglo veinte, Montevideo: Alfa, 1963
Genio y figura de José Enrique Rodó, Buenos Aires: Eudeba, 1966
Letras del continente mestizo, Montevideo: Arca, 1967
Sobre arte y oficios: ensayo, Montevideo: Alfa, 1968
Cuaderno cubano, Montevideo: Arca, 1969
Crítica cómplice, Havana: Instituto Cubano del Libro, 1971
Crónicas del 71, Montevideo: Arca, 1972
Los poetas comunicantes, Montevideo: Biblioteca de Marcha, 1972 [interviews]
Terremoto y después, Montevideo: Arca, 1973
El recurso del supremo patriarca, Buenos Aires: Alfa, 1974
El escritor latinoamericano y la revolución posible, Buenos Aires: Alfa, 1974
Notas sobre algunas formas subsidiarias de la penetración cultural, Mexico City: Tierra Adentro, 1979
Panorama histórico-literario de nuestra América, Havana: Casa de las Américas, and New York: Vitral, 1982
El desexilio y otras conjeturas, Madrid: Ediciones El País, 1984
La cultura, ese blanco móvil, Montevideo: Universidad de la República, 1985
Escritos políticos, Montevideo: Arca, 1985
Noción de patria, Madrid: Visor, 1985
Cultura entre dos fuegos, Montevideo: Universidad de la República, 1986

Compilations and Anthologies
Todos los cuentos de Mario Benedetti, Havana: Casa de las Américas, 1980
Antología poética, prologue by J.M. Caballero Bonald, Madrid: Alianza, 1984

Further Reading

Barros, Daniel, "Tres poetas de hoy: Teillier, Benedetti y Gelman," in his *Poesía sudamericana actual*, Madrid: Miguel Castelote, 1972
Fornet, Ambrosio (editor), *Recopilación de textos sobre Mario Benedetti*, Havana: Casa de las Américas, 1976
Mansour, Mónica, *Tuya, mía, de otros; la poesía coloquial de Mario Benedetti*, Mexico City: UNAM, 1979
Navia Velasco, Carmiña, *Mario Benedetti: una aproximación crítica*, Cali, Colombia: Centro Cultural Popular Meléndez, 1984
Ruffinelli, Jorge (editor), *Mario Benedetti: variaciones críticas*, Montevideo: Libros del Astillero, 1973 [Contains essays by notable creative writers as well as by critics. These include Julieta Campos, Cristina Peri Rossi, Ariel Dorfman, Sebastián Salazar Bondy and Jean Franco]
Valverde, José María, "Verso versus prosa: dos casos en Hispanoamérica," *Revista Canadiense de Estudios Hispánicos* 1 (1976)

Interviews
Alfaro, Hugo, *Mario Benedetti: detrás de un vidrio claro*, Montevideo: Ediciones Trilce, 1986

Best-Sellers

It was not until the 1960s that the term best-seller was used in conjunction with Latin American literature due both to developments in the publishing world and to the emergence of writers who would come to dominate the Latin American literary scene. This period came to be known as the Boom, and the use of the terminology of the market place to describe a literary phenomenon is, as Ángel Rama has said, no accident. Rama notes the changes in the publishing world instrumental in the creation of the Boom in his essay "The 'Boom' in Perspective." While in the 1940s and 1950s it was usual for a publisher to issue 3,000 copies of a novel, by the late 1960s novels by members of "the big four" (Gabriel García Márquez, Mario Vargas Llosa, Julio Cortázar and Carlos Fuentes) could expect to sell at least 20,000 copies. Gabriel García Márquez's *Cien años de soledad* (*One Hundred Years of Solitude*), as Rama notes in the same essay, was consistently selling 100,000 copies per year from 1968, setting a sales record for a Latin American novel and introducing the Latin American novel to an international market.

The high quality of the literature produced in this period along with the new openings for Latin American writers in the book market (stimulated considerably by the interest in Latin American authors shown by the Barcelona publishing house Seix Barral) led to the emergence of Latin American literary superstars, professional writers who became household names in educated circles. Latin American writers, once their reputations were established and translations began to appear, were able to take advantage of developments in the book market. The growth of the literate population, increased distributing power of multinationals and lower prices of paperbacks all combined to guarantee high sales for the few novelists who were able to break into the international market.

Well-known Latin American novelists have, if anything, increased their sales in the 1970s, 1980s and 1990s, probably as their novels have become more accessible and readable. Carlos Fuentes's *Gringo viejo*, 1985 (*The Old Gringo*) has none of the technical difficulties of *La muerte de Artemio Cruz*, 1962 (*The Death of Artemio Cruz*) and Vargas Llosa's exploitation of popular culture and eroticism in *La tía Julia y el escribidor*, 1977 (*Aunt Julia and the Scriptwriter*) has more sales potential than his earlier *La casa verde*, 1966 (*The Green House*). Likewise, García Márquez's *El amor en los tiempos de cólera*, 1985 (*Love in the Time of Cholera*) is an unashamedly romantic tale of enormous popular appeal. The 1970s also saw the emergence of the Argentine writer Manuel Puig whose highly readable explorations of gender and class oppression, sexuality and popular culture have allowed his novels to join the ranks of the international best-sellers.

During this internationalisation of the Latin American novelist, women writers were conspicuous by their absence until the 1980s. While well-established women writers such as Clarice Lispector, Luisa Valenzuela, Elena Poniatowska and Rosario Castellanos have undergone a critical revival due to growing interest by feminist Latin Americanists, the only two Latin American women writers to reach the international best-seller market are Isabel Allende and Laura Esquivel.

DEBORAH A. SHAW

Further Reading

Brown, Meg H., *The Reception of Spanish American Fiction in West Germany: a Study of Best Sellers*, Tübingen: Niemeyer, 1994 [Includes Isabel Allende, García Márquez, Ángeles Mastretta and Vargas Llosa]

Interviews

"Juan José Saer: interviewed by Claudio Canaparo," *Journal of Latin American Cultural Studies*, vol. 4/1 (1995)

Isabel Allende 1942–

Chilean prose writer

Isabel Allende is one of the few writers who has managed to achieve consistently high sales figures while at the same time receiving critical attention in academic circles. Her novels have been translated into many languages and are bought principally by a "non-specialist" readership, while her first novel *La casa de los espíritus*, 1982 (*The House of the Spirits*) was made into a film with a star-studded cast in 1994. How can one account for this previously unknown Chilean writer's dramatic entry onto the international literature shelves? Some of the reasons for her success will be examined here with a focus on some of the common points in Allende's first three novels, novels which established and consolidated her reputation.

Probably the most appealing element of Allende's fiction for a mass readership is her use of magical realism in its most popular form. Latin American writers from the time of the first European conquerors to Miguel Ángel Asturias, Alejo Carpentier and Juan Rulfo through to García Márquez, have long seen Latin America as a land of myth and magic where anything can and usually does happen. An image of Latin America full of larger than life characters whose belief systems are founded on a combination of religion and superstition and who are capable of the best excesses of love and the worst excesses of violence is an image that sells.

Allende draws on this long tradition in her novels, in the view of some critics to the extent of plagiarising García Márquez. Eva, one of Allende's protagonists, best sums up her creator's interpretation of magical realism when she says: "reality is not only what we see on the surface; it has a magical dimension as well, and, if we so desire, it is legitimate to enhance it and color it to make our journey through life less trying." Exotic notions of the continent are confirmed, and "reality" made exciting, different, colourful and magical: all this is wonderful material for fiction.

Herein lies much of the appeal of Allende for an international readership, for she presents an image of Latin America that is always exciting. The novels present a world of extremes: a world of soldiers and guerrillas, of military coups and revolutionary governments, passionate men and women motivated by love, sex and social justice, of poets and torturers, of women with magical powers and men who are either beasts or saints. Add to the list a collection of more or less lovable freaks in the shape of senile old people, a young woman possessed by spirits (*De amor y de sombra*; *Of Love and Shadows*) a hare-lipped Arab, a glamorous transsexual (*Eva Luna*), a woman of surreal beauty and green hair, a repressed lesbian and a sexually perverted sadistic French nobleman (*La casa de los espíritus*) and success is assured.

Allende's novels are also attractive to a female readership through her creation of strong female characters and her conception of magical properties as essentially feminine. Allende, unlike her male fellow-writer García Márquez, emphasises the spiritual dimension of magical realism and makes this the domain of women. Allende creates a series of protagonists with supernatural powers, white witches with feminine virtues whom readers are invited to wonder at and admire: Clara with her clairvoyant powers and her ability to move inanimate objects; Rosa with her green hair and fantastic tapestries; Irene who can predict the future; Evangelina who is possessed by spirits, and Eva who enchants her listeners with the stories she tells them.

The spiritual dimension of Allende's women, as well as providing entertainment, is also of symbolic value. In a society dominated by a militaristic cult of masculinity, the author sees spirituality as a form of feminine resistance. Magical powers can be used to ward off the evil spirits of patriarchy, as Clara shows by retreating into a world of spirituality to escape the violence and negative energy of her husband Esteban Trueba, and through her spirit which returns to give her granddaughter, Alba, strength after she has been imprisoned and sexually abused.

However, women only able to function on a spiritual level are of little use to a female readership and would have a limited appeal as role models. Allende's heroines are successful because they are able to engage with material reality when required by circumstances. Thus, both Irene and Clara, two of the most spiritual characters, are able to return to earthly matters when faced with the harsh realities of social injustice.

Another reason for Allende's mass popularity is the fact that while she adopts elements of feminism, principally in her creation of strong women as protagonists of her novels and in her attacks on the worst excesses of *machista* culture in the form of sexual abuse and militarism, nowhere does she challenge the bases of heterosexual gender relations. On the contrary, her novels depend on the exploitation of the romantic myth for their power to move and intrigue her readership. Romantic love, as in most women's best-sellers, is where ultimate happiness and fulfilment are to be found, and although Allende's women are non-submissive and sexually liberated, their worlds will come to revolve around one man. It is significant that the female characters only become involved with the politics of their country through a romantic involvement with a man: Alba through Miguel; Blanca (to a lesser extent) through Pedro Tercero in *La casa de los espíritus*; Eva through Huberto Naranjo and Rolf Carlé in *Eva Luna*; and Irene through Francisco in *De amor y de sombra*. The overall message is that there is one ideal man out there whom the protagonist will eventually find and without whom she cannot be complete. Allende's appeal is found in the way that she offers her readers a desired reality, the promise of a "new man," gentle, caring, loyal, passionate, driven by political ideals and devoted to one woman.

Neither does Allende frighten off her male readers who in every novel are offered positive role models. They are invited to identify with the new male heroes who are political enough not to be emasculated. There is the additional promise that the new sensitive revolutionary man will be rewarded with the love of a romantic heroine for the 1980s and 1990s, a heroine who is intelligent, spiritual, kind and caring, possessed of a beauty which corresponds to traditional notions of femininity and who has no sexual complexes.

Yet, despite the heavy romantic content of her novels which has laid her open to criticisms of sentimentality and melodrama, Allende takes her fiction beyond the scope of the sugary love story. Story-telling has a clear ideological purpose for Allende, and is used as a vehicle for documenting social and political truths. The narratives are deeply rooted in a specific social and historical context, a context which is never simply there to provide an exotic backdrop to a love story as in the case of Esquivel's first novel. In *De amor y de sombra*, for example, the primary concern of the narrative is to denounce the human rights abuses committed by the military in the Pinochet era in Chile. Similarly, *La casa de los espíritus*, using the format of a family saga, presents an interpretation of modern Chilean history from a broadly socialist perspective: much of the narrative chronicles social inequality and the abuses committed first by old-fashioned conservatives and then by the right-wing military regime. The elation felt by the author when describing the celebratory scenes following the election of the socialist candidate (a reference to the election of Salvador Allende, Isabel's uncle) is unmistakable.

Isabel Allende is not a writer who is likely to appeal to the more intellectual Latin American writers. For example, in an interview given in 1995, the Argentine author Juan José Saer observed that the approval of academia is of much greater importance to Allende than to, say, Borges. He said specifically: "For example, very soon there'll be a flood of these [academic readings] on Isabel Allende. For her, it will be a confirmation and a kind of sacralisation, and I have my doubts about this future consecration." Yet, so-called professional readers/critics are more likely to forgive Allende her idealised notions of romance in the knowledge that she gives so-called non-specialist readers a social insight into human rights abuses in Latin America that they would be unlikely to find in any other of their reading material. At the same time, "non-specialist readers" are able to enjoy novels in which political content is never dry or overly factual but rather highly personalised and fictionalised (build up, suspense, dramatic dénouements, etc.) and interwoven with plenty of anecdote and romance. This having been said, who is to say that "professional readers" do not enjoy a good love story, and that "non-professional readers" are not fascinated to read about Latin American society?

DEBORAH A. SHAW

Biography

Born in Lima, Peru, 2 August 1942; niece of former Chilean President Salvador Allende who died in the course of the military takeover of September, 1973. Attended a private high school in Santiago de Chile, graduated 1959. Secretary, United Nations Food and Agricultural Organization, Santiago, 1959–65. Married Miguel Frías in 1962 (divorced in 1987), one daughter (deceased) and one son. Worked as a journalist, editor, and advice columnist for *Paula* magazine, Santiago, 1967–74; interviewer for Canal 13/Canal 7 television station, 1970–75; worked on movie newsreels, 1973–75; administrator, Colegio Marroco, Caracas, 1979–82; guest teacher, Montclair State College, New Jersey, Spring 1985, and University of Virginia, Charlottesville, Fall 1988; Gildersleeve Lecturer, Barnard College, New York, Spring 1988; taught creative writing at the University of California, Berkeley, Spring 1989. Married William Gordon in 1988, one stepson. Recipient of numerous awards including the Panorama Literario Novel of the Year (Chile), 1983; Author of the Year, 1984, 1986, and Book of the Year, 1984 (Germany); Grand Prix d'Évasion (France), 1984; Colima for best novel (Mexico), 1985; *Mulheres* Best Novel (Portugal), 1987

Selected Works

Novels

La casa de los espíritus, Barcelona: Plaza y Janés, 1982; as *The House of the Spirits*, translated by Magda Bogin, New York: Knopf, and London: Jonathan Cape, 1985

De amor y de sombra, Barcelona: Plaza y Janés, 1984; as *Of Love and Shadows*, translated by Margaret Sayers Peden, New York: Knopf, and London: Jonathan Cape, 1987

Eva Luna, Barcelona: Plaza y Janés, 1987; as *Eva Luna*, translated by Margaret Sayers Peden, New York: Knopf, 1988; London: Hamish Hamilton, 1989

Los cuentos de Eva Luna, Barcelona: Plaza y Janés, 1990; as *The Stories of Eva Luna*, translated by Margaret Sayers Peden, New York: Atheneum, and London: Hamish Hamilton, 1991

El plan infinito, Barcelona: Plaza y Janés, 1991; as *The Infinite Plan*, translated by Margaret Sayers Peden, New York and London: HarperCollins, 1993

Other Writings

Civilice a su troglodita: los impertinentes de Isabel Allende, Santiago de Chile: Lord Cochran, 1974

La gorda de porcelana, Madrid: Alfaguara, 1984 [for children]

Paula, Barcelona: Plaza y Janés, 1994; as *Paula*, translated by Margaret Sayers Peden, New York and London: HarperCollins, 1995 [informal family history]

Further Reading

Antoni, Robert, "Parody or Piracy: the Relation of *The House of the Spirits* to *One Hundred Years of Solitude*," *Latin American Literary Review*, vol. 16/32 (1988)

Arancibia, Juana Alcira, *Evaluación de la literatura femenina de latinoamérica, siglo XX*, Costa Rica: EDUCA, 1985 [Contains several contributions on *La casa de los espíritus*]

Coddou, Marcelo (editor), *Los libros tienen sus propios espíritus*, Veracruz: Universidad Veracruzana, 1986

Coddou, Marcelo, *Para leer a Isabel Allende*, Concepción, Chile: LAR, 1988

Earle, Peter G., "Literature as Survival: Allende's *The House of the Spirits*," *Contemporary Literature*, vol. 28/4 (1987)

Hart, Patricia, *Narrative Magic in the Fiction of Isabel Allende*, Rutherford, New Jersey: Fairleigh Dickinson University Press, and London: Associated University Presses, 1989

Levine, Linda Gould, "A Passage to Androgyny: Isabel Allende's *La casa de los espíritus*," in *In the Feminine Mode: Essays on Hispanic Women Writers*, edited by Noel Valis and Carol Maier, Lewisburg, Pennsylvania: Bucknell University Press, 1990

Meyer, Doris, "Exile and the Female Condition in Isabel Allende's *De amor y de sombra*," *International Fiction Review*, vol. 15/2 (1988)

Moody, Michael, "Isabel Allende and the Testimonial Novel," *Confluencia*, vol. 2/1 (1986)

Riquelme Rojas, Sonia and Edna Aguirre Rehbein (editors), *Critical Approaches to Isabel Allende's Novels*, New York: Peter Lang, 1991

Robinett, Jane, *This Rough Magic: Technology in Latin America Fiction*, New York: Peter Lang, 1994 [Contains two chapters on *La casa de los espíritus*]

Schiminovich, Flora H., "Two Modes of Writing the Female Self: Isabel Allende's *The House of the Spirits* and Clarice Lispector's *The Stream of Life*," in *Redefining Autobiography in 20th-Century Women's Fiction*, edited by Janice Morgan and Colette T. Hall, New York: Garland, 1991

Interviews

García Pinto, Magdalena, *Women Writers of Latin America: Intimate Histories*, Austin: University of Texas Press, 1991

Rodden, John, "'The Responsibility to Tell You': an Interview with Isabel Allende," *Kenyon Review*, vol. 13/1 (1991)

Laura Esquivel 1950–

Mexican novelist

Isabel Allende and Laura Esquivel are the only two Latin American women writers whose names are likely to be known to a non-Latin American and a non-specialist readership. Both Allende's novels and Esquivel's *Como agua para chocolate* (*Like Water for Chocolate*) have vastly outsold novels by the majority of their male contemporaries. *Como agua para chocolate* was the second best-selling novel in Mexico in 1989 while the English translation spent a considerable period in the *New York Times* list of best sellers in 1993. Sales of the novel have also been boosted by Alfonso Arau's screen adaptation of his (now ex-) wife's novel, for which Esquivel wrote the screenplay. The film has been a huge international success, it has won eighteen international awards and was the foreign language film with the highest box office takings in the United States in 1993.

Extraliterary factors are important in the attainment of best-seller status, and literary text cannot be separated from social context. As Resa Dudovitz writes in her book *The Myth of Superwomen*: "The bestseller . . . functions within the popular culture of a particular society as a reflection of contemporary concerns and provides an important understanding of the dominant ideologies of that society." This mode of conceptualising best-sellers is particularly useful in any attempt to understand the phenomenal success of a first novel by an unknown Mexican writer. Various factors are at play in determining the mass appeal of *Como agua para chocolate*: 1. The portrayal of a romantic rural past in the face of ever increasing urban modernisation; 2. The portrayal of a lifelong love affair in an age characterised by relationship breakdowns, serial monogamy and a contradictory belief in the "until death do us part" romantic ideal; 3. The reclaiming of traditional notions of femininity and feminine arts (cookery) in a period of confused gender identities and pre-prepared TV dinners; 4. A sense of perceived authenticity in the shape of "real" Mexican food and "real" Mexican culture at a time when Tex-Mex restaurants are becoming increasingly popular in the

United States and Europe. Esquivel also assures success with the addition of other market-friendly ingredients such as an original narrative formula (the interweaving of a fast-moving storyline and recipes) combined with reassuring use of elements of the familiar genres of fairy tale and soap opera, and a cast of characters whom readers are invited to either cheer or hiss in true pantomime tradition.

As the makers of Hollywood box-office hits have known since the industry's inception, there is nothing that reaches audiences like a good old-fashioned love story. To capture a truly intense sense of romance, artists feel the need to go back in time to a historical period that preceded the sexual revolution, when merely to look longingly at a member of the opposite sex was considered over-bold.

Como agua para chocolate is appropriately set in the home of a family belonging to the land-owning classes in revolutionary and post-revolutionary Mexico. The sexual conservatism of the period is further exacerbated by a Mexican family tradition which decrees that the youngest daughter cannot marry or have children as she has to devote herself to caring for her mother. Tita, the youngest daughter of Esquivel's novel, however, falls in love with Pedro, her childhood sweetheart and what would normally be an extremely conventional relationship (both are of the same class, same ethnic origins, same town and of opposite sex) becomes ideal material for romantic fiction.

Esquivel manages to create an obstacle for her two lovers and to convey the excitement generated by a forbidden love without contravening any of the conservative social values which characterise the ideology within the text, a conservatism upon which its best-seller status depends. As Resa Dudovitz has noted: "women's bestsellers ... rarely propose a world vision which necessitates any radical change of existing social structures." So, in the case of *Como agua para chocolate*, while the reader is given the impression of a heroine who seeks to escape repressive family codes, the temptation to rebel is motivated by Tita's desire to conform to traditional notions of femininity where an ideal woman needs to be wife, mother and nurturer if she is to be fulfilled. Tita's sole desire in life is to marry Pedro, rear his children and provide husband and children with delicious food.

This rather simple, conventional storyline clearly needed spicing up, to use a cooking metaphor, for the novel to reach the spectacular sales figures that it has achieved. This is achieved by the originality of the narrative format, whereby actual recipes are given, and cooking instructions and plenty of culinary metaphors are woven into the telling of Tita's plight; by the use of humour and exaggeration to allow the heavy sentimental nature of the novel to be more easily digested; and by the use of "magical realism" with most of the realism taken out, a proven recipe for success.

Esquivel combines all the clichés of romantic love to humorous effect when she has Tita and Pedro's first orgasm after years of honourable frustration accompanied by spirals of phosphorescent colours which ascend to the sky like delicate Bengal lights. Likewise, the concluding love scene where Pedro enters a tunnel of luminous light which leads to his death in a supreme moment of ecstasy, followed by Tita's self-immolation by eating the contents of a box of matches, has to be read as a parody of representations of romantic love if it is to be rescued from criticisms of being excessively clichéd and literal.

The so-called magical realism of the novel is another major reason for the commercial success of both novel and film. Esquivel and Arau exploited the taste for "magical realism," watering down the realism found in the chronicling of important social events in order to concentrate almost exclusively on the magical as the most entertaining and profitable part of the formula. Two of the most memorable scenes, the wedding banquet at which the bitter tears Tita sheds into the cake causes weeping fits and mass vomiting among the guests, and Gertrudis's abduction at the hands of a revolutionary who picks up the scent of her sexuality released by the aphrodisiac properties of Tita's cooking, take "magical realism" to the level of the purely sensational and provide little if any insight into the workings of Mexican society at a key point in its history.

Both Esquivel and Allende have hit upon the right formula for producing Latin American best-sellers, but while Allende shows that it is possible to write highly entertaining novels without entirely abandoning liberal political and feminist views, Esquivel plays it extremely safe, rooting her story-telling skills within an extremely traditional and conservative ideology.

DEBORAH A. SHAW

See also entries on The Boom, Film, Magical Realism, Translation

Biography
Born in Mexico City in 1950. Worked as a teacher; has also written books for children and film scripts. Named Mexican Woman of the Year in 1992. *Como agua para chocolate* has been translated into 29 languages. Awarded the ABBY (American Booksellers Book of the Year), 1994, the first time the award had been given to a non-US citizen.

Selected Works

Novels
Como agua para chocolate, Mexico City: Planeta, 1989; as *Like Water for Chocolate*, translated by Carol Christensen and Thomas Christensen, New York: Doubleday, and London: Black Swan, 1993
La ley del amor, Barcelona: Plaza y Janés, 1995; as *The Law of Love*, translated by Margaret Sayers Peden, New York: Crown, and London: Chatto and Windus, 1996

Further Reading
Beckman, Pierina E., "Realidad y fantasía en el mundo culinario de Laura Esquivel," *Fem*, vol. 18/136 (June 1994)
Escandón, Carmen Ramos, "Receta y feminidad en *Como agua para chocolate*," *Fem*, vol. 15/102 (June 1991)
Glenn, Kathleen Mary, "Postmodern Parody and Culinary Narrative Art in Laura Esquivel's *Como agua para chocolate*," *Chasqui*, vol. 23/2 (November 1994)
Lawless, Cecilia, "Experimental Cooking in *Como agua para chocolate*," *Monographic Review / Revista Monográfica* 8 (1992)
Lillo, Gastón and Monique Sarfati-Arnaud, "*Como agua para chocolate*: determinaciones de la lectura en el contexto pos-moderno," *Revista Canadiense de Estudios Hispánicos*, vol. 18/3 (Spring 1994)
Marquet, Antonio, "¿Cómo escribir un 'best-seller'? La receta de Laura Esquivel," *Plural* 237 (June 1991)
Oropesa, Salvador A., "*Como agua para chocolate* de Laura Esquivel como lectura del manual de urbanidad y buenas costumbres de Manuel Antonio Carreno," *Chasqui*, vol. 20/2 (November 1991)
Shaw, Deborah A. and Bridget Rollet, "*Como agua para chocolate*: Some of the Reasons for its Success," *Travesía*, vol. 3/1–2 (1994)

Olavo Bilac 1865–1918

Brazilian poet

Olavo Bilac is one of the most anthologized of 19th-century Brazilian poets and is generally described, quite accurately, as both the most famous and the most representative member of the poetic movement Brazilians call Parnassianism. The Parnassianists largely controlled literary society and poetic discourse in Brazil from about 1880 until the rise of *Modernismo* in the early 1920s, almost completely smothering the one serious challenge to their preeminence, Brazilian Symbolism. Bilac's coronation, in 1907, as "The Prince of Brazilian Poets," is indicative both of his contemporary reputation and of the power of the Parnassianist establishment. Bilac's status as the archetypal Parnassianist, however, made him and his works lightning-rods for harsh criticism and satire once the Modernist rebellion began in 1922. Several of Bilac's best-known poems still appear in every anthology of Brazilian poetry, but his reputation has not yet recovered from these Modernist attacks, and no serious critical study of his large and varied production has yet been attempted.

At the end of the 1870s, a number of young Brazilian poets endeavored to break away from Romanticism, producing works they called "scientific poetry," "realist poetry," or, simply, examples of "A idéia nova" [The New Idea]. In real terms, however, the content and form of many of these poems were virtually indistinguishable from those of late-Romantic poets like Antônio de Castro Alves. This search for something new, something more clearly distinct from Romanticism, was reinforced, after 1880, by exposure to the poems of Théophile Gautier, Leconte de Lisle, and other writers linked to the French movement known as Parnassianism, a relatively brief anti-Romantic reaction of the 1860s and 1870s. The young Brazilian poets began to call themselves Parnassianists around 1885, and the prestige inherent in the French origin of the term greatly assisted Olavo Bilac, Raimundo Correia (1859–1911), Alberto de Oliveira (1857–1937), and other members of the group in establishing themselves as the dominant force in Brazilian poetry.

The central problem, and the central irony, of Brazilian Parnassianism is that the poetic ideology these young writers adopted from the French movement, at least as they interpreted and adapted it, was in many ways inherently anti-poetic. That ideology also ran counter, in many cases, to the whole poetic tradition in Brazil and to the personal inclinations of the Brazilian Parnassianists themselves. Bilac's 1886 "Profissão de fé" [Profession of Faith], a work based upon Théophile Gautier's poem "L'Art," published in 1856, was the most influential statement of Brazilian Parnassianist ideology. In that poem, Bilac defines the poet as a craftsman, a goldsmith lovingly and laboriously toiling to create a perfect object; he twists and files and polishes each phrase before setting the rhyme, "like a ruby, into the golden verse." All this effort, Bilac insists, is in the service of the goddess of Form.

As the craftsman metaphor suggests, the Brazilian Parnassianists wholly rejected the Romantic view of poetry as divine inspiration channeled through the genius and the emotions of a few exceptional talents. They argued, rather, that any educated upper-class Brazilian willing to spend the time and energy required to master the movement's detailed and rigidly enforced code of proper versification and metrics could produce a perfect poem. Inspiration and emotion were defined as extraneous to the poetic project; the twin goals were objective description and formal perfection. Many of the titles of Brazilian Parnassianist poems refer to the visual arts and, more specifically, to the imported artistic objects which graced upper-class parlors during the *belle époque*; these poetic objects are still-lifes, watercolors, miniatures, lithographs, even photographs. Moreover, one often finds multiple layers of reproduction in these works – the poetic object reproduces a contemporary lithograph which reproduces a Renaissance painting or a Greek sculpture. The strong undercurrent of exoticism in Brazilian Parnassianism conforms to this model; the countless poetic descriptions of Middle Eastern or Oriental scenes are not works of the imagination, but metrified versions of the hand-colored lithographs or photographs found in popular travel books. At its most extreme, this Parnassianist emphasis upon objective description defined love poetry not as the expression of emotion, but as the careful and detailed reproduction of portions of the beloved object's anatomy. Moreover, objectivity and preoccupation with formal perfection often led to utterly banal but carefully rhymed and metered prose, as in the first stanza of Bilac's poem "Nel mezzo del camin . . ." (published in 1888, in the first edition of his *Poesias*):

Cheguei. Chegaste. Vinhas fatigada
E triste, e triste e fatigado eu vinha.
Tinhas a alma de sonhos povoada,
E a alma de sonhos povoada eu tinha . . .

[I arrived. You arrived. You were tired / And sad, and I was tired and sad as well. / Your soul was filled with dreams, / And my soul too with dreams was filled . . .]

This banality, fortunately, is not typical of Bilac's poetry as a whole, but his works, throughout much of his career, do conform to the model of Brazilian Parnassianism described above, a model he did a great deal to create. There are occasional flashes of real emotion, but objectivity and the constraints of formal perfection far more often serve as a kind of straitjacket, against which he sometimes struggles but which he generally fails to escape. The best of his early poems are found in the *Via láctea* [Milky Way] collection, published as part of his 1888 *Poesias*. In these works, written after the unexpected end of his engagement to marry Alberto de Oliveira's sister, the raw intensity of Bilac's feelings is sometimes able to break through ideology and form and convince us of the authenticity of his emotions. The constant conflict between impulse and constraint in Bilac's verse is perhaps most visible in *O caçador de esmeraldas* [The Emerald Hunter], included in the second edition of his *Poesias* (1902). This long work is Bilac's attempt to force one of the central traditions of Brazilian Romantic verse, the patriotic epic, into the Parnassianist mold.

His topic is the career of Fernão Dias Paes Leme, a 17th-century explorer of the Brazilian interior, but vast landscapes and heroic deeds, in Bilac's hands, become little more than metrified history and static tableaux.

The most satisfying of Bilac's works, for modern readers, is the posthumously-published *Tarde* [Afternoon] of 1919. The poems in this volume make it clear that, despite the poet's public rejection of any challenge to Parnassianist orthodoxy, more recent European intellectual developments (the philosophy of Schopenhauer, the verse of the French Symbolists) had in fact had at least some impact on his ideas and his poetic practice. Moreover, ideology, form and theme finally achieve some sort of balance. These are elegiac poems in which the poet, still nostalgic for the past, expresses his acceptance of aging and the approach of death. He sees himself as beyond passion, and the cold objectivity of Parnassianism makes perfect sense within this context. Form, Bilac insists, is all that survives the death of feeling. His nostalgic scrapbook of poetic photographs of lost youth and lost love convinces us and moves us, and remains, perhaps, the single greatest accomplishment of the Brazilian Parnassianist movement.

DAVID T. HABERLY

Biography
Born Olavo Brás Martins dos Guimarães Bilac in Rio de Janeiro, Brazil, 16 December 1865. Began to study medicine in 1880. First work published in *Gazeta Acadêmica* in 1883. Collaborated with some of the leading writers of the time – Alberto de Oliveira, Aluísio Azevedo, Coelho Neto – from 1886. First travelled to Europe in 1890–91. Secretary General of the third Conferência Panamericana, Rio de Janeiro; Brazilian delegate, 4th Conferência, Buenos Aires, 1910. Member, Academia de Letras, 1896. Died in 1918.

Selected Works

Poetry
Poesias, São Paulo: Teixeira e Irmãos, 1888; 2nd edition, 1902
Crônicas e novelas, n.p., 1894
Sagres, Rio de Janeiro, n.p., 1898
Crítica e fantasia, Lisbon, n.p., 1904
Poesias infantis, Rio de Janeiro: Francisco Alves, 1904
Conferências literárias, Rio de Janeiro: Francisco Alves, 1906
Ironia e piedade, Rio de Janeiro: Francisco Alves, 1916
A defesa nacional, Rio de Janeiro: Liga de Defesa Nacional, 1917
Bocage, São Paulo: Porto, 1917
Tarde, Rio de Janeiro: Francisco Alves, 1919
Bom humor, Rio de Janeiro: Editora Casa Mandarino, 1939

Other Writings
Últimas conferências e discursos, Rio de Janeiro: Francisco Alves, 1977

Compilations and Anthologies
Poesias, São Paulo: Teixeira e Irmão, 1888; 2nd edition, 1902
Os melhores poemas de Olavo Bilac, São Paulo: Global, 1985

Further Reading
Elton, E., *O noivado de Bilac, com a correspondência inédita do poeta a sua noiva*, Rio de Janeiro: Simões, 1954
Jorge, Fernando, *Vida e poesia de Olavo Bilac*, 4th edition, São Paulo: T.A. Queiroz, 1992
Lajolo, M., *Usos e abusos da literatura na escola: Bilac e a literatura escolar na República Velha*, Rio de Janeiro: Globo, 1982
Magalhães, Jr, Raimundo, *Olavo Bilac e sua época*, Rio de Janeiro: Companhia Editora Americana, 1974
Pontes, Eloy, *A vida exuberante de Olavo Bilac*, 2 vols, Rio de Janeiro: José Olympio, 1944

Bildungsroman

"Bildnis" in German is portrait, image, likeness. The related "Bildung" may be translated as shape or shaping, referring both to external form and to the process of formation. While it has lost the strictly religious connotations it had in the Middle Ages (summarisable in the phrase "to fashion in the likeness of God"), "Bildung" retains a moral sense relating to the process of education and acquisition of cultural and social values. "Bildungsroman" is thus the novel of formation or education. The term has left the confines of German studies to be used untranslated in literary criticism in general, a fact which has not always pleased Germanists, who see the Bildungsroman as a national phenomenon.

Theorising about the Bildungsroman (and there is a lot of it, especially in German) often begins with Goethe's *Wilhelm Meisters Lehrjahre*, 1795 (*Wilhelm Meister's Apprenticeship*).

During the 18th century in Germany, a shift took place in the concept of Bildung, away from the religious and towards the humanistic; the individual is increasingly seen as having innate potential (often of an artistic kind) and that potential is to be drawn out and reconciled with his environment, the latter sometimes being conceived in pantheistic terms. But, while nature may provide the seed, it is not enough for the individual to grow passively; instead, he must engage in active self-development: Goethe writes in *Aus meinem Leben: Dichtung und Wahrheit* (*From My Life*) that "[going] to work on one's own moral Bildung . . . is the most advisable thing." Bildung becomes a matter of will; destinies can be shaped. It comes as no surprise to find that the Nazis later sought to appropriate the genre for their own purposes, the individual standing for the nation. Yet while some "novels of education" seem to signal approbation of the process whereby individuals accommodate themselves to the prevailing ethos, many question that ethos or suggest that it is ephemeral.

As "Bildungsroman" becomes part of the general vocabulary of criticism, so its features become less particular. Nowadays, the term is used very generally to refer to novels entailing a dialectic between the individual and the environment; the novel usually has a male protagonist, that protagonist is frequently portrayed in school, the process of growing up is often allied to sexual awakening, and, in keeping with our time, integration into adult life is seen no longer in terms of optimistic affirmation, but sceptically, as a matter of compromise or reconciliation. The narrative is normally in the first person.

That the Bildungsroman should have been so frequently and deliberately the preserve of male protagonists, offering what were often very stereotypical views of passive and irrational female characters, has naturally caught the attention of feminist critics. These appear to be divided as to whether unearthing forgotten novels of female Bildung serves to redress the balance, or whether that is simply a way of capitulating to masculinist standards.

The description Bildungsroman can be applied to a great many Latin American novels. Some examples are: Raul Pompéia's *O ateneu*, 1888 [The Atheneum], a story of a boarding school run by a megalomaniac, the sexual and intellectual awakening of the boy narrator, and the social relationships he develops; two novels that also deal with culture conflict, one of them with a female protagonist: Rosario Castellanos's *Balún Canán*, 1957 (*The Nine Guardians*), which is partly autobiographical and portrays a child of European origin brought up by an Indian nanny, and José María Arguedas's *Los ríos profundos*, 1958 (*Deep Rivers*), also an autobiographically-based story, which tells of a boy torn between his love of the oppressed Quechua people and his Catholic education; Vargas Llosa's *La ciudad y los perros*, 1963 (*The Time of the Hero*) is perhaps the modern novel that best fits the classic model of the Bildungsroman, since it portrays an intelligent boy, surviving by his wits in a cadet school to which he has been sent by an alienated father to rid him of his artistic proclivities, a boy who emerges much the wiser and sadder.

PETER STANDISH

Further Reading

Buckley, Jerome Hamilton, *Season of Youth*, Cambridge, Massachussets: Harvard University Press, 1974

Dorfman, Ariel, *Imaginación y violencia en América*, Santiago de Chile: Editorial Universitaria, 1970 [Contains chapter on *Los ríos profundos* and *La ciudad y los perros*]

Fraiman, Susan, *Unbecoming Women*, New York: Columbia University Press, 1993

Hardin, James (editor), *Reflection and Action: Essays on the Bildungsroman*, Columbia: University of South Carolina Press, 1991

Hart, Stephen M., *White Ink. Essays on Twentieth-Century Feminine Fiction in Spain and Latin America*, London: Támesis, 1993 [Chapter 1 is on formation novels by women]

Kontje, Todd, *The German Bildungsroman: History of a Genre*, Columbia, South Carolina: Camden House, 1993

Pinto, Cristina Ferreira, *O bildungsroman feminino: quatro exemplos brasileiros*, São Paulo: Perspectiva, 1990

Adolfo Bioy Casares 1914–

Argentine prose writer

In 1990, Adolfo Bioy Casares was awarded the Cervantes prize, the highest distinction for writers in the Spanish language. That year also marked the 50th anniversary of *La invención de Morel* (*The Invention of Morel*) the novel by Bioy that opened a crucial decade in the development of the so-called new Latin American narrative. Over more than half a century of literary creation, Bioy Casares's works include seven novels, an even greater number of collections of short stories, books of miscellaneous prose with articles and essays, a novel written with his wife Silvina Ocampo, and several volumes in collaboration with Jorge Luis Borges.

It was Borges who wrote the prologue for *La invención de Morel*, a text that among critics of Spanish American literature has reached a level of popularity and importance equal to that of the novel itself. In this prologue Borges comes down in favor of the adventure story, the novel of "reasoned imagination" while rejecting the psychological and realistic novel. He proposes that a narrative be a "verbal artifice," a work of pure fiction that does not tolerate any superfluous elements. In this sense, Borges qualifies the plot of Bioy Casares's novel as "perfect."

The protagonist of *La invención de Morel* is a fugitive running away from justice who arrives on an apparently uninhabited island. But he soon encounters a number of people, among them a woman, Faustine, and a bearded tennis player named Morel. The fugitive writes in his diary about his efforts to survive the tides that flood part of the island, to find food, and to avoid being discovered by the other inhabitants. He also mentions some strange things that are happening: no one seems to see him or to be aware of his presence; once in a while the people repeat the same words or gestures they had used before; and they disappear as suddenly as they appear. As Borges notes in the prologue, the "fantastic but not supernatural" explanation is that they and their setting are just images formed by Morel's "invention." This consists of machines, activated by the tides, that film, tape record, and then project the complete presence of people and things. The protagonist, in love with Faustine, decides to insert himself into the sequence of projected images with which, facing impending death, he hopes to be able to remain eternally at the side of his beloved. Through the story, Bioy faces the reader with the material and mechanical aspects in the creation of beings and objects by machine and, on the other hand, with the metaphysical reflexion about the refutation of time and the quest for immortality. Without ignoring the importance of these subjects or the author's rich imagination, the fundamental value of this work rests on its compositional techniques, especially on the interplay of narrative levels and points of view.

At the beginning of the novel the protagonist-narrator explains that what we are reading is the journal in which he recorded the strange events that occurred on the island. Every so often there are footnotes written by "the editor," who usually contradicts or criticizes what the protagonist is saying. Also, there is a manuscript by Morel that includes an explanation of his invention as transcribed by the protagonist-narrator. Therefore, we have the "diary" of the fugitive and the "manuscript" of Morel both included in the text "published" by the editor. And we can recognize three sources of information, or three narrative voices – those of the protagonist, the editor, and Morel's – none of them reliable in so far as they try to discredit one another. To this ambiguity one must add the way in which clues and scraps of information are dropped into the narrative to assist readers in unravelling the island's mystery. These are strategies similar to those of a detective story where the reader is invited to participate in the investigation. *La invención de Morel* presents fiction within fiction, a calculated interplay of narrators and characters, verbal repetitions that evoke temporal repetitions, all in order to construct a text that is self-affirming in its autonomous reality as pure literary artifice.

El sueño de los héroes, 1954 (*The Dream of Heroes*) is for many critics, Bioy Casares's best novel, displaying themes and techniques characteristic of his narrative style. Different from the previous novels – *La invención de Morel* and *Plan de evasión* (*A Plan for Escape*) – the action is not set in a remote island but in diverse places in the city of Buenos Aires, a recurrent scene in Bioy Casares's fictions. Very few works in Argentine literature offer such a vivid image of the Buenos Aires of the 1920s and 1930s as this one does. This is not to say that the story always develops in a realistic atmosphere. On the contrary, the central theme revolves around a dream, or a state of mind that is being remembered as magnificent and to which a man tries to return.

The protagonist of the story is Emilio Gauna, a young mechanic who has won some money gambling at the races and decides to spend it with a group of friends and the so-called "doctor" Valerga, a man the young fellows admire for his reported courage. It is the carnival season of 1927, and Emilio and his companions go off on a three-day spree that includes bars, masquerades, and brothels. On the last night, at a ball, Emilio has a brief encounter with a masked woman. They part and, in some confusion, he vaguely remembers a knife duel with Valerga. Later, he awakes in an unfamiliar place

in the middle of a park. The three days of 1927 become an obsession for Emilio and, when in 1930 he again wins at the races, he tries to relive the events that took place three years before. The story ends with Emilio ready to face death in a knife fight with Valerga. Gauna is happy because he discovers that he is not a coward, and he understands the meaning of the dream (or memory) of the mysterious adventure that has haunted him for so long.

Through the reading of *El sueño de los héroes* we can identify frequent patterns in Bioy's narrative. Emilio, the mechanic, and his friends belong to the lower-middle class, the social group that seems to attract especially the author's attention. In his fictions, Bioy provides an accurate characterization of the members of this group on the basis of their actions and habits and, overall, in his rendering of the peculiarities of their language.

The theme of courage, of a young man sacrificing himself while trying to demonstrate his bravery also appears in "Homenaje a Francisco Almeyra" [Homage to Francisco Almeyra], and dissolves into parody in the adventures of Luis Ángel Morales, the protagonist of *Un campeón desparejo* [An Uneven Champion], the novel published in 1993.

Regarding the subjects of dreams, premonitions, and the interconnection of past, present, and future, all central ideas in the plot and narrative structure of *El sueño de los héroes*, it is possible that Bioy found some suggestions in his reading of *An Experiment with Time* by John William Dunne. In "El héroe de las mujeres" [The Women's Hero], the title-story in the volume published in 1978, there are several references to Dunne's ideas. This relation between scientific readings and narrative fictions can be observed in other of Bioy's works.

Finally, we have to mention the predominant theme in all of Bioy Casares's stories, the theme of love with its complexity, inconsistencies and touches of light eroticism. Bioy's fictions offer a parade of confused and unhappy lovers from the fugitive of *La invención de Morel*, who realizes that he has fallen in love with a simulacrum, to Emilio Gauna who only at the end understands that the masked woman of his dream is Clara, his wife. In some situations, the pathetic condition of these lovers is mitigated with the use of humor, a resource that Bioy administers with special ability. Usually it is a veiled humor expressed through irony, witty sayings or light mockery. A frequent character in Bioy's works is that of a man perplexed when facing the vagaries of the amorous relations, and unable to understand the nature of his feelings or to really know the person he loves, as is the case with Lucio Bordenave in *Dormir al sol* (*Asleep in the Sun*) or Nicolasito Almanza in *La aventura de un fotógrafo en La Plata* (*The Adventures of a Photographer in La Plata*). Equally perplexed is the protagonist of *Diario de la guerra del cerdo* (*Diary of the War of the Pig*), a black comedy in the form of a fantasy about the old being persecuted by the young.

Above all, Bioy Casares's narratives are well-told stories supported by structures calculated down to the minutest detail. At the same time, Bioy's considerable gifts as a craftsman are illustrated by his lightness of touch. The vast world of his fictions is rendered in an eloquent style, exemplary in its precise elegance.

MIREYA CAMURATI

Biography

Born in Buenos Aires, Argentina, 15 September 1914, of an upper-class family. Travelled with his family to Europe in 1924 and to the United States in 1929. Attended the University of Buenos Aires in the academic year 1933–34 but became disillusioned with academia and left without completing a course, 1934. Met Jorge Luis Borges in 1932 with whom he collaborated on a number of literary works (under the pseudonyms H. Bustos Domecq and B. Suárez Lynch) and maintained a close friendship until Borges's death. They founded the literary magazine, *Destiempo* in 1936 and the "The Seventh Circle" detective series for Emecé Editores, Buenos Aires, 1943–1956. The year 1932 also marked the beginning of his association with Victoria Ocampo, the founder of the literary journal *Sur*, and then one of the most influential figures in Argentine cultural life. Member of the "*Sur* Group." Married Victoria's sister, Silvina Ocampo in 1940, one daughter. Also wrote film scripts in collaboration with Borges. Recipient of numerous awards including: City of Buenos Aires Municipal Prize, 1941; National Literature Prize, 1969; Argentine Society of Writers Grand Prize of Honour, 1975; Mondello Prize, 1984; Miguel de Cervantes Prize, 1990. Member of the Légion d'Honneur, 1981.

Selected Works

Novels

La invención de Morel, Buenos Aires: Losada, 1940; with stories from *La trama celeste*, as *The Invention of Morel, and Other Stories from "La trama celeste,"* translated by Ruth L.C. Simms, Austin: University of Texas Press, 1964

Plan de evasión, Buenos Aires: Emecé, 1945; as *A Plan for Escape*, translated by Suzanne Jill Levine, New York: Dutton, 1975

El sueño de los héroes, Buenos Aires: Losada, 1954; as *The Dream of Heroes*, translated by Diana Thorold, London: Quartet, 1987; New York: Dutton, 1988

Diario de la guerra del cerdo, Buenos Aires: Emecé, 1969; as *Diary of the War of the Pig*, translated by Gregory Woodruff, New York: McGraw Hill, 1972; London: Allison and Busby, 1989

Dormir al sol, Buenos Aires: Emecé, 1973; as *Asleep in the Sun*, translated by Suzanne Jill Levine, New York: Persea, 1978

La aventura de un fotógrafo en La Plata, Buenos Aires: Emecé, 1985; as *The Adventures of a Photographer in La Plata*, translated by Suzanne Jill Levine, New York: Dutton, 1989; London: Bloomsbury, 1991

Un campeón desparejo, Barcelona: Tusquets, 1993

Short Fiction

17 disparos contra lo porvenir, Buenos Aires: Tor, 1933 [published under the psuedonym Martín Sacastru]

Caos, Buenos Aires: Viau y Zona, 1934

La nueva tormenta, o La vida múltiple de Juan Ruteno, Buenos Aires: Columbo, 1935

Luis Greve, muerto, Buenos Aires: Destiempo, 1937

Seis problemas para don Isidro Parodi, in collaboration with Jorge Luis Borges (published under the pseudonym H. Bustos Domecq), Buenos Aires: Sur, 1942; as *Six Problems for Don Isidro*, translated by Norman Thomas di Giovanni, New York: Dutton, and London: Allen Lane, 1981

El perjurio de la nieve, Buenos Aires: La Quimera, 1945; as *The Perjury of the Snow*, translated by Ruth L.C. Simms, New York: Vanishing Rotating Triangle, 1964

Dos fantasías memorables, in collaboration with Jorge Luis Borges (published under the pseudonym H. Bustos Domecq), Buenos Aires: Oportet y Haereses, 1946

Un modelo para la muerte, in collaboration with Jorge Luis Borges (published under the pseudonym B. Suárez Lynch), Buenos Aires: Oportet y Haereses, 1946

Los que aman, odian, in collaboration with Silvina Ocampo, Buenos Aires: Emecé, 1946

La trama celeste, Buenos Aires: Sur, 1948; with *La invención de Morel*, as *The Invention of Morel, and Other Stories from "La trama celeste,"* translated by Ruth L.C. Simms, Austin: University of Texas Press, 1964

Las vísperas de Fausto, Buenos Aires: La Perdiz, 1949

Historia prodigiosa, Mexico City: Obregón, 1956; augmented edition, Buenos Aires: Emecé, 1961

Guirnalda con amores: cuentos, Buenos Aires: Emecé, 1959

El lado de la sombra, Buenos Aires: Emecé, 1962

El gran Serafín, Buenos Aires: Emecé, 1967

Crónicas de Bustos Domecq, in collaboration with Jorge Luis Borges, Buenos Aires: Losada, 1967; as *Chronicles of Bustos Domecq*, translated by Norman Thomas di Giovanni, New York: Dutton, 1976; London: Allen Lane, 1972

Adversos milagros: relatos, Caracas: Monte Ávila, 1969

Historias de amor, Buenos Aires: Emecé, 1972

Historias fantásticas, Buenos Aires: Emecé, 1972

Nuevos cuentos de Bustos Domecq, in collaboration with Jorge Luis Borges, Buenos Aires: La Ciudad, 1977

El héroe de las mujeres, Buenos Aires: Emecé, 1978

Los afanes, Buenos Aires: Arte Gaglianone, 1983

Historias desaforadas, Buenos Aires: Emecé, 1986

La invención y la trama, Mexico City: Fondo de Cultura Económica, 1988

Una muñeca rusa, Buenos Aires: Tusquets, 1991

Screenplays

Los orilleros; El paraíso de los creyentes, in collaboration with Jorge Luis Borges, Buenos Aires: Losada, 1955

Les Autres, in collaboration with Jorge Luis Borges and Hugo Santiago, Paris: Bourgois, 1974

Other Writings

Prólogo, Buenos Aires: Biblos, 1929

La estatua casera, Buenos Aires: Jacarandá, 1936

Antes del novecientos (recuerdos), Buenos Aires: n.p., 1958

Años de mocedad, Buenos Aires: Nuevo Cabildo, 1963

La otra aventura, Buenos Aires: Galerna, 1968

Memoria sobre la pampa y los gauchos, Buenos Aires: Sur, 1970

Breve diccionario del argentino exquisito (published under the pseudonym Javier Miranda), Buenos Aires: Barros Merino, 1971; augmented editions (as Bioy Casares), Buenos Aires: Emecé, 1978, 1990

Editor, with Jorge Luis Borges and Silvina Ocampo

Antología de la literatura fantástica, Buenos Aires: Sudamericana, 1940; as *The Book of Fantasy*, New York: Viking, and London: Xanadu, 1988

Antología poética argentina, Buenos Aires, Sudamericana, 1941; as *Antología de la poesía argentina*, 1948

Compilations and Anthologies

Adolfo Bioy Casares, edited by Ofelia Kovacci, Buenos Aires: Ministry of Education and Justice, 1963

Páginas, Buenos Aires: Celtia, 1985 [selections]

Anthologies in Translation

A Russian Doll and Other Stories, translated by Suzanne Jill Levine, New York: New Directions, 1992

Selected Stories, translated by Suzannne Jill Levine, New York: New Directions, 1994

Further Reading

Camurati, Mireya, *Bioy Casares y el alegre trabajo de la inteligencia*, Buenos Aires: Corregidor, 1990

Curia, Beatriz, *La concepción del cuento en Adolfo Bioy Casares*, Mendoza: Universidad Nacional de Cuyo, 1986

Gallagher, David P., "The Novels and Short Stories of Adolfo Bioy Casares," *Bulletin of Hispanic Studies*, vol. 52 (1975)

Giacone, Lidia A., *Símbolo y mito en Adolfo Bioy Casares*, Buenos Aires: Agon, 1984

Levine, Suzanne Jill, *Guía de Adolfo Bioy Casares*, Madrid: Fundamentos, 1982

_____ "Parody Island: Two Novels by Adolfo Bioy Casares," *Hispanic Journal*, vol. 4 (1983)

MacAdam, Alfred, "The Mirror and the Lie: Two Stories by Jorge Luis Borges and Adolfo Bioy Casares," *Modern Fiction Studies*, vol. 19 (1973)

_____ "Adolfo Bioy Casares: Satire and Self-Portrait," in his *Modern Latin American Narratives: the Dreams of Reason*, Chicago: University of Chicago Press, 1977

Martino, Daniel, *A-B-C de Adolfo Bioy Casares*, Buenos Aires: Emecé, 1989

Snook, Margaret L., "The Narrator as Creator and Critic in *The Invention of Morel*," *Latin American Literary Review*, vol. 7 (1979)

Suárez Coalla, Francisco, *Lo fantástico en la obra de Adolfo Bioy Casares*, Toluca: Universidad Autónoma del Estada de México, 1994

Tamargo, María Isabel, *La narrativa de Bioy Casares: el texto como escritura-lectura*, Madrid: Playor, 1983

Villordo, Oscar Hermes, *Genio y figura de Adolfo Bioy Casares*, Buenos Aires: Editorial Universitaria de Buenos Aires, 1983

Interviews

Gálvez, Raúl, *From the Ashen Land of the Virgin*, Oakville, Ontario: Mosaic Press, 1989

Ulla, Noemi, *Aventuras de la imaginación: de la vida y los libros de Adolfo Bioy Casares*, Buenos Aires: Corregidor, 1990

Augusto Boal 1931–

Brazilian playwright and drama theorist

During his varied career, Augusto Boal has written plays, essays and novels, worked as a theatre director and drama teacher, and played an active role in Brazilian politics, but it is as a drama theoretician that he has achieved international recognition. The innovative methods and techniques of his Teatro do oprimido (Theater of the Oppressed) have not only been a major force in the development of Latin America's New Popular Theatre, but have also had a huge impact in Europe and North America, where numerous theatre groups have been established to put his theories into practice. Few other Latin American cultural theorists can claim to have had such influence outside the region.

Boal began his work in the theatre in 1956, when, a year after returning from a period of study in the United States, he became artistic director of the Arena Theatre Company in São Paulo. The political atmosphere of the late 1950s and early 1960s in Brazil was highly charged. This was also a time when a wide range of artistic activity was conducted with the objective of stimulating the critical consciousness of the masses in order to help prepare them for political action; Arena was in the forefront of a nation-wide movement to develop a radical popular theatre. In common with many other young dramatists and directors of the period, the starting point for Boal's work was the conviction that the principal task of the artist was to use art to fight for social and political change. Boal opposed traditional, bourgeois theatre, because he saw it as sterile, and essentially reproducing the mechanisms of oppression within society. He advocated instead a new theatre that would articulate the concerns and aspirations of the poor masses, and explore the forms of social change necessary for their interests to be realised. Predictably, some critics have attacked the ideological basis of Boal's theatre, claiming that it compromises artistic creativity. However, no one has done more to revitalize Latin America's theatre, and the enormous appeal of Boal's work among so many is to a large extent explained by the fact that, through its fusion with a diverse range of political, educational and community activities, it has successfully broken theatrical conventions and extended the possibilities of dramaturgy. Significantly, it has encouraged the participation of people who would otherwise have no involvement in the theatre.

With Arena, Boal wrote his first plays, all exploring aspects of political struggle in Latin America, such as *Revolução na América do Sul*, 1960 [Revolution in South America], a satire exploring the exploitation and poverty suffered by Brazil's working classes, and *A lua pequena e a caminhada perigosa*, 1968 [The Small Light and the Dangerous Trek], a short work dedicated to Che Guevara. Boal benefitted from collaboration with other radical playwrights during this period, among them Gianfrancesco Guarnieri and Oduvaldo Viana Filho. Together they experimented with different forms and explored new themes. In plays such as *Arena conta Zumbi* [Arena Tells about Zumbi] and *Arena conta Tiradentes* [Arena Tells about Tiradentes], co-written with Guarnieri in the early 1960s, Boal began to re-examine past struggles in Brazilian history in order to draw lessons for the political conflicts of the present. Most important for Boal's future development, however, were the experiments with new techniques which he carried out with Arena. He described the early years of his work as a "destructive phase," because he placed such emphasis on seeking ways to disrupt the fixed structures and restrictive conventions of bourgeois drama in order to create a more fluid theatre which would stimulate popular participation. He developed techniques which aimed to create disorder, the most notable being the "Joker System," referring to the joker in a pack of cards, and how playing the joker can upset the pattern of the game.

The techniques of this system all served to undermine established forms, bringing about constant changes within a performance in order to increase the possibilities of creative expression.

Given the political objectives of Boal's theatre, it is not surprising that its underlying theories have been strongly influenced by the work of Brecht, which set out the broad ways in which to break from the constraints of bourgeois theatre. It was Brecht who indicated how the theatre might present the world as changeable, not essentially immutable, and how it could employ popular materials, with which the subaltern classes could identify. Most significantly for Boal, Brecht sought to develop a theatre that challenged the traditional relationship between actor and passive spectator. The fundamental concern of Boal's theatre has been to change the spectator into an active participant in order to empower him or her for social and political action.

However, Brecht's work only represented a starting point for Boal, for, although it gives spectators the freedom to think for themselves, power to act is still passed on to the characters in the play. For Boal, that represented an advance at the level of consciousness-raising and the encouragement of critical thinking, but not in terms of action and actually empowering the spectators to act for themselves. That was the crucial issue which Boal set out to address in his theatre. Part of the solution was provided by the Brazilian educationalist, Paulo Freire, for whom all educational and cultural activity was to be conducted with the expressed aim of raising consciousness in order to politicize the marginalized and to enable them to participate in the transformation of their own society. That entailed breaking down the traditional relationship between dominant teacher and passive student, and encouraging the learners to control the course of their own learning. In the process, they would develop a critical awareness of their social experience which would allow them to reflect on the possibilities of change.

The military dictatorship and the resulting political repression forced Boal into exile in 1971, but he continued to develop his new theatre techniques abroad, particulary during extended spells in Argentina and France. His major work, *Teatro do oprimido* (*Theatre of the Oppressed*), published in 1974, represents the crystallization of ten years or more of research and experimentation into methods for transferring theatre-making to the marginalized sectors of society. The techniques presented in the work encourage the spectators to intervene in the dramatic action to change its course. The different alternatives are proposed, discussed and acted out. For Boal, this active participation on the part of those who have long been marginalized is a vital step which can serve as rehearsal for social action.

Boal's approach is exemplified by the techniques of his "Forum Theatre," where a situation is acted out, usually a problem experienced by a member of the group, and then possible solutions improvised. The result is then discussed, and the story acted out again, with the participants invited to intervene in the action to try out an alternative solution. More and more participation is demanded from members of the group, until the stage is reached where, effectively, they direct the entire action. Other exercises serve to develop powers of critical analysis, such as those of *teatro jornal* (Newspaper Theatre), in which reports from newspapers are read in different ways, varying the rhythm and tone, or reading the text in a completely new context, so as to view the content from different perspectives. The group then acts out the information conveyed in the report, and is invited to add elements they think may have been omitted. Building upon that is Boal's *teatro invisível* (Invisible Theatre), where a rehearsed performance which raises social questions is acted out in a public place, concealing the fact that it is a theatrical performance from the onlooking public, who are drawn in as participants of the action. They are thus converted into actors, and become part of a public forum for the debate of social issues and possible solutions.

Boal's theories and techniques have been much debated by drama critics. Some argue that even if the spectators are converted into actors, the fact that they are still operating within certain dramaturgical structures, in front of a public which makes demands upon then, means that they remain subjugated to theatre conventions. Yet Boal's techniques are highly fluid, permitting constant changes of action and of strategies, and giving the participants new scope to assess, evaluate and to act. The aim is to ensure that their involvement in the theatre is accompanied by a high degree of critical awareness. Ultimately, new criteria are required to assess Boal's work, since many of his techniques depart radically from the premises of traditional theatre, and cannot be examined easily with the methods of conventional drama criticism. Meanwhile, Boal's theories on the theatre as a vehicle for liberation continue to be developed in new directions. There is considerable discussion as to the ways in which they can be adapted to new and different contexts in Europe and North America, and Boal himself, elected a city councillor for Rio de Janeiro in 1992, has used his methods among community groups to discuss and assess local problems, and propose legislative solutions. The *Teatro do oprimido* has stimulated a new phase of theatre activity in many parts of Latin America, and has established Boal as the region's foremost drama theorist.

MARK DINNEEN

Biography

Born in the state of Rio de Janeiro, Brazil, 16 March 1931. Graduated in Chemistry; studied theatrical production at University of Columbia, New York. Returned to Brazil in 1955 and became director of the Teatro de Arena in São Paulo, 1956. Held this post until 1971 when he clashed with the military dictatorship as the result of his politically engaged theatre. Arrested, imprisoned and tortured. On his release in the same year he travelled first to Argentina, followed by Chile and Portugal, settling finally in Paris where, from 1978, he directed the Centre for the Study and Dissemination of Active Techniques of Expression, known familiarly as the "Groupe Boal." Experimented with forms of psychodrama. Returned to Brazil in 1986 and became president of the Theatre of the Oppressed centre in Rio de Janeiro. In the early 1990s represented Rio de Janeiro in Brazilian Congress.

Selected Works

Plays

Revolução na América do Sul, São Paulo: Massao Ohno, 1960
Arena conta Tiradentes, in collaboration with Gianfrancesco
    Guarnieri, São Paulo: Livraria Editora Sagrana, 1967

Arena conta Zumbi, in collaboration with Gianfrancesco Guarnieri, et al., *Revista de Teatro*, Rio de Janeiro, 378 (November–December 1970)
Torquemada, in *Teatro latinoamericano de agitación*, Havana: Casa de las Américas, 1972
3 obras de teatro, Buenos Aires: Noé, 1973
O corsário de rei, Rio de Janeiro: Civilização Brasileira, 1985

Novels
A deliciosa e sangrenta aventura latina de Jane Spitfire, espia e mulher sensual, Rio de Janeiro: Codecri, 1977
O suicida com medo da morte, Rio de Janeiro: Civilização Brasileira, 1992

Short Fiction
Crônicas de nuesta America, Rio de Janeiro: Codecri, 1977

Other Writings
Categorías de teatro popular, Buenos Aires: Ediciones Cepe, 1972
Teatro do oprimido y otras poéticas políticas, Buenos Aires: Ediciones de La Flor, 1974; as *Theater of the Oppressed*, translated by Charles A. and Maria-Odilia Leal McBride, New York: Urizen Books, and London: Pluto Press, 1979
Técnicas latinoamericanas de teatro popular, Buenos Aires: Corregidor, 1975

Milagre no Brasil, Rio de Janeiro: Civilização Brasileira, 1976
200 exercícios e jogos para o ator e o não-ator com vontade de dizer algo através do teatro, Rio de Janeiro: Civilização Brasileira, 1977
Stop! C'est magique!, Rio de Janeiro: Civilização Brasileira, 1980
Ciclo de palestras sobre o teatro brasileiro, Rio de Janeiro: Inacen, 1981
Jeux pour acteurs, Paris: La Découverte, 1989; as *Games for Actors and Non-Actors*, translated by Adrian Jackson, London and New York: Routledge, 1992

Compilations and Anthologies
Teatro de Augusto Boal, 2 vols, São Paulo: Editora Hucitec, 1986–90
The Rainbow of Desire: the Boal Method of Theatre and Therapy, translated by Adrian Jackson, London and New York: Routledge, 1995

Further Reading
George, David, *The Modern Brazilian Stage*, Austin: University of Texas Press, 1992 [Chapter 3 is on the theatre in São Paulo in the 1960s]
Schutzman, Mady and Jan Cohen-Cruz (editors), *Playing Boal: Theatre, Therapy, Activism*, London: Routledge, 1994 [Contains both essays and interviews with Boal]

Bolivia

19th- and 20th-Century Prose and Poetry

In cultural terms, Bolivia has long been the poor relation of its neighbours Peru, Argentina and Chile – all of which have a far more prestigious literary tradition. In contrast, such comment as exists on Bolivian literature is almost counterbalanced by investigation of the very reasons for this modest status. Much importance is usually ascribed to the country's isolation from the main centres of colonial power until independence, and afterward as a result of the loss of the Pacific seaboard in 1879. Also blamed is the high indigenous population which has never been entirely Spanish-speaking, much less literate. The absence of a printing-press until late in the colonial era almost certainly had a negative effect, as did the prohibition of books during the same period. Finally, the political instability suffered by the country until recently was another reason for Bolivia's perceived literary backwardness.

The Bolivian novel did not appear until well after that of most other Latin American states. Bolivian literature has been associated, not always unjustly, with a parochialism born of isolation, a debilitating political factionalism and the use of fiction as a polemical mouthpiece. The relatively small available readership has meant that writers have been constrained (and conditioned) by their activities in other professions.

The problems of drawing up a valid Bolivian literary corpus are exacerbated by such issues as reliable attribution, nationality of authors, and the switch from Upper Peru to the Republic. These difficulties stem from the tortuous history of Bolivia's inception and process of self-definition.

However, to place too much emphasis on socio-political factors would be facile: moreover it would be deceptive to present too bleak a picture. Bolivia has produced a rather more valuable body of literature than is generally supposed. One of its most important early writers, and one widely regarded as the progenitor of the nation's literature, was Bartolomé Arzáns de Orsúa y Vela. Arzáns's work is widely regarded as precursor or founder of a national literature. In his monumental *Historia de la Villa Imperial de Potosí* [History of the Imperial Municipality of Potosí] there is an apparent discrepancy between the apocalyptic religious hyperbole favoured by the author and his sense of a burgeoning American identity. However, Potosí was of such economic and political importance by the 18th century that its image as a latter-day Sodom was not entirely inconsistent with its symbolic value as an American icon – one which was used notably by Bolívar. The *Historia* is a multivocal text, built up from a wide range of data including oral sources, biblical references, and the author's personal observations. Another important and long-neglected text, again with its polemical thrust, was the extraordinary Quechua play *Atau Wallpaj p'uchukakuyninpa wankan* [Tragedy of the Death of Atau Wallpa] which deals with the Spanish Conquest from an indigenous perspective.

Colonial Upper Peru, though, was not generally productive on a literary level. The Independence movement provided some creative impetus, notable in the Quechua poetry of Juan Wallparrimachi, and the seditious verses or *pasquines* circulating at the beginning of the 19th century. However, if Arzáns was the founding father of the nation's literature, the origins of the novel in this part of South America are more difficult to identify. While some would attribute even this mantle to Arzáns, others (like Augusto Guzmán in his 1955 survey *La novela en Bolivia*) attribute the first Bolivian novel to an outsider – in this case the Argentine statesman Bartolomé Mitre. In truth, prose fiction in Bolivia did not reach maturity until the late 19th century with the work of Ricardo Jaimes Freyre, Nataniel Aguirre and Alcides Arguedas. Jaimes Freyre, though better-known for the important collections of *modernista* poetry, *Castalia bárbara*, 1899 [Barbarous Castalia] and *Los sueños son vida*, 1917 [Dreams Are Life], wrote stories dealing critically with little-known or deliberately ignored areas of his country's history. Aguirre's novel *Juan de la Rosa* (1885) demonstrates his concern with formal developments and the renunciation of hegemonic narrative positions. The career of Alcides Arguedas was marked by the uneasy coexistence of "sympathetic" mystical-telluric views of the Indian seen in *Wata Wara* (rewritten as *Raza de bronce* [Race of Bronze] in 1919), and the Positivist notion, seen in the 1909 work *Pueblo enfermo* [A Sick People], that Bolivia's traditions of subservience were compounded by the incompetence of the indigenous mind to cope with modern economic and social realities.

The mines have occupied a special place in Bolivian literature, reflecting their economic and cultural importance to the nation. Edgar Ávila Echazú's *Las minas bolivianas: historia, mito y literatura*, 1984 [Bolivian Mines: History, Myth and Literature] traced the discourse of mining and its countercurrents from the beginnings of the Potosí silver boom to the heyday of tin in the 1920s. The nation's vulnerability to outside exploitation appears, in mining literature as elsewhere, to require a solution to the problem of lack of internal cohesion.

Writing on the mines has run the ideological gamut between the Positivist stance of Jaime Mendoza's *En las tierras de Potosí*, 1911 [In the Lands of Potosí], and the doctrinaire Marxist position of a novel such as Roberto Leytón's *Los eternos vagabundos*, 1939 [The Eternal Vagabonds]. Mining literature, in a way that reflects its subject, is often seen in terms of two opposing camps or tendencies. These may be defined by social status and ethnic origin. Apart from social hierarchy, "above" and "below" may be seen as categories determined by an individual's role in the mine. There is a discernible difference between authors with first-hand experience of mining and those without. The first "mining novelist," Jaime Mendoza, is an example of the outsider, at a physical remove from the mine and a cultural distance from its workers. *En las tierras de Potosí* was based on his experiences as a mine doctor, allowing him a pseudo-scientific vantage-point used to fuel a Positivist "Negative Indianism."

At the other end of the spectrum from Mendoza are the short stories of René Poppe, a La Paz writer who once worked in the mines in order to be able to describe the workers' reality. Poppe's work displays an undeniable intimacy with the miners' physical environment, and some understanding of their inter-action with it. The stories in his collection *El paraje del Tío*, 1985 [The Tío's Niche] take place almost entirely below ground, where his characters – the miners themselves and their "deity," the *Tío* – enjoy a certain cultural autonomy and are at least temporarily free from outside interference.

Certainly the mining novel is inextricably bound up with the actual events it portrays: this close link between political reality and fiction has long characterised the Bolivian novel and it will be interesting to see what will result, in cultural as well as social terms, from the waning importance of the mines.

The ruinous Chaco War against Paraguay was a socio-political watershed which spawned its own fictional genre in Bolivia. As Murdo J. McLeod has explained in his 1971 article, "The Bolivian Novel, the Chaco War and the Revolution," the Chaco novel became an opportunity for national self-definition as well as for airing political grievances. A stock feature of most novels discussing the war is the campfire conversation, where the future of Bolivia is discussed by men with a variety of ethnic and geographical origins and who had previously been unaware of each others' existence. Most writing stimulated by the experience of the Chaco had a left-wing bias: one of the most coherent Marxist voices of the era and author of the 1935 novel *Aluvión de fuego* [Torrent of Fire], Oscar Cerruto, was seen as the originator of the Chaco-inspired social novel, and contributed to the process of national self-examination which followed the war.

The approach taken in Néstor Taboada Terán's *El signo escalonado*, 1975 [The Stepped Symbol] is apparently unique. No other novel deals with the era immediately before the conflict and stops short of the event itself, paying more attention to the conditions which made the war a political expedient for Bolivia's rulers. Similarly, Aureliano Belmonte Pool's *Carne de conquista*, 1927 [Flesh of Conquest] is concerned with the internal condition of Bolivia, and proposes ways, five years before the conflict, of avoiding war with Paraguay. Although Cerruto's *Aluvión de fuego* concentrates on conditions at home rather than on the conflict, it deals with social problems contemporary with the war rather than with its causes.

After the Chaco War there were various moves toward a "national literature," a "vernacular school" which set out to express popular concerns. Cerruto lamented the disunity of his country, in which a person from the tropical north, for instance, would hardly recognise a compatriot from the high plains. Augusto Céspedes, a writer of elegant but highly subjective historical fictions, asserts in *Metal del diablo*, 1946 [The Devil's Metal] that the Paraguayan nation had the advantage of "solidez racial y tradición" (racial sturdiness and tradition) over its adversary. This reflects two popular Bolivian misconceptions: one, that the Paraguayan war effort was characterised by solidarity and national unity; the other, that Paraguay could even be considered the victor. Augusto Roa Bastos's novel of 1960, *Hijo de hombre* (Son of Man), explodes both these myths (which nevertheless tell us a good deal about Bolivia's self-image).

There is a constant sense of alienation in most Bolivian social literature, and part of the literary output resulting from the Chaco War was aimed at resolving this national fragmentation: the result was the "exploratory novel" through which it was hoped that Bolivians would become at least theoretically familar with their own geography. This kind of literature, as McLeod points out, had formal political sanction: the post-Revolution MNR (National Revolutionary Movement) government approved of the genre, which usually featured an expedition into the tropics, benefitting Bolivia's long-term purpose of colonising these vast and underpopulated spaces. Today, this investigation of "lo propio" (what is ours) has inevitably become bound up with discussion of the cocaine trade. A novel like Tito Gutiérrez Vargas's *Mariposa blanca*, 1986 [White Butterfly] is an example of the continuing preoccupation with the *Oriente,* or eastern lowlands, and its potential for either national salvation or perdition. The novel's heavily moralising tone plays upon a vision of the lowlands as an Eden from which the people have been estranged through the corrupting effects of the drug trade.

National self-discovery had long been a formal preoccupation of Bolivian Positivists: however, they proposed external scientific investigation rather than any philosophical concern or metaphysical speculation on the essence of the Bolivian character. A fuller kind of exploration, both internal and external, was without doubt stimulated by the trauma of the Chaco.

The mestizo (mixed race) writer occupies an ambiguous position in a country with a majority indigenous population such as Bolivia. This is due to historical as well as social factors: writing has always had an active and instrumental role in the establishment and maintenance of political power. On the other hand, the oral tradition (most often associated with Aymara and Quechua but also strong in Spanish), has allowed local history and identity to develop with a degree of independence from the administrative centre. The role of the *mestizo* writer may be seen to lie in the discursive breach between these two; an assimilation of local or ethnic realities to the requirements of national or supranational identity.

An example of this can be seen in the use of oral historical sources in Bolivia, a remedy not only to the pilfering of historical documents by neighbouring countries and the US (which Arze terms "dependencia documental"); but also to Bolivians' own profligate, uninformed attitude to their cultural patrimony. Oral sources have been used not only by historians but by several novelists: use of such material is seen as not only acknowledging cultural plurality but giving a voice to underprivileged (illiterate) social strata. An important addition to Bolivian literature in this regard has been the recent publication of testimonial documents such as the memoirs of miners' leader Domitila Barrios de Chungara *¡Si me permiten hablar! Testimonio de Domitila, una mujer de las minas bolivianas,* 1977 (*Let Me Speak! Testimony of Domitila, a Woman of the Bolivian Mines*); Ana María Condori's *Nayan Uñatatawi,* 1988 [My Awakening] which tells of the process through which a provincial Aymara-speaking girl reaches political and social awareness; rural union leader Enrique Encinas's view of the 1952 Revolution *Jinapuni – testimonio de un dirigente campesino,* 1989 [That's How it Was: Memoirs of a Peasant Leader]; and, on a far less overtly political level, the stories of Elvira Espejo Ayka's *Ahora les voy a narrar* [Now I'll Tell You a Story], in an Aymara-Spanish bilingual edition by Denise Y. Arnold and Juan de Dios Yapita, 1994.

Indigenist literature in Bolivia has often involved a demagogic stance; such was the case with the most vociferous opponent of Hispanic culture, the early 20th-century poet Franz Tamayo. Himself partly of Aymara descent, Tamayo imbued Indian ethnicity with a telluric mystique which largely derived from Nazism. Guillermo Francovich, who has written extensively on Bolivian art, thought and myth, has linked Tamayo's indigenist supremacism to a Nazi model: Tamayo's political rationale, as dubious in its way as that of Alcides Arguedas, brought equivocal reaction from the Marxist Indian ideologue Fausto Reinaga, who, in *El indio y los escritores de América,* 1968 [The Indian and the Writers of America], abandoned his earlier acceptance of the poet and rejected Tamayo as an oligarch and paternalist. Nevertheless the value of Tamayo's contribution to Bolivian poetry, visible in such work as *Nuevos Rubaiyat,* 1927 [New Rubaiyat] and *Epigramas griegos,* 1945 [Greek Epigrams] is undeniable.

Responses to the degradation of indigenous culture through colonial and state propaganda have come in two essential forms: polemical writing produced by educated Indians such as Reinaga, and literature produced by pro-indigenous elements within the elite group, mostly in the latter half of the 20th century. Most problematic has been the confusion of three inevitably overlapping categories: "nation," "ethnicity" and "class." For many, the solution to such a multifaceted problem lies in a coherent definition of both the social position of the mestizo, and the role, in the future of Bolivia, of *mestizaje* (miscegenation).

The position of Bolivia's intellectuals has followed a pattern dictated by the country's fragmented geographical and social features, its isolation and segregation. Radical ideas have often emanated from the elite; the fiercely anti-Hispanic Tamayo, for instance, and the Marxist Augusto Céspedes, were from landed families. However well-intentioned they may have been, such authors have usually been shackled by ideological loyalties. An exception is the folklorist Rigoberto Paredes Candia (1870–1951), who did ground-breaking work on the mythical beliefs underlying indigenous cultures.

Enrique Finot's *Historia de la literatura boliviana,* 1964 [History of Bolivian Literature] reminds us that Indianism was based not only upon ethnic considerations, but also had its mystic-telluric aspects. If so, it seems equally to reflect notions of class informed by the influx of Marxist ideas during the 1920s and 1930s.

The type of conservative Indigenism favoured by Tamayo and Arguedas was countered, in the early 20th century, by an Indianism more sympathetic to its subject. This can be seen in novels such as Raúl Botelho Gosálvez's *Altiplano,* 1945 [High Plain]; Alfredo Guillén Pinto's *Utama,* 1945 [My House] and, in particular, the work of Jesús Lara (1898–1980) which included indigenist fiction based on ethnographic research and Marxist precepts. The novels *Surumi* (1943) and *Yanakuna* (1952) are examples of his fierce vindication of Indian rights. He also wrote extensively on Indian song, storytelling and dance in *La literatura de los Quechuas,* 1958 [Quechua Literature] and produced an accessible Quechua-Spanish dictionary.

Carlos Medinaceli (1899–1949) was the chief exponent of the influential *novela de cholos* genre (*cholo* = acculturated urban Indian or mestizo) which developed between the Chaco War and the 1952 Revolution. If not truly an example of cultural *mestizaje,* the genre broke new ground in the attention it gave to the neglected urban mestizo as a repository of the Bolivian national character. According to Leonardo García Pabón, Medinaceli noted the poverty of the Bolivian novel and its inability to find what he termed a "genius loci" adequate to its surroundings. Perhaps the biggest failing of the national novel was, for Medinaceli, its adherence to realist and naturalist approaches which served ideological positions rather than producing any perceptive insight. Medinaceli recognised that the Bolivian novel was overtly documentary, but without being true to its subject. *La chaskañawi* [Star-Eyed Woman] controversially dealt with a scandalous affair between a young white man of landed family and a mestiza bar-owner, and opened the way for the examination, through fiction, of the hypocrisies attached to questions of race and class in Bolivia.

The challenge to privilege and vested interests to which Medinaceli's work contributed was to culminate in the 1952 Revolution. This event, though, received little attention from writers - surely a testament to national disappointment at the failures of the new regime to implement worthwhile change. Instead came a period of stifled debate and the stultifying effect on Bolivian intellectual life of a dominant orthodoxy known as "Revolutionary Nationalism." When the miltary regained control in 1964 the result was a prolonged spell of persecution and exile for many of the country's writers. Perhaps the most influential event in the latter half of the 20th century, in terms of Bolivian fiction, has been Che Guevara's guerrilla war in 1967. This provoked several novels, the most celebrated being Renato Prada Oropeza's *Los fundadores del alba*, 1969 [Founders of the Dawn] which nevertheless, in attempting to fuse political content with literary experimentation, falls short on both counts.

Most critics agree on the significance of a 1959 novel, *Los deshabitados* [The Vacant Ones] by Marcelo Quiroga Santa Cruz, which marked a key year in Bolivian writing and stimulated a new phase. Quiroga's novel brought a new approach to subject matter, language and narrative time and space which, although an isolated case, influenced subsequent novelists away from long-standing and anachronistic concerns. The years between 1960 and 1980 saw the last publications of an "old guard" of radical writers who made significant contributions: Arturo Von Vacano, Adolfo Costa du Rels, and Oscar Uzín. Mention must be made of Julio de la Vega's *Matías, el apóstol suplente*, 1971 [Matthew, the Substitute Apostle]. Bolivia's best living poet, Pedro Shimose, whose *Quiero escribir pero me sale espuma*, 1972 [I Want to Write but out Comes Foam] won the Cuban Casa de las Américas prize, continues to live and work in Madrid. However the most notable avant-garde writer of the 1970s is surely Jaime Saenz (1921–86), whose novel *Felipe Delgado* (1979) is a look at urban alienation and social deformation characterised by black humour, a taste for the absurd and grotesque, and an unusual distance from political debate.

More recent literature has echoed Saenz's detachment, or at least adopted a less explicit approach to social issues. An example is Manuel Vargas's *Rastrojos, la novela de Fermín*, 1984 [Leftovers, the Novel of Fermín]. Vargas's work is imbued with the downbeat simplicity of his native Vallegrande, near Santa Cruz in the eastern lowlands. From the city of Santa Cruz itself is José Wolfango Montes, whose satirical novel *Jonas y la ballena rosada*, 1987 (Jonah and the Pink Whale), has been translated into English and filmed. The presentation

of regional identity as a basis for fiction operates in Jesús Urzagasti's *Tirinea* (1969) which weaves the folk traditions of his native Chaco into a modern fable, and is continued in his *En el país del silencio*, 1987 [In the Land of Silence]. Welcome recent publications include Poppe's *El viaje*, 1993 [The Journey], the short stories of Edmundo Paz Soldán, (though written from the US and avowedly owing little to Bolivian models): the poetry of Blanca Garnica, and the irreverent experimental writing of Adolfo Cárdenas Franco.

The problems mentioned above, and the various literary approaches to them, amount to a general picture of social dislocation and failure of communication both in intra-national and international terms. On a discursive level, there appears to be a vacuum caused by mutual incomprehension and distrust among the various local and ethnic groups comprising Bolivian society. So far, literature has been unable fully to address these dilemmas. However, there is reason to believe that new writers, with the backing of such stalwarts as Néstor Taboada Terán (see separate entry) can produce a literature adequate to the country's growing needs.

KEITH J. RICHARDS

Further Reading

Antezana, Luis H., "Panorama de narrativa y poesías bolivianas," *Revista Iberoamericana* 164–65 (July–December 1993)

Cáceres Romero, Adolfo, *Nueva historia de la literatura boliviana*, La Paz: Los Amigos del Libro, 1987

Echeverría, Evelio, *La novela social de Bolivia*, La Paz: Editorial Difusión, 1973

Francovich, Guillermo, *El pensamiento boliviano en el siglo XX*, Mexico City: Fondo de Cultura Económica, 1956

Gisbert, Teresa and José de Mesa, *Esquema de literatura virreinal en Bolivia*, La Paz: Biblioteca de Arte y Cultura Boliviana, 1963

Guzmán, Augusto, *La novela en Bolivia*, La Paz: Editorial Juventud, 1955

Mesa, Carlos D., "Apuntes para una visión socio-histórica de la nueva narrativa boliviana," *Hipótesis*, vol. 18, La Paz (Winter 1983)

Mitre, Eduardo, "Cuatro poetas bolivianos contemporáneos," *Revista Iberoamericana* 134 (1986) [On Oscar Cerruto, Pedro Shimose, Roberto Echazú and Eduardo Camargo]

Ortega, José, *Letras bolivianas de hoy: Renato Prada y Pedro Shimose. Manual de bibliografía de la literatura boliviana*, Buenos Aires: García Cambeiro, 1973

Padden, R.C. (editor), *Tales of Potosí. Selected Translations from "Historia de la Villa Imperial de Potosí" by Bartolomé Arzáns*, Providence, Rhode Island: Brown University Press, 1975

Pastor Poppa, Ricardo, *Escritores andinos: la mina, lo telúrico y lo social*, La Paz and Cochabamba: Los Amigos del Libro, 1987

Poppe, René, *Narrativa minera boliviana*, La Paz: Ediciones Populares Camarlinghi, 1983

Prada, Renato and Pedro Shimose, *Letras bolivianas de hoy*, Buenos Aires: Estudios Latinoamericanos, 1973

Reinaga, Fausto, *El indio y los escritores de América*, La Paz: PIB Editions (Partido Indio de Bolivia), 1969

Rivera-Rodas, Oscar, "Bolivia," in *Handbook of Latin American Literature*, edited by David William Foster, New York: Garland, 1987

Robledo, Angela I., "Brujería, intertextualidad creativa y discurso hispanoamericano en la 'Historia de la Villa Imperial de Potosí,' " *Bulletin of Hispanic Studies*, Liverpool, vol. 69 (January 1992)

Sanjinés, Javier (editor), *Tendencias actuales en la literatura boliviana*, Minneapolis and Valencia: Institute of Ideologies and Literature, 1985

Shimose, Pedro, "Panorama de la narrativa boliviana contemporánea," in *El paseo de los sentidos*, La Paz: Instituto Boliviano de Cultura, 1983

Siles Salinas, Jorge, *La literatura boliviana de la Guerra del Chaco*, La Paz: Ediciones de la Universidad Católica Boliviana, 1969

Tritten, Susan, "Los cholos y la búsqueda de una nueva sociedad," *Revista Iberoamericana*, vol. 18/160–61 (July–December 1992)

Wietüchter, Blanca, "Propuestas para un diálogo sobre el espacio literario boliviano," *Revista Iberoamericana*, vol. 52/134 (January–March 1986)

Zavaleta, René (editor), *Bolivia hoy*, Mexico City: Siglo XXI, 1983

María Luisa Bombal 1910–1980

Chilean prose writer

It has been difficult to accommodate María Luisa Bombal within the Chilean literary mainstream. From the beginning she rejected the contemporary literary dogmas of regionalism in vogue in Chile and her vanguard prose, published first in Argentina, clearly indicated her innovative preoccupation with feminine themes and her desire to subvert traditional narrative technique. Moreover, although always nostalgic about her birthplace, Viña del Mar, Bombal actually lived little of her life in Chile: at the age of thirteen she left for school in France, returning briefly in 1931 only to move on to the brilliant literary scene of Buenos Aires before her long, voluntary exile in the US. Regrettably, her early reputation as an "exotic Bohemian" dogged her literary career both at home and abroad as details of her tumultuous private life were made public. All of this has undoubtedly contributed to a certain marginalization of this original and unconventional figure, although her finely-crafted prose, written "painfully and in silence" often "four, five and even six times over," has enjoyed remarkable success. Her first two novellas, *La última niebla*, 1935 (*The House of Mist*), and *La amortajada*, 1938 (*The Shrouded Woman*), were published in Victoria Ocampo's prestigious journal *Sur* to immediate critical acclaim, first in Hispanic America and then beyond with translations into English, French, Portuguese, Czech, Swedish and Japanese; her much anthologized short story "El árbol," 1939 [The Tree], is now considered a classic in the genre; flattering parallels have been adduced between her poetic prose and that of Juan Ramón Jiménez and Pablo Neruda, or Virginia Woolf and James Joyce; and recent reevaluations of the canon have proposed *La última niebla* as a new founding fiction of modern Latin American writing.

Bombal intended her first novel to be "a sentimental drama" not an excursion into combative feminism. She did, however, initiate the recurring thematic pattern of her fiction in that, in *La última niebla*, the drama turns on a middle-class woman's frustration in a loveless marriage and her gradual alienation from societal norms as she repeatedly asks, but cannot answer, "Why, why is the nature of woman such that a man always has to be the centre of her life?" The lyrical point of view of the first-person narrator is recorded as she translates emptiness and despair into the magical "interior movement" of a series of vital, passionate encounters between the self and the outer world. As a result causal and linear relationships are here displaced by a dynamic network of free-flowing, subjective associations. This transgression or disordering of the "logical" order is clearly apparent in the protagonist's continual substitution of the verb *ver* (to see) by *imaginar* (to imagine), and her use of such vehicles of vision as mirrors, windows, water and, most significantly, the mist itself, to deform or reform the pragmatic copies of reality that vision customarily provides. As Bombal's protagonist observes, the mist "immaterializes" in order that the imagination, prohibited from direct vision, *materialize* a new order. By construing this as the inability to grasp reality, earlier (male) readers found in the "hermetic" world of *La última niebla* evidence only of "an extreme femineity" characterized by both a lack of external action and a sense of individual confinement. More recent criticism has concentrated instead on the "blanks" in coherent, logocentric discourse in Bombal's fragmented and fragmentary narrative, and her deliberate use of ambiguity which permits a plurality of interpretations that question the traditional binary opposition supposed in culture versus nature, or passivity and action, or dream and reason. Alienation is thus viewed positively as an innovative strategy which is both syntactical – making possible the oscillation between reality and otherness in this example of a fantastic narrative – and ideological – critiquing the arbitrariness of prevailing phallocentric standards that govern how to live and die "correctly."

In her second novel, *La amortajada*, Bombal challenged the principle of verisimilitude even more radically by probing into the psyche of a dead woman who fictionalizes her previous existence. Since Ana María cannot speak, this very subjective narration is conducted through memory, free association, and the empathetic manipulation of an anonymous narrator who identifies closely with the experiences of her protagonist. The dominant metaphor here is that of weaving in the numerous references to thread and cloth, and Ana María's tapestry is revealed as a creative stratagem by which an otherwise passive protagonist asserts herself and eludes those realities she finds threatening. From the unravelling of these threads of memory comes spiritual regeneration as Ana María, like another Arachne, finds from within herself the wherewithal to spin the fabric of a new existence, a "life-in-death" rather than her previous "death-in-life." In *La amortajada* Bombal created a novel of greater lyrical intensity than *La última niebla*, but once again her critique of a confined bourgeois existence centred on the alternative of the highly interiorized vision of female experience.

Bombal's reputation was further enhanced by the publication, in 1939 and 1940 in the Argentine journals *Sur* and *Saber Vivir*, of four short stories, of which "El árbol" is undoubtedly the best known. In a series of flashbacks the protagonist, Brígida, recalls episodes from her past as she listens to a concert. Traditional autobiographical techniques are eschewed in favour of a predominantly omniscient third-person narration studded with increasing frequency by Brígida's own thought-quotations. The antagonism thus set up between figural and narrative viewpoint makes for a certain ironic play that permits alternative readings of the text. Middle-class marriage is, as always, the starting point for the Bombalian heroine, and Brígida duly conforms, only to rebel later by separating from her much older husband, Don Luis. From a normative point of view, therefore, Brígida does not adapt – untutored and puerile, she distances herself from coherent social behaviour by separating from the husband who will give her name, status and, eventually, descendants. The psychological corroboration of this failure to conform comes in Brígida's gradual alienation from society as she enters a private dream world. What is different here, however, is that Brígida's mental lucubrations do identify the goal of self-realization and the story ends with her independent declaration in favour of "love, travel and madness." Bombal's innovative narrative technique of "voicing" silence provides an alternative "disorder" to the traditionally male codification of life and art in accordance with the lineage, place and language of power.

After two brief visits to the US in 1937 and 1939, Bombal took up permanent residence there in 1941, working first as a script-writer and then in advertising. In 1944 she married Count Raphael de Saint-Phalle (Fal) and spent the next thirty years in New York. After an initial burst of literary activity that saw, with Fal's help, the revised and augmented translations into English of her novellas as *House of Mist* in 1947, and *The Shrouded Woman* in 1948, Bombal published very little more. Her virtual eclipse from the literary scene after the late 1940s has been, wrongly, attributed to Fal's restraining influence. More likely was the rationalization Bombal later made about a combination of writer's block and separation from her mother tongue. Unable to "repeat" her literary successes, her perfectionism and "real anxiety, anguish even" over language made this a period of self-imposed censure in which she felt "persecuted" by her characters and "confined in prison." Such feelings explain well the nostalgic tone and persistent intratextuality of Bombal's last publications. Thus, in "Washington, ciudad de las ardillas," 1943 [Washington, City of Squirrels], she offered a series of "Christmas cards" to depict the bitter reality of exile into which, as in earlier writings, she incorporated fragments of fairy lore to underscore the distress time passing caused this self-styled "unhappy poet who writes in prose;" while " La maja y el ruiseñor," 1960 [The Princess and the Nightingale], another adult fairy-tale,

echoed the earlier short story "Lo secreto" [The Secret] written in 1941 – and its first version "Mar, cielo y tierra" [Sea, Sky and Land] published in 1940 – in its anecdotal evocation of the sea at Viña, Bombal's "corner of Paradise" and image to conjure up the magic of childhood lost in the adult world.

Although perfectly trilingual the language of composition was clearly an issue for Bombal. Her English translations sold well enough and *House of Mist* even netted handsome film rights, but her "quaint, syrupy prose" lacking "a logical, neat sense of contrivance" met with mixed reviews from the New York critics, who preferred to dwell upon her flamboyant love-life rather than the sensorial rhythms and lyrical intensity of her writing. Bombal railed against the "wasp's nest" that was American literary life and published nothing more in English. Significantly, the struggles of the female artistic consciousness provided the theme of her final publication that appeared in both Spanish and English: the short story "La historia de María Griselda" of 1946 was incorporated two years later into her English version of *The Shrouded Woman*. This was Bombal's last analysis of a female mind trying to comprehend the primary sources of alienation and solitude. The complex narrative is created and sustained by the poetic imagination of a disillusioned woman, Ana María, who not only understands the nature of life's often painful incongruities, but also knows of their destructive impact on the lives of those around her – as evinced in Sylvia's suicide or Alberto's gratuitous violence and alcoholism. As the tale unfolds, the confusion between first- and third-person narrators, in a framework of linear memory sequences outside of time or place, favours a symbiotic relationship between the omniscient self of the poet-novelist and the individual self of the figural mind that develops from this process. Through what is most appropriately read as an "anti-story," the portrait of Griselda the docile, selfless heroine emerges as a dreadful cautionary tale of the female artist who, as victim of her sex and anatomy, can only inspire creativity but not engender it.

Caught herself in a similar paradox, Bombal responded, like all her female protagonists, by silence. Although she continued to write in both Spanish and English until the end of her life nothing appeared in print, neither have her heirs authorized publication or made her manuscripts available for critical comment. In view of this it is worth noting that, according to Sara Vial, the latter include theatre plays, "The Foreign Minister," "Believe Me, Love" and "Dolly and Jekyll and Miss Hyde," a collection of short stories, "Noche de luna" [Moonlit Nights], prose works, "El Señor de Mayo" [The Lord of May], the story of an earthquake in Chile, "Embrujo" [The Spell], and her last novel with a metaphysical theme inspired by and dedicated to Fal, "Y habló Caín" [And Cain Spoke]. Such titles confirm her abiding interest in the theatre, that began in Paris in the late 1920s with her early attempt at melodrama and her sometime dramatic studies at Charles Dullin's Atelier with distinguished French actor Jean Louis Barrault as classmate. Comments in the numerous lectures and interviews given by Bombal in the last years of her life corroborate her continuing search for perfection in narrative technique, and her mid-life predilection for metaphysical and religious themes.

Inevitably, Bombal's novels of female estrangement came under scrutiny during the 1970s but were, at first, given short shrift by orthodox feminists on account of the author's reluctance to categorize her work so explicitly and the seemingly ineluctable fact that by their unprotesting subservience to gender norms her middle-class female protagonists only reinforced traditional images of woman's subordinate role. Most recently, however, this "silence" has been interpreted as one of the typical subversive strategies deployed in vanguard writing by Bombal and other contemporaries like Norah Lange and Teresa de la Parra. Feminist critics now point out how well Bombalian texts, which overflow with rain, mist, ponds and puddles, exemplify the intuition about fluidity as essential to female discourse articulated by French philosopher Luce Irigaray in *Ce Sexe qui n'en est pas un* (*This Sex Which is Not One*), and look to Jacques Lacan's analyses of the "Imaginary" and the "Mirror Stage" to provide insight into Bombal's highly interiorized visions of the subconscious realm of female experience.

Coincidentally, Bombal's first book appeared in the same year as the innovative *Historia universal de una infamia*, 1935 (*A Universal History of Infamy*); much later, the same Borges would assert that "when they name the best names, María Luisa Bombal is never missing from the list." Without question she has won her place among the "new" Latin American writers whose exemplary modernity has made them classics.

K.M. SIBBALD

Biography
Born in Viña del Mar, Chile, 8 June 1910, into a prosperous and cultured family. Father died when María Luisa was ten. Mother and three daughters then settled in Paris. There María Luisa was educated at Notre Dame de L'Assomption and the Lycée La Bruyère, and later the Sorbonne where she studied literature and philosophy. Returned to Chile in 1931 and stayed on family estate in the south of Chile. Settled in Buenos Aires in 1933 where she lived in the home of the then Chilean consul, Pablo Neruda. Married the Argentine painter, Jorge Larco in 1934. After husband's death she moved to New York, 1940. There she married Count Rapahel de Saint-Phalle; one daughter, Brigitte. Led productive literary life in the US but returned to Chile in 1970 after her second husband died. Ignored by Chile's cultural Establishment and never awarded the Chilean National Prize for Literature. Last few years were of isolation and heavy drinking. Died in Santiago de Chile, 6 May 1980.

Selected Works
Some of Bombal's shorter narratives appeared for the first time in the Buenos Aires journal *Sur*, while the longer ones were published by the publishing house of the same name.

La última niebla, Buenos Aires: Sur, 1935; with "El árbol," "Las islas nuevas" and "Lo secreto," Buenos Aires: Editorial Andina, 1973; as *The House of Mist*, New York: Farrar Straus and Giroux, 1947; London: Cassell, 1948 (revised and augmented translation); also in *New Islands and Other Stories*, translated by Richard and Lucía Cunningham, New York: Farrar Straus and Giroux, 1982 [contains *The Final Mist*, "The Tree," "Braids," "The Unknown," and "New Islands"]

La amortajada, Buenos Aires: Sur, 1938; as *The Shrouded Woman*, translated by the author, New York: Farrar Straus and Giroux, 1948

"El árbol," Buenos Aires, *Sur* 69 (September 1939)

"La historia de María Griselda," Buenos Aires, *Sur* 142 (August 1946); Valparaíso, Chile: Universitarias de Valparaíso, 1977

Further Reading
Agosín, Marjorie, *Las desterradas del paraíso: protagonistas en la narrativa de María Luisa Bombal*, New York: Senda Nueva, 1983

Agosín, Marjorie, Elena Gascón-Vera and Joy Renjilian-Burgy (editors), *María Luisa Bombal. Apreciaciones críticas*, Tempe, Arizona: Bilingual Press, 1987

Arancibia, Juana Alcira, *Evaluación de la literatura femenina de latinoamerica, siglo XX*, Costa Rica: EDUCA, 1985 [Contains several contributions on Bombal]

Bastos, María Luisa, "Relectura de *La última niebla*, de María Luisa Bombal," *Revista Iberoamericana* 51 (July–December 1985) [Claims reevaluation of additional founding fiction for Latin American "new" narrative]

Boyle, Catherine, "The Fragile Perfection of the Shrouded Rebellion (Re-reading Passivity in María Luisa Bombal)," in *Women Writers in Twentieth Century Spain and Spanish America*, edited by Catherine Davies, Lampeter, Wales: Edwin Mellen Press, 1993

Fernández, Magali, *El discurso narrativo en la obra de María Luisa Bombal*, Madrid: Pliegos, 1988

Gligo, Agata, *María Luisa*, Santiago de Chile: Andrés Bello, 1984 [A somewhat effusive biography]

Goic, Cedomil, *La novela chilena: los mitos degradados*, Santiago de Chile: Editorial Universitaria, 5th edition, 1991 [Chapter 7 is on *La última niebla*]

Guerra-Cunningham, Lucía, *La narrativa de María Luisa Bombal: una visión de la existencia femenina*, Madrid: Playor, 1980

Kostopulos-Cooperman, Celeste, *The Lyrical Vision of María Luisa Bombal*, London: Támesis, 1988

Masiello, Francine, "Texto, ley, transgresión: especulación sobre la novela (feminista) de vanguardia," *Revista Iberoamericana* 51 (July–December 1985)

Rodríguez-Peralta, Phyllis, "María Luisa Bombal's Poetic Novels of Female Estrangement," in *Modern Latin American Fiction*, edited by Harold Bloom, New York: Chelsea House, 1990

Vidal, Hernán, *María Luisa Bombal: la feminidad enajenada*, Barcelona: Hijos de José Bosch, 1976 [A Jungian study of alienation]

The Boom

During the 1960s, Latin American, or more precisely Spanish American literature quite suddenly came to occupy the forefront of the international literary stage. Reading the fiction of Latin America became fashionable among the elite cultural circles of Europe and the United States and some novels became popular best-sellers. Many of the works in question were in fact written in Europe or the US, by writers in exile, voluntary or otherwise. Several factors contributed to this increased prominence of writers from Latin America: a cluster of fine, technically innovative novels all authored by men. These include Cortázar's *Rayuela* (*Hopscotch*), Fuentes's *La muerte de Artemio Cruz* (*The Death of Artemio Cruz*) and Vargas Llosa's *La ciudad y los perros*, *La casa verde* and *Conversación en La Catedral* (*The Time of the Hero*, *The Green House* and *Conversation in The Cathedral*, respectively). Cabrera Infante's *Tres tristes tigres* (*Three Trapped Tigers*), sought, as its tongue-twisting title indicates, to revitalize the language of literature through word play and the use of the Cuban vernacular. Another major novel to appear in the 1960s was *Cien años de soledad* (*One Hundred Years of Solitude*), to be followed by others over the next decade.

The Cuban Revolution focussed the world's attention on a hitherto relatively unknown subcontinent, while it brought together writers who in the past had often worked in isolation and in ignorance of each other's activities. Hispanic publishers saw the potential in all this and promoted the works of Spanish American writers very effectively in a growing market; translations followed; finally, some of the writers themselves were (or soon became) very adept at keeping in the limelight. It was being recognised that these writers were not simply exotic, but able craftsmen who were well-read in other literatures and ready to lead rather than simply imitate.

The writers of the Boom, mainly authors of prose fiction, do not constitute a formal movement with a clearly defined manifesto; but they can be said to have collectively brought Modernism to Latin America. The concept of magical realism, although its origins predate the Boom, is often invoked in relation to it; that somewhat ill-defined concept is perhaps most meaningfully applied to García Márquez's *Cien años de soledad*. Writers from outside Latin America who influenced those of the Boom include Faulkner, Dos Passos, Virginia Woolf, Proust and Sartre; however, the single most important influence was probably one from Spanish America itself: Jorge Luis Borges. Even if some of the writers of the Boom (García Márquez, for example) disliked Borges, they respected his skills and acquired his respect for the disciplined use of language. The writers of the Boom broke with the established inclination to concentrate on regional or indigenist themes and instead tended to revel in narrative experimentation, self-referentiality and increasing demands made upon the reader. They were much more aware of each others' activities than had been writers before them, and this awareness sometimes gives rise to intertextual allusions. Significant literature had certainly been written earlier in the century (one thinks of the works of Asturias, Carpentier, Onetti, Rulfo and Borges,

to mention only some of the closest precursors who seemed to become assimilated to the Boom in an act of belated recognition) but those works had tended to be written in isolation and to have reached only a limited public.

The Boom was soon caught up in cultural politics, for its stars, at least in the early years, espoused the ideals of the Cuban Revolution, and this spurred the US into trying to steal some of the thunder by seducing them with comfortable visiting posts in its universities. Also important in shaping and promoting the Boom was the role of Seix Barral, a Spanish publishing house which instituted a prize for unpublished novels and awarded it to many of the writers who were to become most famous. Yet, while it is the case that the pre-eminence during the Boom of a few (undoubtedly excellent) novelists, allied with commercial interests, tended to crowd out other writers from Latin America who also deserved attention, it is also true that the Boom gave Latin American literature an international visibility from which many other writers have since profited.

There was no literary manifesto or cohesive credo among the writers of the Boom, but it is noticeable that their novels tended to be formally difficult and challenging for the reader; one of the most extreme examples, and perhaps the novel that marked a turning point, was Donoso's *El obsceno pájaro de la noche*, 1970 (*The Obscene Bird of Night*). For an inclination was soon to develop towards greater accessibility, more simple linear narrative structure, and the incorporation of popular art forms; the work of Manuel Puig is often quoted as leading this transition to what was to be dubbed the "Post-Boom."

PETER STANDISH

See also entries on Magical Realism, The Post-Boom, Prizes, Translation: Spanish America

Further Reading

Donoso, José, *Historia personal del "Boom,"* Barcelona; Anagrama, 1971; as *The "Boom" in Spanish American Literature: a Personal History*, translated by Gregory Kolovakos, New York: Columbia University Press, 1977

Fuentes, Carlos, *La nueva novela hispanoamericana*, Mexico City: Joaquín Mortíz, 1969

Larsen, Neil, "The 'Boom' Novel and the Cold War in Latin America," *Modern Fiction Studies*, West Lafayette, Indiana (Fall 1992)

Lindstrom, Naomi, *Twentieth Century Spanish American Fiction*, Austin: University of Texas Press, 1994 [Chapter 5 is titled "The Boom and its Antecedents, 1950–1970"]

Martínez Torres, Renato, *Para una relectura del boom: populismo y otredad*, Madrid: Pliegos, 1990

Payne, Johnny, *Conquest of the New Word: Experimental Fiction and Translation in the Americas*, Austin: University of Texas Press, 1993 [Chapter 1 is on García Márquez and the Latin American Boom]

Rodríguez Monegal, Emir, *El boom de la novela latinoamericana*, Caracas: Tiempo Nuevo, 1972

Vidal, Hernán, *Literatura hispanoamericana e ideología liberal: surgimiento y crisis: una problemática en torno a la narrativa del Boom*, Buenos Aires: Hispamérica, 1975

Viñas, David, *et al.*, *Más allá del boom: literatura y mercado*, Mexico City: Marcha, 1981

Special Issues of Journals

Review: Latin American Literature and Arts, vol. 33 (September–December 1984)

Latin American Literary Review (LALR), Pittsburgh, Pennsylvania, (January–June 1987)

Jorge Luis Borges 1899–1986

Argentine prose writer and poet

Born in Buenos Aires of mixed English and Argentine stock, Jorge Luis Borges received most of his secondary education in Geneva during World War I and never attended a university. His earliest poetry was written in Europe under the influence of the avant-garde of the period. It was published in little magazines in Spain and France in and after 1919 as part of a Spanish movement called *ultraísmo*, of which Borges co-authored a manifesto in Mallorca in 1921. That same year he returned to Buenos Aires. With a group of friends he launched, through wall-posters, *Prisma I and II* (1921 and 1922), the magazine *Proa* and another manifesto in the review *Nosotros* (1921), Argentine *ultraísmo*. It sought to exclude anecdotic, human content and to strip poetry down to its alleged essence: figurative language. *Ultraísta* poems were supposed to be little more than patterns of novel images, without logical or syntactical connections or punctuation. Borges himself, however, rapidly evolved away from *ultraísmo*, first towards a more nationalistic position, with evocations of suburban Buenos Aires and other Argentine themes, and then towards more profound poetry on themes of solitude, time, the enigma of things and death. Love, sporadically present to begin with, was quickly eliminated. Borges was transforming himself into the metaphysical poet of "pensativo sentir" (thoughtful feeling) he was to become and remain in *Poemas*, 1943 [Poems], amplified in 1954 and 1958, *El hacedor*, 1960 (*Dreamtigers*), *El otro, el mismo* [The Self and the Other], 1969, *Elogio de la sombra*, 1969 (*In Praise of Darkness*), *El oro de los tigres*, 1972 (*The Gold of the Tigers*), *La rosa profunda*, 1975 [The Deep Rose] and *La moneda de hierro*, 1976 [The Iron Coin]. The exception is *Para las seis cuerdas*, 1965 [For the Guitar], simple popular-type songs on Argentine themes. The emphasis on novel imagery gave way to the realization that poetic expression revolves around a few essential metaphors and, as Borges gradually lost his sight, his poetry returned to conventional versification which he could remember more easily. For much of his early manhood Borges was an under-employed intellectual. He worked as a librarian, as the editor of a magazine, *El Hogar*, and of a series of translated detective stories and as a lecturer. He and his family were persecuted by the dictator Perón, but after the latter's fall he became director of the National Library and a member of the Argentine Academy of Letters. His international fame really began when he shared the International Publishers' Formentor Prize along with

Samuel Beckett. Sadly, he never became a Nobel Laureate. Late in life, he married twice and was survived by his second wife, María Kodama.

Borges's early essay collections: *Inquisiciones*, 1925 [Inquisitions], *El tamaño de mi esperanza*, 1926 [The Size of My Hope], and *El idioma de los argentinos*, 1928 [The Language of the Argentines], contain valuable insights into the evolution of his ideas in the 1920s, but were rigidly excluded from his (so-called) *Complete Works* – much else is missing – in his lifetime, and only began to be republished in the 1990s.

In 1933 he published "Hombre de la esquina rosada" (Streetcorner Man), the first of many tales involving knife-fighters from the poor outer districts of Buenos Aires. Thereafter, physical and moral courage remained for him absolute values immune from his otherwise pervasive scepticism. In 1935 he brought out the tales of *Historia universal de la infamia* (*A Universal History of Infamy*), a group of stories adapted from other sources, concerned with evil, cruelty and deceit. These stories do not question reality as those of the 1940s tend to do, and their technique remains linear and generally chronological. By contrast "El acercamiento a Almotasim," 1935 (The Search for Almotasim), takes the form of a spoof book review and by that alone casts doubt on the difference between fiction and non-fiction. At the same time, the quest involved is metaphysical – man's quest for God or the Absolute – which turns out to be circular and ambiguous in its result. Finally, in 1939, Borges wrote one of his most famous tales, "Pierre Menard, autor del Quijote" (Pierre Menard, Author of *Don Quixote*), which marked the beginning of his full maturity as a short-story writer and prefigured his two masterpieces *Ficciones*, 1944 (*Fictions*), amplified in 1956 and *El Aleph*, 1949 (*The Aleph*), amplified in 1952. These short stories, chiefly written in 1940s, mark that decade as the turning point in modern Spanish American fiction and established Borges as a writer of world stature, who figures prominently in discussions both of Modernism and Postmodernism.

His most important and memorable short stories are in a sense fables which explore a world without certainties or ultimate meaning, in which either all may be pure chance, or all perhaps conforms to patterns which we are not programmed to discern. Reality, whether outside ourselves or that of our own personalities, is enigmatic and language is probably not in the end capable of expressing it adequately. The appropriate stance is one of detached, sometimes humorous scepticism. But we are frequently conscious of the strain generated by the discrepancy between viewing the world unwillingly as a chaos and hoping against hope that it is a cosmos, albeit governed by mysterious laws. Borges's most important symbol of life is that of a circular labyrinth. We are born into it; we are alternately comforted and tormented by its deceitful appearance of order; to reach what for each individual is its possible centre is usually to discover a hidden aspect of the self, the futility of the quest, or death. Despite the fundamental Argentinism of some of his tales, most of them, even when set in Argentina, can only be understood in universal, abstract terms. Typical are the "what if ...?" type: what if the world were as the Idealist philosophers proclaim ("Tlön, Uqbar, Orbis Tertius")? what if we were granted immortality ("El inmortal" [The Immortal])? or total recall ("Funes el memorioso;" [Funes the Memorious])? or a simultaneous vision of all things ("El Aleph" [The Aleph])? or the ability to redeem our greatest failing ("La otra muerte" [The Other Death])? Some tales are clear allegories of the human condition: "Las ruinas circulares" (The Circular Ruins), "La Biblioteca de Babel" (The Library of Babel), El congreso (The Congress). Some deal with evil and treachery: "La Casa de Asterión" (The House of Asterion), "La forma de la espada" (The Shape of the Sword), or with the limitations of human knowledge or rationality: "La busca de Averroes" (Averroes's Search), "La muerte y la brújula" (Death and the Compass). To some critics, especially in the 1970s, all Borges's stories deal in the end only with writing and should not be seen primarily as commenting on life and reality; but this view seems reductive. Some of Borges's later stories, such as "La intrusa" (The Intruder), "El indigno" (The Unworthy Friend) or "Historia de Rosendo Juárez" (Rosendo's Tale) deal with the mystery of the individual personality, but this is a more familiar theme than that of the enigma of reality and these tales sometimes seem less successful.

Technically, many of Borges's stories (especially the earlier ones) break completely with old-style realism, rejecting its uncritical use of episodes juxtaposed in chronological order based on the notion of cause and effect. Occasionally, as already noted, Borges used apparently non-fictional forms to blur the distinction between the "imaginary" and the "real"; sometimes he brought "low" fictional forms – the spy story, the detective or mystery story – into "high" literature. Almost always, in his best stories, he used crafty devices – stories within stories, artfully concealed shifts of theme, hidden clues, traps for the unwary reader – to add a puzzle-element which symbolizes the complexity of the real. Often, too, the second part of a story comments ironically on the first part. Borges wrote with extreme meticulousness, often after honing a story in his mind for years. Nothing is there by chance, and no Borges story is fully understood unless all the details fit.

Always the industrious professional writer, Borges published minor fictional works in collaboration with his friend Adolfo Bioy Casares, a couple of screenplays, translations of Virginia Woolf and Kafka, some works of literary history, books on Dante, Buddhism and fantastic animals in literature, sundry miscellanies and dozens of prologues, many of which are uncollected. His other non-fictional works include: Evaristo Carriego, 1930, Discusión, 1932 [Discussion], Historia de la

eternidad [History of Eternity], 1936, and most importantly Otras inquisiciones, 1952 (Other Inquisitions). They reveal Borges's sometimes quirky literary tastes, his sometimes quaint erudition and his general intellectual and philosophical outlook. More than any other single influence, his combination of existential preoccupation and subtly non-realist technique helped to change the entire face of Spanish American fiction. The Cuban author Guillermo Cabrera Infante has asserted that no Spanish American writer escapes the influence of Borges's work.

DONALD L. SHAW

Biography
Born in Buenos Aires, Argentina, 24 August 1899. Educated privately and during World War I at Collège de Genève, Switzerland. Lived in Switzerland with his family, 1914–21. Visited Spain before returning to Argentina in 1921. Co-founding editor of the journals Proa, 1924–26, and Sur, 1931; also associated with Prisma. Served as literary adviser for the publishing house Emecé Editores, Buenos Aires; columnist for El Hogar weekly, Buenos Aires, 1936–39. Municipal librarian, Buenos Aires, (fired from his post by the Péron regime) 1939–46; poultry inspector for Buenos Aires Municipal Market, 1946–54, as a snub from the populist government of Perón. President of the Argentine Writers' Society, 1950–53. Lost his sight (which had always been weak) in 1955. Director of the National Library (after Péron's deposition in 1955), 1955–73. Professor of English Literature, University of Buenos Aires, 1955–70; Norton Professor of Poetry, Harvard University, Cambridge, Massachusetts; visiting lecturer, University of Oklahoma, Norman, 1969. Married Elsa Millan in 1967 (separated in 1970). Married María Kodama in 1986. Recipient of numerous awards including the Buenos Aires Municipal Prize, 1928; Argentine Writers Society Prize, 1945; National Prize for Literature, 1957; Prix Formentor, 1961; Bienal Foundation Inter-American Prize, 1970; Jerusalem Prize, 1971; Alfonso Reyes Prize, 1973; Miguel de Cervantes Prize, 1979. Member of the Argentine National Academy and the Uruguayan Academy of Letters, and Légion d'Honneur. Died in Geneva, 14 June 1986.

Selected Works

Short Fiction
Historia universal de la infamia, Buenos Aires: Tor, 1935; as A Universal History of Infamy, translated by Norman Thomas di Giovanni, New York: Dutton, 1971; London: Allen Lane, 1973 [stories purportedly based on fact]
El jardín de senderos que se bifurcan, Buenos Aires: Sur, 1942
Seis problemas para don Isidro Parodi, in collaboration with Adolfo Bioy Casares (published under the pseudonym H. Bustos Domecq), Buenos Aires: Sur, 1942; as Six Problems for Don Isidro Parodi, translated by Norman Thomas di Giovanni, New York: Dutton, and London: Allen Lane, 1981
Ficciones (1935–1944), Buenos Aires: Sur, 1944; augmented edition, Buenos Aires: Emecé, 1956; as Ficciones, edited and translated by Anthony Kerrigan, New York: Grove Press, 1962, retitled as Fictions, London: Calder, 1965
Dos fantasías memorables, in collaboration with Adolfo Bioy Casares (published under the pseudonym H. Bustos Domecq), Buenos Aires: Oportet y Haereses, 1946
Un modelo para la muerte, in collaboration with Adolfo Bioy Casares (published under the pseudonym B. Suárez Lynch), Buenos Aires: Oportet y Haereses, 1946
El Aleph, Buenos Aires: Losada, 1949; as The Aleph and Other Stories 1933–1969, edited and translated by Norman Thomas di Giovanni, New York: Dutton, 1970; London: Pan, 1973

La muerte y la brújula, Buenos Aires: Emecé, 1951
Crónicas de Bustos Domecq, in collaboration with Adolfo Bioy Casares, Buenos Aires: Losada, 1967; as *Chronicles of Bustos Domecq*, translated by Norman Thomas di Giovanni, New York: Dutton, 1976; London: Allen Lane, 1982
El informe de Brodie, Buenos Aires: Emecé, 1970; as *Dr Brodie's Report*, translated by Norman Thomas di Giovanni, New York: Dutton, 1972; London: Allen Lane, 1974
El congreso, Buenos Aires: El Archibraza, 1970; as *The Congress*, translated by Norman Thomas di Giovanni, London: Enitharmon Press, 1974
El libro de arena, Buenos Aires, Emecé, 1975; as *The Book of Sand*, translated by Norman Thomas di Giovanni (includes *The Gold of the Tigers*), New York: Dutton, 1977; London: Allen Lane, 1979
Nuevos cuentos de Bustos Domecq, in collaboration with Adolfo Bioy Casares, Buenos Aires: La Ciudad, 1977

Poetry
Fervor de Buenos Aires, Buenos Aires: Serrantes, 1923
Luna de enfrente, Buenos Aires: Proa, 1925
Cuaderno San Martín, Buenos Aires: Proa, 1929
Poemas 1922–1943, Buenos Aires: Losada, 1943
Poemas 1923–1958, Buenos Aires: Emecé, 1958
El hacedor, Buenos Aires: Emecé, 1960; as *Dreamtigers*, translated by Mildred Boyer and Harold Morland, London: Souvenir Press, 1963; Austin: University of Texas Press, 1964 [includes prose]
Para las seis cuerdas, Buenos Aires: Emecé, 1965; revised edition, 1970
Elogio de la sombra, Buenos Aires: Emecé, 1969; as *In Praise of Darkness*, translated by Norman Thomas di Giovanni, New York: Dutton, 1974; London: Allen Lane, 1975 [bilingual edition]
El otro, el mismo, Buenos Aires: Emecé, 1969
El oro de los tigres, Buenos Aires: Emecé, 1972
La rosa profunda, Buenos Aires: Emecé, 1975
La moneda de hierro, Buenos Aires: Emecé, 1976
Historia de la noche, Buenos Aires: Emecé, 1977
Adrogué, Argentina: Ediciones Adrogue, 1977 [includes prose]
La cifra, Buenos Aires: Emecé, 1981

Essays and Other Writings
Inquisiciones, Buenos Aires: Proa, 1925
El tamaño de mi esperanza, Buenos Aires: Proa, 1926
El idioma de los argentinos, Buenos Aires: Gleizer, 1928; augmented edition, as *El lenguaje de Buenos Aires*, in collaboration with José Edmundo Clemente, Buenos Aires: Emecé, 1963
Evaristo Carriego, Buenos Aires: Gleizer, 1930; as *Evaristo Carriego: a Book about Old-Time Buenos Aires*, translated by Norman Thomas di Giovanni, New York: Dutton, 1984
Discusión, Buenos Aires: Gleizer, 1932
Las kenningar, Buenos Aires: Colombo, 1933
Historia de la eternidad, Buenos Aires: Viau y Zona, 1936; augmented edition, Buenos Aires: Emecé, 1953
Nueva refutación del tiempo, Buenos Aires: Oportet y Haereses, 1947
Aspectos de la literatura gauchesca, Montevideo: Número, 1950
Antiguas literaturas germánicas, in collaboration with Delia Ingenieros, Mexico City: Fondo de Cultura Económica, 1951
Otras inquisiciones 1937–1952, Buenos Aires: Sur, 1952; as *Other Inquisitions 1937–1952*, translated by Ruth L.C. Simms, Austin: University of Austin Press, 1964; London: Souvenir Press, 1973
El "Martín Fierro," in collaboration with Margarita Guerrero, Buenos Aires: Columba, 1953
Leopoldo Lugones, in collaboration with Betina Edelberg, Buenos Aires: Torquel, 1955

Manual de zoología fantástica, in collaboration with Margarita Guerrero, Mexico City: Fondo de Cultura Económica, 1957; revised edition, as *El libro de los seres imaginarios*, Buenos Aires: Kier, 1967; as *The Imaginary Zoo*, translated by Tim Reynolds, Berkeley: University of California Press, 1969; revised edition, as *The Book of Imaginary Beings*, translated by Norman Thomas de Giovanni, New York: Dutton, 1969; London: Jonathan Cape, 1970
The Spanish Language in South America: a Literary Problem; El gaucho Martín Fierro, London: Hispanic and Luso-Brazilian Councils, 1964 [lecture]
Introducción a la literatura inglesa, in collaboration with María Esther Vázquez, Buenos Aires: Columba, 1965; as *An Introduction to English Literature*, edited and translated by L. Clark Keating and Robert O. Evans, Lexington: University Press of Kentucky, and London: Robson, 1974
Literaturas germánicas medievales, in collaboration with María Esther Vázquez, Buenos Aires: Falbo, 1966
Introducción a la literatura norteamericana, in collaboration with Esther Zemborain de Torres, Buenos Aires: Columba, 1967; as *An Introduction to American Literature*, translated by L. Clark Keating and Robert O. Evans, Lexington: University Press of Kentucky, 1973
Prólogos, Buenos Aires: Torres Agüero, 1975
¿Qué es el budismo? in collaboration with Alicia Jurado, Buenos Aires: Columba, 1976
Borges oral, Buenos Aires: Emecé, 1979 [lectures]
Siete noches, Mexico City: Fondo de Cultura Económica, 1980; as *Seven Nights*, translated by Eliot Weinberger, New York: New Directions, 1984
Nueve ensayos dantescos, Madrid: Espasa Calpe, 1982
Atlas, with María Kodama, Buenos Aires: Sudaméricana, 1985; as *Atlas*, translated by Anthony Kerrigan, New York: Dutton, 1985
Los conjurados, Madrid: Alianza, 1985

Compilations and Anthologies
Obras completas, edited by José Edmundo Clemente, Buenos Aires: Emecé, 9 vols, 1953–60
Antología personal, Buenos Aires: Sur, 1961; as *A Personal Anthology*, edited and translated by Anthony Kerrigan, New York: Grove Press, 1967; London: Jonathan Cape, 1968
Obra poética, 6 vols, Buenos Aires: Emecé, 1964–78
Nueva antología personal, Buenos Aires: Emecé, 1968
Obras completas, edited by Carlos V. Frías, Buenos Aires: Emecé, 1974
Prosa completa, 2 vols, Barcelona: Bruguera, 1980
Borges, a Reader: Selections from the Writings, edited by Emir Rodríguez Monegal and Alastair Reid, New York: Dutton, 1981
Antología poética, 1923–1977, Madrid: Alianza, 1981
Textos cautivos: ensayos y reseñas en El Hogar (1936–1939), edited by Enrique Socerio-Gari and Emir Rodríguez Monegal, Barcelona: Tusquets, 1987
Biblioteca personal: prólogos, Madrid: Alianza, 1988
Páginas escogidas, edited by Roberto Fernández Retamar, Havana: Casa de las Américas, 1988

Anthologies in Translation
Labyrinths: Selected Stories and Other Writings, edited and translated by Donald A. Yates and James E. Irby, New York: New Directions, 1962; augmented edition, 1964; Harmondsworth: Penguin, 1970
Selected Poems 1923–1967, edited by Norman Thomas di Giovanni, New York: Delacorte Press, and London: Allen Lane, 1972
The Gold of the Tigers: Selected Later Poems, translated by Alastair Reid, in *The Book of Sand*, New York: Dutton, 1977; London: Allen Lane, 1979

Further Reading

Aizenberg, Edna, *The Aleph Weaver: Biblical, Kabbalistic and Judaic Elements in Borges*, Potomac, Maryland: Scripta Humanística, 1984

Aizenberg, Edna (editor), *Borges and His Successors: the Borges Impact on Literature and the Arts*, Columbia: University of Missouri Press, 1990

Alazraki, Jaime (editor), *Borges and the Kabbalah and Other Essays on His Fiction and Poetry*, Cambridge: Cambridge University Press, 1988

Balderston, Daniel (editor), *The Literary Universe of Jorge Luis Borges: an Index to References and Allusions to Persons, Titles and Places in His Writings*, New York: Greenwood Press, 1986

Balderston, Daniel, *Out of Context: Historical Reference and the Representation of Reality in Borges*, Durham, North Carolina: Duke University Press, 1993

Barrenechea, Ana María, *Borges, the Labyrinth Maker*, edited and translated by Robert Lima, New York: New York University Press, 1965

Bloom, Harold (editor), *Jorge Luis Borges*, New York: Chelsea House, 1986

Cheselka, Paul, *The Poetry and Poetics of Jorge Luis Borges*, New York: Peter Lang, 1987

Christ, Ronald J., *The Narrow Act: Borges's Art of Allusion*, New York: New York University Press, 1969

Cortínez, Carlos (editor) *Borges the Poet*, Fayetteville: University of Arkansas Press, 1986

Di Giovanni, Norman Thomas, *et al.* (editors), *Borges on Writing*, New York: Dutton, 1973; London: Allen Lane, 1974

Di Giovanni, Norman Thomas (editor), *In Memory of Borges*, London: Constable, 1988

Fishburn, Evelyn and Psiche Hughes, *A Dictionary of Borges*, London: Duckworth, 1990

Friedman, Mary Lusky, *The Emperor's Kites: a Morphology of Borges's Tales*, Durham, North Carolina: Duke University Press, 1987

Isbister, Rob and Peter Standish, *A Concordance to the Works of Jorge Luis Borges 1899–1986*, 6 vols, Lampeter, Wales: Edwin Mellen Press, 1992

Kinzie, Mary and Charles Newman (editors), *Prose for Borges*, Evanston, Illinois: Northwestern University Press, 1974

Lapidot, Ema, *Borges and Artificial Intelligence: an Analysis in the Style of Pierre Menard*, New York: Peter Lang, 1991

McMurray, George R., *Jorge Luis Borges*, New York: Ungar, 1980

Molloy, Sylvia, *Signs of Borges*, Durham, North Carolina: Duke University Press, 1994

Rodríguez-Luis, Julio, *The Contemporary Praxis of the Fantastic: Borges and Cortázar*, New York: Garland, 1991

Rodríguez Monegal, Emír, *Jorge Luis Borges: a Literary Biography*, New York: Dutton, 1978

Sarlo, Beatriz, *Jorge Luis Borges: a Writer on the Edge*, edited by John King, London and New York: Verso, 1993

Shaw, Donald L., *Borges: Ficciones*, London: Grant and Cutler, 1976

_____ *Borges' Narrative Strategy*, Liverpool: Cairns, 1992

Stabb, Martin S., *Borges Revisited*, New York: Twayne, 1991

Sturrock, John, *Paper Tigers: the Ideal Fictions of Borges*, Oxford: Clarendon Press, 1977

Wheelock, Carter, *The Mythmaker: a Study of Motif and Symbol in the Short Stories of Borges*, Austin: University of Texas Press, 1969

Yates, Donald, *Jorge Luis Borges: Life, Work and Criticism*, Fredericton, New Brunswick: York Press, 1985

Bibliographies

Becco, Jorge Horacio, *Borges: bibliografía total 1923–1973*, Buenos Aires: Casa Pardo, 1973

Foster, David William, *Jorge Luis Borges: an Annotated Primary and Secondary Bibliography*, New York: Garland, 1984

Interviews

Alifano, Robert, *Conversaciones con Borges*, Buenos Aires: Atlántida, 1986

Barnstone, Willis (editor), *Borges at Eighty: Conversations*, Bloomington: Indiana University Press, 1982

Burgin, Richard, *Conversations with Jorge Luis Borges*, New York: Holt Rinehart, 1968

Roman, Selden (editor), *Tongues of Fallen Angels: Conversations with Jorge Luis Borges*, New York: New Directions, 1974

Nueva refutación del tiempo

Essay by Jorge Luis Borges

Time, Borges writes at the beginning of *Historia de la eternidad*, 1936 [A History of Eternity], presents perhaps the most vital of all metaphysical problems. For him, the fact that it does so undermines both our confidence in our ability to understand reality and our sense of the unity and continuity of our individual personalities. For we tend to explain reality in terms of chains of causes and effects following one another chronologically. But what if this notion of an on-going line of time linking things understandably together were an illusion, or merely referred to only one of several co-existing dimensions of time? If we could see time in other ways (as a perpetual present, as circular, as spiral, as a web of different time-scales of which we are programmed to recognize only one), our notion of reality might change radically. Time affects our memory, which is our only real link with our past selves, so that awareness of the mystery of time is simultaneously awareness of the mystery of the personality. To question our notion of time is thus to question some of our most ingrained assumptions, and ultimately to suggest that all reality, including that of ourselves, is really just a construct, not something existing objectively.

One of Borges's aims seems to be to question, and thus encourage us to question, the comfortable presuppositions by which we live. His two-part essay "Nueva refutación del tiempo," 1944 and 1946 later republished in *Otras inquisiciones*, 1952 (*Other Inquisitions*), examines arguments which undercut much of what we take for granted in everyday life. It begins from George Berkeley's premiss, that of pure philosophical idealism: all things exist only as they are perceived by the mind. Objects as such exist outside the human mind only because they are continuously perceived by the divine mind. However, Berkeley salvaged the idea of the on-going personal identity of the individual perceiver. Hume, though, went further, replacing individual human identity with a mere flow of perceptions. Borges, taking up the argument in his essay, goes further still. If there is no soul or spirit, if there is no mass or space outside the mind, he asks, how can we defend the idea of continuity, of a before and after for each perception? Each fleeting instant of awareness is completely autonomous; to link them together in series is to cultivate an illusion. On the other hand, it is perhaps possible for the same perception to be shared by different minds, such that each individual "lives" the same "moment," even at what we would normally call different times. The way our intelligence is programmed and the way language itself functions, he admits, imply chronological succession. So it is hard for us to contemplate the idea of time as a delusion or to deny the ideas of an on-going self or an external world with its history. At the beginning of the essay, Borges confesses that he is not personally convinced by the arguments he adduces, calling them word-games. But at the end he utters the anguished wish that they were true and that the world were not a real world in which the fate of the individual is governed by inescapable conditions, among them subjection to time.

DONALD L. SHAW

Editions

First edition: in *Otras inquisiciones 1937–1952*, Buenos Aires: Sur, 1952

Translation: in *Other Inquisitions 1937–1952*, by Ruth L.C. Simms, Austin: University of Texas Press, 1964; London: Souvenir Press, 1973

El jardín de senderos que se bifurcan

Short story by Jorge Luis Borges

Clearly, "Nueva refutación del tiempo" is highly relevant to several of Borges's best-known stories. In "Tlön, Uqbar, Orbis Tertius" reality is reduced to mental perceptions. In "El milagro secreto" (The Secret Miracle) time stops while the protagonist completes a play in which time contains circularities. "La muerte y la brújula" (Death and the Compass) ends with the idea of an Eternal return. But perhaps more interesting is "El jardín de senderos que se bifurcan" (The Garden of Forking Paths). The outer frame of the story is a highly original spy-story which, like the detective-story format of "La muerte y la brújula" situates Borges among the precursors of Postmodernism, one of which features is said to be the blurring of distinctions between "high" and "low" literary genres. Yu Tsun, a Chinese in the pay of Germany in World War I needs to transmit from England to his masters in Berlin the message "Albert," the name of a town in Flanders from which the British are about to launch an attack. To do so he murders an individual named Stephen Albert and is arrested and condemned to death. But before being killed Albert turns out to have solved the mystery of a novel written by one of Yu Tsun's ancestors. "El jardín . . ." is replete with irony. Liddell Hart, whose book on World War I is mentioned at the beginning as one of its sources, points out that the place of the attack was an open secret, so that Yu Tsun's murder of Albert is futile. Worse still Yu Tsun has killed the only man to have explained his ancestor's secret. As elsewhere in Borges, reality ironically refuses to submit to our desire to impose a pattern on it. Plans go wrong; quests fail; man is cut down to size.

During the meeting between Yu Tsun and Albert, the story suddenly changes course. Yu Tsun's ancestor has set out to write a book and to construct a labyrinth. Albert explains that the book *is* the labyrinth. It describes "Un invisible laberinto de tiempo" (An invisible labyrinth of time). Instead of a chain or chains of episodes illustrating a principle of selection by the author, all possible outcomes of each individual episode are followed out, so that each action or decision leads to an ever more complex series of future consequences, all evolving in parallel and intersecting each other. Ts'ui Pên, the author, is described by Albert as obsessed by "el abismal problema del tiempo" (the abysmal problem of time). Hence his intricate novel is in fact a riddle, the answer to which is the word time. Ts'ui Pên, that is, believed time to be like an inextricable network of separate strands of time, criss-crossing each other and all evolving at once. At the peak moment of the story, Yu Tsun is granted a momentary sensation of time pullulating like this all round him. Borges is clearly challenging the reader to take into account that time might well operate in this way and that our limited vision of a single time-flow may well be a simplification, with all that it would entail for our worldview.

But details of the story alert us to the fact that this is only one of several hypotheses. When, near the beginning, Yu Tsun realizes that he alone must undertake the task of transmitting the secret to the Germans and that it will involve his own death, time suddenly freezes: " reflexioné que todas las cosas le suceden a uno precisamente, precisamente, ahora. Siglos de siglos y sólo en el presente ocurren los hechos" (I reflected that everything happens to one precisely, precisely now. Centuries of centuries and things happen only in the present). We detect the similarity with Borges's mention in "Nueva refutación del tiempo" of "nosotros que somos el minucioso presente" (we who are the finely detailed present) and of the fact that "El presente es la forma de toda vida" (The present is the form of all life). Another alternative still remains. Yu Tsun tells us that his ancestor Ts'ui Pên's labyrinthine novel works, and chooses as an example a situation in which an unknown assailant may or may not murder Fang, because of a secret. At the end of the story, Yu Tsun, a foreigner and a stranger, murders Albert for a secret reason. Thus time may be in some cases circular, the same episode repeating itself with minor variations. The last adjective of the tale, "innumerable," referring to Yu Tsun's contrition and weariness after the murder and his arrest, is there to remind us that in all possible dimensions of time evil behaviour will bring remorse and regret.

Time, then, may be "una red creciente y vertiginosa de tiempos divergentes, convergentes y paralelos" (an ever-growing and vertiginous web of divergent, convergent and parallel times), a labyrinth, in fact. If we look at the structure of the tale, we notice that, in making his way from the railway station to Albert's house, Yu Tsun realizes that he has been given directions similar to those for moving through a labyrinth. In other words, a static, spatial labyrinth is evoked to prepare us for the idea of an ever-expanding temporal labyrinth. The second reinforces and amplifies the impact of the first. A maze of country lanes leads us to the disturbing concept of innumerable pasts and presents for each moment in time. Other details of the story are similarly relevant to the theme of the mystery of time. The fact that Yu Tsun writes his confession as he awaits imminent execution reminds us of the infinite preciousness of the here and now. Who more than a man facing death could appreciate the idea of time frozen into an eternal present.

The notion of circular time is alluded to by the circular moon, a circular clock, a circle of lamplight and a gramophone record turning beside a bronze Phoenix.

Typically, Borges in "El jardín . . ." combines a (highly dramatic in this case) realistic-type frame story which deceives us by its reassuring similarity to a familiar genre, with a strange and disturbing core, containing unexpected abstract and quasi-metaphysical considerations. Nor is the core simply inserted into the frame; the two interact functionally. Form and content combine to undercut our complacency in the face of life.

DONALD L. SHAW

Editions

First edition: in *El jardín de senderos que se bifurcan*, Buenos Aires: Sur, 1942

Translation: There are several translations of this story which was included by Borges in *Ficciones*. An accessible one is that by Donald Yates in *Labyrinths: Selected Stories and Other Writings*, New York: New Directions, 1962; Harmondsworth: Penguin, 1970. There are recent reprints.

Brazil

19th-Century Prose and Poetry

At the beginning of the 19th century, Brazil was still part of the Portuguese colonial empire. From the 17th century, this South American colony had relinquished more of its riches to Lisbon than any other, and had already shown strong signs of wanting to become an independent nation. For this reason, it was kept under strict control by the Portuguese government. The most resolute separatist movement had appeared in Vila Rica, in the province of Minas Gerais. The thrust of its ideas derived from reading the French Encyclopedists while pragmatism was influenced by the North American commanders who had been successful in securing the United States' independence from Britain. Joaquim José da Silva Xavier, the movement's presumptive leader, known as Tiradentes, was hanged, while fellow-conspirators, such as the poet Tomás Antônio Gonzaga, were punished effectively through banishment to Africa.

France too gave impetus to the fight for independence. In 1808, Napoleon refused to accept Portugal's decision to support the English cause, and he resolved to invade the country. Immediately, the Prince Regent, Dom João, shifted the capital of the Empire from Lisbon to Rio de Janeiro, by transferring both himself and his entire court to Brazil. As soon as he arrived, he adopted measures essential to the efficient running of State affairs, and this lead quite naturally to a relaxation of both the economic and political constraints to which Brazil had been subjected and which, until that point, had been ruthless. The Prince Regent threw open the doors to the "friendly nations;" he allied himself with England, thus increasing trade with Europe and releasing Brazilian products from the control of Portuguese import taxes. He also launched the Royal Printers which abolished the ban on the publication of books and reading materials in the colony, and made the circulation of news and ideas possible: moreover, he encouraged the establishment of local industry, which until that point had been hampered by legislation and had condemned the

entire country to monocultivation or to mining operations. These activities, such as the sugar plantations in the northeast and the prospecting for gold and diamonds in the central western regions, yielded great profits for, yet did not compete with, the fragile Portuguese economy. In fact they kept it going.

Merchants such as John Luccock, who was in Brazil between 1808 and 1818, together with artists such as Jean-Baptiste Debret, bore direct witness to the level of growth which Rio de Janeiro underwent at this time. The city developed refinements and maturity to receive the Portuguese royal family and their distinguished entourage. By 1821, when they had all returned to Portugal, there was no going back for Brazil, even though the government in Lisbon tried to force it to do so. Members of the ruling classes of the time, together with politicians of the importance of José Bonifácio de Andrade e Silva, opposed the Capital's machinations and persuaded Prince Dom Pedro, the son of Dom João, to head the independence movement, which was begun in 1822 and ratified by 1825.

The new nation, aware that not only political independence, but also symbols and images which would represent this independence were needed, began to search for ways of portraying its individuality and to demonstrate that Brazil really was a separate nation from Portugal. Literature was chosen to fulfil this role, as was described in detail by Ferdinand Denis who had been in Brazil between 1816 and 1819 and had visited Rio de Janeiro and Bahia. In 1826 he published in Paris the *Résumé de l'histoire littéraire du Bresil* [Summary of the History of Brazilian Literature] thus gathering together the literary works of the 17th and 18th centuries which could be attributed to writers born there. By suggesting that "South America must have freedom of expression as well as of government," he summed up the ideas which would set apart the Romantic generation, who had been invited to fulfil the role of providing the nation with its own literary works and thus lend credence to its independent status.

Although it was left to the Romantics to implement this plan, it was the plan itself which was responsible for determining the direction which 19th-century Brazilian literature would take. This in turn gave an outlet to the concept of dualism, which, henceforth, was to be firmly rooted in the country's activities. This dualism comprised the conflict between, on the one hand, the search for a truly national form of expression, free from any possible European influence (superficially Portuguese but French in essence); and on the other, attendance at and use of the most advanced academies and literary styles, which were created and spread within the very same Europe which Brazil had chosen to reject.

France once again played a starring role by helping out in this conflict, as the first Brazilian Romantics graduated from Parisian academies. It was there that, in 1836, Domingos José Gonçalves de Magalhães, together with Manuel Araújo Porto Alegre and Francisco Sales Torres Homem, published the journal *Niterói*. This included the *Ensaio sobre a literatura do Brasil* [An Essay on Brazilian Literature], in which Brazilian poetry was accused of being " a Greek woman clad in French and Portuguese styles and adapted to the climate of Brazil; a Helicon virgin who, while wandering through the world, has ripped her mantle which was made by Homer's own hand; and while sitting in the shade of the South American palm trees, she comforts herself with memories of her homeland, and imagines that she can hear the soft murmuring of Castalia, the tremulous whispering of Lodon and Ismenius, and she mistakes a song-thrush which is warbling amongst the branches of the orange tree, for a nightingale." To try to redress this situation Gonçalves de Magalhães published the verses of *Suspiros poéticos e saudade* [Poetic Sighs and Nostalgia] in the very same year and, again, in Paris. This work is said to announce the arrival of Romanticism in Brazil.

However, it was another Gonçalves, Gonçalves Dias, who set the song-thrush warbling in the shade of the palm trees of South America. Although Gonçalves de Magalhães had been the pioneer of Romanticism, his Neoclassical training as a poet prevented him from breaking the necessary ties with the past. Not even when he returned to writing plays and founded the national theatre with his tragedy *Antônio José, ou o poeta e a inquisição* [Antonio José, or the Poet and the Inquisition] written in 1837 and staged in 1838, nor when he adopted an Indianist style of writing with his 1857 piece entitled *A confederação dos Tamoios* [The Confederacy of the Tamoio Indians] was Magalhães able to produce literary work of some quality. On the other hand, Gonçalves Dias enjoyed the success which had eluded Magalhães: with his 1846 work, *Primeiros cantos* [First Songs], Brazilian poetry discovered the themes and discourse which until this point it had lacked. Now it was equipped to converse in a simple yet lyrical way about the country, about the beauty of nature and about the poet's torments and passions. These were the goals of the poem *Canção do exilio* [The Song of the Exile]. The book's title is also that of the opening text; its verses are remembered, recited and parodied even today by everyone who struggles with the national anthem.

Dias was also responsible for the success of the Indianist theme, the most distinctive product of Romantic aesthetics. Since the first demonstrations during the colonial period, the Indian tribes had been providing plots and characters for novels written about Brazil. The *Carta* (Letter) of Pero Vaz de Caminha begins the series of works by sailors, historians and chroniclers, which refer to the indigenous population of Brazil at the time of the Discoveries. This process continued until the 19th century, when European scientists ventured into the continent's interior in search of research data. In their turn, 18th-century poets such as Basílio da Gama, Santa Rita Durão, Alvarenga Peixoto and Silva Alvarenga, disciples of the reformist ideas of the Encyclopedists and of Jean-Jacques Rousseau, had accorded the Indian the status of most revered symbol of South America in general, and particularly of Brazil.

But Romanticism went further, as Dias wrote poetry with an Indianist theme from the point of view of the savages themselves. Thus, in "I-Juca-Pirama" he portrays the heroes as having strong, manly voices and the features of courageous warriors; men who are both decent and powerful, for whom honour matters above all else. In "Leito de folhas verdes" [The Bed of Green Leaves] he reverses this process by assuming a lyrical style when he, as the narrator, puts himself in the position of an indigenous woman who is waiting for her lover and sees her expectations dashed.

Indianism turned the main desire of the Romantics into a reality, and it generated a style of poetry totally inspired by local themes and characters. This style became popular because of its acceptance by readers and because it was copied for many decades by later generations throughout Brazil. Linked to Rousseau's ideals of the "noble savage," and probably influenced by Rousseau's work, Indianism was a watershed as it classified works, which were written according to its principles, as expressions of Romanticism; equally, it set these works apart from those which had both come before and were to follow. Indianism was the result of stinging criticism levelled at the Brazilian literary world, and this determined its role as the dominating style.

Although Romanticism was not restricted merely to the concept of Indianism, this was indeed the overriding tendency of the era. Between the years 1840 and 1880, it was manifested in the poetry of Gonçalves Dias, in the novels of José de Alencar and in the plays of Martins Pena. Romantic poetry also encompassed other themes, the most notable of these being of an intimate and romantic nature. They tell of hapless lovers, of the loss of childhood innocence, and of the loneliness of the lyrical subject. Álvares de Azevedo, a disciple of Byron, was the first writer to nurture the idea of "the malaise of the era" and in his verses where he courts death, he finds an outlet for his egotistical and lonely subjectivism. Casimiro de Abreu created a more youthful work, which was a resounding success with the public, however here as well, evidence of individualism and ego worship, the writer's main areas of interest, are also apparent. Fagundes Varela stereotyped this style and, indeed, took it to its limits; but in this way a niche was created for poetry of a more social nature, which Castro Alves takes on board.

Alves is responsible for a more energetic style of lyrical poetry, less concerned with the sorrow of the lyrical subject. But his merit lies in the fact that he brought up the subject of slavery. Although he was young when he died, he had enough time to produce powerful poetry such as *Vozes d'África* [Voices from Africa] and *Navio negreiro* [The Slave Ship], his most original and well-known works, which were published posthumously in 1880. In these poems, he condemns the evils of the slave trade and declares the freedom of the blacks to be of pressing importance.

Castro Alves died in 1871, at a time when new writers, such as disciples of Baudelaire and of the French Parnassian school of poetry, eager for a more realist style and uninterested in the heroes who epitomised the national character, began to question the aesthetics of Romanticism. Romanticism lingered because of its ability to support yet another generation of poets, dramatists and novelists, thus spreading its influence over many decades and parts of the country. But precisely for these reasons, its resources were overstretched.

Although Romantic poetry was said to embody the original thought and national character so desired by historians and literary critics, such as Ferdinand Denis and Gonçalves de Magalhães, at the same time it had to distinguish itself from its predecessors and was treated as the inferior style of writers intent on copying the European approach. The Romantic novelists, however, had a different role, and one which was easier to play. Novel-writing began in the 18th century and became popular in the 19th century: thus there were no models to imitate, so the field was open to free artistic expression. However, this freedom was a problem in itself as the would-be novelists lacked a tradition to follow. Consequently, they had to win the public's approval, as the potential readership had little knowledge of the genre.

The Romantic novelists invented the Brazilian novel. Joaquim Manuel de Macedo undertook the task, and the work which launched his career was a great success. A moreninha, 1845 [The Dark-Skinned Girl] was immediately accepted by the Rio de Janeiro public and for many decades remained the favourite reading of young Brazilian women. There are many reasons for its success: the narrative deals with a daily existence with which the reader can easily identify; the narrator puts himself in a position which allows him to talk to both the fictional characters and the reader; the plot is simple and the characters are jolly and appealing. This formula worked well and Joaquim Manuel de Macedo evolved a highly successful career as a writer, to which he added, above all in the 1840s and 1850s, that of chronicler of life in Rio de Janeiro.

In the 1850s, the novel evolved in different ways, and the writer who was principally responsible for this shift was José de Alencar. Although he had made his debut with two senti-mental novels, that is, Cinco minutos, 1856 [Five Minutes] and A viuvinha, 1857 [The Widow], he received public acclaim in Rio de Janeiro for O guarani, 1857 [The Guarani Indian], a historical novel with an Indianist theme. In this novel, Alencar brought the undertaking of Gonçalves Dias to the fictional world: he created a hero of national dimensions, a represen-tative, amongst the indigenous races, of the finest gentlemanly qualities. He achieved the perfect combination of character and the natural backdrop, by appreciating the merits of the Brazilian landscape, in accordance with the maxims of histo-rians and literary critics. He penned a thrilling narrative, full of action, adventure and pace from beginning to end. Finally, he wrapped the whole thing in a mythical enchantment, thus raising the protagonist to the status of timeless symbol and focus of hero-worship by his followers, whether they were other writers or the enthusiastic readers.

With his novel Iracema (Iracema, the Honey-Lips, a Legend of Brazil) published in 1865, José de Alencar continued his Indianist project, embracing it as the way to relate the myths and legends of Brazil to the emerging nation; that is, as the way to bring to life figures from the past, who would serve as guides and role models with which to set standards for present-day behaviour, and with which to set precedents for how the Brazilian people would identify with their past. In his portrayal of the story of the priestess who abandons her tribe and her family because of her love for a Portuguese soldier, Martin, by whom she has a son, (the archetypal Brazilian), Alencar took his lead from the tales of the foundation of the Roman Empire, and compares the future of Brazil with the mighty past of this Empire.

Ubirajara (Ubirajara: a Legend of the Tupi Indians), written in 1874, is Alencar's last indianist romance. In the interim, he had written historical novels, thus defining the nation's history by the use of hero figures, for example in As minas de prata, 1862–66 [The Silver Mines], Alfarrábios, 1873, and A guerra dos mascates, 1873 [The Peddlar's War]. In this same period, he developed the urban novel, recounting in his own way the customs and habits of the Rio de Janeiro middle classes, and levelling criticism, particularly in his novel Senhora, 1875 at the arranged marriages and at the lack of morals exemplified by those who embodied the nation's capitalism. Similarly, the urban romance allowed Alencar to produce fictional leading roles for women; his female characters assumed these roles not only in Senhora, but earlier in Lucíola (1862), Diva (1864) and A pata da gazela, 1870 [The Gazelle's Foot]. These women are colourful characters who are in no way overwhelmed by the male-dominated society in which they are raised.

But the creative efforts of José de Alencar did not stop there; at the beginning of the 1870s, he realised that if fiction was to reflect issues in the country as a whole, then Indianism and the historical novel would not suffice. He understood that in reality the nation was multifaceted, abounding with incidents and with humour, and he sought to portray these facets with all their variation intact. He thus gave the regionalist novel an opportunity to develop, and the first evidence of this is supplied by his novels O gaúcho, 1870 [The Gaucho], O tronco do ipê, 1871 [The Treetrunk] and O sertanejo, 1875 [The Hinterland Dweller].

The other Romantic novelists can be considered only by comparison with Alencar. Notwithstanding this fact, the first to stand out is the journalist Manuel Antônio de Almeida, who, between 1854 and 1855 published the serial Memórias de um sargento de milícias [Memoirs of an Army Sergeant] in the national press, and who, later, compiled the articles into book form. This work, one of the few to deal with people in Rio de Janeiro in the public eye, is teeming with incidents and witticisms, and presents an amusing and nostalgic insight into Court life "in the era of the King," that is, at the time when the Portuguese Prince Regent lived in Brazil.

The other authors were active above all in the 1870s. Viscount de Taunay wrote Inocência in 1872, in which he recounts a story of forbidden love set in the interior of the region of Minas Gerais. Bernardo Guimarães also chooses a rural backdrop for his novels O ermitão de Muquém, 1866 [The Hermit of Muquem], O garimpeiro, 1872 [The Prospector] and O seminarista [The Seminarist] also of 1872.

His most famous romance was *A escrava Isaura*, 1875 [Isaura the Slave Girl], in which he discusses the question of slavery: he surpasses even the abolitionists with his distribution of fictional roles. Franklin Távora was equally accomplished in writing about regional matters, as he showed in his first novel about highway robberies, a theme which was to become popular in Brazilian literature. *O cabeleira*, 1876 [The Bandit] tells the story of a famous bandit from northeastern Brazil, and in order to devise the character, the author, disillusioned with José de Alencar and a defender of the realist style which was beginning to establish itself, examined genuine documents and sources of information in his attempt to stick to the true facts and to avoid fiction and idealism.

The 1870s were a decade of change. Since gaining its independence, Brazil had adopted the monarchy as its method of government, and had chosen Dom Pedro (the son of Dom João VI who had led the independence movement) as its ruler. He reigned between 1822 and 1831 when he was forced, due to disagreements with the country's political leaders, to renounce the throne in favour of his son, who was still a minor. The child, Dom Pedro II, could only ascend to the throne in 1840 when he would reach the age of fourteen. In the interim, the administrative duties fell to the consorts, who were removed from office every time there was a uprising in the provinces. There were many such uprisings, because this period was characterised by the threat of the Brazilian empire being broken up. But this eventuality was avoided with the victory of the royal army and the new sovereign's accession to the throne.

The second reign was calm compared with the rule of Dom Pedro I, followed by the consorts. The monarchist government retained the infrastructure inherited from the colonial period. This was supported by the immense *latifúndios*, the slave trade and monocultivation. However, little by little the country began to modernise, above all because the cultivation of coffee had enabled new social sectors to attain wealth, a shift of power which ultimately transferred the economic focus to São Paulo. The resultant groups comprised the rural oligarchy associated with the cultivation of coffee and the urban middle classes which profited from the exportation of the product; they demanded change and a greater slice of the political action. At odds with the Royal Court, they adopted the Republic as their marching banner; desirous of a more competent work-force both in the towns and in the countryside, they denounced the slave trade and saw a solution to their labour problems in an acceptance of the white European immigrants who were fleeing indigence in Italy and Germany.

The 1870s also witnessed the rise of a new breed of writer who did not admire the Romantic style: Machado de Assis detected their presence in an essay entitled *A nova geração* [The New Generation]. Here he emphasised the recent preference for realist poetry modelled on the French Parnassian style, which was based on the ideas of Baudelaire, and a rejection of the idealist models of the Romantics. Within fiction itself, the appearance of action novels set in Brazil's interior, (and this is how the royal court, where most of the country's readership was based, got to know about these regions), heralded an era of change for Romanticism. Franklin Távora headed the movement which rejected the heroic, complicated and sentimental plots of previous decades and focused his criticism on

José de Alencar, who was thus transformed into the epitome of what to avoid as a role model.

In the 1880s, the transformation seemed complete. Naturalism made a resoundingly successful debut, and was heralded by Aluísio Azevedo who, as a disciple of Émile Zola, described both the private and public depravities of the Second Reign. His debut took place in 1881 with the novel *O mulato* (*Mulatto*); however his main accomplishment was the 1890 novel *O cortiço* (*A Brazilian Tenement*). In his second novel, Azevedo opts for an urban family nucleus, typical of Rio de Janeiro. He uses its members as a backdrop for the depiction of the city's assorted social groups, and also he describes how to rise in the social scale. Adolfo Caminha writes in the same vein as Azevedo, akin to the style of Eça de Queirós, the Portuguese novelist to whom Caminha indirectly pays a tribute in *A normalista*, 1892 [The Training School Student]. With this novel, Caminha intended to expose the corruption of Fortaleza, the capital of Ceará and the book's setting. Another outstanding novel written along the same lines is *O ateneu*, 1888 [The Academy] by Raul Pompéia, which takes place in an upper-class academy. It evokes the atmosphere of student disputes in order to demonstrate forms of outlandish behaviour and how power was expressed in the society of the period.

If the Naturalists had, in their desire to overcome Romanticism, exaggerated the main aspects and in their own way, distorted the reality of the situation, they had, in contrast, given rise to the desire for an entertaining style of literature, intended to expose social problems of the era. This inclination influenced regionalist prose, which abandoned its preoccupation with describing classes of people and regional characteristics, as Alencar, Taunay, Guimarães and even the rebel Franklin Távora had done. Instead, it brought into focus the reasons why certain areas of the interior, especially in the northeast, were underdeveloped. Drought, the subject of many novels in the 1930s, made its debut in this period, as the theme of two novels which were the total antithesis of the idealist perception of Romanticism. The first was *Dona Guidinha do Poço*, 1891 [Dona Guidinha of Poço] by Manuel de Oliveira Paiva, which tells of the conflict on an estate in Ceará, between the powerful landowners and their menials who have had their land taken away and who must endure the whims of their bosses. The second was *Luzia Homem*, 1903 [The Man Luzia] by Domingos Olímpio. This is the story of the difficulties experienced by a group of migrants from the northeast. Even the *sertão*, the arid and remote hinterland of Brazil, plagued by outlaws and rife with inequality, captured the imaginations of the novelists and acquired literary status in the novel *Sertão* [The Hinterland] written in 1896 by Henrique Coelho Neto, and in *Pelo sertão* [For the Hinterland] and *Os jagunços* [The Gunmen], both dating from 1898, by Afonso Arinos de Melo Franco.

However, the most important novelist of the century does not conform to any of these headings or literary styles. Machado de Assis, who began writing prose within a Romantic framework, with *Contos fluminenses*, 1872 [Tales of Rio de Janeiro], *Histórias da meia-noite*, 1873 [Stories at Midnight], *Resurreição* [The Resurrection] of 1872, *A mão e a luva*, 1874 (*The Hand and the Glove*), *Helena* of 1876 and *Iaiá Garcia*, 1878 (*Yayá Garcia*), was the writer who succeeded in turning the outlook of Brazilian literature on its head in the second half of the 19th century. This was due to his capacity for original thought, devoid of any idealisation and totally adverse to any form of classification or strict adherence to aesthetic principles and fashionable political doctrines.

Although in his first works Machado de Assis adheres to the Romantic model of a sentimental narrative with a traditional and well-worn plot, his texts written after 1880 bear the stamp of originality and daring. In 1881 he published *Memórias póstumas de Brás Cubas* (*Epitaph of a Small Winner*). Told by a "defunct novelist" who relates his life in an ironic fashion, it shook the main foundations of Brazilian life at that time. "O alienista" (The Psychiatrist) is from the same year and was included in the publication *Papéis avulsos* [Single Sheets] which depicts the progress of Simão Bacamarte, the doctor who attempts to define the limits between sanity and madness, and ends up succumbing to the latter for want of these limits.

Machado de Assis published his major novels between 1881 and 1908. He divided his time between the novel and writing fables. He brought the latter to a stage of refinement previously unknown in Brazil. He delineated both styles with the attention and care of a true craftsman, and he portrayed the image of society at that time from a satirical point of view, emphasising those characters belonging to the ruling classes as unhappy souls who wander aimlessly and are incapable of creating their own destiny. In *Quincas Borba* (*The Heritage of Quincas Borba* or *Philosopher or Dog?*), published in 1891, he tells the story of a poor teacher from Barbacena in the interior of Minas Gerais, who, finding himself suddenly rich from an inheritance, has no success in Court society. *Dom Casmurro*, published in 1900, is a fictitious autobiography about a man who is tormented by the failure of his marriage. *Esaú e Jacó*, 1904 (*Esau and Jacob*) is the tale of the hostilities between twin brothers who are permanently at loggerheads, and *Memorial de Aires*, 1908 (*Counselor Ayres's Memorial*) is a diary written by an old man who witnesses the end of the slave trade and the beginning of the republican era. In all these novels, Machado de Assis conjures up a world of deception and lack of imagination. His works gave Brazilian literature a face-lift by laying it open to improvements and by solving problems which arose due to Romanticism, the same problems which had prompted him to search for images and symbols which would take into account the life of the nation.

Poetry went in another direction by totally embracing the Parnassian style. The main advocates were Olavo Bilac, Raimundo Correia, Vicente de Carvalho and Alberto de Oliveira. Even though, at the beginning of the second half of the 19th century, Romantic themes had swamped the verses of both aspiring and established poets, it was now the Parnassian model which captured their fertile imagination, providing them with well-defined standards and excellent role models. Only the followers of Symbolism (a style of allegoric poetry which appeared in the last decade of the century) headed by Cruz e Sousa, opposed the Parnassian style. They did so with some success, as Alphonsus de Guimarães, Nestor Vítor and Gonzaga Duque all joined them, together with yet another active generation of young poets in the first decades of the 20th century.

At the end of the century, Brazil's appearance had changed beyond all recognition. It was no longer a Portuguese colony, nor was it a monarchy. The Republic had become firmly established, supported by the foremost writers and intellectuals of the era, such as Raul Pompéia, Euclides da Cunha and Olavo Bilac, although the most brilliant of all, Machado de Assis, regarded it with suspicion and mistrust, as he regarded all ideas which were adopted through fanaticism and ambition. Brazilian literature now seemed to be on a firm footing, and was subjected to constructive criticism by the likes of José Veríssimo and Sílvio Romero. It proffered compositions of different styles: in the area of fiction Machado de Assis, Aluísio Azevedo, Raul Pompéia, Adolfo Caminha and Coelho Neto should be mentioned; in the area of poetry, Olavo Bilac, Cruz e Sousa and Alphonsus de Guimarães.

The topics favoured disclosed a range of interests, touching on both urban and rural issues, the problems of individuals and of the public as a whole. Despite the problems of the slave trade, black and mulatto writers such as Cruz e Sousa and Machado de Assis established their credibility through their novels, and women such as Júlia Lopes de Almeida and Franscisca Júlia began little by little to carve themselves out a niche in the literary world. By the end of the 1890s, these challenges had been replaced by others, and in the next century writers would be propelled to the forefront of Brazilian Modernism and the avant garde.

REGINA ZILBERMAN
translated by Jaine Beswick

20th-Century Prose and Poetry

Brazilian literary production began to occupy an outstanding position in Latin America in the 20th century because it emancipated itself from Europe. This is something which did not yet apply in the 19th century and, even less so, in colonial times. The new phase of its literary history may have resulted in part from the beginning of industrialisation and urban development in the 1920s in São Paulo, which continued on a larger scale, after the 1950s. One can discern four landmarks in Brazilian literature in the 20th century, all of them derived from the vanguard or *modernista* literature which began in the 1920s.

The first of these moments was marked by the "Semana de Arte Moderna" (Week of Modern Art), which took place in the Municipal Theatre of São Paulo, on 13, 15 and 17 February 1922; but it had to be interrupted due to the hostile reaction of the audience to the performances. A group of intellectuals, poets, musicians and painters were interested in disrupting academic art, especially the academic principles of the Parnassian school of poetry, and they decided to present the audience with a true revolution in art. The Week was financed by Paulo Prado, at a time when São Paulo played a leading role in the economy of the country. The city was in the 1920s one of the few important coffee exporters in the world, a situation that lasted until the great economic crisis of 1929. The *modernista* movement was led by São Paulo intellectuals, especially by Mário de Andrade, Oswald de Andrade and his wife the painter Tarsila do Amaral, Menotti del Picchia, Manuel Bandeira and the composer Heitor Villa-Lobos, among others.

The Week of Modern Art echoed the changes that were taking place in Europe and were brought from that continent to Brazil by Graça Aranha, the author of the novel *Canaã* (1902) who, together with Oswald de Andrade, defended the Modernists against the Academics, such as Coelho Neto, an important fiction writer in the 19th century. These changes were represented by the Cubist movement, led by Pablo Picasso, the orchestral and ballet music of Stravinsky, and, especially, the programme recommended by Marinetti in his manifestos of Futurism of 1909 and 1912. In these he urged stylistic simplification and the end to the use of lyrical images, of adjectives and adverbs, which would be replaced by a violent imagery of "words in freedom" related to an age of war, of speed and of machinery. Also the Dada and the Surrealist movements, together with some of Freud's ideas about the non-linear and non-Cartesian workings of the unconscious contributed to a quick demolishing of the precepts of the leading literary schools, and of 19th-century academic art. The French poet Blaise Cendrars visited Brazil in 1924, carrying a Kodak camera. He captured the imagination of Brazilian writers because he held the idea derived from simultaneism and Surrealism that photography could disrupt academic art and traditional aesthetics by replacing them with an instantaneous flash in a transient moment. Cinema stressed this sensation even more – and literature incorporated from it sketchier and briefer plot structures, character delineation and scene descriptions.

Modernist literary magazines still held a prestigious position among intellectuals. Such was the case of the São Paulo magazine *Klaxon* (to blow the horn, in French, after Marinetti's praise of the din made by machinery and the Rio de Janeiro magazine *Festa* [Party], for which Cecília Meireles and Gilka Machado were contributors. Meireles began writing as a post-Symbolist, a trait she always retained even in her most important books published later, such as *Vaga música*, 1942 [Vague Music], or *Mar absoluto*, 1945 [Absolute Sea], and one which not even Mário de Andrade was exempt from, as in his first book, *Há uma gota de sangue em cada poema*, 1917 [Every Poem Has a Drop of Blood]. Gilka Machado scandalized the provincial critics with her erotic poems, as in *Meu glorioso pecado*, 1928 [My Glorious Sin]. However, the most important magazine of the period was the *Revista de antropofagia* [Journal of Anthropophagy]. It ran for only two issues, and it contained the "Manifesto antropófago" [Anthropophagic Manifesto, 1928], which echoed the "Manifesto da poesia pau-brasil," 1924 [The Brazil-wood Poetry Manifesto], both by Oswald de Andrade. In the latter he imagined a parodic solution for the creation of an autonomous Brazilian literature through a metaphor derived from the ritual of anthropophagy. The Brazilian Indians of the past ate the Europeans or their enemies in order to acquire their qualities or their strength. The totem would thus become a taboo. Following the same recipe, only through the overt imitation and absorption of European models and their art, would Brazilian art be able to release itself from the European influence. *Poema pau-brasil*, 1925 [Brazilwood Poem] also achieves this aim, while recovering fragments from the texts by the first European voyagers in Colonial times, and combining them through parody and a series of cuts to ideas which the Indians might express about them.

Mário de Andrade's *Paulicéia desvairada*, 1922 (*Hallucinated City*), a book of poems about São Paulo as a metropolis, was one of the main works of Brazilian Modernism. In fiction, *Macunaíma, o herói sem nenhum caráter*, 1928 (*Macunaíma*) resulted from deep research into Brazilian Indian legends and myths and folklore in general. It immediately became a landmark of Modernism and of Brazilian literature. It built a totally new vision or *paideuma* of the country, as seen from the inside, not through the ethnocentric vision of Europe. The use of parody and intertextuality, the rupture of the realist description of plot and characters and of verisimilitude helped to demolish the old conceptions of art as a definitive, wholesome, coherent structure. It is probably the most complete and also the first piece of anthropological research ever achieved by a Brazilian writer, since the Brazilian Romantic writers used to idealize, not to study or describe accurately the Indian culture. *Macunaíma* is thus the symbol of a struggle for a Brazilian identity and for the establishment of a national culture and language. Mário de Andrade pursued this research in all his books on music, folklore, medicine, in essay style, as in *A escrava que não é Isaura*, 1925 [The Slave Who is not Isaura], in short fiction, as in *Contos novos*, 1956 [New Stories], and in poetry, as in *Remate de males*, 1930 [Strong Evil], among many other works.

Carlos Drummond de Andrade is perhaps the most important Brazilian poet of the 20th century. His first book of poetry *Alguma poesia*, 1930 [Some Poetry] fell in with the spirit of the movement to such an extent that one of its poems, "No meio do caminho" (*In the Middle of the Road*) became almost a motto for it, due to the repetition of a single line derived from its title that symbolized the utmost simplification of the poetic art. His style resembled the fragmented form of the short poems by Oswald de Andrade in *O caderno do aluno de poesia Oswald de Andrade*, 1927 [The Poetry Student Oswald de Andrade's Notebook], where he imitated the naive way in which children express themselves. Writing like an infant, or an Indian untouched by civilisation, would correspond, then, to getting to know the language of the unconscious, as also did Raul Bopp in *Cobra Norato* (1931). After Oswald de Andrade and Carlos Drummond de Andrade, the tone of the poetry written in the country became joke-like, or a "poema-piada" (joke-poem), as it is also called, an inexhaustible form of irreverence towards the long and elevated compositions prescribed by Longinus. Drummond had several phases in his career, such as the political, in *Sentimento do mundo*, 1940 [Feeling about the World] or *A rosa do povo*, 1945 [The People's Rose], or the abstract, as in *Claro enigma*, 1951 [Clear Enigma], and he was also an important short-story writer.

In 1930, the Modernists split into two groups, when writers such as Menotti del Picchia and Cassiano Ricardo moved towards an ideological view of the Indian, calling themselves "Anta" [Tapir], an animal that was supposedly a totem, but which only served as an ideological defence of integralist and Mussolinean ideas. The other group (Mário, Oswald, Tarsila do Amaral, Bopp) carried on with their reading of anthropology, Freud and Marx. These ideological divisions also led São Paulo to the 1930 Revolution, which resulted in the Getúlio Vargas dictatorship (1930–45).

Not every writer accepted the Modernist movement. In spite of being modern in his critical view of Brazilian nationality and identity, Monteiro Lobato defended a rigid Portuguese norm in writing, in opposition to Mário de Andrade, who began to employ Brazilian oral expression or speech and its idioms, a way of writing that was adopted from Modernism and which is still practised in Brazil, as also did Nelson Rodrigues in the theatre. Rodrigues's *Vestido de noiva*, 1943 (*Wedding Dress*) opened a new matter-of-fact tradition for drama present up to now, even on television. Lobato's main legacies are his book of short stories *Urupês* (1918) on the underdevelopment of rural Brazil and its inhabitants, and the series of educational novels for children about everyday life on a farm in the hinterland of São Paulo titled *Sítio do picapau amarelo* [The Yellow Woodpecker Farm], which appeared between 1921 and 1944.

Lima Barreto is perhaps the only truly popular Brazilian writer of the 20th century, if one does not consider the literary quality of Carolina de Jesus's famous *Quarto de despejo* [The Junk Room], *Diário de uma favelada*, 1959 (*Children of Darkness*) or the experimental *Parque industrial*, 1931 [Industrial Park], by Patrícia Galvão. It is in his novels *Recordações do escrivão Isaías Caminha*, 1909 [Memoirs of the Registrar Isaías Caminha] and *Triste fim de Policarpo Quaresma*, 1911 (*The Patriot*) that Barreto establishes himself as a true follower of the great Realist writer Machado de Assis. Both novels criticise fanatical nationalism and the faith in the Republic, existing in Brazil due to the influence of Auguste Comte's Positivism. Although he died in November 1922, Barreto was unaware of the importance of the "Week," but he had a great impact on the ideas and on the Brazilian way of expression as differing from the Portuguese norm.

Os sertões, 1902 (*Rebellion in the Backlands*), by Euclides da Cunha, although published in the 20th century, is a novel written in a rich, ornamental style and is based on 19th-century theories.

In the 1930s, the so-called "Regionalist novel," or the "1930 northeastern cycle of the novel" became prominent in Brazilian letters. It attempted to discuss the social and political under-development of the country, especially in relation to the decaying sugar-cane plantations and the drought in the back-lands of the northeastern region. The backdrop for this literary trend was the growing influence of Marxist ideas on intellec-tuals who encouraged social solutions for Brazil's poor perfor-mance in agriculture, and blamed capitalism in Latin America for the dire situation of its population. The first book of this cycle was actually published in 1928, *A bagaceira* (*Trash*), by José Américo de Almeida, which only featured a farm and the drought region in order to achieve a naive, Romantic setting for a love affair filled with intrigue. *O quinze*, 1930 [The Year Nineteen Fifteen] by Rachel de Queiroz, is the book that actually opened the cycle and first characterized the political consciousness that would define the whole period. José Lins do Rego depicted the decay of the old sugar mills and the impoverishment of the landowners when their property passed into the hands of the industrialists. However, in *Menino de engenho*, 1932 (*Plantation Boy*), *Fogo morto*, 1943 [Dead Fire], or *Usina*, 1936 [The Sugar Mill], he chooses an emotional, personal and confessional tone. Graciliano Ramos was another great writer of this cycle. In his novel *Vidas secas*, 1938 (*Barren Lives*), he employed a vocabulary as lean as the victims of the drought themselves, which resembled a cinema script through its stress on terse dialogue. Two of the novels published by Oswald de Andrade, *Memórias sentimentais de João Miramar*, 1924 (*The Sentimental Memoirs of John Seaborne*) and *Serafim Ponte Grande*, 1933 (*Seraphim Grosse Pointe*) can likewise be interpreted as sensors of this frag-mented and non-linear cinematic vision characteristic of our times. Ramos helped to renovate literary language, ridding it of any ornaments and excesses of imagery. *São Bernardo* (1934) is probably his masterpiece in the sense that it shows the personal conflicts of a landowner and the ill effects that his greedy desire for a large property, typical of his region (the *latifúndio*, or vast estate) had on its impoverished peasants. *Memórias do cárcere*, 1953 (*Jail Prison Memoirs*) is the result of Ramos's political arrest during the Vargas dictatorship. Later, the poetry of João Cabral de Melo Neto, from Pernambuco, employed the same technique of using a very direct vocabulary of political intention to depict poverty and drought in that region. His best-known work is a rhymed one-act Christmas play, *Morte e vida severina*, 1965 [Death and Life of a Common Man], which is about the severe conditions of life of the northeastern population. As a diplomat in Spain, he was able to combine the seven-syllable rhyming scheme of the Spanish *cancionero* (Spanish ballads) with the oral compo-sitions of his native land, either from the *cordel* (stories sold in street fairs) or from the popular *cantadores* (singers). His best poems belong to Concrete poetry, such as *O cão sem plumas*, 1950 [The Featherless Dog], *Uma faca só lâmina*, 1955 (*A Knife All Blade or Usefulness of Fixed Ideas*), and "Tecendo a manhã" [Knitting the Morning] in his *A educação pela pedra*, 1966 [Education through the Stone].

Jorge Amado became known world-wide as a rebellious and political author who situated his novels in the cocoa region of Ilhéus, or in Salvador da Bahia, among very poor characters. He tried to depict the poverty of the region, but imbuing it with a national flavour and sensitivity that only his particular style would permit. Among his most famous novels, which amount to almost fifty, *Capitães da areia*, 1937 (*Captains of the Sands*) and *Seara vermelha*, 1946 [Red Field] correspond to his Marxist phase, whereas *Gabriela, cravo e canela*, 1959 (*Gabriela, Clove and Cinnamon*) opens a new stage – one that even when showing the local political alliances, tends to emphasise the feminine figure in a tropical setting. His short novels *Os velhos marinheiros*, 1961 (*Home is the Sailor*) and *A morte e a morte de Quincas Berro D'Água*, 1962 (*The Two Deaths of Quincas Wateryell*) may be considered as pioneering works of magical realism.

The third great movement in the Modernist phase is marked by the consciousness of language, something that began to emerge in 1945, and was to be stressed in the 1950s. Brazilian literature experienced this shift because the country became more urban, more influenced by the habit of reading of news-papers and books, and more aware of the main intellectual discussions on art and literature. In addition, the growth of federal universities in the main capitals of the country, resulted in a larger and more specialized reading public. The founding of Brasília, in 1972, may be seen as a result of the self-confidence that the country felt from its contribution to modern art and architecture – owing to Lúcio Costa, Joaquim Cardoso and Oscar Niemeyer. The Cubist era founded by the modern art of Brasília symbolised new horizons.

This promising situation in the capitalist scene of the modern world that Brazil experienced in the 1950s may have prompted the appearance of the literary movement known as *Concretismo* (Concrete poetry). Most critics consider that it began in São Paulo, with Augusto de Campos, his brother Haroldo de Campos and Décio Pignatari. Inspired in Arno Holz, its poetic synthesis approaches haiku, or the economy of words present in the media and communication. As in the Cubist flat buildings, this poetry cut out any kind of lyricism or sentimentality, and totally abolished emotion, replacing the old stanzas and lyric elegies with squares, circles and propaganda messages. In 1952 the Concretists founded the magazine *Noigrandes*, which ran to five issues. The Campos brothers also developed a theory of translation that they called transcriation based on the idea of "Make it new," by Ezra Pound, and in part on the translations by Octavio Paz, as in his *Transblanco*.

Guimarães Rosa and Clarice Lispector were the main figures of the period from the 1950s to the 1970s. Rosa presented a dialectical combination between pure love and the countryside view of the bandit (*cangaceiro*) from the north of Minas Gerais, where he was born in the town of Cordisburgo. He chose to employ not a political point of view, but an aesthetic and philosophical perspective on life and on the peculiarity of the idioms of his region. *Grande sertão: veredas*, 1956 (*The Devil to Pay in the Backlands*) is an epic in the form of a novel. It focuses on the farms and the bandit groups that attacked them according to their own sense of law, but it is mainly a travel through words, a research in language similar to the one performed by James Joyce in *Ulysses*, in 1920. Lispector also wrote as if she were in a constant search for words, sometimes from a Heideggerian or Sartrean standpoint; however, her setting was urban and she concentrated on women characters questioning their feminine roles in the domestic space of their homes, as in her outstanding book of short stories *Laços de família*, 1960 (*Family Ties*) or her novel *A paixão segundo G.H.*, 1964 (*The Passion According to G. H.*).

Another group of poets was inspired by Catholic thought and the writings of Santiago Dantas and Jackson de Figueiredo, and opposed the Marxist trend that formed the basis for the political novels begun in the 1930s, defending an aesthetic notion of literature. The main figures of this spiritual movement were Murilo Mendes and Jorge de Lima. Both tended to overwork the word, the expression, to care for the poetic form of the sonnet, the elegy, or even the epic, in the case of Lima's long poem *Canção de Orfeu*, 1952 [Orpheus's Song]. *Crônica da casa assassinada*, 1959 [Chronicle of the Murdered House], by Lúcio Cardoso, depicts the decline of a bourgeois family after the coffee slump that affected plantations in Rio de Janeiro State. In poetry, the so-called "Geração de 1945" (Generation of 1945), was thus called because it emerged after the end of the Vargas dictatorship of "Estado Novo," the death of Mário de Andrade and the end of World War II. It defended a pure aesthetics, rather than the vanguard one proposed by Modernism under the influence of Proust, Eliot, Valéry and Ungaretti, and had two literary magazines: *Revista Brasileira de Poesia* (1942) and *Orfeu* (1947–). Some of its most outstanding authors are Ferreira Gullar, with *Poema sujo*, 1976 (*Dirty Poem*), Affonso Ávila, Ledo Ivo and Thiago de Melo

whose poem *Faz escuro mas eu canto*, 1965 [It is Dark, but I Sing], similar in tone to the political poetry of the Chilean Pablo Neruda, became a political manifesto against the military dictatorship at the time.

The period between the 1970s and the 1990s saw an emphasis on the urban novel and on a postmodern, deconstructive view of utopia and of any optimistic possibilities of social change. At the same time, the population of the country became 85% urban in the 1980s. The imposition in 1964 of a military regime, which lasted until 1984, put an end to all the unrealized projects of social and agrarian reform, and provoked a severe economic crisis later on. The 1970s witnessed the closing down of the Chamber of Deputies and of the Senate, and the end of free elections. While poetry lessened in importance in the literary scene, there was a boom of the short story at the beginning of the 1970s, which was replaced by that of the novel after the 1980s. In the 1970s there was a wave of alternative or "marginal" books by young poets, such as Chacal (pen-name of Ricardo de Carvalho Duarte), Cacaso (pen-name of Antonio Carlos de Brito), Ana Cristina César, Chico Alvim (Francisco Alvim), some of whom sold mimeographed copies of their poems in the streets. They denied the influence of their Modernist predecessors and resented that their generation was unable to effect political change in Brazil; therefore they turned to a personal experience or trip, as did the beat generation in the United States. The 1970s saw the appearance of a great number of novelists and short story writers, most of whom employed magical realism or hyperrealism to depict surreptitiously the political situation of the country under the military dictatorship. Among others, there were Rubem Fonseca, Sérgio Sant'Anna, Ignácio Loyola Brandão. Sant'Anna also employed magical realism, or Surrealism in his *Confissões de Ralfo (uma autobiografia literária)*, 1975 [Confessions of Ralfo, (a Literary Autobiography)] in which fear of madness and the description of a lunatic asylum conveyed the experience of life in the 1970s, but also worked as a psychological reaction to the political events prevailing at the time, a similar setting for Carlos Sussekind (1933–) in *Armadilha para Lamartine*, 1975 [A Trap for Lamartine]. *Roman noir* plots and the techniques of best-sellers allowed Fonseca to break with the emotive background traditionally present in the novel and thus to write crude books about a violent life in a Third World country like Brazil. The short story collection *Feliz ano novo*, 1975 [Happy New Year] by Fonseca, and *Zero* (1975) by Brandão were banned and confiscated by the military regime in the year of their publication. Through hyperrealism they expressed the absurdity of city life strained by violence and lack of perspective due to an incompetent government. In Fonseca's short story "O Cobrador," 1979 [The Bill-Collector], a down-and-out decides to take justice into his own hands and kills all the middle-class professionals that he meets. In the novel *Zero*, Brandão exaggerates the highly bureaucratic structure of the State mounted by the military in order to prevent the ordinary citizens from attaining their most basic rights. Magical realism was present in Dalton Trevisan, whose *O vampiro de Curitiba*, 1965 (*The Vampire of Curitiba and Other Stories*) became a cult book, J. J. Veiga, whose short stories of *Os cavalinhos de Platiplanto*, 1959 [The Little Horses of Platiplanto] introduced magical realism in Brazil, Roberto Drummond, who wrote the fantastic short novel *A morte de D. J. em Paris*, 1979 [The death of D. J. in Paris], João Gilberto Noll, Murilo Rubião, whose short novel *O pirotécnico Zacarias*, 1974 [The Pyrotechnicist Zacharias] became a classic of the fantastic genre, Antônio Torres and Paulo Leminski, with his experimental novel *Catatau* (1975).

Other authors became steadily established in the novel form, such as Autran Dourado, with *Ópera dos mortos*, 1967 (*The Voices of the Dead*), Osman Lins and Érico Veríssimo, whose *O tempo e o vento* (*Time and the Wind*), written between 1949 and 1961, is a classic lyrical novel. In the realist style, there were Antônio Callado's Indian novel *Quarup* (1967), which was made into a film, José Louzeiro, an author of best-sellers that were often filmed and João Ubaldo Ribeiro, an author of very successful novels such as *Viva o povo brasileiro*, 1984 (*An Invincible Memory*).

In the 1990s, Silviano Santiago crossed frontiers of country and sex and infringed the code of nationality while situating his novel *Stella Manhattan* (1985) in New York City. Personal experience became more important than the defence of ideologies in this and other novels which began to be written in the 1980s. The postmodern vogue which focuses on violence and the lack of any sense of belonging in an urban setting is also present in Caio Fernando Abreu's *Onde andará Dulce Veiga?* 1990 [Where Could Dulce Veiga Be?], a pastiche on the life-drama of a transvestite in a big city like São Paulo.

With the collapse of Utopia, typical of the postmodern era, small groups that beforehand could not express themselves were able to publish their books after the 1970s. Women's literature went through a boom then, and so did Black literature, including the one produced by Black women authors. In São Paulo, the group called "Quilombhoje" denounced the prejudice that victimized them through the publication of a magazine with the same title, which dedicates every other issue to poetry or to short stories.

Among women authors, who are mainly urban, white and from the middle class, Lygia Fagundes Telles, Nélida Piñón, Sônia Coutinho, Rachel Jardim, Lya Luft, Patrícia Bins, Márcia Denser, Helena Parente Cunha, Marina Colasanti are authors who have developed a consistent corpus of women's literature since the 1970s. Most of their fiction is a follow-up, in similar style, to the enigmatic and metaphoric prose of Lispector's, and situates women in the confines of the house, from a subjective, self-centered writing of the self. However, it represents a step forward since women have acquired the status of professional writers in Brazil. While Coutinho's plots now center on the crime novel, Ana Miranda has published a successful historical novel on the Baroque poet Gregório de Matos, titled *Boca do Inferno*, 1989 (*Bahia of all the Devils*). Both genres attempt to escape from the idea of self-reference towards a new realistic or historical perspective. All Brazilian literature of the 20th century, in its different facets and phases is, therefore, immersed in the Modernist project begun in the 1920s, and reflects a constant struggle for its identity and autonomous expression.

LUIZA LOBO

See also entries on Concrete Poetry, Modernismo: Brazil, Popular Culture: Brazil, Regionalism: Brazil

Further Reading

General

Cândido, Antônio, *Formação da literatura brasileira: momentos decisivos*, 2 vols, 6th edition, Belo Horizonte: Itatiaia, 1981; as *On Literature and Society*, edited and translated by Howard S. Becker, Princeton, New Jersey: Princeton University Press, 1995

Coutinho, Afrânio (editor), *A Literatura no Brasil*, 6 vols, 3rd edition, Rio de Janeiro: José Olympio, and Niterói: Universidade Federal Fluminense, 1986

Grossmann, Judith, *et al.*, *O espaço geográfico no romance brasileiro*, Salvador, Brazil: Fundaçao Casa de Jorge Amado, 1993

Haberly, David T., *Three Sad Races: Racial Identity and National Consciousness in Brazilian Literature*, Cambridge and New York: Cambridge University Press, 1983

Jozef, Bella, *A máscara e o enigma: a modernidade da representação a transgressão*, Rio de Janeiro: Francisco Alves, 1986

Lajolo, Marisa and Regina Zilberman, *A leitura rarefeita. Livro e literatura no Brasil*, São Paulo: Brasiliense, 1991

Lobo, Luiza, *Crítica sem juízo: ensaios*, Rio de Janeiro: Francisco Alves, 1993

Lowe, Elizabeth, *The City in Brazilian Literature*, Rutherford, New Jersey: Fairleigh Dickinson University Press, 1982

Needell, Jeffrey D., *A Tropical Belle Époque: Elite Culture and Society in Turn-of-the-Century Rio de Janeiro*, Cambridge and New York: Cambridge University Press, 1987

Reis, Roberto (editor), *Toward Socio-Criticism: Selected Proceedings of the Conference "Luso-Brazilian Literatures," a Socio-Critical Approach*, Tempe: Arizona State University / Center for Latin American Studies, 1991

Schwarz, Roberto (editor), *Os pobres na literatura brasileira*, São Paulo: Brasiliense, 1983

Schwarz, Roberto, *Misplaced Ideas: Essays on Brazilian Culture*, edited with an introduction by John Gledson, London and New York: Verso, 1992

Sodré, Nelson Werneck, *História da literatura brasileira: seus fundamentos econômicos*, 6th edition, Rio de Janeiro: Civilização Brasileira, 1978

Zilberman, Regina, *A literatura no Rio Grande do Sul*, Pôrto Alegre, Brazil: Mercado Aberto, 1980

19th Century

Broca, Brito, *Românticos, pré-românticos e ultra-românticos: vida literária e Romantismo brasileiro*, São Paulo: Pólis; Brasília: Instituto Nacional do Livro, 1979

Romero, Sílvio, *História da literatura brasileira*, 2nd edition, Rio de Janeiro: Garnier, 1903; augmented 3rd edition, Rio de Janeiro: José Olympio, 1943

Veríssimo, José, *História da literatura brasileira*, 3rd edition, Rio de Janeiro: José Olympio, 1954 [Stops at Machado de Assis]

20th Century

Bellei, Sérgio Luiz Prado, "Brazilian Culture in the Frontier," *Bulletin of Latin American Research*, vol. 14/1 (January 1995) [Concerned also with Spanish America]

Brito, Mário da Silva (editor), *O Modernismo*, Rio de Janeiro: Civilização Brasileira, 1959

DiAntonio, Robert E., *Brazilian Fiction: Aspects and Evolution of the Contemporary Narrative*, Fayetteville: University of Arkansas Press, 1989

Fitz, Earl E. and Judith A. Payne, *Ambiguity and Gender in the New Novel of Brazil and Spanish America: a Comparative Assessment*, Iowa City: University of Iowa Press, 1993

Jackson, K. David (editor), *Transformations of Literary Language in Latin American Literature from Machado de Assis to the Vanguards*, Austin, Texas: Abaporu Press, 1987

Patai, Daphne, *Myth and Ideology in Contemporary Brazilian Fiction*, Rutherford, New Jersey: Fairleigh Dickinson University Press, and London: Associated University Presses, 1983

Teles, Gilberto Mendonça, *Vanguarda européia e Modernismo brasileiro*, revised 3rd edition, Petrópolis: Vozes, 1976

Dictionaries and Bibliographies

Coutinho, Afrânio and José Galante de Sousa (general editors), *Enciclopédia de literatura brasileira*, 2 vols, Rio de Janeiro: Ministério da Educação, 1990 [Very impressive work with comprehensive coverage of topics as well as of writers]

Foster, David William and Roberto Reis (editors), *A Dictionary of Contemporary Brazilian Authors*, Tempe: Arizona State University / Center for Latin American Studies, 1981

Stern, Irwin (general editor), *Dictionary of Brazilian Literature*, Westport, Connecticut: Greenwood Press, 1988 [Contains very useful and imaginative topics]

Alfredo Bryce Echenique 1939–

Peruvian prose writer

Despite his international success with publishers and reading public alike, Alfredo Bryce Echenique's work has received little in the way of substantial critical attention, as is attested by the Further Reading list at the end of this essay. The most likely explanation for this would appear to be that, having lived in Europe since 1963, he has had his work largely passed over by critics and academics in his native Peru. This was exacerbated by the political situation in Peru in 1970, the year of publication of Bryce Echenique's first (and subsequently widely acclaimed) novel, *Un mundo para Julius* (*A World for Julius*), which portrays a *limeño* oligarchy in decay. In a series of interviews conducted during a visit to Peru in the same year, he refused to place the novel within the context of the left-wing Gobierno Revolucionario de las Fuerzas Armadas (Revolutionary Government of Armed Forces), which had set about undermining the oligarchy since coming to power two years earlier, and brought upon himself a virtual blacklisting by the highly politicised Peruvian academics. In addition to this, the majority of academics in Europe and North America seem until recently to have kept their critical focus firmly on the first wave of the Latin American literary Boom, largely ignoring those authors who belong to what has loosely been called the Post-Boom (those who started to appear in print in the wake of the upsurge of international interest in Latin American literature in the 1960s).

The chronology of Bryce Echenique's work bears witness to a steady rhythm of publication, with a new work appearing every three or four years. The first ten years of his literary career saw the alternate publication of collections of short stories and novels, a feature which is not as arbitrary as might first appear, for the respective novels provided the author with the opportunity to develop more fully the thematic concerns and stylistic features used more tentatively in the preceding short stories. The sense that it is in the novels that Bryce Echenique finds the scope to achieve fullness of thematic and stylistic expression is borne out by the dominance of this genre in his literary production since 1980. As well as the afore-mentioned forms of fictional narrative, Bryce Echenique has published three volumes of chronicles/essays inspired by journeys to the United States, Cuba and various European countries, many of which have first appeared as articles in newspapers and magazines throughout the Spanish-speaking world.

Thematically, Bryce Echenique's early work is characterised by a concern for the emotional and psychological problems of adolescence (*Huerto cerrado* [Enclosed Garden]) and childhood (*Un mundo para Julius*) in a *limeño* society which is governed by convention and strictly observed norms of social behaviour. Structurally and stylistically, the stories of *Huerto cerrado* show certain similarities to those of Ernest Hemingway, a feature which may be explained – together with the use of a central common protagonist in a manner reminiscent of the Nick Adams stories – by Bryce Echenique's undergraduate thesis on "The Function of Dialogue in the Narrative of Hemingway." Perhaps the most pertinent of these parallels are interior monologue, unadorned dialogue, and *style indirect libre*, which comes to constitute the mainstay of the narrative style of *Un mundo para Julius*. It is here in the novel that Bryce Echenique is able to undertake a more profound consideration of the themes initially treated in *Huerto cerrado*, and the scope of the genre enables him to perfect the use of *style indirect libre* to create subtle variations in narrative perspective and to manipulate the relationship between the reader and the novel's various characters.

The subsequent short story-novel coupling of *La felicidad, ja ja*, 1974 [Happiness, Ha Ha] and *Tantas veces Pedro*, 1977 [So Many Times Pedro], represents a largely ignored period of Bryce Echenique's *oeuvre*, yet it is fundamental to an appreciation of the link between his early work and that published since 1980. While a number of the stories of *La felicidad, ja ja* continue to deal with the themes of his earlier works, others show a marked concern with the theme of memory, focused especially on the dichotomy happy childhood/unhappy adulthood. Yet others concentrate on the difficulty of attaining the happiness referred to in the collection's title in a world dominated by the decay of social structures and personal relationships, and it is this aspect in particular which is taken up and given a more thorough consideration in *Tantas veces Pedro*, alongside the self-referential qualities of the earliest of the stories of *La felicidad, ja ja*, "Antes de la cita con los Linares" [Before the Meeting with the Linares]. As was true in the case of the first two works, narrative style and theme are inseparably linked, and in order to treat more effectively the themes of social and interpersonal fragmentation, Bryce Echenique introduces in *La felicidad, ja ja* the use of first- and second-person narrators, as well as experimenting with both spatial and temporal dislocations, with varying degrees of success. The problems encountered in the initial use of these narrative techniques are, on the whole, successfully resolved in *Tantas veces Pedro*, which is set, as are half of the stories of *La felicidad, ja ja*, almost entirely in Europe, reflecting the author's continuing residence in Paris and his growing concern for the problems facing a Latin American in this continent.

The diptych "Cuadernos de navegación en un sillón Voltaire" [Navigational Notebooks in a Voltaire Armchair] consists of two novels: *La vida exagerada de Martín Romaña*, 1981 [The Exaggerated Life of Martín Romaña], and *El hombre que hablaba de Octavia de Cádiz*, 1985 [The Man who Talked about Octavia de Cádiz]. Both are written in the first person which came to dominate *Tantas veces Pedro* and have as their subject matter the search for an idealised love, the question of (cultural) identity, both in the context of a Latin American in Europe and in general terms, and literary creation as a cathartic process. One of the most noteworthy stylistic achievements of these works is the overcoming of the limitations of first-person narration to present the reader with a range of narrative perspectives via techniques such as filtering experience through the eyes of others and recounting episodes with a subjectivity which expands significantly on the conventional features of *style indirect libre*.

The use of these stylistic features and thematic concerns is continued in *La última mudanza de Felipe Carrillo*, 1988 [The Last Move of Felipe Carrillo], which can perhaps be seen as the culmination of the search for a personal narrative voice begun in *Huerto cerrado*. The narrative techniques of the "Cuadernos," born out of the crucial *Tantas veces Pedro*, are used here with similar effectiveness and greater economy, while the more straightforward plot and the return to Peru as a setting mark a synthesis between these and Bryce Echenique's earliest works.

The long-awaited publication of the novel *No me esperen en abril*, 1995 [Don't Wait for Me in April] represents a return to the world of privileged *limeño* society as setting – and to a narrative style which is reminiscent of that of *Un mundo para Julius*, for which Bryce Echenique first made his name, while at the same time bearing witness to the rich variety of techniques employed and polished during the course of his literary production.

DAVID WOOD

Biography

Born in Lima, Peru, 19 February 1939. Parents members of Peruvian oligarchy. Father a banker and mother the granddaughter of a former president of Peru, José Rufino Echenique. Educated at exclusive private schools, the Inmaculado Corazón and Colegio Santa María, both run by US priests and nuns. Later attended boarding school run along British lines, the Colegio San Pablo, which he left in 1956. Pressured by father to study Law at University of San Marcos in Lima, but studied literature at same time. Graduated in 1964 and obtained studentship to study literature at the Sorbonne. Began to work at University of Nanterre in 1967. Married Maggie Revilla in same year but couple later divorced. In late 1970s travelled through the cities of the South in the US, and wrote about Memphis, Atlanta and New Orleans in a personal way. Tired of France and returned to Lima for six months in 1977. Returned to Paris but distraught because of a love affair that ended badly he withdrew to Montepellier in 1980. Abandoned teaching for good in 1984 and moved to Barcelona. Invited as visiting professor to University of Texas (Austin) in 1987. Lectured at several US universities. Moved from Barcelona to Madrid in 1989 where he married Pilar de Vega, a professor of Spanish Linguistics. Contributor to various Spanish and Spanish American journals. Awarded Casa de las Américas Prize, 1968, for *Huerto cerrado*; Peruvian National Literary Award in 1972.

Selected Works

Novels

Un mundo para Julius, Barcelona: Seix Barral, 1970; as *A World for Julius*, translated by Dick Gerdes, Austin: University of Texas Press, 1992

Muerte de Sevilla en Madrid. Antes de la cita con los Linares, Lima: Mosca Azul, 1972

La pasión según San Pedro Balbuena que fue tantas veces Pedro, y nunca pudo negar a nadie, Lima: Libre, 1977; as *Tantas veces Pedro*, Madrid: Catédra, 1981

La vida exagerada de Martín Romaña, Barcelona: Argos Vergara, 1981

El hombre que hablaba de Octavio de Cádiz, Barcelona: Plaza y Janés, 1985

Goig, Madrid: Debate, 1987

La última mudanza de Felipe Carrillo, Barcelona: Plaza y Janés, 1988

No me esperen en abril, Madrid: Anagrama, 1995

Short Fiction

Huerto cerrado, Havana: Casa de las Américas, 1968

La felicidad, ja ja, Barcelona: Barral Editores Peruana, 1974

Dos señores conversan; un sapo en el desierto; los grandes hombres son así, y también asá, Barcelona: Plaza y Janés, 1990 [novellas]

Compilations and Anthologies

Todos los cuentos, Lima: Mosca Azul, 1980

Cuentos completos, Madrid: Alianza, 1981

Magdalena peruana, y otros cuentos, Bogotá: Oveja Negra, 1986

Para que duela menos, edited with an introduction by J.A. Juristo, Madrid: Espasa Calpe, 1995

Other Writings

A vuelo de buen cubero y otras crónicas, Barcelona: Anagrama, 1977; as *Crónicas personales*, Barcelona: Anagrama, 1988 [journalistic pieces]

Permiso para vivir, antimemorias, Barcelona: Anagrama, 1993

Further Reading

Cornejo Polar, Antonio, "*Tantas veces Pedro*," *Revista de Crítica Literaria Latinoamericana* 7–8 (1978) [Extended review which suggests several possible readings of the work]

Ferreira, César and Ismael P. Márquez (editors), *Los mundos de Alfredo Bryce Echenique*, Lima: Pontificia Universidad Católica del Perú, 1994 [Compilation of material from a wide variety of previously published sources, organised into chapters]

La Fuente, José Luis de, *Cómo leer a Alfredo Bryce Echenique*, Madrid: Guías de Lectura Júcar, 1994

Luchting, Wolfgang, *Alfredo Bryce / humores y malhumores*, Lima: Milla Batres, 1975

Ortega, Julio, *El hilo del habla: la narrativa de Alfredo Bryce Echenique*, Guadalajara, Mexico: Universidad de Guadalajara, 1994

Rodríguez Lafuente, Fernando (editor), *Alfredo Bryce Echenique: semana de autor*, Madrid: Ediciones de Cultura Hispánica, 1991

Rodríguez-Peralta, Phyllis, "The Subjective Narration of Alfredo Bryce Echenique's *La vida exagerada de Martín Romaña*," *Hispanic Journal*, vol. 10/2 (Spring 1989)

Un mundo para Julius

Novel by Alfredo Bryce Echenique

Un mundo para Julius, the first novel of Alfredo Bryce Echenique, was a leading contender for the 1970 Seix Barral Prize (it was never awarded following a split within the publishing house), and portrays the problems of a sensitive childhood in an environment which is gradually realized to be increasingly hostile to the ideals of youthful innocence. It also provides the reader with a cross-sectional view of Peruvian society via a dramatis personae of over sixty characters, and more explicitly depicts the decline of the *hacienda*-owning oligarchy. This latter was the only interpretation acceptable to Peruvian critics and academics of the period. This was because Gobierno Revolucionario de las Fuerzas Armadas (Revolutionary Government of the Armed Forces), installedin 1976, had undertaken a significant Agrarian Reform Programme which had greatly weakened the traditional grip of the oligarchy on the Peruvian economy and system of land tenure.

An equally valid interpretation of the work, and one on the whole ignored by critics of the early 1970s, is as a study of child psychology and alienation of the individual. Julius's mother effectively abdicates responsibility for the emotional and social development of her youngest son to the domestic staff, whose values of friendship and freedom of emotional expression he comes to share throughout his early years. These values contrast markedly with those of Julius's widowed mother and his eventual step-father, both of whom are more concerned with the whirl of Lima's exclusive social circles. Susan, Julius's beautiful but *distraite* mother, represents the old aristocratic oligarchy and a relatively caring, but ultimately paternalistic, attitude towards the servants, while the increasingly dominant step-father is a member of the new business class rising to prominence in the Lima of the 1950s within which the novel is apparently set. As the influence of Juan Lucas grows, and eventually comes to dominate the household, relations between the servants and the family become ever more cold and distant, without a substitute emotional and social role model ever being offered to the highly impressionable Julius. Young children are seen as something of an incon-venience by both Susan and Juan Lucas, and until Julius approaches adulthood and can involve himself in the adult world in which his parents are so fully absorbed he seems destined to live in a social and emotional no-man's-land.

The resolution of the question of whether Julius will follow the footsteps of his older brothers into the world of Susan, and more especially of Juan Lucas, or whether he will remain true to his childhood ideals and behaviour is left to the reader, although a close reading of the work provides enough information to arrive at a tentative conclusion. Despite their ruthless hedonism in the latter stages of the work, Julius's older brothers both previously demonstrated emotional sensitivity, as can be seen when Santiago cries disconsolately when he learns that Cinthia, his little sister, is about to die, and Bobby behaves similarly when he loses his first girlfriend. Without being privy to their thoughts and feelings , it would seem that they have both passed from a sensitive, servant-attended childhood to a Juan Lucas style adulthood during the course of their teens, and the manner in which the reader accompanies Julius in his innermost thoughts and emotions makes it all the more tragic that he appears to be simply following the same difficult path.

It is in the last of the novel's five sections, significantly entitled "Retornos" [Returns], that the reader can gather more substantial clues as to the probable outcome of the protagonist's inner turmoil. Until this stage in the work Julius has clung to the memory of his beloved sister as a mentor to whom he could address his thoughts and feelings in times of crisis, but shortly after feeling solidarity with his hitherto loathsome brother Bobby he exorcises the ghost of Cinthia and removes her photograph from his bedside table. Shortly after this he learns that the other emotional mainstay of childhood, his nanny Vilma, is working as a prostitute after having been thrown out of the household to avoid further problems subsequent to her rape by Santiago. When he comes to review his existence and definitively identifies himself in terms of his family, and even Juan Lucas, rather than the servants, unable to see the once beloved Vilma as anything other than a whore, a very conscious decision has been taken to reject those who were his only source of emotional support through his childhood and to accept the values of those who have consistently denied him emotional and social expression and development. Similarly when, as a child of five, Julius entered the servants' quarters for the first time and saw them as small and ugly, he could hardly be held responsible for his thoughts, as he could not be when he was sick during his visit to the shack where Arminda, the laundry maid, was living. At the end of the book, however, as an eleven-year-old, he is perfectly conscious of the decision he takes not to enter the kitchen when he hears that Nilda, ex-cook and friend, has come to visit and bring him a birthday present, and there can be no explanation for his behaviour, other than an acceptance of the values of Juan Lucas and those like him. Such a pessimistic interpretation of the future for the bright and sensitive Julius to whom readers have grown to feel quite attached would also be very much in keeping with the view of the upper echelons of Lima society as corruptor which comes across in Bryce's other early works.

The narrative style and pervasive humour of the work play an important role in reinforcing what is communicated at a thematic level. The major feature in this respect is the use of narrative techniques that develop the conventional *style indirect libre* from which they arise. By allowing the words, and especially the thoughts, of the main characters to enter the narrative in unmediated forms throughout the work, the narrator affords these characters an approbation which comes to influence the manner in which the reader perceives them. This relationship is strengthened by Bryce's keen awareness of the potential of other traditional narrative devices, such as the direct address by the narrator of both reader and certain characters (notably Julius in this case), all of which serves to reinforce the triangular bond established between narrator, reader and characters. It is highly significant that not all of the characters are presented in this fashion, with Juan Lucas and Susan representing the principal exceptions. When, by the end of the novel, they can be seen to have marginalised all of the other characters and dismissed out of hand values which could be taken as positive in numerous other characters, the assorted outcasts from the world of the beautiful people constitute a loose community with the reader and narrator, and it is Susan and Juan Lucas, along with Santiago and Bobby, who come to be seen as isolated, living in a state of complete isolation from those around them and the society in which they live. It would seem that Julius is destined to join them in the cold and shallow world of Lima's aristocracy.

DAVID WOOD

Editions
First edition: *Un mundo para Julius*, Barcelona: Seix Barral, 1970
Critical edition: edited by Julio Ortega, Madrid: Cátedra, 1993
Translation: *A World for Julius*, by Dick Gerdes, Austin: University of Texas Press, 1992

Further Reading
Bensoussan, Albert, "Entrevista con Bryce Echenique," *Ínsula* 308–09 (1972) [Interview in which Bryce discusses the world of *Un mundo* and his literary mentors]
Duncan, Jennifer Ann, "Language as Protagonist: Tradition and Innovation in *Un mundo para Julius*," *Forum for Modern Language Studies*, vol. 16 (1980)
Escajadillo, Tomás Gustavo, "Bryce: elogios varios y una objeción," *Revista de Crítica Literaria Latinoamericana* 6 (1977)
Ferreira, César, "Entrevista con Alfredo Bryce Echenique," *Antípodas* 3 (July 1991)

Fanny Buitrago 1940–

Colombian prose writer

Although Fanny Buitrago has not been overtly political in her writings until her recent collection of stories *¡Líbranos de todo mal!* [Deliver Us from Evil], *la Violencia* (or the civil unrest which took place in Colombia in the 1960s during her formative years as a writer) has always been an important, if not the most important subtext in her work. Rather than give her stories a political context – most of her characters have been demonstrably apolitical – Buitrago's metaphor for characterizing civil unrest is that of the dysfunctional or broken family. This is, in fact, the perfect image for a country, one's political family, that is torn by violent protest and governmental repression, leaving in its wake death and psychological damage.

The symbol of the broken home, sometimes realized as an infertile couple, an abandoned child, a divorced couple, lovers married to people they do not love, is certainly more accessible to the average reader, especially one outside Colombia, than a realistic description of political upheaval. This paradigm of the dysfunctional family extends throughout Buitrago's writings, even to her children's literature. In *La casa del abuelo* [Grandfather's House] and *La casa del arco iris* [Rainbow's House] the children Falsy, Elsy, and Luisito spend time in a pseudo-single parent situation because their father works in the city far from their grandfather's house.

Buitrago has concentrated on fiction rather than poetry, with one award-winning play *El hombre de paja* [Scarecrow], which won her the Cali Theater Festival Prize in 1964, and the libretto for a ballet also to her credit. Buitrago shares many of the other concerns of her fellow Latin American writers: love, death, family honor, the search for personal fulfillment and acceptance, the influence of genetic or racial memory, superstitious beliefs, etc. She also writes about topics of concern to many female writers/readers: rape, or the threat of rape; unwanted pregnancy or its converse, a pregnancy desired in the face of infertility; a woman's place in a male-dominated society; a woman's relation to her child(ren) or spouse. Although there are both male and female characters in Buitrago's writings, most of her protagonists and/or narrators are female. In fact, the world in Buitrago's writings is a woman's world, centered on the eternal triangle of man + woman + child. This triad is uniquely unstable in Buitrago's world view and is seen usually from one of its broken sides: man + woman; woman + child; child + man, thus giving human form to the concept of the dysfunctionality of human interrelations.

To take a concrete example from one of Buitrago's novels, the foundation of the island culture she presents in *Los pañamanes* is based on the legendary cry of women giving birth, "*pañamán*," the "Spanish man," an allusion to the metaphorical rape of the island historically being repeated when illegitimate children are born. The expression then becomes a deep cultural obscenity, abhorrent to all members of the culture, yet the very basis of all their relationships, even generations after the original "rape" of the island. Characters in the novel include illegitimate and/or abandoned children, and marital and other family relationships are consistently strained or destroyed throughout the work.

The collection *Los amores de Afrodita* [The Loves of Aphrodite] consists of four short stories and one novella dealing with various aspects of love. Unfortunately this love is often betrayed for power and/or money. In the story "¡Anhelante, oh anhelante!" [Yearning, oh, Yearning!], one of the few stories with an overt political context, a mother addresses her son whom she feels is about to marry someone inappropriate. After divorcing his first wife, Yiri, to pursue his political ambitions with Maclovia Aranda (the unsuitable one), the son soon discovers that Maclovia's political ambitions are even greater than his, and that she has no real feelings for him. In the end he becomes involved with revolutionaries and is forced to flee the country. From Switzerland he calls home for Yiri, since Maclovia has asked for an annulment. The broken marriage parallels the country broken by revolutionary upheaval.

Whether Buitrago's writings are deliberately set in her coastal island or in fictitious Colombian mainland towns, the action involves the same basic themes of abandonment, marital incompatibility, and social constraints versus personal freedom that form her world view. All these manifestations of the dysfunctional family point again and again to the political unrest which occurred during Buitrago's youth in Colombia. Just as in the refrain popular in the US Civil War ("A house divided against itself cannot stand"), Buitrago demonstrates in her work that relationships and families which are not built on unconditional love will certainly fail; likewise, a country without a firm foundation will crumble from within.

To date, no book-length study of the life and/or works of Fanny Buitrago has been published in the United States, nor has one been listed as published elsewhere in standard reference sources such as the *MLA International Bibliography*. During the past few years several articles have been published which supplement the chapter in an unpublished dissertation by Nancy McCarty. Other articles deal with *Los amores de Afrodita*, *Los pañamanes*, and *El hostigante verano de los dioses* [The Harassing Summer of the Gods], her astounding first novel. The dearth of critical material in the United States on Buitrago is difficult to understand, since her work has earned her so many literary prizes abroad over the years. The fact that her landmark first novel has been reprinted twice in a region of the world not known for major print-runs should be evidence of the significance of that novel, yet no one has undertaken a full-length critical study of *El hostigante verano de los dioses*. However, one of her stories, "Narración de un soñador de tesoros" [Narration of a Dreamer of Treasures], was included in 1993 in a college-level textbook for intermediate students published by Prentice-Hall Publishers in the United States, placing her among twelve authors including Paz, Cela, Cortázar, García Márquez, and Laforet. This points to an increased appreciation of Buitrago's talent and will certainly bring her to the attention of a wider audience.

TERESA R. ARRINGTON

Biography

Born in Barranquilla, Colombia, in 1940. Joined the elitist "nadaísta" (Towards Nothing) group of writers centered on the town of Cali. Member of this group until 1968 when she chose to withdraw from it. She has lived in various parts of Colombia. Her career as a writer started in 1963 and in 1964 her ballet *La garza sucia* was premiered in Buenos Aires. Invited by Iowa State University in 1984 to participate in their International Writing Program. Recipient of the following awards: Cali Theatre Festival Prize, 1964; Argentine Summer Season Prize, 1965; runner-up for Seix Barral Award in 1970; second prize in UNESCO contest for best example of children's fiction, 1988.

Selected Works

Novels
El hostigante verano de los dioses, Bogotá: Tercer Mundo, 1963
Cola de zorro, Bogotá: Monolito, 1970
Los pañamanes, Barcelona: Plaza y Janés, 1979

Short Fiction
Las distancias doradas, Bogotá: Espiral, 1964 [Published with the play *El hombre de paja*]
La otra gente: cuentos, Bogotá: Instituto Colombiano de Cultura, 1973
Bahía Sonora, relatos de la isla, Bogotá: Almanaque Supremo, 1976
Los amores de Afrodita, Bogotá: Plaza y Janés, 1983
¡Líbranos de todo mal!, Bogotá: Carlos Valencia Editores, 1989

Play
El hombre de paja y Las distancias doradas, Bogotá: Espiral, 1964

Children's Literature
La casa del abuelo, Bogotá: Voluntad Unesco, 1979
La casa del arco iris, Bogotá: Carlos Valencia Editores, 1986
Cartas del Palomar, Bogotá: Carlos Valencia Editores, 1988
La casa del verde doncel, Bogotá: Carlos Valencia Editores, 1990

Further Reading

Araujo, Helena, "Siete novelistas colombianas," in her *Manual de literatura colombiana*, vol. 2, Bogotá: Planeta, 1988 [On Buitrago's novel *Cola de zorro*]
Arrington, Teresa R., "Fanny Buitrago," in *Spanish American Women Writers: a Bio-Bibliographical Source Book*, edited by Diane E. Marting, Westport, Connecticut: Greenwood Press, 1990
Bedoya, Luis Iván, "Mitopoética de la cotidianidad femenina en los cuentos de Fanny Buitrago," in *Ensayos de literatura colombiana*, edited by Raymond L. Williams, Bogotá: Plaza y Janés, 1985
Benítez Rojo, Antonio, *The Repeating Island: the Caribbean and the Postmodern Perspective*, translated by James Maraniss, Durham, North Carolina: Duke University Press, 1992 [Chapter 6 is on *Los pañamanes*]
Jaramillo, María Mercedes, "Fanny Buitrago: la desacralización de lo establecido: *El hostigante verano de los dioses, El hombre de paja y Los amores de Afrodita*," in *¿Y las mujeres?: ensayos sobre literatura colombiana*, edited by Jaramillo, Angela I. Robledo and Flor María Rodríguez, Medellín, Colombia: Universidad de Antioquia, 1991

Interviews

Williams, Raymond L., "An Interview with Women Writers in Colombia," in *Latin American Women Writers Yesterday and Today*, edited by Yvette E. Miller and Charles M. Tatum, Pittsburgh: The Review, 1977

C

Cabral de Melo Neto, João

See Melo Neto

Lydia Cabrera 1900–1991

Cuban writer and ethnographer

It may seem ironic that the writer who inspired greatest interest in African-Cuban culture over the last fifty years and who dedicated her life to the recording and creative interpretation of a virtually unexplored African-Cuban heritage should be a white woman, born into one of the most prestigious families in the Cuban Republic. Family connections partly explain the apparent anomaly; Cabrera's brother-in-law, the eminent anthropologist Fernando Ortiz, was the first Cuban to study contemporary African-Cuban culture seriously. She had known him since childhood and it was he who, in his own words, initiated her into "a taste for Afrocuban folklore," as she indicates in "Prejuicio," from *Cuentos negros de Cuba*, 1940 [Black Stories from Cuba]. Cabrera's father, the liberal lawyer and writer Raimundo Cabrera, had founded the newspaper *Cuba y América* in New York and here the young Lydia published articles and illustrations from the age of thirteen. She continued to write for the press when the family returned to Cuba from political exile in 1917. From the start, then, Lydia Cabrera had easy access to the world of print culture. However, more important is the fact that she was a woman. As a girl, Cabrera was in close contact with the black female servants of the household from whom she gathered much of her material (in particular Tula and Teresa M. Omí Tomí); similarly, she was not given a formal education nor expected to pursue a career but was allowed to cultivate her interest in art and antiques and to study Fine Arts in Havana and Paris. It was during her stay in Paris (1927–38) that she became acquainted with the *Négritude* movement and, in 1936, at the insistence of her terminally ill friend, the Venezuelan Teresa de la Parra (who also hailed from a white privileged family and shared her interest in black folk-tales), Cabrera finally wrote down and elaborated on the African-Cuban stories she had heard. These *Contes nègres de Cuba* [Black Stories from Cuba] were published in France that same year; the Spanish version came out in Cuba in 1940. In 1938 Cabrera returned to Cuba and continued to collect African-Cuban stories and to record traditional African-Cuban customs and beliefs with the assistance of her inseparable companion María Teresa de Rojas. This material would be used in a succession of books, published first in Cuba and – after Cabrera's departure from the island in 1960 – in Miami. Clearly, the daughters of white creole families proved to be valuable instruments in the gathering and dissemination of subaltern cultures; in this respect Cabrera's work can be compared to that of Rosario Castellanos and Elena Poniatowska in Mexico.

Apart from Ortiz's pioneering studies, there was little academic interest in African-Cuban culture until the 1930s. During her lifetime Cabrera published over twenty books, all of them related in some way to the African-Cuban world, with the result that she has been compared to Sir James Frazer and her book, *El monte* [The Mountain], to *The Golden Bough*. Yet Cabrera repeatedly denied there was any scientific method to her writings; she was not – nor wished to be – a trained professional. Her approach, that of a journalist, witness or enthusiastic amateur, enabled her to write outside the confines of disciplinary conventions and, as is the case with many female authors, her work cannot be slotted easily into generic classifications. It incorporates the discourses of fiction, song, autobiography, ethnography, linguistics, and testimonial writing. Her four collections of short stories, *Contes nègres de Cuba*, 1936, *¿Por qué? Cuentos negros de Cuba*, 1948 [Why? Black Stories from Cuba], *Ayapá; cuentos de Jicotea*, 1971 [Ayapá. Stories of the Turtle], and *Cuentos para adultos, niños, y retrasados mentales*, 1983 [Stories for Adults, Children, and the Mentally Retarded] and her short autobiographical travelogue, *Itinerarios del insomnio. Trinidad de Cuba*, 1977 [Itineraries of Insomnia. Trinidad in Cuba] have attracted the attention of literary critics, whereas her greatest contributions to anthropological scholarship are the two monographs *El monte*, 1954, and *La sociedad secreta Abakuá*, 1959 [The Secret Society Abakuá] and the linguistic studies *Anagó: vocabulario lucumí*, 1957 [Cuban Yoruba] and *Vocabulario Congo*, 1985 [Cuban Bantu]. *El monte*, however, can also be read as a *testimonio* and as such is of great significance because it is here that the lost voices of the black Cuban women of the first half of the century are recorded. One of the most poignant stories in this book is an account of how Teresa M. Omí Tomí lost her baby daughter because of black magic. Omí Tomí, daughter of a slave and over a hundred years old when Cabrera wrote the book, had been the Cabrera family's seamstress. Before she joined their household she had been brought up among white children and had little knowledge of black religions; consequently, she was unable to protect her child from evil. What she subsequently learned was passed on to Cabrera. The writer acknowledges her debt to her informants in the introduction to *El monte*: "The only value this book has . . . consists exclusively of the part played by the blacks themselves. They are the real authors." She then lists the names of the dozen "real authors" and their associated *orishas* (spirits), including José de Calazán Herrera, Bangoché, alias el Moro, son of Oba Koso and Calixta Morales and Oddeddei, daughter of Ochosi.

There exist several critical studies of the story collections, especially of the early tales such as "Los compadres" [Buddies], "Bregantino Bregantín," and "Chéggue." Unfortunately, criticism is often vitiated by an over-reliance on approaches to literature that stress myth and symbol – the work of Mircea Eliade is a case in point – and by sweeping generalizations about "the African universe," "black thought," and "the primitive mentality." The general view is that Cabrera's stories are creative renderings of black oral traditions told to her by a series of informants. They are set in the past, in a recognizably tropical landscape (Cuba or Africa), and they usually involve a small number of clearly defined and individually named characters which may be human, animal or supernatural. The animals and divine beings are never wholly good or bad but are attributed with human emotions and failings; the narrations in which they feature, therefore, are fables and myths. Some stories incorporate words, refrains and songs in Lucumí or Congo to the extent that a story becomes a bilingual text. It is this mixture of vivid realism, myth and fantasy, the use of animals indigenous to Cuba, particularly the small turtle (*jicotea*), the boa (*majá*), and the vulture (*aura tiñosa*), and the imaginative, almost lyrical, use of language which makes Cabrera's tales such a pleasure to read. The presence of supernatural phenomena alongside realistically portrayed men, women and children suggests that Cabrera was a precursor of Latin American magical realism. Certainly, the narrators show

no surprise at the fantastic events recounted. Detailed analyses of Cabrera's narrative techniques point to the extensive use of anaphora, hypotaxis, simile, metaphor, personification, and other techniques associated with the folk-tale but, at the same time, critics are well aware that these stories are the results of Cabrera's own creative imagination and skill.

A typical story, considered one of the best in Cuban literature, is "Cundió Brujería Mala" [Black Magic Was Spread Around], from *¿Por qué?*, which tells of a woodcutter, Bracundé, who lives near a Congo sorcerer/devil named Indiambo. The devil lusts after Bracundé's wife and, after casting an evil spell (*uemba*) so that Bracundé is put in prison, he kidnaps her and takes her to the mountains in a sack. Once Bracundé is free, with the help of his ancestors, his faithful dog and an angry Axe, he wreaks vengeance on the unfortunate devil who is chopped into pieces. Bracundé and his wife then travel the world scattering the bits of devil as they go. But, the narrator informs us, each chopped-up piece grows into another devil thus explaining why black magic is rife in the world. Cabrera introduces the protagonist with the kind of rhythmic, euphonic prose characteristic of her work:

> Bracundé era leñador. Iba a un monte a cortar leña. En la ceja de este monte, del monte Monte-Munguela, habitaba un brujo congo, Sicongo-lundé-bantúa: congo malo del Congo Real . . . Y este brujo era un diablo y este diablo se llamaba Indiambo.

> [Bracundé was a woodcutter. He used to go to a mountain to cut wood. On the brow of this mountain, of the mountain Mountain-Munguela, there lived a Congo sorcerer, Sicongo-lundé-bantúa: a bad Congo from Royal Congo . . . And this sorcerer was a devil and this devil was called Indiambo].

The dialogue between man and devil continues thus: "Manigualla . . . ¿Kindiambo?" (Who is master?) And Bracundé responded always: "¡Inxambi!" (God) while onomatopoeia connotes the wife's delicate footsteps: "Chiqui chiqui chiquirichí / chiquiri chiquiri chiquirichí . . . " The most striking figure in the story, is the Axe – all-knowing and gleaming on the wall – which finally cuts down the devil in a fit of revenge. The story, just over four pages long, is a typically well-crafted miniature.

Cabrera's later work, written in Miami, becomes increasingly nostalgic as the prospect of returning to Cuba fades. She refers repeatedly to her idyllic childhood on the island to which she would never return. *Trinidad de Cuba*, a digressive potpourri of legends, recipes, and songs is possibly her most subjective work recreating two trips she made to the town in 1923 and 1940. In *Los animales en el folklore y la magia de Cuba*, 1988 [Animals in Cuban Folklore and Magic], a compendium of vignettes, dialogues and stories dedicated to her cats and published just before she died, she alludes to both "the poetic and marvellous inner world of our infancy" and "the unique charm of our lost island" which she hopes to recapture despite the fact that she is living in a country "where time is only money." Cabrera's works have yet to be studied in their full dimension and in their entirety.

CATHERINE DAVIES

Biography

Born in Havana, Cuba, 20 May 1900, into a prominent upper-class family. Her father, Raimundo Cabrera, was a lawyer and writer, involved in the pro-Cuban independence movement. The Cabrera home was a meeting place for leading figures in politics and culture. Educated at home and briefly at a private school. Assimilated legends and magical beliefs of Cuban blacks by listening to family servants. Family went into exile in 1917. When she threatened to kill herself Cabrera's father agreed to allow her to attend the Sorbonne, however, he died before he could fulfil his promise. Determined to be independent, Cabrera set up Havana's first antiques shop. She sold her share in the family business and went to Paris in 1927, where she attended the Ecole du Louvre until 1930. In that time she became aware of the African revival in the arts and of the *Négritude* movement. (Her brother-in-law, Fernando Ortiz (see separate entry), was an outstanding Cuban ethnographer). In Paris, Cabrera also renewed her friendship with the Venezuelan poet and novelist Teresa de la Parra. The latter became ill with tuberculosis in 1932, and Cabrera accompanied her friend to a sanatorium. (Some of Cabrera's African-Cuban stories were written to entertain her sick friend). Cabrera travelled to Spain with de la Parra, but left the country following de la Parra's death and the outbreak of war in 1936. She returned to Cuba in 1939 and became friends with the paleographer María Teresa de Rojas. In the early 1940s Cabrera began to collate and publish stories and articles on African-Cuban culture. Adviser to National Institute of Culture during the 1950s. In 1959 Cabrera left Cuba, and spent the rest of her life in exile in Madrid and Miami. Died in Miami, 18 September 1991.

Selected Works

Short Fiction

Contes nègres de Cuba, Paris: Gallimard, 1936; in Spanish as *Cuentos negros de Cuba*, Havana: La Verónica, 1940
¿Por qué? Cuentos negros de Cuba, Havana: C.R., 1948
Ayapá: cuentos de Jicotea, Miami: Universal, 1971
Cuentos para adultos, niños, y retrasados mentales, Miami: C.R., 1983

Other Writings

El monte: ibgo finda, ewe orisha, vititi nfinda: notas sobre las religiones, la magia, las supersticiones y el folklore de los negros criollos y del pueblo de Cuba, Havana: C.R., 1954

Refranes de negros viejos, Havana: C.R., 1955 [sayings / proverbs]
Anagó: vocabulario lucumí: el yoruba que se habla en Cuba, Havana: C.R., 1957
La sociedad secreta Abakuá, narrada por viejos adeptos, Havana: C.R., 1959
Otán Iyebiyé: las piedras preciosas, Miami: Universal, 1969
La laguna sagrada de San Joaquín, Madrid: R., 1973
Yemayá y Ochún: Kariocha, Iyalorichas y Olorichas, Madrid: C.R., 1974 [legends/myths]
Anaforuana: Ritual y símbolos de la iniciacíon en las sociedad secreta Abakuá, Madrid: R., 1975
Francisco y Francisca: chascarillos de negros viejos, Miami: C.R., 1976
La Regla Kimbisa del Santo Cristo del Buen Viaje, Miami: C.R., 1977
Itinerarios del insomnio, Trindad de Cuba, Miami: C.R., 1977
Reglas de Congo: Palo Monte Mayombé, Miami: C.R., 1979
Koeko, Iyawó, Aprende Novicia: pequeño tratado de Regla Lucumí, Miami: C.R., 1980
La medicina popular de Cuba: médicos de antaño, curanderos, santeros y paleros de hogaño, Miami: C.R., 1984
Vocabulario Congo: el Bantú se habla en Cuba, Miami: Universal, 1985
Supersticiones y buenos consejos, Miami: Universal, 1987
Los animales en el folklore y la magia de Cuba, Miami: Universal, 1988
La lengua sagrada de los ñáñigos, Miami: C.R., 1988

Further Reading

Bueno, Salvador (editor), *Los mejores cuentos cubanos*, vol. 1, Havana: Biblioteca Básica de Cultura, 1959
Castellanos, Isabel and Josefina Inclán (editors), *En torno a Lydia Cabrera (Cincuentenario de "Cuentos Negros de Cuba" 1936–1986*, Miami: Universal, 1987 [Includes several worthwhile articles (Cruz-Valdés, Irizarry, Sánchez Boudy and Zaldívar) and useful bibliographies]
Hiriart, Rosario, *Lydia Cabrera: vida hecha arte*, New York: Eliseo Torres and Sons, 1978
Sánchez, Reinaldo, *et al.* (editors), *Homenaje a Lydia Cabrera*, Miami: Universal, 1977
Valdés-Cruz, Rosa, *Lo ancestral africano en la narrativa de Lydia Cabrera*, Barcelona: Vosgos, 1974

Guillermo Cabrera Infante 1929–

Cuban prose writer

In 1964 Guillermo Cabrera Infante captured readers' imagination with his *Tres tristes tigres* (*Three Trapped Tigers*), a witty tongue-in-cheek unclassifiable text, therefore generally accepted as a "novel." *Tres tristes tigres*, a tongue-twister written in Cabrera Infante's native Cuban dialect mixed with "rejoyced Spunish," would become a milestone in the booming Latin American writing of the 1960s. This work had an interesting history.

In 1964, Cabrera Infante was promising two books: a forthcoming volume of short stories and a novel-in-progress. The first was supposed to be "Ella cantaba boleros" [She Sang Boleros]; it was a book of stories centered on a black night-club singer. Cabrera Infante started writing this "continuing" story in 1961 after his brother's short film *P.M.*, which focused on Havana's night-life, was banned, as a kind of continuation of the film by other means. The manuscript of the promised novel, "Vista del amanecer en el trópico" [View of Dawn in the Tropics], would win, in 1964, the highly sought-after Seix Barral Biblioteca Breve prize which set the pace for the Boom of the 1960s. Almost schizophrenically, one work grew out of dissent from the Cuban Revolution, while the other celebrated it. After Cabrera Infante left Cuba for good in the fall of 1966, although he kept silent on things Cuban until the summer of 1968, his life was in a fix (he was too early for dissidence, which was made popular in the following decade, and Cuban dissidence was unthinkable for the intellectual "Left Bank" anyway). Sitting over the proofs of his novel, he realized that he wanted to publish something else. By coincidence, the Francoist censor had also raised certain objections to the text and Cabrera had to take care of them before the book could be published in Spain. Cabrera Infante seized the occasion, and his work reemerged from its ashes with a new title, *Tres tristes tigres*. Thematically, the novel merged with "Ella cantaba boleros" and shed its previous opportunistic political content. In the new (re)version, Cabrera Infante placed parody in the center to question radically the vexing aesthetic problems of mimetic art. The vignettes of the original version that chronicled the political violence so pervasive throughout Cuban history would be reorganized and updated in 1972 to include the Cuban Revolution of 1959, in order to appear, in 1974, as a separate volume under the old, now only more ironic, title *Vista del amanecer en el trópico* (*A View of Dawn in the Tropics*).

Tres tristes tigres evokes the world of Havana's night-life and popular culture of the late 1950s, which had to disappear, sacrificed as it was by the Revolution to the "train of Modernity," which now continues, squeaking along like a rough bicycle ride. The novel engages in a typical postmodern defense and rescue of a specific local culture; yet, in line with modernist experimentalism, it questions each of its own narrative steps, including the very possibility of reaching its goals through artistic means.

The novel impresses the reader as a "gallery of voices" and as a "concentric chaos" of various points of view, confusing the temporal sequence of the narration and erasing the limits between "reality" and "literature." In the final chapter, "Bachata," a character appears, called Silvestre, who promises to become the "future" author of the work that the reader has already in hand. Throughout the novel, playful Sternian and metanarrative commentaries abound and reveal that what seems to be spontaneous, unmediated oral speech has actually passed through the sieve of literary discourse. "Bachata" even flaunts references to pages of the printed book. Behind the alleged "naturalness" of the human voices "captured in flight," a multifarious textuality appears; and behind this, the various "genealogical" layers of creation that the work puts on display. The creative process of writing is dramatized; it is captured in a state of fermentation; yet, simultaneously, it is presented as the result of a process already completed.

The author has confessed that he writes "armed with scissors and a bottle of glue." In *Tres tristes tigres*, this technique has produced a collage of textual fragments, taking each cut-up from a different story and interweaving them with others in certain patterns. In this fragmentary montage, the first-person narratives are often anonymous or remain separated from the contexts that might explain their meaning (the case of Arsenio and Laura, making their stage debut in "Beginners"). In the contrary direction, one "fact" may engender multiple "literary" versions that are presented in consecutive "drafts," translations and retranslations, or in series of parodies (e.g., the story of the lost walking stick, followed by the corrections made by Mrs Campbell, or the celebrated

literary parodies on the death of Trotsky "as described" by leading Cuban writers, from José Martí to Nicolás Guillén).

Reading *Tres tristes tigres* is like deciphering a Cubist and sometimes Surrealist picture. Narrative discourse, represented world, characters, and even many language elements are cut up into fragments and are playfully exploded. The illusion of representation breaks down continually. Reality turns into theater, movies, literature, fiction, and thus becomes a fierce parody of itself. The anthropomorphic identity of the characters melts away in the wordplay like the watches of Salvador Dalí. One of the central characters of the novel, Bustrófedon, is actually a rhetorical figure; the text offers various examples of "boustrophedonic" writing. This breakdown of referential communication and of the mimetic conventions produces a vacuum of meaning in the very center of the novelistic construction, an emptiness symbolized best by the Sternian blank pages of "Some Revelations." Palindromes and mirror images appear side by side with examples of boustrophedon writing, and link *Tres tristes tigres* closely with Lewis Carroll.

On the surface, the aesthetic quest in *Tres tristes tigres* creates a "baroque body," full of "idle imitations, tricky travesties, embezzled embellishments." However, these "voluptuous volutes" are the result not of superficial playing, but of an agonistic struggle for meaning, representation, and reality through language and playful social discourse (the Cuban *choteo*) that, in turn, impose their own protagonism. The continuous gaming is a part both of the narrative world evoked and of the self-questioning work of art that is emerging. This double "jesture," contradictory yet complementary, is fundamental to the radical aesthetic project embodied by *Tres tristes tigres*.

With the exception of the novel *La Habana para un infante difunto*, 1979 (*Infante's Inferno*) Cabrera Infante's other works do not measure up to *Tres tristes tigres*, and none has matched the latter's international impact and influence on Latin American writing. Yet these other works are not negligible. Different voices of oral discourse and aspects of contemporary urban popular culture are explored in Cabrera Infante's early experimental short stories and vignettes, *Así en la paz como en la guerra*, 1960 (*Writes of Passage*). Cabrera Infante was also an assiduous film critic. His critical close-ups on the new mass culture coming from Hollywood, enriched by narrative passages and Sternian jokes, appeared in *Un oficio del siglo viente* (*A Twentieth-Century Job*), and in *Arcadia todas las noches* [Arcadia Every Night]. The rich leftovers from *Tres tristes tigres* and other short experimental and sharp epigrammatic texts were put together in the whimsical volumes of *O*, 1975, and *Exorcismos de esti(l)o*, 1976 [Midsummer-Style Exorcisms]. *La Habana* is not a trendy novel, but it is a witty and compassionate evocation of life in Havana's lower middle-class milieu during the 1940s and 1950s, covering Cabrera Infante's early teens and his erotic awakening and pursuits. This erotic autobiographical novel shows some picaresque traits and dwells on rather earthy confessions that would have delighted Rousseau. Cabrera Infante collected his political and cultural criticism in a powerful indictment, *Mea Cuba*, 1992

EMIL VOLEK

Biography

Born in Gibara, Cuba, 22 April 1929. Parents were members of the Communist Party and were arrested and imprisoned in 1936 because of their radical political beliefs. Family lived in severe poverty and were obliged to move to Havana in 1941 to find work. Studied at the University of Havana, 1949, and 1950–54. Co-founder of the Cinemateca de Cuba (Cuban Film Archive), 1951. In 1952 the story "Balada de plomo y yerro" [Ballad of Lead and Error] appeared in *Bohemia*; he was jailed and fined on the charge of publishing obscenities and prevented from writing under his own name. Married Marta Calvo in 1953, two daughters. Film critic (under the pseudonym G. Caín), 1954–60, and fiction editor, 1957–60, *Carteles* magazine, Cuba; editor, *Lunes de Revolución* (weekly literary supplement of *Revolución*), 1959–61: closed down by authorities. Divorced and married Mirian Gómez in 1961. Professor of English literature, School of Journalism, Havana, 1960–61; cultural attaché, 1962–64, and chargé d'affaires, 1964–65, Cuban Embassy, Brussels. Returned to Cuba in 1965 to attend his mother's funeral. Left Brussels and moved to Madrid but was ejected by the government for having written anti-Franco articles. Emigrated to England in 1966. Publicly denounced the Castro regime in the Argentine magazine *Primera Plana*, 1968; declared a traitor by the Castro regime. Scriptwriter for 20th Century-Fox and Cupid Productions, 1967–72. The growing pressures of exile resulted in poor health and he suffered a collapse in 1972. Became British citizen in 1979. Visiting Professor, University of Virginia, Charlottesville, Spring 1982. Awards include the Biblioteca Breve Prize (Spain), 1964 for *Tres tristes tigres*; Guggenheim Fellowship, 1970; Foreign Book Prize (France), 1971.

Selected Works

Novels and Short Fiction

Así en la paz como en la guerra: cuentos, Havana: Revolución, 1960; as *Writes of Passage*, translated by John Brookesmith, Peggy Boyars and the author, London: Faber and Faber, 1993

Tres tristes tigres, Barcelona: Seix Barral, 1965; as *Three Trapped Tigers*, translated by Suzanne Jill Levine, New York: Harper, 1971; London: Pan, 1980

Vista del amanecer en el trópico, Barcelona: Seix Barral, 1974; as *A View of Dawn in the Tropics*, translated by Suzanne Jill Levine, New York: Harper, 1978; London: Faber and Faber, 1988

La Habana para un infante difunto, Barcelona: Seix Barral, 1979; as *Infante's Inferno*, translated by Suzanne Jill Levine, New York: Harper, and London: Faber and Faber, 1984

Screenplays (under the pseudonym G. Caín)

Wonderwall, 1968; *Vanishing Point*, 1970

Other Writings

Un oficio del siglo veinte (published under the pseudonym G. Caín), Havana: Revolución, 1960; revised edition, Barcelona: Seix Barral, 1973; as *A Twentieth-Century Job* (as Cabrera Infante), London: Faber and Faber, 1991

O, Barcelona: Seix Barral, 1975

Exorcismos de esti(l)o, Barcelona: Seix Barral, 1976

Arcadia todas las noches, Barcelona: Seix Barral, 1978

Holy Smoke, London: Faber and Faber, and New York: Harper, 1985 [On the cigar]

Mea Cuba, Barcelona: Plaza y Janés, 1992; as *Mea Cuba*, translated by Kenneth Hall and the author, New York: Farrar Straus and Giroux, and London: Faber and Faber, 1994

Further Reading

Cabrera Infante's interviews with Emir Rodríguez Monegal and Rita Guibert are probably the best starting point.

Acosta-Belén, Edna, "The Literary Exorcisms of Guillermo Cabrera Infante," *Crítica Hispánica*, vol. 3/2, (1981)

Álvarez-Borland, Isabel, "The Pícaro's Journey in *La Habana para un infante difunto*," *Hispanófila*, vol. 30 (1987)

———— "*La Habana para un infante difunto*: Cabrera Infante's Self-Conscious Narrative," *Hispania*, vol. 68 (1985)

Cabrera Infante, Guillermo, "Epilogue for Late(nt) Readers," *Review* (Winter 1971–Spring 1972); and various materials in his own complete edition of *Tres tristes tigres*, Caracas: Biblioteca Ayacucho, 1990

Feal, Rosemary Geisdorfer, *Novel Lives: the Fictional Autobiographies of Guillermo Cabrera Infante and Mario Vargas Llosa*, Chapel Hill: University of North Carolina Press, 1986

García Chichester, Ana, "Cultura y vulgaridad en *La Habana para un infante difunto*," *Kentucky Romance Quarterly* (1987)

Hall, Kenneth E., *Guillermo Cabrera Infante and the Cinema*, Newark, Delaware: Juan de la Cuesta, 1989

Hernández-Lima, Dinorah, *Versiones y re-versiones históricas en la obra de Cabrera Infante*, Madrid: Pliegos, 1990

Levine, Suzanne Jill, "Three Trapped Tigers and a Cobra," *Modern Language Notes*, vol. 90/2 (1975)

———— *The Subversive Scribe: Translating Latin American Fiction*, St Paul, Minnesota: Graywolf Press, 1991 [Levine is a translator of Cabrera's work]

Lezra, Jacques, "Squared Circles, Encircling Bowls: Reading Figures in *Tres tristes tigres*," *Latin American Literary Review*, vol. 16 (1988)

MacAdam, Alfred, "Guillermo Cabrera Infante: the Vast Fragment," in his *Modern Latin American Narratives: the Dreams of Reason*, Chicago: University of Chicago Press, 1977

Malcuzynski, M.-Pierrette, "*Tres tristes tigres*, or the Treacherous Play on Carnival," *Ideologies and Literature*, vol. 3/15 (1980)

Merrim, Stephanie, "A Secret Idiom: the Grammar and Role of Language in *Tres tristes tigres*," *Latin American Literary Review*, vol. 8 (1980)

———— *Logos and the Word: the Novel of Language and Linguistic Motivation in Grande sertão: veredas* [by João Guimarães Rosa] *and Tres tristes tigres*, New York: Peter Lang, 1983

———— "*Tres tristes tigres*: antimundo, antilenguaje, antinovela," *Texto Crítico* 33 (1985)

Nelson, Ardis L., *G. Cabrera Infante in the Menippean Tradition*, Newark, Delaware: Juan de la Cuesta, 1983

Siemens, William L., "Heilsgeschichte and the Structure of *Tres tristes tigres*," *Romance Quarterly*, vol. 22/1 (1975)

———— "Women as Cosmic Phenomena in *Tres tristes tigres*," *Journal of Spanish Studies: 20th Century*, vol. 3 (1975)

———— "Guillermo Cabrera Infante: *Tres tristes tigres*," in his *The Worlds Reborn: the Hero in the Modern Spanish American Novel*, Morgantown: West Virginia University Press, 1984

Souza, Raymond D., "Cabrera Infante: Creation in Progress" in his *Major Cuban Novelists: Innovation and Tradition*, Columbia: University of Missouri Press, 1976

Tittler, Jonathan, "Intratextual Distance in *Tres tristes tigres*," *Modern Language Notes*, vol. 93 (1978)

Volek, Emil, "*Tres tristes tigres* en la jaula verbal: las antinomias dialécticas y la tentativa de lo absoluto en la novela de Guillermo Cabrera Infante," in his *Cuatro claves para la modernidad: análisis semiótico de textos hispánicos*, Madrid: Gredos, 1984

Interviews

Guibert, Rita, *Seven Voices: Seven Latin American Writers Talk to Rita Guibert*, New York: Knopf, 1972; a shorter version in Spanish appeared in *Revista Iberoamericana* 76–77 (1971)

Rodríguez Monegal, Emir, "Las fuentes de la narración," *Mundo Nuevo* 25 (1968); the interview is reprinted in his *El arte de narrar: diálogos*, Caracas: Monte Ávila, 1968

Special Issues of Journals

World Literature Today, vol. 61 (Autumn 1987)

Caliban

America as the Other

Caliban, in post-colonial literary criticism, is considered one of the most powerful symbols in the European construction of the New World as its Other. Traditionally, Caliban has been seen as the negative foil to Prospero's culture, Miranda's virtue, Ariel's spirituality in a variety of dyadic interpretations; more recent critical attention has focused on *The Tempest* as "the startling encounter between a lettered and an unlettered culture." For Stephen Greenblatt, the confrontation between Caliban and Prospero dramatises one of the basic elements in the construction of the New World by the coloniser's imagination. The claim made in the play that Caliban had no speech, indeed could not even know his own feelings until given speech, recalls Columbus's declaration in his Journal that he had to name everything in the New World, and also that he would send six native inhabitants to Spain "para que aprendan a hablar" (that they may learn to speak). According to Greenblatt, Caliban's alleged lack of language reflects two important beliefs of the European way of conceptualising the world: first, that the natives had no language other than an unintelligible babble and secondly, that any European language could express the Indian experience in an immediate and unproblematic way. But Shakespeare's Caliban differs from Columbus's natives in that he has no redeeming features of grace, docility or beauty. Caliban is not a noble savage, a being uncorrupted by culture, but "the abhorrent slave," the creature that Aristotle argued had no reason and needed firm government, a sentiment ardently invoked by the Spanish to justify their enslavement of the Indians and the erasure of their cultures.

A near anagram of "cannibal," the name Caliban harks back to Montaigne's famous essay on this topic. Montaigne's interest was to point out the shortcomings of Western civilization, its own barbarous practices. But, with Bartolomé de Las Casas, his was one of the few voices that argued that barbarism was not an absolute concept but was relative to the speaker's situation.

The question of positionality is a crucial point in the contemporary debate about the way Western civilization has set itself up as centre, and constructed an Other according to its own need and for its own self-assertion. This idea was first given prominence with regard to the Orient in Edward Said's seminal work *Orientalism* (1978). Tzvetan Todorov, in *La Conquête de l'Amérique* (1982), discussing this subject with respect to America, examines the manipulative attitudes of Europeans towards the indigenous inhabitants of America. Contemporary theories of literature have brought the question of alterity to the forefront in all discussions of subaltern groups. One of the crucial questions asked is in what way can the centre ever speak of the Other and in turn, by what linguistic means can the Other displace the centre?

Eurocentric assumptions about the centrality and absolute validity of European civilization as opposed to American barbarism were taken as natural by an impressive line of thinkers including Buffon, Voltaire, Hume, Hegel and Schopenhauer: foundational figures in shaping not only European thought, their ideas dominated Latin American self-evaluation. The conflict on these oppositional and hierarchical terms was at the basis of Latin American political thought, expressed most notably in terms of a struggle between civilization and barbarism in Domingo Faustino Sarmiento's polemical work *Facundo*, 1845 (*Life in the Argentine Republic in the Days of the Tyrants*).

At the beginning of the 20th century the thrust of the polemic turned to questions of national identity. The term Caliban came into prominence once more with the writing of José Enrique Rodó's influential essay *Ariel* (1900). The confrontation here, inspired by Shakespeare's *The Tempest* and more particularly by Renan's play *Caliban, suite de "La Tempête"* (1875), was clothed in moral language. Rodó qualified the "colossus of the North," the US, as the base Caliban of the modern age, urging the Latin American nations to seek inspiration in the more ethereal Ariel. Rodó's essay was not a crude polemic against the US: it recognised much of the advances that had been achieved by that nation in terms of material welfare and economic progress and admitted Latin America's comparative backwardness in this respect, but offered different, compensatory values in the stoic tradition of Latin America's cultural heritage. Gerald Martin, in *Journeys through the Labyrinth* (1989) wryly points out that this debate left little space for the Indians, Blacks and Mestizos. Iris M. Zavala, in her discussion of Ariel as part of "The dialogical cultural signs" in *Colonialism and Culture: Hispanic Modernism in the Social Imaginary* (1992), berates Rodó for his uncritical acceptance of the connotations of Shakespeare's characters. She also mentions Caliban as the Other of Darío's symbol of Spanish American *Modernismo*, the swan.

Rodó's essay against the excesses of utilitarianism, pleading for materialism to be tempered by an adherence to moral and spiritual values was misread, and became influential as a spur to a Latin American sense of self-identity based on racial arguments. *La raza cósmica*, 1925 (*The Cosmic Race*) by José Vasconcelos is the best known of a number of writings in this vein.

More recently, and following in the insurrectional footsteps of the Barbadian George Lamming or the Martinican Aimé Césaire, Cuba's leading intellectual Roberto Fernández Retamar inverted once more the symbolism used by Rodó. In his essay *Calibán* (1971) he put forward the idea that while Ariel stands for its intellectual spirit, Latin America is best represented by Caliban, who, though Prospero's slave, remained the island's "rude and unconquerable master." Retamar is aware that in proposing Caliban as the symbol of Latin America he could be accused of perpetuating European linguistic and cultural domination, yet his aim is to use the language of the opponent as an accepted frame of reference in order best to expose and contest its tacit naturalised assumptions and invert its colonialist connotations.

In post-colonial Caribbean (and African) literature, Caliban continues to be used as an important insurrectional symbol. In the words of Rob Nixon, *The Tempest* "came to serve as a Trojan horse, whereby cultures barred from the citadel of 'universal' Western values could win entry and assail those global pretensions from within."

A feminist examination of the failure of *Calibán* to represent women's voices of defiance is awaited. Up to the present the only aspect of the Caliban debate to have been aired by a feminist is what Laura E. Donaldson terms "the Miranda complex." By this she means that in a colonial context the two subalterns, Caliban and Miranda, should have closed ranks against their common oppressor. Instead, Caliban seeks to obtain his revenge on Prospero by attempting to violate Miranda, while she fails to see that as a woman she too is Other and thus continues to support the patriarchal status quo.

EVELYN FISHBURN

See also entries on *Une Tempête* (Aimé Césaire), Civilization and Barbarism, Domingo Faustino Sarmiento, José Vasconcelos

Further Reading

Baker, Jr, Houston, "Caliban's Triple Play," *Critical Inquiry*, vol. 13/1 (1986)

Brown, Paul, "'This thing of darkness I acknowledge mine': *The Tempest* and the Discourse of Colonialism," in *Political Shakespeare: New Essays in Cultural Materialism*, edited by Jonathan Dollimore and Alan Sinfield, Manchester: Manchester University Press, and Ithaca, New York: Cornell University Press, 1985

Casal, Lourdes, "Lo que dice *Calibán*: Relectura," *Areito*, vol. 9/36 (1984)

Condé, Maryse (editor), *L'Héritage de Caliban*, n.p.: Éditions Jasor, 1992

Donaldson, Laura E., *Decolonizing Feminisms*, London: Routledge, 1992

Duchesne Winter, Juan, "Capa de Próspero, piel de Calibán," *Postdata*, San Juan, Puerto Rico, vol. 6/7 (1993)

Fernández Retamar, Roberto, "Calibán," *Casa de las Américas* 68 (September–October 1971); reprinted in his *Para el perfil definitivo del hombre*, Havana: Letras Cubanas, 1981; as *Caliban and Other Essays*, translated by Edward Baker, Minneapolis: University of Minnesota Press, 1989

Greenblatt, Stephen, "Learning to Curse: Aspects of Linguistic Colonialism in the 16th Century," in *First Images of America*, edited by Fredi Chiapelli, Berkeley: University of California Press, 1976

Mannoni, Octave, *Prospero and Caliban: the Psychology of Colonization*, translated by Pamela Powesland, 2nd edition, New York: Praeger, 1956

Melis, Antonio, "Entre Ariel y *Calibán*, ¿Próspero?," *Nuevo Texto Crítico*, vol. 5/9–10 (1992)

Nixon, Rob, "Caribbean and African Appropriations of *The Tempest*," *Critical Inquiry*, vol. 13/3 (1987)

Reid, John T., "The Rise and Decline of the Ariel-Calibán Antithesis in Spanish America," *The Americas*, vol. 34/3 (1978)

Rhys, Jean, *Wide Sargasso Sea*, London: André Deutsch, 1966; New York: Norton, 1967 [Images of Caliban/cannibal explored by Fernández Retamar are also highlighted in this text]

Rodríguez Monegal, Emir, "The Metamorphoses of Caliban," *Diacritics* 7 (September 1977)

Sánchez, Marta E., "Caliban: the New Latin American Protagonist of *The Tempest*," *Diacritics* 6 (1976)

Zavala, Iris M., *Colonialism and Culture: Hispanic Modernism in the Social Imaginary*, Bloomington: Indiana University Press, 1992

Eugenio Cambaceres 1843–1889

Argentine novelist

Three expressions of literature come together in the work of Eugenio Cambaceres: the so-called Generation of 1880, the gauchesque genre, and River Plate Naturalism. Because of its publication date, *Potpourri* could be said to introduce the literary era of the Generation of 1880. Although the themes are urban, certain descriptions of the plains, a natural biological fatalism, and a kind of rootlessness and remoteness, give Cambaceres's characters the pathos found in gauchesque poems.

Cambaceres has been called a pioneer of the Spanish American Naturalist novel and is identified as such in literary history. This is because of his unashamed attachment to Émile Zola, together with diverse related theories (Spencer and Schopenhauer were known in Buenos Aires by then, and Florentino Ameghino had recently arrived from Europe professing and proselytising Darwin-style evolutionism).

Cambaceres wrote four novels. Of these, the first is *Potpourri* – fragmentary, full of inconsistencies, at times burlesque, at times dramatic – an amalgam of themes and its narrative unity is provided by the "realist" precept of the narrator. "I think," says Cambaceres, "as do the disciples of the Realist school, that simply showing the open sores which disfigure the social organism is the most positive reaction we can use against them."

Without Zola's aesthetic density or rigour, but with the same passion for social issues, as well as a few moralistic admonitions under the guise of local colour, *Potpourri* gently tours the imagination of a first-person narrator, with paradoxical autobiographical tinges. "An exploration of society through several Buenos Aires milieus," wrote Benito Varela Jacomé, "it reflects the energy of carnival; criticizes the elections run by demagogues and gangsters; examines the country's educational problems; shows life in the countryside; opposes immigration by creating a grotesque figure of ridicule in the form of a Spanish servant."

As a critical satire of social mores, defamatory and biased, *Potpourri* enjoyed a certain notoriety in Cambaceres's day. His narrator proposes (this is 1882) the principle of separation of Church and State, and denounces the electoral corruption of his very own party, the Conservatives. This may be why the author did not dare sign the first edition; it came out anonymously.

Música sentimental, 1884 [Sentimental Music], Cambaceres's second novel, takes place in France and is the story of a prostitute, Loulou, whose love for Pablo – an Argentine from a wealthy family – changes her life. Here, the allusion to Nana (the protagonist of Zola's novel of that title), is obvious. Despite the autobiographical hint of the first-person narrator, however, the whole nature of the storyteller-witness differs in *Música sentimental* (from *Potpourri*). It shies away from subjective comments, tries to adopt a neutral, distant tone, and also gives more scope to the characters, who express timid opinions in the course of their conversations.

Música sentimental, in fact, demonstrates Cambaceres's evolution and paves the way for his best work, *Sin rumbo*, 1885 [Shiftless]. *Sin rumbo* is the truculent story – the influence of Zola's *Germinal* is obvious – of a wealthy young man who seduces a maid but, on her premature death, and in the name of the daughter she has left him, determines to remake his life. This all ends in fatal failure when, after his daughter's death from diptheria, the hero commits suicide in an apocalyptic finale.

En la sangre, 1887 [In the Blood], Cambaceres's last novel, tells the story of a family of Italian immigrants who have come to Buenos Aires to seek their fortune. The main character, Gennaro, the family's eldest son, is an allegory of social determinism. Of humble origin, despite making a fortune and despite his education, Gennaro ends up as poor as his parents when they first arrived. Cambaceres opposed Sarmiento's programme of importing cheap labour, and in this novel mooted the idea that societies and social classes are a natural phenomenon, biologically determined.

In *En la sangre*, Cambaceres repeats the trajectory of *Sin rumbo*: he presents the protagonist's background, distinguishing between him, his experience and his milieu. There follows a logical and fatal plot development, leading to an inevitable conclusion.

Cambaceres's work is characterized by grand flourishes, a fatalism that comes close to pathos, a taste for vulgarity and a determination to criticize contemporary society until then unknown in Argentine fiction. These are the elements that literary historians will encounter and subsequently elaborate according to their own criteria and agenda. In 1881, Argentine literary history, the history of a "national" literature, was a narrative that had not yet been written. In this sense, Eugenio Cambaceres will be considered historically not so much for his literary production as for the fact that he indicates the end of a given period. Specialists use his work to date both earlier and later stages of Argentine literature, not only in the 19th but also in the 20th century. Cambaceres's biography is

perceived as *ideal* by the authors of Argentine literary history.

His narratives are novelettish and like popular, serialized fiction. They come close to gauchesque poetry and also to the early narratives about *La gran aldea*, 1884 [The Big Village], as Lucio V. López christened Buenos Aires. Cambaceres's narrator is to be found perpetually in this ambiguous position. This shift, like an indiscernible unit, distinguishes all his works and represents, like very few novels of the period, a National Drama that had contained much tragedy and laughter, as applies to these parvenu countries, Argentina among them, invented more by their writers than their statisticians.

CLAUDIO CANAPARO

translated by Ann Wright and Verity Smith

Biography

Born in Buenos Aires, Argentina, 24 February 1843. Son of wealthy French immigrant and an aristocratic Argentine. One of two sons. Travelled frequently to Europe. Read law at university. Visited Europe, lived in Paris. Involved in Argentine politics in 1870s: delegate to the convention of Buenos Aires province, 1871; congressman, 1874. Supported division of Church and State. Important writer in the development of the Argentine novel. Married an Italian, a former opera singer, in 1880s. Died of tuberculosis in Buenos Aires, 14 June 1889.

Selected Works

Novels

Potpourri. Silbidos de un vago, Buenos Aires: Biedma, 1882
Música sentimental. Silbidos de un vago, Paris: Libreria Española y Americana, 1884
Sin rumbo: estudio, Buenos Aires: Lajouane, 1885
En la sangre, Buenos Aires: Sud-América, 1887

Compilations and Anthologies

Obras completas, Sante Fe, Argentina: Castellvi, 1956

Further Reading

Bastos, María Luisa, introduction to *Sin rumbo*, New York: Anaya, 1971
Bazán-Figueras, Patricia, *Eugenio Cambaceres: precursor de la novela argentina contemporánea*, New York: Peter Lang, 1994
Cymerman, Claude, *Diez estudios cambacerianos*, Rouen: Université de Rouen, 1993 [Includes a bio-bibliography]
Epple, Juan, "Eugenio Cambaceres y el naturalismo en Argentina," in *Ideologies and Literature*, vol. 3/14 (1980)
Jitrik, Noé, "Cambaceres: adentro y afuera," in his *Ensayos y estudios de literatura argentina*, Buenos Aires: Galerna, 1970
Lichtblau, Myron I., "Naturalism in the Argentine Novel," in his *The Argentine Novel in the Nineteenth Century*, New York: Hispanic Institute of the United States, 1959
Schade, George D., "El arte narrativo en *Sin rumbo*," *Revista Iberoamericana*, vol. 44 (1978)
_____ "Lo grotesco en la literatura argentina del siglo XIX," in *Estudios de Literatura Argentina*, 2nd series, Buenos Aires, vol. 7 (1982)
Viñas, David, *Literatura argentina y realidad política*, Buenos Aires: Jorge Álvarez, 1964
Williams Alzaga, Enrique, "Aparición de la pampa en la novela *Sin rumbo*, de Eugenio Cambaceres," in *La pampa en la novela argentina*, Buenos Aires: Estrada, 1955

Nellie Campobello 1913–

Mexican prose writer and poet

Among the novelists of the Mexican Revolution, Nellie Campobello is conspicuous not only as the lone woman in the company of such better-known writers as Mariano Azuela, Martín Luis Guzmán and Rafael F. Muñoz, but also for the striking singularity of her work. While her writing shares historical contexts as well as artistic and thematic innovations with other Mexican literature of this period, it also stands out in relief against its textual contemporaries. Much of its singularity stems from Campobello's particular treatment of revolutionary violence and death as filtered through the unflinching gaze of a young female observer.

Although Campobello's work has consistently attracted a small but devoted reading public, particularly in Mexico, the quantity of criticism devoted to her works is still quite low. Her work ranges widely in focus and genre despite the relative brevity of her corpus as a whole, virtually all of which was published in or around the 1930s. Her first publications were in journalism and poetry; her first published book, ¡Yo!, 1929 [I!], was a collection of poems. Her study of Mexican indigenous dance, Ritmos indígenas, 1940 [Indigenous Rhythms], co-authored with her sister Gloria, reflects Campobello's career as a professional dancer and director of the National School of Dance for many years, and also echoes her fascination with rhythm and movement, which pervades her poetry as well as her prose.

Despite the stylistic variety of her writing, Campobello is best known for her autobiographical prose. Her two major literary works, Cartucho, and Las manos de Mamá (published in one volume as Cartucho and My Mother's Hands) draw on her childhood memories of life in the northern Mexican state of Chihuahua during the Revolution. Both works counterpose the author's vivid memories of wartime massacre and injustice with equally powerful images of human tenderness, the latter associated particularly with Campobello's mother. Although often referred to as novels, the two works are better described as memorias (recollections), or estampas (images or prints), a prose style typical of revolutionary literature, characterized by brief portraits of individuals or events, written in simple language and often centering on a striking visual image. The rustic appearance and brevity of Campobello's style, however, belies the brilliant artistic intentionality of her work. Her art utilizes her childhood impressions less for the purposes of historical or autobiographical documentation than as touchstones for artistic creation. However, Campobello blends her artistic intensity with an equally passionate determination to testify to her own vision and experience of the Revolution and to defend those of its leading figures with whom she sympathized. Her hero was Pancho Villa, populist leader in the north later eclipsed by rival Venustiano Carranza, and whom Campobello eulogized in her biographical study, Apuntes sobre la vida militar de Francisco Villa, 1940 [Notes on the Military Life of Francisco Villa]. In her eyes, the maverick Villa was the underdog of the Revolution, suppressed in official historical accounts, and she never missed the opportunity to defend him. In the process, however, Campobello also relinquished critical perspective on her hero, though this is a fault of the biography rather than of the literature.

The objects referred to in the titles of the two autobiographical prose works dominate both of them. They are "cartucho" (cartridge) and the mother's hands, which metonymically evoke the forces that orient Campobello's narration of her childhood. The part, in both cases, stands for a whole, although that whole is absent, shrouded in the past, and the narrator must conjure it in the narrative present: the cartridges, which many revolutionaries wore draped around their chests like armor, are lethal components of one-time explosive revolutionary fervor; the hands are visible representatives and agents of Nellie's deceased mother's strength and maternal care. Violent revolutionary passion and maternal strength, however, are inseparably intertwined in the two works, though the former could be said to dominate Cartucho as the latter preside over Las manos de Mamá. If a father – Pancho Villa – stands behind the cartridge, he is also portrayed in both works as a benevolent, often tender leader; and if the hands of Nellie's mother are a source of family preservation, they will also explode into activity in order to save Nellie's brother from death and to regain custody of her children when they are taken from her.

The metonymic mode of the titles permeates the art and narrative content of the works themselves. Writing decades after the Revolution, Campobello seeks to hold her scattered memories together by repeatedly investing with significance symbolic fragments of the lost wholeness of things. These fragments are often the individuals who died in the Revolution and were forgotten by the victors, their corpses left scattered behind in a national struggle toward cultural and historical cohesion. Frequently, the fragments are also memories of a childhood forever dissipated by war and now reinvoked by a writer who seeks to hold a scattered self together through writing. Finally, the fragments are also those of Campobello's beloved mother, who spent her last breath keeping her family together through violence and hunger and whose many facets are carefully reintegrated in tender invocations.

The structure of Cartucho follows this metonymy through a series of portraits of men – and a few women – associated with Campobello's childhood and who perished in the violence of the Revolution. Particularly in the first half of the novel, the presentation of each portrait tends to follow a similar pattern: a figure passes before the eyes of the young Nellie, who foresees his imminent death; the narrator often catches a small detail of the individual's face or body, which is then reinvoked following his execution – shoes, smiles, fingers, cigars – as if a reminder that death cannot mark a disappearance but always leaves behind a remainder and a memory. Often Nellie herself preserves the corpse as a piece of the departed individual, as when, for example, she grows fond of a body left outside her window for several days; though the whole itself is lost, she labors to keep the remainder intact, as when she carefully deposits into the pockets of a dead man the shards of his own frozen blood. Campobello honors these remainders in a stark, dispassionate prose devoid of sentimentalism.

The presence of Nellie's mother is constant in the pages of *Cartucho*, though her image there remains more in the background in contrast to her centrality in *Las manos de Mamá*. The prose in this latter work is shifting, suggestive and fragmentary, less stark and direct than *Cartucho*, though the metonymical focus of the first work continues with the persistent treatment of the mother's presence by means of the legible peripheries of her hands and skirts. In a similar continuity with the spirit of *Cartucho*, when Nellie's brother loses a hand in gunfire, her mother preserves the fingers in alcohol; Campobello describes them as swimming in the bottle like contented little fishes. The mother in this work becomes a protagonist operating even more actively inside and outside the home, in both masculine and femenine spheres. When her children are taken away from her, she returns courageously to gather them together and then successfully defends before a judge her right to maintain custody of her children. Throughout the text, her hands and skirts are an enclosure protecting young Nellie and her siblings from the horror and hunger of war. The novel begins more slowly than *Cartucho*, but then moves into similar scenes of more rapid-paced violence so pervasive in the earlier work. *Las manos de Mamá* differs from *Cartucho*, however, in its character both as a hymn of devotion to Nellie's mother as well as a eulogy delivered against the attempted erasures of life by death. Rather than verging on nostalgia, *Las manos de Mamá*, like the majority of Campobello's work, is a passionate exercise of rhythm and song against the futility of mere mourning. Or perhaps it could be said that in Nellie Campobello's work mourning and rhythm, longing and invention, seek out their synchrony.

CARL GOOD

Biography
Born at Villa Ocampo in the state of Durango, Mexico, 7 November 1913. Large, prosperous family of three boys and three girls. Family moved to Chihuahua, 1919, and after mother's death, to Mexico City, 1923. Attended the English School. Applied herself seriously to dancing and entered the Department of Fine Arts in 1930 as teacher of dance. Began to teach dance at the National University (UNAM), 1932, and by 1937 she was in charge of the National School of Dance.

Selected Works
¡Yo! Colección de versos, Mexico City: Ediciones L.I.D.N., 1929

Cartucho: relatos de la lucha en el norte de México, Xalapa, Mexico: Ediciones Integrales, 1931; as *Cartucho and My Mother's Hands*, translated by Doris Meyer and Irene Matthews, Austin: University of Texas Press, 1988
Apuntes sobre la vida militar de Francisco Villa, Mexico City: Edición y Distribución Iberoamericana de Publicaciones, 1940
Ritmos indígenas de México, in collaboration with Gloria Campobello, illustrated by Mauro Rafael Moya, Mexico City: n.p., 1940
Las manos de Mamá, illustrated by José Clemente Orozco, 2nd edition, Mexico City: Editorial Villa Ocampo, 1949
Tres poemas, Mexico City: Compañía General de Ediciones, 1957

Compilations and Anthologies
Mis libros, illustrated by José Clemente Orozco, Mexico City: Compañía General de Ediciones, 1960 [Collected works: includes lengthy prologue by Campobello, as well as *Cartucho*, *Las manos de Mamá*, *Apuntes sobre la vida militar de Francisco Villa* and *¡Yo! Colección de Versos*]

Further Reading
Criticism on Campobello is minimal. Her works are consistently mentioned in literary histories of the Mexican Revolution (John S. Brushwood, A. Dessau, M.P. González, Luis Leal, A. Castro Leal, etc.), but usually only in passing. Probably the best treatment of her work is the chapter devoted to Campobello in Martha Robles's book on Mexican women writers. The articles by Meyer, De Beer and Matthews are also good introductions to her work, and Poniatowska provides an excellent, more "literary," treatment of Campobello.

Cazares Hernández, Laura, "Nellie Campobello, novelista de la revolución," *Casa de las Américas* 183 (1991)
De Beer, Gabriella, "Nellie Campobello's Vision of the Mexican Revolution," *The American Hispanist* 4 (1979)
Matthews, Irene, "Daughtering in War: Two "Case Studies" from Mexico and Guatemala," in *Gendering War Talk*, edited by Miriam Cooke and Angela Woolacott, Princeton, New Jersey: Princeton University Press, 1993
Meyer, Doris, "Nellie Campobello's *Las manos de Mamá*: a Rereading," *Hispania* 68 (1985)
____ "Divided Against Herself: the Early Poetry of Nellie Campobello," *Revista de Estudios Hispánicos* 20 (1986)
Parle, Dennis J., "Narrative Style and Technique in Nellie Campobello's *Cartucho*," *Romance Quarterly* 32 (1985)
Poniatowska, Elena, introduction to *Cartucho and My Mother's Hands* by Nellie Campobello, translated by Doris Meyer and Irene Matthews, Austin: University of Texas Press, 1988
Portal, Marta, *Proceso narrativo de la revolución mexicana*, Madrid: Instituto de Cultura Hispánica, 1976
Robles, Martha, *La sombra fugitiva: escritoras en la cultura nacional*, 2 vols, Mexico City: UNAM, 1985

Canon

The Literary Canon in Spanish America

Anthologies and works of reference – such as dictionaries and encyclopedias of literature – are quite reliable guides to the literary canon of a given period because it is not part of their remit to take risks by, say, giving prominence to controversial or experimental works. Thus it is worth noting (though the information will come as no surprise), that until the late 1980s, the entries in dictionaries of literature on Latin American writers were generally confined to (largely) dead, (largely) prosperous and (largely) white men. (This encyclopedia complies to the extent of ending with Zorrilla de San Martín, but departs from the accepted canon by starting with Soledad Acosta de Samper, an author not rescued from oblivion until the 1980s).

Of course, not all the eminent male writers of the canon are dead, since a few of the Boom authors of the 1960s were singled out (or shrewdly singled themselves out) for star treatment and have duly appeared on TV in designer jeans and expensive suits to introduce the culture of their country to the Western world. Some of their works of fiction have become what are known in the publishing world as "hardback heroes;" once they have reached best-seller status and become available as paperbacks, they are subjected to considerable commercial hype by publishers of English translations. This process has involved inevitable tabloid distortions, something which is aggravated when the book is turned into a film with a star-studded international cast (*The Old Gringo*, *The House of the Spirits*, *Chronicle of a Death Foretold*). According to these crude (mis)representations, Latin America is a site of poverty, backwardness and the exotic, that is to say, another bland, consumable manifestation of the "other" whose most obvious expression in the cultural journalese of the North is (of course) magical realism.

But it is not only those who distort for profit who are to blame. In an article of 1992, "On Expanding the Base of Latin American Studies," David Foster addresses this key question: "do Latin American PhD programs in the United States 'capture' the essence of a culture of a foreign land, or do they simply embody in a concrete material sense what Santí calls the discourse of Latinamericanism?" Thus there are Mexican scholars who maintain that in the North their literature of the 20th century has been distorted through too great an emphasis being placed on literary representations of the Mexican Revolution. There are also university teachers who give "readings" of Latin American works without, in certain cases, ever descending from their intellectual eyries in the North to visit the country whose literature they are discussing. For this reason they may offer an invention rather than an illumination, rather like the detective in Borges's "La muerte y la brújula" (Death and the Compass), who insisted on a Jewish solution to a Jewish crime. Those who settle for a virtual reality Latin America based on international congresses and Internet communications are dealers in new forms of sham scholarship: the reality cannot be replaced by information conjured up on a screen.

Teachers of Latin American studies in the North who would like to expand the basis of their courses face very real prac-tical problems. They may, for example, wish to branch out and teach a course on the literature of the Central American countries or other small countries in the region (Paraguay; the Dominican Republic; Bolivia). They are likely to discover that, save in the case of those countries made fashionable by civil war and revolution (Nicaragua; El Salvador), they will not be able to do so because the relevant books will not be available in accessible, inexpensive editions. (Dick Gerdes, in his article on Spanish American literature in translation, included in this volume, gives an illuminating breakdown by country and author of works available in English translation). The same point applies for different reasons to a country like Cuba: purely on political grounds, a *cordon sanitaire* has been drawn round the Island. With the exception of Miguel Barnet, whom it has proved impossible to ignore because he has played a leading role in writing and promoting the fashionable *testimonio* form, the works of Cuba's contemporary writers who are not in exile are not admitted in the canon. It is assumed that nothing worthwhile could be published there under Castro's "tyranny." At the same time, few academics from the US, at least, have been able to visit Cuba since 1959. Thus scholars from this country who wish to challenge the received wisdom on contemporary Cuban Island literature have to work very much against the grain.

The Latin American literary canon rightly gives importance to the authors of the past and within the United States, at least, the Colonial period has now been restored to prominence after decades of neglect, with new emphases such as conventual writing. Again, though, the works of the continent's Colonial and 19th-century writers are not generally available in inexpensive editions. Thus university professors who do not share the (disingenuous?) dismissal by Vargas Llosa of the continent's earlier writers as "primitives" may well be forced as teachers, if not as scholars, to remain within the confines of 20th-century writing. It is important to add, however, that it has been possible to broaden courses synchronically with courses on women writers, the works of other "minorities" and testimonial writing.

In the last two decades of the 20th century there has been at least one hopeful development, that of desktop publishing. This has allowed small, specialized publishers to make a living by concentrating their skills in specific areas. Examples are The White Pine Press and the Curbstone Press (the latter specializing in poetry) in the United States, and Carcanet and Serpent's Tail (publishers of some contemporary Latin American fiction in translation) in the United Kingdom. Also helpful to teachers who wish to give their students the opportunity to investigate the literature of the past are the scholarly and fairly inexpensive Cátedra and Castalia editions published in Spain. These late 20th-century developments could not be more opportune since otherwise canon-formation in the future risks being dictated by market forces and restricted largely to hardback heroes which are "the book of the month" and, preferably, also "the book of the film."

VERITY SMITH

See also entries on Best-Sellers, The Boom, Feminist Literary Theory, Film, The Post-Boom, Prizes, Translation: Spanish America

Further Reading
Achúgar, Hugo, "El poder de la antología/ la antología del poder," *Cuadernos de Marcha* 46 (1989)
Balderston, Daniel, *The Latin American Short Story: an Annotated Guide to Anthologies and Criticism*, Westport, Connecticut: Greenwood Press, 1992 [Pages ix-xx of the Introduction touch on many issues of canon-formation]
Campra, Rosalba, "Las antologías hispanoamericanas del siglo XIX: proyecto literario y proyecto político," *Casa de las Américas* 162 (1987)
Foster, David William, "On Expanding the Base of Latin American Studies," *Latin American Literary Review* 20 (1992)

González Echevarría, Roberto, "Emir y el canon," in *Homenaje a Emir Rodríguez Monegal*, Ministerio de Educación y Cultura, República Oriental de Uruguay, 1987 [Argues that Rodríguez Monegal was responsible for introducing contemporary Spanish American fiction into US university courses]
Hart, Stephen M., "Some Reflections on the Spanish American Literary Canon," *Siglo XX/20th Century* (1994)
Jagoe, Catherine, "Non-canonical Novels and the Question of Quality," *Revista de Estudios Hispánicos* 27 (1993)
Pellón, Gustavo, "The Canon, The Boom and Literary Theory," *Latin American Literary Review* 20 (1992)
Santí, Enrico Mario, "Latinamericanism and Restitution," *Latin American Literary Review* 20 (1992)
Siebermann, Gustav, "Antología computada de poetas latinoamericanos," *La Torre*, Puerto Rico (nueva época) 9 (1989)

Ernesto Cardenal 1925–

Nicaraguan poet, politician, theologian and literary translator

Ernesto Cardenal, whose poetry has been translated into more than a dozen languages, is, without a doubt, one of the most widely-read poets in the world. Because his personal history is so closely allied with the evolution of his poetry and this, in turn, so inextricably linked to the history of Nicaragua, it is almost impossible not to make frequent reference to the linear time of biographical and historical occurrences as a means of understanding Cardenal's extensive literary production.

Thus, one inevitably learns of Cardenal's involvement in the failed attempt to overthrow the dictatorship of Somoza García in April 1954, and how Cardenal transformed these personal experiences into the quintessential Latin American political poem *Hora O* (*Zero Hour*). One considers, too, Cardenal's religious conversion and how he (as Fr. Lawrence) entered a Trappist monastery in Gethsemany, Kentucky, (*Gethsemani, Ky*, Cardenal's book of haiku-like sketches of nature and epiphanies, is from this period), where the renowned Catholic contemplative Thomas Merton was his Novice Master from 1957–59.

Here, in a kind of mutual tutelage, Merton and Cardenal developed virtually all the important themes that would manifest themselves in Cardenal's post-Trappist poetry: history and prophecy, the ethics of Christian and indigenous traditions, and even liberation theology. After Cardenal left the monastery (for health reasons), Merton continued to provide him with a spiritual guidance that shaped his poetry.

Over the next ten years, Cardenal published seminal works that profoundly influenced the development of contemporary Hispanic American poetry. *Epigramas* is a book that links the themes of love and politics with striking originality, but which, like Neruda's *Veinte poemas de amor y una canción desesperada* (*Twenty Love Poems and a Song of Despair*), has not

managed to hold up very well under feminist scrutiny in terms of the way that the two poets portray women. Until the recent definitive edition of *Los ovnis de oro* (*Golden UFOs*) – Cardenal calls this his "Indian poetry" – Cardenal continued to add to the poems on indigenous themes he first published in *Homenaje a los indios americanos* (*Homage to the American Indians*) in 1969. This work describes an ideal Amerindian ethical system based on spirituality, antimaterialism and agrarianism in stark contrast to the destructive and immoral capitalism of consumer societies. In Cardenal's *Salmos* (*Psalms*), the speaker joins a biblical antiquity with the problems of contemporary culture. As the Nicaraguan critic Napoleón Chow has indicated, this interpretation of the Bible in *Salmos* as a means of expressing solidarity with the oppressed and the poor preceded the publication of Peruvian theologian Gustavo Gutiérrez's fundamental book *Teología de la liberación* (*Liberation Theology*) by a full six years. Cardenal later made a significant contribution to the controversies surrounding liberation theology when he published *El evangelio en Solentiname* (*The Gospel in Solentiname*), a work in which peasants from Cardenal's island community (Solentiname) interpret different parts of the New Testament.

Cardenal's ordination as a priest in 1965 not only conferred upon him a definite social status, it also moved him closer to conceiving of himself as a poet-prophet, one capable of speaking in God's voice about justice and morality (as well as their absence). If Solentiname, the community he founded in 1965 on the island of Mancarrón in Nicaragua's Gran Lago (Great Lake), began as a contemplative, perhaps escapist, experiment related to communal experiences in the United States, at the same time, ongoing talks with revolutionary leaders of the Frente Sandinista de Liberación Nacional (FSLN) (such as Tomás Borge and Carlos Fonseca) beginning in 1968 gradually convinced Cardenal to renounce his principles of Gandhian and Mertonian non-violence and to become an international spokesperson for the Frente's program of armed insurrection. The joining of Christian ideals with struggle for social change based on Marxist-Leninist tenets became firmly rooted in Cardenal as well as in his poetry after trips to Chile, where he met Marxist priests, and to Cuba in 1970, where he was deeply impressed with Fidel Castro's experiment in socialism. Cardenal dedicated his *Canto nacional* [National Song] to the FSLN and in it prophesied Nicaragua as "a promised land for the Revolution." For Cardenal, the earthquake that destroyed Managua right before Christmas in 1972 was a disaster of biblical magnitude that provoked the emphatically oracular tone of his long poem *Oráculo sobre Managua* [Oracle over Managua].

Historical figures always have been a major presence in Cardenal's poetry, whether he is describing the conquistadors in the early poem "Proclama del conquistador" [Announcement of the Conquistador] or in *El estrecho dudoso* (*The Doubtful Strait*), indigenous personages such as Nezahualcóyotl or Tahirassawichi, or, from the 19th century, William Walker and the filibusters who occupied Nicaragua, or the national hero A.C. Sandino. The dictator of Nicaragua and his family form such an integral part of Cardenal's poetry that it led some Nicaraguans to joke that Cardenal's poetic muse was Somoza ("Su musa es Somoza"). Cardenal uses these historical figures as a means of establishing an ethical framework by which he judges human actions and prophesies change. Despite a work such as *Vida en el amor* (*Love*) and declarations by critics such as Luce López-Baralt that Cardenal is "the first mystical writer of Hispanic America," Cardenal's fundamental preoccupations as a moralist prevent him from realizing his mystical aspirations in his poetry. This is less true of Cardenal's controversial 600-page poem *Cántico cósmico* (*Cosmic Canticle*), in which the poet distances himself from Catholicism's conception of God in favor of a pot-pourri that includes a cosmic consciousness based on science and a pseudoscience of the poet's own invention, the multiple gods and godhead of a variety of world religions, the heterodox Christianity (Gnosticism) of his compatriot the metaphysical poet Alfonso Cortés, and even atheistic ideas regarding nothingness. This openness to different constructions of the divine is yet another of Cardenal's debts to Merton.

One critic has called *Cántico cósmico* "the most beautiful gem of 20th-century Hispanic American poetry," whereas others are daring to say that the emperor is not wearing any clothes. In any case, the *Cántico* may be considered a summation of Cardenal's work as a poet. It is a culmination of the ideogrammatical compositional technique that Cardenal learned from Ezra Pound, in which fragments from a multitude of sources can be joined in a coherent whole. Because Cardenal incorporates current astrophysical theory (mostly a repetitive, prosaic rehashing of the Big Bang theory as explained by best-selling authors such as Stephen Hawking) to explain the nature of the entire universe and humanity's relation to it, *Cántico cósmico* is also the ultimate extension of Cardenal's concept of so-called "exteriorist" poetry, which he defines as "objective poetry: narrative and anecdotal, made of the elements of real life and concrete things, with proper names

and precise details and exact data and numbers and facts and sayings ... the only poetry that can express Latin American reality, reach the people, and be revolutionary."

Cántico cósmico is considerably weakened by Cardenal's wholesale inclusion of his two least convincing books – the Utopian politicized verse in *Tocar el cielo* [To Touch the Sky] and *Vuelos de victoria* (*Flights of Victory*), written while Cardenal was Minister of Culture in Sandinista Nicaragua. Due to its ambitious attempt to embrace the scientific knowledge of its time, *Cántico cósmico* has been compared to Dante's *Divine Comedy*. Formally, the two poems have little in common: Cardenal's amorphous, poorly-edited text shares none of the precision and refinement of Dante's poem. It has been said, however, that Dante wrote the *Divine Comedy* in order to shore up his own threatened set of beliefs and to preserve a medieval sense of organization (e.g., the Ptolemaic system and a world divided into warring Guelphs and Ghibellines) that he already knew was being replaced by new scientific and political orders. Perhaps Cardenal is faced with a similar situation (in "Cantiga 42," the poet says that the purpose of the *Cántico* is to console himself): the same year that *Cántico cósmico* was published, the Sandinistas lost the elections in Nicaragua and the old Cold War divisions of the world disappeared. With regard to the "science" in Cardenal's poem (the poet states in Cantiga 34, "Obviously, I'm not a scientist"), true astrophysicists have difficulty with Cardenal's "extrapolations and confused concepts." Despite the many moments of Cardenalian brilliance in the *Cántico*, it is perhaps more appropriate to compare Cardenal's poem to Pound's botched magnum opus, the *Cantos*.

STEVEN F. WHITE

Biography
Born in Granada, Nicaragua, 20 January 1925. Studied for Arts degree atUniversidad Nacional Autónoma de México (UNAM), Mexico City, 1943–47, followed by graduate studies at Columbia, 1947–49. Participated in the abortive "April Conspiracy" of 1954, to remove Anastasio ("Tacho") Somoza from power. Underwent religous conversion and studied under Thomas Merton, then in charge of novices at the Trappist monastery of Gethsemani, Kentucky. On leaving Gethsemani in 1959 he travelled to Mexico and stayed at the Benedictine monastery in Cuernavaca, 1959–61. Completed his studies for the priesthood in Colombia and was ordained a priest, 1965. He then founded a Catholic base community, Nuestra Señora de Solentiname, on an island in the Great Lake of Nicaragua. Influenced by the theology of liberation, Cardenal gave his support to the Sandinista revolutionaries. The community at Solentiname was destroyed by Somoza's troops as an act of revenge, 1977. With the triumph of the Nicaraguan Revolution in 1979, Cardenal became minister of Culture. After the defeat of the Sandinistas in the elections of 1990, Cardenal returned to a contemplative life and to writing. Awarded Christopher Book Prize, 1972, and Peace Prize by the German Publishers Association, 1980.

Selected Works

Poetry
Hora O, Mexico City: Revista Mexicana de Literatura, 1960; as *Zero Hour and Other, Documentary Poems*, edited by Donald Walsh, translated by Walsh, Robert Pring-Mill, Paul Borgeson, Jr and Jonathan Cohen, New York: New Directions, 1980

Gethsemani, Ky, Mexico City: Ecuador, 1960

Epigramas, Mexico City: UNAM, 1961; as *Epigramas*, translated by
K.H. Anton, New York: Lodestar Press, 1978

Salmos, Medellín, Colombia: Universidad de Antioquía, 1964; as
Psalms, translated by several leading British poets, London: Sheed
and Ward, and New York: Crossroads, 1981

Oración por Marilyn Monroe y otros poemas, Medellín, Colombia:
La Tertulia, 1965; as *Marilyn Monroe and Other Poems*, edited
and translated by Robert Pring-Mill, London: Search Press,
1975

El estrecho dudoso, Madrid: Cultura Hispánica, 1966; as *The
Doubtful Strait*, translated by John Lyons, Bloomington: Indiana
University Press, 1995

Mayapán, Managua: Ediciones de Librería Cardenal, 1968

Homenaje a los indios americanos, León: Universidad Autónoma de
Nicaragua, 1969; as *Homage to the American Indians*, translated
by Carlos and Monique Altschul, Baltimore: Johns Hopkins
University Press, 1973

Canto nacional, Mexico City: Siglo XXI, 1973

Oráculo sobre Managua, Buenos Aires: Lohlé, 1973

Nostalgia del futuro, Managua: Nueva Nicaragua, 1982

Vuelos de victoria, Madrid: Visor, 1984; as *Flights of Victory /
Vuelos de victoria*, translated by Marc Zimmerman, Maryknoll,
New York: Orbis Books, 1985 [bilingual edition]

Quetzalcóatl, Managua: Nueva Nicaragua, 1985

Los ovnis de oro (poemas indios), Mexico City: Siglo XXI, 1988; as
*Los ovnis de oro / Golden UFOs; Poemas indios / The Indian
Poems*, translated by Carlos and Monique Altschul, edited with
an introduction and glossary by Russell O. Salmon, Bloomington:
Indiana University Press, 1992 [Impressive bilingual scholarly
edition]

Cántico cósmico, Managua: Nueva Nicaragua, 1989; as *The Music
of the Spheres*, translated by Dinah Livingstone, London:
Katabasis, 1990; as *Cosmic Canticle*, translated by John Lyons,
Willimantic: Connecticut: Curbstone Press, 1993

Telescopio en la noche oscura, Madrid: Trotta, 1993

Other Writings

Vida en el amor, prologue by Thomas Merton, Buenos Aires: Lohlé,
1970; as *To Live is to Love*, translated by Kurt Reinhardt, New
York: Herder, 1972; as *Love. Vida en el amor*, translated by
Dinah Livingstone, London: Search Press, 1974

En Cuba, Buenos Aires: Lohlé, 1972; as *In Cuba*, translated by
Donald Walsh, New York: New Directions, 1974

El evangelio en Solentiname, 2 vols, Salamanca: Sígueme, 1976–78;
as *The Gospel in Solentiname*, translated by Donald Walsh, New
York: Orbis Books, 1978–82; as *Love in Practice*, 1 vol., London:
Search Press, 1977

Compilations and Anthologies

Poesía de uso: antología, 1949–1978, Buenos Aires: El Cid, 1979

Antología de poesía primitiva, selected and translated by Ernesto
Cardenal, Madrid: Alianza, 1979

Tocar el cielo: poesías, Managua: Editorial Nueva Nicaragua, 1983

Anthologies in Translation

Apocalypse and Other Poems, edited and translated by Robert
Pring-Mill and Donald Walsh, New York: New Directions, 1977

"With Walker in Nicaragua" and Other Early Poems (1949–1954),
translated by Jonathan Cohen, Middletown, Connecticut:
Wesleyan University Press, 1984 [bilingual edition]

From Nicaragua with Love: Poems (1979–1986), translated by
Jonathan Cohen, San Francisco: City Lights Books, 1986

Further Reading

Since the Sandinistas were defeated in the elections of 1990 there
has been a perhaps inevitable decline of interest in Cardenal's
poetry. This is unfortunate since the many phases of his poetic
production deserve more detailed attention.

Borgeson, Jr, Paul W., *Hacia el hombre nuevo: poesía y pensamiento
de Ernesto Cardenal*, London: Támesis, 1984

Calabrese, Elisa (editor), *Ernesto Cardenal: poeta de la liberación
latinoamericana*, Buenos Aires: García Cambeiro, 1975

Cuadra, Pablo Antonio, "Sobre Ernesto Cardenal," *Papeles de Son
Armadans*, vol. 63 (1971)

Dorfman, Ariel, "Tiempo de amor, tiempo de lucha: la unidad en
los *Epigramas* de Cardenal," *Texto Crítico*, vol. 5/13 (1979)

Urdanivia Bertarelli, Eduardo, *La poesía de Ernesto Cardenal:
cristianismo y revolución*, Lima: Latinoamericana Editores,
1984

Veiravé, Alfredo, *Ernesto Cardenal: el exteriorismo; poesía del
nuevo mundo*, Chaco: Universidad Nacional del Nordeste,
1974

White, Steven F., "Ernesto Cardenal and North American Literature:
the Formulation of an Ethical Identity," in his *Modern
Nicaraguan Poetry: Dialogues with France and the United States*,
London and Toronto: Associated University Presses, 1993

Interviews

Benedetti, Mario, *Los poetas comunicantes*, Montevideo: Biblioteca
de Marcha, 1972

Cántico cósmico

Poem by Ernesto Cardenal

Cántico cósmico is a very ambitious work in which Cardenal
expresses the grandeur of the universe through the history of
different peoples, always in search of God beyond their own
cosmologies. The *Cántico* has on occasion been compared to
Dante's *Divina commedia* (*The Divine Comedy*) and to *De
rerum natura* (*On the Nature of the Universe*) by Lucretius.
Without doubt this is because Cardenal's work is an extensive
compendium of forty-three *Cantigas* (originally, medieval
poems set to music) in which the poet brings together in a
harmonious way human, mythical, religious, philosophical,
political and scientific subjects.

The originality of this "poetic song to the Cosmos" is based
on how the author inserts and recreates the concepts, theories
and models of contemporary physics and astrophysics so as
to give weight and idealism to his literary creation. The
framework for concepts borrowed from physics and astrophysics in relation to the author's spiritual concerns, is as
follows:

> The origin of the Universe: the Big Bang
> The future of the Universe and its significance for Man
> The Earth, its formation, Man
> Life in other possible worlds
> The basic laws of Physics: Mechanics, Thermodynamics,
> Electromagnetism, Nuclear and Quantum Physics.
> The great names of Physics
> A history of Physics

But what is most striking from our point of view is that
profound knowledge and love of the Universe integrated into

a whole, which emerges in the course of the *Cantigas*, creating a magical encounter between astrophysics and poetry.

Writers such as Reinaldo Arenas in his story "El reino de Alipio," 1968 [Alipio's Kingdom], Severo Sarduy in his poetic work *Big Bang* (1973) and Italo Calvino in *Le cosmicomiche*, 1965 (*Cosmicomics*) had already, in one way or another, used scientific knowledge about the heavens in their writings, although not in such an exhaustive way as Cardenal's *Cántico*.

Already in the first *Cantiga*, "The Big Bang," Cardenal writes:

> En el principio no había nada
> > ni espacio
> > > ni tiempo.
> > > > El universo entero concentrado
> en el espacio del núcleo de un átomo,
> y antes aún menos, mucho menos que un protón,
> y aún menos todavía, un infinitamente denso punto
> > matemático.
> > > Y fue el Big Bang.
> La Gran Explosión.

[In the beginning there was nothing / neither space / nor time. / The entire universe was concentrated / in the space of the nucelus of an atom, / and before that even less, much less than a proton, / and even less than that, an infinitely dense mathematical point. / And the Big Bang came to pass. / The Great Explosion]

Currently, the Big Bang is the most commonly accepted cosmological model used to explain the origin and formation of the Universe and, perhaps, its evolution. According to this model, the Universe arose out of an almost punctual configuration whose density tended towards the infinite, some ten or twenty million years ago. It came into being as the result of an explosion which occured simultaneously everywhere. The whole of space filled up from the very beginning and every particle moved away at great speed from all the others. In effect, time and space came into being in that explosion, it being space itself that has expanded from the first moment.

In the hundredth part of a second the Universe was full of electrons, positons, neutrons and photons. The density of this primitive Cosmos may have been four hundred million times greater than that of water, and its temperature of the order of one hundred thousand million degrees kelvin.

Cardenal refers to this scientific knowledge, thus:

> Una centésima de segundo después
> la temperatura era de 100.000 millones de grados
> > centígrados
> aún tan alta que no podía haber ni moléculas ni
> > átomos ni
> núcleos de átomos, sólo partículas elementales:
> electrones, positrones,
> y neutrinos fantasmales sin carga eléctrica y sin masa.

[A split second later / the temperature was of 100.000 million centigrades / still so high that neither molecules nor atoms nor / the nuclei of atoms could exist, only elemental particles / electrons, positrons, / and phantom-like neutrins without electric charge and mass]

The Universe began to expand, to grow cooler, losing density and creating new particles in collisions. In succession, particles formed and were annihilated with a discharge of energy. After three hundred thousand years matter had cooled sufficiently for the electrons to unite with the nuclei, which had been generated. These formed atoms of hydrogen and helium; the photons escaped from the matter producing the cosmic microwave background which can be observed in microwaves. (These were first detected in 1964 and a small anisotropy – COSMOSOMAS – has been confirmed by the satellite COBE and the Institute of Astrophysics of the Canary Islands). The gas that resulted from the effect of gravity started to form clusters which finally would condense to form galaxies and stars.

These ideas too are expressed in the *Cántico cósmico*:

> y este gas por la gravedad se fue juntando, juntando
> > más,
> y después apretándose más en forma de galaxias y
> > estrellas
> del presente universo.

[and this gas owing to gravity began to come together, ever closer, / pressing itself later into the form of galaxies and stars / of the present universe]

This model which we have outlined very briefly is vague in terms of the beginning itself, since the 10 35 seconds. It has been supposed that in the first instants there was a phase of exponential expansion, known as inflation, but we are not going to develop this aspect because Cardenal barely refers to it. But there is an alternative theory which philosophically may seem fairly attractive, one that was put forward by Herman Bondi, Thomas Gold and Fred Hoyle: the Universe, at the time of its creation, was more or less the same as it is now. As it expands so new matter is created and this fills the empty spaces between the galaxies. The problem of the primitive Universe is eliminated since there was no such thing; instead it is infinite and eternal. At the present time other theories which attempt to explain the Universe are being developed; however, the evidence provided by the expansion of the Universe, the wealth of light elements and the fluctuations in the radiation of the cosmic background of microwaves incline contemporary scientists towards the theory of the Big Bang. Some of these facts are expressed in the *Cántico cósmico* with much beauty.

The future of the Universe is another subject of reflection for Cardenal. According to the present Big Bang model the Universe will continue to expand for a time. If the cosmic density of matter is less than than the critical density (the minimum value required to stop its expansion completely), then the Universe's extension will be infinite and it will continue to expand forever; if both densities are equal, the expansion will continue indefinitely, but ever more slowly, tending at the limit to have a zero acceleration of expansion. On the other hand, if the cosmic density is greater than the critical value, the Universe will be finite and its expansion will cease at some point, giving rise to an accelerated contraction that would take it to a state similar to that of its birth, although never the same. The development of this idea may lead to theorizing about a Universe of eternal returns, with successive cycles of expansions and contractions.

Cántico cósmico enquires into this enigma and provides an idealistic, perhaps possible answer:

> ¿Y si el universo entero tiende a ser un sólo ser
> universal?
> ¿Y la última etapa de la evolución
> el superorganismo universal?
> Repitiéndose tras cada Big Bang este universo
> para ser mejor cada vez
> hasta llegar a ser el cosmos perfecto,
> presentes en él todos los tiempos pasados,
> recapitulados todos los seres.

[And if the entire universe inclines towards a sole universal being? / And the last phase of evolution / the universal superorganism? / With every Big Bang this universe repeats itself / to improve on itself each time / until it achieves cosmic perfection, / all past times present in it / all beings recapitulated]

These lines harmonize poetry, philosophy and science. But astrophysics and poetry enter into an almost mystical communion when the relationship between ourselves and the stars is broached. The following lines give concrete expression to this harmony:

> ¿Qué hay en una estrella? Nosotros mismos.
> Todos los elementos de nuestro cuerpo y del planeta
> estuvieron en las entrañas de una estrella.
> Somos polvo de estrellas.
> También somos hijos del sol   (Cantiga 4)

[What is there in a star? Our own selves. / All the elements of our body and of the planet/ were in the womb of a star. / We are stardust . . . / We are also children of the sun]

> . . . .

> ¡Engendrados por las estrellas!   (Cantiga 8)

[engendered by the stars!]

The same ideas recur in other *Cantigas* with new images. Stars are formed by the gravitational compression of the dust and gas of the interstellar medium. As their lives progress, on the basis of hydrogen and helium, they generate different chemical elements through nuclear reactions of fusion. If the star is very massive it may die as a supernova, exploding and enriching the interstellar medium with the elements that it has created in the course of its life and in its spectacular death.

It is thought that the Sun came into being as a result of the death of some star, such as a supernova, when this interstellar space was compressed owing to the shock wave produced by the explosion. The Earth was formed with the Sun, and life – and Man – evolved on the former. Furthermore, advances in spectroscopy have demonstrated that all the chemical elements to be found on Earth, on the Sun, in our bodies and the stars, in the Universe, that is, are the same. Therefore, to some extent it is true to say that we are children of the stars. In the *Cántico cósmico* Cardenal has made clear our intimate relationship with the Universe. This notion of a cosmic connection, of unity in diversity, is one that the Cuban thinker José Martí had already integrated into his philosophy, expressing in 1887 a view that is still relevant today:

> El Universo es lo universo. Y lo universo, lo uni-vario,
> es lo vario en lo uno. La naturaleza "llena de sorpresas"
> es toda una. Lo que hace un puñado de tierra, hace al
> hombre y hace al astro. Los elementos de una estrella
> enfriada están en ungrano de trigo.

[The Universe is what is universal. And the latter, unity in variety, is variety in unity. Nature, "full of surprises" is a whole. What constitutes a fistful of earth, makes humankind and the stars. The elements of a dead star are within a grain of wheat.]

Through the *Cántico cósmico* Cardenal has given expression to our intimate relationship with the Universe. As he says in *Cantiga 6*:

> Soy hijo de la Tierra y del Cielo estrellado
> [I am the child of the Earth and the starry Sky]

María Begoña de Luis

translated by Verity Smith

Editions

First edition: *Cántico cósmico*, Managua: Nueva Nicaragua, 1989

Translation: *Cántico cósmico, English Selections. The Music of the Spheres*, by Dinah Livingstone, London: Katabasis, 1990 [bilingual edition]; also translated as *Cosmic Canticle* by John Lyons, Willimantic, Connecticut: Curbstone Press, 1993

Further Reading

Bondi, Hermann, *Cosmology*, Cambridge: Cambridge University Press, 1952

González Alvarez, Joaquín, *Lo científico en la literatura*, Cuba: Ediciones Holguín, 1991

Luis, María Begoña de, *Introducción a la astrofísica*, Madrid: Universidad Nacional de Educación a Distancia, 1993

Trefil, James S., *The Moment of Creation: Big Bang Physics from Before the First Millisecond to the Present Universe*, New York: Scribner, 1983

Weinberg, Steven, *The First Three Minutes: a View of the Origin of the Universe*, New York: Basic Books, 1977

Alejo Carpentier 1904–1980

Cuban prose writer, musicologist and cultural historian

Alejo Carpentier is rightly considered one of the most important Latin American writers of the 20th century. A man of immense erudition, with his production stretching to fifteen volumes, Carpentier was equally at ease writing on art, architecture or music as he was on literature, history, myth, the African contribution to Cuban culture or the ongoing cultural debate over the identity of Latin America. Carpentier's musical background is ever-present in his works, not only in his countless journalistic articles and important work on the history of Cuban music, *La música en Cuba*, 1946 [Music in Cuba], but in his novels and short stories, many of which also take their form or titles from musical compositions: *El acoso*, 1956 (*The Chase*), *Concierto barroco*, 1974 (*Baroque Concerto*), *La consagración de la primavera*, 1978 [Rite of Spring]. Architecture features prominently in both the imagery he fashions in relation to Europe and America and, in addition, to his scrupulous attention to detail in descriptions of buildings. The visual arts play a vital role, particularly in *El siglo de las luces*, 1962 (*Explosion in a Cathedral*) whose English title is the name of the painting that acts as a recurring motif throughout the novel and whose epigraphs are taken from Goya's series of etchings on the Napoleonic invasion of the Iberian peninsula, "Los desastres de la guerra" [The Disasters of War].

Carpentier has often been labelled one of the most European of Latin American writers. Born of French/Russian parents, he grew up well-versed in French and Russian culture (his mother wrote articles on Russian ballet in Cuban cultural magazines of the 1920s) and lived for long periods in France during his formative years. However, whilst his early writing originated from his involvement with the avant-garde and Surrealist movements, Carpentier's major works, written after his return to Latin America, are characterised by a passionate interest in the New World. In these works, in common with other writers of the Boom period, Carpentier struggles to break through the strictures of the Eurocentric vision in order to find a language and novelistic form adequate to the task of defining the multifaceted reality of Latin America and bringing it within the field of vision of the European. Thus, whilst it is true that we find many echoes of European models, and in particular that of Marcel Proust in his works, his novels as a whole can be seen to reflect his quest to break free from European influences and find a suitable style with which to portray, or as he frequently terms it, to translate, the realities of the New World. In his later writings, and particularly *El recurso del método*, 1974 (*Reasons of State*), he reaches the stage of novelistic development and maturity where he is able to acknowledge openly the influence of his European precursors in his works themselves. In them he asserts in a ludic manner his own independence and that of other Latin American writers with the confidence of an author well aware of the status and influence that Latin American literature has come to enjoy in its own right.

Carpentier was to find his ideal form of expression in his now famous baroque style, with the use of a rich, innovative and at times highly technical vocabulary. His syntactic construction becomes as rich and ornamental as the landscapes and scenes he is describing as he piles up details one after the other, naming or listing every single thing, animate or inanimate, that makes up reality. This concept of naming is integral to Carpentier's approach to communicating the reality of the New World. He considers that, because the conquerors imposed a dominant language and culture on the indigenous populations, the latter have been robbed of both their identity and their own means of expression. Thus there is a need to return to roots and then to begin again from scratch, re-appropriating, and then re-naming every single component that makes up the multi-faceted realities of the New World. Only when this has been accomplished will Latin America be able to assume her true identity and her independence be complete.

In this context Carpentier likens the difficulties of the novelist to those of Columbus and the early chroniclers, who found themselves imprisoned by the confines of their language and terms of reference when it came to describing new realities. The narrator of *Los pasos perdidos* (*The Lost Steps*), is beset by this problem when he seeks to record the phenomena he encounters in the Orinoco/Amazon basins. Similarly Esteban, symbolically employed as a translator in *El siglo de las luces*, finds that he needs to invent new words as he struggles to describe the unique realities of the fantastic world of the Caribbean, whilst in *La consagración de la primavera* Carpentier establishes the parallel between the protagonist Enrique and Hernán Cortés confronted with the completely new realities of Mexico. In his last novel, *El arpa y la sombra* (*The Harp and the Shadow*) Carpentier takes this theme still further, not only drawing parallels with the linguistic problems facing Columbus, but also questioning the veracity of historical records through blistering and irreverent use of parody, as the Pope agonises over whether or not Columbus should be canonised, whilst Carpentier's Columbus, on his death bed, reflects on how many of his texts, and hence the accepted realities of the New World, were nothing more than "un Vasto Repertorio de Embustes" (a vast repertory of lies). By placing himself in the same situation as Columbus and the chroniclers, the first people to record the reality of the New World, Carpentier also effectively puts himself in a position to rewrite this same history and to re-name the reality of Latin America.

Carpentier is probably best known, however, for his concept of "lo real maravilloso" or "the marvellous in the real," which he discusses in his essays and incorporates into his novels, showing how the New World is one in which reality is perceived on a whole new series of levels, contexts and perspectives defying the European imagination – a world in which what constitutes the "marvellous," the "fantastic," or the "magical" in Western eyes actually exists as part of everyday life. Here, Carpentier says, surrealism becomes superfluous – the author does not have to invent the fantastic in his writing, but rather to find a way of expressing the marvellous reality that is already there.

Carpentier introduces his concept of the marvellous real in the prologue of his second novel, *El reino de este mundo*, 1949 (*The Kingdom of this World*), set during Haiti's wars of independence at the end of the 18th century, and seen through the eyes of a Negro slave, Ti Noel. Here, as he recounts the events surrounding the slave rebellions prior to the Bouckman massacre and seizure of power by Henri Christophe, Carpentier juxtaposes the European and Latin American cultural viewpoints – on the one hand the Cartesian and material reality of the French and, on the other, the magical, mainly oral culture of Latin America. Discussions of this and many other issues are found in Carpentier's important collections of essays and lectures, *Tientos y diferencias*, 1964 [Gropings and Differences] and *La novela latinoamericana en vísperas de un nuevo siglo y otros ensayos*, 1981 [The Latin American Novel on the Eve of a New Century and Other Essays].

Closely related to the concept of the "marvellous in the real" is Carpentier's revolutionary treatment of time, history and reality. In his novels he delights in sweeping aside conventional temporal barriers, substituting the traditional linear or diachronic notion of past, present and future with a synchronic vision in which time is depicted as fluid and malleable and different ages are seen as existing simultaneously on the same plane. Carpentier has described Latin America as, "el único continente donde distintas edades coexisten" (the only continent where different ages co-exist). This is the continent where a journey in space also represents one back in time through previous civilisations the further one penetrates the inaccessible interior, giving one, as the narrator of *Los pasos perdidos* discovers, "la estupefaciente posibilidad de viajar en el tiempo, como otros viajan en el espacio" (the amazing possibility of travelling in time just as others travel in space).

The theme of time travel and links between different temporal and geographical planes are constants found throughout Carpentier's works, one of the outstanding examples being his famous short story *Viaje a la semilla*, 1944 (*Journey Back to the Source*) which follows the life of Don Marcial from death to birth, as if a film were being run backwards.

In turn Carpentier projects a vision of the dynamic ongoing spiral of time onto his concept of war and revolution, seeing ideas and revolutionary ideals as being linked throughout the ages, as is illustrated in his short story "Semejante a la noche," 1952 (Like the Night) where wars from different ages are all effortlessly juxtaposed onto the same time plane, or in *El siglo de las luces* and *La consagración de la primavera*, where Carpentier shows how the ideas brought over to the New World from the French and Bolshevik Revolutions have sown the seed for the ongoing revolutionary process culminating in the victory of Fidel Castro in 1959. In his later works Carpentier adopts an increasingly Marxist stance, voicing ever stronger support for the Cuban Revolution. Some critics have questioned the motives of his overt praise for Castro in *La consagración de la primavera*, where some adulatory passages seem to indicate that a desire to win favour has blinded him to the very same need for critical distance when assessing political events which he so advocates in his novels. However, any adverse criticism which political controversy engendered in his later years did not undermine his stature as a writer, as is evidenced by the fact that he was awarded the prestigious Cervantes prize in 1978, two years before his death.

SALLY HARVEY

Biography

Born in Havana, Cuba, 26 December 1904, the son of a Russian mother and a French father. Parents highly educated and very musical. Studied architecture for one year (1922) at the University of Havana. Journalist, Havana, 1921–24, including column on classical music in the *Diario de la Marina*; editor, *Carteles* magazine, Havana, 1924–28. Imprisoned in 1928 for signing a manifesto against the dictator Gerardo Machado. Left for France where he earned his living as a journalist, contributing regularly to the Cuban magazines *Carteles* and *Social*. Director of the Foniric Studios, Paris, 1936–39. Married Marguerite de Lessert, 1933; Eva Frejaville, 1939. Returned to Cuba, 1939. After divorce from second wife, married Lilia Esteban, 1941. Writer and producer, CMZ radio station, Havana, 1939–41; employed as musicologist by the Conservatorio Nacional, Havana, 1941–43; visited Haiti, 1943. Moved to Caracas in 1945 where he worked first in broadcasting and later in an advertising agency. Also wrote regular column on the arts for the newspaper *El Nacional*. After the Cuban Revolution, made director of the Cuban Publishing House, Havana, a post he held from 1963–67; cultural attaché, Cuban Embassy, Paris, from 1968. Deputy, Cuban National Assembly, 1976. Recipient of several awards and honours of which the most important are the Miguel de Cervantes Prize, 1978 and the Medici Prize, 1979. Died in Paris of cancer of the throat, 24 April 1980.

Selected Works

Novels

¡Écue-yamba-Ó! Madrid: Editorial España, 1933

El reino de este mundo, Mexico City: Edición y Distribución Ibero Americana de Publicaciones, 1949; as *The Kingdom of this World*, translated by Harriet de Onís, New York: Knopf, 1957; London: Gollancz, 1967

Los pasos perdidos, Mexico City: Edición y Distribución Ibero Americana de Publicaciones 1953; as *The Lost Steps*, translated by Harriet de Onís, New York: Knopf, and London: Gollancz, 1956

El acoso, Buenos Aires: Losada, 1956; as *The Chase*, translated by Alfred MacAdam, New York: Farrar Straus and Giroux, 1989

El siglo de las luces, Mexico City: Compañía General de Ediciones, 1962; as *Explosion in a Cathedral*, translated by John Sturrock, Boston: Little Brown, and London: Gollancz, 1963

Los convidados de plata, Montevideo: Sandino, 1972

Concierto barroco, Mexico City: Siglo XXI, 1974; as *Baroque Concerto*, translated by Asa Zatz, Tulsa, Oklahoma: Council Oak Books, 1991

El recurso del método, Mexico City: Siglo XXI, 1974; as *Reasons of State*, translated by Frances Partridge, New York: Knopf, and London: Gollancz, 1976

La consagración de la primavera, Mexico City: Siglo XXI, 1978

El arpa y la sombra, Mexico City: Siglo XXI, 1979; as *The Harp and the Shadow*, translated by Thomas and Carol Christensen, San Francisco: Mercury House, 1990

Short Fiction

Viaje a la semilla, Havana: Úcar García, 1944 [novella]

Guerra del tiempo: tres relatos y una novela: El Camino de Santiago, Viaje a la semilla, Semejante a la noche, y El acoso, Mexico City: Compañía General de Ediciones, 1958; as *War on Time* (includes *The Highroad of Saint James, Right of Sanctuary,*

Journey Back to the Source, Like the Night, The Chosen),
translated by Frances Partridge, New York: Knopf, and London:
Gollancz, 1970
El derecho de asilo, Barcelona: Lumen, 1972
Cuentos, Havana: Editorial Arte y Literatura, 1976

Essays

La música en Cuba, Mexico City: Fondo de Cultura Económica,
1946
Tientos y diferencias: ensayos, Mexico City: UNAM, 1964
Literatura y conciencia política en América Latina, Madrid:
Corazón, 1969
La ciudad de las columnas, photographs by Paolo Gasparini,
Barcelona: Lumen, 1970 [On the architecture of Havana]
Letra y solfa, edited by Alexis Márquez Rodríguez, Caracas: Síntesis
Dosmil, 1975 [articles]
Crónicas, 2 vols, Havana: Editorial Arte y Literatura, 1976
Razón de ser, Caracas: Universidad Central de Venezuela, 1976
[lectures]
*Bajo el signo de la Cibeles: crónicas sobre España y los españoles,
1925–1937*, edited by Julio Rodríguez Puértolas, Madrid: Nuestra
Cultura, 1979
El adjetivo y sus arrugas, Buenos Aires: Galerna, 1980
*La novela latinoamericana en vísperas de un nuevo siglo y otros
ensayos*, Mexico City: Siglo XXI, 1981

Compilations and Anthologies

Obras completas, 14 vols, Mexico City: Siglo XXI, 1983

Further Reading

Dorfman, Ariel, *Hacia la liberación del lector latinoamericano*,
Hanover, New Hampshire: Ediciones del Norte, 1984; as *Some
Write to the Future*, translated by the author and George R.
Shivers, Durham, North Carolina: Duke University Press, 1991
[Contains chapter on *El recurso del método*]
Giacoman, Helmy F. (editor), *Homenaje a Alejo Carpentier:
variaciones interpretativas en torno a su obra*, New York: Las
Américas, 1970
González Echevarría, Roberto, *Alejo Carpentier. The Pilgrim at
Home*, Ithaca, New York: Cornell University Press, 1977; 2nd
edition, Austin: University of Texas Press, 1990
Harvey, Sally, *Carpentier's Proustian Fiction: the Influence of Marcel
Proust on Alejo Carpentier*, London: Támesis, 1994
Müller-Bergh, Klaus, *Alejo Carpentier. Estudio biográfico-crítico*,
New York: Las Américas, 1972
Rama, Ángel, *Los dictadores latinoamericanos*, Mexico City: Fondo
de Cultura Económica, 1976 [On *El recurso del método*]
Shaw, Donald L., *Alejo Carpentier*, Boston: Twayne, 1985
Smith, Verity, *Carpentier: los pasos perdidos*, London: Grant and
Cutler, 1983
Volek, Emil, *Cuatro claves para la modernidad: análisis semiótico de
textos hispánicos*, Madrid: Gredos, 1984 [Chapter 3 is on *Los
pasos perdidos*]
Webb, Barbara J., *Myth and History in Caribbean Fiction: Alejo
Carpentier, Wilson Harris and Edouard Glissant*, Amherst:
University of Massachusetts Press, 1992
Wyers Weber, Frances, "*El acoso*: Alejo Carpentier's War on Time,"
PMLA, vol. 77 (4 September 1963)

Bibliographies

García Cananza, Araceli, *Bibliografía de Alejo Carpentier*, Havana:
Letras Cubanas, 1984
González Echevarría, Roberto and Klaus Müller-Bergh, *Alejo
Carpentier: Bibliographical Guide*, Westport, Connecticut:
Greenwood Press, 1983
Rubio, Patricia and Richard A. Young, *Carpentier ante la crítica:
bibliografía comentada*, Veracruz: Universidad Veracruzana, 1985

El reino de este mundo

Novel by Alejo Carpentier

El reino de este mundo, 1949 (*The Kingdom of this World*) is
the introduction to and the opening of Carpentier's grand cycle
of "American novels," closed only by *El arpa y la sombra* (*The
Harp and the Shadow*), in 1979, shortly before his death. In
the celebrated "Prologue" to *El reino*, Carpentier points out,
among the characteristics of the Latin American continent, the
persistence of the mythic worldview, in the Indian and Black
communities; the power of magical belief; the historical abundance of extraordinary events; as well as "virgin landscapes;"
and sums up these special qualities under *lo real maravilloso*
(the marvellous in the real). In this vision, culture, history, and
the poetic presence of nature, together, embody the Latin
American difference from other regions of the world. All of
Latin America is regarded as the land of *lo real maravilloso*.

At mid-point, in *Tientos y diferencias*, 1964 [Gropings and
Differences], Carpentier reinterprets his project in terms of
cultural "contexts," retouches dutifully the social and political
dimension of *lo real maravilloso*, and celebrates the baroque
style as the only "natural" vehicle for the expression of such
a reality. Yet his original "poetics" of the Latin American
reality has been only superficially adapted to the new Marxist
orthodoxy. Carpentier's continued stress on cultural difference
links him rather to such postmodern reassessments as those
found in Antonio Benítez Rojo's *La isla que se repite: El Caribe
y la perspectiva posmoderna*, 1989 (*The Repeating Island: the
Caribbean and the Postmodern Perspective*).

In the Prologue, Carpentier relates "the marvellous" to
Surrealism, but goes to great pains to distance himself from
this bogey of the Stalinist left (this might actually better explain
the history of this text, expurgated in the 1950s and resurrected a decade later, only when its character of manifesto was
fully recognized and Surrealism had become less offensive to
the early *fidelista* Marxism). Carpentier argues that "the
marvellous," pursued only frivolously and superficially by the
Surrealists, "is reality" in America. While his image of
Surrealism, bordering on caricature, and the leap into "reality"
are not completely convincing, and the touch of machismo
would bristle today's sensibilities, the invitation to explore
those aspects of Latin American reality that escape the models
and modes of Western Modernity, proved fruitful and
prophetic. The clash between the Latin American pre-
Modernity and the modern forces of capitalism and imperialism will be at the heart of the aesthetics of "realismo mágico"
(magical realism), from Arguedas's *Yawar fiesta* (1941), right
through to Arenas's *El mundo alucinante* (*Hallucinations*) of
1969 and Vargas Llosa's *El hablador*, 1987 (*The Storyteller*)
among many others. In some cases there is not any docu-
mentable contact with Carpentier's work.

Early criticism took Carpentier's vision for fact. A closer
look, however, reveals many problems and contradictions. *Lo
real maravilloso* is not "reality" nor "Latin American reality"
per se, but only one among many possible models (simulacra)
of the reality (realities) in Latin America, and therefore it can
advance only one among many possible yet all truly Latin
American aesthetics. Although the emphasis of Carpentier's
argument links his "poetics of Latin American reality" rather

obviously to the literary aesthetics of magical realism, there is enough of a margin of ambiguity to ensure that the concepts of *lo real maravilloso*, magical realism, and the fantastic will continue to be happily confused.

Another problem is that "the marvellous" can be recognized only in relation to some dominant norm of "the real;" this norm is, of course, furnished by the modern West. While it could be argued that one's identity is indeed acquired "in the mirror," it is also true that the mirror may be a trap, a family theater with prescribed roles. Is not "the marvellous in the real" then a kitsch for export? Are not all Latin Americans cast in the role of "indians," for the pleasure of Western spectators? Is not the "marvellous reality," connoting many times infrahuman conditions of life, "marvellous" only for the imaginary tourists, foreign or domestic? However, it should be noted that contemporary writers, such as the Argentine Juan José Saer, refuse to play along.

Yet there is also a positive aspect: in many works of magical realism, Western Modernity is, symbolically, defeated; the "indians" and the modern Westerners, and their values, are, though only aesthetically, presented as equal. Through *lo real maravilloso* and magical realism, Latin American pre-Modernity appears to anticipate the Postmodern changes of values, coupled with the disintegration of Eurocentrism. The 1970s and 1980s have added another twist to the aesthetics and politics of *lo real maravilloso*: the growing nostalgic rereading of it as an Edenic, patriarchal past in contrast with the present of rapidly decaying urban landscape, exploding drug "culture," endemic crises, brutal violence on left and right, and spreading ecological disaster.

El reino recreates historical events in Haiti in the period of the French Revolution. The novel is peopled by fictionalized historical characters and verges on an artistic collage and a palimpsest of memoirs, travel books, and historical documents of that period. The narrative is divided into four parts, each relatively autonomous in regard to their elements: the first goes back to the 1750s (the terrorist voodoo campaign of the *mandinga* Mackandal against the white colonists); the second shifts to the French Revolution (the 1791 rebellion of the black slaves led by Bouckman; the bittersweet exile of the plantocracy in Santiago de Cuba; Paulina Bonaparte in Haiti, and the failed French imperial attempt to shore up the colonial regime on the island in 1802); the third focuses on the year 1820 (the downfall of the ruthless black king Henri Christophe, who could be, however, the prototype of the modern, "progressive" dictator); and the fourth goes to the second half of the 1820s (Henri Christophe's family, exiled in Rome, and Paulina Bonaparte's statue; the rise of the mulattoes in Haiti, the new rulers and oppressors of the blacks; Ti Noel's illumination and metamorphosis through voodoo).

What the novel lacks in dramatic center, it gains in epic dimension. The apparent lineal and chronological sequence of the loose episodes is crisscrossed by overlapping compositional grids. The story-line makes an explicit parallel between two cycles of violence and oppression: the colonial *ancien régime* and the first bitter fruit of Independence (Henri Christophe). Towards the end of the novel, a third cycle opens up, that of the "Republican Mulattoes." The book closes with the promise of yet another rebellion of the oppressed. While Mackandal and Bouckman are historical figures, the character of Ti Noel was created by Carpentier just from a name on some historical document (Christmas symbolism and prophecy are readily apparent in the name). Ti Noel becomes the uniting thread for the great part of the novel. First, he is an observer and a marginal participant, a follower of Mackandal; towards the end, he becomes the protagonist tying the loose ends. Parts two and four of the novel highlight the "dialogue" between the European and the American worlds; but this clash of values is underscored throughout the whole text, many times ironically, by the epigraphs and by the allegorical titles of many chapters.

Carpentier creates a new, artistic order by imposing a rigorous pattern of symmetries, counterpoints, and cycles on the flow of history. The omnipresence of voodoo, the selection and arrangement of historical events, the creative fiction that fills in the gaps, and the parody of European high culture and ideals, together, produce *lo real maravilloso*; the repeated conflict between the gamut of oppressors and those who remain oppressed, its "realism;" and the failure of the French Revolution and of the "enlightened" despot, its frustrated Modernity. In the magical realism of Carpentier's novel, voodoo fuels the search for Modernity which, inexorably, represses it.

The author himself, unwittingly disavowing the "Prologue," opts unequivocally for Modernity. In *El reino*, beneath the surface of the "marvellous" history hides an allegoric modern pattern of macrohistory, endowed with all its alleged teleology and promise of the future Utopia. This latent message comes to the fore at the celebrated ending of the novel, through the profession of faith in *The Kingdom of this World*. Yet all this promise rests here on the powers of voodoo. An irony? A postmodern insight?

EMIL VOLEK

Editions

First edition: *El reino de este mundo*, Mexico City: Edición y Distribución Iberoamericana de Publicaciones, 1949

Critical edition: edited by Florinda Friedmann de Goldberg, Buenos Aires: Edhasa, 1978

Translation: *The Kingdom of this World*, by Harriet de Onís, New York: Knopf, 1957; London: Gollancz, 1967 [There are later editions of this uneven translation]

Further Reading

For an excellent introduction, start with Shaw and Young.

Chiampi, Irlemar, *O realismo maravilhoso: forma e ideologia no romance hispano-americano*, São Paulo: Editora Perspectiva, 1980

_____ "Alejo Carpentier y el surrealismo," *Revista de la Universidad de México* vol. 37/5 (1981)

González Echevarría, Roberto, "Isla a su vuelo fugitiva: Carpentier y el realismo mágico," *Revista Iberoamericana* 86 (1974)

_____ *Alejo Carpentier: the Pilgrim at Home*, Ithaca, New York: Cornell University Press, 1977; 2nd edition Austin: University of Texas Press, 1990

Shaw, Donald L., *Alejo Carpentier*, Boston: Twayne, 1985

Volek, Emil, "Realismo mágico entre la modernidad y la postmodernidad," *INTI* 31 (1990); different version in his *Literatura hispanoamericana entre la modernidad y la postmodernidad*, Cuadernos de Trabajo 9, Bogotá: Facultad de Ciencias Humanas, Universidad Nacional de Colombia, 1994

Young, Richard A., *Carpentier: El reino de este mundo*, London: Grant and Cutler, 1983

El siglo de las luces

Novel by Alejo Carpentier

It was not possible for John Sturrock, responsible for the English version of this novel, to provide a literal translation of its title since it would have sounded totally pedestrian and flat. However, he captures the spirit of the work by availing himself of another title, that of a key painting in *El siglo de las luces*. The title of the book in the original Spanish, the "Age of Enlightenment," carries a heavy ironic charge, while the painting, "Explosion in a Cathedral," encapsulates an apparent paradox by depicting a grandiose church captured in the very instant of its collapse. Throughout his work Carpentier uses European artistic expressions to convey the fact that Latin America from the time of the Conquest has been mediated by Europe's gaze.

Carpentier's most ambitious novel, *El siglo* has a considerable canvas which covers the Caribbean basin and western Europe. It tells, in a heavily allegorical way (Carpentier detested realism in both literature and the visual arts), of Latin America's entry into the Age of Independence and Modernity. It begins with three adolescents who are closely related and members of the creole merchant class. They are Carlos and Sofía, who are brother and sister, and their asthmatic cousin, Esteban. When the father of the first two dies unexpectedly, the three young people are able to turn their lives upside down. They break all the rules of both decorum and common sense by living at night and sleeping by day; ordering from Paris crates of scientific equipment which, then, they either do not unpack or put to ludic uses. What matters, though, and Carpentier does not believe in applying a light touch, is that here are three young people, intoxicated with the thought of the *Encyclopédistes* (who nourished the ideas of the French revolutionaries) and who are living in the dark on the eve of the French Revolution. Carpentier offers his readers a Bildungsroman in which Esteban and Sofía grow up by learning what the praxis of the Revolution signifies, particularly when its impact is felt in the New World. These two characters respond to the hard truths of experience in radically different ways: Esteban, sceptical and disgusted, returns to Havana, which had been his point of departure. He vows that he will never again participate in any revolutionary struggle because "No hay más Tierra Prometida que la que el hombre puede encontrar en sí mismo" (The only promised land is that which man may find within himself). Sofía's response is very different in that once she has realized that her lover, Victor Hugues, is a man of straw, she emancipates herself and instead of going back home she proceeds to Madrid. There she is joined by Esteban, whereupon the two of them disappear forever in the course of the uprising against the Napoleonic forces on 2 May 1808. Carlos, Sofía's older brother, travels from Havana to Madrid and tries to piece together the last moments of the two who perished. Sofía, it seems, grabbed a rusty old lance attached to a wall and declared, as she dragged her cousin along behind her: "¡Hay que hacer algo!" (We must do something!). This expression is one of several that are repeated in the novel. This particular one serves to illustrate how Sofía develops from a young girl, who can think only in terms of looking after or supporting "her man," into a mature human being able to accept her responsibilities as a member of a wider community, to the point that she is able to give her life to assist in freeing a people from tyranny. (This notion of individual sacrifice for others is to occupy centre stage in a later and more politicized novel by Carpentier, *La consagración de la primavera* [The Rite of Spring]).

El siglo de las luces reveals the gap between revolutionary theory and practice. Thus slavery is abolished in the early, heady years of the revolutionary process, only to be reintroduced some years later when Napoleon comes to power. But Carpentier makes a point of indicating that some Blacks escape reinslavement and create *palenques*, jungle or bush communities which, in certain cases, lasted for decades. Another point that the author makes here as elsewhere in his writings, concerns what he terms "desajuste cronológico," that is, a time lapse between the exposition of ideas in Europe and their arrival and application in the New World. Thus Victor Hugues orders the destruction of a church in a Caribbean town he is besieging only to discover too late that France is no longer an atheistic state, accepting instead the cult of the Supreme Being. What concerned Carpentier was what he perceived as his continent's cultural dependence on Europe and how aping European fashions (King Henri Christophe in *El reino de este mundo* illustrates this point) does not allow people to develop their own authentic regional being. Julio Ortega has looked at the protagonists in relation to history and concludes that they can only participate in it when they are estranged from it, that is outside their marginal, colonial world. Their estrangement is registered in the repeated use of images from the theatre and the metaphor of spectacle. However, it should be noted that the character most closely connected with theatrical imagery is a Frenchman, Victor Hugues, who struts about giving an imitation of Robespierre, the political role model he cannot outgrow.

Another target for criticism is the emphasis placed by the French revolutionaries on rationalism and the abstract representation of the divine. For Carpentier the cultivation of the life of the spirit was essential to the wellbeing of humankind. As he puts it succinctly in the novel: "El Ser Supremo era un dios sin historia" (The Supreme Being was a god without history), making it clear that religion is an essential aspect of culture and that to seek to deprive people of it is a form of mutilation. Hence the emphasis placed throughout on the guillotine whose blade severs heads, that is, it does away with tradition and also has to be kept sheathed so as to avoid its slow corrosion by the action of nature, or, revolutionary praxis as opposed to theory. The same point is made in the magnificent central chapter (XXIV) through a reference to a piece of glass whose cutting edge has been softened in the course of its long, aimless journey across the Atlantic. Tradition must not be destroyed; some elements of continuity are essential, and the steady rhythms of life survive the turbulence of revolutionary attempts at radical change. Thus when the former slaves burn down the town of Cap Haitien, the disaster is depicted in the background, as though in soft focus. In sharp focus, in the forefront of the image, is a fisherman who mends his nets.

Like other historical novels by Carpentier, *El siglo* is set in a very specific time and place. Yet no dates are given save, with great irony, some from the French revolutionary calendar, and the reason for this is that history is seen in terms of a spiral. There are no exact repetitions; instead a series of similar man-made "acontecimientos" or great events. Thus the Caribbean is represented as the site of a series of invasions: the Caribs travel north into the Caribbean but disaster befalls them when they encounter new arrivals in the region, for the Spanish conquerors have arrived. When Victor Hugues leaves La Rochelle at the head of an expeditionary force to the Caribbean, the author makes a comparison with the first voyage of Columbus. The possibility of human beings attaining perfection, expressed through the upward and expanding movement of the helix, figures significantly in the central chapter, XXIV, when Esteban, in a brief ecstatic interlude outside historical time, contemplates a conch shell and exclaims "Te déum" (Praise God).

VERITY SMITH

See also entry on Magical Realism

Editions

First edition: *El siglo de las luces*, Mexico City: Compañía General de Ediciones, 1962
Critical edition: The closest to one is that published in 1979 by Ayacucho, Caracas. It has a prologue by Carlos Fuentes, and a chronology and bibliographies by Araceli García Carranza
Translation: *Explosion in a Cathedral*, by John Sturrock, Boston: Little Brown, and London: Gollancz, 1963

Further Reading

Labanyi, Jo, "Nature and the Historical Process in *El siglo de las luces*," *Bulletin of Hispanic Studies* 57 (1980) [Bold in conception and persuasive in argument, this article deserves much wider recognition]
Ortega, Julio, *The Poetics of Change: the New Spanish-American Narrative*, translated by Galen D. Greaser, Austin: University of Texas Press, 1984
Souza, Raymond D., *La historia en la novela hispanoamericana moderna*, Bogotá: Tercer Mundo, 1988 [Chapter 1 is on this novel]

Tomás Carrasquilla 1858–1940

Colombian prose writer

Before the 1960s, when Gabriel García Márquez captured the world's attention, Tomás Carrasquilla was Colombia's best-known and most popular writer and for many years Colombian narrative was identified with his name. Although Carrasquilla's narratives were, in the main, written and published in the first decades of the 20th century, his aesthetics is firmly based on literary ideology of the preceding century. Carrasquilla writes in the tradition of 19th-century Realism (*realismo*) and, more specifically, within two common manifestations of that school: first, regionalism (*regionalismo*) – the works are set in a specific locale, in the case of Carrasquilla, in Antioquia, his native province, and second, *costumbrismo* which focuses on the daily life of the people and attempts to reproduce in detail their costumes, tradition and speech in a language that is picturesque and often idiosyncratic to the region. Carrasquilla was hailed early in the century as the "best regionalist writer in America" by the Spanish critic Julio Cejador y Frauca because the Spanish believed that Carrasquilla's work both synthesized and developed the aesthetic concerns of the Realist tradition. In his production – as in that of many other regionalist and costumbrist writers – the evils of the city is a recurring theme.

Frutos de mi tierra, 1896 [Fruits of My Native Land] was his first novel and it received immediate acclaim. Its criticism of the hypocrisy of life in a small town appealed to a wide readership. In this, as in subsequent works, Carrasquilla uses a simple plot peopled with colorful characters. The novel attracts as much for its imitation of the colorful and peculiar language of the characters as for its intrigue. Carrasquilla developed this regionalism in a significant number of short stories and novels. Among the latter, *El Padre Casafús*, 1914 [Father Casafús] is of particular interest. Carrasquilla believed that his novella *Salve, Regina*, 1903 [Hail, Regina] – allegedly written in one week, and published in a volume with other stories – was his best work. The critics, however, point to *La Marquesa de Yolombó*, 1928 [The Marchioness of Yolombó] as his masterpiece. The action of the novel takes place at the end of the 18th century and is an anatomy of colonial society set against a stark background of life dominated by a mining economy. Carrasquilla depicts this world in an ambivalent light – it generated jobs and wealth, but it was centered and sustained by the power of a corrupt nobility in league with an unscrupulous Catholic Church. The wealth it brought was paid for by a social system characterized by gross inequality and racial prejudice, with a parasitic class of nobles backed by a church that often encouraged blatant superstition rather than forgo its institutional wealth and power.

In his last novel, the trilogy *Hace tiempos*, 1935–36 [Long Ago] Carrasquilla examines the transformation of Colombian society in the 19th century from one of mining to one of agriculture and commerce. Bound to this process are religious beliefs both Christian and pagan. Religious syncretism is the abstract representation of the racial miscegenation that occurred in colonial times; it is also an enduring leitmotif in Carrasquilla's work. It is to be found in his first published work, "Simón el mago," 1896 [Simon the Magus] as well as in his best-known short story, "En la diestra de Dios padre," 1897 [In the Right Hand of God the Father].

Carrasquilla ferociously opposed Spanish American *Modernismo* – the literary movement most in vogue in Latin America at the end of the 19th and the beginning of the 20th centuries. The *modernista* school, very strong in Bogotá, returned the favor. The modernists' concern with the purity of language made Carrasquilla's rich patois – the willy-nilly juxtaposition of localisms, vernacular Spanish, colloquialisms, anachronisms and classic Castilian – anathema to the new generation of writers. It also made his work extremely difficult to translate, and is in part the explanation for the paucity of translations of his works.

Carrasquilla is a crucial figure in the production of a national culture in Colombia. His is the creation of a local literature rather than an imitation of foreign, mostly Spanish models. Other writers were to follow his lead. Carrasquilla's work signals the waning of Romanticism in Colombian narrative and it helped establish narrative patterns that would dominate Colombian fiction for decades to come.

Taken altogether, Carrasquilla's literary production is quite varied, consisting of novellas, novels, short stories and *cuadros de costumbres* (brief works that use a "slice of life" to reveal a particular aspect of regional culture). Carrasquilla's work is diverse, but is not of uniform high quality. His output is at times overdrawn and now quite redundant. None the less, it contains much to recommend it and can be of inestimable value to students of Colombian literature and culture.

GILBERTO GÓMEZ OCAMPO

Biography

Born in Santo Domingo, Antioquia, Colombia, 1858, into a middle-class family. Led a largely uneventful life. Enrolled as student of law at Antioquia University in 1876, but studies were interrupted by the outbreak of civil war. Worked at a variety of jobs including as a tailor, a teacher and as a secretary to a judge. Seldom travelled outside Antioquia and remained a bachelor all his life. Lived in Bogotá for two periods (1895 and 1914–19). In 1928, suffered a fall which left him wheelchair bound. By 1934 he was completely blind, and dictated his most famous work, *Hace tiempos*. Awarded the Cruz de Boyacá, Colombia's highest honour, in 1935; Vergara Prize for literature and science, 1937. In 1940, his leg was amputated due to gangrene and this led to his death in the capital of Antioquia, Medellín, in 1940.

Selected Works

Novels

Frutos de mi tierra, Bogotá: Minerva, 1896
Grandeza, Medellín, Colombia: Oficial, 1910
El Padre Casafús, Medellín, Colombia: Oficial, 1914
Entrañas de niño, Medellín, Colombia: Librería de Carlos E. Rodríguez, 1914
El Zarco, Bogotá: Minerva, 1925
Ligia Cruz; Rogelio, Bogotá: Ediciones Colombia, 1926
La Marquesa de Yolombó, Medellín, Colombia: Librería de A.J. Cano, 1928
Hace tiempos: memorias de Eloy Jamboa, 3 vols, Medellín, Colombia: Atlántida, 1935–36

Short Fiction

Salve, Regina, Medellín, Colombia: Atlántida, 1903
Dominicales, Medellín, Colombia: Atlántida, 1934
De tejas arriba, Medellín, Colombia: Atlántida, 1936
Seis cuentos, Mexico City: Andrea, 1959

Critical Editions

Frutos de mi tierra, edited by Seymour Menton, Bogotá: Instituto Caro y Cuervo, 1972
La Marquesa de Yolombó, edited by Kurt L. Levy, Bogotá: Instituto Caro y Cuervo, 1974

Compilations and Anthologies

Obras completas, with an introduction by Federico de Onís, Madrid: Espasa Calpe, 1952
Cuentos de Tomás Carrasquilla, Medellín, Colombia: Bedout, 1956

Further Reading

Levy, Kurt L., *Vida y obras de Tomás Carrasquilla*, Medellín, Colombia: Bedout, 1958
_____ *Tomás Carrasquilla*, Boston: Twayne, 1980
Maya, Rafael, *Los orígenes del modernismo en Colombia*, Bogotá: Nacional, 1961
Mejía Duque, Jaime, *Tomás Carrasquilla*, Bogotá: Procultura, 1990
Rodríguez, R. and Angela Rocío, *Las novelas de Don Tomás Carrasquilla*, Medellín, Colombia: Autores Antioqueños, 1988
Sylvester, Nigel, *The Homilies and "Dominicales" of Tomás Carrasquilla*, Liverpool: Centre for Latin American Studies, University of Liverpool, 1971

Jorge Carrera Andrade 1903–1976

Ecuadorian poet and prose writer

At the heart of Jorge Carrera Andrade's work there is a preoccupation with certain themes: travel, movement, exile, the relationship between human beings and nature. As he himself acknowledged, "el viaje se hizo la razón misma de mi vida" [travelling became the very reason for my life]. Travel in this context takes a more profound meaning than that of simply visiting places, suggesting instead a metaphor for life itself. Exile, equally, has to be understood in a metaphysical rather than a strictly political sense. This is not to say that Carrera Andrade was uninterested in politics. On the contrary, in his early years he became actively involved in the political events in his native Ecuador as the Socialist Party's General Secretary and was even imprisoned as a result of his activities. His commitment to politics was reflected in his early work. He wrote revolutionary poetry and edited an opposition newspaper. Like many other Ecuadorian poets of his generation, Carrera Andrade saw *Modernismo*, which arrived late in Ecuador, as an instrument for the renovation of literary language, as well as a vehicle for the expression of their general sense of dissatisfaction and rebellion. He was, nevertheless, disappointed at the lack of social and political concern expressed in *modernista* writings.

Although an eminent a poet, Carrera Andrade produced a number of works in prose where he dealt with contemporary problems that interested him. Chiefly among his prose works is his history of Ecuador, *El camino del sol* [The Path of the Sun], where he takes a somewhat idealistic view of his country's past. He wrote also accounts of his travels and various volumes of literary history and criticism.

Despite tackling social and political issues, as in his indianist "Cuaderno de poemas indios" [Dossier of Indian Poems], Carrera Andrade cultivated what is essentially a lyrical approach to poetic creation. In his poems he pays close attention to every minute detail as if offering a microscopic view of objects. His poetry, in fact, is characterized by an acute observation of nature. The latter, for Carrera Andrade, is full of signs and portents, as in his poem "Presagios" [Presages]. He sees the objects of nature arranged in meaningful patterns which have to be decoded and understood. The object, hence, becomes an icon, a three-dimensional symbol capable of conveying a message. For Carrera Andrade things are alive and will speak to us if only we listen to them.

This seems to point towards a pantheistic stance on the part of the poet. Instead of seeing nature as the ultimate deity, however, Carrera Andrade's poetry seems to imply that divinity can be found in every object and creature. This is evident in his poem "Cada objeto es un mundo" [Each Object is a World] which brings him close to animism. In poems like "Versión de la tierra" [Earth's Version] or "Taller del tiempo" [Workshop of Time] he seems to support the idea of the existence of secret currents uniting all creatures and objects of nature with human beings. Indeed, he perceives the role of the poet as that of an interpreter of the silent voices of objects, engaging in conversations with them and deciphering their messages for the benefit of others: "interpretar las apariencias del mundo y decifrar el lenguaje de las cosas para darles a entender a los otros hombres, contribuyendo de esa manera a que la vida humana sea digna de vivirse" (to interpret the world's appearances and to decipher the language of things in order to make them understood by other people, and in that way contribute to make human life worth living).

In his poetry Carrera Andrade has managed to reconcile the above aspects with his social concerns through his deep sense of solidarity with all human beings, as evidenced above all in "Hombre planetario" [Planetary Man], where he aspires to be the embodiment of all humankind. This seems to contrast somehow with the more introspective aspects of his work, like his sense of solitude, his aversion to modern civilization, and his metaphysical considerations.

As the title of his poem "Apetito de realidad" [Hunger for Reality] reveals, Carrera Andrade, far from advocating fantasy or a subjective view of the universe, yearns for an ever closer relationship with the physical world inhabited by human beings. This, he implies, can only be achieved through the accurate study of reality. As he confesses in "El objeto y su sombra," reality, for him, has a stronger fascination than dreams or abstractions.

WILLIAM SPINDLER LI

Biography

Born in Quito, capital of Ecuador, 18 September 1903. Attended Catholic schools until 1916 and then transferred to a lay-school, the Instituto Nacional Mejía. Began study of law at University of Quito in 1921, abandoned his studies in 1923. Employed by Ministry of Education, 1924. Appointed General Secretary of Ecuadorian Socialist Party, 1926. In 1928 appointed representative at Fifth International Congress in Moscow, but denied visa in Hamburg and forced to return to Paris. Made Secretary of the Association of Latin American Students in the same year. Visited Paris in 1929, where he worked as private secretary for Gabriela Mistral, then settled in Barcelona. Returned to Quito, 1933. Joined consular service in 1934 and held numerous diplomatic postings: Ecuadorian Chargé d'Affaires in Venezuela, 1943, resigned, 1946; Minister plenipotentiary to United Kingdom, 1947; Permanent delegate to UNESCO, 1951, subsequently editor of their publications in Spanish; Ecuadorian delegate to United Nations, 1960; Ambassador to Venezuela, 1961. From 1969–71 taught Spanish American literature at State University of New York. Died in Quito, 11 November 1976.

Selected Works

Poetry

El estanque inefable, Quito: Universidad Centro, 1922
La guirnalda del silencio, Quito: Imprenta Nacional, 1926
Boletines de mar y tierra, Barcelona: Cervantes, 1930
El tiempo manual, Madrid: Ediciones Literatura, 1935
Biografía para uso de los pájaros, Paris: Cuadernos del Hombre Nuevo, 1937
La hora de las ventanas iluminadas, Santiago de Chile: Ercilla, 1937
Microgramas, Tokyo: Asia-America, 1940
País secreto, Tokyo: Talleres Bunsh-Sha, 1940
Canto al puente de Oakland / To the Bay Bridge, translated by Eleanor L. Turnbull, Stanford, California: Stanford University Press, 1941 [bilingual edition]
Lugar de origen, Caracas: Ediciones al Servicio de la Cultura, 1945
Canto a las fortalezas volantes: cuaderno del paracaidista, Caracas: Destino, 1945
El visitante de niebla y otros poemas, Quito: Casa de la Cultura Ecuatoriana, 1947; as *The Visitor of Mist*, translated by G.R. Coulthard, London: Williams and Norgate, 1950
Aquí yace la espuma, Paris: Editorial Presencias Americanas, 1950
Familia de la noche, Paris: Librería Española de Ediciones, 1953
Moneda del forastero: Monnaie de l'étranger, translated by Jean Mazoyer, Dijon, France: Chambelland, 1958
Hombre planetario, Bogotá: Mito, 1959
Floresta de los guacamayos, Managua: Nicaragüense, 1964
Crónica de las Indias, Paris: Centre de Recherches de l'Institut d'Études Hispaniques, 1965
Poesía última, Havana: Casa de las Américas, 1968
Libro del destierro, Dakar, Senegal: University of Dakar, 1970 [bilingual edition]
Vocación terrena, in the collection *Árbol de fuego* 51, Caracas (1972)
Misterios naturales, Paris: Centre de Recherches de l'Institut d'Études Hispaniques, 1972

Other Writings

Cartas de un emigrado, Quito: Elan, 1933
Latitudes (hombres, viajes, lecturas), Quito: América, 1934
Guía de la joven poesía ecuatoriana, Tokyo: Ediciones Asia-América, 1939
Mirador terrestre, New York: Las Américas, 1943
Rostros y climas: crónicas de viajes, hombres y sucesos de nuestro tiempo, Paris: Ediciones de la Maison de l'Amérique Latine, 1948
Poesía francesa contemporánea, Quito: Casa de la Cultura, 1951
La tierra siempre verde, Paris: Ediciones Internacionales, 1955
El camino del sol, Quito: Casa de Cultura Ecuatoriana, 1958
Galería de místicos y de insurgentes: la vida intelectual del Ecuador, 1555–1955, Quito: Casa de la Cultura Ecuatoriana, 1959
Viaje por países y libros, Quito: Casa de la Cultura Ecuatoriana, 1961
El fabuloso reino de Quito, Quito: Casa de la Cultura Ecuatoriana, 1963
Presencia del Ecuador en Venezuela, Quito: Colón, 1963
Interpretación de Rubén Darío, Managua: Cuadernos Darianos, 1964
Radiografía de la cultura ecuatoriana, Managua: Ministerio de Educación Pública, 1964
Retrato cultural del Ecuador, Paris: Institut d'Études Hispaniques de l'Université de Paris, 1965
Interpretaciones hispanoamericanas, Quito: Casa de la Cultura Ecuatoriana, 1967
Las relaciones culturales entre el Ecuador y Francia, Quito: Edición del Ministerio de Educación Pública, 1967
El volcán y el colibrí, Puebla, Mexico: José M. Cajica, Jr, 1970 [autobiography]
Reflections on Spanish-American Poetry, translated by Don C. Bliss and Gabriella de C. Bliss, Albany: State University of New York Press, 1973

Compilations and Anthologies

Rol de la manzana (1926–1929), Madrid: Espasa Calpe, 1935
Registro del mundo: antología poética, 1922–1939, Quito: Grupo "America," 1940
Poesías escogidas, Caracas: Suma, 1945
Edades poéticas (1922–1956), Quito: Casa de la Cultura Ecuatoriana, 1958
Los primeros poemas de Jorge Carrera Andrada, Lírica Hispana, Caracas, vol. 20/234 (1962)
Mi vida en poemas, Caracas: Casa del Escritor, 1962
Antología poética, Milan: La Goliardica, 1963
Selected Poems of Jorge Carrera Andrada, edited and translated by H.R. Haes, Albany: State University of New York Press, 1973 [bilingual edition]
Obra poética completa, Quito: Casa de la Cultura Ecuatoriana, 1976

Further Reading

Carrera Andrade, a significant poet, man of letters and public figure, does not enjoy critical favour at the present time, something that is reflected in the publication dates of the works cited below.
A critical re-evaluation and theoretical readings are required.

Beardsell, Peter, *Winds of Exile: the Poetry of Jorge Carrera Andrade*, Oxford: Dolphin, 1977
Cuadra, José de la, "Jorge Carrera Andrade," in *Doce siluetas, Obras completas*, Quito: Casa de la Cultura Ecuatoriana, 1958
Liscano, Juan, "Americanos en Europa: país y poesía de Jorge Carrera Andrade," *Cuadernos Americanos*, Mexico, vol. 15 (1956)
Lucio, Francisco, "Jorge Carrera Andrade y *El hombre planetario*," *Cuadernos Hispanoamericanos*, Madrid, 235 (1969)
Ojeda, Enrique, *Jorge Carrera Andrade: introducción al estudio de su vida y de su obra*, New York: Eliseo Torres and Sons, 1971
Reyes, Alfonso, *et al.*, *Jorge Carrera Andrade y la crítica*, Madrid: Espasa Calpe, 1935 [Extracts from newspaper reviews, etc.]
Salinas, Pedro, "Registro de Jorge Carrera Andrade," *Revista Iberoamericana*, vol. 5/10 (1942)
Straub, William J., "Cosmovisión de Jorge Carrera Andrade," *Cuadernos Americanos*, Mexico City, 181 (1972)
____ "Conversación con Jorge Carrera Andrade," *Revista Iberoamericana*, vol. 38/79 (1972)

Cada objeto es un mundo

Poem by Jorge Carrera Andrade

Given below is the complete text of this poem from the section "Taller del tiempo," 1958 [Workshop of Time] in the volume *Hombre planetario* (1959):

"Cada objeto es un mundo"

Arte poético
Comprende, comprende, comprende:
en cada cosa guiña un duende
o una ala invisible se tiende.

Apresa en tus dedos la brisa
que pasa fugaz, indecisa,
No veas el mundo de prisa.
No aprendas efímera ciencia,
que es flor de la humana demencia.
La vida no es sólo apariencia.

Las aves – lección del instante –
nos dan en su escuela volante
la clave de un mundo cambiante.
La rosa es crisol de alegría.
Te ofrece tesoros el día.
Gotea el reloj ambrosía.

Comprende y venera al objeto:
Penetra en ese orbe secreto
y sea la flor tu amuleto.

[Know, know, know: / an invisible wing spreads out / or a sprite winks from every thing. // Grasp the fleeting, undecided breeze in your fingers / Pause to drink in the world. // Do not learn ephemeral science, / for it is a flower of human insanity. / Life is more than appearances. // Birds – lesson of the instant – / give us in their flying school / the key to an ever-changing world. // The rose is a crucible of happiness. // The day offers you treasures. // The clock drips ambrosia. // Grasp and venerate the object: / enter that secret orb / and may the flower be your amulet.]

"Cada objeto es un mundo" is one of the poems by Jorge Carrera Andrade that best express his ideas on the nature of poetry and its relationship to the world of objects. This relates to the poet's view of Nature as a living force present in every object and creature, and to his belief in the possibility of finding and restoring the secret correspondences which bind human beings to this force. In order to achieve this feat, the poet must first learn to decipher the language of objects.

The importance that Carrera Andrade attaches to this poem, as his personal interpretation of poetic art, is evidenced in the insistence with which the first line repeats the word "understand," no less than three times. Carrera Andrade's ideas, as illustrated in this poem, bring him very close to animism, a belief in the presence of the sacred in all things. This is made explicit in the second line which refers to the vital force which, according to the Ecuadorian poet, enlivens all things: a "duende," a kind of forest spirit which hides mischievously behind apparently inanimate things from where it winks at us. The notion of a hidden dimension to all objects is continued in the next line which seems to allude to the existence of angels, with the idea of "una ala invisible" (an invisible wing).

In the next verses Carrera Andrade reaffirms his belief in the possibility of capturing and recording life's transitory experiences, making, as it were, time stand still, through a detailed observation of the world. Such an observation, he suggests, will reveal the true essence of things. He appears to consider the knowledge arrived at through this method as superior to that achieved by "efímera ciencia" (ephemeral science), which he considers a "flor de la humana demencia" (a flowering of human madness) which cannot penetrate beyond the mere appearance of things. In the poem, in fact, he warns against a hasty view of the world: "No veas el mundo de prisa." In a constantly changing universe the only transcendental values are those of Nature itself. This is Nature's lesson delivered in line ten of the poem by the flying birds.

More than a subjective interpretation of the world, the poet seems to be prescribing a search for an intense objectivity based in the appraisal of the intrinsic qualities of objects, in their presence and materiality. Hence the need to penetrate into an "orbe secreto" [secret world] within reality. There, he reassures us, lies the path to the treasures hidden in everyday things like a rose, a recurrent motif in his poetry, a clock, or the day itself. Ultimately, Carrera Andrade's position could be termed idolatrous, in the strictest sense of the word, for his belief in the need to understand Nature's messages as encoded in the iconic language of objects leads him to consider the latter as worthy, not only of comprehension, but of veneration. The final line accentuates the magical, and at the same time lyrical, component of his poetic vision: "sea la flor tu amuleto" (let the flower be your amulet). This poem, like many others by the Ecuadorian poet, seems to bring Jorge Carrera Andrade close to the aesthetic project espoused by some magical realist novelists whose narratives, like Carrera Andrade's poems, emphasize the magical aspects of everyday reality.

WILLIAM SPINDLER LI

Poem transliterated by Verity Smith

Editions
First edition: *Hombre planetario*, Bogotá: Ediciones de la Revista Mito, 1959

Miguel de Carrión 1875–1929

Cuban prose writer and physician

The literary work of Miguel de Carrión belongs to the current of the Naturalist and psychological novel of the first Republican generation. In his thesis novels Carrión tries to show, with a didactic purpose, the evils Cuba faces and which threaten the future of the country. He shares with authors of his generation an acute preoccupation with the problems confronting the newly-formed Republic, finally freed from Spanish colonialism. Among the most important characteristics of his work is the successful psychological development of his female characters, whose creation must have been helped by his experience as a doctor and teacher. As in the Realist novels of Benito Pérez Galdós, in those of the Cuban writer the life of the characters is interwoven with the historical, political and social background of the country, making them a rich source of information on the period.

The recurrent theme in the fiction of Carrión is the love between man and woman; a theme which enables him to bring into the open the prejudices and taboos, the double standards and hypocrisy of the period. Like other writers of his generation, he advocates a liberal education for women and rejects the repressions of a sexual nature which religion imposes on the life of the time. Influenced by the trends of French Naturalism, which emphasizes the fulfilment of physical love for the happiness of the individual, and by his own work as a doctor, he realizes the need for a new type of education which would create men and women free from prejudices, and able to develop mentally and physically in a healthy and harmonious way. His great urge was that Cubans should open their minds to new ways of thinking and truly emancipate themselves from the backwardness and narrow-mindedness of centuries of colonial rule. From this point of view his novels carry great didactic weight.

His first novel, *El milagro*, 1903 [The Miracle] is structured on the polarity of religious-secular life, cloister-country, heaven-earth, and shows the author's concern for the freedom of choice of the individual. The action is set in the country as though to establish more clearly the strength of the dictates of nature which, after a long inner struggle, finally lead the hero to choose a love which is healthy, normal and procreative. In this work, however, the deep social concern of his later novels is not evident.

After years of hard work, dedicated at first to education and later to medicine, in 1917 Carrión published *Las honradas* [Respectable Women], which was a commercial success. The central theme of this novel is the sexual repression of a young married woman who, though educated to hypocritical moral standards, is capable of realizing the social injustices affecting women. All the characters are so well developed psychologically that it is possible to be aware of the psychological background of the period, as also of the social context. *Las honradas* was considered a pornographic novel by those who supported that same intransigent and narrow-minded moral code which Carrión criticizes and attempts to unmask.

Two years later he offset *Las honradas* with *Las impuras* [Fallen Women]. The characters in both novels are interwoven in such a way as to represent a kind of socio-historical saga of Cuban society. They show that morality has nothing to do with the body, whether it be naked or clothed, but rather with a human being's capacity for honesty and understanding. A succession of characters, particularly female ones – who suffer the oppression of an atmosphere and inheritance within the family and socially which conditions them to a life of servility – parade across the pages of both novels. Showing steadfastness and daring in his day, and in order to instruct, in his novels Carrión unveils the intimate life of Cuban society and lays bare the canons of a morality which only produces unhappy homes and frustrated lives. Today his work could undoubtedly be placed within the present feminist trend. Several of his courageous and rebellious female characters fit the definition perfectly.

It is worth mentioning that between the first and last of Miguel de Carrión's novels his frustration and disenchantment with moral, political and social corruption in Cuba becomes evident. In *El milagro*, written almost entirely while he was in exile and published at the birth of the Republic, hope triumphs; the hero is saved and the forces of love are the victors in the vast open space of the countryside. On the other hand, in his last novel, *La esfinge* [The Sphinx], the heroine commits suicide, because she is unable to break through the moral barriers inculcated into her, which makes her repress her instincts and withhold herself from the man she loves. For this novel the author chooses enclosed areas. The ancestral home in Havana is a symbol of the oppressive forces which finally destroy the central character. Carrión may well have portrayed the house in *La esfinge* as a microcosm of Cuba, where the heroine, just as the country, had yielded to the forces of a stifling reality. Compared with his first novel, the author's tone in the final one, shows that he too has surrendered to despair and frustration over the facts of national life.

MARÍA L. NEGRÍN
translated by Patricia James

Biography
Born in Havana, Cuba, 9 April 1875, only son of a physician. Spent the period of the second war of Cuban Independence in the US with his parents. On his return to Cuba in 1898 he became a teacher. In 1903 he founded a journal for teachers, *Cuba Pedagógica*. Married Lucía Rivero Beltrán in 1904; only child, María Antonia, born in 1914. Qualified as a doctor of medicine in 1908 and established a cancer research laboratory, the first of its kind in Cuba. Appointed Professor of medicine at Havana University in 1910. From 1917 to 1929 was Professor of anatomy and physiology at the teacher's training college in Havana. Director of this institution from 1926 to 1928. He was a contributor to *El Heraldo de Cuba* and to several other journals and newspapers. Founder member of the National Academy of Arts and Letters. Died in 1929

Selected Works

Novels
El milagro, Havana: Azul y Rojo, 1903
La última voluntad, Havana: A. Castillo, 1903
Las honradas, Havana: Editorial Librería Nueva, 1917
Las impuras, Havana: Nuestra Novela, 1919
Nochebuena, Havana: Nuestra Novela, 1924
La esfinge, Havana: Comisión Nacional Cubana de la Unesco, 1961

Further Reading
Casey, Calvert, "Carrión o la desnudez," in *Cuba en la Unesco. Homenaje a Miguel de Carrión*, Havana: Comisión Nacional Cubana de la Unesco, 1961
González Muza, L., *La novela y el cuento psicológicos de Miguel de Carrión*, Miami: Universal, 1979
Ibarra, Jorge, *Un análisis psicosocial del cubano: 1898–1925*, Havana: Editorial de Ciencias Sociales, 1985 [Chapter 3 is on the Naturalist novel in Cuba]

Julián del Casal 1863–1893

Cuban poet

Julián del Casal shared with José Martí, Rubén Darío and Manuel Gutiérrez Nájera the initial stages of Modernism in Spanish American literature. His poetic work begins with *Hojas al viento*, 1890 [Leaves in the Wind] The title of this collection refers to the Romantic current then still in vogue among writers in the Hispanic world, but where it was already possible to detect elements belonging to the early stages of a renewal. The main strength of *Hojas al viento* is the need to find unusual literary motifs, thereby shifting the perceptions of both author and reader to barely explored areas of reality and culture. Equally strong is the cultivation of form which, in the best pages of the volume, produces texts in which artistic quality seems to becomes the main subject of the poetry.

In his second book of poems, *Nieve*, 1892 [Snow], Casal reveals a personal assimilation of Parnassian influence, with a special debt to Leconte de Lisle and José María de Heredia, who wrote *Les Trophées* [The Trophies]. The determination to work to exacting standards is evident here in the attention to textual detail of which each poem is the fruit, as well as in the concept of the book as such, divided into five sections that refer to thematic and formal criteria. Throughout the first three sections: "Bocetos antiguos" [Sketches from Ancient Times]; "Mi museo ideal"[My Ideal Museum] and "Cromos españoles" [Spanish Prints], Casal displays his talent at recreating scenes from Græco-Latin mythology, Judeo-Christian tradition, Gustave Moreau's paintings and Iberian folklore, indirectly injecting them with his personality. The second section, based on ten paintings by Moreau, represents the climax of the symbol in Casal. Here he creates the most subtle and significant allusions to a convulsed eroticism. In the last two sections, "Marfiles viejos" [Old Ivory] and "La gruta del ensueño"[The Grotto of Daydreams], the poetic first person, absent in the earlier sections, governs the literary discourse, which gives a steady balance to the structure of the volume. This section has a confessional tone; when the writer uses symbols, he does so in a clear and unequivocal way, stating rather than suggesting, establishing a free and easy, almost conversational discourse.

Casal's third book, *Bustos y rimas*, 1893 [Busts and Rhymes], published soon after his sudden death, brings together a group of biographical sketches in prose [Busts] and another in verse [Rhymes]. The lyrical section carries the voice of "Marfiles viejos" and "La gruta del ensueño" into full maturity. Here, the author's literary personality is consolidated around an aesthetic creed that, sketched out by Casal from his early years as a poet, is defined best in a series of antitheses: the city versus the countryside; sumptuous interiors versus the outdoors in inclement weather; knowledge versus innocence; pain versus joy; and precious worked metals that dull "the radiance of the sparkling stars." With the dark lucidity that brought to him the premonition of his own death, Casal's voice becomes prophetic, entering a world whose unreality threatens not only the poet but reality itself.

Often termed escapist and decadent, Casal's poetry represents a culminating point in the development of Cuban literature. Written with a vocation for cosmopolitanism that reveals itself as a longing for universality, his poetry emerges after a stubborn process of national reinforcement. The place that Casal's poetry takes in this process, characterized by successive breaks that aspire to form a continuity, is truly unique and even contradictory. His voice is not inscribed in the extensive body of Cuban patriotic poetry, in spite of having denounced "los golpes estridentes / del látigo que suena todavía" (the harsh crack of the whip that echoes still); the Island's nature, described by his predecessors in ways ranging from the descriptive to the symbolic, was not to his taste, when he did not renounce it openly. For him Woman, both as a reality and as a poetic subject, represented "centres of disgust." However, "that fine spirit, that timid and tender affection" which, according to José Martí, characterized the poet, constitutes one of the purest values of Cuban culture. Though his poetry contains a range of metric and stanzaic forms that have been acknowledged as characteristic of Spanish American *Modernismo*, while abounding also in expressive resources aimed at renewal, Casal does not possess the stylistic greatness of Martí or Darío. His main contribution to the rise of the new Spanish American poetry was the perfect literary expression of his personality, distinguished by a feeling of extreme and sincere anguish in which Hispanic stoicism and the challenge to an unjust mortality (the term in Spanish is "agonismo") coincide; outlines of a humanist ethics which, in Latin America, tend to blend into a spiritual synthesis, detectable in the work of some of the major writers such as Martí himself and César Vallejo.

EMILIO DE ARMAS

translated by Verity Smith and Tristán White

Biography

Born in Havana, Cuba, 7 November 1863. Attended primary and secondary school in that city. Began to publish poems and articles in newspapers from an early age. Worked in the Treasury and was a student in Faculty of Law but abandoned his studies. Became an important critic on art and literature; also social columnist and commmentator on a wide range of national and international issues. This work complemented his poetic output. Published in *La Habana Elegante* and *El Fígaro*. Lost his modest civil servant's job as the result of criticizing the Captain General and other Spanish dignitaries. Towards the end of 1888 he made a brief journey to Spain, hoping that he might be able to settle in Europe. Returned in January 1889, profoundly disillusioned. Supported independence from Spain and rejected Spanish literary influences in favour of French ones. Died prematurely and abruptly in 1893 of a violent haemorrhage while dining with friends.

Selected Works

Poetry

Hojas al viento: primeras poesías, Havana: El Retiro, 1890
Nieve, Havana: n.p., 1892
Bustos y rimas, Havana: Imprenta La Moderna, 1893

Compilations and Anthologies

The Poetry of Julián del Casal: a Critical Edition, 3 vols, edited by Robert Jay Glickman, Gainesville: University Presses of Florida, 1976

Poesías completas y pequeños poemas en prosa en orden cronológico, edited by Esperanza Figueroa, Miami: Universal, 1993

Further Reading

Armas, Emilio de, *Casal*, Havana: Letras Cubanas, 1981

____ "Julián del Casal y el modernismo," *Revista Iberoamericana*, vol. 56/152–53 (July–December 1990)

Blanco Aguinaga, Carlos, "Crítica marxista y poesía: lectura de un poema de Julián del Casal," in *The Analysis of Hispanic Texts: Current Trends in Methodology*, edited by Mary Ann Beck, *et al.*, New York: Bilingual Press, 1976

Clay Méndez, Luis Felipe, *Julián del Casal: estudio comparativo de prosa y poesía*, Miami: Universal, 1979

Figueroa, Esperanza, *et al.*, *Julián del Casal: estudios críticos sobre su obra*, Miami: Universal, 1974

Geada de Prulleti, Rita, "El sentido de la evasión en la poesía de Julián del Casal," *Revista Iberoamericana* 101 (January–June 1966)

____ "Bibliografía de Julián del Casal," *Revista Iberoamericana* 139 (January–June 1967)

Lezama Lima, José, "Julián del Casal," in his *Analecta del reloj*, Havana: Orígenes, 1953

Loynaz, Dulce María, "Ausencia y presencia de Julián del Casal," in her *Ensayos literarios*, Salamanca: Universidad de Salamanca, 1993

Martí, José, "Julián del Casal," *Obras completas*, vol. 5, Havana: Editorial Nacional de Cuba, 1963

Monner Sans, José, *Julián del Casal y el modernismo hispanoamericano*, Mexico City: Colegio de México, 1952

Montero, Oscar, *Erotismo y representación en Julián del Casal*, Amsterdam: Rodopi, 1993

____ "Julián del Casal and the Queers of Havana," in *¿Entiendes? Queer Readings, Hispanic Writings*, edited by Emilie Bergmann and Paul Julian Smith, Durham, North Carolina: Duke University Press, 1995

Rosario Castellanos 1925–1974

Mexican poet, dramatist and prose writer

Almost inevitably, the work of Rosario Castellanos suffered initially from the effects of her openly feminist stance in an uncompromisingly masculinist culture. Although it is possible to exaggerate the extent to which her work was marginalised by the literary establishment, in particular her later, more overtly feminist work was frequently branded as "caserita" (homespun) and overly domestic in focus (a classic sexist form of attack on women's writing). Thus her work attracted little scholarly attention while she was still alive. However, feminist writers, above all those in Mexico and North America, have acknowledged the huge contribution she made both in opening up the professional literary terrain to women, and as the first contemporary author whose writing covers the whole range of genres, she was imbued with a clear sense of what it was to be female and Mexican.

The other major theme laid out and analysed, especially in her early work and in many of her essays, was the situation of indigenous Mexicans. Here, Castellanos drew not only on her experiences as a child of their oppressors (she had been brought up in a privileged landowning family in rural Chiapas) but also as someone who was herself oppressed, on the grounds of her gender. Her writing on the theme of "race" may in many ways look dated in the light of contemporary theories of difference. However, for its time, drawing as it did on her readings of the work of Frantz Fanon and Simone Weil, as well as her experience of working for the Instituto Nacional Indigenista in her native Chiapas, it effectively re-mapped in the literary sphere the complex relationship between this form of oppression and those of gender and class in 1950s and 1960s Mexico.

Castellanos's first published work as an adult was poetry. In this she was initially influenced by the members of the literary group to which she adhered while at university in Mexico City, which became known as the Generation of 1950. She was also influenced by the work of other poets such as that of José Gorostiza, with its philosophical content and highly allegorical language, as well as by other Latin and North American women writers, for example, Gabriela Mistral and Emily Dickinson, some of whose poetry she translated.

Some critics have argued that the style and concerns of some of her early poetry, *Trayectoria del polvo*, 1948 [Trajectory of Dust], and *De la vigilia estéril*, 1950 [About the Sterile Vigil], with their biblical themes and "Interiorist" trappings, including a heavy reliance on metaphor, underwent a feminist evolution. This involved moving away from what could be categorised as the traditional "feminine" mode of Latin American poetry towards a more original style which adopted the language of an "everyday femininity," albeit with a fiercely ironic, often bitter subtext. This interpretation, if at times based on a rather selective reading of Castellanos's female poetic precursors, is convincing to an extent. In the poetry which Castellanos wrote in the late 1960s and 1970s, ancient mythical settings are replaced by the kind of modern mythical spaces of womanhood which, as contemporary feminists have noted, attempt to pass themselves off as "natural" and "common sense." Frequent use is made of parody and pastiche, replacing elaborate metaphor, to tear holes in the discourses (of psychology, the modern mass media, love and romance, the modern career woman, to name a few) which construct modern femininity. In several poems, Castellanos is expanding what it was possible for a woman poet to write about love, sex, childbearing, while at the same time employing signifiers of an anti-poetic, demythifying stance. Later poems which fall into this category are "Kinsey Report," "Se habla de Gabriel" [Speaking about Gabriel], "Pequeña crónica" [Little Chronicle], and "Entrevista de prensa" [Interview with the Press], all of 1972. However, there are certain constants in Castellanos's poetic work which should not be overlooked and which equally reveal her feminist intentions: the recourse to dramatic monologue, "spoken" by a woman, which is almost always for demythifying purposes, regardless of whether the myths are ancient, metaphor-laden ones (Malinche, Salomé, Dido) or their modern cliché-ridden counterparts (the Spinster, the Divorced Woman, and frequently, Rosario, herself), all with an undercurrent of bitterness and alienation. What changes, then, are not Castellanos's intentions but the poetic possibilities available to her, in an age increasingly influenced by the growth in mass communications and feminist discourses.

Castellanos's narrative work underwent a similar sea-change. Her first novel, *Balún-Canán*, 1957 (*The Nine Guardians*) was a highly original attempt at a fusion of two different prose genres: indigenist writing and autobiographical fiction. The indigenist part of the story – a Tzeltal uprising against the backdrop of the 1930s agrarian reforms in rural Chiapas – was an obvious choice of plot. This is partly because of her childhood experience of this area and of the impact of the reforms implemented during the presidency of Lázaro Cárdenas (1934–40). It was owed also to the resurgence of interest in this genre of writing in the mid-1950s which resulted from the government of Ruiz Cortines's promotion of a neo-Cardenist set of ideals in its rural policy. This backdrop of rural southeast Mexico was to be re-used many times in both of her early collections of short stories, and in her second novel, *Oficio de tinieblas*, 1962 (*Office of Tenebrae*). In her first novel, though, it is the autobiographical part of the story which dominates, with the first-person narration of an unnamed seven-year-old girl, whose life bears many resemblances to known events in the author's childhood, and who describes to the reader how she came to be in a position to take up a pen and write.

This novel of painful self-discovery can clearly be situated in a 20th-century tradition of women's autobiographical writing. *Oficio de tinieblas*, on the other hand, is an ambitious attempt at a more complex depiction of the relationships between the various strata of society in rural Chiapas. Perhaps it is less appealing to readers with its omniscient narrator, broken up only occasionally, as in the first novel, by indigenism's traditional recourse to lyrical passages in the style of pre-Colombian texts, such as the *Popol-Vuh* (the creation myths of the Maya Quiché people).

Both novels and many of the early Chiapas short stories are concerned with the oppression of their women characters – both from the indigenous and mestizo communities and the white ruling class – and much use is made of interior monologue to set out their plight. In Castellanos's last book of stories, *Álbum de familia*, 1971 [Family Album], while the setting shifts to contemporary Mexico City, the feminist concerns are now clearly in the forefront. As with Castellanos's later poetry, her later prose clearly owes a great deal to her knowledge of and commitment to the forms of liberal and then

of radical feminism which were emerging in a Mexico more open to "outside" discourses.

Feminism was not only a discourse from outside. In many of Castellanos's essays and also in her play, *El eterno femenino*, 1975 (*The Eternal Feminine*), she depicts and analyses the pantheon of illustrious female figures from Mexico's past (Adelita, la Malinche, Sor Juana). Much of the time the intention is to assail the various nation-building myths with which they have become associated, and also to carry out the task of "recovering" them for a feminist project. This last is a task that Castellanos had begun back in 1950 when, influenced by Simone de Beauvoir and Virginia Woolf, she wrote her Masters thesis on feminine culture. In her essays, many of which were first published in the major newspapers of the time, for example *¡Siempre!* [Always] and *Excelsior*, this feminist intent and content are conveyed in a highly original style which, like some of her poetry, frequently relies on parody and pastiche. It is the emergence of this style towards the end of her life that certain writers and critics have qualified as Castellanos's greatest contribution to Latin American letters.

CATHERINE GRANT

Biography

Born in Mexico City, 25 May 1925. Grew up in Comitán, state of Chiapas; family moved to Mexico City in 1941, after losing their estate in land reforms. Attended the Universidad Nacional Autónoma de México (UNAM), Mexico City, 1944–50, MA in philosophy 1950; studied at the University of Madrid, 1950–51. Travelled throughout Europe in 1951. Director, Chiapas cultural programmes, 1951–53, and staff member, Institute of Arts and Sciences, both in Tuxtla Gutiérrez. Director, El Teatro Guiñol (puppet theatre) for the National Indigenist Institute, San Cristóbal, 1956–59; the intention behind this venture was to incorporate Indian tribes into Western life. Toured Chiapas, 1956–58. Married Ricardo Guerra in 1958 (divorced), one son. From 1960, journalist for various newspapers and periodicals in Mexico City; press and information director, 1960–66, and Professor of comparative literature, 1967–71, UNAM; Visiting Professor of Latin American literature at the universities of Wisconsin, Indiana, and Colorado, all 1967. Mexican ambassador to Israel, Tel Aviv, and lecturer in Mexican literature, Hebrew University, Jerusalem, 1971–74. Recipient of numerous awards including the Mexican Critics' Award, 1957; Chiapas Prize, 1958; Xavier Villaurrutia Prize, 1961; Woman of the Year Award, Mexico, 1967. Died as result of an electric shock on 7 August 1974.

Selected Works

Poetry

Trayectoria del polvo, Mexico City: n.p., 1948
Apuntes para una declaración de fe, Mexico City: Ediciones de América, 1948
De la vigilia estéril, Mexico City: Ediciones de América, 1950
Presentación al templo: poemas (Madrid, 1951), with *El rescate del mundo*, Mexico City: n.p., 1952
Poemas 1953–1955, Mexico City: n.p., 1957
Al pie de la letra, Xalapa, Mexico: Universidad Veracruzana, 1959
Salomé y Judith: poemas dramáticos, Mexico City: Jus, 1959
Lívida luz, Mexico City: UNAM, 1960
Materia memorable, Mexico City: UNAM, 1969 [poetry and essays]
Bella dama sin piedad y otros poemas, Mexico City: Fondo de Cultura Económica, 1984

Novels and Short Fiction

Balún Canán, Mexico City: Fondo de Cultura Económica, 1957; as *The Nine Guardians*, translated by Irene Nicholson, London: Faber and Faber, 1958; New York: Vanguard Press, 1959

Ciudad real: cuentos, Mexico City: Novaro, 1960; as *The City of Kings*, edited by Yvette E. Miller, translated by Gloria Chacon de Arjona and Robert S. Rudder, Pittsburgh: Latin American Review Press, 1993

Oficio de tinieblas, Mexico City: Joaquín Mortiz, 1962; fragment as *Office of Tenebrae*, translated by Anne and Christopher Fremantle, in *Latin American Literature Today*, 1977

Los convidados de agosto, Mexico City: Era, 1964 [short fiction]

Álbum de familia, Mexico City: Joaquín Mortiz, 1971 [short fiction]

Play

El eterno feminino, Mexico City: Fondo de Cultura Económica, 1975; as *Just Like a Woman*, translated by V.M. Bouvier, 1984; as *The Eternal Feminine*, in *A Rosario Castellanos Reader*, 1988

Other Writings

Sobre cultura femenina, Mexico City: Ediciones de *América*, Revista Antológica, 1950 [essays]

La novela mexicana contemporánea y su valor testimonial, Mexico City: INJM, 1965

Rostros de México, photographs by Bernice Kolko, Mexico City: UNAM, 1966

Juicios sumarios: ensayos, Xalapa, Mexico: Universidad Veracruzana, 1966; revised edition as *Juicios sumarios: ensayos sobre literatura*, 2 vols, 1984

Mujer que sabe latín, Mexico City: UNAM, 1973 [literary criticism]

El uso de la palabra, edited by José Emilio Pacheco, Mexico City: Excelsior, 1974 [essays]

El mar y sus pescaditos, Mexico City: UNAM, 1975 [literary criticism]

Compilations and Anthologies

Poesía no eres tú: obra poética 1948–1971, Mexico City: Fondo de Cultura Económica, 1972

Meditación en el umbral: antología poética, edited by Julian Palley, Mexico City: Fondo de Cultura Económica, 1985; as *Meditation on the Threshold: a Bilingual Anthology of Poetry*, translated by Palley, Tempe, Arizona: Bilingual Press, 1988

Obras, edited by Eduardo Mejía, Mexico City: Fondo de Cultura Económica, 1989

Anthologies in Translation

Looking at the Mona Lisa, translated by Maureen Ahern, London: Rivelin, 1981

A Rosario Castellanos Reader, edited and translated by Maureen Ahern, et al., Austin: University of Texas Press, 1988

Selected Poems , edited by Cecilia Vicuña and Magda Bogin, translated by Bogin, St Paul, Minnesota: Graywolf Press, 1988 [bilingual edition]

Another Way to Be: Selected Works, edited and translated by Myralyn F. Allgood, Athens: University of Georgia Press, 1990

Further Reading

Ahern, Maureen and Mary Seale Vásquez (editors), *Homenaje a Rosario Castellanos*, Valencia: Albatros, 1980

Anderson, Helene M., "Rosario Castellanos and the Structures of Power," in *Contemporary Women Authors of Latin America: Introductory Essays*, edited by Doris Meyer and Marguerite Fernández Olmos, Brooklyn, New York: Brooklyn College Press, 1983

Bigas Torres, Sylvia, *La narrativa indigenista mexicana del Siglo XX*, Guadalajara, Mexico: Editorial Universidad de Guadalajara, 1990 [Chapter 8 is on Castellanos in the context of "new" indigenist writing]

Castillo, Debra A., *Talking Back: Toward a Latin American Feminist Literary Criticism*, Ithaca, New York: Cornell University Press, 1992 [Contains two chapters concerned in part with Rosario Castellanos]

Cypess, Sandra Messinger, "*Balún-Canán*: a Model Demonstration of Discourse as Power," *Revista de Estudios Hispánicos*, vol. 19/3 (1985)

____ "Onomastics and Thematics in *Balún-Canán*," *Literary Onomastic Studies*, vol. 13 (1986)

Dauster, Frank N., *The Double Strand: Five Contemporary Mexican Poets*, Louisville: University Press of Kentucky, 1987

Dorward, Frances R., "The Function of Interiorization in *Oficio de tinieblas*," *Neophilologus*, vol. 69 (1985)

Franco, Jean, "On the Impossibility of Antigone and the Inevitability of *La Malinche*: Rewriting the National Allegory," in her *Plotting Women: Gender and Representation in Mexico*, New York: Columbia University Press, and London: Verso, 1989 [This chapter is on Elena Garro's *Los recuerdos del porvenir* and Castellanos's *Oficio de tinieblas*]

Funival, Chloe, "Confronting Myths of Oppression: the Short Stories of Castellanos," in *Knives and Angels: Women Writers in Latin America*, edited by Susan Bassnett, London: Zed Books, 1990

Grant, Catherine, "Women or Words? The Indigenous *Nodriza* in the Work of Rosario Castellanos," in *Women Writers in Twentieth Century Spain and Spanish America*, edited by Catherine Davies, Lampeter, Wales: Edwin Mellen Press, 1993

Lindstrom, Naomi, "Rosario Castellanos: Women Outside Communication," in her *Women's Voice in Latin American Literature*, Washington, DC: Three Continents Press, 1989

Mandlove, N., "Toward the Ransom of Eve: Myth and History in the Poetry of Rosario Castellanos," in *In Retrospect: Essays on Latin American Literature*, edited by Elizabeth S. Rogers and Timothy J. Rogers, New York: Spanish Literature, 1987

Meyer, Doris (editor), *Lives on the Line: the Testimony of Contemporary Latin American Authors*, Berkeley: University of California Press, 1988

Nelson, Esther W., "Point of View in Selected Poems by Rosario Castellanos," *Revista/Review Interamericana*, vol. 12/1 (1982)

O'Connell, Joanna, *Prospero's Daughter: the Prose of Rosario Castellanos*, Austin: University of Texas Press, 1995

Rodríguez-Peralta, Phyllis, "Images of Women in Castellanos' Prose," *Latin American Literary Review*, vol. 6 (1977)

Scott, Nina M., "Rosario Castellanos: Demythification through Laughter," *Humor*, vol. 2/1 (1989)

Antônio de Castro Alves 1847–1871

Brazilian poet

Antônio de Castro Alves had established his reputation as one of Brazil's greatest poets well before he died of tuberculosis at the age of twenty-four. Much of the poet's renown is based on the belief that his poetry was instrumental in bringing about the abolition of African slavery in 1888. The adulation of his contemporaries is somewhat puzzling, since only one volume of his verse (the 1870 *Espumas flutuantes* [Floating Foam]) had appeared before his death. Some of his other works had been printed in newspapers and magazines, but the most of his poems, along with his one play, *Gonzaga*, were published posthumously. A considerable number of works appeared in print for the first time in Afrânio Peixoto's 1921 edition of Castro Alves's *Obras completas*.

The fact is that Castro Alves, by his own efforts, created a public *persona* which transcended poetry. He became – and still remains – an emblem of talent, suffering, rebelliousness, and humanitarianism, a central figure in Brazil's pantheon of national heroes. He began building that *persona* while still a child, reciting fervent odes on patriotic occasions. He studied at the Faculties of Law in Recife and in São Paulo, but poetry and the amorous adventures which were often the subjects of his verse distracted him from his studies; he had only managed to complete three of the six years of law school by the time he died. His classmates in Recife idolized him as a kind of Student Prince – handsome and beautifully dressed, renowned for his public recitations, his rejection of all constraints on his personal freedom, and his success with women. His greatest conquest came in 1866, when he became the lover of the well-known Portuguese actress Eugênia Câmara. Eugênia was about twenty years older than Castro Alves and, like virtually all actresses in Brazil at the time, was also a prostitute. Eugênia was intelligent and largely self-educated, and had published a volume of her own verse. For more than two years, she was Castro Alves's mentor as well as his mistress and financial support; he wrote a play for her (*Gonzaga*), and toured with her to Bahia, Rio de Janeiro, and São Paulo. During these years, he both perfected his poetic style and learned to present his poems to audiences. Dressed in black, his face powdered dead-white, Castro Alves declaimed his verses on stage or from balconies overlooking public squares; according to contemporary accounts, those who heard these recitations screamed, wept, and fainted.

Many of Castro Alves's most famous poems were clearly written for public performance, and exemplify the poetic style Brazilians call "condoreiro." Like the Andean condor, this poetry of passion and verbal pyrotechnics soars high above the pedestrian concerns of mere mortals. It seeks both to astonish and to enlighten us with a lofty vision of the world and of human history, a vision granted to but a few sublime talents; Castro Alves consistently referred to himself, always in capital letters, as a Poet and a Genius. A number of these impassioned odes, as well as his long dramatic poem "A Cachoeira de Paulo Afonso" [The Paulo-Afonso Waterfall], overtly or implicitly espouse the abolition of African slavery in Brazil. Castro Alves wrote his first abolitionist poem in 1863, when he was sixteen,

and sporadically produced about thirty-five anti-slavery works over the next eight years. Only six of these appeared in print, all in periodicals, before his death, and fewer than eighteen had been printed before the "Golden Law" ended slavery in 1888.

If the relationship between Castro Alves's abolitionist poems and the political fact of Abolition is somewhat problematical, so too is the ideology of those poems. Castro Alves appears to have been almost completely uninterested in politics, and played no role in the anti-slavery Republican Party, founded in 1870 by a group of young men which included some of his colleagues in the Faculty of Law. He almost certainly owned a slave, the son of his slave wet-nurse, who served him throughout his life. Very few of his abolitionist poems deal with the reality of African slavery in contemporary Brazil; rather, Castro Alves presents the history of Africa as inextricably linked to bondage and suffering (in his "Vozes d'Africa" [Voices from Africa]), or chooses to portray slaves during Roman times. Most of the slaves who appear in his poems, in fact, are not called "slaves," but "captives;" they do not represent the millions of blacks who served Castro Alves and his readers, but are universal and timeless emblems of human misery and entrapment. The conflict between the broad themes of Castro Alves's poetry and the specifics of the Brazilian campaign against African slavery is evident in his most famous Abolitionist poem, "O navio negreiro" [The Slave Ship], which was first published in 1880. Written in São Paulo in 1868, this work demands that Brazilians abolish the importation of African slaves – something which British naval superiority in the Atlantic had in fact forced Brazil to do in 1850, eighteen years before Castro Alves produced the poem and thirty years before the poem was published.

In the face of these contradictions and conflicts, how are we to interpret Castro Alves's anti-slavery poems and their impact on the Abolitionist movement in Brazil? There are two answers – one personal, the other essentially political. At the personal level, it seems clear that the most striking feature of these poems for Castro Alves's contemporaries was his willingness to identify with the slaves. Brazilian slave-owners – and virtually all educated Brazilians owned slaves at the middle of the 19th century – did not simply define these blacks as inferior beings destined to serve them; they so completely took their slaves for granted that they were almost unaware of their existence. The drawings of visiting French artists and the accounts of foreign travelers make it clear that slaves were omnipresent and central figures in the daily life of the Brazilian elite. In Brazilian literature of the period, however, as in the consciousness of the readers of that literature, the slave was virtually invisible and irrelevant. Castro Alves made the slaves visible in his poems precisely because his texts make it clear that he identified with them – not as real individuals, but as metaphors for the suffering, isolation, and entrapment which his Romantic ideology taught him were the lot of the true Poet, the role he had so painstakingly created for himself on the stage of life. Castro Alves's early and tragic death was a central component of his definition of the true Poet, an event which he had come to regard as therefore inevitable. His death from tuberculosis and, perhaps, gangrene (he had accidentally shot himself in the foot in 1869) was interpreted by the Brazilian elite as a supreme act of self-sacrifice; shortly after his death in 1871, his contemporaries began to refer to Castro Alves as "The Martyr of the Slaves" or, even, "The Christ of the Slaves." Even those Brazilians who had never read a single poem by Castro Alves, who had never attended one of his recitations, became convinced that this handsome, incredibly talented young member of the elite had in some way laid down his life to free the nation's slaves. This interpretation of Castro Alves's life and death, however flawed and incomplete, none the less made Abolitionism a respectable and acceptable cause, even for those who owned slaves, and laid the psychological groundwork for the end of African slavery in 1888.

DAVID T. HABERLY

Biography
Born on an estate near Curralinho in the state of Bahia, Brazil, 14 March 1847. Secondary education at Colégio Sebrão and Ginásio Baiano. His brother, José Antônio, committed suicide, 1864. Studied law at University of Recife, from 1864. Founder, with fellow students, of an abolitionist society in 1866. Formed relationship with the actress Eugênia Câmara in 1866 and travelled with her to Rio de Janeiro and São Paulo, 1868. Foot amputated, 1869. Died of tuberculosis on 6 July 1871.

Selected Works

Poetry
Espumas flutuantes, Bahia: Camilo Lellis Masson, 1870
A cachoeira de Paulo Afonso, Bahia: Imprensa Econômica, 1876
Vozes d'África – Navio negreiro – Tragedia no mar, Rio de Janeiro: Tipografia da Escola de Serafim José Alves, 1880
Consuelo, São Paulo: Tipografia da Casa Endrizzi, n.d.

Os escravos, Rio de Janeiro: Tipografia da Escola de Serafim José Alves, 1883
Últimas estrofes, Bahia: Tipografia do *Diário da Bahia*, 1895

Play
Gonzaga ou a revolução de Minas, Rio de Janeiro: Cruz Coutinho, 1875

Other Writings
Correspondência, inéditos e dispersos, Bahia: Livraria Progresso Editora, 1956

Compilations and Anthologies
Obras completas de Castro Alves, edited by Afrânio Peixoto, Rio de Janeiro: Francisco Alves, 1921
Poemas revolucionários, São Paulo: Universitária, 1945

Further Reading
Much of the immense bibliography on Castro Alves, partially catalogued by Hans Jürgen Horch, is enormously reverential; the Calmon biography is the most detailed of these texts. Haddad's revisionist study, harshly criticized when it first appeared, has since come to be regarded as fundamental. More recent criticism has focused on the relationship between Castro Alves's Abolitionism and the works of foreign writers, and on his non-Abolitionist lyrics.

Braga, Thomás, "Castro Alves and the New England Abolitionist Poets," *Hispania*, vol. 67 (1984)
Calmon, Pedro, *Castro Alves, o homem e a obra*, Rio de Janeiro: José Olympio, 1973
Haberly, David T., "Heine and Castro Alves: a Question of Influence," *Romanische Forschungen*, vol. 97 (1985)
Haddad, Jamil A., *Revisão de Castro Alves*, 3 vols, São Paulo: Saraiva, 1953
Hill, Telênia, *Castro Alves e o poema lírico*, 2nd edition, Rio de Janeiro: Tempo Brasileiro, 1978
Horch, Hans Jürgen, *Bibliografia de Castro Alves*, Rio de Janeiro: Instituto Nacional do Livro, 1960
Tolman, Jon M., "Castro Alves, poeta amoroso," *Luso-Brazilian Review*, vol. 12 (1975)

Caudillismo and Dictatorship

Caudillismo refers to the exercise of total and arbitrary power by a strong man. After the conquest of Latin America, this system permitted members of native elites to retain a local power base in exchange for loyalty to the colonial regime. In this way, rural populations were kept in the semi-feudal position of retainees. *Caudillismo* – from the Spanish word *caudillo*, a leader or military chieftain – has taken various forms throughout its long history in Latin America. For the most part, *caudillos* have come from the military sector. They have a firm interest in maintaining their power base, maximizing personal gain and defeating rivals. A charismatic personality is a feature common to many leaders of this kind.

The decades following the Wars of Independence in Latin America are known as the age of the *caudillos*. Military chief-tains organized private armies of *gauchos* or *llaneros* and vied for power. The period was chaotic and characterized by intermittent civil wars. A few countries were able to replace this anarchical system with constitutional rule, but in most countries national *caudillos* assumed power and tended to centralize authority. *Caudillaje* thus came to be a system of local rule by a strong political boss. When the Latin American states were founded in the 19th century, the rural and urban subaltern classes persisted as a powerful force in the form of pre-capitalist types of political organization, above all the paternalist institution of *caciquismo* and *coronelismo*. Many of the dictatorships deplored by liberals as "barbarous" during this historical period, however, were more expressive of the culture and interests of rural and regional populations than were the liberal-democratic regimes modeled on those of European nation-states and expressing the interests of the coastal capital cities. A *cacique*, is to this day any strong local leader. (He who establishes his power beyond the locality and who exercises regional or national control is also called a *caudillo*). A *cacique* maintains himself in power by a complex system of nepotism, patronage for his clients, control over local government services, illegal activities, and the use of force. In Peru, *caciques* are known as *curacas*. In Brazil, local bosses are called *coroneis*, and a close equivalent of *caciquismo* is known as *coronelismo*. Traditional and contemporary *caudillos*, charismatic political leaders, and personalist political parties are political expressions of *personalismo*. Peronism (Argentina's Juan and Eva Perón) and Castroism (Cuba's Fidel Castro) are two of many examples where the force of personality has dominated a popularly based political movement. The power of *caudillismo* has been an effective means for mobilizing mass political movements, centralizing the power of the state, and instituting innovative and revolutionary changes. But since the system *caudillismo* sustains is often too dependent on the power and prestige of one man, political succession, institutional stability, and continuity of policy become major and persistent problems in the society.

Some of the more notorious 19th-century *caudillos* include: in Venezuela, José Antonio Paez (1830–36; 1861–63) and Antonio Guzmán Blanco (1870–88); in Argentina, Juan Manuel de Rosas (1829–52); in Mexico, Antonio López de Santa Anna (1829–55). In the 20th century, military men who have established extremely repressive *caudillo*-type personal dictatorships have been: Juan Vicente Gómez in Venezuela; Fulgencio Batista in Cuba; Rafael Leónidas Trujillo in the Dominican Republic; Anastasio Somoza and his son, Anastasio Somoza Debayle, in Nicaragua; François Duvalier and Lieutenant General Rauol Cedras in Haiti; Getítúlio Vargas in Brazil (1930–45) and Augusto Pinochet in Chile. Most literary and "liberal" political writers condemn *caudillos* for their despotism, brutality, cupidity, and antidemocratic stance.

Caudillos flourish in societies held together by strong personal attachments and by patron-client relationships. Such a figure is characterized by a personal style of decision-making. The *caudillo* or dictator figure has inspired a number of novelists to use specific historical figures or the *caudillo* figure as archetype in historical, fictional and semi-fictional accounts.

Caudillo literature has portrayed the dictator/strongman figure since Domingo Faustino Sarmiento's *Facundo*, 1845 (*Life in the Argentine Republic in the Days of the Tyrants*), as each literary text depicts Spanish-American culture and social practice within the framework of diverse literary formats. His paternalistic-authoritarian regime is characterized by both charismatic leadership and terrorist tactics. The literary figure is referred to by a number of synonymous titles or phrases: from the most obvious, *Caudillo* (Chieftain), *Padre* (Father), *Sabio* (Sage), *Señor Presidente* (Mr President), *Primer Magistrado* (First Magistrate), *Supremo* (The Supreme One), *Patriarca* (Patriarch), *Bienhechor* (The Benefactor), *Generalísimo* (The Highest General), *Conductor* (Leader), *Guía* (Guide), *Jefe* (Boss), *Protector* (Protector), *Comandante* (Commander), and *Déspota Ilustrado* (Enlightened Despot). In *Los dictadores latinoamericanos*, Ángel Rama makes the following observation about this figure in Latin American liter-

ature: "More than a historical figure, he is a myth, dreamed about but not thought about, hated but not analyzed." And, giving credence to this perception, the novelist Alejo Carpentier in his *El recurso del método*, 1974 (*Reasons of State*), adds: "nothing walks on this continent as much as a myth." This legendary, recurrent figure is both a myth and a reality for the Latin American writer and is often appropriately portrayed as a blend of the fictional with the historical. The very protean form that the narrative takes reflects the real and surreal images that the figure of the *caudillo* suggests to its Latin American audience. Roa Bastos's *Yo el Supremo*, 1974 (*I the Supreme*), for example, takes on a plethora of formats interwoven in a single work – history, novel, sociological essay, moral philosophy, biographical novel, revolutionary pamphlet, testimonial documentary, poetic prose, autobiographical confession, ideological debate over literary limits, and, finally a linguistic treatise of sorts reflecting on verbal expression and its ability to communicate effectively. At times the protagonist may be a specific historical figure or, in other instances, he may be an archetypical figure, as in García Márquez's *El otoño del patriarca*, 1975 (*The Autumn of the Patriarch*). In this Colombian novel the action takes place in a Latin American country in an advanced state of corruption, anarchy, savagery, and physical exuberance. The time is the modern period, though not specified. Dominating the action is the dictator-general, at first an almost messianic presence loved by the people, appearing suddenly among the peasants like a vision.

Perhaps the best-known of the earlier literary pieces on the *caudillo* figure is Sarmiento's *Facundo*. Sarmiento composed this autobiographical, non-fictional account of his youth using a heterogeneous style encompassing the history of Argentine customs and types, a biography of the gaucho *caudillo* Juan Facundo Quiroga (Rosas's rival *caudillo*), and a political diatribe against the government of the tyrant Manuel Rosas.

Elena De Costa

See also entries on *El Señor Presidente* (Miguel Ángel Asturias), *Los de abajo* (Mariano Azuela), *La muerte de Artemio Cruz* (Carlos Fuentes), *Doña Bárbara* (Rómulo Gallegos), *El general en su laberinto* (Gabriel García Márquez), *Yo el Supremo* (Augusto Roa Bastos), *Pedro Páramo* (Juan Rulfo)

Further Reading

Alexander, Robert J., "Caudillos, Coroneis, and Political Bosses in Latin America," in *Presidential Power in Latin American Politics*, edited by Thomas V. Di Bacco, New York: Praeger, 1977

Azuela, Mariano, *Los caciques*, Mexico City: Editorial de la Compañía Periodística Nacional, 1917; as *The Bosses*, translated by Lesley Byrd Simpson, in *Two Novels of Mexico*, Berkeley: University of California Press, 1956 [fiction]

Brading, D.A. (editor), *Caudillo and Peasant in the Mexican Revolution*, Cambridge: Cambridge University Press, 1980

Brushwood, John S., *The Spanish-American Novel: a Twentieth-Century Survey*, Austin: University of Texas Press, 1980 [Includes critical treatment of many works on *caudillaje* themes]

Calviño, Julio, *La novela del dictador en Hispanoamérica*, Madrid: Cultura Hispánica, 1985

____ *Historia, ideología y mito en la narrativa hispanoamericana contemporánea*, Madrid: Editorial Ayuso, 1987

Canfield, Martha L., *El "patriarca" de García Márquez: arquetipo literario del dictador hispano-americano*, Florence: Opus Libri, 1984

Castellanos, Jorge and Miguel A. Martínez, "El Dictador hispanoamericano como personaje literario," *Latin American Research Review*, vol. 16/2 (1981)

Davis, Harold Eugene, *et al.*, *Revolutionaries, Traditionalists, and Dictators in Latin America*, New York: Cooper Square Publishers, 1973

González Echevarría, Roberto, "The Dictatorship of Rhetoric / The Rhetoric of Dictatorship," in his *The Voice of the Masters: Writing and Authority in Latin American Literature*, Austin: University of Texas Press, 1985

Hamill, Hugh M., *Caudillos, Dictators in Spanish America*, Norman: University of Oklahoma Press, 1992 [Essays on theories underlying the root causes of *caudillismo* and an analysis of various *caudillo* figures in the 19th and 20th centuries. Also includes an excellent bibliography on definitions, theories, and contexts of the *caudillo*, as well as *caudillos* in literature]

Humphreys, R.A., "The Caudillo Tradition," in *Tradition and Revolt in Latin America*, New York: Columbia University Press, 1969

Jitrik, Noé, *Muerte y resurrección de Facundo*, Buenos Aires: Centro Editor de América Latina, 1968

Kern, Robert, *The Caciques – Oligarchical Politics and the System of Caciquismo in the Luso Hispanic World*, Albuquerque: University of New Mexico Press, 1973 [A well-edited collection, with especially good essays on the *cacique* in literature]

Kirkpatrick, S., "*Tirano Banderas* and *El Señor Presidente*: Two Tyrants and Two Visions," in *Proceedings of the 7th Congress of the International Comparative Literature Association*, Stuttgart, Germany: Bieber, 1979

Pacheco, Carlos, *Narrativa de la dictadura y crítica literaria*, Caracas: Ediciones CELARG, 1987

Rama, Ángel, *Los dictadores latinoamericanos*, Mexico City: Fondo de Cultura Económica, 1976

Roniger, Luis, "Caciquismo and Coronelismo: Contextual Dimensions of Patron Brokerage in Mexico and Brazil," *Latin American Research Review*, vol. 22/2 (1987)

Aimé Césaire 1913–

Martinican poet and politician

The short-lived venture of *Légitime Defense* [Legitimate Defence] had a strong Marxist and anti-colonial edge. It was edited by three Martinican students, Etienne Léro, René Ménil and Jules Monnerot when they were together in Paris in 1932. Its publication prompted Aimé Césaire to create his own journal, *L'Etudiant Noir* [The Black Student] in 1934 with Léopold Senghor and Léon Damas "for all black students, regardless of origin, African, Antillean or American." The appearance of this journal was to determine the dual course of Césaire's life.

One can differentiate between Césaire the poet to the politician but not dissociate them. The ambition to define an authentic black culture is encapsulated in the coining of the word *négritude*, around 1935. For Senghor, it is "the whole of the black world's cultural values;" for Césaire, in *Cahier d'un retour au pays natal* (*Return to My Native Land*), it originates in "Haiti, where *Négritude* first stood up and swore by its humanity". Lilyan Kesteloot defines it as "the slave's demand for justice, dignity and humanity."

Cahier d'un retour au pays natal, a cultural milestone, was written in France and first published there in 1939 but achieved recognition under the aegis of André Breton in the bilingual French/English edition of 1947. The themes of *Cahier*, centering on the identity of the black West-Indian, are outlined in *Tropiques*, the journal Césaire founded in 1941 with Ménil and Monnerot after returning to Martinique at the outbreak of World War II.

However, the fame of *Cahier* rests equally on its obscurity and originality, achieving what Ménil called for: "a form originating in Europe awaiting contents originating in Africa." He thereby rejected two centuries of "fake" Antillean literature, based on imitation of French models. His images result from the conscious fusion of numerous sources, owing little, despite what is often alleged, to the Surrealist process of automatic writing.

Césaire's literary vocation and political career run parallel and closely related courses. To quote Ernest Moutoussamy: "His poetic discourse is that of a prophet, his political discourse is that of a realist and as such makes room for compromise." He had seen unification with France as the first step towards independence in the immediate post-war context but after the Left was defeated in June 1946, the decree of unification was found to be ridden with ambiguities. Césaire's career as a deputy, from 1945 until a socialist government was elected in 1981, under François Mitterrand, would be a continuous struggle to ensure that the D.O.M or Overseas Departments be granted in practice the same status as those of mainland France.

His political concern extended to the whole of the colonised world as testified by his support for self-determination and independence in Vietnam, Algeria and Africa. The most famous of those statements is *Discours sur le colonialisme*, 1951 (*Discourse on Colonialism*), in which he denounces humanism and its "universal" values based exclusively on the white civilisation and used as a pretext for world domination: "a civilisation which seeks ways round its principles is condemned to perish."

In 1947, he had launched *Présence Africaine*, journal and publishing house, in order to facilitate cultural exchanges between all areas of the black diaspora, across language divides.

Accused of treason by Frantz Fanon after the unification with France, Césaire has steered an uneasy course marked by growing disillusion with politics. In 1956, after leaving the Communist Party, which he accused of empire building in the Third World in his *Lettre à Maurice Thorez* (*Letter to Maurice Thorez*), he founded the Progressist Martinican Party in order to attend to the needs of his fellow countrymen. Yet he is equally mistrusted by those Martinicans who consider his ultimate commitment to autonomy as dangerously Utopian.

Césaire's literary production, especially his writing for the stage, reflects this disillusion, as neo-colonialism, corruption and nationalism took hold over Africa. *La Tragédie du Roi Christophe*, 1963 (*The Tragedy of King Christophe*) sought to justify strong men such as Nkrumah and Sékou Touré, African leaders who attempted to fill the vacuum left by decolonisation. On the other hand, *Une Saison au Congo*, 1966 (*A Season in the Congo*) takes a deeply pessimistic view of the fate of Patrice Lumumba.

Though revered as a father figure, Césaire's cultural options are also strongly contested by the younger generation of Martinican writers. Whereas he stands firm for *Francophonie* (black literature in French), Bernabé, Chamoiseau and Confiant in their *Eloge de la créolité* of 1992 [In Praise of Creoleness], would like to define their identity by writing in Creole-based French as the way towards a specific Caribbean culture.

DENISE GANDERTON

See also entries on *La Revue du Monde Noir* and *Tropiques* under Journals, Négritude

Biography

Born in Basse-Pointe, Martinique, 25 June 1913. Educated at Lycée Schoelcher, Fort-de France, 1924–31. Won a scholarship to study in France and entered the École Normale Supérieure, renowned for fostering literary careers, in 1935. Graduated in 1936. Co-founder, with Léopold Senghor and Léon Damas, of *L'Etudiant Noir*, Paris, 1934. Married Suzanne Roussi in 1939 (died in 1967). She was to make important contributions to the journal *Tropiques*. Returned to Martinique in 1939 and taught at Lycée Schoelcher until 1945. Editor of *Tropiques*, Fort de France, 1941–45. Elected Mayor of Fort-de-France in 1945, a post he still held in the early 1990s, then member of the Chamber of Deputies in the first post-war government of the IVth Republic until he retired in 1993. Demanded unification with France in 1946. Organised the First Congress of Black writers and artists in Paris in 1956. Awards include: Laporte Prize, 1960; Viareggio-Versilia Prize, 1968; National Grand Prize for Poetry, 1982.

Selected Works

Poetry

Cahier d'un retour au pays natal, Paris: Bordas, 1947 [Early version published in the magazine *Volontés*, 1939]; as *Memorandum on My Martinique*, translated by Ivan Goll and Lionel Abel, New York: Brentano, 1947; as *Return to My Native Land*, translated by Emil Snyder, Paris: Présence Africaine, 1968
Les Armes miraculeuses, Paris: Gallimard, 1946; revised edition, 1970
Ferrements, Paris: Seuil, 1960
Cadastre, Paris: Seuil, 1961; as *Cadastre*, translated by Emile Snyder and Sanford Upson, New York: Third Press, 1973
Moi, laminaire, Paris: Seuil, 1982

Plays

Et les Chiens se taisaient, Paris: Présence Africaine, 1956
La Tragédie du Roi Christophe, Paris: Présence Africaine, 1963; revised edition, 1970; as *The Tragedy of King Christophe*, translated by Ralph Manheim, New York: Grove Press, 1970
Une Saison au Congo, Paris: Seuil, 1966; as *A Season in the Congo*, translated by Ralph Manheim, New York: Grove Press, 1968
Une Tempête, Paris: Seuil, 1969; as *A Tempest*, translated by Richard Miller, New York: Borchardt, 1985

Essays

Discours sur le colonialisme, Paris: Editions Réclame, 1951, Paris: Présence Africaine, 1955; as *Discourse on Colonialism*, translated by Joan Pinkham, New York: Monthly Review Press, 1972
Lettre à Maurice Thorez, Paris: Présence Africaine, 1956; as *Letter to Maurice Thorez*, Paris: Présence Africaine, 1957
Toussaint-Louverture: la révolution française et le problème colonial, Paris: Club Française du Livre, 1960; revised edition, Paris: Présence Africaine, 1962

Compilations and Anthologies

Oeuvres complètes, 3 vols, Fort-de-France, Martinique: Désormeaux, 1976
Aimé Césaire: the Collected Poetry, translated by Clayton Eshleman and Annette Smith, Berkeley: University of California Press, 1983
Lyric and Dramatic Poetry 1946–82, translated by Clayton Eshleman and Annette Smith, Charlottesville: University Press of Virginia, 1990

Further Reading

Arnold, James A., *Modernism and Negritude: the Poetry and Poetics of Aimé Césaire*, Cambridge, Massachusetts: Harvard University Press, 1981
Confiant, Raphael, *Aimé Césaire, une traversée paradoxale du siècle*, Paris: Stock, 1993 [Re-appraisal of Césaire by a member of the Creoleness generation]
Hale, Thomas (editor), *Critical Perspectives on Aimé Césaire*, Washington, DC: Three Continents Press, 1992
Kesteloot, Lilyan, *Aimé Césaire, poète d'aujourd'hui*, Paris: Seghers, 1963
―――― *Les Écrivains noirs de langue francaise*, Brussells: Université de Bruxelles, 1963; as *Black Writers in French*, translated by Ellen Conroy Kennedy, Philadelphia: Temple University Press, 1974 [The fundamental text about *Négritude* and its background]
―――― *Aimé Césaire, l'homme et l'oeuvre*, Paris: Présence Africaine, 1973
Kubayanda, Josephat B., *The Poet's Africa: Africanness in the Poetry of Nicolás Guillén and Aimé Césaire*, New York: Greenwood Press, 1990
Moutoussamy, Ernest, *Aimé Césaire, Député à l'Assemblée Nationale, 1945–1993*, Paris: L'Harmattan, 1993 [Strong defence of Césaire's political career by his colleague, M.P for Guadeloupe]

Une Tempête

Play by Aimé Césaire

Une Tempête is the last of four plays written by Aimé Césaire. In contrast with *La Tragédie du Roi Christophe*, 1963 (*The Tragedy of King Christophe*) and *Une Saison au Congo*, 1967 (*A Season in the Congo*), it is not centered on a specific historical figure and if all Césaire's theatre is political, as Roger Toumson notes, it is on the broader issue of colonisation, by way of a parody of Shakespeare's *The Tempest*.

It was first produced, like its predecessors, by Jean-Marie Serreau who became, in the 1960s, the champion of non-aligned African and Caribbean theatre. Because Césaire's plays were considered as objectionable in France as Soyinka's were in England, backing was initially provided by the Hammamet Festival in Tunisia before it was transferred to the Avignon Festival and subsequently to the Théâtre de la Cité Universitaire, Paris.

Césaire's declared intention was to adapt Shakespeare's *Tempest* for black theatre, so that, as Antoine Régis remarked in *La Littérature franco-antillaise* (1992), "the play's structure, production and even its lyrical moments participate of a single pedagogical purpose."

The title "*A*" *Tempest* points to the choice of a radically different interpretation of Shakespeare's play. Shakespeare's plot is condensed from five acts into three and considerably altered to turn the play into an indictment of the ideology which legitimised the colonial enterprise. From the power struggle between Prospero and his brother Antonio, which underpins the original, he retains the conspiracy which deprived Prospero of his dukedom but assimilates him to Columbus, demoted as viceroy of the Indies by the Spanish sovereigns and accused of heresy and magical practices by the Inquisition. Accordingly, the scene moves to the West Indies and Césaire redefines the central characters on the pattern of the colonial class structure. Prospero and other Europeans stand for white power while Caliban is the black slave, and Ariel the mulatto siding with his master. In accordance with the master-slave dialectics, Shakespeare favours Ariel who shows aspirations to a "civilised" order while giving up on "bestial" Caliban who refuses it, thus justifying the superiority of nurture over nature.

In contrast, Césaire builds his play around the central confrontation between the coloniser and the colonised who contests the legitimacy of the policy of conquest. Caliban denounces the magical (technological) powers used by Prospero to take possession of the island and challenges the superiority of the white civilisation offered as a bonus to inferior beings. He subsumes the revolt of the Rebel of *Et les Chiens se taisaient* [And the Dogs Kept Silent], the struggle for freedom of Christophe in Haiti and the set-back of Lumumba's defeat in *Une Saison au Congo*.

Although Caliban fails to overthrow Prospero by force, he predicts the end of colonial power:

Prospero: Eh bien, moi aussi, je te hais!
　　　　　Car tu es celui par qui, pour
　　　　　la première fois j'ai douté de
　　　　　moi-même.

[I too hate you. For it is through you that for the first time, I have doubted myself.]

(Act 3, scene 5)

In *Une Tempête*, Prospero stays on, with the excuse of defending civilisation and safeguarding its achievements but in reality because he needs his slaves in order to feel superior: "Nous ne sommes plus que deux sur cette île. Plus que Toi et Moi." (Only the two of us left on this island, only You and Me.) (Act 3, scene 4).

Césaire also updates and contextualises *The Tempest* through his choice of resolutely modern language. Prospero's

elevated register when addressing his peers or soliloquising contrasts with the use of slang and colloquialisms when talking to his slaves, coming down to their level: Prospero: " vilain singe. Comment peut-on être si laid!" (Nasty ape. How is it possible to be so ugly!). For which Caliban pays him back in kind: "Avec ton nez crochu, tu ressembles à un vieux vautour." (With your hook nose, you look like an old vulture.) (Act 1, scene 2). To Ariel waxing lyrical, Prospero says: "Écrase! Je n'aime pas les arbres à parole." (Wrap up! I don't like talking trees.) (Act 1, scene 2). Ariel is shown to imitate the high register of his master; Caliban will have none of it:

Ariel: Il m'a promis ma liberté. A terme, sans doubte,
　　　mais c'est la première fois qu'il me l'a promise.
Caliban: Du flan! D'ailleurs ne m'intéresse pas. Ce que
　　　je veux, c'est Freedom now!

(Act 2, scene 1)

[Ariel: He promised to free me. Not just yet, granted, but it is the first time he has made the promise.
Caliban: Rubbish! Anyway, I am not interested in to-morrow. What I want is Freedom now!]

In order to broaden the meaning of the French "liberté," Césaire backs it up with a reference to Black Power. Caliban's description of Prospero's "arsenal anti-émeutes" (riot-squad weaponry) carries a hint of the 1968 Paris riots. The choice of register also indicates that Césaire, in the words of Antoine Régis, is conscious of "writing in French while rejecting the ideological and literary context of the language."

This context is common to all European literature, so that the play is open to a range of other interpretations. Caliban accuses Prospero of having robbed him of everything, including his name. Prospero counters this accusation with a reminder that he could just as well have called him "cannibal" or by derision "Hannibal," alluding to the names the emancipated slaves were given at random from encyclopedias. Whereas Shakespeare used the character of Caliban to deride the "good savage myth" because he believed in the principle of hierarchy, Césaire portrays Prospero as a slave-master who justifies the subjugation of other races on the same principle.

The concept of "identity" which was the cornerstone of European thought until the Renaissance had for consequence that difference could only be construed as inequality. Therefore, Shakespeare's Caliban is the absolute "other," naturally monstrous and inferior because he contradicts the definition of "human" which took white Christian Europeans as the absolute norm. The other can only be defined by reference to it:

Prospero: Tu pourrais au moins me bénir de t'avoir
　　　　　appris à parler

[You could at least thank me for having taught you to speak.]

(Act 1, scene 2)

Another dimension of the play rests with Ariel, pointing to a positive issue to the confrontation. Whereas in order to exist, Caliban can only proclaim what he is not (as Glissant wrote, "Je ne suis qu'en tant que je suis autre" [I only exist through being the other]) Ariel dreams of reconciliation: "J'ai souvent fait le rêve associés, de bâtir un monde merveilleux, chacun apportant en contribution ses qualités propres." (I often had a wild dream that one day, Prospero, you and I, we would undertake like brothers to build a wonderful world where each would contribute his own qualities.) (Act 2, scene 1)

Like the island itself in *Cahier d'un retour*, Ariel would at last accept his multiple identity to assume his destiny.

DENISE GANDERTON

See also entries on America, the invention of; Caliban; Civilization and Barbarism

Editions
First Edition: *Une Tempête*, Paris: Seuil, 1969
Translation: *A Tempest*, by Richard Miller, New York: Borchardt, 1985

Further Reading
Antoine, Régis, *La Littérature franco-antillaise*, Paris: Karthala, 1992
Bradby, David, *Modern French Drama*, Cambridge: Cambridge University Press, 1984
Laville, Pierre, *A. Césaire et J.M. Serreau: un acte politique et poétique*, Les voies de la création théâtrale II, Paris: CNRS, 1970
Nisbet, Anne Marie and Beverley Ormerod, *Négritude et Antillanité, étude d'Une Tempête d'Aimé Césaire*, Kensington: New South Wales University, 1982
Toumson, Roger, *La Transgression des couleurs*, Paris: Caribéennes, 1981

Chicano Literature

Chicano literature (writing by people of Mexican descent residing permanently in the US) is often considered a phenomenon arising at the time of the Civil Rights Movement. While the protest period comprises a moment of intensified literary production yielding an important body of texts, a tradition of Chicano literature dates from well before the 1960s. Philip Ortego refers to that boom of the protest period as a Renaissance, thus stressing a need to recognize earlier texts and to study the relationship between contemporary and prior writings. Since that Renaissance, Chicano literature has earned a world-class reputation and its proliferation over the last two decades attests to a rich and dynamic tradition. As Chicano identity constitutes an ethnic experience of being between two cultures and simultaneously of being a part of the latter, it is no surprise that questions of subjectivity and community have been central concerns in literary production. That is not to say that Chicano literature is monolithic and offers a homogeneous account of the ethnic experience. Rather, the variety of Mexican-American experiences has yielded diverse meditations on identity and community and, thus, the literary tradition is characterized by its heterogeneity. To understand that tradition in relation to the many geographical, socio-historical and cultural contexts of its production, and to situate contemporary writing within an ongoing trajectory, it is helpful to follow Luis Leal's elaboration of four stages in Chicano literary history leading up to the contemporary period: the Hispanic period (1542–1821), the Mexican period (1821–48), the period of transition (1848–1910) and the period of interaction (1910–43).

Here, however, for reasons of space, the period under examination is that defined by Leal as contemporary. Its beginning is marked in 1943 by the events known as the Zoot Suit Riots, sparked by assaults made by US servicemen on Chicanos in Los Angeles. These incidents emphasized the ambiguous status of Mexican-Americans who, although they served their country overseas during World War II, were subject to discrimination

at home. A recognition of the inequity displayed by the riots is crucial for a consideration of Chicano culture as it marks a key moment in the politicization of the latter. That politicized consciousness is fomented by returning Chicano troops whose acute awareness of prejudice led them to take an active role in the organization of Mexican-Americans with a view to the pursuit of civil rights and socio-economic and political empowerment.

Towards the end of the 1960s, amid the climate of protest, the nascent politicization of the 1940s comes to fruition with the activism of different groups whose efforts are collectively referred to as the Chicano Movement. Deriving much of their strategy and rhetoric from the black Civil Rights Movement, Chicanos attempted to direct regional and localized concerns into a cohesive national organization. Yet, the diversity characterizing Chicano identity and its representations undermines any semblance of a unified front reflecting all spheres of experience. The only common factors among the latter were and remain those of US residency and Mexican heritage and, beyond these, Chicano identity resists homogenization. Even Spanish, rather than providing a standard mode of communication, may be ascribed a divisive function, given regional differences and the varying proficiency with which it is spoken and written. Thus, the Movement is best considered an assemblage of separate organizations with localized concerns that have in common the aim of certain forms of empowerment.

A crucial function of the Movement was its catalyzing effect on literary production, particularly poetry and drama. As genres that have traditionally lent themselves to consciousness raising and protest, they evolved in conjunction with the Movement, as expressions of activism and as forums for that very activism. Neither required publication as they were, initially at least, directly available and accessible to the audiences for which they were intended. Poems were distributed and read at political gatherings while theater was conceived and performed contemporaneously with the events which it treated. Luis Valdez's agit-prop *actos* (acts) and "Corky" Gonzales's poem "I Am Joaquín" are two key instances of this politicized literature of the Movement period and comprise the more influential examples of early contemporary cultural production. Both authors were involved with important tendencies in organized political activity. Gonzales was founder/leader of the Denver-based Crusade For Justice; Valdéz and El Teatro Campesino were active in support of the United Farm Workers Union in California. While "I am Joaquín" was read at meetings, the *actos* were performed at sites of protest such as the fieldworker's strikes.

Literature derived from this politically-charged time was generally marked by its alignment with and articulation, at some level, of Movement ideology. Poetry in an innovative, interlingual format provided a popular vehicle for representations of a marginalized socio-cultural and historical experience with the aim of raising consciousness and encouraging self-empowerment. However, poetic representations differed greatly with regard to the terms of community and identity and with regard to the historical and mythical models employed as cultural reference points in the endeavor to provide accounts of the latter. Chicano identity expressed by Alurista, in *Floricanto en Aztlán*, 1971 [Flowerandsong in Aztlán], espouses pan-ethnic solidarity. Employing a largely interlingual syntax, Alurista urged an awareness of a pre-Columbian Chicano heritage and engaged Náhuatl-Mayan philosophy and aesthetics to counter the dominant, Anglocentric worldview which had repressed the Chicano experience.

While certain poets of this period recuperated the pre-Colombian cronotope, others drew upon more recent figures and contexts to provide a cultural axis for a consciousness of community. José Montoya looked to the urban experience of the 1940s and 1950s and to the culture of the Zoot-Suiters, or *pachucos*, for the hero of his 1972 interlingual poem "El Louie" (Louie). By its immortalization of Louie, the deceased focal point of the community that is represented, the poem and its reading perform an elegiac function, guaranteeing the recovery of that community in the present. For Bruce-Novoa, "El Louie" is paradigmatic of Chicano poetry, comprising a recuperation and representation that reaffirms and ensures the continuity of the ethnic heritage and history. That interlingual reaffirmation of identity effected by Montoya is seen in the works of other poets of the Movement period such as Abelardo Delgado, author of *Chicano* (1969), Sergio Elizondo, *Perros y anti-Perros: una épica chicana*, 1972 [Dogs and Anti-Dogs: a Chicano Epic], Tino Villanueva, *Hay otra voz Poems*, 1972 [There is Another Voice Poems], Ricardo Sánchez, *Canto y grito mi liberación*, 1973 [I Sing and Shout My Liberation]), Raúl Salinas, *Viaje/Trip*, 1973 and Angela De Hoyos, *Arise, Chicano! and Other Poems*, 1975.

While much poetry of the late 1960s and early 1970s is linked with Movement ideology, the relationship of narrative with the latter is less direct. Novels could not be written and distributed with the immediacy of poetry and drama. Moreover, prose fiction did not lend itself to oral delivery, least of all in the context of political activism that required uncomplicated, message-oriented works. Furthermore, alongside the popular function and possibilities of poetry and drama, narrative remained inaccessible to a mass audience. Dependent on publication and distribution, narrative supposed a readership with a degree of literacy and leisure that did not include large sectors of the Chicano community at the time. With the institution of the Quinto Sol Press prize for fiction in 1970, works were lauded in so far as they comprised acceptable representations of the Chicano experience. The characteristics of the first three winners, Tomás Rivera's *. . . Y no se lo tragó la tierra*, 1971 (*. . . And the Earth Did Not Part*), Rudolfo Anaya's *Bless Me, Ultima*, 1972 and Rolando Hinojosa's *Estampas del valle y otras obras*, 1972 (*Sketches of the Valley and Other Works*), as well as other sanctioned texts of the period, Richard Vásquez's *Chicano*, 1970 and Ernesto Galarza's *Barrio Boy*, 1971, suggest the criteria for canonicity: an emphasis on community survival; an exploration of the role of the individual as a member of the latter, positioned between opposing ideologies; a representation of the development of the individual as writer of a collective experience; and accessibility of language.

The narrow scope of criteria for canonicity is symptomatic of a repressive tendency within the Movement itself, particularly with regard to issues of gender, as certain dominant factions considered *la causa* (the cause) a male enterprise. A radical politics of ethnic identity precluded issues of sexual politics which were not considered part of the collective agenda. Militant and progressive in the pursuit of racial equality and empowerment, the Movement was conservative and reactionary in relation to questions of gender; a prejudice manifested in the sphere of literary production. Until the mid-1970s, Chicanas had been almost wholly ignored by male-run presses and journals and were published only in so far as they expressed, or left unchallenged, the patriarchal perspective. Consequently, women were prevented from speaking and writing about themselves and their experience of oppression within their ethnic community. In addition to sexual difference, differences of sexuality were not accommodated in a project for community defined by its a heterosexual bias. Homosexuality was taboo given its rejection of the traditional family unit, the preservation of which was prioritized by the Movement as a means of safeguarding cultural heritage and values. Thus, although Chicano author John Rechy had published three novels by 1970, with major presses and to international acclaim, his work was ignored. The refusal to embrace Rechy as a member of the ethnic group was due to his homosexuality and his thematization of the latter in novels such as *City of Night*, 1963 and *Numbers*, 1967.

By the mid-1970s, however, with the waning of the politicization and oppositionality espoused by cultural nationalist factions in the Movement, literature was identified as Chicano more on the basis of the author's heritage than in terms of how that heritage was articulated or manifested itself, if at all. This yielded a more open conceptualization of Chicano literature as Rechy and others were increasingly recognized and accepted as Chicano writers. The shift coinciding with a declining influence of certain ideological currents on the production, publication and reception of literature, declared itself with a flourishing of the kinds of writing repressed by the dominant cultural nationalist discourse of the Movement. This change was heralded above all with the appearance in 1975–76 of important works by women: the collection of short stories *Rain of Scorpions*, 1975 and the play *The Day of the*

Swallows (1976, first published 1971) by Estela Portillo; the novels *Come Down from the Mound* (1975) by Berta Ornelas and *Victuum* (1976) by Isabela Ríos; and the poetry collections *Restless Serpents* (1976) and *La mujer es la tierra*, 1975 (*Woman is the Earth*) by Bernice Zamora and Dorinda Moreno. These works marked the start of two important processes. First, they initiated the articulation of a repressed feminist consciousness with regard to the issue of women's oppression within the ethnic group. Second, the works of Portillo *et al* were pivotal as they ushered in a period in which hitherto unaccommodated literary voices flourished in all genres. Women's writings, regional literature, works not focusing on *la causa* or foregrounding ethnicity in an oppositional sense, and gay writings all began to dispel notions of a monolithic community and literary tradition.

Since the mid-1970s, poetry has moved away from the interlingual and the overtly political to become more introspective, displaying an increasing formal sophistication and a diversification of thematic concerns. Among the more important collections are the following: *The Elements of San Joaquín*, 1977 (Gary Soto); *Bloodroot*, 1979 (Alma Villanueva); *Palabras de mediodía/NoonWords*, 1979 (Lucha Corpi); *Emplumada*, 1981 [Feathered] (Lorna Dee Cervantes); *Women Are Not Roses*, 1984 (Ana Castillo); *Martín and Meditations on the South Valley*, 1987 (Jimmy Santiago Baca); *My Wicked, Wicked Ways*, 1987 (Sandra Cisneros); and *From the Cables of Genocide*, 1991 (Lorna Dee Cervantes). As poetry displays a growing degree of craft, a broadening of thematic and stylistic scope and an accommodation of differences pertaining to gender, sexuality and ideology, narrative has followed a similar trajectory. Writers began to offer different perspectives on Chicano identity, producing more subjective, formally diverse works that did not attempt to speak for the collective, and which largely discarded the previously dominant ethnic Bildungsroman model. Authors started to experiment with other narrative forms and to foster intertextual linkages with works and tendencies from Latin American, United States and Peninsular literary traditions.

While the Quinto Sol prize-winners Anaya and Hinojosa continued to produce, new voices enriched Chicano narrative, breaking fresh structural and thematic ground. In particular, the heterogeneity of Chicano prose is intensified in the late 1970s and early 1980s with narratives which challenge the previously dominant ideology of militant sectors of the Movement. Nash Candelaria's *Memories of the Alhambra*, 1977, rejects Mexican ancestry and problematizes the hitherto familiar depiction of the search for cultural identity and roots. Espousing assimilation, Candelaria anticipates the most polemic text of the 1980s, Richard Rodríguez's *Hunger of Memory* (1982). This sophisticated meditation on language and identity proved controversial due to what many construed as Rodríguez's refusal of responsibility to his ethnic community, his rejection of that which had been achieved with a view to empowering Chicanos and his advocacy of assimilation. The controversy surrounding *Hunger* stemmed from its rejection of bilingual education and affirmative action, two political spoils won through minority activism in the 1960s. To some, Rodríguez was a *vendido* (sell out) and his work without merit while, to other readers, his work added another significant dimension to an already multifaceted Chicano tradition.

Since the early 1980s, numerous works have continued to enrich Chicano prose. *The Rain God*, 1984 (Arturo Islas), *Face*, 1985 (Cecile Piñeda), *The Hidden Law*, 1992 (Michael Nava) and *The Rag Doll Plagues*, 1992 (Alejandro Morales) are some of the novels which stand out, along with the autobiographical narratives *Living Up the Street*, 1985 (Gary Soto), *A Beautiful, Cruel Country*, 1987 (Eva Antonia Wilbur-Cruce) and *Always Running*, 1993 (Luis Rodríguez). Within this corpus of prose, as with poetry, the Chicana contribution has been significant. Continuing the work begun by writers such as Portillo, recent fiction has increasingly addressed the status of women within the ethnic group and has sought to negotiate feminine subjectivity and to provide representations of the latter. Moreover, diverse works by Sandra Cisneros (*The House on Mango Street*, 1984), Sheila Ortiz Taylor (*Faultline*, 1982), Ana Castillo (*The Mixquiahuala Letters*, 1986), Denise Chávez (*The Last of the Menu Girls*, 1986) and Alma Villanueva (*The Ultraviolet Sky*, 1988) explore issues of gender and sexuality both within the specificity of the minority experience and, simultaneously, within a broader, trans-ethnic feminist context.

In addition to the novel, a varied body of essayistic prose has flourished. Alongside Richard Rodríguez's *Days of Obligation* (1992) and Rubén Martínez's *The Other Side* (1992) an outstanding contribution is Cherríe Moraga's *Loving in the War Years / Lo que nunca pasó por sus labios*, 1983 [What Never Passed His/Her Lips]. A hybrid, bilingual, autobiographical narrative documenting the oppression of Chicanas from a lesbian perspective, Moraga's work critiques the heterosexual hegemony and the homophobia of the patriarchal ethnic community. Yet, the most important work of the last decade is Gloria Anzaldúa's *Borderlands/La Frontera: the New Mestiza* (1987), a text that defies genre categories. This bilingual and interlingual work blends the lyrical and the prosaic, theoretical commentary and autobiographical insight, to propose a more accommodating conceptualization of Chicano ethnicity. Anzaldúa rejects the binary logic of Western thought that underlies strategies of domination and according to which identity is constructed in unitary terms through its repression of differences. In place of a repressed model of subjectivity, Anzaldúa proposes a *mestiza*, or border consciousness, which refuses confinement to one identity and permits simultaneous residence in plural communities through multiple alliances and identifications.

WILSON NEATE

Further Reading

Critical Studies

Bruce-Novoa, Juan, *Chicano Poetry: a Response to Chaos*, Austin: University of Texas Press, 1982

—— (editor), *RetroSpace: Collected Essays on Chicano Literature*, Houston: Arte Público Press, 1990

—— "Shipwrecked in the Seas of Signification: Cabeza de Vaca's *Relación* and Chicano Literature," in *Reconstructing a Chicano/a Literary Heritage: Hispanic Colonial Literature of the Southwest*, edited by María Herrera Sobek, Tucson: University of Arizona Press, 1993

Candelaria, Cordelia, *Chicano Poetry: a Critical Introduction*. Westport, Connecticut: Greenwood Press, 1986

Leal, Luis, "Mexican American Literature: a Historical Perspective," in *Modern Chicano Writers*, edited by Joseph Sommer and Tomás

Ybarra-Frausto, Englewood Cliffs, New Jersey: Prentice-Hall, 1979

Neate, Wilson, "Re-writing/Re-reading Ethnicity: the Lesson of Chicana Poetry," in *Gender, Self, and Society*, Frankfurt: Peter Lang, 1993

Pérez Torres, Rafael, *Movements in Chicano Poetry: against Myth, against Margins*, Cambridge: Cambridge University Press, 1995

Rodríguez del Pino, Salvador, *La novela chicana escrita en español: cinco autores comprometidos*, Ypsilanti: Bilingual Press, 1982

Saldívar, Ramón, *Chicano Narrative: the Dialectics of Difference*, Madison: University of Wisconsin Press, 1990

Sánchez, Marta, *Chicana Poetry: a Critical Approach to an Emerging Literature*, Berkeley: University of California Press, 1985

Tatum, Charles N., *Chicano Literature*, Boston: Twayne, 1982

Villanueva, Tino, "Sobre el término 'chicano,'" in his *Chicanos: antología histórica y literaria*, Mexico City: Fondo de Cultura Económica, 1980

Yarbro-Bejarano, Yvonne, "Chicana Literature From a Chicana Feminist Perspective," *Chicana Creativity and Criticism: Charting New Frontiers in American Literature*, edited by María Herrera Sobek and Helena María Viramontes, Houston: Arte Público, 1988

Poetry and Narrative

Acosta, Oscar Zeta, *The Autobiography of a Brown Buffalo*, San Francisco: Straight Arrow Books, 1972

Arias, Ron, *The Road to Tamazunchale*, Reno, California: West Coast Poetry Review, 1975

Brito, Aristeo, *El diablo en Texas*, Tucson, Arizona: Editorial Peregrinos, 1976

Candelaria, Cordelia, *Ojo de la cueva/Cave Springs*, Colorado Springs: Maize Press, 1984

Castillo, Ana, *Sapogonia*, New York: Bilingual Review/Press, 1990

Cisneros, Sandra, *Woman Hollering Creek and Other Stories*, New York: Random House, 1991

Méndez, Miguel M., *Peregrinos de Aztlán*, Tucson, Arizona: Editorial Peregrinos, 1974

Morales, Alejandro, *Caras viejas y vino nuevo*, Mexico City: Joaquín Mortiz, 1975

Romero, Leo, *Celso*, Houston: Arte Público, 1985

Ulibarrí, Sabine, *Mi abuela fumaba puros y otros cuentos de Tierra Amarilla*, Berkeley, California: Quinto Sol, 1977

Children's Literature

Feminists are apt to say that literature for children tends to be dismissed by university teachers and scholars as an area suitable only for attention by women. It is certainly true that up to the present children's literature in Latin America has attracted very little critical interest in the English-speaking world, a point that emerges with sharp clarity in the list of texts recommended for further reading at the end of this article. However, within the continent the importance of children's literature has been widely recognised by intellectuals who are also creative writers, ethnographers or pedagogues. Borges once gave an interviewer to understand that all great literature eventually becomes children's literature, adding that he hoped that in the long run his own work would be read by children and, indeed, his personal bestiary, *El libro de los seres imaginarios* (*The Book of Imaginary Beings*), is certainly accessible to young readers. Other writers of continental stature who have either written children's literature or recognised its importance, are Domingo Faustino Sarmiento (Argentina), José Vasconcelos (Mexico), Horacio Quiroga and Juana de Ibarbourou (Uruguay), Marta Brunet and Gabriela Mistral (Chile), Monteiro Lobato (Brazil), Salomé Ureña (Dominican Republic) and both José Martí and Eliseo Diego in Cuba. To these one might add the Peruvian writer and ethnographer, José María Arguedas, whose Castilian versions of popular tales and poems of the Quechua people include material accessible to children and adolescents.

Why, then, has literature for the young in Latin America attracted the attention of many of its most distinguished writers? One very important reason is that it is a foundational literature in the sense that governments in newly-independent countries seek to inculcate a sense of nationhood into schoolchildren. In the case of provinces or regions remote from the capital, this involves accepting the notion of central government, of a culturally dominant metropolis and a periphery whose own culture is tamed by being turned into folklore. Scholars working in the area of cultural studies in Latin America have noted how folklore was discovered in the early decades of the 20th century when modernising states were seeking ways to achieve partial integration of their rural populations. This form of research and cultural appropriation finds its way into children's books and school texts either directly through, say, compilations of popular tales and poetry, or in a more mediated way by the adaptation of indigenous or regional originals. However, there is one crucial example of resistance to the centre by a writer, precisely when and where the process of absorbing the regions into the national mix was in its most acute phase. The author in question was Horacio Quiroga, a Uruguayan by birth, who spent most of his adult life in Argentina. For much of the time he chose to live in a wild tropical part of the country, writing short stories which centre on human beings in relation to their natural environment. Quiroga's most famous collection of stories for children is *Cuentos de la selva* (*South American Jungle Tales*), and an interesting point about this book is that in 1919 the Uruguayan Ministry of Education considered its suitability as a school text but turned the text down because it was thought not to be didactic. At the end of the 20th century its didacticism is perfectly obvious because Quiroga was several generations ahead of his time in his concern for the environment and his awareness of the danger to species in the wild caused by humans encroaching on the animals' natural habitat. This is the theme of many stories for adults and also of "La guerra de los yacarés" [The War of the Alligators] from *Cuentos de la selva*. In fact, all Quiroga's animal stories are accessible to young people, but the essential difference between these and the ones he wrote specifically for children is that the latter display a delicate sense of humour altogether lacking in the sombre stories for adults. In his stories Quiroga attempted also to educate his readers about snakes, so as to counteract the horror of them inculcated by film-makers and both elite and popular writers in the West.

The emergent nation state in Latin America needed to safeguard itself against the cultural imperialism of the United States. At the end of the 19th century the Cuban José Martí regularly warned Latin Americans that the increasing economic power of the US placed them in danger of losing their independence once more. And Martí too wrote for the young by founding in 1889 a magazine, *La Edad de Oro* [The Golden Age]. Only four issues appeared, not because the magazine was not well received, but because Martí fell out with his financial backer. Thus scholars have only a limited amount of material to work on, but all the same, certain points emerge clearly. For example, the opening article of the first issue is devoted to the subject of liberty. This is "Tres héroes" [Three Heroes], which centres on leading figures of the wars of independence in Latin America, Simón Bolivar, Hidalgo and San Martín. Another article, "La ruinas indias" [Indian Ruins], serves to awaken interest in the continent's pre-Columbian past, while "La Ilíada de Homero" [Homer's Iliad], shows how important it was to Martí that children should also be introduced to the European classics. This was a belief shared by the Mexican José Vasconcelos who was Minister of Education in the early 1920s after the decade of revolution in his country. He chose to emphasize Hispanic and Catholic elements so as to combat influences from the Protestant North and, like Martí, he believed that children should be introduced to the works of Homer because the epic was appropriate to childhood as the dawn of life.

Children's literature was not, of course, only fashioned or commissioned by educators intent on forming young minds in a particular way. The children of the creole elite learned the lore of other cultures, such as the African or the Amerinidian, from their nannies. This oral tradition was particularly strong in Brazil where, in addition, written expressions of the popular such as "literatura de cordel" (literature on a string, because that was the way it was sold in markets) appealed to children because of its strong and lurid narrative line.

The 1959 Revolution in Cuba brought children's literature into prominence, as had applied earlier in the case of Mexico. Since that time officials in the cultural sphere have given the impression that with the exception of Martí, children's literature in Cuba was the invention of the Revolution. Certainly it is true that it had never before been promoted to such an extent nor received generous subsidies, but the official line requires some qualification. The children's theatre in Havana, the Guiñol Nacional, was opened in 1955 and there was some interesting work for children being published in the 1940s and 1950s, particularly by Anita Arroyo, Hilda Perera-Soto and Emma Pérez. Anita Arroyo's children's stories are fascinating in ideological terms because as an educated member of the

bourgeosie she was sensitively aware of social injustice, but at the same time she had a very real vested interest in the status quo. Thus, like some 19th-century English writers (Dickens, George Eliot), she thought that social conditions could be improved by individual acts of philanthropy. A particularly clear example of her political naiveté is the story "Islas de diamantes" [Diamond Islands] in which a golden-hearted gringo gives a beach urchin an extraordinary experience by taking him on a flight from Varadero to Havana. In another story, "La rosa de conchas" [The Conch Shell Rose], a gringo buys an urchin a set of new clothes which transform him, readers are told, in a most amazing way. At the end of this story the fortunes of the poor family are left to chance in a literal sense as the good gringo buys them a set of lottery tickets. Since the Cuban Revolution there has been an explosion of talent in the sphere of children's writing in Cuba. Among the most important contributors to its success have been Eliseo Diego, Mirta Aguirre, Enid Vian, Dora Alonso, Julia Calzadilla and many others, including book illustrators and stage designers. It is likely that one reason for the popularity of this form of activity in Cuba since 1959 is that it is "safe" in the sense that there is no need for the creative people involved to practice self-censorship.

The globalization of US mass culture alarms Latin American intellectuals and this includes, of course, its impact on the young. In 1971 Ariel Dorfman and Armand Mattelart published *Para leer al Pato Donald: comunicación de masa y colonialismo* (*How to Read Donald Duck: Imperialist Ideology in the Disney Comic*). At the time it made a great impact but read now, although it is a well-researched study, it seems strident, over-earnest and dualistic. As has been pointed out in a more recent study on popular and mass culture in Latin America, namely *Memory and Modernity* by William Rowe and Vivian Schelling (1991), the "alien" culture may be assimilated in such a way as to produce active, creative results. Thus the authors of this work remind us that the residents of *barrios* or shanty towns in Mexico City appropriated the figure of Superman, turning him into *Superbarrio*, a character who dresses like the American original and who fights for their right to running water, electric light and sewage.

VERITY SMITH

Further Reading

This is divided into three sections: 1. Anthologies and histories of children's literature that cover the continent; 2. Works by writers and pedagogues about literature for children in Latin America; 3. Works of fiction and non-fiction for children from some of the countries of the continent.

1.
Bravo Villasante, C., *Historia y antología de la literatura infantil iberoamericana*, 2 vols, Madrid: Doncel, 1966
Schultz de Mantovani, Fryda, *Sobre las hadas (Ensayos de literatura infantil)*, Buenos Aires: Editorial Nova, 1959

2.
Brunet, Marta, "El mundo mágico del niño," a special issue of *Atenea* (Santiago de Chile), 1959
____ "Cuentos para niños," in *Obras completas*, Santiago de Chile: Zig-Zag, 1963
Dorfman, Ariel and Armand Mattelart, *Para leer al Pato Donald:*

comunicación de masa y colonialismo, Valpairaíso, Chile: Ediciones Universitaria de Valparaíso, 1971; as *How to Read Donald Duck. Imperialist Ideology in the Disney Comic*, translated by David Kunzle, New York: International General, 1975

Meireles, Cecília, *Problemas de la literatura infantil*, 3rd edition, Rio de Janeiro: Nova Frontera, 1984

Sarmiento, Domingo Faustino, "Cuentos para niños," in *Obras completas*, vol. 29, Buenos Aires: Juan Roldán, 1914

Vasconcelos, José, *De Robinson a Odiseo. Obras completas*, Mexico City: Libreros Mexicanos Unidos, vol. 2, 1958

Zilberman, Regina, *Literatura infantil: autoritarismo e emancipaçao*, São Paulo: Ática, 1982

3.

Aguirre, Mirta (Cuba), *Juegos y otros poemas*, Havana: Gente Nueva, 1974

Arroyo, Anita (Cuba), *El pájaro de lata*, Havana: Cultural Sociedad Anónima, 1946

Corona, Pascuala (Mexico), *Cuentos mexicanos para niños*, Mexico City: Porrúa, 1945

Ibarbourou, Juana de (Uruguay), *Chico Carlo*, Montevideo: Barreiro y Ramos, 1944

____ *Los sueños de Natacha*, Montevideo: Ediciones Liceo, 1945

Martí, José (Cuba), *La Edad de Oro*, San Salvador: Ministerio de Educación, 1955

Mistral, Gabriela (Chile), "Rondas" and "Jugarretas," in *Poesías completas*, Madrid: Aguilar, 1958

Quiroga, Horacio (Uruguay), *Cuentos de la selva*, Buenos Aires: Sociedad Cooperativa Editora "Buenos Aires," 1918; as *South American Jungle Tales*, translated by Arthur Livingston, New York: Duffield, 1922; London: Methuen, 1923

Rego, José Lins do (Brazil), *Histórias da Velha Totônia*, Rio de Janeiro: José Olympio, 1936; subsequent editions as *Estorias da Velha Totônia*

Walsh, María Elena (Argentina), *El reino del revés*, Buenos Aires: Fariña, 1963

____ *Cuentopos de Gulubú*, Buenos Aires: Fariña, 1966

Chile

19th- and 20th-Century Prose and Poetry

Nineteenth-century Chilean literature sought to create a national mode of expression while maintaining an extensive dialogue with the literature of Spain, the rest of Europe and North America. There was also an intense relationship with French literature, with particular emphasis on its ideology. The 19th century falls into three distinct stages, each identifying with the major literary tendencies of the period: Neoclassicism 1800–45; Romanticism 1845–90; and Naturalism 1890–1935. These periods coincide with moments of historical, political and social transformation in Chile: first, the struggle for independence and the anarchy it involved; second, the establishment of the republic; and last, the social upheavals resulting from industrialization. Common to all these periods is the utilitarian concept of literature, which perceives literature as an instrument for change and which can influence the social structure. Literature is an expression of society and its collective concerns, and as such is realistic. It sets out faithfully and efficiently to depict changing conditions. It is deterministic and historicist, portraying the collapse of the old regime and the introduction of a new order. Its ultimate aim is to point the way to rationality, freedom and progress.

In terms of literary history, the period of independence and anarchy (1810–45) runs parallel to a Neoclassicism inspired by the Italianate tendencies predominating in Spain. The most obvious influence in poetry and theatre is Metastasio. Outstanding among the first Neoclassical generation was Juan Egaña (1768–1836), a Catholic intellectual, professor of Rhetoric and dean of the Royal and Pontifical University of San Felipe, author of *Cartas Pehuenches* [Andean Letters] and personal memoirs, *El Chileno consolado en los presidios o Filosofía de la religión*, 1826 [A Chilean Finds Consolation in Prison or Philosophy of Religion], written during his incarceration at Juan Fernández. He was a poet who emulated Metastasio, like Meléndez Valdés, who translated his *Zenobia*, for the salon of the wife of the governor Muñoz de Guzmán. A senator and member of the 1813 Junta, he drafted the Constitution of 1823. Among his contemporaries was Camilo Henríquez (1769–1825), a priest of La Buena Muerte and man of letters whose reading included Raynal, Rousseau and Voltaire. He was the author of a proclamation of freedom, signed with the anagram Quirino Lemachez, and editor of Chile's first newspaper, the weekly *Aurora de Chile* (1812–14). He also wrote two dramas not intended for production. The first, inspired by Rousseau, was *Camila o la patriota de Sur América* [Camila or the Patriot of South America]. The second, *La Inocencia en el asilo de las virtudes* [Innocence in the Sanctuary of the Virtues] drew its inspiration from Jansen. The political satire that flourished in the press encouraged debate and also gave rise to the most extensive literary outpourings of the period, from such writers as Camilo Henríquez, José Joaquín de Mora and Antonio José de Irisarri. Those in power, and the Chilean character, were the main butts of the satire. The dominant figure of the Neoclassical period, whose influence endured into the following period, its greatest poet and the most distinguished figure in 19th-century humanism, was Andrés Bello (1781–1865). The leading figure of the third generation of Neoclassicists was Antonio José de Irisarri (1786–1868), satirical poet and author of the novels *El cristiano errante*, 1847 [The Wandering Christian] and *Historia del Perínclito Don Epaminondas del Cauca*, 1863 [The History of the Highly Illustrious Don Epaminondas of Cauca]. Irisarri was also an eminent philologist. Mercedes Marín del Solar

(1804–1860), a disciple of Andrés Bello, was the leading woman writer of the 19th century. Among her poetry is the *Poema fúnebre a la muerte de Diego Portales*, 1837 [Elegy on the Death of Diego Portales], written to mark the statesman's death.

Romanticism developed during the formation of the autocratic republic and the ensuing crisis (1845–1890). The literary output of this time was inhibited by the anti-liberal climate and the classical education of the young writers. The 1842 movement, which provided a starting point for the new generation, was centred on the reforms attempted by the old San Felipe University which was abolished to make way for the University of Chile, which, under the leadership of Andrés Bello, organized the country's entire educational and cultural system. These liberal, innovative and combative activities centred on proscribed Argentine writers, in particular Domingo Faustino Sarmiento and Vicente F. López, who aggressively incited Chilean youth to challenge Bello's authority. The outlook of the young Chileans was, however, no less romantic than that of their detractors, nor were the genres they cultivated – scenes from everyday life, narrative poems, sentimental lyric poems – out of step with the new trends. José Victorino Lastarria's address to the Literary Society on 3 May 1842 is credited with being the starting point of the new movement and the first declaration of intent to instigate a distinctly Chilean literature. Lastarria was later to lose much of his influence in the light of the new demands of Naturalism and Positivism. Of the shorter literary forms, the one most cultivated by this first generation and throughout the period was the *artículo de costumbres*. The inspiration for articles of this kind came from two Spanish authors, Mariano José de Larra and Mesonero Romanos, and they consisted of scenes from everyday life and portraits of social types which served to describe the characteristics of the various social strata. The genre was developed by the leading writers of the period, the most important of whom was José Joaquín Vallejo (1811–1858), writing under the pen-name "Jotabeche." Lastarria, Alberto Blest Gana, Daniel Barros Grez and many others cultivated this type of work. "Jotabeche" outshines the rest through the scope and continuity of his work and the humour and artistry of his description and characterisation of types. In some cases, his narrative style emulates that of the short story and anticipates the *tradición* of Ricardo Palma. His contributions to *El Mercurio de Valparaíso* made him the best-known writer of his time. The most important novelist of the 19th century was Alberto Blest Gana (1830–1920). He produced a cycle of historical novels, covering events beginning with the period known as the Spanish Reconquest, 1814–18, described in *Durante la Reconquista* [During the Reconquest]. The 1835 victory over the Peruvian-Bolivian Confederation is the subject of *El loco Estero*, 1875 [Estero the Madman], while *Martín Rivas* (1862) deals with the civil war of 1851, and *Los transplantados*, 1875 [The Expatriates] focuses on Spanish Americans in Paris at the turn of the century. Like Balzac, Blest Gana saw himself as the chronicler and custodian of his time. His most popular work is *Martín Rivas* (*Martín Rivas* in the English version). This is the novel that every Chilean has read and of which the largest number of editions have been published. A popular genre of the period was the serial novel, of which Daniel Barros Grez (1834–1904) is the most outstanding writer. His series, *Las aventuras del maravilloso perro Cuatro Remos*, 1883 [The Adventures of Four-Legs the Wonder Dog], is still read today. In the realm of travelogues, memoirs and autobiography, Vicente Pérez Rosales's *Recuerdos del pasado*, 1882 [Memories of the Past], are the most important memoirs of the 19th century. He orders events from childhood to maturity, in Chilean, Brazilian and French settings: the Silvela School in Paris and his teacher Leandro Fernández de Moratín; crossing the Andes and the bands of gaucho guerillas; finally, the German colonization of the south. It is still an enjoyable read and its interest as both history and personal memoir has not dwindled. Lastarria's *Recuerdos literarios*, 1885 [Literary Recollections] are vital to the understanding of the literary history of the period. The most notable examples of travel literature are Sarmiento's *Viajes* [Journeys] and *Páginas de mi diario durante tres años de viaje*, 1856 [Pages from My Diary during Three Years of Travel] by Benjamín Vicuña Mackenna (1831–86), biographer, chronicler and historian, and the most prolific writer of the time. The outstanding contemporary political essayist was Francisco Bilbao (1823–57), whose essays include *Sociabilidad chilena* [Chilean Sociability]. History books were the most relevant intellectual expression of the period, represented by the immense works of Miguel Luis Amunátegui (1828–88), Diego Barros Arana (1830–1907) and Vicuña Mackenna.

In poetry, Salvador Sanfuentes (1817–60), Guillermo Blest Gana (1829–1905), Eusebio Lillo (1826–1910) and Guillermo Matta (1826–99) were the leading Chilean Romantic poets. Among Sanfuentes's narrative poems is *El campanario*, 1842 [The Bell Tower], in which, motivated by liberal political ideas, he tells of the struggle for independence and recounts native legends, using both themes to lay the foundation of a national poetry centred on Indian affairs and the history of the homeland. Guillermo Blest Gana and Eusebio Lillo were the most distinctly lyrical of the sentimental poets. Blest Gana's *Armonías*, 1884 [Harmonies] is about love, sadness, reminiscence and nostalgia, and includes protest, letters, humour and a few Indian verses. Guillermo Matta was a civic poet who drew his inspiration from Auguste Comte's "religion of humanity," devoting his poetry to the glorification of scientists and thinkers, modern heroes who give the poetry a lingeringly prosaic and intellectual flavour. Only a few poems and certain verses from the work of these poets survive.

The Naturalist novel developed out of Lastarria's *¡Salvad las apariencias!*, 1884 [For the Sake of Appearances] and by virtue of its absence from the work of Blest Gana, who explicitly rejects Naturalism in his techniques of characterisation. The period was to last from 1890 until 1935, through three generations, each adopting a different approach to Naturalism. The first attempts to portray a crude form of reality were bedroom scenes. These were later abandoned in the face of serious criticism by the press. On a socio-political level, the movement coincided with industrialization, social advancement and enrichment, and the establishment of the first workers' organizations, and what contemporary bourgeois liberals called "the social question." The Revolution of 1891 deeply affected the realities of Chilean life. The period 1890–1935 witnessed a blend of Modernism – with its Parnassian, Symbolist and Decadent elements – and Naturalism. Vicente Grez (1847–1909) whose novels include *El ideal de una esposa*,

1887 [A Wife's Ideal], a portrait of temperamental incompatibility and jealousy, was the most outstanding novelist of the first Naturalist generation. Luis Orrego Luco (1866–1947) was Chile's leading *modernista*. A contemporary of Rubén Darío, Orrego Luco was responsible for receiving the poet on his arrival in Santiago. His most important novel *Casa grande*, 1908 [The Big House] is a love story which ends with an elegantly-executed crime brought about by a clash of temperaments, social change and the moral and economic collapse of the upper class. However, the most original expression of Naturalism came with the *mundonovista* generation, enhanced by elements other than the influence of Zola and Taine. From his European vantage point, Francisco Contreras, poet and prose writer, created the concept and coined the word *mondovisme* (New Worldism) in the *Mercure de France*. His foreword to *El pueblo maravilloso*, 1927 [The Marvellous People] traces the development of this type of novel. Mariano Latorre is the most convincing and lucid representative of the regionalist movement. His narrative takes as its setting the many and varied geographical locations suggested by the title of his anthology *Chile, país de rincones*, 1947 [Chile, Land of Crannies], in which, using the argument of the determinism of environment, he rejects the possibility of literature advocating the unity of a land which encompasses seven types of different and conflicting landscapes: desert, transversal valleys, longitudinal valleys, mountain range, coast, forest and the south. His novel *Zurzulita* (1918) anticipates the so-called "American exemplary novels" or "novels of the homeland." However, for the protagonist the drive for regeneration of the land is not the result of expectation or desire, but of the triumph of violence and peasant cunning. The *mundonovista* novel explores different aspects of the conflict between the rural and urban attitudes. Eduardo Barrios (1884–1963), developed the psychological novel, beginning with the Naturalistic form of *Un perdido*, 1918 [A Lost Soul], through the Decadence of *El hermano asno*, 1922 (Brother Asno), to the contemporary psychological insight of *Los hombres del hombre*, 1950 [Man's Many Faces] and the robust rural expression of *Gran señor y rajadiablos*, 1948 [Great Lord and Hell-raiser]. Fernando Santiván (1886–1973) shows understanding of social problems and sympathy towards the emancipation of the lower classes in *El Crisol* [The Melting Pot]. Joaquín Edwards Bello (1887–1968) describes the world of a seaport in his novel *Valparaíso, la ciudad del viento* [Valparaíso, the Windy City] which was to appear in various versions. It was published under this title in 1931, then in 1943 as *En el viejo almendral* [In the Old Almond Grove] and then simply as *Valparaíso* in 1955. Other notable novelists are Augusto D'Halmar (1882–1950) following in the steps of Zola in *Juana Lucero* (1902) and, in the Decadent tradition, *Pasión y muerte del cura Deusto* [The Passion and Death of Father Deusto] and in many novellas. There are two writers who, each in their different way, are something of a phenomenon. One is Pedro Prado (1886–1952) author of the novels *Rapa Nui, un juez rural* [A Country Magistrate] and especially *Alsino* (1920). The latter is the novel of a *mundonovista* artist and poet, who derives his poetry from its natural source. The second is Jenaro Prieto (1889–1946), author of *El socio*, 1928 [The Partner], an ironic challenge to the aggressive tendencies of the avant-garde, especially in its parody of imagist language.

The short story was a popular genre of the period. An outstanding member of the first generation was Daniel Riquelme (1854–1912) whose *Bajo la tienda* [Under Canvas] carries echoes of the Pacific Campaign. Baldomero Lillo (1867–1923) with his collections *Sub terra* (1904) and *Sub sole* (1907), Federico Gana (1867–1926), with *Días de campo*, 1926 [Days in the Country] and Rubén Darío (1867–1916), with his stories in *Azul*, 1888 [Blue] are examples of Naturalistic and Decadent tendencies. Mariano Latorre (1885–1955), author of many volumes of stories, is the *mundonovista* and *criollista* short story writer *par excellence*. Augusto d'Halmar, Eduardo Barrios, Pedro Prado, Olegario Lazo Baeza all handle the short story with great dexterity. In literature by women, novels of the period brought to the fore the first authors to gain prominence in the world of letters. They wrote under pseudonyms and were members of the upper class. They included "Shade," Mariana Cox de Stuven (1871–1914) author of *Un remordimiento*, 1909 [A Sense of Remorse] and *La vida íntima de María Goetz*, 1909 [The Intimate Life of María Goetz], and "Iris," Inés Echeverría de Larraín (1868–1949), with her cycle of novels in the style of memoirs, *Cuando mi tierra nació*, 1930 [When My Country Was Born], *Cuando mi tierra era niña*, 1942 [When My Country Was a Young Girl], and *Cuando mi tierra fue moza*, 1943–46 [When My Country Was a Young Woman]. The celebrations in 1910 of the centenary of Independence provoked reflection on the state of the nation expressed in essays like those of Nicolás Palacios, *Raza chilena*, 1911 [Chilean Race], Alejandro Venegas, Dr Valdés Canje *Sinceridad o Chile íntimo en 1910* [Sincerity or Inside Chile in 1910], Francisco A. Encina (1874–1965), *Nuestra inferioridad económica*, 1911 [Our Economic Inferiority]. Armando Donos, Augusto D'Halmar, and Fernando Santiván all produced interesting memoirs. In *La fronda aristocrática*, 1928 [The Aristocratic Frond], Alberto Edwards (1873–1932) presents the deepest insight into the socio-political phenomenon of Chile. Literary history, criticism, bibliography and other disciplines were dominated by the distinguished and multi-talented writer José Toribio Medina (1852–1930), whose vast output seems hardly conceivable for one man.

In poetry, the first – 1882 – generation of poets included José A. Soffia and Luis Rodríguez Velasco, who took their inspiration from Bécquer and Campoamor, as well as from Classicism and the first manifestations of the French Parnassians. The *modernista* generation of 1897, whose sensibility began early in Chile with the publication of Darío's *Azul*, issued its first publication to coincide with its participation in the 1887 Varela Competition, taking second prize in the poetry section, in which the winner was Eduardo de la Barra with his heroic *Canto a las glorias de Chile* [Ballad to the Glories of Chile]. Rubén Darío was to live in Chile between 1887 and 1889 and his work would influence the poets of his own generation and the whole period. Pedro A. González (1863–1903) was the most outstanding *modernista* poet with his *Ritmos*, 1895 [Rhythms] and *Poesías* [Poems] (1905). Julio Vicuña Cifuentes, Antonio Bórquez Solar and Gustavo Valledor Sánchez also produced notable works. As for the younger – 1912 – generation, Pedro Prado (1886–1952), in his *Flores de cardo*, 1909 [Flowers of the Thistle], marks the shift of sensibility away from Modernism and towards the intimacy and simplicity that were the hallmarks of the new generation. Prado's books of poetic prose has resonances of Rabindranath Tagore and Omar Khayyam. With the Mexican Antonio Castro Leal, he was joint author of *Fragmentos*, 1922 [Fragments], an apocryphal book bearing the signature of Karez-y-Rosham. *Los pájaros errantes*, 1915 [Birds of Passage], *Otoño en las dunas*, 1940 [Autumn in the Dunes], *Esta bella ciudad envenenada*, 1945 [This Beautiful Poisoned City], *Más que una rosa*, 1946 [More than a Rose] revert to the sonnet and other traditional forms. Carlos Pezoa Velis (1879–1908) represents the *sencillismo* (cultivated simplicity) of his generation with the inclusion of popular themes in poems such as "Pancho y Tomás [Pancho and Thomas], "Nada" [Nothing], and others, in his posthumous anthology. Gabriela Mistral (1889–1957) detaches herself from the trends followed by others of her generation and creates her personal brand of poetry, taking advantage of the innovations of the avant-garde. Her great books, *Desolación*, 1922 [Desolation], *Ternura*, 1924 [Tenderness], *Tala*, 1938 [Felling], *Lagar*, 1954 [Winepress], and *Poema de Chile*, 1967 [Poem of Chile] transformed her into the leading figure in contemporary Chilean and Spanish American letters. Other outstanding poets of the group include Carlos R. Mondaca (1881–1928), Diego Dublé Urrutia (1877–1967), Manuel Magallanes Moure (1878–1924), Max Jara (1886–1965), Jorge González Bastías (1879–1950), who together made up a generation whose diverse forms of expression are all within the simple spirit of elemental motifs and unpretentious sentiments.

Chilean literature during the contemporary era (1935–95) is enhanced by the international status acquired by such major figures as Gabriela Mistral, winner of the Nobel Prize for Literature in 1945, the first to be awarded after World War II and the first to be accorded to a Spanish American writer, and Pablo Neruda (1904–73) who was awarded the Nobel Prize in 1971, Neruda is the most widely-read writer in Spanish and his work has been translated into many languages. Vicente Huidobro (1893–1948) was a writer of considerable literary importance, who influenced Spanish and Latin American poetry and the French and European avant-garde. His premature death limited the extent of his work. All these poets were affected to a greater or lesser degree by the socio-political situation, and the new factional alignments of left and right leading to the turmoil which was to shape the fate of the nation throughout the period between 1938 and 1980. The avant-garde period and the political realignment of left and right is marked by Huidobro's early militancy and his equally precocious rejection of the foolhardy pact between the Soviet Union and Germany in 1939, followed by his condemnation of ideological divisions and the affirmation of "el hombre total" (the whole man). In this respect, the only parallels were Gabriela Mistral, who denounced the Cold War in "La Palabra Maldita" [That Accursed Word], and later the essays of Lihn, Valdés and Hunneus which censured sectarianism in *La cultura en la sociedad en vías al socialismo* [Culture in a Society Moving Towards Socialism]. Avant-garde writers of the period clearly registered their rejection of the status quo, not only in the world of letters but also in contemporary society and the world at large. As well as Huidobro and Neruda, others including Parra, Lihn and Arteche wrote poems dealing unequivocally with the current situation. Postmodern poetry of the present day defies such classification and embraces allusions to current events, imitations of journalistic and advertising styles, and its own interpretation of different ethnic cultures.

Among the first generation of the literary avant-garde, the generation of 1927, it was Vicente Huidobro more than anyone else in the world of Hispanic letters, who defined *creacionista* poetry, which champions the autonomy of poetry and inspired a poetic language independent of everyday language, while staying close in its selection of vocabulary and linguistic content of its process of subversion. His poetic work, whose autonomy is not at odds with its specific context, presents a critical vision of modernity and its plans for democratization and secularization, the introduction of technology and distortion of the environment. In *El espejo de agua*, 1916 [The Mirror of Water], *Poemas árticos*, 1918 (*Arctic Poems*), *Ecuatorial*, 1918 [Equatorial], *Altazor* (1931), *Temblor de cielo*, 1931 [Heaven Trembling], *Ver y Palpar*, 1941 [Seeing and Feeling] and *El ciudadano del olvido*, 1941 [Citizen of Oblivion], Huidobro moves increasingly towards autonomy of vocabulary and subject matter. Pablo Neruda was the poet with the greatest influence on the language thanks to simple, sentimental works like *Crepusculario*, 1923 [Where Twilight Dwells] and some of the *Veinte poemas de amor y una canción desepserada*, 1924 (*Twenty Love Poems and a Song of Despair*) of which millions of copies have been sold and the poems set to music and sung by the unprivileged. His most ambitious and disparate work is *Canto general*, 1950 (*Canto General*), which in fifteen poems traces the political history of America from pre-Columbian civilization up to the modern dictatorships. Linked by an autobiographical thread, the various sections of the *Canto* tell of political militancy and the persecution suffered as a result. The crowning moment comes with *Alturas de Macchu Picchu* (*The Heights of Macchu Picchu*), one of the greatest poems ever written in Spanish. Stimulated by the transformations introduced by the new trends, he wrote *Estravagario* (*Extravagaria*) along the lines of anti-poetry and *Odas elementales* (*The Elemental Odes*) in the style of the youthful *poetas láricos* (poets of the hearth or of provincial settings), following the prototype of *Materias* [Materials] in Gabriela Mistral's *Tala*. He left eight posthumous books, which developed and expanded on the playful, mythical and ideological themes of his previous work. Pablo de Rokha (1894–1968) was the thunderously aggressive poet of ideological opposition. Inspired by Marx and Mao, his language is savage, prosaic and violent. Other important, but less striking, members of this generation were Ángel Cruchaga Santa María (1893–1964), whose early works were mystical and closer to Neruda, his *Rostro de Chile*, 1955 [Face of Chile] filling the gaps in *Canto general*, and Rosamel del Valle (1900–65) whose early work bore strong resemblances to Huidobro but who later turned to Surrealism, contributing to the magazine *Mandrágora*.

The second avant-garde generation, the generation of 1942, was Surrealist and anti-poetic. The young poets founded the *runrunismo* and *agú* movements and their periodicals *Mandrágora* (1938), *Leit Motif*, *Ariel* (1925), and others. The outstanding figure of this second avant-garde generation is Nicanor Parra. His (anti-) poetry proclaims the precedence of the spoken language over the written, through speeches, sermons, debates and vernacular sayings, partisan slogans, etc., although he also produced a variety of written genres, such as statements, political speeches, newspaper articles, advertising slogans, news bulletins, stories in various styles, lending a prosaic dimension to his antipoetry, which was also expressed in popular forms like folk song, advertising, postcards, painting and photography. Irony and humour are the dominant stylistic devices in his satire which targets populist politics, dictatorship and repression in equal measure. Later he devoted himself to the protection of the environment, writing so-called "eco-poems." Alongside Parra, the most outstanding figure is Gonzalo Rojas (1917–), 1992 winner of the National Prize for Literature and the Queen Sofía Poetry Prize in the same year. His impassioned and sensual poetry has matured with the poet. His major works are *Contra la muerte*, 1964 [Against Death], *Oscuro*, 1977 [Dark], *Transtierro*, 1979 [Hinterland], *Del relámpago*, 1981 [From the Lightning], and *Materia de testamento*, 1988 [Clauses from a Will]. His basic themes are eroticism, freedom, death and mystery, the cryptic and the conspicuous. Other outstanding poets of this generation include Humberto Díaz Casanueva (1906–92), whose works include the exceptional *Requiem* (1945), *La estatua de sal*, 1947 [The Salt Statue], *Los penitenciales* [Penitential] (1960) and *Sol de lenguas*, 1969 [The Light of Language]. He is a poet who combines poetry and erudition. The most important phenomenon of this generation is the Surrealist group Mandrágora [Mandrake] formed around 1938 by Braulio Arenas, Enrique Gómez Correa and Jorge Cáceres. They were briefly joined by Gonzalo Rojas, Humberto Díaz Casanueva and several poets of the previous generation. Among the Surrealists, Braulio Arenas (1913–88) produced the most extensive and coherent work, although in his later years he moved away from Surrealism. He was awarded the National Prize for Literature in 1984. The magazines *Mandrágora*, *Leitmotif* and his books, including *El AGC de la Mandrágora*, trace the history of the movement and help explain it. Among his most important books are *Discurso del gran poder* [Discourse on Might], *Luz adjunta* [Adjoining Light] and *Poesía* [Poetry].

The third avant-garde generation, the generation of 1957, was defined by ideological and political tensions and permeated by the singularly barbed and sceptical attitudes of the 1980s. Among its leading and diverse representatives are Enrique Lihn (1929–88), Miguel Arteche (1926–) and Armando Uribe Arce (1933–). Lihn was a poet, novelist and playwright, whose poetic works are the most worthy of recognition. His poetry proclaims the precedence of the written language over the spoken, we speak as we write, but paradoxically seeks to show the domination of the printed word over our literary practices. *La pieza oscura*, 1963 [The Dark Room], *La musiquilla de las pobres esferas*, 1969 [A Little Music from the Lower Spheres], *París, situación irregular*, 1977 [Paris, an Unusual Situation], *Diario de muerte*, 1989 [Diary of Death], display highly individual features marked by irony, disillusion, and self-conscious criticism of his own poetry. Miguel Arteche represents a totally different outlook with the biblical and religious references of his tormented view of the world, reminiscent of Quevedo, and the curious nature of his visions. His most striking works are *Destierros y tinieblas*, 1963 [Exile and Twilight], *Otro continente*, 1957

[Another Continent], *Quince poemas*, 1961 [Fifteen Poems], *Noches*, 1976 [Nights] and *Fénix de madrugada*, 1994 [Dawn Phoenix]. Last, Armando Uribe Arce has produced only a few books of short, humorous and ironic poems: *Los obstáculos*, 1960 [Obstacles], *No hay lugar*, 1971 [There is No Room], *Por ser vos quien sois*, 1989 [Since You Are Who You Are]. Other notable poets of the period are Luis Oyarzún (1920–72) and Ludwig Zeller (1927–).

With the relaxation of political and ideological tension, a new period began around 1980, rejecting the affectation and detachment of the pre-avant-garde poets. The generation of 1972 includes Jorge Teillier (1935–), Oscar Hahn (1938–), Manuel Silva Acevedo (1942–), Juan Luis Martínez (1943–93), Waldo Rojas (1943–) Gonzalo Millán (1947–) and Rodrigo Lira (1949–81). Teillier is one of several important "poets of the hearth" or "poets of provincial settings," using a muted rhetoric and straightforward subjects. Some of their output was to be affected by exile, worldly experience and scepticism. Others are dissidents such as Martínez, Rodrigo Lira and Gonzalo Millán, whose work is characterized by the confluence of different cultural and artistic forms.

Numbering among the outstanding representatives of the current generation of 1987 is Raúl Zurita (1951–), whose work is the most extensive, most widely recognized and translated. He is the author of *Anteparaíso*, 1982 [Antiparadise], *Purgatorio*, 1979 [Purgatory], *Canto a su amor desaparecido*, 1985 [Song to a Lost Love], *El amor de Chile* [The Love of Chile) and *Vida nueva*, 1994 [New Life]. Another notable poet is Diego Maquieira (1951–), author of *La Tirana*, 1983 [The Tyrant] and *Los Sea-Harrier*, 1993 [Sea Harriers].

Poetry written by women is a growing phenomenon. The unsurpassed works of Gabriela Mistral are the most distinguished expression of feminine poetry, defying categorization. Other women poets include María Monvel, Teresa Wilms Montt, Winett de Rokha (1895–1951) and Marta Brunet (1897–1967) who in her *Aleluyas para los más chiquitos* [Alleluias for the Very Young] tackles the difficult genre of children's poetry, similar to the Mistrailan "jugarretas" (nursery rhymes). There are many other women poets among whom Delia Domínguez (1931–), Sara Vial (1931–) and Rosa Cruchaga (1931–) stand out.

Popular poetry presents the exceptional case of the living voice of folk tradition which inspires the widely published works of Violeta Parra (1917–67), including *Violeta*, *Décimas* [Ten-line stanzas], *Veintiuno son los dolores* [Twenty-one Forms of Pain], *Virtud de los elementos* [The Virtue of the Elements] and others included in numerous anthologies. Apart from the popular poetry tracked down in towns and villages, and brought to a wide audience by Violeta Parra and her brother Roberto, others, such as Julio Vicuña Cifuentes, Raquel Barros, Manuel Dannemann and Inés Dolz, have guaranteed the survival of folk ballads, while the popular poetry of soldiers, religious festivals and songs celebrating the human and the divine, have been collected by Juan Uribe Echevarría.

A new phenomenon is ethnic poetry and literature. Indigenous poetry, that is, poetry written by Araucanian Indians in Spanish or Mapudungún and sometimes published in a bilingual version. This new trend is represented by Elicura Chihuailaf (1958–) in *En el país de la memoria*, 1988 [In the Land of Memory] and the youthful Leonel Lienlaf (1970–) with his *Se ha despertado el ave de mi corazón*, 1989 [The Bird in My Heart Has Awakened]. Another variation is poetry written in Spanish by descendants of the colonialists using Araucanian words and phrases, as in *Karra Maw'n* (1984) by Clemente Riedman (1953).

The contemporary novel shows how this genre has been transformed by narrative subjectivity, new levels of reality, self-examination and strange allegories and allusions illuminating new contexts. Manuel Rojas (1896–1973) was the first to use a subjective narrative position in an early novel *Lanchas en la bahía*, 1932 [Boats in the Bay]. The novel was innovative in taking as its subject the common people, the marginal world of the outcast, and the development of the protagonist in the midst of desperate conditions. The same applies to his four-part cycle *Hijo de ladrón*, 1951 (*Born Guilty*), *Mejor que el vino*, 1964 [Better than Wine], and his last novel *La oscura vida radiante*, 1971 [A Life of Darkness and Light]. *Hijo de ladrón* is the finest, and is undeniably among the most distinguished of all Spanish American novels. Its autobiographical story, its narrative style and technique display considerable originality. *La oscura vida radiante* invokes the political situation of 1920, and describes political agitation with an ideological fervour not previously seen in his work *Punta de rieles*, 1960 [Where the Rails Cross], is an innovative novel in the form of a conversation in which two characters exchange the intimate details of their personal lives and a double play on words both spoken and undisclosed. Rojas was also one of the more important writers of short stories, striking for their anecdotal and emotive style rather than for any other narrative virtue. Of the novels of Benjamín Subercaseaux (1902–73), which include *Daniel*, *Rahab* and *Jemmy Button*, the last is his most ambitious. It tells of the voyage aboard the "Beagle," of Captain FitzRoy, who rounds up a group of Yaghan Indians and takes them to the Royal Court of England. Having been educated there, they return to their homeland where they integrate fully and forget all about their European training. It is a culturally and ethnically diverse, anthropologically pessimistic novel. The novels of Juan Marín (1900–63) *Viento negro*, 1944 [Black Wind] and *Paralelo 53 Sur* [Parallel 53 South] were denied recognition when first published, because of the denunciation of the exploitation in the coal mines in the former, and criticism of international interests in the Chilean petrochemical industry in the latter. Other notable novelists of this generation are Salvador Reyes (1899–1970) and Carlos Sepúlveda Leyton (1894–1944), author of *Hijuna*, 1934 [Bastard], *La fábrica*, 1935 [The Factory] and *Camarada*, 1938 [Comrade]. The most prominent woman writer of the period is Marta Brunet (1897–1967), author of *Montaña adentro*, 1923 [Into the Mountain], *Humo hacia el sur*, 1946 [Smoke in the South], *María Nadie*, 1957 [María Nobody], *Amasijo*, 1962 [Hotchpotch], and among other works, two volumes of short stories, *La mampara*, 1946 [The Screen] and *Raíz del sueño*, 1949 [Root of Sleep]. The main theme of her work is the role and experience of women. Another important writer is Alberto Romero (1896–1981), best remembered for his novel *La viuda del conventillo*, 1930 [The Widow from the Slums].

Among the leading novelists of the 1942 generation are Carlos Droguett (1912–), María Luisa Bombal (1910–80) and Nicomedes Guzmán (1914–64). Droguett's novels include *Los*

asesinados del Seguro Obrero, 1940 [Murders at the Dole Office] and his more elaborate version, *Sesenta muertos en la escalera*, 1940 [Sixty Corpses on the Staircase] (1940), *Eloy* (1960), *El compadre*, 1967 [The Buddy], *Patas de perro* [Dog's Paws] (1965), *Todas esas muertes*, 1971 [So Many Deaths] and *El hombre que trasladaba ciudades* [The Man Who Moved Cities]. His novels of colonial times *Supay el cristiano*, 1967 [Supay the Christian] and *Cien gotas de sangre*, 1961 [One Hundred Drops of Blood] complete his obsessive and self-imposed task of portraying Chile's bloody history. His most notable successes are *Eloy* and *El compadre*. The first is the story of a murderer at bay in the mountains, while the second records popular dismay at the death of the President, a character modelled on Pedro Aguirre Cerda. One of the leading Spanish American storytellers is María Luisa Bombal, author of *La última niebla* (*The House of Mist*), *La amortajada* (*The Shrouded Woman*) and *La historia de María Griselda* [The Story of María Griselda], and a handful of other masterly short stories available in collections. All are stories of women forlornly defending their identity and their right to genuine love. Representing a distinctly Chilean version of Neorealism, a modified version of Socialist Realism, Nicomedes Guzmán (1914–64), a writer of working-class origins, produced novels based on his personal experiences, such as *Los hombres oscuros*, 1939 [Men of Darkness], *La sangre y la esperanza*, 1943 [Blood and Hope] and *La luz viene del mar*, 1951 [The Light Comes from the Sea]. Another remarkable figure is that of Juan Godoy (1911–81), author of *Angurrientos*, 1940 [The Greedy], *La cifra solitaria*, 1945 [The Solitary Number] and *Sangre de murciélago*, 1959 [Bat's Blood]. Oscar Castro, Daniel Belmat, Francisco Coloane, Reinaldo Lomboy and Volodia Teitelboim are important novelists of the period. This generation's short stories were inspired by Surrealism and by the debate surrounding new writing in Chile, in which Braulio Arenas, Droguett and Miguel Serrano participated. The leading short story writers are María Luisa Bombal, whose work includes the masterly story "El árbol" (The Tree), and Oscar Castro.

The generation of 1957 began to publish in 1950, but the latter date gave the group its name. Their most important member and Chile's outstanding contemporary writer is José Donoso. His works include *Coronación*, 1957 (*Coronation*), *El obsceno pájaro de la noche*, 1970 (*The Obscene Bird of Night*), *Casa de campo* (*A House in the Country*) and *La desesperanza* (*Curfew*). His most recent novel, the first in ten years, is *Donde van a morir los elefantes*, 1995 [The Elephants' Graveyard] which mingles humour, disillusion and metanarrative. Donoso's *El lugar sin límites* (*Hell Has No Limits*), *Este Domingo* (*This Sunday*), *El jardín de al lado* (*The Garden Next Door*) and *La misteriosa desaparición de la condesita de Loria* [The Mysterious Disappearance of the Young Countess of Loria], are novels of sexuality, disaffection and exile, whose influences include that of the erotic novel. He has also written several novellas and collections of short stories, as well as *Historia personal del Boom* (*The "Boom" in Spanish American Literature: a Personal History*), an ingenious exercise in literary history. Jorge Edwards is the author of *Los convidados de piedra* [The Stone Guests], which alludes to recent political events in Chile, *El museo de cera* [The Wax Museum] and *La mujer imaginaria* [The Imaginary Woman]. He has also produced *Cuentos completos* [Complete Short Stories], collected in several volumes. The small output of Jorge Guzmán (1930–), author of *Job-Boj* (1968) and *Ay Mama Inés*, 1963 [Oh, Mother Inés], is of exceptional quality. *Job-Boj* tells two interwoven and contrasting stories of people in different situations, and *Ay Mama Inés* is an example of the new Latin American historical novel, conforming to the evolution of the genre and telling the story of Inés Suárez, mistress of Pedro de Valdivia, conqueror of Chile. Other outstanding writers of this generation are Enrique Lafourcade (1927–), Guillermo Blanco (1926–), and Hugo Correa (1926–), who specializes in science fiction. Margarita Aguirre and Mercedes Valdivieso (1925–93) are the leading women writers of the generation.

The present period, which began in about 1980 is already far removed from the activities of the avant-garde and the confrontation between left and right that typified their youth. Three generations can be distinguished, already dissolved in the spirit of the postmodern. Among the outstanding representatives of the generation of 1972 is Antonio Skármeta (1940–), a skilful storyteller whose works include *Desnudo en el tejado* [Naked on the Roof], *Novios y solitarios* [Couples and Singles], *Tiro libre* [Fire at Will], and novels with resonances in actual events, such as *Soñé que la nieve ardía* (*I Dreamt the Snow was Burning*), about Allende's last days in Chile, *La Insurrección* (*The Insurrection*), dealing with the time leading up to the Sandinista Revolution in Nicaragua, and *Match Ball*, a parody of sports reporting and tabloid journalism, set in the world of international tennis. The novels of Mauricio Wacquez (1939–) explore the realm of sexuality. They include *Frente a un hombre armado*, 1981 [Face to Face with a Gunman], *Paréntesis*, 1982 [Parenthesis], and *Ella, o El sueño de nadie*, 1983 [She, or The Dream of Nobody]. Cristián Hunneus (1937–85), was the author of *Cuento de cámara* [Chamber Stories], *La casa de Algarrobo* [The House of Algarrobo] and the novels *El cuarto de los niños*, 1980 [The Children's Room]. The last is an account of childhood unfolding predominantly as a metanarrative commentary, and *El verano del ganadero*, 1983 [The Summer of the Rancher], an erotic novel narrated by the central character, Gaspar Ruiz, a device distancing the narrative from the controlling hand of the real author. Other novelists of this generation include Carlos Morand (1936–), José Luis Rosasco (1935–), Poli Délano (1936–), Patricio Manns (1937–), and Francisco Simón Rivas (1943–). Among the younger members of the group, Luis Sepúlveda (1949–), author of the novels *Un viejo que leía novelas de amor*, 1992 [An Old Man Who Read Romantic Novels] (1992) and *Nombre de torero*, 1994 [Name of a Bullfighter], has succeeded in interpreting the literary concerns of the new society. He projects an ecological vision defending cultural and ethnic differences against the violence of society and the powers that be, while writing a well-told story. This period has brought to the fore a large number of women writers, who have assertively established a new and different literary environment. Isabel Allende (1942–), Diamela Eltit (1949–) and Ana María del Río (1948–) form an exceptional group of novelists who have elevated the status of women in 20th-century literature. With *La casa de los espíritus* (*The House of the Spirits*), Isabel Allende has reached a wide audience and her fame has increased even further with the translation of the novel into several languages. *Eva Luna*, 1987, *El plan infinito*, 1991 [The Infinite Plan] and *Paula* (1994) clearly draw on the territory explored in her first novel. Diamela Eltit's publications begin with a series of anti-novels on marginal subjects, unlike those usually forming the basis of the novel. These include *Por la patria*, 1986 [In the Name of the Fatherland] and *Lumpérica*, 1983 [Lumpen/America]. Among her later novels is *Vaca sagrada*, 1991 (*Sacred Cow*), where she modifies her strategies, turning to the ideology of the body and the act of writing, producing a novel of eroticism stained by the blood of woman. *Los vigilantes*, 1994 [The Vigilantes], is a monodic novel in the form of letters, a feminist allegory in a unique setting. Ana María del Río, is a novelist and short story writer, author of *De golpe, Amalia en el umbral*, 1991 [Suddenly, Amalia is on the Doorstep]. In her feminist novel *Siete días de la señora K*, 1992 [Seven Days in the Life of Mrs K], she attempts to revive women's experience of discovering their bodies and autoeroticism, tempered by the disillusion with such experience taken from the work of María Luisa Bombal. In general terms, this is her most accomplished work. Her latest novel is *Tiempo que ladra*, 1994 [Barking Time].

The present generation (that of 1987) comprises novelists born between 1950 and 1964 who are just beginning to achieve prominence. They include Gonzalo Contreras (1958–), author of *La ciudad lejana* [The Distant City], Arturo Fontaine (1952–), author of *Oír su voz*, 1992 [To Hear His/Her Voice], Marcela Serrano (1951–) and Pía Barros (1956–), the most skilled and aggressive of the feminist writers with her *El tono menor del deseo*, 1991 [Desire in a Minor Key]. Alberto Fuguet (1964–) emerges as the most innovative figure in his short stories and novels *Mala onda* (1991) and *Por favor, rebobinar*, 1994 [Rewind, Please].

Reportage-style literature, arising from political events in Chile between 1973 and 1985, deals with international politics, internal repression and exile. The most important works of this kind are *Tejas Verdes* (*Tejas Verdes*), by Hernán Valdés, and Jorge Edwards's *Persona non grata*. Ethnic literature, focusing on indigenous cultures, includes *La reina de Rapa-Nui* [The Queen of Rapa-Nui], by Pedro Prado, about the Easter Islanders, and *Ranquil* (1942), by Reynaldo Lomboy (1910–74), the story of a massacre of Indians during colonial expansion. *El vado de la noche*, 1955 [The Night Ford] by Lautori Yankas (1902–), and other works of lesser significance, deal with different periods in the history and aspects of the lives of Chile's indigenous Araucanian Indians. This period has also seen the emergence of a number of works revealing the spirit of the descendants of the frontiersmen of long ago. Collectively, these have come to be known as the literature of "bad conscience" or "guilty conscience." Patricio Manns (1937–) and Luis Vulliamy are the leading exponents of this tendency. Another aspect of ethnic literature is that collected by Rodolfo Lenz in his *Estudios araucanos* [Araucanian Studies], and more recently in *Cuentos mapuches de Chile*, 1987 [Mapuche Tales from Chile], stories told orally in Spanish, and carefully compiled by the great folklorist Yolando Pino Saavedra, as part of his extensive research into the Chilean folk tale.

CEDOMIL GOIC

translated by Isabel Varea

Further Reading

Concha, Jaime, *Poesía chilena*, Santiago de Chile: Editorial
   Quimantú, 1973
Fein, John M., *Modernismo in Chilean Literature: the Second
   Period*, Durham, North Carolina: Duke University Press, 1965
Fleak, Kenneth, *The Chilean Short Story: Writers from the
   Generation of 1950*, New York: Peter Lang, 1989
Goic, Cedomil, *La novela chilena: los mitos degradados*, Santiago de
   Chile: Editorial Universitaria, 1968; 5th edition, 1991
Jara, René, *Los límites de la representación: la novela chilena del
   golpe*, Madrid: Hiperión, 1985
____ *El revés de la arpillera: perfil literario de Chile*, Madrid:
   Hiperión, 1988
Promis Ojeda, José, *La novela chilena actual: orígenes y desarrollo*,
   Buenos Aires: García Cambeiro, 1977
____ *La novela chilena del último siglo*, Santiago de Chile: Editorial
   La Noria, 1993
Rodríguez Fernández, Mario, *El modernismo en Chile y en
   Hispanoamérica*, Santiago de Chile: Editorial Universitaria, 1962

Silva Castro, Raúl, *Historia crítica de la novela chilena*, Madrid:
   Ediciones Cultura Hispánica, 1960

Bibliographies

Foster, David William, *Chilean Literature. A Working Bibliography
   of Secondary Sources*, Boston: G.K. Hall, 1978
Goic, Cedomil, *Bibliografía de la novela chilena del siglo XX*,
   Santiago de Chile: Editorial Universitaria, 1962
Muñoz González, Luis, *Diccionario de movimientos y grupos
   literarios chilenos*, Concepción, Chile: Universidad de Concepción,
   1993

Special Issues of Journals

Review: Latin American Literature and Arts, vol. 49 (Fall
   1994)
Revista Iberoamericana 168–69 (July–December 1994) [On 20th-
   century Chilean literature]

Antonio Cisneros 1942–

Peruvian poet

Antonio Cisneros is a member of an influential generation of Latin American poets that began publishing their first collection of poems in the 1960s. What brings these poets together to constitute a generation is the belief that writers must embrace the moral imperative of being truthful and of engaging with their reality; therefore, they must insist on saying what needs to be said rather than what it is possible to say within the constraints of poetic writing. In Cisneros's preface to his anthological *Poesía, una historia de locos* [Poetry, a History of the Mad], the writer's ideal should be to say what one wishes to express and not simply what it is acceptable to say. He is addressing one of the principles which defined the new poetic practice of his generation.

Cisneros is one of the most important voices of the "Sixties Generation." His poetry is iconoclastic, acerbic, highly critical of his cultural heritage, and up to a point, quite contemptuous of Latin American reality. His is a strident version of conversational poetry, keenly observant of the injustice of traditional social demarcations, which he denounces fiercely. One of his main concerns is the Peruvian national experience, a theme that dominates *Comentarios reales de Antonio Cisneros*, 1964 [Royal Commentaries of Antonio Cisneros], his third book of poems, and the first widely acclaimed work by him to introduce a new poetic expression and a new narrative tone. It is uncommon for a book of poems to receive such a national broad-based acclaim as this volume did in Peru. The collection reviews the history of Peru backwards, or in Cisneros's words, a Brechtian vision of history, meaning that history is here told from the viewpoint of the common people, thus superseding the perspective of the national heroes and monuments erected to commemorate them. This early work speaks accurately to the historical decade of the 1960s in Peru, when guerilla uprisings in the Sierra region, and in Ayacucho in particular, had been defeated. Cisneros, although sceptical of Socialist Realism's worth, had fewer reservations about the political convictions that provoked it. Thus he joined the second phase of the political uprising in the Ayacucho area, in a gesture similar to other Peruvian intellectuals of his generation. It should be remembered that the decade of the 1960s, marked as it was by the Cuban Revolution of 1959 and of its leader, Fidel Castro, was crucial in the development of many Latin American artists and writers, one of the reasons for grouping them within a generation. The other book of poems that is connected to this concern is *Crónica del Niño Jesús de Chilca*, 1981 [Chronicle of the Child Jesus of Chilca]. This volume's central theme is also historical; this time it centres on a community of coastal Peru, 100 kilometres outside Lima, which shares the same linguistic features of Cisneros, according to the poet's description. Whereas his *Comentarios reales*, is a chronicle in dialogue with the idea of Spanish chronicles of the Conquest of America, in *Crónica del Niño Jesús de Chilca* he assumes an anthropological approach. This applies in the sense that the poet replicates the social sciences' methodology of interviewing informants whose testimony is transcribed, imitating their linguistic idiosyncrasies. These poems chronicle the birth, existence and impending death of the Niño Jesús de Chilca religious community, and the disappearance of a way of life in the area. Both of these books, set apart as they are by almost twenty years, reflect Cisneros's concerns with Peruvian sociopolitical reality.

In between these two major books, Cisneros wrote four volumes of poetry whose titles reflect considerable change in tone and theme as this poetry is informed by new experiences and new perception of unencountered realities. *Canto ceremonial contra un oso hormiguero*, 1968 [Ceremonial Song against an Anteater], displays the aesthetics of the "Sixties Generation," in that it exposes a very vital and critical Latin American perspective of Western culture, written after the poet made his first trip outside of Peru for an extended visit to England, where he arrived on board a cargo ship. His first encounter with European culture and the confrontation with it is what nurtures this volume of well crafted poems. Cisneros considers this collection of poems the first set in which he felt free to speak of themes not addressed before – such as speaking freely of Peru as well as of England, of highly personal themes as well as of his cultural background – all conceived within a new poetic language. Cisneros considers this period of his life quite important for himself as well as for the world. He was attempting to reinvent a rigid and death-bound Leftist political movement by addressing a range of liberatory movements: feminism, free love, communitarianism, and other heterodoxies that arose during the 1960s together with the outrageousness of popular English rock artists like The Beatles, The Rolling Stones or Bob Dylan in the United States. *Agua que no has de beber* [Water You Will Not Drink] and *Como higuera en un campo de golf* [Like a Fig Tree on a Golf Course], construct a dramatic personal mythology, the former, in a sense, anticipating the latter. Cisneros regards both as pushing too far into the construction of an individualistic poetry that he describes as "Anglo-Saxon and French permissiveness" because of what this phrase connotes about solidarity and the individual. *El Libro de Dios y de los húngaros*, 1978 [The Book of God and of the Hungarians] marks another dramatic change of pace and theme in Cisneros's poetic evolution. This collection of poems is constructed with political, religious, and travel material, whose poetic voice reveals great fragility as well as great maturity. It is a striking volume in that the reader witnesses the reconversion of the poetic voice – and of the poet Cisneros himself – to Christianity, a development in Cisneros's trajectory of a quite unusual nature. However, this dramatic turn of events is a part of the significant shifts that constitute the imprint of this outstanding Peruvian poet. This volume took by surprise both Cisneros's associates in the Left, and those in the political right, another feature of Cisneros's character as a writer and as an individual. *Monólogo de la casta Susana*, 1986 [Chaste Susan's Monologue], also articulates the profound belief in God which, as the poet himself has pointed out, began in his second book of poems *David* (1962). Recently, Eduardo Urdanivia Bertarelli has studied this important element in Cisneros's most recent poetry. The poetry of Antonio Cisneros will continue to evolve as it has in the past twenty years, and it will continue to challenge the use and articulation of poetic language in Spanish American literature. This poet bears the mark of a great writer.

MAGDALENA GARCÍA PINTO

Biography

Born in Lima, Peru, 27 December 1942. Educated at Catholic University, Lima; Universidad Nacional de San Marcos, Lima, PhD, 1974. Lecturer in literature, University of Huamanga, Ayacucho, 1965; University of Southampton, England, 1967–70; University of Nice, France, 1970–72; Universidad Nacional de San Marcos, Lima, since 1972. Exchange professor, University of Budapest, 1974–75. Awarded the National Poetry Prize (Peru), 1965, for *Comentarios reales*, and the Casa de las Américas Prize, 1968, for *Canto ceremonial contra un oso hormiguero*. Apart from his creative work, he wrote a series of demographic and social studies for the Bolivian Centro de Investigaciones Sociales in the 1970s.

Selected Works

Poetry
Destierro, Lima: Cuadernos del Hontanar, 1961
David, Lima: El Timonel, 1962
Comentarios reales, Lima: La Rama Florida/Universitaria, 1964
Canto ceremonial contra un oso hormiguero, Havana: Casa de las Américas, 1968
Agua que no has de beber, Barcelona: Milla Batres, 1971
Como higuera en un campo de golf, Lima: Instituto Nacional de Cultura, 1972
El libro de Dios y los húngaros, Lima: Libre-1, 1978
Crónica del Niño Jesús de Chilca, Mexico City: Premià, 1981
Monólogo de la casta Susana y otros poemas, Lima: Instituto Nacional de Cultura, 1986
El arte de envolver pescado, Lima: Caballo Rojo, 1990
Las inmensas preguntas celestes, Lima: Campodónico, 1992

Other Writings
El libro del Buen Salvaje. Crónicas de viaje/ Crónicas de viejo, Lima: PEISA, 1994

Compilations and Anthologies
The Spider Hangs Too Far from the Ground, translated by Maureen Ahern, William Rowe and David Tipton, London: Cape Goliard, 1970 [Contains poems from several collections]
Helicopters in the Kingdom of Peru, translated by Maureen Ahern, William Rowe and David Tipton, Bradford, England: Rivelin/Equatorial, 1981 [as above]
Por la noche los gatos: poesía, 1961–1986, Mexico City: Fondo de Cultura Económica, 1989; as *At Night the Cats*, edited and translated by Maureen Ahern, William Rowe and David Tipton, New York: Red Dust, 1985
Land of Angels, translated by Maureen Ahern, William Rowe and David Tipton, Portree, Isle of Skye: Aquila, 1985
Propios como ajenos: poesía, 1962–1989, Lima: PEISA, 1989
Poesía, una historia de locos: 1962–1986, Madrid: Hiperión, 1990

Further Reading
Bueno, Raúl, "Antonio Cisneros entre las aguas del Pacífico Sur," *Revista de Crítica Literaria Latinoamericana*, vol. 18/35 (1992)
Cornejo Polar, Antonio, "La poesía de Antonio Cisneros," *Revista Iberoamericana* 140 (July–September 1987)
Higgins, James, *Hitos de la poesía peruana siglo XX*, Lima: Milla Batres, 1993 [Chapter 4 has a section on Cisneros]
Russel Lamadrid, Enrique, "La poesía de Antonio Cisneros: dialéctica de creación y tradición," *Revista de Crítica Literaria Latinoamericana*, vol. 11 (1980)
Urdanivia Bertarelli, Eduardo, " . . . y blanquearé más que la nieve. Poesía y experiencia de fe en la obra de Antonio Cisneros," *Revista de Crítica Literaria Latinoamericana*, vol. 18/35 (1992)

Interviews
Ortega, Julio, "Entrevista con Antonio Cisneros," *Hispamérica*, vol. 13/37 (1984)

Special Issues of Journals
INTI, Revista de Literatura Hispánica, "Catorce poetas hispanoamericanos de hoy," 18–19 (1983–84)

Civilization and Barbarism

This traditional dichotomy was made prominent in Latin America with the publication of Domingo Faustino Sarmiento's monumental work *Civilización y barbarie: vida de Juan Facundo Quiroga*, 1845 (*Life in the Argentine Republic in the Days of the Tyrants*). It became the key concept in all evaluation and self-evaluation of Latin America, the principal metaphor through which its reality was perceived and conveyed. Eventually the referents of each of the terms changed, but the dual and oppositional formula remained constant. The origins of the terms are interesting to note: *civilization* harks back to its Greek meaning of *city* whereas *barbarism*, also Greek in origin, was simply the way the Greeks referred to those whose language was not Greek and pronounced Greek badly. By the time these terms came to be used by Sarmiento they had become clearly hierarchical: the worst and the best stages in the evolution of nations. But Sarmiento simply highlighted and adapted a trope that had prevailed in connection with America from the time of the conquest, and even before, when the constricted imagination of medieval Europe had felt the need for an idealised Other against which to measure itself. This took the form of both an Utopia that would serve to show up Europe's own imperfections, and its opposite, a place of savagery which would allow it to exult in its own superiority. Recent studies of the first writings about the newly discovered continent reveal a carefully constructed text to reflect this dual position. For instance, in his letters, Columbus simultaneously enthuses over the beauty, docility and good-nature of the natives he has come upon (as if to fulfill expectations of having reached the Indies), whilst at the same time warning against the natives' lack of disciplined behaviour and barbaric cannibalistic practices (in justification of conquest and colonization). But under colonialism, it is almost exclusively the latter image of barbarism that is made to predominate, the indigenous population demonized and their cultures ignored or erased. At best, the attitude was of America as a *tabula rasa* awaiting the imprint of civilization. Only some lone voices, such as Bartolomé de Las Casas pointed out that barbarism was a subjective criterion, dependant upon the speaker's position.

Antoniello Gerbi, in his *La disputa del Nuevo Mundo*, 1960 [The Dispute of the New World] traces the continuously Eurocentric debate concerning the New World, highlighting the uninterrupted flow of theories on the inferiority of America, from Buffon's assertion that America is a more recent and still immature continent where animals fail to reach their full growth potential, to Cornelius De Pauw's view that things degenerate in America's unhealthy climate and Hegel's unflinching acceptance of these ideas. These became foundational beliefs, later developed by theories of environmental and biological determinism which, together with the racial pyramid of Positivist thought, were the philosophical ideas that exerted the greatest influence in the political thought of post-independence American states.

From Mexico to Argentina, the dynamics of history were seen as a conflict between native barbarism and cosmopolitan civilization. Sarmiento, in *Facundo*, declared that these key terms were transitional, adding that since barbarism was the earlier one, it would be eradicated by the inevitable forward march of progress. The conditions most conducive to barbarism were those of life on the pampas, where the extension of the territory and its rigours made human communication difficult if not impossible, and allowed for the rule of brute force by the local petty tyrants, the *caudillos*. It was a primitive, retrograde way of life which had become a stumbling block in the development of the nation. Hispanic colonial rule, with its insistence on traditional, conservative values and blind authoritarianism, had done little to alter this basic picture but was now seen to provide a stepping stone to a more progressive system, a civilization based upon the European model. Sarmiento's ideal civilization was that of the industrialized Anglo-Saxon countries of northern Europe, their chief virtues being their democratically elected government and their liberal *laissez-faire* policies. Reason, order, system, strategy are some of the key words that describe civilization; another is cosmopolitanism with a decidedly European bent. Literary critics have often pointed out that *Facundo's* narrative style does not support the clear-cut division of the political message arguing that the romantic exuberance of Sarmiento's prose betrayed an ambivalence in his position. There is much truth in this concerning the artist's æsthetic sensibility, but little as regards the politician. Sarmiento's ruthless political programme was, at the time of writing *Facundo*, unequivocal: he advocated massive immigration, preferably from the industrialised countries of northern Europe in order to "whiten the desert" and bring Argentina nearer to the coveted way of life which he termed "civilization." The first step to achieve this was to be the wholesale extermination of the gauchos and their way of life, or, at best, their absorption into the new order. (He was to reverse his ideas once his desired policies were put into execution.) José Hernández, in his epic poem in two parts, *Martín Fierro* (1872 and 1879), depicts this extermination, but in his version barbarism is imposed upon the gaucho by the policies of a centralized government whose methods are corruption, treachery and forcible conscription. Barbarism is also depicted as the natural condition of the Indians who have become the new cultural underdogs.

The most famous fictionalised attempt to dramatise the conflict between the dual forces of civilization and barbarism is found in *Doña Bárbara* (1928) by Rómulo Gallegos. In this novel, nature, represented in its unbridled barbarism by the eponymous heroine, is defeated by the forces of enlightenment and the promise of a new dawn (her rival and victor is called Santos Luzardo, *luz* being the Spanish for "light").

Sarmiento's ideas, though continuing to be influential throughout the sub-continent, were beginning to be questioned in the face of events once they had become implemented. The Cuban José Martí, at first an admirer of Sarmiento, moved the debate surrounding civilization and barbarism on to a moral plane. Taking the US as an example of a nation that followed the path of "civilization," he suggested that whilst the economic and political advances of industrialising countries such as the US were undisputed, Latin America had other, more valuable spiritual assets which it ought not to betray. Arguing against the crude importation of ideas from Europe and the

US, Martí wrote in his essay "Nuestra América" (Our America) of 1891: "No hay batalla entre la civilización y la barbarie, sino entre la falsa erudición y la naturaleza." (It is not a question of a battle between civilization and barbarism, but between false learning and Nature). These sentiments were echoed by the Uruguayan José Enrique Rodó, whose essay *Ariel* inspired a new generation with a measure of pride in their Latin American cultural heritage.

In the first decades of the 20th century, when the advantages of this new American promise had already begun to disappoint, the debate evolved around the problems attendant upon the encroachment of Modernism. A new aesthetic flourished in the literary movement called *criollismo* (creolism), which spread across the sub-continent this time aligning wisdom with a mythical past golden age in which those who had previously been held to be barbarians became the new repositories of civilization.

In Ricardo Güiraldes's Bildungsroman *Don Segundo Sombra* (1926), a complete *volte face* has taken place, with the eponymous gaucho becoming the highest exponent of civilization. As a result of the vertiginous growth of the city, the rural countryside has once again become the seat of "true" civilization, and gaucho life is presented as one of seamless physical and spiritual harmony.

Sylvia Molloy, in her study of autobiography, *At Face Value* (1991), draws parallels between Sarmiento and the Mexican José Vasconcelos. For the latter, barbarism equalled ignorance which he and his party as self-appointed educators of the nation sought to eradicate. The polarized forces of nativism or *indigenismo* and universalism became the conflicting forces in a search for national identity.

In recent years, feminists have adapted Sarmiento's worn terminology to the situation of women in Latin America. The most important study on these lines is Francine Masiello's *Between Civilization and Barbarism: Women, Nation and Literary Culture in Modern Argentina* (1992), an exploration of the positioning of women in the changing cultural constructions of the nation. Masiello's revisionist reading suggests the "collapse of these false dichotomies." The construction of women, either as the civilizing influence of the homemaker and thus supporter of the patriarchal state, or as feared exponent of barbarism, irrational and anarchic creatures threatening the nation's stability finds little support in the extensive documentation of women's writing of the last hundred years. These reveal, instead a more fluid cultural history in which the distinctions of the official binary account are constantly blurred.

The opposition between civilization and barbarism reappears in Borges's "Poema conjetural" [Conjectural Poem] as stages in the discovery and acceptance of one's inner destiny. In *Out of Context* (1993), Daniel Balderston expands upon this idea in his penetrating reading of Borges's story "Historia del guerrero y de la cautiva" (Story of the Warrior and the Captive) in which he examines the strongly contested connotations of civilization and barbarism and its wide historical context. Even when emptied of its traditional values, the dualism of the trope continues to attract writers and critics as a powerful metaphor to express the contradictions of Latin America.

EVELYN FISHBURN

See also entries on *Doña Bárbara* (Rómulo Gallegos), *Don Segundo Sombra* (Ricardo Güiraldes)

Further Reading

Alonso, Carlos J., *The Spanish American Regional Novel*, Cambridge: Cambridge University Press, 1989

Brushwood, John S., *Genteel Barbarism: Experiments in the Analysis of Nineteenth Century Spanish-American Novels*, Lincoln: University of Nebraska Press, 1981

Fernández Retamar, Roberto, "Algunos usos de civilización y barbarie," in his *Para el perfil definitivo del hombre*, Havana: Letras Cubanas, 1981; as *Caliban and Other Essays*, translated by Edward Baker, Minneapolis: University of Minnesota Press, 1989

Fitz, Earl E., *Rediscovering the New World: Inter-American Literature in a Comparative Context*, Iowa City: University of Iowa Press, 1991

González Echevarría, Roberto, *The Voice of the Masters: Writing and Authority in Modern Spanish American Literature*, Austin: University of Texas Press, 1985

Greenblatt, Stephen, *Marvelous Possessions: the Wonder of the New World*, Oxford: Oxford University Press, and Chicago: University of Chicago Press, 1991

Lojo de Beuter, María Rosa, *La "barbarie" en la narrativa argentina (siglo XIX)*, Buenos Aires: Corregidor, 1994

Martínez, Tomás Eloy, "A Culture of Barbarism," in *Argentina in the Crisis Years (1983–1990): from Alfonsín to Menem*, edited by Colin M. Lewis and Nissa Torrents, London: Institute of Latin American Studies, 1993

Masiello, Francine, *Between Civilization and Barbarism: Women, Nation and Literary Culture in Modern Argentina*, Lincoln: University of Nebraska Press, 1992

Salomon, Noël, *Realidad, ideología y literatura en el "Facundo" de D.F. Sarmiento* Amsterdam: Rodopi, 1984

Svampa, Maristella, *El dilema argentino: "Civilización o Barbarie." De Sarmiento al revisionismo peronista*, Buenos Aires: El Cielo por Asalto / Imago Mundi, 1994

Viñas, David, *Indios, ejército y frontera*, Mexico City: Siglo XXI, 1982

Williamson, Edwin, *The Penguin History of Latin America*, Harmondsworth: Penguin, 1992 [Chapter 8 is on Civilization and Barbarism]

Colombia

19th- and 20th-Century Prose and Poetry

Until the publication of Gabriel García Márquez's *Cien años de soledad* (*One Hundred Years of Solitude*) in 1967, the history of Colombian literature was dominated by the development of five distinct historical and cultural traditions: the Caribbean coast, Greater Antioquia, the Cundinamarca-Boyaca Highlands, Greater Tolima and the Western Valley. Geographical barriers contributed to this development of regional literatures associated with ideological constants related to each region's cultural and socioeconomic history. Instead of considering Colombian literature as a continuous and cohesive development within a global, national literary tradition characterized by successive and distinct literary movements, the country's regional literary evolution has tended to emphasize separate traditions and individual writers and/or works produced within each region. For example, within the Greater Antioquia region, the novelist Tomás Carrasquilla, produced Realist and *costumbrista* fiction in considerable quantity between 1896 and 1935. In the Greater Valley the most important work has long been considered Jorge Isaacs's *María* (1867). In the Greater Tolima region, which has been closely associated with the Cundinamarca-Boyaca Highlands, José Eustasio Rivera's novel, *La vorágine*, 1924 (*The Vortex*), considered a classic novel of Colombian literature, belongs to the elitist, writing culture which has dominated much of the country's literary traditions and history until the 1970s.

When García Márquez's *Cien años de soledad* appeared in 1967, it marked a decisive turning point in Colombian and Latin American literature. In a sense, the novel turned the whole idea of regionalism inside out by situating the story of the Buendía clan in the remote town of Macondo which has since acquired mythic proportions. Suddenly, the margin-ocentric displaced the traditional centers of literary dominance, and the Caribbean coastal region, which had long been isolated geographically and culturally from the interior throughout much of Colombia's history, assumed a new literary prominence. *Cien años*'s transcendent regionalism not only enabled the coastal literature to participate in a more national and international tradition, but it also initiated a re-evaluation of Colombian literary traditions.

With the Declaration of Independence in 1810 and complete independence from Spain in 1824, political power passed from the Spanish to the national aristocracy and military leaders. Both of these groups were of creole origin, that is, citizens of Spanish descent who were born in New Granada. These leaders often occupied second-tier political military posts in the Spanish colonial system, so they frequently lacked the governing experience necessary to ensure a smooth transition from colonialism to independence. In Colombia the political battle lines were quickly drawn between the Liberals and the Conservatives, each of which had diametrically opposed political agendas. The Liberals advocated regional autonomy, reduced power for the Catholic Church, and free international commerce. Conservatives, many of whom belonged to the landed aristocracy, favored a strong central government and

church, on which their political power and wealth directly depended.

The 19th century witnessed the rise of many charismatic *caudillos*, or strongmen (see entry on Caudillismo and Dictatorship), whose lack of political experience and leadership helped fuel the numerous bloody civil wars which ravaged not only Colombia but many of the fledgling independent countries of Latin America. The Liberal/Conservative paradigm, under many different names, has dominated much of Colombian and Latin American history up to the present day. In Colombia, two of the most internecine conflicts were The Thousand Days War (1899–1902) and the period designated as *la Violencia* (The Violence), 1948 to 1965, during which an undeclared civil war claimed the lives of some 200,000 to 300,000 people. Since most of the violence took place in the countryside, Colombia experienced a tremendous emigration to the cities. This period also profoundly marked literary production, giving rise to what some have called the Novela de la Violencia (the Novel of Violence).

Even after the establishment of the Frente Nacional (National Front) in 1958, a bipartisan agreement between the Liberals and Conservatives to alternate in political power for four years during sixteen years to restore order and peace and create a controlled democracy, the powerbrokers remained the same. The goals of the successive governments were the pacification of the country, economic development, political stability and unification of the country. The Cuban Revolution of 1959 helped spawn the formation of guerrilla movements in Colombia, the most important of which are Las Fuerzas Armadas Revolucionarias de Colombia (The Armed Revolutionary Forces of Colombia), El Ejército de Liberación Nacional (The National Liberation Army) and M-19 which disbanded in the late 1980s. The other recent significant development in Colombia is the creation of drug cartels in the 1980s, the most notable of which are the Medellín and Cali cartels. While the Colombian government was finally able to destroy the Medellín cartel after waging a bloody and costly war, the Cali cartel continues to function along with many other microcartels which grow, process and export cocaine and, more recently, heroin. While the guerillas and the drug barons talk of peace and surrender with successive Colombian governments, their sophisticated organization in cells and extensive networks enable them to reap enormous illicit profits.

This sociopolitical situation creates enormous distortions in Colombian society and its economy and it adversely affects the development of literature beyond regional boundaries. Gabriel García Márquez, in spite of his international status, is still considered by Colombians a *costeño* writer, that is, a writer from the Caribbean coast. Indeed, of all the regions of Colombia, the coastal region stands in sharpest contrast to the interior, which usually refers to the highlands region of which Bogotá is the center. Unlike the highlands region, which represented the repository of traditional Hispanic traditions and values (Bogotá traditionally portrayed itself as the "Athens of Latin America") and where writing and political power were the most closely wedded, the Caribbean coast, with its oral traditions, heterogeneous cultures, African influence, its more radical geographical isolation, tropical climate and proximity to the ocean, has developed distinct literary traditions.

Two famous *costeño* poets, Candelario Obeso (1849–84) and Luis Carlos López (1883–1950), incorporated popular language and themes into their poetry. Obeso was the first Colombian poet to attempt to write authentic African-American poetry by using everyday language and colloquial expressions. His one published book of poetry, *Cantos populares de mi tierra*, 1877 [Popular Songs of My Land], employs colloquial language and speech patterns which contrast with the prevailing literary language of the Hispanic Romantic poetry of the period. Luis Carlos López, who came from Cartagena, incorporated local customs, traditions and language into his poetry. He also introduced another dominant costeño cultural element into his poetry – humor – which not only permeates coastal literary traditions but constitutes one of the hallmarks of the coastal region's most famous writer, Gabriel García Márquez.

In spite of these and other innovations, literary production remained closely allied to the elite writing culture. Juan José Nieto (1804–66) from Cartagena, was not only a novelist but also one of Colombia's important political and military leaders of the 19th century. Two of his novels, *Ingermina, o la hija de Calamar*, 1844 [Ingermina, or the Child of Calamar] and *Los moriscos*, 1845 [The Moors], deal successively with the conquest of the Calamar Indians and the expulsion of the Moors from Spain, both clichéd themes of official history. Nevertheless, beginning in the 1920s, new works started to appear which had little to do with the establishment. In 1927, José Felix Fuenmayor (1885–1966) published *Cosme* in which a character of the same name, living in Barranquilla, employs humor and irony to mock many traditional institutions. By the 1940s and 1950s writers like Álvaro Cepeda Samudio (1926–72), Héctor Rojas Herazo (b. 1921), Alfonso Fuenmayor (b. 1927) and García Márquez were expanding the horizons of Colombian literature by searching for new modes of literary expression. A group of young writers and intellectuals, which would later be called the Barranquilla Group (García Márquez, Cepeda Samudio, Fuenmayor and Germán Vargas), avidly read the works of Franz Kafka, Ernest Hemingway, William Faulkner, Virginia Woolf and others, discussed them and initiated their own writing experiments.

Two of the more important works to emerge from this group are Cepeda Samudio's *La casa grande*, 1962 [The Big House] and García Márquez's *Cien años de soledad*. *La casa grande* centers on a family during the famous massacre of the banana workers in Ciénaga in 1928. The complex narrative structure of the novel reveals the generational conflicts and the political upheaval caused by this seminal event in Colombian labor history. García Márquez's *Cien años de soledad* combines and completes much of his earlier work and constitutes the totalizing novel which not only encompasses Colombian and Latin American history, but also extends into the realm of myth and timelessness. The novel, which is the chronicle of the Buendía family living in the remote town of Macondo, achieves universality by intensifying and concentrating everything in a few characters and a small fictional space. It is a totalizing novel which communicates to readers on many levels, and William Faulkner's mentorship in this novel and other works by García Márquez has served the latter well.

Antioquia, while not as geographically isolated as the Coastal region, nevertheless remained rather underdeveloped during the colonial period and its literary traditions did not start to flourish until well after the founding of Medellín in 1616. The 18th century saw a cultural and economic upsurge under the leadership of Juan Antonio Mon y Velarde (1784–87). During the late 19th century Antioquia experienced a significant economic growth accompanied by considerable increase in its literary production.

The first major novelist, Tomás Carrasquilla (1858–1940), represents the middle-class Antioquian writer who did not belong to the elite class which had dominated Colombian literature until the 20th century. Between 1896 and 1935 Carrasquilla produced a large number of Realist and *costumbrista* works. His three major works are *Frutos de mi tierra*, 1896 [Fruits of My Land], *Grandeza*, 1910 [Greatness] and *La marquesa de Yolombó*, 1928 [The Marchioness of Yolombó]. Following the lead of the European Realist and Naturalist writers, Carrasquilla tied his description of his characters to their environment. He paid particular attention to local customs, character types, the common people and local color.

One of the most innovative figures of Antioquian literature is León de Grieff (1895–1976) who created a new poetic language in Colombian poetry. He belonged to a literary group called *Los Nuevos* (The New Ones) and his own exploration of avant-garde literature contributed to his new poetic language. His *Libro de signos*, 1930 [The Book of Signs] created new technical innovations in poetic language.

The 20th-century Antioquian novel has generally remained more traditional, and one of the most important figures is Manuel Mejía Vallejo. His best-known novel, *El día señalado*, 1964 [The Appointed Day], contains two narratives: a third-person account of a town and the unwanted presence of government troops, and a first-person story of personal vengeance. The main theme of the novel is *la Violencia* in Antioquia, and the novel succeeds in surpassing the status of a simple protest novel.

Bogotá and the highlands region have been the dominant cultural loci since the colonial period and have continued to dominate in all the literary spheres since independence. Culture has remained the most strictly Hispanic in Bogotá. In the late 19th and early 20th centuries Bogotá underwent a period of conflict, growth and the incipient phases of modernization. The combination of traditional Hispanic cultural values and the effects of modernization also dichotomized literary production into conservative and modern, experimental spheres. This region has been the center of major poetic movements in the 20th century – *Los Nuevos*, *Piedra y Cielo*, *Mito* and *Nadaísmo* – as well as the repository of important novelists such as José María Vargas Vila (1860–1933), Clímaco Soto Borda (1870–1919), Eduardo Zalamea Borda (1907–63), Tomás Vargas Osorio (1908–41) and Eduardo Caballero Calderón (b. 1910).

Costumbrismo flourished in the highlands region and José María Vergara y Vergara (1831–72) and José María Samper (1828–88) were its main exponents. 19th-century poetry was dominated by the Romantic verse of Rafael Pombo (1833–1912). Miguel Antonio Caro (1843–1909) and José Asunción Silva (1865–96) represent opposite tendencies in poetic language at the turn of the century. While Caro's poetic inspiration derived from classical sources, Silva drew his inspiration from Baudelaire, Verlaine, Rimbaud and other 19th-century European poets. Silva died at the age of thirty-one and his poetry was only posthumously appreciated in Colombia. During the mid-1930s the *Piedra y Cielo* group formed in Bogotá and its young poets began to effectuate an important renovation of Colombian poetry. Its two major figures are Eduardo Carranzas (b. 1913), who is the traditionalist, and Arturo Camacho Ramírez (b. 1910), the avant-gardist. The *Piedra y Cielo* group concentrated on the universe of poetic metaphors, somewhat in line with the French Symbolist poet Stéphane Mallarmé who sought to create a poetic language which did not name but suggest objects or reality. Other poetic movements of the succeeding decades continued to bring innovations to Colombian poetry.

The 20th-century novel of the highland region was closely linked to the official literary language of the power elite. José María Rivas Groot (1863–1923) and José Manuel Marroquín (1856–1918) embodied the conservative values in their fiction. The thorn in the side of the Conservative political and literary hegemony was José María Vargas Vila, whose many novels and other writings openly expressed his anticlerical and anti-institutional stance. Another contrast to the official literary language is the work of José A. Osorio Lizarazo (1900–64) whose proletarian novels coincided with the rapid industrialization of Bogotá and also its worst economic crisis of the 20th century. Eduardo Zalamea Borda published *Cuatro años a bordo de mí mismo*, 1934 [Four Years with Myself] which chronicles the rites of passage into manhood of the narrator as he travels from the urban culture of Bogotá to the coastal Guajira area. This novel contrasts the folkloric, rural traditions of the coast with the urban culture of Bogotá. Eduardo Caballero Calderón exemplifies the cultural values of the elite culture in Bogotá in which writing and power are indissolubly linked.

Greater Tolima, which includes the area of the Department of Huila, closely mirrors the literary traditions of the highland paradigm. The literary tradition of this region resembles the highland model. In spite of having two important cities, Ibagué and Neiva, no independent cosmopolitan center has evolved in the region. The region's most important writer is José Eustasio Rivera (1889–1928) whose 1924 novel, *La vorágine* (*The Vortex*), has become a classic of Colombian and Latin American literature. As Raymond L. Williams points out, "the predominant subject is not a fictional world projecting a simulacrum of 1924 rural Colombia – with its vacuous women and bedraggled workers – but rather the self in the process of writing. Lacking traditional subject matter, Cova's most fully developed and central subject is writing: its dynamism is found in the narrator's striving for a form of written expression." The novel is the mature expression of a writing culture whose close links to Bogotá confine writing to a specific sociocultural domain.

The other event which deeply affected the Tolima region was *la Violencia* and Tolima was a focus point of this phenomenon during the 1950s. While many of the novels it spawned are of dubious literary value, the novel of Jorge Eliécer Pardo (b. 1945), *El jardín de las Hartmann*, 1978 [The Garden of the Hartmann Ladies], transcends the limits of protest literature to depict the violence in more generic terms.

The Western Valley region, centered in the Valle del Cauca, which includes Popayán to the south and the Chocó region to the north, shares the cultural heterogeneity of the Coastal region. Popayán has long been a bastion of traditional values while the Valle del Cauca, with Cali as its center, has had both the traditional aristocracy and more popular traditions. The Chocó, which was opened to mining in the 18th century, has remained isolated and sparsely populated, and is a center of African traditions. The region's abundant resources and fertile land have brought it economic prosperity, and the region underwent a significant economic transformation during the early part of the 20th century. *La Violencia* also deeply affected the region and, since the 1980s, one of the most significant factors has been the rise to prominence of the Cali drug cartel. Although the poetic tradition of Western Valley has not been as strong as that of the highland region, its novelistic tradition has always been strong and independent, influenced by a combination of cultural and historical forces and by a mixture of oral and written culture.

The most important novel of the 19th century is the Romantic novel *María* (1867) by Jorge Isaacs (1837–95). While Isaacs's novel is primarily the product of his involvement in the writing culture of the Western Valley, it is nevertheless a well-conceived work whose intimate connection with the natural world is sensitively portrayed. The novel's oedipal structure, the themes of childhood and separation and the attention to sensorial images related to nature make it a more authentic rendition of many archetypal Romantic themes than certain European models which never surpass the vague and pervasive feeling of melancholy.

The creation of a literature rooted more in oral traditions has also played an important role in the Western Valley region. Its most distinguished 20th-century novelist is Gustavo Álvarez Gardeazábal (b. 1945) whose novels are deeply racinated in the history and oral traditions of the Valle del Cauca, primarily the city of Tuluá, where he has also served as mayor. His first two novels, *La tara del papa*, 1971 [The Pope's Defect] and *Cóndores no entierran todos los días*, 1972 [Condors Don't Bury Everyday], are squarely situated in the historical context of *la Violencia* of the Valle del Cauca. He draws on the oral tradition in *El bazar de los idiotas*, 1974 [The Idiots' Bazaar] in which he creates humorous and critical effects by parodying a variety of languages. More recently, Álvarez Gardeazábal has started a new cycle of novels which veer away from the regional tradition. Another important writer who draws on oral sources is Andrés Caicedo (1951–77) whose only novel, *Que viva la música*, 1977 [Let the Music Roll On] depicts the frenetic life of a young woman who, obsessed by music and leading a nocturnal existence in Cali, is caught up in the sociocultural ambiguities which confront many young people.

Colombian literature since the publication of *Cien años de soledad* has developed in new directions and it is more difficult to consider it in purely regional terms. García Márquez's universal critical and popular appeal has given Colombia increased national and international exposure. One interesting development for Colombian literature has been the creation of the Association of North American Colombianists in 1983. This group of American and Colombian academics has helped disseminate Colombian literature through its meetings in Colombia and the United States. Writers such as R. H. Moreno-Durán, Albalucía Ángel and Fanny Buitrago have lived abroad for many years and their work reflects the influence and cultural traditions of other countries. García Márquez, who has also spent much of his career abroad, has cast a long shadow over Colombian and Latin American literature. His enormous impact on the literature of his continent has continued unabated, and his work has incorporated and reshaped many of the elements of Modernism and Postmodernism. García Márquez, along with many other Latin American like Carlos Fuentes, Mario Vargas Llosa and Augusto Roa Bastos, have helped propel Latin American literature to the forefront of worldwide literary prominence. The formerly Latin American literary marginocentric has displaced the traditional literary centers.

The progressive blurring of regional boundaries in Colombian literature of the last twenty-five years has produced a literature which also tends to efface the dividing line between official and popular culture. Fanny Buitrago situates much of her short fiction and novels in the Caribbean coast, and oral culture plays an important role. Her novels include *El hostigante verano de los dioses*, 1963 [The Harassing Summer of the Gods], *Cola de zorro*, 1970 [Fox's Tail], *Los pañamanes*, 1979 [The Pañamanes] and *Los amores de Afrodite*, 1983 [The Loves of Aphrodite]. Manuel Zapata Olivella's *Changó, el gran putas*, 1983 [Changó, the Baddest S.O.B] is an ambitious novel about the African diaspora which covers several continents and six centuries of African and African-American history. He incorporates oral traditions, collective memory and myth in his sweeping and ambitious novel.

Colombian literature has surpassed its regional boundaries and has responded to factors which lie beyond the grasp of the elite writing culture. It not only incorporates a much wider gamut of cultural elements but it also participates much more extensively in the international discourse of Latin American literature.

ROBERT L. SIMS

See also entries on Fanny Buitrago, Tomás Carrasquilla, Gabriel García Márquez, Jorge Isaacs, José Eustasio Rivera

Further Reading

Deas, Malcolm, *Del poder y la gramática, y otros ensayos sobre historia, política y literatura colombianas*, Bogotá: Tercer Mundo, 1993

Galeano, Juan Carlos, "El nadaismo y 'la violencia' en Colombia," *Revista Iberoamericana* 164–65 (July–December 1993)

Gómez Ocampo, Gilberto, *Entre "María" y "La vorágine:" la literatura colombiana finisecular*, Bogotá: Fondo Cultural Cafetero, 1988

Jaramillo, María Mercedes and Angela I. Robledo (editors), *Escritura y diferencia. Autoras colombianas del siglo veinte*, Colombia: Universidad de los Andes y Universidad de Antioquia, 1994

Jiménez, David P., *Historia de la crítica literaria en Colombia*, Bogotá: Centro Editorial Universidad Nacional de Colombia, 1992

Karsen, Sonja, *Ensayos de literatura e historia iberoamericana*, New York: Peter Lang, 1988 [Chapter 3 has sections on Jorge Isaacs, Guillermo Valencia and *Cien años de soledad*]

Kohut, Karl (editor), *Literatura colombiana hoy. Imaginación y barbarie*, Frankfurt: Vervuert Verlag, and Madrid: Iberoamericana, 1994

Menton, Seymour, *La novela colombiana: planetas y satélites*, Bogotá: Plaza y Janés, 1975

Meyer-Minnemann, Klaus, *La novela hispanoamericana del "fin de siècle,"* Mexico City: Fondo de Cultura Económica, 1991 [Chapter 6 has sections on Vargas Vila]

Romero, Armando, *El nadaísmo colombiano o la búsqueda de una vanguardia perdida*, Bogotá: Tercer Mundo, 1988

Williams, Raymond L., *Una década de la novela colombiana: la experiencia de los setenta*, Bogotá: Plaza y Janés, 1981

____ *The Colombian Novel 1844–1987*, Austin: University of Texas Press, 1991

Colonial Literature

New Granada

The conquest of present day Colombia began in 1508, when Alonso de Ojeda arrived in Cartagena. Like his fellow Spanish explorers Diego de Nicuesa, Martín Fernández de Enciso and Gonzalo Fernández de Oviedo (1478–1557), Ojeda wrote about the conquest of the northern "Terra Firma" zone of Colombia. He made valuable contributions to the ethnography and natural sciences of that region of America in *Sumario de la natural historia de las Indias*, 1526 [A Summary of the Natural History of the Indies] and *Historia natural y general de las Indias* [The Natural and General History of the Indies], whose first part was published in 1535. Gonzalo Jiménez de Quesada (1499 or 1509(?)–79) narrated the expedition from the Caribbean coast and the foundation of Santa Fe de Bogotá (1538) in his *Epítome de la conquista del Nuevo Reino de Granada*, 1550 [Epitome of the New Kingdom of Granada's Conquest]. Jiménez de Quesada also referred to the American theme in other works that remain lost: "Los ratos de Suesca" [Suesca Times], "Historia general de las Indias" [General History of the Indies], and "Diferencia de la guerra de dos mundos" [Differences in Warfare from Two Worlds].

The *Epítome*, as well as other tales of expeditions that will be mentioned, fit within the general characteristics of the chronicles of the Indies. Like them, they reveal the establishment of a nascent capitalism and a period of ideological and political upheavals. Thus they inscribed apparently incongruent and diverse aspects related to Spanish impositions. Reading them shows medieval, humanist and renaissance mentalities, or how they distance themselves or adjust to a providentialist historiography. Fray Pedro de Aguado, the first writer exclusively concerned with the New Kingdom of Granada, posited in his *Recopilación historial*, 1582 [Collected Historical Writings] that the basic goal of the Spanish empire was to expand Christianity in the New World. Aguado consequently adheres to Utopian ideals and reneges from the Machiavellian concepts which other authors would adopt. These chronicles also register the confrontation between the conquerors and the Amerindians, a relevant and well-known theme in the formation of Spanish American literature. In this regard, Jiménez de Quesada emphasized the need to "debarbarize" the Amerindians.

On the other hand Aguado, carried away by his moralizing attitude, presented the natives as victims of Spanish injustice and cruelty. A similar attitude was assumed by Joan de Castellanos (1522–1607) in his verse chronicle *Elegías de varones ilustres de Indias*, 1589 [Elegies of Celebrated Men of the Indies]. Castellanos alluded to the "painful cases of the conquest." Nevertheless, he underlines the "deeds" of his compatriots. Aguado employed Adam-like metaphors, while other chroniclers availed themselves of cannibalistic descriptions. Jiménez de Quesada mentions the abruptness of the New World landscape, although other texts present the land with images inspired in the notion of paradise.

Fray Pedro Simón (1574–1626(?)), in his providentialist *Noticias historiales de las conquistas de Tierra Firme en las Indias Occidentales* [Historical Notices of the Conquest of Terra Firma in the Western Indies] revealed the conflicts and struggles among the Spaniards. For this reason, the second and third part of his work were not published along with the first in 1627. It is worth repeating that most of the chronicles were self-proclaimed "true stories," which refute the validity of other texts which called themselves "truthful." This description is due to several causes. Sometimes the authors are interested in acquiring fame or in obtaining colonial territories that were in litigation. Other times the dispute centers on how to write history from the perspective of what has been "seen, lived or heard," like Aguado and Simón. Or, "truth," in telling came from the author's use of other narratives or testimonies, as is the case with "official" chronicles. Thus, the variety of "true histories" displaces the medieval notion of a single "truth." As a consequence the chroniclers employ narrative strategies that would facilitate acquisition of personal benefits, as textualized (despite their differences) in Cortés and Bernal Díaz del Castillo. In any case, powerful self-images are constructed and, like Jiménez de Quesada, who emphasized the riches of the emerald and salt mines, magnify the booty obtained. Naturally, as critics have argued over the last thirty years, the use of such sources blurs the frontier between history and fiction.

After the first half of the 16th century colonial society is consolidated. Regal and hierarchical, it is a society attached to homogenizing Spanish principles and Counter-Reformation proposals. Despite this, the literature of the period insinuates a process of crossbreeding and the awakening of a Spanish American conscience. The colonial chronicles of this period do not recreate intrepid deeds but rather everyday events. They recount what took place in the ecclesiastical and civil administrations as well as notable episodes within religious orders and anecdotes from the provinces. One such tales is Lucas Fernández de Piedrahita's (1624–88) *Noticia historial de las conquistas del Nuevo Reino de Granada*, 1688 [Historical Notice of the New Kingdom of Granada's Conquests]. This deeply moralizing work is a chronological re-ordering of other published and unpublished histories of the region. One of its sources is Jiménez de Quesada's "Compendio historial de las conquistas del Nuevo Reino" [Historical Compendium of the Conquests of the New Kingdom]. A work like Juan Flórez de Ocáriz's (1626–?) *Genealogías del Nuevo Reino de Granada*, 1674 [Genealogies of the New Kingdom of Granada] deals with a basic concern of the incipient creole society: it establishes new ancestries, whose origins are constituted by individuals who transported Catholicism and Iberian customs to the New World. Another chronicle of the period, *Historia de la Provincia de San Antonino del Nuevo Reino de Granada*, 1701 [History of the New Kingdom of Granada's San Antonino Province], by Alonso de Zamora (1635–1717), tells the history of the Dominican order in that land and relates matters of general interest. Zamora's text is remarkable in terms of the physical description of the New Kingdom. As in other American territories, the missionary work of the religious orders involved translating catechisms, philological treatises and grammars. Some of the latter date back to the first half of the 17th century and deal with the native languages of the New Kingdom of Granada. Most notable among them are the books by fathers Bernardo Lugo and José Dadey on the Chibcha language and the research by brothers Francisco Varaix and Luis Zapata de Cárdenas on the Muisca language.

The society of 17th-century New Granada also partook of the Baroque. It was thus marked by a tendency toward excess, which combined penitence and lavishness, sensuality and asceticism. This is particularly evident in *El carnero*, 1636 (*The Conquest of New Granada*) by Juan Rodríguez Freyle (1566–1640?), another moralizing chronicle. However, it is a work that combines fun with sin, while subtly discovering and criticizing the social reality of Santa Fe de Bogotá by relating "cases." These are stories of scandalous events, most of them sexual in nature, which Rodríguez Freyle incorporates to the story of the first hundred years of colonialism in New Granada. Yet, those "cases" are also important because they are fabricated by employing very elaborated aesthetic procedures.

The Baroque period produces other types of text. One of them, the *Desierto prodigioso y prodigio del desierto* [The Wonderful Wilderness and Wonders of the Wilderness], written around the mid-17th century is, according to Héctor Orjuela, the first Spanish American novel. This complex work by Pedro de Solís y Valenzuela (1624–1711) has multiple narrators and is organized by superimposing narrative levels. Thus, what comes together are "prodigious" tales, an autobiography and some stories that its author tells, poems, ascetic prose, biographies and theater.

Many writers, among them Pedro Tobar y Buendía, Basilio Vicente de Oviedo, Juan Bautista de Toro and Fernando de Vergara Azcárate produce religious works in prose and verse. Nevertheless, outstanding among them is Francisco Álvarez de Velasco y Zorrilla (1647–1708), whose conceptist *Rhytmica sacra, moral y laudatoria*, 1703 [Sacred, Moral and Laudatory Rhytmics] shows different and innovative metric combinations.

Of course, the most canonical of these authors was Hernando Domínguez Camargo (1606–1659). Some of his poetry and a brief text in which poetry alternates with verse is *Inventiva apologética* [An Inventive Apologetic], included in Jacinto de Evia's *Ramillete de varias flores poéticas*, 1676 [A Cluster of Various Poetic Flowers]. The *Inventiva* is a literary and theological treatise, full of malice and wit, written by Domínguez Camargo in order to attack the author of a critique against one of his poems devoted to Christ. His best-known work, the unfinished *Poema heroico de San Ignacio de Loyola*, 1666 [Heroic Poem of Saint Ignatius of Loyola], is made up of 1200 octaves that encompass the birth of the saint up to the founding of the Society of Jesus. The *Poema* follows the Góngora model and, according to present day criticism, enriches that model. It does so by showing the poet's mythological erudition and his various knowledge not only of theological but of natural sciences, games of chance, hunting and culinary arts.

Convents were a key site for the colonial life of New Granada, since their relations with the outside world were quite singular. They had close ties with the various levels of political and economic power. But, at the same time, managed to stay away from them. They thus became spaces for literature and, above all, for literature written by women. Those texts, according to contemporary feminist criticism which has devoted special attention to research on conventual writing, are clear early examples of "feminine writing."

Some priests wrote about the lives of the religious women who took confession with them. Those writings became the "lives" of nuns. These texts could very well have been autobiographical tales whose probable authors gave them to their confessors, who turned them into biographies. Some of these narrations are the life of Madre Catalina María de la Concepción, founder of the Convent of Santa Clara de Cartagena; the life of Madre Francisca María del Niño Jesús (1723); and that of Sor María Gertrudis Theresa de Santa Inés. These works, however, have been attributed respectively to fathers Luis de Jodar, Pedro Pablo de Villamor and Andrés Calvo de la Riba.

Within the context of conventual writing, there were autobiographies by nuns whose authorship was not usurped by their confessors. One of them is *Su vida* [Her Life], by Francisca Josefa de Castillo y Guevara (1672–1741). This is a text that interlinks dreams and fantasies with everyday details, without being concerned about chronology. It also includes childhood memories, details about the author's family and the misfortunes of her existence in the cloisters of Santa Clara, together with intimate testimonies, mystical experiences and pious thoughts. Another one of her works is *Afectos espirituales* [Spiritual Passions], which, like *Su vida*, can be read as autobiographical, mystical and hagiographical. But this is clearly a more poetic text whose literary elaboration surpasses *Su vida*. Another nun who produced an autobiographical text

was Jerónima Nava y Saavedra (1669–1727), who finished writing her "spiritual life" in 1727. Her narrative, due to critics' carelessness, was attributed to Juan de Olmos and was edited and published in 1994, under the title *Autobiografía de una monja venerable* [Autobiography of a Venerable Nun].

The writing of chronicles persisted into the 18th century. Generally written by priests, their purpose was to give prominence to the missionary work of the various religious orders settled in the New Kingdom of Granada. They are *Historia de las misiones de los llanos de Casanare y los ríos Orinoco y Meta*, 1728 [History of the Casanare Plains and Orinoco and Meta Rivers Missions], by Juan Rivero (1681–1736); *Historia de la Provincia de la Compañía de Jesús del Nuevo Reino de Granada en la América*, 1741 [History of the Province of the Society of Jesus in America's New Kingdom of Granada], written in Spain by José Cassani (1673–1750); *El Orinoco ilustrado, historia natural, civil y geográfica de este gran río y sus caudalosas vertientes*, 1741 [The Illustrated Orinoco: the Natural and Political History of this Great River and its Mighty Sources] by José Gumilla (1686–1750); and *Floresta de la Santa Iglesia Catedral de Santa Marta*, 1739 [Collected Delights from the Santa Marta Cathedral] by José Nicolás de la Rosa.

Toward the middle of the 18th century the colonial system began to disintegrate. The way of life, once austere, gave way to frivolous behavior. Rococo, the style that corresponds to these circumstances, had its representative in the poet Francisco Antonio Vélez Ladrón de Guevara (1721–?). The society of New Granada, now guided by Enlightenment ideas, became interested in questioning the present, planning the future and writing about it. New literary genres were produced to replace the scarce production in poetry and prose fiction. The Enlightment also entered feminine cloisters. In one of them, the convent of La Enseñanza, María Petronila Cuéllar (1761–1814) wrote *Riego espiritual para nuevas plantas*, 1805 [Spiritual Watering for New Plants], a manual for the education of the novitiate. There were also numerous essays, administrative reports, travel books and, finally, open pamphlets and critiques of the Spanish regime. The crisis in the Iberian peninsula, Bourbon politics, the rigidness and inefficiency of the colonial apparatus, the introduction of the printing press, the creation of newspapers, the Botanical Expedition that was undertaken, and the consolidation of Spanish American conscience by mestizos and creole groups explain those changes.

Some of the books which diagnosed society and proposed alternatives to transform it were *Descripción del Reyno de Santa Fe de Bogotá*, 1789 [Description of the Kingdom of Santa Fe de Bogotá], by Francisco Silvestre, the *Pensamientos políticos y memorias sobre la población del Nuevo Reino de Granada*, 1808 [Political Thoughts and Memoirs Concerning the New Kingdom of Granada] by Pedro Fermín de Vargas (1762–1811). By the same token, Antonio Nariño (1765–1823) translated and published *The Rights of Man and of the Citizen* in 1794; a text which was essential for the development of the struggle for Independence in Colombia. Camilo Torres, Francisco José de Caldas, Jorge Tadeo Lozano and Francisco Antonio Zea, outstanding authors and politicians were also active participants in the process of rupture from Spain which culminated in 1819.

From 1980 on the tendencies of international criticism, which contend to revise literary canons and recover ignored or marginal texts, have provided a creative impulse to research on the colonial literature of New Granada. This is buoyed by the increasing interest among Colombian scholars, in various disciplines, who carry out tremendous effort toward reconstructing the country's past. Colombia's colonial literary history is thus undergoing a period of rewriting and expansion.

ANGELA I. ROBLEDO

See also entry on Conventual Writing

Further Reading

Cobo Borda, Juan Gustavo and Santiago Mutis Durán (editors), *Manual de historia de Colombia*, 2 vols, 2nd edition, Bogotá: Procultura e Instituto Colombiano de Cultura, 1982 [Volume 1 is on the colonial period]

Gómez Restrepo, Antonio, *Historia de la literatura colombiana*, 3 vols, 4th edition, Bogotá: Litografía Villegas, 1956–57

González Echevarría, Roberto, *Myth and Archive: a Theory of Latin American Narrative*, Cambridge and New York: Cambridge University Press, 1990 [Chapter 2 is concerned in part with Rodríguez Freyle's *El carnero*]

Jaramillo de Zuleta, Pilar, *En olor de santidad. Aspectos del convento colonial 1680–1830*, Santa Fé de Bogotá: OP Gráficas, 1992

Orjuela, Héctor, *Estudios sobre literatura indígena y colonial*, Bogotá: Instituto Caro y Cuervo, 1986

Robledo, Angela I., "Antes de la Independencia," in *¿Y las mujeres? ensayos sobre literatura colombiana*, edited by Robledo, María Mercedes Jaramillo and Flor María Rodríguez, Medellín, Colombia: Universidad de Antioquia, 1991

Tovar Zambrano, Bernardo, *La colonia en la historiografía colombiana*, 3rd edition, Bogotá: ECOE, 1984

Vergara y Vergara, José María, *Historia de la literatura en Nueva Granada*, 3 vols, Bogotá: Biblioteca de la Presidencia de Colombia, 1958

Colonial Literature

New Spain

With the conquest of the Aztecs in 1521, the Spaniards immediately began to rebuild the former city of Tenochtitlán, which they called Mexico, and to transform it into a major cultural center in the New World. As the capital of the new Viceroyalty of New Spain, it was the seat of the region's colonial administration and the focal point of religious efforts to convert the area's Amerindian population. Spain's physical presence in New Spain, however, was only the beginning of the colonization process; its ultimate success would rest on the effectiveness of the Spaniards to communicate their beliefs and values to the conquered, thus imposing European culture upon them.

In order to incorporate this new viceroyalty within the Spanish empire in a systematic and harmonious manner, therefore, a conceptualization of the conquest was set forth by officialdom in which the Peninsular-born male Spaniard was portrayed as the dominant figure in a society that was paternalistic and protective of Indians, blacks, mestizos, women, and even American-born Spaniards, or creoles. This hegemonic vision of the New World pervaded Spain's ideology in the Indies and made Utopia a principal theme of colonial discourse.

The first works of literary merit produced by the Spaniards in New Spain were chronicles and histories that generally followed the principles of Renaissance historiography. Creative literary devices were clearly utilized within the historical framework of these persuasive and often eloquent accounts, and they usually provided moral instruction and paradigms of identity for New Spain's residents to follow. In this regard, these writings were meant to play a positive and unifying role in the formation of Mexican society that would confirm Spain's absolute authority.

With the intention of maintaining Spain's preeminence in the New World and reaffirming its belief in Utopianism there, official restrictions were placed on the exportation of books to New Spain and the writing of works about America. As early as 1506 Ferdinand prohibited the transfer of works of fiction to the viceroyalty, and the prohibition was restated twenty-five years later by Juana la Loca, who identified chivalric novels such as *Amadís de Gaula* [Amadis of Gaul] as being especially detrimental to the welfare of newly converted Indians. Both civil and ecclesiastical authorities were responsible for this censorship, and severe punishment was meted out, in some cases, to those who violated their rules. In 1556 the first *Index* was published in Spain, in 1560 the Council of the Indies required all printers and vendors of books with an American theme to have a license, and in 1571 the Inquisition was established in Mexico City. Despite all of these measures, however, books that were supposedly prohibited flowed into New Spain, according to extant ship manifests, and circulated freely among members of the viceroyalty's readership. Although relatively few writers, printers, or book dealers suffered the consequences of violating these restrictions, efforts to enforce strict censorship did influence literary production in New Spain. Even the great poet Sor Juana Inés de la Cruz expressed a desire to avoid any problems with the Inquisition in her famous letter to the bishop of Puebla, and the development of the entire genre of the novel was greatly restricted until the early part of the 19th century when José Joaquín Fernández de Lizardi wrote his picaresque narrative *El Periquillo Sarniento* (*The Itching Parrot*).

The military subjugation of New Spain's Indians was immediately followed by the area's religious conquest, which was zealously undertaken by the Catholic Church, the right arm, as it were, of the Spanish state. Friars from the Dominican, Franciscan, Mercedarian, and Augustinian orders and the Society of Jesus engaged in the conversion on a grand scale and established schools, libraries, and universities. In 1538 the first printing press arrived in the New World at the request of Mexico's first bishop, Friar Juan de Zumárraga. Vocabularies and dictionaries of Amerindian languages along with doctrinal Christian works comprised the first publications produced. Many of New Spain's earliest writers were members of religious communities, and they sought to document their role in the progress of the evangelization as well as to preserve elements of indigenous culture. Among them was Friar Toribio de Benavente who became known as Motolinía, or "poor one" in the Náhuatl language. His principal work *Historia de los indios de Nueva España* (*History of the Indians of New Spain*) is noted for its description of an early performance of missionary theater that took place in Tlaxcala in 1538. The play, or *auto*, as it was called, depicts Adam and Eve in the garden of Eden at the time of the Fall. The brief dramatic work was designed to incorporate new converts more closely within the Catholic Church by enabling them to participate in Christian ceremonies. For that reason, it was performed by Indian actors speaking their own language. This piece closes with a religious carol, or *villancico*, in which Eve's purportedly deceitful actions are reiterated. These ten lines of poetry were probably some of the first written in Spanish in New Spain, and constituted, in some cases, the initial words that Indians learned in Spanish.

Another Franciscan, who studied and wrote about New Spain's Indians, was Friar Bernardino de Sahagún, a professor of Latin at the Academy of Santa Cruz de Tlaltelolco, which was founded in 1536 by the Flemish friar Pedro de Gante. His *Historia general de las cosas de Nueva España* (*General History of the Things of New Spain*), although only parts of it are extant, is considered to be his most notable work and provides a valuable source of information on the ancient Aztecs.

Adding to the knowledge of pre-conquest Mexico are several accounts written by Indian historians who had been educated in the schools established by the first friars. The *Crónica mexicana* [Mexican Chronicle] by Don Hernando de Alvarado Tezozomoc is particularly worthy of mention because of the penetrating view it presents of the nature of the Indian and its inclusion of elements from the *Códice Ramírez* [Ramírez Codex], an anonymous manuscript that reflects on the events surrounding the conquest from the indigenous perspective. Don Fernando de Alva Ixtlilxóchitl, another descendant of Aztec royalty, who was able to interpret the hieroglyphics of antiquity, wrote the *Historia chichimeca* [History of the Chichimecas], a work that complements the accounts of Tezozomoc and other Indian historians by unveiling the rich culture of a neighboring tribe of the politically dominant Aztecs.

Although the conquest of Mexico was essentially complete with the fall of Tenochtitlán, many of the issues that it posed were left unresolved. Paramount to the wellbeing of its Spanish participants were the rewards granted by the Crown to the conquerors for their loyal service in the Indies. Many years after serving in the ranks of Hernán Cortés's army, Bernal Díaz del Castillo endeavored to claim for the common soldier the spoils of victory he felt that were due. In his *Historia verdadera de la conquista de la Nueva España* (*True History of the Conquest of New Spain*), he presents a compelling case for the just compensation of his comrades at arms and at the same time provides the most thorough and lively description of the Spanish campaigns against the Indians. Contradicting Francisco López de Gómara's *Historia general de las Indias* (*General History of the Indies*), which the historian had based on the *Cartas de relación* (*Letters*) written by Cortés himself, Bernal Díaz focuses on the accomplishments of his fellow soldiers without diminishing the stature of his captain. In a forthright and colloquial manner, he recounts his many adventures to the reader, and his creative portraits of Moctezuma and Doña Marina, the Indian woman who served as Cortés's translator when he arrived in Tenochititlán, are unmatched by any other eyewitness account. In this respect, his history marks an initial phase in the evolutionary development of the novel.

Apart from the many chronicles and histories, only several of which have been mentioned here, residents of New Spain cultivated other forms of literary expression, and their works often extolled the viceregal capital for its splendor or recounted the heroism of the conquest in verse. Francisco de Terrazas was probably the first poet of Spanish descent to be born in Mexico, and his poetry generally demonstrates the influence of Italianate rhyme in the New World. Cervantes praised his talent by referring to him as the "new Apollo" in the sixth book of *La Galatea*. In his sonnet "Dejad las hebras de oro ensortijado" [Surrender the Golden Curls], for example, Terrazas exalts feminine beauty and charm and follows precisely the Renaissance concept of womanhood in which a lady's loveliness is compared to the rare beauties of nature. Inspired by Alonso de Ercilla's epic *La Araucana*, he also wrote a long poem entitled *Nuevo Mundo y Conquista* [New World and Its Conquest], a work that remained unfinished at the time of his death.

Another significant contributor to the development of poetry in New Spain was Bernardo de Balbuena. Describing the city of Mexico as a paradise in a constant state of springtime, he focuses principally on its physical aspects that eloquently come alive with his erudite language and meticulous description. This elegant tableau depicts the capital at the end of the 16th century and introduces Mexican readers to the initial intricacies of the Baroque.

Although Mexico City was for many Spaniards the realization of the Utopian dreams they had for their American territories, it represented the great disparity that existed in other sectors of colonial society as well, especially when comparing the lot of Peninsular-born Spaniards to that of creoles. Several anonymous works, one beginning "Viene de España" [He Comes from Spain] and "Minas sin plata" [Mines without Silver] convey the resentment and anger of some creoles at being denied access to the wealth and power bestowed routinely on those actually born in Spain. These satiric poems are important in the history of literature, as they represent the emergence of a popular culture in New Spain and the glimmer of a national consciousness that would increase as the colonial period progressed.

The conversion of New Spain's native population was the principal impetus in the development of the theater, and indeed the Catholic Church would play a role in the performance of theatrical works throughout the colonial era, as plays were an integral part of religious festivities. By the close of the 16th century, however, the dramatist Fernán González de Eslava began introducing lay elements into his *coloquios*, or colloquies, a measure that would signal the advent of a separate secular theater in New Spain. Although this new trend in drama precipitated the construction of theaters throughout New Spain, the viceroyalty boasted few outstanding dramatists during the 17th and 18th centuries. Juan Ruiz de Alarcón, who left Mexico for Spain and is considered among the Golden Age dramatists, and Sor Juana Inés de la Cruz are the only real exceptions.

González de Eslava's *coloquios*, which are divided into acts and are accompanied by dedicatory poems and interludes, afforded the playwright the opportunity of incorporating current customs and events within the context of episodes taken from the Bible. An excellent example of this is his *Coloquio VII* in which Teresa and Diego, a married couple living in New Spain, have a spat over the new law prohibiting the production of silk in the viceroyalty because it was already produced in Spain. When Teresa insists that she must have it to make her dresses, she forces Diego to accompany her aboard a ship bound for China. The prophet Jonah, who is on his way to Nineveh, is also a passenger, and when a storm breaks unexpectedly during the voyage, both Teresa and Jonah think that they are responsible for this manifestation of God's wrath. Jonah ultimately hurls himself into the ocean to restore calm seas, and a contrite Teresa promises to be an obedient wife. Although all of González de Eslava's colloquies are morally didactic and inspired by some aspect of religious doctrine, comedy is a characteristic of his work. Slapstick, buffoons, and a distorted yet amusing form of speech called *sayagués* contribute moments of levity to his works and temper the seriousness of these pieces with entertaining frivolity. The inclusion of a comic character in the cast of a religious play was not uncommon and was also employed by the Mexican born playwright Juan Pérez Ramírez in his *Desposorio espiritual* [Spiritual Betrothal of Pastor Peter and the Mexican Church].

The Baroque had a profound influence on the literature of New Spain during the 17th century, and the sheer challenge of its odd metrical forms and complex metaphors inspired numerous writers to try their skills at literary composition. Although aspiring poets were especially fascinated by the ambiguity and contradiction of such rhetorical adornment, the extravagance and affectation that characterized their works won them little distinction. The *Triunfo Parthénico* [Parthenic Triumph] compiled by Don Carlos de Sigüenza y Góngora provides a sampling of works by New Spain's poets written for one of the many competitions in which learned people engaged. This particular compilation was assembled in 1682 to celebrate the Immaculate Conception, and the quality of its entries exemplifies the general mediocrity that pervaded the 1600s.

A rare exception to the stylistic decadence of the 17th century was the literary production of Sor Juana Inés de la Cruz, who used the elaborate excesses of the time to create a space in which to express the concerns of a female intellectual. Her prose, poetry, and drama represent the pinnacle of literary creativity from both the viceregal court and Catholic convents in New Spain whose excellence remained unmatched throughout the entire colonial period.

Having been invited to the court of the viceroy of the Marquis of Mancera because of her precocity, she wrote extensively for its members. The sonnet "Este que ves . . ." [This (portrait) That You See . . .] is particularly beautiful, and the sensitivity of her love poetry has given rise to much speculation about her personal life. Among her other notable works are the long poem *El primero sueño* (*Sor Juana's Dream*), in which she imitates the extreme style of the Spanish Baroque poet Luis de Góngora, and the riotous comedy *Los empeños de una casa* [The Trials of a Noble House], in which she follows the tradition of the Golden Age dramatist, Pedro Calderón de la Barca. Although she ultimately decided to leave the court because of its artificiality, she continued to write secular works after entering the convent, the only viable alternative for a single woman during the colonial period who did not wish to remain with her family. Her desire to continue writing non-religious works, however, brought her into conflict with the bishop of Puebla, Don Manuel Fernández de Santa Cruz, and provoked the writing of her famous letter *Respuesta a Sor Filotea de la Cruz* (*The Answer*), in which she defends her inclination to study and write and speaks out on behalf of education for women. Although she did write many works of a profane nature, those with a religious theme are no less meritorious. Her *auto sacramental*, *Divino Narciso* [Divine Narcissus], in which Sor Juana brilliantly blends mythology and theology, is considered to be a masterpiece.

Although Sigüenza y Góngora did not distinguish himself as a poet, despite his many efforts, his ability to document and write history was exceptional, and the artistry with which he composed his works puts him in second place, after Sor Juana, as a literary figure of importance in 17th century New Spain. As an outstanding intellectual of his time, he was a professor of mathematics at Mexico's university and was appointed royal cosmographer by Charles II. Among his works of literary merit is his *Infortunios de Alonso Ramírez* [Misadventures of Alonso Ramírez], which possesses definite novelistic features that in some respects characterize the Spanish picaresque. He also participated in a scientific expedition to Florida's Gulf coast and prepared a plan for the defense of Pensacola against the pirates. His most important scientific work, however, is his *Libra astronómica y filosófica* [Astronomical and Philosophical Terms], in which he countered the theory of the Jesuit Father Kino, who believed that comets such as the one that appeared over Mexico City in November of 1680 would bring disaster.

The interest in Mexican history, especially in the ancient past, continued during the 18th century. Departing from the scholasticism and Gongorist rhetoric of their immediate predecessors, historians such as Don Francisco Clavijero and Don Mariano Fernández de Echeverría y Veytia applied modern methods of thought and investigation to the task of piecing together the heritage of pre-conquest cultures and civilizations. Aided by his exceptional linguistic ability in Amerindian languages and basing his work on the careful research accomplished by Sigüenza y Góngora and other historians like him, Clavijero sought to provide a rich and varied panorama of the life of the Aztecs and their neighboring tribes. The picture presented in Clavijero's outstanding book, *Historia antigua de México* [Ancient History of Mexico] is completed by Veytia's *Historia antigua* [Ancient History], which deals with additional indigenous groups to inhabit the territory that later became known as the Viceroyalty of New Spain. Veytia is also recognized for his study of Mexico's prominent female religious figures, most notably the Virgin of Guadalupe.

Throughout the viceregal period, classical culture was a major influence in New Spain's literature, and it inspired the composition of a number of works in Latin. Beginning in the 16th century with Francisco Cervantes de Salazar's *Diálogos* [Dialogues], this tradition continued during the last one hundred years of Spain's rule and flourished among members of religious orders such as the humanists Francisco Javier Alegre, Rafael Landívar, and Diego José Abad. Landívar is the most important of these writers, and his *Rusticatio Mexicana* [A Rural Life in Mexico], which was influenced by Virgil's *Georgics*, is probably the most striking example of neo-Latin poetry in which the viceroyalty of New Spain is described.

By the end of the 18th century, it was clear that residents of New Spain had formulated their own identity separate from that of the Spaniards and that the imposition of colonial administration must be lifted and the viceroyalty dissolved. Mexicans had developed a national consciousness that was no longer compatible with the cultural and ideological goals of Spain, and they adamantly moved toward revolution. The novelist and essayist José Joaquín Fernández de Lizardi, known among his contemporaries as "the Mexican Thinker," is the embodiment of this new spirit, and the freedom he expresses in his many works, which marks the advent of the independence era, is both political and artistic.

JULIE GREER JOHNSON

See also entries on José Joaquín Fernández de Lizardi, Sor Juana Inés de la Cruz

Further Reading

Arenal, Electra and Stacey Schlau (editors), *Untold Sisters: Hispanic Nuns in Their Own Writings*, Albuquerque: University of New Mexico Press, 1989

Cypess, Sandra Messinger, *La Malinche in Mexican Literature: from History to Myth*, Austin: University of Texas Press, 1991

Foster, David William (editor), *Mexican Literature: a History*, Austin: University of Texas Press, 1994 [Chapter 2 covers the colonial period]

Franco, Jean, *Plotting Women: Gender and Representation in Mexico*, New York: Columbia University Press, and London: Verso, 1989

Johnson, Julie Greer, *Women in Colonial Spanish American Literature: Literary Images*, Westport, Connecticut: Greenwood Press, 1983

____ *The Book in the Americas: the Role of Books and Printing in the Development of Culture and Society in Colonial Latin America*, Providence, Rhode Island: John Carter Brown Library, 1988

____ *Satire in Colonial Spanish America: Turning the New World Upside Down*, Austin: University of Texas Press, 1993

Leonard, Irving A., *Baroque Times in Old Mexico. Seventeenth-Century Persons, Places and Practices*, Ann Arbor: University of Michigan Press, 1966

Merrim, Stephanie (editor), *Feminist Perspectives on Sor Juana Inés de la Cruz*, Detroit: Wayne State University Press, 1991

Myers, Kathleen (editor), *Word from New Spain: the Spiritual Autobiography of Madre María de San José (1656–1719)*, Liverpool: Liverpool University Press, 1993

Paz, Octavio, *Sor Juana Inés de la Cruz, o, Las trampas de la fe*, Mexico City: Fondo de Cultura Económica, 1982; as *Sor Juana, or, The Traps of Faith*, translated by Margaret Sayers Peden, Cambridge, Massachusetts: Harvard University Press, and London: Faber and Faber, 1988

Perelmuter Pérez, Rosa, *Noche intelectual: la oscuridad idiomática en el Primer Sueño*, Mexico City: UNAM, 1982

Pupo-Walker, Enrique, *La vocación literaria del pensamiento histórico en América, desarrollo de la prosa de ficción: siglos XVI, XVII, XVIII, y XIX*, Madrid: Gredos, 1982

Ross, Kathleen, *The Baroque Narrative of Carlos de Sigüenza y Góngora: a New World Paradise*, Cambridge: Cambridge University Press, 1994

Sabat de Rivers, Georgina, *El sueño de Sor Juana Inés de la Cruz*, London: Támesis, 1977

Vogeley, Nancy, "Defining the Colonial Reader: *El Periquillo Sarniento*," PMLA 102 (1987)

Colonial Literature

Peru

When we speak of Peruvian colonial literature, we must credit Inca literature as a valuable foundation. The first Spanish priests understood that the only way to teach religion to the natives was by learning their language and their traditions and giving them a new Catholic meaning. This was the main reason for the syncretism that still endures in Peruvian and Latin American culture. In addition, the Inca's oral tradition was recreated not only for the chroniclers but also for literary authors. As Dick Gerdes states in his essay on Peruvian literature in the *Handbook of Latin American Literature* (1992), it is clear that an examination of colonial literature must go beyond the study of "white" male writers: "The project for the future will be to incorporate all canon strata, dominant and popular, written and oral, male and female, into a literary canon in which modern critical perspectives will help us to appreciate Peruvian literature."

When the Spanish arrived in the New World, they encountered a people and environment unknown to them and all other Europeans. They recorded their new experiences in the form of chronicles. At first these works were considered to be simply historical documents, but they recently have come to be seen as literary works. The rhetorical styles of the chronicles were strongly influenced by the triumphant, providential, and paternalistic modes. With Francisco Pizarro's arrival in Peru in 1532, the Inca civilization changed abruptly for both the so-called "colonized Indian" and the European colonizer. Styles intermingled and informed one another; agendas emerged and changed; and the telling of history became also the creation of colonial selves.

There are three groups of chroniclers: the Spanish, the mestizos, and the Inca. Among all the Spanish chroniclers Pedro Pizarro (1515–87) was one of the few who wrote exclusively about Peru. In his *Relación del descubrimiento y conquista del Perú* [Account of the Discovery and Conquest of Peru], he describes the fratricidal savagery of the Spanish civil wars and lavishes praise on his conqueror cousin. Pizarro's narrative style is lively and has the authority of an eye-witness who describes Pizarro's arrival on Peruvian soil, Atahualpa's capture, and the Inca's way of life, especially their dances. Another well-known chronicler is José de Acosta (1540–1600). He deserves mention because he was a defender of the native Peruvians against the Spanish excesses and cruelties. His *Historia natural y moral de las Indias*, 1500 [Natural History of the West Indies] is a study which more accurately approaches the culture and the organization of the Inca Empire. Acosta, like Father Bartolomé de Las Casas, writes about the emperors of Mexico and Peru, recognizing their monarchical skills. Besides providing an incisive philosophical, ethnographical and historical study of the New World, he reveals himself as a skillful scientist writing brilliantly about the natural richness of Peru and of Latin America.

Among the mestizo chroniclers, El Inca Garcilaso de la Vega is the first famous Peruvian writer. He asserts in his *Comentarios reales de los Incas*, 1609 (*Royal Commentaries of the Incas*), the significance of knowing the Peruvian native culture and language in writing about the Incas. He relates how his Inca relatives and his mother introduced him to the history and customs of his Inca heritage, thus making clear that he could speak about his ancestors with authority. He wrote *La Florida del Inca*, 1605 (*The Florida of the Inca*), which describes Hernando Soto's expedition to Florida. The second part of the *Comentarios Reales* is *Historia General del Perú*, 1619 [General History of Peru] which narrates the bloody civil war among the Spaniards.

Garcilaso's *Comentarios reales* is considered a classic work and is the beginning of the Latin American literary canon. The text was conceived as a penetrating exploration of personal and Peruvian identity. Because of the native uprising during the 18th century, the Spanish Crown banned the reading of Garcilaso's seminal work, and it was secretly confiscated all over Peru.

Another colonial author was Francisco de Ávila (1573–1647), a mestizo born in Cuzco. Ávila studied at the Jesuit College in Cuzco, Peru, and graduated in 1606. he was the author of *El manuscrito de Huarochirí* [The Huarochiri Manuscript] which was translated by José María Arguedas, and given the title *Hombres y dioses de Huarochirí*, 1966 [Huarochiri Men and Gods]. Ávila's *Manuscrito* is a chronicle of magical origins about the gods, traditions, and legends of the Andean people. Ávila's work, and it helps us to understand the importance of indigenous traditions. It has been compared to the *Comentarios reales* of El Inca Garcilaso de la Vega, in its presentation of the Inca's religion and customs. Furthermore, *El manuscrito de Huarochirí* has a subtext that suggests that the European and Andean religions are of equal value, correcting the belief that one is superior to the other.

Before examining what have been called "Indian" chroniclers, it should be noted that it is more accurate to call them "native" chroniclers and that accuracy is important. It is not appropriate to continue the tradition of misdesignation that began with Columbus.

Among the native chroniclers are Titu Cusi Yupanqui, Joan de Santacruz Pachacuti Yamqui Sallqamaygua and Felipe Guaman Poma de Ayala. (The work of only the first two will be examined because there is a separate essay on Guaman Poma in this encyclopedia). Titu Cusi Yupanqui (1529–70), whose Spanish name was Diego de Castro, wrote the *Relación de la conquista del Perú* [Account of the Conquest of Peru] and *Hechos del Inca Manco Inca II* [The Deeds of Inca Manco Inca II]. The former was not published until 1916, perhaps because it was not popular during its time as it was a direct and passionate defense of the native people. This chronicle was inspired by the abusive treatment of the natives by the ruling Spanish. In *Hechos del Inca Manco II*, Cusi Yupanqui writes of the last Incan King of Cuzco, Manco Inca, and his rebellion in 1535. He presents Manco Inca as a heroic warrior who battled bravely against the European invasion. His style of narration is vivid, and his rhetoric is dramatic and captures the attention of the reader.

Joan de Santacruz Pachacuti Yamqui Sallqamaygua was a bilingual native who wrote *Relación de Antigüedades deste Reyno del Pirú* [Account of the Antiquities of the Kingdom of Peru]. It was first published in English in 1873. His work has a distinctly evangelical tone because he was a convert to Catholicism. Although Santacruz Pachacuti condemns the idolatry of some Andean people, he rescues the Incas' faith and compares it to Spanish Catholicism. He writes with great beauty about native traditions and mythology. But Santacruz Pachacuti is also important because he is the first to reveal and include Inca poetry. His chronicle interweaves the religious and liturgical hymns of Sinchi Roca, Manco Cápac, and Huascar. In writing about Manco Capac's hymn, Santacruz Pachacuti emphasizes its lyrical form and use of metaphor. Sinchi Roca's hymn is also beautifully described. It was composed by the Inca to honor his first-born child in the same way one would honor God's Son.

Besides the chronicle, other literary forms flourished during colonial times. Poetry and drama in their diverse expressions were used to teach religion. Juan de Espinoza Medrano (1629–88) is perhaps the most notable writer of the period. He was known as "El Lunarejo" and wrote extensively in drama, lyric, and prose. Among his dramatic works are *El hijo pródigo* [The Prodigal Son], a religious allegory in both

Quechua and Spanish. *Amar su propia muerte* [Love Your Own Death] based on a passage from the Old Testament, and *El rapto de Proserpina* [Proserpine's Abduction], were both extensively presented in colonial times. "El Lunarejo" was a faithful disciple of Góngora. The Peruvian writer dedicated *El apologético en favor de D. Luis de Góngora, Príncipe de los poetas líricos de España* [The Apologetics of Don Luis de Góngora, Prince of the Spanish Lyric Poets] to his teacher. Among his prose, *La novena maravilla* [The Ninth Wonder] has aroused new critical interest. Other writers, such as Pedro Peralta Barnuevo (1664–1743) with *Pasión y triunfo de Cristo*, 1737 [Passion and Triumph of Christ], and Pablo de Olavide (1725–1803) and his *El Evangelio en triunfo*, 1798 [The Triumph of the Gospel], are considered to be Espinoza Medrano's disciples.

Drama was a popular genre during colonial times. Besides the religious plays the most well-known dramatic play is represented by *Ollantay*. Although it was first published in Cuzco in 1837, the truth is that this play had been transmitted by oral tradition for countless generations. Some critical editions have credited the play to Antonio Valdez, a Sicuani (Cuzco) priest who knew the native Quechua and could have transcribed the work. *Ollantay* is an epic play in three acts which narrates the plebeian general Ollantay's rebellion against King Inca Pachacutec when he is not allowed to marry the Princess Cusi Coyllur. *Ollantay* recreates Inca times and is considered the most representative play of colonial times.

La muerte de Atahualpa [The Death of Atahualpa Inca] is another bilingual play. This dramatic play has only one act and is written in verse and prose it has native and Spanish characters. Among the natives are the Inca King Atahualpa, Huáscar his brother, three Coyas or Inca Queens, and other minor characters. The Spanish are represented by Francisco Pizarro, as a diplomatic ambassador and Father Valverde as the preacher. The play recounts the fateful encounter between Atahualpa and Pizarro.

In addition to the *Ollantay* and *La Muerte de Atahualpa* there are also some others plays such as *Usca Paucar* [Paucar the Beggar], an anonymous play written in the 18th century. *Usca Paucar* is a Quechua-Christian play dedicated to the Virgin of Copacabana. This play is divided into three acts and deals with the trials of its protagonist Paucar, a rebel beggar Inca. Although *Usca Paucar* was very poor and, as a former noble, untutored in any trade, he could not accept any help because he was arrogant and proud of his origin. Moreover, in the end he was convinced by his love of Koirtica to join the Procession honoring the Virgin Mary and was led to conversion and happiness; as in other Spanish colonies, the majority of plays had religious purposes and relied on allegory to communicate their message.

In general the most popular genre during colonial times was the lyric. For a time it was believed that this form reigned supreme until the discovery of the first Peruvian novel, written by José de Acosta, *Peregrinación de Bartolomé Lorenzo*, 1666 [Bartolomé Lorenzo's Peregrination]. For many years the novel was forgotten, but in 1899 it was rediscovered by Cesáreo Fernández Duro who published it in the *Boletín de la Real Academia de la Historia* in the same year. The most recent edition was published in Peru by the well-known literary critic José de Arrom in 1982, and in 1994 a study of this first Peruvian novel was included in *Historia de la literatura peruana* by César Toro Montalvo.

Peregrinación de Bartolomé Lorenzo is a biography, but Acosta also includes some fictional passages that partake of the picaresque genre and make the novel interesting. Furthermore, Acosta enriches his narration with the language of the native people and his descriptions of American flora and fauna. *Peregrinación* is a short but dense novel of about thirty-five pages. Divided into five chapters and written in a picaresque style, Acosta's novel may be compared to that of the Mexican writer Singuenza y Góngora's *Infortunios de Alonso Ramírez*, 1690 [The Misfortunes of Alonso Ramírez]. However, the Peruvian novel also has a humanitarian message – throughout the text, the reader can perceive Bartolomé Lorenzo's charitable and kind intensions toward the native people. In many passages of the novel Bartolomé Lorenzo avoids joining his fellow Spanish commanders in attacking the native villages. For this reason he is persecuted and ordered to be hanged; but, because some Jesuit priests come to his aid, he is able to escape his doom. Indeed, Bartolomé Lorenzo then entered a monastery.

Satire was another popular genre in the colony. It was used as a didactic form to point up certain social and political problems and to entertain the audience at the same time. These satirists used language in an ironic and humorous manner, and the preferred targets of their criticism were lascivious women, false virgins, doctors, cheats, lower-class people (especially slaves), and even priests. Esteban de Terralla Landa and Juan del Valle y Caviedes enjoyed misrepresenting and mocking a wide range of people in their works. By criticizing everyone, the satirist subverted and deconstructed the social conventions of the colony. Hardly anyone could escape becoming a target of colonial satirists such as Mateo Rosas de Oquendo (16th century), Juan del Valle y Caviedes (17th century), and Alonso Carrió de la Vandera and de Terralla Landa (both 18th century).

During the Classic period, some colonial female authors emerged alongside their male counterparts. These include Amarilis, whose real name was never revealed. Amarilis wrote her *Épistola de Amarilis a Belardo*, 1621 [Epistle from Amarilis to Belardo]. Another woman writer was Clarinda, whose name was uncovered in the 19th century by Ricardo Palma. Prior to that time her writing had appeared anonymously in 1608. Her only known text is *Discurso en loor de la poesía*, 1608 [A Discourse in Praise of Poetry], a sensual poem of neoplatonic provenance. Besides the lay women authors, many nuns were writers. Santa Rosa de Lima (1586–1617) is well-known for her exquisite poetry. Others include Sor Antonia Lucía del Espíritu Santo (1646–1709), whose work was compiled by Josefa de la Providencia; María Manuela de Santa Ana (1695–1793) a recent discovery whose manuscripts are still unpublished; Juana de Herrera y Mendoza (18th century); Josefa de Azaña y Llano (1696–1748); Josefa Bravo de Lagunas y Villela (18th century); and Juana Calderón Badillo (1726–1809). These women wrote mostly spiritual autobiographies of literary as well as historical interest. The works of nuns are particularly relevant because they reveal importants facts about life within the convent and beyond its walls. Also much conventual literature portrays the microcosm within which nuns had considerable independence. Although they were subject to the orders of their superiors, they could deal freely with philosophical, spiritual and historical issues and they could record their thoughts in their writing.

The list of women's names makes it clear that there are a substantial number of female writers; yet, the anthologies and other collections represent a heavily male tradition. There is a need to improve the circulation of knowledge about Peruvian women's literature because women play an important part in the construction of culture at all times.

It is also important to refer to the transitional literature before Peruvian independence; of particular relevance in this context is *Carta a los españoles americanos* [Letter to the Spanish Americans] written by the ex-Jesuit Juan Pablo Viscardo y Guzmán (1747–98). *Carta a los españoles americanos* was published in Paris on the eve of the third century of the Discovery of America. It is considered fundamental because it served to raise the consciousness not only of the Peruvians but also the entire Americas as well. In addition, *Carta a los españoles americanos* is considered a historic document seminal for the independence of all the South American nations.

El Mercurio Peruano, 1792 [The Peruvian Mercury] was a newspaper founded by many patriotic intellectuals of *La Sociedad Amantes del Perú* [Society of Supporters of Peru]. *El Mercurio Peruano* is another foundational component of colonial literature which shaped the consciousness for independence. It transmitted the ideas of the Enlightenment and also provided, although tenuously, the opportunity for intellectual and social change. In this important newspaper is reflected the transcendental nationalist spirit epitomized by some well-known collaborators, Hipólito Unanue, Baquíjano y Carrillo, Peralta Barnuevo, José de Riva-Agüero, among others.

Another literary form was the *pasquines* (pasquinades). These were anonymous, satirical texts and lampoons, written in verse and prose, sometimes with drawings. The pages were printed and pasted on the walls of public buildings in the most important cities such as Lima, Arequipa, Cuzco and Puno, and in the small villages as well. The *pasquines* used popular language and their role was to exalt the Peruvians' awareness of political and social issues. They were banned and prohibited because their texts were considered subversive and against the principles of the Spanish crown Another purpose of the *pasquines* was to criticize the administration in general.

Some of these *pasquines* also discussed the brave actions of Túpac Amaru's uprising and several poems in the form of *pasquines* are dedicated to him. For instance, Melchor de Paz in his *Diálogo sobre los sucesos del Perú* [Dialogues about the Events in Peru] includes some *pasquines* from Arequipa written in 1870. The verses criticizes the Spanish King and exalt Tupac Amaru's deeds. There is one well-known poem, a *décima* to Tupac Amaru King of the American Continent, which was read in differents parts of the Viceroyalty such as La Plata,

Oruro, and Nueva Granada. It has a libertarian tone and was illuminating, especially to the oppressed people of the colony. García Márquez was to draw on the tradition of the *pasquines* in an early novel, *La mala hora* (*In Evil Hour*).

As the culmination of "colonial" literature, the "*pasquines*" are, in a sense, symbolic of much that has existed in Peruvian writing from the beginning. The telling of histories, the wry and unfettered wit, the spirit of rebellion, the hungry quest for spiritual and intellectual enlightenment, and the constant renegotiation in the diverse and exciting literature have all been present in the diverse and exciting literature of Peru. Whether we read the chroniclers, marvel at the fables of the Incas, laugh with the satirists, delve into the newly discovered treasures of women's writing, or explore the many other literary forms discussed, we are tapping into a tradition rich in conflict, wonder, and brilliance.

In conclusion, the literature of colonial Peru is a vast field that offers many interesting possibilities for continued study. This study will shed light not only on the nature of colonialism and its interaction with the native cultures of the region, but also on these issues in the larger context of colonialism throughout the world.

ELIA J. ARMACANQUI-TIPACTI

See also entries on El Inca Garcilaso de la Vega, Felipe Guaman Poma de Ayala

Further Reading

Adán, Martín, *De lo barroco en el Perú*, Lima: San Marcos, 1976 [Study by a prominent 20th-century poet]

Adorno, Rolena (editor), *From Oral to Written Expression: Native Andean Chronicles of the Early Colonial Period*, Syracuse, New York: Syracuse University Press, 1982

Barreda y Laos, Felipe, *Vida intelectual del virreinato*, Lima: Universidad Mayor de San Marcos, 1964

Bermúdez-Gallegos, Marta, *Poesía, sociedad y cultura: diálogos y retratos del Perú colonial*, Potomac, Maryland: Scripta Humanística, 1992

Chang-Rodríguez, Raquel, "Sobre los cronistas indígenas del Perú y los comienzos de una escritura hispanoamericana," *Revista Iberoamericana* 120–21 (1982)

Chang-Rodríguez, Raquel (editor), *Cancionero peruano del siglo XVII*, Lima: La Católica, 1983

Gerdes, Dick, "Peru," in *Handbook of Latin American Literature*, edited by David W. Foster, New York: Garland, 1987; 2nd edition, 1992

Harrison, Regina, "The Language and Rhetoric of Conversion in the Viceroyalty of Peru," *Poetics Today*, vol. 16/1 (1995)

Higgins, James, *A History of Peruvian Literature*, Liverpool: Cairns, 1987 [Chapter 2 covers the colonial period]

Lohmann Villena, Guillermo, *El arte dramático en Lima durante el virreinato*, Madrid: Escuela de Estudios Hispanoamericanos de la Universidad de Sevilla, 1945

Miró Quesada, Aurelio, *El primer virrey-poeta en América (Don Juan de Mendoza y Lima, Marqués de Montesclaros)*, Madrid: Gredos, 1962

Concrete Poetry

Concrete poetry was an international avant-garde movement in poetry in the 1950s and 1960s. The prime exponents of this spatially and visually oriented minimalism were the co-founders Swiss-Bolivian poet Eugen Gomringer and the Brazilian Noigandres group: Augusto de Campos, Haroldo de Campos and Décio Pignatari. This cosmopolitan movement owes a great deal to their organizational, theoretical, and creative initiatives. The conceptualization and practice of concrete poetry, in fact, developed more intensively in Brazil than anywhere else, quite remarkable for a peripheral South American nation with natural operational restrictions. Brazilian concrete poetry is widely cited, and its supporting essays are recognized as the richest contribution to the theory of concrete poetry. In terms of local impact, it is noteworthy that while in many countries concrete poetry had a relatively modest impact, *poesia concreta* comprised the most provocative and distinctive development in Brazilian lyric after Modernism. Beyond national frontiers, concrete ventures have attracted more attention for Brazilian poetry than any other contemporary manifestation. In terms of recognition, repertories of broadly-conceived concretism – encompassing theory, literary criticism, poetry, and translations by the Noigandres poets and associates – has been to Brazil what the writings of Octavio Paz are to Mexico, or the poetry and memoirs of Pablo Neruda to Spanish America.

As a movement, Brazilian concrete poetry lasted from the mid-1950s to the late 1960s, in three stages of development. In the first "organic" or "phenomenological" stage (1953–56), depersonalization, spatialization and visual shaping were key procedures. The second division (1956–61) is that of "classical," "high" or "orthodox" concrete poetry, when the Noigandres poets and their colleagues used ultra-rational principles of composition. The foundational document – the "pilot plan for concrete poetry" (1958) – comprised a compilation of interdisciplinary ideas from earlier manifestos and articles. The concrete platform was built of universal and national planks. Select features of the experimental works of key modern authors of both the "old" and "new" worlds were adopted. Cornerstones were Mallarmé's "prismatic subdivision of ideas," Pound's ideogrammatic method, and Joyce's concept of "verbivocovisual" word-ideogram. Other essential points of departure were e.e. cummings's typography and atomization of words and Apollinaire's vision of *calligramme*. National resources were the synthetic, Cubist poetry of Oswald de Andrade and his celebrated manifestos, as well as the architectonic verse of João Cabral de Melo Neto. In a third phase, 1962 on, more open notions of "invention" prevailed. Diverse practices included semantic variations, collages, creative advertisements, and lexically-keyed semiotic poems.

Since about 1960, the term "concrete poetry" has been used worldwide to refer to various kinds of verbal (and some nearly non-verbal) experiments on the printed page that are not rightly comparable to high concrete poetry, which was profoundly poetic and conceptual. Since some later visual poetry – including Brazilian – may appear to be "against" language, it must be kept in mind that classical Brazilian material was founded *on* literary language and is often *about* words. The Noigandres poets did cite Pound's notion that poetry is more like painting and music than literature, but they first sought to be true to his characterization of great literature as "language charged with meaning to the utmost possible degree."

Brazilian concrete poetry, from its inception to unresolved current debates, has lived a stormy and controversial life. In the 1950s, it was attacked for its lack of an orienting affectivity, and its non-linear, non-discursive structure was held to be self-defeating. It was frequently said that the concrete project was doomed to be a blind alley, since it proclaimed the end of the "historical cycle of verse." In the early 1960s, objections to concrete poetry's assaults on natural syntax, conventional lyricism, and verse-making gave way to protests based on political attitudes and ideology. In the phase of invention, concrete poets responded overtly to Brazil's climate of nationalism and activism, in essays and creative texts alike. Early concrete poetry had included notable examples of social discourse (land reform, cultural imperialism), and later examples proved no inherent contradiction between concrete techniques and social aims. Many still challenged the appropriateness of an experimental avant-garde in a severely imbalanced, underdeveloped country such as Brazil. Appealing to the gains of Modernism, the Noigandres poets defended their right to aesthetic research and recalled Oswald's critical re-elaboration of foreign information in national terms. In the context of the developmentalism of the 1950s, it is instructive to note that concrete poetry reversed the normal flow of cultural information from metropolis to colony and became an export product. Still, while there are indeed pertinent social factors in concretism, the vocation of the Noigandres poets was always primarily poetic, and concrete poetry was above all a textual enterprise.

New Brazilian poetry of the 1970s was markedly pluralistic. While the informal discursivity of so-called marginal poetry garnered attention, the lasting effects of concretism cannot be overlooked in other ventures. Since the late 1960s, song was a recognized channel for poetry, and Augusto de Campos's interest in innovative popular music (MPB) prompted experimentation that included concrete concepts. Varied products of verbal art fell under the sign of "intersemiotic creation," from constructivist lyric to different youthful experiments with visuality and graphics. Preference for semiosis over emotivity implied clear but non-restrictive recognition of concretist ideals. In many lyrical pursuits, fracture, paronomasia and concision figured prominently. The most evident impact of concrete poetry may be found in a propensity toward brevity, which is reflected in the popularity of haiku. To whatever degree concrete poetry was a factor in new lyric of the 1970s, the value of the term "post-concrete" is primarily chronological. Late in the decade the Noigandres poets increased their visibility and circulation with the publication of their collected poems: Haroldo de Campos, *Xadrez de estrelas*, 1975 [Stars' Chess], Décio Pignatari, *Poesia pois é poesia*, 1976 [Poetry for That is What it Is], and Augusto de Campos, *VIVA VAIA*, 1979 [Long Live Catcalls].

Since 1975, only the work of Augusto de Campos shows palpable continuity with concrete poetry. His poems are enriched with such non-verbal elements as typeface, color, and layout, and there is a return to words and phrases without renouncing the visual syntheses of concrete poetry. Augusto's most provocative poem was the timely "pós-tudo," 1984 [post-everything], which pondered the dilemma of those who pursue innovation in the late century, questioned Postmodernism as fashion, and touched off an extended polemic in Brazil about the legacy of concrete poetry, something that is discussed by Gonzalez and Treece in their study, *The Gathering of Voices* (1992).

Four decades after the inaugural exhibition of concrete poetry in Brazil, there is adequate perspective to judge its development and impact. The historical chapter of concrete poetry as a vanguard movement has long been closed, but concretism's attention to materiality, linguistic substance, and modernity remains in vigor. Problematic aspects of the formulation of concrete poetry include the sanctification of certain critical references (e.g., Pound) and the elevation of rupture and textual radicalization to self-justified values. In addition, the Brazilians' portrayal of concrete poetry as the result of an organic evolution of literary forms was illusory; instead it was the product of contrived invention and conscious elaboration. Similarly, the Noigandres poets' declaration of the end of verse, far from being prophetic, was mostly a manifesto phrase of iconoclasm. Conventional poetry of self-expresssion continued forcefully in Brazil, but concrete poetry both affected the shape and extension of verse and spawned other poetic vanguards, such as *neo-concretismo* (1957), *poesia praxis* (1962), and *poema processo* (1967), as well as non-denominational experimentation in the 1970s and 1980s.

Concrete poetry represents the most solidly theorized and carefully practiced organized modality of poetry in Brazil. The Noigandres poets merit recognition, with and beyond concrete poetry, for creating new textual modalities, offering alternate

(e.g., analogical, visual) models of expressivity, initiating a major rethinking of poetic structuring, and for the pursuit of uniqueness and rigor. In a broader sense, the leaders of *poesia concreta* set new parameters for the discussion of modernity, creating an option to aestheticism and ethnically-driven nationalism. With its insistence on theory, historical reconsiderations, and alternative tradition, the concrete vanguard took on a civilizing mission that proved to be a national project of modernity, thus joining what Antônio Cândido called the *tradição empenhada*, the national and continental tradition of engagement. With its front-line integration into international circuits and proactive emphasis on a modernizing exploitation of intellectual and technical resources regardless of origin, Brazilian concretism helped reconfigure the nation in cultural terms.

CHARLES A. PERRONE

Further Reading

Bann, Stephen (editor), *Concrete Poetry: an International Anthology*, London: London Magazine Editions, 1967

Perrone, Charles A., *Seven Faces: Brazilian Poetry Since Modernism*, Durham, North Carolina: Duke University Press, 1996 [See chapter 2]

Solt, Mary Ellen (editor), *Concrete Poetry: a World View*, Bloomington: Indiana University Press, 1970 [The introduction has essential documentation and includes major manifestos]

Williams, Emmett, *An Anthology of Concrete Poetry*, New York: Something Else Press, 1967 [Each example has a critical commentary alongside the lexical key]

Special Issues of Journals

"The Changing Guard II," *Times Literary Supplement*, London (3 September 1964) [This issue of *TLS* features international experimental poetry and avant-garde movements. Articles by Max Bense, the Brazilian theorists and others]

Poetics Today vol. 3/3 (1982) [Articles by Claus Clüver, Jon Tolman, *et al.*, and translations of key articles by the Noigandres poets]

Maryse Condé 1934–

Guadeloupean novelist, playwright and essayist

Although Maryse Condé remains outside the recent French Antillean *antillanité* and *creolité* literary movements, her discourse in its polyphonic nature and wide range addresses the predominant preoccupations of the Antillean writer. Within the context of the complex and traumatic West Indian heritage of slavery, colonization and assimilation, Condé's fictional characters are searching for an identity which reflects that of a larger community. And, as a black woman writer from a geographically, culturally and politically marginal world, Condé self-consciously attempts to represent the interrelated

issues of race, gender and class. In her fiction – eleven novels over twenty years – Condé weaves together the cultural and historical confluences of Europe, Africa and America in a pattern similar to her personal itinerary as well as reminiscent of the "golden triangle" of the Atlantic slave trade. With a cynical distance which seemingly reflects her ideological independence, she explores the multi-layered hybridity and multifarious contradictions of the system of relationships in the Antilles while expanding it beyond her native island to the larger West Indian community as well as to the global world.

Indeed, if Condé belongs to the French Antilles, she refuses to be compartimentalized as an Antillean in order to maintain a freedom devoid of the boundaries of restrictive definitions. Condé's nomadism, which translates into a transcultural and intercultural approach, along with her systematic exploration and recontruction of history, are the most striking characteristics of her fictional work.

In the first stage of her writing, the myth of Africa as maternal figure of the original genealogy – the return to the authentic past – is her main source of inspiration. With *Hérémakhonon*, 1976 (which ironically means "welcome home" in Malinké), and *Une Saison à Rihata*, 1981 (*A Season in Rihata*), Condé questions and challenges Aimé Césaire's vision of *Négritude* through two Guadeloupean female protagonists in search of their African roots. Mirroring the antinomies of their colonial backgrounds, these exiles are unable to define a role for themselves on the African soil and to break free from a westernized frame of reference. With these novels, Condé initiates her narrative technique involving multiple points of view which convey the unsolvable conflicts experienced by the heroines and which reflect their historical collective condition. The quest for the African past is also the main focus of *Ségou*, 1984 (*Segu*), the two-volume saga of the Bambara empire of Segu. In this award-winning best-seller, Condé recreates a high civilization of a precolonial Africa that practiced slavery well before the Europeans and entertained extensive contacts with the Christian and Islamic worlds. The political and religious conflicts which eventually dissolved the Bambara empire lead to the dispersion of the children of Nya to Brazil and the Caribbean, and consequently to the emergence of the African diaspora. Thus, Condé challenges again Césaire's claim of his Bambara heritage as one confiscated solely by the Europeans.

During the decade between *Hérémakhonon* and *Ségou*, Condé published several theoretical essays on Aimé Césaire's poetry and on Antillean culture and literature, and she particularly examined the historico-cultural significance of early women novelists of the French Antilles, thus reflecting her activity as university professor in France and in the United States. However, after *Ségou*, Condé focused almost exclusively on her creative writing and resolutely turned to the African diaspora with *Moi, Tituba sorcière noire de Salem*, 1986 (*I, Tituba, Black Witch of Salem*), a historical subject which begins her series of fictional works set in the New World. The novel's female protagonist asserts her presence and her role within the puritanical and racist US society of the 17th century, as well as within the institution of sugarcane plantations in Barbados. Tituba's first-person narrative – the story of her escape from erasure by colonial and patriarchal forces – allows Condé to rewrite a new Caribbean history from a woman-centered point of view.

The revision of history, also by a woman narrator, and the elusive pursuit of "authenticity" confront the characters of *La Vie scélérate*, 1987 (*The Tree of Life*). In this novel, Condé reconstructs the story of her own family through a multicultural narrative which explores the historical and cultural significance of race, gender and class relations in the diverse contexts of the New World – Panama, the US, Jamaica, Haiti – and of France. She raises unrelentingly the questions of exile, estrangement from the motherland, relations to the "others" of the diaspora and to the whites, and a return to roots. Through the young female narrator, Condé also examines the reality of the West Indian woman within the present structures of power and her role as a writer.

The nature of writing and the failure of achieving a completed story is also central to *Traversée de la mangrove*, 1989 (*Crossing the Mangrove*). Written as a detective novel, the book never solves the mystery – the death of the central hero – because the multi-voiced narrative technique unceasingly disrupts and contradicts the telling of his past. The hero's individual story, which is constructed like a puzzle with missing pieces, remains as elusive as the collective history of the island he inhabits. Through the characters acting as traditional storytellers, *Traversée* explores the diversity of the voices of the community and suggests the impossibility of retrieving the collective history. This obsessive quest forms also the underlining narrative of *Les Derniers Rois Mages*, 1992 [The Last Magi] which, as with *Tituba*, deals with a historical subject revised by the imaginary of the writer. And, as with Condé's other novels, the themes of exile, dispossession, psychological dislocation, and the search for African roots are predominant. The Martinican-born descendant of an African king lives in exile on a South Carolina island while the hero's African-American wife is investigating her own heritage in the French Antilles.

The relation between the Caribbean, Africa and America, and the destiny of the spiritually dispossessed remain Condé's concern throughout her fiction up to her recent work, *La Colonie du Nouveau Monde*, 1993 [The Colony of the New World]. In this novel, the author continues her exploration of exile and of the yearning for belonging in relation to establishing identity in a totally foreign world. With her usual irony, she uncovers the great futility pursued by the "colony," a marginal group of diverse people attempting to save a community going through an inexorable process of metamorphosis and final disintegration.

Condé has also written several plays in which characters, invested with symbols, represent the confrontation of traditional African or Antillean values with new ideas imported from abroad. However, these themes find a more developed and effective treatment in her novels.

If Condé's fiction departs from Guadeloupean perspectives, it expands far beyond her island to represent universal problems. Her large international readership, especially in the English versions of her novels, demonstrates her major role in revising our understanding of the world.

MARIE-AGNÈS SOURIEAU

See also entry on Francophone West Indies for more information about the *Créolité* and *Antillanité* movements

Biography

Born in Pointe-à-Pitre, Gaudeloupe, 11 February 1934. Attended the Sorbonne, Paris, MA, PhD in comparative literature 1976. Married Mamadou Condé in 1958 (divorced 1981), four children. Instructor, École Normale Supérieure, Conakry, Guinea, 1960–64, Ghana Institute of Languages, Accra, 1966–68, and Lycée Charles de Gaulle, Saint Louis, Sénégal, 1966–68. Programme producer for the French Services of the BBC, London, 1968–70. Assistant at Jussieau,

1970–72, lecturer at Nanterre, 1972–80, and course director at the Sorbonne, 1980–85, all University of Paris. Editor for the publishing house Présence Africaine, Paris, 1972; programme producer, Radio France Internationale, from 1980. Married Richard Philcox, her translator into English, in 1982. Fulbright scholar, 1985–86. Since 1990, Professor, University of California, Berkeley. Awarded the Prix Littéraire de la Femme, 1986; Boucheron Prize, 1986; Rockefeller Foundation Fellowship, 1987; Guggenheim Fellowship, 1987–88; Académie Française Prize, 1988.

Selected Works

Novels

Hérémakhonon, Paris: Union Générale d'Éditions, 1976; as *Heremakhonon*, translated by Richard Philcox, Washington, DC: Three Contintents Press, 1982

Une Saison à Rihata, Paris: Laffont, 1981; as *A Season in Rihata*, translated by Richard Philcox, London: Heinemann, 1988

Ségou; les murailles de terre, Paris: Laffont, 1984; as *Segu*, translated by Barbara Bray, New York: Viking, 1987

Ségou II: la terre en miettes, Paris: Laffont, 1985; as *The Children of Segu*, translated by Linda Coverdale, New York: Viking, 1989

Pays mêlél Nanna-ya, Paris: Hatier, 1985

Moi, Tituba, sorcière noire de Salem, Paris: Mercure, 1986; as *I, Tituba, Black Witch of Salem*, translated by Richard Philcox, Charlottesville: University Press of Virginia, 1992

La Vie scélérate, Paris: Seghers, 1987; as *The Tree of Life*, translated by Victoria Reiter, New York: Ballantine, 1992; London: Women's Press, 1994

Traversée de la mangrove, Paris: Mercure, 1989; as *Crossing the Mangrove*, translated by Richard Philcox, New York: Anchor Books, 1995

Les Derniers Rois Mages, Paris: Mercure, 1992

La Colonie du Nouveau Monde, Paris: Laffont, 1993

La Migration des cœurs, Paris: Laffont, 1995

Plays

Dieu nous l'a donné, Paris: Oswald, 1972

Mort d'Oluwémi d'Ajumako, Paris: Oswald, 1973

Pension les Alizés, Paris: Mercure, 1988

An Tan Revolisyon, Pointe-à-Pitre: Conseil Régional, 1989

The Hills of Massabielle, produced New York, 1991

Essays and Other Writings

La Civilisation de bosalle, Paris: L'Harmattan, 1978

Le Profil d'une oeuvre: cahier d'un retour au pays natal, Paris: Hatier, 1978

La Parole des femmes: essai des romancières des Antilles de langue française, Paris: L'Harmattan, 1979

Haïti chérie, Paris: Bayard, 1987 [for children]

Guadeloupe, photographs by Jean Du Boisberranger, Paris: Richer/Hoa Qui, 1988

Victor et les barricades, Paris, Bayard, 1989 [for children]

Further Reading

Bruner, David K., "Maryse Condé: Creative Writer in a Political World," in *L'Esprit Créateur* (Summer 1977)

Bruner, David K. and Charlotte Bruner, "Buchi Emecheta and Maryse Condé: Contemporary Writing from Africa and the Caribbean," *World Literature Today*, vol. 59/1 (1985)

Flannigan, Arthur, "Reading Below the Belt: Sex and Sexuality in Françoise Éga and Maryse Condé," *French Review* (December 1988)

Hewitt, Leah Dianne, *Autobiographical Tightropes: Simone de Beauvoir, Nathalie Sarraute, Marguerite Duras, Monique Wittig, and Maryse Condé*, Lincoln: University of Nebraska Press, 1990

Ngaté, Jonathan, "Maryse Condé and Africa: the Making of a Relcalcitrant Daughter?" *Current Bibliography on African Affairs*, vol. 19/1 (1986–87)

Smith, Arlette M., "Maryse Condé's *Hérémakhonon*: a Triangular Structure of Alienation," *College Language Association Journal* (September 1988)

Snitgen, Jeanne "History, Identity and the Constitution of the Female Subject: Maryse Condé's *Tituba*," *Matatu*, vol. 3/6 (1989)

Interviews

Clark, VeVe A. and Cecile Daheny, "'Je me suis réconcilié avec mon île' / 'I have made peace with my island': an Interview with Maryse Condé," *Callaloo* (Winter 1989)

Pfaff, Françoise, *Entretiens avec Maryse Condé*, Paris: Karthala, 1993

Special Issues of Journals

World Literature Today, vol. 67/4 (Autumn 1993)

Conventual Writing

Writing by the nuns of Spanish America is an exciting field of research that has come into its own in the past fifteen to twenty years. After centuries of neglect, scholars are beginning to realize the importance of these texts; as Arenal and Schlau noted: "these texts contain almost the only record we have of the consciousness of early modern women in Hispanic lands." This statement requires one qualification: the women in question were exclusively white and of the middle or upper classes. Women of other races could be nuns' servants, but not nuns themselves, at least not until the 18th century, when the daughters of the Indian nobility in Mexico finally had a convent of their own.

In colonial times the great majority of women were totally illiterate, though nuns often had some degree of literacy. There were also many, many religious communities in Spanish American cities, as the daughters of the upper and middle classes had but two options in life: marriage or the convent. For a daughter to enter a convent presupposed paying a dowry to the order, but once she was a nun, her spiritual and bodily well-being was assured. As religion permeated all aspects of colonial society, most women who took the veil were dutiful Catholics, but not all of them had a true religious calling. Furthermore, since nuns were perpetually enclosed within the walls of their convents, life within a religious community was often full of contention, strife, politics and even physical violence.

What did nuns write? All kinds of religious literature: devotional meditations, prayers, poetry, songs, plays to be performed on religious holidays, descriptions of mystical experiences, letters, records of the founding of convents, and spiritual autobiographies. It is the last of these that has attracted the most scholarly attention in recent years.

Pioneering research in this field of conventual writing was done by historians Josefina Muriel and Asunción Lavrin, but as colonial documents are often interdisciplinary in nature, more recently literary scholars, especially feminists, have been drawn to the spiritual autobiographies of Spanish American nuns. For years the only text under consideration in this genre was Sor Juana Inés de la Cruz's *Respuesta a Sor Filotea*, 1691 (*The Answer*) but now there are a number of other autobiographies available. Besides Arenal and Schlau's study, *Untold Sisters*, which covers life stories by nuns in both Spain and Spanish America, there are three other works which are very useful when read in terms of comparison and contrast, especially since the nuns who authored them were more or less contemporaries: Madre María de San José (Mexico, 1656–1719); Francisca Josefa de la Concepción de Castillo, known as "La Madre Castillo" (Colombia, 1671–1742); and Ursula Suárez (Chile, 1666–1749).

Writing by nuns is not readily accessible to the modern reader for several reasons. First of all, the religious setting and its language are frequently unfamiliar to our more secular age. Because nuns had little formal education, their spelling and grammar are often whimsical, their punctuation erratic, and their vocabulary colloquial. (These factors make the texts of special interest to historians of the language, however.) One must also understand the conditions under which these autobiographies were produced. The great model for these nuns was the autobiography of St Theresa of Ávila (1515–82). Because of her extraordinary qualities as a mystic and reformer, she had been ordered by her confessors to write down her life story, something she did not want to do, and did in a hurry. She was canonized in 1622, only forty years after her death, and her life, reforms and great devotion had an enormous impact on Spanish America. Many confessors looked at the nuns under their spiritual guidance, and urged those who also showed exceptional qualities to write down their lives. No, not urged – ordered. Many nuns found writing a harrowing task, and no wonder: because of their lack of education, they felt inferior setting pen to paper; what they wrote became the property of their confessor, and could be shown to the Inquisition; and the act of writing ran counter to all the Church had taught them. Exemplary nuns were to be silent and self-effacing, and were told to discipline both their flesh and their will in the service of God. Then to ask them to write their autobiography, the most self-affirming kind of writing there is, was extremely conflictive for many of these women. All three of the nuns under discussion here recorded their fear and revulsion at writing, though how much of this was formulaic is not certain.

Another problem was the women's relationship to the confessors who not only ordered them to write, but had complete control over the texts the nuns produced. Their spiritual fathers could edit and publish them under their own name, burn them, forget them, or lose them. This happened to María de San José, whose previous confessor lost ten out of thirty notebooks she had written; a subsequent confessor ordered her to rewrite the missing part. Ursula Suárez's confessor would give her only enough paper for each day's writing, then take the pages away and not let her see them again, all the while insisting that she continue telling her life story. She was thus unable to give her autobiography any kind of inner cohesion. Because the nuns were aware of possible scrutiny by the Inquisition, they wrote circumspectly and within carefully delineated parameters, but in spite of this their stories have very personal touches, ranging from relationships with their families and sister nuns, to open ire at male and female superiors.

With all the emphasis on religion in this time, one would think that families would be glad when a daughter wanted to become a nun. This was not always the case. Some had to overcome a great deal of family hostility towards their choice of the religious life. Ursula Suárez's mother was determined that her well-born daughter should marry well, while María de San José's family simply could not afford the entrance dowry. For nearly thirty years she lived a religious life of fasting, devotion and penance within her family, which did not always find this behavior easy to live with. Because María de San José had to wait so long before she was able to enter a convent, her life story is an excellent account of daily life on a small Mexican ranch in the late 17th century.

All of these women experienced visions, heard God speak to them, and felt the ecstasy of direct communion with their Lord. As nuns were considered the brides of Christ, these visions and experiences at times took on decidedly erotic overtones. Yet mystical experiences also gave them the power of authority, as their confessors could not dispute that which the nuns had heard, seen, and felt. But how could they be sure it was God and not the Devil who spoke through them? We forget today how very dark the nights were for the people of earlier centuries, how filled with shadows, and fear of the Evil One. All three women attested to seeing the Devil, and, illustrative of the racism endemic to colonial society, said he appeared either as a Black or an Indian man. La Madre Castillo even attested to seeing the Devil dressed as a cleric glare at her balefully, then go into the cell of a sister nun.

Many nuns reported having visions, yet, instead of being hailed as a blessing, often led to fights with their sisters, who were jealous or thought it was a device to get attention. La Madre Castillo, who seemed to have been generally quite unpopular, suffered under this greatly, as she was physically attacked and verbally abused by other nuns in her convent. Ursula Suárez also had battles, but hers were political, as she was the ringleader of one faction in her convent. In spite of frequent strife, all three of these women became leaders in their communities: La Madre Castillo and Ursula Suárez were elected abbesses, and María de San José was selected to be one of the founders of a new convent of her order.

Spiritual autobiographies by nuns thus reveal a great deal of information about a significant sector of colonial Spanish American women: their concept of themselves in relationship first to their families and then to their communities, the manner in which female orders governed themselves, and finally the tactics of submission and subversion by means of which they navigated, in the words of Arenal and Schlau, "being a woman author who asserts her own authority even as she declares obedience to God's and her confessor's will."

NINA M. SCOTT

See also entries on Colonial Literature: New Granada, New Spain and Peru; Sor Juana Inés de la Cruz; Mystics

Further Reading

Conventual Writings
Arenal, Electa and Stacey Schlau (editors), *Untold Sisters: Hispanic Nuns in Their Own Work*, Albuquerque: University of New Mexico Press, 1989
Castillo, Francisca Josefa de, *Obras completas*, with an introduction by Darío Achury Valenzuela, Bogotá: Talleres Gráficos del Banco de la República, 1968
Myers, Kathleen (editor), *Word from New Spain: the Spiritual Autobiography of Madre María de San José (1656–1719)*, Liverpool: Liverpool University Press, 1993
Nava y Saavedra, Jerónima, *Jerónima Nava y Saavedra (1669–1727): autobiografía de una monja venerable*, critical

edition and introduction by Angela I. Robledo, Cali, Colombia: Universidad del Valle, 1994
Suárez, Ursula, *Relación autobiográfica*, prologue and crítical edition by Mario Ferreccio Podestá, Concepción, Chile: Universidad de Concepción, 1984

Critical Studies
Benítez, Fernando, *Los demonios en el convento: sexo y religión en la Nueva España*, Mexico City: Era, 1985
Franco, Jean, *Plotting Women: Gender and Representation in Mexico*, New York: Columbia University Press, and London: Verso, 1989
Gallagher, Ann Miriam, "The Indian Nuns of Mexico City's *Monasterio* of Corpus Christi, 1724–1821," in *Latin American Women: Historical Perspectives*, edited by Asunción Lavrin, Westport, Connecticut: Greenwood Press, 1978
Lavrin, Asunción, "Women and Religion in Spanish America," in *Women and Religion in America: the Colonial and Revolutionary Periods*, vol. 2, edited by Rosemary Radford Ruether and Rosemary S. Keller, San Francisco: Harper and Row, 1981
McKnight, Kathryn J., "Voz, subjetividad y mística en la Madre Castillo: tres elementos de una escritura femenina conventual," *Texto y Contexto* 17 (September–December 1991)
Muriel, Josefina, *Cultura femenina novohispana*, Mexico City: UNAM, 1982

Julio Cortázar 1914–1984

Argentine prose writer

Author of eight collections of short stories, five novels and a number of other books that are less easy to categorize, Julio Cortázar is one of the four most notable writers of the Boom and Argentina's most influential and famous modern writer after Borges. In fact, it was the publication of one of Cortázar's early stories, "Casa tomada" (The House Taken Over), in the journal *Sur*, on the advice of Borges, that brought the younger author to public attention. Cortázar had previously published poetry under the pseudonym of Julio Denis, and a verse play, *Los reyes* [The Kings], inspired by the myth of the Minotaur; but it was as a short story writer that he first made his name, and many still regard him as a master of that genre above all others.

Cortázar was something of a polyglot, and translated *Robinson Crusoe* and the stories of Edgar Allan Poe into Spanish; Poe's influence is visible in a number of the Argentine's tales. The first collection, of which "Casa tomada" was to be part, was *Bestiario*, 1951 [Bestiary]. It established a broad pattern that was to be followed in various guises for a long time thereafter: ordinary human beings in ordinary situations become caught up in extraordinary developments. Also evident is the influence of Alfred Jarry, for whom, as is well known, the rules were less interesting than the exceptions; Cortázar's debt to the French Symbolists and Surrealists has been demonstrated in a number of studies.

"Casa tomada" deals with a middle-aged brother and sister living alone and in comfort in a large family house; one day, one of them hears a noise in another part of the house and, concluding that the premises have been invaded, they confine their movements to "this side," only to find themselves ever more constrained by the (always unidentified) invaders; eventually, the couple flee. The sense of there being two sides, one of which is unknown, beyond reach or forbidden, is something of a constant in Cortázar: his characters are often caught in designs that they can neither understand nor influence, often feel the need to go beyond the comfortably knowable and into the realm of the indefinable, the "other side." Cortázar's interest in Buddhism and the Vedanta may be at play, for the other side, even when it involves death, is often seen as a complementary mode of existence. Critics have had a field day with the ambiguities of "Casa tomada," seeing it (for example) as a story about incest or as political allegory. That, too, is symptomatic: the impossibility of arriving at a single, unequivocal interpretation, as also the determination to try to do so, have been hallmarks of Cortázar criticism.

In *Bestiario* there are resonances and parallels between stories that suggest that there is more of an overall authorial design than can be discerned in the later collections. Many of the characters in *Bestiario* seem to have a monstrous dimension which is repressed and must be released; in the title story a young girl senses that a tiger is roaming through her house; in another its narrator starts to vomit rabbits. The fantastic and mysterious loom large in the subsequent story collections, *Final del juego* (*End of the Game*) and *Las armas secretas* (*Secret Weapons*) – 1956 and 1959 respectively. In "La noche boca arriba"(The Night Face Up) a hospital patient who has been in a motorcycle crash becomes a sacrificial victim on an Aztec pyramid; in "Lejana" [The Distant Woman] the soul of a young woman in Buenos Aires transmigrates to an old woman in Budapest; in "Las armas secretas," one of Cortázar's most accomplished and unsettling stories, a young Frenchman, increasingly possessed by the personality of a Nazi who had raped a French girl years earlier, comes to threaten to rape his own girlfriend. All three of the previous examples demonstrate Cortázar's interest in the idea of the double and in portraying links (he was to coin the term "figuras") between people in different times and places. Perhaps the prime example of this is the title story of *Todos los fuegos el fuego*, 1966 (*All Fires the Fire*), in which two tales of passion unfold, one in a Roman arena, one in the Paris of the 1960s, revealing increasing parallels and correspondences until they come to a common end by fire (hence the title can be understood to mean that all fires are particular instances of a general and timeless phenomenon: fire).

Despite all the fantastic elements there are also stories that are broadly realistic, such as those dealing with childhood and adolescence, both of which themes the author treated with masterly sensitivity: "Los venenos" (The Poison), "Final del juego" and "La señorita Cora" are examples.

In his later books of stories Cortázar continues to plumb the human psyche, and to experiment with techniques in doing so. For example, the theme of the transition from adolescence to adulthood, which had already given rise to some formal fireworks in the last story mentioned, is more daringly explored in "Vd. se tendió a tu lado" (You Lay Down at Thy Side) from the collection *Alguien que anda por ahí*, 1977 (*A Change of Light and Other Stories*). "Clone," from *Queremos tanto a Glenda*, 1981 (*We Love Glenda So Much*), deals with a chamber choir (one of its members is Gesualdo – a clear reference to the Neapolitan composer and murderer) and its form is based on the disposition of "voices" in the different movements of Bach's "Musical Offering." Indeed, music is a considerable force in Cortázar's literature: he makes many references to the classical and jazz repertoire, uses musical structures as metaphors, takes the inspiration for one of his most famous stories, "El perseguidor" (The Pursuer), from the life of Charlie Parker.

It was above all the liberating power of improvisation in jazz, the ability to break free of the pattern (even if it was to return to it eventually) that appealed to Cortázar. In many of his writings he portrays people as victims of routine, and advocates the case for breaking the pattern of the predictable; in one of his less easily classified books (and that itself is surely significant) he describes the behaviour of the "famas," who are well organised, conventional and dull beings as compared with the lively and unpredictable "cronopios" (of whom Cortázar, of course, is one!). In *Los premios*, 1960 (*The Winners*), the first-published of his novels (he had written one earlier, but it was published posthumously) a group of competition winners find that their prize is to spend time on a ship anchored in the

estuary of the River Plate close to Buenos Aires. They learn that a part of the ship is forbidden territory, and react to this news in a variety of ways, some passively acquiescing and some not. The novel combines sociopolitical criticism with a certain amount of metaphysical speculation; it also has a mysterious authorial presence in the person of Persio, hovering above and seeking a coherent design in the narrative. Here can be seen the seeds of what was to come.

Unable to tolerate the Peronist regime, Cortázar had left Argentina in 1951. Though he lived in France for some three decades, his creative writing was always in Spanish, and in a variety of it that is both accessible and easily recognisable as the language of the River Plate. It was in Paris and Buenos Aires that he set the novel that many regard as the greatest of the century in Latin America: *Rayuela*, 1963 (*Hopscotch*; see separate essay, below). The hopscotch figure is like a mandala, symbolizing the searches in which the various characters are involved, but also representing the challenge facing the reader. The latter is presented at the outset with an invitation to read the novel in at least two possible ways: the first is the conventional way, entailing beginning at the beginning and stopping at a line of asterisks, which, says the author rather scornfully, stand for "FIN" (The End); one might perhaps call this the "fama" reading. The second involves jumping about the book and including apparently extraneous material that is left out in the other reading. Needless to say, the second reading is the more challenging, demands more reader participation in the construction of the novelistic experience, and is the role Cortázar favours: that of the "lector cómplice" (participatory reader). Once again, we find the notion that there is "another side" to be discovered, reflected in the formal division of the book into three parts, the first of which is labelled "Del lado de allá" (That Side), the second "Del lado de acá" (This Side), while the third is "De otros lados (capítulos prescindibles)"(From Other Sides [dispensable chapters]). Buenos Aires is set against Paris. The protagonist, Oliveira, is an intellectual seeking a transcendental perspective; the Cartesian world-view is undermined; bridges are extended between opposites. To this metaphysical dimension is added literary speculation by the characters, in the shadow of a fantasmal author-figure called Morelli (some of whose precepts are to be read about in the "extraneous" chapters). Ponderous as all this may sound, the potential for pedantry and pretentiousness is avoided thanks to an iconoclastic humour that has few equals in Latin American literature. Cortázar is certainly concerned about the big issues, and every bit an intellectual, but he is also often very funny indeed.

From a chapter in *Rayuela* was to come the idea for his next novel, *62: modelo para armar*, 1968 (*62: a Model Kit*), which takes reader participation a stage further by providing the elements with which to build a narrative. His last novel *Libro de Manuel*, 1973 (*A Manual for Manuel*), is concerned with reconciling aesthetic concerns with politically engaged literature, to make creative writing accessible and socially meaningful to the public without compromising the use of language. In that novel a manual is being composed for the child Manuel, a sort of collage of press clippings about politically sensitive issues.

Once a fervent supporter of the Cuban Revolution (although his enthusiasm was reduced by the events of 1968), a frequent critic of the politics of the Southern Cone, and a champion of the Sandinistas (giving them the royalties of some of his last books), Cortázar was a man of impressive political strength, but equally strong as a defender of literature on its own terms. He faced many pressures to write more explicitly political literature, but was no more willing to compromise his writing than he was to abandon his struggle for a better society. Much of his work can in fact be read as political allegory; some of those in power found him explicit enough to have his books prohibited. For all that, he takes his place in literary history as a highly inventive and skilled writer who had much to say about existential and literary matters.

PETER STANDISH

Biography

Born in Brussels, Belgium, 26 August 1914. Family returned to Argentina, 1918. Attended the Escuela Normal de Profesores Mariano Acosta (teachers training college), Buenos Aires, degree as primary-level teacher, 1932, degree as secondary-level teacher, 1935; University of Buenos Aires, 1936–37. Married Aurora Bernárdez in 1953 (separated); lived with Carol Dunlop in later years. Taught in secondary schools in Bolívar, Chivilcoy, and Mendoza, 1937–44; professor of French literature, University of Cuyo, Mendoza, 1944–45, and imprisoned briefly for involvement in anti-Peronist demonstrations at the university, 1945. Manager, Cámara Argentina del Libro [Publishing Association of Argentina], Buenos Aires, 1946–48; passed examinations in law and languages, and worked as translator, Buenos Aires, 1948–51. Travelled to Paris on a scholarship, 1951, and took up permanent residence there. Writer and freelance translator for UNESCO, from 1952; visited Cuba, 1961, Argentina, Peru, Ecuador, and Chile, all 1973, Nicaragua and (after the lifting of a seven-year ban on his entry into the country) Argentina, 1983. Visiting lecturer, University of Oklahoma, Norman, 1975, and Gildersleeve lecturer, Barnard College, New York, 1980. Acquired French citizenship (in addition to existing Argentine citizenship), 1981. Member, Second Russell Tribunal for investigation of human rights abuses in Latin America, 1975. Recipient of numerous awards including Médicis Prize (France), 1974 for *Libro de Manuel*, and Rubén Darío Order of Cultural Independence (Nicaragua), 1983. Died of leukemia in Paris, 12 February 1984.

Selected Works

Short Fiction

Bestiario, Buenos Aires: Sudamericana, 1951
Final del juego, Mexico City: Los Presentes, 1956
Las armas secretas, Buenos Aires: Sudamericana, 1959
Historias de cronopios y de famas, Buenos Aires: Minotaura, 1962; as *Cronopios and Famas*, translated by Paul Blackburn, New York: Pantheon, 1969; London: Boyars, 1978
Todos los fuegos el fuego, Buenos Aires: Sudamericana, 1966; as *All Fires the Fire and Other Stories*, translated by Suzanne Jill Levine, New York: Pantheon, 1973; London: Boyars, 1979
El perseguidor y otros cuentos, Buenos Aires: Centro Editor de América Latina, 1967
Ceremonias, Barcelona: Seix Barral, 1968 [Contains *Final del juego* and *Las armas secretas*]
La isla a mediodía y otros relatos, Estella: Salvat, 1971
Octaedro, Buenos Aires: Sudamericana, 1974
Alguien que anda por ahí y otros relatos, Madrid: Alfaguara, 1977
Un tal Lucas, Buenos Aires: Sudamericana, 1979; as *A Certain Lucas*, translated by Gregory Rabassa, New York: Knopf, 1984

Queremos tanto a Glenda, Madrid: Alfaguara, 1981; as *We Love Glenda So Much and Other Tales*, translated by Gregory Rabassa, New York: Knopf, 1983; London: Harvill Press, 1984
Deshoras, Buenos Aires: Sudamericana, 1983
El examen, Buenos Aires: Sudamericana, 1986
Divertimento, Buenos Aires: Sudamericana, 1986

Novels

Los premios, Buenos Aires, Sudamericana, 1960; as *The Winners*, translated by Elaine Kerrigan, New York: Pantheon, and London: Souvenir Press, 1965
Rayuela, Buenos Aires: Sudamericana, 1963; as *Hopscotch*, translated by Gregory Rabassa, New York: Pantheon, 1966; London: Collins Harvill, 1967
62: modelo para armar, Buenos Aires: Sudamericana, 1968; as *62: a Model Kit*, translated by Gregory Rabassa, New York: Pantheon, 1972; London: Calder and Boyars, 1976
Libro de Manuel, Buenos Aires: Sudamericana, 1973; as *A Manual for Manuel*, translated by Gregory Rabassa, New York: Pantheon, 1978; London: Harvill Press, 1984

Poetry

Presencia, Buenos Aires: El Bibliófilo, 1938 [Published under the pseudonym Julio Denis]
Pameos y meopas, Barcelona: OCNOS, Editorial Llibres de Sinera, 1971
Salvo el crepúsculo, Madrid: Alfaguara, 1984

Plays

Los reyes, Buenos Aires: Gulab y Aldabahor, 1949
Nada a Pehuajó, y Adiós, Robinson, Mexico City: Katun, 1984

Essays and Other Writings

La vuelta al día en ochenta mundos, Mexico City: Siglo XXI, 1967; as *Around the Day in Eighty Worlds*, translated by Thomas Christensen, San Francisco: North Point Press, 1986
Buenos Aires, Buenos Aires, photographs by Alicia d'Amico and Sara Facio, Buenos Aires: Sudamericana, 1968 [includes English translation]
Último round, Mexico City: Siglo XXI, 1969
Literatura en la revolución y revolución en la literatura, in collaboration with Oscar Collazos and Mario Vargas Llosa, Mexico City: Siglo XXI, 1970
Viaje alrededor de una mesa, Buenos Aires: Cuadernos de Rayuela, 1970
Prosa del observatorio, in collaboration with Antonio Gálvez, photographs by Cortázar, Barcelona: Lumen, 1972
Humanario, Buenos Aires: La Azotea, 1976 [on the photographs of Alicia D'Amico and Sara Facio]
París: ritmos de una ciudad, photographs by Alecio de Andrade, Barcelona: Edhasa, 1981; as *Paris: the Essence of an Image*, translated by Gregory Rabassa, New York: Norton, 1981
Los autonautas de la cosmopista; o, un viaje atemporal París – Marsella, in collaboration with Carol Dunlop, Barcelona: Muchnik, 1983
Nicaragua, tan violentamente dulce, Buenos Aires: Katun, 1983; as *Nicaraguan Sketches*, translated by Kathleen Weaver, New York: Norton, 1989
Argentina: años de alambradas culturales, edited by Saúl Yurkievich, Buenos Aires: Muchnik, 1984
Policrítica en la hora de los chacales, Concepción, Chile: LAR, 1987
Fantomas contra los vampiros multinacionales, Buenos Aires: GenteSur, 1989

Compilations and Anthologies

Cuentos, edited by Antón Arrufat, Havana: Casa de las Américas, 1964
La casilla de los Morelli y otros textos, edited by Julio Ortega, Barcelona: Lumen, 1973 [miscellany]

Los relatos, 3 vols, Madrid: Alianza, 1976
Cortázar: iconografía, edited by Alba C. de Rojo and Felipe
    Garrido, Mexico City: Fondo de Cultura Económica, 1985
Cartas a una pelirroja, edited by Evelyn Picon Garfield, Madrid:
    Orígenes, 1990
Cuentos completos (1945–1982), 2 vols, Madrid: Alfaguara, 1994
Julio Cortázar: siete cuentos, edited by Peter Beardsall, Manchester:
    Manchester University Press, 1994 [Part of a series intended for
    students, with a long introduction]
Obra crítica, edited by Saúl Yurkievich, Jaime Alazraki and Saúl
    Sosnowski, 3 vols, Madrid: Alfaguara, 1994

Anthologies in Translation
End of the Game and Other Stories, translated by Paul Blackburn,
    New York: Pantheon, 1967; London: Collins Harvill, 1968;
    retitled as *Blow-Up and Other Stories*, New York: Collier,
    1968
A Change of Light and Other Stories, translated by Gregory
    Rabassa, New York: Knopf, 1980; London: Harvill Press,
    1984

Further Reading
Alazraki, Jaime, *En busca del unicornio: los cuentos de Julio
    Cortázar*, Madrid: Gredos, 1983
____ *Hacia Cortázar: aproximaciones a su obra*, Barcelona:
    Anthropos, 1994
Boldy, Steven, *The Novels of Julio Cortázar*, Cambridge and New
    York: Cambridge University Press, 1980
Burgos, Fernando (editor), *Los ochenta mundos de Cortázar:
    ensayos*, Madrid: EDI-6, 1987
Carter, E. Dale (editor), *Otro round: estudios sobre la obra de Julio
    Cortázar*, Sacramento: California State University, 1988
Cedola, Estela, *Cortázar: el escritor y sus contextos*, Buenos Aires:
    Edicial, 1994
García Canclini, Néstor, *Cortázar: una antropología poética*, Buenos
    Aires: Nova, 1968
Giacoman, Helmy F. (editor), *Homenaje a Julio Cortázar*, New
    York: Las Américas, 1972
Ivask, Ivan and Jaime Alazraki (editors), *The Final Island: the
    Fiction of Cortázar*, Norman: University of Oklahoma Press,
    1978
Lagmanovich, David (editor), *Estudios sobre los cuentos de Julio
    Cortázar*, Barcelona: Hispamérica, 1975
Lastra, Pedro (editor), *Julio Cortázar*, Madrid: Taurus, 1981
MacAdam, Alfred, *El individuo y el otro: crítica a los cuentos de
    Julio Cortázar*, Buenos Aires and New York: La Librería,
    1971
Nino, Hugo (editor), *Queremas tanto a Julio: 20 autores para
    Cortázar*, Managua: Editorial Nueva Nicaragua, 1984 [includes
    essays by Ramírez, Galeano, Gelman, Benedetti, Monterroso,
    Skármeta, Amado, Rulfo]
Ortega, Julio, *Letras hispanoamericanas de nuestro tiempo*, Madrid:
    Porrúa Turanzas, 1976 [Chapter on *Octaedro*]
Ortiz, Carmen, *Julio Cortázar: una estética de la búsqueda*, Buenos
    Aires: Almageste, 1994
Picon Garfield, Evelyn, *¿Es Julio Cortázar un surrealista?* Madrid:
    Gredos, 1975
____ *Julio Cortázar*, New York: Ungar, 1975
Puleo, Alicia H., *Como leer a Julio Cortázar*, Madrid: Júcar, 1990
Rein, Mercedes, *Julio Cortázar: el escritor y sus máscaras*,
    Montevideo: Diaco, 1969
Sosnowski, Saúl, *Julio Cortázar: una búsqueda mítica*, Buenos Aires:
    Noé, 1973
____ "Pursuers," in *Modern Latin American Fiction*, edited by
    Harold Bloom, New York: Chelsea House, 1990
Stavans, Ilan, *Julio Cortázar: a Study of the Short Fiction*, New
    York: Twayne, 1996
Viñas, David, *De Sarmiento a Cortázar*, Buenos Aires: Siglo XX,
    1970

Yovanovich, Gordana, *Julio Cortázar's Character Mosaic: Reading
    the Longer Fiction*, Toronto: University of Toronto Press, 1991
Yurkievich, Saúl, *Julio Cortázar: mundos y modos*, Madrid:
    Muchnik, 1994
Zamora, Lois Parkinson, *Writing the Apocalypse: Historical Vision
    in Contemporary United States and Latin American Fiction*,
    Cambridge and New York: Cambridge University Press, 1988
    [Chapter on Cortázar]

Interviews
González Bermejo, Ernesto, *Conversaciones con Cortázar*, Barcelona:
    Edhasa, 1978; as *Revelaciones de un cronopio: conversaciones
    con Cortázar*, 1986
Guibert, Rita, *Seven Voices: Seven Latin American Writers Talk to
    Rita Guibert*, New York: Knopf, 1972
Prego, Omar, *La fascinación de las palabras: conversaciones con
    Julio Cortázar*, Barcelona: Muchnik, 1985

Bibliographies
Mundo Lo, Sarah, *Julio Cortázar: His Works and His Critics, a
    Bibliography*, Urbana, Illinois: Albatross, 1985

Special Issues of Journals
Books Abroad, vol. 50/3 (1976)
Casa de las Américas, vol. 25/145–46 (1984)

Rayuela

Novel by Julio Cortázar

Published in 1963, Cortázar's second novel is one of the principal works of the Latin American new narrative. It is also
characteristic of the River Plate: its roots in the metaphysical
tradition are evident; it is a Buenos Aires odyssey, following
Roberto Arlt's *Los siete locos* (*The Seven Madmen*) and
Leopoldo Marechal's *Adán Buenosayres*; and it is an instance,
and a critique, of the traditional connections of educated and
affluent citizens of the River Plate republics with European
high culture, and especially with Paris.

In *Rayuela*, Western ways of thinking are explicitly criticised. More precisely, the habit of establishing categories,
which are then accepted unquestioningly as real (this includes
the passive reception of literary genres, as well as dictionary
definitions) is perceived as dangerous and inhibiting, and is
undermined, using reference to many modes of thought,
including modern western science, as well as poetry, Zen,
wordplay, and the absurd.

The construction of *Rayuela* virtually guarantees an active
reader or "lector cómplice", and hence multiple readings.
There are two narrative sections: chapters 1–36 – "Del lado
de allá" (That side) – which are set in Paris, and chapters
37–56 – "Del lado de acá" (This side) – set in Buenos Aires;
the third section, chapters 57–155 – "De otros lados, capítulos
prescindibles" (Other places, optional chapters) – is a heterogeneous collection of texts. The author states in a "tablero
de dirección" (table of instructions) that *Rayuela* is many
different books, and proposes two principal readings: sequentially, ending at chapter 56; a hopscotch progress beginning
at chapter 73, thereafter jumping at the end of each chapter
to another, as directed.

The hopscotch has multiple significance. The notion of quest is implicit: in the game one progresses by stages from "earth" to "heaven." However, the fact that hopscotch is a game implies that the quest requires childlike qualities, and that it is never conclusive; it is neither a place nor an allegorical map, merely a pattern. Its abstract, formal, repeatable nature (there are in *Rayuela* two real hopscotches, one in a Paris street, the other in a Buenos Aires lunatic asylum) on the one hand suggests the underlying patterns (*figuras*), often found in Cortázar's stories – "La noche boca arriba" (The Night Face Up), for example – or Borges's unseen labyrinths: "La muerte y la brújula" (Death and the Compass). Conversely, the pattern's ubiquity and the unpredictability of the game suggest a surreal, rather than a causal universe (or narrative).

Reading sequentially, chapters 1 to 36 present the life of Horacio Oliveira, an Argentine intellectual misfit, in 1950s Paris where he has fled to escape what he considers a backward, derivative society. Oliveira, who mistrusts all linguistic and social structures and signs, is engaged on a search for meaning, his "kibbutz of desire." The main foci of his existence are his Uruguayan companion, Maga, (the name means "enchantress") and a circle of friends known as the "Club de la Serpiente" (Serpent Club). Maga's conventional tastes and intellectual naivety coexist with instinctive apprehension of reality. As Oliveira observes: while he defines and describes, but cannot touch metaphysical rivers, she swims in them with the natural grace of a swallow in flight. The couple eschew definite assignations, instead staging chance encounters on the hopscotch of central Paris. Bridges, which link territories but do not belong in them, hold special fascination. The Club is the forum for intense discussion, and for drinking and listening to jazz. (References to jazz abound in *Rayuela*, and it is the subject of Cortázar's story "El perseguidor" (The Pursuer), where the jazzman inhabits a complementary, non-rational reality). In *Rayuela* however, jazz (like sexual encounters) does not open a way through the inhibiting incrustation of culture. The resolution of the Paris section is triggered by the parting of Oliveira and Maga, and the death of her child, Rocamadour. This leads to Maga's disappearance – perhaps suicide – and the Dantesque descent of Oliveira, who is arrested engaging in fellatio with a bag lady below a bridge over the Seine, and as a result of this transgressive act is deported. The dénouement contains some memorable episodes: the concert of the absurd, brave modernist pianist, Berthe Trépat (chapter 23); the sustained tension of the reunion of the Club while, unknown to Maga, Rocamadour lies dead in the same room (chapter 28).

Back in Buenos Aires, Oliveira associates with a long-time friend, Traveler, and his wife Talita. Tension grows, as it emerges that Traveler and Oliveira are doubles, and Talita resembles the lost Maga. Bridges continue to be important, notably the absurd physical and psychic bridge constructed between Oliveira and Traveler, which Talita straddles (chapter 41); a second key notion is of a porous reality, which is pierced by tunnels, rather like the wormholes of modern cosmology. This section also ends with Oliveira's descent, this time into a comically-portrayed lucid lunacy: after kissing Talita/Maga in the basement morgue of the lunatic asylum where the three work, he expects Traveler's attack, and barricades himself in

his room. In fact, through "finding" Maga, Oliveira has crossed a threshold, and his real fear is the reimposition of a dead, absurd order, personified by the Arltian caricatures who own the asylum, rather than Traveler. The story ends in suspension: any attempt to invade Oliveira's territory might provoke him to cross a second threshold, making a final leap onto the "heaven" square of a hopscotch below.

In the second proposed reading, the Paris and Buenos Aires chapters are encountered in the same relative order (except the deleted chapter 55, whose material is incorporated elsewhere), usually alternating with single chapters or series from the third section. As Steven Boldy puts it, the "optional" chapters are the culture (in the broadest sense) linking Paris and Buenos Aires (sections). The inserted texts may be poems, press cuttings etc., which resonate with allusions elsewhere in *Rayuela*, specific digressions, such as conversations or introspections, or new narrative branches, for example that detailing Oliveira's relationship with a second lover, Pola. The ending also changes: while the sequential reading ends with the suspension of events, the second skips over the suspended events to a new stalemate of chapters 58 and 131, whose circling includes the theoretical, as well as the narrative aspects of *Rayuela*.

Chapter 22, in which an old man (subsequently revealed as an author, Morelli) is reported to have been run down in the street is, in terms of *Rayuela's* own metaphors, the bridge linking these two aspects. Morelli's thoughts are presented, directly or through the Club's commentary; and he possesses a collection of texts – chapters of the novel's third part (some labelled "Morelliana") – which are to be assembled by the "lector cómplice"/the Club into a book.

Essentially, these chapters from the third section accompany the narrative with discussion of perception and representation, both in relation to (the) narrative, and in the broader context of occidental thought. The argument begins at chapter 73 with a declaration of the fluidity or arbitrariness of signs, one example used being Picasso's car/ape sculpture, although given the concept of underlying *figuras*, Mambrino's helmet (*Don Quixote*, Book 1, chapter 21) is perhaps there too. A dismantling of language and genre culminates, near the end of the Paris section, in a group of chapters (particularly chapter 99) which is a kind of Morelli/Cortázar "manifesto." Then, in the Buenos Aires half of the narrative, manifestly absurd analytical structures, such as Ceferino's taxonomy, accompany and contrast with dissolution of categories in thought, as Oliveira approaches and crosses the sanity/madness threshold.

Cortázar and Morelli reiterate the principle that the reader is essential in the novel's writing. This being the case, the suggested readings, like the bridges and tunnels, are also metaphors, and Morelli's injunction to assemble a collection of texts a literal suggestion, not (only) a pointer to discovery of foreseen alternative structures (see Borges's story, "Examen de la obra de Herbert Quain" (Examination of Herbert Quain's Works). Secondly, chapter 115 includes the Morellian statement that he does not place characters in contexts, but, rather creates situations in the characters; he is concerned not with representation, but with the flow of mind. In the light of these principles, the multitudinous references – frequently simply namings – to jazz, painting, philosophy and literature, among other subjects, may be accepted as proof of the inevitability of multiple and autonomous readings/writings, rather than as a challenge for a painstaking Pierre Menard (chapter 22 leads us to Morelli; and see Borges's story "Pierre Menard, autor del Quijote" [Author of the *Quixote*]).

PAUL JORDAN

Editions

First edition: *Rayuela*, Buenos Aires: Sudamericana, 1963
Critical edition: edited by Julio Ortega, Saúl Yurkievich and Andrés Amorós, Madrid: Cátedra, 1984
Translation: *Hopscotch*, by Gregory Rabassa, New York: Pantheon, 1966; London: Collins Harvill, 1967

Further Reading

Barrenechea, Ana María, "La estructura de *Rayuela* de Julio Cortázar, in *Julio Cortázar*, edited by Pedro Lastra, Madrid: Taurus, 1981
Boldy, Steven, *The Novels of Julio Cortázar*, Cambridge and New York: Cambridge University Press, 1980 [Chapter 2 is on *Rayuela*]
Hussey, Barbara, "*Rayuela*: Chapter 55 as Take-(away)," in *Modern Latin American Fiction*, edited by Harold Bloom, New York: Chelsea House, 1990

Costa Rica

19th-and 20th-Century Prose and Poetry

According to Abelardo Bonilla in *Historia y antología de la literatura costarricense*, 1957–61 [History and Anthology of Costa Rican Literature], when news of independence from Spain reached Costa Rica from Guatemala, it did not occasion significant expressions of patriotism because this geographic area, which had had little contact either with Spain or with the rest of Spanish America, already perceived itself as a nation. This precocious sense of independence was due in part to lax governing by the Spanish authorities, for whom Costa Rica was not a source of great wealth or power. The absence of mines and a relatively small indigenous population were factors that kept this province, so distant from the seat of government in Guatemala, from becoming an area of large-scale exploitation of natural resources, or of large plantations. The indigenous population, estimated to have been 50,000 in 1502, by 1810 had decreased to 8,000. The total population of Costa Rica, in fact, in the early years of Central American independence, was 50,000. Most Costa Ricans were farmers and lived in the central highlands in or near the cities of Cartago (the capital), San José, Heredia, and Alajuela.

By 1848, when Costa Rica officially established itself as an independent nation and not a part of a Central American confederation, its population had doubled (100,000) and its intellectuals and politicians had taken up the challenge of defining a national identity. Among the characteristics widely accepted as conforming to the Costa Rican national identity are: patriarchal, peace-loving, passive, conciliatory, timid, respectful of law and human rights, orderly, hard-working, democratic and homogeneous. Someone once called Costa Rica "the Switzerland of the Americas," and this image, with its connotations of fair-skinned Europeanness, has also become commonplace, along with the observation that there is very little indigenous influence in popular culture. It is possible to read the literary history of Costa Rica as a dialectic of the nurturing and rejection of these myths of identity.

Writers during the second half of the 19th century, which encompassed the initial period of nation formation from 1848–89, tended to be doctors, lawyers and/or politicians, who wrote political speeches, essays on education, law, history and science, and texts appropriate for use in the newly founded schools. Newspapers were an important forum for the diffusion and debate of ideas and the exchange of opinion. The first printing press was brought to Costa Rica in 1830. The first printed newspapers were *El Noticioso Universal*, 1833–35 [The Universal News], *Correo de Costa Rica*, c.1833 [The Post of Costa Rica], and *La Tertulia*, 1834 [The Gathering]. A hand-written newspaper, *La Tertulia Patriótica* [The Patriotic Gathering], had circulated in 1824, published by Rafael Francisco Osejo, perhaps the most noteworthy intellectual of the pre and early independence period in Costa Rica. A native of Nicaragua, he went to Costa Rica in 1814 to establish the first institution of higher learning, the Casa de Enseñanza de Santo Tomás (The House of Teaching of St Thomas). Before its opening, young men from Costa Rica typically studied at the University of León in Nicaragua or the University of San Carlos in Guatemala. Osejo wrote the first locally-produced textbooks: *Aritmética*, 1830 [Arithmetic] and *Geografía*, 1833 [Geography], and was instrumental in composing the country's first Law of Public Instruction in 1832. Between 1840 and 1850 the Escuela Normal (Teachers' Training College) was founded, as well as the Liceo de Niñas (School for Girls). Costa Rica's democratic attitude toward public education is well-known and admired internationally, and Osejo is the first in an illustrious line of educators and political leaders who have maintained a tradition of free and equal access to public education. This prioritizing of public education has had an obvious salutary effect on the literary expression of the nation.

Osejo's successor, José María Castro Madriz, was the founder and rector of the University of Santo Tomás, as well as president of Costa Rica from 1847 to 1849, and again from

1866 to 1868. His speech at the inauguration of the University, and the University's statutes, which he composed and which establish the institution's collective and autonomous character, are important cultural documents that reflect the essential independence and egalitarianism at the heart of Costa Rican national identity. Castro Madriz's legacy was continued in the second half of the 19th century in the work of Jesús Jiménez (1823–1925), statesman and educational administrator, Julián Volio (1827–89), whose articles on topics of politics and education appeared in such publications as *La República* [The Republic], and *El Noticiero* [The News], and Mauro Fernández (1843–1905), who, as Minister of Education from 1886–89, was responsible for promulgating the General Law of Public Education of 1886. He also made the controversial decision to close the University of Santo Tomás in 1888, arguing that the country lacked a sufficient foundation at the primary and secondary levels to support a university. It was reopened in 1940.

Also contributing to the cultural atmosphere of the second half of the 19th century were numerous intellectuals from Europe, Latin America, and the United States who spent time in Costa Rica involved in research, teaching, journalism, and publishing. Among them were various German scientists such as Alejandro von Frantzius, who studied and wrote on the flora, fauna and geography of Costa Rica; the Cuban revolutionary Antonio Zambrano, who lived in Costa Rica from 1876–1906 and is credited with popularizing there the ideas of Positivism, which deeply influenced much of the narrative of the time. The visits in 1891 of the famous Nicaraguan *modernista* poet, Rubén Darío, and the Cuban writer and revolutionary José Martí, also served as a stimulus to local intellectuals. Numerous Central American writers have, at various times, lived in Costa Rica and participated in literary life. Of note in the late 19th century were Salvadorean Alberto Masferrer and Guatemalan Máximo Soto Hall, who founded the first newspaper in Costa Rica with sections devoted to literature and art, *El Diario de Costa Rica*, 1885 [The Costa Rica Daily]. The presence and influence of foreign writers, particularly from other Central American countries, has continued to the present. Many Nicaraguans, for example, such as Sergio Ramírez and Daisy Zamora, spent time in Costa Rica during the Sandinista war against Somoza in the 1970s. Manlio Argueta of El Salvador and Mario Morales of Guatemala are but two more of the numerous examples of Central American writers who have sought and found refuge in Costa Rica.

The most common forms of written expression during the 19th century were to be found in the numerous newspapers and periodicals that carried interviews with public figures and articles and essays of a polemical nature on political, social, and cultural topics. It was customary for contributors to use pseudonyms, due to the incendiary nature of much of their writing. Most of these periodicals were published at irregular intervals and were short-lived. Not until late in the century were there daily newspapers, such as the above-mentioned *El Diario de Costa Rica*, *La Prensa Libre* [The Free Press] and *El Heraldo de Costa Rica* [The Herald of Costa Rica]. These daily publications often included reviews, literary criticism, short stories and poems, and promoted literary expression through the sponsorship of literary contests and prizes. Pío Víquez (1848–99) was one of the most prominent journalists of this time. He founded and directed *El Heraldo de Costa Rica* and was known for his humorous and iconoclastic articles that included travel narratives, sketches of daily life, and commentary on art and politics.

With the exception of a brief and tantalizing summary of the literary accomplishments of Manuela Escalante, who lived in San José during the first half of the 19th century, there are no Costa Rican women writers of this period discussed or anthologized in the histories of Costa Rican literature. Whether this is due to an absence of women dedicated to writing at this time, or to a critical practice that has ignored or been blind to women's literary presence, will be resolved only if scholars take on the task of researching this phenomenon.

One of the few records currently available to scholars interested in Costa Rican poetry of the 19th century is *Lira costarricense*, 1890 [Costa Rican Lyre], an anthology of poetry from the second half of the century compiled by Máximo Fernández. Among the poets included are Emilio Pachecho Cooper (1865–1905), Justo A. Facio (1859–1931), and José María Alfaro Cooper (1861–1939) Alfaro Cooper's extensive religious poem *La epopeya de la cruz*, 1921 [The Epic of the Cross], is the only example in Costa Rican literature of epic poetry. There are no women poets in the anthology.

One of the first Costa Rican writers to publish a work of fiction in book form was Manuel Argüello Mora (1845–1902). His *Costa Rica pintoresca*, 1899 [Picturesque Costa Rica] includes three historical narratives: "Margarita," Elisa" and "La trinchera" [The Trench]. "Elisa Delmar imaginatively recounts the life of an illegitimate daughter of one of Costa Rica's heroes of the campaign against William Walker during 1856–57.

Literary historians agree that the dominance of *costumbrismo* is the distinguishing characteristic of Costa Rican narrative until well into the 20th century. *Costumbrismo* in Costa Rica is diverse in tone, technique, and degree of criticism of the national reality, but what all *costumbrista* texts have in common is that they focus on the customs, language, and social patterns of Costa Rica. They are descriptive and colloquial. The following three early practitioners of *costumbrismo* display the trends that later costumbrist writers would follow.

Manuel González Zeledón (1864–1936), who used the pseudonym Magón, is one of *costumbrismo*'s most beloved writers. He began publishing sketches of Costa Rican life in 1885 in the periodical *La Patria* [The Fatherland]. In 1910 he moved to the United States where he lived until shortly before his death in 1936. His stories and sketches, most of which are based on his own life and retold with humour, irony, and nostalgia, paint a picture of life in Costa Rica in the 19th century that sentimentalizes the patriarchal structure and locates national identity in language and folklore. His descriptions of market scenes, rural celebrations, and everyday interactions are full of affection and good humour.

In Aquileo J. Echeverría's (1866–1909) short stories, *Crónicas y cuentos míos* [My Chronicles and Stories], published posthumously in 1934, one can see the influence of the *modernista* aesthetic of musical, sensual prose, but he is remembered primarily for his *Concherías*, a term he invented to describe *costumbrista* sketches in verse that reproduce the regional speech of the *conchos* or rural Costa Ricans.

Joaquín García Monge's brand of *costumbrismo* is often described as realist because he flavours his descriptions of rural as well as urban Costa Rican life with a Naturalist perspective and a denunciation of society's ills. This is apparent in *El moto*, 1990 [The Orphan] and *La hijas del campo*, 1900 [Daughters of the Countryside]. Besides his contribution to the novel, García Monge is an important figure in Costa Rican literature because he founded and directed the *Repertorio Americano*, 1919–58 [American Repertory], an influential and unusually long-lived cultural journal of international circulation. He encouraged Costa Rican writers and published their essays, stories, and poems alongside the submissions of illustrious writers from Spanish America and Spain and translations of offerings by Europeans and North Americans.

The beginnings of *costumbrismo* were concurrent with the widespread popularity in much of Spanish America of *Modernismo*, whose aesthetics and ideology were radically different from *costumbrismo*'s regional focus and folksy diction. These differences inspired a literary debate regarding the use of popular speech in literature. Those who argued for its appropriateness included Carlos Gagini (1865–1925), a short story writer and philologist, whose *Diccionario de barbarismos y provincialismos de Costa Rica*, 1892 [Dictionary of Costa Rican Idioms and Regionalisms], reedited in 1919 as *Diccionario de Costarriqueñismos* [Dictionary of Typical Costa Rican Speech], bears testimony to a national trend to embrace, as central to the national identity, all that could be considered typically Costa Rican, even and especially if it did not coincide with the cultural norms of the metropolis. Fernández Guardia articulated the opposing point of view, insisting that the Spanish language not be deformed by elevating regional expressions and "mispronunciations" to the status of literary language. Those who argued for a home-grown thematic and aesthetic proved unquestionably to be in the majority. The desire for Costa Rican literature to be more cosmopolitan, eurocentred, or universal, has remained a weak, yet constant, counterpoint to the more prevalent impulse to observe, describe, and define the local scene. This has been true of poetry as well as prose, evidenced by the extreme popularity of the *costumbrista Concherías*, as compared to the minor influence of *Modernismo*. The foremost *modernista* poet was Rafael Cardona, whose *Poema de las piedras preciosas*, 1914 [Poems of the Precious Stones], although published after the popularity of *Modernismo* had waned in most of Spanish America, is clearly *modernista* in theme, language, and musicality.

The cultivation of coffee was introduced in 1804, and in 1844 the first shipments to England initiated a period of economic growth that gradually transformed Costa Rica into a capitalist economy with an extensive transportation and communication infrastructure. In 1897 banana cultivation began, and the Atlantic coast became the scene of large-scale investment in this crop. The social displacement, alienation, and oppression occasioned by the new system or large plantations devoted to coffee and banana production, often owned by foreign companies, and by the exigencies inherent in an export economy, became a persistent theme in much Costa Rican narrative from the end of the 19th century well into the 20th. The writers who explored this painful side of Costa Rican reality include many of the country's most acclaimed novelists and short-story writers. Noteworthy among those who came to be known as the Generation of 1940 are Carlos Luis Fallas (1909–66), whose novel *Mamita Yunai*, 1941 [Mommy United Fruit], is based on his personal experiences as a worker and union organizer on the banana plantations; Fabián Dobles (b. 1918), author of *Ese que llaman pueblo*, 1942 [What the People are Called] and *El sitio de las abras*, 1950 [Where the Clearings Are]; Joaquín Gutiérrez (b. 1918), whose novel *Puerto Limón* deals with the situation of workers on the Atlantic Coast.

But not all Costa Rican writers were content to cultivate the various types of *costumbrismo* and Social Realism. Yolanda Oreamuno (1916–56) published in 1943 in *Repertorio Americano* "Protesta contra el foklore," [Protest against Folklore], a critique of *costumbrista* literature that she claimed had become shallow through repetition. She argues for a literature that embraces the urban environment and the psychological suffering caused by the bureaucratic and technological changes of contemporary society. Her novel, *La ruta de su evasión*, 1949 [The Route of Their Escape], incorporates the then experimental techniques of stream of consciousness and interior monologue. The text is a complex and tortuous introspection by characters located in no explicitly defined time or place.

Oreamuno was a pioneer because she dared to challenge the literary Establishment and because she was a woman attempting to forge a place for herself in Costa Rican letters. She was preceded by a handful of literary foremothers. One of the first was María Fernández de Tinoco (1877–1961), a novelist and archaeologist as well as a founding member of the Theosophical Society of Costa Rica. This esoteric belief system was popular among Costa Rican intellectuals in the early years of the 20th century. Among its adherents were José Basileo Acuña and Rafael Cardona. Given the virtual extinction of the indigenous population of Costa Rica, Fernández de Tinoco's two novels, *Zulai* (1909) and *Yonta* (1909), which advance an esoteric theory to explain the origin of pre-Colombian civilizations in the New World, are anomalies. None the less, the author has the distinction of being the first woman in Costa Rica to publish a literary text.

María Isabel Carvajal (1888–1949), who used the pseudonym Carmen Lyra, wrote *Bananos y hombres*, 1931 [Bananas and Men], a Social Realist novel, but is best known for *Los cuentos de mi tía Panchita*, 1920 [My Aunt Panchita's Stories], still read and loved by Costa Rican children. She was instrumental in legitimizing children's literature among Costa Rican writers. Other practitioners of this genre include Lilia Ramos (1903–88), Carlos Luis Sáenz (1899–1984), and Marilín Echeverría (writing under the pseudonym Lara Ríos). Carvajal also contributed to Costa Rican literary life by befriending and encouraging many young writers. A teacher and an active member of the Communist Party, her home in San José doubled as a print shop for political and educational publications and a gathering place for Latin American political exiles as well as Costa Rican students and intellectuals.

Luisa González (b. 1904) was a writer, educator and political activist who founded, with Carmen Lyra, the first preschool in Costa Rica. Among her literary accomplishments are the editing of *Nuestra Voz* [Our Voice], a newspaper for women, and *A ras del suelo*, 1970 [Ground Level], an autobiographical narrative that portrays her childhood in a poor neighbourhood in San José.

Following Yolanda Oreamuno's example, a number of women have enriched Costa Rican narrative with innovative and arresting fiction. Carmen Naranjo (b. 1931), a prominent figure in Costa Rican cultural life, has written many novels, including *Los perros no ladraron*, 1966 [The Dogs Did Not Bark], a critique of bureaucracy, and *Diario de una multitud*, 1974 [Diary of a Crowd], a collage of urban voices. She has also written poetry and essays. Her short stories are perhaps her most successful writing. They address such themes as political corruption, lost idealism, ambiguous sexuality, and women's struggle for autonomy. Anacristina Rossi's (b. 1952) *María la noche*, 1985 [Maria the Night], won the national award for the novel in 1985. Its exploration of feminine sexuality and its lyricism appear again in her latest works: *La loca de Gandoca*, 1992 [The Madwoman of Gandoca], an ecological novel based on actual happenings, and *Situaciones conyugales*, 1993 [Conjugal Situations], a collection of short stories. Linda Berrón has written short stories and a novel, *El expediente*, 1989 [The File], a playful and ironic love story with a feminist twist. She directs the recently established publishing company, "Mujer" [Woman], devoted to publishing works by and about women.

Tatiana Lobo was born in Uruguay but now makes Costa Rica her home. Her excellent collection of stories, *Tiempo de claveles*, 1989 [Time of Carnations], was followed by the ambitious and imaginatively conceived historical novel *Asalto al paraíso*, 1992 [Assault on Paradise]. Lobo's novel represents a high point in a contemporary trend in the Costa Rican novel to reconsider and redefine their history and national identity, questioning official versions and foregrounding previously marginalized or ignored groups, events, and regions of the country. Other examples are *Así en la vida como en la muerte*, 1975 [In Life as in Death], by Gerardo César Hurtado (b. 1949); *Breve historia de todas las cosas*, 1975 [A Brief History of Everything], by Marco Tulio Aguilera Gurramuño; and Samuel Rovinski's *Ceremonia de casta*, 1975 [Family Ritual].

Following the Civil War of 1948, there was a decade of relatively little literary production. The themes that most fiction writers gravitated to in the 1960s and 1970s were the various existential crises occasioned by urban growth. Some examples are Julieta Pinto's *A la vuelta de la esquina*, 1975 [Around the Corner] and Alfonso Chase's *Mirar con inocencia*, 1975 [To Look Innocently].

The lives of the African-Caribbean inhabitants of the Atlantic Coast entered Costa Rican literature through the novels of Carlos Luis Fallas. In *Mamita Yunai*, for example, their socio-economic situation is emphasized. Quince Duncan (b. 1940), Costa Rica's first African-Caribbean writer, has broadened and deepened this presence by introducing the identity issues related to being a minority ethnic group within a country that has historically seen itself as homogeneous. Among his novels are *Hombres curtidos*, 1971 [Hardened Men] and *Kimbo*, 1989. Eulalia Bernard, an African-Caribbean poet, has published *Ritmohéroe*, 1982 [Rhythmhero], a collection of poems that express with irony, honesty, and affection, the daily life of her people, seen through the lens of an acute political awareness.

Costa Rica's poetry of the 20th century is more difficult to categorize than its fiction. Numerous poets have experimented with an intensely subjective and intimate expression on the one hand, or have followed the various Spanish American trends such as exteriorism and conversational poetry, which communicate an attitude of solidarity and anti-elitism. Poets who represent the former include Isaac Felipe Azofeifa (b. 1909), Mario Picado Umaña (b. 1928), and Alfonso Chase (b. 1945). Julieta Dobles (b. 1943) and Laureano Albán (b. 1942) tend towards the latter generalization. A third trend has been to incorporate classical and biblical or pre-Colombian myths in a poetry that strives for transcendence, such as *Quetzalcoatl* (1947), by José Basileo Acuña. Recent women's poetry is often openly celebratory of female sexuality and questioning of gender roles. A precursor was Eunice Odio (1922–74), whose *Los elementos terrestres*, 1948 [Terrestrial Elements] is a collection of eight long poems that project a mystical-erotic vision of gender relations. A more recent example is *La estación de fiebre*, 1982 [The Season of Fever], by Ana Istarú (b. 1960).

Costa Rica in the 1990s has become a most desirable tourist destination. The national identity myth that Yolanda Oreamuno, ever the iconoclast, openly criticized in 1939 in "El ambiente tico y los mitos tropicales" [The Tropical Myths and the Costa Rican Environment]: That Costa Rica is a tropical paradise populated by beautiful women and peace-loving men, blessed with beautiful beaches, exuberant tropical nature, and a climate of eternal spring; that the nation is a democracy, committed to egalitarianism and public education, disinterested in bearing arms; that Costa Rica is "the Switzerland of Central America" i.e. homogeneously white – these national myths have survived and continue to be exploited. None the less, as Costa Rican literature travels through the 20th century from *costumbrismo* through Naturalism and Social Realism, grappling with change and the pressures of the modern world, it has often painted a different picture. Costa Rica as seen through its literature is more complex, less homogeneous, less complacent and less egalitarian than the myth.

Abelardo Bonilla (1899–1969) has been extremely influential in determining the Costa Rican literary canon. In his exhaustively researched and generously inclusive *Historia y antología de la literatura costarricense*, 1957 [History and Anthology of Costa Rican Literature], he established coherent parameters and offered judicious evaluations that subsequent scholars, critics, and literary historians have followed with only minor deviations. Magza Zavala and Seidy Araya, in their provocative *La historiografía literaria en América Central*, 1995 [Literary Historiography in Central America], examine Bonilla's aesthetic and political assumptions and offer suggestions for future literary historians searching for more timely ways to organize, evaluate, and make sense of the literature not only of Costa Rica but of Central America.

JANET N. GOLD

Further Reading

Baeza Flores, Alberto, *Evolución de la poesía costarricense, 1954–1977*, San José: Editorial Costa Rica, 1978

Bonilla, Abelardo, *Historia y antología de la literatura costarricense*, 2 vols, San José: Editorial Universitaria, 1957–61

Castro Rawson, Margarita, *El costumbrismo en Costa Rica*, San José: Editorial Costa Rica, 1966

Duncan, Quince (editor), *El negro en la literatura costarricense*, San José: Editorial Costa Rica, 1975

Garnier, Leonor (editor), *Antología femenina del ensayo costarricense*, San José: Ministerio de Cultura, Juventud y Deportes, 1976

Martínez, Luz Ivette, *Carmen Naranjo y la narrativa femenina en Costa Rica*, San José: EDUCA, 1987

Menton, Seymour, *El cuento costarricense*, Mexico City: Andrea, and Lawrence, Kansas: University of Kansas Press, 1964

Monge, Carlos Francisco, *La imagen separada: modelos ideológicos de la poesía costarricense, 1950–1980*, San José, Costa Rica: Ministerio de Cultura, 1984

Portuguez de Bolaños, Elizabeth, *El cuento en Costa Rica*, San José: Antonio Lehmann, 1964

Sandoval de Fonseca, Virginia, *Resumen de literatura costarricense*, San José: Editorial Costa Rica, 1978

Segura Méndez, Manuel, *La poesía en Costa Rica*, San José: Editorial Costa Rica, 1963

Sotelo, Rogelio, *Valores literarios de Costa Rica*. San José: Imprenta Alsina, 1920

____ *Literatura costarricense: antología y biografías*, San José: Librería e Imprenta Lehmann, 1927

Valdeperas, Jorge, *Para una nueva interpretación de la literatura costarricense*, San José: Editorial Costa Rica, 1979

Zavala, Magda and Seidy Araya, *La historiografía literaria en América Central (1957–87)*, San José: Editorial Fundación, 1995

Special Issues of Journals
Revista Iberoamericana 138–39 (January–June 1987)

José de la Cuadra 1903–1941

Ecuadorian prose writer and journalist

Best known for his short stories, José de la Cuadra is one of the most illustrious Ecuadorian writers in terms of technical expertise and political commitment. He was an active member of the Generation of 1930 and of the Group of Guayaquil. As a lawyer, professor and social activist, he steadfastly served the popular classes, especially the *montuvios* – lowland peasants, inhabitants of the costal region of Ecuador – whose world, customs, and language he carefully observed in his pioneering essay, *El montuvio ecuatoriano*, 1937 [The Ecuadorian Montuvio].

Four historical events were key in the development of Cuadra's progressive political and literary ideology: the popular uprising of 15 November 1912, in the course of which an estimated 1,000 workers were massacred in Guayaquil; the July Revolution of 1925, led by a group of young, progressive military officers; the founding of the Socialist Party in 1926; and the publication in 1930 of Demetrio Aguilera Malta, Joaquín Gallegos Lara and Enrique Gil Gilbert's *Los que se van: cuentos del cholo i del montuvio* [The Disappearing Ones: Tales of Halfbreeds and Hillbillies], a seminal work in modern Ecuadorian fiction. Cuadra's belief in the writer's responsibility to criticize injustice prompted him to formulate, for the first time in Ecuador, the foundations of a popular committed literature of "denunciation and protest."

The Ecuadorian coast, known for its brutal exploitation of peasants, is the setting of Cuadra's work. Although the agricultural bourgeoisie of Guayaquil controlled this region throughout the 19th century, there existed simultaneously a social organization, ruled by peasant *caciques*. The latter, however, were displaced by the expansion of the urban bourgeoisie at the beginning of the 20th century. The demise of *caciquismo* ended a way of life shared by many peasants of the Ecuadorian lowlands. The fascinating world of the *montuvio*, on the border of myth and history, was rescued for future generations by the writers of the Generation of 1930. They were urban middle-class intellectuals of popular extraction, who sought the institutionalization of an Ecuadorian national language drawing from different popular idioms.

Of Cuadra's early books, *El amor que dormía*, 1930 [Love Sleeping] is characterized by a certain pompousness in a Romantic and *modernista* vein. However, in some of the stories of *Repisas*, 1931 [Display Case], Cuadra had already perfected many elements of his writing: realistic crudeness of language and themes, an ample register of popular voices, a tragic conception of human destiny, and the unconditional demand for justice. The last trait is evident, for example, in the strange vengeance exacted by a retarded boy, as recounted in "Chumbote." The twelve short stories of *Horno*, 1932 [Oven] adumbrate Cuadra's mature work with its faithful representation of the world-view of the *montuvio*. We find there as well a kind of linguistic synthesis, a laconic expressiveness – effective antidotes to what Alfredo Pareja Diezcanseco called the "baroque excesses of tropicalism" · which turn such stories as "Banda de pueblo" (Travelling Musicians), "La Tigra" (The Tigress), "Olor de cacao" (The Scent of Cocoa) into masterpieces. "Banda de pueblo" has been hailed by Jorge Enrique Adoum as the greatest short story in Spanish.

After this book, Cuadra's language would express a bitter irony, stripped of rhetorical flourishes, reproducing in a succinct style the speech of his characters. Cuadra's last work in this genre, *Guásinton*, 1938 [Washington], is a collection of fourteen diverse stories linked by a sparse style and a sharp psychological analysis. In this work, Cuadra explores the collective consciousness of the *montuvios* as he searches for symbols that convey the human condition and imprint it in collective memory. Thus he presents such memorable figures as the mythical-legendary alligator, Guásinton, "feudal lord of the Montuvian waters," or men with tragic destinies like the healer and miracle-worker, Camilo Franco.

Of particular importance for the subsequent development of the Latin American narrative was Cuadra's short excursus into the realm of the novel, *Los Sangurimas*, 1934 [The Sangurimas] and the unfinished *Los monos enloquecidos*, 1931 [The Mad Monkeys], published posthumously in 1951. In *Los Sangurimas* Cuadra emerges as the precursor of magical realism in Spanish America, anticipating by thirty three years García Márquez's classic *Cien años de soledad*, 1967 (*One Hundred Years of Solitude*), a work considered to be the epitome of the genre. *Los Sangurimas* superimposes various levels of reality: mythic, legendary, magical, hyperbolic, symbolic, historical, and sociological. It is a polysemic re-creation of coastal peasants' lives, which proceeds from the sociological principles Cuadra himself develops, three years later, in his essay *El montuvio ecuatoriano*. This work can be considered one of the main contributions to the social thought regarding Ecuador's indigenous peoples, as well as a theory of national culture.

It was a long and difficult process of experimentation which led Cuadra towards the mythical-legendary world view finally expressed in *Los Sangurimas*. For example, the mythical and circular structure of time is present in short stories like "Guásinton," "Cubillo, buscador de ganado" (Cubillo, the Cattle Rustler), and "Galleros" (Cock Fighters), where the reader can detect the artistic use of elements of popular culture such as fables, folk-accounts, and superstitions. The tragic symbolism of "Banda de pueblo" is a key part of the transition from traditional realism towards a magical one: nine hallucinating beings – eight men and one child – anti-heroes of the tropics, musicians roaming through coastal villages, transcend their apparent simplicity to become fantastic characters, hyperbolic creatures who flirt insolently with death and life. Finally, "La Tigra," a story written after *Los Sangurimas*, presents the intertwining of multiple levels of reality, using the theme of the virile woman. The young Pancha, having witnessed the violent death of her parents, seeks to avenge them and protect the virginity of her younger sister, Sarita, by becoming "Francisca the Tigress." Cuadra explores the dilemma of personal freedom, the psychology of a sado-masochistic woman, the fixation of hatred. There seems to be a kind of fatalism at work as Pancha becomes a male-devouring woman. The metaphorical structure, the poetic intensity, the linguistic economy, the interaction of lineal and circular plots, the closed and oppressive space, and the ritualized sexual orgies make "La Tigra" a clear precursor of the magical-realistic tradition.

But it is *Los Sangurimas* that provides a synthesis of Cuadra's world-view in techniques and concerns. It is both a personal and collective story, a dialectical interplay between fiction and reality, clearly showing Ecuadorian particularities within Spanish America. Various narrative levels are superimposed, driving the novel in many directions both temporally and spatially. On the surface, the novel appears simple and traditional. It begins with a prologue in which Cuadra develops "La teoría del matapalo" [The Theory of the Matapalo]. The matapalo, a large, robust tree growing in the coastal plains of Ecuador, serves as a metaphor for the world view of the

Montuvian people, whose way of life is centered around violence and *machismo*. The three central parts of the novel are entitled: (1) "El tronco añoso" (The Old Tree-trunk), which recounts the life of the lecherous patriarch Nicasio Sangurima, the mythical reincarnation of the *matapalo*; (2) "Las ramas robustas" (The Sturdy Branches), which present the stories of four of Nicasio's many children: Colonel Eufrasio (an illiterate, womanizer, a looter, and the murderer of his brother), the lawyer Francisco (a despised and corrupt traitor), Father Terencio (the drunken and opportunistic exploiter of his parishioners), and the farmer Ventura (an egotistical, greedy, and subservient man, "un grandísimo pendejo" [a big fool]); (3) "Torbellino en las hojas" (Whirlwind in the Leaves), which narrates the generational conflict set in motion by incestuous relationships: intense fighting divides the family, and the section ends with homicide and the profanation of the magical world the characters inhabit. In the epilogue, entitled "Palo abajo" (The Fallen Matapalo), we witness Nicasio's madness and the final destruction of the Sangurima family and the matapalo tree.

Time and space in the novel have a mythical and cyclical life of their own. Violence, solitude, lack of love and of communication also emerge as cyclical and of mythical proportions. They are unavoidable and their consequences imply destruction as illustrated by the contrapuntal repetition of key elements: life, death, water, soil, shadow, and light, which give life to Cuadra's magical realist style.

Cuadra's literary world, as a saga of the *Montuvian* people, is a legacy of intense aesthetic and social significance. As he once said, "A people without a mythical past is like a man who has never been a child." Thus the mythical past and the conflictual present are rendered with tenderness, solidarity, humanity, on the one hand, and with crudity, corrosive irony, and bitter humor, on the other. His unforgettable characters are complex human beings, rather than Manichean creatures. Cuadra's threefold commitment – to his people, his art and his ideology – bears testimony and becomes a testament: a written proof of the socio-political meaning of literature.

PABLO A. MARTÍNEZ

Biography
Born in Guayaquil, Ecuador, 3 September 1903. Attended Vicente Rocafuerte High School, Guayaquil; entered University of Guayaquil as a student of law in 1921, obtaining his first degree in 1927. Studied for a doctorate in law. Participated actively in student organizations and founded the Universidad Popular, intended for the underprivileged, in 1925. Married Inés Múñez del Arco Andrade in 1928. He was also a teacher in secondary and tertiary education; a civil servant who held important posts such as General Secretary of Public Administration. Professor of Penal Law at the University of Guayaquil; 1937. In addition he represented his country as consul in Argentina and Uruguay. Died in Guayaquil in 1941.

Selected Prose Works
Oro de sol, Guayaquil: El Telégrafo, 1924
Perlita Lila (recuerdos), Guayaquil: Mundo Moderno, 1925 [memoir]
Olga Catalina, Guayaquil: Mundo Moderno, 1925
Sueño de una noche de Navidad, Guayaquil: Artes Gráficas "Senefelder", 1930 [Published under the pseudonym Ortuño Zamudio]

El amor que dormía, Guayaquil: Artes Gráficas "Senefelder," 1930 [short fiction]
Repisas (narraciones breves), Guayaquil: Artes Gráficas "Senefelder," 1931 [short fiction]
La vuelta de la locura, Madrid: Dédalo, 1932
Horno, cuentos, Guayaquil: Tipografía y Librería de la Sociedad Filantrópica, 1932 [short fiction]
12 siluetas, Quito: América, 1934 [Sketches of his own generation of Ecuadorian authors]
Los Sangurimas, novela montuvia ecuatoriana, Madrid: Cenit, 1934 [novella]
El montuvio ecuatoriano (ensayo de presentación), Buenos Aires: Imán, 1937 [An essay on the people of Cuadra's own region]
Guásinton; relatos y crónicas, Quito: Talleres Gráficos de Educación, 1938 [short fiction]
Palo de balsa, Quito: América, 1938

Los monos enloquecidos, Quito: Casa de la Cultura Ecuatoriana, 1951

Compilations and Anthologies
Obras completas, edited by Jorge Enrique Adoum, with a prologue by Alfredo Pareja Diezcanseco, Quito: Casa de la Cultura Ecuatoriana, 1958
Cuentos, with a prologue by Jorge Enrique Adoum, Havana: Casa de las Américas, 1970

Further Reading
Robles, Humberto E., *Testimonio y tendencia mítica en la obra de José de la Cuadra*, Quito: Casa de la Cultura Ecuatoriana, 1976
——— "De San Borondón a Samborondón (José de la Cuadra), *Nuevo Texto Crítico*, vol. 4/8 (1991)

Cuba

19th-and 20th-Century Prose and Poetry

Cuban literature is generally said to begin with Silvestre de Balboa, who was born in the Canary Islands and was the city clerk of Puerto Príncipe (Camagüey). At the beginning of the 17th century he wrote a historical epic poem in royal octaves, *Espejo de paciencia* [Mirror of Patience], inspired by the kidnapping of the bishop Fray Juan de las Cabezas y Altamirano by the French pirate Gilberto Girón. This poem is accompanied by six laudatory sonnets written by separate authors and a motet composed by Balboa himself, all of which form an exceptional and early illustration of the importance that poetry was beginning to have in the country's life.

The foundation of various educational institutions represented an important step forward in the cultural life of the country, in whose capital a printing press had been established in the first few years of the 17th century. In 1722 the Seminario de San Basilio was founded in Santiago de Cuba, and in 1728 the University of Havana. The year 1773 saw the creation, also in Havana, of the Colegio Seminario de San Carlos, one of the most significant institutions as regards the country's cultural life during its long colonial period. This century also gave rise to another important aspect of Cuba's intellectual life: the emigration of leading figures, who left the country in search of a more favourable cultural environment. During this period, three Cubans dedicated to religious oratory achieved public recognition in Mexico: Brother José Manuel Rodríguez, José Julián Parreño and Francisco Javier Conde y Oquendo. However, no truly outstanding literary figures emerged in the course of this century.

Cuban literature's second period, which began around 1790, includes the island's transformation from trading post to colony, and the emergence of a national identity, with some serious expressions in the fields of poetry and reflexive prose,

and, to a lesser extent, those of narrative and drama, the latter genre meriting the mention of the work by Santiago Pita, *El príncipe jardinero y fingido Cloridano* [The Gardener Prince and Fake Cloridano], printed in Seville in 1730. There emerged, also, a current that would manifest itself forcefully and constantly in the country's literature: *costumbrismo*, the genre depicting customs and manners. Journalism began in 1790 with the publication of the *Papel Periódico de la Havana* [The Havana Periodical Paper], and became the principal vehicle for literary diffusion in Cuba during the greater part of the 19th century.

The first important poet was José María Heredia (1803–39), whose pro-independence ideas led to his early exile. Heredia, a cultured poet inheriting a Neoclassical tradition, and who displayed an intense Romantic style, is one of the first great names in Spanish American literature. Amongst the most notable of his compositions are "En el Teocalli de Cholula" [In the Teocalli of Cholula], "Niágara", "Himno del desterrado" [The Hymn of the Exile], "Inmortalidad" [Immortality], "A mi esposa" [To My Wife] and "A Emilia" [To Emilia]. Heredia's poetry, published in New York in 1825, exerted a productive influence on the literary life of the country during the first half of the 19th century.

In the field of prose writing, the most notable figures of this time were Francisco de Arango y Parreño (1765–1837), Father Félix Varela (1787–1853), José Antonio Saco (1797–1879), José de la Luz y Caballero (1800–62) and Domingo Delmonte (1804–53). Together they developed the nation's intellectuality in such areas as the economy, sociology, education, philosophy and literary criticism.

Alexander von Humboldt described Arango y Parreño – whose work focused principally on the country's economy

– as an eminent statesman. Félix Varela excelled in the field of philosophy, and served as Cuba's representative to the Spanish Cortes (Parliament). Because of his political convictions, he was sentenced to death in 1823, during the second of Ferdinand VII's absolutist political reactions. Having managed to escape, he spent the rest of his life in exile in the United States, where he supported the idea of Cuban independence, and where his work within the Catholic Church was so distinguished that he achieved the post of vicar-general of New York. José Antonio Saco was one of the century's most notable figures of the Cuban intelligentsia. In his works, the central preoccupation was the country's identity, for which he postulated an evolutionary process the best result of which would lead to independence, and the least desirable, to the annexation of Cuba by the United States.

On these foundations, the second division of this period began, in 1834, when the literature of the country grew in strength while undergoing a transformation. Lyrical poetry, established by the previous works of innumerable poets, and wholly dignified by Heredia, came to the forefront of literary life, and *costumbrismo* manifested itself emphatically and with ingenuity.

After Heredia's death in exile, three poets came to dominate this initial stage of Romanticism in Cuba: Gabriel de la Concepción Valdés (1809–44), José Jacinto Milanés (1814–63) and Gertrudis Gómez de Avellaneda (1814–73). Valdés, who became famous under the pseudonym Plácido, is the first Cuban writer of any consequence with mixed Spanish and African origins. Plácido came from the stream of versifiers that ran throughout Cuban literature, and he brought to the country's poetry an air of fine transparency that stands out in some of his best compositions, such as "Jicotencal," "A una ingrata" [To an Ungrateful Woman], "La luna de enero" [The January Moon], "Égloga cubana" [Cuban Eclogue], "La flor del café" [Coffee Blossom], "La flor de caña" [Cane Blossom] and "La flor de la piña" [Pineapple Blossom]. The strong desire for liberty expressed in other exceptional poems – "El juramento" [The Oath] and "Muerte de Gesler" [The Death of Gesler] – together with his condition as a free mulatto, in a slave-owning society, led to his being persecuted, and to his execution by firing squad, at the hands of the colonial government.

José Jacinto Milanés brought a feeling of melancholic intimacy and an expression of unblemished sensitivity to his best poems: "La fuga de la tórtola" [The Escape of the Turtledove], "La madrugada" [Dawn], "El mar" [The Sea], "El beso" [The Kiss], "De codos sobre el puente" [Resting on the Side of the Bridge], "Bajo el mango" [Below the Mango Tree] and "Invierno en Cuba" [Winter in Cuba]. He was one of the first representatives of Romantic theatre in Latin America, with his plays *El conde Alarcos*, 1838 [Count Alarcos] and *Un poeta en la corte*, 1846 [A Poet at Court].

It is in the person of Gertrudis Gómez de Avellaneda that Cuban literature had its first great woman writer. Already established in Spain, she gained a high degree of fame as a poet and a dramatist. Her style is forceful and, on occasion, declamatory, but it was provoked by genuine feelings, which she manifested above all in her collected letters. As a dramatist, she wrote a play of unquestionable quality in the tragedy *Baltasar* (1858). Her novel *Sab* (1841), set in Cuba, is a telling indictment of the horrors of slavery. Among her poems, the most notable are: "Al partir" [When Leaving], "Imitando una oda de Safo" [Imitating one of Sappho's Odes], "A él" [To Him], "La pesca en el mar" [Fishing at Sea], "Serenata de Cuba" and "La vuelta a la patria" [Return to the Homeland].

During this period, Cirilo Villaverde began to write his novel *Cecilia Valdés*, the most important example of the narrative genre in 19th-century Cuban literature. Although he completed the final version in 1879, it was not published until 1882. At the same time journalism grew in diversity through an incalculable number of publications, most of them short-lived; and academic oratory and the theatre strengthened their presence in the cultural life of the country.

Two quite different poets brought this literary period to its conclusion: Joaquín Lorenzo Luaces (1826–67) and Juan Clemente Zenea (1832–71). They both distanced themselves from Spanish influences in order to embrace other literatures, especially French and English, as sources for their cultural education.

Lorenzo Luaces developed two forms of expression arising from a growing tendency to differentiate between the Cuban and Spanish cultures: creole and ciboneyist (a term that relates to the Ciboney Indians) poetry and drama. However, the most abiding elements of his work can be found in compositions of a careful formal elaboration, in which he reveals himself as a precursor of Julián del Casal: "La concha de Venus" [Venus's Shell], "La fuente del amor" [The Fountain of Love], "La salida del cafetal" [On leaving the Coffee Plantation] and "La muerte de la bacante" [The Death of the Bacchante]. On the other hand, Creolism and Ciboneyism were no more than a attempt to consolidate an authentically popular form of poetry, which would take shape in the literary work of Juan Cristóbal Nápoles Fajardo (1829–62). Using the pseudonym El Cuculambé, Nápoles Fajardo published *Rumores del Hórmigo* [Rumours of the Hórmigo] in 1856. This book became a model for the country's popular poets, and its mode of expression is, almost exclusively, the ten-line stanza (*décima*). (It is a type of poetry that continues to be cultivated successfully to the present day in both its learned and popular forms).

Clemente Zenea was a Romantic poet, writing with refined expression and an elegiac style. Some of the best examples of truly lyrical verse in 19th-century Cuban poetry can be ascribed to him. His poetic voice penetrates the depths of feeling, and succeeds in reaching some of the mysteries of the soul. Linked, while still a youth, to the cause of Cuban independence, he lived in exile in the United States, where he practised revolutionary journalism. He returned to Cuba in order to meet the leader of the Revolution, Carlos Manuel de Céspedes. Zenea was taken prisoner while trying to return to the United States and was shot by the colonial government. Among his best poems are the narrative poem "Fidelia," "Sobre el mar" [On the Sea], "Retorno" [The Return], "A mi amada" [To My Beloved], "Oriente y ocaso" [Sunrise and Sunset], "Nocturno," "En días de esclavitud" [In the Days of Slavery], "A una golondrina" [To a Swallow] and "En Greenwood."

With the outbreak of the Ten Years War in 1868, the third period of Cuban literature began, which, spanning the successive attempts to gain independence, extended to the establishment of the Republic in 1902. Two intellectual currents characterize this period: one of a pro-independence stance, essentially revolutionary; and one advocating autonomy, believing in gradual change, and having as its basis a Positivist philosophy.

This period embraced the literary output of two generations, structured, approximately, around the year 1860. The attempts to liberate Cuba from Spanish domination, or to loosen the constraints placed upon the island by Spain, mark the polemical, and frequently declamatory, style of the literature of this time. Moreover, the influence of French literature is palpable, many writers having turned to it as a further example of their aspirations for liberty. Romanticism was diluted little by little, until the best from this deep current flowed into a new form of expression, *Modernismo*, which emerged as the first specifically Spanish American literary movement. In Cuba, José Martí (1853–95) and Julián del Casal (1863–93) were the two foremost figures of this movement.

The status of pioneer of the Modernist movement is assigned to José Martí. Modernist traits can be seen even in some of his early prose – as in the short story "Hora de lluvia" [The Time for Rain], published anonymously in 1875 in the Mexican publication *Revista Universal* [Universal Magazine] – and it takes clearer shape in his first book of poems, *Ismaelillo* [Little Ishmael] of 1882. In this work he fuses together the most vibrant currents of popular and anonymous Spanish poetry with his own innovative conception of the literary image as an expression of plastic fantasies springing from one's consciousness. He wrote almost all of his *oeuvre* in exile, with the imperative of taking the pro-independence revolution forward, to which he dedicated a significant part of his oratorical and journalistic writings, and for which he died in combat. During his long stay in the United States, he produced a large body of articles on that country, which constitute a beautiful and expressive literary portrait of life in North America. These articles and *Ismaelillo* greatly influenced Rubén Darío's *Azul*, 1888 [Blue], and dazzled Domingo Faustino Sarmiento. Martí's *Versos libres* [Free Verses] – a work that, because of its posthumous publication, became more of a poetic cycle than a book – responds to the development of poetic art discernible in *Ismaelillo*, and progresses from the most robust sources to be found in Romanticism to a modernity that surpasses text-book *Modernismo*, in effect preparing the ground for the poetry of the 20th century. The *Versos sencillos*, 1891 [Simple Verses] constitute Martí's most successful attempt to render visual art as verbal imagery. As a literary and art critic his work is as acute as it was ahead of its time, and this can be attributed to the integrative quality of his thought, which led him to construct opinions of a universal applicability from specific valuations. He wrote his last great pages in a notebook, in which he jotted down his impressions of the military campaign, in the middle of a war of independence.

Julián del Casal, taking as starting points his rejection of the colonial milieu in which he lived and the models offered him by the French poetry of the time, produced literary work marked by the bitterness and desperation of his feelings, and by structural composition of the highest quality. His poetic art is based around the ever more polarized opposition of art and reality which he ends up by rejecting in an absolute and self-destructing manner. He worked on sonnets as one might paint with words, and his three books – *Hojas al viento*, 1890

[Leaves in the Wind], *Nieve*, 1892 [Snow] and *Bustos y rimas*, 1893 [Busts and Rhymes], with a poetry section and another of prose writings – make him one of the most exceptional poets of Cuban literature.

During this period, besides the revolutionary oratory of Martí and Manuel Sanguily (1848–1925), there was a flowering of pro-autonomist oratory, notably in the figure of Rafael Montoro (1852–1933). The field of literary criticism produced an abundance of important writers, particularly Enrique Piñeyro (1839–1911), whose broad intellectual background and wide range of ideas fused with his capacity for sharp analysis.

Enrique José Varona (1849–1933) stands out as one of the most eminent figures of 19th-century Cuban literature. He devoted himself to literary criticism and to thought and his longevity allowed him to continue his intellectual development during the republican period.

The War of Independence (1895–98) quickly came to an end once the United States entered the conflict. North American troops combined with the Ejército Libertador de Cuba (Cuban Liberation Army) to defeat the colonial forces. There followed four years of administration by the United States, designed to serve as a period of transition between the colonial regime and the republican one. It was brought about through the adoption of a liberal constitution, limited by the Platt Amendment, which allowed the United States the right of intervention in the island's affairs in exceptional circumstances. The island officially became the Republic of Cuba on 20 May 1902.

The fourth period of the literary history of Cuba thus began with the establishment of the republic, and continued until the republican regime was replaced by the revolutionary one, on 1 January 1959.

At the end of the 19th century the development of poetry was briefly disrupted after the death of its two principal exponents of *Modernismo*, Martí and Julián Casal. The most representative poetic voices of this particular moment are collected in the anthology *Arpas cubanas*, 1904 [Cuban Harps], but the poetry of the new century did not take off in Cuba until the arrival of two innovative figures: Regino Boti (1878–1958) and José Manuel Poveda (1888–1926). Boti, inspired by a serious concern with form, assumed consciously the task of enriching Cuban poetry, something which he achieved in *Arabescos mentales* (1913) and in later books such as *El mar y la montaña*, 1921 [The Sea and the Mountain] and *La torre del silencio*, 1926 [The Tower of Silence]. Poveda was a poet and prose writer with hyperaesthetic sensibility; his texts are characterized by a nervous imagination and a formal care, which take shape in his *Versos precursores* (1917).

The other leading poet of this period was Agustín Acosta, who evolved from a *modernista* position and displayed a fluid use of language. His poetry tends towards a profundity of thought and uncomplicated expression, and on some occasions a strong social resonance. Among the most notable compositions of his considerable *oeuvre* are *Ala*, 1915 [Wing], *La zafra*, 1926 [The Sugar Cane Harvest], *Los camellos distantes*, 1936 [Distant Camels], *Últimos instantes*, 1941 [Last Instants] and *Las islas desoladas*, 1943 [Desolate Islands].

Essay writing, one of the strongest strands of Cuban literature, extends and diversifies during the 20th century. However, during the early years of this period the overriding preoccupation was the exploration of nationhood, which was studied from a variety of perspectives, ranging from the socioeconomic to the metaphysical. In the first generation of republican writers, the most prominent essayists include Jesús Castellanos (1879–1912), Luis Rodríguez Embil (1879–1954), Emilio Gaspar Rodríguez (1889–1939), Fernando Lles (1883–1949), José Antonio Ramos (1885–1943), Francisco José Castellanos (1892–1920), Medardo Vitier (1886–1960) and Fernando Ortiz, who produced a monumental piece of research and analysis of Cuban culture, which he defined as the result of the transculturation of Hispanic and African roots.

In the second republican generation the essay form tended towards barbed criticism and polemic, although there is space also within the genre for the expression of the imagination. Given the political role of this generation in the country's disturbed history, the essay was one of its principal literary manifestations. The leading figures were: Rafael Suárez Solís, José María Chacón y Calvo, Miguel Ángel Carbonell, Félix Lizaso, José Antonio Fernández de Castro, Jorge Mañach, Juan Marinello, Francisco Ichaso, Antonio Sánchez de Bustamante y Montoro and, right on the chronological edge of the generation, José Antonio Portuondo and Mirta Aguirre.

During the first few decades of the 20th century, Cuban narrative did not offer works of any particular interest, but was rather a period of gradual growth towards maturity, in which it is possible to call attention to some key moments. Jesús Castellanos, an excellent writer of narrative of the *modernista* school, marks the transition between the 19th and 20th centuries with a careful prose style which serves as a vehicle of expression for his critical viewpoint and disenchantment with reality. Historical narratives, inspired above all by the recent War of Independence, make up the principal output of such writers as: Emilio Bacardí (1844–1922), Raimundo Cabrera and Luis Rodríguez Embil. Reflections of social preoccupations can be seen in the work of José Antonio Ramos, Carlos Loveira (1882–1928), Luis Felipe Rodríguez (1888–1947) and Enrique Serpa. An interest in the psychological is present in the work of Miguel de Carrión (1875–1929), and in the short stories of the painter Carlos Enríquez.

Carlos Loveira was the author of novels that are fundamental for an understanding of the social reality of his era: *Generales y doctores*, 1920 [Generals and Doctors], *Los ciegos*, 1922 [The Blind] and *Juan Criollo*, 1927 [John the Creole]. Miguel de Carrión portrayed women successfully, which was the most important aspect of his novels with a psychological bent, such as: *Las honradas*, 1917 [Respectable Women] and *Las impuras*, 1919 [Fallen Women]. Luis Felipe Rodríguez, from a poor background, put together the best of his narrative work around 1924 in *La conjura de la ciénaga* [The Conspiracy of the Swamp], a work that would reach its definitive form with the title *Ciénaga* in 1937.

The short story and the novel were developed by writers such as Alfonso Hernández Catá; Federico de Ibarzábal; Carlos Montenegro; and Lydia Cabrera, whose splendid research into African-Cuban culture culminated in her book *El monte* [The Mountain]; Lino Novás Calvo; Félix Pita Rodríguez; Dora Alonso; and Onelio Jorge Cardoso, a narrator who transformed the range of topics to be found in the countryside into a veritable art form.

The third decade of the century witnessed the rise of a new generation of poets including the pioneering figure Mariano Brull (1891–1956). His *Poemas en menguante*, 1928 [Waning Poems], introduced pure poetry into Cuba, sustained by the thesis of the Frenchman Henri Brémond, and influenced by Paul Valéry. Brull was the creator of the *jitanjáfora*, a playful style of verbal invention, where poetry is reduced to the pure beauty of words stripped of meaning. His work comprises the following books: *Canto redondo*, 1934 [Round Song]; *Solo de rosa*, 1941 [Rose Solo]; *Tiempo en pena*, 1954 [Time in Sorrow] and *Nada más que*, 1954 [No More Than], where he offers self-contained and intense metaphysical texts.

A number of women poets came to the fore during this period. The most outstanding of them are Emilia Bernal, Dulce María Loynaz (b. 1902), Serafina Núñez (b. 1913), Carilda Oliver Labra (b. 1924) and Rafaela Chacón Nardi (b. 1926). Loynaz's poetry is of an intensely intimate nature, and shows great attention to form. Her *Obra lírica* (1955), which does not attach itself to any particular school, was honoured, in Spain, with the Miguel de Cervantes Prize. Her exceptional literary talents are confirmed in her poetic novel *Jardín* (1951) and in her travel book *Un verano en Tenerife*, 1958 [A Summer in Tenerife].

Other poets of the time include Ramón Rubiera, Enrique Loynaz (one of Dulce María's brothers) and Andrés Núñez Olano, whose works, although not as innovative as those of Brull, nor of a quality as refined as those of Dulce María Loynaz, are worthy of consideration from the point of view of their markedly personal lyricism. Another group of poets stands out, whose sentimental tone, tempered by irony and a colloquial style, sets them apart from the previous authors; they are José Zacarías Tallet, María Villar Buceta, and Rubén Martínez Villena (1899–1934), the latter a poet of great sensibility and a pure stylistic talent. Such poets have in common a critical outlook that directs them towards poetry with a social content, especially so in Manuel Navarro Luna, Regino Pedroso and Félix Pita Rodríguez.

Three poets of stature dominate the literary scene from the 1930s: Eugenio Florit (b. 1903), Emilio Ballagas (1908–54) and Nicolás Guillén (1902–89). The first, of Spanish origin, produced a very considerable lyrical output that situates him among the foremost figures of pure poetry in Cuba, with brilliant texts, where personal feeling is expressed in an ever purer manner. Of note among his works are *Doble acento*, 1937 [Double Accent]; *Reino*, 1938 [Kingdom]; *Cuatro poemas*, 1940 [Four Poems]; *Poema mío*, 1947 [My Poem], which constitutes the first compilation of his poetry. *Conversación a mi padre*, 1949 [Talking at My Father]; *Asonante final*, 1950 [Final Assonant] and a book of poems as recent as *Hasta luego*, 1992 [See You Later], ratify his highest qualities as a lyrical poet.

Emilio Ballagas is another of the chief voices of Cuban poetry. His lyricism has a strong emotional vein, which takes shape in his book *Sabor eterno*, 1939 [Eternal Taste], where he collected – among other texts of exceptional quality – "Elegía sin nombre" [Elegy without a Name] and "Nocturno y Elegía" [Nocturne and Elegy], two of the most abiding love poems of all time in the history of Cuban poetry. In his last book, *Cielo en rehenes* [Sky in Hostages], he chose to restrict himself to the sonnet form, which allowed him to achieve a

more controlled form of expression, in which the love sentiment fuses with religious emotion. Ballagas also developed
poetry with an African-Cuban theme in *Cuaderno de poesía
negra*, 1934 [Black Poetry Notebook], and also wrote some
social poetry.

But it was Nicolás Guillén who brought together and took
to the highest plane these two strands; the African-Cuban and
the social, with a type of poetry displaying a forceful quality
of expression, and deeply rooted in Spanish popular verse and
the sonority of the Cuban way of speaking. His extensive
output reaches culminating points in *Motivos de son* [Son
Motifs] (1930), *Sóngoro cosongo* (1931), *West Indies, Ltd.*
(1934), *El son entero*, 1947 [The Entire Son] and, above all,
in his *Elegías* (1958). His poetry benefits from its thematic
diversity, in which themes of love and eroticism occupy an
important place alongside collective actions. He was able to
combine refinement of form with a popular style, which turned
him into a poet of national importance.

The first great moment for stylistic renovation – as regards
expression and structure – in the Cuban novel, comes about
with the work of Enrique Labrador Ruiz (b. 1902), a writer
with fine creative flair and with deep Cuban roots. His short
stories, which he called *gaseiformes*, deconstruct and reform
the narrative with surprising mastery: *El laberinto de sí mismo*,
1933 [His Own Labyrinth], *Cresival* (1936) and *Anteo*
(1940). His "misty" novels – *Carne de quimera*, 1947 [Illusory
Flesh] and *Tráiler de sueños*, 1949 [Dream Trailer] – are
equally original and innovative. The novel *La sangre hambri-
enta*, 1950 [Hungry Blood] and his collection of short stories
El gallo en el espejo, 1953 [The Rooster in the Mirror] are
his most mature works, revealing his capacity for continual
innovation and searching, characteristics also of *El pan de
los muertos*, 1958 [The Bread of the Dead]. The profound
feeling of liberty that runs throughout his work caused him
to leave Cuba and he died in exile in the United States. This
meant that his work, and even his name, were silenced by the
Cuban authorities, practically erasing him from the country's
literary history.

Alejo Carpentier, perceived by many Cubans as a
"European," produced solid, well-crafted narratives of a
thematic richness that turned him into one of the most internationally renowned of Cuban writers. His novels and short
stories are notable as much on account of their verbal density
as because of their imaginative plots and frequent use of
American themes. Among his principal works are *El reino de
este mundo*, 1949 (*The Kingdom of this World*); *Los pasos
perdidos*, 1953 (*The Lost Steps*); *Guerra del tiempo*, 1958
(*War on Time*); and *El siglo de las luces*, 1962 (*Explosion in
a Cathedral*), a work displaying an epic style and quality, which
represents the height of his literary production.

The poetry of the third republican generation is characterized by the accentuated autonomy of lyrical expression as
contrasted with social expression, from which the majority
of new poets distance themselves in order to undertake the
search for Cubanness, which turns towards not only the roots
of nationhood, but also to metaphysical and universal dimensions. The poet José Lezama Lima (1910–76), was central to
this enterprise. He founded various journals, culminating with
Orígenes (1944–56), around which a group of poets of the
highest calibre gathered.

Lezama Lima's literary production is one of the most controversial in Latin American literature. His was a poetic concept
of reality sustained in the image, the image itself conceived as
the incarnation of poetic essence, at the same time as it is the
expression of significant knowledge. Lezama became known
through his poem *Muerte de Narciso*, 1937 [The Death of
Narcissus]; there then followed: *Enemigo rumor*, 1941 [Hostile
Rumour]; *Aventuras sigilosas*, 1945 [Stealthy Adventures]; *La
fijeza*, 1949 [Fixedness]; *Dador*, 1960 [The Giver] and
Fragmentos a su imán [Fragments to Their Magnet], published
posthumously in 1977. His novel *Paradiso* (1966), in which
he developed his concept of the image as a reproductive force
in the poetic universe, brought him international acclaim. At
the same time it became the initial cause for the ostracism to
which he was subjected by the Cuban regime, whose authorities rejected the strong eroticism of certain passages in the
work, and above all its treatment of homosexuality.

Together with Lezama Lima, the first group of poets involved
with *Orígenes* are: Virgilio Piñera (1912–79), Ángel Gaztelu
(b. 1914), Justo Rodríguez Santos (b. 1915) and Gastón
Baquero (b. 1918). Virgilio Piñera's literary work began with
poetry – *Las furias*, 1942 [The Furies] and *La isla en peso*,
1943 [The Corporeal Island] – but he achieved his best results
in the field of narrative, and, above all, in the theatre. Ángel
Gaztelu, the author of *Gradual de laudes*, 1955 [Gradual for
Lutes], is a poet of genuine and transparent mysticism. Justo
Rodríguez Santos, by way of contrast to the other members
of the group, stands out because of his classical verse style,
which finds its principal form of expression in the sonnet.
Gastón Baquero is one of the greatest voices of Cuban poetry,
the author of works of the highest quality, such as "Palabras
escritas en la arena por un inocente" [Words Written in the
Sand by an Innocent]. His free verse conforms to a way of
thinking that hovers over reality as though it were to observe
it from a participating distance.

The second *Orígenes* group brings together Eliseo Diego
(1920–94), Cintio Vitier (b. 1921), Octavio Smith (1921–86),
Fina García Marruz (b. 1923) and Lorenzo García Vega (b.
1926). Eliseo Diego's poetry is uncomplicated yet profound,
and carefully worked, and expresses an almost unfathomable
compassion for living and inanimate things. All his works are
of a sustained quality, though of particular note are *En la
Calzada de Jesús del Monte*, 1949 [In Jesus del Monte
Boulevard] and *El oscuro esplendor*, 1966 [The Dark
Splendour]. Cintio Vitier's poetry – which the poet groups in
three phases: *Vísperas* [Eves], *Testimonios* [Testimonies] and
Nupcias [Nuptials] – follows successive paths of expressive
inquiry as a result of deep metaphysical, philosophical and
social preoccupations. At the same time, his work as a critic
and essayist has broadened the range of his influence. As a
student of Cuban poetry and the work of José Martí, he has
written texts that are of great importance to the national
culture, among which *Lo cubano en la poesía*, 1957
[Cubanness in Poetry] is the most notable.

Fina García Marruz's poetry has unveiled some of the
deepest recesses of the everyday. Her poetic discourse is heavily
charged with meaning and the image reaches the unsurpassable quality of identifying itself with the reality named. Among
her principal works are *Las miradas perdidas*, 1951 [The Lost
Gazes] and *Visitaciones*, 1970 [Visitations]. Octavio Smith is

an author whose work is brief and to the point. His first book, *Del furtivo destierro*, 1946 [From the Furtive Exile], contains some of his best poems. *Estos barrios* [These Neighbourhoods] and *Crónicas y andanzas* [Chronicles and Adventures] complete his *oeuvre*. Lorenzo García Vega is a poet and prose writer with a strong imaginative projection. His best books include: *Suite para la espera*, 1948 [Waiting Room], the novel *Espirales del cuje*, 1952 [Tobacco-frame Spirals], the essay collection *Los años de "Orígenes,"* 1979 [The *Orígenes* Years], *Variaciones o como veredicto para sol de otras dudas*, 1993 [Variations or as a Verdict for a Sun of Other Doubts] and *Collages de un notario* [A Notary's Collages].

Virgilio Piñera's efforts as a dramatist reinvigorated the theatrical genre in Cuba. As a writer of short stories, Piñera was not only an excellent creative artist, but he also influenced the authors of the next generation. His rich imagination and the capacity to express the essential elements of reality, come together with a wide literary culture and an irreverent attitude, which make him one of the sharpest figures of 20th-century Cuban literature. He wrote the novels *La carne de René*, 1952 (*René's Flesh*) and *Pequeñas maniobras*, 1963 [Small Manoeuvres], but his most important narratives appear in *Cuentos fríos*, 1956 (*Cold Tales*) and *Cuentos*, 1964 [Stories], books that bring together texts of universal significance.

The fifth period in the history of Cuban literature commenced in an abrupt fashion when, on the 1st January 1959, a popular Revolution overturned the military dictatorship governing the island. The complex events that followed the Revolution gave rise to the establishment of a Marxist regime, officially proclaimed in 1961. An ever widening group of people was affected by the economic and political measures adopted by the regime, and exile became the only option for thousands of citizens, especially professionals from the sectors of medicine, law, and education. The country entered a period of increasing subordination to the Soviet Union, and literature, as well as art and culture in general, remained under the patronage and supervision of the State. The slogan "Within the Revolution, everything; without the Revolution, nothing" indicated the pattern of censorship that the Cuban authorities were to apply to any cultural manifestation. Established writers such as Gastón Baquero, Enrique Labrador Ruiz, Lydia Cabrera and Agustín Acosta, left Cuba. Others, such as José Lezama Lima and Virgilio Piñera – after enjoying, initially, some prestige – became victims of ostracism until the end of their lives. By way of contrast, figures such as Cintio Vitier, Eliseo Diego and Fina García Marruz, after remaining silent during the first few years of the political process, adhered to it and continued to write and publish important works. Nicolás Guillén, having, for a long time, been a Marxist militant, was exalted to the status of national poet. A sanitized interpretation of Carpentier's work also merited official praise and the prestige of an institute devoted to the promotion of his work. Dulce María Loynaz sank (or so she maintains) into a prolonged silence, equivalent to being an internal exile.

The profound and often violent transformation of the economic and political structures in these years coincided, approximately, with the arrival of the fourth literary generation of the century, composed of figures born around 1930. In general terms, this generation adopted an attitude of hostile and open criticism towards the preceding one, blaming it for having written a literature of evasion. Political slogans now took the place of literary images, and realism with a social content became the principal mode in the field of narrative, while the colloquial and the prosaic dominated in poetry. The substantial resources directed at literature and art by the State favoured the growth, without precedent, of new writers.

The most outstanding poets of this generation are Rolando Escardó (1925–1960), Ana Rosa Núñez (b. 1926), Roberto Friol (b. 1928), Francisco de Oraá (b. 1929), Roberto Fernández Retamar (b. 1930), Pablo Armando Fernández (b. 1930), Fayad Jamís (1930–88), Pedro de Oraá (b. 1931), José Álvarez Baragaño (1932–62), Heberto Padilla (b. 1932), César López (b. 1933); Rafael Alcides (b. 1933), Alberto Rocasolano (b. 1933), Antón Arrufat (b. 1935), Manuel Díaz Martínez (b. 1936), Armando Álvarez Bravo (b. 1938), Juana Rosa Pita (b. 1939); Miguel Barnet (b. 1940), Belkis Cuza Malé (b. 1942), Guillermo Rodríguez Rivera (b. 1943) and Nancy Morejón (b. 1944).

In the field of narrative, the most notable figures are Guillermo Cabrera Infante, Calvert Casey, José Lorenzo Fuentes, Severo Sarduy, José Soler Puig, Manuel Cofiño, Norberto Fuentes, Lisandro Otero, Hilda Perera, Jesús Díaz and Reinaldo Arenas. This generation found itself already split for political reasons towards the end of the 1960s, when the contradictions between official requirements and the natural development of intellectual life created a crisis around the poet Heberto Padilla, which produced a tightening of state control over art and literature. These pressures were most marked in the narrative genre, where stories dedicated to the guerrilla battles and the activities of the state's security forces were promoted. While writers such as Lisandro Otero and Roberto Fernández Retamar – the latter with a wide output as both a poet and an essayist – identified wholly with the official line, other authors, such as Juana Rosa Pita, Ana Rosa Núñez, Sarduy, Padilla himself, Cuza Malé, Cabrera Infante, Álvarez Bravo and Arenas, left Cuba. In exile, some of these authors wrote works that have brought them international recognition.

Towards the end of the 1970s and early 1980s another literary group began to emerge, composed both of writers living on the island and writers in exile, especially in the United States or Spain. This wave was to be characterized by its evident thematic and stylistic break with the preceding one, and by its giving rise to a literature where the values of subjectivity and of the image oppose, implicitly, the prevailing assumptions.

Among the poets of this set that have achieved literary maturity on the island, the most notable are Lina de Feria (b. 1944), Delfín Prats (b. 1945), Luis Rogelio Nogueras (1945–85), Alberto Serret (b. 1947), Raúl Hernández Novás (1948–93), Aramís Quintero (b. 1948), Raúl Rivero, Lourdes González (b. 1952), Luis Álvarez (b. 1950), Reyna María Rodríguez (b. 1952), Lourdes Rensoli (b. 1952), María Elena Cruz Varela (b. 1953), Cira Andrés (b. 1954), Jorge Yglesias (b. 1956), Chely Lima (b. 1957), Daína Chaviano (b. 1957) and Alberto Lauro (b. 1959). The literature of this group has had to negotiate censorship, and, in some cases, oppose it. Delfín Prats's poetry was banned in Cuba for over ten years. María Elena Cruz Varela suffered acts of violence, and was imprisoned because of her defence of political freedom, and Raúl Hernández Novás, a poet of enormous talent, committed suicide in 1993.

In exile the poets most worthy of note are José Kozer, Reinaldo García Ramos (b. 1944), Esteban Luis Cárdenas (b. 1945), Amando Fernández (1949–94), Lourdes Gil (b. 1950), Carlos A. Díaz Barrios (b. 1950), Andrés Reynaldo (b. 1953) and Roberto Valero (1955–94). The narrative of this group, like the poetry, contains a wide thematic range, and in it the inner being of its characters is given prominence, together with a stylistic treatment in which the realism is enriched by a conscious attention to formal values. The works of Carlos Victoria (b. 1950) – published while in exile – stand out, as do those of Senel Paz, Francisco López Sacha, Reinaldo Montero, Roberto Urías and Alejandro Querejeta. The best examples of dramatic writing in this generation are in the works of Abelardo Estorino, José Triana (b. 1931), Antón Arrufat and Abilio Estévez; and Rine Leal emerges as the outstanding critic of this genre.

The early 1990s have been painfully difficult for Cuban writers – as for all those who live in the island – because of acute shortages and a loss of peace of mind resulting from the collapse of the economy. However, in the middle of the decade it can be said that matters have improved considerably, an improvement that applies as much to the health of cultural journals as to book publishing. Several worthwhile short story writers have either consolidated their reputations or emerged on the scene in the course of this decade. Many anthologies, which include the work of different age groups have appeared, among which are *Fábula de ángeles*, 1994 [Fable of Angels], edited by Salvador Redonet and Francisco López Sacha. This volume, quite unselfconsciously, excludes women contributors completely, assigning to women a totally traditional image, via an erotic design on the book's cover. Apparently, not even the term "tokenism" has yet entered the vocabulary of some editors in Havana. A further development in publishing has been the emergence of the Pinos Nuevos [Young Pines] series intended for those who have not previously published in book form. This series of slender, inexpensive volumes includes both fiction and criticism, and was made possible by the financial assistance of an Argentine publisher. Where genre writing is concerned, one serious talent has emerged over the last few years, namely that of Leonardo Padura Fuentes (b. 1955), previously a journalist, literary critic (particularly of the work of Carpentier and of crime fiction) and writer of "serious" narrative. Padura plans a tetralogy of hardboiled or *noir* novels, and published the third of these, *Máscaras* [Masks], in 1996. Unsurprisingly, this intelligent, well-crafted work won him the Spanish Premio Gijón for the best "novela negra" of 1995. Padura's genre writing is boldly critical of corruption in high places (junior ministers, career diplomats, etc.), and he consciously deflates the political rhetoric with which his own generation grew up.

In spite of the rifts created in Cuban literature by the political circumstances of the last thirty-seven years, the salient values of this body of literature, as much on the island as off it, confirm its essential unity.

EMILIO DE ARMAS

translated by Luis González Fernández

Note: The penultimate paragraph was written by the editor after her return from Cuba in April 1996.

Further Reading

Lists of this kind, particularly on contemporary Cuban writing, are sometimes marred by a Montague versus Capulet (that is, Miami versus Havana) approach which is inimical to serious scholarship. The list below seeks to provide interesting, worthwhile and provocative items regardless of their place of publication.

Benítez Rojo, Antonio, *La isla que se repite: el Caribe y la perspectiva posmoderna*, Hanover, New Hampshire: Ediciones del Norte, 1989; as *The Repeating Island: the Caribbean and the Postmodern Perspective*, translated by James Maraniss, Durham, North Carolina: Duke University Press, 1992

Bernard, Jorge L. and Juan A. Pola (editors), *Quienes escriben en Cuba*, Havana: Letras Cubanas, 1985 [Interesting because it shows the rehabilitation of some authors silenced in the 1970s]

Bunck, Julie M., *Fidel Castro and the Quest for a Revolutionary Culture in Cuba*, University Park: Pennsylvania State University Press, 1994

Campuzano, Luisa, *Quirón o el ensayo y otros eventos*, Havana: Letras Cubanas, 1988 [Included because it contains a first, sketchy outline of women's writing in Cuba since 1959]

Fowler, Victor, "Poesía joven cubana: de la maquinaria al ontologismo goticista," *Journal of Hispanic Research*, London, vol. 2/2 (Spring 1994)

Huertas, Begoña, *Ensayo de un cambio. La narrativa cubana de los 80*, Havana: Casa de las Américas, 1993

Kutzinski, Vera M., *Sugar's Secrets: Race and the Erotics of Cuban Nationalism*, Charlottesville: University Press of Virginia, 1993

Loynaz, Dulce María, "Influencia de los poetas cubanos en el Modernismo," in her *Ensayos literarios*, Salamanca: Universidad de Salamanca, 1993

Mateo Palmer, Margarita, "La literatura caribeña al cierre del siglo," *Revista Iberoamericana*, vol. 59/164–65 (July–December 1993)

Menton, Seymour, *Prose Fiction of the Cuban Revolution*, Austin: University of Texas Press, 1975

Navarro, Desiderio, *Ejercicios del criterio*, Havana: Unión, 1989 [Regarded as something of a maverick by more sedate island critics, Navarro played a key part in promoting interest in literary theory – particularly that emanating from Eastern Europe and the USSR – in Cuba in the 1980s]

Ortega, Julio, *Relato de la utopía*, Barcelona: La Gaya Ciencia, 1973

Pérez Firmat, Gustavo, *The Cuban Condition: Translation and Identity in Modern Cuban Literature*, Cambridge and New York: Cambridge University Press, 1989

Plaf, Ineke, *Novelando La Habana*, Madrid: Orígenes, 1990

Prats Sariol, José, *Estudios sobre poesía cubana*, Havana: UNEAC, 1980

Rodríguez Castro, María Elena, "Listening to the Reader: the Working Class Cultural Project in Cuba and Puerto Rico," in *A History of Literature in the Caribbean*, vol. 1: Hispanic and Francophone Regions, edited by A. James Arnold, Amsterdam and Philadelphia: Benjamins, 1994

Rodríguez Coronel, Rogelio, *La novela de la revolución cubana*, Havana: Letras Cubanas, 1986 [A classic example of a critical work ruined by the attentions of the censor. It is included here for its historical interest since it was written in the 1970s, the darkest period in post-revolutionary letters]

Santí, Enrico Mario, *Escritura y tradición: texto, crítica y poética en la literatura hispanoamericana*, Barcelona: Laia, 1987 [Chapters on Desnoes, Lezama Lima, Martí, Severo Sarduy and Cintio Vitier]

Smith, Verity, "Obedezco pero no cumplo: una introducción a la labor de los poetas de Holguín," *Cuban Studies*, Pittsburgh, 22 (1992) [Focuses on a dynamic group of artists and writers, and seeks to demonstrate that Cuban literary life in the 1980s was by no means limited to Havana]

Stoner, Lynn K., *From the House to the Streets: the Cuban Woman's Movement for Legal Reform 1898–1940*, Durham, North Carolina: Duke University Press, 1991

Vitier, Cintio (editor), *La crítica literaria y estética en el siglo XIX cubano*, Havana: Biblioteca Nacional José Martí, 1974

Vitier, Cintio, *Crítica cubana*, Havana: Letras Cubanas, 1988

Williams, Lorna V., *The Representation of Slavery in Cuban Fiction*, Columbia: University of Missouri Press, 1994

Zurbano, Roberto, *Los estados nacientes. Literatura cubana y postmodernidad*, Havana: Pinos Nuevos, 1996

Anthologies

Pérez Sarduy, Pedro and Jean Stubbs (editors), *Afrocuba. An Anthology of Cuban Writing on Race, Politics and Culture*, Melbourne, Australia: Ocean Press, 1993

Bibliographies

Foster, David William, *Cuban Literature: a Research Guide*, New York: Garland, 1985

Maratos, Daniel C. and D. Hill Marnesba, *Escritores de la diáspora cubana; manual bibliográfico / Cuban Exile Writers: a Bibliographical Handbook*, Metuchen: New Jersey: Scarecrow Press, 1986 [bilingual edition]

Martínez, Julio A. (editor), *Dictionary of Twentieth Century Cuban Literature*, Westport, Connecticut: Greenwood Press, 1990 [Includes lengthy topics and a useful appendix on major literary journals. Quite comprehensive coverage of women writers]

Special Issues of Journals

Latin American Literary Review, vol. 8/16 (Spring–Summer 1980) [Special issue on literature of the Hispanic Caribbean with articles on general topics and individual writers such as Reinaldo Arenas, Rafael Barnet, Lydia Cabrera, René Marqués and Severo Sarduy. Also contains poems and short stories in English translation]

Revista Iberoamericana, vol. 55 (January–June 1990) and vol. 56 (July–December 1990)

Letras cubanas 20 (December 1994) [The section "Prosas profanas" is devoted to narrative by women]

Cuban Writing in the United States

Cuban writers outside the island have consistently pursued their literary endeavour. Their writing is not disconnected from the place which nurtured their first images and the rituals of their culture. Allegories and tropes bear the marks of a national identity that constitutes its leitmotif. Cuban poet José Lezama Lima believed that it was the common vision, myths and traditions that linked the social group and conformed a nation. "If the vision is ever lost," he wrote, "the people will be scattered, the nation dispersed." Yet he also believed that Cubans were "a people inhabited by a living image." To this, Cuban author Cabrera Infante has added that "we all carry Cuba within us, like a mysterious music, like a singular vision."

Exile writing in the US bears testimony to precisely the indelible presence of that vision from a distance. The historical conditions which led to exile itself cannot be ignored and they form the focal point of contemporary Cuban literature. The Revolution officially sanctioned a bifurcation of the country's literary discourse. This rupture served to legitimize what was written and published inside Cuba, while the literature produced outside the island would carry with it the stigma of the fugitive. Only recently have these two discourses begun to be reintegrated, and there have been many gestures toward that restoration from both sides.

Contrary to how it may be perceived, Cuban writing in the US is highly heterogenous, in content as well as style. The reasons for this are varied. Authors of several generations are represented, as are the members of all social classes and races. In addition, a writer's arrival to US shores can be dated as late as the mid 1990s, as in the cases of María Elena Cruz Varela and Norberto Fuentes; or it can go as far back as the 1960s, as in the cases of Lorenzo García Vega (a member of the Orígenes group) and Lydia Cabrera. Another complicating factor is the internal division that sets aside, on the one hand, those writers who began to publish while still living in Cuba. Until recently, they have been regarded, in their country and abroad, as the true heirs of the national literary canon. On the other hand, there are those who began their writing career after they abandoned the island. They consider themselves the real exile writers. This self-definition is based on the fact that they were deprived of the proper channels and the institutions of their trade. They had no access to publishing houses nor did they encounter, once in the US, any interest in their work. They had no writers' union, no national award. They had to create the mechanisms that allowed them to publish and distribute their books in a country where the dominant language was not Spanish. In spite of their efforts, the global literary community still questions their legitimate Cuban heritage.

Beyond all their aesthetic diversity, Cuban exile literature is shaped within the political coordinates of expatriation. It is within this alternate Cuban space, this extra-territorial reality, that its identity is built. Despite the individual writer's desire or interests, historical reasons condition, transcend and interpret the literary text. When the Revolution defines as a hegemonic discourse all that is written inside the island, it succeeds in relegating the one produced abroad to a state of illegitimacy. The perception that others have of this writing inserts the writer within an inescapable political context.

This is why exile as a condition of being is what ultimately defines Cuban writing in the US, more than the classifications of language or generation. It is a literature that harps on the themes of displacement and loss, reflecting the anguish of marginalization. Yet, far from being marginal, it is an organic discourse, full of history and of images arising from Cuba's literary traditions and cultural codes. There are, indeed, historical precedents for this phenomenon. The first territorial displacements in the island's difficult history occurred in the aftermath of Spain's domination, late in the 19th century. Cuba's most prominent writers of the last century – José María Heredia, Cirilo Villaverde, José Martí, Juan Clemente Zenea – lived and wrote their major works in the US.

Since dispersion and displacement conform to a pattern in the nation's history, Cuban writers in the US believe their exile to be temporary. This rationale, enhanced by a strong sense of national identity and a self-determination to continue writing in Spanish, implies a resistance to US cultural hegemony. Unlike other Hispanic authors in North America, Cubans have shown little interest in incorporating their writing into mainstream society. The insistence on the usage of Spanish, particularly, has relegated their work to the indifference and alienation of their milieu. The passage from one place and its culture to a strange environment, between conflicting languages, has acted as a threat to the self. Therefore, the recurrence of themes which have been naively perceived as stubbornness of memory and nostalgia for the past, merely affirm the vital experience of resisting dissolution and fragmentation through a continuity.

A chronology of Cuban exile literature reveals various degrees of consciousness and development throughout its different periods. Four major, significant transitions occur between 1959 and 1995. These intervals loosely correspond to each decade. The 1960s, for example, can be viewed as the "dark ages" of Cuban writing in the US. Few books were published, and writers were more concerned with gathering in small groups (usually isolated pockets in Miami and New York) for readings of their work. They also funded modest literary magazines. Poet and journalist Mauricio Fernández played a significant role then, editing several short-lived journals and organizing cultural functions. As a contrast, authors in the island were experiencing Cuban literature's first golden era, when Carpentier, Lezama, Piñera, Padilla, Triana, Vitier, Diego and Arrufat, published their major works.

The situation gradually changed during the 1970s. Cuban literary reviews in the US achieved a level of excellence. *Escandalar*, *Enlace*, *Exilio* and others, were edited by the emerging and established voices of Lorenzo García Vega, Octavio Armand, José Kozer, Mauricio Fernández and Lourdes Casal. Poetry was the most prolific genre of the period, and Orlando Rossardi edited the first anthology of poets from inside and outside the island. The works of Kozer and Armand, of Isel Rivero, Pura del Prado, Rafael Catalá, Martha Padilla, Omar Torres, Mercedes Cortázar, Dolores Prida and Ivan Acosta became better known. Three books proved to be the most influential of that decade. *El sitio de nadie*, 1972 [Nobody's Place], a novel by Hilda Perera, portrayed the predicaments of the Cuban middle classes, shaken by an idealized version of the Revolution and disrupted by exile life in Miami. *El caso Padilla*, 1972 [The Padilla Case], by Lourdes Casal, was a compilation of documents, declarations, articles, letters, interviews and other pertinent information concerning Heberto Padilla's controversy over official cultural policy, his book *Fuera del juego* (*Sent off the Field*), which won the Casa de las Américas Prize in 1968, his incarceration in 1971, and

his public self-criticism at the Union of Artists and Writers in Havana. In 1978, Lorenzo García Vega published *Los años de Orígenes* [The Orígenes Years], his subjective and polemic account of that generation of writers. Perera, Casal, and to a lesser extent García Vega, succeeded in striking a tender political chord in the collective psyche of the Cuban exile community, which the poetry collections had failed to address.

When the Mariel Harbour boat-lift operation began in 1980, the exodus of new and established writers to the US was once again renewed. After twenty years, the two separate branches of Cuban discourse met and tried to merge. As a result, exile literature was revitalized linguistically and thematically. For the new arrivals, it meant the freedom to explore areas such as homosexuality in their texts, as well as an access to books that were unavailable at home. A healthy curiosity for the Other, and a desire to be heard produced several journals during that decade. First, there were *Linden Lane* (edited by Belkis Cuza and Heberto Padilla) and *Mariel* (founded by Reinaldo Arenas, Reinaldo García Ramos and Carlos Victoria); then, *Lyra* (Iraida Iturralde and Lourdes Gil) and *La nuez* [The Nut] by Rafael Bordao. A more coherent, articulate vision of Cuban literature in the US began to emerge.

In 1988, the first major international conference on Cuban literature outside the island was held at Rutgers University, New Jersey. Author and art curator Ileana Fuentes directed this project where writers and critics met for several days of lectures, readings and panel discussions. The event acted as a catalyst for a series of similar efforts, some as ambitious and others more geographically and financially restricted. Three conferences were held: one in Miami and two in New York, at the Ollantay Centre for the Arts. In the period between 1987 and 1994 two poetry anthologies and a first collection of essays, exclusively on the topic of Cuban writing, were published. The Latin American Writers Institute of New York had Lourdes Gil as guest editor for a special issue on the subject of Cuban writing in the US. The more significant books of that decade, all published in 1989, were *La isla que se repite* (*The Repeating Island*), a collection of essays on identity in the Caribbean by Antonio Benítez Rojo; *La mala memoria* [A Poor Memory], Heberto Padilla's account of his participation in the revolutionary process; and *El portero* [The Porter], a first novel on life in exile, by Reinaldo Arenas.

In the last decade of the 20th century, Cuban discourse appears to be steering in a new direction. *Revista Iberoamericana* of the University of Pittsburgh, edited by Alfredo Roggiano and Enrico Mario Santí, gathered together the literature from inside and outside the island in a two volume edition. *Michigan Quarterly Review* also published two volumes on the subject, edited by anthropologist and author Ruth Behar. This attempts to reevaluate Cuban discourse and proposes alternate ways for the future of a nation that no longer fits its insularity. The approach is not popular in many sectors of the exile community, nor is it totally accepted inside the island. Further interest in the issue was stated at two international conferences of Cuban writers from outside and inside the island, celebrated in Stockholm and Madrid in 1994. Four writers living in the US participated: Heberto Padilla, Lourdes Gil, José Kozer and Orlando Rossardi. Though new perspectives stretching beyond ideologies, generations and geography are being sought, the political reality of a divided nation adds to what is already a complex question.

LOURDES GIL

Further Reading

Critical Studies

Colecchia, Francesca and L. González Cruz (editors), *Cuban Theater in the United States*, Tempe: Arizona: Bilingual Press, 1992

Monge Rafulls, Pedro (editor), *Lo que no se ha dicho*, New York: Ollantay Press, 1994

Sánchez Boudy, José, *Historia de la literatura cubana (en el exilio)*, Miami: Universal, 1975

Vázquez Díaz, René (editor), *Bipolaridad de la cultura cubana*, Stockholm: Olof Palme Center, 1994

Fiction

Excludes writers with separate entries in the book. Works published before the author went into exile are not listed.

Benítez Rojo, Antonio, *El mar de las lentejas*, Barcelona: Plaza y Janés, 1984

_____ *Estatuas sepultadas y otros relatos*, Hanover, New Hampshire: Ediciones del Norte, 1984

Cuza Malé, Belkis, *El clavel y la rosa*, Madrid: Instituto de Cooperación Iberoamericana, 1986

Fernández, Amando, *Los siete círculos*, León: Ayuntamiento de León, 1988

García Ramos, Reinaldo, *Caverna fiel*, Madrid: Verbum, 1993

García Vega, Lorenzo, *Los años de Orígenes*, Caracas: Monte Ávila, 1978

Gil, Lourdes, *Neumas*, New York: Senda Nueva de Ediciones, 1977

_____ *Vencido el fuego de la especie*, Somerville, New Jersey: SLUSA, 1983

_____ *Empieza la ciudad*, Coral Gables, Miami: La Torre de Papel, 1993

Iturralde, Iraida, *Tropel de espejos*, Madrid: Betania, 1989

Kozer, José, *El carillón de los muertos*, Buenos Aires: Último Reino, 1987

_____ *Carece de causa*, Buenos Aires: Último Reino, 1988

_____ *De donde oscilan los seres en sus proporciones*, Tenerife, Canary Islands: H.A. Editor, 1990

Montes Huidobro, Matías, *Desterrados al fuego*, Mexico City: Fondo de Cultura Económica, 1975

_____ *Segar a los muertos*, Miami: Universal, 1980

_____ *Ojos para no ver*, Miami: Universal, 1981

Núñez, Ana Rosa, *Poesía en éxodo*, Miami: Universal, 1970

Padilla, Heberto, *El hombre junto al mar*, Barcelona: Seix Barral, 1981

_____ *Legacies: Selected Poems*, New York: Farrar Straus and Giroux, 1982 [Bilingual selection of poems translated by Alastair Reid and Andrew Hurley]

_____ *La mala memoria*, Barcelona: Plaza y Janés, 1989

Perera Soto, Hilda, *El sitio de nadie*, Barcelona: Planeta, 1972

Robles, Mireya, *Hagiografía de Narcisa la bella*, Hanover, New Hampshire: Ediciones del Norte, 1985

Rodríguez Santos, Justo, *Los naipes conjurados*, Madrid: Playor, 1979

Valero, Roberto (pseudonym of Julio Real), *Desde un ángulo oscuro*, Madrid: Playor, 1982

_____ *En fin la noche*, Madrid: Playor, 1983

Victoria, Carlos, *Dharma*, Miami: Universal, 1985

_____ *Las sombras en la playa*, Miami: Universal, 1992

Anthologies

Burunat, Silvia and Ofelia García (editors), *Veinte años de literatura cubano-americana*, Tempe, Arizona: Bilingual Press, 1988 [Divided into several sections which include African-Cuban, Roots and Family; Politics and Revolution]

Casal, Lourdes, *Itinerario ideológico: antología de Lourdes Casal*, Miami: Instituto de Estudios Cubanos, 1982

Espina Pérez, Darío (editor), *Poetisas cubanas contemporáneas*, Miami: Academia Poética, 1990

Hospital, Carolina (editor), *Cuban American Writers: los atrevidos*, Princeton, New Jersey: Linden Lane Press, 1988

Lázaro, Felipe (editor), *Poetas cubanos en Nueva York*, Madrid: Betania, 1988

_____ *Poetas cubanas en Nueva York / Cuban Women Poets in New York*, Madrid: Betania, 1991 [bilingual edition]

Bibliographies

Maratos, Daniel C. and D. Hill Marnesba, *Escritores de la diáspora cubana: manual bibliográfico/ Cuban Exile Writers: a Bibliographic Handbook*, Metuchen, New Jersey: Scarecrow Press, 1986 [Introductory essays on "Exile in the Cuban Literary Experience" and "Cuban Short Fiction of the Diaspora"]

Cultural Dependency

Cultural dependency is said to occur when a society follows external models of culture at the expense of its ability to develop its own. Dependency implies not merely mutual influence, which would permit an exchange of cultural traits, but an unequal interaction in which the stronger partner enjoys an advantage and is able to promote its own cultural forms as the most desirable. In most cases, the phrase refers to the reliance of an economically disadvantaged nation or region on more powerful foreign countries. However, it can equally well apply to the situation within a single region or country, as less populated and cosmopolitan areas turn to the nearest cultural capitals to lead them in cultural matters. For example, the major literary and arts centers of Latin America, such as Buenos Aires, Mexico City and São Paulo, come under the sway of European and US modes. At the same time, they exert a considerable influence not only on the rest of the country but also on neighboring nations with less sophisticated cultural resources. The discussion of cultural dependency should include its inverse, cultural autonomy. The latter does not imply puristic isolation from foreign influences, but rather the ability to assimilate new elements, including those from other regions, without their displacing the local culture's own cultural products and dampening its creativity.

Although the term cultural dependency only gained currency in the 1960s, the phenomenon has long been in existence. The Spanish and Portuguese colonization of the New World created severe inequalities between cultures. Native groups lost not only the lands they once governed but also many of their cultural practices, especially such elite skills as astronomy, cosmology and writing. While the writing of Mesoamerican peoples and the notational system of the Inca empire survived some time after the conquest, they eventually died out as new generations were not trained in their use. Since then, native communities have depended on the Roman alphabet, and often on European languages, to transcribe their groups' traditional knowledge in durable form. Oral transmission has been a conduit not just for traditional learning but also for rebellion. As Jean Franco notes in *Minnesota Review* (1975), while writing was a blocked outlet, oral expression allowed native peoples "to maintain a consciousness of their past and build up resentment and subversion over long periods."

Descendants of Spaniards and Portuguese were also at a cultural disadvantage *vis-à-vis* the colonial powers, who understandably wished to prevent the development of an independent New World identity. Spain's controls over New World culture included censorship, the Inquisition, and restrictions on printing presses and the importation of books. Novels were forbidden lest they overstimulate the inhabitants of the New World. For *criollos*, American-born offspring of Spaniards, talk allowed for backbiting and the mockery of ecclesiastical and viceregal authorities. Among colonial-era documents that convey this anti-authoritarian talk is the *Lazarillo de ciegos caminantes desde Buenos Aires hasta Lima* [Guide for Blind Travelers from Buenos Aires to Lima] by Concolorcorvo (real name Alonso Carrió de la Vandera, born c.1715, died after 1778), published clandestinely in 1775 or 1776. This work satirizes authorities and the attitude that would later be called cultural dependency. For example, it ridicules a New World dweller ignorant of the land he inhabits, convinced that only European affairs are of any consequence.

Paradoxically, the colonials' desire to imitate the mother country at times produced an original, unique New World expression. The ardor with which Latin American architects, artists and writers threw themselves into baroque creation resulted in a uniquely Latin American Baroque.

The majority of Latin American countries declared their political independence early in the 19th century. As independence became a reality, many intellectuals realized that political decolonization was only the beginning of constructing new national and Pan-American identities. During this era, a good deal of poetry was written to promote nationalistic sentiment and to stress the differences between the Old and New Worlds. Europe often appeared as an exhausted, decadent continent, while Latin America, uncontaminated by excessive sophistication, was a virtuous fresh start. The 1826 poem *A la agricultura de la zona tórrida* [To the Agriculture of the Torrid Zone], by Andrés Bello, epitomizes the campaign to convince Latin Americans that they are entrusted with a unique cultural mission. In Bello's vision, the newly freed inhabitants of the New World are to shun the strife and urban decadence of

Europe and to stand out as a decentralized, pacific culture. Independence-era intellectuals made proposals to strengthen Latin America's cultural independence from Europe. Pre-conquest Indian civilizations were idealized as emblems of the New World; place names changed; the unsullied American landscape, with its unique flora and fauna, was celebrated. Pedro Henríquez Ureña, in his *Ensayos en busca de nuestra expresión* [Essays in Search of Our Expression], whose core essays appeared in 1928, reminds readers of the many Utopian schemes to make Latin American culture unique, such as the proposed development of new linguistic strains that would allow the New World to divorce itself from Spanish and Portuguese. Yet the European linguistic legacy proved inevitable in literature and general intellectual discussion. With specialized exceptions, such as Indian-language material transcribed in Roman alphabet, Latin American literature today exists in the language of the conquerors.

Starting in the 1870s, Latin American economies became more engaged with those of Western Europe and the United States. The new trade relations disadvantaged Latin America, which exported raw materials while relying on more industrialized countries for manufactured goods. The region was dependent in the sense that economically stronger countries set the agenda; it was also vulnerable to depressions caused by drops in commodity prices. Yet its traders and financiers enjoyed unprecedented prosperity, importing luxury items and modern conveniences. Culturally, as well, Latin America grew closer to continental Europe and the United States; in particular, educated Latin Americans were pre-occupied with following literary developments in France. It was during this period that Spanish American literary Modernism arose. Though criticized for its imitative dependency on foreign tendencies, Spanish American Modernism was the first original literary movement generated in Latin America. Critics from Octavio Paz to Ángel Rama have examined this paradox. In Rama's analysis, Spanish American Modernists, fearful of inhabiting a cultural backwater, rushed pell-mell to acquire the latest European trends. In their zeal, they mixed together literary novelties considered incompatible in Europe as well as the established Romanticism and Realism, creating an original fusion. While Modernism was long perceived as above the fray of social relations, many researchers now study it as part of the transition the region was undergoing through strengthened trade and cultural exchange and campaigns for modernization and internationalization.

The 20th century brought novel forms of cultural exchange and influence. New media came to Latin America, starting with telegraph, radio, telephone and cinema. From the mid-1950s, forms of communication proliferated. Nations wielded influence less via industrial might than up-to-the-minute expertise in communications and marketing. Poorer countries depended less on Western Europe and more on US and transnational corporations. As such forms as transistor radios and televisions spread even to rural areas, observers expressed concern that they were inhibiting locally produced culture and imparting an outlook at odds with local realities. To use a much-cited example, international satellite newscasts, at a high level of technical sophistication, often displaced reportage originating in Latin America. Critics were disturbed that the satellite broadcasts reflected a US view, with Latin American issues receiving meager and poorly informed coverage. Herbert Schiller's 1969 *Mass Communications and American Empire* documents the basis for such concerns.

The Chilean Ariel Dorfman deserves mention for his ability to spread concepts of cultural dependency to a broad audience. Dorfman and Armand Mattelart's popular *Para leer al Pato Donald*, 1971 (*How to Read Donald Duck: Imperialist Ideology in the Disney Comic*), shows how Donald Duck stories justify the US practice of investing abroad after exhausting domestic opportunities. Dorfman and his students sought to counter such influences by producing comics reflecting Chile's concerns.

A common objection to the concept of cultural dependency is that it promotes an isolationist cultural ideal. While some nationalistic purists may well use the term cultural dependency, most educated observers realize that interregional exchange is inevitable. To criticize cultural dependency is not to object to all outside influences. Rather, the goal is to support the creativity of regional cultures, which can evolve by adapting foreign elements if they are not overwhelmed by them.

NAOMI LINDSTROM

See also entries on Andrés Bello, Ariel Dorfman, Modernismo: Spanish America

Further Reading

Cândido, Antônio, "Literatura y subdesarrollo," in *América Latina en su literatura*, edited by César Fernández Moreno, Mexico City: Siglo XXI, 1972

Casals, Lourdes (editor), *El caso Padilla: literatura y revolución en Cuba*, Miami: Universal, 1970 [See, in particular, documents 15 and 16]

Castro, Fidel, *Palabras a los intelectuales*, Havana: Consejo Nacional de Cultura, 1961

Dorfman, Ariel and Armand Mattelart, *Para leer al Pato Donald*, Valparaíso, Chile: Universitarias de Valparaíso, 1971; as *How to Read Donald Duck: Imperialist Ideology in the Disney Comic*, translated by David Kunzle, New York: International General, 1975; revised edition, 1984 [This content analysis of Disney comics, concerned with economic as well as cultural dependency, spread concepts of dependency to a general intellectual public]

Fernández Retamar, Roberto, *Para una teoría de la literatura hispanoamericana*, revised edition, Mexico City: Nuestro Tiempo, 1977 [1st edition, 1975]

Franco, Jean, "Dependency Theory and Literary History: the Case of Latin America," *Minnesota Review* 5 (Fall 1975)

Henríquez Ureña, Pedro, *Ensayos en busca de nuestra expresión*, Buenos Aires: Raigal, 1928

Rama, Ángel, *Transculturación narrativa en América Latina*, Mexico City: Siglo XXI, 1982 [Rama is the literary critic who has achieved the most significant results in examining dependency and related phenomena in Latin American writing]

____ *Las máscaras democráticas del modernismo*, Montevideo: Fundación Ángel Rama, 1985

Santiago, Silviano, *Uma literatura nos trópicos: ensaios sobre dependência cultural*, São Paulo: Perspectiva, 1978

Schiller, Herbert I., *Mass Communications and American Empire*, New York: A.M. Kelley, 1969; revised edition, Boulder, Colorado: Westview Press, 1992

Vidal, Hernán (editor), *Literatura hispanoamericana e ideología liberal: surgimiento y crisis: una problemática en torno a la narrativa del Boom*, Buenos Aires: Hispamérica, 1975

D

Roque Dalton 1935–1975

Salvadorean, poet, prose writer and revolutionary

Few lives conform to the stereotypical image of the Latin American romantic revolutionary intellectual as neatly as Roque Dalton's. As a political activist and guerrilla fighter, Dalton's existence was one of imprisonment, torture, close brushes with death, periods of exile and clandestine returns to El Salvador. As a writer, he is best known for his poetry, the medium which he loved and the medium in which he felt he could express himself most comfortably. Yet Dalton also worked in a variety of other literary forms including drama, the essay, the monograph, history and journalism. In both his prose and his poetry, he often manipulated and stretched genre parameters in his never-ending search for creative self-expression. Finally, as a Don Juan, Dalton was reported to have loved women . . . and to have had affairs with hundreds of them. Dalton's death was no less dramatic than his life. Caught up in the midst of the ideological battles of El Salvador's notoriously sectarian left, he was accused of revisionism, charged with treason, and tried and executed by former comrades. "Lógica Revi" [(Per)Verse Logic], a poem that ends with the chilling prediction that "Una crítica al Partido Comunista Salvadoreño / solo la puede hacer un agente de la CIA. / Una autocrítica equivale al suicidio." (Only a CIA agent / can criticize the Salvadorean Communist Party / Self-criticism is equivalent to suicide), thus makes for prophetic reading.

What most strongly characterises Dalton's work is his unrelenting quest to find the universal in the Salvadorean and the Salvadorean in the universal; he was driven by a compulsive need to find a way of being Salvadorean within a larger world and obsessed with finding ways to communicate his findings to his compatriots. Often lonely and isolated – he spent nearly thirteen years in exile (in Mexico, Cuba and Prague) and other periods in prison – Dalton's writing is fiercely patriotic, and bursts with love and longing for his country and his people. Yet Dalton is neither excessively didactic nor excessively morose. He possessed a biting wit and a devastating sense of humour, and, despite his commitment to the convictions for which he lived and died, was rarely one to take himself or his circumstances too seriously. Rather, he mocks, jokes and lets his audience have a laugh at his expense, but never without the sting in the tail, never in the absence of a message or a

deeper meaning. These traits are evident in a verse titled "Taberna" that he wrote during his exile in Prague: "Ironizar sobre el socialismo parece ser aquí un buen digestivo / pero te juro que en mi país primero hay que conseguirse la cena." (Here, to speak ironically about socialism / seems to be a great way to aid digestion / but I can tell you that in my country / we have yet to eat our dinner).

Dalton's life was coloured by the popular uprising of 1932 which was led by the communist leader Agustín Farabundo Martí. The insurrection failed, and 30,000 people, most of whom were unarmed Indians, peasants and workers, were massacred under the presidency of General Maximiliano Hernández Martínez. As Dalton wrote in a poem entitled "Todos" [Everyone] he therefore belonged to a generation that was deemed half-dead and half-alive because, at that time, "to be a Salvadorean is to be half-dead." Events such as the massacre had been erased from official history, and because of this Dalton vowed to uncover and resuscitate what he called the hidden history of his country, *Las historias prohibidas del Pulgarcito* [The Prohibited Stories of Tom Thumb]. The title is taken from the nickname given to the smallest of the five Central American republics by the Chilean poet Gabriela Mistral. In this work, Dalton constructs an account of El Salvador from the time of the conquest through 1969, the year of the so-called "Soccer War" with Honduras. Dalton has pieced together a counterhegemonic or countercultural history of El Salvador by interspersing his own poetry with actual government documents, fragments of text taken from Spanish chronicles, verses from popular songs, letters and newspaper reports.

Even at his most political, Dalton never sought to hide the personal qualities that fuelled his convictions. This is evident in *Miguel Mármol: los sucesos de 1932 en El Salvador* (*Miguel Mármol*). Here, in Dalton's recording of the testimony of the most legendary of El Salvador's older generation of communists, the personal and the political are tightly interwoven. As a result of the interactions that occurred in the course of its making – between interviewer and interviewee, old guard and new-generation communist, oral "folk" historian and academically-trained historian – the text is enriched with an extraordinary ideological and strategical complexity and vigour. Dalton's own historical and political interpretations and analyses appear alongside Mármol's, and the theoretical debates of the old and the new left are as crucial to the narrative as the eyewitness accounts of the development of the revolutionary process in El Salvador and the stories about the daily lives of the peasants and workers. *Miguel Mármol* is therefore not strictly a testimonial but a new kind of polemical literary form that is revolutionary as literature as well as revolutionary in its political message. Dalton's friend and fellow writer Manlio Argueta has called the man who survived twelve near-death experiences "a living document," and the book is considered to be essential reading for anyone interested in people's history.

Dalton was a great admirer of José Carlos Mariátegui, the brilliant revolutionary intellectual who sought to adapt Marxism-Leninism to the circumstances of his native Peru. In his efforts to "decolonize" European Marxism and to show how Marxist theory was applicable to El Salvador, Dalton, like Mariátegui, changed its packaging by (re)presenting it in a way that was consistent with the national reality of his country. Thus, a poem such as "La gran burguesía" [The Grand Bourgeoisie] paints a portrait of this social sector that is recognizable to the Salvadorean reader: "Los que producen el aguardiente / y luego dicen que no hay que aumentar el sueldo / a los campesinos / porque todo se lo van a gastar en aguardiente ... (Those who produce liquor / and who then say that we musn't raise the salaries / of the peasants / because if we do then they'll just go and spend it all on liquor ...)

In some instances, as John Beverley points out, this repackaging may present problems for the English-speaking reader because its very "Salvadorean-ness" compromises its universality. This could be a negative feature of Dalton's work were it not for the numerous aids that he provides by way of a guide. Thus, while certain cultural references or colloquialisms may be unknown – and seemingly untraceable – the concepts contained elsewhere explain Dalton's motivations and reasoning in no uncertain terms. The essay "Poesía y militancia en América Latina" or the shorter "El problema de hablar de Lenin en América Latina con el agravante de hacerlo desde un poema" [The Problem of Speaking about Lenin in Latin America and the Added Injury of Doing So in a Poem] are therefore good starting points for the new reader.

Where Dalton does connect easily and directly with his public, it is often because his humanitarianism and his openness about himself and his politics are so appealing. Outside of his poetry, this is most apparent in the "semi-autobiographical novel" entitled *¡Pobrecito poeta que era yo!* [What a Dud Poet I Was!]. Dalton preferred to view his life as being representative of the lives of many others of his generation, and this is a fictionalised account of a life that Dalton never considered to be specifically his. Dalton-as-Dalton is therefore absent from his own "autobiography," and the book is instead arranged around the diaries of several different characters. What is expressed elsewhere in poetry here appears in a Joycean-style stream of consciousness prose. Sarcastic, honest, moving – and at times unremittingly funny – its lighter side tells of Dalton's bouts of drunkenness and his search for good meals, good poetry and "good" women during his years as a law student and aspiring poet. But the other side of the life of

an increasingly committed militant communist living under a repressive military government is also portrayed here in all its horror. Full of Dalton's opinions on national culture (what he referred to as both a *Reader's Digest* culture and as "a load of shit") and of his self-critical philosophical and psychoanalytical interpretations of his episodes of existential and patriotic angst, *¡Pobrecito poeta* reads as a sort of politicised Central American version of *The Catcher in the Rye*.

The role of the intellectual and the role of cultural practices within a revolutionary process represent other constant themes in Dalton's work. As a middle-class revolutionary intellectual and militant within a highly polarised society, these issues were close to his heart. He attempted to work through them in his essays and his poetry, maintaining that honest intellectuals who lived their lives in the struggle could become "proletarianized" to some extent by being aware of their class position and of "the eminently bourgeois character" of the expressive means that they had at their disposal. Some of these reflections appear in *Un libro rojo para Lenin* [A Red Book for Lenin]. Here, Dalton plays with Lenin's notion of Party literature and its relevance and applicability to El Salvador and Latin America. While Dalton queried these ideas, he never wavered from his belief that the cultural field ought to be as important in the revolutionary process as the battlefield; as far as he was concerned, his poetry and his gun were weapons of equal importance. In so far as he worked through his political ideas both as a poet and as a guerrilla fighter, it must be said that in few other lives have communist revolutionary theory and action been so very closely linked.

JENNY SHUBOW

See also entries on Guerrilla Poetry, José Carlos Mariátegui

Biography

Born in El Salvador, 14 May 1935. Attended Jesuit primary and secondary schools in San Salvador and university in Chile, Mexico and El Salvador. Unable to complete law school due to imprisonment and exile. Joined the Communist Party of El Salvador in mid-1950s. Co-founder of the important Círculo Literario Universitario in San Salvador; editor of "La Jodarría," a satirical-political journal; visited USSR as delegate to a youth conference. Exiled to Mexico in 1961; first visit to Cuba, where he was to live eventually and where he worked with *Casa de las Américas*. Lived in Prague from 1965 to 1967. Late 1960s and early 1970s, visited North Korea and North Vietnam, where he worked in a bicycle factory and underwent military training. Made several clandestine journeys to El Salvador; in 1973. Following a split in the Communist Party, joined the Ejército Revolucionario del Pueblo (People's Revolutionary Army). Recipient of numerous literary awards for his poetry, including: Central American Poetry Prize (co-recipient, with Otto René Castillo), 1955; Central American Award of the University of San Salvador, 1956, 1958, 1959; International Literature Prize of the International Union of Students, 1961, Casa de las Américas Prize, 1969. Assassinated by a rival guerrilla faction, on 10 May 1975, four days before his 40th birthday.

Selected Works

Poetry
La ventana en el rostro, Mexico City: Andrea, 1961
El turno del ofendido, Havana: Casa de las Américas, 1962
Poemas, San Salvador: Editorial Universitaria, 1968

Taberna y otros lugares, Havana: Casa de las Américas, 1969
Los pequeños infiernos, Barcelona: Llibres de Sinera, 1970
Poemas clandestinos, San José, Costa Rica: EDUCA, 1980; as
Poemas clandestinos / Clandestine Poems, translated by Jack
Hirschman, San Francisco: Solidarity Publications, 1984 [This
bilingual edition contains an interesting – if occasionally
inaccurate – introduction by Margaret Randall]
Un libro levemente odioso, Mexico City: Siglo XXI, 1988

Prose Poetry or Collage Poetry
Las historias prohibidas del Pulgarcito, Mexico City: Siglo XXI,
1974
Un libro rojo para Lenin, Managua: Editorial Nueva Nicaragua,
1986
Prosoemas, Madrid: La Idea, 1987

Essays
"Poesía y militancia en América Latina," Havana: Casa de las
Américas 20–21 (1963); as *Poetry and Militancy in Latin
America*, translated by James Scully, Willimantic, Connecticut:
Curbstone Press, 1981 [The "Afterword" is a very useful critical
essay by the translator]
El Salvador: (monografía), Havana: Biblioteca Nacional José Martí,
1963
¿Revolución en la revolución? y la crítica de derecha, Havana: Casa
de las Américas, 1970 [A critique of Regis Debray's highly
influential essay, and a defense of the essay against the right-wing
attacks it received]

Compilations and Anthologies
Poesía escogida, San José, Costa Rica: EDUCA, 1983
Poesía militante / Militant Poetry, translated by Arlene Scully and
Jack Scully, London: El Salvador Solidarity Campaign, 1983
[Together with a small collection of poems, this includes an
English translation of an excerpt from "Poetry and Militancy in
Latin America"]
Poems, translated by Richard Schaaf, Willimantic, Connecticut:
Curbstone Press, 1984
Con manos de fantasma: antología, Buenos Aires: Nueva América,
1987
En la humedad del secreto: antología poética de Roque Dalton,
edited by Rafael Lara Martínez, San Salvador: Conculura, 1994

Other Writings
El intelectual y la sociedad, with others, Mexico City: Siglo XXI,
1969 [Transcription of a round-table discussion held in Havana
on 2 May 1969]
Miguel Mármol: los sucesos de 1932 en El Salvador, San José,
Costa Rica: EDUCA, 1972 [testimonial]; as *Miguel Mármol*,
translated by Kathleen Ross and Richard Schaaf, Willimantic,
Connecticut: Curbstone Press, 1987 [Manlio Argueta's prologue
provides important background material]
¡Pobrecito poeta que era yo!, San José, Costa Rica: EDUCA, 1976
[semi-autobiographical novel]
Los helicópteros: pieza teatral en varias escenas, in collaboration
with Peperuiz, San Salvador: Editorial Universitaria, 1980 [play]

Further Reading
Achúgar, Hugo, "The Book of Poems as a Social Act: Notes Toward
an Interpretation of Contemporary Hispanic American Poetry," in
Marxism and the Interpretation of Culture, edited by Cary
Nelson and Lawrence Grossberg, London: Macmillan, and
Urbana: University of Illinois Press, 1988
Benedetti, Mario, "Una hora con Roque Dalton," in his *Los poetas
comunicantes*, Montevideo: Marcha, 1972
___ *Poesía trunca*, Havana: Casa de las Américas, 1977
Beverley, John and Marc Zimmerman, *Literature and Politics in the
Central American Revolutions*, Austin: University of Texas Press,

1990 [This book, like the authors' other joint and single
publications, provides what is perhaps the most useful and
important assessment of Dalton's context and work]
Pring-Mill, Robert, "Both in Sorrow and in Anger: Spanish
American Protest Poetry," *Cambridge Review*, vol. 91/2195 (20
February 1970) [Pring-Mill's articles are important for an
understanding of political poetry in Spanish America]
___ "The Scope of Spanish-American Committed Poetry," in
Homenaje a Rodolfo Grossman, Frankfurt: Peter Lang, 1977
___ "The Nature and Functions of Spanish American POESÍA DE
COMPROMISO," *Bulletin of the Society for Latin American
Studies* 31 (October 1979)
Zimmerman, Marc, *El Salvador at War: a Collage Epic. A Book of
Insurrection, War and U.S. Intervention*, Minneapolis: MEP
Publications, 1988

Poems

By Roque Dalton

As a revolutionary poet, Roque Dalton's lifelong mission was
to heighten the political awareness of his audience through
denouncing the atrocities and injustice perpetrated by El
Salvador's long string of military dictatorships. Real experiences and real people, real places and real dates appear time
and time again in these pages; Dalton wanted his fellow
Salvadoreans to learn their history. Poetry was therefore not
simply a means of denouncing the inhumane, but also a vehicle
for teaching the reader about the actual strategies for effecting
social and political change that were being played out on the
battlefield in El Salvador and other parts of the world. The
revolutionary theories of Guevara and Fanon and the concrete
examples of Cuba and Chile appear alongside the lessons to
be learned from the failures of El Salvador's own revolutionary
movements. For example, "Maneras de morir" [Ways of
Dying], written in the aftermath of the 1973 coup in Chile, is
meant to provoke a rethink about how political and social
change might be brought about in Latin America:

El Comandante Ernesto Che Guevara
llamado por los pacifistas "el gran aventurero de la
    lucha armada"
fue y aplicó sus concepciones revolucionarias
a Bolivia.
En la prueba se perdió su vida y la de un puñado de
    héroes.
Los grandes pacifistas de la vía prudente
también probaron sus propias concepciones en Chile:
los muertos pasan ya de 30 mil.
Piense el lector en lo que nos dirían
si pudieran hablarnos de su experiencia
los muertos en nombre de cada concepción.

[Commander Ernesto Che Guevara / whom the pacifists
call / "the great adventurer of the armed struggle" / went
and applied his revolutionary conceptions / to Bolivia. /
In putting them to the test he lost his life and that of a
handful of heroes. / The great pacifists of the prudent
way / also tried out their conceptions in Chile: / more
than 30,000 people have already died. / Let the reader

think about what they would say to us / those who have
died for each of these concepts / if they could tell us
about their experiences.]

Full of unveiled party political messages and obsessed with
communicating the need to fight for revolutionary change, this
poetry escapes the agit-prop label only because Dalton's love
for his country and his people comes through so clearly and
consistently. This, rather, is didactic political poetry at its best
– and at its most didactic and political.

Despite his many commitments as a guerrilla in the midst
of a guerrilla war, Dalton was a prolific writer. Margaret
Randall (1990) estimates that apart from his prose he produced
some 800 pages of poetry and prose-poetry. In these pages,
elements taken from Salvadorean popular culture, the hard
political rhetoric of the committed left-wing intellectual and
Dalton's own artistic genius work together to depict an alternative or unofficial version of Salvadorean reality. Dalton's
work must therefore be read as a search to define and express
"lo salvadoreño," what Gramsci referred to as the "national-
popular." For example, the country's name (which translates
as "The Saviour" or "The Redeemer") has long been the basis
for many jokes. As a result, a verse that draws upon this living
tradition and this sense of humour must be read as being affectionately critical rather than just critical: "Todo es posible en
un país como éste que, entre otras cosas, tiene el nombre más
risible del mundo: cualquiera diría que se trata de un hospital
o de un remolcador. (Everything is possible in a country like
this / one that, among other things, has the most ludicrous
name in the world: / who wouldn't think that it refers to a
hospital or a tugboat." From "Sir Thomas").

Indeed, although it is revolutionary in style as well as
content, Dalton's poetry often drew upon extant Salvadorean
and Latin American traditions (Salarrué's use of the vernacular, Náhuatl poetry's humanism, Otto René Castillo's fierce
patriotism, Nicanor Parra's "anti-poetry"). References to oral
as well as written traditions are apparent: what is often an
idiosyncratic rambling verse is interspersed with popular
Salvadoran sayings, dirty jokes and phrases from songs, as well
as with borrowings in direct quotation from a variety of
national and international printed sources. Together they
contextualize the poetry, thereby helping the poet to connect
with his audience by providing them with common cultural
references which they can relate to. Because of this, when
Dalton uses his collage-poems to portray his interpretation of
the state of the nation or, equally potently, as a space in which
he can present his vision of what the nation could and should
become, both images come across as identifiably and unequivocally Salvadorean:

El Salvador será un lindo
(y sin exagerar) serio país
cuando la clase obrera y el campesinado
lo fertilecen lo peinen lo talqueen
le curen la goma histórica
lo adecenten lo reconstituyan
y lo echan a andar.

[El Salvador will be a lovely / (and without exaggerating)
serious country / when the working class and the
peasants / fertilize it brush it up powder it / cure its

historical hangover / make it presentable reconstruct it /
and set it on its way.]

(from "El Salvador será"/El Salvador Will Be)

Similarly, when highlighting – as he so often did – the contradictions of capitalism and underdevelopment, he is at the same
time contributing to the Salvadorean tradition of finding
delight in paradox and absurdity. In a country with a highly
developed vernacular and with a highly politicised population,
Dalton's use of Salvadorean slang alongside Marxist-Leninist
phraseology and concepts seems to make perfect sense.

Dalton's poetry draws on his studies in Mesoamerican
anthropology and world history. The commitment to humanity
which is also evident in his work must certainly have been
influenced by his religious education; "like almost all revolutionaries," he once said, "I was educated in a Jesuit school."
Although Dalton considered the religious themes that surface
in his work to be vestiges of "the conflict that existed in
my youth between my revolutionary consciousness and my
Christian consciousness," his later poetry shows that while this
Christian consciousness might have merged with his revolutionary one, it never disappeared altogether. ("Los hongos"
[Mushrooms], a very long poem that Dalton worked on
between 1966 to 1972, is dedicated to Ernesto Cardenal, the
Nicaraguan revolutionary poet and Trappist monk, "as our
problem, a problem of Catholics and Communists"). As
Poemas clandestinos (Clandestine Poems), the title of one of
his most well-known collections of poems, makes clear, his
poetry was also conditioned by several periods of imprisonment and torture and by the nearly thirteen years spent in exile
and the secret returns to his homeland: "No confundir," he
wrote of himself and of the comrade-poets of the so-called
"Committed Generation," "somos poetas que escribimos desde
la clandestinidad en que vivimos" (Let's set the record straight:
we are poets who write from the clandestinity in which we
live), from "Sobre nuestra moral poética" [On Our Poetic
Morality]. Yet despite the harshness of the circumstances of
his life, Dalton never lost his almost child-like love for his
homeland and his people: "País mío vení /papaítopaísa solas
con tu sol / todo el frío del mundo me ha tocado a mí / y tu
sudando amor amor amor (Come to me, my country /
Daddyland, alone with your sun / Here I am feeling all the
cold in the world / and there you are sweating love love love),
from "Temores" [Fears].

Dalton's poetry is warm, tender, intimate, honest, self-paro-
dying and eminently human; it is telling that he should have
rejected Neruda (for being mechanical) in favour of the more
complex Vallejo. He was firmly committed to writing poetry
that was "beautiful" – indeed, what he wrote on aesthetics
shows that he was unwavering in his belief that a work of art
must not just serve a political function, but that it first and
foremost must be good as art. He regarded "the privilege
of beauty" to be but one more privilege that needed to be
expropriated from the bourgeoisie through class struggle. Nor
was all of his poetry purely political. Dalton was moderately
self-obsessed, and he himself was a common theme for his
work. This is evident in poems such as "Huelo mal" [I Stink],
"27 años" [27 Years Old], "Buscándome líos" [Looking for
Trouble] and "No siempre fui tan feo;" [I Wasn't Always
So Ugly]. (His face had borne the brunt of football injuries,

beatings in prison, an attack carried out on him during his lengthy exile in Prague – and, it is said, the odd punch meted out by a jealous husband or two). He also wrote a good deal of love poetry. Yet even in these poems Dalton is seeking to connect with others, to show that he was no different from anyone else, that, "Yo, como tú, / amo el amor, la vida, el dulce encanto / de las cosas . . .". (I, like you, / love love, life, the sweet enchantment / of things . . .".) (in "Como tú;" [Like You]). Finally, although his is often gallows humour, Dalton must surely rank as one of the funniest writers that Latin America has ever produced. His mastery of the pun and the subversive and his joyously carnivalesque qualities make the frequent comparisons with Brecht (whom Dalton admired enormously) fully warranted.

JENNY SHUBOW

Rubén Darío 1867–1916

Nicaraguan poet, prose writer and journalist

Most scholars would agree that the *modernista*s's search for originality in poetic expression, together with the forging of a Latin American project of intellectual autonomy so much discussed in the continent since Independence, was pushed forward with Rubén Darío. He, in a contradictory fashion, refused to be the head of a movement that none the less seized the imagination of writers in the American continent as well as in Spain. Darío provided a then stultified linguistic vehicle with renewed combinations of rhythm, rhyme and a richness of lexicon that reinvented the Spanish language, and made it more malleable to modern poetic practice. Thus the Spanish poet Gerardo Diego noted the liberating influence of the Nicaraguan poet in the Peninsula in the construction of a language endowed with an enhanced poetic expression suitable for the new generation's needs and aspirations to linguistic renovation.

Darío grounded the formal aspect of what he conceived as innovative in his poetic system on the abandonment of usual orderings and common clichés; on directing attention to interior melody in order to develop a successful rhythmic expression; on novelty in the choice of adjectives; on a careful study of the etymological meaning of the words; on the appropriate application of erudition and lexical refinement, and on appropriation and recasting of thematic and poetic concerns from French Symbolist, Parnassian, and Romantic poetics.

Darío's poetics embodied the *modernista* spirit, and spearheaded this movement which has been defined from different perspectives. For Federico de Onís, Spanish American *Modernismo* was the Hispanic form of the Western crisis of letters and spirit that began to take place around 1885 and ended during the second decade of the 20th century. For the Mexican poet, Octavio Paz, *Modernismo* is an erotics of language and a consciousness of linguistic expression. More recently another poet, José Emilio Pacheco, perceptively interpreted *Modernismo* as an attempt to break away from centuries of humiliation to begin a process of reconstruction and development similar to those of the main urban cultural centres in Western culture. It is in this context that Darío needs to be situated and read.

However, even closer to the present, the Uruguayan critic Ángel Rama asked a very pointed question: Why is it that Darío is still alive today, when his aesthetics has been abolished, and his ornate lexicon, themes and poetics superseded? Rama credits Darío with changing the perception of intellectual work by rejecting the view that art was merely expression; instead literature should be regarded as a process of rigorous intellectual engagement that required serious and arduous preparation. Darío was in Rama's words "the perfect example of this reevaluation of intellectual work that set a great divide" in Latin American literary history.

In addition, Darío is the best counter-example to the argument that only urban, cosmopolitan areas can be the site of innovation and change in Latin American culture. Born in Metapa, then a small town in a small Central American country, in a sense, marginal twice over, Darío mastered the poetic forms of the European literary tradition, ventured into the forms and themes of 19th-century European culture, and appropriated them for Spanish American literature. Although he wrote poems during his formative years, such as *Epístolas y poemas*, 1885 [Epistles and Poems], it is with the publication of *Azul*, 1888 [Blue] in Santiago de Chile, that *Modernismo* is recognized as a new artistic movement, a recognition that tended to blur partly the contribution of José Martí and Julián del Casal (Cuba), José Asunción Silva (Colombia) and Manuel Gutiérrez Nájera (Mexico) to *Modernismo*, a misreading that has been appropriately addressed by present-day literary criticism.

Jorge Luis Borges, in assessing the importance of Darío in Spanish American letters, enlightened Darío's contribution to his generation by stating that "Darío renovated everything: subject matter, vocabulary, meter, the magic of certain words, the poet's sensibility and that of the reader. Its flavour has not ceased and will never cease. Those of us who at some point rejected him now understand that we are his followers. We can call him the liberator." Without Darío, Spanish American turn-of-the-century literary production would not have achieved the originality and legitimization that it has today.

During his years in Santiago de Chile (June 1886 to February 1889) the young Darío explored a cornucopia of poetic possibilities: from the patriotic hymn, "Canto épico a las glorias de Chile," [Epic Song to the Glories of Chile] to romantic rhymes ("Oto-ñales") to satiric poems in (Abrojos [Thistles]) to the sensual poetry of Azul, as well as a successful incursion into the short story through widely acclaimed texts included in Azul, Darío's first important collection. Ángel Rama finds it useful to think of these poems as belonging to two different categories: one group are "realist poems" in which the poet ruminates over ideas about the world, and in the other "artistic poems," he constructs the world within its own contradictions.

Prosas profanas y otros poemas, 1896 (Prosas profanas and Other Poems) is his second great collection. It is a display of a sensually charged reading of culture new to Spanish American letters. Poems that made a mark as in the case of "Era un aire suave" (There Was a Softness in the Air). It was also a compendium of musical rhythms and metrical combinations not yet heard in Spanish, although Darío's mastery of versification came from the great poetry of the Spanish Medieval and Renaissance traditions, somewhat obscured by the decadence of the Spanish spirit in later centuries.

Cantos de vida y esperanza, 1905 [Songs of Life and Hope] continue the spirit and themes of Prosas profanas. This time, however, "it is the crisis of the aestheticism of Prosas profanas," comments Enrique Anderson Imbert. Darío's reflection on himself as a Spanish American poet, and as a man of his time, laconically remarks in the opening lines of this most moving book of poemas: "Yo soy aquel que ayer no más decía / el verso azul y la canción profana … (I am the one who only yesterday sang the blue verse and the profane song). These are poems of a mature poetic voice that has not renounced his earlier obsessions; rather, there is a reckoning of what must prevail from the poetic edifice he had constructed thus far. Darío envisioned the "selva sagrada" (sacred forest) as an all encompassing artifice that includes the world in its totality. The aspiration to a harmonious unity is the overriding force in this book; a force that was taken up by the poets that followed Darío, like the Mexican Octavio Paz.

El canto errante, 1907 [The Wandering Song] is preceded by one of the most lucid prologues, where he enunciates more explicitly than in the prologues to Prosas profanas and Cantos de vida y esperanza, his thoughts on poetry: "Poetic form will not disappear; it will expand, modify itself, following an ever-changing development in the eternal rhythm of the centuries." His other books of poems are Poema del otoño y otros poemas, 1910 [Autumn Poem and Other Poems], Canto a la Argentina y otros poemas, 1914 [Song to Argentina and Other Poems]; his prose collections include El mundo de los sueños, 1917 [The World of Dreams], La vida de Rubén Darío escrita por él mismo [The Life of Rubén Darío Written by Himself], Los raros, 1896 [The Eccentrics], España contemporánea, 1901 [Contemporary Spain], Letras, 1911 [Letters].

MAGDALENA GARCÍA PINTO

Biography

Born Félix Rubén García Sarmiento in Metapa, Nicaragua, 18 January 1867. Adopted the pseudonym Rubén Darío by 1880. Travelled to Chile, 1886 where he spent three years. This stay considerably broadened his intellectual horizons. Returned to Central America, 1889. Married Rafaela Contreras in 1890 (died 1892), one son; later married Francisca Sánchez, one son. Secretary of the Nicaraguan delegation for the celebration of the 400th anniversary of the discovery of American, Spain, 1892; Colombian consul in Buenos Aires, 1893–94; visited Paris, June 1893; journalist in Buenos Aires; visited Madrid, 1899; travelled to France and Italy, April 1900. Nicaraguan consul in Paris, 1903–07; secretary, Nicaraguan delegation at the Pan-American conference, Rio de Janeiro, 1906; correspondent for Latin American papers, such as La Nación (Buenos Aires) in various parts of Latin America as well as in Paris and Madrid; also served Guatemala in various diplomatic and representative functions. Led an increasingly dissipated life and died of cirrhosis of the liver in Nicaragua, 6 February 1916.

Selected Works

Poetry

Epístolas y poemas, Managua, Nicaragua: Tipografía Nacional, 1885

Abrojos, Santiago de Chile: Imprenta Cervantes, 1887

Azul, Valparaíso: Excélsior, 1888; revised and augmented edition, Guatemala: La Unión, 1890; "definitive" edition, Buenos Aires: Biblioteca de la Nacion, 1905

Prosas profanas y otros poemas, Buenos Aires: Imprenta Pablo E. Coni e hijos, 1896; revised edition, Paris: Charles Bouret, 1901; as Prosas profanas and Other Poems, translated by Charles B. McMichael, New York: Nicholas L. Brown, 1922

Cantos de vida y esperanza, "Los cisnes," y otros poemas, Madrid: Tipografía de la Revista de Archivos, Bibliotecas y Museos, 1905

El canto errante, Madrid: Pérez Villavicencio, 1907

Poema del otoño y otros poemas, Madrid: Biblioteca Ateneo, 1910

Canto a la Argentina y otros poemas, Madrid: Clásica Española, 1914

Sol del domingo: poesías ineditas, Madrid: Sucesores de Hernando, 1917

Other Writings

A. de Gilbert: biografía de Pedro Balmaceda, San Salvador: Imprenta Nacional, 1890

Los raros, Buenos Aires: Talleres de La Vasconia, 1896; revised and augmented edition, Barcelona: Maucci, 1905

Castelar, Madrid: B. Rodríguez Serra, 1899

Peregrinaciones, Paris: Charles Bouret, 1901

España contemporánea, Paris: Garnier Hermanos, 1901

La caravana pasa, Paris: Garnier Hermanos, 1902

Tierras solares, Madrid: Leonardo Williams, 1904

Opiniones, Madrid: Librería de Fernando Fe, 1906

El viaje a Nicaragua, Madrid: Biblioteca Ateneo, 1909

Todo al vuelo, Madrid: Renacimiento, 1912

La vida de Rubén Darío, escrita por el mismo, Barcelona: Maucci, 1916

Compilations and Anthologies

El mundo de los sueños: prosas póstumas, Madrid: Libreria de la Vivda de Pueyo, 1917 [journalism]

Obras completas, edited by Alberto Ghiraldo and Andrés González-Blanco, 21 vols, Madrid: Biblioteca Rubén Darío, 1923–29

Impresiones y sensaciones, edited by Alberto Ghiraldo, Madrid: Biblioteca Rubén Darío, 1925

Poesías completas, edited by Alfonso Méndez Plancarte, Madrid: Aguilar, 1952; revised edition, edited by Antonio Oliver Belmás, 2 vols, Madrid: Aguilar, 1967

Cartas de Rubén Darío: epistolario inédito, edited by Dictino Álvarez Hernández, Madrid: Taurus, 1963

Escritos dispersos, edited by Pedro Luis Barcia, 2 vols, La Plata: Universidad Nacional de La Plata, 1968–73

Cuentos fantásticos, edited by José Olivio Jiménez, Madrid: Alianza, 1979

Textos socio-políticos, edited by Jorge Eduardo Arellano and
Francisco Valle, Managua: Biblioteca Nacional, 1980
Cuentos, edited by José Emilio Balladares, San José, Costa Rica:
Libro Libre, 1986
Poesías inéditas, edited by Ricardo Llopesa, Madrid: Visor, 1988

Anthologies in Translation
Eleven Poems, translated by Thomas Walsh and Salomón de la
Selva, New York: Putnam, 1916
Selected Poems, translated by Lysander Kemp, Austin: University of
Texas Press, 1965

Further Reading
Anderson Imbert, Enrique, *La originalidad de Rubén Darío*, Buenos
Aires: Centro Editor de America Latina, 1967
Ellis, Keith, *Critical Approaches to Rubén Darío*, Toronto:
University of Toronto Press, 1974
Giordano, Jaime, *La edad de ensueño: sobre la imaginación poética
de Rubén Darío*, Santiago de Chile: Editorial Universitaria, 1971
Henríquez Ureña, Max, *Breve historia del Modernismo*, Mexico
City: Fondo de Cultura Económica, 1954
Ingwersen, Sonya A., *Light and Longing: Silva and Darío:
Modernism and Religious Heterodoxy*, New York: Peter Lang,
1986
Pacheco, José Emilio, prologue to *Antología del Modernismo,
1884–1921*, Mexico City: UNAM, 1970
Paz, Octavio, *Cuadrivio*, Mexico City: Joaquín Mortiz, 1965
Perus, Françoise, *Literatura y sociedad en America Latina: el
Modernismo*, Mexico City: Siglo XXI, 1976
Rama, Ángel, *Rubén Darío y el Modernismo (circunstancia
socioeconómica de un arte americano)*, Caracas: Biblioteca de la
Universidad Central de Venezuela, 1970
_____ Prologue to Rubén Darío, *Poesía*, Caracas: Biblioteca
Ayacucho, 1977
Salinas, Pedro, *La poesía de Rubén Darío*, 2nd edition, Buenos
Aires: Losada, 1957
Skryme, Raymond, *Rubén Darío and the Pythagorean Tradition*,
Gainesville: University Presses of Florida, 1975
Torres, Edelberto, *La dramática vida de Rubén Darío*, 6th edition,
San José, Costa Rica: EDUCA, 1982
Watland, Charles D., *Poet-Errant: a Biography of Rubén Darío*,
New York: Philosophical Library, 1965
Zavala, Iris M. (editor), *Rubén Darío: el Modernismo*, Madrid:
Alianza, 1989

Bibliographies
Arellano, Jorge Eduardo, *Bibliografía activa de Rubén Darío*,
Managua: Biblioteca Nacional Rubén Darío, 1981
Woodbridge, Hensley C., *Rubén Darío: a Selective Classified and
Annotated Bibliography*, Metuchen, New Jersey: Scarecrow Press,
1975

Nocturno XXXII

Poem from *Cantos de vida y esperanza* by
Rubén Darío

Nocturno
A Mariano de Cavia

Los que auscultasteis el corazón de la noche,
los que por el insomnio tenaz habéis oido
el cerrar de una puerta, el resonar de un coche
lejano, un eco vago, un ligero ruido. . .

En los instantes del silencio misterioso,
cuando surgen de su prisión los olvidados,
en la hora de los muertos, en la hora del reposo,
sabréis leer estos versos de amargor impregnados. . .

Como en un vaso vierto en ellos mis dolores
de lejanos recuerdos y desgracias funestas,
y las tristes nostalgias de mi alma, ebria de flores,
y el duelo de mi corazón, triste de fiestas.

Y el pensar de no ser lo que yo hubiera sido,
la pérdida del reino que estaba para mí,
el pensar que un instante pude no haber nacido,
y el sueño que es mi vida desde que yo nací.

Todo esto viene en medio del silencio profundo
en que la noche envuelve la terrena ilusión,
y siento como un eco del corazón del mundo
que penetra y conmueve mi propio corazón.

[You who have sounded the heart of the night / who,
gripped by insomnia, have heard, / a clicking door, a
rattling coach / a long way off, a muffled echo, the
merest sound . . .

In the instants of mysterious silence / when the forgotten
rise from their prisons / at the hour of the dead, at the
hour of repose / you will know how to read these lines
in bitterness steeped . . .

As though in a glass, I pour into them my sorrows / of
distant memories and grave misfortunes / and my soul,
light-headed on flowers, harks back sadly / and my heart
grieves jaded by pleasure

And I think how I am not / what I might have been /
the loss of the kingdom that was there for me / and the
thought that for an instant I might not have been born
/ and how my life has been a dream since my birth

All this comes in the midst of the deepest silence / in
which night envelops earthly illusion / and I feel like an
echo of the world's heart / that pierces and moves my
own heart.]

There is an apparent irony in the fact that this poem is dedicated to Mariano de Cavia, a well known Spanish journalist
of the period (that is the first decade of the 20th century) who
specialized in articles on linguistic refinements and subtleties.
This is because although the poem shows Darío at the heights
of his powers (*Cantos de vida y esperanza* was published in
1905), it is also, with one exception, written in rather plain
language. Not, of course, that this "Nocturno" is simple in
technical terms; on the contrary, translating it reveals the extent
of the poet's technical confidence and competence. However,
what stands out here is that for Darío the period of defamil-
iarizing the language of literature in Spanish is over. There are
no verbal pyrotechnics, no imported, exotic language; gone are
the excesses (including the kitsch) of *Azul* and *Prosas profanas*.
Within the new plain(er) language there is one term taken from
scientific discourse that stares out threateningly from the first
line. This is the verb *auscultar*, to auscultate in English,
although it has been rendered in the translation of the poem
by the unscientific "to sound," since the more learned term

would never be used by a doctor when addressing a patient in the English-speaking world. But it is important to take due note of this scientific term because it shows that Darío in his maturity is still experimenting with language and, in this respect, despite the poem's old-fashioned confessional tone, is moving towards the avant-garde. A few years later – in 1913 – Stravinsky was to shock to the core a Parisian audience with his ballet *The Rite of Spring*, in which rhythm dominates over melody and harmony; in 1917, T.S. Eliot challenged conventional "poetic" language by the use, again, of a scientific term im his poem "The Love Song of J. Alfred Prufrock." This is where he writes: "Let us go then, you and I, when the evening is spread out against the sky / Like a patient etherised upon a table." Darío too is experimenting, not only with words but with silence, suggested here by the use of unfinished lines that leave the interlocutor(s) to work out, as in a casual conversation, what has been left unsaid.

The title, "Nocturno," is an apparently straightforward verbal sign denoting a dreamy and gentle musical composition appropriate to the night. In the still night the poet establishes at once an intimacy with his readers or interlocutors by assuming that they will empathize with him: "Los que auscultásteis el corazón de la noche." They too, in their maturity, will have experienced insomnia and this type of sadness, provoked by an awareness of past indulgence and squandered talent. Where *is* the poet? Granted that Darío is talking to us in such a relaxed manner, we want to know where the conversation takes place, but the information is withheld, for the poem is not anecdotal and the poet is indifferent to local colour. The setting, though, is urban and, like the verb of the first line, this is potentially alienating granted the poet's hostility to modern bourgeois society.

The poem, in keeping with its title, is intensely musical, something else that emerges clearly when a translation is attempted. A strong, almost compulsive rhythm is established, one that is based on inner rhymes (line 4), on enjambment, that is, of running one line straight into the next one (lines 3–4 of the poem), the use of alliteration and of the repetition of often plain words and their cognates : *pensar; nacer / nacido; triste*, and the most dominant of all, the beating heart. By the time Darío wrote this "Nocturno," the dissipated life to which he alludes in it was undermining his health and death, or *Ella* (She) as he often referred to it, began to haunt him; so it is not surprising that the spirit of the dead, rising from their graves, should be evoked in the second stanza. The dreamlike quality of the traditional nocturne is thus disturbed by powerful, dark emotions.

Like many other poems by Darío, this "Nocturno" is a much quoted classic and phrases from it such as the opening line and "triste de fiestas," are as well known in the Spanish-speaking world as certain lines from Shakespeare's sonnets. Yet its modernity prevents it from being a safe, conventional poem. Exasperated by the sillier excesses of Spanish American *Modernismo*, the Mexican poet Enrique González Martínez exclaimed: "Tuércele el cuello al cisne" (Twist the swan's neck), a remark aimed at Darío who used swans consistently in his poetry in either a decorative or a thoughtful way. Arguably, though, in a poem like this "Nocturno," Darío was engaged in throttling his own swan.

VERITY SMITH

See also entries on Julián del Casal, Manuel Gutiérrez Nájera, José Martí, Modernismo: Spanish America, José Asunción Silva

Editions

First edition: *Cantos de vida y esperanza. "Los cisnes" y otros poemas*, Madrid: Tipografía de la Revista de Archivos, Bibliotecas y Museos, 1905

Critical edition: *Azul . . . Cantos de vida y esperanza*, edited by J. María Martínez, Madrid: Cátedra, 1995

Note: There appears to be no translation of this collection – an unlikely gap.

Del Paso, Fernando

See Paso

René Depestre 1926–

Haitian poet and prose writer

René Depestre, the most celebrated contemporary Haitian poet, has spent most of his adult life in political exile. But, despite his absence from his native island, he remains essentially Haitian, identifying with his deprived countrymen, unrelentingly returning to the mythology of his heritage and expressing the obsessive, often painful memories, associated with his homeland. His early literary career was dedicated to the cause of socialist humanism and Haiti's liberation from oppression. Jacques Roumain had a profound impact on his political thinking and poetic inspiration, as on most of the intellectuals of Depestre's generation.

From his first revolutionary volume of verse, *Étincelles*, 1945 [Sparks], published at the age of nineteen, Depestre demonstrated his commitment to the restoration of his people's dignity and to all the oppressed of the world. Heir of ardent Haitian patriots such as Makandal, Louverture, Dessalines and Roumain, Depestre became the leading voice for the radical young generation, expressing his bitterness and rage for his country's exploitation and deprivation. But his communist orientation, and his use of poetry as a vehicle for his politics forced him to exile. Indeed, for Depestre, the intellectual's responsibility is to dispense knowledge to the masses and to give them hope by initiating revolt. In linking poetry and revolution, he developed a new literary radicalism. After the failed student revolution of 1946, Depestre was exiled in France. Later, in 1958, he chose to live in Cuba, then in France again when Haiti yielded to the excesses of the Duvalier dictatorships.

Traduit du grand large, 1952 [Translated from the High Sea] is a volume of poetry written during Depestre's Cuban exile. It is a long and devastating song relating the miseries of his handcuffed island and of the whole planet under the maddening North American imperialist violence. But as the poet unfolds the world map of racism and oppression, he also depicts a magnificent portrait of a liberated humanity, inspired by the example of socialist countries where the people have overthrown the dictatorship of injustice, hunger and illiteracy.

In *Minerai noir*, 1956 [Black Ore], the poet exposes the plight of Blacks reduced, as the title reveals, to objects of material exploitation. In this poem, Depestre expresses painful memories of his homeland, personified as a female captive: she is a zombi, an essential figure of dispossession in Haitian mythology. Depestre's poetic inspiration reveals the tension between his unattainable, mythic past and his present sense of alienation, between his individual quest and his visceral attachment to his lost land. This tension is most evident in his subsequent collection of poetry, *Journal d'un animal marin*, 1964 [Diary of a Marine Animal] where the poet must confront his permanent condition of exile, reexamine his life of errancy, and consider the problematics of being elsewhere. His sense of alienation leads him to reevaluate his identity as necessarily an unstable composite of elements, as a constant process of transformation.

Pursuing his political reflections in his poem, *Un Arc-en-ciel pour l'Occident chrétien*, 1967 (*A Rainbow for the Christian West*), Depestre attests to the great wrath that shakes the foundations of the world. The poet is a "new Negro" who is proud of his disruptive marooning powers. He is able to conjure up the fighting divinities of Haitian Voodoo mythology as well as the great revolutionary heroes of the past. But the poet-hougan becomes powerless when at the end of his crusade he encounters a neo-colonial world ready to sacrifice humanity with "atomic gods" to economic greed. Only wisdom and goodwill of all peoples may save humanity from barbarity and hatred. The poet's anger has transcended and transformed itself into a song of love and hope.

The question of race and origins determined Depestre's political vision. Early, he rejected the concept of Indigenism and *Négritude* – the latter transformed to "noirisme" by François Duvalier in support of his fascist politics – for a universal authenticity. Along with several members of the short-lived *Haïti Littéraire* – such as Anthony Phelps, Jacques-Stéphen Alexis, René Philoctète, Franck Étienne – Depestre shifted from the notion of a timeless Haitian essence or cultural authenticity to the concept of an open-ended, ever-changing cultural identity. "I have a whole system of roots . . . I have multiple identities," he said in a 1992 interview. His collection of essays entitled *Bonjour et adieu à la négritude*, 1980 [Hello and Goodbye to Negritude], reflects the poet's rejection of the ideology of authenticity and his urge to liberate aesthetics by demythifying the process of literary creation.

In *Le Mât de cocagne* (*The Festival of the Greasy Pole*), Depestre, satirizing the Duvalier regime, violently criticizes the axioms of the *Négritude* ideology. However, *Poète à Cuba*, 1976 [Poet in Cuba], dedicated to the great writer Jacques-Stéphen Alexis, tortured and murdered by François Duvalier's henchmen, marks a turning point in Depestre's ideological commitment. The poet is still dedicated to the "dezombification" of his people (i.e., their liberation from bondage), but he redefines the revolution through an exploration of his erotic obsessions and anxieties. He attempts to comprehend himself and his transitory world through a celebration of woman, a composite muse who takes him far away from his revolutionary project. He transforms the political into the erotic.

In this respect, *Alléluia pour une femme-jardin* [Hallelujah for a Garden-Woman, first published in Cuba in 1973 and reprinted in France in 1981] articulates Depestre's new paradoxical pursuit. His search for the lost Eden, his need to repossess the beauty of his native land, becomes embodied in a long list of beautiful women to be possessed and lost, or simply disposed of. In this collection of stories the writer articulates the use and abuse of woman's image in the Caribbean through what he calls his "géolibertinage."

The myth of the island woman as the vessel of his sexual vigor remains Depestre's obsession in his two subsequent volumes. In *Hadriana dans tous mes rêves*, 1988 [Hadriana in All My Dreams], he reimagines, through the technique of magical realism, the marvelous realm of his native Jacmel. The confusion between reality and the imaginary leads to an allegorical representation of the mystery of woman. His last published volume, *Éros dans un train chinois*, 1993 [Eros in a Chinese Train], expresses through an aesthetic that Depestre calls "erotico-magical realism," his boundless love for women of different cultures, their beauty and fertility. Unfortunately, his image of the female tends to represent a new kind of exploitation.

With his erotic imagination, Depestre attempts to apprehend the world and to recreate a liberated, triumphant Haiti. If Depestre has succeeded in transcending the narrowness of his national identity to embrace a world perspective on erotic ecosystems, his revolutionary projects in socialist and militant humanism belong to a lost past.

MARIE-AGNÈS SOURIEAU

Biography

Born in Jacmel, Haiti, 29 August 1926. Attended the Lycée Pinchinat, Jacmel, and the Lycée Pétion, Port-au-Prince, 1939–44; the Sorbonne and the Institut d'Études Politiques, University of Paris, 1946–51. Journalist in Haiti, various Latin American countries, and Cuba; co-founder, with Jacques Stephen Alexis of the Haitian Communist Party. Participated in the Haitian Revolution in 1946; imprisoned, then expelled from Haiti in 1946; expelled twice from France, once from Cuba, then lived in Chile, Argentina, and Brazil, 1951–55. Married Edith Sorel in 1950 (divorced 1961). Returned to Haiti in 1958; moved to Cuba in 1959 where he was a teacher and editor until 1978. Married Nelly Campano in 1962, with whom he has two sons. Worked for Ministry of External Relations, National Cultural Council, and Radio Havana; expelled from Cuba in 1978; member of the Secretariat, 1979–86, attaché to the Office of the Director General, 1979–82, and to the Office of Culture, 1982–86, UNESCO, Paris. Became French citizen in 1991. Awarded the Goncourt Prize, 1982; Société des Gens de Lettres Prize, 1988; Académie Royale Prize (Belgium), 1988.

Selected Works

Poetry

Étincelles, Port-au-Prince: Imprimerie de l'État, 1945
Gerbe de sang, Port-au-Prince: Imprimerie de L'État, 1946
Végétations de clarté, Paris: Seghers, 1951; as *Vegetations of Splendor*, translated by Jack Hirschman, Chicago: Vanguard, 1981
Minerai noir, Paris: Présence Africaine, 1956

Journal d'un animal marin, Paris: Seghers, 1964
Un Arc-en-ciel pour l'Occident chrétien, Paris: Présence Africaine, 1967; as *A Rainbow for the Christian West*, translated by Jack Hirschman, Fairfax, California: Red Hill Press, 1972
Cantate d'octobre à la vie et à la mort du commandant Ernesto Che Guevara, Havana: Instituto del Libro, 1968; revised edition, Algiers: SNED, 1969
Poète à Cuba, Paris: Oswald, 1976
En État de poésie, Paris: Les Éditeurs Français Réunis, 1980
Journal d'un animal marin: choisi de poèmes, 1956–1990, Paris: Gallimard, 1990
Au Matin de la négritude, Luxembourg: Euroeditor, 1990
Anthologie personnelle: poésie, Arles: Actes Sud, 1993

Novels

Le Mât de cocagne, Paris: Gallimard, 1979; as *The Festival of the Greasy Pole*, translated by Carrol F. Coates, Charlottesville: University Press of Virginia, 1990
Alléluia pour une femme-jardin, Paris: Gallimard, 1982
Hadriana dans tous mes rêves, Paris: Gallimard, 1988
Éros dans un train chinois: neuf histoires d'amour et un conte de sorcier, Paris: Gallimard, 1990

Other Writings

Por la revolución, por la poesía, Havana: Instituto del Libro, 1969; as *Pour la Révolution, pour la poésie*, Montreal: Leméac, 1974
Influencia del África en las literaturas antillanas, in collaboration with Henry Bangou and George Lamming, Montevideo: ILAC, 1972
Problemas de la indentidad del hombre negro en las literaturas antillanas, Mexico City: UNAM, 1978
Bonjour et adieu à la négritude: travaux d'identité, Paris: Laffont, 1980

Further Reading

Dayan, Joan, "'Hallelujah for a Garden-Woman': the Caribbean Adam and His Pretext," *French Review* (March 1986)
Ferdinand, Joseph, "The New Political Statement in Haitian Fiction," in *Voices from Under: Black Narrative in Latin America and the Caribbean*, edited by William Luis, Westport, Connecticut: Greenwood Press, 1984
Kundera, Milan, "The Umbrella, the Night World and the Lonely Moon," in *The New York Review* (19 December 1991)
Levilain, Guy Viêt, *Cultural Identity, Négritude, and Decolonization: the Haitian Situation in the Light of the Socialist Humanism of Jacques Roumain and René Depestre*, New York: American Institute for Marxist Studies, 1978

Detective Fiction

Although Latin American writers are not prolific when it comes to producing detective fiction, the region is the source of a significant body of works that follows or plays with the conventional formulas of the British whodunit and North American hard-boiled narrative. The development of the genre in Latin America is governed in large part by a marketplace saturated with translations from abroad. Publishers often have been reluctant to support native authors, since foreign works are cheaper to produce and their sales are easier to predict. That circumstance has changed in some respects since the 1970s due to shifting views of what constitutes literary expression. The genre has flourished, for example, in post-revolutionary Cuba, and in Argentina the lowbrow status of the hard-boiled model lent itself to the form's use in questioning official discourses of authority. Despite these recent developments, the detective fiction sections of bookstores from Mexico City to Buenos Aires continue to be dominated by Agatha Christie novels and the like in Spanish and Portuguese.

Latin America's detective fiction is best characterized by a sense of estrangement, resistance, and invention. The genre evolves there as if it were itself a mystery, not to be solved, but rather explored. The aim is not mastery, as Sherlock Holmes would have it, but rather elaboration. Because of its origins and ideological perspective, the genre is, in a sense, an unusually visible reminder of the phantom hand that rests on Latin America's shoulders, the imperial grip that defines a colonized reality. The imported genre is an incongruent model that demands to be scrutinized. As such, detective fiction functions also as an invitation to reinvention. The formulas of the two main detective fiction models – the tidy, British murder puzzle and the more violent and variable hard-boiled tale associated with the United States – are ideologically and culturally loaded tropes that provoke. As might be expected, strictly formulaic detective fiction is relatively rare in Latin America, as are serial writers. The constraints of the genre and the discouragements of the market create an environment where authors are less likely to satisfy conventions than they are to experiment with them.

Latin America's centers of detective fiction writing are Argentina, Brazil, Cuba and Mexico. Other countries, especially Chile, Colombia and Peru, have also produced notable texts. The earliest works are from Argentina and date from the late 19th-century, only a few decades after what is generally regarded as the birth of the genre with the publication of Edgar Allan Poe's "Murders in the Rue Morgue" (1841). Outside of Argentina, detective fiction does not emerge significantly until the 1920s. Throughout Latin America, detective fiction has been cultivated by some of the region's leading intellectuals and public figures. Among those contributing to the genre are: in the River Plate, Eduardo Ladislao Holmberg, Horacio Quiroga, Jorge Luis Borges, Adolfo Bioy Casares, Enrique Anderson Imbert, Marco Denevi, Osvaldo Soriano and Ricardo Piglia; in Brazil, Afrânio Peixoto, Maximiniano Coelho Neto, Jorge Amado, João Guimarães Rosa, Rubem Fonseca; in Cuba, Lino Novás Calvo; and in Mexico, Rodolfo Usigli, José Emilio Pacheco, Jorge Ibargüengoitia, Vicente Leñero. In Colombia and Peru respectively, Gabriel García Márquez and Mario Vargas Llosa are significant cultivators of the genre.

The absence of women on these lists is consistent with the gendered history of literary culture in Latin America. Two other aspects help to explain women's relative absence from the field. First is the historical record that finds the British whodunit model to be the one most cultivated by women authors anywhere until late in the 20th century. That precedent, however, is set in another context. The whodunit's potential to inspire is undermined by the difficulty evident throughout the history of the genre in Latin America of adapting the model to another register. The strongest detective fiction by women writers there emerges as an expression of an oppositional voice. Like Latin American literature in general, most detective fiction that reaches the reading public is produced by representatives of the dominant, white, male society, although these authors often use the form to question

some of the values and attitudes that affirm that culture. Among the few women who have experimented with the genre are: from Argentina, Silvina Ocampo, María Angélica Bosco, Syria Poletti, Angélica Gorodischer, Gloria Pampillo; from Brazil, Maria Alice Barroso; and from Mexico, María Elvira Bermúdez.

Apart from the few formulaic works produced in Latin America, and the Cuban post-revolutionary genre, the region's detective fiction typically falls into three categories: parody, documentary narrative, and anti-detective fiction. These three modes or intentions frequently occur together as well, in various combinations. An example of parody is Glauco Rodrigues Corrêa's *Crime na baia sul*, 1980 (*The South Bay Crime*), which pokes fun at Brazilian paternalism and provincialism, while also satirizing the whodunit formula by questioning its crime-to-official solution inevitability. An example of the fusion of detective and documentary fiction is Rodolfo Walsh's *Operación masacre*, 1957 [Operation Massacre]. Here, the author incorporates detective fiction devices into a text that attempts to document an extralegal execution that the Argentine government denies ever occurred. The conventions that entertain by producing suspense are engaged here instead for the purpose of challenging and denouncing. The "solution" to Walsh's mystery is knowledge and committment to social change. In Vicente Leñero's anti-detective novel *Los albañiles*, 1963 [The Bricklayers], the solution is eliminated altogether. The principle of closure is replaced by an overwhelming sense of duplicity generated by the hierarchical structure that, for Leñero, describes Mexican culture. One final group of works of detective fiction from Latin America are the Cuban texts that emerge in the post-revolutionary period. These are intended to promote the values of the Revolution, and they often lose out in the translation of a genre steeped in capitalist tradition. Some authors, however, have been successful in exploiting conventional strategies while projecting a socialist perspective. Among these are Ignacio Cárdenas Acuña, Juan Ángel Cardi, and Arnaldo Correa.

AMELIA SIMPSON

Further Reading

General

Simpson, Amelia, *Detective Fiction from Latin America*, Rutherford, New Jersey: Fairleigh Dickinson Press, 1990 [This comprehensive study of the genre in Latin America gives an historical overview followed by an analysis of selected texts]

Simpson, Amelia, (editor and translator), *New Tales of Mystery and Crime from Latin America*, Rutherford, New Jersey: Fairleigh Dickinson Press, 1992 [An introduction that discusses the genre and introduces the eight stories that follow. These are from Argentina, Mexico, Brazil, and Cuba. Authors include Ricardo Piglia, Ignácio de Loyola Brandão, and Rubem Fonseca. Most are published here for the first time in English]

Sklodowska, Elzbieta, *La parodia en la nueva novela latinoamericana (1960–1985)*, Amsterdam and Philadelphia: Benjamins, 1991 [Chapter 5 is on varieties of detective fiction]

Argentina

Hernández Martín, Jorge, *Readers and Labyrinths. Detective Fiction in Borges, Bustos Domecq, and Eco*, New York: Garland, 1995

Lafforgue, Jorge and Jorge B. Rivera (editors), *Asesinos de papel*, Buenos Aires: Calicanto, 1977 [This important anthology includes introductory remarks about detective fiction in Argentina, a series of observations about the genre by Jorge Luis Borges, Marco Denevi, Ricardo Piglia and others, and stories by authors such as Horacio Quiroga, Leonardo Castellani, Velmiro Ayala Gauna and Adolfo Pérez Zelaschi]

Rivera, Jorge B. (editor), *El relato policial en la Argentina*, Buenos Aires: Eudeba, 1986 [A valuable introduction by Rivera is followed by stories by seven writers including Rodolfo J. Walsh, Juan Carlos Martini and Eduardo Goligorsky. The authors' responses to written interview questions are also included]

Brazil

Amâncio, Moacir (editor), *Chame o ladrão: Contos policiais brasileiros*, São Paulo: Edições Populares, 1978 [The introduction to this anthology angrily protests social conditions in Brazil, and the stories, which are examples of detective fiction broadly defined, support that view]

Medeiros e Albuquerque, Paulo de, *O mundo emocionante do romance policial*, Rio de Janeiro: Francisco Alves, 1979 [The book focuses on the foreign detective fiction Brazilians mostly read. There is one chapter, however, on detective fiction written by Brazilians]

Cuba

Navarro, Desiderio, "La novela policial y la literatura artística," in *Cultura y marxismo: problemas y polémicas*, Havana: Letras Cubanas, 1986

____ "Aspectos comunicacionales de la literatura masiva. El caso de la novela policial en la América Latina," in *Ejercicios del criterio*, Havana: Unión, 1989

Nogueras, Luis Rogelio, *Por la novela policial*, Havana: Unión, 1982 [This thoughtful, short book argues for the genre's validity in a post-capitalist setting, and analyzes some specific texts]

Mexico

Torres, Vicente Francisco, *El cuento policial mexicano*, Mexico City: Diógenes, 1982 [This anthology of Mexican detective stories by authors such as Antonio Helú, María Elvira Bermúdez, and Pepe Martínez de la Vega includes a useful, historical introduction]

Augusto D'Halmar 1882(?)–1950

Chilean prose writer

Augusto D'Halmar began his literary career in Chile in the early 1900s and quickly gained prominence as one of the country's foremost writers. His works reflect the influence of several different literary movements in Latin America, including Naturalism, Spanish American Modernism, and Vanguardism. He was also an avid reader and follower of such authors as Tolstoy, Oscar Wilde, Alphonse Daudet, and Pierre Loti, among others, whose style is evident throughout his works. He was such an avid admirer of Tolstoy that he even established a short-lived Tolstoyan agricultural colony. He was the recipient of the first National Literature Prize awarded in Chile (1942). Both his works and his adventurous life as a traveler and foreign diplomat helped to create a sort of mystique about him throughout Chile, aided by a twenty-six year absence from the country.

D'Halmar's first work was the Naturalist novel *Juana Lucero, o los vicios de Chile*, 1902 [Juana Lucero, or the Vices of Chile]. Both the topic and the style of the novel were greatly influenced by Émile Zola's novel *Nana* (1880). *Juana Lucero* is the story of a young girl who falls prey to prostitution and societal prejudice and eventually dies a tragic death. It is not the author's most memorable text. However, it is important for having introduced Naturalism to Chilean letters, and it provoked considerable debate throughout Chilean society. The novel also predated more lasting Latin American Naturalist novels of the time that took up the prostitute-as-heroine theme such as *Santa* (1903) by the Mexican Federico Gamboa, and *Nacha Regules* (1919) by the Argentine writer Manuel Gálvez.

D'Halmar is best known as a novelist, but he is also the author of numerous short stories that can best be characterized as marking the period of transition between Naturalism and Modernism in Chile. After *Juana Lucero*, the author abandoned his adhesion to the stricter tenets of Naturalism and introduced many elements of the fantastic into his stories. Of all the author's short stories, two in particular express his mastery of this genre. Both "En provincia" [In the Provinces] and "A rodar tierras" [Rolling Across the Land], demonstrate the author's superb narrative ability. Imbued with suspense, fantasy, and a complex psychological portrayal of the protagonists, "En provincia" is considered by Mario Ossea as one of the best short stories in Chilean literature. It is a tale about adultery in a small town in southern Chile told in the first person by the narrator, a lonely bachelor used by his boss's wife to give her the child that her husband could not. "A rodar tierras" is an allegorical tale that is much more fantastic in nature, and it is said to have been influenced by Hans Christian Andersen. The story narrates the history of a piece of thistle-down that errantly blows across the land. The narrative voice is seemingly directed toward a juvenile audience. The author employs the simple tones and narrative style characteristic of children's literature. None the less, the story is a telling allegory of man's wandering upon the earth, and of life's lack of direction or meaning. The story is actually quite reflective of D'Halmar's own life story and was in fact considered by the author to be his only and best autobiography, as he himself makes clear in "Cuento como cuento un cuento" [Telling How I Tell a Tale].

With *La lámpara en el molino*, 1914 [The Lamp in the Mill], D'Halmar further abandoned the limitations of realism which confined his earlier works. *La lámpara* makes use of a far more poetic language, of surreal imagery, and the imaginative presentation of people, places, and events that go beyond the merely descriptive confines of realist prose. Evident in the text is an effort to seek out beauty, lyricism, and the metaphysical. *Imaginismo* as it was called, was in part the heir of Modernism, but D'Halmar is largely held responsible for initiating this literary style into Chilean letters. Subsequent writers who carried on this tradition include Pedro Prado and María Luisa Bombal. *La lámpara* is based on the events surrounding the controversial courtship and marriage of D'Halmar's sister.

D'Halmar's early works are all representative of Chilean reality in that the places, people, and customs all tend to be taken directly from the national environment and from his own personal experiences. However, the works of the second phase of his production differ greatly in that they were all conceived and written during his twenty-six year absence from the country. D'Halmar's travels and employment as a Chilean diplomat literally took him around the globe. The exotic places, people, and experiences he encountered became the subject matter of his books. His residence in Spain led to his most famous novel, *La pasión y muerte del cura Deusto*, 1924 [The Passion and Death of Father Deusto], and his collection of essays, *La Mancha de Don Quijote*, 1934 [Don Quixote's La Mancha], based on that famous region of Spain, home to one of literature's most memorable characters. In *Mi otro yo*, 1924 [My Other Self], D'Halmar uses India as the backdrop for the novel, giving very lengthy and detailed descriptions of the country and customs of the people. The novel itself is not a very tidy narration, but is does give insight into the author's passion for exotic travel and adventure.

D'Halmar enjoyed great success as an author during his lifetime. He came to be one of the most influential of 20th-century Chilean writers; his texts were widely read, reprinted, and used as models for younger writers. Although he played such an important role in the history of Chilean letters, both the author and his works for the most part have remained forgotten for the past thirty years. Recently, however, there has been a renewal of interest in his writing because of the open treatment of homoerotic themes found throughout the majority of his texts. In the past this topic, as well as the author's own homosexuality, conveniently had been glossed over, mentioned in highly euphemistic terms, or neatly explained away by most critics, in spite of an often overt textual presence. Indeed, as David Foster has demonstrated, at least ten of D'Halmar's works deal either directly or indirectly with homosexuality and largely involve older male/younger male relationships that inevitably end in tragedy. The work that most openly addresses this issue, *La pasión y muerte del cura Deusto*, contains all the characteristics of a tragic love story. The novel was written during the author's residence in Spain, and it takes place in Seville. The basic plot revolves around the personal conflict between religiosity and homosexual desire as experienced by a Basque priest who finds himself overwhelming attracted to an Andalusian boy. His desire eventually leads him to commit suicide rather than succumb to his physical yearnings and a love that must not be. *La pasión y muerte* is also the author's best novel in terms of narrative style, structure, and

the psychological development of the characters. For Ramón Acevedo it is the most complex and original Modernist novel of Hispanic America, although it was published quite some time after the zenith of Modernism. Other texts by D'Halmar dealing with homosexuality include *La sombra de humo en el espejo*, 1924 [The Shadow of Smoke in the Mirror] and *Nirvana* (1918), both autobiographical in nature in which the author recounts his travels in the Orient, the Far East, and Europe and his experiences with servant boys and guides. A third text, *Los alucinados*, 1935 [The Hallucinated], is a collection of four short stories all dealing with male homosexual relationships.

DARRELL B. LOCKHART

Biography

Born Augusto Geommine Thomson in Santiago de Chile on 23 April 1882(?). Illegitimate son of a French adventurer and merchant captain, Auguste Geommine, and of Manuela Thomson Cross, only child of a distinguished lady of Scottish ancestry, Juana Cross. D'Halmar much affected by his illegitimacy granted the high social standing of his mother's family. Childhood spent in Valparaíso on the coast in the home of his maternal grandmother. Brought up in female household; pampered; lacked a male role model. Had two sisters after his mother married, but latter died young. Returned to Santiago where he attended school. This was an unhappy experience, and he had to endure the nickname "Margarita." Able to live by his pen as a journalist because his grandmother supplemented his income. In 1903 he decided to establish a Tolstoyan colony with two friends. This ended in 1905 since they were not able to adapt to a simple, agricultural life. Stayed in the country at San Bernardo where he worked in a very modest capacity at the railway station. Joined there by his grandmother and sisters. Idyllic period of his life. In 1907 became consul general in Calcutta after travelling widely in Europe. Left India after a few months because of ill health. Consul in Etén on the north coast of Peru. Returned to Chile in 1915 and then became war correspondent for Buenos Aires newspaper, *La Nación*. Travelled to France in 1917. Wounded at front and almost died from septicemia. Recovered and settled in Madrid in 1918 where he spent the next 16 years. Felt very much at home in Spain but returned to Chile in 1934 where he was greeted with enthusiasm. First writer to be awarded Chilean National Prize for Literature after its creation in 1942. Died of cancer of the throat on 27 January 1950.

Selected Works

Juana Lucero, o los vicios de Chile, Desterrados del ideal y de la suerte no despertéis al que sueña, Santiago de Chile: Imprenta Turín, 1902
La lámpara en el molino, Santiago de Chile: Imprenta New York, 1914
Gatita, Santiago de Chile: Imprenta Universitaria, 1917
Nirvana, Barcelona: Casa Editorial Maucci, 1918 [travel book]
Mi otro yo, Madrid: Ediciones de la Novela Semanal, 1924
La sombra del humo en el espejo, Madrid: Editora Internacional, 1924 [Volume about his travels in Europe, Egypt and the Far East]
La pasión y muerte del cura Deusto, Madrid: Editora Internacional, 1924
La Mancha de Don Quijote, Santiago de Chile: Ercilla, 1934
Capitanes sin barco, Santiago de Chile: Ercilla, 1934
Los alucinados, Santiago de Chile: Ercilla, 1935

Compilations and Anthologies

Cristián y yo, Santiago de Chile: Nascimento, 1946

Further Reading

Acevedo, Ramón L., *Augusto D'Halmar: novelista (estudio de "Pasión y muerte del cura Deusto")*, San Juan, Puerto Rico: Editorial Universitaria, 1976 [An excellent analysis of D'Halmar's most famous text, which also provides insights into his other works. Places the author's work within the framework of Spanish American Modernism]

Díaz Arrieta, Hernán, "Augusto D'Halmar," in his *Los cuatro grandes de la literatura chilena durante el siglo XX*, Santiago de Chile: Zig-Zag, 1962

Espinoza, Enrique, "El hermano errante," prologue to *Antología de Augusto D'Halmar*, Santiago de Chile: Zig-Zag, 1963

Foster, David William, *Gay and Lesbian Themes in Latin American Writing*, Austin: University of Texas Press, 1991

Foster, Stephen Wayne, "Latin American Studies," *Cabiron and Gay Books Bulletin* 11 (1984)

Muñoz Medina, Guillermo, "La generación de 1900 y Augusto G. Thomson," *Atenea* 135 (1935)

Orlandi, Julio and Alejandro Ramírez, *Augusto D'Halmar: obra-estilo-técnica*, Santiago de Chile: Editorial del Pacífico, 1942

Ossea, Mario, "Sobre siete cuentos maestros de la literatura chilena," *Atenea*, vol. 25 (1948)

Urbistondo, Vicente, "Augusto D'Halmar" in *El naturalismo en la novela chilena*, Santiago de Chile: Andrés Bello, 1955

Villanueva, Alfredo, "Augusto D'Halmar," in *Latin American Writers on Gay and Lesbian Themes: a Bio-Critical Sourcebook*, edited by David William Foster, Westport, Connecticut: Greenwood Press, 1994

Dias, Antônio Gonçalves

See Gonçalves Dias

Eliseo Diego 1920–1994

Cuban poet, prose writer and literary translator

One of modern Cuba's most renowned authors, Eliseo Diego began his literary career as a member of the Orígenes group of poets. Writers like Ángel Gaztelu, Cintio Vitier, Fina García Marruz, Gastón Baquero, Virgilio Piñera, Justo Rodríguez Santos, Octavio Smith and others, gathered around the journal (*Orígenes*) founded by poetic oracle José Lezama Lima to practice what Roberto Fernández Retamar (1954) has designated *trascendentalismo*, that is, the aesthetic of distancing oneself from surrounding reality to pursue metaphysical explorations through a cosmopolitan and frequently complex baroque style. Diego, however, represents within the group a visionary clarity and an attachment to relatively simple forms that transform him into something of an anomaly. In her excellent preface to the Uruguayan edition of *Divertimentos y versiones*, 1967 [Divertimentos and Versions], Ida Vitale clarifies this contradiction when she emphasizes that Diego "does not appear to have been overtaken by the Surrealist torrent that captivated and defined Labrador Ruiz or Lezama Lima." Instead, Diego exudes a false *naïveté* based on a literary attitude permanently attached to a sense of wonderment when confronting the most trivial matters. A prolific writer, he reflects as well a remarkable thematic continuity throughout his ample literary production. Love, death, tedium, nostalgia and, above all, time reappear insatiably to promote what Vitale has called the "trama unitaria" [unitarian structure] of his works. As a result, Diego at times seems reiterative, monotonous and, paradoxically, somewhat dense despite his characteristic tonal and stylistic simplicity, a writer whose poetry and prose must be absorbed in small dosages.

Despite Vitale's assertions, Diego is firmly entrenched within the artistic taste of the *Orígenes* generation. Cintio Vitier (1970) has argued correctly that Lezama Lima's creative family, over which he presided for decades as paternalistic coryphaeus, was far more diverse than one may presume. If writers like Gaztelu, Virgilio Piñera and Baquero pursue Lezama's teleological baroque over which metaphor presides as an ever-changing and always surprising deity and cultural and speculative themes retain predominance, Octavio Smith, Lorenzo García Vega and, of course, Eliseo Diego evidence a second, more mundane attitude. According to Vitier, they have in common " a more intimate approach to poetry, a dependence upon quotidian reality and a search for an intuitive center located in memory." In Diego's case, an inherent lyrical nostalgia for a familial and national past as well as for objects, feelings, experiences, relies precisely on what one of his poetic voices has named "el prodigio feliz de la memoria" (the happy portent of memory). In his Proustian looking back, the writer frequently creates an almost child-like dreamy ambiance where reality and unreality intermingle in bewildering fashion. Hence, as Antonio Fernández Ferrer (1993) aptly concludes, not only Diego's prose but also his poetry fit regularly within the mold of fantastic literature.

Diego's second and third books, *Divertimentos* (1946) and *En la Calzada de Jesús del Monte*, 1949 [In Jesus del Monte Boulevard], still convey the essence of his creative persona. The first work is a collection of brief narrative pieces akin in spirit to the fable and the fairy tale. From his beginning as a writer, Diego evinced an interest in children's stories which finally resulted in translations of the tales of Hans Christian Andersen (1965) and the Grimm brothers (1966). In *Divertimentos*, their influence as well as that of Jonathan Swift, Lewis Carroll and other authors associated at least tangentially with such fiction is revealed particularly in the ingenuous lyrical tone of anecdotes laden with parabolic significance. Nevertheless, as José Lezama Lima has pointed out (1970), these *divertissements* possess a grotesque quality that transforms them into imagistic conceptions closer to the Goya of joyous tapestries than to the evangelically evanescent Murillo. They embrace what Lezama terms a "bewitching clarity" that forces the reader to amble between translucent story and the potentialities of metaphor. The sisters who bring about someone's demise by cutting a thread on a perpetually unfinished decorative cloth in "De las hermanas" (About the Sisters); the numerous obstacles that Don Rigoberto Rodríguez employs unsuccessfully to impede death's deliberate approximation in "De la pelea" (About the Struggle); the Lazarillo-like character of "De los pasteles" (About the Pastries), whose pact with the Devil to guarantee him access to pastries meant for the Bishop fails because of Satan's own gluttony, are texts representative of Diego's prodigious imagination. It allows him to transcend poetic reality by interspersing successfully heterogeneous psychological, marvelous and fantastic elements. This collection exemplifies as well the impossibility to categorize Diego's writings in a conventionally generic manner. His poetry oftentimes resembles prose, his prose resembles poetry. Antonio Fernández Ferrer (1993) maintains that, for Diego, poetry and prose are inseparable. They correspond to a self-same creative attitude and to a homologous world view that require identical responses from readers. For instance, a book like *Versiones* (1970), traditionally defined as prose-poetry in critical studies and literary dictionaries, is included as fiction in Ida Vitale's edition of *Divertimentos y versiones*.

En la Calzada de Jesús del Monte is a fundamental book in the annals of contemporary Cuban poetry. Cintio Vitier (1949) asserts that through a discursive lyrical approach fluctuating between psalm and testimony, Diego undertakes the task of toning down ("sosegar") poetry, while providing a physical background ("espaciar") for it. The poet pretends to place readers within the context of individual remembrance and immediate concreteness to make them reflect on their temporality, on their mortality. "La calzada más bien enorme de Jesús del Monte" (The more or less enormous boulevard of Jesús del Monte) symbolizes a spatial stability that will inevitably supersede a poetic voice which, albeit conscious of its own impermanence, finds solace in the endurance of familiar places, objects, reconstructed lives and circumstances through iterative and, in a sense, communicative memory. By sharing a past, by inscribing it literarily, one secures continuity through descrip-

tion. At the same time, the conceived artifact becomes, as Diego himself attests (1992), "un nuevo objeto dentro de la realidad" (a new object within reality), enriching it by becoming a symbol to be reinterpreted and apprehended in changing circumstances.

In 1968, Eliseo Diego published a curious compendium of prose and poetry: *Muestrario del mundo o Libro de las maravillas de Boloña* [A Sampling of the World or Book of the Marvels of Boloña]. Mixing prose, free verse and conventional poetic stanzas (couplets, sonnets, traditional *décimas* or ten-line strophes, etc.), Diego elaborates a series of intuitive images based on etchings produced by the 19th-century Cuban printer José Severino Boloña. The poet's fascination with time, death, memory, cyclical nature, chance, and so forth makes itself manifest through a myriad lyrical descriptions far more provocative than the pre-text whence they emanate. At times, Diego's style gains archaic qualities to convey the colonial nature of the reconstructed etchings. In the fragment entitled "Intercálase la historia del anticuario [Here You Find Intercalated the Story of the Antiquarian] for example, his writing becomes more *antique* than the anecdote itself, resembling the rhetorical tone of apologues conceived by medieval Spanish author Don Juan Manuel or the ingenuousness of Indo-Arabic tales. In the story, an antiquarian is so given to his art of refurbishing and in some cases recreating objects that he rejects Aladdin's lamp upon finding it. There is nothing he requires but his craft. The tale's significance emerges from its metaphorical virtue, from its intent to reproduce Diego's own artistic process *vis-à-vis* his pre-text. In other texts within the collection, the writer intends to formulate prolonged existential metaphors. Such is the case of the poem "Riesgos del equilibrista" [Risks of the High Wire Artist] in which the poetic voice expands on Boloña's image to illustrate the precariousness of human life in the uncomfortable movement between the darkness from which one emerges and the one into which one disappears.

Eliseo Diego's numerous other books give evidence of a creative evolution dependent upon similar motifs and a consistent poetic view based at least partly on his religiosity. A writer who works in a socialist society, he has nevertheless defined his public role as follows: "I am a very religious man, I am Catholic, and for me one of the most fascinating concepts in the world is the problem of good and evil. The artist's responsibility is to make use of his creative gift in the best possible manner, always trying to contribute to future well-being, to children's welfare, to humor, to what is called goodness and beauty. That is the way in which the artist will fulfill his social responsibility." Such a quasi theological commitment to an art based on the elevation of the trivial and insignificant to sublime spheres, defines Diego as an inimitable writer, one who has developed a highly personal style and a patently recognizable creative intuition.

JORGE FEBLES

See also entry on *Orígenes* under Journals

Biography

Born in Havana, Cuba, 2 July 1920. His mother was Cuban by birth, but raised in New York and so her first language was English. Attended primary and secondary schools in Havana. Studied law at

University of Havana (1941), but gave it up in 1943. Married Bella García Marruz, sister of the poet Fina García Marruz. Member of the editorial board of the Spanish literary journal, *Clavileño* and founder member of the Cuban journal *Orígenes* from 1944 to 1947. Taught English at night school. Inspector of English Instruction at Ministry of Education, until 1954. Completed his studies in Education in 1959. In 1959 and 1960 he taught British and US literature in courses at Casa de las Américas. Worked in Department of Children's Literature and Storytelling at the National Library in Havana, 1962–70. Placed in charge of public relations at the UNEAC (Union of Artists and Writers) in 1963. Appointed editor of one of UNEAC's magazines, *Unión*, 1970; also served as member of their publications committee. Frequently judge of literary contests in Cuba. Travelled to Eastern Europe and to USSR. Translated literary texts from English and Russian (using a transliteration in the case of the latter). In 1979 awarded Maxim Gorky International Prize for his translations of poetry from the Russian. Awarded National Prize for Literature in 1986, and Juan Rulfo Prize in 1993. Died in 1994.

Selected Works

Poetry and Short Fiction
No attempt has been made to separate the genres since the author often mixed prose and poetry in one volume.

En las oscuras manos del olvido, Havana: Clavijo, 1942
Divertimentos, Havana: Orígenes, 1946
En la Calzada de Jesús del Monte, Havana: Orígenes, 1949
Por los extraños pueblos, Havana: Úcar García, 1958
El oscuro esplendor, Havana: Belic, 1966
Divertimentos y versiones, Montevideo: ARCA, 1967
Muestrario del Mundo o Libro de las maravillas de Boloña. La Habana, 1836–1967, Havana: Instituto de Libro, 1968
Versiones, Havana: Unión, 1970
Nombrar las cosas, Havana: Unión, 1970
Noticias de la Quimera, Havana: Unión, 1975
Los días de tu vida, Havana: Unión, 1977
La casa del pan, Havana: Letras Cubanas, 1978
Un almacén como otro cualquiera, Havana: Letras Cubanas, 1978
A través de mi espejo, Havana: Unión, 1981
Soñar despierto, Havana: Gente Nueva, 1988
Libro de quizás y de quién sabe, Havana: Letras Cubanas, 1989
Cuatro de oros, Mexico City: Siglo XXI, 1991

Translations
Poems, translated by Kathleen Weaver and Eliseo Diego, New York: Center for Cuban Studies, 1982

Conversación con los difuntos, Mexico City: Ediciones del Equilibrista, 1991 [Translations by Eliseo Diego of the poetry of other writers]

Compilations and Anthologies
Inventario de asombros, Havana: Letras Cubanas, 1983
Poesía, Havana: Letras Cubanas, 1983
Prosas escogidas, Havana: Letras Cubanas, 1983
Entre la dicha y la tiniebla. Antología poética, 1949–1985, Mexico City: Fondo de Cultura Económica, 1986
Veintiséis poemas recientes, Mexico City: Ediciones del Equilibrista, 1986
Eliseo Diego [Antología poética], Mexico City: UNAM, 1987
Poesía y prosa selecta, Caracas: Biblioteca Ayacucho, 1992
La sed de lo perdido, edited by Antonio Fernández Ferrer, Madrid: Siruela, 1993 [An excellent collection of Diego's prose and poetry which permits readers to familiarize themselves with texts illustrative of the writer's aesthetic evolution]

Further Reading
Fernández Ferrer, Antonio, "La claridad hechizada de Eliseo Diego," preface to *La sed de lo perdido*, Madrid: Siruela, 1993
Lezama Lima, José, "Otra página sobre los *Divertimentos* de Eliseo Diego," in *Tratados en La Habana: ensayos estéticos*, Santiago de Chile: ORBE, 1970 [A brief review of *Divertimentos* that appeared initially in *Orígenes*. Lezama makes profound comments about the grotesque qualities of the book]
Vitale, Ida, "Un poeta en verso y prosa," preface to *Divertimentos y versiones*, Montevideo: ARCA, 1967 [A perceptive critical analysis of the poet's aesthetics]
Vitier, Cintio, "La poesía de la memoria en Diego," in *Lo cubano en la poesía*, Havana: Letras Cubanas, 1970 [An excellent analysis of *En la Calzada de Jesús del Monte*]
Zaldívar, Gladys, "El arte narrativo de Eliseo Diego en *Divertimentos y versiones*," in her edition of *Cinco aproximaciones a la narrativa hispanoamericana contemporánea*, Madrid: Playor, 1977

Interviews
Bejel, Emilio, "Eliseo Diego," *Escribir en Cuba. Entrevistas con escritores cubanos: 1979–1989*, Río Piedras: Editorial de la Universidad de Puerto Rico, 1991 [A detailed interview with Eliseo Diego. The poet discusses his relationship with the Orígenes group, the religious substratum of his works, his conception of poetry and other aesthetic notions]

Special Issues of Journals
La Gaceta de Cuba, Havana (July 1990)
Casa de las Américas, vol. 34/194 (January–March 1994)

Dominican Republic

19th- and 20th-Century Prose and Poetry

To a great extent, the literature of the Dominican Republic has been engaged in the struggle against the political oppression that has held Hispaniola in its grip since 1492 when this island – now Haiti and the Dominican Republic – became part of the then nascent Spanish empire. Since then, in the Dominican Republic, the literary text has served as an instrument of protest against abuses by governments concerned most often with exploiting the people and the land. Dominican literature has tried to come to terms with the historical realities of a nation that has suffered from a particularly disturbing history. Moreover, it expresses a people's search for a national identity. Hispaniola was first settled by Spaniards, but also passed under the colonial rule of England and France. As the native inhabitants were obliterated, Africans were brought over by force to work the plantations. Dominicans came to share their Caribbean island with Haiti, a country that invaded and annexed the Dominican Republic in the 19th century. The countless changes in government led a 19th-century Dominican priest to write: "Spanish I was born yesterday / in the afternoon I became French / Ethiopian I was in the night / today English I am, they say. / My Lord, what in the end will I be?" In the 20th century, Hispaniola has still been preyed upon by foreign forces; the United States has made its presence felt on the island through business enterprises and military interventions. Finally, as one considers a history of Dominican literature one cannot forget that all aspects of Dominican life were profoundly affected by the brutal dictatorship of Rafael Leonidas Trujillo which lasted from 1930 to 1961.

It is hard to determine at what precise moment a body of Dominican literature with an identity of its own began to emerge. However, here as elsewhere, poetry is the first genre to establish itself. Leonor de Ovando (died c.1610) is one of the first if not the very first poet of America. It is known that she was born on the island, became a Dominican nun, and prioress of the Regina Monastery. Of her literary work five sonnets and a composition written in blank verse are extant. Other early Dominican female poets are Manuela Aybar "La Deana" (1790–1850) and Josefa Antonia Perdomo (1834–96). Salomé Ureña Henríquez (1850–97) was the first woman in the Dominican Republic to write nationalistic poetry with topics such as Spain's rule of her country and the injustices of the various despotic and corrupt governments that dominated the island in the 19th century. Ureña's work, both literary and social, aimed at the foundation of a Dominican nationality. Through her poetry she tried to inspire Dominicans to work towards a better country. Moreover, influenced by Puerto Rico's Eugenio María de Hostos (1839–1903) she herself contributed to the progress of her country by establishing the first Teachers' Training College for Women. She has been grouped with other nationalistic poets known as "Dioses Mayores" [The Greatest Gods] that include Gastón Deligne (1861–1914) and José Joaquín Pérez (1845–1900). Deligne harshly criticized Spanish American *modernismo* in his "Ars Nova Scribendi," 1897 [Art of New Writing]. Pérez's poetry,

as his *Fantasías indígenas*, celebrates the native inhabitants of the island.

Tomás Hernández Franco (1904–52), Héctor Incháustegui Cabral (1912–79), Manuel del Cabral (1912), and Pedro Mir (1913) have been classified as the Poetas Independientes del 40 (Independent Poets of the 1940s). In *Yelidá*, Hernández Franco exposes his ideas about the superiority of the Caribbean mulatto while telling the story of a young Norwegian sailor who marries a black prostitute: "la esposa de Erick madam Suquí / rezaba a Legbá y a Ogún por su hombre blanco / rezaba en la catedral por su hombre rubio" (the wife of Erick madame Suquí / prayed for her white man to Legbá and Ogún / she prayed for her blond man in the cathedral). The tone of Héctor Incháustegui Cabral's poetry is pessimistic. Through it he examines his country and the injustices that abound there. He expresses his dissatisfaction in poems like "Canto triste a la patria bien amada" [Sad Song to the Beloved Mother Country] in which he states, "Patria, palabra hueca y torpe / para mí, mientras los hombres / miren con desprecio los pies sucios y arrugados, / y maldigan las proles largas, / y en cada cruce de caminos claven una bandera/ para lucir sus colores nada más . . ." (Motherland, empty and crude word / for me, while men / look at dirty and wrinkled feet with contempt, / and curse the abundant progeny, / and at every crossroads bury a flag / only to show off its colors). Unlike other Dominican poets, his protest was not directed at the figure of Trujillo but at the bourgeoisie which he accused of hypocrisy, superficiality, and indifference in "Invitación a los de arriba [Invitation to Those at the Top]. In *Diario de la guerra* [Diary of War] he offers the reader a vision of death and destruction as he describes the effects of the 1963 war on Dominican society. Manuel del Cabral's poems deal with social issues and with the role that Africans played in the history of the Americas. He praises Africans and attempts to return to their descendants a sense of self-esteem and love for their heritage. He alludes to the injustices blacks have suffered in the poem "Ellos" [They]: "Ellos comen cuando pueden / pero por ellos comemos cuando queremos. / Ellos son zapateros pero están descalzos. / Ellos nos visten pero están desnudos" (They eat when they can / but because of them we eat when we want. / They are shoemakers but are barefoot. / They dress us but are naked). His *Compadre Mon* [Friend Mon] is an epic poem in praise of the common Dominican man personified in the figure of Don Mon and may be compared to José Hernández's *Martín Fierro*. Pedro Mir has been forced by the oppressive political situation of his country, namely the dictatorship of Trujillo, to use his poetry as an instrument of resistance against despotism and social injustices. Prominent in his poetry is the image of the victimized Dominican peasant. In *Hay un país en el mundo* [There is a Country in the World] he creates a sociohistory of his country while presenting a problem common to Latin American capitalist countries, that is, the polarity that exists between the rich and the poor. In this poem he calls the Dominican Republic, "País inverosímil" [Unimaginable Country] and insists that "los campesinos no tienen tierra" (the peasants own no land). History is an important element in many of Mir's works. *El gran incendio*, 1969 [The Great Fire], *Las raíces dominicanas de la doctrina de Monroe*, 1974 [The Dominican Roots of the Monroe Doctrine], *La noción de período en la historia dominicana*, 1981–83 [The Concept of Period in Dominican History] , and *Historia del hambre*, 1987 [History of Hunger] are all dedicated to Dominican history, and even his novel, *Cuando amaban las tierras comuneras*, 1978 [When Communal Lands Were Loved] explores the significance of his country's troubled history. In "Contracanto a Walt Whitman" (*Countersong to Walt Whitman*) Mir criticizes Whitman's vision of the United States developed in *Leaves of Grass*. Mir's concern for Dominican women is shown in "Poema del llanto trigueño" [Poem of the Mulatto Weeping] and "Amén de mariposas" [Butterflies' Amen]. In the first of these, the exploitation of working Dominican women is presented through the colors black and white. The second is an elegy for the death of the Mirabal sisters who were assassinated on Trujillo's orders on 25 November 1960. In his introduction to *Countersong to Walt Whitman and Other Poems*, Silvio Torres-Saillant has written, "In the Dominican Republic no one lays a more legitimate claim to intimacy with the yearnings of the Dominican people as well as with the texture of their collective voice than Pedro Mir." Undoubtedly, Mir remains popular and highly esteemed among Dominicans living on and off the island.

Aída Cartagena Portalatín (1918–94) belonged to La Poesía Sorprendida [The Surprised Poetry], a movement that began in 1943 when a journal of the same name was established. The members of this movement included among others Franklin Mieses Burgos (1907–76), Freddy Gatón Arce (1920), and Manuel Rueda (1921). Gatón Arce was one of the founders and co-directors of the magazine and editions published by La Poesía Sorprendida. His "Vlía" represents a first attempt at automatic writing and Surrealism in the Dominican Republic and has been compared in its importance to Aimé Césaire's *Cahier d'un retour au pays natal* (*Return to My Native Land*). Manuel Rueda established in 1953 the collection "La Isla Necesaria" [The Necessary Island] in which his sonnets "Las Noches" [The Nights] were published. In his poems, as in "Canto de regreso a la tierra prometida" [Song of Return to the Promised Land] a concern over the division of Hispaniola is expressed: "Medias montañas / medios ríos, / y hasta la muerte / compartida" (Half mountains / half rivers, / and even death / shared). Cartagena Portalatín began to publish in the 1940s when the dictator Trujillo was in power and any overt criticism of him or his system of government could bring immediate death. This situation made her write poetry whose message of protest is veiled. For example, in "Como llorar la muerte de una rosa" [How to Cry the Death of a Rose] from her collection *Del sueño al mundo*, 1945 [From Slumber into the World] she questions why people do not show pain at the death of others, but she hides her criticism within a poem that pretends to be about the fleeting beauty of a rose. In her work, both prose and poetry, she refers to her struggle as a woman living and writing in a male dominated society.

La Poesía Sorprendida group was followed by the Generations of 1948 and 1960. Straddling these two generations is Marcio Veloz Maggiolo (1936) whose poetry is marked by a striving to understand man's relationship with God and nature. Jeannette Miller (1944) started her literary work as part of the Generation of 1960, and her work is still mostly scattered in newspapers and magazines except for three volumes of poetry, *El viaje*, 1967 [The Voyage], *Fórmulas para combatir el miedo*, 1977 [Formulas to Fight Against Fear] and *Fichas de identidad/Estadía*, 1987 [Identity Records/Sojourn]. The death of Trujillo and the war in 1965 mark a moment of change in Dominican literature. After 1965 various poetry groups emerged: El Puño, La Isla, La Máscara, La Antorcha, etc., (respectively: The Fist, The Island, The Mask and The Torch). The poetry produced by these groups became known as Joven Poesía or Poesía de Postguerra (Young Poetry or Postwar Poetry). Some of the poets that participated in this movement were Norberto James Rawlings (b. 1965), Enriquillo Sánchez (b. 1947), Mateo Morrison (b. 1947), Cayo Claudio Espinal (b. 1955), and Soledad Álvarez (b. 1950).

Since the 1980s there has been what Bruno Rosario Candelier has called in his *Ensayos literarios*, 1986 [Literary Essays] "un boom femenino." Among the most recent Dominican women poets are Carmen Sánchez, Sherezada (Chiqui) Vicioso, Aurora Arias, Ylonka Nacidit-Perdomo, Ángela Hernández and Sabrina Román. These poets have incorporated into their work an element that has often been denied in Dominican society, the African heritage of the island. As Daisy Cocco De Filippis has put it in "*Indias y trigueñas* No Longer: Contemporary Dominican Women Poets Speak": "The rejection of the African element in Dominican poetry is expressed in the representation of women in a constant antinomy between a virginal and submissive white woman and a sensual and sinful negress or mulatto woman." De Filippis also reminds us that the Black woman has been usually Haitian in Dominican poetry such as in Manuel del Cabral's poetry and Tomás Hernández Franco's *Yelidá*. Perhaps taking their directive from Cartagena Portalatín, who was a Black poet and was not afraid to celebrate her African descent in her writings, now female poets have begun to change the image of women in Dominican poetry.

Although it has been stated that the quality and volume of poetry far outweighs those of prose, the novel, short story, drama, and essay have been successfully cultivated in the Dominican Republic. As with poetry, these genres have been practiced both by men and women. The novel appears on the island in the 19th century with Amelia Francisca de Marchena (1850–(?)) who published *Madre culpable* (1893) and *Francisca Martinoff* (1901). Furthermore, since the 19th century short stories have been written by Dominicans such as Máximo Gómez (1833–1905), Virginia Elena Ortea (1866–1903), Pedro Henríquez Ureña (1884–1946), and José Alcántara Almánzar (b. 1946). Where theater is concerned, the group *Los Trinitarios*, used the stage to promote independence during the 19th century. Members of the Poesía Sorprendida and Generación del 48, Manuel Rueda, Héctor Incháustegui Cabral, and Máximo A. Blonda (b. 1931), also have produced socially engaged plays in the 20th century. For example, social issues like the significance of the frontier with Haiti and the political situation of the country after Trujillo's death are the main topics of Blonda's *Pirámide 179*, 1969 [Pyramid 179] and Franklin Domínguez's *Se Busca un hombre honesto*, 1964 [Looking for an Honest Man]. Camila Henríquez Ureña

(1894–1973) has been considered a Cuban writer even though she was born and died in the Dominican Republic. The reasons for this are likely to be that she emigrated with her family, Francisco Henríquez Carvajal and Salomé Ureña, to Cuba as a young girl and that her adoptive country provided her with a far more developed cultural milieu than her birthplace. She travelled extensively in her life and held teaching positions at various universities in the United States and Cuba. Throughout her career she wrote essays on a variety of literary figures such as Goethe, Shakespeare, Lope de Vega, and Gabriela Mistral. Her works were collected and published in Cuba in 1982 under the title *Estudios y Conferencias*.

Dominican critics, such as Pedro Paix (b. 1952) in *La narrativa yugulada*, 1981 [Strangled Narrative], have stated that their country has not evolved culturally to the point that it can serve as fertile ground for the development of the novel. Yet, in spite of these assertions, the novel has taken root in the Dominican Republic and there are examples, both from the past and the present century, that have been worthy of international attention.

The 19th century in the Dominican Republic, as in the rest of Latin America, was a time of nation building. The new nations had to legitimize themselves and the concerns of these young nations were translated by their writers into novels that explored national identities. As part of this search, writers like Manuel de Jesús Galván (1834–1910) looked at the customs, ethnic backgrounds and history of their people and wrote novels such as *Enriquillo, leyenda histórica dominicana*, 1882 (*The Cross and the Sword*). This text has a political and cultural significance in the history of the Dominican Republic since it established a cultural identity for Dominicans as descendants of the intermarriage of noble Indians and Spaniards while excluding Africans from their culture. Other novels that share similar concerns are Federico García Godoy's *Rufinito* (1908), *Alma dominicana*, 1911 [Dominican Soul], and *Guanuma* (1908–14), and Tulio Cestero's *La sangre*, 1914 [Blood].

In the 20th century there have been two major female voices in Dominican prose, Aída Cartagena Portalatín and Hilma Contreras. Cartagena Portalatín's best-known prose work is an experimental novel, *Escalera para Electra*, 1969 [A Staircase for Electra]. This novel received an honorable mention in Spain's Seix Barral Prize competition for best novel of the year. Moreover, it was the first prose text after the fall of Trujillo to search for a new definition of national identity. Hilma Contreras's talent was recognized by Juan Bosch in 1937 when she sent him the short story "La desjababa." He wrote back praising her, "al país le nace una escritora cabal, no una principiante, ni siquiera una aficionada feliz. Un fruto sazonado" (a complete writer has been born to this country, not a beginner, not even a happy amateur. A ripe fruit). In 1953 she published her first volume of short stories, *Cuatro cuentos* [Four Stories] and, in 1986, a novel, *La tierra está bramando* [The Earth is Roaring]. In 1993 she was honored by the Dominican National Library which organized a conference to celebrate her eightieth birthday and published a collection of her short stories, *Facetas de la vida* [Facets of Life]. Moreover, Dominican women are now willing to try their hand at genres like science fiction usually considered off limits for Hispanic women. One such writer is Altagracia Moreta Feliz who in

1992 published *El extraño fenómeno de los 500 años* [The Strange Phenomenon of the 500 Years], a didactic science fiction novel which in adapted form has become required reading in Dominican schools.

Juan Bosch (b. 1909) was a political exile from 1937 to 1961; in 1963, after Trujillo's death and promising to establish a democracy, he was elected president of the Dominican Republic. Because he opposed Trujillo, Bosch was ignored by Dominican critics while the dictator lived, and afterwards, critics have often been overwhelmed by Bosch's political life, so that his works remain mostly unstudied. He has written prose since the 1930s and one of his early works, *La mañosa*, 1936 [The Wily One] is a political novel in which a mule becomes the main character in a text that portrays the confusion of a country involved in a civil war. The text also speaks to economic concerns since it portrays the exploitation of a country for the financial benefit of the powerful few. He has published many essays of political and historical significance for the Dominican Republic, among these are *De Cristóbal Colón a Fidel Castro (El Caribe, frontera imperial)* [From Christopher Columbus to Fidel Castro (The Caribbean, Imperial Frontier)] and *El estado: sus orígenes y desarrollo* [The State: its Origins and Development]. In the second, Bosch traces the origins and developments of the state since its beginnings in Mesopotamia to the formation of the Nazi state in 1934. The importance of Bosch's short stories cannot be denied and after Trujillo's death, Aída Cartagena Portalatín in her 1969 anthology, *Narradores dominicanos* [Dominican Narrators], described Bosch as "the best example of the Dominican short story writer." His two collections, *Cuentos escritos en el exilio*, 1976 [Stories Written in Exile] and *Cuentos*, 1983 [Stories], have influenced many other Dominican writers. His texts have motivated younger Dominicans to emulate him or to rebel against his traditionalism expressed in stories whose main topic is the peasant and his problems. Among the writers Bosch has influenced is José Alcántara Almánzar who has become one of the best modern Dominican short story writers.

Pedro Mir's prose includes works like *La noción de período en la historia dominicana*, 1981 [The Concept of Period in Dominican History], an essay which dates the beginning of Dominican literature to the 17th century and a novel, *Cuando amaban las tierras comuneras*, 1978 [When Communal Lands Were Loved]. In his novel, Mir examines the relationship of the Dominican Republic and the United States and the historical significance of the "tierras comuneras" [common lands]. Among the important characteristics of the novel is the rejection of grammar. Sentences may go on for several pages and punctuation symbols are non-existent. The narrator not only rejects grammar, he also states that his narration rejects the standard rules of literature and places it within the boundaries of common public documents like birth and death certificates. The novel portrays the heroic struggles of the common Dominican people against other nations and shows how as similar historical situations recur, the people answer each new challenge with actions that seem repetitions of those carried out before but which in fact achieve progress. Throughout the text references are made to the cyclical nature of history.

Marcio Veloz Maggiolo's *De abril en adelante*, 1975 [From April On] also holds a significant place in Dominican letters as it was a finalist for the Seix Barral Prize. Maggiolo's text seeks to deal with the historical events of April 1965. His novel, *Los ángeles de hueso*, 1967 [Angels of Flesh and Blood], attempts to transform Dominican narrative and his collection of short stories, "La fértil agonía del amor," won the Dominican Republic's National Award for Short Stories in 1980. Yet another example of an internationally acclaimed Dominican novel is Pedro Vergés's *Sólo cenizas hallarás (bolero)*, 1980 [You Will Only Find Ashes (Bolero)]. This novel explores the effects of Trujillo's repressive regime and his legacy on the personal lives of Dominican's struggling to better themselves within a repressive society.

After Trujillo's death and a change in the United States' immigration laws of 1965, a greater number of Dominicans went to the United States. Some have permanently settled there while others continue to travel back and forth between the island and the mainland. From this population of Dominicans living in the United States a new body of literature, sometimes written in English, sometimes in Spanish, or a combination of both, is emerging. For example, Julia Álvarez has published two volumes of poetry *Homecoming* (1984) and *The Housekeeping Book* and two novels, *How the García Girls Lost their Accents* (1991) and *In the Time of the Butterflies* (1994), all originally written in English, that have rapidly come to the attention of critics. The first of the novels tells the story of three sisters and their parents, who, forced out of the Dominican Republic by Trujillo's regime, must change a life of luxury in their native land for exile in the United States. The second is a fictional account of the life and assassination of the Mirabal sisters. Another work acclaimed by critics is Viriato Sención's first novel, *Los que falsificaron la firma de Dios*, 1992 [Those Who Forged God's Signature]. This Spanish language novel, written in the New York's South Bronx, has been, according to Silvio Torres-Saillant in *Brújula/Compass* 16 (1993), "hailed as the most important text in the Dominican literary market today" and "a significant achievement in a place where literary artists have too often and too easily spoken of the apathy of their home public." Other Dominicans living and writing in the United States are Leandro Morales, Manuel Marshall, and Luis Manuel Ledesma. Moreover, among these immigrants literary groups such as the *Círculo de Escritores Dominicanos en Nueva York* and *Grupo Literario Pensum* have begun to publish collections of works by Dominican writers living in the United States.

LINDA M. RODRÍGUEZ

Further Reading

Primary Sources

Cabral, Manuel del, *Cuentos*, Buenos Aires: Ediciones Orión, 1976

Cabral, Manuel del (editor), *10 poetas dominicanos, tres con vida y siete desenterrados*, Santo Domingo: Publicaciones América, 1980

Cartagena Portalatín, Aída, *La tierra escrita: elegías*, Colección Baluarte 15. Ediciones Brigadas Dominicanas, Santo Domingo: Editora Arte y Cine, 1967

___ *Escalera para Electra*, Santo Domingo: Editora Taller, 1975

___ *Tablero: doce cuentos de lo popular a lo culto*, Biblioteca Taller 109, Santo Domingo: Editora Taller, 1978

___ *Culturas africanas: rebeldes con causa*, Santo Domingo: Editora Taller, 1986

De Filippis, Daisy Cocco (editor), *From Desolation to Compromise. A Bilingual Anthology of the Poetry of Aída Cartagena Portalatín*, Colección Montesinos no. 10, Santo Domingo: Editora Taller, 1988

Francisco, Ramón, *Literatura Dominicana 60*, Colección Contemporáneos, no. 7, Santiago: Universidad Católica Madre y Maestra, 1969

Galván, Manuel de Jesús, *Enriquillo, leyenda histórica dominicana (1503-1533)*, Mexico City: Porrúa, 1986; as *The Cross and the Sword*, translated by Robert Graves, Bloomington: Indiana University Press, 1954; London: Gollancz, 1956

Mena, Miguel, *Reunión de poesía, poetas de la crisis*, Santo Domingo: Ediciones Armario Urbano, 1985

Mir, Pedro, *El gran incendio: los balbuceos americanos del capitalismo mundial*, 2nd edition, Santo Domingo: Ediciones Taller, 1974

___ *Cuando amaban las tierras comuneras*, Mexico City: Siglo XXI, 1978

___ *¡Buen viaje, Pancho Valentín! (Memorias de un marinero)*, Biblioteca Taller 130, Santo Domingo: Editora Taller, 1981

___ *La noción de período en la historia dominicana*, Santo Domingo: Universidad Autónoma de Santo Domingo, 1981

___ *Countersong to Walt Whitman and other Poems*, translated by Jonathan Cohen and Donald D. Walsh, Washington, DC: Azul Editions, 1993

Moreta Feliz, Altagracia, *El extraño fenómeno de los 500 años*, Santo Domingo: Grafideas, 1992

Sención, Viriato, *Los que falsificaron la firma de Dios*, Santo Domingo: Editora Taller, 1992

Critical Studies

Alcántara Almánzar, José, *Estudios de poesía dominicana*, Santo Domingo: Editora Alfa y Omega, 1979

Baeza Flores, Alberto, *La poesía dominicana en el siglo XX, generaciones y tendencias, poetas independientes, La poesía sorprendida, suprarrealismo, dominicanidad y universalidad (1943-1947) II*, Colección Estudios no. 22, Santiago: Universidad Católica Madre y Maestra, 1977

Calder, Bruce J., *The Impact of Intervention: the Dominican Republic During the United States Occupation of 1916-1924*, Austin: University of Texas Press, 1984

Cruz, Josefina de la, *La sociedad dominicana de finales de siglo a través de la novela*, Literatura y Sociedad, no. 1, Ciudad Universitaria: Editora Universitaria, 2nd edition, 1986

Davis, Lisa E., "Revolución socialista en las Antillas: *Cuando amaban las tierras comuneras* del dominicano Pedro Mir," in *Latin American Fiction Today: a Symposium*, edited by Rose S. Minc, Upper Montclair: Montclair State College, and Takoma Park, Maryland: Hispamérica, 1979

De Filippis, Daisy Coco (editor), *The Women of Hispaniola: Moving Towards Tomorrow*, Selected Proceedings of the 1993 Conference, New York: York College, 1993

García Cabrera, Estela, "La conquista y colonización de América a la luz de Manuel de Jesús Galván," *Revista de la Universidad Católica de Puerto Rico* 61 (October 1987)

Gutiérrez, Franklin (editor), *Aproximaciones a la narrativa de Juan Bosch*, New York: Ediciones Alcance, 1989

Guzman, Catherine, "Onomatology in Aída Cartagena Portalatín's Fiction," *Literary Onomastics Studies*, vol. 10 (1983)

Henríquez Ureña, Camila, *Estudios y conferencias*, Havana: Letras Cubanas, 1982

Henríquez Ureña, Pedro, "Enriquillo," in his *Obra crítica*, Mexico City: Fondo de Cultura Económica, 1960

Laguna-Díaz, Elpidio, "Cuando amaban las tierras comuneras: visión mitopoética de una historia," *Hispamérica: Revista de Literatura* 31 (1982)

Mateo, Andrés L. (editor), *Manifiestos literarios de la república dominicana*, Santo Domingo: Editora Taller, 1984

Piña Contreras, Guillermo, *Enriquillo: el texto y la historia*, Santo Domingo: Editora Alfa y Omega, 1985

Sommer, Doris, "History and Romanticism in Pedro Mir's Novel, *Cuando amaban las tierras comuneras*," *Revista de Estudios Hispánicos*, Río Piedras, Puerto Rico, 6 (1979)

_____ "Good-Bye to Revolution and the Rest: Aspects of Dominican Narrative Since 1965," *Latin American Literary Review*, vol. 8/16 (1980)

_____ *One Master for Another. Populism as Patriarchal Rhetoric in Dominican Novels*. Lanham, Maryland: University Press of America, 1983

_____ "El otro Enriquillo," *Revista de Crítica Literaria Latinoamericana*, vol. 9/17 (1983)

_____ "Not Just Any Narrative: How Romance Can Love Us to Death," in *The Historical Novel in Latin America*, edited by Daniel Balderston, Gaithersburg, Maryland: Hispamérica, 1986

Sosa, José Rafael (editor), *La mujer en la literatura: homenaje a Aída Cartagena Portalatín*, Santo Domingo: Editora Universitaria, 1986

Torres-Saillant, Silvio, "La literatura dominicana en los Estados Unidos y la periferia del margen," in *Punto y Coma*, vol. 3/1–2 (1991)

_____ "Literatura y libertinaje: el oficio en la emigración," *Trasimagen*, vol. 1/1 (1993)

_____ "Dominican Literature and Its Criticism: Anatomy of a Troubled Identity," in *A History of Literature in the Caribbean*, edited by A. James Arnold, vol. 1, Amsterdam and Philadelphia: Benjamins, 1994

Bibliographies
Olivera, Otto, *Bibliografía de la literatura dominicana*, Lincoln, Nebraska: Society of Spanish and Spanish-American Studies, 1984

Special Issues of Journals
Revista Iberoamericana 142 (1988) [Includes articles by Efraín Barredas, Margarite Fernández Olmos, Neil Larson and Doris Sommer]

José Donoso 1924–1996

Chilean prose writer

When Chile awarded its Premio Nacional de Literatura (National Prize for Literature) in 1990 to José Donoso, his native country recognized not only the importance of his work within the Chilean context but also the place of preeminence his writing has achieved in Latin American letters in the 20th century. One of the most articulate spokesmen for contemporary Latin American literature and culture, Donoso is among the renowned group of Boom writers who began to receive wide recognition in the 1960s (i.e., Julio Cortázar, Carlos Fuentes, Gabriel García Márquez and Mario Vargas Llosa). He has been known mainly as a fiction writer, and his novels, novellas, and short stories have been read all over the globe. He has, in addition, also published works of poetry and drama, as well as a widely read memoir about the Boom of the Latin American novel, *Historia personal del "Boom"* (*The "Boom" in Spanish American Literature: a Personal History*).

Donoso's contributions to Latin American literature, and to 20th-century fiction as a whole, lie mainly in the area of prose fiction, if not also in the realm of fictional poetics. His writing has examined the social and cultural realities of Latin America, and especially of Chile, while also addressing timeless questions about the nature of literature and the writer's art. Both in his "realist" and "reflexive" writing Donoso has looked with a critical eye at the social and political forces that shape modern Latin American reality and at the literary and linguistic strategies that sustain contemporary narrative fiction. Consequently, his novels inventively engage modern literary theory and criticism as much as they perceptively analyze Chilean and Latin American history, society and culture. Donoso's steady literary production since the 1950s and the sustained critical attention paid to his work for more than three decades confirm his place of preeminence within the Latin American tradition and his enduring contribution to modern literature. Indeed, acknowledgment of his work has come in the form of various awards, fellowships, and academic appointments, as well as with the international success of his individual texts.

Donoso's literary production has been varied, as evidenced by the diverse literary models with which his writing has been engaged and the disparate thematic motifs that have informed his many works of fiction. He has given his readers elaborate political allegory in *Casa de campo* (*A House in the Country*), clever erotic farce in *La misteriosa desaparición de la marquesita de Loria* [The Mysterious Disappearance of the Young Marchioness of Loria], and a personal, politico-literary documentary in *La desesperanza* (*Curfew*); he has presented introspective meditations on exile in *El jardín de al lado* (*The Garden Next Door*), searching queries about sexual identity in *El lugar sin límites* (*Hell Has No Limits*), incisive evaluations of modern bourgeois culture in *Tres novelitas burguesas* (*Sacred Families: Three Novellas*), and critical reflections on writing and authorship in *El obsceno pájaro de la noche* (*The Obscene Bird of Night*), *Casa de campo*, *El jardín de al lado* and *Taratuta* (*Taratuta; Still Life with Pipe*). All of these works have drawn on Donoso's vast knowledge of European and US literature, art and music, while also remaining rooted in the experience of Latin American culture. He has become an international literary figure whose works resonate with equal force outside and inside the borders of his native Chile.

Donoso's literary career began in Chile in the 1950s with the publication of *Veraneo y otros cuentos* [Summer Vacation and Other Stories]; included in *Charleston and Other Stories* in 1955, and *Coronación* (*Coronation*) in 1957. The focus on Chilean society and culture through tales revolving around upper-middle-class households is evident in these mostly realist texts and also shapes the stories and critical perspectives of *Este domingo* (*This Sunday*) and *El lugar sin límites*, both published in 1966. It has been widely held, by both critics and the author himself, that in his next novel, *El obsceno pájaro de la noche*, published in 1970 but written over a period of eight years, Donoso takes a significant turn away from realist representation and toward a reflexive interrogation of literature and language. This thematically and technically complex novel, arguably Donoso's Boom-era masterpiece, is at once the culmination of earlier meditations on the established familial and class structures underlying Chilean, and also Latin American, social order and the beginning of his critical inquiry about the procedures and principles of narrative fiction. The dual focus on Latin American reality and on literary problems also informs some of his most important and successful later works. For example, *Casa de campo* is both a political allegory dealing with the rise and fall of Allende in Chile and a literary meditation about the art of writing novels in the 20th century; *El jardín de al lado* thematizes the question of exile, as experienced by Donoso and many of his compatriots in recent decades, and experiments with techniques of narrative surprise; and *Taratuta* involves itself with a story about the Russian Revolution, which at the same time resonates meaningfully for the Latin American context and interrogates the relation between history and literature more generally.

While Donoso's writing contains many significant ideas about Latin American history, politics, and culture, and many of his works of fiction inventively engage current issues in narrative poetics and criticism, his writing overall is essentially literary. In addition, Donoso's personal memoir of the Boom years, first published in 1971 and expanded in 1983 to include an authorial update and also an account by Donoso's wife, provides an inside view of the literary phenomemon as experienced by its writers rather than by its critics and readers. Though his view is personal and idiosyncratic, as the title of the essay underscores, it also speaks of a group experience and cultural phenomenon that has been much analyzed by others, and which, his essay reminds its readers, can be seen from a variety of perspectives. Other, perhaps more critically instructive, self-analyses can be found in the many interviews Donoso has granted to critics over the years, and especially in "Ithaca: the Impossible Return," where, in speaking about his own art, language, and life, he inevitably seems to speak for other Latin American authors as well. Written just before he returned to live in Chile after a seventeen-year self-exile, the essay ends with the following observation: "Just as it was necessary, at one point, to leave Chile, and introduce a distance, an *ausencia*, a linguistic silence so I could write – an experience shared with so many novelists of my generation – I may have to go back to the first Ithaca I came from [i.e., Chile] in order to write about the uprooted and lonely people, younger than I, to

whose breed, with its debilitated national identity and lost national vernacular, I now seem to belong." Throughout his career, Donoso's writing has continually interrogated questions about national identity and language, about the people, history, and culture to which his work is attached; more important, perhaps, is that his literary production has offered some of the most varied and adventurous responses to those questions within modern Latin American literature.

LUCILLE KERR

Biography

Born in Santiago de Chile, 5 October 1924. Attended the Grange School, Santiago; University of Chile Instituto Pedagógico, 1947; Princeton University, New Jersey, A.B., 1951. Worked as a shepherd in Patagonia. Taught English at the Catholic University of Chile in 1954 and journalism at the University of Chile; staff member at *Revista Ercilla*, Santiago, 1959–64. Married María del Pilar Serrano in 1961, one daughter. Worked at Colorado State University, Fort Collins, 1969; literary critic for the magazine *Siempre*, 1964–66; participant in Writers' Workshop, University of Iowa, Iowa City, 1965–67. Recipient of numerous awards including: City of Santiago Prize, 1955; Chile-Italy Prize for journalism, 1960; William Faulkner Foundation Prize, 1962; Guggenheim Fellowship, 1968 and 1973; Critics' Prize (Spain), 1979; Encomienda con Placa de la Orden de Alfonso X el Sabio, 1987; National Prize for Literature (Chile), 1990; Woodrow Wilson Foundation Fellow, 1992. Died in Santiago de Chile, 7 December 1996.

Selected Works

Novels and Short Fiction

Veraneo y otros cuentos, Santiago de Chile: Editorial Universitaria, 1955

Dos cuentos, Santiago de Chile: Guarda Vieja, 1956

Coronación, Santiago de Chile: Nascimento, 1957; as *Coronation*, translated by Jocasta Goodwin, New York: Knopf, and London: Bodley Head, 1965

El charlestón, Santiago de Chile: Nascimento, 1960; as *Charleston and Other Stories*, translated by Andrée Conrad, Boston: Godine, 1977

El lugar sin límites, Mexico City: Joaquín Mortiz, 1966; as *Hell Has No Limits*, translated by Hallie D. Taylor and Suzanne Jill Levine, in *Triple Cross*, New York: Dutton, 1972

Este domingo, Santiago de Chile: Zig-Zag, 1966; as *This Sunday*, translated by Lorraine O'Grady Freeman, New York: Knopf, 1967; London: Bodley Head, 1968

El obsceno pájaro de la noche, Barcelona: Seix Barral, 1970; as *The Obscene Bird of Night*, translated by Hardie St Martin, New York: Knopf, 1973; London: Jonathan Cape, 1974

Cuentos, Barcelona: Seix Barral, 1971

Tres novelitas burguesas, Barcelona: Seix Barral, 1973; as *Sacred Families: Three Novellas*, translated by Andrée Conrad, New York: Knopf, 1977; London: Gollancz, 1978

Casa de campo, Barcelona: Seix Barral, 1978; as *A House in the Country*, translated by David Pritchard, New York: Knopf, and London: Allen Lane, 1984

La misteriosa desaparición de la marquesita de Loria, Barcelona: Seix Barral, 1980

El jardín de al lado, Barcelona: Seix Barral, 1981; as *The Garden Next Door*, translated by Hardie St Martin, New York: Grove Press, 1992

Cuatro para Delfina, Barcelona: Seix Barral, 1982

Seis cuentos para ganar, Santiago de Chile: Cochrane-Planeta/Teleduc, 1985

La desesperanza, Barcelona: Seix Barral, 1986; as *Curfew*, translated by Alfred MacAdam, New York: Weidenfeld and Nicolson, 1988; London: Picador, 1990

Taratuta; naturaleza muerta con cachimba, Madrid: Mondadori, 1990; as *Taratuta; Still Life with Pipe*, translated by Gregory Rabassa, New York: Norton, 1993

Donde van a morir los elefantes, Buenos Aires: Alfaguara, 1995

Poetry

Poemas de un novelista, Santiago de Chile: Ganymedes, 1981

Plays

Sueños de mala muerte, Santiago de Chile: Editorial Universitaria, 1985

Este domingo: versión teatral de la novela homónima, Santiago de Chile: Andrés Bello, 1990 [Adapted from his novel of the same title]

Essays

Historia personal del "Boom," Barcelona: Anagrama, 1971; augmented 2nd edition, Barcelona: Seix Barral, 1983; as *The "Boom" in Spanish American Literature: a Personal History*, translated by Gregory Kolovakos, New York: Columbia University Press, 1977

Further Reading

Achúgar, Hugo, *Ideología y estructuras narrativas en José Donoso, 1950–1970*, Caracas: Centro de Estudios Rómulo Gallegos, 1979

Adelstein, Miriam (editor), *Studies on the Works of José Donoso: an Anthology of Critical Essays*, Lampeter, Wales: Edwin Mellen Press, 1990

Castillo-Feliú, Guillermo (editor), *The Creative Process in the Works of José Donoso*, Rick Hill, South Carolina: Winthrop College, 1982

Cerda, Carlos, *José Donoso: originales y metáforas*, Santiago de Chile: Planeta, 1988

Cornejo Polar, Antonio (editor), *Donoso: la destrucción de un mundo*, Buenos Aires: García Cambeiro, 1975

González Mandri, Flora, *José Donoso's House of Fiction: a Dramatic Contruction of Time and Place*, Detroit: Wayne State University Press, 1995

Gutiérrez Mouat, Ricardo, *José Donoso: impostura e impostación; la modelización lúdica y carnavalesca de una producción literaria*, Gaithersburg, Maryland: Hispamérica, 1983

Luengo, Enrique, *José Donoso: desde el teatro al metatexto*, Concepción, Chile: Aníbal Pinto, 1991

McMurray, George R., *José Donoso*, Boston: Twayne, 1979

Magnarelli, Sharon, *Understanding José Donoso*, Columbia: University of South Carolina Press, 1993

Quinteros, Isis, *José Donoso: una insurrección contra la realidad*, Madrid: Hispanova, 1978

Sarrochi, Augusto C., *El simbolismo en la obra de José Donoso*, n.p.: La Noria, 1992

Solotorevsky, Myrna, *José Donoso: incursiones en su producción novelesca*, Valparaíso, Chile: Universitarias de Valparaíso, 1983

Vidal, Hernán, *José Donoso: surrealismo y rebelión de los instintos*, San Antonio de Calonge, Spain: Aubi, 1972

Interviews

"Ithaca: the Impossible Return," *City College Papers* 18, New York: City College (1982)

Casa de campo

Novel by José Donoso

Donoso's *Casa de campo* tells the story of a very large Chilean family in the 19th century and presents the ruminations of the 20th-century narrator-author who tells that story. It is a text that focuses as much attention on the telling of that story as on the story that is told. It is a text that can be read allegorically, to figure either recent Chilean history or the history of Spanish America more generally, or reflexively, to analyze the narrative procedures and critical principles that govern the reading and writing of novels such as Donoso's *Casa de campo*.

The events of the fiction involve the Ventura y Ventura family, which comprises numerous adults and children who spend their summers together at the family property called Marulanda; their servants, who accompany the family to their summer home; and the native population that resides around Marulanda and on whose labor the family wealth has been built. The key events in the story are the picnic excursion taken by the adults and the servants away from the house and what transpires among the children during their absence, which is simultaneously perceived as a period of one year by the children and one day by the adults. Critics have proposed that the setting and events correspond to Chile's political history from around 1970, when Salvador Allende was elected President, to 1973, the date of the military coup and Allende's death. In that reading, Marulanda has been equated with Chile; the Ventura y Ventura adults with the oligarchy; the family's children with the Chilean middle class; the natives with the country's lower classes or proletariat or even Communists; the family's servants with the Armed Forces; the servants' leader (the Mayordomo) with Pinochet; Adriano Gomara (who became a Ventura by marrying into the family) with Allende, and his rise to a position of leadership over the children during the parents' absence with Allende's election in 1970; the return of the servants and the death of Adriano at the novel's end with the military coup of September 1973; and the foreigners who accompany the adults on their return and to whom the adults arrange to sell their property with North Americans.

Casa de campo's political allegory is a powerful, and apparently overriding, concern of the whole novel. Indeed, in this text Donoso seems to have aimed to speak more directly about a specific set of historical events in Chilean, and also Latin American, history rather than to focus on more circumscribed social and cultural issues that had dominated some of his earlier works. As important as the allegorical content of the novel is, however, it is not the only significant topic taken up here by Donoso. Indeed, *Casa de campo* also presents a complex meditation on modern literary language and narrative technique; it is also a playful consideration of the art of writing and narrating novels. The novel explores such topics in the pages in which the narrator, who identifies himself also as the novel's author, speaks openly to the reader about the decisions he has had to make in telling the Venturas' story and about the critical concepts and notions of which he is aware as he composes his text. The narrator-author talks about verisimilitude, about the psychology of fictional characters, about the language deployed by different entities, about the author's relation to the reader, and about the real-world models on which his fiction supposedly has been based. All the while this narrator-author emphasizes the text's status as artifice and the unreality of its story, which, he confesses near the end of the text, none the less manages to seduce its knowledgeable creator into its narrative web. *Casa de campo* artfully moves between what might appear to be opposing thematic interests and discursive forms; however, under Donoso's sure hand these seemingly diverse topics and techniques coalesce to produce one of the author's most accomplished works of fiction and a text that exemplifies the extraordinary inventiveness that has characterized Latin American narrative in recent decades.

LUCILLE KERR

Editions
First edition: *Casa de campo*, Barcelona: Seix Barral, 1978

Translation: *A House in the Country*, by David Pritchard, New York: Knopf, and London: Allen Lane, 1984

Further Reading
Baker, Rilda L., "Perfil del narrador desenmascarado en *Casa de campo*," *CHISPA '81: Selected Proceedings, February 26–28, 1981*, edited by Gilbert Paolini, New Orleans, Louisiana: Tulane University, 1981
Gutiérrez Mouat, Ricardo, "*Casa de campo* y la novela del dictador," *Kañina*, vol. 7/2 (1983)
Íñigo Madrigal, Luis, "Alegoría, historia, novela (a propósito de *Casa de Campo* de José Donoso), *Hispamérica* 21 (1978)
Kerr, Lucille, "Conventions of Authorial Design: José Donoso's *Casa campo*," *Symposium* 42 (1988)
MacAdam, Alfred, "José Donoso: *Casa de campo*," *Revista Iberoamericana*, vol. 47/116–17 (1981)
Murphy, Marie, *Authorizing Fictions: José Donoso's "Casa de Campo,"* London: Támesis, 1992

Ariel Dorfman 1942–

Chilean prose writer and dramatist

It may be one of the more delightful ironies of Latin American literature that Ariel Dorfman should be best known for one of his earliest works and one of his latest works, both through genres with which one does not immediately identify this enormously talented writer. *Para leer al pato Donald*, 1971 (*How to Read Donald Duck*) is a biting sociological interpretation of Walt Disney's comics in terms of US imperialism, which has become a handbook of de-colonisation. More recently his provocative play *La muerte y la doncella*, 1992 (*Death and the Maiden*) has gained for Dorfman an international reputation, admired by critics both in the stage version seen in London and Broadway, and more recently in the Roman Polanski film version. The irony resides in the fact that, sandwiched between these two book-end popular works of political ideology and Pinochet-inspired drama, lies a whole solid corpus of literary writings, critical essays, short fiction, poetry, drama and especially novels, for which he is not at all well known, because of their complexity (both formal and thematic) and challenging propositions. One of the reasons why Dorfman has not gained a popular following is because the complexities of his work force the reader to participate in the creative process. In addition, Dorfman needs to write about politics which influences our lives, and its concomitant themes in Latin America, like exile and alienation.

Dorfman's first novel *Moros en la costa*, 1973 (*Hard Rain*), is much more a fictional collage of book reviews, film scripts, letters, interviews and other miscellaneous pieces which capture the times of the Allende Marxist experiment, with its socio-economic and cultural reforms, all rendered in an obscure but challenging manner by the author's attempt to modify and modernise the structure of the novel. It owes much formally to Cortázar's *Rayuela* (*Hopscotch*) and resembles his *Libro de Manuel*, 1973 (*A Manual for Manuel*) despite Dorfman's criticism of the latter which he considered a political failure. As an early statement of Dorfman's ideological stand and experimental approach to language, *Moros en la costa* is a dense work which certainly achieves his aim of provoking the active reader's collaboration.

Viudas, 1981 (*Widows*), if more structurally traditional, is very much a novel in the Dorfman tradition, concerned as he was (in exile) with the political implications of his country under Pinochet. Dorfman's original intention had been to have it published under a pseudonym, since he was *persona non grata* in Chile, to obviate the censor's rules. However, since it was set in a Greek village suffering from Nazi oppression during World War II, the political (editorial) strategy proved also to be a successful literary device because it ensured aesthetic distancing. Setting it in Greece gave it tragic overtones (Antigone, Trojan women) which it might not have achieved otherwise, if set realistically in Chile. The timeless, yet timely, story of the bereaved women and the disappeared men makes a powerful contribution to the universal cry for human rights.

More directly concerned with Pinochet's Chile, although set in an unnamed country, *La última canción de Manuel Sendero*, 1982 (*The Last Song of Manuel Sendero*) is another complex work. Linked to his first novel by the revolutionary form of the text, it has multiple narrative voices and several layers of plot, including that of the two main characters writing a film script about Pinochet (cf., the two-thousand-year legend of the dragon Pinchot), and the babies (including the son of Manuel Sendero) who refuse to be born into an evil world full of victims, oppressors, and abuse of power. This is a powerful novel about Dorfman's favourite themes, exile, dictatorship, human love, solidarity, which represents the best of his ideas while pushing literary and formal boundaries to the limit, thus daring his readers to jump into the creative act of composition. Dorfman insults no one's intelligence in this rewarding, labyrinthine novel which transcends borders and epochs.

With the publication of *Máscaras*, 1988 (*Mascara*), Dorfman has produced another provocative study of the soul of dictatorship, which conjures up comparisons with Kafka and Orwell, without being overtly a political novel, since it is not set in Chile or even in Latin America. In this inventive story, which is not obviously about human rights but more about betrayal and deception, alienation and memory, Dorfman has created a nondescript character who is not remembered or recognised by anyone, not even his own family. His encounters with a plastic surgeon and his amnesiac lover change his invisibility (not to mention his life) forever. This is a disturbing novel, difficult to understand (even for Dorfman, he admits), notwithstanding the "sort of epilogue" which, rather than helping the reader with its clues and hints, only confuses us more with its quirky ideas on identity, personality and politics.

One of the themes of *Máscaras*, the absence of trust and the need to confide in others, becomes paramount in Dorfman's recent novel *Konfidenz* [Confiding] which was published in 1994 with little fanfare, so taken up were the critics with the filming of *La muerte y la doncella* and its director, Roman Polanski. As in all of his novels, Dorfman is concerned here with the effect of dictatorship, exile and political corruption on human beings. With something of the tone and spirit of his previous novels, *Konfidenz* is at once a political allegory (about truth and betrayal) and a story of personal love between two people who have never met, thrown together by tyranny and approaching war. The unwary reader might assume that it is another novel about Chilean exiles, notwithstanding the title, before the plot unfolds to reveal details about the anti-fascist protagonists who are, in fact, Germans conspiring in Paris against Nazism just before the outbreak of war in 1939. The personal life of the heroine, her love for her fiancée, the links with the political organisation and its ambivalent, ambiguously named members and their need to confide and trust in each other, all demand an attentive reading. The intrusion of anonymous voices and characters, the role of the narrator, the author and, of course, the accomplice-reader, all contribute to the work's fascination and sophistication.

Dorfman's recent commercial success may tempt him to write with less intellectual rigour. Will he be able to sustain his writing on popular culture (Disney, Reader's Digest, Lone Ranger, children's literature, etc.) and literary criticism – original essays on Roa Bastos, Neruda, Asturias, García Márquez, Carpentier, Cardenal, Borges, testimonial literature and much more, in revealing studies like *Imaginación y violencia en América* (1970), and *Hacia la liberación del lector latinoamericano*, 1984 (*Some Write to the Future*). Five collections of short stories capture the essence of life in Chile under Pinochet's dictatorship – human dramas as they affect children, prisoners, doctors, censors, soldiers and their families.

If Dorfman seems best known in the mid-1990s for *La muerte y la doncella*, an irony that will not be lost on him, given his views on popular literature and the demands he puts on his readers, at least he is consistent in his themes. The Pinochet abuses cannot and should not be forgotten by the families of the disappeared or those who survived the institutionalised torture like the protagonist of this hit play. Pauline never forgets the brutal humiliation of doctor Miranda, who tortured her whilst listening to Schubert's music, nor does she forget the voice. In the post-dictatorship days, when her neo-liberal husband, the lawyer Gerardo, now commissioned to investigate the atrocities of the previous regime, brings home his new friend the doctor, Pauline, with horror, recognises the voice of her torturer. Or does she? Set on revenge, she takes the law into her own hands, despite the protests and the advice of her fair-minded do-gooder husband. Dorfman's preoccupation with this theme, which runs like a leitmotif through all his work, is matched only by his dramatic presentation and theatrical skill – not to mention the convincing ambiguity and the accomplice-reader's doubts. Dorfman deals with some important moral issues here – especially the dilemma for the victims of oppression (and the author) who have to live in peace with the now pardoned oppressors and torturers. As he wrestles with truth and lies, reality and imagination, Dorfman creates not only powerful drama but also demands from his compatriots an examination of conscience. With the success of *La muerte y la doncella* and the stage version of *Viudas*, and several other plays in gestation, Dorfman's work for the stage is unlikely to prove ephemeral.

With democracy restored to Chile, although the dragon Pinchot still hovers in the shadows, Dorfman can now spend half his life in his own country, and the other half as a distinguished professor and a literary celebrity in the US. Given the many fragments and contradictions in his own make-up, Dorfman is clearly a multifaceted figure. But the pain and grief of the Pinochet years remain, and will be reflected in his continuing work, which is at root still political.

JOHN WALKER

Biography

Born in Buenos Aires, Argentina, 6 May 1942. Lived in the United States for ten years; moved to Chile in 1954; became Chilean citizen in 1967. Graduated from the University of Chile, Santiago, in philosophy (summa cum laude) 1967. Married María Angélica Malinarich in 1966; two sons. Research scholar, University of California, Berkeley, 1968–69; Professor of Spanish-American studies, University of Chile, 1970–73; exiled from Chile by Pinochet regime, 1973; research fellow, Friedrich Ebert Stiftung, 1974–76; taught Spanish American literature at the Sorbonne, Paris, 1975–76; head of scientific research, Spaans Seminarium, University of Amsterdam, 1976–80; Fellow, Woodrow Wilson Center for International Scholars, Washington, DC, 1980–81; Visiting Fellow, Institute for Policy Studies, Washington, DC, 1981–84; Visiting Professor, University of Maryland, College Park, 1983; Visiting Professor, 1984, and since 1985 (spring semesters) Research Professor of literature and Latin American studies, Duke University, Durham, North Carolina. In the late 1980s he contributed regularly to *Los Angeles Times*, *The Nation*, and *Village Voice*. Recipient of numerous awards including: Chile Films Award, for screenplay, 1972; Israeli Alternative Theatre Festival Prize, 1987; Kennedy Center-American Express New American Plays Award, 1988; *Time Out* Award (London), 1991 for *Death and the Maiden*; Olivier Award (London), 1992 for *Death and the Maiden*.

Selected Works

Novels and Short Fiction

Moros en la costa, Buenos Aires: Sudamericana, 1973; as *Hard Rain*, translated by the author and George R. Shivers, London and Columbia, Louisiana: Readers International, 1990

Cría ojos, Mexico City: Nueva Imagen, 1979; as *My House is on Fire*, translated by the author and George Shivers, New York: Viking, 1990

Viudas, Mexico City: Siglo XXI, 1981; as *Widows*, translated by Stephen Kessler, New York: Pantheon, and London: Pluto, 1983

La última canción de Manuel Sendero, Mexico City: Siglo XXI, 1982; as *The Last Song of Manuel Sendero*, translated by the author and George R. Shivers, New York: Viking, 1987

Dorando la píldora, Santiago de Chile: Ediciones del Ornitorrinco, 1985

Travesía: cuentos, Montevideo: Banda Oriental, 1986

Cuentos paramilitares: la batalla de los colores y otros cuentos, Santiago de Chile: Emisión, 1986

Máscaras, Buenos Aires: Sudamericana, 1988; as *Mascara*, New York: Viking, 1988

Konfidenz, New York: Farrar Straus and Giroux, and London: Hodder and Stoughton, 1995

Plays

Widows, produced 1988 [Adapted from his novel *Viudas*]

Death and the Maiden, London: Nick Hern Books, 1991; New York: Viking Penguin, 1992; as *La muerte y la doncella*, Buenos Aires: Ediciones de La Flor, 1992 [First published in English]

Poetry

Aus den Augen Verlieren/Desaparecer, Bonn: Lamuv, 1979; as *Missing*, translated by Edith Grossman, London: Amnesty International British Section, 1982

Pruebas al canto, Mexico City: Nueva Imagen, 1980

Pastel de choclo, Santiago de Chile: Sinfronteras, 1986

Last Waltz in Santiago and Other Poems of Exile and Disappearance, translated by the author and Edith Grossman, New York: Viking, 1988

Essays and Other Writings

El absurdo entre cuatro paredes: el teatro de Harold Pinter, Santiago de Chile: Editorial Universitaria, 1968

Imaginación y violencia en América, Santiago de Chile: Editorial Universitaria, 1970

Para leer al Pato Donald, in collaboration with Armand Mattelart, Valparaíso, Chile: Universitaria de Valparaíso, 1971; as *How to Read Donald Duck: Imperialist Ideology in the Disney Comic*, translated by David Kunzle, New York: International General, 1975; revised edition, 1984

Ensayos quemados en Chile: inocencia y neocolonialismo, Buenos Aires: Ediciones de La Flor, 1974

Superman y sus amigos del alma, in collaboration with Manuel Jofré, Buenos Aires: Galerna, 1974

La última aventura del llanero solitario, San José, Costa Rica: Ciudad Universitaria Rodrigo Facio, 1979

Reader's nuestro que estás en la tierra: ensayos sobre el imperialismo cultural, Mexico City: Nueva Imagen, 1980; enlarged edition, as *The Empire's Old Clothes: What the Lone Ranger, Babar, and Other Innocent Heroes Do to Our Minds*, New York: Pantheon, and London: Pluto Press, 1983; revised edition, as *Patos, elefantes y héroes: la infancia como subdesarrollo*, Buenos Aires: Ediciones de La Flor, 1985

Hacia la liberación del lector latinoamericano, Hanover, New Hampshire: Ediciones del Norte, 1984; as *Some Write to the Future*, translated by the author and George R. Shivers, Durham, North Carolina: Duke University Press, 1991

Sin ir más lejos: ensayos y crónicas irreverentes, Santiago de Chile: Pehuén, 1986

Los sueños nucleares de Reagan, Buenos Aires: Legasa, 1986

La rebelión de los conejos mágicos, Buenos Aires: Ediciones de La Flor, 1987 [for children]

Chile from Within, 1973–1988, in collaboration with Marco Antonio de la Parra, photographs by Paz Errazuriz, *et al.*, New York: Norton, 1990

Further Reading

As yet, there has been no sustained criticism of Dorfman's work, apart from Oropesa's modest monograph. However, there have been a fair number of book reviews of individual works, and his critical and sociological works have been highly regarded for many years.

Galán, Eduardo, "*La muerte y la doncella. ¿Perdonar los crímenes del fascismo?*" *Primer Acto* (May–June 1993)

Graham-Yool, Andrew, "Dorfman: a Case of Conscience," *Index on Censorship*, vol. 20/6 (June 1991)

Jara, René, *Los límites de la representación. La novela chilena del golpe*, Madrid: Fundación Instituto Shakespeare, 1985

Kapka, Paul, "On Exile and Return. An Interview with Ariel Dorfman," *The Bloomsbury Review*, vol. 9/6 (1989)

Oropesa, Salvador, *La obra de Ariel Dorfman: ficción y crítica*, Madrid: Pliegos, 1992

Vidal, Hernán, *Cultura nacional chilena, crítica literaria y derechos humanos*, Minneapolis: Ideology and Literature, 1989

Interviews

Incledon, John, "Liberating the Reader: a Conversation with Ariel Dorfman," *Chasqui*, vol. 20/1 (May 1991)

Autran Dourado 1926–

Brazilian prose writer

Autran Dourado stands out as one of the most important contemporary Brazilian writers. Since 1947, he has authored more than twenty books, including novels, short stories, novellas, and essays dealing with the poetics of the narrative. Obsessed by the baroque heritage of his native state of Minas Gerais, skilful in the use of stream of consciousness, a skilled craftsman, he has written many of his books employing *blocos* (blocks), a technique that he outlines in his *Uma poética de romance*, 1973 [A Poetics of the Novel].

A significant portion of his fiction is set in Minas Gerais, probably by the turn of the century or in the first three decades of this century, when politics was chiefly a conflict between the two most powerful local families, in a social environment dominated by colonels (chieftains) and landlords; in this setting, honour was an indisputable value, passion was repressed, sex was a matter for men in the brothels. The main exceptions to this general background are *Os sinos da agonia*, 1974 (*The Bells of Agony*), whose plot takes place in 18th-century Minas Gerais, and *A serviço del-Rei*, 1984 [On His Majesty's Service], a kind of contemporary account of the intricacies of power, based on his experiences as the Presidency's Press Secretary.

Three of his novels, *Ópera dos mortos*, 1967 (*The Voices of the Dead*), *Lucas Procópio*, 1984 and *Um cavalheiro de antigamente*, 1992 [An Old-Fashioned Gentleman] reconstitute the story of the family Honório Cota. In the first one, Rosalina inherits the tradition of the *sobrado* (mansion) a kind of sacred space, in the words of Maria Lúcia Lepecki, in opposition to the profane space of the town. In the house both lineages – the one her grandfather, the passionate Lucas Procópio, and that of her father, the secluded João Capistrano – mingled together. Silence reigns in the house, and its only linkage with the small town is through Quiquina, a black servant who is a deaf mute. When Juca Passarinho arrives and settles in the house to work as an odd-job man, the prevailing order is disturbed: he talks too much, he is from another social stratum, he tries to change things (in the mansion the watches were stopped each time someone died). When he becomes Rosalina's lover, she begins to suffer a process of double and divided personality: a passionate woman who speaks uninterruptedly (not about him and not to him) during the night and the boss during the day. At the end, Rosalina goes mad, her unborn child is buried by Quiquina, who restores the sacred order in the *sobrado* and expels Juca. The patriarchal order is disappearing, there are no heirs, the silence and conversation symbolizes the impossibility of historicity within the *sobrado*. As language is primarily a form of socialization, within a space in which language is frozen there is no social transformation possible.

Despite the fact that Quiquina belongs to both another social group and a different ethnicity, the truth is that she is totally absorbed by the values of the mansion. There is no continuation for the seignorial class due to the absence of heirs and due to the impossibility of forging another agent of social transformation. In this regard, *Ópera dos mortos* portrays the impasse of social reproduction among the dominant elites in Brazil, during the transition from the agrarian "aristocracy" into the new urban sectors.

Senra argues that Autranian fiction is built labyrinthically, focusing on characters that are always on the margins of society, surrounded by the pomp of a baroque and decadent Minas Gerais, with its social injustice and moral depravity. "I continue more and more bent towards the past and a Minas that weighs inside of me," he said once in an interview with Senra (1983). In Dourado's novels the mythic is used for the purpose of criticizing, among other things, a state of social immobility. The author's obsession with the phantoms of the *mineiro* past, nevertheless, seems to suggest that his fiction is somehow trapped in the critique that it is aiming to tackle. Be that as it may, incommunicability, death, decadence, madness, solitude are among the main themes that act as vertebrae for his production, undoubtedly one of the most outstanding in Brazilian contemporary literature.

ROBERTO REIS

Biography

Born Waldomiro Autran Dourado in Patos, Minas Gerais, Brazil, 18 January 1926. Childhood in Monte Santo and São Sebastião do Paraíso, Minas Gerais. Began to write short stories at age 16. Moved to Belo Horizonte; journalist. Law degree. Moved to Rio de Janeiro, 1954. Press Secretary of President Juscelino Kubitschek, 1955–60. Awarded the Goethe Literary Prize, Germany, 1982, among others. Books translated into several languages. In 1990s living in Rio de Janeiro, retired as deputy attorney in the Justice Department.

Selected Works

No attempt has been made to divide these works into separate genres because this would run contrary to the author's intentions.

Teia, Belo Horizonte, Brazil: Edifício, 1947
Sombra e exílio, Belo Horizonte, Brazil: João Calazans, 1950
Tempo de amar, Rio de Janeiro: José Olympio, 1952
Três histórias na praia, Rio de Janeiro: Ministério da Educação e Cultura, 1955
Nove histórias em grupo de três, Rio de Janeiro: José Olympio, 1957
A barca dos homens, Rio de Janeiro: Autor, 1961
Uma vida em segredo, Rio de Janeiro: Civilização Brasileira, 1964; as *A Hidden Life*, translated by Edgar H. Miller Jr, New York: Knopf, 1969
Ópera dos mortos, Rio de Janeiro: Civilização Brasileira, 1967; as *The Voices of the Dead*, translated by John Parker, London: Peter Owen, 1980; New York: Tapingler, 1981
O risco do bordado, Rio de Janeiro: Expressão e Cultura, 1970; as *Pattern for a Tapestry*, translated by John Parker, London: Peter Owen, 1984
Solidão solitude, Rio de Janeiro: Civilização Brasileira, 1972
Os sinos da agonia, Rio de Janeiro: Expressão e Cultura, 1974; as *The Bells of Agony*, translated by John Parker, London: Peter Owen, 1988

Novelário de Donga Novais, Rio de Janeiro: DIFEL, 1976
Armas e corações, Rio de Janeiro: DIFEL, 1978
Três histórias no internato: conto, São Paulo: Editora Nacional, 1978
As imaginações pecaminosas, Rio de Janeiro: Record, 1982
A serviço del-Rei, Rio de Janeiro: Record, 1984
Lucas Procópio, Rio de Janeiro: Record, 1984
Violetas e caracóis, Rio de Janeiro: Guanabara, 1987
Um artista aprendiz, Rio de Janeiro: José Olympio, 1989
Monte da Alegria, Rio de Janeiro: Francisco Alves, 1990
Um cavalheiro de antigamente, São Paulo: Siciliano, 1992

Essays

Uma poética de romance, São Paulo/Brasília: Perspectiva/INL, 1973
"Matéria de carpintaria," *Cadernos da PUC*, vol. 9 (1975)
Novelas do aprendizando, Rio de Janeiro: Nova Fronteira, 1980 [On *Teia* and *Sombra e exílio*]
O meu mestre imáginario, Rio de Janeiro: Record, 1982

Compilations and Anthologies

Autran Dourado: seleção de textos, notas, estudos biográfico histórico e crítico e exercícios, edited by Ângela Marie de Freitas Senra, São Paulo: Abril Educação, 1983

Further Reading

Campos, Maria Consuelo Cunha, "Coronéis e jagunços na ficção de Autran Dourado," *Revista Brasileira de Língua e Literatura*, vol. 2/6 (1980)
Chaves, Flávio Loureiro, "Os sinos da agonia," *Minas Gerais*, *Supplemento Literário* 435 (1974)
Lepecki, Maria Lúcia, *Autran Dourado*, São Paulo/Brasília: Quíron/INL, 1976
Patai, Daphne, *Myth and Ideology in Contemporary Brazilian Fiction*, Rutherford, New Jersey: Fairleigh Dickinson University Press, and London: Associated University Presses, 1983 [Chapter 8 is on Dourado]
Reis, Roberto, *A permanência do círculo – hierarquia no romance brasileiro*, Niterói/Brasília: EDUFF/INL, 1987
Senra, Ângela Maria de Freitas (editor), *Autran Dourado*, São Paulo: Abril, 1983 [Série Literatura Comentada]

Drummond de Andrade, Carlos

See Andrade

Oswald Durand 1840–1906

Haitian poet

Oswald Durand has traditionally been considered Haiti's national poet and, until quite recently, was unanimously hailed by his countrymen as "the Haitian Verlaine" or even "the Haitian Victor Hugo." Present-day critics have tended to temper this adulation. In particular, they have criticized his imperfect versification and his tendency to use the same images and turns of phrases in different poems. Throughout his life, Durand contributed numerous poems to newspapers and reviews. Only in 1896, when he was fifty-six, did a selection of his work appear in the two volumes of *Rires et pleurs* [Laughter and Tears] published in Paris. Four years later, a twenty-page brochure of his *Quatre nouveaux poèmes* [Four New Poems] appeared in Haiti, but it is likely that the major part of his production is still buried in 19th-century periodicals, most of which have become extremely rare.

Be that as it may, several of Durand's poems have become classics: most literate Haitians know them, often by heart. Whatever their formal qualities or shortcomings, these poems strikingly illustrate important aspects of the Haitian collective psychology, and of Haitian attitudes towards life. Thus, Durand was one of the first poets who dared to allude directly to the color prejudice through which class distinctions are, to a large degree, expressed in Haiti. The obviously auto-biographical *Le Fils du noir* [The Black Man's Son] is the first-person lament of a dark-complexioned man whom a light-colored young woman has rejected as a suitor simply because of his pigmentation. Like most of his readership, Durand was phenotypically a *mulâtre* rather than a *noir* (the Black man's son is careful to remind us that his dead mother was as white as his beloved). This overly sentimental poem, which expresses neither resentment nor revolt but only plaintive sorrow and resignation, hardly constitutes a threat to the status quo. To be sure, color tensions and rivalries in Haiti were much less virulent in the 19th century than they became later, and were expressed with particular discretion, all the more since, at the time Haitians were proclaiming their patriotism and unity before foreign racism and especially before the first ominous manifestations of US imperialism in the Caribbean.

This patriotism is given expression in many of Durand's poems. The famous *Ces Allemands!* [These Germans!] for example, was written right after the Kaiser sent two warships to Haiti to enforce a German national's abusive claims on the national treasury. The government was forced to comply, and the German crew piled insult upon injury by befouling a Haitian flag before sailing away. Durand compares his country's humiliation to that of the French, who were also ransomed by the enemy after their defeat in the Franco-Prussian war. In *Ode à la France* [Ode to France], another denunciation of the Prussian barbarians, the poet invokes and celebrates the spirit of Napoleon Bonaparte. This is surprising, at the very least, since Napoleon had condemned Toussaint Louverture, the greatest hero of Haiti's struggle for independence, to die of cold and starvation in the Fort de Joux in the Jura mountains.

Another well-known poem deals with an epidemic that was destroying coconut palms around 1880. Since the coconut palm appears on the Haitian coat of arms, it becomes, in *La Mort de nos cocotiers* [The Death of Our Coconut Palms], a synecdoche for the whole country. Durand expresses the fear that the tree dying of sickness symbolizes the country, dying of partisan politics and corrupt government. This lamentation on the state of the nation and the criminal irresponsibility of its leaders has been a traditional theme in Haitian letters practically since Independence, and Durand illustrates it with an ingenious and felicitous conceit.

But not all of Durand's poems are suffused with this typically Haitian pessimism; many express the sensuality and *joie de vivre* which are equally typical of the Haitian collective sensibility. Durand was famous for his appreciation of attractive ladies and strong drink, and many of his poems are celebrations of the beauty of Haitian women. In *Nos payses* [Our Country's Women], for example, he compares them favorably to their White sisters both in physical appearance and amorous expertise. The poet exalts the different phenotypes found in Haiti, the Griffonnes et négresses, et jaunes mulâtresses (light and dark and high-yellow girls), whom he claims to have loved with equal abandon. He tends to describe them in a typical Haitian manner, that is by comparing them to tropical fruit. So that his mistress Idalina's mouth ". . . notre caïmitte / Elle imite / Le violet pur et beau" (As purple as our lovely caymitos) and her breasts suggest "Deux sapottes veloutées / Surmontées / De deux grains de raisin noir" (Rising above twin sapodillas / Two black grapes or maybe raisins).

Just as Durand celebrated his country's women, so was he inspired by its landscapes. He was the first to introduce systematically in his verse the flora and fauna of the island. Until then, Haitian poets preferred to pretend that Haiti (like France) was covered with oaks and apple trees where larks and nightingales sang, rather than with royal palms and mango trees where pipirits and madam saras nestled. In the same way,

Durand could be called one of Haiti's first *costumbristas*: he delighted in describing everyday scenes of urban and rural Haitians at work and play. As the critic Louis Morpeau put it twenty years after Durand's death, he can be considered the most Haitian, the most instinctively African-Latin, the most original of our poets, because he commemorated our splendors and bewailed our wretchedness, because he felt, and skillfully expressed the captivating charm of our country, its very soul.

Another of Durand's claims to fame is his supposedly autobiographical Creole poem, *Choucoune*. Several Haitian poets had occasionally composed in the vernacular before him, invariably in the comic or lightly erotic vein, and Durand in fact contributed numerous compositions of that kind to newspapers. Indeed, he innovated by also composing rather clever advertisements for various Port-au-Prince stores and businesses. Although he carefully collected his Creole poems in several notebooks which were never published and seem to have disappeared, only two poems in the vernacular were included in the one hundred and sixty-eight titles collected in his *Rires et pleurs*: a short fable in the manner of La Fontaine, *Lion aq bourrique* (The Lion and the Donkey), and *Choucoune*. The latter is probably the best-known of all Haitian poems: it was set to music by Mauléar-Monton, a compatriot of Durand's, and, under its English title *Yellow Bird*, is still played and sung by West Indian orchestras all over the world. Of course, only Creole speakers can appreciate the original lyrics. The poem is in fact a kind of pastoral variation on the theme of *Le Fils du Noir*: Petit-Pierre (the name denotes a Haitian of lower social status) bemoans the faithlessness of Choucoune, a beautiful *marabou* (a woman with dark skin, European features and long silky hair) who was about to marry him when a young white man came on the scene and seduced her away. The refrain expresses Petit-Pierre's sorrow with a pungent Creole expression which probably dates back to the times of slavery: dé piéds-moin lan chaîne! (my two feet are in chains!). Significantly, unlike the French-language *Le Fils du Noir*, the poem is not an expression of despair. Indeed it is full of half-humorous, half-salacious details: Choucoune has "tété dubout (firm breasts), li pas gros femm', li grassett'" (she is not a stout woman, she is plump) and when her jilted lover sees her some time later, "Li va fai' yon p'tit qat'ron . . . p'ti ventr'-li bien rond!" (She's about to have a little mulatto . . . her stomach is nice and round !). The description of the White seducer is also humorous and somewhat bitter-sweet: unlike Petit-Pierre, he is rich enough to sport a pocket-watch, he has red hair, a nice pink face, and above all "bell' chivé" (good, that is silky, not woolly hair). But what immediately wins Choucoune over is that "li parlé francé," and not Creole, the lowly, inferior, lower-class language which every Haitian speaks but which the upper classes denigrate: that a Haitian who speaks French is superior to one who speaks Creole only seemed obvious to Durand's readers who, by definition, belonged to the former group. No doubt they identified with the White seducer, and found it perfectly natural that a pretty peasant girl would prefer him to her rough-hewn betrothed. Yet, while not revolutionary, the poem is somewhat disturbing, as evidenced by the fact that it has often been anthologized in bowdlerized versions.

LÉON-FRANÇOIS HOFFMANN

Biography

Born in Cap-Haïtien, Haiti, in 1840. His mother was Aristie de Vastey, a relative of general Thomas-Alexandre Dumas (father of Dumas *père*). Both parents were killed in the 1842 earthquake; raised by his grandmother in the border town of Ouanaminte. Largely self-educated, having received only elementary schooling and two years of secondary formal education. Worked as a tinsmith and was encouraged by Demesvar Delorme, one of the most famous Haitian men of letters of the day, to submit his poetry to newspapers. In 1860 he was teaching at a primary school when he married Virginie Sampeur, whom he deserted a few years later. His wife's lament, *L'Abandonnée* [The Abandoned Woman], appears in most anthologies of Haitain poetry. In 1866 he was named director of the lycée (academic secondary school) in the provincial town of Gonaïves. Having somehow displeased the government, he spent some time in prison in 1883 under sentence of death, but two years later was freed and elected to the lower chamber of the legislature, where he enjoyed six consecutive terms and served as the publisher of the official journal, *Le Moniteur*, and the satiric review *Les Bigailles*. In 1905, at the urging of the novelist Frédéric Marcelin, who was at the time Minister of Finance, the Haitian Parliament awarded Durand a monthly retirement pension of 225 gourdes. Died in 1906 and was given a state funeral.

Selected Works

Fiction

Rires et pleurs (1869–1896), 2 vols, Paris: Imprimerie de Crété, 1896
Quatre nouveaux poèmes, Cap-Haïtien: Imprimerie Librairie La Conscience, 1900

Further Reading

Douyon, Ernest, *L'Année d'Oswald Durand*, Port-au-Prince: Imprimerie de l'Abeille, 1905 [A volume in honour of Durand containing, in particular, speeches to the legislature in support of a motion granting the poet a pension]
Fignolé, Jean-Claude, *Oswald Durand, essai critique*, Port-au-Prince: Imprimerie Les Presses Port-au-Princiennes, 1968 [A revisionist essay stressing, through an analysis of selected poems, the limitations of Durand's poetry]
Fleischmann, Ulrich, "Die vieldeutige Liebe zu Choucoune," in *Frankophone Literaturen ausserhalb Europas*, edited by Janos Riesz, Frankfurt: Peter Lang, 1987; Spanish translation as "El ambiguo amor por Choucoune," in *Anales del Caribe*, Havana 7–8 (1987–88) [An analysis of Durand's most famous poem]
Viard, Félix, *La Dernière étape : Oswald Durand et ses admirateurs*, Montpellier: Éditions des Nouvelles Annales, 1906 [A compendium of critical essays and personal reminiscences by the author's friends]

E

Esteban Echeverría 1805–1851

Argentine poet and prose writer

Among Latin America's finest and best-known Romantic writers, Esteban Echeverría was largely responsible for the introduction into Argentina, and the Southern Cone in general, of the movement he personifies. He is also an early example of the strong tendency among Latin American writers of the 19th century to become important political figures, a regional characteristic which in more muted fashion continues today. As in the case of José Martí and (to some extent) Pablo Neruda, it is somewhat difficult to separate the value of his strictly literary contributions from what he represents to Latin American intellectual history as a whole: just as he, and they, would have had it.

Echeverría was born in Buenos Aires in 1805, to a family of modest economic resources, further reduced with the death of his father when the poet was still a young child. His formal education, in part due to his limited opportunities, was never completed, even though he studied Law and Social Sciences in Paris, using such savings as he had accumulated working in a dry-goods store while pursuing his own readings in diverse areas, together with the study of French. Echeverría's time in France, along with the influence of English Romanticism, was to mark permanently both Echeverría's life, and Spanish American Romanticism. In Paris he came to know many of the major literary figures of the time – Hugo and both the Dumas (father and son), for example – and was much inspired by the passions and innovations of the new style which was sweeping the European continent in all the arts. Schiller, Goethe and Byron in particular, were his most enduring Romantic inspirations.

Upon his return to Buenos Aires in 1830, he set the pattern for his adult life, participating simultaneously in the promotion of the new art he brought from his European experience and in actively opposing the dictatorial regime of Juan Manuel de Rosas, the subject of Echeverría's most acclaimed single piece, the short story *El matadero* (*The Slaughter House*), often described as the first example of the short story genre in Spanish America. It is, along with his essays, his best writing for many modern readers: mordant, allegorical, denunciatory and clearly political, accusing Rosas and his Federalist cohorts of turning the capital city, and the country itself, into nothing less than a place of bestial carnage. (Echeverría was a Unitarian, that is, one who favored a strong central government in Buenos Aires and progressive schemes of modernization on a European model). *El matadero* uses effectively mordant sarcasm and blunt, polar symbolism to denounce Rosas and his deeds and to portray favorably the Unitarian cause. The story then is, aside from its artistic merit, a classic illustration of fictional narrative addressing real social issues in Spanish America.

El matadero and all of Echeverría's best works were written after 1830, in spite of his active participation in the Asociación de Mayo he helped found, in political forums and in his abundant essays and speeches. (One of the best-known of the latter was to this same association, on its inauguration.) He also theorized about writing, especially in the Romantic vein ("Classicism and Romanticism," for example), and continually stressed the urgent need for an independence which went beyond mere political separation from Spain and promoted artistic and intellectual liberation as well from any foreign models: "We are independent, but not free," he wrote. And like a good and dedicated Romantic, his strongly moralistic foundations were expressed in prose and verse in which the national territory, history and character were the models on which to base the Argentina he wished to see, both in reality and in his country's literature.

El matadero, along with several poetic works, stands in esteem today despite what now seems a somewhat simplistic and at times over-wrought melodramaticism: that is to say that Echeverría both introduced Romanticism, and was the exponent of both its greatest and most valuable passions, and its tendencies toward qualities now more often seen as "unrealistic." This sin – if it is a sin – lies in the very nature of the entire movement, in its glorification of the individual, the homeland and emotional commitment, along with persistent conflicts with lived, politicized and all-too-fallible realities. In this tonality, he produced his best-known work, "Elvira, o La novia del Plata" [Elvira, or The Bride of the River Plate]; his passionate *Los consuelos* [Consolations], his dramatic and Byronesque *La cautiva* [(The Captive], along with his *Rimas* [Rhymes]. While a good part of his work was only published posthumously, largely for political reasons, Echeverría was nevertheless a visible, oft-quoted and influential artistic and political figure for two decades.

Echeverría was largely responsible for introducing to Spanish America what soon became Romantic commonplaces: the portrayal of nature as reflective of the characters' mental and spiritual state, and its strong personification and use in fore-shadowing; the hyper-pure leading characters; the extreme moral dichotomy between typologized antagonists; use of varied verse-forms; abundance of vivid and active adjectives, subordination of realistic plot to apparently-fortuitous events, and more. All these qualities may be exemplified in the following passages from *La cautiva*, which (the first two stanzas) introduce and then (the last one) close an Indian attack on the "Christian" (white) settlers of the pampa. The "subhuman" and cruel Indians approach:

El crepúsculo, entretanto,
con su claroscuro manto,
veló la tierra; una faja,
negra como una mortaja,
el occidente cubrió;
mientras la noche bajando
lenta venía, la calma
que contempla suspirando,
inquieta a veces el alma,
con el silencio reinó . . .

Bajo la planta sonante
del ágil potro arrogante
el duro suelo temblaba.
Y envuelto en polvo cruzaba [el clamor]
como animado tropel,
velozmente cabalgando;
víanse lanzas agudas,
cabezas, crines ondeando,
y como formas desnudas
de aspecto extraño y cruel . . .

The bloody attack over, the Indians withdraw in raucous celebration:

. . . y bajo el callo
del indómito caballo,
crujiendo el suelo temblaba;
hueco y sordo retumbaba
su grito en la soledad.
Mientras la noche, cubierto
el rostro en manto nubloso,
echó en el vasto desierto,
su silencio pavoroso,
su sombría majestad.

[Nightfall, meantime, /with its chiaroscuro cloak, / o'er-looked the land; a band, / black as a winding-cloth, / covered the West; / while the descending night / slowly came, for the calm / it contemplates sighing, / restless at times its soul, / in silence assumed its reign. // Under the resounding hooves / of the daring and agile mounts / the firm soil shook. / And wrapped in dust there crossed / in animated throng, /swiftly riding [the horde's sound]; / sharp spears gleamed, / heads and manes undulated, /

and things like naked forms / of strange and cruel appearance. // . . . and under the hooves / of the un-mastered horse / the earth creaked and shook; / their screams in the solitude / empty and dully resounded. / While the night, its face / covered in cloudy cloak, / threw o'er the vast desert, / its fearsome silence, / its dark majesty.]

Echeverría, unlike many of his contemporaries in the Unitarian movement, was able to spend most of his time in his native land, being exiled only later in his life, when he joined those who had preceded him to Montevideo after an unsuccessful attempt to oust Rosas. Through his final months, suffering from the probable tuberculosis which had afflicted him since his youth (and possibly contracted during the ten years he himself called "degenerate"), he continued to write. At the time of his death in 1851, he was correcting the manuscript of *La cautiva*. Echeverría stands today as a model of intelligent and reasoned political commitment, the man most responsible for the introduction of Romanticism into Spanish America – where it became arguably the most dominant literary movement ever – and the author of works which, in denouncing the failings of his own times, announce his own lasting faith that humankind can and surely will produce better days to come, through social commitment and art alike: for Echeverría, as a thoroughgoing Romantic, these two passions are one, inseparably the responsibility and hence the grand opportunity for nothing less than personal and national glory.

PAUL W. BORGESON, JR

Poem translated by Paul W. Borgeson, Jr

See also entry on Caudillismo and Dictatorship

Biography

Born José Esteban Antonino Echeverría in Buenos Aires, Argentina, 2 September 1805. Studied Latin, French, philosophy and drawing during a foundation year at the University of Buenos Aires. Visited Paris in 1825. There, over a period of five years, he delved into a range of subjects in an unmethodical way. Returned to Buenos Aires via London, 1830. Profoundly depressed by state of Argentina on his return. Withdrew into himself. This proved to be a productive period for him as a writer. Joined the literary group that met in the back room of the bookseller Marcos Sastre, 1838. Formed the "Asociación de la Joven Generación Argentina," 1838. Involved in abortive insurrection against the strongman, Manuel de Rosas, 1839, and fled to Montevideo. Poverty and poor health prevented him from further involvement in bringing down Rosas. Died 19 January 1851.

Selected Works

Poetry
Elvira, o, la novia del Plata, Buenos Aires: Argentina, 1832
Los consuelos, Buenos Aires: Argentina, 1834
Rimas, Buenos Aires: Argentina, 1837
La guitarra, Montevideo: n.p.,1842
La insurrección del sud, Montevideo: Cornecio de Plato, 1849
El ángel caído, in *Obras completas*, vol. 2, Buenos Aires: Imprenta y Librería de Mayo, 1871

Prose Narratives
"El matadero," in *Revista del Río de la Plata*, Buenos Aires, 1871; in book form, Buenos Aires: Imprenta de la Universidad, 1926; as *The Slaughter House*, translated by Ángel Flores, New York: Las Américas, 1959
"El peregrinaje de Gualpo," in *Revista del Río de la Plata*, Buenos Aires, 1873
"Cartas a un amigo," in *Revista del Río de la Plata*, Buenos Aires, 1873

Essays
Dogma socialista, Montevideo: Nacional, 1846

Compilations and Anthologies
Obras completas, edited by Juan María Gutiérrez, 5 vols, Buenos Aires: Imprenta y Librería de Mayo, 1870–74; 2nd edition, Buenos Aires: Zamora, 1972
La cautiva, La guitarra y otros poemas, Buenos Aires: Plus Ultra, 1975
Antología de prosa y versos, edited by Osvaldo Pellettieri, Buenos Aires: Editorial de Belgrano, 1981
Obras escogidas, edited by Beatriz Sarlo and Carlos Altamirano, Hanover, New Hampshire: Ediciones del Norte, 1991

Further Reading
Bogliolo, Rómulo, *Las ideas democráticas y socialistas de Esteban Echeverría*, 3rd edition, Buenos Aires: La Vanguardia, 1937

Bucich, Antonio, *Esteban Echeverría y su tiempo*, Buenos Aires: Virtus, 1938
Ghiano, Juan Carlos, *"El matadero" de Echeverría y el costumbrismo*, Buenos Aires: América Latina, 1968
Jitrik, Noé, *El fuego de la especie: ensayos sobre seis escritores argentinos*, Buenos Aires: Siglo XXI, 1971
Katra, William H., *The Argentine Generation of 1837: Echeverría, Sarmiento, Alberdi, Mitre*, Rutherford, New Jersey: Fairleigh Dickinson University Press, 1996
Mantovani, Juan, *Echeverría y la doctrina de la educación popular*, Buenos Aires: Perrot, 1957
Mercado, Juan C., *Building a Nation: the Case of Esteban Echeverría*, Lanham, Maryland: University Press of America, 1995
Moreno Davis, Julio, *Esteban Echeverría, su vida y su pensamiento*, Panama City: n.p., 1972
Palcos, Alberto, *Historia de Esteban Echeverría*, Buenos Aires: Emecé, 1960
Pupo-Walker, Enrique, "Originalidad y composición de un texto romántico: "'El matadero' de Esteban Echeverría," in *El cuento hispanoamericano ante la crítica*, Madrid: Castalia, 1973
Roggiano, Alfredo, "Esteban Echeverría y el romanticismo europeo," in *Actas del Sexto Congreso Internacional de Hispanistas*, Toronto: Department of Spanish and Portuguese, University of Toronto, 1980
Sosnowski, Saúl, "Esteban Echeverría: el intelectual ante la formación del estado," *Revista Iberoamericana* 114–15 (1981)

Ecuador

19th- and 20th-Century Prose and Poetry

The modern name Ecuador, bestowed upon the nation by the members of the National Assembly in 1830, rather belies the pre-Hispanic and colonial heritage of the country. Much more descriptive are previous designations such as the Kingdom of the Shyris (referring to the indigenous peoples who populated the region) or the colonial demarcations of the territory (when Ecuador was called the Audience of Quito). Despite Ecuador's reduced size since 1942, Benjamín Carrión's idea of the "patria pequeña" (small fatherland) asserts that Ecuador is capable of major contributions to world culture, nevertheless: "El Ecuador no podrá competir con las grandes potencias en el aspecto material, pero podrá hacerlo en las faenas del espíritu" (Ecuador cannot compete with major nations as far as material goods are concerned, yet it can compete in matters of spirituality).

It is an Ecuadorian, José Joaquín Olmedo, who is cited in numerous literary anthologies for writing the rousing text of the military victory against Spain which secured the independence of the colonies. His epic poem *La victoria de Junín, Canto a Bolívar*, 1825 [The Victory at Junín, Song to Bolívar] immortalizes the heroic deeds of Simón Bolívar and links the victorious general to the accomplishments of the traditional warrior-kings of the Incas. A defender of the rights of the indigenous population, Olmedo also argued vociferously as a delegate to the courts at Cádiz. Olmedo, for a number of decades dominated the literary scene. His measured poetry describes another epic battle, the successful campaign of General Flores against rebellious armies of citizens. His letters, in addition to his poetry, assure him international recognition.

Newly conscious of their national identity in the aftermath of independence from Spain, several Ecuadorians are credited with establishing the origins of their nation: Pedro Fermín Cevallos wrote a history of Ecuador up to 1845; Pablo Herrera published a history of Ecuadorian literature in 1860, as did Juan León Mera in 1868. The literature of the early republic often features the essays of Ecuador's politicians, especially the presidents. In the 19th century, Vicente Rocafuerte's and García Moreno's speeches and long essays are preserved, as are Luis Cordero's verses of Quichua poetry. These same writers contributed to the regional magazines devoted to the arts and the exploration of social issues: *La Unión Literaria*, 1893 [The Literary Union, Cuenca] and *Revista Ecuatoriana*, 1890 [Ecuadorian Magazine, Quito]. One of the earliest feminist essays was published in the highly regarded *Revista de la*

Sociedad Jurídico-literaria, 1904 [Journal of the Judicial-Literary Society] where Marietta de Veintimilla argued against male superiority and encouraged women to become writers.

Federico González Suárez's *Historia general de la República del Ecuador*, 1890 [General History of the Republic of Ecuador] took him ten years to write for he gathered up books and manuscripts, consulted the archives of Spain and the Americas, and even undertook archeological excavations. The four volumes were shaped by his view of history: "In looking back at our ancestors we can suggest a way of bettering our national character, because a nation, however virtuous it may be, can also improve itself." González Suárez's legacy surpasses the chapters and pages he wrote. He fomented a valuable contribution to Ecuadorian culture in acquiring an impressive research library and in founding the Ecuadorian Society of American Historical Studies, 1909, later the National Academy of History). The nucleus of young intellectuals he gathered in the Archbishop's Palace became outstanding contributors to museum collections and library holdings, in addition to writing monographs on Ecuadorian culture: Jacinto Jijón y Caamaño, Carlos Manuel Larrea and José Gabriel Navarro.

An attempt to summarize the literary tendencies of the 19th century calls attention to the excesses of Romanticism and the cool presence of Neoclassic decorum. Dolores Veintimilla de Galindo embodies the Romantic ideal prominent in the century. Her scant production of intensely personal verse (ten poems) and prose (three texts) is rendered more poignant by the taking of her own life in 1857. Another romantic figure is seen in Marietta Veintimilla who assumed command of Ecuadorian troops and accepted presidential duties if pressed into service by her uncle, Ignacio Veintimilla, who governed Ecuador from 1876 to 1883. Later, in exile, she wrote *Páginas del Ecuador*, 1890 [Pages on Ecuador], a hybrid of novel and memoir.

Juan Montalvo also reflects the political tensions defining the 19th century; much of his writing was undertaken in exile. Montalvo oscillates between Romantic ardor in his polemical pamphlets and a Neoclassic manner in his didactic essay. Much to Montalvo's chagrin, Juan León Mera's skill as a writer and his choice of indigenous themes brought Mera recognition from the Spanish Academy. The success of Mera's *Cumandá* (1879), a novel inspired equally by French literature as well as the tropical forests of Ecuador, intensified the rivalry between the two writers, both native sons of Ambato. Mera's prominence as the foremost Ecuadorian literary spokesperson was challenged by other contemporaries. In his essays, Remigio Crespo Toral took exception with Mera's depictions of Ecuador as a country steeped in indigenous lore. Instead, Crespo's poetry embraced religious themes, Bolívar's last thoughts, and improved relations between Spain and the Americas. Julio Zaldumbide, known as the "philosophical poet," also criticized Mera's position: "Our nation is not Incan, and thus that kind of poetry cannot be our national poetry nor can you be proclaimed our national poet because you do not think and feel as the American populace thinks and feels." Zaldumbide, diplomat and cabinet-level appointee, wrote intensely self-searching meditative verse. Another statesman-poet, Numa Pompilio Llona, similarly avoided themes of nation to craft finely-honed sonnets reflecting Parnassian esthetics and Golden Age motifs.

General Eloy Alfaro's victorious march up the Sierra from the coastal plains in 1895 would decisively affect literary production at the turn of the century. An advocate of separation of church and state, Alfaro's liberal policies are reflected in the increasingly realistic observation of socio-economic problems in Ecuadorian literature. *A la costa* [To the Coast], published by Luis A. Martínez in 1904, uses climactic and ecological factors to explain character development. More importantly, Martínez portrays an entire society, coast and highlands, subject to unjust and obsolete economic and social controls. The graphic realism so characteristic of *A la costa* was continued by three young writers from Guayaquil (Gallegos Lara, Aguilera Malta, Gil Gilbert) in their collection of short stories *Los que se van*, 1930 [Those Who Leave]. The choppy, incisive and occasionally lyrical prose highlights the dialectical speech and customs of the coastal inhabitant, the *montuvio*. All three of these authors, along with José de la Cuadra and Alfredo Pareja Diezcanseco, formed the influential writers collective, the "Grupo de Guayaquil." Nela Martínez, an active member of this group whose work is dispersed in numerous publications, deserves more critical attention.

Demetrio Aguilera Malta and Alfredo Pareja Diezcanseco both served as Ecuador's representatives in diplomatic as well as literary circles and, despite these obligations, they were the most prolific writers of the "Guayaquil Group." In his early novels, *Don Goyo*, 1933 and *La isla virgen*, 1942 [The Virgin Island], Aguilera Malta describes lyrically the mythical belief systems of the coastal inhabitants who at the same time realistically confront the ruling class's exploitation of their environment. Although later novels *C.Z.* (*Canal Zone*), 1935 and *Madrid*, 1936, venture beyond the enclosed regional themes of the Ecuadorian coast, Aguilera returned to this location in his *Siete lunas y siete serpientes*, 1970 (*Seven Serpents and Seven Moons*). Aguilera Malta also made an unjustly under-regarded contribution to the novel of dictatorship with his *El secuestro del general*, 1973 (*Babelandia*). Pareja Diezcanseco was the first of the Guayaquil group to narrate the novel of the city and thus present the complexities of factory workers and wealthy industrialists, a growing middle class, street peddlers and domestic workers, and the claustrophobic confines of incarceration explored in *La casa de los locos*, 1929 [House of Fools]; *Río arriba*, 1931 [Up River]; *El muelle*, 1933 [The Dock]. Although Pareja embarked upon a project of defining the nation in his history of Ecuador (1946) and in his novelistic renditions of the colonial artist Miguel de Santiago and President Eloy Alfaro, he experimented with myth and magical realism in *Las pequeñas estaturas*, 1970 [The Small Ones] and *La manticora*, 1974 [The Manticore].

In the Andean region of Ecuador, writers described the plight of the downtrodden Indian inhabitants, paralleling the efforts of the writers on the coast. Gonzalo Zaldumbide's early novel *Egloga trágica* [Tragic Elegy], written in 1910–11 and finally published as a novel in 1956, shows little sympathy for the Indian; Agustín Cueva characterizes it as a "swan song" of the ruling landowner class. However, literary interest in the Indian was heightened by the powerful sociological analysis written by Pío Jaramillo Alvarado, *El indio ecuatoriano*, 1922 [The Ecuadorian Indian]. Jorge Icaza's *Huasipungo*, 1934 (*The Villagers*) depicted the government official, priest, and landowner as oppressors of the Indian, much as did Fernando Chávez in a previous novel. The crude vocabulary and brutal descriptions of living conditions common to Icaza's style are occasionally relieved by passages of intense lyricism adapted from the Quichua oral tradition, as when Andrés mourns the death of his wife. Icaza's novel, despite its pessimistic theme, was enormously successful and inspired many imitators. Alfonso Barrera Valverde's lyrical novel *Dos muertes en una vida*, 1971 [Two Deaths in One Life] moves beyond the indigenous theme to depict the *campesino* of indigenous heritage who leaves the countryside to obtain a university degree and thus contemplates a new identity as a mestizo of Indian and Spanish heritage. It is possible that indigenous narrative and poetry will be infused with new insights, given heightened cultural consciousness among Indians and the successful protest marches coordinated by CONAIE (the Confederation of Indigenous Nations of Ecuador) in 1990 and 1992. For instance, Ariruma Kowii, a native of Otavalo, recently has published two books of Quechua poetry.

The Esmeraldas province has inspired both Adalberto Ortiz (*Juyungo*, 1934) and Nelson Estupiñán Bass's *Cuando los guayacanes florecieron*, 1954 [When the Guayacan Trees Bloomed] to portray the traditional rhythms and lyrics of the African Ecuadorian population along with narratives of social unrest and a quest for equality. Antonio Preciado's poetry, reflective of Esmeraldas, has received numerous prizes and is widely translated. Laura Hidalgo has collected and analyzed the traditional *décimas*, popular verses sung in the northwestern coastal cities of Ecuador.

While much of Ecuadorian literature takes a long, hard look at social injustice and economic hardship, there is a significant body of work that departs from this theme. In disseminating the writings of Henri Barbusse, Gabriele D'Annunzio and José Enrique Rodó, Gonzalo Zaldumbide provided the intellectual foundation for Ecuador's generation of "decapitated" *modernista* poets of the turn of the century: Borja, Noboa Caamaño, Fierro, and Silva. Zaldumbide's admiration for French literature and culture is paralleled in Alfredo Gangotena's work, written primarily in French. Well received by Jean Cocteau, Max Jacob and Tristan Tzara, Gangotena's poetry received wider dissemination with translations written by Gonzalo Escudero and Filoteo Samaniego (1956). Similarly, César Dávila Andrade, a member of the poetic literary circle called "Elán," cultivated a personal and hermetic style, which ended with despair in his final years in Caracas. His poetry reflects a meditative contemplation of natural surroundings and the place of humans within it; however, in *Boletín y elegía de las mitas*, 1954 [Bulletin and Elegy of Work Gangs] he does engage in a more ideologically outspoken defense of the Indian.

In the 1920s and 1930s, the vanguardist manifestos published in literary magazines articulated the esthetic and social concerns of many writers. Decidedly modern illustrations, innovative typography, and audacious Modernist themes distinguish the internationally-oriented Guayaquil magazines of the 1920s (*Savia, Los hermes, Singulus*). Unfortunately, *Motocicleta* [Motorbike], a key magazine of these years, has not yet turned up (1996) despite intensive research. Among its contributors was Hugo Mayo; *El zaguán de aluminio*, 1982 [The Aluminum Vestibule] recovers some of his provocative

vanguardist poetry. Often, these publications focused on regional issues. In Loja, *Hontanar*, 1931 [Hontanar] and *Bloque*, 1935 [Block] emphasized indigenous themes under the guidance of Carlos Manuel Espinosa, while G. Humberto Mata in Cuenca wrote poems laced with Quechua words for *Mañana*, 1928 [Tomorrow]. In Quito, *Lampadario* changed its name to *Elán* in 1932, yet the orientation of the journal was steadfast. In 1931 their stated objective was "To make art out of its social function, extracting it from our own reality." *Nervio* (1934) was the organ of the socialist writers of A.N.D.E.S in Quito. Despite the activity of these literary circles, Jorge Icaza remained unattached to any group while Jorge Carrera Andrade's essays and poetry were eagerly sought by these periodicals.

Pablo Palacio was one of the first writers to capture the fragmentation of Ecuadorian society. In fact, some critics laud Palacios as a precursor of vanguardism and the founder of Ecuadorian literature, assertions much debated by Agustín Cueva. A glance at the titles of his brief narratives reveal the psychologically oriented, subjective themes that characterize his work: *Un hombre muerto a puntapies*, 1927 [A Man Kicked to Death], *Vida del ahorcado*, 1932 [Life of a Hanged Man], along with *Déborah* (1927). This self-reflexiveness allows him to address the central questions of literary representation, although this same piercing inquiry causes significant disruptions in a coherent narrative framework. Eschewing regional stereotypes, Palacio decenters reality and presents a universal dilemma, according to Patricia Varas: "What we end up with is one individual, alone, encapsuled in a cement block."

As in the 19th century, the question of identity surfaces in contemporary Ecuadorian literature and essay. With the creation of the Casa de la Cultura (the Ecuadorian Cultural Endowment) in 1944, selected writers and artists have received national recognition and funding. However, in the 1960s, writers and critics proposed an alternative model for the legitimization of culture in the nation. The Frente Cultural (Cultural Front) challenged the official line in their journals *La bufanda del sol* [The Muffler of the Sun] and *Pucuna* [Blowgun]. Members of this collective, Raúl Pérez Torres and Ivan Egüez, with dazzling narrative techniques closely evaluated their society. They both highlight political events in their narratives – the massacre of sugar mill workers in 1977 and the aftermath of the Peruvian invasion in the time of Galo Plaza – with consciously crafted prose. Pérez, recipient of three prizes for narrative, uses stream of consciousness and multiple narrators in first/second/third persons to mock bourgeois conventions. Egüez in *La Linares*, 1975 [The Linares Woman] contrasts the official government version of events with the gossipy whisper of testimony from the masses. In poetry, Ulises Estrella's *Peatón de Quito*, 1994 [Footsteps through Quito] is a demythifying glance at Ecuadorian history, along with Humberto Vinueza's *Un gallinazo cantor bajo un sol de a perro*, 1970 [A Buzzard Singer Beneath A Scorching Sun].

In recent poetry and narrative, the everyday language of life is exalted. Julio Pazo's prizewinning book of poetry, *Levantamiento del país con textos libres*, 1982 [A Bettering of the Country Through Free Texts] emphasizes Andean foods ("sancocho" soup with its common ingredient, potatoes) and popular culture (the singer Carlota Jaramillo), while Euler Granda includes dialog recovered from the sounds of the city, recast in poetic form (*Poemas con piel de oveja*, 1993 [Poems in Sheepskin]. Women writers also observe their surroundings and are not silent about controversial topics such as abortion (Laura Pérez's *Sangre en las manos*, 1959 [Blood on One's Hands], lesbianism and rape (the short stories of Eugenia Viteri), the confusion of *mestizaje* (creolization) in Mary Corylé, and subversions of sexual categories (the title story of Lucrecia Maldonaldo's *No es el amor quien muere*, 1994 [It's Not Love Who Dies]. Currently, the literary group Mujeres del Atico (Women of Atico) has attracted attention through their sponsorship of cultural events and their newspaper editorials published in *El Telegráfo* (The Telegraph, Guayaquil). Cecilia Ansaldo Briones is one of the participants. Her anthology of Ecuadorian short stories *Cuento contigo*, 1993 [I'm Counting on You] is a useful guide to the genre and her critical essays are always insightful.

Television has encouraged an appreciation of Ecuadorian themes with the airing of a mini-series based on *Cumandá* and "*La Tigra*" (The Tiger). In addition, the publication of "Clásicos Ariel" (Ariel Classics) and Colección Antares (the Antares Collection) has made Olmedo, Mera, and Icaza (as well as other writers) available in low cost, mass-produced editions with excellent critical commentary appended. As in many nations, appropriations to the humanities have been slashed and therefore publications have been curtailed. Nevertheless, *Cultura*, the journal of the Central Bank of Ecuador, continues to provide insightful commentary as does the new magazine *Kipus* [Incan Knots], published by the Andean University Simón Bolívar. With the continuing sponsorship of regional workshops, the Casa de la Cultura (Ecuadorian Cultural Endowment) is providing a venue for little-known but gifted writers. Thus, literature and the arts may begin to reflect the multicultural society so often mentioned in the speeches of presidents Borja and Sixto Durán in recent years.

REGINA HARRISON

Further Reading

Adoum, Jorge Enrique, "Las clases sociales en las letras contemporáneas de Ecuador," in *Panorama de la actual literatura latinoamericana*, Havana: Casa de las Américas, 1969

Carvajal, Ivan, *et al.*, *Historia, cultura y política en el Ecuador*, Quito, Ecuador: El Conejo, 1988

Carrasco, Adrián, *et al.*, *Estado, nación y cultura. Los proyectos históricos en el Ecuador*, Cuenca, Ecuador: IDIS, Universidad de Cuenca, 1988

Cueva, Agustín, *Entre la ira y la esperanza: Ensayos sobre la cultura nacional*, Quito, Ecuador: Editorial Casa de la Cultura, 1967

____ *Sobre nuestra ambigüedad cultural*, Quito, Ecuador: Editorial Universitaria, 1974

____ *Literatura y conciencia histórica en América Latina*, Quito, Ecuador: Planeta, 1993

Handelsman, Michael, *Amazonas y artistas: un estudio de la prosa de la mujer ecuatoriana*, 2 vols, Ecuador: Núcleo del Guayas, 1978

____ *El modernismo en las revistas literarias del Ecuador: 1895–1930*, Cuenca, Ecuador: Casa de la Cultura Ecuatoriana, 1981

____ *Incursiones en el mundo literario del Ecuador*, Guayaquil: Universidad de Guayaquil, 1987

Heise, Karl H., "*El grupo de Guayaquil*": arte y técnica de sus novelas sociales, Madrid: Playor, 1975

Ribadeneira, Edmundo, *La moderna novela ecuatoriana*, Quito, Ecuador: Editorial Universitaria, 1981

Rojas, Ángel F., *La novela ecuatoriana*, Mexico City: Fondo de Cultura Económica, 1948

Sacoto, Antonio, *The Indian in the Ecuadorian Novel*, New York: Las Américas, 1967

____ *Sobre el ensayo ecuatoriano contemporáneo*, Quito: Banco Central, 1988

____ *Novelas claves de la literatura ecuatoriana*, Cuenca, Ecuador: Universidad de Cuenca, 1990 [Includes *Cumandá*; *Entre Marx y una mujer desnuda*; *Huasipungo*; several works by Aguilera Malta]

Tinajero, Fernando, *De la evasión al desencanto*, Quito, Ecuador: El Conejo, 1983 [Iconoclastic response to Ecuadorian letters]

____ *Aproximaciones y distancias*, Quito, Ecuador: Planeta, 1986

Waag, C. Michael, "Political Satire through Popular Music and a Popular Vision of Reality: *La Linares*, a New Novel from Ecuador," *Perspectives on Contemporary Literature* 13 (1986)

Compilations and Anthologies
Rodríguez Castelo, Hernán, *Lírica ecuatoriana contemporánea*, 2 vols, Quito, Ecuador: Círculo de Lectores, 1979

Special Issues of Journals
Casa de las Américas, Havana, 127 (July–August 1981)
Revista Iberoamericana 144–45 (July–December 1988)

Jorge Edwards 1931–

Chilean prose writer

By tradition, Latin American intellectuals are often granted or assume diplomatic posts. With this in mind, it is not surprising to discover that Jorge Edwards joined the Chilean Ministry of Foreign Relations in 1960. Edwards, by then a recognized short-story writer, became the first diplomatic representative to be sent to Cuba by the Allende government. This brief and stormy appointment of only three and a half months culminated in his enforced resignation and departure from Cuba. The experience marked a turning point in Edwards's career as a writer since it provoked him into writing the work for which he is perhaps best known, *Persona non grata*. Work on this book began in early 1971, continued in Paris, and was completed in Spain toward the end of 1973. Within five months of its publication, this historical chronicle or testimony, which Edwards describes as "a non-fiction political novel" of post-revolutionary Cuba had sold out two editions. *Persona non grata* sets itself apart from other social documents of the period, since it chronicles social repression from the viewpoint of the artist who speaks his conscience in a police state. Since the work is, in part, the autobiography of an intellectual, it offers a richness of unique perspectives – a single authorial voice which calls upon other renowned figures to comment upon a multiplicity of related topics. Fidel Castro, of course, is an important figure in the narrative as are his brother Raúl, Che Guevara briefly, Salvador Allende, as well as a number of writers, such as Carlos Fuentes, Mario Vargas Llosa, Pablo Neruda and several Cuban ones. Indeed, the book's publication resulted in a political scandal and intellectual debate in Latin America that caused Mario Vargas Llosa (by then hostile to Cuba) to comment that Edwards had "broke[n] the sacred taboo among intellectuals: the untouchability of the Cuban Revolution." *Persona non grata*, although not limited to these topics, includes reflections on the following: Chile during the Allende years, socialism in Latin America, the role of the writer-diplomat, freedom of speech and conscience of the writer in the newly-formed society as he attempts to critique that society, the Chilean Revolution and the diverse interpretations of socialism taken by Cuba and Chile, charismatic leadership and its advantages and pitfalls, the plight of the artist in a repressive society, foreign intervention in Chilean and Cuban internal political affairs, the Latin American need for independence from foreign control and exploitation, and the fate of the bourgeoisie and the intelligentsia in Cuba. An open-structured, polyhistoric, or multi-perspective narrative, *Persona non grata* is replete with testimonial formats: chronicles, anecdotes, diary excerpts, self-reflections, rhetorical questions, personification, demythification, critical commentary, analysis, and synthesis. These forms of pseudofiction are presented as undisguised autobiography, often underscored through typographical variation or quotation marks in the text. The work placed Edwards in a type of "literary exile" from those of his peers who, like Julio Cortázar, still supported the Cuban Revolution. This sector of the Left condemned the book, and mass demonstrations ensued at the work's publishing houses in Germany and France. Edwards was harshly criticized and isolated from his contemporaries both in their native countries and those living abroad in exile. The publication of this book, more than any of his other writings, was to have a lasting impact on Jorge Edwards the man and the writer. It was at this point that Edwards began to question the role of the intellectual in the political affairs of the state, particularly as they relate to artistic creation. In short, the demarcation between literary creation and testimonial or historical accounts, between fiction and reality, became even further narrowed with the publication of *Persona non grata*.

As regards Edwards's other prose works – namely his short story collections and novels – they are characterized by autobiographical elements and a lyrical mood, together with social criticism, particularly of the Chilean middle class. In the epigraph to his short story "Adiós, Luisa," Edwards reveals his "symphonic" approach to his craft: "The writer is a public researcher: he alters what he begins, stubborn and unfaithful, he is unfamiliar with anything else but this single artistry: that of themes and their variations." His themes in these shorter narratives generally are the product of his own experiences placed in a social context: childhood, solitude, lack of communication, and, most significantly, an existentialist focus on sociopolitical, familial, and cosmic order. Revolution-counterrevolution, order-disorder, harmony-disharmony in all their personal and social manifestations are examined repeatedly in Edwards's narratives. These existentialist themes of self and society of the so-called Generation of 1950 group of writers of which Jorge Edwards is considered a member, are most apparent in his short story collections *El patio*, *Gente de la ciudad* [City Folk] and *Las máscaras* [Masks] and his novel *El peso de la noche* [The Weight of the Night]. The writers of this group share an intellectual curiosity for the works of Camus, Kafka, Proust, Jean-Paul Sartre and an artistic appreciation of the poetic works of fellow Chileans Vicente Huidobro and Pablo Neruda. Their protest in the form of "peaceful anarchy" exposes social ills in their literary works through a variety of styles. Jorge Edwards's works of social realism focus on autobiographical themes with a sharp criticism of bureaucracy and middle-class decadence and loss of values. His works portray an authoritarian Chilean society operating on rigid norms which place sanctions on personal rebellion and individual freedoms. All the while Edwards creates a subtle poetic mood, despite his biting censure. Just as Edwards's experimentation with new narrative techniques of time and simultaneity and the limits between reality and fantasy are apparent in later works, a sense of "time lost" in the Proustian sense provides the backdrop to his short stories and novels. As figures resigned to empty, ritualistic, and sordid lives, many of his characters incapable of enduring the pain of their suffering or of altering their lives, seek escape in alcoholism, denial, and fantasy. The themes of bourgeois decadence and decaying conservatism are recurrent concerns in all of his works. Social, political and moral order are sharply contrasted with disorder, adventure, and individual and social excesses; familial degeneration becomes a reflection of social disintegration. Edwards portrays alcoholics as examples of social degeneration and believes that alcohol is the "opium of the Chilean people" that has become an integral part of all facets of societal interactions.

Like García Márquez, Edwards was entertained by the stories of an older person (his mother) as a child. Indeed, the strong female characters prevalent in some of his works are fictional counterparts to this maternal figure – the grandmother Cristina in *El peso de la noche;* the protagonist of *La mujer imaginaria* [The Imaginary Woman] varied characters in *Los convidados de piedra* [The Stone Guests]. The artistry in the prolific writings of Jorge Edwards perhaps lies most in his ability to blend the personal with the social, the anecdotal with the historical, and the real with the imaginary. His recently developed interest in the historical novel is a testimony to his diverse stylistic talents in this regard. Throughout his narrative career Jorge Edwards has never lost sight of his national heritage. Regardless of his travels abroad, Edwards's major concern is an almost sociological study of the Chilean people, their personal lives and social interactions, their impact upon individual lives (such as the novelist's own life), as well as the profound effect of class and group dynamics on the nation as a whole in its pendulum movements to embrace different degrees and forms of order from social revolution to military dictatorship to a restoration of democratic rule.

ELENA DE COSTA

See also entry on Testimonial Writing

Biography

Born in Santiago de Chile, 29 July 1931. Relatives were owners of the important daily newspaper *El Mercurio* to which he contributed for a time. Educated by Jesuits at the Colegio de San Ignacio de Santiago preparatory school; studied Law and Philosophy at the University of Chile where he came in contact with a number of writers and poets. Received law degree in 1958; studied Political Science at Princeton University, New Jersey, a year later. Foreign political appointments include: 1960, secretary of Chilean embassy and representative for European affairs (as Chilean delegate to General Agreement on Tariffs and Trade, otherwise known as GATT), served in Paris; 1962, named Secretary to the Chilean Ambassador in France and to the European Common Market (Brussels); 1967, Advisor for Cultural Affairs and Chairman of Department for Eastern European Affairs in Chile (Ministry of Foreign Relations); 1970, attaché to Chilean embassy in Lima, Peru, and first diplomatic representative of Salvador Allende's socialist government in Havana, Cuba, at the end of the same year; 1971, enforced departure from his post in Havana; subsequently sent to Paris to assist the Chilean ambassador, Pablo Neruda, in the capacity of Advisory Minister; 1973, expelled from the diplomatic corps by General Augusto Pinochet. Political views are currently expressed as President of the Committee for Freedom of Expression of the Chilean Commission on Human Rights. In 1980 Edwards was accepted into the Chilean Academy of the Language. In 1985 he assumed teaching posts in the United States at the University of Fort Collins, Colorado and Vanderbilt University in Nashville, Tennessee.

Selected Works

Short Fiction

El patio, Santiago de Chile: Carmel Soria, 1952

Gente de la ciudad, Santiago de Chile: Editorial Universitaria, 1961
Las máscaras, Barcelona: Seix Barral, 1967
Temas y variaciones, Santiago de Chile: Editorial Universitaria, 1969

Novels

El peso de la noche, Barcelona: Seix Barral, 1964
Los convidados de piedra, Barcelona: Seix Barral, 1978
El museo de cera, Barcelona: Bruguera, 1981
La mujer imaginaria, Barcelona: Plaza y Janés, 1985
El anfitrión, Santiago de Chile: Planeta, 1987
Fantasmas de carne y hueso, Barcelona: Tusquets, 1993

Testimonial Writing

Persona non grata, Barcelona: Seix Barral, 1973; as *Persona non grata: a Memoir of Disenchantment with the Cuban Revolution*, translated by Andrew Hurley, New York: Paragon House, 1993 [An earlier translation was published in 1977]

Other Writings

Desde la cola del dragón, Chile y España 1973–1977, Barcelona: Dopesa, 1977 [Collection of articles and essays about Chilean and Spanish culture, politics and society published in Spanish newspapers]
Adiós, poeta, Barcelona: Tusquets, 1990 [Memoir of Pablo Neruda]

Compilations and Anthologies

Temas y variaciones. Antología de relatos, Santiago de Chile: Editorial Universitaria, 1969
Cuentos completos, Barcelona: Plaza y Janés, 1990

Further Reading

Alegría, Fernando, *Nueva historia de la novela hispanoamericana*, Hanover, New Hampshire: Ediciones del Norte, 1986
Jara, René, *Los límites de la representación*, Madrid: Hiperión, 1985
Jara, René and Hernán Vidal, *Testimonio y literatura*, Minneapolis, Minnesota: Institute for the Study of Ideologies and Literature, 1986
Lafourcade, Enrique, *Cuentos de la Generación del 50*, Santiago de Chile: Nuevo Extremo, 1959
Lihn, Enrique, "Jorge Edwards: la aventura y el orden en la nueva narrativa chilena," prologue to the anthology of short stories by Jorge Edwards, *Temas y variaciones*, Santiago de Chile: Editorial Universitaria, 1969
Osses González, Pedro, *Acercamiento a Jorge Edwards*, Santiago de Chile: Editorial La Noria, 1992
Peralta, Jaime, *Cuentos chilenos de la Generación de 1950*, Madrid: Ínsula, 1963
Promis Ojeda, José, *La novela chilena actual*, Buenos Aires: García Cambeiro, 1977
Shaw, Donald L., *Nueva narrativa hispanoamericana*, Madrid: Cátedra, 1981
Skármeta, Antonio, "Narrativa después del golpe," in *Primer coloquio sobre literatura chilena (de resistencia en el exilio)*, Mexico City: UNAM, 1980
Turner, John H., review of *Persona non grata*, *Chasqui*, vol. 4/1 (November 1974)
Vargas Llosa, Mario, "Un francotirador tranquilo," in his *Contra viento y marea (1962–1982)*, Barcelona: Seix Barral, 1983

Interviews

Gliemmo, Graciela, *Las huellas de la memoria. Entrevista a escritores latinoamericanos*, Buenos Aires: Beas, 1994

José María Eguren 1874–1942

Peruvian poet

Alongside the work of César Vallejo, that of José María Eguren is the other literary landmark critics refer to in discussions about modern poetry in Peru. In the introduction to his *Antología de la poesía peruana,* 1965 [Anthology of Peruvian Poetry], in which he traces a history of the poetic tendencies of this century, Alberto Escobar calls them the "founders" of the tradition.

Eguren's first poems appeared in 1899, during the great social changes of the western world at the end of the century. His first book was published a few years before World War I, a period which saw the close of the *belle époque* and the expansion of the society of masses. In contrast with these agitated years, Eguren lived a life isolated from the artistic milieu of his era, his few contacts with other writers were, nevertheless, fundamental. He established friendships with authors of earlier and later generations, predominantly with those representing dissonant voices in a conservative environment. His friendship and interaction with Manuel González Prada, José Carlos Mariátegui and Martín Adán testify to his knowledge of the literature of his contemporaries and his immersion in the aesthetic preoccupations of his time. In his works, Eguren assembles the different ways in which Spanish American *Modernismo* and European poetry give form to the definitive universal expansion of capitalism and of bourgeois values.

Eguren's biographers have underlined the importance of his childhood in the outskirts of Lima, the city where he was born, as well as the years he spent living by the sea. These circumstances have been used by his critics to explain the poet's constant inclination toward nature and his detailed contemplation of the rural landscape and Lima's foggy coastal shores.

Eguren's style is most certainly sensorial and meticulous to the point of miniaturization. With regard to sound, his verses create a refined musicality. The use of synesthesia and a rich vocabulary contribute to this effect, as one can appreciate in the initial lines of the poem "Avatara" from his collection *La canción de las figuras,* 1916 [The Song of Figures], "Sweet Orpheons were echoing . . . / The lamplighter painted / a violet evening star, / and we saw crystal sadness on the balconies." Visually, Eguren's images are unstable, mysterious, surrounded by scenery full of vagueness and crepuscular shadows. Eguren also draws upon Nordic mythological imagery to create poetic scenographies for memorable characters, such as, for example, those that appear in the texts "Los reyes rojos" [The Red Kings], "Syhna la blanca" [Syhna, the White One], "La tarda" [The She-Evening] or "La niña de la lámpara azul" [The Girl with the Blue Lamp]. The predominance of sensorial images; an interest in nature and the sea; the title of his first volume, *Simbólicas,* 1911 [Symbolics]; and elements reminiscent of Charles Baudelaire and Edgar Allan Poe, have permitted a Symbolist reading of his work. The voice of Eguren imposes itself subtly and full of suggestion as, for example, at the end of the poem "El bote viejo" [The Old Boat], from his collection *Sombra,* 1929 [Shadow]: "And in the depths of the night, / on a delicate glistening wave, / the dying boat departed / towards faraway ports."

The critics never cease to mention Poe – a poet with whom Eguren was certainly familiar – in many of the readings of the Peruvian's work. There are, in fact, numerous common elements between the two writers: medieval and gothic settings, speculative wanderings, hair-raising situations, an atmosphere of death, an infantile tone and rigorous formality, among others. Eguren eclectically appropriated whatever he might need. These same elements are also shared by the Bolivian poet Ricardo Jaimes Freyre, his contemporary. But the previous comparisons are sustained, especially if the analysis goes beyond thematics and stylistic tools, paying special attention to the "founding" function these poets played in the cultural life of their nations, undergoing a move from an aristocratic rural society to a democratic industrial society.

Contemporary commentators on Poe, William Carlos Williams and T.S. Eliot, for example, have emphasized the "originality" of Poe's work (as being novel and creating space for novelty) in the English language. Just as Poe is a cultural founder of the first modern project of a democratic, industrial and capitalist nation, Eguren plays a similar role in the formation of a modern nationality in Peru. The complex imagery created by these writers consists of people, places and settings that have not previously existed anywhere, neither spatially nor temporally, the origins of which reside in language itself. This new type of poetic language, that has marked the western poetry of the 20th century, possesses forms and contents that capture the readers' attention. The poem is no longer a stylized or ornamented reflection of an already existing reality. The language signals the artificial nature of the poem as a work of art that proposes to sustain itself on its own, without being obliged to reflect or to reproduce any previously known reality. The geography, the setting, the protagonists and the objects of this poetry have vague contours making them unrecognizable. Eguren's poetry proposes to broaden the reader's parameters of perception, thus allowing a new consideration of sensory reality, a type of modern "consciousness."

These poetics precede the reorganization of the world at the beginning of the 20th-century when, along with industrial production and mass society, wars are carried out which result in the redefining of territories and the determining of economic relationships between the modern nations. It is in light of this context that the characters of Eguren's poetry are animated, as in the poem "El caballo" [The Horse], where this figure, killed in "an ancient battle," "At the leaden corner / of the barricade, / with empty eyes / and with horror, comes to halt. // Later its slow steps / are heard / along deserted roads, / and ruinous town squares." The atmosphere of infantile evocations, decadence and disintegration in Eguren's poems, is an expression that accompanies a process of modernization that has two faces: military destruction and the promise of technological progress. The contemplation of nature as well as the treatment of childhood take on particular importance in the works of Eguren, especially if one considers that these refer to the experience of the years of the Pacific War (1879–83), Chilean military occupation and the biggest economic crisis in

19th-century Peru. At the end of the war, Eguren's family left the *hacienda* where they lived in the outskirts of Lima, and moved to the town of Barranco, on the shores of the Pacific. This town and the neighboring beach resort of Chorrillos were residential zones ransacked and burned by the occupying troops.

Along with his literary work in verse, Eguren left a series of texts in prose that were collected and published posthumously under the title *Motivos estéticos*, 1959 [Aesthetic Motives]. In these he elaborates his ideas on art, poetry, and the manner in which the artist gives form to modernity. Eguren sees the poet as one who "guides his contemporaries toward civilization," saying also that: "The poet should consecrate his artistic aptitudes toward breaking through the limits reached up to that time, if this is not achieved he will remain there; but under no circumstances is he allowed to turn his head because the defeated will defeat him." Eguren's conception of modernity finds its roots in the "specialized" work of the writer, which he understands as the person who dedicates himself to the production of new forms of language and interpretations of his world.

The work of Eguren also includes painting and photography. His watercolors develop themes and depict environments similar to those found in his poetry. In photography, Eguren was a dedicated technician who constructed miniature cameras and experimented with microfilm.

Those active in the circuit of cultural propagation in Peru chose to shun Eguren who, therefore, was valued by only a few of his contemporaries. Now he is considered one of the most difficult and fascinating writers of Spanish America. Even with *Modernismo* and avant-garde in the past, his work still offers unexplored facets for his critics.

Luis Rebaza-Soraluz

Biography
Born in Lima, Peru, 7 July 1874. Brought up with seven siblings on an estate near Lima. Happy childhood in close proximity with nature. Educated at Jesuit school, La Inmaculada, in Lima. After the death of his parents, he moved to Barranco (then a small village close to Lima) with his two unmarried sisters, Susana and Angélica. Began to publish poetry in magazines in 1899. Took up painting and photography. Published poetry in Mariátegui's journal, *Amauta* (see entry on José Carlos Mariátegui). Lived a retired life with his sisters until his patrimony ran out around 1928. Moved house and obtained employment as librarian in Ministry of Education. Health declined and he died in Lima, April 1942.

Selected Works

Poetry
Poesías, Lima: Biblioteca Amauta, 1929 [Contains *Simbólicas*, 1911; *La canción de las figuras*, 1916; *Sombra* and *Rondinelas*]

Prose
Motivos estéticos: notas sobre el arte y la naturaleza, Lima: Universidad Nacional Mayor de San Marcos, 1959

Compilations and Anthologies
Poesías escogidas, selected by Manuel Scorza, with an introduction by José Carlos Mariátegui, Lima: Patronato del Libro Peruano, 1957
Obras completas, edited by Ricardo Silva-Santisteban, Lima: Mosca Azul, 1974

Further Reading
Adán, Martín, "Eguren," in his *De lo barroco en el Perú*, Lima: Universidad de San Marcos, 1968
Higgins, James, *Hitos de la poesía peruana*, Lima: Milla Batres, 1993 [Chapter 1 is on Eguren]
Mariáteguí, José Carlos, "Eguren," in his *Siete ensayos de interpretación de la realidad peruana*, Lima: Amauta, 1928; as *Seven Interpretative Essays on Peruvian Reality*, translated by Marjory Urquidi, Austin: University of Texas Press, 1971
Ortega, Julio, *José María Eguren*, Lima: Editorial Universitaria, 1965
Silva-Santisteban, Ricardo (editor), *José María Eguren: aproximaciones y perspectivas*, Lima: Universidad del Pacífico, 1977

El Salvador

19th- and 20th-Century Prose and Poetry

The literary history of El Salvador is characterised by two salient features: small clusters of writers who stand out like beacons among their contemporaries and the critical, often tragic nexus between literature and politics throughout its embattled history since Central American independence in 1821. This general framework for surveying modern Salvadorean literature yields three immediate insights. First, with very few exceptions, El Salvador's literary canon does not seem to have left behind many significant schools or movements. Second, as if in confirmation of Carlos Fuentes's thesis that in history "centuries" are not to be measured in years but by epochs, Salvadorean history – including that of its literary development since independence – falls into three clear-cut periods: a very long 19th century until the Great Massacre of 1932; a very short 20th century from 1932 to the signing of the Peace Accords of 1992, and since then the possibility, at least, of a New Dawn of political reconciliation. Third, because the novel, as Georg Lukács has argued, is quintessentially a bourgeois genre, and El Salvador has to this day remained trapped at a feudal stage of development, the country has produced very few novelists, or for that matter, novels of note. Poetry has in fact been the principal genre, with important contributions in areas such as the short story, the essay, literary journalism, literary criticism and, to a much lesser extent, theatre.

Among the poets who flourished in the first fifty years after independence, the most prominent was Miguel Álvarez Castro (1795–1856). He wrote patriotic and pastoral verse, his best known compositions being "Al ciudadano José del Valle" [Ode to José del Valle, Citizen] and "A la muerte del Coronel Pierzon" [Upon the Death of Colonel Pierzon]. Another important name is that of José Batres Montúfar (1809–44), the "Salvadorean Leopardi," and one of the principal links between Neoclassicism and Romanticism in Central America. Apart from his lyrical poetry in the madrigal or elegiac manner, Batres Montúfar is also remembered for his *Tradiciones de Guatemala* (1845), evocative short stories and verses about life, courtship and intrigue in the colonial era.

A Spanish poet from Santander, the florid and grandiloquent Fernando Velarde, spent some time in El Salvador in the 1870s, bringing with him his *Cánticos del Nuevo Mundo*, 1860 [Songs from the New World], a collection which helped to ignite the romantic imagination in the republic. Inspired by the currents of passion, liberty and pantheism flowing from Europe, Salvadorean Romantics sang principally of the self, love and country. Among the leading exponents of Romantic verse were Juan J. Cañas (1826–1918), who penned the national anthem; Francisco E. Galindo (1850–96), whose "sonorous thought" and "words of gilded rose" were praised by Rubén Darío; and Antonia Galindo (1858–93), the first woman poet of renown, whose verses combined personal feeling with a universal sympathy, as exemplified in "A mi madre" [To My Mother]. A significant development during this period was the first regular appearance of literary criticism in the cultural pages of the country's newspapers. Joaquín Méndez (1868–1942) founded La Juventud [Youth], a society of scientific and literary enquiry, which published a monthly journal, *La Juventud Salvadoreña* [Salvadorean Youth], in its heyday in the 1890s. The literary and cultural revival taking place towards the end the 1800s was given a significant fillip by the foundation of the National Library in 1870, the establishment of the Academy of Language in 1876, and the creation of the Academy of Science and Literature in 1888, which for a brief period published a monthly journal, *Repertorio Salvadoreño* [Salvadorean Index]. Some of the leading intellectuals in the country wrote for *Repertorio Salvadoreño*, which also attracted contributions by international names of the calibre of Ricardo Palma, Julián del Casal and Rubén Darío.

In 1882 *Modernismo* (Spanish American Modernism) made a grand entrance in the field of Salvadorean letters via Francisco Gavidia, who introduced Rubén Darío himself to the revolutionary application of the rhythms of the French Alexandrine to Spanish verse. Gavidia (1863 or 1865–1955) is in fact the first major figure in the history of Salvadorean literature, his output in poetry, drama, philology, the essay and fiction spanning almost eighty years. It is, however, as a modernist and epic poet that Gavidia excelled, and such compositions as his translation of Victor Hugo's "Stella," "La ofrenda del bramán" [The Brahman's Offering], "La defensa de Pan" [In Defence of Pan], and "Sóter o tierra de preseas"

[The Saviour or The Land of Jewels] are worthy of inclusion in any anthology of Spanish verse. Although capable of extreme exoticism, Gavidia was also responsive to his time and place in history: he could sing just as easily of fauns, princesses and swans as of the native *senzontle*, the Indian maiden Xochitl or the clay figurines of the Christ of Esquipulas. His poems may narrate the deeds of Apollo, Orpheus and Euridice but they also celebrate the cause of liberty embodied in national heroes like Francisco Morazán and José Matías Delgado. His interest in autochthonous Salvadorean themes is also evident in his dramatic works, especially in *La princesa Cavek*, 1913(?) [Princess Cavek] and *Cuento de marinos*, 1947 [Seafarers' Tale]. He excelled as a writer of short fiction, his most impressive collection being *Cuentos y narraciones*, 1947 [Stories and Tales], in which he skilfully blends personal memory and national history. He wrote his own epitaph in the final verses of "*Turris Babel*": " ¡Poeta! / Tú de nuevo edifica / No la torre . . . el idioma" (Poet! Your task is to rebuild not the tower but language).

A small but impressive list of writers, mainly poets, joined Gavidia in the late 1800s and early 1900s in creating a modern Salvadorean literary tradition, among them the two Romantics *par excellence*, José Calixto Mixco (1880–1901) and Armando Rodríguez Portillo (1880–1905), whose melancholy verses presaged their early deaths by suicide. Carlos Bustamante (1890–1952), a follower of Darío, in his early years wrote sonorous verses redolent of *modernista* colour and panache. During this period the beginning of a modern Salvadorean theatre was also forged, with plays by J. Emilio Aragón (1887–1938) and José Llerena (1895–1943). However, the only figure to rival Gavidia in stature was Alberto Masferrer (1868–1932), who exerted a profound influence nationally through a series of moral and philosophical treatises based on an eccentric brand of Tolstoyan christianity, oriental mysticism, theosophy and parapsychology, and which he applied in magisterial fashion to Salvadorean reality. Written in a polished, clear, poetic style, his main publications included *Las siete cuerdas de la lira*, 1926 [The Seven Strings of the Lyre], *El dinero maldito*, 1927 [Wretched Money] and *El mínimum vital*, 1929 [Life's Minimum]. He dabbled in poetry and theatre, and he wrote a novel, *Una vida en el cine* [A Life in the Cinema], with a feminist theme. In 1926 he founded a newspaper, *Patria*, a section of which, "Vivir," showcased the work of up-and-coming writers. As a literary critic he encouraged the imitation of the French masters, but warned that European models should be read creatively and critically in the search for an original Salavadorean voice, thus anticipating Alejo Carpentier's quest for an autochthonous identity for Latin America via its European heritage. By lending his name and prestige to the candidature of the Labour Party's Arturo Araujo in the presidential elections of 1929–30, Masferrer sealed his political fate. He ended his life a sad and broken man two years later during the barbarous regime of Maximiliano H. Martínez, the antithesis of everything Masferrer stood for intellectually and politically.

The most important literary movement in El Salvador following the golden years of *Modernismo* was *costumbrismo* [literature of manners and customs], embodied in prose by Arturo Ambrogi (1875–1936) and by José María Peralta Lagos (1873–1944), and in poetry by Alfredo Espino (1900–28).

A precocious talent who began his career as an obsessive modernist nicknamed "la Señorita Azul" [The Blue Miss], Ambrogi later found another and more lasting voice as the verbal painter of El Salvador's rural spirit. In his most famous book, *El libro del trópico*, 1918 [The Book of the Tropics], in a series of short stories and vignettes, he combines impressionistic brushstrokes to describe the countryside with an authentic feel for the nuances and registers of Salvadorean Spanish. On occasions he manages to enter the consciousness of his humble characters and to penetrate the depths of their hearts, as in the case of "Bruno," a tale of a *campesino's* (peasant's) thwarted love. Ambrogi also won further acclaim for his travel book, *Sensaciones de Japón y de China*, 1915 [Impressions of Japan and China]. Peralta Lagos, alias T.P. Mechín, wrote two famous books, *Burla burlando*, 1923 [Mocking the Mocked] and *Brochazos* [Brushstrokes], festive descriptions of Salvadorean customs and types. He also wrote a short novel, *Doctor Gonorreitigorrea* (1926), a satire of Salvadorean society and the play *Candidato* [Candidate], a satire of the presidential campaign of 1930–31 that was to have such dire consequences for Salvadorean history. Ambrogi and Peralta had their poetic counterpart in Alfredo Espino, long-since regarded as El Salvador's national poet. His posthumous volume, *Jícaras tristes* [Cups of Sadness], full of a gentle, nostalgic love of country, have become compulsory reading for Salvadorean expatriates and exiles.

Times of great political convulsion and moral disturbance, according to Mario Vargas Llosa, tend to provide a stimulus for literary creativity – and this is exactly what occurred in El Salvador following the Great Slaughter of 1932, when General Martínez ordered the massacre of about four per cent of the population in order to save the country from an alleged Communist insurrection. For the next fifteen years or so a brilliant nucleus of intellectuals did not so much oppose, as offer passive resistance, to the military-oligarchical regime in command. Among creative writers the doyen was undoubtedly Salarrué (pen name for Salvador Salazar Arrué, 1899–1975). Beginning his career as a novelist with *El Cristo negro*, 1922 [The Black Christ], and ending it as a poet with the collection *Mundo nomasito*, 1975 [My Little World], Salarrué earned international acclaim for his book of regionalist short stories, *Cuentos de barro*, 1933 [Clay Stories], some of which have become Salvadorean classics, such as "Somos malos" [We're Evil] and "La repunta" [The Flood]. A confirmed theosophist and a master of narrative technique, as well as possessing an incomparable ear for the sounds and rhythms of Salvadorean Spanish, Salarrué manages to impart to his stories an air of magic and superstition that antedates the magical realism of subsequent generations. He also wrote *Cuentos de cipotes*, 1945 [Kids' Stories], a highly original collection of stories *about* children *for* children *and* adults narrated in an eccentric style that seeks to imitate the playful, cheeky, sometimes incomprehensible voice of Salvadorean *cipotes* (urchins or kids) talking to each other.

A number of fine poets of multifarious hues and tendencies participated in the literary renaissance heralded by Salarrué. Claudia Lars (pseudonym for Carmen Brannon, 1899–1974) is not only considered El Salvador's outstanding woman poet, but also the country's foremost lyrical voice, comparable in quality to Gabriela Mistral and Alfonsina Storni. Her best known collections of this period are *Estrellas en el pozo*, 1934 [Stars in the Well], *Romances del norte y sur*, 1947 [Ballads of the North and the South] and *Sonetos* (1947). Like Salarrué, she continued writing until the end of her life, but even as El Salvador plunged ever deeper into fratricidal conflict, Claudia Lars never lost sight of of her country's place in the universal scheme of things, as demonstrated by *Nuestro pulsante mundo*, 1969 [Our Pulsating World], in which she responds with eyes of wonder to Paul McCartney and to the conquest of space. Throughout his long life Vicente Rosales y Rosales (1894–1980) wrote varied poetry of cosmic, mythological and mystic themes, but is best remembered for a collection with the eccentric title of *Eutorpologio Politonal*, 1938 [From Euterpe, the Muse of Music and Lyric Poetry, Logos and Polytonal], in which he applied a personal theory of comparative theory and music to versification. In the 1940s, Lydia Valiente (1900–76) wrote poetry about her intensely felt proletarian ideals, while Serafín Quiteño (1899–1952) produced one outstanding collection, *Corasón con S*, 1941 [Heart written with an S], that conveys powerfully felt emotions.

Among novelists two names stand out in Salarrués generation: Alberto Rivas Bonilla (1891–?) and Miguel Angel Espino (1902–68). In 1936 Rivas Bonilla published *Andanzas y malandanzas* [Adventures and Misadventures], a picaresque tale of the trials and tribulations of canine life in rural El Salvador; whether it is an allegory of existence in the dehumanising environment of the time is for the reader to determine. Espino, on the other hand, is remembered for two novels, *Trenes*, 1940 [Trains] and *Hombres contra la muerte*, 1947 [Men against Death]. Written in the style of a fictional autobiography, *Trenes* makes compelling reading for two reasons: it is an ode to woman in her multiple avatars (virgin, mother, courtesan, goddess), as well as a metanovel anticipating the self-conscious narratives of the post-boom. *Hombres contra la muerte*, by contrast, is a novel of the jungle inspired by José Eustasio Rivera's *La vorágine*, 1924 (*The Vortex*). Highly praised for its power and lyricism, it denounces the exploitation of forest workers in Belize. One other figure stands out during this traumatic period of El Salvador's history: Alberto Guerra-Trigueros (1898–1950), one of the most influential intellectuals of his generation. Owner and director of *Patria* and a disciple of Masferrer, Guerra-Trigueros used his newspaper as a tribune to denounce imperialism in Central America and dictatorship in El Salvador. He published *Poesía versus Arte*, 1942 [Poetry versus Art] and *El libro, el hombre y la cultura*, 1948 [The Book, Man and Culture], in which he expounded his humanistic views on art and culture. Guerra-Trigueros, more than anybody else, paved the way for the next generation of committed writers who were to rise to prominence following the so-called "revolution of 1948."

Between 1948 and 1956 the promise of a new political and social deal was not fulfilled because of yet another period of authoritarian rule. Salvadorean intellectuals, many of whom had opposed the Martínez dictatorship, were prompted to express their anger and disenchantment, with poetry as their principal medium. Patriotic, irreverent, rebellious, iconoclastic, many of them forced into exile, they composed powerful verses denouncing social injustice and the cynicism of the Salvadorean establishment. "Monólogo en dos preguntas" [Monologue in the Form of Two Questions], by Antonio Gamero (1917–74), in which the poet is exalted as the singer of proletarian hopes and aspirations, and the suggestively titled *10 sonetos para mil y más obreros* [10 Sonnets for a Thousand Workers and More], by Oswaldo Escobar Velado (1919–61), convey the aesthetic that lay at the heart of this kind of poetry in El Salvador. Pedro Geoffroy Rivas (1908–79) wrote his anti-bourgeois lament, "Vida, pasión y muerte del anti-hombre" [Life, Passion and Death of Anti-Man] in 1936–37 when he was in gaol in Mexico for anti-government activities, and it was to become the anthem for committed writers in El Salvador from the 1950s to the present. One of its verses, "¡Pobrecito poeta que era yo!" [What a Dud Poet I Was!] was to be immortalised by Roque Dalton in the title of his celebrated novel.

Not all Salvadorean intellectuals, however, have been politicised, with some notable figures refusing to have their creative work "contaminated" by what they have considered the stench of politics. Perhaps the outstanding representative of this school of thought was Raúl Contreras (1896–1973), a poet who had made an impression as far back as 1925 with *La princesa está triste* [The Princess is Sad], a play-in-verse glossing Rubén Darío's renowned poem. Contreras found renewed fame in the late 1940s and in the 1950s as Lydia Nogales, the pseudonym he used to compose some of the most beautiful and perfectly crafted verses (especially sonnets) in the history of Salvadorean literature. Lydia's mysterious, dream-like allure is captured in the sonnet "Inesperada" [The Unexpected One]: "Yo soy la Novia que jamás se entrega; corporal y sutil, cálida y fría, / que a sí misma se ignora todavía, / siendo principio y fin, alfa y omega." (I am the unattainable bride, of flesh and yet subtle, warm and cold, I am she who doesn't yet herself know, I am the beginning and the end, alpha and omega). By the mid-1950s the apparition of Lydia Nogales had split the Salvadorean literary establishment into two camps: the "pro-nogalists" who believed in an art of truth and beauty beyond politics, and the "anti-nogalists," who, rejecting what they considered the view of the artist in an ivory tower, called for a new aesthetic built upon the music of hammers, saws and hoes. This division has in fact continued to condition and inform the outlook of creative writers in El Salvador throughout the succession of military and civilian presidents, juntas, dictators and the civil war that have racked the country since then.

An outstanding literary figure beyond politics was Hugo Lindo (1917–85), who, while suffering intensely the Salvadorean tragedy, chose to devote his creative energies to the task of preserving and continuing what he deemed the beauty of Latin America's literary heritage in his war-torn country. As a poet, he wrote polished verses of metaphysical dimension with subtle transitions from the natural to the spiritual world. Some of his best poetry has been published in a bilingual edition by Elizabeth Gamble Miller (*Sólo la voz/ Only the Voice*, 1984). He is acknowledged as the pioneer of science fiction in El Salvador with the collection of short-stories *Guaro y champán*, 1947 [Liquor and Champagne], a genre he explored further in *Espejos paralelos*, 1974 [Parallel Mirrors]. His major novel, *¡Justicia, señor Gobernador!* [Give us Justice, Mr Governor!], is a fine psychological study of a judge who, during the trial of a child murderer, reviews the country's social and economic iniquities, coming to the scandalous conclusion that it is God who is guilty of the crime and all other crimes in El Salvador.

Hugo Lindo was also a literary critic who did much to dignify the profession in El Salvador, crowning his career in this area with a meticulous two-volume edition of the select works of Salarrué (1969–70). In a country where, outside the cultural pages of the principal newspapers (*La Prensa Gráfica*, *El Diario de Hoy* and *Diario Latino*) literary criticism has had scarce outlets and few professional practitioners, the outstanding critic has been Luis Gallegos Valdés (1917–?). The country's most prolific and far-ranging critic, his masterpiece is *Panorama de la literatura salvadoreña*, 1981 [Panorama of Salvadorean Literature], which is obligatory reading for any scholar specialising in this field. Another outstanding critic is Matilde Elena López (1922–), who has written numerous articles on poetry, her main publication being *Estudios sobre poesía*, 1970 [Poetry Studies]. Edmundo Barbero contributed more than anybody to promote the appreciation and the study of theatre in El Salvador, and his *Panorama del teatro en El Salvador*, 1970 [Panorama of Theatre in El Salvador] is an invaluable volume.

From the mid-1950s to the present very few intellectuals in El Salvador have not been influenced by Sartre's Existentialism, on the one hand, and Castro's Revolution, on the other. The consequence has been the appearance of successive generations of committed writers, their degree of commitment ranging from the purely verbal, to the spiritual, to the ideological and in some extreme cases, to the militant. The moral leader for assuming commitment with one's time and place in history was the historian, dramatist, editor and poet Italo López Vallecillos (1932– ?). López Vallecillos utilises poetry sensitively as a vehicle to explore the depths of existential dilemmas in a godless milieu, as in these verses from "Arriba, Abajo," 1954 [Up, Down]: "Y entre las nubes y el polvo/que camino, yo, el solitario, el hombre de la duda, sin Dios" (And between the clouds and the dust that I tread, go I, lonely, man of doubt, without God). López Vallecillos shows in his poetry that it is indeed possible to be a committed poet without blatant sloganeering, as does the playwright Walter Béneke (1928–) in *Funeral Home*, 1954, with its dramatic depiction of alienation in an absurd world.

The supreme model of revolutionary commitment in El Salvador was Roque Dalton (1935–75), for whom poetry was as militant an expression of the armed struggle as Che Guevara's rifle. In his best-known and most admired collection, *Taberna y otros lugares*, 1969 [In a Tavern and Other Places], he explored the ineluctable nexus between poetry and politics, a subject over which he agonised and which he finally summarised with deceptive simplicity in "Arte Poética 1974": Poesía / Perdóname por haberte ayudado a comprender / que no estás hecha sólo de palabras" (Poetry, forgive me for having helped you to understand that you are not made solely of words). Dalton was also an accomplished novelist, producing two important works, *Miguel Mármol* (1972), which set the tone for future testimonial narratives in Latin America, and *¡Pobrecito poeta que era yo!*, 1976 [What a Dud Poet I Was!], a verbal and stylistic extravaganza in which the reader perceives the despair of a man seeking to find a justification for being a writer in a country like El Salvador: "¡Qué

risa! Es terriblemente rídiculo ser un escitor salvadoreño . . ."
(What a joke! It's horribly absurd to to be a Salvadorean writer
. . .) It is no exaggeration to say that since Gavidia, no writer
has left such an indelible influence in El Salvador, morally and
creatively, as Dalton, whose tragic death at the hands of fellow-
Communists brought to a premature end the life of one of the
most talented writers Latin America has produced in the
modern era.

Other writers of Dalton's generation have produced works
of diverse merit and sensibility. Roberto Araujo (1937–) earned
fame in the 1960s as the poet of Chalatenango, the forgotten
province of El Salvador, and he has also written a major play,
Jugando a la gallina ciega, 1970 [Blind Man's Bluff], which
combines elements of the grotesque and of horror most effectively. Roberto Cea (1939–), a prolific and versatile writer, has
written verses that range from the mythical and the magical
in *Todo el códice*, 1968 [The Entire Codex], to the erotic in
Mester de picardía, 1977 [The Picaresque Craft], to the political and historical in *Los herederos de Farabundo*, 1981
[Farabundo's Heirs]. Alfonso Quijada Urías (1940–) is a poet
who earned Dalton's admiration for *Estados sobrenaturales y
otros poemas*, 1971 [Supernatural States and Other Poems], in
which he explores the fears and neuroses of being alive in
Central America in the 1960s. Alvaro Menéndez Leal (alias
Menen Desleal, 1931–) is an iconoclastic writer who, apart
from fantastic fiction, is the author of *Luz negra*, 1966 [Black
Light], an absurdist play in which the main characters are two
severed heads; it is the most widely translated and performed
play by a Salvadorean.

However, apart from Dalton, only two other modern writers
have succeeded in consistently transcending the borders of El
Salvador with their works, and not insignificantly, their most
important output has been published elsewhere: Claribel
Alegría (1924–) and Manlio Argueta (1935–). Alegría,
Nicaraguan by birth, brought up in El Salvador, now divides
her time between Nicaragua and Mallorca and has retained a
profound Salvadorean consciousness. She has written
numerous collections of poetry, including *Sobrevivo*, 1978 [I
Survive], which won the Casa de las Américas prize in 1978.
It is as a novelist that she has won most acclaim, particularly
for *Cenizas de Izalco*, 1966 (*Ashes of Izalco*), written jointly
with her husband, Darwin J. Flakoll. She has earned a reputation as one of Latin America's best writers of testimonial
fiction, depicting the fate of peasants and women in war-
ravaged Central America. Manlio Argueta, who lived in exile
in Costa Rica between 1972 until very recently, and has now
returned to El Salvador to work in the national university, has
written some of the best examples of war literature in Central
America. His novel, *Un día en la vida*, 1980 (*One Day of Life*)
is without doubt one of the most technically competent and
psychologically harrowing depictions of the effects of civil war
on the peasant population of El Salvador. Both Alegría and
Argueta have compiled important anthologies that have done
much to promote the literary talent of El Salvador abroad,
including *New Voices of El Salvador* (1962) by the former, and
Poesía de El Salvador, 1983 [Poetry of El Salvador], by the
latter.

During the last civil war (1982–92) a number of writers,
spanning different generations and encompassing a wide

range of perspectives, responded to the carnage with varying
degrees of anger, pain, bewilderment or defiance. Poetry and
short fiction were the favoured genres, particularly among the
younger writers, with Ricardo Lindo (1947–), Miguel Huezo
Mixco (1954–), Horacio Castellanos Moya (1957–) and
Jacinta Escudos (1961–) being the most prominent. However,
among the writers who chose to remain in El Salvador during
these years and who survived, physically and creatively, one
name undoubtedly stands out: David Escobar Galindo (1943–),
poet, novelist, dramatist, short-story writer and literary critic.
Escobar Galindo has been producing poetry of the highest
quality since 1963, when he was still a student. His best collections, *Duelo ceremonial por la violencia*, 1971 [Ceremonial
Wake for Violence], *Trenos por la violencia*, 1977 [Lament for
Violence], *Sonetos penitenciales*, 1982 [Penitential Sonnets]
and *Oración en la guerra*, 1989 [Prayer in War], treat the
theme of violence from the point of view of an anguished
humanist, as conveyed by "Penitential Sonnet I" : "Igual que
en el soneto de Quevedo / miré los muros de la patria mía, /
y en lugar de la justa simetría / sólo hay desorden, crápula,
remedo." (Just like Quevedo in his famous sonnet, I beheld
the walls of my dear country, and where there should be
glorious symmetry saw only chaos, dissipation and parody).
His short novel *La estrella cautiva*, 1985 [The Captive Star],
is a subtle study of psychological agony and erotic intrigue set
against the background of political mayhem in the city of San
Salvador. Since 1988 Escobar Galindo has been writing a very
popular series of weekly short stories, *Historias sin cuento*
[Stories without a Plot], in *La Prensa Gráfica*, which focus
upon the joys and sorrows of daily life in the towns and villages
of El Salvador. An analysis of these stories, written in the
elegant, controlled style of a superb literary craftsman aiming
to write for a wide audience, irrespective of class or ideology,
reveals the subtle transition that appears to be occurring in
Salvadorean literature as writers move out of a dark era into
a more promising one.

In the mid 1990s it is too early, however, to claim that an
"aesthetic of peace" is replacing the "literature of war."
Nevertheless, there are signs of a literary reawakening.
Testimonial literature by ex-combatants from both sides, but
particularly by ex-guerrillas, is flourishing in the form of war
memoirs, journals, novels and short-stories. Exiled writers
such as Manlio Argueta have returned to work alongside those
who, like David Escobar Galindo and Roberto Cea, suffered
the war years at home. Literary and cultural magazines of
quality are being published once again: *Cultura*, *Amate*,
Tendencias, *Paradoxa*, *Ars*, all of which receive the support
of the government or that of a university or a foundation.
Books of literary criticism are appearing in the university
bookshops and critics of quality and experience, such as
Rafael Rodríguez Díaz, are now focusing their attention on
Salvadorean writers and topics objectively and dispassionately.
Foreign critics are also now devoting more time and space to
Salvadorean writers. In the final analysis, it seems as if after
years of marginalisation and neglect reflecting the country's
turbulent history, Salvadorean literature may be set to enter a
new period of creativity.

Roy C. Boland

Further Reading

Criticism on Salvadorean literature is scarce. Some of the most important works of criticism have been published by Salvadorean writers and have already been cited in the article. Since El Salvador made the headlines during the civil war, more attention has been paid to its literary output, especially in the US and Europe. For articles and books on the major writers (Salarrué, Roque Dalton, Claribel Alegría) it is advisable to consult the Further Reading section of the entry on each one of these authors, and the MLA Bibliography. The following publications provide useful anthological or critical material:

Escobar Galindo, David, *Indice de la poesía salvadoreña*, 2nd edition, San Salvador: UCA Editores, 1987 [An excellent anthology of Salvadorean poetry, with notes and prologue]
____ *Después de medianoche/After Midnight*, translated and edited by Roy C. Boland, Santa Tecla: Ricaldone, 1987
Guillén, Orlando, *Hombres como madrugadas: la poesía de El Salvador*, Barcelona: Antropos, 1985

Huezo Mixco, Miguel, "Acerca de una estética extrema," in *Letraviva*, San Salvador: Istmo Editores, 1994 [A provocative personal commentary on the evolution of Salvadorean literature from independence to the period immediately after the civil war of 1982–92]
Jaramillo Levi, Enrique and Leland H. Chambers, *Contemporary Short Stories from Central America*, Austin: University of Texas Press, 1994
Paschke, Barbara and David Voldenpesta (editors), *Clamor of Innocence: Central American Short Stories*, San Francisco: City Lights Books, 1989
Rodríguez Díaz, Rafael, *Temas salvadoreños*, San Salvador: UCA Editores, 1992 [Contains some penetrating analyses of important authors and developments in Salvadorean literature]
Santos, Rosario (editor), *And We Sold the Rain: Contemporary Fiction from Central America*, Peterborough: Ryan Publishing, 1989
Yanes, Gabriela, *Mirrors of War*: Literature and Revolution in *El Salvador*, London: Zed Books, 1985

Salvador Elizondo 1932–

Mexican prose writer

The work of Salvador Elizondo chronicles in a very consistent – and persistent – manner the drama of writing. The stage, for most of the time, is the vast universe of literature, art and cinema. There is no Mexican Revolution, little or no local colour, very few rounded characters, and absolutely no social comment. Instead, we have a series of books, or *literary projects*, that continually mirror the act of writing, each project seeking to purify this act and cleanse it from the external world itself or from that literature which arrogantly boasts a faithful depiction of it. Needless to say, to take an active part in this rarefied world of writing on writing, the reader and the critic are obliged, in their turn, to participate in the purification process by throwing off old habits and acquiring the graceful stance of the scribe.

At an early stage in his writing career, certain critics turned Elizondo into the renegade of Mexican letters. It was a quick-and-ready solution for those who had problems reading him or situating him within a recognisable literary context. A short autobiography Elizondo wrote for *Bellas Artes* in 1966 provided further comfort for the disconcerted: a demented writer fond of alcohol. That, they said, explained the macabre and sadistic world invoked in *Farabeuf*.

The variety of critical approaches to Elizondo's work is due to the greater or lesser degree to which critics have sought to overcome inadequate methods and tackle what might seem, in the case of Elizondo, a much less attractive proposition, that is, to analyse the writings of a man who presents no specific social context nor easily identifiable themes.

Farabeuf was published in 1965, won the Villaurrutia Prize, and established Elizondo as one of Mexico's leading writers. To piece together a storyline serves little purpose. Like an involved poem where the meaning behind the constellation of images is not immediately apparent, *Farabeuf* has to be read slowly and painstakingly. Certain scenes are repeated, over and over again, with slight variations each time. Like the woman at the end of the hallway of the house in Paris, the reader must be attentive to the changes, to the modifications in the text. *Farabeuf* does not ask the reader to suspend his disbelief – there are no traditional rewards for getting through the text – but instead to give himself or herself up totally to the experience of reading. Then, and only then, will the secret be revealed, will the emotion be undeniably felt.

For Elizondo the ideal novel would be that which reveals a prodigious and arduous interplay between the mind or spirit, on the one hand, and writing, on the other. Subsequently, the idea of genre assumes a much broader scope, encompassing not only possibilities defined within certain categories but any possibility whatsoever. In an introduction to Elizondo's complete works, published in 1994 by El Colegio Nacional, Adolfo Castañón draws our attention to the author's versatility in exploring a vast range of narrative forms and techniques, from the dialogue and commercial letter, to the simulated essay and taxonomical description. Indeed, in his writings Elizondo moves expertly in and out of the world of literature and styles, using the whole range of literary -and non-literary conventions to fabricate his own fictions. In *Narda o el verano*, 1966 [Narda or the Summer] and *El retrato de Zoe y otras mentiras*, 1969 [Zoe's Portrait and Other Lies], he reveals unquestionable talent as a weaver of tales and fabulations, quite prepared at any given moment to subvert tradition and to declare greater loyalty to personal goals, while in *El grafógrafo*, 1972 [The Graphographer] the scribe has gone one step further, this time banishing the world of literature from his study and replacing it with a mirror: "Escribo. Escribo que escribo. Mentalmente me veo escribir que escribo ..." (I'm writing. I write that I'm writing. Mentally I see myself writing that I'm writing ...)

Refreshed by this literary purge, unburdened perhaps by an endeavour that can go no further unless it is the blank page, Elizondo adds significantly to his own literary tradition in subsequent years with *Miscast*, *Cámera Lúcida*, *La luz que regresa* [The Returning Light], and *Elsinore*. Whether it is theatre or autobiography, personal myth or invented machine, each piece of writing is developed and executed with consummate skill. In these later writings, furthermore, there is evidence of a more playful approach, a touch of light humour has crept into that on-going and utterly coherent meditation on the art and craft of writing.

DERMOT CURLEY

Biography
Born in Mexico City, 19 December 1932. Attended primary school in Mexico City. Secondary education in the US and Canada. Tertiary education in United Kingdom; Cambridge graduate. Spent time also in France and Italy. Returned to Mexico and studied plastic arts at La Esmeralda and San Carlos; studied English literature at Universidad Nacional Autónoma de México (UNAM), Mexico City, 1952–53. Began to work at this university in 1964. Held scholarship of the Mexican Writers Center in 1963–64 and studied Chinese. Member of the editorial boards of two cultural magazines, *Plural* and *Vuelta*. Literary translator from English, French, German and Italian. Major awards include Villaurrutia Prize, 1965 for *Farabeuf*. Member of the Mexican Academy of the Language since 1976, and of the Colegio Nacional since 1981.

Selected Works
Because of the experimental nature of Elizondo's creative writing, no attempt has been made to divide it into different genres.

Poemas, Mexico City: privately printed, 1960
Farabeuf, o la crónica de un instante, Mexico City: Joaquín Mortiz, 1965; as *Farabeuf, the Chronicle of an Instant*, translated by John Incledon, New York: Garland, 1992
Narda o el verano, Mexico City: Era, 1966
El Hipogeo Secreto, Mexico City: Joaquín Mortiz, 1968
El retrato de Zoe y otras mentiras, Mexico City: Joaquín Mortiz, 1969

El grafógrafo, Mexico City: Joaquín Mortiz, 1972
Miscast, o, Ha llegado la señora Marquesa: comedia opaca en tres actos, Mexico City: Oasis, 1981
Regreso a casa, Mexico City: UNAM, 1982
Cámera Lúcida, Mexico City: Joaquín Mortiz, 1983
La luz que regresa, Mexico City: Fondo de Cultura Económica, 1985
Elsinore: un cuaderno, Mexico City: Equilibrista, 1988

Other Writings
Luchino Visconti, Mexico City: UNAM, 1963
Salvador Elizondo: nuevos escritores mexicanos del siglo veinte presentados por sí mismos, Mexico City: Empresas Editoriales, 1966
Cuaderno de escritura, Guanajuato: Universidad de Guanajuato, 1969
Contextos, no. 79 of Sep-Setentas, Mexico City: Sepsentas, 1973
Teoría del infierno y otros ensayos, Mexico City: El Colegio Nacional/ Ediciones del Equilibrista, 1992

Further Reading
Bradu, Fabienne, "*Cámera Lúcida*," *Vuelta* 83 (October 1983)
Bell, Steven M., "Literatura crítica y crítica de la literatura: teoría y práctica en la obra de Salvador Elizondo," *Chasqui*, vol. 11/1 (1981)
____ "Postmodern Fiction in Spanish America: the Examples of Salvador Elizondo and Nestor Sánchez," *Arizona Quarterly*, vol. 42/1 (1986)
Castañón, Adolfo, "Las ficciones de Salvador Elizondo," introduction to *Salvador Elizondo: Obras*, vol. 1, Mexico City: El Colegio de México, 1994
Curley, Dermot, *En la isla desierta: una lectura de la obra de Salvador Elizondo*, Mexico City: Fondo de Cultura Económica, 1989
Glantz, Margo, "*Farabeuf*: escritura barroca y novela mexicana," in her *Repeticiones: ensayos sobre literatura mexicana*, Xalapa, Mexico: Universidad Veracruzana, 1979
Jará, René, *Farabeuf. Estrategias de la inscripción narrativa*, Xalapa, Mexico: Universidad Veracruzana, 1982
McMurray, George R., "Salvador Elizondo's *Farabeuf*," *Hispania* 50 (1967)
Poniatowska, Elena, "Entrevista a Salvador Elizondo," *Plural*, vol. 4/9 (1975)
Ruffinelli, Jorge, *El lugar de Rulfo y otros ensayos*, Xalapa, Mexico: Universidad Veracruzana, 1980 [chapter on Elizondo]
Sotomayor, Aurea M., *El Hipogeo Secreto: la escritura como palindromo y cópula*, *Revista Iberoamericana* 112–13 (1980)

Diamela Eltit 1949–

Chilean prose writer

Diamela Eltit has established an international reputation as a writer intent on testing the limits of language. The aggressive nature of her production, with its cultivation of "bad taste," disturbs the reader. As a polemical intellectual, and as a member of the new literary scene of *la avanzada* (a cultural movement of resistance to the Pinochet dictatorship identified as the "progressive avant-garde"), Eltit provoked ambivalent reactions from the traditional critics of both the right and the left with her first novel *Lumpérica*, 1983 [Lumpen/America] labeled as snobbish, obscure, and cryptic. Having written four fictional works under the Pinochet regime, and being part of the 1980 post-coup literary generation, Eltit confronts the official cultural space, and its essentialist, hegemonic, and authoritarian paradigms.

Eltit excludes from her texts mimetic representation, conventional modes of expression and the comfort of a linear plot. Thus, *Lumpérica* places at the center of the narrative a female misfit who suffers from bleeding and convulsions. Through this character the author offers her vision of the contemporary metropolitan scene. Eltit uses cinematic techniques to describe grotesque events among the down-and-outs in a square in Santiago de Chile. As the text opens, a narrator, named diamela eltit, reveals the plaza as a public space, and illuminates its different faces at night. It focuses on "La Iluminada" (a character performing on camera under a neon light, described as "el luminoso"), who puts on display the promiscuity, solitude and marginality of these vagrants in a public square which is also the site of bestial and orgiastic rituals. Other fragments involve the interrogation of an anonymous character about the plaza's inhabitants, a manifesto which uses a range of discourses (ludic, prosaic, poetic) about the formulation of a literary image, and the capricious deconstruction of multiple stories that might have taken place it the square. In another fragment of the text, the reader is presented with scattered phrases related to the act of writing, thoughts on an imaginary discourse about the plaza, and graffiti inscribed on the ground. In the next section, writing is explored as an act of protest, failure, fiction, official imprisonment. It is also reflected upon as an act of copulation, masturbation, escape, achievement, abandonment, and erosion.

Simultaneously, a rebellious voice at the bottom of the page cuts across the text telling another story which captures a lesbian scene. Abrupt cuts juxtapose interrogation, an inserted photograph of Diamela Eltit, alluding to her tortured sculptured-body, and the plaza as morning arrives. *Lumpérica* demands alert readers who are required to reconstruct the plot and to be aware of their own dependency on official modes of representation when consuming cultural products.

In *Por la patria* [In the Name of the Fatherland], the mestizo protagonist Coya-Coa performs in her imagination an act of incest with the Father and the Mother. In the first part the poor are abused by soldiers, threatened by the arrival of tanks, and the continuous occupation of the shantytown by the police force. This culminates with Coya's arrest. The second part depicts Coya and three other females who have been rounded up, as they are being held in a prison where they suffer torture and are interrogated by the villanous traitor, Juan. Women, the lumpen, and the American continent bring Latin American subjectivity into a carnivalesque political and ideological arena. This is a response to the dictatorship's official discourse which demanded silent acceptance, sacrifice and imposed an official version of history in the name of the nation.

El cuarto mundo (*The Fourth World*) concerns an incestuous relationship between twins. At the same time, it dismantles the process of creating a novel. Feminine, masculine, and androgynous voices dramatize acts of violence and lust in a house, while transient miserable *sudacas* (derogatory term coined in Spain to refer to undocumented Latin American workers) invade the city. In *El padre mío* [Father of Mine] three fragments from 1983, 1984, 1985 (framed by the Preface of a certain diamela eltit), involve a soliloqy uttered by a schizophrenic indigent from the slum of Conchalí in Santiago. This experimental sociological text, of course, mocks the national mythology constructed by an authoritarian regime.

Vaca sagrada (*Sacred Cow*) takes the form of an inquiry into identity and representation as the reader is required to associate different scenes, starting with the inscription of the bodily fluids of the female protagonist, and then moving on to the psycho-sexual relationship between her and Manuel, a walk in a demonic city, Manuel's decision to return to the fearful South, and Manuel, Sergio, Ana, and Francisca's meaningless relationships. Through the elusive characters, the text captures the range of representations of body, language, gender, culture and ideology.

El infarto del alma [A Soul's Shock] deals with madness, writing and culture, as it juxtaposes her prose with documentary photographs (by Paz Errázuriz) of indigent couples in a public hospital for the chronically insane.

Eltit's most recent narrative, *Los vigilantes* [The Vigilantes], is noteworthy for its elaborate visual compositions, and its experiments with fragmentary prose and disintegrating language which goes beyond *Lumpérica's* explorations. More than a narrative, this performance-text connects incoherent and contradictory scenes conveying the characters' perceptions, and the reader's assumptions. An oppressed mother exchanges letters with an absent father, writing impulsively and frenetically while her son, her former male companion, her mother-in-law, a man with a limp and the neighbours look on watchfully. Three chapters, "BAAM," "Amanecer"[Dawn], and "BRRR," which differ in length, style, point of view, subject matter, and treatment, tell the story of the mother. Predictably, the tone is grotesque, and the setting is one of urban decay; it is winter and the predominant colour is an icy blue.

Although Eltit embodies some of the innovations of the Latin American Post-Boom writers, a hallmark of her works is her use of artistic, cinematic, and video-clipping techniques, as part of her own aesthetic and political agenda. Deserving attention are her assimilation and transformation of Severo Sarduy's Neobaroque marking of the text, and the use of the body as a multiple signifier, the ludic use of language characteristic of Guillermo Cabrera Infante, and the somber tones conveyed by Rulfo's and Arguedas's marginal characters.

MAGDALENA MAÍZ-PEÑA

Biography

Born in Santiago de Chile in 1949. Stayed in Chile after military coup; joined resistance groups and actively protested against the regime. Member of the 80s Post-Coup Generation (writers born between 1948–57, who started publishing under the dictatorship). Studied for an arts degree at the University of Chile. Performance and video artist known for her work with Santiago's down-and-outs; also a film director. A founder of CADA (Colectivo de Acciones de Arte / Political and Artistic Co-op). Organizer of El Congreso Internacional de Literatura Femenina Latinoamericana, the most important literary event during the dictatorship, Santiago de Chile, August 1987. Taught literary theory at Brown University, Providence, Rhode Island, and at the National University of Chile. Promoter of the cultural project "Educación para la Democracia" (Education for Democracy); Cultural attaché at Chilean Embassy in Mexico when Patricio Alwyn was president of Chile. Currently professor at the Universidad Tecnológica Metropolitana, Mexico City. Awarded Guggenheim grant, 1985 and a Social Science Research Council scholarship, 1988.

Selected Works

Novels
Lumpérica, Santiago de Chile: Ediciones del Ornitorrinco, 1983
Por la patria, Santiago de Chile: Ediciones del Ornitorrinco, 1986
El cuarto mundo, Santiago de Chile: Planeta, 1988; as *The Fourth World*, translated by Dick Gerdes, Lincoln: University of Nebraska Press, 1995
El padre mío, Santiago de Chile: Francisco Zegers Editor, 1989
Vaca sagrada, Santiago-Buenos Aires: Planeta, 1991; as *Sacred Cow*, translated by Amanda Hopkinson, London and New York: Serpents Tail, 1995
Los vigilantes, Santiago-Buenos Aires: Sudamericana, 1994

Short Fiction
"Diez noches de Francisca Lombardo," in *El muro y la intemperie*, edited by Julio Ortega, Hanover, New Hampshire: Ediciones del Norte, 1989
"Lujuria: aunque me lavase con agua de nieve," in *Los siete pecados capitales*, edited by Mariano Aguirre, Santiago de Chile: Grijalbo, 1995

Further Reading
The collection of critical essays edited by Juan Carlos Lértora is indispensable reading. It contains some of the best critical essays written on Diamela Eltit's work by the editor, Julio Ortega, Sara Castro-Klarén, Nelly Richard, Raquel Olea, María Inés Lagos, Ivette Malverde Disselkoen, Guillermo García Corales, Marina Arrate and Fernando Moreno. Each of the essays illuminates Eltit's writing either by focussing on one of her works or by postulating innovative theses. Critical information is contained in the outstanding bibliography compiled by Patricia Rubio.

Brito, Eugenia, *Campos minados; literatura post-golpe en Chile*, Santiago de Chile: Cuarto Propio, 1990
Cánovas, Rodrigo, "Apuntes sobre la novela *Por la patria* (1986) de Diamela Eltit," *Acta Literaria* 15 (1990)
Lértora, Juan Carlos (editor), *Una poética de literatura menor: la narrativa de Diamela Eltit*, Santiago de Chile: Paratextos / Editorial Cuarto Propio, 1993
Norat, Gisela, "Diálogo fraternal. *El cuarto mundo* de Diamela Eltit y *Cristóbal Nonato* de Carlos Fuentes," *Chasqui*, vol. 23/2 (1994)
Richard, Nelly, *Margins and Institutions. Art in Chile since 1973*, Melbourne, Australia: Paul Foss and Paul Taylor, 1986
Santos, Susana, "Diamela Eltit: una ruptura ejemplar," *Feminaria Literaria*, vol. 2/3 (1992)
Tierney-Tello, Mary Beth, "Re-Making the Margins: from Subalterity to Subjectivity in Diamela Eltit's *Por la patria*," *Monographic Review / Revista Monográfica* 8 (1992)

Interviews
Ortega, Julio, "Resistencia y sujeto femenino: entrevista con Diamela Eltit," *La Torre*, Puerto Rico, vol. 4/14 (1990)

Erotic and Homoerotic Writing

The literary expression of the erotic is through the body, which can be either the physiological or the textual body. Therefore, erotic writing can be thought of as the literary production focused on the materialization of the human body by depicting non-genitally-based sexual pleasure; in other words, pornography for the well-to-do. On the other hand, eroticism can be implied in the act of writing itself: the Barthesian pleasure experienced by the author while writing and the reader when facing the text. In works by the River Plate writers Julio Cortázar, Cristina Peri Rossi and Sylvia Molloy; the Cubans José Lezama Lima and Severo Sarduy, both conceptualizations of erotic writing are exemplified.

Studies by theorists such as Stanley Fish and Wolfgang Iser, emphasizing the creative role of the reader, have opened up new ways of viewing texts, even canonical ones. From this perspective, eroticism may be discerned in texts as far back as the colonial period, for example in works by Sor Juana Inés de la Cruz.

The Nicaraguan *modernista* poet, Rubén Darío, with his symbolic representation of sexuality and his erotic interpretation of the world, provides the most conventional representation of eroticism within the parameters of western culture, namely heterosexuality. Darío created a new poetic language for the expression of the erotic in Latin American literature which continued right through the 20th century. In his work the woman's body is the object of male desire and is represented as an artificial construct. However, in later texts, for example, in the poetry of Pablo Neruda, the female body appears as a component of Nature and in harmony with it.

Women had to work against the grain of an entirely masculine canon and thus the inscription of an erotic female subject in Latin American writing does not appear until the first decades of the 20th century in the poetry of Delmira Agustini. The center of her texts is the search for a language to express eroticism outside the patriarchal tradition: a unique experience which is born in the woman's body. During the 20th century the following Argentine writers: Griselda Gambaro, Silvina Ocampo, Alejandra Pizarnik, and Ana María Shua, have written erotic texts with the purpose of inscribing the female erotic, previously excluded from the canon. Similarly, as David Foster has demonstrated, homosexuality has been erased from the patriarcal linguistic and literary codes, although there exists now a considerable production which is creating a language appropriate to the homosexual erotic experience; both gay male and lesbian.

Influenced by the work of Monique Wittig and Hélène Cixous, some writers have depicted a non-phallic eroticism. Among them are the Mexicans Sabina Berman, Sara Levi-Calderón, María Luisa Mendoza; the Mexican American, Cherríe Moraga, and Reina Roffé, Cristina Peri Rossi and Silvia Molloy from the River Plate countries. In Latin America, as elsewhere, lesbianism developed together with mainstream feminism thanks to intercontinental gatherings and an exchange of ideas from the late 1970s. This political basis opened a space for the representation of women bodies in literature, depicting either lesbian or male homosexual eroticism.

Although until recently homosexuality has been represented only timidly and obliquely in Latin American letters, homoerotism appears in 1895 in the novel, *Bom-Crioulo* [The Good Creole] by the Brazilian Adolfo Caminha. Also, during the 1920s, the Colombian Porfirio Barba Jacob wrote highly homoerotic texts. However, gays have been the "scapegoats" of oppressive regimes as appear in the texts by Mario Vargas Llosa (Peru), Manuel Puig (Argentina), and in the works of Reinaldo Arenas, who left Cuba in 1980 because he was unable to publish his works there. In particular, his homoerotic writing was distasteful in a highly militarized, macho society. A new homoerotic writing is being developed by writers such as Luis Zapata (Mexico), an author who explores textually the possibilities of fusing the erotic pleasure of writing with the act of writing about eroticism.

Erotic writing depicting either homosexuality or heterosexuality, represents a resistance discourse whose end would be to question the cultural construction of gender, sexuality and the body.

ANA MARÍA BRENES-GARCÍA

See also entries on Delmira Agustini, *Rayuela* (Julio Cortázar), Rubem Fonseca, Cristina Peri Rossi, *El beso de la mujer araña* (Manuel Puig)

Further Reading

Critical Studies

Barthes, Roland, *Le Plaisir du Texte*, Paris: Seuil, 1973
Bergmann, Emilie and Paul Julian Smith (editors), *¿Entiendes? Queer Readings, Hispanic Writings*, Durham, North Carolina: Duke University Press, 1995
Foster, David William, *Gay and Lesbian Themes in Latin American Writing*, Austin: University of Texas Press, 1991
Foster, David William (editor), *Latin American Writers on Gay and Lesbian Themes: a Biographical and Critical Sourcebook*, Westport, Connecticut: Greenwood Press, 1994
Foster, David William and Roberto Reis (editors), *Bodies and Biases: the Representation of Sexualities in Hispanic Cultures and Literatures*, Minneapolis: University of Minnesota Press, 1995
Sarduy, Severo, *Escrito sobre un cuerpo: ensayos de crítica*, Buenos Aires: Sudamericana, 1969; as *Written on a Body*, translated by Carol Maier, New York: Lumen, 1989
Wittig, Monique, *Le Corps lesbien*, Paris: Les Éditions de Minuit, 1973

Anthologies

Coutinho, Edilberto (editor), *Erotismo no romance brasileiro*, Rio de Janeiro: Editorial Nórdica, 1979
___ *Erotismo no conto brasileiro: antología*, Río de Janeiro: Civilizaçao Brasileira, 1980
Denser, Márcia (editor), *O prazer é todo meu; contos eróticos femeninos*, 2nd edition, Rio de Janeiro: Record, 1982
Fernández Olmos, Margarite and Lizabeth Paravisini-Gebert (editors), *El placer de la palabra. Literatura erótica femenina de América Latina: antología crítica*, Mexico City: Planeta, 1991
Giardinelli, Mempo and Graciela Glemmo (editors), *La Venus de papel. Antología de cuentos eróticos argentinos*, Buenos Aires: Beas, 1993
Jaramillo Levi, Enrique (editor), *El cuento erótico en México*, Mexico City: Diana, 1975
Lovera De-Sola, R.J. (editor), *Eróticos erotómanos y otras especies*, Caracas: Alfadil Ediciones, 1983

Texts by Spanish American Authors

Berman, Sabina (Mexico), *El teatro de Sabina Berman*, Mexico City: Editores Unidos, 1985
Calderón, Sara-Levi (Mexico), *Dos mujeres*, Mexico City: Diana, 1991
Gambaro, Griselda (Argentina), *Lo impenetrable*, Buenos Aires: Torres Agüero, 1984
García, Luis Manuel (Cuba), *Habaneceres*, Havana: Casa de las Américas, 1990
Lezama Lima, José (Cuba), *Paradiso*, Havana: Unión, 1966; translated by Gregory Rabassa, New York: Farrar Straus and Giroux, and London: Secker and Warburg, 1974
Mendoza, María Luisa (Mexico), *De ausencia*, Mexico City: Joaquín Mortiz, 1974
Molloy, Sylvia (Argentina), *En breve cárcel*, Barcelona: Seix Barral, 1981; as *Certificate of Absence*, translated by Daniel Balderston and the author, Austin: University of Texas Press, 1989
Monasterios, Rubén (Venezuela), *Encanto de la mujer madura y otros relatos obscenos*, Caracas: Línea Editores, 1987
Montero, Mayra (Cuba), *La última noche que pasé contigo*, Barcelona: Tusquets, 1991
Nandino, Elías (Mexico), *Erotismo al rojo blanco*, Mexico City: Editorial Domés, 1983
Paz, Senel (Cuba), *El lobo, el bosque y el hombre nuevo*, Havana: Edición Homenaje, 1991
Roffé, Reina (Argentina), *Monte de Venus*, Buenos Aires: Corregidor, 1976
Roffiel, Rosa M. (Mexico), *Amora*, Mexico City: Planeta, 1989
Sarduy, Severo (Cuba), *Cobra*, Buenos Aires: Sudamericana, 1972; translated by Suzanne Jill Levine, New York: Dutton, 1975
Steimberg, Alicia (Argentina), *Amatista*, Barcelona: Tusquets, 1989
Vargas Llosa, Mario (Peru), *Elogio de la madrastra*, Barcelona: Tusquets, 1988; as *In Praise of the Stepmother*, translated by Helen Lane, New York: Farrar Straus and Giroux, 1990; London: Faber and Faber, 1991
Viñas, David (Argentina), *Los años despiadados*, Buenos Aires: Letras Universitarias, 1956

Esquivel, Laura

See Best-Sellers

The Essay

The essay form acquired prominence in Spanish America in the second half of the 19th century, and it has flourished through most of the 20th. Traditionally classified as a minor genre, its perspectives and techniques are nevertheless apparent in works ranging from diaries and formal or informal letters to lectures and speeches, meditative poems and a variety of narrative forms.

Its pervasiveness is evident in as diversified works as José Joaquín Fernández de Lizardi's *El Periquillo Sarniento*, 1816 (*The Itching Parrot*), arguably as much a social essay as a social novel; José Gorostiza's long poem *Muerte sin fin*, 1939 (*Death without End*); José Asunción Silva's posthumous novel-as-diary, *De sobremesa*, 1925 [Table Talk]; many of Jorge Luis Borges's short stories, Ernesto Sábato's existential novel *Sobre héroes y tumbas*, 1961 (*On Heroes and Tombs*); and Gabriel García Márquez's biographical novel *El general en su laberinto*, 1989 (*The General in His Labyrinth*).

In Latin America, then, the essay has always been more than a marginal form of writing; it is a frequently used exploratory procedure. From Christopher Columbus's diaries and Hernán Cortés's letters to Emperor Charles V to José Martí's critiques of North American life in the 1880s and Julio Cortázar's whimsicalities in *La vuelta al día en ochenta mundos*, 1967 (*Around the Day in Eighty Worlds*), the essay has been a basic though often covert literary practice.

Like both poets and philosophers, essayists explore more than they invent. The essay writer's task could be defined as that of balancing inquisitiveness, insightful observation, and the skills of persuasion. By his title *Essais* (1580, and subsequent revised editions) Michel de Montaigne implies a process of inquiry akin to testing or trying out. He lays no claim to "knowledge" as such, demonstrating instead an insatiable curiosity. To think, Montaigne reminds us, is to inquire. Appropriately enough, *pensador* (thinker) and *pensamiento* (thought) are terms commonly appplied in the Hispanic world to discursive writers and what they write. The *pensador* aspires to combine the philosopher's quest for meaning with the moralist's convictions and the literary or art critic's judgment. Significantly, all the selections in José Gaos's *Antología del pensamiento en lengua española en la edad contemporánea*, 1945 [Anthology of Thought in the Spanish Language in the Contemporary Era] are essays.

The relatively static, authoritarian colonial period (1500–1810) was not a propitious time or atmosphere for essayists, two memorable exceptions being the polemical Spanish missionary Fray Bartolomé de Las Casas (1474–1566) and Mexico's leading intellectual of the 17th century, Sor Juana Inés de la Cruz (1651(?)–95). It is in the aftermath of Hispanic American wars for independence from Mexico to the Southern Cone that important essays begin to appear.

Political and social turbulence through most of the 19th century created both a precarious environment and a cultural incitement for Hispanic American writers, and much of the leading essayists' work was produced in exile and in the context of quite bizarre power struggles in their homelands. Andrés Bello (1781–1865) of Venezuela, the Argentines Domingo Faustino Sarmiento (1811–88) and Juan Bautista Alberdi (1810–84), the Ecuadorian Juan Montalvo (1832–89), Puerto Rico's Eugenio María de Hostos (1839–1903), and the Cuban José Martí (1853–95) all lived and wrote abroad for extensive periods.

The six authors just mentioned were also political activists. Bello helped Simón Bolívar organize his independence movement in northern South America; Sarmiento wrote *Civilización y barbarie: vida de Juan Facundo Quiroga*, 1845 (*Life in the Argentine Republic in the Days of the Tyrants*) in hopes of overthrowing the Argentine strongman Juan Manuel de Rosas. Sarmiento himself served as president from 1868 to 1874. Martí and Hostos were active organizers of the liberation, respectively, of Cuba and Puerto Rico from Spain. It is generally agreed that Sarmiento and Martí (also a poet) were the two most important Hispanic American essayists of the 19th century. Both showed a strong romantic temperament; both considered their chief function as writers – prolific as they were – to be an instrument of political action and cultural persuasion. Sarmiento's best writing, apart from *Facundo*, is to be found in *Viajes por Europa, Africa y América*, 1845–1847, 1849–51, [Journeys through Europe, Africa and the United States] and in *Recuerdos de provincia*, 1850 [Memoirs of Provincial Life]. Martí lived in New York from 1879 to early 1895 (the year of his death in Cuba as a participant in a rebel military action against the colonial Spanish forces). Much of his production was collected posthumously under the titles *Escenas norteamericanas* and *Escenas neoyorquinas* [North American Scenes and New York Scenes]; his most frequently anthologized piece is "Nuestra América," 1891 (Our America).

Bridging the gap between a predominant idealism among 19th-century essayists and the predominant skepticism of their 20th-century successors were the Uruguayan José Enrique

Rodó (1871–1917) in *Ariel* (1900), the Mexican José Vasconcelos (1882–1959) in *La raza cósmica*, 1925 (*The Cosmic Race*) and *Indología*, 1926 [Indiology], the Dominican Pedro Henríquez Ureña (1884–1946) in *Seis ensayos en busca de nuestra expresión*, 1928 [Six Essays in Search of our Style]; the spiritual Peruvian Marxist José Carlos Mariátegui (1895–1930) in *Siete ensayos de interpretación de la realidad peruana*, 1928 (*Seven Interpretative Essays on Peruvian Reality*), and the Mexican Alfonso Reyes (1889–1959) in *Última Tule*, 1942 [The Last Thule], which includes "Notas sobre la inteligencia americana," 1939 [Notes on the Hispanic American Mind]. Most of what is thought and expressed in these works constitutes an ideological sequel to Martí's above-mentioned essay, "Nuestra América." In a judicious mixture of hope and foreboding they point to inherent differences between Americans of North and South and insist on the need for Latin American cultural autonomy.

Beginning in the 1930s, the major authors undertake a closer examination of Latin America's history and its future, often arriving at a generally unfavorable comparison of its situation with that of Europe and the United States. Accordingly, a principal theme is cultural disillusionment, as in Antonio S. Pedreira's skeptical assessment of Puerto Rico's possibilities for the future in *Insularismo*, 1934 [Island Isolation], *Radiografía de la pampa*, 1933 (*X-Ray of the Pampa*) by Ezequiel Martínez Estrada (1895–1964) with his revisionist view of Argentina and the New World as a historical wasteland. H.A. Murena (1924–75), an Argentine compatriot and close reader of Martínez Estrada, is just as pessimistic in *El pecado original de América*, 1954 [Latin America's Original Sin]. Carlos Rangel (1929) deplores a Hispanic American tendency to blame the United States for Hispanic America's problems in *Del buen salvaje al buen revolucionario*, 1976 [From the Noble Savage to the Good Revolutionary].

On a more abstract and deeper existential level is *Historia de una pasión argentina*, 1937 [History of an Argentine Passion], a quest for a national (though not nationalist) sense of spiritual identification by the novelist and essay writer, Eduardo Mallea (1903–82). Sebastián Salazar Bondy (1924–64) unleashes an entertaining diatribe on Peruvian society in *Lima la horrible*, 1964 [Beastly Lima]. With his sensibility as one of this century's most profound poets, Octavio Paz analyzes Mexicans' personality "masks" from the conquest to modern times in *El laberinto de la soledad*, 1950 (*The Labyrinth of Solitude*). *Posdata*, 1970 (*The Other Mexico: Critique of the Pyramid*), serves an an appendix to *El laberinto*, and is a criticism of the repression that occurred in Mexico City in October, 1968. That violence also motivated an important testimonial work by Elena Poniatowska, *La noche de Tlatelolco*, 1971 (*Massacre in Mexico*). Paz's best essays on poetics and the poet's experience are *El arco y la lira*, 1956 (*The Bow and the Lyre*) and *Los hijos del limo*, 1974 (*Children of the Myre*). Jorge Luis Borges (1899–1986) also has original thoughts on literary creativity and on modern culture in *Discusión*, 1932 [Discussion], *Otras inquisisiones*, 1952 (*Other Inquisitions*), and *Historia de la eternidad*, 1936 [A History of Eternity].

Increasingly, the memoir and testimonial writing have become a significant variation of the Hispanic American essay.

Among many other essays, Alfonso Reyes (1889–1959), the leading Hispanic American humanist of our time, wrote "Oración del 9 de febrero," 1930 [Reflections on the 9th of February], *Pasado inmediato*, 1941 [The Immediate Past], *Parentelia*, 1954 [My Family], and a posthumous *Diario*, 1911–1930 (1969).

With a temperament and ambitions comparable to those of Domingo Faustino Sarmiento, José Vasconcelos reflects on his achievements and failures as an educator and politician in a four-volume *Memorias* (1936–39). It is rich in anecdote, autobiography, and biographical allusions. Critics are generally agreed that the first volume (*Ulises criollo* [A Mexican Ulysses]) is the most coherent and convincing.

Stylistically more refined than Vasconcelos and with keen perceptiveness, Victoria Ocampo (1890–1979) wrote and published ten series (i.e., volumes) of *Testimonios* [Testimonies] between 1935 and 1977; she also founded and directed the prestigious Argentine literary journal *Sur* (1931–80) in which the work of many of the world's leading writers appeared. Her testimonies constitute an expansive and sensitive autobiography. The Venezuelan Mariano Picón-Salas (1904–65) wrote graceful impressionistic essays, e.g., *Gusto de México*, 1952 [A Taste of Mexico], *Comprensión de Venezuela*, 1976 [Understanding Venezuela] , and a lively and thoughtful testimony of his youthful years in exile, *Regreso de tres mundos*, 1959 [Return from Three Worlds]. Luis Cardoza y Aragón (1904–93), the Guatemalan poet and art critic, lived mostly in Mexican exile after 1944. In addition to *Guatemala, las líneas de su mano*, 1955 [Guatemala, the Lines on Her Hand], a historical revision similar in some ways to Paz's *El laberinto de la soledad*, he wrote a long memoir that includes vivid portraits of many of his contemporaries, *El río. Novelas de caballería*, 1989 [The River. Chivalric Novels] and has virtually nothing to do with chivalric novels. Two other residents in Mexico, the Guatemalan Augusto Monterroso and the Puerto Rican José Luis González, have published lively accounts of their formative years, respectively, *Los buscadores de oro*, 1993 [The Gold Seekers] and *La luna no era de queso*, 1988 [The Moon Wasn't Made of Cheese].

Four writers with an intense political view of Latin American problems are the Mexican novelist Carlos Fuentes, author of *Tiempo mexicano*, 1971 [Mexican Time] and the more personal *Myself with Others* (1988); Roberto Fernández Retamar, the Cuban poet who wrote a late sequel (and socialist reconstruction) of Rodó's *Ariel: Calibán: apuntes sobre la cultura en nuestra América*, 1971 (*Caliban: Notes on Culture in Our America*); the Chilean Ariel Dorfman, who satirizes US cultural imperialism in *La última aventura del Llanero solitario*, 1979 and *Patos, elefantes y héroes*, 1985 [Ducks, Elephants and Heroes]; and Elena Poniatowska who wrote a many-faceted testimony of the 1985 earthquake in Mexico City, *Nada, nadie*, 1988 [Nobody, Nothing] that provides us with interesting reflections on Mexican society and authorities in a moment of collective stress.

As this survey has intended to show, the essay of the past two centuries has adjusted sensitively and well to the circumstances, preferences and crises of Latin American life.

PETER G. EARLE

Further Reading

Critical Studies

Alazraki, Jaime, "Tres formas del ensayo contemporáneo: Borges, Paz, Cortázar," *Revista Iberoamericana* 118–19 (1982)

Anderson Imbert, Enrique, "Defensa del ensayo" [1945], in his *Los domingos del profesor*, 2nd edition, Buenos Aires: Ediciones Gure, 1972

____ "Misión de los intelectuales en Hispanoamérica," in his *Estudios sobre letras hispánicas*, Mexico City: Editorial Libros de México, 1974

Clemente, José Edmundo, *El ensayo*, Buenos Aires: Ediciones Culturales Argentinas, 1961

Earle, Peter G., "On the Contemporary Displacement of the Hispanoamerican Essay," *Hispanic Review*, vol. 46 (1978)

____ "El ensayo hispanoamericano, del Modernismo a la Modernidad," *Revista Iberoamericana* 118–19 (1982)

____ "Essay," in *A History of Literature in the Caribbean*, edited by A. James Arnold, *et al.*, vol. 1, Amsterdam and Philadelphia: Benjamins, 1994

Earle, Peter G. and Robert G. Mead, Jr, *Historia del ensayo hispanoamericano*, Mexico City: Andrea, 1973

Giordano, Jaime, "El ensayo hispanoamericano de las últimas generaciones," *Mundo* 1 (1987)

Gómez-Martínez, José Luis, "El ensayo y su función social," *Diálogos* 69 (1976)

____ "El ensayo como género literario: estudio de sus características," Part I in *Abside*, 40 and 42 (1976 and 1978)

____ *Teoría del ensayo*, Mexico City: UNAM, 2nd edition, 1992

Lévy, Isaac J. and Juan Loveluck (editors), *Simposio: el ensayo hispánico*, Columbia: University of South Carolina Press, 1984

Levy, Kurt L. and Keith Ellis (editors), *El ensayo y la crítica literaria en Iberoamérica*, Toronto: University of Toronto Press, 1970

Loveluck, Juan, "El ensayo hispanoamericano y su naturaleza," in *Los Ensayistas* 1 (1976)

Mead, Jr, Robert G., *Breve historia del ensayo hispanoamericano*, Mexico City: Andrea, 1956

Meyer, Doris (editor), *Reinterpreting the Spanish American Essay: Women Writers of the 19th and 20th Centuries*, Austin: University of Texas Press, 1995

Oviedo, José Miguel, *Breve historia del ensayo hispanoamericano*, Madrid: Alianza, 1991

Picón-Salas, Mariano, "En torno al ensayo," *La Nueva Democracia* 42 (1962)

Rey de Guido, Clara, *Contribución al estudio del ensayo en Hispanoamérica*, Caracas: Biblioteca de la Academia Nacional de la Historia, 1985

Roy, Joaquín, "Del ensayo y la crítica," *El Urogallo* 35–36 (1975)

Stabb, Martin S., *In Quest of Identity. Patterns in the Spanish American Essay of Ideas, 1890–1960*, Chapel Hill: University of North Carolina Press, 1967

____ *The Dissenting Voice: the New Essay of Spanish America, 1960–1985*, Austin: University of Texas Press, 1995

Vitier, Medardo, *Del ensayo americano*, Mexico City: Fondo de Cultura Económica, 1945

Anthologies of the Hispanic American Essay

Giordano, Jaime (editor), *La identidad cultural de Hispanoamérica*, Santiago de Chile: Ediciones del Maitén, 1986

Mejía Sánchez, Ernesto (editor), *El ensayo actual hispanoamericano*, Mexico City: Andrea, 1971

Ripoll, Carlos (editor), *Conciencia intelectual de América: antología del ensayo hispanoamericano (1836–1959)*, 3rd edition, New York: Torres, 1974

Skirius, John (editor), *El ensayo hispanoamericano del siglo XX*, Mexico City: Fondo de Cultura Económica, 1981

F

Fagundes Telles, Lygia

See Telles

Feminism

Early feminism in Latin America was first conceived as a feminist critique of society in that it was a political and social movement that struggled for women's rights such as suffrage, labour laws to improve working conditions, obtain better wages, and access to education. This critique also examined the role of institutionalized religion in women's lives and argued for less rigid religious views on women as well as for the passing of a divorce law. There were feminist movements that advocated similar programs in most countries and reached similar solutions, when successful as in the case of Argentina and Uruguay. The changes advocated by Latin American feminists were implemented gradually, and changes were incorporated into societies in diverse fashions.

In many cases, progressive movements were thwarted by the rise of the political right. This development, and/or the rise of militarism, manifested itself in social and political programs that eventually led to the exclusion of women from participation in public culture. Consequently, the advances that had been made were put on hold in many instances. As Francesca Miller argues in her article "Latin American Feminism and the Transnational Arena," Latin American women's contribution to feminism has been insistently "shrouded" in superficial assumptions on the nature of its originality, which has been underestimated.

The pioneers who participated in international activities and debates came from Argentina, Chile, Uruguay and Brazil. The most recent wave of feminism in Latin America has been partially influenced by similar manifestations in the United States and Western Europe in the 1960s, when new awareness brought women's rights to the fore once more. This time, however, it came with a renewed sense of urgency and staying power, which may allow women's lives to be altered more substantially

in these societies. On the one hand, consciousness-raising activities have been unevenly practised in the subcontinent as women mobilized more openly in Argentina, Uruguay, Chile, Mexico or Cuba than in Honduras, Ecuador or the Dominican Republic; on the other, the Guatemalan Quiché activist Rigoberta Menchú has become a prominent universal voice against the excesses committed against her community, even though Guatemala's manifestations of a feminist movement are insignificant. Menchú achieved international recognition, and in 1992 she was awarded the Nobel Peace Prize for her unabated work against militarism, racism, sexism, and classism, the four feared male riders of Latin American women's apocalypse.

Historically, there were feminist organizations and movements that began to develop in the last quarter of the 19th century and continued into the 20th century in most Latin American countries. However, more effective were those in Argentina, Uruguay, Chile, Mexico and Cuba, where upper- and middle-class women joined the new European immigrants. Many of them were proponents of socialist, syndicalist, and/or anarchist ideas during the various waves of immigration to the American continent which accelerated its pace towards the end of the 19th century, reaching its peak early in the 20th century. Thus, it can be said that feminism is linked strongly to its European roots. The impact of feminist activities taking place in the US did not reach these movements until the 1920s. At its inception, Latin American feminists sought to better conditions for workers, including women (10% of the non-agricultural force) and children; fought for the improvement and expansion of the educational system; and struggled to obtain women's suffrage. The last was granted in piecemeal fashion until fully passed in the 1940s and expanded throughout the American subcontinent.

Argentina was a pioneer in this regard, although suffrage was only incorporated into the national constitution in 1947. By the late 1860s Argentina had began to develop a public school system intended to reach a large segment of the population. Women, Domingo Faustino Sarmiento argued during his presidency (1868–74), should be educated to become Argentina's teachers because they are best suited for the profession. A culture, he said, is best judged by the level of education accessible to its female population.

When the Socialist Party was founded in Argentina in 1896, women were admitted as full members, and later they founded Socialist Women's Centres. The Socialist Party advocated reforms in the Civil Code for universal suffrage and for the equality of rights of the sexes, divorce, legal equality for legitimate and illegitimate children. Feminism and socialism are strongly linked at this point in history. Socialist feminists such as Elvira López, Ernestina López de Nelson and Elvira Rawson de Dellepiane contributed to women's education and helped enlarge the ranks of feminism.

Carolina Muzzilli, a factory worker, reported in *La Prensa* on the general working conditions facing female labourers, characterized by long hours, inadequate machinery, unhealthy conditions and physical and sexual abuse. A group of distinguished feminists of immigrant stock dedicated most of their lives to this movement. Among them were the medical doctors Alicia Moreau de Justo (France/Argentina, 1885–1986), Julieta Lantieri, Elvira Rawson and Cecilia Grierson, who attended the School of Medicine at the University of Buenos Aires.

Alicia Moreau de Justo argued that industrial development had made of the feminist movement a necessity granted that women were entitled to profit from their own labour. Work, she pointed out, is not incompatible with motherhood and mothering. She criticized the Argentine-Spanish heritage that constructed the "child-doll personality" that denied women their inalienable civil rights.

In 1910 – the year when several Latin American nations celebrated the centennial of their independence from Spain – the First International Feminist Congress of Argentina sponsored by the Argentine Association of University Women was held in February. Women from the interior of Argentina, from Uruguay, Chile, Peru, Italy and the United States attended this congress; in April, the National Council of Women also took place. Julieta Lantieri founded the National Feminist Party in Argentina whose main objective was the franchise. Active in educational improvements for young women, feminists had substantial impact in this country's quality of education. The Civil Code was finally amended in 1926 to include women's rights, the most important of the political gains of this movement.

The other area in which Argentine women contributed to the improvement of women's and children's lives was through philanthropy – The Society of Beneficence is the most notable example. Argentina's early feminist impulse towards female education and civil rights gave women the platform from which to demand parity with men; however, not all classes were included in the movement's leadership. None the less, the substantial gains obtained by the early wave of feminists set up the scene for the emergence of the Peronist feminist movement in the 1940s, during which suffrage and better pay were obtained. Under the charismatic Eva Perón, women entered the political arena with confidence, and were able to influence the drafting of progressive legislation for women.

Doctors Moreau and Luisi travelled throughout Latin America to help women's organizations, and Dr Moreau addressed the International Congress of Women Workers in Washington, DC. She was an advocate of government-sponsored day-care centres, comprehensive maternity protection, equal pay and a forty hour working week. She spoke against the white slave trade in South America, about the opposition to sex education in public schools and in the army.

A different case is Brazil, an agricultural state, heavily dependent on slave labour systems. But during the second half of the 19th century, incipient groups of feminists began to have access to the printed media in South Central Brazil – the most progressive region of this country – to struggle for women's rights, in spite of living in seclusion and being subjected to the authority of father, or husband. Some conditions improved when urban areas began to expand, and a new urban elite appeared on the social horizon. With modernization and industrialization, and São Paulo at the centre of progress, social changes began to take place. Women were offered for the first time limited access to education, and thus a small segment of the female population acquired literacy. According to the 1872 census in Brazil its population had reached ten million inhabitants of which about one million free men, half a million free women, less than 1,000 male slaves and 500 female slaves were literate. In Rio de Janeiro Joana Paula Manso de Noronha founded *O Jornal das Senhoras* [The Ladies' Journal] – devoted to fashion, literature, fine arts, theatre and criticism – to educate the public, and women in particular, about women's issues. She argued that women's destiny was not located only at home with her husband and children, and as a means of acquiring wealth for men. She also issued an invitation to women to collaborate in her periodical, remarking, to make it easier, that contributions would be published anonymously. Women naturally reacted positively to this invitation, and the ensuing publication lasted four years. Violante Atabalipa Ximenes de Bivar e Velasco and Gervasia Nunezia Pires dos Santos were the other editors of this pioneering periodical, which closed in December of 1855. In 1862 a second publication entitled *O Bello Sexo* [The Fair Sex] appeared in Rio de Janeiro with a more progressive group of collaborators who did not need to hide their identity any longer. Other publications include *O Sexo Feminino* [The Feminine Sex] which appeared in 1873 and was edited by Francisca Senhorinha da Motta Diniz, a lady from Campanha in the state of Minas Gerais. This publication was directed "to the education, instruction, and emancipation of women." Its objective was to demand rights for women by appealing to their support and by training them to change their attitudes toward themselves; only by changing oppressive conditions could women achieve parity with men. *Miosótis* [Forget-Me-Not] appeared in Recife in 1875. *Eco das Damas* [The Ladies' Echo], edited by Amelia Carolina da Silva Couto, was published in Rio de Janeiro in 1879, and disseminated the United States model of moral and material improvement for women. By 1890 some improvement was noted in the most developed urban areas of coastal Brazil. Josephina Alvares de Azevedo was a member of a new wave of Brazilian feminists who objected strongly to the patriarchal structure of their society. She published a periodical entitled *A*

Familia [The Family], which encouraged women to take charge of their own lives. Feminism in Brazil was mainly concerned with improving the legal status of women, with the role of women in the family, access to education, the abolition of slavery, the introduction of female suffrage, and divorce. By 1891, when Brazil became a republic, women's issues were brought to the constitutional convention. Suffrage was not achieved then, but the movement continued in Brazil, and the law was passed in 1932 making Brazil the third country in the Western Hemisphere to grant women the right to vote. The other two were the United States and Ecuador.

In Mexico, feminism manifested itself first in the State of Yucatán. The women's liberation movement flourished there partly because of its contact with populous urban areas outside of Mexico City, partly on account of it being more open to European contact and thirdly, because the region was already a centre of revolutionary activity and social protest. In Mérida, the capital city of Yucatán, feminists pushed for women's rights as early as 1870 when Rita Cetina Gutiérrez founded the feminist society *La Siempreviva* [The Everlasting Flower], which supported the education of women to enable them to become teachers of younger generations. Two feminist congresses were held in this city in 1916, where female teachers demanded an end to bigotry, intolerance, and religious conservatism. Some laws favouring women were included in the Mexican Constitution of 1917. Present at the first Pan American Conference of Women held in Maryland (1923) were Hermila Galiando, the most radical of Mexican feminists, and Elena Torres who was elected vice-president for North America of the Pan American league for the Elevation of Women. The Maryland congress, attended by professional women from the US, Mexico and Cuba, was dominated by the delegation from Yucatán led by Elvia Carrillo Puerto, that wanted to open a debate on birth control, female sexuality, sex education in the schools, and white slave traffic. Much was done to oppose them but they were able to open these serious issues to debate, although most were not accepted. The feminist struggle in Mexico intensified in the crucial period of social ferment in the early years of the 20th century. This spanned the end of the Porfirio Díaz regime, the outbreak of the Mexican Revolution and beyond it into the decade of 1930–40. Women were to be found in the middle of the armed struggle as combatants, as support groups for the armies, as drafters of plans and propaganda and as couriers. Their role of *soldaderas* (camp followers) has usually been highlighted in detriment to other central war activities outlined above. As María Antonieta Rascón points out, Mexican histiography has focused primarily on *heroines* and *femmes célebres*, usually connected to famous men, thus minimizing the participation of working women and other women's groups that are not linked to the dominant class. Women participated in the revolutionary war that started in 1910, the first social revolution of the century, before the Chinese Revolution of 1911 and the Russian Revolution of 1917. When the Mexican revolutionary platform became part of the constitutional text of 1917, however, women were not included in the definition of citizen. Most women's issues remained unaddressed. Perhaps for this reason, women were also active as leaders of the backlash to the Revolution, the *Cristero* rebellion, that took place in the state of Jalisco at the end of the 1920s. (The role of the female leader in that political movement of the extreme right is represented melodramatically in *Pensativa* (1945), a novel by Jesús Goytortúa).

In the second wave of feminism, the goals and objectives of Western feminists shifted since the struggle now was to focus on the total liberation of women. As Simone de Beauvoir remarked in 1972, women had not won the struggle, and since 1950 women had not gained anything. The movement then became radicalized. For Latin American society in general, the decade of the 1960s presents a complex picture. On the one hand it saw an increase in militarism and a growing intolerance of liberation movements such as feminism. On the other, it experimented in populist political movements. The Cuban Revolution has succeeded in overturning the historical course for the island of Cuba. The oppressed masses began to express their plight more overtly, partly fostered by the discourse of the Cuban Revolution, partly by an opening in the ranks of the Catholic Church with a new message, that of the theology of liberation. In the early and mid 1970s, Argentina, Chile and Uruguay became the victims of a new totalitarian ideology disseminated by the military class; Central American countries were under strong dictatorships of the political right; others like Bolivia and Paraguay were under military regimes. None of these regimes favoured the cause of women. On the contrary, they became prey to the hardening rule of patriarchal power and, therefore, fighting these powers became a central concern of women affiliated to progressive political movements. It is in the 1980s, when elected democratic administrations come to power, that feminism is slowly revitalized in many of these nations. A great task ahead for Latin American feminists is that they need to confront the specific problems the region faces today. It is likely that feminism, currently under attack by the general rise of the political right in all Western countries, will be revitalized in Latin America in the near future.

MAGDALENA GARCÍA PINTO

Further Reading

For additional items see also the Further Reading lists for the entries on Feminist Literary Theory and Women's Writing

Bergmann, Emilie, *et al.*, *Women, Culture, and Politics in Latin America. Seminar on Feminism and Culture in Latin America*, Berkeley: University of California Press, 1990

Carlson, Marifran, *¡Feminismo! The Woman's Movement in Argentina from Its Beginnings to Eva Perón*, Chicago: Academy, 1988

Lavrin, Asunción (editor), *Latin American Women: Historical Perspectives*, Westport, Connecticut: Greenwood Press, 1978

Lavrin, Asunción, *Women, Feminism and Social Change in Argentina, Chile and Uruguay, 1890–1940*, Lincoln: University of Nebraska Press, 1995

Macías, Ana, *Against all Odds: the Feminist Movement in Mexico to 1940*, Westport, Connecticut: Greenwood Press, 1982

Randall, Margaret, *Gathering Rage: the Failure of the Twentieth Century Revolutions to Develop a Feminist Agenda*, New York: Monthly Review Press, 1992

Stoner, Lynn K., *From the House to the Streets. The Cuban Woman's Movement for Legal Reform 1898–1940*, Durham, North Carolina: Duke University Press, 1991

Feminist Literary Theory

Since the end of the 1970s feminist literary theory has played an increasingly important role in the development of contemporary Latin American cultural studies. During this time it has persistently interrogated androcentric critical assumptions and helped open up the canon to previously neglected women writers. In the British and North American academies the polemic surrounding the early advances of feminist criticism was eased by a more or less liberal consensus. In Latin America no such consensus existed and there were fewer women academics able and inclined to support its creation. These difficult beginnings have left their mark on feminism and feminist literary theory alike, and help to explain why so many of Latin America's leading feminist writers – for example Sylvia Molloy (Argentina) and Cristina Peri Rossi (Uruguay) – continue to live and work elsewhere. Within Latin America, class has been the key analytic concept for the majority of radical academics since the 1960s, and early feminist criticism was censured as a bourgeois distraction from cross-gender analysis and activism. Although this tendency is less marked today, a number of leading feminist writers – among them Elena Poniatowska (Mexico) and Beatriz Sarlo (Argentina) – retain a clear class or anti-capitalist dimension in their work. For many younger critics in particular, however, this dimension is less crucial. Sarlo's base at Buenos Aires University is also home to Lacanian-inspired psychoanalytic critics and a gender research group influenced less by Marx than by Michel Foucault and Judith Butler.

A rather different objection to feminism comes from writers like Julieta Campos (Cuba/Mexico) and Isabel Allende (Chile), who share some feminist concerns but see writing as an activity which they undertake as human beings rather than as women. Since its beginnings in the 1970s Latin American feminist criticism has challenged this view of writing as ungendered. Early examples used strategies adapted from Kate Millett's *Sexual Politics* to expose patriarchal assumptions in Latin American male-authored texts. Results were uneven, however, and many readers were uneasy with this application of Northern critical procedures and categories to Latin American writing. The 1975 Congress of Latin American Women Writers soon gave a recognizably Iberoamerican inflection to individual feminist concerns, with its focus on women's broader social roles. The conference also underlined the tension between two very different critical tendencies in Latin American cultural studies. One of these foregrounds the text's status as a *representation* of (for example) gender relations and engages with those relations *as words*. The other treats these representations as a more or less transparent window onto the relations and events depicted. This second tendency has traditionally been more marked in Latin American non-feminist critical writing. It also appears in some feminist criticism, however, despite the basic feminist premise that analytic and representational categories are not transparent, objective or universal, but derive their authority from patriarchal networks of domination and exclusion.

This premise was the starting point for the feminist reconstitution of the canon. The process involved establishing a corpus of texts by new as well as previously neglected women writers, and included not only standard "authorized" genres but also previously marginalized ones (such as testimonials, autobiographies and private letters) particularly associated with women writers. Essential to this process were the many anthologies of Latin American women's writing which began to be published from the late 1970s. As a result of what has been termed the continuing "boom" in women's writing, such anthologies remain popular today, many of them in translation for Anglo-European consumption. The most recent and useful of these is Sara Castro-Klarén, Sylvia Molloy and Beatriz Sarlo's *Women's Writing in Latin America: an Anthology,* which combines a wide range of writers, texts and genres with excellent critical and biographical introductions. Collections of interviews – particularly those edited by Evelyn Picon Garfield and Magdalena García Pinto – have also been an invaluable resource for feminist critics.

One question which this process inevitably raised, and which many of these interviews addressed, was whether women's writing was essentially different from men's. Influential writers like Clarice Lispector (Brazil), Cristina Peri Rossi and Julieta Campos had all rejected the notion of a specific and clearly differentiated women's writing. The 1982 Congress of Latin American Writers provided a platform for leading critics and writers to explore this question in detail. Rosario Ferré (Puerto Rico) and Josefina Ludmer (Mexico) were unwilling to accept the hypothesis of a fixed women's nature that could be deduced from or reflected in stable stylistic differences. Other delegates underlined the risks of perpetuating women's dependency by defining their writing in relation to men's – for example as a marginal other. Sara Castro-Klarén took a rather different line. She began by observing that the large number of texts being produced by Latin American women writers had so far failed to generate any continent-specific theoretical positions. In fact, Josefina Ludmer's own contribution, "Las tretas del débil" or "The Strategies of the Weak," is widely acknowledged to have begun this process. Unlike Ludmer, however, Castro-Klarén urged feminists wishing to subvert patriarchal representational assumptions to adapt French feminist theories for the purpose.

Ten years later the application of non-Latin American feminist critical assumptions to Latin American texts is more widespread, but its remains controversial. However, critics like Jean Franco (UK) reject calls for theoretical purity as alien to the continent's tradition of critical bricolage (a "do it yourself" approach). At the same time she reminds feminists who advocate non-theoretical, "common sense," approaches to texts of the extent to which these approaches are themselves grounded in unexamined, patriarchally-influenced notions of distance and objectivity which feminist theory has helped to discredit. The publication in 1986 of Franco's "Apuntes sobre la crítica feminista y la literatura hispanoamericana" [Notes on Feminist Criticism and Latin American Literature] took this debate a stage further and clarified its terms. While criticism rescues lost texts or re-evaluates forgotten ones, she contended, theory has a broader, explicitly political, role in the exploration of power relations and for this purpose the critical application of any theory is warranted. Three years later her full-length study, *Plotting Women,* used a range of theories to link the claims of life practices and textuality, political power and marginality. Her analysis focused on the inherently political nature of women's collective reality, at a time when women's experience of a dislocated existence within male paradigms was increasingly seen as offering a standpoint for non male constructed knowledge.

The early feminist concern for solidarity had tended to minimize differences among women, focusing instead on differences between men and women or (in the case of psychoanalytically-inspired feminism) on different aspects of individual women. However the 1980s saw a growing focus on the specificity of Latin American women and their writing. Chilean sociologist Hernán Vidal, co-ordinator of the 1988 Conference on Cultural and Historical Grounding for Hispanic and Luso-Brazilian Feminist Literary Criticism, was one of several speakers to contrast the more privatized and individualistic concerns of Northern feminism and the more social, public and structural orientation of Latin American critics. As suggested above, such generalizations are inevitably reductive. At the same time they leave Latin Americanists who are also Northern feminists out of the picture – a key omission, since the only full-length studies towards a specifically Latin American literary theory have come from this group.

The first of these attempts came four years later with US critic Debra Castillo's *Talking Back: Toward a Latin American Feminist Literary Criticism*. It starts from the undesirability of subjecting the diversity of Latin American women's writing to a single, overarching theoretical framework. Instead (following Ludmer) Castillo takes such conventionally negative features of specific Latin American and Latino women's texts as silences and superficiality, and redeploys them as ingredients in her critical recipe. Exploiting the work of poststructuralist, postmodern, postcolonial and French feminist theorists, she attempts to engage not only with women writers from the middle classes but also, by a complex process of double voicing, with urban poor, Indian and other less audible women.

In a 1992 essay, Jean Franco marks a critical shift away from the ethical and political complexities of representing other women towards a more pragmatic attempt to engage with them. This was in part a response to the growing importance for international feminism of Latin America's new social movements. In her own full-length study of Latin American feminist criticism published a year later, US critic Amy Kaminsky's emphasis on political practice and women's agency takes this move towards engagement a stage further. Like Vidal she believes that the "political" and the "aesthetic" have been constructed as antithetical in the US academy and the "political" marginalized in its literary discourse. Suggesting that (particularly lesbian) sexuality has been similarly marginalized in Latin America, she attempts to bridge these differences by undertaking a feminist "demetaphorization" of the language of sexuality for Latin Americanists and a "dethetorization" of the language of politics for (North American) feminists.

Clearly, North/South tension has been a key factor in the development of Latin American feminist literary theory. However no survey of this theory can neglect the influential critique directed at such binary oppositions by Latin American women writers who have grown up in the US. By celebrating their hybrid status as *latinas* – and in the case of Gloria Anzaldúa and Cherríe Moraga as lesbian *latinas* – these women have opened up a rich vein of theoretical possibilities which has yet to be fully explored.

ANNY BROOKSBANK JONES

Further Reading

Castillo, Debra A., *Talking Back: Toward a Latin American Feminist Literary Criticism*, Ithaca, New York: Cornell University Press, 1992

Davies, Catherine and Anny Brooksbank Jones, *Latin American Women's Writing: Feminist Readings on Theory and Crisis*, Oxford: Clarendon Press, 1996

Franco, Jean, "Apuntes sobre la crítica feminista y la literatura hispanoamericana," *Hispamérica*, vol. 15/45 (1986)

____ *Plotting Women: Gender and Representation in Mexico*, New York: Columbia University Press, and London: Verso, 1989

____ "Going Public: Rehabilitating the Private," in *On Edge: the Crisis of Contemporary Latin American Culture*, edited by Franco George Yúdice and Ángel Flores, Minneapolis: University of Minnesota Press, 1993

Jehenson, Myriam Y., *Latin-American Women Writers: Class Race and Gender*, Albany: State University of New York Press, 1995

Kaminsky, Amy K., *Reading the Body Politic: Feminist Criticism and Latin American Women Writers*, Minneapolis: University of Minnesota Press, 1993

Lindstrom, Naomi and Carmelo Virgillo (editors), *Woman as Myth and Metaphor in Latin American Literature*, Columbia: University of Missouri Press, 1985

Rodríguez, Ileana, *House/Garden/Nation: Space, Gender and Ethnicity in Post-Colonial Latin American Literatures by Women*, translated by Rodríguez and Robert Carr, Durham, North Carolina: Duke University Press, 1994

Sblodowska, Elzbieta, "La escritura femenina: una contra-corriente paródica," in her *La parodia en la nueva novela hispanoamericana(1960–1985)*, Amsterdam and Philadelphia, Benjamins, 1991

Smith, Paul Julian, *Representing the Other: Race, Text and Gender in Spanish and Spanish American Narrative*, Oxford: Clarendon Press, and New York: Oxford University Press, 1992

Vidal, Hernán, *Cultural and Historical Grounding for Hispanic and Luso-Brazilian Feminist Literary Criticism*, Minneapolis: Institute for the Studies of Ideology and Literature, 1989 [See, in particular, the article by Naomi Lindstrom]

Special Issues of Journals
Revista Iberoamericana, vol. 51/132–33 (1985)

Macedonio Fernández 1874-1952

Argentine experimental prose writer

During the last few decades, Macedonio Fernández's work has attained extraordinary renown and has become a real revelation to the younger generations of writers, who consider him the most authentic forerunner of the avant-garde break with tradition and the innovative linguistic features of the contemporary novel. Furthermore, knowledge of his aesthetic and philosophical theories – only partly disseminated until a few years ago – has opened up new research perspectives to critics, thus intensifying interest in his work in a remarkable way through studies and newspaper articles which try to grasp his complex creative activity from very different angles.

The renown which Macedonio's personality has acquired is clearly justified as soon as we come into contact with the peculiar expressive subtlety of his theorizings and stories, which make him one of the most original writers of Argentine literature. The many and sometimes disconcerting nuances in Macedonio Fernández's writing primarily surprise by the contrasting directions of their expression and by the dense network of theorising relating to artistic tasks which progressively become interwoven in the literary text itself. Fact and fiction are thus brought together on the same linguistic level, which from the basis of that duality, unexpectedly severs the usual relationships of discourse, and presents us with a fresh anti-rhetorical proposition opposed to conventional form.

Although in many passages of his theorizings Macedonio puts forward three specific genres – poetics, serious prose and humorous prose – he never places them in a regular order nor does he present them as inflexible or unquestionable models; instead they are linked only by the mutually exclusive procedures they share in their execution. He seeks to retain that which has not yet ended, that which flows creatively and, therefore, in the dynamic uncertainty of that which can continue because closure is not in sight. To develop all the time, not to reach a conclusion somehow, means giving in neither to the stillness of death nor to what it already closed and defined for ever. All his written work – not only that of literary intent, but also his newspaper articles, essays, speeches, toasts and even his letters – is in a fragmented and unorganized style but is essentially conditioned by a search for permanence which establishes an order beyond logical correlations and seemingly expressive subtleties.

Fernández's preoccupation with renewal, so passionate and persistent, grows stronger in the course of time and is more obvious in his post-1940 work, where an inseparable fusion between his theories and technical achievements is evident. He displays at one and the same time two levels of writing: theoretical reflection and fiction – and he interrelates or confuses them intentionally. He thus puts forward a real questioning of his own task as a writer, showing it clearly even in its as yet unconnected primary material – in its interminable growth from the amorphism of the creative purpose – while he moves towards a concrete expression that is realized.

Apart from critical research and theories published independently, those observations on the task itself form part of his short stories or poems through insistent processes – notes, annotations, letters, postscripts, prologues, characters' or narrators' digressions etc. – which convey his articulation of the plot. This is a way of openly displaying the framework of the creative work and, at the same time, not throwing himself fully into the magic and liberating world of fantasy, ruled only by its fictitious implications.

Between what was promised and what was sketched, there are also innumerable prologues of his much proclaimed *Museo de la Novela de la Eterna* [Museum of the Novel of the Eternal]. Here he feigns narrative weakness, and stubbornly perseveres in going beyond the limits of Aristotelian verisimilitude and mimesis so as to project himself towards a free and subjective concept of creative activity. That idealistic attitude, which challenges a true copy of the world around us, spurs him on to the purpose of capturing a bright and radiant memory of a higher reality free from spatial and chronological ties.

Not even causality or the sequential order of things is relevant to Macedonio in that illusory space achieved by "indirect techniques of emotional arousal," where time can be turned back and the past, immersed in the present, constitutes an unceasing present in which reality and dreams, fact and fiction are fused into an enlarged experience that goes beyond the senses, without relativist frontiers. In it the author's much desired relationship would at last take place with the hypothetical reader – "minimal," "casual" "who reads only the first page" or "only one story" etc. Such a reader, on being incorporated into the novel as an additional character, allows the author to prolong his creative plan into an indefinable future, which will have to renew that interminable task with each new reader who identifies him or herself with the work, thus safeguarding its perennial nature.

Macedonio Fernández is surrounded by an aura of legend that tends to make his work seem esoteric. This results from his self-denial as a professional writer, his lack of concern at having his work published, his determination to keep his writing uninfluenced by the trends of the time, his way of living, remote from literary circles – except during the years when he was connected with the Martín Fierro group and with the Neoromantic generation.

The reissue of his out-of-print books, as well as the appearance of previously unpublished material, offer a very different image of his aesthetic works and his literary output dating from the 1960s. In this sense, the dissemination of *Museo de la Novela de la Eterna* and of his *Teorías* has been of fundamental importance to clarify apparently obscure or unconnected aspects of his creative activity. These demonstrate his steadfast, though hidden, continuity of a task and an attitude which is forever dedicated to enquiry. From the very first of his publications, that analytical capacity, open to the provocative stimulation of philosophical meditation which is always part of his essential preoccupations, is concentrated on the search for a sense of purpose, as contrasted with the contradictory fortunes of our existence.

All the attempts at expression which Macedonio Fernández has left us in visible form are expressed on those basic lines. But what is visible is only a minimal portion of what can be surmised. His fundamental preoccupations spring from the need to decipher the mysterious interrelations which join life to death, sleep to waking, the past to the future, and our limited being to the radiant eternity which sustains us in some irrevocable way.

NÉLIDA SALVADOR

translated by Patricia James

Biography
Born in Buenos Aires, Argentina, 1 June 1874. Son of wealthy parents and thus had private income, but studied law at University of Buenos Aires. Taught himself philosophy and political theory. Doctorate in Jurisprudence, 1897. With Leopoldo Lugones and other friends decided to establish a socialist colony in Paraguay, but they lost heart en route and never reached their destination. Married Elena de Obieta in 1901. Corresponded with William James and began to think about the application to literature of a systematically irrationalistic philosophy. From an early age he published anti-Establishment articles. Withdrew from public life, but gave up his hermit-like existence for a time in the 1920s when Borges and others were forging the avant-garde in Argentina. Borges sought to involve him so that young writers might learn how a radical aesthetic might be developed, and appointed him co-editor of the literary journal *Proa* in 1922. Died on 10 December 1952, leaving a vast assortment of writings in a state of disorder.

Selected Works
No attempt has been made to place the works of this very experimental author in different generic categories.

No todo es vigilia la de los ojos abiertos, Buenos Aires: Gleizer, 1928
Papeles de recienvenido, Buenos Aires: Cuadernos del Plata, 1929
Una novela que comienza, Santiago de Chile: Ercilla, 1941

Papeles de recienvenido; Continuación de la nada, Buenos Aires: Losada, 1944
Poemas, Mexico City: Guaranía, 1953
Museo de la Novela de la Eterna, Buenos Aires: Centro Editor de América Latina, 1967
Cuadernos de todo y nada, Buenos Aires: Corregidor, 1972

Compilations and Anthologies
Macedonio Fernández, Buenos Aires: Ediciones Culturales Argentinas, 1961 [Selection and prologue by Jorge Luis Borges]
Museo de la Novela de la Eterna, Caracas: Biblioteca Ayacucho, 1982 [A scholarly edition by César Fernández Moreno with extracts from all the author's works]
Obras completas, 8 vols, Buenos Aires: Corregidor, 1974–89 [Includes previously unpublished works such as letters, and *Adriana Buenos Aires; última novela mala*]

Further Reading
Borinsky, Alicia, *Macedonio Fernández y la teoría crítica: una evaluación*, Buenos Aires: Corregidor, 1987
Engelbert, Jo Anne, *Macedonio Fernández and the Spanish American New Novel*, New York: New York University Press, 1978
García, Germán Leopoldo, *Hablan de Macedonio Fernández: entrevistas*, Buenos Aires: Carlos Pérez, 1968
Isaacson, José, *Macedonio Fernández, sus ideas políticas y estéticas*, Buenos Aires: Belgrano, 1981
Jitrik, Noé, *La novela futura de Macedonio Fernández*, Caracas: Universidad Central de Venezuela, 1973
Kaminszain, Tamara, "Invenciones de Macedonio Fernández," in her *El texto silencioso: tradición y vanguardia en la poesía sudamericana*, Mexico City: UNAM, 1983
Lindstrom, Naomi, *Macedonio Fernández*, Lincoln, Nebraska: Society of Spanish and Spanish-American Studies, 1981
Salvador, Nélida, *Macedonio Fernández: precursor de la antinovela*, Buenos Aires: Plus Ultra, 1986
Schiminovich, Flora, *La obra de Macedonio Fernández: una lectura surrealista*, Madrid: Pliegos, 1986
Tripoli, Vicente, *Macedonio Fernández: esbozo de una inteligencia*, Buenos Aires: Colombo, 1971

José Joaquín Fernández de Lizardi 1776–1827

Mexican prose writer

Though it is for *El Periquillo Sarniento* (*The Itching Parrot*) that José Joaquín Fernández de Lizardi is remembered, he also published three other novels, *Noches tristes*, 1818 [Sad Nights], *La Quijotita y su prima*, 1818 [Little Miss Quixote and her Cousin] and *Don Catrín de la Fachenda* (1832). When the freedom of the press was reinstated in 1820 Fernández de Lizardi began to support even more vigorously the Independence cause, and he joined the liberal-leaning Partido Federal, though his ideas were too radical for many of his contemporaries. Two months before his death he published a scathing pamphlet on the evils afflicting Mexico, a fitting testimony to the reforming zeal that characterized his life and work.

El Periquillo Sarniento is Fernández de Lizardi's masterpiece and has been canonized as the first Spanish American novel. It echoes the picaresque novel (for example *Lazarillo de Tormes*) in that it describes the misadventures of a young man driven on by hunger and poverty to make a way in the world, in which he must cheat to survive; it also has a liberal amount of slapstick humour (good examples of which occur during his residency as a doctor's assistant in Tula, and the episode when he attempts to steal jewellery from a corpse). Like the protagonist of *Lazarillo de Tormes*, Periquillo experiences a series of apprenticeships – in a ranch, a monastery, a barber's shop, a pharmacy – thereby learning a variety of trades which range from the socially prestigious (doctor's assistant, sacristan's assistant) to the dubious (croupier, cardsman) to the illegal (thief). The important part of these learning experiences is that they are all based on deception. Those elements which *El Periquillo Sarniento* shares with the great Spanish classic are effective. However, unlike *Lazarillo de Tormes*, Fernández de Lizardi's novel inserts long, moralizing passages which expatiate on the moral meaning of the events described and, for the modern reader at least, reduce their impact. Another important influence, evident to good effect in the prologue to the second volume is Cervantes; like *Don Quixote*, the second volume opens with a discussion between the editor and a personage called Conociemiento (Knowledge) about the reputation that Periquillo now has as a result of the publication of the first volume, as if to underscore that Periquillo is a real-life person.

The society which *El Periquillo Sarniento* describes is in flux. The second half of the 17th century in the Spanish colonies saw, in particular, a displacement of power from the hands of the church, the monarchy, and the land-owning elite to a new self-aware professional class of doctors, lawyers and merchants; a key date is 1778 when Charles III's Decree of Free Trade allowed the twenty-four ports of Spanish America to trade between themselves directly without any need for Spain as an intermediary. *El Periquillo Sarniento* is sensitive to these changing social phenomena and gives a vivid picture of a society under the Bourbons (whose family succeeded to the throne in 1713) which, gradually, was becoming more economically and politically independent from Spain; an indication of this change of ambience is evident in the opening pages of the novel. The novel's prologue describes an imaginary conversation between the author and a friend who tries at first to persuade the former to dedicate his work to a wealthy patron (preferably a member of the nobility) but then advises him to dedicate it to his readers since "ellos son los que costean la impresión, y por lo mismo sus mecenas más seguros" (they are the ones who pay for the printing, and are therefore more reliable sponsors). In *El Periquillo* we see at work what Perry Anderson calls "the national imagination" as encapsulated by the "movement of a solitary hero through a sociological landscape of a fixity that fuses the world inside the novel with the world outside." It is not by chance that the first Spanish-American novel should refer to a new mode of production (capital-based entrepreneurial book production) and, by implication, to the new class from which it sprang, since the 19th-century novel is an outgrowth of the bourgeoisie. In Spanish America, as elsewhere, the growth of the new professional classes, including doctors, lawyers, merchants, suppliers and indeed, printers, was accompanied by a parasitic group of unqualified and dishonest professionals; it is these latter that *El Periquillo Sarniento* sets out to satirize.

Most critics agree that the main aim of *El Periquillo* is to identify the abuse of power in the professions in colonial New Spain. What is intriguing, however, is that the protagonist is used not so much as a means whereby the hypocrisy and corruption of others is exposed; rather he becomes himself a butt of ridicule. In Part I, chapter 1, for example, the narrator, Pedro Sarniento, takes great pains to list the circumstances of his upbringing which explain his wayward ways: his parents' lack of education, their lack of concern for his upbringing and,

in particular, their frequent recourse to wet-nurses: what nowadays would be called an unsettled domestic environment. The didacticism underlying these details becomes only too clear when the narrator refers to the way in which old wives' tales affected him as a young child, and the narrative beings to creak under its self-imposed burden of moralism: "estaba persuadido de que los muertos se aparecían a los vivos cada rato, que los diablos salían a rasguñarnos y apretarnos el pescuezo con la cola cada vez que estaban para ello, que había bultos que se nos echaban encima, que andaban las ánimas en pena mendigando nuestros sufragios, y creía otras majaderías de esta clase que los artículos de la fe. ¡Gracias a un puñado de viejas necias que, o ya en clase de criadas o de visitas, procuraban entretener al niño con cuentos de sus espantos, visiones y apariciones intolerables! ¡Ah, qué daño me hicieron estas viejas! ¡De cuántas supersticiones llenaron mi cabeza!' (I was persuaded that the dead appeared to the living at every opportunity, that devils popped up to scratch up and to throttle us with their tail any time they wanted to, that there were forms which jumped on top of us, that souls in purgatory wandered around begging for our intercessions, and I believed in other absurdities of the kind, apart from the articles of faith. Thanks to a bunch of foolish old women who, whether they were maids or simply visiting, sought to entertain the child with their stories of horror, visions and monstrous apparitions! Oh, what harm those old women did me! How they filled my head with superstitious notions!" [Part I, chapter 1]). It could be argued that the moralistic intention of this passage (which is typical of many others) is over-transparent, and Pedro Sarniento's credibility as a narrator is diminished as a result.

The rationale behind the many episodes of Sarniento's life emerges at the end of the novel. In Book III, chapter 3, the narrator is shipwrecked on an unidentified island in the Landrone Isles in the Pacific Ocean and he finds himself forced to justify the laws and customs of his native land to a sceptical Chinese chieftain (who may well be Fernández de Lizardi's spokesman). In describing his society's customs, Pedro Sarniento manages to make them appear absurd (for example, the concept of a paid army, although, here, history supports New Spain rather than Fernández de Lizardi), and the notion that a nobleman cannot work: "yo soy noble en mi tierra, y por eso no tengo oficio alguno mecánico, porque es bajeza en los caballeros trabajar corporalmente" (I am a nobleman in my land, and thus I have no trade, for it is a sign of low birth to perform manual labour) (Part III, chapter 3). In addition to these absurdities, Pedro Sarniento's stupidity is triumphantly revealed when, in the same chapter, he not only fails to recognise a plant but diagnoses its medicinal function in precisely the wrong way. The narrative of events finally runs against Pedro Sarniento and he is humiliated by the Chinese chieftain: "yo me fui bien avergonzado con mi protector, pensando cómo aprendería al cabo de la vejez algún oficio en una tierra que no consentía inútiles ni vagos Periquillos" (I felt ashamed of myself before my protector, wondering how I should learn some trade while now so old in a land which did not look favourably on useless, vagabond Periquillos). When we ask the question: at what or whom is the satire being directed?, the answer must surely be the European customs of Spanish-American society, since Europeans are specifically mentioned by the Chinese chieftain. In its rather heavy-handed way, therefore, Fernández de Lizardi is satirizing the European infrastructure of the Spanish colonies through the voice of the chieftain, and through the actions and words of Periquillo. The novel's satire is clumsy as a result in that it is directed at the narrator of the story, Pedro Sarniento himself, who does not even try to justify the way he lives (surely not a human trait).

There are some scenes in the novel, however, which show Fernández de Lizardi's consummate skill in allowing irony to emerge from events rather than commentary. A good example is the frequently anthologized scene in Part II, chapter 6, in which Sarniento decides to become a doctor, takes on Andrés as his assistant and, with the luck of the devil, manages to revive a tax-collector (*alcabalero*) who is on his death-bed. Sarniento's oft-repeated use of Latin to hoodwink his audience and hide his ignorance when faced with medical symptoms, is effectively done. In this vignette Fernández de Lizardi offers a convincing picture of colonial society in which half-learned Latin tags are used to confound the populace and fleece the poor.

STEPHEN M. HART

Biography

Born in Mexico City, 15 November 1776. Lizardi was of Spanish descent, a *criollo* in a racially mixed society. Although his father was a physician, the family lived in fairly poor conditions. Educated at the College of San Ildefonso, from 1793; possibly received his degree there; in 1798 he completed advanced course in Rhetoric and returned to Tepoltzotlán. Little is known of his life over the next decade. Contributed to *Diario de México*. Bought printing press, 1810. Viceroy's representative, Taxco, 1810: Lizardi turned over the city's arms and amunitions to insurgent forces and was subsequently imprisoned in 1811. In October 1812, founded his own newspaper, *El Pensador Mexicano* [The Mexican Thinker], a name he also adopted as a pseudonym; through the paper's columns Lizardi attacked corruption. Newspaper lasted until 1814. Worked as a political journalist during this period. Founded many other newspapers during his lifetime, including *Las Sombras de Heráclito y Demócratico* (1815), *Alacena de Frioleras* (1815-16) and *El Hermano de Perico que Cantaba la Victoria* (1823). Published some 280 pamphlets. Imprisoned in March 1821; excommunicated from the Catholic Church, 22 February 1822. Spent his last years in abject poverty and suffered from tuberculosis. Died in Mexico City, 27 June 1827.

Selected Works

Novels

El Periquillo Sarniento, Mexico City: Valdés, 1816; edited by Jefferson Rea Spell, 3 vols, Mexico City: Porrúa, 1949; as *The Itching Parrot*, translated by Eugene Pressly, edited with an introduction by Katherine Anne Porter, New York: Doubleday, 1942

Noches tristes y día alegre, Mexico City: Zúnigar Ontiveros, 1818-19

La Quijotita y su prima, Mexico City: Zúnigar Ontiveros, 1818; modern edition, with an introduction by María del Carmen Ruiz Castañeda, Mexico City: Porrúa, 1967

Don Catrín de la Fachenda, Mexico City: Valdés, 1832; edited by Jefferson Rea Spell, Mexico City: Cultura, 1959

Plays

El fuego de Prometeo, Mexico City: Valdés, 1811

Auto mariano para recordar la milagrosa aparición de Nuestra Madre y Señora de Guadalupe, Mexico City: Valdés, 1813

La Pastorela en dos actos, Mexico City: Valdés, 1817

El Unipersonal de Don Agustín de Iturbide, emperador de México, Mexico City: Ontiveros, 1823

El negro sensible, Mexico City: Ontiveros, 1825

El grito de libertad en el pueblo de Dolores, Mexico City: Ontiveros, 1827

La tragedia del padre Arenas, Mexico City: Ontiveros, 1827

Other Writings

Fábulas, Mexico City: Ontiveros, 1817

Ratos entretenidos, Mexico City: Ontiveros, 1819

Calendario histórico y político; por El Pensador Mexicano; para el año bisiesto de 1824, Mexico City: Ontiveros, 1824

Calendario para el año de 1825, dedicado a las señoritas americanas, Mexico City: Ontiveros, 1825

Calendario histórico y pronóstico político; por El Pensador Mexicano; para el año del Señor de 1825, Mexico City: Ontiveros, 1825

Testamento y despedida del Pensador Mexicano, Mexico City: Ontiveros, 1827

Heroínas mexicanas, Mexico City: Rea, 1955 [on women writers]

El Pensador Mexicano, Mexico City: UNAM, 1962

Testamento del Pensador Mexicano, Mexico City: Echániz, 1963

Compilations and Anthologies

Obras, 10 vols, Mexico City: UNAM, 1963-81

Further Reading

Altamirano, Ignacio Manuel, *La literatura nacional: revistas, ensayos, biografías y prólogos 1.*, edited by José Luis Martínez, Mexico City: Botas, 1949

Bueno, Salvador, "El negro en El Periquillo Sarniento: Antirracismo de Lizardi," *Cuadernos Americanos*, vol. 183 (1972)

Cros, Edmond, "The Values of Liberalism in *El Periquillo Sarniento*," *Sociocriticism* 2 (1985)

Dehesa y Gómez Farías, María Teresa, *Introducción a la obra dramática de José Joaquín Fernández de Lizardi*, Mexico City: UNAM, 1961

Franco, Jean, "La heterogeneidad peligrosa: escritura y control social en vísperas de la independencia mexicana," *Hispamérica*, vol. 12/34 (1983)

Godoy, Bernabé, *Corrientes culturales que definen al "Periquillo,"* Guadalajara, Mexico: Editorial Universidad, 1938

McKegney, James C., "El Pensador Mexicano – Reactionary," *Revista de Letras*, vol. 3/9 (1971)

_____ "Dos obras recién descubiertas de Lizardi," *Historiografía y Bibliografía Americanistas*, vol. 16 (1972)

Moore, Ernest R., "Una bibliografía descriptiva: *El Periquillo Sarniento* de J. J. Fernández de Lizardi," *Revista Iberoamericana*, vol. 10/20 (1946)

Palacios Sierra, Margarita, *Estudios preliminares e índices del periodismo de José Joaquín Fernández de Lizardi*, Mexico City: UNAM, 1965

Pawlowski, John, "*Periquillo* and *Catrín*: Comparison and Contrast," *Hispania*, vol. 58 (1975)

Radin, Paul, *The Opponents and Friends of Lizardi*, San Francisco: California State Library, 1939

Salomon, Noël, "La crítica del sistema colonial de la Nueva España en *El Periquillo Sarniento*," *Cuadernos Americanos*, vol. 21/138 (1965)

Spell, Jefferson Rea, *The Life and Works of José Joaquín Fernández de Lizardi*, Philadelphia: University of Pennsylvania Press, 1931

_____ "The Historical and Social Background of *El Periquillo Sarniento*," *Hispanic American Historical Review*, vol. 36/4 (1956)

_____ "The Intellectual Background of Lizardi as Reflected in *El Periquillo Sarniento*", *PMLA*, vol. 71/3 (1956)

Vogel, Nancy, "The Concept of 'the people' in *El Periquillo Sarniento*," *Hispania*, vol. 70 (1987)

_____ "Defining the 'Colonial Reader': *El Periquillo Sarniento*," *PMLA*, vol. 102 (1987)

Bibliographies

Radin, Paul, *An Annotated Bibliography of the Poems and Pamphlets of J.J. Fernández de Lizardi: the First and Second Periods (1808–27)*, San Francisco: San Francisco State Library, Sutro Branch, 1940

_____ "An Annotated Bibliography of the Poems and Pamphlets of J.J. Fernández de Lizardi (1824–27)," *Hispanic American Historical Review*, vol. 26 (1946)

Rosario Ferré 1942–

Puerto Rican prose writer, poet and feminist critic

During the 1970s in Puerto Rico, the impact of the international women's movement was strongly felt. In addition, the growing prominence of Latin American literature and the questioning of national and social identities helped foster a new group of women writers, among them the highly regarded Rosario Ferré. As co-founder and editor of the literary journal *Zona de Carga y Descarga* [Loading and Unloading Zone] from 1971 to 1975, she published her first pieces of fiction and essays here, and actively engaged in literary debates. Along with the general trend in Latin American literature to incorporate fantasy as a means of questioning established concepts, and the tendency to ever greater precision and experimentation in literary language, Ferré and other women writers of the Island such as Olga Nolla, Ana Lydia Vega and Carmen Lugo, created new modes of figuring female sexuality and reversed many of the myths of female roles.

Ferré achieved notoriety with her first book, *Papeles de Pandora*, 1976 (*The Youngest Doll*), a collection of stories and poetry characterized by humor, mystery, fantasy or grotesque touches. Her prestige has steadily increased as she has also proven her ability to write insightful essays, literary criticism, children's stories and a short novel. Not only has Ferré mastered a wide range of genres, she writes about a large number of subjects and utilizes in-depth research in her literary studies. The complex literary resonances in her poems and prose have produced a growing body of Ferré criticism and an international reputation.

As younger writers like her begin to write in an increasingly ironic tone the story of love and politics in a decomposing society, Ferré makes the feminist view of the colonized body a central issue. Her mother's patrician background made her privy to the nostalgic narrative of the land-owning classes' "paradise island," as well as the northward-looking view of her wealthy father, ex-Governor of the country, Luis Ferré. Her writing also reflects the life experiences of a woman who dramatically altered her role as housewife and mother to venture into writing as a necessary source of meaning – a narrative about submission and rebellion woven into the political circumstances of her country. Her study of the Puerto Rican, Julia de Burgos's poetry, and of the lives and works of so many feminists, including Sylvia Plath, Lillian Hellman, Virginia Woolf and Simone de Beauvoir, brings into focus a major preoccupation during her emerging self-definition as a woman and writer noted in *Papeles de Pandora*, and the collection of essays, *Sitio a Eros* [Besieging Eros], the second, expanded edition. The enigma of love which her title suggests, a version of the title of a book of essays written by the Russian revolutionary and writer, Alexandra Kollontai, is a central topic around which Ferré's book revolves. The search for an ideal love in the face of the bourgeois constraints of marriage, and the impulse to create, which requires an independence from the fetters of most love relationships, provoke her sometimes into the use of scathing irony or parody, registers present in all except her most recent work. A daring use of sexual language, and a humorous, playful rhythm in a style suggestive of Nicolás Guillén, characterize some of her stories.

In the collection of poems, *Fábulas de la garza desangrada*, 1982 [Fables of the Bleeding Heron], Ferré sets out to rewrite women's myths, particularly love myths, to some extent as a dialogue with 19th-century women poets like Christina Rossetti and others, in which even these poets expressed their eroticism as a reflection of the beloved, a point noted by José Miguel Oviedo. As Margarite Fernández Olmos has discussed, Ferré reinvents metaphors and characters from the Western tradition, including biblical figures like Salomé and Mary Magdalene, literary figures like Dante's Francesca and Cervantes's Dorotea, and classical protagonists like Medusa, Ariadne or Antigone, along with Puerto Rican literary figures such as Julia de Burgos or her own invented heroines: Catalina or Rosario. The many references to women in the broader tradition of Western culture of this collection is akin to *Sitio*'s discussion of the lives and work of women writers, often surprisingly productive and authentic despite the restrictions of patriarchal society.

The scrutiny of women's images and their reverse projection, displays a distinctly personal and self-reflexive style, less explicitly political than her next works. The women who have traditionally been portrayed as the (sexual) object, become the subject (of sex), often taking on sexually aggressive roles or other deliberately transposed roles. In one poem "Odalisca," the slave serving the sultan is transformed. Her breasts become eyes, linked to religious architecture, connoting identity, vision, self-scrutiny and the mirror image which is the central conceit of the book. The Other (the female) as created by the male imagination is examined and dismantled, while the seeing eye constructs its space. What remains after the act of love is the solitary breast/female I/ eye (of god) as the center of the world and female writing. This goddess-like quality applies to other poems in Ferré's collection; thus the poetic speaker of the poem "Fábula de la garza desangrada" engenders and multiplies herself. The entire female body is endowed with sight, all of her orifices and parts become a symphony of sensual eyes via the tactile, the expressive and the visual.

In other poems, the game of reversals also unites mirror images, sexuality and textuality, and plays between feminine and masculine grammatical gender or role stereotypes. Female body images become blurred with male images in an androgynous play that nevertheless retains the specificity of the female body. The Catalina of one poem has her own harem of men draped over divans for her pleasure. This female rides her men like horses, penetrating them from behind, in direct appropriation of a supposedly male prerogative. In a poem which refers to the Roman goddess of the arts of cooking and the hearth, the home is invested with everything but ordinary domesticity. Making love in that context becomes writing, a violent passion linked to death. Throughout the collection, the women rather than the men play the active roles and transgress against norms. In so far as Ferré demonstrates that we are all written by language, she also shows her male as subject to disappearance by the gaze and invention of the female. He too is a wounded heron, whose voice can become mute and whose blood can be dissolved in the ink of the poet's pen. The lament against the image of the female in the mirror becomes a song dedicated to ephemeral versions and visions, fragmentary beings reflected and reconstructed in mirrors and pages.

The author's next work, like the earlier *Papeles*, takes place within a clearly drawn Puerto Rican society. *Maldito amor*, 1986 (*Sweet Diamond Dust*) includes a short novel giving the collection its name, and three other stories, "El regalo" (The Gift), "Isolda en el espejo" (Isolda in the Mirror), and "La extraña muerte del capitancito Candelario" (The Strange Death of the Cute Captain Candelario). The narratives span nearly one hundred years, from 1898, the year of the United States invasion of the Island, and continue into an invented future. The novel tells a melodramatic family saga within the context of the Puerto Rico's transition from a Spanish-affiliated, sugarcane agricultural base to an economy dependent upon the United States. The position of women *vis-à-vis* men, be it the father or husband, is implicitly paralleled to that of Puerto Rico as a colony. The precious, diminutive pearl-island, engulfed within the vast ocean, is like the first, feminine protagonist, the tiny Elvira with her bull of a man, Don Julio. Ferré parodies the romantic plot: the powerful attraction Elvira feels for the gallant male, the subordinate status of Elvira as the supportive mate, an overwhelming passion brought within bounds via the legitimation of marriage, and her eventual death – a final silence. The author's ironic and humorous use of 19th-century plots and omniscient narration writes beyond the traditional marriage-or-death endings of romance.

Beneath the smug dominance of the older aristocracy associated with Spain and now with the American-affiliated upper class, the challenging gesture at the end of the novel, allies a marginal group which includes women, blacks and servants, linking the possibility of independence from the United States with the breakdown of racial and class barriers. The question of power (on the level of discourse, at least) is not unambiguously in anyone's hands, since the last female narrator's point of view undercuts the omniscient frame's authority. The appropriation of voice, via the specificity of first person accounts and previously absent racial and class markers, signals the problematics of identity, both of the colony which does not know who/whose it is and of the women who likewise speak within the confines of a patriarchal society.

In her most recent work, *Las dos Venecias*, 1992 [The Two Venices], Ferré moves to a more tranquil space, at once the dreamlike place where wealthy, Puerto Rican honeymooners travel, the imagined paradise her mother evoked in her stories and the cradle song of the book's title, and the place of writing. *Papeles*'s irate view of marriage and class divisions, and the parodic rebellion in *Maldito amor* against romantic myths, are replaced with the harmonious yet vital space of flowing water: canals, island, urban and female geography blending in a new writing. The collection includes autobiographical essays and poetry, and voyages through her childhood in Puerto Rico to evocations of a wide variety of paintings and literary works. The title of the book discussed in the first essay establishes her major thesis: the journey of marriage initiated in the honeymoon can endanger the fixed identity as conceived by a young woman enclosed in her father's house, or it can be accepted as a rite of passage into the open space of the canal, of the house without walls. There she discovers the freedom of transformations of all kinds in opposition to stable identities and places. The author talks of her own fears of dispersion as her body became a place of passages rather than the self-sufficient adolescent body, feelings only relieved when years later she began to write. While writing did not restore her sense of wholeness, it allowed the adventure of interior voyages, into her own channels, making her dispersion flow as rivers and ocean waves, words leading to other words, just as her body's birth canal brought other lives.

The Venetian bridge of Rialto is converted in Ferré's book into a feminine character (thus the masculine word "el puente" (the bridge) becomes a woman (Rialta) rowing through Venice, the apparently immobile becoming an impulse forward through the city, museums, experiences and dreams. The eternal transformations from mist, to rain, to bodies of water, tears, as well as the changes from life to death, or from reality to dreams, permit the author to consider a variety of topics, as her experiences through various residences, readings and paintings.

Here, as in *Maldito amor*, Ferré combines the interior, the emotions and passions of women with the social forces of the world exterior to the kitchen, a goal described in her essay "La cocina de la escritura." In *Venecias*, she posits a relationship between the interior of women with the external, the political and geographic sense of Puerto Rico as a Caribbean island. In contrast to her earlier view that there is no discernible women's writing style as such, rather only a propensity for certain themes as lived experiences, with this work, she implicitly embraces the fluid, multiple "feminine" writing which some French theorists have made their signature. The flow of geography and the dual character of the island people, who stand on the shore and are renewed by the forces of the visiting peoples, or are renewed by the voyages outward, expresses a more hopeful view of Ferré's early themes. The contradictory, bittersweet ebb and flow of the relationship between men and women in all cultures, and between dominant and oppressed cultures, between stability and change, seemingly suggests new strengths and definitions of the self and other in her two most recent works.

MARIE MURPHY

See also entry on Ana Lydia Vega

Biography
Born in Ponce, Puerto Rico, 28 July 1942 (some sources say 1938 or 1940). Father a former governor. Attended Manhattanville College, Bronx, New York; University of Puerto Rico, San Juan, where she met Mario Vargas Llosa and the critic Ángel Rama; University of Maryland, College Park, awarded PhD, 1986. Married Benigno Trigo in 1960 (divorced); one daughter and two sons. Founder and editor of the journal *Zona de Carga y Descarga* , 1971–75, in which her first works appeared.

Selected Works

Short Fiction
Papeles de Pandora, Mexico City: Joaquín Mortiz, 1976; as *The Youngest Doll*, Lincoln: University of Nebraska Press, 1991
El medio pollito: siete cuentos infantiles, Río Piedras, Puerto Rico: Huracán, 1976
Los cuentos de Juan Bobo, Río Piedras, Puerto Rico: Huracán, 1981
La mona que le pisaron la cola, Río Piedras, Puerto Rico: Huracán, 1981
La caja de cristal, Mexico City: La Máquina de Escribir, 1982; as "The Glass Box," translated by the author and Kathy Taylor, *Massachusetts Review*, 3–4 (Fall–Winter 1986)
Las dos Venecias, Mexico City: Joaquín Mortiz, 1992

Novel
Maldito amor, Mexico City: Joaquín Mortiz, 1986; revised edition, as *Sweet Diamond Dust*, translated by the author, New York: Ballantine, 1988

Poetry
Fábulas de la garza desangrada, Mexico City: Joaquín Mortiz, 1982
Sonatinas, Río Piedras, Puerto Rico: Huracán, 1989

Essays
Sitio a Eros: trece ensayos literarios, Mexico City: Joaquín Mortiz, 1980; revised and augmented edition, as *Sitio a Eros: quince ensayos literarios*, 1986
El acomodador: una lectura fantástica de Felisberto Hernández, Mexico City: Fondo de Cultura Económica, 1986
El árbol y sus sombras, Mexico City: Fondo de Cultura Económica, 1989
El coloquio de las perras, San Juan, Puerto Rico: Cultural, 1990
Cortázar, el romántico en su observatorio, San Juan, Puerto Rico: Cultural, 1991

Further Reading
Davis, Lisa E., "La puertorriqueña dócil y rebelde en los cuentos de Rosario Ferré," *Sin Nombre*, vol. 4 (January–March 1979)
Fernández Olmos, Margarite, "Sex, Color and Class in Contemporary Puerto Rican Women Authors," *Heresies*, vol. 3 (1982)
____ "From a Woman's Perspective: the Short Stories of Rosario Ferré and Ana Lydia Vega," in *Contemporary Women Authors of Latin America: Introductory Essays*, edited by Fernández Olmos and Doris Meyer, New York: Brooklyn College Press, 1983
____ "Rosario Ferré," in *Spanish American Women Writers: a Bio-Bibliographical Source Book*, edited by Diane E. Marting, New York: Greenwood Press, 1990
Guerra-Cunningham, Lucía, "Tensiones paradójicas de la femineidad en la narrativa de Rosario Ferré," *Chasqui*, vol. 2/3 (February–May 1984)
Gutiérrez Mouat, Ricardo, "La 'loca del desván' y otro intertextos de *Maldito amor*," *Modern Language Notes* 109 (March 1994)
Lagos-Pope, María Inés, "Sumisión y rebeldía: el doble o la representación de la alienación femenina en narraciones de Marta Brunet y Rosario Ferré," *Revista Iberoamericana* 132–33 (July–December 1985)
Méndez-Clark, Ronald, "La pasión y la marginalidad en (de) la escritura: Rosario Ferré," in *La sartén por el mango*, edited by Patricia Elena González and Eliana Ortega, Río Piedras, Puerto Rico: Huracán, 1984
Ortega, Julio, *Reapropriaciones: cultura y nueva escritura en Puerto Rico*, Río Piedras, Puerto Rico: Universidad de Puerto Rico, 1991 [Contains two articles on Ferré's work]
Oviedo, José Miguel, "La palabra apasionada de Rosario Ferré," *La Gaceta* del Fondo de Cultura Económica, vol. 161 (May 1984)
Sotomayor Miletti, Aurea María, "Rosario Ferré: el revés del bordado," in *De lengua, razón y cuerpo (Nueve poetas contemporáneas puertorriqueñas): antología y ensayo crítico*, San Juan: Instituto de Cultura Puertorriqueña, 1987

Interviews
García Pinto, Magdalena, *Women Writers of Latin America: Intimate Histories*, Austin: University of Texas Press, 1991 [Lengthy interview with Rosario Ferré]

Adonias Filho 1915–1990

Brazilian prose writer

The work of Adonias Filho focuses principally on the southern part of Bahia, a zone of cocoa-bean plantations. The preferred characters of his books are those rugged men and women who are trying to colonize the land and are involved in violent struggles against one another and against the nature that surrounds them. His works express a tragic sense of life by means of characters lacerated by love, violence and death.

The critic Fred Ellison has described Filho's novels as "neo-naturalistic." In *Corpo vivo*, 1962 [Live Body], perhaps his best-known work, Cajango finally abdicates his determination to revenge his family when his love for Malva pacifies his hatred. The end of the novel is mythical: the couple will seek refuge in the mountains, a passage that is expressed by the future tense, a verbal form that, in Brazilian Portuguese, tends to translate a time that is not within our immediate reach.

This impression may be further developed by reading *O forte*, 1965 [The Fortress], a novel that portrays an old building erected during colonial times. It is now about to be destroyed by the engineer, one of the two main characters in the novel, the other being Olegário. The latter is a black man who helped to build the fortress, who took part in the wars in which the fortress defended Bahia against invaders, and who is still alive to witness its demolition. Since the novel covers a period of over two hundred years, its historical and documentary intent (even assuming that the story is invented and that such a fortress never really existed) is obviously compromised by the internal inverosimilitude of a character who is more than two hundred years old.

This contradiction helps us to classify Adonias's fiction in a more intelligent way: instead of being regionalist (if by that we understand social and political commitment), the stage in which his novels and short stories take place is in fact a *templum*, a space in which mythical (and not historical) plots are narrated. In other words, this short-circuit opens the way for a more ideological reading of his novelistic production.

If one were to pursue this avenue, the probable conclusion would be that Adonias's works are still tributaries of what we might call a patriarchal *epistème* (search for origins): in *Luanda, Beira, Bahia* (1971), the main character engages in a search for his father (and the African traditions of his ancestors) in Portugal and in Africa; in *Corpo vivo*, it is a family matter of family that detonates the narrative.

But maybe it is in *Memórias de Lázaro*, 1952 (*Memories of Lazarus*) that the quest motive is clearest: Alexandre leaves the valley seeking to repeat his father's journey. The novel ends up by portraying an extremely closed society, in which the contrast between the two spaces (the violent valley and the jungle, where Alexandre first found love and compassion) are neutralized to install immobility.

Adonias Filho also wrote a book on the cocoa region of southern Bahia (which serves as a substratum to understand a large portion of his fiction) and essays on the writers of the 1930s. The latter suggest both his literary debts and his possible differences from that group of writers. His works may still be considered tributaries of that hierarchical and authoritarian pattern, the difference being that now, in light of the decline of the agrarian sectors, the only way of restoring the patriarchal order is by means of myths.

ROBERTO REIS

Biography

Born in Lima de Aguiar in Itajuípe, near Ilhéus, Bahia, Brazil, 27 November 1915. Spent his formative years on his parents' cocoa plantation. Moved to Rio de Janeiro in 1936. Director of the newspaper, *A Noite*; National Theatre Service; National Library; National Institute of Books; and the National Press Agency. President and member of the Federal Culture Council; president of the Brazilian Press Association. Awarded the Paula Brito Prize. Member of the Brazilian Academy of Letters. Died in Itajuípe, 4 August 1990.

Selected Works

Novels

Os servos da morte, Rio de Janeiro: José Olympio, 1946
Memórias de Lázaro, Rio de Janeiro: O Cruzeiro, 1952; as *Memories of Lazarus*, translated by Fred P. Ellison, Austin: University of Texas Press, 1969
Corpo vivo, Rio de Janeiro: Civilização Brasileira, 1962
O forte, Rio de Janeiro: Civilização Brasileira, 1965
Luanda, Beira, Bahia, Rio de Janeiro: Civilização Brasileira, 1971
As velhas, Rio de Janeiro: Civilização Brasileira, 1975
Noite sem madrugada, São Paulo: Difel, 1983 [detective fiction]
O homem de branco, Rio de Janeiro: Bertrand Brasil, 1987 [fictionalized biography]

Short Fiction

Léguas da promissão, Rio de Janeiro: Civilização Brasileira, 1968
O Largo da Palma, Rio de Janeiro: Civilização Brasileira, 1981

Children's Literature

Uma nota de cem, Rio de Janeiro: Ouro, 1973
Fora da pista, Rio de Janeiro: Civilização Brasileira, 1978

Other Writings

Modernos ficcionistas brasileiros, Rio de Janeiro: O Cruzeiro, 1958
O romance brasileiro de 30, Rio de Janeiro: Bloch, 1969
Sul da Bahia: chão de cacau, Rio de Janeiro: Civilização Brasileira, 1976
O auto dos ilhéus, Rio de Janeiro: Civilização Brasileira, 1981 [folk pageant]

Further Reading

Ellison, Fred P., "The Schizophrenic Narrator and the Myth of Renewal" in *Memórias de Lázaro*," in *From Linguistics to*

Literature: Romance Studies Offered to Francis M. Rogers,
Amsterdam: Benjamins, 1981
Jukes, Lauro, "O índio interior de Adonias Filho," *Correio do
Povo, Caderno de Sábado* (8 May 1971)
Patai, Daphne, "Adonias Filho: the Myth of Malevolence," in *Myth
and Ideology in Contemporary Brazilian Fiction*, Rutherford,
New Jersey: Fairleigh Dickinson University Press, and London:

Associated University Presses, 1983
Reis, Roberto, "A selva como templo," *Minas Gerais, Suplemento
Literário* 654 and 655 (1979)
____ "O maravilhoso caminho," *Linguagens*, vols 1 and 2
(1982)
____ *A permanência do círculo – hierarquia no romance brasileiro*,
Niterói/Brasília: EDUFF/INL, 1987

Film

Brazil

Brazil was the first country in Latin America to import the French *cinématographe* in July 1896. Since that time the Brazilian industry as well as other ones in the region have been in a dependent relationship to foreign, particularly US, film industries (a situation described in greater detail in the article on film in Spanish America). Given the intense competition from abroad, Brazilian films have often stressed the specificity of local culture, sometimes relying on the adaptation of national or regional literature. While sharing this preoccupation with other countries in the region, the Brazilian industry also has some unique features, particularly its tie to the local music industry and its recurring interest in carnival and carnivalesque parody.

As noted by John King in *Magical Reels*, the arrival of cinema coincided with the establishment of the Republic (1889) and a series of other changes like urbanization and Italian immigration that favored its sustained development. Spurred on by the modernization of Rio de Janeiro, the exhibition sector expanded quickly, supplied by imported films from France and Italy. When Brazilian filmmakers entered the business they focused on the local and immediate. First producing actualities, they then turned toward fictional films based on real-life crimes and sometimes adapted operas like Carlos Gomes's *O guarani* (1916) and literary classics like José de Alencar's, *A viuvinha*, 1914 [The Little Widow], *Iracema* (1917) and *Ubirajara* (1918). São Paulo had a thriving production center tied to its Italian immigrants and there were also a number of "regional cycles" in Cataguases, Recife, and other places. The film industry was so successful between 1908–1912 that critics have called it the *Bela Época*. The short-lived era ended when US companies penetrated the Brazilian market in the early 1910s and began to push their films more aggressively by establishing distribution franchises.

As in other countries in the region, the conversion to sound around 1930 had both positive and negative effects. Many of the undercapitalized production companies did not survive. At the same time, Adhemar Gonzaga's Cinédia studio (established in 1930) rose on the basis of films that took advantage of the new sound technology. Some of Cinédia's earliest sound productions *Alô, alô Brasil* (1935) and *Alô, alô carnaval* (1936) capitalized on the success of two popular phenomena:

carnival and radio. The titles themselves were take-offs on the opening address of contemporary radio programs. Both films had minimal plots and highlighted performances of popular carnival songs by radio stars like Carmen Miranda. Films featuring carnival crystallized into a genre called the *chanchada* which became a mainstay of not only Cinédia but also of Atlântida studio. The broad appeal of the *chanchadas*, which combined musical numbers and comic plots, guaranteed the survival and relative success of Brazilian production, given the overwhelming competition from the US. As the only Portuguese-speaking country in the region, the Brazilian industry also circumvented the challenge posed by the Argentine and Mexican industries whose strength came in part from exporting their films to the less-developed industries in other Spanish-speaking countries.

The success of the *chanchadas* did not please all Brazilians. In the late 1940s, a group of São Paulo businessmen, disgusted by what they saw as the vulgarity of *chanchadas*, established Vera Cruz studio to produce films with Brazilian themes and Hollywood production values. Like the recently established Museum of Modern Art and the Brazilian Comedy Theatre, Vera Cruz was an attempt to create a "high quality" national product. Given its goal, it is not surprising that some of its eighteen films were adaptations of national literature like Maria Dezzone Pacheco Fernandes's *Sinhá moça*, 1953 [Young Lady] with Osvaldo Sampaio and Tom Payne. However, the Vera Cruz productions never achieved the popular success enjoyed by the *chanchadas*. Failing to recuperate their production costs quickly enough, the studio went bankrupt within a few years.

After the fall of Vera Cruz studio, Brazilian filmmakers lost faith in their ability to establish a national film industry through a system of mass production. While many established directors argued for the continued efficacy of commercial cinema at several conferences on national cinema in the early to mid-1950s, a number of young filmmakers proposed a more radical solution. Cineastes like Glauber Rocha, Carlos Diegues, Joaquim Pedro de Andrade, and Leon Hirszman called for small-scale films produced by individuals rather than by large companies. The films they made following this model became known as Cinema Novo (New Cinema). Never a cohesive movement, Cinema Novo defined a loose affiliation of directors who shared a common outlook on the way to revitalize

Brazilian cinema. Influenced by leftist cultural organizations, they wanted to make films about and for the popular sectors and not for the middle classes as had Vera Cruz. They followed the lead of Nelson Pereira dos Santos whose *Rio 40 graus*, 1955 [Rio 40 Degrees] broke traditional filmmaking practice by foregrounding the life of the urban poor. Subsequent films by other cineastes dealt with other marginalized aspects of Brazil like the migrant laborers of the northeast (an extremely impoverished region), the historical experiences of African Brazilians, and the struggles of the urban working class. The young cineastes also experimented with formal strategies. In 1962, for example, dos Santos adapted a Graciliano Ramos novel *Vidas secas* (*Barren Lives*) from the 1930s, about a family forced to migrate across the drought-ridden *sertão* (backlands) in search of work and food. Luiz Carlos Barreto, the film's cinematographer, did not use special lenses to filter the hard northeastern sunlight; as a result, the film appears overexposed and conveys the blinding force of the elements which so shaped the family's destiny. Glauber Rocha called these formal innovations "Uma estética da fome" ("An Aesthetic of Hunger") in his 1965 manifesto where he argued that truly revolutionary films must register the underdevelopment of Latin America not only in their themes but also in their structure and stylistic aspects.

By the late 1960s, however, the Cinema Novistas changed their approach as a result of poor box-office returns and increased political repression. Influenced by trends in the other arts (particularly music and theatre), Cinema Novo entered its "Tropicalist" phase. Films like the colorful *Macunaíma* (1969, Joaquim Pedro de Andrade), adapted from Mário de Andrade's novel of the same name, resurrected the cannibalist metaphors at the center of the 1920s Modernist movement. They critiqued Brazil's dependent position in the world economy through carnivalesque parody and allegory. Filmmakers increasingly used literary classics as a source for films: *São Bernardo* (1973, Leon Hirszman) based on the Ramos novel; *Iracema* (1974, Jorge Bodanzky/Orlando Senna); *Lição de amor*, 1975 [Lesson of Love], directed by Eduardo Escorel, also based on a novel by Mário de Andrade; *Dona Flor e seus dois maridos*, 1976 (*Dona Flor and Her Two Husbands*), directed by Bruno Barreto, *Tenda dos milagres*, 1977 (*Tent of Miracles*) by Nelson Pereira dos Santos, and *Gabriela*, 1983, by Bruno Barreto, all three based on novels by Jorge Amado. Many of those films expressed social critique in an allegorical format that appealed to audiences and also avoided direct confrontation with the military government.

The Brazilian film industry continued to produce adaptations in the 1980s, encouraged by a 1982 state directive establishing an annual prize for films based on literary works by deceased authors. In *Magical Reels*, King notes how the state strategy "neutralized ideological debates" by relegating any discussion of the present to the level of allegory. Nevertheless, there were some piercing critiques in films set in the past. Nelson Pereira dos Santos's *Memórias do cárcere*, 1984 (*Jail Prison Memoirs*) based on the notebooks written by Ramos while in jail was a particularly acute discussion of state repression and cross-class alliance produced a year before the country's return to democracy. The prize also may have encouraged directors to look outside the realm of politics to critique other sources of oppression as in Suzana Amaral's *A hora da estrela*, 1985 (*The Hour of the Star*), an adaptation of Clarice Lispector's novella about the experiences of a poor young woman from the northeast who emigrates to Rio. Literary adaptations also took advantage of the popularity of certain novels like those of best-selling author Jorge Amado to enhance their commercial appeal. The adaptations of *Dona Flor* and *Gabriela* also capitalized on the star-power of Sônia Braga and the conventions of the successful *pornochanchada*, a type of soft-core porn that emerged in the 1970s.

If directors like dos Santos used literary adaptations to appeal to a wider segment of the population, others featured the innovative work of top recording artists. Carlos Diegues's latest film, *Veja essa canção*, 1994 (*Rio's Love Songs*), is the most extreme example of how films have been shaped by the commercial success of contemporary Brazilian music; its four episodes are based on the lyrics to songs by Jorge Ben, Chico Buarque, Gilberto Gil and Caetano Veloso. The film industry's reliance on music to increase its commercial viability is more important now than ever before as a result of increasingly high production costs, the loss of state subsidies, the rise of TV and, more particularly, of TV Globo, the fourth largest private network in the world. Unlike the situation in the US and more recently in Europe, the Brazilian TV industry has not relied on film production companies for their programming. Thus, while forging some alliances with the literary and music industries, Brazilian film has recently encountered competition inside its national borders.

LAURA PODALSKY

Spanish America

1996 marked the centennial anniversary of film in Spanish America. The *cinématographe* arrived in the region less than a year after the first public screening in Paris – appearing in Buenos Aires and Montevideo in July 1896, and in Mexico City one month later. Functioning as both projector and camera, the machines allowed the foreign cameramen who had brought them to make the first films in the region. Local entrepreneurs quickly entered the business as both filmmakers and theatre owners. In the one hundred years since its appearance, the cinema has become a major cultural force in every Spanish American country. While the types of films produced have varied over time and from country to country, the various Spanish American film industries share a number of characteristics relating to their status within the world market that make their development quite different from that of other cultural products like literature. Spanish American dependence on imported cinematic technologies did not wane after the 1890s. Today, Spanish American countries still import both raw film stock and other equipment essential to the production process. Thus, the regional film industry is greatly affected by shifts in the larger economy (e.g., changes in the balance of trade, the exchange rate, and the rate of inflation). Furthermore, within many Latin American countries, US distribution companies have dominated the local market since the late 1910s. The recent emergence of Blockbuster video outlets in major urban centers like Mexico City and Buenos Aires suggests a parallel development in the area of video distribution. Given this precarious position, local filmmakers have often made films which emphasized the specificities of local culture, demonstrating a recurring interest in both documentary forms and representing the nation.

These tendencies are also linked to film's introduction to Spanish America at a number of interesting historical conjunctures. As noted by John King in his book *Magical Reels*, the early development of the industry coincided with the establishment of the independent republic of Cuba and with a more general period of modernization in Argentina as well as in Mexico. It was in countries like Argentina and Mexico that cinema spread most quickly, supported by the solidification of the local infrastructure (e.g., electrification for a stable exhibition sector and the growth of transport lines, both within and between urban centers, for the circulation of both films and cameramen) and by an urbanized population that provided ready audiences. In this early period, several local entrepreneurs became involved in multiple aspects of the growing industry – capitalizing on their success in the exhibition business to become film producers like Enrique Rosas in Mexico or distributors like Max Glucksmann in Argentina. The early films produced by local filmmakers emphasized local sites as well as important government events. This type of production crystallized into weekly newsreels by companies like Film Revista Valle (1917–30) in Argentina and Revista Semanal de México (established in 1919). Other filmmakers began making fiction films based on local crimes like *La banda del automóvil gris* [The Grey Car Gang], made in Mexico in 1919, Enrique Rosas) and on nationalist themes found in local history or 19th-century literature like the Cuban *El capitán mambí*, 1914 [The Mambi Captain], directed by Enrique Díaz Quesada; *Amalia* (1914), an Argentine film by Enrique García Velloso, based on José Mármol's novel of the same name; *Nobleza gaucha*, 1916 [Gaucho Nobility], made in Argentina by Eduardo Martínez de la Pera, Ernesto Gunche, and Humberto Cairo which used intertitles taken from José Hernández's epic poem *Martín Fierro*; the Mexican *Santa*, 1918 [Saint], made by Luis Peredo and based on the Federico Gamboa novel of the same title; and *María* (Colombia, 1922, Alfredo del Diestro and Máximo Calino) based on the famous 19th-century novel by Jorge Isaacs. Despite their relative success, domestic productions were overwhelmed in number by French and Italian imports and, after World War I and the end of the Motion Picture Patents War, by US productions.

The introduction of sound technology in Spanish America concentrated the film industry by raising production costs to levels beyond the means of artisan-filmmakers and delivered a fatal blow to regional production (e.g., in places like Yucatán and Guadalajara). At the same time, the conversion to sound cut into Hollywood's hold over Spanish-language audiences and a studio system arose in both Argentina and Mexico. The studios gained a foothold in the Spanish American market by doing what Hollywood could not; they produced films which foregrounded emblems of national identity like music and dance. In the early 1930s, Argentine filmmakers capitalized on the success of tango in dance halls and radio shows and made films which mixed melodrama and musical numbers. The success of these films was brief. During World War II, the already faltering Argentine industry was almost paralyzed when the US restricted the sale of raw film stock to Argentina to punish its supposed support of the Axis. While the Argentine

industry stagnated, the Mexican film industry flourished with direct support from the US. The Mexican studios specialized in *comedias rancheras* (ranch comedies), family melodramas, and films about the Revolution of 1910. Having created a number of popular genres, the Mexican industry did not rely on adaptations of local literature during this "golden age" although there were a few exceptions [e.g., two other versions of *Santa* (1931, Antonio Moreno and 1943, Norman Foster) and one of Mariano Azuela's *Los de abajo* (1939, Chano Ureta)]. In fact, Mexican films were successful not only within the country but also in the larger Spanish-language market. The Mexican government eventually created a distribution agency, Pel-Mex, in 1945 to aid further the exportation of their films to the rest of Spanish America. Other Spanish American countries produced films only sporadically. Like the Argentines and Mexicans, filmmakers in these countries tried to distinguish their productions from those of the competition by highlighting the specificity of national culture. Cuban films from both the 1930s and the 1950s featured African-Cuban rhythms while Bolivian productions often focused on indigenous culture. Unable to compete with imported films from the US and Mexico or to recuperate their production costs on the small domestic market, these efforts were short-lived. Even Mexico's success was relative. While it was able to foster a healthy domestic industry as well as to corner an important part of the larger Spanish-language market, Mexico was never able to threaten Hollywood's hegemony.

By the late 1950s and early 1960s, filmmakers in many Spanish American countries as well as in Brazil began to advocate a new type of filmmaking in response to both the crisis in local production and the contemporary political climate. Registering the revolutionary fervor present in Latin American following the 1959 Cuban Revolution, political groups in various Latin Amerian countries criticized the influence of the US on the region, the structure of their national economies, and the marginalized status of the poor and of particular racial and ethnic groups. A new generation of filmmakers took an active role in the politicized atmosphere and used their medium to help shape the debate. They argued that the dominance of imported Hollywood cinema had an alienating effect on the local population and simply furthered US neo-imperialism. The young filmmakers also renounced the older Latin American cinema as merely imitative and called for a new type of cinema that would address the problems of their nations in a more "authentic" manner. Influenced by Italian Neorealism, they favored films informed by documentary impulses. After training at the Centro Sperimentale in Rome, Fernando Birri established a school for documentary filmmaking in Santa Fe, Argentina in 1956. For the next four years, Birri collaborated with his young students on films about the socio-economic conditions of the surrounding area. From 1959 to the mid-1960s, filmmakers in Cuba produced hundreds of newsreels and documentaries about the progress of the Revolution and about regions of the country that had been previously ignored. The filmmakers in these and other countries shared a desire to use film to explore the issue of national identity and to unite the people of their country.

Despite these shared goals, their work emerged in and responded to very different social and political contexts. After 1959, Cuban cineastes placed their cameras in service of the

Revolution which was radically restructuring both the social and the economic order of the island along socialist principles. The film industry itself was nationalized and all aspects of the business (production, distribution, and exhibition) were placed under the control of ICAIC, the state film agency. The anti-imperialist stand of the Cuban Revolution served as an inspiration for leftist movements throughout Latin America. While many Latin American cineastes supported particular political and social movements in their respective countries, they often faced opposition from conservative administrations. Two Peronist militants in Argentina used film to protest the repressive actions of the military government (1966–73). Fernando Solanas and Octavio Getino produced *La hora de los hornos*, 1966–68 [The Hour of the Furnaces] to diagnose the social and economic ills of their country and to advocate the return to power of exiled leader Juan Perón. Solanas and Getino made their film covertly and screened it at secret locations to avoid government repression. This type of "guerrilla filmmaking" emerged from their belief that the camera should be used like a gun; by "shooting" the problems of society, films could further the fight for social justice and revolutionary change. Similar efforts by filmmaking collectives arose in the late 1960s and early 1970s in both Bolivia (Grupo Ukumau) and in Chile (Equipo Tercer Año or Third Year Team).

These national cinematic movements developed in relative isolation until the late 1960s. At that time, these filmmakers finally coalesced as a group during several film festivals held in different Latin America countries. At the 1968 festival in Mérida, Venezuela, various Latin American filmmakers drafted a resolution in which they called for a "cinema of reality." Rejecting the notion of cinema as entertainment or escapism, the filmmakers felt that the medium should register the poverty and underdevelopment of the region and the very specific social and economic problems of each country. These principles formed the basis of what came to be called New Latin American Cinema.

While this generation of filmmakers agitated for social change, only the Cubans managed to restructure the film industry in their country. In other countries, the lack of structural change limited the radicalizing possibilities of the films. Often circulating on the margins of the commerical industry, the films of the New Latin American Cinema did not effectively challenge the domination of US imports. Eventually their inability to reach mass audiences on a consistent basis, the continuing difficulty of obtaining financing for stylistically experimental films, and a number of other factors forced film-makers to redirect their efforts. The highly politicized atmosphere of the 1960s did not continue into the 1970s. Military governments seized power in Argentina, Bolivia, Brazil, Chile, and Uruguay and violently repressed not only the more militant guerrilla groups but also numerous leftist filmmakers – many of whom went into exile. In the 1980s, democratic administrations returned to many Latin American countries but were strapped with an economic crisis that diminished the capacity of state film agencies like INC (Argentina, established 1956) and Embrafilme (Brazil, 1969–90) to support actively the local industry through low-interest loans and other types of subsidies.

In the face of this general crisis, filmmakers have tried different strategies in the 1980s and 1990s to overcome these multiple difficulties. Several filmmakers resuscitated older, popular genres like the melodrama in films like *Camila*, directed by María Luisa Bemberg (Argentina, 1984), and another Argentine film, *La historia oficial*, 1984 [The Official Version], directed by Luis Puenzo. Others experimented with newer ones like the thriller-adventure film as in *Johnny Cien Pesos*, or *One Hundred Pesos Johnny* (Cuba-Mexico-Chile, 1993, Gustavo Graef Marino). Films like these three managed to package social criticism in commercially-viable formulas. While still calling on their audiences to examine critically their own society, these films did not advocate immediate political action as did many Latin American films in the late 1960s and early 1970s. Instead, they made themselves more accessible to larger sectors of the population by using intense emotion or comedy to protest social inequalities and injustice. While attracting wider audiences, the technical sophistication of these films also raised production costs and forced filmmakers to find financial backing outside their own countries. At the same time, the film industry as a whole faced stiff competition from television and video. However, these trends have also created some new options. Recently some cineastes have financed their work through agreements with either film companies or TV stations in Spain, Germany, and England. A number of contemporary Latin American directors repeatedly finance their films this way like Ruy Guerra, Miguel Littín, and María Luisa Bemberg, whose film *Yo, la peor de todas*, 1990 [I, the Worst of All] was based on Octavio Paz's *Sor Juana, o las trampas de la fe* (*Sor Juana, or, the Traps of Faith*). While providing both much-needed funds and access to wider distribution, the co-productions often need to address audiences across different borders. As scholars B. Ruby Rich and Kathleen Newman note, the rise of the co-production marks a turn away from the national toward the global – a shift linked to changes in the world economy.

Globalizing tendencies are also evident in the increasingly noticeable intersection of the literary and film industries, particularly evident in the rise of Gabriel García Márquez as a major force shaping Spanish American film. As mentioned above, the film industry has often drawn on the literary world. National literary classics were adapted to the screen from the 1910s onward and the classic Mexican industry claimed not only its own literary traditions (e.g., *Los de abajo*, *Pedro Páramo*) but also those of other countries (e.g., the Venezuelan novel *Doña Bárbara*; the Colombian *María*; and the French *Nana*). However, Spanish American writers never worked directly for studios as did US writers like James M. Cain and William Faulkner. It was only after the studio era that a significant number of writers became involved with the film industry – either having their work repeatedly used as a source for films (e.g., Augusto Roa Bastos, Beatriz Guido, Julio Cortázar, Manuel Puig, Gabriel García Márquez); being involved in the film-making process themselves as screenwriters, directors, or actors (e.g., Antonio Skármeta, Mario Benedetti, Manuel Puig, Carlos Fuentes, Gabriel García Márquez); or being fascinated by, and sometimes formally schooled in, film-making (e.g., Jorge Luis Borges; Guillermo Cabrera Infante, Manuel Puig). In many of these cases, the involvement of the Spanish American author in the film industry arose out of a general post-Boom celebration of literature as both industry and art form and a more specific positioning of the author as star.

Those shifts in the field of literature dovetailed with the needs of both the contemporary Spanish-language and world film industries.

Gabriel García Márquez epitomizes these trends. In 1987, he was named head of the Fundación del Nuevo Cine Latinoamericano, a foundation designed to foster co-productions. While perhaps linked to his personal friendship with Fidel Castro, García Márquez's position is attributable also to his canonical status in the world of literature and to his marketability, which lend prestige and his fund-raising capacity to the fledgling institution. García Márquez's ability to bridge the literary and film industries was established the following year when he brokered a deal with Televisión Española (RTVE) to produce the *Amores difíciles* [Difficult Loves] series of six films which played on the success of the *telenovela*, the newest format for melodrama and a staple of Latin American television. Based on scripts written by García Márquez, the films were directed by prestigous directors from several Latin American countries as well as Spain (Colombian Lisandro Duque, Cuban Tomás Gutiérrez Alea; Argentine Fernando Birri; Brazilian Ruy Guerra; Mexican Jaime Humberto Hermosillo; and Spaniard Jaime Chavarri). García Márquez's ability to anchor the interest of so many parties by seemingly guaranteeing both the artistic quality and the marketability of the individual films attests to his status in the international cultural marketplace.

Since 1988, producing films around a Spanish American literary star has become more commonplace not only in the Spanish-language world but also in the US: Argentine Manuel Puig's *El beso de la mujer araña* became *Kiss of the Spiderwoman* (1985, Hector Babenco); Mexican Carlos Fuentes's *El gringo viejo*, *The Old Gringo* (1989, Luis Puenzo); and Chilean Isabel Allende's *La casa de los espíritus*, *House of the Spirits* (1993, Bille August). These films confirm that globalization is also a trend in Hollywood where many major companies are owned by Japanese and Australian media firms. Directed by prestige filmmakers with transnational credentials (Babenco is Argentine-born but lives in Brazil; Puenzo is Argentine; August is Swedish) and starring US actors, these films capitalize on the star-authors of their source-texts who are well-known to educated readers throughout the world and whose popularity helps to sell the films. These combinations of film and literature actually work to increase the sales of both products. This is particularly evident in two recent cases. The success of the film *Como agua para chocolate*, 1993 (*Like Water for Chocolate*), a Mexican production directed by Alfonso Arau, made the English-language translation of Laura Esquivel's source novel a bestseller in the United States. Perhaps more provocative is *Kiss of the Spider Woman*, a virtual entertainment franchise. First a novel, then a film, the text re-emerged most recently in the form of a hit Broadway musical.

While not the only type of films being produced today, these adaptations indicate the globalization of cultural industries and, more specifically, the fostering of a pool of transnational writers and directors as well as a niche market of transnational elite audiences who act as both readers and spectators. The films produced in conjunction with US companies also demonstrate new hegemonic practices and place an ironic twist on the historical function of the literary adaptation. Cultural specificity is a feature of co-productions like *Alsino y el condor*, 1982 [Alsino and the Condor], a film directed by Miguel Littín which involved Nicaragua, Costa Rica, Mexico and Cuba, and *Tangos, el exilio de Gardel*, 1985 [Tangos: Gardel's Exile], a Franco-Argentine production directed by Fernando Solanas. On the other hand, many of the US-backed productions co-opt Spanish American literature and erase all cultural specificity. This is a far cry from the way that literary adaptations had been used starting in the silent era to distinguish the Spanish American films from their foreign competition.

LAURA PODALSKY

Further Reading

Carboné, Giancarlo (editor), *El cine en el Perú: 1897–1950. Testimonios*, Lima: Universidad de Lima, 1992

Chanan, Michael, *The Cuban Image: Cimena and Cultural Politics in Cuba*, London: British Film Institute, and Bloomington: Indiana University Press, 1985

Fregoso, Rosa Linda, *The Bronze Screen: Chicana and Chicano Film Culture*, Minneapolis: University of Minnesota Press, 1993

García Riera, Emilio, *Historia del cine mexicano*, Mexico City: Consejo Nacional de Fomento Educativo, 1986

Johnson, Randal and Robert Stam (editors), *Brazilian Cinema*, Rutherford, New Jersey: Fairleigh Dickinson University Press, 1982; augmented edition, New York: Colombia University Press, 1995

King, John, *Magical Reels: a History of Cinema in Latin America*, London: Verso, 1990

King, John, Ana López and Manuel Alvarado (editors), *Mediating Two Worlds: Cinematic Encounters in the Americas*, London: British Film Institute, 1993

Pick, Zuzana M., *The New Latin American Cinema: a Continental Project*, Austin: University of Texas Press, 1993

Torrents, Nissa, "The Cinema that Never Was," in *Argentina in the Crisis Years: 1983–1990*, edited by Colin M. Lewis and Nissa Torrents, London: Institute of Latin American Studies, 1993

Rubem Fonseca 1925–

Brazilian prose writer

One of Brazil's best-selling contemporary authors, Rubem Fonseca stands out as an urban satirist whose prose exposes the underbelly of society where white and blue collar crime symbolize the inequities of a corrupt and unjust world. Noted for his wry use of parody, intertextuality, humor, and profanity, Fonseca also dramatizes the role of the artist as an irreverent marginal, struggling to violate the image of the status quo in society as well as in art. Owing to his unabashed use of sex and violence, he has also become a very controversial writer, particularly due to his indefatigable defiance of oppressive standards of good taste and morality. In this vein, he can be considered an ethical and aesthetic vanguardist because his fiction challenges conventional notions of high culture and bourgeois codes that censure alternative lifestyles and forms of expression. Nowhere is this better dramatized than in his novel *A grande arte*, 1983 (*High Art*), a *tour de force* parody of "high art" in which the skill of wielding a stiletto becomes another kind of artistic expression. By infusing his prose with taboo words and actions, Fonseca affirms an anti-repressive stance that harbors socio-political agendas and fosters a radical aestheticism frequently asssociated with postmodern literature. In doing so, he provides a disturbing yet entertaining side to the Brazilian scene with the aim of offering other perspectives that will dislodge the reader's customary optic.

Writing since the early 1960s, Fonseca gained notoriety during the repressive years of the military's reign (1964–85), especially when his story collection, *Feliz ano novo*, 1975 [Happy New Year] was banned by General Ernesto Geisel's regime. Watched over vigilantly by the regime's censor during the 1970s, an era when fiction represented the only means for evoking the other reality behind the image and propaganda of socio-political order promoted by the military's authoritarian program, Fonseca's fiction, along with that of other writers of this period, experimented with new ways of demonstrating how tyranny, corruption, and evil were insidiously linked to the imposition of absolute power and control. By breaking through the crust of hierarchical behavior and jolting the reader into another way of thinking via an alien code of ethics, Fonseca deconstructs the notion of all absolutist postures. This stance dismantles rigid aesthetic and social codes, even to the point of implicating (author)itarian artists who profess to be fair and impartial, as one of his protagonists states in *Bufo & Spallanzani* (1985), a novel about the abuses of all kinds of power. Creating characters who often operate outside the Law, Fonseca exposes the blind application of universal value and moral systems that do not accommodate the harsh injustices and singular circumstances of local realities. Also, in focusing upon the theme of cultural production, Fonseca subverts notions that Brazilian fiction should have to adhere to canonical Eurocentric standards of literature and so he has his prose engage in a playful intertextuality wherein foreign literature is shown to relate to Brazilian art and not vice versa.

A consummate storyteller, evident in his six best-selling collections, Fonseca has been consistent in his scatological thematics where the body becomes the vehicle for expressing uncanny sentiments about the fear and threat of modern urban living in a society of too many have-nots. However, most of his narratives juxtapose social criticism with metaliterary commentary. In his famous collection, *Feliz ano novo* [Happy New Year], insights into Fonseca's aesthetics may be gleaned from the story "Intestino grosso" [Large Intestine] which takes the form of an interview with a famous Brazilian writer. Here, the writer discusses his radical approach to fiction and his use of the body and eroticism which he explains is designed for the expressed purpose of disclosing to the reader a special kind of "carnal knowledge." The fictional writer believes in confronting the forbidden, especially sexual desires and social taboos, instinctual behavior often camouflaged behind restrictive social conventions. This line of thinking is enhanced further with Fonseca's deft use of metafiction which points to what is behind the mask of literary and political illusion, thereby also referring indirectly to the mechanics of censorship and exposing the logic of the censor's mind. According to the writer-protagonist, the repression of the forbidden tends to justify and perpetuate the practice of many forms of censorship.

A staple in all of Fonseca's narratives, metafiction also represents Fonseca's continual dialogue with other literary voices. This practice is flagrantly developed in his collection, *Romance negro*, 1992 [Black Romance] where there appear innumerable allusions to internationally known writers such as Joseph Conrad, Stephen Crane and P.D. James. Of course, this volume's title also pays homage to the other strong feature in Fonseca's work, his appropriation of the detective novel genre. The elements of pulp and *noir* pervade Fonseca's fiction and interestingly these flourish alongside discussions of erudite art. The juxtaposition of popular/mass culture and high art forces the reader to rethink the role of aesthetics within a social context and, by extension, the implied positioning and subjectivity behind the construction of all culture. In using the detective frame, Fonseca at the same time subverts this genre because invariably his detectives never get their man. In other words, the authoritative final ending, when all is supposedly solved, never occurs. Frequently the detection remains in the hands of the reader who realizes that there may be many truths behind all the deceptions. Even though Fonseca employs many of the devices common to the *roman noir* – fast action, page-turning plot, lurid violence – his self-conscious narrators are always involved in some form of artistic expression. His novel *Vastas emoções e pensamentos imperfeitos*, 1988 [Vast Emotions and Imperfect Thoughts] shows the relationship between dreams, art, reality, and the cinema in order to underscore how artistic truths emerge amid the montage of fantasy. Here, Fonseca also uses intertextuality to illustrate how various forms of art speak to each other.

Fonseca's preference for narrative hybridity is also apparent in his mix of erudite art, popular detective fiction and the historical novel. In order to reread Brazilian history with other eyes while simultaneously illustrating how the problems of the

Brazilian present are analogous to those of the past, Fonseca has written two novels that reflect this historical posture – *Agosto*, 1990 [August] and *O selvagem da ópera*, 1994.

With *Agosto*, Fonseca relates the corrupt dramas and political abuses occuring during the weeks prior to President Getúlio Vargas's suicide on 24 August 1954 in order to mark this date as a turning point in Brazilian history between an old-fashioned type of politics and a modern but corrupt style of political intrigue and dishonesty. And with *O selvagem*, relating the vicissitudes in the life of Carlos Gomes, the 19th-century Brazilian composer of nationalistic operas such as *O guarani*, Fonseca again takes up the theme of artistic creation across several genres – historical biography, film script, and the novel. His work has been translated into several languages and transposed to other artistic mediums: for example, the story "Lúcia McCartney," was adapted for the stage in 1987, and *A grande arte* was made into a feature length film in 1991, with an international cast. In these ways, Rubem Fonseca is not only reaching a wider audience, but is also crossing several artistic borders, an act repeatedly manifested in his dynamic prose.

NELSON H. VIEIRA

Biography
Born in Minas Gerais, Brazil, in 1925, to Portuguese parents. Family moved to Rio de Janeiro when he was eight. Later studied law at University of Rio de Janeiro and public administration at New York and Boston. Varied career which has included being a criminal lawyer, university teacher, researcher and executive in a multinational company. Has actively supported authors' rights and served as Secretary of Culture for the state of Rio de Janeiro from 1980 to 1981. Awarded Brazilian Goethe Prize for Fiction in 1985.

Selected Works

Short Fiction
Os prisioneiros, Rio de Janeiro: GRD, 1963
A coleira do cão, Rio de Janeiro: GRD, 1965

Lúcia McCartney, Rio de Janeiro: Olivé, 1969
O homem de fevereiro ou março, Rio de Janeiro: Artenova, 1973 [anthology]
Feliz ano novo, Rio de Janeiro: Artenova, 1975
O cobrador, Rio de Janeiro: Nova Fronteira, 1979
Romance negro e outras histórias, São Paulo: Companhia das Letras, 1992 [anthology]

Novels
O caso Morel, Rio de Janeiro: Artenova, 1973
A grande arte, Rio de Janeiro: Francisco Alves, 1983; as *High Art*, translated by Ellen Watson, New York: Harper and Row, 1986; London: Collins, 1987
Bufo & Spallanzani, Rio de Janeiro: Francisco Alves, 1985; as *Bufo and Spallanzani*, translated by Clifford E. Landers, New York: Dutton, 1990
Vastas emoções e pensamentos imperfeitos, São Paulo: Companhia das Letras, 1988
Agosto, São Paulo: Companhia das Letras, 1990
O selvagem da ópera, São Paulo: Companhia das Letras, 1994

Further Reading
Barzun, Jacques, "Venus at Large," *Encounter*, vol. 26/3 (March 1966)
Coutinho, Afrânio, "Erotismo na literatura brasileira: o caso Rubem Fonseca," *Encontros com a Civilização Brasileira* 10 (April 1979)
Hook, Sydney, "Pornography and the Censor," *New York Times Book Review*, 12 April, 1964
McKeon, Richard, "Canonic Books and Prohibited Books: Orthodoxy and Heresy in Religion and Culture," *Critical Inquiry*, Chicago, vol. 2/4 (Summer 1976)
Sant'Anna, Sérgio, "A propósito de *Lúcia McCartney*," *Minas Gerais*, *Suplemento Literário*, Belo Horizonte (December 1969)
Silva, Deónisio, *O caso Rubem Fonseca: violência e erotismo em "Feliz Ano Novo,"* São Paulo: Alfa-Omega, 1983
Tolman, Jon, "The Moral Dimension in Rubem Fonseca's Prose," *New World* 1 (1986)

Foundational Literature

The term foundational literature, generally refers to those works which seek to explain and evoke in imaginative terms, the birth of the modern nation state. In a concealed way, its function is therefore political and historical. Indeed, Andrés Bello, the 19th-century Venezuelan nationalist claimed that in the absence of adequate documents, and in countries where historical evidence was scattered, narrative literature became its substitute for history. Bello's assertion is echoed in the opinion of a later essayist, the Peruvian, José Carlos Mariátegui, who claimed that the nation was an abstraction which could not be defined scientifically.

The more recent interest among Western scholars in the links between literary creativity and the evocation of national identity derive from Benedict Anderson's linking of the emergence of print in newly independent states with the concept of an "imagined community," which itself owes something to Ernest Gellner's theory that nations do not exist prior to their invention by nationalism. Taking this idea a little further, Timothy Brennan concluded that the inventive process of national foundation, depends on "an apparatus of cultural fictions in which imaginative literature plays a decisive part." In the specific case of Latin American literature, the most exhaustive study of the links between nationalism and creative literature is that provided by Doris Sommer, who sees the apparently domestic romances of the mid-19th century as reflecting, on an allegorical level, the conciliatory nationalism of the generation of writers following that of the leaders of independence.

Foundational literature, then, closely accompanied the consolidation of the still fragile nation state, and corresponded very closely with the Romantic movement, the influence of which was most strongly felt in Latin America between the 1830s and the 1860s. Romantic love, however, underwent a change on its journey across the Atlantic to the New World, for it divested itself of individualism, as well as of the impossibility of attainment. Preserving the sentimentality of Romanticism, writers gave erotic passion and emotion a public function: love of freedom and of country . Sometimes, as in the case of the Brazilian novels, *O guarani*, 1857 [The Guaraní Indian], or *Iracema*, 1865 (*Iracema, the Honey-Lips, a Legend of Brazil*) by José de Alencar, or of *Enriquillo*, 1882 (*The Cross and the Sword*) by the Dominican novelist, Manuel de Jesús Galván, the setting was the early colonial period, but the romantic relationships which form the central focuses of the works, represent an attempt to bridge a divide between apparently incompatible positions. Thus, in *O guarani*, the attachment between the Indian hero, Peri, and the white maiden, Cecília, reconciles slave and mistress, nature and civilisation, paganness and Catholicism. The departure of the couple into the wilderness as orphans, and with the blessing of Cecília's father, a Portuguese nobleman who is to die a little later, serves as an allegory of Brazil's essentially conciliatory independence process. Galván, for his part, delves back to the dawn of conquest to give us a vision of rebellion, romance and reconciliation, which points to the political disturbances of the Dominican Republic in the second half of the 19th century, as it was tossed politically between Spain, Haiti, and the United States.

Elsewhere, romance was situated in the contemporary age. In the Argentine José Mármol's *Amalia* (1855), the love of Eduardo and Amalia symbolises the reconciliation between city and province, liberal Buenos Aires and conservative backlands, during and after the fall of Juan Manuel Rosas, whose role in the novel is to prohibit their love.

In some countries, the issue of the abolition of slavery was the wound inhibiting national unity, and this was reflected in novels such as *Sab* (1841) by the Cuban writer Gertrudis Gómez de Avellaneda, and *A escrava Isaura*, 1875 [Isaura the Slave Girl] by the Brazilian, Bernardo Guimarães. In the Cuban novel, the slave Sab, in his silent passion for his mistress, Carlota, is obliged to witness her marriage to the son of an English slave trader, who mistreats her. The novel allegorises the misguided alliance between the Cuban nationalists and the British, who were seen as using Cuba for their own interests, and posits a solution to national disunity through a more robust alliance of blacks and creoles, independent of the society of the *latifundia*, and which is symbolised by the garden which Sab creates and tends in the middle of the plantation.

In the Brazilian novel the situation is reversed in that it is the tale of lust on the part of a Rio coffee planter for a slave woman. Spurned by the woman he considers no more than chattel, he persecutes her, only for her to be rescued by an aristocrat from Recife, who ultimately takes her as his wife. The union of northeastern liberalism and a near white woman of proven conservative, Portuguese pedigree (her father is a "miguelista" who sought refuge in Brazil after the return of the liberals in Portugal), represents the reconciliation between south and north, native Brazilian and Portuguese, the old creole aristocracy and the more recent émigrés from the Old World.

Less often, the marriage of opposites as a symbol of national reconciliation, was lampooned. In Machado de Assis's end of the century novel, *Dom Casmurro* (1899), the romantic engagement of rural aristocracy and urban petite bourgeoisie, in the form of the childhood sweethearts, Bento and Capitu, leads to jealousy and separation, reflecting to some extent the social changes which would find their political expression in the abolition of slavery, the overthrow of the monarchy, and the inception of the republic in 1889. Gone is the concept of a national family, mirrored in the reward of domestic bliss. Indeed, Machado's novel portends the rather more parodic view of national foundation which is a feature of contemporary Latin American fiction.

Sommer suggests that foundational fiction does not die out with Romanticism, but is adapted to the more socially grounded literature of the 20th century, moulded by Realist and Naturalist priorities, and political populism. Thus, a novel like *Doña Bárbara* (1929) by the Venezuelan writer, Rómulo Gallegos, in the manner of Mármol's work, effects a reconciliation between the modernising, liberal values of the city and the rural, anarchic world of the plains, in the characters of the city-educated, Santos Luzardo and the indomitable plainswoman, Bárbara, but this only occurs after barbarism has been defeated, and the hero has established his conjugal rights over the land, by marrying Bárbara's daughter, Marisela. What happens in Gallegos's novel also occurs in the Colombian José Eustacio Rivera's *La vorágine*, 1923 (*The Vortex*), or the Brazilian Jorge Amado's *Terras do sem fim*, 1943 (*The Violent Land*): the emphasis is by this time on domination rather than reconciliation, the re-affirmation of patriarchy over the somewhat more feminised novels of the high period of foundational literature in the 19th century.

DAVID BROOKSHAW

Further Reading

Anderson, Benedict, *Imagined Communities: Reflections on the Origin and Spread of Nationalism*, London and New York: Verso, 1983

Bhabha, Homi K. (editor), *Nation and Narration*, London and New York: Routledge, 1990 [See, in particular, Timothy Brennan's "The National Longing for Form" and Doris Sommer's "Irresistible Romance: the Foundational Fictions of Latin America"]

Masiello, Francine, *Between Civilization and Barbarism: Women, Nation and Literary Culture in Modern Argentina*, Lincoln: University of Nebraska Press, 1992

Sommer, Doris, *Foundational Fictions: the National Romances of Latin America*, Berkeley: University of California Press, 1991

Francophone West Indies

Although the countries of the Francophone West Indies – Haiti, Martinique and Guadeloupe – initially shared a history of French colonialism and African slave labour, their political and cultural paths have diverged over the past two centuries. The story of Haiti is one of extremes, epitomized by the dramatic shift from the cruelties of slavery to the triumphant expulsion of the French at the start of the 19th century, when Haiti became the first black republic in the world. These extremes continue to be evident in the violent topplings of regimes which have marked the decades of Haiti's independence, and in the enormous socio-economic gap between the middle class and the vast urban and rural proletariat. The typical Haitian writer of recent decades has lived and worked in exile. In Martinique and Guadeloupe, where no slave revolt was ever successful, French cultural and political hegemony has always been a fact of life. France's Eastern Caribbean possessions were maintained as sugar-producing colonies until the abolition of slavery in 1848, and prolonged in this tradition by indentured labour until the decline of the sugar industry in the present century. Today Martinique and Guadeloupe, now accorded the status of Overseas Departments of France, no longer produce wealth but are consumer societies wholly subsidized by the metropolis. The financial advantages of their quasi-colonial situation bring them into sharp contrast with the independent, but economically disadvantaged Caribbean states that surround them; and nowhere is this difference more marked than in Haiti, universally recognized as the poorest country in the western hemisphere.

These differences in socio-political background explain the differing tendencies in Francophone Caribbean literature. European influences were, however, very evident in the early stages of all French West Indian writing: metropolitan models set the tone for a curiously distanced presentation of the tropical landscape, while the racial hierarchies of the colonial era produced a particular sensibility alive to class and caste distinctions, to the oppressive interplay between power, birth and skin shade. At the same time, an undercurrent of loss has always been apparent in the themes of isolation, exile, and nostalgia for an Africa still discernible in folk tradition. Haitian writing also bears the particular imprint of black revolutionary triumph, proudly evoked, yet tempered by the desire for international recognition. In the mid- and late 20th century, the theme of exile has taken on a different cast for considerable numbers of Haitian writers who have fled – mainly to Canada and the United States – in order to escape political tyranny and to seek freedom of expression. This North American dimension is largely absent in the literature of the French Overseas Departments, where, despite the privileged position of Africa at the height of the *Négritude* movement, Paris has remained the natural point of reference overseas. For these islands, France is the uncontested source of public education, media information, cultural trend-setting, scholarships and exchanges, as well as the chief agent for the publication and diffusion of literary works. Even those contemporary Martinican or Guadeloupean writers who deplore the detrimental effects of all-pervasive metropolitan French culture upon creole folkways and traditions, are generally obliged to

do so through the medium of their Parisian publisher. Such cultural protest is, moreover, largely confined to intellectual circles; voting trends clearly indicate that the average French West Indian does not perceive close association with France as anything other than an advantage.

Literature and public affairs have long been intertwined in Haiti. The internal political turmoil which has marred her independence has also made her vulnerable to foreign intervention, most strikingly illustrated in the lengthy US military occupation (1915–34) which re-introduced a humiliating power hierarchy based on white superiority. The reaction of journalists and intellectuals to those years marked the birth of modern Haitian literature. Critical essays, anti-American poetry and militant fiction all contributed to the rise of the Indigenous Movement, dedicated to the promotion of national consciousness. A key factor in its doctrine was the necessity of solidarity between the largely mulatto Haitian elite – from which most writers came – and the generally darker-skinned, illiterate and impoverished masses that the bourgeoisie had traditionally ignored. The population was inadvertently drawn together by the colour prejudice of the US occupying forces, which knew no class distinctions. Alongside this internal spur to nationalist protest, many Haitians found a renewed source of racial pride through awareness of the intense wave of interest in African art and culture which occurred in Europe during the 1920s. Popularized by the Haitian journal *La Nouvelle Ronde* and then by such influential thinkers as Jean Price-Mars (*Ainsi parla l'oncle*, 1928 (*So Spoke the Uncle*), this focus on African culture encouraged a poetic view of the Haitian proletariat and a flowering of such magazines as *La Revue Indigène*. The Indigenous Movement fostered the revival of the peasant novel, of which Jacques Roumain, with *Gouverneurs de la rosée*, 1944 (*Masters of the Dew*), was to become the finest exponent. Roumain discreetly deployed unique Haitian features such as Creole speech, traditional folklore and customs, and the centrally important voodoo religion in his portrayal of the neglected peasant majority. But overriding the nationalist theme of fidelity to African roots – and accompanied by grave doubts about the essential passivity of voodoo beliefs in a context crying out for social action – is Roumain's conviction that Marxism offered the best solution to the glaring inequalities of Haitian society. Founder, in 1934, of the short-lived Haitian Communist Party, Roumain used Marxism in his political writings to justify his criticism of the Haitian regime and his vision of economic reform. The profoundly allegorical and didactic *Gouverneurs de la rosée* adapts Marxism to a rural Caribbean setting, stressing the need for individual effort, peasant solidarity, and full appreciation of the African heritage of dignity, strength and physical grace.

Roumain's nationalist themes – together, paradoxically, with his ultimate move beyond Indigenism – and his long political exile made him a role model for successors like René Depestre, and for those still younger poets who felt themselves living the condition of exiles within Duvalier's Haiti. Depestre and Jacques-Stéphen Alexis, both left-wing thinkers, both emotionally attuned to the world of the Caribbean folk, were both to be forced, like Roumain, into actual exile. In tribute to Roumain, Alexis created the character of Pierre Roumel, the idealized Marxist mentor of the naive slum hero in *Compère Général Soleil*, 1955 [Comrade General Sun], the first novel in which an urban proletariat strikingly replaces the peasantry as the focal point of ideological reform. The experience of forced expatriation enhanced these Haitian writers' appreciation of the savour and variety of their native land, while also encouraging them to take a wider Caribbean view of their identity. Cubans, Dominicans and Puerto Ricans are sympathetically portrayed in Alexis's novels, while Depestre, in *Bonjour et adieu à la négritude*, 1980 [Hello and Goodbye to Negritude], advances the concept of a pan-Caribbean identity which he calls, in a purely geographical sense, *américanité* [Americanness]. Strong parallels with modern tendencies in Latin-American literature are visible in Alexis's theory of magical realism, on which he published a seminal paper, "Prolegomena to a Manifesto on the Marvellous Realism of the Haitians," in *Présence Africaine* (8 October 1956). Alexis's sense of national identity encompasses not only his African ancestry, but also the indigenous Indian ancestors whom he claimed as part of his spiritual legacy, and who in pre-Columbian times linked the Caribbean archipelago with Latin America. His brand of magical realism, which seems at home in a country where the supernatural and the everyday are frequently intermingled, is increasingly present in Haitian fiction, which infuses its portrayals of rural life with fantastic, dreamlike episodes that bring the Haitian novel close to many contemporary Latin-American counterparts.

The exterior circumstance of political tyranny has constantly intervened in the working conditions of Haitian writers. Roumain's years of separation from his native land, the brutal killing of Alexis upon his attempt to bring about the overthrow of Duvalier, the imprisonment and frequently the torture of critics of the regime in power, have consistently maintained a climate hostile to intellectual freedom. It is not yet clear how literary life may be affected by the restoration to power of President Aristide in 1994. Rare was the dissenting voice that managed to make itself heard with impunity during the long Duvalier dictatorship. Marie Chauvet, Haiti's best-known woman writer, was forced to leave for the United States after the publication of her trilogy *Amour, colère et folie* [Love, Anger and Madness] in 1968. Pierre Clitandre, editor of the opposition newspaper *Le Petit-Samedi-Soir*, was exiled to the United States in 1980, the year in which his *Cathédrale du mois d'août* (*Cathedral of the August Heat*) – a novel protesting conditions in the slums of the capital – appeared in Haiti. Young writers' groups such as *Haïti Littéraire* disappeared altogether. Some eluded reprisals: the novelist Franketienne, for instance, whose denunciation of Papa Doc in *Les Affres d'un défi*, 1979 (*Defiance and Dread*) is effectively veiled in the rituals of the voudou temple and the cockpit. Other writers who remained in Haiti, such as Jean-Claude Fignolé (*Les Possédés de la pleine lune*, 1987 [Those Possessed by the Full Moon]), avoided directly political themes, focusing on lyrical evocations of peasant culture and spiritual beliefs. Jan J. Dominique, who left Haiti but chose to return, in *Mémoire d'une amnésique*, 1984 [Memory of an Amnesiac], used the device of a child eyewitness to present brutal events with a false naivety, all political commentary remaining implicit. Many artists opposed to the military regime of the

early 1990s turned away from the dangerous written word to the less compromising medium of folksong and popular music.

Those who went into exile have not seen their geographical remoteness as a diminishing of their commitment to Haiti. Jean Métellus, who lives in Europe, has expressed in an interview his intimate sense of relationship with his own country: "In fact, I am a Haitian exile who has never left Haiti, and Haiti has never left me. For many years, my imagination has linked me to my native land." Other writers have echoed his sentiments and developed socio-political themes which are key elements in Métellus's work also: dispossession, political blunders and betrayals, the lyrical imagination and tenacious will of a vast, oppressed proletariat. Some, like the dramatist Syto Cavé, have returned home to resume contact with the popular culture from which their work springs. Others, like Roger Dorsinville after long years in Africa, came back tragically too late to find the Haiti they had lost. The journal *Chemins Critiques* [Critical Roads], launched in 1986 after the overthrow of the younger Duvalier, has attempted to create a zone of free debate for Haitian intellectuals. Important areas of discussion in literary circles, both in Haiti and abroad, include the function of the writer in a largely illiterate population, the appropriate place of Creole in literature, and the danger of being restricted to "exotic" subjects (voodoo, slum violence) in order to satisfy a foreign public in search of sensationalism. A recent remarkable example of the powerful, but not sensationalist, treatment of a voodoo theme is Lilas Desquiron's novel *Les Chemins de Loco-Miroir*, 1990 [The Roads of Loco-Miroir]. The most striking feature of late 20th-century Haitian writing is the number of writers who are based in Francophone Canada. There is an older generation of established writers who fled to Quebec in the 1960s to escape Duvalierism: Emile Ollivier, whose novel *Mère-Solitude*, 1983 [Mother Solitude], is a rich backward glance at the complex essence of Haiti; Anthony Phelps, Gérard Etienne and others. A more disparate group includes the feminist novelist Nadine Magloire, and the provocative, ironic Dany Laferrière, author of *Comment faire l'amour avec un Nègre sans se fatiguer*, 1985 [How to Make Love with a Negro without Getting Tired]. A new generation of writers who have spent their formative years in Quebec, such as the poet Joël Des Rosiers, is now attempting to determine and express an emerging Haitian-Canadian identity.

In Martinique and Guadeloupe, the longer period of colonial rule imposed French culture upon a population of mixed origins – African, Indian, Chinese, Syrian/Lebanese, as well as European. Although Creole is spoken everywhere, French is the educational and literary norm. Questions of race and language are thus tied to the issue of cultural identity, which has preoccupied successive literary movements in these islands. In the first half of the 20th century, the theory of *Négritude*, developed by three colonial students who had met in Paris: the Martinican Aimé Césaire, the Guyanese L.-G. Damas and the Senegalese Léopold Sédar Senghor, exalted an African cultural identity long repressed and despised in the West Indies, where the assumption of white superiority over black had been basic to the whole system of slavery. No subsequent Caribbean writer has escaped the influence of Césaire's key text of 1939, *Cahier d'un retour au pays natal* (*Return to My Native Land*), which gave a poetic form to the militant demands of *Légitime Défense* and *L'Etudiant Noir* [The Black Student], movements launched by West Indian and African students in France in the early 1930s. Césaire was not the first 20th-century black writer to convey in violent images his anger at white colonial oppression, or to express his yearning, passionate desire for reconciliation with ancestral Africa. But his dense, searing text became the cornerstone of modern Francophone West Indian literature, and his theme of black cultural exile was picked up by many writers concerned with the search for identity: Xavier Orville, Vincent Placoly, the younger Simone Schwarz-Bart. The privileged position which Césaire accorded to Africa in his works – a step intended as a corrective to Europe's long dismissal of African civilization – has been opposed, however, on the grounds that it encourages West Indians to bypass their own country in their quest for spiritual roots. This issue is still being publicly debated by younger writers like Raphaël Confiant and Patrick Chamoiseau, whose *Créolité* movement regards Africa as a detour in the search for Caribbean identity (see, for example, Confiant's controversial attack on Césaire's ideology in *Aimé Césaire: une traversée paradoxale du siècle*, 1993 [Aimé Césaire: a Paradoxical Journey through the Century]. In the political sphere, Césaire's approval of Departmental status for the islands – which, in 1946, appeared to be a vast improvement upon their colonial situation – has been criticized by more radical, pro-independence writers in later decades.

Another notion of cultural identity followed *Négritude*, and was to have a profound influence on the later *Créolité* movement. This was *Antillanité* (Caribbeanness), a concept put forward by Edouard Glissant, whose figure has dominated Francophone West Indian writing in the second half of the 20th century. Viewing the recovery of African identity as a practical impossibility due to the intervening, alienating centuries of slavery, Glissant has preferred to focus his attention not on a distant, imagined continent but on the real country of his birth. His vision of Martinique's destiny is of a collective realization of national unity, composed of two sorts of solidarity: a self-reliant cooperation within Martinique to replace her increasing dependence on France, and a sense of fraternity and common purpose binding the Francophone islands to the entire Caribbean archipelago. Many of these ideas are resumed in his major collection of essays, *Le Discours antillais*, 1981 (*Caribbean Discourse*), and in novels such as *Malemort* (1975), *La Case du commandeur*, 1981 [The Driver's Hut], and *Tout-Monde*, 1993 [All the World]; they are the core of the recurrent motifs in his fiction, poetry, drama and theoretical writings since 1956. In founding the journal *Acoma* in the early 1970s, Glissant provided a forum for psychological and socio-economic debate about Martinique and Guadeloupe. His own works aim at restoring, not the total emotional affiliation with Africa which was the goal of *Négritude*, but an understanding of the forgotten centuries of history and culture which belonged to the slaves of the Francophone West Indies and their descendants. For him, this supremely important past lies waiting to be rediscovered in a landscape which is emblematic of Caribbean authenticity, bearing the imprint of centuries of patient survival. Beyond reconciliation with the landscape itself lies the possibility of the birth of a Martinican nation.

Glissant's insistence on certain themes – the value of history, the imperfections of Caribbean folk memory, collective destiny, independence and contingency, the effects of time and exterior influences upon a people's culture and destiny – has had a marked effect upon succeeding generations of novelists, dramatists and essayists in this region. The Guadeloupean writer Daniel Maximin features in his novels *L'Isolé Soleil*, 1981 (*Lone Sun*), and *Soufrières* (1987), the theme of reconciliation with the past and the notion of an underlying cultural unity that links the islands in the Caribbean sea. Younger writers in Martinique today such as Patrick Chamoiseau and Raphaël Confiant acknowledge the influence of Glissant not only by direct allusions to his work, but also in their close attention to his directives regarding folk history and oral tradition. Chamoiseau and Confiant are particularly concerned with the promotion of the Creole language (long regarded as the vernacular of the ill-educated, fit only for comic usage) in serious literature, and the development of strategies for incorporating modified forms of Creole within works that, for financial reasons, must remain accessible to a non-Creole-speaking public. These writers share a preference for popular milieux – the locus of choice for a panorama of collective history – and they show dazzling virtuosity in transforming a French narrative by the insertion not only of Creole expressions, but of "Creolized" French words, Creole social concepts and West Indian modes of thought. Chamoiseau's novels – *Chronique des sept misères*, 1986 [Chronicle of the Seven Misfortunes]; *Solibo magnifique*, 1988 [Magnificent Solibo]; *Texaco* (1992) – and those of Confiant – *Le Nègre et l'amiral*, 1989 [The Black Man and the Admiral]; *Eau de café*, 1991 [Coffee Water]; *L'Allée des soupirs*, 1994 [The Path of Sighs] – afford a fascinating study of how two quite different stylists have come to grips with the triple challenge of remaining faithful to West Indian folkways, turning in a bravura linguistic performance and retaining an audience in France. Along with Jean Bernabé of Guadeloupe, Chamoiseau and Confiant co-authored in 1989 a short, provocative manifesto entitled *Eloge de la Créolité* (*In Praise of Creoleness*). In it they echo Glissant's theme that the Francophone West Indian islands can never assume a true Caribbean identity unless they move beyond their present state of cultural and socio-economic dependence upon France. The notion of *Créolité* is based on the assumption of a natural affinity between Francophone Creole countries (Haiti, Guadeloupe, Martinique, St Lucia, Dominica and Guyane) whatever their political affiliations. A narrower concept than Glissant's *Antillanité*, it is primarily the underpinning of a linguistic and literary programme which accords a privileged place to traditional oral culture, Caribbean racial diversity, magical realism, and the writer who speaks as and with the collective voice of the common people.

The two best-known women writers in the French West Indies, both from Guadeloupe, have not chosen to adhere strictly to a socio-cultural literary programme. Like their male counterparts, they are interested in questions of racial ancestry and cultural identity; but they pursue these questions in a personal and independent way. Simone Schwarz-Bart's celebrated second novel, *Pluie et vent sur Télumée Miracle*, 1972 (*The Bridge of Beyond*), conveys the essence of a peasant community without ever actually employing Creole dialogue. Rather, the author's richly metaphoric French text contains frequent echoes of Creole proverbs and habitual expressions that re-create the social ambience of rural Guadeloupe. Her play *Ton Beau capitaine*, 1987 (*Your Handsome Captain*), relates the ending of a proletarian love story through a counterpoint of poignantly restrained French-speaking voices and insistent, wailing Creole song. Maryse Condé, probably the most prolific and idiosyncratic of Guadeloupean novelists, is sceptical and sardonic when she touches on the West Indian search for cultural identity. Yet a theme she has made particularly her own is the fate of the African diaspora in the New World: in novels such as *La Vie scélérate*, 1987 (*The Tree of Life*), or *Les Derniers Rois Mages*, 1992 [The Last Magi], she traces the attractions and misunderstandings that may arise between those linked by race but springing from different cultural backgrounds. There are indications that younger women writers may now be tending towards a more deliberate choice of literary school. Gisèle Pineau, for instance, has experimented with two types of text: one a short, realistic novella (*Un Papillon dans la cité*, 1992 [A Butterfly in the Housing Estate], about a young girl's move from the West Indies to Paris, obviously intended for metropolitan consumption, with its few, carefully annotated snatches of Creole; and the other (*La Grande drive des esprits*, 1993 [The Long Wandering of the Spirits]), a richly detailed fictional history of a Guadeloupe peasant family, in some respects resembling the novels of the *Creolité* school through its frequent use of untranslated Creole dialogue, its pursuit of a multitude of different life stories, and its casual acceptance of the supernatural as a feature of everyday life.

While many contemporary Haitian writers have been forced to look beyond their country's frontiers, adapt to exile, compromise with unfamiliar cultures, and find ways of assimilating a second identity, writers in Martinique and Guadeloupe are obliged to accept a *de facto* metropolitan French affiliation, since they depend on France for their literary survival. The current popularity of the *Creolité* movement shows, however, that there are fears in these islands that an essentially Creole social reality may be in the process of disappearing,

submerged by metropolitan influences. There exists, therefore, an ardent desire to maintain in the Eastern Caribbean, and to promote in the wider Francophone community, a sense of Martinican and Guadeloupean cultural identity.

BEVERLEY ORMEROD

See also the entries on *La Revue du Monde Noir* and *Tropiques* under Journals

Further Reading
There is little work by critics that treats the Caribbean as a regional entity with a common colonial past and neo-colonial present. This results from a tradition of university departments that specialize in a particular language, such as French or Spanish. There is a real need here for a comparatist's outlook.

Arnold, James A. (editor), *A History of Literature in the Caribbean: Volume I, Hispanic and Francophone Regions*, Amsterdam and Philadelphia: Benjamins, 1994 [Comprehensive coverage of different genres and movements by established scholars]

Berrou, Rapael and Pradel Pompilus, *Histoire de la littérature haïtienne*, 2 vols, Port-au-Prince, Haiti: Editions Caraïbes, 1975–77

Corzani, Jack, *La Littérature des Antilles Guyane-Françaises*, 6 vols, Fort-de-France: Désormeaux, 1978

Dash, J. Michael, *Literature and Ideology in Haiti, 1915–1961*, London: Macmillan, and Totowa, New Jersey: Barnes and Noble, 1981

Hoffmann, Léon-François, *Le Nègre romantique: personnage littéraire et obsession collective*, Paris: Payot, 1973

____ *Le Roman Haïtien, idéologie et structure*, Sherbrook: Éditions Naaman, 1982

Ormerod, Beverley, *An Introduction to the French Caribbean Novel*, London: Heinemann, 1985

Régis, Antoine, *La Littérature franco-antillaise*, Paris: Karthala, 1992 [Sections on Alexis, Césaire, Glissant, Roumain and literary movements]

Special Issues of Journals
Callaloo, vol. 15/2–3 (1992) [Highly recommended for coverage of Haitian literature and visual arts]

Gilberto Freyre 1900–1987

Brazilian sociologist, writer and polymath

Few 20th-century Brazilian writers have had such a profound impact on the study of the nation's social history and cultural development as Gilberto Freyre. A scholar of wide interests, his approach broke down traditional barriers between academic disciplines, to incorporate sociology, literature, anthropology, history and social psychology. The principal achievement of his most significant work was that, through the application of new theories in the social sciences, it presented a radical reassessment of Brazilian history, which offered a positive vision of the nation's cultural formation. In doing so, it gave considerable impetus to a wide variety of research into all levels of Brazilian reality. However, it is also highly controversial work, both in terms of the methodology employed and the conclusions drawn, and it has generated heated debate between Freyre's supporters and his critics.

Freyre was the descendant of a traditional, plantation-owning family in northeast Brazil, and had to contend with the reality of social and economic decline in the region, with the disintegration of the traditional patterns of life which had revolved around the *casa grande* (literally big house) of the plantation owner. Much of Freyre's work was a response to that process of regional decline, and, with it, the decline of his own social class. It was in this context that Freyre sought to reaffirm northeastern cultural values, and, at a time of intense debate over the question of national culture, demonstrate that the authentic spirit of Brazilian cultural identity was located in the rural interior of that region. It was, Freyre argued, a distinct identity forged by the social relations particular to the patriarchal plantation regime. Deep nostalgia for a past age orientated Freyre's approach to his work, and frequently resulted in a romantic view of regional traditions. He saw the traditional plantation life of the northeast as having been essentially harmonious, centring on a more benign form of slavery. Such views would come under increasing attack from other scholars later in the century.

Shortly after returning to Brazil from his studies in the United States and Europe, Freyre launched the northeast Regionalist Movement in his native Recife, in 1926, with the objective of affirming and promoting the cultural values of the region. It succeeded in stimulating sociological enquiry into northeastern social life and cultural traditions, and played an influential role in the development of regionalist literature throughout the following decade. José Américo de Almeida and José Lins do Rego, for example, both acknowledged the importance which Freyre's regionalist thought had for their writing. However, the movement was characterized by conservatism. Freyre saw the popular culture of the northeast, embracing living conditions, diet and art forms, as being in a state of steady decline, even extinction, suffocated by the relentless process of cultural massification, and thus in need of protection by those with the necessary intellectual and financial resources. For this purpose, he proposed regional museums, craft shops, folkloric festivals, and even a restaurant to promote the region's culinary tradition. It was a paternalistic view of the popular classes and their particular forms of cultural expression, emphasising the notion of defending regional traditions from modernization and cosmopolitanism. The dynamism of popular culture, which explains its ever-changing forms, was nullified, and what was promoted were folkloric traditions primarily associated with a past age. There was a contradiction running through Freyre's regionalist philosophy. Addressing the need felt to elaborate a distinctly Brazilian cultural identity, Freyre looked to traditional forms of popular culture to provide the necessary materials. He was, however, unable to extricate himself from the restrictive ideology of his social class in order to come to a deeper understanding of the conditions of life experienced by the social sectors largely responsible for the production of that popular culture. The result is a detached vision of the popular classes, which are frequently viewed as ingenuous and compliant.

Freyre's reputation was largely established through the historical studies of patriarchal rural society which he published in the 1930s, especially *Casa grande e senzala*, 1933 (*The Masters and the Slaves*), which defined the main themes and preoccupations that would structure the rest of his scholarship. The book played a major role in combating negative interpretations of Brazilian reality through the positive promotion of the country's culture and racial composition. Earlier

writers had challenged the biological determinism which Positivist philosophy stressed as the major determinant explaining the differences between peoples, but *Casa grande e senzala* did much to consolidate the shift to cultural factors as the basis for explanation, as opposed to racial characteristics. It helped to provide a new sense of optimism and national pride, which many Brazilians were seeking. Freyre continued his historical research in *Sobrados e mucambos* (*The Mansions and the Shanties*), published three years later in 1936, this time examining the decline in the power of the traditional landed aristocracy and the expansion of the cities. Both works rely on detailed examination of daily social life, but are also characterised by a fluid literary style, intimate, even colloquial at times, which strongly conveys the author's personality. Though admired by some critics, it was criticized by others who argued that it compromised the scientific basis of Freyre's work. Most arguments, however, focused on the thesis of his writings. Freyre advanced the notion of an essential cultural homogeneity which had resulted from the process of miscegenation and which provided the basis for national integration and unity. He thereby contributed towards the elaboration of an ideology of national culture, which disguised the deep class and racial divisions within 20th-century Brazilian society. Indeed, Freyre played a major role in promoting Brazil as a "racial democracy;" a notion that was soon countered by others who produced evidence of racial inequality and prejudice at many levels of Brazilian society.

The central idea of racial, social and regional differences harmoniously integrated into a unified national structure was further developed in later works. The Portuguese, he argued, were well equipped to adapt to the new demands made upon them by life in the tropics, where, instead of simply implanting their own values and customs, they moulded themselves to the new natural and social conditions encountered, developing new perceptions, responses and values, which effectively constituted a new culture. In particular, Freyre alleged that the lack of prejudice of the Portuguese enabled them to mix freely with other races, and a symbiotic relationship developed between African and Portuguese which changed both. This was the basis for Freyre's concept of *Luso-tropicalismo*, developed in such works as *O mundo que o português criou*, 1940 [The World the Portuguese Created] and *Integração portuguesa nos trópicos*, 1958 (*Portuguese Integration in the Tropics*) promoting the cultural, and hence political, unity of the Portuguese speaking world. It became one of Freyre's most controversial theories, and was strongly condemned by critics as a myth which, stressing racial and social equality, served to justify Portuguese colonialism. It was indeed used for precisely that purpose by interested parties in reference to Portuguese-speaking Africa. In the latter part of his life, Freyre and his ideas became increasingly associated with right wing political current, both in Brazil and abroad, further polarizing critical responses to his work.

Freyre later turned his hand to fiction, writing what he termed "seminovels:" novels constructed within a historical framework. *Dona Sinhá e o filho padre*, 1964 (*Mother and Son*) and *O outro amor do Dr Paulo*, 1977 [Dr Paulo's Other Love] examined human relationships against the backcloth of the political and social changes taking place in 19th-century Brazilian society, which he had covered earlier, and with considerably more success, in his historical surveys. It was as a social historian that he left his mark on Brazilian intellectual life. Many of his ideas have been effectively countered, some even discredited, but his pioneering role cannot be denied. His work established a firm basis for the sociological study of Brazilian life and culture for many decades.

MARK DINNEEN

See also entries on Fernando Ortiz, Regionalism: Brazil

Biography

Born in Recife, Pernambuco State, Brazil, 15 March 1900. Attended the American Colégio Gilreath in Recife to 1917; Baylor University, Waco, Texas, 1918–21; studied anthropology under Franz Boas at Columbia University, New York, 1921–22. Travelled in Europe, 1922–23. Co-organizer of the Regionalist Artistic Movement's Congress in Recife, 1926; private secretary to the Governor of Pernambuco, Recife, 1927–30, whom he accompanied into exile in Portugal, 1930; editor of *A Província*, Recife, 1928–30; Assistant Professor of Sociology at the Escola Normal in Recife, 1928. Travelled to Africa, 1930. Visiting Professor, Stanford University, California, 1931; Professor of Sociology, Faculty of Law, Recife, 1935, and appointed to the Chair of Sociology and Social Anthropology, Federal University in 1935; Visiting Professor, Columbia University, New York, 1938. Married Maria Magdalena Guedes Pereira in 1941; one daughter and one son. Representative for Pernambuco, National Assembly, 1946, and in the House of Deputies, 1947–50. Brazilian Ambassador to the United Nations General Assembly, 1949; Founder, Joaquim Nabuco Institute, Recife, 1949. Member of São Paulo Academy of Letters, 1961, and of the Brazilian Academy of Letters, 1962; Visiting Professor, Indiana University, Bloomington, 1966. Recipient of numerous awards including: Machado de Assis Prize, 1963; Aspen Award, 1967; La Madonnina International Literary Prize (Italy), 1969; José Vasconcelos Gold Medal (Mexico), 1974; Moinho Santista Prize, 1974. Awarded the KBE (Knight Commander, Order of the British Empire) in 1971 and Commander, Légion d'Honneur in 1986. Died 18 July 1987.

Selected Works

Novels and Short Fiction

Assombrações do Recife velho, Rio de Janeiro: Condé, 1955
Dona Sinhá e o filho padre, Rio de Janeiro: José Olympio, 1964; as *Mother and Son*, translated by Barbara Shelby, New York: Knopf, 1967
O outro amor do Dr Paulo, Rio de Janeiro: José Olympio, 1977

Poetry

Talvez poesia, Rio de Janeiro: José Olympio, 1962
Gilberto poeta: algumas confissões, Recife: Ranulpho, 1980
Poesia reunida, Recife: Pirata, 1980

Sociological and Other Academic Works

Casa grande e senzala, Rio de Janeiro: Maia and Schmidt, 1933; revised edition, 2 vols, Rio de Janeiro: José Olympio, 1943; as *The Masters and the Slaves: a Study in the Development of Brazilian Civilization*, translated by Samuel Putnam, New York: Knopf, 1946; London: Secker and Warburg, 1947
Guia prático, histórico e sentimental da cidade da Recife, Recife: privately printed, 1934; revised editions, Rio de Janeiro: José Olympio, 1942, 1961, 1968
Artigos de jornal, Recife: Casa Mozart, 1935
Sobrados e mucambos, São Paulo: Nacional, 1936; as *The Mansions and the Shanties: the Making of Modern Brazil*, translated by Harriet de Onís, New York: Knopf, 1963

Mucambos do nordeste, Rio de Janeiro: Servico do Patrimônio Histórico e Artístico Nacional, 1937
Nordeste, Rio de Janeiro: José Olympio, 1937
Olinda: 2° guia prático, histórico, e sentimental de cidade brasileira, Rio de Janeiro: José Olympio, 1939
Açúcar, Rio de Janeiro: José Olympio, 1939
Um engenheiro francês no Brazil, Rio de Janeiro: José Olympio, 1940; revised 2nd edition, 2 vols, 1960
O mundo que o português criou, Rio de Janeiro: José Olympio, 1940
Região e tradição, Rio de Janeiro: José Olympio, 1941
Uma cultura ameaçada, Rio de Janeiro: Casa do Estudante do Brasil, 1942
Ingleses, Rio de Janeiro: José Olympio, 1942
Problemas brasileiros de antropologia, Rio de Janeiro: Casa do Estudante do Brazil, 1943; revised edition: Rio de Janeiro: José Olympio, 1954
Na Bahia em 1943, Rio de Janeiro: Artes Gráficas, 1944
Perfil de Euclides e outros perfis, Rio de Janeiro: José Olympio, 1944
Sociologia, 2 vols, Rio de Janeiro: José Olympio, 1945
Brazil: an Introduction, New York: Knopf, 1945; revised edition as *New World in the Tropics: the Culture of Modern Brazil*, 1959 [written in English]
Quase política, Rio de Janeiro: José Olympio, 1950; revised edition, 1966
Aventura e rotina, Rio de Janeiro: José Olympio, 1953
Um brasileiro em terras portuguesas, Rio de Janeiro: José Olympio, 1953
Sugestões para uma nova política no Brasil: a rurbana, Recife: Secretário de Educação e Cultura, 1956
Integração portuguesa nos trópicos, Lisbon: Ministério do Ultramar, 1958; as *Portuguese Integration in the Tropics*, translated anonymously, Lisbon: Silvas, 1961
A propósito de frades, Salvador: Universidade da Bahia, 1959
A propósito de Morão, Rosa e Pimenta, Recife: Estadual, 1959
Ordem e progresso, 2 vols, Rio de Janeiro: José Olympio, 1959; as *Order and Progress: Brazil from Monarchy to Republic*, edited and translated by Rod W. Horton, New York: Knopf, 1970; London: Secker and Warburg, 1972
Brasis, Brasil, e Brasília, Lisbon, 1960; revised edition, Rio de Janeiro: Record, 1968
O Luso e o trópico, Lisbon: Committee for the Commemoration of the Vth Centenary of the Death of Prince Henry the Navigator, 1961
Vida, forma, e cor, Rio de Janeiro: José Olympio, 1962
Homen, cultura, e trópico, Recife: Imprensa Universitária, 1962
O escravo nos anúncios de jornais brasileiros do século XIX, Recife: Universidade Federal de Pernambuco, 1963; revised edition, São Paulo: Nacional, 1979
Retalhos de jornais velhos, Rio de Janeiro: José Olympio, 1964
O Recife, sim! Recife, não!, São Paulo: Arquimedes, 1967
Sociologia da medicina, Lisbon: Fundação Gulbenkian, 1967
Como e porque sou e não sou sociólogo, Brasília: Editora Universidade de Brasília, 1968
Contribuição para uma sociologia da biografia, 2 vols, Lisbon: Academia Internacional da Cultura Portuguesa, 1968
Oliveira Lima, Don Quixote gordo, Recife: Universidade Federal de Pernambuco, 1968
A casa brasileira, Rio de Janeiro: Grifo, 1971
Nós e a Europa germânica, Rio de Janeiro: Grifo, 1971
Além do apenas moderno, Rio de Janeiro: José Olympio, 1973
A presença do açúcar na formação brasileira, Rio de Janeiro: M.I.C., 1975
O brasileiro entre os outros hispanos, Rio de Janeiro: José Olympio, 1975
Tempo morto e outros tempos: trechos de um diário de adolescência e primeira mocidade 1915–1930, Rio de Janeiro: José Olympio, 1978

Alhos & bugalhos, Rio de Janeiro: Nova Fronteira, 1978
Heróis e vilões no romance brasileiro, São Paulo: Cultrix, 1979
Oh de casa! Recife: Instituto Joaquim Nabuco de Pesquisas Sociasis, 1979
Arte, ciência, e trópico, São Paulo: Martins, 1980
Pessoas, coisas e animais, Rio de Janeiro: Globo, 1981
Insurgências e ressurgências atuais: cruzamentos de sins e nãos num mundo em transicão, Rio de Janeiro: Globo, 1983
Médicos, doentes e contextos sociais, Rio de Janeiro: Globo, 1983

Compilations and Anthologies
Obras reunidas, 12 vols, Rio de Janeiro: José Olympio, 1959–66
Selta para jovens de Gilberto Freyre, 1971; as *The Gilberto Freyre Reader*, translated by Barbara Shelby, New York; Knopf, 1974
A condição humana e outros temas, edited by Maria Elisa Dias Collier, Rio de Janeiro: José Olympio, 1972
Cartas do próprio punho sobre pessoas e coisas do Brasil e do estrangeiro, edited by Sylvio Rabello, Rio de Janeiro: Conselho Federal de Cultura, 1978
Prefácios desgarrados, edited by Edson Nery da Fonseca, 2 vols, Rio de Janeiro: Cátedra, 1978
Tempo de aprendiz, edited by José Antônio Gonsalves de Mello, São Paulo: Ibrasa, 1979 [articles]

Further Reading

Barros, Homero do Rego, *Gilberto Freyre, agora e sempre*, Recife: Fundação Joaquin Nabuco, 1987
Chacon, Vamirech, *Gilberto Freyre: uma biografia intelectual*, Recife: Fundação Joaquim Nabuco, 1993
Claudina, Assis, *O monstro sagrado e o amorelinho comunista: Gliberto Freyre, Dom Helder e a revolução de 64*, Recife: Opcão, 1985
Coutinho, Edilberto, *A imaginação do real: uma leitura da ficção de Gilberto Freyre*, Rio de Janeiro: José Olympio, 1983
D'Andrea, Moema Selma, *A tradição re(des)coberta; o pensamento de Gilberto Freyre no contexto das manifestações culturais e/ou literárias nordestinas*, Campinas: Unicamp, 1993
Loos, Dorothy Scott, "Gilberto Freyre as a Literary Figure: an Introductory Study," *Revista Hispánica Moderna* 32 (1968)
Matos, Potiguar, *Gilberto Freyre: presença definitiva*, Recife: Fundação Gilberto Freyre, 1988
Mazzara, Richard A., "Gilberto Freyre and José Honório Rodrigues: Old and New Horizons for Brazil," *Hispania* (May 1964)
Menezes, Diogo de Melo, *Gilberto Freyre*, Rio de Janeiro: C.E.B., 1944
Pereira, Nilo, *Gilberto Freyre visto de perto*, Recife: Fundação Joaquim Nabuco, 1986

Casa grande e senzala

A social history of northeast Brazil by Gilberto Freyre

The major work of Gilberto Freyre, *Casa grande e senzala*, published in 1933, launched a new phase in the study of Brazil's social history. Armed with new anthropological theories obtained whilst studying abroad, Freyre reanalysed Brazil's social and cultural formation. In the process he challenged existing negative interpretations of national identity, and presented an alternative view of a unique society in which miscegenation had produced a distinct, and favourable, Brazilian national character. Such was the impact of the work, and the acclaim which it received, that it was many decades

before it was seriously challenged by critics, but eventually many would argue that the book idealized Brazil's social development, and thereby concealed many of the conflicts and contradictions that it had generated.

The ideology of racial determinism still played an influential role in Brazilian intellectual life in the early decades of the 20th century. It appeared to prove scientifically the inevitability of the superiority of some races – and by extension some nations – over others. The racist dogma asserted that miscegenation weakened all races, but especially the white race, and led to degeneration. The logical conclusion was that the inferiority of the Brazilian *mestiço* would condemn the nation to perpetual underdevelopment. The theory was assimilated by many Brazilian scholars and writers, and engendered a pervasive pessimism with regard to the country's future. *Casa grande e senzala* played a significant part in breaking such assumptions. Through his detailed study of the nation's social history, Freyre argued that Brazil had benefited considerably from the distinctive contributions of the three formative races – Amerindian, Portuguese and African – and the resultant culture was dynamic and full of positive potential. It was this optimistic interpretation, involving the rejection of any notion of the inferiority of certain races on the one hand, and the appreciation of the contribution of the previously denigrated negro on the other, that led to the book being hailed as innovative, and even radical, in the 1930s, when fascist doctrine was rife. Central to Freyre's thesis was the work of the anthropologist Franz Boas, under whom he studied in the United States. Boas argued that the differences between peoples were not to be explained by innate racial characteristics, but rather by cultural factors. Perhaps the major contribution of *Casa grande e senzala* to Brazilian social history was that it consolidated the shift to culture as the centre of analysis, rather than race, highlighting the role of cultural rather than racial syncretism.

Unlike Boas, however, Freyre ascribed to all human groups certain psychological traits, which he saw as resulting from the interaction between race and environment. As a result, he conceived national identity, which he did not distinguish from race, to be formed essentially by psychological characteristics, which, though scientifically unverifiable, could be identified by intuition. The result is a highly subjective interpretation of Brazil's cultural development, around which Freyre moulds his documentary evidence, undermining its objective value in the process. The high degree of subjectivity evident in *Casa grande e senzala* has been one of the most controversial aspects of the work. Although some critics have argued that it gives the work power and individuality, and produces a successful fusion of scholarly research and creative literature, others have demonstrated how it leads to significant distortions in Freyre's interpretation, and results in the idealization of the social experience of the poor and oppressed sectors of Brazilian society.

Freyre's assertion that the cultural behaviour of the Brazilian is largely determined by psychological qualities, rather than by socio-economic realities, permitted him to mask questions of class divisions in Brazil. *Casa grande e senzala* reinforces the mythology of an all inclusive national culture. The theme of a common psyche, developing through the process of miscegenation, to unify the race, and hence the nation, is repeated throughout the work. For Freyre, the basic psychological unity has been reinforced by certain objective factors that have further contributed to cultural homogeneity, namely the Catholic Church and the patriarchal family. It is this overall vision of unity, the harmonious formation of a national culture, that enabled Freyre to universalize his interpretation of Brazilian development, and present it, not as the perception that one particular social class has of its own history, but as an objective study of the Brazilian population as a whole. However, Freyre's ideological approach can clearly be traced to his roots in the old, plantation owning aristocracy of northeast Brazil, a class being edged from power by new social forces. That provides the key for another interpretation of *Casa grande e senzala*: that it represents a reaction to the decline of Freyre's own social class, and an attempt to redeem it through a favourable interpretation of Brazil's social history. It is in this context that the work gives such prominence to the role of the traditional rural oligarchy in the process of national development. Freyre saw the old patriarchal regime, based on slave labour, as having been an essentially positive force in Brazil's socio-economic history, laying down the foundation for national identity and the development of a unique racial democracy by creating an atmosphere that encouraged miscegenation rather than racial segregation. It was in the patterns of life which centred on the *casa grande*, Freyre argued, that the most authentic expression of Brazilian national character was to be found. The contribution of the rural elites is thereby projected into the future, linking them positively to the modernizing capitalist development that, by the 1930s, was reshaping the social and economic structures of the nation. Historical evidence that is incompatible with this vision of harmonious social evolution, such as social uprisings, class antagonism and the brutality of the slave system, is either ignored or incorporated into the work in an appropriately attenuated form.

The focus of *Casa grande e senzala* is very much the Brazilian northeast. However, Freyre could not isolate himself from national political realities, particularly with the process of centralization of economic and political power in the centre-south of Brazil exposing ever more clearly the decline and dependence of the northeast. Ultimately, Freyre has to express

himself within a national context, and deal with the issue of national culture. Freyre, however, is unable to reach any real understanding of the process of articulation between the regional and the national, and tends simply to extend his conclusions on the northeast to the national level. In the preface to one edition of the work, he states that the observations he made in other regions of Brazil confirmed his findings on the northeast. That position inevitably results in contradictions. He argues at one point that different regions produce different psychological types, but still seeks to define the typical national character. Ideological restrictions hindered him from understanding the significance of northeastern socio-economic development within a more global context, and his vision remained essentially parochial.

Casa grande e senzala presents an extremely detailed examination of life in the rural northeast, which gives new prominence to a wide range of cultural traditions, from practices of child rearing, to clothing, to cooking. More significantly, it emphasises the relationship between social classes, and recognizes the role that each has played in Brazilian history. It therefore offered a broader perspective of the nation's cultural development than had hitherto been available. However, the theoretical limitations of the work, and contradictions in the methods applied, make it extremely problematical. For some critics, its main value resides in its literary merits, rather than in what it offers in terms of social and cultural analysis.

MARK DINNEEN

Editions

First edition: *Casa grande e senzala*, Rio de Janeiro: Maia and Schmidt, 1933
Translation: *The Master and the Slaves: a Study in the Development of Brazilian Civilization*, by Samuel Putnam, New York: Knopf, 1946; London: Secker and Warburg, 1947

Further Reading

Marques, Ruy João, *Casa grande e senzala: Gilberto Freyre e medicina*, Recife: Pernambuco, 1983
Medeiros, Maria Alice de Aguiar, *O elogio da dominação: relendo "Casa grande e senzala,"* Rio de Janeiro: Achiame, 1984

Carlos Fuentes 1928–

Mexican prose writer

Together with Juan Rulfo, Carlos Fuentes is the most important prose writer in 20th-century Mexico. Since the short stories of *Los días enmascarados* [The Masked Days], he has published twenty novels and collections of shorter fiction, as well as essays and plays. While his writing is often intensely Mexican in diction and theme, it is also characterized by a distinct cosmopolitanism both in its literary modernity and in its awareness of the relation between cultures. Mexican

identity is often seen to be forged as a dialogue with other very different cultures, such as those of England, Spain, France and the US. *Gringo viejo* (*The Old Gringo*), for example, plays with the Hollywood vision of the Mexican Revolution (1910–17) and with the clichéd Mexican view of puritanical North American protestantism. *Cumpleaños* [Birthday] is set in London, while *Una familia lejana* (*Distant Relations*) presents a hypothetical Carlos Fuentes who has settled in France and writes in a gallicized, Proustian fashion. In the vast *Terra Nostra* it is the whole history and literature of Golden Age Spain which is seen as the living memory and hence future of Spanish America.

His first novel was *La región más transparente* (*Where the Air is Clear*), a brilliant and complex evocation of the Mexico City of the 1940s and 1950s as the aggressive capitalism of the Ávila Camacho and Miguel Alemán regimes displaced the idealistic rhetoric of the post-revolutionary period. It makes ample use of the Anglo-American Modernism of Dos Passos, Lawrence and Faulkner to orchestrate a symphony of strikingly Mexican voices from all the social strata of the city. A further force in this novel is the shaping presence of Ancient Mexican mythology. He returns to the theme of Mexico City in the novellas of *Agua quemada* (*Burnt Water*) and at much greater length in his 1987 novel *Cristóbal nonato* (*Christopher Unborn*), a grotesque, bitterly satirical vision of post-earthquake (1984) Mexico projected onto a 1992, where much of the national territory had been lost, sold or invaded, and where the Spanish language itself is bursting at the seams with Anglicisms. The whole is saved by a nostalgic affection for Mexico and a fiercely inventive prose style.

Perhaps Fuentes's best-known novel, *La muerte de Artemio Cruz* (*The Death of Artemio Cruz*) is a successful work which traces the path of a series of patriarchs and their families through Mexican history since Independence. The narration is separated into three alternating voices in the past, present and future, tenses, which gives an ambiguous and plural perspective on the career of Artemio Cruz, from bastard son of a Veracruz landowner through the Revolution to immense wealth and power as a tyrannical and corrupt business magnate. In many of his works the dilemmas of identity and freedom are played out in the arena of the family and over various generations, often involving complex questions of inherited memory and intricate doublings over time. In the same year as *La muerte de Artemio Cruz*, the novella *Aura* uses a haunting second-person narration to explore similar questions in a decidedly gothic or fantastic manner. A young historian, Felipe Montero, stays at the house of a very old lady, reminiscent of the old Empress Carlota of Mexico, in order to edit the memoirs of her husband, a general of Emperor Maximilian. The historian is seduced by the beautiful young Aura, who turns out to be a magical projection of the old witch Consuelo, and Felipe comes more and more to reincarnate the dead general. The whole question of literary genealogy, the rewriting of previous texts and traditions and the relation with the literary predecessor is metaphorically played out in such games.

In the late 1960s, Fuentes seemed to move in a rather different direction with a couple of novels, *Cambio de piel* (*A Change of Skin*) and *Zona sagrada* (*Holy Place*), which are far more carnivalesque, irreverent and mockingly self-referential than anything before. And yet they combine this style with an often harrowing exploration of evil and violence throughout history and latent in every individual. In the first of these novels, the disquieting reversals, narrative inconsistencies and jarring combinations of style tend to deprive the reader of any stable position from which to view and judge. The authority of the author and reader is dramatized in the novel in scenes where an authoritarian ego figure is seen to enclose, annihilate or disqualify by turning into spectacle anything radically different or "other" which may threaten it. Women are seen as witches; the Jews enclosed in Treblinka are made to sing; the Mexican working class are reduced to picturesque mariachis; madness and violence becomes a spectacle to reassure the viewer of his own normality. *Zona sagrada* is an agile novelized version of the relation between the Mexican actress María Félix and her son. Here the conventional order is associated with the structures of Greek myth, to be mocked, reversed and fragmented by a narrative characterized by transformation, modern ritual and amusing juxtapositions of high and low culture.

Terra Nostra must surely be one of the most ambitious fictional enterprises in the Spanish language. It ranges from the Roman Empire at the time of Christ, Counter Reformation Spain, a mythical account of the Conquest of Mexico, guerrilla warfare in Veracruz, to an apocalyptic view of Paris in 1999. Principally, however, it is set in the severe, enclosing architecture of the monastery-palace of El Escorial, where King Felipe, an amalgam of various monarchs but strongly reminiscent of Felipe II, pits his notion of a unity of race and belief against a world which refuses to be still and unambiguous. Against the architecture of the monastery is set the dizzying combinations of the texts presenting the figures of Celestina, don Juan and don Quijote, while an inextricable web of narrators disallows any sense of centredness and stability.

Following this *tour de force* of erudition and stamina, Fuentes produced a spy thriller, *La cabeza de la hidra* (*The Hydra Head*), an amusing and exciting, lightly parodic novel about rival Arab and Israeli interests in Mexico's oil reserves. The intricate doubling and twinning of the thriller plot become something altogether more high literature in the labyrinthine layering of identity and intentionality in the next novel, *Una familia lejana*. A Faustian pact to recover the past generates a maze-like quest over generations and between Mexico and France in which the plot reflects fragments of texts by a series of French writers, often of Spanish American origin, such as Supervielle.

Some of Fuentes's more recent fiction has been realist in a more conventional but never naive manner. The four, loosely linked novellas of *Agua quemada* depict adolescents facing the future in four different areas and distinct social classes within Mexico City. Their semi-autonomous status within the collection reflects a fragmented society, held together mainly through the exercise of violence passed from one generation to another. *La campaña* (*The Campaign*) is the first novel of a planned trilogy on Continental Spanish American history, and follows the Independence movement through the adventures and travels of the protean Baltasar Bustos. There is a constantly ironic confrontation in the novel between the texts of the French Enlightenment which helped to inspire the movement and the complex racial and social realities which resist being interpreted through their prism. Other works, such as the shorter fiction of *El naranjo o los círculos del tiempo* (*The Orange Tree*) or *Constancia y otras novelas para vírgenes* (*Constancia and Other Stories for Virgins*), and especially the latter, parade their artifice in a much more openly postmodern way, with a vigorous often grotesque humour which combines memorably with a sense of tragedy, loss and exile.

Over the last twenty years or so, Fuentes has steadily published some major collections of essays. *La nueva novela hispanoamericana* [The New Spanish American Novel] is one of the clearest expositions of the concerns and interests of the novelists of the so-called Boom of literature in the late 1960s. *Cervantes o la crítica de la lectura* (*Don Quixote, or the Critique of Reading*) offers excellent insights into the writing of *Terra Nostra*, together with its bibliography, while *Geografía de la novela* [Geography of the Novel] situates Spanish American culture within a new decentred and plural cultural world.

STEVEN BOLDY

Biography
Born in Panama City, 11 November 1928. As a child lived in the United States, Chile, and Argentina; returned to Mexico at age 16. Attended Colegio Francisco Morelos; Universidad Nacional Autónoma de México (UNAM), Mexico City, LL.B. 1948; Institut des Hautes Études Internationales, Geneva. Member, then Secretary, Mexican delegation, International Labor Organization, Geneva, 1950–52; assistant chief of press section, Ministry of Foreign Affairs, Mexico City, 1954; press secretary, United Nations Information Center, Mexico City, 1954; secretary, then assistant director of cultural department, UNAM, 1955–56; Head of Department of Cultural Relations, Ministry of Foreign Affairs, 1957–59. Married the film star Rita Macedo in 1959 (divorced in 1966), one daughter. Married Sylvia Lemus in 1973, one son and one daughter. Mexican Ambassador to France, 1974–77. Fellow, Woodrow Wilson International Center for Scholars, 1974; Virginia Gildersleeve Visiting Professor, Barnard College, New York, 1977; Norman Maccoll Lecturer, 1977, and Henry L. Tinker Lecturer, Columbia University, New York, 1978. Professor of English, University of Pennsylvania, Philadelphia, 1978–83; Fellow of the Humanities, Princeton University, New Jersey; Professor of comparative literature, 1984–86; Bolívar Professor, Cambridge University, 1986–87; Robert F. Kennedy Professor of Latin American studies, since 1987, Harvard University, Cambridge, Massachusetts. Editor, *Revista Mexicana de Literatura*, 1954–58, *El Espectador*, 1959–61, *Siempre*, from 1960, and *Política*, from 1960. President, Modern Humanities Research Association, since 1989. Recipient of numerous awards including: Mexican Writers' Center Fellowship, 1956; Biblioteca Breve Prize, 1967; Xavier Villaurrutia Prize, 1975; Rómulos Gallegos Prize (Venezuela), 1977; Alfonso Reyes Prize, 1979; Mexican National Award for Literature, 1984; Miguel de Cervantes Prize, 1987; Rubén Darío Prize, 1988; Instituto Italo-Latino Americano Prize, 1988; New York City National Arts Club Medal of Honor, 1988; Order of Cultural Independence (Nicaragua), 1988. Member, El Colegio Nacional, since 1974; American Academy and Institute of Arts and Letters, 1986.

Selected Works

Novels
La región más transparente, Mexico City: Fondo de Cultura Económica, 1958; as *Where the Air is Clear*, translated by Sam Hileman, New York: Farrar Straus and Giroux, 1960; London: André Deutsch, 1986

Las buenas conciencias, Mexico City: Fondo de Cultura Económica, 1959; as *The Good Conscience*, translated Sam Hileman, New York: Noonday Press, and London: André Deutsch, 1961

La muerte de Artemio Cruz, Mexico City: Fondo de Cultura Económica, 1962; as *The Death of Artemio Cruz*, translated by Sam Hileman, New York: Noonday Press, and London: Collins, 1964; also translated by Alfred MacAdam, New York: Farrar Straus and Giroux, 1991

Aura, Mexico City: Era, 1962; as *Aura*, translated by Lysander Kemp, New York: Farrar Straus and Giroux, 1965; London: André Deutsch, 1990

Zona sagrada, Mexico City: Siglo XXI, 1967; as *Holy Place*, translated by Suzanne Jill Levine, in *Triple Cross*, New York: Dutton, 1972

Cambio de piel, Mexico City: Joaquín Mortiz, 1967; as *A Change of Skin*, translated by Sam Hileman, New York: Farrar Straus and Giroux, and London: Jonathan Cape, 1968

Cumpleaños, Mexico City: Joaquín Mortiz, 1969

Terra Nostra, Barcelona: Seix Barral, 1975; as *Terra Nostra*, translated by Margaret Sayers Peden, New York: Farrar Straus and Giroux, 1976; London: Secker and Warburg, 1977

La cabeza de la hidra, Mexico City: Joaquín Mortiz, 1978; as *The Hydra Head*, translated by Margaret Sayers Peden, New York: Farrar Straus and Giroux, 1978; London: Secker and Warburg, 1979

Una familia lejana, Mexico City: Era, 1980; as *Distant Relations*, translated by Margaret Sayers Peden, New York: Farrar Straus and Giroux, and London: Secker and Warburg, 1982

Gringo viejo, Mexico City: Fondo de Cultura Económica, 1985; as *The Old Gringo*, translated by Margaret Sayers Peden, New York: Farrar Straus and Giroux, 1985; London: André Deutsch, 1986

Cristóbal nonato, Mexico City: Fondo de Cultura Económica, 1987; as *Christopher Unborn*, translated by the author and Alfred MacAdam, New York: Farrar Straus and Giroux, and London: André Deutsch, 1989

La campaña, Madrid: Mondadori, 1990; as *The Campaign*, translated by Alfred MacAdam, New York: Farrar Straus and Giroux, and London: André Deutsch, 1991

Diana, o la cazadora solitaria, Mexico City: Alfaguara, 1994; as *Diana, the Goddess Who Hunts Alone*, translated by Alfred MacAdam, New York: Farrar Straus and Giroux, 1995; retitled as *Diana, the Lonely Huntress*, London: Bloomsbury, 1995

La frontera de cristal: una novela en nueve cuentos, Mexico City: Alfaguara, 1995

Short Fiction
Los días enmascarados, Mexico City: Los Presentes, 1954

Cantar de ciegos, Mexico City: Joaquín Mortiz, 1964

Chac Mool y otros cuentos, Estella: Salvat, 1973

Agua quemada, Mexico City: Fondo de Cultura Económica, 1981; as *Burnt Water*, translated by Margaret Sayers Peden, New York: Farrar Straus and Giroux, 1980; London: Secker and Warburg, 1981

Constancia, y otras novelas para vírgenes, Madrid: Mondadori, 1989; as *Constancia and Other Stories for Virgins*, translated by Thomas Christensen, New York: Farrar Straus and Giroux, and London: André Deutsch, 1990

El naranjo o los círculos del tiempo, Mexico City: Alfaguara, 1993; as *The Orange Tree*, translated by Alfred MacAdam, New York: Farrar Straus and Giroux, and London: André Deutsch, 1994

Plays
Todos los gatos son pardos, Mexico City: Siglo XXI, 1970

El tuerto es rey, Mexico City: Joaquín Mortiz, 1970

Los reinos originarios, Barcelona: Seix Barral, 1971 [includes *Todos los gatos son pardos* and *El tuerto es rey*]

Orquídeas a la luz de la luna, Barcelona, Seix Barral, 1982; as *Orchids in the Moonlight*, translated by the author, in *Drama Contemporary: Latin America*, edited by George W. Woodyard and Marion Peter Holt, 1986

Ceremonias del alba, Mexico City: Siglo XXI, 1991 [new version of *Todos los gatos*]

Poetry
Poemas de amor: cuentos del alma, Madrid: Cruces, 1971

Essays and Other Writings

The Argument of Latin America: Words for North Americans, n.p: Radical Education Project, 1963

Paris: la revolución de Mayo, Mexico City: Era, 1968

La nueva novela hispanoamericana, Mexico City: Joaquín Mortiz, 1969

El mundo de José Luis Cuevas, Mexico City: Tudor, 1969

Casa con dos puertas, Mexico City: Joaquín Mortiz, 1970

Tiempo mexicano, Mexico City: Joaquín Mortiz, 1971

Cuerpos y ofrendas, Madrid: Alianza, 1972

Cervantes o la crítica de la lectura, Mexico City: Joaquín Mortiz, 1976; as *Don Quixote or, the Critique of Reading*, translated anonymously, Austin: University of Texas Institute of Latin American Studies, 1976

High Noon in Latin America, Los Angeles: Manas, 1983

Juan Soriano y su obra, in collaboration with Teresa del Conde, Mexico City: Institute of Fine Arts, 1984

On Human Rights: a Speech, Dallas: Somesuch Press, 1984

Latin America: At War with the Past, Montreal: CBC Enterprises, 1985

Palacio Nacional, in collaboration with Guillermo Tovar y de Teresa, Mexico City: Presidencia de la República, Dirección General de Comunición Social, 1986

Gabriel García Márquez and the Invention of America, Liverpool: Liverpool University Press, 1987 [lecture]

Valiente mundo nuevo, épica, utopía y mito en la novela hispanoamericana, Madrid: Mondadori España, 1990

The Buried Mirror: Reflections on Spain and the New World, Boston: Houghton Mifflin, and London: André Deutsch, 1992

Return to Mexico: Journeys Behind the Mask, photographs by Abbas, New York: Norton, 1992

El espejo enterrado, Mexico City: Fondo de Cultura Económica, 1992

Geografía de la novela, Mexico City: Fondo de Cultura Económica, 1993

Tres discursos para dos aldeas, Buenos Aires: Fondo de Cultura Económica, 1993

Nuevo tiempo mexicano, Mexico City: Aguillar, 1994; as *A New Time for Mexico*, translated by the author and Marina Gutman Castaneda, New York: Farrar Straus and Giroux, 1996

Compilations and Anthologies

Selected Literary Essays, New York: Farrar Straus and Giroux, 1986

Myself with Others: Selected Essays, New York: Farrar Straus and Giroux, and London: André Deutsch, 1988

Further Reading

Befumo Boschi, Liliana and Elisa Calabrese, *Nostalgia del futuro en la obra de Carlos Fuentes*, Buenos Aires: García Cambeiro, 1974

Boldy, Stephen, "Carlos Fuentes," in *Modern Latin American Fiction: a Survey*, edited by John King, London: Faber and Faber, 1987

Brody, Robert and Charles Rossman (editors), *Carlos Fuentes: a Critical View*, Austin: University of Texas Press, 1982

Durán, Gloria, *La mágia y las brujas en la obra de Carlos Fuentes*, 1976; translated as *The Archetypes of Carlos Fuentes: from Witch to Androgyne*, Hamden, Connecticut: Shoestring Press, 1980

Durán, Víctor Manuel, *A Marxist Reading of Fuentes, Vargas Llosa, and Puig*, Lanham, Maryland: University Press of America, 1993

Faris, Wendy, *Carlos Fuentes*, New York: Ungar, 1983

Feijoo, Gladys, *Lo fantástico en los relatos de Carlos Fuentes*, New York: Senda Nueva de Ediciones, 1985

[Carlos Fuentes] *Carlos Fuentes. Premio "Miguel de Cervantes" 1987*, Barcelona: Anthropos/Ministerio de Cultura, 1988

García Gutiérrez, Georgina, *Los disfraces: la obra mestiza de Carlos Fuentes*, Mexico City: Colegio de México, 1981

García Núñez, Fernando, *Fabulación de la fe: Carlos Fuentes*, Xalapa, Mexico: Universidad Veracruzana, 1989

Giacoman, Helmy F. (editor), *Homenaje a Carlos Fuentes: variaciones interpretativas en torno a su obra*, New York: Las Américas, 1971

González, Alfonso, *Carlos Fuentes: Life, Work, and Criticism*, Fredericton, New Brunswick: York Press, 1987

Gyurko, Lanin, "Carlos Fuentes," in *Dictionary of Literary Biography: Modern Latin American Fiction Writers*, vol. 113, edited by William Luis, Detroit: Gale Research, 1992

Hernández de López, Ana María, *La obra de Carlos Fuentes: una visión múltiple*, Madrid: Pliegos, 1988

Ibsen, Kristine, *Author, Text and Reader in the Novels of Carlos Fuentes*, New York: Peter Lang, 1993

Ordiz, Francisco Javier, *El mito en la obra narrativa de Carlos Fuentes*, León: Universidad de León, 1987

Ramírez Mattei, Aida Elsa, *La narrativa de Carlos Fuentes*, Río Piedras, Puerto Rico: Universidad de Puerto Rico, 1983

Simson, Ingrid, *Realidad y ficción en Terra Nostra de Carlos Fuentes*, Frankfurt: Vervuert Verlag, 1989

Velarde, Agustín, *Carlos Fuentes y "Las buenas conciencias"*, Mexico City: Buena Prensa, 1962

Zamora, Lois Parkinson, *Writing the Apocalypse: Historical Vision in Contemporary U.S. and Latin American Fiction*, Cambridge and New York: Cambridge University Press, 1988 [Contains chapter on *Terra Nostra*]

Bibliographies

Dunn, Sandra L., "Carlos Fuentes: a Bibliography," *Review of Contemporary Fiction*, vol. 8 (1988)

Foster, David William, *Mexican Literature: a Bibliography of Secondary Sources*, Metuchen, New Jersey: Scarecrow Press, 1992

Interviews

King, John, "Carlos Fuentes: an Interview," in his *Modern Latin American Fiction: a Survey*, London: Faber and Faber, 1987

Special Issues of Journals

World Literature Today, vol. 57/4 (1983)

Agua quemada

Collection of novellas by Carlos Fuentes

The title of Fuentes's 1981 collection of four novellas, *Agua quemada*, refers us to Mexico City, and indeed it is one of three of his works dedicated to that city, together with *La región más transparente*, 1958 (*Where the Air is Clear*) and *Cristóbal Nonato*, 1987 (*Christopher Unborn*). One of the two epigraphs of the work indicates that the title comes from a poem by Octavio Paz, which talks of violence and alienation, and goes on to say "se rompió el signo" (the sign was broken) alluding to a fracturing of language. The other epigraph, from Alfonso Reyes, nostalgically asks " Is this 'la región más transparente del aire' (the place where the air is clearest). What have you done, then, with my high metaphysical valley?" The quotation links the collection directly to the earlier novel, and suggests a sense of loss. Whereas the first novel's reference to von Humboldt's description of the crystal-clear air of the city is somewhat ironic in the bustling metropolis of the 1950s with three million inhabitants, it is positively sarcastic for the smog-filled and traffic-congested city of eight million when the stories were set at the end of the 1960s, and even more so for the twenty million plus megapolis of the late 20th century.

The epigraphs underline the subterranean continuity of Fuentes's work but also the change in his country. At the end of *La región*, an important scene of recognition brings together a large number of characters from this sprawling novel into an overall pattern of coherence. At the end of the final story of *Agua quemada*, Bernabé Aparicio sees his long-lost father in a cemetery, and chooses not to speak to him, musing: "Let him not come back. A vague memory, a not knowing is enough." This loss and separation is reflected in the "narrative quartet" form chosen here in preference to the totalizing form of the novel. In fact three of his recent works have consisted of collections of short stories or novellas, linked internally by formal patterns and by often ironic parallels which mockingly ape a lost unity rather than unify. Whereas, however, the 1989 *Constancia* is a positively postmodern affirmation of a decentralized world, the tone of *Agua quemada* is altogether more elegiac.

Each of the four stories explores a family drama in a different, carefully mapped out area of Mexico City. In "El día de las madres" (Mother's Day), the Vergara family came from a career in the Revolution and later administrations to farming and eventually to drug producing, and live in a mansion in the elite Lomas de Chapultepec. In "Estos fueron los palacios" (These Were the Palaces), the family of Luis has come down from an opulent background in Veracruz State to bureaucratic drudgery and a downtown *vecindad*, or tenement. In "Las mañanitas" (Sunny Mornings), Federico Silva, the last member of a long-established semi-aristocratic family, lives in a traditional mansion in Colonia Roma hedged in by skyscrapers. In "El hijo de Andrés Aparicio" (The Son of . . .) the Aparicio family have been forced from their previous decent home to a shack in a shanty town on the dusty outskirts. The links between the families are documented in detail – two characters work in a petrol station owned by another; a character in one story used to be the maid of a family from another, etc. – but are so flimsy and so quickly disappearing as to point to dispersal rather than to any real community.

What does link the stories and families is the same thing which separates and fragments them: violence of various sorts. The unspoken political backroun to the collection is the massacre of many students by the authorities in Tlatelolco before the Olympic Games in 1968, which both went unpunished and was repeated on a smaller scale in 1971, an incident which is portrayed in "El hijo de Andrés Aparicio." In each of the stories an adolescent or youth strives to affirm his freedom within a complex pattern of family inheritance and determinism. In the first Plutarco wishes to outdo his businessman father by emulating his grandfather, who was a hero of the Revolution. His final attempted act of liberation, when he humiliates a prostitute by having sex with her in front of a band of mariachis in full tune, simply confirms a pattern by repeating his father and grandfather's earlier murder of his mother. Silva, in the third story, tries to avoid both children and the working classes in the street only to be murdered by his symbolic children, the hippies, when he insults their mother. The violence takes on its full political dimension in the final story when the youth from the shantytown ends up as a murderous fascist thug in the paramilitary group of the man who had been the life-long enemy of his father, a left-wing agrarian engineer.

STEVEN BOLDY

Editions

First edition: *Agua quemada,* Mexico City: Fondo de Cultura Económica, 1981
Critical edition: edited by Steven Boldy, Manchester: Manchester University Press, 1995
Translation: *Burnt Water*, by Margaret Sayers Peden, New York: Farrar Straus and Giroux, 1980; London: Secker and Warburg, 1981

Further Reading

Boling, Becky, "Parricide and Revolution: Fuentes's 'El día de las madres' and *Gringo viejo*," *Hispanófila*, vol. 32/95 (1989)
Fuentes, Sylvia, "Estos fueron los palacios," an interview with Carlos Fuentes, in *Espejo de escritores*, edited by Reina Roffé, Hanover, New Hampshire: Ediciones del Norte, 1985
García Gutiérrez, Georgina, "Post scriptum" in her edition of Carlos Fuentes, *La región más transparente*, Madrid, 1982 [The whole of her "Introducción," pp. 11–142, is most informative]
Van Delden, Maarten, "Carlos Fuentes' *Agua quemada*: the Nation as Unimaginable Community," *Latin American Literary Review*, vol. 21/42 (July–December 1993)

Aura

Novella by Carlos Fuentes

Sooner or later, everybody finds his or her "consolations" withered, the "aura" of hope fading, and some pages of life desiring to be revisited. Behind this age-old theme, Carlos Fuentes conjured a powerful artistic wizardry, a poetic vision, and a subtle art of narrative deception. His novella *Aura* has kept its readers spellbound since its publication in 1962.

Aura tells the story of a young historian, Felipe Montero, who stumbles on a lucrative advertisement for a private secretary which looks tailor-made for him. The next day, we find him reading the same ad and walking in the run-down old part of Mexico City, noting the confusion of street numbers accumulated from different periods. Felipe enters the dilapidated house on Donceles 815, "formerly 69," and is summoned, through dark corridors, to an old lady, who seems to know that he is coming. He must stay to edit and "complete" the memoirs of her late husband, General Llorente, who left Mexico after the collapse of the empire of the ill-fated Maximilian in 1867, and who died in exile in France sometime at the end of the 19th century, "sixty years ago."

Felipe notices a lot of strange things about the house. He becomes irresistibly attracted to the old woman's young niece Aura, a dream-like figure who appears to act mechanically or in strange synchrony with her aunt, Señora Consuelo. His work on the General's papers alternates with sensual thoughts and advances. At night, his nightmarish dream turns into Aura making love to him. The second day and night are full of rituals. Felipe is frightened by the strange behavior of both women as they sacrifice a he-goat; Felipe barricades himself in his room and dreams his second nightmare. That night he is invited to Aura's bedroom. First, he examines the plants in the patio and recalls old psychoactive recipes for which they may be used. Aura now looks like a woman in her forties, but Felipe is not surprised; not even when he finds Consuelo present at their lovemaking ritual. Next morning he has a weird feeling that he has engendered his own double; but, as is usual with him, he goes back to some routine and forgets. Aura appears willing to elope with him, but he baulks. She will wait for him in her aunt's bedroom. Reviewing the third batch of papers and photographs, Felipe realizes that Aura is the young Consuelo, and he is . . . General Llorente.

The first story only exists as a pretext for a second story, that of a startling self-discovery and a double "recovery." The dead General's memoirs appear as a part of this second story, leading Felipe towards his old identity. Historical, linear time, a lifetime, a century of time vanish into "bodiless dust." When he enters the house, Felipe steps into a time warp, a world where present and past, history and fiction, the self and the other implode. Some wish to see in this a return to the Mother, to the womb. Does reality melt into fantasy here, or does it leap into the fantastic? The first story just opens the Pandora's box of many other latent stories, depending on how the reader reads the story and its narrator-protagonist, Felipe Montero.

Criticism has celebrated *Aura* as a powerful love story: lovers, separated by death, are reunited; death and old age are exorcised. Yet, in the final scene, Felipe can embrace only his Aura turned Consuelo. The desired Aura is exhausted; Consuelo cannot keep her "alive" for more than three days. "Together" they will try to conjure back the fleeting aura of youth. The mismatch of the "lovers" could not be greater: under the romantic and *gothic* veil, *Aura* reveals a baroque and absurd face. Instead of the voluptuous 69 (the original number of the old house), the story ends with a kiss on the withered cheek.

One crucial strategic choice made by the author is the use of the "second person" narrative. This strikingly experimental technique has created considerable confusion. Who speaks to whom? Is Felipe the narrator? Is he the narratee? Is he a reliable whatever he might be? Is the text addressed to the reader? Like the seven blind men, critics have come up with all kinds of answers; some multiply possible speakers, others reduce everything to Consuelo's or Felipe's dream. Since the speaking "I" remains unveiled, besides Felipe, both General Llorente and Consuelo have been advanced for this "opening;" only Aura is sorely missing to complete the paradigm. There is no textual basis to cast General Llorente in this role; it would even contradict the stance he assumes in his memoirs regarding Consuelo's "experiments." Consuelo is, of course, the powerful *mover* behind the story; yet her powers seem limited: Aura ages fast; Felipe does not look or act like another aura of hers, and she needs to check his profile for its "fit." More importantly, narrative discourse does not impress as a *hypnotic*, manipulative discourse, but rather as a reflection, from within, of the character's consciousness: "Parece dirigido a ti, a nadie más. Distraído, dejas que" (It seems to be addressed to you and nobody else. Distraught, you let). Yet the "natural" conclusion – i.e., that Felipe speaks to himself – does not put the problem completely to rest.

The narrative follows the train of Felipe's thoughts and actions, basically in the present tense: "Lees ese anuncio" (You read the ad). Occasionally, the future is used for immediate action: "Tú releerás" (You will read it again). The story is thus presented through Felipe's immediate vision; he is groping for sense in the strange, yet familiar world he has immersed himself in. From the very beginning, the second person splits him into two selves; the unknown puts his sanity to the test. Is he reliable or not? According to the answer, the fantastic is swapped for dreams or madness. Felipe and the reader are left in the dark. It is this narrative irony that creates the uneasy alliance between them *vis-à-vis* Consuelo, who "knows," not that any reader would mistake him or herself for the addressee of the second-person discourse. The reader is closer to grasping the sense of the strange signs reported by Felipe (e.g., the lovemaking ritual with black mass overtones); yet his final revelation comes as a surprise. This (mis)leading of the reader is fundamental to the narrative strategy of *Aura*.

This illusion of immediacy and of simultaneity between narrating and narrated times is broken only once, at the very beginning. The third paragraph summarizes, in the future tense and in less than a line, the rest of the first day: "Vivirás ese día, idéntico a los demás" (You will spend that day, just like the other days). There follows another ellipsis, this time without a summary, between his rereading of the advertisment the next morning and walking towards his destiny later that afternoon. This double ellipsis and one summary, intensified by the future tense, transgress the simultaneity of the narration. For Felipe, the omitted time is routine, oblivion; therefore, he could still be the narrator and protagonist in one person, speaking to himself simultaneously with the action. But the cleavage in the flow of discourse also creates an "opening" for manipulation "from behind" by a narrator who is or is not Felipe himself, though none of the other characters could fit this role. In the second case, Felipe as character would be the "center of consciousness," engaged in a dialogue by either the distant, remembering self or some other narrator. These two or three possibilities are not reducible to any one: we find here a radical ambiguity and transgression, one of many carefully disseminated throughout the text.

The only thing we can discard at this point is the suggestion that Felipe is the narratee, i.e., the framing narrative function of somebody to whom the story is being told. True, he is engaged by the discourse, yet he is not the receiver of the story, but an actor-narrator or co-narrator within the story told in such peculiar way. The confusion between discourse and narrative functions, between primary and secondary modeling systems, comes from French structuralism.

Another detail, clearly beyond Felipe's control in either narrative role, is the segmentation into chapters. Although there is an identical number of days and chapters (five), these do not coincide, creating (similar to enjambment in verse) an intricate rhythmic narrative pattern which helps to mix up the flow of "real" time. But this, together with other metatextual elements, such as the epigraph from Jules Michelet, the title of the novella, and any intertextual play beyond the knowledge of the narrator (and even of the "real" author), can be attributed to the "implied author," which is for us the last authority within the text, controlling the semantic interplay of the subordinate levels and their elements.

The epigraph opens another Pandora's box, that of intertextual play. Projected on the text, it strengthens the role of Consuelo. But it is also just the tip of an iceberg: it leads to Michelet's *La Sorcière*, 1878 (*Satanism and Witchcraft*, 1939), a surprising Borges-like investigation of the "invention" of modern-day sorcery. The names of the characters, Felipe, Consuelo, Aura, are found there; the code of witchcraft as explained there is superimposed on the ordinary contemporary reality. But it would be an error to try to reduce the irreducible polysemy and guessing game to the triviality of one specific, determinate meaning, be it witchcraft or psychoanalysis. This is only one important facet of the playful expansion of the literary "reality" in Fuentes's work. The absurd twists in communication recall the black humor of Rulfo's *Pedro Páramo* (1955), for which Fuentes wrote the screen adaptation. On second thought, many more elements of this novel find their crafty "reincarnation" in *Aura*. The tragic story of love, death, and madness in the historical Maximilian and Carlota, and its Pirandellian stage version by Rodolfo Usigli, *Corona de sombra*, 1943 (*Crown of Shadows*), are also closer intertexts for *Aura* than James, Dickens, or Pushkin, identified by the author himself.

EMIL VOLEK

Editions

First edition: *Aura*, Mexico City: Era, 1962

Critical edition: edited by Peter Standish, Durham, England: University of Durham, 1986

Translation: *Aura*, by Lysander Kemp, New York: Farrar Straus and Giroux, 1965; London: André Deutsch, 1990

Further Reading

Alazraki, Jaime, "Theme and System in Carlos Fuentes' *Aura*," in *Carlos Fuentes: a Critical View*, edited by Robert Brody and Charles Rossman, Austin: University of Texas Press, 1982

Fuentes, Carlos, "How I Wrote One of My Books," in *World Literature Today*, vol. 57/4 (1983), and in his *Myself with Others*, New York: Farrar Straus and Giroux, and London: André Deutsch, 1988

Geasler Titiev, Janice, "Withcraft in Carlos Fuentes' *Aura*," *Revista de Estudios Hispánicos*, vol. 15 (1981)

Hernández de López, Ana María (editor), *La obra de Carlos Fuentes: una visión múltiple*, Madrid: Pliegos, 1988 [Contains items on *Aura*]

Merino, Blanca, "Fantasía y realidad en *Aura* de Carlos Fuentes," *Literatura Mexicana*, vol. 2/1 (1991)

Standish, Peter, "Intention and Technique in Fuentes' *Aura*," *Iberoamerikanisches Archiv*, vol. 6 (1981)

Zamora, Lois Parkinson, "A Garden Inclosed: Fuentes' *Aura*, Hawthorne's and Paz's 'Rapaccini's Daughter,' and Uyeda's *Ugetsu Monogatari*," *Revista Canadiense de Estudios Hispánicos*, vol. 8 (1984)

La muerte de Artemio Cruz

Novel by Carlos Fuentes

La muerte de Artemio Cruz, 1962 (*The Death of Artemio Cruz*) is one of the early and most popular novels of the Latin American Boom. Thematically, it explores the issue of Mexican identity whilst, stylistically, it experiments with new novelistic techniques associated with modern writers such as James Joyce. The novel consists of thirty-eight fragments. These fragments may be further subdivided into twelve groups of three fragments each (with two final fragments that close the novel). Each of these three fragments is characterized by a different form of narration: first person singular, present tense (Artemio's stream-of-consciousness on his deathbed), second person singular, future tense (Artemio's alter ego speaks to him reminding him of all the wrong choices he has made in his life), and third person singular, preterite tense (an omniscient narrator who objectively narrates past events). These last fragments are dated (ranging from 1889 to 1955) but do not appear in chronological order. Moreover, within each fragment episodes are non-chronologically narrated and superimposed upon each other without transitional statements.

When the novel opens, Artemio, seventy-one years old, is dying. As he lies in his bed suffering great physical pain, he reviews his life as a series of choices between what Joseph Sommers calls two almost equally unacceptable options with which life has presented him. According to Sommers in *Yáñez, Rulfo, Fuentes: la novela mexicana moderna*, it is this lack of any *real* choice that makes Artemio Cruz a tragic character. He consistently chooses the path of self-gain at the expense of others, because the forsaken choice, the path to love, selflessness, authenticity, would have almost always led to death or poverty. Artemio's dilemma, while individual, is also collective: he is seen as representative of all Mexicans who, due to the country's social and political development, must be either "chingadores" (motherfuckers) or "chingados" (fucked over). Variations of this word, "santo y seña de México" (Mexico's password), form an entire section on Mexican identity in the novel. The origins of this concept are found in Octavio's Paz's landmark essay of 1950, *El laberinto de la soledad* (*The Labyrinth of Solitude*), a reflection on Mexican identity, where the meaning of the word "chingar" is discussed and Mexicans are defined as "hijos de la chingada" (children of the fucked mother).

The novel traces Artemio's participation in the 1910 Mexican Revolution and his rise to a position of wealth and power by taking advantage of the desperate situation of Don Gamaliel Bernal. The peasants refuse to work Gamaliel's land because he refuses to give them any of their own to till; moreover, they stop repaying the loans they owe him. Artemio offers him a quarter of the profits if he turns the loans over to him. He also gets the peasants to till Gamaliel's land by giving them dry farming tracts to cultivate under the guise of agrarian reform. Artemio marries Gamaliel's daughter, Catalina, and thus gains control of Gamaliel's estate, but there is never any genuine communication between them. Once again, his possibility for love and fulfilment is thwarted, just as his relationship with his first love, Regina, was cut short by her murder during the Revolution. Later in life he loses his chance for an authentic relationship with his mistress, Laura, because he doesn't have the necessary integrity to leave his wife and commit himself to her.

Fuentes employs a variety of formal techniques characteristic of the Modern or "New Novel" to communicate meaning to the reader. These include a variety of different types of dialogue, interior monologues, leitmotifs, enumerations, sensorial descriptions, symbols, wordplay, oxymorons and cinematographic techniques such as flashbacks, fadeouts, and superimposition of images. The most interesting symbols and/or leitmotifs are the mirror and the mask. Both refer to the process of introspection that the characters – Artemio in particular – undergo.

The range of meanings Fuentes assigns to the mask is another novelistic element that originates in Paz's essay, *El laberinto de la soledad*. The book's second chapter titled "Máscaras mexicanas" (Mexican Masks) asserts that the Mexican is a being who "se encierra y se preserva" (locks himself up and saves himself) and that they always establish a wall between the self and reality. Fuentes repeats this mask motif both explicitly and implicitly throughout his novel, thus illustrating this interpretation of Mexican nature through the actions of his characters. Thus when Artemio visits Don Galamiel to seize his lands and usurp the place of Gamaliel's son, Bernal, he thinks about the irony "de ser él quien regresaba a Puebla, y no el fusilado Bernal" (that it was he rather than the executed Bernal who had returned to Puebla), and this amuses him because it was "en cierto modo, una mascarada, una sustitición, una broma que podía jugarse con la mayor seriedad" (in a way a masquerade, a sleight-of-hand, a joke that could be played with the greatest seriousness).

This example leads us to perhaps the most important and least studied of the novel's techniques: its use of oxymorons. Words are constantly paired with their opposites to convey a paradox. For example, when Catalina and Artemio meet for the first time we are told "Ella se extrañó de la fortaleza con que sucumbía, del poder de su debilidad" (She was surprised at the strength with which she succumbed, the power of her weakness). The oxymoron is not a mere stylistic device, but rather is used to convey the essence of Mexican identity as embodied in the character Artemio Cruz. In one passage, Artemio's wish to have been born in the United States focuses on the essential differences between Mexicans and their northern neighbors: "por más que lo intentes, no puedes ser como ellos . . . ¿Tu visión de las cosas, en tus peores o en tus mejores momentos, ha sido tan simplista como la de ellos? Nunca. Nunca has podido pensar en blanco y negro, en buenos y malos, en Dios y Diablo: admite que siempre, aun cuando parecía lo contrario, has encontrado en lo negro el germen, el reflejo de su opuesto: tu propia crueldad, cuando has sido cruel, ¿no estaba teñida de cierta ternura?" (no matter how much you try, you cannot be like them . . . was your vision of things . . . ever as simplistic as theirs? Never. Never have you been able to think in black and white, good guys versus bad guys, God or the Devil: admit that always, even when it seemed just the opposite, you've found the germ, the reflection of the white in the black. Your own cruelty, when you've been cruel, hasn't it always been tinged with a certain tenderness?)

Both Mexican identity and the choices with which Artemio Cruz is faced intertwine with historical events portrayed in the novel. Nelson Osorio in his article in *Homenaje a Carlos Fuentes* [In Honour of Carlos Fuentes] notes that Mexican history is depicted as a cycle in which the "users" obtain their wealth and power by taking advantage of the "used." Ireneo Menchaca, the wealthy landowner who fathered Artemio with the Indian servant Isabel Cruz, obtained the Cocuya estate by joining General Santa Anna. Gamaliel Bernal obtained his land when Juárez auctioned off the properties formerly owned by the Catholic clergy, and Artemio acquires his property when Porfirio Díaz's government falls, the Mexican Revolution triumphs, and the supposed agrarian reform is realized. He sells the revolutionary ideals short in favor of personal gain by giving the dry farming land to the Indians and keeping the best land for himself. His later business dealings, such as selling rights to exploit the sulphur mines to the United States for two million dollars, also show his betrayal of the principles of the Revolution. In each case the victors receive power and wealth, while the masses remain poor and abused. This reinforces the notion of Mexicans as either "chingadores" or "chingados." It also places the character Artemio and his decisions within a historical and political context which is evaluated and criticized as much as the character is. Although Artemio Cruz is criticized throughout the novel, the character, product of the Mexican socio-political context, and painfully cognizant of the wrong choices he made in his life, is not a totally unsympathetic figure. He is the oxymoron Fuentes relies on so heavily in the novel: tender and cruel, weak and strong, tough and vulnerable: all of life's opposites rolled into one tragic survivor. Artemio Cruz is both pitied and denounced in *La muerte de Artemio Cruz*.

HELENE CAROL WELDT-BASSON

See also entries on The Boom, *El laberinto de la soledad* (Octavio Paz)

Editions
First edition: *La muerte de Artemio Cruz*, Mexico City: Fondo de Cultura Económica, 1962
Translation: *The Death of Artemio Cruz*, by Alfred MacAdam, New York: Farrar Straus and Giroux, 1991

Further Reading
Ezquerro, Milagros, Eva Golluscio de Montoya and Michèle Raymond, *Manual de análisis textual*, Toulouse: France-Ibérie Recherche, 1988 [chapter on *La muerte*]
Gyurko, Lanin, "Self, Double and Mask in Fuentes's *La muerte de Artemio Cruz*, *Texas Studies in Literature and Language*, vol. 16/2 (Summer 1974)
____ "Women in Mexican Society: Fuentes's Portrayal of Oppression," *Revista Hispánica Moderna*, vol. 38 (1974–75)
____ "Artemio Cruz and Citizen Kane: a Comparative Analysis," in *Carlos Fuentes: a Critical View*, edited by Robert Brody and Charles Rossman, Austin: University of Texas Press, 1982
Shaw, Donald L., "Narrative Arrangement in *La muerte de Artemio Cruz*," in *Contemporary Latin American Fiction*, edited by Salvador Bacarisse, Edinburgh: Scottish Academic Press, 1980

G

Eduardo Galeano 1940–

Uruguayan essayist, journalist and historian

The work of Eduardo Galeano is perhaps one of the most problematical among recent Latin American authors in terms of categorisation and critical study, for he is neither simply an essayist, nor a journalist nor a historian, but rather a combination of the three whose writing has an undeniably literary quality. The virtual critical vacuum within which Galeano finds himself is due not to the quality of his work, for he has published two works, *Las venas abiertas de América Latina*, 1971 (*The Open Veins of Latin America*) and the trilogy *Memoria del fuego*, 1982–86 (*Memory of Fire*), which are widely recognised to be of seminal value. Instead, the reason appears to be the uncertainty with which literary critics confront works which are clearly documents of economic and socio-cultural history. Similarly, Galeano's work carries too much of the creativity and conscious interpretation of events common to much of contemporary Latin American fiction to attract conventional historians. This unique vision of Latin America arises from Galeano's experiences of life and the written word, central to which is a twelve-year period of exile, first in Argentina and later in Spain, to escape persecution by the increasingly brutal Uruguayan, and subsequently Argentine, military regimes of the 1970s, whose censure of him arose from his position as editor-in-chief of *Época* and his critical, politically committed journalism.

Despite the common motifs encountered throughout Galeano's work, there are also clear lines of development. His global concerns might best be summarised by his own words in the foreword to *Memoria del fuego*, where he states that "quisiera contribuir al rescate de la memoria secuestrada de toda América, pero sobre todo de América Latina: quisiera preguntarle de qué diversos barros fue nacida, de qué actos de amor y violaciones viene" (I would like to contribute to the rescue of the kidnapped memory of all America, but especially that of Latin America: I would like to ask her from what earth was she born, from what acts of love and rape she rises). This he does in his early works through a denunciation of the economic, social and political injustices of the continent, while in subsequent publications the tone of the denunciation becomes less directly confrontational or negatory, and is modified to assimilate a more creative and literary aspect within the narration of historical events and cultural traditions.

Las venas abiertas de América Latina takes the form of a series of essays which represent critical analyses of the exploitation of resources such as gold, silver, sugar, rubber, cotton, minerals and oil since the arrival of the Spanish at the end of the 15th century. The essays frequently foreground the economic imperialism of first the European powers, and more recently of the United States, via a wealth of facts and figures which serve as the framework for sections that concern themselves with the political and social ramifications of such a system. Despite the subjectivity and informality of the narrative, evidenced in the use of deliberately loaded nouns and adjectives which correspond to emotional reactions, and despite Galeano's own perception of the work as having been written "en el estilo de una novela de amor o de piratas" (in the style of a novel about love or about pirates), the sheer volume and density of the factual information, all of which is of equal importance to the overarching structure of the work, mean that *Las venas* is not a text whose reading can be undertaken lightly: it demands to be read from cover to cover with the same urgency with which it was written.

Memoria del fuego shares with *Las venas* a preoccupation with the portrayal of injustices, even if here the focus is more social than politico-economic, but the manner of presentation has an additional goal, as is outlined by the author in *El descubrimiento de América que todavía no fue*, 1986 [The Discovery of America that Still Has Not Been], namely that of contributing to "revelar la voz de los que no tienen voz" (bring forth the voice of those who have no voice). In order to achieve this Galeano synthesises works by scores of Spanish chroniclers, colonial authors, modern historians and anthropologists, and most importantly indigenous traditions, with his own vision of the Americas to produce challenging recreations of events and beliefs. The opening section of the first volume of *Memoria del fuego*, entitled "Primeras voces" (First Voices), goes beyond the scope and the chronological boundaries of *Las venas* to present the beliefs and traditions of the indigenous peoples in pre-Columbian times, thereby taking a significant first step in breaking away from conventional histories of the region and familiarising the reader with the perspective which permeates the three volumes. The structure of the work is similarly unconventional, each. volume consisting of hundreds of self-contained scenes which portray events and conditions over the course of the region's colonial history and republican independence, and while most have their source in the historical and anthropological documents mentioned above, a significant number are taken from non-literary sources, such as oral tradition, letters, songs, newspaper advertisements and graffiti, which are particularly relevant to the stated aims of the work. Galeano himself is aware of the manner in which this work, and others, defy easy categorisation. However, his conscious rejection of conventional literary forms, themselves products of the very culture whose dominance and vision he is challenging, comes over as a strength rather than a shortcoming, and represents a totally appropriate questioning of traditions of form which parallels the positing of an alternative vision of the continent, its peoples and its history.

The move away from the realm of the hard facts and figures which proved illuminating in *Las venas abiertas de América Latina* has led to a far more subjective mode of expression more suited to the rejection of objective (or pseudo-objective) history and the incorporation of more individual forms of cultural expression, such as folklore and oral narrative. This empowering of those who traditionally have no voice within the framework of the established cultural hierarchy reaches its height to date in Galeano's recent work, the ambitious *Las palabras andantes*, 1993 (*Walking Words*), which self-consciously attempts to produce a synthesis of oral tradition and concise insights into Latin-American reality through transcribed oral narratives and intercalated *ventanas* (windows), illustrated by prints from woodcuts typical of the popular *literatura de cordel* (literature on a string: it was thus displayed for sale). The prints are, however, more than mere illustrations, and their importance as cultural manifestations is equal to that of the texts they accompany. The inherent contradictions of recording modes of expression which are taken from outside the realm of the written word within what is ultimately a literary project are not easily overcome, but *Las palabras andantes* admirably serves to give a voice to a sector of the population who have traditionally been denied any form of access to the conventional vehicles of cultural expression, and to bring to the attention of the book-reading (predominantly middle-class) public a range of values and a culture which might otherwise have remained unknown.

One of the features of the structure of Galeano's works is the ease with which the reader can gain access to individual texts and achieve a high level of engagement with relative facility. This is especially true of more recent works, in which the reader is presented with a series of short episodes or images that bind together to form the collage text. It is, however, possible to enjoy the individual elements in their own right as well as for their contribution to the orchestrated whole, owing to both the subject matter and the highly personal, even intimate, style which to some extent manages to recreate the context of their original production and overcome in part the contradictions mentioned above. Such a fragmentary view of Galeano's recent works is supported by the author's words in a television interview from 1992 in which he affirms that the

stories of *Memoria del fuego* "me enseñaron a ver el universo por el ojo de la cerradura: descubrí la historia grande a través de las historias chiquitas" (taught me to view the universe through a keyhole: I discovered History through little histories).

The questioning of traditional Eurocentric perspectives which accompanied the recent quincentenary celebrations of the "Discovery," and the consequent upsurge of interest in Latin American perceptions of their own historical process and culture, are fused in Galeano's work with the narrative voice of one of the authors of the post-Boom, whose writings continue in the line of the acclaimed narratives of García Márquez, Cortázar, Fuentes and others. It must only be a matter of time before the ability of Galeano to unite these two threads, and give a characteristically Latin American voice to such topical concerns, leads to the considered appraisal his work calls for.

DAVID WOOD

See also entry on *Marcha* under Journals

Biography
Born in Montevideo, Uruguay, 3 September 1940, into a middle-class Catholic family of Welsh, German, Spanish and Italian ancestry. Son of Eduardo Hughes and Ester Galeano. Educated in Uruguay until age 16. Sold his first political cartoon at the age of 14 to socialist newsaper, *El Sol*. Worked at a variety of menial jobs in adolescence which gave him an early interest in trade union and socialist politics. Editor-in-chief, *Marcha*, Montevideo, 1961–64; editor of the daily, *Época*, Montevideo, 1964–66; editor-in-chief, University Press, Montevideo, 1965–73. As a result of the military coup of 1973, he was first imprisoned and then forced to leave Uruguay. Founder of *Crisis* magazine, Buenos Aires, Argentina, 1973, editor-in-chief, 1973–76. After the military coup of 1976 in Argentina, he received death threats. Moved to Spain where he lived until he was able to return to Uruguay in 1984. Continues to reside there in the 1990s. Principal awards include: Premio Casa de las Américas, 1975, for *La canción de nosotros*, and in 1978, for *Días y noches de amor y de guerra*; American Book Award of the University of Washington, Seattle, 1989, for *Memoria del fuego*. *Las venas abiertas de América Latina* has been translated into 20 languages and has well over 50 Spanish-language editions, making it one of Latin America's best-selling books of all time.

Selected Works
Like a fellow-Uruguayan author, Mario Benedetti, and other Latin American writers of the Left, much of Galeano's work transcends orthodox genres; thus no attempt has been made to place his works in different categories.

Los días siguientes, Montevideo: Alfa, 1963
China 1964: crónica de un desafío, Buenos Aires: Jorge Álvarez, 1964
Guatemala: clave de Latinoamérica, Montevideo: Ediciones de la Banda Oriental, 1967; published under the title *Guatemala, país ocupado*, Mexico City: Nuestro Tiempo, 1967; as *Guatemala: Occupied Country*, translated by Cedric Belfrage, New York: Monthly Review Press, 1969
Reportajes: tierras de Latinoamérica, otros puntos cardinales, y algo más, Montevideo: Tauro, 1967
Los fantasmas del día del léon, y otros relatos, Montevideo: Arca, 1967
Su majestad el fútbol, Montevideo: Arca, 1968 [anthology]

Las venas abiertas de América Latina, Montevideo: Universidad de la República, 1971; as *The Open Veins of Latin America*, translated by Cedric Belfrage, New York: Monthly Review Press, 1973

Siete imágenes de Bolivia, Caracas: Fondo Editorial Salvador de la Plaza, 1971

Violencia y enajenación, Mexico City: Nuestro Tiempo, 1971

Crónicas latinoamericanas, Montevideo: Girón, 1972

Vagamundo, Buenos Aires: Crisis, 1973

La canción de nosotros, Havana: Casa de las Américas, 1975

Conversaciones con Raimón, Barcelona: Granica, 1977

Días y noches de amor y de guerra, Barcelona: Laia, 1978; as *Days and Nights of Love and War*, translated by Judith Brister, New York: Monthly Review Press, and London: Pluto Press, 1983

La piedra arde, Salamanca: Lóguez, 1980 [children's fiction]

Voces de nuestro tiempo, San José, Costa Rica: Universitaria Centroamericana, 1981

Memoria del fuego, 3 vols, 1982–86; as *Memory of Fire*, 3 vols, 1985–88

   1. *Los nacimientos*, Mexico City: Siglo XXI, 1982; as *Genesis*, translated by Cedric Belfrage, New York: Pantheon, 1985

   2. *Las caras y las máscaras*, Mexico City: Siglo XXI, 1984; as *Faces and Masks*, translated by Cedric Belfrage, New York: Pantheon, and London: Quartet, 1987

   3. *El siglo del viento*, Mexico City: Siglo XXI, 1986; as *Century of the Wind*, translated by Cedric Belfrage, New York: Pantheon, and London: Quartet, 1988

Aventuras de los jóvenes dioses, Buenos Aires: Kapelusz, 1984 [children's fiction]

Ventana sobre Sandino, Managua, Nicaragua: Raiti, 1985

Contraseña, Buenos Aires: Sol, 1985

El descubrimiento de América que todavía no fue y otros escritos, Barcelona: Laia, 1986

El tigre azul y otros artículos, Santiago de Chile: Amerinda, 1988

El libro de los abrazos, Madrid: Siglo XXI, 1989; as *The Book of Embraces*, edited and translated by Cedric Belfrage and M. Schafer, New York: Norton, 1991

Nosotros decimos no: crónicas (1963–1988), Mexico City: Siglo XXI, 1989; revised edition, as *We Say No (1963–1991)*, translated by Mark Fried, et al., New York: Norton, 1992

América Latina para entenderte mejor: con Agustín Cueva en Panamá, Panama City: Universidad de Panamá, 1990

Las palabras andantes, Madrid: Siglo XXI, 1993; as *Walking Words*, translated by Mark Fried, New York: Norton, 1995

Úselo y tírelo: el mundo del fin, Buenos Aires: Planeta, 1994 [ecology]

El fútbol a sol y sombra, Madrid: Siglo XXI, 1995

Compilations and Anthologies

Entrevistas y artículos (1962–1987), Montevideo: Ediciones del Chanchito, 1988

Palabras: antología personal, Buenos Aires: GenteSur, 1990

Ser como ellos y otros artículos, Montevideo: Ediciones del Chanchito, 1992

Amares. Antología preparada por el autor, Madrid: Alianza, 1993

Further Reading

Galeano's work is often ignored in academic publications. The secondary bibliography is limited to a small number of articles which tend to focus either on his subjective view of history or on the political aspect of his writing in exile. The most substantial of these articles, together with two books, appear below.

Bach, Caleb, "Eduardo Galeano: in Celebration of Contradiction," *Americas*, vol. 44/5 (1992)

Barros-Lémez, Alvaro, "Cantares que de gente en gente quedan: América Latina, lucha exilio y narrativa en la obra de Eduardo Galeano," *Escritura: Revista de Teoría y Crítica Literarias*, vol. 12/23–24 (1987)

Crespi, Roberto, "State Terror, the Radical Nationalist Intellectual, and the Class Question," *Latin American Perspectives*, vol. 13/4 (1986)

Fishlin, Daniel, "Eduardo Galeano and the Politics of Style," *Ariel: a Review of International English Literature*, Calgary, Canada, vol. 24/4 (1993)

Lovell, W. George, "Re-Membering America: the Historical Vision of Eduardo Galeano," *Queen's Quarterly*, vol. 99/3 (Fall 1992)

Martin, Gerald, "Hope Springs Eternal: Eduardo Galeano and the History of Latin America," *History Journal Workshop* 34 (1992) [Critical of Galeano's more recent work for what is perceived as its false optimism]

Palaversich, Diana, "Eduardo Galeano's *Memoria del fuego* as Alternative History," *Antípodas* 3 (1991)

_____ "Eduardo Galeano: entre el postmodernismo y el post colonialismo," *Indiana Journal of Hispanic Literatures*, vol. 1/2 (1993)

_____ *Silencio, voz y escritura en Eduardo Galeano*, Frankfurt: Vervuert Verlag, 1995

Rosencof, Mauricio, *El vendedor de reliquias. Sobre "Memorias del fuego" de Eduardo Galeano*, Montevideo: Arca, 1992 [Written by a friend of Galeano who experienced the horrors of Uruguay's military dictatorship]

Saad, Gabriel, "Eduardo Galeano: la literatura como una pasión latinoamericana," *Cuadernos Hispanoamericanos* 324 (June 1977)

Saz, Sara, "Breath, Liberty, and the Word: Eduardo Galeano's Interpretation of History," *SECOLAS Annals: Journal of the Southeastern Council on Latin-American Studies* 21 (March 1990)

Vogel, H., "Eduardo Galeano como historiador," in *Foro hispánico. La nueva novela histórica hispanoamericana*, Amsterdam: Rodopi, 1991 [Highly critical of Galeano's historiography]

Wilson, S.R., "El Cono Sur: the Tradition of Exile, the Language of Poetry," *Revista Canadiense de Estudios Hispánicos*, vol. 8/2 (1984)

Interviews

Henríquez-Lagarde, Manuel, "Las huellas de la pelea," *Casa de las Américas*, vol. 30/174 (1989)

Price, Greg, *Latin America: the Writer's Journey*, London: Hamish Hamilton, 1990

Rómulo Gallegos 1884–1969

Venezuelan prose writer

Rómulo Gallegos's third novel, one of the few to have been translated into English, *Doña Bárbara*, 1929, (drastically revised 1930) marks the peak of the regionalist novel in Spanish America. The regionalists' aim was to try to explain and interpret the specifically Spanish American reality they saw, especially in the undeveloped interior of the continent. In performing this function, they tended to avoid obtrusive narrative experimentation, relying on the setting to provide novelty and attraction.

Doña Bárbara, then, is the paradigmatic novel of a quest for the "cultural essence" of some given area of Spanish America (and, by extension, perhaps of Spanish America itself). In Gallegos, signs of this quest began to appear twenty years earlier with his early essays in the Caracas magazine *La Alborada* [Reveille] on social and political themes, including the failure of the Venezuelan educational system to correct what he regarded as the pernicious cultural legacy of Spain: indiscipline, impulsiveness, self-indulgence, lack of moral responsibility, excessive individualism and the like. In his political essays Gallegos called for an end to violence as a factor in political change, civic consciousness and respect for law, and an end to dictatorship. In his early short stories he similarly criticized the use of arbitrary force to settle social differences, cynical dishonesty in public affairs and other forms of behaviour which he thought stood in the way of national progress. Already, however, we notice two features which were to survive in his later work. One is a tendency to confuse cultural with racial characteristics. The other is a certain ambivalence with regard to some of the features which he consciously intended to attack, especially individual force of character. With part of his mind he rejected it, but with another part he saw it as a sign of the abounding energy of a young society.

In his first novels *Reinaldo Solar* (1920) and *La trepadora*, 1925 [The Social Climber], written while he was, characteristically, earning his living as a teacher before his voluntary exile in 1931 for political reasons, Gallegos reached out towards a new type of semi-symbolic fictional character which could be used to illustrate aspects of the national situation and to incorporate an implicit lesson. Reinaldo Solar is young, attractive, cultured and idealistic, but afflicted with a sense of alienation and moral crisis which leads him to search for new values. He struggles fruitlessly to impose a direction on his life, but we are aware that, unlike them, it is only as a social being and a citizen that he would be able to achieve full self-realization. He fails largely because of personality defects which reflect the ills of the Venezuelan national character that Gallegos had postulated in his earlier writings. Nevertheless, he dies fighting for progress. In *La trepadora* the problem is expressed in terms of the taming of an imperfectly socialized, aggressively individualistic figure, Hilario Guanipa, by his wife and daughter, so that he eventually becomes a useful and responsible member of the directing class. The fact that his daughter, Victoria, successfully marries into the landed gentry, prefigures the theme of social integration (on a strictly limited scale) which also underlies the love-plot in *Doña Bárbara*.

Doña Bárbara was a best-seller for many years. Inspired by a surprisingly brief trip to the vast savannas of the Venezuelan interior where it is set, its theme is the threat to the country from the barbarous social conditions in the outback and the attraction exerted by their macho values on the young, intellectual elite of the country. Initially, it seems that the task confronting the hero, Santos Luzardo, is that of bringing the cattle-ranching economy of the plains under proper legal control and developing its productivity. But the reader's attention is quickly diverted from this practical task to that of overcoming the primitive, violent and anti-social mentality and customs of the plains people and especially of their leading representative, the local landowner, Doña Bárbara. The struggle between Bárbara and Santos provides the dramatic interest of the novel, while the latter's efforts to overcome the attraction of macho self-assertion, which exerts itself even more powerfully as the conflict develops, deepens the symbolism of his character.

The characters of Santos and Bárbara evolve symmetrically, his towards greater machismo and potential violence, hers towards greater femininity and readiness to make concessions. A feature of the novel, however, is that these evolutions never really cross. There is only one real confrontation between the two characters, marking the central point of this exceptionally well-constructed plot. Santos, that is, never feels emotionally or sexually attracted to Bárbara, which is a pity, since it would have been the ultimate test of his personality. As it is, Santos's love is reserved for Marisela, Bárbara's daughter, the symbol of all that is potentially salvageable in the soul of Venezuela. However, we should notice that by marrying her, after narrowly avoiding a descent into barbarous violence himself, Santos is marrying his cousin, a member of the landowning elite. This is not in any real sense symbolic of fusing either classes or races in Venezuela.

In his later work, Gallegos never again reached the creative level of *Doña Bárbara*. His subsequent novels were *Cantaclaro* (1934), *Canaima*, 1936, *Pobre negro*, 1937 [Poor Black], *El forastero*, 1942 [The Stranger], *Sobre la misma tierra*, 1943 [On this Very Earth], *La brizna de paja en el viento*, 1952 [The Wisp of Straw in the Wind] and the posthumous *Tierra bajo los pies*, 1971 [Earth under One's Feet]. Already in *Cantaclaro*, now written in exile, the confident assertion of man's mastery over nature and over his own natural instincts becomes more muted, and merely nostalgic, folkloric interest often takes first place. The railway, a symbol of progress in *Doña Bárbara*, gives way to a multiplicity of dirt tracks, none of which really leads in a positive direction. The plains as a "symbolic space," that is, take on once more a threatening, unconquered and at times curiously unreal aspect, in which courage and sacrifice have little meaning. At the end of *Cantaclaro*, Martín Salcedo, the surviving figure of patriotic aspiration, leaves the plains to seek another, unidentified, path towards his country's salvation. In *Canaima*, Gallegos fustigates the rape of natural resources in Venezuelan Guyana and once more explores the terrible attraction of violent self-assertion in the hero, Marcos Vargas. We are conscious that Gallegos has receded from his belief in the relative ease with which national characteristics could be reconciled with progressive politics. He was to find that belief brutally contradicted in real life when, after the death of the dictator Gómez, he returned from exile in 1936 and resumed his interrupted political career, becoming Minister of Education in the new government of López Contreras. In 1947 he was elected President of Venezuela as the leader of the Democratic Action party with an overwhelming majority but after less than a year in office his government was overthrown by a military coup under Pérez Jiménez. It meant exile for the second time. He was not to return to Venezuela until 1958.

Symbolically, *Pobre negro*, whose theme is the need to integrate the blacks in Venezuela into the national family is set in the past and the issues are seen from a comfortable historical distance. Nevertheless, in the more discursive sections of the novel Gallegos sharply criticizes both the selfish greed of the old propertied oligarchy and the ideological bankruptcy of the progressives, which he saw as having perpetuated the country's divisions. Interestingly, this is possibly the first novel in Spanish America written by a man to call for the liberation of women from their traditional passive social role. Gallegos's remaining novels continue the pattern of "civic" writing already described. *El forastero* is concerned with local tyranny and its powers of survival and *Sobre la misma tierra* with the betrayal of the country for the benefit of foreign oil interests (which were to assist in engineering his fall from the Presidency in 1948). *La brizna de paja en el viento*, written in exile, applies Gallegos's by now characteristic vision of Latin America as dominated by the struggle between forces of good and evil, idealism and greedy violence, civilization and barbarism, to the political revolutionary activity of Cuban university students in Havana in the 1940s (in which Fidel Castro first emerged as a figure of importance). But by now the formula had begun to seem naive and hackneyed and the structure of the novel too subordinate to the didactic intention. A similarly simple dualism is visible in *Tierra bajo los pies*, whose theme is the land problem in post-revolutionary Mexico.

Like the others in the regionalist movement, Gallegos seems nowadays to have seen Latin American reality too unambiguously. But *Doña Bárbara* remains the most important and popular Spanish American novel before García Márquez's *Cien años de soledad* (*One Hundred Years of Solitude*).

DONALD L. SHAW

Biography

Born in Caracas, Venezuela, 2 August 1884. Attended Colegio Sucre, Caracas, 1901–04, degree 1905; studied law at the Central University of Venezuela, Caracas, 1905. Co-founder of the journal, *La Alborada* [Dawn Song], 1909, in which many of his essays appeared. Contributed stories to *El Cojo Ilustrado*, 1910–14, *La Revista*, 1915–16, *Actualidades*, 1919 (publisher and editor, 1919–21), *La Lectura Semanal*, 1922, and *La Novela Semanal*. Married Teotiste Arocha in 1912 (died in 1951), one daughter. Director, Colegio Federal de Barcelona de Venezuela, 1912; deputy director, 1912–18, then director, 1922–30, Colegio Federal de Caracas (renamed Liceo Andrés Bello); deputy director, Escuela Normal de Caracas, 1918–22; senator for the state of Apure,

1930–31; resigned post in New York, and went into self-imposed exile, 1931–36 during the dictatorship of Juan Vicente Gómez. Moved to Spain, 1932, and worked for a cash register company; on return to Venezuela, in 1936, appointed Minister for Public Education under President Eleazar López Contreras: resigned after six weeks because of opposition to his reforms; congressional deputy, 1937–40; founder, 1941, and president, 1941–47, Action Party; elected chairman, Caracas City Council, 1941; elected President of Venezuela, 1947: toppled by a military coup in the same year, imprisoned briefly, then lived in exile in Cuba, 1948, and Mexico, 1949–58, before returning to Venezuela in 1958. Honorary President, Venezuelan College of Professors, 1958; Honorary President, Action Party, 1958. Awarded the National Prize for Literature, 1958; Alberdi-Sarmiento Prize (Argentina), 1959; America Prize (Mexico), 1967. The prestigious literary prize that bears his name was created by the Venezuelan government in 1964. Died in Caracas, 5 April 1969.

Selected Works

Short Fiction
Los aventureros, Caracas: Bolívar, 1913
La rebelión y otros cuentos, Caracas: Librería y Editorial del Maestro, 1946
Cuentos venezolanos, Buenos Aires: Austral, 1949
La doncella; El último patriota, Mexico City: Montobar, 1957

Novels
El último solar, Caracas: Imprenta Bolívar, 1920; retitled as *Reinaldo Solar* in all subsequent editions
La trepadora, Caracas: Tipografía Mercantil, 1925
Doña Bárbara, Barcelona: Araluce, 1929; as *Doña Bárbara*, translated by Robert Malloy, Magnolia, Massachusetts: Peter Smith, 1948 [the most recent edition]
Cantaclaro, Barcelona: Araluce, 1934
Canaima, Barcelona: Araluce, 1936; as *Canaima*, translated by Jaime Tello, Caracas: North American Association of Venezuela, 1984
Pobre negro, Caracas: Elite, 1937
Sobre la misma tierra, Caracas: Elite, 1943
La brizna de paja en el viento, Havana: Selecta, 1952

Essay
Una posición en la vida, Mexico City: Humanismo, 1954

Compilations and Anthologies
Obras completas, 2 vols, with a prologue by Jesús López Pacheco, Madrid: Aguilar, 1959–62

Further Reading
Understandably, much of the criticism on Gallegos's work concentrates on *Doña Bárbara*. Readers should refer to the essay on this novel for items concerned exclusively with it. The list given below is of more general studies.

Alonso, Carlos J., *The Spanish American Regional Novel*, Cambridge: Cambridge University Press, 1990 [Chapter on Gallegos]
Dunham, Lowell, *Rómulo Gallegos: vida y obra*, Mexico City: Andrea, 1957
Prieto, Luis B., *et al.*, *Relectura de Rómulo Gallegos*, Caracas: Centro de Estudios Latinoamericanos Rómulo Gallegos, 1980
Rodríguez, Ileana, *House/Garden/Nation: Space, Gender and Ethnicity in Post-Colonial Latin American Literatures by Women*, translated by Rodríguez and Robert Carr, Durham,

North Carolina: Duke University Press, 1994 [Includes chapter on Gallegos, José Eustasio Rivera and the Nicaraguan Omar Cabezas]

Rodríguez Alcalá, Hugo, *Nine Essays on Rómulo Gallegos*, Riverside: University of California Press, 1979

Doña Bárbara

Novel by Rómulo Gallegos

Rómulo Gallegos served his country as a teacher, Minister of Education, and briefly as President of the nation. As a writer, educator, and political figure, he epitomizes the struggle against tyranny in Latin America. Among his novels, *Doña Bárbara* (published in Spain in 1929) best represents his ideas and ideals. The conflict on the Venezuelan *llanos* (plains) between Santos Luzardo and Doña Bárbara is a microcosmic re-enactment of Sarmiento's archetypal struggle between civilization and barbarism. In Gallegos's work, as in other Spanish American novels written around the same time, this basic dichotomy manifests itself in a series of duelling oppositions: urban versus rural, European (i.e. white) versus mestizo, rational thought versus superstition, progress versus tradition. Doña Bárbara, the personification of the *llanos*, is one of the most memorable characters in all of Spanish American literature. From her base of operations at the ranch El Miedo (literally, "The Fear") she exerts absolute control over her fiefdom by means of her sexuality, sorcery, and brute force. Santos Luzardo, on the other hand, is an idealized figure. Raised and educated in the city, he is the embodiment of Gallegos's liberal agenda. His local efforts to preserve the decaying Altamira estate and bring the enlightened ways of the city to the benighted countryside mirror the novelist's endeavors on the national level. Luzardo proposes to civilize the *cacica* (rural boss), Doña Bárbara, and her illegitimate daughter, Marisela, just as he aims to restore order to the *llanos*. Along the way he falls victim to the spell of his adversary and the land itself, but eventually he prevails. Luzardo's education of and subsequent marriage to Marisela is emblematic of national restoration and unification. Ironically, Gallegos's nemesis, the dictator Juan Vicente Gómez, expressed great admiration for the novel. Failing to recognize himself in the portrayal of the tyrannical eponymous character, he was apparently unaware that the book's subject matter was intended as a repudiation of his regime.

Gallegos wrote his next two novels, *Cantaclaro* and *Canaima* during his self-imposed exile in Spain. Both emphasize setting at the expense of other narrative elements. *Cantaclaro*, like *Doña Bárbara*, relates legends and superstitions, incorporates aspects of *costumbrismo*, and offers a poetic treatment of the landscape. Florentino, the roving singer of the title, seems a permanent fixture of the plains, inseparable from the environment of which he is a product. For *Canaima* Gallegos chooses a jungle setting in the Orinoco basin. Once again, he develops his narrative within the context of the "man versus nature" theme. Setting out from the city in search of adventure, the protagonist, Marcos Vargas ultimately enters the jungle and casts his lot with the Indians. The migration of his mestizo son back to the city reverses the path taken by Marcos, thereby signalling a victory for the forces of civilization. Both *Cantaclaro* and *Canaima* are characterized by folkloric and sociological content and a lack of structural unity. The novelist's preoccupation with the problems of his country evidently outweighed his concern for narrativity.

In *Doña Bárbara* and other novels Gallegos utilizes many of the trappings of 19th-century Realism – linear narration, omniscient narrator, action scenes, lengthy descriptions, *costumbrismo* – but his style is poetic rather than strictly realistic. Although he grew up under the influence of Rodó and Spanish American *Modernismo*, he eschewed the escapist tendencies of that earlier generation, focusing instead on his country's geographical, social, and political realities. His novels paint a portrait of Venezuela's rural regions – the plains, jungles, and mountains – with their distinctive flora, fauna, climate, customs, popular legends, and superstitions. Despite nature's seductive and bewitching aspects, the environment proves to be an inhospitable zone that must be tamed. Frequently, the influence of the landscape is so powerful that setting overshadows character development and plot.

Gallegos's characters often resemble mere idealizations, personifications, or caricatures, rather than flesh-and-blood individuals. Doña Bárbara, for example, is frequently referred to as "la devoradora de hombres" (the Devourer of Men), and Dr Payara in *Cantaclaro* is known as "el diablo del Cunaviche" (the Devil of the Cunaviche). Name symbolism serves as a primary rhetorical device in his novels; in the final analysis, however, rather than contributing to character development, it actually hinders his efforts by causing readers to notice characters more for what they represent than for what they appear to be. Besides the two most obvious examples, the names of the antagonists in *Doña Bárbara*, other symbolic appellations from that novel include the moniker of Mister Danger, a transparent reference to the threats posed by North American imperialism, and the names of the two ranches, Altamira (High Sights) and El Miedo, neither of which leaves the reader with any doubt as to its significance.

From the standpoint of literary history Rómulo Gallegos is considered an icon of the regional novel, a sub-genre that was one of the mainstays of Spanish American literature for much of the first half of the 20th century. The destiny of the Venezuelan nation, its progress toward the future, is the real theme of his work and the ultimate meaning behind his allegories. The solutions to the country's problems, as set forth in his novels, lie in education and racial and political unification. In his selection of autochthonous themes and materials as subjects worthy of literary treatment, Gallegos employs one of the defining characteristics of regionalism and contributes to the creation of a national identity.

MELVIN S. ARRINGTON, JR

Editions

First edition: *Doña Bárbara*, Barcelona: Araluce, 1929
Critical edition: edited by Efraín Subero, Caracas: Biblioteca Ayacucho, 1977
Translation: *Doña Bárbara*, by Robert Malloy, Magnolia, Massachusetts: Peter Smith, 1948 [the most recent edition]

Further Reading

Alonso, Carlos J., *The Spanish American Regional Novel*, Cambridge: Cambridge University Press, 1990 [Chapter 4 is on *Doña Bárbara*]

Bermúdez, Manuel (editor), *"Doña Bárbara" ante la crítica*, Caracas: Monte Ávila, 1991

Brushwood, John S., "The Year of *Doña Bárbara*," in his *The Spanish American Novel*, Austin: University of Texas Press, 1975

Michalski, André S., *Doña Bárbara*: un cuento de hadas," *PMLA*, vol. 85 (1970)

Osorio, Luis Enrique, *et al.*, *"Doña Bárbara" ante la crítica*, Caracas: Monte Ávila, 1991

Shaw, Donald L., *Gallegos: Doña Bárbara*, London: Grant and Cutler, 1972

Sommer, Doris, "Love *of* Country: Populism's Revised Romance in *La vorágine* and *Doña Bárbara*," in her *Foundational Fictions: the National Romances of Latin America*, Berkeley: University of California Press, 1990

Manuel Gálvez 1882–1962

Argentine prose writer, dramatist and poet

As the author of novels like *La maestra normal*, 1914 [The Training College Teacher], *El mal metafísico*, 1916 [The Metaphysical Ill], *La sombra del convento*, 1917 [The Shadow of the Convent] and *Nacha Regules* (1919), Manuel Gálvez has gained a reputation in Argentine literary circles for presenting the social problems of his country in a convincingly realistic manner. As early as 1916, in a letter to Julio Cejador, the young Gálvez was already confirming the ambitious literary project then in hand: "From now on I will write only novels. I have a vast plan, and I intend to reflect the multiple life of this complicated country of ours." This prudent decision to devote his life to fiction, despite his talents in the field of poetry, drama (less so) and of course the essay, was to the benefit of Gálvez and his country. In 1910 he had already formulated in essay form, in *El diario de Gabriel Quiroga* [The Diary of Gabriel Quiroga], an examination of the key themes of Argentine history (federalism versus unitarianism, immigration, civilisation versus barbarism and Buenos Aires versus the provinces).

The fruits of the seeds sown in the early essays began to appear thematically in the fiction published in the second decade of the century. Following his designated scheme, Gálvez situated his first novel, *La maestra normal*, in La Rioja province, which he knew well from his school-inspector travels. His treatment of the love affair between the sentimental schoolteacher Rasalda and the visitor Solís from Buenos Aires, captures the time and place through the use of *costumbrismo* and Social Realism while also introducing something of the converse idealism which was to be a characteristic of Gálvez's later novels. Despite the praise of Miguel de Unamuno, *La maestra normal* provoked opposition from supporters of the system then in use in teacher's training colleges for primary school teachers, and generated much antipathy between the provinces and Buenos Aires. The capital was to be the setting of *El mal metafísico*, subtitled *Vida romántica* [A Romantic Life], a realistic treatment of a phase in Gálvez's own life. Between 1900 and 1910 Gálvez lived many of the experiences of the sentimental poet, Carlos Riga, in a bohemian group of artists (easily identified) struggling against the philistinism and materialism of *porteño* or city society. Riga, an apathetic provincial youth destroyed by the cold city, is yet another symbol of the idealism and spiritual love manifest in Gálvez's early novels, characterised as, and much praised for their Social Realism.

As promised in his 1916 plan, Gálvez placed his next novel, *La sombra del convento* in yet another part of the country, this time in the provincial city of Córdoba, noted for its beautiful churches and Jesuit-dominated schools, not to mention its religious authoritarianism and narrow-mindedness. The young protagonist José Alberto Flores, despite a series of struggles against these conservative forces, marries into one of these families after a felicitous conversion. In *Nacha Regules* Gálvez returns to the Buenos Aires setting to treat in Zolaesque fashion the ills of society, this time city prostitution. Despite the naturalistic tone of the work, Nacha is redeemed through the love of the saintly Monsalvat, who shares the romantic idealism of his literary predecessors and rescues Gálvez and his novel from bleak determinism, thus preparing the way for future (Catholic) novels.

Although *La tragedia de un hombre fuerte*, 1922 [The Tragedy of a Strong Man] belongs to this early period, and deals in a more subtle way with the long-term debate over civilisation and barbarism – in this case the struggle between the interior's perceived *espíritu estático* and the coastline's *espíritu dinámico* – one notes, beneath the surface of the socio-economic problems, a growing awareness of Gálvez's ideology, presented through the figure of the protagonist Victor Urgel. For the maturing Gálvez, moved by his own anguish in the face of the moral turpitude of his country during the *década infame*, Victor incarnates this awareness of metaphysical problems – the solitude described not only as a product of the geographical ambience (the isolation and the vastness of the pampa), but also as a universal phenomenon i.e. the spiritual solitude, expressed in all its existentialist dimensions (lack of communication, alienation, angst) as an essential part of the human condition. In this sense, *La tragedia* represents a subtle change in Gálvez's fiction.

This exploration of the national character, coupled with his interest in the Argentine solitude which transcends geographical barriers, this weaving of the ideological strand with the metaphysical concerns, was not to appear again so fully drawn till 1938, with the publication of *Hombres en soledad* [Men in Solitude], a novel about the possible regeneration of Argentina by means of the 1930 military coup of General Uriburu. Gálvez was to take up again this theme of spiritual solitude and political regeneration in *El uno y la multitud*, 1955 [The Individual and the Multitude] in the final days of the Perón dictatorship – this time to narrate the events which Argentina suffered between 1942 and 1947, that is the conflict during World War II between the two opposed groups of neutralists and supporters of the Allies. In the last years of his life, the conservative nationalist Gálvez, who had flirted with fascism in the 1930s (*Este pueblo necesita*, 1934 [This Nation Needs]) and Peronism in the 1940s, was well into his "theological," ultra-Catholic stage. Novels like *Perdido en su noche*, 1958 [Lost in His Dark Night], and *La locura de ser santo* [The Madness of Being a Saint], published posthumously in 1967, speak more to his own search for sanctity, which left him well out of step, not only spiritually and morally but also culturally and artistically, with the rest of his countrymen.

By the time of his death in 1962, some of the Boom novelists had already made their mark. There was no place, it appears, for a literary, ideological, conservative, religious dinosaur. More than thirty years later, at the end of the century, it seems time for a revaluation of Manual Gálvez, whose sixty volumes of fiction, biography, poetry, essay and drama have made a significant contribution to Argentine life and letters. Recent news of the new Fundación Manuel Gálvez, plus plans for filming *La maestra normal*, and publishing new editions of *Hombres en soledad* and *El uno y la multitud* in the series Colección Identidad Nacional, may point the way to possible rehabilitation of this writer, who has in the past often been judged more for his politics and ideology, than for his imaginative gifts.

JOHN WALKER

Biography

Born in the town of Paraná, Argentina, 18 July 1882. Attended Franciscan secondary school in Buenos Aires, completing his studies in 1897. In 1903 he began to work as a law clerk in a criminal court in Buenos Aires. Took degree in law in 1904. First trip to Europe in 1905. Inspector of secondary schools and of teachers' training colleges 1906–31; resigned. Married the writer, Delfina Bunge, in 1910; three children. In the same year travelled to Paris as a delegate to International Congress on Unemployment. Joined staff of important journal, *Nosotros* [Us], in 1912, and also contributed to *Revista de América*, *Caras y Caretas* and *La Nación*. Founded two publishing houses: Editorial Pax (1919) and Biblioteca de Novelistas Americanos (1920). Founded Argentine chapter of the PEN Club in 1930. Took leading part in founding the Argentine Academy of Letters and became a member of it in 1931. Candidate for Nobel Prize in 1932. Wife died in 1952 and he married María Elena Gaviola Salas in 1954. Awarded the Buenos Aires Municipal Prize, 1919, for *Nacha Regules*. Died in Buenos Aires, 14 November 1962.

Selected Works

Novels

La maestra normal, Buenos Aires: Sociedad Cooperativa Nosotros, 1914
El mal metafísico, Buenos Aires: Sociedad Cooperativa Nosotros, 1916
La sombre del convento, Buenos Aires: Sociedad Cooperativa Nosotros, 1917
Nacha Regules, Buenos Aires: Pax, 1919; as *Nacha Regules*, translated by Leo Ongley, New York: Dutton, 1922
La tragedia de un hombre fuerte, Buenos Aires: Biblioteca de Novelistas Americanos, 1922
Historia de arrabal, Buenos Aires: Agencia General de Librería y Publicaciones, 1922
El cántico espiritual, Buenos Aires: Agencia General de Librería y Publicaciones, 1923
La pampa y su pasión, Buenos Aires: Agencia General de Librería y Publicaciones, 1926
Una mujer muy moderna, Buenos Aires: Gleizer, 1927
Los caminos de la muerte, Buenos Aires: La Facultad, 1928
Humaitá, Buenso Aires: La Facultad, 1929
Jornadas de agonía, Buenos Aires: La Facultad, 1929
Miércoles santo, Buenos Aires: La Facultad, 1930; as *Holy Wednesday*, translated by W.B. Wells, London: Bodley Head, and New York: Appleton, 1934
El gaucho de Los Cerrillos, Buenos Aires: La Facultad, 1931
El General Quiroga, Buenos Aires: La Facultad, 1932
Cautiverio, Buenos Aires: Sociedad Amigos del Libro Rioplatense, 1935
La noche toca a su fin, Buenos Aires: Cabaut y Compañía, 1935
Hombres en soledad, Buenos Aires: Club del Libro, 1938
La ciudad pintada en rojo, Buenos Aires: Instituto Panamericano de Cultura, 1948
La muerte en las calles: novela de las invasiones inglesas, 1806–1807, Buenos Aires: El Ateneo, 1949
Tiempo de odio y angustia, Buenos Aires: Espasa Calpe Argentina, 1951
Han tocado a degüello, Buenos Aires: Espasa Calpe Argentina, 1951
Bajo la garra anglo-francesca, Buenos Aires: Espasa Calpe Argentina, 1953
Y así cayó don Juan Manuel, Buenos Aires: Espasa Calpe Argentina, 1954
Las dos vidas del pobre Napoleón, Buenos Aires: Losada, 1954
El uno y la multitud, Buenos Aires: Alpe, 1955
Tránsito Guzmán, Buenos Aires: Theoría, 1956
Perdido en su noche, Buenos Aires: Sudamericana, 1958
Me mataron entre todos, Buenos Aires: Emecé, 1962
La locura de ser santo, Buenos Aires: Puma, 1967

Short Fiction

Los mejores cuentos, Buenos Aires: Patria, 1919
Luna de miel y otras narraciones, Buenos Aires: Biblioteca de Novelistas Americanos, 1920

Poetry

El enigma interior, Buenos Aires: privately printed, 1907
El sendero de humildad, Buenos Aires: Moen y Hermano, 1909
Poemas para la recién llegada, Buenos Aires: Theoría, 1957

Plays

El hombre de los ojos azules: comedia en tres actos, Buenos Aires: La Facultad, 1928
Calibán: tragicomedia de la vida política, Buenos Aires: privately printed, 1943

Biographies

Vida de Fray Mamerto Esquiú, Buenos Aires: Tor, 1938
Vida de Hipólito Yrigoyen, Buenos Aires: Tor, 1939
Vida de don Juan Manuel de Rosas, Buenos Aires: El Ateneo, 1940
Vida de don Gabriel García Moreno, Buenos Aires: Difusión, 1942
Vida de Aparicio Saravia, Buenos Aires: privately printed, 1942
Vida de Sarmiento, Buenos Aires: La Universidad, 1947
José Hernández, Buenos Aires: La Universidad, 1945
Don Francisco de Miranda, Buenos Aires: Emecé, 1947
El santito de la toldería: la vida perfecta de Ceferino Namuncurá, Buenos Aires: Poblet, 1947

Essays

El diario de Gabriel Quiroga: opiniones sobre la vida argentina, Buenos Aires: Moen, 1910
Argentina, Buenos Aires: Sociedad Cooperativa Nosotros, 1913
La inseguridad de la vida obrera: informe sobre el paro forzoso, Buenos Aires: Alsina, 1913
El espíritu de aristocracia y otros ensayos, Buenos Aires: Agencia General de Librería y Publicaciones, 1924
Este pueblo necesita, Buenos Aires: García Santos, 1934
La Argentina en nuestros libros, Santiago de Chile: Ercilla, 1935
España y algunos españoles, Buenos Aires: Huarpes, 1945
El novelista y las novelas, Buenos Aires: Emecé, 1949

Memoirs

Amigos y maestros de mi juventud, 1900–1910, Buenos Aires: Kraft, 1944
Recuerdos de la vida literaria, Buenos Aires: Hachette, 1961
En el mundo de los seres ficticios, Buenos Aires: Hachette, 1961
Entre la novela y la historia, Buenos Aires: Hachette, 1962
En el mundo de los seres reales, Buenos Aires: Hachette, 1965

Other Writings

La vida múltiple, Buenos Aires: Sociedad Cooperativa Nosotros, 1916
El solar de la raza, obra premiada por el gobierno de la República Argentina, Madrid: Saturnino Calleja, 1920
El espiritualismo español, Buenos Aires: Bayardo, 1921

La casa colonial, edited by Guillermo Rivera, Oxford and New York: Oxford University Press, 1939
La gran familia de los Laris, Buenos Aires: Universitaria de Buenos Aires, 1973

Compilations and Anthologies

Obras escogidas, Buenos Aires: Aguilar, 1949
Biografías completas, 2 vols, Buenos Aires: Emecé, 1962

Further Reading

After decades of neglect, Gálvez *appears* to have been receiving a little more attention from the critics in the last few years – a prerequisite for both rehabilitation and revisionary readings. To be appreciated by modern readers Gálvez's work must be seen in the context of his period. Thus it is not surprising that the direction of more recent criticism is often ideological and political.

Agresti, Mable Susana, *Literaturas y realidades: la visión del país en algunas novelas de Manuel Gálvez*, Mendoza: Universidad Nacional de Cuyo, 1981
Anzoátegui, Ignacio B., *Manuel Gálvez*, Buenos Aires: Ediciones Culturales Argentinas, 1961
Borello, Rodolfo A., *El peronismo (1943–1955) en la narrativa argentina*, Ottawa: Dovehouse Editions, 1991
Desinano, Norma, *La novelística de Manuel Gálvez*, Santa Fe, Argentina: Universidad Nacional del Litoral, 1965
Jiménez, Luis A., *Literatura y sociedad en la narrativa de Manuel Gálvez*, Buenos Aires: Peña Lillo, 1990
Lichtblau, Myron I., *Manuel Gálvez*, Boston: Twayne, 1972
Olivari, Nicolás and Lorenzo Stanchina, *Manuel Gálvez: ensayo sobre su obra*, Buenos Aires: Agencia General de Librería y Publicaciones, 1924
Puente, Joseph E., *Estudio crítico-histórico de las novelas de Manuel Gálvez*, Miami: Universal, 1975
Quijada, Mónica, *Manuel Gálvez: 60 años de pensamiento nacionalista*, Buenos Aires: Centro Editor de América Latina, 1985
Szmetan, Ricardo, *La situación del escritor en la obra de Manuel Gálvez*, New York: Peter Lang, 1994

Griselda Gambaro 1928–

Argentine dramatist and prose writer

Although Griselda Gambaro began her career as a fiction writer, she was to become best known as a playwright. But many of the themes developed in her plays have their origins in her narratives. The examination of violence in both its universal and national contexts, either as punishment for posing a threat to an existing authority or simply as a gratuitous act – this is the major concern present in all of Gambaro's work to date. For reasons of brevity, this essay will focus on Griselda Gambaro the dramatist, but this in no way is meant to undermine the value of her significant contributions to the narrative genre.

In common with so many other contemporary dramatists in Latin America, in her plays Gambaro's goal is a fusion of sociopolitical commitment with verbal and non-verbal expressions of violence. This is achieved by the portrayal of the harsh realities of societal repression and resistance – torture, both physical and psychological, the subsequent numbing of individual and communal responsiveness, and the ultimate collapse of basic human interaction. Violence becomes both an expression of the characters' environment as well as an increasingly disturbing part of their own psyche. This is revealed in their own violent behaviour towards others or in their failure to control the violence around them. With their origins in the Argentine genre, *el grotesco*, or the grotesque, which is rooted in the works of Armando Discépolo (1887–1971), Gambaro's dramatic production becomes combative theatre. It is theatre which demands the collaboration, the complicity, the active response and participation of its audience (the third element in the victim/victimizer triangle) in the expectation that the human condition can change or be changed by active intervention.

The perpetrators of violence are stripped of human attributes through demystification, buffoonery, ridicule and dehumanization, whilst passive bystanders (including the drama's real-life audience) are equally condemned as accomplices of the oppressors. The identification between oppressor-oppressed, which results from the inability to see man's inhumanity to man as a threat to the victim's very survival, has tragic consequences as in *Los siameses* [The Siamese Twins] and *El desatino* [The Absurdity]. But when the oppressed unite against their oppressors, a sense of revolutionary optimism prevails as in *La malasangre* [Bad Blood] and *Del sol naciente* [The Rising Sun].

Since the 1960s Griselda Gambaro has studied what is for her a country suffering from schizophrenia, one that lives two lives. Thus in classifying her prolific theatrical production, Diana Taylor has aptly categorized Gambaro's plays of the 1960s (including *Las paredes*, *Los siameses*, and *El campo*) as "theatre of crisis;" her work of the 1970s (*Decir sí*, *El despojamiento*, and *Información para extranjeros*), respectively "Saying Yes," "Dispossession" and "Information for Foreigners," as "drama of disappearance, obsessed with the 'missing'," and the more recent plays of the 1980s (including *La malasangre*, *Del sol naciente*, and *Antígona furiosa*) as "theatre of crisis analysis, differentiating victims from victimizers."

While the earlier plays of the 1960s are in two acts, Gambaro's later plays are fragmented, very short one-acts like *Decir sí*, *El despojamiento*, or the episodic *Información para extranjeros* (A Chronicle in Twenty Scenes, 1971–73, first published in 1987). Indeed, Gambaro depicts the birth of a national consciousness – an awareness of a country's own social ills and the need to combat – the painful psycho-social growth of contemporary Argentina.

Gambaro's dramatic theory took shape during her years in exile since in this time she was unable to write for the theatre. She has said that the dramatic text is born in an immediate confrontation with a locale and with the conflicts of that world: "Every theatre piece is a settling of accounts, an immediate encounter with the society." And, underscoring the necessity of the audience for the appropriate rendering of the performance text, Gambaro stated in 1989 that theatre "is a learning experience and an exchange ... with all the modes of expression of a community." As a collective phenomenon, it is the physical presence of the audience that is necessary to complete a given performance text. But, as Gambaro herself asserts, theatre cannot be a panacea for the social ills it depicts. It is only when the audience is affected as *individuals* that change can be brought about. And it is within this framework of conveying a moving moral message on the personal level (i.e., a familiar universal tragedy brought to the level of each reader/spectator) that Gambaro's *Antígona furiosa* can best be understood – a *universal* drama without temporal or spatial boundaries speaking to the *individual* conscience. The piece was written in 1985 and 1986, during and shortly after the trial of the Dirty War commanders when, out of political

expediency, President Carlos Menem granted them an executive pardon. It deals with passivity in the face of repression, popular compliance with terror. As a retelling of the Sophoclean tragedy as well as a dramatization of the struggle by the Mothers of the Plaza de Mayo to recover their children's corpses, *Antígona furiosa* demonstrates that crimes of national conscience are not limited to Latin America or even to her native Argentina but move across cultural boundaries. The play represents a pivotal point in Gambaro's dramaturgy in the sense that it demonstrates how her protagonists have developed from a state of passive acquiescence to authority in the roles of victim-accomplices to one of raised consciousness and even to being capable of rising above their desperate situations by acts of rebellion against repression even in the face of their own death.

As a playwright, Griselda Gambaro is keenly aware of the role of representation (social and theatrical) in maintaining or dismantling the political structure. Gambaro's *Información para extranjeros* (written in the period 1971–1973) most acutely illustrates this sentiment. More so than in any of her other dramatic pieces, *Información para extranjeros* confuses art-as-truth and art-as-fiction as it interplays with the breakdown of the barriers between stage and audience. The dramatist describes this manipulation between "reality" and "theatre" as a "guided tour of the places of repression and indignity" due to the significance that leading, following, and bearing witness play as audience members are given personal "guides" with narration ("Explanation: For Foreigners," readings of newspaper articles that appeared in the Argentine press during this period, the "official story" of events) through spaces used for detention and torture. As Gambaro gives new meaning to *environmental theatre* in this work by placing acts of political violence within familiar places – public streets, private houses, directly in the lives of audience members themselves – she exposes the secret and dark places of prisons and torture chambers hidden from view for all to see and, in some measure, "experience." Due to its demanding staging requirements, not to mention a participatory audience, the only performances of this work to date have been at English-language workshops and readings in the United States. The Argentine public has not been particularly receptive to a performance text that wages "assaults" against passivity and inaction, not to mention the implicit social criticism of a people who allowed government-sponsored terrorism in the form of kidnapping, torture, and death to paralyze them.

ELENA DE COSTA

Biography

Born in Buenos Aires, Argentina, 28 July 1928. Parents were Italian immigrants; father a Post Office employee. After leaving high school in 1943 she worked as a clerk for a publishing house and a sports club, 1947–56. Married the sculptor Juan Carlos Distéfano; two children, Andrea (b. 1961) and Lucas (b. 1965). Taught drama at the Universidad Nacional del Litoral, Santé Fé, 1969. Spent year in Rome, 1970. Associated with the Centro de Experimentación Audiovisual del Instituto Torcuato di Tella. Lived in Barcelona, 1977–80, to avoid the worst years of the military dictatorship. She had been forced into exile when one of her novels, *Ganarse la muerte* [Asking for Death] was banned by the direct decree of

General Jorge Rafael Videla, such a ban amounted to a death threat. On her return to Buenos Aires she collaborated with the Teatro Abierto (Open Theatre) and produced political plays. Guggenheim Award in 1982 enabled her to travel to Mexico, the US and France. Recipient of numerous awards including the Emecé Prize, 1965, for *El desatino*, the Revista Teatro XX Prize in the same year for *El desatino* and four first prizes for her play *El campo* in 1968.

Selected Works

Plays
Madrigal en ciudad, Buenos Aires: Goyanarte, 1963
El desatino, Buenos Aires: Editorial del Instituto Di Tella, 1965
Una felicidad con menos pena, Buenos Aires: Sudamericana, 1967
Los siameses, Buenos Aires: Insurrexit, 1967
El campo, Buenos Aires: Insurrexit, 1967
La gracia, in *El Urogallo* 17, Madrid (1972)
Nada que ver con otra historia, Buenos Aires: Noé, 1972
Sólo un aspecto, in *La palabra y el hombre* 8, Mexico City (1973)
El nombre, in supplement of *El Cronista*, Buenos Aires (September 1975)
Ganarse la muerte, Buenos Aires: Ediciones de La Flor, 1976
Dios no nos quiere contentos, Barcelona: Lumen, 1979
Decir sí, Buenos Aires: Editorial Teatro Abierto, 1981
El despojamiento, in *Tramoya*, Mexico City, 21–22 (1981)
Nada que ver. Sucede lo que pasa, Ottawa: Girol Books, 1983
Lo impenetrable, Buenos Aires: Torres Agüero, 1984
Antígona furiosa, Gestos 5 (1988)

Compilations and Anthologies
Teatro: Las paredes, El desatino, Los siameses, Buenos Aires and Barcelona: Argonauta, 1979
Teatro: Real envido, La malasangre, Del sol naciente, vol. 1, Buenos Aires: Ediciones de La Flor, 1984
Teatro: Dar la vuelta, Información para extranjeros, Puesta en claro, Sucede lo que pasa, vol. 2, Buenos Aires: Ediciones de La Flor, 1987
Teatro: Antígona furiosa y otras piezas breves, vol. 3, Buenos Aires: Ediciones de La Flor, 1989
Teatro: Las paredes, El desatino, Los siameses, El campo, Nada que ver, vol. 4, Buenos Aires: Ediciones de La Flor, 1990

Anthologies in Translation
Information for Foreigners: Three Plays, edited and translated by Marguerite Feitlowitz, Evanston, Illinois: Northwestern University Press, 1992

Novels and Short Fiction
La cola mágica, Buenos Aires: Ediciones de La Flor, 1976 [stories for children]
Conversaciones con chicos, Buenos Aires: Timerman, 1976
Un poco de historia, Un río que sólo corre de noche, Buenos Aires and Barcelona: Argonauta, 1988
Después del día de fiesta, Buenos Aires: Seix Barral, 1994

Other Writings
"Disyuntivas de un autor teatral que se convierte en novelista," *La Opinión*, Buenos Aires (March 1977)
"¿Es posible y deseable una dramaturgia específicamente femenina?" *Latin American Theatre Review*, vol. 12/2 (Fall 1980)
"Discépolo, nuestro dramaturgo necesario," *Revista del Teatro Municipal General San Martín*, Buenos Aires, vol. 2/3 (1981)
"Algunas consideraciones sobre la mujer y la literatura," *Revista Iberoamericana* 51 (1985)
"Algunas consideraciones sobre la crisis de la dramaturgia," *En busca de una imagen: ensayos críticos sobre Griselda Gambaro y José Triana*, edited by Diana Taylor, Ottawa: Girol Books, 1989

Further Reading
Albuquerque, Severino J., *Violent Acts: a Study of Latin American Theatre*, Detroit, Michigan: Wayne State University Press, 1991
Cypess, Sandra Messinger, "The Plays of Griselda Gambaro," in *Dramatists in Revolt*, edited by Leon F. Lyday and George W. Woodyard, Austin: University of Texas Press, 1975
Feitlowitz, Marguerite, "Crisis, Terror, Disappearance: the Theater of Griselda Gambaro," *Theater; Yale School Drama*, (Summer–Fall 1990)
Foster, David William, "Argentine Sociopolitical Commentary, the Malvinas Conflict, and Beyond: Rhetoricizing a National Experience," *Latin American Theatre Review*, vol. 22/1 (Spring 1979)
Gladhart, Amalia, "Nothing's Happening: Performance as Coercion in Contemporary Latin American Theatre," *Gestos: teoría y práctica del teatro hispano* 9 (18 November 1994)
Kubiak, Anthony, *Stages of Terror: Terrorism, Ideology and Coercion as Theatre History*, Bloomington: Indiana University Press, 1991
Lewis, Ward B., "Exile Drama: the Example of Argentina," in *Latin America and the Literature of Exile*, Heidelberg: Carl Winter Universitätsverlag, 1983
Nigro, Kirsten F., "Griselda Gambaro vista desde lejos: primeros textos y contextos culturales," *Teatro argentino de los '60*, Buenos Aires: Ediciones Corregidor, 1989
Rosen, Carol, *Plays of Impasse: Contemporary Drama Set in Confining Institutions*, Princeton, New Jersey: Princeton University Press, 1983
Taylor, Diana, "Theater and Terror: Griselda Gambaro," in her *Theatre of Crisis. Drama and Politics in Latin America*, Lexington: University Press of Kentucky, 1991

Interviews
Betsko, Kathleen and Rachel Koening (editors), *Interviews with Contemporary Women Playwrights*, New York: Beech Tree Books, 1987
Picon Garfield, Evelyn (editor), *Women's Voices from Latin America: Interviews with Six Contemporary Authors*, Detroit, Michigan: Wayne State University Press, 1985

Ventura García Calderón 1886–1959

Peruvian prose writer

Although Ventura García Calderón spent his early years in his native Peru, from 1906 until 1959 he lived in Europe and for the most part in Paris. As a youth García Calderón read José Enrique Rodó's influential essay *Ariel* and Rubén Darío's *Prosas profanas*, widely circulated works that could both underscore and create conflict for the Americanism which García Calderón consistently expressed in his literary endeavours. His work is of a transitional nature, having its beginnings in the Spanish American *modernista* or post-modernist period of Darío and Juan Ramón Jiménez.

García Calderón is a master of prose creation. He is best known as the author of *La venganza del cóndor*, 1924 [The Condor's Revenge] and *Cunetos peruanos*, 1952 [Peruvian Stories] but was also extremely prolific in other cultural areas. He produced numerous articles of literary criticism and chronicles which were a cross between literary analysis, reviews of cultural events, historical reflections and fiction. His prose style was fundamentally *modernista* and attracted readers' attention even in the presence of such contemporaries as Gutiérrez Nájera, Martí and Darío. The influence of D'Annunzian decadence is evident in *Frívolamente*, 1908 [Frivolously] and *Cantilenas*, 1920 [Ballads]. In the former one finds multifaceted portraits of the Paris he knew as an American observer, situated between Anatole de France and Paul Verlaine, by his own confession. The world described is one of sensuality; particularly in relation to women and other aspects of nightlife, and is suggestive yet restrained by subtle references to honour, love for country, and faith. The details of daily and artistic existence in the French capital are sometimes linked to the Hispanic, often to the concept of a Latin character, and a very sensitive human response to the immediate surroundings. Women figure frequently in García Calderón's short articles and they range from the scorned (writers) to the idealized (mystics, female representations in works of art), but are always clearly portrayed from a patriarchal and conservative perspective. *Cantilenas* is a volume of mixed genres – prose and poetry – with *modernista* tones.

Although he may be considered weak politically, and less than faithful to his responsibilities, as a diplomat (he lost his post in 1921 and only regained it in 1930), García Calderón was true to his vocation as a writer and strove to show European readers that Latin Americans were more than picturesque individuals. One of the expressions of his commitment was a constant attention to American literary production. In 1910 he published *Del romanticismo al modernismo*, an anthology of Peruvian writers from Romanticism to Modernism accompanied by critical commentaries. In 1910 he published *Dolorosa y desnuda realidad* [Painful, Naked Truth], a collection of short stories influenced by Oscar Wilde, J.-K. Huysmans and Leconte de Lisle.

García Calderón became associated with the *Revue Hispanique* in Paris, which resulted in the publication of literary histories of Latin American countries. The five volumes which appeared include two authored or co-authored by him, these being considered the best of the collection: *La literatura peruana* [Peruvian Literature] and *La literatura uruguaya* [Uruguayan Literature] with H. Barbagelata. The twelve-volume *Biblioteca de Cultura Peruana*, 1939 [The Library of Peruvian Culture] was perhaps the culmination of the author/ diplomat's effort to create a respected space for American writing in Europe. Before and after this, numerous volumes appeared, including critical studies or editions of Latin American writers (Valle Caviedes, El Lunarejo), European authors (Montherlant, Wilde), creative fiction, chronicles and verse. Several of his works appeared in French: *Danger de mort*, 1926 [Mortal Danger], *Couleur de sang*, 1930 [The Colour of Blood], *Le Sang plus vite*, 1936 [The Swiftest Blood] and *Amour indien*, 1944 [Indian Love] are but some of these.

Ironically, but perhaps also to his liking, García Calderón is best remembered as the author of *La venganza del cóndor*, in which he views the Peruvian highlands from a distant Europe and through the lenses of Arielist cultural concepts and Riva Agüeró's desire to foment a greater understanding of Peruvian culture. The Indian reality in these stories is beautiful, nostalgic and false. The suggestion of idealized forms and peoples resembles the world of Chateaubriand and potentially noble savages, but the content reveals a familiarity with the Quechua world that is only expressible by the author in terms of sadness and exoticism. The period of the conquest, with the display of military and sexual prowess on the part of Spanish soldiers, is the most valued, and thus validates the hierarchical perspective of historical violence as an inevitable result of the clash between superior European cultures and lesser native American ones. The fall from past glory of Peruvian civilization provides the perfect literary theme: mysterious, distant, imperial grandeur, tragic, lyrical, in a word, dramatic. This viewpoint, conflictive in its vacillation between delicate description and truculent action, presented from an external viewpoint, is in one sense a step backward in the development of a national Peruvian literature, and its ideology is vastly different from that of García Calderón's contemporary, López Albújar.

While throughout his life García Calderón continued to investigate the American cultural identity and to illustrate his love for Lima through titles such as *Vale un Perú*, 1939 [Worth a Gold Mine], *La Perichole*, 1940 [Madam Perichola], or *Instantes del Perú*, 1941 [Peruvian Moments], in which a spicy humour prevails, he also is torn by his other cultural ties to the immediate context, which is illustrated by publications such as *Cette France que nous aimions*, 1945 [The France We Loved]. He forever revels in language – the mestizos' contribution to Spanish in America – as evinced by the pamphlet *El nuevo idioma castellano* [The New Castilian Language], but perhaps did not truly understand the Peru to which he was always attached, if not by birth, by choice. On the one hand, his great aesthetic sensitivity à la Darío helped him imagine what was distinctly sad, and autochthonous about his distant country; on the other, his megalomania and bohemian nature left him suspended in a world that was Peruvian, Spanish and French, in changing order.

Kathleen N. March

See also entry on Paris

Biography

Born in Paris, 1886, where he was to spend much of his life. Educated at the School of the Sacred Heart in Lima and later at University of San Marcos where he studied Law, Literature and Politics. Served in Peruvian consular service in various West European capitals. Later settled in Paris where he ran the Excelsior publishing house. Wrote and published in French as well as in Spanish. Represented Peru at League of Nations in 1930 and appointed Peru's permanent delegate at UNESCO in 1949. Died in 1959.

Selected Works (in Spanish)

Novels

Baja el clamor de las sirenas, Paris: América Latina, 1919
Aguja de marear, Paris: Garnier, 1936

Short Fiction

Dolorosa y desnuda realidad, Paris: Garnier, 1910
Cuentos, Lima: *Literatura Peruana*, vol. I/II (1923)
La venganza del cóndor, Madrid: Mundo Latino, 1924 [Contains "La venganza del cóndor," "La llama blanca" and 22 other stories]; as *The White Llama*, translated by Richard Phibbs, London: Golden Cockerell Press, 1938
Cuentos peruanos, Madrid: Aguilar, 1952

Other Writings

Frívolamente (crónicas), Paris: Garnier, 1908
Del romanticismo al modernismo: prosistas y poetas peruanos, Paris: Ollendorf, 1910
Cantilenas, Paris: Brujas, 1920 [poems]
En la verbena de Madrid (crónicas), Paris: Ediciones America-Latina, 1920
Semblanzas de América, Madrid: Biblioteca Ariel, 1922
Sonrisas de París (crónicas), Buenos Aires: Nuestra América, 1926
Los románticos, Paris: Desclée de Brouwer, 1938
La Périchole, Paris: n.p., 1940
Instantes del Perú, Paris: Garnier, 1941
Nosotros, Paris: Garnier, 1946

Compilations and Anthologies

Obras escogidas, edited by Luis Alberto Sánchez, Lima: Edubanco, 1986
Obra literaria selecta, prologue by Luis Alberto Sánchez, chronology and bibliography by Marlene Polo Miranda, Caracas: Biblioteca Ayacucho, 1989

Further Reading

Hommage à Ventura García Calderón, edited by Henri Lefèvre, Paris: Lefèvre, 1947

Gabriel García Márquez 1928(?)–

Colombian prose writer

Born in Aracataca in the northern, Caribbean, region of Colombia, Gabriel García Márquez was brought up by his grandparents until the age of eight. The influence of rural popular culture, which reached him above all through the stories he heard from his grandmother, has been primordial in his work. Another main source has been his grandfather, who fought with the Liberals in the War of a Thousand Days, a civil war that took place at the very end of the 19th century. After being sent to school in the cold highlands, he became a journalist, working for *El Espectador,* which included a period spent as European correspondent. These separations from the places of his childhood convinced him of his identity as a Caribbean writer. Subsequently, he has lived mainly in Barcelona and Mexico. He has had close contacts with Cuba, and unlike for example Marío Vargas Llosa, he continued to support the Cuban Revolution. He was awarded the Nobel Prize for Literature in 1982.

Márquez's earliest writings consist of journalism, of which *Cuando era feliz e indocumentado*, 1973 [When I was a Young Unknown] offers a selection from the 1950s. Short stories written between 1947 and 1953 are collected in *Ojos de perro azul*, 1972 [Eyes of the Blue Dog]: the influences here are Kafka and Poe and it was not until he discovered the same tone of voice in his grandmother's stories and in Kafka's that he was able to find the language of his mature work, capable of conveying the natural and the supernatural, the everyday and the marvellous, without division. His first novel, *La hojarasca*, 1955 (*Leaf Storm*), establishes an aristocratic vision of Macondo, the imaginary region of much of his fiction of the 1950s and 1960s. The title refers to the arrival in the region of the "Banana Company" (historically, the United Fruit Company), which for the local aristocracy signifies the apocalyptic demise of their world, their values and of time itself. The key historical referents of *El coronel no tiene quien le escriba*, 1957 (*No One Writes to the Colonel*) are the War of a Thousand Days and the modern period of *la Violencia*, when civil war conditions dominated the country between 1949 and 1962 and left more than 200,000 dead. The Colonel of the title is still waiting, in 1956, for the state pension he was promised for fighting in the 19th-century civil war. The other source of hope, in a novel which counterposes the humiliating drudgery of survival under political and social oppression to the Colonel's sense of trascendence, is a fighting cock, which "must win." Amid sensations of history being as uncontrollable as the lottery or the weather, these two objects sustain symbolically the possibility of change. Humour and fatalism collide in this short but multi-layered book: in one discarded version the cock was to have ended up in a stew. The same atmosphere of oppressive political violence is explored in *La mala hora*, 1962 (*In Evil Hour*), but the emphasis is on satirical exposure of the corrupting penetration of power into everyday life. The political regime has come to rely more on social amnesia than military violence. It is the poor who remember those killed in political murders, who embody the truth masked by the "caring" language of the regime. The main characters are middle-class people, *gente decente*, whose concern for appearances is mockingly juxtaposed with the hidden violence of the social order. A collection of stories published in 1962 – *Los funerales de la Mamá Grande* (*Big Mama's Funeral*) – deploys informal and carnavalesque aspects of popular culture for humorous demolitions of the pretensions of social authority. The title story, which is a mock sermon ridiculing power, directs a local oral sense of history against the distortions of official written history.

With *Cien años de soledad*, 1967 (*One Hundred Years of Solitude*), the history of Macondo is placed on a epic level, from its mythic/historical foundation to its final disappearance. This extraordinary novel stands in the same kind of importance for Latin American literature as *Don Quixote* does for Spanish. Reopening narrative fiction to earlier, pre-novelistic modes, it also exposes the bourgeois family chronicle, historical backbone of the genre, to the onslaught of other varieties of knowledge and experience which do not fit with the bourgeois notion of civilisation. Above all, it includes the vast world of popular beliefs and practices. Loose application of the term Magical Realism is not necessarily useful given the historical and social particularity of magic in this novel: García Márquez has stressed that everything that happens in it is perfectly normal in a Colombian context. The failure of epic foundation, played out as the destruction of a family through inward-turning incestuous desire, is in a sense the failure to found viable Latin American nation-states in the post-colonial period. The structure of fatalism in which the family are trapped collides with García Márquez's socialist politics, as he was careful to stress in his Nobel Prize acceptance speech. On the other hand, the text can be read on many levels: as a Latin American satire on Western civilisation; as a compendium of the possibilities of Latin America; as a critique of the liberal (i.e. bourgeois) history of Colombia; as a "postmodern" exploration of the limits of narrative fiction.

The stories of *La increíble y triste historia de la cándida Eréndira y de su abuela desalmada*, 1972 (*Innocent Erendira and Other Stories*) continue to undermine the usual – European, enlightened – division between the real and the irrational, for instance in the account of how a very old man with huge wings turns up on the beach after a Caribbean storm. The title story, a farcical allegory of capital accumulation, reveals García Márquez's concern with the economics of regions marginally integrated into the world capitalist system. His next major work was a response to the historical legacy of dictatorship in Latin America, sharpened by a personal need to confront the isolation of personal fame by analysing desire for power. The dictator in *El otoño del patriarca*, 1975 (*The Autumn of the Patriarch*) is both a myth and an amalgam of actual historical figures. It is the voice of the people which supplies him with power by constructing him as dominant

figure, but the same voice parodies and unmasks the imagery of power.

García Márquez's declared fascination with Greek tragedy shows above all in the short novel *Crónica de una muerte anunciada*, 1981 (*Chronicle of a Death Foretold*), which recounts the murder of a man for allegedly violating the law of honour. Investigation reveals the whole town to be responsible. But it is the form of the plot, with its chains of coincidences that carries the tragic dimension, not people's accounts of their actions. The result is all the more disturbing: the mechanism of fatalism is not in people's consciousness. *El amor en los tiempos del cólera*, 1985 (*Love in the Time of Cholera*) appears to move in a very different direction. It celebrates a love affair without tragedy or wastage, one which flowers in old age, after a lifetime of waiting. Nevertheless, time as wastage haunts the edge of the scene, in the form of the forests being devoured as fuel by the river-boat where the lovers find themselves, revealing a recurrent concern in García Márquez's writing with processes of decadence and renewal, both in the individual psyche and over the longer terms of history. In a subsequent novel, he continues to make the past his subject, but paradoxically regenerating the vision of Latin American unity. *El general en su laberinto*, 1989 (*The General in His Labyrinth*) traces Bolívar's final journey down the Magdalena river, his destruction in soul and body as forces of division and dictatorship grow up around him, wrecking his plan of making Latin America into a single federated State, a massive force for an alternative vision of the future.

Doce cuentos peregrinos, 1992 (*Strange Pilgrims*) is a collection of short stories which deal with "the strange things that happen to Latin Americans in Europe" as events that place routine attitudes at an edge where securities of cultural interpretation become thin. Humour – as in all of García Márquez's work, a key feature – is used to explore what those securities seek to control and the effects of time swing between devastation and repetition, without renewal. His recent novel *Del amor y otros demonios* (*Of Love and Other Demons*), is set in Colombia in the 18th century, towards the end of the colonial period, in a society that is both sumptuous and decaying and that in subtle ways continues alongside the modern world of the late 20th century. African religions brought by slaves, inquisitional Catholicism and loss of faith (a phenomenon of the changing times) coexist, and in their midst the miraculous, a theme that has interested García Márquez since he began writing, is handled ambiguously: it is both what cannot be explained or accommodated by belief systems and what the Church uses for authoritarian control. Fascination with religion in a society that is falling apart makes this clearly an end of 20th-century novel.

WILLIAM ROWE

See also entries on The Boom, Caudillismo and Dictatorship, The Historical Novel, Magical Realism

Biography
Born in Aracataca, Colombia, 6 March 1928(?). Attended Colegio San José, Barranquilla, 1940–42; Colegio Nacional, Zipaquirá, to 1946; studied law and journalism at the National University of Colombia, Bogotá, 1947–48; University of Cartagena, 1948–49. Journalist, 1947–50, 1954. European correspondent in Rome and

Paris, for the newspaper *El Espectador*, 1955. Lost his post when this newspaper was closed down by the dictator Rojas Pinilla. Travelled to USSR. Journalist for *El Heraldo*, Barranquilla, 1950–54; founder, Prensa Latina (Cuban press agency), Bogotá: worked in Prensa Latina office, Havana, 1959, and New York, 1961. Married Mercedes Barcha in 1958; two sons. Lived in Venezuela, Cuba, the United States, Spain and Mexico; returned to Colombia in 1982. Founder, 1979, and since 1979 president, Fundación Habeas. Also founder of Film School near Havana. Recipient of numerous awards including: Colombian Association of Writers and Artists Award, 1954; Concurso Nacional de Cuento Short Story Prize, 1955; Chianciano Prize (Italy), 1968; Foreign Book Prize (France), 1970; Rómulo Gallegos Prize (Venezuela), 1972; Neustadt International Prize, 1972; Nobel Prize for Literature, 1982; Los Angeles *Times* Prize, 1988.

Selected Works

Novels and Novellas

La hojarasca, Bogotá: Sipa, 1955
El coronel no tiene quien le escriba, Mexico City: Era: 1957; as *No One Writes to the Colonel*, translated by J.S. Bernstein, in *No One Writes to the Colonel and Other Stories*, New York: Harper and Row, 1968; London: Jonathan Cape, 1971
La mala hora, Madrid: Pérez, 1962; as *In Evil Hour*, translated by Gregory Rabassa, New York: Avon Books, 1980; London: Jonathan Cape, 1980
Isabel viendo llover en Macondo, Buenos Aires: Estuario, 1967
Cien años de soledad, Buenos Aires: Sudamericana, 1967; as *One Hundred Years of Solitude*, translated by Gregory Rabassa, New York: Harper and Row, and London: Jonathan Cape, 1970
El negro qui hizo esperar a los ángeles, Montevideo: Alfil, 1972 [novella]
El otoño del patriarca, Barcelona: Plaza y Janés, 1975; as *The Autumn of the Patriarch*, translated by Gregory Rabassa, New York: Harper and Row, 1976; London: Jonathan Cape, 1977
El último viaje del buque fantasma, Parets del Vallés: Polígrafa, 1976 [novella]
Crónica de una muerte anunciada, Bogotá: Oveja Negra, 1981; as *Chronicle of a Death Foretold*, translated by Gregory Rabassa, New York: Knopf, and London: Jonathan Cape, 1982 [novella]
El rastro de tu sangre en la nieve: el verano feliz de la señora Forbes, Bogotá: W. Dampier Editores, 1982 [novella]
El amor en los tiempos del cólera, Bogotá: Oveja Negra, 1985; as *Love in the Time of Cholera*, translated by Edith Grossman, New York: Knopf, and London: Jonathan Cape, 1988
El general en su laberinto, Bogotá: Oveja Negra, 1989; as *The General in His Labyrinth*, translated by Edith Grossman, New York: Knopf, 1990; London: Jonathan Cape, 1991
Del amor y otros demonios, Mexico City: Diana, 1994; as *Of Love and Other Demons*, translated by Edith Grossman, New York: Knopf, 1995; Harmondsworth: Penguin, 1996

Short Fiction

Los funerales de la Mamá Grande, Xalapa, Mexico: Universidad Veracruzana, 1962; as *Big Mama's Funeral*, translated by J.S. Bernstein, in *No One Writes to the Colonel*, New York: Harper and Row, 1968
Ojos de perro azul: nueve cuentos desconocidos, Buenos Aires: Equis, 1972
La increíble y triste historia de la cándida Eréndira y de su abuela desalmada: siete cuentos, Barcelona: Seix Barral, 1972; as *Innocent Erendira and Other Stories*, translated by Gregory Rabassa, New York: Harper and Row, 1978; London: Jonathan Cape, 1979

Doce cuentos peregrinos, Bogotá: Oveja Negra, 1992; as *Strange Pilgrims: 12 Stories*, translated by Edith Grossman, New York: Knopf, and London: Jonathan Cape, 1993; retitled as *Bon Voyage, Mr President and Other Stories*, Harmondsworth: Penguin, 1995

Plays

Viva Sandino, Managua: Nueva Nicaragua, 1982; as *El asalto: el operativo con que el FSLN se lanzó al mundo*, 1983
El secuestro, Salamanca: Lóquez, 1982 [screenplay]
María de mi corazón (*Mary My Dearest*), in collaboration with J.H. Hermosillo, 1983 [screenplay]
Eréndira, n.p.: Les Films du Triangle, 1983 [screenplay]
Diatriba de amor contra un hombre sentado, Santafé de Bogotá: Arnago, 1994

Other Writings

La novela en América Latina: diálogo, in collaboration with Mario Vargas Llosa, Lima: Milla Batres, 1968
Relato de un náufrago que estuvo diez días, Barcelona: Tusquets, 1970; as *The Story of a Shipwrecked Sailor*, translated by Randolph Hogan, New York: Knopf, and London: Jonathan Cape, 1986
Cuando era feliz e indocumentado, Caracas: El Ojo del Camello, 1973
De viaje por los países socialistas: 90 días en la "Cortina de Hierro," Cali, Colombia: Macondo, 1978
Crónicas y reportajes, Bogotá: Oveja Negra, 1978
Periodismo militante, Bogotá: Son de Máquina Editores, 1978
La batalla de Nicaragua, in collaboration with Gregoria Selser and Daniel Waksman Schinca, Mexico City: Bruguera Mexicana, 1979
García Márquez habla de García Márquez, Bogotá: Rentería, 1979
El olor de la guayaba, Bogotá: Oveja Negra, 1982; as *The Fragrance of Guava*, Plinio Apuleyo Mendoza in Conversation with Gabriel García Márquez, translated by Ann Wright, London: Verso/New Left, 1983
La soledad de América Latina; brindis por la poesía, Cali: Corporación Editorial Universitaria de Colombia, 1983
Persecución y muerte de minorías, in collaboration with Guillermo Nolasco-Juárez, Buenos Aires: Juárez, 1984
La aventura de Miguel Littín, clandestino en Chile: un reportaje, Bogotá: Oveja Negra, 1986; as *Clandestine in Chile: the Adventures of Miguel Littín*, translated by Asa Zatz, New York: Holt, 1987; London: Granta, 1989
El cataclismo de Damocles = The Doom of Damocles, San José, Costa Rica: Universitaria Centroamericana, 1986 [bilingual edition]
Textos costeños, Buenos Aires: Sudamericana, 1987
Noticia de un secuestro, Buenos Aires: Sudamericana, 1996

Compilations and Anthologies

Todo los cuentos 1947–1972, Barcelona: Plaza y Janés, 1975
Obra periodística, edited by Jacques Gilard, 4 vols, Buenos Aires: Bruguera, 1981–83 [Contains vol. 1: *Textos costeños*; vols 2–3: *Entre cachacos*; vol. 4: *De Europa y América (1955–1960)*]

Anthologies in Translation

Leaf Storm and Other Stories, translated by Gregory Rabassa, New York: Harper and Row, 1972
Collected Stories, translated by Gregory Rabassa, New York: Harper and Row, 1984; revised edition, London: Jonathan Cape, 1991
Collected Novellas, translated by Gregory Rabassa and J.S. Bernstein, New York: HarperCollins, 1990

Further Reading

Bell-Villas, Gene H., *Gabriel García Márquez: the Man and His Work*, Chapel Hill: University of North Carolina Press, 1990

Earle, Peter G. (editor), *Gabriel García Márquez*, Madrid: Taurus, 1982

Fuentes, Carlos, *Gabriel García Márquez and the Invention of America*, Liverpool: Liverpool University Press, 1987

Hart, Stephen M., *Crónica de una muerte anunciada*, London: Grant and Cutler, 1994

Janes, Regina, *Gabriel García Márquez: Revolution in Wonderland*, Columbia: University of Missouri Press, 1981

McGuirk, Bernard and Richard Cardwell (editors), *Gabriel García Márquez: New Readings*, Cambridge and New York: Cambridge University Press, 1987

McMurray, George R., *Gabriel García Márquez*, New York: Ungar, 1977

McMurray George R., (editor), *Critical Essays on Gabriel García Márquez*, Boston: G.K. Hall, 1987 [Interesting selection of articles and reviews of works up to *Crónica de una muerte anunciada*]

McNerney, Kathleen, *Understanding Gabriel García Márquez*, Columbia: University of South Carolina Press, 1989

Minta, Stephen, *Gabriel García Márquez, Writer of Colombia*, London: Jonathan Cape, 1987

Oberhelman, Harley D., *Gabriel García Márquez: a Study of the Short Fiction*; Boston: Twayne, 1991

Ortega, Julio (editor), *Gabriel García Márquez and the Powers of Fiction*, Austin: University of Texas Press, 1988

Penuel, Arnold M., *Intertextuality in García Márquez*, New York: Spanish Literature Publications, 1994

Sims, Robert L., *The First García Márquez: a Study of His Journalistic Writing from 1948 to 1955*, Lanham, Maryland: University Press of America, 1992

Vargas Llosa, Mario, *Gabriel García Márquez: historia de un deicidio*, Barcelona: Seix Barral, 1971

Williams, Raymond L., *Gabriel García Márquez*, Boston: Twayne, 1984

Bibliographies

Fau, Margaret Eustella, *Gabriel García Márquez: an Annotated Bibliography 1947–1979*, Westport, Connecticut: Greenwood Press, 1980

Fau, Margaret Eustella and Nelly Sfeir de González, *A Bibliographical Guide to Gabriel García Márquez 1979–1985*, Westport, Connecticut: Greenwood Press, 1986

Sfeir de González, Nelly, *A Bibliographical Guide to Gabriel García Márquez, 1986–1992*, Westport, Connecticut: Greenwood Press, 1994

Special Issues of Journals

Special Issue: Gabriel García Márquez, Latin American Literary Review, edited by Yvette Miller and Charles Rossman, vol. 13/25 (January–June 1985)

El amor en los tiempos del cólera

Novel by Gabriel García Márquez

El amor en los tiempos del cólera is García Márquez's version of the 19th-century romantic novel. For this reason the novel is much more traditional in form and, perhaps, considerably easier to read, than some of the author's earlier major works. Set in the north of Colombia, in and around a town which bears much resemblance to Cartagena, its time sequence stretches over some sixty years between the late 1870s and early 1930s, covering most of the life of its two main characters. The narrative starts around 1930, recapitulating the events of the previous fifty years and then moves on to the conclusion two years later.

According to the romantic tradition on which García Márquez is drawing, the love affair central to the plot undergoes many vicissitudes and set-backs. In addition, the relationship between the two lovers is offset by the presence of a third, the heroine's husband. In this triangle, however – and this is one of the many ironies of the book – the heroine is neither in love with the man she marries nor – after a very brief adolescent romance – with her lover. And the lover – puny, myopic and constipated, and always attired in black – spends half a century squandering his passion over more than 600 sexual affairs, while waiting for his beloved to come around to loving him. Which she finally does – as a seventy-two-year-old widow.

Thus romantic love is apparently debunked and debased by the author's detached, humorous treatment. A famous example of this is an early episode in which the young heroine receives a love letter from the very hands of her passionate lover just as a bird dropping falls on it. To relieve her blushing embarrassment, however, the young man smilingly comments that it is meant to bring good luck. And the reader becomes aware of how many of the romantic clichés with which the narrative abounds are here repeated as a kind of private joke, a wink between the writer and the reader, a complicity of which the very characters seem to be apart.

This "tongue in cheek" style is evident from the very title associating love with cholera. In fact the symptoms of love – dizziness, sickness and diarrhoea – are not unlike those of the illness often fatal and endemic in Latin America. For love and death, true to the romantic tradition, go hand in hand. Or do they?

In the initial episode we read of a suicide – a man misleadingly named Saint-Amour – and we are led at first to believe that he took his life because of unrequited love. That is not the case: it appears that he was well loved and that the suicide was prompted by his desire to die before being overtaken by the infirmities of old age. While Saint-Amour is never mentioned again in the course of the text, it becomes obvious that his death is intended to pose a challenge to the concept of love being stronger than old age and death. Yet this challenge is taken up and defied at the conclusion of the novel when the two lovers – now in their seventies – having finally consummated their bond, will remain on the boat going up and down the Magdalena river under the yellow flag of "Cholera aboard" for "toda la vida" (forever).

More romantic than the Romantics the author, who has denied the capacity to love to so many of his earlier male characters, is presenting the protagonist Florentino as "todo amor" (all love). His outlandish sexual behaviour is a manifestation of his being "un solitario necesitado de amor" (a solitary man in need of love). Towards the end, confronted by his aging beloved, Fermina, he answers "de inmediato sin un temblor en la voz: Es que me he conservado virgen para ti" (without hesitation in a steady voice: "I have remained a virgin for you"). She chooses to accept this, even though she doesn't believe him. On equal terms, the reader is asked to accept all these affairs were but a manifestation of his love. And such love seems to be García Márquez's final answer to gerontophobia, when the aging couple finally realizes that "el amor era el amor en cualquier tiempo y en cualquier parte, pero tanto más denso cuanto más cerca de la muerte" (love was love any time and any place, but more solid the closer it came to death).

Readers of García Márquez will find in this book many of the traits which they have grown to recognize in the work of this writer, such as humorous hyperboles, an abundance of scatological details, liturgical dates encoding major events of the plot, and – here even more than previously – a choice of names whose meanings are clearly related to the characters: Fermina, the loyal steadfast wife; Florentino, the conquering lover and, incidentally, a reminder of Europe at the time of the Renaissance; America, his young charge whom – like the conquered continent – he seduces, exploits and then abandons driving her to death; Nueva Fidelidad (New Fidelity), the boat which will take the aging lovers on their journey to the end of their lives. Equally the readers will find in the descriptions of many journeys over the Sierra and across the wild selva, a rich background of vegetable and animal life, often endowed with a symbolic role. References to the act of reading, and even more so of writing, also abound: Florentino is an avid reader and a professional writer of love letters; hence the allusions to the "decoding of the message" when the lovers communicate by telegraph.

Less obvious perhaps than in other works, but still subtly present in the narrative are the allusions to the political life of Latin America – repeated references to wars and violence and the disturbing sight of the bodies of unknown victims. Of more prominence here, is the comment on Colombian society: the heroine's husband, Urbino, a doctor and member of the upper classes is presented as a caricature of the servility to European cultural values – he reads *Le Figaro*. Urbino is confronted and replaced by the working class Florentino, member of the mestizo/mulatto population of Colombia, while poverty, filth and despair rage around the rich man's house. Urbino's parodic death is a symbol of the failure of the liberal dream in Colombian politics.

More novel is the apparently feminist line which García Márquez takes us in the denunciation of married life within the patriarchal system, an example of which is the one Urbino offers to Fermina. The sense of liberation and "finding herself" which she experiences upon his death is further illustrated by the recurrent image of the manatees. Spotted on the shores of the river, the manatees are both symbols of motherhood and of androgyny, for their species is said to be without a male.

The primary aim of the book remains, however, a celebration of life, of the spontaneity of human emotions and their illogicality. The symbol of cholera, of terror, is displaced by a symbol of love, "un estado de gracia" (a state of grace).

PSICHE HUGHES

Editions
First edition: *El amor en los tiempos del cólera*, Bogotá: Oveja Negra, 1985
Translation: *Love in the Time of Cholera*, by Edith Grossman, New York: Knopf, and London: Jonathan Cape, 1988

Further Reading
Monsiváis, Carlos, "*El amor en los tiempos del cólera*: la novela extraordinaria de un Premio Nobel que no deja que ésto lo sojuzgue," Mexico City, *Proceso* 477 (23 December 1985)
Romero, Armando, "Gabriel García Márquez: *El amor en los tiempos del cólera, Revista Iberoamericana* 137 (October–December 1986)

Cien años de soledad

Novel by Gabriel García Márquez

Cien años de soledad is an epic historical novel which charts the fortunes of a small Colombian town (Macondo) from its founding as an isolated outpost at the start of the 19th century, through its experience of civil and ecclesiastical authorities, the prolonged civil wars between Liberals and Conservatives, the invasion by the Banana Company which represents a period of neo-colonial domination by the US, the strike by the workers, the massacre and the slow erosion of the town in the 20th century until a devastating wind erases it from the face of the earth. While these events parallel a chronological period in Colombian history, the "cien años" also represent a metaphorical hundred years which reach back to the period of Discovery and Conquest as well as forward to post-colonial attempts to heal a history of fragmentation and oppression.

Central to this latter aim is García Márquez's use of parody. At the same time as there is a demonstrable historicity to the events of the novel, the mass of information in the form of dates, names, events, wars, governments, family lines etc., reads like a parody of the historical novel which serves to undermine both the totalizing nature of the genre, and the metanarrative of "history" itself. As Michael Wood demonstrates in his study, *Gabriel García Márquez: One Hundred Years of Solitude*, the linear chronology of the historical novel is fragmented structurally, by sequences of loops and flashbacks and constant narrative interruptions, and also syntactically, by the use of multiple tenses in a single sentence. The novel's opening sentence is typical of the way in which a notion of time is displaced to suggest the interconnections between past, present and future: "Muchos años después, frente al pelotón de fusilamiento, el coronel Aureliano Buendía había de recordar aquella tarde remota en que su padre lo llevó a conocer el hielo. (Many years later, as he faced the firing squad, Colonel Aureliano Buendía was to remember that distant afternoon when his father took him to discover ice).

The word "después" immediately provokes the question, "later than what?" and the search for the present time is further problematized by the phrase "aquella tarde remota" which sets in the distant past an event that is about to be described. Despite the immediacy of "frente al pelotón de fusilamiento," the use of "había de recordar" again blurs the reader's perspective, reminding us of our dependency on the narrator's memory, and the power of prophecy. The verbal form "había de" is used throughout the novel and is, in some ways, its most characteristic device. It looks both forward and backward, pointing to a place where the future of the story will have become (what it always was) the past of the narrator and the present of the reader.

The reader experiences the novel, then, as a kind of schizophrenic journey backwards and forwards in time and this is further complicated by the blurred distinctions between the living and the dead, the physical and spiritual worlds. Various characters return from the dead to play a key part in the text, notably Prudencio Aguilar and Melquíades, while various of the Buendías retain the ability to communicate with an ancestral spirit world. Much of this journeying, or attempt to journey, beyond fixed categories is staged for comic effect, as with Amaranta preparing to carry the mail to the dead, or Melquíades's return from death "porque no pudo soportar la soledad" (because he could not bear the solitude), and as Clive Griffin reminds us, it is important to remember the comic exuberance which uplifts the novel throughout, defining it as much as a celebration, as a critique, of character and event. Indeed, the ability to do both is central to its aims and it is perhaps the novel's deliberate focus on simultaneous possibilities which has generated such diverse, and sometimes contradictory, critical responses.

Underpinning this method is the complex patterning of oppositional categories. Characters and events are structured through the pairing of oppositions, such as myth and history, oral and written traditions, scientific knowledge and intuitive wisdom. At the same time, these patterns are variously interchangeable which causes the disruption of binary thought and focus, instead, on their dynamic interplay. José Arcadio Buendía, the head of the family and the founder of Macondo, is the embodiment of the scientific method, meticulously working out schemes for social improvement and greater knowledge, and is directly contrasted with Úrsula, the enduring matriarch, who emphasizes the need to cultivate intuitive, even spiritual, insight. He plays the "masculine" to her "feminine" and his endeavours to subject every new discovery to strict rational criteria, such as stripping down the piano to discover its "magia secreta," become the source of much comedy for the reader. The intimacy with which these two characters combine, however, reminds us that it is the *interplay*, rather than the separation of these categories which is dynamic. Colonel Aureliano and Remedios the Beauty are, in their different ways, lessons in the dangers of a single perspective; Aureliano representing the extreme isolation of the materialist while Remedios, unable to interact with the formal world, levitates as pure spirit out of Macondo and into the clouds. This lesson is reinforced by the presence of Melquíades who serves to cross-culturize notions of scientific knowledge and intuitive wisdom. He is introduced as a mysterious and supernatural being who "parecía conocer el otro lado de las cosas" (seemed to know the other side of things). But although he drifts in and out of Macondo in marvellous and unpredictable ways, his insights always remain rooted in the earth. As Floyd Merrell points out, Melquíades signifies a specifically Eastern knowledge which, though in direct contrast to José Arcadio's Western framework, is none the less scientific. The limitations of José Arcadio's scientific paradigms are exposed, then, through the intuitive (though not unscientific) perspectives of both Úrsula and Melquíades. These perspectives do not, however, invalidate José Arcadio's struggle to comprehend reality, beneficial as it was to the modernization of Macondo.

Nor can the characters of Úrsula and Melquíades be confined to the terms of this equation. Úrsula, for instance, also represents the oral tradition while Melquíades, as keeper of the archive, has been described as a figure of Borges.

Subject positions are constructed as mobile, then, with each new relationship serving to relativize a series of interconnecting debates and ideas. Running parallel with the story of Úrsula, for instance, is that of Pilar Ternera, the prostitute and keeper of the brothel who is marginalized in the novel's social structures but central to its narrative strategies. Not until the arrival of Amaranta Úrsula, the product of both Úrsula (her great, great grandmother) and Pilar Ternera (great grandmother), do we detect a disruption of the madonna/whore dichotomy that had separated her ancient grandmothers. But the novel rarely offers a synthesis of this kind and the need to find such resolution is symptomatic of the dangers of reading myth as history. Myth has a dual function in the novel – as a process of demystifying "myths" in the pejorative sense of "what is not real," such as the Banana Company's declaration that no one was killed in the historic strike; and as a structuring principle and genuinely alternative perspective to disrupt the closed linearity of the historical narrative. For at the core of the palimpsestic historical novel which is *Cien años de soledad*, lies a primitive creation myth founded in violence and incest which completes its circular trajectory in the transgression of taboo and the birth of a child with a pig's tail. According to the myth, the act of transgression which, at the level of content, signals the destruction of community is also that which, at the level of form, instigates its transformation and evolution. The complexities of the novel's metafictional/mythical/historical ending, and the multiperspectives it demands of the reader cannot easily be reduced, but it is as a myth that the final apocalypse of the Buendías, instigated by both Amaranta Úrsula and Aureliano Babilonia, can be read as a liberation and a renewal. This is consistent with the function of Melquíades's manuscript which cannot be read by the Buendías until they have translated (transgressed) and decoded (deconstructed) historical parameters finally to reveal the perspectives through which the text/their own identity can be deciphered. It is these, formerly eclipsed, perspectives which generate the "magical realism" of the text – "lo real maravilloso" in a genuinely Carpenterian sense of a hybridized reality that responds to myth as well as history.

Critics who have preferred to stress the importance of history have tended to interpret solitude as alienation, or as nostalgia (Saldívar, Gerald Martin) rather than as "la soledad compartida" (shared solitude), or, as Michael Bell expresses it, solitude as solidarity. As critical attention shifts to García Márquez's later work, *Cien años* will also inevitably be re-read in the light of this retrospective, perhaps more rigorously post-modernizing, lens (see Carlos J. Alonso). While negotiating such diverse critical contexts, the reader should perhaps remember Dorfman's comment: "*One Hundred Years of Solitude* situates itself in the impossible middle between what is inside and outside, between life and death, between history and imagination. This means that the reader, ultimately, gets to choose."

PATRICIA MURRAY

Editions

First edition: *Cien años de soledad*, Buenos Aires: Sudamericana, 1967

Critical edition: edited by Jacques Joset, Madrid: Cátedra, 1987

Translation: *One Hundred Years of Solitude*, by Gregory Rabassa, New York: Harper and Row, and London: Jonathan Cape, 1970

Further Reading

Alonso, Carlos J., "The Mourning After: García Márquez, Fuentes and the Meaning of Postmodernity in Spanish America," *Modern Language Notes* 109 (1994)

Bell, Michael, *Gabriel García Márquez: Solitude and Solidarity* London: Macmillan, 1993

Dorfman, Ariel, "Someone Writes to the Future: Meditations on Hope and Violence in García Márquez," in *Some Write to the Future: Essays on Contemporary Latin American Fiction*, translated by the author and George R. Shivers, Durham, North Carolina: Duke University Press, 1991

Griffin, Clive, "The Humour of *One Hundred Years of Solitude*," in *Gabriel García Márquez: New Readings*, edited by Bernard McGuirk and Richard Cardwell, Cambridge: Cambridge University Press, 1987

Ludmer, Josefina, "*Cien años de soledad*": *una interpretación*, Buenos Aires: Tiempo Contemporáneo, 1972

Martin, Gerald, "On 'Magical' and Social Realism in García Márquez," in *Gabriel García Márquez: New Readings*, edited by Bernard McGuirk and Richard Cardwell, Cambridge: Cambridge University Press, 1987

Saldívar, José David, "Ideology and Deconstruction in Macondo," in *Latin American Literary Review*, vol. 13/25 (1985)

Wood, Michael, *García Márquez: One Hundred Years of Solitude*, Cambridge: Cambridge University Press, 1990

El general en su laberinto

Novel by Gabriel García Márquez

Gabriel García Márquez's *El general en su laberinto*, 1989 (*The General in His Labyrinth*) is a historical novel that portrays the life of Simón Bolívar. The action takes place in 1830, the year of Bolívar's death and dwells on the journey by river that he made during the last few months of his life. The narration of this journey is constantly broken by evocations of earlier events. These "flashbacks" narrate in a non-chronological way the major episodes of both Bolívar's political career and his personal life. There is a constant see-saw between Bolívar's various loves and important historical events in the era of Latin American independence from Spain and Latin America's subsequent formation into nation states. The present Bolívar: elderly, infirm, and no longer in power, is contrasted with the earlier Bolívar: young, vibrant, and heroic.

García Márquez's choice of Bolívar, undisputed hero of Latin American independence, as the subject of his novel is an interesting one, because it breaks with the Latin American tradition of focusing on figures whose historical roles are ambiguous, such as Dr Francia in Augusto Roa Bastos's *Yo el Supremo* (*I the Supreme*). Daniel Balderston in his introduction to *The Historical Novel in Latin America* asserts that traditionally the purpose of the historical novel in Latin America has been to elucidate the role of such ambiguous

historical figures. Thus, García Márquez's choice of Bolívar as a subject immediately raises questions about his intentions with regard to this revered historical figure.

Recent criticism on *El general en su laberinto* has divided itself into two opposing camps. On the one hand, Gerald Martin in *Journeys through the Labyrinth* and Seymour Menton in *Latin America's New Historical Novel* state that García Márquez's goal is to offer a historically accurate portrait of Bolívar without questioning the validity of the notion of history and the pretensions of his own text to simulate it. Others, notably Roberto González Echevarría in his article of 1991, "García Márquez y la voz de Bolívar" [García Márquez and Bolívar's Voice], believe that the novel imitates historical texts in order to show the similarity between fiction and history in the process of textual production. According to González Echevarría, novels such as *El general en su laberinto*, largely based on historical documents, are "archival fictions" whose main topic is the reflection on the origins of narrative discourse.

Perhaps the reason for this dissension is that paradoxically, García Márquez attempts to accomplish both of these opposing goals at once: to provide historically accurate information about Bolívar and yet simultaneously to question the validity of the (supposed) objectivity of historical texts. With regard to the first goal, many critics focus on the importance of the issue of accuracy in historical fiction. For example, both Noé Jitrik and William Katra in their essays in *The Historical Novel in Latin America*, focus on the educational value of historical reference within fiction.

García Márquez employs various techniques in order to instruct the reader about historical fact. The chief tool that *El general en su laberinto* uses to teach the reader about the life of Simón Bolívar is the educational summary. For example, García Márquez compresses Bolívar's actions over several years during the war for independence after his self-imposed exile in Jamaica into a single paragraph. Another example is the passage that summarizes Bolívar's handling of money matters, both personal and professional, before and during his presidency.

A second important technique is the use of historically-based "paratexts" to aid the reader in the separation of fact from fiction. The literary theorist Gérard Genette in *Palimpsestes* employs the term "paratextuality" to refer to the use of any supporting materials in a literary work that comment upon it, such as prefaces, introductions, epigraphs, footnotes, blurbs, and illustrations. *El general en su laberinto* incorporates a number of paratexts: it begins with an epigraph, ends with a section titled "Acknowledgments," includes a chronology of Bolívar's life and a map of Bolívar's travels during 1830 (the year of his death). These paratexts bear a relationship to history and ultimately serve the function of historical clarification.

In the "Acknowledgments" section, García Márquez thanks the historians Eugenio Gutiérrez Cely and Fabio Puyo and recognizes his debt to their book, *Bolívar día a día* [Bolivar Day by Day]. The direct reference to a historical source proves to be extremely important, for if readers decide to consult this book they can indeed distinguish between much of what is true and false in the novel. *Bolívar día a día* proves to be more than just a source of historical confirmation; it is a major historical intertext (a text either directly or indirectly alluded to within the novel).

None the less, it is entirely possible that the reader of the novel will not choose to delve into the novel's historical sources, despite the very real incentives. Thus, García Márquez includes within the novel itself, a chronology of Bolívar's life compiled by Vinicio Romero Martínez, another historian mentioned in the acknowledgments section. Most of the novel's events are documented in this chronology and it even includes a few excerpts from Bolívar's letters. In this way the reader can ascertain that much of García Márquez's fiction has historical validity as well, without ever consulting historical sources outside the novel.

Despite all this emphasis on historical fact and accuracy, an in-depth analysis of *El general en su laberinto* also confirms the opposite viewpoint; García Márquez does indeed question the objectivity of historical texts by underscoring their similarity of construction to historical novels. In the "Acknowledgments" section García Márquez speaks of corrections designed to make *El general en su laberinto* conform to historical reality and maintain the so-called "rigor de esta novela" (the exactitude of this novel). However, if we compare the novel to historical sources such as *Bolívar día a día*, it becomes clear that García Márquez alters historical details in order to contradict his stated pretensions to historical accuracy, as well as to highlight his dedication to purely novelistic development.

Frequently, García Márquez uses a historical episode as a mere departure point for his novelistic development. Although there is a shred of historical fact at the core, the greater part of the passage is fictitious. This blending of fact and fiction contains an implicit statement about the nature of textual production, whether historical or novelistic. The two constantly overlap; there is no such thing as pure truth or history.

Some of the most incredible episodes of the novel are in fact historically-based and thus confirm the age-old adage that truth is stranger than fiction. This use of historical episodes that seem fictitious is another way in which the author blends history and fiction and thus shows how historical texts are similar to novels. Many of the details of the assassination attempt on Bolívar's life in 1828 seem absurd, but are actually true, such as Bolívar's escape through the balcony wearing his lover's (Manuela Sáenz's) rain slippers. Such details are authentic as recounted in a letter by Manuela reproduced in *Bolívar día a día*.

El general en su laberinto is a more complicated novel than it appears to be on the surface. García Márquez manages simultaneously to clarify history while he confuses the borders of history and fiction in order to underscore the similarities of construction between the two. Thus, the ultimate subjectivity of any text is brought to light, but with a technique so subtle as to be imperceptible to the reader unless he carefully compares the novel to its sources. García Márquez outlines historical sources in the novel precisely for this reason: he wishes to encourage the comparison between fiction and history. However, his debunking of history as absolute truth does not preclude the novel's educational value. Most readers will learn something about Simón Bolívar, a hero both sung and demystified by this novelistic portrayal, just as history itself is both exalted and deconstructed within its pages.

To portray the tyrant in his decrepitude, as Márquez does in *El otoño del patriarca* (*The Autumn of the Patriarch*) is, of course, laudable in the eyes of Spanish American readers. But to represent a school text book hero well past his glory days is truly shocking.

HELENE CAROL WELDT-BASSON

Editions

First edition: *El general en su laberinto*, Bogotá: Oveja Negra, 1989
Translation: *The General in His Labyrinth*, by Edith Grossman, New York: Knopf, 1990; London: Jonathan Cape, 1991

Further Reading

González Echevarría, Roberto, "García Márquez y la voz de Bolívar," *Cuadernos Americanos* 28 (1991)

Menton, Seymour, "The Bolívar Quartette, or Varieties of Historical Fiction," in his *Latin America's New Historical Novel*, Austin: University of Texas Press, 1993

Ortega, Julio, "El lector en su laberinto," *Hispanic Review*, vol. 60/2 (1992)

Rincón, Carlos, "Metaficción, historia, posmodernismo: a propósito de *El general en su laberinto*." *Nuevo Texto Crítico*, vol. 5/9–10 (1992)

Weldt-Basson, Helene Carol, "The Purpose of Historical Reference in Gabriel García Márquez's *El general en su laberinto*," *Revista Hispánica Moderna*, vol. 47 (1994)

Fina García Marruz 1923–

Cuban poet

Critical appreciation of the work of Fina García Marruz has tended to focus on her membership of the group of writers and artists who, under the tutelage of José Lezama Lima, were associated with the review *Orígenes* between 1944 and 1956. While it is true that García Marruz (married to fellow poet and critic Cintio Vitier) was certainly the only woman in the group, unlike her male companions she has not received the recognition she so clearly deserves. This is due to unwarranted diffidence on her part, to the fact that the kind of poetry she wrote did not fit easily into the post-revolutionary Cuban cultural scene, and that marriage to Vitier, who published her work, nevertheless reduced the scope for independent critical evaluation. A sense of propriety has restrained him, for example, from discussing her poetry at length. García Marruz published her first book of poems in 1942 but it was with the exceptionally beautiful *Las miradas perdidas*, 1951 [The Lost Gazes] that she first made her name in Cuba and Spain. It was on the basis of this collection that Carmen Conde included García Marruz in her book *Once grandes poetisas hispanoamericanas* [Eleven Great Spanish American Women Poets] in 1967. After the Revolution of 1959 García Marruz remained in Cuba and published a second outstanding collection, *Visitaciones* [Visitations], in 1970. Apart from a perceptive commentary by Eliseo Diego, however, the book passed virtually unnoticed. She would have to wait until the 1980s when, in a cultural climate more propitious for women writers, a selection of her poetry (*Poesías escogidas*, 1984) was published, giving rise to a spurt of critical analyses including the only book-length study of her work to date (Arcos, 1990). Her essays on poetry and poetics, some dating back to 1959, were collected and published in the same decade (*Hablar de la poesía*, 1986 [Speaking of Poetry]). This book includes insightful studies of the work of poets such as Bécquer, Sor Juana Inés de la Cruz and José Martí as well García Marruz's own discerning and somewhat cryptic reflections on poetry itself. The quality and significance of her work is now widely acknowledged in Cuba, particularly among younger poets who have rejected social realist paradigms in favour of the more esoteric aesthetics of the Orígenes group as a whole. Proof of their dedication and enthusiasm are the 200 booklets containing García Marruz's more recent poems ("Créditos de Charlot," 1990 [Charlie Chaplin Credits], produced by hand during the first phase of the "special period in peacetime" when publishing in Cuba came almost to a standstill.

As one might expect from a poet of her generation, García Marruz writes in the tradition of classical Spanish and Spanish American poetry. Like all the Orígenes poets she was much influenced by Juan Ramón Jiménez (whom she met when she was thirteen), by María Zambrano who lectured on poetry and philosophy at Havana University in the early 1940s, and by the master himself, José Lezama Lima. In *Las miradas perdidas* she cultivates the sonnet and, although in her later work she experiments more freely with form, her poetry is always polished and precise. However, quite unlike Lezama, she prefers a clarity of style, a certain lucid simplicity and penetrating vision which is more reminiscent of the poetry of Unamuno or Jorge Guillén. What García Marruz did share with the other Orígenes poets was their Catholic faith and their concept of poetry as a religion, a prophesy, a vehicle of spiritual knowledge. As she explains in her essays, for her, poetry is the revelation of divine grace, the Word made flesh; poetry is a gift which enables the poet to apprehend what is beyond the world of experience, to glimpse another dimension of reality, the underlying unity behind all diversity and change. But poetry is also manifested and made substance in the situations and objects of everyday life. In this sense García Marruz's vision is rooted both in the transcendental idealism of St Agustine and in St Thomas's reconciliation of reason with faith. She follows in the path of Catholic thinkers such as Henri Bergson and Simone Weil. Generally speaking, however, apart from some noticeable exceptions (for example, the much celebrated *Transfiguración de Jesús en el Monte*, 1947 [Transfiguration of Jesus on the Mount], whose subject is, in any case, epiphany) her poetry is not overtly devotional.

What is most striking about García Marruz's poetry is its curious blend of the homely and the metaphysical. Her poetry is firmly grounded in a woman's experience of ordinary, domestic routine yet it is interspersed with moments of profound philosophical insight. The overriding theme of *La miradas perdidas* is the fragility of memory (see, for example, "Versos del que se olvida" [Verses of the One who Forgets], "Recuerdos imaginarios" [Imaginary Memories]). The poems in this collection reconstruct a rosy (or rather lilac) vision of the childhood home with its magical interior spaces (interiores mágicos), its lamps, mirrors, portraits and windows looking out onto symbolical landscapes. The poet's mother off to the theatre in her feathered hat, her aunt bringing her milk in the morning, the sound of the piano, the smell of bread, a walk through the city's parks, are vivid scenes – snapshots in time – which, on reflection, offer the poet a dazzling glimpse of the secret of life (see "Una dulce nevada está cayendo / detrás de cada cosa, cada amante" [A sweet snowfall is falling/ behind each thing, behind each loved one]). The home and its contents thus function as a microcosm of the universe and acquire deep symbolic value, what García Marruz calls "lo misterioso en lo cotidiano" (the mystery of everyday life). Several poems foreground the constant struggle with language and autopoiesis itself ("Yo os amo, palabras, madres tristes" [I love you, words, sad mothers], "Me queda grande y chica la palabra" (The word is too big or small for me) although the poet avoids gratuitous experimentation with language. Her poetry is crystalline, written with maximum poetic economy without a hint of the darker, surreal or oneiric aspects of reality.

Visitaciones is a more varied collection of poems and poetic prose and contains her widely acknowledged elegy "En la muerte de Ernesto Che Guevara" [On the Death of Che Guevara] written in 1966. Again the presence of the home and the family (mother, husband, sons, and friends) is crucial although the poet's angle of vision is more panoramic. She describes local figures (the road sweeper, a drunkard, a child smiling, the housemaid) and intrinsically Cuban landscapes. She also includes poems to Martin Luther King and Ho Chi Minh, and poems written in Mexico and Spain. As in *Las miradas perdidas*, what is of particular interest for feminist critics is the way in which the childhood home is reconstructed through objects (clocks, jugs, lamps, plates) and spaces (patios, terraces, windows, doors) as a lost paradise. Of similar interest is the inscription of the poet's elusive mother who is always associated with light, colour, openings, and the new day. In "Pequeñas canciones" [Little Songs] the mother's hands are "luces tan perdidas / albas que vuelven /-vuelan y vuelven" (lights so lost / dawns that return / fly and return); in "Alegres y cortas melodías" [Happy, Short Melodies] she enters the house in her flower printed dress, "¡Qué fuerte daba el sol! / Cómo entrabas en casa" (How the sun shone! / How you came in the house!); her protection and nurturance is represented by her bed, "tu lecho amplio y suave / allí quiero dormir" [your wide and soft bed / that's where I wish to sleep] and in "Música ilusa" [Illusory Music] by her hands "¿Qué me sostiene? / El recuerdo / de tu mano / dándome algo / que he olvidado" (What sustains me? / The memory of your hand / giving me something / I have forgotten). Images of the mother are built up through repeated and detailed listings of parts of her body, material attributes, and domestic surroundings (hands, printed dress, long hair, multicoloured handbag, red sunshade), but her face is never mentioned. She is, after all, no more than the music of her piano, "los valses y canciones que sólo la memoria y el amor oyen ya" (the waltzes and songs that only memory and love hear now). Clearly, Julia Kristeva's notion of the maternal semiotic – the music and rhythms of poetic language affording a momentary glimpse of the inexpressible pleasure of the pre-oedipal union between mother and child – is particularly relevant in this context.

Interesting in this respect are the explicit connections García Marruz makes between the home, the mother, and the mother tongue. The poem "Español" [Spanish] (in the section of *Vistaciones* dedicated to Spain) is a eulogy to the Spanish language whose words and rhythms are reclaimed and affirmed by the poet as her means of self-identification, her source of her strength:

> . . . híncheme, tómame,
> me vuelve a no sé que tiempo inmemorial
> y ya no huyo: méceme, la gran habla madre . . .
> ¿Cuándo insegura, trémula,
> niña aún, sin memoria,
> busqué tu pecho de firmeza,
> como se hunde la cabeza sollozante del hijo
> en el regazo innumerable? ¿Cuántas veces
> las marchas y oberturas, los dúos
> de la zarzuela que escuchaba
> a mi madre, en las tardes habaneras
> de distinta nostalgia, me sacaron de mi secreto huir,
> me devolvieron
> al desafío alegre, el dar a lo hecho pecho,
> rompiendo las visiones nocturnas
> con el bregar de la casa, la limpieza
> del atareo matinal?

[fill me, take me, / to I know not what eternity / and I shall not flee: rock me, great mother tongue . . . / When did I unsure, trembling, / still a girl, without memory, / seek your breast of strength, / like a sobbing child buries its head / in the bountiful mother's lap? How many times / did the marches and overtures, the duos / and operettas that I heard / from my mother, in the Havana evenings / of a different nostalgia, draw me out of my secret hideaway, bring me back / to the happy challenge, gritting my teeth, / dissolving nightime visions / in the wrangling house, the cleaning / of morning chores?]

Shy and retiring as ever, in the mid 1990s García Marruz is still writing in her Havana home. Her work urgently demands serious critical attention which focuses not so much on Catholic and Cuban issues but on the fact that the voice here is that of a woman.

CATHERINE DAVIES

Poem translated by Catherine Davies

Biography

Born in Havana, Cuba, 28 April, 1923. Active member of Orígenes group of poets and contributor to their journal of the same name. Married to distinguished critic, poet and Martí scholar, Cintio Vitier. Awarded doctorate in Social Sciences by Havana University in 1961. Worked as a researcher at both the National Library and the Center for Martí Studies in Havana. Two children, Sergio, and José María, both composers. The latter wrote the music for the film version of *Fresa y chocolate*, 1992 (*Strawberry and Chocolate*). Principal awards include the Cuban Premio de la Crítica and the Premio Nacional, 1990.

Selected Works

Poetry
Poemas, Havana: Úcar García, 1942
Transfiguración de Jesús en el Monte, Havana: Orígenes, 1947
Las miradas perdidas: 1944–1950, Havana: Úcar García, 1951
Los versos de Martí, Havana: offprint of the *Revista de la Biblioteca Nacional José Martí*, 1968
Visitaciones, Havana: Instituto del Libro, 1970
Los Rembrandt de l'Hermitage, Havana: UNEAC, 1992

Other Writings
Flor oculta de la poesía cubana: siglos XVIII y XIX, in collaboration with Cintio Vitier (editors), Havana: Editorial Arte y Literatura, 1978
Hablar de poesía, Havana: Letras Cubanas, 1986

Compilations and Anthologies
Poesías escogidas, edited by Jorge Yglesias, Havana: Letras Cubanas, 1984

Further Reading
Arcos, Jorge Luis, *En torno a la obra poética de Fina García Marruz*, Havana: UNEAC, 1990 [Reviews criticism on García Marruz's work to date]
——— "Obra y pensamiento poético de Fina García Marruz," *Revista Iberoamericana*, vol. 56/152–53 (July–December 1990) [A shorter version of the book]
Bobes, Marilyn, "Fina García Marruz: elogio de la serena perfección," *Casa de las Américas* 149 (1985) [Interesting for a woman's reading of *Poesías escogidas*]
Cardenal, Ernesto, *Poesía cubana de la revolución*, Mexico City: Extemporáneos, 1976

Conde, Carmen, "Fina García Marruz," in her *Once grandes poetisas hispanoamericanas*, Madrid: Cultura Hispánica, 1967
Fernández Retamar, Roberto, *La poesía contemporánea en Cuba (1927–1953)*, Havana: Orígenes, 1954

Kristeva, Julia, *La Révolution du langage poétique: l'avant garde a la fin du XIX siècle*, Paris: Seuil, 1974; as *Revolution in Poetic Language*, translated by Margaret Waller, New York: Columbia University Press, 1984

Juan García Ponce 1932–

Mexican prose writer and dramatist

Juan García Ponce is one of the most prolific writers in contemporary Spanish-American literature and a leading figure of the Mexican literary generation born between 1930 and 1940. A prize-winning dramatist, poet and essayist, García Ponce is mainly an author of prose fiction. Octavio Paz said of him "García Ponce is not an essayist who writes novels, but a novelist who writes essays." García Ponce began his literary career within a group which eventually established the *Revista Mexicana de Literatura* [Journal of Mexican Literature; second era: 1959–65], assuming its directorship along with Tomás Segovia. Writing within thematic and formal contemporary European and North American literary trends, he avoided, along with other writers of his generation, the limitations of an isolating nationalism. His literary production is noteworthy not because of extravagant formal experiments, but because of its daring themes relating life and art. His narrative system revolves around solitude, the nostalgia of lost innocence, love, desire, and their confluence in eroticism. From *Imagen primera*, 1963 [First Image] to *Inmaculada o los placeres de la inocencia*, 1989 [Inmaculada or the Pleasures of Innocence], García Ponce explores eroticism as a means to a reality that transcends the original one to offer a glimpse of a truly sacred and profane love. The short story "El gato" (The Cat) included in *Encuentros*, 1972 (*Encounters*) is a classic example of his thematic uniqueness. A couple in the story find a cat and incorporate the cat's intrusive presence into its erotic games. The cat, as a silent witness of their passion, becomes so indispensable in their love-making that the lovers cannot perform without it. The theme of a voyeuristic third, functioning as an element of erotic intensification and as a complement of the couple, reappears constantly in his narrative works. Variations on this theme fluctuate according to specific situations from homoeroticism to incestual relationships, as in the short stories, "Tajimara" in *La noche*, 1963 [The Night] and "Imagen primera" in the book of the same name, and in the novel *Figura de paja*, 1964 [Straw Figure]. *Figura de paja* explores the erotic relationship between two women and a man, dealing with situations such as homosexuality, masochism, sexual ambivalence, the moral ambiguity of desire, and tragic death through suicide. In García Ponce's works, incest, a love triangle, or a compulsive voyeuristic ceremony, more that being a pretext to explore sexuality, become a means to explore the pluridimensionality of eroticism in the human condition. García Ponce reflects about transgression, deviation, and the presence of a third

party as erotic alternatives of communication. Other novels such as *La casa en la playa*, 1966 (*The House on the Beach*), *La cabaña*, 1969 [The Cabin], *La vida perdurable*, 1970 [Enduring Life], *La invitación*, 1972 [The Invitation] and *Unión*, 1974 [Union] are focused on the limitations of individual identity, its consequences in erotic-sentimental relationships, and in the impossibility of fulfilment in the fragmentary monotony of everyday life. The novels relate sexual encounters and affective separations, presenting characters through the gaze of an obsessive narrator who filters their consciousness and projects their perceptions. *Crónica de la intervención*, 1982 [Chronicle of the Intervention] represents his most ambitious and successful narrative project. The text presents overlapping public, private, intimate, historical and social spheres: the Tlatelolco massacre of students on the 2nd of October 1968, and the erotic-emotional experience of a middle-class group of friends in Mexico City. The main character, Esteban, tries to identify a woman he finds in a stack of fading photographs. Two identical women (María Inés/Mariana) with different identities, seem to become one. Is this a fusion effect, or is this the unification of complementary beings into one? Does the text imply that the superposition of photographs is melding a third identity in María Inés? The relationship between Mariana and her lover Anselmo, shared by Esteban later on, becomes an erotic ritual in which all participate, always being watched by an individual or a group. Mariana and María Inés become synthesized in a sacred form of eroticism, a sacramental bid of passion, body, blood, spirit, and mysterious presence who embodies the desires of others. García Ponce's novel displays the simultaneous fusion and annulment of subjectivities as a couple copulates, while a third gaze registers their union, thus providing a totality. *Crónica de la intervención* combines García Ponce's skills as novelist and critic. The metamorphosis of Eros makes his texts a direct or indirect homage to García Ponce's literary tradition, from the erotic mystic San Juan de la Cruz of the 16th century to Robert Musil, Georges Bataille and Pierre Klossowski in the 20th.

García Ponce's protagonists deal with obsessions, abandonment, fears, and phobias. Solitude, isolation, and despair are momentarily overcome by ecstatic instants of continuity. These instants are sacred, divine or poetic, according to the nature of the erotic particulars and participants. His characters, lonely, sad, depressed and unsatisfied, live empty lives while they witness other people like them who, in their own loneliness, are waiting for the encounter that will reveal an incomprehensible cohesiveness that brings together erotic and mystic unity. From García Ponce's perspective, events, protagonists, situations, and places are not new but, rather, interchangeable. The situations he describes remain at best secondary in importance, symbols of something deeper: the manifestations of man's inner life that is the source of what is unique and different in him. In this narrative world, the gaze of the third observer is what unites and separates narrator, characters, and world. The gaze filters the consciousness that relates the stories, registering the subjectivity of events and characters. García Ponce's prose is clear, mysteriously transparent, and natural, his narrative techniques are indirect, and his dialogues are dense. Although one can say that he combines stylistic devices taken from painting and theater, his narrative disdains the spectacular experimental apparatus employed by other writers of the same generation. His predisposition to erotic themes, his unorthodox approach to characters, his exploration of the violation of the moral norms of the collectivity place García Ponce in the vein of the so called contemporary vital irrationalists. It could be said that the most salient situation in his works is a fear to surrender to existential emptiness. García Ponce departs from the fact that solitude is inherent in the human condition; but instead holds that the search for wholeness with the world in modern times is not futile. Most of the ideas he explores emphasize the interpretation, rather than the description of human experience. The tension between rational encounters with fixed reality and experiences with an infinite domain of feelings inspire his personal treatment of the modern condition. His vital preoccupation centres on the situation that creates alienation, isolation and introversion. His protagonists are introverted and lonely people seeking for meaning, identity and completeness in their lives. His unease with the restraints of traditional social, political, ethical, and cultural systems gives his work endless possibilities. By positioning the reader between objective and subjective reality, between illusion and certainty, between rationality and emotions, he forces his audience to confront life as a venture of endless possibilities. García Ponce does not hide his desire to be controversial and to disturb the good bourgeois by portraying middle-class protagonists violating moral prescriptions. In his works the reader, the writer and the characters are fused in a literary *ménage à trois*, in which to witness lovemaking is as important as to participate in it. For García Ponce, literature like eroticism is an act of contemplation as well as an act of possession.

LUIS H. PEÑA

Biography

Born in Mérida, state of Yucatán, Mexico, 22 September 1932. Studied drama in Mexico City. Fellow of the Centro de Escritores Mexicanos, 1957–58. Contributor and editor of very influential journals such as *Universidad de México*, 1958–66, literary supplements, such as "México en la Cultura," *Plural*, 1973–76, *Vuelta*, 1976; founder of "Diagonales," 1985. His major awards include: Literary Prize of Mexico City, 1956; Xavier Villaurrutia Award, 1972; and the National Prize for Literature, 1989. Recipient of the Great Cross of Honor (Austria), 1987.

Selected Works

Short Fiction

Imagen primera, Xalapa, Mexico: Universidad Veracruzana, 1963
La noche, Mexico City: Era, 1963
Encuentros, Mexico City: Fondo de Cultura Económica, 1972; as *Encounters*, translated by Helen Lane, Hygiene, Colorado: Eridanos Press, 1989
Figuraciones, Mexico City: Fondo de Cultura Económica, 1982
El gato y otros cuentos, Mexico City: Fondo de Cultura / SEP, 1984
Tajimara y el gato, edited by Eduardo M. Vázquez, Mexico City: UNAM, 1986

Novels

Figura de paja, Mexico City: Joaquín Mortiz, 1964
La casa en la playa, Mexico City: Joaquín Mortiz, 1966; as *The House on the Beach*, translated by Margarita Vargas and Juan Bruce-Novoa, Austin: University of Texas Press, 1994
La presencia lejana, Montevideo: Arca, 1968
La cabaña, Mexico City: Joaquín Mortiz, 1969
La vida perdurable, Mexico City: Joaquín Mortiz, 1970
El nombre olvidado, Mexico City: Era, 1970
La invitación, Mexico City: Joaquín Mortiz, 1972
Unión, Mexico City: Joaquín Mortiz, 1974
Crónica de la intervención, 2 vols, Barcelona: Bruguera, 1982
Inmaculada o los placeres de la inocencia, Mexico City: Fondo de Cultura Económica, 1989

Essays

Rufino Tamayo, Mexico City: Galería Misrachi, 1967
Desconsideraciones, Mexico City: Joaquín Mortiz, 1968
La aparición de lo invisible, Mexico City: Siglo XXI, 1968
Nueve pintores mexicanos, Mexico City: Era, 1968
Entrada en materia, Mexico City: UNAM, 1968; as *Entry into Matter: Modern Literature and Reality*, translated by David Parent and Juan Bruce-Novoa, Normal, Illinois: Applied Literature Press, 1976 [collection of poems and essays]
El reino milenario (Robert Musil, el hombre sin cualidades), Montevideo: Arca, 1970
Teología y pornografía. Pierre Klossowski en su obra: una descripción, Mexico City: Era, 1975
La errancia sin fin: Musil, Borges, Klossowsky, Barcelona: Anagrama, 1981
Imágenes y visiones, Mexico City: Vuelta, 1989

Further Reading

Batis's study is an indispensable general overview. Bruce-Novoa explores the intertextuality of García Ponce's production. Rama analyzes García Ponce's work in the Spanish American literary tradition.

Batis, Huberto, "La obra literaria de Juan García Ponce," *Revista de Bellas Artes* 21 (1968)
Bell, Steven M., "Juan García Ponce," *Hispamérica* 43 (1986)
Bruce-Novoa, Juan, "Drama to Fiction and Back: Juan García Ponce's Intratext," *Latin American Theatre Review*, vol. 16/2 (1983)
____ "Writing and the Visual Arts in Mexico: the Generation of Juan García Ponce," *Review* 39 (1988)
Rama, Ángel, "El arte intimista de García Ponce," in *Nueva novela latinoamericana* 1, edited by Julio Lafforgue, Buenos Aires: Paidós, 1969–72

El Inca Garcilaso de la Vega 1539–1616

Peruvian chronicler

El Inca Garcilaso de la Vega has often been called "the first truly American writer," in so far as he belonged to the first generation of mestizos (mixed European and Amerindian blood) born in Peru after the Spanish conquest; he was the first to celebrate this dual heritage in literature. In 1560 at the age of twenty-one, Garcilaso de la Vega left his native Cuzco for Spain and was never to return to his Peruvian homeland. The character of the literary vocation he developed some twenty years later was shaped by this fact, as well as by his residence, for his first thirty years in Spain, in the ancient Roman and feudal town of Montilla in the province of Córdoba before moving to the city of Córdoba about 1588–90.

His major literary works are his Castilian translation of the Italian text of León Hebreo's *Dialoghi d'amore* [Dialogues of Love] (Madrid, 1590), his *La Florida del Inca* (*The Florida of the Inca*) (Lisbon, 1605), based on the oral accounts of survivors of the De Soto expedition as well as published sources, and his *Comentarios reales de los Incas* (*Royal Commentaries of the Incas*), based on his boyhood recollections, information gathered from childhood friends in Cuzco, and a host of published and unpublished writings on the conquest and cultures of Peru (Lisbon, 1609; Córdoba, 1617). The *Diálogos de amor* consist of three dialogues between "Filón" and "Sofía" in which love and its object are described, the concepts of the good and the beautiful analyzed, and the origin and birth of love are identified. The *Florida*, divided into six books, covers the six years of the expedition (1538–43), from Hernando De Soto's receipt of a grant from the emperor Charles V in April 1538, to conquer Florida, through the discovery in October, 1543, by Diego Maldonado and Gómez Arias that the governor and more than half of the hundreds of men on the expedition had perished. The *Comentarios reales* narrates the rise and fall of the Inca empire, from the legendary dawn of its civilization through the Spanish conquest to the execution of the last Inca prince, Tupac Amaru, in 1572.

Always suffering a hiatus between the composition and publication of his works, by the late 1580s Garcilaso had translated León Hebreo's *Dialoghi d'amore* and written his *Historia de la Florida*; the *Primera parte* of his *Comentarios reales de los Incas* was approved for publication by the Holy Office in 1604, and the *Segunda parte* was finished about 1612–13 and published posthumously under a title (*Historia general del Perú*; *General History of Peru*) that Garcilaso had not chosen.

The characterization of Garcilaso's literary production has been disputed since the middle of the 19th century and particularly after the beginning of the 20th. What kind of relationship did his translation of Hebreo's 1502 synthetic, neoplatonist treatise on love bear to his historical narratives? And how historically reliable were his narratives of the De Soto expedition to Florida and of Inca civilization and history? In the struggle to lend dignity to the occasionally embattled works of Garcilaso, literary critics have made exaggerated claims about the historicity of his narrative works or his contribution to Renaissance culture on the basis of his translation of Hebreo's neoplatonist dialogues. Yet the unique and lasting significance of Garcilaso's works does not lie in such conventional, canonical categories. Furthermore, to place undue weight on the fictional (sometimes fantastic) quality of his work is to trivialize the substantial contribution he made to Spanish American literary and cultural history and to assess incorrectly the power that his works hold for readers today.

The major thrust of Garcilaso's works is as a memorialist, and the role of the celebration of memory is the key to their understanding. The critic Mariano Ibérico Rodríguez (quoted in José Durand, *El Inca Garcilaso, clásico de América*), is responsible for this little-studied insight, observing that the *Comentarios reales* consist not of the transcription of what Garcilaso read but rather "the transmission of what he heard in an atmosphere of emotionally charged recollection." No doubt animated by this possibility in hearing Gonzalo Silvestre's vivid accounts of his adventures on the De Soto expedition used for *La Florida*, Garcilaso then turned to his own recollections of the myths and legends of Inca origins he had heard from his maternal uncle in Quechua as a child. Using those moving accounts as a point of departure for his *Comentarios reales*, his prior study of León Hebreo helped him solve the problem of how to articulate mythic and allegorical understanding with literal accounts of historical events, allowing him to argue for the deeper meaning of such mythical accounts without insisting upon their credibility.

Also significant for the development of Garcilaso's haunting representation of lost worlds was his affinity for certain aspects of learned tradition: philology for the study of language etymology and usage as a key to cultural understanding; the practice of interpretive commentary and gloss as the centerpiece of his literary vocation; and antiquarianism with its appreciative study of monuments and relics for their insight into the past.

Garcilaso's vision was thoroughly an idealized one in his accounts of the firm and just establishment of civilization by the Inca lords in the Andes and of the heroism and bravery of the Spanish *conquistadores* in Florida and Peru. His identity as an heir to both the Inca dynasty and the Spanish nobility assured the heroic breadth of his vision. Nevertheless, his marginal status in aristocratic Spanish society (and no doubt his recollection of his Inca relatives considering him the son of an enemy) undercut this ideal vision of heroic duty and just reward, of honors received for honorable conduct, and of justice prevailing in spite of the vicissitudes of personal fortune.

The injustice of the destruction of the Inca empire – that realm "destroyed before it came to be known" – colors his recollected memories with more intense, richer, and also darker hues. Yet the highly modulated bitterness that occasionally shows through Garcilaso's lines is not the anguish of a spokesman for "the Indians of Peru." If he discovers common cause with them by the time he pens his prologue to the *Historia General del Perú*, it is not because he sees himself as one of them (as his rhetorical claims about his modesty as "an Indian" might lead the reader to believe), but rather because, despite being an Inca aristocrat, he feels that his experiences have put him in the same humble position as they. Notwithstanding the profoundly aristocratic bearing of the narrator Garcilaso, the enormous subtlety and affective range of his work – tempering rage with the poignancy of loss – speaks meaningfully to readers today. His works are appreciated as emblems of cultural contradiction and cultural identity and as monuments to time, memory and loss.

ROLENA ADORNO

Biography
Born in Cuzco, capital of the Incan Empire, 12 April 1539; the illegitimate child of an Inca princess, Isabel Suárez Chimpu Ocllo and a Spanish captain. He left Peru for Spain when he was twenty-one and never returned to his native land. His position in Spain was relatively privileged owing to his father's status and he adapted to European ways without undue difficulty. Died in Cordoba, 23 April 1616.

Selected Works
Comentarios reales de los Incas, vols 2–4 of *Obras completas del Inca Garcilaso de la Vega*, edited by Carmelo Sáenz de Santa María, Biblioteca de Autores Españoles, Madrid: Atlas, 1963–65; as *Royal Commentaries of the Incas and General History of Peru*, translated by Harold V. Livermore, foreword by Arnold J. Toynbee, 2 vols, Austin, University of Texas Press, 1966
Diálogos de amor de León Hebreo, translated by Garcilaso de la Vega, with an introduction and notes by Miguel de Burgos Núñez, Seville: Padilla Libros, 1989
La Florida del Inca, prologue by Aurelio Miró Quesada, bibliographical study by José Durand (editor), and notes by Emma Susana Speratti Piñero, Mexico City: Fondo de Cultura Económica, 1956; as *The Florida of the Inca*, translated by John Grier Varner and Jeannette Johnson Varner, Austin: University of Texas Press, 1988

Further Reading
Durand, José, *El Inca Garcilaso, clásico de América*, Mexico City: SepSetentas, 1976
Jákfalvi-Leiva, Susana, *Traducción, escritura y violencia colonizadora: un estudio de la obra del Inca Garcilaso*, Foreign and Comparative Studies/Latin American Series, No. 7, Syracuse, New York, Maxwell School of Citizenship and Public Affairs, 1984
Miró Quesada, Aurelio, *El Inca Garcilaso y otros estudios garcilasistas*, Madrid: Cultura Hispánica, 1971
Porras Barrenechea, Raúl, *El Inca Garcilaso en Montilla (1561–1614)*, Lima: Instituto de Historia, Editorial San Marcos, 1955
Varner, John Grier, *El Inca: the Life and Times of Garcilaso de la Vega*, Austin: University of Texas Press, 1988
Zamora, Margarita, *Language, Authority, and Indigenous History in the "Comentarios reales de los Incas"*, Cambridge and New York: Cambridge University Press, 1988

Comentarios reales de los Incas

A personal account of Inca history by Garcilaso de la Vega

The *Comentarios reales de los Incas* of Garcilaso de la Vega narrates the history of the Incas from their legendary origins in an age of barbarity through the execution of the last Inca prince, Tupac Amaru. Published in Lisbon in 1609, the *Primera parte* (*First Part*) takes the story from the Inca establishment of civilization in the Andes through the death of the legitimate heir to the Inca's throne, Huascar Inca, at the time of the Spanish invasion near the end of 1532. (At its apogee at that time, the Inca empire extended from the northern border of present-day Ecuador through the Andes to Mendoza in west-central Argentina and the Maule River in central Chile.) The *Segunda parte* (*Second Part*), which appeared posthumously (Córdoba, 1617) under the title *Historia general del Perú* (*General History of Peru*), narrates the fall of the empire from the first Spanish efforts to reach Peru from Panama in the mid-1520s and Pizarro and Almagro's arrival at the Inca empire in 1532 through to the execution of Tupac Amaru by the fifth Spanish viceroy of Peru, Francisco de Toledo, in 1572. Garcilaso ended his account with notes concerning Toledo's death in 1584 and that of Tupac Amaru's captor, Martín García de Loyola, in 1598, as well as a reminder that the petitions he had sent to the Spanish court on behalf of the last descendants of the Incas, whom he had named at the conclusion of the *Primera parte*, had not been acted upon.

Emphasizing his identity as the son of an Inca (princess) and a Spanish conquistador, Garcilaso made the claim at the end of his work that in the *First Part* he had fulfilled his obligation to his maternal homeland and relatives, but that in the *Second Part* he had only partially completed the task of telling "the brave deeds of the valorous Spaniards who won that very rich empire." In effect, the rise and fall of Inca civilization is the framework that embraces his narration of the Inca conquests of other Andean nations and, ultimately, the Spanish conquest of the Incas.

This structure of the work, however, does not reveal its generic character; the *Comentarios reales* is neither a history of the Incas nor a novelistic representation of the same. (In the wake of William Hickling Prescott's 1847 assessment of the work as historically dubious, Marcelino Menéndez Pelayo identified it in 1894 as a "Utopian novel;" he rectified this view slightly but not substantially in his 1913 posthumous version in deference to the defense of the reliability of Garcilaso's work as history by José de la Riva-Agüero.) Instead, the descriptive character of the title "*Commentaries*" and Garcilaso's claims in the proem to the *First Part* to the effect that he intended to provide a "commentary and gloss" to the histories written by Spanish authors, offers the key to a more valid assessment.

With origins in antiquity and the Middle Ages, the commentary was recognized as an independent genre by the 16th century. Its chronological limits were commonly the author's lifetime; unlike a formal history, it was free to add events to a narrative account, or to omit them, and it was not bound by a single thesis or theme. Ostensibly, its goal was to inform, not to explain or persuade. Not confined to the type of commentary defined by Julius Caesar pertaining to his own military exploits, as an interpretive work the *Comentarios reales* ranges broadly over a wide field of topics, correcting and contradicting accounts of other historians, complementing previously treated topics with additional information and adding altogether new topics of interest (such as the clusters of chapters devoted to the flora and fauna native to Peru and those brought to the Andes by the Spaniards).

The "text" that Garcilaso comments on is the body of extant writing on the Indies and particularly Peru and it includes the mythical and allegorical accounts of Inca origins that Garcilaso learned through the oral traditions of his mother's relatives. Although the *Comentarios reales* stands as an independent work in its own right both then and now, it was understood by Garcilaso and the readers of his day as a contribution to a larger dialogue that debated such topics as the worthiness of Inca civilization, the right of the Spanish to conquer and colonize the Indies, and the aptitude of native Andeans to assimilate European customs and the Christian religion.

Despite its appearance as a grand history and an encyclopedia of Andean customs and cultures, Garcilaso's *Comentarios reales* is a vast and highly personal essay on the character of Inca civilization and the consequences of its fall. The central question that Garcilaso addresses is therefore not "What happened?" between the days of the first Inca and the last, but rather "What is the meaning of all that has happened?" His orientation is philosophical rather than historical or belletristic, and his translation of Leone Hebreo's (Judah Abrabanel's) 1502 *Dialoghi d'amore* [Dialogues of Love] from Italian to Castilian provides the key to his outlook. Hebreo's work was not only a treatise on Neoplatonic love but, as John Charles Nelson indicates in his *Renaissance Theory of Love*, "a detailed analysis of philosophical doctrine centering on a restatement of the Neoplatonic position." In translating the *Dialoghi*, Garcilaso studied not only how its author brought together the worlds of Hellenism and Hebraism but also how he articulated the epistemological systems of Plato and Aristotle, that is, the allegorical, mythical forms of understanding of the former and the encipherment of esoteric meanings and systematic logic of the latter.

Both in content and in method, the synthesizing conceptualization of Hebreo was appropriated by Garcilaso, who had learned its rationale and technique for articulating the meanings of the myths of the ancient Incas with their equivalents in the European tradition of documentary and written history. The heart of Garcilaso's project was to bring together disparate Andean and European ways of conceiving the world, history and time, and of making the Andean world intelligible and acceptable to the European reader. Yet Garcilaso apprehended the lost Inca world more by appreciation than through understanding, and when he plunged into the narration of the reigns of the twelve Incas, he had probably exceeded his originally expressed goal of explaining Inca rites and Andean customs and correcting certain European misunderstandings about them.

A significant dimension of 16th-century commentary was that devoted to biblical and poetic exegesis. The philological character of these types of interpretation was likewise of great import to Garcilaso, who corrected European misunderstandings of Andean concepts and ideas through his analysis of Quechua etymology and usage. More than the occurrence or meaning of events that he had (or had not) witnessed and could (or could not) vouchsafe, the domain of his expertise lay with the recollected knowledge of his native Quechua and the effort involved to reveal Andean meanings. For Garcilaso, the word – not the event – was central to understanding and memorializing the synchrony of Inca society despite the imponderability of its historical fortunes.

For all of the above reasons, Garcilaso rightly called his work "*Commentaries*" and it is useful for late 20th-century readers to keep the concept in mind. Notable events in the history of the work's reception include its official prohibition in 1782, when it was seen as subversive, having been implicated as promoting in the preceding years the most serious native Andean insurrection to threaten Spanish rule in the Andes during the entire viceregal period. In more recent times, the *Comentarios reales de los Incas* has been taken to represent the birth of consciousness and it stands today as a sublime symbol of the contested and conflicted concept of, the inauguration of a tradition of critical and meta-critical American writing, and a call to Utopian thinking to question the history that has condemned the contemporary Andean to the margins of modern, "developed" society.

ROLENA ADORNO

Editions

Primera parte de los Comentarios reales, Lisbon: Pedro Crasbeeck, 1609

Historia General del Perú, Córdoba: Andrés Barrera, 1617

Historia General del Perú, Madrid: Oficina Real y a costa de Nicolás Rodríguez Franco, 1722

Primera parte de los Comentarios reales, Madrid: Oficina Real y a costa de Nicolás Rodríguez Franco, 1723

Comentarios reales de los Incas, edited by Ángel Rosenblat, Buenos Aires: Emecé, 1943

Historia General del Perú, edited by Ángel Rosenblat, Buenos Aires: Emecé, 1944

Comentarios reales de los Incas, vols 2–4 of *Obras completas del Inca Garcilaso de la Vega*, edited by Carmelo Sáenz de Santa María, Biblioteca de Autores Españoles 133–35, Madrid: Atlas, 1963–65

Royal Commentaries of the Incas and General History of Peru, translated by Harold V. Livermore, 2 vols, Austin: University of Texas Press, 1966

Further Reading

González Echevarría, Roberto, *Myth and Archive: a Theory of Latin American Narrative*, Cambridge and New York: Cambridge University Press, 1990 [Chapter 2 is on the *Comentarios*]

MacCormack, Sabine, "Religion and Philosophy: Garcilaso de la Vega and some Peruvian Readers, 1609–1639," in *Religion in the Andes*, Princeton, New Jersey: Princeton University Press, 1991

Elena Garro 1920–

Mexican prose writer and dramatist

Elena Garro began her writing career as a journalist; subsequently she has written novels, short stories and plays. Her first novel *Los recuerdos del porvenir*, 1963 (*Recollections of Things to Come*) which is also the first work she wrote, is undoubtedly her most important contribution to Spanish American letters in general, and to Mexican fiction in particular.

Garro's work explores the magical and the fantastic as they coexist with objective dimensions of reality. In her early works (*Los recuerdos del porvenir* and the short stories of *La semana de colores* [The Week of Colors]), the pre-Columbian Mexican tradition, especially its conception of cyclical time, contribute to the creation of worlds which weave magic and myth with history. In her later novels – *Testimonios sobre Mariana* [Mariana's Testimonies] and *La casa junto al río* [The House by the River] – the fantastic replaces myth, creating as in her earlier fiction, eccentric worlds characterized by the rupture of unity and the prevalence of multivalence. The ambiguity of her fictive worlds is underscored by the way in which surreal events are presented as if they were an integral part of ordinary or common experience.

Her treatment of time is one of the primary elements contributing to such difuseness. The characters in several short stories of *La semana de colores*, for example, may simultaneously exist in two historical periods. Thus, in "La culpa es de los tlaxcaltecas" (Blame the Tlaxcaltecs), whose protagonist escapes an unhappy and oppressive marriage to join her imaginary Aztec lover in a remote past. The characters of "El día que fuimos perros" [The Day We Were Dogs] live in "one day which has two days inside." *Los recuerdos del porvenir* is, however, the work which most decisively questions the linearity of time. Its characters experience multiple chronologies: the time of history corresponding to the Cristero War of the late 1920s which submits the inhabitants of Ixtepec to the indiscriminate violence of the invading army; the time of a forever lost Indian past which places the town "in a dimension of reality which remains still;" the timelessness of mythical time as experienced by Julia, the evasive lover of General Rosas, and Hurtado the outsider who rescues her after introducing the Moncada siblings to poetry and the realm of the imaginary; finally, the subjective time of the Moncadas who experience "a new and melancholic time where gestures and voices begin to move in the past."

Felipe Ángeles and *Y Matarazo no llamó* [And Matarazo Did Not Call], much like *Los recuerdos del porvenir*, criticize the arbitrariness and opportunism of political power. Felipe Ángeles, a "documentary-drama" recreates the farcical trial of one of the greatest albeit forgotten heroes of the Mexican Revolution. General Ángeles was a salient strategist and diplomat whose intelligence and integrity were feared by his military peers and political rivals. Forced into self-imposed exile he returned to Mexico in 1919 only to be accused of treason by the Carranza forces and shot later that year. The play exposes the violation of his rights to due process, and bitterly criticizes the military leaders who sacrifice the revolu-

tionary ideals, and the best individuals among them in their lust for power.

The main characters of her thriller *Y Matarazo no llamó*, which is probably her least successful novel, reveal the plight of two ordinary citizens who aid a group of workers on strike. Victims of their naïveté they are used by the political forces on the Left, and singled out as scapegoats by the security forces which are faced with increasing social unrest. Both characters are accused of committing crimes of which they are innocent. Appearances, however, prevent them from claiming their innocence, and they ultimately pay with their lives.

Some of her works of fiction, *La casa junto al río*, *Testimonios sobre Mariana*, *Reencuentro de personajes* [The Characters Meet Again] and the short stories of *Andamos huyendo Lola* [Lola, We Are on the Run], refer more specifically to the situation of women who despite their efforts often fail to find a space for themselves in a male dominated society. Both Mariana, the main character of *Testimonios sobre Mariana*, and Verónica, of *Reencuentro de personajes*, are destroyed by their male counterparts. The principal objective of Mariana's husband, a brilliant, young Mexican anthropologist is to punish his wife for her silent but firm resistance to his overpowering personality. He submits her to physical, verbal and psychological abuse, constantly humiliating and harassing her in public. Verónica, on the other hand, becomes entangled in a sado-masochistic relationship with a bisexual man, who reduces her to passivity by means of constant harassment, verbal abuse and persecution.

The female characters of *Andamos huyendo Lola* suffer the effects of political forces and exclusionary government policies. Most of them are women in exile escaping persecution in their countries of origin, but unable to find a living space abroad. Unable to return to their homelands, they become the victims of poverty, isolation and uprootedness in foreign lands.

La casa junto al río tells the story of a Mexican women who returns after her father's death to his home town in Asturias, hoping to renew the family ties severed by the civil war. She encounters, however, the hostility of the locals, understanding too late that her relatives will kill her in order to lay claim to her sizeable inheritance the existence of which she ignored. As with most of her other women characters, Consuelo is unaided in her struggle against forces which will ultimately defeat her.

A study of the stylistic richness and structural complexities of most of Garro's work, especially of her novels, lies beyond the scope of this thematic survey. Her works, however, are best understood and fully appreciated in a thorough consideration of their technical and stylistic sophistication. Her fiction, especially *Los recuerdos del porvenir*, *Testimonios sobre Mariana* and the short stories of *La semana de colores*, are central to the understanding of the development of contemporary Mexican fiction in general, and of Mexican's women's writing in particular.

PATRICIA RUBIO

Biography

Born in Puebla, Mexico, 15 December 1920. Attended the Universidad Nacional Autónoma de México (UNAM), Mexico City. Married Octavio Paz (see separate entry) in 1937, one daughter. Choreographer for Teatro de la Universidad; writer and reporter, championing the disadvantaged. Accompanied Paz on his diplomatic posting to Paris, 1945–51. In Paris she associated with writers of the Surrealist group including André Breton. Divorced from Paz in 1959, lived in Paris until 1963 then returned to Mexico. Continued work as a writer and reporter. Named as one of the instigators of the student demonstrations in Tlatelolco and imprisoned for nine days, 1968. Fled to the United States and then Spain where she lived in obscurity for several years. Returned to Paris in 1980. Awarded the Xavier Villarrutia Prize, 1964 for *Los recuerdos del porvenir*.

Selected Works

Novels

Los recuerdos del porvenir, Mexico City: Joaquín Mortiz, 1963; as *Recollections of Things to Come*, translated by Ruth L.C. Simms, Austin: University of Texas Press, 1969
Testimonios sobre Mariana, Mexico City: Grijalbo, 1981
Reencuentro de personajes, Mexico City: Grijalbo, 1982
La casa junto al río, Mexico City: Grijalbo, 1983
Y Matarazo no llamó, Mexico City: Grijalbo, 1991
Inés, Mexico City: Grijalbo, 1995

Short Fiction

La semana de colores, Xalapa, Mexico: Universidad Veracruzana, 1964 [English-language version of "La culpa es de los tlaxcaltecas" is to be found in *Short Stories by Latin American Women: the Magic and the Real*, edited by Celia Correas de Zapata, Houston, Texas: Arte Público Press, 1990]
Andamos huyendo Lola, Mexico City: Joaquín Mortiz, 1980

Plays

Un hogar sólido y otras piezas en un acto, Xalapa, Mexico: Universidad Veracruzana, 1958; 2nd augmented edition, 1983
La señora en su balcón, Mexico City: Colección Teatro Mexicano, 1960
Felipe Ángeles, Mexico City: Difusión Cultural / UNAM, 1979

Other Writings

Memorias de España, 1937, Mexico City: Siglo XXI, 1992

Further Reading

Anderson, Robert K., "Myth and Archetype in *Recollections of Things to Come*," *Studies in Twentieth Century Literature*, vol. 9/2 (1985)
Balderston, Daniel, "The New Historical Novel: History and Fantasy in *Los recuerdos del porvenir*," *Bulletin of Hispanic Studies*, vol. 66 (1989)
Callan, Richard J., "Analytical Psychology and Garro's *Los pilares de doña Blanca*, " in *Latin American Theatre Review*, vol. 16/2 (1983)
Cypess, Sandra Messinger, "Visual and Verbal Distances in the Mexican Theatre: the Plays of Elena Garro," in *Woman as Myth and Metaphor in Latin American Literature*, edited by Naomi Lindstrom and Carmelo Virgillo, Columbia: University of Missouri Press, 1985
Dauster, Frank N., "Elena Garro y sus 'Recuerdos del porvenir'," *Journal of Spanish Studies: Twentieth Century*, vol. 8/1–2 (1980)
Galvín, Delia V., *La ficción reciente de Elena Garro, 1979–1983*, Querétaro, Mexico: Universidad Autónoma de Querétaro, 1988
Kaminsky, Amy, "The Uses and Limits of Foreign Feminist Theory: Elena Garro's *Los recuerdos del porvenir*," in her *Reading the Body Politic*, Minneapolis: University of Minnesota Press, 1993
Meyer, Doris, "Alienation and Escape in Elena Garro's *La semana de colores*," *Hispanic Review*, vol. 55 (1987)
Mora, Gabriela, "A Thematic Exploration of the Works of Elena Garro," in *Latin American Women Writers Yesterday and Today*, edited by Yvette Miller and Charles Tatum, Pittsburgh: Latin American Review Press, 1977
Rubio, Patricia, "Funciones del nivel descriptivo en *Los recuerdos del porvenir*," *Cahiers du Monde Hispanique et Luso-Brésilien*, vol. 49 (1987)
Stoll, Anita (editor), *A Different Reality: Essays on the World of Elena Garro*, Lewisburg, Pennsylvania: Bucknell University Press, 1990
Taylor, Kathy, *Elena Garro: the Inversions of Fiction,"* in her *The New Narrative of Mexico*, Lewisburg, Pennsylvania: Bucknell University Press and London: Associated University Presses, 1994

Juan Gelman 1930–

Argentine poet

Since his first collection in 1956, *Violín y otras cuestiones* [Violin and Other Issues], Juan Gelman has published almost twenty books of poems, as well as numerous anthologies and compilations. His poetry impresses in the same way as that of Juan Ortiz, by its regularity, consistency and uniformity, and is comparable also because Gelman establishes in his early works the entire poetic universe which he went on to cultivate for more than twenty years.

This initial corporal unity in the output of Gelman applies to his first four works: from *Violín y otras cuestiones* to *Gotán* (1962). It is a unity that can be thought of literally as a human body, an extension of the poet's physical anatomy. These first four works can thus be linked to the four fundamental schemes of Gelman's poetry, namely: the senses, represented by *Violín* (1956); sensation and feeling, represented by *El juego en que andamos*, 1959 (The Kind of Game We're In) and *Velorio del solo*, 1961 [Solo's Wake]; the act of naming represented by *Gotán* (1962).

The rest of Gelman's works can thus be divided into these three major schemes. *De cólera buey*, 1965 [About the Bullock's Rage] to *Relaciones*, 1973 [Relations] is the poetry of naming, of speaking and assigning names to things, of *showing.* From *Hechos y relaciones,* 1980 [Deeds and Relations] to *Hacia el sur,* 1982 [Towards the South] is the poetry of sensations and, above all, of feeling: the poet does not merely establish a mode of feeling, but rather poeticizes feeling itself. In the phase from *Composiciones,* 1986 [Compositions] to the most recent work, the senses are rendered poetically.

According to this hypothetical division, each *poetic scheme* can also be linked to three verbal operations, which might constitute the substance of each of them: understanding, attending to and comprehending, respectively. Firstly the "understanding" of names, words, utterances; then the "attending" to sensations and the sensibility, paying attention, being attentive, alert, apprehending; and finally "comprehending" the senses, explaining them and applying them, rendering them and using them.

Gelman's poetry combines the "very stuff of existence," a prodigious sense of the commonplace, unsuspected meanings in the most trivial objects, an unerring verbal facility and the innocence we would all wish to derive from the flux of events. Such a perception is, of course, subject to evolution: Gelman has met each new development, each new social and poetic horizon, with grace and fortitude. He has thus encountered both success and failure, but above all he has been able to create a characteristic and original *poetic idiom.* The notion of poetry as the deployment of a language, rather than the art of composing lines or verses, is a conception Gelman originally derived from Juan L. Ortiz, and which he then passionately developed.

The poems of Gelman, following the pattern of his books, work on two levels. On the first level, language is used to *translate* a state, a situation, a feeling, an inspirational idea. This is manifested, at least until *Gotán,* by the use of colloquial forms and modes, and by the exploration of ulterior meanings in the realm of trivial and ordinary objects, in the pure dimension of the "day-to-day." With great musicality and beauty, Gelman exploits the hidden significance of the commonplace. As the poet's active engagement with Argentine politics increased, turning him into a public figure, this aspect of his work most clearly manifests itself as a choice of subject-matter. Having withdrawn from political life, Gelman, in his recent works (e.g. *Anunciaciones* [Annunciations] and *Salarios del impío*), suggests a reappraisal of his former preoccupation with language and a reworking of his own experiences through poetic creativity, no longer as a choice of subject-matter but rather as the structure of a language for which Gelman justifiably claims all creative rights.

The second level is a constant throughout Gelman's work which, although it has fluctuated according to his various aesthetic experiences, constitutes the backbone of his production: his poetry makes no claims to be placed in any established tradition, rather it constructs its own world, a private imaginary based particularly on two essential influences: César Vallejo and Juan L. Ortiz.

Gelman, the only contemporary of Borges who has managed to write without feeling the need to allude to his work, has created an open poetic universe, laying the foundations for a *poetics,* that is to say a word-stock, a grammar, an entire conception of poetic creation. Rather than simply writing poems, Gelman has established a poetic idiom with tones, nuances and varying degrees of felicity; this is his fundamental link with César Vallejo and Juan L. Ortiz. This level of linguistic expression ultimately manifests itself intellectually in the notion of "grammatical plurality" which Gelman defends and demands for Spain's former colonies (and not merely for their literature). For Gelman, the coexistence of three or four different grammars in 17th-century Spain is what articulates his approach to literature: to create is to reinvent language itself from moment to moment and from era to era. Gelman thus shows his desire to overcome *by practical means* the disappearance of the cultural and philosophical context which sustained poetry in classical terms. Gelman, in this sense, is concerned more with the *poetic sentiment* than with poetry.

Gelman's journalistic pieces, some of which date back as far as the 1960s, have generally been linked to the first of the two levels. His work as a translator and his preoccupation with language are related to the second level.

Though these two expressive levels are constant throughout his poetry, Gelman perpetually renews them in his works. From his first publications in 1956 up to those of the 1990s, he has unceasingly explored poetic alternatives, for in attempting to invent a language it is as if he felt an imperious need to *name poetically* certain places in as many ways as possible.

Gelman is one of the few Argentine poets who has paid scant attention to classical verse forms, though he knows and can use them. Instead, he continually composes harmonious lines and stanzas whose value lies not merely in their being avant-garde (as is the case with much contemporary Argentine poetry), but rather in their balance, in the tone achieved by the combination of sound, of meter, of punctuation, of expressiveness (he has an unusual gift for exploiting the *pictographic significance* of a word, without resorting to the "concrete" excesses of certain so-called "avant la lettre" writing) and finally of meaning (the right term would be "language:" reading Gelman one senses that *to signify is in fact to invent a language,* not merely to favour an idiom.

Gelman's proximity to the tango, to the English, French and Italian languages, and to painting, is evident throughout his work and further confirms the dual nature of his poetry. His lines on the tango, the echo of the *milonga* (another popular Argentine dance) in certain poems, the translations (both real and spurious), the considerable and undenied influence of Proust and Quevedo, the enlightenment of many of his works and the *plastic* fashion in which many are written, all these are quintessential to this permanent exile, native of both Buenos Aires and Santa Fe, who has managed to see in each of his mundane homes, despite the misfortunes which have befallen him, the flowers of which Baudelaire spoke: "Criaturas o abandonos que // / me juntás siéndome / yo vivo // ya no yo / sino vos / paloma // que te dejás / das / transformás (Creatures or derelictions that you bring to me, myself being / alive no longer I / but rather you, / dove who releases / gives / transforms).

In short, Juan Gelman has created a language for "those secret catastrophes of the heart" which inhabit every corner of South America: "no es para quedarnos en casa que hacemos una casa // no es para quedarnos en el amor que amamos // y no morimos para morir // tenemos sed // y paciencias de animal." (We are not building a house in order to stay at home", he says in the poem *Habits*, "nor do we love in order to stay in love / nor die in order to die / we have thirst / and animal patience.")

CLAUDIO CANAPARO

translated by Ian Craig

Biography

Born in Buenos Aires, Argentina, 3 May 1930. Imprisoned in early 1960s with other Argentine intellectuals. Editor of the magazine *Panorama* in 1969, and of the cultural supplement of newspaper *La Opinión* (1971); member of editorial staff of *Crisis* (1973). Fled to Europe in 1975. His two children and his son's pregnant wife were kidnapped by a paramilitary group in Argentina. Gelman's daughter, Nora Eva, turned up but his son and daughter-in-law were among the disappeared. Returned to Argentina in 1988; took up permament residence in Mexico City, 1989. Awarded the International Mondello Poetry Prize, 1980.

Selected Works

Poetry

Violín y otras cuestiones, Buenos Aires: Gleizer, 1956
El juego en que andamos, Buenos Aires: Nueva Expresión, 1959
Velorio del solo, Buenos Aires: Nueva Expresión, 1961
Gotán, Buenos Aires: La Rosa Blindada, 1962
De cólera buey, Havana: La Tertulia, 1965
Los poemas de Sidney West, Buenos Aires: Galerna, 1969
Fábulas, Buenos Aires: La Rosa Blindada, 1971
Relaciones, Buenos Aires: La Rosa Blindada, 1973
Hechos y relaciones, Barcelona: Lumen, 1980
Si dulcemente, Barcelona: Lumen, 1980
Citas y comentarios, Madrid: Visor, 1982
Hacia el sur, Mexico City: Marcha, 1982
Composiciones, Barcelona: Llibres del Mall, 1986
Anunciaciones, Madrid: Visor, 1988
Interrupciones, Buenos Aires: Libros de Tierra Firme, 1989
Cartas a mi madre, Buenos Aires: Libros de Tierra Firme, 1989
Salarios del impío, Buenos Aires: Libros de Tierra Firme, 1993
En abierta oscuridad, Mexico City: Siglo XXI, 1994
Dibaxu, Buenos Aires: Seix Barral, 1994

Compilations and Anthologies

Obra poética, Buenos Aires: Corregidor, 1975
De palabra (Poesía 1971–1987), Madrid: Visor, 1994
Hacia el sur y otros poemas, Buenos Aires: Espasa Calpe, 1995

Further Reading

Achúgar, Hugo, "La poesía de Juan Gelman o la ternura desatada," *Hispamérica* 41 (1985)
Boccanera, Jorge, *Confiar en el misterio: viaje por la poesía de Juan Gelman*, Buenos Aires: Sudamericana, 1994
Borinsky, Alicia, "Interlocución y aporía: notas a propósito de Alberto Girri y Juan Gelman," *Revista Iberoamericana* 125 (1983)
Dalmaroni, Miguel, *Juan Gelman, contra las fabulaciones del mundo*, Buenos Aires: Almagesto, 1993
Giordano, Jaime, *Dioses, Antidioses: ensayos críticos sobre poesía hispanoamericana*, Concepción, Chile: Lar, 1987
Murray, Frederic W., *The Aesthetics of Contemporary Spanish American Social Protest Poetry*, Lampeter, Wales: Edwin Mellen Press, 1990 [Sections of chapter 6 are on Gelman's poetry]
Olivera-Williams, María Rosa, "Poesía del exilio: el Cono Sur," *Revista Hispánica Moderna*, vol. 41/2 (1988)

Interviews

Benedetti, Mario, "Juan Gelman y su ardua empresa de matar la melancolía," in his *Los poetas comunicantes*, Montevideo: Biblioteca de Marcha, 1972
Mero, Roberto, *Conversaciones con Juan Gelman: contraderrota, Montoneros y la revolución perdida*, Buenos Aires: Contrapunto, 1987

Asomos

Poem from *Hechos y relaciones* by Juan Gelman

Asomos

podrías estar avanzando a empujones por un río de
    tristeza / con
la tristeza al cuello / los ojos
ciegos ya de tristeza / el alma
como pez en tristeza / ninguna

orilla a la vista / o
calor o sol como mano o tibieza sobre
la nuca / y entonces podría
ser o saltar la poesía del fondo enredada en los pies/

consolación / memoria /
triste tal vez / pero ya no tristeza / dolor
tal vez / pero memoria / consolación / abrigo /
suavidad de los días o lomo

donde descansa el corazón salvaje
y turbio y triste como la tristeza
y furiosa cabeza
asomada a este viaje

Note: In the transliteration given below, two slashes (//) indicate a new line. A number indicates a new stanza. This system is necessary in order to respect the poet's use of a single slash to break up the lines of the poem.

[You might be elbowing your way along a river of sadness / with // sadness at your throat/ your eyes // blinded now by sadness / your soul // like a fish steeped in sadness / not a (2) shore in sight / Nor // heat nor sun like a hand or warm breath on // the nape of the neck / and then poetry might be // or leap up from the depths entangled committing the whole self (3) solace / memory / sad perhaps / but no longer sadness / pain // perhaps / but memory / solace / shelter // the softness of the bareback days (4) where the wild heart rests // and turbid and sad like sadness // and furious head // looking out at this journey].

The poem suggests two readings; one following the graphic scansion of each line. For the sake of convenience we might term this the *classic* one; another in which the scansion is established by the slash [/]. This can be termed the *alternative* reading.

The classic reading invites meaning, it awakens in us a curiosity of the senses ("la tristeza al cuello / los ojos", "la nuca / y entonces podría"). We have the impression of a proliferation, one which we vaguely intuit has an order. This consists of enumerations, alternating between the description of actions or states of mind, blurring the two without providing a solution ("ser o saltar . . .").

The alternative reading favours rhythm, scansion expressed as sound, and the power of the word. This reading brings together the meaning of those apparently unconnected lines offered by the previous reading.

It is by combining, alternating or approaching these two readings simultaneously that unexpected meanings arise which affect the poem's rhythm. In addition, this counterpoint renders useless punctuation marks and the rules of standard grammar (such as words in upper or lower case) to such an extent that we barely notice their absence: the pauses, intakes of breath, the impact of the metaphors is made by combining the meaning of words (lexicon = idiolect) and the two scansions (tone = music = voice). In this way an undoubtedly poetic effect is obtained: words uncover new possible scansions and the scansions uncover new meanings in the words. Thus the poem may be read and reread in different keys, since the two initial scansions have given way to a range of alternatives and words whose original meaning left no room for doubts and which now are ambiguous, moving fans.

In "Asomos," each classic line represents a *figure (figura)*, in general an "object" clad in feeling, affection or a state of mind, that is, personalized in some way. Furthermore, the alternative lines *disintegrate* (when they are submitted to close scrutiny) bodies, things and feelings so as to allow a semantic and morphological *plasticity*. Its paradoxical final destiny does not consist only of allowing us to participate in a physical proximity, but at the same time to reintegrate objects and beings, now merged and endowed with a whole range of visual and auditive senses. Thus, for example, the title which at the beginning of our (classic) reading is "Asomos" (to see something; place oneself above something; glimpse; see imperfectly; spy; hide bashfully; look out of) in a second reading, is: "A/somos" (We *can* be; we are still what we were; we no longer are but we may be; ourselves in; we are for such a thing; in this we are). It would be possible to analyze "Asomos" in its entirety in the same way: "asomos" (state) and a somos (so we are) are constantly intermingled.

Metaphors appear as inverted or absurd representations: necks that carry sadness, rivers and eyes endowed with sadness, furious heads. And always inscribed as a state of mind and a feeling of being/exisiting/acting is sadness. To such an extent that sadness overcomes its own condition and abandoning its condition as name almost turns into a noun (or an adjective rendered as a noun): "triste como la tristeza" "triste tal vez / pero ya no de tristeza."

The symbolic indentification between verbs expressing a state and verbs expressing an action ("ser," to be and "saltar," to jump or leap) renders in aesthetic terms a nebulous condition somewhere between sentir/querer (to feel/to want). Thus poetry "wells up entangled giving everything it's got." Body, eyes, necks, hands, heart and head (the last signifying thought, of course) fight, argue and are linked to memories, forms of solace, days, journeys, forms of warmth, fish, sun and river banks.

In effect, to the tú/vos (Castilian "thou" and its colloquial Argentine equivalent) implied in the poem (the narrator addresses this person when he is not thinking aloud); that is to say, he may be addressing someone else or himself, two alternative present themselves. One is to let himself go:

> . . . por un río de tristeza / con
> la tristeza al cuello / los ojos
> ciegos ya de tristeza / el alma
> como pez en tristeza / ninguna
>
> orilla a la vista . . .

The other is to pick up that state-of-sadness and make it speak, utter, chatter, offering solace, remembering, contemplating via memory:

> donde descansa el corazón salvaje
> y turbio y triste como la tristeza
> y furiosa cabeza
> asomada a este viaje

Heart (feeling); body (matter), memory, sadness and journey shape the poetic cycle: the ground is *covered* in the right direction or going the wrong way, wholly or partly, "asomamos" (we look out at) and our senses of smell, touch, hearing and sight are engaged. That very bitter taste, surely, can be left behind.

CLAUDIO CANAPARO

translated by Verity Smith

Editions
First edition: *Hechos y relaciones*, prologue by Eduardo Galeano, Barcelona: Lumen, 1980

Mempo Giardinelli 1947–

Argentine prose writer

Mempo Giardinelli was born in Resistencia, a town in the Chaco province, but since culture in Argentina is so centralized, his career as a writer evolved in Buenos Aires. None the less, from his very first novel, the Chaco region's own special history and language helped inform his writing. His first novel, *La revolución en bicicleta*, 1980 [Revolution on a Bicycle], tells of the patient wait of an old Paraguayan army major, who after having been involved in different skirmishes, ends up vegetating in exile in the north of Argentina. While he waits for the call to arms again, his life ticks away. It is the recurring theme of the old warrior stubbornly refusing to accept his fate, the best known fictional example of which is probably Gabriel García Márquez's colonel in *El coronel no tiene quien le escriba* (*No one Writes to the Colonel*) who also lives "waiting" until the very end. In Giardinelli's case, what distinguished *La revolución en bicicleta* was its humour as well as the wit and freshness of its prose. It was not actually the first novel Giardelli wrote. *Toño tuerto rey de ciegos* [Toño One-Eyed King of the Blind] was his first, but for some obscure reason it was not published until 1983 when it appeared under the title *¿Por qué prohibieron al circo?* [Why Did They Ban the Circus?]. The latter tells the story of a remote town in the north of Argentina, tightly ruled both by tradition and an iron-clad political structure of exploitation. Set in the sawmills and cotton plantations, with workers enslaved by armed guards and administrative bureaucracy, it is typical of the neo-feudal landowning regime which gave birth to novels of social protest in the River Plate area such as Alfredo Varela's *El río oscuro* [The Dark River] and Enrique Amorim's *Los montaraces* [The Wild Ones].

El cielo en las manos, 1981 [Grasping the Sky] tackled more intimate themes, less social and political. It could be called a story of an erotic obsession, the tale of a voyeur in love with the feminine image he glimpsed as an adolescent, and which he rediscovers in a mature woman, not now as an image but as real flesh, blood and spirit. It illustrates the adolescent myth of the eternal woman, Aurora (the name is symbolic), who appears at the very dawn of the hero's erotic sensitivity. This passion and confused sexuality reappear again in a detective novel which won the 1983 Mexican National Prize for the Novel: *Luna caliente* [Hot Moon]. It is both a tribute to the "noir novel" (a genre about which Giardinelli wrote a book) and Clouzot-style horror films like *Les Diaboliques*.

The period from *¿Por qué prohibieron al circo?* to *El cielo con las manos* mirrors the author's own personal circumstances. Giardinelli lived in political exile in Mexico from 1976 to 1984 and went through the agony of the writer who loses contact with his natural local audience and has to begin communicating with another, constructing different cultural and linguistic codes. Aware of the importance of language, knowing the novel is above all language, and in his case, language "in crisis," Giardinelli has dealt intelligently with the novel itself as a theme. The narrator describes his generation, much as Giardinelli could describe his, as a "lost" generation and concentrates its crisis on the problem of language: "I now

find that being a loser, frustrated, a friend to defeat, is unbearable. Only memories have any consistency. Like Argentina, Buenos Aires, or my province the Chaco, which are now pure memory. The same happens with language, diluted by Mexicanisms, despite efforts to maintain an Argentine identity. So we speak a hybrid mixture of Argymex or something of the sort. But we don't pronounce Argentine properly, nor Mexican. That's no use either. It's not even useful for saying all these things." The image of mass exile is also there, that of the Argentine diaspora of the 1970s caused by the military dictatorship: "Here we are, scattered round the world as if we came from an ant hill which someone kicked." However, this realization of loss is a challenge for Giardinelli rather than a reason for defeat.

This is seen clearly in his next novel, *Qué solos se quedan los muertos*, 1985 [Lonely Are the Dead], which is a double tribute: to the country that offered him a home for several years and to the aforementioned hardboiled or "tough guy" US fiction. The Mexican stage of Giardinelli's life ended in 1985. He returned to Buenos Aires when the dictatorship collapsed. Althought he published his detective novel in Buenos Aires, it is a decidedly "Mexican" book, without doubt the best example of transculturation produced by the thousands of Argentines in Mexico between 1973 and 1985. *Qué solos se quedan los muertos* is, on the one hand, a novel about Mexican violence related to drug trafficking and gangsterism, and on the other, an examination of the vanity and self-worship of the Argentine exiles themselves, an analysis and discussion, if not of the essence, at least of the phenomenon of Argentine failure abroad. If Giardinelli can marry two such disparate aspects and do it persuasively and with ease, it is because he has the ingredients to hand. He tells the story of an Argentine journalist who is asked for help by a woman who was his lover ten years earlier. As he looks for this woman, from the time he gets her message, the hero is submerged in the Zacatecas underworld, caught up in an expected and violent intrigue of crime and drug trafficking.

In 1986, Giardinelli published *La entrevista* [The Interview] in Madrid, a small collection including three short stories written between 1979 and 1984. It is a book of secondary importance but at least one of the stories, with its strong references to Jorge Luis Borges, demonstrates that Giardinelli's work is tending towards the baroque, further and further removed from his original realism, he is increasingly partial to literary references, and eager to show that literature is a "construct" not a register of reality. The first story seems like a Borgesian joke and is basically a tribute to Borges, a mixture of adoration and disdain, love and hate, for a classic father figure. It is clear from the very first lines when the narrator refers to "este viejo insólito al que tanto he admirado y, claro, tanto detesto todavía."(this extraordinary old man whom I have admired so much and, yes, still hate). The story tells how an American editor asks the narrator to interview Borges, except that the ficticious Borges is 130 years old and we are in the year 2028.

In 1991 Giardinelli published his most ambitious, personal and beautiful work: *Santo oficio de la memoria* [The Holy Office of Memory]. It is, at the same time, the best example of his baroque writing. More than a novel in the traditional sense, it is a profound exploration of the experience of family life. Set in an Argentine family from the Chaco, it recounts their lives but is also a kaleidoscope of multiple aspects of the culture which makes up what we could call the writer's own personal mythology. It contains, in greater or lesser detail, references to contemporary culture, probably more familiar to the writer than to his characters. They range from Gardel to García Márquez, the films of Eliseo Subiela, the poetry of T.S. Eliot, the literature of Armonía Somers and Tito Monterroso, as if a book of notes were mixed with the lives of his characters, creating an attractive, magnetic tale, in which writer and characters speak in unison with the reader. This novel received the 1993 Rómulo Gallegos Prize, the most prestigious prize for Latin American literature.

JORGE RUFFINELLI

translated by Ann Wright

Biography

Born in Resistencia, Chaco, Argentina, 2 July 1947. Studied law at the University of Buenos Aires but did not complete studies. Made his reputation as a journalist in early 1970s, contributing to *Semana Gráfica, Siete Días* and *Panorama*, among other publications. Left Argentina in 1976 because of military dictatorship. Lived in Mexico City from 1976 to 1985 where he worked as editor and publisher. Returned to Argentina in 1985 and settled in the Chaco again in 1993, commuting frequently to Buenos Aires. Awarded the Mexican National Prize for the Novel in 1983 for *Luna caliente* and the Rómulo Gallegos Prize in 1993, for *Santo oficio de la memoria*.

Selected Works

Novels and Short Fiction
La revolución en bicicleta, Barcelona: Pomaire, 1980
El cielo con las manos, Hanover, New Hampshire: Ediciones del Norte, 1981
Vidas ejemplares, Hanover, New Hampshire: Ediciones del Norte, 1982
¿Por qué prohibieron el circo? Mexico City: Oasis, 1983
Luna caliente, Mexico City: Oasis, 1983
Qué solos se quedan los muertos, Buenos Aires: Sudamericana, 1985
La entrevista, Madrid: Almarabu, 1986
Santo oficio de la memoria, Barcelona: Grupo Editorial Norma, 1991
El castigo de Dios: cuentos, Buenos Aires: Tesis, Grupo Editorial Norma, 1993
Imposible equilibrio, Buenos Aires: Planeta Argentina, 1995

Compilations and Anthologies
Cuentos: antología personal, Buenos Aires: Puntosur, 1987

Other Writings
El género negro, 2 vols, Mexico City: UNAM, 1984
Así se escribe un cuento, Buenos Aires: Beas, 1992 [Collection of interviews with several Latin American writers]

Further Reading

Gutiérrez Mouat, Ricardo, "La narrativa latinoamericana del posboom," *Revista Interamericana de Bibliografía*, vol. 38 (1988)
Kohut, Karl (editor), *Un universo cargado de violencia. Presentación, aproximación y documentación de la obra de Mempo Giardinelli*, Frankfurt: Vervuert Verlag, 1990
Marcos, Juan Manuel, "Mempo Giardinelli in the Wake of Utopia," *Hispania*, vol. 70/2 (1987)
Ruffinelli, Jorge, "Mempo Giardinelli al encuentro de territorios posibles," *Hispamérica*, vol. 40 (1985)

Oliverio Girondo 1891–1967

Argentine poet

Oliverio Girondo epitomized the ways a poet adapted to the different avant-garde movements crossing over from Europe to Latin America from the early 1920s to the 1950s. Girondo was a perpetual experimenter who was never satisfied with a particular way of writing, and sought to push poetic innovation to the limits, without ever being a slavish imitator of European fashions, or sacrificing his poetic voice to mere stylistic originality. At the core of his poetics lay an attempt to search for his own elusive self and voice.

His first collection of poems, *Veinte poemas para ser leídos en el tranvía*, 1922 [Twenty Poems to be Read in the Tram], published in Paris, caught the modern mood of the times in its title, mocking a more serious view of poetry. The poems reflect the cosmopolitan Girondo's travels (Venice, Seville, Brest, Rio de Janeiro, etc.) and read like photographic snapshots, often capturing absurd moments, and reveal his relish in shocking his readers with erotic outbursts. This is a visual poetry where the instant of perception is liberated from common sense and logic. Girondo was writing against his serious elders wearing what he called the solemn "frock coat." He deliberately sought to express the new freedom and acceleration of modern city life following the French poet Apollinaire's Cubist poetics of simultaneity, colloquial language and humour. Girondo was aware from the start of his poetic career that he was a Latin American who sought to "oxigenate" the Spanish language. Everyday life was what seized his imagination. In 1924 he said in an interview that his aim was "To look at the daily spectacle of life with our own eyes. To see what is moving, what is pathetic, what is unusual and what is grotesque in a pair of gloves." The poem "Plaza" [Square], written in Buenos Aires in 1920, has the poet simply watching what happens on the street as people walk by. The last verse has a woman calling for help as "sus mellizos se están estrangulando en su barriga" (her twins are strangling each other in her belly). Jorge Luis Borges defined these demythifying poems thus: "Girondo is a violent man. He stares at things for a long time and then knocks them over with a slap."

Thanks to his wealth Girondo was able to travel and live abroad at whim as a typical bohemian of those days. He was the force behind the Buenos Aires avant-garde magazine *Martín Fierro* (1924–27), that united many of Argentina's creative minds from Borges to the visual artist Xul Solar and Norah Lange, whom Girondo later married. Girondo wrote the manifesto for this group that appeared in number 4, 1924, of the magazine. In this aggressive piece he defined the new sensibility as a preference for a Hispano-Suiza car over a Louis XV chair in a tone that derived from Spanish *ultraísmo* and Italian Futurism. However, Girondo was especially aware of the differences between Latin America and Europe, and sought to defend a native or criollo (creolist) modernity.

His next important collection, *Espantapájaros* [Scarecrow] appeared in 1932, and marked an impressive change in Girondo's poetics from mocking comments on social life to prose explorations of his inner dreamscape. Girondo was a close follower of the French Surrealists, without ever adopting their orthodoxies or joining their groups. The book explores the poet's realization of how pointless and false the world is, and how poetry should aspire to be "badly written" to catch inner realities. These prose poems are packed with vivid and contradictory self-dramatizations. Poem 8 summarises Girondo's theory of poetic self as an unstable, ever-changing one: "I do not have a personality: I am a cocktail, a conglomeration, a mass meeting of personalities."

From the 1940s to his death Girondo's poetry became more sombre, and delved even deeper into the elusive self. Poem 1 from *Persuasión de los días* [Persuasion of the Days], 1942, ends: "No soy yo quien escribe estas palabras huérfanas" (It is not I who write these orphan words). This sense of breaking into deeper inner strata is confirmed in Girondo's last magnificent collection, with its neologistic title, *En la masmédula*, 1954 [In the MoreMarrow], where Girondo takes up the challenge of César Vallejo's *Trilce* (1922) and systematically shatters syntax and creates a new hybrid language to reach a more real and psychic voice in the rubble of conventional words. His poetics are summarised as "subvoces que brotan del intrafondo eufónico" (subvoices that burst from the euphonic intradepths) where the poet's "egohueco" (Egohollow) shouts its "pure No." The title of another poem, "Invitación al vómito" [Invitation to Vomit], asks the reader to share the poet's nausea with the world and language as it is, and sick it

up in order to find perhaps some therapeutic rebirth. These difficult poems are close to Surrealist automatic writing where sound helps break down petrified sense in a liberational urge to go beyond the frustrations and impotences of social life. It is fitting that Girondo translated Arthur Rimbaud's *Una temporada en el infierno* (*Une Saison en enfer*) with the Argentine Surrealist poet Enrique Molina in 1959, for by the 1950s Girondo had become the mentor to a group of younger, angry writers who collectively subscribed to the Rimbaudian formulation of poetry as a descent into the inner hell of the false social self.

JASON WILSON

Biography

Born in Buenos Aires, Argentina, 17 August 1891, into an upper-middle-class family. During his childhood spent much time in Europe with his family, attending schools in London and Arcueil, France. Co-founder, with Evar Méndez and Samuel Glusberg, of the manifesto of the avant-garde magazine *Martín Fierro*, 1924. Travelled widely: visited Chile, Peru, Cuba, Mexico, United States, France and Spain, 1924–25. Settled permanently in Buenos Aires in 1931. Married the poet Nora Lange (see separate entry) in 1946. The couples' home became an important centre of literary activity in Buenos Aires. Died in Buenos Aires, 24 January 1967.

Selected Works

Poetry
Veinte poemas para ser leídos en el tranvía, Argenteuil: Coulouma, 1922
Calcomanías, Madrid: Espasa Calpe, 1925
Espantapájaros, Buenos Aires: Proa, 1932
Persuasión de los días, Buenos Aires: Losada, 1942
Campo nuestro, Buenos Aires: Sudamericana, 1946
En la masmédula, Buenos Aires: Losada, 1954
En la masvida, Barcelona: Llibres de Sinera, 1972

Short Fiction
Interlunio, Buenos Aires: Sur, 1937

Compilations and Anthologies
Oliverio Girondo, edited by Aldo Pellegrini, Buenos Aires: 1964
Veinte poemas para ser leídos en el tranvía, *Calcomanías*, and *Espantapájaros*, Buenos Aires: Centro Editor de América Latina, 1966
Obras completas, Buenos Aires: Losada, 1968
Antología, edited by Aldo Pellegrini, Buenos Aires: Argonauta, 1986

Further Reading

Becco, Horacio Jorge, "'El Vanguardismo' en la Argentina (1920–1930)," in *Cuadernos del idioma*, Buenos Aires, 4 (April 1966)
Borges, Jorge Luis, "Oliverio Girondo," in *Segunda Época*, Buenos Aires, vol. 2/18 (26 June 1925)
Kaminszain, Tamara, *El texto silencioso. Tradición y vanguardia en la poesía sudamericana*, Mexico City: UNAM, 1983 [Chapter 1 is on Girondo]
Schwartz, Jorge, *Vanguarda e cosmopolitismo na década de 20: Oliverio Girondo e Oswald de Andrade*, São Paulo: Perspectiva, 1983

Alberto Girri 1919–1991

Argentine poet and literary translator

Alberto Girri was the first Argentine poet to live professionally from poetry, which he was able to do from 1967 onwards. He began publishing poems in 1940, but only did so regularly as from his first collection, *Playa sola*, 1946 [Beach Alone]. From this point until his death he was to publish around forty different books. He also published stories, and was a fine translator of Anglo-American poetry with volumes on Robert Lowell, Wallace Stevens, Stephen Spender, Theodore Roethke, etc. Indeed, one of the principal themes of his work is the poet's ethical response to art and life, with an austere, puritan rejection of what he called the Spanish Baroque tradition of verbosity.

Girri grew up as a poet under the shadow of Victoria Ocampo's prestigious international magazine *Sur* to which he first contributed in 1948 and whose editorial board he later joined. He shared Jorge Luis Borges's taste for literature in English, for defining the Argentine literary tradition as the whole Western literary canon, for writing from a critical metaphysical position, often alluding to philosophical texts or Buddhism or the Tao or Gurdjieff, and for creating a rigorous use of language, verging on aphorism. Girri's debt to Borges was enormous, and offered him a literary space that was not typical in an Argentina that tended to look towards France (Surrealism) as a source for poetic models.

One of Girri's key words is "consider" (another is "examine") where he asks his reader to share a journey of introspection, akin to meditation, working away from the surface ego and social self that often ends with Girri's liberating sarcasm or exasperation. At a level of poetics Girri views the poem as a mental space (epitomized in his collections *Casa de la mente*, 1970 [The House of the Mind] where the poet cleans language of its dross, sharpens mental perceptions, suggests a deeper reality open to the mental senses and close to silence. The phrase "investigating into reality" summarises his poetics. Many poems move from a general statement or abstraction or cultural premiss to a specific, direct insight or experiential truth; a move from idea to object. It has been called an intellectual poetry, which it is, but it is also a therapeutic poetry that restores to language its "attentiveness" to a reality outside words. Girri's poetry explores the delusions of consciousness, and ponders the value of the poem itself, and the process of reading, and trying to make sense of life as in the title poem of the collection *En la letra, ambigua selva*, 1972 [In the Letter, Ambiguous Jungle]. He often defined poetry as a "criticism of language." The message of the poem "Cuenta regresiva" [Regressive Account] from *Poesía de observación* (1973) is "belief or metaphysics / (there is no reason for priority) / always derive / from the anguish of a body." However, the language used is plain and colloquial, with a notable absence of figuration and obvious musicality close to prose, as Ezra Pound often recommended.

A critique of his poetry would have to address the monotony, the variations on a theme, and the sheer bulk, as well as the dense, even elitist cultural inter-textuality assuming a Borgesian richness of allusions. Later poets have also criticised Girri's

mentalist-spiritual leanings (though these affirm the concept of "nada" [Nothingness]), and his tendency to didactic endings. Girri listed his own failings in *Diario de un libro*, 1972 [Diary of a Book], as being too analytical, and writing too much about poetry itself.

The moral influence he exercised as the result of living a life of austerity as a poet in Argentina was enormous, despite his claim that poetry works beyond ideologies. His critical response to demolishing Spanish rhetoric and his dedication to a literal and faithful translation, with notes, of crucial Anglo-American modernists have enriched the Latin American poetic tradition. As Saúl Yurkievich (1978) noted, Girri's work transcends local circumstances and is an "antidote to certain Latin American failings" such as pompous tellurism, neo-popularism and confessional pyschologism.

JASON WILSON

Biography

Born in Buenos Aires, Argentina, 27 November 1919. Educated at the Faculty of Arts at the University of Buenos Aires. Married Leonor Vassena in 1958. Contributed to the magazine *Sur* for many years. Translated works by several major US and British poets into Spanish: John Donne, T.S. Eliot, Robert Lowell, Stephen Spender and Wallace Stevens. Awarded the Buenos Aires Municipal Prize for Poetry, 1955; National Prize for Poetry, 1967, and the Gran Premio de la Fundación Argentina para la Poesía, 1976. Died in 1991.

Selected Works

Poetry

Playa sola, Buenos Aires: Nova, 1946
Coronacíon de la espera, Buenos Aires: Botella al Mar, 1947
Trece poemas, Buenos Aires: Botella al Mar, 1949
El tiempo que destruye, Buenos Aires: Botella al Mar, 1952
Escándalo y soledades, Buenos Aires: Botella al Mar, 1956
Examen de nuestra causa, Buenos Aires: Sur, 1956
Línea de la vida, edited by H.A. Murena, Buenos Aires: Sur, 1957
La penitencia y el mérito, Buenos Aires: Sur, 1957
Elegías italianas, Buenos Aires: Sur, 1957
Propiedades de la magia, Buenos Aires: Sur, 1959
La condición necesaria, Buenos Aires: Sur, 1960
El ojo, Buenos Aires: Losada, 1964
Envíos, Buenos Aires: Sudamericana, 1967
Casa de la mente, Buenos Aires: Sudamericana, 1970
Valores diarios, Buenos Aires: Sudamericana, 1970
En la letra, ambigua selva, Buenos Aires: Sudamericana, 1972
Poesía de observación, Buenos Aires: Sudamericana, 1973
Quien habla no está muerto, Buenos Aires: Sudamericana, 1975
Bestiario, Buenos Aries: La Garza, 1976
El motivo es el poema, Buenos Aires: Sudamericana, 1976
Árbol de la estirpe humana, Buenos Aires: Sudamericana, 1978
Lo propio, lo de todos, Buenos Aires: Sudamericana, 1980
Homenaje a W.C. Williams, Buenos Aires: Sudamericana, 1981
  [Includes Girri's Spanish versions of poems by William Carlos Williams]
Los Diez Mandamientos, Buenos Aires: Estudio Abierto, 1981
Borradores, Buenos Aires: Galería Rubbers, 1982
Lírica de percepciones, Buenos Aires: Sudamericana, 1983
Monodias, Buenos Aires: Sudamericana, 1985

Existenciales, Buenos Aires: Sudamericana, 1988
1989/1990, Buenos Aires: Fraterna, 1990
Juegos alegóricos, Buenos Aires: Fraterna, 1993

Other Writings
Diario de un libro, Buenos Aires: Sudamericana, 1972
Notas sobre la experiencia poética, Buenos Aires: Losada, 1983
Cuestiones y razones, Buenos Aires: Fraterna, 1987

Compilations and Anthologies
Poemas elegidos, Buenos Aires: Losada, 1965
Coronación de la espera, Trece poemas, La penitencia y el mérito, Propiedades de la magia, Buenos Aires: Centro, 1967
Prosas, Caracas: Monte Ávila, 1977

Further Reading
Alberto Girri: homenaje, Buenos Aires: Compañía de A. Diaconú, 1993
Borinsky, Alicia, "Interlocución y aporía: notas a propósito de Alberto Girri y Juan Gelman," *Revista Iberoamericana* 125 (1983)

Crespoe de Arnaud, Bárbara, "Alberto Girri," in *Historia de la literatura argentina*, vol. 5, *Los Contemporáneos*, Buenos Aires: Centro Editor de América Latina, 1982
Pascoe, Muriel Slade, *La poesía de Alberto Girri*, Buenos Aires: Sudamericana, 1986
Suárez, María Victoria, *Alberto Girri: existencia y lógica poética*, Buenos Aires: Corregidor, 1987
Sucre, Guillermo, *La máscara, la transparencia*, Caracas: Monte Ávila, 1975
Vittor, Luis Alberto, *Simbolismo e iniciación en la poesía de Alberto Girri*, Buenos Aires: Fraterna, 1990
Yurkievich, Saúl, "Alberto Girri: la elocuencia de la lucidez," in his *La confabulación con la palabra*, Madrid: Taurus, 1978
____ "Alberto Girri: fases de su creciente," in his *A través de la trama: sobre vanguardias literarias y otra concomitancias*, Barcelona: Muchnik, 1984

Interviews
Encuesta a la literatura argentina contemporánea, Buenos Aires: Centro Editor de América Latina, 1981

Margo Glantz 1930–

Mexican prose writer, critic and literary translator

As the critic Magdalena García Pinto has suggested, Margo Glantz's literary production consists of two forms of expression which continuously overlap, sustaining an incessant intertextual dialogue: that of her creative writing, and that of literary criticism. In the latter she adopts a sociocultural approach which involves an obsessive reading of the body, memory, history and cultural practices. As a member of the generation of the 1950s, Glantz has not received yet the critical recognition that she deserves because she is a writer in the dissenting tradition.

As a student of the Chronicles of the conquest, the Baroque theater, English 19th-century literature, travel diaries, avant-garde European theater, and contemporary Latin American and Mexican literature, Glantz playfully incorporates the knowledge derived from her wide-ranging readings into her creative works. Ingenuity and wit overlap to make up original narratives full of extraordinary events, fictional, historical and mythological characters, with both unusual and ordinary endings. As Glantz has said in an interview with the Chilean writer Mercedes Valdivieso, her creative works reflect her relationship to the world, and to herself, equating states of mind and modes of writing.

Her first fictional work, *Las mil y una calorías. Novela dietética*, 1978 [One Hundred and One Calories. A Dietetic Novel], is an experimental exercise of the imagination that combines fragments of verse and fantastic stories for the reader to link together and to interpret according to their own taste and readings. "Historias de escrituras y cerebros" (Stories of Writings and Brains) is one of the best examples of her exuberant imagination, posing challenging questions related to the conceptualization of sexuality and writing. *Doscientas ballenas azules*, 1979 [Two Hundred Blue Whales] deals with an interior amniotic voyage in the placenta, and the feminine theme of interior productivity and instintive consciousness are conveyed through a vast repertoire of visual and sensorial imagery. *No pronunciarás*, 1980 [Do not Invoke the Name], is a ludic narrative piece, which explores the act of naming using parody and irony. For Glantz, naming becomes a pretext to investigate the significance of the name, identity, biography, historical anecdote, cultural practice. This imaginary and analytical composition encompasses from the naming of animals by Adam, the associative power of names to qualities and disposition, the anecdotical interpretation of names at certain historical moments, the magical power of names, to cultural practices such as naming and colonization, naming and acculturation, marriage and the changing of names. *Las genealogías*, 1981 (*The Family Tree*) is her best-known work. It deals with personal and collective identity, memory, culture and the process of acculturation, the autobiographical impulse and the textual construction of the subject. Glantz gives voice to her father Jacobo Glantz, to her mother Lucía, to herself and her ancestors, and even to her daughter Renata entering a room while she listens to tapes, and edits the (auto)biography. The Other, the others, and the narrator/protagonist weave a textual tapestry on tapes with forgotten memories, real and imaginary stories, framed conversations, old photographs, and nostalgic recollections, while recording Jewish cultural history in the process of being Mexicanized.

In *La lengua en la mano*, 1983 [The Tongue in the Hand] Glantz combines her skills as writer and critic elaborating a sophisticated study on eroticism centered on the representation of the tongue, hand, the foot, and their relationship to writing. Taking Georges Bataille and Roland Barthes's studies into consideration, Glantz proposes an interpretative discourse debating the body and genre, the body and gender, the body and social class, the body and moral discourse in 19th-century Mexican literature. Her infatuation with the grammar of the body and cultural interpretation leads her also to investigate tattooing, mutilation and fragmentation. Her *De la amorosa inclinación a enredarse en cabellos*, 1984 [About the Loving Temptation to get Entangled in Hair], merges cultural articles, from the newspapers *Uno Más Uno* (Mexico) and *Zona Franca* (Caracas), regarding the hair as a symbol of love, eroticism and filial relationships. Her semiotic approach becomes a dynamic inquiry as she considers the hair as a symbol of love, lust, frivolity, repression, liberation, life and death. Her intellectual biography, *Síndrome de naufragios*, 1984 [Shipwreck Syndrome] depicts natural and personal calamities and misfortunes such as hurricanes, floods, epidemics and divorce. The text merges catastrophic events so that the biblical flood intrudes in a divorce. In this way Glantz conceptualizes the relationship of writing and fragmentary representation. Her cultural project *El día de tu boda*, 1982 [Your Wedding Day] is a sociological treatise and cultural essay on the postcard, the epistolary genre, and the love-letter. It ascertains her versatility, inventiveness and experimental aesthetic pursuit, being also an homage to Roland Barthes and Walter Benjamin.

Some of her most recent critical works include essays on Núñez Cabeza de Vaca, and on the Malinche myth. Glantz's creative works provide the reader with valuable insights; each one has posed serious literary questions ahead of their time. Her texts encourage readers to be aware of the resistance of a text to be catalogued within a specific genre, and of the proliferation of demands intertextuality imposes on them. Her prose also questions the function of thematic obsession as an interpretative tool enhancing the semantic possibilities of the text, the sociological value of mixing discourses from different traditions and modes of expression, and the critical importance of reading a variety of cultural artifacts. It is important to note that *Las genealogías*, as Erna Pfeiffer suggests, pioneered the Mexican feminine genealogical novel centering on the problematics of identity and origin being followed by *Las hojas muertas*, 1987 [Dead Leaves] by Barbara Jacobs, *Antes* [Before] and *Mejor desaparece*, 1988 [Better That She Should Disappear] by Carmen Boullosa, *La flor de Lis*, 1988 [The Fleur-de-Lis] by Elena Poniatowska, *La familia vino del norte*, 1988 [The Family Came from the North] and *Héctor* by Silvia Molina, some short stories by Ethel Krauze, and *La bobe* (1990) by Sabina Berman. The value of her critical works is still hard to assess, but one can say that her preface to the anthology *Onda y escritura en Mexico*, 1971 [Writing and the New Wave in Mexico] is representative of her role as an avant-garde analyst of Mexican literature and as a leading literary critic in contemporary Mexico. Her introduction was considered one of the most polemical essays of the decade, igniting a cultural and political debate on the new defiant and subversive mode of expression she named "literatura de *la Onda*" (new wave literature).

As a first-generation immigrant, and a Judeo-Mexican writer, she has explored vital issues of this hybrid culture. Ahead of her contemporaries, Glantz called attention to the representation of the female body, the importance of the gaze within the text, and of how a phallocentric view of the world permeates the culture that she tries to understand, and from which she departs as she writes.

MAGDALENA MAÍZ-PEÑA

See also entry on Jewish Writers

Biography

Born in Mexico City, 26 January 1930 of Jewish parents from the Ukraine. Attended the Sorbonne, Paris, received doctorate, 1958; also studied history of art at the Louvre and English literature at Central London Polytechnic. Leading intellectual who has been involved in policy-making in significant cultural projects, through the Universidad Nacional Autónoma de México and her work for several important publishing houses. Director, Cultural Institute of Mexico-Israel, 1964–67; director, literature program, Instituto Nacional de Bellas Artes, 1964–67; professor of literature at UNAM. Has taught at universities in the US and is a contributor to important cultural journals such as *Filosofía y Letras* and the *Revista Iberoamericana*. Has also translated works by Georges Bataille, Tennessee Williams, Henry Fielding and Antonin Artaud. Cultural attaché at the Embassy of Mexico in London, 1986–88. Recipient of the Premio Villaurrutia, 1984 for *Síndrome de naufragios*.

Selected Works

Novels

Las mil y una calorías. Novela dietética, Puebla: Premiá, 1978

Doscientas ballenas azules, Mexico City: La Máquina de Escribir, 1979

No pronunciarás, Mexico City: Premiá, 1980

Síndrome de naufragios, Mexico City: Joaquín Mortiz, 1984

Las genealogías, Mexico City: Martín Casillas, 1981; as *The Family Tree: an Illustrated Novel*, translated by Susan Bassnett, London: Serpent's Tail, 1991

Short Fiction

La guerra de los hermanos. Leyenda de la Coyolxauhqui, illustrated by María Figueroa, Colección del Jicote Argüendero, Mexico City: Penélope, 1982

"Todas las rosas," in *Mujeres en espejo. Narradoras latinoamericanas siglo XX*, vol. 2, edited by Sara Sefcovich, Mexico City: Folios Ediciones, 1985

Essays

Tennessee Williams y el teatro norteamericano, Mexico City: UNAM, 1964

Onda y escritura en México: Jóvenes de 20 a 33, Mexico City: Siglo XXI, 1971 [Critical edition with a lengthy introduction by Margo Glantz]

Repeticiones; ensayos sobre literatura mexicana, Xalapa, Mexico: Universidad Veracruzana, 1979

Intervenciones y pretexto; ensayos de literatura comparada e iberoamericana, Mexico City: UNAM, 1981

El día de tu boda, Mexico City: Cultura/SEP, 1982

La lengua en la mano, Mexico City: Premiá, 1983

De la amorosa inclinación a enredarse en cabellos, Mexico City: Océano, 1984

Erosiones, Mexico City: UNAM, 1984

Borrones y borradores; reflexiones sobre el ejercicio de la escritura,
Mexico City: UNAM, 1992
Esguince de cintura, Mexico City: Consejo Nacional para la Cultura
y las Artes, 1994
La Malinche, sus padres y sus hijos, Mexico City: UNAM, 1994

Further Reading
Agosín, Marjorie, "Dialogando *Las genealogías* de Margo Glantz,"
Las hacedoras: mujer, imagen, escritura, Santiago de Chile:
Cuarto Propio, 1993
García Pinto, Magdalena, "La problemática de la sexualidad en la
escritura de Margo Glantz," *Coloquio Internacional: escritura y
sexualidad en la literatura hispanoamericana*, with an
introduction by Alain Sicard and César Fernández Moreno,
Madrid: Centre de Recherches Latino-Americaines / Fundamentos,
1990
Glemma, Graciela, "La transgresión que no cesa," *Feminaria*,
Buenos Aires, vol. 3/6 (1990)
Lindstrom, Naomi, "*No pronunciarás* de Margo Glantz: los
nombres como señas de la imaginación cultural," *Revista
Iberoamericana*, vol. 56/150 (1990)

Ocampo, Aurora (editor), "Margo Glantz," in *Diccionario de
escritores mexicanos. Siglo XX*, vol. 3, Mexico City: UNAM,
1993
Otero-Krauthammer, Elizabeth, "Integración de la identidad judía en
Las genealogías de Margo Glantz," *Revista Iberoamericana*, vol.
51 (1985)

Interviews
García Pinto, Magdalena, "Entrevista con Margo Glantz," in her
*Historias íntimas: conversaciones con dieiz escritoras
latinoamericanas*, Hanover, New Hampshire: Ediciones del Norte,
1988; as *Women Writers of Latin America: Intimate Histories*,
translated by Magdalena García Pinto and Trudy Balch, Austin:
University of Texas Press, 1991
Miller, Beth, *A la sombra del volcán: conversaciones sobre la
narrativa mexicana actual*," Xalapa, Mexico: Universidad
Veracruzana, 1990 [Contains interview with Margo Glantz]
Pfeiffer, Erna, "Tenemos que reescribir el mundo: Margo Glantz,"
in her *Entrevistas; diez escritoras mexicanas desde bastidores*,
Frankfurt: Vervuert Verlag, 1992

Edouard Glissant 1928–

Martinican prose writer, poet and dramatist

Edouard Glissant is an outstanding example of the second
generation of black Caribbean writers who have struggled to
come to terms with the fragmented, unsatisfactory heritage
with which they have to work, and whose efforts have gone
into creating a language that attempts to rescue the past and
offer fresh opportunities for the future. One of Glissant's
teachers at secondary school was Aimé Césaire, whose ideas
on *Négritude* and revindication of a specific black Caribbean
tradition have been taken a stage further by these younger
writers. While continuing Césaire's search for a specific
Caribbean identity, they were unable to accept his sometimes
simple oppositions, and have, as in the case of Glissant, found
that there are no easy answers.

Another, very different writer from the Caribbean – Jean
Rhys – wrote in her novel *Wide Sargasso Sea*: "how can rivers
and mountains and sea seem unreal?" This is the drama that
Glissant often enacts in his own work: how he, as a black
writer on a small island, nominally a part of France, can come
to feel so dispossessed. He feels uneasy with the sea because
his ancestors were brought across it against their will: its presence serves as a constant reminder of the homeland of which
they were robbed. The sea also emphasizes the distance with
France, still governing Martinique and pretending, at least on
some levels, that the island is no different from anywhere in
metropolitan France itself – "Of course there are problems
here," says a character in *Malemort*, "but a Frenchman's a
Frenchman, whether he's a Breton, an Alsatian or a West
Indian." Glissant also finds himself cut off from the landscape
of mountains and rivers of the Caribbean islands because, once

again, his ancestors were never allowed to feel it belonged to
them in any way.

This sense of the lack of a home extends in Glissant to the
use of language itself. French is the tongue he has learnt from
the masters, but which he stubbornly uses to name, to subvert,
to create meanings that will serve him and his fellows rather
than those who seek to control the language in order to reinforce their power. In this sense, Glissant learnt the subversive
power of language from French Surrealist poets like André
Breton or René Char, a power that he endows with a prophetic
dignity and despair in many of his poems.

Although Glisssant's work has become increasingly
pessimistic, his most infuential work in many ways remains his
early novel *La Lézarde* (*The Ripening*) which focusses more
on the possibilities of revolt. Based on the events of 1945,
when a generation of young Martinicans believed they could
achieve political change through revolution, the novel traces
the story of Thael from the hills, who has been chosen as the
instrument of a revolutionary group to kill the reactionary
Garin. As Thael, like the river moves down from the hills to
the life of society in the plains, he acquires knowledge that is
painful but at the same time unavoidable. The plot is summarized as follows by Beverley Ormerod in *An Introduction to
the French Caribbean Novel*: "The fiction is built on traditional, archetypal motifs: the departure from a known region
into the unknown; the encounter with an alluring woman; the
questing journey through a mysterious forest; the descent, in
darkness, to a magic spring; the tests of skill and endurance;
the killing which frees imprisoned waters and lifts a curse from

a community; the final, difficult return of the hero enriched and matured by his initiatory experiences." As a whole, the book is remarkable for the way that the landscape and the characters are linked not only at the level of the plot but also at that of language and sensibility, through a style that is richly meditative.

Later novels follow a similar theme of quest. In *Le Quatrième Siècle* [The Fourth Century], the different choices of two families who arrived on the same slave ship from Africa are explored: one whose members accept their fate as slaves, the others who immediately flee to the hills and live the clandestine existence of *marrons*, or runaways. By the time of the later novel *Malemort*, the rebellion and cautious optimism of these earlier works has gone. Now the same river of *La Lézarde* is choked and overgrown, and has lost its way to the sea.

Glissant has also written plays in which he attempts to reclaim history for those who have suffered rather than dictated it. In the preface to his *Monsieur Toussaint* he wrote "For those who know of their own history only that obscure and diminished portion to which they have been relegated, the recovery of the near or distant past is an absolute necessity ... a passionate determination to unveil the past which has been deformed or obliterated by others may sometimes give us a better sense of the meaning of the present".

It is in Glissant's poems, particularly in the collection *Le Sel noir* [Black Salt], that the reader is most aware of how this same process is enacted through language itself. Words in the poems carry their own weight of history, which is brought into the present and renewed through both a startling use of imagery and of poetic voice, endowing them with a sudden immediacy of poetic meaning.

NICK CAISTOR

Biography
Born in Sainte-Marie, Martinique, 21 September 1928. Attended the Lycée Schoelcher, Fort-de-France, and studied under Aimé Césaire, 1939–45. Moved to France in 1946. Enrolled at the Sorbonne and also studied ethnology at the Musée de l'Homme. Worked at the Centre National de la Recherche Scientifique, Paris. Contributor to *Présence Africaine*, from 1947; active in left-wing political and cultural groups from the early 1950s, including the Société Africaine de Culture. Co-founder, with Paul Niger, of the Front Antillo Guyanais, c.1959 until it was dissolved by Charles De Gaulle in 1961. Glissant was forbidden to return to Martinique from 1959 to 1965 and prevented from travelling to Algeria. Returned to Martinique, 1965; founder and director, Institut Martiniquais d'Études, from 1967; editor of the quartely review *Acoma*, 1970–73. Awarded the Renaudot Prize, 1958 for *La Lézarde* and the Veillon Prize, 1965 for *Le Quatrième Siècle*.

Selected Works

Novels
La Lézarde, Paris: Seuil, 1958; as *The Ripening*, translated by Frances Frenaye, New York: Braziller, 1959; also translated by J. Michael Dash, London: Heinemann, 1985
Le Quatrième Siècle, Paris: Seuil, 1964
Malemort, Paris: Seuil, 1975
La Case du commandeur, Paris: Seuil, 1981
Mahagony, Paris: Seuil, 1987
Tout-monde, Paris: Gallimard, 1993

Play
Monsieur Toussaint, Paris: Seuil, 1961; as *Monsieur Toussaint*, translated by Joseph G. Foster and Barbara Franklin, Washington, DC: Three Continents Press, 1981

Poetry
Un Champ d'îles, Paris: Dragon, 1953
La Terre inquiète, Paris: Dragon, 1954
Les Indes: poèmes de l'une et l'autre terre, Paris: Seuil, 1956; as *The Indies*, translated by Dominique O'Neill, Toronto: Gref, 1992 [bilingual edition]
Le Sel noir, Paris: Seuil, 1960
Le Sang rivé, Paris: Présence Africaine, 1961
Boises, Paris: Acoma, 1979
Pays rêvé, pays réel, Paris: Seuil, 1985

Essays
Soleil de la conscience, Paris: Seuil, 1956
L'Intention poétique, Paris: Seuil, 1969
Le Discours antillais, Paris: Seuil, 1981; as *Caribbean Discourse*, translated by J. Michael Dash, Charlottesville: University Press of Virginia, 1989
Poétique de la relation, Paris: Gallimard, 1990

Compilations and Anthologies
Poèmes complets, Paris: Gallimard, 1994

Further Reading
Cailler, Bernadette, *Conquerants de la nuit nue: Edouard Glissant et l'H(h)istoire antillaise*, Tubingen: G. Narr, 1988
Case, Frederich, "The Novels of Edouard Glissant," in *Black Images* 2 (Autumn–Winter 1973)
Ormerod, Beverley, *An Introduction to the French Caribbean Novel*, London: Heinemann, 1985
Radford, Daniel, *Edouard Glissant*, Paris: Seghers, 1982
Roget, Wilbert J., "The Image of Africa in the Writings of Edouard Glissant," *College Language Association Journal*, vol. 21 (1978)
Silenieks, Juris, "Glissant's Prophetic Vision of the Past," *African Literature Today*, vol. 11 (1980)

Special Issues of Journals
World Literature Today (Autumn 1987)

Gertrudis Gómez de Avellaneda 1814–1873

Cuban prose writer, poet and dramatist

Although Gertrudis Gómez de Avellaneda was born and educated in Cuba, she spent most of her literary career in Spain. In her lifetime she was highly popular and acknowledged as an outstanding authoress in what was a male-dominated literary world, but her acclaim dwindled after her death. However, scholarly research in recent years has been shedding considerable light on her persona and literary output, resurrecting, to some extent, the critical esteem she still deserves within both Cuban and Spanish literature. All Avellaneda's output reflects the personal conflicts in her unconventional early life, and the feelings and concerns she experienced as a woman torn between her instinctive individualism and eventual conformity.

Avellaneda first became known as a lyric poet in Madrid in the early 1840s. From the first, one of her main themes was love, both temporal and spiritual. In her poem "A él," 1845 [To Him], written at a time when she felt an unrequited passion for a certain Ignacio de Cepeda, she identifies with and abandons herself to the power of amorous infatuation: "¡Poder que me arrastras! ¿Serás tú mi llama? / ¿Serás mi océano? ¿mi sierpe serás? . . . / ¿Qué importa? Mi pecho te acepta y te ama, / Ya vida, ya muerte le aguarde detrás." (Force that carries me away! Will you be my flame? / Will you be my ocean? Will you be my serpent? . . . / Who cares? My heart accepts and loves you, / Whether life or death awaits beyond). The pain provoked by her frustrated love appears in numerous poems: "La serenata del poeta" [The Poet's Serenade], "El cazador" [The Hunter], "La venganza" [Vengeance], among others. As a consequence of her disillusionment with sexual love, Avellaneda entered a more spiritual phase which was similarly reflected in her poetry: "Las contradicciones" [The Contradictions], "Al mar" [To the Sea], "A una acacia" [To an Acacia], "Dios y el hombre" [God and Man]. Not only did many incorporate deep disappointments in her early amorous experiences, but they also demonstrated the melancholy sentiments she had for the idealised Cuban homeland she had left when she was twenty-two years old. These feelings are evident in the enthusiastic and constant references to the natural history of the island, and the unbridled admiration she lavished on her Cuban compatriots. Poems like "Al partir" [On Leaving], which she wrote when she first left Cuba in 1836, and "La vuelta a la patria" [Return to the Homeland], written twenty-three years later when she returned to Cuba, are packed with patriotic sentiments for Cuba expressed in exalting metaphors: "Perla del mar" [Pearl of the Sea], "Hermosa Cuba" [Beautiful Cuba], "Patria feliz" [Joyous Homeland], "Edén querido" [Beloved Eden]. All display the rose-tinted, and even somewhat mawkish, sentiments of the typical expatriate.

Avellaneda was also a popular and famous dramatist. She wrote numerous plays whose main themes were historical, such as *Munio Alfonso*, 1844, *Egilona*, 1845, or historical-biblical, such as *Baltasar*, 1858, *Saúl*, 1849, as well as comedies, such as *La hija de las flores* [The Daughter of the Flowers], 1852, *La aventurera*, 1853 [The Adventuress], among others. Each

demonstrates a preoccupation with the three major philosophical currents of the Romantic period: freedom, morality and justice. In many of her tragedies she used the subjects, characters and ideas of outstanding English, French and Spanish writers, such as Shakespeare, Byron, Emile Augier, Madame de Staël, George Sand, Manuel José de Quintana, and others. In *La aventurera*, Avellaneda defends the fallen woman as a victim of a chauvinist society in a serious attempt to condemn prevailing social canons. Avellaneda clearly identifies with her character, as she too had suffered the opprobrium of a censorious society when she rejected the restrictive cultural values that her own society attempted to place upon her. Her personal desire for independence encouraged her to defy conventional patriarchal society by refusing an arranged marriage. She indulged in love affairs and had an illegitimate child. In like vein, she did not restrain herself from voicing her emancipating ideas on marriage, divorce and chauvinism in a covert manner in some of her fictional work. While on occasion her plays and poems are devices for her anti-chauvinism, it is in her novels that her concerns are most consistently and directly expressed. Two novels, in particular, stand out: *Sab*, 1841 and *Dos mujeres*, 1842 [Two Women]. In *Sab*, Avellaneda uses slavery as a metaphor to denounce simultaneously the servitude of black people and white women alike. Sab, the mulatto protagonist, writes: "¡Oh, las mujeres! ¡Pobres y ciegas víctimas! Como los esclavos, ellas arrastran pacientemente su cadena y bajan la cabeza bajo el yugo de las leyes humanas. Sin otra guía que su corazón ignorante y crédulo eligen un dueño para toda la vida." (Oh, women! Poor, blind victims! Like slaves, they patiently drag their chains and bow their heads under the yoke of human laws. With no other guide than their uneducated and naively gullible heart, they choose (when marrying) a master for life). In *Dos mujeres*, she goes still further and presents the idea of a man who genuinely loves two women, his wife, and his lover. In this, Avellaneda attempts to reveal the institution of marriage as something mutable, with the societal concept of adultery as a sinful and punishable act contrasted with the reality of simultaneous, virtuous and multiple love.

A strident feminism appears in Avellaneda's later articles, collectively entitled "La mujer," 1860 [Woman], for the literary magazine *Álbum cubano*, which she founded and edited when she returned to Cuba. These articles, both claiming and seeking to justify equality of rights, appear to have been written as a result of her application for membership of the Spanish Royal Academy being turned down on the grounds of her gender. In spite of her efforts to promote equal rights for women, Avellaneda was ultimately defeated by the very chauvinistic society in which, against the odds, she had largely succeeded and which she had so often attacked. Her novels *Sab* and *Dos mujeres* were not only banned in Cuba, because they were considered a danger to conventional notions of the moral fabric of society, but were also excluded eventually by Avellaneda herself from the final edition of her *Obras literarias* [Literary Works]. She possibly felt defeated by a censorious and critical society and thus obliged to exclude both works. It would seem that in her later years Avellaneda's more strident feminism mellowed and she lapsed into populist prose once again. In the end she decided to accept the norms imposed by a patriarchal society, just as, of course, most of her fellow women did. Nevertheless, as her posthumously published autobiography and personal letters indicated, she privately continued to feel different from other women: "Ya he dicho mil veces que no pienso como el común de las mujeres, y que mi modo de obrar y de sentir me pertenecen exclusivamente." (I have said a thousand times that I do not think like the rest of women, and that my ways of behaving and feeling belong exclusively to me).

The populist, sentimental works of Avellaneda, which appear now perhaps a little tawdry, should be seen in relation to their historical context. That same context ought, similarly, to show Avellaneda as a feminist pioneer in Hispanic cultures. She bravely attempted to challenge the discriminatory society in which she lived. And even if in the end the weight of social pressure forced her to conform, the reality of those anti-chauvinist works she did achieve, suffice to guarantee her critical acclaim.

BRIGIDA PASTOR

Biography
Born in Puerto Príncipe in the province of Camagüey, Cuba, 23 March 1814. Nicknamed "Tula." Eldest of five children and only daughter, but only she and her brother Manuel survived. Was most fortunate in her education and among her tutors was the poet José María Heredia who encouraged her to write. Father died when Tula was nine and mother remarried ten months later. Tula disliked her stepfather. Family left for Europe in 1836. Stayed in Corunna where Tula was briefly engaged to Francisco Ricafort. Settled with her brother, Manuel, in Seville. Met Ignacio de Cepeda and began to publish poems using pen name "La Peregrina" (The Pilgrim). First play, Leoncia, produced in Seville in 1840. Had passionate love affair with Gabriel García Tssara and bore him a child, but he abandoned them, and the little girl died when less than a year old. Married Pedro Sabater in 1846; he died less than four months later and she sought solace in a convent in Bordeaux. In 1853 she applied for membership of the Royal Spanish Academy, but her application was rejected on account of her gender. (The first woman member was to be admitted in 1977). Married Colonel Domingo Verdugo y Massieu in 1855; he was stabbed and seriously wounded in 1858. In 1859 Verdugo attached to staff of new Governor General of Cuba. Couple travelled to the island where in 1860 Tula founded and edited the shortlived women's magazine, Álbum cubano de lo bueno y lo bello [Cuban Album of the Good and the Beautiful]. Husband died in 1863, after which she returned to Seville. Moved to Madrid in 1869 where she died of diabetes on 1 February 1873.

Selected Works

Individual Works
Devocionario nuevo y completísimo en prosa y verso, Seville: D.A. Izquierdo, 1867
Poesías líricas de la Señora Doña Gertrudis Gómez de Avellaneda, Madrid: Leocadio López, 1877
El artista barquero, 2 vols, Havana: "El Pilar" de Manuel de Armas, 1890

Autobiografía y cartas de la ilustre poetisa hasta ahora inéditas, Huelva, Spain: Imprenta Miguel Mora, 1907
Cartas inéditas y documentos relativos a su vida en Cuba de 1859 a 1864, Matanzas, Cuba: Imprenta La Pluma de Oro, 1912
Diario de amor, Madrid: Aguilar, 1928

Critical Editions
Baltasar, edited by Carmen Bravo Villasante, Havana: Consejo Nacional de Cultura, 1962
Sab, edited by Carmen Bravo Villasante, Havana: Consejo Nacional de Cultura, 1965; Salamanca, Spain: Anaya, 1970

Compilations and Anthologies
Obras literarias de la señora Gertrudis Gómez de Avellaneda, 5 vols, Madrid: Imprenta de M. Rivadenera, 1868–69
Obras de doña Gertrudis Gómez de Avellaneda, 6 vols, Havana: Imprenta de A. Miranda, 1914

Translations
Cuahtemoc, the Last Aztec Emperor, translated by Mrs Wilson W. Blake, Mexico: F.P. Hoeck, 1898 [Translation of Guatimozín, último emperador de Méjico]
Belshazzar, translated by William Freeman Burbank, London: B.F. Stevens and Brown, 1914 [Translation of Baltasar]
The Love Letters, translated by Dorrey Malcolm, Havana: Juan Fernández Burgos, 1956
Sab and Autobiography, translated by Nina M. Scott, Austin: University of Texas Press, 1993 [Critical edition and excellent translation]

Further Reading
Cabrera, Rosa M. and Gladys B. Zaldívar, Homenaje a Gertrudis Gómez de Avellaneda: memorias del simposio en el centenario de su muerte, Miami: Universal, 1981
Figarola Caneda, Domingo and Doña Emilia Boxhorn, Gertrudis Gómez de Avellaneda: biografía, bibliografía e iconografía, incluyendo muchas cartas inéditas y publicadas, escritas por la gran poetisa o dirigidas a ella, y sus memorias, Madrid: Sociedad General Española de Librería, 1929
Gold, Janet N., "The Feminine Bond: Victimization and Beyond in the Novels of Gertrudis Gómez de Avellaneda," Letras Femeninas 15 (1989)
Guerra, Lucía, "Estrategias femeninas en la elaboración del sujeto romántico en la obra de Gertrudis Gómez de Avellaneda," Revista Iberoamericana 132–33 (1985)
Harter, Hugh A., Gertrudis Gómez de Avellaneda, Boston: Twayne, 1981
Kirkpatrick, Susan, Las Románticas: Women Writers and Subjectivity in Spain, 1835–1850, Berkeley: University of California Press, 1989 [Gómez de Avellaneda's work is considered here because she is claimed by both Spain and Cuba]
Luis, William, Literary Bondage: Slavery in Cuban Narrative, Austin: University of Texas Press, 1990
Núñez, Ana Rosa, Ensayo de un diccionario de pensamiento vivo de la Avellaneda, Miami: Universal, 1975
Pastor, Brigida, "Cuba's Covert Cultural Critic: the Feminist Writings of Gertrudis Gómez de Avellaneda," Romance Quarterly, vol. 42/3 (1995)
Picon Garfield, Evelyn, Poder y sexualidad: el discurso de Gertrudis Gómez de Avellaneda, Amsterdam: Rodopi, 1993
Schlau, Stacey, "Stranger in a Strange Land: the Discourse of Alienation in Gómez de Avellaneda's Abolitionist Novel Sab," Hispania 69 (1986)
Sommer, Doris, Foundational Fictions: the National Romances of Latin America, Berkeley: University of California Press, 1991 [Chapter on Sab]

Antônio Gonçalves Dias 1823–1864

Brazilian poet

Antônio Gonçalves Dias was proud of the coincidence of his birth and that of a newly-independent Brazil: he was born in Caxias, in the province of Maranhão, just ten days after the last armed conflict of the independence process, a brief skirmish between Brazilians and Portuguese loyalists, took place in the same small city. He never publicly admitted another coincidence, however: he was the illegitimate son of a Portuguese immigrant and a *cafuza* (mixed African and Indian) mother, and was therefore, like Brazil itself, a product of the three national races.

Despite his illegitimacy, his mixed ancestry, and his decidedly Indian appearance, Gonçalves Dias enjoyed remarkable success in academic and public life. He attended the University of Coimbra, in Portugal, where he belonged to a group of student poets who styled themselves "medievalists." He then went on to become the most famous Brazilian poet of his time, the nation's first serious ethnographer, a leading specialist on education and on colonial history, a professor at the premier national secondary school, and a friend of the Emperor, Peter II. Gonçalves Dias visited Europe several times, usually at the Emperor's expense, to research educational organization and Brazilian history. His works were widely known and admired in Portugal, France and Germany, and he was the first Brazilian writer to appear in a European encyclopedia of world literature. A key member of the prestigious Brazilian Institute of History and Geography, the oldest surviving learned society in Latin America, Gonçalves Dias was enormously influential in the process of constructing a viable national past for the new nation. He wrote a dictionary of the Tupi Indian language, and the native artifacts he gathered during a nine-month expedition to the Amazon formed the core of the collection of the Brazilian National Museum.

Most of Gonçalves Dias's poetry appeared in four volumes between 1846 and 1857. In very general terms, his verse can be divided into three broad categories: Romantic set-pieces, largely autobiographical lyrics, and works dealing with the Middle Ages – but it is important to understand that this last category includes a sizable body of poems about what Gonçalves Dias defined as Brazil's medieval past, the world of the Indian. The verses included in first of these categories are the least interesting. Obviously influenced by the poetry of Lamartine and Hugo, these verbose dramatic narratives and hymns to the beauty of nature are surprisingly un-Brazilian in both theme and detail.

The lyrics included in these volumes are very different indeed. Their language is simple and highly musical, purified of the ponderous adjectivization found in his more consciously romantic poems. Many of them deal with unhappy love, and reflect Gonçalves Dias's miserable marriage and his enduring and unconsummated love for another woman, the sister of his best friend. Others sing the beauties of nature in Brazil and the poet's longing, during his frequent stays in Europe, for his homeland. The tone, the vocabulary, and the metrics of many of these works are intensely non-literary and convincingly authentic; portions of several of these poems have passed directly into popular culture, recited or sung by individuals entirely unaware of their origins, and have been collected by 20th-century folklorists. The most popular and beloved of all Brazilian poems, in fact, is Gonçalves Dias's "Canção do exílio" (Song of Exile), written while he was a student in Portugal, which almost all of the nation's inhabitants know by heart.

The most complex and intriguing of Gonçalves Dias's poetic works are his recreations of the medieval past. One group of recreations focuses on Brazil's Indian past, both before and just after the arrival of the Portuguese in 1500, and includes both brief lyrics and narratives and his epic poem *Os timbiras* [The Timbira Indians], published in Germany in 1857; Gonçalves Dias described this last work as both an American *Genesis* and a Brazilian *Iliad*. His other medieval text, the *Sextilhas de Frei Antão* [Brother Antony's Sextets], published in 1848, is a painstaking recreation of the language and society of 15th-century Portugal.

In all of these works, Gonçalves Dias has a double purpose: at one level, these poems are but one aspect of the central goal of his life – to use history to construct a distinctive national identity for Brazilians, and to create a literature capable of expressing that identity. His idealized knights and damsels, clothed in armor and damask or in breechcloths, housed in Portuguese castles or communal dwellings in the limitless forests of the Amazon, were all designed to give the readers of a new nation a sense of pride in their heroic transatlantic history. At the same time, Gonçalves Dias was acutely conscious of his non-European origins and highly sensitive to the racial prejudice he felt he encountered even among his friends. His Indianist poems, therefore, also allowed him to escape from the white-dominated society of the Empire into an imaginary realm, the world of his native ancestors. The poet's intense personal identification with that world gives these works a unique power and authenticity; nothing comparable to the best of these poems was produced anywhere in the Americas in the 19th century. Gonçalves Dias wrote and published his Indianist verses well before his 1861 expedition to the Amazon and his encounter with the reality of native life in trading-posts and villages along the river, a reality very different from the world he had imagined and described; he insisted, in his diary of the expedition, that the natives he met were not real Indians at all, but half-breeds.

The same duality of purpose can be seen in the *Sextilhas de Frei Antão*. Writers in Portugal, some of whom resented the very idea that Brazil might possess a national literature of its own, had criticized the style and syntax of Gonçalves Dias's early poems. In response, he immersed himself in medieval texts and produced these verse narratives in something approximating 15th-century Portuguese. The *Sextilhas* thus represent both a recreation of Brazil's heroic Portuguese past and a reply to those who had questioned the validity of his work and of Brazilian literature in general. These verses, however, are also designed to continue the very personal project Gonçalves Dias had begun in his Indianist verses – the redemption, through poetry, of all of his ancestors, whether Amerindian, Portuguese or African. In Brother Antony's narratives, both Christians and Moors are paragons of beauty, virtue, and heroism; love between Europeans and Africans is sanctified and even glorified by the Church and by society. Beyond his remarkable talent and originality, it is the inclusiveness of Gonçalves Dias's vision of the national past that sets him apart as the greatest poet of 19th-century Brazil.

DAVID T. HABERLY

Biography
Born in Caxias, Maranhão, Brazil, 10 August 1823. Illegitimate son of a Portuguese shopkeeper and a *cafusa* (woman of mixed Indian and African race). Spent most of his childhood with his mother on a small cotton farm. Educated in Caxias, 1830–36. Visited Europe with father in 1837. Funded by his stepmother, he studied law and modern languages in Coimbra, Portugal. Read the French Romantics, Victor Hugo, Chateaubriand, and the Portuguese writers, Alexandre Herculano and Almeida Garrett. Travelled to Lisbon in 1838. Returned to Maranhão penniless in 1845 and concentrated on writing. Embarked on several unhappy love affairs; developed syphilis, before eventually marrying. Travelled around Europe and the interior of Brazil while employed on academic and diplomatic missions in the 1850s. Died in a shipwreck on 3 November 1864.

Selected Works

Poetry
Primeiros cantos, Rio de Janeiro: Tipografia Universal do Laemmert, 1846
Segundos cantos, Rio de Janeiro: Monteiro, 1848
Últimos cantos, Rio de Janeiro: Paulo Brito, 1851
Os timbiras, Leipzig: Brockhaus, 1857

Play
Leonor de Mendonça, Rio de Janeiro: Villeneuse, 1847

Other Writings
Dicionário da Língua Tupi, Leipzig: Brockhaus, 1858

Compilations and Anthologies
Cantos, 3rd edition, Leipzig: Brockhaus, 1860
Obras póstumas, 6 vols, edited by Antônio Henriques Leal, São Luís do Maranhão: Imprenta por B. de Matos, Tipografía do Rua da Paz, 1868–69
Poesias completas, edited by F. J. da Silva Ramos, São Paulo: Saraiva, 1950, 1957
Poesias, edited by Manuel Bandeira, Rio de Janeiro: Agir, 1960
Os melhores poemas de Gonçalves Dias, edited by José Carlos Garbuglio, São Paulo: Global, 1991

Further Reading
Despite his unquestioned importance, few major studies of Gonçalves Dias's verse have appeared during the last decades.

Bandeira, Manuel, introduction to Gonçalves Dias's *Poesia completa e prosa escolida*, Rio de Janeiro: Aguilar, 1959
Driver, David M., *The Indian in Brazilian Literature*, New York: Hispanic Institute, 1942
Haberly, David T., "The Songs of an Exile," in *Three Sad Races: Racial Identity and National Consciousness in Brazilian Literature*, Cambridge and New York: Cambridge University Press, 1983
Matos, Cláudia, *Gentis guerreiros: o indianismo de Gonçalves Dias*, São Paulo: Atual Editora, 1988
Montello, Josué, *Para conhecer melhor Gonçalves Dias*, Rio de Janeiro: Bloch, 1973

Manuel González Prada 1844–1918

Peruvian poet and essayist

Manuel González Prada represents the emergence of modern critical thinking in the history of Peruvian letters. In his speech in the Ateneo de Lima (1886), collected in *Páginas libres* [Free Pages], González Prada launched a polemical attack on the "archaic," "reactionary," "lackey" poetics of the Romantics and called for a radical, politically-minded literature that would address the problems of the nation. With the foundation of the progressive literary association "Círculo literario" (Literary Circle) in 1886, González Prada hoped to encourage the production of a modern, national literature which would lead the voices of dissent against the official liberal program. The virulent conflict, unleashed between the Romantics and González Prada following his speech, represents clearly the historical conflict of two divergent generations and of two radically different forms of literary poetics. González Prada and the writers that gathered around him, amongst them Clorinda Matto de Turner, had indeed, para-phrasing the celebrated writer of *Tradiciones peruanas*, Ricardo Palma, the "petulance" to militate for the political party of their ideological choice. González Prada believed that a writer should be a "soldier of truth" whose mission was to produce a "literature of combat" and he conceived artistic space as the battlefield where the political and economic elites were to be confronted by an army of subversive intellectuals. The Romantics, on the other hand, visualised literature as a neutralising space or "poetic retreat" where "sterile struggles" were conciliated, thus providing writers and readers with a refuge from the avatars of public life. González Prada disparaged delicacy of expression and demanded a tough, aggressive and "virile" language to counteract the "impotent" and "effeminate" language of the previous generation of writers. González Prada's raging "literature of disillusion" as it came to be known later, emerged with overwhelming force in the midst of an intensely military and revengeful atmosphere after the War of the Pacific and its sequel of economic disaster, moral disintegration and profound humiliation.

In his essays he also developed a vision of an alternative anti-oligarchic modernity to the one proposed by the "Aristocratic Republic," a term which in itself indicates the essential paradox of the period in which Prada lived and worked. He saw the official national discourse, with its images of a sovereign, egalitarian nation as a farce, "un remedo" (a poor imitation), which aimed at legitimizing the subordination of Indians not at emancipating them. A modern idea of nation, he claimed, was incompatible with the existence of immense structures of exclusion, of citizens with no rights, enslaved in colonial institutions masquerading under a modern name. In his essay "Nuestros indios" [Our Indians], collected in *Horas de lucha* [Hours of Struggle] he states that "nuestra forma de gobierno se reduce a una gran mentira, porque no merece llamarse república democrática un estado en que dos o tres millones de individuos viven fuera de la ley" (our form of government is nothing but a sham, because a state which includes two or three million subjects living outside the law does not deserve to be called a democratic republic). González Prada called for the incorporation of the indigenous population as the centre for the construction of a Peruvian, rather than a creole identity as clearly expressed in his "Discurso en el Politeama," 1888 [Speech in the Politeama] : "no forman el verdadero Perú las agrupaciones de criollos y extranjeros que habitan la faja de tierra situada entre el Pacífico y los Andes; la nación está formada por las muchedumbres de indios diseminadas en la banda oriental de la cordillera" (the authentic Peru is not constituted by the group of creoles and foreigners who live in the strip of land situated between the Pacific and the Andes: the nation is constituted by the mass of Indians scattered on the eastern slopes of the mountains). González Prada takes the debate on the Indian question one step further by adding that the problem would not disappear with education but with land tenure and weapons: "a la violencia respondería con la violencia" (violence would elicit violence). He thus anticipated the political projects developed thirty years later by Haya de la Torre and José Carlos Mariátegui.

FRANCESCA DENEGRI

See also entries on Juana Manuela Gorriti, Clorinda Matto de Turner, Ricardo Palma

Biography

Born in Lima, Peru, in 1844. Father exiled to Chile where Manuel attended English School in Valparaíso. Transferred in 1857 to Santo Toribio Seminary, but found the regime very strict. Moved to Convictorio de San Carlos in 1860. Obliged to study law but preferred to dedicate himself to agriculture in the Valle de Cañete, 1870. Fought against the Chileans at the battle of Miraflores. Defeat of Peruvians in the war against Chile caused him to reflect on the negative characteristics of his countrymen. President of Literary Club, 1885. This became the National Union in 1891 and was a centre for political radicals. Appointed director of National Library in 1912, after Ricardo Palma retired. González Prada's chief concern was the education of the unprivileged. Died in 1918.

Selected Works

Essays

Páginas libres, Paris: Dupont, 1894
Horas de lucha, Lima: Tipografía "El Progreso Literario," 1908
Bajo el oprobio, Paris: Typographie L. Bellenand et Fils, 1933
Anarquía, Santiago de Chile: Ercilla, 1937
Nuevas páginas libres, Santiago de Chile: Ercilla, 1937
Figuras y figurones, Paris: Typographie L. Bellenand et Fils, 1938
Propaganda y ataque, Buenos Aires: Imán, 1939
Prosa menuda, Buenos Aires: Imán, 1941
El tonel de Diógenes, Mexico City: Tezontle, 1945
Ortometría: apuntes para una rítmica, Lima: Universidad de San Marcos, Dirección Universitaria de Biblioteca y Publicaciones, 1977

Poetry

Minúsculas, Lima: Cien Ejemplares, 1901
Presbiterianas, Lima: Imprenta "El Olimpo," 1909 [published anonymously]
Exóticas, Lima: Tipografía de "El Lucero," 1911
Trozos de vida, Paris: Typographie de L. Bellenand et Fils, 1933
Baladas peruanas, Santiago de Chile: Ercilla, 1935
Grafitos, Paris: Typographie de L. Bellenand et Fils, 1937
Libertarias, Paris: Typographie de L. Bellenand et Fils, 1938
Baladas, Paris: Typographie de L. Bellenand et Fils, 1939
Letrillas, edited by Luis Alberto Sánchez, Lima: Milla Batres, 1975

Compilations and Anthologies

Poemas desconocidos, edited by Elsa Villanueva, Lima: Clépsidra, 1973
Sobre el militarismo: antología; Bajo el oprobio (selections), edited by Bruno Podestá, Lima: Horizonte, 1978
Cantos de otro siglo, Lima: Universidad de San Marcos, Dirección Universitaria de Biblioteca y Publicaciones, 1979
Textos: una antología general, edited by Jorge Ruedas de la Serna, Mexico City: UNAM, 1982
Obras, 4 vols, edited by Luis Alberto Sánchez, Lima: Copé, 1985–86

Further Reading

Chang-Rodríguez, Eugenio, *La literatura política de González Prada, Mariátegui y Haya de la Torre*, Mexico City: Andrea, 1957
____ "El ensayo de Manuel González Prada," *Revista Iberoamericana*, vol. 42/95 (1976)
____ "González Prada y el anarquismo," in *Opciones políticas peruanas*, Lima: Normas Legales, 1987
Mariátegui, José Carlos, "González Prada," in *Siete ensayos de interpretación de la realidad peruana*, Lima: Amauta, 1928; as *Seven Interpretative Essays on Peruvian Reality*, translated by Marjory Urquidi, Austin, Texas: University of Texas Press, 1971
Mead, Robert G., "Manuel González Prada: Peruvian Judge of Spain," *PMLA*, vol. 68/4 (1953)
Rovira, Catherine, *Semblanza y circunstancia de Manuel González Prada*, Miami: Universal, 1993
Sánchez, Luis Alberto, *Mito y realidad de González Prada*, Lima: Villanueva, 1976

José Gorostiza 1901–1979

Mexican poet and critic

José Gorostiza is assured of a lasting place at the heart of the Mexican literary canon. He belongs to that select band of writers whose reputation rests mainly on one work and whose output, though slim, nevertheless manages to be a source of endless fascination. *Muerte sin fin* (*Death without End*), his 1939 poem, is among the finest in the Spanish language, and takes its place alongside Eliot's *The Wasteland* (1922) or Valéry's *Le Cimetière marin* (1920) as one of the pinnacles of sustained poetic achievement in the 20th century.

In the early part of the 20th century, debates on the virtues of championing a national discourse as opposed to articulating a universal literary language raged among intellectuals in Mexico. As one of the most prominent members of the Contemporáneos group of writers and thinkers, Gorostiza's literary stance in the late 1920s and early 1930s was firmly on the side of the "universal" Western literary canon. Indeed the overwhelming impression left by Gorostiza's work is of a language suspended in time and space, a literary landscape of absolutes. This is a poetry of timeless essences which commands our attention as an example of the triumph of the human intellect. The elements of Gorostiza's eclecticism are many and varied: Catholic philosophy and esoteric mysticism; French poetry and German philosophy; Mexican images of death and the music of classical verse.

Gorostiza's early work is characterised by certain key influences. As with many other young Latin American poets of the first decades of the 20th century, the influence of Darío and other *modernistas* is never absent. López Velarde casts an unmistakable shadow. In addition, Gorostiza's profound interest in Eastern mysticism, fuelled both by readings of the *Rubaiyat* of Omar Khayam and of the work of Rabindranath Tagore, imbue even his earliest writings with a sense of religious transcendence.

Gorostiza's first published collection of poetry, *Canciones para cantar en las barcas*, 1925 [Boating Songs], can be read as a poetic essay on the musicality of language. The art of prosody can seldom have appeared so effortless: there is rhythmic sophistication in these poems; their resonant counterpoints are as compelling as they are haunting. The language is brilliant in its simplicity, moderating flights of poetic fancy with an ear for the music of colloquial expression. It would be easy, therefore, to write off these early poems as youthful exercises in the rhetoric of poetry. But the simplicity is deceptive. In every stanza's sparing use of language, a close reading uncovers layers of ambiguity. As the undulating ebb and flow of the rhythms lull us gently into a sense of the familiar, the image of something darker lurks indistinctly in the gloom. That something, inevitably, is death.

If death is never far away from Gorostiza's early poetry, it becomes positively central to his mature output. *Muerte sin fin*, as its title suggests, represents an intense meditation on the topic. It is impossible to overstate the importance of this poem in Mexican literature. For over a decade, Gorostiza had published no verse, and when the poem appeared in 1938, it seemed to come from nowhere. Many of the concerns and the unmistakable voice were reminiscent of the work of other members of the Contemporáneos group, especially Xavier Villaurrutia. But from the outset, it was apparent that here was something more, a poem worthy of standing alone at the centre of the Mexican canon.

The poem has probably been subjected to more interpretation that any other single Mexican text, with the exception of Juan Rulfo's *Pedro Páramo*. It is as complex as it is compelling. Its network of allusions spreads out from the image of a simple glass of water, and embarks upon a series of speculations on the "essences" of human existence: life, love, death and God. By specifically calling on human intelligence to guide him, Gorostiza creates a verbal texture in which such ideas become tangible. In an epic theological struggle with the infinite and with contingency, the poem's interrogation of Being and of the essence of time is rigorous to the point of intellectual violence, every stanza glimpsing apocalyptic catastrophe. The insistent and inescapable call of death and the devil threaten throughout to send us spiralling into a nihilistic nightmare. But language, intelligence and irony remain intact in a conclusion which ultimately reifies poetry itself and the depth and penetration of its own peculiar logic. The meaning of meaning undergoes a radical, inexorable shift.

Muerte sin fin belongs to the tradition of long poetic explorations which includes Luis de Góngora's *Soledades* (*The Solitudes*) and the *Primero sueño* (*Sor Juana's Dream*) of Sor Juana Inés de la Cruz. It recalls the work of Eliot, Valéry and Guillén; but it also has philosophical antecedents. In the reification of concepts and the positing of a realm of the intellect, the pulse of a contemporary Platonism can be discerned, pumping new life into the sounds and images of 20th-century Mexico. Some have even convincingly suggested that the theological world of the poem belongs to a Cabbalistic universe of divine emanations, in which at the court of transcendent divinity Intelligence presides majestically, and in which the World triumphs in its role in the fundamental principles of creation.

Such readings suggest that the poem is dealing with a universal set of ideas as opposed to evoking a Mexican reality. But the truth is that *Muerte sin fin* is without doubt a Mexican poem. Although the tone of the poem is suffused with the high-flown and philosophical discourses of European traditions, there are constant references to the speech-patterns, sounds, sights and beliefs of Mexico. There is evidence that by the time of completing the poem, Gorostiza had modified the hostility which he had once felt towards the social-realists' demands for a nationalistic literature, and it is fair to say that *Muerte sin fin*, amongst other things, stands as the consummate poetic act of balancing the universal and the Mexican.

Although some other poems appeared in 1964 in a retrospective volume entitled *Poesía*, Gorostiza's poetic reputation rests chiefly on *Muerte sin fin*. Its influence has been far-reaching, especially on Octavio Paz, whose *Piedra de sol* (*Sun Stone*), another high-point of Mexican learned poetry, is unquestionably indebted to Gorostiza's poetics.

Apart from his poetry, Gorostiza also wrote lucid and uncompromising prose, in which the intellectual honesty of the poems is exercised on topics such as music, theatre, painting, and literary theory. The prose style is uncomplicated and yet refined. In *Notas sobre poesía*, 1955 [Notes on Poetry], Gorostiza articulates brilliantly his personal poetics in which poetic form is elevated to a position of singular pre-eminence, and in which the poet is like a prophet embarking on a delicate mission, enacting miracles in the name of the divine. From another writer, such a claim might seem bombastic or arrogant. Coming as it does from the author of *Muerte sin fin*, it seems eminently reasonable.

MAURICE BIRIOTTI

Biography

Born in Villahermosa, Tabasco, Mexico, 10 November 1901. Educated at Instituto Científico y Literario, Aguascalientes (founded student paper, president, student association); Escuela Nacional Preparatoria (National Preparatory School). Co-editor, with Enrique González Rojo, *Revista Nueva*, 1920. Head of department of Fine Arts, Ministry of Education. Sponsor, Teatro de Orientación. Founder of the journal *Contemporáneos*. Served in the diplomatic corps in London, 1927–28; on his return to Mexico City taught at the Universidad Nacional Autónoma de México (UNAM). Third secretary, and private secretary to foreign minister, Mexican Legation, Copenhagen, 1937–39. Secretary, Mexican legation, Rome, 1939, holding the same position later in Guatemala and Cuba. A Mexican representative at the founding of United Nations in San Francisco (1947), and the establishment of UNESCO in London. Delegate, 9th Interamerican Conference, Bogotá, 1949. Served as foreign ambassador to the Netherlands and Greece; Mexican representative, United Nations, subsecretary to the Ministry of Foreign Affairs, 1953–63, head of this ministry, April to November 1964. Head, National Commission on Nuclear Energy, 1965–70. Awarded the National Literature Prize, 1968. Died in Mexico City, 16 March 1979.

Selected Works

Poetry
Canciones para cantar en las barcas, Mexico City: Cultura, 1925
Muerte sin fin, Mexico City: Cultura, 1939; as *Death without End*, translated by Laura Villaseñor, Austin: University of Texas Press, 1969

Compilations and Anthologies
Poesía, Mexico City: Fondo de Cultura Económica, 1964
Prosa, edited by Miguel Capistrán, Guanajuato, Mexico: Universidad de Guanajuato, 1969
Cauces de la poesía mexicana y otros textos, edited by José Emilio Pacheco, Mexico City: UNAM, 1988

Further Reading

Gelpí, Juan G., *Enunciación y dependencia en José Gorostiza: estudio de una máscara poética*, Mexico City: UNAM, 1984
Paz, Octavio, "Muerte sin fin," in his *Las peras del olmo*, Mexico City: UNAM, 1957
_____ *Los hijos del limo*, Barcelona: Seix Barral, 1974; as *Children of the Mire*, translated by Rachel Phillips, Cambridge, Massachusetts: Harvard University Press, 1974; revised edition, 1991
Sheridan, Guillermo, *Los Contemporáneos ayer*, Mexico City: UNAM, 1985
Xirau, Ramón, *Tres poetas de la soledad: Villaurrutia, Gorostiza, Paz*, Mexico City: Robredo, 1955

Juana Manuela Gorriti 1818–1892

Argentine prose writer and feminist

A distinguished writer of narrative fiction and renowned organizer of 19th-century cultural life in Lima and Buenos Aires, Juana Manuela Gorriti, like so many other intellectual women of her time, has slipped into oblivion and only a few of her works are readily available to today's readers. Born and brought up within a landowning family torn by the ideological conflicts of civil war, she learned early in her life about the relentless overlapping of the personal and the political, a conflict she explored later in her work. Her first novella, "La quena," 1845 [The Reed Flute], included in her first collection of stories *Sueños y realidades*, 1865 [Dreams and Realities], found its source of inspiration in the historic theme of the conquest. However, unlike other contemporary Indianist romances where the conquest is treated as epic, Gorriti's work attempted to rewrite history from the point of view of the marginalised: women and the Indians. Rejecting his father's Christian, Hispanic tradition, the first generation mestizo hero identifies with his mother's Quechua culture and is punished for it. Gorriti consistently used the family unit as an allegory of the nation. Hence in "La quena," the potentiality of family relations is destroyed by conflicting ideological forces embodied in the struggle between Spanish father and mestizo son, and between Spanish father and creole daughter. Her reading of the problem of family life in a continent founded on rape and colonisation was extended to republican settings in her Peruvian story "Si haces mal no esperes bien" [Do Not Expect Good if You Do Evil] and in her Argentine battle narratives. In "El guante negro" [The Black Glove], "La novia del muerto" [The Dead Man's Bride], "El lucero del manantia" [The Star of the Spring] and "El pozo del Yocci" [The Well of

Yocci], the national struggle between the forces of civilization and barbarism is embodied in uncompliant wives, daughters and mothers who engage in dramatic and often violent confrontation with *rosista* patriarchs, not seldom paying with their own lives. Their dissenting voices enter the territory of the fantastic as their defeated ghosts appear in the epilogue roaming the deserted battlefields where the nation's future was being fought out.

Gorriti's work was also a critical response to the "Argentine Generation of 1837," the liberal intelligentsia devoted to the project of national progress. By weaving the logic of dreams, intuition and Fatum into historical narratives, she was successful at undermining the chronological, rational discourse revered by liberal intellectuals, whilst at the same time writing women into national history. In the story "Güemes: recuerdos de la infancia" [Güemes: Childhood Memories], which purports to narrate the defeat of General Lavalle's army by Rosas's forces from a feminine perspective, the discourse of Fatum, rich in omens, dreams and presentiments, creeps in to undermine the progress of the chronological battle narrative which has no benefit of hindsight. As a result, the historical narrative is impaired as the signs of death are scattered throughout the text even before the hero prepares to march into the battlefield.

Gorriti was also successful in exploring the personal and private stories of women and inserting them into narratives about the nation's historical past and present. Thus the ideological differentiation between the public sphere of men and the private, domestic sphere of women was blurred. This practice of deconstructing the distinctions established by the dominant binary system of thought is taken to the very heart of her narrative strategy in her novel *Peregrinaciones de una alma triste* [Peregrinations of a Sorrowful Soul], anthologised in *Panoramas de la vida*, 1876 [Panoramas of Life]. The heroine, a modern Scheherazade languishing in her domestic prison where she must remain under prescription of her authoritarian medical doctor, decides to take responsibility for her own health and to find a less oppressive cure. This she finds in travelling and writing about her experiences in her long journey across the subcontinent. The stories of the Mocovi and the Guarani Indians of the Chaco, the laments of women in search of their dead sons and husbands in the Argentine pampas, and the plight of the black slaves of Brazil, are all integrated in a kaleidoscopic narrative through the voice of the heroine/narrator who reminisces about her experiences for the benefit of her interlocutor/reader. The narrator/heroine's journey into independent womanhood and health is thus achieved through direct contact with the different indigenous groups that she meets alone in her "peregrination." These groups, represented within specific racial, religious, sexual and cultural identities, stand in opposition to the idea, so intensely explored by contemporary intellectuals, of unified and discrete national identities.

Although the concept of nation, modernity and progress is subtly dismantled in Gorriti's narrative fiction, her later work explored modern themes particularly when they touched women's lives. This is particularly clear in *Oasis en la vida*, 1888 [An Oasis in Life], where the argument for savings and investment is interwoven with a love story between a male writer and a working woman. However, much of Gorriti's work deals with the irrational in history, and this is perhaps why it has not been included in a canon of Latin American literature written from a modern, positivist and masculinist perspective.

FRANCESCA DENEGRI

Biography

Born at Horcones ranch, province of Salta, in northwest Argentina, 15 June 1818. Both parents of Spanish descent. Father fought in War of Independence against Spain. Seventh of eight children. Early years spent on army base at Horcones where her father was the commanding officer. Self-taught because she did not take to the convent school where she was sent at an early age. Married Bolivian army officer, Manuel Belzú, in 1833 when she was fourteen. Couple settled in La Paz. Belzú exiled for conspiracy in 1845 and couple, with their two daughters, settled in Lima. When Belzú returned to Bolivia, Juana Manuela did not accompany him. Instead, she opened a primary school and another for young ladies to support her family. Two more children born to her while she was in Lima. Organized successful literary salon or "veladas literarias." Unique occasions owing to the inclusion of women and their concerns: education and job-training. Belzú assassinated in La Paz where Gorriti pronounced an oration at his wake in the presence of a crowd of several thousands. Granted pension in Argentina as daughter of General Juan Ignacio Gorriti. Founded the newspaper *La Alborada* [The Dawn]. Died in Buenos Aires of pneumonia, 6 November 1892.

Selected Works

A detailed breakdown of the contents of each of the volumes listed below is to be found in *Women Writers of Spanish America: an Annotated Bio-Biographical Guide*, edited by Diane E. Marting, Westport, Connecticut: Greenwood Press, 1987

Un año en California, Buenos Aires: El Nacional, 1846
Sueños y realidades, 2 vols, Buenos Aires: Casavalle, 1865
Biografía del general Don Dionisio de Puch, Paris: n.p., 1868
El pozo del Yocci, Paris: n.p., 1869
Panoramas de la vida; colección de novelas, fantasías, leyendas y descripciones americanas, Buenos Aires: Casavalle, 1876
Misceláneas; colección de leyendas, juicios, pensamientos, discursos, impresiones de viaje y descripciones americanas, Buenos Aires: Imprenta de M. Biedma, 1878
El mundo de los recuerdos, Buenos Aires: Félix Lajouane, 1886
Oasis en la vida, Buenos Aires: Félix Lajouane, 1888
La tierra natal, Buenos Aires: Félix Lajouane, 1889
Cocina ecléctica, Buenos Aires: Félix Lajouane, 1890
Perfiles (Primera parte), Buenos Aires: Félix Lajouane, 1892
Veladas literarias de Lima, 1876–1877; tomo primero, veladas I a X, Buenos Aires: Imprenta Europea, 1892
Lo íntimo de Juana Manuela Gorriti, Buenos Aires: Ramón Espasa, 1893
El tesoro de los incas (leyenda histórica), Buenos Aires: Universidad de Buenos Aires, Instituto de Literatura Argentina, 1929

Compilations and Anthologies

Narraciones, edited with a prologue by W.G.Weyland, Buenos Aires: Ediciones Estrada, 1946
Relatos, edited with a prologue by Antonio Pagés Larraya, Buenos Aires: Editorial Universitaria de Buenos Aires, 1962

Further Reading

Guerra-Cunningham, Lucía, "Visión marginal de la historia en la narrativa de Juana Manuela Gorriti," *Ideologies and Literature*, vol. 2/2 (Fall 1987)

Masiello, Francine, "On Gender, Marriage and the State: Juana Manuela Gorriti;" and "On Money, Marriage and Publicity: the Commerce of Women's Fiction," in her *Between Civilization and Barbarism: Women, Nation and Literary Culture in Modern Argentina*, Lincoln: University of Nebraska Press, 1992

Pratt, Marie Louise, "Barbarous Words," in her *Imperial Eyes. Travel Writing and Transculturation*, London and New York: Routledge, 1992

Scott, Nina M., "Juana Manuela Gorriti's *Cocina ecléctica*: Recipes as Feminine Discourse," *Hispania* (May 1992)

Yeager, Gertrude, "Juana Manuel Gorriti: Writer in Exile," in *The Human Tradition in Latin America. The Nineteenth Century*, edited by William H. Beezley and Judith Ewell, Wilmington, Delaware: Scholarly Resources, 1989

Graça Aranha, José Pereira da

See Aranha

Felipe Guaman Poma de Ayala Died c.1615

Chronicler of the colonial period

The *Nueva Corónica y Buen Gobierno* (*Letter to a King*), a 1,200-page address to the King Philip III of Spain, was written shortly after the conquest, between the late 16th and early 17th centuries. It was rediscovered in 1908 at the Royal Library in Copenhagen. The details of its route to this unlikely resting-place is only one of the mysteries surrounding the book and its author, Felipe Guaman Poma de Ayala.

We know of Guaman Poma that he was a 16th-century Quechua-speaking *ladino* (or Spanish-acculturated) Indian from the Ayacucho region of the Peruvian southern Andes. Despite the scale of this work, and the space its author devotes to presenting himself and his background, little can be taken for granted as reliable autobiographical information. The reason for this has to do with the *Nueva Corónica's* very discursive premise: Guaman Poma was moved to write to the king to complain of colonialist abuses, and to vindicate pre-Columbian Andean culture, as well as to better his own and his family's position under the new regime. Therefore he indulges in much of the self-aggrandisement common in petitionary literature of the era. Among his family, he claims, is a "saint," his half-brother Martín de Ayala: an ambassador and Inca's "deputy" – his father Guaman Mallqui; and a *Coya* (an indigenous term usually, if inaccurately translated as "queen") in the form of his mother, doña Juana. Guaman Mallqui, it is argued, represented the Inca Huáscar in welcoming the conquistador Pizarro on his first arrival in Peru. He also saved the life of a Spanish captain in battle, according to his son. Most of these claims, historians agree, are highly dubious. They are also arguably essential to the success of his enterprise.

The author, then, is speaking from a position, albeit false, of equal validity in both Andean and European cultures: he is close to religious sanctity (Martín's "sainthood"), is linked to the indigenous nobility through both parents, and has associations with loyalty to the Spanish crown through both diplomatic and military channels. Accordingly, Guaman Poma is obliged to vindicate his position according to two quite disparate cultural traditions, primarily using the tools of the newly dominant culture: the Spanish language, which he handles with great inventiveness as well as some discomfort, and the technique of writing. European historiography is also employed, as are the humanist ideas of Bartolomé de Las Casas and other opponents of Spain's exploitation of the Indies.

The *Nueva Corónica* is also notable for its illustrations: around four hundred ink drawings, displaying both European Baroque influences and the traces of indigenous visual codes, bolster the author's main arguments. These can be summarised as follows: indigenous Andean culture is essentially valid – despite alleged Devil-worship among the first Incas, proto-Christian elements can be seen in native religious tradition. Guaman Poma supports his position with a wealth of ethnographic detail, including descriptions of ritual, Quechua song and dance, and agricultural cycles. He nevertheless defends the central authority of the Spanish monarchy as a global organising principle, and presents a *Mapamundi* arranged along the same lines as the Inca realm: divided into four parts, with a strong and immutable centre (Castile, rather than the Inca capital Cuzco). However, Guaman Poma is bitter and fiercely satirical in his attack on the crown's representatives in the Indies: one of his drawings characterises both ecclesiastical and secular authorities as wild, rapacious beasts consuming the hapless Indian, whose depiction is similar to that given by Las Casas. Guaman Poma argues for ethnic segregation in order to preserve not only identity but also morality: only vice and corruption can result from the proximity of Indian and Spaniard. Into this equation comes the Negro, given a separate chapter in which Guaman Poma adopts a sympathetic tone, despite the usual role of African slaves as henchmen forcing the Indians to serve Spain.

Guaman Poma's stance on most issues, then, is ambivalent. His defence of indigenous culture must be seen in contrast to his participation in 16th-century extirpation campaigns. The list of Inca rulers incorporated into the work implies approval of the dynasty, but favours certain rulers at the expense of others. Reasons for this are varied: the Incas had overrun Guaman Poma's home province of Lucanas and made enemies there, as elsewhere in the Andes, and he had no interest in the kind of pro-Cuzco stance taken by Peru's other great Andean mestizo chronicler, El Inca Garcilaso de la Vega, whose mother belonged to the Inca nobility. The author is also at pains to distance himself from those who opposed the Spanish invasion, although he maintains that indigenous resistance was minimal and factional. Paradoxically, Inca forms of social organisation are largely praised and often held up as a model for the future of the colony. However, the outlook is bleak and the author has recourse to the image of a "world upside-down," then common in European satire, to render the cataclysm which had befallen the inhabitants of Spain's new possessions.

Other aspects of the *Nueva Corónica*, appear less self-contradictory: the anti-clericalism which might appear to undermine Guaman Poma's claims to Christian rectitude was common enough in Spain and elsewhere in Europe at the time. This, like several of his stances, seems to have been borrowed from his reading of contemporary Spanish thinkers. As is the case with other indigenous writings or testimonies of the early colonial era such as those by Pachacuti Yamqui or Titu Cusi, Guaman Poma has to maintain a credible discursive position whilst appeasing those in power. This leads to a form of presentation which is eclectic and multi-faceted, using a gamut of literary styles and a sometimes bewildering juxtaposition of arguments. Nevertheless this is one of the most powerful and illuminating documents to have emerged since the conquest; voicing outrage and despair whilst addressing the future of the Andean region as inescapably subject to foreign domination; assimilating outside influences whilst minimising their damage. Guaman Poma's document contains many of the salient features of later Latin American literature and is one of the most powerful examples of the indigenous use of writing as a response to the Spanish presence and an assimilation of new political and social realities.

KEITH J. RICHARDS

Biography

The available information on Guaman Poma's life is very sketchy. His date of birth is not known and it is only *thought* that he died in Lima in 1615. He felt intensely the suffering and deprivations of his own (Inca) people and travelled around the viceroyalty of Peru recording his experiences. He only returned home in old age, declaring then that he wished to travel to Spain to make the king aware of the unjust treatment of his fellow Indians. But he was unable to realize this intention owing to ill health. The manuscript of his *Nueva Corónica y Buen Gobierno* was discovered in 1908 by Robert Pietschmann in the Copenhagen Royal Library.

Work

Nueva Corónica y Buen Gobierno, 1612; modern edition, edited by Franklin Pease, Mexico City: Siglo XXI, 1980; as *Letter to a King: a Picture History of the Inca Civilization*, edited and translated by Christopher Dilke, London: Allen and Unwin, 1978

Further Reading

Adorno, Rolena (editor), *From Oral to Written Expression: Native Andean Chronicles from the Early Colonial Period*, Syracuse, New York: Syracuse University, 1982

____ *Writing and Resistance in Colonial Peru*, Austin, Texas: Dolphin Press, 1986

Bendezú, Edmundo, "La mitología de Huamán Poma," in his *La otra literatura peruana*, Mexico City: Fondo de Cultura Económica, 1986

Harrison, Regina, *Signs, Songs and Memory in the Andes*, Austin: University of Texas Press, 1989

López-Baralt, Mercedes, "La metáfora como *traslatio*: del código verbal al visual en la crónica ilustrada de Guaman Poma," *Nueva Revista de Filología Hispánica*, vol. 36/1 (1986)

____ *Icono y conquista*, Madrid: Hiperión, 1988

Ortega, Julio, "El cronista indio Guaman Poma y la conciencia cultural pluralista en el Perú colonial," *Nueva Revista de Filología Hispánica*, vol. 36/1 (1986)

____ "Guaman Poma y la producción del texto," in his *Crítica de la identidad: la pregunta por el Perú en su literatura*, Mexico City: Fondo de Cultura Económica, 1988

Ossio, Juan M. (editor), *Ideología mesiánica del mundo andino*, Lima: Ignacio Prado Pastor, 1973

Salomon, Frank, "Chroniclers of the Impossible: Notes on Three Peruvian Indigenous Chroniclers," in *From Oral to Written Expression: Native Andean Chronicles from the Early Colonial Period*, edited by Rolena Adorno, Syracuse, New York: Syracuse University, 1982

Guatemala

19th- and 20th-Century Prose and Poetry

Guatemala is the largest of the Central American republics and the most Indian of all the countries of Latin America. Its landscapes – lakes, volcanoes, maize-planted valleys, cloud-forest – are among the most beautiful in the world. Yet its history must be reckoned one of the most violent and sombre in the region. In the 20th century, events have taken such a tragic turn that most writers have been forced into active political commitment. In few countries has it been more dangerous to record opinions in writing: exile or death have been the normal rewards.

Nevertheless Guatemala has a very rich cultural history for a country of its size. It was at the centre of Central American life throughout the colonial period: indeed, in a curious way it replicated within Central America itself the impact of Mexico on the whole of Middle America including Guatemala. Moreover Guatemala was the focal point of the maize-based Maya empire attacked and destroyed by Cortés's most ruthless subordinate, Pedro de Alvarado, after 1524. It was there that extraordinary semi-mythological "chronicles" such as the *Popol Vuh* or "Quiché Bible" and "dramas" like the *Rabinal Achí* were written down in the decades after the conquest, and these works have formed a crucial point of departure for contemporary Guatemalan literature and culture which only in the 20th century has that country begun fully to assimilate. Their importance can hardly be overstated, however, precisely because the whole history of the country has been dominated by the desperate struggle of the "Ladinos" (whites first and mestizos later) to subjugate the "Indian" majority. Guatemalan literature reflects this struggle both materially – there have been few "Indian" writers, even though the country's foundational works are, as we have seen, Indian – and thematically.

No other Latin American republic had either the cultural antecedents or the nascent literary tradition which Guatemala was developing during the colonial period. Not surprisingly, this allowed the growth of a distinctly conservative literary mode in the 19th century, despite the influence of leading independence intellectuals like José Cecilio del Valle (1777–1834, born in Honduras), and Pedro Molina (1777–1854). The outstanding Guatemalan writer of the period was undoubtedly José Batres Montúfar (1809–1944), who in his brief romantic life wrote accomplished lyrics and remarkable comic narrative poems called *Tradiciones de Guatemala* [Guatemalan Traditions] which in many respects anticipate the Peruvian Ricardo Palma's much admired stories *Tradiciones peruanas*, and are scarcely inferior to them. *Don Pablo* and *El relox* [The Clock] are among the best known. Batres Montúfar's only rival, in terms of literary achievement, is another Romantic poet, Juan Diéguez (1813–66).

Guatemalan fiction truly begins with Antonio José de Irisarri (1786–1868), author of two novels *El cristiano errante*, 1847 [The Wandering Christian] and *Historia del perínclito Epaminondas del Cauca*, 1863 [History of the Incomparable Epaminondas of the Cauca], and, more importantly, with José Milla y Vidaurre (1822–82), author of *costumbrista* and historical novels mainly based on the colonial period, though other

works such as *Un viaje al otro mundo pasando por otras partes*, 1874 [A Journey to the Other World and Other Destinations] are also noteworthy. Milla is to Guatemalan literature what Dickens is to English literature, and it was he who invented Guatemala's national representative figure, Juan Chapín. Guatemala also had, in Ramón A. Salazar (1852–1914), a novelist of Realist intentions; in Enrique Martínez Sobral (1875–1950), a disciple of Zola, with titles like *Humo* [Smoke] and *El alcohol*; and in Máximo Soto Hall (1871–1944), a similarly styled writer who initiated the anti-imperialist novel with *El problema* (1899) followed by *La sombra de la Casa Blanca* [The Shadow of the White House] in 1927.

Central America, together with the Caribbean, was one of the focal points of Spanish American *Modernismo*, thanks largely but not uniquely to the joint influence, both complementary and contrasting, of the Nicaraguan Rubén Darío and the Cuban José Martí, both of whom made subsequently mythologized visits to Guatemala at important moments of their own lives. The major contributions made by Darío and Martí to poetry in Spanish, and the award to the Guatemalan Miguel Ángel Asturias in 1967 of the first Nobel Prize ever given to a Latin American novelist, have helped to ensure that the role of these small Balkanized or island republics has not been a minor one. Guatemalan *modernista* poets include Domingo Estrada (1855–1901) and María Cruz (1876–1915); but Guatemala's main claim to fame in this period was the work of the extraordinary Enrique Gómez Carrillo (1873–1927), undoubtedly the most influential prose writer of turn-of-the-century Latin America – despite the fact (or more likely because of it) that it was in Paris, not Latin America, where he spent most of his life. Reputedly a great lover and undeniably a scandalously fluent producer of facile but intoxicating chronicles about the delights of the Old World, Gómez Carrillo was the metaphorical seducer of an entire generation of young Guatemalan – and not only Guatemalan – would-be literati.

In the colonial period Guatemalan literature, like that of all Spanish America, was dominated by Spanish concepts – not only of genre and style but also of what was considered appropriate and indeed permissible within the colonial context. In the 19th century other notions began to be more influential: Scott's view of the historical novel, for example, or French ideas about literary schools and movements. Later, *Modernismo* arrived and provided a crucial miscegenation of French and Spanish American currents. After this writers began to be grouped into "generations" – showing the continuing influence of Spanish attitudes – and then, after the avant-garde decade of the 1920s, with its multifarious "isms," they also became organized in "movements."

The key writer of the 1910 Generation – the last pre-modern generation, one might say – was Rafael Arévalo Martínez (1884–1975). Although active in many literary forms – poetry, novel, essay, autobiography – Arévalo Martínez is immortalized as a short story writer, above all for "El hombre que parecía un caballo," 1914 [The Man Who Looked Like a Horse], inspired by his relationship with the bohemian Colombian poet Porfirio Barba-Jacob. This curious work, transitional between the *modernista* short story and the fictions of Borges, has appeared in numerous anthologies of Latin American short fiction.

For all his success and influence within Guatemala, however, the prolific Arévalo Martínez is a transitional figure, not one installed within post World War I modernity. Guatemala had been gradually transformed between 1871 and 1885 by the Liberal policies of Justo Rufino Barrios, who had curtailed clerical power, modernized and centralized the economy, and initiated a new agricultural pattern based first on coffee and later on, bananas. Between 1898 and 1920 the country was ruled by the ruthless Manuel Estrada Cabrera, who carried out a "Porfirian'" policy of severe repression combined with rapid economic modernization. It was his regime that Miguel Ángel Asturias later depicted in *El señor Presidente*, 1946 (*The President*). As early as 1904 Cabrera allowed the penetration of the United Fruit Company – permanently demonized, in its turn, by Asturias's *Trilogía bananera* or Banana Trilogy. This consisted of *Viento fuerte*, 1949 (*The Cyclone*); *El papa verde*, 1954 (*The Green Pope*) and *Los ojos de los enterrados*, 1960 (*The Eyes of the Interred*). The company monopolized the route to the Gulf coast and its only port, Puerto Barrios, as well as controlling International Railways of Central America. After Cabrera fell, the 1920s saw a confused period of dubiously elected governments, usually headed by soldiers. In 1931 Colonel Jorge Ubico, a nationalist right-wing soldier, came to power and held it until 1944. Ubico, a fascist sympathiser, used vagrancy laws to direct Indian labour to seasonal work on the coast once the debt peonage system was ended.

It was this violent, ideologically confusing and disarticulated period which provided the background for the rise of the so-called Generation of 1920, without doubt the most important in Guatemala in the 20th century. It included César Brañas (1900–76), much admired inside the country though almost unknown elsewhere; Flavio Herrera (1895–1968), author of successful, melodramatically naturalistic novels like *El tigre*, 1935 [The Tiger] and *La tempestad*, 1935 [The Storm]; Alfonso Orantes (1898–); Carlos Samayoa Aguilar (1899–1978); Carlos Samayoa Chinchilla (1898–1973), author of *Madre milpa*, 1934 [Mother Maizefield] and the documentary *El dictador y yo*, 1950 [The Dictator and I] about his experience working for Ubico; Arqueles Vela (1898–1977); Alberto Velázquez (1891–1968); Carlos Wyld Ospina (1891–1956), author of the documentary *El autócrata*, 1929 [The Autocrat], about Estrada Cabrera, and several influential works of fiction, *El solar de los Gonzagas*, 1924 [The Ancestral Home of the Gonzagas], *La tierra de las Nahuyacas*, 1933 [The Land of the Nahuyacas], stories, *La Gringa* (1935) and *Los lares apagados*, 1958 [The Cold Hearths], stories; and two important writer-journalists, Clemente Marroquín Rojas (1897–1978) and David Vela (1901–).

Without a doubt, however, the two giants of the generation were Miguel Ángel Asturias (1899–1974) and Luis Cardoza y Aragón (1904–92), both of whom spent most of their adult lives outside Guatemala (as did the two outstanding writers of later generations, Mario Monteforte Toledo and Augusto Monterroso). Asturias is the author of *Leyendas de Guatemala*

(1930), *El señor Presidente*, *Hombres de maíz*, 1949 (*Men of Maize*), an authentic Latin American literary monument, the *Trilogía bananera* (1950–60; mentioned above, and *Mulata de tal*, 1963 (*Mulatta*). Asturias is unarguably the most important novelist to have emerged from Central America. Cardoza y Aragón was a leading poet, essayist and art critic, editor of the influential *Revista de Guatemala* after the 1944 Revolution. The essay *Guatemala: las líneas de su mano*, 1955 [Guatemala: the Lines of Her Hand] is probably his best-known work, though collections of poetry like *Luna Park* (1923), *Pequeña sinfonía del Nuevo Mundo*, 1948 [Brief Symphony of the New World] and *Quinta estación*, 1972 [Fifth Season] were also influential.

Several members of the 1920 Generation were able to escape the country and to profit from interaction with the international avant-garde. The 1930 Generation was less fortunate and was forced to live through the dark years of the 1930s under the dictatorship of Ubico (1931–44). It was at this point that a number of young writers formed a group called "los Tepeus," which, without rejecting the 1920s avant-garde, took a more considered and programmatic approach to social and political matters through the development of a creolist, regionalist and indigenist mode. These writers included Alfredo Balsells Rivera (1904–40), the leading poet of the 1930s and author of *El venadeado y otros cuentos* [The Ambush and Other Stories], published posthumously in 1958; Francisco Méndez (1907–62), author of the much underrated *Cuentos de Joyabaj*, 1957 [Tales of Joyabaj]; Miguel Marsicovétere y Durán (1912–) and Oscar Mirón Álvarez (1910–38). However the best-known members of the generation were Mario Monteforte Toledo (1911–) and Manuel Galich (1913–), both of whom took an active part in the 1944 Revolution and both of whom eventually became government ministers. Galich was a student leader in the 1940s, became a leading dramatist and testimonialist exiled after 1954, and spent his later years as an influential theatre critic and revolutionary doctrinaire in Cuba. Monteforte is one of Guatemala's most colourful intellectual figures, an outstanding academic and essayist but best known for indigenist novels like *Anaité* (1948), *Entre la piedra y la cruz*, 1948 [Between the Stone and the Cross] and *Y vinieron del mar*, 1963 [And they Came from the Sea], and for political novels like *Donde acaban los caminos*, 1953 [Where the Roads End] and *Una manera de morir*, 1957 [A Way of Dying].

The "Acento" Group, founded in 1943 by members of the Generation of 1940, was perhaps the first explicitly political literary group in Guatemala and openly supported the 1944 Revolution. It included Otto Raúl González (1921–), director of the review also called *Acento*. He was exiled in Mexico after 1954, but was finally recognized as one of the nation's leading poets when he won the Premio Nacional Literario Miguel Ángel Asturias in 1990. Other important members were Raúl Leiva (1916–75), assistant editor of Cardoza's *Revista de Guatemala*, exiled in 1954 to Mexico and author of *Palabra en el tiempo*, 1975 [Word in Time]; Enrique Juárez Toledo (1922–), poet and diplomat; Carlos Solórzano (1922–), a playwright and teacher-critic who spent most of his adult life in Mexico; Carlos Illescas (1918–), an excellent poet and yet another writer forced into exile in Mexico; and Augusto Monterroso (1921–), widely considered to be Guatemala's outstanding short-story writer of the century, author of astonishingly original collections like *Obras completas y otros cuentos*, 1959 [Complete Works and Other Stories], *La oveja negra y demas fábulas*, 1969 [The Black Sheep and Other Fables], *Movimiento perpetuo*, 1972 [Perpetual Motion] and several other important works. He is compared frequently – and never unfavourably – to Jorge Luis Borges and Juan José Arreola.

The 1944–54 Revolution, led by Juan José Arévalo and Jacobo Arbenz, was the most important political event in the history of 20th-century Guatemala. It allowed the belated assimilation of some of the literary discoveries of the 1920 Generation, including the combined effect of the 1920s avant-garde and, more particularly, the kinds of cultural policy initiated by the Mexican Revolution. The "Grupo Saker-ti" (1948–54), formed by the artists and writers of the Revolution itself, was perhaps the most cohesive and influential of all Guatemala's literary groups, a liberal-left coalition associated closely though not exclusively with the Guatemalan Communist Party (PGT). The name means "dawn" in Maya-Quiché. Its 1950 manifesto called for a "democratic, nationalist and realist" art form. The group included Miguel Ángel Vázquez (1922–), a key writer of the Revolution, whose output included poetry and the 1976 novel *La semilla del fuego* [The Seed of Fire]; Abelardo Rodas (1930–80); Roberto Paz y Paz (1927–), author of the novel *La inteligencia* (1967); Julio Fausto Aguilera (1928–); and Oscar Arturo Palencia (1932–81), associated with the movement both as political activist and poet, exiled from his country and murdered on his return in 1981. Saker-ti was also supported by established writers like Monterroso, Leiva, Juárez Toledo and Illescas. Other writers of this period included a vigorous dramatist Hugo Carrillo (1928–), who adapted several of Asturias's novels for the stage as well as writing plays of his own, the journalist and essayist Jaime Díaz Rozzotto, and one of the most popular poets of the century, Werner Ovalle López (1928–68).

The 1954 US-backed invasion and coup led by Castillo Armas was a decisive event in the history of Latin America – Che Guevara was an impotent spectator and drew far-reaching conclusions – and a catastrophe for democracy in Guatemala for decades to come. It led inexorably to forty years of renewed violence and, eventually, to nationwide horror on a scale unknown since the conquest. A whole generation of Guatemalan writers went into exile, mainly to Mexico, most never to return for any significant period of time. The new generations were effectively orphaned; and they rebelled against their new masters.

For this reason the post-1954 generation has been called the "Committed Generation." It united around the opposition to the military regimes which followed the Castillo Armas coup and remained a more or less cohesive group until around 1970. It coincided with the early guerrilla campaigns of the now legendary César Montes and Luis Turcios Lima of the FAR, Bernardo Alvarado Monzón of the PGT and Marco Antonio Yon Sosa of the MR-13 from the early 1960s. Writers included the essayists José Luis Balcárcel and Roberto Díaz Castillo; Arqueles Morales (1936–89), once Asturias's secretary in Argentina, who lived in Nicaragua after the 1979 Revolution and died in Cuba; the poet Leonor Paz y Paz (1932–); and the campaigning social novelist José María López Valdizón

(1929–75), author of *La sangre del maíz*, 1966 [Blood of the Maize]. However the great figure of the generation, and an example beyond the borders of Guatemala, was the poet Otto René Castillo (1936–67), a member of the PGT who, exiled in Eastern Europe, joined the guerrilla group FAR and was eventually tortured and murdered by the army in Zacapa. His *oeuvre* is a classic of revolutionary romanticism, including *Vámonos patria a caminar*, 1965 [Come Walk with Me, My Country], whose title poem has become a Guatemalan revolutionary anthem, and *Informe de una injusticia*, 1975 [Report on an Injustice].

After the death of Otto René Castillo in 1967, the "Grupo Nuevo Signo" was set up in 1968, oriented more to social and cultural matters generally than to politics as such, and turning again to Indian and regional concerns. Its founders included Luis Alfredo Arango (1935–), a neo-indigenist poet who won the National Literary Prize in 1988; Francisco Morales Santos (1940–), later the first president of the Community of Guatemalan Writers (1988), whose poetry is collected in *Archivador de pueblos*, 1977 [Archivist of Towns]; the younger poet Delia Quiñónez (1946–), author of *Barro pleno*, 1968 [Fullness of Earth]; and veterans José Luis Villatoro (1932–), poet of the everyday, non-magical Indian, as in *Pedro a secas*, 1968 [Just Pedro], Julio Fausto Aguilera (1929–), formerly of Saker-ti, and Roberto Obregón (1940–70), author of *Poesía de barro*, 1966 [Poetry of Clay], a member of the Committed Generation, like Castillo, who met a similar tragic fate when he disappeared on the Salvadorean border in 1981. Nuevo Signo was closely associated with the university journal *Alero*, one of Latin America's best at the time, and sought a new form of social, colloquial, "unpoetic" poetry, as an antidote to the supposedly exotic view of the Indians conveyed by writers like Asturias.

Up to this point few women have been mentioned – indeed, it remains the case that women novelists are extremely rare in Guatemala. But there have been many women poets and, as elsewhere in Latin America in the 1970s, women's writing began to take on a perceptibly feminist note. Important examples are Delia Quiñónez, already mentioned; Luz Méndez de la Vega (1929–), author of *Eva sin Dios*, 1979 [Eve without God]; Alaíde Foppa, born in Spain to a Guatemalan mother and an Argentine father, exiled to Mexico after 1954, author of the very audacious *Elogio de mi cuerpo*, 1970 [In Praise of My Body] and *Las palabras y el tiempo*, 1979 [Words and Time], and "disappeared" on a brief visit to the country in 1980; Margarita Carrera (1929–), who wrote *Del noveno círculo*, 1977 [About The Ninth Circle] and *Siglo veinte*, 1985 [Twentieth Century]; Aída Toledo, author of *Realidad más extraña que el sueño*, 1994 [Truth Stranger than Fiction]; Julia Esquivel, a poet both religious and political who has taken refuge in Mexico; and Caly Domitila Cane'k, a social worker and teacher who ran a Cakchiquel radio programme and is now exiled in the US. But undoubtedly the best-known recent woman poet is the redoubtable Ana María Rodas (1937–), whose *Poemas de la izquierda erótica* [Poems of the Erotic Left] exploded on the literary scene in 1973 and questioned the machismo not only of the right but of the heroic guerrillas in poems that were cynical, bitter and unyielding. She later became the third president of the Guatemalan community of Writers (1990).

A similarly sceptical group of poets formed the "Grupo Moira" in the 1970s, led by the charismatic Manuel José Arce (1935–85), who was also an excellent playwright and a polemical, crusading journalist; together with Luz Méndez, mentioned above, teacher, feminist poet and a key member of the "RIN-78" group later in the same decade. Other noteworthy poets of the last two decades are José Barnoya (1931–), Edwin Cifuentes (1926–), Rafael Gutiérrez (1958–) and Enrique Noriega (1948–), iconoclastic author of *Oh banalidad* and *Libreta del centauro copulante*, 1994 [Notebook of the Copulating Centaur].

In February 1976 Guatemala City was devastated by a massive earthquake, adding to the sense of catastrophe in a country where it was becoming more dangerous than ever to be a writer. In 1978, with General Lucas García in power, a number of influential literary figures founded the Grupo Editorial "Rin-78" in an attempt to take safety in numbers and achieve solidarity without appearing too overtly political. It was what Beverley and Zimmerman have called "a kind of literary popular front," unity within diversity, bringing together many Nuevo Signo, feminist and younger writers, and has been very effective in its own terms. Another significant advance was the emergence of the literary supplement *Tzolkin* in 1986: it was government-sponsored (Cerezo was in power) and edited by Marco Vinicio Mejía Dávila, who was replaced in 1987 when *Tzolkin* was reorganized and made more conservative in the wake of a failed coup. One reaction to this reverse was the founding in 1987 of the "Rial Academia": set up against the literary status quo and state cooptation, it was iconoclastic and parodic rather than explicitly political. Members included Vinicio Mejía Dávila, Marco Augusto Quiroa (1937–), Eduardo Villagrán, René Leiva (1947–) and Carlos René García Escobar (1948–), anthropologist, novelist and critic. In 1988 the Community of Guatemalan Writers was founded by many of the writers already mentioned and others including Dante Liano (1948–), Max Araujo (1950–), Francisco Albizúrez Palma, Guatemala's most prolific contemporary critic and Hugo Cerezo Dardón (1920–), a veteran with a highly varied production.

In the last analysis, however, just as Nicaragua is above all a land of poets, so Guatemala is less a country of essayists and poets than of narrators – though the last forty years have tested the literary imagination of even the most audacious and resolute. The key figures in the early 1970s were still Asturias, Monteforte Toledo and Monterroso (by then associated with the Boom and frequently compared to Borges or Cortázar). But in the mid-1970s a post-Boom style began to develop, as younger writers, crucified between the seductions of the Latin American Boom, the Mexican *Onda* and the demands of political commitment, sought their own new way of writing. Miguel Ángel Vázquez wrote *La semilla del fuego*, already mentioned, a retrospective assessment of the Ubico regime (a later novel, *Operación Iscariote*, 1989 [Operation Iscariot] – looked at the end of the Arbenz era). Carlos Cojulén Bedoya (1914–) wrote *¡Violencia!* (1979), a curiously melodramatic novel about the misadventures of a young Guatemalan girl of her times. The decisive work however was by Marco Antonio Flores (1937–), *Los compañeros*, 1976 [The Comrades], a largely autobiographical novel which expresses his disillusionment with the guerrilla dream of the 1960s. Flores broke with the revolu-

tionary romanticism of the Cuban-inspired left and went into self-exile in Mexico, concentrating thereafter on poetry. By contrast Mario Roberto Morales (1947–) has wrestled more persistently with the tension between hedonism and commitment, mere juvenile rebellion and the call of the guerrilla struggle. *Los demonios salvajes*, 1978 [The Crazy Devils], *El esplendor de la pirámide*, 1986 [Splendour of the Pyramid] and *Señores bajo los árboles*, 1994 [Lords Beneath the Trees] record one of the most interesting trajectories in recent Guatemalan narrative. Edwin Cifuentes (1926–), an older writer, published the linguistically ambitious *El pueblo y los atentados* [The People and the Violence] in 1979. The best known of the younger novelists is Arturo Arias (1950–), whose *Después de las bombas* [After the Bombs) and *Itzam na* (1981) were perhaps the most ambitious new novels of the era. In 1989 Arias, who wrote the script for the internationally successful movie *El Norte*, published the even more audacious *El jaguar en llamas* [Jaguar in Flames]. Luis de Lión Díaz (1939–84), an indigenist – indeed, Indian writer – wrote a landmark novel entitled *El tiempo principía en Xibalbá* [Time Began in Xibalbá] shortly before he tragically "disappeared" in 1984.

Other recent works of narrative fiction are *Ida y vuelta*, 1983 [Return Journey] by Francisco Albizúrez Palma, *Hogar, dulce hogar*, 1983 [Home, Sweet Home] by Mario Alberto Carrera, *El tren no llega*, 1984 [The Train Never Comes] by José Luis Perdomo, *Vida en un pueblo muerto*, 1984 [Life in a Dead Town] by William Lemus, *La llama del retorno*, 1984 [Flame of Return] by Carlos René García Escobar, *Grito, susurro y llanto*, 1985 [Shouts, Whispers and Tears] by Armando Bendaña, *Panzos y otras historias*, 1984 [Panzos and Other Stories] by José Barnoya, *Cuentos para contar corriendo*, 1984 [Stories Told on the Run] by Catarino Mateo, *En los sueños no todo es reposo*, 1987 [Dreams Aren't Always Restful] by Fernando González Davison, *Los cómplices*, 1988 [The Accomplices) by Francisco Nájera, *El filo de la locura*, 1988 [Edge of Insanity] by Roberto Quezada and *La princesa de onix*, 1989 [The Onyx Princess] by Franz Galich.

Despite the efforts of creative writers to rise above the brutal realities of recent Guatemalan history, few have been able to do so for long. That is why Guatemala is one of the privileged homes of *testimonio*, that documentary style of first-person narrative which has been particularly potent in Latin America since the 1960s. The most famous example, without doubt, is *Me llamo Rigoberta Menchú y así me nació la conciencia* 1983 *(I, Rigoberta Menchú)* by Rigoberta Menchú (1959–), daughter of a Quiché leader burned alive in the Spanish Embassy in 1980, she was awarded the Nobel Peace Prize in 1992. Other examples of the genre are *Los días de la selva*, 1980 *(Days of the Jungle)* by the poet Mario Payeras (1937–95), about his experiences as a guerrilla with the EGP in the mountains, and the later *El trueno en la ciudad*, 1987 [Thunder in the City], which recounts his growing disillusionment with the revolutionary movement; *Tiempo de sudor y lucha*, 1987 [Time of Sweat and Struggle] by the journalist and PGT militant Miguel Ángel Albizures, about the epic strike by Coca-Cola workers in Guatemala City; and *Testimonio*, 1990 [Witness] by Víctor Montejo, a former rural teacher in Huehuetenango.

Despite, or even because of, the defeat of the guerrilla movements and the Indian "holocaust" of the last thirty years, it is difficult to believe that Guatemalan affairs can be quite as sombre in the decades to come. In literature two developments must be counted as positive. Firstly the legacy of Miguel Ángel Asturias, for many years now a conflictive figure on both left and right, has finally been assimilated into the culture and his influence is both managed and acknowledged with increasingly less controversy, not to say anxiety. Secondly, in addition to Rigoberta Menchú, one or two Indian poets and novelists have emerged at last, and many more can be expected to do so as time goes by. Enrique Luis Sam Colop (1955–), an Indian lawyer-poet from Quezaltenango, writes in Quiché; Luis de Lión, mentioned above, was an example of a successful Indian novelist; and Caly Domitila Cane'k is a Cakchiquel Indian who writes testimonial poems in Spanish. As we enter the new post-modern and deterritorialized world of the future, it may be that Guatemalan literature has the means to come to terms, just in time, with its national past.

GERALD MARTIN

Further Reading

Albizúrez Palma, Francisco and Catalina Barrios, *Historia de la literatura guatemalteca*, 3 vols, Guatemala: Editorial Universitaria, 1981–87

Albizúrez Palma, Francisco, *Grandes momentos de la literatura guatemalteca*, Guatemala: Editorial José de Pineda Ibarra, 1983

Beverley, John and Marc Zimmerman, *Literature and Politics in the Central American Revolutions*, Austin: University of Texas Press, 1990

Liano, Dante, *Ensayos de literatura guatemalteca*, Rome: Bulzoni, 1992

Zimmerman, Marc and Raúl Rojas, *Guatemala: voces desde el silencio. Un collage épico*, Guatemala: Palo de Hormiga, 1993

Zimmerman, Marc, *Literature and Resistance in Guatemala: Textual Modes and Cultural Politics from "El señor Presidente" to Rigoberta Menchú*, 2 vols, Athens: Ohio University Press, 1995

Guerrilla Poetry

The very designation "guerrilla poetry" raises difficult questions of definition. There *was* a generation of young people who became revolutionary guerrillas during the 1960s and 1970s; many of them *were* poets, though their work did not necessarily arise directly out of their experiences of armed struggle. What can be said is that their work, in its great diversity, had in common a profound idealism and a personal commitment to the struggle for change which, in a majority of cases, sadly brought their early death. This is also true of others, of course, who paid an equally high price for their political allegiances, albeit while they were involved in different arenas of political action.

There is a further common characteristic which gives the category of "guerrilla poetry" a less circumstantial meaning. Curiously, it is a feature more associated with Romantic poetry than with social or Realist writing – the perception of the poet, and the guerrilla him or herself, as a heroic but marginalised figure endowed with a great vision. That idea of change through sacrifice is embodied in the *guerrillero*/poet; and poetry is elected as the form most appropriate to visionary insight, rather than because of its brevity or ease of composition. Yet even within that frame, this body of work embraces great contrasts of style and language.

In 1959, the Cuban Revolution produced a new form of political organization – guerrilla warfare. The overthrow of the Batista regime at the hands of the 26th July Movement, led by Fidel Castro, transformed the political environment in the whole of Latin America, and placed social change on the historical agenda once again. For many young revolutionaries in Latin America the Cuban experience provided a new model of "armed propaganda" with which a small number of dedicated and well organized armed opponents could overthrow even the most entrenched regimes. This form of action was symbolised above all by one figure, Che Guevara, the Argentina doctor of medicine and second in command to Castro whose face became the icon of the young *guerrilleros*.

Guerrilla groups began to be formed in imitation of Cuba. They arose in Peru, in Colombia, Nicaragua, Argentina, Uruguay, Guatemala and El Salvador – and for a brief moment, in Paraguay. Each had their poets.

The Peruvian poet Javier Heraud was a university student before he joined the guerrillas of the Ejército de Liberación Nacional or ELN (Army of National Liberation). He was killed in 1963, when barely twenty-one. His poetry, of which there is a substantial amount, is urgent and lyrical, written in brief lines and in a direct and simple language. Much of it concerns the landscape of his native Peru, its rivers and mountains. In those mountains, of course, he lived his brief political life – and there he saw the country he was fighting to recapture. His actions and his poetry could perhaps both be encapsulated in his concept of "Arte poética": – "la poesía es / un relámpago maravilloso, / una lluvia de palabras silenciosas . . . / el canto de los pueblos oprimidos, / . . . Y la poesía es entonces, / el amor; la muerte, / las redención de los hombres" (poetry is a wonderful bolt of lightning / a rain of silent words / the song of oppressed people / . . . so poetry is / love, death / the redemption of all men).

Otto René Castillo was a Guatemalan, born in 1936. He studied in Europe and was a recognised poet when he returned to fight with the Fuerzas Armadas Revolucionarias or FAR (Armed Revolutionary Forces). He was captured and killed in March 1967. His poetry has a sharp sense of irony not unlike that of the Salvadorean Roque Dalton (with whom he shared a poetry prize in 1955) – best summarised in his satire on "Los intelectuales apolíticos." His best known work, however, is the title poem from the collection "Vámonos patria a caminar"[Come Walk with Me, My Country]. It is a kind of personal manifesto: "Vámonos patria a caminar, yo te acompaño / Yo bajaré los abismos que me digas / Yo beberé tus cálices amargos / Yo me quedaré ciego para que tengas ojos / Yo me quedaré sin voz para que tu cantes" (Come walk with me, my country, I'll go with you / I'll descend into whatever abyss you tell me to / I'll drink your bitter cups / I'll become blind so that you may see / I'll lose my voice so that you can sing).

Roque Dalton was one of the most significant figures of the period. Incisive and broad in his writing, he spent time in Europe and in Cuba – experiences that find their place in his poetry. But his recognisable style marries a conversational tone, a sense of history and a savage sense of irony – sometimes directed even at himself. In "Buscándome líos" [I'm Looking for Trouble] he paints a poignant picture of his first political meeting ... He also wrote under a number of different pseudonyms, to provide a kind of single-handed chorus to the development of resistance in his country, El Salvador. Tragically, and wastefully, he was killed by his own comrades in 1975, as a result of internal disputes. Dalton was an enemy of grandiloquent language – and excessive seriousness. It is the directness and the humour of his writing that gives it its special power.

Nicaragua has more than its share of guerrilla poets – indeed more than its share of fine poets for a small and culturally undeveloped country. Nicaraguan students were inspired, as others were, by Cuba – and particularly so since Nicaragua had been dominated by a single family dynasty – the Somozas – since 1936. The regime was remorseless in its repression of all opposition, so Nicaragua has a long list of dead poets – among them Fernando Gordillo, Ricardo Morles, Leonel Rugama – to add to those who continued to write until the Sandinista Revolution of 1979 overthrew the Somoza regime. Outstanding among the living was (and is) Ernesto Cardenal, the poet/priest who formed a generation of writers and artists. His non-symbolic *exteriorista* style embraced every language

and experience in poetry; and Rugama, among others, skilfully used the language of advertising and journalism to denounce his own society. Since 1979, a new generation of poets – many of whom were involved in the struggles to overthrow Somoza – has emerged, most sensitive and searching among them the group of women poets like Rosario Murillo, Vidaluz Meneses and Gioconda Belli. Gordillo's "Un joven muerto" [A Dead Youth] may stand as a commentary on a whole generation whose heroism cannot be questioned, even if the tactics they adopted proved to be often misguided or naive. "Un joven muerto, no hiere el corazón de un rifle. / Ni hace sufrir las sombras de la nada / pero por sus heridas, un poco de cade / uno se ha escapado, para no volver. / La soledad del héroe, es su mayor / martirio. / Hacedle compañia." (A dead youth cannot pierce the heart of a rifle. / He cannot make the shades of nothingness suffer. / But through his wounds, a little from each / one has escaped never to return. / The solitude of the hero is his greatest / martyrdom. / Stay and keep him company).

There were other fine poets who died for their commitment to a political cause – Francisco (Paco) Urondo was killed, Juan Gelman lost his family, Jaime Suárez Quemain was murdered in El Salvador. The list is long and tragic. But it was not a mere coincidence that so many of them wrote poetry – what moved them all were the highest and most humane of ideals.

MIKE GONZALEZ

See also entries on Gioconda Belli, Ernesto Cardenal, Roque Dalton

Further Reading

Castillo, Otto René, *Poemas*, Havana: Casa de las Américas, 1971

Gonzalez, Mike and David Treece, *The Gathering of Voices: the Twentieth-Century Poetry of Latin America*, London and New York: Verso, 1992 [A comprehensive analysis of 20th-century poetry in Spanish America and Brazil]

Gott, Richard, *Guerrilla Movements in Latin America*, London: Thomas Nelson, 1970 [Useful on historical background. Chapter 3 of Part 4 is titled "The Death of Javier Heraud at Puerto Maldonado"]

Heraud, Javier, *Poemas*, Havana: Casa de las Américas, 1970

Márquez, Robert (editor), *Latin American Revolutionary Poetry / Poesía revolucionaria latinoamericana*, New York: Monthly Review Press, 1974 [bilingual anthology]

Nicolás Guillén 1902–1989

Cuban poet

Nicolás Guillén was born of two generations of mulattoes in 1902, but it was not until 1930 that he was born into his artistic fullness. His brother poet from the United States, Langston Hughes, was the spiritual midwife for this new birth. Confused by the systematic distortions spawned by slavery, the slave trade, and European colonial expansion, Guillén had lain slumped in what Amilcar Cabral, inspired by Frantz Fanon, has termed the "Capitulation Phase." He saw himself as just another Latin American poet in the tradition of the great Darío. As the exaggerated liberalism of the 1920s roared in the north, in the south the US tightened its grip, and the young mulatto poet was shocked to see his race-based class privileges evaporate before his very eyes. So, in the words of Fanon in *Les Damnés de la terre* (*The Wretched of the Earth*) he began to "remember what he [was]." In January 1930 Hughes paid a visit to Havana, and the two met. Shortly afterwards, on the 20th of April, the Cuban spoke "en negro de verdad" [authentic Black] for the first time when his eight *Motivos de son* [Son Motifs] were published in the *Ideales de la raza* [Ideals of the Race] section of the *Diario de la Marina* newspaper.

The collection entitled *Sóngoro cosongo*, which appeared in 1931, was the poet's first after finding the new voice that was sounded with his dramatic passing into the "Revitalization Phase," according to the Cabral schema. Conscious of the immense significance of the work, Guillén opened it with a brief prologue defiantly proclaiming his artistically "born again" poetry to be "versos mulatos" permeated with quintessential Cubanness, "*color cubano*." Mainstream critics consistently consider the works of this phase to be Guillén's best, and indeed, these may well be the most representative of his artistic genius. He did, however, evolve into the "Radicalization Phase," the fighting phase. The publication of his collection *West Indies, Ltd.* in 1934 marks his entry into this final phase of development for the native artist. "*Sabás*," arguably Guillén's most powerful poem, belongs to this collection. It was written in that very year and significantly was dedicated to Hughes.

In May 1937 the collection *Cantos para soldados y sones para turistas* [Songs for Soldiers and *Sones* for Tourists] was published in Mexico. Entirely consistent with the revolutionary, fighting phase of development it turned out to be the final expression of that particular period of the poet's ongoing artistic evolution. In the very month of May, the poet, again in Mexico, wrote "*España, poema en cuatro angustias y una esperanza*" [Spain, a Poem in Four Anguished Voices and One of Hope]. The long work was published immediately in Mexico and then at the end of August in Valencia, Spain. Significantly, there in Valencia that very same year, Guillén formally joined the Communist Party, thereby entering what might be termed the "post-colonial" phase.

In recent years there has been a major thrust in the United States to validate the category "biracial," sometimes indistinguishable from "multiracial." Even at his most radical stage Guillén, by opting for *mulatez* [mulattoness] over *Négritude*, fell short of developing what is viewed today as an African consciousness. Furthermore, by joining the Communist Party he officially subsumed his race consciousness – at best a *mulatez* – to a class consciousness, and would later expressly repudiate *Négritude*, the Afrocentricity of the 1930s. Richard L. Jackson, the first North American scholar in modern times to present a clear understanding of Latin American racism, equates *mulatez*, a form of *mestizaje,* with "ethnic lynching." The fact is that the poet Nicolás Guillén is recognized in the circles of those who read and study literature today as a "black" Latin American poet. The works of his "Revitalization" phase are those that compel the interest of the academy. As was indicated in the entries on "African-Caribbean Literature" and "African-American Literature (Central and South America)" it is only by employing the analytical tools proffered by the new Afrocentric scholarship that the researcher will reap the full harvest of appreciation and hence enjoyment of the literary output of any African-ancestored writer.

If, as Derek Walcott would put it, "the poet never lies," then *Sóngoro cosongo* should not really be different from the work of Guillén the post-colonial *Poeta Nacional* of Fidel's Cuba. The poem "Sensemayá," with the subtitle "Poem to Kill a Snake" first appeared in the 1934 collection *West Indies, Ltd.* and has become a signature work for the poet and for so-called "African-Cuban" poetry, but it has been shown to be remarkably similar in form and content to a poem of ancient Kemet that was inscribed indelibly (almost) in hieroglyphs on the walls of a pyramid tomb of Teta, a pharaoh of the Sixth Dynasty. It represents one of two instances when the Cuban poet was satisfied with the first version of a work: when he composed the original *son* poems written in the course of one night of true inspiration; and when "Sensemayá," burst forth spontaneously but based on his recollection of carnival chants he had heard as a youth.

In marked contrast, the poet's "Elegía a Jesús Menéndez," written between 1948 and 1951 and finally published in the 1958 collection *La paloma de vuelo popular* [The Dove of the People's Flight], is perhaps his most carefully crafted work. The poem is correctly Marxist-Leninist, rooted in the atheistic contemporary European intellectual tradition. However, the poet gets the best of both worlds for this modern Marxist hero is a suffering servant, a messiah in the cast of his divine namesake. Furthermore it is quite clear that Guillén consciously incorporates traditional West African religious symbolism into his aesthetic. Jesús Menéndez is presented as a manifestation of Shango, "the great Yoruba ancestor and military leader who has been raised to the ranks of the *orishas* (divinities) . . . becoming . . . the god of thunder."

Henry Louis Gates, Jr is one of those contemporary mainstream scholars who have acknowledged the pivotal importance of another Yoruba *orisha*, Legba, the Trickster. Legba's is the discourse of the "signifying monkey," or in the popular parlance of the contemporary Caribbean: the "mamaguyer" the "broad-talker" the "shit-talker." It is Legba who inspires those tea meetings in Nevis in the Leeward Islands which Roger D. Abrahams depicts as, "a remarkable combination of pageant, mock fertility ritual, variety show, and organized mayhem." It is clearly Legba who inspired the poem "Digo que no soy un hombre puro" [I'm No Pure Man, I Say] that first appeared in 1968 and was included in the second edition of the 1972 collection, *La rueda dentada* [The Cogwheel]. In this poem "the artist's purpose appears to be the signaling to the world that the old poet still retains the vibrancy of youth. It is this same purpose that prompted the extreme experimentation of the book *El diario que a diario.*" Legba's connection to a book like *El gran zoo* (1967) is much more readily grasped. From the dawn of recorded history African civilizations have evinced a deep appreciation for the links between the supernatural and the various parts of the natural, this latter including the plant, animal, and human kingdom. So African literature throughout the ages is replete with totemic representations of the Trickster: the spider, the rabbit, the land turtle (*jicotea*), the (signifying) monkey, etc. Some of Guillén's finest expressions of political satire are to be found in the pages of this book penned by the National Poet of a Communist nation.

El diario que a diario, 1972 (*The Daily Daily*), Guillén's final book, is the same kind of work as the novel *Mumbo Jumbo* (1972) by the African American Ishmael Reed, a consummate parody. According to Gates, "In six demanding novels [including *Mumbo Jumbo*], Reed has criticized, through signifying, what he perceives to be the conventional structures of feeling that he has received from the African-American tradition." Employing the selfsame pastiche format, the Cuban's book parodies and signifies on our received notions of his nation's history, and is sustained artistically by its irony and sarcasm. It is an experimental work, but the experimental form is not divorced from the content, as the poet is manifestly seeking a new way to express his central poetic vision.

Guillén is, then, more than just the token "Black" poet to be trotted out every time the specter of racism rises menacingly. He has, in fact, plumbed the depth of his "sous-réalité" to speak "en negro de verdad," in an authentic African voice. In the course of Nancy Morejón's *Conversación con Nicolás Guillén*, which was first published in 1970, the poet declared: "My poetry has always been internally consistent." This, of course, is just another way of expressing the Walcottean declaration. Unfortunately this internally consistent, authentic African voice has yet to be fully understood by the mainstream.

IAN ISIDORE SMART

Biography

Born in Camagüey, Cuba, 10 July 1902. Attended the Instituto de Segunda Enseñanza, Camagüey, to 1920; studied law at the University of Havana, 1920 and 1921–22: abandoned studies. Worked for *El Nacional* as printer and typesetter while taking evening classes, 1918–19; contributed to the magazines, *Camagüey Gráfico* (this magazine published his first poems), 1919, *Orto*, 1920 and 1927, *Las Dos Repúblicas*, 1920, and *Alma Mater*, 1922. Co-founder and editor of *Lis*, 1923; editor, *El Camagüeyano*, 1923; typist, Ministry of the Interior, Havana, 1926; contributor, *Diario de la Marina*, from 1928, editor, *Información* and *El Loco*, from 1934; worked in the Havana Ministry of Culture, 1935–36; editor, *Mediodía*, 1936–38; travelled to Spain and attended pro-Republican conferences, 1937; joined National Committee of the Cuban Communist Party, 1938, and worked on its journal *Hoy*, from 1938 to 1950 when it was closed by the authorities, and from its revival in 1959. Stood for mayor in Camagüey, 1940, but not elected. Travelled to Haiti, 1942, and throughout Latin America on a lecture and recital tour, 1945–48; co-editor, *Gaceta del Caribe*, 1944; travelled widely throughout Europe (East and West), USSR, and China, attending conferences and cultural events, 1948–52. Contributed to *La Última Hora*, 1952; arrested twice for activities against the Batista regime, 1952; left Cuba for Chile, 1953, and, though based in Paris, 1955–58, continued travelling widely during the 1950s; lived in Buenos Aires, 1958–59. Returned to Cuba, from virtual exile, after the Castro Revolution in 1959, and thereafter combined career as writer with attendances at numerous international conferences, lectures, and cultural events, often in other countries of the socialist bloc, and often in an official capacity as Cuban ambassador at large or president of the Cuban Union of Writers and Artists (UNEAC) (appointed 1961); member, Central Committee of the Communist Party of Cuba, from 1975; had leg amputated, June 1989. Recipient of numerous awards including: International Lenin Peace Prize, 1954; Viareggio Prize (Italy), 1972; Cuban National Prize for Literature, 1983; Maurice Bishop Prize, 1989. Died in Havana, 16 July 1989.

Selected Works

Poetry

Motivos de son, Havana: Rambla, Bouza y Compañía, 1930
Sóngoro cosongo: poemas mulatos, Havana: Úcar García, 1931
West Indies, Ltd: poemas, Havana: Úcar García, 1934
España: poema en cuatro angustias y una esperanza, Mexico City: México Nuevo, 1937
Cantos para soldados y sones para turistas, Mexico City: Masas, 1937
El son entero; suma poética 1929–1946, Buenos Aires: Pleamar, 1947
Elegía a Jacques Roumain en el cielo de Haití, Havana: Ayón, 1948
Elegía a Jesús Menéndez, Havana: Páginas, 1951
Elegía cubana, Havana: n.p.,1952
La paloma de vuelo popular. Elegías, Buenos Aires: Losada, 1958
Buenos días, Fidel, Mexico City: Gráfica Horizonte, 1959
Poesías, Havana: Comisión Nacional Cubana de la UNESCO, 1962
Poemas de amor, Havana: Cuadernos de Poesía, 1964
Tengo, Havana: Universidad Central de Las Villas, 1964; as *Tengo*, translated by Richard J. Carr, Detroit, Michigan: Broadside Press, 1974
Che comandante, Havana: Instituto Cubano del Libro, 1967
El gran zoo, Havana: Unión, 1967; translated as "The Great Zoo," in *¡Patria o muerte!: The Great Zoo and Other Poems*, 1973
Cuatro canciones para el Che, Havana: Consejo Nacional de Cultura, 1969
El diario que a diario, Havana: Unión, 1972; revised edition, 1979; as *The Daily Daily*, translated by Vera M. Kutzinski, Berkeley: University of California Press, 1989
La rueda dentada, Havana: Unión, 1972
El corazón con que vivo, Havana: Unión, 1975
Poemas manuables, Havana: Unión, 1975
Por el mar de las Antillas anda un barco de papel, Havana: Unión, 1977
Música de cámara, Havana: Unión, 1979
Coplas de Juan Descalzo, Havana: Letras Cubanas, 1979
Sol de domingo, Havana: Instituto Cubano del Libro, 1982
El libro de los sonetos, Havana: Unión, 1984

Other Writings

Páginas vueltas; memorias, Havana: Unión, 1982

Compilations and Anthologies

Sus mejores poemas, Havana: Biblioteca Básica de Cultura Cubana, 1959 [Contains selections from *Motivos de son*, *Sóngoro cosongo*, *West Indies, Ltd.*, *Cantos para soldados y sones para turistas*, *España*, *El son entero*, and *La paloma de vuelo popular*]

Los mejores versos, Buenos Aires: Nuestra América, 1961

Antología mayor: el son entero y otros poemas, Havana: Unión, 1964

Antología clave, Santiago de Chile: Nascimento, 1971

Obra poética 1920–1972, edited by Ángel Augier, 2 vols, Havana: Instituto Cubano del Libro, 1972–73; revised edition, 1985

Prosa de prisa 1929–1972, edited by Ángel Augier, 3 vols, Havana: Instituto Cubano del Libro, 1975–76

Summa poética, edited by Luis Íñigo Madrigal, Madrid: Cátedra, 1976

El libro de las décimas, edited by Nancy Morejón, Havana: Unión, 1980 [selection]

Anthologies in Translation

Cuba Libre: Poems by Nicolás Guillén, translated by Langston Hughes and Ben Frederic Carruthers, Los Angeles: Ward Ritchie Press, 1948

Man-Making Words: Selected Poems, translated by Robert Márquez and David Arthur McMurray, Amherst: University of Massachusetts Press, 1972

¡Patria o muerte!: The Great Zoo and Other Poems, edited and translated by Robert Márquez, New York: Monthly Review Press, 1973 [bilingual edition]

Further Reading

Studies that provide the cultural context for Guillén's work

Abrahams, Roger D., *The Man-of-Words in the West Indies: Performance and the Emergence of a Creole Culture*, Baltimore: Johns Hopkins University Press, 1983

Cobb, Martha, *Harlem, Haiti, and Havana: a Comparative Critical Study of Langston Hughes, Jacques Roumain, and Nicolás Guillén*, Washington, DC: Three Continents Press, 1979

Fanon, Frantz, *Les Damnés de la terre*, Paris: Maspero, 1961; as *The Wretched of the Earth*, translated by Constance Farrington, New York: Grove Press, 1965; Harmondsworth: Penguin, 1967

Gates, Jr, Henry Louis, *The Signifying Monkey: a Theory of African-American Literary Criticism*, Oxford and New York: Oxford University Press, 1988

Jackson, Richard L., *The Black Image in Latin American Literature*, Albuquerque: University of New Mexico Press, 1976

Kubayanda, Josaphat B., *The Poet's Africa: Africanness in the Poetry of Nicolás Guillén and Aimé Césaire*, New York: Greenwood Press, 1990

Kutzinski, Vera M., *Against the American Grain: Myth and History in William Carlos Williams, Jay Wright and Nicolás Guillén*, Baltimore: Johns Hopkins University Press, 1987

_____ *Sugar's Secrets: Race and the Erotics of Cuban Nationalism*, Charlottesville: University Press of Virginia, 1993 [Chapters 5 and 6 discuss Guillén]

Studies of Guillén's poetry

Ellis, Keith, *Cuba's Nicolás Guillén: Poetry and Ideology*, Toronto: University of Toronto Press, 1983

Morejón, Nancy, *Nación y mestizaje en Nicolás Guillén*, Havana: Unión, 1982

Pérez Firmat, Gustavo, *The Cuban Condition: Translation and Identity in Modern Cuban Literature*, Cambridge and New York: Cambridge University Press, 1989 [Chapters 4 and 5 are on Guillén]

Ruffinelli, Jorge, *Poesía y descolonización: viaje por la poesía de Nicolás Guillén*, Mexico City: Oasis, 1985

Smart, Ian Isidore, *Nicolás Guillén, Popular Poet of the Caribbean*, Columbia: University of Missouri Press, 1990

Williams, Lorna V., *Self and Society in the Poetry of Nicolás Guillén*, Baltimore: Johns Hopkins University Press, 1982

Sóngoro cosongo

Collection of poems by Nicolás Guillén

As from his first important collection of poems, *Motivos de son*, 1930 [Son Motifs], Guillén demonstrated an independence from the *negrista* poetry of his contemporaries (Ballagas, Palés Matos) in tone and style, while not entirely in thematic consideration. The *son* form which predominates in this volume, is one of the basic forms of Cuban music, containing African and Spanish elements, accompanied by guitar, its relative the *tres*, with three pairs of strings, which initiates the rhythm, bass, bongo drums, maracas, *claves* (two small rounded sticks of hard wood), and trumpet. The provocative and lively rhythms of the *son* musical form were appropriately adapted by Guillén in his *poemas-son* (son-poems) in order to capture the spirit of the African-Cuban culture as well as to serve as a counterpoint to a people determined to be joyous despite the extreme poverty and racism in which they lived. The characters that inhabit his *Motivos de son* and subsequent works present themselves to us in their own language, using the unique rhythmic expressions of their musical heritage. Rather than being caricatures of what the black is perceived to be, they show us who he really is – a complex web of wants and needs left unsatisfied, potentials left unfulfilled by the social inequities the typical African-Hispanic was forced to endure by the dominant white European culture in Cuba.

The following year marks the publication of Guillén's second major collection of poetry, *Sóngoro cosongo* (1931), which, as its title suggests, continues the persistent and primitive rhythms of the previous book's poem-sounds with its popular phonetics, folkloric resonances, and adaptations of motifs from popular songs and dances. The title of this second book is taken from the *jitanjáfora* (an extra-semantic phenomenon that relies heavily for meaning on context and on onomatopoeic association) that form the *estribillo* (refrain or chorus) of the poem "Si tí supiera" [If You Knew] of the first book. But the fifteen poems in *Sóngoro cosongo* give more emphasis to the sources of national unrest – racial disharmony, imperialistic intervention, and the socioeconomic impoverishment of oppressed blacks. In fact, the book opens with an admonishment to the reader that the poems will be upsetting to many because they deal with blacks and other popular classes. After identifying the verses as "mulatto" and stating that Cuba is culturally "mestizo," Guillén closes his second volume of poetry on a hopeful note of a soon-to-be-realized day when "the definitive color" will be "Cuban color." Thus, the thematic disunity and national unrest which mark the text come full circle in an ardent aspiration for harmony among all Cubans, regardless of color. So diverse is the treatment of subject matter in *Sóngoro cosongo* that the structure of the book itself may be viewed as a commentary on the social unrest and disunity that Guillén saw all around him. Some of the poems depict black life in its daily celebratory pursuits – physical celebrations which, all too often, serve as distractions to the black's existence on the fringes of society (the poems "Quirino," "Rumba," and "Canto negro" serve as examples). The elemental beauty of the black woman, while celebrated in "Mujer nueva" [New Woman] and the two madrigals, is placed in jeopardy as the black woman becomes victimized by violent eruptions of repressed anger and frustrations on the part of the black man in "Chévere." This point-counterpoint motif continues in the musical beauty with undercurrents of violence in the two poems "Velorio de Papá Montero" [Funeral Wake for Papá Montero] and in "Secuestro de la mujer de Antonio" [Abduction of Antonio's Wife], not to mention the muscles (an allusion to the physical and violence) that have made the black boxer successful in Guillén's portrayal of the boxer, whose physical prowess is overshadowed by the fact that he is perceived only as entertainment for others, in "Pequeña oda a un negro boxeador cubano" [Little Ode to a Black Cuban Boxer]: And the contrast between the African-Cuban prior to his transport to Cuba, stressing his African roots, and his initiation into slavery and social injustice is made apparent in the poems "Llegada" [Arrival] and "Canción del bongó" [The Song of the Bongo Drum].

But Guillén's intent was not to divide Cubans further but, rather to unite them in his quest for a national identity in *Sóngoro cosongo*, while, at the same time, both singing the praises of his African heritage and denouncing the exploitation of the black by Cubans of European ancestry. In his controversial prologue to this second book of poetry, Nicolás Guillén proudly proclaims: ". . . these are mulatto verses. They partake perhaps of the same elements that enter into the ethnic composition of Cuba where we are all a little mixed . . . The African input into this country is . . . profound and . . . many capillary currents criss-cross in our well-irrigated waterways. I think therefore that a creole poetry among us will not be realized completely with the omission of blacks . . . The spirit of Cuba is *mestizo*. And from the spirit to the skin the definitive color will come to us. Some day they will say: "Cuban color." These poems wish to hasten that day." What Guillén accomplishes in his poetry is to fortify historical memory, to strengthen collective identity, and to create a new poetic circuit based on musical rhythms, linguistic discourse, and experienced realities (both past and present) of the African-Cuban. In this way his poetry validates and renews internalized recollections of an ancestral past, which have progressively receded through the experiences of displacement or exile, cultural assimilation, not to mention the experience of slavery. What *Sóngoro cosongo* achieves over Guillén's first volume of poetry is a demonstration that the celebration of life that is so much of a part of the African heritage, even in the midst of adversity, can be shared with all Cuban citizens in the cementing of a national unity wherein cultural differences are recognized within the context of a common national Cuban identity, regardless of race.

Because of the political repression under Cuban dictator Gerardo Machado, who was in power from 1925 to 1933, aggravated by the social consequences of the Great Depression of the 1930s, Guillén's writing, such as *Sóngoro cosongo* and *West Indies, Ltd.* (1934) began to delve more into social realism. Guillén's African-Hispanic *negrismo* (blackness) therefore emerged largely against a backdrop of Caribbean self-review and self-recognition. It served as an intellectual and cultural attempt to affirm a Cuban affinity with Africa as well as to express faith in a Caribbean national identity. Due, in part, to Guillén's *Négritude* poetic discourse, a greater awareness of the shared heritage from Africa arose in Cuba and beyond – the black experiences *vis-à-vis* the European ordering of Caribbean society; the intellectual awakening of the marginalized blacks of the Caribbean and elsewhere; the more perceptible role of African customs, music, oral tradition and ontological systems; and the kindling of creativity among black poets nearly everywhere. In fact, Nicolás Guillén is a forerunner of present-day committed poetry. While Guillén was proclaiming his blackness in the Cuba of the 1930s and 1940s, there were few creative Cuban artists who viewed writing as a social responsibility and a discursive challenge to the mainstream ethos. And, from a stylistic perspective, Guillén's poetry was antithetical to classical European literary tradition, representing, instead, a postcolonial oppositional discourse of the Third World with an identifiable African-Caribbean flavor. As Nancy Morejón proclaims in her book *Nación y mestizaje en Nicolás Guillén* Africa is not *in* but is *part of* Cuba and Guillén is merely voicing and validating this reality in his pre-revolutionary poetry. Guillén's celebration of the black situation in *Sóngoro cosongo* is founded not just in contemporary Cuba, but in the Cuba of the last four hundred years. Each poem in this volume is linked to memories of either the immediate or remote past, as well as on reflections on the social and racial destiny of blacks in a context in which Africa encounters Europe, and exclusionary practices encounter the *other* in a spirit of hoped-for unity and common brotherhood for all Cubans.

ELENA DE COSTA

Editions

First edition: *Sóngoro cosongo: poemas mulatos*, Havana: Úcar García, 1931

Further Reading

Martínez Estrada, Ezequiel, *La poesía afrocubana de Nicolás Guillén*, Montevideo: Arca, 1966

White, Clement A., *Decoding the Word: Nicolás Guillén as Maker and Debunker of Myth*, Miami: Universal, 1993

Bernardo Guimarães 1825–1884

Brazilian novelist and poet

Bernardo Guimarães, born in the interior province of Minas Gerais, was sent to the Faculty of Law in São Paulo in 1847. He began his literary career there, one member of a group of student poets and bohemians who sought to imitate Byron and other European Romantics in both their verses and their lifestyle. Guimarães's early poems, collected in *Cantos de solidão* [Songs of Solitude], first appeared in 1852, the year of his graduation. He spent much of the next fifteen years as a municipal judge in a small town in the very distant interior, in what is now the state of Goiás. In 1867, Guimarães moved back to Minas Gerais, where he found work as a schoolteacher. He continued to write and occasionally publish poetry, but after about 1865 concentrated on the production of prose fiction. Guimarães's reputation today, as in his own time, is largely based on his 1875 novel *A escrava Isaura* [Isaura, the Slave Girl], one of the great best-sellers of 19th-century Brazil.

These biographical details are important because they tell us a great deal about Guimarães's position within 19th-century Brazilian literature. Despite his education in São Paulo and a couple of forays to Rio de Janeiro, he preferred to spend his life in the interior – working a little, but primarily devoting his time to riding, hunting, fishing and conversation. His love of these rural pursuits comes through clearly, both in his poetry and his fiction. Moreover, Guimarães's regionalism is very firmly based on real experience and on his affection for specific landscapes and ways of life; other regionalist fiction of the time, particularly that of José de Alencar, is primarily the product of a little reading and a great deal of imagination.

Bernardo Guimarães, unlike almost all other Brazilian writers of the 19th century, published substantial amounts of both poetry and prose. This division of labors, in part, reflects his constant desire for popularity; Guimarães did not begin publishing fiction until after other writers had established the Brazilian novel and created a market for national fiction. It is also the product, however, of his easy versatility. He appears to have been able to write, almost effortlessly, in any style he chose. His poetry is far more varied, in form and in content, than that of any of his contemporaries; the same versatility allowed him to produce Indianist fiction, historical novels, and novels set in both urban and rural environments. The downside of this versatility, however, is a certain technical and intellectual laziness, visibile in both his poetry and his prose. One of Guimarães's late poems, the "Hino à preguiça" [Hymn to Laziness], published in 1883, humorously pleads guilty to this charge. It is this fundamental unwillingness to challenge his readers' expectations and to polish his texts that has relegated Guimarães, despite all his talent, to secondary status in both poetry and prose.

Thus Guimarães's early lyrics, written while he was in law school, seem both artificial in tone and metrically sloppy, particularly when compared to the very similar works produced by his much younger friend and fellow-student, Manuel Antônio Álvares de Azevedo (1831–52), the great poet of their generation. Guimarães's complaints of world-weariness and despair ring false, the product of his readings in European literature rather than real experience; in sharp contrast, his best poems of the period from 1847 to 1865 reflect his love of the good things in life (a good cigar, a comfortable hammock, for example) and his nostalgia for the world he had left behind in Minas Gerais – his favorite horse, a sunset, the landscapes that he loved. His later verse concentrates on these simple pleasures, but also contains a number of elegies for his friends and celebrations of family anniversaries or local political events.

As a novelist, Guimarães has often been described as above all a story-teller – equally at home swapping tales in a rural bar or writing simple narratives designed for unsophisticated readers. None of his novels really broke new ground, in theme or in style; structurally, even works written in the late 1870s are indistinguishable from Brazilian novels published thirty years earlier. His heroes and heroines are uniformly and wholly pure and noble; his villains are uniformly and wholly evil. Guimarães presents his characters, and the hero and heroine fall in love at first sight; the machinations of their enemies produce a few obstacles to happiness, but everything is quickly and simplistically resolved. The best of these texts are his regionalist novels, where the mechanical plots are interrupted by vivid descriptions of rural landscapes and customs.

The most famous of Guimarães's novels, however, is *A escrava Isaura*, a work which may have been influenced by Harriet Beecher Stowe's *Uncle Tom's Cabin* (widely read in translation in Brazil) and, perhaps, by Dion Boucicault's 1861 play, *The Octoroon*. Isaura, the incredibly lovely, cultured and noble mulatto heroine, is the color of ivory. She successfully rejects the lustful advances of her master, Leôncio, and is finally saved by her true love, Álvaro, a free-thinking aristocrat and millionaire who destroys Leôncio, frees her, and proposes marriage. *A escrava Isaura* is often described as an abolitionist work, but it is rather difficult to see how it contributed to the end of African slavery in Brazil. Guimarães does not appear to regard slavery, as an institution, as evil; the problem, rather, is that Isaura (unlike the other slave girls Leôncio owns) is fully white in appearance, character, and refinement, and therefore does not deserve to be enslaved.

The popularity of *A escrava Isaura*, despite its stereotypical characterization and hackneyed plot, is suggestive of certain realities in 19th-century Brazilian society and in Guimarães's own life. The plot is driven by Leôncio's obsessive efforts to seduce Isaura; her success in resisting his advances, thereby maintaining her purity for Álvaro, is one of the most unrealistic aspects of the novel. Real slaves, like Rosa (a minor character in the text), were unable to resist seduction or rape by their masters. The novel's undercurrent of sexual exploitation and violence directed towards subservient women, whether white or of color, is a reflection of the realities of Brazilian life. That reflection, moreover, is far more explicit elsewhere in Guimarães's life and work. As a young man in São Paulo, he was one of the founders of the student Epicurean Society, which hired local prostitutes for extravagant orgies of sex and violence; according to the recollections of some of the participants, those orgies led to the death of at least one of the women. Clear reflections of the darkest sort of eroticism appear in several of his poems as well – in the extremely pornographic "Elíxir do pajé" [The Shaman's Potion], which has circulated widely in manuscript form for at least a century, or in the published "Orgia dos duendes" [The Ghosts' Orgy], works in which, as Antônio Cândido has noted (*Formação da literatura brasileira*, 1975), the combination of pan-sexuality and sadism recalls the paintings of Hieronymus Bosch.

DAVID T. HABERLY

Biography

Born Bernardo Joaquim da Silva Guimarães in Ouro Prêto in the state of Minas Gerais, Brazil, 15 August 1825. Studied law at University of São Paulo, where he founded the student Epicurean Society. After graduating he practiced law in Minas Gerais and Goiás where he got to know the hinterland. Spent some time in Rio, working as a journalist. Returned to Ouro Prêto in 1867, where he married and began his career as a writer. Earned his living as a teacher, journalist and lawyer. Died in Ouro Prêto, 10 March 1884.

Selected Works

Poetry
Cantos de solidão, São Paulo: Tipografia Liberal, 1852
Poesías, Rio de Janeiro: Garnier, 1865
Novas poesias, Rio de Janeiro: Garnier, 1876
Folhas de outono, Rio de Janeiro: Garnier, 1883

Novels and Short Fiction
O ermitão de Muquém, Rio de Janeiro: Garnier, 1866
Lendas e romances, Rio de Janeiro: Garnier, 1871
O garimpeiro, Rio de Janeiro: Garnier, 1872
Histórias da província de Minas Gerais, Rio de Janeiro: Garnier, 1872
O seminarista, Rio de Janeiro: Garnier, 1872
A escrava Isaura, Rio de Janeiro: Garnier, 1875
Maurício ou os paulistas em São João del Rei, Rio de Janeiro: Garnier, 1877
A ilha maldita, Rio de Janeiro: Garnier, 1879
O pão de ouro, Rio de Janeiro: Garnier, 1879
Rosaura, a enjeitada, Rio de Janeiro: Garnier, 1883
O bandido do rio das Mortes, Belo Horizonte, Brazil: Imprensa Oficial de Belo Horizonte, 1904

Compilations and Anthologies
Poesias completas, edited by Alphonsus de Guimarães filho, Rio de Janeiro: Instituto Nacional do Livro, 1959
Histórias e tradições da província de Minas Gerais, edited by Alphonsus de Guimarães filho, Rio de Janeiro: Civilização Brasileira, 1976 [Contains *A cabeça do Tiradentes*, *A filha do fazendeiro*, *Jupira*]

Further Reading
Relatively little has been published on Guimarães's poetry and prose, as these listings suggest.

Andrews, Jr, Norwood, "Modern Classification of Bernardo Guimarães's Prose Narratives," *Luso-Brazilian Review*, vol. 3 (1966)
Cândido, Antônio, *Formação da literatura brasileira*, 5th edition, vol. 2, Belo Horizonte, Brazil: Itatiaia, 1975
Magalhães, Basílio de, *Bernardo Guimarães*, Rio de Janeiro: Anuário do Brasil, 1926

A escrava Isaura

Novel by Bernardo Guimarães

Born in 1825, Bernardo Guimarães's life spanned the heights of a Brazilian Romanticism which declined later than its European counterpart. His best known novel, *A escrava Isaura*, 1875 [Isaura, the Slave Girl] reflects many of the characteristics of the movement both in its general European parameters and in the specific way in which these parameters were adapted to convey a Brazilian reality. The work exhibits the contradictions which such adaptations invariably entailed.

A escrava Isaura is Bernardo Guimarães's fifth novel. Together with his other writings, it is at present judged by most critics a minor manifestation of Brazilian Romanticism. However, it offers the attentive reader a fascinating insight into some of Brazilian society's central contradictions at that time. The nation was then in the process of articulating itself as an autonomous geographical, ethnic and cultural entity in the first half-century after its political independence. Brazil declared independence from Portugal in 1822 and among the major political events that mark its emergence as a nation in the century that followed, can be included the abolition of slavery in 1888, and the declaration of the Republic in 1889.

The central themes of *A escrava Isaura* are slavery and abolition, with Isaura, its heroine, as the sublime martyr who, but for her slave status is indistinguishable from her paradigmatic European precursors. For example, in his novels, Samuel Richardson embarks upon what is ostensibly, and no doubt in good faith, an anti-slavery campaign which echoes similar abolitionist literary efforts in the United States of America prior to 1870. However, given its undisguised politically reformist mission, contradictions arise in the course of the Brazilian novel over the author's treatment of themes such as enslavement and the human right to freedom. These point to the wider contradictions then plaguing a country which purported to have adopted European liberal convictions while continuing to rely on slavery as the basis of its economy.

Isaura is a beautiful and pious young slave who, thanks to the indulgence of her mistress, is also brought up to be educated and refined. Her physical appearance, it is repeatedly implied, owes little to the few drops of black blood responsible for her enslaved status, and much to a European (and Christian or Marian) canon of beauty which, in the course of the novel explicitly or implicitly reiterates that Isaura, while technically black, is in fact in heart and soul, and skin, as white as the then-prevailing racist assumptions of white superiority and black sub-humanity could require a heroine to be. Isaura's sufferings escalate following the death of her kind (albeit enslaving) mistress, when she finds herself at the mercy of the latter's lustful and evil son, Leôncio, now her master and intent upon besieging her indomitable chastity. Leôncio's persecutions become increasingly violent and Isaura, herself in love with a well-to-do young man, Álvaro, undergoes many vicissitudes, which include her near-torture by Leôncio, her escape aided and abetted by her white father, recapture, and eventual rescue by Álvaro, who, exhibiting miraculous timing reappears just as events are reaching a desperate contingency. By means of the expedient of redeeming the various debts which Leôncio, inveterate gambler and dissipator of his inherited fortune has accumulated, Álvaro exercises his right to ruin the latter, thus acquiring absolute rights to his property, goods and chattels, including Isaura, whom he naturally releases and marries, leaving Leôncio to compound his sins by the ultimate one of suicide.

Isaura, the vehicle for enlisting a 19th-century audience's sympathy in the cause of abolition, acts at the end of the novel as the cathartic means toward the moral end of the anti-slavery campaign. However, to a 20th-century reader, the novel's plot and assumptions, even taking into account the readerly expectations of its contemporary audience, exhibit areas of ideological difficulty and contradiction which, for that very reason, render this work more complex, albeit unintentionally so, than its simplistic plot structure might otherwise indicate.

The author's insistence upon Isaura's whiteness, which according to the then-prevailing notions on the wider associations of race carries moral implications as well as pigmentational ones, exposes a persistent belief in the undesirability of any dimension of blackness pertaining to the heroine, in the view of even this self-declared abolitionist writer. This belief, almost universally apparent in the early abolitionist novel of the two Americas, results here in the creation of a heroine who is only indiscernibly black, vastly unrepresentative of the wider plight of slaves, and who could be said to amount to no more than an instance of special pleading on behalf of one single individual, one uniquely undeserving of an enslaved destiny, while leaving uncontested the fate of the larger collectivity of other slaves in the novel, and the moral standing of the institution as a whole.

Furthermore, Isaura's own understanding of the significance of slavery leads her not only to apply to herself on occasion racist notions which classify her as – for example – unworthy of the love of a white man, but, equally, sometimes to see herself as distinct from other slaves. This is because she is whiter than they, and therefore especially or solely entitled to a right to freedom which does not automatically accrue to her darker and hence less deserving fellow sufferers. This separatist position reflects the views endorsed by other characters in the novel, including, remarkably, some of the other slaves.

This disturbing but unequivocal impasse in the novel's abolitionist motivation is further confirmed by the characterization of Leôncio. The latter, irredeemably evil in a straightforward manner which is typical of Romanticism's sometimes rather cardboardish attempts at psychological delineation, adds to his sins (he is a slave owner) others seen to be equally damning: gambling, dissipation of his inherited fortune, bad property

management and libertine behaviour resulting in his failure to promote the welfare of the family as the nucleus of bourgeois stability. These flaws, undermining as they do the sacrosanct areas of marriage, work, property and inheritance, become, in the context of the novel, necessary elements in the construction of a case against Leôncio. In his depiction as a wholly reprehensible character, the fact that he owns and brutalizes slaves would not be seen as sufficiently damning in itself.

From a 20th-century perspective, Isaura begins and ends the novel in positions which only differ from one another technically: if, in its opening pages she is the oppressed slave acquired by purchase and stripped of her (white) heritage, freedom and right to identity, at its culmination she is the archetypal 19th-century wife, acquired by means of an equally clear slave-market but also matrimonial purchase (by Álvaro). At the end she is stripped of her black heritage (whitened by marriage to the latter), and, by implication, deprived also of other dimensions of freedom and right to identity, namely the freedom to be black but not a slave, and the right to a black identity without stigma or oppression. Isaura's technical release from slavery, therefore, purchased at the price of the erasure of her black roots, becomes analogous to the deaths through cultural consumption of the numerous Blacks and Indians who, in the pages of Brazilian Romanticism, disappeared beyond any possibility of recovery under the impact of a movement which, paradoxically, sought to reclaim them as its heroes.

MARIA MANUEL LISBOA

Editions
First edition: *A escrava Isaura*, Rio de Janeiro: Garnier, 1875

Further Reading
To date, *A Escrava Isaura* has received very little critical attention.

Alphonsus, João, "Bernardo Guimarães, romancista e regionalista," in *O romance Brasileiro*, Rio de Janeiro: O Cruzeiro, 1952
Casassanta, Mário, "A escrava Isaura, um panfleto político," *Mensagem* 5 (15 September 1939)
Christian, Barbara, "Shadows Uplifted," in *Feminist Criticism and Social Change: Sex, Class and Race in Literature and Culture*, edited by Judith Newton and Deborah Rosenfelt, New York and London: Methuen, 1985 [An illuminating discussion of images of black women in abolitionist literature]
Magalhães, Basílio de, *Bernardo Guimarães (esboço biográfico e crítico)*, Rio de Janeiro: Anuário do Brasil, 1926

João Guimarães Rosa 1908–1967

Brazilian prose writer

Arguably the most important Brazilian fiction writer of the 20th century, Guimarães Rosa cultivated letters while serving as a medical doctor in his home state of Minas Gerais and subsequently as a career diplomat in Europe, Latin America, and Brazil itself. His production spans all fictional genres from the extremely brief and concise *crônica* (mini-essay) through short stories of all dimensions and novellas to the gigantic expanse of his single novel, *Grande sertão: veredas*, 1956 (*The Devil to Pay in the Backlands*). A polyglot, well read in numerous literatures both ancient and modern, he created via the pages of his fiction a series of stylistic and linguistic innovations akin to those introduced by James Joyce in English literature: neologisms of many kinds, a sort of "telegraphic syntax," hyperbaton, widespread lexical borrowings from many tongues, and intermixing of multiple levels of language usage (from colloquial to erudite) in a single locution. He consistently favored an orally based story-telling style echoing medieval and ancient Middle Eastern patterns, and once said that the language he was really searching for was the one spoken by humanity prior to the Tower of Babel.

Guimarães Rosa's works, in chronological order, are: *Magma*, 1934 (which won the Brazilian Academy of Letters Prize for poetry, but was never published); *Sagarana*, 1946: nine fairly long short stories; *Corpo de baile*, 1956 [Corps de Ballet]: seven novellas (subdivided, beginning with its third edition in 1964, into three volumes, with the titles *Manuelzão e Miguilim* [Big Manuel and Mikey], *Noites do sertão* [Nights in the Backlands] and *No Urubuquaquá, no Pinhém* [In the Urubuquaqua and Pinhem Area]); *Grande sertão: veredas*, 1956; *Primeiras estórias* (*The Third Bank of the River and Other Stories*), short stories published in 1962; *Tutaméia*, 1967 [Nothing Much]: very short stories and essay-like "prefaces"; *Estas estórias*, 1969 [These Stories], published posthumously: short stories of a length similar to those of *Ave, palavra* [Hail Word, or Bird, Word], also published posthumously, in 1970: miscellanea of fictional pieces (*crônicas*), poetry, and very short stories. Publishing initially as a poet before embarking upon his illustrious fictional career, Guimarães Rosa shows in his last posthumous collection the permanence of the poetic vein in his writing. His prose works themselves are interlaced with snatches of verse, and sections of a number of his stories (when read aloud) are discovered to be written in iambic or dactylic rhythm, usually in imitation of sounds of nature such as the hoofbeats of cattle and horses.

The publication of *Sagarana* in 1946 was a "bombshell" in a Brazilian literary world characterized by picturesque regionalism that reproduced and interpreted the everyday life of the rural and urban masses in accordance with a fairly simplistic code of socioeconomic and/or political premises. While obviously a regionalist in theme, treating primitive human existence in the most remote areas of Minas Gerais and Bahia, Guimarães Rosa flouted all the stereotypes of regionalist fiction with his inclusion of introspective, metaphysical dimensions hitherto excluded from the genre's paradigm. His stylistic innovations and reworking of the Portuguese literary language

suggested a possible kinship with the Mário de Andrade of *Macunaíma* (1928), but Rosa denied such a affiliation on the basis of Mário's irreverent iconoclasm. Guimarães Rosa would come to be known as a "universal regionalist" or "surregionalist," whose work was like no other and would be the watershed of 20th-century letters.

Sagarana's nine stories, all set in the backlands of central Brazil, present the cowboys, politicians, animals, landscapes, tensions, problems and entertainment of the area. Its protagonists include a small donkey who saves the lives of a couple of humans during a flood, a wayward but irresistible husband, two old friends dying of malaria, two "man hunters" in a love triangle, a pair of chess-playing friends engaged in an equally slow-moving courtship, a voodoo practitioner and his taunting neighbor, a bully and the timid rival who bests him with the aid of a spell, a herd of talking oxen who wreak exemplary vengeance on their cruel master with the subconscious help of their child guide, and a cruel husband turned saint through the intervention of a pair of humble "good samaritans." The last of these narratives – "A hora e vez de Augusto Matraga" (Augusto Matraga's Day in the Sun) – has become a classic in its own right and has been made into a film. *Sagarana* establishes the author's unflagging empathy for his region in its best and worst aspects and his confidence in the outworking of cosmic justice (with mercy) through the activity of children, animals and other unsung heroes. And set right in the middle of "São Marcos" (St Mark), a story of syncretistic religion and amorous doggerel verse, is an intercalated "position statement" on the logic of neologisms and the necessity for linguistic refreshing and renovation; this encapsulated mini-treatise proved prophetic of what Guimarães Rosa was to practice throughout his entire literary career, and finds an *a posteriori* echo in *Tutaméia*, the last collection published during the author's lifetime.

Corpo de baile's seven novellas show a degree of occasional interweaving, especially regarding several of their protagonists (e.g., Miguilim) who appear as children in the early pieces and as adults in later ones. Guimarães Rosa's re-creation of the world as observed through the nonjudgmental perception of children is without equal in modern literature. His psychological sensitivity shows in the treatment of the superstitions, fears, fantasies, erotic urges, suspense and tenderness that flow through the collection as well as in the oneiric atmosphere that reigns in at least half of the pieces, giving them a surrealistic quality not present in most of Rosa's other works.

Grande sertão: veredas, published the same year as *Corpo de baile* in a veritable marathon of literary activity, is a 600-page monologued novel without chapter division, narrated in the first-person singular by its protagonist Riobaldo, a retired ex-bandit chieftain, to a presumed narratee of higher education, whose opinion he seeks especially regarding his (not) having made a pact with the Devil to defeat a rival *jagunço* leader and to avenge the death of his own former chief. Riobaldo's lengthy blow-by-blow narration of his youth and outlaw career, with its numerous violent encounters and its psychological vicissitudes, is enriched by vivid descriptions of the landscape, fauna, flora and everyday rural life of Minas Gerais and Bahia. This work of epic proportions – sometimes classified as a Brazilian prose epic because of its themes of honor, the hero and his absent love, the quest involving purification through a series of journeys and trials, the appearance of a traitor, the homogeneous action of a heterogeneous group under an inspired leader, and the interpolation within the main narrative of numerous tangential episodes told for moralistic purpose or entertainment – may also be read as an allegory of the battle between Good and Evil. The secondary figure, Diadorim (also called Reinaldo), comrade of Riobaldo and eventual slayer of the villainous Hermógenes, arouses Riobaldo sexually while at the same time acting as his human "guardian angel," Riobaldo's anguish over his apparent homosexuality is transformed into despair of another sort when his best friend dies in the encounter with Hermógenes: Diadorim is a young woman, masquerading as adolescent male warrior to avenge her own father's death.

Though this single monumental novel by Guimarães Rosa has attracted the majority of analytical commentary to date, his 1962 story collection, *Primeiras estórias*, ranks in second place. Marking the author's definitive return to his preferred genre of short fiction, the delightful little stories of this collection are structured around "epiphanies" in the lives of children and other relatively powerless members of society. Courage to prevail in the face of adversity marks the careers of a number of these protagonists (e.g., Soroco with his demented mother and daughter, Uncle Man'Antônio and his motherless brood, the disfigured old war veteran whose horse drinks beer, the benevolent street-cleaning beggar woman, a bewildered child on an airplane between the stressful and the unknown, entry-level manual laborers in a starch company, and a frightened adolescent caught among feuding thugs), while other more liminal figures such as the "A menina de lá" (The Girl from Beyond), "Um moço muito branco" (A Very Pale Young Man), the guiding cow of "Sequência" (Sequence), and the characters in "Nenhum, nenhuma" (No Man, no Woman) bring reconciliation, stability, and peace into a troubled world by their very presence. Two stories of the *Primeiras estórias* collection – "O espelho" (The Mirror) and "A terceira margem do rio" (The Third Bank of the River) – challenge the reader with existential dramas and serious questions of conscience, while others such as "Pirlimpsiquice" (Hocus-Psychosis), "Partida do audaz navegante" (Voyage of the Audacious Navigator), "Famigerado" (Renowned), and "Darandina" display the hilarious results of childish and elderly creativity in a rather pedestrian world.

Tutaméia, subtitled "Third Tales," is the last volume of fiction published in Guimarães Rosa's lifetime and reveals his high degree of metaphysical sensitivity and artistic awareness. The forty tiny "anecdotes of abstraction" that comprise this volume, arranged essentially in alphabetical order (except for the J-G-R of the author's own initials), are intercepted at four points by longer essays (labeled "prefaces") which treat theoretical or abstract qualities such as the nature of imagination and originality, the concept of the genre of *estória* (tale), the rationale of neologisms in everyday and erudite language, and the author's own perspective on inspiration and the essence of life.

The posthumous collection of nine *Sagarana*-length short stories entitled *Estas estórias* was prepared in part under Guimarães Rosa's supervision. These stories are not set exclusively in the interior of Brazil, as was most of the author's previous prose, however, but expand to include a humorous coastal episode and a rather tense adventure in an Andean country. Nevertheless, their style, pace, and density approach those of *Sagarana*.

Ave, palavra, a posthumous miscellanea of prose and poetry, is comprised of fifty-five brief entries ranging from vignettes of zoos in Italy, France, Germany, and Brazil to memoir-like pieces of urban cosmopolitan setting as well as rural context, reflecting the author's decades of professional diplomatic activity and his international consciousness. There is a "one world" quality about these literary titbits, among the least colloquial and most cerebral of his writings.

Guimarães Rosa has suggested that his works be read simultaneously on three levels: first, their underlying charm (enchantment); second, their "level-lying" common meaning; and third their "overlying" metaphysical idea. He has created a very personal, stylized Portuguese literary language involving a quintessentially oral base and a dynamically eclectic morphological/lexical component. He has revolutionized Brazilian regionalist fiction and has compassionately drawn into focus, without partisan program nor schematic simplification, a complex rural population previously almost ignored in the national literature, thus achieving universal status for the most authentic of Brazilian literary forms.

MARY L. DANIEL

Biography

Born in Cordisburgo, Minas Gerais, Brazil, 27 June 1908. Attended the Colégio Arnaldo, Belo Horizonte and the Medical School of Minas Gerais, Belo Horizonte from 1925 to 1930. Worked in the Statistical Service, Minas Gerais, 1929–31. Married Lygia Cabral Pena in 1930; two daughters. Doctor in private practice serving the rural population of Itaguara, Minas Gerais, 1931–32. Volunteered as military medical officer, Belo Horizonte in 1932. Served as a medical officer in the Ninth Infantry Battalion, Barbacena in 1934. In the same year he passed civil service examinations and joined Ministry of Foreign Affairs. Married Aracy Moebius de Carvalho in 1938. Posted to Hamburg as vice-consul in 1938. He was interned briefly in Baden-Baden, following Brazil's entry into World War II, 1942. Secretary for the Brazilian Embassy in Bogotá, Colombia, until 1944. Returned to Brazil and became Director of the Ministry of State's Documentation Service. In 1946 he was secretary of the Brazilian Delegation to the Paris Peace Conference. Secretary-general, Brazilian Delegation to Ninth Pan-American Conference, Bogotá, 1948; principal secretary, Brazilian Embassy, Paris, 1949–51; cabinet head, Ministry of Foreign Affairs, Rio de Janeiro, 1953–58; head of Frontier Demarcation Service, 1962–67. Vice-President, First Latin American Writers Conference, Mexico City, 1967. Awarded the Brazilian Academy of Letters Poetry Prize, 1936; Carmen Dolores Barbosa Prize, 1957; Paula Brito Prize, 1957. Elected to the Brazilian Academy of Letters in 1963. Died 19 November 1967.

Selected Works

Short Fiction

Sagarana, Rio de Janeiro: Universal, 1946; revised edition, 1951; as *Sagarana: a Cycle of Stories*, translated by Harriet de Onís, New York: Knopf, 1966

Corpo de baile: sete novelas (contains *Manuelzão e Miguilim*; *No Urubuquaquá, no Pinhém*; *Noites do sertão*) 2 vols, Rio de Janeiro: José Olympio, 1956; 3 vols, Rio de Janeiro, 1964–66

Primeiras estórias, Rio de Janeiro: José Olympio, 1962; as *The Third Bank of the River and Other Stories*, translated by Barbara Shelby, New York: Knopf, 1968

Os sete pecados capitais, with others, Rio de Janeiro: Editora Civilização Brasileira, 1964 [novellas]

Campo geral, Rio de Janeiro: Sociedade dos Cem Bibliófilos do Brasil, 1964

Tumaméia: terceiras estórias, Rio de Janeiro: José Olympio, 1967

Estas estórias, Rio de Janeiro: José Olympio, 1969

Ave, palavra, Rio de Janeiro: José Olympio, 1970 [poetry and prose]

Contos, edited by Heitor Megale and Marilena Matsuola, São Paulo: Nacional, 1978

Novel

Grande sertão: veredas, Rio de Janeiro: José Olympio, 1956; as *The Devil to Pay in the Backlands*, translated by James L. Taylor and Harriet de Onís, New York: Knopf, 1963

Further Reading

Coutinho, Eduardo de Faria (editor), *Guimarães Rosa*, Rio de Janeiro: Civilização Brasileira, 1991

Daniel, Mary L., *João Guimarães Rosa: travessia literária*, Rio de Janeiro: José Olympio, 1968

Filho, Adonias, *et al.*, *Guimarães Rosa*, Lisbon: Instituto Luso-Brasileiro, 1969

Guimarães Rosa, João, *Em memória de João Guimarães Rosa*, Rio de Janeiro: José Olympio, 1968

Leonel, M. da Graça, *Guimarães Rosa alquimista: processo de criação do texto*, São Paulo: Universidad de São Paulo, 1985

Rodríguez Monegal, Emir, "En busca de Guimarães Rosa," *Mundo Nuevo*, vol. 20/4–24 (1968)

Santos, Wendel, *A construção do romance em Guimarães Rosa*, São Paulo: Ática, 1978

Vincent, Jon S., *João Guimarães Rosa*, Boston: Twayne, 1978

Xisto, Pedro, Augusto de Campos and Haroldo de Campos, *Guimarães Rosa em três dimensões*, São Paulo: Conselho Estadual de Cultura, 1970

Grande sertão: veredas

Novel by João Guimarães Rosa

The work of Guimarães Rosa could be considered as the culmination of some of the most important trends of Brazilian literature. There is no doubt that his fiction portrays the "sertão dos gerais." This consists of the inland part of his native state of Minas Gerais, the one that neighbours the states of Goiás in the west and Bahía in the north, and the human plethora that inhabits this region, especially the *vaqueiros and jagunços* (cowboys and bandits). Guimarães Rosa's work is considered as a documentary of cultural habits, social practices, and dialects, as well as a farewell to a traditional and rural Brazil about to disappear.

But the landscape in Guimarães Rosa transcends the documentary dimension, as it is charged with metaphysical, symbolic and magical connotations. The two banks of the São Francisco river, for instance, delimitate two contrasting dimensions of human experience. It becomes an axis in the *sertão* while making it equal to the world itself (e.g., *Sertão-Mundo*).

In this sense, Guimarães Rosa's work is a tributary of the Brazilian regionalist novel, but it also surpasses this tradition, by giving to the picturesque detailed notations of the environment a universal and philosophical weight in which the most common dramas of human kind are enacted.

Also visible in Guimarães Rosa is the heritage of baroque language and the point of arrival of a baroque tradition within Brazilian literature. Guimarães Rosa explored the potentialities and the limits of the Portuguese language, by incorporating words from other languages (he spoke six and could read in fourteen other languages), revitalizing disused terms and expressions, utilizing the "dialects" of the backlands, creating neologisms, experimenting with alliterations, and forging new syntactical connections. The final result is that his diction is a trademark. Hard to imitate and impossible to translate without a considerable loss of its poetic force, it requires an effort of recreation into the target language. He turns Portuguese inside out, confers on it a new expressive stature, and liberates language, in his own words, "from the mountains of ashes under which it lay."

But the care taken with language reaches beyond the aesthetic and the ludic in that, for Guimarães Rosa, language possesses a metaphysical dimension. To quote the title of a famous story of his, all of Rosa's rivers have "three banks." Words have their own "third bank." Guimarães Rosa sees language as a weapon in the defence of human dignity. By renovating language, the world is renovated. The sense of life may be recovered via a reconstruction of language whereby the latter has restored to it its naming and creative power, the original act of *poiesis* by which being is founded through the word. Concomitantly, Guimarães Rosa rejects Cartesian rationality in favour of a greater role for intuition, revelation, inspiration, enchantment, and magic. As a consequence, there is a rejection of certain weaknesses of Western thought and its reliance on binary oppositions: reason versus emotion, good versus evil, and so on. Rosa shows how "everything is and nothing is," how each thing carries within it its own contrary, and how the "third bank" may be seen as a privileged space, a Utopian territory in which contradictions are abolished. Neither this bank nor that bank and both at the same time, the "third bank" is the place where the subject wanders, where he explores the different-same waters of the river of life, free from the confines of temporality.

A recent study has added another aspect to this discussion, by affiliating Guimarães Rosa to the post-structuralist debate: according to Avelar (1994), in Rosa oppositions are problematized, but they are not resolved in a synthesis; instead, they are called upon to be in a constant contradictory and paradoxical tension. In other words, meaning is always deferred. In this regard, it may well be said that his writing goes against the mainstream of patriarchal writing, inasmuch as it decentres and problematizes meaning.

All the above remarks suit perfectly *Grande sertão: veredas*, the 460-page saga of Riobaldo Tatarana through the *sertão*, nurtured by his quest for the existence of the devil and for the meaningfulness of his life. An *ex-jagunço*, now a landowner, the narrator tells, in a long monologue, to an educated listener (who never replies explicitly, his reactions being understood by the protagonist's discourse), the story of his life, his love for Diadorim, the difficulties of overcoming the *Liso do Sussuarão* (a sort of hell), his fights on the side of Zé Bebelo and against Hermógenes, an incarnation of evil, until he himself becomes Chief Urutù Branco. A poor translation of this incredible mosaic could reduce it to the level of a simple Western: adventures in the backlands of Brazil. But there is a parade of good and evil, life and death, love and hate, doubts and certainties, and a number of pairs that portray the human struggle in search of its ultimate meaning. All this is permeated by the attraction between Riobaldo and Diadorim. It is easy to imagine the transgressive quality of such love, since we are among *jagunços*, for whom manhood is an unquestionable matter of honour. But, at the end, Diadorim, murdered in a duel, reveals his true female identity. Perhaps paying tribute to the conservative nature of Brazilian society, *Grande sertão* steps back from the issue of homosexuality.

Not many socio-critical studies on *Grande sertão* are available. It is hard to ascertain to what extent the novel underscores or installs a rupture with the patriarchal and seignorial tradition that prevails in most of Brazilian literature. Maybe this question also has its "third bank." In this case, the novel is both rupture and allegiance at the same time, and its powerful poeticity relies precisely on this point.

ROBERTO REIS

Editions

First edition: *Grande sertão: veredas*, Rio de Janeiro: José Olympio, 1956

Critical edition: *Grande sertão*, 4th edition, Rio de Janeiro: José Olympio, 1965 [Includes introduction and notes]

Translation: *The Devil to Pay in the Backlands*, by James L. Taylor and Harriet de Onís, New York: Knopf, 1963

Further Reading

Albergaria, Consuelo, *Bruxo da linguagem no "Grande sertão"*, Rio de Janeiro: Tempo Brasileiro, 1977

Avelar, Idelber, "Os paradoxos do vazio e da ausência em *Grande sertão: veredas*," *Brasil/Brazil*, Brown University, vol. 7/11 (1994)

Cândido, Antônio, "O homen do avessos," in his *Tese e antítese*, São Paulo: Nacional, 1964 [Perceptive analysis of this novel]

____ "Jagunços mineiros de Cláudio a Guimarães Rosa," in *Vários escritos*, São Paulo: Duas Cidades, 1970

Coutinho, Eduardo de Faria, *The "Synthesis" Novel in Latin America: a Study of João Guimarães Rosa's "Grande sertão: veredas,"* Chapel Hill: University of North Carolina Press, 1991

Galvão, Walnice Nogueira, *As formas do falso*, São Paulo: Perspectiva, 1972

Lorenz, Günter, "Diálogo com Guimarães Rosa," in *Guimarães Rosa*, edited by Eduardo de Faria Coutinho, Rio de Janeiro/Brasília: Civilização Brasileira/INL, 1983

Perrone, Charles A., "Lyrical Passage(s): Verse, Song and Sense in *Grande sertão: veredas*," *Luso-Brazilian Review* vol. 27 (1990)

Reis, Roberto, "O sertão humano," *Ibero-Amerikanisches Archiv*, vol. 7/4 (1981)

Rosenfield, Kathrin Holzermayr, "*Grande sertão: veredas* – o caos ordenado: à memória dos 25 anos da morte do autor," *Brasil/Brazil* 5-7 (1992)

Utéza, Francis, *João Guimarães Rosa: metafísica do "Grande sertão,"* translated by José Carlos Garbuglio, São Paulo: Universidade de São Paulo, 1994

Special Issues of Journals

Coutinho, Eduardo de Faria (editor), "Guimarães Rosa," *Fortuna Crítica* 6, Rio de Janeiro: Civilização Brasileira, 1983

Ricardo Güiraldes 1886–1927

Argentine prose writer and poet

Ricardo Güiraldes belonged to the Argentine land-owning elite, and he enjoyed all the luxuries of life that it afforded him, including extensive travel abroad. His travels literally took him around the globe, with periodic residency in Paris. His travel experiences are greatly evident in his works, either as direct portrayals of his adventures, or as influenced by foreign literary movements and authors. His status as a privileged member of society initially proved to be somewhat of a hindrance to him as an author: neither Güiraldes nor his early works were considered to be of any lasting value. Rather than being received as a serious author, he was more often criticized for being a member of the wealthy elite who could afford the luxury of dabbling in literature, for which he had little talent. Güiraldes would eventually align himself both ideologically and artistically with the Florida group of writers, whose members included Jorge Luis Borges, Leopoldo Marechal and Oliverio Girondo. The writers of the Florida group concentrated on the creation of a new literary aesthetic that departed from the conventions of *Modernismo*. In contrast to the bourgeois writers of Florida were the more proletarian writers of the Boedo group, who were far more intent on using literature as a social weapon than as an art form. In spite of the difficulties that Güiraldes encountered at first, he was a tireless writer and participant in the Buenos Aires literary scene. While he only published six books during his lifetime, eight more were published posthumously. His complete works include poetry, novels, short stories, journalistic commentaries and other miscellaneous items.

Güiraldes published his first two books in 1915: *El cencerro de cristal* [The Crystal Cow Bell], a collection of poetry and poetic prose, and *Cuentos de muerte y de sangre* [Tales of Death and Blood]. *El cencerro* displays the influence of the

Franco-Uruguayan poets Jules Laforgue and Jules Supervielle, both of whom Güiraldes admired greatly. Both books were received poorly by the critics and the public alike, either meeting with complete indifference or outright disdain. The negative reaction to *El cencerro de cristal* caused Güiraldes in anguish to throw the remaining copies down the well at La Porteña, the family ranch. The volume contains forty-six pieces divided into five sections. The common theme is Nature, through rural descriptions, tales and sketches in which the author mixes impressionistic compositions with humor and irony. The poems are largely simplistic and lack both poetic depth and artistic creativity. None the less, the volume offers insights into Güiraldes's early stages of writing. The stories included in *Cuentos de muerte y de sangre* – some of which were first published in periodicals such as *Plus Ultra* and *Caras y Caretas* [Faces and Masks] – follow a more folkloric vein in that they are meant to be read or told as camp-fire stories. Furthermore, many are not solely of Güiraldes's own invention, but rather come from oral tradition. Events and figures from Argentine history are either alluded to or directly mentioned in the tales. In the story "Al rescoldo" [Huddled around the Embers], the figure of Don Segundo Sombra (protagonist of the famous novel by Güiraldes of the same name) first appears taking on his role as a master story-teller. Many of the stories revolve around instances of extreme violence and/or death. Following the campfire style stories are a series of other tales grouped under the subtitles "Antítesis" [Antithesis], "Aventuras grotescas" [Grotesque Adventures], four vignettes that are admittedly *cursi* (exaggeratedly emotive) to the point of being preposterous, and "Trilogía cristiana" [Christian Trilogy], three interesting stories that call into question the adherence to religious beliefs.

Raucho: momentos de una juventud contemporánea, 1917 [Raucho: Moments of Contemporary Youth] is a loosely auto-biographical novel that Güiraldes began to write in 1911 while in Paris. Güiraldes referred to *Raucho* as "an autobiography of a diminished self." It contains many events that the author himself experienced in his youth. The narrator recounts his experiences away from home while attending school, the summer vacations spent in the country and, later as an adult, the exotic tales of night life in the exclusive clubs of Paris that many young and wealthy Argentine men enjoyed surrounded by friends, women and frivolous excess. The novel, however, revolves primarily around the virtues of the land, in particular the Argentine pampa. *Raucho* is essentially a Romantic text by virtue of the focus on idyllic rural scenes, the valorization of a telluric force, and the purity of the pampa; likewise, the portrayal of the city as destructive and debilitating. The negative effects of the city experienced as a young boy attending school in Buenos Aires or as an adult in Paris, a city that literally causes Raucho to fall ill, are placed in direct contrast with the country and the healing properties of Nature. The pampa not only offers physical health, but more importantly soothes the soul and nurtures spiritual well-being. *Raucho* is not a significant contribution to Güiraldes's works, mainly because of the rather simplistic view it presents by way of an un-polished narrative style. Nevertheless, the text offers an early example of the themes and technique that the author later perfected in his masterpiece, *Don Segundo Sombra* (see essay below). *Raucho* represents a concerted effort by Güiraldes to create a specifically Argentine text that attempts to define the national character as pertaining to creole tradition.

Rosaura, a novella, continues many of the same romantic tendencies that were put forth in *Raucho*. The text first appeared under the title *Un idilio de estación* [A Seasonal Idyll] in the 3 May, 1918 issue of *El Cuento Ilustrado*, a literary publication edited by Horacio Quiroga. Güiraldes republished the work as a separate volume under the title *Rosaura* in 1922. However, the dedication to his sister Lolita, indicates that it was completed in 1914. The plot is quite simple and highly sentimental in its depiction of events that unfold on the site of the train depot of a small town on the pampas. The progression of the plot corresponds to the seasons of the year. The author again pits the deceiving pretentiousness of city life against the simplicity of a rural existence. A principal and recurring symbol throughout the narration is the train that for Rosaura represents change and progress, as well as introducing adventure into the monotony of small-town life. It is also the agent of the innocent young protagonist's destruction since Rosaura falls desperately in love with a stranger who arrives by train one day. The stranger, Carlos Ramallo, turns out to be a wealthy landowner who attends a ball where he dances with Rosaura. She allows her imagination to create an elaborate future with Carlos, but then discovers that it can never be. While in a hysterical emotional state, Rosaura meets her tragic end beneath the wheels of the train. There is a marked change in Güiraldes's prose style in *Rosaura* in that the tone and discourse are much more sentimental. The author employs more delicate adjectives to create exquisitely lacy descriptions, and seems deliberately to avoid the use of more masculine expressions. For example, there is an obvious absence of discourse related to gaucho practices and earthy or rustic customs.

Xaimaca is considered to be one of the best novels written by Güiraldes, excluding *Don Segundo Sombra*. In 1916–17 Güiraldes travelled to the West Indies with his wife Adelina del Carril and another couple during which time he took extensive notes that later became the novel which he completed in 1919 and published in 1923. *Xaimaca* is structured around three separate narrative segments. The first is in the form of a travelogue in which the narrator provides lengthy descriptions of travel itineraries that record the journey's progress from Buenos Aires to Mendoza, across the Andes mountains to Chile, from Valparaíso to Panama, on to Jamaica, and finally Cuba. The second part recounts the experiences of the travellers during the trip. The third segment establishes the novelistic plot involving the romance of Marcos Galván, the narrator, and Clara Ordóñez, which blooms rapidly, only to be suddenly disrupted by Clara's brother. The novel is the most lyrical of all Güiraldes's writings, and it is extremely impressionistic in its style and use of language. The novel displays a more polished discursive technique than in previous works, indicative of the author's maturation as a narrator.

Following the death of Güiraldes, his wife sent two manuscripts, both collections of her husband's poetry, to the publisher Colombo. The result was the publication in 1928 of *Poemas solitarios* [Solitary Poems], written between 1921 and 1927, and *Poemas místicos* [Mystic Poems]. *Poemas solitarios* is a collection of twelve poems of intensely reflective content. *Poemas místicos* is comprised of only seven poems of a prominently religious nature in relation to death. Jorge Luis Borges has commented that the poems are seemingly a "dialogue between Ricardo Güiraldes, a creole gentleman, and Jesus Christ." *El sendero* [The Path] published in 1932 in Holland is a collection of short observations, commentaries and meditations that the author wrote down on cards. These personal notes were never meant for publication, but they provide an insight into the author's feelings and emotions and reveal many of his motivations and influences. *Pampa* is a minor collection of six poetic compositions that reveal Güiraldes's attachment to the land and environment that were central to his writing. *Pampa* was published in 1954 with a preface by Horacio Becco. The volume of his complete works, *Obras completas* (1962) is an invaluable collection of the author's writings. It includes not only his literary texts, but also the notes, commentaries, and letters that Güiraldes exchanged with many of his contemporaries.

DARRELL B. LOCKHART

Biography

Born in Buenos Aires, Argentina, 13 February 1886. Member of landowning oligarchy. Spoke French before Castilian. Learned to play the guitar at a very young age. Preferred life on the pampas to school work. Finished secondary education in 1904 and entered Faculty of Architecture at University of Buenos Aires. Travelled to Paris in 1910 where he stayed until 1912. Married Adelina del Carril in 1913: considered a suitable (and successful) match. Travelled with friends to the Caribbean via Chile in 1916. Returned to Paris in 1919. Began to write *Don Segundo Sombra* in Paris in late 1920; published it in new wave literary journal, *Martín Fierro*. In 1923 he founded his own publication, *Proa* [Prow] which lasted two years. Hogkin's disease diagnosed in 1926, the year which saw the publication of *Don Segundo Sombra*. Güiraldes amazed by novel's success. Awarded National Prize for Literature in the same year. Last journey to Paris in March 1927. Died in Paris, 8 October 1927.

Selected Works

Short Fiction

Cuentos de muerte y de sangre; Aventuras grotescas; Trilogía cristiana, Buenos Aires: Librería La Facultad, 1915
Seis relatos, Buenos Aires: Proa, 1929

Novels

Raucho: momentos de una juventud contemporánea, Buenos Aires: Librería La Facultad, 1917
Rosaura, San Antonio de Areco, Argentina: Establecimiento Gráfico Colón, 1922 [novella]
Xaimaca, Buenos Aires: Agencia General de Librería y Publicaciones, 1923
Don Segundo Sombra, Buenos Aires: Proa, 1926; as *Don Segundo Sombra*, translated by Patricia Owen Steiner, Pittsburgh: University of Pittsburgh Press, 1994

Poetry

El cencerro de cristal, Buenos Aires: Librería La Facultad, 1915
Poemas místicos, San Antonio de Areco, Argentina: Establecimientos Gráficos Colón, 1928
Poemas solitarios, San Antonio de Areco: Establecimientos Gráficos Colón, 1928
Pampa, Buenos Aires: Ollantay, 1954

Other Writings

El sendero: notas sobre mi evolución espiritualista en vista de un futuro, Maastricht, Holland: A.A.M. Stols, 1932 [limited edition]
Semblanza de nuestro país, Mar del Plata: Talleres de la Escuela de Artes Gráficas "Pablo Tavelli," 1972

Compilations and Anthologies

Obras completas, edited by Juan José Güiraldes and Augusto Mario Delfino, Buenos Aires: Emecé, 1962
Don Segundo Sombra. Prosas y poemas, edited by Alberto Blasi and Luis Harss, Caracas: Biblioteca Ayacucho, 1983

Further Reading

Ara, Guillermo, *Ricardo Güiraldes*, Buenos Aires: La Mandrágora, 1961
Battistessa, Ángel José, *Ricardo Güiraldes: en la huella espiritual y expresiva de un argentino (1886–1986)*, Buenos Aires: Corregidor, 1987
Bordelois, Ivonne, *Genio y figura de Ricardo Güiraldes*, Buenos Aires: Eudeba, 1967
Curet de De Anda, Miriam, *El sistema expresivo de Ricardo Güiraldes*, Río Piedras: Editorial Universitaria, Universidad de Puerto Rico, 1976
Ghiano, Juan Carlos, *Ricardo Güiraldes*, Buenos Aires: Pleamar, 1966
Liberal Villar, José R., *Vida y obra de Ricardo Güiraldes: ensayo y antología*, Buenos Aires: Corregidor, 1980
Pastoriza de Etchebarne, Dora, *Elementos románticos en las novelas de Ricardo Güiraldes*. Buenos Aires: Perrot, 1957
Previtali, Giovanni, *Ricardo Güiraldes and "Don Segundo Sombra": Life and Works*, foreword by Adelina del Carril de Güiraldes, preface by Jorge Luis Borges, New York: Hispanic Institute in the United States, 1963; revised and enlarged Spanish version as *Ricardo Güiraldes: biografía y crítica*, translated from the English by Pablo Max Ynsfran, Mexico City: Andrea, 1965
Soler Canas, Luis M., *Güiraldes y su tierra*, Buenos Aires: Castaneda, 1977

Special Issues of Journals

Chasqui, vol. 6/2 (1977) [Special issue dedicated to Güiraldes on the fiftieth anniversary of his death]

Don Segundo Sombra

Novel by Ricardo Güiraldes

Ricardo Güiraldes published his novel *Don Segundo Sombra* in 1926. Some seven years in the writing, it was his most accomplished work, earning him the prestigious National Literature award and marking the culmination of his career as a writer. On its release, the novel received the enthusiastic praise of such authors as Leopoldo Lugones (who had been ruthlessly critical in his dismissal of Güiraldes's early works) and Jorge Luis Borges, along with other members of the Florida literary clan. *Don Segundo Sombra* quite literally became an instant classic of Argentine literature. Since its initial publication the novel has enjoyed innumerable reprintings, is used as an essential text in virtually all Argentine schools, has been translated into more than ten languages (including Yiddish and Czech), and was made into a motion picture in 1969 by Manuel Antín.

Don Segundo Sombra is structurally and thematically a Bildungsroman, that is, a narrative about individual development. In this respect it resembles Rudyard Kipling's novel *Kim*, to which it was compared by Borges. It is narrated in the first person by an adult narrator who nostalgically reminisces about the character-shaping events of his life. As a young orphan, Fabio Cáceres is taken under the tutelage of a much older and wiser mentor in the character of Don Segundo Sombra, the gaucho who guides Fabio through his apprenticeship on the rugged pampas and his initiation into manhood. The title character in the novel was loosely based on Segundo Ramírez, a ranch hand employed during Güiraldes's youth on the family *estancia* (cattle ranch). *Don Segundo Sombra* tells the tale of Fabio's voyage of transformation from the abandoned *guacho* (orphaned animal or illegitimate child) to the noble gaucho. The twenty-seven chapters of the novel are divided equally into a tripartite narrative structure that encompasses the three major time periods in the protagonist's life. The first section is dedicated to the boy's adolescent adventures in the small town where he has been left to live with his two aunts. The second describes in detail his association with Don Segundo Sombra, his progress towards becoming a man, a gaucho, and also his interest, to a certain degree, in the social and cultural aspects of life. In the third and final section, now a hardened gaucho, he learns the identity of his father, upon whose death he inherits both land and responsibility, neither of which he initially wants to accept since it would also mean the end of his freedom. In the end, however, Fabio foregoes the gaucho lifestyle to take on the responsibilities of his inheritance. Nevertheless, the character ends up with the best of both worlds; he has the heart and virtues of the gaucho and the wealth and power of an *estanciero*, most likely indicative of how Güiraldes viewed his own position. The novel is rich in detailed depictions of life on the cattle ranches, the various tasks of the ranch hands and the customs of the country folk, as well as lengthy descriptions of the awesome beauty and power of Nature.

Don Segundo Sombra contains far less of the flowery language, rhetorical ramblings and ornamentalism that characterized his earlier works. Nevertheless, the novel is highly lyrical in nature and the influence of Asian thought and culture (which Güiraldes studied in some depth) is evident in the subtle mysticism expressed not only through the characters, but also in the lengthy descriptions of the land. However, what is most evident about the work is that it directly reflects the general sociopolitical milieu of Argentina in the 1920s, from the perspective of the oligarchy. *Don Segundo Sombra* is an allegory of the country, detailing its past and prescribing a future based on telluric ideals. The text presents the basic perception that a redemption of Argentine identity – viewed as being seriously threatened by the large influx of various immigrant groups – must be based on a return to the values of Argentina's rural past. While the text is in essence an elegiac farewell to a way of life that, in fact, had disappeared several decades before, Güiraldes proposes that Argentines can retain many aspects of that life. Without a doubt, *Don Segundo Sombra* presents a highly romanticized version of the gaucho way of life, one that had disappeared by the time Güiraldes published his novel. It presents the positive aspects of the ranch hands' work, while negating the very destruction of the gaucho way of life brought about by the landed aristocracy to which Güiraldes belonged. This view is patently obvious in the char-

acter of Don Segundo Sombra himself. He is truly a shadowy figure, an anachronistic ghost from the past who was in actuality "más una idea que un hombre" (more an idea than a man). Don Segundo Sombra is the quintessential gaucho, the summation of all the heroes of the gauchesque literary tradition lionized by such authors as Hilario Ascasubi (1807–75), José Hernández (1834–86), Bartolomé Mitre (1821–1906) and Leopoldo Lugones (1874–1938). But *Don Segundo Sombra* also fits nicely into a much larger literary scheme in formation at the time throughout Latin America; that of the so-called "novela de la tierra" (novel of the land). In *Don Segundo Sombra* and other similar novels of the period like *La vorágine* (*The Vortex*) by Colombian José Eustasio Rivera (1889–1928) and *Doña Bárbara* by Venezuelan Rómulo Gallegos (1884–1969), the land is perhaps the principal protagonist of the text. These authors all sought to portray the land as having a life force of its own, capable of influencing or directly acting upon those who chose to inhabit the vast expanses of prairie or dense jungle from which seemed to emanate a spiritual energy, which can either make the human protagonists stronger and wiser, or lead them to their destruction. In the case of *Don Segundo Sombra*, the harshness as well as the beauty of the land play an active role in shaping the physical and spiritual development of the young character into a man. The idyllic symbiotic relationship of man to Nature is personified in the larger-than-life figure of Don Segundo Sombra.

Don Segundo Sombra is decidedly conservative in its justification of the privileged position of the oligarchy, politically charged in its anti-Liberal commentaries, and it is highly xenophobic in its portrayal of immigrants. In principle, the novel spoke eloquently to a wide audience of Argentines, who in the 1920s were experiencing drastic changes in the political and social physiognomy of the country, and many of whom felt that Argentina was changing for the worse. A return to the idyllic rural setting (much more a myth than reality), the rejection of modern urban living, and the recovery of rapidly vanishing creole values, traditions, and in particular hegemony, were seen as the solution to the growing pains the country was experiencing. *Don Segundo Sombra* is very much a text about men, masculinity and the continuity of patriarchal ideals. Furthermore, it is exceedingly misogynistic in its treatment of the female characters, almost all of whom are considered to be contemptible, irrelevant as human beings, or threatening to the freedom of men. The only young female character who is not associated with denigrating qualities perhaps suffers an even greater humiliation. Aurora, the young girl with whom Fabio has a romantic liaison, is nothing more than a symbol of his initiation into manhood, whereby rape is implicitly justified as necessary for the maturation of the male. Undercurrents of machismo, violence, authoritarianism and eroticism, all revolving around power struggles and death, permeate the narration. Homosocial relations between the male characters have also been the focus of contemporary interpretations of the novel (cf. Christopher Leland).

Despite modern readings that are quick to identify the often facile political motivations that underlie the narrative, *Don Segundo Sombra* continues to be valued for its outstanding literary merit. Güiraldes is most often associated with the Latin American avant-garde writers. Likewise, *Don Segundo Sombra* is one of the most representative and original novels of the period. However, the novel does not adhere strictly to a definition of the avant-garde because it does not incorporate the striking experimentalism and metaphoric expression characteristic of this movement. Güiraldes created a gaucho narrative that effectively portrayed an image of the national character long sought after. *Don Segundo Sombra* was one of the first texts to incorporate successfully authentic rural speech into a prose work that was artistically sound. Rural popular culture also predominates in several instances in the form of the musical couplets of the *payadores* (gaucho minstrels) that are bantered among the gauchos. Rural folklore is transmitted through Don Segundo Sombra, an accomplished story teller, through whom Güiraldes intercalates two folktales into the narration (chapters 12 and 21). The novel is replete with numerous *costumbrista* sketches of rural life, characters and nature, all of which are designed to endear the reader to the virtues of the pampas. The psychological development of the protagonists, by which the message of the exalted gaucho heritage is transmitted, comprises the prime motivation of the narrative. Through *Don Segundo Sombra* Güiraldes proposed a characterization of collective Argentine identity based on creole tradition, language and customs within a highly stylized narrative structure. The adult Fabio Cáceres who retells the experiences that formed him as a youth, does so with refined language and sophisticated modes of expression foreign to the gaucho, lending a sense of lyrical realism to the narrative that in fact consists of a false poetic portrayal of the real nature of gaucho life. None the less, the novel has stood the test of time as a work of art, continuing to attract readership and criticism both nationally and internationally. When praised for his work, Güiraldes proudly exclaimed "we have all written *Don Segundo Sombra*. It was in us, and we are elated to have it in print."

DARRELL B. LOCKHART

See also entries on José Hernández and *Martín Fierro*, Regionalism: Spanish America

Editions

First edition: *Don Segundo Sombra*, Buenos Aires: Proa, 1926
Critical edition and translation: *Don Segundo Sombra*, translated by Patricia Owen Steiner and edited by Gwen Kirkpatrick, Pittsburgh: University of Pittsburgh Press, 1995 [There is an earlier translation by Harriet de Onís: New York: Farrar and Rinehart, 1935. There are also other critical editions]

Further Reading

Alonso, Carlos J., *The Spanish American Regional Novel: Modernity and Autochthony*, Cambridge and New York: Cambridge University Press, 1990 [Chapters 2 and 3 refer to this novel]
Dellepiane, Ángela B., introduction to her critical edition of *Don Segundo Sombra*, Madrid; Castalia, 1990
Donahue, John, *Don Segundo Sombra y El Virginiano: gaucho y cowboy*, Madrid: Pliegos, 1987
Leland, Christopher Towne, "The Failure of Myth: Ricardo Güiraldes and *Don Segundo Sombra*," in his *The Last Happy Men: The Generation of 1922, Fiction, and the Argentine Reality*, Syracuse, New York: Syracuse University Press, 1986
Liberal Villar, José R. *"Don Segundo Sombra" de Ricardo Güiraldes: motivaciones y análisis literario*, Buenos Aires: F.A. Colombo, 1969
Pinto, Luis C., *"Don Segundo Sombra," sus críticos y el idioma*, 2nd revised and augmented edition, Buenos Aires: Nueva Vida, 1956
Rodríguez Alcalá, Hugo, *Quince ensayos*, Asunción, Paraguay: Criterio, 1987 [Contains three relevant chapters: on *Doña Bárbara* and *Don Segundo Sombra*; Jorge Luis Borges's opinion of this novel and, a third, on Güiraldes in the context of the intellectual ambience of the period]

Ferreira Gullar 1930–

Brazilian poet

Few Latin American poets of the 20th century have created such exceptional works as those of Ferreira Gullar. Among living Brazilian poets he has no equal. Vinícius de Moraes claimed that Gullar is the last great Brazilian poet, and Sérgio Buarque de Holanda wrote in *Toda poesia* that the only other modern Brazilian author of comparable greatness is João Guimarães Rosa, a writer of prose fiction.

Most Brazilians know Ferreira Gullar best as the author of *Poema sujo*, 1976 (*Dirty Poem*). Many others know him also for a career that spans decades of self-reflective innovation and endeavor not only as a poet but also as a playwright, journalist and art critic. In retrospect, he wrote much of what preceded *Poema sujo* in unknowing preparation for what was

to become his most important work. For instance, *A luta corporal*, 1954 [The Body's Struggle], reveals much of the ideological and esthetic framework of *Poema sujo*.

Gullar grew up in São Luís, Maranhão, in one of the poorest states of Brazil where large land holdings sustain a near feudal relationship between the rich and the poor. Some poems from *A luta corporal*, such as "As peras" [The Pears], suggest the injustice and inexorable decay implicit in a socio-economic system with a medieval taint. And other poems from the same book reflect his pursuit of what he calls "essential poetry." This is poetry that he sees as existing outside of the bounds of preconceived form and that subverts normal syntax, as well as linguistic and literary conventions. In *Indagações de hoje*

[Inquiries about Today] Gullar cited an example of this: "Cerne claro, cousa / aberta; / na paz da tarde ateia, bran- / co, / o seu incêndio." (Pallid heartwood, solid / open; / in the peace of the afternoon fans, white- / hot, / your fire).

In the early 1960s Gullar joined the *Centro Popular de Cultura* [Popular Culture Center] a leftist popular arts organization. This provoked an esthetic revolution for Gullar, and he began writing folk ballads, a learned version of the traditional *literatura de cordel*. He hoped not only to reach another audience but also to discover a purity of expression unlike his earlier approach to "essential poetry." Although his involvement in this organization was short-lived, his demotic commitment had the effect of altering his awareness of society and its relation to art.

Shortly after the military coup of 1964, the police closed the Popular Culture Center, and Gullar with others formed a theater company called *Grupo Opinião* (Opinion Group). From this association he became subject to searches, and in 1968 he was jailed for a time. In 1970 Gullar went into hiding, and in 1971 he left the country and began a six-year period of exile.

By 1975 he had published *Dentro da noite veloz* [Within the Rapid Night], with a stance more confrontational than anything that had preceded it. "Poema brasileiro" [Brazilian Poem], for instance, addresses the problem of infant mortality, "Não há vagas" [Not Hiring] notes the crushing weight of an inhumane economic system, "Exílio" continues his exposé of Brazilian living conditions, and "Maio 1964" [May 1964] reflects some of the horror and fear that he has felt: "Estou aqui. O espelho / não guardará a marca deste rosto, / se simplesmente saio do lugar / ou se morro / se me matam. / Estou aqui e não estarei, um dia, / em parte alguma." (I am here. The mirror / will not hold the image of this face, / if I just move from this spot / or if I die / or if they murder me. / I am here but some day / will not be anywhere).

By 1975, Gullar had little hope that he would ever see his family again. He felt it was time to assess his life and circumstances, and, in response, he composed his long, autobiographical *Poema sujo*. In combination with the esthetic and thematic content reminiscent of his previous works, the powerful intimacy and sense of desperation in *Poema sujo* galvanized a generation. It opens with a conspicuous reference to Gullar's experimental verse of the 1950s. Where he would earlier work with the deep, dark sounds and associations of the blue sea in his neo-*concretista* period, and where he would earlier subvert clarity and convention to elicit a desired sensation as he was seeking the "essential poem," on the first page of *Poema sujo* he returns to the style of his earlier work:

turvo turvo / a turva / mão do sopro / contra o muro / escuro / menos menos / menos que escuro / menos que mole e duro menos que fosso e muro: menos que furo / escuro / mais que escuro: / claro / como água? como pluma? claro mais que claro claro: coisa alguma / e tudo / (ou quase) / um bicho que o universo fabrica e vem sonhando desde as entranhas / azul / era o gato / azul / era o galo / azul / o cavalo / azul / teu cu."

[muddled muddled / the muddled / hand of the wind / against the wall / dull / less less / less than dull / less than supple and stable less than a well and a wall: less

than a hole / dull / more than dull / bright / like water? like a feather? bright more than bright right: nothing at all / and all / (or nearly all) / a creature sired by the universe has been dreaming from its belly / blue / the cat / blue / the cock / blue / the colt / blue / your bum.]

Toward autobiographical completeness, he has begun at his watery beginning, suggesting the "essential" moment of his conception.

Tracing the events of his life, the poem moves from sequences of recall to moments of introspection. As it evolves, it gathers focus, clarity and detail and tells stories of innocence and experience in a poetic account of all that he judged formative. And, while the poem began with reliance on the ephemeral suggestiveness of words, it concludes with a sharply articulated statement on his exile: "a cidade está no homem / quase como a árvore voa / no pássaro que a deixa / cada coisa está em outra / de sua própria maneira / e de maneira distinta / de como está em si mesma / a cidade não está no homem / do mesmo modo que em suas / quitandas praças e ruas". (A city is in a man / almost as a tree flies / in the bird that drops it / everything is in another / in its own / and different way / of being in itself / a city is not in a man / the way it is in these / plazas streets and trees).

By the time Gullar published *Na vertigem do dia*, 1980 [In the Dizziness of Daylight], he had passed the crisis that had precipitated the writing of *Poema sujo*, but many of the concerns he had remained with him. His magnificent "Bananas podres" [Rotten Bananas] strongly recalls his autobiographical work. In certain ways it surpasses and fills out the portions of *Poema sujo* to which it corresponds, as do other autobiographical elements that also appear in this collection.

Barulhos [Noises], published in 1987, reveals a subtle shift in his perspective. Where many of his works have focused on his past and on particularly outrageous conditions and events, *Barulhos* takes a look at death and at the way that the ones we most love keep slipping from our reach. In this vein, he gives clear voice to the classical *ubi sunt* motif in "Onde estão?" [Where Are They?]: "Mas e os mortos, / onde estão? / O Vinícius, por exemplo, / e o Hélio? a Clarice?" (But the dead, / where are they? / Vinícius, for example, / and Hélio? Clarice?). And, although in both his life and works political militancy has receded in recent years, his sympathies and solidarity remain clearly expressed in this book, as well as in other writing, for those who have tried to change the world through political word and action.

LELAND GUYER

Biography

Born José Ribamar Ferreira in São Luís, Maranhão, Brazil in 1930. Married Theresa Aragão, three children. Lived in Rio de Janeiro, 1951–71. Worked mainly as a poet, journalist and art critic, his life has had a strong political engagement. Joined the Brazilian Communist Party in 1964; arrested for political reasons, 1968. In 1970 he began a year of clandestine existence. Left Brazil, 1971, and lived in exile in Buenos Aires, Lima, Santiago and Moscow. Returned to Brazil in 1977 and has been living in Rio de Janeiro since this time.

Selected Works

Poetry

Um pouco acima do chão, São Luís do Maranhão: privately printed, 1949
A luta corporal, Rio de Janeiro: Civilização Brasileira, 1954
Poemas, Rio de Janeiro: Edições Espaço, 1958
João Boa-Morte, cabra marcado p'ra morrer, Rio de Janeiro: CPC-UNE, 1962
Quem matou Aparecida? Rio de Janeiro: CPC-UNE, 1962
A luta corporal e novos poemas, Rio de Janeiro: José Álvaro, 1966
Dentro da noite veloz, Rio de Janeiro: Civilização Brasileira, 1975
Poema sujo, Rio de Janeiro: Civilização Brasileira, 1976; as *Dirty Poem/Poema sujo*, edited and translated by Leland Guyer, Lanham, Maryland: University Press of America, 1990
Egberto Gismonti, Rio de Janeiro: Som Livre, 1979
Na vertigem do dia, Rio de Janeiro: Civilização Brasileira, 1980
Barulhos, Rio de Janeiro: José Olympio, 1987
O formigueiro, Rio de Janeiro: Europa, 1991

Plays

A saída? Onde fica a saída? Rio de Janeiro: Grupo Opinião, 1967
Dr. Getúlio, sua vida e sua glória, Rio de Janeiro: Civilização Brasileira, 1968
Um rubi no umbigo, Rio de Janeiro: Civilização Brasileira, 1979
Se correr o bicho pega, se ficar o bicho come, Rio de Janeiro: Civilização Brasileira, 1981

Other Writings

Teoria do não-objeto, Rio de Janeiro: Edição SDJB, 1959
Cultura posta em questão, Rio de Janeiro: Civilização Brasileira, 1964
"A obra aberta e a filosofia da praxis," *Revista Civilização Brasileira*, vol. 21/22 (1968)
Vanguarda e subdesenvolvimento: ensaios sobre arte, Rio de Janeiro: Civilização Brasileira, 1969
Arte brasileira hoje, Rio de Janeiro: Paz e Terra, 1973
Uma luz do chão, Rio de Janeiro: Editora Avenir, 1978
Sobre arte, Rio de Janeiro: Avenir Editora and Palavra e Imagem Editora, 1982
Argumentação contra a morte da arte, Rio de Janeiro: Revan, 1982
Etapas da arte contemporânea: do cubismo ao neo-concretismo, São Paulo: Livraria Nobel, 1985
Crime na flora, Rio de Janeiro: José Olympio, 1986
A estranha vida banal, Rio de Janeiro: José Olympio, 1989
Indagações de hoje, Rio de Janeiro: José Olympio, 1989

Translations

Brazilian Poetry (1950–80), edited by Emanuel Brasil and William Jay Smith, Middletown, Connecticut: Wesleyan University Press, 1983

Compilations and Anthologies

Antologia poética, 4th edition, São Paulo: Summus Editorial, 1979
Antologia poética, recording, read by the author, with musical accompaniment by Egberto Gismonti, Rio de Janeiro: Som Livre, 1979
Toda poesia, edited by Sérgio Buarque de Holanda, Rio de Janeiro: Civilização Brasileira, 1981
Os melhores poemas de Ferreira Gullar, edited by Alfredo Bosi, 2nd edition, Rio de Janeiro: Global Editora, 1985

Further Reading

Alves, Guilherme, "Ferreira Gullar: uma luta corporal com a palavra," *Minas Gerais*, Belo Horizonte, "Suplemento Literário" (26 March 1983)
Aquino Filho, Jorge de, "Os rumos da poesia brasileira, III: Que a poesia brasileira seja variada, rica e generosa," *Minas Gerais*, Belo Horizonte, "Suplemento Literário" (16 April 1983)
Barbosa, Alaor, "*Toda poesia*, de Ferreira Gullar," *Minas Gerais*, Belo Horizonte, "Suplemento Literário" (26 February 1983)
Campos, Paulo Mendes, "Ferreira Gullar: o *Poema sujo*, a pátria distante," *Jornal do Brasil*, Rio de Janeiro (14 August 1976)
Guyer, Leland, "An Interview with Ferreira Gullar," *Discurso Literário* 5 (1987)
_____ "*Poema sujo*: Last Will and Testament," *Selecta* 8 (1987)
Hohlfeldt, A., "Four Modern Brazilian Poets: Moacyr Felix, Ferreira Gullar, Affonso Romano de Santanna, and Carlos Nejar," *Europe, Revue Littéraire Mensuelle* 60 (1982)
Jozef, Bella, "A Review of the 1985 Literary Year in Brazil," *Colóquio: Letras* 90 (1986)
Kern, M.L., "Non-Alignment and Concrete Art in Brazil," *Estudos Ibero-Americanos* 8 (1982)
Kovadloff, Santiago, "Ferreira Gullar: o fogo solidário," translated by Fernando Ribeira Machado, *Encontros com a Civilização Brasileira* 9 (1979)
Merquior, José Guilherme, "A volta do poema," *Jornal do Brasil*, Rio de Janeiro (22 November 1980)
Müller-Bergh, Klaus, "Feijoada, Coke and the Urbanoid: Brazilian Poetry since 1945," *World Literature Today* 53 (1979)
Osiel, M.J., "Going to the People: Popular Culture and the Intellectuals in Brazil," *Archives Europeennes de Sociologie* 25 (1984)
Stelzer, O., "Art Education through Manual Practice," *Zeitschrift fur Asthetik und Allgemeine Kunstwissenschaft* 26 (1981)
Traba, Marta, "The Fine Arts in Latin America: a National Tradition, *Revista Hispanoamericana de Literatura* 8 (1979)
Vilaça, Alcides, "Em torno do *Poema sujo*," *Encontros com a Civilização Brasileira* 9 (1979)

Manuel Gutiérrez Nájera 1859–1895

Mexican poet and journalist

Manual Gutiérrez Nájera, one of Mexico's best-known writers of the 19th century, has traditionally been considered one of four precursors of the Modernist period of Spanish American literature (1875–1925). It was customarily believed that the genesis of *Modernismo* lay in innovations in poetry, thus it was Nájera's poetic production that received the attention of the critics for a long time. In the past few years, however, after careful examination of the modernist writers' prose works, scholars have discovered not only that the first signs of *Modernismo* are to be found in prose, but that Nájera's major contribution to the modernist enterprise were his prose pieces. This self-taught journalist who published his first article when he was only thirteen years old, was responsible for introducing the *crónica* (a prose genre derived from the French *chronique*) in Mexico. Nájera's literary production is divided into three genres: poetry, short fiction, and *crónicas*. An indefatigable writer who spent his entire life working for a multitude of Mexican newspapers and magazines, he is said to have published approximately 1,500 prose pieces under different pseudonyms. Of these, he put together only one collection of short stories in his lifetime: *Cuentos frágiles*, 1883 [Fragile Stories], a landmark in the evolution of the Spanish American short story. Nájera also contributed to the dissemination of *modernista* aesthetics with the publication of articles devoted to art (such as "El arte y el materialismo" [Art and Materialism]) and the foundation, in conjunction with Carlos Díaz Dufóo, of *Revista Azul* (1894), one of the most important *modernista* publications in Latin America. As regards his poetic production, el Duque Job (his favourite pen name) did not assemble his verses in book form; his first collection of poems was published posthumously by friends in 1896. As much in prose as in poetry, among Nájera's major influences were the French Romantics Victor Hugo, Alfred de Musset and Gérard de Nerval, and the Parnassians Leconte de Lisle and José María Heredia. Because of Nájera's love and admiration for the French writers of the period, he was often accused of being a Francophile who demonstrated little interest in national affairs, an accusation, it suffices to say, launched against most Spanish American *modernistas* which was far from the truth.

What credits Nájera with being the first important short-story writer in the Spanish American Modernist period are principally the short stories that appear in *Cuentos frágiles* and the posthumous *Cuentos color de humo*, 1898 [Smoked-Coloured Stories]; thereafter, some eighty-seven other fictional pieces were added to these two collections. The core of his narrative production arises from personal experience plus diverse readings of foreign literature which Nájera was often in the habit of translating and adapting to his own needs. Many of these short stories began as *crónicas* or were inserted in the corpus of a *crónica* in order to make it more entertaining and alive to the public. In consequence, they display the formal aspects of the *crónicas*, like the presence of partially verifiable facts and manifold thematic unities, for instance. The writing of short stories liberated the writer's imagination from the daily constraints of journalism. Nájera's short fiction explores the psychological aspects of human existence, especially those that are located on the opposite pole of the rational, and occasionally delves into the psyche of a character or narrator, as for example in "La balada de Año Nuevo" [New Year's Ballad], the first short story of *Cuentos frágiles*. Plot, in most of these stories, occupies a subsidiary position to the treatment of human emotion. In countless of them the narrator shows a unique affinity for women and defence-less children. Some of his best known short stories are "La mañana de San Juan" [The Morning of St John's Day], "La novela del tranvía" [The Novel of the Streetcar], "Los amores del cometa" [The Loves of the Comet], "Historia de un peso falso [History of a False Peso] and "Juan el organista" [John the Organist]. "La mañana de San Juan" is indubitably his best story. In it the characteristically poetic nature of Nájera's prose serves the purpose of reconstructing a rather dramatic story in which children meet a sad end. In another fine story, "La novela del tranvía," the narrator, a passenger who by means of humorous language imagines the lives of fellow passengers as he observes them carefully, could be said to be the perfect incarnation of *El Duque Job* himself. The emphasis here does not reside either in what the passengers do for a living or in what they look like; what most interests the narrator is their possible thoughts and, most importantly, how he himself reacts to them.

The *crónicas* are undoubtedly the best part of Gutiérrez Nájera's prose production. Given their large quantity as well as their varied scope, it is not easy to reach a coherent definition of this portion of his prose writing. It suffices to say, none the less, that the writer made ample use of the French *chronique* and adapted it comfortably to national aesthetic needs. Each of them constitutes a masterpiece, intelligently and elegantly crafted, but lacking in stylistic unity. Essentially, Nájera's *crónicas* are literary (unlike Martí's, which tend more to the political), not only because many of his short stories proceed from them, but because several are almost indistinguishable from prose poems. The writer did not express a strong interest in politics (even though he was for a time actively involved in them) and hence most of his *crónicas* are devoid of any clear ideological intent, this despite the fact that Nájera was writing at the heights of Porfirio Díaz's long dictatorship. In a number of *crónicas*, however, Nájera does allude to some of the evils that were undermining society, such as unemployment, prostitution and alcoholism; but he never attacked directly the Mexican authorities. Far more important than informing the public was to entertain it with fantasies and exaggerations. Nájera published his *crónicas* under various pseudonyms: Fru-Fru, M. Can-Can, Fritz, Junius, Pomponet, Ignotus, Omega, among others. At the same time, he frequently transposed an isolated section of a *crónica* into another *crónica* through the slight alteration of the original text. Nájera went as far as using texts written by others but publishing them as his own. In the series of *crónicas* entitled "Platos del día [Today's Specials], "Cosas que hacen falta" [Things that Are

Missing] and "Pláticas doctrinales" [Doctrinal Chats], the narrator indulges in the use of humour and satire. Of great quality and sensibility are the uncounted *crónicas* dedicated to dramatic performances, literary essays and social events, composed with a simplicity and elegance worthy of any of the modernist writers that would come after him. Among his last *crónicas* are found two series of seven "sermons" called "Cuaresmas del Duque Job" [Duke Job's Lent], written with a humorous and intelligent language and addressed to women. These "sermons" are characterized by a very personal style: in them, Nájera displays the full scope of his lexical knowledge and writes with a mellifluous rhythm that makes for a very enjoyable reading. In the mid-1990s a significant number of his *crónicas* have yet to be published.

With his poetry, Gutiérrez Nájera declared war on a poetic tradition that had run its course. To accomplish the uprooting task he had no choice but to turn to French literature. Aided especially by Musset, he was able to infuse a breath of fresh air into the tired verse of Spanish America. From Musset and other French Romantics and Parnassians, he learned to set his verses to music and to refine his poetic expression. It has even been claimed that, at least with respect to poetry, Nájera is more of a Romantic than a *modernista*, particularly because the major themes of his verse possess predominantly Romantic overtones and, ultimately, in view of the fact that he did not innovate Spanish metric. In most of his poems he, in effect, uses verses of eight and eleven syllables. It must be underscored that Nájera's Modernism in poetry is demonstrated by his alacrity to create beautiful and colourful objects by means of words; similarly, there is a conscious effort on the part of the poet to resist rhetorical and classical models. As regards the constructing of his verse, Nájera followed, almost to the tee, Wilde's dictums on aesthetics. He wrote poetry from 1875 until the very year of his death. In his youth, his beacons were Bécquer and Campoamor; as time elapsed, Gautier, Mendès, Coppée, and the French writers aforementioned, began to exert their influence on him. Nájera's poetry is marked by an existential angst encountered in all Spanish American *modernistas*; in addition to this , moreover, a permeating and more immediate note of pain and suffering fills his verse. Outstanding representatives of this elegiac phase include "Mis enlutadas" [In Mourning] and "Nada es mío" [Nothing is Mine]. Francisco G. Guerrero divides Nájera's poetic production into various stages: love and religious themes play a key role in the first phase; in this phase there is no novelty in the use of adjectives and images. Later, however, Nájera's poetry begins to display some of Modernism's nascent attributes: heavy utilization of colours, especially white; insertion of French words in his strophes; use of synesthesia; and inclusion of elements of the Catholic rite in preponderately pagan contexts. Among his best poems are "La duquesa Job," 1884 [Duchess Job], "Tristissima nox," 1884 [Saddest Night], "Mariposas," 1887 [Butterflies], "La serenata de Schubert," 1888 [Schubert's Serenata], and "De blanco, 1888 [In White].

J. AGUSTÍN PASTÉN B.

Biography

Born in Mexico City, 22 December 1859. Lived prosaic life. Never travelled abroad and seldom left Mexico City. Travelled, instead, in his imagination. Father a journalist, editor and man of letters. Mother instilled religious fervour into her son. Taught himself to read and write and had lessons from private tutors. Began journalistic career at the age of sixteen. In 1888, appointed deputy to National Congress for Texcoco. Married Cecilia Maillefert with whom he had two daughters: Cecilia and Margarita. Co-founder, with Carlos Diaz Dufóa, of the *Revista Azul* (1894) and director of the newspaper *El Partido Liberal*. In 1895 was elected president of the Associated Press of Mexico, but he died before being able to occupy this post.

Selected Works

Poetry
Poesías, Mexico City: Oficina Impresora del Timbre, 1896
Poesías completas, prologue by Francisco González Guerrero, Mexico City: Porrúa, 1966

Short Fiction and Sketches (*crónicas*)
Cuentos frágiles, Mexico City: Biblioteca Honrada, 1883
Hojas sueltas, prologue by Carlos Díz Dufóo, Mexico City: Antigua Imprenta de Murguía, 1912
Cuentos color de humo y Cuentos frágiles, Madrid: América, 1920
Obras inéditas. Crónicas de "Puck," selected by E.K. Mapes, New York: Hispanic Institute, 1943
Divagaciones y fantasías: crónicas de M.G. N., edited by Boyd G. Carter, Mexico City: Secretaría de Educación Pública, 1944
Cuaresma del Duque Job y otras artículos, edited by Francisco González Guerrero, Mexico City: Chapultepec, 1946
Crónicas y fantasías, prologue by Salvador Novo, Mexico City: W.M. Jackson, 1948
Escritos inéditos de sabor satírico, "Plato del día," edited by Boyd G. Carter, Columbia: University of Missouri Press, 1972

Compilations and Anthologies of Prose Works
Cuentos completos y otras narraciones, prologue, edition and notes by E.K. Mapes, Mexico City: Fondo de Cultura Económica, 1958
Obras, Crítica literaria I: Ideas y temas literarios. Literatura mexicana, compiled by E.K. Mapes; edited by Ernesto Mejía Sánchez, Mexico City: UNAM, 1959

Further Reading

Bondy, Liselotte, *El dolor en la poesía de Manuel Gutiérrez Nájera*, Mexico City: UNAM, 1962
Carter, Boyd G., *En torno a Gutiérrez Nájera y las letras mexicanas del siglo XIX*, Mexico City: Botas, 1960
____ "Gutiérrez Nájera y Martí como iniciadores del Modernismo," *Revista Iberoamericana* 28 (1962)
Gálvez, Marina, "Manuel Gutiérrez Nájera," in *Del neoclasicismo al modernismo*, edited by Luis Íñigo Madrigal, Madrid: Cátedra, 1987 [Volume 2 of *Historia de la literatura hispanoamericana*, 2 vols, 1982–87]
Gómez del Prado, Carlos, *Manuel Gutiérrez Nájera: vida y obra*, Mexico City: Andrea and East Lansing: Michigan State University, 1964
González, Anibal, *La crónica modernista hispanoamericana*, Madrid: Porrúa Turanzas, 1983
Kosloff, Alexander, "Técnica de los cuentos de Manuel Gutiérrez Nájera," *Revista Iberoamericana*, vols 19 (1954) and 20 (1955)
Mapes, E. K., "The First Published Writings of Manuel Gutiérrez Nájera," *Hispanic Review*, vol. 5/3 (1937)

_____ "The Pseudonyms of Manuel Gutiérrez Nájera," *PMLA* 4 (1949)

Pearsall, Priscilla, "Manuel Gutiérrez Nájera: Modernity and the Destruction of the Romantic *Angel consoladora*," in her *An Art Alienated from Itself: Studies in Spanish American Modernism*, Valencia: Artes Gráficas Soler, 1984

Schulman, Ivan, "José Martí y Manuel Gutiérrez Nájera: iniciadores del modernismo," *Revista Iberoamericana*, vol. 3/57 (1964)

_____ *Génesis del modernismo: Martí, Nájera, Silva, Casal*, Mexico City: El Colegio de México, 1966

Walker, Nell, *The Life and Works of Manuel Gutiérrez Nájera, The University of Missouri Studies*, vol. 2/2 (1927)

Martín Luis Guzmán 1887–1976

Mexican novelist, essayist and journalist

One of Mexico's best observers of the Mexican Revolution (1910–20), Martín Luis Guzmán is known above all for three works: *El águila y la serpiente* (*The Eagle and the Serpent*), *La sombra del caudillo* [The Shadow of the Tyrant], and *Memorias de Pancho Villa* (*Memoirs of Pancho Villa*). Although he was offered high military rank by several revolutionary leaders, Guzmán steadfastly retained his civilian status, occupying administrative posts in both the army and the government during the upheaval. Thus, he was perhaps able to portray prominent military figures with greater objectivity. He also served as Villa's personal secretary, a post that accorded him a unique vantage point for two of his books.

El águila y la serpiente has been referred to as a novel, but it is in reality an autobiographical chronicle of Guzmán's experiences between 1913 and 1915. With a sharp eye for detail and a keen sense of psychology, the author describes, among many others, Generals Venustiano Carranza and Álvaro Obregón, the former emerging as an egotist interested only in political power and the latter eliciting the label "farsante" (charlatan). But Guzmán's fascination with Pancho Villa stems from a mixture of awe, respect and fear. Portrayed as the incarnation of primitive instinct and destruction, Villa nevertheless displays unquestionable military genius and a deep sympathy for Mexico's downtrodden. He also obviously respects Guzmán, allowing him to search for his family in the final pages of the book, but begging him not to abandon him as so many others had done. Guzmán's does in fact abandon Villa and ends his chronicle shortly before the latter's defeat by Obregón.

Several chapters of *El águila* can be read separately as short stories. These include "La fiesta de las balas" (The Fiesta of Bullets), in which one of Villa's officers shoots three hundred prisoners; "Pancho Villa en la cruz" (Pancho Villa on the Cross), which describes Villa's torment after being persuaded that his order to shoot a large number of prisoners is unjustified; and "La muerte de David Berlanga" (The Death of David Berlanga), depicting the stoic demeanor of a young man condemned to death for having censured the wanton behavior of Villa's men in the Mexican capital. The eponymous eagle and serpent represent emblems of Mexico, suggesting not only the nation's search for identity but also the idealism (eagle) and the earthy reality (serpent) of the Revolution.

A roman-à-clef, *La sombra del caudillo* dramatizes events that occurred during the regimes of Presidents Obregón (1920–24) and Plutarco Elías Calles (1924–28), the tyrant of the title being a composite of these two leaders. After a series of complex political machinations, Ignacio Aguirre, the protagonist and minister of war, announces his candidacy for president against the candidate chosen by "the tyrant," an act that ultimately leads to Aguirre's assassination. (Aguirre embodies characteristics of General Adolfo de la Huerta, who led an unsuccessful uprising against Obregón in 1923, and General Francisco Serrano, who was shot by Calles for declaring his candidacy for president in 1927.) Although the "tyrant" makes only rare appearances in the novel, his dark shadow shrouds the entire nation in a nebulous, unstable political ambience replete with shifting alliances, intrigues and violence. Guzmán's principal theme is the betrayal of the ideals of the Revolution by politicians interested only in power and personal gain. Despite Aguirre's fatal flaws (he accepts bribes and lacks political acumen), he emerges as a courageous protagonist whose relations with his idealistic friend and alter ego, Axkaná, increase his appeal to the reader. Thus, although the novel ends with the murders of Aguirre and most of his followers, the badly wounded Axkaná – and presumably the revolutionary ideals he represents – manages to survive.

El águila y la serpiente and *La sombra del caudillo* both depict love affairs in their introductory chapters that foreshadow and allegorize the future action, enhancing the structural unity of the two works. In addition, both books are characterized by the author's masterful literary style, an artistic combination of luminous description, impressionistic imagery and classical elegance.

In order to write his *Memorias de Pancho Villa*, Guzmán consulted Villa's service records, his personal files, documents in the national archives and the notes he himself took on the many personal conversations he had with Villa. Guzmán's purpose in writing the memoirs was twofold: to present a panorama of the Revolution and to vindicate the memory of the oft-maligned leader who, in Guzmán's view, fought solely for social justice. Presented as Villa's first-person account, although Guzmán admits to having taken some liberties with the general's use of language, the memoirs begin with Villa's escape to the mountains when, at the age of seventeen, he shot a landowner for raping his sister. Soon thereafter he joined the Revolution under the banner of Francisco Madero and rose to the rank of general. The book ends in April 1915 shortly after Villa's defeat by Obregón in the battle of Celaya. Memorable in these pages are Villa's high esteem for Madero, his scorn for Carranza and Obregón, and his personal bravery in countless battles throughout northern Mexico. But the reader is also struck by the many acts of cruelty Villa committed, seemingly without remorse, during the bloodiest phase of the Revolution.

The winner of several major literary prizes, Martín Luis Guzmán remains one of Mexico's most important writers of the 20th century. His works are among the most readable of his nation's literature.

GEORGE R. McMURRAY

Biography

Born in Chihuahua, Mexico, 6 October 1887. Son of Colonel Martín Luis Guzmán y Rendón, an instructor at the Military Academy in Chapultepec. Mother Carmen Franco Terrazas. Started periodical *Juventud* [Youth] in Veracruz at the age of thirteen. Formed part of the El Ateneo group with Alfonso Reyes and other intellectuals of the period. In 1913 was staff officer of General Ramón Iturbe. Envoy of Venustiano Carranza, 1914. Later in 1914 he joined the forces of Pancho Villa. Imprisoned in the faction-ridden period by Carranza in Mexico City. From 1915–20 in voluntary exile, first in Spain and then in the US. On his return appointed editor-in-chief of *El Heraldo de México* and named private secretary to Alberto Pani, secretary of external relations in the government of Obregón. Founded *El Mundo* (1922) and went into exile again (1925–36) in Spain. Wrote for *El Universal* on his return to Mexico, and founded periodical *Tiempo* (1942). In 1958 awarded both the Manuel Ávila Camacho Prize and the National Prize for Literature. Died in Mexico City, 22 December 1976.

Selected Works

La guerrilla de México, Madrid: Imprenta Clásica Española, 1915
A orillas del Hudson, Mexico City: Botas, 1920
El águila y la serpiente, Madrid: Aguilar, 1928; as *The Eagle and the Serpent*, translated by Harriet de Onís, New York: Knopf, 1930; New York: Dolphin Books, 1965
La sombra del caudillo, Madrid: Espasa Calpe, 1929
Aventuras democráticas, Madrid: Compañía Iberoamericana de Publicaciones, 1931
Mina el mozo, héroe de Navarra, Madrid: Espasa Calpe, 1932
Filadelfia, paraíso de conspiradores, Madrid: n.p., 1933
Memorias de Pancho Villa, 4 vols, Mexico City: Botas, 1938–40; as *Memoirs of Pancho Villa*, translated by Virginia H. Taylor, Austin: University of Texas Press, 1965
El liberalismo mexicano en pensamiento y acción, 15 vols, Mexico City: Empresas Editoriales, 1947–50
Muertes históricas, Mexico City: Compañía General de Ediciones, 1958
Islas Marías, novela y drama, Mexico City: Compañía General de Ediciones, 1959

Compilations and Anthologies

Obras completas, Mexico City: Compañía General de Ediciones, 1961
Castro Leal, Antonio, *La novela de la revolución mexicana*, 6th edition, Mexico City: Aguilar, 1965 [Volume 1 contains *El águila y la serpiente* and *La sombra del caudillo*]

Further Reading

These studies concentrate on theme, style, structure and, in the case of *La sombra del caudillo*, on the real-life identity of the characters.

Abreu Gómez, Emilio, *Martín Luis Guzmán*, Mexico City: Empresas Editoriales, 1968
Bruce-Novoa, Juan, "Martín Luis Guzmán's Necessary Overtures," *Discurso Literario*, vol. 4/1 (1986)
Gyurko, Lanin, "Martín Luis Guzmán," in *Latin American Writers*, edited by Carlos A. Solé and María Isabel Abreu, New York: Scribner, 1989
Leal, Luis, "*La sombra del caudillo*, roman à clef," *Modern Language Journal*, vol. 36/1 (January 1952)
Portal, Marta, *Proceso narrativo de la revolución mexicana*, Madrid: Editorial Cultura Hispánica, 1977 [Chapter 5 has a section on Guzmán]

H

Felisberto Hernández 1902–1964

Uruguayan short story writer

Felisberto Hernández's bizarre stories have always attracted a small group of admirers as well as a number of detractors. In his lifetime, some critics celebrated Hernández's originality, humour and subsivenes: so at first did Jules Supervielle (the Uruguayan-born French poet) and later Ángel Rama. But his stories were more negatively received by others who, like Emir Rodríguez Monegal in a famous review (1948), attacked Hernández's flawed Spanish and the unorthodox sexuality depicted in his tales.

In the River Plate in particular, perceptions of Hernández's work have often been related to perceptions of the man. The favourable accounts of his character tend to come from those who knew Hernández personally but who were not his sexual partners (e.g. the critics Norah Giraldi de Dei Cas and Washington Lockhart, and Hernández's daughter Ana María Hernández de Elena). Less positive versions are expressed by those who were lovers or wives (Paulina Medeiros, Reina Reyes) or who wrote from the Left whilst bearing in mind Hernández's involvement with anti-communist campaigns (the strongest example is Tomás Eloy Martínez's lively 1977 article). The relevance of biographical information is invited not only by the parallels between Felisberto's life and the tribulations of his characters, but also by the meditative and overtly personal tone of his writing. This led a contemporary critic, Carlos Martínez Moreno (1964), to open a well-balanced article on Hernández by noting the excessive use of the first person pronoun in his stories.

It is usual to divide the work of Felisberto Hernández into three roughly chronological groups. Three preoccupations characterise all of Hernández's stories, although a particular one commands each period. They are the workings of the mind, memory and eroticism. His early work consists of "coverless books." These comprise a set of short and cheaply produced texts, but the lack of covers also relates to the books' goal to encourage the reader's active participation, as stated explicitly in the second of them, called precisely *El libro sin tapas*, 1929 [The Book without Covers]. These early texts are concerned with matters of philosophy and psychology, and, in particular, issues of perception. They are also imbued with humour. "Historia de un cigarrillo" [The Story of a Cigarette],

displays some common features. In this mini-story the narrator gradually allocates intention to his cigarettes, corresponding to their "pequeño espíritu" (small souls). He becomes preoccupied in particular by the behaviour of the one cigarette which manages to avoid being smoked first by falling flat on the bottom of the packet and eventually by dropping into a puddle of water on the floor. The narrator's declared "obsesión" with this cigarette is consistent with similar preoccupations with shapes and patterns in other early texts (e.g., "El vestido blanco" [The White Dress], of the same collection). It is also an instance of the personification of objects which continues throughout Hernández's work, a famous example being "El balcón," 1945 [The Balcony], where the female protagonist falls in love with the balcony where she spends most of her time and through whose painted glass windows she perceives the world. Much of the early material can be understood at least partly by bearing in mind the dominance in contemporary philosophy of subjectivist theories such as those of Bergson, Whitehead and William James. Hernández knew their work, but he was probably more influenced by the ideas of their local counterpart, Carlos Vaz Ferreira (1872–1958), who was his mentor and friend.

The second group of texts is made up of three novellas, *Por los tiempos de Clemente Colling*, 1942 [For the Times of Clemente Colling], *El caballo perdido*, 1943 [The Lost Horse], *Tierras de la memoria* [Lands of Memory] (posthumous but probably of 1944). In these works Hernández reminisces over his childhood and adolescence. The difficulties involved in such an enterprise are dramatised in *El caballo perdido*, which, according to his daughter, was the author's favourite text. Whilst the first half of the story is devoted to the experiences of the narrator as a boy in the living room of his piano teacher Celina, the second half is concerned with the problems of attempting to recover the boy's perspective. The narrator recalls the child's ability to perceive the whole through any one of its parts: "Cuando el niño miraba el brazo desnudo de Celina sentía que toda ella estaba en aquel brazo" (When the child looked at the naked arm of Celina he felt that all of her was contained in that arm). Although such experience is now difficult, it can occasionally be achieved when the viewpoint of the child is fleetingly reenacted: "Hay un solo instante en que los ojos de ahora ven bien: es el instante fugaz en que se encuentran con los ojos del niño" (There is only one instant when the eyes of today manage to see in the right way: the brief instant when they meet the eyes of the child). Much of Hernández's work attempts to depict mental experience which is close to that of a child and which differs from the logical and goal-oriented thinking of the adult. The latter has lost the capacity to see the "mystery" of things: "Las partes han perdido la misteriosa relación que las une" (The parts have lost the mysterious links that keep them together). "Mystery" is in fact one of a set of key terms which Hernández uses to denote the gains of an alternative perception.

The celebration of childhood is consistent with a general picture of infantilism in Hernández which was already noted by Rodríguez Monegal in his early review. The phenomenon also occurs in the third phase of his production, where the texts seem more interested in telling a plot than in reflection. This last group of texts comprises the stories of *Nadie encendía las lámparas*, 1947 [No One Turned the Lights On] and a few others which were published separately afterwards. In these stories eroticism, which was already conspicuous in the first part of *El caballo perdido* (e.g., when the boy touches the bust of a statue of a woman in Celina's living room), now often assumes a central role. Some of the bizarre situations depicted in the collection include the woman in love with her balcony already mentioned, as well as the female sleepwalker who steps on a man that is lying on the floor in a room full of glass cabinets ("El acomodador," [The Usher]) and the man who touches girls' faces and a set of mundane objects in a dark tunnel in his country house, with the aim of generating new meanings and sensations to be recollected afterwards ("Menos Julia" [All But Julia]). The most outrageous text in this sense is "Las Hortensias" [The Hortensias], the story of a man who becomes increasingly interested in dolls as a replacement for his wife and who goes as far as having them filled with hot water to enhance their similarity to humans. Infantile too is the overt preference of the male protagonists of the later stories for large and passive matrons who are prepared to let the narrator desire them without making demands of mutuality in return. Two examples of this ideal woman are Ursula, in the eponymous tale, who is likened to a dairy cow, and Señora Margarita, of the last text published in Hernández's lifetime, *La casa inundada*, 1960 [The Flooded House], whom the narrator splits into two: the innocent one who in his fantasy belongs to him alone, and the one who is still attached to the memory of her stranded husband. He prefers the former because "(en ella) mi imaginación podía intervenir libremente" (on her my imagination could intervene freely). When women refuse to act maternally and instead demand commitment on the part of the narrator, he tends to flee (as in "Las Hortensias" and "Menos Julia").

The future of Felisberto Hernández studies seems bright. One current tendency in criticism focuses on the richness and ambiguity of his writing (a recent example is the article by Stephanie Merrim on the subject of the "other" in Hernández's short fiction). There is still much to explore as regards the peculiarity of the mind depicted in his texts, an issue which continued to preoccupy Hernández until his death, as shown in his dense and unfinished *Diario del sinvergüenza* [Diary of the Scoundrel], where he ponders the relationship between his mind and his body (the scoundrel of the title). Reina Reyes's short essay on the man Hernández, where she claims he was a schizophrenic, is an interesting source in this respect. A return to more negative evaluations of Hernández is also likely in the light of gender studies.

Two important monographs on Hernández are Lasarte (traditional) and Echavarren (Lacanian), both in Spanish. Although full-length studies in English are still to come, an international homage to Felisberto Hernández took place in Washington, DC, in April 1993. Part of the explanation for the relatively little attention Hernández's work has received outside the River Plate lies in the lack of readily accessible editions of his work, until recently jealously guarded by Hernández's family (see Ana María Hernández de Elena's prologue to Hernández's *Narraciones fundamentales* [1993]). Two editions of *Nadie encendía las lámparas*, one recent (Cátedra's Letras Hispánicas series) and the other imminent (Colección Archivos) will no doubt encourage teachers and critics to explore this unusual writer. It is fortunate that several of his collected short stories are now available in English since his quirky sense of humour and fondness for the absurd in "ordinary" urban contexts are bound to appeal to an Anglo-Saxon readership.

GUSTAVO SAN ROMÁN

Biography

Born in Montevideo, Uruguay, 20 October 1902; father from Canary Islands, mother Uruguayan. Attended primary school in Montevideo; no further academic training, although in later life he was befriended by the philosopher Carlos Vaz Ferreira and important local psychiatrists. Learned piano from early age, tutored by teachers who appear in his stories. Played piano on tours around Uruguay and Argentina, often to accompany silent films at the cinema. In 1940s writing took over from piano as main activity. Worked intermittently as minor civil servant, but remained on low income most of his life; often needed support from friends to publish his books. Lived in Paris on a French government scholarship, 1946–48. In 1956 he made anti-communist radio broadcasts, and wrote two anti-communist newspaper articles, 1958. Married four times: 1) María Isabel Guerra in 1925 (separated 1931); 2) Amalia Nieto in 1937 (separated 1943); 3) María Luisa Las Heras in 1949 (separated 1950); 4) Reina Reyes in 1954 (separated 1958). Relationships with Paulina Medeiros (1943–48) and María Dolores Roselló (1960–64). Particularly close to his mother throughout his life. Died in Montevideo, 15 January 1964.

Selected Works

Short Fiction
Fulano de Tal, Montevideo: José Rodríguez Riet, 1925
El libro sin tapas, Montevideo: Rocha: Imprenta "La Palabra," 1929
La cara de Ana, Montevideo: Mercedes, 1930
La envenenada, Montevideo: Florida, 1931
Por los tiempos de Clemente Colling, Montevideo: González Panizza Hermanos, 1942
El caballo perdido, Montevideo: González Panizza Hermanos, 1943
Nadie encendía las lámparas, Buenos Aires: Sudamericana, 1947
Las Hortensias, Montevideo: Imprenta La Gaceta Comercial, 1950
La casa inundada, Montevideo: Alfa, 1960
Tierras de la memoria, Montevideo: Arca, 1965

Compilations and Anthologies

Obras completas, 6 vols, edited by Norah Giraldi de Dei Cas and
José Pedro Díaz, Montevideo: Arca, 1967–74

Narraciones fundamentales, edited by Walter Rela, Montevideo:
Relieve, 1993 [Includes an up-to-date secondary bibliography]

Translations

"El cocodrilo," as "The Crocodile," translated by Stephanie
Merrim, *Fiction*, vol. 5/1 (1976) [Special issue devoted to the
Uruguayan cultural journal, *Marcha*]

"A Windy Morning"[Una mañana de viento], "El balcón" [The
Balcony] and "Just Before Falling Asleep" [paragraph from "Mi
primer concierto en Montevideo"], translated with an
introduction by Luis Harss, *Review* 20 (Spring 1977)

Piano Stories, translated by Luis Harss, with an introduction by
Italo Calvino, New York: Marsilio, 1993 [Contains *Nadie
encendía las lámparas*, *La casa inundada*, *Las Hortensias*, and
Explicación falsa de mis cuentos]

Further Reading

Echevarren, Roberto, *El espacio de la verdad. Práctica del texto en
Felisberto Hernández*, Buenos Aires: Sudamericana, 1981

Giraldi de Dei Cas, Norah, *Felisberto Hernández: del creador al
hombre*, Montevideo: Ediciones de la Banda Oriental, 1975

Lasarte, Francisco, *Felisberto Hernández y la escritura de "lo otro,"*
Madrid: Insula, 1981

Lockhart, Washington, *Felisberto Hernández. Una biografía literaria*,
Montevideo: Arca, 1991

Martínez, Tomás Eloy, "Para que nadie olvide a Felisberto
Hernández," *Plural*, vol. 6/7 (1977)

Martínez Moreno, Carlos, "Un viajero falsamente distraído,"
Número, 2nd period, vol. 2/3–4 (1964)

Medeiros, Paulina, *Felisberto Hernández y yo*, Montevideo:
Biblioteca de Marcha, 1974

Merrim, Stephanie, "Felisberto Hernández's Aesthetic of 'lo otro':
the Writing of Indeterminacy," *Revista Canadiense de Estudios
Hispánicos*, vol. 11/3 (1987)

Reyes, Reina, "Mi imagen de Felisberto Hernández," in *¿Otro
Felisberto?*, edited by Ricardo Pallares and Reina Reyes,
Montevideo: Imago, 1983

Rodríguez Monegal, Emir, review of Felisberto Hernández's, *Nadie
encendía las lámparas*, *Clinamen*, Montevideo 5 (1948)

Sicard, Alain (editor), *Felisberto Hernández ante la crítica actual*,
Caracas: Monte Ávila, 1977 [Contributions by Jaime Concha,
Juan José Saer and Jason Wilson]

Special Issues of Journals

Escritura, Caracas, 13–14 (1982)

José Hernández 1834–1886

Argentine writer and politician

José Hernández, a writer and political figure of the second half
of 19th-century Argentina, is by far best known as the author
of the great poem *Martín Fierro*. Hernández, who suffered as
a child from pulmonary problems, was raised on a ranch near
Buenos Aires where he came to know first-hand and for many
years the gauchos who worked for his father's cattle-raising
operation. While Hernández was assuredly not himself a
gaucho, he came to know their speech, customs and mannerisms as if he were, and his identification with rural life and
the values the gauchos represented – freedom above all from
the restrictions, oppression and subordination imposed by the
nearby capital city – led him to defend the provinces in their
struggle for self-determination against the inevitable domination of Buenos Aires. In this cause Hernández, who in time
became a Senator, published a journal, *El Río de la Plata*, in
which, although it lasted less than a year, he espoused his views
and defended the rural way of life, whose traditions contained
the national essence of Argentina. He also published in
numerous other periodicals of the time. In his essays and
addresses he not only opposed, in the highest Romantic tradition, forces which were almost certainly bound to defeat him
and which for a time exiled him to Brazil, but also the most
powerful and prestigious politicians of his time, Domingo
Faustino Sarmiento and Bartolomé Mitre among them. His
pro-countryside campaigns and writings moderated in his latter

years, although it is not fully clear whether this is owed to a
moderation of his social view or a simple recognition that
change was on its way: that it could not be resisted, but merely
accommodated and humanized as best as could be managed.

Hernández, in spite of a certain prominence in Argentine
politics of his time, is nevertheless remembered as the poet who
wrote *Martín Fierro*: so much so that the character of Fierro
is often associated with Hernández himself, something which
the poem itself would seem to encourage, due to brief moments
of apparent authorial intervention. To whatever degree the
relationship of Fierro to Hernández is valid as a projection
fusing both his own aspirations and a view of Argentina's past
and future – it is said he was often called "Senator Martín
Fierro" – it may be said that most readers know and care
rather less about the author than about his creation: as with
Cervantes and Don Quixote. Both authors' realities are
subsumed into those of their creations.

Hernández's formal education was limited to elementary
school, so that like so many Spanish American writers he was
essentially self-taught. This fact underscores the credibility of
his character Fierro, who also learned more from life itself than
from other, indirect and hence unreliable, sources. (One may
contrast here the outrageously picaresque world-view offered
by the character Vizcacha with the moralizations and sage
advice of Fierro to his sons near the end of the poem.) This

difference between Hernández and other Latin American Romantics, such as those who authored the "cuadros de costumbres" (short sketches of local color and customs) is crucial, for in his great poem sheer intellect is always balanced and enriched by the Pampa and first-hand experience. Hernández thus avoids the dull ontological generalizations of certain other Romantic (and Neoclassic) writers. This "materialistic" quality of his poem is one of its major characteristics, and enables its relatively simple examples and teachings to achieve a credibility quite rarely, if ever, achieved by his more abstractly sententious contemporaries. It is also a major component of his work's artistic value, which far surpasses that of earlier gaucho poems, a description which is hardly adequate to Hernández's great *Martín Fierro*, for while it is, in setting, a gaucho poem, it goes far beyond the terrain explored by his predecessors to become a great deal more, being also a philosophy of life, a song from the heart of Argentina and a vision and a plan for the future.

Just as Hernández's political program sought to defend a dual Argentina – countryside and city in approximate counterbalance – his poem sought and found a dual audience. The first part, the *Ida* [Departure] is principally destined for the reader in Buenos Aires, largely ignorant of life in the countryside and even more mistrustfully so of the gauchos whose basic manual labor provided their sustenance. He explicitly wrote of Fierro as a "type" (which he is, although a fundamentally different type from any known before) who would represent gaucho life and values to the city-dwelling reader and vindicate a tradition Hernández considered as valuable as it was unknown. The second and final part of the poem, the *Vuelta* [Return] was explicitly aimed at the gaucho as well as at the reader in Buenos Aires, for the advice Fierro gives his sons is also clearly given to the latter-year gaucho for his survival and integration into Argentina's future. As Hernández wrote, one of his objectives was to bring even reading itself, long associated only with the upper classes and the cities, to the gaucho: the book is intended to "despertar la inteligencia y el amor a la lectura en una población casi primitiva, a servirle de provechoso recreo, después de fatigosas tareas, a millares de personas que jamás han leído" (awaken the understanding and the love of reading in a nearly primitive people, to serve as a useful entertainment, after arduous chores, for thousands of people who have never read). It is part of the popular tradition that the gauchos believed the poem to have been written by one of themselves, and that they would recite long passages from it. It is more certain that Hernández's poem has both entered and helped form the Argentine national identity – not without conflict and inconsistencies, be it said, for Argentines, like their great narrator Jorge Luis Borges, simultaneously tend to be book-inspired intellectuals and dancers of tangos, both gauchos and political philosophers. Socio-economic history makes clear that Hernández's side largely lost the struggle for Argentina's development; cultural history makes equally clear that as long as Martín Fierro lives – as long as *Martín Fierro* is read – the gaucho's and Hernández's ideals will persist. The character Martín Fierro and the poem in which he is given birth give eloquent and moving expression to the contradictions and aspirations of the intimate life of his nation, and much of Latin America.

PAUL W. BORGESON, JR

Biography

Born in the hamlet of Caserío de Perdriel in the province of Buenos Aires, Argentina, 10 November 1834. His fortunes as a child were very mixed. First of all, because his parents travelled a good deal and left him with an aunt. José was separated from her at the age of six and developed a strong sense of orphanhood. Placed next in the care of his paternal grandfather close to Buenos Aires. Attended school run by a gifted teacher, Pedro Sánchez, in Barracas, 1841–45. But period of formal education was brief. His mother died in 1843 and he was then sent to live with his father in the pampas. Father in charge of vast cattle ranches and José was captivated by the prairies and the life of the gauchos. He learned the skills of the plainsmen. After the fall of Rosas (1852), Hernández was recruited into the Federalist army. For many years he lived equally by the sword and the pen. Fought against the Unitarians, who wanted to fashion a centralized nation state with all the power radiating from Buenos Aires. Worked also as a soldier, politician, civil servant and journalist. Fought in several battles against the Unitarians. This period of civil war was a painful experience to him and he referred to it as the "nine terrible years" (between the battle of Caseros, 1852, when Rosas's forces were defeated, to Pavón in 1862). Married Carolina González del Solar in 1863 and worked as a lawyer and teacher of Spanish literature at a secondary school. Founding editor of the newspaper *El Río de la Plata*, Buenos Aires, August 1869 to April 1870. This was his most ambitious journalistic undertaking. As late as 1868 he took part in the armed resistance of Evaristo López, governor of the remote province of Corrientes. Went into exile in the south of Brazil in 1872 where he came into contact with the Brazilian gauchos. Forced into exile again, seeking refuge this time in Uruguay, when he fell foul of the Unitarian president of Argentina, Domingo Faustino Sarmiento. Returned to Argentina in 1875 and prospered as a landowner. Elected to Chamber of Deputies and later to Senate. Died 21 October 1886, while fulfilling his duties as senator.

Martín Fierro

Narrative poem by José Hernández

Martín Fierro is the greatest single work of Spanish American Romanticism, and among the very finest writings in Spanish at any time or in any country. Aside from its universally recognised merit as an outstanding work of literature, this long poem's impact is such that for many readers it is one of two works (together with Domingo Faustino Sarmiento's *Facundo*) which define Argentine national identity. The poem and its character are both born of specifically Argentine roots, and persist today as a firmly implanted symbol of the romantic side of the national psyche. In this sense, the poem may be compared, for example, to the relationship of *Don Quixote* or *The Cid* to Spain, for these, like *Martín Fierro*, are works which serve their respective countries as symbols both mythical and epic in character.

El gaucho Martín Fierro is the formal title of the poem published by José Hernández in 1872, although it is often referred to as the *Ida* [Departure], since at its conclusion the eponymous hero and his gaucho companion Sergeant Cruz have left white civilization in disgust at their mistreatment by the authorities, to live amid the Pampa Indians. Seven years later, Hernández published *La vuelta de Martín Fierro* [Martín Fierro's Return] the continuation and conclusion of the entire work. The two sections together form a single poem which marks the passing of the 19th century (the *Ida*) and then in the *Vuelta* announces the beginning of the 20th century. For the Martín Fierro who returns to white lands (Cruz dies during their self-exile) is only in part the same gaucho who departed, and the conjoining of the two parts plaintively reflects both the melancholy of loss and the promise of the coming Modernity. In sum, it appears that the gaucho must "die" – that is, change, evolve, integrate himself – so that the new Argentine society, of which Fierro himself is among the first prototypes, may emerge. Hernández foresaw that neither the Indians, against whom the gauchos were conscripted to fight and whose values are portrayed as still more vile than those of the Spanish-speaking society, nor the traditional gauchos – independent, self-reliant, with a unique cultural, linguistic and even racial heritage – will survive the changes of time.

The evolution of Martín Fierro is clearly a paradigm of the changes already taking place in Argentina when the poem was written. As the result of government policy, by the 1880s the traditional gaucho and his way of life had been laid to rest. Hernández's simultaneous lament for the Romantic past – valor, honesty, personal merit and the belief in justice – and the ambivalent welcome given to the inevitable future is one of the poem's most fundamental and appealing characteristics, both as a work of poetry and as allegory of Argentine society at a time of transition.

The poem's plot is typically Romantic in its reliance upon fortuitous encounters of characters and the loose stringing together of events, less a matter of causality than of the hope that the presence of the random in life may not preclude the finding of some sense and a personal place within it. Also much in the tradition of the Romantic movement, characterization is much more important and convincing than plot, that of Fierro foremost, but even that of Cruz, the black gauchos who appear in both parts and the vividly popular characters of Vizcacha and Picardía, the latter of whom turns out to be a long-lost son of Cruz. All major characters in Hernández's creation both rely on recognizable typologies, which they then turn to the poem's internal needs, and establish new types: Picardía and Vizcacha, notably, are traditional picaroons who adapt to the changing and morally subjective experience of the Pampa; and Fierro, in his turn, has a good deal of the epic hero in him, yet this poem's generic classification is elusive. Epic and picaresque characteristics have been mentioned, along with social criticism and historical underpinnings; yet even more obvious, and more enjoyable in the actual reading, are the highly lyrical passages in which Fierro, principally, sings – the entire poem is sung with guitar accompaniment – of love, loss, fate and faith. Plot, finally, becomes clearly secondary to both characterization and, best of all, the experience of language itself, the level at which Hernández reaches his greatest powers.

Martín Fierro is among the first serious poems written in what is largely popular Spanish, long considered by a society still stratified by class as unworthy of great themes and high literature. Hernández had lived among gauchos as a child, and had both learned much about their lives and absorbed their way of speech, which he remarkably makes the exclusive level of style for his poem. The radical nature of this departure should not be underestimated: for decades to come, popular language will (when it appears at all) tend to be relegated to a secondary, "picturesque" level of cultural curiosity. Yet *Martín Fierro* uses it to tell the entire tale, with no authorial intromission of the formal language of the Buenos Aires metropolis for which the poem – the *Ida* in particular – was in part written. Few authors indeed, until the works of Juan Rulfo in the 1950s, will use only spoken-style speech to achieve the degree of lyrical beauty which poetic tradition only associated with the speech of the educated. Hernández, through Fierro, teaches us that the untutored can see truths to which formal education can blind us; that we can express all human thought and emotion in language that is ours, not the Others'; that, finally, until language actually belongs to and is remade by its user, neither intellectual nor esthetic freedom can be achieved.

Several metrical forms are used in *Martín Fierro*, the most common being the "hernandina," named for the poem's author (although he did not invent the form). All forms are popular in use, with frequent open rhymes and an improvisational connotation proper to the spontaneous story-telling and "duels" of singers in the Pampa *pulperías* (bars). Rhetorical resources are believably modest, with a great reliance on simile rather than metaphor, especially those relating to Nature, the gaucho's real guide and model for human life: Fierro's young children are "como los pichones / sin acabar de emplumar" (like nestlings whose feathers haven't yet formed); he himself, in his fury at their disappearance, wanders "como el tigre / que le roban sus cachorros" (like a jaguar whose cubs have been stolen). Yet for many readers the most revelatory moments of this marvelous poem's expressive power come when Fierro, late in the *Vuelta*, wins an improvisational verbal duel with the brother of the black gaucho he had fought and killed in the *Ida*, posing and answering questions of each other until one finally cannot answer. Fierro here answers what "quantities" are, by saying that "Dios / no crió cantidá ninguna. / El ser de todos los seres / sólo formó la unidad; / lo demás lo ha criado el hombre / después que aprendió a contar" (God / created no quantities. / The Being of all Beings / formed only unity; / mankind made up the rest / after he learned to count). Fierro, simply and directly, tells us here that division and isolation, which he has lived in his own flesh for years, are creations not of God but of humankind. Similarly, he tells us in a simple and meaningful way what time itself is: no astrophysical or subconscious abstraction, but only "tardanza / de lo que está por venir" (the delay / in that which is to come). Fierro, finally, teaches the educated reader just as he does the gaucho himself, and becomes as much a model in understanding of life as he is the supreme gaucho.

One striking characteristic of *Martín Fierro* is its frequent use of humor, something hardly characteristic of the Romantic movement, which – when it is used at all – typically used it from outside the thing rendered comical, such as in the mockery of rustic simplemindedness and unsophistication one finds in some gaucho poems which preceded Hernández's masterpiece. In *Martín Fierro*, by contrast, humor not only provides necessary contrast between scenes and situations, but it always comes from within the gaucho subculture. It serves, then, not to distance but to conjoin and to allow the reader to share in the experience. (Vizcacha and Picardía, gaucho versions of the Golden Age *gracioso*, or comic servant, are the principal examples of humor, yet the reader is so "seduced" by Fierro's gaucho ethic that we judge him from Fierro's own point of view.) It is also to be noted that such are Hernández's skill and resourcefulness that his use of humor in no way diminishes the lyricism of his portrait of nature or the heroism of his characters: Fierro himself uses it on several occasions and achieves a greater credibility, a richer humanity, for it.

Martín Fierro enjoyed unprecedented popular success, although critical reaction lagged somewhat behind. Within two years of publication it had gone through nine printings, and in its first three decades 60,000 copies had been sold. It is today one of the relatively few works, especially of poetry, not only to be known but actually to be read, by a wide readership of all classes. Its multiple dimensions, rich creativeness, fusion of traditional literary modes and insightfulness into human nature and historical and cultural forces and – above all – its marvelous, flexible and unmatched use of the language of real people, rendering its characters and their plights equally real, make of *Martín Fierro* one of the greatest literary creations of the Spanish language.

PAUL W. BORGESON, JR

Editions

First edition: *El gaucho Martín Fierro. Contiene al final una interesante memoria sobre el camino trasandino*, Buenos Aires: Imprenta de La Pampa, 1872

La vuelta de Martín Fierro, Buenos Aires: Imprenta de Pablo F. Coni, 1879

Critical editions: There are several. Among the more recent and accessible of both the *Ida* and the *Vuelta* is that by Luis Saínz de Medrano, Madrid: Cátedra, 1987

Translations: There are several. For details see Jason Wilson, *An A to Z of Modern Latin American Literature in English Translation*, London: Institute of Latin American Studies, 1989. The most recently published English version is *The Gaucho Martín Fierro*, translated by Frank Carrino, Alberto Carlos and Norman Mangouro, Albany: State University of New York, 1974

Further Reading

Aragón, Roque Raúl and J. Calcetti, *Genio y figura de José Hernández*, Buenos Aires: Universitaria de Buenos Aires, 1972

Azeves, Ángel Hector, *La elaboración literaria del "Martín Fierro,"* La Plata: Universidad Nacional de La Plata, 1960

Battistessa, Ángel, *Jose Hernández y "Martín Fierro" en la perspectiva del tiempo*, Buenos Aires: Academia Argentina de Letras, 1972

Borello, Rodolfo, *Hernández: poesía y política*, Buenos Aires: Plus Ultra, 1973

Borges, Jorge Luis and Adolfo Bioy Casares, prologue to *Poesía gauchesca*, Buenos Aires: Fondo de Cultura Económica, 1955

Isaacson, José (editor), *Martín Fierro: cien años de crítica*, Buenos Aires: Plus Ultra, 1986

Martínez Estrada, Ezequiel, *Muerte y transfiguración de Martín Fierro*, 2 vols, Buenos Aires: Fondo de Cultura Económica, 1948; revised edition, 1958

Unamuno, Miguel de, "El gaucho Martín Fierro," *La Revista Española*, vol. 1/1 (1894)

Julio Herrera y Reissig 1875–1910

Uruguayan poet, prose writer and dramatist

One of the major poets of 20th-century Uruguay, Herrera y Reissig also wrote essays such as "Conceptos de crítica" [Critical Concepts], "El círculo de la muerte" [The Circle of Death], short stories, "El traje lila," "Delicias fúnebres" and "Mademoiselle Jaquelin (sic)" [respectively: The Lilac Dress, Funereal Delights and Mademoiselle Jacquelin], three plays, and other prose writings.

From a privileged background, and a member of a prominent political family, Julio Herrera was born with a serious heart condition that caused his premature and much regretted death at the age of thirty-five. None the less, in his short but eventful life he was one of the poetic voices of Spanish American Modernism that developed an original expressive system and who left an indelible mark on Modernist discourse in a manner not unlike that of Rubén Darío, the Nicaraguan poet whose personality and work shaped much *fin-de-siècle* poetic production.

Julio Herrera had read with great care the Latin and Greek poets during his formative years; he also had extensive in-depth knowledge of Golden Age Spanish and 19th-century French poetry, both of which provided an advantageous platform from which to elaborate and develop a poetic praxis to challenge the *modernista* canon. His poetry brings a stronger sense of formalism to Darío's metrical, rhythmic and rhyme-innovative procedures in Spanish versification. He also reintroduced pastoral themes treated with parodic and humorous wit.

Herrera is considered a late *modernista* whose work illustrates well the contradictions of this important period of Spanish American literary history. As Gwen Kirkpatrick remarks: "Julio Herrera y Reissig filled his short life ... with a dazzling output of verse and prose which startled its early readers and continues to evoke astonishment even among contemporaries." Kirkpatrick is referring to his skilful mastery of versification, remarkable ability in the manipulation of language, and daring experimentation with classic and modern poetic forms. Herrera's literary material incorporated elements from diverse and often apparently unrelated semantic fields with pleasurable irreverence when mixing elements from science, technology, mythic pastoral figures and the erotic. All are linked by a skilful management of sonorous lexical items, set by unexpected metaphors and original alliterations.

Herrera was strongly attracted to the poetry of French Symbolist Albert Samain (1858–1900), as other *modernistas* before him, but he remains a remarkably original creator in the use of tropes involving accumulation of detail to produce the effect of overloading, well exemplified in the poems of *Los parques abandonados* [The Deserted Parks].

In August, 1899, Herrera began to publish *La Revista*, a magazine of literature and science to provide the new generations of Uruguayans with a space where they might present new ideas. He published twenty-two issues; however, the magazine ceased to appear when the poet's heart condition worsened, rendering him unable to continue with this worthy enterprise. His acute illness led him to find relief in morphine, a common drug used for heart disease. Herrera took advantage of this situation and romanticized the use of drugs. He spoke of the importance of experimenting with narcotics. In his short story "Delicias fúnebres," he describes his experience with this type of artificial paradise.

He and a group of his friends and colleagues met to discuss their intellectual concerns in a place he named "The Tower of the Panoramas," mostly an imaginary forum of Herrera's creative imagination. It required, as Hugo Achúgar indicates, adherence to certain aesthetic-ideological principles that united these writers. Among its members were Horacio Quiroga, César Miranda and Roberto de las Carreras.

The books of poems compiled by the poet himself include the following titles and dates, according to the 1961 edition of the *Poesías completas* of Julio Herrera y Reissig by Roberto Bula Píriz: *Los Peregrinos de piedra*, 1903 [The Stone Pilgrims], *Los éxtasis de la montaña. Eglogánimas*, 1904–07 [Mountain Ecstacies], *La torre de las esfinges*, 1909 [The Sphinxes' Tower], *Los parques abandonados*, 1902–05 [The Deserted Parks], and *Las campanas solariegas*, 1907 [Manor House Bells]. Additional poems left unpublished by Herrera's untimely death, and numerous new titles are included in this edition.

Herrera's lyric production bears witness to the rapid transformation and modernization of Uruguay. In his valuable study of the impact of *Modernismo* on Uruguayan society, Hugo Achúgar attests to the importance of Julio Herrera y Reissig's literary production thus: "His passion for Art, his aesthetic adherence and his zeal for certain canonical Modernism texts were fully assumed [by the poet] . . . [His poetic work] aims at the construction of a universe and at its very destruction". This statement is best exemplified in his most remarkable collection of poems, *Los peregrinos de piedra*.

MAGDALENA GARCÍA PINTO

Biography

Born in Montevideo, Uruguay, on 9 January 1875. Sixth of nine children. Father lost his wealth in 1882 and family had to leave their luxurious home. Suffered from a heart condition from his childhood. Published first poems in 1898. In 1899 began to work as secretary of the Minister of Education (Instrucción Pública); resigned after 18 months. In 1904 made his one journey abroad, to Buenos Aires, where he spent five months and worked in the Census Office. On his return to Montevideo, appointed to editorial board of the newspaper *La Democracia*. Married Julieta de la Fuente in 1908. By 1909 he was gravely ill and living in poverty through being unable to work. Died in 1910.

Selected Works

Poetry
Los peregrinos de piedra, Montevideo: O.M. Bertani, 1910; as *Los éxtasis de la montaña*, La Plata, Argentina: Calomino, 1943
Las pascuas del tiempo, Montevideo: O.M. Bertani, 1913
La vida y otros poemas, Montevideo: O.M. Bertani, 1913
El teatro de las humildes, Montevideo: O.M. Bertani, 1913
Las lunas de oro, Montevideo: O.M. Bertani, 1915
Ciles alucinada, San José, Costa Rica: Alsino, 1916
Ópalos (poemas en prosa), Buenos Aires: Glusberg, 1919
Los parques abandonados, Buenos Aires: América, 1919

Other Writings
"*Epílogo wagneriano*" a "*La política de fusión*," Montevideo: García y Compañía, 1902
Prosas: crítica, cuentos, comentarios, Montevideo: García y Compañía, and Valencia: Cervantes, 1918
El renacimiento en España, Montevideo: García y Compañía, 1919

Compilations and Anthologies
Poesías completas y páginas en prosa, edited with an introduction by Roberto Bula Píriz, Madrid: Aguilar, 1961
Herrera y Reissig: antología, estudio crítico y notas, edited by Rogelio Mirza, Montevideo: Arca, 1975
Poesías, Mexico City: Porrúa, 1977
Poesía completa y prosa selecta, edited by Alicia Migdal, Caracas: Biblioteca Ayacucho, 1978

Further Reading
Achúgar, Hugo, *Poesía y sociedad. (Uruguay 1880–1911)*, Montevideo: Arca, 1985
Amestoy Leal, Beatriz, *Poética de lo imaginario: la mujer y su configuración imaginaria en la poesía de Julio Herrera y Reissig*, Montevideo: Trilce, 1991
Bula Píriz, Roberto, introduction to *Poesías completas y páginas en prosa de Julio Herrera y Reissig*, Madrid: Aguilar, 1961
Hahn, Oscar, "Herrera y Reissig o el discreto encanto de lo cursi," *Texto Crítico* 5 (1979)
Kirkpatrick, Gwen, *The Dissonant Legacy of Modernismo. Lugones, Herrera y Reissig and the Voices of Modern Spanish American Poetry*, Berkeley: University of California Press, 1989
Rama, Ángel, *Las máscaras democráticas del modernismo*, Montevideo: Arca, 1985
Sucre, Guillermo, *La máscara, la transparencia. Ensayos sobre poesía hispanoamericana*, Caracas: Monte Ávila, 1975
Vilariño, Idea, *Julio Herrera y Reissig*, Montevideo: Técnica, 1974
Yurkievich, Saúl, *Celebración del modernismo*, Barcelona: Tusquets, 1976

Special Issues of Journals
Caballo Verde para la Poesía, Madrid, 5 (1937)

Fernand Hibbert 1873–1928

Haitian novelist and dramatist

Fernand Hibbert, a member of the *Génération de la Ronde*, stands out in the history of the Haitian novel by virtue of the eloquence of his satirical wit. The literary movement of La Ronde (The Circle), whose other members include Frédéric Marcelin, Justin Lhérisson and Antoine Innocent, falls between the Patriotic Movement (1860–98) and the Indigenous Movement formed after the American occupation in 1915. The Génération de la Ronde differs from its predecessors through the production of a literary discourse which aims for the universal and which draws from the French Realist tradition. The times of turmoil of the "bayonets," which marked a period of economic and political disaster in Haiti, constitutes the socio-political background from which Fernand Hibbert draws the inspiration for his depiction of Haitian life during the years preceding 1914.

Strongly influenced by French literature, Hibbert's writing evokes the skepticism of Renan as well as that of Anatole France. Likewise, following the example of Balzac, Hibbert creates an *étude de moeurs*. Further, the reappearance of some characters from novel to novel, or from tale to tale (as is the case of *Masques et visages* [Masks and Faces]), as well as, in particular, the opening scene of *Les Thazar* [The Thazars] – where the mansion Thazar is depicted with the same narrative technique as the Vaquer pension in *Le Père Goriot* (*Old Goriot*) – attest to the influence of the French master of the Realist novel over Hibbert. However, unlike Balzac, who varies his depiction of social classes from one novel to another, Hibbert sets his scenes primarily in Port-au-Prince and focuses almost exclusively on the greedy and malicious merchant bourgeoisie and on the corrupt and conspiratorial world of local politicians. Only a handful of characters, acting as the author's spokesmen, retain a sense of dignity, in what may be called "scenes of Haitian life."

The action, in Hibbert's novels, often unfolds to the rhythm of conversations. These shed much light on the Haitian political, social and economic situation at the turn of the century. Whether trivial or serious, these conversations usually have the same objective: when illustrating the political or sentimental schemes of the bourgeois circles, they underscore the author's latent criticism of the society, and when presenting the views of the writer's spokesmen, they reveal equally caustic opinions. Some of these conversations may seem rather technical or philosophical, and therefore at first, not congruent with the smooth unfolding of the action. Yet, these same conversations often contain the very elements which feed the characters' consciences and which guide the action to the final outcome. Therefore, in *Séna* (1905), Hibbert's first novel, while the eponymous character Séna acts as the central figure in the first part, which takes place in Port-au-Prince, his role becomes overshadowed in the second part of the novel by the author's spokesman, Dehli, as a consequence of the latter's erudition and discursive power over his companions. The attention given to Dehli's conversations is such that, by the end of the book, his discussions become the only real justification for Séna's rather sudden conversion to altruism.

The prevalence of social and political satirical discourse characterizes Hibbert's works. His satirical vision finds its niche in a series of recurring themes: cases of adultery, matchmaking, political conspiracies, and financial schemes.

With regard to the social scene, Hibbert's satire lends itself to several rather comical and finely crafted episodes. In the series of adulteries, the reader is at a loss when trying to figure out which character to pity the most – whether it be the husband, the wife, or the lover, since the author seems intent on ridiculing every single one of them. Thus, for example, in *Les Simulacres*, 1923 [The Pretenses], Hibbert's last novel, Mr. Hélénus Caton, after having committed "several crimes" and having spent "a year . . . in the ministry," to ensure his wealth for his late years, becomes cuckolded before being deprived by his wife's lover of a healthy sum of money that he had himself acquired in not too honorable a fashion. The cheating wife, Céphise, after having made the most of her charms, is threatened with kidnapping by her handsome lover. Last, the Cuban lover Pablo Alcantaro is double-crossed by Dehli, the very man whose confidence he thought he had won, before being extradited to his own country. In conclusion, all of the characters have their fair share of misfortune, each time shattering the confidence they had in their actions.

In the series of matchmaking incidents, the union with a foreigner often stands as the common rule. This model recurs with some variations in *Les Thazar*, *Séna*, and in a few tales of *Masques et visages*. The most representative example is certainly that of the young Cécile Thazar who, preferring a German to the Haitian man she loves, justifies her actions in the following materialistic terms: " J'épouse Schlieden parce que je ne veux pas de la vie petite, mesquine, tracassière des ménages sans fortunes . . . Evidemment tu n'es pas un pauvre diable, mais tu es Haïtien, et ton petit avoir est à la merci du plus infime bouleversement" (I am marrying Schlieden because I do not want [any of] the bothersome, petty and small life of destitute households . . . Obviously, you're not a poor devil, but you are Haitian, and your meager assets are at the mercy of the slightest upheaval).

Functioning as a variation on the theme of matchmaking with a foreigner, the subject of a journey to Paris occurs often. Many dream about it, some accumulate money towards realizing that transatlantic experience, and a few return from their voyage enriched or ruined. However, the theme of foreign experience becomes tainted with political nuances in *Les Simulacres*, Hibbert's only novel written after the American occupation in 1915. Here, the author's point of view is twofold. It first finds its voice in the spokesman Brion, who considers the American intervention to have occurred only to the extent that the government prior to the occupation consisted of "shams." He points out: "en ce moment, nous avons la liberté d'écrire, les autres libertés viendront. Le développement du pays par le travail et le commerce es imminent (vu que les Américains y ont un intérêt sérieux par le fait qu'ils détiennent toute notre dette publique)." (at this time, we have the freedom to write; other freedoms shall come. The development of the country through work and trade is imminent [since the Americans have a vested interest given that they hold our public debt])." The opinion of the second spokesman, Delhi, stands in counterpoint; he regrets "the situation prior to the Occupation" which after all was "not so bad" when considering the trade-off: "Ce pays n'a plus d'honneur, plus de vie publique, plus de commerce, plus de souvenirs, plus de littérature, plus de gaieté; tout a sombré dans l'Américain!" (This country has no more honor, no more public life, no more trade, no more memories, no more literature, no more mirth; everything has foundered before the American!")

In the public sector, the satirical wit of the Haitian author does not abate. On the Hibbertian political scene, each one in turn benefits from the advantages of his position until the next term, that is, most generally, until the advent of a new government. Although such a pattern recurs in Hibbert's work, the turbulent political situation in Haiti at the turn of the century is displayed with the utmost cynicism in *Le Caïman* [The Caiman], a one-act comedy, unpublished until the 1988 Deschamps edition. The title already announces the misunderstanding, since the caiman does not refer to the animal, but to a Haitian meal prepared with lamb meat. Indeed, this meal plays a noteworthy role in the distribution of ministerial seats. Further, this very meal, once enjoyed by the future president Vilmoret at the Dametois's table entitles the head of the household to a seat in the government. Thereupon, anything goes and even before the official announcement is given, Dametois is solicited for money in his own home by his future subordinates.

As for the financial schemes, they dominate Hibbert's work, whether they take place in the family, government or administrative circles. The two-act comedy, *La Réclamation Hopton* [The Hopton Complaint], perceptively illustrates the administration's financial meandering. After a false accusation of conspiracy, several months of being stranded, numerous encounters with lawyers and administrators, and several climatic developments, the Pennsylvanian Hopton fails to recover his two trunks impounded by the customs office. Hopton's grievance results in $1,000 in compensation, on behalf of the state of course, in order to dismiss the wrongdoing of its own administrators. However, as one of the characters exclaims, "If we didn't laugh in this country, well . . . we'd choke to death. We laugh so as not to choke. *That is the question.*"

Humour is the next principal facet of Hibbert's work. One finds humour in the circumstances, in the language, and in the onomastics, since humour is evidenced in every line and even between the lines. It is that humour which keeps Hibbert's stories from becoming sordid. The circumstances have their own share of facetiousness, and several of these have already been mentioned. As for the language used, the following definition from *Les Simulacres* will provide us with better insight: "Par l'action du milieu, le français que nous parlons et écrivons n'est pas plus français de France que l'anglais des Etats-Unis n'est l'anglais des Iles Britanniques – et j'ajoute que rien n'est plus ridicule qu'un puriste haïtien . . . " (Through the influence of the environment, the French that we speak and write is no more the French of France than the English spoken in the United States is the English of the British Isles, – and I shall add that nothing is more ridiculous than a Haitian purist

. . .). Indeed, the author uses creolisms, regional terms or expressions, and sometimes even a few americanisms, which invariably color his writing. As another source of constant humour, one finds the onomastic: the reader encounters incongruous nicknames (Rorrotte, Chacha), some strongly charged names (Lamertume [Bitterness]; Mme Veuve Dutemple [Mrs Church Widow]) and some unexpected famous names (Lafayette Oscar, Rothschild).

This brief exposition on the works of Fernand Hibbert would be incomplete should mention not be made to the attention given to history. Hibbert's work is most of all a testimony that intends to be realistic and objective, and there is no doubt that it offers an inexhaustible wealth of social and economic insights into Haitian life at the turn of the century. However, one must add to this testimony the account of an episode of Haiti's history, the siege of Miragoâne in 1833, related in *Romulus* (1908). This historical novel recounts the ten-month civil war of opposition between Bazelais's partisans and government troops. Although embellished, this work presents an important historical source on Haitian history, were it only for the notes at the bottom of the pages, which not only add more details, but also include excerpts from the *Moniteur* and from the Treasury Department's report.

Yet the historical narration is intended to be more than a mere testimony. With equal respect to other themes presented in Hibbert's work, the historical narration fits within Hibbert's critical approach of Haitian politics. As illustrated in the following excerpt from *Le Manuscrit de mon ami* [My Friend's Manuscript] (a sociological essay first published in 1910 as a series in the weekly journal *Le Matin*), to write is to commit oneself: "Si tu t'étais contenté de souffrir et de chercher en gémissant sans écrire, c'est à dire sans agir, ton existence serait ignorée aujourd' hui et ta chair pourrie se serait mêlée à la terre maternelle comme tant d'autres chairs d'hommes." (If you had been content to suffer and to search without writing, that is, without acting, your existence would be ignored today and your rotten flesh would have mingled with the maternal soil as has the flesh of so many men).

Far from belonging to those quickly forgotten men, Fernand Hibbert initiates, along with his friends of *La Ronde*, a long tradition of political criticism widely embraced to this day.

MARIE-MAGDELEINE CHIROL

Biography
Born in Miragoàne, Haiti, 8 October 1873. Completed his education in Paris: Collège Saint-Martial, studied law at the *École des Sciences Politiques* and at the *Collège de France* in Paris. Accountant at the Haitian Ministry of Finance, 1894. Professor of History, 1904, and of French Language and Literature, 1907, at the Lycée Piéton. Head of Division in the Foreign Affairs Ministry, 1912. Minister Plenipotentiary of Haiti in Havana, 1916–20. State Secretary for Public Instruction to the Cabinet of President Dartiguenave, 1921–22. Died in 1928.

Selected Works
The volumes listed under Novels and Plays are to be found in the collection *Esquisses d'hier, tableaux d'aujourd'hui*, 7 vols, Port-au-Prince: Deschamps, 1988

Novels

Séna, Port-au-Prince: L'Abeille, 1905; Port-au-Prince: Deschamps, 1988 [First published as a series in the periodical *Le Soir*]

Les Thazar, Port-au-Prince: L'Abeille, 1907; Port-au-Prince: Deschamps, 1988

Romulus, Port-au-Prince: L'Abeille, 1908; Port-au-Prince: Deschamps, 1988

Masques et visages, Port-au-Prince: L'Abeille, 1910; Port-au-Prince: Deschamps, 1988

Le Manuscrit de mon ami, Port-au-Prince: L'Abeille, 1923; Port-au-Prince: Deschamps, 1988 [First published in 1910 as a series in the periodical *Le Matin*]

Les Simulacres, Port-au-Prince: L'Abeille, 1923; Port-au-Prince: Deschamps, 1988

Plays

Une Affaire d'honneur; La Réclamation Hopton; Le Caïman, Port-au-Prince: Deschamps, 1988

Other Writings

"Une Mulâtresse fille de Louis XIV," *La Ronde*, Port-au-Prince, (July 1901)

"Le Néronisme de Rochambeau," *La Ronde*, Port-au-Prince, (September 1901)

"Un Nègre à la cour de Louis XIV," *La Ronde*, Port-au-Prince, (October 1901)

"La Bacchante," *La Ronde*, Port-au-Prince, (15 January 1902)

Further Reading

Berrou, Raphaèl, *Histoire de la littérature haïtienne*, Port-au-Prince: Caraïbes, 1975

Gaillard, Roger, "Hibbert: sexualité des personnages et érotisme du romancier," in *Conjonction* 122–23 (1974)

Gindine, Yvette, "Satire and the Birth of Haitian Fiction (1901–1905)," in *Caribbean Quarterly*, vol. 21/3 (1975)

Hoffmann, Léon-François, *Le Roman haïtien: idéologie et structure*, Sherbrooke, Quebec: Editions Naaman, 1982

The Historical Novel

Granted that almost two centuries have elapsed since independence, it is possible to affirm that the historical novel in Spanish America is one of constant production, with the variations that are characteristic of successive aesthetic trends, and which has currently achieved an important presence through the radical transformation of its concepts and structures. This fact is symptomatic of the persistent need to resolve questions of national identity in Latin America.

The production of the novel in Spanish America arises in relation to the organization of the nation-states, both because it is the space in which projects are proposed and because of the importance of creating a national literature. But perhaps the historical novel is the one which concentrates most directly on questions that are the result of the foundational reality, given the function of the historical as an interpretive model of real processes and, consequently, a legitimizer of the new status quo. According to 19th-century concepts of history, the novel can articulate an interpretation of time in which the study of the past serves to isolate the idiosyncratic features of each country. Representations of colonial society would allow authors to demonstrate weakness and strengths and thus integrate the role of each facet into the future social whole. The first example was the anonymous novel *Jicoténcal*, published in Philadelphia in 1826, and written following 18th-century models. However, the genre established itself in Spanish America via imitations of historical novels by European writers such as Sir Walter Scott, Alfred de Vigny and Alexandre Dumas *père*, among others, and with them also came the controversy concerning the consistency of such narratives. The long debate over the possible harmonizing of the opposite principles of historical truthfulness and fictional invention is well known. The subcontinent saw an early manifestation in the work of the Cuban José María Heredia, *Ensayo sobre la novela*, 1832 [Essay on the Novel], in which he posed and rejected this type of novel because of its irreconcilable terms. There was an abundance of historical narrative and there were wide, uneven debates over this issue. Argentine intellectuals of the Asociación de Mayo [May Association], statesmen, historians and writers were the ones who elaborated formulations of great relevance. During their period of exile in Chile, they participated in a widespread polemic concerning the historical theme. Soon after writing his historical novel *La novia del hereje* 1842 [The Heretic's Betrothed], with a prologue that contains a definition of the genre, Vicente Fidel López wrote his *Memoria sobre los resultados generales con que los pueblos antiguos han contribuido a la civilización de la humanidad* [Historical Overview of the General Results with which the Ancient Peoples Contributed to Human Civilization] and *Curso de Bellas Letras* [Course in Fine Arts] in 1845, in which he explains his idea of history in relation to certain schools of historiography. He takes Walter Scott as his point of reference and following Thierry tends to favor a history that knows how to combine documentation with imagination. The historian, according to López, should be faithful to the facts, but should also know how to represent dramatic situations with art and style. In his 1882 polemic with Bartolomé Mitre, López notes that the historical novel and history should share the same goal.

The novel spread throughout the continent, as is shown by *El Inquisidor mayor*, 1852 [The Chief Inquisitor] by the Chilean Manuel Bilbao, to *Enriquillo, leyenda histórica dominicana*, 1882 (*The Cross and the Sword*) by the Dominican Manuel de Jesús Galván. However, in Colombia and Mexico there was a broader response, or it may seem so due to the existence of in-depth studies of the genre for these two countries. In Mexico the civil conflicts and the French invasion of Maximilian sharpened the interest in the past and the viewpoints that argued over the model of national construction. The novels of Justo Sierra, Juan A. Mateos and Riva Palacios, who were liberal politicians, usually deal with the theme of the Inquisition as a means of proclaiming the freedom of ideas and attacking the great power of the Catholic Church.

The new historical novel responds to the changes brought about by Postmodernism. Its importance is the symptom of a new crisis in the definition of the nation in Latin America, because the very concept of national identity is questioned. Now it is not a matter of knowing either what that past was like or what it teaches the present, but rather of invalidating cognitive worth and declaring that knowledge inconsistent. Theoretical goals of historiographical discourse as well as the values of the traditional historical novel have become relative. The first solution sought to harmonize truthfulness and fiction, but the current leveling of both discourses, considering the importance of the fictional in the historical discourse, allows the former to be diluted, and this now produces a text which is not faithful, and which admits the inexhaustible possibilities of the multiple. If the historical novel today, situated in the new sophistry of Postmodernism, from which it takes ideas such as the multiplicity of the self or the critique of the subject, does not overcome that neosophistic theoretical barrier, it will not have the ability to reach truth and will remain trapped in the dazzle of verbal pyrotechnics.

Alejo Carpentier is the writer who, in *El reino de este mundo*, 1949 (*The Kingdom of this World*), describes the passage from a documented narrative to another in which invention is dominant: *Concierto barroco*, 1974 (*Baroque Concerto*) and *El arpa y la sombra*, 1979 (*The Harp and the Shadow*). Nevertheless, the works which mark the point of no return are *Yo el Supremo*, 1974 (*I the Supreme*) by the Paraguayan Augusto Roa Bastos and *Terra Nostra* (1975), by the Mexican Carlos Fuentes. The younger exponents of this sceptical approach to history include writers such as Abel Posse, Fernando del Paso and Sergio Ramírez. *Yo el Supremo* is a historical novel which doubly questions historical representation and the representation of the novel itself. Undergoing a constant undermining of its narrative structures, it ends with the impossibility of affirming anything. Historiography and the historical novel are incapable of capturing truth and the only thing that is told is that something is being told. Thus history or the empty spots it leaves are rewritten through irony, parody, the grotesque, the collision of styles, anachronisms. This current tendency of fiction is accompanied by a critical revision of the colonial texts, particularly in the work of mestizo authors, focusing on their rhetorical complexities and relegating Positivist criteria to a secondary level.

In the same manner, certain critical tendencies deny both the existence of historical process and its theoretical representation. Consequently, their exponents do not accept the concept of the historical formation of a "nation." Again, other critics have begun to develop a theory concerning national identities in Latin America and refuse to allow the concept of this historical process to be discarded. Their argument involves a rejection of monological principles, that is, a belief in a homogeneous and implicitly authoritarian reality. Instead, they propose a discourse which is articulated so as to portray the differences or heterogeneous features of national identity. Thus, the nation cannot be theorized according to its perceived essences or individual characteristics: "the Argentine" or "the Peruvian." Its existence is affirmed, but it is defined in terms of the variety of characteristics, of factors which may appear and disappear, leaving their mark, yet not necessarily "eternal."

LUIS MARTUL TOBÍO

See also the entry on Brazil: 19th-Century Prose and Poetry, for information about the Bazilian historical novel

Further Reading

Fiction

Galván, Manuel de Jesús, *Enriquillo, leyenda histórica dominicana*, 1882; critical edition, Mexico City: Porrúa, 1976; as *The Cross and the Sword*, translated by Robert Graves, Bloomington: Indiana University Press, 1954; London: Gollancz, 1956

Gómez de Avellaneda, Gertrudis, *Guatimozín, último emperador de Méjico*, Madrid: Espinosa, 1846; as *Cuahtemac, the Last Aztec Emperor*, translated by Mrs Wilson W. Blake, Mexico: F.P. Hoeck, 1898

Criticism

Balderston, Daniel (editor), *The Historical Novel in Latin America: a Symposium*, Gaithersburg, Maryland: Ediciones Hispamérica, 1986

Chang-Rodríguez, Raquel and Gabriela de Beer (editors), *La historia en la literatura iberoamericana*, Hanover, New Hampshire: Ediciones del Norte, 1989

Hermans, H. and M. Steenmeijer, *La nueva novela histórica hispanoamericana*, Amsterdam: Foro Hispánico, 1990

Menton, Seymour, *Latin America's New Historical Novel*, Austin: University of Texas Press, 1993

Meyer-Minnemann, Klaus, *La novela hispanoamericana del fin de siècle*, Mexico City: Fondo de Cultura Económica, 1991 [Contains a section on *La gloria de Don Ramiro*]

Sblodowska, Elzbieta, "La novela histórica revisitada: parodia y reescritura," in her *La parodia en la nueva novela hispanoamericana (1960–1985)*, Amsterdam and Philadelphia: Benjamins, 1991

Souza, Raymond D., *La historia en la novela hispanoamericana moderna*, Bogotá, Colombia: Tercer Mundo, 1988 [See, in particular, the introduction, "La historia en la imaginación literaria latinoamericana"]

Honduras

19th-and 20th-Century Prose and Poetry

Some literary historians have denied the existence of a specifically Honduran literature during the first decades of Central American independence, and have advanced social, economic and political instability to explain the paucity of literary production during the period from independence to the so-called liberal reform in the 1870s. One could argue, however, that it was precisely this instability regarding their future – whether they would become part of a Mexican empire, if they would join with the other Central American provinces to form a Central American federation, or to what extent they would become sovereign and independent nations – that was the reality and the raw material that informed and inspired the first literary expression of the Honduran people. The Central American provinces achieved independence from Spain in 1821. This date signified a transfer of power from the colonial elite to the wealthy and powerful provincial criollos, who then engaged in their own local as well as regional power struggles for several decades. These power struggles, as well as more altruistic meditations on themes of importance to the emerging nation, such as health, education, agriculture, laws and good government, inspired numerous poems, essays, tracts and speeches. One of the earliest and most important of these was the text of the last testament of Francisco Morazán (1792–1842), native of Tegucigalpa and fervent promoter of Central American union, who served as president of Central America from 1830–38, during its brief life as a regional federation. His last words, dictated to his son in the hours before his execution in Costa Rica, are an impassioned call to the youth of Central America not to let the flame of liberty die. He declares that he does not deserve to die for what he considers to have been patriotic deeds, and nobly forgives his executioners. Other examples of these historico-literary texts are the speech delivered by Dionisio de Herrera (1780–1850), Honduras's first head of state, at the opening of the first legislative assembly (Comayagua, 1825), and "Meditaciones de un pueblo libre" [Thoughts of a Free People], written in 1822 by the illustrious statesman and president of Honduras from 1848–52, Luan Lindo (c. 1790–1857).

One individual stands out for his exemplary participation in regional politics as well as his voluminous writings on topics of practical and philosophical importance. José Cecilio del Valle (1777–1834), known as "El Sabio" [The Sage], was instrumental in drawing up the first Central American constitution in 1824. He was born in Choluteca, Honduras, studied in Guatemala, and worked and published in both Honduras and Guatemala. He wrote essays on a wide variety of topics, including laws and government, freedom of the press, statistics, agriculture, geography and astronomy, and maintained correspondence with intellectuals from England and America. His essay "Los maestros" [Teachers] is a good example of his vision, erudition and clarity of expression. In it he explains the importance of teachers to the well-being and progress of the nation, outlines a national plan for the preparation and evaluation of teachers, and argues for the establishment of a government fund to support public schools and teachers. He declares in favor of an organic approach to education in which theory is not divorced from observation of phenomena. In other essays he reiterates this concern. When he writes about "Estadística" [Statistics], for example, it is to exhort Hondurans not only to appreciate the importance of this science, but to compile statistical information about their own country, the better to know it, and consequently the better to govern it. Although his life and work are not as widely known as some of his contemporaries from other Latin American countries, he can be counted among such great 19th-century humanists as Venezuela's Andrés Bello.

Two factors, one political, the other geographical, stand out as significant in having determined during the colonial period the nature of the geographical region that would become the nation of Honduras. These factors continued to be significant to cultural life in the 19th century. One was the political and cultural dominance of Guatemala, which had been the seat of government during colonial rule. The University of San Carlos in Guatemala City had traditionally been the preeminent institution of higher learning in Central America, and continued to be for many years after independence, until the other countries were able to establish and build up their own national universities. The Honduran National University was founded in 1847, but it took many years for it to grow to a size and prestige that would tempt young intellectuals to stay at home rather than go to study in one of the Guatemalan universities or the University of León in Nicaragua.

The second factor is topography and natural resources. Honduras was and continues to be the most sparsely populated of the Central American countries. The mountain range that cuts through the country effectively separates the north and south coasts and the rugged terrain has made transportation and communication difficult. The capital was moved in 1880 from Comayagua to Tegucigalpa, in the mineral-rich central mountains. Its location created a physical and cultural isolation that either kept Hondurans on the margins of regional and international cultural movements, or motivated them to leave the country to pursue an education or to be in touch with more cosmopolitan circles.

The years immediately following independence were characterized by a series of firsts in Honduran cultural life. In 1822 the first public elementary school was opened in Tegucigalpa. In 1829 the first printing press was brought to Honduras by Francisco Morazán, and it was used to print the first newspaper, La Gaceta del Gobierno [The Government Gazette], in 1830. Around this same time José Cecilio del Valle began Honduras's first periodical, El Amigo de la Patria [The Friend of the Fatherland].

The leading cultural figure in Tegucigalpa at this time was the well-read and eloquent man of letters, Father José Trinidad Reyes (1797–1855). Besides being a tireless and prolific scholar, he was also a poet, playwright and gifted composer. He is remembered for having brought the first piano to Tegucigalpa, and he wrote the scores himself for his pastorelas. These were traditional plays to celebrate the Nativity. The opening scenes typically take place in the countryside, and Father Reyes used these scenes of dialogue among country-folk to moralize or to project his political opinions through his characters. He was also known for his *cuandos* (whens), biting and witty satirical verses that get their name from the final word of each ten-line stanza. Among his essays, "Ideas de Sofía Seyers" [Sophia Seyers's Ideas] is of particular interest for its clever defense of women's education. His many accomplishments include the distinction of being the founder of the Honduran National University and the University Library.

The presidency (1876–83) of Marco Aurelio Soto (1846–1908) marked the beginning of the period known as the liberal reform. His attempt to organize, open and modernize the country led to an increase in foreign investment and the transformation from a subsistence to an export economy. In the socio-cultural realm, his government was responsible for the creation of the National Library and Archives and for improved transportation and communication due to the creation of a national postal and telegraph system and the construction of a southern highway. Soto's advisers and ministers included noted intellectuals such as Ramón Rosa (1848–93) and Adolfo Zúniga, (1836–1900), who worked indefatigably to establish public schools of primary and secondary education throughout the country, to reorient public education away from a clergy-dominated scholasticism and toward an emphasis on science and technology, and to create teachers' colleges to train a new generation of educators. Rosa was an eloquent essayist and biographer. His biographical subjects include José Trinidad Reyes, José Cecilio del Valle and Francisco Morazán.

The willingness to devote public revenues to education and culture was a revolutionary concept in Honduras, and it soon bore fruit. The relative stability and openness of Honduran society at this time, as well as government sponsorship of study abroad, allowed for more international cultural exchange. This was reflected in the styles and themes adopted by the new generation of writers. The late 19th and early 20th centuries saw a proliferation of literate individuals who, while maintaining active participation in government, commerce or medicine, found time to write verses that reflected the themes and styles of Romanticism. Few poets devoted themselves exclusively to a literary occupation. The modern phenomenon of publishing companies did not exist then, rather, if financially able and so inclined, one might have one's own book printed and distribute it among friends. Other ways of sharing one's poetic expression were through literary periodicals of mostly ephemeral existence, such as *El Guacerique*, which survived for five issues around 1875, and by giving copies of one's poems to friends or composing verses as gifts for special occasions or as remembrances in personal albums.

Among the late-19th-century poets are Adán Cuevas (1852–95), Carlos F. Gutiérrez (1861–99), Lucila Estrada de Pérez (1856–?), Josefa Carrasco (1855–1945) and Manuel Molina Vigil (1853–83). Critical opinion in Honduras often singles out from this group, José Antonio Domínguez (1869–1903), for the depth and quality of his poetry. His themes are quintessentially Romantic: beauty, freedom, idealism, the drama of nature, but the musicality of his verse connects him as well to Spanish American *Modernismo*. His most important work, "Himno a la materia" [Hymn to Matter], is an ambitious long poem that addresses the philosophical question of humanity's spiritual and material nature.

Honduran writers at the turn of the century were aware of the then popular *Modernismo*, and many tried their hand at it, few with any great success, perhaps because its preciousness and exoticism were so far removed from their reality. One exception was Juan Ramón Molina (1875–1908), who achieved international acclaim and is considered one of Central America's finest *modernista* poets. His collected lyrics were published in 1911 as *Tierras, mares y cielos* [Lands, Seas and Skies].

Hondurans in the first decades of the 20th century kept themselves informed of international literary trends largely through the efforts of their pre-emminent man of letters Froylán Turcios (1875–1943). He founded and/or directed numerous newspapers and literary journals, notably *Esfinge* [Sphinx] and *Ariel*, which published the work of Honduran writers as well as excerpts from classics of world literature, and the *Boletín de la Defensa Nacional* [Bulletin of National Defence], an important political paper that denounced the occupation of Tegucigalpa by US Marines in 1924. Besides novellas, short stories and poetry, Turcios chronicled his most interesting life in *Memorias* [Memoirs], published posthumously in 1980.

Narrative fiction made its appearance at the turn of the century with the publication of the first Honduran novel, by the prolific Lucila Gamero de Medina (1873–1964). A practicing physician, essayist, feminist and active Pan-Americanist, Doña Lucila published numerous novels during her long and productive life. The first two were published in Tegucigalpa in 1893: *Amalia Montiel* and *Adriana y Margarita* [Adriana and Margarita]. Her best known work is *Blanca Olmedo* (1903), a romantic novel that was controversial because of its open attack on the Catholic clergy. Carlos F. Gutiérrez's novella, *Angelina* (1898), had enjoyed the reputation for being Honduras's first novel, until it was shown that Gamero's novels predated his.

Much Honduran prose, particularly but not exclusively of the first half of the 20th century, conforms to the styles and themes of *costumbrismo*, also known as *criollismo*, which delights in local color and folk ways and attempts to recreate the customs, language and landscape primarily of the countryside, although urban characters are treated as well. Noteworthy among the authors who have cultivated an anecdotal style that idealizes the Honduran country dweller is Víctor Cáceres Lara, whose short stories have been collected in *Tierra ardiente*, 1970 [Burning Earth]. Marco Antonio Rosa (1899–1983) in his novel, *Tegucigalpa, ciudad de remembranzas*, 1968 [Tegucigalpa, City of Memories], evokes a bygone time with romantic nostalgia, as he chronicles life in the Honduran capital when it was a sleepy provincial town with a well-defined class system. Daniel Laínez (1914–59) portrayed the literati and other urban eccentrics of Tegucigalpa with a touch of black humor in *Estampas locales*, 1948 [Local Sketches] and *Manicomio* [Insane Asylum], published posthumously in 1980. Medardo Mejía (1907–81), in *Comizahual, leyendas, tradiciones y relatos de Honduras*, 1981 [Comizahual, Legends, Traditions and Stories of Honduras], employs irony, sarcasm and humor to deconstruct the social patterns of Honduran society.

Also numerous have been narratives that combine the descriptive and folk-oriented impulse of *costumbrismo* with a denunciation of the exploitation of national territory by foreign interests, in particular the Standard and Cuyamel Fruit Companies on the north coast. Paca Navas de Miralda (1900–69), who had distinguished herself as a folklorist with the publication of *Ritmos criollos*, 1947 [Creole Rhythms], published in 1951, *Barro* [Clay], a novel set in a town newly established for workers of an international fruit company. It details the lives of families who leave their homes in the interior of the country, attracted by the hope of a more prosperous life on the coast. The novel weaves together scenes of traditional domesticity and daily life, and descriptions of the hard work and suffering of the transplanted families, with conversations intended to record the actual speech of this population. Other novels of this genre are more denunciatory, such as *Trópico* [Tropics], written in 1948 and published posthumously in 1971, by Marcos Carías Reyes (1905–49). Ramón Amaya Amador (1916–66), a self-taught writer and journalist from a working-class family, was himself a worker on the north coast banana plantations for many years. In 1943, he founded *Alerta* [Alert], a weekly newspaper dedicated to defending the interests of the workers. Due to subsequent political persecution by the government of Tiburcio Carías Andino, he lived much of the rest of his life in exile. His novel *Prisión verde*, 1950 [Green Prison], has become a classic example of socially committed writing in Honduras. Another novel worthy of mention is *Peregrinaje* (published in English as *Enriqueta and I*, 1944), by Argentina Díaz Lozano (1914–). Told from the point of view of a young girl who traverses Honduras with her widowed mother, a school teacher who moves from job to job until she finally settles in the capital, it is a charming blend of *costumbrismo* and autobiography. Díaz Lozano is one of Honduras's most prolific authors, with over sixteen titles published, including poetry, novels and biography. Her forte is historical fiction.

Many contemporary fiction writers tend to be experimental in technique and wide-ranging in theme, although the Honduran milieu prevails. The short story remains the preferred genre, even though many accomplished short story writers have written novels as well. Marcos Carías Zapata (1938–), for example, began his career with a book of stories, *La ternura que esperaba*, 1970 [The Hoped for Tenderness], and has subsequently turned to longer fiction, of note, *Una función con móbiles y tentetiesos*, 1980 [Performance with Mobiles and Roly-Poly Toys], a linguistic and structural *tour de force* that attempts to reflect the multi-level sensorial reality of contemporary Tegucigalpa.

While most of the current generation of fiction writers ascribe to a politically progressive ideology, they have as a group not expressed their commitment in propagandist prose. Some have dealt with political themes such as the war between Honduras and El Salvador of 1969, for example Eduardo Bähr (1940–) in *El cuento de la guerra*, 1973 [The War Story], and Julio Escoto (1944–) in *Días de ventisca, noches de huracán*, 1980 [Days of Blizzard, Nights of Hurricane], but language and narrative technique play an equally important role with political urgency, which was usually not the case with the committed writers of the past. The predilection for magical realism that infected so many Latin American writers influenced by García Márquez's astounding fame, can be seen in contemporary Honduran narrative, but this tendency has developed national idiosyncracies that distinguish it from its predecessors and counterparts. Among these qualities are deeply complex if eccentric characters, trapped in a world bounded by poverty, historical misfortune and the absence of any real hope for change. One also finds an intriguing blend of the tragic and the comic, and the persistent and intrusive presence of the military. Among the best of the current fiction writers are Roberto Castillo (1950–), Horacio Castellanos Moya (1957–), Julio Escoto and Jorge Luis Oviedo (1957–). Of these, Julio Escoto has been the most prolific, and has achieved a well-deserved international reputation. His most recent novel, *Madrugada*, 1993 [Daybreak], is an ambitious work that explores the Honduran and Central American national identity throughout its history of conquest, colonization and exploitation.

Like the narrative, Honduran poetry has grown and changed during the 20th century, responding to internal realities as well as to international literary trends. The poets who came to be known as the Generation of 1935 participated in one of the most creative and diverse periods in Honduran literary history. Their penchant for gathering in local cafés and the bohemian self-concept they shared contributed to their group identity, although they published no literary manifesto, as was common among vanguard groups of the time. Inflamed by the Republican cause during the Spanish Civil War and personally affected by the dictatorship (1933–49) of Tiburcio Carías Andino, poets such as Claudio Barrera (pseudonym of Vicente Alemán, 1912–71), Jacobo Cárcomo (1916–59) and Daniel Laínez (1914–59) turned to social and political themes after an initial period of experimentation with avant-garde techniques. Laínez is known for his use of rural themes and speech. Barrera and Cárcamo both fled the dictatorship and spent time in Mexico, as did many other writers, artists and intellectuals. Most of the poets of this generation experimented with the themes and rhythms of the then popular *negrista* poetry, which is not surprising considering the large African-Caribbean population on the north coast.

The work of the next important generation of poets, the Generation of 1950, is characterized by two predominant themes: the desire for social justice and the beauty, passion and complexity of the love relationship. Pompeyo del Valle's (1929–) *La ruta fulgurante*, 1956 [The Shining Path] exemplifies this first tendency, while Oscar Acosta's (1933–) *Formas del amor*, 1959 [Forms of Love] is an outstanding example of the latter. Roberto Sosa (1930–) is the most distinguished poet of this group. His finely crafted and deeply sensitive poetry has been widely translated. His work is permeated with compassion and a sense of sorrow and outrage at injustice. Among his volumes of poetry are *Un mundo para todos dividido*, 1971 [A World for All Divided], *Los pobres*, 1979 [The Poor], and *Secreto militar*, 1985 [Military Secret]. His collected works were published in 1993.

A firm footing in the country's social and political reality is a constant in the poetry of the later 20th century. Following in the footsteps of Roberto Sosa, poets such as Rigoberto Paredes (1948–) and José Luis Quesada (1948–) never forget that they are Honduran, but their tone is significantly different from their predecessors. Paredes's *Las cosas por su nombre*,

1978 [Things by Their Names] and *Materia prima*, 1985 [Raw Material] are informed by a mocking and ironic irreverence, while Quesada's *La memoria posible*, 1990 [Possible Memory] is anguished, serious and reflective. José Adán Castelar (1940–), like the novelist Ramón Amaya Amador, is of humble extraction and worked on the banana plantations of the north coast. His poetry expresses the daily life and concerns of the Honduran working class and denounces their exploitation by the military and by foreign interests. Other active and noteworthy poets of this time are David Díaz Acosta (1951–), José González (1953–) and Juan Ramón Saravia (1951–).

Women writers of Honduras are still perceived as marginal or exceptional, although today's young men and women are beginning to confront this prejudice. The first woman to publish a volume of poetry in Honduras was Clementina Suárez (1902–91), whose *Corazón sangrante*, 1930 [Bleeding Heart] brought her widespread notoriety. Recognized now as Honduras's foremost woman poet, Suárez struggled throughout her life to create a place for herself in Honduran and Central American literary history. She began her career writing romantic sonnets, but later turned to free verse to express her social commitment and to celebrate love, sexuality, motherhood and freedom. She continues to be an inspiration to new generations of women writers who admire her lifelong dedication to her art as well as her strength and independence. Other women who have written noteworthy poetry in this century are Victoria Bertrand (1907–51), Eva Thais (pseudonym of Edith Tarrius López, 1931–) and Ángela Valle (1927–). Noteworthy among the current generation are María Eugenia Ramos (1959–), Aída Ondina Sabonge (1958–), Aleyda Romero and Yadira Eguiguren. Ramos's *Porque ningún sol es el último*, 1989 [Because No Sun is the Last] expresses in language that is often colloquial, an acute social awareness. Sabonge's first published volume, *Declaración doméstica*, 1993 [Domestic Statement], displays a strong, intelligent voice, conscious of her femininity and her feminism. Romero and Eguiguren, the youngest of this new generation of women poets, have not yet published their work in book form.

Finally, mention must be made of the work of three writer-scholars whose efforts have been significant in the appreciation and professionalization of Honduran letters. Rafael Heliodoro Valle (1891–1959), poet, journalist, historian, anthologist and bibliophile, compiled numerous important bibliographies and wrote serious studies that have served scholars in their study of Honduran culture, among them, *Historia de la cultura hondureña* [History of Honduran Culture], published posthumously in 1981. Rómulo E. Durón (1865–1942) collected the literature of Honduras of the 19th century in *Honduras literaria*, 1896–99 [Literary Honduras]. And Helen Umaña (1942–) has contributed significantly to the understanding and appreciation of Honduran literature through her excellent critical studies, including *Literatura hondureña contemporánea*, 1986 [Contemporary Honduran Literature] and *Narradoras hondureñas*, 1990 [Honduran Women Novelists].

JANET N. GOLD

Further Reading

Argueta, Mario R., *Diccionario crítico de obras literarias hondureñas*, Tegucigalpa: Guaymuras, 1993

Cárdenas Amador, Galel (editor), *Primer simposio de literatura hondureña*, Tegucigalpa: Universidad Nacional Autónoma de Honduras, 1991

Durón, Rómulo E., *Honduras literaria*, 2 vols, Tegucigalpa: Ministerio de Educación, 1896–99

Gold, Janet N., *Clementina Suárez: Her Life and Poetry*, Gainesville: University Presses of Florida, 1995

López Lazo, José D., *Voces de la literatura hondureña actual*, Tegucigalpa: Universidad Nacional Autónoma de Honduras, 1994

Martínez, José Francisco, *Literatura hondureña y su proceso generacional*, Tegucigalpa: Universidad Nacional Autónoma de Honduras, 1987

Paredes, Rigoberto and Manuel Salinas Paguada (editors), *Literatura hondureña*, Tegucigalpa: Editores Unidos, 1987

Salinas Paguada, Manuel, *Cultura hondureña contemporánea*, Tegucigalpa: Universidad Nacional Autónoma de Honduras, 1991

Sosa, Roberto (editor), *Diálogo de sombras*, Tegucigalpa: Editorial Guaymuras, 1993

Umaña, Helen, *Literatura hondureña contemporánea (ensayos)*, Tegucigalpa: Guaymuras, 1986

—— *Narradoras hondureñas*, Tegucigalpa: Guaymuras, 1990

—— *Ensayos sobre literatura hondureña*, Tegucigalpa: Guaymuras, 1992

Valle, Rafael Heliodoro, *Historia de la cultura hondureña*, Tegucigalpa: Universidad Nacional Autónoma de Honduras, 1981

Vicente Huidobro 1893–1948

Chilean poet and prose writer

Although Vicente Huidobro is known primarily as a poet, his constant search for innovation led him to experiment with other literary genres, including fiction, drama, critical essays on film and literature, and journalism (as a World War II correspondent). Huidobro even wrote a screenplay called "Cagliostro," based on the life of an 18th-century mystic, for which he won a $10,000 prize in 1927. Because Huidobro was born into a patrician South American family (his family residence in Santiago de Chile at the corner of the Alameda and San Martín was a sumptuous, European-style palace), he was independently wealthy throughout his life. This biographical fact helps explain Huidobro's mobility as a literary (and political) activist and tireless promoter of his own work. He was a ubiquitous figure, living in order to create aesthetic conflicts, to crusade for converts to his artistic ideals and to joust with anyone or anything (including the entire universe) in disagreement with him. His many travels between Europe and the American continent enabled him to remain in the public eye through conferences, controversial manifestos and literary magazines. He also appeared at key historical periods (e.g., in France during the artistic effervescence of Cubism, in Chile as the Popular Front came into being, and in Spain throughout the Spanish Civil War) and was able to insert himself with an uncanny, natural ease in these varied contexts.

Huidobro was a bilingual poet, who composed a third of his production in French, including early versions of his long poem *Altazor* (the title is an invention by Huidobro based on the Spanish words for "high" and "hawk"), a masterpiece of 20th-century poetry, which exists in a superb English translation by Eliot Weinberger (1988). Huidobro travelled to Paris in December 1916 and, over the next two years, began producing avant-garde literature in conjunction with Guillaume Apollinaire, Juan Gris, Pablo Picasso, Max Jacob, Jacques Lipchitz, Diego Rivera, Jean Cocteau, Pierre Reverdy, Robert Delaunay and others in works such as *Horizon carré* [Square Horizon], *Poemas árticos* (Arctic Poems), *Ecuatorial* [Equatorial], and *Tour Eiffel* [Eiffel Tower]. There is a facsimile edition of this last work included with the truly magnificent 400-page issue of *Poesía* dedicated to Huidobro, which was edited by René De Costa and published by Spain's Ministry of Culture in 1989. Huidobro was not only an integral part of this pioneering epoch when Paris was the cultural capital of the world, but also, as Octavio Paz says, the bridge between the French vanguard and the poetry of the Spanish language.

Huidobro is a transitional figure as well in that he links the *modernista* aesthetics of Nicaraguan poet Rubén Darío (1867–1916) with the avant-garde poetics of the Hispanic American *vanguardistas*. For example, Huidobro's "Arte poética" [Ars Poetica] from *El espejo de agua*, 1916 [The Mirror of Water] with its conception of the poet as "un pequeño dios" (a little god), is a reduced-scale version of Darío's desperate hymn to artistic elitism in "¡Torres de Dios! ¡Poetas! . . ." [Towers of God! Poets!], which he wrote in Paris in 1903. Huidobro may have moved away from Darío's traditional alexandrines and innovative rhythms in order to explore the new precisions of *vers libre* and concrete poetry, but something of Darío's lyrical voice survived in his poetry, even in the fragmentation and collapse of language in *Altazor*. Huidobro's first calligrammes (poems in the shape of a chapel and a triangle) resemble the typographical experimentation of Guillaume Apollinaire (even though, as René De Costa points out, they predate the 1918 publication of Apollinaire's *Calligrammes* by six years), yet at the same time make use of Darío's refined vocabulary, solemn tone and exotic themes.

Although fundamentally lyrical poems, Huidobro's *Ecuatorial* (1918) and *Altazor* (begun in 1919, but not published until 1931) have a great deal in common in terms of their avant-garde method of composition. Huidobro's preoccupation with metaphor as a way of joining the dissimilar as well as with word-collage, which he used to create striking, layered juxtapositions in addition to a new graphic sense of the printed page, led him to formulate the tenets of what he called *creacionismo*. Creationism was Huidobro's poorly-defined and shortlived (late teens through the first years of the 1920s) attempt to militantly create an artistic movement around himself and his own publications as well as to expropriate an aesthetic already embodied in Cubism. *Altazor* might be considered the brilliant result of another kind of failure. René De Costa has called this long poem by Huidobro "a text in discontinuous progress, suddenly brought to a conclusion, frozen as an 'open work'." The long period of its composition (twelve years) and its rough, unfinished appearance bespeak a work that leaves literary difficulties unresolved, thereby creating a new, visionary poetics. This is one of the 20th century's most radical poems in linguistic terms. There are powerful metamorphoses of the word operating in this work (which is divided into seven Cantos), especially in the "golondrina" (swallow) and "ruiseñor" (nightingale) sections of Canto IV. The metaphorical extravagance of the "molino" (mill) in Canto V is classic Huidobro. Since the subtitle of *Altazor* is "A Voyage in a Parachute," it is only appropriate that Canto VII ends in a primal scream – as if the parachute (of faith in God and redemption? of belief in the poetic word?) had failed to open for Huidobro, the aerial poet. Indeed, as one critic has suggested, *Altazor* is an abandonment of the poetic modes of expression embodied in Symbolism, Modernism, Creationism and Surrealism. In Canto VII, this disarticulation of language becomes a new anti-language that is composed solely of sound and fragments of words.

Despite the preponderance of metaphysical and ontological themes in *Ecuatorial* and *Altazor*, Huidobro's legacy is also one of playfulness. Huidobro's marvelous experiments, as Eliot Weinberger has pointed out, are part of his conception of poetry as "a divine game of language."

STEVEN F. WHITE

Biography

Born Vicente García Huidobro Fernández in Santiago de Chile, 10 January 1893, into a wealthy aristocratic family. Attended the

Jesuit-run Colegio San Ignacio, Santiago; Berthelot Lyceum. Married Manuela Portas Bello in 1912. Founded the journals *Musa Joven* and *Azul*, 1912–13. Moved to Paris in 1916 and associated with the leading literary figures of the time. Contributed to French avant-garde literary magazines; co-founder, with Pierre Reverdy and Guillaume Apollinaire, of the journal *Nord-Sud*, 1917. Travelled widely throughout Europe immediately after World War I: visited Madrid in 1918. Actively involved in *ultraísmo*, a Hispanic vanguard poetry movement, with Gerardo Diego, Juan Larrea and Jorge Luis Borges. Returned to Chile in 1925; founder, *Acción, Dario de Purificación Nacional*, Santiago. Candidate in the Presidential election. Began a relationship with Ximena Amunátegui; Huidobro announced their affair in *La Nación* provoking a scandal; he was obliged to leave the country. Returned to Chile secretly in 1928 and kidnapped Ximena. Joined Republican forces during Spanish Civil War (1936–38). Returned to Chile, 1938. Served with the Allied Forces during World War II; sustained serious head wound. Died in Cartagena, as a delayed result of his injury, 2 January 1948.

Selected Works

Poetry

Ecos del alma, Santiago de Chile: Imprenta Chile, 1911
Canciones en la noche, Santiago de Chile: Imprenta Chile, 1913
La gruta del silencio, Santiago de Chile: Imprenta Universitaria, 1913
Adán, Santiago de Chile: Imprenta Universitaria, 1914
El espejo de agua, Buenos Aires: Orión, 1916
Horizon carré, Paris: Paul Birault, 1917
Ecuatorial, Madrid: Imprenta Pueyo, 1918
Hallali: poème de guerre, Madrid: Jesús López, 1918
Poemas árticos, Madrid: Imprenta Pueyo, 1918; as *Arctic Poems*, translated by William Witherup and Serge Echeverría, Santa Fe, New Mexico: Desert Review Press, 1974
Tour Eiffel, Madrid: Imprenta Pueyo, 1918
Automne régulier, Paris: Librairie de France, 1925
Tout à coup, Paris: Au Sans Pareil, 1925
Altazor, o, el viaje en paracaídas, poema en VII cantos, Madrid: Iberoamericana, 1931 (originally published in various periodicals); as *Altazor, or, a Voyage in a Parachute*, translated by Eliot Weinberger, St Paul, Minnesota: Graywolf Press, 1988
Temblor de cielo, Madrid: Plutarco, 1931
El ciudadano del olvido (1924–1934), Santiago de Chile: Ercilla, 1941

Novels

Mío Cid Campeador, hazaña, Madrid: Compañía Iberoamericana de Publicaciones, 1929; as *Portrait of a Paladin*, translated by Warre B. Wells, London: Eyre and Spottiswoode, 1931; New York: Liveright, 1932
The Mirror of a Mage, translated by Warre B. Wells, London: Eyre and Spottiswoode, and Boston: Houghton Mifflin, 1931 (English translation published before Spanish original); *Cagliostro, novela-film*, Santiago de Chile: Zig-Zag, 1934
Papá; o, el diario de Alicia Mir, Santiago de Chile: Walton, 1934
La próxima (historia que pasó en poco tiempo más), Santiago de Chile: Walton, 1934

Tres inmensas novelas, in collaboration with Hans Arp, Santiago de Chile: Zig-Zag, 1935
Sátiro o, el poder de las palabras, Santiago de Chile: Zig-Zag, 1939

Essays

Pasando y pasando: crónicas y comentarios, Santiago de Chile: Imprenta Chile, 1914
¡Finis Britannia! Une redoutable société s'est dressée contre l'impérialisme anglais, Paris: Fiat Lux, 1923
Manifestes, Paris: Editions de la Revue Mondiale, 1925
Vientos contrarios, Santiago de Chile: Nascimento, 1926

Compilations and Anthologies

Saisons choisies, Paris: La Cible, 1921 [poetry and prose]
Últimos poemas, Santiago de Chile: Talleres Gráficos Ahués, 1948
Obras completas, 2 vols, introduction by Hugo Montes, Santiago de Chile: Andrés Bello, 1976
Poética y estética creacionistas, edited by Vicente Quirarte, Mexico City: UNAM, 1994

Translations

The Selected Poems of Vicente Huidobro, edited and translated by David M. Guss, New York: New Directions, 1981
The Poet is a Little God, translated by Jorge García-Gómez, San Bernadino, California: Borgo Press, 1990 [Contains translations from *El espejo de agua*, *Poemas árticos* and *Ecuatorial*]

Further Reading

Admussen, Richard L. and René De Costa, "Huidobro, Reverdy and the *editio princeps* of El espejo de agua," *Comparative Literature* 24 (1972)
Camurati, Mireya, *Poesía y poética de Vicente Huidobro*, Madrid: Cambeiro, 1980
Concha, Jaime, "*Altazor*, de Vicente Huidobro," *Anales de la Universidad de Chile* 73 (1965)
____ *Vicente Huidobro*, Madrid: Júcar, 1980
De Costa, René, *Vicente Huidobro y el creacionismo*, Madrid: Taurus, 1975
____ *En pos de Huidobro: siete ensayos de interpretación*, Santiago de Chile: Editorial Universitaria, 1980
____ *Vicente Huidobro: the Careers of a Poet*, Oxford: Clarendon Press, and New York: Oxford University Press, 1984
Forster, Merlin H., "Elementos de innovación en la narrativa de *Tres inmensas novelas*," in *Prosa hispánica de vanguardia*, edited by Fernando Burgos, Madrid: Orígenes, 1986
Neghme Echeverría, Lidia, "El creacionismo político de Huidobro en *En la luna*," *Latin American Theatre Review*, vol. 18/1 (1984)
Picon Garfield, Evelyn, "Tradición y ruptura: modernidad en *Tres novelas ejemplares* de Vicente Huidobro y Hans Arp," *Hispanic Review*, vol. 51 (1983)
Schwartz, Jorge, "Vicente Huidobro o la cosmópolis textualizada," *Eco*, 202/1 (1978)
Yúdice, George, *Vicente Huidobro y la motivación del lenguaje*, Buenos Aires: Galerna, 1978

Special Issues of Journals

"Vicente Huidobro y la vanguardia," *Revista Iberoamericana*, vol. 45/106–07 (1979)

I

Juana de Ibarbourou 1892–1979

Uruguayan poet and prose writer

Juana Fernández is known by her married name, de Ibarbourou, which is a Basque term meaning "head of the valley." She was one of the pioneers of a literary tradition for women in Latin America, and her literary career spanned some fifty years. Her work is connected to the production of Alfonsina Storni (Argentina) and Gabriela Mistral (Chile) because all three of them wrote in the first decades of the 20th century and found a "room of their own" through their writing. They questioned the prejudices and conventions of the conservative middle class from within its own ranks. As women enclosed in a patriarchal society they wrote from the margins focusing on their own difference, creating a new poetic language on the margins of male poetic discourse.

Juana de Ibarbourou was a self-educated writer who started her literary career with a book of poems, *Las lenguas de diamante*, 1919 [Diamond Tongues], followed by a narrative text, *El cántaro fresco*, 1920 [The Fresh Earthen Vessel], and a second collection of poems, *Raíz salvaje*, 1922 [Savage Root]. In her early poetry Ibarbourou used free verse and focused on the female body and its sensuality, as is exemplified in some poems from *Las lenguas de diamante*, such as "Salvaje"[Savage], "Ofrenda" [Offer], or in the verses from "Te doy mi alma" [I Give You My Soul]: "Desnuda y toda abierta de par en par / Por el goce de amar" (Naked and wide open / for the enjoyment of loving). The emphasis on female sensuality and erotic pleasure is also the main focus of one of her predecessors and fellow uruguayan, Delmira Agustini. They both break the silence of woman's sexual desire by giving it a voice through their poems. In de Ibarbourou's poems the female body becomes the place of receiving and giving in to the lover, and also the site where is conceived a harmony with Nature. In "La buena criatura" [The Good Creature], the subject of the utterance considers water to be her sister, and her hands literally to bloom in "El dulce milagro" [Sweet Miracle]. The images of Nature fused with Culture within her body are constant, both in her poems and narrative, giving a sense of wholeness.

Juana de Ibarbourou had a son in 1917, Julio César Ibarbourou, and her experience of maternity became a source of creativity, as is shown through her *Diario de una joven madre* [Diary of a Young Mother], or in her autobiographical text *Chico-Carlo*, 1944 [Kid Carlo], where she recalls some of her own childhood friends and memories. The plays, *Los sueños de Natacha*, 1945 [Natacha's Dreams], and *Puck*, are also examples of children's literature. She also wrote her own version of some traditional children's stories such as "Caperucita roja" [Little Red Riding Hood] or created new ones as in "La primera lección" [The First Lesson].

The passing of time and the inevitability of death appears as another of her themes, materialized in her poems from "Vida-Garfio" [Hook-Life], included in *Las lenguas de diamante*, to her later texts *Perdida*, 1950 [Lost], *Elegía*, 1967 [Elegy] and *La pasajera*, 1967 [The Woman Passenger]. Her battle against time is displayed in the theme of "carpe diem," exemplified in "Laceria" [Wretchedness], and the famous verses "Tómame ahora que aún es temprano / y que llevo dalias nuevas en la mano" (Take me now while it is still early / and I carry fresh dahlias in my hand) from "La hora" [The Hour], both poems from her first book. Her own fight against death, added to the death of her father, mother and husband, generates the development of a religious mysticism appearing in some narrative texts, *Loores de Nuestra Señora*, 1934 [Praise to Our Lady], *Estampas de la Biblia*, 1934 [Bible Prints], and *San Francisco de Asís*, 1935. These narrative works have been the center of attention of literary criticism, to the detriment of her early texts.

As a feminist, de Ibarbourou gives a voice to bourgeois Latin American women by writing from that particular perspective. That is to say, by inserting her identity as a female lover and as a mother into the hegemonic literary discourses of the day. Her social status as a married woman meant that her personal discourse was accepted and integrated into the public one. Her success culminated in her election as the "Woman of the Americas" by the Union of American Women of New York in 1953 and through being nominated for the Nobel Prize in 1958.

ANA MARÍA BRENES-GARCÍA

Biography

Born Juana Fernández in Melo, Uruguay, 8 March 1892 (some sources give 1895). Family lived in several military posts in the interior before settling in the capital, Montevideo, 1918. Self-educated. Married Lucas Ibarbourou in 1913, who died in 1942; one son. Nominated, "Juana de América," 1929. Member of the Uruguayan Academy of Letters, 1947. President, Uruguayan Writers Association, AUDE, 1949. Elected, "Woman of the Américas" by Union of American Women of New York, 1953. Nominated for Nobel Prize, 1958. Emeritus member, National Academy of Letters, 1960. Died in Montevideo, 15 July 1979. Granted state funeral.

Selected Works

Poetry

Las lenguas de diamante, Buenos Aires: Cooperativa Editorial Limitada, 1919
Raíz salvaje, Montevideo: Editorial Maximino García, 1922
La rosa de los vientos, Montevideo: Palacio del Libro, 1930
Perdida, Buenos Aires: Losada, 1950
Azor, Buenos Aires: Losada, 1953
Oro y tormenta, Santiago de Chile: Zig-Zag, 1956
Elegía, San Juan: Universidad de Río Piedras de Puerto Rico, 1967
La pasajera, Buenos Aires: Losada, 1967

Prose Works

El cántaro fresco, Montevideo: Editora Uruguaya, 1920
Loores de Nuestra Señora, Montevideo: Barreiro y Ramos, 1934
Estampas de la Biblia, Montevideo: Barreiro y Ramos, 1934
San Francisco de Asís, Montevideo: Imprenta Rosgal, 1935
Juan soldado, Buenos Aires: Losada, 1971

Children's Literature

Chico Carlo, Montevideo: Barreiro y Ramos, 1944
Los sueños de Natacha, Montevideo: Ediciones Liceo, 1945

Compilations and Anthologies

Juana de Ibarbourou: obras completas, edited by Dora Isella Russell, 2nd edition, Madrid: Aguilar, 1960
Obras, 5 vols, Montevideo: Instituto Nacional del Libro, 1992

Further Reading

Arbeleche, Jorge, *Juana de Ibarbourou*, Montevideo: Editorial Técnica, S.R.L., 1978
Castro, Juan Jesús, *Cronología de la vida y obra de Juana de Ibarbourou*, Montevideo: El Galeón, 1992
Irving, Evelyn, "La literatura infantil de Juana de Ibarbourou," in *Proceedings of the International Literature Conference: Homage to Agustini, Ibarbourou, Mistral, Storni*, Calexico: Institute for Border Studies, San Diego State University, 1991
Pickenhayen, Jorge Oscar, *Vida y obra de Juana de Ibarbourou*, Buenos Aires: Plus Ultra, 1975

Jorge Ibargüengoitia 1928–1983

Mexican prose writer, dramatist and journalist

A follower of Rodolfo Usigli – one of Mexico's best-known dramatists – Jorge Ibargüengoitia began his literary career as a playwright. In 1954 his play *Susana y los jóvenes* [Susana and the Young People] was performed with relative success, and was followed one year later by *Clotilde en su casa* [Clotilde at Home]. These two works set the pattern found in most of his plays, dealing satirically with the daily life of the Mexican upper-middle classes and bourgeoisie. After this brief period of success, Ibargüengoitia wrote ten further plays, the great majority of which were not performed. The last in this little known series is *El atentado*, 1964 [The Assassination] which, despite receiving an award, also failed to reach the stage. In this play, Ibargüengoitia breaks with his previously preferred themes and tackles a historical subject for the first time: "The death," according to the author himself, " in 1928 of a Mexican president (General Álvaro Obregón) at the hands of a Catholic." This work, which lays bare the various machinations of the ruling classes and the military, was subject to government censorship for over fifteen years and could only be produced in 1975. This was Ibargüengoitia's last play. It was, however, the documentary research undertaken for *El atentado* which inspired his first novel, *Los relámpagos de agosto*, 1964 (*The Lightning of August*).

This novel, written in 1962 and published in 1964, reconstructs a period of Mexican history through the "memoirs" of a revolutionary general. It is here that Ibargüengoitia finally succeeds in voicing not only a social criticism of established morality – already present in his dramatic works – but also, simultaneously and with great refinement, critically penetrating Mexican history – with all its myths and time-honoured truths – and the use of power by the governing classes. This novel displays all the concerns and themes which Ibargüengoitia develops with sustained quality in his prose works until his tragic death in 1983.

La ley de Herodes [Herod's Law], his second prose work, was published in 1967, by which time Ibargüengoitia was also writing as a journalist. Despite being a collection of short narratives, this work is held together by a favourite theme of the author's: the upbeat record of urban life and humour. In this book, he produces a detailed account of daily life in the Mexican capital, which includes various autobiographical elements.

Maten al león, 1969 [Kill the Lion], is his second novel. Intended originally as a film script based on *El atentado*, this is a classic in which Ibargüengoitia depicts, with heavy irony, the figure of the Latin American patriarchal dictator (as have, among others, Asturias, Roa Bastos and García Márquez). However, Ibargüengoitia differs in approach from the others by producing a farce in which the dictators appear as ridiculous and obtuse as their enemies. It is in this work, as with *Los relámpagos de agosto*, that Ibargüengoitia best elaborates one of his predominant themes: a caricature of the Mexican Revolution, an ironic and disrespectful reading of the disaster unleashed by it and the possible ideas and causes behind the event.

Estas ruinas que ves, 1975 [These Ruins You See], his third novel, continues the more or less autobiographical tone already begun in *La ley de Herodes*. "*Estas ruinas que ves*," notes the critic Jaime Castañeda Iturbe, "becomes a novelistic account of customs, whose common factor is eroticism, a subject which the author treats with the iniquity and humour that characterise his work. Indeed, the episodes and anecdotes described not only amuse and entertain, but possess the lucid and demythologising quality of his other novels."

Las muertas, 1977 (*The Dead Girls*), the plot for which Ibargüengoitia alludes to in *Estas ruinas que ves*, is the narrative of a police incident involving a group of women from the Bajío area, dealing in the white slave trade, known as "Las Poquianchas." *Las muertas* is without a doubt Ibargüengoitia's most refined work, but perhaps not his most probing. The novel's main virtue is its success in combining different time levels, not only when dealing with events which occur simultaneously within the plot, but in relation to the temporal diversity of the characters themselves. The means for achieving this is as simple as it is awkward: the story is divided into various temporal segments, each described by a different character.

Dos crímenes (*Two Crimes*), Ibargüengoitia's fifth novel, published in 1979, is perhaps his most astute, probing and, from the point of view of narrative rhythm, his most sustained work. Despite dealing once again with the police, as he did in *Las muertas*, and despite being dominated throughout by intrigue, Ibargüengoitia succeeds in displaying humour, irony and a fluent narrative which constantly surprises the reader.

Los pasos de López, 1982 [Lopez's Footsteps], his last novel, is set at the beginning of the Mexican War of Independence and originates, as did *Los relámpagos de agosto*, from a play entitled *La conspiración vendida* [The Bought Conspiracy] which Ibargüengoitia had been commissioned to write in 1959. In similar vein to his first novel, *Los pasos de López* explores a historical account. His aim, which he undoubtedly achieves, is, in his own words, "to reveal history as a Sphinx without a secret, a vacant or disproportionate pedestal; but without bitterness, without hate ... " All the great myths of post-revolutionary Mexico are knocked off their pedestal and made to seem trivial and ordinary in a readable and amusing manner. The assertion which underlies the entire novel is a view which Ibargüengoitia defends lucidly and with humour: that the Mexican Revolution was a political movement, led from above and based on unclear principles.

Apart from his work as a novelist, Ibargüengoitia was a prolific journalist, but unlike other Latin American writers, came to journalism through his literature. He wrote for the *Revista de la Universidad de México*, the cultural supplement of *¡Siempre!*, *Diálogos* and other journals. However, his contributions to *Excelsior* and *Vuelta* had the most impact. His work as a columnist provided material for four anthologies. *Viajes*

en la América ignota, 1972 [Travels into Unknown America] and *Sálvese quien pueda*, 1975 [Every Man for Himself] were both published during his lifetime. *La casa de usted y otros viajes* [Your House and Other Journeys] and *Instrucciones para vivir en México* [Instructions for Living in Mexico] appeared posthumously.

In this dual role as novelist and journalist, Ibargüengoitia transformed the history of Mexico into a literary narrative, a series of novels. It was his main area of concern, be it through its characters or through the institutions which they exploited. This notion of a *reality* constructed through literature sets the author apart from his contemporaries and at the same time explains the misunderstanding which has resulted in his belated recognition as a storyteller. *Las muertas*, for example, seen by critics as the adaptation of a police report into a literary form, is in fact true historical narrative: the past in its only possible present form, that is to say, a tale of past events interpreted through the eyes of the present. Continuing with the same example, *Las muertas* is more than the literary version of an event recorded by the press, it is the construction of the event itself, the exploration of its meanings and the placing of the plot in historical perspective.

Ibargüengoitia wrote books imbued with humour and a rare talent, whose ironic, sarcastic and insistently critical plots do not diminish their effect but instead breathe life into and embellish the stories of contemporary Mexico. Ibargüengoitia's books are among those where the literary is thought and written simultaneously and where the aesthetic aim is also a concept close to events, both past and future.

CLAUDIO CANAPARO

translated by Carol Tully

Biography

Born in Guanajuato, Mexico, 22 January 1928. Studied engineering and then switched to Faculty of Arts at Universidad Nacional Autónoma de México (UNAM), 1951–54, specialized in drama and awarded MA in 1957. Granted scholarship by Mexican Writer's Centre (1954) and by Rockefeller Foundation (1955), to study drama in New York. Professor of Dramatic Theory and Composition at UNAM (1955–56) and of Language and Literature at Monterrey Institute for Foreign Studies (1963). Taught at the University of the Americas, 1965–66, and at the University of California, 1968. Contributor to several cultural publications including *Revista de la Universidad de México* and *Excelsior*. Member of the editorial board of *Vuelta*. Recipient of several national prizes for his plays and novels; twice winner of the Casa de las Américas prize: 1963 for *El atentado*, and 1964 for *Los relámpagos de agosto*. Died in a plane crash in Spain, 27 November 1983. Three other Spanish American literary figures – Ángel Rama, his wife Marta Traba and the Peruvian writer Manuel Scorza – died in the same accident.

Selected Works

Plays

Susana y los jóvenes, in *Teatro mexicano*, Madrid: Aguilar, 1955
Llegó Margó, in *Teatro mexicano del siglo XX*, vol. 2, Mexico City: Fondo de Cultura Económica, 1956
Clotilde en su casa, in *Teatro mexicano del siglo XX*, vol. 3, Mexico City: Fondo de Cultura Económica, 1956
Ante varias esfinges, in *La palabra y el hombre* 15 (July–September 1960)

El tesoro perdido, in *Universidad de México* (August 1960)

El viaje superficial, in *Revista Mexicana de Literatura* (June–September 1960); in book form with *Pájaro en mano*, Veracruz, Mexico: Universidad de Veracruz, 1964

El loco amor viene, cultural supplement of newspaper *Novedades* (1961)

El atentado, Havana: Casa de las Américas, 1964

La conspiración vendida, in *Revista de Bellas Artes* 3 (May–June 1965)

Novels and Short Fiction

Los relámpagos de agosto, Havana: Casa de las Américas, 1964; as *The Lightning of August*, translated by Irene del Corral, London: Chatto and Windus, and New York: Avon, 1986

La ley de Herodes, Mexico City: Joaquín Mortiz, 1967

Maten al león, Mexico City: Joaquín Mortiz, 1969

Estas ruinas que ves, Mexico City: Novaro, S.A., 1975

Las muertas, Mexico City: Joaquín Mortiz, 1977; as *The Dead Girls*, translated by Asa Zatz, London: Chatto and Windus, and New York: Avon, 1983

Dos crímenes, Mexico City: Joaquín Mortiz, 1979; as *Two Crimes*, translated by Asa Zatz, London: Chatto and Windus, and New York: Avon, 1984

Los conspiradores, Barcelona: Aros Vergara, S.A., 1981

Los pasos de López, Mexico City: Océano, 1982

Journalism

Viajes en la América ignota, Mexico City: Joaquín Mortiz, 1972

Sálvese quien pueda, Mexico City: Joaquín Mortiz, 1975

Compilations

Teatro, 3 vols, Mexico City: Joaquín Mortiz, 1989

Further Reading

González, Alfonso, *Euphoria and Crisis: Essays on the Contemporary Mexican Novel*, Fredericton, New Brunswick: York Press, 1990

Torres, Vicente Francisco, "Jorge Ibargüengoitia desnuda al rey," *Texto Crítico* 30 (1984)

Jorge Icaza 1906–1978

Ecuadorian prose writer and dramatist

Jorge Icaza was a bookstore owner by profession. A resident of Quito, he visited his uncle's Riobamba hacienda in the sierra in 1912. He atttributed the inspiration for his best-known work, *Huasipungo* 1934 (*The Villagers*) to this contact.

The early years of the 20th century were ones of political and economic chaos in Ecuador. The liberal groups of the coast contrasted with those of the conservatives in the highlands. When cocoa prices plunged, the decades of the 1920s and 1930s saw numerous uprisings of peasants, workers and artisans. Some works, such as Luis A. Martínez's *Al la costa* 1904 [To the Coast], portrayed the conservatism of the religious and land-owning groups. In the same year as the massacre in Guayaquil (1922), Pío Jaramillo's *El indio ecuatoriano* [The Ecuadorian Indian] appeared.

Intellectuals, especially of the Generation of 1930, were located in the sierra and on the coast as well: Demetrio Aguilera Malta, José de la Cuadra, Gilberto Gil, Gallegos Lara and Pareja Diezcanseco in Guayaquil, and Humberto Mata, Fernando Chaves and Jorge Icaza in Quito. While the influence of Positivist thought on literature was slow in disappearing, new approaches became evident. Ecuador, a country whose population was mostly indigenous at the turn of the 20th century – and still is – had, previous to 1900, seen few works that dealt with this group. Of these, *Cumandá* (1879) by Juan León Mera, was the best known. This *indianista* or romantic and religious perspective, was never able to provide an accurate portrayal of stark Andean economic and racial conditions. The Mexican and Russian Revolutions of 1910 and 1917, respectively, along with World War I, had brought social concerns to the forefront of literature as well, with indigenous

rights entering debates in the 1920s. Icaza's generation sought to produce an authentic Ecuadorian literature amid the cultural clashes. This literature would be one with greater focus on the plight of the mestizos, more in line with the Mexican José Vasconcelos's *La raza cósmica* (*The Cosmic Race*) concept than the socialist José Carlos Mariátegui's statements that an indigenous literature would develop when Indians wrote it, implying that such a literature could come into being.

Nevertheless, writers of the 1930s and 1940s in Ecuador have been considered members of the *indigenista* school in their treatment of native characters. It is in this aesthetic and political context that the emphatic, harsh style of Jorge Icaza first captured the attention of readers. When he began his career, Icaza declared that he had read Marx, Lenin, Freud, and Russian novelists such as Tolstoy and Dostoevsky, concerned with themes of social redemption. The plight and the language of Quechua Indians in Ecuador was taken by his public to be a daring portrait of national reality. While recognized as the author of short stories and plays, and although his novels show dramatic characteristics in the structure of scenes and dialogues, *Huasipungo* continues to be the most widely cited work, and the one that established his fame primarily as a novelist. It has also contributed to his perceived role as "Defender of Indians," in which capacity he traveled to other countries.

Huasipungo is the story of the circumstances which provoke an Indian uprising, led by Andrés Chiliquinga after his mate Cunshi dies from eating tainted meat. The characters are representative of the main groups which live, work, and otherwise interact in the Andean highland. The landowner, Pereira, deals with the political and religious leaders in order to maintain his control over the Indian workers, and is aided by the *cholo* type who has lost his class and ethnic identity. The Indians are considered less than human, and are forced not only to work under the cruelest of conditions, but also to tend to the needs of the *patrón*'s family, down to nursing his unmarried daughter's child. They are starving and ignorant, the condition which leads to the retrieval of spoiled meat after it has been buried, and subsequently to Cunshi's death and Andrés's maddened rebellion. The final words of the novel, uttered in Quechua, have become famous as the expression of Indian protest, although it is admittedly difficult to feel much will come of any movement, given the negative characterization of the people throughout the novel.

Later works, except for *Huairapamushcas* (*Hijos del viento*), 1948 [Sons of the Wind], focus more on the figure of the mestizo or person of mixed-blood: *Cholos*, 1937 [Half-Bloods], *En las calles*, 1935 [In the Streets], a novel whose theme is the 1932 civil war, *Media vida deslumbrados*, 1942 [Blinded for Half Their Lives], *El chulla Romero y Flores*, 1958 [The Chulla Romero and Flores], and the trilogy *Atrapados*, 1972 [Trapped]. Icaza's short stories – *Barro de la sierra*, 1933 [Sierran Clay], and *Seis veces la muerte*, 1954 [Six Times Death] are also set in indigenous communities. The mestizo characters are seen through a Freudian perspective which takes stock of the negative effects of the indigenous heritage – effects only justifiable from a middle- or upper-class viewpoint.

Icaza's Indians and mestizos have come to represent character types which in turn represent social classes and collective behaviours. While the Quechuas are brutally oppressed, the mixed bloods are caught between the memory of that oppression and the hope of upward mobility. From the racial and economic elements derives a moral pattern, seen as one of inferiority complex (on the psychological level) and betrayal (on the ethical). Its is essentially the clash of guilt (caused by Spanish origins) versus shame (Indian heritage), also called ancestral ghosts. The style of expression that has become Icaza's trademark includes the distortion of Latin American or Ecuadorian Spanish through phonetic, morphosyntactic and lexical features, to represent the Indians' speech. The result reinforces the idea that communication and respect among social groups is difficult and does not take into account that to be truly realistic the Quechuas would have to be seen as speaking their native language rather than Spanish. Interestingly, this feature of Icaza's fiction has also resulted in strongly contradictory evaluations by critics. One group of critics sees Icaza's naked portrayal of injustice as an effective, realistic "call to arms." Another sees his attitude as dehumanizing and too ambivalent, signifying a fatalistic, prejudiced belief in the eternal suffering of the Indians, an Existential condition as it were, part of an inherited and unalterable hierarchy. The contrasting viewpoints still question the role of violence, incoherent or nearly incoherent speech, and the ugliness of poverty in representing Latin American history by means of literary creation. How real is too real? Is there any hope for improvement in the conditions that are so negative? Can the Indians whose social awareness is so limited really become the social equals of other groups?

Icaza will always be read for his blatant style of portraiture, applicable to much of the Andean area, and for his unfor-

giving, insistent revelation of intergroup relationships as characterized by exploitation, fear and lack of communication. The highland population is comprised of the Indians, the mestizos, and the "unholy Trinity of the Indian," as designated by the Peruvian Manuel González Prada: the clergy, the politicians, and the wealthy landowners. The author himself was satisfied that his work was a service to the lower-class people. Not every reader agrees.

KATHLEEN N. MARCH

Biography

Born in Quito, capital of Ecuador, 10 July 1906. After being widowed, Icaza's mother married a politican who was persecuted by the government. Family fled to country estate of a relative. Studied medicine at Central University of Quito, but forced to abandon studies in 1924 on the death of his stepfather and mother. Entered civil service and worked in the Treasury of the province of Pichincha. Acted in the National Theatre (Compañía Dramática Nacional) where he met the most distinguished Ecuadorian actress of the period, Marina Moncaya, whom he later married. Wrote plays which were published in small editions and made no impact on the public. Around 1937 gave up job in civil service and bought a bookshop in Quito. Co-founder, with other writers, Ecuadorian Syndicate of Artists and Writers and was for several years its general secretary. Entered politics amd joined the Concentración de Fuerzas Populares.Travelled to China, USSR and Cuba. Awarded National Prize for Literature in 1936. Died 26 May 1978.

Selected Works

Novels

Huasipungo, Quito: Imprenta Nacional, 1934; as *The Villagers*, translated by Philip Dulsey, Carbondale: Southern Illinois University Press, 1964
En las calles, Quito: Imprenta Nacional, 1935
Cholos, Quito: Litografía e Imprenta Romero, 1937
Media vida deslumbrados, Quito: Editorial Quito, 1942
Huairapamushcas (Hijos de viento), Quito: Casa de la Cultura Ecuatoriana, 1948
El chulla Romero y Flores, Quito: Casa de la Cultura Ecuatoriana, 1958
Atrapados, 3 vols, Buenos Aires: Losada, 1972

Short Fiction

Seis relatos, Quito: Biblioteca de Relatistas Ecuatorianos, 1952

Compilations and Anthologies

Obras escogidas, edited by F. Ferrándiz Alborz, Mexico City: Aguilar, 1961

Further Reading

Albán Gómez, Ernesto, "Presente y futuro de *Huasipungo*," *Mundo Nuevo*, Paris, 49 (1970)
Benedetti, Mario, "Temas y problemas," in *América latina en su literatura*, edited by César Fernández Moreno, Mexico City and Paris: Siglo XXI, 1972
Cueva, Agustín, *Jorge Icaza*, Buenos Aires: Centro Editor de América Latina, 1968
____ "En pos de la historicidad perdida (Contribución al debate sobre la literatura indigenista del Ecuador)," *Revista de Crítica Literaria Latinoamericana*, Lima, vol. 4/7–8 (1978)
Lorente Medina, Antonio, *La narrativa menor de Jorge Icaza*, Valladolid, Spain: Universidad de Valladolid, 1980
Sackett, Theodore Alan, *El arte en la novelística de Jorge Icaza*, Quito: Casa de la Cultura, 1974
Vetrano, Anthony J., *La problemática psico-social y su correlación lingüística en las novelas de Jorge Icaza*, Miami: Universal, 1974

Identity

There are entire library shelves stacked with studies on identity in relation to Latin America as to other parts of the world. There are so many factors that shape cultural identity: language, ethnicity, gender, geopolitical factors such as patterns of economic migration or prolonged periods of exile, with its concomitant immersion in another culture, that here it is necessary to be extremely selective. What will be provided is a historical mapping of the subject with a list of related entries given at the end. The latter includes authors who provide examples of the literary representation of different ethnic groups in the "New World." Although the scope of this article is limited to Spanish America, much of it is relevant to Brazil, and for this reason some Brazilian writers figure also in the list provided at the end.

In forming an idea of Latin American identity it is essential to consider the continent's history from pre-Columbian times. The European conquerors, over the generations, virtually destroyed the culture of the pre-Columbian civilizations: the Aztecs, Mayas and Incas. Thus the native Americans who survived this experience became acculturated because their collective historical memory was almost wiped out. Yet this process was never completed since the home, for example, became a site of resistance, a place where the family could have an informal altar to their old gods. In the same way, the *palenques* or fortified bush communities constructed by runaways, acted as sites of resistance to the slave-owning plantocracy. Cultural identity survived also through religious syncretism (which involved the appropriation of elements of Christianity by peoples of other cultures to mask their own magical beliefs), through local *fiestas*, the cult of Virgins with indigenous colouring (the Virgen de Guadalupe in Mexico; the Virgen del Cobre in Cuba) and the part played by the local *curanderos* (healers), sometimes described as "witch doctors." However, as William Rowe and Vivian Schelling point out in *Memory and Modernity*, despite this process of counter-acculturation in which women played a prominent part because of its modest, domestic scale, what the indigenous survivors lost was "an organized semantic memory."

Independence caused the liberal intellectuals of the creole elite to create new versions of the continent's past. Thus Joaquín de Olmedo in his laudatory poem to Bolívar, *La victoria de Junín, Canto a Bolívar*, 1825 [The Victory at Junín, Song to Bolívar], evokes an ideal vision of the Indian past. Bolívar, for his part, like his fellow-liberator, San Martín, was disturbed by the fact that these Spanish Americans, now divided into separate nations, seemed to deny an "Hispanic" ideal as the two of them had visualized it. It was Bolívar who wrote in his *Carta de Jamaica* [The Jamaica Letter] in 1815: ". . . más nosotros . . . que no somos indios ni europeos, sino una especie media entre los legítimos propri-etarios del páis y los usurpadores españoles: en suma, siendo nosotros americanos por nacimiento y nuestros derechos los de Europa, tenemos que disputar éstos a los del país y que mantenernos en él contra la invasión de los invasores." (. . . we are, moreover, neither Indian nor European, but a species midway between the legitimate proprietors of this country and the Spanish usurpers. In short, though Americans by birth we derive our rights from Europe, and we have to assert these rights against the rights of the natives and at the same time we must defend ourselves against the invaders).

The European invaders could not help Latin Americans in a self-defining process. Their earlier role was played out and, in theory, it was now left to Latin Americans to create (and in the case of the subject peoples, to protect) their own identity. But although the European powers accepted the hegemony of the US in their hemisphere, and settled for economic penetration instead, Europe continued to exercise considerable influence in the sphere of culture. This is because the creole elite looked to Europe for cultural models, adopting a "copy cat" manner which the Cuban writer Alejo Carpentier brings out extremely well in his novels *El reino de este mundo* (*The Kingdom of this World*) and *El recurso del método* (*Reasons of State*). The former is a key text on Latin American identity since it includes a reflection on how European culture is made incongruous by being introduced in an indiscriminate way into a setting alien to it. In *El reino*, Carpentier inverts the terms of Sarmiento's Civilization versus Barbarism dichotomy by supporting the world picture of a people with magical beliefs (the black slaves), and criticizing the sceptical rationalism of the French. Finally, through his interpretation of the black tyrant, Henri Christophe, Carpentier considers the price that is paid by those who *choose* acculturation (as opposed to those who have it thrust upon them).

The efforts at nation-building in the post-independence period created a tension between the regions and the metropolis. In Argentina, Sarmiento fostered a racist ideology in which native Americans and those of mixed race were seen as accountable for the continent's alleged backwardness. This was the thinking behind the genocide of the Indians of the Argentine plains, completed by General Roca in his military campaign of 1879. The modern nation state, in the opinion of Sarmiento and other like-minded Argentines, should be "whitened" by encouraging massive immigration from Europe. One result of this huge influx was that the cultural products imported from Europe in the 19th century by the elite, which were limited to its high culture, now had to compete with the popular culture introduced by the poor of Europe's South. In the former slave-owning societies, a further ingredient was added to the continent's already powerful racial cocktail by the arrival of bonded labourers from China and the Indian sub-continent, many of whom settled in Latin America after they had bought back their freedom.

United States hegemony has had a powerful effect on Latin American identity. This is partly because, like the continent's two international languages, Castilian and Portuguese, it unites many of their people; in this case, in a common bond of hatred or deep resentment of the *gringo* who controlled the economy (and the politics) of the smaller Latin American republics, particularly of those in their "backyard." In addition, the United States through its aggressive exportation of popular (mass) culture has tended at different periods to overwhelm different expressions of local culture, something which has applied notoriously in the case of cinema.

Yet at the end of the 20th century it is much more appropriate to speak of transculturation than of acculturation. The former is a term coined by the Cuban anthropologist Fernando Ortiz, which seeks to describe cultural transformation in terms of a synthesis of systems tending to produce new and differentiated cultural hybrids. Relevant here is the quiet reclamation by Mexicans of the southwest of the United States, a region that was formerly a part of their own nation. Relevant also are the other Hispanic "beacheads" in the US: Cubans in Miami and New York, Puerto/Nuyoricans and refugees from Central America and Haiti. Their presence in the US is not new but their numbers now permit them to alter the official culture of the host country by, for example, making parts of it bilingual. They are creating new versions of cultural *mestizaje*, having arrived from a continent always marked by cultural exchange and hybridity, even when authority attempted to stamp out these complex processes.

Another factor that affects identity is sexuality. The question of homosexuality was generally taboo until the 1970s (the Argentine author, Manuel Puig, was in the vanguard in this respect) but at the end of the 20th century it is debated openly. It is a factor which, allied with ethnicity, language and gender can tend to fragment the collective identity of formerly more cohesive (Hispanic) groups. Thus the writer Gloria Anzaldúa described herself in the following terms at a reading of her work given at the University of Kentucky in 1993: "a Chicana *tejana* feminist dyke-*patlache* poet, fiction writer and cultural theorist." Yet, perhaps such fragmentation may be conceived positively in the context of Postmodernism, as a plurality of identities which incorporates difference.

VERITY SMITH

Listed here are some of the entries on authors who have written about ethnic groups, and topics that relate to this subject: America, the Invention of; José María Arguedas; Caliban; Alejo Carpentier (*El reino de este mundo*); Rosario Castellanos; Chicano Literature; Civilization and Barbarism; Film: Spanish America; Gertrudis Gómez de Avellaneda; Bernardo Guimarães; Indianism; Indigenism; Clorinda Matto de Turner; Juan León Mera, Fernando Ortiz; Octavio Paz (*El laberinto de la soledad*); Domingo Faustino Sarmiento; Transculturation; Juan Zorrilla de San Martín

Further Reading

Allen, Jr, David H., "Rubén Darío frente a la creciente influencia de los Estados Unidos," *Revista Iberoamericana*, vol. 33/64 (1967)

Carpentier, Alejo, "Problemática de la actual novela latinoamericana," in his *Tientos y diferencias*, Mexico City: UNAM, 1963 [A key essay on the problems faced by Latin American authors in representing their own culture(s) to those from beyond its boundaries]

Gutiérrez Girardot, Rafael, *La imagen de América en Alfonso Reyes*, Madrid: Insula, 1955

Lafaye, Jacques, "Los abismos de la identidad cultural," in *Past and Present in the Americas*, edited by John Lynch, Manchester: Manchester University Press, 1982

Levine, Robert M., *Race and Ethnic Relations in Latin America and the Caribbean, an Historical Dictionary and Bibliography*, Metuchen, New Jersey: Scarecrow Press, 1980

Lipp, Solomon, *U.S.A - Spanish America: Challenge and Response*, London: Támesis, 1994 [Contains several chapters on Identity]

Ryan-Ransn, Helen, *Imagination, Emblems and Expressions: Essays on Latin American, Caribbean and Continental Culture and Identity*, Bowling Green, Ohio: Bowling Green State University Popular Press, 1993

Sacoto, Antonio, "El indio en la obra literaria de Sarmiento y Martí," *Cuadernos Americanos*, Mexico City, 156 (January–February 1968)

Sarmiento, Domingo Faustino, *Conflicto y armonías de las razas en América*, in *Obras*, 5th edition, Buenos Aires: Espasa Calpe, 1939

Schuttle, Ofelia, *Cultural Identity and Social Liberation in Latin American Thought*, Albany, New York: State University of New York Press, 1993

Smith, Paul Julian, *Representing the Other: "Race," Text and Gender in Spanish American Narrative*, Oxford: Clarendon Press, and New York: Oxford University Press, 1992

Stabb, Martin S., *In Quest of Identity: Patterns in the Spanish American Essay of Ideas, 1890–1960*, Chapel Hill: University of North Carolina Press, 1967

Valenzuela, Victor M., *Anti-United States Sentiment in Latin American Literature and Other Essays*, Bethlehem, Pennsylvania: n.p., 1982

Vargas Llosa, Mario, "La amistad difícil," *Ideas*, University of Miami, vol. 2/1 (1988)

Yurkievich, Saúl (editor), *Identidad cultural de Iberoamérica en su literatura*, Madrid: Alhambra, 1986

Zea, Leopoldo, "Identity: a Latin American Philosophical Problem," *Philosophical Forum* 20 (1988–89)

Indianism

Brazil

Indianism in Brazil, like other nativist tendencies in Latin American literature, owes its origins to European and, to some extent also, to North American influences. In Europe, the figure of the American Indian gained some prominence among the Romantics at the end of the 18th century. They in turn relied on more ancient portrayals of primitive man. The myth of the Noble Savage had entered the imagination of writers in Western Europe ever since the 16th century, via such works as

Sir Thomas More's *Utopia*, Michel Montaigne's essay, "Des cannibales," 1580 [About Cannibals], and Jean-Jacques Rousseau's *Julie ou la nouvelle Heloïse*, 1761 (*Eloisa: or, a Series of Original Letters*). This was later transposed into the novels and plays of Chateaubriand and Victor Hugo in France, and in turn into the novels of James Fenimore Cooper, in North America. At the same time, visions of innocence and youthful romance within the bosom of Nature, were exploited by such writers as Bernardin de Saint-Pierre, whose *Paul et Virginie* (1788), was widely read by the Brazilian Romantics.

The influence of Romanticism was also felt more directly in Brazil, as a result of the visit of the French liberal idealist, Ferdinand Denis from 1816 to 1819. Denis was instrumental in urging local writers to take an interest in their own natural environment and their country's aboriginal inhabitants. Not that there had been a total absence of Indianist literature before this. Indeed, Basílio da Gama's *O Uraguai* (1769), and José de Santa Rita Durão's *Caramuru* (1781), were both epic poems modelled on Camões's *Os lusíadas*, 1572 (*The Lusiads)* in which a nascent interest in and even admiration for the Brazilian Indian is discernible.

It is ironic that one of the first newspapers to be published in Brazil during the years when the Portuguese monarch was resident in Rio (1808–21), was named after the tribe of Indians which had once inhabited the area: *O Tamoio*. Equally ironic, perhaps, was the assumption of an Indian name, Guatimozim, by the first emperor of Brazil, the Portuguese born, Pedro I. However, native American names were fashionable in the early years of independence, indicating as they did, a separate tradition from that of the Old World.

It took two decades for the euphoria of independence to pass, by which time the creole elite, which had switched so painlessly from Portuguese to Brazilian sovereignty, began to seek to explain national identity as somehow deriving from a reconciliation of opposites: the European conqueror on the one hand, and the native American on the other. If the latter had all but disappeared from the seaboard area by the 19th century, he nevertheless performed a vital function in the myth of origin, by which the creole elite sought to legitimise itself.

The high period of Brazilian Indianism lasted from the mid-1840s, coinciding with the publication of Gonçalves Dias's *Poemas americanos*, to the mid-1870s, and the appearance of José de Alencar's novel, *Ubirajara*. Dias went on to compile a Tupi-Portuguese dictionary, and to begin an epic, *Os Timbiras*, which he never finished. Like Dias, whose mother was an Indian, Teixeira e Sousa was also a man of mixed descent, whose long, melodramatic poem, *Os três dias de um noivado*, 1844 [The Three Days of an Engagement], is set in the Indianist mould, but provides a more far-reaching criticism of the marginalisation of all people of colour in Brazil.

By the 1850s, Indianism received royal sanction when the emperor himself commissioned a work from the aristocratic "court" poet, Domingos José Gonçalves de Magalhães. The resulting *A confederação dos Tamoios*, 1856 [The Confederacy of the Tamoio Indians] was a highly conservative poetic medallion to the foundation of Rio de Janeiro, modelled to some extent on the Camonian epic. It is perhaps more well known for the harsh criticism it received from the author whose name would become synonymous with Indianism, José de Alencar.

Alencar is generally regarded as the father of the Brazilian novel, but is remembered most for his Indianist works, in particular, *O guarani*, 1857 [The Guarani Indian], and *Iracema*, 1865 (*Iracema, the Honey-Lips, a Legend of Brazil*). Both of these novels are set at the dawn of the colonial era, and the central focus of their plots is the mutual attraction between opposites: white heroine and Indian brave, in the case of the first novel, white soldier and Indian maiden in the second. Within the greater or lesser complexity of their respective plots, Alencar portrays the tragic consequences of miscegenation, colonial greed in the form of the bad colonizer,

savage Indians who resist colonial rule, and are therefore contrasted with the good Indian, who allies himself to the colonial mission of introducing Christianity where pagan beliefs existed before.

Alencar betrays in his work the contradictions of a man who was deeply conservative in his social and political beliefs, but who at the same time was, as a northeasterner at the court of Rio, somewhat of a marginal figure. The dedication that the Indian, Peri, lavishes on the white girl, Ceci, in *O guarani*, corresponds to the devoted service a good slave shows for his mistress (fittingly Alencar opposed the rapid abolition of slavery during the 1850s). The attraction Peri feels is that of Nature personified in the face of Christian culture in its purest form: Ceci is no more than the Virgin Mary Peri glimpsed on a chapel wall. If the end of the novel sees them escaping into the wilderness, Peri's terrain, we are left in little doubt that Ceci's tutelage of her beloved will continue, that of an elder sister over a younger but dedicated brother. Moreover, the two flee with the blessing of Ceci's father, the noble Portuguese "fidalgo," Dom Antônio, in an allegory of Brazil's essentially conciliatory independence process.

In *Iracema*, the Portuguese warrior, Martim, falls in love with the Tabajara virgin, Iracema, whose name is conveniently an anagram for America, and whose tribe is an enemy of the Portuguese. The two settle by the banks of a river, and have a child. In due course, Martim goes off to war again. By the time he returns, Iracema has died. Their son, Moacyr, has been saved, and is taken by his father to be brought up in the bosom of civilisation, the first true Brazilian. What has appealed to readers down the years is the tragic story of love between opposites. What the novel upholds, however, are the conciliatory and sentimental myths that underpin Brazil's self-image as a racially democratic nation: miscegenation did occur, but this was balanced by an irreversible whitening process which somehow safeguarded the elite's greater loyalty to European cultural values.

Ultimately, Alencar's most lasting contribution to the development of Brazilian literature, was his use of language: by Brazilianising his written Portuguese, and by incorporating native terms into his novels, Alencar scandalised the academicians of Portugal, but set his country's literature on an independent course, a feat recognised by subsequent generations of cultural nationalists.

Apart from Alencar and Gonçalves Dias, the only other writer who made an original contribution to Brazilian Indianism, was the poet, Joaquim de Sousa Andrade (Sousândrade), whose long poem, *Guesa errante*, 1874–77 [Wandering Inca] is at once a heartfelt defence of Indian culture and a condemnation of the effects of European colonisation, a diatribe against the imperial government and a defence of republicanism, and an anguished cry of exile from a man who spent many years of his life in the United States.

Nineteenth-century Indianism passed with the end of Romanticism after about 1875. On the one hand, the considerable influence of Social-Darwinist theories turned writers away from an idealistic portrayal of the Indians, towards one that tended to be openly disparaging of Brazil's non-European ethnic components. On the other hand, in keeping with the new literary priorities of the Realists, more tangible symbols of a native identity were sought, such as the various forms of mestizo, and the mulatto. It was not until the Modernist movement of the 1920s that the Indian reappeared in literature, but by now writers no longer glorified the Noble Savage. On the contrary, under the influence of Freud, it was the cannibal who was used as a positive image in the struggle to affirm national cultural innocence and irreverence. Most representative of this trend was the Rabelaisian anti-hero of Mário de Andrade's Surrealist novel, *Macunaíma* (1928), or Raul Bopp's Amazonian poem, *Cobra Norato* (1931).

Although Indianism as a movement was a phenomenon of the 19th century, authors have continued to focus periodically on the theme of the Indian, even in more recent times. Chief among these are Antônio Callado, whose cult novel of the 1960s, *Quarup* (1967), amalgamated indianist concerns with a criticism of the dictatorship, Darcy Ribeiro, whose novel, *Maíra* (1976), reflects the author's experience as an anthropologist, and João de Jesus Paes Loureiro, whose Amazonian poems, *Cantares amazônicos* (1985), are worthy successors to the poetry of Gonçalves Dias and Sousândrade.

DAVID BROOKSHAW

Further Reading

Brookshaw, David, *Paradise Betrayed: Brazilian Literature of the Indian*, Amsterdam: CEDLA, 1989

Driver, David Miller, *The Indian in Brazilian Literature*, New York: Hispanic Institute, 1942

Haberly, David T., *Three Sad Races: Racial Identity and National Consciousness in Brazilian Literature*, Cambridge and New York: Cambridge University Press, 1983

Treece, David, "Victims, Allies, Rebels: Towards a New History of Nineteenth-Century Indianism in Brazil," *Portuguese Studies*, vol. 2 (1986)

Spanish America

Indianism, a term invoked to distinguish the romantic depiction of native American peoples, contrasts with Indigenism, a term coined to describe a more realistic assessment of native peoples within a national setting. A useful definition of both terms is found in José Carlos Mariátegui's *Siete ensayos de interpretación de la realidad peruana*, 1928 (*Seven Interpretative Essays on Peruvian Reality*): "Los indigenistas auténticos – que no deben ser confundidos con los que explotan temas indígenas por mero exoticismo – colaboran conscientemente o no, en una obra política y económica de reivindicación – no de restauración ni resurrección" (Authentic indigenists – who should not be confused with those who exploit indigenous themes for its mere exoticism – collaborate, consciously or unconsciously, for political and economic platform of vindication – not for a restoration or resurrection of the Indian).

From the first letter penned about the "New" World, a heavy dose of exoticism permeates the early images of the Indians. Columbus's description of the peoples he encountered in the Americas now strikes the reader as exotic: the admirable orderliness of Indian communities, their generous giving of gifts, and their well-formed bodies. Later, of course, daily contact with these "amenable" savages would alter the overly idealized images. In the battles of conquest and invasion, the Spanish made contact with fierce warriors who often repelled their advances. Yet with the decimation of the indigenous populations due to disease and increased tribute demands, the image of the Indian in literature was portrayed against a backdrop of a nostalgia for the splendor of the ancient civilizations or of pristinely poetic, nomadic tribal units. As Hayden White notes: "It is significant, I think, that the idolization of the natives of the New World occurs only *after* the conflict between the Europeans and the natives had already been decided and when, therefore, it could no longer hamper the exploitation of the latter by the former."

European philosophers shaped reconsideration of the native of the Americas for, with allusions to the natural state of the Indians, European manners and institutions were held up to criticism. Thus, in the 18th century, in the writings of Rousseau, the theme of the Noble Savage is firmly established and the natural goodness of an indigenous egalitarian society becomes the ideal. Chateaubriand's search for this ideal society stimulated his travel in North America; his failure to encounter the ideal community did not dissuade his efforts to create a literary version of his romantic vision. His novel *Atala* provided a model for subsequent mention of Indians in narrative and verse.

Literary works which celebrated Indianism proliferated in 19th-century Latin America, when the break with Spain was declared and the newly liberated authors were intent on defining their particular vision of American lands and native peoples. José Joaquín Olmedo's use of the Incan ruler Huayna Capac in his "*Canto a Bolívar*," 1825–26 [Ode to Bolívar] competes with the heroism of the rebellious commander Bolívar. In the poem, the Inca yearns for a just and beneficent government to rule in the recently liberated colonies, one in which Indians and those of Spanish descent will be equal: "¡Oh pueblos, que formáis un pueblo solo / y una familia, y todos son mis hijos!" (Oh peoples, who form one nation / one family, all of you my children). Of course, this prophecy did not come to pass. Esteban Echeverría's *La cautiva*, 1837 [The Captive] documents the actions of the "indio malón" (the ransacking and raiding Indian) who roamed the pampas.

The attempt to forge a new Latin American identity separate from the legacy of Spain fostered reconsideration of the continent. Writers observed the countryside surrounding them and found less reason to constantly compare nature in the Americas to that of Europe. Instead, with evocative descriptions of tropical forest scenery and of majestic Andean peaks, poets and novelists captured the interest of both Europeans and their own South American reading public.

Thus, the Amerindian customs of the native inhabitants likewise are observed and written down, conceived as an original contribution to creation of a particularly South American literature. The assertion by the Ecuadorian Juan León Mera that Indian themes are worthy of literature now strikes us as anachronistic, yet in the 19th century his comment represented a departure from accepted topics: "Todo lo indígena existe como recuerdo y como historia, y no veo inconveniente para que pueda servir en una obra poética, sea como tema principal, sea accesoriamente" (All Indianness exists as memory and as history and I do not see any problem in its appearance in works of poetry, as a main theme or as a secondary theme). Mera's statement also reveals a major shortcoming of the indianist orientation; they often chose to depict historical themes and nostalgic remembrances of vanished peoples. The Cuban writer Gertrudis Gómez de Avellaneda is intrigued by the Aztec past in her novel *Guatimozín* (1846) as is her compatriot Gabriel de la Concepción Valdés who idealizes Incan royalty in *Cora*.

One of the best examples of the historical use of Indian themes to create a national identity is José Joaquín Pérez's *Fantasías indígenas*, 1877 [Indian Fantasies] where the natives are innocents, slaughtered by the cruel Spanish soldiers on the island of Santo Domingo. Similarly, the Uruguayan writer Juan Zorrilla de San Martín laments the fate of another "disappeared" race in his *Tabaré* (1888): "Ni las manchas siquiera / de vuestra sangre nuestra tierra guarda" (Not even one drop of your blood remains in our land). The Indian protagonist, Tabaré, rather much embodies this assertion, for he is described by Zorilla as a blue-eyed melancholic warrior who does not wear warpaint or pierce his lips as the other males of the tribe. His soul is Christian, for his mother – blond and blue-eyed as well – has raised him in the faith despite her liaison with the mighty Indian chief Caracé. His fate is sealed, within the confines of the poem that is, when he falls in love with Blanca, a non-Indian. He dies in her arms, in the end, "an unfortunate mestizo who would like to forget the Indian half of him and is desperately attracted to the fair race," to quote the critic Carmelo Virgillo.

Similar plotting is found in the Ecuadorian novel of nation, *Cumandá* (1879), written by Juan León Mera. Here, the Indian protagonist, Cumandá, in living with the Záparos, allows the author to fill the narrative with picturesque details of indigenous customs (funerary rites, courtship, settlement patterns). The reader might suspect her true origins, for as Tabaré, she is described by means of non-Indian markers, light skin and a "civilized" demeanor. It comes as no surprise that she turns out to be the abducted daughter of an Andean landowner, torn from the bosom of her family in a raid of revenge by the highland Indians. Her death late in the novel also buries the controversial themes of racial integration and incest which are latent in the novel, for Cumandá (the supposed Indian) is in love with her own brother, Carlos (a non-Indian), from whom she was separated in childhood.

In assessing Indianist perspectives it may benefit us more to "look attentively at representational practices" rather than to distinguish between good and false representations of indigenous peoples, as Stephen Greenblatt suggests in *Marvelous Possessions*. Thus, in the creation of Tabaré or Cumandá there lingers the European-derived sense of superiority coupled with a sensitivity to the passing of an age of innocence. *Indigenista* writers such as Clorinda Matto de Turner, Jorge Icaza and José María Arguedas in the 20th century would go forth to probe the confines of race. Unlike the indianists, the endings to their *indigenista* novels provide a narrative of the future embroiled in conflict and turmoil, with no easy answers.

REGINA HARRISON

See also entries on Juan León Mera, Juan Zorrilla de San Martín

Further Reading

Greenblatt, Stephen, *Marvelous Possessions: the Wonder of the New World*, Oxford: Oxford University Press, and Chicago: University of Chicago Press, 1991
Sommer, Doris, *Foundational Fictions: the National Romances of Latin America*, Berkeley: University of California Press, 1991

Indigenism

Indigenism is a term used especially in art and literature, and it refers to the portrayal of the status, identity and culture of indigenous peoples. A concern among writers with the plight of Indians in Latin America is first evident in Fray Bartolomé de Las Casas's tale of the destruction of the Indies (1542), an account of the cruelty and abuses perpetrated by the conquering Spaniards that gave rise to what became known as the "leyenda negra." The 16th and 17th centuries also saw Ercilla y Zúñiga's epic of the wars with the Araucanians and the *Comentarios reales* (*Royal Commentaries of the Incas*) by Garcilaso de la Vega, often referred to as "el inca Garcilaso" because he was son of a Spaniard and an Inca princess; his text is a recollection of the pre-conquest Inca world. Also significant is a long illustrated letter, addressed to Philip III by another Inca, Guaman Poma de Ayala. However, *indigenismo* is a term primarily used in reference to the late-19th and 20th centuries, and Clorinda Matto de Turner, specifically her novel *Aves sin nido*, 1889 (*Birds without a Nest*) is usually credited with being its first major exponent.

Indigenist writing seeks to portray and in some way reassert the values and importance of indigenous peoples of Latin America. Not surprisingly, these countries with the largest Indian populations have produced most of the writers concerned. The term indigenism is sometimes restricted to the Andean countries and to a particular period in their literary history: roughly the 1920s and 1930s. Notable novels from that time are the Bolivian Alcides Arguedas's *Raza de bronce*, 1919 [Bronze Race], the Ecuadorian Jorge Icaza's *Huasipungo*, 1934 (*The Villagers*), the Peruvian Ciro Alegría's *El mundo es ancho y ajeno*, 1941 (*Broad and Alien is the World*). However, such temporal and geographical limitations are rather false: José María Arguedas and others have continued the tradition of indigenist writing in Peru, while Central America and Mexico are clearly an equally relevant part of the picture, having produced novels such as Miguel Ángel Asturias's *Hombres de maíz*, 1949 (*Men of Maize*) and Rosario Castellanos's *Balún Canán*, 1957 (*The Nine Guardians*) and *Oficio de tinieblas*, 1962 [*Tenebrae*]. Perhaps, too, certain works of what is now called testimonial literature, straddling the documentary, or quasi anthropological approach and the imaginative one, should be considered manifestations of indigenist writing: Ricardo Pozas's *Juan Pérez Jolote* (1948) was first published in an anthropological journal, and purports to be the story of an Amerindian told by himself; Rigoberta Menchú, the Mayan woman who won a Nobel prize for peace, tells her story through Elisabeth Burgos in *Me llamo Rigoberta Menchú*, 1985 (*I, Rigoberta Menchú*).

For the most part, however, the Indians have not spoken for themselves, but instead Spanish-speaking writers have attempted to speak for them. The results have sometimes been patronising, or over-exotic, quite frequently romanticising (the term Indianism is sometimes used in this regard); at worst the works are social tracts rather than novels. One of the most controversial was *Huasipungo*, which, while raising public awareness of the hard facts surrounding the exploitation of Indians, also portrayed them in a distasteful light. Yet many such writers were aware of these pitfalls and strove to find innovative ways of bridging the cultural divide. Thus legends, myths and concepts from Indian life are incorporated, the individual is downplayed in favour of the collective, and, more adventurously, attempts are made to reshape Spanish as a means of expressing Indian language and thought (rather than simply peppering the narrative with Indian words). The most innovative and fruitful works have been those of Asturias and

José María Arguedas: *Los ríos profundos* (*Deep Rivers*), *Yawar fiesta* (*Yawar Fiesta*), *Todas las sangres* [*Everyone's Blood*]. Arguedas was himself a product of two cultures, and spoke from the heart. Vargas Llosa, a great admirer of Arguedas, makes his own attempt at conveying an Indian world view in *El hablador*, 1987 (*The Storyteller*), with some success. Manuel Scorza's cycle of five novels, the last of which, *La tumba del relámpago* [*Requiem* for a Lightning Bolt] was published in 1979, is an attempt to portray a political struggle from an Indian perspective by the use of mythical narrative.

PETER STANDISH

Further Reading

Bigas Torres, Sylvia, *La narrativa indigenista mexicana del siglo XX*, Guadalajara, Mexico: Editorial Universidad de Guadalajara, 1990 [Chapter 1 is an introduction to the subject in Spanish America; chapter 2 introduces the subject in 20th-century Mexico]

Díaz Polanco, Hector, *Indigenismo, modernización y marginalidad: una revisión crítica*, Mexico City: Juan Pablos Editor, 1979

Kristal, Efraín, *The Andes Viewed from the City: Literary and Political Discourse on the Indian in Peru 1848–1930*, New York: Peter Lang, 1987 [The introduction is titled "Indigenismo and Politics"]

Lindstrom, Naomi, *Twentieth-Century Spanish American Fiction*, Austin: University of Texas Press, 1994 [Chapter 4, "Realism and Beyond," is relevant to this subject]

Rodríguez-Luis, Julio, *Hermenéutica y praxis del indigenismo*, Mexico City: Tierra Firme, 1980

Scheben, Helmut, "Indigenismo y Modernismo," *Revista de Crítica Literaria Latinoamericana* 18 (1979)

Jorge Isaacs 1837–1895

Colombian novelist and poet

Like most Colombian writers of the 19th century, Jorge Isaacs considered himself a poet. But he only published one slim volume of verse and his fame rests solidly on his extraordinary novel *María*, in which we can clearly detect poetic elements. Indeed, this powerful work of Romanticism shimmers with a tremulous lyricism, and in the tradition of sentimental literary works, overflows with emotion. The author tells us that he himself felt this emotion deeply. Before publishing the book in 1867, he confessed to some friends: "I have experienced the emotion of my book, but will the public feel it too?" The answer has been a resounding yes. Ever since *María* appeared, both reading public and critics have welcomed the novel enthusiastically. Its editorial success has also been phenomenal, with countless editions appearing in Latin America and in Spain; it is undoubtedly one of the most widely read books of Hispanic literature. For many years critics were moved by its thematic features, the romantically tragic love

story. Since about 1950, they also have begun to appreciate more and more the virtues of its narrative technique. At the end of the 20th century, some feminists and other critics like Doris Sommer, have begun to raise serious questions about Isaacs – his role in society – and *María*, questioning both, when earlier the critical voices were all but unanimous in their praise. While recognizing that some things in the book have become hopelessly dated, like the raven of ill omen which appears croaking in various scenes, *María* can still interest and move readers deeply.

Many aspects of the novel have an autobiographical slant, beginning with the confessional first-person narration by Efraín, who serves the dual role of protagonist and narrator of the entire volume. Isaacs's father, like Efraín's, was Jewish, emigrated from Jamaica, and converted to Catholicism when he married a Colombian lady of the landed upper class. It seems significant that the protagonist, Efraín, has a Jewish name, as did María before her conversion (Ester). Doris Sommer dwells on this Jewishness, pointing out perspicaciously how it pervades and gives another dimension to the text. Isaacs lived during his formative childhood years in a beautiful country estate bought by his father called "Paradise," and he repeatedly and nostalgically evokes this lovely countryside in *María*. Near the beginning of the novel – in Chapter 2 – we are told by Efraín that "Así el cielo, los horizontes, las pampas y las cumbres del Cauca, hacen enmudecer a quien los contempla." (The sky, the horizons, meadows and peaks of the River Cauca leave those who contemplate them speechless). Allusions to nature recur throughout the novel, most often in a Romantic fashion, reflecting the joy or the sadness felt by Efraín and María. Isaacs captures nature in all its beauty and power, but in this essentially tragic story fraught with obstacles and perils it comes across most frequently as somber, echoing the sobs and the weeping of the characters.

The love story told in retrospect by Efraín some years after the event makes up the heart of the novel. The love between Efraín and María is based on the clearest precepts of Romantic ideals: it is a first love for both of them and this mutual attraction emerges when they are still children. Second cousins, they grow up in the same happy household. But, as the reader soon learns, their love is doomed never to be consummated in a physical union of the two lovers. From the beginning of the novel, María's fatal illness (epilepsy) and premature death hover menacingly throughout. The initial scene, describing Efraín's leaving to go to school in Bogotá, is filled with foreboding and copious tears – an important leitmotif in the novel – and prefigures his last leave-taking, the journey to London to study medicine, across the immense ocean which separates the lovers forever. Both young people's love is unconditional, another strong Romantic element. Efraín swears to love María forever, and now, some years later, he is still bitterly lamenting her loss. María's love for Efraín is undying: she goes to her grave before her loved one, hastening home from England, can reach her side. Throughout the book, the reactions of Efraín and his beloved María to external factors become converted into the main action in this sentimental romance.

The secondary action of the novel describes realistic scenes of local customs. Large chunks of *María* are devoted to these descriptions of local color, often found in the Romantic 19th-century Spanish American novel. If we examine these realistic episodes carefully, which seem at first glance to break the novel's unity or distract from the main sentimental story, we find that they are interlaced with the other parts of the book. Most of them have to do with other pairs of lovers who marry happily, contrasting cruelly with Efraín and María, or in the case of the wretched African lovers Nay and Sinar, whose love is consummated physically, but who are separated forever by the sea, a sad comparison with what happens to Efraín and María. The parallel romantic and realistic currents in the 19th-century novel fuse harmoniously here.

There is a whole range of characters representing the various inhabitants of the Cauca Valley where the novel takes place: José and his family represent the humble, hardworking honest *criollo*; in Bruno and Remigia we are given a slice of life of two black slaves, and with Custodio and his daughter Salomé mulattos are described. In addition, there are two wealthy landowning families, Carlos's and Emigdio's – both friends of Efraín who contrast with him and his romantic impulses, especially Emigdio, who has gone rather native and wallows in realism. All the most important characters, however, form part of the protagonist's family, typical landowning proprietors with strong familial bonds, dominated by the figure of the father. This paternalistic structure assumes an important role in the novel's plot, for Efraín unquestioningly obeys his father, even when he doesn't want to. The only racial element unrepresented in *María* are the Indians.

Almost all these characters with the exception of Efraín are stereotypical figures. They are also idealized, like María's black nursemaid Feliciana/Nay, whose tragic history is recounted in a dramatic short novel interpolated in the main novel (a technique reminiscent of that used by Cervantes in *Don Quixote*). And because we see everything through Efraín's narrative eye, María has scant opportunity to show herself: only in conversations, and in parts of letters she writes to Efraín while he is studying in London which are reproduced in the text. All the characters serve as background or frame for the two lovers, especially Efraín.

Another remarkable quality of the characters in *María* is their good nature, their kindness. Unlike the realistic novels of the period, where many of the characters are bad or marred by flaws, here nobody has execrable characteristics. This is especially true of Efraín and María; their extreme goodness puts into relief even more their tragic destiny. One might assume that their personalities remain static and unchanged. However, by the novel's end, Efraín has changed from a happy adolescent to a grieving mature man.

Joy or sadness is determined in both principal characters by external forces. Human relationships in this novel all seem exempt from serious problems or conflicts. The real antagonists facing Efraín are María's fatal illness and death. The novel, then, can be reduced to Efraín's confrontation with the existence of evil, translated into terms of pain, grief, sickness and death. We watch Efraín's stumbling process, the passage marking an adolescent's steps toward maturity. The novel thus can be read as a process of maturation taken by a young man confronting the frightening presence of death in his life. This reading contradicts those critics who dismiss *María* as a lachrymose, overly-sentimental romance and one can understand why the novel continues to be read with pleasure, for it deals delicately with a theme of great universal impact.

Isaacs shows skill in portraying his characters. They all speak naturally, whether in elegant, simple or realistic language. The novel is also full of what Anderson-Imbert calls "the physiology of love:" tears, swoons, blushes and blanching. María is the typical pale romantic heroine. Still, we get to know her not only through Efraín's doting eyes, but also as she takes part in the novel's action: putting flowers in her beloved's room, caring for the father when he falls seriously ill, playing with the youngster Juan, in her letters, and when she listens mesmerized to Efraín's reading from Chateaubriand's *Atala* (another significant prefigurative scene of the tragedy to come near the beginning of the book).

Despite the title bearing her name, it is Efraín, rather than María, who is the protagonist of the novel. It is his life's story being unfolded in retrospect and he appears in practically every scene, while María is often absent. We watch Efraín in action, we see him happy and sad, we watch him suffer, doubt and love. Nobody else comments on him, for he is the sole narrator. As the novel advances, we get a good spiritual portrait of Efraín, who is just like many other Romantic young men his age, so we can sympathize and perhaps identify with him. The novel has thus attained what Isaacs sought to do: it recounts for us the tragic story of two adolescents. We contemplate their ill-fated love, take pity on them with all their suffering, and in the end, we have traversed a rather complex road of universal human experience.

GEORGE D. SCHADE

Biography

Born in Cali, Colombia, 1 April 1837. Descendant of English Jews and Spanish immigrants who left Jamaica to improve their prospects in Colombia. Educated at Colegio del Espíritu Santo, Bogotá, 1848 – left without graduating. Enlisted in the army of Colonel Tejada against the revolutionary General Melo, in 1854. Married Felisa González Umaña in 1856. Fought against General Tomás Cupriano de Mosquera, 1860–61. Began to write poetry in the early 1860s. Manager of the family ranch, 1860–63, but this venture failed. Fled to Bogotá, 1863. Construction inspector, Buenaventura-Cali road, November 1864. Representative of Congress, 1866–69. Managed a drapery store. Director, *La República*, July to December 1867. Secretary, House of Representatives, 1868–70. Colombian consul, Chile, 1870–72. Returned to Colombia in 1873 and bought a ranch, which failed and bankrupted him. Appointed superintendent of state institutions in Cauca Valley by his cousin, César Canto. Co-director, with Canto, of *El Programa Liberal*. Fought on government side during the Revolution, 1876–77. Secretary to governor of the Cauca Valley, 1877; resigned in 1878 and was elected to federal congress, Bogotá. Travelled to Antioquia, 1879. Director of the political paper *La Nueva Era*, 1879. Declared himself the president of Antioquia, served for one month in 1880. Expelled from congress for revolutionary activities. Nominated member of the commission to study mineral wealth along the unexplored regions of the Atlantic Coast, 1881. Given 3000 pesos by General Roca in 1884 to live in Argentina, but did not leave Colombia. In 1886, given rights to exploit coal deposits but could not raise the necessary capital. Studied the tribes of the Magdalena, published study in 1887. Died in Ibagué, 17 April 1895. Remains moved to Medellín in 1904.

Selected Works

Novels
María, novela original, Bogotá: Gaitán, 1867; as *Maria, a South American Romance*, translated by Rollo Ogden, New York: Harper, 1890
"Camilo," 6 chapters of an unfinished novel, *Boletín de la Academia Colombiana*, Bogotá, vol. 2 (1937)

Poetry
Saulo, Bogotá: Echeverría, 1881

Plays
"Paulina Lamberti," *Bolívar*, no. 12 (1952) [Unpublished in Isaacs's lifetime]

Other Writings
A mis amigos y los comerciantes del Cauca, Cali: Hurtado, 1875
La revolución radical en Antioquia, Bogotá: Gaitán, 1880

Compilations and Anthologies
Poesías de Jorge Isaacs, Bogotá, Imprenta de El Mosaico, 1864
Poesías completas, Barcelona: Maucci, 1920
Obras completas, 2 vols, Medellín, Colombia: Montoya y Montoya, 1966

Further Reading

Anderson-Imbert, Enrique, prologue to *María*, Mexico City: Fondo de Cultura Económica, 1951; also published as "La romántica *María* de Isaacs," in his *Crítica interna*, Madrid: Taurus, 1960
McGrady, Donald, *Jorge Isaacs*, New York: Twayne, 1972
Magnarelli, Sharon, *The Lost Rib: Female Characters in the Spanish American Novel*, Lewisburg, Pennsylvania: Bucknell University Press, and London: Associated University Presses, 1985 [a feminist reading]
Molloy, Sylvia, "Paraíso perdido y economía terrenal en *María*" *Sin Nombre*, vol. 14/3 (1984)
Sommer, Doris, *Foundational Fictions: the National Romances of Latin America*, Berkeley: University of California Press, 1991 [Includes chapter on *María*]
Zanetti, Susana, *Jorge Isaacs*, Buenos Aires: Centro Editor de América Latina, 1967

J

Ricardo Jaimes Freyre 1868–1933

Bolivian poet and historian

Ricardo Jaimes Freyre's literary output includes poetry, plays and short stories. An outstanding example of the last is "Justicia india" [Indian Justice], also known by the title "En las montañas" [In the Mountains]. In addition, he published a treatise on metrics, *Leyes de versificación castellana* [Rules of Spanish Versification], the only tract of its kind written by a practitioner of Spanish American *modernista* poetry. Seeking to liberate Hispanic verse from the stifling regularity of its metrical patterns, he defended free verse and called for a new method of scanning a line – by measuring feet rather than simply counting syllables. He was a socialist, and occasionally, as in "Justicia india," he revealed a concern for societal problems. But it was as an "ivory tower" *modernista* poet that he made his most enduring contributions. Not at all modest when speaking of his achievements, he once observed: "hubo tres grandes innovadores de las letras en América: Rubén Darío, Lugones, y Yo" (There were three great innovators in Spanish American literature: Rubén Darío, Leopoldo Lugones, and I).

The appearance in 1899 of *Castalia bárbara* [Barbarous Castalia], his first and most famous poetry collection, coincided with the apogee of the first phase of *Modernismo*. The title recalls Leconte de Lisle's *Poèmes barbares*, a work published in 1862 that evoked legends and traditions from other cultures, including the Nordic. Inspired by this French volume, Jaimes Freyre introduced a new strain of escapism into Hispanic poetry, the world of Scandinavian mythology. Castalia was the fountain that flowed from Mount Parnassus, the mythic source of poetic inspiration for the Greeks. However, Jaimes Freyre's Castalia was not the serene spring of classical Greece but, rather, a barbaric one that proffered violent motifs from Norse mythology.

In these poems, especially in the first section, also called "Castalia bárbara," he summons the Norse gods and recreates Valhalla and other thematic material from the Wagnerian cycle. "Aeternum Vale" [Eternal Farewell] is an apocalyptic vision of the twilight of the old gods – Odin, Thor, etc. – and the coming of a new deity, "un Dios silencioso que tiene los brazos abiertos" (a silent God with open arms). In "Los héroes" [The Heroes] he offers a hyperbolic portrait of fierce Germanic warriors as if they were comic book supermen: "los anchos pechos, los sangrientos ojos / y las hirsutas cabelleras blondas" (broad chests, bloodthirsty eyes, and bristly blond hair). "El Walhalla" captures the sights and sounds of battle and furnishes a textbook example of synesthesia, a favorite *modernista* device, in its opening phrase "Vibra el himno rojo" (The red hymn echoes). The poem concludes with an orgiastic scene in the great hall: "Hay besos y risas. / Y un cráneo lleno / de hidromiel, en donde apagan, / abrasados por la fiebre, su sed los guerreros muertos." (Amidst laughter and kisses, the dead warriors, parched with fever, quench their thirst from a skull filled with mead).

Erotic imagery and themes dominate the second portion of this collection, "País de sueño" [Dream Country]. Several poems in this section treat the Middle Ages, a period attractive to Jaimes Freyre precisely because of its historical and spatial remoteness. The centerpiece of Part Three, "País de sombra" [Shadow Country], is "Las voces tristes" [The Sad Voices], in which he sketches a frigid, inhospitable terrain that lacks human warmth. The sensation of physical and emotional coldness conveyed by this poem is a by-product of his literary elitism and aloofness. Here, the harshness of the climate has a direct bearing on tone and outlook: "sobre el vasto desierto / flota una vaga sensación de angustia, / de supremo abandono, de profundo y sombrío desaliento" (floating over the vast desert is a vague sensation of anguish, of supreme abandonment, of deep, dark discouragement). "Las voces tristes" also clearly illustrates one of Jaimes Freyre's favorite techniques, the irregular combination of long and short lines, with verses ranging in length from two syllables to eighteen.

One final poem in *Castalia bárbara*, "Siempre" [Always], often identified by its initial verse, "Peregrina paloma imaginaria" (Imaginary Wandering Dove), merits comment because it encapsulates one of the major tenets of the *modernista* aesthetic, the obsession with the pursuit of a lofty, elusive ideal. The linking of whiteness, the dove's flight, and images of light and the sacred points to a higher plane beyond the grasp of mere mortals who bathe in "el mar glacial de los dolores" (the glacial sea of sorrows).

Jaimes Freyre's second and final volume of poetry, *Los sueños son vida*, 1917 [Dreams Are Life], conveys traditional themes such as love, beauty, and human emotions utilizing an assortment of verse forms. His subject matter ranges from Greek mythology and native American civilizations to a panegyric on Tolstoy. These poems also contain some of the best examples of his *modernista* imagery: "un collar de perlas" (a pearl necklace), "los senos de Cleopatra" (Cleopatra's breasts), "princesa errante" (errant princess), "viviente escultura" (living sculpture), "sueño de mármol" (dream of marble) and "rostro níveo" [snow-white face]. Lexical items such as "talismán" and the titles "Eros" and "El rubí" [The Ruby] also place this collection firmly within the *modernista* camp. "Lo fugaz" [That Which is Fleeting], the best-known selection, juxtaposes the rose, one of the most readily-identifiable images of beauty in all of poetry, with its antithesis, a dark, muddy swamp. As the flower dies, its scattered petals give off a perfume that sweetens the noxious waters. Despite the transitory nature of life, ideal beauty, symbolized by the rose, is eternal.

Ricardo Jaimes Freyre, the intellectual of the *modernista* group, created a poetic world detached from the common experiences of daily life. His fantastic settings were geographically and temporally remote from and thematically antithetical to the Spanish American social and political realities of his time. Jaimes Freyre's poetry is rich in its variety of musical sounds and metrical forms, including free verse. In the history of Spanish American literature he is best remembered for his unique themes based on Nordic mythology, his formal and technical renovation of Hispanic poetry, and his theoretical formulations on versification.

MELVIN S. ARRINGTON, JR

Biography
Born in Bolivia, 12 May 1868. Both parents were writers. Much of his life spent in Argentina, his adopted country. Close friend of Rubén Darío with whom he founded the *Revista de América*, 1894. Moved to the province of Tucumán in northwest of Argentina in 1900, where he taught literature and history at the University of Tucumán. Interest turned increasingly to early history of this province. Returned to Bolivia in early 1920s where he held a number of high-level government posts including those of Minister of Education and of Foreign Affairs. Also served as ambassador to United States, Chile and Brazil, as well as being Bolivia's representative at the United Nations. Died in Argentina, 24 April 1933.

Selected Works

Poetry
Castalia bárbara, Buenos Aires: Juan Schurër, 1899
Los sueños son vida, Buenos Aires: Sociedad Cooperativa Editorial Limitada, 1917

Prose Narratives
Note: It is not possible to provide full publication details for the items listed below because at the time of publication there is no collection of Jaimes Freyre's prose fiction.

"Zoe," Buenos Aires, 1894
"Los viajeros," Buenos Aires, 1900
"Zaghi, mendigo," Buenos Aires, 1905
"En las montañas," Caracas, 1906
"En un hermoso día de verano," Buenos Aires, 1907
Los jardines de Academo [unfinished novel], n.d.

Plays
La hija de Jefte, La Paz: Tipografía de El Siglo Industrial, 1889
Los conquistadores, Buenos Aires: Perroti, 1928

Other Writings
Historia de la edad media y de los tiempos modernos, Buenos Aires: n.p.,1895
Tucumán en 1810, Tucumán, Argentina: n.p., 1909
Historia de la República de Tucumán, Buenos Aires: Coni Hermanos, 1911
Leyes de la versificación castellana, Buenos Aires: Coni Hermanos, 1912
El Tucumán del siglo XVI, Buenos Aires: Coni Hermanos, 1914
El Tucumán colonial, Buenos Aires: Coni Hermanos, 1915
Historia del descubrimiento de Tucumán, Buenos Aires: Coni Hermanos, 1916

Compilations and Anthologies
Poesías completas, edited by F. Díez de Medina, La Paz: Ministerio de Educación y Bellas Artes, 1957

Further Reading
Carrilla, Emilio, *Ricardo Jaimes Freyre*, Buenos Aires: América, 1963
Castañón Barrientes, Carlos, *Cuentos de Ricardo Jaimes Freyre*, La Paz: n.p., 1975
Cortés, Darío Alvaro, "Los cuentos de Ricardo Jaimes Freyre," *Cuadernos Americanos* 256 (1984)
Francovich, Guillermo, *Tres poetas modernistas de Bolivia*, La Paz: Editorial Juventud, 1971
Gosalvez, Bothelo Raul, "Ricardo Jaimes Freyre en el modernismo americano," *Cuadernos Americanos* 156–57 (1968)
Jaimes-Freyre, Mireya, *Modernismos y 98 a través de Ricardo Jaimes Freyre*, Madrid: Gredos, 1969

Jewish Writing

Mexico, Central America and the Spanish-Speaking Caribbean

In the early 16th century, the New World was known as a safe-haven for Latino-speaking Jewish colonists escaping the Holy Inquisition. Many were *conversos* and *marranos* (e.g., crypto-Jews) who had come with Columbus looking for a promised land, while others simply had Jewish blood in their veins, which they were afraid to acknowledge. Cuba and Mexico in particular were considered places where the lack of pure blood ("pureza de sangre") was common. And while these escapees seldom declared their Judaism, people like Juan Ruíz de Alarcón and even Sor Juana Inés de la Cruz were rumoured to have Jewish ancestors. The literature of the time available to us is in the form of theological tracts, diaries, correspondence, family chronicles and edicts. It refers to personalities like the Carvajal family in Mexico, whose odyssey was recorded in book form, in 1944, by the historian Alfonso Toro. But the growth of a solid Jewish literary tradition, from the Rió Grande to Panama, as well as in the Spanish-speaking Caribbean, is not a result of an Iberian-Jewish presence, which had all but disappeared by the time the US–Mexican war was declared. Instead, it was a product of Yiddish-speaking Eastern-European immigrants arriving from the end of the 19th century to the end of World War II. They came from small rural towns, known as *shtetls*, and were fervent readers of novels by Sholem Aleichem and I.L. Peretz. While the switch to Spanish took place immediately, it wasn't until the second and third generation that distinguished novelists, essayists, playwrights and poets began to flourish in the region.

Yiddish poetry flourished in Mexico City and Havana in the early decades of the 20th century, a time when the Jewish community was important enough to have daily newspapers in Yiddish, as well as publishing houses. The first works of fiction by Jewish writers in Spanish were published in the 1960s but, unlike their US counterparts, they were not widely read and had trouble getting published. But just as Cuba was becoming an established Jewish cultural centre, things changed radically with the Revolution of 1959. Most Cuban Jews, granted their prosperity, chose exile, and whatever infrastructure has been created then was dismantled. Instead, Mexico, with a wealthy community of 50,000 members, has, since the 1960s, become an attractive magnet to Jewish writers, second only to Argentina and Brazil.

Ironically, most of what is available by Jewish writers in Mexico is eclipsed by the work of gentile ones with crucial Jewish motifs: Carlos Fuentes, for instance, is responsible for several novels that have a Jewish cast or Jewish symbols, including *La cabeza de la hidra* (*The Hydra Head*). Likewise, Homero Aridjis's *1492: Vida y tiempos de Juan Cabezón de Castilla* [*1492: the Life and Times of Juan Cabezón de Castilla*] is a well-known novel on the arrival of *conversos* in Mexico, while José Emilio Pacheco's *Morirás lejos* [*A Distant Death*] is an exploration of the Holocaust in a Mexican setting. Because of their authors' fame, books like these have eclipsed important works by Jewish writers. Among the most prominent Jewish writers in Mexico are three women: Margo Glantz (b. 1930; see separate entry), Angelina Muñíz-Huberman (b. 1937), and Esther Seligson (b. 1941). While space limitations make it impossible to offer an analysis of their work, it is important to mention that the first, a daughter of the Yiddish poet Jacob Glantz and the author of *Genealogías* (*The Family Tree: an Illustrated Novel*), is mainly a literary critic and recorder of the past, whereas the other two are best known as novelists and short-story writers. Muñíz won the prestigious Xavier Villaurrutia Prize for *Huerto cerrado, huerto sellado* [*Enclosed and Sealed Garden*]. Her themes are metaphysical: an alchemist's search for God; the inner sexual thoughts of Sor Juana; and the redemptive quest of a man who is challenged to cross a river. Muñíz is a writer highly influenced by Borges and also by Rabbi Nahman of Bratslav, a leader of existential Hasidism. She has also edited anthologies and critical volumes on Kabbalah in the Hispanic world. Seligson, on the other hand, is a theatre critic; she is also the author of *La morada en el tiempo*, 1982 [*A Dwelling Place in Time*], an attempt to rewrite the Bible. Her writing is metaphorical, obscure, perhaps even evasive. Like the creatures of Frida Kahlo, herself a descendant of Hungarian Jews, Seligson's characters are not bound by the physical laws of time and space and perceive fantastic visions of eternity. Among the younger Mexican Jewish writers is Ilan Stavans (b. 1961), an essayist and short-story writer who settled in the United States. He is the author of *Talia y el cielo* [*Thalia and the Sky*] and *La pianista manca* (*The One-Handed Pianist and Other Stories*), both of which exemplify his passion to establish a bridge between Eastern European letters and the Latin American imagination.

The most distinguished of all is José Kozer (b. 1940), a major poet to emerge from the Cuban diaspora since the Cuban Revolution. Starting with *Padres y otras profesiones* [*Parents and other Professions*], published in his thirties, he has produced a solid poetic *oeuvre* of more than half a dozen collections. His work often deals with his early life in Santos Juárez, a neighbourhood in Havana where he grew up, but not with New York, where he has resided since he went into exile in 1960.

When compared to Mexico and Cuba, the Jewish communities in Central America (Costa Rica, Honduras, Panama, Guatemala) have always been small. Their sharpest increase took place before and during World War II, when governments accepted small numbers of refugees from Eastern Europe. As a result of its small numbers, literature among members of these communities has remained a local affair. As in the case of Mexico, gentile Central American writers have also dealt with Jewish themes and their work is considerably more prominent than that of their Jewish counterparts. For instance, Rubén Darío, the celebrated *modernista* poet, wrote in the following stanza from his poem "Canto a la Argentina" [Song to Argentina] these lines which are much better known than anything by a native Jewish author from this area: " ¡Cantad judios de la pampa! Mocetones de ruda estampa, dulces Rebecas de ojos francos, Rubenes de largas guedejas, patriarcas de cabellos blancos, y espesos como hípicas crines; cantad, cantad, Saras viejas y adolescentes Benjamines, con voz de vuestro corazón: ¡Hemos encontrado a Sión! [Sing Jews of the Pampa! Young men of rugged appearance, sweet Rebbeccas with honest eyes, Reubens of long locks, patriarchs of white, dense, horse-like hair. Sing, sing old Sarahs and adolescent Benjamins with the voice of our heart: We have found Zion!].

Jewish writers from Central America include Samuel Rovinski (b. 1936) and a couple of Guatemalans of distinction: Victor Perera (b. 1934), a Sephardic Jew who emigrated to the United States at an early age, is the author of *Rites. A Guatemalan Boyhood*, and is also respected as an activist who defends the rights of native Indians on the Guatemala-Mexico border. The second is Alcina Lubitch Domecq (b. 1953), another Guatemalan who is responsible for *El espejo en el espejo: o, La noble sonrisa del perro* [The Mirror's Mirror: or, The Noble Smile of the Dog] a novel clearly influenced by Lewis Carroll and Borges, which describes the adventures of an eight-year-old Jewish girl left alone in a battlefield, and *Intoxicada* [Intoxicated], a collection of what the American critic Irving Howe once called "short shorts."

There is little indication that Jewish writers from Latin America as a whole have read and are influenced by each other. When acknowledged, their role models come from abroad (Eastern Europe, Russia, the US), and are often writers like Sholem Aleichem, Isaac Babel, Franz Kafka, Bruno Schulz and Isaac Bashevis Singer: Americans like Saul Bellow and Phillip Roth; or contemporary Israeli writers such as A.B. Yehoshua and Amos Oz. But as the Jewish communities in the region come of age, a sense of maturity and stylistic development can be felt among the new literary generation. Happily, young writers in the 1990s are beginning to look to their native Jewish predecessors as cornerstones in the shaping of a Hispanic-Jewish literary identity.

ILAN STAVANS

Further Reading

See the Further Reading section at the end of the following essay for critical studies in this field. Provided below are creative works only.

Glantz, Margo (Mexico), *Las genealogías*, Mexico City: Martín Casillas, 1981; as *The Family Tree: an Illustrated Novel*, translated by Susan Bassnett, London: Serpent's Tail, 1991

Kozer, José (Cuba), *Padres y otras profesiones*, New York: Villa Miseria, 1972

____ *De Chepén a la Habana*, in collaboration with Isaac Goldemberg, New York: Bayú-Menoráh, 1973

____ *La garza sin sombras*, Barcelona: Llibres del Mall, 1985

____ *De donde oscilan los seres en sus proporciones*, Tenerife, Canary Islands: H.A. Editores, 1990

Lubitch-Domec, Alcina (Guatemala), *El espejo en el espejo: o La noble sonrisa del perro*, Mexico City: Joaquín Mortiz, 1983

____ *Intoxicada* (Mexico), Mexico City: Joaquín Mortiz, 1988

Muñiz-Huberman, Angelina (Mexico), *Huerto cerrado, huerto sellado*, Mexico City: Oasis, 1985

____ *De magias y prodigios*, Mexico City: Fondo de Cultura Económica, 1987

Perera, Victor (Guatemala), *Rites: a Guatemalan Boyhood*, San Diego: Harcourt Brace Jovanovich, 1986

Seligson, Esther (Mexico), *La morada en el tiempo*, Mexico City: Editorial Artifice, 1981

Stavans, Ilan (Mexico), in collaboration with Zuri Balkoff, *Talia y el cielo: o El libro de los ensueños*, Mexico City: Plaza y Valdés, 1989

____ *La pianista manca*, Caracas: Alfadil Editores, 1991; as *The Invention of Memory and Other Stories*, Albuquerque: University of New Mexico Press, 1995

____ (editor), *Tropical Synagogues. Short Stories by Jewish-Latin American Writers*, New York: Holmes and Meier, 1994

Toro, Alfonso, *La familia Carvajal*, 2 vols, Mexico City: Editorial Patria, 1944

South America

Jewish writing in South America did not really begin until the 20th century. Yet it is important to recognize that since the Spanish Conquest there has been a Jewish presence in Latin America, manifested in the writings of scholars and theologians. The history of the Sephardim during the Inquisition is retold and imaginatively reinterpreted by contemporary Jewish writers.

Religious animosity towards New Christians had been eroded by the late 19th century, when Latin American countries achieved independence. In Colombia, Jorge Isaacs, of Sephardic-English descent, wrote *María* (1867), considered the finest example of the Romantic novel in Spanish America. Although María is a Catholic, her bucolic romance with her Christian cousin is doomed to failure. *María* has been explained as a parable, with an undercurrent of lyricism and fatalism that stems from the Jewish tradition.

The corpus of Jewish writings in South America – from the beginning of the 20th century, spans three to four generations – and is mostly made up of Eastern European Ashkenazi writers who enriched the process of cultural adaptation by adding their experience directly to the literary heritage of their adopted countries. Most writers are Argentine, because Argentina has by far the largest Jewish community. Its most celebrated author was Alberto Gerchunoff, a journalist for the Buenos Aires liberal paper *La Nación*. Gerchunoff wrote *Los gauchos judíos*, 1910 (*The Jewish Gauchos of the Pampas*), on the occasion of the country's first centenary: These twenty-six vignettes have become a classic of Argentine literature. The preface idealizes life in the early Jewish settlements by emphasizing the virtue of honest work on the land, far from pogroms and persecution.

Gerchunoff's descriptions of man's struggle with nature and the brutal conditions of rural life were followed by the works of Rebeca Mactas, José Pavlotzky, Marcos Alpersohn, Samuel Tarnopolsky and José Rabinovich. Rabinovich was a prolific novelist and playwright, noteworthy for his testimonial, caustic style. These writers also evoked Hispanism, hoping to give respectibility to the immigrant and help him integrate his national allegiance with his Mediterranean-Hispanic-Hebrew tradition.

The Yiddish language of this first generation leaves the intimacy of the *shtetl*, and under a renewed cultural impetus becomes a polished, literary language. Yiddish papers thrive, Yiddish theatres increase their repertoires.

The generation of the 1940s and 1950s, from the rapidly growing Jewish centers, contributed to new literary trends. Among the social critics, Bernardo E. Koremblit is prominent for his erudite analyses of the intellectual's role in working towards reform. Among the novelists, Bernardo Verbitsky's *Es difícil empezar a vivir*, 1941 [It's Hard to Start a Life], portrays

Jewish life in Buenos Aires in the 1930s, when fascism was on the rise. Through the eyes of a curious adolescent, Verbitsky unfolds a life of corruption and anti-Semitic injustices.

In addition to broadening the social vision of Latin American literature, Jewish authors strongly contributed to a new genre: psychological drama. Its major exponent, Samuel Eichelbaum, designed careful plots for his "superrealist" dramas that dwell on the hidden aspects of the human psyche and on universal dilemmas. Of his plays on Jewish themes, *El judío Aarón*, 1926 [Aaron the Jew], probes the polemics among agricultural colonists, and *Nadie la conoció nunca*, 1926 [No One Ever Knew Her], touches upon Jewish prostitution.

In his plays *El teatro soy yo*, 1933 [I Am Theatre], and *Pan criollo*, 1938 [Creole Bread], César Tiempo (pseudonym for Israel Zeitlin) develops conflicts with dramatic force and realism. His poems idealize the harmony of Argentine and Jewish culture, and glorify the Sabbath day.

The pseudonym of Samuel Glusberg – Enrique Espinoza, honoring Baruch Spinoza and Heinrich Heine, as befits a cosmopolitan thinker closely attached to his heritage. An eminent essayist, Glusberg also edited two reviews, *América* and *Babel*. His short stories about Jews in Buenos Aires are collected in *La levita gris*, 1924 [The Grey Coat].

In *Mester de judería*, 1924 [Crafted Jewish Verse], Carlos Grumberg directed his rage at the world's indifference to the extermination of the Jews during the Holocaust. The writings of Lázaro Liacho in *Pan de Buenos Aires*, 1935 [Bread of Buenos Aires], depict relationships between Jews and Christians in Argentina; in later years Liacho turned to metaphysical and religious themes.

The polemical style of David Viñas is illustrated in *Los dueños de la tierra*, 1959 [The Owners of the Land], an ideological examination of the governing classes, based on a historical incident. Like Viñas's own father – a judge under President Yrigoyen — the protagonist is sent to mediate a labor conflict. When the army intervenes and massacres the workmen, they become, ironically, the real "owners of the land" where they are buried.

While earlier writers were careful to maintain a "purebred," classical language – Spanish or Portuguese – in order to establish their credentials as legitimate Latin American authors, the second generation (of Pedro Orgambide and Noé Jitrik) no longer felt the need to justify themselves for their Jewishness, and came to be perceived in subtler, more universal terms.

The third wave of writers, from the 1960s onward, experienced a return to centuries-old roots as a way to reconnect with their past. Those who sought to insert themselves into a national discourse that excluded them, linked various periods of political strife and inserted their individual "petite histoire" into the collective history of their country. They invented myths of illustrious ancestors, and utopian dreams of assimilation into a space that history had previously denied them. Most representative, and ahead of his generation in Argentina, was Germán Rozenmacher, whose "knight of the Indies," *Simón Brumelstein* (1987), escapes from his drab existence into his imaginary kingdom of Chantania. Similar solutions are sought by the protagonist of Jorge Goldemberg's *Krinsky* (1977) and of Osvaldo Dragún's *Arriba, Corazón*, 1987 [Forward, Corazón], who break linear chronology as they trace their Ashkenazi ancestry. Mario Szichman in *A las 20:25 la señora*

entró en la inmortalidad, 1981 [At 20:25 the Lady Entered Immortality], provides an apocryphal aristocratic lineage for his Jewish immigrant characters. Moacyr Scliar in *A estranha nação de Rafael Mendes*, 1983 [The Strange Nation of Rafael Mendes] and Marcos Aguinis in *La gesta del marrano*, 1992 [The Saga of the "Filthy Pig"], draw on real events of Sephardic history to write their novels. With *Mil años un día*, 1986 [A Thousand Years One Day], and against the background of the military repression in Argentina, Ricardo Halac gives a modern twist to the meaning of the 1492 Edict of Expulsion against the Jews. Isaac Chocrón introduces Sephardic values and customs into Venezuelan sensibility in his plays *Clíper*; *Animales feroces*, 1963 [Wild Animals], and novels *Rómpase en caso de incendio* [Break in Case of Fire].

The devastating impact of the Chilean and Argentine military dictatorships among Jewish writers is reflected in the plays of Ariel Dorfman and Aída Bortnik, and in the poetry of Marjorie Agosín, and Alicia Portnoy. Mario Goloboff succeeds in recreating the atmosphere of anguish resulting from a century of repression, within the Jewish gaucho tradition initiated by Gerchunoff. Goloboff advances the saga of the Jewish pioneers into the 21st century with his novel *Comuna Verdad*, 1995 ["The Truth" Commune].

A long tradition of journalism has resulted in research on Jewish communities by Argentine historians like Boleslao Lewin, by essayists Bernardo Korenblitt, Ismael Viñas, Jacobo Timerman, León Rozitchner, and Elio Brailovsky, and by the highly poetic essays of Santiago Kovadloff. In Brazil, journalists Zevi Guivelder, Alberto Dines, and Patricia Finzi are also editors of leading journals. Their topics range from analyses of the effects of Nazism to reflections on the contemporary alienation of Jewish youth.

Over the past three decades, as South American countries witnessed a growth in extreme nationalism, anti-imperialism, and anti-Semitism, Israel became a strong presence in the consciousness of Jewish writers like Ricardo Feierstein, author of *Mestizo*, 1993, who regards himself and his contemporaries as those of the "Generation of the Desert," deprived of active participation in the shaping of Jewish history yet bearing its burden.

A great number of authors who reside abroad through forced or voluntary exile continue writing in their own tongues. Far from losing their identity with their country, they strengthened it, and at the same time, they reaffirmed their links with Judaism: in France, Alicia Dujovne-Ortiz, Luisa Futoransky, Mario Goloboff; in Spain, Arnoldo Liberman, and Mario Satz; in the US Alicia Borinsky, Marjorie Agosín, Nora Glickman; in Mexico, Juan Gelman; in Israel, Samuel Pecar and Oded Sverdlik.

A preference for religious, biblical, kabbalistic and metaphysical poetry characterizes the works of Eliahu Toker (who still writes in Spanish and in Yiddish), José Isaacson, Manuela Fingueret, Rubén Kanalestein and Humberto Costantini.

Humor has been a constant feature among South American Jewish writers, exemplified in Samuel Pecar's sketches of Buenos Aires's Jews and in Isaac Goldemberg's picaresque adventures of a Peruvian Jew in *La vida a plazos de Jacobo Lerner*, 1976 (*The Fragmented Life of Don Jacobo Lerner*). The parody of the "Yiddishe mame" stereotypes is presented in Alicia Steimberg's novel *Cuando digo Magdalena*, 1992

[When I Say Magdalena], and in Diana Raznovich's play *Casa Matriz* [Matrix House]; the depiction of Jewish immigrants' machinations in a drug-ridden Colombia is illustrated in the novels of Azriel Bibliowicz; the happy combination of Brazilian magical realism with Jewish irony is unanimously praised in the novels of Moacyr Scliar, like *O exército de un hómen só*, 1973 [The One-Man Army].

The boom in women's literature since the 1960s includes a high proportion of Jewish writers who chose to reveal their conflicted identities in autobiographical, satirical, intellectual fiction, though never at the expense of intimacy and conviviality. Brazilian novelist Clarice Lispector and Argentine poet Alejandra Pizarnik increased their international reputation posthumously. As professionals and intellectuals, Jewish women experiment in various genres. Venezuelan journalist Alicia Freilich-Segal wrote the novel *Cláper* (1987), to observe her father's generation as it related to her own. Women writers have recently begun to fill anthologies and are now the subjects of numerous critical studies. These include: Luisa Futoransky, Tamara Kamenszain, Alicia Steimberg, Alicia Dujovne-Ortiz, Aída Gelbrunk, Nora Glickman and Ana Maria Shúa.

NORA GLICKMAN

Further Reading

DiAntonio, Robert and Nora Glickman (editors), *Tradition and Innovation: Reflections of Latin American Jewish Writing*, Albany: State University of New York Press, 1993

Glickman, Nora (editor), *Argentine Jewish Writers: Critical Essays*, New York: Modern Jewish Studies Books, 1993

Glickman, Nora and G.F. Waldman (editors), *Argentine Jewish Theatre: a Critical Anthology*, Lewisburg, Pennsylvania: Bucknell University Press, 1996

Kaminszain, Tamara, "Dos apéndices," in her *El texto silencioso: tradición y vanguardia en la poesía sudamericana*, Mexico City: UNAM, 1983

Lindstrom, Naomi, *Jewish Issues in Argentine Literature: From Gerchunoff to Szichman*, Columbia: University of Missouri Press, 1989

Lockhart, Darrell B., *Latin American Jewish Writers: a Critical Dictionary*, New York: Garland, 1996

Senkman, Leonardo, *La identidad judía en la Argentina*, Buenos Aires: Editorial Pardés, 1983

____ *Pluralismo e identidad: lo judío en la literatura latinoamericana*, Buenos Aires: Milá, 1986

Vieira, Nelson H., *Jewish Voices in Brazilian Literature: a Prophetic Discourse of Alterity*, Gainesville: University Presses of Florida, 1995

Special Issues of Journals

"Latin American Jewish Writers," *Folio*, SUNY-Brockport, vol. 17 (1987) [Guest editor, Judith Morganroth Schneider]

Journals

It must be emphasized that all it is possible to offer here is a tiny selection of the many interesting cultural journals of Latin America, both past and present.

Marcha (1939–1973)

Marcha was founded in Montevideo, Uruguay, on 23 June 1939 by the economist and journalist Carlos Quijano. From its early days, in a tide of anti-fascism, it was the proponent of a fusion of economic, political and aesthetic debate. Quijano himself had been both a member of parliament and a professor of political economy, and was the cohesive force around whom, in the pages of *Marcha*, the post-war generations of Uruguayan writers would form. Anti-imperialist, nationalist, with an emphasis on Latin American rather than European culture, and (when the time came) pro-Cuban, this weekly magazine was to become an enduring and influential left-wing rallying point for Latin American intellectuals over the next three decades or more.

Together with its importance in creating a platform for free-thinking commentary and analysis within Uruguay, *Marcha* was in a position to greet, and nurture, the new tide of innovative writing that was to flourish in Latin America as the Boom of the 1960s. Juan Carlos Onetti had joined the newly-founded weekly in 1939 as literary editor, with his own humorous column, and the eminent Uruguayan critic Emir Rodríguez Monegal, later to become one of the foremost commentators of the Boom, was literary editor from 1944 to the mid-1950s. From 1958 to 1968 the position was held by Ángel Rama, notoriously an adversary of Monegal's "literato puro" stance, and an advocate of the re-evaluation of literature and culture from a sociological, Marxist-theoretical standpoint. In the early 1960s the magazine was directed by a youthful Eduardo Galeano (1961–64) and towards the end of the decade *Marcha* could count on regular contributions from writers such as David Viñas, Mario Vargas Llosa, Mario Benedetti, Manuel Maldonado Denis and Roberto Fernández Retamar. This kind of range, together with the breadth and scope of Quijano's editorial columns, and Rama's groundbreaking analyses of Latin American culture, were to earn *Marcha*'s reputation as one of the great 20th-century magazines to come out of the continent.

Marcha's demise was one of the results of the horrific military coup of 27 June 1973. The *Marcha* team were already aware that in the prevailing climate of repression and censorship the magazine's fate was probably sealed, and the time came towards the end of that year with the publication of the winning entry of a *Marcha* short story competition. The story, "La guardaespaldas" by Nelson Marra, was taken by the military to be a direct indictment of the regime, and Marra was arrested, closely followed by Quijano, Onetti, and Hugo Alfaro, the chief editor of the magazine. Another competition judge and a notable contributor, Jorge Ruffinelli, was in Mexico at the time of the arrests and judged fit not to return. The most chilling aspect of reprisals relating to *Marcha* personnel was the disappearance in August 1977 of the magazine's deputy editor, Julio Castro. Following his release Carlos Quijano went into exile in Mexico, where he later renewed the magazine as *Cuadernos de Marcha*, which continued to publish items from earlier collaborators such as Rama.

FRANK McQUADE

Further Reading

Alfaro, Hugo (editor), *Antología de "Marcha"* (1939), Montevideo: Biblioteca de Marcha, 1970

Rama, Ángel, *La generación crítica, 1939–1969*, Montevideo: Arca, 1972

Ruffinelli, Jorge, "Ángel Rama, *Marcha*, y la crítica literaria latinoamericana en los años 60," *Casa de las Américas*, vol. 34/192 (July–September 1993)

Mundo Nuevo (1966–1971)

Founded in Paris in 1966 by the noted Uruguayan literary critic Emir Rodríguez Monegal, *Mundo Nuevo* was the flagship for the latest writing of the 1960s in Latin America. Its purpose was to provide a critical forum for discussion of the avant-garde writers of the period, and this in large part meant a celebration of the so-called Boom. In its earlier days at least, under the direction of Rodríguez Monegal, the review was an elegant showcase of new Latin American writing, and its wide-ranging newsletter sections, *Brújula* [Compass] and *Sextante* (appropriate metaphors of navigation and exploration in the context of the magazine's self-styled role as a vehicle for cultural debate) brought together items concerning conferences, translations, literary awards, and critical reviews. The opening "Presentación," and the first article of the first issue, a dialogue between Rodríguez Monegal and Carlos Fuentes, set the pace for the review, with its emphasis on the new cultural dawn of Latin American letters, the cosmopolitan perspective of the Latin American intellectual, with a certain Eurocentric celebration of Latin America most obviously underpinned by Monegal's insistence that the magazine should be based in Paris, to avoid the possible cultural parochialism that might result from projecting it from a more obvious Latin American base such as Mexico City or Buenos Aires. The magazine's declared ideological neutrality did not prevent it from including political issues, some polemical, such as Vargas Llosa's open letter concerning the Siniavski-Daniel censorship affair in Russia, and the United States' involvement in Vietnam and Puerto Rico. *Mundo Nuevo* was notable for its presentation of new pieces of Latin-American literature, often before their full publication. The second issue includes a chapter from *Cien años de soledad* (*One Hundred Years of Solitude*), and later issues would include forthcoming works by Severo Sarduy, José Donoso and Cabrera Infante.

In spite of its claims to ideological neutrality in the name of liberal, artistic purity, the magazine was dogged almost from the outset by attacks from the Left, particularly in Cuba. In 1966 the *New York Times* broke the story of the infiltration of supposedly liberal intellectual journals by the CIA, by means of allegedly dummy funding organizations, such as the Congress for Cultural Freedom. This body did indeed fund in part the magazine, and was shown to have backing itself from the CIA. In spite of Monegal's repeated claims in an extensive defence in the magazine, and in subsequent years, the ideological mud stuck. In its first few years *Mundo Nuevo* continued to be a rich promotional vehicle for Latin American writing and literary debate, but its quality deteriorated with the removal of the magazine to Buenos Aires in 1968, and Monegal's resignation. In spite of some interesting debates on, for example, "la nueva novela" in Latin America, it ceased to be a force after this time, and the magazine folded with issue 58 when the Ford Foundation withdrew its support in 1971.

FRANK McQUADE

Further Reading

Frenk, Susan F., "Two Cultural Journals of the 1960s: *Casa de las Américas* and *Mundo Nuevo*," *Bulletin of Latin American Research*, vol. 3/2 (1984)

MacAdam, Alfred, "The Boom: a Retrospective," *Review* 33 (1984) [Interview with Emir Rodríguez Monegal]

McQuade, Frank, "*Mundo Nuevo*: la nueva novela y la guerra fría cultural," *América* (Cahiers du CRICCAL), vol. 9/10 (1992)

Orígenes (1944–1956)

This influential arts review, the most prestigious of its day in the Spanish Caribbean, was an extension of the literary group, mainly poets, headed by José Lezama Lima. The magazine was founded in Havana by Lezama and José (Pepe) Rodríguez Feo in 1944, and ran to a total of forty-two issues until its demise in 1956. Its early editors comprised Lezama Lima, Rodríguez Feo, Mariano (Rodríguez) and Alfredo Lozano. With the thirty-sixth issue, the wealthy Rodríguez Feo, who funded the review, withdrew his patronage after an editorial conflict with Lezama (concerning the publication of an article by Juan Ramón Jiménez).

Orígenes provided a focal point for many of the most promising poets and critics in Cuba in the 1940s and 1950s, and featured poetry, short stories and critical essays on contemporary art, music and philosophical trends. Also included were numerous illustrations by notable Cuban artists of the day, and cover illustrations include work by Amelia Peláez, Wifredo Lam, René Portocarrero, Alfredo Lozano, and "Mariano." This variety and vitality was informed, however, by a coherent and unifying aesthetic vision, principally that of the transcendental status of the creative artist, and the durability of artistic creation in the face of the taints of the outside world; in essence a hermetic and apolitical position. The opening editorial, penned by Lezama, is a strident assertion of the supremacy of pure artistic creation:

> No le interesa a ORÍGENES formular un programa, sino ir lanzando las flechas de su propia estela . . . La libertad consiste para nosotros en el respeto absoluto que merece el trabajo por la creación, para expresarse en la forma

más conveniente a su temperamento, a sus deseos o a su frustración, ya partiendo de su yo más oscuro, de su reacción o acción ante las solicitaciones del mundo exterior, siempre que se manifieste dentro de la tradición humanista, y la libertad que se deriva de esa tradición que ha sido el orgullo y la apetencia del americano.

[*Orígenes* is not interested in establishing a platform but, instead, in dispatching the arrows of its own shooting star trail . . . Freedom, for us, consists in the total respect that creative work deserves, to express itself in the form most appropriate to its temperament, desires or frustrations, either taking as its point of departure the darkest recesses of the subject, its reaction or action in the face of the demands of the outside world, so long as it expresses itself within the humanist tradition, and the freedom derived from this tradition which, for Americans, has been a source of pride and yearning.]

Orígenes published only original work, by both Cuban and foreign writers. Apart from the extensive contributions of its editorial committee, it also published pieces by Alejo Carpentier, Roberto Fernández Retamar, Samuel Feijoó, Eugenio Florit, Enrique Labrador Ruiz, Lydia Cabrera, Virgilio Piñera, to name but a few. Among its foreign contributors were Juan Ramón Jiménez, Vicente Aleixandre, Albert Camus, Luis Cernuda, Macedonio Fernández and Carlos Fuentes. The cosmopolitan and international edge to the magazine was enhanced by Rodríguez Feo's extensive translation work, of writers such as Georges Braque, Albert Camus, T.S. Eliot, Anaïs Nin and Wallace Stevens.

Issue thirty-five appeared in two forms as the result of the editorial split between Lezama Lima and Rodríguez Feo. The rift was complete when Lezama succeeded in registering the magazine under his directorship, and Rodríguez Feo went on to found his new, short-lived but significant magazine project, *Ciclón*. This review, in its brief life from 1955 to 1958, continued the work of *Orígenes* in the late 1940s in one important respect: it published the newest and most innovative writing. However, funded by a gay man, it was for its time quite bold on the subject of homosexuality and published the work of a group of young Cuban homosexual writers such as Calvert Casey, Antón Arrufat and Severo Sarduy.

Orígenes was to have continuing financial problems in this period until its demise, with its fortieth issue, in 1956.

FRANK MCQUADE

Further Reading
The entire run of *Orígenes: revista de arte y literatura*, is most readily available in the facsimile edition by Equilibrista, Mexico, and Ediciones Turner: Madrid, 1989, with an introduction and author index by Marcelo Uribe.

Barquet, Jesús A., "El grupo *Orígenes* y España," *Cuadernos Hispanoamericanos* 513 (1993)
García Vega, Lorenzo, *Los años de Orígenes*, Caracas: Monte Ávila, 1978
Martínez, Julio A. (editor), "Orígenes," in his *Dictionary of Twentieth Century Cuban Literature*, Westport, Connecticut: Greenwood Press, 1992
Rodríguez Feo, José, *Mi correspondencia con Lezama Lima*, Havana: Unión, 1989

Plural (1971–1976)

Plural appeared in October 1971, under the directorship of the renowned poet and critic Octavio Paz, as a monthly cultural journal funded by the leading Mexican newspaper, *Excelsior*. It was forced to close in July 1976 when the government of Luis Echeverría intervened in *Excelsior* to change its political focus. Until that moment, Octavio Paz had full editorial control over *Plural* and its orientation reflected in great measure Paz's "pluralist" interests in literature, criticism, art, philosophy, and political and historical movements. The immediate historical context helped to define the debates on contemporary issues in the magazine. Paz had resigned his ambassadorship in India in 1968 as a protest at the massacre of students in Tlatelolco and he kept a critical distance from the new president of Mexico, Echeverría, who sought to heal the breach with the intellectual community in the aftermath of Tlatelolco by pouring money into intellectual and cultural activities. Many writers were convinced by Echeverría's cultural and political policies (Carlos Fuentes became ambassador in Paris), but Paz warned against intimacy with the "philanthropic ogre," his name for the Mexican state. Some of Mexico's most prominent intellectuals – Paz himself, Fuentes, Daniel Cosío Villegas, Gabriel Zaid, Gastón García Cantú, Víctor Fores Olea and Luís Villoro – analysed the Mexican political system, the need for reform in the Partido Revolucionario Institucional, the role of the intellectual, in trenchant fashion. Events in Latin America, in particular the spread of authoritarian regimes, were also featured and a strong criticism was made of the repressive nature of state socialism in the USSR and the Eastern bloc countries.

Plural was primarily a cultural journal, publishing new writing and criticism in the arts. A group of Mexican and Spanish American writers – Juan García Ponce, Salvador Elizondo, Alejandro Rossi, Mario Vargas Llosa, Severo Sarduy, Damián Bayón – was joined by the most significant names in contemporary criticism: Roman Jakobson, Claude Lévi-Strauss, George Steiner, Roland Barthes, Norman O. Brown, Susan Sontag, Harry Levin. Paz's international reputation and contacts, the editorial skills of the magazine's staff, which included the critics Tomás Segovia and José de la Colina and the artist Kasuya Sakai, and the resources of *Excelsior* all helped to guarantee the quality of the contributors and made *Plural* one of the world's finest journals in its day. With the closure of *Excelsior*, Paz started up the magazine *Vuelta* with certain members of the *Plural* group and *Vuelta* continued under his editorship into the 1990s.

JOHN KING

Further Reading
Camp, Roderic A., *Intellectuals and the State in Twentieth-Century Mexico*, Austin: University of Texas Press, 1985

Punto de Vista (1978–)

In November 1994, the Argentine cultural journal *Punto de Vista* brought out its fiftieth issue. This marked more than sixteen years of unbroken publication, a considerable achievement in a cultural field of short-lived little magazines. Since its outset, the journal has been the project of Buenos Aires-based intellectuals, under the directorship of the cultural critic Beatriz Sarlo. It began in March 1978, as a response to one of the darkest moments in Argentine history, when a brutal military dictatorship had fractured the cultural field, imposing strict censorship. It was one instance of the development of a "catacomb" culture, where small groups sought to keep intellectual discussion alive in the interstices of state terror. No names of editorial staff appeared on the first issues, for security reasons. Issue 6 (July 1979) published the name of Sarlo as managing editor, whilst the less severe political conditions of the early 1980s allowed for the appearance of the journal's first editorial (Issue 12, July 1981). This spoke for the first time openly, about the need – in a situation of economic, political and ideological crisis – to develop "points of view," to open up new spaces for the discussion and circulation of ideas. There was also an urgent need to reconceptualise socialist culture in Argentina, in the aftermath of the populism, ideological Manicheism, and political radicalism of the early 1970s, which had been caught up in a spiral of violence and culminated in military dictatorship (1976–82). In these first issues, the emphasis was on a rereading of Argentine literature in a nuanced way and the introduction to Argentina of critics such as Raymond Williams and Richard Hoggart who offered a way out of linguistic or semiological formalism and traditional sociology through a complex analysis of the relationship between literature, ideology, language and experience.

As dictatorship was replaced by democracy, the journal could develop its strategy of avoiding the "simplistic versions of history" and "clichés of populism," terms which appear as a leitmotif in many issues. It has intervened in political discussions, speaking out against the Falklands/Malvinas war, supporting the early democratic openings of President Alfonsín (1983–88), contesting the harsh neo-liberal reforms and media manipulation of President Menem (1989–), and promoting the opposition to Menem, the "Frente Grande," in the 1995 elections. It has also carried forward important debates about modernity and postmodernity in the cultural field. The core group of contributors, Beatriz Sarlo, Carlos Altamirano, María Teresa Gramuglio, Juan Carlos Portantiero, Hilda Sábato and Hugo Vezzetti have continued this work of critical "modernisation" and have been joined by a number of younger critics in the fields of literature, history, philosophy, plastic arts and media studies.

JOHN KING

Further Reading

King, John, "Las revistas culturales de la dictadura a la democracia," in *Literatura argentina hoy: de la dictadura a la democracia*, edited by Karl Kohut and Andrea Pagni, Frankfurt: Vervuert Verlag, 1989

Masiello, Francine, "La Argentina durante el Proceso: las múltiples resistencias de la cultura," in *Ficción y política. La narrativa argentina durante el proceso militar*, edited by René Jara and Hernán Vidal, Buenos Aires: Alianza, 1987

La Revue du Monde Noir (1931–1932)

As a student in Paris in November 1931, the Martinican Paulette Nardal with the help of Haitian Dr Léo Sajous,

established the international, bilingual (French/English) periodical *La Revue du Monde Noir / The Review of the Black World*, whose six issues were unprecedented and audacious. The review proposed to serve as a voice for black intellectuals and friends of Blacks, to express the cultural richness of Africa and black civilization, and to create a moral and intellectual bond among Blacks throughout the world without distinction of nationality. The underlying assumption of this ambitious project was that a return to the authentic values of Africa – the "awakening of race consciousness," as Paulette Nardal put it – would ensure a repossession of black pride that had always been denied by the white world. Revalorization of black culture thus became linked to a racial anthropology.

"The Nardals were *Négritude* at work," remembers the Martinican novelist Joseph Zobel, who named Paulette "the godmother of *Négritude*." Indeed, Paulette Nardal and her sisters Andrée and Jane (under the pen-name Yadhé) can be considered the precursors of the *Négritude* movement which reached its peak in the late 1930s with the literary and philosophical works of Aimé Césaire, Léon Gontran Damas and Léopold Sédar Senghor.

The review counted such contributors as the Haitian "indigenist" Jean Price-Mars; the anthropologists Delafosse of France, Frobenius of Germany, and Bernelot-Moens of the Netherlands; the Antillean intellectuals Louis Achille, Félix Eboué, Gilbert Gratiant, René Maran; and Americans Georges Gregory, Langston Hughes, Claude McKay and John Matheus. Among the women contributors, aside from the Nardal sisters, were Roberte Horth from French Guyana, Magd Raney (or Marie-Magdeleine Carbet) from Martinique, and Margaret Rose Martin and Clara Shepard from the United States.

Articles ranged from literary and artistic subjects to the social, political, scientific and philosophical. Despite Paulette Nardal's later claim, the goal of the editors and contributors was more political than literary. They challenged the historical ambiguities based on racial, social and cultural prejudices. Their search for identity was based on racial solidarity and its power for change. Articles on African anthropology prevailed, followed by those signed by black writers from the United States, who published samples of their own work and wrote about the "negro" artistic happenings in Paris. They also introduced the Cuban writers Regino Pedroso and Nicolás Guillén.

Paulette Nardal had planned to publish an edition of *The Review of the Black World* in Spanish, but the periodical had to be abandoned in April 1932 for lack of financial support. Some suspected that, in spite of its moderate and conciliatory tone, colonial pressure hastened its end. The review, however, paved the way for two provocative Martinican journals, the one-issue *Légitime Défense* [Legitimate Defence] founded in Paris in 1932 by René Ménil and Etienne Léro, and the more moderate *L'Etudiant Noir* [The Black Student] published in 1934, also in Paris, by Césaire, Damas and Senghor.

Despite the lack of unity of the articles, *The Review of the Black World* did try to raise among black intellectuals of all origins the consciousness of their common blackness and its potential as a unifying force, as well as of the richness and diversity of their cultures.

MARIE-AGNÈS SOURIEAU

Sur (1931–1970)

The Argentine magazine *Sur* was published regularly between 1931 and 1970, and irregularly thereafter, until the death of its founder, Victoria Ocampo, in 1978. It was one of the longest running, and certainly the most significant cultural journal to appear in Argentina and, arguably, in Latin America, in the 20th century. Although it was conceived primarily as a literary magazine, its scope was always broader, offering an elegant fusion of fiction, philosophy, plastic arts, history and social commentary. *Sur* defended a tradition of aristocratic Argentine liberalism, inherited from the 19th century, against attacks from nationalist and authoritarian regimes at home and abroad: the spread of totalitarian regimes, both Nazi and communist, during the 1930s; the threat of Hitler in the war years; the growth of what contributors perceived as fascism in Argentina under Perón; the Marxist shadow in Latin America after the Cuban Revolution. In *Sur*'s view, the intellectual had a right to protect the conditions in which art could act as a civilising force, yet these cultural standards could only be maintained by a like-minded clerisy, a "spiritual" aristocracy.

Victoria Ocampo conceived of the journal as a "bridge" between the cultures of Argentina and, by extension, Latin America, and those of Europe and North America. In order to open up the cultural field to new currents in literature and culture, *Sur* translated and published the key writers and intellectuals of the 20th century, from Faulkner and Virginia Woolf to Sartre and Malraux, from Le Corbusier to Lacan. Whilst the bulk of these translations were of European authors, North American writers and movements were also covered extensively. Latin American authors, outside Argentina, were not published systematically, especially in the Boom years of the 1960s.

Sur also disseminated the work of the finest Argentine writers of the period: the short stories of Jorge Luis Borges, Adolfo Bioy Casares, Silvina Ocampo and José Bianco, who ran *Sur*'s editorial office. The poetry of Alberto Girri; the essays of Eduardo Mallea, Julio Cortázar and H.A. Murena; the literary criticism and *testimonios* of Victoria Ocampo. It also included and encouraged younger critics. As the magazine developed into a cultural institution with considerable power, it became the butt of strong criticism, especially in the ideologically and politically polarised climate of the 1960s. Yet its detractors provided no lasting alternative strategy, and *Sur* can be seen today as one of the most significant publications in Latin American culture.

JOHN KING

Further Reading

King, John, *Sur: a Study of the Argentine Literary Journal and Its Role in the Development of a Culture 1931–1970*, Cambridge and New York: Cambridge University Press, 1985

Tropiques (1941–1945)

During World War II, back in Martinique after eight years of study in Paris, Aimé Césaire, with his wife Suzanne and René Ménil, founded the journal *Tropiques*. From April 1941 to October 1945, fourteen issues, of sixty to eighty pages each, appeared in Fort-de-France under extremely difficult material conditions. Though isolated because of its geographic insularity, the economic blockade and the Vichy government censorship, the journal had a profound impact as the hidden voice of *Négritude* aimed at all the colonized people in the world.

While in Paris in the 1930s, Aimé Césaire, René Ménil and many Antillean intellectuals became aware of belonging to a larger community and an ancient heritage and of the need to overcome alienation. They discovered the Harlem Renaissance writers along with Leo Frobenius's anthropological work on the grandeur of African civilization. In *L'Etudiant Noir* [The Black Student] Césaire began to articulate the political and cultural identity of the black people, which he called *Négritude*. And a few years later, in his celebrated *Cahier d'un retour au pays natal*, 1939 (*Return to My Native Land*) he expressed the intolerable reality of his people, their "negritude," through a new poetic language that tapped the forbidden zones of the unconscious.

Because of fascist domination of Martinique, *Tropiques* could not be overtly political. It was founded as a cultural or indigenous review whose purpose was to raise native consciousness of and pride in Martinique's unexplored African heritage and its autochthonous richness. But the hidden political goal of the editors was to liberate their people from their traumatized past, and educate them in the rich potential of their culture. Therefore, the first objective of *Tropiques* was an existential quest aimed at finding concrete answers to the specifically Martinican psychology and natural environment. Articles ranged from anthropological to folkloric to fauna and flora-related subjects. The contents of Césaire's poems and of René Ménil's essays were very similar in their celebration of life, their questioning and Surrealist approach to existence. Indeed, Surrealist techniques allowed the uncovering of what had been repressed by shame and, therefore, had a reintegrating power.

Further, Surrealism became a method to critique rational bourgeois Western philosophy. Upon fleeing the Vichy regime for the United States, André Breton, author of *Manifeste du surréalisme* (1924) came across the first issue of *Tropiques*: there he found an affirmation of his own values. Césaire recalled his meeting with Breton in a 1978 interview with Jacqueline Leiner: "Breton brought us courage . . . he shortened our research and our hesitations. I realized that most of the problems I was struggling with had been resolved by Breton and Surrealism . . . The meeting with Breton was a confirmation of the truth that I found on my own." Indeed, Césaire's Surrealist poems published in the journal were eventually collected in the volume *Les Armes miraculeuses*, 1946 [The Miraculous Weapons]. The philosopher René Ménil published Surrealist-framed essays such as "Introduction au merveilleux" [Introduction to the Marvelous], while Suzanne Césaire wrote articles praising Breton, the "maître penseur" (mastermind), and his poetic influence on the social and aesthetic identity of the Antilleans. Thus, the concept of *Négritude* coincided with the Surrealist quest of putting humankind in touch with its deepest, repressed desires: for the Martinicans, this quest led to their black, African, Antillean specificity. Numerous texts or poems by Breton, Lautréamont, Mallarmé, Péguy,

McKay and Picabia expressed the universality of the Surrealist experience and its meaning for Martinican consciousness.

Moreover, *Tropiques* wanted to echo the intellectual developments of the New World and put Martinique at the center of international exchanges. Thus, literary news from Venezuela, Curaçao and Mexico was reported. Cuban writers and artists such as Lydia Cabrera, Wilfredo Lam, Alejo Carpentier, and the Chilean Jorge Cáceres published short stories and folktales.

Against colonization and its coercive assimilation, *Tropiques* attempted to define the identity of "this ambiguous being, the Antillean," to borrow Suzanne Césaire's words. Despite its limitations in history and anthropology, the journal opened new avenues for rethinking Antillean culture and society, and, in particular, the political situation of the region.

MARIE-AGNÈS SOURIEAU

Vuelta (1976–)

Founded in November 1976 in Mexico by Octavio Paz, *Vuelta* – in the mid 1990s – is one of the most prominent and dynamic cultural journals in Latin America, and embodies some of the typical struggles and dichotomies of a modern liberal magazine as it attempts to protect its aesthetic values from the temptations of political doctrine. After five years of nurturing the innovative monthly *Plural*, funded by and linked with the newspaper *Excelsior*, Octavio Paz was able to draw on the support of former contributors and subscribers to create a new magazine following the complex shift of allegiances in the aftermath of the resignation of the newspaper's editor Julio Scherer. *Vuelta* is in many ways a continuation of *Plural*, being essentially a literary magazine, with an additional range of items on the other arts, politics, current affairs and historical issues, notably in the essays of Enrique Krauze. Paz himself is a regular and vigorous contributor of his poetry, essays on art and culture, and extensive personal memoirs, and other regular contributors have included Gabriel Zaid, Juan García Ponce, Guillermo Sheridan and Guillermo Cabrera Infante. When making claims for the journal, Paz is reminiscent of other magazine directors (for example, Rodríguez Monegal with *Mundo Nuevo*) in declaring the freedom and integrity of his publication in the face of ideological pressures. Such claims for aesthetic autonomy may be sustainable, but always emerge a little battered in reality, and *Vuelta* has irked the Latin American Left with its criticisms of the Sandinistas, and the Castro regime in Cuba. Paz has expressed exasperation at this perception of the magazine as adversarial or elitist in tone, and urges that it be seen as a totality, and most importantly as a dialogue. In this respect *Vuelta* is an extension of *Plural*, which itself was in the tradition of earlier 20th-century Mexican publications such as *Contemporáneos*, *Tierra Nueva*, *Taller* and *Revista Mexicana de Literatura*. In its concentration on literary and aesthetic values of a "high" order it is challenged in the field of Mexican letters by the more sociological and current affairs-centred journal *Nexos*. Paz clearly sees his own and other comparable liberal intellectual journals as the conscience of the intellectual elite, promoting national culture, and opening up world literature to Mexico, in an atmosphere of debate and exchange, free of ideological complacency and dogma. This is an old polemic, which in Mexico is compounded by the positing of a "liberal" identity in a context where this can be seen to be a reaffirmation of the old order, and Paz's skirmishes with PRI in the 1960s and his series of essays in *Vuelta* in the mid-1980s are complicated by his later realignment with a now-discredited Carlos Salinas. The long-standing belief, however, in the intellectual journal as a powerful communicator of ideas, and a safeguard against doctrinaire inflexibility, is still forcefully presented in this eloquent and elegant literary showcase of contemporary Latin American letters.

FRANK McQUADE

Further Reading
King, John, "The Periodicals: *Vuelta*," *Times Literary Supplement* 4541 (1990)
Paz, Octavio, "Historia y prehistoria de *Vuelta*," *Pasión crítica*, Barcelona: Seix Barral, 1985

Sor Juana Inés de la Cruz 1651(?)–1695

Mexican writer and woman of ideas

The Spanish colonies in America, although established by military conquest and built upon the ruins of the Aztec and the Inca empires, had brought from Europe certain Utopian and pastoral dimensions, allowing Spanish missionaries to set up new experimental communities, and Spanish women, as well as their *criollo* daughters, to run plantations and businesses, and to assert their financial and social independence in ways not often possible in metropolitan Spain. In the sphere of letters, however, few texts written by colonial women have survived, and most of these were produced in convents, where women had more opportunity to educate themselves, to read, and to write. A Jeronimite convent near the viceroy's court in Mexico City provided a home, a library and a study for one of the greatest of all colonial writers, who was also a woman: Juana Inés Asuaje y Ramírez, more generally known by her religious name, Sor Juana Inés de la Cruz. A viceroy's wife, her beloved friend María Luisa Manrique de Lara – Countess of Paredes in her own right, and Marchioness of Laguna by her husband – and other admirers made sure that her works were published in Madrid: *Inundación castálida*, 1689 [Castalian Inundation], the first edition of the first volume of her works, sold well and was highly appreciated, winning for Sor Juana fame and recognition as a learned woman in her own times. Her work is a reflection of both her erudition and of the struggle she carried on to win general acknowledgement of the intellectual equality between the sexes.

Except for a few poems published in Mexico, the bulk of Sor Juana's works were published in Spain in three different volumes: the first in 1689, the second in 1692, and the third posthumously in 1700. All of these editions were frequently reprinted, which gives an indication of the extent of the readership she had in the late 17th and early 18th centuries. Her works are evidence of her wide readings in philosophy, theology, history, science and literature. We can also clearly perceive her concern with the status of women and of New World culture. As a poet, she cultivated a wide range of forms, meters and themes, most of them typical of the period; her witty plays on words and ideas – also typical of the *conceptismo* and *culteranismo* of Baroque literature, and with an ornate style marked by conceits – are an integral part of her poetic personality, which has an unusual freshness and enthusiasm.

Her works include many different types of poetry, dramatic works in verse, and prose works of a more doctrinal or autobiographical sort. Her secular lyric poetry is her best-known and most important form. For example, there are such highly original works as her verse portrait of the Countess of Paredes; her sonnet on a painting of herself considered as a vain attempt to save her body from annihilation; the Baroque fascination with complex machines, as is the case of a poem devoted to a marquis on his birthday, concerning a clock or hourglass, which mechanically measures the ineffable passing of human time; several "carpe diem" sonnets centered on the image of the rose; poems on hope and the vanity of human illusions; verses on fidelity in love, always seen as a feminine characteristic (she, significantly, devotes five of her sonnets to female heroines who sacrificed their lives for their honor: Porcia, Lucretia, Julia and Tisbe); the many stanzas of the *romance* (ballad) to the Duchess of Aveiro where she expresses her "feminism" and her *criollismo* and the ones belonging to the "Villancicos de Santa Catarina" [Carols to St Catherine of Alexandria]; poems on absence and the sufferings of love, reflected in Nature, despite its appearance of insensibility; or, on love's passion resolved in the rhetoric of tears; and poems on our imagination, within which we can imprison a beloved person. Her most famous and popular poem is a bitingly witty criticism of men's unfairness in blaming women for the sinfulness that men themselves provoke and promote.

Among her devotional writings are the *Ejercicios de la Encarnación* [Exercises on the Incarnation], in which she presents in prose the Virgin Mary as a model of feminine power and wisdom, almost on the same level as God. Her "villancicos," or carol sequences, written for festive performance in cathedrals, allow us a glimpse of her religious and social sensibility; this popular genre, with many different voices, permitted the poet to speak for marginal social groups such as blacks, Indians and women, and to make fun of masculine clerical types such as arrogant students: the consciousness of her own marginality, as a woman, as a *criolla*, and as an illegitimate child, gave her an understanding of what it meant to be discriminated against. In such songs, then, she presents religious women as both intellectual and devout, as in the portrayals of the Virgin Mary and of St Catherine of Alexandria in her carols mentioned before. Her black voices speak a special dialect of Spanish, and her Indians speak Náhuatl, to address God and to complain about how they are treated by Spanish representatives of the Church or State.

Sor Juana's long poem entitled *El Sueño* (Sor Juana's Dream) occupies a unique place among her works. In her highly significant autobiographical *Respuesta* (The Answer, see separate essay, below) she refers to the *Sueño* as the only poem that she had written for her own pleasure. It is a compendium of contemporary scholastic and scientific knowledge, ranging from the Ancient philosophers and the Church Fathers to Florentine hermetic wisdom and the then recent ideas of Athanasius Kircher and perhaps even of Descartes. It draws on Renaissance poetic topology or commonplaces, recast in Spanish Baroque forms. The narrative structure of the *Dream* consists of three steps of falling asleep, dreaming, and waking up and its protagonist, the Soul, struggles with the problematic of scientific knowledge. It concerns the intellectual adventure of the Soul searching for total comprehension of the universe, an enterprise that represents the highest ambition growing out of human love for scientific knowledge. (See my essay on this poem, below.)

In 1690 the Bishop of Puebla published and sent to Sor Juana her critique of a Portuguese Jesuit's sermon, along with a letter of his own, with the pseudonymous signature of a nun. In her critique (*Carta atenagórica* or *Crisis sobre un sermón*) [Athenagoric Letter or Crisis over a Sermon], Sor Juana had refuted, in a highly sophisticated and learned way, the argument of Father Antonio de Vieira, in which he rejected interpretations by the Church Fathers and proposed his own. The Bishop – a typical cleric of his time – reveals in his letter, although it is subtly ambiguous, his admiration for Sor Juana's intelligence as he urges her to use it in the study of divine rather than secular matters. All of this provided her with an excuse for a full-scale defense of her life and literary career in *La respuesta a Sor Filotea*. This eloquent and warmly human document explains fully the nun's intellectual vocation by recalling her childhood eagerness to learn to read and write, her adolescent rejection of marriage and her choice of the convent as a place to study; she cites many famous women from the Bible and from classical antiquity in her defense of feminine access to study and to writing. She implies that women as scientists have empirical advantages when she asserts, "If Aristotle had done some cooking, he would have written even more." All of this is relevant to the Bishop's apparent reprimand; it is a feminist *apologia* that was unique in the 17th-century Hispanic world: she claimed the right to dissent from the opinions of Father Viera, just as everybody else had the right to differ from her opinions. (And in the *Carta de Monterrey* [Monterrey Letter], a letter discovered relatively recently (by Father Aureliano Tapia Méndez),which Sor Juana wrote to her confessor Father Antonio Núñez de Miranda, long before writing her *Respuesta*, we find her defending her rights in even stronger terms.)

Neptuno alegórico [Allegorical Neptune], a very Baroque piece of writing, is, for the modern reader, a difficult work; it is an official "relación" or explanation of the triumphal arch erected in November of 1680 for the reception of the new viceroy, the Marquis of La Laguna, and his wife. In her poetic description of the arch Sor Juana presents the mythological figure of Neptune as an allegorical model for the viceroy. This is a highly learned text in which she displays her most arcane erudition and ingenuity.

Sor Juana's theatrical works consist of several *loas* (short dramatic prologues), largely mythical and allegorical; three *autos sacramentales*, or allegorical dramatizations of sacramental theology in the Calderonian tradition (even surpassing Calderón in *Divino Narciso*), written, with their *loas*, for the feast of Corpus Christi; and two full-length "cape and sword" plays in the tradition of Lope de Vega. The *loas* that precede her *autos* are especially interesting for their presentation of Aztec feminine characters, who defend pre-Christian religious practices. *El cetro de José* [Joseph's Sceptre] is based on a story from the Bible; *El mártir del Sacramento San Hermenegildo* [The Martyr of the Sacrament St Hermenegildo] is hagiographic; and *Divino Narciso* [Divine Narcissus] is an ingenious allegorization of the pagan mythological Narcissus as the redeeming Christ. In *Divino Narciso* the Narcissus (Christ), having rejected the advances of Echo (the Devil), who is the rival of Human Nature, sees the latter reflected in the Fountain of Grace (the Virgin Mary), which unites God with Human Nature at the moment of the Incarnation; then Narcissus, in love with himself as reflected in Human Nature, falls into the fountain and drowns, allegorically crucified.

The three *loas*, or dramatic prologues, written for these *autos sacramentales* have a particular importance for us, for in those belonging to *El cetro de José* and *Divino Narciso* we can hear the voice of Sor Juana as very much that of a woman born in the New World; we see the world of Aztec culture in female allegorical figures: women here have political roles, and represent the historical voices of their communities. In the *loa* for *San Hermenegildo*, Sor Juana presents herself among a group of students as an able scholastic teacher; she criticizes the traditional dogmatism of antiquated European ideas devised by men and shows how new ideas and discoveries displace them; she emphazises the value of doubt as a basis for the advancement of science.

One of the secular plays, *Amor es más laberinto* [Love is More a Labyrinth], was written in collaboration with Juan de Guevara; the other, *Los empeños de una casa* [Trials of a Noble House], has strong leading female characters, especially that of Leonor, an autobiographical figure. The comic character Castaño, a mulatto servant from the New World, speaks satirically of the machismo of white Spaniards in a metatheatrical scene parodying the "cape and sword" comedy as a literary genre.

From the baroque intellectual world of her convent cell Sor Juana wrote about her deep concerns as both a woman and a *criolla*. She is a key figure for the understanding of colonial Mexico; and her lucid and advanced ideas remain exemplary for us today.

GEORGINA SABAT DE RIVERS

Biography
Born Juana Ramírez de Asbaje (or Asuaje) in San Miguel de Nepantla, Viceroyalty of New Spain (now Mexico), 12 November 1651 (some sources give 1648). Largely self-educated. Invited to attend the court of the Spanish Viceroy, the Marquis of Mancera and his wife Doña Leonor Carreto, in Mexico City, c.1659, and subsequently wrote poetry for official events. Entered the Carmelite convent in Mexico City on 14 August 1667 but stayed for only three months. In 1669 she entered the Jeronymite Convent of Santa Paula, Mexico City, and adopted the religious name Sor Juana Inés de la Cruz. Continued her intellectual pursuits and her international reputation grew. Around 1690 came under increasing pressure from the Church authorities to concentrate on theology and cease writing profane works. Chose to abandon writing and lead a life of complete seclusion c.1693. Died of the plague, 17 April 1695.

Selected Works

Collected Works
[Works] 3 vols, 1689–1700
  Volume 1: *Inundación castálida*, Madrid, 1689 [includes verse and the play *El Neptuno alegórico*]; as *Poemas*, Madrid, 1690
  Volume 2: *Segundo volumen de las obras*, Seville, 1692 [includes "El sueño"; the autos *El cetro de José*, *El mártir del Sacramento San Hermenegildo*, *Divino Narciso*; the comedies *Los empeños de una casa*, *Amor es más laberinto*; and *Crisis sobre un sermón: Carta atenagórica*]
  Volume 3: *Fama y obras póstumas*, Madrid, 1700 [includes *La respuesta a Sor Filotea*]

Compilations and Anthologies
Obras completas, edited by Alfonso Méndez Plancarte, 4 vols, Mexico City: Fondo de Cultura Económica, 1951–57
Poesía, teatro y prosa, edited by Antonio Castro Leal, Mexico City: Porrúa, 1965
Obras selectas, edited by Georgina Sabat de Rivers and Elias L. Rivers, Barcelona: Noguer, 1976
Obra selecta, edited by Lusi Sáinz de Medrano, Barcelona: Planeta, 1987

Anthologies in Translation
The Pathless Grove: Sonnets, translated by Pauline Cook, Prairie City, Illinois: Decker Press, 1950
A Woman of Genius: the Intellectual Autobiography of Sor Juana Inés de la Cruz, translated by Margaret Sayers Peden, Salisbury, Connecticut: Lime Rock Press, 1982
Sor Juana Inés de la Cruz: Poems, edited and translated by Margaret Sayers Peden, Binghampton, New York: Bilingual Press, 1985 [bilingual edition]
Selected Sonnets, translated by Sandra Sider, Saskatoon: Peregrina, 1987
A Sor Juana Anthology, translated by Alan S. Trueblood, Cambridge, Massachusetts: Harvard University Press, 1988 [bilingual edition]

Further Reading
Aguirre, Mirta, *Del encausto a la sangre: Sor Juana Inés de la Cruz*, Havana: Casa de las Américas, 1975
Alfau de Solalinde, Jesusa, *El barroco en la vida de Sor Juana*, Mexico City: Instituto de Estudios y Documentos Históricos, 1981
Bénassy-Berling, Marie-Cécile, *Humanismo y religión en Sor Juana Inés de la Cruz*, translated by Laura López de Belair, Mexico City: UNAM, 1983
Cox, Patricia, *El secreto de Sor Juana*, Mexico City: Populibros La Prensa, 1971
Daniel, Lee A., *The Loa of Sor Juana Inés de la Cruz*, Fredricton, New Brunswick: York Press, 1994

Flynn, Gerard C., *Sor Juana Inés de la Cruz*, New York: Twayne, 1971

Galeano Ospina, Carlos E., *Juana de Asbaje: aproximación a la autobiografía de la décima musa*, Medellin, Colombia: Secretaría de Educación y Cultura, 1976

Guilarte, Cecilia G. de, *Sor Juana Inés de la Cruz: claro en la selva*, Buenos Aires: Ekin, 1958

Ludmer, Josefina, "Las tretas del débil," in *La sartén por el mango. Encuentro de escritoras hispanoamericanas*, edited by Patricia Elena González and Eliana Ortega, Río Piedras, Puerto Rico: Huracán, 1984

Maza, Francisco de la and Elías Trabulse, *Sor Juana Inés de la Cruz ante la historia*, Mexico City: UNAM, 1980

Merrim, Stephanie (editor), *Feminist Perspectives on Sor Juana Inés de la Cruz*, Detroit: Wayne State University Press, 1991

Montross, Constance M., *Virtue or Vice?: Sor Juana's Use of Thomistic Thought*, Washington, DC: University Press of America, 1981

Paz, Octavio, *Sor Juana Inés de la Cruz, o las trampas de la fe*, Mexico City: Fondo de Cultura Económica, 1982, as *Sor Juana or the Traps of Faith*, translated by Margaret Sayers Peden, Cambridge: Massachusetts, Bel Knap Press, 1988; retitled as *Sor Juana: Her Life and World*, London: Faber and Faber, 1988

Pérez, María Esther, *Lo americano en el teatro de Sor Juana Inés de la Cruz*, New York: Torres, 1975

Pfandl, Ludwig, *Sor Juana Inés de la Cruz: la décima musa de México*, translated by Juan Antonio Ortega y Medina, Mexico City: UNAM, 1963

Poot Herrera, Sara (editor), *Y diversa de mí misma/entre vuestras plumas ando. Homenaje internacional a Sor Juana Inés de la Cruz*, Mexico City: El Colegio de México, 1994

Sabat de Rivers, Georgina, "*Ejercicios de la Encarnación*: sobre la imagen de María y la decisión final de Sor Juana," in *Estudios de literatura hispanoamericana. Sor Juana Inés de la cruz y otros poetas barrocos de la Colonia*, Barcelona: PPU, 1992

——— "Apología de América y del mundo azteca en tres loas de Sor Juana," *Revista de Estudios Hispánicos. Letras coloniales*, Universidad de Puerto Rico (1992)

Tavard, George H., *Juana Inés de la Cruz and the Theology of Beauty*, Notre Dame, Indiana: Notre Dame University Press, 1991

Trabulse, Elías, *Sor Juana Inés de la Cruz: ante la historia*, Mexico City: UNAM, 1980

Divino Narciso

Auto by Sor Juana Inés de la Cruz

The Spanish word *auto* is a generic term applied to a religious drama, usually dealing with Christmas and Eucharistic themes; *auto* is a form of the word *acto* or act, used for other theatrical productions and their subdivisions. The *auto* was derived from the liturgy in the Middle Ages, from scenes or "mysteries" that were dramatized in monasteries and churches. Characteristically, a cart or wagon was used in them for carrying religious paintings and images in procession. Valbuena Prat has given us a clear-cut definition of the *auto* as "a dramatic composition, in one act, which is allegorical and refers to the Eucharist."

Between 1680 and 1691, at the latest, Sor Juana wrote three *autos sacramentales*, preceded by their *loas*: *El mártir del Sacramento San Hermenegildo* [The Martyr of the Sacrament St Hermenegildo], *Divino Narciso*, and *El cetro de José* [Joseph's Sceptre], probably in that order, to judge by the

growing attention paid in the *loas* to the discovery of America and to Aztec culture. But *Divino Narciso* was published before the others (and perhaps this indicates that its literary superiority was immediately recognized).

In this *auto* the author introduces us to the Aztec world with the characters named Occidente, who is dressed as an Indian youth, and America, a strong, brave Indian maiden in fancy costume. Sor Juana mentions clothing typical of the Indians, blankets and *huipiles* (women's tunics) and a dance called "tocotín," as well as feathers and rattles, showing that she was familiar with the Indian customs of her native land. Her musical choruses present an *apologia* for ancient Mexico in the ceremony of *teocualo* or the eating of the god, which the nun presents as an Aztec rite that prefigures Christian communion. In this rite an image of the god Huitzilopchtli was raised up and on it was made a dough combining grains and seeds with human blood, which was then handed out in small pieces to those present. We also find the characters named Christian Religion and Zeal, the latter dressed as a military officer surrounded by soldiers, giving us an aggressive view of religion. In the subsequent dialogues between the two groups, the Spaniards echo the sermons of religious chroniclers, denouncing the diabolical character of the false pagan rites, such as *teocualo*, as well as other commonplaces such as the power of Occidente and the beauty and wealth of America.

In their speeches, America and Occidente protest against the inequality of the two groups' forces, which pitch "monstruous Centaurs," or men on horseback, and "fiery balls of lead" against mere arrows; and they defend their gods and their own freedom to continue worshipping them. We should note that in this whole passage Sor Juana deliberately endows her Indians with the same kind of free will that was being discussed by European theologians, as well as the same qualities of rational knowledge which the latter presupposed were theirs exclusively. What the nun makes obvious is the impossibility of communication between the two cultures; she also questions the right, so often disputed by Spanish theologians, of the Crown and the Church to conquer and evangelize the new continent. The *loa* ends, as might have been expected, with America and Occident consenting to attend the *auto* to become better informed about the meaning of the Christian Eucharist; thus the *loa* leads directly into the following *auto*. The final words of the *loa*, nevertheless, sung during an Aztec dance performed by all the cast – Indians and Spaniards together – may well disconcert us: "¡Dichoso el día / que conocí al gran Dios de las Semillas!" (Happy the day that I came to know the great God of Seeds), the God that has been mentioned throughout the *loa* with the name Quetzalcoatl-Huizilopochtli, in this ambiguous hymn, is now being converted into the Christian God.

In *Divino Narciso* we find ideas taken from Ovid's *Metamorphoses* combined with passages from the Bible, especially the *Song of Songs*, and lines from St John of the Cross, as well as from Calderón, the 17th-century Spanish dramatist who raised the *auto sacramental* to its highest level. Sor Juana gave form to revisionist ideas about Narcissus, circulating in her time, which transformed this traditionally frivolous and selfish figure figure into that of Christ. She presents him as falling in love, not with his own reflection in the water, but with Human Nature, who is hidden behind him and whom he sees reflected; all of this takes place in an Arcadian, pastoral world of Paradise, in which, nevertheless, Evil also exists. Human Nature, a feminine character, is representative of the human race created in the image and likeness of God; Narcissus tells her at one point, "and I kept thee as precious to my eyes." Echo represents fallen angelic nature, that is, Lucifer. In this play, Echo and Human Nature both appear as shepherdesses competing for the love of Narcissus (Christ). Echo retains the attributes that, according to Greek mythology, Juno had given her as a punishment: she is presented as incapable of expressing her own ideas and able only to repeat the final words of those speaking to her (hence her name); she is, as Octavio Paz says, "God's monkey." She is also mute like the evil spirit of the New Testament whom Jesus silenced. Echo is accompanied by two characters, Pride and Self-Love, who sum up the sins most to be feared by any Christian since they led the most intelligent and beautiful angel, Lucifer, to attempt to compete with God. Human Nature, on the other hand, is presented within the biblical tradition of man's fall from grace in Paradise, the source of original sin, as well as of other subsequent betrayals.

Narcissus, weary of fleeing from Echo, reaches a spring or fountain (the source of grace), the waters of which have never been muddied, and he sings the song that begins:

Ovejuela perdida,
de tu dueño olvidada,
¿a dónde vas errada?
[Little lost sheep,
forgetful of thine owner,
where dost thou wander?]

This is just a sample of the lovely poetry found in the play. As he approaches to have a drink of water, he sees the reflection of Human Nature hidden in the bushes behind him and falls in love with her, which is to say, in terms of the fable, he falls in love with himself at the same time, since she has been created in his image and likeness:

De mirar su retrato
enamorado muere
que aun copiada su imagen
hace efecto tan fuerte.

[From looking at her picture / he is dying of love / for even a copy of his image / has a powerful effect.]

Narcissus plunges into the spring and at that moment is transformed into a white flower, the narcissus or Eucharistic Host. Thus Narcissus-Christ dies for Human Nature, in a metaphor of the Crucifixion, in order to redeem her from sin and to make possible her return to Paradise. The knowledge of one's self, reflected in the spring, which led (according to Tiresias' prophecy) to the death of the mythological Narcissus, in Sor Juana's play leads him to resurrection. As Paz expresses it: "knowledge does not kill: it brings back to life." And Christ continues, in sacramental form, to give strength to the human race throughout the ages.

The fountain of grace, which is the source of baptismal water, cleansing the human being from original sin, is also the personification of the Immaculate Virgin Mary, born without original sin, through whom redemption is achieved by means of the Incarnation. Mary, always pure, conceives Jesus by the Holy Spirit; Christ combines divine and human nature within his single person. In this way Sor Juana emphasizes the importance of Mary's role as partner in the redemption of the human race.

Finally, after the elevation of the Host, the play ends with the Latin liturgical hymn "Pange, lingua, gloriosi / Corporis mysterium" written by Thomas Aquinas for the celebration of Corpus Christi. The nun's deep respect for sacramental doctrine probably inhibited her from introducing the usual comic character, or "figura del donaire," which we find in Calderón's *autos sacramentales*, despite her great ability to merge the sacred and the profane. At the same time, Vossler draws our attention, in this *auto*, to a diffuse sensuality which brings a note of everyday simplicity to the seriousness of the subject-matter.

Sor Juana's open, syncretistic spirit, in the Jesuit tradition, brought in, at the beginning of this play, characters named Synagogue and Paganism, whom Human Nature claims as her children. They represent human beings whose choruses sing (in the case of Synagogue), "Praise the Lord of all men," and (in the case of Paganism), "Applaud Narcissus, ye streams and flowers," reminding us of her use in the *loa* of the Aztec hymn to the God of Seeds. By bringing in Synagogue and Paganism, the author emphasizes the teachings of the Old Testament as well as the pagan source of the original Narcissus story.

Divino Narciso contains a wide range of poetic forms and meters; in the play we find some of the most beautiful verses that Sor Juana ever wrote. Here her poetry, although in tone closer to that of Garcilaso de la Vega than to that of Calderón, nevertheless has the Baroque intellectual trademark of the latter. Sor Juana created, in her *Divino Narciso*, one of her three masterpieces, along with the *Sueño* (*Sor Juana's Dream*) and the *Respuesta* (*The Answer*). The Mexican nun's ability to synthesize the elements of her wide range of knowledge takes us from an Aztec religious rite, as prefiguration of the Eucharist, to the myths of ancient Greece, and from there to the familiar theological world of her scholastic education, producing this masterpiece of the Baroque allegorical *auto sacramental*.

GEORGINA SABAT DE RIVERS

Editions

First edition: *Divino Narciso*, Mexico City, 1690
Critical edition: *Obras completas de Sor Juana Inés de la Cruz*, vol. 3, edited by Alfonso Méndez Plancarte, Mexico City: Fondo de Cultura Económica, 1951

Further Reading

Checa, Jorge, *El Divino Narciso* y la redención del lenguaje," *Nueva Revista de Filología Hispánica*, vol. 38/1 (1990)
Merrim, Stephanie, "Narciso *desdoblado*: Narcissistic stratagems in *El Divino Narciso* and the *Respuesta a Sor Filotea de la Cruz*," *Bulletin of Hispanic Studies*, vol. 64 (1987)

Primero sueño

Poem by Sor Juana Inés de la Cruz

This poem, almost one thousand lines long, is Sor Juana's most important and significant work in verse; she herself remarks on its unique character in her *Respuesta*, 1691 (*The Answer*) when she calls it, probably exaggerating, the only one of her works that she had written on her own initiative and for her own pleasure. The *Primero sueño* was first published in 1692, in the second volume of Sor Juana's complete works. We do not know exactly when it was written, but given its high level of intellectual and poetic sophistication it must belong to the fully mature period of her life.

The *Sueño* is written in a Spanish metrical form known as the *silva*, an irregular combination of 7- and 11-syllable lines without consistent rhyme-schemes or stanzas. In her poem Sor Juana draws on all her readings in science and poetry; she gives us a wide-ranging sample of scholastic philosophy, modern technology and scientific theories, and her own personal experiments and thought. In this respect the *Sueño* and the *Respuesta* are closely related and shed light on one another from the point of view of the author's intellectual development; both of them reflect her most vital concerns and interests, one in the form of poetic fiction and the other in more literal autobiography. It is worth considering first the literary tradition on which Sor Juana draws in the *Sueño*, and then indicating her more personal concerns, especially a woman's concerns, as they are reflected in the text.

One of the primary ancient traditions from which Sor Juana's poem derives is that of the dream/vision, with its view of the world and human life from on high, at a philosophical distance. Other classical commonplaces on which writers drew were the battle between light and darkness, personified by the Sun and the Night; the ideas of sleep as the illusory cure for one's waking ills and of sleep, like death, as the leveler that comes to all of us, regardless of social rank. In addition to these classical *topoi*, in Sor Juana's *Sueño* we find many others that are typical of Renaissance poetry, related to the law, to astrology, to history, mythology and religion, and even to anatomy.

We should take note of the ambiguity of the word "sueño" in Spanish. Deriving simultaneously from the Latin words "somnium" (dream) and "somnus" (sleep), it does not always distinguish clearly between these two meanings: in modern Spanish, "tengo sueño," for example, means "I am sleepy," while "tuve un sueño" means "I had a dream." Thus "sueño" is as often the image of death (*somnium imago mortis*) as of life (life as a dream, as in the case of Calderón's famous play *La vida es sueño*, from which Segismundo may awaken into eternity); the human subject is not always sure whether he or she is dreaming. This motif is frequently related to themes of love, such as the fulfilment of erotic desires while one is asleep; it is also related to moral and philosophical questions concerning life, its brevity and its anguish. Dreams may seem to warn us of an impending disaster or to anticipate future happiness; as a temporary death they teach us how to make the most of life or to achieve eternal glory. This whole familiar and complex Renaissance tradition is touched upon, either explicitly or allusively, in Sor Juana's *Sueño*, adapted innova-

tively to a dream that is neither amorous nor mystical, but intellectually scientific: Sor Juana's dream, while she is asleep, is an attempt to resolve an inner crisis concerning the possibilities of knowledge and concerning her own identity as a woman, a crisis that vitally preoccupies her while she is awake.

Sor Juana's work is the only great poem in 16th- and 17th-century Hispanic literature that is clearly devoted to turning scientific thought into poetry, a poetry in some ways comparable to that of Lucretius' *De rerum natura* (*On the Nature of the Universe*); it brings into sharp focus vaguely scientific ideas that appear in a scattered way in previous Renaissance and Baroque poetry written in Spanish. The value of her poem lies not so much in the validity of its scientific ideas as in its problematic epistemology, the human mind striving in a dynamic way to comprehend the universe.

The poem begins with a densely Baroque description of nightfall, deriving from geometric shadows in planetary space: "Piramidal, funesta, de la tierra / nacida sombra, al cielo encaminaba / de vanos obeliscos punta altiva / escalar pretendiendo las estrellas ... " (A pyramidal, funereal shadow born of the Earth pushed its sharp point of empty obelisks toward Heaven, trying to climb to the stars ...). The Earth's shadow slowly invades the elemental domains of the animals (earth), of the fish (water) and of the birds (air) with a sleep that overwhelms them all. We should note that the poet features, from the start, cosmic entities that are mythologically or grammatically feminine; and some of these nocturnal figures are well-known for having broken laws established by masculine figures, "the law of the father."

As we read on, the stillness of the external world invades the human body, which is now "muerto a la vida y a la muerte vivo" (dead to life and alive to death); as it sleeps, only its heart, lungs and stomach maintain life "con mudas voces" (with silent voices). The inner world of human dreams, continuing the activity of the mind while awake, gives rise to the elaboration of new images. Sor Juana explains this in her *Respuesta* with the following words:

> ni aun el sueño se libró de este continuo movimiento de mi imaginativa; antes suele obrar en él más libre y desembarazada, confiriendo con mayor claridad y sosiego las especies que ha conservado del día, arguyendo, haciendo versos, de que os pudiera hacer un catálogo muy grande, y de algunas razones y delgadezas que he alcanzado dormida mejor que despierta.

> [not even sleep freed me from the continual movement of my imagination; on the contrary, it usually moves more freely and unobstructedly in sleep, bringing together more clearly and calmly the impressions that it has retained from daytime, creating arguments and verses of which I could make you a long catalogue, as well as of some subtle processes of reasoning that I follow better while asleep than awake].

The central section of the poem, coming after this, is dense and difficult as it recounts the Soul's problematic search for knowledge. This epistemological investigation is carried out on two levels, one abstract and the other personal.

As the body goes to sleep, the Soul, grammatically feminine but functionally asexual and created in the image of God, begins its solitary adventure. (In other literary dream-journeys, such as that of Dante's *Divine Comedy*, for example, the protagonist usually has a companion or guide.) The Soul is presented as being primarily an intellectual entity with Aristotelian characteristics; with the help of the imagination it converts into mental concepts fragmentary images that have been received through the senses, a process that the poet compares with what "la azogada luna," or mirror, on top of the Pharos of Alexandria, does with the images of ships at sea. The Soul, now completely separated from its body, rises to cosmic heights and is able to look at everything, even itself; from such heights, compared to Atlas and Olympus, the Pyramids and the eagle flying up toward the sun, the Soul strives to embrace, to comprehend, in an intuitive Platonic vision, the whole of creation; but, dazzled by the Sun, it strives in vain "y por mirarlo todo, nada vía" (and because it stares at everything, it sees nothing).

The Soul slowly recovers from this first failure and tries again, using this time a discursive method based on Aristotle's ten categories, moving systematically from the simple to the complex, rising step by step, inductively arriving at general ideas. In this way Sor Juana begins to explain the limits of human understanding. The poem now moves slowly upward, from mineral to vegetable to animal; the Soul seems to be succeeding in its attempt to reach the peak of knowledge, but then falls back, only to attempt to rise again. It finally falls into disillusion: the human intellect is excessively daring in trying to understand everything, for it cannot really comprehend even the simplest phenomena: the subterranean flow of water, the color and perfume of a flower. Such phenomena are associated with mythological figures that are female, such as Arethusa, Proserpine and Ceres, frustrated by the male figures of Alpheus and Pluto: there is a feminist agenda underlying this scientific quest, making it clear to the modern reader that Sor Juana, as a woman, was protesting against the intellectual barriers raised against her by male ecclesiastics and their well-established misogynistic tradition.

To compensate for defeat in the search for full knowledge, the poet evokes the mythological figure of Phaeton, the illegitimate young son of Apollo, the sun god: Phaeton had failed in his attempt to control the Sun's chariot, but was nevertheless glorious in defeat. Similarly, intellectually daring, the nun's challenge to authority and incomprehensible reality, although condemned in advance to defeat, is a glorious attempt that, when punished, inspires further daring: "Tipo es, antes, modelo . . . / que alas engendra a repetido vuelo / del ánimo ambicioso" (He is, rather, a model and example . . . which gives wings to further flights of the ambitious spirit). Phaeton not only represents the overcoming of Sor Juana's own illegitimacy in her struggle against her father, but sets an example of rebellion for her "arrogant spirit," which can be applied to the defense of her status as a woman and a native of the New World (*criolla*).

The dawn epilogue of the *Sueño* balances in perfect symmetry its nightfall prologue. But before the arrival of the Sun (mentioned without the proper name of Apollo or Phoebus), Venus and Aurora appear, preceding him as they bring light to the world. Before the Sun imposes himself once more as the source of daytime, there is a battle between him – personifying the authority of the absent, nameless father –

and Night, the perhaps terrible mother, but nevertheless the person who has given birth to the dream. Night, an Amazon armed with an awesome scepter, loses her battle against the Sun, but her defeat, like the defeat of Phaeton by the same Sun, is not definitive: she "segunda vez rebelde determina / mirarse coronada" (in rebellion once more decides to achieve her crown), and to do so, taking courage from defeat, she withdraws to the other side of the globe that the Sun has left unprotected ("la mitad del globo que ha dejado / el Sol desamparada"). If the Sun represents masculine authority, Night represents its female counterpart; if daytime has been occupied by the Sun, Night rules over a shadowy world of dreams in regular cosmic rotation. This is the solution that, in a patriarchal society, the nun proposes, in order to support her profound conviction concerning the intellectual equality of man and woman. The tense Baroque alternation of light and darkness with which Sor Juana concludes her dream-poem, rejecting paternal authority and asserting herself as a combatant in the figures of Phaeton and Night, will continue to take place, night after night, as a projection of the experiences of her daily life. Hence, in the final line of her long poem, Sor Juana's voice shifts from the generic human Soul to her own first-person self, in the feminine gender, when the sunlight awakes her and she becomes fully conscious that a new day has arrived: "quedando a luz más cierta / el mundo iluminado, y yo despierta" (leaving the world illumined / by a more positive light, and me awake).

Finally, this poems contains many of Sor Juana's personal concerns, as a *criolla* woman, as a colonial subject. The presence of the eagle and of nocturnal birds in the poem may well be related to Aztec mythology; the mention of two pyramids: "montes dos artificiales" (two artificial hills), and not the three Egyptian ones, may well indicate that she was thinking of Teotihuacán, with its pyramids of the Sun and of the Moon. In any case, Sor Juana, as a woman and as an intellectual, takes on in this poem the loftiest and most problematic aspirations of the human mind: the desire to understand the whole of reality. Her defeat and her victory belong to all of us. The *Primero Sueño* sums up a splendid tradition and is a link joining the Iberian peninsula to the magic world of America, and its future literary development.

GEORGINA SABAT DE RIVERS

Editions

First edition: *Segundo Volumen de las Obras*, Seville, 1692
Critical edition: *Sor Juana Inés de la Cruz. El sueño*, edited with an introduction and notes by Alfonso Méndez Plancarte, Mexico City: Fondo de Cultura Económica, 1951
Translation: *Sor Juana's Dream*, by Luis Harss, New York: Lumen Books, 1986 [bilingual edition]

Further Reading

Arrayo Higaldo, Susana, *El primero sueño de Sor Juana: estudio semántico y retórico*, Mexico City: UNAM, 1993
Sabat de Rivers, Georgina, *El sueño de Sor Juana Inés de la Cruz: tradiciones literarias y originalidad*, London: Támesis, 1977

Respuesta a Sor Filotea

Epistolary autobiography by
Sor Juana Inés de la Cruz

> Entréme religiosa, porque aunque conocía que tenía el estado cosas ... muchas repugnantes a mi genio, con todo, para la total negación que tenía al matrimonio, era lo menos desproporcionado y lo más decente que podía elegir en materia de la seguridad que deseaba de mi salvación ...

> [I became a nun, because even though I was aware that that state had many aspects ... that were in opposition to my character, it was the most fitting and seemly state I could choose with respect to the assurance of my salvation that I desired ...]

The above passage is one of the most famous from the epistolary autobiography Sor Juana Inés de la Cruz wrote to "Sister Philotea" in March of 1691. Her explanation as to why she entered the religious life is startling in its candor; her recounting of what she had to relinquish in the process is heartrending: "cedieron y sujetaron la cerviz todas las impertinencillas de mi genio, que eran de vivir sola; de no querer tener ocupación obligatoria que embarazase la libertad de mi estudio, ni rumor de comunidad que impediese el sosegado silencio de mis libros." (all the impertinent little quirks of my character bowed their heads and surrendered, which were to live alone; not to have forced obligations which would interrupt the freedom of my study, nor the noise of a community which would interfere with the tranquil silence of my books). What is clear from the quotation is that she entered the convent not because she had a strong religious calling, but because it was the one place where she could continue her studies.

The *Respuesta a Sor Filotea* is one of the most passionate and unique documents to come out of Western literature, the cry of a supremely intellectual woman for the right to use her mind in the way men of her time could. Before discussing its content it is important to establish the circumstances under which this document came to be.

Sor Juana's fame as one of the leading intellectuals and poets of the viceroyalty of New Spain had been established long ago. She wrote a great deal of the religious literature nuns were expected to produce, but she was also ambitious and vitally interested in matters outside the Church. She wrote courtly love poetry, secular drama and witty satiric verse that often deeply offended the churchmen that were her superiors, most especially the overtly misogynistic Archbishop of Mexico, Francisco Aguiar y Seixas. Sor Juana had for years endured stinging criticism of her literary activities, but around 1690 this became increasingly strident. One ally in the Church hierarchy was the Bishop of Puebla, who had published a religious treatise Sor Juana had composed, but simultaneously sent her a letter of admonition to mend her ways. Since God had given her a supreme intellect, he wrote, she had the obligation to devote it exclusively to His service. Should the nun fail to remember this, her mortal soul stood in danger of condemnation. The Bishop knew that his message was a strong one, and, in order to soften the impact, he signed it with the name

of "Sister Philotea," making it appear that here was one nun speaking to another. When Sor Juana drafted her reply, however, she was fully aware that she was being spoken to by a male superior, but for tactical reasons she continued the fiction of the female addressee. It is important to remember that these were not private letters, but ones that would circulate among many readers. Both "Sor Philotea" and Sor Juana were fully aware of this, and it conditioned their respective responses.

In spite of his admonitions, the Bishop may have been giving Sor Juana the opportunity to apologize for her past offences and promise to mend her ways in the future. If this was his objective, it failed. Instead of an apology, she went on the offensive in an all-out attempt to justify her right to an intellectual vocation. In so doing, she has left us an extraordinary autobiography.

The uninitiated reader may at first find her style daunting: long, convoluted sentences, and an apparent lack of inner organization. Perelmuter Pérez (1983), however, showed that in fact Sor Juana adhered closely to Quintilian's rules of rhetoric: her letter has an *introduction*, a *narration* of the facts of the case, *proof* of her own position and refutation of countercharges, and a *conclusion*.

In the *introduction* (paragraphs 1–5) there are conventional phrases of gratitude and humility at the favor Sister Philotea has done Sor Juana by writing to her. She says she can find no way to reply to "vuestra doctísima, discretísima, santísima y amorosísima carta" (your overwhelmingly learned, prudent, holy and loving letter). The English translation in no way renders the excessiveness of the string of superlatives of the original. Is Sor Juana being overtly humble or covertly mocking?

The *narration* (paragraphs 6–29) is the most extensive part of the epistle. There are various recurrent themes, but front and center is Sor Juana's appropriation of the Bishop's reason for admonishing her: that her intellect is a gift of God. She refers to "este natural impulso que Dios puso en mí" (this natural impulse God installed in me), implying in several places in her letter that if God is the author of her intelligence, then how can it be sinful to make use of it? Sor Juana establishes that an insatiable hunger for knowledge was with her from the moment she began to think rationally, and that she was prepared to risk all in order to learn. There are two telling episodes in her childhood that illustrate this. When she was barely three, she sneaked off to school with her older sister, lied to the teacher that her mother wanted her to learn to read, and proceeded to master this skill with lightning speed; she said nothing to her mother until the deed was done, although she feared being whipped for her lie. When she was eight, she heard that there was a university in the capital, and begged her mother to let her dress as a boy and go; on being turned down, she devoured the books in her grandfather's library in spite of frequent scoldings and punishment. Several important lessons were thus learned early: hunger for knowledge involved punishment, which she risked; she was prepared to lie to get what she wanted; her gender was the main obstacle to her intellectual goals.

In the *narration* Sor Juana recounts the problems she had in deciding on the religious life, the stresses involved in living in community, and her immense solitude at always having to study alone: "teniendo sólo por maestro un libro mudo, por condiscípulo un tintero insensible" (having but a mute book for a teacher, an unfeeling inkwell for a fellow student). The nun defends her interest in secular matters by noting that they are the stepping stones to theology, the highest science, and recounts the unrelenting criticism she has suffered over the years. To prove that she *cannot* stop using her mind, she cites how when she is cooking, she observes the interaction of ingredients in a scientific way, thus turning the kitchen, that archetypal female space, into a laboratory. "Pero Señora," she slyly asks her ficticious counterpart, "¿qué podemos saber las mujeres sino filosofías de cocina?" (But my Lady, what can we women know except kitchen philosophies?)

In the *proof* section (paragraphs 30–45), Sor Juana first enumerates a long list of illustrious women predecessors, a familiar tactic many early women writers used to legitimize actions the world might see as aberrant, then goes on to the crux of the problem: the Church's inconsistent stand on the role of women within its ranks. She goes straight to St Paul's dictum for women to be silent in church, manipulating both St Paul and St Jerome's words to suit her purposes. To her credit, Sor Juana was concerned not only for her own intellectual life, but for that of other Mexican women of her class. Many parents feared that daily contact with male tutors might ruin their daughters' reputations, and thus left them illiterate; Sor Juana was appalled by this, and suggested using older learned women as instructors, a pedagogical concern that was, predictably, ignored.

She also took exception to the criticism levelled at her for critiquing the sermon of Antonio Vieira, a famous Jesuit preacher. "Mi entendimiento tal cual ¿no es tan libre como el suyo, pues viene de un solar?" she queried. (My mind, such as it is, is it not as free as his, as both come from the same source?) Sor Juana also claimed that almost all she had ever written had been because others had demanded this of her – patent falsehood.

In the *conclusion* (the last two paragraphs) Sor Juana very cleverly covers herself by begging Sor Philotea's pardon for being so familiar with her: "que a veros sin velo, no sucediera así" (for had I seen you without your veil, it would never have happened like this). Sor Juana gives her sister licence to adjust the style of the letter, and thus avoid any possible affront.

This brief summary cannot begin to do justice to the conceptual, stylistic and human richness of the *Respuesta*. It is a document that has inspired and challenged critics for many years, and will continue to do so.

NINA M. SCOTT

Editions

First edition: in *Fama y obras póstumas del Fénix de Méjico*, Madrid, 1700

Critical edition and translation: *The Answer/La Respuesta. Including a Selection of Poems*, edited and translated by Electa Arenal and Amanda Powell, New York: Feminist Press at the City University of New York, 1994

Further Reading

Perelmuter Pérez, Rosa, "La estructura retórica de la *Respuesta a Sor Filotea*," *Hispanic Review* 51 (1983)

Scott, Nina M., "Sor Juana Inés de la Cruz: 'Let Your Women Keep Silent in the Churches,'" *Women's Studies International Forum* 8 (1985)

―― "'La gran turba de las que merecieron nombres:' Sor Juana's Foremothers in *La Respuesta a Sor Filotea*," in *Coded Encounters: Writing, Gender and Ethnicity in Colonial Latin America*, edited by Scott, Francisco Javier Cevallos Candau, Jeffrey A. Cole and Nicomedes Suárez Araúz, Amherst: University of Massachusetts Press, 1994

L

Land and Literature

The identification with a specific geographic space is the main component of the identity of a community. In the case of Latin American countries, the land between the Straight of Magellan and the Mexican border with the US, has been the focus of its most significant writers in marking their American difference. The Argentine pampa, the jungles of Central America and Brazil, the Andes in Chile, Peru and Bolivia, the Amazon river, or the coffee and banana plantations of Colombia have figured prominently in the works of Spanish American writers, who have endowed nature with a range of significances and created symbolic landscapes. The land connected to literature depends on the perspective, or the "gaze" of the author who depicts it: it can be observed from outside or from inside, as the Other to be dominated by the western subject, or as the source of life to be protected from the barbarism of civilization.

The first texts by Europeans about Latin American land are written by 16th-century travellers: outsiders who are impressed by the landscape and depict it as a new place to be possessed, as in the texts by Christopher Columbus. During the colonial period, travellers, missionaries and conquerors centered their writing in the American land. Among these are Bernardo de Balbuena, el Inca Garcilaso de la Vega, Juan de Castellanos, Pedro de Oña, Juan de Ercilla, Sebastião da Rocha Pita, and Gonçalves Días.

However, the Venezuelan humanist Andrés Bello is considered the first Latin American author to transform the land into literature from an insider's view in his poems, *La agricultura de la zona tórrida* [The Agriculture of the Torrid Zone] and *América*. Naming the elements that constitute the American land, he proposes a conscious intention of literary emancipation parallel to the political one in such verses as: "tiempo es que dejes ya la culta Europa / que tu nativa rustiquez desama / y dirijas el vuelo donde te abre / el mundo de Colón su grande escena" (it is time for you to leave educated Europe / that your native rusticity disloves / and to direct your flight to where Colombus's world / opens its great scene for you).

During the 19th-century period of independence from Spain, the land is the main element consolidating the different national identities, and the principal writers of each emergent country devote parts of their production to the evocation of their native land. Among these are José Martí (Cuba), Juan Bautista Alberdi and Domingo Faustino Sarmiento (Argentina), Jorge Isaacs (Colombia). Towards the end of the 19th century, however, the trend among Spanish American *modernista* writers was either to neglect the representation of their own natural sourroundings in favour of others perceived as exotic (Europe, the Orient) or to construct picturesque pre-Columbian settings.

A narrative with a telluric tendency develops afterwards. It is called "the novel of the land" and starts with *La vorágine*, 1924 (*The Vortex*) by José Eustasio Rivera, where the Amazon jungle controlled by unknown laws dominates human beings, and ends by devouring them, as is shown in the last words of this novel: "¡Se los tragó la selva!" (The jungle swallowed them!). This tendency is continued by Teófano Cuéllar (Bolivia) in *La borrachera verde*, 1937 [The Green Drunkenness] and by Jorge Amado (Brazil) in *Terras do sem fim*, 1943 (*The Violent Land*). Also, rural Mexico provides the setting for Mariano Azuela's account of the early years of the Revolution, *Los de abajo*, 1916 (*The Underdogs*), and one of the main characters of *Doña Bárbara*, 1929 and *Canaima*, 1935, by Rómulo Gallegos the Venezuelan, is American Nature. These are novels in which certain "primitive" elements associated with nature (through gender, ethnicity or poverty) are seen as obstacles in the formation of the modern (masculine) nation state.

The relationship between land and human beings has taken different paths in the last decades. In *Los pasos perdidos* (*The Lost Steps*) by the Cuban writer Alejo Carpentier, the jungle is no longer an uncontrollable being, but its characteristics alter according to individual perception and perspective (according to how it is "read"), factors which can transform it into a paradise or hell. Other 20th-century writers: Miguel Ángel Asturias (Guatemala), João Guimarães Rosa (Brazil), Horacio Quiroga (Uruguay) and Ciro Alegría (Peru), have developed a different perspective to look at the land, what Fernando Ainsa calls a literary "colonization" from within, and what could be considered as a fusion between the Subject and the Other. For example, in the texts by Asturias written from the perspective of the Maya Quiché Indians, human beings have a bush soul, they are born as plants, the land is the mother, origin and end of life; maize is sacred and should not be grown as a cash crop. This relationship is also obvious in the texts by Ciro

Alegría who affirms in one of his poems: "Pacha Mama, a ti te hirieron mil pedruscos / destrozando tu ternura de madre, / desde entonces te volviste amarga de lágrimas indias / y tu alegría de dar la estamos buscando" (Pacha Mama, a thousand stones hurt you / destroying your motherly tenderness, / since then you have grown bitter with Indian tears / and we are searching for your happiness of giving). This same connection between women and land has been part of Latin American literature in Juana de Ibarbourou's texts since the first decades of the 20th century, and it is notable in works by the Nicaraguan poets Gioconda Belli and Rosario Murillo. The former is author of the poem "Metamorfosis," where the female subject becomes part of nature, "metamorfoseada, / espinosa, / sola, / hecha naturaleza" (and in my metamorphosis / thorny / alone / at one with nature). Also in Nicaragua, Pablo Antonio Cuadra analyzes the landscape in *Tierra que habla* [Land that Talks], and tries to recover native culture and its implications with the land in *El jaguar y la luna* [The Jaguar and the Moon].

Contemporary ecological concerns about the destruction of the Earth and of humanity with it by "civilization," cross national boundaries and universalize land as the place where we all live. This thinking is apparent in the works of the Mexican Homero Aridjis, author of "Descreación" [Uncreation] and "Murió el último caballo" [The Last Horse Died], and in poems like "12.34" by Roberto Juarroz. The two writers consider both the barbarism implicit in our civilization and the ignorance of the land: "acepto mi pobreza de hombre / sin dios en el firmamento y sin futuro en la vida" (I accept my poverty as a man / without god in the firmament and without a future in life) or "ignoramos la función de la tierra" (we ignore the function of the land).

ANA MARÍA BRENES-GARCÍA

Further Reading

Critical Studies

Ainsa, Fernando, *Identidad cultural de Iberoamérica en su narrativa*, Madrid: Gredos, 1986

D'Elía, Miguel Alfredo, *La literatura del Brasil: el sentido de la tierra en la narrativa*, Buenos Aires: Platt Establecimientos Gráficos, 1948

Ebanks, Gerardo M., *La novela de la tierra*, Montevideo: Centro de Estudios de Literatura Latinoamericana, 1968

León Hazera, Lydia de, *La novela de la selva hispanoamericana*, Bogotá: Instituto Caro y Cuervo, 1971

Morínigo, Mariano, *Estudios sobre nuestra expresión*, Tucumán, Argentina: Ediciones del Cardón, 1965

Seminario Internacional de literatura Hispanoamericana, *La naturaleza y el hombre en la novela hispanoamericana*, Antofagasta, Chile: Universidad del Norte, 1969

Verdevoye, Paul (editor), *Identidad y literatura en los países hispanoamericanos*, Buenos Aires: Ediciones Solar, 1984

Fiction

Alegría, Ciro (Peru), *El mundo es ancho y ajeno*, Santiago de Chile: Ercilla, 1941; as *Broad and Alien is the World*, translated by Harriet de Onís, New York: Farrar and Rinehart, 1941; London: Merlin Press, 1973

Aridjis, Homero (Mexico), *Imágenes para el fin del milenio*, Mexico City: Joaquín Mortiz, 1990

Columbus, Christopher, *Textos y documentos completos*, edited by Consuelo Varela, Madrid: Alianza, 1982

Cuadra, Pablo Antonio (Nicaragua), *Obra poética completa*, 5 vols, San José de Costa Rica: Asociación Libro Libre, 1983–89

Cunha, Euclides da (Brazil), *Os sertões*, Rio de Janeiro: Laemmert, 1902; as *Rebellion in the Backlands*, translated by Samuel Putnam, Chicago: University of Chicago Press, 1944

Juarroz, Roberto (Argentina), *Duodécima poesía vertical*, Buenos Aires: Carlos Lohlé, 1991

Murillo, Rosario (Nicaragua), *Las esperanzas misteriosas*, Managua, Nicaragua: Vanguardia, 1990

Norah Lange 1906–1972

Argentine poet and prose writer

A certain notoriety came early to Norah Lange. From the cultural gatherings held at the family home on Tronador Street, immortalized in Leopoldo Marechal's novelized memoirs *Adán Buenosayres* (1948), came the intimacy with her cousin, Jorge Luis Borges, and others in the Argentine vanguard movements. This led to Lange's consecration as "the Muse of the Ultraists" on the publication, in 1924, of her first collection of poems, *La calle de la tarde* [The Street at Evening]. After a first meeting in 1926 with fellow poet and rich playboy, Oliverio Girondo, the brilliant bionomy "Noraliverio Olinora" enlivened Argentina's literary scene throughout the 1930s with unbridled gaiety as, together with the Martín Fierro group, they waged "war against solemnity" in their attempts to reintegrate art in the praxis of life. Quite typical of those years were Lange's mock serious banquet speeches, later collected as *Estimados congéneres*, 1968 [Esteemed Companions], outrageous performances by the orator who blended nonsense, metaphor and cacophony into a true live art experience. The long relationship with Girondo, her acknowledged first and most demanding critic – they were eventually married in 1946 – also provided the leisure and the discipline Lange needed to polish the subtle, innovative writing style of her mature novels published in the 1950s.

Superficially, little in theme and subject matter distinguishes Lange's three books of poetry from the conventional aesthetic of the Latin American "poetesses" in the period 1916–30, which predominantly male critics have typified as a subjective, monotonous infantilism. Lange creates an intimate, enclosed world of house and garden wherein the female subject, languidly awaiting the dynamic presence of the male other, is doomed to view from window or doorway the city only he possesses because her external reality never reaches beyond the crucifixes, rosaries and altars that translate the suffering of her adolescent love. Nevertheless, if Borges chauvinistically pointed out the "little girl" quality here, he also, and quite rightly, praised "the noble prodigality" of Lange's metaphors and "the sparseness" of her poetry, both characteristics she would make the virtues of her prose.

In her later years Lange disclaimed as "bad" and "superficial" her first incursions into prose, *Voz de la vida*, 1927 [Voice of Life], and *45 días y 30 marineros*, 1933 [45 Days and 30 Sailors]. The former is an epistolary novel exploring passion and adultery from the woman protagonist's point of view, whilst the latter (and the only writing by Lange not in the ambiguous first person she found so "comfortable") describes the sexual tightrope walked between the Captain, officers and crew by the lone woman passenger on board the ship from Buenos Aires to Oslo. Published to mixed reviews on account of what was perceived as their unsuitable subject matter for a lady novelist, these learning exercises are not without interest today, precisely on account of their vanguard feminism. They also point to what Lange would develop further: the autobiographical theme, a gendered discourse, and the valuable lesson that "I could do what I wished with language."

Cuadernos de infancia, 1937 [A Childhood Scrapbook], is undoubtedly Lange's best-known work. Unanimous critical acclaim led to official recognition and prestigious prizes for what would become a recommended reader for several generations of Argentine schoolchildren. Like the later, less overtly autobiographical, *Antes de que mueran*, 1944 [Before They Die], *Cuadernos de infancia* is a series of vignettes or flashback memories of Lange's early childhood, dating from the family move to Mendoza late in 1910 or early 1911 until the return to Buenos Aires on her father's death in 1915. Although the first-person narrator is without name, her five sisters and brother are strongly reminiscent of Lange's own large family, prompting critics to wax enthusiastic about a tenderly poetic evocation of growing up in an exceptional and unorthodox family. Sylvia Molloy's thought-provoking analysis in *At Face Value: Autobiographical Writing in Spanish America* suggests, however, that *Cuadernos de infancia* has been widely misread. Rather than writing a "safe," feminine fiction in line with the conventional memoir of childhood that is tinged with smug nostalgia for a pre-adolescent golden age, Lange made over into narrative strategy the ultraist flair for the truncated metaphor, the visually disturbing, and the linguistic experimentation, that is her hallmark. This is a performance similar to her contemporaneous speeches or self-styled "anatomical essays," in that she foregrounds eccentricity rather than conformity, defiance not passivity, and fragmentation as opposed to consolidation. It signals a deliberate and noteworthy break with the recurring patterns in Argentine autobiographical writing that, for example, a contemporary of Lange, María Rosa Oliver, prolonged so effectively in *Mundo, mi casa*, 1970 [World, My House]. *Cuadernos de infancia* begins with disruption as Lange describes the move to Mendoza that triggers her childhood memories, which are here characterized as "cut-outs" and seen as if through "a fogged window." This arbitrary, ludic design continues throughout the multi-fissured text which has no dates and only a single, fleeting reference to any historical context, distorts genealogy and patronymics, and is systematically unsentimental in avoiding any depiction of home and the daily routine as a protected and protective space. The child's spying eye acts as an unexpectedly candid camera and the resulting snapshots intrigue rather than explain, enticing the reader to enter into this game of literary voyeurism that centres on the elucidation of disquieting private fears and personal manias.

In reinscribing her vanguard self into her childhood memories Lange elaborated a narrative technique based on her "favourite pastime: spying on others' intimacy." She exploited this to great advantage in the ritual of the quotidian, "the possibilities that move behind the words," and the deft depiction of psychological undercurrents in her last two novels, *Personas en la sala*, 1950 [People in the Drawing-Room] and *Los dos retratos*, 1956 [The Two Portraits]. These works placed Lange alongside José Bianco, Felisberto Hernández and Juan Carlos Onetti, as practitioners of the "novel of ambiguity" that explores the problems of self and identity. Both novels are about literary creation by women: the anonymous adolescent in *Personas en la sala* imagines, elaborates on and annotates the story behind the faces of three women outlined one stormy night in the window of the empty house opposite. Another adolescent, Marta in *Los dos retratos*, peers into the mirror that reflects both the faces of the family and those depicted in two photographs hung in the dining-room in order to reconstruct what happened on the afternoon the photographs were taken. Each retires to a room of her own in which to pursue a succession of fantasies that answer a compulsive need to visualize her own self. As each character builds up her story, at once ambiguous and ambivalent as it moves between reality and dream, different moments in time and space, first and third person narrative, and the enigmatic, symbiotic relationships between the characters, the narrator's self is fractured or splintered in what becomes an open-ended text which may be read in a variety of ways. Thus, in *Personas en la sala*, the three women are projections of the narrator which point up the repression, solitude and boredom typical of female marginalization and silence that gradual empowerment (the act of narration) ends (as the narrator eliminates the women at the end of her narration). Similarly, in *Los dos retratos*, Marta corrects her own "off-centre" position, is too young to be reflected either at the family table or in the photographs. What she does is to construct her version of love, intrigue and jealousy between family members, in a text at play with itself as Lange explores the complexity of the creative process which authors a female identity. Lacanian pyschoanalytical criticism will certainly enrich any reading of Lange's obsessive use of dreams, mirrors, portraits and photographs to frame the textual construction-deconstruction-reconstruction carried out in these novels, but no single interpretation should strait-jacket what the author herself saw as the possibilities of "magic" in her "pure voyeurism."

If both her poetry and prose were on the whole well received by their contemporary readers Lange has, nevertheless, been a victim of her own legendary literary status, for scholarly evaluation has come late, and from outside Argentina. With the advent of feminist criticism Lange is now credited, together with María Luisa Bombal and Teresa de la Parra, with writing from a vanguard perspective that both subverts and transforms the traditionally male codification of the Latin American novel in accordance with the lineage, place and language of power. Yet to come are the English translations of her novels and the wider recognition Lange's finely-crafted writing deserves.

K.M. SIBBALD

Biography

Born in Argentina, 23 October 1906; of Norwegian descent. Published first volume of poetry, *La calle de la tarde*, at the age of 18. Early member of the *ultraísta* movement, centred around Borges in Buenos Aires during the early 1920s and 1930s. Married the avant-garde poet Oliverio Girondo (see separate entry) in 1946. Their home in Buenos Aires became the centre of avant-garde activity. Contributed to the journals *Martín Fierro* and *Proa*. Awarded Buenos Aires Literary Prize, 1937 for *Cuadernos de infancia*. Died on 6 August 1972.

Selected Works

Poetry

La calle de la tarde, prologue by Jorge Luis Borges, Buenos Aires: J. Samet, 1924
Los días y las noches, Buenos Aires: El Inca, 1926
El rumbo de la rosa, Buenos Aires: Proa, 1930

Prose Works

Voz de la vida, Buenos Aires: Proa, 1927
45 días y 30 marineros, Buenos Aires: Tor, 1933
Cuadernos de infancia, Buenos Aires: Losada, 1937
Discursos, Buenos Aires: Ediciones CAYDE, 1942
Antes de que mueran, Buenos Aires: Losada, 1944
Personas en la sala, Buenos Aires: Sudamericana, 1950
Los dos retratos, Buenos Aires: Losada, 1956
"El parecido," *Claudia* 113 (October 1966)
Estimados congéneres, Buenos Aires: Losada, 1968
"La mano en el retrato," *La Nación* (28 December 1969)

Further Reading

Lindstrom, Naomi, "Norah Lange: presencia desmonumentalizadora en la vanguardia argentina," *Crítica Hispánica*, Pittsburgh, vol. 5/2 (1983)
Masiello, Francine, "Texto, ley, transgresión: especulación sobre la novela (feminista) de vanguardia," *Revista Iberoamericana* 51 (July–December 1985)
Miguel, María Esther de, *Norah Lange*, Buenos Aires: Planeta, 1991 [An uneven, not always reliable, literary biography]
Molloy, Sylvia, *At Face Value: Autobiographical Writing in Spanish America*, Cambridge and New York: Cambridge University Press, 1991
Nóbile, Beatriz de, *Palabras con Norah Lange*, Buenos Aires: Carlos Pérez Editor, 1968
Percas, Helena, *La poesía femenina argentina (1810–1950)*, Madrid: Ediciones Cultura Hispánica, 1958

Enrique Larreta 1873–1961

Argentine prose writer and dramatist

Enrique Larreta's family had a financially secure position which allowed the author to travel to Europe as a youth and to develop aristocratic tastes and sensibilities; these inclinations are artistically conveyed in his writings. Larreta's first novel, a short work entitled *Artemis*, dealt with life in ancient Greece; it appeared in 1896 in the periodical *La Biblioteca*. On a trip to Spain in 1903 he visited Ávila, where he painstakingly researched his most famous novel, *La gloria de don Ramiro (una vida en tiempos de Felipe II)* (*The Glory of Don Ramiro. A Life in the Times of Philip II*), a work he completed and published in 1908. His next significant novel, *Zogoibi* (1926), a depiction of gaucho life on an *estancia* (ranch) in Argentina, contrasted the snobbery of the upper classes with the simple customs of the country people. Larreta also produced a handful of non-fiction works and dramas, most of which he wrote in the 1920s and 1930s. His volume of poems, *La calle de la vida y de la muerte*, 1941 [The Street of Life and Death], combines characteristics of Symbolism and Impressionism. He also went on to write several other novels but none of his works achieved the critical acclaim and popularity of *La gloria de don Ramiro*.

Larreta's masterpiece, an impressionistic work written in an elegant, ornate style, is widely recognized as the most outstanding novel of Spanish American *Modernismo* and one of the best historical novels in the Spanish language. In it he presents the theme of the eternal struggle (in Christian cultures) between the flesh and the spirit. Ramiro, who embodies this conflict, is caught between the two career options for pursuing personal glory in Golden Age Spain, the way of the cross (as a monk) or of the sword (as a conquistador). *La gloria de don Ramiro* attempts to recreate the language, the tense co-existence of cultures – one Christian and the other Islamic – and the heroic spirit that typified the age of Philip II.

The novel tells the story of Ramiro, the son of a Castilian woman and a Moor. Born in 1570, Ramiro (who would have been a contemporary of another character of fiction, Don Quixote), receives a strict education in preparation for an ecclesiastical career but forsakes the calling when he falls in love with Beatriz. Enlisted to unmask a conspiracy hatched by the *moriscos* (Moorish converts to Christianity who were often suspected of secretly adhering to their former faith), Ramiro comes under the influence of Aixa, a *morisca* seductress, and subsequently gets a taste of witchcraft, astrology and the black arts. He returns to the Christian sector and tries to win the affections of Beatriz, but she rejects him. In a highly charged emotional scene, Ramiro strangles Beatriz with her rosary.

He flees to Toledo and there witnesses an *auto da fé* and the burning of the beautiful Aixa. After this incident he withdraws from the world and attempts to lead the life of an ascetic. Soon, however, he feels the call of adventure and sails to America as a soldier of fortune. At the age of thirty-five, after repenting and expiating his sins, he dies. The novel's final scene takes place in Lima where Santa Rosa prays over Ramiro's body.

Thanks to his eye for detail and obsession with historical accuracy, Larreta succeeds in conveying through colors and other sense impressions the feel and essence of Spanish life in the last quarter of the 16th century. The novel rings true especially in its use of the language of the period. Forms such as *fiyo* (*hijo*, son); *quitalles* (*quitarles*, to take away from them); the phrase *hartos años ha* (*hace muchos años*, many years ago); *aína* (an obsolete word meaning "quickly" or "immediately"); *mesma* (*misma*, same); *cobdicia* (*codicia*, greed); *bisagüelo* (*bisabuelo*, great-grandfather); *agora* (*ahora*, now) and other archaic usage help make the work convincing as a historical novel. However, Larreta's cultivation of archaic language distances modern readers from the text.

The best examples of *modernista* prose are found in descriptions of art objects, fabrics, etc., and in passages that relate Ramiro's erotic escapades among the *moriscos*, specifically his relationship with the enchanting Aixa. As Ramiro watches her bathe, he becomes fascinated with her beauty and eventually submits to the desires of the flesh. These sensually charged scenes culminate in the bewitching dance Aixa performs for Ramiro. The novelist describes her rhythmic movements with carefully selected olfactory, visual and auditory imagery. Aixa enters a trance and the dance ends when she swoons, a sequence that implies close parallels between erotic ecstasy and mystical rapture.

Larreta, like all the other *modernistas*, viewed literature as its own justification rather than as a tool for achieving social or political goals. Advancing the slogan "art for art's sake," the *modernistas* devoted themselves to the pursuit of an ideal (always unattainable) and the exploration of things far removed from routine experience. In their search for absolute beauty and perfection of form they openly expressed their disdain for the mundane. This escape from reality led to a cultivation of the erotic and the exotic (foreign and distant). Inevitably, eroticism and exoticism came to be associated with the Other. Despite his attention to detail and concern for accuracy in describing places, buildings, interior designs, etc., Larreta's evocation of Spanish settings and Moorish culture bears the unmistakable imprint of his cultural preconceptions regarding alterity. In other words, the *moriscos* of Golden Age Spain were "exotic" precisely because of their otherness. This notion of what constituted the exotic defines the tone of *La gloria de don Ramiro*. The novel's exaltation of sensuality and its assault on the senses make it the *modernista* novel *par excellence*.

MELVIN S. ARRINGTON, JR

Biography

Born in Buenos Aires, Argentina, 4 March 1873, into a privileged family of Uruguayan and Basque stock. Secondary education at the Colegio Nacional in Buenos Aires. Obtained doctorate in law. Taught medieval and modern history at the Colegio Nacional. Travelled to Spain with his wife Josefina Anchorena Castellanos. Dazzled by the walled city of Ávila in Castile. By 1903 had completed the plan of *La gloria de don Ramiro*. Moved to France in 1907. Appointed ambassador to France in 1910. Returned to Argentina in 1916 and devoted himself thereafter to writing and to painting. Made corresponding member of the Spanish Royal Academy. Honours include the Grand Cross of Alfonso the Wise, the Legion of Honour and the Grand Cross of Isabel the Catholic. Awarded the Miguel de Cervantes Prize, 1949. Died in Buenos Aires, 6 July 1961.

Selected Works

Short Fiction
Artemis, Buenos Aires: La Biblioteca, II, 1896

Novels
La gloria de don Ramiro, Madrid: Suárez, 1908; as *The Glory of Don Ramiro*, translated by L.B. Walton, New York: Dutton, and London: Dent, 1924
Zogoibi, Buenos Aires: Roldán, 1926
Orillas del Ebro, Madrid: Espasa Calpe, 1949
El Gerardo; o la torre de las damas, Buenos Aires and Madrid: Aguilar, 1953
En la pampa, Buenos Aires and Madrid: Aguilar, 1955

Poetry
La calle de la vida y de la muerte, Buenos Aires: Espasa Calpe, 1941

Plays
La lampe d'argile, Paris: n.p., 1915
El linyera, Buenos Aires: Roldán, 1932
Santa María del Buen Aire, Madrid: Suárez, 1935
Pasión de Roma, Buenos Aires: Rosso, 1937
La que buscaba Don Juan, Buenos Aires: Rosso, 1937
Tenía que suceder, Buenos Aires: Al Ateneo, 1943
Jerónimo y su almohada, Madrid and Buenos Aires: Espasa Calpe, 1944
Clamor, Buenos Aires: Espasa Calpe, 1959

Essays
Historiales, Buenos Aires: Losada, 1921
Las dos fundaciones de Buenos Aires: Buenos Aires: Viau y Viau, 1933
Tiempos iluminados, Buenos Aires: Espasa Calpe, 1939
La naranja, Buenos Aires: Al Ateneo, 1947

Compilations and Anthologies
Obras completas, Madrid: Plenitud, 1948 [Carelessly edited; reproduces errors of Austral editions]
Obras completas, 2 vols, Buenos Aires: Claridad, 1959

Further Reading
The majority of studies on Larreta that have appeared to date have a disappointingly old-fashioned critical apparatus. An exception is the study by Gabriela Ibieta, which recognizes the relevance of Edward Said's *Orientalism* to aspects of *La gloria de don Ramiro*.

Alonso, Amado, *Ensayo sobre la novela histórica: el modernismo en la "Gloria de don Ramiro,"* Buenos Aires: Instituto de Filología, 1942 [Classic study of this novel]

Borello, Rodolfo, "Modernismo y narrativa. Enrique Larreta," in *Historia de la literatura argentina*, vol. 3, edited by Susana Zanetti, Buenos Aires: Centro Editor de América Latina, 1981

Campanella, Hebe N., *Enrique Larreta: el hombre y el escritor*, Buenos Aires: Marymar, 1987 [Considers in detail biography, plays and novels]

Colón Ortíz, P., *Cumbres del Modernismo en Hispanoamérica: Enrique Larreta*, San Juan, Puerto Rico: Huracán, 1983 [Disappointingly old-fashioned critical apparatus]

Ghiano, Juan Carlos, *Análisis de "La gloria de don Ramiro,"* Buenos Aires: Centro Editorial de América Latina, 1968 [Brief introduction with a sharp critical edge]

Ibieta, Gabriela, *Tradition and Renewal in "La gloria de don Ramiro,"* Potomac, Maryland: Scripta Humanística, 1986 [Modern critical approach which notes relevance of Edward Said's *Orientalism* to the construction of the Moorish world in this novel]

Jansen, André, *Enrique Larreta, novelista hispanoargentino*, Madrid: Labor, 1967

Meyer-Minnemann, Klaus, *La novela hispanoamericana del "fin de siècle,"* Mexico City: Fondo de Cultura Económica, 1991 [Chapter 8 has sections on *La gloria de don Ramiro*]

José Lezama Lima 1910–1976

Cuban poet and prose writer

José Lezama Lima's production is among the most complex and disquieting to have emerged from the literature of Spanish America. His verbal scheme is based upon the formulation of a poetic system in which the image appears as the substance of the creative will. His literary work constitutes a prodigious textual edifice where poetry, the essay, short stories, and the novel are structured around an organising nucleus which is Lezama's poetics. Furthermore, this represents the thematic centre of all his work that develops out of itself with an ever widening and integrating movement through a dazzling multiplicity of images whose internal logic would prove almost imperceptible to the majority of the writer's contemporaries: this would confer on Lezama the title of Neobaroque writer, and the accusation of being almost incomprehensible.

This concept of poetic writing radically contradicted the process of continuity which, stemming from a point of ephemeral vanguardism and going through solid pure poetry – Mariano Brull, Eugenio Florit and Emilio Ballagas – had established itself as a patently perceptible condition in the Cuban lyric poetry of the period.

The first stage in the work of Lezama Lima consists of the poem *Muerte de Narciso*, 1937 [The Death of Narcissus] and the book *Enemigo rumor*, 1941 [Hostile Rumour]. It is characterized by a luscious use of language, which extends through a successive series of metaphors whose sense, often hidden behind the beauty of the verbal forms, nevertheless responds to a perfectly fathomable logic. In both texts, the poet's discourse settles on two planes that reflect each other – deciphering and obfuscating one another at the same time, like Narcissus before the mirror: the mirror of sexual experience and of poetic experience, taken on like the two poles between which a powerful creative current is formed. All the language of *Enemigo rumor* seems to hide and reveal this complementary polarity, and the subsequent tensions with which the poetry occupies that space, expressing and extending its limits in order to offer itself new methods of resistance.

The second stage of Lezama's work encompasses three titles: *Aventuras sigilosas*, 1945 [Stealthy Adventures]; *La fijeza*, 1949 [Fixedness]; and *Dador*, 1960 [Giver]. During this period, the reader's growing difficulty in understanding Lezama's writings is accentuated. It is a difficulty that responds to the author's essential outstanding literary quality and which does not reside only in a deliberate desire to write poetry out of new formal concepts, but in the need for consciousness and for spiritual transcendence, which runs throughout his work, and which appears to come to him from a radiating centre of intense originality. The reliance on metaphors that has been highlighted by the critics of Lezama's work is one of the forms in which this thirst is manifested.

In *Aventuras sigilosas* – a poetry collection that, like *Dador*, refers back to the field of narrative or drama – the poet explores, using a rich variety of images, the unconditioned creative path that comes to constitute poetry, according to the system devised by Lezama. In these books, Lezama Lima's thought process is unfolded – with absolute coherence – around a fundamental concept: "el genitor por la imagen" (the begetter through the image), the being that acts outside causality and creates starting from within himself. "Impregnation, conjugation, germination," affirms Lezama, "are more subtle forms of creation than causal developments." Mastery over these forms leads "the begetter of the image," that is to say, the poet, to adorn the quasi-divine condition which some primitive communities bestow upon him, attributing to him a fecund knowledge that, in the same fashion as St Augustine's *logos spermatikos*, bursts into the culture: "como un toro germinativo" (like a breeding-stock bull), as Lezama says. The idea concerns a concept based on the creative force of the word, that itself refers back to St John's formulation ("In the beginning was the word"), a coming together of Christian faith and Greek thought at the outset of an innovative vision of the world.

The language of these three books – in which Lezama exhibits and develops the elements that form his poetic practices – is exceptionally rich. This can be traced to that kind of "transcendental materialism" on which his aesthetic concepts are grounded, which culminate in a formulation of a philosophical quality. Only in this manner can the far-reaching element that he attributes to his own system be explained; an element that aspires to establish itself in a real poetic reinterpretation – that is to say, essential – of the world. We find ourselves faced with a case of exceptional quality: that of a contemporary poet who not only draws on the great myths in order to extract from them features of literary value long since abandoned by Western culture, but who utilizes those same features freely, integrating and modifying them according to the hypotheses of a thought process that, though it may appear delirious at root level and in its proposals – nothing less than advocating the poetic systematization of the world – is irrefutably logical within its own terms of reference.

A type of poetry that barricades itself in, it reveals its codes and apparently arbitrary means throughout the second stage of his literary career, transforming itself into a language as oracular as it is coherent. Poetry, assumed by Lezama as a metaphor for creation, aspires to embody the reality of this creation, governed by its own laws that transcend causality as a creative factor.

The publication in 1966 of his novel *Paradiso* brought Lezama international critical attention, and the censure of the Cuban authorities, who rejected the strong erotic content of some passages in the novel, and, above all, the important space occupied by homosexuality among his other themes. Strictly speaking, the novel constitutes the exposition of the author's philosophy, organized around his poetic system of the world.

In the same year, Julio Cortázar published an essay "Para llegar a Lezama Lima" [To reach Lezama Lima], analyzing *Paradiso*. "Lezama is not only hermetic in the literal sense," writes Cortázar, "for which reason the best of his work proposes the seizure of essences by way of the mythical and the esoteric in all of their historic, psychic, and literary forms, vertiginously combined within a poetic system ... but he is also hermetic in a formal sense, as much because of the candour which makes him believe that the most heteroclitic of his metaphorical series will be perfectly understood by everyone, as because of the fact that his form of expression is of baroque style of an original nature."

The third and last stage of Lezama's work comprises two works published posthumously: the novel *Oppiano Licario*, dedicated to the character that dominates the end of *Paradiso*, and who reappears in this new text as the embodiment of the author's thoughts; and the poem collection *Fragmentos a su imán* [Fragments to Their Magnet], where he opens up, through the use of the traditional Lezamian style, a sense of communicative urgency which appears to transcend the co-ordinates of the writer's poetic system, when, in reality, it actually takes it to its culminating point

The full development of his ideas and of his poetic discourse allows Lezama access, in *Fragmentos a su imán*, to a level of communication that appears to contradict, at certain points, the hermeticism of his previous books, when, in fact, the conversational texts of this collection of poems are the last result of that hermeticism. It is presented in *Fragmentos a su imán* as the unveiling and delivery of the author's thoughts, guided by the all-consuming desire to reach an absolute, a

palpable possession in its verbal manifestation; as if the text were able to become texture, in flesh that becomes habitable like a body.

EMILIO DE ARMAS

translated by Luis González Fernández

Biography

Born in Havana, Cuba, 19 December 1910 (some sources give 1912). Grew up in the Fort Barrancas military camp, Pensacola. Educated at the Instituto de Havana, until 1928; University of Havana, degree in law 1938. Worked briefly in private law practice after graduation; worked for the Higher Council for Social Security, from 1938; director, Department of Culture, Ministry of Education, from 1945. Travelled to Mexico, 1949, Jamaica, 1950. Director, Department of Literature and Publications, National Council of Culture, Havana, from 1959, and adviser, Cuban Centre for Literary Investigation. Editor or co-editor, *Verbum* (with Guy Pérez de Cisneros), 1937, *Espuela de Plata*, 1939–41, *Nadie Parecía*, 1942–1944, *Orígenes*, 1944–1956. The last of these was a most important literary journal, funded by the wealthy José (Pepe) Rodríguez Feo, a Harvard graduate with a marked interest in literature. It was because Rodríguez Feo and Lezama Lima fell out that *Orígenes* ceased publication. One of six vice-presidents, Cuban Union of Artists and Writers (UNEAC), 1959–1962. Married María Luisa Bautista in 1965. His novel *Paradiso* withdawn from circulation after its publication in Cuba. As creative writing in Cuba grew ever more bureaucratized and sovietized, so Lezama Lima fell out of favour. Died (obscurely) on 9 August 1976. There was a great revival of interest in his work, particularly among young writers in Cuba, in the late 1980s.

Selected Works

Poetry

Muerte de Narciso, Havana: Úcar García y Cía, 1937
Enemigo rumor, Havana: Espuela de Plata, 1941
Aventuras sigilosas, Havana: Orígenes, 1945
La fijeza, Havana: Orígenes, 1949
Dador, Havana: Instituto Nacional del Libro, 1960
Fragmentos a su imán, Havana: Arte y Literatura, 1977

Novels

Paradiso, Havana: Unión, 1966; revised edition, edited by Julio Cortázar and Carlos Monsiváis, Buenos Aires: Ediciones de La Flor, 1968; as *Paradiso*, translated by Gregory Rabassa, New York: Farrar Straus and Giroux, and London: Secker and Warburg, 1974
Oppiano Licario (incomplete), Havana: Arte y Literatura, 1977; edited by César López, Madrid: Cátedra, 1989

Essays and Other Writings

Coloquio con Juan Ramón Jiménez, Havana: Dirección Nacional de Cultura, 1938
La pintura de Aristides Fernández, Havana: Dirección Nacional de Cultura, 1950
Analecta del reloj, Havana: Orígenes, 1953
La expresión americana, Havana: Instituto Nacional de Cultura, 1957 [lectures]
Tratados en La Habana, Havana: Universidad Central de la Villas, 1958
La cantidad hechizada Havana: Unión, 1970
Introducción a "Los vasos órficos," Barcelona: Seix Barral, 1971
Las eras imaginarias, Madrid: Fundamentos, 1971

Compilations and Anthologies

Antología de la poesía cubana, 3 vols, Havana: Consejo Nacional de Cultura, 1965

Lezama Lima: los grandes todos, Montevideo: Arca, 1968

Poesías completa, Havana: Instituto del Libro, 1970

Obras completas, edited by Cintio Vitier, 2 vols, Mexico City: Aguilar, 1975–77

El reino de la imagen, edited by Julio Ortega, Caracas: Biblioteca Ayacucho, 1981 [selected essays]

Poesía completa, Havana: Letras Cubanas, 1985

Poesía, edited by Emilio de Armas, Madrid: Cátedra, 1992

Further Reading

Bejel, Emilio, *José Lezama Lima: Poet of the Image*, Gainesville: University Presses of Florida, 1990

Cortázar, Julio, "Para llegar a Lezama Lima," in his *La vuelta al día en ochenta mundos*, Mexico City: Siglo XXI, 1967; as *Around the Day in Eighty Worlds*, translated by Thomas Christensen, San Francisco: North Point Press, 1986

de Villa, Álvaro and José Sánchez-Boudy, *Lezama Lima: Peregrino inmóvil (Paradiso al desnudo): un estudio crítico*, Miami: Universal, 1974

Goytisolo, José Augustín (editor), *Posible imagen de José Lezama Lima*, Barcelona: Llibres de Sinera, 1969

Levinson, Brett, *Secondary Moderns: Mimesis, History and Revolution in Lezama Lima's "American Expression,"* Lewisburg, Pennsylvania: Bucknell University Press, 1996

Lutz, R.R., "The Inseparability of Opposites in José Lezama Lima's *Muerte de Narciso*," *Romance Quarterly*, vol. 31/3 (1984)

Márquez, Enrique, *José Lezama Lima: bases y génesis de un sistema poético*, New York: Peter Lang, 1991

Molinero, Rita V., *José Lezama Lima, o el hechizo de la búsqueda*, Madrid: Playor, 1989

Ortega, Julio, "Reading *Paradiso*," in his *Poetics of Change: the New Spanish-American Narrative*, translated by Galen D. Greaser, Austin: University of Texas Press, 1984

Pellón, Gustavo, *José Lezama Lima's Joyful Vision: a Study of "Paradiso" and Other Prose*, Austin: University of Texas Press, 1989

Pérez Firmat, Gustavo, "Descent into *Paradiso*: a Study of Heaven and Homosexuality," *Hispania*, vol. 59/2 (1976)

_____ "The Strut of the Centipede: José Lezama Lima and New World Exceptionalism," in his *Do the Americas Have a Common Literature?* Durham, North Carolina: Duke University Press, 1990

Ruiz Barrionuevo, Carmen, *El paradiso de Lezama Lima: elucidación crítica*, Madrid: Insula, 1980

Sabatini, A., "On Reading *Paradiso*," *Latin American Fiction Today* (1980)

Sarduy, Severo, "Dispersión/falsas notas. Homenaje a Lezama," *Mundo Nuevo*, vol. 24/5–17 (1968)

Santí, Enrico Mario, "Párridiso," *Modern Language Notes*, vol. 94/2 (1979)

Schwartz, Ronald, "Lezama Lima: Cuban Sexual Propensities," in his *Nomads, Exiles, and Emigrés: the Rebirth of the Latin American Narrative 1960–80*, Metuchen, New Jersey: Scarecrow Press, 1980

Simón, Pedro (editor), *Recopilación de textos sobre José Lezama Lima*, Havana: Casa de las Américas, 1968

Souza, Raymond D., *The Poetic Fiction of José Lezama Lima*, Columbia: University of Missouri Press, 1983

Suárez Galbán, Eugenio (editor), *Lezama Lima*, Madrid: Taurus, 1987

Valdiviesco, Jaime, *Bajo el signo de Orfeo: Lezama Lima y Proust*, Madrid: Orígenes, 1980

Vitier, Cintio (editor), *Paradiso*, Madrid: Archivos, 1988 [Contains essays by leading scholars and writers]

Vizcaíno, Cristina and Eugenio Suárez Galbán, *Coloquio internacional sobra la obra de José Lezama Lima*, 2 vols, Madrid: Fundamentos, 1984

Waller, Claudia Joan, "José Lezama Lima's *Paradiso*: the Theme of Light and Resurrection," *Hispania*, vol. 56 (1973)

Zaldívar, Gladys, *Novelística cubana de los años 60: "Paradiso"; "El mundo alucinante"*, Miami: Universal, 1977

Bibliographies

Ulloa, Justo C., *Sobre José Lezama Lima y sus lectores: guía y compendio bibliográfico*, Boulder, Colorado: Society of Spanish and Spanish-American Studies, 1987

Interviews

Bravo, Armando Álvarez (editor), *Órbita de José Lezama Lima*, Havana: UNEAC, 1966 [interviews and selected texts]

Justin Lhérisson 1873–1907

Haitian prose writer and poet

Although he also wrote poetry and was an amateur historian, Justin Lhérisson's place in Haitian letters is assured by his two short novels, *La Famille des Pitite-Caille*, 1905 [The Pitite-Caille Family] and *Zoune chez sa ninnaine*, 1906 [Zoune at Her Grandmother's].

The plot of *La Famille des Pitite-Caille* (in Créole *pitit-kay* means "intimate friend of the family" or "one of ours") is simple: a man of the people, Éliézer Pitite-Caille becomes rich thanks to the skill of his wife Velléda, a renowned fortune-teller and brewer of love potions, whose clients include high society ladies. The Pitite-Cailles move to a fashionable neigh-

borhood and send their children to be educated in France. Disaster strikes when Éliézer decides to run for the Chamber of Deputies. Boutenègre, an unscrupulous ward heeler, exploits his ambition and cheats him out of his fortune. His popularity disturbs the clique in power, and they have Pitite-Caille arrested, beaten and thrown in jail. When, prematurely aged by his stay in prison, he is finally allowed to return home after the election, he swears to give up politics. But, falsely accused of plotting against the government, he is arrested and abused once again. Éliézer Pitite-Caille is finally released but dies of apoplexy soon after. What is left of his fortune is squandered by his children, and his widow is forced to become the concubine of an army general.

Pitite-Caille's adventure allows Lhérisson to depict (for the first time in Haitian literature) the details of an electoral campaign, with its required masonic initiations, recruitment of bodyguards and political workers, organization of "spontaneous" support rallies, and sponsoring of banquets and open-air dancing for the voters. All this is recounted with a broad humor that provokes guffaws and belly laughter but constitutes also, for the attentive reader, a penetrating and anguished critique of the unsavory nature of Haitian politics. The plot of *Zoune chez sa ninnaine* can be summarized in a few sentences : Mme Florida Boyotte, a Port-au-Prince store-keeper, takes in and raises her goddaughter Zoune, the daughter of poor peasants from the hills. Once the child has grown into an attractive adolescent, she is coveted by Mme Boyotte's good-for-nothing lover, police officer Cadet Jacques. Despite entreaties, gifts and threats, Zoune rejects Cadet Jacques's attentions. She finally complains to her godmother after he attempts to rape her, but the wretch claims that the girl encouraged him and Zoune is thrown out by her *ninnaine* ("godmother" in Créole).

La Famille . . . and *Zoune . . .* are novellas rather than true novels. More than the works of those of Lhérisson's contemporaries (Frédéric Marcelin, Fernand Hibbert and Antoine Innocent) who have been dubbed, like him "national" or "realist" writers, they mark an important stage in the quest for literary "Haitianness."

Lhérisson is the first novelist to have chosen his protagonists not from the upper classes but from the commercial petty bourgeoisie whose daily life and particular manners he chronicles. For example, *La Famille . . .* includes the first description not only of electoral practices and malpractices but of a whole series of Haitian traditions, such as the promise made to the voodoo spirits to provide, as an expression of thanksgiving for a prayer answered, a good meal (in Créole *tchiampan*) to prisoners in the central jail. This allows Lhérisson to describe in detail the appalling living conditions and the abuses of all kinds that are inflicted on the inmates. After *La Famille . . .*, and up to the present day, numerous Haitian writers have followed suit and protested against arbitrary arrest and the disgraceful conditions which reign in the penal establishments.

Before Lhérisson, if peasant life was described at all, it was in an edulcorated manner, as far removed from reality as the pastoral novels and poems of the Baroque period. In the first pages of *Zoune . . .*, rural life is for the first time described as it was (and remains) in actuality: exhausting, precarious, brutalizing, and steeped in distrust, ignorance and superstition. To be sure, Lhérisson's voice remains sardonic: he thus chooses ridiculous names for Zoune's parents: Maréchal Ticoq for her father, an indefatigable womanizer and Sor Poum (Madam Fart) for her mother, who is afflicted with chronic flatulence; but that does not prevent the novelist from exposing the great and criminal injustice of which our peasant brothers are the unfortunate victims: everything for the city folk, nothing for the country people; everything for our sarcastic and lazy urbanites and nothing for the "black hands who give us our white bread."

But above all, Lhérisson's fame rests on having created a new genre, the literary *audience*. What Haitians call *audience* is the custom of getting together to comment on the latest happenings in the neighborhood or in the Republic, to exchange gossip and to tell stories and jokes. The talent of the *audiencier* consists of finding an original point of view, in selecting picturesque images, in modulating the levels of expression, in sprinkling pauses and changes of rythm in the delivery, in alternating seriousness and buffoonery, high rhetoric and pungent colloquialisms. Since *audience* is by nature oral and performative, its written version cannot help but consist in large measure of either monologue or dialogue: under Lhérisson's pen, the genre constitutes itself half-way between narrative and theater. By transcribing this authentically Haitian "oraliture," by adopting its apparent artlessness and its verbal acrobatics, and even by incorporating the onomatopoeias and suggesting the mimicry which are essential components of any good *audience*, Lhérisson founded a tradition which writers of the next generation, such as Jacques Roumain, Jacques-Stéphen Alexis, Francis-Joachim Roy and later Gary Victor would illustrate brilliantly and which, in more or less explicit ways, informs most modern Haitian fiction.

Being informal, *audience* in its oral and written forms requires the use of vernacular, that is to say of Créole, either in its "pure" form or mixed with French and preferably with Haitian French, in accordance with the speaker's place in the social scale. Justin Lhérisson, an extraordinarily gifted *audiencier*, perfected the technique consisting of amalgamating French (especially for the narrative voice) with créolised French and pure Créole for most of the dialogues. The drawback (if it is a drawback) is of course that Lhérisson's *audiences* are completely intelligible only to Haitians and to those rare foreigners who understand Créole. This explains why, in contradistinction to most Haitian works of fiction, Lhérisson's novels were not published in Paris but in Port-au-Prince. His public was for all intents and purposes limited to his compatriots, not composed of the broad spectrum of readers of French, whatever their nationality.

To be sure, *La Famille des Pitite-Caille* was published with explanatory footnotes provided by the author; but these notes, which gave the French equivalent of certain lower-class popular expressions, were aimed at Haitian readers who, belonging by definition to the literate aristocracy, might not be familiar with them. In the same way *mutatis mutandis*, Victor Hugo and Balzac had annotated for their middle-class readers certain Parisian underworld slang expressions. The intrusion of Créole into Haitian literature, for which purity and elegance of French were a matter of principle and pride, did not, of course, please everyone. Reviewing *Zoune* for the December 1906 issue of *Le Petit Haïtien*, Édouard Fanfant wrote: "We understand that in a Haitian novel, in a novel which describes our way of life, some Créole words can find their place . . . But that they should be lavished indiscriminately, under the pretext of local color, of national literature is inadmissible. No, national literature does not consist in peppering the French text with Créole expressions. That would be too easy! And besides, when larded with Créole phrases, the style takes on a grotesque tone."

For a long time, the writers who followed Lhérisson's example risked being accused of contaminating French elegance with Créole vulgarity. Only recently have Haitian novelists (and even poets) felt justified in amalgamating in the same text their country's two official languages.

It should be noted in passing that, while vodùn is hardly mentioned in Lherisson's fiction and in that of most of his contemporaries, he published a seminal article in 1905 entitled *Le Marronnage et le vaudou* [Runaway Slaves and Vodùn], which affirms and celebrates the role of the folk religion under the colonial regime in inspiring resistance to slavery and the struggle for national independence.

Lhérisson's two short novels have become classics and have often been reprinted in Haiti and even abroad. As Pradel Pompilus pointed out:

> Haitians are attracted to *Pitite-Caille* and to *Zoune* because they find in them the true expression of their national identity, and foreigners by the evocation of a landscape and society profoundly different from their own.

LÉON-FRANÇOIS HOFFMANN

Biography

Born in Port-au-Prince, Haiti in 1873. He studied at Lycée Pétion, the country's top public secondary school, where he later taught the history and geography of Haiti. After obtaining his law degree, while only twenty years old, he founded in 1893 a literary and humoristic review, *La Jeune Haïti* [Young Haiti], to which he contributed poems, as he did to the famous *La Ronde* [The Circle]. Founder and editer, until his death, of an important daily newspaper, *Le Soir*. Became famous for the articles, filled with double entendres, in which he subtly criticized and satirized the government, and for his penetrating literary criticism. Published two undistinguished collections of poetry in the Parnassian mode, and wrote the words to *La Dessalinienne* (music by Nicolas Geffrard) which was adopted in 1903 as Haiti's national anthem. Died in 1907, while composing a sequel to his 1906 novel *Zoune chez sa ninnaine*.

Selected Works

Poetry

Myrtha, poème érotique, Port-au-Prince: Imprimerie Haïtienne, 1892
Les Champs de l'aurore; primes rimes, Port-au-Prince: Imprimerie de la Jeunesse, 1893
Passe-temps; poésies, Tours: Imprimerie Deslis Frères, 1893

Novels

La Famille des Pitite-Caille, Port-au-Prince: Imprimerie Auguste A. Héraux, 1905
Zoune chez sa ninnaine, Port-au-Prince: Imprimerie Auguste A. Héraux, 1906

Other Writings

Les Enseignements de l'histoire, Port-au-Prince: Imprimerie H. Amblard, 1894
"Le Marronnage et le vaudou," *Bulletin Officiel du Département de l'Instruction Publique*, Port-au-Prince, vol. 5/7 (April 1905) and vol. 5/8 (May 1905)
Manuel d'histoire à l'usage des écoles de la république, in collaboration with Wilson Bellegarde, Port-au-Prince: n. p., 1907

Further Reading

Joassaint, Erick, *Haïti, Golimin et les autres: une lecture de Justin Lhérisson*, Port-au-Prince: Presses de l'Imprimerie Nouvelle, 1986
Pompilus, Pradel, "Permanance de Justin Lhérisson," *Conjonction*, Port-au-Prince, 143 (May 1979)
Roméus, Wilhem, "En lisant Justin Lhérisson," *Le Nouvelliste*, Port-au-Prince (23 and 27–28 August 1977) [Stresses the subversive dimensions of Lhérisson's writings]

Libraries

Major Research Collections

The largest Latin American research collections are, of course, in the United States. The Library of Congress, in Washington, DC, is estimated to contain around a million titles relevant to Latin America and the Caribbean, over 60,000 of them in the fields of languages and literature. The Library's Hispanic Division also maintains the Archive of Hispanic Literature on Tape (see below). Also in Washington is the Columbus Memorial Library of the Organization of American States, with approximately 300,000 monograph titles in all, 25,000 of them in languages and literature.

The New York Public Library was recorded in 1991 as having over 36,000 titles classified as Latin American literature, followed closely by the University of California, Los Angeles, with over 33,000, and the University of Wisconsin (Madison), with over 29,000, whilst the Nettie Lee Benson Collection at the University of Texas (Austin), the largest collection in total of Latin American titles after the Library of Congress, reported over 25,000. Other specialist Latin American collections with strong holdings in literature are at the Universities of Indiana and New Mexico, with over 24,000 each, the University of North Carolina (Chapel Hill), the Widener Library at Harvard University, the University of Pittsburgh, Pennsylvania State University and the University of Illinois.

Partly as a consequence of cooperative acquisitions policies such as the Farmington Plan (1948–73) and the Latin American Cooperative Acquisitions Program (LACAP) (1961–73), many of these libraries have particular regional strengths; Florida and Miami, for instance, in Caribbean materials, Tulane in Central America, Cornell in the countries of the Southern Cone, Texas in Mexico. The Library of Congress, Columbia, New York University and Wisconsin have good coverage of Brazil, whilst the Morland-Spingarn Research Center Library at Howard University, in Washington, DC, has strong holdings of Haitian, African-Cuban, and African-Brazilian publications. Chicano material is collected by San José State University, and Mexican pulp literature at the University of Minnesota. The University of New Mexico (Albuquerque) collects Brazilian "literatura de cordel" and small press publications (largely little magazines, alternative press and avant-garde material). Latin American drama is well represented at the University of Kansas, whilst the Ruth S. Lamb Collection of Latin American Imprints (predominantly theater and drama) is housed in the Ella Strong Denison Library at Scripps College, Claremont, California, and the Frank Melville Memoral Library of the University of New York at Stony Brook contains the Amunátegui Collection of [Chilean and Latin American] Theatre Pamphlets. For contemporary Latin American literature (but especially *Modernismo*), the major resource (after the Library of Congress) is the New York Public Library. The University of Illinois maintains a major specialist collection of works by and about Gabriel García Marquez and the University of Virginia (Charlottesville) has a Jorge Luis Borges collection. A descriptive catalogue of this collection was published in 1993. The Library of Caribbean Research of the Research Institute for the Study of Man (New York) collects systematically in the area of English-speaking Caribbean literature.

Incunabula and early materials are held at Harvard University Library, the John Carter Brown Library of Brown University, the Lilly Library at the University of Indiana, the Newberry Library, Chicago, and Yale University Library. The Godoy Collection of Paraguayan Letters is at the University of California, Riverside, and the José Toribio Medina Collection is at the University of Connecticut. Finally, Princeton University Library possesses an outstanding collection of modern literary manuscripts and correspondence, including major collections of the papers of Reinaldo Arenas, Miguel Ángel Asturias, Guillermo Cabrera Infante, José Donoso, Jorge Edwards, Mario Vargas Llosa and others.

As far as European libraries are concerned, the available statistics are much less informative; they cover total holdings, but do not distinguish specific subject areas. However, a survey of European collections published in 1978 identified the Iberoamerikanisches Institut Stiftung Preussischer Kulturbesitz in Berlin as the largest European collection of Latin Americana, with an estimated total of 470,000 books and 2,700 periodicals, followed by the library of the Centro Iberoamericano de Cooperación in Madrid, with approximately 450,000 books and over 7,000 serials. In 1987 a survey of the British Union Catalogue of Latin Americana (BUCLA), which, unfortunately, contains relatively little information about holdings acquired before 1965, indicated, nevertheless, that the largest British collections were to be found at the University of Oxford (in the Bodleian Library, together with the Taylor Institution Library, which specialises in languages and literatures, and the Library of the Modern Languages Faculty), the British Library, the Albert Sloman Library at the University of Essex, the University of London Library, and the Library of the Hispanic and Luso-Brazilian Councils, at Canning House, London. In France the largest Latin American holdings were to be found in the Institut des Hautes Études de l'Amérique Latine, Paris, and in Italy at the Istituto Italo-Latinoamericano, Rome.

Though most of these collections will have continued to grow in the last fifteen years, it seems unlikely that their relative rankings will have changed very much. However, libraries vary in their collecting patterns, and the largest collections in terms of total numbers of volumes or titles may not always have the richest holdings in the field of literature. Nevertheless, it is safe to say that in the UK the most important collections of incunabula and early material as well as modern publications are held in the British Library and the Bodleian Library, Oxford. Good collections of modern Latin American literature are also to be found at the Taylorian Institution (University of Oxford), the University of London Library, King's College, London, University College, London, and the John Rylands University Library of Manchester.

There are few general guides to noteworthy holdings in Latin American and Caribbean libraries. However, the Biblioteca Julio Jiménez Rueda in Mexico City, which supports the Centro de Estudios Literarios of the Universidad Nacional Autónoma de México (UNAM), is reported to have complete sets of the publishers' series Letras Mexicanas (Fondo de Cultura Económica), Escritores Mexicanos (Porrúa) and Ficción (Universidad Veracruzana). In Rio de Janeiro, important literary collections exist in the Biblioteca Plínio Doyle, which is a research division of the Casa Fundação Rui Barbosa, and the Oficina Literário Afrânio Coutinho. The Instituto de Estudos Brasileiros of the Universidad de São Paulo houses Mário de Andrade's library, whilst the libraries and archives of Sérgio Buarque de Hollanda and Oswald de Andrade have been deposited at the Universidade Estadual de São Paulo, Campinas.

The prime collection in the English-speaking Caribbean is probably the West Indies Collection in the Library of the University of the West Indies, Mona, Jamaica, which has a collection of literary manuscripts, notably those of Roger Mais. Jamaica is also the home of the other major collection of English-language Caribbeana, the West India Reference Library in Kingston.

Audio-Visual Materials

The outstanding collection in this area is the Archive of Hispanic Literature on Tape, which is part of the Hispanic Division of the Library of Congress (see above), and since its inception in 1943 has recorded readings by over 600 Latin American and Caribbean literary figures. Despite its title, "languages include Spanish Catalan, Portuguese, French, Zapotec, Náhuatl, Quechua, and . . . English." Reproduction tapes for non-commercial use can be supplied.

A number of commercial audio and videotapes featuring Latin American writers reading from their own works, as well as dramatizations of novels or productions of works by Latin American playwrights have been produced by various organizations, and these are available in many research libraries. The University of Virginia, for instance, has a notable collection of videotapes, including many Latin American feature films. The Instituto Cervantes (New York) has a collection of Spanish-language films, including over 350 Latin American titles.

In the UK, the Library of the Institute of Latin American Studies of the University of London houses the Nissa Torrents Video Collection, which includes Latin American feature films as well as documentaries about writers and their work. The

National Sound Archive of the British Library has acquired Latin American literary recordings produced in Mexico and Argentina, and NSA staff have also themselves recorded readings by contemporary Latin American writers.

The Museu da Imagem e Som in Rio de Janeiro has recordings of readings by a number of Brazilian authors; a selective discography was published in 1977.

Library Catalogues

Most major libraries now provide a digitized online catalogue accessible via the Internet (see also Information Technology, below), but with certain limitations. To date (1996) few libraries have converted all their catalogue records to be available online; in particular, older acquisitions and special collections acquired before the late 1970s or early 1980s, when most online catalogues were initiated, are often recorded only in on-site card catalogues. The card catalogues of a number of major libraries were, however, published in printed format in the 1960s and 1970s; these included the Library of the Hispanic and Luso-Brazilian Councils at Canning House, London, the Nettie Lee Benson Collection at the University of Texas, the Institute of Jamaica West India Collection, the Ticknor Collection at Boston Public Library, the Oliveira Lima Library of the Catholic University of America, the Library of the Hispanic Society of America, the shelflist of the Latin American literature collection in the Widener Library at Harvard, and the Latin American and Caribbean collections at the Universities of Miami (Coral Gables) and Florida. These catalogues are usually available at other major research libraries in the US and the UK, and they provide a useful supplement to online catalogues in cases where the catalogue records of older holdings have not yet been digitized. Although digitization is leading to increasing standardization of classification systems for the arrangement of collections, some libraries, particularly in the UK, still make use of sometimes rather idiosyncratic locally-devised systems.

Inter-Library Loan/Document Delivery

Most libraries participate in a scheme which allows them to borrow from another library material which they do not already hold but which is required by one of their patrons. The conditions covering these schemes vary from country to country, but usually operate at an international as well as at a national level. Document delivery is usually defined as the provision of the content of a text (usually, but not always, a periodical article) in electronic format, via the Internet. (See Information Technology, below.)

Union Catalogues

These record the holdings of several libraries, and are particularly useful to locate unusual or rare items. Some are on-line databases, such as OCLC (Online Computer Library Center), RLIN (Research Libraries Information Network), and CURL (Consortium of University and Research Libraries) (see Information Technology, below). The National Union Catalog produced by the Library of Congress, and published in 753 volumes from 1967 to 1980 (and with regular supplements in print, and latterly in microform) contains locations for most research libraries in the US. It is widely available in other major libraries in both the US and UK. The *British Union Catalogue*

of Latin Americana, a card catalogue, was maintained from 1966 to 1988 by the Institute of Latin American Studies of the University of London. It contains entries for some, though by no means all, of the holdings of most of the UK libraries which collected Latin American material during that period; some of these libraries, but again not all, also submitted retrospective information.

PAT NOBLE

Further Reading

Bray, David B. and Richard E. Greenleaf, with the assistance of Bruce D. Tobias, *Directory of Latin American Studies in the United States*, New Orleans, Louisiana: Tulane University, Roger Thayer Stone Center for Latin American Studies, 1986

Covington, Paula H. (editor), *Latin America and the Caribbean: a Critical Guide to Research Resources*, Westport, Connecticut: Greenwood Press, 1992

Dorn, Georgette Magassy, "El Archivo de literatura hispánica de la Biblioteca del Congreso," *Revista Interamericana de Biblioteconomía*, vol. 39/1 (1989)

Grow, Michael, *Scholar's Guide to Washington, DC, for Latin American and Caribbean Studies*, Washington, DC: Smithsonian Institution Press, 2nd edition, 1992

Harvard University Library, *Latin American literature: Classification schedule, classified lists by callmarks, author and title lists, chronological listing* (Widener Library shelflist, 21), Cambridge, Massachusetts: Harvard University Press, 1969

Heintze, James R., *Scholars' Guide to Washington, DC, for Audio Resources*, Washington, DC: Smithsonian Institution Press, 1985

Hellman, Ronald G. and Beth Kampler Pfannl (editors), *Tinker Guide to Latin American and Caribbean Policy and Scholarly Resources in Metropolitan New York*, New York: Bildner Center for Western Hemisphere Studies, 1988

Jackson, William V., *Library Guide for Brazilian Studies*, Pittsburgh, Pennsylvania: University of Pittsburgh Book Center, 1964

____ *Resources for Brazilian Studies at the Bibliothèque Nationale*, Austin, Texas: Jackson, 1980

____ "American Library Resources for Latin American Studies," *Harvard Library Bulletin* 1–4 (Winter 1990–91)

Lindvall, Karen, *Research in Mexico City: a Guide to Libraries and Research Centers*, San Diego: University Library, University of California, 1977

Macdonald, Roger and Carole Travis, *Libraries and Special Collections on Latin America and the Caribbean: a Directory of European Resources*, London: Athlone Press, 2nd edition, 1988

McNeil, Robert A. and Barbara V. Valk (editors), "Libraries and Their Use," in *Latin American Studies: a Basic Guide to Resources*, 2nd revised edition, Metuchen, New Jersey: Scarecrow Press, 1990

Melville, Annette, *Special Collections in the Library of Congress: a Selective Guide*, Washington, DC: Library of Congress, 1980

Mesa Lago, Carmelo, *Latin American Studies in Europe*, Pittsburgh, Pennsylvania: University of Pittsburgh Center for Latin American Studies, 1979(?)

Noble, Pat and Ann Wade (editors), *The Future of Latin American Research Collections in the United Kingdom: Reports and Papers of Two Workshops*, London: Institute of Latin American Studies, SCONUL, 1993

Sable, Martin, *The Latin American Studies Directory*, Detroit, Michigan: Blaine Ethridge, 1981

"Seminar on the Acquisition of Latin American Library Materials," in *Library Resources on Latin America: New Perspectives for the 1980s: Final Report and Working Papers of the Twenty-fifth Seminar on the Acquisition of Latin American Library Materials ... 1980*, edited by Dan C. Hazen, Albuquerque, New Mexico: SALALM, 1981

Siefer, Elisabeth, *Estudios recientes sobre America Latina: institutos y bibliotecas en la República Federal de Alemania y Berlin Occidental*, Hamburg: ADLAF, 1971

Souza, Sebastião de, *Discografia da literatura brasileira*, Rio de Janeiro: Cátedra, 1977

Tatum, Charles, "An overview of Chicano Library Materials: Abstract and Bibliography," in *Library Resources on Latin America: New Perspectives for the 1980s: Final Report and Working Papers of the Twenty-Fifth Seminar on the Acquisition of Latin American Library Materials*, edited by Dan Hazen, Madison, Wisconsin: SALALM Secretariat, 1981

Williams, Sam P., William V. Jackson and James W. Henderson, *Guide to the Research Collections of the New York Public Library*, Chicago: American Library Association, 1975

Information Technology

Information technology may be defined as the use of computer technology for the organization, analysis and dissemination of information and data. As such, its application to the humanities is recent, and it has not yet been adopted as widely as in the sciences. However the growth of the worldwide communications network known as the Internet, which now links the computer systems of most large organizations, and allows an unprecedented degree of immediate and flexible access to important sources of information, especially the catalogues of major research libraries, is already transforming it into an indispensible new tool and means of communication for the serious scholar in any discipline.

It is becoming easier and easier to access the system; virtually all major research institutions and major corporations are linked up, whilst many cities, in the US particularly, have set up local networks, or "freenets." Increasingly, public libraries provide computer facilities with network access, and "cyber-cafes" offering public access terminals on a commercial basis at hourly rates have been set up in both the US and the UK. The pace of change in this field has in all respects been very rapid, and new facilities and resources seem to appear almost daily; the following is a necessarily brief summary of the situation as it appeared at the time of writing (1996).

The applications of information technology to research method may be said to fall into three major categories: those which can be carried out on an independent personal computer or word processor; those which require a personal computer equiped with a CD-Rom drive; and finally those which are dependent on a link to the worldwide computer network known as the Internet, or to one of the national, regional, or commercial networks which provide a "gateway" to the Internet itself.

The first category, which comprises the production of text (word processing), and of bibliographies and catalogues, together with the analysis of text (e.g. word counts, indexing, etc.), is becoming commonplace, and needs no elaboration. Familiarity with the second category, the use of CD-Roms, particularly as vehicles for reference tools such as encyclopedias and cumulative indexes, is not yet as widespread, although the number of multimedia products now on sale to the public is growing fast. For research purposes, CD-Roms offer many of the benefits of online databases, such as keyword searching and the printing out of information, at lower cost than is incurred by direct access through commercial host services, though with some loss of currency. Major databases such as the *MLA Bibliography* and *Scholarly Book Reviews*, and the catalogues of some libraries (for instance, the British Library and the French Bibliothèque Nationale, and a number of Mexican research libraries) are published on CD-Rom as well as in hard copy or as an online service, and are increasingly acquired by many institutions in preference to the printed format. At the time of writing (1995), the number of CD-Roms exclusively devoted to Latin American studies is small, but *Latin American Studies* includes the catalogue of the Nettie Lee Benson Collection at the University of Texas, the *Hispanic American Periodicals Index*, and the *Handbook of Latin American Studies (HLAS)* from volume 50 onwards, whilst *Biblioteca sin fronteras* contains the holdings on Latin America of a number of Spanish libraries.

The third category, however, comprising direct interactive access through the computer networks to library catalogues, text archives, and other informational databases, together with fast and efficient communication either within a group or person-to-person (electronic mail), is still unfamiliar to many people outside academic communities, although these facilities are already easily available even from a home computer for the price of a local phone call, plus at most a small monthly subscription.

The basic requirement for access to online databases is connection to a computer network (either a local one or the Internet itself), and this is achieved via a mainframe computer operated by a service provider, which may be either a large institution such as a university, a local public network (a freenet), or a nationwide commercial organization such as Compuserve or CIX. An individual user can connect to the service provider either through a terminal linked directly to a mainframe computer via an internal network (such as are provided in most research libraries), or through a personal or laptop computer, which may be located anywhere provided it is linked to a mainframe through the telephone or optical fibre cable network by means of a device known as a modem.

Since the whole of this technology is still at a relatively early stage of development, methods of connection to the Internet can vary considerably from institution to institution. Various projects are under way, however, aimed at establishing an industry standard, and it is to be hoped that by the beginning of the 21st century this will have been achieved.

Information Resources Available

The most important of these resources are the catalogues of major research libraries, most of which are available for consultation online (though an important caveat needs to be entered here – at the time of writing many libraries, particularly in the UK, have in their online computerized catalogues records only for material acquired since the installation of the system; earlier material is often recorded only in their traditional onsite card catalogues [see also the section on Libraries]). Most major research libraries also contribute information to shared databases which act as union catalogues allowing for the location of rare or unusual items; important examples of these are RLIN (Research Libraries Information Network), OCLC (Online Computer Library Center), and CURL (Consortium of University and Research Libraries); a Europe-wide bibliographical database, CERL, is also projected. Many libraries offer facilities for patrons to conduct their own searches of these union catalogues as well as of the online catalogues of other libraries.

There are a number of general online indexes to periodical literature, of which the most important are UnCover, which is part of the database produced by CARL (Colorado Alliance of Research Libraries), FirstSearch (an OCLC service) and BIDS (Bath Information and Data Services) which includes the Arts and Humanities Citation Index. UnCover may be accessed directly by individuals via the Internet, but FirstSearch is a subscription service available in libraries, whilst BIDS is a service funded by the British Higher Education Funding Councils for the benefit of members of British research institutions, and requires a password. The *Hispanic American Periodicals Index* offers an online service to subscribers, and the *MLA Bibliography*, *Arts and Humanities Search*, and *Dissertation Abstracts On-Line* may be searched through commercial database hosts such as DIALOG.

Also available online are full text versions of many newspapers, periodicals, journals, often including graphics and sound. There are also several projects, amongst them the Gutenberg Project and the Oxford Text Archive, to create text archives of monograph material, in effect libraries in digitized form. The Gutenberg Project has the stated aim of creating an archive of one million texts by the year 2000, and in early 1995 the Library of Congress met with directors of libraries belonging to the Association of Research Libraries, to discuss the creation of a National Digital Library, with the aim of converting important collections to digital formats.

Digitized texts are one way of preserving the contents of publications in poor physical condition, but they also have certain other advantages over printed copies, in that they allow for keyword searching and programmed textual analysis. They may be published in CD-Rom format, or archived in computers accessible online, or both. Texts stored on one computer can be transmitted to another via a service known as FTP (file transfer protocol), usually in a compressed format, which may be read with the aid of special, freely available software. However, a new project, Alex, initiated in July 1994, aims not only to index the texts offered by the Gutenberg Project and a number of other text archives, but allows for fulltext retrieval as well. Systems like this, which provide electronic document delivery, supplement traditional inter-library loan services, and may eventually replace them.

At present, most of the texts available in this way have been transcribed from printed originals now out of copyright, or in poor condition, but it seems likely that as time passes more and more periodicals, particularly academic journals, and perhaps also experimental writing for which only restricted circulation is anticipated, will be published and distributed principally by electronic means. Increasing interest in this format is being expressed by commercial publishers; however, questions of copyright and text integrity will need to be resolved before real growth in this area can take place.

A common criticism of the resources available on the Internet is that of information overload, "drinking from a fire-hose" as it has been described, and discrimination needs to be exercised as much in this as in any other medium. Various projects are now being developed to provide organized access and structured indexes. The most widely available at the moment are "gophers," which are essentially indexes arranged in hierarchical menus, but also offer keyword searching of all the Internet resources listed, by means of such specialist finding tools such as Archie, Veronica and Jughead, as well as providing direct connection to other databases. Many also have provision for files of information to be downloaded into an enquirer's electronic mail account.

A recent development is the World Wide Web (WWW), which allows graphics, speech and music, as well as text to be stored and retrieved into a personal computer equipped with the appropriate software. The Library of the University of Texas WWW server, for example, can display and transmit maps, documents and pictures of artifacts from its collections. Text displayed in the World Wide Web format also contains highlighted words which provide direct links to other relevant documents and information sources.

The Web allows all sorts of individuals and organizations to set up their own "homepages" for online reference, and a recent development is the appearance of online versions of booksellers' and publishers' catalogues. Early 1995 saw the creation of an electronic clearinghouse, the Internet Bookshop, which allows users of the World Wide Web system to look up books in print, browse the file by subject, and obtain a list of booksellers and publishers able to supply whatever title is selected.

Among the most useful online resources for Latin American studies are:

1. Library catalogues: the catalogues of the major research libraries in the United States (see the essay on Major Research Collections), especially MELVYL, the catalogue of the libraries of the University of California (and one of the easiest to use) together with the Library of Congress database, LOCIS, and the catalogue of the Library of the University of Texas at Austin which contains the holdings of the Nettie Lee Benson Collection.
2. Indexes and databases: Handbook of Latin American Studies (available as part of LOCIS); MLA (via DIALOG (also on CD-Rom), available in many libraries, subscription only); HAPI, Hispanic American Periodicals Index (online directly at UCLA, by subscription only, or on CD-Rom as part of *Latin American Studies*); UnCover (available via CARL).
3. Electronic journals: most literary electronic journals carry material of the "little magazine" type, and none of these have any Latin American relevance at present, but one of the longest established, *Postmodern Culture*, occasionally publishes material on Latin American or Caribbean modern writers; it is indexed in the *MLA Bibliography*.

Electronic Mail

The fact that Electronic mail (also known as e-mail) is now extensively used by individual scholars and universities, has resulted in the electronic mailing list. An e-mail list operates by means of a master list of subscribers which is held on a computer; a copy of any individual message sent to the list is forwarded by the host computer to all members simultaneously. Each mailing list has a specific focus. Some mailing lists have thousands of subscribers worldwide, others may be confined to the members of one institution or even department. Lists allow informal discussion of topics of common interest to take place over different time zones, and can also be very valuable for posting enquiries, as well as for the rapid dissemination of information, project reports, conference announcements, etc., Catalogues and indexes of lists are available from various sources, both printed and online. There are a wide range of lists specific to individual countries of Latin America, and at present two general lists without restrictions on membership: LASNET, based at the University of Texas, and LATAM-INFO, part of the British Networked Information Services Project (NISP).

USENET "newsgroups" are similar to mailing lists in that they allow multilateral communication via electronic mail, but differ in that messages are not sent directly to individual subscribers, but are posted in sequence on a common database where they can be read via any computer equipped with the appropriate software. Newsgroups are divided into sub-groups, or "hierarchies"; there are several in the sub-group SOC which focus on Latin American topics or countries. Many library catalogue gophers provide access to these newsgroups, as do commercial suppliers of Internet access.

PAT NOBLE

Further Reading

New guides to online resources on the Internet and to the various search tools are appearing almost daily, but one of the earliest, and still one of the most useful, is:

Krol, Ed, *The Whole Internet: User's Guide and Catalog*, Sebastopol, California: O'Reilly and Associates, 2nd edition, 1994

Also recommended:

Laquey, Tracy, *The Internet Companion: a Beginner's Guide to Global Networking*, Reading, Massachusetts: Addison-Wesley, 2nd edition, 1994

Okerson, Ann (editor), *Directory of Electronic Journals, Newsletters, and Academic Discussion Lists*, 4th edition, Washington, DC: Association of Research Libraries, 1994 [The printed version of an online directory which is regularly updated, and is available on many gophers, including BUBL]

Smith, Richard J. and Mark Gibbs, *Navigating the Internet*, Indianapolis, Indiana: Sams Publishing, 1994

Technology, the Environment and Social Change: Papers of the Thirty-Eighth Annual Meeting of the Seminar on the Acquisition of Latin American Library Materials . . . Guadalajara . . . 1993, Albuquerque, New Mexico: SALALM Secretariat, 1995 [Contains a number of papers on information technology and its implications for Latin America and Latin American studies, including papers and resource lists by Molly Molloy]

Especially for Latin Americanists based in the UK:

Miller, Rory and Pat Noble, *Information Technology for Latin Americanists*, Liverpool: Society for Latin American Studies and Advisory Council on Latin American and Iberian Information Resources, 1994

Up-to-date texts of many guides to the Internet which have been published in printed form are often available on the Internet itself, through gophers, and may be downloaded by FTP or e-mail; BUBL is also a very useful source of general information about the latest proposals, technical developments, and new information services.

Most broadsheet newspapers and serious journals publish regular columns or sections on information technology, and these are excellent sources of information for the most recent developments, while *College & Research Library News* has a regular feature, *Internet News*, which offers valuable tips on new research resources. There are also a number of commercial journals catering for non-academic users of the Internet.

Enrique Lihn 1929–1988

Chilean poet and prose writer

Enrique Lihn's literary works began to appear in the late 1940s and acquired prominence during the 1960s. Although his poetry stands out above the rest of his work, his artistic activity is multifaceted. Lihn dedicated himself to other written genres as well (narrative, drama, essay) and he used visual media and both fine and applied arts (drawing, hand crafting of books, publicity).

His interest in different modes of communication and in diverse languages is a characteristic he shares with various Spanish American poets of his generation. Other predominant characteristics are the presence of "intertextualities" (the insertion into his texts of cultural references or the work of other authors), as in the poem "Apología y condenación de Las

Ramblas" [Apology and Condemnation of Las Ramblas]: "Levantando el brazo inducido por una descarga eléctrica, habló / *¿Padre por qué me has abandonado?* (Lifting his arm induced by an electric charge, he spoke: *Father why have you abandoned me?*); the "conversational" language (in which the pragmatic function takes priority and codes common to those used in everyday life are used), as, for example, in the poem "Noche de paz" [Silent Night] from *Al bello aparecer de este lucero*, 1983 [To the Beautiful Appearance of this Bright Star]: "No soy tu Papá Noel ni estás posando junto a mí / para la eternidad de una postal en familia / ni estamos menos separados que los vivos de los muertos." (I am not your Santa Claus nor are you posing at my side / for the eternity of a family postcard / nor are we less distant than the living from the dead); the constant variation of a limited number of themes (for example in the poems "El insomnio" [Insomnia] and "Carne del insomnio" [Flesh of Insomnia], or in "Barca de los convalescientes" [Ship of Convalescents] and "Hospital de Barcelona" [Barcelona Hospital]); and the reduction of the space between the non-specialized reader and poetry.

The artistic, structural and stylistic operations that Lihn performs reduce the prestige and the redeeming function of poetry, desacralizing it. Colloquial language and that of mass media communication play an important role in establishing a precise context for communication, an experience common to both the poet and the reader. An example of this is an experiment carried out during the 1950s by Lihn, Nicanor Parra and other writers, called *Quebrantahuesos* [Osprey], a satirical collective news board crafted out of clippings taken from a variety of journalistic materials. Another facet of this was a "Spectacle-Discourse" (whose text was published later with illustrations and photographs) performed by Lihn in December of 1977. Before the eyes of the spectators, the writer went through a process of transformation into the farcical fictional character Gerardo de Pompier. In the years of the military dictatorship that had deposed president Salvador Allende, Lihn drew upon both experiences in order to create and read poems from his collection *El Paseo Ahumada*, 1983 [The Ahumada Promenade], in public, on one of the most central commercial streets of Santiago. In the texts, "The Penguin" – a beggar who plays a drum – recites a discourse containing various intermingled speakers who deplore the economic situation of the unemployed reduced to selling odds and ends among the luxurious stores that the government had helped build in order to promote an image of false national prosperity. The voices say "Su ayuda es mi sueldo . . . / Su calculadora en mi mano a la que le falta un dedo con el que me prevengo de los errores del cálculo . . . / Su aparición en el Paseo Ahumada es mi estreno en sociedad . . . / Su dos más dos son cuatro es mi dos menos dos." (Your help is my salary . . . / Your calculator is my hand missing a finger that I use to prevent miscalculations . . . / Your appearance in the Promenade Ahumada is my debut in society . . . / Your two plus two is my two minus two).

Throughout Lihn's work there is a constant ironic and corrosive tone that immediately grabs one's attention. The speaker of his poems assumes, for a few instants, the optimistic and hopeful attitudes that have traditionally found a place in the lyric genre, in order to take them to the point of absurdity later. Lihn affirmed, in a preface opening his collection *La musiquilla de las pobres esferas*, 1969 [A Little Music from the Lower Spheres], that he wrote "poetry against poetry; a poetry, as Huidobro would have said, 'skeptical of itself'."

As is the case with other Spanish American poets of his generation (Ernesto Cardenal, Juan Gelman, José Emilio Pacheco, Antonio Cisneros), Lihn creates irony by drawing upon contrasts, for example in "La guitarrista más hermosa del mundo" [The Most Beautiful Guitarist in the World]: "La guitarrista más hermosa del mundo / toca en E 50 St. y 5 Ave. por unos centavos que recoge / en el cajón de su guitarra, forrado de púrpura por dentro / como un cardenal asesinado" (The most beautiful guitarist in the world / plays on East 50th St and 5th Ave for a few pennies she gathers / in her guitar case, lined with purple / like an assassinated cardinal). The

presence of an unforeseen twist in an everyday experience jars the reader into accepting a dialogue. Among his recurrent themes one finds temporality (old age, deterioration, sickness and death); writing ("Porque escribí" [Because I Wrote], "Si se ha de escribir correctamente poesía" [If You Are Going to Write Poetry Correctly . . .]; love; painting ("Woman Bathing in a Shallow Tub," "Kandinsky 1904," "Catedral de Monet" [Monet's Cathedral]); and travelling – as can be observed in the titles of his books *Escrito en Cuba*, 1969 [Written in Cuba], *Paris, situación irregular*, 1977 [Paris, an Unusual Situation], *A partir de Manhattan*, 1979 [As from Manhattan].

According to Lihn, the poet is a conscious producer of his craft. His work consists of manipulating language. Lihn's poetry uses biographical elements and a language of colloquial expressions and structures. Personal expression is thus made into that of a public person. He has said that his poetic speaker "writes, inscribing himself" in a "situation." The "situation" of Lihn's poetic subject is the context of Spanish America, which Lihn understands as that of a mimetic culture that follows European models with disastrous results. Lihn's poetry seeks to make evident the lack of unity in a reality that depends upon Europe and the United States. "Situated poetry," as Lihn prefered to call it, is also an answer to the problem of how to bring poetry closer to the non-specialized reader and how to create an intersection between the circumstances of everyday life (presented as continuous) and critical reflection (atemporal). The irony of his poems undermines the traditional distances established between the individual, his circumstances and the optimistic discourses that explain these circumstances, justify them or give them some meaning. Thus the individual's attention is deflected from the tensions and confrontations of life experiences.

Lihn's critics see "La pieza oscura" [The Dark Room], the title poem of his third collection, 1963, as the moment in which Lihn effectively explores the role of memory. The text is centered on the perturbing discovery of sexuality experienced by a group of children playing in the dark. In the volume *Conversaciones con Enrique Lihn*, edited by Pedro Lastra, Lihn says that the verses of "La pieza oscura" point toward a moment that involves "the readiness of a child to become an adult before this occurs and with this begins a process of constant degradation. I believe that these poems [of the collection *La pieza oscura*] presuppose a sort of negative philosophy of existence that conceives life as that process: time is the irreversible illness whose conclusion is death."

Lihn's novels and short stories have a strong experimental style. His characters are presences that become absurd and ironic, to the point that language comes forth as the protagonist. The title of his first novel is a good example: *Batman en Chile; o, El ocaso de un ídolo; o, Solo contra el desierto rojo*, 1973 [Batman in Chile, or the Fall of an Idol, or Alone against the Red Desert]. In his second novel: *La orquesta de cristal*, 1976 [The Crystal Orchestra], a millionaire orders the composition of a symphony and the fabrication of crystal instruments for an entire orchestra that was to appear in public in the Paris of 1900. The story is the chronicle of the orchestra's fate from its origin to its destruction by the Nazi occupation in 1942. The chronicle ends and is destroyed on that date, nevertheless it had been quoted "a priori" by the characters since 1900. *El arte de la palabra*, 1980 [The Art of the Word], takes place in the imaginary Republic of Miranda, and its revolves around entanglements involving a congress of writers.

In 1988, Enrique Lihn was hospitalized with incurable cancer. Given only a few months to live, Lihn continued to write until his last moments of lucidity, reworking his themes and maintaining in his writing the same critical attitude characteristic of his "negative philosophy of existence." The poems of his *Diario de muerte* [Diary of Death] were compiled and edited by Adriana Valdés and Pedro Lastra, his close friends and collaborators.

LUIS REBAZA-SORALUZ

Biography

Born in Santiago de Chile, 3 September 1929. Reared by his maternal grandmother. Enrolled at School of Fine Arts, University of Santiago de Chile, in 1941; left after one year; later arts reviewer and editor of the university's journal of fine art. Travelled to Europe in 1965 on UNESCO scholarship to take a course in museum curatorship. Returned to Chile in 1968 and edited cultural journals, including *Cormarán* and *Alerce*. Worked for the publishing house Casa de las Américas, 1967–68 after winning their poetry prize in 1966 for *Poesía de paso*. Research professor of literature, University of Chile, 1972. Travelled to US and Paris, 1975. Died 24 July 1988.

Selected Works

Poetry

Nada se escurre, Santiago de Chile: Colección Orfeo, 1949
Poemas de este tiempo y de otro, Santiago de Chile: Ediciones Renovación, 1955
La pieza oscura, 1955–1962, Santiago de Chile: Editorial Universitaria, 1963
Poesía de paso, Havana: Casa de las Américas, 1966
Escrito en Cuba, Mexico City: Era, 1969
La musiquilla de las pobres esferas, Santiago de Chile: Editorial Universitaria, 1969
Por fuerza mayor, Barcelona: Ocnos-Editorial Llibres de Sinera, 1975
París, situación irregular, Santiago de Chile: Aconcagua, 1977
A partir de Manhattan, Santiago de Chile: Ganymedes, 1979
Estación de los Desamparados, Mexico City: Premiá Editora, 1982
El Paseo Ahumada, Santiago de Chile: Ediciones Minga, 1983
Al bello aparecer de este lucero, Hanover, New Hampshire: Ediciones del Norte, 1983
Pena de extrañamiento, Santiago de Chile: Sinfronteras, 1986
Diario de muerte, Santiago de Chile: Editorial Universitaria, 1989

Short Fiction

Agua de arroz, Buenos Aires: Centro Editor de América Latina, 1968
La república independiente de Miranda, Buenos Aires: Sudamericana, 1989

Novels

Batman en Chile; o, El ocaso de un ídolo; o, Solo contra el desierto rojo, Buenos Aires: Ediciones de La Flor, 1973
La orquesta de cristal, Buenos Aires: Sudamericana, 1976
El arte de la palabra, Barcelona: Pomaire, 1980

Compilations and Anthologies

Algunos poemas, Barcelona: Ocnos-Editorial Llibres de Sinera, 1972 [Consists of an anthology of the first four books together with the collection *Album de toda especie de poemas*]

Translations

This Endless Malice; 25 Poems, translated by Serge Echeverría and William Witherup, Northwood Narrows, New Hampshire: Lillabulero Press, 1969 [Contains *La pieza oscura* and *Poesía de paso*]
If Poetry is to be Written Right; Poems, translated by Dave Oliphant, Texas City: Texas Portfolio Press, 1977
The Dark Room and Other Poems, edited by Patricio Lerzundi, translated by Jonathan Cohen, John Felstiner and David Unger, New York: New Directions, 1978 [bilingual edition]

Further Reading

Bocaz, Luis, "La poesía de Enrique Lihn," in *Poesía chilena (1960–1965)*, edited by Carlos Cortínez and Omar Lara, Santiago de Chile: Trilce, 1966
Cánovas, Rodrigo, *Texto y censura: las novelas de Enrique Lihn*, Santiago de Chile: CENECA, 1986
Goic, Cedomil, "Enrique Lihn: *La pieza oscura*. 1955–1966," *Anales de la Universidad de Chile* 128 (September–December 1963)
Ibáñez Langlois, José Miguel, *Poesía chilena e hispanoamericana actual*, Santiago de Chile: Nascimento, 1975
Lastra, Pedro (editor), *Conversaciones con Enrique Lihn*, Santiago de Chile: Atelier, 1990
Libertella, Hector, *Nueva escritura en Latinoamérica*, Caracas: Monte Ávila, 1977
Peña, Juan Andrés, *Conversaciones con la poesía chilena*, Santiago de Chile: Pehuén, 1990 [Chapter 4 is an interview with Lihn]
Rojas, Waldo, " Lihn ¿aún poeta joven?" *Atenea*, Universidad de Concepción, Chile, vol. 166/417 (July–September 1967)
Sucre, Guillermo, "Poesía crítica: lenguaje y silencio," *Revista Iberoamericana*, vol. 37/76–77 (July–December 1971)

Special Issues of Journals

Review 23 (1978)

Baldomero Lillo 1867–1923

Chilean prose writer

Naturalism was a literary extension of European thought and philosophy of the late 19th century transferred to Latin America, especially through the novels of Zola. Under the influence of thinkers like Auguste Comte, Herbert Spencer, Saint-Simon and Jeremy Bentham, Positivism and Utilitarianism, coming in the wake of the Industrial Revolution in Europe, were supposed to raise the level of life for the working classes and help them to escape the stranglehold of the Catholic Church. The new ideas, coupled with the social sciences, the growing industrial wealth in the hands of the magnates, supported by the progressive young *científicos* (technocrats), were to provide the greatest possible happiness for the greatest number of people. This was particularly true of Chile whose rich mines and natural resources attracted a huge proletariat from all over the world. Positivist Chilean thinkers like Francisco Bilbao and José Victorino Lastarria propagated new doctrines readily received by the people. However, the Utopias and the New Jerusalems were not to be within the grasp of the masses. The "progress and order" message of the new thinkers produced a state of affairs that militated against the poor, but gained profit for a few industrialists, while the masses toiled in factories and mines. Such grievous injustices provoked new ideas on the rights of man, fraternity, solidarity, and produced a useful source of literary raw material for Baldomero Lillo.

At the beginning of the 20th century, Lillo gained a deserved reputation as a writer who devoted his life and his literature to the miners working in inhuman conditions below ground. Though not read much today, his mining stories of *Sub terra* (1904) created the image of Lillo as a *comprometido* (or engaged) writer whose stories, steeped in the bleakest Naturalism, followed the Zolaesque tradition in their description of the conditions of the workers exploited by the capitalist system. Through their portraits of a downtrodden people, these stories provided the enemies of capitalism with a great deal of material to wage a propaganda war and situated Lillo the humanitarian in the ranks of the socialists and other radical groups who struggled to overthrow the government and the forces of reaction.

Because *Sub terra* was written when Lillo himself was working in the mines and shared his fellow-workers' circumstances, it was a true cry from the heart. Allegedly less concerned with the form of his work than with the experiences he wanted to portray, Lillo produced a series of stories destined to improve the life of his companions. The gruesome details of underground life have been well documented in stories like "La compuerta número 12" [Hatch No. 12] which relates the tragic story of an eight-year-old boy forced to work down the mine by his grief-stricken father who needs the boy's tiny wage to feed the family's other children. Tied to the mine-cage so that he cannot escape, the child, crying for his mother, is as much a prisoner of the mining company as his wretched father is dying of tuberculosis but obliged to continue working for fear of losing his job. "El chiflón del diablo" (The Devil's Pit), another much anthologised story, depicts something of the

same hopeless situation when a young miner, having lost his job, accepts a position in the dangerous mine of the title. His poor mother, who has already lost her husband and two sons to the site, is so overcome with grief on receiving news of the accident which kills her last son that she jumps into the pit, a desperate gesture of helplessness. Death by suicide, accident, company indifference and heartlessness, or hunger and neglect; the fate of the miner is always the same. In "El grisú" [Firedamp] it is exploitation, explosion, and gruesome death. In "Los inválidos" [The Disabled] an old miner uses the example of the tied up pit pony, wounded, tired, awaiting death, to show the miners their fate in life. The young husband in "El pago" [Payment] stands in line on pay day, only to be told that *he* owes money to the company, as his wife and babies wait at home for food.

Depressing as all of these stories are, they are rescued from a totally negative and numbing Naturalism by their pleas for justice. Although Lillo does not spare the reader the horrible details of death, misery and human deprivation, his stories advocate mercy and justice. Beneath the surface of the grim details is the humanitarian voice of the author crying out against the bosses and the system for pity and humanity in the name of the miners, and of all the exploited people of the world. Lillo's stories seem to beg compassion for individual miners, society and even the human race in the face of life's evils. The object of his rage extends beyond individual bosses and society's leaders to providence itself which permits the young and the innocent to suffer and die in the face of existential evil.

The tendency to see Lillo only as an engaged author producing works of social protest and denunciation does a great disservice to Lillo the artist. Critics have underscored the propagandistic elements of *Sub terra* as a socio-economic document, whilst neglecting the positive elements of his *costumbrismo minero* and the fine, effective use of natural phenomena which he introduced to highlight the hopelessness of their situation – the beauty of the sun (contrasted with the dark life of the underground mine), a sun which exists for them only in dreams, or as an ironic reminder of a merciless God. Although it may seem at first glance that in this first collection the pathetic and political elements triumph over the aesthetic qualities, Lillo's work was not yet complete.

In 1907 Lillo published another collection, *Sub sole*, which promoted him, perhaps unwillingly, from the ranks of the writers of social protest to the level of those who transcend geographical and chronological frontiers. Although there are two mining stories in the second collection, the situation of the underground workers is not the predominant theme. One finds also costumbrist-type stories, others dedicated to marine life, to the portrayal of Indians, humorous stories, and most importantly, some of a symbolic nature.

In *Sub sole* there are four symbolic stories that might be labelled *modernista*, but with a difference. Lillo, however, does not belong to the Art for Art's sake world of his contemporaries, since, according to him, the writer cannot fulfill his artistic duties divorced from the real world of actuality. But there is no doubt that Lillo was influenced by his *modernista* mentors, although this aspect of Lillo's work has not generally been treated by experts in the field (Fernando Alegría, Ricardo Latcham, Max Henríquez Ureña), even those devoted to *Modernismo* in Chile (John M. Fein, Mario Rodríguez Fernández).The *modernista* aspects of Lillo's work should not be ignored. In fact, one of the characteristics of this movement in Chile is the co-existence of various currents within the movement, in many cases even in the same writer who produces without emotional or aesthetic conflict a mixture of creole, social and decadent poetry, e.g., Carlos Pezoa Vélez, Pedro Antonio González, Antonio Bórquez Solar. This anomaly was possible in the Chilean movement which could not boast of a single leader or one outstanding *modernista* writer.

Although Darío published his *Azul* [Blue] in Chile in 1888, he had no disciples, and there was little interest shown in his work. Perhaps driven too much by just anger in *Sub terra*, Lillo had little recourse to his artistic spiritual mentors. However, in his new collection, *Sub sole*, by means of fantasy, imagination, symbolism and allegory, Lillo wrote stories, four philosophical parables in particular, to propagate again his humanitarian ideas under a surface of *modernista* prose. In these stories, by means of the inevitable princesses, fairies, spirits, kings, colours, jewels and music, one sees revealed the other side of the coin, the artistic Lillo. However, this does not cancel out, rather it confirms, the image of the engaged – but now more subtle – writer.

The first story of the collection, "El rapto del sol" [The Abduction of the Sun] is a parable against the ambition and pride of an all-powerful king, indifferent to the problems of his oppressed people. The word "Humanidad," which ends the tale, is the key to our interpretation of the story and the link with *Sub terra*. In spite of its *modernista* style, language, and imagery, the story highlights the plight of the ordinary man, and removes Lillo from the elitist position of his fellow-*modernistas*. The only solution for the world, according to Lillo, is a rebirth of universal love, when the capitalist grasps the hand of the proletariat. Only when Humanity conquers in the class-stuggle will peace triumph in the world. Complementing this story is the significantly titled "El oro" [Gold] in which Lillo chooses the well-worn symbols of the eagle and the sun to draw parallels with the first story. Here again the message is solidarity and brotherly love, although the language and the images are *modernista*, including a preference for the Rubenian *esdrújulo* (a word accented on the antepenultimate syllable).

But perhaps the most *modernista* of these stories from the stylistic point of view is "Las nieves eternas" [The Eternal Snows] which narrates the life of a drop of water, in a perfect cycle from its mountain birth melted by the sun, carried by a hurricane, turned into vapour, then snow and back to its mountain home. Thus Lillo depicts the *modernista* escape towards light and colour, through formal and thematic characteristics. In reality, however, the drop's pilgrimage is a symbol of life itself, with all its vicissitudes, a manifestation of the human vices depicted in the two previous stories. The cycle inevitably ends in death – and here this little poem in prose is linked with the Zolaesque determinism of *Sub terra*. Beneath the lyrical language of "Las nieves eternas" the picture is still the same – a Darwinian vision of the world in which only the fittest survive.

Even more explicit is the theme of "Irredención" [Non-Redemption], a title which emphasies the almost religious sentiments of Lillo towards those who abuse and exploit human life. This story is not only about the punishment of vanity, but also about the destruction of life and the human seed, as in the princess's nightmare world where flowers are destroyed. The story underscores the value of life – the princess destroys flowers, the mine bosses kill children – for Lillo, an unforgivable sin, from which there is no redemption. In spite of the religious terminology of the story, the most horrible aspect of the crime for Lillo (hardly an orthodox Catholic) was in the human field, and it is this hatred of man's inhumanity to man which constitutes the basis of his protest both in *Sub terra* and *Sub sole*.

Notwithstanding the formal and technical characteristics of these symbolic stories, the philosophical parables which link Lillo to the *modernista* movement, the message is unchanging. By temperament and artistic vision, Baldomero could not surrender totally to the artificial world of the ivory tower. In both collections, his voice is still raised in protest against selfishness, pride, hatred and greed. To counteract these vices which cause life's suffering, even a century later, Baldomero Lillo offers us human solidarity and universal love.

JOHN WALKER

See also the entry on Bolivia for further information on mining literature

Biography

Born at port of Lota, Chile, 6 January 1867. Father was employed at the foundry in Lota. Was a sickly child who attended school only irregularly but was avid reader. Started working in a store at an early age and later ran the store at the Buen Retiro mine. This allowed him to observe directly the wretched life of the miners. Married Natividad Miller. Moved to Santiago de Chile in 1898. Won short story contest in 1903. *Sub terra* appeared in 1904, and made him famous not only in intellectual circles but also among students and workers. Wife died in 1912, after which he took care of their four children. Retired in 1917 to live on his farm at San Bernardo. Died from tuberculosis on 10 September 1923.

Selected Works

Short Fiction

Sub terra: cuadros mineros, Santiago de Chile: Moderna, 1904
Sub sole, Santiago de Chile: Imprenta y Encuadernación Universitaria, 1907
Relatos populares, edited by José Santos González Vera, Santiago de Chile: Nascimento, 1942
El hallazgo y otros cuentos del mar, Santiago de Chile: Ercilla, 1956
Pesquisa trágica. Cuentos olvidados, Santiago de Chile: Luis Rivano, 1963

Compilations and Anthologies

Obras completas, Santiago de Chile: Nascimento, 1968
   [Contains biographical outline by Raul Silva Castro and reviews of *Sub terra* and *Sub sole* which appeared in the wake of their publication]

Translations
The Devil's Pit and Other Stories, translated by Esther S. Dillon and
Ángel Flores, Washington, DC: Pan American Union, 1959

Further Reading
The paucity of book-length criticism, and the dates of the few
articles dedicated to Lillo, highlight the neglect of his short
fiction.

Alegría, Fernando, "Introducción a los cuentos de Baldomero Lillo,"
in his *Las fronteras del realismo: literatura chilena del siglo XX*,
Santiago de Chile: Zig-Zag, 1962

Latcham, Ricardo, "El naturalismo de Baldomero Lillo," in his
Antología, Santiago de Chile: Zig-Zag, 1965
Orellana, Carlos (editor), *El nuevo cuento realista chileno*, Santiago
de Chile: Editorial Universitaria, 1962
Sedgwick, Ruth, "El mensaje social de Baldomero Lillo," in
*Memoria del segundo congreso internacional de catedráticos de
literatura iberoamericana*, Berkeley: University of California Press,
1941
_____ "Baldomero Lillo y Émile Zola," *Revista Iberoamericana*, vol.
7/14 (February 1944)
Walker, John, "Baldomero Lillo, ¿Modernista comprometido?,"
Cuadernos Hispanoamericanos, vol. 95/283 (1974)

Lins do Rego, José

See Rego

Clarice Lispector 1920–1977

Brazilian prose writer

Considered one of the major writers in Portuguese, Clarice
Lispector fascinates the reader with her unique style. Blending
an intuitive, spontaneous writing with an elaborate aesthetic
and technique, her entire production provokes with endless
questions about the meaning of existence, the profound dimensions of the ego, and the nature of subjectivity, gender and
writing. Her versatile legacy includes short stories, novels, journalistic productions and chronicles, translations and children's
literature.

Born in Tchetchelnik, Ukraine, Lispector was two months
old when she arrived with her parents in Brazil. The family
lived in the northeast and later moved to Rio de Janeiro. In
1943, she graduated from law school and married a fellow
student whose diplomatic career would lead them abroad.
They resided in Europe and the United States before returning
to Brazil. These migrations inside and outside the country reinforce the awareness of being a foreigner that installs an alternate central or marginal outsider within herself. As Diane E.
Marting states in *Clarice Lispector: a Bio-Bibliography* (1993),
the writer's closeness to diplomatic circles might have been the
reason for her reticence to reveal her political opinions,
however, it is still unexplained why Lispector resented questions about her age, her accent, her family's immigration to
Brazil and her Judaism (she tried to blend into the Catholic
majority rather than to hold on to her roots). Perhaps a hidden

Clarice is always confronting the other one while both of them
are woven into the more autobiographical narrative voices.

Her first novel, *Perto do coração selvagem*, 1944 (*Near to
the Wild Heart*), is partly autobiographical and is innovative
in terms of the ways language is used and the meaning attributed to linguistic expression. The short stories of *Laços de
família*, 1960 (*Family Ties*), and *A legião estrangeira*, 1964
(*The Foreign Legion*), confirm this trend. Here the author
employs a cinematic slow motion, which focuses on close-ups
of the characters through stream-of-consciousness, rather than
on developing a strong narrative line. *A maçã no escuro*, 1961
(*The Apple in the Dark*), Lispector's longest novel, in which
the male protagonist, Martim, realizes that the world is like
an apple that cannot be explained, anticipates topics that will
be addressed later in her most studied work, *A paixão segundo
G.H.*, 1964 (*The Passion According to G.H.*). In this novel,
with affection but in an essayistic tone, the female protagonist, the nameless G.H., sets up a confessional first-person
narration that establishes a dialogue with somebody unknown
and invisible. When she unexpectedly encounters a cockroach,
she understands that in order to achieve the essence of existence beyond conventions, she will have to cannibalize the
disgusting creature. The consequent Sartrean nausea is brilliantly described as well as the tension between self and non-
self. From the simplicity of an apple up to the rite of sacrifice

and purification, Lispector's fiction displays an intertextuality based on myths and biblical references.

Due to Lispector's extraordinary exploration of the feminine condition from a Latin American woman's perspective and voice, she can be aligned with other important female writers, such as the Venezuelan Teresa de la Parra, the Chilean María Luisa Bombal, the Mexican Elena Poniatowska and the Argentine Luisa Valenzuela. Lispector, whose books have been translated into several languages, can also be placed with innovative Brazilian writers such as Waldomiro Autran Dourado and Adonias Filho. Influenced by her readings of Monteiro Lobato, Herman Hesse, Katherine Mansfield, Virginia Woolf, Albert Camus and Jean-Paul Sartre, she creates the characters' inner world that flows in a river of metaphysical interrogations.

Lispector's talent is capable of melting silence, words, textures and music into a poetic prose that constitutes a sensual quest for the experience of feeling, thoughts and things rather than for a rational search of an absolute truth. This quest was relevant to the argument advanced by the French feminist Hélène Cixous, who proposed the study of Lispector as an ideal example of *l'écriture féminine*. In *Coming to Writing* (1991), Cixous argues that feminine writing goes beyond binarisms that dichotomize emotion and reason, masculine and feminine, conscious and unconscious. To write the body, rejecting divisions of gender, implies a Lyotardean libidinal economy as an exchange between materiality and affection, as a post-modern sensibility: the wor(l)d is fruit, felt, and tasted. Lispector, for whom to live is to write, magically combines flesh, spirituality and a state of mind.

While dying of cancer, Lispector wrote a masterpiece which is also her most socially committed work, *A hora da estrela*, 1977 (*The Hour of the Star*). Playing a last mystical ritual, Lispector's language and writing can succeed over death. A narrative hermaphroditism unites the ugly, marginal and insignificant Macabéa with the male narrator, Rodrigo, S.M. The feminine subjectivity becomes the centre that attacks, through different voices, the patriarchal values of an abusive, cruel society. A film based on this novel and directed by Suzana Amaral received the first prize at the Havana Film Festival in 1986. This is another indication of an escalating interest in Clarice Lispector and a homage to her gifted singularity.

ANDREA YANNUZZI

Biography

Born in Tchetchelnik, Ukraine, 10 December 1925. Family moved to Brazil in 1926 (Lispector was 2 months old) and settled in Recife in 1927. Attended the Ginásio Pernambuco from 1935 to 1936; Colégio Sílvio Leite in 1937, and later Colégio Andrews; National Faculty of Law, Rio de Janeiro from 1941 to 1944, received law degree, 1944. Edited and contributed to *Agência Nacional* and *A Noite*, while still a student, 1941–44. Married Mauri Gurgel Valente in 1943; two sons. Left Brazil because of her husband's diplomatic postings and lived in Europe, mainly Naples and Berne until 1952, and in the US from 1952 to 1959. After separating from her husband she returned to Rio de Janeiro in 1959. Awards include: Graça Aranha Foundation Prize, 1944; São Paulo Carmen Dolores Barbosa Prize, 1962; Golfinho de Ouro Prize, 1969. Died 9 December 1977.

Selected Works

Novels

Perto do coração selvagem, Rio de Janeiro: A Noite, 1944; as *Near to the Wild Heart*, translated by Giovanni Pontiero, Manchester: Carcanet, and New York: New Directions, 1990

O lustre, Rio de Janeiro: Editora Agir, 1946

A cidade sitiada, Rio de Janeiro: A Noite, 1948

A maçã no escuro, Rio de Janeiro: Francisco Alves, 1961; as *The Apple in the Dark*, translated by Gregory Rabassa, New York: Knopf, 1967; London: Virago, 1985

A paixão segundo G.H., Rio de Janeiro: Editora do Autor, 1964; as *The Passion According to G.H.*, translated by Ronald W. Sousa, Minneapolis: University of Minnesota Press, 1988

Uma aprendizagem ou o livro dos prazeres, Rio de Janeiro: Sabiá, 1969; as *An Apprenticeship, or the Book of Delights*, translated by Richard A. Mazzara and Lorri A. Parris, Austin: University of Texas Press, 1986

Água viva, Rio de Janeiro: Editora Artenova, 1973; as *The Stream of Life*, translated by Elizabeth Lowe and Earl E. Fitz, Minneapolis: University of Minnesota Press, 1989

A hora da estrela, Rio de Janeiro: José Olympio, 1977; as *The Hour of the Star*, translated by Giovanni Pontiero, Manchester: Carcanet, 1986

Um sopro do vida: pulsações, Rio de Janeiro: Nova Fronteira, 1978 [A Breath of Life is the only full-length narrative text published after the author's death.]

Short Fiction

Alguns contos, Rio de Janeiro: Ministério de Educação e Saúde, 1952

Laços de família, Rio de Janeiro: Francisco Alves, 1960; as *Family Ties*, translated by Giovanni Pontiero, Austin: University of Texas Press, 1972

A legião estrangeira, Rio de Janeiro: Editora de Autor, 1964; as *The Foreign Legion*, translated by Giovanni Pontiero, Manchester: Carcanet, 1986

Felicidade clandestina: contos, Rio de Janeiro: Sabiá, 1971

Onde estivestes de noite, Rio de Janeiro: Artenova, 1974

A via crucis do corpo, Rio de Janeiro: Artenova, 1974

A bela e a fera, Rio de Janeiro: Nova Fronteira, 1979

Children's Fiction

O mistério de coelho pensante (uma estória policial para crianças), Rio de Janeiro: José Álvaro, 1967

A mulher que matou os peixes, Rio de Janeiro: Sabiá, 1968; as *The Woman who Killed the Fish*, translated by Earl E. Fitz, *Latin American Literary Review*, vol. 11/21 (July–December 1988)

A vida íntima de Laura, Rio de Janeiro: José Olympio, 1974

Quase de verdade, Rio de Janeiro: Rocco, 1978

Essays and Other Writings

Para não esquecer, São Paulo: Ática, 1979

A descoberta do mundo, Rio de Janeiro: Nova Fronteira, 1984; as *Discovering the World*, translated by Giovanni Pontiero, Manchester: Carcanet, 1992 [Newspaper articles published between 1967 and 1976]

Anthologies in Translation

Soulstorm, translated by Alexis Levitin, New York: New Directions, 1989

Further Reading

Castillo, Debra A., "Negation: Clarice Lispector," in her *Talking Back: Toward a Latin American Feminist Criticism*, Ithaca, New York: Cornell University Press, 1992

Cixous, Hélène, "Reading Clarice Lispector's 'Sunday before Going to Sleep,'" in *Modern Latin American Fiction*, edited by Harold Bloom, New York: Chelsea House, 1990

____ *"Coming to Writing" and Other Essays*, edited by Deborah Jenson, translated by Sarah Cornell, Cambridge, Massachusetts: Harvard University Press, 1991

Douglass, Ellen H., "Myth and Gender in Clarice Lispector: Quest as a Feminist Statement in 'A imitação da rosa'," *Luso-Brazilian Review*, vol. 25/2 (Winter 1988)

Fitz, Earl E., *Clarice Lispector*, Boston: Twayne, 1985

Jozef, Bella, "Clarice Lispector: la recuperación de la palabra," *Revista Iberoamericana*, vol. 50/126 (January–March 1984)

Lindstrom, Naomi, "Clarice Lispector: Articulating Women's Experience," in her *Women's Voice in Latin American Literature*, Washington, DC: Three Continents Press, 1989

Lobo, Luiza, "Leitor," in *Palavras da crítica: tendências e conceitos no estudo da literatura*, edited by José Luis Jobim, Rio de Janeiro: Imago, 1992

Nunes, Benedito, *Leitura de Clarice Lispector*, São Paulo: Quíron, 1973

Nunes, Benedito (editor), *Clarice Lispector: "A paixão segundo G.H.,"* Critical edition, Trinidade, Brazil: UFSC/UNESCO, 1988

Patai, Daphne, "Clarice Lispector and the Clamor of the Ineffable," *Kentucky Romance Quarterly*, vol. 27/2 (1980)

Peixoto, Marta, *Passionate Fictions: Gender, Narrative and Violence in Clarice Lispector*, Minneapolis: University of Minnesota Press, 1994

Pontiero, Giovanni, "Clarice Lispector: an Intuitive Approach to Fiction," in *Knives and Angels: Women Writers in Latin America*, edited by Susan Bassnett, London: Zed Books, 1990

Senna, Marta de, "Clarice Lispector's 'A imitação da rosa': an Interpretation," in *Portuguese Studies*, vol. 2 (1986)

Bibliographies

Marting, Diane E. (editor), *Clarice Lispector: a Bio-Bibliography*, Westport, Connecticut: Greenwood Press, 1993 [Contains essays on all the main aspects of Lispector's work by important scholars. A major contribution to Lispector studies]

A hora da estrela

Novel by Clarice Lispector

Throughout her work, and particularly in *A hora da estrela* (1977), Lispector dwells repeatedly on the process whereby the everyday, the linguistically, intellectually and emotionally comprehensible, are set adrift. These elements are stripped of cohesion and abandoned as the disorderly remnants of an old order now rendered unimaginable. In this new reality, the narrative's focus of attention is the unfolding subjectivity of the main characters, of the world seen through their often uncomprehending eyes. The familiar is abruptly defamiliarized and is subsequently destroyed. The characters, confronted with information they are unable to process, are perceptually impotent, and their condition becomes metonymical of their inadequate intellectual capacity, and even of their existence.

In *A Hora da estrela* all readerly expectations are challenged from the opening lines, or even prior to that, in the long list of possible alternative titles, some of which challenge the chronology and genre position of the work, depicting it as alternatively fact, pulp fiction, etc. Similarly, assertions concerning the absolute interpretative freedom allegedly bestowed upon the reader are problematized in the very moment of being made, by alternating with proclamations of an omnipotent authorial status as *Deus ex machina*, itself at once questioned by the visible spectacle of the author/narrator at points losing control over narrative events.

The plot, in so far as any plot can be said to survive Lispector's refusal of linearity in this as in other works, revolves around the female protagonist, Macabéa. Macabéa shares that common denominator linking all of of Lispector's main characters, namely a dangerous relationship with language, which she variously subverts and violates, but which also threatens to destroy her. Her identity is the product of a figure of speech which is not hers but the narrator's. The latter is not identified and on at least one occasion appears interchangeable with the equally elusive figure of Olímpico, Macabéa's boyfriend and assassin. The triangular relationship, indeed, is almost entirely linguistically enacted within a framework of words and word games. In this process, language becomes the instrument whereby each character may or may not acquire definition (and the possibility of survival) by means of the erasure of the other. Thus the male narrator's writing gradually emerges as the act of murdering Macabéa, and he variously experiences this murder as sin, crime or self-defence against his own existential evanescence.

The narrator and Olímpico's enduring presence depends on the successful linguistic establishment of a binary structure which will rephrase Macabéa as the absent counterpart to their present, tangible selves. He writes as an act of despair, which is also a sacrificial ritual with Macabéa as the burnt-offering, requiring his atonement (for the sacrifice of her life in exchange for his) by means of a sackcloth-and-ashes penance. Thus, at various points he confesses himself to be both guilty of and remorseful for her death. He fears that in writing about her he will vouchsafe her identity at the price of his own and to avoid this he must relocate her in antithesis to himself, previous to her linguistic or narrative murder. To this purpose, the descriptions of Macabéa as the narrative progresses witness his ever more insistent identification of her with images of evanescence, void and absence. Both the narrator and Olímpico, whether or not they are one and the same person, a point which remains debatable to the end, grow in garrulousness as Macabéa fades into silence. Their speech ever more obsessively affirms its power to save or destroy her, to bestow upon her a future or to consign her to oblivion.

Macabéa is twice condemned to death by the narrative and its narrator. She is first declared tubercular and on this occasion the narrator, experiencing one of several moments of frightening identification with her, an identification which threatens to carry him into her void, combats the danger by declaring himself in love with her as his *other* half. This means also his antithesis, the dumping ground for that which in him is vulnerable and whose danger he contains, consigning it to her and demarcating *it*, and *her*, as that from which he differs and is distanced. At this moment, when she is narratively condemned, Olímpico experiences her death and silence in conjunction with her. He combats the engulfing fusion by reasserting himself as her demiurge in a creator-creature pairing which grants him the power of imposing upon her a death of his choosing. He must become her murderer rather than allowing her to die of her own volition (illness) because only by becoming her murderer can he also become the inheritor of the life he stole from her.

He reiterates, only immediately to withhold, the power he possesses of awarding her life instead of death, and at that moment Macabéa, "grávida de futuro" (pregnant with a future) is run over by a car and dies. In the moment of her dying the narrator claims his right to resurrection, or possibly immortality, at the price of her death, and acknowledges his role in bringing the latter about. It is at this moment, however, that he paradoxically also acknowledges the universal nature of mortality, including his own death, foreseen in this moment of insight. The novel concludes with a question – will I die, too? – and with an answer – yes – which in a final linguistic sleight of hand appears as the affirmation of the ultimate negation, omnipresent death and omnipresent disappearance.

Lispector's fiction is peppered with moments of epiphany or revelation. Not, however, the revelation of transcendental or divine meaning, or solutions, but only the conclusion that any meaning attained is likely to be so temporary and dispersed as to relinquish the right to self-definition as meaningfulness. This realization, in works such as A hora da estrela, potentially leads to a temporary or indefinite suspension of sanity, or establishment of madness, and in particular of female madness, as the status quo.

The latter point elicits the question of whether or not it is possible to identify a measure of social and political concern in Lispector's work. This question is all the more pertinent given her undoubted preferential casting of women and the materially dispossessed as central to the process of subjective fragmentation at the heart of her fiction. There have been successful critical interpretations of her work based on the assumption of a preoccupation with both feminist and class issues and with the problem of disenfranchisement from power

in her writing; all these points are clearly central to A hora da estrela. For these reasons, but also, or possibly primarily for her quasi-Wittgensteinian investigation of the limitations of language in structuring understanding, Clarice Lispector continues to be one of the great voices of modernity within and outside Brazil.

MARIA MANUEL LISBOA

Editions

First edition: A hora da estrela, Rio de Janeiro: José Olympio, 1977
Translation: The Hour of the Star, by Giovanni Pontiero, Manchester: Carcanet, 1986

Further Reading

Cixous, Hélène, "The Hour of the Star: How Does One Desire Wealth or Poverty?" in Reading with Clarice Lispector, edited and translated by Verena Andermatt Conley, Minneapolis: University of Minnesota Press, and London: Harvester Wheatsheaf, 1990

DiAntonio, Robert E., "Clarice Lispector's A hora da estrela: the Actualization of Existential, Religious, and Sociopolitical Paradoxes," in his Brazilian Fiction: Aspects and Evolution of the Contemporary Narrative, Fayetteville: University of Arkansas Press, 1989

Fitz, Earl E., "Points of View in Clarice Lispector's A hora da estrela," Luso-Brazilian Review, vol. 19/2 (Winter 1982)

Gálvez-Breton, Mara, "Post-Feminist Discourse in Clarice Lispector's The Hour of the Star," in Splintering Darkness: Latin American Women Writers in Search of Themselves, edited by Lucía Guerra-Cunningham, Pittsburgh: Latin American Review Press, 1990

Guidin, Márcia Lígia, A hora da estrela – Clarice Lispector, São Paulo: Ática, 1994

Peixoto, Marta, "A hora da estrela," in Clarice Lispector: a Bio-Bibliography, edited by Diane E. Marting, Westport, Connecticut: Greenwood Press, 1993

Literacy Campaigns

Brazil

Paulo Freire was born in 1921 in Recife, a port on the north-eastern coast of Brazil that has had more than its share of poverty. As a young man, influenced by the Christian Personalist movement, he became passionately committed to the poor and their struggle to better themselves economically and educationally. This distinguished Brazilian educator is best known for his work in developing literacy campaigns in Third World countries such as his native Brazil, Angola, Guinea-Bissau, Nicaragua, Chile and Tanzania. None the less many of his ideas are applicable to the struggles of ethnic minority groups worldwide. In addition, Freire was special advisor in education to the World Council of Churches in Geneva, and prior to the military coup against the Allende government, he

was a UNESCO consultant at Chile's Institute of Research and Training in Agrarian Reform (ICIRA).

Paulo Freire's work with adult literacy began in the 1950s when he worked as a teacher and advocate among the people of the slums in his native Brazil. It was while he did this work that he became involved in literacy training, gradually focusing his attention on adult literacy, especially among the poor of Recife. Between 1947 and 1959, Freire's involvement with adult literacy intensified, resulting in his dissatisfaction with the traditional methods for dealing with illiteracy that posited an authoritarian relationship between teacher and pupil. His criticism of the prepared primers for literacy education caused him to conclude that such materials contained a hidden curriculum consisting of knowledge, attitudes, and values espoused by the dominant culture which illiterates were to learn in conjunction with the rudiments of literacy. In the early 1960s Freire plunged into various reform movements in northeast Brazil, having been given the responsibility of an adult literacy effort in Recife by its mayor, Miguel Arraes in 1962. These attempted reforms were centered on the Popular Culture Movement, which pushed for the democratization of culture through discussions (Freire's *culture circles*) on such themes as nationalism, remission of profits, economic development, and literacy. Moreover, students and activists like Freire attempted to raise class consciousness (Freire's famed *conscientización / conscientização*). Although incitement to revolt was never the direct objective of Freire as an educator, his work undeniably contained the seeds of social revolt because it gave the people an understanding of the oppressive reality of their lives. Between June 1963 and March 1964, Freire's literacy program was extended to the entire nation by Paulo de Tarso, Brazil's Minister of Education, and, subsequently Freire was appointed Secretary of Education and General Coordinator of the National Plan of Adult Literacy. Training programs, using the Freirean method for adult literacy education, were initiated in almost all the state capitals throughout Brazil (Rio Grande do Norte, São Paulo, Bahia, Sergipe, and Rio Grande do Sul). This national campaign was modeled after Cuba's literacy campaign of 1961, which had almost eliminated illiteracy in the island. But such endeavors ended abruptly with the fall of President João Goulart's government owing to a military coup in 1964. However, the Popular Culture Movement, together with the Supervisory Agency for Agrarian Reform (SUPRA), were successful in mobilizing rural and urban workers in northeastern Brazil. Literacy, however, remained the key to all the reform movements in northeast Brazil since only literates were permitted to vote.

Francisco Weffort, in his introduction to the Portuguese version of Freire's *Education as the Practice of Freedom* (1969) contends that there is a high correlation between illiteracy and socioeconomic stagnation, and maintains that the power elites of the country were purposely fostering this situation in order to maintain the status quo. At the center of Freire's writing and teaching lies a moral commitment to a set of democratic practices that engages all citizens in common governance. He posits that these practices can never be inherited but must be learned and relearned by each successive generation. In espousing these views, Freire emerged as one of the most outspoken proponents of the "critical pedagogy" movement. At the heart of this amalgam of educational philosophies lies a belief in the centrality of education in determining political and social relations. As practiced by Freire in countries throughout the Third World, the doctrines of critical pedagogy were used by colonized citizens to analyze their roles in relations of oppression and to devise programs for revolutionary change to provide a voice for the "culture of silence." The impoverished and oppressed elements in society were encouraged to look critically at their world in a dialogical encounter with others. When given the proper tools of literacy and critical awareness or consciousness of their situation, the downtrodden gradually perceive their personal and social reality and deal critically with it through social activism. Coming to a new awareness of self, a sense of dignity and identity, the once oppressed members of society are stirred by new hope – *liberated* both to speak and to act in a thoughtful and responsible

manner, *actively* transforming their environment rather than passively responding and adapting to changes and decisions made for them. Armed with such a critical perspective, once illiterate and powerless individuals seek to change the structures of society that had once served to oppress them. During the 1970s and 1980s the philosophies of critical pedagogy were adapted throughout the industrialized world as a means of addressing power imbalances there. As a result, much of the vocabulary of "empowerment," "dialogue," and "voice" has entered the lexicon of Western social reform movements. At the same time the principles of critical pedagogy have undergone significant modifications that adapt them to the needs of contemporary technocratic societies. Paulo Freire's principle of "education as cultural action" has been adapted to fit a variety of projects where learning forms part of a social conflict situation. Freire sees knowledge as embedded in social practice and inseparable from political life. His theories are thus highly relevant to those working in education and those concerned with the theology of liberation.

Despite its short-lived application in Brazil in the early 1960s, Freire and the Popular Culture Movement followed a specific methodology which met with a high degree of acceptance and success among the population. Visual aids were used to dramatize various issues under discussion among marginalized groups of the population in the famous "Centros Populares de Cultura" (Centers of Popular Culture) in Brazil. His specific work on education and literacy campaigns were geared toward the empowerment of the masses in order to become agents of social change. Freire developed his doctrine through a critique of what he called the "banking concept of education," the traditional method of making students ingest information passively, not allowing a critical response to the "deposits received, filed and stored." This stress on the passive storage of information further prevents the subject from applying it in a creative way and acting upon what was learned. He proposed instead a method of learning centered around each individual's experience, where the educator drops the role of the all-knowing paternalistic provider of knowledge and adopts a more humble role of "facilitator": a mediator between the students and the world, who proposes alternatives for finding solutions – solutions which ultimately will have to be chosen and executed by the students.

Subsidized, in part, by the United States-sponsored Alliance for Progress and the Aid for International Development (AID) program for his literacy project in Angicos, a city of the Rio Grande do Norte, Freire and his team were able to teach three hundred workers to read and write in forty-five days. After members of the Communist Party infiltrated the rank and file of the Catholic-led Popular Culture Movement, Freire transferred his populist method to the cultural extension service of the University of Recife. Paulo Freire the educator became the radical social reformist after the military coup in 1964 and his arrest and subsequent exile in Chile. After his twenty-year exile he moved first to Chile, then emigrated to the United States before returning to Brazil. In his *Pedagogy of the Oppressed* (1970), written a number of years after the Brazilian experience, Freire indeed shows himself to be concerned with education as a means for promoting revolutionary action, particularly in countries like Brazil where revolution appears to be the only means of bringing about adequate social and political change through the establishment of a truly participatory democracy.

More recently, Latin American liberation theologians have taken note of the work of Paulo Freire with Gustavo Gutiérrez openly praising Freire's Pedagogy of the Oppressed. Indeed, Freire's theological and educational ideas parallel those of Latin American theologians of liberation. On a number of occasions Freire refers to the Christian base communities (comunidades de base) that are prevalent in Brazil and sees his literacy methods as operative in their educational efforts. For example, in these communities there is a rereading of the gospel which makes it relevant to life in society, an emphasis on social justice issues affecting both the individual and the community, and an encouragement to think critically and to take an active part in shaping the future through discussion groups, literacy training, participation in the duties of citizenship and the exercise of free speech. And another liberation theologian, Juan Segundo, has adopted Freire's concept of conscientizing evangelization by viewing the gospel as a liberating interpretation of history in which men and women are the subjects rather than the objects of history. Of the connection between literacy training and evangelization Juan Segundo writes as follows in *The idea of God*: "An evangelization committed to man's liberation is deeply tied up with the new form of literacy training, i.e., one incorporated within a process of consciousness-raising . . . as a process of liberation . . . "

ELENA DE COSTA

See also entry on Augusto Boal

Further Reading

Primary Sources

Freire, Paulo, *Educação como pratica da liberdade*, Rio de Janeiro: Paz e Terra, 1967; translated as *Education, the Practice of Freedom*, London: Writers and Readers Publishing Cooperative, 1976

_____ *Pedagogy of the Oppressed*, translated by Myra Bergman Ramas, New York: Herder and Herder, 1970

_____ *Cultural Action for Freedom*, Cambridge, Massachusetts: *Harvard Educational Review* and Center for the Study of Development and Social Change, 1970; Harmondsworth: Penguin, 1972

_____ *Education for Critical Consciousness*, translated by Myra Bergman Ramos, New York: Seabury Press, 1973; London: Sheed and Ward, 1974 [includes *Education as the Practice of Freedom* and *Extension or Communication*]

_____ *Pedagogy in Process: the Letters to Guinea-Bissau*, translated by Carman St John Hunter, New York: Seabury Press, 1978

_____ *The Politics of Education: Culture, Power, and Liberation*, translated by Donald Macedo, South Hadley, Massachusetts: Bergin and Garvey, 1985

Freire, Paulo and Donaldo Macedo, *Literacy: Reading the Word and the World*, South Hadley, Massachusetts: Bergin and Garvey, 1987

Freire, Paulo and Antonio Faundez, *Learning to Question: a Pedagogy of Liberation*, translated by Tony Coates, New York: Continuum, 1989

Gutiérrez, Gustavo, *A Theology of Liberation: History, Politics and Salvation*, translated by Sister Claridad Inda and John Eagleson, Maryknoll, New York: Orbis Books, 1973

Segundo, Juan, *Our Idea of God*, translated by John Drury, Maryknoll, New York: Orbis Books, 1974

Shor, Ira and Paulo Freire, *A Pedagogy for Liberation: Dialogues on Transforming Education*, South Hadley, Massachusetts: Bergin and Garvey, 1987

Critical Studies

Arraes, Miguel, *Brazil: the People and the Power*, translated by Lancelot Sheppard, Harmondsworth: Penguin, 1969

Dave, R.H., A. Ouane and A.M. Ranaweera (editors), *Learning Strategies for Post-Literacy and Continuing Education in Brazil, Colombia, Jamaica, and Venezuela*, Hamburg: Unesco Institute for Education, 1986

Elias, John L., *Conscientization and Deschooling: Freire's and Illich's Proposals for Reshaping Society*, Philadelphia: Westminster Press, 1976

Livingstone, David (editor), *Critical Pedagogy and Cultural Power*, South Hadley, Massachusetts: Bergin and Garvey, 1987

McCann, Dennis, *Christian Realism and Liberation Theology: Practical Theologies in Creative Conflict*, Maryknoll, New York: Orbis Books, 1981

Walsh, Catherine E. (editor), *Literacy as Praxis: Culture, Language, and Pedagogy*, Norwood, New Jersey: Ablex, 1991

Cuba and Nicaragua

Each of the two popular socialist revolutions in Latin America (Cuba and Nicaragua) produced an aggressive and impressive literacy campaign that profoundly changed the educational and political nature of its respective population.

The Cuban Literacy Campaign was undertaken during an eight month period in 1961. It was the first of many national mobilizations that Castro would order and, indeed, it provided both a model and source of organizational and logistical training and experience for many subsequent national campaigns, including the famous sugar cane harvests. The program was directed primarily at adults. Its immediate goal was educational, but in a longer view it was political.

At the time of the Revolution, Cuba's population suffered from a 24% illiteracy rate, primarily in the rural sector. Fewer than 50% of the children between the ages of seven and fourteen attended school. Indeed, only about 12.8% of Cuba's 6.4 million citizens had received an education. Castro knew well the plight of the rural peasants and, in particular, their need for basic education. His view was simple: a country with a high illiteracy rate would be hard to govern. Thus, one of the new government's first priorities was to address the problem of illiteracy.

In April 1961, after a brief period of training, over 100,000 students were organized into literacy brigades and sent to all parts of the countryside. For adolescents (the campaign involved secondary school students from the age of thirteen), especially, the literacy campaign was an exciting event, that filled them with hope and a sense of adventure. Indeed, the process of learning was (and was certainly intended as) a two-way one since the more privileged urban young were to learn about the wretched conditons in which the rural population attempted to survive. Armed with books, tablets, and pencils, and under the direction of experienced teachers, these young brigades reduced the national illiteracy rate to an officially reported 3.9% in less than a year.

In addition to providing almost immediately a literate (in certain instances semi-literate) adult population, the literacy campaign produced an early social cement between young revolutionaries from the cities and the adult rural population. Moreover, the campaign provided both a national view of unity and purpose and martyrs since several young *brigadistas* were killed by counter-revolutionaries. In all, the literacy campaign to this day stands as one of the greatest accomplishments of the Castro government. That the Cubans understand the crusade's revolutionary importance is validated by the support and popularity of the Museum of Literacy in Havana. It should be noted that the campaign produced many written *testimonios* (Dora Alonso's *El año 61* [The Year 1961]; Araceli Aguililla's *Por llanos y montañas* [Across Plains and Up Mountains] and at least one entertaining and worthwhile novel in Manuel Pereira's *El capitán Veneno*, 1979 [Captain Poison].

The Nicaraguan Literacy Crusade began in March 1980, and lasted some five months. It was the first national project of the Sandinista government. It began with 85,000 teachers (of whom 60% were women), a figure that grew eventually to nearly 100,000. It shared characteristics and problems with the earlier Cuban campaign: formidable logistical obstacles because of the roughness of the terrain and the absence of any infrastructure and, on the positive side, the same determination to break down divisions between the urban young and the impoverished peasants. In the case of Nicaragua, the massive program launched in 1980 had long been contemplated by the Sandinista National Liberation Front (FSLN) prior to assuming power in 1979. In fact, it had been articulated as a political objective as early as 1969 by Sandinista leaders.

Under the direction of the Minister of Education, the Jesuit Fernando Cardenal (brother of the poet Ernesto Cardenal), with the collaboration of Brazilian educator Paulo Freire as consultant, the National Literacy Crusade was carefully planned and extensively supported through international agencies and foreign governments. It is difficult to overstate the immense fervour and commitment of those who participated as volunteers. Utilizing a military command structure, the crusade was organized into "brigades," "columns," and "squadrons." They took their fight against illiteracy to the various "fronts" of the "battlefield." Their primary weapon was a basic reader entitled *El amanecer del pueblo* [Dawn of the People].

When the Sandinistas took control of the government in 1979, Nicaragua's illiteracy rate was nearly 50%. In some rural areas it was as high as 90%. But government estimates at the end of the five-month crusade put the national level of illiteracy at only 13%. This stunning success resulted in the crusade winning the 1980 UNESCO Literacy Prize.

Unquestionably, the National Literacy Crusade was a major act of the Nicaraguan reconstruction. Similar in many ways to the Cuban Literacy Campaign some twenty years earlier, it forged a national consciousness by introducing enthusiastic urban youth to their country's rural poor. The crusade integrated previously excluded groups into the mainstream of the Revolution, and it helped strengthen emerging mass organizations that supported the Sandinista efforts. Viewed as a coalescing political event, the National Literary Crusade set the political and social tone for the subsequent years of Sandinista rule.

SAM L. SLICK

Further Reading

Arnove, Robert, *Education and Revolution in Nicaragua*, New York: Praeger, 1986

Black, George and John Bevan, *The Loss of Fear: Education in Nicaragua before and after the Revolution*, London: Nicaragua Solidarity Campaign, 1980

Bunck, Julie Marie, *Fidel Castro and the Quest for a Revolutionary Culture in Cuba*, University Park: Pennsylvania University Press, 1994 [Chapter 2, "Castro and the Children," concerns the literacy campaign]

Centro de Estudios Sobre América (editor), *The Cuban Revolution into the 1990s: Cuban Perspectives*, Boulder, Colorado: Westview Press, 1992

Fagen, Richard R., *The Transformation of Political Culture in Cuba*, Stanford, California: Stanford University Press, 1969

Gillette, Arthur, *Cuba's Educational Revolution*, London: Fabian Society, 1962

Hershon, Sheryl L. and Judy Butler, *And Also Teach Them to Read*, Westport, Connecticut: Lawrence Hill, 1983

MacGaffey, Wyatt and Clifford R. Barnett, *Cuba: Its People, Its Society, Its Culture*, Westport, Connecticut: Greenwood Press, 1974

Miller, Valerie, *Between Struggle and Hope: the Nicaraguan Literacy Crusade*, Boulder, Colorado: Westview Press, 1985

Literary Theory

Contrary to the aspirations of some of its its principal practicioners (e.g., Ángel Rama, Alejandro Losada, Antônio Cândido), literary theory has never encompassed the entire continent. A "Latin American" literary critical practice might more effectively be described as a fabric, the interwoven threads of which offer intricate patterns for analysis and re-elaboration. The threads to be pulled in its reading, by no means hanging loose, are to be chosen or unravelled by the individual analyst or appropriator, according to the sociological, cultural, ideological or literary perspective adopted.

The first, still contentious figure, Ángel Rama, provides a basic frame of the discursive fabric of Latin America, a structure whose elaboration Rama attributes to the labour of the intellectuals, the compilers of the cultural works, the "weavers, in the grand historical workshop of Latin American society." For Rama as well as for some of his contemporaries (e.g., Losada, Cândido), the operational unit in any critical approach is "Latin America," a conceptual whole they inherit from previous discourses but which they survey aware of its nature *qua* construct, as a project which demands the careful tracking down and identification of the diversity encompassed. This complex pattern leads Rama and Losada, drawing on the work of cultural anthropologists, to adopt regional and sub-regional units, the definition of which relies on the traditional dimensions of geography and ethnicity together with the more relevant aspects of historical and economic development. Their objective is to map the diversities that have been articulated and to form them into a global network; to write the literary history of the subcontinent while posing questions about its own chronology and periodization, to re-enact differently the colonial Utopian project not of discovering but of *writing* "Latin America." The means are the critic and the written word, a semiotic effect which from colonial times displaced the orality of pre-colonial Latin America. In the suggestive title of Rama's masterpiece, *La ciudad letrada*, 1984 [The Lettered City], published after his death, he reveals the writer's task of weaving and writing in the construction of society and culture in Latin America. According to Rama, the materiality of the word captures the ambiguity of cultural life in colonial and post-colonial Latin America: on the one hand, in its subjection to and perpetuation of authority; on the other, in its subversive potential arising from the multiple economical structures that decentralized power in colonial times. The word and its artificer, the writer, are the agents of violent displacement of the oral cultures though, paradoxically, they become the agents of transformation and survival of that repressed orality in a process Rama calls "transculturación" (transculturation). Transculturators like Gabriel García Márquez, João Guimarães Rosa and José María Arguedas perform the act of translating modernity by recreating the pre-Columbian orality rediscovered through the eyes of the innovating forces coming from abroad. To Rama, transculturation legitimates cultural modernity in Latin America in that it provides a solid source for the "independence," "originality" and "representativeness" of Latin American literature.

Ángel Rama's argument for modernity through the notion of transculturation resonates in some of his contemporaries, who also tackle the controversial issue of the originality of Latin America's critical production. To the Brazilian literary critic, Roberto Schwarz, modernity brings ideas to Latin America, specifically Brazil, which when placed in the context of the new soil become "misplaced" and fictitious. Schwarz exemplifies this process in his analysis of the discrepancy produced in Brazil by the establishment of the modern nation sustained by the structure of slavery. Misplacement of ideas produces a hierarchical society in which unequal access to education and the written word invalidates all claims of representativeness of the cultural production made by one class. The divide between the elites and the masses, between modernity and old systems constitutes for Schwarz the touchstone of the debate on cultural representation in Brazil. Together with one of his Brazilian contemporaries, Alfredo Bosi, Schwarz

problematizes the representativeness of the Brazilian literary canon in so far as it marginalizes other forms of cultural expression which they label as "cultura popular" (popular culture).

Recognizing the plurality inherent in cultural forms in Latin America and the abyss existing between intellectuals and the illiterate population ("o pesadelo da história" [history's nightmare] in Haroldo de Campos's words), other Brazilian literary critics, such as Silviano Santiago and de Campos himself, elaborate on the issue of the originality of Latin American literature through the notions of "entre-lugar" (in-betweenness) and "tradução" (translation). In a foundational article, "O entre-lugar do discurso latino-americano" [The In-Betweenness of Latin American Discourse], Santiago describes the Latin American writer as operating in a plural textual site traversed by different memories, different languages, different histories. The colonial encounter, Santiago contends, brings to the colonized an other history and an other culture which displace the native memory and culture. This displacement produces a feeling of "outsiderness" in the Latin American subject, who incorporates the new memory, in a replicating process, as a fiction going on in some other time, some other place. Being no longer either in the native *locus* or wholly assimilated to the new culture, the Latin American subject inhabits a place in-between, from which he interprets the universal literary tradition in a distinctive manner. He reads the signs of tradition capturing the plurality of meaning his in-betweenness allows him to perceive. His reading or translation of the tradition is "never an innocent one; it could never be so."

Relating the Latin American original and differential character to the Baroque experience of colonial times, to the mastery of complex semiotic codes ever since Latin American literature emerged, Haroldo de Campos pursues the creative character of Latin America through the development of the notion of translation as "transcriação" (transcreation), a notion he applies both to the general process of literary creation (cultural translation) and to the specific recreation of a foreign work of art in a new language and cultural context. Translation is for de Campos a means to *create* tradition, recreating the work of the other but also projecting one's own tradition into the tradition of the other, a process he pinpoints in writers such as Jorge Luis Borges and in his own translation project. In tune with the Mexican critic Octavio Paz, de Campos proposes a view of tradition as a constellation of "signs in rotation," in which synchronic and diachronic dialogues take place between writers. The Latin American author, they contend, selects his precursors from the universal literary repertoire and thus creates his own literary tradition, legitimate and representative of his own self.

The selection of a tradition is for the Argentine critic Ricardo Piglia a process the Argentine – or the Latin American writer – performs as an act of translation, as an appropriation of the culture of the other (the European culture) in such a way that the notion of originality and authorship are subverted. In his famous novel, *Nombre falso* (Assumed Name), Piglia enacts a literary plagiarism by introducing a short story allegedly written by Roberto Arlt as an original literary piece. The subtle play Piglia produces between the text and the paratext reveals to the reader the falseness of Piglia's contention. The attribution of authorship and originality, Piglia implies, is ultimately a subtle power-structure, clearly to be seen in the exclusive originality and superiority claimed as the property of "central," as distinct from "peripheric" cultures. Using the Borgesian stratagem of borrowing and recreating, and the intriguing plots of Roberto Arlt, Piglia (re)creates a detective quest which resembles the Latin American writer's search for original authorship and, resonantly, for the "ex-tradition of Latin America."

In an analogous detective search through the archives and images of the past, the Argentine literary critic Beatriz Sarlo interrogates modernity and its multifaceted aspects in Argentina. Her search keeps history close at hand in a two-directional process whereby history illuminates fiction and is in turn illuminated by it. Sarlo works with the images of Argentine fictional discourse and elaborates from them a new reading of tradition. In the textuality of the Argentine fabric, Sarlo gazes, for instance, at the desert and its emptiness as a generation of Argentine intellectuals saw it in order to account for the desire and necessity which led that generation to populate the pampa, to fill in the cultural void, to implant a tradition. Sarlo also looks at the image of the gaucho, mythical foundation of a past in order to sustain a rapidly advancing modernity. Fiction records, for Sarlo, those images and concerns which enable the critic to reconstruct both the past and, ultimately, the social imaginary of the nation.

The intricate relationship between fiction and critical discourse pursued by Sarlo illustrates an approach to Latin American literary theory at a microlevel of analysis, unravelling the threads of modernity which contributed in Latin America to the construction of the different nations. This micro-reading brings back on stage Ángel Rama's contention, now transposed into new dimensions, regarding the role of the word in the construction of Latin America, a task he judged as being still, and ever, in process, performed by the work of the Latin American critic. As the theorizings of the writers and critics discussed above seem to imply, a continuous thread in the yet-to-be compiled Latin American history of literary theory undoubtedly reveals the Janus-faced nature of this task: for Latin American theorists, the construction of literary theories is inextricably related to the contruction of Latin American identities.

ADRIANA SILVINA PAGANO

See also entry on Ricardo Piglia

Further Reading

Campos, Haroldo de, "Tradición, traducción, transculturación: historiografía y ex-centricidad," translated by Nestor Perlongher, in *Filología*, vol. 22/2 (1987)

____ "Da razão antropofágica: diálogo e diferença na cultura brasileira," in his *Metalinguagem e outras metas*, São Paulo: Perspectiva, 1992

Cândido, Antônio, *A educação pela noite e outros ensaios*, São Paulo: Ática, 1987

Iturri, Guillermo Mariaca, "El canon de la modernidad: Ángel Rama," *Casa de las Américas*, vol. 34/192 (July–September 1993)

Lienhard, Martin, Ineke Phaf and José Saravia Morales, "Alejandro Losada," in *Revista Iberoamericana*, vol. 43/160–61 (July–December 1992)

Paz, Octavio, *Los signos en rotación y otros ensayos*, Buenos Aires: Sur, 1965

Piglia, Ricardo, *Nombre falso*, Buenos Aires: Siglo XXI, 1975; as *Assumed Name*, translated by Sergio Waisman, Pittsburgh: Latin American Literary Review Press, 1995

____ *Crítica y ficción*, Santa Fe, Argentina: Universidad Nacional del Litoral, 1986

____ "Memoria y tradición," in 2° *Congreso ABRALIC*, Belo Horizonte, UFMG, 1 (1991)

Rama, Ángel, *Transculturación narrativa en América Latina*, Mexico City: Siglo XXI, 1982

____ *La ciudad letrada*, Hanover, New Hampshire: Ediciones del Norte, 1984

Santiago, Silviano, "O entre-lugar do discurso latino-americano," in his *Uma literatura nos trópicos*, São Paulo: Perspectiva, 1978

____ "A pesar de dependente, universal," in his *Vale quanto pesa*, Rio de Janeiro: Paz e Terra, 1982

Sarlo, Beatriz, "En el origen de la cultura argentina: Europa y el desierto. Búsqueda del fundamento," in 1° *Seminário Latino-Americano de Literatura Comparada*, Pôrto Alegre, Brazil: UFRGS, 1986

____ *Una modernidad periférica: Buenos Aires, 1920 y 1930*, Buenos Aires: Nueva Visión, 1988

Schwarz, Roberto, "Nacional por subtração," in *Que horas são?* São Paulo: Companhia das Letras, 1988

____ *Misplaced Ideas. Essays on Brazilian Culture*, translated by John Gledson, London and New York: Verso, 1992

Special Issues of Journals
Casa de las Américas, Havana, vol. 34/192 (July–September 1993) [Issue devoted to Ángel Rama]

Enrique López Albújar 1872–1966

Peruvian writer

There is a definite indigenist intent in the best-known of Enrique López Albújar's publications, *Cuentos andinos* [Andean Tales] and *Nuevos cuentos andinos* [New Andean Tales]. He is also the author of the regionalist novel *Matalaché* and shorter pieces. The latter work is linked to the urban realism that developed in Peru among members of the generation of 1954–55.

Tomás Escajadillo is insistent in his identification of López Albújar as founder of the movement of indigenist narrative, and in the difference in vision of the indigenous world as depicted by this writer and that by his countryman Ventura García Calderón, with whom in fact he has been compared frequently. When *Cuentos andinos* appeared, it was during a period of searching by both writers and public for a national literature in Peru, a reaction to the exoticism of Spanish American modernist works. There was a sense that the Indian, who was an unavoidable part of Latin American reality, had been treated in too picturesque or distant a manner until then. The stories of *Cuentos andinos* at times resemble novels in their condensed narrative style. Their language is brusque and direct, synthesizing thoughts and actions. While the author was an outsider to what he observed and described, readers sensed the depth and breadth of his sensitivity to Quechua reality. It is generally felt that the native population's psychology is not probed to a great degree, but it is skilfully suggested. The effect of the author's profession is seen in the way the oppression of the people is of less interest to him than is the observable behaviour of individuals, a behaviour which can be analyzed and evaluated for its correctness.

A spiritual follower of Manuel González Prada, López Albújar served as a bridge between the end-of-century Realists and the later *indigenistas*. He portrays neither horrors nor sentimental lamentation and does not stylize characters, thus giving greater narrative sensitivity to the world represented in the stories. Ideologically, López Albújar remained independent, but was essentially a liberal of the Durand group, believing in a liberal government. While his work as a judge did not allow him to make altogether positive observations about the Indians, they are nevertheless not portrayed as a depraved group and in fact are not even submissive, but rebellious. One senses that their pre-Columbian beliefs and ethics have survived even though the author still sees the need to integrate them into Western and Specifically Peruvian civilization. López Albújar's *indigenismo* is not Positivist, but rather is linked generally to criminal actions and individual cases. Despite the restricted perspective, the native characters are closer to being "flesh and blood" than those found in the works of earlier authors. In addition, they offer a more careful portrait of social organization through the protagonists.

López Albújar's Andean tales appear to have influenced works such as Ciro Alegría's *El Mundo es ancho y ajeno*, 1941 (*Broad and Alien is the World*). The second group of Andean stories may be less successful from a literary perspective, but as a whole they attribute greater social awareness to the Indians and their communities. This has been thought to be the result of the previous appearance of prose works by other Peruvian writers César Vallejo, José María Arguedas and Ciro Alegría.

Matalaché is considered to be the first *negrista* novel of Peru, and it earned the author the designation of a writer concerned with race and social equality. It is a little-studied work, significantly set in 1816, just prior to Peruvian independence. The parallel with human freedom and that of Latin America is evident. The intention to write a novel with historical content and social commitment is noted in the subtitle "Novela retaguardista" [Novel of the Rear Guard]. Although López Albújar did experiment with short compositions in the Futurist style of Marinetti, he ultimately opted for social concerns over aesthetic experiments of avant-garde writing. It may be the author's own mulatto background and experience which impressed racial concerns upon his writing. In any event, he was instrumental in making racial themes a legitimate part of Peruvian literature and national sentiment.

KATHLEEN N. MARCH

Biography

Born in Chiclayo, Peru, 23 November 1872. Spent childhood in Piura on northern coast of Peru. Studied law at the University of San Marcos, graduated in 1894. Founded the newspaper *El Amigo del Pueblo* [The Friend of the People]. Later wrote for important newspapers in Lima and Buenos Aires. Active in politics and imprisoned for a short time as a result of writing a poem that was considered insulting to General Cáceres. Practised law in Piura and Lima. Editor of *La Prensa*. Appointed judge in Huánuco in the Andes, 1917–23. Returned to Piura in 1923 and became Director of Cultural Education for a brief period. Appointed judge of the superior court in Tacna, 1931 and lived there until 1947 when he retired to Lima. Died in Lima, 6 March 1966.

Selected Works

Novels and Short Fiction

Cuentos andinos, Lima: Opinión Nacional, 1920
Matalaché, Piura: El Tiempo, 1928
Calderonadas, Chiclayo: El Tiempo, 1930
Nuevos cuentos andinos, Santiago de Chile: Ercilla, 1937
Las caridades de la Señora de Tordoya, Lima: Mejía Baca, 1955

Other Writings

Miniaturas; álbum de bellezas limeñas, Lima: Gil, 1895 [early verse]
De mi casona, Lima: Lux, 1924 [Memoirs of his childhood in Piura]
Los caballeros del delito, Lima: Compañia de Impressiones y Publicidad, 1936 [study of Peruvian banditry]
De la tierra brava: poemas afroyungas, Lima: Peruana, 1938 [poetry]
El hechizo de Tomayquichua, Lima: Peruanidad, 1943
Memorias, Lima: Villanueva, 1963 [memoirs]

Compilations and Anthologies

Los mejores cuentos, Lima: Patronato del Libro Peruano, 1957
La mujer Diógenes. Cuentos de arena y sol. Palos al viento, Lima: CONUP, 1972

Further Reading

Cáceres Cuadros, Tito, *Indigenismo y estructuralismo en López Albújar*, Lima : UNSA, 1981
Cornejo, Raúl Estuardo, *López Albújar, narrador de América: trayectoria vital*, Madrid: Anaya, 1961
Escajadillo, Tomás G., *La narrativa de López Albújar*, Lima: CONUP, 1972

Ramón López Velarde 1888–1921

Mexican poet and essayist

Modern Mexican poetry begins with Ramón López Velarde. He is undoubtedly one of the most genuine poetic voices to inhabit that hard-to-classify period in Spanish American literature that stretches from Modernism to the vanguard poets. As a major representative of Spanish American *postmodernismo* (that is, the period that followed *Modernismo*), he is the first writer in Mexico to thematize the Mexican province in a new way. But he ought not be reduced to being the poet of the province. López Velarde was above all the creator of a new poetic language; this alone distinguishes him from González Martínez, for example. The value of his verse resides in having rescued from oblivion the simple and the minuscule by means of a deceivingly prosaic language. If, in his haiku, José Juan Tablada delves into the small and colourful, and Carlos Pellicer manages to compose beautiful symphonies to nature, López Velarde turns inward; consequently, the themes of his poetry are his conscience, his anguish, his vacillations, his childhood memories, his feelings of guilt, etc. His poetry constitutes one of the most dramatic confessions in Mexican letters. As regards the themes, they were not new to Mexican poetry; what was new was the sensibility with which he approached them. One theme stands out among all: love, or, as Octavio Paz, one of his best critics states, "la pasión de amor" (the passion of love). Other prominent themes are women, sensuality, religion and death. Though López Velarde was not a great reader, he felt the influence of Baudelaire, Lafforgue, Góngora, Quevedo, Darío, Herrera y Reissig, Francisco González León (1862–1945) – a minor Mexican poet who wrote about life in the provinces – and especially Leopold Lugones, from whom he learned to create surprising metaphors by avoiding clichés and commonplaces.

López Velarde's literary production is rather small, since he published only two books of poetry in his lifetime: *La sangre devota*, 1916 [Consecrated Blood] and *Zozobra*, 1919 [Anguish]. Posthumous works include his collection of poetry *El son del corazón*, 1932 (*Song of the Heart*), and two prose collections: *El minutero*, 1923 [The Minute Hand], and *El don de febrero y otras prosas*, 1952 [February's Gift and Other Prose Writings]. Generally speaking, *La sangre devota* is characterized by a partially *modernista* atmosphere which gradually becomes a timid exercise in avant-garde experi-

mentation via the use of obscure metaphors and colloquialisms in the second half of the book. In *Zozobra* and *El son del corazón*, clearly more complex texts than *La sangre devota*, López Velarde reaches the maturity of his style not by abandoning the themes of province, woman or impossible love, but by complicating them formally by means of new avant-garde imagery. In all of his literary production, however, there are certain paramount concerns that never leave the poet's imagination. The most significant is the struggle that the lyric voice wages between the thorough idealization of woman, woman as the pure love object, and woman as primarily a creature of flesh and blood who makes the staunchly Catholic López Velarde unreservedly give in to the temptations of the flesh. From this perennial conflict, in effect, emanate not only the attendant dilemma of an incessant wavering between good and evil but also the linguistic contradictions as well as the unusual juxtapositions of adjectives which are part and parcel of his style.

The most vivid incarnation of the poetic voice's spiritual predicament in the early poems (written between 1905 and 1912 and not included in *La sangre devota*) and in the poems of *La sangre devota* is Fuensanta, an almost mystical figure from the province who arguably becomes the archetype of woman in the poetry of López Velarde. Fuensanta's real name was Josefa de los Ríos, and she had a love relationship with the poet which ended abruptly and definitively. In his verse, she represents impossible love; the lyric voice describes her as a chaste and pure woman very much like the ideal woman of the courtly love tradition. It is not an accident, therefore, that critics have found parallels between the poetry of López Velarde and that of his compatriot, Amado Nervo. *La sangre devota* has been portrayed as a passionate spiritual biography. In the process of the transfiguration of Fuensanta, the poet does not know whether to venerate her or to desire her, for she in fact simultaneously embodies mystical temptation and physical attraction. This is especially evident in "En las tinieblas húmedas" [In the Moist Darkness], where a state of absolute confusion and conflict prevail, and also in "Pobrecilla sonámbula [Poor Sleepless One], where Fuensanta is depicted as an intangible being, a phantom who walks in her sleep. Thematically, in López Velarde's first poetic phase eroticism is always associated with religious and liturgical themes; hence, verbs such as to venerate, to revere, or to canonize, as well as nouns belonging to the Catholic rite and to the Bible, abound. Formally, this first phase is characterized by the use of an intimate and authentic language very different from the *modernistas*' often superficial expression. Among the best poems of *La sangre devota* are "Mi prima Agueda" [My Cousin Agueda], "¿Qué será lo que espero? [I Wonder What It Is I Want?] and "Y pensar que pudimos . . ." [To Think We Could Have . . .].

Three years elapsed between the publication of *La sangre devota* and *Zozobra*. During this time López Velarde moved to the capital and abandoned politics, utterly disillusioned after the death of his friend and hero Francisco L. Madero. Fuensanta and the province continue to be present in *Zozobra* and *El son*, but they are transformed. The erotic aspects of love which begin to surface in a number of poems of *La sangre devota* seem to overcome the poetic voice in these two texts as the lyric succumbs to the pleasures of the flesh in a desperate attempt to attain impossible love. Of the many women who are poeticized in these two collections of poems, María Nevares, with whom López Velarde corresponded for a good many years, plays a fundamental role. *Zozobra* represents the poet's highest literary achievement. It has been called López Velarde's most personal book. One of the best poems of the collection is the first one, "Hoy como nunca" [Today as Never Before], which functions as a type of thematic bridge between *Zozobra* and *La sangre devota*. Here the lyric voice invokes Fuensanta and reminisces about the past as he sinks deeper and deeper into a sea of desperation; this poem also introduces the theme of death, one of the most prevalent themes in López Velarde's second poetic phase. In *Zozobra* the poet reacts strongly against sentimentalism. This is especially discernible in the abundance of rare adjectives, juxtapositions of dissimilar realities, combinations of surprising words and horrific images of death as in the best paintings of Hieronymus Bosch. Some of the most successful poems of *Zozobra* are "La mancha púrpura [The Purple Stain], "Tierra mojada" [Wet Land], "El retorno maléfico" [Evil Return], "Hormigas" [Ants] and "La última odalisca" [The Last Odalisque], the last of these being one of López Velarde's most hermetic poems.

El son del corazón represents the final stage in the spiritual and aesthetic evolution of the artist. The presence of tangibly identified women disappears, and the women who do appear, such as Ligia and Zoraida, constitute symbolic representations of the now distant Fuensanta, who is not mentioned by name. In the poems of *El son* woman is in effect spiritualized and made less concrete. Availing himself of cosmic images, the more mature and reflexive poet re-elaborates the major themes of his previous works. There is a certain attitude of resignation even, as the lyric voice comes to accept the corruptibility of the flesh. The outstanding poem of *El son* is "La suave patria" [The Gentle Homeland], though "Treinta y tres" [Thirty Three] and "El sueño de los guantes negros" [The Dream of the Black Gloves] are equally excellent compositions. Going back to Othón before him, López Velarde evokes in "La suave patria" not the most typical but rather the most intimate and lyrical aspects of the homeland. In this sense, López Velarde was much more than the poet of the Mexican Revolution, as José Vasconcelos liked to think.

In *El minutero* and *El don de febrero* are contained a series of prose pieces that López Velarde wrote for different Mexican magazines and newspapers. According to Allen W. Phillips, López Velarde's prose is not inferior to his poetry: rather, thematically and formally both poetry and prose run parallel to each other. Phillips underlines above all the lyrical quality of López Velarde's prose and links it to the prose writings of Martí instead of to the most flamboyantly fancy compositions of Darío. The poet's prose writings encompass prose poems, two short stories, literary and political articles and other prose pieces that are more difficult to classify. In the end, it must be clear that this part of López Velarde's literary production, and especially his prose poems, offer an exceptional insight into the major aspects of his poetry.

J. AGUSTÍN PASTÉN B.

See also entry on José Juan Tablada

Biography

Born in Jerez (now Ciudad García) in the state of Zacatecas, Mexico, 15 June 1888. First born of nine children. Educated at the Seminario Conciliar de Zacatecas, 1901–02; the Seminario Conciliar de Santa María de Guadalupe de Aguascalientes, 1902–05; and the Instituto Científico y Literario de Aguascalientes, 1905–07. Entered law school in San Luis Potosí in 1908 and graduated in 1911. While a student co-founded the little magazine, *Bohemio*. Contributed to various newspapers and from 1909 his signature became well known in the provinces. Moved to Mexico City shortly after graduating and spent the rest of his life there. Contributed articles to several metropolitan journals and was active also in the administration of Cultura, an important publishing house for intellectuals of the period. Died prematurely of bronchial-pneumonia in 1921.

Selected Works

Poetry

La sangre devota, Mexico City: Revista de Revistas, 1916
Zozobra, Mexico City: México Moderno, 1919
El son del corazón, Mexico City: Bloque de Obreros Intelectuales, 1932; as *Song of the Heart*, translated by Margaret Sayers Peden, Austin: University of Texas Press, 1995

Prose

El minutero, Mexico City: Imprenta Murguía, 1923
El don de febrero y otras prosas, edited by Elena Molina Ortega, Mexico City: Imprenta Universitaria, 1952

Compilations and Anthologies

Obras completas, Mexico City: Nueva España, 1944
Poesías completas y El minutero, edited by Antonio Castro Leal, 8th edition, Mexico City: Porrúa, 1983
"La suave patria" y otros poemas, edited by Emilio de Armas, Havana: Editorial Arte y Literatura, 1983
Obras, edited by José Luis Martínez, augmented 2nd edition, Mexico City: Fondo de Cultura Económica, 1990

Further Reading

Clark, Stella T., "La realidad desfamiliarizada en la poesía de Ramón López Velarde," *Hispania* 2 (1988)
De la Fuente, Carmen, *López Velarde: su mundo intelectual y afectivo*, Mexico City: Federación Editorial Mexicana, 1971
Espejo, Beatriz, "Ramón López Velarde, un pesimista lujurioso," *Revista Iberoamericana* 148–49 (1989)

Gálvez de Tovar, Concepción, *Ramón López Velarde en tres tiempos*, Mexico City: Porrúa, 1971

Leiva, Raúl and Jorge Ruedas, *La prosa de López Velarde*, Mexico City: UNAM, 1971

Noyola Vázquez, Luis, *Fuentes de Fuensanta. La ascención de López Velarde*, Mexico City: La Impresora, 1947

Molina Ortega, Elena, *Ramón López Velarde. Estudio biográfico*, Mexico City: Imprenta Universitaria, 1952

Monterde, Francisco, "Ramón López Velarde y la provincia," *Cuadernos Americanos* 3 (1974)

Murray, Frederic W., *La imagen arquetípica en la poesía de Ramón López Velarde*, Chapel Hill: University of North Carolina Press, 1972

Paz, Octavio, "El camino de la pasión," in *Cuadrivio*, Mexico City: Joaquín Mortiz, 1965 [One of the most lucid analyses of López Velarde's poetry]

Phillips, Allen W., "Una amistad literaria: Tablada y López Velarde," *Nueva Revista de Filología Hispánica* 3–4 (1961)

____ *Ramón López Velarde, el poeta y el prosista*, Mexico City: Instituto Nacional de Bella Artes, 1962 [Indubitably the best comprehensive study on López Velarde's poetry and prose to date]

____ "Otra vez Fuensanta: despedida y reencuentro," *Revista Iberoamericana*, vol. 78 (1972)

Ruiz Soto, Alfonso, "Los poemas en prosa de López Velarde," *Cuadernos Americanos* 12 (1988)

Segovia, Tomás, "Ramón López Velarde o el amor más allá de la muerte," *Vuelta* 150 (1989)

Suárez, Bernardo, "El impresionismo en la prosa de Ramón López Velarde," *Cuadernos Americanos* 2 (1974)

Villaurrutia, Xavier, "Encuentro con Ramón López Velarde," *El libro y el pueblo* 12 (1934)

Zaid, Gabriel, "Un amor imposible de López Velarde," *Vuelta* 110 (1985)

Carlos Loveira 1882–1928

Cuban prose writer

Perhaps because his own life was dedicated to the workers' struggles of his time, Carlos Loveira was able to expose – as were few other writers of his generation – the evils of the incipient Republic: the favouritism, the economic dependence, the dishonesty and corruption of those in power, the administrative incompetence and, in particular, the Cuban people's feeling of frustration over the failure of their struggle.

One of his first books, *De los 26 a los 35: lecciones de la lucha obrera*, 1917 [From 1926 to 1935: Lessons of the Workers' Struggle], is, in a sense, a foretaste of his works of fiction, in which autobiographical details abound. In it he advocates social changes, but considers that all change should be gradual and non-violent; he rejects the introduction of foreign ideologies into Latin America.

His Naturalist novels, in which scenes of local customs abound, portray the social problems of Cuba in the first decades of the 20th century. Often the thesis the author tries to express breaks into the discourse with digressions and observations which render the characters lifeless and slow down the narrative. *Los inmorales* [The Immoral Ones], Loveira's first novel, appeared in the Havana journal *Cuba Contemporánea* (1913–27). According to the author himself, he wrote the novel as propaganda in favour of divorce, and it is a clear attack on the prevailing social and economic order and the hypocrisy of contemporary moral conventions. This magazine also published his second novel *Generales y doctores*, 1920 [Generals and Doctors], in which he satirizes the ruling class but fails to give an objective perspective because he turns it into a sermon on what he considers to be the solutions to the country's problems; the thesis drowns the plot. Similarly *Los ciegos*, 1922 [The Blind], is a novel expressed in the pamphleteering tones of Socialist propaganda, in which the workers are depicted as

idyllic characters. In *La última lección* 1924 [The Last Lesson], he criticizes the position of women and advocates their emancipation. His last novel, *Juan Criollo*, 1927 [John the Creole] is regarded as the best of his literary works. Here the characters develop more independently and the omniscient author does not interrupt the discourse so much. In this novel Loveira also discards the authoritarian tone which characterizes his previous works and the style is lighter.

The failures which mark Cuba's political history: the Ten Years War (1868–78), thwarted by the Zanjón pact; US intervention in the War of Independence which, in Loveira's opinion, delayed the natural process of historical evolution of Cuban nationality, mark his work with a strong pessimistic tone. His deterministic world view also influenced the creation of his characters whose attitude and evolution are determined by their social class. This feeling of frustration, which was shared by other authors of the period, was also due to the introduction of the Platt Amendment, which allowed the US to intervene in Cuba's political problems whenever it wished; a humiliating Amendment which left a feeling of great bitterness in the intellectuals of the day, who were even more embittered by the second North American intervention of 1906.

Another characteristic of Loveira's novels, particularly noticeable in *Juan Criollo*, is eroticism, through which the author portrays the vices of that time: corruption and prostitution, abuse by the rich and powerful, orphanhood. Eroticism is shown as an evasion, as national escapism. The author seems to say that through sex his characters find consolation to appease their inner frustration, born of the lack of faith in the future of the country and its people and most of all in the lack of national identity. In his novels, and especially in this last one, the author tries to answer his agonizing question: "Why is Cuba like this?"

In Loveira's novels an intense criticism of all the social institutions of the country, especially the Catholic Church, is apparent. In short, the author seems to say that every Republican institution perpetuates the legacy of corruption bequeathed to it by centuries of colonial rule. He realizes that a republic cannot be built on the evils of a colony. Loveira's characters, disillusioned and worn out by years of struggle and frustration, react with the cynicism and desperation of a society whose national conscience is in crisis. Loveira offers no hope of this crisis being overcome. His characters do not transcend social conditions, they are anti-heroes, roguish – picaresque elements are particularly evident in his last novel – who allow themselves to be carried on the current of opportunism and, as in *Lazarillo de Tormes*, they shelter in any port, degraded by the very society they denounce and reject. His novels cover a historic period when the Republican conscience was being shaped, and even today they are relevant as a literary metaphor to analyse the problems of Cuban society and people. Loveira gradually brought these problems into the open in all his work, finally summing them up in the character of Juan Criollo, who, for the author, was a symbol of Cuba.

María L. Negrín

translated by Patricia James

Biography

Born in El Santo, Santa Clara, Cuba, 21 March 1882. Of humble origin. Father died when Carlos was three years old. Brought up by the family for whom his mother worked as a cook; went to New York with them and there became a street vendor of sweets and fruit. At the age of sixteen joined up and returned to Cuba to fight for independence. At the end of the war he worked on the construction of the central railway. Also worked on the building of the Panama Canal. Returned to Cuba in 1908 and founded the Cuban League of Railway Employees in 1910. Founded the trade paper *El ferrocarrilero* [The Railway Worker] and published other short-lived newspapers and magazines. Left for Yucatán in 1913 where he created the Department of Labour for this state. Became Secretary of the Pan-American Labour Federation with headquarters in Washington, DC. In 1917 returned to Cuba for good as Head of the Department of Colonization and Labour of the Ministry of Agriculture. Member of the Academy of Philosophy and Art, 1926. Died 26 November 1928.

Selected Works

Novels
Los inmorales, Havana: Cuba Contemporánea, 1919
Generales y doctores, Havana: Cuba Contemporánea, 1920
Los ciegos, Havana: Imprimería El Siglo XX, 1922
La última lección, Havana: Imprimería y Papelería de Rambla Bouza, 1924
Juan Criollo, Havana: Cultural, 1927

Other Writings
El movimiento obrero en los Estados Unidos, Washington, DC: The Law Reporter, 1915
La Federación Panamericana del Trabajo, Washington, DC: The Law Reporter, 1916
El socialismo en Yucatán, Washington, DC: The Law Reporter, 1916
De los 26 a los 35: lecciones de la lucha obrera, Washington, DC: The Law Reporter, 1917
"Un gran ensayista cubano: Fernando Lles," *Anales de la Academia Nacional de Artes y Letras*, vol. 10 (1926)
"Adrián del Valle: escritor y periodista de Cuba," *Cuba Contemporánea*, vol. 43/71 (1926)

Further Reading

Loveira's work is not widely read outside Cuba; hence the paucity of critical material in English.

Aguirre, Mirta, "Carlos Loveira. *Generales y doctores*," *Cuba Socialista*, Havana, vol. 3/21 (May 1963)
Herrera, Lourdes S., *La novelística de Carlos Loveira*, New York: Las Américas, 1983
Marqués, Sarah, *Arte y sociedad en las novelas de Carlos Loveira*, Miami: Universal, 1977
Owre, J. Riis, "*Juan Criollo*, after Forty Years," *Journal of Inter-American Studies*, vol. 9 (1967)
Pérez Firmat, Gustavo, *The Cuban Condition: Translation and Identity in Modern Cuban Literature*, Cambridge and New York: Cambridge University Press, 1989 [Chapter on *Juan Criollo*]

Dulce María Loynaz 1902–

Cuban poet, prose writer and literary critic

In common with the work of so many other women writers in Latin America, that of Dulce María Loynaz has only recently been recognised and brought to the attention of a wider reading public. Above all, being awarded the highly prestigious Cervantes Prize for Literature in 1992, helped to rescue her work from the oblivion in which it had lain since the 1950s. In the course of that decade, persuaded by a supportive husband, she published most of what she had written up to that point in Spain where her work then enjoyed a brief popularity in literary circles. She herself was partly to blame if her name was subsequently forgotten, at least in her homeland, because she expressed hostility to the Cuban Revolution by holding herself aloof and declaring (incorrectly) that she was no longer writing. Age and the changed circumstances of her country, she said, had caused her inspiration to dry up. As with other Latin American women writers of her generation, class and religion were in conflict with Loynaz's feminism. Her patrician background, coupled with her Catholicism prevented her from appreciating the real gains made by Cuban women after the Revolution. Thus unlike, say, Renée Méndez Capote, another Cuban woman writer of same class and generation but with progressive political views, Loynaz was not able to adapt to the new situation and to give younger women writers in Cuba a support from which they might well have benefited. This is because women's progress in the socio-economic sphere after 1959 was not matched by more prestige in what remains to this day a largely white and male-dominated sphere of letters.

Loynaz is best known, and perhaps rightly so, as a poet. Her poetry tends to be inward-looking but this does not prevent her from tackling grand themes such as love of country. Her patriotism is passionately felt, in that her family history is inseparable from the founding of the Cuban state. Loynaz's father, General Enrique Loynaz del Castillo, fought in the second war of Independence against the Spanish (1895–98), and she later edited his memoirs. She was born in the year in which Cuba became, theoretically at least, an independent country. These were the factors that prevented her from taking the easy way out after the Cuban Revolution for, unlike her second husband, she was not prepared to leave Cuba. In writing what are effectively love poems to her island, the intimate tone characteristic of Loynaz's verse saves them from the pomposity and empty rhetoric which often mars poetry of this kind. Understandably, the prose poem "Isla mía" [My Island] from *Poemas sin nombre*, 1953 (*Poems without Name*), is the most famous in this category, together with "El Almendares" [The Almendares] from the collection *Juegos de agua* [Water Play]. In "Isla Mía," in particular, she applies to Cuba a wide range of cultural references from the Bible and Greek mythology. In so doing, however, she does not show the cultural subservience towards Europe characteristic of earlier generations of Latin American writers. Hers is a self-confident blend of images from different sources in a poem which shows also a loving and knowledgeable regard for nature.

Loynaz was a feminist, and overtly so in speeches and articles devoted to other Spanish American women poets. But in her poetry such feelings are expressed covertly and therefore a feminist reading is only one of several possible interpretations. The emphasis on liquidity in the poems of *Juegos de agua* is relevant to the argument advanced by the French philosopher Luce Irigaray in *Ce Sexe qui n'en pas un*, 1977 (*This Sex Which is Not One*). Here she associates femaleness and liquidity, referring to the need to accept the changeable movements of liquids as appropriate metaphors for female discourse. This line of thought can be applied most fruitfully to Loynaz's creative work. A theme of her poetry, related to her condition as a woman, is a yearning for freedom frustrated by forms of enclosure. Release comes from the creative act itself, as is made clear in the poem from *Juegos de agua* that begins with the lines "I am free in my verse, it is my sea." On the other hand, many poems from this collection such as "Aquarium," "Water Play," and "Water in the Park" express the poet's frustration over her incarceration.

Both the water imagery and the theme of imprisonment appear also in Loynaz's bold, avante-garde novel, *Jardín* [Garden], a work that she wrote over a period of several years (1928–35). Her approach here is decidedly feminist because she rejects the realist novel with its insistence on plot, characterisation and sequential time as inappropriate to her purpose. In the Prelude to the novel she writes: "This is the incoherent and monotonous story of a woman and a garden. Unlike Einstein's theories, time and space do not exist. Garden and woman are in any meridian of the world – the most curved or the most taut. And on any level – the highest or the lowest – of time's circumference. There are many roses." Such a statement, dangerously essentialist for contemporary feminists, shows in the context of its period a boldness belied by the fact that she made no attempt to publish this work until 1951. *Jardín*, described by the author as a "lyrical novel," is in many ways deliberately obscure, although a knowledge of Loynaz's poetry helps readers to unravel its meaning. In any event, certain points can be grasped very readily: the writer rejects the modern world that is swallowing up nature (expressed, of course, by the garden); the protagonist, Barbara, is isolated; she yearns for freedom but ends up marrying and "settling down." At the end of the novel Barbara seeks to return to her garden, but it is too late: her condition is irrevocably post-lapsarian, and she cannot return to the (barbaric) Eden she abandoned for a more "civilised" world (Europe). All that escapes destruction is a lizard, a hint that a new start is possible. *Jardín* is a bold experimental novel for a woman to have written at this time in Latin America, and for this reason it is unfortunate that Loynaz allowed it to collect dust in a drawer for so many years.

Winning the Cervantes prize has provoked an unprecedented surge of interest in Loynaz's production and a growing number of her works has been either hastily reprinted or assembled for publication. Yet to come are English translations of her work, and the seriously scholarly attention that it undoubtedly deserves.

VERITY SMITH

Biography

Born in Havana, Cuba, 10 December 1902. Educated by tutors at home; attended the University of Havana, doctorate in civil law, 1927. Married twice: 1) her cousin, Enrique de Quesada y Loynaz in 1938 (divorced in 1943); 2) the social columnist, Pablo Álvarez de Cañas in 1946 (died in 1974). After the Cuban Revolution embarked on history of El Vedado (residential district of Havana), but her failing eyesight is making it difficult for her to finish it. TV documentary, "Una mujer que no existe" [A Non-Existent Woman] shown on Cuban television in 1990. Member of the Cuban Academy of the Language, 1959; Corresponding Member, Royal Academy of the Spanish Language, 1968, Emeritus Member, Cuban Union of Artists and Writers (UNEAC). Awarded the Cross of Alfonso X (Spain), 1947; Cuban National Prize for Literature, 1987; Miguel de Cervantes Prize, 1992. Centre for Information and Promotion of the work of the Loynaz family opened in Pinar del Río, Cuba, 1990.

Selected Works

Poetry

Versos, 1920–1938, Havana: Úcar García, 1938
Juegos de agua, Madrid: Editora Nacional, 1947
Poemas sin nombre, Madrid: Aguilar, 1953; as *Poems without Name*, translated by Harriet de Onís, Havana: Editorial José Martí, 1993

Carta de amor a Tut-ank-Amen, Madrid: Nueva Imprenta Radio, 1953

Obra lírica. Versos (1928–1938), Madrid: Aguilar, 1955

Últimos días de una casa, Madrid: Imprenta Soler Hermanos, 1958

La novia de Lázaro, Madrid: Betania, 1991

Poemas náufragos, Havana: Letras Cubanas, 1992

Bestiarium, Havana: Ministerio de Cultura y UNEAC, 1992

Novel

Jardín, Madrid: Aguilar, 1951; Barcelona: Seix Barral, 1992

Other Writings

Un verano en Tenerife, Madrid: Aguilar, 1958; Havana: Letras Cubanas, 1994

Yo fui feliz en Cuba . . . : los días cubanos de la Infanta Eulalia, Havana: Letras Cubanas, 1993

Ensayos literarios, Salamanca: Ediciones Universidad de Salamanca, 1993

Fe de vida. Evocación de Pablo Álvarez de Cañas, Pinar del Río, Cuba: Ediciones Hermanos Loynaz, 1994

Compilations and Anthologies

Poesías escogidas, edited by Pedro Símon, Madrid: Visor, 1993

Poesía completa, Havana: Letras Cubanas, 1993

Antología lírica, edited by María Asunción Mateo, Madrid: Espasa Calpe, 1993

Further Reading

Araújo, Nara, "El alfiler y la mariposa," *Unión*, Havana, vol. 7/20 (July–September 1995)

Campuzano, Luisa, "Últimos textos de una dama: crónicas y memorias de Dulce María Loynaz," *Casa de las Américas* 201 (October–December 1995)

González Castro, Vicente, *La hija del general*, Havana: Letras Cubanas, 1991

Loynaz, Dulce María, *Dulce María Loynaz. Premio de literatura en lengua castellana Miguel de Cervantes 1992*, Madrid: Ministerio de Cultura, 1993

Núñez, Ana Rosa (editor), *Homenaje a Dulce María Loynaz, Premio Cervantes 1992*, Miami: Universal, 1993

Rodríguez, Ileana, *House/Garden/Nation: Space, Gender, and Ethnicity in Post-Colonial Latin American Literature by Women*, translated by Rodríguez and Robert Carr, Durham, North Carolina: Duke University Press, 1994 [Chapter on *Jardín*]

Simón, Pedro (editor), *Dulce María Loynaz*, Havana: Casa de las Américas y Letras Cubanas, 1991 [Comprehensive and well-documented volume in the Valoracíon Múltiple series, but the articles on the author's work show a marked critical conservatism]

Smith, Verity, "'Eva sin Paraíso': una lectura feminista de *Jardín* de Dulce María Loynaz," *Nueva Revista de Filología Hispánica*, Mexico, vol. 41/1 (1993)

Special Issues of Journals

Anthropos, Barcelona, edited by Nara Araújo, 151 (1993)

Leopoldo Lugones 1874–1938

Argentine poet and prose writer

The literature of Leopoldo Lugones is inextricably linked with Spanish American *Modernismo*. Together with José Martí and Rubén Darío, Lugones is considered to be one of the principal figures of that literary movement. His early poetry had a far-reaching influence both within Argentina and abroad. Lugones began his literary career as a poet, but he later came to be the most productive author of *modernista* prose fiction. Likewise, he wrote extensive essays, political commentaries and historical treatises, as well as literary and cultural analyses. His strong and wide ranging ideological stances – from socialism in his youth to fascism in his later years – are readily apparent in his writing.

As a poet he gained almost immediate prominence with his 1897 collection *Las montañas del oro* [The Golden Mountains]. Although to the present-day reader *modernista* poetry, and in particular that of Lugones, seems overcharged with baroque language, exotic imagery, and overstated metaphors, at the time of its publication *Las montañas* was highly praised as being poetically innovative and, more importantly, for defining the exalted role of the poet within society. The

volume is loosely modeled after a poetic journey that takes the reader on a Dantean voyage from the summit to the darkest depths, and back again into the light. The poem's *modernista* characteristics are not only evident in the language and style of the verse, but also in the traditional poetic imagery that is skillfully enmeshed with urban, technological and scientific images of a new age. Lugones continued his calculated experimentation with lexical and rhythmic form in subsequent volumes that were equally astounding examples of his skill for poetic composition. *Los crepúsculos del jardín*, 1905 [Garden Twilights] is widely considered to be one of the texts from the period that most thoroughly exemplifies the conventions of *Modernismo*. The poet's deliberate focus on exotic scenes, intense emotion and physical love all combine to make the text highly erotic in nature. *Lunario sentimental*, 1909 [Sentimental Lunar Calendar] marked the beginning of Lugones's break with *Modernismo*. More than just a collection of poetry, *Lunario* comprises a rather eclectic assortment of poems, short stories and even short plays that all revolve around the central theme of the moon. The volume provoked quite a controversy when it appeared, since it in essence mocked the excesses of Modernism, while it also ridiculed the high-brow culture of those to whom it catered.

When Lugones was placed in charge of cultural commemorations for the first centenary of Argentine independence from Spain, he took on the responsibility of commissioning appropriate works that would hail the occasion. Rubén Darío contributed his *Canto a la Argentina* [Song to Argentina], and Lugones offered his own *Odas seculares* [Centennial Odes]. *Odas* is significant not only because of the occasion for which it was written, but more importantly because it marked a change in direction for the poet himself. For the first time, Lugones based his poetry on specifically Argentine themes. The ten separate compositions that make up the volume are steeped in the imagery of the people, places and history of Argentina, which is indicative of his progressive movement toward his later famous nationalist stance. Lugones published several subsequent volumes of poetry, none of which ever gained for him the critical acclaim that greeted his earlier compositions. His only book published outside of Argentina was a collection of tender love poems titled *El libro fiel*, 1912 [The Faithful Book] that the poet wrote to his wife. His last two collections, *Poemas solariegos*, 1928 [Ancestral Poems] and *Romances del Río Seco* [Río Seco Ballads], published posthumously in 1938, follow the same strong interest in Argentine themes.

Lugones was as skilled a prose writer as he was a poet, publishing in both genres simultaneously. In spite of the fact that Argentina did not become the subject matter of his poetry until 1912, his first prose work, *La guerra gaucha*, 1905 [The Gaucho War] deals with the most Argentine of all literary motifs, that of the gaucho. *La guerra gaucha* is truly a remarkable text in many ways. The twenty-three interrelated episodes, which could be considered short stories independent of one another, narrate the struggles for independence in northern Argentina as they were experienced by the gaucho soldiers, in particular the adventures of Martín Güemes, a 19th-century gaucho hero. The narrative is exceedingly complex in its use of metaphor, lyrical structure and the exorbitant use of arcane lexicon, all of which are employed to give elaborate descriptions of battles, hardships and human suffering. The text is in fact so complex that it even prompted such a sophisticated reader as Jorge Luis Borges to criticize Lugones's convoluted and baroque prose style. In spite of its difficult narrative style, the novel has enjoyed numerous reprintings and was made into a motion picture; it continues to be a classic of Argentine literature. Notwithstanding the virtues of his first prose work, Lugones later proved to be an even better master of the short story. In 1906 Lugones published his first volume of short stories, *Las fuerzas extrañas* [Strange Forces]. The narrative of this second prose work is far less encumbered by the elaborate syntactic and lexical entanglements of the previous experiment. Likewise, the twelve stories, joined by a treatise on cosmogony, diverge from the author's intense patriotism in *La guerra gaucha* to focus on elements of the supernatural, the forces of nature, pseudo-scientific experiments gone awry, and the occult.

The topic of the fantastic was very much in vogue in Buenos Aires at the turn of the century, and its influence on literature was only part of the entire picture. Séances, consultations with mediums, experimenting with ouija boards, and the study of theosophy and Kabbalah were all popular activities. Such authors as Edgar Allan Poe and Guy de Maupassant were widely read and assimilated by *modernista* writers. Lugones was no exception. Indeed, his characteristically hair-raising tales attest to the fact that he was a master of suspense and horror. Almost all the characters of *Las fuerzas extrañas* inevitably suffer cruel deaths as the result of having tampered with the forces of nature, a fate that reflects society's angst over the modernization of culture. In most of the stories the author employs a narrative framing device that presents the story as non-fiction. His tales often included fictional testimonies, legal documents, diary entries, or the discovered fragments of lost manuscripts that lent credence to the action. Lengthy theoretical hypotheses and scientific data of the author's own invention were also used to give the perception of authenticity. Lugones's "Ensayo de una cosmogonía en diez lecciones" [Essay on Cosmogony in Ten Lessons] is perhaps the most coherent summation of the Modernists' relation with the occult. It is essentially a treatise in which the author outlines the beliefs and attitudes concerning the doctrine of animism. Lugones continued and expanded his interest in the fantastic with his 1924 collection of short stories, *Cuentos fatales* [Fatal Stories], all based on the author's interest in Oriental studies, in particular Egyptology. He hired an Arabic tutor to learn the language and became an amateur expert on the subject. The stories of *Cuentos fatales* include Lugones himself and his tutor as characters and draw widely on the occult doctrines and ancient belief systems of the Arab world. Lugones also wrote one full-length conventional novel, *El ángel de la sombra*, 1926 [The Angel of Darkness]. However, it was never successful and is in fact a largely forgotten item of the author's abundant literary corpus. An interesting aspect of the novel is its treatment of the topic of suicide, foreshadowing the author's own death.

Of Lugones's vast essayistic writings, *El payador*, 1916 [The Gaucho Minstrel] deserves the most mention. It is actually the compilation of a series of public lectures Lugones gave in 1913 at the Teatro Odeón in Buenos Aires, which were attended by the most distinguished personalities of Buenos Aires society, including president Roque Sáenz Peña. In *El payador* Lugones begins by discussing the nature of epic poetry and ancient Greek culture, with the intention of later proving that *Martín Fierro* (the gauchesque poem written by José Hernández, and most famous work of all Argentine literature) an epic poem in its own right and representative of gaucho culture (poetry, music, language) can be directly linked to the lineage of Hercules. It is a very lengthy, in-depth, and at times tedious analysis. Nevertheless, it is significant because it marks a profound change in the author's ideological trajectory, abandoning the socialism of his earlier years for nationalism. In *El payador* Lugones attempts to construct an image of national identity based on creole ideals and the continuance of Hispano-Catholic hegemony in Argentina, one of the fundamental issues of Argentine nationalist ideology. Subsequent essays such as *La patria fuerte*, 1930 [The Strong Homeland] and *La grande Argentina*, 1930 [Heroic Argentina] reveal his strongly fascist ideals.

Lugones is a truly monolithic figure in Argentine letters, provoking both admiration and disdain. His works have greatly influenced subsequent generations of writers throughout Latin America and his literature continues to entice literary critics for its sophistication and originality.

DARRELL B. LOCKHART

Biography

Born in the province of Córdoba, Argentina, 13 June 1874, to privileged parents. Family's wealth lost in crash of 1890 and moved to Córdoba City in 1892. Employed by city council. By 1894 he had established a reputation as a poet and orator. Organized student strikes in 1895. Settled in Buenos Aires where he founded the newspaper *La Montaña*. Appointed Post Office archivist, 1899. In 1903 headed government mission to the Jesuit ruins of Misiones in the northeast of Argentina. First official trip to Europe in 1906 to study educational methods in Sweden and France. Returned to Europe during World War I and established the *Revue Sud-Américaine*, Paris. On his return to Argentina in 1915 appointed director of the National Teachers' Library, a post he was to hold for the next 23 years. Returned to France in 1919 at the invitation of the French government to visit the devastated war zones. Underwent change of ideology in 1920s as the result of disillusionment with liberal politicians. Supported the military coup of General Uriburu in 1930. Committed suicide in 1938.

Selected Works

Poetry

Las montañas del oro, Buenos Aires: Kern, 1897
Los crepúsculos del jardín, Buenos Aires: Moen, 1905
Lunario sentimental, Buenos Aires: Moen, 1909
Odas seculares, Buenos Aires: Moen, 1910
El libro fiel, Buenos Aires: Piazza, 1912
El libro de los paisajes, Buenos Aires: Otero y García, 1917
Las horas doradas, Buenos Aires: Babel, 1922
Romancero, Buenos Aires: Babel, 1924
Poemas solariegos, Buenos Aires: Babel, 1928
Romances del Río Seco, Buenos Aires: Centurión, 1938

Novels and Short Fiction

La guerra gaucha, Buenos Aires: Moen, 1905
Las fuerzas extrañas, Buenos Aires: Moen, 1906
Cuentos, Buenos Aires: Babel, 1916
Cuentos fatales, Buenos Aires: Babel, 1924
El ángel de la sombra, Buenos Aires: Gleizer, 1926

Essays

La reforma educacional, un ministro y doce académicos, Buenos Aires: n.p., 1903
El imperio jesuítico: ensayo histórico, Buenos Aires: Compañía Sudamericana de Billetes de Banco, 1904
Didáctica, Buenos Aires: Otero y García, 1910
Las limaduras de Hephaestos: 1. Piedras liminares, 2. Prometeo, Buenos Aires: Moen, 1910
Historia de Sarmiento, Buenos Aires: Otero y Compañía, 1911
Elogio de Ameghino, Buenos Aires: Otero y Compañía, 1915
El payador: 1. Hijo de la pampa, Buenos Aires: Otero Impresores, 1916
Mi beligerancia, Buenos Aires: Otero y García, 1917
La torre de Casandra, Buenos Aires: Talleres Gráficos "Atlántida," 1919
Las industrias de Atenas, Buenos Aires: Talleres Gráficos "Atlántida," 1919

Estudios helénicos, 4 vols, Buenos Aires: Babel, 1923–24
Filosofícula, Buenos Aires: Babel, 1924
La organización de la paz, Buenos Aires: La Editora Argentina, 1925
Nuevos estudios helénicos, Buenos Aires: La Editora Argentina, 1928
La patria fuerte, Buenos Aires: Taller Gráfico de L. Bernard, 1930
La grande Argentina, Buenos Aires: Babel, 1930
Política revolucionaria, Buenos Aires: Anaconda, 1931
El estado equitativo (ensayo sobre la realidad argentina), Buenos Aires: La Editora Argentina, 1932
Roca, Buenos Aires: Coni, 1938

Compilations and Anthologies

Obras poéticas completas, 2nd edition, Madrid: Aguilar, 1952
"El payador" y antología de poesía y prosa, edited by Guillermo Ara, Caracas: Biblioteca Ayacucho, 1979
Antología poética, selected by Jorge Luis Borges, Madrid: Alianza, 1982

Further Reading

Alva Negri, Tomás, *Lugones: planteamientos para una crítica*, Berlin: Colloquium Verlag, 1984
Barcia, Pedro Luis, "Introducción biográfica y crítica," *Cuentos fantásticos*, by Leopoldo Lugones, Madrid: Clásicos Castalia, 1987
Bischoff, Efraín V., *Aquel rebelde Leopoldo Lugones (sus primeros 22 años: 1874–1896)*, Córdoba: Junta Provincial de Historia de Córdoba, 1981
Borges, Jorge Luis, in collaboration with Betina Edelberg, *Leopoldo Lugones*, Buenos Aires: Ediciones Troquel, 1955
Capdevila, Arturo, *Lugones*, Buenos Aires: Aguilar, 1973
Fraser, Howard M., *In the Presence of Mystery: Modernist Fiction and the Occult*, Chapel Hill: North Carolina Studies in the Romance Languages and Literatures/University of North Carolina at Chapel Hill, 1992 [An excellent study in which the author analyzes the influence of the occult on the *modernista* fiction of Lugones, Darío and Nervo]
Ghiano, Juan Carlos, *Análisis de "La guerra gaucha,"* Buenos Aires: Centro Editor de América Latina, 1967
Gramuglio, María Teresa, "Literatura y nacionalismo: Leopoldo Lugones y la construcción de imágenes de escritor," *Hispamérica*, vol. 22/64–65 (1994)
Irazusta, Julio, *Genio y figura de Leopoldo Lugones*, Buenos Aires: Eudeba, 1968
Jitrik, Noé, *Leopoldo Lugones: mito nacional*, Buenos Aires: Ediciones Palestra, 1969
Kirkpatrick, Gwen, *The Dissonant Legacy of Modernismo: Lugones, Herrera y Reissig and the Voices of Modern Spanish American Poetry*, Berkeley: University of California Press, 1989 [A superb analysis of Lugones's early poetry within the context of *Modernismo*]
Lermón, Miguel, *Contribución a la bibliografía de Leopoldo Lugones*, Buenos Aires: Marúa, 1969
Lugones, Leopoldo, *Mi padre: biografía de Leopoldo Lugones*, Buenos Aires: Ediciones Centurión, 1949 [biography by Lugones's son]
Martínez Estrada, Ezequiel, *Leopoldo Lugones: retrato sin retocar*, Buenos Aires: Emecé, 1968
Metz, Allan, *Leopoldo Lugones y los judíos: las contradicciones del nacionalismo argentino*, Buenos Aires: Milá, 1992 [An interesting approach to Lugones's nationalism and his controversial relationship with the Jewish community of Argentina]
Phillips, Allen W., "La prosa artística de Leopoldo Lugones en *La Guerra Gaucha*," *La Torre*, Puerto Rico, vol. 5/17 (1957)

M

Joaquim Maria Machado de Assis 1839–1908

Brazilian prose writer

The literary production of Machado de Assis spans the last stages of the Brazilian Romantic movement and the emergence in Brazil, in the wake of analogous earlier developments in Europe, of the Realist "New Idea." In his works he was responsible both for divulging and questioning this new approach in a tantalizing manner. Machado both engages with and to a large extent questions the central tenets of Realism, including the optimistic notion of the possibility of an accessible truth as upheld by Positivism. His writing spans most of the literary genres but excels in particular in the sphere of the novel and short story.

Machado shared with many authors of his period in Brazil and Europe alike a reformist concern. In his case this finds expression not in prescriptive formulae for social modification but instead in an irony which seeks to denounce wrongs through laughter. His targets are both some of the more pernicious premises of 19th-century Realist thought, and also the specifically Brazilian adaptations of these principles. Works such as *Memórias póstumas de Brás Cubas* (*Epitaph of a Small Winner*) and *Quincas Borba* (*The Heritage of Quincas Borba* or *Philosopher or Dog?*), for example, parody certain concepts central to Realist thought, such as Darwinism and natural selection. The reader is made aware that dangers lurk under the comic surface: the sanctioning within society of a so-called law of nature (the survival of the fittest), unrestrained by any measure of collective or individual responsibility or altruism.

Such considerations are applied throughout his work to specific problems; for example, the interaction of the sexes, the races, social classes, nations or continents. In the last case, his particular concern is the interaction between Europe as a whole and Brazil as a nation on the periphery of European concerns. However, since Europe profoundly influenced Brazilian society, political life, ideology and mores, Machado's universality (that is, the appreciation of his work in the Western world) is ensured. At the same time, he preserves his interest in the local and his status as, in his own definition, "a man of his epoch and of his country."

To the reader of later periods, Machado's voice offers a remarkably contemporary ressonance, and a common denominator of scepticism regarding the possibility of transcendence or attainable truth. All this indicates, much more clearly than any 19th-century optimism, a modern awareness of fragmentation and loss. His is a reflection on the society of his period which offers a savage commentary on the moral contradictions of Brazil. The young nation felt compelled to adopt European models uncritically and superficially, and to promote industrialization without conviction, liberalism while preserving slavery, and scientism devoid of moral responsibility.

Machado's scepticism concerning the possibility of human goodness, which is intimately linked to his disavowal of the notion of truth in human relations, becomes particularly visible in his later novelistic work. It is customary to divide Machado's production into two phases; the first encompasses his first four novels, some short fiction, a few plays, much of his poetry and a considerable number of his *crônicas* (journalistic sketches) and critical writing. The second includes the last five novels and a substantial number of short stories, as well as contributions to the other genres. Although some of the concerns already outlined are adumbrated in the earlier works, it is in later novels, and in particular in those in which first-person narration is used, namely *Memórias póstumas de Brás Cubas*, *Dom Casmurro* and *Memorial de Aires* (*Counselor Ayres' Memorial*), that he resorts to certain discursive tactics and methods. These are deployed so that the reader's expectations of a reliable narrative voice and the veracity of the plot are undermined at the end. It is also in the later works that certain areas of specific social concern, and in particular identifiable recurring preoccupations with issues of class and gender, of poverty and female exclusion, of marginalization on grounds of material or sexual status, emerge as the products of a lifelong meditation.

The body of his work offers to the contemporary reader an uncannily modern insistence on issues such as power and disempowerment, treated in a manner that conforms more easily to inclusion within a late 20th-century gaze than to an optimistic, reformist late 19th-century understanding. His numerous female characters in their roles as mothers, daughters and sisters, wives, widows and mistresses, and men in antithetical roles as masters or slaves, rich or poor, are shown to be perceptually mediated by a gaze, usually that of a narrator, and on closer investigation seen to be distorting and often deliberately so, a mendacious falsifier of reality. That reality, therefore, becomes itself inacessible in a universe of fiction in which the interference of the perceptual and narrative processes is everything, and in which themes of ressurrected classical tragedy, such as murder, kinslaying, incest, betrayal and retribution exist side by side with a contemporary treatment of areas of debate around the issues of sex, class and race.

Machado de Assis emerges as both a "man of his epoch and of his country," the chronicler of the Brazilian local, and as an articulator of universal myths and concerns. His voice, representative both of 19th-century contemporaneity and of prophetic wisdom, foretells the dilemmas of a modernity which both formally and thematically he anticipated by at least half a century, in his depiction of a universe ideologically decentred and devoid of the possibility of transcendental truth.

MARIA MANUEL LISBOA

Biography

Born in Rio de Janeiro, Brazil, 21 June 1839. Worked as a clerk and later typographer's apprentice at the National Press, 1854–58; salesman and proofreader, Paulo Brito Bookshop. Published his first works in periodicals including *A Marmota Fluminense*, *Correio Mercantil*, *Diário do Rio de Janeiro* and *A Semana Ilustrada*. Married Carolina de Novaes in 1869 (died in 1904). Clerk, then Director of accounting division, Ministry of Agriculture, Commerce and Public Works, 1873–1908. Member, and censor, 1862–64, Conservatório Dramático Brasileiro. Granted the Order of the Rose, 1888. Founding president, Academia Brasileira de Letras, 1897–1908. Died 29 September 1908.

Selected Works

Novels

Ressurreição, Rio de Janeiro: Garnier, 1872
A mão e a luva, Rio de Janeiro: Gomes de Oliveira, 1874; as *The Hand and the Glove*, translated by Albert I. Bagby, Jr, Lexington: University Press of Kentucky, 1970
Helena, Rio de Janeiro: Garnier, 1876; as *Helena*, translated by Helen Caldwell, Berkeley: University of California Press, 1984
Iaiá Garcia, Rio de Janeiro: G. Vianna, 1878; as *Yayá Garcia*, translated by R.L. Scott-Buccleuch, London: Peter Owen, 1976
Memórias póstumas de Brás Cubas, Rio de Janeiro: Tipografica Nacional, 1881; as *Epitaph of a Small Winner*, translated by William L. Grossman, New York: Noonday Press, 1952; London, W.H. Allen, 1953; as *Posthumous Reminiscences of Bras Cubas*, translated by E. Percy Ellis, Rio de Janeiro: Instituto Nacional do Livro, 1955
Quincas Borba, Rio de Janeiro: Garnier, 1891; as *The Heritage of Quincas Borba*, translated by Clotilde Wilson, London: W.H. Allen, 1954; retitled as *Philosopher or Dog?*, New York: Noonday Press, 1954
Dom Casmurro, Rio de Janeiro: Garnier, 1899; as *Dom Casmurro*, translated by Helen Caldwell, New York: Noonday Press, and London: W.H. Allen, 1953; also translated by R.L. Scott-Buccleuch, London: Peter Owen, 1992
Esaú e Jacó, Rio de Janeiro: Garnier, 1904; as *Esau and Jacob*, translated by Helen Caldwell, Berkeley: University of California Press, and London: Peter Owen, 1966
Memorial de Aires, Rio de Janeiro: Garnier, 1908; as *Counselor Ayres' Memorial*, translated by Helen Caldwell, Berkeley: University of California Press, 1972; as *The Wager: Aires' Journal*, translated by R.L. Scott-Buccleuch, London: Peter Owen, 1990

Short Fiction

Contos fluminenses, Rio de Janeiro: Garnier, 1872
Histórias da meia-noite, Rio de Janeiro: Garnier, 1873
Papéis avulsos, Rio de Janeiro: Lombaerts, 1882
Histórias sem data, Rio de Janeiro: Garnier, 1884
Várias histórias, Rio de Janeiro: Laemmert, 1896
Páginas recolhidas, Rio de Janeiro: Garnier, 1899
Relíquias de Casa Velha, Rio de Janeiro: Garnier, 1906

Plays

Desencantos: fantasia dramática, *Poesias completas*, Rio de Janeiro: Paula Brito, 1861
Quase ministro, Rio de Janeiro: Serafim José Alves, 1864(?)
Os deuses de casaca, Rio de Janeiro: Tipografia do Imperial Instituto Artistico, 1866
Tu, só tu, puro amor, Rio de Janeiro: Lombaerts, 1881

Poetry

Crisálidas, Rio de Janeiro: Garnier, 1864
Falenas, Rio de Janeiro: Garnier, 1870
Americanas, Rio de Janeiro: Garnier, 1875

Compilations and Anthologies

Poesias completas, Rio de Janeiro: Garnier, 1901
Teatro, Rio de Janeiro: Garnier, 1910 [Includes *O caminho da porta*; *O protocolo*; *Quase ministro*; *Os deuses de casaca*; *Tu, só tu, puro amor*; *Não consultes médico*; *Lição de botânica*]
Crítica, edited by Mário de Alencar, Rio de Janeiro: Garnier, 1910
Obras completas, 31 vols, Rio de Janeiro: W.M. Jackson, 1937–42
Adelaide Ristori, edited by Barbosa Lima Sobrinho, Rio de Janeiro: Academia Brasileira de Letras, 1955
Obra completa, edited by Afrânio Coutinho, 3 vols, Rio de Janeiro: Aguilar, 1959–62

Anthologies in Translation

The Psychiatrist and Other Stories, translated by Helen Caldwell and William L. Grossman, Berkeley: University of California Press, and London: Peter Owen, 1963
The Devil's Church and Other Stories, edited and translated by Jack Schmitt and Lorie Ishimatsu, Austin: University of Texas Press, 1977; Manchester: Carcanet, 1985

Further Reading

The bibliography on Machado de Assis is extensive. The following recommended works will be useful in following up the aspects of his work emphasized above.

Caldwell, Helen, *Machado de Assis: the Brazilian Master and His Novels*, Berkeley: University of California Press, 1970
Maia Neto, José Raimundo, *Machado de Assis, the Brazilian Pyrrhonian*, West Lafayette, Indiana: Purdue University Press, 1994
Pereira, Lúcia Miguel, *Machado de Assis: estudo crítico e biográfico*, São Paulo: Editora Itatiaia, Editora da Universidade de São Paulo, 1988
Romero, Silvio, *Machado de Assis: estudo comparativo da literatura brasileira*, São Paulo: Unicamp, 1992
Schwarz, Roberto, *Ao vencedor as batatas: forma literária e processo social nos inícios do romance brasileiro*, São Paulo: Duas Cidades, 1977
――― *Um mestre na periferia do capitalismo*, São Paulo: Duas Cidades, 1990
Stein, Ingrid, *Figuras femininas em Machado de Assis*, Rio de Janeiro: Paz e Terra, Coleção Literatura e Teoria Literária, 1984
Xavier, Therezinha Mucci de, *A personagem feminina no romance de Machado de Assis*, Rio de Janeiro: Presença Edições, Coleção Atualidade Crítica, 1986

Bibliography
Sousa de Galante, José, *Bibliografía de Machado de Assis*, Rio de Janeiro: Instituto Nacional do Livro, 1955

Dom Casmurro

Novel by Joaquim Maria Machado de Assis

First published in 1899, *Dom Casmurro* is the third and most famous novel of the mature phase of Machado de Assis and also, to borrow the novel's term, "the most oblique and dissembling" of all his novels.

At a first reading of *Dom Casmurro* the innocent reader is immediately led into a trap: this being to pass judgement on the character Capitu, accused by her husband and childhood sweetheart Bento Santiago, the "casmurro" [aloof] narrator of these memoirs, of committing the crime of adultery with his best friend Escobar. In this sense the book belongs in a certain category of the 19th-century novel, namely that concerned with the psychological study of feminine adultery, of which *O primo Basílio* [Cousin Basílio] and *Madame Bovary* are examples.

However, a more careful reading will certainly reveal that *Dom Casmurro*, if it is a study at all, is a study of jealousy based on the account of a husband committed to convincing himself and the reader of his wife's guilt. If in the beginning this remains unnoticed, it is probably because readers allow themselves to be impressed by the poetic and social prestige of the narrator. In fact, how can one not trust a distinguished gentleman, already in his sixties, alien to the practical issues in life, a well-educated prose writer who is obsessed by reminiscences of his childhood, of his first sweetheart?

Readers begin to grow suspicious only when eventually they consider the possibility that since the case is being made by a very interested party, it may well be biased. After all, readers know that Bento has no concrete proof of adultery, and that the alleged similarity between his son Ezequiel and Escobar is not that marked, in a narrative that presents a succession of physiognomic resemblances and coincidences of all sorts.

Once that initial suspicion is aroused the next step is to note the tendentious way in which the narrator organizes the evidence of Capitu's supposed guilt. This is established on the basis of what seems to be his main argument. He wants to convince us that the behaviour of the girl with the eyes of an "oblique and sly" gipsy already predicted the future unfaithfulness of the woman: "e tu concordarás comigo; se te lembras bem da Capitu menina, hás de reconhecer que uma estava dentro da outra, como a fruta dentro da casca" (and you willl agree with me. If you remember Capitu the girl, you must admit that one was inside the other, as the fruit is inside the husk).

Again, the only image of the girl Capitu that is available to the reader is the picture sketched by the narrator. And so we realize that it is not by chance that he spends two-thirds of the novel portraying her, colouring with the brightest colours her supposed slyness. Accordingly, if one takes a closer look at this delineation of character, one will notice that both the account of Capitu's behaviour and the very narrative organization of these memoirs have the rigour of a premeditated account. Bento tells the reader that he had already reached the middle of the book and "the best of the narrative [is] still to come." In addition, his main goal is to persuade us to condemn his spouse out of hand. After all, it is not a coincidence that Machado de Assis attributes to the husband the profession of lawyer and, therefore, ability in the art of persuasion.

Given all these considerations, what initially readers thought of as the evocation of sincere memories reveals itself as a disguised effort against Capitu. It is the self-justification of a jealous husband, haunted by the responsibility: "Aí vindes outra vez, inquietas sombras?" (Come ye again, restless shades?) – of having cast out his wife and son until death. His reconstruction of the past is biased and generous to himself, since its aim, by persuading himself and the reader of Capitu's guilt, is to free himself from these "restless shades." In brief, after a more careful reading of the "oblique and dissembling" pages of *Dom Casmurro*, we are able to see the prosecutor turned into the culprit who is acting as his own advocate.

Machado de Assis thus daringly anticipates what was then an unusual type of narrator, "the narrator put in context," i.e., the narrator of a story whose drama is completely elucidated only from the moment one takes into account the active bias of the narrator created by the author. This means that behind the story told by the narrator there lies hidden another story told by the author, and to understand this other story in its entirety it is above all important to notice the distance between both points of view. Then the narrator, "disidentified" from the author, loses his status as a voice above any suspicion, to be situated on the same level as the other characters, and therefore a questionable character as well.

In the specific case of *Dom Casmurro*, from the moment the authority of the narrator is questioned his narration reveals itself as the very opposite, i.e., as an unwilling statement against himself. It is the narrator who is presented to the reader as the one to be judged. In this way, throughout *Dom Casmurro*, instead of the truth about Capitu the only truth presented by Machado de Assis is the one about the "casmurro" narrator of these memoirs.

TERESINHA V. ZIMBRÃO DA SILVA

Editions

First edition: *Dom Casmurro*, Rio de Janeiro: Garnier, 1899
Critical edition: Rio de Janeiro: Instituto Nacional do Libro, 1969
Translation: There are several available and a further one is to be published in the late 1990s. At present the most modern is that by R.L. Scott-Buccleuch, London: Peter Owen, 1992

Further Reading

Only after the publication of Helen Caldwell's study did Machadian critics realize the unreliability of the narrator in *Dom Casmurro*. Up to that point they were lost in discussions about Capitu's guilt.

Caldwell, Helen, *The Brazilian Othello of Machado de Assis*, Berkeley: University of California Press, 1960
Gledson, John, *The Deceptive Realism of Machado de Assis: a Dissenting Interpretation of Dom Casmurro*, Liverpool: Cairns, 1984
Santiago, Silviano, "Retórica da verossimilhança," in his *Uma literatura nos trópicos: ensaio sobre dependência cultural*, São Paulo: Perspectiva, 1978
Schwarz, Roberto, "A poesia envenenada de Dom Casmurro," in *Novos Estudos CEBRAP*, vol. 29 (March 1991)

Magical Realism

From the 1960s, through to the 1990s, magical realism became a much-used term in the discussion of Latin American literature. For some critics, it advertised what made the Latin American novel different from European traditions; for others, more narrowly but more usefully, it defined a specific direction that arose in the Latin American novel around the mid-20th century and that could be distinguished from Social Realism as its counterpart. This second meaning is the one that will be addressed here. Even in this case, though, the term has come to be used extremely loosely, without clarity as to the meaning of its two components (magic and realism). The only way to achieve that clarity is to place the words in a context of social and cultural history. Before doing that, however, a brief account is needed of how magical realism – as a term and as a way of writing – arose.

The key examples here are Alejo Carpentier, Miguel Ángel Asturias, Juan Rulfo and Gabriel García Márquez. In the preface to his novel *El reino de este mundo*, 1949 (*The Kingdom of this World*), Carpentier proposes that "lo real maravilloso" defines the most accurate way of seeing the history of Latin America. The main characteristic of the marvellous in the real is the way in which European myths and dreams, from the Fountain of Eternal Youth to Surrealism's desire to make dream into reality, have found their real counterparts in Latin America. The marvellous in Latin America is not a mere literary fabrication, "presupone una fe" (it assumes a belief) – it is a question of people actually believing in such things as El Dorado, the city of the Golden Man, which was still being sighted, as Carpentier points out, in the 20th century.

As a method for writing novels in the 20th century, marvellous realism (though Carpentier does not actually use the term) involves juxtaposing European and native – in Carpentier's case, African-Caribbean – perceptions of events. The best example in Carpentier's novel is the burning at the stake of Mackandal, leader of a slave revolt. In the white version, he is seen to be consumed by the flames. In the black one, he shoots up into the sky untouched by the fire. With this method, events themselves can become ambiguous, because told from more than one narrative position, a device which responds to a situation of cultural duality. This duality between colonial and native cultures pertains in most of Latin America, giving wide relevance to Carpentier's method.

Magical realism, as the words indicate, is the proposal of a method for giving to magic the status of reality. The main difficulty is the definition of magic. Rather than trying to arrive at a theory of it (there is no consistent theory of magical realism), it is better to trace the various ways of writing associated with it. Although the expression was first used in German art criticism in the 1920s, its Latin American meaning is different and dates from the 1950s. Works like Asturias's *Hombres de maíz* (*Men of Maize*), Rulfo's *Pedro Páramo* and above all García Márquez's *Cien años de soledad* (*One Hundred Years of Solitude*) became its defining examples. What distinguished these novels was the treatment of native and popular beliefs as valid knowledge rather than as exotic folklore. This meant that these beliefs would penetrate the language used for narrating and readers would not be able to rely on Western scientific-rational ideas associated with Progress to interpret what they read. The first few pages of any of the novels mentioned above will make that clear: in *Pedro Páramo*, for example, it emerges that all the characters are dead.

In opting against the rationalism of progress, these and other similar writers are adopting the ways of seeing, speaking and thinking of the regional societies which had not been modernised. In the case of García Márquez, it is the Caribbean coast of Colombia, specifically its oral traditions (full of "superstition"), which supplies a view of the world that challenges the usual Western ideas of modernity by validating magical attitudes. Neoliberal thinking of the 1980s and 1990s, as personified say in Vargas Llosa, has argued that these attitudes are "archaic" and stand in the way of progress.

However, the novels in question suggest a different way of looking at the issue. Instead of characterising the ethnic or mestizo cultures of the regions as "backward," they propose that in Latin America modern and non-modern societies exist alongside each other, without one being superior to the other, and that it is in their creative as opposed to destructive interaction that the possibilities of an alternative, transcultural, modernity are to be found (these arguments are elaborated by J. Martín-Barbero in *Procesos de comunicación y matrices de cultura* and Ángel Rama in *Transculturación narrativa en América Latina*).

García Márquez's methods are a mixture of this type: on the one hand Kafka and, on the other, folk-tales and popular oral memories. This mixture of the avant-garde and the non-modern is equally to be found in Asturias, Rulfo and Guimarães Rosa, or in the films of Glauber Rocha. To call their materials magical is to draw attention to their incompatibility with those programmes of rational enlightenment and modernization which virtually all governments of the last two centuries have imposed. Historically, the "superstitions" that these artists treat seriously in their works arose during the colonial period, in the interstices of the colonial societies, where actual everyday life was governed more by a mixture of native, black African and popular Spanish beliefs than by the official version of orthodox Christian belief. This mentality continues, for example, in popular Catholicism, where saints, many of them unrecognised by the Vatican, are treated as capable of miracles, and the dead are believed to continue their lives on the earth at certain times and places.

Much criticism of magical realism ignores the fact that such a collection of beliefs is not necessarily a release but a suffocating trap (Rulfo's characters are trapped inside the hell of popular catholicism) or more broadly a form of social control (as it is in García Márquez, particularly for the women). Magical realism in its beginnings was not a type of literary fantasy – European critics compared it with the literature of the fantastic – but a presentation of the social imagination of particular groups. Thus García Márquez has often insisted that what seems fantastic to certain readers and critics is actually an ordinary, everyday reality. It seems fantastic or exotic if you are not aware of the social and historical context.

In the 1980s, magical realism became a genre formula, transferable to scenarios that lacked the particular historical characteristics outlined above, and was even adopted as a model by non-Latin American writers (such as Angela Carter). The Chilean novelist Isabel Allende uses in her narratives magic as an amalgam of styles from previous writers like García Márquez. The term "magical" becomes problematic when it no longer includes a recognition that modern societies also use magic in that they use hidden forms of control which include what is called News, something that García Márquez learned when he was a journalist. In this light, the classic theories of realism, such as Lukács's, which often underlie definitions of magical realism, for example, that of Gerald Martin in *Journeys through the Labyrinth*, become untenable.

Historically, magical realism has to do with the Latin American experience of modernization, in particular with the massive migration of rural populations to cities, which produced a confrontation between urban and rural cultural universes. Removed from this base, magic becomes wish-fulfillment or drug (William Empson's word for the Edwardian taste in magic). Latin America inherited two forms of reason that disallowed magic: medieval scholasticism and the Reason of the French Enlightenment. The first engaged in extirpating idolatry (i.e., native religions) in the colonial period, the second in eradicating superstition so as to achieve modernity. Magical realism, which draws on popular rather than erudite traditions, opens up an alternative way of looking at things.

Not all literature that explores native cultures can be called magical realist. If the marvellous, as Carpentier points out, requires faith, then it can only be experienced by a believer, in which case it is no longer marvellous. Thus the effect of the marvellous or the magical, as something capable of being experienced by a reader, arises from a dramatized juxtaposition of rationality and beliefs that do not fit. Where a writer extensively uses native cultural forms as bases for narrative, then the novel ceases to be a European, erudite form upholding a rational world that can be played off against magic. In this sense, the novels of José María Arguedas, for instance, should not be called magical realist, a fact that helps to define the limits of the concept and get rid of some of the confusions it has caused.

WILLIAM ROWE

See also entries on Best-Sellers: Isabel Allende, *El reino de este mundo* (Alejo Carpentier)

Further Reading

Alexis, Jacques-Stéphen, "Du Réalisme merveilleux des Haïtiens," *Présence Africaine* 8–10 (June–November 1956)

Chiampi, Irlemar, *El realismo maravilloso: forma e ideología en la novela hispanomericana*, Caracas: Monte Ávila, 1983

Faris, Wendy B. and Lois Parkinson Zamora (editors), *Magical Realism: Theory, History, Community*, Durham, North Carolina: Duke University Press, 1995

Larsen, Ross, *Fantasy and Imagination in the Mexican Narrative*, Tempe, Arizona: Center for Latin American Studies, 1977 [Chapter 7 is on Magical Realism in Mexico]

Yates, Donald A. (editor), *Otros mundos, otros fuegos: fantasía y realismo mágico en Iberoamérica*, Pittsburgh: Latin American Studies Center of Michigan University, 1975 [Published conference papers with contributions on the history of the term, etc., by excellent critics such as Emir Rodríguez Monegal]

Eduardo Mallea 1903–1982

Argentine prose writer

When Eduardo Mallea died in 1982, he died a bitter man, his friends say. Whilst Argentine contemporaries like Borges, Sábato and even Cortázar in exile, were being praised by the world's press and the academy's scholars, Mallea suffered in silence, underestimated even by his compatriots. That he also wrote about his suffering – "He escrito siempre con sufrimiento" (I have always written with suffering) he said in *Notas de un novelista*, 1954 [Notes of a Novelist] – is the stuff of his fiction of ideas which deal with human passions. Mallea's novels were too intellectual, too much like fictionalised essays, his critics claimed, to attract a wide public. Suspect too for some was his apparent concern for *hondura* (depth) rather than *belleza* (beauty), a charge that at times undermined the reputation of the artist, if boosting the image of the thinker, concerned as he was with man's place in the universe and the human condition.

If such terms orient the reader towards the existentialist ideas emanating from France in the late 1930s and 1940s (Camus, Malraux, Sartre), it is no coincidence. But Mallea never lost sight of the fact that he was an Argentine. In 1937 he published his *Historia de una pasión argentina* (History of an Argentine Passion), a seminal essay important not only as a résumé of Mallea's key ideas on *argentinidad*, the national identity, and the search for the soul of his country, but also because it contains the aesthetic and philosophical seeds of the rest of his fictional output – not to mention the spiritual autobiography of the author. *Historia de una pasión argentina* is the work of a thinker (*pensador*) in a long tradition that starts in the 19th century with Sarmiento, Alberdi and Mitre, and continues in the 20th with Martínez Estrada, Gálvez, Scalabrini Ortiz and others. All these men of ideas tried to penetrate to the *alma de la raza* (the soul of the race), to analyse and explain the phenomenon of *civilización/barbarie*, and other "guiding fictions," to repeat the phrase of Nicolas Shumway in his recent study, *The Invention of Argentina*. Like Gálvez, faced with the conduct of the corrupt conservative oligarchy of the 1930s, and the growing materialism, philistinism and lack of spiritual values, Mallea sought to examine the Argentine character through his concept of the two Argentinas, visible and invisible. The visible Argentina is represented by the cold, hard city of Buenos Aires, unnatural, artificial, deceitful, pretentious, with no substance, as opposed to the invisible Argentina to be found in the hinterland, close to nature, warm, hospitable, authentic, the source of Argentina's true nature which had been corrupted by a selfish, greedy society, tempted by quick progress and easy profits, which can only undermine the hidden values of the true Argentina. This important essay was to influence many of Mallea's novels, like *Fiesta en noviembre*, 1938 (*Fiesta in November*), *Todo verdor perecerá*, 1941 (*All Green Shall Perish*), *Chaves*, 1953 (*Chaves and Other Stories*) and others, but none so obviously and so closely as his key novel *La bahía de silencio*, 1940 (*The Bay of Silence*). The fact that his view of the two Argentinas turned on its head Sarmiento's classic opposition of civilisation and barbarism or city and country in *Facundo*, 1845 (*Life in the Argentine Republic in the Days of the Tyrants*) reinforced by Martínez Estrada's gloomy and pessimistic view as expressed in *Radiografía de la pampa*, 1933 (*X-Ray of the Pampa*), enhances Mallea's position as a revolutionary thinker on the Argentine way of being.

It is always a very dangerous practice to describe in general terms the art of any writer, which is usually a complex and evolving process. However, at the risk of simplifying a complicated procedure, one can state without too much fear of contradiction that Mallea operates at two levels which one can loosely call the "universal" (that is, Western) and the national. Universal in this context signifies that Mallea is a modern writer who deals with contemporary problems of existence, which implies a group of concepts like lack of communication, especially between the sexes, solitude, isolation, the search for a meaning in life, that is, the themes of his French existentialist mentors. On the national level, Mallea is clearly concerned with the aforementioned themes of *argentinidad*, the national character, and the search for the identity of his people.

The universal current is noted early in Mallea's fiction by way of a literary line which can be traced directly from his first early work, *Cuentos para una inglesa desesperada*, 1926 [*Tales for a Desperate Englishwoman*], and through to works of the 1940s and 1950s, characterised by what Myron Lichtblau identifies as emotional mutism, in which Mallea describes the human condition without underscoring the geographical, historical background or the Argentine way of being. What interested the young Mallea, and was to persist throughout his work, was the condition of alienated, anguished characters suffering in an impersonal, indifferent, inhospitable society the effects of inner silence–not unlike the visible Argentina portrayed in *Historia de una pasión argentina*, as symbolised by Buenos Aires, *la ciudad-cáncer* (cancer city), to cite Roberto Arlt's phrase.

Running parallel with this tendency, then, is the other Mallean concern, the national problem, which can be traced in another line from *Historia de una pasión argentina* up through *La bahía de silencio* and on into the 1970s, for example, *En la creciente oscuridad*, 1973 [*In the Growing Darkness*]. However, it should be added that one of the merits of *La bahía de silencio* resides in the fact that Mallea transcends the purely regional by commenting on the human condition within the framework of what appears to be essentially an Argentine novel. Although there is a certain similarity between Mallea and Gálvez, writing at the same time on similar problems of the 1930s, Mallea is a more profound thinker and perhaps a more conscious artist, despite the tendency of critics to classify his work as philosophical essays disguised as fiction.

If at times Mallea gives the impression of being more concerned with expressing truth in human terms rather than the fulfilment of aesthetic needs, he is no primitive in the field of literature and literary theory, as his critical essays in *Notas de un novelista* and *Poderío de la novela*, 1965 [*Power of the Novel*] indicate.

As Donald Shaw has noted in the introduction to his edition of *Todo verdor perecerá*, the fundamental idea in Mallea, as in his contemporaries Gálvez and Barrios, is that the real proof of the artistic value of any writer can be found in the depth of his metaphysical perspective: "Toda obra grande es, por dentro, de planteo y paisaje general. Por eso un gran escritor es un escritor de paso ancho." (Every great work is, essentially, made up of ideas and general background. Therefore a great writer is a writer who takes broad steps). Thus, if Mallea, in his search for individual, national or "universal" (i.e., Western) authenticity, allows his metaphysical concerns to take precedence over the so-called formal aspects of the novel, one ought not to consider any digressions as a sign of his inability to write worthwhile narratives. Mallea's novels are far from being boring and formless, as some critics have unjustly described *La bahía de silencio*, perhaps his most important and most influential novel.

One can appreciate this key novel fully only in the light of Mallea's concept of the two Argentinas. *La bahía de silencio* is the search by the (possibly autobiographical) protagonist Martín Tregua for a group of kindred spirits and a set of spiritual values on which to found the regeneration of his country. At the same time, he desires to establish certain moral precepts, permanent and stable, on which he can also construct a personal vision of life which might then have some meaning. If the novel appears to end on a tragic note, in the sense that Tregua never really finds his authentic Juan Argentino, or solves his own personal problems, it may be deemed a failure, but only for the want of suitable witnesses who cannot or will not listen to Tregua's message of hope and regeneration. But the title of the novel also implies the *positive* act of waiting. That bay of silence, it should be remembered, is a waiting place for those optimists who can drift outward – and upward. On a final positive note, then, one can argue that Mallea's novels, like Tregua's work, because of the very fact that they have been written, will have permanent metaphysical and aesthetic value.

Mallea need not have died so embittered. His considerable output of novels and essays make a valid contribution to Argentine literature and thought, through their treatment of the key questions of *argentinidad* and national identity, at the same time as dealing with the transcendental problems of the human condition which help us to examine, if not to decipher, the mystery of existence. Mallea's thought-provoking work will continue to be read after more popular and best-selling novels gather dust on library shelves.

JOHN WALKER

Biography

Born in Bahía Blanca, a coastal town in the province of Buenos Aires, Argentina, 14 August 1903. Father a surgeon in local hospital. At the age of seven sent to school run by an Australian where he mixed with the children of immigrants and became proficient in English. Family moved to the capital in 1916. Studied law at University of Buenos Aires but did not complete the course. Joined staff of *La Nación* in 1928 and began to edit its literary supplement in 1931. Invited to lecture in Rome and Milan in 1934. Attended international congress of PEN club in 1936. President of Society of Argentine Writers in 1940. Joined editorial board of *Sur* (see separate entry under Journals). Married the poet Helena Muñiz Larreta in 1944. After the fall of Perón in 1955, appointed Argentine delegate to UNESCO. Ambassador to France from 1955 to 1958. Elected to Argentine Academy of Letters in 1960. Died in Buenos Aires, 14 August 1982.

Selected Works

Novels and Short Fiction

Cuentos para una inglesa desesperada, Buenos Aires: Gleizer, 1926
La ciudad junto al río inmóvil, Buenos Aires: Sur, 1936
Fiesta en noviembre, Buenos Aires: Amigos del Libro Argentino, 1938; as *Fiesta in November*, translated by Alis de Solá, London: Calder and Boyars, 1969
La bahía de silencio, Buenos Aires: Sudamericana, 1940; as *The Bay of Silence*, translated by Stuart Edgar Grummon, New York: Knopf, 1944
Todo verdor perecerá, Buenos Aires: Espasa Calpe, 1941; as *All Green Shall Perish*, translated by John B. Hughes, London: Calder and Boyars, 1967
Las águilas, Buenos Aires: Sudamericana, 1943
Rodeada está de sueño, Buenos Aires: Espasa Calpe, 1944
El retorno, Buenos Aires: Espasa Calpe, 1946
Los enemigos del alma, Buenos Aires: Sudamericana, 1950
La torre, Buenos Aires: Sudamericana, 1951
Chaves, Buenos Aires: Losada, 1953; as *Chaves and Other Stories*, translated by María Mercedes Aspiazu, London: Calder and Boyars, 1970
La sala de espera, Buenos Aires: Sudamericana, 1953
Notas de un novelista, Buenos Aires: Emecé, 1954
Simbad, Buenos Aires: Sudamericana, 1957
Posesión, Buenos Aires: Sudamericana, 1958
La razón humana, Buenos Aires: Losada, 1959
La guerra interior, Buenos Aires: Sur, 1963

El resentimiento, Buenos Aires: Sudamericana, 1966
La barca de hielo, Buenos Aires: Sudamericana, 1967
La red, Buenos Aires: Sudamericana, 1968
La penúltima puerta, Buenos Aires: Sudamericana, 1969
Gabriel Andaral, Buenos Aires: Sudamericana, 1971
Triste piel del universo, Buenos Aires: Sudamericana, 1971
En la creciente oscuridad, Buenos Aires: Sudamericana, 1973

Essays

Conocimiento y expresión de la Argentina, Buenos Aires: Sur, 1935
Nocturno europeo, Buenos Aires: Sur, 1935
Historia de una pasión argentina, Buenos Aires: Sur, 1937; as *History of an Argentine Passion*, translated by Myron I. Lichtblau, Pittsburgh: Latin American Literary Review Press, 1983
Meditación en la costa, Buenos Aires: Imprenta Mercatali, 1939
Notas de un novelista, Buenos Aires: Emecé, 1954
La razón humana, Buenos Aires: Losada, 1959
La vida blanca, Buenos Aires: Sur, 1960
Las travesías, 2 vols, Buenos Aires: Sudamericana, 1961–62
Poderío de la novela, Buenos Aires: Aguilar, 1965

Compilations and Anthologies

Obras completas, 2 vols, Buenos Aires: Emecé, 1961

Further Reading

Like many other (male) post-Boom writers, Mallea has suffered neglect at the hands of critics, preoccupied with Postmodern problems.

Foster, David William, *Currents in the Contemporary Argentine Novel*, Columbia: University of Missouri Press, 1975 [Chapter on Mallea]
Lewald, H. Ernest, *Eduardo Mallea*, Boston: Twayne, 1977
Lichtblau, Myron I., *El arte estilístico de Eduardo Mallea*, Buenos Aires: Goyenarte, 1967
Lichtblau, Myron I. (editor), *Mallea ante la crítica*, Miami: Universal, 1985
Polt, John H.R., *The Writings of Eduardo Mallea*, Berkeley: University of California Press, 1959
Rodríguez Monegal, Emir, *Narradores de esta América*, Caracas: Monte Ávila, 1969
Shaw, Donald L., "Narrative Technique in Mallea's *La bahía de silencio*," *Symposium*, vol. 20/1 (1966)
Villordo, Oscar H., *Genio y figura de Eduardo Mallea*, Buenos Aires: Editorial Universitaria, 1973

Marcha

See Journals

Leopoldo Marechal 1900–1970

Argentine prose writer, dramatist and poet

Leopoldo Marechal belongs to the so-called "Martín Fierro" generation. He worked for *Proa* magazine, sponsored by Ricardo Güiraldes and promoted by the supporters of *ultraism*, together with Borges, González Lanuza and Oliverio Girondo.

In his first book of poems, *Los aguiluchos*, 1922 [The Eaglets], the youthful images show Victor Hugo's influence and contain references to 19th-century French poetry. Pantheism, technical dexterity and metaphoric discoveries would be refined in his later works. In *Días como flechas*, 1926 [Days Like Arrows], which is marked with a sensual vocabulary, he manages to convey a personal voice celebrating his own self and the joy of the world.

Odas para el hombre y la mujer, 1929 [Odes for Men and Women] is a balanced work which closes a first phase. He wants to interpret the harmony of the world, intensifying the mythology of the countryside, transformed into an ideal territory.

Cinco poemas australes, 1937 [Five Austral Poems], an elegy in which he recalls the time of his childhood, is a lyrical interpretation of Argentine places and traditions, where he allows himself to give in to expressive, intrinsic values. His vehemence is not spoilt by stanzas of controlled ardour. *Laberinto de amor*, 1935 [Labyrinth of Love], in paired alexandrines and *Sonetos a Sophía y otros poemas*, 1940 [Sonnets to Sophia and Other Poems] of simple contraction, with themes of a transcendental purpose and a more cerebral content, are restricted to a set metre.

Little by little he combines man's universal experiences with those of his national circumstances. He shows a high degree of synthesis where verse and expressive rigour meet. He made use of several traditions to merge them into a cumulative compactness: the poetry of the Old Testament, Spanish lyrics, the ancient and the modern, in a profound relationship with American Baroque.

El poema de Robot, 1966 [Robot's Poem] is a meditation on a scientific circumstance typical of our times, creators of monsters. It is about the author's thoughts when faced with the tangible and dehumanized reality with which he has to live. The proud "formal aristocracy" of all his work is retained as is poetic purism over spontaneous emotionalism. He wants to establish a philosophy and an ethic of being. His language oscillates between classical in form and modern in concept, in an attempt to summarize all knowledge up to the present time. He gathers together all popular wisdom in the telluric dimension of his verses. He uses capital letters to emphasize the importance of the element he wants to exalt. He instils his experiences and his beliefs into his conceptual poetry.

El heptamerón (1966) is his "summa poetica." The seven days are considered with reflections on aesthetics and morality, together with philosophical preoccupations. It is his most complete allegorical/metaphysical statement. With ethical rigour he takes stock of his life and demonstrates that one's native country is either a complete and certain entity or it is nothing. Previous generations have bequeathed Utopias, "they taught us the mother country was / I do not yet know what

wise paradise / of indefatigable wheatfields and repetitive cows." Salvation lies in the Cross, which compromises "the vertical of the saint, the horizontal of the hero."

Marechal's finest works are his novels: *Adán Buenosayres* (1948), *El banquete de Severo Arcángelo*, 1966 [Severo Arcángelo's Banquet], and his posthumous work *Megafón, o la guerra*, 1970 [Megaphone or War]. With the first, which is easy to read, Marechal set out to write an epic in prose, something like a synthesis of national life. The hero's symbolic journey is developed over a series of interior and exterior encounters jointly with other characters. It is a soul's adventure towards darkness and towards light, containing a rich range of themes, a multiplicity of tones and purposes and a variety of levels of meaning, with an abundance of lyrical and dramatic elements. The novel begins with a metaphysical awakening in a room in Villa Crespo and takes place over a period of three days. The main character succumbs to memories of his childhood, reminiscences about his ancestors, of inconsequentially heroic lives. His private diary (the sixth book of the novel), "Copybook with Blue Covers," discloses biographical details. The character has imagined himself as an ascetic, a quack, a boxer, a gangster, a pioneer in Patagonia, a founder of cities.

If, in *Adán Buenosayres* the lyrical element abounds, in *El banquete* this element disappears and action is the shaping factor. Its thrity-three chapters (symbolizing the life of Christ), attempt to prove man's precarious nature, and his decadence throughout history. Because there is no omniscient narrator, dramatic devices abound, latent in all the episodes of the novel where objective reality is ignored. Arcángelo is the intermediary between heaven and earth and in *Megafón* the fictitious narrator "L .M." is openly the character Leopoldo Marechal. Megafón, " a man of the day before yesterday and a man of the day after tomorrow," Argentine man, leader and prophet, combines three manifestations: the warrior, the civilizer and the mystic, to fight inertia and indifference. Leopoldo Marechal knew and admired Gnostic metaphysics, occultism, Hinduism, Platonic idealism, the speculations of the cabbala, in a philosophical syncretism similar to that of his character Samuel Tesler. Nevertheless, he used this character to make fun of many ideas which he did not share. He combines the rationalist lines of St Thomas with the oracular and prophetic guidance of oriental religions and the latest theories of contemporary science. In the world proposed by Marechal as an alternative to current reality, man retains his spiritual dignity and his metaphysical hope, his essential optimism and his eclectic deism. Truth exists independently from us, and the essence of a human being is the point of departure of philosophical speculation and precedes existence. Opposing the fragmented vision of man and of the ordinary world in 20th-century narrative, he starts from a paradigm, that of an integral image of the human being and puts it forward as an example of salvation.

Marechal insists that the fall of the soul is equal to the break-up of the whole person, to its dispersal in multiplicity, to its progressive individualization. Human existence ranks with the banishment from Paradise, it is the soul's exile in the sentient world. Adam feels a "lost taste of Eden," even though he many consider that the creation of the world is the result of a loving divine will. Defining himself as "Christian without strings," Marechal's intention was to demythologize reality in order to attempt to rescue a legitimate order from false substitutes.

BELLA JOZEF

translated by Patricia James

Biography

Born in Buenos Aires, Argentina, 11 June 1900. Attended the Escuela Normal de Profesores Mariano Acosta, Buenos Aires, until 1915, where he obtained a teaching qualification. Elementary schoolteacher, c.1920–40; also journalist from 1922. Travelled to Spain and France in 1926, and established contact with several avant-garde artistic groups; was also friendly with Jorge Luis Borges. Active in pro-Peronist politics, from 1943, and held official posts during Juan Perón's two periods in office, 1946–55, including: director-general, Ministry of Education Department of Culture, 1944–45; head, Santa Fe province education council, 1944; president, National Commission for Tradition and Folklore, 1947–55; director-general of Higher Education and the Arts, 1948–55; largely ostracized in artistic and political spheres for his Peronism, 1955–65; visited Cuba, 1967. Contributed to *La Nación*, *Sol y Luna*, *Proa*, and *Martín Fierro*. Vice-president, Argentine Society of Writers, 1938–39. Awards include: Buenos Aires Prize, 1929; National Poetry Prize, 1940. Died 26 June 1970.

Selected Works

Novels

Adán Buenosayres, Buenos Aires: Sudamericana, 1948
El banquete de Severo Arcángelo, Buenos Aires: Sudamericana, 1966
Megafón, o la guerra, Buenos Aires: Sudamericana, 1970

Poetry

Los aguiluchos, Buenos Aires: Gleizer, 1922
Días como flechas, Buenos Aires: Gleizer, 1926
Odas para el hombre y la mujer, Buenos Aires: Libra, 1929
Laberinto de amor, Buenos Aires: Sur, 1935
Cinco poemas australes, Buenos Aires: Cursos de Cultura Católica, 1937
El centauro, Buenos Aires: Sol y Luna, 1940; as *The Centaur*, translated by Richard O'Connell and James Graham-Luján, in *New Directions 8* (1944)
Sonetos a Sophía y otros poemas, Buenos Aires: Sol y Luna, 1940
El viaje de la primavera, Buenos Aires: Emecé, 1945
El heptamerón, Buenos Aires: Sudamericana, 1966
El poema de Robot, Buenos Aires: Americalée, 1966
"Tres poemas sobre la Pasión," in *La poesía religiosa argentina*, by Roque Raúl Aragón, Buenos Aires: Culturales Argentinas, 1967
Canto de San Martín, Buenos Aires: Castañeda, 1979
Poemas de la creación, Buenos Aires: Castañeda, 1979

Plays

Antígona Vélez, Buenos Aires: Citerea, 1965
Las tres caras de Venus, Buenos Aires: Citerea, 1970
La batalla de José Luna, Santiago de Chile: Editorial Universitaria, 1970
Athanar (Sainete Alquímico), in *Megafón*, Buenos Aires: Sudamericana, 1970
Don Juan, Buenos Aires: Castañeda, 1978

Other Writings

Historia de la calle Corrientes, Buenos Aires: Municipalidad, 1937
Descenso y ascenso del alma por la belleza, Buenos Aires: Sol y Luna, 1939; revised edition, 1965 [definitive version]
Vida de Santa Rosa de Lima, Buenos Aires: Emecé, 1943
"Prólogo," in *Cántico espiritual*, by St John of the Cross, Buenos Aires: Emecé, 1944
"Proyecciones culturales del momento argentino," in *Argentina en marcha*, Buenos Aires: Sudamericana, 1947
Cuadernos de navegación, Buenos Aires: Sudamericana, 1966

Compliations and Anthologies

Antología poética, with a preface by Juan Carlos Ghiano, Buenos Aires: Espasa Calpe, 1950
Antología poética, with a preface by Alfredo Andrés, Buenos Aires: Ediciones de La Flor, 1969
"El beatle final" y otros páginas, edited by Ángel Núñez, Buenos Aires: América Latina, 1981
Poesía (1924–1950) por Leopoldo Marechal, Buenos Aires: Del 80, 1984

Further Reading

Alonso Gamo, José, "Marechal," in *Tres poetas argentinos: Marechal, Molinari, Bernárdez*, Madrid: Ediciones Cultura Hispánica, 1951
Andrés, Alfredo, *Palabras con Leopoldo Marechal*, Buenos Aires: C. Peréz, 1968 [interview and anthology]
Cavallari, Hector, "Leopoldo Marechal: de la metafísica a la revolución nacional," *Ideologies and Literature*, vol. 2/9 (1979)
_____ "*Adán Buenosayres*: discurso, texto, significación," *Texto Crítico* 16–17 (1980)
Centro de Investigaciones Literarias Buenosayres, "Pruebas y hazañas de *Adán Buenosayres*," in *Nueva novela latinoamericana*, vol. 2, edited by Jorge Lafforgue, Buenos Aires: Paídos, 1972
Chiesi, Bernardo, *La espiritualización del Eros en la obra de Leopoldo Marechal*, Buenos Aires: Centro de Estudios Latinoamericanas, 1982
Cortázar, Julio, "Leopoldo Marechal: *Adán Buenosayres*," *Realidad* 14 (1949)
Coulson, Graciela, *Marechal: la pasión metafísica*, Buenos Aires: García Cambeiro, 1974
Cricco, Valentín, *et al.*, *Marechal, el otro: la escritura testada de Adán Buenosayres*, Buenos Aires: Serpiente, 1985
Del Corro, Gaspar Pío, "Leopoldo Marechal: la visión metagónica," in *La mujer: símbolo del mundo nuevo*, edited by Vicente Cicchitti, *et al.*, Buenos Aires: García Cambeiro, 1985
Jitrik, Noé, "*Adán Buenosayres*: la novela de Leopoldo Marechal," *Contorno* 5–6 (1955)
Stabb, Martin S., "Argentine Letters and the Peronato: an Overview," *Journal of Inter-American Studies and World Affairs*, vol. 13/3–4 (1971)

Marianism

Marianism and machismo constitute a binary model for gender relationships in Latin America; while machismo is the cult of virility and agressiveness, Marianism is the cult of motherhood and of female spiritual superiority over men. As L.P. Stevens notes, Marianism is closely linked to machismo in terms of "reciprocal arrangements" whereby Latin American women benefit from social and economic advantages. The stereotype of women as suffering mothers has been a useful ideological tool for reinforcing customs and beliefs which reduce women to the private realm of the house and the family. A private space from where some female writers have acquired a voice through a production focused on motherhood, such as *Lecturas para mujeres* [Readings for Women] by Gabriela Mistral or *Diario de una joven madre* [Diary of a Young Mother] by Juana de Ibarbourou. Nevertheless, while the white woman has traditionally followed this traditional model, David Foster points out in the introduction to his *Latin American Writers on Gay and Lesbian Themes* that the "indian and the black woman did not follow this pattern of socialization," and therefore, "they are both coded outside [either] as whores [or] as hysterics."

Both Marianism and machismo were promoted at the time of the Spanish Empire through its institutions (the state, the church and the army) to sustain class, race and gender domination. The base of this cultural construct originates, on the one hand, in the precolonial myths of the mother goddess who was seen as the source of life and, on the other hand, in the role played by the Virgin Mary as the self-sacrificing and long-suffering mother in the Catholic tradition. Mary provides also a model for chastity which deprives women of sexual pleasure limiting them to reproduction. Although Marianism differs from Mariolatry, which is the cult of the Virgin Mary, it is thought of as a synchretism of the ancient pre-colonial myths and the Christian ones, as is exemplified in the figure of the Mexican Virgin of Guadalupe, who first appeared on Mount Tepeyacac, where the Aztec deity of Tonantzin ("Our mother") had been worshipped. This cult of Mary the mother-virgin is represented in the text written by the Uruguayan poet Juana de Ibarbourou, *Loores de Nuestra Señora* [Praise to Our Lady].

One of the most popular novels of 20th-century Latin American literature, *Cien años de soledad* (*One Hundred Years of Solitude*), contains a parodic version of the Catholic belief in the Assumption of the Virgin Mary. This occurs when Remedios la Bella, who has magic powers over men, is elevated into heaven before dying. Also, the Virgin's place is taken by one of the characters in Mario Vargas Llosa's play, *La señorita de Tacna* (*The Young Lady from Tacna*) where a woman decides to become the mother of her sister's children, and so she is both virgin and mother taking the position of Mary, the woman who escapes mortality and is deprived of sexuality.

It is important to note that the most popular Spanish term for a lesbian is *marimacho* (originally a word for tomboy). This is a linguistic/cultural fusion of the female (María) and the macho which, by moving away from gender polarization, forms an androgynous being without a defined position within the sexual hierarchy.

Military governments in Latin America have used the Marianism/machismo model to limit women to their homes and to reproduction from the 1970s. These same governments have directed torture and violence to the realms of the most sacred places: the church and the home. Their political atrocities have displaced women from the privacy of their homes to the public space where they insist on the social implications of their role as mothers. In countries like Argentina, Bolivia, Chile, El Salvador, Guatemala, Honduras and Nicaragua, Marianism has been used in the last decades as the conscious female appropiation of their motherhood: an expression of the power of "private" voices transfered to the public realm of political action. This displacement is exemplified in some testimonial texts. One of them by a Bolivian woman, Domitila Barrios de Chungara, *¡Si me permiten hablar! Testimonio de Domitila, una mujer de las minas bolivianas* (*Let Me Speak! Testimony of Domitila, a Woman of the Bolivian Mines*), where a woman has the political voice of the Trade Unions and faces the government to defend the rights of all women's husbands and children.

The most notable example of Marianism in contemporary Latin America is the case of the mothers of the Plaza de Mayo in Buenos Aires who began to meet every Tuesday, starting in 1976, relying on their identity as mothers of the disappeared to justify their political stance. This happened also in Chile during Pinochet's dictatorship (1973–90). These women have rearticulated the motherhood discourse and in the name of their sacred condition demand that human rights be respected in their countries. The mothers in both countries have tried to keep their discourse as a resistance to the main patriarchal tradition. Therefore, their voices have not been integrated yet into literary production.

Ana María Brenes-García

Further Reading

Critical Studies

Chaney, Elsa, *Supermadre: Women in Politics in Latin America*, Austin: University of Texas Press, 1979

Del Campo, Alicia, "Resignificación del marianismo por los movimientos de mujeres de oposición en Chile," in *Poética de la población marginal: sensibilidades determinantes*, edited by James V. Romano, Minneapolis: Prisma Institute, 1987

Fabj, Valeria, "Motherhood as Political Voice: the Rhetoric of the Mothers of Plaza de Mayo," *Communication Studies* 44 (1993)

Foster, David William (editor), *Latin American Writers on Gay and Lesbian Themes: a Bio-Critical Sourcebook*, Westport, Connecticut: Greenwood Press, 1994

Kristeva, Julia, "Stabat Mater," in *Contemporary Literary Criticism*, edited by Robert Con Davis and Ronald Schleifer, 2nd edition, New York: Longman, 1989

Montecino, Sonia, *et al.*, *Historias testimoniales de mujeres del campo*, Santiago de Chile: Círculo de Estudios de la Mujer, 1983

Stevens, E.P., "Marianismo: the Other Face of Machismo in Latin America," in *Female and Male in Latin America*, edited by Ann Pescatello, Pittsburgh: University of Pittsburgh Press, 1973

Valenzuela, María Elena, *La mujer en el Chile militar: todas íbamos a ser reinas*, Santiago de Chile: Ediciones Chile y América, 1987

Creative and Testimonial Works

Barrios de Chungara, Domitila, ¡Si me permiten hablar! Testimonio de Domitila, una mujer de las minas bolivianas, Mexico City: Siglo XXI, 1977; as Let Me Speak! Testimony of Domitila, a Woman of the Bolivian Mines, translated by Victoria Ortiz, New York: Monthly Review Press, 1978

Mistral, Gabriela, Lecturas para mujeres, Mexico City: Secretaría de Educación, 1923

Russell, Dora Isella (editor), Juana de Ibarbourou: obras completas, 2nd edition, Madrid: Aguilar, 1960

Vargas Llosa, Mario, La señorita de Tacna, Barcelona: Seix Barral, 1981; as The Young Lady from Tacna, translated by David Graham-Young, in Three Plays, London: Faber and Faber, 1990

José Carlos Mariátegui 1894–1930

Peruvian man of ideas

The significance of José Carlos Mariátegui for the whole of Latin America is as great as it is underestimated. His central contribution was in the sphere of political theory and organization. He edited the most important cultural journal of the 1920s, Amauta, and founded the Peruvian Socialist Party in 1928 on the basis of the comprehensive analysis of Peruvian history and social development presented in the best known (and most integrated) of his collections of writings – the Siete ensayos de interpretación de la realidad peruana, 1928 (Seven Interpretative Essays on Peruvian Reality). He was also the founder of the Peruvian Trade Union Congress (the CGTP) and its most respected leader – the counsel to the movement contained in his First of May Address of 1925 is a key document in the birth of Peruvian trade unionism. In 1929, already so sick, with the disease that was to cause his premature death in early 1930, that he could not attend in person, he wrote three key documents for the Congress of Latin American Communist Parties organized by the Comintern at Montevideo. These documents on the questions of race, anti-imperialism and political organization were in many ways prophetic.

Latin America therefore lost its three finest political and trade union leaders within a few years – Mella of Cuba, Recabarren of Chile and Mariátegui of Peru. They were sorely missed in the subsequent decade. But while all three had a lasting impact on the political life of Latin America, Mariátegui's role in its cultural history was second to none. That role was enshrined in the journal he founded and edited and whose brief existence belied its authority – Amauta. In its pages the issues and debates that concerned progressive artists and intellectuals elsewhere in the world were made known to a Latin American audience, but they were also seen in relation to the central questions of Latin American culture.

Mariátegui was not a spare-time cultural critic; nor was his interest in literature and art limited to a youthful pre-political phase, as some critics have suggested. What he called the "myth" of an age – a concept borrowed from the French theorist Georges Sorel – was the key to his exploration of culture. A revolutionary political analysis, in Mariátegui's view, contained both an analytical and a visionary element; it was these components which he found in combination in Marxism. The vision captured the society towards which a transforming activity was directed; for Mariátegui, that activity was informed by cultural traditions and experiences both national and international. The pages of Amauta and of his trade union journal Labor gave space to a constant advocacy of the indigenous cause. Amauta also reproduced the writings of the indigenists – like Valcárcel, for example – side by side with articles stemming from cultural debates in the revolutionary movement in Europe and the United States. Henri Barbusse, Louis Aragon, Vladimir Mayakovsky, Trotsky and Serge Lunacharsky were all published in the journal.

In these debates and discussions two elements met. On the one hand, the search for cultural traditions – chiefly the collectivism of the Indian communities; on the other, a continuing discussion of the role of committed intellectuals in forging a national culture.

From a much earlier stage Mariátegui was also absorbed by the visionary qualities of artistic forms and movements not necessarily committed to social transformation, yet which should also be seen as critical of a narrow and unequal social order. In his youth, and in his reports for journals like Mundial (Lima) Mariátegui was first and foremost an iconoclast, identifying with the bohemian poets and artists who had colonised Lima's central avenue, the Jirón de la Unión. He was one of a group who scandalised Lima's conservative elite by inviting a Russian ballerina to dance at midnight in a cemetery – like the great Russian poet Mayakovsky, he was first a revolutionary artist and only later a political revolutionary. But there was no break between the two, rather a movement from revolutionary thought through theory (discussed in the collection Ideología y política) to political action. One of his seminal Siete ensayos, for example, addresses "El proceso de la literatura" [The Process of Literature]. Here he seeks "el sentido profundo de una literatura " (the deep sense of a literature), and finds that "se instaura el proceso de la literatura nacional" (the process of forging a national literature has begun). In confronting modernity, the "colony" – the intellectual dependence on the metropolis – must be broken, just as the great poet Manuel González Prada had enjoined Peruvian youth to break with Spain. The problem was that many writers and artists identified with those new currents that in Europe represented a withdrawal from a rejection of the older cultural traditions. For the Latin American, Mariátegui insists, that it not enough; but neither should it be rejected. The finest and most stimulating artists, and those who will provide the building blocks of a new national culture, are not limited to one field or another, but rather borrow from many, be they national or cosmopolitan. The important thing is to find new forms, that break the imposed mould of thought and permit the construction in the imagination of a world that will be built in the reality. It was in this sense that Mariátegui was no enthusiast about the work of César Vallejo, for example.

The years after Mariátegui's death have shown how major a lacuna he left behind. There is a tragic irony in the fact that this revolutionary humanist and organizer of broad vision has been claimed as their own by a series of organizations characterised by sectarianism and the narrowest of nationalisms. The whole body of Mariátegui's work was broad in its horizons, catholic in its embrace and open in its understanding of the complex and eclectic nature of national cultures – seeing both complexity and openness as the material from which a new world could be forged. At the same time these insights were interwoven with the practical business of organizing trade unions, and building an organization of revolutionaries.

MIKE GONZALEZ

Biography
Born in Moquegua, Peru, 14 June 1894. Fell ill in 1902; spent most of 1903 bedridden. Studied French in 1905. From 1914 began to submit articles to newspapers and journals under the name Juan Croniqueur. Began to study Latin, Universidad Católica, Lima, 1917. Journalist, El Tiempo, 1918–1919. Travelled to Europe, 1919. Associated with leading European intellectuals, including the Communist leader Antonio Gramsci. Wrote his experiences in a series of articles for El Tiempo. Married Anna Chiappe in 1921; one son, Sandro (future president of the cabinet of Peru, 1980–1985). Returned to Peru in March, 1923. Organised an exhibition of Peruvian/Italian art, Lima, 1923. Lecturer, González Prada People's University, 1923; general editor, Claridad, 1923. Contributor to the journals Variedades, Lima, 1908–32, Mundial, Lima, 1920–31. Right leg amputated, 1923. Leading intellectuals and artists met at his house during the 1920s. Co-founder, with brother Julio César, of the Minerva publishing house. Founder (with help of American Popular Revolutionary Alliance, and communist and socialist parties), Amauta, September 1926; published Labor, November 1928–29. Organiser, Partido Socialista del Perú (Peruvian Socialist Party), 1928. Helped labour leaders to establish the organizing group of the Confederación General de Trabajadores del Perú (Peruvian General Federation of Workers, CGTP), 17 May 1929. Travelled to Argentina, 1930. Died in Lima, 16 April 1930.

Selected Works
La escena contemporánea, Lima: Minerva, 1925
Siete ensayos de interpretación de la realidad peruana, Lima: Amauta, 1928; as Seven Interpretative Essays on Peruvian Reality, translated by Marjory Urquidi, Austin: University of Texas Press, 1971
Defensa del marxismo, Santiago de Chile: Nacional y Extranjeras, 1934

El alma matinal y otras estaciones del hombre de hoy, Lima: Amauta, 1950
La novela y la vida: Siegfried y el profesor Canella, Lima: Amauta, 1955
El artista y la época, Lima: Amauta, 1959
Historia de la crisis mundial: conferencias (1923–1924), Lima: Amauta, 1959
Signos y obras, Lima: Amauta, 1959
Temas de nuestra América, Lima: Amauta, 1960
La organización del proletariado, Lima: Amauta, 1967
Cartas de Italia, Lima: Amauta, 1969
Crítica literaria, Buenos Aires: Jorge Álvarez, 1969
Ideología y política, Lima: Amauta, 1969
Figuras y aspectos de la vida mundial, Lima: Amauta, 1970
Peruanicemos al Perú, Lima: Amauta, 1970
El proletariado y su organización, Mexico City: Solidaridad, 1970
Temas de educación, Lima: Amauta, 1970
Fascismo sudamericano: los intelectuales y la revolución y otros artículos inéditos (1923–24), Lima: Amauta, 1975
Las tapadas, in collaboration with Julio Baudoin, Lima: Amauta, 1976

Compilations and Anthologies
Ediciones populares de las obras completas de José Carlos Mariátegui, 20 vols, Lima: Amauta, 1959–70

Translations
The Heroic and Creative Meaning of Socialism. Selected Essays of José Carlos Mariátegui, edited and translated by Michael Pearlman, Atlantic Highlands, New Jersey: Humanities Press, 1995

Further Reading
Aricó, José (editor), Mariátegui y los orígenes del marxismo latinoamericano, Mexico City: Siglo XXI, 1978
Barrenechea, Ana María, "El intento novelístico de José Carlos Mariátegui," in her Textos hispanoamericanos, Caracas: Monte Ávila, 1978
Belaúnde, Victor Andrés, "En torno a los Siete ensayos de José Carlos Mariátegui," in his La realidad nacional, Lima: Villanueva, 1980
Chang-Rodríguez, Eugenio, Poética e ideología en José Carlos Mariátegui, Madrid: Turanzas, 1983
Cornejo Polar, Antonio, "Apuntes sobre la literatura nacional en el pensamiento crítico de Mariátegui," in Mariátegui y la literatura, by Xavier Abril, et al., Lima: Amauta, 1980
Forgues, Roland, Mariátegui: la utopía realizable, Lima: Amauta, 1995
Melis, Antonio, Mariátegui en Italia, Lima: Amauta, 1981
Posada, Francisco, Los orígenes del pensamiento marxista en Latinoamérica: política y cultura en José Carlos Mariátegui, Havana: Casa de las Américas, 1968
Salazar Bondy, Augusto, "El pensamiento de Mariátegui y la filosofía marxista," in Historia de las ideas en el Perú contemporáneo, Lima: Francisco Moncloa, 1965
Stabb, Martin S., "The New Humanism and the Left," in his In Quest of Identity: Patterns in the Spanish American Essay of Ideas, 1890–1960, Chapel Hill: University of North Carolina Press, 1967
Terán, Oscar, Discutir Mariátegui, Mexico City: Katún, 1985
Vanden, Harry E., National Marxism in Latin America: José Carlos Mariátegui's Thought and Politics, Boulder, Colorado: Lynne Rienner, 1986
Wise, David O., "Labor (Lima, 1928–1929), José Carlos Mariátegui's Working Counterpart to Amauta," Revista de Estudios Hispánicos, vol. 14/3 (1980)

José Mármol 1817–1871

Argentine prose writer and poet

José Mármol was the most versatile writer of the talented Generation of 1837, with journalistic articles, essays, and drama to his credit, but excelling most in lyrical poetry and the novel. In 1839 – at the age of twenty three – he spent six days incarcerated by the regime of the Argentine dictator, Juan Manuel de Rosas, and later passed into exile, which would last till the fall of the strongman, Rosas, in 1852. In Montevideo he forged personal and ideological ties not only with Esteban Echeverría, Juan Bautista Alberdi, and Juan María Gutiérrez, the guiding spirits of the Romantic generation's "Asociación de Mayo," but also with Florencio Varela, leader of the exiled Unitarian Party. The trials of political persecution and exile constitute the central focus of his literary production, most of which was written during the exile period. After 1852 Mármol would serve the province of Buenos Aires, then the united country, in several important capacities – provincial representative, national senator, director of the National Library, delegate to constitutional conventions, ambassador – yet his arrogant and tempestuous personality often impeded fruitful results.

His literary production had a decidedly political focus. Like that of the other renowned 1837 militants, his most important writings played a part in the ideological and propagandistic campaign to discredit Rosas and to promote the liberal, social and political order that would follow on the tyrant's downfall. Mármol's writing, born of political expediency, exuded the political and civic passion that he lived in those trying days. Few internalized better than he the tenets of Romantic versification, that made light of grammatical correctness and favored instead robust, sonorous verses. In the poetic competitions of 1841 held in Montevideo, Mármol's patriotic poem, "Al 25 de mayo," [To the 25th of May] won the highest honors, gaining him instant renown among his exiled compatriots as "bard of democracy." Domingo Faustino Sarmiento, who appreciated any politically inspired writing, called Mármol "poet of maldition" whose verses made him "the most impassioned enemy of tyranny." But Echeverría, for whom political intentions were viewed as a contaminating force in artistic matters, surely had Mármol in mind when he denounced his fellow exiles on account of their opportunistic and demagogic writings in the pages of Montevideo's press.

Mármol's intense interior life also found expression in lyric poetry, a genre that attracted few writers or readers in the conflict-ridden environment of mid-century Argentina. In 1844, a near-death experience in a storm while aboard a schooner attempting to navigate around Cape Horn en route to Chile, provided the inspiration for the resonant Romantic verses of *Cantos del peregrino*, 1847 [Songs of the Pilgrim], whose title, tone and content reveal the poet's debt to Byron's *Childe Harold's Pilgrimage*. The narrative thread uniting the distinct parts of this fragmentary work is the sea voyage from Brazil to Montevideo of the exiled Carlos, during which time he poetically contemplates his interior world and the tempestuous natural forces. Here the Romantic creed predominates: the poet is a prophet exiled from an imperfect and impure humanity

whose words bespeak the message of the gods. Mármol's other important poetic work, *Armonías*, 1851 [Harmonies], also from his period in exile, utilized the gamut of meters associated with the Hispanic Romantic canon in expressing profound feelings for nature and man's striving for a more just social order.

Without doubt Mármol's most lasting legacy in the canon of Argentine and Latin American literature is his novel, *Amalia*, parts of which were published in instalments in the Montevidean press in 1851, and then in its entirety in Buenos Aires in 1855. It is the finest work of narrative fiction by any writer of his generation, and is rivaled only by Sarmiento's biography cum essay, *Facundo*, 1845 (*Life in the Argentine Republic in the Days of the Tyrants*) in presenting a sociological, historical, and ideological interpretation of Argentine -politics and society during the Rosas period. In depicting the persecution and terror experienced by the members of the young generation of intellectuals at the hands of Rosas's henchmen, Mármol was able to draw upon his own experiences between 1839 and 1840: his brief incarceration, months of clandestine opposition, and a harrowing escape to Montevideo. Also of documentary value are the literary portraits offered in the novel of the diabolical sister of the dictator, and his enchanting daughter, Manuelita; Cuitiño, a blood-thirsty military official reputed to be Rosas's preferred executioner; the *mazoqueros* (literally, corn huskers), or band of thugs hired to persecute the regime's alleged enemies; and Florencio Varela, Mármol's erstwhile friend and liberal supporter in Montevideo.

Typical of the variant of Romanticism that prevailed in Hispanic America, the novelistic action of *Amalia* centers on a series of oppositions: love versus hate, spirit versus body, Christianity versus satanism, liberty versus oppression, civilization versus barbarism. Characterization predictably follows a melodramatic pattern: Daniel Bello and Eduardo Belgrano, the leading male characters, are physically and morally "beautiful," and incarnate the most idealized values of Mármol's generation; Amalia, the female protagonist, is remarkable only on account of her transcendental spirituality: with a body enjoying "celestial resplendence" and a sensitivity pointing toward an "diaphanous, bluish space," she more resembles an idea associated with the Argentine ideal than a flesh-and-blood woman. On the other hand, the figures associated with the Rosas regime – with the exception of Manuelita – are depicted in deformed, darkened, animalistic terms. The novelistic action revolves around a conspiracy planned by the young men, their discovery by a paid informer of the regime, and their brutal assassination.

An ideolological reading of the novel reveals several interesting facets of Mármol's world view and his place within the society that would emerge after the fall of Rosas. First, there is the author's recalcitrant unitarianism and, as such, the total war he declared on the federalist creed and its followers in the country's interior. Not uncommon, for an intellectual of the period, was his fervent support of the Europeanized culture of

Buenos Aires, and a corresponding disdain for what he considered to be the brutish customs and values of the country's Hispanic, Indian, and mixed-raced peoples, in addition to its large black slave population. But Mármol's extreme unitarian beliefs and adherence to the "monarchic principle" many times led him to oppose not only the compromise politics of the more moderate members of his generation – Echeverría, Alberdi, Gutiérrez, V. F. López – but also the republicanism of Sarmiento.

Lastly, the failed rescue at the end of the novel by Bello's father suggests the contradictory nature of Mármol's politics in the post-1852 era. The protagonist's father, who nearly saves the lives of the youths and, as such their liberal revolt, was "a true federalist; cattle rancher, business partner of the Anchorena; and enjoying wide prestige in the countryside." He was, in fact, a member of the very class that had supported Rosas's rise to power and had benefitted so enormously under the dictator's rule. This novelistic conclusion has confused generations of readers unschooled in the political intricacies of the period. Yet more realistically than any of the other important literary writings by Mármol and his generational peers, it suggests the unlikely alliance that was to reign supreme in Buenos Aires and then the rest of the country in the post-Rosas period. That ruling coalition joined two groups: the liberal intelligentsia, primarily of unitarian extraction, who had spent fifteen exile years in mortal opposition to Rosas; and the cattle-ranching latifundists, primarily of federalist extraction, who had been the mainstay of the Rosas regime.

WILLIAM H. KATRA

See also entry on Civilization and Barbarism

Biography

Born in Buenos Aires, Argentina, 2 December 1817. Studied at the Colegio de Ciencias Morales and the Universidad de Buenos Aires, 1828–40. Imprisoned briefly in 1939; exiled in Montevideo and Río de Janeiro, 1840–52. Edited the newspaper *La Semana*, Montevideo. Returned from exile in 1852. Held to traditional catholic beliefs and believed firmly in unitarian government, with power concentrated in Buenos Aires. Representative for provincial senate of Buenos Aires, 1854–62; delegate for Buenos Aires Constitutional Convention, 1853, and member of municipal governing board of Buenos Aires, 1856. Director of National Library, 1858–71; delegate for Santa Fe Constitutional Convention, 1859; member of National House of Representatives, 1860; Ambassador to Brazil and other posts in national diplomatic corps, 1860–70. Died in Buenos Aires, 9 August 1871.

Selected Works

Poetry
Cantos del peregrino, Buenos Aires: n.p., 1847
Armonías, Buenos Aires: Ross, 1851

Plays
El poeta, Buenos Aires: n.p., 1842
El cruzado, Barcelona: n.p., 1851

Novel
Amalia, Buenos Aires: Tor, 1855; as *Amalia: a Romance of the Argentine*, translated by Mary J. Serrano, New York: Dutton, 1919, reprinted New York: Gordon Press, 1977

Compilations and Anthologies
Obras poéticas y dramáticas, Paris: Bouret, 1875
Poesías completas, edited with an introduction by Rafael Alberto Arrieta, 2 vols, Buenos Aires: Studium, 1946–47

Further Reading

Blasi Brambilla, Alberto, *José Mármol y la sombra de Rosas*, Buenos Aires: Pleamar, 1970

Brushwood, John S., *Genteel Barbarism. Experiments in the Analysis of Nineteenth- Century Spanish American Novels*, Lincoln: University of Nebraska Press, 1981 [Chapter 3 is on *Amalia*]

Cuthbertson, Stuart, *The Poetry of José Mármol*, Boulder: University of Colorado, 1935

Dámaso Martínez, Carlos, "Nacimiento de la novela. José Mármol," in *Historia de la literatura argentina*, vol. 1: *Desde la colonia hasta el romanticismo*, edited by Josefina Delgado *et al.*, Buenos Aires: Centro Editor de América Latina, 1980

Ghiano, Juan Carlos, prologue to *José Mármol, Asesinato del Sr. Dr. D. Florencio Varela. Manuela Rosas*, Buenos Aires: Casa Pardo, 1972

Giannangeli, Liliana, *Construcción a la bibliografía de José Mármol*, prologue by Juan Carlos Ghiano, La Plata: Universidad Nacional de la Plata, 1972

Katra, William H., *The Argentine Generation of 1837: Echeverría, Alberdi, Sarmiento, Mitre*, Rutherford: Fairleigh Dickinson University Press, 1996

Rojas, Ricardo, "El poeta José Mármol," in *Historia de la literatura argentina*, vol. 6, part II: *Los proscriptos*, Buenos Aires: Kraft, 1960

Sommer, Doris, *Foundational Fictions: the National Romances of Latin America*, Berkeley: University of California Press, 1991 [Chapter 3 is on *Amalia*]

Vidal, Hernán, "*Amalia*: melodrama y dependencia," *Ideologies and Literature*, vol. 1/1 (February–April 1977)

René Marqués 1919–1979

Puerto Rican dramatist and prose writer

René Marqués, a staunch defender of all things Puerto Rican, widely acknowledged as a gifted and prolific writer whose works have advanced the cause of Puerto Rican letters, early on abandoned the traditional family career in agronomy in favor of writing. In doing so, Marqués none the less continued a family tradition, for his relatives included several writers, among them Padrina Padilla de Sanz a poet and short story writer who regularly wrote articles advocating women's rights and Puerto Rican independence. As happened with several Latin American dramatists of his generation, a grant from the Rockefeller Foundation at a critical point in his artistic development – in his case in 1949 when he was thirty – afforded Marqués the opportunity to leave the island to immerse himself in his craft.

Marqués produced a copious body of work which encompasses a book of poetry, fifteen plays, two volumes of essays, five volumes of short stories and two novels as well as an anthology of short stories, which he edited. This does not include the countless pedagogical articles written while he worked for the Division of Community Education of the Department of Education, nor the numerous reviews and articles of literary criticism published in journals and newspapers such as *Asomante* and the *Diario de Puerto Rico*.

Though most would agree that the major contribution of Marqués to Latin American letters lies in his drama, one cannot relegate his fiction to second class status. His novel *La víspera del hombre* [The Eve of Manhood], considered by many to have autobiographical overtones, follows the young Piruelo in his progression from childhood to manhood. This is a two-part journey: a geographic one as he leaves the stability of the coffee plantation where he has lived all his life; and a spiritual one as he discovers his true self in his growth to adulthood. The novel also focuses on the impact of the sale of the plantation where he had worked and the economic repercussions on his family as well as on him as an individual. *La mirada* [The Glance], his second novel, also with a young man as its protagonist, chronicles his search for meaning in an essentially senseless world. Many of the concerns voiced in his novels are echoed in Marqués's short stories, all marked by a certain poetic technique which transforms several of them into prose poems. A number of Marqués's plays find their source in his short stories, as for example, *Un niño azul para esa sombra* [A Blue Child for that Shadow] which recalls " El niño en el árbol" [The Boy in the Tree] and " La sala" [The Living Room].

Time plays a significant role in Marqués's dramas. Its function is not limited to the customary indication of the passage of time. The author's recourse to the flashback in certain works juxtaposes past, present and future. At times, as in *Un niño azul para esa sombra*, different levels of time coexist, i.e., present time or the reality in which the action takes place, and internal time, the individual, personal reality in which the protagonist exists. However, in its inexorable march time plays its most menacing role, for those characters who hesitate to take a stand, or to come to a decision, find that time has run out leaving them to the mercy of their circumstances.

The theater of Marqués, an innovative one rich in its use of symbol, repeats long standing preoccupations of the Puerto Rican author. Two in particular inform his theater and by extension his complete literary corpus: a loathing of anything which might defile or destroy Puerto Rican culture, and freedom for the island from its semi-colonial status and dependence on the United States. This freedom is more than political or economic. For the author it is also the liberty to maintain individual as well as national identity free from external adulteration. Much of this translates into criticism of the United States in his writings. The dilemmas of the characters in the majority of his plays, the notable exception being his biblical dramas, result from what he perceives as the political and economic leverage the United States exercises over his homeland. In *La carreta* (*The Oxcart*), a rural Puerto Rican family abandons the countryside to seek a better life in San Juan. Disillusioned, they move to New York only to find more heartache, and eventually return to the peace and stability of their rural home. *La muerte no entrará en palacio* [Death Will Not Enter the Palace], though set in an unnamed South American country, addresses the regime of Muñoz Marín and its acquiescence to the United States. *Un niño azul para esa sombra*, a study in the juxtaposition of temporal realities, recounts the sad tale of Michelín, who, devastated by the breakdown in his parents' marriage, resents his father's absence and his mother's passionate devotion to all things American to such a degree that he eventually takes his life. Even the tragic fate of the three Burkhart sisters in *Los soles truncos* (*The Fanlights*) results, for Marqués, from the clash between the two cultures and the dominance of the United States rather than from the failure of the sisters to cope with present reality. *Juan Bobo y la Dama de Occidente* [Johnny the Fool and the Lady from the West], a pantomime-ballet, enunciates more clearly than other works by Marqués the motivation and nature of his anti-Americanism. While acerbic in its denunciation of the United States, a thoughtful reading of this play, with the accompanying introductory material, suggests that although Marqués directed his criticism against what he perceived as the preeminence of the United States in Puerto Rican life, he was none the less cognizant of almost five hundred years of Puerto Rican colonialism with less than twenty per cent of this subjugation transpiring at the hands of the United States, a fact which prompts one to wonder whether he would not have protested with equal vehemence had Spain continued to control the island. Moreover, scrutiny of Marqués's theater reveals that the thrust of his protest is directed not so much at the political /economic circumstances of this supremacy as at the cultural annihilation perpetuated in its name. He resented the anglicization of Puerto Rican life, the substitution of Puerto Rican values for others. In his works Marqués sought to reaffirm the historical and cultural individuality of his homeland, and to renew the appreciation of and confidence in the Puerto Rican way.

FRANCESca Colecchia

Biography

Born in Arecibo, Puerto Rico, 4 October 1919. Attended the College of Agriculture and Mechanical Arts at Mayagüez, Puerto Rico: degree in agronomy, 1942. Married Serena Velasco in 1942 (divorced in 1957), two sons and one daughter. Worked for the Department of Agriculture, 1944–46. Wrote literary reviews for newspapers and journals including *El Mundo*, *Asomante* and *Diario de Puerto Rico*. Spent a year in Spain with his wife and family in 1946 and studied literature at the University of Madrid. Founder and president of the theatre group Pro-Arte de Arecibo, 1947. Studied drama at Columbia University, New York on a Rockefeller Foundation grant; took additional courses at Erwin Piscator's Dramatic Workshop, 1949. Returned to San Juan in 1950; writer, 1950, and editorial director, 1953–69, for the Department of Education. Co-founder, with José M. Lacomba, and director of the Teatro Experimental del Ateneo, 1951: left board of the Ateneo following the controversy over *La Carreta*, 1953. Awarded a Guggenheim grant in 1954, accepted in 1957. Writer for the radio station WIPR, 1958. Co-founder, with Eleizer Curet Cuevas, the Club del Libro de Puerto Rico, 1959. Professor of Literature, University of Puerto Rico, 1969–76. Recipient of numerous awards including: Premio del Cuento del Ateneo, 1948; Premio Ateneo Puertorriqueño, 1958; Premio de Teatro del Ateneo Puertorriqueño, 1961 and 1963; Faulkner Foundation Iberian American Prize, 1962; Diploma of Honor, Institute of Puerto Rican Culture, 1979. Died in San Juan, 22 March 1979.

Selected Works

Plays

El hombre y sus sueños, Asomante, vol. 4/2 (April–June 1948)
Juan Bobo y la Dama de Occidente, Mexico City: Los Presentes, 1956
El sol y los Mac Donald, Asomante, vol. 13/1 (January–March 1957)
Los soles truncos, in *Teatro Puertorriqueño, Primer Festival*, San Juan, Puerto Rico: Instituto de Cultura Puertorriqueña, 1959; as *The Fanlights*, translated by Richard John Wiezell, in *The Modern Stage in Latin America: Six Plays*, edited by George W. Woodyard, New York: Dutton, 1971
Un niño azul para esa sombra, Barcelona: Rumbos, 1961
La casa sin reloj, Xalapa, Mexico: Universidad Veracruzana, 1962
La carreta, Río Piedras, Puerto Rico: Cultural, 1963; as *The Oxcart*, translated by Charles Pilditch, New York: Scribner, 1969
El apartamiento, in *Teatro Puertorriqueño, Séptimo Festival*, San Juan, Puerto Rico: Instituto de Cultura Puertorriqueña, 1965
Mariana o el alba, Río Piedras, Puerto Rico: Cultural, 1965
Sacrificio en el Monte Moriah, Río Piedras, Puerto Rico: Antillana, 1969
David y Jonatán; Tito y Berenice: dos dramas de poder, amor y desamor, Río Piedras, Puerto Rico: Cultural, 1970

La muerte no entrará en palacio, Río Piedras, Puerto Rico: Cultural, 2nd edition, 1970
Vía crucis del hombre puertorriqueño, San Juan, Puerto Rico: Antillana, 1971
Carnaval afuera, carnaval adentro, Río Piedras, Puerto Rico: Antillana, 1971

Short Fiction

Otro día nuestro, San Juan, Puerto Rico: Imprenta Venezuela, 1955
En una ciudad llamada San Juan, Mexico City: UNAM, 1960
Purificación en la calle del Cristo, Río Piedras, Puerto Rico: Cultural, 1972 [Includes *Los soles truncos*]
Ese mosaico fresco sobre aquel mosaico antiguo, Río Piedras, Puerto Rico: Cultural, 1975 [First published in *Sin Nombre*, vol. 2/3 (1972); this edition includes photographs by Jorge Rigan]
Inmersos en el silencio: cuentos, Río Piedras, Puerto Rico: Antillana, 1976

Novels

La víspera del hombre, Río Piedras, Puerto Rico: Cultural, 1959
La mirada, Río Piedras, Puerto Rico: Antillana, 1975

Other Writings

Peregrinación, Arecibo, Puerto Rico: n.p., 1944 [poetry]
Cuentos puertorriqueños de hoy (anthology), 2nd edition, Río Piedras, Puerto Rico: Cultural, 1959
Ensayos (1953–1966), San Juan, Puerto Rico: Antillana, 1966; revised and augmented edition, 1972
El puertorriqueño dócil y otros ensayos, Río Piedras, Puerto Rico: Antillana, 1975

Compilations and Anthologies

Teatro, 3 vols, Río Piedras, Puerto Rico: Cultural, 1970–71

Further Reading

Barradas, Efraín, "El machismo existencialista de René Marqués: relecturas y nuevas lecturas," *Sin Nombre*, San Juan, Puerto Rico, vol. 7/3 (October–December 1977)
Caballero Wanguemert, María M., *La narrativa de René Marqués*, Madrid: Playor, 1988
Montes-Huidobro, Matías, *Persona: vida y máscara en el teatro puertorriqueño*, San Juan, Puerto Rico: Centro de Estudios Avanzados de Puerto y el Caribe, 1986 [Includes critical studies on all of Marqués's theater]
Pilditch, Charles R., *René Marqués; A Study of His Fiction*, New York: Plus Ultra, 1977
Reynolds, Bonnie Hildebrand, *Space, Time, and Crisis: the Theatre of René Marqués*, York, South Carolina: Spanish Literature, 1988

José Martí 1853–1895

Cuban poet, essayist and political thinker

The first period of José Martí's literary development started in his adolescence, through to the year 1880, and includes everything that he wrote prior to his sojourn in Venezuela (1881), during which the first notable changes in his style become perceptible. In this period Martí's poetic output was considerable, and it can be subdivided into two phases: the poems written in Cuba and in Spain (during his first deportation to that country), from 1868–73; and the poems written in Mexico and Guatemala (1875–77). This was a long period of literary training in which one can perceive a personal poetic voice that struggles for expression among the strong influences of late examples of Spanish Romanticism and some signs of turn-of-the-century Neoclassicism, displaying a preference for long poems, of amorous and sometimes social content. Martí wrote various pieces for the theatre during this period, and a collection of political writings among which the most notable are *El presidio político en Cuba* [Political Imprisonment in Cuba] and *La república española ante la revolución cubana* [The Spanish Republic in the Face of the Cuban Revolution].

The second period of Martí's literary career started in 1881 and lasted until approximately 1888. The year 1881 was fundamental in Martí's literary experience, and was marked by such works as *El centenario de Calderón* [Calderón's Centenary], and especially by *El carácter de "La Revista Venezolana"* [The Thrust of the Venezuelan Review] – a veritable theoretical textbook on Spanish American literary *Modernismo*. The year also saw the arrival of his collection of poems *Ismaelillo* [Little Ishmael] – published the following year – which Martí believed was his first really accomplished poetic effort, and which is, at the same time, the first precise example of *Modernismo*. There are evident signs of *Ismaelillo* in Rubén Darío's *Azul . . .* [Blue], published in 1888, in the same way that this book would influence some aspects of the poetry written by Martí at a later date. This period covers the first few years of his residence in New York, where he practised journalism, writing for some important North American and Latin American publications. This allowed him to develop an impressive collection of articles centering on the most diverse aspects of life in the United States; articles, indeed, that considerably influenced Darío, and that served as a cultural bridge between Anglo-Saxon America and Hispanic America. The powerful charge of expression found in Martí's articles makes one think about that part of his output which, apparently, is most dissimilar to them: his poetry, and especially his *Versos libres* [Free Verses], which Martí never published. This collection of poems, or better still, this expression of his poetic voice, came about, according to the author himself, when he was twenty-five years old, in 1878. There is sufficient evidence to affirm that it accompanied him, as an intense and well used method of shaping – through words – the most personal part of his thought, throughout the decade of the 1880s at least. The *Versos libres* respond, in a considerable way, to the mark of modern urban life as Martí came to know it in the United States, especially in New York. Its convulsed quality is a reflection of that context, and its real modernity derives from it.

The language used in these poems is a far cry form the strong Hispanic vein that runs through *Ismaelillo*, and that reappears in *Versos sencillos*, 1891 [Simple Verses] in order to adopt a line of expression that can be recognised as essentially *different*: the lyrical density of *Ismaelillo* is abandoned in *Versos libres* in favour of a desire that aspires to encompass everything within the poem, thereby transcending the traditional thematic frontiers between poetry and prose. The relationship between text and context is much more apparent and extensive in *Versos libres* than in any other area of Martí's poetic *oeuvre*, and, consequently, the typically modern contentious quality of poetry manifests itself in this book with unaccustomed force. Referring to the relationship between Martí and Spanish American Modernism, Octavio Paz says, in *Los hijos del limo* (*Children of the Mire*), that a poem from this book, "Dos patrias" [Two Homelands]: "condenses that whole movement and announces, too, the arrival of contemporary poetry."

Martí's third period of literary development commenced around 1889, and includes such works as: the production of the children's literature magazine *La Edad de Oro* [The Golden Age]; critical pieces on literature and art – as in his lecture "Heredia" and "La exhibición de pinturas del ruso Vereschagin" [The Exhibition of Paintings by the Russian Vereschagin]; articles on "The International Washington Congress" and "The American Conference," and the vibrant patriotic address "Vindicación de Cuba." This period is enriched considerably by his third book of poems, *Versos sencillos*, his revolutionary speeches – that constitute one of the culminating moments of 19th-century oratory – and his political documents, among which the most notable, because of its complex and completely rigorous prose, is "El manifiesto de Montecristi." In 1895, with an apparently unsurpassable quality, Martí produced the extraordinary *Diario de campaña* [Campaign Diary], a text where the fusion between the epic and the lyrical reaches an intensity of dramatic proportions.

From a strictly literary point of view, *Versos sencillos* represents the most important work from this period and is considered to be the culmination of Martí's poetic *oeuvre*. In the brief and essential prologue that he wrote for the book, the author himself highlighted the originality of the formal methods that govern the realization of these poems structured around a traditional scheme: the octosyllabic quartet with consonant rhymes, but effected by using profoundly innovative procedures. Among these the most noteworthy are: the repetition of the rhyme in order to create an "echo" effect; the taking advantage of graphic values for expressive ends; and the visible suppression of the rhyme in those parts of the poem where it is required by emotional intensity, substituting it by the aforementioned "echo" effect, placing it within the line of verse.

Throughout his work, Martí's language assumes the expression of the "visions" produced by the awareness within the poet's consciousness, striving to lock them up whole inside images. Martí lends the verse, as an entity, an aggressive, denuding, and penetrating function, attributing to it – in the prologue that he wrote for the publication of *Versos libres* –

essentially sensory qualities: auditory (containing a vibrant and difficult sonorousness); visual (statuesque, fleeting); and tactile (statuesque, vibrant, and overwhelming). It concerns the means used to transfer to the verbal language the artist's "visions," that is, the plastic images through which a process of learning and understanding of reality, in some of its most rich and varied forms, took shape in the poet's consciousness. The exposition of this process is conceived by Martí as an authentic spectacle, that is to say, as an expression that can be visualized; as Martí himself postulated in 1881, writing in the *Revista Venezolana*: "es fuerza que se abra paso esta verdad acerca del estilo: el escritor ha de pintar como el pintor. No hay razón para que el uno use de diversos colores, y no el otro." (It is necessary for this particular truth about style to break through: the writer must paint like the painter. There is no reason why one should use a variety of colours and not the other). But this aesthetic statement does not exhaust itself in a pictorial sense whose literary implications would not be able to transcend the 19th century. To paint in words is, for Martí, to make the reader see using the word as the substance of the poetic image: "el deleite del alba que origina el penetrar anhelante y trémulo en lo por venir" (the pleasure of the daybreak that begins the wishful and timid penetration of the forthcoming), in such a way that "la frase suene como escudo, taje como espada y arremeta como lanza" (the phrase sounds like a shield, slashes like a sword, and pierces like a spear), as Martí himself would characterize the emergence of a literature capable of expressing "la grande América nueva, sólida, batallante, trabajadora y asombrosa" (the great America, new, solid, persevering, industrious, and astounding). The ultimate reach of Martí's literature constitutes, in its origins and in its greatest achievements, a proposed poetic language for that America; a poetic language that would not just be a mere aesthetic achievement for him, but the ethical testimony of an artist who consciously assumes the expression of a new age. No other Latin American 19th-century writer believed himself to be, like Martí, immersed in the accelerated and ever-changing flow of history. The capacity to express this flow, with a use of language that appears to come from the very nucleus of the process, gave him access to an originality that makes him one of the outstanding figures of Latin American literature.

EMILIO DE ARMAS

translated by Luis González Fernández

Biography
Born in Havana, Cuba, then a Spanish colony, 28 January 1853. Attended the Municipal Boys' School, Havana, 1865–66; Instituto de Havana, 1866–69; University of Madrid, 1873; University of Zaragoza, degree in law, 1873, arts degree, 1874. After the first Cuban war against Spain, 1868, Martí devoted himself to revolutionary politics. Collaborated in the publication of the underground periodicals *El Diablo Cojuelo* and *La Patria Libre*, 1869; arrested for subversion, 1869, and sentenced to six years hard labour, sentence commuted and exiled to Spain in 1871. Moved to Mexico, 1875, via France and England. Contributed to *Revista Universal*, 1875–76, and founded the Alarcón Society, both in Mexico City. Married Carmen Zayas Bazán in 1876, one son. Visited Cuba briefly in 1877. Teacher of languages and philosophy in Guatemala, 1876–77; returned again to Cuba: worked in a law office, and taught literature at the Liceo de Guanabacoa; arrested on suspicion of anti-government activity, and deported again to Spain,

1879; travelled to France in the same year, then sailed to the US. Lived in New York, 1879–95; journalist for the *New York Sun*, c.1880. Critical of country's economic structure and painfully aware that its economic might threatened the liberty of the Latin American states. Travelled to Venezuela and founded the *Revista Venezolana*, Caracas, 1881. Correspondent for various Spanish American newspapers in New York, including *El Partido Liberal* (Mexico), *La Opinión Nacional* (Venezuela), from 1881, *La Nación* (Argentina), from 1882 and *La República* (Honduras), from 1886, *El Economista Americano* (New York), 1887 and *La Opinión Pública* (Uruguay), from 1889. Translator for the publishing house, Appleton, New York, from 1882; contributing editor, *La América*, New York, from 1883. Consul for Uruguay, New York, 1887–91; North American representative of the Free Press Association of Argentina, from 1888; founding editor of the children's magazine, *La Edad de Oro* [The Golden Age], 1889 (ran for four issues); Spanish teacher, Central High School, New York, 1890; consul for Argentina and Paraguay, 1890–91, and Paraguay, from 1890; founder, *Liga de Instrucción*, Tampa, Florida, 1891; in last years his involvement in Cuban revolutionary politics intensified: co-founder, Cuban Revolutionary Party and the revolutionary journal *Patria*, both 1892, travelled constantly throughout Central America, the Caribbean and Florida, helped organize the invasion of Cuba, 1895 (named Major General of the Army of Liberation in the island). Killed in action at Dos Ríos, 19 May 1895. Regarded as model Cuban patriot and, for this reason, has become an icon.

Selected Works

Poetry
Ismaelillo, New York: Thompson and Moreau Press, 1882
Versos sencillos, New York: Louis Weiss, 1891

Poetry Anthologies
Poesías, edited by Juan Marinello, Havana: Cultural, 1928
Versos de amor (inéditos), edited by Gonzalo de Quesada y Miranda, Havana: n.p., 1930
Flores del destierro (versos inéditos), edited by Gonzalo de Quesada y Miranda, Havana: Molina y Cía, 1933
Poesías completas, edited by Rafael Esténger, Havana: Librería Económica, 1953
Major Poems, edited by Philip S. Foner and translated by Elinor Randall, New York: Holmes and Meier, 1982 [bilingual edition]
Poesía completa, edited by Eliana Dávila, Havana: Letras Cubanas, 1985
Antología poética, edited by María Esther Cantonnet, Montevideo: Casa del Estudiante,1987

Novella
Amistad funesta, New York: n.p., 1885 [Published under the pseudonym Adelaida Real]

Plays
Amor con amor se paga, Mexico City: n.p., 1876; as *Love is Repaid by Love*, translated by Willis K. Jones, in *Archivos de José Martí*, vol. 2, Havana: 1947
Adúltera: drama inédito, Havana: n.p., 1935

Collected Works
Obras completas, edited by Gonzalo de Quesada y Miranda, 74 vols, Havana: Trópico, 1936–53
Obras completas, 28 vols, Havana: Editorial Nacional de Cuba, 1963–73

Compilations and Anthologies
Artículos desconocidos, Havana: Universo, 1930

Epistolario, edited by Félix Lizaso, 3 vols, Havana: Cultural, 1930–31

Obras escogidas, edited by Rafael Esténger, Madrid: Aguilar, 1953

Páginas de José Martí, edited by Fryda Schulz de Mantovani, Buenos Aires: Universitaria, 1963

Escritos desconocidos, edited by Carlos Ripoll, New York: Torres, 1971

Ensayos sobre arte y literatura, edited by Roberto Fernández Retamar, Havana: Instituto Cubano de Libro, 1972

Nuestra América, edited by Hugo Achúgar, Caracas: Biblioteca Ayacucho, 1977

Nuevas cartas de Nueva York, edited by E. Mejía Sánchez, Mexico City: Siglo XXI, 1980

Dos congresos; Las razones ocultas, edited by the Centro de Estudios Martianos, Havana: Editorial de Ciencias Sociales, 1985

Martí y el Uruguay: crónicas y correspondencia, Montevideo: Universidad de la Republica, 1988

Epistolario, edited by Luis García Pascual and Enrique H. Morena, Havana: Editorial de Ciencias Sociales, 1993

Anthologies in Translation

The America of José Martí: Selected Writings, translated by Juan de Onís, New York: Noonday Press, 1953

Martí on the USA, edited and translated by Luis A. Baralt, Carbondale: Southern Illinois University Press, 1966

Inside the Monster: Writings on the United States and American Imperialism, edited by Philip S. Foner and translated by Foner, Elinor Randall, *et al.*, New York: Monthly Review Press, 1975

On Education: Articles on Educational Theory and Pedagogy, and Writings for Children from the Age of Gold, edited by Philip S. Foner and translated by Elinor Randall, New York: Monthly Review Press, 1979

Our America: Writings on Latin America and the Struggle for Cuban Independence, edited by Philip S. Foner and translated by Elinor Randall, New York: Monthly Review Press, 1979

On Art and Literature, edited by Philip S. Foner and translated by Elinor Randall, New York: Monthly Review Press, 1982

Political Parties and Elections in the United States, edited by Philip S. Foner and translated by Elinor Randall, Philadelphia: Temple University Press, 1989

Further Reading

Abel, Christopher and Nissa Torrents (editors), *José Martí: Revolutionary Democrat*, Durham, North Carolina: Duke University Press, and London: Athlone Press, 1986

Agramonte, Roberto, *Martí y su concepción del mundo*, Rio Piedras: Universidad de Puerto Rico, 1971

Arias, Salvador, *Acerca de "La Edad de Oro,"* Havana: Centro de Estudios Martianos, Letras Cubanas, 1980

Cantón Navarro, José, *Algunas ideas de José Martí en relación con la clase obrera y el socialismo*, Havana: Instituto Cubano del Libro, 1970

Carbonell, Néstor, *Martí, carne y espíritu*, 2 vols, Havana: Edicion-Homenaje a la República de Cuba en el Cincuentenario de su Independencia, 1951–52

Esténger, Rafael, *Vida de Martí: biografía*, Santiago de Chile: Ercilla, 1936

González, Manuel Pedro, *José Martí: Epic Chronicler of the United States in the Eighties*, Chapel Hill: University of North Carolina Press, 1953

Gray, Richard B., *José Martí: Cuban Patriot*, Gainesville: University Presses of Florida, 1962

Jiménez, José Olivio, *José Martí: poesía y existencia*, Mexico City: Oasis, 1983

Kirk, John M., *José Martí: Mentor of the Cuban Nation*, Tampa: University Presses of Florida, 1983

Marinello, Juan, *Once ensayos martianos*, Havana: Comision Nacional Cubana de la Unesco, 1964

Martínez Estrada, Ezequiel, *Martí: El héroe y su acción revolucionaria*, Mexico City: Siglo XXI, 1966

Mistral, Gabriela, *La lengua de Martí*, Havana: Secretaría de Educación, 1934

Rama, Ángel, "Indagación de la ideología en la poesía (Los dípticos seriados de *Versos sencillos*)," *Revista Iberoamericana*, vol. 46/112–13 (1980)

Rexach, Rosario, *Estudios sobre Martí*, Madrid: Playor, 1985

Ronning, C. Neale, *José Martí and the Emigré Colony in Key West: Leadership and State Formation*, New York: Praeger, 1990

Schulman, Ivan, *Martí, Darío y el modernismo*, Madrid: Gredos, 1969

Vitier, Cintio, *Los versos de Martí*, Havana: Universidad de la Havana, 1969

Vitier, Cintio and Fina García Marruz, *Temas martianos*, Havana: Biblioteca Nacional José Martí, 1969

Bibliographies

Peraza Sarausa, Fermín, *Bibliografía martiana (1853–1953)*, Havana: Comisión Nacional Organizadora de los Actos y Ediciones del Centario y del Monumento de Martí, 1954, supplemented with *Bibliografía martiana (1954–63)*, by Celestino Blanch y Blanco, 1965

Ripoll, Carlos, *Archivo José Martí*, New York: Torres, 1971

Nuestra América

Essay by José Martí

"Nuestra América" (Our America), José Martí's seminal essay on Spanish American character, history and destiny, first appeared in the January 1891 issue of New York's *La Revista Ilustrada* [The Illustrated Review], edited by Elías de Losada. According to Vernon Chamberlain and Ivan Schulman (*La Revista Ilustrada de Nueva York: History, Anthology, and Index of Literary Selections*, 1975), it is one of four contributions that the Cuban writer made to the *Revista* during its 1886 to 1893 run. Additionally, Chamberlain and Schulman conclude that the Cuban also translated André Theuriet's novella "Un idilio de Pascua" [A Christmas Romance] which appeared under the pseudonym M. de S. in the May 1892 issue. An identical version of "Nuestra América" was published later in *El Partido Liberal* [The Liberal Party], expanding the audience for ideas that Martí saw fit to print in *La Revista Ilustrada* because, as Chamberlain and Schulman attest, he sympathized with the editor's fervent Latin Americanism. Martí himself wrote the following to Elías de Losada: "Me pareció el periódico, cosa mía, por la tolerancia y el pensamiento americano, del bueno, que Ud. pone en él" (The newspaper appeared my very own because of its tolerance and the fine American spirit with which you imbue it).

Martí's "Nuestra America" is regularly considered his most cohesive appraisal of the defining features of a region which he circumscribes within the essay to those lands that extend from the Rio Bravo to Patagonia. He espouses ideas that, in Chamberlain's and Schulman's opinion, lie at the core of his Spanish Americanism. The essay synthesizes an ideological evolution which began during Martí's initial encounter with Latin America as a continent. After a period of exile in Spain due to anticolonialist activities in Cuba, the writer returned to the New World. Between 1875 and 1878, Martí resided first in Mexico and then in Guatemala. According to Cintio Vitier in his *Temas martianos: segunda serie* (1982), this epoch is crucial in the formulation of the Martí's belief, clearly articulated in "Nuestra América," that "El gobierno ha de nacer del país. El espíritu del gobierno ha de ser el del país. El gobierno no es más que el equilibrio de los elementos naturales del país" (Government should emanate from the country itself. The spirit of the government has to be the spirit of the country. Government is no more than the equilibrium of a country's natural elements). This and other similar pan-nationalist notions evolve particularly during Martí's stay in the United States (1879–95). Vitier and others have argued that the writer's political conception undergoes a transformation based on the recognition of North American expansionist ambitions. If Martí focuses his organizational activities on securing Cuba's independence from Spain, a nation representative of old Europe's decadence, his more ambitious pedagogical and propagandistic concerns center on enunciating the need to avoid dangers explained in "Nuestra America." In essence, these risks are internal and external in nature. Latin America must struggle against regionalistic fervor and a limiting world view which promote a general malaise at the same time that they make the continent look with envy toward Europe and the United States. Similarly, New World Hispanic nations must unite to combat the inherent racism of the North Americans and their imperialist impetus. Martí emphasizes the need to come to terms with the continent's multi-racial identity. Long the basis of perceived inferiority, this polyvalent ethnicity should be reexamined in all its manifestations and recognized as the substance of innate originality. He teaches: "No hay odio de razas, porque no hay razas" (There is no racial hatred, because there are no races). Through this dictum he preaches a unity founded on a color-blindness that refutes what he terms "razas de librería" (bookstore races) and that allows for the absolute integration of peoples within and outside national borders. Only then could Latin America forge an effective barrier against Anglo-Saxon expansion, a barrier emerging from self-discovery and from acknowledgement of the collective need to upgrade submerged indigenous and African populations.

When Martí crafts "Nuestra América" as a fundamental expression of his pan-Latin Americanist doctrine, he is more aware than ever of the dangers posed by Manifest Destiny. As David Saville Muzzey indicates in his study *James G. Blaine: a Political Idol of Other Days* (1934), on October 2, 1889, North American Secretary of State James G. Blaine convened an International American Conference in Washington to discuss such topics as "the establishment of regular communications between ports of commerce, the formation of an American customs union, a uniform standard of weights and measures, uniform copyright and patent laws, the adoption of a common monetary (silver) unit, and, most important of all, the agreement on a general plan of arbitration for the settlement of controversies in which the honor or independence of several states was not involved." At its closing on April 19, 1890 representatives from the seventeen nations that eventually agreed to participate came together on only one item, identified by Alice Felt Tyler in *The Foreign Policy of James G. Blaine* (1965) as "the establishment of an International Bureau of American Republics, which was destined to be a permanent

and very valuable agent for the collection and dissemination of information." In part, the Conference's failure resulted from Latin American distrust of United States intentions in the era of Manifest Destiny. Perceiving these deliberations among the nations of the Americas as essential to Cuba's political destiny, José Martí followed them with anguish from distant New York City. The conversations coincided with Florida Senator Wilkinson Call's introduction of a controversial bill that would permit his country to seek the Island's independence from Spain under the tutelage of a voucher nation responsible for guaranteeing indemnification. To Martí, this initiative conceived by Cuban annexationist José Ignacio Rodríguez, a personal friend of Call's who had in fact crafted it, was tantamount to granting the United States sovereignty over the Island. As a result, he worked feverishly behind the scenes and through his articles in *La Nación* of Buenos Aires to prevent the Conference delegates from voicing their approval of Call and Rodríguez's machinations. To Martí, the Congress's abject failure represents Latin American recognition of the imperialist objectives of the United States and, in Cuba's case, the temporary victory of his message that "Cambiar de amos no es ser libre" (To change masters is not to be free). Two years later, Martí served as Uruguay's representative to the International Monetary Conference, again held in Washington under the auspices of the United States. Its hidden intention was to impose a silver standard on Latin America. As Jorge Mañach documents in his *Martí, el apóstol* (1933), Martí addressed the Conference on behalf of Argentina, Brazil, Chile and Uruguay. He argued vehemently in favor of bimetallic standards, and he admonished those present about the danger of falling prey to new imperialist intentions imposed by devious means.

All these realities which he experienced within the *monster*, as Martí referred to the United States in a frequently mentioned letter to Mexican Manuel Mercado, integrate the dialogic substratum of "Nuestra América," a text in which the writer dialectically opposes Blaine's Pan-Americanism by contrasting it implicitly with his own Pan-Latin Americanism. The writer rejects any illogical political or economic dealings between Spanish America and that "pueblo emprendedor y pujante que la desconoce y la desdeña" (enterprising and powerful nation that neither knows it nor respects it). With pragmatic, albeit somewhat romantic, nationalism – based on perceived commonalities which he details in the essay – Martí justifies the inferior socio-economic and political position of the Spanish-speaking continent through a brief critical overview of its colonial past, from which Latin America emerged only after violent and yet unfinished revolutionary upheaval. A destructive conquest and its aftermath resulted in the repression and impoverishment of indigenous peoples, while rampant mercantilism promoted a new marginal population by the institution of African slavery. In his discourse, Martí advocates the need to rediscover the Other's voice in order to define in more complete fashion Latin American identity. If Todorov in his *The Conquest of America* (1982) proclaimed the contemporary crisis of that ethnocentric period in European history when conquered voices were interpreted and transformed to distort their difference through assimilation into a cultural mainstream, Martí preached in 1891 the need to reconstruct the history of Spanish America by rescripting its most distant past and by teaching this rescripted past regardless of complexity, even at the expense of conventional hegemonic historiography. He wrote: "La historia de América, de los incas acá, ha de enseñarse al dedillo, aunque no se enseñe a los arcontes de Grecia. Nuestra Grecia es preferible a la Grecia que no es nuestra" (The history of America, from the Incas to the present, must be taught thoroughly, even if we do not teach about Grecian Magistrates. Our Greece is preferable to a Greece that is not ours). The writer excuses as well the predominance throughout 19th-century Latin America of what Sarmiento named "caudillos bárbaros," or "primitive chieftains." A natural biproduct of lands whose intrinsic realities are repudiated by ruling classes, *caudillos* emerge extemporaneously from areas whose idiosyncracies they more or less understand. However, Martí maintains, as soon as they betray those forces which forged them, the very masses that supported their struggle for power rise in rebellion to destroy them. Hence, it stands to reason that those civilian groups more apt to govern well must first study "los factores reales del país" (the real elements of a country) so that just and democratic systems are summoned forth as if by acclamation in the Americas.

Martí's exuberantly poetic prose – often baroque in nature, inspired by classical models, always intensely personal – produces what Miguel de Unamuno felicitously described as a "prophetic, biblical style." An abundance of rhetorical complexities more admirable that lucid, renders his writing almost untranslatable and sometimes difficult to assimilate at an intellectual level. None the less, Martí's writing never fails to affect the reader emotionally or aesthetically. In the specific case of "Nuestra América," however, Martí tempers his prose to formulate a visionary, coherent and powerfully convincing manifesto which, despite its conciseness, represents one of the outstanding political texts in Latin American letters.

JORGE FEBLES

Editions

First edition: *Nuestra América*, *La Revista Ilustrada*, New York (January 1891)

Critical edition: in *Nuestra América*, prologue by Juan Marinello; selection and notes by Hugo Achúgar; chronology by Cintio Vitier, Caracas: Biblioteca Ayacucho, 1977

Translation: *Our America*, by Elinor Randall, New York: Monthly Review Press, 1979

Further Reading

Agramonte, Roberto, *Las doctrinas educativas y políticas de Martí*, Río Piedras: Editorial de la Universidad de Puerto Rico, 1981

Iduarte, Andrés, *Martí, escritor*, Mexico City: Joaquín Mortiz, 3rd edition, 1982 [Despite its dated approach, Iduarte's book is extremely informative regarding Martí's life and works]

Portuondo, José Antonio, *Martí, escritor revolucionario*, Havana: Editora Poética, 1982

Vitier, Cintio and Fina García Marruz, *Temas martianos*, Havana: Biblioteca Nacional José Martí, 1969

Zea, Leopoldo, *et al.* (editors), *José Martí a cien años de Nuestra América*, Mexico City: UNAM, 1993

Versos sencillos

Collection of poems by José Martí

In October 1891, José Martí published *Versos sencillos* [Simple Verses], a brief collection consisting of forty-six untitled compositions whose deceptive facility illustrates the author's creative maturity. Although the book is composed essentially of traditional octosyllabic quatrains arranged according to diverse consonantal rhyming patterns (abba; abab; aabb), it constitutes, nevertheless, a fundamental text in the development of Spanish American *Modernismo*. According to Federico de Onís (*España en América*, 1955) this late 19th and early 20th-century literary movement synthesizes the Hispanic version of a world-wide attitudinal crisis that, beginning in 1885, manifested itself in the arts, science, religion, politics, and finally, in every sphere of public life. Hence, *Modernismo* reflects Western modernity, described conventionally in light of shared universals: a break with tradition, rejection of empty rhetoric, a sense of historical discontinuity, the advent of psychologism, and so forth.

As Ángel Rama has detailed in a fundamental essay (*Revista Iberoamericana*, 1980), the book's genesis must be taken into account to understand both its form and content. *Versos sencillos* was written during a particularly difficult period in Martí's life. For years, he had lived apart from his wife, Carmen Zayas Bazán, and his son José, on whom he had based his first significant poetic collection, *Ismaelillo*, 1882 [Little Ishmael], and to whom the work is dedicated. "Hijo, espantado de todo me refugio en ti" (Son, horrified by everything I seek refuge in you), the poet wrote in the anthology's preface. The couple's definitive separation came about after Carmen's brief visit to New York in October 1890. Additionally, as José Miguel Oviedo has clearly delineated in *La niña de Nueva York: una revisión de la vida erótica de José Martí*, 1989 [The New York Girl: a Revision of Martí's Erotic Life], since 1880 the Cuban had been romantically entangled with Carmen Mantilla, a married woman not widowed from Manuel Mantilla until 1885. Martí and Carmita's daughter, María, on whom the writer lavished much fatherly love, is the protagonist of several "versos sencillos."

In addition to this complicated personal life that had a tremendous impact on the psyche of a sensitive man intent on abiding by a strict moral code based, as Oviedo reminds us, on "lealtad, honestidad y pureza de corazón" (loyalty, honesty and purity of heart), Martí's political commitments had taken a heavy physical toll. Intensely devoted to the cause of Cuba's freedom, for over ten years he had been involved in organizational efforts to secure the country's liberation by force. As a result, he suffered great anguish during the International American Conference of 1889, when he feared that Cuba would fall prey to the United States' annexational whims. Pressure proved overbearing and the poet fell ill. Martí explains in the oft quoted preface to the *Versos sencillos* that, during August 1890, he sojourned in the Catskill Mountains under medical orders. There he wrote feverishly, surrounded by a natural ambience which he transcribed lyrically with transcendental ardor derived from his much admired Ralph Waldo Emerson. Several months later, he read the poems at a social gathering. The enthusiasm with which they were received by friends led to their publication, because the author sought to prove his love for "la sencillez" (simplicity) and his belief in "la necesidad de poner el sentimiento en formas llanas y sinceras" (the necessity to express sentiment in plain and sincere forms), as he says in *Versos sencillos*.

Its title notwithstanding, Martí's collection encompasses often difficult compositions whose symbolic complexity has been lucidly explained in Ivan Schulman's seminal *Símbolo y color en la poesía de José Martí* (1960). As this critic explains, words like "wing," "eagle," "sun," "star," often paralleled to antithetical notions such as "abyss," "worm," "coal," "vulture" "yoke," are presented in polar manner to characterize a dualistic reality. In their struggle for hegemony, these contradictory elements sometimes reconciled permitting the advent of positive natural and human forces. In *Versos sencillos*, the reader also observes Martí's further development of a personal emblematic color scheme akin to those formulated by other poets of his generation.

José Juan Arrom has studied at length Martí's compositional method in *Versos sencillos* (*Certidumbre de América*, 1971). Arrom argues that, given the politically-charged state of mind Martí describes in his preface, he sought to direct poetic preoccupations and images through strophes and meters intrinsically Hispanic in nature. Essentially, the *Versos sencillos* fit within the tradition of the Spanish "copla," broadly defined as octosyllabic verses organized in stanzas of varied lengths. Unaffected in tone and spirit and often meant to be sung, these lyrics constitute a common corpus to which Martí consciously or unconsciously referred, as Arrom demonstrates convincingly by juxtaposing analytically specific textual fragments. This traditional nature of the *Versos sencillos* has ensured their permanence in Cuban folklore, to the point that several strophes have been widely disseminated in song. Popular composer Joseíto Fernández's world-renowned "Guantanamera," for instance, consists merely of a monotonous peasant *guajira*, whose refrain surrounds various "versos sencillos," often altered at the discretion of the interpreter. By seeking inspiration in this inherently Hispanic creative form, Martí not only makes the political statements that Arrom and Rama claim for the anthology, but he also retrieves in *modernista* fashion a conventional meter not in vogue, one whose medieval roots represent the endurance of poetry and music.

Versos sencillos evolves around a variety of motifs which may develop logically within certain texts, or may appear fortuituously intertwined in some, or may be presented confrontationally in others to suggest ideological tensions. Predominant among these motifs are love, honor, country, death, innocence, exile, nature, virtue, friendship, often fragmented to elucidate secondary notions that amplify the collection's quasi pedagogical tone. Ideas emanate from a highly confessional poetic voice whose individuality is, nevertheless, obscured at times by an eloquent commitment to humankind, to the cosmos, and to transparent historico-political circumstances. Ivan Schulman has explained that this lyrical entity is neither the anonymous poetic *I* of popular song, nor the Romantic *I* struggling against an evil and insensitive world. Rather, it is that symbiotic I associated with the modern poet, in whose persona soul and exterior reality coalesce to shape a voice ambiguous as well as elusive (*Ismaelillo, Versos libres, Versos sencillos*). Texts generally evince antithetical structures

that underline internal and external conflicts. This reflects a sense of crisis resolved explicitly or implicitly by the didactic voice which, by reading itself, guides the reader through ideological and imagistic frameworks. For instance, poem 23 states: "Yo quiero salir del mundo / por la puerta natural: // en un carro de hojas verdes / a morir me han de llevar. // No me pongan en lo oscuro a morir como un traidor: // yo soy bueno, y como bueno / moriré de cara al sol" (I would like to leave this world // through the natural door: // In a cart made of green leaves // they will take me to my death. // Do not place me in the darkness / to expire like a traitor: / I am good, and like a good man // I will die facing the sun). Positive natural images ("green leaves," "sun") are positioned antagonistically to the feared darkness which Martí conventionally associated with betrayal, with corruption, with the most negative human features. By defining itself as "good," the poetic voice not only ascertains its right to "the burial of the just" and to look the sun in its face, but indirectly as well it enunciates a universal tenet: whoever is good deserves an identical honor.

Another ideological juxtaposition emphasized by Rama in his lengthy essay departs from the predominant airiness of the previous example. Martí at times permits traditional visions of ugliness and beauty to coexist in order to create tensions resolved intellectually by the reader's recognition of their merely objective representation. Rama analyzes in particular the following stanzas: "En el bote iba remando / por el lago seductor / con el sol que era oro puro / y en el alma más de un sol. // Y a mis pies vi de repente / ofendido del hedor / un pez muerto, un pez hediondo / en el bote remador" (I was rowing in a boat / on the seductive lake / with the sun that was pure gold / and in my soul more than one sun // Suddenly, at my feet I saw / offended by its stench / a dead fish, a stinking fish / in the rowboat). For Rama, by allowing beauty and ugliness to share realistically the same poetic structure, Martí subverts individual consciousness, signifying in Emersonian fashion that natural elements belong outside what this critic calls "standard evaluative cultural systems."

A key motif in the collection, love and its concomitant image, woman, manifests itself at the core of several compositions. Poems 16 to 21 deal with the romantic convention of the *femme fatale*, perceived by the poetic voice in traditionally mysoginist manner, a proclivity in the author's work that Jacqueline Cruz has studied in a controversial essay published in *Hispania* (1992). Eve as the root of all evil, regardless of her individual physical attributes, reappears ephemerally in several compositions. She also provides the substance for many other texts. Noteworthy examples of both possibilities are 1, 4, 10, 13, 14, 16, 33, 36, 37, 38, 41, 42, and one of Martí's most enticing poems, 43, in which he craves an erotic encounter with an archetypal temptress. Powerfully sensual, the text focuses in *modernista* fashion on the woman's red tresses, which the poetic voice longs to spread thread by thread over her naked back. More Patonic in nature is Martí's best-known composition, the suggestive 9, "La niña de Guatemala" [The Girl from Guatemala]. This lyrical dramatization of the fleeting relationship between the *real author* and María García Granados, a young woman who was his student when Martí resided in Guatemala, this "melodious game," as Gabriela Mistral aptly designated it, may be described none the less as a confessional text through which the poet seeks to extirpate a sense of guilt emanating from María's death from pneumonia shortly after he returned to Guatemala with his wife, Carmen Zayas Bazán.

Versos sencillos epitomizes Martí's creative maturity. An essential volume in the development of Spanish American *modernista* poetry, it reveals as well the political commitment that cost the writer his life. Honor and duty, perceived by the lyric voice as the need to sacrifice for an ideal irrevocably entwined with Cuba's fate, are guiding tenets that force the poet textually as well as historically to forsake verse. Darío, who questioned the island's right to claim a man destined to be an artist, rectified himself at the end of an essay included in *Los raros*, 1896 [The Eccentrics] by resurrecting Martí's voice. Here Darío recreates dramatically number 45 of the *Versos sencillos*. Dressed in the heroic stone vestments with which the Cuban poet had envisioned dead heroes reborn to punish a moment of weakness on the part of his lyrical alter ego, Martí bursts on the scene to address the essayist: "Yo quiero, cuando me muera / sin patria, pero sin amo / tener en mi tumba un ramo / de flores, ¡y una bandera!" (I would like, when I die / without country, but without master / to have placed upon my tombstone / a bouquet of flowers and a flag!) [José Martí]). Martí's dual identity as an aesthete devoted to a political cause and a poet who chose to become a prophet for the Americas is reflected powerfully in the *Versos sencillos*, a collection that cements his reputation as arguably the most provocative Spanish American *modernista* author.

JORGE FEBLES

Editions

First edition: *Versos sencillos*, New York: Louis Weiss, 1891

Critical edition and translation: *José Martí: Major Poems: a Bilingual Edition*, edited with an introduction by Philip S. Foner and translated by Elinor Randal, New York and London: Holmes and Meier, 1982 [Contains selection of poems from *Versos sencillos*]

Further Reading

Ballón, José, *Autonomía cultural americana: Emerson y Martí*, Madrid: Pliegos, 1986

Barroso, Leopoldo, "El prólogo de los *Versos sencillos*: ¿Qué quiso decir Martí?," *Círculo: Revista de Cultura* 18 (1989)

García Ronda, Denia, "Las antinomias en '*Versos sencillos*'," *Universidad de La Habana* 228 (1986)

Hernández-Chiroldes, Alberto, *Los " Versos sencillos" de José Martí: análisis crítico*, Miami: Universal, 1983

Oviedo, José Miguel, *La niña de Nueva York: una revisión de la vida erótica de José Martí*, Mexico City: Fondo de Cultura Económica, 1989

Radamés de la Campa, Antonio, "En los cien años de los *Versos sencillos*," *Círculo: Revista de Cultura*, 21 (1992)

Rivera-Meléndez, Blanca, *Poetry and Machinery of Illusion: José Martí and the Poetics of Machinery*, Ithaca, New York: Cornell University Press, 1992

Ezequiel Martínez Estrada 1895–1964

Argentine essayist and poet

Although his first publications were five very short essays that appeared in Buenos Aires between 1916 and 1918, Ezequiel Martínez Estrada formally began his literary career as a premeditative poet in the rarefied tradition of Leopoldo Lugones's lexical gymnastics, Edgar Allan Poe's phantasmal visions, and the mythological evocations of Rubén Darío. Between 1918 and 1929 he produced six volumes of poetry which were not then, nor have been since, much appreciated by literary historians and critics. Nevertheless, there was an emotional harmony between the poet's lyric intuitions and a sombre view of the world that was to permeate his prose from 1930 to his late writing.

His life's work was a steady progression from the cerebral toward the emotional, as one can tell by a successive reading of three of his key essays: *Radiografía de la pampa*, 1933 (*X-Ray of the Pampa*), *Muerte y transfiguración de Martín Fierro*, 1948 [Death and Transfiguration of Martin Fierro], and his posthumous *Martí, revolucionario*, 1967 [Martí the Revolutionary]. A tone of disillusionment dominates

Radiografía, but at the same time the historical vision of Argentine's discovery, exploration and settlement is clear and perceptive. The second work (his longest) is also written in a historical perspective, based on a close, expansive reading of José Hernández's narrative poem *Martín Fierro* (see separate entry). In the frustrated life of the gaucho protagonist, Martínez Estrada finds a symbol of modern Argentina's political and social disorientation, a departure toward indeterminacy. José Martí, the essayist, poet and political organizer who died in 1895 during the second Cuban War of Independence, is portrayed as one of the Western world's last heroes. "He was not a philosopher," says Martínez Estrada in his essay, "but a thinker in action, who wanted to change the world rather than understand (i.e., accept) it."

In a way reminiscent of the Spaniard Miguel de Unamuno's spiritual reiterations, Martínez Estrada had (and cultivated) a tragic sense of life. He persistently stressed a love-hate relationship with his country; and one feels that his late sojourn in Cuba (1960–62) was, in addition to an opportunity to do

intensive research on the life and work of Martí and an enthusiastic endorsement of the 1959 Revolution, a form of symbolic
exile in protest against the political state of affairs then prevalent in Argentina and several other Latin American countries
(it was even rumoured in the press, erroneously, that Martínez
Estrada had planned to adopt Cuban citizenship.

His pessimism has often been seen as excessively nihilistic.
Juan José Sebreli, for example, in a book written from a
Marxist point of view (*Martínez Estrada: una rebelión inútil*,
1960) [Martínez Estrada: a Useless Rebellion], sees him as an
out-of-touch romantic who arbitrarily dismissed all possibility
of historical progress. Dardo Cúneo, another compatriot,
writes: "Martínez Estrada can be legitimately criticized for
picking out elements of Argentine reality and evaluating the
worst of them in such a way as to indicate that they contain
the whole truth." Possibly Martínez Estrada himself wanted to
correct these impressions with his biography of a militantly
optimistic 19th-century Cuban writer.

Although the author of *Radiografía de la pampa* published
his works in four forms (poetry, essay, short story, drama),
the essay, which E.B. White has identified as the genre of
"congenitally self-centred" writers, was his basic instrument.
His continual suggestion of a symbiotic relationship between
his country and himself was both his poetic strength and his
rational weakness (like Domingo Faustino Sarmiento a century
before him). His visions were more compelling than his
thoughts: the pampa; evocations of the gaucho as a predetermined victim and pariah; colonization of the pampa regions
and South America in general as an implicit search for
paradise; his view of Buenos Aires as the temporary abode
described in one of the twenty-five essays comprising *La cabeza
de Goliat*, 1940 [Goliath's Head]: "We had a past without art,
lacking in substance and without dignity, for things were not
built, as in Rome, to last for ever, but only to remain the short
time that our adventure would last."

Radiografía de la pampa was Martínez Estrada's foundation work; its basic themes would be further developed over
the next two decades in *La cabeza de Goliat*, *Sarmiento*,
Muerte y transfiguración de Martín Fierro and *El mundo
maravilloso de Guillermo Enrique Hudson* [The Marvellous
World of William Henry Hudson]. *Radiografía*'s six parts
correspond to its six main topics: collective disillusionment;
collective solitude; primitive forces ("telluric," "mechanical"
and "psychic") which Martínez Estrada thinks have caused
Argentina's historical "erosion" more than its evolution;
Buenos Aires, social and political exploiter of the nation; fear,
an inhibitive force that has repeatedly provoked violence in the
guise of "defence"; pseudostructures, or forms and functions
that unintentionally reveal an illusory existence based on self-
interest.

Muerte y transfiguración de Martín Fierro expands on the
psychological and cultural inferences of *Radiografía*. The
author takes over José Hernández's protagonist, a rural Argentine mass-man of the 19th century who, in contrast to Ulysses,
Faust and Don Quixote, is a restless symbol of the ordinary.
Hernández defended him as a representative victim; Martínez
Estrada, in full sympathy with Martín Fierro's unspoiled nature
and generally good intentions, considers him as the 20th-
century Argentines' ancestor who anticipates their spiritual
insecurity, and their tendency to resent their historical fate.

In *Sarmiento*, which preceded *Muerte y transfiguración*, and
El mundo maravilloso de Guillermo Enrique Hudson, which
followed it, the author opposes Sarmiento's good-civilization
versus bad-ruralism thesis in a Neoromantic defense of natural
man. William Henry Hudson, who grew up on the pampas,
was an accomplished naturalist and writer who nostalgically
relived his youthful years in *Far Away and Long Ago* (1918),
The Purple Land (1885) and *Idle Days in Patagonia* (1893).
Martínez Estrada found a congenial soul in Hudson, who
shared the belief that man was progressively enslaved through
his own inventiveness and that his only alternative was a return
to nature.

Like many of his essays, Martínez Estrada's short stories are
based on dilemmas that allow no solutions. The longest one,
"Sábado de Gloria," 1944 [Holy Saturday] is the nightmarish,
Kafkaesque account of a government office worker's attempts
to finish his assignments by early afternoon the Saturday before
Easter so that he and his family can leave on the 1.30 train
for their vacation; but it's almost four o'clock when another
employee tells him he's wanted on the telephone, and there the
story ends. The author's own dull experience as a part-time
postal employee in Buenos Aires from 1916 to 1946 was undeniably the motivation for that tale. In "La inundación" [The
Deluge], also published in 1944, over a thousand inhabitants
of a remote village take refuge in a large, unfinished church
on a hill during a flood. One recalls Noah's Ark, but the theme
is human survival (or demise) in the contemporary world. The
rains continue day after day; food becomes scarce; 200 hungry
dogs are outside. A doctor, an aged priest, and a mad prophet
can't attend to the people's needs. But then, on the last page,
heavy drops begin to fall once again on the anxious, uplifted
faces.

One wonders to what extent Martínez Estrada enjoyed or
suffered his vocation. The reader senses that authorship for
him was both an indulgence and a torture. In an autobiographical letter (1945) that Victoria Ocampo asked him to
write for her journal *Sur* he declares that "to prolong life
beyond puberty is a fatal error that one pays for with survival
itself" and that in his fiftieth year he could remember no
instance in which he was able "to experience a child's innocence."

PETER G. EARLE

Biography

Born in San Juan de la Esquina, province of Santa Fe, Argentina, 14
September 1895. Eldest of three sons. Moved to Goyena in south of
province of Buenos Aires where father ran a general store. Sent to
Buenos Aires at the age of twelve where he attended the Colegio
Avellaneda, but largely self-taught because he was unable to finish
his formal education. Employed by Post Office, 1914. Published first
articles in the magazine *Nosotros*, Buenos Aires, 1917. Married the
portrait painter and restorer Agustina Marconi in 1921. From 1923
taught at the Colegio Nacional, a school of the University of La
Plata. Visited Italy and France, 1927. Lost his teaching post when
Perón was elected president, 1945. Afflicted by painful skin
complaint, 1952, which was to last five years. Travelled to Mexico,
1959, where he worked in the School of Political Science,
Universidad Nacional Autónoma de México (UNAM). Went to
Cuba, February 1960 to receive a Casa de las Américas award for
his essay, *Análisis funcional de la cultura*. Stayed in Cuba from
September 1960 until November 1962 to write an extensive

biography of José Martí (see separate entry) commissioned by the Cuban government. Died of abdominal cancer in Bahía Blanca, 3 November 1964.

Selected Works

Poetry

Poesía, Buenos Aires: Argos, 1947 [A collection of six previously published volumes: *Oro y piedra*, 1918; *Nefeliba*, 1922; *Motivos del cielo*, 1924; *Argentina*, 1927; *Títeres de pies ligeros*, 1929; *Humoresca*, 1929]

Essays

Radiografía de la pampa, Buenos Aires: Babel, 1933, edited by Leo Pollmann, *et al.*, Madrid: Colección Archivos, 1991; as *X-Ray of the Pampa*, translated by Alain Swietlicki, Austin: University of Texas Press, 1971
Sarmiento, Buenos Aires: Argos, 1946
La cabeza de Goliat microscopía de Buenos Aires, 2nd augmented edition, Buenos Aires: Emecé, 1947; Madrid: Revista de Occidente, 1970
Panorama de los Estados Unidos, 2nd edition, Buenos Aires: Emecé, 1947; edited by Joaquín Roy, Buenos Aires: Torres Aguero, 1985 [Contains "Diario de Viaje" and "Diagrama de los Estados Unidos"]
Muerte y transfiguración de Martín Fierro. Ensayo de interpretación de la vida argentina, 2 vols, Mexico City: Fondo de Cultura Económica, 1948; revised edition, 1958
El mundo maravilloso de Guillermo Enrique Hudson, Mexico City: Fondo de Cultura Económica, 1951
El hermano Quiroga, Montevideo: Instituto Nacional de Investigaciones y Archivos Literarios, 1957
Diferencias y semejanzas entre los países de la América Latina, Mexico City: Escuela Nacional de Ciencias Politicas y Sociales, 1962; critical edition, Caracas: Biblioteca Ayacucho, 1990
Martí revolucionario, prologue by Roberto Fernández Retamar, Havana: Casa de las Américas, 1967

Compilations and Anthologies

Antología, Mexico City: Fondo de Cultura Económica, 1964
Leer y escribir, edited by Enrique Espinoza, Mexico City: Joaquín Mortiz, 1969
Cuentos completos, Madrid: Alianza Editorial and Fundación Ezequiel Martínez Estrada, 1975
Antología, Havana: Casa de las Américas, 1986

Translations

Holy Saturday and Other Stories, translated by Leland H. Chambers, Pittsburgh: Latin American Literary Review Press, 1988

Further Reading

Adam, Carlos, *Bibliografía y documentos de Ezequiel Martínez Estrada*, La Plata: Universidad Nacional de la Plata, 1968
Anderson Imbert, Enrique, "Martínez Estrada en 1926," *Sur* 295 (July–August 1965) [Testimony in an issue commemorating Martínez Estrada]
Avellaneda, Andrés, "Martínez Estrada: historia de un profeta argentino," in Avellenada, *et al.*, *Ocho escritores por ocho periodistas*, Buenos Aires: Timerman Editores, 1976
Borello, Rodolfo, *El peronismo (1943–1955) en la narrativa argentina*, Ottawa: Dovehouse Editions, 1991 [Section on Martínez Estrada]
Canal Feijóo, Bernardo, "Radiografías fatídicas," *Sur* 37 (1937)
Cúneo, Dardo, "Sobre Ezequiel Martínez Estrada," in his *Aventura y letra de América Latina*, Buenos Aires: Pleamar, 1964
Earle, Peter G., *Prophet in the Wilderness. The Works of Ezequiel Martínez Estrada*, Austin: University of Texas Press, 1971
—— "Las soledades de Martínez Estrada," in *Idea/Imágenes*, cultural supplement of *La Nueva Provincia*, Bahía Blanca (30 September 1993)
Fernández Retamar, Roberto, "Razón de homenaje," in *Casa de las Américas* 33 (November–December 1965) [Introduction to an issue commemorating Martínez Estrada]
Maharg, James, *A Call to Authenticity: the Essays of Ezequiel Martínez Estrada*, University of Mississippi: Romance Monographs, 1977
Morsella, Astur, *Martínez Estrada*, Buenos Aires: Plus Ultra, 1970
Murena, H.A., "Martínez Estrada: la lección de los desposeídos," in his *El pecado original de América*, Buenos Aires: Editorial *Sur*, 1954
Orgambide, Pedro de, *Genio y figura de Ezequiel Martínez Estrada*, Buenos Aires: Eudeba, 1980
Rivera, Juan Manuel, *Estética y mitificación en la obra de Ezequiel Martínez Estrada*, Madrid: Pliegos, 1987
Sebreli, Juan José, *Martínez Estrada: una rebelión inútil*, augmented 3rd edition, Buenos Aires: Catálogos, 1986
Stabb, Martin S., "Ezequiel Martínez Estrada: the Formative Writings," *Hispania*, vol. 49 (1966)
Viñas, David, "Ezequiel Martínez Estrada, hace tiempo y allá lejos," in *Cuadernos Americanos* 6 (1982)
Weinberg de Magis, Liliana, *Ezequiel Martínez Estrada y la interpretación del "Martín Fierro,"* Mexico City: UNAM, 1992

Carlos Martínez Moreno 1917–1986

Uruguayan prose writer

Like other members of the Uruguayan "Generation of 1945," Carlos Martínez Moreno has been overshadowed by Juan Carlos Onetti and Mario Benedetti. However, the publication of a monographic study by Kenton Van Stone in 1994, may bring Martínez Moreno's work the critical attention it deserves at home as well as abroad.

At ease with the different demands of essay, short story and full-length novel, Martínez Moreno looked beyond Uruguay for his subject matter. Spain provides the setting for the early "El niño que prepara su muerte" [The Child Who Prepares His Death] and "La pareja del Museo del Prado" [The Couple in the Prado Museum], from the collection *Los días por vivir* [Days for Living]. The Cuban Revolution gave rise to *El paredón* [The Execution Wall] and the fruitlessness of the United States' military intervention in Vietnam is the subject of "Para un cadáver en Khe Sanh" [To a Corpse in Khe Sanh]. But much of his literary production is set in and pertains very clearly to the River Plate region. Martínez Moreno's prose fiction as a whole might be considered a metaphor for Uruguay, if not Latin America as a whole, dealing as it does with decay and decline, the disintegration of human relationships – "El lazo en la aldaba" [The Wreath on the Door Knocker], a Christmas story without a happy ending – and abject failure ("La última morada" [The Last Dwelling Place]). Rubén Cotelo draws our attention to "the obstinate and recurring presence of certain symbols of pessimism and frustration."

While Martínez Moreno is deeply concerned with social and political themes, the specificities of concrete events are subordinated in his narrative to their effects on the people who participate in them. Whether the scions of upper-class families (Eugenio in *Con las primeras luces* [With the First Lights], or Carlos Juárez, one of the pampered, wealthy young described in "El simulacro" [The Simulacrum], whether they are drug traffickers (*Coca*) or petty thieves for whom violent crime is the only way of life, as in *Tierra en la boca* [Eating Earth], Martínez Moreno's characters are trapped in a spiral of impotent degradation, living out their lives in "quiet desperation," sometimes even madness, as in "El ciclo del señor Philidor" [Mr Philidor's Cycle] and "El prisionero" [The Prisoner]. Accused by critics of despising the characters he creates, rather he is pitiless in stripping away the veils of pretence with which people delude others and, worse still, themselves. These attacks on hypocrisy are not necessarily without humour. The eponymous narrator-protagonist of "El invitado" [The Guest] observes his host and hostess first pretending that the maid has not dropped the soup tureen, then ignoring the appearance of "otro personaje. Es enorme, negro y lustroso" (. . . another character. He is enormous, black and shiny), the family pet, Ponciano, who first licks up the asparagus soup then vomits all over the porcelain shards. Along with symbols of pessimism and frustration, we also find the recurring motifs of eyes, vision, looks, perceived appearance as opposed to sordid, inner reality, particularly in "Los sueños buscan el mayor peligro" [Dreams Seek the Greatest Danger]. Much emphasis has been placed on the density and rigour of Martínez

Moreno's language. Sometimes convoluted in his descriptive passages, he is entirely successful in conveying an impression of authentic speech, whether that heard in the elegant drawing-rooms of the the upper classes or the rougher but no less meaningful parlance of the slums and shanty towns.

Martínez Moreno's writing is also full of references to the visual arts and literature. It is difficult to know how far we should trust the voice of the narrator-protagonist of "El simulacro," but one affirmation does stand out. When faced with the choice between a book on political history and the literary magazine *Caras y Caretas* (a famous Argentine magazine in which an earlier Uruguayan writer, Horacio Quiroga published his short stories), he would prefer the latter, a view possibly shared by the author. Arguably, such allusions do not constitute an empty display of authorial erudition, but may fulfil several purposes, social criticism being the predominant one. In the self-conscious "Los prados de la conciencia" [The Meadows of Conscience], the narrator-protagonist pokes fun at his peers, the participants in a writers' congress in New York, recommends to Pérez, whom he has singled out for close attention "no elijas la profesión de escritor" (Don't choose the profession of writer) and unexpectedly informs the reader that: "Mis lecturas hacen las veces de mi gusto, de mi experiencia y de mi vida" (My reading stands in for my taste, my experiences and my life). "El salto del tigre" [The Tiger's Leap] contains what may well be the Uruguayan equivalent of Cervantes's book-burning scene. There is no doubt that Martínez Moreno makes use of irony, ostensibly for humorous effects, though normally with more satirical intentions in mind. "Cuatro o cinco islas" [Four or Five Islands] with its idea of using an island as a reformatory for minors, shares the tone of Swift's *A Modest Proposal*.

Finally, one should consider those aspects of Martínez Moreno's narrative that demand further investigation. The most obvious is his socio-political comment, but equally rewarding might be a close reading of his works to disentangle the web of intertextualities, as exemplified by the Lear motif in "Cordelia" (1956), or the Jamesian reminiscences of "Los aborígenes" [The Natives]. Within the Uruguayan canon, an obvious point of comparison for stories like "Paloma" (translated into English as "The Pigeon" in 1966 and still being included in anthologies as recently as 1993), is Mario Benedetti's collection of short stories *Montevideanos* with its emphasis on stultifying routine, limited aspirations and petty-mindedness. Another path to explore is his use of *roman noir* or "tough guy" fiction, arising no doubt out of his experiences as journalist and criminal lawyer. *La otra mitad* [The Other Half] deals with adultery, murder and suicide, *Tierra en la boca* with murder and theft. "El careo" [The Confrontation], another short story that appears in various anthologies, shows a murderer condemned out of his own mouth.

PATRICIA ANNE ODBER DE BAUBETA

See also entry on Mario Benedetti

Biography
Born in Colonia del Sacramento, Uruguay, 1 September 1917.
Family bankrupted in 1920. Moved to Montevideo, 1925. Reporter
for *El País*, 1938; staff member, *El Diario*, 1943 and began
contributing to *Marcha* (see entry under Journals). Won short story
competition, 1944. In 1952 covered Bolivian Revolution and became
friends of its leaders, Paz Estensoro and Siles Suazo. Joined the
Leftist coalition, the Broad Front, 1971. Resisted both growing
threat of military rule and the path of violent resistance chosen by
the urban guerrillas. Awarded the Mexican Premio Latinoamericano
del Cuento, 1977, for "La máscara." Home bombed by right-wing
death squad, 1978. Left Uruguay and went to Spain initially, settling
later in Mexico. Professor of political science, Universidad Nacional
Autónoma de México (UNAM). Died of heart attack in Mexico
City, 6 February 1986.

Selected Works

Novels
El paredón, Barcelona: Seix Barral, 1963
Con las primeras luces, Barcelona: Seix Barral, 1966
La otra mitad, Mexico City: Joaquín Mortiz, 1966
Coca, Caracas: Monte Ávila, 1970
El color que el infierno me escondiera, Mexico City: Nueva Imagen,
    1981; as *El infierno*, translated by Ann Wright, London: Readers
    International, 1988

Short Fiction
Los días por vivir, Montevideo: Asir, 1960 [Contains "Los sueños
    buscan el mayor peligro," "Cuatro o cinco islas," "Los días
    escolares," "El invitado," "La pareja del Museo del Prado,"
    "La serpiente"]
Cordelia, Montevideo: Colección Letras de Hoy, no. 7, 1961 [short
    story, written 1956]
Los aborígenes, 2nd edition, Montevideo: Alfa, 1964 [Contains
    "Los aborígenes," "Paloma," "El careo," "El ciclo del Señor
    Philidor," "Tenencia alterna," "El violoncello," "La fortuna de
    Oscar Gómez"]
Las cuatro. Novelas cortas, Montevideo: Alfa, 1967 [Contains "La
    última morada," "El lazo en la aldaba," "El salto del tigre,"
    "Cordelia"]
La sirena y otros cuentos, Buenos Aires, CEDAL: 1968
Los prados de la conciencia, Montevideo: Alfa, 1968 [Contains
    "Los prados de la conciencia," "El prisionero," "La muñeca,"
    "Las bebidas azules," "Ignotus," "¡Adiós Papá!," "La sirena,"
    "El simulacro"]
Las bebidas azules, Caracas: Monte Ávila, 1969 [Contains "Las
    bebidas azules," "Los aborígenes," "Paloma," "La muñeca,"
    "¡Adiós papá!," "El violoncello," "El simulacro," "La fortuna de
    Oscar Gómez," "La sirena," "Para un cadáver en Khe Sanh"]
De vida o muerte, Buenos Aires: Siglo XXI, 1971
Tierra en la boca, Buenos Aires: Losada, 1974
Animal de palabras, Montevideo: Arca, 1987

Essays on Literature and Art
Los narradores de 1900: Carlos Reyles, Montevideo: CEDAL, 1968
El aura del Novecientos, Montevideo: CEDAL, 1969
Las vanguardias literarias, Montevideo: Arca y Editores Reunidos,
    1969
Montevideo en la literatura y en el arte, Montevideo: Nuestra
    Tierra, 1971
Ensayos, 2 vols, Montevideo: Cámara de Senadores, 1994
Crítica teatral, Montevideo: Cámara de Senadores, 1994
Literatura americana y europea, Montevideo: Cámara de Senadores,
    1994

Translations
"The Pigeon," translated by Giovanni Pontiero, in *Spanish Short
    Stories/Cuentos Hispánicos 1*, Harmondsworth: Penguin, 1966

Further Reading
It should be noted that there is only one published full-length study
on Martínez Moreno's work. The two unpublished ones appear in
the secondary bibliography of Kenton Van Stone's monograph of
1994.

Aínsa, Fernando, *Los novelistas del 45*, Montevideo: CEDAL, 1968
____ *Tiempo reconquistado*, Montevideo: Géminis, 1977
Benedetti, Mario, *Literatura uruguaya siglo XX*, Montevideo: Alfa,
    1963
Erro-Orthmann, Nora, "Entrevista: Carlos Martínez Moreno,"
    Hispamérica, vol. 15/45
Fontana, Hugo, "Carlos Martínez Moreno: testigo de cargo,"
    Revista Iberoamericana, vol. 58 (1992)
Lewald, H. Ernest and Doris Stephens, "Trends in the Uruguayan
    Short Story in the 1970s," *Revista Internacional de Bibliografía /
    Inter-American Review of Bibliography* 30 (1980)
Paganini, Alberto, *Los cuentistas del 45*, Montevideo: CEDAL,
    1968
Rama, Ángel, *La generación crítica*, Montevideo: Arca, 1972
Real de Azúa, Carlos, *Antología del ensayo uruguayo
    contemporáneo*, Montevideo: Universidad de la República,
    1964
Rodríguez Monegal, Emir, *Literatura uruguaya del medio siglo*,
    Montevideo: Alfa, 1966
Rossell, Avenir, "El habla popular montevideana," *Texto Crítico*,
    vol. 3/6, Mexico City (January–April 1977)
Ruffinelli, Jorge, "Carlos Martínez Moreno la energía que no cesa,"
    Palabras en orden, Veracruz, Mexico: Universidad Veracruzana,
    1985
Stone, Kenton Van, *Utopia Undone: the Fall of Uruguay in the
    Novels of Carlos Martínez Moreno*, Lewisburg, Pennsylvania:
    Bucknell University Press, 1994
Visca, Arturo S., *Antología del cuento uruguayo. Los del cuarenta y
    cinco*, Montevideo: Ediciones de la Banda Oriental, 1968
Young, Richard, "War is Hell: Dante in Uruguay," in *Literature and
    War*, edited by David Bevan, Amsterdam: Rodopi, 1990

Marxism and Culture in Spanish America

In Latin America as in other parts of the world, Marxism manifests itself as a multifaceted phenomenon. On the political plane, and that of social struggle – *praxis* was the term used in the 1960s – Marxism gave rise to, or stimulated, the creation of the region's communist parties, most of which were founded during the 1920s, partly as a result of the efforts of the Third International (1919). The communist parties of Mexico and the three Southern Cone countries were founded around 1920; and in 1928, José Carlos Mariátegui founded the Peruvian Socialist Party which was, for all intents and purposes, a communist organization. As a vision of mankind and society, the ideology devised by Marx and Engels has inspired the thoughts and actions of countless anonymous militants, of political and syndicalist leaders, and of the odd hero or two, or perhaps martyrs. (For example, Ernesto "Che" Guevara, the Argentine-born revolutionary who was assassinated in Bolivia in 1967 whilst trying to promote a guerrilla army of liberation in the South of the subcontinent; also, Salvador Allende, the constitutional president of Chile, who died in 1973 whilst fighting insurgent officers attempting a *coup d'état*). In its aesthetic and cultural orientation, Marxism has exerted a strong influence on the best of Latin American art, ranging from the mural paintings by the Mexican artists (Diego Rivera, David Alfaro Siqueiros, and to a lesser extent José Clemente Orozco) to the vast epic of Neruda's *Canto general* (1950). Equally worthy of note is the expression of Marxism in popular music and social protest songs (such as those by the Argentine Atahualpa Yupanqui; the Uruguayans Daniel Viglietti and Alfredo Zitarrosa; the Mexican Amparo Ochoa; and the cantata *Santa María de Iquique* [The Virgin Mary of Iquique] by the Chilean Luis Advis, etc.). In fact, at least five of the greatest contributions to the world's artistic repertory to have come from Latin America display signs, some of them direct, others less so, of Marxist thought and sensibility: 20th-century ultramodern and revolutionary poetry (Vallejo, Guillén, Neruda, Cardenal); the realist, social, or (before these) historical novel, before and after the Boom (Asturias, Arguedas, Roa Bastos, and the later works of Carpentier); Mexican mural art and the indigenist painting of the Ecuadorian Oswaldo Guayasamín; Brazilian architecture as conceived by Oscar Niemeyer; and the protest song (mentioned above) that peaks, as well as garnering an ample continental following, after the Cuban Revolution of 1959. A potent symbol of this alliance between art and ideological commitment is the political affiliation of the Brazilian novelist Jorge Amado, or of Nobel Prize winners such as the Guatemalan Miguel Ángel Asturias (1967), and the Chilean Pablo Neruda (1971), all of whom were communists for most of their lives.

Marxist ideas began to spread and to make themselves felt in Latin America during the final decade of the 19th century. The names of Marx and Engels were not unknown to the European immigrants (and to the Arab immigrants from the Middle East, to a lesser extent). Their names circulated in urban areas, spreading their message of social change to the mining regions of northern Mexico and Tampico, and to the salt and coal mines in Chile. Marx is known, in particular, as the activist of the First International (1864); the anarchist

diatribe at this point surely contributes to his popularity. Engels, who died in 1895, is seen in the light of his contribution to the Second International (1889), the seed and guide of various Latin American socialist parties (the Socialist Party of Argentina, founded in 1896 by Justo; and the Socialist Workers Party of Chile, founded in 1912 by Recabarren).

If one divides Latin American Marxism into rough periods, it is possible to note a decisive change occurring with the advent of World War I or, more particularly, with the coming of the Russian Revolution. Before 1914 or 1917, Marxism coexists in an indiscriminate ideological amalgam with Evolutionism on the one hand and the anarchist creed on the other. The latter impregnated the early life of many communist leaders and even the lives of some founder members of the Party (Elías Lafertte and Braulio León Peña in Chile stand out in this respect); the former, the Evolutionist and pro-science atmosphere, not only blurs the frontiers between Positivism and Marxism, but, worse still, reinforces Marx's anti-peasant prejudices, according to the well-known and distasteful analogy of *The 18th Brumaire* in which the conservative French peasants and their smallholdings are compared to "sacks of potatoes." By adopting this line, one risks condemning the rural, that is, almost all of Latin America, as uncivilised and backward.

After 1917 and with the help of Lenin, Marxism evolved and took a more and more definite shape, sailing with ease through the no longer hazardous reefs of Positivism and anarchism. The good communist's bedside book, or, more appropriately, those to be placed at the sword's hilt, are Lenin's most accessible publications (*Imperialism; the Highest Stage of Capitalism*, and to a lesser extent, *The State and Revolution*), and later, Stalin's *Problems of Leninism* (1924; 1947). Later still, a book ubiquitous in all the cells and schools for the formation of executive committees, *The Fundamental Lessons of Marxism*, written by the French normalist (*normalien*) and militant Georges Politzer. After World War II, Marxism entered academic circles little by little, becoming a matter for debate in universities among economists, historians, literary critics and sociologists, of all kinds. From 1959, and as a direct result of the Cuban Revolution and in response to the explosive worldwide situation, Marxist thought enjoyed a great degree of dissemination as much in specialist publications as in newspapers, magazines, and other forms of mass media. The Central American revolutions of the most recent decades, the Sandinistas of Nicaragua and the FMLN (Frente Farabundo Martí para la Liberación Nacional) of El Salvador, have been the objects of study and reflection by the Chilean-Cuban Marta Harnecker, who analyzes the transformations that have brought about the alliance between Marxism and guerrilla forces with diverse ideologies (Christian, social-democrat, and fundamentally independent organizations).

So that it might not appear unilateral, a description of the origins and reach of Marxism must take into account and put some emphasis on the context of its reception, that is, on the specific regions, countries and socio-historical circumstances in which the ideas and practice of Marxism will develop. In this sense, more than of Marxism, it is possible to talk in terms of

Marxisms in Latin America, because of the manifest variety and ramifications of the phenomenon. Some light is shed on this question by a comparison of three relevant individual and national cases; those of the Cuban Julio Antonio Mella (1903–29); the Chilean Luis Emilio Recabarren (1876–1924); and the Peruvian José Carlos Mariátegui (1894–1930). Mella forged himself a path as a student leader at university. During his short period of exile in Mexico, before his assassination at the hands of Gerardo Machado's henchmen, his main contributions went to the magazine created by Diego Rivera, *El Machete*. The predominant feature of these contributions is an anti-imperialist sentiment, that follows and makes topical once again Martí's ideas in a post-revolutionary Mexico that paints clearer still the condition of his country of origin, Cuba, bound to the United States by the Platt Amendment (1902). By contrast, Recabarren worked as a typographer from his early teens, and from his affiliation to the Democratic Party (1894) up to the founding of the Communist Party of Chile (1922), his principal fields of action were the urban masses in Santiago and Valparaíso, and the miners in the north of the country. There he formed *mancomunales*, a type of class-based organization that, surpassing the limits of the mutualist and anarchist guilds, pointed the way already towards the workers' federations that followed on a national scale. Throughout his life, until his suicide in 1924, Recabarren was the tenacious creator of the Chilean workers' press and an indefatigable supporter of the popular theatre of political expression. As for Mariátegui (see separate entry), after what he himself described as his *modernista* and Bohemian "Stone Age" (1914–18), and after his productive Italian years (1919–23), he went on to analyze with impressive maturity the situation of both his country and the world, an analysis that culminates in his *Siete ensayos de interpretación de la realidad peruana*, 1928 (*Seven Interpretative Essays on Peruvian Reality*). This is probably one of the few Marxist contributions to the study of a particular social structure, in this case, that of Peru.

It would be inappropriate in a short article to evaluate and pass judgement on the effects of Marxism, separating the wheat from the chaff. Was it a powerful force in the 20th century, or an alarming accumulation of weaknesses, as some would have us believe? Does it still have a future in the midst of an *intelligentsia* reduced to impotence owing to a complete lack of political strategy? However, from a neutral or impartial base, it would be difficult to deny its having been an important, if not decisive, component in the cultural life of Latin America. Besides those literary figures already mentioned, much of the less well-known fiction would be inconceivable without the Marxist perspective. The profile of a culture does not depend only on its peaks, but, to use a Taoist metaphor,

on "the spirit of the valley" as well! The Ecuadorian novels of the 1930s, a significant portion of the indigenous writing from the Andes, Mexican fiction by such writers as Mauricio Magdaleno and José Mancisidor, novels by the Costa Ricans Carlos Luis Fallas and Joaquín Gutiérrez, and narratives from the Argentines Raúl Larra and David Viñas, among many others, make this point clear. As regards essay writing, besides the fundamental works of the Chilean Volodia Teitelboim and the Argentine Héctor Agosti (who edited and translated Gramsci in the 1950s), recent years have given rise to: the Mexicans Eli de Gortari and Jaime Labastida in the fields of epistemology and philosophy; the Ecuadorian Agustín Cueva writing in the field of political and cultural sociology; studies on cultural criticism in Brazil, whose pivotal point resides in Roberto Schwartz; and literary criticism in Cuba in a continuous line from Juan Marinello and José Antonio Portuondo to Roberto Fernández Retamar; and in Puerto Rico, the works of José Luis González, etc. These examples alone would suffice to prove the current vitality of Marxism which, while having a manifold influence over the actions of the masses, has stimulated a significant number of intellectuals: artists, journalists, professionals, the last of these, as one might expect, especially in the variegated field of the social sciences.

JAIME CONCHA

translated by Luis González Fernández

Further Reading

General

Aricó, José, *Marx y América Latina*, Lima: Centro de Estudios para el Desarrollo y la Participación, 1980

Fernández, Osvaldo, "Sobre los orígenes del marxismo en América Latina," *Araucaria de Chile* 23 (1983)

Pan, Luis, *Juan B. Justo y su tiempo*, Buenos Aires: Planeta, 1991

Taibo II, Paco Ignacio, *Los bolshevikis: historia narrativa de los orígenes del comunismo en México, 1919–1925*, Mexico City: Joaquín Mortiz, 1986 [At once an entertaining and disturbing history of the early years of the Communist Party in Mexico]

Works on/by Individual Marxists

Guevara, Ernesto, *Obra revolucionaria*, edited by Roberto Fernández Retamar, Mexico City: Era, 1967

Mariátegui, José Carlos, *Siete ensayos de interpretación de la realidad peruana*, Lima: Amauta, 1928; as *Seven Interpretative Essays on Peruvian Reality*, translated by Marjory Urquidi, Austin: University of Texas Press, 1971

Recabarren, Luis Emilio, *Escritos de prensa*, edited by Ximena Cruzat and Eduardo Devés, 4 vols, Santiago de Chile: Nuestra América, 1985–87

Tibol, Raquel, *Julio Antonio Mella en "El Machete,"* Mexico City: Fondo de Cultura Económica, 1968

Clorinda Matto de Turner 1852–1909

Peruvian prose writer, dramatist and translator

In contrast to the other members of the first generation of women writers in Peru, Clorinda Matto did not grow up savouring the cultural pleasures of European modernity that the liberal elite enthusiastically incorporated into 19th-century Lima. She was born in the city of Cuzco to a family of landowners and spent a good proportion of her childhood on her family's estate in Calca, where she attended the local school and learned Quechua, a skill she put to use later in her life with the translation of the New Testament into the language of the ancient Incas. Her experiences as a girl growing up in the Urubamba valley, isolated from the guano-booming capital, Lima, and rich in Quechua traditions, became central to her work as a journalist and novelist. Her commitment to forging a Peruvian identity which would incorporate at its heart elements of Quechua culture, was reflected in her two novels on life in the Peruvian Andes, *Aves sin nido*, 1889 (*Birds without a Nest*) and *Índole*, 1892 [Human Nature]. If it is true that Matto did not remain altogether invulnerable to the dazzling effects of the "civilizing lights" emanating from European modernity, her Andean background erupts in her work to provide a vision of national identity which was alien to the homogenizing images of a white, western, modern Peru constructed by the ruling liberal elite. Arriving in Lima for the first time as a literary visitor at the age of twenty-three, at a time when literature was still enmeshed in the poetics of Romanticism, Clorinda Matto found herself within a society that was relatively tolerant of women writers, but with its eyes firmly turned towards Europe.

Her first novel, *Aves sin nido*, narrates the experience of an enlightened creole couple in a small and remote Andean town where they witness at first hand the economic, social and sexual exploitation to which the local religious and political authorities subject the Indians. The book provoked intense controversy, unleashing a flood of critical reviews in the national literary press. Her supporters praised it for its timely courage and progressive stance towards the Indians and compared it with Harriet Beecher Stowe's *Uncle Tom's Cabin*, but the general consensus of the reading public was that the book was offensive for its anti-Catholic spirit and defamatory intentions. The book was later banned, Matto was excommunicated and her effigy burned in a public demonstration. The title of the novel alludes to the story of Margarita and Manuel who, having fallen in love, discover that they are brother and sister, both children of the Bishop of Killac and Indian mothers. They are then, birds that have no nest, no identifiable father, and in the last instance, no identifiable origin or identity.

Her second novel, *Índole*, is also set in an Andean village where the narrator observes and compares two opposite models of family life: one represented by a newly wed Indian couple, and another by a creole family in the process of disintegration. Despite the unequal conditions under which the dominant and the subordinated groups interact in Matto's first two novels, the salient feature of this Andean world is an openness to the Other, practised by all the social groups concerned: Indians, masters and creole outsiders. The artistic power of these scenes of cultural interchange, suggests the author's allegiance to an Andean social order which stands in stark contrast to the segregating practices of the Lima of *Herencia* [Heredity], the sequel to *Aves sin nido*. However much the enlightened creole characters of the first two novels rhapsodise about the Edenic Lima, its reality, as presented in *Herencia*, totally contradicts their dreams and shows just how deceived they had been. Where both Killac and Rosalina are characterised by the close cultural dependence between Indians and *notables*, or gentry, manifested particularly in domestic life, i.e. food, dress, forms of housekeeping, language of affection, festivities and forms of personal relations, the Lima of *Herencia* is marked by the barriers – cultural, social and spatial – that divide the three social actors represented by the bourgeoisie, the middle class and the destitute working class. The clusters of traditional Andean cultural practices represented in her first two novels provide a model, albeit not fully articulated, or what modern critics would define as transculturation.

The unfavourable reaction which her novels and her journalistic work provoked in the Lima reading public can be partly explained in political terms as part of the profound schism between the ever conflicting Andean and creole worlds which makes Peru, to this day, a nation divided by violence. Matto was indeed a promoter of Andean values in a nation intent on seeing itself as creole. However, a Christian feminist subtext emerges in Matto's work which caused further controversy. For *Aves sin nido* is also the story of a group of women, creole, mestizo and Indian, who together resist oppression despite the belief of the local authorities that "las mujeres no deben mezclarse nunca en cosas de hombres, sino estar con la aguja, las calcetas y los tamalitos" (women should never interfere with men's affairs, but should keep to their sewing, knitting and cooking). It is the home, not the public sphere, which is presented as the centre of potential revolutionary power, whence a combative morality spreads out into the community threatening the stability of an age old order. It is the female characters who appropriate the language of the New Testament to exhort and proselytise, and who directly confront the oppressors thus unleashing the plot. Matto's intense and clear commitment to feminist concerns was more explicit in her journalistic work, particularly in her contributions to *El Perú Ilustrado* of Lima, and *El Búcaro Americano* [The American Vase] of Buenos Aires, two leading cultural journals where she worked as director, and in her founding of a publishing house staffed by women and devoted to the publication of works written by contemporary women throughout the continent.

Francesca Denegri

Biography

Born Grimanesa Martina Matto Usandiravas in Cuzco, Peru, 11 November 1852. Parents owned small estate where Matto and her two brother spent their childhood. Spoke fluent Quechua for this reason. Formal education in Cuzco where she edited the school newspaper. Mother died in 1862 and in 1868 Clorinda left school in order to run the family household. Married the English physician,

John Turner in 1871. Visited Lima in 1877 where she was drawn into the intellectual circle and salon organized by Juana Manuela Gorriti (see separate entry). During war between Peru and Chile (1879–83), Matto's home turned into a hospital. Husband died in 1881 leaving her heavily in debt. Moved to Arequipa in 1883. Edited the daily newspaper, *La Bolsa*, 1884–86 [The Stock Exchange]; first woman in America to hold such a post. Moved to Lima in 1886. Deeply influenced by the ideas of Manuel González Prada who supported Indian education and was hostile to the Catholic Church. Editor-in-chief, *El Perú Ilustrado* [Cultured Peru], Lima's most important literary magazine, 1889. Excommunicated by archbishop of Lima as result of both articles in *El Perú Ilustrado* and her novel, *Aves sin nido*. Resigned as editor in 1891 and founded feminist press, "La Equitativa," staffed entirely by women, in 1892. A political enemy, Nicolás de Piérola, took over government in 1895. As a result Matto's home was destroyed; her press sacked and her manuscripts lost. She took flight and settled in Buenos Aires where she undertook a translation of the Bible into Quechua at the request of the American Bible Society. Founded and edited the bimonthly *El Búcaro Americano* [The American Vase], a social and literary magazine that encouraged contributions from women. Died of pneumonia on 25 October 1909, leaving a part of her estate to the Women's Hospital in Cuzco.

Selected Works

Novels

Aves sin nido, Buenos Aires: Lajouane, 1889; as *Birds without a Nest: a Story of Indian Life and Priestly Oppression in Peru*, translated by J.H. Hudson, London: Charles J. Thynne, 1904

Índole (novela peruana), Lima: Imprenta "La Equitativa", 1892

Herencia (novela peruana), Lima: Masias, 1895

Play

Hima-Sumac: drama en tres actos y en prosa, Lima: Imprenta "La Equitativa," 1892

Other Writings

Perú – tradiciones cuzqueñas, Arequipa: Imprenta de "La Bolsa," 1884

Tradiciones cuzqueñas, vol. 2, Lima: Imprenta de Torres Aguirre, 1886

Elementos de literatura según el Reglamento de Instrucción Pública para uso del bello sexo, Arequipa: Imprenta de "La Bolsa," 1889

Bocetos al lápiz de americanos célebres, Lima: Bacigalupi y Compañía, 1889

Leyendas y recortes, Lima: Masías, 1895

Analogía: segundo año de gramática castellana en las escuelas normales, según el programa oficial, Buenos Aires: n.p., 1897

Boreales, miniaturas y porcelanas, Buenos Aires: Alsina, 1909

Viaje de recreo: España, Francia, Inglaterra, Italia, Suiza, Alemania, Valencia, Spain: Sempere y Compañía, 1909

Further Reading

Brushwood, John S., *Genteel Barbarism: Experiments in the Analysis of Nineteenth-Century Spanish-American Novels*, Lincoln: University of Nebraska Press, 1981 [chapter on *Aves sin nido*]

Cornejo Polar, Antonio, "Los usos de la ficción: tres novelas andinas de la formación de la nacionalidad," in his *Escribir en el aire: ensayo sobre la heterogeneidad socio-cultural en las literaturas andinas*, Lima: Horizonte, 1994

Kristal, Efrain, "The Political Dimension of Clorinda Matto de Turner's 'Indigenismo,'" in his *The Andes Viewed from the City: Literary and Political Discourse on the Indian in Peru 1848–1930*, New York: Peter Lang, 1987

Lemoine, Joaquín, *Clorinda Matto de Turner*, Lima: Imprenta y Librería de Benito Gil, 1887

Lewis, Bart L., "Art, Society and Criticism: the Literary Theories of Mercedes Cabello de Carbonera and Clorinda Matto de Turner," *Letras Femeninas*, vol. 10/12 (1984)

Manrique, Nelson, "Clorinda Matto y el nacimiento del indigenismo literario," *Debate Agrario*, Lima (January–July 1989)

Marting, Diane E. (editor), *Spanish American Women Writers: a Bio-Bibliographical Source Book*, New York: Greenwood Press, 1990

Masiello, Francine, *Between Civilization and Barbarism: Women, Nation and Literary Culture in Modern Argentina*, Lincoln: University of Nebraska Press, 1992 [Chapter 3 has material on this author]

Miller, Martin C., "Clorinda Matto de Turner and Mercedes Cabello de Carbonera: Societal Criticism and Morality," in *Latin American Women Writers: Yesterday and Today*, edited by Yvette E. Miller and Charles M. Tatum, Pittsburgh: The Review Press, 1977

Tauro, Alberto, *Clorinda Matto de Turner y la novela indigenista*, Lima: Universidad de San Marcos, 1976

Mayan Literature

The Maya were the only people of America's high cultures who developed a glyph-writ language (a partly ideographic, partly phonetic mode of writing) capable of recording events. But by the time the Spanish conquistadors arrived in Yucatán, where the Maya were then concentrated, many of the great Maya city-states and sacred cities – Tikal, Uaxactun, Copán, and Palenque – were deserted. The Maya codices known as the *Dresden*, the *Paris*, and the *Tro-Cortesiano* antedate the Conquest. Also, among the Mayas, as among the peoples of Central Mexico, there were schools in which the ancient wisdom and knowledge contained in the painted books were passed on and preserved through oral tradition or memorization. As a result of this method of cultural transmission, important literary works have survived from several Mayan groups. Certain scribes who lived through the conquest and recalled the pre-Hispanic teachings transcribed many texts in the alphabet brought by the conquerors or simply transmitted orally information based on the ancient codices to a Spaniard, thereby sometimes compromising the text's consistency. Humanist friars such as Andrés de Olmos and Bernardino de Sahagún were able to rescue and thus preserve this cultural-literary heritage of the Mayas. Among the Mayas of Yucatán and the Quichés and Cakchiquels of Guatemala (the Maya Indians comprise numerous linguistic and sociocultural groups including the Chontal, Chorti, Huastec, Ixil, Jacalteca, Kanjobal, Kekchi, Lacandon, Mam, Mopan, Tzeltal, Tzotzil and Tzutuhil, in addition to the Cakchikel and Quiché). There were also scribes, usually descended from priests or nobles, who began to transcribe the traditions of the pre-Hispanic centers of learning and the content of the ancient codices. The work of these custodians of the culture thus preserved various chronicles, some books on native medicine (notably the *Libro de medicina* [Book of Medicine], the *Cuaderno de Teabo* [Teabo Notebook], the *Noticias de varias plantas* [Information about Various Plants], the *Libro de los médicos* [Book of Doctors], and the *Ritual de los Bacaab* [Ritual of the Bacaab], all by unknown authors), and a whole series of texts called the *Chilam Balam*, written in the Maya language of Yucatán in Latin script.

The eighteen known books of *Chilam Balam* are undoubtedly the most significant portion of what remains of early Mayan literature. The volume contains prophecies of the days, the years, and longer periods of time. Within its pages there are also mythical and historical passages, hymns and songs, as well as valuable accounts of tradition and ancient wisdom interspersed with ideas demonstrating the influence of Christianity, mainly of biblical origins. And the best known of these texts is the *Chilam Balam of Chumayel*, of which only a late version exists, copied at the end of the 18th century. The indigenous testimonies contained herein are descriptions rather than explanations of events during the conquest, asserting that all of these occurrences came to pass because the Indians had lost control of communication. The language of the gods had either become unintelligible, or else these deities fell silent. "Understanding is lost, wisdom is lost"(*Chilam Balam*, 22). "There was no longer any great teacher, any great orator, any supreme priest, when the change of rulers occurred upon their arrival" (*Chilam Balam*, 5). The *Chilam Balam* reiterates their piercing question which can no longer receive an adequate response: "Where is the prophet, where is the priest who will give the true meaning of the language of this book?"(*Chilam Balam*, 24).

The Quiché and Cakchiquel peoples have also left a rich literary legacy with their famous *Popol Vuh* (*Book of the People*), the *Títulos de los Señores de Totonicapán* [Titles of the Lords of Totonicapán], and the pre-Hispanic play, the *Rabinal Achí*. The *Popol Vuh*, referred to by some as the "Mayan Bible," is based on the oral traditions of the Maya-Quiché of Guatemala. It is a chronicle of their history which also includes sections on mythology, religion and cosmogony. Despite the relatively late date of transcription (Etiénne Brasseur de Bourbourg's French translation of 1862), the *Rabinal Achí* piece (originally known as the *Baile del Tun-a-tun* [Dance of the Tun-a-Tun] refers to the Mayan year of 360 days and perhaps the play's annual performance at a festival or ceremony; the term also refers to a sacred native drum used as an accompaniment in the music/dance format of the drama) is authentically indigenous and the only literary work of its

kind considered untainted by European or other more recent influence, particularly the taint of the late-medieval Spanish stage conventions found in extant versions of other important pre-Columbian dramas (i.e., the Quechuan *Ollantay* of Peru and the Náhuatl *Güegüence* of Nicaragua). Its purity is perhaps due, in part, to the isolation of the Quiché Mayas of Rabinal in Guatemala. The form and structure of the *Rabinal Achí* is significant in that it points to certain literary conventions apparent in Maya poetry: parallelism, phonic enchantment, repetitions, rhythm resulting from the reiteration of key words. The play also provides an insight into the structure that might have informed other dramatic Maya pieces: dance accompanied by music to punctuate and separate the "episodes," monotonous, simple and repetitious music, retrospective exposition through dialogic exchanges, abundant reiterations to underscore the theme, the participation of large bodies of persons continually on stage (paralleling the presence of the Greek chorus), and the use of speech conventions and exact repetitions of dialogue by the responding character so as to aid oral transmission. The Mayas' love of dramatic performances (solemn religious representations, diverting masquerades, or mere pantomimes) was not discouraged by the conquerors. On the contrary, the Spaniards (particularly the missionaries) cultivated drama as a means of instructing converts in religion (the "miracle plays" or *autos sacramentales*) or conveying cultural values. The more intelligent natives were even allowed to compose the text of such plays. What was saved from oblivion of the pre-Hispanic theatre, fragmentary as it is, still gives a glimpse of the richness and uniqueness of native American drama which had its beginnings in the sacred feasts and developed in isolation its own original forms of expression.

From these literary texts, several principal subjects of native Maya literature are apparent: myths and legends, sacred hymns, various kinds of epic, lyric, and religious poetry, early forms of theatre, chronicles and history based on the ancient annals, speeches and discourses, religious doctrines, and even the tenets of what may be called pre-Hispanic philosophy. In their ancient myths and sacred hymns, in particular, the Mayas show certain similarities in comparison with literary texts of the Náhuas. There had been many contacts between the two cultures ever since the Teotihuacán period and especially in Toltec days when the Náhuas migrated southward, and so, this provides a plausible explanation for parallelism in themes and styles between the two cultures. The native Maya language provides not only an adequate but a rich and elegant medium for communication. By the juxtaposition of roots or morphemes and the use of a number of suffixes and prefixes, it was possible for these literary "custodians of the culture" or "artists of the word" to express any idea with both precision and eloquence, however abstract and complex it might have been. Using the formulaic conventions of oral tradition, the same themes recurred, but they were stitched together or "rhapsodized" differently in each rendition even by the same poet, depending on audience reaction, the mood of the poet or the occasion, and other social and psychological factors. While Mayan poetry and prose was situational, purposeful, instructive in thematic content, recalling cosmological myths and legends about the gods and culture heroes, it also was the expression of creative imagination in its structural format. The old chronicles frequently mention lyric poetry and songs, especially those composed in the Náhuatl and Maya tongues. From the Mayas there is some lyric poetry preserved as part of religious celebrations and festivals in *The Book of the Songs of Dzitbalché* and also some poems scattered through the various books of the aforementioned *Chilam Balam* as well as in the *Popol Vuh* of the Quichés. But the Mayas did not have a Sahagún or a team of well-trained Indian scholars who devoted their time to collecting and preserving the old texts and traditions, and many of their literary compositions were lost. From what remains of their work, however, it is evident that the existence of a rich lyric poetry in the early days of indigenous Mexico is a testimony to the idea of poetry and art as a gift of the gods, as the survival of man on earth, a way to discover divinity, a possible wealth for mankind among the main pre-Columbian cultures of Mexico. The structure of such poetic compositions – repetition of ideas, expression of sentiment in parallel form to reinforce a single idea, the abundant use of metaphors – are similar to the structure of theatre pieces such as the already discussed *Rabinal Achí*. Indeed, such indigenous lyric poetry is considered to be a forerunner of a very ancient form of dramatic presentation, with groups of singers carrying on a chanted dialogue among themselves. As regards thematic content, prophecies and predictions about the *katúns* and chronicles and lyric accounts of the Spanish Conquest, together with other songs, are found in the various Yucatec books of *Chilam Balam*. Of a different flavor, more delicate and sensitive in expression, are many of the poems, sacred hymns and more personal lyric compositions in *The Book of the Songs of Dzitbalché*. And there are a number of lyric compositions scattered throughout the *Popol Vuh*. The critic-translator of the *Popol Vuh*, in a discerning analysis of the conceptualization of the creation myth in this Maya text, emphasizes the primacy given the aural sense in the Maya imagining of things both in thematic content and in lyric expressiveness: "In the beginning, there was a murmurous hush which slowly defined itself into the rippling of water, of softly shifting winds, of the tiny noise of insects, as the sounds of the world separated themselves and came into being" (from *The Spoken Word and the Work of Interpretation*). Walter Ong is among several commentators who have studied the different sensibilities shaped by primary dependence on what he calls "chirographic" as against the oral mode. One of his key discriminations in distinguishing the sensibility of a literary form from an oral culture arises from his claim that writing, by fixing thought, allows "study": the systematic and sequential analysis of ideas. And so, the glyph-writing format of the Maya, just as the pictographs among the Aztecs, served to generate discourse and to aid thoughtful analysis, as well as to record received information.

ELENA DE COSTA

See also entries on Aymara Literature, Náhuatl Literature, Quechua Literature

Further Reading

Anthologies, critical editions, and important Mayan literary texts

Barrera Vásquez, Alfredo, *El Libro de los Libros de Chilam Balam*, Mexico City: Fondo de Cultura Económica, 1948; as *The Book of Chilam Balam de Chumayel*, translated and edited by Ralph L. Roys, Washington, DC: Smithsonian Institution, 1933; Norman, Oklahoma: University of Oklahoma Press, 1967 [The more recent edition is particularly recommended since it is a bilingual Maya/English one]

Barrera Vásquez, Alfredo, *The Maya Chronicles*, Washington, DC: Publication 585 of the Carnegie Institution of Washington, 1949; reprinted, New York: Johnson, 1970

Crónicas indígenas de Guatemala, edited by Adrián Recinos, Guatemala City: Editorial Universitaria, 1957

Monterde, Francisco, *Teatro indígena prehispánico. Rabinal Achí*, preface by Georges Raynaud, Mexico City: Imprenta Universitaria, 1955

Popol Vuh: the Sacred Book of the Ancient Quiché Maya, English version by Delia Goetz and Sylvanus G. Morley, from the Spanish translation by Adrián Recinos, Norman: University of Oklahoma Press, 1950; also translated by Dennis Tedlock as *Popol Vuh: the Definitive Edition of the Mayan Book of the Dawn of Life and the Glories of Gods and Kings*, New York: Simon and Schuster, 1985

Critical works or commentaries on Mayan literature

Brinton, Daniel G., *Aboriginal American Authors and Their Productions*, Chicago: Checagou Reprints, 1970

Brotherston, Gordon, *Book of the Fourth World: Reading the Native Americas through Their Literature*, Cambridge and New York: Cambridge University Press, 1992

Correa, Gustavo, Calvin Cannon, W.A. Hunter and Barbara Bode (editors), *The Native Theatre in Middle America*, Middle American Research Institute, Publication 27, New Orleans: Tulane University, 1961

Edmonson, Munro S. (editor and translator), *Heaven Born. Mérida and its Destiny: the Book of Chilam Balam of Chumayel*, Austin: University of Texas Press, 1986

León-Portilla, Miguel, *Pre-Columbian Literatures of Mexico*, translated by the author and Grace Lobanov, Norman: University of Oklahoma Press, 1969

_____ *Cantos y crónicas del México antiguo a través de sus códices y tradiciones*, Madrid: Historia 16, 1986

Ong, Walter J., *The Presence of the Word: Some Prolegomena for Cultural and Religious History*, New Haven, Connecticut: Yale University Press, 1967

_____ *Rhetoric, Romance, and Technology: Studies in the Interaction of Expression and Culture*, Ithaca, New York: Cornell University Press, 1977

_____ *Orality and Literacy: the Technologizing of the Word*, London and New York: Methuen, 1982

Tedlock, Dennis, *The Spoken Word and the Work of Interpretation*, Philadelphia: University of Pennsylvania Press, 1983

Von Hagen, Victor W., *World of the Maya*, New York: New American Library, 1960

Wolff, Werner, *El mundo simbólico de mayas y aztecas*, Mexico City: SEP, 1963

Cecília Meireles 1901–1964

Brazilian poet

Cecília Meireles is considered one of the most important poets of the second phase of the Brazilian Modernist movement. Her first three books of poetry, *Espectros* [Spectrums], *Nunca mais . . . e poema dos poemas* [Never Again and the Poem of Poems] and *Baladas para el-rei* [Ballads for the King] were written in the Symbolist tradition, although the poet later chose to dissociate herself from these earlier volumes and to date her poetic contribution to literature from the book which followed a fourteen-year silence and was published in 1939, *Viagem* [Journey].

Meireles's poetry was profoundly influenced by two events: first, the death of her parents and three older brothers, and second, the suicide of her first husband Fernando Correia Dias in 1934. She felt that experiencing so many deaths gave her an opportunity to see the transitory nature of life and provided for her what she referred to as an intimacy with death. Her poetry reflects this intimacy as well as an overriding concern with loneliness. The silence and solitude that were such an integral part of her childhood forced her to develop her imagination and to create magical worlds that would serve her well in her development as a poet.

Another element that had a profound effect on Meireles was that of being raised by her Portuguese grandmother. This upbringing later made its way into her poetry in the form of the traditional rhythms and poetic patterns associated with the Portuguese lyrical tradition that remained a constant throughout her literary career. This adhesion to Portuguese poetic forms was considered to be at odds with the growing Brazilian nationalism and dedication to innovation that was so prevalent during the first phase of Brazilian *Modernismo*.

Meireles's first association with Brazilian Modernism came by way of the publication of *Festa* [Party] a journal that sought to create a poetry that would be more spiritual, universal, and harmonious in terms of form and content than the poetry written by the early Modernists. It reflected the concerns of the second phase of Modernism which did not have the irreverent and experimental character of the first phase. From 1930, poetry in Brazil began to present a greater equilibrium and more maturity as well as an abundance of religious and mystical themes. Meireles fitted right in with the growing body of poetry being produced during that time, composing a lyric poetry infused with a certain mysticism and a melancholic tone.

Viagem, which received the Poetry Prize from the Brazilian Academy of Letters in 1939, was considered by many to show her full maturity as a poet. The volume consists of twelve poems that may be interpreted as twelve stages of a spiritual trajectory. The title refers to this journey, where life and poetry join together to the extent that poetry and nature are also fused.

Meireles travelled a great deal and her travelling became an integral part of her poetry, as was seen in some of her later volumes such as *Poemas escritos na Índia* [Poems Written in India] and *Poemas italianos* [Italian Poems]. *Doze noturnos de Holanda* [Twelve Dutch Nocturnes] is also comprised of poetry that Meireles composed while travelling and reflect the mysteries of the night as well as her typical themes of music and melancholy. In a figurative sense, the image of the night in some way is involved in each of the poems of *Doze noturnos*, and there is a persistent existential anxiety. In the poems, animate and inanimate objects become shadowy and produce doubt and anguish. The poem "Noturno" may be noted for its reflection of metaphysical anguish and the poet's bewilderment at the eternal cycle of life and death.

In *Giroflê, Giroflá*, Meireles joins together various sketches (crônicas) from her trips to India and Italy in a highly poetic prose. The title refers to an operetta written by Charles Lecoq; to a French word for the Indian clove (giroflé); and also alludes to language games played by children. In the text highly suggestive words are transformed into symbolic allusions to the countries she visited. In particular, India exerted a considerable influence on the poet after her journey there in 1953, when she was invited to participate in a symposium on the work of Gandhi.

There are other themes that may be considered emblematic of the author, such as the passing of time, the transitory nature of matter and the meaninglessness of life. All these components form some of the most unique and rich poetry in the history of Brazilian literature.

MELISSA A. LOCKHART

Biography

Born Cecília Benevides Meirelles in Rio de Janeiro, Brazil, 7 November 1901. Father died three months before her birth. Mother, an elementary school teacher, died when Cecília was three. The three other children of this marriage died before Cecília was born. Raised by maternal grandmother and her nanny, Pedrina. The former told her stories from her birthplace, the Azores, while from the latter she learned Brazilian folk songs and games. Her grandmother's house was surrounded by lush vegetation which allowed Cecília to live close to nature. Death and solitude fed her creative imagination. Graduated with honours from elementary school and awarded a Gold Medal of Merit. Married the painter Fernando Correia Dias in 1921; three daughters, Maria Elvira, Maria Matilde and Maria Fernanda. Established a children's library in 1934. Travelled to Portugal with her husband in 1935 where she lectured in Brazilian literature at several Portuguese universities. Husband, who suffered from acute depression, committed suicide on their return to Rio. Married Heitor Grillo in 1940. From the 1940s to her death, she was active in several related fields, publishing around twelve books; working on literary translation from Spanish, English and French; lecturing abroad; broadcasting on cultural subjects and organising symposia on folklore, a field in which she was a recognized authority. Awarded the Brazilian Academy of Letters Prize, 1939 for *Viagem*. Died in Rio de Janeiro, from cancer, 9 November 1964.

Selected Works

Poetry

Espectros, Rio de Janeiro: Leite Ribeiro e Maurillo, 1919
Nunca mais . . . e poema dos poemas, Rio de Janeiro: Leite Ribeiro, 1923
Baladas para el-rei, Rio de Janeiro: Brasileira Lux, 1925

Viagem, Lisbon: Ocidente, 1939
Vaga música, Rio de Janeiro: Irmãos Pongetti, 1942
Mar absoluto e outros poemas, Pôrto Alegre, Brazil: Globo, 1945
Retrato natural, Rio de Janeiro: Livros de Portugal, 1949
Amor em Leonoreta, Rio de Janeiro: Hipocampo, 1951
Doze noturnos de Holanda e O aeronauta, Rio de Janeiro: Livros de Portugal, 1952
Romanceiro da inconfidência, Rio de Janeiro: Livros de Portugal, 1953
Pistóia, cemitério brasileiro, Rio de Janeiro: Philobiblion, 1955
Pequeno oratório de Santa Clara, Rio de Janeiro: Philobiblion, 1955
Canções, Rio de Janeiro: Livros de Portugal, 1956
Solombar, Rio de Janeiro: Livros de Portugal, 1956
Romance de Santa Cecília, Rio de Janeiro: Philobiblion, 1957
A rosa, Salvador, Brazil: Edição Dinamene, 1957
Metal rosicler, Rio de Janeiro: Livros de Portugal, 1960
Poemas escritos na Índia, Rio de Janeiro: Livrario São José, 1962
Ou isto ou aquilo, São Paulo: Editora Giroflê, 1964
Crônica trovada da cidade de Sam Sebastiam do Rio de Janeiro no quarto centenário de sua fundação pelo Capitão-Mor Estácio de Saa, Rio de Janeiro: José Olympio, 1965
Poemas italianos, São Paulo: Instituto Cultural Ítalo-Brasileiro, 1968
Ou isto ou aquilo e poémas inéditos, São Paulo: Edições Melhoramentos, 1969

Prose

Giroflê, Giroflá, Rio de Janeiro: Civilização Brasileira, 1956
Quadrante 1 e quadrante 2, Rio de Janeiro: Editora do Autor, 1962–63
Escolha o seu sonho, Rio de Janeiro: Record, 1964
Vozes da cidade, Rio de Janeiro: Record, 1965
Inéditos, Rio de Janeiro: Bloch, 1968
Olhinhos de gato, 2nd edition, São Paulo: Editora Moderna, 1980
O que se diz e o que se entende, Rio de Janeiro: Nova Fronteira, 1980

Compilations and Anthologies

Obra poética, Rio de Janeiro: Aguilar, 1958
Antologia poética, Rio de Janeiro: Editora do Autor, 1963
Flor de poemas, Rio de Janeiro: Nova Fronteira, 1972
Cecília Meireles, Petrópolis: Vozes, 1973
Seleta em prosa e verso de Cecília Meireles, edited by Darcy Damasceno, Rio de Janeiro: José Olympio, 1973
Cânticos, poesias inéditas, São Paulo: Editora Moderna, 1981

Translations

Cecília Meireles. Poemas em Tradução/ Poems in Translation, edited with an introduction by Henry Keith and Raymond Sayers, Washington, DC: Brazilian-American Cultural Institute, 1977

Further Reading

García, Rubén, "Symbolism in the Early Works of Cecília Meireles," *Romance Notes* 21 (1980)
Igel, Regina, "Cecília Meireles," *Letras Femeninas*, vol. 1/1 (1975)
Nist, John, "The Poetry of Cecília Meireles," *Hispania* 46 (1963)
____ *The Modernist Movement in Brazil: a Literary Study*, Austin: University of Texas Press, 1967
Peixoto, Marta, "The Absent Body: Female Signature and Poetic Convention in Cecília Meireles," *Bulletin of Hispanic Studies* 65 (1988)
Sadlier, Darlene, "Metaphor and Metamorphosis: a Study of the Sea Imagery in Cecília Meireles's 'Mar Absoluto,'" *Kentucky Romance Quarterly* 27 (1980)
____ "Looking into the Mirror in Cecília Meireles's Poetry," *Romance Notes* 23 (1982)
____ *Imagery and Theme in the Poetry of Cecília Meireles: a Study of "Mar absoluto,"* Madrid: Porrúa Turanzas, 1983
Stackhouse, Kenneth A., "The Sea in the Poetry of Cecília Meireles," *Luso-Brazilian Review* 18 (1982)
Vilar, Amélia, *Uma voz do Brasil: Cecília Meireles*, Porto: Costa Carregal, 1965

João Cabral de Melo Neto 1920–

Brazilian poet

Traditional historiography always points out João Cabral de Melo Neto's poetry as being an exception within the so-called Generation of 1945 – a generation that restored the "great themes" of poetry and that, moved by a formalistic preoccupation (accusing the Modernists of being careless about the formal aspects of poetry), revived fixed forms, like the sonnet. This kind of characterization is still superficial and does not do justice to the author of *Uma faca só lâmina* (*A Knife All Blade*).

Within Brazilian poetry, Melo Neto's works are unique in many other ways. First of all, while most of Brazilian poetry (including here popular music lyrics) seems to have inherited a certain lyrical sentimentalism from the Portuguese, Cabral fits into a tradition of Constructivist art (he admires Mondrian, Le Corbusier, Miró, Valéry, Jorge Guillén, among others); his writing is much more like that of an engineer or an architect than one who attempts to explore the inner soul of a subject. Poetry is a product of intelligence and perseverance, and not of inspiration and chance. Luiz Costa Lima (1968) has described Cabral's poetry as "antilyrical," after suggesting that modern Brazilian poetry has followed a trajectory from a more emotional tone (Manuel Bandeira, 1886–1968), via Carlos Drummond de Andrade's irony (1902–88), and culminating in Melo Neto's "anti-lyricism." João Alexandre Barbosa (1974) synthesizes Lima's concept by arguing that Melo Neto's poetry eliminates lyricism so as to instal its search.

This could be extended to the problem of representation. In Melo Neto, language is pushed to its limits in order to problematize its possibilities of representing reality. In most, if not all, of Melo Neto's poems there is a procedure that has been called the "rectification of metaphors" where the language of the poem is always testing and revising the images that were used to symbolize reality, each time going deeper or assessing its content from another perspective. The major consequence of that procedure is that meaning acquires a plural potential, allowing the poem to be interpreted from different angles.

Also, one may say that there is a poetics of reading inscribed in Melo Neto's poetry. Signs like "pedra" (rock) are symbols of obstacles to the reader, who should go through the poem not as a transparency of reality, but as something *espesso* (thick), as an object made out of words, that creates and represents reality but also is a reality in itself. Instead of the image of a dreamer, who wonders while reading the poem, Melo Neto's text calls for patient, alert and lucid readers, who will open their eyes to the reality portrayed therein.

This is important because many of Melo Neto's poems talk about the poverty and the misery of northeastern Brazil, combining an extremely sophisticated poetic diction with social consciousness. The geographic descriptions provided by his texts are loaded with ethical (and political) implications: northeastern people do not have the minimum standards required to be recognized as human beings. In the series of poems describing cemeteries, what is at stake is the presence of death within a reality of hunger, social injustice and high rates of infant mortality. The ethic engraved in this poetry is a "morality of resistance," it is when there is no human thread in the northeastern backlander that he should be able to achieve survival in such adverse conditions.

As a diplomat, Melo Neto spent most of his adult life abroad, in Spain, in Africa, in other Latin American countries. A significant number of his works talk about Spain and compare it with Brazil's northeast. Elements of Spanish culture have penetrated deeply Melo Neto's poetics, such as the "palo seco" of Andalusian *cante jondo*: the "canto a palo seco" means a poetry that is reduced to its very bones, without any excrescence. By the same token, the tension and the eroticism that electrifies the dance of the *bailadoras* may well sum up the whole drama of the mimesis, trying to find the proper way to encapsulate within the precariousness of language the sensual movement of the dancer.

It must be added that Melo Neto also combines forms of popular poetry (such as the *cordel* literature: hand-made booklets of poems sold in fairs and hung on a string) with an acute awareness of modern art and the problematics of modern poetry (the issue of communication, the crisis of representation) – he has written several poems, which discuss both Brazilian and foreign artists. Melo Neto also goes against the mainstream of Brazilian cultural discourse when he denies essentialistic views, advocating a Nietzschian notion of reality that is anchored in the physicality of the world. Moreover, Melo Neto also touches upon the issue of historicity, not only because he wrote poems about historical figures (like Frei Caneca): although a subject is often absent from his poems, in his few erotic works there seems to occur a fusion between the voice of the enunciator and the loved being represented. If it could be said that love is the starting point of history – since

it implies a socialization between two partners – this socialization is definitely present in Melo Neto's erotic poetry.

ROBERTO REIS

Biography

Born in Recife, Pernambuco, Brazil, 9 January 1920; into a traditional Pernambucan family. Spent childhood in Poço do Aleixo (São Laurenço da Mata), his grandmother's estate, becoming familiar with the *catinga* (scrub) and the backlands that later would feature prominently in his poetry. Family moved to Recife, 1930. Settled in Rio de Janeiro in 1942. Joined the diplomatic corps, 1945. Married Stella Maria Barbosa in 1946. Worked as diplomat in Barcelona, London, Seville, Marseille, Geneva, Berne, Dakar, Asunción, Quito; ambassador to Ecuador, 1982. Elected to Brazilian Academy of Letters, 1968; Awarded the Neustadt International Prize for Literature, 1992. Currently retired, living in Rio de Janeiro.

Selected Works

Poetry

Duas aguas, poemas reunidos, Rio de Janeiro: José Olympio, 1956
Terceira feira, Rio de Janeiro: Editora do Autor, 1961
Museu de tudo, Rio de Janeiro: José Olympio, 1975
A escola das facas, Rio de Janeiro: José Olympio, 1980
Auto de frade: poema para vozes, Rio de Janeiro: José Olympio, 1984
Agrestes, 2nd edition, Rio de Janeiro: Nova Fronteira, 1985
Crime na Calle Relaton, Rio de Janeiro: Nova Fronteira, 1987
Sevilha andando, Rio de Janeiro: Nova Fronteira, 1989

Translations

A Knife All Blade or Usefulness of Fixed Ideas, translated by Kerry Shawn Keys, Camp Hill: Pennsylvania: Pine Press, 1980
Selected Poetry 1937–1990, edited by Djelal Kadir, translated by Elizabeth Bishop, Hanover, New Hampshire: University Press of New England, 1994

Compilations and Anthologies

Poesias completas (1940–1965), Rio de Janeiro: Sabiá, 1968
Obra completa, edited by Marly de Oliveira, Rio de Janeiro: Editora Nova Aguilar, 1994

Further Reading

Barbosa, João Alexandre, "Linguagem e metalinguagem em João Cabral," in *A metáfora crítica*, São Paulo: Perspectiva, 1974
_____ *A imitação da forma: uma leitura de João Cabral de Melo Neto*, São Paulo: Duas Cidades, 1975
_____ "Balanço de João Cabral," in his *As ilusões da modernidade*, São Paulo: Perspectiva, 1986
Lima, Luiz Costa, *Lira e antilira*, Rio de Janeiro: Civilização Brasileira, 1968
Merquior, José Guilherme, "Nuvem civil sonhada – ensaio sobre a poética de João Cabral de Melo Neto," in his *A astúcia da mímese*, Rio de Janeiro: José Olympio, 1972
Nunes, Benedito, *João Cabral de Melo Neto*, Petrópolis: Vozes, 2nd edition, 1971
Reis, Roberto, "Os dentes do poema," *Revista Letras*, vol. 29 (1980)
Senna, Marta de, *João Cabral: tempo e memória*, Rio de Janeiro: Antares, 1980

Special Issues of Journals

World Literature Today (Autumn 1992)

Murilo Mendes 1901–1975

Brazilian poet

In speaking of the poetry of Murilo Mendes, critics are fond of citing the three events that Mendes himself recalls as being crucial in his development as a writer: the passage of Halley's comet in 1910 apparently awakened Mendes to his vocation as a poet; in 1917 he ran away from school in Niterói to see a performance by Nijinsky at the Municipal Theater in Rio de Janeiro; and in 1921 he established a friendship with the painter Ismael Nery, whose premature death in 1934 provoked a spiritual crisis in Mendes and his conversion to Catholicism. Perhaps what these events have in common is the idea that the other-worldly can be perceived in this world and embodied as a source of spiritual guidance: a communion of the cosmic and the social. Like the famous comet, the poetry of Mendes possesses a definite luminosity and is capable of inspiring the kind of panic associated with the end of the world as we know it. Like the legendary Russian dancer, Mendes detaches himself from time and space in his writing in order to achieve a universal spirit that defies gravity in a search for grace. The religious quality that marks Mendes's work (linked to a rather vague philosophy that Nery called Essentialism) enables the poet to channel his anguish and passion and to demonstrate the power of the Christian values of love and charity.

Although Mendes collaborated with the first literary magazines (*Revista de Antropofagia* [Cannibal's Journal] and *Verde* [Green]) that grew from the landmark and controversial "Week of Modern Art" in São Paulo in 1922, Mendes is also part of a Catholic renaissance of the same period led by Jackson de Figueiredo and Tasso de Silveira and associated with the magazines *A Ordem* [Order] and *Festa* [Party]. Mendes was much younger than the first champions of the Brazilian Modernist movement (including Mário de Andrade, Manuel Bandeira and Oswald de Andrade) and did not publish his first book, *Poemas*, until 1929. For this reason, he belongs to a second phase of Brazilian Modernism, which was less encumbered by the propaganda of manifestos and freed of the predominance of what Alfredo Bosi has characterized as the Modernists' initial aesthetics of a return to a primitive matriarchy based on a misunderstood and poorly-assimilated Freudian model. Mendes remained true to Modernism's rebellious spirit in that he was a believer in modernity conceived of as *liberation*, and was therefore drawn to the irrational force of Surrealism. Mendes's use of this language, however, gave him access to the subconscious world and a way of expressing an equilibrium between the transcendent qualities of eternal life and the banality of our everyday lives. For this reason, Manuel Bandeira in a well-known poetic homage called Mendes a "Conciliator of contraries/ One who incorporates the eternal in the contingent."

With the exception of *História do Brasil* [History of Brazil] and *Convergência* [Convergence], there is an amazing consistency in the themes and tone of Mendes's poetry. The poet himself realized this when he excluded the flippant, almost disposable poetry linked so closely to linear time and historical figures of *História do Brasil* from the major gathering of his work *Poesias* (1959). *Convergência*, poems written from 1963–66, is also an anomalous work, and seems produced in response to the veiled criticism of Brazilian Concretist poet Haroldo de Campos, who wrote an article in 1963 in which he characterizes Mendes as a perhaps overly cautious vanguardist, who has eschewed the "experimental laboratory" of the younger Brazilian poets. However, Mendes's attempt to metamorphose himself and become a Concrete poet in *Convergência* is somewhat unconvincing, though his series of "Murilogramas" are interesting literary homages and imitations.

A poetic language laden with biblical images and embedded in an often oneiric montage of *realia* is at the core of much of his poetry. For example, Mendes, in collaboration with his compatriot Jorge de Lima, produced *Tempo e eternidade* [Time and Eternity], an orthodox effort to recreate Christianity in 20th-century poetry, drawing on the poetics of Neosymbolist French poets such as Charles Péguy and Paul Claudel. Most readers, however, prefer the spiritual intensity, marvelous enigmas and Zen-like paradoxes of works such as *O visionário* [The Visionary] (with its striking image of the poet as a new Prometheus chained to Rio de Janeiro's Sugar Loaf Mountain, his liver eaten away by airplanes), *As metamorfoses* [The Metamorphoses], and the remarkable *Poesia liberdade* [Freedom Poetry], composed during World War II. Before leaving for Europe where he would live for some twenty years, Mendes paid tribute to his roots in Minas Gerais by constructing in verse of perfectly-sculpted lines a Baroque representation of a city that is part of the Patrimony of Humanity: *Contemplação de Ouro Preto* [Contemplation of Ouro Preto].

Murilo Mendes is one of the most complex voices of Brazilian Modernism. The poet has created a fascinating hybrid poetry that moves from a youthful anarchistic spiritual despair to a more mature visionary connection to a metaphysical world. With the 1994 publication of Mendes's *Poesia completa e prosa* [Complete Poetry and Prose], the work of this world-class poet is finally more accessible.

STEVEN F. WHITE

Biography

Born in Minas Gerais, Brazil, in 1901, where he received his primary and secondary education. Ran away from school in 1917 to Rio de Janeiro to see performance by the Russian ballet dancer, Nijinsky. Back in Minas, he worked as a telegraphist, pharmacist's assistant, book-keeper and notary's clerk. Worked at the Treasury in Rio de Janeiro. In 1957 he was appointed Professor of Brazilian Literature at the University of Rome. He seldom returned to Brazil thereafter and, as a result both of his voluntary exile and of his work being translated into several European languages, he became better known in Europe than in his homeland. Recipient of the Graça Aranha Foundation Prize and the Etna-Taormina International Prize for Poetry (1972). Died in Lisbon, 15 August 1975.

Selected Works

História do Brasil, Rio de Janeiro: Ariel, 1932
Tempo e eternidade, in collaboration with Jorge de Lima, Pôrto Alegre, Brazil: Edição de Livraria do Globo, 1935
A poesia em pânico, Rio de Janeiro: Guanabara, 1938
O visionário, Rio de Janeiro: José Olympio, 1941
Mundo enigma, Rio de Janeiro: Edição de Livraria do Globo, 1945
Poesia liberdade, Rio de Janeiro: Agir, 1947
Janela do caos, Paris: Union, 1949
Contemplação de Ouro Preto, Rio de Janeiro: Ministério da Educação e Cultura, Serviço de Documentação, 1954
Parábola e Siciliana, Rome: Sciascia, 1959
Tempo espanhol, Lisbon: Círculo de Poesia, 1959
Murilogramas, Rio de Janeiro: José Olympio, 1965
Convergência, São Paulo: Duas Cidades, 1970
Poliedro, Rio de Janeiro: José Olympio, 1974

Compilations and Anthologies

Poemas: 1924–1929, Juiz de Fora, Brazil: Dias Cardosa, 1930
Poesias: 1922–1955, Rio de Janeiro: José Olympio, 1959
Poesia completa e prosa, Rio de Janeiro: Editora Nova Aguilar, 1994

Further Reading

Araújo, L. Correa do, *Murilo Mendes*, Petrópolis: Vozes, 1972
Bandeira, Manuel, "The Sardonic Braziliano," *Americas* (September 1954)
Campos, Haroldo de, "Murilo e o mundo substantivo," *Metalinguagem*, São Paulo: Cultrix, 1976 [Contains short section on Mendes's work]
Guimarães, J. Castañon, *Murilo Mendes*, Rio de Janeiro: Nova Fronteira, 1986

Juan León Mera 1832–1894

Ecuadorian prose writer and poet

Until recently Juan León Mera has been identified as a Romantic writer, author of a single novel, *Cumandá*, because it is one of the foundations for the formation of this genre in Latin America and it established the novel in Ecuador. This evaluation has changed in recent years as a result of the appearance of studies on key points of this work, which include the intellectual activity of its author in a more global and precise manner. Nevertheless, that significance had not gone unnoticed by his contemporaries, as Alcalá Galiano remarked in 1903: ". . . I can affirm that Mera's literature is not mere literature, but rather a very subtle political and social philosophy, adorned with the rainment of wit and a nimble style."

Mera began his career, not as a novelist but as a poet, writing *Poesías*, 1858 [Poems], *La virgen del sol*, 1861 [The Virgin of the Sun], *Poesías devotas y nuevo mes de María*, 1867 [Devout Poems and the New Month of Mary]. The choice of genre is not accidental; at that time it was the medium of expression with which the dominant culture identified, and in letters it represented the continuums of colonial society within the republic. His themes were the conventional ones, which followed the official criteria of the period: the family, patriotism, educational satire and, especially, religion. For the young man, born in Ambato, of a social class that had declined in status and with no contact with the capital, poetry was the first rung in the social ladder, and he strove hard to achieve this ascent. His education had three characteristics: he was self-taught, as he was unable to attend the university; had very few intellectual contacts – F. Cevallos and Julio Zaldumbide – and he had a Catholic upbringing, which led him to forsake his early liberalism for conservatism.

As a writer and politician he concentrated on the promotion of both political and cultural structures, but always within the boundaries of conservative thought and in agreement with the established cultural canon. His incursions into poetry and narrative, painting, literary criticism, biography, epistolary writing, and also into history, pedagogy, geography, folklore, and journalism, derived from the idea of a project for renewal to which the intellectual was morally bound. This explains a work such as *Ojeada histórico-crítica sobre la poesía ecuatoriana*, 1868 [Historico-Critical Overview of Ecuadorian Poetry], in which he analyzes the reasons for the underdevelopment of writers and shows a new direction which does not have a decisive impact on the cultural context because of his eclecticism. His is an edifying literature in accordance with the conservative nature of the society and the moderation of Ecuadorian Romanticism. Thus it is significant that Mera and the intellectuals around him continued to study the Spanish classics – and also that Mera was interested in the critical commentaries of Valera, Pereda and Alarcón. Mera and his fellow-writers continued to respect the notion that Castilian should remain "pure." Furthermore, in his adoption of literary Americanism as a formula for national cultural independence, Mera expressed his desire for integration into the Hispanic American world. The last is seen as a unit in which the reason for being a part of "the American reality" would be the contribution to the fabrication of that whole. Thus Mera developed native elements: indigenous folklore, nature, historical anecdotes, local customs. In addition to indianist narrative he wrote legends, stories and local color articles: "Entre dos tías y un tío," 1891 [Between Two Aunts and an Uncle], *Tijeretazos y plumadas*, 1903 [Snips and Penstrokes].

Not long after the publication of his *Poesías*, Mera began his political career. From 1861 on he held important offices and was to become the most outstanding intellectual of the Conservative party, collaborating in the modernization project for the State that was promoted by the dictator García

Moreno, with whom he closely identified. This project sought to endow the State with real power, defined as having a divine origin. Their goal was to be achieved with the support of the landowners in the regions and the union of Church and State. The Catholic Church was charged with keeping a vigilant eye on ideology and education. After the assassination of the dictator, together with the social changes that then took place, this particular expression of power was jeopardized. Thus Mera tried to find a formula that would allow the system of large landholdings common to the highlands to continue despite the threat presented by the liberal sectors of the coast, but he was unable to make his influence felt. His *La Dictadura y la Restauración* [The Dictatorship and the Restoration], written in 1884 but published in 1932, is an example of his role as ideologue, although the reaction of members of his political party was adverse.

In *Cumandá* (1879), Mera brings together a a Romantic concept of the novel and an ideological interpretation of the country. The work's lineage may be traced back to Chateaubriand and sentimental and indianist narratives. There are no signs of linguistic unorthodoxy, since the intention of the author is to write correctly – especially because the novel is dedicated to the Spanish Academy – following established models, leaving originality for themes, according to the tenets of literary Americanism. Thus the action is articulated with the familiar mixtures of narrative lines, changes of rhythm, unexpected turns, including the final anagnorisis and temporal counterpoints, supporting a story of love, hate, revenge, sin and repentance. The main plot narrates the love between the Indian Cumandá and the creole Carlos, impeded by the adversities which culminate in the death of the young woman. Linked to this story are the description and symbolization of nature and the sequences protagonized by Indians, including folklorish scenes.

Cumandá belongs to the period following on the dictatorship of García Moreno (1860–75) in which Mera is aware of the decline of both power in the sierra and of his model for the State. The novel tries to offer a formula for saving a world deep in sin (violence) because of landowners like Orozco and the interruption of the Jesuits' civilizing mission when they were expelled. The sacrifice of an innocent Cumandá, a "white" Indian, allows for the reconciliation in orthodox Catholic terms between Orozco, father of the heroine and by then a Dominican priest, and Tongana, the Indian who had abducted Cumandá. At the same time it impedes the act of incest between the two young people. That is, the social solution must be found through reconciliation in Catholic terms. Religion acts as a moral guide so that material conditions change as a result. The solution Mera proposed is ineffective in societal terms since it consisted of a Jesuit model of civilization that was unacceptable to the landowners of the highlands. In 1895 the liberals come to power; a year earlier Mera had died, forgotten by the members of his own party.

LUIS MARTUL TOBÍO

Biography

Born in Ambato, Ecuador, 28 June 1832. Abandoned by father and brought up by his mother in abject poverty; largely self-taught. Began to paint water colours which he sold to travellers. When he was able to visit Quito, made friends with the painter Antonio Salas, and mixed with younger writers such as Julio Zaldumbide. Involved in politics and journalism; became provincial governor, a deputy in the national Congress and president of the Senate. Composed song adopted as national anthem in 1865. Civil war and injustices of Ecuador's society influenced his writing. Died in Ambato, 13 December 1894.

Selected Works

Novels and Short Fiction
"Los novios de una aldea ecuatoriana," serialized in *La Prensa*, Guayaquil, Ecuador (February–April 1872)
Cumandá, o, un drama entre salvajes, Quito: J. Guzmán Almeida, 1879
Por qué soy cristiano, Quito: Imprenta de la Universidad, 1891
"Entre dos tías y un tío," *Revista Ecuatoriana*, Quito, Ecuador, nos. 9–30 (1891)
"Un matrimonio inconveniente," *Revista Fe*, Quito, Ecuador, nos. 58–60 (October–December 1893); in book form, Quito: El Conejo, 1984

Poetry
Poesías, Quito: Bermeo, 1858
La virgen del sol, leyenda indiana, Quito: n.p., 1861
Poesías devotas y nuevo mes de María, Quito: Bermeo, 1867

Other Writings
Ojeada histórico-crítica sobre la poesía ecuatoriana desde su época más remota hasta nuestros días, Quito: Sanz, 1868
La escuela doméstica; artículos publicados en "El Fénix," Quito: Nacional, 1880

Compilations and Anthologies
Novelitas ecuatorianas, Madrid: n.p., 1909; Guayaquil, Ecuador: Publicaciones Educativas Ariel, 1974
Obras escogidas, Quito: Casa de la Cultura Ecuatoriana, 1948
Novelas cortas, Ambato, Ecuador: Imprenta Municipal, 1952

Further Reading

Guevara, Darío O., *Juan León Mera o el hombre de cimas*, Quito: Ministerio de Educacion Pública, 1944
Sacoto, Anthony, *The Indian in the Ecuadorian Novel*, New York: Las Américas, 1967
Sevilla, Carlos A., "Aspectos de la personalidad de Juan León Mera," *La Casa de Montalvo*, Ambato, Ecuador, nos. 57–58, (1953)
Sommer, Doris, *Foundational Fictions: the National Romances of Latin America*, Berkeley: University of California Press, 1991 [Chapter 8 is on *Cumandá, Enriquillo* and *Tabaré*]

Special Issues of Journals
La Casa de Montalvo, Ambato (June–August 1933)

Mestizo

Racial terminology in Latin America has often involved a confused and unequal use of terms and references to reflect many multi-racial cultures and peoples. The Spanish Crown contributed to this confusion early on with its near obsessive goal of identifying and categorizing the racial (caste) origin of the New World colonial population. In the final analysis, mestizo has been used to describe a variety of mixed-blood groups. Current clinical and popular usage, however, define a mestizo as a product of white European and Indian blood lines.

Unlike their British colonial counterparts in North America, who came with entire families to seek a new life, Spaniards often came to the New World without their women. Thus, Spaniards began the process of miscegenation (white and Indian) from the first moments of the conquest, seeking to couple with indigenous women, and that comingling of blood continues to this day in virtually every nation in Latin America. In the case of the Aztec empire, the Indian woman who represents this union and the creation of the mestizo is Doña Marina or La Malinche, given by her parents to Hernán Cortés and reviled as betrayer of the race until recent feminist re-visions by, among others, Rosario Castellanos (see separate entry) and the US critic Sandra Messinger Cypess.

This process of miscegenation between Spaniards (or in modern times other European blood lines, including British, German and Italian) and the indigenous populations, referred to in Latin America as *mestizaje*, has played a varied social and political role throughout the history of Latin America. Its primary importance has been in Mexico, most of Central America, and in many South American countries, particularly the Andean countries and Paraguay where the indigenous population is considerable.

In Spanish colonial society mestizos formed a major category in the social caste system, positioned above Indians and blacks, but distinctly inferior to both creoles and Spaniards. Mestizos were often shunned by Indians. On the other hand, they were often mistrusted by the creole and Peninsular authorities who questioned their loyalty to the throne. After the Wars of Independence and throughout most of the 19th and early 20th centuries the mestizo's role in society stayed much the same. In many areas mestizos continued to have a stigma attached to them that suggested they were somehow bastard offspring. Still, mestizos have not generally suffered from the same level of racial discrimination that has been visited upon many Indian groups in Latin America. Moreover, during the last sixty to seventy years the mestizo has assumed a leadership role in many Latin American countries. Unlike Indians, mestizos now hold a wide variety of professional and political positions and live in socially differentiated towns and neighbourhoods, integrating with people of European extraction.

It is in Mexico where the mestizo and *mestizaje* are most heralded. Indeed, an entire historical mythology has sprung up in Mexico surrounding the mysterious and wondrous nature of the mestizo who is, in the final analysis, the modern Mexican. This new attitude is largely the result of the Mexican Revolution in which the majority of revolutionary military and political leaders were mestizos. Encouraged to some extent by the writings of the Mexican philosopher José Vasconcelos (see separate entry), who posited the notion of the "cosmic race," this fusion of the great European (Spanish) heritage with the sturdy and admirable Indian races of pre-Columbian Mexico has become a sort of national sacred event – providing for the creation of a New Man. But it was the Mexican philosopher Andrés Molina Enríquez in his *Los grandes problemas nacionales* [Great National Problems] who most elaborated the view of the mestizo's racial importance and started a tradition in Mexican historiography.

Mestizos come in a variety of complexions, tending to be more Indian-looking than European, or more European-looking than Indian. The result: there is no one particular mestizo physiognomy. But in addition to using the term mestizo to denote racial features, the term is also associated with culture (*mestizaje cultural*) – indicating variously a way of life, a psychological disposition, customs, and so forth. In addition, the status of being a mestizo often suggests political and economic (commercial) distinctions in society. Thus, discussions of the mestizo in Latin American literature and letters often are not anthropologically or racially based, but rather sociologically and politically focused. This is apparent, for example, in the term *cholo*, meaning a mestizo, but also a "civilized" (that is, integrated) Amerindian.

SAM L. SLICK

See also entries on *La muerte de Artemio Cruz* (Carlos Fuentes), El Inca Garcilaso de la Vega, Felipe Guaman Poma de Ayala, Identity, "Nuestra América" (José Martí), Fernando Ortiz, *El laberinto de la soledad* (Octavio Paz), José Vasconcelos

Further Reading

Anzaldúa, Gloria, *Borderlands / La Frontera: the New Mestiza*, San Francisco: Spinsters / Aunt Lute Book Company, 1987

Browman, David L. and Ronald A. Schwartz (editors), *Peasants, Primitives and Proletariats: the Struggle for Identity in South America*, The Hague: Mouton, 1979

Cuadra, Pablo Antonio, "Rubén Darío y la aventura literaria del mestizaje," *Cuadernos Hispanoamericanos*, Madrid, 398 (August 1983)

Cypess, Sandra Messinger, *La Malinche in Mexican Literature: from History to Myth*, Austin: University of Texas Press, 1991

Liss, Sheldon B. and Peggy K. Liss (editors), *Man, State, and Society in Latin American History*, New York: Praeger, and London: Pall Mall Press, 1972

Morner, Magnus (editor), *Race and Class in Latin America*, New York: Columbia University Press, 1970

Needler, Martin C., *An Introduction to Latin American Politics: the Structure of Conflict*, Englewood Cliffs, New Jersey: Prentice-Hall, 1977

Olaechea Labayen, Juan B., "El vocabulario racial de la América española y en especial la voz *mestizo*," *Boletín de la Real Academia Española*, Madrid, vol. 65/234 (January–April 1985)

Paz, Octavio, *El laberinto de la soledad*, Mexico City: Cuadernos Americanos, 1950; as *The Labyrinth of Solitude: Life and*

Thought in Mexico, translated by Lysander Kemp, New York: Grove Press, 1978; Harmondsworth: Penguin, 1985 [Chapter 4 of this gloomy book is titled "Los hijos de la Malinche," and in it Paz argues that the Mexican male subject has been constituted as a violent rejection of this shameful mother]

Race and Class in Post-Colonial Society: a Study of Ethnic Group Relation in the English-Speaking Caribbean, Bolivia, Chile and Mexico, Paris: UNESCO, 1977
Rodríguez, Ileana, "El texto literario como expresión *mestizo-creole*, *Casa de las Américas*, Miami, vol. 21/126 (May–June 1981)

Metafiction

From the moment pen was first put to paper certain writers have played with the conceited idea of immortalising themselves not only through their works but in their works. Curtailed by conventions – for example, the omniscient narrator is never omniscient enough – many writers take it upon themselves to invent new rules (not always for the same reason) that allow their appearance, brief or prolonged, on the stage of their own making. This gesture, once innovation and today yet another convention, is one of many visible in the technical repertoire of modern-day creators of fiction.

Metafiction is, in the general sense, all that fiction which tends to reflect or comment, either directly or indirectly, on its own fictitious composition. In so doing, such writing breaks necessarily with realist conventions, experimenting with subject matter, style, temporal sequences and any other category that once might have been sacrosanct to the Realist School. Of course, this break can be playful, political, philosophical or simply aesthetic, depending on the aims of the writer in question. This trend away from the traditional categories of the novel is very much evident in contemporary Latin American fiction.

Since the beginning of the 20th century Latin American narrative has witnessed a variety of trends, perhaps the most prominent being the move, particularly since the middle of the century, away from traditional Realist writing. If Latin American literature was to respond to the many aspects and levels of its own reality, then creative autonomy would represent a crucial ingredient in communicating such a rich and heterogenous universe. The Boom, as we know it today, implied a revision of definition of the real in a phenomenological sense. While Realism tended to exalt Life and diminish Art, some Latin American writers, seeing little or no future in the regionalist novel and its mimetic narrative, opted for a different kind of writing that would come to grips with a more comprehensive definition of reality. This would include not only the knowable and familiar, the social and political, but also the individual's personal and secret conceptions of life and of writing. In fact, objective reality is often questioned or totally rejected, while the subjective levels of dream and fantasy become the writer's scenario.

This growing conviction of the writer's freedom to select his or her field of vision and the tools with which to communicate it is frequently accompanied by the parallel conviction that the literary text is essentially a work of composition involving craft and artifice. This emphasis on the formal dimension of writing, intuitively practiced by all writers, becomes a conscious path taken by others and the *raison d'être* of their work. For these, narrative becomes the play on words and literary and novelistic conventions, a goal which frequently implies the attempted annihilation of fixed meanings or, in more extreme cases, of words having any referential meaning at all.

There is, however, no clear-cut chronological calendar in Latin America for this development towards more conscious craft and artifice in the novel. Nor do all writers have exactly the same motives for abandoning realist techniques and a clearly defined social and political backdrop. Moreover, the intensity with which they embrace technical innovation and change varies greatly and for different reasons.

In Argentina a pioneer of metafiction was Macedonio Fernández who remains little known because the experimental nature of his writing means that the reader has to struggle to achieve understanding. He is, in Barthes's term, "writerly" rather than "readerly" and thus it is not surprising that Borges, in particular, should have admired his work and devised ways of presenting metafiction which appealed to the imagination and made it intellectually exciting. It is Borges's interest in metafiction that accounts for him being the first Latin American writer to be taken up by the French intelligentsia. Borges was seen as relevant partly because he rejected realism and stressed the artificiality of literary creation. He argued that since the universe is, in any event, beyond the understanding of human beings it cannot be captured by them on paper. Thoughts can be conveyed on paper only through a series of words, an organization which places them in time, and any chronological order is artificial, since the material world is not reducible to semiotic signs. This is a point Borges illustrates through the fable of the map makers and the empire. The cartographers, desperate to make their synoptic version of the empire as accurate as possible, keep increasing the size of the map until it is as large as the territory itself, for they have learned that any synopsis (an encyclopedia, for instance) involves distortion. It follows from this that language, too, is an inadequate instrument to convey "reality" since it is at one remove from it; nor is it possible to reconcile the way intelligence seeks to structure the universe in a (vain) attempt to comprehend it, with the infinite matter it seeks to circumscribe and reduce to words. These metafictive concerns proliferate in Borges's work; a few relevant stories are the following. In "Pierre Menard, autor del Quijote" (Pierre Menard, Author of the Quixote), a diffident, minor French writer of the early 20th century decides to immerse himself so completely in the atmosphere of Cervantes's Spain that he will be able to *rewrite the Quixote* using exactly the same words that Cervantes used. Menard is able to achieve this bizarre objective in a partial way by a perfect reproduction of certain parts of this classic novel. But Borges's point is that the same words do not have the same meaning when read in a different century: time has altered their sense irrevocably. "El Aleph" (The Aleph) illustrates the writer's plight as a being living in time. The protagonist is able to see the universe in its entirety, but this revelation, of course, is outside of chronological time. How then can he convey this experience on paper? In "Emma Zunz," Borges dwells on the distinction between the verisimilar and the real by stressing the artificiality of narrative. To save her life after committing a murder, Emma Zunz tells the police a story which is quite credible and in which, as Borges puts it drily: "sólo eran falsas las circunstancias, la hora y uno o dos nombres propios" (all that was false were the circumstances, the time and one or two proper nouns). In "La muerte y la brújula" (Death and the Compass), a pseudo-detective story, the investigator of a series of murders acts like a critic with a fixed idea. He decides that a Jewish murder requires a Jewish solution and turns himself into an instant scholar on Judaic culture. This obsession is his downfall since a character who bears the detective a grudge is able to use the knowledge of his obsession to destroy him.

Another Argentine author of metafiction is Julio Cortázar whose novel *Rayuela* (*Hopscotch*) is one of the 20th-century's monuments of self-conscious fiction in Spanish America. Since there is a separate entry on this text in the encyclopedia, the other examples that will be given here are *Tres tristes tigres*, 1967 (*Three Trapped Tigers*) by Guillermo Cabrera Infante and *Máscaras*, 1996 [Masks] by a fellow-Cuban, Leonardo Padura Fuentes, who makes an innovative use of the *noire* genre in his novels of the 1990s.

Cabrera, like Borges, is a ludic writer, but he believes more than Borges in the liberating potential of language. Specifically, he believes that language can be released from its servitude to Western Reason by being used playfully and creatively. With this objective in mind, Cabrera Infante like Cortázar, thought it of the utmost importance for authors to free themselves from "correct" Castilian and to reclaim the vernacular. This explains Cortázar's insistence on using River Plate Spanish and why Cabrera Infante sees fit to alert the readers of *Tres tristes tigres* to the fact that "El libro está en cubano." (The book is in Cuban Spanish). This emphasis accounts for the parodies of different island authors, exposing what is perceived as their contrived prose style. However, the written word, even when

"Cuban," is seen as but an inadequate substitute for the spoken vernacular. Pursuing the subject of the inadequacies of written language, Cabrera, who assisted with the English translation of *Tres tristes tigres*, also presents its readers with different forms of poor translation in the two versions of the "Tale of a Walking Stick" told by a couple of US tourists visiting Havana in the 1950s. The first version is a pedantic one with footnotes, and the second is that of Mrs Campbell, one of the main characters of the story who corrects the translation of the tale told about her and her husband.

Leonardo Padura Fuentes is a postmodern writer who has shrewdly exploited the climate of tolerance of the transitional period in Cuba (one which, for example, allows authors to publish abroad), to focus on corruption in high – and other – places in the island's contemporary society. His recent novel, *Máscaras*, unsurprisingly, won the Spanish Premio Gijón for the best crime novel of 1996. Its subject matter is bold, for it involves the death of a transvestite in a wood close to Havana, a crime which, as a detective on the case observes, is of a type associated with a "developed" country. In addition, it transpires that the victim has been killed by his own father, a trusted diplomat who has frequently served his country abroad. *Máscaras* is also a metafictive novel in several ways. It reflects on cultural policy since the Cuban Revolution, with particular reference to the silencing at the end of the 1960s of all but those writers prepared to follow the most orthodox Party line – the latter being those offered as models to aspiring writers of the protagonist's generation. In addition the detective, Mario Conde, is a failed writer, and a story of his is inserted in the fiction. There is also a composite, homosexual character, Alberto Marqués, based on the playwrights Antón Arrufat and Virgilio Piñera. The complexities, sophistication and implied social criticism of *Máscaras* shows how far crime fiction in Cuba has evolved since the 1970s when it served as a propaganda tool in the Cold War.

Other 20th-century Latin American writers of metafiction who have an entry in this volume are: Reinaldo Arenas (see the article on *Arturo la estrella más brillante* [*Arthur the Brightest Star*]), Julio Cortázar, José Donoso, Salvador Elizondo, Manuel Puig (parody), Augusto Roa Bastos (*Yo el Supremo* [*I the Supreme*]) and Mario Vargas Llosa (particularly in *La tía Julia y el escribidor* [*Aunt Julia and the Scriptwriter*]).

DERMOT CURLEY AND VERITY SMITH

Further Reading

Waugh, Patricia, *Metafiction. The Theory and Practice of Self-Conscious Fiction*, London and New York: Methuen, 1984

Mexico

19th-Century Prose and Poetry

In 19th-century Mexico, all official academic poetry still adhered anachronistically to the pastoral artifices of Neoclassicism. When this finally gave way to the impetus of Romanticism, the form of sentimental lyricism and its political neutrality continued. It was the Cuban José María Heredia (1803–39) who introduced Romanticism to Mexico. He brought together groups of young Mexican poets and gave them space in newspapers such as *El Iris* (1826), *La Miscelánea* (1832) and *La Gaceta Especial de la República* which he himself edited.

In the 1850s a disagreement arose concerning cultural dependency. On the one hand, conservative literary circles (members of the academies of San Juan de Letrán and La Lengua) maintained that Mexican literature should remain faithful to Spanish models. On the other hand, Liberals such as Ignacio Ramírez (1818–79) and Franciso Zarco (1829–69) (members of the Liceo Hidalgo) favoured a nationalist perspective enriched by the presence of other forms of European literature. As a result, three forms of Romanticism were created in poetry, one a Hispanophile conservative form, another anti-Spanish liberal form, open to other European models and a third, eclectic form, combining moral conservatism with a sense of nationalism and an openness to models from all over Europe.

The Hispanophile faction favoured a form of Romanticism that was conservative in theme and adhered strictly to classical rules of form. Although its themes were social it avoided political commitment, and the love conventions of the Spanish canon were followed. Critical opinion holds that it is mediocre poetry, lacking in spirit and poetic imagination since its adherents had resorted, it was claimed, to clichés and pallid sentimentalism. On the other hand, it is acknowledged that this poetry has an impressive command of rhetorical resources and classical metres, as well as a certain originality in its treatment of religious themes. To date there has been no thorough examination of the theoretical implications of a double religious and erotic code in the lyrical poetry of Manuel M. Flores, J. Arcadio Pagaza, Antonio Plaza and José Joaquín Pesado.

The liberal poetic wing was made up of poets of a younger generation: José María Heredia, Rodríguez Galván (1816–42), Fernando Calderón (1809–45) and Ignacio Ramírez. These poets began their creative life in the Academy of San Juan de Letrán and went on to the Liceo Hidalgo in its first period, under the leadership of Francisco Zarco from 1851–70. Until its closure in 1882, the Liceo Hidalgo was the most significant literary institution in Mexico. Among the array of poets and writers who gathered there the most outstanding were: Guillermo Prieto (1818–97) who tried, with Riva Palacio, to popularize poetry and to poeticize the popular in the style of Fernández de Lizardi. They used the resources of the oral tradition of the ballad (*romance/corrido*), satirical poetry and the "jácara virreinal," a picaresque ballad of the colonial period. They thus secured the attention of the masses.

Eclectic Romanticism was favoured by Ignacio Manuel Altamirano when he took over the Liceo Hidalgo. In his manifesto "La literatura nacional" (1870), which would be part of the canon for several generations, he proposed the modulation of the sentimental tone and a return to the formal rigour of Classicism. He believed that if landscape constituted a state of the soul, then the spirit of the race could be defined through the reproduction of the features of diverse regions. He recommended national models above foreign ones, and he included in that category the European icons of both the conservatives and the liberals, erasing the old disagreement between the two.

Among the followers of Altamirano, Salvador Díaz Mirón (1853–1928) stands out owing to his thematic complexity, the intensity of his tone and his refinement of form. Contemporary criticism was unanimous in declaring him the best Mexican Romantic poet.

With the Restored Republic (1867–77) came the pragmatic Positivist ideology of order and progress, austere Republican morality and indifference towards art. The teaching of literature was considered one of the three least important subjects in the official education programme of Gabino Barreda, which was in force from 1862 to 1912. During the first five presidencies of Porfirio Díaz (1876–96), lyric poetry was the least favoured genre, and there were no poets in positions of middle to high political or administrative responsibility. Against this materialism and in the face of the Realist canon, *Modernismo* arose.

Spanish American Modernist poetry is not a stylistic tendency but rather a complex and coherent aesthetic expression, with its own well defined epistemology. It explores new intuitive and empirical ways of perceiving the poetic world and seeks to convey it via appropriate lyrical resources. Notable examples of such are the symbol, the metaphor and synaesthesia. Its poetic theory is made plain in the debate that Amado Nervo (1870–1919) and other Mexican poets continued for more than a decade with academician Salado Álvarez (1867–1931). This debate has been most effectively examined by Luis Mario Schneider in *Ruptura y continuidad de la literatura mexicana, en polémica*.

It is inaccurate to see Modernism as an anti-scientific reaction; conversely it looks to Physics and Experimental Psychology to find arguments to take apart the materialism of the positivist theories. In the same way, it is imprecise to contrast Realism as the literature of the masses with Modernist poetry as that of the elite, despite the fact that both aspired to these respective goals. With very few exceptions, all Mexican 19th-century literature was elitist, since even at the end of the century more than 87 % of the population was still illiterate.

The Mexican Modernist lyric can be divided into three periods which correspond to the positions of three very influential magazines in Latin America. The initial period is represented by the *Revista Azul* [Blue Journal] (1894–96). This became the most influential magazine of poetry in the Spanish language. Contributors included: the Cuban Julián del Casal, the Colombian José Asunción Silva (1865–96), the Uruguayan Julio Herrera y Reissig (1875–1910), the Bolivian Ricardo Jaimes Freyre (1868–1933), the Spaniards Salvador Rueda (1857–1933) and Ramón del Valle-Inclán (1868–1936), the Mexicans Salvador Díaz Mirón, Agustín F. Cuenca (1850–84),

Justo Sierra and Laura Méndez de Cuenca (1853–1928). The publication was edited by Amado Nervo, Manuel Gutiérrez Nájera (1859–95) and Carlos Díaz Dufoo (1861–1941).

The *Revista Moderna* covered the most thriving period in which a balance was sought between formal preciosity and a greater insistence on existential and philosophical problems. With Jesús Valenzuela as their patron and the teaching of Nervo as their inspiration, the following published their best texts: Manuel José Othón (1858–1906), Luis G. Urbina (1868–1934), Efrén Rebolledo (1877–1929) with his first books of poetry and José Juan Tablada (1871–1945).

The postmodernist poets emerged through the magazine *Savia Moderna* [Modern Sap]. In this magazine a number of more minor writers who showed some aesthetic inconsistency were published, for example Maria Enriqueta Camarillo (1875–1968). It is worth noting the influence of the "Ateneo de la juventud," above all in the reaction against the aestheticism of the first period of Modernist poetry. Two poets of great talent stand out: Enrique González Martínez (1871–1952) and Ramón López Velarde (1888–1921). These two favoured a return to humanist idealism and to the neopopularism that the avant-garde poets of the Contemporáneos group (1928–32) were to develop later. The work of Dolores Bolio (1880–1950), who perceptively reopened the problematic woman question, should be noted among these alternatives.

In poetry and in narrative, Mexican Modernism laid the foundations for the avant-garde movement. It is evident in all 20th-century Mexican lyric poetry, whether in the avoidance of ordinary settings (as in the Generación de Contemporáneos) or in the adherence to some of its principles such as the rejection of bourgeois materialism and of transnational capitalism.

From the first days of Mexican independence attempts were made to erase the Spanish presence, and Mexico's pre-Hispanic heritage was revitalized as a sign of the new nationality. In 1827 Valentín Gómez Farías and Carlos María Bustamante issued a federal decree in which the Mexican Indian and all that was native was declared a symbol of Mexican nationality. The decree soon lost force. During the governments of Juárez and Díaz, the Mexican Indian was eradicated as a figure of national identity and was replaced by the mestizo (racially mixed). These presidents undertook all kinds of campaigns (including military ones) against the indigenous communities who would not use their land for the extensive cash crops of capitalism, and who did not participate in the manufacturing drive. As a consequence, the Indian disappeared from all official novels during these governments.

The novel was the instrument that was used to spread the liberal political concept of social and racial identity. In the first period of the Romantic novel (1810–69), four main forms predominate: historical, costumbrist, sentimental and serialized. However, none of these was a pure or independent narrative form.

The historical novel was the least widespread but the most political. It was the only form which systematically favoured Rousseau's theme of the Indian as the good primitive man, and denounced the atrocities of the Spanish conquest or indeed the intolerance and authoritarianism of the colonial period. It supported the official stance of the Indian as an icon of nationality. In these novels, the structure of the plot was weak and the narrative techniques were basic and ineffective. A para-

digmatic case is *Jicoténcal* (1826) published anonymously in Philadelphia, which Luis Leal has put forward as the first historical novelistic text in the Spanish language. In *Netzula* (1832) by José María Lafragua (1813–76), the Romantic theme of racial and social equality for all gives way to sentimentalism. From then on, in the 19th-century novel, texts inspired by Rousseau lost their political dimension and held on only to the narrative convention which showed admiration for uncultivated nature, and which presented the native as a fatal victim of history and destiny. The Positivist ideal of progress based on the urban values of institutional work and order was to predominate.

As Mexico did not have a Middle Ages, its authors sought to recreate the colonial period. Examples of such would be Ignacio Rodríguez Galván (1816–42) in *La hija del oidor*, 1836 [The Judge's Daughter] or the failed attempt of Mariano Meléndez y Muñoz in *El misterio*, 1836 [The Mystery], set in the court of Philip II. They both lacked sufficient force and accuracy to capture either the atmosphere or the characters. The former constructed the action around the devices of the serialized novel, and the latter relied on a profusion of detail and the conventions of melodrama.

The *costumbrista* novel renewed the search for the nation's soul and drew on aspects of society which it considered representative. It was based on the novelistic tradition started by Lizardi, which frequently resorted to prettification or redundant scenes. However, the costumbrist form gave the novels verisimilitude, as well as variety of plot and anthropological interest. The costumbrist proclivity for detail and affected sentimentalism detracted from the main thrust of the action, gave a slow heavy pace to the storyline, often interrupted the plot and caused the characters (even the major ones) to grow blurred. The costumbrist genre through José Tomás de Cuéllar (1830–94) became an independent narrative genre, and following the influence of Altamirano, became an integral part of Realism.

The sentimental novel was the most widespread and most characteristic of conventional Romantic sensibility. All the internal and structural elements of the texts were designed to achieve the melodramatic effect of the amorous conflict. It was perhaps the only form of the novel to remain pure, without resorting to history, costumbrist scenes or the resources of the serialized novel. This form imposed on the others the plot of an immortal and unrealized love to provoke the tension within the novel.

The influence of the sentimental did not disappear during the 19th century. Paradigmatic tales of this narrative form are *Amor secreto*, 1843 [Secret Love] by Manuel Payno (1810–94) and *La sensitiva*, 1859 [The Sensitive Girl] by Juan Díaz Cobarrubias (1837–59). In her study of the 19th-century novel in Latin America, *Foundational Fictions* (1991), Doris Sommer has pointed out that if one takes the woman as a double sign of desire and individual political aspiration (Eros and Polis), and if one takes the family as a substitute structure for government, since Romantic texts only present love relationships interrupted by the authoritarianism of patriarchal figures, the following conclusions can be drawn: the young generation was cut off from the project of the nation, there was great fear of change in the intellectual establishment, and the social classes remained impermeable, all of this in a country that was supposed to be in the process of developing.

Since the serialized novel did not aim for the verisimilitude of the historical novel, it was able to escape from political propaganda, finding an expression for the novelesque through the legendary and ended up in the realms of the fantastic. Although it aimed for a strictly novelistic space, it fell into the conventions of the serialized genre. It was however more flexible and critical than the other forms. These were the novels that were most read in the 19th century as they were published in weekly episodes in newspapers or independent booklets. The first time that the theory of the serialized novel was expressed in Mexican Literature was in the prologue to *La hija del judío* [The Jew's Daughter] by Justo Sierra O'Reilly (1814–61), a story which can be taken as a model of the subgenre in its conservative form.

The serialized novel has been mistakenly scorned for the exaggerated and contrived nature of its plot, as well as for its supposed superficiality. However *Astucia, el jefe de los hermanos de la hoja o los charros contrabandistas de la rama*, 1865–66 [Artful Astucia, the Chief of the Brothers of the Blade] or by Luis Gonzaga Inclán (1816–75) and *Los bandidos de Río Frío*, 1889–91 [The Bandits of Río Frío] by Manuel Payno are novels that under the trivial appearance of adventure included a second code in which the objectives of the governments of Juárez and Porfirio Díaz were questioned. In *Astucia* the vulnerability of fiscal control and the law is exposed and society is replaced by an idealized community of smugglers. During the presidencies of Juárez (1858–72) (who was of native American descent), the representation of the Indian disappeared from the novel, in a country where a third of its population were indigenous but which was convincing itself of its claims to modernity. During the xenophobic dictatorship of Díaz, *Los bandidos de Río Frío* gave visibility to the Indian as a marginalized social entity who had been reduced to nomadism and banditry owing to agrarian policy. Both novels document the failure and corruption of the campaigns to bring peace to the country and to attract foreign investment.

As in politics, in the novels of the first period (1810–68), there were no influential masters, and not even a dominant canon. The novel remained more isolated than poetry and more adrift. There was no clear differentiation between the novel, the novella and the short story. However in the second period (1868–1911), Altamirano was responsible for the re-emergence of the novel and its re-structuring and shaping into what was known as the national novel. This made use of the empirical realism of costumbrism and the Mexicanist tradition in theme, space and type, as had been initiated by Lizardi and continued by Luis G. Inclán. It incorporated into one the contributions of nearly all Romantic European novelists.

Although the national novel preserved the sentimentalism of the Romantic spirit, it introduced a more restrained tone and presented marriage as a compensatory alliance for characters who worked for progress and social stability. The characters evolved even if they were predictable. They were created in pairs in binary opposition, for example the European character opposite the native or character of mixed race. Under the guiding hand of Altamirano the Mexican novel showed greater rigour in the design of its narrative structure and in the formation of its characters. There was a preoccupation with a sense of variety and proportion of tone and style. It is important to stress the independence of the national novel from European

models and to note that it was a tradition that continued for more than forty years. The problem was that the transmission of reality resulted in a convention that was tied to the politics of Juárez and later Porfirio Díaz.

Mexican Realism involved a serious misrepresentation of reality, and perhaps for this reason contemporary criticism was united in questioning the use of the term "Realism." The different generations of Realist novelists promoted the two phases of the project of Díaz's regime. On the one hand they supported the programme of depoliticization (*porfirismo* 1876–88) through the repression or discrediting of revolts, as in *La bola*, 1887 [The Riot] and *La guerra de tres años*, 1891 [The Three-Year War] by Emilio Rabasa (1856–1930) and *El Zarco*, 1901 (*El Zarco, the Bandit*) by Altamirano. At the same time they presented government bureaucracy as a corrupt activity and thus an aspiration unworthy of the majority, as in *La gran ciencia*, 1887 [The Great Science] and *Moneda falsa*, 1888 [Counterfeit Money] by Rabasa. In the same manner the Realists promoted Porfirio Díaz's programme by portraying social immobility as stability, political neutrality as Porfirio-styled peace and progress as an unquestionable absolute. This was the picture portrayed in the novels of José López Portillo y Rojas (1850–1923), Rafael Delgado (1853–1914) and Ángel de Campo (1868–1908).

The world was painted as a self-satisfied one. Authors selected certain aspects of a reality which had by then become a literary cliché and a stereotype. Although certain social and political blemishes were denounced, they were shown to be exceptions or individual cases which did not alter the upward direction of the system. The exploitation of those working on the plantations, the company stores and repressive authoritarianism were only denounced as vices in the case of feudal landowners, who were seen as antagonistic to the national project of modernity (capitalist land-owning), or such issues were set in periods long before Díaz's government.

The Realist novelists considered mimesis to be of artistic merit, that is to say that they took as a starting point the assumption that reality was rational, ordered, unalterable and describable. They made gratuitous use of generalizations. They debased the social function of Altamirano's novelistic tradition and the theory of European Realism, often converting this into an aesthetic diversion with a huge false impact. The fact that they narrated in the past tense reinforced their perspective of a stable world closed to change. The characters in their works were inconstant and static, and were psychologically at odds with themselves. Owing to the lack of any profound sense of irony, poetic subjectivity was not erased, and this resulted in a naive and childishly sentimental world.

Surprisingly, as the Realist short story was considered a minor genre, it was less subject to aesthetic and moral conventions, and more flexible regarding narrative technique. It thus allowed irony and in some cases, for example the short stories of López Portillo y Rojas compiled by Emmanuel Carballo in *Cuentos completos*, 1965 [Complete Short Stories], Vicente Riva Palacio in *Los cuentos del general*, 1896 [The General's Stories] and Ángel de Campo in *Apuntes y ocios*, 1896 [Notes and Leisure], moral principles and social structures were rigorously questioned. The technique of the short story, whilst it had tinges of humour, became more flexible and more creative in its production of character and linguistic strategy.

It is difficult and unhelpful to draw a clear line between Mexican Realism and Naturalism, as both share aesthetic and ideological features, besides which both incorporate into their texts expressive formulas taken from Spanish American Modernism and even Romanticism. In Realism and Naturalism there were obvious Romantic features: a sentimental plot in which psychological tension and narrative interest were combined, and also characterization through physical, psychological, moral, ethnic, social and political contrasting. From Romanticism, they also took the rather simplistic technique of basing narrative conflict around contrasting categories of moral forces that were at odds with each other. They also made use of the tendency towards melodrama via exaggerated emotionality and the contrived theatricality of the story's organization.

In Mexico, as in the rest of Spanish America, the Naturalists distanced themselves from the method of Zola's *Le Roman experimental*, 1870 (*The Experimental Novel*), since they emphasized the artistic production of the material they had gathered and not the effectiveness of a purely scientific report. On the one hand they concealed symbols, allegories and other interpretations with spiritual significance, whilst at another level their descriptions were subject to apparent objective rigour.

The atmosphere was not favourable to Naturalism because Mexico lacked a sizeable middle class, as well as a major industry and metropolis. As Carballo has pointed out, Mexican Naturalism captured the new forms of the colonial period and perceived the beginning of underdevelopment. So it opened the way for other topics traditionally excluded from Realism, such as sexuality, anarchism and proletarianism, the issue of the dialectic of exploitation and poverty and with it other perspectives of strategies of authority and power. The protagonist of *Pacotillas*, 1900 [Shoddy Goods] by Porfirio Parra, because he is of mixed race and is middle class, represents the model of identity and the model of Porfirio Díaz's official programme, which owing to the lack of opportunities and the repression of the dictatorship was linked with mental alienation and death. The (female) protagonist of *Santa* (1903) by Federico Gamboa is put forward consistently throughout the story as an allegory of the Mexican identity expelled from the countryside, who arrives in the city only to be prostituted by foreign companies. This was a clear allusion to the economic and political strategies of Porfirio Díaz. The Naturalist novel made the most fundamental and systematic criticism of the corruption of political principles, of laws, institutions and the procedures of Porfirio Diaz's government. Surprisingly only *Tomochic* by Frías mentions Díaz as the cause of the nation's ills, an accusation which cost Frías persecution and exile.

In some senses, the atypical nature of Mexican Naturalism was due to a reaction against the novelistic strategies of the form of Realism inspired by Altamirano. Gamboa, distancing himself from the Realist canon in *Metamorfosis* (1899) and *Santa* created great ideological ambiguity through a dyglossic discourse, composed of at least two narrative codes in tension. This confirmed another facet of the novelistic modernity of Mexican Naturalism.

Owing to the repression of Díaz's dictatorship and the materialism of the national project, Modernism pointed to the self-awareness of the individual as a being who was socially alienated, spiritually oppressed and psychologically dislocated. The result was that modernist novels took the form of psychological or metaphysical exploration and their authors avoided placing them in an objective or realistic time and space. Modernism was the first convention to take an anti-canonical stance towards Realism, subverting its narrative conventions, and it thus caused the emergence of the following: the novella, the chronicle, the short story-essay, the short story-myth, the short story-aphorism, the suppression of action, decharacterization, the parody of the omniscient narrator, and as a final result the short Modernist novel which fused all the diverse experimental genres.

As a result of their scope and atypicality short modernist novels in Mexico were confused with the short story form. However, over twenty were published, among which the following deserve mention: ten novels by Amado Nervo (1870–1919), *Querens* (1891) by Pedro Castera (1838–1906), *Nikko* (1898), *Hojas de bambú*, 1910 [Bamboo Leaves], *El enemigo*, 1900 [The Enemy], *Salamandra* (1919) by Efrén Rebolledo (1877–1929); *Claro-obscuro*, 1894 [Light and Shade] by Ciro B. Ceballos (1873–1948), *El espejo de amarilis*, 1899 [Amyrillis's Mirror] by Laura Méndez de Cuenca (1853–1928) and *Un adulterio*, 1903 [An Adultery] by Rubén M. Campos (1876–1945). To understand the aesthetics of the Modernist narrative it is essential to consider the outstanding volumes of short stories by Carlos Díaz Dufoo, Alberto Leduc (1867–1908), Dolores Bolio (1880–?), Laura Méndez de Cuenca and Bernardo Couto Castillo (1880–1901).

The narrators and poets of the Mexican Modernist movement made use of the same influences (already mentioned) which allowed a great imaginative freedom. This was enriched by a new reading of Eastern mythological, Nordic and Greco-Latin tales, which they then adapted to their *fin-de-siècle* sensibility. They transgressed all sense of reality by presenting a plot and resolution of an archetypal or fantastical nature. Irony, parody and humour linked to eroticism were other elements which transgressed the binary moral categories of Realism.

In Realism love was expressed within legal boundaries and social institutions, and in Naturalism it was presented as a deviation from the norm and a transgression of marriage. However, in Modernism love was exposed beneath all forms of eroticism as a perversion to any moral and legal principle, and it was given an aesthetic ontological dimension, and even a sacred value. Eroticism in the Modernist narrative was not only the fundamental theme but the most outstanding structural resource. It was the element which dissolved morals, reason, work, stability, evolution, identity and the national project. It questioned the certainty of reality, the nature and apprehension of time and space as well as the knowledge and control of human beings and their environment.

It can thus be said that the definitive feature of modernity in the Mexican novel of the 20th century was the creation and re-structuring of the novelistic world, free from the old necessity to faithfully reproduce reality. The creation of a strictly novelistic space in Modernism was achieved via fantasy, ambiguity, eroticism, a hostility to the epic manner, irony and an anti-narrative stance. All these features anticipated the experimentalism of avant-garde literature and subverted the ideology and narrative forms that had been persistently used throughout the 19th century.

MARIO MARTÍN
translated by Jo Glen

Further Reading

Alegría, Fernando, *Historia de la novela hispanoamericana*, 4th edition, Mexico City: Andrea, 1974

Altamirano, Ignacio Manuel, "La literatura nacional," in *Crítica de la novela mexicana del siglo XIX*, edited by Emmanuel Carballo, Mexico City: UNAM, 1989

Brushwood, John S., *Mexico in Its Novel: a Nation's Search for Identity*, Austin: University of Texas Press, 1966

____ *Genteel Barbarism: Experiments in the Analysis of Nineteenth-Century Spanish-American Novels*, Lincoln: University of Nebraska Press, 1981

Carballo, Emmanuel, *Letras mexicanas del siglo XIX*. Mexico City: Universidad de Guadalajara, 1991

García Barragán, María G., *El naturalismo literario en México*, 2nd edition, Mexico City: UNAM, 1993

Hale, Charles A., *The Transformation of Liberalism in Late Nineteenth-Century Mexico*, Princeton, New Jersey: Princeton University Press, 1989

Larroyo, Francisco, *Historia comparada de la educación en México*, 6th edition, Mexico City: Porrúa, 1962

Leal, Luis *"Jicoténcal, primera novela histórica en castellano," Revista Iberoamericana*, vol. 25/49 (January–July 1960)

Lukács, Georg, *The Theory of the Novel: a Historico-Philosophical Essay on the Forms of Epic Literature*, translated by Anna Bostock, London: Merlin Press, 1978

Martín, Mario, "Nineteenth Century Prose Fiction," in *Mexican Literature: a History*, edited by David William Foster, Austin: University of Texas Press, 1994

Promis Ojeda, José, *La novela experimental / La novela moderna*, Santiago de Chile: Universidad Católica de Chile, 1968

Ramos, Julio, *Desencuentros de la modernidad en América Latina*, Mexico City: Fondo de Cultura Económica, 1989

Schneider, Luis Mario, *Ruptura y continuidad: la literatura mexicana en polémica*, Mexico City: Fondo de Cultura Económica, 1975

20th-Century Prose and Poetry

Few Latin American countries can match the quality of present-day Mexican literary production; probably none could offer comparable diversity. If we look at the line-up of undisputed representative "complete writers," that is, those who excel at both creative writing and critical reflection, with the exception of Borges, we can make the following observation. This role in the 20th century would seem to fall to the Mexicans: Alfonso Reyes, Octavio Paz, Carlos Fuentes and, at a later stage, possibly José Emilio Pacheco. By contrast, Mexican literature has not attracted the same high level of criticism as the other major centers (e.g., Argentina and Brazil).

20th-century Mexican literature presents a rich canvas woven from the influences of, and responses to, social upheavals (such as the Revolution of 1910, the massive migration and emigration, the infamous Tlatelolco massacre of 1968, and the ongoing deep political and economic crisis of the country), international literary and cultural currents (the avant-garde movements, postmodern culture), and Mexico's own plural, historical and cultural heritage, enriched subsequently by several waves of refugees seeking haven or new home (interwar and war immigration, especially after the Spanish Civil War, and Latin American diaspora from the Southern Cone in the 1970s). Mexico has also fascinated numerous first-class foreign writers; *The Plumed Serpent* (1926) by D.H. Lawrence; *Under the Volcano* (1947) by Malcolm Lowry; or the works by the enigmatic B. Traven, to name just a few, all are part of Mexican heritage and have left their influence on Mexican literature.

The mask of orderly progress and successful modernization Mexico was displaying at the beginning of the century was shattered by the Revolution of 1910, and the country seemed to be falling prey, once again, to its violent demons. The young intellectuals grouped around the Ateneo de la Juventud (1909) were the first to sense that there was something rotten about Mexican "Modernity," and they turned against its ageing bulwark, the philosophy of Positivism, the scientific warranty on which was expiring all over Europe at that time. The new, Neoromantic philosophies and literary currents (such as Symbolism or Vitalism) directed the attention towards the land, culture and metaphysics. Elsewhere in Latin America, the allegorical and visionary "Novel of the Land" was born out of this confluence; in Mexico, the mystique of the land was overwhelmed by history.

The young Mexicans turned to the many aspects of their culture and history dormant under the "modern varnish," and became the first contemporary thinkers of *mexicanidad* and educators of post-revolutionary Mexico. Under José Vasconcelos as Minister of Education in the early 1920s, mass education and national values in arts, geared to the Mexican history of *mestizaje*, flourished. Alfonso Reyes evoked old Mexico in exquisite prose in his "Visión de Anáhuac," 1915 [Vision of Anáhuac], which later became a kind of poetic "script" for some murals of Diego Rivera. But Reyes was an accomplished man of letters, a career diplomat; his literary tastes were refined and cosmopolitan; after he returned to his country permanently in the late 1930s, he set international standards for higher education, founding the Colegio de México in 1940 with the help of Spanish intellectuals who found refuge in Mexico. In poetry, Ramón López Velarde evoked the traditional slow-paced everyday life of the provinces, and, in his poem "El retorno maléfico," 1919 [Evil Return], expressed "an intimate reactionary sadness" over the destruction caused by the Revolution. López Velarde is renowned for his precise use of colloquial language which opened up a new universe for Mexican poetry; Salvador Novo (1904–74), Efraín Huerta (1914–82), Jaime Sabines (b. 1926), and José Emilio Pacheco (b. 1939) after 1968, among others, would continue to explore this path.

The Revolution of 1910 left its indelible mark on Mexican narrative which has lasted up to present. Mariano Azuela (1873–1952) produced not only the most highly acclaimed work of the first cycle (up to the mid-1940s) of the "Novel of the Revolution," *Los de abajo*, 1915 (*The Underdogs*), but chronicled assiduously the unfolding Mexican post-revolutionary human tragicomedy. (In the second cycle, this role, at times enlarged to include all Latin America and the Hispanic world, would be assumed by Carlos Fuentes). In spite of the circumstances of its first appearance, i.e., being written in midst of the war and published as a serial in a newspaper in El Paso, Texas, *Los de abajo* is a narrative carefully planned and masterfully executed with attention to the smallest detail. Naturalistic symbolism; mythical closure; a narrative line cut to the bone and yet amazingly polymorphous; a discourse that combines lyricism, rough language and satire, all contribute to the continued vitality of this novel. The effaced narrator lets his characters engage, among themselves and sometimes including the landscape, in a truly polyphonic dialogue. This continually rejuvenating text also strikes one by being completely saturated with Mexican popular culture; many passages read like echoes of popular and revolutionary *corridos*; the ever-present elements of colloquial language aim beyond any simple naturalistic imitation and introduce a popular world-view, metaphors, the picaresque, folk wisdom and values. Through the dense and multifarious use of these elements, *Los de abajo* seems to anticipate the forms of postmodern writing which explored Latin American popular cultures in the guise of the *novela del lenguaje* (language novel) from the 1960s to the 1980s.

Several other works from this cycle stand out from the rubble; some of them have been called "novels" by default. The hybrid eye-witness narratives assembled by Martín Luis Guzmán in *El águila y la serpiente*, 1928 (*The Eagle and the Serpent*); some of Nellie Campobello's short stories from *Cartucho; relatos de la lucha en el norte de México*, 1931, showing the utter absurdity of revolutionary violence as seen from a young girl's point of view; some powerful pages of José Vasconcelos's memoirs, started in 1935 with the first instalment of his *Ulises criollo* (abridged as *A Mexican Ulysses*); and José Rubén Romero's (1890–1952) vintage picaresque novel *La vida inútil de Pito Pérez*, 1938 (*The Futile Life of Pito Pérez*).

In the second cycle, the novels of the Revolution become more conscious of their literary status, more experimental as narratives and more ambitious as symbolic structures, although especially in the feminist testimonial texts fiction and experiment may be softened for the powerful revisionist values their works bring along. It might be worthwhile noting that some dramatic texts by the avant-garde playwright Rodolfo Usigli (1905–79), such as *Corona de sombra; pieza antihistórica en tres actos*, 1943 (*Crown of Shadows*), have anticipated, and perhaps stimulated, this coming complexity in the novel, and specifically foreshadowed some early postmodern writing of Carlos Fuentes (b. 1928), such as his outstanding novella *Aura*, 1962, or the later "historical novel" *Noticias del imperio*, 1987 [News of the Empire], by Fernando del Paso.

The second cycle opens with a powerful indictment of gloomy prerevolutionary provincial life: in Agustín Yáñez's *Al filo del agua*, 1947 (*The Edge of the Storm*) the Revolution bursts in at the very end of the novel as a promise of change. It is implied that bright prospects lie ahead. By contrast, other novels of this cycle concentrate on the turbulent period following the outbreak of the Revolution and after. Not much happiness is to be found in *Pedro Páramo*, 1955, by Juan Rulfo; his slim novel actually includes important elements of sly parody of *Al filo del agua* as well as of *El laberinto de la soledad*, 1950 (*The Labyrinth of Solitude*), by the poet and essayist Octavio Paz, which exerted so powerful an influence on the Mexican novel and subsequent thinking about Mexico. Paz's presence is felt strongly in the early narrative of Carlos Fuentes, especially in his masterpiece novel *La muerte de Artemio Cruz*, 1962 (*The Death of Artemio Cruz*). *Los recuerdos del porvenir*, 1963 (*Recollections of Things to Come*), by Elena Garro, anticipates the free mingling of imagination and the fantastic with reality which will characterize the magical realism (*realismo mágico*) of Gabriel García Márquez and, later, of Isabel Allende. The panoply of female women characters in this novel also foreshadows later feminist revisionist narrative. In a playful fictional key, Jorge Ibargüengoitia satirizes mercilessly the unsettled post-revolutionary period in his biting and hilarious novel *Los relámpagos de agosto*, 1964 (*The Lightning of August*).

Ibargüengoitia's joyfully irreverent attitude towards the Revolution opened the doors for the testimonial novels written by Mexican women writers such as Elena Poniatowska, in *Hasta no verte, Jesús mío*, 1969 (*Until We Meet Again*); and Ángeles Mastretta (b. 1949), in *Arráncame la vida*, 1985 (*Mexican Bolero*). Both novels feature strong women as their protagonists, thus questioning the stereotypes of traditional Mexican woman as outlined in *El laberinto de la soledad*. They are also incisive as a radical revisionist history of the Revolution from the feminist/feminine perspective. Mastretta's fictionalized *roman-à-clef*, based in great part on oral testimonies, dares to unravel the mystique of the times of the "untouchable" Lázaro Cárdenas. The clever recipe book and family saga *Como agua para chocolate*, 1989 (*Like Water for Chocolate*), written by Laura Esquivel, is only the latest (re)version of the "Novel of the Revolution;" it combines the new feminist self-assured writing with the spice of Allende's magical realism in a sagacious and salacious postmodern cooking. In the same way that avant-garde art obliged its readers to relearn to read and focus on the *mise-en-abîme* of endlessly proliferating, dense autotelic symbolic structures, intertextual spiderwebs, and metaliterary obstructs (Roland Barthes called this aseptic cabbalistic encounter with the text "bliss"), postmodern writing rediscovers some "simple pleasures" of reading which are, of course, anything but simple.

The avant-garde winds of change blew to Mexico first from the East. The traveler through the Orient José Juan Tablada toyed with the conciseness and imagist metaphoricity of the Japanese haiku, and he explored the ideographic, visual poetic space in *Li-Po y otros poemas*, 1920 [Li-Po and Other Poems]. However, not unlike Apollinaire's earlier *Calligrammes* (1918), the somewhat adolescent art of painting objects with words and typography, the combining of words and images into visual structures, and the even more complex exploration of textual spatial dimensions, all coexist in *Li-Po* with still traditional poetic motifs and wordwork. For example, Tablada's New York partakes of a different century from that of the Peruvian Carlos Oquendo de Amat or Federico García Lorca. Tablada's poetry, at least on the surface, and his commentary on the visual arts both float freely with the artistic currents of the first half of the 20th century.

The first true, though ephemeral, avant-garde school, the *estridentista* (strident) movement, sputtered in the maritime province of Veracruz between 1921 and 1927. At that time, the ports were still the neuralgic points of the countries, being the places of first encounter and exchange of information. Yet one wonders whether the donkeys lazing in the streets of sleepy Xalapa, rather than being dutifully *épatés*, were not getting hiccups from all that futurist, Bolshevik-proletarian vertigo that was descending upon them. The founder of the movement, Manuel Maples Arce (1898–1963), wrote a vociferous visionary poem "Urbe; super-poema bolchevique en 5 cantos," 1924 [City; Bolshevik Super-Poem in 5 Cantos], where naive politics is further drowned in *ultraísta* metaphors. The *estridentistas* are best remembered in Mexican literary folklore for the one-liner that ends their Manifesto of 1923, *¡Viva el Mole de Guajolote!*, raising the favorite Mexican national dish of turkey with chili sauce as their banner.

In the meantime, the more serious members of the avant-garde generation gathered strength around literary journals such as *La Falange*, 1922–23 [The Phalanx], and *Ulises*, 1927–28 [Ulysses]. From the very beginning, they resisted the nationalistic "turn" imposed on Mexican culture by the Revolution and, instead of celebrating *mestizaje*, strove to express "the Latin soul of America" as opposed to the rival "winter civilization" of the North. (It is surprising then that their journals turned out to be the main conduits to Latin America for translations of contemporary North-American poetry.) The major achievement of this group was the journal *Contemporáneos*, 1928–31 [Contemporaries], which then gave the name to the whole generation.

The poets and critics around *Contemporáneos* were a loose grouping of heterogeneous voices, including Bernardo Ortiz de Montellano (1899–1949), the editor; José Gorostiza (1901–79); Jaime Torres Bodet (1902–74); Xavier Villaurrutia (1903–50); Salvador Novo; and Gilberto Owen (1905–52). Carlos Pellicer (1899–1977), who was after Torres Bodet the secretary to Vasconcelos, is also peripherally included among the Contemporáneos. In their activities, the "contemporaries" put on display their exclusive concentration on literature and avoided politics as ostentatiously. Some were career diplomats or held important government posts. It was enough of a scandal that a number of their inner group were more or less openly homosexual. Not surprisingly, Gide and Proust were their heroes, and theater benefited from their interests. Homoeroticism among the Contemporáneos group was vocally denounced, for example, by Maples Arce, who seems to be one of the first specimens of Latin American "*machismo-leninismo.*"

The "contemporaries" did for poetry (and for theater) what the second cycle did for the novel. Literature acquired in them autotelic status and their aim was the highest quality of production possible. Their literary aesthetics followed rather the conservative, intellectual strand of the avant-garde, i.e., the line of symbolism evolving into so-called "pure poetry," under the influence of Paul Valéry and Juan Ramón Jiménez. Therefore, the group had little time for Dadaism or for Surrealism; only much later did Villaurrutia show some affinity with the latter, perhaps under the influence of his intimate friend, the Peruvian Surrealist César Moro who lived in Mexico during the war years. This horizon of aesthetic interests then limited the scope of contemporary literature disseminated by the journal; yet within its own terms of reference, *Contemporáneos* was a first-class achievement. Among the "contemporaries," the intellectual purification of poetry was taken to its limit by Gorostiza in his hermetic *Muerte sin fin*, 1939 (*Death without End*), which is a 20th-century version of Sor Juana's philosophical poem *Primero sueño*, 1692 (*Sor Juana's Dream*). Death was also high on the mind of Villaurrutia in his famous *nocturnos* (nocturnes). By contrast, Pellicer celebrated the sunny "tropics" with "hands full of color."

The poets of the next generation rallied around the journal *Taller* [Workshop], 1938–41. As if programmatically, *Taller* concentrated on Mexican literature; yet it also showed a certain continuity by including the Contemporáneos. The initial literary aesthetics of the group was also somewhat ambiguous: they felt attraction to "pure art," yet expressed a willingness to subordinate art to broader social goals. It is no surprise then that the two generations mingled later in *El hijo pródigo*, 1943–46 [The Prodigal Son]. Among the *talleristas*, Efraín Huerta came closest to emphasizing exclusively the political dimension; later in his career he was recognized for his playful satirical, humorous, erotic, and otherwise *pungent poemínimos* (minipoems). The major poet to emerge from the Taller group was Octavio Paz who, in 1990, became the first Mexican Nobel prizewinner for literature. Paz formulated the disjuncture faced by the artist in his "Ética del artista" [Ethics of the Artist] as early as 1931, which was his first printed essay and the first manifesto of his creed, and he has tried to reconcile the opposites ever since. The very fruitfulness of his poetry and critical commentary consisted in the fact that he never abandoned completely one stance for the other, and both were continually being reborn in him within new intellectual and social contexts. "Ética," surprisingly, contained already the seeds of Paz's romantic revolt against Modernity.

The Spanish Civil War seemed to push Paz up the slope of political action and poetry. Yet his stay in Spain in 1937 was not without reverses; forty years later he finally raised the veil on some of his experiences in the notes to "Elegía a un compañero muerto en el frente de Aragón," 1937 [Elegy for a Comrade Killed at the Aragonese Front], in *Poemas*, 1979. (Elena Garro, who was his wife at that time, is much more outspoken in her *Memorias de España 1937*, 1992 [Memories of Spain]). During the war years and shortly thereafter, Paz underwent the first metamorphosis: the contact with the US and his diplomatic travels all over the world drew him to intercultural problems; and the close friendship with the French Surrealists after the war made him a participant in the larger agenda of one of the most "postmodern" among the avant-garde movements. Towards the end of the 1940s, a stream of brilliant works started to pour out: his selected poems *Libertad bajo palabra*, 1949 [Freedom on Parole, partial translation in *Early Poems, 1935–1955*], early postmodern reflection on the Mexican soul, history, and culture in *El laberinto de la soledad*, 1950; parasurrealistic poems in prose, *¿Aguila o sol?*, 1951 (*Eagle or Sun?*); philosophy of modern (his) poetry, *El arco y la lira*, 1956 (*The Bow and the Lyre*); and the poetic summation of that period in *Piedra de sol*, 1957 (*Sun Stone*).

The 1960s brought a second metamorphosis for Paz: signs in (almost) aleatoric rotation and visual poetry combined with structuralism, semiology, deconstruction and Buddhism in one hallucinating poetic nirvana. Paz not only speaks about love, but he eroticizes the page in *Blanco*, 1967, included in *Ladera este*, 1969 (*East Slope*, in *The Collected Poems, 1957–1987*). Perhaps the sharpest expression of his new poetics appeared in a hybrid volume of poetry in prose, metacriticism, and ritual journey in one, *El mono gramático*, 1974 (*The Monkey Grammarian*). A casual introduction to Mexican popular picaresque turned into an exploration of world's major civilizations in *Conjunciones y disyunciones*, 1969 (*Conjunctions and Disjunctions*). *Los hijos del limo*, 1974 (*Children of the Mire*), gives a magisterial overview of the history of modern poetry.

The savagery of Tlatelolco brought Paz back to earth and to his Mexico in crisis. His immediate reaction to the massacre and his public rebuke of the Government turned him into the conscience of the Mexican intelligentsia. The *Posdata to El laberinto*, 1970 (*The Other Mexico*), started the process of his intellectual and physical return, and the literary and political journals, *Plural*, 1971–76, and *Vuelta* [Return], 1976 to the present, marked the road. Yet Paz's postmodern vision and politics came too early to his country, torn among minuscule Utopian factions (fictions), a dreadful social reality, and the pragmatics of slick corruption. History must have seemed like a better bet, and Paz's audacious postmodern re-reading of an end of an epoch emerges in *Sor Juana Inés de la Cruz o Las trampas de la fe*, 1982 (*Sor Juana, or The Traps of Faith*). Love was the first and is also the last refuge of the poet; in 1993, his meditation on love in modern Western culture, *La doble llama* (*The Double Flame*), appeared in print.

It took more time for the narrators of Paz's generation to reach maturity. Together with Paz, Juan Rulfo, Juan José Arreola (b. 1918), and José Revueltas (1914–76) could be considered the founders of contemporary Mexican literature. Rulfo expressed his stark vision of the Mexican countryside in and after the Revolution at the beginning of the 1950s. His fame is based on just two slim volumes: the short stories *El llano en llamas*, 1953 (*The Burning Plain and Other Stories*), and the novel *Pedro Páramo* (1955). Rulfo's work offers a deceptive façade of apparent simplicity; but behind his rustic, taciturn characters and their halting speech lies an accomplished master of modern narrative techniques; and behind the apparent realism lurks parody, satire, the grotesque and the absurd. *Pedro Páramo* stretches this line to the limit and achieves almost surrealistic qualities. Yet the array of experimental techniques in Rulfo's work is never an end in itself, but only a means to achieve a merciless exploration of recent Mexican history and traditional cultural values. From this perspective, *Pedro Páramo* can be seen as an oneiric appendix to, and sly rebuttal of, Paz's famous *El laberinto de la soledad*.

Arreola became famous for his parodistic, absurdist, and Kafkaesque short fictions, collected in various versions of his *Confabulario*, 1952 (*Confabulario and Other Inventions*). Later Arreola's short pieces got even shorter, in his whimsical minifictions, aphorisms, sharp quotes, and "cute" observations (following the lead of Ramón Gómez de la Serna's *greguerías*). Arreola's trademark was his prodigious verbal mastery and economy; through his literary workshops he was teacher to a whole generation of younger Mexican writers. By contrast, Revueltas was a radical political activist by nature, carrying "revolt" in his very name. Yet he seemed to always come either too early or too late. One generation earlier, his idiosyncratic Marxism could have been celebrated like that of the Peruvian José Carlos Mariátegui; by the 1940s the expectations had changed. *Los días terrenales*, 1949 [Earthly Days], earned Revueltas the ire of the Stalinists, because the novel dared to question what would later be called, and officially criticized by the same Stalinists, as "sectarian attitudes." After a severe dressing down by his comrades in which the then "faithful" Pablo Neruda also participated with insults typical of the times, Revueltas recanted, but later he turned into an acerbic critic of the Mexican Communist Party. Revueltas had a hard time fitting into the minuscule leftist splinter groups so typical in

Latin America, warring more among themselves rather than with their "class" enemy. (Vargas Llosa captured a personal version of this atmosphere in his partly autobiographic *Historia de Mayta*, 1984 [*The Real Life of Alejandro Mayta*]). Finally in 1968 the opportunity seemed to knock on Revueltas's door as he became involved in the Mexican students' unorthodox rebellion; yet even he proved able to lead them only to Tlatelolco. Today it is almost painful to read his own utopian "organizational charts" for the "revolution" which neither the country nor the student body were ready to follow; if those *organigramas* were not soaked in young blood, they would look just like any other pages of fantastic literature. The posthumous collection of these materials, titled *México 68: juventud y revolución*, 1978 [Mexico 68: Youth and Revolution], furnishes an important dimension otherwise missing in Elena Poniatowska's *La noche de Tlatelolco*, 1971 (*Massacre in Mexico*), focusing on the human tragedy of those who went one step too far. While in prison for his role in the student movement, Revueltas wrote what is undoubtedly his literary masterpiece, the novella *El apando*, 1969 [Solitary Confinement], a powerful naturalistic and visionary parable of socialized brutality and human degradation. *El apando* reads like a distant echo of "El matadero" (*The Slaughter House*) by the Argentine Esteban Echeverría. What appeared as a hideous exceptional situation is espoused in Revueltas's work as normal daily reality. In this sense, *El apando* was also a prophecy of what was to come to Latin America in the following decades.

Unmistakable seeds of diversification appeared in the next generation, especially through the strength of women's writing. Yet the overshadowing figure was, and is, Carlos Fuentes. Fuentes consolidated the modernization of Mexican and Latin American narrative. In his own version of magical realism, Fuentes magnified Paz's insight of the massive survival of "old Mexico" under modern varnish by his own infusion of myth and ritual (e.g., the themes of cyclical return and the double), obliging the reader to follow simultaneously different strands of meaning, not readily reducible one to another. The emerging polymorphous vision of reality was channeled, in the first cycle of his great narratives, by the ideal of the "totalizing novel": *La región más transparente*, 1958 (*Where the Air is Clear*), uncovers modern Mexico City and its many subcultures; *La muerte de Artemio Cruz*, 1962 (*The Death of Artemio Cruz*), revisits the period from the Revolution to the present; *Terra Nostra*, 1975, plays with the whole of Hispanic culture, from the discovery of the New World to the apocalyptic end of Western civilization. Yet, at the same time, Fuentes writes early postmodern short fiction, such as the capriccio on themes from Mexican history and the history of modern witchcraft, *Aura*. This latter strand is then further explored both in his shorter and longer fiction: *Zona sagrada* (*Holy Place*) and *Cambio de piel* (*A Change of Skin*), both from 1967, *Cumpleaños*, 1969 [Birthday], and *Una familia lejana*, 1980 (*Distant Relations*). In Mexico, only Fernando del Paso dared to take up the challenge of the "totalizing novel," but without any overwhelming success. Fuentes managed to make a smooth transition to post-Boom writing, and his spy thriller *La cabeza de la hidra*, 1978 (*The Hydra Head*); and the string of novels as diverse as *Gringo viejo*, 1985 (*The Old Gringo*), *Cristóbal nonato*, 1987 (*Christopher Unborn*) and *La campaña*, 1990 (*The Campaign*), have further enriched his grand cycles of present-day Mexican and Latin American "human comedy." Paradoxically, *Cristóbal nonato* is a fully postmodern narrative which, however, pokes fun at and takes to task some early postmodern cultural trends.

A group of writers took the modernization of narrative a step further towards the exploration of narrative and language structures as self-sufficient artefacts. Similar to the French *nouveau roman*, some literature useful for writers and critics was produced. In Mexico, the trend was anticipated by Josefina Vicens (1911–88), who, according to experts, wrote the best novel about nothing in *El libro vacío*, 1958 (*The Empty Book*). For sure, Vicens still reads like Dostoyevsky in comparison with, for example, Salvador Elizondo (b. 1932), who has achieved a certain fame by taxing his readers' endurance to the limit in a series of hermetic *grafógrafos* (graphograph-manias). Yet even Elizondo was returned to life through the magnificent theatrical (per)version of his postmodern political divertimento *Miscast*, 1981. Juan Vicente Melo (b. 1932) has also shown a "nocturnal obedience" to this type of literature. Juan García Ponce (b. 1932) early on and Sergio Pitol (b. 1933) more recently were able to find their way out of a literature turned upon and against itself. Hugo Hiriart (b. 1942) put this vogue of literary *préciosité* on its head and wrote a hilarious pastiche of chivalresque novel and other lost Utopias in *Galaor*, 1972 [Galahad].

Vicente Leñero (b. 1933) straddles the line between the experimental novel and theater and documentary literature and political commentary. The novelist and playwright Jorge Ibargüengoitia stands apart in this panorama, because he used rather traditional means, though ones which until recently were almost absent from Latin American writing, such as humor, parody, and satire (aggravated by sarcasm). Political and cultural commentary in Mexico also profited from the "new journalism," represented by Elena Poniatowska and Carlos Monsiváis (b. 1938). The *crónica* (sketch) became one of the most versatile and ubiquitous genres in present-day Mexican literature and journalism: Cristina Pacheco (b. 1941) explored popular classes and their traditional values; Guadalupe Loaeza dissected the *reinas* (queens) from the swanky Polanco neighborhood; Juan Villoro (b. 1956) chronicled the sentimental journey of the post-Tlatelolco generation; and in his *Ucronías*, 1990 [Uchronies], Oscar de la Borbolla (b. 1953) added a crisp fictional "turn" to this literary-journalistic "reporting."

Marco Antonio Montes de Oca (b. 1932) and Jaime Sabines illustrate the two competing currents in contemporary Mexican poetry: the experimental line echoing Octavio Paz and the down-to-earth line of colloquial poetry. Sabines is a poet who when stumbling on a stone, does not hesitate to protest against the *pinche piedra*; his modern elegy on the death of his father strikes a powerful chord with the distant voice of Jorge Manrique. In the later members of this generation, their "rebellious spike" (*La espiga amotinada*, 1960) seems to have rather pinched the wheels of their poetic Volkswagen.

The novelist, poet, and essayist Rosario Castellanos (1925–74) came to be considered the founding figure for contemporary Mexican women's writing. In her consciously feminist work, cut short by her early death, she discussed topics placed later in the center of feminist discourse, such as women and language or cultural difference. Castellanos was also exemplary in transcending middle-class feminism and reaching out,

through the narrative, towards the underprivileged indigenous people in Chiapas where she grew up as a child. Her experimental text in dramatic form, *El eterno femenino*, 1975 [The Eternal Woman] is a kind of encyclopedia of feminist topics in traditional Mexican culture and history. Elena Poniatowska, the most recognized woman writer in Mexico today, negotiates the line between journalism and fiction; her fiction proves that she is an accomplished storyteller, and this shows even in the string of her great testimonial and documentary narratives for which she has been especially praised, from *Hasta no verte, Jesús mío*, 1969 (*Until We Meet Again*), through *La noche de Tlatelolco*, 1971 (*Massacre in Mexico*) to *Tinísima*, 1992 [Tina Modotti]. The sly masterpiece novella *Querido Diego, te abraza Quiela*, 1978 (*Dear Diego*), is a homage to and a demythification of the "fabulous life" of Diego Rivera, chipping away at the macho image of one of the best known Mexican artists of the 20th century.

With Garro, Castellanos, Poniatowska, Mastretta, Esquivel, and a host of others, women's writing in Mexico comes to the fore. The group of first-generation Mexican Jewish women writers has been very active. Coming from different parts of the world, they have focused on their double heritage and sometimes conflictive identity. Esther Seligson (b. 1941) delved into timeless Jewish history in her pastiche of biblical narrative *La morada en el tiempo*, 1981 [The Abode in Time], and she revisited Penelope's story in her outstanding novella *Sed de mar*, 1987 [Thirst of the Sea]. Following the international success of Alex Haley's *Roots*, 1976, Margo Glantz inaugurated this genre in Mexico with the documentary chronicle of her family *Las genealogías*, 1981 (*The Family Tree: an Illustrated Novel*); originally the work was published as an essay but the novelistic element hidden in it won. The feminist playwright Sabina Berman (b. 1953) evokes her childhood in the novella *La bobe*, 1990 [Grandma]; she also wrote openly lesbian poetry in *Lunas*, 1988 [Moons]. Angelina Muñiz-Huberman (b. 1936) recalls the experience of the Republican children taken to the Soviet Union and her first years in Mexico in *Dulcinea encantada*, 1992 [Enchanted Dulcinea]. Rosa Nissán recreated, from a child's point of view, the world of the Lagunilla market and of the conflictive interculturality in her sparkling *Novia que te vea*, 1992 [Bride that Could See You]. Myriam Moscona (b. 1955) took up her Sephardic origin in her poetry.

The genre of documentary family saga spread among non-Jewish women writers. Silvia Molina (b. 1946) published *La familia vino del norte*, 1987 [The Family Came from the North]; earlier she was recognized for her autobiographical novel-diary *Mañana debe seguir gris*, 1977 (*Gray Skies Tomorrow*), dealing with her love affair with the ill-fated poet José Carlos Becerra (1937–70). Poniatowska recalled her coming to Mexico in *La "Flor de Lis,"* 1988 [The "Flor de Lis"]. Bárbara Jacobs (b. 1947), sometimes appended to the Jewish writers for her Middle-Eastern origin, evoked her father in *Hojas muertas*, 1988 (*The Dead Leaves*). Yet Mexican women's writing cannot be tied to any such specific themes. María Luisa Puga (b. 1944) used her travels in Africa for the novel *Las posibilidades del odio*, 1978 [The Possibilities of Hatred]. Martha Cerda (b. 1948), from Guadalajara, put all the worlds of Mrs Rodríguez into her proverbial bag, in *La señora Rodríguez y otros mundos*, 1990 [Mrs Rodríguez and

Other Worlds]. The versatile playwright, poet, and novelist Carmen Boullosa (b. 1954) based her dense novellas *Mejor desaparece*, 1987 [Better Get Out of Sight], and *Antes*, 1989 [Before], on autobiographical elements; in 1993 she surprised readers with a masterpiece multigenre pastiche *La milagrosa* (*The Miracle-Worker*), uncannily prophetic about the bloody 1994 presidential campaign.

In the 1960s, while still "modernizing" along the lines of 19th-century industrialization, Mexico was hit by the early forms of emerging postmodern culture. The mass of middle-class teenagers, themselves a product of Mexico's "progress" and urbanization, adopted international pop and countercultural toys for their newborn leisure culture; *la Onda* (the new wave) spread on these wavelengths like a brushfire. Various generational gaps appeared. The parents were appalled by the new sexual freedom, drugs and rock music. The older "progressive" intellectuals charged that songs in English and teenage game-playing in "Spanglish" implied a sellout to US imperialism; the Government shrank at the very idea of freedom. The young split between those who, although dressed like hippies, continued to pursue contemporary high culture and those who set out to explore the new cultural space and forms. Tlatelolco would dampen the joyful iconoclasm of Mexican youth and bring these two groups closer together. Yet the literary side of *la Onda*, was not any direct equivalent of the social phenomenon of that name; it was a sophisticated writing, saturated by the literary self-consciousness of the Boom aesthetics and by the experiments with the *novela del lenguaje* ("language novel," inaugurated by the Argentine Julio Cortázar's *Rayuela*, 1963). That is why such prime *Onda* writers as Gustavo Sainz (b. 1940) and José Agustín (b. 1944) could (plausibly) deny their belonging to that movement; both outgrew their work of the 1960s, but it was difficult for them to retain their original freshness. Only much later some populist authors resorted to surfing, with neo-naturalistic dedication, the low- and underclass language. *La Onda* as a social phenomenon survived Tlatelolco and culminated in the rock festival of Avándaro, 1971 (the Mexican equivalent of Woodstock), after which a clampdown on countercultural phenomena followed. In an experimental collaborative "script for a cinematic rock opera," *Ahí viene la plaga*, 1985 [The Plague is Coming; title of the Mexican translation of one of Elvis Presley's songs], José Agustín, José Buil and Gerardo Pardo take stock of that roller-coaster period. Whatever its limitations and contradictions might be, *la Onda* helped to shatter the grip of the elite establishement over cultural production.

José Emilio Pacheco and Homero Aridjis (b. 1940), both poets and novelists, illustrate some alternatives to the *Onda* literature. Pacheco wrote a highly experimental, yet also highly charged, novel juxtaposing crucial events of Jewish diaspora and persecution, *Morirás lejos*, 1967 [You Will Die Far Away]. Tlatelolco inspired in him some powerful palimpsests over the voices of the vanquished from the conquest and from Poniatowska's testimony. His masterpiece novella, or prose poem, *Las batallas en el desierto*, 1981 (*Battles in the Desert and Other Stories*), which fictionalizes his own sentimental education and evokes a neighborhood and times now buried by the earthquake of 1985 and by history. It disproves the claims that postmodern writing is all surface, without histor-

ical dimension and social critique; all that is missing in *Las batallas* is an overarching allegory, didactic purpose, and total-izing (totalitarian?) ideology. Aridjis turned to the historical novel in *1942*; *Vida y tiempos de Juan Cabezón de Castilla*, 1985 (*1942; The Life and Times of Juan Cabezón of Castile*), and he pursued ecological activities and topics which in Mexico lead to apocalyptic vision, as in *El último Adán*, 1985 [The Last Adam], and *La leyenda de los soles*, 1993 [The Legend of the Suns]; the latter blends myth, ecological and human wasteland, political satire, lyricism and the fantastic into a prophetic postmodern end-game.

Other writers of this generation have already well-estab-lished records. In the north, the novelists Jesús Gardea (b. 1939), Gerardo Cornejo (b. 1937), Ricardo Elizondo (b. 1950), or Daniel Sada (b. 1953). From Xalapa, Luis Arturo Ramos (b. 1947). In the center, René Avilés Fabila (b. 1940), Agustín Monsreal (b. 1941), Joaquín-Armando Chacón (b. 1944), Héctor Manjarrez (b. 1945), Humberto Guzmán (b. 1948), Marco Antonio Campos (b. 1949), Luis Zapata (b. 1951), Fabio Morábito (b. 1955). In and out of the center, Federico Campbell (b. 1945), Hernán Lara Zavala (b. 1946), Carlos Montemayor (b. 1947). And let us not forget the "incurable" poet David Huerta (b. 1949).

Since the 1970s no predominant mode of writing has been established; Mexican writers have ceased to feel bound to the "Mexican" reality only; anything can be attempted, provided that high quality literature outcome is achieved. The result has been an enormous diversification. If Octavio Paz's selective *Poesía en movimiento* [Poetry in Movement], 1966, expressed the tenor of the 1960s, Gabriel Zaid's "busload of Mexican poetry" (*Omnibus de poesía mexicana*, 1971), is typical of the more inclusive postmodern tastes. At the end of the century, Mexican literature offers signs of robust health. Scores of new talented writers have appeared. Literature is now free to discover and rediscover new realities; a strong current of women's writing has especially contributed to this. An explo-sion of regional literature has also changed the literary land-scape: we are witnessing the revival of traditional centers (Guadalajara, Xalapa); emergence of northern borderlands and beyond (the US Southwest and Chicano culture), all with a production informed by contemporary models. Mexico City itself has turned into a hub of "satelite" subcultures. An array of minority cultures has emerged: indigenous cultures (as yet less noticeable in nationally visible cultural production); a strong group of writers focusing on their Jewish heritage; and a space opening up for gay/lesbian writers. This enormous diversity of elements coming in all possible combinations has produced a vibrant culture that no crisis could quell.

EMIL VOLEK

Further Reading

Bigas Torres, Sylvia, *La narrativa indigenista mexicana del siglo XX*, Guadalajara: Universidad de Guadalajara, 1990

Brushwood, John S., *Narrative Innovation and Political Change in Mexico*, New York: Peter Lang, 1989

Dauster, Frank N., *The Double Strand: Five Contemporary Mexican Poets*, Lexington: University Press of Kentucky, 1987

Duncan, J. Ann, *Voices, Visions and a New Reality: Mexican Fiction since 1970*, Pittsburgh: University of Pittsburgh Press, 1986

Fernández, Jesse and Norma Klahn (editors), *Lugar de encuentro: ensayos críticos sobre poesía mexicana actual*, Mexico City: Katún, 1987

Forster, Merlin H. and Julio Ortega (editors), *De la crónica a la nueva narrativa mexicana: coloquio sobre literatura mexicana*, Mexico City: Oasis, 1986

Foster, David William (editor), *Mexican Literature: a History*, Austin: University of Texas Press, 1994

Gibbons, Reginald (editor), *New Writing from Mexico*, Evanston, Illinois: Northwestern University, 1992

Kohut, Karl (editor), *Literatura mexicana hoy: del 68 al ocaso de la revolución*, Frankfurt: Vervuert Verlag, 1991

___ (editor), *Literatura mexicana hoy, II: Los de fin de siglo*, Frankfurt: Vervuert Verlag, 1993

Lara Zavala, Hernán (editor), *Ruptura y diversidad*, Mexico City: UNAM, 1990

Schneider, Luis Mario, *México y el surrealismo (1925–1950)*, Mexico City: Arte y Libros, 1978

___ *El estridentismo: México, 1921–1927*, Mexico City: UNAM, 1985

Sheridan, Guillermo, *Los contemporáneos ayer*, Mexico City: Fondo de Cultura Económica, 1985

___ *Índices de Contemporáneos: Revista mexicana de cultura (1928–1931)*, Mexico City: UNAM, 1988

Steele, Cynthia, *Politics, Gender and the Mexican Novel, 1968–1988: Beyond the Pyramid*, Austin: University of Texas Press, 1992

Anthologies

Domínguez Michael, Christopher (editor), *Antología de la narrativa mexicana del siglo XX*, 2 vols, Mexico City: Fondo de Cultura Económica, 1989–91

Ocampo, Aurora M., *La crítica de la novela mexicana contemporánea: antología*, Mexico City: UNAM, 1981

Bibliographies

Foster, David William, *Mexican Literature: a Bibliography of Secondary Sources*, 2nd edition, Metuchen, New Jersey: Scarecrow Press, 1992

Ocampo, Aurora M., *Diccionario de escritores mexicanos, siglo XX: desde las generaciones del Ateneo y novelistas de la Revolución hasta nuestros días*, Mexico City: UNAM, 1988 [Up to 1995, only 3 volumes have appeared]

Gabriela Mistral 1889–1957

Chilean poet

Gabriela Mistral was the pseudonym of Lucila Godoy Alcayaga, born in 1889 and raised in an isolated mountain valley of Chile's semi-arid north. Although the celebration of her public figure and her wanderings as a diplomat presented her with ample opportunity to mingle with wealthy socialites and the cultural elite, Mistral never hesitated to identify herself as a mestiza of Basque, Indian and possibly Jewish antecedents, whose family belonged to "la clase media baja campesina que lindaba con la tierra" (the rural lower-middle class, close to the land). These identifications persist throughout her writings and underlie her lifelong concern with peace, education, the rights of children, the struggle for social justice on behalf of the dispossessed and respect for the land. Her poetry dwells on suffering and loss while finding reason for hope in individual and communal experience of ordinary life, and in nostalgia for the remote past.

Melancholy poetry and socially-conscious prose were Mistral's trademarks from her earliest publications in local newspapers, while she was an adolescent. Her refusal to tone down her publications in response to criticism led local authorities to bar her from entering secondary school. At the age of sixteen she began to support herself and her mother by working as a teacher's aide in a rural school. Her frequent moves from one school to another in Chile exposed her to the complex and volatile social situation. The first of Chile's major poets to come from outside a small, Europe-oriented elite, Mistral's meteoric advancement as a teacher and educator in the state-run schools of Chile was owed to her extensive publications, which were directed at a diverse audience of schoolteachers, administrators, children and fellow poets. Despite her lack of a professional degree, in 1921 Mistral was placed in charge of Chile's most prestigious secondary school for girls. Such successes in a woman from an obscure background earned her more than a few enemies. Never one to forget the ill-will of others, by 1926 she resolved to leave Chile, subsequently returning for only two brief visits, in 1938 and 1954. Her disinclination to settle in any one place and her fascination with seeing new landscapes worked in her favor. Supporting herself through journalism and lecture tours she became known, in Fernando Alegría's phrase, as "a walking educational mission."

In late adolescence and young adulthood Mistral claimed the Colombian Vargas Vila and the Nicaraguan Rubén Darío as her models. Only the influence of the latter persisted, in her attention to metrical form and her celebration of poetry as "song." Although she initiated epistolary contact with Darío (as she did with most of the leading Latin American writers of her time), intellectually and temperamentally Mistral was from her early twenties a loner who preferred to reside outside of any particular literary or political group. Her political and artistic independence, coupled with the mindless exaltation of her as a symbolic mother for schoolchildren, has tended to dissuade most attempts to relate her work to any larger frameworks in Latin American cultural production. Among her various accomplishments, she was with José Martí one of the originators of children's literature in Latin America. Partly as an extension of her work with the League for Intellectual Co-operation, she was deeply familiar with European and American folklore. Her "Sonetos de la muerte," dating from about 1914, have been favorably compared to the verses of Quevedo. She singlehandedly invented, first in verse, then in prose, the "Recado" [Message] as a popular form for conveying the qualities of an impromptu oral presentation in compact, vivid prose. Other demonstrable influences on her poetry are the aboriginal traditions of the Americas, the tragedies of Aeschylus, the biblical Psalms, and the verses of Dante. She read very widely in history, devotional literature from East and West, and philosophy. In her journalism she was particularly interested in biography, novels and travel writing.

A substantial portion of the published poetry of Mistral, from her earliest poems published in teachers' magazines and the theosophist journals, to her posthumously-published *Poema de Chile*, aimed to remedy the scarcity of interesting and instructive reading material available for use in the schools. It is virtually impossible to generalize about her school-based work except to point out that while some of it is occasional verse, other items are complex attempts to render philosophical ideas in the form of songs. From the 1930s onward, that school-based or didactic work increasingly concentrates on exploring the natural history of the Americas.

Mistral postponed until 1922 the publication of her first book-length collection of verse, *Desolación* [Desolation]. Scarpa explains the postponement as a result of the poet's sensivity to criticism, her vulnerability as a woman and as a schoolteacher, and her very high standards with respect to her work: less than a fifth of the poetry that Mistral had finished up to 1922 appears in *Desolación*, and many of the verses that appear in that text were subsequently included in revised versions, in *Lecturas para mujeres*, 1923 [Readings for Women] and subsequently in the first edition of *Ternura*, 1924 [Tenderness]. In effect, these divisions and repetitions show the poet's awareness of the increasing segmentation of the audience for poetry. As writing for children came to be regarded as a distinctly specialized subfield, Mistral sought not so much to distance herself from the readers of "children's" or "educational" texts, as to bridge the gap between "popular" and "elite" cultural production. Crucial to Mistral's success in this endeavor was her developing the figure of the poet as a spiritual teacher, almost a guru, who confronts injustice and decadence, who identifies with the suffering of others, and who finds communion with the natural world.

Retreat from society and closeness to the natural world brings purification and relief, in such early poems such as "La maestra rural" [The Rural Schoolmistress] and "La mujer fuerte" [The Strong Woman], and in the poet's later celebration of American landscapes. As Jaime Concha points out, Mistral's rejection of urban life and her romantic exaltation of country life are stances that Mistral shares with other early 20th century poets in Chile. Yet her work deeply diverges from that of her male contemporaries (and friends) Pedro Prado, Magallanes Moure and Eduardo Barrios, partly in her class-specific affiliation with the public (state) schools, and even more tellingly in her rejection of heterosexual love.

Writing about the body of the mother from within a deliberately female perspective provided Mistral with an alternative to poetic traditions in which woman is constructed solely in terms of satisfying male desire. Because Mistral never married and never had children, critics for many years wrote of her interest in writing for children and mothers as symptomatic of a tragic, laudable, or pathological longing for physical maternity. Only in her first volume of verse does she even allude to heterosexuality, however; in her writings on art and the role of the artist she clearly associates male-female sexual relations with pain, suffering and the degradation of both partners. In contrast to this negative view are her lyrical descriptions of the maternal body, appearing in "Poemas de las madres" (Poems of Mothers), her earlier cradle songs, and "Recuerdo de la madre ausente" (Memory of the Absent Mother). The sexual identification of the speaker is never an easy or straightforward matter in any of Mistral's earlier verses, while in the later verses the speaker turns attention on the remote past, description of people and places.

Mistral left Chile for Mexico in 1922, where the Minister of Education, José Vasconcelos, called her to assist in the development of the nation's school system. Her writings from Mexico and later show her discovery of "Americanism," and her interest in the indigenous past subsequently colors her relation to European history. Concurrent with the development of Americanism in her work is her increased productivity as a journalist, and a tendency away from the forced syntax evident in *Desolación*, which some Chilean critics criticized as twisted or arhymical, and others as an attempt to draw attention to herself. Mistral returned to Chile in late 1924 with the apparent intention of starting her own school, along the principles of the Belgian educator Decroly, but by the following, politically very tumultuous year she was thoroughly disillusioned by what she saw as the shallowness of Chile.

Because inflation and the whims of the Chilean government made it impossible for her to depend on the pension from her twenty years' service in the public schools, Mistral supported herself during her subsequent residence in Europe by writing some fifty or more newspaper and magazine articles a year, over the next ten years. Her dependence on this income prevented her from publishing another full-length volume of verse, *Tala* [Felling] until 1938. With poems such as "Dos himnos: cordillera y sol de trópico" (Two Hymns: Mountain Range and Tropic Sun), this second volume represents a fuller extension of the Americanist concern increasingly evident in her journalism. While her older contemporaries preferred *Desolación* for its lyrical intensity, her younger critics preferred the explicit concern with recent history, cultural geography and the more sustained elegiac modes, in the first section of *Tala*. A constant in both volumes, as well as in Mistral's next major collection, *Lagar* [Wine Press] is the poet's preoccupation with death, which along with childhood and landscape, is one of Mistral's greatest themes.

In Mistral's poetry the expression of loss moves swiftly from personal desolation, to survey, in prophetic witness, the scarred common terrain. Where *Tala* arises out of the Spanish Civil War, *Lagar* shows the poet's confrontation of World War II and the Holocaust. It is out of this prophetic witness that her commitment to pacifism emerges alongside her ever-present struggle for social justice on behalf of those who have been driven from the land: indians, farmworkers, abandoned women, refugees. Of all the volumes that Mistral published in her lifetime, her last work, *Lagar*, is at once her most hopeful, and her most pessimistic. The opening series of poems, entitled "Locas Mujeres" [Madwomen] show the continual effort to transcend individual personality, to comprehend the whole, and to seek an absolutely spare, unadorned language that will precisely name the absence of identity which the poet seeks. Like the volumes that preceed it, *Lagar* is the work of a poet who sought continuously to remake herself. Beyond fashions or fads, her only interest in innovation was in the dogged commitment to put past successes behind her, to explore unfamiliar territory.

Popular religiosity exerted a strong influence on Mistral's verse and thinking. Much has been written about her wide-ranging interest in religious expression, her belief reincarnation, her unorthodox attitude towards suicide, her belief in natural and herbal remedies. One reason for the relative neglect of her work is that at a time when many Latin American intellectuals were increasingly drawn to Marxism, Mistral joined the lay order of the Franciscans. Not a devout churchgoer, Mistral's admiration for St Francis is none the less evident in her "Motivos de San Francisco" (Motifs of Saint Francis) and her unique combination of spiritual and material values appears in her "Elogios de las cosas de la tierra" (Elegies of the Things of the Earth). Franciscanism also enters into her uncompleted epic-romance, *Poema de Chile* [Poem of Chile] which the poet worked on throughout the last ten years of her life, piecing it together as a kind of memory book against which to shore up the now-vanished landscape of a pre-industrial, purely agrarian Chile. The narrative of *Poema de Chile* has the poet returning to her native land, as a haunt, accompanied by two equally spectral figures: a little boy from the Atacama desert, in Chile's far north, and a huemul, or Andean deer.

There is to date no collected, critical edition of Mistral's poetry. While the *Poesías completas* that Mistral supervised in the last year of her life has been criticized for typographical and other errors, it includes crucial aspects such as dedications to individual poems, aspects that the popular paperback and schooltext editions lack. One challenge facing textual editors of Mistral's verses will be to confront the impossibility of deciding on anything resembling a "definitive reading" for texts which she regularly, repeatedly revised, and which were published in multiple versions during her lifetime. In her later years her precarious health and her constant travelling meant that many of her poems lay unfinished, in multiple manuscript versions. Two volumes of poetry, *Poema de Chile* and *Lagar II*, incomplete at her death, were subsequently published from these papers. With more than two decades of editorial labors by Scarpa, Céspedes, Calderón and Jaime Quezada, it seems probable that all but a few of the hundreds of essays that she wrote and published throughout Latin America are now in reliable texts.

Mistral would draw our attention for the originality of her thought and for the extraordinary story of her life's journey, from a childhood spent in miserable poverty, to world renown, even if she had not written so much, and even if so much were not written about her. Even outside of her remarkable poetry and her lucid, wide-ranging prose she was during her own lifetime a monumental figure for Latin America. Of this woman who was the first Nobel Laureate from Latin America, who accepted that prize in the name of all those who work on behalf of Latin American culture, it can be no small task to comprehend the whole.

ELIZABETH HORAN

Biography

Born Lucila Godoy Alcayafa in Vicuña, Chile, 6 or 7 April 1889. Attended rural primary school taught by her elder, half-sister, Emelina, in the village of Montegrande; Vicuña state secondary school, 1898–1901. First works published in the newspapers, *La Voz de Elqui* and *Diario Radical de Coquimbo*, 1905; began using the pseudonym Gabriel Mistral in 1908. Worked in schools throughout Chile: La Serena and nearby, 1906–10; Barrancas (now Pudahuel, Santiago, 1910); Traiguen, 1910; Antofagasta, 1911; Los Andes, 1912–18; Punta Arenas, 1918–20; Temuco, 1920; Santiago, 1921–22. Worked for José Vasconcelos in Mexico, 1922–24. Resided primarily in Europe (France and Italy), 1925–34, working for the League for Intellectual Co-operation of the League of Nations. Visiting Professor, Barnard College, New York City and Vassar College, Poughkeepsie, New York, 1930, followed by lecture tour of Central America. Entered Chilean Foreign Service, 1933: served in Madrid, where she was named Chilean consul, second class, with right to choose her residence, by special act of the Chilean legislature, 1936. Moved to Lisbon, 1936. Travelled throughout Brazil, Argentina, Chile, 1938. From 1939 to 1940 lived in Nice, then moved to Brazil, where she lived in Rio de Janeiro in 1940, Niteroi in 1941, Petrópolis, 1942–45. Travel and residence in the United States, Mexico and Italy, 1946–57. Awarded the Nobel Prize for Literature, 1945; Franciscan Americas Prize, 1950; National Prize for Literature, Chile, 1951. Died in Hempstead, New York, 10 January 1957. Buried in Montegrande, Chile. Casa-Museo Gabriela Mistral established in Vicuña, Chile, 1982. Microfilming of Gabriela Mistral collection for the Library of Congress and the Organization of American States, completed 1982.

Selected Works

Poetry

Desolación, New York: Instituto de las Españas, 1922; revised edition, Santiago de Chile: Zig-Zag, 1926

Lecturas para mujeres, Mexico City: Secretaría de Educación, 1923 [includes prose]

Ternura, Madrid: Saturnino Callejas, 1924; revised edition, Buenos Aires: Espasa Calpe, 1945

Tala, Buenos Aires: Sur, 1938

Lagar, Santiago de Chile: Pacífico, 1954

Motivos de San Francisco, edited by César Díaz-Muñoz Cormatches, Santiago de Chile: Pacífico, 1965

Poema de Chile, edited by Doris Dana, Santiago de Chile: Pomaire, 1967

Lagar II, Santiago de Chile: Biblioteca Nacional, 1992

Correspondence

Gabriela Mistral Epistolario. Cartas a Eugenio Labarca 1915–1916, edited by Raúl Silva Castro, Santiago de Chile: Anales de la Universidad de Chile, 1958

Cartas de amor de Gabriela Mistral, edited by Sergio Fernández Larraín, Santiago de Chile: Andrés Bello, 1978

Cartas a Lydia Cabrera: correspondencia inédita de Gabriela Mistral y Teresa de la Parra, edited by Rosario Hiriart, Madrid: Torremozas, 1988

Epistolario de Gabriela Mistral y Eduardo Barrios, edited by Luis Vargas Saavedra, Santiago de Chile: Universidad Católica, 1988

Gabriela Mistral y Joaquín García Monge: una correspondencia inédita, edited by Magda Arce, Santiago de Chile: Andrés Bello, 1989

Tan de usted: epistolario de Gabriela Mistral con Alfonso Reyes,
edited by Luis Vargas Saavedra, Santiago de Chile: Hachette and
Universidad Católica, 1991

*En batalla de sencillez: epistolario de Gabriela Mistral a Pedro
Prado*, edited by Luis Vargas Saavedra, M. Ester Martínez Sanz
and Regina Valdéz Bowen, Santiago de Chile: Dolmen, 1993

Compilations and Anthologies

Selected Poems, translated by Langston Hughes, Bloomington:
Indiana University Press, 1958

Poesías completas, edited by Margaret Bates, Madrid: Aguilar, 1958

Selected Poems, translated by Doris Dana, Baltimore: Johns Hopkins
University Press, 1971

Gabriela anda por el mundo, edited by Roque Esteban Scarpa,
Santiago de Chile: Andrés Bello, 1978

Gabriela piensa en . . . edited by Roque Esteban Scarpa, Santiago de
Chile: Andrés Bello, 1978

Materias: prosa inédita, edited by Alfonso Calderón, Santiago de
Chile: Editorial Universitaria, 1978

Prosa religiosa de Gabriela Mistral, edited by Luis Vargas Saavedra,
Santiago de Chile: Andrés Bello, 1978

Recados para América: textos de Gabriela Mistral, edited by Mario
Céspedes, Santiago de Chile: Epesa, 1978

Croquis mexicanos, edited by Alfonso Calderón, Santiago de Chile:
Nascimiento, 1979

Elogio de las cosas de la tierra, edited by Roque Esteban Scarpa,
Santiago de Chile: Andrés Bello, 1979

Grandeza de los oficios, edited by Roque Esteban Scarpa, Santiago
de Chile: Andrés Bello, 1979

Magisterio y niño, edited by Roque Esteban Scarpa, Santiago de
Chile: Andrés Bello, 1979

Reino: poesía dispersa e inédita, en verso y prosa, edited by Gastón
von Demme Bussche, Valparaíso, Chile: Universidad Católica,
1983

Gabriela Mistral en La Voz de Elqui, edited by the Museo Gabriela
Mistral de Vicuña, 1992

Further Reading

The studies by Scarpa and Bahamonde include valuable primary
sources such as letters, variant readings of early poems, and texts of
poems that the poet excluded from her collected works. Of the
various biographical studies, the earliest, by Figueroa, is extremely
uneven but provides information not included elsewhere. The
attention to dates in Gazarian Gautier's biography make it one of
the most reliable. Teitelboim's biography is more up-to-date in terms
of references to more recent publications, but includes no new
factual material. While the poet's letters are among the more useful
sources for understanding her relation to her milieu, a number of
books include anecdotal details about her later life: Ladrón de
Guevara gives interesting descriptions of the writer's work habits,
while Alegría, Concha, and Samatan all contain convincing analyses
of her complex and conflicted relationship with Chile. The poet's
centenary in 1989 sparked many fine reassessments of her poetry
and prose, too numerous to list here, which appeared in a variety of
special issues of Chilean magazines and in edited collections. The
repetitive, uninformative, or cliché-ridden celebrations of her life are
being gradually replaced by serious scholarly studies, among which
the collections of correspondence edited by Luis Vargas Saavedra
and Patricia Rubio's monumental annotated bibliography, are the
most important.

Alegría, Fernando, *Genio y figura de Gabriela Mistral*, Buenos
Aires: Universitaria, 1966

Bahamonde, Mario, *Gabriela Mistral en Antofagasta: años de forja
y valentía*, Santiago de Chile: Nascimento, 1980

Concha, Jaime, *Gabriela Mistral*, Madrid: Júcar, 1986

Figueroa, Virgilio, *La divina Gabriela*, Santiago de Chile: Impreso El
Esfuerzo, 1933

Fiol-Matta, Licia, "The 'Schoolteacher of America': Gender,
Sexuality, and Nation in Gabriela Mistral," in *¿Entiendes? Queer
Readings, Hispanic Writings*, edited by Emilie Bergmann and Paul
Julian Smith, Durham, North Carolina: Duke University Press,
1995

Gazarian-Gautier, Marie-Lise, *Gabriela Mistral: the Teacher from
the Valley of Elqui*, Chicago: Franciscan World Herald Press,
1975

Horan, Elizabeth, *Gabriela Mistral: an Artist and Her People*,
Washington, DC: Organization of American States, 1994

Ladrón de Guevara, Matilde, *Gabriela Mistral: rebelde magnífica*,
Santiago de Chile: Araucaria, 1957

Loynaz, Dulce María, "Gabriela y Lucila," in her *Ensayos literarios*,
Salamanca: Universidad de Salamanca, 1993 [The view of a
Cuban woman poet who was a contemporary of Mistral]

Una palabra cómplice: encuentro con Gabriela Mistral, Colectivo
Isis Internacional, Santiago de Chile: Casa de la mujer La
Morada, Isis Internacional, 1990

Samatan, Marta Elena, *Gabriela Mistral: campesina del Valle de
Elqui*, Buenos Aires: Instituto Amigos del Libro Argentino, 1969

Scarpa, Roque Esteban, *Una mujer nada de tonta*, Santiago de
Chile: Nascimento, 1976

——— *La desterrada en su patria*, 2 vols, Santiago de Chile:
Nascimento, 1980

Silva Castro, Raúl, *Producción de Gabriela Mistral de 1912 a 1918*,
Santiago de Chile: Anales de la Universidad de Chile, 1957

Taylor, Martin C., *Sensibilidad religiosa de Gabriela Mistral*,
translated by Pilar García Noreña, Madrid: Gredos, 1975

Teitelboim, Volodia, *Gabriela Mistral pública y secreta*, Santiago de
Chile: BAT, 1992

Bibliographies

Rubio, Patricia, *Gabriela Mistral ante la crítica: bibliografía
anotada*, Santiago de Chile: Dirección de Bibliotecas, Archivos y
Museos, 1995

Modernismo

Brazil

Modernism in Brazil started in the 1920s and should not be confused with the eponymous movement that took place in the previous generation (and therefore during the epoch of Symbolism and Parnassianism in Brazil) in the Spanish American countries. Corresponding primarily to what became known as the avant-garde in those countries, the Brazilian movement equally benefited from the formal experimentation to which writers of the European avant-garde had dedicated themselves since the first decade of the 20th century. However, in the young Brazilian nation, in addition to the preoccupation with purely aesthetic renewal, there was the desire to construct a literary code that was essentially Brazilian. Thus, if on the one hand Brazilian Modernism converged with the European avant-garde in their rupture with the previous literature through a revolutionary reflection on language, on the other hand, in their nationalism, the Modernists rescued and deepened one of the dearest proposals of Romanticism. Accordingly, as José de Alencar incorporated the indigenous vocabulary to the romantic prose of *Iracema* (*Iracema, the Honey-Lips*), Manuel Bandeira for instance would incorporate spontaneous speech of the people in his modern poetry of free verse.

A decisive event for the definition of the movement was the "Week of Modern Art" held in São Paulo from 11 to 17 February, 1922. There and then converged the diverse avant-garde tendencies that had been taking shape in the country for some time, making possible the consolidation of groups and proposals, and the publication of books, magazines and manifestos. Among the "isms" imported from Europe to Brazilian territory, at least two of them are noteworthy: Futurism, whose programme was based on experimenting with language towards one more appropriate for the civilization of technology and speed; and Primitivism, which in turn proposed experimenting with language from the liberation and projection of the forces of the individual and collective unconscious, and so valued marginal elements such as those of popular origin repressed by the formality of academic literature. These two trends, to a certain degree distinct in Europe, curiously merged in Brazil, acquiring new features, especially in the hands of the two most expressive writers of this first moment in Modernism: Oswald de Andrade and Mário de Andrade. Such a curious fusion between the Futurist and Primitivist programmes reveals itself as a natural development when one considers the context of the movement, i.e., a country in which the civilized and primitive coincided. So the Modernist writers, many of them from urban centres under modernization like Rio de Janeiro and São Paulo, thus aimed to conciliate their desire to align themselves with the audacity of modernity, whose most radical expression was Futurism, with their awareness of the fact that the unconfessedly black and indigenous roots of Brazil required a forcefully Primitivist aesthetics.

This very willingness to experiment with modern forms of expression and at the same time discover symbols and allegories capable of suggesting the repressed elements of Brazilian nationality – such as the Black, the evil of the wild man (in contrast to the idealized "noble savage"), the mulatto, the

"malandro" – surfaces in the poems from *Pau-brasil* [Brazil-Wood] by Oswald and the novel by Mário de Andrade, *Macunaíma*. Brazilian Modernism thus proposed to keep pace with the literature of the civilized metropolis, but adopting a different attitude to that of movements since Independence. Earlier writers had seen the wildness of the country as a disadvantage. However, in the hands of Modernist writers, this supposed deficiency turned to be seen as a primary source for the production and exportation of good literature. Just as brazil-wood was the first Brazilian product to be exported to Europe, the same was intended for the poetry inspired by it: a quality national production to compete in the international literary market. So the wild and primitive aspect of the nation, previously considered a reason for embarassment *vis-à-vis* the "civilized" metropolis (or at most as romantic idealization), was from then on manifestly incorporated as a source of inspiration, and a very original one, instead of being regarded as an obstacle to the elaboration of culture. It was also intended that the originality of this native source was such that, when combined with the necessary European source, the former would have the power to transform the latter so that the literature inspired in both would result in something essentially Brazilian. The manifestos "Poesia pau-brasil" [Brazil-Wood Poetry] and "Antropófago" [Cannibal] constitute the perfect Oswaldian translation of this Modernist proposal.

As the 1930s drew near, paralleling the vogue for Social Realism in Western literature, a movement for rehabilitating regionalist values took place in the northeast of Brazil. This second moment of Brazilian Modernism, even though as a whole opposing the most precursory aspects of the first, benefited much from the incorporation of colloquial speech, of lexic and syntactic regionalism and "Brazilianism" created by the prose of the generation of 1922, who paved the way to much more complex forms of narrating the day-to-day. The new group was able to reconcile some of the aesthetic achievements of the previous group with their own interest in their regional reality. Traditional regionalism could then be redefined by an updated artistic language. The movement gathered around Gilberto Freyre who, with his studies on certain repressed aspects of the Brazilian colonial past, above all *Casa grande e senzala* (*The Masters and the Slaves*), motivated writers like José Lins do Rego to search in the present of the region for the prolongation of those unconfessed Brazilian roots. In this sense these regionalists gave continuity to the Primitivism of the 1922 generation, whose own experimentalism extended, albeit in a different way, to the most expressive name of this second moment: Graciliano Ramos. In fact, each of his novels possesses its own language, thus revealing the writer's preoccupation with finding new forms of expression. Parallel to the regionalist prose, poetry as well in this second moment of the Brazilian modernism was contaminated by the concern with social reality. So, if in the most formal aspects Carlos Drummond de Andrade and Murilo Mendes needed only to proceed on the route of aesthetic liberation previously proposed, in the thematic aspect however they introduced politics in free verse.

Modernism renewed the language of Brazilian poetry and prose, freeing them from their academic past, and from the rejection of many ethnic and historic issues. It provided its writers with a coherent programme for literary autonomy, in addition to their maturing with respect to aesthetic problems concerning the representation of social reality. It paved the way, after all, for the germination, from the mid 1940s, of literature with the vitality and complexity by the likes of João Cabral de Melo Neto, Guimarães Rosa and Clarice Lispector.

TERESINHA V. ZIMBRÃO DA SILVA

Further Reading
For a long time critics had a tendency to underrate the achievements of the first phase of Brazilian Modernism in favour of the second. This situation has been reversed in the last thirty years or so because the application of concepts like carnivalization and parody allowed a productive re-reading of the works by Oswald de Andrade and Mário de Andrade.

Andrade, Mário de, *Aspectos da literatura brasileira*, 3rd edition, São Paulo: Martins, 1972

Bosi, Alfredo, "Pré-Modernismo e Modernismo" in *História concisa da literatura brasileira*, São Paulo: Cultrix, 1970

Brito, Mário da Silva, *História do Modernismo brasileiro. 1. Antecedentes da Semana de Arte Moderna*, 5th edition, Rio de Janeiro: Civilização Brasileira, 1978

Cândido, Antônio, "Literatura e cultura de 1900 a 1945," in *Literatura e sociedade*, São Paulo: Companhia Editora Nacional, 1973

Fitz, Earl E., "The Five (Six?) Faces of American Modernism," in his *Rediscovering the New World: Inter-American Literature in a Comparative Context*, Iowa City: University of Iowa Press, 1991 [An overview of all the cultural movements of this name in the Americas]

Guelfi, María Lucía Fernandes, *Novíssima: contribução para o estudo do Modernismo*, São Paulo: Universidade de São Paulo, Instituto do Estudos Brasileiros, 1987

Teles, Gilberto Mendonça, *Vanguarda européia e Modernismo brasileiro*, Petrópolis: Vozes, 1978

Modernismo

Spanish America

This is a mainly poetic movement whose major creative impulse lasted from the 1880s to around 1915. It should not be confused with Brazilian *Modernismo* or European and Anglo-American Modernism.

The critical approach to *Modernismo* has undergone a change, due to a re-evaluation of the impact of Romanticism on the history of ideas, research on the Spanish branch of the movement and its European origins, and studies of Rubén Darío's relationship with intellectual currents of his time. The result has been to explode two well-established myths. One was that popularized by Federico de Onís, according to which *Modernismo* expressed a novel crisis of sensibility occurring in the mid-1880s. The other was fashioned by Spanish poets and critics, Pedro Salinas, Dámaso Alonso and Manuel Machado among others, and presented *Modernismo* as characterized by little more than formal, technical innovations in poetic diction. Nowadays *Modernismo* is seen as representing a more intensified stage in the evolution of romantic intellectual and spiritual malaise. The *modernistas*' preoccupation with beauty and the religion of art, that is, now tends to be interpreted as part of a response to cosmic disenchantment inherited from the Romantics. Another aspect of the debate about *Modernismo* concerns the relative importance of Darío and José Martí as founders and leaders of the movement. Martí preceded Darío chronologically as an innovator, but his innovations were chiefly important for prose. The real shift came in poetry and, after the publication in 1888 of his *Azul*, was led without question by Darío.

To seek the origins of *Modernismo* we must look mainly in two directions. If we agree with José Enrique Rodó, himself an outstanding *modernista*, that to come to terms with the movement is primarily "a question of ideas," we must see that behind it lay the recognition that later 19th-century thought, and in particular Positivism, had failed to find an answer to the legacy of Romantic doubt and scepticism, intensified by Schopenhauerian pessimism. But the fact that all over Europe writers and intellectuals seemed to be groping towards a new set of ideal values – Ferdinand Brunetière's *La Renaissance de l'idéalisme* for instance, came out in 1896 – had not passed unnoticed across the Atlantic. Two years later, José Asunción Silva, one of the first *modernista* poets, was writing in his novel *De sobremesa* [Table Talk], which contains a compendium of early *modernista* attitudes, about an "idealist renaissance of art." It was brought about, he asserted, by a reaction against Naturalism, and was heavily influenced by Wagner, Verlaine, Puvis de Chavannes and Gustave Moreau, among others. Darío had already proclaimed in his poem "El cisne" [The Swan] in *Prosas profanas* (1896) that, following Wagner's lead, the new poetry had given birth to "la Helena eterna y pura que encarna el ideal" (the eternal and pure Helen who incarnates the ideal). Thus, in *Modernismo*, a longing for new, hopeful ideals struggled – in the end unsuccessfully – against what Rodó in *Ariel* (1900) called "the challenge of the Sphynx," i.e. of ultimate why-questions. For this reason, the typical *modernista* fictional heroes, such as José Fernández in Silva's *De sobremesa*, Juan Jerez in Martí's *Amistad funesta*, 1885 [Fatal Friendship], Tulio Arcos in Manuel Díaz Rodríguez's *Sangre patricia*, 1902 [Patrician Blood] are young men in the grip of a personal crisis of hopes and beliefs from which they try to escape by seeking a new, life-enhancing ideal. For the *modernista* poets, this ideal took the form of a worship of beauty, an attempt to overcome inner disquiet by living the life of art. They found inspiration in the evolution of French poetry from Théophile Gautier (whom both Manuel Gutiérrez

Nájera and Darío imitated) through Baudelaire (not forgetting the influence of Poe, which he transmitted) to both Parnassianism and Symbolism. This is the second direction in which the origins of *Modernismo* can be sought.

In their quest to regenerate post-Romantic poetry in Spanish, they evolved new formal techniques of prosody, imagery, symbolism and poetic diction generally, to express on the one hand, a crisis of confidence in the human condition and on the other their aspiration towards new ideals, chief among them that of beauty as the only absolute. Among the most important representatives of the movement apart from those already mentioned, were Julián del Casal, Manuel González Prada and Salvador Díaz Mirón. In the later phase of *Modernismo*, we find such poets as Julio Herrera y Reissig, Leopoldo Lugones, José Santos Chocano, Amado Nervo, Guillermo Valencia, Ricardo Jaimes Freyre and Enrique González Martínez, but in their work we can usually discern a transition towards Neoromanticism (Nervo), Americanist *mundonovismo* (Chocano), Neosymbolism (González Martínez) and, especially in Lugones, towards an even newer type of less ornamental imagery which portended the avant-garde, soon to appear in the 1920s.

Up to the 1880s, poetry in Spanish had chiefly expressed ideas and emotions (until Bécquer in Spain, sometimes rather stridently). With *Modernismo*, sensations became prominent. Poems appeared which expressed reactions to sights and sounds; visual, acoustical and even olfactory images were foregrounded as the senses came to be regarded as worthy of exploration. This had two important results. First, there was a clear shift in the depiction of women. In place of the angelic, desexualized, consoling, Romantic stereotype, we find women presented often very erotically as genuine sex-objects. This broke, for the first time in Spanish America, a very strong literary taboo. Second, other avenues having failed, the senses, along with the visionary insight of the true artist, were perceived (by Darío especially) as opening doors of perception onto a higher reality, hidden from the common man, a view which has survived in the work of Octavio Paz.

In terms of the renovation of forms and poetic technique, *Modernismo* represents the peak of the process which began with the Romantics' experimentation with mixed verse-forms (*polimetría*) and novel diction. Darío and his fellow-poets foregrounded the cult of beauty by using obtrusively musical rhythms, highly ornamental imagery designed to beautify banal or ugly reality, audacious rhymes, synaesthesia (the combination of two sense-impressions into one) and systematic use of new rhythmical and metrical patterns, often with lines of fourteen syllables or longer. A whole new range of symbols came into use. They included above all, that of the swan, whose snowy plumage symbolized pure beauty, but whose neck, shaped like a question mark, symbolized the enigma of existence. But present also was that of the centaur, representing the unity of the flesh, the mind and the spirit, and alluding to the paganism of classical times, in which the *modernistas* saw an age when beauty and sensuality were untrammelled by any Christian sense of sin. References to exotic foreign lands and cultures played a part in the *modernistas*' fierce rejection of the philistinism of the late 19th century in Spanish America and elsewhere. Not only classical Greece, medieval Italy and late 18th-century France, but also China, India and Scandinavia provided poetic scenarios. Important, too, were poetic evocations of the other arts, especially music, sculpture and painting, imitated from the French "transpositions d'art." As time went on, specifically Spanish American themes began to be increasingly employed. These would lead eventually, through Chocano, in the direction, for example, of Caribbean "black" poetry such as that of Cuba's Nicolás Guillén, Neruda's *Canto general* and Cardenal's *Homenaje a los indios americanos* (*Homage to the American Indians*).

It is important to notice, however, that sporadically pessimistic, the *modernistas* did not as yet envisage a random world, unpredictable and unintelligible, even absurd, as was to be the case later with Neruda and Vallejo, both of whom, like Paz, had strong roots in *Modernismo*. Thus *modernista* poems remained carefully structured verbal artefacts, with the logical nexuses still in place, using regular verse-forms and generally avoiding difficult or disturbing imagery. To that extent their poetry still reflected a world in which beauty was not divorced from goodness and truth and in which the survival of a formal aesthetic order pointed reassuringly to the survival of a moral order and of epistemological confidence. *Modernismo* was harshly rejected by many in the next generation of poets, notably by Borges, but what was rejected was its increasingly artificial-seeming aestheticism. Its existential disquiet lived on and is still with us.

DONALD L. SHAW

See also entries on Rubén Darío, Julio Herrera y Reissig, Ricardo Freyre, Enrique Larreta, Leopoldo Lugones, José Martí, José Asunción Silva, José Juan Tablada

Further Reading

Cardwell, Richard and Bernard McGuirk, *¿Qué es el modernismo? Nueva encuesta, nuevas lecturas*, Boulder, Colorado: Society of Spanish and Spanish-American Studies, 1993

Carter, Boyd, "El *modernismo* en las revistas literarias: 1894," *Chasqui* (1979)

Davison, Ned J., *The Concept of Modernism in Hispanic Criticism*, Boulder, Colorado: Pruett Press, 1966

Earle, Peter G., "El ensayo hispanoamericano: del *modernismo* a la modernidad," *Revista Iberoamericana*, vol. 48/118–19 (1982)

Fraser, Howard M., *In the Presence of Mystery: Modernist Fiction and the Occult*, Chapel Hill: University of North Carolina Department of Romance Languages, 1992

González, Aníbal, *La crónica modernista hispanoamericana*, Madrid: Porrúa Turanzas, 1983

—— *La novela modernista hispanoamericana*, Madrid: Gredos, 1987

Gullón, Ricardo, *Direcciones del modernismo*, Madrid: Gredos, 1963

Hart, Stephen M., "Current Trends in Scholarship on *Modernismo*," *Neophilologus* 71 (1987)

Henríquez Ureña, Max, *Breve historia del modernismo*, Mexico City: Fondo de Cultura Económica, 1954

Íñigo Madrigal, Luis (editor), *Historia de la literatura hispanoamericana*, vol. 2: *Del Neoclasicismo al Modernismo*, Madrid: Cátedra, 1987

Jitrik, Noé, *Las contradicciones del modernismo: productividad poética y situación sociológica*, Mexico City: El Colegio de México, 1978

Lindstrom, Naomi, *Twentieth-Century Spanish American Fiction*, Austin: University of Texas Press, 1994 [Chapter 1 is on *modernista* prose fiction]

Litvak, Lily, *El modernismo*, Madrid: Taurus, 1975
Pérus, Françoise, *Literatura y sociedad en América Latina: el modernismo*, Havana: Casa de las Américas, 1976
Rama, Ángel, *Las máscaras democráticas del modernismo*, Montevideo: Fundación Ángel Rama, 1985
Schulman, Ivan (editor), *Nuevos asedios al modernismo*, Madrid: Taurus, 1987
Zavala, Iris M., *Colonialism and Culture. Hispanic Modernisms and*

the Social Imaginary, Bloomington: Indiana University Press, 1992
Zimmerman, Marc, "Françoise Pérus and Latin American Modernism: the Interventions of Althusser," *Praxis: a Journal of Culture and Criticism*, Los Angeles, 6 (1982)

Special Issues of Journals
Revista Iberoamericana (January–June 1989)

Augusto Monterroso 1921–

Guatemalan/Mexican prose writer

Augusto Monterroso's grandfather, general Antonio Monterroso, was a friend of writers and poets, amongst them Porfirio Barba Jacob. His father, Vicente Monterroso, one of the most moving characters in *Los buscadores de oro* [The Gold Seekers], was equally passionate about literature and alcohol. He "lived always immersed in his dreams and with absolute certainty he died wrapped in them." Paradoxically, Augusto Monterroso, partly as a result of his family's itinerant life, constantly on the move between Honduras and Guatemala, and partly because of his proverbial shyness and laziness, frequently referred to in his writing, left school without completing his primary education. In 1937 he started working as a clerk at a butchers. But the family's artistic and intellectual legacy was not lost, and in the few spare hours he had every day, he started reading Lord Chesterfield, Madame de Sevigné, Horace, Juvenal and Phaedrus, the translator of Aesop's fables into Latin verse. These authors, and others, would exert a profound influence on Monterroso's writing. This self-educated man is one of the most sophisticated readers in Latin American literature, equally familiar with the classics as well as with modern and contemporary writers.

Indeed, many will be tempted to identify Monterroso with a writer he often quotes: Jorge Luis Borges, an author with whom he shares a passion for literature. Both writers have been able to bring life into literature through the use of their imagination; they both feel a special attachment towards English literature and, in both, humour is an essential ingredient. More than anything else, what brings them together is a unique talent to create a style of prose writing that is simultaneously contemporary and timeless: the very quality attributed to classic writers, regardless of the specific time into which they were born. However, dissimilarities are no less in evidence. Borges had an intellectual, scholarly and philosophical imagination. His language has the perfection of things that are stable, emphasised by his detachment. Monterroso, if not a political writer, never ignores political reality precisely because he never ignores reality. In contrast to Borges's detachment, Monterroso's personal life, his own personality, are constantly present in his literature. While, on the one hand, Monterroso shares Borges's scepticism, on the other, he is a moralist. Moreover, he takes paradox to its limits, in the process creating a paradoxical language: if he

is a classic, it is not because he wants to create a timeless language but because of what could be described as his radical wisdom.

Paradoxical yet again, Monterroso leans on classic tradition to modify and even to reverse, in book after book and without destroying them, the different literary genres. In the very title of *Obras completas (y otros cuentos)* the author underlines the writer's ability to tease literary conventions through paradox: this collection of short stories undoubtedly constitutes his first collected works, or *obras completas*, but the title also refers to the title of one of the short stories included. In this instance, the break with tradition is limited. The opposite could, indeed, be argued: Monterroso reveals his extraordinary talent as a storyteller. More than modifying, he is challenging and excelling. It also contains what arguably could be considered as the shortest and most brilliant short story ever written, a line admired, amongst many others, by Italo Calvino, and one which has ensured Monterroso's fame more than the rest of his work considered as a whole: "When he woke up, the dinosaur was still there." In this book we find many of the characteristic features in Monterroso's writing: the use of parody, paradox and nonsense, the frequent literary references incorporating the creative world of the imagination and ridiculing the pomposity in the worst tradition of Latin American writing, political ethos without a political discourse, the subtle presence of the writer that permeates his writing with irony, sarcasm, scepticism, melancholy and, more than anything else, the common-sense philosophy that allows the author to unmask conventional beliefs and attitudes.

Such common sense, carried gently, albeit relentlessly, to its logical conclusion, led Monterroso to subvert moral conventions in *La oveja negra y demás fábulas*, 1969 (*The Black Sheep and Other Fables*) and, consequently, to subvert the fable as a conventional genre. While the nonsensical aspect is emphasised and, therefore, humour is fully developed as the narrative activator, there is also a deeper and more compassionate understanding of human nature. While keeping his sarcasm for the wicked – often politicians and/or bad writers – Monterroso accepts resignedly that stupidity is part of the human condition, and a fable becomes a mirror in which we see ourselves undisguised. This subtle amalgam of humour and compassion, literature and life, scepticism and moral outrage demand to be developed in their full potential, a wider space, that is to say, the space provided by the novel. *Lo demás es silencio* [The Rest is Silence] is Monterroso's most complex book. Once again, the structured conception of the novel disintegrates, in the same way that Cervantes – the ultimate model for Monterroso as well as for other contemporary novelists – disintegrated the novel of chivalry. Ambiguity is here the logical and even exacerbated consequence of Monterroso's need to unmask conventions and highlight and accept contradictions. Eduardo Torres, the main character, a man of letters, is, just like Don Quixote, a parody, yet at the same time the instigator of the parody of other writers. San Blas, where the action of the novel takes place, could be San Ángel, a residential and sophisticated neighbourhood in Mexico City, perhaps Mexico City itself, or even a more general mirror of Latin America's parochial culture. The popularity of *Obras completas (y otros cuentos)* and *La oveja negra y demás fábulas* has overshadowed *Lo demás es silencio*, probably his most important book.

In books of essays like *Movimiento perpetuo* and *La palabra mágica* [The Magic Word], the compilation of interviews in *Viaje al centro de la fábula* [Journey to the Centre of the Fable], the diary *La letra e* [The Alphabet Letter] or the autobiographical *Los buscadores de oro*, it is impossible to distinguish the illuminating and original discourse from invention. Monterroso's books are always truthful, imaginative, entertaining and funny. In questioning our conventional perception of literary genres and of human nature, he has created his own unmistakeable, inimitable and idiosyncratic genre.

JUAN ANTONIO MASOLIVER

Biography

Born in Tegucigalpa, Honduras, 21 December 1921, but of Guatemalan nationality. Educated at Guatemalan National University. Did not settle in Guatemala until 1936. As a member of the "Generation of 1940," he was active in the opposition to Jorge Ubico's dictatorship through the Association of Young Guatemalan Artists and Writers. After his arrest by the police of Ubico's successor, General Federico Ponce Valdés, he went to Mexico as a political exile in 1944, where he stayed until 1953. Attended classes at the Arts Faculty of Universidad Nacional Autónoma de México (UNAM). University teacher in Mexico. Married Dolores Yáñez in 1953; and was appointed consul and First Secretary at the Guatemalan Embassy in La Paz (Bolivia) by the left-wing government of President Jacobo Arbenz Guzmán. After the US intervention and the fall of the Arbenz government in 1954, Monterroso went to Santiago de Chile as a political exile. Made friends with Pablo Neruda, and worked with him on his magazine *Gaceta de Chile*. In the *El Siglo* [The Century] newspaper, he published what would become his most famous as well as most often translated short story, "Mr Taylor," later included in his *Obras completas (y otros cuentos)*. In 1956 he returned to Mexico where he was to settle permanently. Married Milena Esguerra in

1962. Married the Mexican writer Bárbara Jacobs in 1976. Awarded the Xavier Villaurrutia Prize, 1975 (normally accorded only to a Mexican citizen); the Mexican Premio Nacional de la Crítica, 1992; the Premio Letterario Istituto Italo-Latino Americano, 1993. Order of the Águila Azteca, 1988.

Selected Works

No attempt has been made to divide Monterroso's works by genre since their rule-breaking nature would make this a counter-productive exercise.

La oveja negra y demás fábulas, Mexico City: Joaquín Mortiz, 1969; as *The Black Sheep and Other Fables*, translated by Walter Bradbury, New York: Doubleday, 1971
Animales y hombres, San José, Costa Rica: Editorial Universitaria Centroamericana, 1972
Movimiento perpetuo, Mexico City: Joaquín Mortiz, 1972
Lo demás es silencio: la vida y la obra de Eduardo Torres, Mexico City: Joaquín Mortiz, 1978
Viaje al centro de la fábula: con Jorge Ruffinelli . . . et al., Mexico City: UNAM, 1981
Mr Taylor & Co., Havana: Casa de las Américas, 1982
La palabra mágica, Mexico City: Era, 1983
La letra e (fragmentos de un diario), Mexico City: Era, 1987
Esa fauna, Mexico City: Era, 1992
Los buscadores de oro, Barcelona: Anagrama, 1993

Compilations and Anthologies

Obras completas (y otros cuentos), Barcelona: Anagrama, 1990
Sinfonía concluida y otros cuentos, Caracas: Monte Ávila, 1994
Complete Works and Other Stories, translated by Edith Grossman, Austin: University of Texas Press, 1995

Further Reading

The dearth of critical material on the work of Augusto Monterroso (as opposed to its quality) indicates that his literary production is undervalued.

Campos, Marco Antonio (editor), *La literatura de Augusto Monterroso*, Mexico City: UNAM, 1988 [Includes essays by, among others, Julieta Campos, Noé Jitrik, Juan Antonio Masoliver, José Miguel Oviedo, Ángel Rama and Saúl Sosnowski]
Corral, Wilfrido H., *Lector, sociedad y género en Monterroso*, Xalapa, Mexico: Centro de Investigaciones Lingüístico-Literarias de la Universidad Veracruzana, 1985
Roux de Caicedo, Lina de, *Augusto Monterroso: la fábula en Monterroso, lugar de encuentro con la verdad*, Bogotá: Serie de Escritores de las Américas, 1991
Ruffinelli, Jorge (editor), *Monterroso*, Xalapa, Mexico: Centro de Investigaciones Lingüístico-Literarias de la Universidad Veracruzana, 1976 [articles by Jorge Ruffinelli, José Miguel Oviedo, Alí Chumacero, Ángel Rama and others]

Interviews

Gliemmo, Graciela, *Las huellas de la memoria: entrevistas a escritores latinoamericanos*, Buenos Aires: Beas, 1994
Price, Greg, *Latin America. The Writer's Journey*, London: Hamish Hamilton, 1990

Vinícius de Moraes 1913-1980

Brazilian poet

Vinícius de Moraes is one of the outstanding Brazilian poets of the 20th century; furthermore, his engagement in various artistic fields situates him among the major figures in Brazil's cultural life. The musical activity in which Vinícius, as he is also known to Brazilians, engaged almost exclusively in his maturity increased his popularity within his own country as well as abroad. Vinícius's contribution to Brazilian popular music involved a genuine revolution in the late 1950s, for he was, jointly with Antônio Carlos Jobim and João Gilberto, one of the creators of the new *bossa nova* rhythm, originated from traditional *samba*. If, on the one hand, the involvement of Vinícius with music brought him international fame – he wrote the words to the famous song "A garota de Ipanema" (*The Girl from Ipanema*) – on the other, it proved prejudicial to his earlier poetic production which, unjustly, has been underrated by literary critics.

Vinícius de Moraes is the great poet of love and women, of love's happy moments but also of its bitter torments. Woman is undoubtedly central to his poetry; she figures first as the ethereal woman of the early books, becoming in his later works the carnal and sensual inspiration for his erotic poetry, one of the most passionate in Brazilian literature. The vicissitudes of love are the predominant theme of Vinícius's work. None the less, the poet also showed his interest in themes taken from everyday life in the big city, in the problems of Brazil's poor, and expressed his concern over the most urgent issues of his time: some of Vinícius's best-known poems condemn the tragedy of the concentration camps victims of World War II and the launching of the atomic bomb. Vinícius de Moraes's profound sensitivity enabled him to discover poetry both in the tumult of the spirit and in the bustle of the outside world.

The poet's interest in the external world does not make itself apparent right from his first books. The author himself points out two distinct periods in his work: the first, of a marked transcendental and mystical mood, the second, characterised by his immersion in the material world. *O sentimento do sublime* [The Sense of the Sublime], as he titled his first three books – written between 1933 and 1936 – when organising the edition of his complete works, is filled with the influence of the poet's Jesuit education. The themes revolve around a strong feeling of sin and the aspiration of ascent from earthly existence.

But the human and worldly Vinícius de Moraes that the public grew to love, overcame this phase of mystic torment and turned to daily life, to the poetry of love, of ordinary people. His later book *Poemas, sonetos e baladas*, 1946 [Poems, Sonnets and Ballads], is a synthesis of the wide range of themes and metres explored during the second phase of his literary career. By conferring on the book the new title *O encontro do cotidiano* [Encountering the Everyday], Vinícius made clear the new outlook which marks this collection of poems. The variety of poetic forms employed is a sign of change and of Vinícius's urge to experiment with different metrical forms. The long biblical verse of his early years is replaced by shorter metres. In *O encontro do cotidiano*, he makes use of Modernist free verse and composes ballads of Iberian influence as well as sonnets. It was two of the most beautiful of Vinícius's sonnets – "Soneto de fidelidade" (Sonnet of Faithfulness) and "Soneto de separação" (Sonnet of Separation), of *O encontro do cotidiano*, which rendered immortal the fundamental theme to his work.

The final tercet of "Soneto de fidelidade" includes some of Vinícius's best-known verses on the experience of love: "Eu possa me dizer do amor (que tive): / Que não seja imortal, posto que é chama / Mas que seja infinito enquanto dure." (May I be able to say of the love I had: / May it not be immortal, for it is flame / But be it infinite while it lasts). The sonnet form turned out to be the perfect receptacle for his intensely dramatic poetry, which thrives on oppositions, explores conflicting imagery, and focuses on the movements, on the turmoil of emotions. The "Soneto de separação" offers an example of such dramatic tension in his poetry. In a succession of stanzas the poet describes the lovers' ever increasing pain as they part. The imagery is plastic and dynamic, these being characteristics of his verse, of which the first quatrain gives an example: "De repente do riso fez-se o pranto / Silencioso e branco como a bruma / E das bocas unidas fez-se a espuma / E das mãos espalmadas fez-se o espanto." (Suddenly laughter turned to tears / Silent and white like mist / And foam issued from their joined mouths / And terror rose from their upturned palms).

Vinícius was born in the city of Rio de Janeiro and his work reveals his strong attachment to his origins, not only as a *carioca* but especially as a Brazilian. His poetry speaks of the life in the tropical country, giving us pictures of the carefree life of the more fortunate classes as well as images of abject poverty. In "Balada das meninas de bicicleta" [Ballad of the Girls on Bicycles], also included in *O encontro do cotidiano*, the poet watches a group of young girls, beautifully bronzed from their life on the beach, as they ride their bicycles along the sea-front in the *zona sul* of Rio, the most opulent part of the city. "Balada no Mangue" [Ballad in Mangue], by contrast, is devoted to the poor women who find the sole means of livelihood in prostitution in Mangue, at the time the poem was written a well-known red-light district in the vicinity of the docks area of Rio de Janeiro.

Vinícius de Moraes owes his fame to his poetry and his lyrics but he achieved wide recognition for his dramatic production. His much acclaimed play *Orfeu da Conceição* (1954) was adapted for the film *Orfeu negro* [Black Orpheus], which won the Oscar for best foreign film in 1959.

SARA BRANDELLERO

Biography

Born in Rio de Janeiro, Brazil, in 1913. Studied law; spent a year at Oxford University, England, 1938–39. Consul, Brazilian legations, Los Angeles, Paris, Montevideo. Film critic from the 1940s. Interested in music, especially jazz. Collaborated with Antônio Carlos Jobim and João Gilberto in 1962; worked with the former on the musical version of *Orfeu da Conceição* (*Black Orpheus*) in

1965. Left diplomatic service in 1969, and became a composer, lyricist and singer. Outspoken critic of the military dictatorship of the late 1960s and 1970s. Died in 1980.

Selected Works

Poetry

O caminho para a distância, Rio de Janeiro: Schmidt, 1933
Forma e exégese, Rio de Janeiro: Irmãos Pongetti, 1935
Ariana, a mulher, Rio de Janeiro: Irmãos Pongetti, 1936
Novos poemas, Rio de Janeiro: José Olympio, 1938
Cinco elegias, Rio de Janeiro: Irmãos Pongetti, 1943
Poemas, sonetos e baladas, São Paulo: Gaveta, 1946
Livro de sonetos, Rio de Janeiro: Livros de Portugal, 1957
Para viver um grande amor, Rio de Janeiro: Autor, 1962
O operário em construção e outros poemas, 4th edition, Lisbon: Publicações Dom Quixote, 1975

Plays

Orfeu da Conceição, Rio de Janeiro: Autor, 1956
As feras: tragédia em tres actos, Rio de Janeiro: Serviço Nacional de Teatro, Ministério de Educação e Cultura, 1968

Compilations and Anthologies

Antologia poética, Rio de Janeiro: Noite, 1949; revised edition, 1960
Obra poética, Rio de Janeiro: Aguilar, 1968
Poesia completa e prosa, Rio de Janeiro: Aguilar, 1974
As coisas do alto: poemas de formação, edited by Jose Castello, São Paulo: Companhia das Letras, 1993
Jardim noturno: poemas inéditos, edited by Ana Miranda, São Paulo: Companhia das Letras, 1993

Other Writings

Para uma menina com uma flor: crônicas, Rio de Janeiro: Editora do Autor, 1966
The Girl from Ipanema, translated by Gregory Rabassa, Merrick, New York: Cross-Cultural Communications, 1982 [song lyric]

Further Reading

Lyra, Pedro, *Vinícius de Moraes. Poesia*, Rio de Janeiro: Agir, 1983
Moraes, Vinícius de, *Poesia completa e prosa*, Rio de Janeiro: Nova Aguilar, 1987 [The anthology includes a selection of the most significant studies written on the poet's work]
Sant'Anna, Affonso Romano de, *Música popular e moderna poesia brasileira*, Petrópolis: Vozes, 1986 [Includes an interesting study of the origins and characteristics of the *bossa nova* movement and gives special attention to the role of Vinícius de Moraes in the renewal of Brazilian popular music]

Nancy Morejón 1944–

Cuban poet, literary critic and translator

Nancy Morejón is the most internationally successful and widely translated Cuban woman poet of the post-revolutionary period. Born into a respectable, black, working-class family, she participated in the Revolution while studying French language and literature at Havana University. Many of her poems confirm her early political commitment. Morejón was the first black woman poet in Cuban history to be given the opportunity to publish widely and to acquire a professional status as a writer, critic and translator. Influenced by the Black movement in the United States (particularly Angela Davis) and by the example of her literary mentor, the mulatto poet Nicolás Guillén, Morejón was one of the first Cuban women to celebrate blackness in poetry. Nevertheless, like Guillén, Morejón has always refused to separate black politics from the wider revolutionary process. In her view there is not a distinct African Cuban identity but a Cuban identity which cannot be understood without taking into consideration the black cultures of America. As she wrote in *Nación y mestizaje*: "it is impossible to engage in an exclusively cutaneous critique" of literature. This assimilationist approach (in some ways peculiar to Latin America) was particularly favoured in Cuba after 1959 when emphasis was laid on the need for a homogenous, syncretic national identity. So, while Morejón focuses on the experiences of black Cubans (particularly women) in her poetry, and while she is keen to inscribe Cuban culture within a Pan-Caribbean framework, she is always careful to do so within the parameters of Cuban revolutionary thought.

Morejón's most renowned and widely translated poems are those which foreground the black Cuban woman participating in the long struggle for personal and collective freedom. In "Mujer negra" (Black Woman) from *Parajes de una época*, 1979 [Places of an Age], a mythical black woman recounts her transhistorical experience, from the crossing of the Atlantic as a slave to the part she plays with the revolutionary forces in the Sierra Maestra, until she and her people are finally free. Similarly, in "Amo a mi amo" (I Love My Master) from *Octubre imprescindible*, 1983 [Essential October], an 18th-century female slave voices her gradual awareness of the oppression to which she is submitted. She runs away from the white master she loved and, inspired by the sounds of African drums, plots cruel revenge. In these poems Morejón draws a clear connection between the slave's fight for freedom against capitalism and that of the postcolonial Cuban nation. In other words, she articulates in her poems the complex interplay of class, race, nation and gender. Although she would probably not consider herself a feminist, she firmly accepts Alice Walker's term "womanist." She stated in an interview; "in my literature it is very important that I am a woman. It would be a nonsense to say I am not, or that I think women don't write in a very special mode and with a special experience and charge." Other poems that focus on black Cubans and African Cuban culture include "Los ojos de Elegguá" (Eleggua's Eyes) in *Richard trajo su flauta*, 1967 [Richard Brought His Flute], "Madrigal para cimarrones" (Madrigal for Runaway Slaves),

"Güijes" (Sprites), from *Octubre imprescindible*, and "Negro" (Blackman) and "Mundos" (Worlds) in *Piedra pulida*, 1986 [Polished Stone]. Morejón also writes about contemporary Africa; for example, the seven poems in the collection *Baladas para un sueño*, 1989 [Ballads for a Dream] are an eloquent protest against apartheid. One of Morejón's most successful poems is "Freedom Now," published as early as 1967. It is dedicated to "the struggle of the blacks in the US":

en el sur de los Estados Unidos
se fabrican ferrocarriles ganchos lámparas
ganchos pintura de uña para señoritas
cremas y helados de chocolate
tinte plateado autos edificios de propiedad horizontal

televisores escuelas *democráticas* . . .
ciudades misteriosas llenas de gente
que lincha negros y pisa cucarachas
                    (from *Richard trajo su flauta*)

In the south of the States
they manufacture railroads hooks lamps
hairpins fingernails polish for elegant señoritas
lotions and chocolate ice cream
platinum tints cars condominium properties
televisions *democratic* schools . . .

strange cities full of people
who lynch negroes and step on
cockroaches
                    (*Where the Island Sleeps like a Wing*)

Poems such as these, written from an African-Hispanic and often womanist perspective, are of great significance not only because they provide a bridge between the Cuban and the Caribbean literary traditions (Morejón is a specialist in French and English Caribbean writing), but also because they constitute some of the rare examples of black, feminist poetry written in Spanish.

However, to read Morejón purely (or even primarily) as a black poet is shortsighted in the extreme. Apart from wider political issues, for example, the war against Vietnam, nuclear arms, the Soviet space programme, the missile crisis in Cuba, the Nicaraguan Revolution, and the American invasion of Grenada, she has written a book on dance (*Elogio de la danza*, 1982 [In Praise of Dance]) and numerous poems which describe people and scenes from her home-town, Havana. Arguably, the most important themes in her work are the family and love. Her early collection *Richard trajo su flauta* opens with three poems dedicated to her paternal grandmother, her parents and her maternal grandmother respectively. The family home often figures as a space which provides loving support for the young woman despite generational differences. In the title poem "Richard trajo su flauta," for example, the poet's grandfather laments the passing of traditional Cuban music while she and her friends sit around listening to recordings of American jazz (Count Basie, Duke Ellington, and Nat King Cole). Morejón's poem to her mother ("Madre" [Mother]), published in *Piedra pulida*, is particularly moving: "Mi madre no tuvo jardín / sino islas acantiladas / flotando, bajo el sol, / en sus corales delicados" (My mother had no garden / only cragged cliff-edged islands / floating under the sun / in reefs of delicate coral).

Here, as in many poems, Morejón makes full use of imagery associated with the sea. What most clearly distinguishes *Piedra pulida* from earlier collections, however, is the shift away from the urban landscape (streets, patios, the port) of the early Morejón, to rural landcapes and natural imagery. Trees, leaves, plants, rivers and mountains create an imaginary landscape as lush as the Cuban countryside itself. Water and greenery suggest life and love, as in, for example, "La planta infiel" (The Unfaithful Plant) and "Lianas, peces y algas" (Lianas, Fish and Seaweed). Apart from these key themes in Morejón's work and the moral import of her poetry, the reader is struck by constant hankering for perfection, beauty, and art (as the title Polished Stone suggests). It is this concern for poetry as an aesthetic which has prevented Morejón from lapsing into propagandistic verse despite the often overtly political themes and her preference for free verse. As she says, "I think poets should create to teach people to see beauty . . . one of our duties is to create an awareness that beauty is a very concrete thing, but something that could be found in everyday life" (*Ours the Earth*).

CATHERINE DAVIES

Biography

Born in old part of Havana, Cuba, 7 August 1944, where she continued to live with her parents in adulthood. First African-Cuban student to take a degree in Faculty of Arts at Havana University where she majored in French. Graduated in 1966 and specializes in translation of French narrative and poetry. Worked for the Ministry of the Interior, on cultural brigades, in publishing and in the Havana headquarters of UNEAC (Cuban Union of Artists and Writers). Frequently represents her country at literary festivals, poetry readings and congresses. In the early 1990s appointed director of the publishing house associated with the Fundación Pablo Milanés in Havana. This centre was closed by the authorities in 1995 because it was perceived as a cultural "palenque" or centre for black intellectuals who might prove unreliable. Recipient of several Cuban awards for literature and criticism, of which the most important to date is the Premio de la Crítica, 1986.

Selected Works

Poetry
Mutismos, Havana: El Puente, 1962
Amor, ciudad atribuida, Havana: El Puente, 1964
Richard trajo su flauta, Havana: UNEAC, 1967
Parajes de una época, Havana: Letras Cubanas, 1979
Poemas, Mexico City: UNAM, 1980
Elogio de la danza, Mexico City: UNAM, 1982
Octubre imprescindible, Havana: UNEAC, 1983
Cuaderno de Granada, Havana: Casa de las Américas, 1984; as *Grenada Notebook*, translated by Lisa Davis, New York: Círculo Cubano de Nueva York, 1984 [bilingual edition]
Piedra pulida, Havana: Letras Cubanas, 1986
Baladas para un sueño, Havana: UNEAC, 1989
Paisaje célebre, Caracas: Fundarte, 1993

Essays
Lengua de pájaro, in collaboration with Carmen Gonce, Havana: UNEAC, 1971 [testimonial]
Nación y mestizaje en Nicolás Guillén, Havana: UNEAC, 1982
Fundación de la imagen, Havana: UNEAC, 1988

Translations
Where the Island Sleeps like a Wing. Selected Poetry by Nancy Morejón, translated by Kathleen Weaver, San Francisco: Black Scholar Press, 1985

Ours the Earth. Poems by Nancy Morejón, edited and translated by
J.R. Pereira, University of the West Indies: Mona, 1990

Further Reading
Barnet, Miguel, "The Poetry of Nancy Morejón," introduction to
the anthology *Where the Island Sleeps like a Wing*, San
Francisco: Black Scholar Press, 1985
Barradas, Efraín, "La negritud hoy: nota sobre la poesía de Nancy
Morejón," *Areíto*, vol. 6/24 (1980)
Boyce Davies, Carole and Elaine Savory Fido (editors), *Out of the
Kumbla. Caribbean Women and Literature*, Trenton, New Jersey:
Africa World Press, 1990 [Interview with Morejón]
Busby, Margaret (editor), *Daughters of Africa; an International
Anthology of Words and Writings by Women of African Descent
from the Ancient Egyptian to the Present*, London: Jonathan
Cape, and New York: Pantheon, 1992
Captain-Hidalgo, Yvonne, "The Poetics of the Quotidian in the
Works of Nancy Morejón," *Callaloo*, vol. 10/4 (1987)
Castro-Klarén, Sara, Sylvia Molloy and Beatriz Sarlo (editors),
Women's Writing in Latin America. An Anthology, Boulder,
Colorado: Westview Press, 1991
Davies, Catherine, "Writing the African Subject. The Work of Two
Cuban Women Poets," *Women. A Cultural Review*, vol. 4/1
(1993)
Fernández Olmos, Margarite, "El género testimonial:
approximaciones feministas," *Review / Revista Interamericana*,
vol. 2/1 (1981)
Finn, Julio, *Voices of Negritude*, London: Quartet, 1988
Marting, Diane E. (editor), *Spanish American Women Writers:
a Bio-Bibliographical Source Book*, Westport, Connecticut:

Greenwood Press, 1990 [Contains a full and useful chapter on
Morejón]
Moore, Carlos, "Congo or Carabalí?: Race Relations in Socialist
Cuba," *Rethinking Cuba* [special issue], *Caribbean Review*, vol.
15/2 (1986)
Randall, Margaret, *Breaking the Silences: an Anthology of 20th-
Century Poetry by Cuban Women*, Vancouver: Pulp Press, 1982
[Provides a bio-bibliographical sketch and translations of
Morejón's poetry]
Rodríguez, María Cristina, "Women Writers of the Spanish
Speaking Caribbean. An Overview," in *Caribbean Women
Writers*, edited by Selwyn R. Cudjoe, Wellesley, Massachusetts:
Calaloux, 1990
Rosegreen Williams, C., "Rewriting the History of the Afro-Cuban
Woman: Nancy Morejón's 'Mujer Negra'," *Afro-Hispanic Review*,
vol. 8/3 (1989)
Salgado, María, "La poesía tradicional y el compromiso ideológico
en la creación femenina de la segunda promoción de la
revolución cubana," in *La historia en la literatura
iberoamericana*, edited by Raquel Chang-Rodríguez and
Gabriella de Beer, Hanover, New Hampshire: Ediciones del Norte,
1989
Waldman, Gloria Feiman, "Affirmation and Resistance: Women
Poets from the Caribbean," in *Contemporary Women Authors of
Latin America: Introductory Essays*, edited by Doris Meyer and
Margarite Fernández Olmos, Brooklyn, New York: Brooklyn
College Press, 1983
Walker, Alice, *In Search of Our Mothers' Gardens: Womanist Prose*,
San Diego: Harcourt Brace, 1983; London: Women's Press,
1984

Félix Morisseau-Leroy 1912–

Haitian playwright, poet and novelist

Félix Morisseau-Leroy was one of the first, most vocal and most articulate champions of a Haitian literature in Creole. Not that he advocated abandoning French altogether: indeed, as is the case with many contemporary Haitian authors, Morisseau-Leroy's works in French, whether in poetry, prose fiction or plays, alternate with those he composed in the national language.

The performance in Port-au-Prince of his *Antigone en créole* created a sensation in 1953. While Creole plays had been written and performed in Haiti since colonial days, they were almost invariably farces whose bawdy double entendres and slapstick were intended to provoke guffaws rather than to elicit reflection. They were almost never deemed worthy of publication and the only traces of them that remain are in occasional announcements and newspaper reviews.

Legend has it that Morisseau-Leroy's *Antigone* was the outcome of a bet with friends who argued that Creole was fit only for colloquial and trivial expression and quite incapable of expressing higher conceits. He is supposed to have wagered that, in the same way Racine and Goethe adapted Euripides' *Iphigenia* in French and German, he would adapt Sophocles' *Antigone* into Creole. Morisseau-Leroy actually went further than his predecessors, since he transposed the action from a

palace in Thebes to a voodoo temple in the imaginary Haitian mountain village of Tèb, and transformed the original characters into Haitian peasants; as he explains in the Foreword to the printed version:

> This is a story that was told a long long time ago, and has already been told in many countries and translated into many languages ... I kept what I could from the original story, and then I added to it the sun of Haiti, a certain way the Haitians understand life and death, courage and sorrow, luck and misfortune. I added the saints, the souls of the dead, the spirits of voodoo, the spirits who watch over the roads, the cemeteries, the doors, the trees, the fields, the sea, the rivers, who rule over rain, wind, storms in Haiti, and who much resemble what people call the Greek gods ... And then I let Antigone, Ismène, Marraine, Roi Créon, Tirésias, Hémon, Filo, speak exactly the way a Haitian would speak in their place.

Despite the grumbling of traditionalists, *Antigone*, performed under the direction of Morisseau-Leroy by peasants from the village of Morne Hercule, was very well received in Port-au-Prince. In 1959, the company was invited to Paris where the play was presented in the Théâtre des Nations series to a somewhat perplexed French public, which was unaccustomed to classical tragedies in voodoo settings.

The success of *Antigone* encouraged other playwrights to adapt foreign classics for performance in Creole: Franck Fouché's *Oedipe Roi* was staged shortly afterward (although never published); he also adapted García Lorca's *Yerma* (which was published). Corneille's *Le Cid* would later be transposed into Creole by Nono Numa under the title *Compère Général Rodrigue*, Molière's *Tartuffe* by Lyonel Desmarattes as *Mouché Défas*, etc. At the same time, serious original plays were beginning to be written in Creole and performed in both Haiti and the Haitian diaspora. Contemporary Creole playwrights such as Frankétienne and Sito Kavé owe much to Morisseau-Leroy's 1953 initiative.

In 1978, Morisseau-Leroy published a sequel to *Antigone* entitled *Roua Kréon*. While less famous than its predecessor, since it was only published abroad in a photocopy edition by an émigré group, *Roua Kréon* could be considered the better play. King Créon and his niece, Antigone, are dead and the bumpkin prince Hémon has ascended the throne. Hémon is occasionally inspired to be a good king and to alleviate his people's misery. But his father – who in the underworld has become an evil voodoo spirit – regularly possesses Hémon before he can take any action and, through him, Créon perpetuates his nefarious reign. The play was written at a time when young Jean-Claude Duvalier (whether by conviction or under pressure from the international community) was making timid moves to liberalize the dictatorial system put in place by his father. Morisseau-Leroy's message is clear: so long as the system is not destroyed completely, it will remain as repugnant as under the dreaded *Papa Dok*.

Morisseau-Leroy's most famous collection of poems is *Diacoute* [Satchel]; this work was first published in Port-au-Prince in 1953 then, with additional items, in Dakar (the poet was in African exile at the time) as *Diacoute 2* in 1972; and, with further additions, in Miami, where he had settled, as *Dyakout 1, 2, 3 . . .* in 1983. In this third version, all the poems are transcribed according to the rules legislated in 1979. Once Creole was recognized as a fully-fledged language, and no longer as merely a simplified, debased form of French, Morisseau-Leroy could write: "No one can claim any longer that French is the language of the Haitian people." The author explains that in his Creole poems: "In *Dyakout 1*, in *Dyakout 2*, in *Dyakout 3*, it is the common people of Haiti who speak. All I do is put on paper what they are saying."

His poems, composed in simple, direct verse, have become very famous among Haitians. They express the resentment of the Haitian poor at the injustice and abuse perpetrated upon them by the ruling classes and the foreigners, who are held equally responsible, in poems such as "Touris, pa pren pòtre" (Tourist, Don't Take My Picture) or "F.M.I" (International Monetary Fund), for the conditions which force poor Haitians to become *Botpipèl* (Boat people).

Written in French, Morisseau-Leroy's first novel, as well as his 1977 collection of poems *Kasamansa*, are suffused with leftist ideology. While the former is a lucid analysis of the forces which conspire to keep Haitian peasants downtrodden, the latter are little more than ideologically determined paeans to his racial brothers, Pushkin and Nkruma, as well as to the

martyred President Allende, and are in no way comparable in quality to his poetry in Creole.

LÉON-FRANÇOIS HOFFMANN

Biography

Born in the southern village of Grand-Gosier, Haiti, 1912. Studied at the state secondary school in the nearby town of Jacmel, then in Port-au-Prince. After graduating from the Law School, he attended Columbia University, New York, from which he received a Master's degree in education. Teacher and an administrator in the Ministry of Education, where he was named *Chef de division* in 1941. Editor of *Le Matin*, one of the important Port-au-Prince dailies, and was a frequent contributor of poetry and essays to Port-au-Prince periodicals. Like so many intellectuals of his generation, he went into exile under the Duvalier dictatorship. With the writers Jean Brierre, Gérard Chenêt and Roger Dorsinville among others, he spent many years in West Africa, first in Nigeria, then in Ghana with a UNESCO mission from 1960 to 1967, then in Senegal, where he organized theater workshops and staged performances for the Ministry of Culture. In 1981, when his eyesight began to fail, he joined relatives in Miami, and only returned to visit Haiti after the fall of Jean-Claude Duvalier.

Selected Works

Poetry in French
Plénitude, Port-au-Prince: Imprimerie N. Telhomme, 1940
Gerbe pour deux amis, in collaboration with Roussan Camille and Jean F. Brierre, Port-au-Prince: Imprimerie H. Deschamps, 1945
Natif-natal, un conte en vers, Port-au-Prince: Éditions Haïtiennes, 1948
Kasamansa, Dakar: Nouvelles Éditions Africaines, 1977

Poetry in Creole
Diacoute 1, Port-au-Prince: Éditions H. Deschamps, 1953
Diacoute 2, Montreal: Éditions Nouvelle Optique, 1972
Kasamansa, Dakar: Nouvelles Éditions Africaines, 1977
Vilbonè (Happytown), Miami: Jaden Kreyòl, 1982
Dyakout 1, 2, 3, ak twa lòt poèm, Miami: Jaden Kreyòl, 1983

Plays
Antigone en créole, Pétionville: Culture, 1953 [in Creole]
Doguicimi, tragédie, Accra, Ghana: Mimeo, 1961 [in French]
Jadinkreyol, Dakar: Nouvelles Éditions Africaines, 1977
"*Roua Kréon*" ak "*Pèp-la*," Dakar: Jadan Kreyòl, 1978 [in Creole]

Prose Fiction
Récolte, Port-au-Prince: Éditions Haïtiennes, 1946 [novel]
Ravinodyab - La Ravine aux Diables, contes haïtiens, Paris: L'Harmattan, 1982 [tales in bilingual French and Creole versions]

Other Writings
Le Destin des Caraïbes - El destino del Caribe, Port-au-Prince: Imprimerie Telhomme, 1941 [essay in bilingual French and Spanish versions]
"Pourquoi ils écrivent en créole," *Optique*, Port-au-Prince, 5 (July 1954), reprinted in Robert Cornevin, *Le Théâtre haïtien*, Montreal: Léméac, 1973 [An eloquent defense of Creole as a fully-fledged language and the authentic means of expression of the Haitian people]

Further Reading
Apart from occasional newspaper reviews there are, surprisingly, no biographical or critical studies, and even very few articles, devoted to Morisseau-Leroy either by Haitians or by foreigners.

Silenieks, Juris, "Toward *créolité*: Postnegritude Developments," in *A History of Literature in the Caribbean*, vol. 1: Hispanic and Francophone Regions, Amsterdam and Philadelphia: Benjamins, 1994 [on theater]

César Moro 1903–1956

Peruvian poet and painter

César Moro is the pen-name of Alfredo Quíspez Asín. Born in Lima, Moro went into voluntary exile in Paris in 1925, where he met André Breton and joined the Surrealist movement that had inaugurated a new literary and artistic period of great influence in Western art and literature, Surrealism. Moro became an active member of this movement in Paris (1925–33), where he stayed for nine years until his return to Peru. He had read extensively on Marxism, anthropology, psychoanalysis and the writings of Sigmund Freud; he had learned and mastered French, the language in which he wrote all of his poems except those of *La tortuga ecuestre* [The Equestrian Turtle]. Back in Lima he organized the First Surrealist Painting Exhibition in 1935, challenging what he understood to be the false morality of the Peruvian middle-class, and naturally, caused great scandal in the city. To add to the confrontation, the catalog of the exhibition was framed with a typical Surrealist phrase of the period by Francis Picabia: "Art is a pharmaceutical product for imbeciles." During these years, he coined the phrase "Lima, la horrible" (beastly Lima) that has been used many times by other Peruvian poets.

In 1938 Moro traveled to Mexico, where he continued to be an active member of the movement sponsored by André Breton. He invested considerable energy into launching a Surrealist magazine. The first effort translated in a one-page publication entitled *El uso de la palabra* [About Utterance], with only one issue published in December of 1939. In his study of Peruvian poets, James Higgins argues that "the rejection of the alienating reality in which he was born and brought up in order to assume another felt to be more authentic is perhaps the key to his life and career." Higgins is referring to Moro's homosexuality, never acknowledged overtly by anyone and yet a factor which brought substantial alienation to Moro. But there is a further aspect of this alienation that is the mark of his poetic language. By producing work written in a language other than Spanish, Moro's poetry is at an obvious disadvantage with regard to the general reading public. This question seems to take on a dimension of its own when set against the context of Peru then and today, a country of great importance at the end of the 20th century still suffers from high levels of illiteracy. How would a poet of Moro's profile be read in his own country under these circumstances? It would be indeed be difficult.

Moro believed in the merging of reason and purpose of poetry and life, and it was one of the strong appealing forces that brought this Peruvian poet to the Surrealist fold. After four years in Peru, he left again. This time his voluntary exile took him to Mexico, where he met most of the members of the Contemporáneos group of poets, Carlos Pellicer, Salvador Novo and Gilberto Owen, and, most importantly, cherished the friendship of two homosexual poets, Agustín Lazo and Xavier Villaurrutia in particular. The issue of his homosexuality remains still today faintly implied. However, the voice that speaks through these poems is that of a homosexual subject, a voice that when disguised, is unable to find its truth. In this sense, it can be said that Moro was forced into a double exile, that of his poetic ideology articulated by the tenets of the Surrealist movement, and that of his homosexual disposition. In James Higgins's reading of Moro's poetry, he quite pointedly asserts that the poet "chooses the figure of the madman to embody his poetics, as deployed in the poem entitled "A vista perdida"(Lost from View)." The madman does not abide by the "rational" laws that are the cause of Moro's alienation; he can display freely what is repressed, and so he does in Moro's texts. It is accurate to think of Moro's poetics as quite radical and iconoclastic, both characteristics that explain why he is still a marginal figure in the larger picture of Latin American poetry.

Recently, there has been more attention dedicated to his work, but much is in need of scholarly attention. As is the case with Vicente Huidobro, for example, some of Moro's poems are in French; thus, his poetry remains unread by most Latin American critics. During his stay in Mexico, Moro published in the magazine *El Hijo Pródigo* [The Prodigal Son], and in *Dyn*, a journal directed by the Surrealist artist Wolfgang Paalen. He also collaborated in other prestigious Mexican journals such as *Estaciones* [Stations/Seasons], *Letras de México* [Mexican Letters] and *Poesía*. He met and shared concerns with Wolfgang and Alice Paalen, Leonora Carrington and Remedios Varo, all Surrealist artists who were working in Mexico at the time.

Moro's poetic works were published posthumously by André Coyné, a French scholar who met Moro after he returned to Peru from Mexico. They became close friends, and when the Peruvian poet died in 1956, Coyné published the first complete version of *La tortuga ecuestre y otros poemas* in 1957. He also compiled a volume containing most of the critical writings of Moro under the title of *Los anteojos de azufre* [The Sulphur Spectacles] published in 1958. In 1980, the Instituto Nacional de Cultura published the first of two volumes Moro's complete poetic works.

MAGDALENA GARCÍA PINTO

Biography

Born Alfredo Quíspez Asín in Lima, Peru, 19 August 1903. Educated at Jesuit Colegio de la Inmaculada, Lima. Lived in Paris from 1925. Member of the Surrealist movement; worked on *Le Surréalisme*. Prominent painter; held exhibition, Brussels, 1925, Paris, 1927. Although initially wrote in Spanish, most of later works written in French. Returned to Peru, 1933. Formed a Peruvian Surrealist group; founder of the Surrealist journal, *El Uso de la Palabra*, 1939. Persecuted by the police following publication of a work in support of Republican Spain. Travelled to Mexico in 1938 where he lived until 1940. Organised the International Surrealist Exhibition with André Breton (1940). Eventually broke away from Breton's conception of Surrealism. Returned to Peru in 1948; worked as a lecturer and as a curator. Died in Lima (under mysterious circumstances), 10 January 1956.

Selected Works

Poetry

Lettre d'amour, Mexico City: Dyn, 1944
La chateau de grisou, Mexico City: Tigrondine, 1943
Trafalgar Square, Lima: Tigrondine, 1954
Amour à mort, Paris: Le Cheval Marin, 1957; as *Amour à mort /
Love Till Death*, translated by Frances LeFevre, New York:
Vanishing Rotating Triangle Press, 1973 [bilingual edition]

Compilations and Anthologies

La tortuga ecuestre y otros poemas (1924–1949), Lima: Tigrondine,
1957
Los anteojos de azufre, edited by André Coyné, Lima: San Marcos,
1958
La tortuga ecuestre y otros textos, edited by Julio Ortega, Caracas:
Monte Ávila, 1976

The Scandalous Life of César Moro: In His Own Words, translated
by Philip Ward, New York: Oleander Press, 1976
Antología esencial, Lima: Ediciones Zendas, 1976
Obra poética, edited by Ricardo Silva-Santisteban, Lima: Instituto
Nacional de Cultura, 1980

Other Writings

Versiones del surrealismo, edited by Julio Ortega, Barcelona:
Tusquets, 1974

Further Reading

Coyné, André, *César Moro*, Lima: Imprenta Torres Aguirre, 1956
Higgins, James, *The Poet in Peru: Alienation and the Quest for
Super-Reality*, Liverpool: Cairns, 1982
Ortega, Julio, *Figuración de la persona*, Barcelona: Edhasa, 1971
Schreiber, M., *Bibliografía de César Moro*, Lima: Escuela Nacional
de Bibliotecarios, 1963

Mulatto

Latin America has a varied and mixed population in terms of racial ancestry. In the main, the ethnic population groups are native Indians, Whites, Blacks and people of mixed ancestry. The white population of Latin America is of European descent. Blacks were brought from Africa to the then "New World" as slaves from as early as the 1500s through to the 1800s. The term "mixed ancestry" applies to people of dual (or in the case of Latin America in the 1990s) multi-ethnic racial ancestral mixtures. Through the centuries, many Whites, Blacks and Indians in Latin America have intermarried/interbred and as a result, most Latin Americans today are of an ethnically mixed ancestry. One of the largest groups of peoples of mixed ancestry are mulattoes (*mulato* in Spanish). Mulattoes are people of mixed black and white descent. Originally, the term designated the first cross between European and African; it still does so, but definition now depends largely on the country. In some countries of Latin America today, mulatto may refer to any degree of African-European inter-mixture and sometimes, as in the case of Brazil, can refer to a person of mixed-blood of any origin.

One unofficial criterion seems to be that mulatto is equated with fair-skinned people throughout the countries of Latin America. However, it is to be noted that in the case of Brazil, the category is even further broken down to "mulato claro" i.e., light-skinned and "mulato oscuro" i.e., dark-skinned, while in the Caribbean, mulatto (mulato) is synonymous with "trigueño" a wheat-coloured or light-skinned individual while "moreno" is the term used for a darker-ancestry. In Latin America mulattoes are numerous but, specifically, can be found in large numbers in Brazil where some 38% of the population of 155,356,073 (July 1991), is considered to be of mixed ancestry; Panama where 70% of the population of 2,476,281 (July 1991) is officially listed as mixed in ancestry and throughout the islands of the Caribbean, where, in particular, Cuba stands out with a population of 10,732,037 (July 1991) that is 51% mulatto.

Although the people of Latin America share many traditions and values that proceed from a common colonial heritage, there are a great many local differences in their way of life. Most Latin American countries have a class system based largely on ancestry. Peoples of mixed ancestry, including mulattoes, usually make up most of the middle class and to a limited extent they also penetrate the upper class. However, in the context of Latin America, it must be noted that social position is not decided solely on the basis of ancestry so that being a mulatto does not restrict a person to a low social status, nor does it entitle a person to affiliation to a higher class or economic circumstance; yet in many societies, it can be the benchmark of social acceptance.

Mulatto, like most other racial categorizations can be pejorative in meaning in most countries of Latin America, depending on the intonation of the speaker, but it should also be noted that mulatto is a term which can be, and is often, used by people of mixed ancestry as well as Blacks who are light-skinned to refer to themselves. Finally, in literature the mulatto woman has been promoted as a (masculinist) feminine ideal, because of her remarkably uncommon beauty and her (alleged) extremely powerful sexuality. Specifically the ideal of "mulatez," i.e., being a mulatto, can be found in abundance in the popular poetry of Cuba. Examples of the representation of the *mulata* in the Island's literature are provided by Cirilo Villaverde in his novel *Cecilia Valdés*, by Martín Morúa Delgado in *Sofía* (1891), and the poets Nicolás Guillén and Luis Palés Matos (the latter, a Puerto Rican) in the 20th century.

NICOLE ROBERTS

See also entries on Nicolás Guillén, Mestizo, *Cecilia Valdés* (Cirilo Villaverde)

Further Reading

Berzon, Judith R., *Neither White nor Black: the Mulatto Character in American Fiction*, New York: New York University Press, 1978

Cohen, David and Jack P. Greene (editors), *Neither Slave nor Free: the Freedman of African Descent in the Slave Societies of the New World*, Baltimore: Johns Hopkins University Press, 1970

Jackson, Richard L., "'Mestizaje' vs. Black Identity: the Color Crisis in Latin America," *Black World*, vol. 24/9 (1975)

Kutzinski, Vera M., *Sugar's Secrets: Race and the Erotics of Cuban Nationalism*, Charlottesville: University Press of Virginia, 1993 [On *mulatez* in Cuban literature in relation to gender]

Martínez-Alier, Verena, *Marriage, Class, and Colour in Nineteenth-Century Cuba: a Study of Racial Attitudes and Sexual Values in a Slave Society*, Ann Arbor: University of Michigan Press, 1989

Martínez-Echazabal, Lourdes, *Para una semiótica de la mulatez*, Madrid: Porrúa Turanzas, 1990

Rodríguez, Ileana, "The Birth of Mulatto Countries," in chapter 4 of her *House/Garden/Nation: Space, Gender and Ethnicity in Post-Colonial Latin American Literatures by Women*, translated by Rodríguez and Robert Carr, Durham, North Carolina: Duke University Press, 1994

Mundo Nuevo

See Journals

Álvaro Mutis 1923–

Colombian prose writer and poet

The Colombian writer Álvaro Mutis first made his name in his own country as a poet. He began publishing poetry in 1948, with the unmemorable volume *La Balanza* [The Scales], followed by *Los elementos del desastre*, 1953 [The Elements of the Disaster]. A collected volume of his poems, *Summa de Maqroll el Gaviero*, was first published in 1973, since when he has diversified into short stories and novellas, most of them based on this figure of Maqroll el Gaviero or "the Lookout." Mutis's poems show a renovating spirit not often seen in Colombian poetry of the 1950s, still at that time much influenced by Spanish American Modernism, which by then was little more than a thoroughly outmoded Romanticism. Influenced by the French Surrealists, Mutis brought poetry into the modern day, into a time of despair and lack of meaning, in which chance and death are the most powerful forces. This sense of tragedy was conveyed however in a scrupulous, densely imaged language – often in prose poems (again from the French 20th-century tradition), and often imbued with a bitter humour at human frailty. From the French poetic tradition Mutis also learnt that poetry is as much a way of seeing the world as a matter of rhyme or verses, and he has written many prose poems and short Surrealist pieces. His poetry has been described by Octavio Paz as "rich without any ostentation or waste ... showing a love of words, desperation with words, a hatred of words: the extremes of a poet."

The poetry collection dedicated to Maqroll the Lookout introduces Mutis's most interesting creation, a figure who dominates his prose work. Mutis published the first of the Maqroll series in 1986: *La nieve del almirante* [The Snow of the Admiral], and he is present as a secondary character in one of his later works of fiction, *La última escala del tramp steamer*, 1989 [The Tramp Steamer's Last Port of Call]. Maqroll is a mythic figure in a world that no longer believes in myths. He is a sailor, a flying Dutchman condemned to travel the world fulfilling a duty that he imposes on himself because that is no more absurd than any other reason for living. Maqroll is a figure from Conrad or Rudyard Kipling, stripped of any idea of glory. In his wanderings, he provides Mutis with the outsider who can judge the experience of Europe and its civilisation as lived by Latin Americans, who feel themselves part of it yet distinct. His eponymous hero also casts a cold eye on the history of Latin America, where the perpetual if inexplicable turmoil is balanced by the overwhelming beauty of the landscape. Mutis also relishes the Arab tradition he senses he has inherited via Spain, and the wanderings of Maqroll ultimately link back to a figure like that of Sinbad in the *Arabian Nights*. Mutis's fiction constantly reaches out from the contemporary world into one of myth, retelling stories he feels to be eternal. As he says at the end of *La última escala del tramp steamer*: "Men – I thought – change so little, they go on being so much the same that there has only been a single love story since the dawn of time, repeated an infinite number of times without ever losing its terrible simplicity, its irredeemable misfortune."

NICK CAISTOR

Biography

Born in Bogotá, Colombia, 25 August 1923. Lived in Brussels as a child, educated there. Visited Colombia to stay with his wealthy plantation-owning grandfather. After the assassination of Jorge Eliécer Gaitán (1947), a book of which he was co-author, was burnt. Member of the Mito group, which published the journal *Mito*, 1953–63. Has lived in Mexico since 1956. Awarded Colombia's National Poetry Prize and the Mexican El Águila Azteca, 1989.

Selected Works

Novels and Short Fiction

Diario de Lecumberri, Xalapa, Mexico: Universidad Veracruzana, 1960
La mansión de Araucaima; relato gótico de tierra caliente, Buenos Aires: Sudamericana, 1973
La nieve del almirante, Madrid: Alianza, 1986
Ilona llega con la lluvia, Madrid: Mondadori, 1987
Un bel morir, Bogotá: Oveja Negra, 1989
La última escala del tramp steamer, Colombia: Arango, 1989

Poetry

Los elementos del desastre, Buenos Aires: Losada, 1953
Los emisarios, Mexico City: Fondo de Cultura Económica, 1984
Crónica regia; y Alabanza del reino, Madrid: Cátedra, 1985
Un homenaje y siete nocturnos, Mexico City: Ediciones del Equilibrista, 1986
Amirbar, Madrid: Siruela, 1990
El último rostro, Madrid: Siruela, 1990

Compilations and Anthologies

Los trabajos perdidos, Mexico City: Era, 1965
Obra literaria, Bogotá: Procultura, 1985

La muerte del estratega: narraciones, prosas y ensayos, Mexico City: Fondo de Cultura Económica, 1988
Summa de Maqroll el Gaviero: poesía 1948–1988, Mexico City: Fondo de Cultura Económica, 1990
Obra poética, Bogotá: Arango Editores, 1993

Translations

Maqroll: Three Novellas, translated by Edith Grossman, New York: HarperCollins, 1992; London: Picador, 1993
The Adventures of Maqroll: Four Novellas, translated by Edith Grossman, New York: HarperCollins, 1995

Further Reading

Balza, José, "Mutis: disoluciones y mudanzas," *Inti*, Rhode Island, 34–35 (Fall–Spring 1991–92)
Eyzaguirre, Luis, "Álvaro Mutis o la transitoreidad de la palabra poética," *Inti*, Rhode Island 18–19 (Fall–Spring 1983–84)
_____ "Transformaciones del personaje en la poesía de Álvaro Mutis," *Revista de Crítica Literaria Latinoamericana*, Lima, vol. 18/35 (1992)
García Aguilar, Eduardo, *Celebraciones y otros fantasmas: una biografía intelectual de Álvaro Mutis*, Santafe de Bogotá: T-M Editores, 1993
Homero, J., "Tres novelas de Álvaro Mutis," *Vuelta*, vol. 13/152 (July 1989)
Mutis Durán, Santiago, *Tras las rutas de Maqroll el Gaviero*, Madrid: Proartes, 1988

Interviews

Balboa, Rosina, "Entrevista con Álvaro Mutis: perseguidor de nostalgias," *Quimera: Revista de Literatura,* Barcelona, 108 (1991)
Quiroz, Fernando, *El reino que estaba para mí: conversaciones con Álvaro Mutis*, Barcelona: Grupo Editorial Norma, 1993

Mysticism

Traditionally, Latin American literature has been perceived as a monopoly of male writers. However, the research into women's writing (especially that which dates from the mid-1970s) makes it possible to argue that over the centuries women too have been making contributions. Because the education of lay women was banned during colonial times, the majority of women writers were nuns. Convents were the only enclaves where women with intellectual aspirations could cloister themselves and be free from patriarchal control. In addition, being a nun gave a woman a special status in society.

Many nuns were mystics and were ordered by their confessors and the abbesses of their convents to write about their spiritual experiences. The purpose of this writing was to serve as a "vida exempla" for other sisters and also to encourage their vocation. In general mystics' works were characterized by hybrid narration. They are valuable primary sources for historians as well as literary critics because they contain not only descriptions of the women's mystical experiences, but also unique portrayals of the events of their times.

While the importance of rescuing women's voices from the past is recognized, often the emphasis has been on the writings of a few well-known nuns. Although this is necessary, it is important also to continue along the path made by researchers such as the Mexican scholar, Josefina Muriel. Thus this article will concentrate on the work of two authors, of whom one needs further study while the other was discovered only in the early 1990s. The first is Sister María Magdalena de Lorravaquio Muñoz (1576–1636), whose works were compiled and edited by Josefina Muriel, and the second is a little-known mystic, Sister María Manuela de Santa Ana (1695–1793).

Sister María Magdalena de Lorravaquio Muñoz wrote her autobiography, *Libro en que se contiene la vida de la madre María Magdalena, monja profesa del convento del Señor San Jerónimo de la ciudad de México, hija de Domingo de Larravaquio y de Ysabel Muñoz su legítima mujer* [A Book Containing the Life of Mother María Magdalena, Professed Nun of the Convent of St Jerome in Mexico City, Legitimate

Daughter of Domingo de Lorravaquio and Ysabel Muñoz His Lawful Wife]. Sister María Magdalena's autobiography exhibits the characteristics common to the writings of all mystics.

As already noted, these women wrote because they were ordered to do so by their confessors. Indeed, Sister María Magdalena did not have previous writing experience. She credits her skill to Jesus Christ and the Virgin Mary, and uses the rhetoric of humility to describe her life. A characteristic of her writing is the spiritual yet sensuous tone of the narratives. Sister María Magdalena often refers to the tenderness of her love for Jesus Christ. Many nuns' writings were read with skepticism, and "false mystics" were punished by the confiscation and burning of their works. But Sister María Magdalena was a genuine mystic, well-known in her time and allowed to create freely and to discuss her religious and actual world. Sister María Magdalena was successful partly because her writing was safe from the meticulous censorship of the Inquisition.

Sister María Magdalena's autobiography contains a microcosm of historical and social events as seen from the convent. The most interesting of her observations on society refer to social class. Because her own background was middle class rather than patrician, Sister María Magdalena sided with the poor. She narrates how she spent her time teaching the slaves and the Indian women in the convent. The following account makes clear her role as a teacher: "enseñar la doctrina cristiana a todas las mozas de servicio que quieren aprenderla. Después de esto dispongo todo lo necesario para el servicio de mis necesidades y de las hermanas que conmigo están. . ." (to teach Christian doctrine to all the young maidservants who wish to learn it. After this I arrange what is necessary for my own needs and those of the other sisters who are with me).

Here we have an invaluable record of women's communal relations, of women helping and fostering the advancement of other women. This small example suggests the great value of the study of the body of women's mysticism. These texts are not simply accounts of spiritual transfigurations, but vital preservations of the activities of and relations between women. María Madgalena died prematurely at the age of fifty after a protracted and painful illness. Yet she joined thousands of other women writers of her day in providing precious links in the almost invisible chain of women's history.

The work of the second nun, Sor María Manuela de Santa Ana, is not yet known but it serves to illustrate that women have at all times played a significant role in society. Two valuable manuscripts written by her have been found. The first is a short but dense autobiography, "Vida" [Life] and the second manuscript contains some confessional letters and a long poem both compiled in "Correspondencia espiritual y poesías" [Spiritual Letters and Poetry].

The "Vida" is a mirror of the religious life both within and the outside convent walls. It follows the traditional rules of autobiography, but it also has a unique narrative style. "Vida" has embedded within it another text, "Las Capillas" [The Chapels]. This subtext is like St Theresa's *Castillo interior* [Interior Castle] but the narration of "Las Capillas" differs from that of St Theresa because Sister María Manuela's spiritual unions are very sensual. In this sense, her writing more closely resembles the spiritual eroticism found in the work of both Sor Juana Inés de la Cruz and in that of the Spanish mystic, San Juan de la Cruz. Sister María Manuela continues the tradition of allegory present in *The Song of the Songs*.

The historic accounts of Sister María Manuela have a profound impact on many present day readers because of her descriptions of the most important events of her time, such as the Jesuits' expulsion from all Peru. Her comments about the Jesuits are significant because they protected and defended indigenous people against exploitation by the Spanish. If the Inquisition and Sister María Manuela's confessors would have carefully read her autobiography, we probably would not have her works today. She narrates the expulsion of the Jesuits as follows: "Dos años antes del estrañamiento de la compañía de Jesús, lo veía con los ojos del alma acabada. Y que no había Jesuitas y todo lo que han en nada desecho." (Two years before the estrangement of the Company of Jesus, I saw with sorrow through the eyes of my soul what would take place. And that there would no longer be any Jesuits in this land, and that everything they had done would be cast down).

In conclusion, the autobiographies of Sister María Magdalena and Sister María Manuela have a great deal of interest as both literature and history. Their texts offer us distinctive styles of writing the self that enrich our research. Furthermore, the examination of these works provides us with the real facts that highlighted women's presence in the construction of colonial society.

ELIA J. ARMACANQUI-TIPACTI

See also entry on Conventual Writing

Further Reading

Arenal, Electa, " 'Leyendo yo y escribiendo ella': the Convent as Intellectual Community," *Journal of Hispanic Philology* 13 (1989)

Armacanqui-Tipacti, Elia J., "Sor María Manuela de Santa Ana: a Peruvian Window on the World," *The Monographic Review/Revista monográfica*, vol. 9 (1993)

Benítez, Fernando, *Los demonios en el convento. Sexo y religión en la Nueva España*, Mexico City: Era, 1985

Giles, Mary E. (editor), *The Feminist Mystic and Other Essays on Women and Spirituality*, New York: Crossroad, 1982

Lavrín, Asunción, "Female Religious." *Cities and Society in Colonial Latin America*, edited by Louisa S. Hoberman and Susan M. Sorolow, Albuquerque: University of New Mexico Press, 1986

Myth

Definitions of myth are always necessarily partial and dependent on the needs of a particular discipline as it attempts to focus an area of study. Although our increasing awareness of the multi-dimensional nature of myths has demanded interdisciplinary perspectives, the processes of colonialism and postcolonialism continue to impose a Eurocentric framework on scholarly attempts to elucidate the formation, transmission and functioning of myth in culture. The Americas have been a particular rich area for the study of myth, inspiring works like Lévi-Strauss's *Structural Anthropology*, but recent work (such as Gordon Brotherston's *Image of the New World*, 1992), reminds us that the diversity of language systems that exist(ed) in the Americas are still little understood and severely question and problematize some of the categories (such as that between oral and written traditions) that are used to underpin theories of myth. Since the conception that we have of myth has to be revised continually in the light of modern scholarship, and since the "texts" that have been preserved are still in the process of being fully interpreted, any commentary must be tentative in its use of conceptual and disciplinary boundaries and able to anticipate a further shifting of such borders.

In his essay "The Problem of Defining Myth," Lauri Honko offers a definition based on the criteria of form, content, function and context. Like Mircea Eliade in *Myth and Reality*, Honko emphasizes that myth expressed a "truth," a sacred narrative that tells how something came into existence, a pattern for behaviour or an institution, and as such establishes the paradigms for all significant human acts. Myth has a strong performative element. The knowledge it reveals is not an external, abstract knowledge but one that can be experienced ritually, either by ceremonially recounting the myth or by performing the ritual for which it is the justification. For Honko, "the ritual acting out of myth implies the defence of the world order; by imitating sacred exemplars the world is prevented from being brought to chaos." The re-enactment of a creative event, for example, the healing wrought by a god in the beginning of time, is the common aim of myth and ritual. In this way the event is transferred to the present and its result, i.e. the healing of a sick person, can be achieved once more here and now." In this context, myth is synonymous with history – in its documentation of the creation and development of a society – and is also a form of science as it combines with medical practice in the healer's role as shaman, bearer of the soul. Myth is a language, then, that both records a narrative and intervenes in the present as a "lived" experience.

These dual functions are vividly portrayed in Jorge Sanjines's *La nación clandestina* [The Secret Nation], a film set in the Bolivia of 1952–89, which simultaneously charts the attacks on a indigenous way of life by both government and guerilla forces, and the ritual re-enactment of the myth of "The Great Dancer" by one of its members as a defence of their culture against such attacks. In its content, the film gives voice to the continued presence of Amerindians in the Americas and their – often clandestine – preservation of ancient customs and institutions. In its form, Sanjines exploits the cyclical structures and narrative ambivalence of myth to fragment the linear story of urban conquest and domination, and to displace the certainties of a colonial world-view. Confronted by this disjunction of place and discourse, punctuated only by the melody of the pan pipes, the audience is forced to weave together the scenes of (indigenous) myth and (colonial) history, thus themselves actively engaging in the ritual dance and producing with it a new, hybrid reality.

It is as a radical post-colonial tool, writing/talking back to history and to the process of colonialism, that myth finds its most powerful manifestation in the literature of the Americas. Eduardo Galeano's *Los nacimientos* (*Genesis*), for example, compiles a range of myths from the Great Lakes to Tierra del Fuego, gathering peoples as diverse as the metropolitan Aztecs and Incas, the confederacies of the Iroquois and Cherokee in the Appalachians and the loosely organized and widespread language family of the Guarani and Tupi in Brazil and Paraguay. All relating to a "creation" of some sort and based on documentary evidence (with details included in a glossary), these extracts are collectively entitled "Primeras voces" [First Voices] and provide insight into some of the Amerindian texts through which its people have represented themselves. Introduced as if apparently timeless, these poetic tales of creation and destruction, climate and government, retribution and trauma and healing and worship, built on an interconnectedness between man and the gods, animal and landscape, gradually accumulate into a vital context which throws into sharp relief the "Viejo Nuevo Mundo" (Old New Word) that follows. The use of dates in this second section introduces the historical framework of the colonizers (1492–1700) intent on conquest and domination, but the reader, empowered by the perspectives of the early context, is now suspicious of this totalizing discourse and its claims to power. Galeano's re-presenting of ancient Amerindian myths not only allows those worlds to be recreated in their own voice, it also enables the reader to recognize their continued presence in the "Viejo Nuevo Mundo," increasingly hybridized perhaps, but nevertheless providing an alternative and equally valid approach to a shared post-colonial reality.

Of course there are problems with this kind of literary representing of myth. Anthropologists have been particularly wary of literature's use of the poetics of myth and have emphasized the need to interpret myth, or the *series* of myths which inevitably structure the oral transmission of any one variant, in a focused ethnographic context. (Compare Lévi-Strauss's methodology in *The Raw and the Cooked*). There is also the danger in a project like Galeano's that the specificity of different Amerindian cultures and epochs may be lost in the political need to assemble a coherent resistance to colonial genocide. Writers like Miguel Ángel Asturias, José María Arguedas and Augusto Roa Bastos have preferred to focus on their own native ancestry and on specific texts (like the Maya-Quiché creation myths, the *Popol Vuh*, which inspired Asturias's *Hombres de maíz / Men of Maize*) in their attempts to use the strategies of myth and mythic texts to reshape a Latin American aesthetic. Attempts at gauging the "authenticity" of myth in any of these texts (whether literature, anthropology or any other contemporary discipline) is a futile exercise, however. The "documentary evidence" has often been through more than one translation process, the translators and native guides themselves straddling periods of cultural transition and acculturation. No interpretative process can be ideologically free and the translation from oral to written mediums is inevitably subject to change.

Nor is Amerindian myth the only resource available to the contemporary writer of the Americas. The continent's history of conquest and migration, including enforced slavery and indentured labour, has caused the displacement and transplantation of various mythological systems. The African-Hispanic novels of Nelson Estupiñán Bass (Ecuador), Quince Duncan (Costa Rica), Carlos Guillermo Wilson (Panama) and Manuel Zapata Olivella (Colombia) reveal the creative syncretism that emerges out of the need both to preserve African traditions and to re-interpret these traditions from a New World perspective. Zapata Olivella's *Changó, el gran putas* [Shango, the Baddest SOB] for example, specifically calls on Shango, the hero-god of the Yoruba, in an attempt to re-appropriate myths of slavery. Although the novel has its roots in Africa, "soul-force" – the power of the spirits of ancestors to give strength and direction to the living – a ritual which parallels the Amerindian use of myth, the emphasis is on the "nuevo Muntu Americano" (the new American man) who becomes a voice of hope for the wider cross-cultural community.

In the Circum-Caribbean, writers as diverse as Alejo Carpentier and Wilson Harris have, in their own times, formulated cross-cultural, New World perspectives that seek to inactivate the dynamic resources of myth to challenge the "one-sided conquistadorial realism" (Harris) of the colonizer's history. Carpentier defines his notion of "lo real maravilloso" (the marvellous in the real) in direct relation to the cross-cultural landscape of the Americas and the creative possibility for dialogue and dialectic which it represents. Though drawing on the very tangible myths of an African, Arawak and Christian heritage, Harris has also argued for the continued significance of eclipsed cultures, like that of the Carib, as "absent presences" which resonate powerfully throughout the cross-cultural imagination of the Americas. These two writers (the former a Cuban who wrote in Spanish, the latter a Guyanese writing in English) also remind us of the colonial demarcating of a shared mythical heritage and the artificiality of such geographical and disciplinary boundaries. Within these academic boundaries a genre such as magical realism may be confined to the past and associated with the stars of the Latin American Boom (like Gabriel García Márquez and Carlos Fuentes), when novels as diverse as *La Maravilla* [The Marvel] by the Chicano writer Alfredo Véa, Jr and the Trinidadian Lawrence Scott's *Witchbroom* demonstrate that the dual perspective of this genre, which attempts to respond to myth as well as to history, continues to offer an appropriate way forward for the post-colonial writer of the Americas.

Myth is central to both the writing and the vision of literature in the Americas, then, providing a catalyst for the experimentation and innovation of form and mapping a wider comparative and cross-cultural terrain than "Latin American" sometimes implies. At the same time as its influence is broad, however, we must also remember that myth retains a specificity of meaning for tangible and coherent Amerindian communities that are still little understood, or respected, so that our engagement with the ongoing translation process must be politicized if it is to be adequate.

PATRICIA MURRAY

Further Reading

Bierhost, John (editor and translator), *The Hungry Woman: Myths and Legends of the Aztecs*, New York: Morrow, 1984 [Bierhost is the translator of numerous other native American myths]

Brotherston, Gordon, *Image of the New World: the American Continent Portrayed in Native Texts*, London: Thames and Hudson, 1979

_____ *Book of the Fourth World: Reading the Native Americas through Their Literature*, Cambridge and New York: Cambridge University Press, 1992 [Contains a full bibliography of the editions and availability of native texts]

Carpentier, Alejo, "De lo real maravilloso americano," in his *Tientos y diferencias*, Mexico City: UNAM, 1964

Eliade, Mircea, *Myth and Reality*, translated by Willard R. Trask, New York: Harper and Row, 1963

Erdoes, Richard and Alfonso Ortiz (editors), *American Indian Myths and Legends*, New York: Pantheon, 1984

Galeano, Eduardo, *Memoria del fuego 1: Los nacimientos*, Madrid: Siglo XXI, 1982; as *Memory of Fire 1: Genesis*, translated by Cedric Belfridge, New York: Pantheon Books, 1985; London: Methuen, 1987

Harris, Wilson, "History, Fable and Myth in the Caribbean and Guianas," in *Explorations: a Selection of Talks and Articles 1966–1981*, edited by Hena Maes-Jelinek, Aarhus: Dangaroo Press, 1981

_____ "The Absent Presence: the Caribbean, Central and South America," in *The Radical Imagination: Lectures and Talks by Wilson Harris*, edited by Alan Riach and Mark Williams, Liège: Liège Language and Literature, 1992

Honko, Lauri, "The Problem of Defining Myth" in *Sacred Narrative: Readings in the Theory of Myth*, edited by Alan Dundes, Berkeley: University of California Press, 1984 [A useful collection of essays that contains various approaches to myth by Jung, Freud, Campbell, Lévi-Strauss, Malinowski etc., as well as commentaries on them. Many of the essays use myths of the Americas as their source material].

Jackson, Richard L., "The Black Novel in Latin America Today," *Revista de Literatura Latinoamericana*, vol. 16/2–3 (1987)

Kirk, G.S., *Myth: Its Meaning and Functions in Ancient and Other Cultures*, Cambridge: Cambridge University Press, and Berkeley: University of California Press, 1970

Knab, T.J. and Thelma D. Sullivan, *A Scattering of Jades: Stories, Poems and Prayers of the Aztecs*, New York: Touchstone, 1994

Lévi-Strauss, Claude, *The Raw and the Cooked: Introduction to a Science of Mythology*, translated by John and Doreen Weightman, New York: Harper and Row, 1969

Murray, David, *Forked Tongues: Speech Writing and Representation in North American Indian Texts*, Bloomington: Indiana University Press, 1991 [Although focusing primarily on North American texts, provides useful contexts and insights, especially on the theory and translation of myth]

Sajines, Jorge, "Problems of Form and Content in Revolutionary Cinema," in *Twenty-Five Years of the New Latin American Cinema*, edited by Michael Chanan, London: British Film Institute, 1983

Scott, Lawrence, *Witchbroom*, Oxford: Heinemann, 1992

Véa, Jr, Alfredo, *La Maravilla*, New York: Plume, 1994

Young, Robert, *White Mythologies: Writing History and the West*, London: Routledge, 1990

Zapata Olivella, Manuel, *Changó, el gran putas*, Bogotá: Oveja Negra, 1983

N

Náhuatl Literature

Indigenous literature is expressed in various forms of poetry and prose: great epic poems recalling cosmological myths and legends about the gods and cultural heroes, sacred hymns, and a variety of religious poetry often lyrical and sometimes dramatic, chronicles and historical accounts based on the ancient annals, and, finally, stories of creative imagination and instructive texts covering numerous topics. The greatest wealth of preserved literary texts (due to the efforts of friars and native survivors) has come down to us from the Náhuas of Central Mexico. Náhuatl literature (the literature of the people of the empire which sprawled across much of modern Mexico, collectively referred to as the "Mexica") covered all aspects of life, for its aim was to help the memory to retain the whole accumulated knowledge of earlier generations, their religious ideas, myths, ritual, divination, medicine, history, law, as well as rhetoric and lyric and epic poetry. Prose was used for instructive treatises, mythical and historical narratives and verse for religious or profane poems. Many accounts or descriptions of events were in the form of poetry or rhythmic verses, since this format was easier to commit to memory. Some of these poems were veritable sagas, and others reflections upon the brevity of life or the uncertainty of fate, satisfying this culture's appetite for philosophico-moral rhetoric. In contrast to the delicate sensitivity of the poems and legends of Maya literature, the often forceful expressions of Náhuatl literature reflect the mentality of the Aztecs, a people obsessed by a mystico-militaristic concept of life. Ritual was a major tool in the creation of an imperial people – a highly elastic and dynamic expressive mode, more akin to street theatre and collective popular representation of familiar "performance texts." Such extended dramatized performances (they often lasted days), recruiting different groups of participants from different social levels in complex sequence, were themselves sculpted successions of choreographed sentiments loosely organized around a theme, and made the more powerful for being repeatable, public, and participatory through the ritual aesthetic. Books or written accounts, using a compromise between ideogram, phoneticism and simple representation or pictography, served merely as prompters to the memory, since historical accounts, hymns and poems had to be learned by heart for transmission. For this reason, certain prompts were used such as phonetic parallels, assonances and alliterations.

The Náhuas had both a strong tradition of oral history before the conquest and a tradition of written record-keeping. In the 16th century when the conquest narratives were composed and recorded, the oral tradition still remained strong and the written texts show evidence of its influence. The repetition of information in slight variation and the relative lack of autonomy of the Náhuatl texts obviously come from the oral tradition. In contrast to their written counterpart, oral texts depend on reiteration and speaker intervention for their effectiveness in transmission. Such written texts demonstrate their origins in an orally constituted sensibility and tradition. This is apparent in Náhuatl and other early indigenous compositions in the oral drive to use formulaic expression, the oral mnemonic drive to exploit balance, the oral drive to redundancy, and the oral drive to narrate rather than simply to juxtapose. And, given poetic license and the variability allowed in multiple authorship and diverse time sequences of construction, in addition to the different polities that participated in different ways, as allies or enemies of the Spaniards, it is not surprising that no unified native account of the conquest exists. Obvious examples of differing points of view are Diego Muñoz Camargo's *Historia de Tlaxcala* and the conquest chronicle of Tenochtitlán-Tlatelolco compiled under the direction of Bernardino de Sahagún in the *Florentine Codex*. Much of the Sahagún material has the resonance of confident memory: the chants to the gods in their archaic Náhuatl; the formal exhortations of parents to children; the midwife's prayer for the newborn child, spoken when no male was present – all these as part of the memories of the elderly. Native conquest narratives, including those of Náhuatl literature, tend to be more a means for gaining insight into the native cosmogony than for constructing a historically accurate chronicle of events.

In the indigenous mind all art forms were intimately inter-related, as were all manifestations, activations or clarifications of the divine text sustained by the sacred impulse. The poet-singers and musicians as well as the scribes indicated the text's sacred elevation through the richness of metaphor. Indeed, there is a suggestion in some poems that the processes of chant and inscription were simultaneous, the "text" as much sung as painted. Sung poetry was referred to in Náhuatl *xochi-cuicatl*, "flower-song" (humans, like flowers and song, exist only ephemerally in the world), and in the painted books the speech-scrolls which indicated the words were colored the deep blue-green of jade, of quetzal plumes, an incomparably precious commodity. Poetry, rather than being an individual-istic art form as is the case in most cultures, can be said to represent collective understandings among Amerindians, who have a long tradition of song-poems as public, and publicly shaped, performances. Such poetry, although often composed by a single poet, was an arrangement of shared formulae more than the creative outpouring of an individual. The symbology and styles within the strongly marked genres (warrior songs, burgeon songs, songs of lamentation and love) were very much prescribed, indeed, and particular songs entered the repertoire only upon acceptance by the general population. Thus, songcraft or sung poems remained a popularly based art in Náhuatl aesthetics, as was the case among other pre-Columbian indigenous peoples. The Aztecs themselves divided poetry into various categories depending on subject matter: religious songs or hymns, war-songs, flowery, bantering songs, etc. As was previously mentioned, artistic forms were not strictly divided into separate genres. And so, poem and song were synonymous, for the poem was always sung or at the very least declaimed to the accompaniment of musical instru-ments. And, in turn, these poems were not only sung, but "acted" in dramatic fashion, that is, each of the verses repeated on numerous occasions throughout the performance text accompanied a given phase of a ritual ceremony, some set action of the priests or some specific masked dance. Thus, in the combination of recital, song, dance and music there were also to be found the elements of a dramatic art with actors in costume to represent historical or mythical heroes, dialogue, and, at times, exchanges between the characters and a choir. Even mimed songs, some of them sung by women, were inserted into these compositions of ballets and tragedies. The ancient Mexicans' passionate love of oratory and poetry, music and dancing, had free rein at feasts, banquets and innumer-able ceremonies. Dancing was not only a form of entertain-ment or a rite; it was a means of expressing worthiness and favor with the gods by paying homage to them with one's entire body. The simplicity of instrumental accompaniment – the conch, the trumpet, the flute and some percussion – primarily provided a basic rhythm for singing and dancing. This perpetual theatre of Náhuas consisted of performances and sacrifices throughout the year coinciding with different religious festivals. It was the richness and eloquence of the Mexican language (Náhuatl had become the common tongue of the whole vast country by the beginning of the 16th century) which was exploited to its fullest potential in the rhetorical and poetic style of indigenous literary achievements. Reading their words, we note the poise of the cadences and the prac-ticed balance of the repetitions and parallelisms. Náhuatl was and is a language rich in metaphor, and the Mexica took delight in exploring veiled resemblances, sometimes speaking literally and, more often, speaking metaphorically. Plays like the Maya-Quiché Rabinal Achí were frequent among both the Mayas and Náhuas. Fray Diego de Durán writes about Náhuatl schools for dance, making a clear distinction between the plays presented in festivals to honor the gods (a serious cosmic responsibility for the preservation of their people) and others which he specifically called "farces, interludes, and songs of much mirth" performed for sheer entertainment.

The "Anales" of Tlatelolco, possibly transcribed into European script in the post-conquest period (1528), is the first indigenous document written in European script that we have. Although written only seven years after the Spanish Conquest, this composition seems to have remained intact, without outside influence or contamination. The two great collections of Náhuatl "song-poems" are *La colección de cantares mexi-canos* [Collected Mexican Songs] and *Manuscrito de los romances de los señores de la Nueva España* [Manuscript of the Ballads of the Lords of New Spain]. In addition, there is the *Libro de los coloquios* [Book of the Debates], which is lyrical in flavor despite its dialogue form, and was written down (and some say possibly composed) in the 1560s. These give some access, through their patterns of verse, their insis-tent metaphors, and their mournful evocation of mood, to pre-conquest sensibility. Most post-conquest Náhuatl texts, however, result in a hybridization of indigenous and European thought and forms.

ELENA DE COSTA

Further Reading

Anthologies, critical editions and individual texts

Baudot, Georges and Tzvetan Todorov (editors), *Relatos aztecas de la Conquista*, Mexico City: Grijalbo, 1990 [Baudot provides new translations of the Náhuatl texts (although not the originals). His preface to the Náhuatl and Spanish texts indicates the provenance of the writers and any relevant biographical material that is known. Todorov's interpretative essay deals with the "modalities of the narrative – narrators, genres, and styles" – and discusses the histories themselves]

Correa, Gustavo, *et al.*, *The Native Theatre in Middle America*, New Orleans: Tulane University, 1961

Garibay, Angel María K. (editor), *Poesía náhuatl*, 3 vols, vol. 1, *Romances de los señores de Nueva España*; vols 2 and 3, *Cantares mexicanos* (incomplete), Mexico City: UNAM, 1964–68

León-Portilla, Miguel, *Quince poetas del mundo azteca*, Mexico City: Diana, 1994

Sahagún, Bernardino de, *Códice florentino*, Mexico City: Secretaría de Gobernación, 1979

Critical Studies

Brotherston, Gordon, *Book of the Fourth World: Reading the Native Americas through Their Literature*, Cambridge and New York: Cambridge University Press, 1992

Garibay, Ángel María K., *Historia de la literatura Náhuatl*, vols 1–5, Mexico City: Porrúa, 1987

____ *Panorama literario de los pueblos Náhuas*, Mexico City: Porrúa, 1987

Kartunnen, Frances, "Náhuatl Literacy," in *The Inca and Mexica States 1400–1800: Anthropology and History*, edited by George A. Collier, Renato I. Rosaldo and John D. Wirth, New York: Academic Press, 1982

Launey, Michel, *Introducción a la lengua y la literatura Náhuatl*, Mexico City: UNAM, 1992

León-Portilla, Miguel, *Aztec Thought and Culture: a Study of the Ancient Náhuatl Mind*, translated by Jack Emory Davis, Norman: University of Oklahoma Press, 1963

____ *The Broken Spears: the Aztec Account of the Conquest of Mexico*, translated by Lysander Kemp, Boston: Beacon Press, 1966

____ *Pre-Columbian Literatures of Mexico*, translated by the author and Grace Lobanov, Norman: University of Oklahoma Press, 1969

____ *Native Mesoamerican Spirtuality: Ancient Myths, Discourses, Stories, Doctrines, Hymns, Poems from the Aztec, Yucatec, Quiché-Maya and Other Sacred Traditions*, New York: Paulist Press, 1980

María y Campos, Armando de, *Representaciones teatrales en la Nueva España*, Mexico City: Costa-Amic, 1959

Ong, Walter J., *The Presence of the Word: Some Prolegomena for Cultural and Religious History*, New Haven, Connecticut: Yale University Press, 1967

____ *Orality and Literacy: the Technologizing of the Word*, New York and London Methuen, 1982

Schroeder, Susan, *Chimalpahin and the Kingdoms of Chalco*, Tucson: University of Arizona Press, 1991 [Chimalpahin is a significant native writer-annalist whose work (written in his native language) transcends conquest history. He wrote to glorify the history of his home polity of Amaquemeca (modern Amecameca). Schroeder's study contains lengthy passages in Náhuatl with English glosses, and emphasizes the importance of understanding native categories within the indigenous context]

Soustelle, Jacques, *The Daily Life of the Aztecs on the Eve of the Spanish Conquest*, translated by Patrick O'Brian, London: Weidenfeld and Nicolson, 1961; New York: Macmillan, 1962

Todorov, Tzvetan, *The Conquest of America: the Question of the Other*, translated by Richard Howard, New York: Harper and Row, 1984

Nationalism in Spanish America

Before the 19th century the literary works written in Hispanic America that manifested an inherently local focus constituted only a small exception to the rule. One looks in vain for a realistic depiction of American types and customs in the colonial literary canon. Ercilla's Araucanian characters, only Indian in name, possessed the values and character of their Virgilian literary models. Ruiz de Alarcón merits inclusion in the elite of Golden Age dramatists, yet his finely crafted plays hardly reveal their American origin. Sor Juana, in her brilliant poetic and epistolary writings, depicts a superior intellect that seems to rise largely above geographical determinants. Lonely exceptions to this pattern were Guaman Poma de Ayala and El Inca Garcilaso de la Vega. The latter, after a lifetime of attempting to assimilate himself to European norms, proclaimed in the prologue to his monumental work, *Comentarios reales de los Incas* (*Royal Commentaries of the Incas*), a spiritual link with his Peruvian *patria* (homeland). In actual fact, nationalism – understood in the sense of a priority granted to American goals and forms – was not in vogue. Instead, the mutually supporting ideas of monarchy and empire in political thought, scholasticism in religion, and Neoclassicism in literature, joined together in prescribing centralized, Old World norms. This was not to be altered by the advent of Enlightenment ideas that did not challenge universalist structures in the priority now granted to an enshrined Reason. In short, colonial elites had little motivation for challenging the vertical conception of the universe that justified the derivative nature of their institutions and art.

In contrast to what occurred in the United States, political independence for the newly emancipated Hispanic republics in the early decades of the 19th century largely pre-dated the spread of a nationalist consciousness. As a result, the region's intellectuals and writers emerged into the post-independence period with many previous conceptions largely unmodified. Yet there were changes: local elites increasingly followed British rather than Spanish leadership in the organization of their banking and trade practices; in the realms of philosophy, art and literature, they now emulated French models and condemned "retrograde" Hispanic influences. In spite of these changes, what remained largely unaltered was the doctrinaire nature of their thought. In culture, government, and fashion, their ideas of progress and the good life led them to continue preaching the necessity of imposing Europe-derived structures in the hope of replacing these with the perceived deficiencies in lifestyle and beliefs of the continent's then largely rural society.

There were exceptions to this diffusionist model, however. In the correspondence of Venezuela's Simón Bolívar (1783–1830) one finds a passionate expression of the dual ideals of Hispanic American independence and nationhood. In the Río de la Plata region, the highly popular gauchesque verses by Bartolomé Hidalgo (1788–1822) promoted the independence cause among the largely unlettered population and also set a standard for a future national literature by portraying the rural population's customs, feelings and social types. Similar was the contribution of Mexico's fiery journalist, José Joaquín Fernández de Lizardi, who defended that country's struggle for independence through his journalism. He also published what has come to be regarded as Hispanic America's first novel, *El Periquillo Sarniento*, 1816 (*The Itching Parrot*), which attacked Spanish influences and demonstrated sociological awareness of his Mexican homeland.

During the first three to four decades after independence, most Hispanic American republics experienced devastating internecine struggles that usually pitted modernizing urban elites against more traditional rural sectors. Urban intellectuals, the primary porters of the written culture, continued to call for more intimate links with France, Britain, and the centers of what they called civilization. At the same time, they condemned the Hispanic traditions and *nativista* (localist) art forms of the poncho-clad rural inhabitants on account of an anachronistic barbarism. For those elites, cultural parameters were inextricably linked to political criteria. Argentina's Domingo Faustino Sarmiento, writing in *Facundo*, 1845 (*Life in the Argentine Republic in the Days of the Tyrants*), attacked the dictator Rosas, among other reasons, for the latter's defence of "the American principle." The promotion of nationalism, in his eyes, was equivalent to the obstruction of progress and modernity.

The spread of Romantic ideas among Hispanic American elites that began toward the end of the 1830s, accounts at least in part for a change of attitute that made increasingly acceptable the study and literary treatment of national reality. Although Sarmiento and his renowed cohorts of the Argentine Generation of 1837 opposed aspects of an American, or nationalist politics, it was they who expressed most authoritatively the imperative for a truly national orientation in Hispanic Americans' literary and intellectual endeavors. Yet their advocacy was ambiguous. Esteban Echeverría, the foremost advocate and literary practitioner of this group, urged in *Dogma socialista* (1838) a fusion of urban and rural, unitarian and federalist, European and American orientations. None did more to disseminate the pragmatic new ideas emanating from European intellectual circles, yet it was he who most strenuously called for a science, a literature, and a government that would be based on the lived experiences and real needs of his countrymen. His disciple, Juan Baustista Alberdi (1810–84), succinctly expressed this thought: "A people must first acquire a philosophy before they can achieve a nationality."

Under the sign of these ambiguities, the first indications of a national literature began to appear. The poem, "Silva a la agricultura en la zona tórrida," 1826 [Song to Tropical Agriculture], by the Venezuelan Andrés Bello and Alberdi's lyrical essay, *Memoria descriptiva sobre Tucumán*, 1834 [Descriptive Report on Tucumán], although heeding the Romantic call to turn away from the themes of classical antiuity and focus lyrical attention on the beauty of the American landscape, nevertheless betray the Neoclassical orientations of their creators. Echeverría's long narrative poem, *La cautiva*, 1837 [The Captive], celebrates the savage American landscape that nearly consumes the Europeanized protagonist, Brián, and his diaphanous consort, María. Sarmiento's very original character sketches of the pathfinder and the gaucho outlaw appear within a work – *Facundo* – whose main thrust was an attack on rural society and "American barbarism."

Advancing into the second half of the century, many countries still suffered from tragic civil struggles between different social, ethnic and racial groups vying for hegemony. In this setting, writing often assumed the advocate's role of defending the rights of minority groups within the emerging national fabric: Gertrudis Gómez de Avellaneda (1814–73), wrote *Sab* to attack slavery and to project a humanized image of Cuba's black population; the monumental gauchesque poem, *Martín Fierro* (published in two parts, the first in 1872 and the second in 1879), by José Hernández, attacked the abuses to Argentina's rural population at the hands of urban society; and Juan León Mera (1832–94) in *Cumandá, o, un drama entre salvajes*, 1879 [Cumandá or a Drama among Savages], defended the place of indigenous people within a larger conception of Ecuadorian nationality.

By the latter decades of the century, social peace had been gained in the majority of the Hispanic American republics, but often at a terrible price. Now, the militancy of previously rebellious minorities, often rural groups, had been broken, and urban elites were firmly in control of governmental authority. Given this setting, the production of many writers must be viewed, at least in part, as an attempt to legitimize these new social and political realities. Representative literary works sought to "violently forget" recent struggles and disseminate a positive historical memory of earlier pursuits of nationality. In *Enriquillo, leyenda histórica dominicana*, 1882 (*The Cross and the Sword*), Manuel de Jesús Galván (1834–1910), embellished the Dominican Republic's Indian and mestizo origins. In Peru, the historico-literary essays of *Tradiciones peruanas* (1872–1910), by Ricardo Palma (1833–1919), celebrated the glories of Lima's colonial past. The literary archeology undertaken by Chile's Alberto Blest Gana (1830–1920) and Mexico's Ignacio Manuel Altamirano (1834–93), participated in establishing harmonious views of their respective country's colonial and early republican past. More political was Uruguay's Eduardo Acevedo Díaz (1851–1924), whose historical novels had the "revisionist" mission of contradicting previous accounts and highlighting the uniqueness of the early independence leader, José Gervasio Artigas and, as such, his own small country's contributions to the emancipation struggle. With *Tabaré*, 1888 (*Tabaré: an Indian Legend of Uruguay*), mythification approached a fanciful extreme, since Juan Zorrilla de San Martín (1855–1931) projects an Indian and mestizo identity onto Uruguay, a land where the Amerindians had already disappeared.

Evidence of the success enjoyed by the intellectuals in their quest to enhance nationalist sentiment was the wide diffusion in many of the region's cities – very apparent by the 1890s – of a pulp literature and popular culture celebrating rural or creolist themes. Argentina was the first country to witness the rise of a national theater catering for the aesthetic tastes of all the different social classes, that featured as protagonist the honorable gaucho outlaw, Juan Moreira. Hispanic America's urban reading public began to favor, for the first time, local writers expounding on mythified or folkloric national themes.

Approaching the end of the century, new historical factors account for yet another wave of nationalist sentiment in the literature of the region. Writers associated with the movement called *Modernismo* (Spanish American Modernism), in their desire for artistic, philosophical, and spiritual renovation, echoed the material advances and political maturity of their societies. But they also expressed discomfort before a new threat to the region's political and cultural integrity: the bullish and expansive Anglo-American republic to the north. José Enrique Rodó, in his seminal essay *Ariel* (1900), communicated the Hispanic Americans' spiritual superiority – the flipside to their defensive inferiority – in contrast to the crass materialism that reigned in the United States. Similar was the denouncement of Big-Stick imperialist ventures in Panama in poems like "A Roosevelt" [To Roosevelt], by the most outstanding of the region's Modernist poets, the Nicaraguan Rubén Darío (1867–1919). The crowning effort of this continental wave of indignation was "Nuestra América" (Our America), an essay by Cuba's José Martí (1853–95) that resonated with passionate pan-Hispanic sentiment.

WILLIAM H. KATRA

See also entries on Andrés Bello, Esteban Echeverría, José Martí, Domingo Faustino Sarmiento

Further Reading

Anderson, Benedict, *Imagined Communities: Reflections on the Origins and Spread of Nationalism*, London: Verso, 1983; revised edition, 1991

Barbero, María Inés and Fernando Devoto, *Los nacionalistas, 1910–1932*, Biblioteca Política no. 9, Buenos Aires: Centro Editor de América Latina, 1983

Bhaba, Homi K. (editor), *Nation and Narration*, London and New York: Routledge, 1990

Katra, William H., *The Argentine Generation of 1837: Echeverría, Sarmiento, Alberdi, Mitre*, Rutherford, New Jersey: Fairleigh Dickinson University Press, 1996

Masiello, Francine, *Between Civilization and Barbarism: Women, Nation, and Literary Culture in Modern Argentina*, Lincoln: University of Nebraska Press, 1992

Romero, José Luis, *Las ideologías de la cultura nacional y otros ensayos*, Buenos Aires: Centro Editor de América Latina, 1982

Négritude

Négritude, sometimes described as "the Afrocentricity of the 1930s," is the name given to a Black literary movement which, beginning in the 1930s, continued into the 1950s. The movement began among French-speaking Caribbean and African writers, and its leading figures include Aimé Césaire, a Martinican writer; to whom is attributed the first use of the term *Négritude*, Léopold Senghor , who became the first president of the Republic of Sénégal in 1960 and Léon-Gontran Damas (1912–78), from French Guiana.

The *Négritude* writers held various traits and ideologies in common: they were all Black, from former French colonies and at the time all living in Paris. They were much encouraged by the example of Black Americans in Paris who were involved in asserting their distinctive culture. On the other hand, it was a time when Francophone Blacks still aspired to assimilation. The concept of *Négritude* evolved between 1933 and 1935 as a protest over thwarted political aspirations. As writers, they felt the need to examine critically Western values and thought, and in so doing they began to reassess Black African culture. They theorized that assimilation was ideological and that the assumption behind it was the inherent superiority of European culture and civilization over its African equivalents. Indeed in some circles (despite the importance given, particularly after World War I, to "primitive" art) it was even assumed that Africa had no history or culture. Thus, their awareness of cultural identity increased as they dwelt on the suffering, mental bondage and humiliation of Black peoples, not only during times of slavery but also under colonial rule.

This inspired in them the following views later expounded in their works: that all Africans and people of colour must look to the richness of their past, to their cultural heritage and in so doing could choose values and traditions invaluable to them in their modern world; that it was the challenge of committed Black writers to exceed the boundaries of the African as subject matter and to infuse their readers with the desire for political freedom and freedom of thought; that *Négritude* means all aspects of Black African cultural, social, economic and political values and as such the value and dignity of Black African traditions and her peoples must be reasserted;

and that African life with its oral tradition and its mystic value would hold its rightful place in literary and cultural circles, especially when compared with the materialism and soulnessness of Western culture. In 1934, Senghor, Damas and Césaire co-founded the magazine *L'Etudiant Noir* [Black Student] and it was Senghor who was later to write the following statement on the methods and objectives of *Négritude* writers:

> Pour asseoir une révolution efficace, *notre* révolution, il nous fallait d'abord nous débarasser de nos vêtements d'emprunt – ceux de l'assimilation – et affirmer notre être, c'est à dire notre *négritude*. Cependant la Négritude, même définie comme 'l'ensemble des valeurs culturelles de l'Afrique noire,' ne pouvait nous offrir que le début de la solution de notre problème, non la solution elle-même.

> [To establish an effective revolution, *our* own revolution, we first had to cast off our borrowed clothes – the clothes of assimilation – and to assert our being, which meant asserting our *négritude*. Yet Négritude even when defined as "all the cultural values of black Africa," could only provide us with the beginnings of a solution to our problem, not the solution itself].

In a sense, the *Négritude* literary movement was one of the greatest contributions to Black writers the world over as it empowered them. Their stories began to hold meaning for Black readers and others alike. The meanings held importance. The legacies live on, as in the 1990s Black writers, globally, continue to struggle against class inequality, racism, discrimination, and even the environment, as they wrestle to throw off the yokes (both internal and external) of colonialist partisan prejudice and discrimination.

NICOLE ROBERTS

See also the entries on Aimé Césaire, Francophone West Indies, *La Revue du Monde Noir* under Journals

Further Reading

Critical Works

[Aimé Césaire's *Discours sur le colonialisme* is essential reading]

Arnold, James A., "Négritude Then and Now," in *A History of Literature in the Caribbean*, edited by James A. Arnold, vol. 1: Hispanic and Francophone Regions, Amsterdam and Philadelphia: Benjamins, 1994

Depestre, René, *Bonjour et adieu à la négritude: travaux d'identité*, Paris: Laffont, 1980

Markovitz, Irving L., *Leopold Sédar Senghor and the Politics of Négritude*, London: Heinemann Educational, and New York: Atheneum, 1969

Piquion, René, *Les Trois grands de la négritude, Damas, Césaire, Senghor*, Port-au-Prince: Henri Deschamps, 1964

Senghor, Leopold Sédar, *Anthologie de la nouvelle poesie nègre et malgache de langue française*, Paris: Presses Universitaires de France, 1948

——— *Liberté*, 5 vols, 1964–93:
  1. *Négritude et humanisme*, Paris: Seuil, 1964
  2. *Nation et voie africaine du socialisme*, Paris: Seuil, 1971
  3. *Négritude et civilisation de l'universel*, Paris: Seuil, 1977
  4. *Socialisme en planification*, Paris: Seuil, 1983
  5. *Le Dialogue des cultures*, Paris: Seuil, 1993

——— *Pour une Relecture africaine de Marx et d'Engels*, Dakar: Nouvelles Éditions Africaines, 1976; Paris: Presses Universitaires de France, 1977

——— *Ce que je Crois, négritude, francité et civilization de l'universel*, Paris: Grasset, 1988

Washington Ba, Sylvia, *The Concept of Négritude in the Poetry of Leopold Sédar Senghor*, Princeton, New Jersey: Princeton University Press, 1973

Works by creative writers

[(except Césaire, who has a separate entry)]

Damas, Léon-Gontran, *Retour de Guyane*, 1938
——— *Poèmes nègres sur des airs africains*, Paris: GLM, 1948
——— *Graffiti*, Paris: Seghers, 1952
——— *Black Label, poèmes*, Paris: Gallimard, 1956
——— *Névralgies*, Paris: Présence Africaine, 1965
Senghor, Leopold Sédar, *Chants d'ombre*, Paris: Seuil, 1945
——— *Hosties noires*, Paris: Seuil, 1948
——— *Chants pour Naett*, Paris: Seghers, 1949
——— *Ethiopiques*, Paris: Seuil, 1956
——— *Nocturnes*, Paris: Seuil, 1961
——— *Poèmes*, Paris: Seuil, 1964
——— *Selected Poems*, edited and translated by John Reed and Clive Wake, London: Oxford University Press, and New York: Atheneum, 1964
——— *Prose and Poetry by L.S. Senghor*, translated by John Reed and Clive Wake, London: Oxford University Press, 1965
——— *Elégie des Alizés*, Paris: Seuil, 1969
——— *Lettres d'hivernage*, Paris: Seuil, 1973

Pablo Neruda 1904–1973

Chilean poet

Among the most prolific of Latin American poets, Pablo Neruda was and arguably is the most widely read of the Spanish American poets. Indeed, operating within the domain of a notoriously esoteric and elitist genre, Neruda managed, more than any other Latin American poet to date, to popularize poetry. His *Veinte poemas de amor y una canción desesperada*, 1924 (*Twenty Love Poems and a Song of Despair*), alone has sold over a million copies since it first appeared in print. On the one hand, this unusual cultural phenomenon was largely due to Neruda's background; on the other hand, it was a result of his involvement in national and international politics.

The son of a railroad worker, Neruda was born and raised in rural southern Chile, where he developed a keen interest, that would last his entire life, in natural phenomena: the sea and forest would always be generators for his poetry. However, nature would never be static or idyllic; nor would it be a romantic refuge from society. Even in his early poetry – *Crepusculario*, 1923 [Where Twilight Dwells], *El hondero entusiasta* [The Enthusiastic Diver], written in 1923, and *Veinte poemas de amor* – Neruda depicts nature's energy and movement and his insatiable desire to portray the material world's complexity. However, it is also a source of anxiety and sadness

for him. The poet had the opportunity to live in southern Chile at the very historical moment when the industrialization of the countryside was taking place, and his father's work placed Neruda the child at the axis of these socio-economic changes. His father's work on the railroad as well in the lumber industry, furnished the young poet with a special vantage point for appreciating the conflicts that that socio-economic development wrought in a rural region in which the indigenous (Araucan) population had been exterminated. Nevertheless, Neruda's early poetry is also marked by a Romantic and abstract search for conjugal love. In *Crepusculario* and *El hondero entusiasta*, and even in *Veinte poemas*, clearly he is searching for an earthly Ideal, so he cannot consummate his passion. One could maintain that erotic passion becomes entwined with the conscious desire to express the natural and social environment that surrounds him in language.

Two volumes of poetry written from 1925 to 1935, *Residencia en la tierra* (*Residence on Earth*), represent a qualitative leap with respect to his previous poetic production. These works are punctuated with constant references to the anguish or "ennui" of existence (as a reading of "Walking Around" attests) and to the menacing effects of an omnipresent nature. Since Neruda was always prone to be a critical realist at heart, it is difficult, if not impossible, to interpret this poetry as anything other than a real, largely autobiographical testimony of his social condition in the Orient. Having become part of the underpaid Chilean diplomatic corps in the Orient, and working variously in Rangoon, Ceylon, Java and Singapore, Neruda – as his poetry of these years and his memoirs affirm – felt alienated because he was neither a representative of the British Empire in the Orient nor a natural citizen of these regions, he could not speak the native languages nor English fluently, his position as a bureaucrat was dreadfully boring, the socio-economic exploitation of the population by the ruling class and the British was brutal, and the climate was suffocating him. In the *Residencias*, time and death become obsessively destructive in exercising their dominion over the human subject. Until the second half of the book two, nature is an autonomous, creative, and destructive force with which the poetic speaker cannot identify. The frailty of human life and the incessant movement of nature horrifies Neruda. The poet sees his own existence objectified before him in nature. This proved to be very a valuable and humbling experience that allowed the poet – especially after 1935 – to question the guiding principles of art under capitalism. Although his early participation in anarchist activities in Chile certainly played a key role here, from this moment on, the ivory tower that bourgeois society offers its literati, did not seduce him.

It is worth noting that at the end of this period of nostalgia and social alienation, specifically in "Entrada a la madera" (Opening to Wood), Neruda came to grips with the situation: nature, from that moment on, became a source of amazement and discovery rather than an antagonist. Significantly, these "Tres cantos materiales" (Three Material Songs) – of which "Entrada a la madera" is a part – were first published in Spain, where Neruda had arrived as the new consul of Barcelona and, a few months later, Madrid. This biographical material is indispensable in order to understand the next phase in Neruda's poetic work. For the poet arrived in Spain the same year that miners in Asturias took political power and set up a commune for ten days in this northern province. This was a period of increasing class conflict between the rural bourgeoisie, the Catholic Church, and the military on the one hand and, the liberal, Socialist, and Communist working and middle classes on the other hand. Neruda stayed in Madrid until late 1936, when he was discharged from his post as consul, and when the Spanish Civil War intensified.

Published on Republican territory during the war against fascism, *España en el corazón* [Spain in the Heart] – originally published in Chile in 1937 – was the product of Neruda's open engagement with progressive and leftist political causes. A landmark in his *oeuvre*, in this book Neruda documented the central conflicts taking place in the Iberian peninsula. Thus, he dedicates several poems to specific battles (such as "El Jarama" [The Jarama River]), blistering critiques of the Nationalists, the socio-economic causes that had led to the war, and the dehumanization of war caused by the Nationalists. In sum, the socio-political, and even existential or ontological dimensions, and Neruda's own perseverance challenged the alienation that plagued him so in the *Residencias*. The poet became a participant and writer of a Neorealist account of the making of history.

España en el corazón acts as a bridge between the Neruda of the *Residencias* and his magnum opus, *Canto general*, 1950 (*Residence on Earth*). In the intervening years, from 1937 to 1949, Neruda published relatively little compared to other moments in his life because he participated very actively in progressive and leftist politics. Having left Spain for France, he began coordinating support among the intelligentsia for the Republican cause. Moreover, he organized a mission to ship Spanish refugees to Chile during the waning moments of the civil war. Once he arrived in Chile he worked busily for the Popular Front's presidential campaign, which triumphed in 1938.

Beginning in 1940 he spent three years in Mexico as a consul once again. Surrounded by left-wing artists and writers in Mexico under the progressive Lázaro Cárdenas regime, and concerned by the strength of fascism in Europe, Neruda's political consciousness underwent another qualitative leap, expressed in his "Canto de amor a Stalingrado" (A Love Song for Stalingrad) and "Nuevo canto de amor a Stalingrado" (A New Love Song for Stalingrad). For Neruda, as for many other left-wing intellectuals, the fight against Franco's Nationalist forces became an integral part of the struggle against fascism worldwide. These two poems, which the poet read in public in Mexico, narrate the defence of the Soviet Union against the invading German armies and they suggest the degree to which Neruda committed himself to socialism. Unsurprisingly, then, after returning to Chile Neruda joined the Communist Party in 1945, a few months after he was elected senator for the mining area of northern Chile. Thus, during these years Neruda's commitment to humanitarian and socialist causes deepens.

Canto general, then, is the culmination of this period of increased political activity and awareness. This book is an attempt to re-write Latin American history from the vantage point of the oppressed, beginning with the American continent's indigenous civilizations, extending to the brutality of the conquest, the wars of independence, leading up to the various dictatorships established in the 1930s and 1940s, and the resistance to them on the part of peasants and workers. Neruda's poetic method in this work underwent a significant transformation as did the conception of poetry in Latin America. *Canto general* is a *tour de force* that depends on a great deal of knowledge about Latin American geography, history and politics, all of which is represented in particular and general abstractions that illuminate the driving forces at work in the region. While it is true that Neruda's unique poetry – like that of Ernesto Cardenal – is capable of approximating the socio-historical developments in a Neorealist form, it is also true that Neruda's work acquires a philosophical depth that surpasses that of his earlier books of poetry. Throughout *Canto general*, but especially in the cases of "Alturas de Macchu Picchu" (*The Heights of Macchu Picchu*) and "La tierra se llama Juan" (The Earth's Name is John), Neruda discovers that labor is the driving instrument of history. Human labor is the materialization of culture from the Inca, Maya and Aztec civilizations to reformist capitalist states in the 1940s. Hence, Neruda valorizes the peasant and worker as the architects of Latin American history. In maintaining this, the poet refuses to accept as legitimate the division of labor and the privileging of intellectual over manual labor in capitalism. It follows that workers' economic and political power would be the basis of an egalitarian society.

This is a theme that he continues to develop in his three volumes of odes, *Odas elementales*, 1954 (*Elemental Odes*), *Nuevas odas elementales*, 1956 and *Tercer libro de las odas*, 1957. However, Neruda shifts the focus in the works from a historical-geographical panorama of Latin America, to a philosophical meditation on the productivity of nature and human beings, including an account of how the latter transforms the former into labor. So, in short verses and long poems, he dedicates odes to the atom or to the onion with the intent of learning more about the universe and nature, a learning process that we can appreciate as readers. While Neruda still concentrates on the central role that labor has to play in human society – seen for instance in "El hombre invisible" (The Invisible Man) – poetry's obligation is to attempt to write (a labor) history. The poet (the "hombre invisible" or "hombre sencillo") [the invisible or humble man] is a worker; he is not a privileged spokesperson for society, nor a high priest of culture. Most importantly, in the *Odas elementales*, to the chagrin of many (though not all) critics, the language is realist, it is tangible, it is readable. Few intellectuals and artists of any political persuasion in Latin America have been able to meditate philosophically through the medium of a language accessible to most people, but this is Neruda's great achievement in the *Odas*.

It is important to touch on one last work in Neruda's long list of poetic productions, which sets the tone for the rest of his books – even though almost every one of his works renews his world view and his poetic theory. As in the case of most Communists in the world, Neruda was deeply shaken by Khrushchev's revelation of the crimes committed during the Stalin regime in the Soviet Union. *Extravagario*, 1958 (*Extravagaria*), published two years after the Twentieth Party Congress, represents a notable change in the tone and themes in Neruda's poetic repertoire. Nature, time, death and solitude take center stage again in his poetry. The poet turns inward in an attempt to rediscover his youth: the fragility of human existence, the limitations of human knowledge, the tragically contradictory nature of society and history. Unlike his previous works, humor and questions also play a central role in *Extravagario*. Yet this is clearly a hiatus in his work, a time for rethinking and self-critiquing his Marxist beliefs while presenting the reader with a purview on his view of daily life and our own mortality.

GREG DAWES

Biography

Born Neftalí Ricardo Reyes Basoalto in Parral, Chile, 12 July 1904; Pablo Neruda became his legal name, 1946. Attended a school for boys in Temuco, 1910–20; Instituto Pedagógico, Santiago in the 1920s. Married María Antonieta Hagenaar in 1930 (separated 1936), one daughter. Lived with the Argentine painter Delia del Carril in 1930s and 1940s; she encouraged his interest in the politics of the Left. They married in 1943, but the marriage was not recognized in Chile, separated, 1955. Married the Chilean singer Matilde Urrutia in 1966. In Chilean consular and diplomatic service: consul in Rangoon, 1927, Colombo, 1928, Batavia, 1930, Singapore, 1931. This was a very depressing period of his life. Consul in Buenos Aires, 1933, Barcelona, 1933, Madrid, 1935–36; had to resign from this post because he sided with the Spanish

Republicans. As consul in Paris, 1939, helped Spanish refugees by re-settling them in Chile; Consul-General, Mexico City, 1940–43; elected to Chilean Senate as member of the Communist Party, 1945; attacked President González Videla in print, and was in exile after 1947; returned to Chile after the victory of the anti-Videla forces, 1952. After Salvador Allende was elected President in 1970, named Ambassador to France, 1971–72 (resigned because of ill health). Co-editor, with Manuel Altolaguirre, *Caballo Verde para la Poesía*, Spain, 1935–36, and *Aurora de Chile*, 1938. Member of the World Peace Council, from 1950 and President of the Union of Chilean Writers, 1957–73. Recipient of numerous awards including: National Literature Prize, 1945; Stalin Peace Prize, 1953; Viareggio-Versilia Prize for cultural understanding, 1967; Nobel Prize for Literature, 1971. Died of cancer on 23 September 1973. His death was probably accelerated by the Pinochet coup earlier that month.

Selected Works

Poetry
Crepusculario, Santiago de Chile: Claridad, 1923
Veinte poemas de amor y una canción desesperada, Santiago de Chile: Nascimento, 1924; as *Twenty Love Poems and a Song of Despair*, translated by W.S. Merwin, London: Jonathan Cape, 1969; New York: Grossman, 1971 [bilingual edition]
Anillos, Santiago de Chile: Nascimento, 1926
Tentativa del hombre infinito, Santiago de Chile: Nascimento, 1926
El hondero entusiasta, Santiago de Chile: Empresa Letras de Santiago, 1933
Residencia en la tierra (1925–1931), Santiago de Chile: Nascimento, 1933
Residencia en la tierra (1925–1935), Madrid: Cruz y Raya, 1935; as *Residence on Earth*, translated by Ángel Flores, Norfolk, Connecticut: New Directions, 1946; also translated by Donald D. Walsh, New York: New Directions, 1973; London: Souvenir Press, 1976
España en el corazón: himno a las glorias del pueblo en la guerra 1936–1937, Santiago de Chile: Ercilla, 1937
Tercera residencia, Buenos Aires: Losada, 1947
Canto general, Mexico City: Océano, 1950; as *Canto General*, translated by Jack Schmitt, Berkeley: University of California Press, 1991
Los versos del capitán: poemas de amor, privately printed, 1952; as *The Captain's Verses*, translated by Donald D. Walsh, New York: New Directions, 1972
Las uvas y el viento, Santiago de Chile: Nascimento, 1954
Odas elementales, Santiago de Chile: Nascimento, 1954; as *Elementary Odes*, translated by Carlos Lozano, New York: Massa, 1961; as *Elemental Odes*, translated by Margaret Sayers Peden, London: Libris, 1990
Nuevas odas elementales, Buenos Aires: Losada, 1956
Tercer libro de las ódas, Buenos Aires: Losada, 1957
Extravagario, Buenos Aires: Losada, 1958; as *Extravagaria*, translated by Alastair Reid, London: Jonathan Cape, 1972; New York: Farrar Straus and Giroux, 1974
Navegaciones y regresos, Buenos Aires: Losada, 1959
Cien sonetos de amor, Buenos Aires: Losada, 1960; as *One Hundred Love Sonnets*, translated by Stephen Tapscott, Austin: University of Texas Press, 1986 [bilingual edition]
Canción de gesta, Santiago de Chile: Ediciones Austral, 1960; as *Song of Protest*, translated by Miguel Algarín, New York: Morrow, 1976
Las piedras de Chile, Buenos Aires: Losada, 1960; as *Stones of Chile*, translated by Dennis Maloney, Fredonia, New York: White Pine Press, 1986
Cantos ceremoniales, Buenos Aires: Losada, 1960
Plenos poderes, Buenos Aires: Losada, 1962; as *Fully Empowered*, translated by Alastair Reid, New York: Farrar Straus and Giroux, 1975; London: Souvenir Press, 1976

Memorial de Isla Negra, 5 vols, Buenos Aires: Losada, 1964; as *Isla Negra: a Notebook*, translated by Alastair Reid, New York: Farrar Straus and Giroux, 1970; London: Souvenir Press, 1981 [bilingual edition]

Arte de pájaros, privately printed, 1966; as *Art of Birds*, translated by Jack Schmitt, Austin: University of Texas Press,1985

La casa de arena, Barcelona: Lumen, 1966; as *The House in the Sand: Prose Poems*, translated by Dennis Maloney and Clark M. Zlotchew, Minneapolis: Minnesota: Milkweed Editions, 1990

Las manos del día, Buenos Aires: Losada, 1968

Fin del mundo, Buenos Aires: Losada, 1969

Aún, Buenos Aires: Losada, 1969; as *Still Another Day*, translated by William O'Daly, Port Townsend, Washington: Copper Canyon Press, 1984

La espada encendida, Buenos Aires: Losada, 1970

Las piedras del cielo, Buenos Aires: Losada, 1970; as *Stones of the Skies*, translated by James Nolar, Port Townsend, Washington: Copper Canyon Press, 1987

Geografía infructuosa, Buenos Aires: Losada, 1972

Incitación al Nixoncidio y alabanza de la revolución chilena, Santiago de Chile: Quimantú, 1973; as *A Call for the Destruction of Nixon and Praise for the Chilean Revolution*, translated by Teresa Anderson, Cambridge, Massachusetts: West End Press, 1980

2000, Buenos Aires: Losada, 1974; as *2000*, translated by Richard Schaaf, Washington, DC: Azul, 1992 [bilingual edition]

El mar y las campanas, Buenos Aires: Losada, 1974; as *The Sea and the Bells*, translated by William O'Daly, Port Townsend, Washington: Copper Canyon Press, 1988

Elegía, Buenos Aires: Losada, 1974

El corazón amarillo, Buenos Aires: Losada, 1974

El libro de preguntas, Buenos Aires: Losada, 1974

Jardín de invierno, Buenos Aires: Losada, 1974; as *Winter Garden*, translated by William O'Daly, Port Townsend, Washington: Copper Canyon Press, 1986

La rosa separada, Buenos Aires: Losada, 1974; as *The Separate Rose*, translated by William O'Daly, Port Townsend, Washington: Copper Canyon Press, 1985

Defectos escogidos, Buenos Aires: Losada, 1974

El fin del viaje, Buenos Aires: Losada, 1982

Anthologies of Poetry in Translation

Selected Poems, translated by Ángel Flores, privately printed, 1944

Selected Poems, translated by Ben Belitt, New York: Grove Press, 1961

Early Poems, translated by David Ossman and Carlos B. Hagen, New York: New Rivers Press, 1969

A New Decade: Poems 1958–67, translated by Ben Belitt and Alastair Reed, New York: Grove Press, 1969

Five Decades: Poems 1925–1970, translated by Ben Belitt, New York: Grove Press, 1974

Late and Posthumous Poems 1968–1974, translated by Ben Belitt, New York: Grove Press, 1988

Play

Fulgor y muerte de Joaquín Murieta, Santiago de Chile: Zig-Zag, 1967; as *The Splendour and Death of Joaquín Murieta*, translated by Ben Belitt, New York: Farrar Straus and Giroux, 1966; London: Alcove Press, 1973

Other Writings

Comiendo en Hungría, in collaboration with Miguel Ángel Asturias, Barcelona: Lumen, 1969; as *Sentimental Journey around the Hungarian Cuisine*, translated by Barna Balogh, 1969 [poetry and illustrations]

Confieso que he vivido: memorias, Buenos Aires: Losada, 1974; as *Memoirs*, translated by Hardie St Martin, New York: Farrar Straus and Giroux, and London: Souvenir Press, 1977

Para nacer he nacido, Buenos Aires: Losada, 1977; as *Passions and Impressions*, translated by Margaret Sayers Peden, New York: Farrar Straus and Giroux, 1983

Compilations and Anthologies

Poesía política: discursos políticos, 2 vols, Santiago de Chile: Austral, 1953

Obras completas, edited by Margarita Aguirre, Alfonso M. Escudero and Hernán Loyola, 3 vols, Buenos Aires: Losada, 4th edition, 1973

Further Reading

Agosín, Marjorie, *Pablo Neruda*, Boston: Twayne, 1986

Anderson, David G., *On Elevating the Commonplace: a Structuralist Analysis of the "Odes" of Pablo Neruda*, Valencia: Albatros Hispanófila, 1987

Bizzaro, Salvatore, *Pablo Neruda: All Poets the Poet*, Metuchen, New Jersey: Scarecrow Press, 1979

De Costa, René, *The Poetry of Pablo Neruda*, Cambridge, Massachusetts: Harvard University Press, 1979

Durán, Manuel and Margery Safir, *Earth Tones: the Poetry of Pablo Neruda*, Bloomington: Indiana University Press, 1981

Felstiner, John, *Translating Neruda: the Way to Macchu Picchu*, Stanford, California: Stanford University Press, 1980

Perriam, Christopher, *The Late Poetry of Neruda*, Oxford: Dolphin Books, 1989

Poirot, Luis, *Pablo Neruda: Absence and Presence*, translated by Alastair Reid, New York: Norton, 1990

Reiss, Frank, *The Word and the Stone: Language and Imagery in Neruda's "Canto General,"* London: Oxford University Press, 1972

Rodríguez Monegal, Emir, *El viajero inmóvil: introducción a Pablo Neruda*, Buenos Aires: Losada, 1966

Rodríguez Monegal, Emir and Enrico Mario Santí (editors), *Pablo Neruda*, Madrid: Taurus, 1980

Santí, Enrico Mario, *Pablo Neruda: the Poetics of Prophecy*, Ithaca, New York: Cornell University Press, 1982

Teitelboim, Volodia, *Neruda: an Intimate Biography*, translated by Beverly J. DeLong-Tonelli, Austin: University of Texas Press, 1991

Bibliography

Woodbridge, Hensley C. and David S. Zubatsky, *Pablo Neruda: an Annotated Bibliography of Biography and Critical Studies*, New York: Garland, 1988

Alturas de Macchu Picchu

Canto II of Pablo Neruda's *Canto general*

"Alturas de Macchu Picchu" postulates, in a lengthy poem with twelve different functioning units or sections, a new conception of poetry in the Latin American context. In this new poetics the borderline traditionally dividing poetry from history and politics is effectively erased, so that poetry becomes yet another vehicle for acquiring knowledge about the world. Yet this position does not involve any exaltation of the place of poetry as a form of expression that is somehow more "pure" or privileged than others. On the contrary, after 1935, Neruda always associates poetry with other forms of human labor, especially manual labor. Manual work maintains a direct contact with nature and transforms it. From Neruda's Marxist point of view, labor is the foundation of human societies, and laborers are its architects. Ironically, the prevailing ideas of bourgeois revolutions – especially the French and American examples – are based on a fundamental belief in core human equality, yet capitalism produces equalities that give credence to the writings of the Enlightenment, but it also generates acute social and economic inequalities that contradict the rhetoric of the American and French Revolutions. Infused by Social Darwinist ideas, capitalism tends to portray the existing class differences and conflicts as something natural. In this way the economic benefits accrued by the capitalists at the expense of the working population, are deemed to be intrinsically part of human nature. Neruda's materialist philosophy and social analysis, expressed succinctly in "Alturas de Macchu Picchu," argues that Social Darwinism distorts human nature – which is always changing and open – on the level of social analysis so that the interests of the ruling class take precedent over those of working people, when the reverse should be true.

What makes Neruda's case particularly interesting, is that his poetry up to 1935, consists of a double movement. On the one hand, his underdeveloped poetic theory recorded his own individual misery due to social and economic alienation in the Orient. Following in the tracks of bourgeois aesthetics, the socio-historical factors that lead the poetic speaker to wallow in his solitude appear only as indirect causes. His creed, as it appears in section II, was: "mátala y agonízala con papel y con odio" (kill and agonize it with paper and hate). On the other hand, Neruda endeavors to record this alienating period in his life as vividly as possible. So it is that, paradoxically, his struggle with his own mortality, with the objectivity of time, and with his own social alienation provides the impetus for him to discover the materialist grounding of our existence as human beings:

> hundí la mano turbulenta y dulce
> en lo más genital de lo terrestre
> Puse la frente entre las olas profundas
> descendí como gota entre la paz sulfúrica
> y, como un ciego, regresé al jazmín
> de la gastada primavera.
>
> (Section I)

[I plunged my turbulent and sweet hand / into the most earthly reproductive organs / I placed my forehead among the deep waves / I descended like a water drop among the sulphuric peace / and, like a blind man, I returned to the jasmin / of the worn human spring.]

The speaker's senses serve as the guides to discover his place in nature and his own mortality. Yet, according to Neruda's account, from 1925 to 1935 particularly, he is blind because he carried out this ontological search while overlooking the decisive importance of human nature. Indeed, as he indicates at the end of sections II and V, this poetic theory and practice only enable him to seize a partial, masked purview of society. The protagonist perceives the effects of human suffering due to our mortality as a species, but he cannot discern the social factors that impede human flourishing (such as a core human equality).

However, section VI, signals a decisive moment in this poetic autobiography. Visiting the Incan ruins of Macchu Picchu in Peru allows Neruda to speculate about the direction of his poetry after 1935. It is by recognizing the central significance of manual labor in the construction of the ruins and of Incan civilization that Neruda begins to conceive his own traditionally intellectual labor – according to bourgeois society – as manual labor:

> Miro las vestiduras y las manos
> el vestigio del agua en la oquedad sonora
> la pared suavizada por el tacto de un rostro
> que miró con mis ojos las lámparas terrestres
> que aceitó con mis manos las desparecidas
> maderas: porque todo, ropaje, piel, vasijas
> palabras, vino, panes
> se fue, cayó a la tierra.
>
> (Section VI)

[I look at the garments and the hands / the vestige of water in the sonorous cavity / the wall smoothed by the touch of a face / that looked with my eyes at the earthly lamps / that greased with my hands the disappeared wood / because everything, clothing, skin, pottery / words, wine, bread, left, fell to the earth.]

We can benefit from two decisive insights here. First, the speaker observes and reflects on the grandeur of this labor (the ruins), and not on the destruction wrought by the Spanish conquest of the Incan empire. He identifies himself and confuses his own destiny with the vanquished, not the conquerors (thus, he states that an Incan "*miró* con *mis* ojos" [looked with *my* eyes]). Second, the Incans' manual labor leaves traces of their history on the product of their labor. Engraved with the Inca's own social authorship, the architecture, becomes ruins due to the conquest. These structures are the social and the sensual (i.e., of the senses) result of their work. Thus, in examining this architectural landscape, Neruda pays homage to the Inca laborers (the slave, the serf, the miserable one, as he underscores it in section X) and not to the Inca monarchy.

As a vital residue of the Inca civilization, the ruins, fruit of Inca labor, have their own forgotten version of history to tell. The shape, surface, and texture of the stones, as well as their architectural arrangement, attest to the mores and values of Inca civilization and to the labor of their authors. In spite of the existence of a nobility during the Inca empire, Neruda notes that the society was collective in its orientation: "la ciudad como un vaso se levantó en las manos / de todos" (section VII) (the city like a cup was raised in the hands of all) and generally egalitarian when compared to other social systems. The Spanish conquerors thought that they had erased Inca history by subjugating and destroying the fabric of their civilization and by murdering its inhabitants and dismantling its cities. However, Neruda makes it clear that the regenerating vestiges of this destruction contain their own history, embodied in Machu Picchu. While the vanquished appear to be silenced, Neruda suggests in section VIII that, if one investigates further, there is an Inca version of history to be told if one can interpret the socio-historical and anthropological signs. In sections VIII through XII the poet pleads with Incas to reveal to him this buried history, a history which Neruda reconstructs in the rest of the *Canto general* as a complex and conflictive struggle between classes, individual destinies within the social context, and developed and underdeveloped nations. Re-examining Inca civilization from the point of view of the oppressed enables him to rewrite the central struggles in Latin American history.

This meditation on history is also a reflection on poetry. As regards the form, the poet's method at this stage of his work is not unlike that prior to 1936. Conscious empiricism continues to be the source for discoveries about human nature. However, from 1936 on, the content of Neruda's poetry reflects his capacity to encompass and approximate our knowledge in various fields. On the basis of his own reading as well as his personal and political experience, he is able to adduce various central characteristics about the human species, society (specifically capitalism), history, and universal laws. This method allows Neruda to analyze the internal relations that exist among these fields of human knowledge.

Neruda's poetics also parts company with many of his contemporaries by acting as a vessel for those who create value in capitalism: the laborers. In section XII of "Alturas de Macchu Picchu," Neruda recuperates and reconstructs a history of Inca civilization based on the works and lives of the oppressed. This he does with inordinate interest in objective and subjective detail: "contadme todo, cadena a cadena, / eslabón a eslabón, y paso a paso" (tell me everything, chain by chain, link by link, and step by step). The poet's own empowerment, then, does not come, as it does in bourgeois society, from his favored class (and social) position, in which he attempts to instruct the "masses" on societal and moral values. Rather, the poet like any other worker, attempts to learn from his fellow workers, from their transformation and construction of history. Challenging the notion of the division of labor, Neruda pleads with the Incas to "habladme toda esta larga noche / como si yo estuviera con vosotros anclado" (speak to me all this long night / as if I were anchored with you).

GREG DAWES

Editions
First edition: *Canto general*, Mexico City: Océano, 1950
Translation: *The Heights of Macchu Picchu*, by John Felstiner, in his *Translating Neruda: the Way to Macchu Picchu*, Stanford, California: Stanford University Press, 1980 [bilingual edition]

Further Reading
Goic, Cedomil, "Alturas de Macchu Picchu," in *Pablo Neruda*, edited by Emir Rodríguez Monegal and Enrico Mario Santí, Madrid: Taurus, 1980
Yurkievich, Saúl, "Mito e Historia," in *Pablo Neruda*, edited by Emir Rodríguez Monegal and Enrico Mario Santí, Madrid: Taurus, 1980

Nicaragua

19th- and 20th-Century Prose and Poetry

In the 19th and 20th centuries – arguably up to 1979 – Nicaragua's sovereignty was constantly in jeopardy due to the presence of British and American financial and strategic interests. Largely because of those interests Nicaragua was an underpopulated, underproductive agricultural nation dominated by oligarchies. Compared to other Central American countries it suffered from a lack of specialization and investment concentrated in agricultural products. The persistent vying for political power that took place between León liberals and Granada conservatives reflected the interests of town versus country to be sure, but the bourgeoisie had not managed to develop fully as a class and, consequently, always needed to contest the power of the landowners. In this context the arts suffered from unproduction. Until the last fifteen years, poetry, a concise and brief literary form compared to other genres, was the main arena of cultural activity.

Paradoxically, 19th-century Nicaraguan literature was dominated by one of Latin America's most heralded poets of this period, Rubén Darío (1867–1916). Having grown up in one of the most underdeveloped countries in Latin America, this well-traveled poet would become the spokesperson for the *modernista* literary movement, which had to grapple with the impact of European and US imperialism in the hemisphere. Where the Romantic and Neoromantic poets had chosen to emulate European literary form and content in the mid- to late 19th century, Darío wanted to imitate Symbolist and Parnassian poetry to perfection and then create a uniquely Latin American literary identity.

His poetic works can be judged as contradictory attempts to come to grips with the onslaught of modernity which, for Darío, can be both attractive and inhumane. Thus, in "A Roosevelt," from *Cantos de vida y esperanza*, 1905 [Songs of Life and Hope], he assailed the US version of modernity which places economic gain above all else. By meddling in Latin American affairs North Americans, he charged, unite the "cult of Hercules with the cult of Mammon." Yet in this and other cases, Darío upholds anachronistic values – the traditional beliefs of Catholicism for instance – in the face of US capitalist industrialization.

Darío turned to spirituality to defend his values against the advance of modernity in the hemisphere. Poetry protects its own territory from the sciences by becoming self-reflexive, by highlighting the formal specificities of the genre for fear that the content will be invaded by the new. However, Darío distinguished between European and US influence. The United States was "Primitive and modern, simple and complicated" because of its lack of history – relative to Europe and Latin America – and its one-dimensional pragmatism which did not valorize religion and art. Unlike the United States, Darío maintained, France had found a place for the artist. He was particularly influenced by transcendental symbolism – Mallarmé, Valéry and Verlaine – precisely because it seemed to unite religious beliefs with art and because, in so doing, it sidestepped the fundamental and stark realities of industrialization.

Darío's first major work, written in a Europeanized and relatively modern Chile, *Azul*, 1888 [Blue], established a similar dichotomy between daily life and the realm of art. In "El velo de la reina Mab" [Queen Mab's Veil] he interweaves scenes of various artisans/artists who attempt to persuade Queen Mab of their virtue, a virtue which is directly connected to their insatiable search for the Ideal. In spite of its attempt to shun everyday life, the very purpose of the story arises from the marginal status art occupied at the turn of the century in Latin America. If the artist was unable to find a wealthy patron, then he was forced to work as a journalist and eek out a living. For all its parading of the Classical tradition and the virtues of sculpture, painting, music, the narration returns to Darío's dilemma in the late 1900s: "Yo escribiría algo inmortal; mas me abruma un porvenir de miseria y de hambre" (I would write something immortal; but a future of hunger and misery overwhelms me).

The next major literary period was the "vanguardia" (avant-garde), which included José Coronel Urtecho (1906–), Manolo Cuadra (1907–57), Joaquín Zavala Urtecho (1910–71), Pablo Antonio Cuadra (1912–), Luis Alberto Cabrales (1901–74), Luis Downing (1914–) and Joaquín Pasos (1914–47). All were from oligarchical families living in Granada who had held conservative political convictions. Ultra-nationalist and firmly Catholic, the *vanguardistas* both followed in the footsteps of and took issue with Rubén Darío's work. They shared his general belief in the primary importance of art – which, here too, attained a religious aura – and in the urgency of modernization. But they claimed to break with Darío's anachronistic ideas: the reliance on Classical myths, precious images and monarchist ideas. In its place one vanguardist tendency, led by Pablo Antonio Cuadra – whose *Poemas nicaragüenses*, 1934 [Nicaraguan Poems] was this movement's most salient work – attempted to incorporate popular songs, lyrics, legends and indigenous history into the conversational poetry they wrote. Influenced by the New American Poetry and by the French poets Apollinaire, Paul Claudel and Jules Supervielle, another tendency, led principally by Coronel Urtecho and Pasos, practiced a type of Futurist and Dadaist poetry in which free verse was the formal vehicle. Both currents in this vanguard, however, were generally united in their political and aesthetic persuasions. They wanted to express "Nicaraguanness" through Catholic faith and Castilian language. While the indigenous past was something they cherished, they also fully accepted their Spanish heritage.

The *vanguardistas* felt that the bourgeoisie could be the socio-economic agent of Nicaraguan development, but its anachronistic ideas and values held it back. Since for the members of this group, modernization necessarily involved a spiritual or ethical transformation as well – where art was seen as playing a fundamental role – they ridiculed the bourgoisie's pecuniary obsession, its individualism, apathy and anti-intel-lectualism. At various moments their political ideology wavered between fascism, monarchism and populism (where the model was, ironically, Augusto Sandino's national liberation movement during the US occupation of Nicaragua). With very few exceptions the vanguardista members ended up supporting Somoza García's rise to power as a military figure and later as the actual or *de facto* dictator of Nicaragua from 1936 to 1956.

Pablo Antonio Cuadra would go on to become one of Nicaragua's most revered poets and most imposing cultural figures. Having held key posts on Nicaragua's most important mainstream newspaper, *La Prensa* [The Press] and on the editorial board of *El pez y la serpiente* [The Fish and the Serpent] – a significant publishing house for creating writing – Cuadra has had more of an impact on Nicaraguan literati than any other poet except Ernesto Cardenal. As his *Poemas nicaragüenses* attest, in traveling abroad Cuadra seemed to lose a sense of himself in the geographical and historical differences that he encountered. His search for meaning continued in *Canto temporal*, 1943 [Temporal Song], written, ironically when Cuadra had become a partisan of fascism in Europe and Central America. Yet the themes that fill this book of poetry point to the isolation and despair of the speaker. He emerged out of this crisis by becoming more devoutly Catholic. *Libro de horas*, 1946 [Book of Hours] expressed his renewed religious convictions very well. *Canto temporal* had already signaled his commitment to traditional Christian values, but *Libro de horas* clearly marked his return to morals and to a religious conception of art: the poet becomes a prophetic figure.

In the next decade Cuadra published three works of poetry. *Poemas con un crespúsculo a cuestas*, 1949 [Poems with Dusk on My Back] was even more introspective and self-congratulatory than his previous books. In poems like "Pablo y Antonio" he gave primacy to a prophetic view of the poet and his creation once again, while exalting Catholic moral values. Written coterminously with Ernesto Cardenal's *Epigramas*, Cuadra's book by the same title, composed between 1957 and 1963, also critiques the authoritarianism of the Somoza dictatorship. However, Cuadra's most significant work during the 1950s and 1960s is *El jaguar y la luna*, 1958 (*The Jaguar and the Moon*). Based on extensive research and reading on the ancient Central American Maya and Aztec mythology and history, this book recovers these cultural roots while referring to then contemporary socio-political matters, such as the ruthlessness of the military dictatorship. In *Cantos de Cifar y del mar dulce*, 1969 (*Songs of Cifar and the Sweet Sea*) the poet relies on the epic tradition as the basis of his poetry, expressing himself through *carpe diem*, political and metapoetical themes. It is perhaps *Esos rostros que asoman en la multitud*, 1964 [Those Faces that Become Visible in the Crowd] that constituted Cuadra's most committed efforts to make popular songs, lyrics, and stories part of his poetic corpus while taking a firmer stand against the United States' support of the Somoza regime. It marks most clearly a transformation in his political beliefs: he was then an ardent supporter of liberalism and an opponent of US imperialism. *Siete árboles contra el atardecer*, 1977 [Seven Trees against the Sunset] revisited many of the themes brought up in *Esos rostros*. Written during a much more intense socio-political time, when the Sandinista National

Liberation Front (FSLN) was waging guerrilla warfare against the Somoza regime, this work deepens Cuadra's historical research into the ancient Maya seeds of liberation. Like *El jaguar y la luna*, it interweaves the ancient struggles for social justice with those mapped out in Nicaragua just prior to the Revolution of 1979. By contrast, *Tun – la ronda del año*, 1988 [Tun – as the Year Passes], pointed to his adherence to liberalism and his disenchantment with the revolutionary Sandinista government. The poet appears as a messianic figure, and art the domain from which to critique society's ills. Poetry itself surfaces from nature in a mysterious way and serves as the area in which a "democratic" alternative to "authoritarianism" can be elaborated.

Ernesto Cardenal (1925–), Carlos Martínez Rivas (1924–) and Ernesto Mejía Sánchez (1923–85), or the generation of the 1940s, perhaps had the most significant impact on Latin American literature of any Nicaraguan literary figures since Rubén Darío. With García Somoza still in power during this period, the economic modernization that had taken place had benefited the oligarchy and the bourgeoisie while creating little space or hope for culture. Influenced by periods spent in Europe, this generation either avoided the problems dictatorship posed, or they critiqued it. Martínez Rivas composed his *La insurrección solitaria*, 1953 [Solitary Insurrection] in Paris, where he visited Surrealists, became associated with Octavio Paz and became engulfed in a type of Christian existentialism. In the post-World War II era of despair, in which he perceived the disappearance of the individual, the poet turned to Christianity as the only redeeming hope. Other-worldly belief, which connects with Darío's Platonism, pervades this poetry. When it comes into contact with daily life – which becomes a penance – it searches out contemplative perfection and purity in the sexist image of "woman."

Working in the late 1940s Mejía Sánchez began to develop very intense and brief poetic poems. *La carne contigua*, 1948 [Contiguous Flesh] dealt with the family and its relation to society, principally via the question of incest. Several works in the 1950s, *La impureza* [Impurity], written in 1950, published in 1972; *El retorno*, 1950 [The Return], and *Contemplaciones europeas*, 1957 [European Contemplations] showed the poet's mastery of word play and verbal allusions while underscoring such themes as solitude, purity, good and evil, the importance of human love, the crucifixion, the passage of time, the joy of life and poetry itself. Mejía Sánchez took a moral stance in the face of social injustice in his poetry and personally when he opposed the Somoza dictatorship in the 1950s.

Regarded as one of Latin America's outstanding poets, Cardenal wrote a more socially committed poetry at around the same historical period. He studied at Columbia University in New York and later became a Trappist monk in Gethsemani, Kentucky, where his life changed dramatically thanks to Thomas Merton, an influential theologian in the 1960s who was his mentor in the monastery. In his *Epigramas* (1961), Cardenal employed this concise Roman poetic form to denounce the dictatorship of Somoza Debayle and to write love poems. This book is highlighted by ingenious word play and syntactical inversions which help underscore the political content.

Gethsemani, Kentucky (1960) and *Salmos*, 1964 (*Psalms*), are products of Cardenal's religious conversion. Consisting of a series of short and dense poems, the first work counterposes Trappist collective life to life under multinational capitalism, underlining the waste, competition and alienation that the system produces for most of the world's inhabitants. *Psalms* marks one further step toward left-wing politics and Liberation Theology. Having lived with Camilo Torres in Colombia and spent time in Cuernavaca, Mexico – both havens for radical theology during these years – Cardenal came to recognize more clearly the affinities between Christianity and socialism. In *El estrecho dudoso*, 1966 (*The Doubtful Strait*) and *Homenaje a los indios americanos*, 1969 (*Homage to the American Indians*), Cardenal presents well-documented and researched material in narrative poems. Both books could be seen as anthropological, historical, theological and poetic tracts on native American life before and after the conquest. A significant advance in Cardenal's thinking is evidenced in *Canto nacional*, 1973 [National Song]. Using various film techniques, the poet interlaces his texts with references to history, politics, and plant and animal life in order to trace the struggle against the Somoza dictatorship and for national (and socialist) liberation in Nicaragua.

After a long period of belief in non-violence, the Christian base community Cardenal helped found, Solentiname, became involved in the national liberation struggle, which led to the assassination of several of the community's members and the destruction of the community. In 1979 when the Sandinista popular Revolution triumphed, Cardenal was made Minister of Culture. His own poetic production suffered somewhat, but popular poetry workshops, in which peasants, workers and soldiers participated sprung up all over revolutionary Nicaragua with the support of the Ministry of Culture. A major democratization of the political, economic and cultural realms took place during these years, especially between 1979 and 1988.

In the meantime Cardenal published a book of short poems, *Vuelos de victoria*, 1984 (*Flights of Victory*), which interweaves revolutionary, theological and evolutionary ideas. Basing his poetry on scrupulous scientific research, and collaborating his radical reading of the Bible with his Marxist understanding of political and economic systems, *Flights of Victory* could be regarded as the prelude to Cardenal's latest masterpiece, *Cántico cósmico*, 1989 (*Cosmic Canticle*), which explores these issues in a complex 600-page epic poem. In contrast to the notorious division between science and poetry, where critics and poets alike consider poetry to be the realm of subjectivity and irrationalism in opposition to the "objective rationality" of the sciences, Cardenal breaks down the barriers between these two spheres of human knowledge much as he had done with history and poetry.

Relegated to a marginal status in literary circles prior to the Sandinista Revolution in spite of the growth and size of the women's movement in Nicaragua, works published by women dramatically increased in number after 1979. Two very different yet indispensible forerunners to the literary production during the Revolution are Michele Najlis (1946–) and Ana Ilce Gómez (1945–). Najlis's *El viento armado*, 1969 [The Armed Wind] was composed in the midst of the struggle against the Somoza regime and US imperialism. Following the "personal politics" of the 1960s, Najlis suggested that individual liberation enables one to become committed to other socio-political causes. Since 1969, Najlis has published *Augurios*, 1981 [Augury], a didactic social poetry which reflects on the impact of the Revolution, and *Ars combinatoria* (1988), which is a highly experimental, heterogeneous poetic text that combines fables, short narratives and prose.

A poet of equal stature, but less explicitly political, Ana Ilce Gómez gained the immediate respect of critics and poets with the publication of *Las ceremonias del silencio*, 1975 [The Silent Ceremonies]. As a subtle meditation on sexism and the exploitation of women in patriarchal Nicaragua – a reading which seems to escape every male critic and poet – *Las ceremonias del silencio* documents the secondary status that women were and are relegated to in Nicaragua. Women reproduce socially (housework) and biologically but this is not judged by patriarchy to be essential, socially vital work. Ilce attacks this sexism in her haunting portraits of alienated women who can only find emptiness when they search for social recognition or family love.

The thematic traces of the poetry of Najlis and Ilce can be identified in the poetic and narrative works of Gioconda Belli (1948–), although Belli writes more openly about and poeticizes women's sexuality. Belli's first book of poetry, *Sobre la grama*, 1974 [On the Grass] represents the hypocrisy of male sexism in Nicaragua. In 1978 Belli won the Casa de las Américas poetry prize for *Línea de fuego* [Line of Fire], which made a more explicit link between sexual liberation and Sandinista political beliefs. These poems make public – for the first time in verse – the pleasures of sex and eroticism from a woman's point of view; the personal anguish she felt due to the political repression and its effect on her family; and the manner in which her own "individual" stances unite with her Sandinista populist socialism. These two themes are even more successfully intertwined in *De la costilla de Eva*, 1987 (*From Eve's Rib*). Here too the reader encounters physical descriptions of love scenes from a woman's vantage point. But Belli also denounces US-sponsored atrocities in Nicaragua with a socially justified moralism. Since 1987, Belli has dedicated herself completely to writing novels. *La mujer habitada*, 1988 (*The Inhabited Woman*), deals with the participation of women in the armed struggle in the years leading up to the Revolution. Lavinia, the protagonist, breaks out of the role traditionally assigned to wives and lovers of guerrillas by joining and participating in the organization. Belli's second novel, *Sofía de los presagios*, 1990 [Sophia of the Presages], is more liberal feminist in approach. The protagonist is a gypsy adopted by a family of mixed class background who marries a bourgeois traditionalist who expects her to fulfil the conventional gender roles of reproduction and housework. Sofía rebels against this status by using contraceptives to prevent childbirth and by falling in love with another man. After her father passes away, Sofía inherits his money and becomes a landowner in her own right.

The other principal tendency in women's poetry today is led by Daisy Zamora (1950–). Zamora's testimonial poetry critiques patriarchal institutions and gender relations within the workplace. Using irony and parody as critical realist tools, her poetry denounces the sexual division of labor, patriarchal insistence on reproduction, as well as the physical subjugation of women in Nicaragua. Her second and third books of poetry are more mature and provocative than *La violenta espuma*,

1981 [The Violent Foam], Zamora's first work. *En limpio se escribe la vida*, 1988 (*Clean Slate*), consists of a series of vignettes on the working conditions of waitresses, housewives, seamstresses and the like. In these conversational, realist poems she depicts women as they are working – as they are being physically exploited. Zamora particularly assails the exploitation of women in familial relations. In Zamora's autobiographical meditations on familial and gender relations in *A cada quien la vida*, 1994 (*Life for Each*), she critiques the submissiveness, passivity and traditional "mothering" of women of her own and her mother's generation as well as the objectification of women as objects of pleasure and beauty under Sandinismo and under the current capitalist system in Nicaragua.

In the last decade the novel has become the second most important genre in Nicaragua. The most distinguished novelist, short-story writer and essayist is Sergio Ramírez (1942–). *¿Te dió miedo la sangre?* 1983 (*To Bury Our Fathers*) is a rewriting of Nicaraguan history under the first years of the Somoza dictatorship. Told through six intertextual stories narrated in the first-person, this novel attempts to represent the political views of various sectors of the national population. Ramírez's techniques create a narrative, class and political distance between the people and the semi-oligarchical Somoza dictatorship. His most ambitious novel, *Castigo divino*, 1988 [Divine Punishment], is a historical novel based on meticulous documentation of bourgeois life in León in the 1930s. Centered on an unusual crime, Ramírez aims to show the hypocritical bourgeois reaction that it provoked.

As an outgrowth of the guerrilla struggles in the 1960s and 1970s, Nicaragua, perhaps because of the success of the Sandinista revolution, has won fame in the Americas and Europe for its testimonial literature. Here we can mention only the most renowned narratives. Omar Cabezas's *La montaña es algo más que una inmensa estepa verde*, 1982 (*Fire from the Mountain*), is a first-person narrative of a middle-class university student – Cabezas himself – who becomes involved with the guerrillas, first on campus, and then in the jungles of Nicaragua. The mountain, symbol of Sandino's struggle against the US military presence and national sovereignty, becomes the home for rethinking national identity and for understanding revolutionary consciousness more fully. In *Canción de amor para los hombres*, 1988 [A Song of Love for All], Cabezas describes in detail the everyday life of the guerrillas during the revolutionary struggle. Whereas *La montaña es algo más que una inmensa estepa verde* had been almost the equivalent of a lengthy news dispatch, his second work is a more conscious reflection on the significance of this period of his life some nine years after the Revolution proved victorious.

Lastly, Tomás Borge's *La paciente impaciencia*, 1989 (*The Patient Impatience*), which won the Casa de las Américas prize for testimonial literature, should probably be considered more strictly as an autobiography, published some ten years after the Revolution. As in the case of Cabezas, by this stage Borge has had the time to reflect on his experiences in jail, in the armed struggle, and in his capacity as a major leader of the revolutionary government, which he narrates in a realist and poetic discourse.

GREG DAWES

Further Reading

Arellano, Jorge Eduardo, "Ocho poetas mayores de Nicaragua: notas críticas," *Cuadernos Hispanoamericanos* 14 (1985)

_____ "El movimiento nicaragüense de vanguardia," *Cuadernos Hispanoamericanos* 468 (1989)

Beverley, John and Marc Zimmerman, *Literature and Politics in the Central American Revolutions*, Austin: University of Texas Press, 1990

Craven, David, *The New Concept of Art and Popular Culture in Nicaragua since the Revolution in 1979*, Lampeter, Wales: Edwin Mellen Press, 1989

Hodges, Donald, *The Intellectual Foundations of the Nicaraguan Revolution*, Austin: University of Texas Press, 1986

Oviedo, José Miguel (editor), *Musas en guerra. Poesía, arte y cultura en la nueva Nicaragua (1974–1986)*, Mexico City: Joaquín Mortiz, 1987

Pailler, Claire, *Mitos primordiales y poesía fundadora en América Central*, Paris: Editions du Centre Nationale de la Recherche Scientifique, 1989 [Contains four chapters on Nicaraguan poetry]

Verani, Hugo J., "Manifiestos de la vanguardia en Nicaragua," *Revista de Crítica Literaria Latinamericana*, vol. 8/15 (1982)

White, Steven F., *Culture and Politics in Nicaragua: Testimonies of Poets and Writers*, New York: Lumen Books, 1986

_____ *Modern Nicaraguan Poetry: Dialogues with France and the United States*, Lewisburg, Pennsylvania: Bucknell University Press, and London: Associated University Presses, 1993

Anthologies

White, Steven F. (editor), *Poets of Nicaragua: a Bilingual Anthology 1918–1979*, Greensboro, North Carolina: Unicorn Press, 1982

Special Issues of Journals

Revista Iberoamericana 157 (October–December 1991)

Rafael Núñez 1825–1894

Colombian poet, journalist and statesman

Born in the Caribbean city of Cartagena, Rafael Núñez was a popular, often imitated poet of his time. He was also a leading politician, first in the Liberal Party then, toward the end of his life, a staunch defender of conservative causes. As was often the case at the time, Núñez began his literary career as a journalist. His newspaper columns and articles are among his best writing, especially those that deal with literary and cultural topics. However, Núñez's concerns were eclectic and typical of public figures, ranging broadly over politics, economics, sociology and literature. His periods of service as consul in Liverpool and Le Havre exposed him to liberal ideas and ideals that informed his work as journalist and publicist. His *Ensayos de crítica social*, 1860–74 [Essays on Social Criticism] and *Reforma política en Colombia*, 1885 [Political Reform in Colombia] were very influential, as was his essay *La crisis económica*, 1886 [The Economic Crisis]. Núñez wrote for several Colombian newspapers as well as for *El Nacional* of Lima and *El Continental* of New York. Throughout his life he contributed poems to various magazines and newpapers both in the Americas and in Europe. The works were gathered in one volume, *Poesías*, and published by Hachette in Paris (1889). This is the only authorized edition of his poetry.

Núñez's early poetry is characterized by philosophical search and profound indecision as reflected in his famous poem "Que sais je?" [What Do I Know?] in which the religious implications of 19th-century Positivism clash with the certainties of Roman Catholicism. In later years Núñez embraced orthodox Catholicism and was recognized by Pope Leo XIII, who considered him one of the most influential members of the Church in America.

Much of Núñez's poetry is based on the romance of love and the comfort it offers in times of conflict. His aesthetics and style show him to be a late adherent of the Romantic movement; as such his poetry lacks innovation and is quite derivative. While the sincerity of his emotions is not doubted, modern critics regularly remark on the lack of technical virtuosity that afflicts his work. Rafael Maya, for instance, calls his poetry "Romanticism of the first type: very ardent as a feeling but somehow rudimentary in its expression."

Although influential and imitated, Núñez was not a skilled poet and today his literary fame rests chiefly on the fact that he wrote the lyrics to a march that subsequently became the national anthem of Colombia. The text of the "Himno Nacional" [National Anthem] is a symbolic expression of an a-historical struggle for ideological dominance in the context of the "Regeneración," the name given by historians to the violent conservative takeover in 1885–86, of which the then-conservative Núñez was the leader. Military victory is the overarching theme of the anthem: this motif is presented on several referential levels (battles in Greece, the War of Independence against Spain earlier in the century), but no reference is made to the immediate violent events which gave rise to the poem. It does not, for example, mention the word "Colombia" (or its earlier, colonial version, "Nueva Granada"), a clear indication that Núñez sought to provide the text with an a-historic immanence thereby giving the anthem a meaning that transcends mere partisanship. The hymn is also an effective vehicle for the glorification of Simón Bolívar as father of the country, the hero who defeated the powerful Spanish army and vanquished nature, here represented by the mighty Andean mountains.

In politics Núñez was a man to be reckoned with. He was president on several occasions (1880–82, 1884–86 and 1887–94), with the notorious Conservative revisionist Marco Antonio Caro (himself a poet) as his vice-president. In matters of literary aesthetics, Núñez shows indifference – if not outright hostility – to innovation. He professed disgust for the budding Spanish American *Modernismo*. Nevertheless, Rubén Darío – the recognized father of *Modernismo* – and José Asunción Silva, were among his protegés. Darío visited him in 1892. Núñez arranged for Darío to be appointed Colombian Consul General in Buenos Aires, a position that was handsomely paid and enabled Darío to visit New York and his beloved France for the first time.

Núñez's literary work, vastly outdated by the beginning of the *modernista* movement, is none the less a significant example of the prevalence of written culture over orality in the mainstream culture of 19th-century Colombia. More important, however, is that his poetry, together with Caro's, remains a prime example of the drastic denial both of *Modernismo* and modernity in Colombia in the second half of the 19th century, and as such, it contributed to make Colombia a nation without a literary avant-garde.

GILBERTO GÓMEZ OCAMPO

Biography

Born in Cartagena, Colombia, 28 September 1825. Doctor of law; practised law for 20 years. Journalist for several Colombian newspapers, and contributed to *El Nacional* (Lima), and *El Continental* (New York). Politician, initially in the Liberal Party, but towards the end of his life supported more conservative program. Secretary of State during the government of Tomás Cipriano de Mosquera. Consul, Le Havre, and Liverpool, England, in the 1860s. Returned to Colombia in 1874. Elected President of Colombia, 1880–82, 1884–86, and 1887–94. Responsible for Constitution of 1886 which restored power of Catholic Church. Died in Cartagena, 18 September 1894.

Selected Works

Political Writings

Arreglo de las deudas flotantes, de tesorería, Bogotá: Imprenta del Estado, 1856
Ensayos de crítica social, Rouen: Cagniard, 1874
¡Alocución bolivarense! Los enemigos de toda moral y de todo sano principio, Cartagena: Imprenta de J.P. Durán, 1885
Reforma política en Colombia, Bogotá: Imprenta La Luz, 1885
Escritos políticos, edited by Gonzalo España, Bogotá: El Áncora Editores, 1986

Compilations and Anthologies

Poesías, Bogotá: Imprenta La Luz, 1885
Poesías de Rafael Núñez, Paris: Hachette, 1889
Los mejores artículos de Rafael Núñez, Bogotá: Minerva, 1936 [prose]
Poesías, Cartagena: Dirección de Educación Pública de Bolívar, 1946

Further Reading

Miramón, Alberto, *La angustia creadora en Núñez y Pombo*, Bogotá: Caro y Cuervo, 1975

O

Silvina Ocampo 1903(?)–1993

Argentine prose writer, poet and literary translator

Silvina Ocampo is one of the Latin American masters of the grotesque, along with Virgilio Piñera in Cuba and Felisberto Hernández in Uruguay. Her stories and some of her poems tell of a world upside down – the transvestite saint Teodora in the 1984 book of poems *Breve santoral* [Short Book of Saints], the children who build a world to their measure in the story "La raza inextinguible" [The Invincible Race] – a world where extreme acts of cruelty express love, where the finding of lost possessions becomes the source of disquieting misfortune, where a character's knowledge of the future is interpreted by others as a blatant lack of sensitivity.

Ocampo's current reputation rests largely on two collections of stories, *La furia*, 1959 [The Fury], and *Las invitadas*, 1961 [The Guests]. Her first book of stories, though, dates from 1937: *Viaje olvidado* [Forgotten Journey] consists of impressionistic stories about childhood, told from a less harrowing point of view than that of the later collections (it earned a rather quizzical review in *Sur* from her sister Victoria). Her last two books of stories, *Y así sucesivamente*, 1987 [And So On], and *Cornelia frente al espejo*, 1988 [Cornelia in the Mirror], are strange but less violent than the stories of *La furia* and *Las invitadas*.

The title story of *La furia* is typical of the core of Ocampo's writing. A man is writing a memoir of the events that led to his incarceration for the murder of a little boy named Cintito. He murdered the boy for refusing to stop beating on a toy drum in a place where noise of this kind was most unwelcome – the hotel with rooms rented by the hour where the narrator had taken Winifred, Cintito's nursemaid. Winifred abandons the narrator with the boy after telling him the terrifying story of her life, especially of the incidents that culminated years before in the death of Winifred's best friend, Lavinia, burned to death during a ceremony where the two little girls were dressed up as angels. Winifred's love for Lavinia was a cruel love: to "cure" her of her irrational fears she subjected her to ever more drastic frights, and there is every reason to assume that Winifred deliberately set Lavinia's costume on fire. When the narrator objects that Winifred was cruel to Lavinia, Winifred replies that she will be cruel to him too, a statement chilling in its accuracy.

Another story from the same collection, "La casa de los relojes" [The Clock House], is equally perverse. Couched as the composition of a schoolboy writing to his teacher about "what I did in my summer vacation," the boy's memoir begins with swimming and other adventures, to culminate in the story of an unforgettable party. Wenceslao the watch repairman, who lives in a shack erected on the flat roof of the narrator's building, is a hunchback not much accustomed to society, and he sheepishly appears at the baptismal party in a rumpled suit. One of the neighbours, the co-owner of a laundry and by now rather drunk, offers to press Wenceslao's suit. When they get to the laundry, the offer to press the suit turns into an offer to press the suit while Wenceslao is wearing it, thus pressing the deformity of the back also. Days later the boy purports not to fully understand what he has seen, and tells his teacher that his mother has told him simply that Wenceslao "went away." The horror of the story is deftly conveyed through the use of an seemingly innocent narrator.

"Tales eran sus rostros" [Thus Were Their Faces], the first story in *Las invitadas*, turns from grand guignol to the terror of the sacred. This is the story of secret communication among schoolchildren identified late in the story as deaf mutes, and of their teachers' efforts to capture their secret. When the children throw themselves (or fall accidentally) from an airplane, one of the teachers sees that they have sprouted wings. A comment by the narrator provides a poetics of the story: "En realidad no se sabe si era horrible y se volvía hermoso, o si era hermoso y se volvía horrible" (In reality, we don't know whether it was horrible and then became beautiful, or whether it was beautiful and became horrible). The uncertainty shared by the teachers and the narrator as to the nature of the event has to do with a perceived contradiction between the categories of "beauty" and "horror," which in Ocampo's work seem more to imply each other than to represent mutually exclusive semantic fields.

Ocampo's poetry plays on the same contradictory nature of experience. In the poetic sequence "Los árboles de Buenos Aires" [The Trees of Buenos Aires] in *Amarillo celeste*, 1972 [Sky-Yellow], the trees are simultaneously innocent and wise and lascivious and friendly and frightening. The saints' lives retold in *Breve santoral,* similarly, are full of unresolved tensions. Santa Teodora, for instance, dresses as a man and becomes a monk, only to be accused falsely of fathering a child. Unwilling to defend herself against the unjust accusation, her saintliness is revealed only upon her death, when her body is being washed and her female nature is revealed. It is fitting that Ocampo's book of religious poems (illustrated with Norah Borges's trademark angels) should reveal the story of a transvestite saint.

Among Ocampo's less-known works are a detective novel she wrote in collaboration with her husband, Adolfo Bioy Casares, *Los que aman, odian,* 1946 [Those Who Love, Hate]; a verse drama written with Juan Rodolfo Wilcock about life in ancient Rome, *Los traidores,* 1956 [The Traitors]; several books of stories for children; and a significant body of translations of poetry from French and English, including many poems of Emily Dickinson. She also collaborated with Bioy Casares and with Borges on two anthologies. The first was the famous *Antología de la literatura fantástica,* 1940 (*The Book of Fantasy*), a project that Noemí Ulla has claimed to have been Ocampo's idea originally, though Bioy and Borges were to explore the fantastic much more thoroughly in the following years than she herself. The second, the *Antología poética argentina,* 1941 [Anthology of Argentine Poetry], features the opening of one of her most popular poems, "Enumeración de la patria" [Enumeration of the Nation].

It has sometimes been argued that Ocampo was overshadowed in her lifetime by her more famous sister and husband. A more compelling explanation is that her work frightens or shocks many readers, with its focus on cruelty, deceit, metamorphosis, violence and sexual ambiguity. Her work is now being discovered anew, as has also happened with her peers in the grotesque, Felisberto Hernández and Virgilio Piñera, who have only been fully recognized after their deaths.

DANIEL BALDERSTON

See also entries on Adolfo Bioy Casares, Felisberto Hernández, Victoria Ocampo, Virgilio Piñera

Biography
Born in Buenos Aires, Argentina, in 1903(?). Sister of the writer Victoria Ocampo (see separate entry). Studied painting in Paris with Giorgio de Chirico and Fernand Léger. Married Adolfo Bioy Casares in 1940; one daughter. Awarded the Municipal Prize for Poetry, 1945; National Poetry Prize, 1962 for *Lo amargo por dulce;* Club de los XIII Prize, 1988; PEN Club Gold Pen. Died in November 1993.

Selected Works

Novels and Short Fiction
Viaje olvidado, Buenos Aires: Sur, 1937
Los que aman, odian, in collaboration with Adolfo Bioy Casares, Buenos Aires: Emecé, 1946
Autobiografía de Irene, Buenos Aires: Sur, 1948
La furia y otros cuentos, Buenos Aires: Sur, 1959
Las invitadas, Buenos Aires: Losada, 1961
El pecado mortal, Buenos Aires: Editorial Universitaria, 1966
Informe del cielo y del infierno, Caracas: Monte Ávila, 1970

Los días de la noche, Buenos Aires: Sudamericana, 1970
Canto escolar, Buenos Aires: Fraterna, 1979
Y así sucesivamente, Barcelona: Tusquets, 1987
Cornelia frente al espejo, Barcelona: Tusquets, 1988

Children's Fiction
El caballo alado, Buenos Aires: Ediciones de La Flor, 1972
El cofre volante, Buenos Aires: Estrada, 1974
El tobogán, Buenos Aires: Estrada, 1975
La naranja maravillosa: cuentos para chicos grandes y para grandes chicos, Buenos Aires: Orión, 1977

Poetry
Enumeración de la patria y otros poemas, Buenos Aires: Sur, 1942
Espacios métricos, Buenos Aires: Sur, 1945
Los sonetos del jardín, Buenos Aires: Sur, 1946
Poemas de amor desesperado, Buenos Aires: Sudamericana, 1949
Los nombres, Buenos Aires: Emecé, 1953
Pequeña antología, Buenos Aires: En, 1954
Lo amargo por dulce, Buenos Aires: Emecé, 1962
Amarillo celeste, Buenos Aires: Losada, 1972
Árboles de Buenos Aires, in collaboration with Aldo Sessa, Buenos Aires: Librería la Ciudad, 1979

Play
Los traidores, in collaboration with Juan Rudolfo Wilcock, Buenos Aires: Losada, 1956 [in verse]

Compilations and Anthologies
La continuación y otras páginas, Buenos Aires: Centro Editor de América Latina, 1981
Breve santoral, Buenos Aires: Ediciones de Arte Gaglianone, 1984
Páginas, Buenos Aires: Celtia, 1984
Las reglas del secreto: antología, edited by Matilde Sánchez, Mexico City: Fondo de Cultura Económica, 1991

Editor, with Jorge Luis Borges and Adolfo Bioy Casares:
Antología de la literatura fantástica, Buenos Aires: Sudamericana, 1940; as *The Book of Fantasy,* New York: Viking, and London: Xanadu, 1988
Antología poética argentina, Buenos Aires: Sudamericana, 1941

Translation
Leopoldina's Dream, translated by Daniel Balderston, New York, and Harmondsworth: Penguin, 1988 [collection of short fiction]

Further Reading
Aponte, Barbara A., "The Initiation Archetype in Arguedas, Roa Bastos and Ocampo," *Latin American Literary Review,* vol. 11/2, (1982)
Gálvez, Raúl, *From the Ashen Land of the Virgin: Conversations with Bioy Casares, Borges, Denevi, Etchecopar, Silvina Ocampo, Orozco, Sábato,* Oakville, Ontario: Mosaic Press, 1989
Klingenberg, Patricia N., "A Portrait of the Writer as Artist: Silvina Ocampo," *Perspectives on Contemporary Literature,* vol. 13 (1987)
____ "The Twisted Mirror: the Fantastic Stories of Silvina Ocampo," *Letras Femeninas,* vol 13/1–2 (1987)
____ "The Mad Double in the Stories of Silvina Ocampo, *Latin American Literary Review,* vol. 16/32 (1988)
Ulla, Noemí, *Invenciones a dos voces: ficción y poesía en Silvina Ocampo,* Buenos Aires: Torres Agüero, 1992

Victoria Ocampo 1890–1979

Argentine writer and patron of culture

Victoria Ocampo was the most influential woman of letters and cultural promoter in 20th-century Argentina. She founded, financed and was the main editor of the literary journal *Sur* (1931–70) which served as a bridge between the cultures of the Americas and Europe. Writing dominated her life, as she remarked in an early published volume: "my only ambition is to write one day, no matter how well or poorly, but as a woman." Her extensive *oeuvre* bears witness to an ambition fulfilled: a six-volume autobiography (a genre in Argentina previously dominated by men), published posthumously; ten volumes of *Testimonios*, which record and express her very personal views on literature and life, placing her private, female, presence firmly in the public sphere; critical works on figures from Virginia Woolf and T.E. Lawrence to Borges and translations of contemporary literature from several languages. She was brought up in an aristocratic household, as trilingual in English, French and Spanish and would not feel confident writing in Spanish until the 1930s. Yet she viewed this linguistic schizophrenia as positive: equating her story, as she often did, with the history of Argentina, she always asserted that the polyglot could expand the boundaries of the Argentine nation, opening it up to enriching, heterodox ideas. She followed these principles, cultivating friendships all over the world with the most significant cultural figures of the day, inviting them to her homes in Argentina or, when they could or would not travel – as was the case of Virginia Woolf – offering them the hospitality of publishing in her "house" journal, *Sur*. She had both the advantages and disadvantages of wealth and background, and sought to open up new opportunities for women in a closed male society.

The world of her childhood and adolescence was both cosseted and claustrophobic. She was born into one of the wealthiest and most powerful families in Argentina and would always defend the cultural values of that liberal aristocratic tradition. Yet she saw from an early age, in a world hemmed in by nannies and servants, that the power of her class was male: women were excluded from male institutions, either political or cultural. The smoking room or the club were the spaces in which this power resided and Victoria Ocampo battled against convention to find "a room of her own" in Woolf's celebrated phrase (from an article that *Sur* would publish in the 1930s). She married early and disastrously and although the marriage lasted for only a few months, she was forced to keep up the appearance of respectability for over a decade, hiding from family and friends a longstanding love affair with a cousin of her husband, in a society where divorce was forbidden. Her autobiography would later explore in great detail these first forty years of her life, expressing with unusual frankness the struggle for control over her own body and desires. Her first published work, an essay on Dante, would also seek to explore, through metaphor, the nature of "profane" and "sacred" love. This first text, from 1920, showed what would become a constant in her writing: the essay form (itself an incursion into male territory: women were supposed to write about feelings in poetry, not about ideas in

essays), which stressed quotation, translation and interpretation of the canon, an active process of engagement with the literary work in an accessible, almost conversational, style.

Her first contract with cultural life came not through an immersion in the avant-garde experimentalism of the 1920s but through meeting writers who came to Buenos Aires: Tagore, Ortega y Gasset, Count Keyserling. She later wrote about the advantages of becoming part of an aristocracy of the spirit and the drawbacks of being taken as a muse or emblem of male fantasy. By the late 1920s she was aware that she could take control of her life, living openly on her own, travelling to Europe and the United States and mixing with the most significant artists and intellectuals of the day. Her wealth, in a world of impecunious artists, cast her naturally in the role of Maecenas, and it was another traveller to Buenos Aires, the North American Waldo Frank, who encouraged her to channel her passions and her talents into a concrete cultural endeavour, the periodical *Sur*, which set the standards for intellectual life in Argentina for some forty years. In *Sur*, the journal and the publishing house, can be charted her developing interests in literature, modernist art and architecture, feminist issues and her conception of culture as a dialogue between cultivated minorities across the world. Although she was never actively involved with political parties, her increasing prominence in the public sphere (as the best known woman in Argentina after Eva Péron) made her the target of opposition. She was outspoken in her rejection of Péron, and was locked up by the regime for some days in 1953. She also turned her face against the Cuban Revolution and the political and cultural radicalisation of the 1960s and 1970s in Argentina, which caused a younger generation to dismiss her as a cultural "oligarch." But the more measured criticism of the last fifteen years, since her death in 1979, especially the growth of feminist criticism, has recognised her importance both as a disseminator and as a creative writer. She was elected to the Argentine Academy in 1977, the first woman to receive this recognition, and her acceptance speech told of the double lineage of her family. She was descended, she said, from both the Spanish conquistadors and from an indigenous woman, Agueda. In the figure of Agueda she stressed her own American roots but also her *female* relationship to history. Argentine culture, for her, was a mixture of the European and the American, the modern and the traditional and it was a culture that had been deaf, for too long, to the voices of its women. Victoria Ocampo was one of the clearest of these voices.

JOHN KING

See also entries on *Sur*, under Journals; Silvina Ocampo

Biography

Born in Buenos Aires, Argentina, 7 April 1890. Eldest of six daughters; her youngest sister, Silvina, became a writer of fiction Family were members of oligarchy and very Francophile. Travelled to Europe in 1896 and again in 1908. Married Luis Bernardo de Estrada in 1912. Couple decidedly incompatible and theirs became a stage marriage. Long relationship with another man, but this was never made public so as not to bring shame on her family. Espoused cause of women's rights. First publications were articles in *La Nación* in early 1920s. Founder of the journal *Sur*, 1931 and the publishing house of the same name. Ran these for forty years as sole financial backer. Arrested and imprisoned for one month in 1953. This was the first time (apart from with her servants) that she came into close contact with women from other social classes. First woman to be admitted to Argentine Academy of Letters, 1977. Died on 27 January 1979.

Selected Works

De Francesca a Beatrice, Madrid: Revista de Occidente, 1924
La laguna de los nenúfares, Madrid: Revista de Occidente, 1926
Testimonios I, Madrid: Revista de Occidente, 1935
Domingos en Hyde Park, Buenos Aires: Sur, 1936
Testimonios II, Buenos Aires: Sur, 1941
San Isidro, con un poema de Silvina Ocampo, Buenos Aires: Sur, 1941
338171 T.E. (Lawrence de Arabia), Buenos Aires: Sur, 1942
Testimonios III, Buenos Aires: Sudamericana, 1946
Soledad sonora, Buenos Aires: Sudamericana, 1950 [Fourth volume of *Testimonio*]
El viajero y una de sus sombras: Keyserling en mis memorias, Buenos Aires: Sudamericana, 1951
Virginia Woolf en su diario, Buenos Aires: Sur, 1954
Testimonios V, Buenos Aires: Sur, 1957
Habla el algarrobo, Buenos Aires: Sur, 1959
Tagore en las barrancas de San Isidro, Buenos Aires: Sur, 1961
Testimonios VI, Buenos Aires: Sur, 1963

Juan Sebastián Bach, el hombre, Buenos Aires: Sur, 1964
Testimonios VII, Buenos Aires: Sur, 1967
Diálogo con Borges, Buenos Aires: Sur, 1969
Diálogo con Mallea, Buenos Aires: Sur, 1969
Testimonios VIII, Buenos Aires: Sur, 1971
Testimonios IX, Buenos Aires: Sur, 1975
Testimonios X, Buenos Aires: Sur, 1977

Further Reading

Bergmann, Emilie, *et al.* (editors), *Women, Culture and Politics in Latin America*, Berkeley: University of California Press, 1990
Dyson, Ketaki, *In Your Blossoming Flower Garden: Rabindranath Tagore and Victoria Ocampo*, New Delhi: Safutya Academi, 1988
King, John, "Victoria Ocampo: *Sur* y el peronismo, 1946–1955," Madrid, *Revista de Occidente* 37 (1984)
Lugo-Ortiz, Agnes I., "Memoria infantil y perspectiva histórica: *El archipiélago* de Victoria Ocampo," *Revista Iberoamericana*, vol. 53/140 (July–September 1987)
Masiello, Francine, *Between Civilization and Barbarism: Women, Nation and Literary Culture in Modern Argentina*, Lincoln: University of Nebraska Press, 1992
Meyer, Doris, *Victoria Ocampo: Against the Wind and the Tide*, New York: Braziller, 1979
____ "Letters and Correspondence in the Essays of Victoria Ocampo," *Revista Interamericana de Bibliografía*, Washington, DC, vol. 42/2 (1992)
Molloy, Sylvia, "Dos proyectos de vida: *Cuadernos de infancia* de Nora Lange y *El archipiélago* de Victoria Ocampo," *Filología*, Buenos Aires, vol. 20/2 (1985)

Juan Carlos Onetti 1909–1994

Uruguayan prose writer

Juan Carlos Onetti lived a sedentary and reclusive life, and during his last decades there were very few attractions which could distract him from staying in his bedroom (first in Montevideo, then in Madrid). In that bedroom he read thousands of novels (from high brow to pulp fiction works), and wrote some of his most important short stories and novels. In reality, he seemed to belong to his own fictional world, because the characters of his invention were also daytime dreamers, used to sharing reality with imaginative endeavors, and imagining for themselves lives different from those they were living. Onetti started to write short stories in such a fashion, in the 1930s, when some of them ("Avenida de Mayo-Diagonal-Avenida de Mayo," "El posible Baldi" [The Possible Baldi]) told how a bureaucrat, a bank employee, dreamed of a life full of adventures that was possible at a turning point when he chose instead to be sedentary. Such characters feel nostalgic about a kind of life much more interesting and thrilling than their own boring lives. A similar scenario is depicted in Onetti's first novel, *El pozo*, 1939 (*The Pit*). Before going to sleep every night, its main character imagines himself immersed in different adventures in exotic places, as a way of compensating for his

dull present. This process went yet further a decade later, in his best novel, *La vida breve*, 1950 (*A Brief Life*). Its protagonist, Juan María Brausen, is a script-writer who is asked to write a story and gets lost in his imagination thinking about a fictional place, the town of Santa María. In (his) "real" life, he starts inserting himself in a strange fiction which could develop into a possible murder and when he needs to escape from the police, he moves into that imaginary region. Thus, in 1950 Onetti founded Santa María, a coastal town imprecisely located in Argentina but also with traces of old provincial Uruguayan towns. The rest of his important novels take place in Santa María, but this town is never again mentioned as imaginary. The only ironic stance from the author was to name Juan María Brausen, the script writer from *La vida breve*, as the patriarchal founder of the small city.

While working as an assistant editor on the highly regarded Uruguayan journal, *Marcha*, Onetti promoted a radical transformation of River Plate literature (that is, of Argentina and Uruguay): writers should forget the all-pervasive literary theme of the countryside, and start developing stories about the cities. They had at least a metropolis, Buenos Aires, and a middle-sized but culturally very active city, Montevideo, and the characters should not be the gauchos any more, a type that had disappeared, but the urban citizens with their own array of different professions and trades. Onetti wrote programmatic articles on this subject, under a pseudonym, and published his urban short stories and novels. In this sense, he was continuing a then recently established Argentine trend, which had important practitioners like Eduardo Mallea and Roberto Arlt. Onetti felt closer to Arlt, whose literary imagination was, like his, a mixture of "Boys Own" adventures with picturesque characters, and a sense of the surrounding urban reality. They started what is considered the urban novel in South America.

Onetti wrote an unconventional narrative, stylistically and because of his themes. His style is difficult, elliptical and in many instances ambiguous because of long and sinuous phrases. He admired William Faulkner very much, and took from him the complexity of syntax besides the construction of a "saga" and an imaginary space. What Yoknapatawpha and the Comptons meant for Faulkner, Santa María and Larsen and Díaz Grey and Jorge Malabia, among other characters, meant for Onetti. Onetti continued one novel into the other, changing significantly the role of his characters, but Larsen has a special place because he is at the center of his narrative. Larsen was also supposed to be unconventional because of his peculiar enterprises: to fund a whorehouse near Santa María, in *Juntacadáveres*, 1964 (*The Body Snatcher*), or to rebuild an abandoned shipyard, as in *El astillero*, 1961 (*The Shipyard*), an enterprise owned by a madman. Many of Onetti's novels and short stories lack the "logic" of human enterprises, hopes and desires, because these are the components of bourgeois life. Onetti's more anarchistic view of the world advanced against the grain, but behind the uniqueness and unconventionalities the reader finds a very moving sentiment for humanity, a compassion which has its roots in religion. Pain, grief, compassion for the other are feelings to be found in novels such as *Tan triste como ella* [Sad as She], *Para una tumba sin nombre* (*A Grave with No Name*), or short stories such as "Jacob y el otro" (Jacob and the Other), "El infierno tan temido" (Hell Most Feared), "Un sueño realizado" (A Dream Come True).

Among other dichotomies that make his novels so complex and mesmerizing, purity as opposed to corruption is crucial to the understanding of his literature. Onetti used the archetype of childhood to symbolize purity, and depicted adulthood as a longer and dramatic age of decay. His novels and short stories abound in adult men trying desperately to find some kind of salvation. To compromise, to accept social hypocrisies, and simulacra implied to lose onself. In "El infierno tan temido," a father commits suicide to prevent his daughter's virginity being lost. The town's gossip about a former athlete visited by two women proved to be false and a product of slander. In "Bienvenido, Bob" (Welcome, Bob), an older man feels hurt when Bob, the brother of his young fiancée, despises him just because of his age, so he only has to wait until Bob grows old, to welcome him into his "corrupted" reality. There are no evil people in Onetti's literature, only people wasted by the simple fact of living.

Onetti's international reputation, and the fact that he was considered the most distinguished Uruguayan writer, did not prevent his imprisonment in 1974. He and other authors had awarded a literary prize to Nelson Marra for a short story that the military considered offensive. He was liberated three months later, and the following year he moved definitively to Spain and refused to go back to his country even when democracy was restored. In 1985, the new president of Uruguay travelled to Spain to present Onetti with the National Literary award but was not able to get even a promise that the author would return to his native country. In Madrid Onetti wrote several novels and short stories, each of them more pessimistic than the previous ones, to the point that in *Dejemos hablar al viento* [Let the Wind Speak], he had Santa María destroyed by fire. His literary style became paradoxically more and more allegorical and hermetic at the same time that his books sold quickly and made him a popular writer. In 1980, he received the Cervantes prize handed to him by Juan Carlos, the King of Spain.

JORGE RUFFINELLI

Biography

Born in Montevideo, Uruguay, 1 July 1909. Lived in Buenos Aires, 1930–34 and 1941–55. Began publishing his work in 1933, but he attracted little critical attention outside Uruguay until the mid-1960s. Married four times: 1) his cousin María Amalia Onetti, 1930 (one son); 2) his cousin María Julia Onetti, 1934; 3) Elizabeth María Pekelharing, 1945 (one daughter); 4) Dorotea Muhr in 1980, after living together for 25 years. Edited the weekly journal *Marcha* in Montevideo, 1939–42, and *Vea y Lea*, Buenos Aires, 1946–55; editor for Reuters News Agency, Montevideo, 1941–43, and Buenos Aires, 1943–46. Manager of an advertising company in Montevideo, 1955–57; Director of Municipal Libraries, Montevideo, 1957. In 1974 he was imprisoned by the military dictatorship for being a member of the jury that awarded a literary prize to a story by Nelson Marra, which the authorities considered to be pornographic and subversive. Incarcerated briefly in mental institution. Forced to move to Madrid, and became Spanish citizen in 1975. Worked at a number of odd-jobs including waiter, salesman and doorman. Recipient of numerous awards including: National Literature Prize, 1962; William Faulkner Foundation Ibero-American Award, 1963; Casa de las Américas Prize, 1965; Italian-Latin American Institute Prize, 1972; Miguel de Cervantes Prize, 1980. Died in Madrid, 30 May 1994.

Selected Works

Novels

El pozo, Montevideo: Signo, 1939; as *The Pit*, translated by Peter Bush, published with *Tonight*, London: Quartet, 1991

Tierra de nadie, Buenos Aires: Losada, 1941; as *No Man's Land*, translated by Peter Bush, London: Quartet, 1994

Para esta noche, Buenos Aires: Poseidon, 1943; as *Tonight*, translated by Peter Bush, published with *The Pit*, London: Quartet, 1991

La vida breve, Buenos Aires: Sudamericana, 1950; as *A Brief Life*, translated by Hortense Carpentier, New York: Grossman, and London: Serpent's Tail, 1976

Una tumba sin nombre, Montevideo: Marcha, 1959; retitled as *Para una tumba sin nombre*, with *El pozo*, Montevideo: Arca, 1974; as *A Grave with No Name*, translated by Peter Bush, published with *Farewells*, London: Quartet, 1992

La cara de la desgracia, Montevideo: Alfa, 1960

El astillero, Buenos Aires: Fabril, 1961; as *The Shipyard*, translated by Rachel Caffyn, New York: Scribner, 1968; also translated by Nick Caistor, London: Serpent's Tail, 1992

El infierno tan temido, Montevideo: Asir, 1962

Tan triste como ella, Montevideo: Alfa, 1963
Juntacadáveres, Montevideo: Alfa, 1964; as *The Body Snatcher*,
    translated by Alfred MacAdam, London: Quartet, and New York:
    Pantheon, 1991
Los rostros del amor, Buenos Aires: Centro Editor de America
    Latina, 1968
La muerte y la niña, Buenos Aires: Corregidor, 1973
Dejemos hablar al viento, Barcelona: Bruguera, 1979

Short Fiction
Un sueño realizado y otros cuentos, Montevideo: Número,
    1951
Los adioses, Buenos Aires: Sur, 1954; as *Farewells*, translated by
    Peter Bush, published with *A Grave with No Name*, London:
    Quartet, 1992
Jacob y el otro: un sueño realizado y otros cuentos, Montevideo:
    Banda Oriental, 1965
La novia robada y otros cuentos, Buenos Aires: Centro Editor de
    América Latina, 1968
Tiempo de abrazar y los cuentos de 1933 a 1950, Montevideo:
    Arca, 1974
Tan triste como ella y otros cuentos, Barcelona: Lumen, 1976
Cuentos secretos: Periquito el Aguador y otras máscaras,
    Montevideo: Biblioteca de Marcha, 1986
Presencia y otros cuentos, Madrid: Almarabu, 1986
Cuando entonces, Madrid: Mondadori, and Buenos Aires:
    Sudamericana, 1987
Cuando ya no importe, Madrid: Alfaguara, 1993; as *Past Caring*,
    translated by Peter Bush, London: Quartet, 1995

Essays
Requiem por Faulkner y otros artículos, Montevideo: Arca,
    1975

Compilations and Anthologies
Cuentos completos, Buenos Aires: Centro Editor de América Latina,
    1967; revised edition, Buenos Aires: Corregidor, 1974
Novelas y cuentos cortos completos, 2 vols, Caracas: Monte Ávila,
    1968
Obras completas, Mexico City: Aguilar, 1970

Anthologies in Translation
Goodbyes and Other Stories, translated by Daniel Balderston,
    Austin: University of Texas Press, 1990

Further Reading
Adams, M. Ian, *Three Authors of Alienation: Bombal, Onetti,
    Carpentier*, Austin: University of Texas Press, 1975
Aínsa, Fernando, *Las trampas de Onetti*, Montevideo: Alfa, 1970
Curiel, Fernando, *Onetti: obra y calculado infortunio*, Mexico City:
    UNAM, 1980
Jones, Yvonne Perier, *The Formal Expression of Meaning in Juan
    Carlos Onetti's Narrative Art*, Cuernavaca: Cidoc, 1971
Kadir, Djelal, *Juan Carlos Onetti*, Boston: Twayne, 1977
Lewis, Bart L., "Juan Carlos Onetti and the Auto-Referential Text,"
    Hispanófila, vol. 96 (1989)
Ludmer, Josefina, *Onetti: los procesos de construcción del lenguaje*,
    Buenos Aires: Sudamericana, 1977
Millington, Mark, *Reading Onetti: Language, Narrative and the
    Subject*, Liverpool: Cairns, 1985
Molina, Juan Carlos, *La dialéctica de la identidad en la obra de
    Juan Carlos Onetti*, New York: Peter Lang, 1982
Ruffinelli, Jorge, *Juan Carlos Onetti*, Montevideo: Marcha,
    1973
Verani, Hugo J., *Onetti: el ritual de la impostura*, Caracas: Monte
    Ávila, 1981
Verani, Hugo J. (editor), *Juan Carlos Onetti*, Madrid: Taurus,
    1987

Interviews
Chao, Ramón, *Un possible Onetti*, Barcelona: Ronsel, 1994

Special Issues of Journals
Crisis, Buenos Aires, 6 (1974)
Review, New York, 16 (1975)

El astillero

Novel by Juan Carlos Onetti

El astillero (*The Shipyard*) was published in 1961, after it won
the prize for best novel awarded by the Buenos Aires publishing
house, Fabril. The novel forms part of the saga of Santa María
which Onetti began creating more or less from the publication
of *La vida breve*, 1950 (*A Brief Life*). This novel was followed
by *Para una tumba sin nombre*, 1959 (*A Grave with No
Name*), *Juntacadáveres*, 1964 (*The Body Snatcher*), *La novia
robada*, 1968 [The Stolen Bride] and *Dejemos hablar al viento*,
1979 [Let the Wind Speak].

The plot of *El astillero* is simple: the owner of a bankrupt
shipyard, unable to accept either the passing of time or the
demise of his business, employs a manager, Larsen, to "administer" and "organise" the yard, along with the two other
surviving employees. The obvious result of this is a chimera
and an allegory of failure. The owner, in a state of delirium,
cannot see that the shipyard has been abandoned for years and
that the chances of it ever working again are extremely remote.
In fact, this character, Jeremías Petrus, cannot even see that
the yard has been closed and has lain derelict for some time.
Larsen, despite being aware of all this, accepts the post, for
which – incidentally – he is never paid. The novel centres on
the development of this character in relation to this situation,
his own past and the characters (Jeremías Petrus, his daughter
Inés, the maid Josefina, the employees Gálvez and Khun and
Gálvez's wife) who represent the life of Puerto Astillero, where
most of the action takes place.

The most common misinterpretation of *El astillero* stems
from a peculiarity of Onetti's work which requires the reader
to distinguish between the chronology of the publication of
Onetti's novels and the chronology of the saga of Santa María,
the imaginary town which gives life to Onetti's fiction. *El
astillero* was published before *Juntacadáveres*, but in the
chronology of Santa María, events in *Juntacadáveres* precede
those of *El astillero*.

Leaving aside certain elements of the plot, *El astillero*
comprises the story of Larsen, creating a type of sentimental
biography. The character first appears, albeit in vague form,
in Onetti's second novel, *Tierra de nadie*, 1941 (*No Man's
Land*), and can also be recognised elsewhere as Junta Larsen,
Juntacadáveres, or Carreño. *El astillero* underlines Larsen's
role as more than a character. He functions as a type of "narrative voice," running through the stories which make up the
Santa María saga. Larsen's importance lies not in his physical
presence, which could even be regarded as secondary when
compared to that of other characters, but in his function as a
type of parameter with respect to certain modes of behaviour,
situations and attitudes which are, at least in a figurative,

imaginary sense, practically unique to him. The other characters are judged in relation to him and it is in *El astillero*, more than any other novel in the Santa María series, that this tendency is particularly pronounced.

El astillero is divided into eighteen chapters. In order to reinforce the notion of the characters experiencing different, often contradictory feelings simultaneously, Onetti alternates the moods and settings through which they pass. He creates situations and contexts which, while appearing each time to be different, are possessed of an individual logic and direction.

The corpse collector is the main character in *El astillero*, but at the same time he is more: Larsen is a discursive model forming a mental and personal base for each element in Onetti's cosmonogy. This is no minor achievement when one considers that *El astillero*, as previously mentioned, constitutes an "internal biography" of Larsen, relating his rise, fall and ambiguous disappearance. *El astillero* does not deal with attachment or feeling but explains, contextualises and suggests a sentimental discourse for the description of sentimentalism and its characters. This discourse is not so much verbal as imaginary. More than a *macró* (pimp), Larsen is a sentimentalist. The novel is a sentimental narrative which describes the ideas and concepts of a sentimental world.

Larsen is a sentimentalist because, while recognising his fate (the fate of humanity is one of Onetti's favourite themes), he nevertheless continues to pursue tastes and preferences which can do little to alter his situation and indeed serve to worsen it. This image of the pursuit of pleasure, despite an awareness of imminent demise, is Larsen's most outstanding characteristic as well as being a permanent feature of Onetti's novels. "Como si fuera cierto" (As if it were true), says the narrator, "que todo acto humano nace antes de ser cometido, preexiste a su encuentro con un ejecutor variable. Sabía que era necesario e inevitable hacer. Pero no le importaba descubrir el porqué" (that every human action was born before its realisation, exists prior to its encounter with a variable subject. He knew it was necessary and inevitable that he did it. But he wasn't interested in finding out why). This lucid unbelief, the province of the sceptic, is what makes it possible constantly to pardon the figure of Juntacadáveres, and at the same time, the novel itself.

The narrator suggests that Larsen is a failed artist and that it is as such that he involuntarily attempts to rationalise his situation and to show a sentimental world that he belongs to it, at least occasionally. There is something in Larsen's character which condemns him to persistent failure. It is not a deficiency but instead an excess: the collector is ingenuous but lacks malice and a certain slyness. His innocence is pure, or more specifically, grave, serious, determinant, fatal, even malevolent. Larsen's artistic failure is the result of an excess of understanding, pity and compassion; he is too clearheaded to be creative. This could be described as the *Larsen complex* and is an attitude relevant to both life and art with the character's

self-image based not on an assessment of what he believes himself to be, but instead on what he knows he is not and never can be: "Ese señor que – piensa Larsen de sí mismo – me mira en el espejo." (That gent – thinks Larsen about himself – who looks at me in the mirror). Larsen's radical sentimentalism merits wider consideration: an artist would have been able to oscillate between the belief in an image and the certainty of a condition, but not Larsen who, in this respect, is an excessively lucid character.

El astillero constitutes the most successful metaphor for the sentimental imperfection of the inhabitants of the universe of Santa María, in particular, and the stories of Onetti in general. This is a depiction of sentimental imperfection which particularly includes failure, or more precisely, human existence as failure. *El astillero* is a metaphor for the gap between that which remains and that which has disappeared, between people possessed of excessive ingenuity and characters with no understanding. Onetti's great achievement has been in creating, without stereotypes and with sustained depth, a narrative where the most ingenuous brutality and ignorance manage to coexist with the most sordid and sterile lucidity, a game (like Queca with the street plan of Paris in *La vida breve*) where the animalistic and pure saves the rationalist from angst and audacity and where the sordid and cruel cries out desperately to the innocent.

Discretion without resentment, isolation without caprice: Onetti's characters seem to disbelieve the possibilities of history and place themselves in a *tempo,* described as destiny, which leads them irredeemably along a path which, although already written, must be repeated in order to conjure up a sense of boredom and weariness. "Cuando él decide algo" (When he decides something), says Gálvez's wife, summarising the dominant message of the Santa María stories, and of *El astillero* in particular, "yo me entero y entonces conozco lo que me va a pasar. Es así; yo sé, además, que tiene que ser así."(I pick up on it and then I know what's going to happen to me. That's the way it is, and what's more, I know that's the way it has to be).

CLAUDIO CANAPARO

translated by Carol Tully

Editions

First edition: *El astillero*, Buenos Aires: Fabril, 1961
Translation: *The Shipyard*, by Rachel Caffyn, New York: Scribner, 1968; also translated by Nick Caistor, London: Serpent's Tail, 1992

Further Reading

Musselwhite, David, "*El astillero en Marcha*," *Nuevos Aires*, 11 (1973)
Turton, Peter, "Lo rectilíneo y lo circular en *El astillero*," *Texto Crítico*, vol. 2/4 (1976)

Orality

Traditional oral culture is often seen in counter-distinction with modern rational culture, based on an abstract form of communication: writing. Orality, in opposition to written language, has recently become associated with resistance movements of the oppressed in Latin American literature. Theirs is the collective voice of a semi-literate or illiterate people, with a purely oral history, consisting of traditional tales, proverbs, prayers and formulaic expressions. These are features of works such as the ancient Guatemalan drama of epic proportions *Rabinal Achí* as well as other oral genres. Psychodynamic elements of orality, including onomatopoeic sounds, form part of the linguistic scaffolding of such novels as *La cofradía del mullo del vestido de la Virgen Pipona*, 1985 (*The Sisterhood of the Sacred Vestments of the Plump Virgin*) by the Ecuadorian Alicia Yánez Cossío. Latin American texts ranging from myth and legend to the contemporary testimonial form of *Rigoberta Menchú* and Violeta Parra's song-text poetry demonstrate the extent to which literate thought and expression have emerged from orality in varieties of Latin American writing. The spoken word acquires power as an instrument of action and dominance over described reality. Even a very sophisticated writer, such as Octavio Paz, recognizes the importance of orality in poetry when he pays homage to the oral tradition and primary oral cultures. In an article published in *Vuelta* (1991) he reminded his readers that: "La poesía comenzó antes de la escritura. Es un arte esencialmente verbal y que entra no sólo por los ojos y el entendimiento sino por los oídos. La poesía es algo que se dice y se oye." (Poetry began before writing. It is essentially a verbal art that enters not only through the eyes and understanding but also through the ears. Poetry is something that is verbalized and is heard). Other poets who share a similar view of the oral nature of poetry, and who incorporated it into their verses in a very deliberate manner, are Violeta Parra (Chile), whose song-texts were the inspiration for the *Nueva Canción* (New Song) musical movement in Latin America, Nicolás Guillén (Cuba) and his *son*-poems which use onomatopoeia to re-create African-Cuban instrumentation and ritual ceremonial sounds, and Miguel Ángel Asturias (Guatemala) in those verses and narratives in which he draws on the culture of the Mayas. Apart from the lexical and morphological inventiveness of popular speech, there is an exceptional use of the sensuousness of sound in these texts. Indeed, the living tradition of oral protest poetry of the contemporary era has its origins in the popular protest poetry and songs which were sung in oral performance by the *payador* or *gaucho* balladeer and kept alive in print in the legendary gauchesque literature. The *corridos* of the Mexican Revolution and post-revolutionary Mexico are one such example of the impact that the oral tradition had on Spanish American protest poetry.

Critics such as Walter J. Ong (*Orality and Literacy*) believe that the main interest a writer might have in orality is based not only on sounds and the spoken word that determine forms of expression in a community, but also on the process of human thought itself. If it is true, as he says, that we know what we can remember, it is worth identifying the mental processes that humans use in order to remember things,

namely, important events. In addition to the importance given to certain elements that define orality such as repetition, rhythm and other syntactical aspects, it should be noted that in oral cultures many constructions are aggregative rather than analytic, that is to say, remembered information is not systematized individually but in groups or series of related groups by means of parallelisms, antitheses and epithets. So, too, oral cultures depend heavily on repetition and redundancy in order to sustain an unbroken process of thought, i.e., copious repetition of linking phrases that at the same time to reinforce the orality of the text; the multiple use of different types of oral cultural texts: popular and religious songs; children's sayings and games; formal talks and conferences for celebrating homages; word games; puns; moral sayings; prayers; legends and gossip.

The proverb maintains collective moral values. The nature of the oral is to create fluidity, excess, verbosity that, on another level, impedes the critical recognition of certain options for action and thus maintains the status quo of the community. Thus, a new language characterized by polyphonic communication, the collective voice of the populace, emerges from this intersection between the oral and the written, language as speech and language as written code. This language refuses to be a written, literary language, and can only be the reemergence of a spoken language, of a new colloquy. Replacing the shattered established literary and rationalist language, the new one is announced as an Adamic language in some forms of contemporary Latin American literature. This "poetics of change" as Julio Ortega refers to it, deconstructs both the notion of the text within the literary tradition and its role in the natural language. Indeed, in 1976 the literary critic Jean Franco acknowledged orality's significance to the literary domain when she wrote "No study of Latin American literature, even in the 20th century, is balanced unless the oral performance is taken into account and unless there is some notion of the dialectics or oral and written literatures."

The Mexican critic Miguel León-Portilla writes at great length about the colorful expressions of pre-Columbian literature. The rhythmic style of many of these texts (the sacred Mayan *Popol Vuh* or "Book of the People" and the pre-Hispanic play *Rabinal Achi*, for example) is similar to the mythical accounts and poems of other primarily oral peoples and cultures. Their form of expression, which frequently repeats the same idea in parallel form, indicates that such texts were memorized in the pre-Hispanic centers of learning and recited during important religious festivals. In pre-Columbian society orally preserved and transmitted myths form the seed of what was to become their religious thought. Recited during festivals and ceremonies or sung to the accompaniment of flutes, conch-shells, and drums, they were also the beginning of religious drama. Pre-Hispanic imaginative and didactic prose (chronicles and history, descriptions and narrative texts, speeches, and admonitions) follow many of the stylistic procedures which are frequent in other forms of pre-Hispanic composition, such as parallel expressions, which repeat the same idea in different ways, the often observed rhythm of phrases, and the constant use of metaphors and idiomatic expressions, undeniable characteristics of both indigenous languages and orality. We are reminded by Walter J. Ong in *Orality and Literacy* that the oral nature of these elements relates them directly to the production of sound, and their aural reception unifies and internalizes sounds perceived by human beings.

Despite revealing the traces and scars of translation, as well as the liberating tropes that come from code switching, Latin American testimonial texts retain an unmistakable oral quality through the edited and polished version that reaches the reader. It is often the case that these stories are orally transmitted through a mediating voice (that of a social worker or anthropologist), who is responsible for transcribing and organizing the recorded material. Such works, prevalent in Latin American letters of recent years, give recognition (and sometimes prominence) to the voice of the unprivileged. As a device, orality helps to account for the testimonial's construction of a collective self. For, unlike the private moment of autobiographical writing, testimonies are public events which strive to renew an interpersonal rhetoric (as opposed to producing a personal and distinctive style as part of the individuation process of traditional autobiography). The life stories of the Guatemalan Indian Rigoberta Menchú (*Me llamo Rigoberta Menchú* (*I, Rigoberta Menchú: an Indian Woman in Guatemala*), and the Bolivian miner's wife Domitila Barrios de Chungara (*¡Si me permiten hablar! Testimonio de Domitila, una mujer de las minas de Bolivia* (*Let Me Speak! Testimony of Domitila, a Woman of the Bolivian Mines*) are two such examples of this literary form. In this context it is worth noting that in Latin America, it became common, as from the 16th century, for members of the dominant culture to interview subalterns: Spanish prelates recorded native accounts of religious practices and historical memory; confessors appropriated the visions of (illiterate and learned) nuns by recording them on paper.

For primarily oral cultures, such as the Andean or indigenous cultures of Central America, for example, meanings are registered and transmitted non-textually – through theatre, oral poetry, music, pilgrimage, artefacts, narratives (myths and legends, popular stories). These are often ways to preserve native knowledge in fields such as cosmology and history. And so it is oral tradition that provides the working material (musical devices, formulaic patterns, the figurative language characteristic of folk speech) for the practitioners of the Latin American popular theatre collectives today. Theatre facilitators such as the Nicaraguan Alan Bolt and the Honduran Jesuit Jack Warner and his Teatro La Fragua (Forge Theatre) exemplify the current trend to take theatre to the people, returning it to its roots of origin as a relationship between oral tradition and sociopolitical commitment. With borrowings from the aforementioned *Popol Vuh*, and both traditional and contemporary folklore rooted in oral tradition, such artists attempt to reawaken the people's awareness of their historical roots.

At the same time, they mirror a contemporary and thus directly meaningful circumstance in a performance text for an illiterate or semi-literate audience. It is in this context that we see the coincidence of two concepts of popular orality: the use of traditionally oral forms of communication with themes originating in oral culture, in conjunction with a modern medium enlisted in the service of raising the political as well as the cultural consciousness of a subordinate class and validating its needs and demands.

ELENA DE COSTA

Further Reading

Adorno, Rolena (editor), *From Oral to Written Expression: Native Andean Chronicles of the Early Colonial Period,* Syracuse, New York: Syracuse University Press, 1982

Benjamin, Walter, "The Storyteller and Artisan Cultures," in *Critical Sociology: Selected Readings*, edited by Paul Connerton, Harmondsworth: Penguin, 1976

Fabregat, Claudio Esteva, "Reflejos morales en la literatura oral: el caso de los hispanos de Nuevo México," *Étnica* 18 (1982)

Finnegan, Ruth, *Literacy and Orality: Studies in the Technology of Communication*, Oxford and New York: Blackwell, 1988

Franco, Jean, "Latin American Literature in a Social Context," *Association of Departments of Foreign Languages* 7 (March 1976)

Honko, Lauri and Vilmos Voigt (editors), *Genre, Structure and Reproduction in Oral Literature*, Budapest: Akadémiai Kiadó, 1980

León-Portilla, Miguel, *Pre-Columbian Literatures of Mexico*, translated by the author and Grace Lobanov, Norman: University of Oklahoma Press, 1969

Minc, Rose S. (editor), *Literature and Popular Culture in the Hispanic World: a Symposium*, Gaithersburg, Maryland: Hispamérica, 1981

Olrik, Axel, *Principles for Oral Narrative Research*, translated by Kirsten Wolf and Jody Jensen, Bloomington: Indiana University Press, 1992

Olson, David R. and Nancy Torrance (editors), *Literacy and Orality*, Cambridge and New York: Cambridge University Press, 1991

Ong, Walter J., *Orality and Literacy: the Technologizing of the Word*, New York and London: Methuen, 1982

Rowe, William and Vivian Schelling, *Memory and Modernity. Popular Culture in Latin America*, London and New York: Verso, 1993 [Refer to readings on oral poetry and storytelling/oral transmission]

Stahl, Sandra Dolby, *Literary Folkloristics and the Personal Narrative*, Bloomington: Indiana University Press, 1989

Wilbert, Johannes and Karin Simoneau (editors), *Folk Literature of the Ge Indians*, Los Angeles: Latin American Center Publications, 1978

____ *Folk Literature of the Mataco Indians*, Los Angeles: Latin American Center Publications, 1982

____ *Folk Literature of the Toba Indians*, Los Angeles: Latin American Center Publications, 1982

____ *Folk Literature of the Bororo Indians*, Los Angeles: Latin American Center Publications, 1983

Orígenes

See Journals

Olga Orozco 1920–

Argentine poet

Olga Orozco established her reputation as a somewhat atypical member of the Argentine "Generación del 40" with her first book of poetry, *Desde lejos* [From Afar], which was published in 1946, the year of Juan Perón's first election as president. Her most recent book, *Con esta boca en este mundo* [With this Mouth in this World], was published to much acclaim in Buenos Aires in 1994. For a body of published work which has spanned almost five decades, Orozco's poetic voice is remarkable, among other reasons, not only for its longevity, which no doubt accounts for much of its current resonance in her country, but also for its consistency. Orozco's poetic universe, which she elaborates in eleven original books over a period in which the changes and shifts in Argentine society have been immense, seems to have remained relatively free from the common pressures to respond either to changing poetic fashions or to external political events.

While Orozco is mainly known as a poet, she has also published two books of prose fiction: *La oscuridad es otro sol*, 1967 [The Darkness is Another Sun] and *La luz es un abismo*, 1973 [The Light is an Abyss]. As Orozco has affirmed about the first of these volumes, her prose work gathers together autobiographical stories based on incidents from her early childhood in Toay in La Pampa province. These texts set in this distant small town – which are added to by the three previously unpublished stories which appeared in the later collection – share the same first-person narrator, the young girl Lía (Olga), as well as the same gallery of secondary characters, based on family members and friends. They also share the same focus: meditations on intimate events – both the traumatic and the everyday – conveyed in a language which cannot but reveal the verbal and conceptual traces of early Catholic indoctrination mixed with other related traditions of popular superstition and magic.

In many respects, while Orozco's prose texts could be set easily in the modern Argentine short story tradition, with their echoes particularly of the work of Silvina Ocampo and of some early texts by Julio Cortázar (both friends of Orozco), they have more often been read as providing a useful explicatory framework for her poetry which has been seen as "difficult," in other words, as philosophically, lexically and syntactically complex. From her first book to her last, Orozco's long poems fill the pages with words, spilling over the line and exceeding the margins. In their subject matter, her poems juxtapose the two realms which are present in her prose texts: the orthodox and the unorthodox realms of the religious and the supernatural. In their form, they point constantly to the ritual and invocatory possibilities of poetry.

From her third book of poems onwards, *Los juegos peligrosos*, 1962 [Dangerous Games], this "other worldly" aspect comes to the fore in her work. But it is in her 1977 collection, *Cantos a Berenice* [Songs to Berenice], ostensibly a series of poems addressed to her cat, where Orozco's usual subject matter – the proximity of the supernatural world to the everday world – is cast solidly in specifically feminine terms, in this case, revolving around the relationship between the witch and her familiar. While Orozco would never claim to have been influenced by feminism, in this aspect her work shows similar esoteric and occult concerns present in the work of several European Surrealist women poets and writers, such as Leonora Carrington and Valentine Penrose. These writers belong to the same generation as Orozco and have attracted much recent feminist critical comment. This particular aspect of Orozco's work merits a good deal more attention.

Her last four books of poetry have been increasingly involved in a more conventional religious exploration, with meditations on the process of aging, and on being surrounded by, and of communing with, the dead. While Orozco's poetry has never openly tackled political themes, it is clear, however, that like the work of others from subsequent poetic generations in Argentina, her work, which speaks of silence, death and metaphysical anguish, has had a political resonance for its contemporary readers. Her recent book, *Con esta boca en este mundo*, with its abundant Eliotesque allusions, ends with a poem titled "Les jeux sont faits" [The Dice Are Thrown] which is a particularly good example of how these modern connotations arise: "Todo lo que recuerda mi boca fue borrado de la memoria de otra boca; / se alojó en nuestro abrazo la ceniza, se nos precipitó la lejanía, / y soy como la sobreviviente pompeyana / separada por siglos del amante sepultado en la piedra" (Everything my mouth remembers was wiped from the memory of another mouth; / has lodged in our embrace, distance pounced on us, / and I am like a Pompeian survivor / separated by centuries from the lover buried in the stone).

CATHERINE GRANT

Biography

Born in Toay, in the province of La Pampa, Argentina, 17 March 1920. Father Sicilian. Moved to Bahía Blanca in 1928 and then to Buenos Aires in 1936. Attended University of Buenos Aires, 1938, where she studied in the Faculty of Arts. Friends of Oliverio Girondo, Norah Lange and Alberto Girri (see separate entries). Travelled in South America, 1947–54; Europe, 1969–70; Africa, 1974–76. Awarded fellowship in Italy, 1976. Recipient of several awards, including: First prize of the Argentine Association of Poetry, 1971; National Arts Prize,1980; Premio Fundación Alfredo Fortabal, 1987; Argentine Writers Society, 1989, and the Laurel Wreath of the University of Turin, 1989.

Selected Works

Poetry

Desde lejos, Buenos Aires: Losada, 1946
Las muertes, Buenos Aires: Losada, 1952
Los juegos peligrosos, Buenos Aires: Losada, 1962
Museo salvaje, Buenos Aires: Losada, 1974
Cantos a Berenice, Buenos Aires: Sudamericana, 1977
Mutaciones de la realidad, Buenos Aires: Sudamericana, 1979
La noche a la deriva, Mexico City: Fondo de Cultura Económica, 1984
En el revés del cielo, Buenos Aires: Sudamericana, 1987
Con esta boca, en este mundo, edited by Jacobo Sefamí, Mexico City: Universidad Autónoma Metropolitana, 1992

Short Fiction

La oscuridad es otro sol, Buenos Aires: Losada, 1967
La luz es un abismo, Montevideo: Vintén, 1993

Compilations and Anthologies

Las muertes; los juegos peligrosos, Buenos Aires: Losada, 1972
Veintinueve poemas, Caracas: Monte Ávila, 1975

Obra poética, Buenos Aires: Corregidor, 1979
Poesía: antología, edited by Telma Lazzani Bystrowicz, Centro editor de América Latina, 1982
Páginas de Olga Orozco seleccionadas por la autora, Buenos Aires: Celtia, 1984 [Contains secondary bibliography selected by the author, comments on her work by Guillermo Sucre, Juan Liscano, Enrique Molina and Alejandra Pizarnik, and an interview with Alicia Dujovne Ortiz]
Poemas, Medellín, Colombia: Departamento de Bibliotecas, Universidad de Antioquía, 1984
Antología poética, Madrid: Ediciones de Cultura Hispánica, 1985

Further Reading

Campanella, Hebe N., "La voz de la mujer en la joven poesía argentina: cuatro registros," *Cuadernos Hispanoamericanos* 300 (1975)
Colombo, Stella Maris, *Metáfora y cosmovisión en la poesía de Olga Orozco*, Rosario, Argentina: Cuadernos Altheia de Investigación y Ensayo, 1983
Gómez Paz, Julieta, "Nostalgia del paraíso," in *Cuatro actitudes poéticas: Alejandra Pizarnik, Olga Orozco, Amelia Biagoni y María Elena Walsh*, Buenos Aires: Conjunta, 1977
____ *Dos textos sobre la poesía de Olga Orozco*, Buenos Aires: Tekné, 1980
Lindstrom, Naomi, "Olga Orozco: la voz poética que llama entre mundos," *Revista Iberoamericana* 132–33 (1985)
Liscano, Juan, "Olga Orozco y sus juegos peligrosos," in *Descripciones*, Buenos Aires: Ediciones de La Flor, 1983
Lojo, María Rosa, *Olga Orozco: la poesía como viaje heroico*, Buenos Aires: América Latina, 1988
Tacconi, María del Carmen, "Para una lectura simbólica de Olga Orozco," *Sur* 348 (1981)
Torres de Peralta, Elba, *La poética de Olga Orozco: desdoblamiento de Dios en máscara de todos*, Madrid: Playor, 1987

Fernando Ortiz 1881–1969

Cuban criminologist, ethnographer and anthropologist

Fernando Ortiz is regarded in Cuba as her leading intellectual between the death of José Martí in the Second War of Cuban Independence (1895–98) and the Cuban Revolution of 1959. Various Communist intellectuals associated with the revolutionary regime have seen him as an intellectual mentor, who, though not a Communist himself, had open, pluralistic attitudes which assumed mature shape during the "Popular Front" period of the mid-1930s. Both a nationalist and an internationalist, Ortiz argued that since reformist intellectuals and politicians had so dismally failed to guarantee *cubanidad* (Cubanness) between 1898 and 1959, a new generation was entitled to experiment with bolder revolutionary solutions. Educated in law in Madrid, Ortiz was influenced by the stress on an orderly evolution of society, as propounded by John Stuart Mill, by Positivist traditions both Comtean and Spencerian, and by the Functionalism of Durkheim. Ortiz

studied too in Barcelona, where he was influenced by the protest of the "Generation of 1898" against the vacuousness and sterility then prevailing in Spanish intellectual life. Ortiz's interests were broad, extending from law and criminology to archaeology, ethnography and anthropology. Between 1906 and 1916 Ortiz was a member of the House of Representatives, acquiring a reputation for moral probity by refusing offers of a share in the national lottery, one of the perquisites of office that brought the politics of the pseudo-republic into disrepute. Ortiz then withdrew from day-to-day politics, but continued to take part in public life as president of the Sociedad Económica de Amigos del País (Economic Society of Friends of the Country), director of the vigorous periodical *Revista Bimestre Cubana* [Cuban Bimonthly Review] and editor of *Ultra*. He was also an institutional innovator, founding the Sociedad del Folklore Cubano. He wrote occasional political pamphlets, with Ramiro Guerra y Sánchez and Emilio Roig y Leuschenring, making trenchant critiques of Cuba's internal organization and external relationships. The total output of Ortiz is voluminous. His complete works merit collection and publication.

Ortiz used Positivistic ideas and methods to undertake rational diagnoses of society and to devise practical solutions to perceived problems. For Ortiz, unlike some Mexican intellectuals, Positivism was an instrument for change, not a weapon of the status quo. Ortiz looked to the formation of a patriotic and disinterested meritocracy, and, influenced by the Italian socialist criminologist Enrico Ferri, was animated by the view that social cohesion and the quality of civic life would best be assured by a penal code designed to constrain despotism. From his boyhood experience of a clerical schooling and his observation of the identification of the Catholic Church with Spanish colonialism in the 1890s, Ortiz derived a powerful anti-clericalism and a hostility to all forms of superstition and religious fanaticism. This was observed in both his pioneering studies of African-cult practices in Cuba and his historical study of "folk" Catholicism in the 17th century. Ortiz was careful, however, to stress that an irrational belief in the supernatural and a regression into primitive behaviour could be seen among Spanish immigrants (rich and poor) as well as among African-Cubans.

A second major theme in Ortiz's writings is patriotic citizenship. His concern was to awaken Cubans to a greater awareness of the vitality of their national heritage through political pamphlets, works of philology and anthropological writings. Rejecting both an uncritical absorption of US culture and the alternative of Pan-Hispanism propagated from Spain, Ortiz looked to the evolution of a strong, independent republic inextricably linked with the notion of patriotic citizenship. The emancipation of an independent, sovereign Cuba was deferred by the failure of the intelligentsia to maintain the quality of leadership set by Martí and the patriotic heroes of the 1890s. Ortiz warned in 1924 of a national decline evident in poor literacy rates and falling school attendance disclosed by census data. Essential prerequisites of a strong republic included a thorough education reform, agrarian reform and the fragmentation of the large landed estates, and constitutional changes, above all clean, honest elections. It was characteristic of Ortiz that he chose to publish a selection of the writings against annexation to the United States by the Cuban intellectual of the mid-19th century, José Antonio Saco, to coincide with the peak of US hegemony and the entrenchment of the dictatorship of President Gerardo Machado. It was equally typical of Ortiz that he sought to revive memories of Martí in the year of the centenary of his birth (1953), shortly after Fulgencio Batista thwarted aspirations to democratic consolidation by seizing power in a coup.

The third main theme of Ortiz's writings is ethnicity and race. Ortiz sought to arouse awareness of the Indo-Cuban past through his archaeological inquiries. But his studies of the African-Cuban present had more immediate and long-term impact. The customs, traditions, music, dance and folklore of African-Cubans were too glibly dismissed as being picturesque; they all merited rigorous study as invigorating features of national life. In a series of powerful studies, both historical and contemporary, of African-Cuban themes, Ortiz had the civic objective of demolishing racist orthodoxies, and of undermining the regulation of political rights and the mediation of citizenship by the state along ethnic lines. An efflorescence of African-Cuban militancy during the inter-war period, supported by advocates of an inclusionary *cubanidad* like Ortiz's, did much to stimulate a public openness to the creative vitality of the politically committed poetry of Nicolás Guillén and the work of other lesser figures who lived the life of African-Cubans in their poetry. The democratic cosmopolitanism of Ortiz was manifest in his endorsement of rebuttals by democrats of Fascist and Nazi social theories, and in his reflections upon both the Holocaust and segregationism in the Deep South. For Ortiz there were no "predestined," "chosen" or damned races, only racism, a tragic reality founded in a pernicious myth of superiority.

The discourse of Fernando Ortiz had three main strands. One was an invigorating eclecticism that reflected the strengths of Cuban intellectual traditions, and upon which the revolutionary regime drew in the 1960s and 1970s. A second unitary thread was a commitment to the concept and practice of patriotic citizenship and to the accountability of intellectuals and politicians. A third feature was his contribution to the international debate on themes of ethnicity and race, and, with regard to Cuba, to the question of constructing a national identity where the contributions of all ethnic groups were equally recognized.

CHRISTOPHER ABEL

Biography

Born in Havana, Cuba, 16 July 1881. Childhood spent in Menorca (Balearics) where he completed his secondary education. Studied law, first at the University of Havana, and later at Barcelona and Madrid. Obtained doctorate in law in 1901. Worked in Cuban consular service in various European countries. Started to teach law at Havana University in 1909. Among the founders of the Universidad Popular (intended for the unprivileged) in 1914. Editor of *Revista Bimestre Cubana*, 1910–59. Elected president of the Sociedad Económica de Amigos del País in 1923. A founder of the Society of Cuban Folklore in 1924 and of their journal, *Archivos del Folklore Cubano*, in the same year. Lived in Washington from 1931 to 1933 when he took an active stand against the Cuban dictator, Gerardo Machado. Founded the Society for African-Cuban Studies in 1937. Began series of seminars on ethnography at Havana University in 1942. Received honorary doctorates from the universities of Columbia, Cuzco and Santa Clara (Cuba). Died in 1969.

Selected Works

Ortiz's output is vast, and as indicated in Christopher Abel's article on him, as yet there is no edition of his complete works. Thus what is given here is a selection of his publications, which concentrates on those most likely to interest students of literature. Details of a bibliography are also provided below.

Hampa afro-cubana. Los negros brujos, Madrid: Librería de F. Fé, 1906
El caballero encantado y la moza esquiva, Havana: Imprenta La Universal, 1910
La reconquista de América. Reflexiones sobre el panhispanismo, Paris: Ollendorf, 1910
Entre cubanos, Paris: Ollendorf, 1913
Un catauro de cubanismos, Havana: n.p., 1923
Glosario de afronegrismos, Havana: Imprenta El Siglo XX, 1924

La fiesta afrocubana del Día de Reyes, Havana: Imprenta El Siglo XX, 1925

"Los negros curros," *Archivos del Folklore Cubano*, vol. 2 (1926–27); vol. 3 (1928)

"Más acerca de la poesía mulata. Escorzos para su estudio," *Revista Bimestre Cubana*, vol. 37 (1936)

"La cubanidad y los negros," *Estudios Afrocubanos*, vol. 3 (1939)

"América es un ajiaco," *La Nueva Democracia*, vol. 21/11 (1940)

Contrapunteo cubano del tabaco y el azúcar, Havana: J. Montero, 1940; as *Cuban Counterpoint: Tobacco and Sugar*, translated by Harriet de Onís, New York: Knopf, 1947

"Del fenómeno social de la transculturación y de su importancia en Cuba," *Revista Bimestre Cubana*, vol. 46 (1940)

"Los factores humanos de la cubanidad," *Revista Bimestre Cubana*, vol. 21 (1940)

"Por la integración de blancos y negros," *Revista Bimestre Cubana*, vol. 51 (1943)

El huracán. Su mitología y sus símbolos, Mexico City: Fondo de Cultura Económica, 1947

"La 'tragedia' de los ñáñigos," *Cuadernos Americanos*, vol. 52/4 (1950)

La africanía de la música folklórica de Cuba, Havana: Publicaciones del Ministerio de Educación, 1950

"Los negros y la transculturación," *La Nueva Democracia*, vol. 31/1 (1951)

"Cubanidad y cubanía," *Islas*, Santa Clara, vol. 6/2 (1964)

Further Reading

Barnet, Miguel, "La segunda africanía," *Unión*, vol. 5/3 (July–September 1966)

_____ "Los estudios del folklore en Cuba," in his *La fuente viva*, Havana: Letras Cubanas, 1983

Coronil, Fernando, "Challenging Colonial Histories: *Cuban Counterpoint* / Ortiz's Counterfetishism, " in *Critical Theory, Cultural Politics and Latin American Narrative*, edited by Steven M. Bell, Albert H. Le May and Leonard Orr, Notre Dame, Indiana: University of Notre Dame Press, 1993

Gutiérrez de la Solana, Alberto, "En torno a Fernando Ortiz, lo afrocubano y otros ensayos," in *El ensayo y la crítica en Iberoamérica*, edited by Keith Ellis and Kurt L. Levy, Toronto: University of Toronto Press, 1970

Ibarra, Jorge, "La herencia científica de Fernando Ortiz," *Revista Iberoamericana*, vol. 56/152–53 (July–December 1990)

Marinello, Juan, "Don Fernando Ortiz: notas sobre nuestro tercer descubridor," *Bohemia*, Havana, vol. 61/16 (18 April 1969)

Miscelánea de estudios dedicados a Fernando Ortiz, Havana: Sociedad Económica de Amigos del País, 1956

Pérez Firmat, Gustavo, *The Cuban Condition: Translation and Identity in Modern Cuban Literature*, Cambridge and New York: Cambridge University Press, 1989 [Chapters 1 and 2 are on Ortíz]

Serrano, Carlos, "Miguel de Unamuno y Fernando Ortiz: un caso de regeneracionismo transatlántico," *Nueva Revista de Filología Hispánica*, vol. 35/1 (1987)

Bibliographies

García Carranza, Araceli, *Bio-bibliografía de don Fernando Ortiz*, Havana: Biblioteca Nacional José Martí, 1970

Juan L. Ortiz 1896–1978

Argentine poet

Juan L. Ortiz's poetry only began to be widely known and read in Argentina – aside from a few honourable exceptions – in the 1960s. Moreover, the thirteen books of verse collected in *En el aura del sauce*, 1970–71 [In the Aura of the Willow] were only available in limited editions published by the author, and some of them, such as *El junco y la corriente* [The Rush and the Stream] or *El Gualeguay* [The Gualeguay River], had never actually appeared in book form before. *En el aura del sauce*, published in three volumes, more or less amounts to Ortiz's complete works. It includes published but little-known collections, as well as previously unpublished works.

The most arresting feature of Ortiz's work is its consistency, continuity and uniformity. From 1924, the date of his first known compositions, to 1970, Ortiz wrote and rewrote almost uninterruptedly his "conception of the world" (in Lucien Goldmann's phrase), that is the world of the Argentine seaboard, its constituent parts, its characteristics, its people. Ortiz was a virtuoso of monotony, for despite having written about the same figures and scenarios for almost fifty years, he always achieved difference and variation, always found that

"something extra" in a line or verse which distinguishes invention from mere repetition. In this characteristic Ortiz is unparalleled in Argentine literature.

In the case of Ortiz, more so than for other Argentine poets, it is difficult to separate the life from the work. The poet's entire existence as a discreet, taciturn administrator, withdrawn into a context of provincial tranquillity, seems to be manifested in his poems and throughout his entire production. This tranquillity, this tender solitude and withdrawal, accompanies the continual presence of the coastal landscape, a presence which in its turn constitutes the essence of his poetry.

The search for harmony between certain objects, nature and the human presence is a characteristic of Ortiz's poetry. This imperative recurs throughout his work, and indeed gives it poetic unity and coherence. Since this harmony can only be achieved provisionally and on rare occasions, Ortiz asserted, the poet's task is to search and to question unceasingly. In his poetry, Ortiz attempts to draw back the veil from each entity and feature of the coastal cosmos; he has attempted to capture that mystery, that nakedness where the poetic essence of each entity and feature is to be found. Ortiz has striven to see beneath the surface, to a realm in which the harmony between objects, nature and the human presence is realized.

El agua y la noche [The Water and the Night], Ortiz's first work, was published in 1933. It was followed by *El alba sube*, 1937 [The Dawn Rises], *El ángel inclinado*, 1938 [The Bowed Angel] and *La rama hacia el este*, 1940 [The Branch Bending to the East]. These four works form a unity which might be described as the basis of Ortiz's vision of the banks of the river and its people. Here the poet establishes the inhabitants, atmosphere and situations of the poetic universe which all his subsequent works were to inhabit.

It was in *El aire conmovido*, 1949 [The Unquiet Air], however, that Ortiz managed to liberate poetry from the shackles of the poetic line – perhaps the most interesting poetic achievement of his work – in order to yoke it to language as a whole. Poetry would thus no longer be a technical problem of versification – as it continued to be for most Argentine poets of the era – becoming rather a problem of language and expression: "Mirábamos el río, las islas, este río, estas islas. / Dos o tres notas, sólo, que jugaba apaciblemente / hasta el infinito, sin elevarse mucho, / en el brillo natural como rocío persistente. / Una gracia quieta, quieta, de melodia algo aérea, / que se veía morir, sin embargo." (We watched the river, the islands, this river, these islands. / Just two or three notes, which played peacefully / into infinity, rising just a little, / in the splendour of nature like persistent dew. / A still, still grace, with an airy melody, / which nevertheless was visibly dying).

This affirmation of language itself as the very stuff of poetry – which as well as being the mark of his own work represents the poetic legacy taken up by writers such as Juan José Saer or Juan Gelman, to name two very different examples – is striven for by employing words in order to sound out their vital pulse: as Hugo Gola states in his prologue to *En el aura del sauce*, "Ortiz demonstrates in his work that he merely liberates the poetic treatment of the Word; anything else would be continued slavery. He thus situates himself, involuntarily, at the vanguard of a literature which strives to push back the confines of verse, breaking down all barriers and making language merely the raw material of poetry."

The period spanning *La mano infinita*, 1951 [The Infinite Hand] to *La orilla que se abisma*, 1970 [The Abysmal Bank] and *El Gualeguay* (1970) – via *La brisa profunda*, 1954 [The Deep Breeze], *El alma y las colinas*, 1956 [The Soul and the Hills] and *De las raíces y del cielo*, 1958 [From the Roots and from Heaven] – can be defined as the second phase of Ortiz's poetic output, in which the poetic universe of the seaboard, whose foundations were laid in his first four books, is more fully realized.

Generally literary critics have subsumed Ortiz's works under the three headings of philosophically idealistic verse, the poetry of love for nature, and that of social commitment.

Ortiz, though he loathed dull provincialism, was much more than a mere imitator of Buenos Aires personalities or theories, as some have asserted. His autodidactic education and subtle irony gave him a remarkable lucidity from a young age (in the early years of the century, when Louis Aragon had hardly begun to be known in Buenos Aires, Juan José Saer recounts, "Ortiz had already translated a couple of his novels"). Despite his long-standing sympathy for communism, Ortiz was a liber-

tarian spirit, free of aesthetic or social prejudices. The only creed he professed was an unparalleled curiosity and innocence, which he managed to convey in his verses with candour and wit. "The outstanding feature of his character," adds Saer in relation to Ortiz, "was his generosity of spirit, a kind of cosmic compassion which caused him to consider every living thing worthy of friendship, solace and nurture."

Imprisoned in the vastness of the seaboard, Ortiz made an art of monotony, a contemplative virtue of descriptive and allegorical reiteration: "In Ortiz thematic reiteration does not constitute repetition," concludes Hugo Gola, "but rather observance of a "formal law of fantasy" which applies throughout Ortiz's work. His insistence reveals an ever-renewed desire to capture images which call to him and force him to repeat tirelessly his expressive litany, so as to overcome inevitable despair, the bitter taste of ashes."

Amidst unimagined vicissitudes, Ortiz has been a stalwart of integrity and asceticism. Devoted to anonymity and indifferent to formal and officious culture, he has painstakingly constructed a poetic world whose originality marks it as his own. Many of his verses bear a stamp which is quite unmistakable: ". . . alma, / ¿por qué tiritas, / si la melancolía, no lo ves? pasa a su cielo, allá, / casi enseguida / encima del platino que pareciera el *en sí* / del río . . . " (. . . soul, / why do you shiver, / when melancholy, don't you see? passes on to its heaven, there, / almost in an instant / over the platinum which seems the very essence of the river . . .), in *La orilla que se abisma*; or "Alma, inclínate / ante los cariños idos . . ." (Soul, bow down before departed affections . . .) in *El alma y las colinas*; or that unforgettable ode to one of his many greyhounds in *La brisa profunda*: "Ay, oigo todavía tu llamado, tu súplica latida como desde una medrosa pesadilla / mientras mi corazón lo mismo que tus flancos, sangra, sangra, y marzo, entre las cañas sigue lloviendo sobre ti . . ." (I can still hear you calling, howling your entreaty as if from a fearful nightmare / whilst my heart, like your flanks, bleeds and bleeds, and March, amidst the sugar canes, still rains over you . . .).

As suggested previously, it is almost impossible not to link the works of *Juanele* (as his friends called him) with the story of his life. The pervasive sense of authenticity in all the poet's descriptions is perhaps the principal evidence for such a link: here is a man who has wrought a means of writing out of existence itself, forged a daily necessity out of harmony. This is perhaps why his readers have been avid but few: to capture and to breathe these poems, the *image* of the poet is necessary. Where it intersects with the image of the poet himself, poetry is in fact just one more element of an entire contemplative harmony: in Ortiz, poetry is a tool for such a contemplation, for an acute and vigilant reflection on life.

"No olvidéis que la poesía / si la pura sensitiva," says the poet, "o la ineludible sensitiva / es asimismo, o acaso sobre todo, la intemperie sin fin / tendida, humildemente, para el invento del amor" (Do not forget that poetry, / whether purely sensitive or inescapably sensitive / is also, perhaps above all, hard and endless vistas, / crossed, or crucified, if you prefer, by endless calls / and laid out, humbly, for the invention of love).

Such a conception of poetry, and its relation to the life of the poet, is perhaps the reason why Ortiz's legacy, evident in a long and disparate generation of writers he influenced, has been that of a man of letters rather than that of a public poet.

Since the poet's death in provincial obscurity during a dictatorship, his works have come to form a fitting biographical testimony; the verses now define Ortiz, not vice versa. The Argentine seaboard and Juan L. Ortiz have thus become so inextricably linked that it is impossible to talk about one without referring to the other, for he has been in a certain sense the founder of its handful of myths and the bearer of its joys.

CLAUDIO CANAPARO

translated by Ian Craig

Biography

Born in Puerto Ruiz, province of Entre Ríos, Argentina, 11 June 1896. Youngest of ten children. Father ranch mananger. Began secondary education in Gualeguay, 1910. Started to spend time in Buenos Aires, attending lectures at Arts Faculty, 1913. Published in the anarchist newspaper, *La Protesta*. Returned to Gualeguay, 1915, and lived there until 1942. Employed by local registry office. Married Gerarda Irazusta in 1924. Known by his many friends and admirers as "Juanele." Retired in 1942, and settled for good in Paraná. Travelled to China, 1957. Awarded the Prize of Honour by the Argentine Poetry Foundation and the "Minuán de Oro" by the municipality of Gualeguay to mark his 80th birthday in 1976. Died at his home on 2 September 1978.

Selected Works

All Ortiz's books of poems are the traditional "slim" volumes. Thus, although they are all listed here, readers are likely to find the Complete Works in 3 volumes more useful.

Poetry

El agua y la noche, Buenos Aires: Biblioteca Editorial P.A.C, 1933
El alba sube, Buenos Aires: Rumbo, 1937
El ángel inclinado, Buenos Aires: Feria, 1938
La rama hacia el este, Buenos Aires: AIAPE, 1940
El álamo y el viento, Buenos Aires: Sauce, 1947
El aire conmovido, Buenos Aires: Sauce, 1949
La mano infinita, Buenos Aires: Llanura, 1951
La brisa profunda, Buenos Aires: Este, 1954
El alma y las colinas, Buenos Aires: Este, 1956
De las raíces y del cielo, Buenos Aires: Este, 1958

Complete Works

En el aura del sauce, 3 vols, Rosario, Argentina: Biblioteca, 1970–71

Further Reading

Ara, Guillermo, *Suma de poesía argentina (1538–1968)*, Buenos Aires: Guadalupe, 1971
Beracochea, Roberto, *El paisaje de Gualeguay y sus poetas*, Paraná: Mesopotamia, 1977
Kamenszain, Tamara, *El texto silencioso (tradición y vanguardia en la poesía sudamericana)*, Mexico City: UNAM, 1983
Sadí Grosso, Luis, *Poesía argentina. Poemática entrerriana contemporánea*, Paraná: Nueva Impresora, 1958
Salas, Horacio, "Juanele. El último de los olvidados," *Análisis* (29 January 1969)
Serra, Edelweis, *El cosmos de la palabra. Mensaje poético y estilo de Juan L. Ortiz*, Buenos Aires: Noé, 1976
Veiravé, Alfredo, *Juan L. Ortiz: la experiencia poética*, Buenos Aires: Lohlé, 1984 [reliable monograph]

Oswald de Sousa Andrade, José

See Andrade

Miguel Otero Silva 1908–1985

Venezuelan prose writer and poet

It has been said that during Miguel Otero Silva's long tenure as one of Venezuela's most prominent narrators, he took his country's literature to a new level using innovative narrative techniques. An exception is found in his first novel *Fiebre*, 1939 [Fever], where Otero Silva narrates in linear form the difficult moments of the political turmoil that Venezuela experienced in 1928 of which he was a protagonist, as were many other university students. Absent from its pages are the techniques – such as the experimentation with time – that were already used by writers of this period and initiated by Proust, Joyce, Faulkner and Virginia Woolf. The primary concern of the author in this youthful work is not of an aesthetic nature; rather, he seeks to engage with the suffering of a generation of people under a dictatorship.

It was sixteen years before Otero Silva's next novel, *Casas muertas*, 1955 [Dead Houses] appeared, and this was the first to receive national and international recognition. During the years of literary silence, Otero Silva's time was absorbed as editor-in-chief of *El Nacional*, the Caracas newspaper that he founded. In *Casas muertas* the author begins to use a chronological structure in a novel that apparently has a circular development. Apparently, because the last chapter is not narrated retrospectively as were the previous eleven; instead it projects itself away from the text to give birth to a new theme that will be fully developed in his next novel *Oficina no. 1*, 1961 [Office Number 1]. Even though there is perfect continuity between both works, in the second novel Otero Silva makes use of the double narrative plane and the flashback, techniques previously used in Venezuelan narrative by Enrique Bernardo Núñez. Both novels are preoccupied with the decay of the agricultural way of life in Venezuela and the sudden imposition of a new way of life based on the wealth created by the petroleum industry.

Following *Oficina no. 1*, Otero Silva published *La muerte de Honorio*, 1963 [Honorio's Death], *Cuando quiero llorar no lloro*, 1970 [I Can't Cry When I Want to], *Lope de Aguirre, príncipe de la libertad*, 1979 [Lope de Aguirre Prince of Liberty] and lastly, *La piedra que era Cristo*, 1984 [The Rock that Was Christ].

Even though it is correct to state that all of Otero Silva's novels incorporate elements of Venezuela's contemporary history, *Lope de Aguirre, príncipe de la libertad* is the only one of his works that can be classified as a historical novel. It is in this work that the author is most concerned with historical truth but, on the other hand, he is not simply recounting the life of Lope de Aguirre, since the author presents an ideological reinterpretation of this historical figure's life. Lope de Aguirre is a figure which has fascinated writers and artists both from Latin America and Europe. He is the protagonist of *Daimón* by the Argentine writer, Abel Posse; a source for the composite figure of the tyrant in Valle-Inclán's brilliant avant garde novel, *Tirano Banderas* (*The Tyrant*) and the protagonist of the extraordinary film *Aguirre the Wrath of God* by the German director, Werner Herzog.

It is a common denominator of all Otero Silva's novels to make use of characters that represent the ordinary people, many of whom are known only by their first name. More than characters, they are recognisable types that are at the forefront of Venezuela's ever evolving history since they are found in the markets, political prisons, shanty towns, streets, and therefore are easily identifiable with the reader's own experience.

JOSÉ B. ALVAREZ IV

Biography

Born in Barcelona, Venezuela, 26 October 1908. Attended primary school at Puerto La Cruz. Moved to Caracas, 1914. Secondary education, Liceo San José. His first poem, "Estampa" [Print], published in a magazine, 1924. Studied engineering at Caracas University, graduating in 1924. Participated in student rebellion against the strongman, Juan Vicente Gómez, and had to leave the country in the late 1920s. Founded the satirical-political magazine *El morrocoy azul*, 1941, and the newspaper *El Nacional*, 1942. Private visit to USSR, 1965. Appointed member of the Venezuelan Academy of the Language, 1972. Died in Caracas, 28 August 1985.

Selected Works

Novels

Fiebre, Caracas: Elite, 1939
Casas muertas, Caracas: Pasa, 1955
Oficina no. 1, Buenos Aires: Losada, 1961
La muerte de Honorio, Buenos Aires: Losada, 1963
Cuando quiero llorar no lloro, Caracas: Tiempo Nuevo, 1970
Lope de Aguirre, príncipe de la libertad, Barcelona: Seix Barral, 1979
La piedra que era Cristo, Bogotá: Oveja Negra, 1984

Poetry

Agua y cauce: poemas revolucionarios, Mexico City: México Nuevo, 1937
La mar que es el morir, Caracas: Arte, 1965
Poesía completa, Caracas: Monte Ávila, 1972

Other Writings

Elegía coral a Andrés Eloy Blanco, Caracas: Tipografía Vargas, 1958
México y la revolución mexicana. Un escritor venezolano en la Unión Soviética, Caracas: Dirección de Cultura, Universidad Central de Venezuela, 1966
Andrés Eloy Blanco: homenaje en el LXXVIII aniversario de su natalicio, Caracas: Ediciones del Congreso de la República, 1974

Further Reading

Araujo, Orlando, "¿Qué buscaba Miguel Otero Silva?" in his *Narrativa venezolana contemporánea*, Caracas: Tiempo Nuevo, 1972
Barnola, Pedro Pablo, "Miguel Otero Silva y *Casas muertas*," in his *Estudios crítico-literarios*, Caracas: Monte Ávila, 1970
Barrientos, Juan José, "Aguirre y la rebelión de 'Los Marañones,'" *Cuadernos Americanos*, vol. 2/2 (1988)
Fauquié Bescós, Rafael, "Sobre Miguel Otero Silva," *Revista Nacional de Cultura*, vol. 47/260 (1986)

Guaramato, Oscar, *et al.*, *Miguel Otero Silva y su tiempo*, Cumaná, Venezuela: Universidad de Oriente, 1986

Larrazábal Henríquez, Osvaldo, "*Lope de Aguirre, príncipe de la libertad*: una novedosa novela de Miguel Otero Silva," *Revista Iberoamericana*, vol. 60/166–67 (1994)

Marbán, Jorge, "Transfiguración histórica y creación literaria en el *Lope de Aguirre* de Otero Silva," *Revista Iberoamericana*, vol. 51/130–31 (1985)

Márquez Rodríguez, Alexis, *Acción y pasión en los personajes de Miguel Otero Silva y otros ensayos*, Caracas: Academia Nacional de la Historia, 1985

Pacheco, Carlos, "Retrospectiva crítica de Miguel Otero Silva," *Revista Iberoamericana*, vol. 60/166–67 (1994)

Pastor, Beatriz, "Las metamorfosis de *Lope de Aguirre*," *Estudios*, vol. 1/1 (1993)

Paz Castillo, Fernando, *Miguel Otero Silva: su obra literaria*, Caracas: Dirección de Cultura, Universidad Central de Venezuela, 1975

Szichman, Mario, *Miguel Otero Silva: mitología de una generación frustrada*, Caracas: Universidad Central de Venezuela, 1975

Zemskov, Valerii Borisovich, "Héroes, historia, ironía: algunos rasgos de la semblanza de Miguel Otero Silva," *América Latina*, Moscow, 1–2 (1981)

Interviews

"El compromiso esencial del artista es luchar por la paz del mundo (entrevista)," *América Latina* 12 (1980)

"Miguel Otero Silva: 'El escritor debe defender la justicia'," *América Latina* 12 (1981)

P

José Emilio Pacheco 1939–

Mexican poet, prose writer and translator

The work of José Emilio Pacheco is not confined to one genre. It includes poetry, the novel, the short story, theatre, the chronicle, translation. Activities that imply not only the production but also investigation and dissemination of culture. Since its beginnings during the early 1960s, in the field of literary journalism, his work has received increasing recognition, confirmed by national journalism and literature awards. Outside Mexico, Pacheco's prestige allowed him to establish an international network of artistic and academic interchange that is evident in his poetry. Poems like "Turner's Landscape," "D.H. Lawrence y los poetas muertos" [D.H. Lawrence and the Dead Poets] or "'Birds in the Night' (Vallejo y Cernuda se encuentran en Lima)" [Vallejo and Cernuda Meet in Lima] call for a communal meeting of different cultural traditions. Pacheco's Spanish versions of poetry written in other languages are regularly included in his own books under sections entitled "Approximations," "Imitation," "Reading of . . .".

His critics regard him as the most important poet of his generation, and agree that his work, especially from *No me preguntes cómo pasa el tiempo*, 1969 (*Don't Ask Me How the Time Goes By*), succeeds in widening poetry's traditionally small circle of readers reducing the distance between the language of the specialist and that of the average inhabitant of the Latin American metropolis. The means he uses have been described in terms of "conversational language," "collage," "ready-made," "graffiti."

The first concept describes the predominant presence of linguistic forms that prioritize communication and resemble those used to transmit pragmatic information in everyday exchange, as in the case of the poem "Hoy mismo" [Right Now]: "Mira como las cosas que se van / Recuérda las / porque no volverás / a verlas nunca." (Take a good look at things as they go / Remember them / for you will never / see them again). "Collage" refers to the presence of diverse objects in an environment that is conventionally alien to them. In Pacheco's poetry, this is evident in the inclusion or insertion of epigraphs and titles (lines taken literally from other writers) or of codes disassociated from poetry (journalistic, historical, mathematical and biological language) – as is the case of the poem "Tema y variaciones: los insectos" [Theme and Variations: Insects]:

"El esfex de alas amarillas ataca / al saltamontes / Abre con su aguijón tres orificios / Pone sus huevecillos en las heridas / a fin de que al nacer los esfex / se coman vivo al prisionero que fue su tierra y cuna." (The yellow winged esfex attacks / the grasshopper / It opens three holes with its stinger / Lays its small eggs in the wounds / so that the newborn esfex / may eat alive / the prisoner that was their land and cradle.) These lines also shed light on the concept of "ready-made". The critic José Miguel Oviedo has described it as Pacheco's skilful use or manipulation of an object not "made" with artistic aims, but rather "found" for that purpose. The poet succeeds in rapidly bringing the reader and the poem together by means of the anomaly effected by reproducing the object in a foreign context. This operation suggests other contents and provokes a revision of its original meaning. Lastly, the concept of "graffiti" emphasizes the efficiency with which ephemeral writing reaches the reader. Presented in a space where the written word's capacities for recording and transcending are not justified, the graffiti's presence produces an impact because of its irony, which makes it stand out and gives it meaning by contrast. These mechanisms, that appeal to and reach the reader in various degrees, permit Pacheco to exercise a philosophical and social criticism (abstract and concrete) in which the traditional heights of specialization and its languages are reduced in order to allow a common ground of opinion for different types of readers.

This multiple presence of writing, voices and images previously created by others, has been understood as "intertextuality". Michael Doudoroff finds that the most interesting thing about this phenomenon in Pacheco's work is how the writer neutralizes the borders that conventionally divide literary experience from other types of experiences. The intertextualities of his poems allow Pacheco to establish a variety of places and moments in which to situate an experience, and the reflection and analysis that it provokes. In the synthetic mention of cities, landscapes, historical scenarios and characters, or cultural references, readers gain access to a cosmopolitan world that also reaches them through their familiarity with mass media (radio, TV, films) and the products of the consumer society surrounding them. The distance between poetry and the average citizen is thus reduced. This dissolving of borders allows the construction of poems as sharp "literary" comments originating from a vast spectrum of non literary themes (a street scene, travels, the reading of a book, a newspaper article, a machine, all things as being in constant motion and faced with the inevitability of their eventual disappearance, as in poems such as "Conversación romana" [Roman Conversation]. The sum of these reveals the unified vision underlying his multifaceted interests.

Despite the presence of highly communicative language, José Emilio Pacheco does not actually follow the tracks of "conversational" poetry, that reached its peak in Spanish America during the 1960s (Ernesto Cardenal – a poet to whom Pacheco pays homage – is one of its most prestigious figures), but rather, circulates among different languages and voices, making use of codes found primarily in dialogue while, at the same time, employing specialized vocabulary or words forgotten in everyday speech.

With regard to his versions in Spanish of other writers' works, Pacheco has said in the introductory note to his book *Tarde o temprano*, 1980 [Sooner or Later]: "In some way they are not, as one might believe, 'translations of translations', but rather poems based on other poems. I consider these pieces a collective work that should be anonymous and, to me, it seems abusive to sign it." The same criteria that can be used to explain the presence of intertextuality can be applied to his other stylistic devices. Universal poetry seen as a flowing process of continual becoming, the writing of an author is but one more contribution, always limited and ephemeral as is one's life in cosmic terms. In the poem "A quien pueda interesar" [To Whom It May Concern], Pacheco writes: " La poesía que busco / es como un diario / en donde no hay proyecto / ni medida." (the poetry I seek / is like a journal / that has no project / nor measure.)

Already in *El reposo del fuego*, 1966 [The Resting Place of Fire], the idea of an ephemeral life/work was contained in the image of the rapid combustion of the flame: "Arden las llamas / mundo y fuego /Mira/ la hoja al viento / tan triste / de la hoguera. Es hoguera el poema / y no perdura / Hoja al viento también / también tristísima." (the flames burn / world and fire. / Look at / the leaf in the wind / so sad / of the bonfire. // The poem is a bonfire / and it does not last / A leaf in the wind / too / also very sad). According to Pacheco's poetics, the project of every human being is a constant beginning with no possibility of completion. As with the nature of the flame, the goal is to burn for an instant. Completion is just an appearance, the abandonment of a project halfway through, because even short-term human achievements are deceptively projected toward transcendence. Human beings suffer from a terrible illusion of immortality. Before reaching its impossible finale everything disintegrates. The object of all existence is a constant beginning that will be taken over by another builder whose reason for being is to collaborate in the construction of a monumental building of beginnings. This idea can be traced throughout his later work, for example in the volume *Miro la tierra* [I Look at the Earth], thus entitled in memory of the earthquake that destroyed part of Mexico City in 1985: "Todos sufrimos la derrota / somos víctimas del desastre / Pero en vez de llorar actuemos // Con piedras de las ruinas hay que forjar / otra ciudad, otro país, otra vida." (We all suffer the defeat / we are victims of the disaster / But instead of crying let us act // With stones from the ruins we must forge / another city, another country, another life).

In Pacheco's narrative, the novella *Las batallas en el desierto*, 1981 (*Battles in the Desert*), earned him the unanimous recognition of his critics. The motives and results contained in the rest of his works can be found in its plot. An adolescent, Carlitos, falls in love with Mariana, the young mother of his best friend, Jim. While Carlitos's love suffers repression from family, the metropolis, Mexico City during the 1940s, changes and the country undergoes economic modernization. The narration interweaves childhood memories, recounted by the now adult character, with the more immediate actions of Carlitos as a child. Writing about this novel, Hugo Verani says: "The story, apparently trivial, comes out strongly imprinted with a will to demythify childhood as a golden age and to question the established order: that of the Mexican bourgeoisie and its values." Here, childhood is just one more beginning with the illusion of completion, with adulthood it begins to crumble halfway through.

Pacheco's social and philosophical criticism has attracted the attention of those who see modernization as a threat to the global ecological balance. A number of his poems dealing with nature, especially animals and insects as victims of the human search for immortality and well-being, have been collected in anthologies such as *Fin de siglo y otros poemas*, 1984 [End of the Century and Other Poems], and *Álbum de zoología*, 1991 (*An Ark for the Next Millennium*), and have awakened a renewed interest in his work.

LUIS REBAZA-SORALUZ

Biography

Born in Mexico City, 30 June 1939. Attended the Universidad Nacional Autónoma de México (UNAM), Mexico City, 1957–64; left without a degree. Married; two daughters. Worked on *México en la Cultura*, 1958–61 and served as editor, 1962–71; editorial secretary, *Revista de la Universidad de México*, 1959–65. Contributed to the journals *Revista Mexicana de Literatura*, *Cuadernos del Viento* and *Pájaro Cascabel*. Lecturer, University of Maryland, College Park; University of Illinois, Urbana; universities in Toronto and New York; and University of Essex, Colchester, England. Editor of the critical review, *Diálogos*, and cultural sections of *Excelsior* and *Novedades* newspapers. Awarded the Enrique Lihn Prize, 1966; Magda Donato Prize, 1968; National Poetry Prize, 1969 for *No me preguntes cómo pasa el tiempo*; Guggenheim Fellowship, 1970; Xavier Villaurrutia Prize, 1973. Elected to the Colegio Nacional, 1986.

Selected Works

Poetry
Los elementos de la noche, Mexico City: UNAM, 1963
El reposo del fuego, Mexico City: Fondo de Cultura Económica, 1966
No me preguntes cómo pasa el tiempo: poemas, 1964–1968, Mexico City: Joaquín Mortiz, 1969; as *Don't Ask Me How the Time Goes By: Poems, 1964–1968*, translated by Alastair Reid, New York: Columbia University Press, 1978 [bilingual edition]
Árbol entre dos muros/Tree Between Two Walls, translated by Ed Dorn and Gordon Brotherston, Los Angeles: Black Sparrow Press, 1969 [bilingual edition]

Irás y no volverás, Mexico City: Fondo de Cultura Económica, 1973
Islas a la deriva, Mexico City: Siglo XXI, 1976
Ayer es nunca jamás, Caracas: Monte Ávila, 1978
Desde entonces: poemas 1975–1978, Mexico City: Era, 1980
Tarde o temprano, Mexico City: Fondo de Cultura Económica, 1980 [Includes translations of other poets' work]
Los trabajos del mar, Mexico City: Era, 1983
Fin de siglo y otros poemas, Mexico City: Fondo de Cultura Económica, 1984
Alta traición, Madrid: Alianza, 1985
Álbum de zoología, Guadalajara: Cuarto Menguante, 1985; *An Ark for the Next Millennium*, translated by Margaret Sayers Peden, Austin: University of Texas Press, 1993 [selections]
Miro la tierra: poemas 1983–1986, Mexico City: Era, 1986
Ciudad de la memoria: poemas 1986–1989, Mexico City: Era, 1989
El silencio de la luna: poemas 1985–1993, Mexico City: Era, 1994

Short Fiction

La sangre de Medusa, Mexico City: Porrúa, 1958
El viento distante y otros relatos, Mexico City: Era, 1963
El principio del placer, Mexico City: Joaquín Mortiz, 1972
Las batallas en el desierto, Mexico City: Era, 1981; as *Battles in the Desert and Other Stories*, translated by Katherine Silver, New York: New Directions, 1987
La sangre de Medusa y otros cuentos marginales, Mexico City: Era, 1990

Novel

Morirás lejos, Mexico City: Joaquín Mortiz, 1967

Other Writings

Poesía modernista, Mexico City: SEP/UNAM, 1982
Crónica del puerto de Veracruz, in collaboration with Fernando Benítez, Xalapa, Mexico: Gobierno del Estado de Veracruz, 1986

Anthologies in Translation

Signals from the Flames: Selected Poetry, edited by Yvette Miller and translated by Thomas Hoeksema, Pittsburgh: Latin American Literary Review Press, 1980
Selected Poems, edited by George McWhirter and translated by Thomas Hoeksema, *et al.*, New York: New Directions, 1987 [bilingual edition]

Compilations and Anthologies

José Emilio Pacheco: selecciones, edited by Luis Antonio de Villena, Madrid: Júcar, 1986

Further Reading

Aguilar, Helene J.F. de, "Inspiration and Its Agents," *Parnassus*, vol. 14/2 (1988)
Cluff, Russell M., "Immutable Humanity within the Hands of Time: Two Short Stories by José Emilio Pacheco," *Latin American Literary Review*, vol. 10/20 (1982)
D'Lugo, Carol Clark, "Narrative and Historical Commitment in Pacheco's *Morirás lejos, Chasqui*, vol. 19/2 (1990)
Dourdoroff, Michael J., "José Emilio Pacheco: an Overview of the Poetry," *Hispania*, vol. 72/2 (1989)
Duncan, Cynthia, "The Fantastic as a Vehicle of Social Criticism in José Emilio Pacheco's 'La fiesta brava,'" *Chasqui*, vol, 14/2–3 (1985)
Duncan, J. Ann, "The Themes of Isolation and Persecution in José Emilio Pacheco's Short Stories," *Ibero-Amerikanisches Archiv*, vol. 4/3 (1978)
_____ "The Novel as Poem and Document: José Emilio Pacheco's *Morirás lejos*," *Ibero-Amerikanisches Archiv*, vol. 6/4 (1980)
Forster, Merlin H., "Four Contemporary Mexican Poets: Marco Antonio Montes de Oca, Gabriel Zaid, José Emilio Pacheco, Homero Aridjis," in *Tradition and Renewal: Essays on 20th-Century Latin American Literature and Culture*, Urbana: University of Illinois Press, 1975
Gordon, Samuel, "Los poetas ya no cantan, ahora hablan: aproximaciones a la poesía de José Emilio Pacheco," *Revista Iberoamericana*, vol. 56/150 (1990)
Gullón, Agnes M., "Dreams and Distance in Recent Poetry of José Emilio Pacheco," *Latin American Literary Review*, vol. 6/11 (1977)
Hancock, Joel, "Perfecting a Text: Authorial Revisions in José Emilio Pacheco's *Morirás lejos*," *Chasqui*, vol. 14/2–3 (1985)
Hoeksema, Thomas J., "José Emilio Pacheco: Signals from the Flames," *Latin American Literary Review*, vol. 3/5 (1974)
_____ "A Poetry of Extremes," *Review*, vol. 23 (1978)
Jiménez de Báez, Yvette, Diana Morán and Edith Negrín, *Ficción e historia. La narrativa de José Emilio Pacheco*, Mexico City: El Colegio de México, 1979
Negrín, Edith, "José Emilio Pacheco y el palimpsesto de la historia: a propósito de la tercera edición de *La sangre de Medusa*, *Literatura Mexicana*, vol. 2/1 (1991)
Olivera Williams, María-Rosa, "*Ciudad de la memoria* de José Emilio Pacheco: hacia la creación de un único poemario," *Literatura Mexicana*, vol. 2/2 (1991)
Verani, Hugo J. (editor), *José Emilio Pacheco ante la crítica*, Mexico City: UNAM, 1987; revised edition as *La hoguera y el viento: José Emilio Pacheco ante la crítica*, Mexico City: Era, 1993

Ricardo Palma 1833–1919

Peruvian prose writer

Though he began his literary career as a dramatist and poet, Ricardo Palma remains best known as the author of *Tradiciones peruanas* [Peruvian Traditions], collected in ten volumes and a supplement published over a period of nearly forty years (1872–1910). Many individual pieces had appeared in journals from as early as 1851, and many were extensively rewritten before republication, a practice which has created complex bibliographical problems for scholars.

The *tradición* as a genre was Palma's creation. Among its formal predecessors, Quevedo's *Sueños* come first, followed by the "letters" of 18th-century writers such as Montesquieu, Voltaire and Cadalso, Larra's essays, and Spanish *costum-*

bristas such as Estébanez Calderón and Mesonero Romanos; all of these offered possible models for describing aspects of social behaviour, though only occasionally from a historical perspective. On the other hand, Bécquer's *leyendas*, most of which were written during the decade before the publication of the first series of *Tradiciones peruanas*, showed how the late Middle Ages and the Renaissance could become the settings for romantic short stories as well as for full-scale novels in the manner of Sir Walter Scott.

The distinctive feature of the *tradición* is the historical note with which Palma interrupts his brief narratives, often drawing the reader's attention to the device as he does so. These notes supply information drawn from chronicles or histories, or from their documentary sources, concerning the principal figures of the period in which the anecdote is set, and especially the viceroy of the day, whose titles and honours are listed in full, as a preliminary to a brief outline of his career. The majority of these notes concern colonial Peru, with occasional excursions into the pre-Columbian era or the more recent period since Independence; a few draw on the history of a foreign nation, usually one of Peru's neighbours. The information is offered for its own sake, and contributes little or nothing to a better appreciation of the *tradición*'s particular anecdote, while its fragmentary presentation – brief notes spread across many *tradiciones* – prevents any possibility of its constituting a coherent popular history of Peru.

The *tradiciones* cover the entire range of Peruvian society, from viceroy to beggar, observed in a wide variety of situations. Courtiers, officials, clergy, lawyers, merchants, tradespeople, artists and rogues, all take their turn as the focus of Palma's attention. Some of the rarer crafts require explanation; the author's lively curiosity ensures that it is given with due attention to detail. At other times, as with the legal and medical professions, Palma can rely on common prejudice to do the work for him; the reader needs no prompting or direction as to ambiences such as these.

The historical notes in the *tradición*, especially when supported by archival documents, could be seen as authenticating the narrative they accompany. In many instances the anecdote indeed has a core of fact, but Palma has glossed and reworked his material to create an aesthetically pleasing text which is neither true history nor wholly fiction. Elsewhere the fictional element predominates, embroidering standard folktale motifs. As might be expected of the colonial period, many deal with matters of honour lost or impugned and vengeance taken, a rich source of material, already thoroughly exploited in Spanish Golden Age drama: the quarrel may be occasioned by direct verbal or physical insult, or arise from some misconduct with women, whether actual or merely perceived, or be the result of violating conventions of rank or social status; and vengeance may be swift and instinctive, taken in the heat of the moment, or coldly calculated and executed long after the event. Other *tradiciones* owe more to the picaresque repertoire of tricks and deceptions, generally practiced for personal gain but at times as returns in kind for the malicious actions of other people. A third source of material, again predictable in the context, is religion, and especially miracles attributed to the intervention of those saints who were the objects of popular devotion; punishment for sacrilegious acts against them is a particularly common theme.

Palma was fascinated by popular turns of phrase and many *tradiciones* are devoted to explaining their origin with a picturesque character in a specific situation. His love of language is reflected in the style he developed for the *tradición*, jocular and ironic, full of allusion and wordplay, switching easily from echoes of Golden Age authors to contemporary colloquialisms. Palma's highly individual style charmed his readers, but also discouraged imitation; the form he created, the *tradición*, effectively died with him.

RON KEIGHTLEY

Biography

Born in centre of Lima, Peru, 7 February 1833. Illegitimate son of Pedro Palma and Guillerma Carrillo, both *pardos* (mulattos). Mother died in Palma's childhood, a period of considerable political upheaval. Published early poems in the newspaper *El Comercio*, 1848. Took part in conspiracy against president Ramón Castilla in 1860, later an ally and friend. Spent next three years in exile in Chile. This experience broadened his intellectual horizons and gave him an interest in history. Travelled to Europe in 1864 and visited London, Paris and Venice. Acted as personal secretary to José Balta during latter's presidency which started in 1868. Later Palma was both deputy and senator for several terms. Married Cristina Román in 1876. Named corresponding member of Royal Spanish Academy of the Language, 1878. Home in Miraflores burnt down by Chilean troops during war of 1879–83. Lost the manuscript of a work in progress, "Los Marañones," as well as books and documents. Named director of National Library in 1883 and became known as "the begging librarian" because the library had been sacked by Chilean troops. Travelled to Spain in 1892. Last years spent in semi-retirement. Gave up directorship of National Library in 1911 and died at his home in Miraflores on 6 October 1919.

Selected Works

Poetry
Armonías: libro de un desterrado, Paris: Librairie de Charles Bouret, 1865
Pasionarias, Le Havre, France: Typographie Alphonse Lemale, 1870
Verbos y gerundios, Lima: Benito Gil, 1877
Filigranas, Lima: Imprenta Benito Gil, 1892

Prose Works
Corona patriótica, Lima: Tipografía del Mensajero, 1853
El demonio de los Andes, New York: Imprenta "Las Novedades," 1883
"Libro nuevo," in Clorinda Matto de Turner, *Tradiciones cuzqueñas*, Lima: Imprenta Torres Aguirre, 1886
Cachivaches, Lima: Imprenta Torres Aguirre, 1900

Compilations and Anthologies
Tradiciones, 6 vols, Lima: n.p. 1872–83
Epistolario, 2 vols, edited by Raúl Porras Barrenechea, Lima: Editorial Cultura Antártica, 1949
Tradiciones peruanas completas, edited by Edith Palma, Madrid: Aguilar, 1952 [There are several later editions. Apart from including *all* the Tradiciones, this volume carries *Anales de la Inquisición de Lima*, *La bohemia de mi tiempo*, and *Neologismos y americanismos*]
Cartas inéditas de Ricardo Palma, edited by Rubén Vargas Ugarte, Lima: Carlos Milla Batres, 1964

Translations
The Knights of the Cape, translated by Harriet de Onís, New York: Knopf, 1945 [Includes the title story and 37 other *Tradiciones*]

Further Reading

Andreu, Alicia G., "Una nueva aproximación al lenguaje en las *Tradiciones peruanas* de Ricardo Palma," *Revista de Estudios Hispánicos*, vol. 23/2 (1989)

Compton, Merlin D., *Ricardo Palma*, Boston: Twayne, 1982

Durán Luzio, Juan, "Ricardo Palma: cronista de una sociedad barroca," *Revista Iberoamericana*, vol. 53/140 (1987)

González, Aníbal, "Ricardo Palma's *Tradiciones peruanas*," in his *Journalism and the Development of Spanish American Narrative*, Cambridge: Cambridge University Press, 1993

Martínez Tolentino, Jaime, *Literatura hispánica e hispanoamericana. Tres autores revalorados: Ricardo Palma, Julián del Casal y Jacinto Benavente*, Kassel: Reichenberger, 1992

Porras Barrenechea, Raúl, "Palma romántico," in *Tres ensayos sobre Ricardo Palma*, Lima: Mejía Baca, 1954 [Contains poems by Palma not included elsewhere]

Tanner, Roy L., "Ricardo Palma and Francisco Quevedo: a Case of Rhetorical Affinity and Debt," *Kentucky Romance Quarterly*, vol. 31/4 (1984)

Panama

19th- and 20th-Century Narrative and Poetry

Just as Central American literature in general is one of the least known literatures of Latin America, so Panamanian letters, in particular, have been the least disseminated and internationally recognised. To the world, Panama is the country of the Canal, the Isthmus with its corridor linking two oceans: a stop-over point. To the Panamanian, this special geographical situation has been the defining feature of the nation's economic, political, social and cultural history.

Panamanian literature begins before Panama became an independent country. On 28 November 1821 the Isthmus broke away from the Spanish empire and on 24 February 1822 it was incorporated into Colombia. From the outset Panama suffered the consequences of living under Colombian rule, and separatist feeling developed. The physical distance between the two countries led to the stagnation of Panama's political, economic and cultural life, and to neglect in the areas of health and education. From the beginning, therefore, the Isthmus thought of itself as an appendage independent of Colombia.

The introduction of printing in 1821, at the end of the colonial era, facilitated the publication of newspapers in which the intellectual and literary output of the Republic's writers appeared. Mariano Arosemena (1794–1868), politician, journalist, diarist and one of the signatories of the Act of 1821, began to publish his ideas on the future of the Isthmus in the first newspapers of the era. A complete version of his *Apuntamientos históricos* [Historical Summaries], which appears in fragmentary form in newspapers during 1868 and 1869, was published in 1949. The work narrates the political, cultural and social history of Panama in the first forty years of the 19th century. Its value lies in its minutely detailed account of the events of the era, making it an indispensable source for students of the period.

The author's son, Justo Arosemena (1817–96), a doctor of law, representative, senator, diplomat and, briefly, President of the Federal State of Panama, is perhaps the most important figure in Panamanian political thought of the 19th century. In 1852, Justo Arosemena put forward a constitutional reform project to the Colombian congress. The project proposed making the Isthmus a federal state, autonomous with respect to home affairs, but dependent on the central government with regard to currency, foreign affairs, weights and measures, the Army and Navy, and the naturalization of foreign citizens. The project was turned down. Arosemena continued to campaign tenaciously by penning newspaper articles. In his works *Comentario al proyecto de acto reformatorio*, 1852 [Report on the Reform Act Project] and *El estado federal de Panamá*, 1855 [The Federal State of Panama], he argues brilliantly in favour of Panamanian national interests and the creation of the federal state. In 1855 the Colombian Congress drew up the Additional Act of the Constitution, in which Panama is designated a federal state (though it was returned to provincial status in 1885), thanks to the eloquent reasoning of Arosemena. Despite his duties as a public servant, Arosemena's output was prolific, and included numerous essays, as well as political, legal and moral treatises.

In the second decade of the 19th century a group of poets formed which Rodrigo Miró has called the first literary generation of Panama. It included Gil Colunje (1831–99), Tomás Martín Feuillet (1832–62) and Amelia Denis (1836–1911). This era is characterized by large-scale social upheavals and feverish commercial activity, caused by an influx of North Americans spurred on by the discovery of gold in California, by the building of the Trans-Isthmus railway, and by the construction of the Panama Canal by the French. Gil Colunje launched his career with a sketch for a novel, *La verdad triunfante*, 1849 [Triumphant Truth], which originally appeared in instalments. Though Rodrigo Miró grants the work scant literary merit and concentrates on its documentary interest, Ramón Luis Acevedo identifies *La verdad triunfante* as the first Central American Romantic novel. However, Colunje is firmly established in the history of Panamanian letters as a poet. He wrote one of the key poems of the period, the ode "28 de noviembre" [28 November]. In it the poet sings to liberty from colonial subjection, to Bolívar and his American dream of a Great Colombia, and he closes with a prophetic characterization of the "American Isthmus" as a means of linking the two worlds. Tomás Martín Feuillet developed a poetic style which was lyrical and emotive without being sentimental, not dissimilar to that of Bécquer, though without the latter's sobriety. Occasionally Feuillet produced surprising comic verses, in which he criticized the commercialism of the era. His ballad "Retrato" [Portrait], in which he describes himself humorously and in detail, is of documentary value. The female representative of the Romantic period is Amelia Denis, who lived in Guatemala for several decades with her first husband, and for long periods in Nicaragua with her second. In Guatemala she wrote for various newspapers under the pseudonym "Elena." The two principal themes of her poetry are domestic life and social injustice. The poem which secured her place in the Panamanian literary canon is "Al cerro Ancón" [To Ancón Hill], inspired by her last visit to Panama in 1906. Drawing on personal recollections, the poet paints a melancholy picture of the nation's loss of territory to the United States because of the construction of the Canal. The work is prescient, for in the location of the title one of the most violent confrontations between Panama and the United States was to take place, decades later, over the question of respect for Panamanian sovereignty. "Al cerro Ancón" introduces the theme of the Canal, which was to reappear, more or less insistently, throughout 20th-century Panamanian literature.

The beginning of the *modernista* period was marked by Darío Herrera (1870–1914), more accomplished as a prose writer than as a poet, who was one of the first writers to turn his hand to the short story. His poetic output is Parnassian in character, and is largely made up of descriptive evocations of the era. Some of his poems are monotonous. His stories are more descriptive than narrative and his prose is meticulous. He published a single volume of short stories, *Horas lejanas*, 1903 [Distant Hours]. *Lejanías*, 1971 [Distant Places] is a partial collection of his poetic works. The rest of his literary output, which consists of chronicles, stories, verses and criticism, is scattered throughout newspapers and journals of the continent. The principal woman writer of the period is Nicole Garay (1873–1928). Though some critics compare Garay's poetry to that of Amelia Denis, seeing parallels in the common focus on social issues, her verses are in fact very different. Garay's work bears a decidedly modernist stamp. Some of her poems are pictorial compositions whose antecedents are clearly Parnassian. Her poem "Esplín" [Spleen] is characterized by a sense of weariness with life, a malaise suffered by many *modernistas* such as Julián del Casal and Julio Herrera y Reissig. Garay's work evinces a rebelliousness absent in Denis, and contains more daring images, musicality and Symbolist undertones.

The struggle against centralized Colombian rule came to a head in the Thousand Days War (1889–1902), in which Panama fought in the ranks of the liberal party. The failure of the French Canal and, later on in 1903, the Colombian Senate's rejection of the Herrán-Hay Treaty, which envisaged the building of a Canal using North American capital, provoked a resurgence of Panamanian separatist feeling, particularly among the commercial bourgeoisie. Aware of the trading interests of the Isthmus, this group saw the beginning of a prosperous future in the North American proposal. The United States took advantage of the climate of discontent to facilitate

Panama's separation from Colombia on the 6th of November 1903. Almost immediately, the Hay-Bunau Varilla Treaty with the United States, in which Panama conceded almost all rights and privileges as well as a strip of its territory in perpetuity, was signed and ratified. From this moment on, the political and economic life of the Isthmus has revolved around the Canal, which was opened in 1914. Henceforward Panamanian history is characterized by frequent negotiations for more equitable treaties and by defence of territorial sovereignty and national interests. There have been several violent confrontations with the United States over its interference in Panamanian affairs, the most recent being the US invasion of Panama on 20th December 1989.

The first generation of poets of this new historical era are Ricardo Miró (1883–1940), María Olimpia de Obaldía (1891–1985), Gaspar Octavio Hernández (1893–1918) and Demetrio Korsi (1899–1957). Miró is considered to be Panama's greatest poet. The National Literature Competition, founded in 1942, is named after him. Though the *modernista* influence is evident in the poet's imagery, verse forms and use of rhythm, Miró's poetry is more sober and intimate. Nationalism is a recurrent theme in his work. Particularly worthy of note is his poem "Patria" [Homeland], in which the poetic narrator forges a sense of national identity using personal experiences and intimate recollections, similar to the nostalgia for home. His works include *Preludios*, 1908, *Los segundos preludios*, 1916 [Second Preludes], *La leyenda del Pacífico*, 1919 [The Legend of the Pacific], *Versos patrióticos y recitaciones escolares*, 1925 [Patriotic Verses and School Readings], *Caminos silenciosos*, 1929 [Silent Paths], *El poema de la reencarnación*, 1929 [Reincarnation Poem] and *Obra literaria de Ricardo Miró: novela y cuento*, 1984 [The Writings of Ricardo Miró: Novels and Short Stories]. The poetry of María Olimpia de Obaldía, the first woman to gain admission to the Panamanian Academy of the Language (from 1951 to 1985), is simple and emotive. The poet revels in the treatment of exclusively female experiences such as motherhood, childbirth and breast-feeding. The sensuality of love is subtly alluded to in her work, but the poet stops short of eroticism. Gaspar Octavio Hernández was an exponent of different *modernista* styles. A certain preciousness, exoticism and the evasion of reality are evident in some of his poems. Others, however, are fervently patriotic and nationalistic, and protest at North American interference in the affairs of the Isthmus. Hernández's work also includes a small selection of popular and comic verse, which were the stock in trade of Demetrio Korsi. Korsi is the chronicler of the life of the urban people. In technical terms, his poems show avant-garde tendencies in their experimentation with free verse.

The arrival of the avant-garde in Panama is marked by the publication of the collection *Onda*, 1929 [Wave] by Rogelio Sinán (1904–94), the pseudonym of Bernardo Domínguez Alba. Sinán is the outstanding figure in 20th-century Panamanian literature, and the best-known internationally. He turned his hand to all genres, having come to prominence as a master of the short story in works such as *A la orilla de las escuelas maduras*, 1946 [On the Brink of the Mature Schools], *La boina roja*, 1954 [The Red Beret] and *El candelabro de los malos oficios*, 1982 [Candelabra of Dead End Jobs]. *Plenilunio*, 1947 [Full Moon], published in the heyday of Creolism in

Panama, is perhaps one of the first Spanish American novels to focus entirely on the subject of metafiction and the active participation of the reader. The author/narrator, of the type one finds in Pirandello or Unamuno, initially addresses a female narratee, who withdraws to a bedroom since the author is being visited by the characters. The characters constantly discuss the story's style, and rebel against the ending, which they propose to rewrite, but which ultimately remains incomplete. The author thus suggests one of the most important principles of the aesthetics of reception, namely that the creative potential of different readings and interpretations of a work is infinite. Sinán's second novel, *La isla mágica*, 1979 [The Magical Island], sustains the ludic tone of *Plenilunio*, but in a different way. In the earlier work the author establishes a metaphysical game which challenges the reader. In *la isla mágica*, playfulness is evident in the size of the story, in the multiple names ascribed to a single character, in the way religious imagery is used to describe genital organs or sexual acts, in Pipe the black man's ruses to deflower maidens, and, above all, in a series of comic scenes of ordinary folk. This work is wholly characteristic of the new Panamanian novel of the 1970s.

Sinán also revitalized Panamanian poetry. The avant-garde was still unknown in Panama when *Onda* appeared. Avant-garde and post avant-garde literature took off as a result of Sinán's energy. Demetrio Herrera (1902–50) achieved fame when he published *Kodak*, 1937, which shows the influence of *ultraísmo* (a Spanish avant-garde movement of the 1920s). Herrera's poetic voice is that of the social rebel who chronicles the life of the slums. The post avant-garde poets include Ricardo J. Bermúdez (1914–), Esther María Osses (1916–90), Stella Sierra (1917–) and Diana Morán (1932–87).

The group of poets who began to publish in the 1960s is made up of Ramón Oviero, Moravia Ochoa and Bertalicia Peralta. These poets were decisive in condemning the North American invasion in 1989 (*La voz aún no quemada* [Our Still Unburned Voice, 1990]). Oviero's work since 1961 is collected in *Inventariando*, 1985 [Making an Inventory]. Ochoa has published *Ganas para un poco vivir*, 1975 [Desirous of a Little Living] and *Me ensayo para ser una mujer*, 1983 [I Am Rehearsing to Be a Woman]. The best of Peralta's work includes *Sendas fugitivas*, 1962 [Fleeing Paths] and *Piel de gallina*, 1982 [Goose Flesh]. The younger generation of poets consists of Manuel Orestes Nieto, Giovanna Benedetti, Pedro Correa (1955–) and Consuelo Tomás (1957–). Manuel Orestes Nieto won the Casa de las Américas prize for his collection *Dar la cara* [Facing Up] in which he testifies to the damage caused to the country by the US occupation of the Canal. *Rendición de cuentas*, 1990 [The Reckoning] is a collection of the author's output over twenty years. Consuelo Tomás is a poet and author of short stories. She has published five poetry collections and a book of stories, *Cuentos rotos*, 1991 [Torn Tales]. In 1994 she won Miró prizes in the poetry section, for *Agonía de la reina* [Queen's Agony], and the short story section, for *Inauguración de la fe* [Inauguration of Faith]. Tomás is one of the most promising young writers of the Isthmus. Popular humour and the grotesque are features of her work.

From the second decade of the 20th century, the short story begins to replace poetry as the dominant genre. Initially, peasant life is the most common subject matter. The rural theme is most effectively explored by Graciela Rojas Sucre, in *Terruñadas de lo chico*, 1931 [Smallholdings], and by Gil Blas Tejeira, in *El retablo de los duendes*, 1945 [The Goblin's Altarpiece] and *Campiña interiorana*, 1947 [Heartlands]. The Creolist short story tradition began with José María Sánchez. His stories, set in Boca del Toro, describe the atmosphere of the exuberant natural setting in which the United Fruit Company establishes itself, and in which a colony of blacks from the British West Indies lives and works. *Tres cuentos*, 1946 [Three Stories] and *Shumio-Ara* (1948) are especially noteworthy. In *Los clandestinos*, 1957 [Illegal Aliens], César A. Candanedo describes aspects of life in Darién and in the banana growing area of Chiriquí. With the works *Campo adentro*, 1947 [Inland] and *Luna de Veraguas* [Veraguas Moon], Mario Augusto Rodríguez became the representative of "Cholo" or mixed race literature. Carlos F. Chang Marín began as a poet but achieved fulfilment in prose. The Creolist tradition is continued in *Faragual* (1961), though the work also explores self-consciousness and the complexity of discourse in the story "Seis madres" [Six Mothers]. The work of Renato Ozores marks a shift from rural to urban settings. Part of his short story output is collected in *Un incidente y otros cuentos*, 1947 [An Incident and Other Stories] and *El dedo ajeno*, 1954 [The Other's Finger]. In the 1960s and 1970s, the literary preoccupation with city life is accompanied by the first stylistic innovations and experiments in Panamanian fiction. The best contemporary exponents of the short story appear on the scene at this time: Pedro Rivera, Dimas Lidio Pitti, Enrique Jaramillo Levi, Moravia Ochoa and Bertalicia Peralta. These writers consolidate their reputations in the 1980s. In the 1990s, along with Tomás, Antonio Paredes Villegas is worthy of particular note. In *El duende y otros cuentos*, 1993 [The Goblin and Other Stories], Paredes deconstructs popular myths using empirical discoveries.

The novel came late to Panama. Poetry dominated the national literary output for many decades, until the short story began to gain ground in the 1920s and 1930s. It was not until the 1940s that the novel began to develop as a genre in Panamanian letters. The chief exponent of the Canal novel is Joaquín Beleño. His trilogy on the subject consists of *Luna verde*, 1951 [Green Moon], *Gamboa Road Gang* (1959) and *Curundú* (1961). *El desván*, 1954 [The Attic] by Ramón H. Jurado, is a psychological novel concerning the preoccupation with the human inability to communicate, which was a central theme in Spanish American fiction of the era. It is narrated by an unreliable and unauthoritative narrator, who, by establishing a distance between himself and the reader, obliges the latter to participate actively. In *El ahogado*, 1957 [The Drowned Man], Tristán Solarte (1924) interweaves the life of the protagonist with the myth of the "tulivieja." The story appears to be recounted by a traditional third person narrator, but this is an illusion, since an enigma remains ultimately unresolved: who killed the protagonist? This feature suggests a more experimental type of fiction, in keeping with the changes beginning to take place in Spanish American literature of the period.

In the 1960s, while the canon of the Spanish American new novel was being established, Panamanian output was prolific (twenty five novels, as against fifteen in the 1950s) but traditional in character, apart from the exceptions mentioned above. The principal figures to emerge in this decade, Justo Arroyo and Gloria Guardia, have remained dominant to the present day. Arroyo's *La gayola*, 1966 [The Slammer] brings the Panamanian novel into line with the Boom of Spanish American fiction which, in the case of Panama, takes off in the 1970s. As well as Guardia and Arroyo, Panama's Boom generation includes Enrique Chuez, Saúl Trinidad Torres, Dimas Lidio Pitti and Rafael Pernett y Morales. Arroyo has been one of the most active writers of contemporary fiction in Panama. In the 1970s he published *Dedos*, 1971 [Fingers], *Dejando atrás al hombre de celofán*, 1973 [Leaving Behind the Cellophane Man] and *El pez y el segundo*, 1979 [The Fish and the Second]. In structural terms, *Dedos* is the most innovative. In it the author experiments with all the formal techniques assimilated from the Spanish American new novel: multiple viewpoints, rupture of the chronological order, switching of narrative styles and defamiliarization of the creative act. Arroyo has also published another novel *Geografía de mujer*, 1981 [A Woman's Geography], and two volumes of short stories *Capricornio en gris*, 1972 [Capricorn in Grey] and *Rostros como manchas*, 1992 [Faces like Stains]. Gloria Guardia's *Tiniebla blanca*, 1961 [White Shadow] is very much a first novel, without formal innovations, but it firmly established the author in Panamanian literary circles. *El último juego*, 1976 [The Last Game], with its multiple viewpoints which establish semantic polyphony in the text, clearly belongs to the stylistic current of the Spanish American new novel. The story is built around the conflict caused by the treaty which ratified the continued presence of military bases in Panama. Guardia is presently working on a short story collection to be entitled *La estatua de libertad y otras fábulas* [The Statue of Liberty and Other Fables]. In *Las averías*, 1972 [The Breakdowns], by Enrique Chuez, *Marcha forzada*, 1973 [Forced March] by Saúl Trinidad Torres, and *Estación de navegantes*, 1975 [Navigators' Station] by Dimas Lidio Pitti, the mechanisms of poetry are used to suggest multiple interpretive possibilities. Rafael Pernett y Morales initiates the use of street humour and of playful and parodic tones in Panamanian fiction. *Loma ardiente y vestida de sol*, 1973 [Burning Loma and Dressed in Sun] sets a precedent in the Panamanian novel by making a working class area (Loma) both the protagonist and the setting of the work. *Estas manos son para caminar*, 1977 [These Hands Are for Walking] is a kind of "antibildungsroman" which achieves the goal of exposing the corruption and hypocrisy of the country's ruling class by narrating from the viewpoint of a social climber.

To complete the account of contemporary Panamanian fiction by women, in the last two decades two outstanding women writers can be added to the names of Consuelo Tomás, Gloria Guardia, Moravia Ochoa and Bertalicia Peralta. Rosa María Britton, novelist, short story writer, dramatist and essayist, is one of the most prolific writers of recent years. In her novels *El ataúd de uso*, 1983 [The Accustomed Coffin], *El señor de las lluvias y el viento*, 1985 [Lord of the Wind and the Rains] and *No pertenezco a este siglo*, 1992 [I Do Not Belong to this Century], she experiments with unreliable narrators and antagonistic narrative voices, as well as drawing on popular myths and glossing the history of the nation as part of Colombia. Isis Tejeira explores the shaping of the female subject in an oppressive patriarchal society in *Sin fechas fija*, 1982 [No Fixed Date]. She has also published a book of short stories entitled *Está linda la mar y otros cuentos* [The Sea is Fine and Other Stories]. In the novels of the 1990s, historical revisionism is the dominant tendency. In *Cuando perecen las ruinas*, 1991 [When the Ruins Perish], Rogelio Guerra Ávila recounts the abandonment of the town of Chagres which took place as a result of the 1903 Treaty. Enrique Chuez's *Operación causa justa*, 1991 [Operation Just Cause] is a chronicle or testimony of the North American invasion of Panama in 1989. The historical background of Britton's most recent work, mentioned above, is the era of political turmoil in Colombia between independence from Spain and 1904.

This account would be incomplete without mentioning Rodrigo Miró, whose role as a historian and anthologizer of Panamanian literature has been essential to the nation's literary development.

CARMEN S. ALVERIO

translated by Ian Craig

Further Reading

Acevedo, Ramón Luis, *La novela centroamericana*, Río Piedras, Puerto Rico: Editorial Universitaria, 1982

Jamieson Villiers, Martin E., "Literatura panameña actual," *Cuadernos Hispanoamericanos* 407 (1984)

Jaramillo Levi, Enrique (editor), *Poesía panameña contemporánea (1929–1979)*, Mexico City: Liberta-Sumaria, 1980

El mago de la isla. Reflexiones críticas en torno a la obra literaria de Rogelio Sinán, by several authors, Panama City: Instituto Nacional de Cultura, 1992

Miró, Rodrigo, *Aspectos de la literatura novelesca en Panamá*, Panama City: Impresora Panamá, 1968

___ *La literatura panameña (origen y proceso)*, San José, Costa Rica: Imprenta Trejos Hermanos, 1972

___ *Itinerario de la poesía en Panamá (1502–1974)*, Panama City: Editorial Universitaria, 1974

Sepúlveda, Mélida Ruth, *El tema del Canal en la novelística panameña*, Caracas: Universidad Católica Andrés Bello, 1975

Paraguay

19th- and 20th-Century Prose, Poetry and Literature in Guarani

When surveying Paraguayan literature over time and across the contemporary spectrum, the reader is taken with the diversity and richness of work produced by what is supposedly one of South America's least developed and most benighted societies. Indeed, any careful perusal of this literature gives the lie to pseudo-scientific and ethnocentric notions, popular in certain scholarly circles since the late 19th century, that Paraguay is a cultural wasteland, permanently incapacitated for "progress" by centuries of war and dictatorship. The fact is that those evils have not extinguished the artistic impulses of Paraguay's people. Indeed, one can, without seeming to justify the country's suffering, venture to say that it has been a raw material from which the best Paraguayan writers have produced works of undoubted genius.

What has been missing in Paraguay's literature is not quality but the recognition of quality. To observe the struggles of Paraguayan writers is to confirm the half-serious witticism that "publishing in Paraguay is like remaining unpublished." Paraguay has a viable publishing industry, but readership within the country is limited, and most Paraguayan writers have received scant attention in the wider Latin American and world literary markets. Foreign readers and foreign editors have tended to dismiss Paraguay as a far-flung bit of exotica of little importance beyond its own borders. This is true to the small extent that it recognizes the country's unique qualities, but utterly false in undervaluing their universal appeal. Paraguay *is* an anomaly, and its story is worth telling precisely for that reason. In terms of language alone, the country has much to teach us. Most Paraguayans speak some form of Guarani, two-thirds to three-quarters are bilingual, and a small minority speaks only Spanish. The country is thus unique, in Latin America and perhaps in the world, in that its population has opted to preserve an indigenous language despite extensive European immigration and extensive intermarriage between the indigenous population and Europeans. The incongruities which flow from these facts deserve recognition in the world of ideas, for they reveal much about the encounter between Western and non-Western cultures that has molded and shaken our planet for the past five centuries.

Perhaps the chief incongruity of Paraguay's linguistic reality is that Spanish, despite its smaller number of speakers, remains very much the language of power. Government is carried on mostly in Spanish, as are the major functions of education and commerce. Guarani is primarily a language of home and street, and while it has a considerable written tradition, this literature cannot attract enough readers to sustain its practitioners economically. Writers in Guarani have the same problem as their colleagues in Spanish, except to a much greater degree. In general, they must write as an avocation, and forget any dreams of a reputation outside the country. No survey of Paraguay's literature, however, should ignore the Guarani component, which is absolutely essential as a symbol of Paraguayan nationalism and as a distinct vehicle for interpreting the country's reality. For all the obstacles to publishing in the indigenous language, enough writers have overcome them to make their efforts an ongoing and vital part of the nation's culture. This is particularly true in poetry and the theater.

The incorporation of Guarani literature into the national literature of Paraguay is somewhat problematical because its aboriginal referent both *exceeds* the current boundaries of the country and *precedes* its existence as a historical entity. There are Guarani-speaking native communities in neighboring countries as well as within Paraguay, and their presence obviously predates the political construct that bears that name. Given this fact and the numerous miseries they have suffered at the hands of the national government, indigenous Guarani speakers do not necessarily identify themselves with Paraguay. However, unlike the Quechua and Aymara literatures of the Andean region, Guarani literature cannot, on the whole, be considered in isolation from the literature of the modern nation-state in which it struggles to endure. Centuries of war, illness, poverty and assimilation have reduced the aboriginal communities to a small percentage of Paraguay's population, while their ancestral tongue has spread and survived as the nation's majority language. Most Guarani speakers, therefore, are non-indigenous persons whose self-identification is wholly and unabashedly Paraguayan. Guarani literature has a certain indigenous underpinning, but rarely does this "deep structure" explicitly challenge the national cultural ethos which overlays it. Myths and other aboriginal motifs are often employed in validating that ethos, not contradicting it, and the Guarani language itself is frequently a literary emblem of fierce patriotism.

Another sector of the population that has struggled against literary disenfranchisement is women. As in other Latin American nations, men have dominated the writing arts in Paraguay, regarding them as an extension of the power they wield in the political and economic spheres. Women writers have generally been obliged to operate from the interstices of this structure, confining their material to themes considered "appropriate" to feminine concern or exploiting an occasional opportunity to be the "exceptional woman" of "genuine influence" in matters normally left to men. Nevertheless, female writers have asserted themselves in sufficient numbers to merit attention as a distinct force in Paraguayan literature, and are doing so increasingly *as women*. That is, there is a growing consciousness of writing explicitly or implicitly in the cause of women. This is not to say that no debate exists as to the proper feminist relationship with men, nor is it to claim that Paraguayan feminism follows a North American or European model. Paraguayan women writers are slowly carving a place for themselves, but they are accomplishing this according to the realities and peculiarities of their own society.

It is sometimes said that Paraguay simply had no literature before the 20th century. While this is a patent falsehood, there is truth in the notion of Paraguay's literary *paucity* prior to 1900. For the literary historian, therefore, the task is largely to understand the reasons for this scarcity and to identify the literary production which did in fact take place.

The Horsemen of the Apocalypse have been frequent visitors to Paraguay, and disasters that would seem hyperbolic in many other countries are here the stuff of history. From 1864 to 1870, Paraguay fought and lost the War of the Triple Alliance, quixotically taking on the combined forces of Brazil, Argentina and Uruguay, and suffering in the process a population reduction of over seventy-five per cent! Of the 1,300,000 Paraguayans alive at the war's outset, only 300,000 remained by the end, most of them women and children. This alone suffices to explain the dearth of writers in the last decades of the century. Genocide simply erased many of the country's potential literati. It must be added, however, that Paraguay's nucleus of writers was never very robust even before the war, owing in part to the muzzle of dictatorship. During the regime of Dr José Gaspar Rodríguez de Francia from 1814 to 1840, literary expression was strictly forbidden even as the country enjoyed a degree of economic prosperity. No class of literati, therefore, was allowed to exist in the critical first decades of the country's independence. Francia's successors Carlos Antonio López and his son Francisco Solano López attempted to reverse this condition, but in the end their efforts were decimated by the war. The elder López promoted cultural institutions, including the *Academia Literaria* and the *Aula de Filosofía*. Students were sent overseas, journals were founded, and an interest in European Romanticism took hold. Journalism was generally an organ of the government, but at least one finds in it the potential for a serious interest in the art of writing.

What literature preceded the War of the Triple Alliance, and what managed to survive it, was dominated by chronicles and historical essays. In colonial times, Ruy Díaz de Guzmán (1558–1629) set this trend in motion with his account of European settlement in the Río de la Plata region. Following Díaz's example and having a strong desire to make sense of their unique evolution as a people, Paraguayans have always been a nation of historiographers and analytical essayists. Writers of the López and post-López eras, including Crisóstomo Centurión (1840–1903) and Natalicio Talavera (1839–67), continued the colonial tradition of recording and commenting on the events of their time.

Paraguayan historiography in the 19th century was often – and unscientifically – bound up with the nation's new-found interest in Romanticism. The same ambience which encouraged analyses of the meaning of events also gave birth to a Romantic sentimentalization of the nation's history. Romanticism in Paraguay, however, did have themes other than patriotism, and did produce work in genres other than the essay. Diógenes (1857–1920) and José Segundo Decoud (1848–1909), along with Fulgencio R. Moreno (1872–1933) and the transplanted Bolivian Tristán Roca (1826–68), all produced non-historiographical essays, especially in literary criticism, and among the poets and narrators whose work set important precedents for later writers in these genres, one may cite Centurión, Moreno, Roca and Talavera, as well as Victorino Abente y Lago (1846–1935), Adriano M. Aguiar (1859–1913) and Enrique D. Parodi (1857–1917).

Along with its relative scarcity of works, Paraguayan literature before 1900 was noted for the belatedness with which foreign literary influences arrived in the country. European Romanticism came late to Latin America in general, but even later to Paraguay. Thus cynics have suggested that Paraguay's writers were not only slavish in imitating foreign models, but hopelessly behind time in doing so. A more generous and correct view is that Romanticism was simply a matrix within which Paraguayans sought, as in everything else, to find meaning in their unique circumstances. Parodi and Roca, for example, contributed to interest in the nation's Guarani heritage. One must conclude, however, that praiseworthy as their efforts were, the Romantics' nod to Guarani culture did not come close to recognizing its true importance. All around these makers of *literature* there abounded, and still does, a vast "proto-literature," the Guarani oral tradition, which even now has only begun to be acknowledged. The Romantics' work foreshadowed the 20th-century recognition of the indigenous language as a basis for Paraguay's originality and identity, but much remains to be done in this area.

Narrative fiction has been the least prolific genre in Paraguayan literature, and the most affected by the nation's historical and political context. The historical essay was predominant until the mid-century, and what narrative production there was tended to emphasize romantic and nationalistic themes: the exaltation of the past, the affirmation of Paraguayan spiritual values, and the commemoration of the heroic struggle to survive the catastrophic War of the Triple Alliance (1864–70). This traditional framework was initiated by the Argentine Martín de Goycoechea Menéndez (1877–1906), who glorified the war and endowed the national literature with a mythic air. Other narratives of the traditionalist type are the historical *costumbrista* works of Natalicio González (1897–1966), Teresa Lamas de Rodríguez Alcalá (1887–1975), Concepción Leyes de Chaves (1891–1985) and Carlos Zubizarreta (1904–72).

Between 1932 and 1935, Paraguay fought another war, the Chaco War with Bolivia, which nevertheless had positive consequences for the literary sphere. The nation's reality intruded on the consciousness of writers, and significant new themes – war, agrarian problems, political persecution, exile, and so forth – found their way into subsequent narratives. Exemplars of this thematic innovation are *Cruces de quebracho*, 1934 [Quebracho Wood Crosses] by Arnaldo Valdovinos (1908–91), *Ocho hombres*, 1934 [Eight Men] by José Santiago Villarejo, and especially *El guajhú*, 1938 [The Howl] by Gabriel Casaccia (1907–80). The first three were inspired by the Chaco War, and the last, Casaccia's work, is a collection of stories which gives the *coup de grâce* to totally false, romantic and idealized literary images of the Paraguayan *campesino*.

Despite these advances, Paraguayan narrative fiction only began to achieve distinction and international renown in the 1950s with the appearance in Buenos Aires of three works: Casaccia's novel *La babosa*, 1952 [The Gossiping Woman], the novel *Follaje en los ojos*, 1952 [Leaves in the Eyes] by José María Rivarola Matto and the story collection *El trueno entre las hojas*, 1953 [Thunder among the Leaves] by Augusto Roa Bastos (1917–). These works broke with the dominant trend toward narcissism and mythification in literature, and reclaimed for fiction the critical realism that had been practically eclipsed since Rafael Barrett (1876–1910) initiated it in the essay genre at the turn of the century.

Historical and political circumstances over the last fifty years have impeded Paraguayan narrative production, but they also help to explain it. In that interval the country has suffered a bloody civil war (the Revolution of 1947) and lived through the second longest dictatorship in the history of the Americas (that of General Stroessner, 1954–89). It should surprise no one, therefore, that the works currently best known were conceived and published in exile, for it is only at some remove from repression and censorship that writers have been able to express themselves freely and develop unfettered an artistically wrought narrative style in tune with contemporary historical conditions and containing significant socio-political material. The works of expatriate authors – Rubén Bareiro Saguier (1930–), Gabriel Casaccia, Rodrigo Díaz-Pérez (1924–), Augusto Roa Bastos, Lincoln Silva (1945–) and others – are where one finds the most honest articulation of Paraguay's contemporary problems. Casaccia, the progenitor of contemporary Paraguayan narrative, critically re-created several decades of moral and political corruption in three novels: the aforementioned La babosa, La llaga, 1963 [The Wound] and Los herederos, 1975 [The Inheritors]. In another of his novels, Los exiliados, 1966 [The Exiles], Casaccia devoted himself to the theme of political exile, practically unexplored in fiction composed within Paraguay's borders. Augusto Roa Bastos, awarded the Cervantes Prize in 1989, and well known as one of Latin America's most outstanding writers, examines the nation's past and present within a historical and political framework in Hijo de hombre, 1960 (Son of Man), a novel steeped in the pain of being Paraguayan. Hijo de hombre has become one of the most important texts of contemporary Latin American fiction. Roa's best-known novel, however, is his second one, Yo el Supremo, 1974 (I the Supreme), narrated from the ubiquitous perspective of Paraguay's first dictator Dr José Gaspar Rodríguez de Francia, one of the most controversial figures in the history of the nation.

The theme of dictatorship, hard to include in narratives written within Paraguay, is implicitly or explicitly present in the fear that torments innumerable characters in the fiction of exile. And it intrudes directly in the reality of jail, torture and persecution portrayed in stories by Rubén Bareiro Saguier collected in Ojo por diente, 1973 [An Eye for a Tooth] and El séptimo pétalo del viento, 1984 [The Seventh Petal of the Wind], in stories by Rodrigo Díaz-Pérez contained in Entrevista, 1978 [Interview] and Hace tiempo . . . mañana, 1989 [Some Time Ago . . . Tomorrow], and in Lincoln Silva's novels Rebelión después, 1970 [Rebellion Afterward] and General General, 1975 [General General]. Also products of exile are the story collection El collar sobre el río, 1987 [Necklace Over the River] by Carlos Garcete (1918–) and the novel El invierno de Gunter, 1987 [Gunter's Winter] by Juan Manuel Marcos (1950–) – both inspired by the problems of the nation – as well as the collection of short poetic narratives Ultimo domicilio conocido, 1990 [Last Known Address] by Ester de Izaguirre (1923–).

As for narrative production written within Paraguay between 1960 and 1989, it is important to point out the negative impact of dictatorial repression and of the censorship and self-censorship that prevailed in every corner of the country. These factors do much to explain the limited number of works published in Paraguay until now. As Guido Rodríguez Alcalá says in an essay published in 1980, given Paraguay's political and cultural context, "the surprising thing is not that not much [literature]

is produced, but that any is produced at all." Even though narrative activity during this time is relatively scant and the works that have been published do not get the international attention lavished on those of exiled authors, Paraguay's internal narrative corpus does have a number of works and writers of considerable merit who have received important national prizes and distinctions. Between 1960 and the mid-1980s, internal narrative production ranged from costumbrista chronicles to fictions which explicitly criticized diverse aspects of the social, political and historical context of the time. Among the representative works of the period one should mention are Imágenes sin tierra, 1965 [Images without Land] by José-Luis Appleyard (1927–), El laberinto, 1972 [The Maze] by Augusto Casola (1944–), Crónicas de una familia, 1966 [Chronicles of a Family] and Andresa Escobar, 1975 by Ana Iris Chaves de Ferreiro (1922–93), La mano en la tierra, 1963 [Hand in the Soil] and El espejo y el canasto, 1981 [The Mirror and the Basket] by Josefina Pla (1909–), Caballero, 1986 [Caballero] by Guido Rodríguez Alcalá, Las musarañas, 1973 [The Shrews] and El contador de cuentos, 1980 [The Teller of Tales] by Jesús Ruiz Nestosa (1941–). Beginning in the mid-1980s, some works have appeared in which certain open wounds of Paraguayan reality are laid bare and criticism often becomes a scathing denunciation of Stroessner's repressive and asphyxiating dictatorship which lasted from 1954 to 1989. Of these works the following deserve particular mention: Celda 12, 1991 [Cell 12] by Moncho Azuaga (1953–), La seca y otros cuentos, 1986 [The Drought and Other Stories] and Los nudos del silencio, 1988 [The Knots of Silence] by René Ferrer (1944–), Diagonal de sangre, 1986 [Diagonal of Blood] and La isla sin mar, 1987 [Island without Sea] by Juan Bautista Rivarola Matto (1933–91), Sin testigos, 1987 [No Witnesses] by Roberto Thompson Molinas (1928–) and En busca del hueso perdido: tratado de paraguayología, 1990 [In Search of the Lost Bone: a Treatise on the Paraguayan Way] by Helio Vera (1946–). Virtually all of these works have won, or been finalists for, important national competitions in narrative fiction.

The self-assertion of women narrators has been particularly significant since the 1980s, revealing in their voices a wide variety of styles and themes. Besides the aforementioned René Ferrer's works, we may note, among others, the following novels by Neida Bonnet de Mendonça (1933–): Golpe de luz, 1987 [Blow of Light]; La vera historia de Purificación, 1989 [Purificación's True Story], and La niña que perdí en el circo, 1987 [The Child I Lost at the Circus]. A further novel to be noted is Esta zanja está ocupada, 1994 [This Ditch is Occupied] by Raquel Saguier (1940–); while valuable collections of short fiction include La oscuridad de afuera, 1987 [The Darkness Outside] by Sara Karlik (1935–); and Tierra mansa y otros cuentos [Gentle Earth and Other Tales] by Lucy Mendonça de Spinci (1932–).

That narrative fiction is primarily an urban middle-class art form seems to be confirmed by the fact that little of it has been produced in Guarani. A notable exception is the Guarani novel Kalaíto Pombéro, 1981 [Kalaíto Bogey-Man] by Tadeo Zarratea (1947–). Other Guarani works of fiction draw on the country's rich oral tradition. Miguelángel Meza and Rubén Rolandi, among others, have produced compilations of folk-tales in Guarani.

Although Paraguay in recent decades has not been fertile soil for artistic creation in general, poetry has always been the most prolific genre in Paraguayan letters. The temporal framework of current Paraguayan poetry, if by this we mean what has been written since 1960, falls almost entirely within the thirty-five years of General Stroessner's dictatorship. The resulting political, economic and cultural condition of Paraguay, and the varying degrees of censorship imposed by the tyrant on writers, have diminished both the quantity and quality of poetic composition within the country. Arbitrary arrests, ideological persecution and political repression resulted in exile for almost a million Paraguayans, a third of the population, including many writers and artists. "For these reasons," explains Giuseppe Bellini, "the literature of Paraguay has been built more from the contributions of exiles than from those of writers who lived in their country." In fact, the two internationally most renowned Paraguayan poets, Hérib Campos Cervera (1905–53) and Elvio Romero (1926–), have written practically all of their work as exiles in Buenos Aires.

Regarded as the most important poet of the generation of 1940, Campos Cervera is also one of three writers from that group – the others are Josefina Pla and Augusto Roa Bastos – who have had a broad impact on contemporary Paraguayan literature as a whole. As witnesses to the cruel events of the Chaco War of 1932–35 with Bolivia, and in some cases as combatants in it, the members of the generation of 1940 all shared a concern for literary renewal during the harsh decade that led up to the bloody Revolution of 1947. The facts of life and survival in the Paraguay of that time forced these writers to a new awareness of the national reality, and their work reflects a renewed critical disposition. These poets, whose ranks also include Oscar Ferreiro (1921–), Ezequiel González Alsina (1919–89) and Hugo Rodríguez-Alcalá, have produced an introspective poetry which plumbs the depths of the intimate and has its roots in the ways of human beings, their ideals, dreams, doubts and anxieties. Frequently this poetic introspection discloses collective suffering and the anguish of expatriation; introspection becomes solidarity and there emerges a kind of testimonial poetry representative of human values. Such is the case in the work of Campos Cervera and that of numerous other poets influenced by him.

Of the works that bear Campos Cervera's influence, special mention needs to be made of Elvio Romero's poetic collections, among them *Destierro y atardecer*, 1975 [Exile and Evening] and *El poeta y sus encrucijadas*, 1991 [The Poet and His Crossroads]. The best-known Paraguayan poet at this time, Romero has produced work which is part poetic diary, part tormented witness to repression, and part denunciation of decades of Paraguayan suffering. Also in the vein of social protest are the works of expatriate writers like Rodrigo Díaz-Pérez and Rubén Bareiro Saguier, and those of others like Jorge Canese (1947–).

In the 1950s there arose a group of poets whose debt to the generation of 1940 (among them Roa Bastos, Campos Cervera and Romero) was real but indirect, since the older writers had been forced into exile after the Civil War of 1947. This generation of 1950 – which includes Bareiro Saguier, Díaz-Pérez, Martínez and Villagra Marsal, has pursued other genres as well, particularly fiction, and has collaborated in producing *Alcor*, an important literary journal founded in 1955 by Bareiro Saguier and Julio César Troche. The generation of 1950 witnessed the violence and hatred of the 1947 conflict, and their works are often melancholy intimations of love, death, childhood, existential anguish, and nostalgia for an imagined lost paradise.

Many of these themes are also present in the poetry of those who wrote in Guarani. Carlos F. Abente (1915–), Gumercindo Ayala Aquino (1910–72), Narciso R. Colmán ("Rosicrán") (1876–1954), are among those who maintained the Guarani poetic tradition in the early and middle decades of the century.

Beginning around 1960, a number of other groups appeared, all of them reacting in one degree or another to the conditions imposed by dictatorship. One of these groups, the so-called generation of 1960, began under the leadership of Josefina Pla and included writers born between 1937 and 1943 such as Esteban Cabañas, Miguel Ángel Fernández, Francisco Pérez-Maricevich and Roque Vallejos. Their works, like those of others not in the group, reflect an acute awareness of the country's political and economic problems and express this awareness in simple, clear, essential verse, free of hollow rhetoric. Another group of the 1960s appeared toward the end of the decade, in rough simultaneity with the student unrest of 1968: this was the "*Criterio* group," so named for its publication of the journal *Criterio* (1966–71, 1976–77). Most of the *Criterio* group's members, who included Juan Manuel Marcos, Emilio Pérez Chaves, René Dávalos, Nelson Roura and others, were born between 1943 and 1950. Primarily students, their poetics of political liberation and social conscience incurred a wave of repression which resulted in the group's complete dispersal.

The work of Guarani-language poets in this period deserves separate mention. The Stroessner regime sought political gain by instituting certain policies promoting the Guarani language, but this did not make it easier for writers seeking to publish in the indigenous language from the 1960s to the 1980s. Among those poets whose production in this period was partly or entirely in Guarani, we may cite Susy Delgado, Félix Giménez Gómez ("Félix de Guarania"), Juan Maidana (1917–82), Carlos Martínez Gamba (1942–) and Miguelángel Meza (1955–). Others who have published primarily in the 1990s include Wilfredo Máximo Acosta (1953–) and Zenón Bogado Rolón (1954–). The latter is noted for his vehement poetic defense of Paraguay's indigenous peoples.

Political repression was a constant throughout the 1970s, at the end of which decade there appeared a group of poets whose ill luck was to have been born and raised entirely in the Stroessner era, that is, after 1954. It was also their fortune, however, to witness the end of dictatorship in 1989, and to incorporate this experience in their maturation as artists. These young writers comprise the generation of 1980. Most of them have participated in the Manuel Ortiz Guerrero Poetry Workshop sponsored by the Spanish Embassy in Paraguay, resulting in the publication of several volumes of collective effort. *Y ahora la palabra*, 1979 [And Now the Word] and *Poesía Taller*, 1982 [Workshop Poetry] are just two of the volumes produced by the workshop.

As in narrative fiction, the last ten to fifteen years of Paraguayan poetry have witnessed an expansion of output by female writers. Young poets like Delfina Acosta, Lourdes Espínola, Nila López and Mabel Pedrozo have claimed a place in the poetic "fraternity" which until recently included women only under unusual circumstances.

The first half of the century produced scarcely any playwrights whose reputation transcended the borders of Paraguay. A possible exception is Josefina Pla, author (alone or with Roque Centurión Miranda (1900–60)) of a number of plays, and scholarly criticism of Paraguayan drama in general. As in other Latin American countries, historical, political and socioeconomic factors offer some explanation of why theater has been and remains the least fertile literary genre in the 20th century. Nevertheless, the two decades before the Chaco War saw unprecedented interest in theater, and numerous authors, of whom the most renowned is José Arturo Alsina (1897–1984), produced dramas and comedies predominantly popular in tone and content. Alsina was born in Argentina but lived in Paraguay from early childhood; hence despite the influence of European playwrights in some of his plays, for example Ibsen in *El derecho de nacer* [The Right to Be Born] and Pirandello in *La ciudad soñada* [Dream City], his work is essentially a product of the Paraguayan milieu.

Of enormous cultural significance for this bilingual nation was the career of Julio Correa (1890–1953), a writer of great talent whose work in the 1930s opened up the Paraguayan stage to productions in Guarani. Correa's plays demonstrated what should have been obvious all along: that serious dramatic discourse regarding Paraguay's historical and political context, and the Chaco War in particular, was possible and desirable in the country's majority language. Among Correa's contemporaries, a number of playwrights – including Roque Centurión Miranda, Francisco Barrios and Luis Rufinelli (1889–1973) – followed his lead in producing works in Guarani.

Over the last four decades, the best-known playwrights include Ernesto Báez, Ovidio Benítez Pereira, José María Rivarola Matto, Julio César Troche, Mario Halley Mora – the most prolific dramatist of the period – and Alcibiades González Delvalle – perhaps the most polemical. Halley Mora's work is interesting in that it includes a number of pieces in *yopará*, the blend of Spanish and Guarani spoken in many parts of Paraguay. The Paraguayan stage receives support from two important institutions: the Ateneo Paraguayo, and the Escuela de Arte Escénico de Asunción, founded in 1948 by Centurión Miranda. These bodies are part of the creative potential which has characterized the Paraguayan stage in recent years. Among the many individuals who figure prominently in that ferment, one may mention José Luis Appleyard, Ramiro Domínguez and Ezequiel González Alsina (1919–89), all of them writers and critics; Manuel E. B. Argüello (1924–), actor, writer and essayist; Agustín Núñez, critic and director; Gloria Muñoz (1949), playwright and theatrical scriptwriter; and Edda de los Ríos (1942–), actress, playwright and international advocate for Paraguayan theater. Muñoz and Núñez collaborated in 1991 on a successful stage version of Roa Bastos's novel *Yo el Supremo*.

The essay has been a rich and influential literary form in Paraguay throughout the century, and particularly so in the mid-1950s, when fiction, especially by exiled writers, began to incorporate historical themes which had belonged to the essayist. The essay thus became an important source of narrative material. As elsewhere in Latin America, the historical, political and cultural context of the end of the 19th century and the first four decades of the 20th century was conducive to the essay's prosperity as a genre, both at that time and subsequently. The contextual coordinates of that prosperity are, paradoxically, the very disasters which the essay has so often decried in the course of Paraguay's 19th- and 20th-century history. While theater was diminished by these factors because it requires labor-intensive collaboration by numerous artists, the essayist has the comparatively easier task of committing thoughts to paper and finding a publisher. Thus the very conditions which weakened the stage created a need which essayists moved to fill.

Paraguayan literature is generally thought to have taken a significant leap forward around the turn of the century, with the work of a group of intellectuals known as the "generation of 1900." These writers, most of them born around the time of the War of the Triple Alliance, sought by the prolific production of essays and poetry to do for Paraguay what their Spanish contemporaries in the "generation of 1898" did for Spain: to promote the country's spiritual reconstruction by reaffirming certain national values on the one hand and reinterpreting certain lessons of the past on the other. Among the most representative of this group are Cecilio Báez (1862–1941), Manuel Domínguez (1868–1935), Eloy Fariña Núñez (1885–1929), Blas Garay (1873–99), Manuel Gondra (1871–1927), Alejandro Guanes (1872–1925), Fulgencio R. Moreno (1872–1933) and Juan E. O'Leary (1879–1969). All were journalists, all except Domínguez were poets, and all except Guanes cultivated the historical essay in varying degrees.

At least as important for Paraguayan letters as the generation of 1900 was their contemporary Rafael Barrett (see separate entry). Often excluded from Paraguayan literary histories on the grounds that he was born and raised in Europe, Barrett's work actually deserves mention in any account of the country's written tradition. His efforts as a crusading journalist are strongly identified with Paraguay and exerted a profound influence on his peers, both in the essay genre and in fiction.

Around 1915 there emerged another group of essayists. Continuing the work of historical research and reinterpretation begun by the generation of 1900, this group included Justo Pastor Benítez (1895–1963), Arturo Bray (1898–1977), Natalicio González and Pablo Max Ynsfrán (1894–1972). Beginning in the 1930s, these writers were joined by two historians of distinction: Julio César Chaves (1907–89), author of one of the best-known biographies of the dictator Francia, and Efraím Cardozo (1906–75), one of the signers of the pact which ended the Chaco War and a profound expert on its causes and evolution. Since that time, many other essayists of importance have appeared in the disciplines of historiography and philosophy, among whom one may mention Osvaldo Chaves (1918–91), Bacón Duarte Prado (1915), Adriano Irala Burgos (1928), Epifanio Méndez Fleitas (1917–85) and Hipólito Sánchez Quell (1907–86). Of Paraguay's cultural historians and literary critics, some of the most productive are Raúl Amaral (1918–), Rubén Bareiro Saguier, Carlos R. Centurión (1902–69), Juan Manuel Marcos, Francisco Pérez-Maricevich, Josefina Pla and Hugo Rodríguez-Alcalá.

Paraguayan essayists generally write for an urban, upper-and middle-class readership, and have for this reason practiced their art almost entirely in Spanish. Little expository prose has been written in Guarani, and there exists in the general population a mistaken notion that the indigenous language is unsuited to such purposes. Of those who have defied this myth, a few, including Pedro Encina Ramos and Darío Gómez Serrato, are compiled in Fray Antonio Guasch's *El idioma guaraní: gramática y antología de prosa y verso*, 1983 [The Guarani Language: Grammar and Anthology of Prose and Verse].

TERESA MÉNDEZ-FAITH AND TRACY K. LEWIS

Further Reading

Amaral, Raúl, *El modernismo poético en el Paraguay (1901–1916)*, Asunción, Paraguay: Alcándara, 1982

———, *El romanticismo paraguayo 1860–1910*, Asunción, Paraguay: Alcándara, 1985

Bareiro Saguier, Rubén, *et al.*, *Literatura guaraní del Paraguay*, Caracas: Biblioteca Ayacucho, 1980

Bellini, Giuseppe, *Historia de la literatura hispanoamericana*, Madrid: Castalia, 1985

Cardozo, Efraím, *Apuntes de historia cultural del Paraguay*, Asunción, Paraguay: Universidad Católica, 1985

Díaz Pérez, Viriato, *Literatura del Paraguay*, Palma de Mallorca: Luis Ripoll, 1980

Guasch, Antonio S.J., *El idioma guaraní: gramática y antología de prosa y verso*, Asunción, Paraguay: Ediciones Loyola, 1983

Lewis, Tracy K., "Indígena e indigenista en la literatura guaranítica paraguaya: ¿un fracaso de etiquetas?" in *Past, Present, and Future: Selected Papers on Latin American Indian Literatures*, edited by Mary H. Preuss, Culver City, California: Labyrinthos, 1991

Méndez-Faith, Teresa, *Paraguay: novela y exilio*, Somerville, New Jersey: SLUSA, 1985

———, *Breve antología de la literatura paraguaya*, Asunción, Paraguay: El Lector, 1994

———, *Breve diccionario de la literatura paraguaya*, Asunción, Paraguay: El Lector, 1994

Pérez-Maricevich, Francisco, *La poesía y la narrativa en el Paraguay*, Asunción, Paraguay: Editorial del Centenario, 1969

Rodríguez-Alcalá, Hugo, *Historia de la literatura paraguaya*, Mexico City: Andrea, 1970

———, "El vanguardismo en el Paraguay," *Revista Iberoamericana* 118–19 (1982)

Para-Literature

The term "para-literature" is used as a substitute for "popular literature" to designate all works which have not been canonized by institutions; that is to say, the mass of texts constituting the popular novel of the 19th century, the melodrama, the detective novel in its various forms, the romance novel, the western, the tale of terror, science fiction, the spy novel, the pornographic novel, etc.

It is important to assume the existence of a literature/para-literature dichotomy and to reconsider both these categories in relation to each other; thus, an understanding of what is para-literature will allow a greater comprehension of the literary phenomenon.

Thus, with the realization that literature and para-literature are an indissoluble pair, it is important to define these two phenomena in theoretical terms, for which we shall base ourselves primarily on Jakobson's function scheme. In a literary text, the dominant function is by definition the poetic function, which focuses on the message itself – the text – which is not a means to an end but an objective in its own right. In para-literature, on the other hand, the predominance of the poetic function has been replaced by the conative function, which emphasizes the addressee of the message, in as much as it tries to produce a certain effect on the reader – an effect which varies from one para-literary form to another. It is, thus, possible to recognize a dominant conative-emotive function in the romance novel and in the melodrama, a dominant conative-cognitive function in the classic detective novel, a dominant conative-sensual function in the erotic novel. What is important in each case is that there be a persuasive effect on the addressee. The effectiveness of the conative function requires and arouses an intensification of the phatic function, the latter being the function which maintains contact between the addresser and the addressee.

The consequences arising from this difference of dominant function are manifold. Let us concentrate, firstly, on the concept of "contemplative distance" or "esthetic distance," a necessary factor in literary comprehension. This comprehension would be unfortunate in a case where, for certain reasons, the reader were to suppress the distance and, identifying with the work, were to narcissistically substitute the object of contemplation for his own ego or introduce characters or events from the novel into the exigencies of real life. In para-literary experience, however, contemplative distance is voided and the message is reduced to a means of successfully imposing certain effects on the addressee.

The notion of distance is related to another concept, that of "disinterest," in the Kantian sense. In the case of literature, there is a mutual disinterest on the part of the text, which does not seek to impose itself on the reader by means of effects previously elaborated in the work itself, and on the part of the reader, who does not use the text as a means of self-gratification but rather as an object of contemplation; an artistic text would thus transcend any intention of ideological imposition, causing opening effects at certain levels. Paradoxically, this respectful disinterest would be the manifestation of the most intense interest in the actualization of the esthetic object as such.

The predominance of the poetic function results in the polysemy of the poetic text, its indeterminacy and unpredictability, and, with that, its vast flow of information. The para-literary text, on the other hand, contains a minimal degree of information, given its essentially predictable and transparent meaning; it is defined in this sense as a "narrative of redundancy."

Because of its redundancies, a para-literary work is a pleasure-inducing text, belonging to Barthes's "texte de plaisir" (text of pleasure) category: a text which produces contentment, which satisfies, which is rooted in culture and related to a comfortable practice of reading. This production of pleasure is understandable from a Freudian perspective, according to which pleasure is attributed to the parsimony of psychic outpouring and, for that reason, the encounter with a known element evokes a pleasurable effect.

A para-literary work thus fully satisfies the reader's "horizon of expectations". According to Jauss, the distance between the horizon of expectation and the work itself – between the already familiar nature of the esthetic experience to date and the change in horizon necessitated by receiving a new work – determines the artistic character of a literary work: as this distance decreases and the consciousness of the reader does not require the horizon of a heretofore unknown experience, the work approaches the sphere of entertainment.

It may be inferred from what has been said that a para-literary text enjoys a high degree of readability, in Barthes's sense; namely, its reader is conceived as eminently receptive and passive. In the case of those para-literary forms which provoke activity on the part of the reader whether to anticipate or infer the unfolding of the plot or to attempt to solve enigmas – think of a feuilleton and a detective story, such activity would be pleasurable, not exhausting.

The greatest contrast between para-literary phenomena and a writable text – that which, according to Barthes, unlike a readable text, requires the reader's participation, his constructive effort – can be appreciated by having recourse to the metaphoric and metonymic poles. Para-literature is metaphoric; it seeks to discover meaning(s) and, more frequently, one single major meaning. The writable text, by contrast, is resistant to metaphor; it is conspicuously metonymic: wherein associations, contiguities, accumulations are clearly noted.

In a literary text, the units are not repeatable, for when a unit is repeated, it is no longer the same; it becomes something else. Para-literature, on the other hand, is the very realm of repetition – which is felt as such, which is not transformed, thus creating a redundant effect – both in the intertextual area (concerning the text itself) and in the relationship between the text and its genre; the proliferation of clichés, the presence of stereotyped characters, is a clear manifestation of what we are discussing; the Freudian perspective, which has already been noted with respect to the pleasurable effect produced by what is known, is also valid for the aspect to which we are now referring.

Also with regard to the process of rereading, there are noticeable differences between the literary and para-literary work. In the case of the latter, rereading, which the simplicity of the literary text renders unnecessary, would not be an enriching expansion of the first reading, although the pleasure of repetition could be produced thereby. As regards a critical rereading or meta-reading of the para-literary work, this would permit a dismantling of the text, which would uncover the textual strategies put into play. This operation, however – unlike what happens in a literary work, in which a major subtlety in understanding the text, must produce a more clear-cut reception of the message – would be to the detriment of the dominant conative function, which itself would be weakened or eliminated, resulting in a destructive exposure of the text.

It is understandable that, given its aims, para-literature should prefer to use myths conceived as intentionally concealing, misleading instances rather than myths understood as instances which reveal in an ontological sense. Just as literature can provoke an occurrence or emergence of truth, i.e., ontological unconcealment, a para-literary text precludes any opening, enclosing us in the facile excitation and satisfaction of one's own ego.

Once we have grasped the differences between literature and para-literature, it is important to understand that both revitalize each other. Literature incorporates para-literary models and procedures, producing thereby intentional effects of rupture. The following cases should be noted by way of example:

Literary texts which disguise themselves paratextually as being manifestations of para-literary genres: *Boquitas pintadas* (*Heartbreak Tango*), by Manuel Puig, calls itself a feuilleton in its subtitle; *The Buenos Aires Affair*, by the same author, follows the same procedure by calling itself a "novela policial" [detective novel].

Literary works which, without having recourse to an explicitly disguising statement, constantly refer in all or part of their plot development to a para-literary genre, in which they are included, thus acquiring meaning, totally or in part. The first case corresponds to "La Muerte y la brújula" (Death and the Compass), by Jorge Luis Borges and its relationship to the detective genre; the second case is that of *La misteriosa desaparición de la marquesita de Loria* [The Mysterious Disappearance of the Young Marchioness of Loria], by José Donoso, a novel in which the erotic para-literary model is eliminated by the intervention of another genre, the fantastic, which is defined precisely by its unresolvable, ambiguous nature and which is therefore incompatible with the nature of para-literature.

Literary texts which incorporate para-literary microtexts into their structure, creating an intertextual dialogue between the macrotext and its microtexts: newspaper articles and commercials in *Libro de Manuel* (*A Manual for Manuel*), by Julio Cortázar; radio dramas in *La tía Julia y el escribidor* (*Aunt Julia and the Script Writer*), by Mario Vargas Llosa; recounting of sentimental movies in *El beso de la mujer araña* (*The Kiss of the Spider Woman*), by Manuel Puig.

MYRNA SOLOTOREVSKY

See also entries on Detective Fiction, Pornography, Science Fiction

Further Reading

Barthes, Roland, *Mythologies*, Paris: Seuil, 1957; selections as *Mythologies*, translated by Annette Lavers, London: Jonathan Cape, 1972; New York: Hill and Wang, 1973

Dorfman, Ariel, *Reader's nuestro que estás en la tierra: ensayos sobre el imperialismo cultural*, Mexico City: Nueva Imagen, 1980

_____ *El comic es algo serio*, Mexico City: Eufesa, 1982

Foster, David William, *From Mafalda to Los Supermachos: Latin American Graphic Humor as Popular Culture*, Boulder, Colorado: Lynne Rienner, 1989

Franco, Jean, "What's in a Name? Popular Culture Theories and Their Limitations," *Studies in Latin American Popular Culture* 1 (1982)

Greenberg, Clement, "Avant-Garde and Kitsch," in *Mass Culture: the Popular Arts in America*, edited by Bernard Rosenberg and David Manning White, Glencoe, Illinois: The Free Press, 1960

Gubern, Román, *La imagen y la cultura de masas*, Barcelona: Bruguera, 1983

Hinds Jr, Harold E. and Charles M. Tatum (editors), *Handbook of Latin American Popular Culture*, Westport, Connecticut: Greenwood Press, 1985

Jameson, Fredric, "Ideology, Narrative Analysis and Popular Culture," *Theory and Society* 4 (1977)

Kunzle, David, "Nationalist, Internationalist and Anti-Imperialist Themes in the Public Revolutionary Art of Cuba, Chile and Nicaragua," *Studies in Latin American Popular Culture* 2 (1983)

Mattelart, Michèle, *La cultura de las opresión femenina*, Mexico City: Era, 1977

Minc, Rose S. (editor), *Literature and Popular Culture in the Hispanic World*, Gaithersburg, Maryland: Hispamérica, 1981

Solotorevsky, Myrna, *Literatura – paraliteratura: Puig, Borges, Donoso, Cortázar, Vargas Llosa*, Gaithersburg, Maryland: Hispamérica, 1988

Paris

In "El otro cielo" (The Other Heaven), an excellent though underrated story by Julio Cortázar (in the collection *Todos los fuegos el fuego; All Fires the Fire*), the author sketches a shadowy figure who lives in a bohemian quarter of Paris (c.1870), an aspiring artist known only generically as "el americano." This character dies in a garret (of course) before the story ends, alone and unrecognised. "El otro cielo" is narrated by a young Argentine who, when the story opens, is able by a leap of the imagination to transfer himself from contemporary Argentina (c.1945) to an exciting (because dangerous) bohemian Paris of the 1870s. The execution in Paris of a serial "Jack the Ripper" type killer, who occupies the forefront of the Parisian part of the story, and the inglorious death of "el americano" – also in Paris– are followed by the figurative death in Buenos Aires of the narrator. The latter loses his creative ability as the result of marriage and the mediocrity that automatically ensues – in the author's view – from the institutionalization of the erotic and its consequent loss, together with the proletarization of Argentine society implied by Juan Perón coming to power in 1945. Thereafter, the Argentine narrator, now sipping his mate in a domestic setting, can no longer "connect" to a Parisian arcade in the 1870s.

Cortázar, who lost his university post during Perón's first presidency, was to settle for good in Paris in 1950. But many of his stories and his experimental novel *Rayuela* (*Hopscotch*), display a self-conscious unease over becoming a (Latin) American in Paris. For Cortázar, the dilemma faced by Latin American artists of an earlier period who settled in Paris is that if they remained there they risked losing their roots and becoming imitators of European styles; alternatively, to stay at home meant stultification on the rim of Western culture. Cortázar said in an interview given to Karl Kohut shortly before his death, that the intelligentsia of the French metropolis no longer exercised a powerful influence on Latin American artists and writers: the child had emerged from the shadow cast by the Gallic father and Paris had become a comfortable place of residence for Latin American artists or writers in exile, a city where they were guaranteed a community of fellow-exiles. This might explain why in *Rayuela*, as Jean Franco has pointed out, Paris is seen through the lens of the Surrealist writers, since they really did exercise a powerful influence on a generation of Spanish Americans in Paris.

Cortázar's life and work are useful illustrations of the delicate and intricate links forged by Latin American intellectuals who spent periods of their life in Paris. Apart from Cortázar, the Spanish American writer who responded most sensitively and thoughtfully to the experience of spending many years in Paris was the Cuban Alejo Carpentier. During the eleven years that he spent in this city (1928–39), Carpentier earned his living as a journalist, sending home to Cuba articles on a most considerable range of cultural and political topics. Among the most interesting are the many he devoted to artists of the Surrealist movement, because their poetics had a considerable impact on the development of his own poetics and aesthetics. Carpentier also learned while in Paris that the French were both ignorant of and indifferent to Latin America. He vowed, therefore, to act as propagandist for his continent. Paris figures in this author's fiction from the moment that this city first penetrated the consciousness of Latin American intellectuals, namely at the time of the French Revolution. Parts of Carpentier's finest novel, *El siglo de las luces* (*Explosion in a Cathedral*), take place in Paris and describe how two young Cubans respond to that maelstrom. But in the first half of the 19th century Paris had to compete with London since Britain was perceived as a country of relatively enlightened ideas and political tolerance, and therefore one which provided a haven for revolutionaries such as Karl Marx. Paris had its heyday in the *belle époque*, that is in the years preceding World War I and also in the 1920s. The *belle époque* forms the background of Carpentier's dictatorship novel, *El recurso del método*, 1974 (*Reasons of State*) in which the sybaritic "president for life" of a representative Latin American state spends all the time he can living it up in Paris, returning to his banana republic only when he must crush a coup against him. He winds up in old age as an exile in Paris, at which point Carpentier uses avant-garde art of the 1920s to show that the protagonist is a relic of an earlier age: "We have no bananas today" is the mocking line from a popular song of the period that greets the ex-dictator at the beginning of his Parisian exile.

A Latin American author closely associated with Paris in the *belle époque* is Rubén Darío, the leading Spanish American *modernista* poet, who projects in some of his early works a naughty "gay Paree" image of Paris complete with foaming champagne and *garconnières*. Inside the latter, a figure like the Carolina of "De invierno" [About Winter], from the collection *Prosas profanas*, 1896 [Profane Poems], waits to warm the poet up in this chilly (and for him) exotic, setting: "Abre los ojos, mírame con su mirar risueño, / y en tanto cae la nieve de Paris." (She opens her eyes, gives me a radiant smile / and all the while the snow falls over Paris). Clearly, few are the (extant) Latin American writers who produced such engaging rubbish, and at the other end of the spectrum is the Peruvian César Vallejo who in his poem "París, octubre 1936," bids a farewell to life (he was to die two years later) in terms which, with much irony, encompass the plight of someone like Cortázar's character, "el americano." Vallejo begins this poem with the following lines: "De todo esto, yo soy el único que parte. / De este banco me voy, de mis calzones, / de mi gran situación, de mis acciones, de mi número hendido parte a parte, / de todo esto yo soy el único que parte." (I'm taking my leave of all of this / I'm leaving this park bench, my boxer shorts, / my grand situation, my actions, / my number split asunder, / I'm the only one to leave it all).

Despite earlier activity, as in the case of US writers, the period when Paris proved most magnetic to Latin Americans was the 1920s. This was a time when there was a concentration of intellectual talent there in the form of students, diplomats, journalists and playboys. Among them were members of the oligarchy, such as the Argentine Ricardo Güiraldes, who supposedly introduced Parisian polite society to the tango; two women writers, who were also emotionally very close: the Venezuelan Teresa de la Parra and her Cuban friend Lydia Cabrera, the ambassador of Ecuador, Gonzalo Zaldumbide, the Guatemalan Miguel Ángel Asturias who, in a way that was typical of the period, came to Europe to learn about the history of his own continent – in his case, that of the Mayan Indians.

In the interview Julio Cortázar gave to Karl Kohut mentioned above, he said that Paris ceased being an important influence on Latin American writers after World War II. But this remark is limited to male writers since for some women writers a transformative experience has been their encounter with French feminism. A striking example is provided by the Cuban poet Zoé Valdés whose first collection, *Respuestas para vivir* [Answers for Living] won the "Roque Dalton" prize in 1982, before she went to work in Paris as the assistant of Alfredo Guevara, who then headed the Cuban delegation to UNESCO. Her second volume of poetry, *Todo para una sombra*, 1986 [Everything for a Shadow] shows how the knowledge she acquired there of French feminist theory radicalized her perception of gender and heterosexual relations. The Peruvian poet Blanca Varela, who spent several years living in Paris, is another contemporary author whose self-awareness as both a Latin American creative writer and a woman increased as a direct result of this experience.

VERITY SMITH

See also entries on Alejo Carpentier, *Rayuela* (Julio Cortázar), Surrealism

Further Reading

It seems strange that so important, interesting and varied a subject as this has not yet merited a single detailed study. There is scope here for several, but right now all that exist are very partial accounts such as chapters about Paris in the experience of a particular writer or an account of, say, Parisian literary journals of the 1920s which focused on Latin America.

Carpentier, Alejo, *Crónicas*, 2 vols, Havana: Editorial Arte y Literatura, 1975 [A selection of Carpentier's journalism from the period 1928–39, which he spent in Paris]

Cheymol, Marc, *Miguel Ángel Asturias dans le Paris des Années Folles*, Grenoble: Presses Universitaires de Grenoble, 1987 [Chapter 2 is on Spanish American journalism in Paris in the early decades of the 20th century]

Cortázar, Julio, *París: ritmos de una ciudad*, photographs by Alecio de Andrade, Barcelona: Edhasa, 1981; as *Paris: the Essence of an Image*, translated by Gregory Rabassa, New York: Norton, 1981

Kohut, Karl, *Escribir en París*, Barcelona: Hogar del Libro, 1983 [Includes interviews with Cortázar, Roa Bastos and Severo Sarduy, which focus on the experience of exile in Paris]

Molloy, Sylvia, *La Diffusion de la littérature hispano-américaine en France au XXème siécle*, Paris: PUF-CNRS, 1972

Otero, Lisandro, "Los años de París," *Casa de las Américas*, Havana, vol. 34/192 (July–September 1993 [Fragment of yet unpublished memoirs, "Hago constar"]

Patout, Paulette, *Alfonso Reyes et la France*, Paris: Klincksieck, 1978

―――― "Teresa de la Parra, París y *Las memorias de Mamá Blanca*," in *Las memorias de Mamá Blanca*, edited by Velia Bosch, Paris: UNESCO, 1988

Samurovic-Pavlovic, Liliana, *Les Lettres hispano-américaines au "Mercure de France," (1897–1915)*, Belgrade: University of Belgrade, 1969

Ugarte, M., *La Jeune littérature hispano-américaine*, Paris: Sansot, 1907

Nicanor Parra 1914–

Chilean poet

"Qué es la antipoesía?" (What is antipoetry?) asks the speaker in Nicanor Parra's poem "Test." The many alternatives given to the reader include, "Una tempestad en una taza de té? / Una mancha de nieve en una roca? / Un azafate lleno de excrementos humanos? / ... Un ataúd a gas de parafina? / Una capilla ardiente sin difunto? / Marque con una cruz / La definición que considere correcta." (A tempest in a teapot? / A snowy spot on a rock? /A tray covered with human excrement? / ... A coffin that runs on kerosene? / A funeral parlor without a corpse? / Put an X / Next to the answer you think is correct." The irreverent and humorous work that Parra published as *Poemas y antipoemas*, 1954 (*Poems and Anti-Poems*) has had a marked effect on poetry from Hispanic America as well as from the United States and England when his poems were translated into English in the 1960s. The term *antipoesía* or antipoetry, as Parra's claim to originality, is misleading, given literature's ongoing tradition of breaking with tradition. For example, as different as Nicanor Parra and the Chilean poet Vicente Huidobro are in terms of their poetry, Huidobro also called himself an "antipoet" due to the ways he was working against tradition, while at the same time depending on that tradition as a means of providing the creative tension in his work. As one might expect, the four decades that have passed since the resoundingly successful publication of the *Poemas y antipoemas* have called forth plenty of anti-antipoets.

If one considers Parra's first book *Cancionero sin nombre* [Song Book without a Name], a work published in 1937 that Parra now disowns and will not allow to be republished in anthologies of his poetry, it is clear that he produced the antipoems by writing against himself, in much the same way that his countryman Pablo Neruda completely remade his poetry at least half a dozen times throughout his life. The major difference between these two poets, however, is that Parra, once he found his "antipoetic" voice, has maintained it with very little real variation. Although the poems from Parra's first book are largely unsuccessful imitations of Lorca's *Romancero gitano* (*Gypsy Ballads*), they occasionally give an indication of the poet Parra will later become. In "El Matador" [The Matador], for example, the speaker of the poem tells his supposedly shocked listener that he is going to " eat an angel" and that "two priests of sperm" are going to hunt down the speaker in the afternoon "por provocar a los santos / por desorden en la calle / por derramar en la iglesia / un litro y medio de sangre." (for having provoked the saints / for being disorderly in the street / for spilling in the church / a litre and a half of blood). This poem contains some of the same violent, surreal humor that appears in Neruda's poem from the early 1930s, "Walking Around."

Generally speaking, Parra's antipoetry is *anti-lyrical* in that it is more prosaic and colloquial than traditional poetry. The Mexican poet José Emilio Pacheco has pointed out that the conversational poetry that became so prevalent in Hispanic America in the 1960s has an antecedent in the unacknowledged work of three poets that Pacheco calls "the other vanguard." Pedro Henríquez Ureña, Salomón de la Selva and Salvador Novo were contemporaries of Huidobro, César Vallejo and Neruda, but were influenced by the so-called New Poetry from the United States in the first decades of the 20th century. In any case, Parra uses the most colloquial forms of speech to demystify absolutes, to cut through rhetoric and to deflate the overly solemn and the sacred.

Often he writes about everyday things by means of personae immersed in the banal, sometimes absurd, situations of the human condition. For example, in his well-known poem "Soliloquio del Individuo" (Soliloquy of the Individual), the speaker is the collective consciousness of the individual from the Stone Age to the contemporary world. In order to satirize our times more effectively as well as to make his audience laugh and blush by means of black humor, scandal and vulgarity, Parra adopts the persona of an ascetic itinerant preacher he calls the Christ of Elqui in *Sermones y prédicas del Cristo de Elqui*, 1977 (*Sermons and Homilies of the Christ of Elqui*), followed by a sequel two years later, and resurrected again in 1983.

As a writer, Parra is less a loose cannon than a sniper. He has maintained an anarchist's stance in his politicized poetry, which holds no ideology sacred. The Chilean left, for example, was unforgiving of the political position of Parra in his *Artefactos* (1972) during the Allende years and the way Parra gloated over the vanquished supporters of the Popular Unity government at the time of the military coup in 1973. Parra remained in Chile during the military dictatorship and eventually began to use the written and spoken word as a means of criticizing Pinochet, albeit in somewhat predictable, unconvincing ways, such as the poems in *Chistes parRa desorientar a la policía*, 1983 [ParRa's Jokes to Mislead the Police]. It is quite likely that the collective public art actions taken in the early 1980s by a new Chilean art avant garde (that included poet Raúl Zurita) to protest the dictatorship were influenced by the legendary *Quebrantahuesos* [Bonebreakers] of 1952–53. Ronald Kay, in an act of literary archeology, presented some of these texts in 1975 in the magazine *Manuscritos*. The *quebrantahuesos*, conceived by Nicanor Parra with a heavy dose of absurd humor and social satire, were collages assembled from newspapers and exhibited at the corner of Bandera and Ahumada streets in the heart of downtown Santiago on a weekly basis.

Although Parra continues to use his brilliant, mordant humor as a basis for much of his more recent work, such as the epigrammatic *Ecopoemas*, 1982 [Ecopoems], he also confounds those who try to categorize his poetry by writing a beautifully lyrical, melancholy, ontological poem such as "El hombre imaginario" (The Man He Imagined). Taken as a whole, Parra's poetry (often imitated, but never equalled) certainly embodies some of the most important characteristics of 20th-century Hispanic American poetry.

STEVEN F. WHITE

Biography

Born in San Fabián, Chile, 5 September 1914. Brother of the song writer Violeta Parra (see separate entry). Attended the University of Chile, Santiago, degree in mathematics and physics, 1938; studied advanced mechanics, Brown University, Providence, Rhode Island, 1943–45; studied cosmology at Oxford University (British Council grant), 1949–51. Married Ana Troncoso in 1948 (marriage dissolved); later married Inga Palmen; seven children. Secondary school teacher, 1938–43. Director, School of Engineering, 1948–49; and Professor of theoretical physics, University of Chile, 1952–91. Visiting Professor, Louisiana State University, Baton Rouge, 1966, and New York, Columbia, and Yale universities, 1971. Awarded the City of Santiago Prize, 1937, for *Cancionero sin nombre*, and in 1954 for *Poemas y antipoemas*; Writers' Union Prize, 1954; National Literature Prize, 1969 for *Obra gruesa*; Guggenheim Fellowship, 1972; Juan Rulfo Prize, 1991.

Selected Works

Poetry

Cancionero sin nombre, Santiago de Chile: Nascimento, 1937
Poemas y antipoemas, Santiago de Chile: Nascimento, 1954
La cueca larga, Santiago de Chile: Editorial Universitaria, 1958
Versos de salón, Santiago de Chile: Nascimento, 1962
Canciones rusas, Santiago de Chile: Editorial Universitaria, 1967
Poesía rusa contemporánea, Santiago de Chile: Ediciones Nueva Universidad, 1967
Poemas, Havana: Casa de las Américas, 1969
Los profesores, New York: Antiediciones Villa Miseria, 1971
Artefactos, Santiago de Chile: Universidad Católica de Chile, 1972
Sermones y prédicas del Cristo de Elqui, Santiago de Chile: Universidad de Chile Estudios Humanísticos, 1977; as *Sermons and Homilies of the Christ of Elqui*, translated by Sandra Reyes, Columbia: University of Missouri Press, 1984 [Includes translations of poems from *Nuevos sermones y prédicas del Cristo de Elqui*]
Nuevos sermones y prédicas del Cristo de Elqui, Valparaíso, Chile: Ganymedes, 1979
Poema y antipoema a Eduardo Frei, Santiago de Chile: América del Sur, 1982
El anti-Lázaro, Santiago de Chile: Gráfica Marginal, 1982
Ecopoemas, Santiago de Chile: Gráfica Marginal, 1982
Coplas de navidad, Santiago de Chile: Ediciones del Camaleón, 1983
Chistes parRa desorientar a la policía, Santiago de Chile: Galería Época, 1983

Compilations and Anthologies

Obra gruesa, Santiago de Chile: Editorial Universitaria, 1969
Antipoems: antología 1944–1969, edited by José Miguel Ibañez-Langlois, Barcelona: Seix Barral, 1972
Poesía política, Santiago de Chile: Bruguera, 1983
Hojas de Parra, edited by David Turkeltaub, Santiago de Chile: Ganymedes, 1985
Fotopoemas sobre textos de Nicanor Parra, photographs by Sergio Marras, Santiago de Chile: Ornitorrinco, 1986
Nicanor Parra: biografía emotiva, edited by Efrain Szmulewicz, Santiago de Chile: Rumbos, 1988
Poemas para combatir la calvicie: muesta de antipoesía, edited by Julio Ortega, Mexico City: Fondo de Cultura Económica, 1993

Anthologies in Translation

Anti-Poems, translated by Jorge Elliot, San Francisco: City Lights, 1960
Poems and Antipoems, edited by Miller Williams, translated by Fernando Alegría, *et al.*, New York: New Directions, 1967; London: Jonathan Cape, 1968 [bilingual edition]
Emergency Poems, translated by Miller Williams, New York: New Directions, 1972; London: Boyars, 1977 [bilingual edition]
Antipoems: New and Selected, edited by David Unger, translated by Lawrence Ferlinghetti, *et al.*, New York: New Directions, 1985 [bilingual edition]

Other Writings

Discursos, in collaboration with Pablo Neruda, Santiago de Chile: Nascimento, 1962

Further Reading

Barrow, Geoffrey R., "Generic Composition in Latin American Poetry: Nicanor Parra and Diatribe," *Selected Proceedings of the 35th Annual Mountain Interstate Foreign Language Conference*, Greenville, South Carolina, 1987
Borgeson, Jr, Paul W., "Lenguaje hablado / lenguaje poético: Parra, Cardenal y la antipoesía," *Revista Iberoamericana* 118–19 (1982)
Flores, Ángel (editor), *Aproximaciones a Nicanor Parra*, Barcelona: Ocnos, 1973
Goic, Cedomil, "La antipoesía de Nicanor Parra," in *Historia y crítica de la literatura hispanoamericana*, vol. 3, *Época contemporánea*, edited by Goic, Barcelona: Crítica, 1991
Grossman, Edith, *The Antipoetry of Nicanor Parra*, New York: New York University Press, 1975
López Mejía, Adelaida, "Nicanor Parra and the Question of Authority," *Latin American Literary Review*, vol. 18/38 (1990)
Melnykovich, George, "Nicanor Parra: Antipoetry, Retraction and Silence," *Latin American Literary Review*, vol. 3/6 (1975)
Montes, Hugo and Mario Rodríguez (editors), *Nicanor Parra y la poesía de lo cotidiano*, Santiago de Chile: Pacífico, 1970
Morales, Leónidas, *La poesía de Nicanor Parra*, Santiago de Chile: Andrés Bello, 1972
Ortega, Julio, "Voces de Nicanor Parra," *Revista de Literatura* 108 (1991)
Salvador Jofre, Álvaro Luis, *Para una lectura de Nicanor Parra: el proyecto ideológico y el inconsciente*, Seville: Universidad de Sevilla, 1976
Yamal, Ricardo, *Sistema y visión de la poesía de Nicanor Parra*, Valencia: Albatros-Hispanófila, 1985

Interviews

Lerzundi, Patricio, "In Defense of Antipoetry: an Interview with Nicanor Parra," *Review*, vols 4 and 5 (1971–72)
Morales, Leónidas T., *Conversaciones con Nicanor Parra*, Santiago de Chile: Editorial Universitaria, 1990

Teresa de la Parra 1889–1936

Venezuelan prose writer

Born in Paris at the end of the 19th century to a family of diplomats, Teresa de la Parra's early years were spent on a sugar mill plantation in the Venezuelan countryside, an idyllic childhood which she nostalgically recounted in her *Las Memorias de Mamá Blanca (Mamá Blanca's Souvenirs)*. Parra's early writings were first published around 1915 when some of her short fiction appeared in the magazine *El Universal*. Included in *Obras (Narrativa, Ensayos, Cartas)* [Oeuvre (Narrative, Essays, Letters)] are three of these short stories: "Historia de la señorita Grano de Polvo Bailarina del Sol," "El genio del pesacartas" and "El ermitaño del reloj" [respectively: The Story of Miss Speck of Dust Dancer of the Sun, The Genie of the Letter Scales, The Hermit of the Clock]. Considered as examples of literature of the fantastic, these three stories are clearly allegorical of the artist's position in society, more specifically of women artists.

In "Grano de Polvo," a puppet relates to his master (a poet) the story of a beautiful speck of dust who used to dance in a ray of sunlight. The ballerina can no longer practice her art because he is keeping her "safe" inside his wallet, afraid that he may lose her forever if she were to be released. Parra's feminism is already evident in this early story. When at the urging of the poet the puppet finally allows her to dance in the sunlight, Miss Speck of Dust forever eludes her captor and finds her freedom by allowing a monstrous bug to swallow her. The tone of this story is one of biting irony, from the straightforward denunciation of possessive male love to the horrifying solution found to the fragile dancer's imprisonment.

Parra returned to Caracas in 1919 and remained there until 1923. The impact postcolonial Caracas had on Parra's sensibility is recorded in her novel *Ifigenia: diario de una señorita que escribió porque se fastidiaba (Iphigenia: the Diary of a Young Lady Who Wrote because She Was Bored)*, published in Paris on her return in 1924, quickly followed by a French translation (1926). Undoubtedly Parra's most controversial work, *Ifigenia* was heralded following its publication as either a charmingly "feminine" new work by a female author or as a book of dubious merit, subversively dangerous to young ladies. Parra herself was obliged to explain her own position regarding the novel's feminist premises, which she defended as "moderate" in her essay "Influencia de las mujeres en la formación del alma americana" [The Influence of Women in the Forging of the American Soul].

In the novel, the narrator María Eugenia struggles to bridge the gap between her European upbringing and the provincial society she encounters back at home. Forced to return to Caracas after the death of both parents, the young woman must gradually relinquish her progressive ideas (tied to the figure of the young and liberal Gabriel) and indeed her identity, in order to settle into the society she has inherited (as personified by the patriarchal figure of her uncle Eduardo and the pious women of the family). Initially rebellious and outspoken, family pressures lead the young woman to accept the older and conservative Leal as her future husband. A repulsive choice, it is clear that Leal would eventually crush her spirit, since during their courtship he either mocks or ignores all expressions of María Eugenia's intelligence and individuality. The question of a woman's "duty" in such a society is evident in her arbitrary choice of Leal over Gabriel. Indeed, if we consider the implications of the novel's title (that is *Ifigenia* rather than *María Eugenia*, in reference to the main character), we find that the heroine's ironic rejection of freedom in favour of family alludes to the classical theme of a daughter's sacrifice. In Racine's drama *Iphigénie* (1674), the heroine is at the center of a power struggle between her father Agamemnon and her betrothed Achilles. Agamemnon has offered Iphigénie's life in sacrifice to the gods, in exchange for the fate of Troy. Iphigénie's submissiveness, however, as revealed in her long reply to Agamemnon, is meant to underscore her father's wrong and cruel disposal of her existence as though a commodity. In Parra's novel, as María Eugenia falls prey to Leal, her submission to her family's wishes is also an act that reveals as evil and fatal what becomes the only choice left to a dutiful and honour bound young woman. Thus, ironically, Parra's heroine becomes the tragic victim of a self-imposed punishment.

Parra's other novel *Memorias de Mamá Blanca*, narrates different aspects of a little girl's childhood in rural Venezuela. In the novel's prologue a narrator relates the story of her friendship with an old woman (Blanca) whose memoirs of the past she has inherited. Young Blanca's memoirs are loosely structured, with chapters devoted to her sisters, to an old black farm hand named Vicente Cochocho, and also to the family's painful move to the city. Notably absent from the family for long periods of time, Blanca's father is a sometimes benevolent, sometimes testy and distant figure who strives to bring "order" and authority to the *hacienda*. His confrontation with Blanca's adored old Cochocho inserts a strong note of social criticism, as it reveals the old man's dignity and determination. A most important aspect of the novel, the relationship between Blanca and her mother, is presented through the latter's obsession with her daughter's straight hair. While the five other sisters, who have been graced with beautiful curls are not required to go through the "curling" process, Blanca alone is singled out as needing special attention. Time spent alone with her mother is a transforming experience for Blanca, since in the process of attempting to beautify her daughter's hair, the mother instills in the young girl her passion for language and for story-telling. The mother's poetic and creative spirit is thus transferred onto the daughter, a theme later echoed in feminist novels, most singularly in Isabel Allende's *La casa de los espíritus (The House of the Spirits)*. One further point worth noting about the *Memorias*, is that in the very masculine (and male-dominated) world of Latin American intellectuals in Paris, this work was perceived as important enough to be translated at once into French and it appeared, in a version by Francis de Miomandre (who had also translated *Ifigenia*), in the same year as the Spanish version, 1929.

It has been the task of a new generation of critics and readers to bring Teresa de la Parra's writing out of obscurity. Her work is important not only to a complete understanding of contemporary writing by women but it is of equal value to comprehend vanguardist narrative and its impact on the literature that followed.

ANA GARCÍA CHICHESTER

Biography

Born Ana Teresa Parra Sanojo in Paris, 5 October 1889. Early childhood spent in Venezuela. Educated at the School of the Sacred Heart in Godella, Valencia (Spain), 1902–09. Recognized in 1922 by the newspaper *El Luchador* [The Fighter] for her short story *Mamá X*. Awarded annual prize of the Casa Editora Franco-Ibero-Americana (Paris) for the Spanish edition of *Ifigenia* in 1924. Lectured on Bolívar, in Havana, 1927, and on the role of women in Latin American history, in Bogotá and Barranquilla, Colombia, 1930. From 1931–36 was in and out of the sanatorium at Fuenfría, Spain, suffering from tuberculosis. Died in Madrid, 23 April 1936 in the company of her intimate friend, the Cuban writer Lydia Cabrera. Remains moved to the Parra Sanojo family gravesite at the Almudena cemetery in Caracas.

Selected Works

Novels

Diario de una señorita que se fastidia, Caracas: Imprenta Bolívar, 1922
Ifigenia: diario de una señorita que escribió porque se fastidiaba, Paris: Franco-Ibero-Americana, 1924; as *Iphigenia: the Diary of a Young Lady who Wrote because She Was Bored*, translated by Bertie Acker, Austin: University of Texas Press, 1994
La Mamá X, Caracas: Tipografía Moderna, 1923
Las Memorias de Mamá Blanca, Paris: Editorial "Le Livre Libre," 1929; as *Mamá Blanca's Souvenirs*, translated by Harriet de Onís, Washington, DC: Pan American Union, 1959; revised by Frederick H. Fornoff, Pittsburgh: University of Pittsburgh Press, 1993

Other Writings

Cartas, Caracas: Cruz del Sur, 1951
Epistolario íntimo, Caracas: Imprenta Nacional, 1953
Tres conferencias inéditas, Caracas: Garrido, 1961
Cartas a Lydia Cabrera: correspondencia inédita de Gabriela Mistral y Teresa de la Parra, edited by Rosario Hiriart, Madrid: Ediciones Torremozas, 1988 [Important also on issue of gender]

Compilations and Anthologies

Obras completas, Caracas: Arte, 1965
Obras (Narrativa, Ensayos, Cartas), Caracas: Biblioteca Ayacucho, 1982

Further Reading

Aizenberg, Edna, "El Bildungsroman fracasado en Latino América: el caso de *Ifigenia* de Teresa de la Parra," *Revista Iberoamericana*, vol. 51/132–33 (1985) [A study of *Ifigenia* as a truncated Bildungsroman]
Bosch, Velia (editor), *Teresa de la Parra ante la crítica*, Caracas: Monte Ávila, 1980
Gambarini, Elsa Krieger, "The Male Critic and the Woman Writer: Reading Teresa de la Parra's Critics," in *In the Feminine Mode: Essays on Hispanic Women Writers*, edited by Noel Valis and Carol Maier, Lewisburg, Pennsylvania: Bucknell University Press, and London: Associated University Presses, 1990 [Examines the reaction of male readers and critics to Parra's work, and explains why it has been rejected by many who try to influence the Latin American literary canon]
Lemâitre, Louis Antoine, *Between Flight and Longing: the Journey of Teresa de la Parra*, New York: Vantage Press, 1986 [biography]
Masiello, Francine, "Texto, ley, transgresión: especulación sobre la novela (feminista) de vanguardia," *Revista Iberoamericana*, vol. 51/132–33 (July–December 1985) [Discusses the feminist avant-garde novel, focusing primarily on the work of Norah Lange, María Luisa Bombal and Teresa de la Parra]
Meyer, Doris, " 'Feminine' Testimony in the Works of Teresa de la Parra, María Luisa Bombal and Victoria Ocampo," in *Contemporary Women Authors of Latin America: Introductory Essays*, edited by Meyer and Margarite Fernández Olmos, Brooklyn, New York: Brooklyn College Press, 1983
Molloy, Sylvia, "Disappearing Acts: Reading Lesbian in Teresa de la Parra," in *¿Entiendes? Queer Readings, Hispanic Writings*, edited by Emilie Bergmann and Paul Julian Smith, Durham, North Carolina: Duke University Press, 1995
Picón Salas, Mariano, *Formación y proceso de la literatura venezolana*, Caracas: Monte Ávila, 1984 [Contains short section on Teresa de la Parra's letters]
Rodríguez, Ileana, *House/Garden/Nation: Space, Gender and Ethnicity in Post-Colonial Latin American Literature by Women*, translated by Rodríguez and Robert Carr, Durham, North Carolina: Duke University Press, 1994 [Chapter 2 is on Teresa de la Parra, with particular reference to *Ifigenia*]

Las memorias de Mamá Blanca

Novel by Teresa de la Parra

In *Las memorias de Mamá Blanca* (1926) Teresa de la Parra explores certain aspects of elite creole society in rural Venezuela in the early part of the 20th century. Published at a time when Social Realism was a strong influence in Latin American fictional writing, this novel has received some criticism for its nostalgic and idyllic portrayal of post-colonial upper-class society. Such appraisal seems unjust. Since the memoirs are narrated by a young Blanca Nieves (Snow White), blatant criticism of any aspect of society would have created a discrepancy in the narrative voice which any careful author would have avoided. To read this novel as a frivolous evocation of Parra's social milieu is to ignore some of its most subtle and penetrating passages in which, without altering the book's evocative and lyrical style, economic disparity and social injustice are disclosed.

The novel's prologue is by a "writer" who claims to have in her possession Mamá Blanca's manuscript, written toward the end of her life. This pre-textual narrative is a philosophical treatise on the nature of loves that transcend blood lines, loves that are often wrongly judged and misunderstood by others (undoubtedly Parra's lesbian proclivities are of relevance here). Pointing out only that a "mysterious spiritual affinity" had been established between the two women (old Mamá Blanca and the young writer), the prologue's narrator describes her love for Mamá Blanca as one in which, "as in all true loves, from beginning to end, I was looking for myself;" meaning that in Mama Blanca, an artist without a profession, she had found a mirror of her own dismantled soul.

It is important to remember that one of the most salient features of the feminist novel of the vanguardist period (including the work of Norah Lange and María Luisa Bombal), is the emphasis on "lateral" bonds of love as opposed to family ties, and on the friendship among women as essential to the fabric of female life. Parra's novel adheres to these and other vanguardist tenets: first, there is the figure of the father who remains distant throughout the novel; secondly, the single most influential figure in little Blanca's early childhood is unquestionably her own mother who, far from taking control over this family of women (there are six little girls in all), behaves much like an older sister. In addition, the novel rejects a strictly linear development, in favour of a more episodic structure, which highlights little Blanca's memories of Vicente Cochocho (the old black farmhand), Cousin Juancho (an endearing charlatan), and the sisters' favorite pastimes. As in many feminist fictional narratives that have followed, it is the inner world of women, the daily concerns of domestic life, and the interrelationships within the female members of the family that become the main subject of the novel.

One of the most important sections of the memoirs deals with Blanca's admiration for her mother, who is far from a figure of authority or discipline. That role is reserved to Blanca's father, who appears only occasionally to bring "order" to an otherwise chaotic and whimsical household. The mother's role is that of teacher, and it is through her magnificent talent for story-telling that Blanca becomes familiar with European novels and romances. These tales become distorted and embellished as Blanca's mother responds to her daughter's request to make the stories more pertinent to her everyday rural experience. By juxtaposing European myth with Venezuelan images, mother and daughter engage in the kind of counter-discursive practice that was at the center of vanguardist literary production. The transformation of Snow White into a Venezuelan "Blanca Nieves," pokes gentle fun at the controversy between civilization (gentility) and barbarism that had been debated in the earlier part of the century and also, more significantly, points the way of the future for Latin American literature.

ANA GARCÍA CHICHESTER

Editions

First edition: *Las memorias de Mamá Blanca*, Paris: Editorial "Le Livre Libre," 1929

Critical edition: edited by Velia Bosch, Paris: UNESCO, 1988 [Text preceded by illuminating articles on various aspects of the novel]

Translation: *Mamá Blanca's Souvenirs*, by Harriet de Onís and revised by Frederick H. Fornoff, Pittsburgh: University of Pittsburgh Press, 1993

Further Reading

Coloquio internacional: escritura y sexualidad en la literatura hispanoamericana, Madrid: Fundamento, 1990 [Contribution by Nissa Torrents on the *Memorias*]

Sommer, Doris, *Foundational Fictions: the National Romances of Latin America*, Berkeley: University of California Press, 1991 [Chapter on the *Memorias*]

Violeta Parra 1917–1967

Chilean song writer

Within the context of Latin American cultural fiction, Violeta Parra constitutes one of Latin America's most innovative and original figures. However, after her death in 1968, Parra became better known as a folk singer than as a poet and it was not until the 1980s that literary critics became interested in incorporating her lyrical discourse into the Latin American literary canon.

The life and the literary production of Violeta Parra are almost inseparable and are surrounded by a constant myth. She was born in 1907 in a small town in the south of Chile called San Carlos. Her relatives were musicians and circus folk of especially humble origin, a situation which never allowed her access to the culture of the elite. This and the fact that Parra was born in rural Chile, will be the most important foundation of her artistic legacy. From her childhood, she sang the melodies she heard her parents and other peasant families sing and she began her life as a folk singer, traveling through the neighboring areas and singing in the most loyal peasant tradition of the south of Chile.

In the 1950s, Parra migrated to Santiago where she sang regularly in bars on the outskirts of the city. That was a time when her singing developed along with her compositional skills and she began writing her own songs in which she incorporated many traditional elements of Chilean folklore, together with elements of her own imagination. At the end of the 1970s Parra began to have a very important part as the author of her own compositions which were sung in cafes throughout the capital; these were the result of her own initiative and that of her sons.

During the 1970s, Parra participated in the great political and cultural debate that mobilized students worldwide but which coincided, in Chile, with the so-called Movement of the New Chilean Song, a rescue "phenomenon" which focused on indigenous music as well as the politics of cultural reevaluation based on Chilean identity. In this phase of renewal, Parra promoted the country's indigenous instruments, including those of northern Chile along the border with Bolivia.

Parra began to compose memorable poetry with a strong political theme, based on a social vindication, a concern for the workers, the dispossessed, students and women. The themes of love and disenchantment are also ever-present.

In Parra's work, her songs as well as her poems and letters are collected in a book *Toda Violeta Parra* [All of Violeta Parra], we can see a marked preoccupation with women's role and her relationship with Latin American patriarchal society. *Las décimas* represents her ultimate autobiography written in verse. There are various poems in which we can see woman as a victim due to her gender, but also due to man's domination, violation and physical abuse.

Parra represents an extraordinary phenomenon within Latin American and Chilean culture. Not only was she a great folk singer who, working in precarious conditions, managed to collect more than three thousand songs throughout the country. She also was a great rescuer of the national culture which she considered to be embedded in folk music. Parra reawoke a sleeping cultural identity in the continent and also vindicated the cultural projects of the young and of women. Together with her work as a composer and a folk singer, she dedicated herself to making tapestries and pottery. Only rarely has Latin America produced an artist with such multiple talents as well as one of the few authors to have worked in the realm of genuinely popular culture with an essentially modern outlook.

Among her most remarkable works is the already mentioned *Las décimas*, an autobiography written in a form of verse that follows the traditional *décima*, consisting of ten lines. It also incorporated the struggle of a peasant woman attempting to become part of a patriarchal society, the conflicts of the country and the city and the role of working women.

Through her art Parra represents a fundamental link between the traditional and the modern, between the native perspective of the period and her internationalist outlook. Now that at long last her work is being taken seriously, it is emerging as one of fundamental importance in the Latin American culture.

MARJORIE AGOSÍN

See also entry on María Elena Walsh

Biography

Born in San Carlos, Ñuble, in the south of Chile, 4 October 1917. Daughter of a *campesino* and a music teacher, sister of the poet Nicanor Parra (see separate entry). Moved to Santiago de Chile, 1930. By the age of twenty she was composing popular songs and singing at local fairs and in taverns. Married a railway worker, Luis Cereceda in 1937. Their daughter, Isabel, born in the same year; followed by son, Ángel. Worked with Spanish theatrical company, 1945. Separated from Cereceda and married again, 1949; two daughters. Director of the Museum of Popular Art, Concepción, 1950–51. Worked with her children in a circus. Career took off when she sang on the radio, 1953. Participated in the work of rescuing Chile's authentic rural music. Awarded Caupolicán prize for outstanding folklorist of the year, 1953. Invited to International Conference of Communist Youth in Poland, 1953; travelled to USSR; spent two years in France where she made her first recordings. Returned to Chile, 1956 and made her first LP there. Moved to Concepción, in the south of Chile, under contract to the university, 1957. Continued her research on Chilean song there. Returned to Santiago, 1958, and began to work in pottery, painting and *arpillera* work (the last consists of creating images on sackcloth). Travelled to Europe, 1961, spending three years in France. Tapestries exhibited in the Museum of Mankind Paris, 1963, hers being the first individual show by a Latin American artist to be held there. Made documentary for Swiss TV, Returned to Santiago, 1964, where she installed herself in a large tent on the outskirts of Santiago: "la Carpa de la Reina" (Queen's Tent). Travelled to Bolivia, 1966. Committed suicide in her tent/home, 5 February 1967.

Selected Works

Publications

Poésie populaire des Andes, Paris: François Masperó, 1965 [The only collection of her songs and poems to be published in her lifetime. Bilingual edition]

Las décimas: autobiografía en versos chilenas, Santiago de Chile: Pomaire, 1970 [Introduction by Pablo Neruda, Pablo de Rokha and Nicanor Parra]

21 son los dolores: antología amorosa, edited by Juan Andrés Piña, Santiago de Chile: Aconcagua, 1976 [Anthology of poems and songs about love]

Violeta del pueblo, edited by Javier Martínez Reverte, Madrid: Visor, 1976

La guitarra indócil, Barcelona: Júcar, 1978 [A French edition appeared in 1977]

Cantos folklóricos chilenos, Santiago de Chile: Nascimento, 1979

El libro mayor, Barcelona: n.p., 1981 [Includes some of her letters and the text of an interview for Swiss television]

Compilations and Anthologies

Toda Violeta Parra, edited by Alfonso Alcalde, Buenos Aires: Ediciones de La Flor, 1974

Selected Discography (78 rpm records are not listed)

Cantos de Chile, Paris: Le Chant du Monde, 1956

Acompañada de guitarra, Santiago de Chile: Odeon, 1957

La cueca presentada por Violeta Parra, Santiago de Chile: Odeon, 1959

La tonada presentada por Violeta Parra, Santiago de Chile: Odeon, 1959

Toda Violeta Parra, Santiago de Chile: Odeon, 1961

Recordando a Chile, Santiago de Chile: Odeon, 1965

Carpa de la Reina, Santiago de Chile: Odeon, 1966

Las últimas composiciones de Violeta Parra, Santiago de Chile: RCA, 1966

Canciones reencontradas en París, Santiago de Chile: Dicap, 1971

Canciones, Violeta Parra, Havana: Casa de las Américas, 1971

Décimas, Santiago de Chile: Alerce, 1976

Further Reading

Agosín, Marjorie and Inés Dölz Blackburn, *Violeta Parra: santa de pura greda: un estudio de su obra poética*, Santiago de Chile: Planeta, 1988

____ *Violeta Parra o la expresión inefable: un análisis crítico de su poesía, prosa y pintura*, Santiago de Chile: Planeta, 1992

Canépa-Hurtado, Gina, "La canción de lucha de Violeta Parra y su ubicación en el complejo cultural chileno entre los años 1960 a 1973," *Revista de Crítica Literaria Latinoamericana*, vol. 9/17 (1983)

Epple, Juan Armando, "Notas sobre la cueca larga de Violeta Parra," *Cuadernos Americanos*, vol. 124/3 (1979)

Huasi, Julio, "Violeta de América," *Casa de las Américas* 65–66 (1971)

Lindstrom, Naomi, "Construcción folklórica y desconstrucción individual en un texto de Violeta Parra," *Literatura Chilena: creación y critica*, vol. 9/33–34 (1985)

Oviedo, Carmen, *Mentira todo lo cierto: tras la huella de Violeta Parra*, Santiago de Chile: Editorial Universitaria, 1990

Pérez Ocampo, Gustavo, *Gracias a la vida: diálogo con Violeta Parra*, Peru: Lluvia, 1989

Pring-Mill, Robert, *"Gracias a la vida": the Power and Poetry of Song*, London: Department of Hispanic Studies, Queen Mary and Westfield College, 1990

Subercaseaux, Benjamín, *Gracias a la vida: Violeta Parra, testimonio*, Buenos Aires: Galerna, 1976

Las décimas

Autobiography in verse by Violeta Parra

Las décimas by Violeta Parra is a binding and essential work for the author and it constitutes one of the richest contributions to Latin American popular poetry of the 20th century. In this work she uses the structure of popular poetry and includes customs, popular sayings, proverbs and tableaux of country life.

This work presents the autobiography of the poet and certain recurrent themes such as religious faith, death, time, fate and disillusion as related to religious faith and to hope in general. The topic of death, treated by and linked to the medieval Spanish tradition, appears frequently in this work, especially as the motif or framework of her childhood: "La muerte se acerca limpia/ya se oye su cascabel" (Death approaches cleanly / you can her its bell).

Parra's obsession with learning about and confronting death is linked to her predisposition in *Las décimas* to write about certain ritualistic forces such as the ceremonies in the cemeteries that she recreates, as well as the constant reflections on death which appear in the song books of the 15th century and the "Coplas," the lament on the death of his father, written by Jorge Manrique.

Together with this invocation and recreation of death, we find in this autobiography descriptions of traditional feasts, such as those of San Juan and of the Cruz de Mayo, where Parra brings together, with great dexterity, the pagan and religious elements so characteristic of national folklore. She describes vividly the ceremony of the Cruz de Mayo (the May cross) where, following the traditions of the brotherhoods founded by the Spanish crown, rural Chileans maintain the cult of the cross which is venerated and decked out. Parra recreates this experience through her verses: "Festín de luz y de plata / la noche del dos de mayo / petardos gritos y rayos / inolvidables fogatas." (Feast of light and silver / the night of May the second / fireworks shouts and lightning / unforgettable bonfires).

Las décimas, not only have a great expressive richness of a historical nature, especially the re-elaboration of folk elements and the articulation of the religious themes in a poetic way, but these poems also document the originality with which Parra works with the poetic text, recreates it giving it a sense and a vision of the world where she creates, almost always, an antagonistic relationship with the objects that surround it such as love and deception, but at the same time the possibility of redeeming one's self, of finding faith through song and creation.

The autobiographical component of *Las décimas* is also very revealing because, on the one hand, Parra presents these women's need for independence in their lives as well as the importance of reevaluating and rethinking the feminine. At the same time, Parra's texts speak to us constantly of physical ugliness, of the marks left by chicken pox and deception.

On the one hand, these poems show her reflecting on woman's physical beauty; they critique the degree of objectification to which women are subjected by men. However, at the same time, Parra addresses the same question from other angles, implying that woman's identity is associated to her beauty, and therefore, that her physical appearance is very important. This dichotomy is always always present in Parra's texts along with the re-elaboration of certain elements related to femininity, such as clothes, colored ribbons and fabrics.

Together with the autobiographical element, *Las décimas* restore the leitmotif that attempts to vindicate the dispossessed and especially, the life of women who have had to submit, to become dependent on others. The element of social justice and of rejection and loneliness become memorable in poems such as "Se llevan a Teresa" [They Are Taking Teresa] where Parra assumes the voice of the seer that witnesses a rape, a crime in which Teresa's body is cruelly dragged through town. This theme, as well as the social preoccupation, the marginalization of the peasant woman and unemployment, will reach their culminating point in Parra's later creations.

Throughout *Las décimas*, we manage to see Parra's way of living with all its contradictions and her speculations on life and death, as well as her desire to redeem her historical circumstances through her creativity. The structures of these *décimas* is very interesting because, although they follow the traditional form, Violeta Parra defines and recreates herself by creating one of the most fascinating works of literature of her time.

MARJORIE AGOSÍN

Editions

First edition: *Las décimas: autobiografía en versos chilenos*, Santiago de Chile: Pomaire, 1970

Fernando del Paso 1935–

Mexican prose writer

Known as a practitioner of the encyclopedic and historical novel, Fernando del Paso is an immoderate writer who belongs to a literary generation that grew up under the spell of Carlos Fuentes. His are always all-knowing, all encompassing fictional narratives bringing to mind images of excess and portraying its creator as a gluttonous, Epicurean artist given to dissipation. And indeed, much like his idols, Joyce, Rabelais and Laurence Sterne, del Paso's three major books – *José Trigo* (1966), *Palinuro de México*, 1977 (*Palinuro of Mexico*), and *Noticias del Imperio*, 1987 [News of the Empire] – are gargantuan in scope and stylistic playfulness. Their length varies between 500 and 1,250 pages, and the plot is often made to appear secondary and inconsequential. The development of a storyline is not what matters; the main purpose being not to entertain but to challenge, to perplex and obfuscate. The novels do not have a linear structure but, in Georges Perec's words, they approach life "horizontally;" that is, instead of narrating one storyline or more chronologically and realistically from point A to point C, they devote their energy and space to describing a bulk of atemporal experiences, which are often presented arbitrarily. And as far as their linguistic dimension goes, it is fair to say that language is used less as a conduit and more as a primary protagonist and as an inexhaustible pyrotechnics' machine, a powerful volcano spewing out all sorts of ingenious pirouettes, riddles, rhymes, and puns. In short, their Utopian objective is to embrace reality as a whole, to leave absolutely nothing out, which results in an awesome array of information organized capriciously, with shifting viewpoints, and a multiple and often confusing cast of characters.

Del Paso's baroqueness explains why he is so perfectly at home with his native culture: he is a consummate impersonator, and a writer's writer, but one still fighting to keep a sense of originality. As he himself has claimed, "Tristram Shandy is my Jesus Christ, Joyce my Virgin Mary and the Spanish language my canvas." His remarkable literary status was established with the appearance of his first novel, *José Trigo*, about a railway strike and the migration of workers from rural areas to urban centers. Three years later he was part of the University of Iowa's Writing Program, where he first drafted *Palinuro de México*. Since then he has written very little fiction. *Noticias del Imperio* (1987) is a rich historical novel about the French intervention in Mexico, and particularly about Maximilian of Hapsburg, his wife Carlota of Belgium, and their ill-fated reign in Mexico (1862–67), known as "the Second Mexican Empire." In addition, he has published a biography of Juan José Arreola, a crucial figure in Mexican letters, instrumental in shaping the art of a number of writers, among them the poet and essayist José Emilio Pacheco. Del Paso's second novel remains the most puzzling. Published in 1977, *Palinuro de México* belongs to a time in Latin American letters, between the early 1960s and the late 1980s, when readers couldn't satisfy their hunger for encyclopedic novels. Not surprisingly, it has been compared to Julio Cortázar's *Rayuela* (*Hopscotch*), Augusto Roa Bastos's *Yo el Supremo* (*I the Supreme*), José Lezama Lima's *Paradiso*, and Guillermo Cabrera Infante's *Tres*

tristes tigres (*Three Trapped Tigers*), although, as the British critic Gerald Martin once rightly argued, its linguistic texture is "insufficiently demanding to stretch the reader's consciousness to the dimensions required by del Paso's Ulyssean perspective." Unlike its counterparts in the Hispanic world, the novel is more accessible but also less rewarding in linguistic terms – more conventional and less nightmarish.

The novel defies easy summary. The plot, if any, circles around a certain Palinuro, whose main obsession is the act of creation in its multiple expressions: artistic invention, sexual intercourse and procreation, health and sickness, recreation, acculturation, as well as transmigration. The scenario allows del Paso the opportunity for long disquisitions on history, time, and the meaning of things. In short, the book is about everything and nothing – medicine, eschatology, resistance and affirmation, linguistic and psychological emigration, atemporal love, Mexican history from pre-Colombian times to the 1968 student massacre in Tlatelolco Square, in which Palinuro dies ("*Acta est Fabula*: The Comedy is Over"). Its characters are ambiguous and evasive: Palinuro and Estefania, its protagonists, are in turns siblings, cousins, lovers, and mere companions. Their ancestors, Uncle Esteban, Grandmother Altagracia, Aunt Clementina, Mamá Clementina, Uncle Federico, are globe-trotting figures whose stage fluctuates between London, Prague, the Crimea, Paris, and Mexico City. Innumerable references (names, places, entire scenes) pay tribute to *Alice in Wonderland* and Laurence Sterne. Chapter 25, entitled "Palinuro on the Stairs; or, The Art of Comedy," is an autonomous play using *commedia dell'arte* characters such as Harlequin and Scaramouche. In 1992, del Paso published the segment separately, as an independent volume (*Palinuro en la escalera*). The point of view shifts constantly: at times Palinuro tells the story; at other times he talks of himself and those around in the second and third person; and in a vampiresque twist, he becomes an anonymous entity and his cousin Walter assumes the narration. A colorful parade of historical and literary figures keep on resurfacing: "Che" Guevara, Ambrose Bierce, Jonathan Swift, Ho Chi Min; and scores of Latin American luminaries: José Asunción Silva, Rubén Darío, Pancho Villa, and others. Nothing is certain – except, perhaps, the novel's concrete existence.

Del Paso's Mexico is at once mythical and mythological. In *Noticias del Imperio*, and less patently so in his other two narratives, time is cyclical: history is a spiral leading to nothingness. In fact, his novels can be read as a parodic reading of a Diego Rivera mural: color, lots of color surrounding omnipresent luminaries; and the message: an amorphous, indecipherable, vacuous collective identity made of various races, religions, and political backgrounds. But the novel is not an inconsequential quagmire. It reflects the rapid national modernization and deep collective introspection that took place in Mexico from the end of World War II to 1968. As the nation's capital became an all-encompassing octopus, with tentacles everywhere, the Partido Revolucionario Institucional, the corrupt ruling party in power since 1929, solidified its bureaucratic power. The result was a sense of suffocation, the perception that, on the road to being, in Octavio Paz's words, a "contemporary of the rest of humankind," Mexico was selling its soul to the devil. It was losing whatever authenticity it once had. In 1958 Fuentes published *La región más transparente* (*Where the Air is Clear*), an ambitious examination of the social and political tension ubiquitous in Mexico City. Shortly after, a new anti-Establishment generation, modeled after the Beatniks in the United States and the French *noveau roman*, which became known as *la Onda* (New Wave) appeared in Mexico. Leading writers of this group were José Agustín and Gustavo Sainz, who promoted an anarchic, spontaneously written, loosely structured fiction, with innumerable links to foreign cultural influences, one contaminated by history, autobiography and non-fiction. Del Paso analyzes the destruction and renewal in the country's culture and ponders where it is going and at what cost. He reflects on the increasing openness of Mexico to the outside world, its cosmopolitanism, the democratic spirit developing in the populace, which results in conflagration and tragedy.

His contribution walks hand-in-hand with Fuentes's, whose work champions encyclopedism in Mexico. Two years before the appearance of del Paso's *Palinuro*, Fuentes published *Terra Nostra*, a narrative pilgrimage from 1492 to the 21st century with the Spanish language as its leading star; and in 1987, *Cristóbal nonato* (*Christopher Unborn*) an anti-Utopian apocalyptic vision, a nine-month long literary pregnancy, which culminated in an overpopulated Mexico City on 12 October 1992. Clearly, Fuentes's goal, which he easily achieved, was to insert Mexico in the torrent of international fiction, to bring his native country to the international literary banquet. Not surprisingly, his books pay homage to infinite novelistic playfulness. But Fuentes's charismatic personality and the seriousness with which he undertakes his itinerant role of "cultural ambassador of Hispanic America," have somehow eclipsed *Palinuro de Mexico*. Del Paso isn't Fuentes: his vision is less pedantic and more intimate and legible. While he also establishes a dialogue with his Mexican contemporaries (including Salvador Elizondo, the *la Onda* writers, and Fuentes himself), he does not reprimand, lecture, or look down on his readers. Instead, he creates a game of mirrors through which his troubled native country is perceived as a reflection,

an addition, an appendix to a global European and American consciousness.

ILAN STAVANS

Biography

Born in Mexico City, 19 April 1935. Attended the Universidad Nacional Autónoma de México (UNAM), Mexico City: received BA in biological and economic sciences. Fellow of the Mexican Center for Writers, 1964–65; Guggenheim Fellow in 1970. Lived in London for eight years where he worked for the BBC World Service. Diplomat: cultural attaché at the Mexican Embassy in Paris. Received the Xavier Villarrutia Prize, 1966 for *José Trigo*; Prix du Meilleur Roman Étranger (France), 1975; Rómulo Gallegos Prize (Venezuela), 1977 for *Palinuro de México*.

Selected Works

Novels

José Trigo, Mexico City: Siglo XXI, 1966
Palinuro de México, Mexico City: Joaquín Mortiz, 1977; as
  Palinuro of Mexico, translated by Elisabeth Plaister, London:
  Quartet, 1989
Noticias del Imperio, Mexico City: Diana, 1987

Poetry

Sonetos de lo diario, Mexico City: Cuadernos del Unicornio, 1958

Play

Palinuro en la escalera, Mexico City: Diana, 1992

Other Writings

Memoria y olvido. Vida de Juan José Arreola (1920–1947), Mexico
  City: Consejo Nacional para la Cultura y las Artes, 1994

Further Reading

Fiddian, Robin W., "*Palinuro de México*: a World of Words,"
  Bulletin of Hispanic Studies, vol. 58 (2 April 1981)
_____ "James Joyce y Fernando del Paso," *Ínsula*, vol. 39/455
  (October 1984)
Orrantia, Dagoberto, "The Function of Myth in Fernando de Paso's
  José Trigo," in *Tradition and Renewal: Essays on 20th Century
  Latin American Literature and Culture*, edited by Merlin H.
  Forster, Urbana: University of Illinois Press, 1975
Stavans, Ilan, "*Palinuro of Mexico*," introduction to Elizabeth
  Plaister's English translation, London: Quartet, 1989

Octavio Paz 1914–

Mexican poet, prose writer, and literary translator

Poetry

Octavio Paz is one of the most outstanding poets of Spanish America. Although he has written more than twenty books of poetry, there is a unifying factor in his work: the poems always reflect on themselves, they are self-referential, even if their main subject is different. That is, Paz can write about love, history, past recollections, myths, but the poems none the less refer to how words intertwine with these same subjects. The word is situated at the center of his poetry. From this foundation, other common features derive: silence (as opposed to utterance), as the final stage in poetic achievement; absence, as the representation of the impossibility of finding true presences, the true Word; history, as a fault or fall from Edenic harmony; eroticism, in contrast to absence, as a clear path to find the true other, a natural elimination of differences; and the construction of the poetic persona. Although Paz might use complex theory and thought, his poems are founded on basic images belonging to nature: the tree, water, wind, stone, birds, earth, etc. His poems use a clear syntax, a transparency that confronts enigmas, and which speaks to the reader with wisdom and simplicity.

Paz began publishing poetry in 1933 – the year in which he published his first book, *Luna silvestre* [Rustic Moon] – but he has expressed uncertainties about the quality of his early work. One of the seven poems of this collection (quoted by Alberto Ruy Sánchez in *Una introducción a Octavio Paz*) announces one of Paz's recurring themes – words emerging from the beloved. Nevertheless, Paz did not, in the end, approve of the lyricism of this book and it was never reprinted. The same thing happened with a book of very different tone, *¡No pasarán!* 1936 [They Shall Not Pass!], inspired by the Spanish Civil War. Paz came to despise its social rhetoric and eliminated it from later anthologies and compilations. Very few poems of this kind survived Paz's revisions. "Elegía a un joven muerto en el frente" (Elegy to a Young Man Killed on the Front) is one of them.

Libertad bajo palabra, 1935–1957, 1960 (in *Early Poems, 1935–1955*) was the first compilation of Paz's poetry. The homonymous poem became the prologue to the entire volume. In it, the speaker assumes the invention of the word, the poem itself, as the reinvention of the world: "Invento la víspera, la noche, el día siguiente que se levanta . . . invento el terror, la esperanza, el mediodía . . . Invento la quemadura y el aullido, la masturbación en las letrinas . . . invento la desesperación, la mente que me concibe . . . Contra el silencio y el bullicio invento la Palabra, libertad que se inventa y me inventa cada día."(I invent evening, night, the next day rising . . . I invent terror, hope, noon . . . I invent the burn and the howl, masturbation in latrines . . . I invent despair, the mind that conceives me . . . Against silence and noise I invent the Word, freedom that invents itself and invents me every day). The Word (in capital letters because it refers to the absolute in language) predominates even over the persona that creates it, acquiring autonomy. But in Paz's poetry, language is never set free as in Surrealism. Paz has always been concerned with poetic form. His poems are well structured and maintain a formal equilibrium. Nevertheless, it could be argued that Surrealism was a major influence on Paz's work. "Surrealism is an attitude of the human spirit . . . It is the concrete exercise of freedom. Surrealism tries to eliminate the differences," says Paz. The compilation *Libertad bajo palabra* ends with one of the most celebrated poems by Octavio Paz, and probably the best-known of Latin America in the second half of the 20th century: "Piedra de sol," 1957 ["Sunstone"]. This is a circular poem: it starts with the same lines with which it ends. That is, at the end of the poem the reader is forced to begin again. Its title is taken from the Aztec stone of the same name. In the first part, the analogy of the poem brings together nature, words, and love: "Voy por tu cuerpo como por el mundo . . . voy por tus ojos como por el agua . . . voy por tu frente como por la luna . . . voy por tu vientre como por tus sueños . . . voy por tu talle como por un río / voy por tu cuerpo como por un bosque." (I travel your body, like the world . . . I travel your eyes, like the sea . . . I travel your forehead, like the moon . . . I travel your belly, like your dreams . . . I travel your length, like a river / I travel your body, like a forest). But soon the poetic persona finds himself alone, in search of the other, an elusive subject that is both generalized and nullified. Then, a long series of images (resembling, in tone, those used by Neruda in "Alturas de Macchu Picchu") present dualities: life and death, happiness and anguish, creation and destruction: "grieta en la roca, reina de serpientes / columna de vapor, fuente en la peña / circo lunar, peñasco de las águilas." (crack in the stone, queen of snakes / column of mist, spring in the rock / lunar circus, eyrie of eagles). The poem becomes, at this point, autobiographical. There are specific references to Paz's travels. Also, in the middle of the poem there is a concrete place and date: "Madrid, 1937." His personal history is extended to social circumstances, since there is an obvious connection to the Spanish Civil War (1936–39), and to Paz's visit to Spain, and to his participation in the Second Congress of Antifascist Writers in Valencia (1937). In the second part of "Sunstone," love rises above the violence and atrocities of war: " el mundo cambia / si dos, vertiginosso y enlazados / caen sobre la yerba . . . / tiempo total donde no pasa nada / sino su propio trascurrir dichoso." (The world changes if two, dizzy and entwined, fall / on the grass . . . total time where nothing / happens but its own ecstatic passing). "Sunstone" presupposes that love, freedom, and poetry (the famous triad of Surrealism) can transform the world. If history appears as a destructive force, circularity and a challenge to linear time is offered through the images of nature and its metaphor of woman. The poem ends with its beginning.

With *Salamandra*, 1958–1961, 1962 (*Salamander*), Paz breaks with the traditional presentation of poetry. Paz uses some of the typographical innovations of French Cubism, linked in particular to Apollinaire and Reverdy. The images are reduced to the minimum. This is an example from "Pares y nones" (Odd or Even): "Invisible collar de miradas / a tu garganta encadenada" (invisible necklace of glances / fastened around your throat). *Salamandra* was written in Paris. Paz later served as the Mexican ambassador to India (1962–68). Those years resulted in *Ladera en este* (1962–1968), 1969 [East Slope], a volume that clearly links Eastern myths and philosophy to his poetry. Calm and tranquility suffuse the poems to transparency. The words and metaphors used by Paz are simple, but at the same time the poet denotes vast knowledge, lucidity, and wisdom. *Ladera este* was accompanied by notes explaining and clarifying references (places, religious figures, myths, etc.) that were new to Mexican readers. In a way, some of the Indian myths used by Paz confirmed concepts (i.e., creation/destruction, human and divine dualities, etc.) previously expressed in relation to Mexican and European motifs. But Paz penetrates into the subject of silence and the state of transcendental peacefulness. "El día en Udaipur" [The Day in Udaipur], for example, presents duality in two alternating columns, and concludes with a Buddhist notion of nothingness: "Esto que he visto y digo, el sol, blanco, lo borra." (What I've seen here, what I say / the white sun erases). Both *Salamandra* and *Ladera este* seem to culminate in a single poem, *Blanco*, 1967 [White], although *Blanco* was published two years earlier than *Ladera*. *Blanco* brings together Paz's readings of Mallarmé (Paz has written extensively on "*Un coup de dés*" [A Throw of the Dice]), John Cage's theories on music and silence, and Eastern philosophy. *Blanco* is, like "Piedra de sol," one of the best-known and acclaimed poems by Paz. The English edition clarifies the title. "*Blanco*: white; blank; an unmarked space; emptiness; void; the white mark in the center of a target." Analogy seems to be the dominant theme: poem, woman and world are identified and fused. The first edition was published as a long single sheet (printed in three columns and in different colors), folded and packed in a box. Paz included an explanatory note, observing that the poem could be read in six different ways, which include three basic themes: the center column as a text on language ("the passage of the word from silence to silence"), the lefthand column as a text on the four traditional elements (earth, air, water and fire), and the righthanded column as a text on four variations of human knowledge: sensation, perception, imagination and understanding. What this note does not say is that the poem as a whole is also, and primarily, a love poem.

Another period in Paz's poetry would open after his return to Mexico in 1969. Besides the continued reflection on language and poetry, the following books present long poems based on memories of childhood and youth. Two poems are of particular relevance: "San Ildefonso Nocturne" – from *Vuelta*, 1976 (*Return*), and *Pasado en claro*, 1975 (*A Draft of Shadows*). Autobiography becomes an important element of these poems. Memory is used as an elusive way to evoke an unattainable past. Again, the self-reflective nature of these poems makes the itineraries an illusion of words. In *Pasado en claro* "Names: they vanish / in a pause between two words." Paz's recent book of poetry, *Árbol adentro*, 1987 (*A Tree Within*), presents the poet's preoccupations in a variety of ways. Many of Paz's poems are based on paintings by Joan Miró, Marcel Duchamp, Antoni Tapies, Robert Rauschenberg and Roberto Matta. *Árbol adentro* ends with a love poem, "Carta de creencia" [Letter of Testimony]. Again, as in the beginning, Paz attributes to love the creation of language and,

thus, of life. The "Coda" says: "Tal vez amar es aprender / a caminar por este mundo / Aprender a quedarnos quietos / como el tiulo y la encina de la fábula / Aprender a mirar / tu mirada es sembradora. Plantó un árbol / Yo hablo porque tu meces los follajes." (Perhaps to love is to learn / to walk through this world / To learn to be silent / like the oak and the linden of the fable / To learn to see / Your glance scatters seeds / It planted a tree / I talk/ because you shake its leaves).

JACOBO SEFAMÍ

Biography

Born in Mexico City, 31 March 1914. Attended the Universidad Nacional Autónoma de México (UNAM), Mexico City, 1932–37. Married Elena Garro (see separate entry) in 1937; divorced in 1959. Co-founder and editor of literary review *Barandal* [Balustrade] 1931–32; editor of *Cuadernos del Valle de México* [Notebooks from the Valley of Mexico], 1933–34. Travelled to Yucatán, 1937. Attended the Second International Congress of Anti-Fascist Writers in Spain, 1937. Returned to Mexico City in 1938. Editor of the magazine, *Taller*, 1938–41; co-founder, *El Hijo Pródigo* [The Prodigal Son], 1943. Left Mexico at the end of 1943 and moved to the United States: lived in San Francisco and later New York for two years. Joined the Mexican Diplomatic Corps in 1945 and held a number of posts: Secretary, 1946, and Extraordinary and Plenipotentiary minister, 1959–62, Mexican Embassy, Paris, 1945–51; Chargé d'Affaires, 1951, later posted to Secretariat for External Affairs, Mexican Embassy, Tokyo; Mexican Ambassador to India, 1962–68. Resigned his diplomatic post in protest over the massacre of students at Tlatelolco, 1968. Married Marie José Tramini in 1964; one daughter. Visiting Professor of Spanish American Literature, University of Texas, Austin, and Pittsburgh University, Pennsylvania, 1968–70; Simón Bolívar Professor of Latin American Studies, 1970, and Fellow of Churchill College, 1970–71, Cambridge University; Charles Eliot Norton Professor of Poetry, Harvard University, Cambridge, Massachusetts, 1971–72. Honorary member, American Academy of Arts and Letters, 1972. Editor of *Plural*, 1971–76 and *Vuelta* [Return] since 1976. Regent's fellow, University of California, San Diego. Recipient of numerous awards including the following major ones: Guggenheim Fellowship, 1944; International Grand Prize for Poetry (Belgium), 1963; City of Jerusalem Prize, 1977; Grande Aigle d'Or (Nice), 1979; Neustadt International Prize, 1982; Miguel de Cervantes Prize, 1982; Federation of German Book Trade Peace Prize, 1984; Gran Cruz de Alfonso X el Sabio, 1986; Nobel Prize for Literature, 1990.

Selected Poetry

Luna silvestre, Mexico City: Fábula, 1933
¡No pasarán!, Mexico City: Simbad, 1936
Raíz del hombre, Mexico City: Simbad, 1937
Bajo tu clara sombra y otros poemas sobre España, Valencia: Españolas, 1937; revised edition, Valencia: Tierra Nueva, 1941
Entre la piedra y la flor, Mexico City: Nueva Voz, 1941
A la orilla del mundo y primer día: bajo tu clara sombra, Raíz del hombre, Noche de resurrecciones, Mexico City: Companía Editora y Librera Ars, 1942
Libertad bajo palabra, Mexico City: Tezontle, 1949
¿Aguila o sol? Mexico City: Tezontle, 1951; as *Eagle or Sun?* translated by Eliot Weinberger, New York: October House, 1970; London: Peter Owen, 1990
Semillas para un himno, Mexico City: Tezontle, 1954
Piedra de sol, Mexico City: Tezontle, 1957; as *Sun Stone*, translated by Muriel Rukeyser, New York: New Directions, 1963; as *The Sun Stone*, translated by Donald Gardner, New York: Cosmos, 1969
La estación violenta, Mexico City: Fondo de Cultura Económica, 1958

Agua y viento, Bogota: Mito, 1959
Libertad bajo palabra: obra poética 1935–1958, Mexico City: Fondo de Cultura Económica, 1960; revised edition, 1968
Salamandra, 1958–1961, Mexico City: Joaquín Mortiz, 1962
Viento entero, New Delhi: Laxton Press, 1965
Vrindaban, Madurai, New Delhi: Laxton Press, 1965
Blanco, Mexico City: Joaquín Mortiz, 1967; as *Blanco*, translated by Eliot Weinberger, New York: The Press, 1974
Discos visuales, Mexico City: Era, 1968 [four poems printed on paper disks]
Ladera este (1962–1968), Mexico City: Joaquín Mortiz, 1969
La centena: poemas 1935–1968, Barcelona: Seix Barral, 1969
Topoemas, Mexico City: Era, 1971
Renga: a Chain of Poems, in collaboration with Jacques Roubaud, Edoardo Sanguinetti, and Charles Tomlinson, [Polyglot poem in English, French, Italian and Spanish]; with English translation by Tomlinson, New York: Braziller, 1972; Harmondsworth: Penguin, 1979
Pasado en claro, Mexico City: Fondo de Cultura Económica, 1975
Vuelta, Barcelona: Seix Barral, 1976
Poemas 1935–1975, Barcelona: Seix Barral, 1978
Airborn/Hijos del aire, in collaboration with Charles Tomlinson, London: Anvil Press, 1981
Poemas recientes, n.p., Institución Cultural de Cantabria de la Diputación Provincial de Santander, 1981
Instante y revelación, photographs by Manuel Álvarez Bravo, Mexico City: Círculo, 1982; New York: Grove Weidenfeld, 1985 [bilingual edition]
Árbol adentro, Barcelona: Seix Barral, 1987; as *A Tree Within*, translated by Eliot Weinberger, New York: New Directions, 1988

Anthologies and Compilations
Lo mejor de Octavio Paz: el fuego de cada día, Barcelona: Seix Barral, 1989
Obras completas, 14 vols, Mexico City: Fondo de Cultura Económica, 2nd edition, 1994

Poetry Anthologies in Translation
Selected Poems, translated by Muriel Rukeyser, Bloomington: Indiana University Press, 1963
Configurations, translated by Muriel Rukeyser, *et al.*, New York: New Directions, and London: Jonathan Cape, 1971
Early Poems, 1935–1955, translated by Muriel Rukeyser, *et al.*, New York: New Directions, 1973
A Draft of Shadows and Other Poems, edited by Eliot Weinberger, translated by Weinberger, Elizabeth Bishop and Mark Strand, New York: New Directions, 1979 [bilingual edition]
Selected Poems, translated by Charles Tomlinson, Harmondsworth: Penguin, 1979 [bilingual edition]
Selected Poems, edited and translated by Eliot Weinberger, New York: New Directions, 1984
Cuatro chopos/The Four Poplars, translated by Eliot Weinberger, Purchases: State University of New York, 1985
The Collected Poems of Octavio Paz, 1957–1987, edited and translated by Eliot Weinberger, New York: New Directions, 1987; Manchester: Carcanet, 1988 [bilingual edition]

Further Reading
Fein, John M., *Octavio Paz. A Reading of His Major Poems, 1957–1976*, Lexington: University Press of Kentucky, 1986 [Close readings of poems in *Piedra de sol, Salamandra, Blanco, Ladera este, Pasado en claro* and *Vuelta*]
Gimferrer, Pere, *Lecturas de Octavio Paz*, Barcelona: Anagrama, 1980 [Close readings of long poems: *Piedra de sol, Blanco, Pasado en claro* and "San Ildefonso Nocturne"]
Phillips, Rachel, *The Poetic Modes of Octavio Paz*, London: Oxford University Press, 1972

Ruy Sánchez, Alberto, *Una introducción a Octavio Paz*, Mexico: Joaquín Mortiz, 1990
Santí, Enrico Mario, prologue to *Libertad bajo palabra 1935–1957*, edited by Santí, Madrid: Cátedra, 1988
Sucre, Guillermo, "Paz: La vivacidad, la transparencia," in *La máscara, la transparencia*, Caracas: Monte Ávila, 1975 [One of the key essays on Paz, based primarily on poetic language's self-reflection]
Wilson, Jason, *Octavio Paz*, Boston: Twayne, 1986

Bibliographies
Verani, Hugo J., *Octavio Paz: bibliografía crítica*, Mexico City: UNAM, 1983

Interviews
Verani, Hugo J. (editor), *Pasión crítica: conversaciones con Octavio Paz*, Barcelona: Seix Barral, 1985

Essays

Octavio Paz's essays cover an astonishing range of subjects. Aztec art, Tantric Buddhism, Mexican politics, neo-Platonic philosophy, economic reform, avant-garde poetry, structuralist anthropology, utopian socialism, the dissident movement in the Soviet Union, sexuality and eroticism: these are but some of the topics Paz has explored in his essays. He is as comfortable writing in sweeping terms about such large issues as the nature of religion or the end of modernity as he is drawing delicate character sketches of people he has known in the course of his very long life. He is both deeply immersed in Mexican history and culture, having produced in *El laberinto de la soledad* (*The Labyrinth of Solitude*) – see separate essay – one of the most influential interpretations of the Mexican character ever written. Paz is also steeped in the Western tradition as a whole, as one can see from a work such as *Los hijos del limo*, 1974 (*Children of the Mire*), a history of modern poetry from German Romanticism to the 1960s avant-garde that remains unparalleled in its reach.

Yet it would be wrong to describe Paz as an eclectic thinker. What strikes the reader of Paz's essays is not just the ease with which he moves between different topics, but also the extraordinary depth and consistency of vision he has maintained throughout his many varied projects. At a very early age, in the 1930s, Paz came into contact with two complex and occasionally interrelated phenomena that expressed the longing for a grand social and spiritual transformation that has resided at the heart of modernity: avant-garde aesthetics and revolutionary politics. Since then – that is, for almost six decades now – Paz has conducted in his essays an ongoing meditation on these two cornerstones of the modern era. Even though Paz's disenchantment with revolutionary politics set in very soon, the left, especially the Marxist left, continued to perform the role of implicit interlocutor in his political essays. And even though the direct link between political and artistic practice also snapped in Paz's mind very early in his career, his writings on poetry are even now imbued with a profoundly utopian spirit.

By the time the Cold War began, Paz had already decisively spurned the Soviet model. This did not mean, however, that he immediately embraced the democratic-capitalist alternative to communism. In *El laberinto* Paz approached the two opposed blocs as simply different versions of the same general phenomenon, which later, following Raymond Aron, he would label "industrial civilization." *El laberinto* contains pages of passionate denunciation of the dehumanization afflicting modern societies, both East and West. Subsequent collections of essays, such as *Corriente alterna*, 1967 (*Alternating Current*), and *Posdata*, 1970 (*The Other Mexico*), also bristle with distaste for the materialism and soullessness of the Western democracies. Even in the 1980s and 1990s, by which time Paz had become an influential supporter of the neo-liberal economic policies pursued by successive Mexican governments, he continued to write unflinchingly in texts such as *Tiempo nublado*, 1983 (*One Earth, Four or Five Worlds*), *La otra voz*, 1990 (*The Other Voice*), and *Itinerario*, 1993 [Itinerary], of the weaknesses of liberal democracy, as well as of the havoc wrought by the free-market system. Yet by this time he had also become adamant in his insistence that Mexico needed to become modern if it wished to survive and flourish under current global conditions. He continued to sound a note he had favored for a long time, which was that Mexico should find its "own path" to modernity, but by the 1980s such vague protestations began to have a rote quality to them. In practice, the policies Paz supported meant that Mexico was becoming increasingly aligned with the US economic model.

The persistent ambivalence about modernity may have something to do with the fact that in Mexico modernity is often regarded as an alien imposition, and therefore as a problem. Yet in diagnosing the social, economic, political and ecological disasters it has brought about, Paz drew considerable inspiration from a specific tradition within modernity itself. Ever since *Posdata*, a long essay Paz wrote shortly after resigning as Mexico's ambassador to India to protest the massacre by the Mexican Army of hundreds of peaceful demonstrators in the Plaza Tlatelolco in Mexico City in October 1968, "criticism" has been Octavio Paz's watchword. In *Posdata* Paz presented a devastating critique of the Mexican political system as well as of the nation's cultural imaginary. As a cure for the nation's ailments, Paz offered as a first step the practice of criticism itself, arguing that it was only by ensuring the possibility of free inquiry and open debate that the nation could even begin to think about ways to resolve its problems. What Paz was calling for, in other words, was the creation of a public sphere. As founder and editor of two important monthly reviews based in Mexico City, *Plural* (1971–76) and *Vuelta* (1976–) Paz went on to make a crucial contribution to the forging of such a space for intellectual discussion.

At the end of *Posdata*, Paz describes criticism as an "acid" that corrodes the myths of a nation. It brings to light a culture's subconscious, making it the object of rational debate. It serves to free a people of their blind submission to a set of cultural fantasies. Paz believes that criticism in this sense originated in the Enlightenment. In fact, he has often argued that many of the weaknesses of Latin America's political and intellectual tradition are the result of the absence in Latin America of an Enlightenment. From this, it is clear that Paz sympathizes with the demystifying effects of modernity. And yet in his writings on poetry, Paz appears not as the level-headed spokesman for a rationalized, disenchanted world, but as the impassioned defender of poetry's visionary powers. Over the years, Paz has returned repeatedly to the idea that the function of poetry in the modern world has been to serve as an antidote to modernity

itself. The Romantic rebellion against the Enlightenment first established this pattern, according to Paz. Where the Enlightenment spoke in the name of reason, the Romantics spoke for all that was repressed by reason. What is remarkable about Paz is how he has tried to straddle this divide, to take on both the cause of the Enlightenment and the cause of Romanticism.

In "Poesía de soledad y poesía de comunión," 1942 [Poetry of Solitude and Poetry of Communion], Paz posits a stark conflict between poetry and the modern world. Paz speaks of how modern society robs people of their humanity, turning them into commodities or instruments. Under such circumstances, the task of poetry is to restore the world that has been lost to humanity, the world of dreams and innocence, of eternity and ecstasy. Because of its opposition to the dominant norms of modern society, poetry is a fundamentally dissident, sacrilegious activity. It is not surprising, then, that "Poesía de soledad" celebrates the tradition of the *poète maudit* embodied in figures such as Novalis, Nerval, Baudelaire and Lautréamont. Over the course of his career, Paz was to maintain this view of poetry as a profoundly transgressive activity. Yet he also undertook over the years a gradual reappraisal of the very target of modern poetry's foundational act of transgression: the Enlightenment.

To begin with, this was a matter of recognizing that the Enlightenment helped prepare the way not only for the rationalization and hence dehumanization of the world, but also for the rooting of the social order in the profoundly emancipatory activity of criticism. If poetry was an act of rebellion, then it was a mode of criticism, and as such it was an integral part of the project of modernity. The initial reappraisal of the Enlightenment led inevitably to a modified view of the modern world itself. Some of its constitutive elements – democracy, criticism, the free market – even came to be regarded by Paz as attractive and desirable. But what did this mean for poetry? Could it continue to blaspheme against the very world Paz was now defending? Or did the changes in Paz's political views allow him to envision the building of a new kind of bridge between poetry and modernity?

In *La otra voz* Paz argues that the tradition of liberalism that flowed out of the Enlightenment has brought immense benefits to humanity. Yet he also thinks that liberalism cannot answer some of the most important questions about human life. This is where poetry comes in: it reminds us of that vast zone of reality that is ignored and suppressed in the modern world. Clearly, Paz continues to believe in the profound importance of poetry to society. But whereas in his early work poetry was thought to be able to give us a "new man," in his late work poetry discloses a buried world, the world of what Paz calls the "other" voice, yet without being able to provide more than a temporary respite from the iron hand of the market. By the 1990s the function of poetry is no longer to transform life, but to make it more complete.

MAARTEN VAN DELDEN

Selected Essays

El laberinto de la soledad, Mexico City: Cuadernos Americanos, 1950; revised edition, Mexico City: Fondo de Cultura Económica, 1959; as *The Labyrinth of Solitude: Life and Thought in Mexico*, translated by Lysander Kemp, New York: Grove Press, 1961; London: Allen Lane, 1967

El arco y la lira: el poema, la revelación poética, poesía e historia,
Mexico City: Fondo de Cultura Económica,1956; revised edition,
1967; as *The Bow and the Lyre: the Poem, the Poetic Revelation,
Poetry and History*, translated by Ruth L.G. Simms, Austin:
University of Texas Press, 1973

Las peras del olmo, Mexico City: UNAM, 1957

Tamayo en la pintura mexicana, Mexico City: UNAM, 1959

Cuadrivio, Mexico City: Joaquín Mortiz, 1965 [on Darío, López
Velarde, Pessoa, Cernuda]

Los signos en rotación, Buenos Aires: Sur, 1965

Puertas al campo, Mexico City: UNAM, 1966

Claude Lévi-Strauss o, el nuevo festín de Esopo, Mexico City:
Joaquín Mortiz, 1967; as *Claude Lévi-Strauss: an Introduction*,
translated by J.S. and Maxine Bernstein, New York: Cornell
University Press,1970; retitled as *On Lévi-Straus*, London:
Jonathan Cape, 1970

Corriente alterna, Mexico City: Siglo XXI, 1967; as *Alternating
Current*, translated by Helen Lane, New York: Viking Press,
1973; London: Wildwood House, 1974

Marcel Duchamp o, el castillo de la pureza, Mexico City: Era,
1968; as *Marcel Duchamp or, the Castle of Purity*, translated by
Donald Gardner, New York: Grossman, and London: Cape
Goliard, 1970

México: la última década, Austin: University of Texas Institute of
Latin American Studies, 1969

Conjunciones y disyunciones, Mexico City: Joaquín Mortiz, 1969;
as *Conjunctions and Disjunctions*, translated by Helen Lane, New
York: Viking Press, 1974; London: Calder and Boyers, 1975

Posdata, Mexico City: Siglo XXI, 1970; as *The Other Mexico:
Critique of the Pyramid*, translated by Lysander Kemp, New
York: Grove Press, 1972

Las cosas en su sitio: sobre la literatura española del siglo XX, in
collaboration with Juan Marichal, Mexico City: Finisterre,
1971

Los signos en rotación y otra ensayos, edited by Carlos Fuentes,
Madrid: Alianza, 1971

Traducción: literatura y literalidad, Barcelona: Tusquets,
1971

Apariencia desnuda: la obra de Marcel Duchamp, Mexico City: Era,
1973; as *Marcel Duchamp: Appearance Stripped Bare*, translated
by Rachel Phillips and Donald Gardener, New York: Viking Press,
1979

El signo y el garabato, Mexico City: Joaquín Mortiz, 1973

Solo a dos voces, in collaboration with Julián Ríos, Barcelona:
Lumen, 1973

La búsqueda del comienzo; escritos sobre el surrealismo, Madrid:
Fundamentos, 1974

Teatro de signos/transparencias, edited by Julián Ríos, Madrid:
Fundamentos, 1974

Los hijos del limo: del romanticismo a la vanguardia, Barcelona:
Seix Barral, 1974; as *Children of the Mire: Modern Poetry from
Romanticism to the Avant-Garde*, translated by Rachel Phillips,
Cambridge, Massachusetts, Harvard University Press, 1974,
revised edition, 1991

El mono gramático, Barcelona: Seix Barral, 1974; as *The Monkey
Grammarian*, translated by Helen Lane, New York: Seaver, and
London: Peter Owen, 1981

Xavier Villaurrutia en persona y en obra, Mexico City: Fondo de
Cultura Económica, 1978

El ogro filantrópico: historia y política 1971-1978, Barcelona: Seix
Barral, 1979

Rufino Tamayo, in collaboration with Jacques Lassaigne, Barcelona:
Polifrafía, 1982; in English, New York: Rizzoli, 1982

Sor Juana Inés de la Cruz o, Las trampas de la Fe, Mexico City:
Fondo de Cultura Económica, 1982; as *Sor Juana or, The Traps
of Faith*, translated by Margaret Sayers Peden, Cambridge,
Massachusetts: Belknap Press, 1988; retitled as *Sor Juana: Her
Life and World*, London: Faber and Faber, 1988

Tiempo nublado, Barcelona: Seix Barral, 1983; as *One Earth, Four
or Five Worlds: Reflections on Contemporary History*, translated
by Helen Lane, San Diego: Harcourt Brace, and Manchester:
Carcanet, 1985

Sombras de obras: arte y literatura, Barcelona: Seix Barral, 1983

Günter Gerzo (in Spanish, English, and French), in collaboration
with John Golding, Neuchâtel: Griffon, 1983; Montclair, New
Jersey: Abner Schram, 1984

Hombres en su siglo y otros ensayos, Barcelona: Seix Barral, 1984;
as *On Poets and Others*, translated by Michael Schmidt, New
York: Seaver, 1986; Manchester: Carcanet, 1987

Convergences: Essays on Art and Literature, translated by Helen
Lane, San Diego: Harcourt Brace, and London: Bloomsbury, 1987

México en la obra de Octavio Paz, 3 vols, Mexico City: Fondo de
Cultura Económica, 1987
    1. *El peregrino en su patría: historia y politica de México*
    2. *Generaciones y semblanzas: escritores y letras de México*
    3. *Los privilegios de la vista: arte de México*

Primeras letras (1931-1943), edited by Enrico Mario Santí,
Barcelona: Seix Barral, 1988

La otra voz; poesía y fin de siglo, Barcelona: Seix Barral, 1990; as
The Other Voice: Poetry and the Fin-de-siècle, translated by
Helen Lane, New York: Harcourt Brace, 1991; Manchester:
Carcanet, 1992

Pequeña crónica de grandes días, Mexico City: Fondo de Cultura
Económica, 1990

In Search of the Present, San Diego: Harcourt Brace, 1990 [Nobel
lecture]

One Word to the Other, translated by Amelia Simpson, Mansfield,
Texas: Latitudes Press, 1992

Itinerario, Mexico City: Fondo de Cultura Económica, 1993

Un mas all erótico: Sade, Mexico City: Vuelta, 1993

La llama doble, amor y erotismo, Barcelona: Seix Barral, 1993; as
The Double Flame: Love and Eroticism, translated by Helen
Lane, New York: Harcourt Brace, 1995; London: Harvill Press,
1996

Vislumbres de la India, Barcelona: Seix Barral, 1995

Essays in Translation

The Siren and the Seashell and Other Essays on Poets and Poetry,
translated by Lysander Kemp and Margaret Seyers Peden, Austin:
University of Texas Press, 1976

*The Labyrinth of Solitude, The Other Mexico, Return to the
Labyrinth of Solitude, Mexico and the United States, and The
Philanthropic Ogre*, translated by Lysander Kemp, Yara Milos
and Rachel Phillips, New York: Grove Press, 1985

Further Reading

Surprisingly, in the light of Paz's stature and notoriety, there are still
relatively few detailed and systematic studies of his essays. Much
more critical attention has been paid to his poetry. There are signs,
however – in Fernando Vizcaíno's recent book, for example – that
the impact Paz has had on the intellectual debate in Mexico,
especially in the last twenty-five years, is beginning to result in an
increased focus on Paz's career as an essayist and intellectual.

Aguilar Mora, Jorge, *La divina pareja: historia y mito en Octavio
Paz*, Mexico City: Era, 1978 [Still the most reliable attack on a
much vilified author]

Krauze, Enrique, "Octavio Paz: Facing the Century. A Reading of
Tiempo nublado," translated by Sonja Karsen, in *Salmagundi*
70-71 (Spring–Summer 1986). [A well-informed essay that offers
a much broader account of Paz's ideological development than
the title indicates]

Ruy Sánchez, Alberto, *Una introducción a Octavio Paz*, Mexico
City: Joaquín Mortiz, 1990

Vizcaíno, Fernando, *Biografía política de Octavio Paz, o, La razón
ardiente*, Málaga: Algazara, 1993

El laberinto de la soledad

Essay by Octavio Paz

Following the seminal meditation *El perfil del hombre y de la cultura en México*, 1934 [Profile of Man and Culture in Mexico], by the philosopher Samuel Ramos, young Octavio Paz embarked, in his polymorphous *El laberinto de la soledad*, 1950 (*The Labyrinth of Solitude*), on a search through and for the Mexican soul. The essay appeared at a time when Mexico was consolidating its post-Revolution and the economic benefits of World War II, with every intention of stepping into the "first world"; and when the young artist, under the influence of post-war Surrealism, was opening a new, "violent station" in his poetry and was longing to put Mexican literature on the world stage. In a way, *El laberinto* symbolizes Mexico and the poet's coming of age. The book dazzled, hit home, and hurt. To some it was a Bible of *mexicanidad*, of being Mexican; to others it was an obscene gesture to the mother country. In time, this instant classic became a Mexican institution. Similar to other great Latin American essays, like Sarmiento's *Facundo* (*Life in the Argentine Republic in the Days of the Tyrants*), it turned into a standard mimetic referent, a simulacrum of reality, for future literary (and academic) fictions.

El laberinto is the work of a keen analyst of culture, of a poet, and of a visionary, surprising at every turn. Paz starts with his personal experience: in the United States, where he lived on two occasions and had the chance to see the *pachucos*, his "estranged" Mexican countrymen, settled in-between the two cultures; and in Spain, during the Civil War, where he witnessed – he says – the man in the image he wishes man to have, to break the circle of solitude and to open up to the extraordinary and the transcendent. Going from personal experience to myth, the first chapter is a miniature preview of the whole. The next three chapters focus on Mexican traditional culture (social ritual, *fiesta*, language, popular symbols and myths). Paz shows the syncretic nature of many social values, and, sometimes, even a smooth transition from Mesoamerican pre-Columbian values to those brought in by the Spanish conquistadors. The old Mexico appears to be well and alive under layers of modern varnish. The following two chapters turn to Mexican history, tracing the genealogy of social alienation from the conquest to the Mexican Revolution. Paz envisions modern Mexican history as a string of repressions and partial revivals of the "true" Mexican being. This binary myth-paradigm produces striking insights as well as some marvels. Conquest is, of course, a neat repression; but the 16th and early 17th century colony, with its "participatory structures" and syncretism at work, appears, surprisingly, as a kind of revival and is even posited as a certain idealized Origin (how could he do this to the Aztecs!). On the other hand, it is imperative for the Revolution to be presented as a reversal of the mid-19th-century Reform which, according to the same blueprint, was designed as the most radical incarnation of the modern European project in Mexico. This underlying logic also explains why there is not much history on the image of the Revolution, exalted as a *fiesta*, as an immersion of Mexico in its old self, and as "a return to the mother." The next chapter gives a quick review of contemporary Mexican high culture. Then, vision and History turn into vision and myth

again: "The Dialectic of Solitude" gives an overarching closure to the spiritual odyssey through personal, collective, and universal labyrinths of solitude and solidarity.

For the second edition, in 1959, Paz completed the paradigm of symbols, opposing the Virgin of Guadalupe to the "violated Mother," La Malinche, the *Chingada*; and added a new chapter to update the historical dimension of the book. "The Present Day" is a strikingly iconoclastic "supplement." The *fiesta*-image was left behind as Paz focused on the *historical* Revolution and its mixed record. This partial demystification alone would not be that problematic. Paz was actually very cautious in his judgments, looking as he was all the time for signs for optimism. Where he crossed the line was when he turned on the sacred contemporary revolutions and their icons, from Russia to the emerging "Third World." He also chastised contemporary intelligentsia for its failure to analyze "the new reality confronting us," and even dared to invoke the name of Trotsky in positive terms. Orthodox Marxists were outraged, and Paz, like his surrealist mentors, was dutifully blacklisted. What went unnoticed was that, following his criticism of left and right, he went on to declare bankrupt the whole project of Modernity, diagnosing the end of Eurocentrism and "the general collapse of Faith and Reason, of God and Utopia." In this context, the words referring to Mexicans as being "contemporaries of all mankind" meant that they were actually stepping into a brave new world of post-Modernity.

Paz reacted strongly to the massacre of students at Tlatelolco square in October 1968, resigned from his post of ambassador in protest, and poured out his bitter reflections on Mexican past and present in *Posdata*, 1970 (*The Other Mexico: Critique of the Pyramid*), meant as a "postscript" to *El laberinto*. It was not a complete surprise to see that Aztecs and PRI, the Mexican Government party of "institutionalized revolution," shared his ire. Throughout the years, he continued updating and expanding his vision of Mexico. All these works make up the first volume of his *México en la obra de Octavio Paz*, 1987 [Mexico in the Work of Octavio Paz]. Brilliant as they may be, these later writings have not retained the freshness, scope of vision and transgressive innocence of the first.

In the decades after the publication of *El laberinto*, Mexico went through dramatic changes: rampant urbanization, population explosion, industrialization, rapidly deteriorating ecology, accelerated by the devastating earthquake and economic crisis of the 1980s. These changes were bound to call into question a work dated in the late 1940s, and to push the poet's words back to poetry and myth. The fall of the Berlin Wall buried under its debris more than one of the traumas charring "The Present Day." What is remarkable, then, is actually the resilience of *El laberinto*, especially of its first half.

It has been noted that the most thorough meditation about *mexicanidad* starts from the vision of the *pachucos*. However, instead of celebrating the fact that Paz gives them an early recognition and puts them in the origin of his quest, the Mexican-American intelligentsia of the 1970s and 1980s preferred to feel offended. Paz could not anticipate the present-day orthodoxy of "political correctness;" he is describing his experience and his feeling of estrangement when he sees himself in the "mirror" of the *pachuco*. Is the latter a future image of an "Americanized" Mexico? Yet the *pachuco* does not cease to be Mexican; and his acting up in face of an alien overwhelming culture even draws certain admiration, thus becoming a symbol of Mexican struggle with North-American civilization. Paz will return many times to this counterpoint. This interest in marginal and other cultures reappears when he assumes the limits of his voice and recognizes the existence of a *plurality* of Mexicos, living side by side in different historical times. "Past epochs never vanish completely, and blood still drips from all their wounds, even the most ancient."

The three chapters on traditional culture direct the reader to Mexican intrahistory (in Miguel de Unamuno's sense of the word). Unlike Ramos, Paz does not exert moral indignation over the low, and does not repress it; he enjoys both the high and the low, the kitsch and the exquisite; his best intuitions come from the verb that would be unpronounceable for the philosopher. This inspiration is not unique: Paz's influential meditation on world cultures, *Conjunciones y disyunciones*, 1969 (*Conjunctions and Disjunctions*), which takes *El laberinto* to a universal dimension, originated from a similar source. The symbolism of *chingar* (sexual penetration) and *fiesta* anticipates the present craze for carnival, although the postmodern version of it is a rather hermetic intellectual exercise and re-enactment on the page. Further, unlike Ramos, Paz does not sit comfortably at the rhetorical and moral distance of an enlightened pedagogue: he struggles, agonizes, mimics contradictory voices, contradicting himself. His symbols are not allegories, but flow and change (the Revolution). When he refers to Mexican women, does he impersonate tradition? Does he accept it as his? Does he identify with it? Or do some protestations reflect the sarcastic voice of his then wife, Elena Garro, who became one of the founders of Mexican feminism? Finally, unlike Ramos, Paz is not interested to just make the Mexican functional in modern society; for him, this would only produce another alienation and repression. Once again following the path of Surrealism and its radical critique of Modernity, the solution, for Paz, lies in reconciliation of the contraries, the high and the low, the intellectual and the erotic, the strange and the normal, the transcendence and the intranscendental.

In *El laberinto*, Paz attempts to square the triangle of Mexican traditional culture, full of masks, rituals and symbols; the painful History, specifically Mexican but universal in its pursuit of Modernity; and the universal dimensions – lacks and needs, fears and desires – of any human being. Nowadays, the aesthetic structures of *El laberinto* are more visible, and History continues reshuffling its pragmatic values. It would be easy to criticize facets of its awesome pyramidal structure, its visionary excesses, psychoanalytic shell, latent binary biases and, in general, how the poet produces poetic myths. What makes it stay alive is how much of it exceeds its matrix and what new values are foregrounded in time. The interest in and recognition on equal terms of marginal and alien cultures; carnivalization and popular culture accepted and analyzed without bias; strategic use of shifting symbols; polymorphous character, radical ambiguity of meaning, irreducible to any one "origin;" unambiguous assault on the modern project and Eurocentrism; both in ideology and form, this magnificent and still uncomfortable work shows many signs of an early postmodern text.

EMIL VOLEK

Editions

First edition: *El laberinto de la soledad*, Mexico City: Cuadernos Americanos, 1950
Critical edition: edited with an introduction by Enrico Mario Santí, Madrid: Cátedra, 1993 [Highly recommended]
Translation: *The Labyrinth of Solitude: Life and Though in Mexico*, by Lysander Kemp, New York: Grove Press, 1961; London: Allen Lane, 1967

Further Reading

Bartra, Roger, *La jaula de la melancolía: identidad y metamorfosis del mexicano*, Mexico City: Grijalbo, 1987
Mermall, Thomas, "Octavio Paz: *El laberinto de la soledad* y el sicoanálisis de la historia," *Cuadernos Americanos* 156 (1968)
Oclio, Elena Baca, "The 'distaff' perspective in Paz's *El laberinto de la soledad*," *Publications of the Arkansas Philological Association*, vol. 6/2 (1980)
Palazón, María Rosa, "Sobre *El laberinto de la soledad*," *Punto de Partida* 11 (1968)
Rangel-Guerrero, Daniel, "*The Labyrinth of Solitude* Revisited," *Proceedings of the Pacific Northwest Conference on Foreign Languages*, vol. 28/2 (1977)
Toro, Fernando de, "*El laberinto de la soledad* y la forma del ensayo," *Cuadernos Hispanoamericanos* 343–45 (1979)
Urrello, Antonio, "*El laberinto de la soledad*: dicotomía e indentidad," in his *Verosimilitud y estrategia textual en el ensayo hispanoamericano*, Mexico City: Premiá, 1986

Cristina Peri Rossi 1941–

Uruguayan prose writer and poet

Bearing in mind that until recently Latin American women writers suffered from a significant lack of recognition, Cristina Peri Rossi's fiction is well-known and read beyond academic circles. The Argentine writer Julio Cortázar has been most appreciative of her work, perhaps acknowledging an affiliation between them through Surrealism; she is widely recognized in Spain where she has lived in Barcelona since 1972; and her works have been translated into English, German, French, Czechoslovakian and Yiddish.

Peri Rossi's first thirty-one years, spent in her native Uruguay, were marked by the general mistrust towards women whose writing did not consist, as she says, "of certain laudatory lines composed for official occasions to recognize the achievements of public figures." This attitude, and above all the threat presented by the dictatorship of Bordaberry (who militarized all civil institutions and officially abolished any recognition of human rights) forced her to leave the country in 1972. Though she now frequently visits her home, she has chosen not to return to Uruguay on a permanent basis, because, she says, she now feels estranged from her own country. Exile – a frequent theme in the work of many Latin American writers – is a characteristic of life: "We are all exiled from *La nave de los locos* (*The Ship of Fools*), this is the true condition of man." This sense of alienation and estrangement contributes to the hallucinatory perspective of many of the situations described in her fiction: "The category in which the universe manifests itself is the category of hallucination," she writes, quoting Gottfried Benn in an epigraph to her collection of short stories, *El museo de los esfuerzos inútiles* [The Museum of Useless Efforts].

Peri Rossi's works include poetry, short fiction and novels. She says she works on three typewriters at the same time, moving from one to the other, as the impulse takes her. There are three main components to the thematics of her work: the political, be it in terms of national politics or of feminist protest and non-conformity to established canons; the erotic and the questioning of sexuality and gender distinctions; third, the continuous dialogue with language.

With reference to the first, the political, many of her earlier short stories denounce the oppression and persecution of totalitarian regimes. "Los trapecistas" [The Trapeze Artists] from *Indicios pánicos* (an ambiguous title in Spanish meaning both Signs of Panic and Vestiges of Pan) tells of the despair of a man who feels compelled to denounce his lover to the authorities. While in "Anuciación" [Annunciation] from *La rebelión de los niños* [The Children's Rebellion] we read of a child on a beach confronting the guns of the military to protect a guerrilla woman who appears to him as an image of the Virgin.

Political subtexts can also be read in the story of the long distance runner in *El museo de los esfuerzos inútiles* who, being expected to beat the existing speed record, when approaching the end of the race chooses to lie on the grass verge by the track and look up at the sunlight playing among the tree tops. Breaking out of the role imposed on him, he exemplifies the right to question and, if appropriate, refuse to comply with society's expectations.

The feminist intent is evident, for example, in *La nave de los locos* in a "fragment from the unpublished Confessions of Eve," a subversive reading of the patriarchal myth of the creation; or in the macabre journey of a coach load of women coming to London to seek an abortion.

The erotic theme figures frequently in Peri Rossi's work, scrutinized in its various manifestations and aberrations, such as the fallacious belief in a life-long monogamous marriage or the inability to put a stop to a relationship that is finished. There is also the question of the prohibition of love, which intensifies desire to the extent of compelling the individual to take refuge in the imaginary interior space of wish-fulfilment, more powerful than the material world, as in the story "Una pasión prohibida" [A Forbidden Passion]. Yet loving is an essential condition of reality: "El infierno es no poder amar" (Hell is not being able to love), says one of Peri Rossi's characters in *La nave de los locos*.

The questions of sexuality and gender emerging from the erotic theme have long preoccupied Peri Rossi, who sees the latter not as "the simple result of biological elements," but as what "is socially thrust upon us by our parents and by society." Hence, our sexual role is often an "imposition on our behaviour," and Peri Rossi's characters strive to break loose from these pre-conditions by experimenting with a multiple sexuality and/or periodically acknowledging an absence of sexuality, or reversing the traditional roles, thus subverting the sexual hierarchy.

Peri Rossi's further preoccupation with language is evident in both her poetry and prose. In her stories from *La rebelión de los niños*, language figures as a form of social oppression, being institutionalized and posing a permanent dialectical crisis between its official and personal usage. Against such oppression, the arbitrary nature of language is emphasized: "Así supe que el sonido es una geometría que podemos componer y el significado, apenas una referencia ostensible a las cosas que aprendimos a nombrar de niños, en el tiempo de la obediencia" (So I learnt that the sound is a geometry that we can make up and its meaning only a visible reference to the objects which we learn to name in our childhood at the time of obedience) says Oliveiro in *El libro de mis primos* [My Cousins' Book].

Elsewhere, especially in the poems, the pleasure of words is described in erotic terms: "Las mujeres son todas pronunciadas y las palabras son todas amadas" (Women are all pronounced, words are all loved) goes a line from *Evohé*; or "Leyendo el diccionario / he encontrado una palabra nueva / con gusto, con sarcasmo la pronuncia / la palpo, la apalabro, la manto, la calco, la pulso / la digo, la encierro, la lamo, la toco con las / yemas de los dedos . . ." (Reading the dictionary / I have found a new word / with pleasure, with sarcasm I pronounce it / I feel it, I engage it, I cover it, I press it, I push it / I say it, I enclose it, I lick it, I touch it with the tips of my fingers . . .).

Her erotic association with language is also a feature of her poetry. One of her later collections, *Babel bárbara* [Barbarian Babel] consists mainly of love poems, dedicated to a woman aptly named Babel, based on the connection between writing and desire. The poem "Amar" [To Love] begins: "Amar es trahir – traducir – (To love is to betray – to translate –) a much more poignant comparison in Spanish given the similarity of the words meaning to betray and to translate.

"The act of loving and the act of writing hold something in common," says Peri Rossi, "namely the ludic element." Her novel of 1992, *La última noche de Dostoievski* (*Dostoyevsky's Last Night*), is a metaphor of this association. It tells of a journalist, a compulsive gambler, who seeks help from a psychoanalyst to overcome his compulsion. Games of chance have for him an erotic attraction – and so has the psychoanalyst. The solution, the only possible solution, will be for him to turn to that other activity which shares many attributes with gambling, in particular, pleasure: writing.

PSICHE HUGHES

Biography
Born in Montevideo, Uruguay, 12 November 1941. Attended the State University. Studied music and biology but graduated in comparative literature and became teacher of literature at the age of 22. Exiled from Uruguay in 1972 and settled in Barcelona. In 1980 she received a grant from the DAAD (Deutsche Akademische Aussendienst) to study in Berlin. Awarded a Guggenheim Foundation grant, 1994. Works for the Madrid newspaper *Diario 16*. Recipient of the following awards: Inventarios Provisionales Prize, 1976; City of Palma de Mallorca Prize, 1979; Benito Pérez Galdós Prize,1980; City of Barcelona Prize, 1991.

Selected Works

Novels
El libro de mis primos, Montevideo: Biblioteca de Marcha, 1969
La nave de los locos, Barcelona: Seix Barral, 1984; as *The Ship of Fools*, translated by Psiche Hughes, London: Allison and Busby, and Columbia, Louisiana: Readers International, 1989
Solitario de amor, Barcelona: Grijalbo, 1988
La última noche de Dostoievski, Madrid: Mondadori, 1992; as *Dostoevsky's Last Night*, translated by Laura C. Dail, New York: Picador, 1995

Short Fiction
Viviendo, Montevideo: Alfa, 1963
Los museos abandonados, Montevideo: Arca, 1969
Indicios pánicos, Montevideo: Nuestra América, 1970
La tarde del dinosaurio, Barcelona: Planeta, 1976
La rebelión de los niños, Caracas: Monte Ávila, 1980
El museo de los esfuerzos inútiles, Barcelona: Seix Barral, 1983
Una pasión prohibida, Barcelona: Seix Barral, 1986; as *A Forbidden Passion*, translated by Mary Jane Treacy, Pittsburgh: Cleis Press, 1993
Cosmoagonías, Barcelona: Laia, 1988
La ciudad de Luzbel, Montevideo: Trilce, 1993

Poetry
Evohé: poemas eróticos, Montevideo: Girón, 1971; as *Evohé: poemas eróticos = Erotic Poems*, translated by Diana P. Decker, Washington, DC: Azul, 1994
Descripción de un naufragio, Barcelona: Lumen, 1974
Diáspora, Barcelona: Lumen, 1976
Lingüística general, Valencia: Prometeo, 1979
Europa después de la lluvia, Madrid: Fundación Banco Exterior, 1987
Babel bárbara, Caracas: Angria, 1990
Otra vez Eros, Barcelona: Lumen, 1994

Other Writings
Fantasías eróticas, Madrid: Temas de Hoy, 1991
Acerca de la escritura, Zaragoza, Spain: Universidad de Zaragoza, 1991

Further Reading
Castillo, Debra A., "(De)ciphering Reality in 'Los extraños objetos voladores,'" *Letras Femeninas*, vol. 13/1–2 (1987)
Chanady, Amaryll B., "Cristina Peri Rossi and the Other Side of Reality," *Antigonish Review*, vol. 54 (1983)
Kaminsky, Amy, "Gender and Exile in Cristina Peri Rossi," in *Continental, Latin American and Francophone Writers*, edited by Eunice Myers and Ginette Adamson, Lanham, Maryland: University Press of America, 1987
____ "Cristina Peri Rossi and the Question of Lesbian Presence," in her *Reading the Body Politic: Feminist Criticism and Latin American Women Writers*, Minneapolis: University of Minnesota Press, 1993
Mora, Gabriela, "Enigmas and Subversions in Cristina Peri Rossi's *La nave de los locos*," in *Splintering Darkness: Latin American Women Writers in Search of Themselves*, edited by Lucía Guerra-Cunningham, Pittsburgh: Latin American Literary Review Press, 1990
Narvaez, Carlos Raul, "Critical Approaches to Cristina Peri Rossi's *El libro de mis primos*," *Dissertation Abstracts International*, vol. 44/12 (June 1984)
Olivera-Williams, María Rosa, "*La nave de los locos* de Cristina Peri Rossi," *Revista de Crítica Literaria Latinoamericana*, vol. 11/23 (1986)
Rodríguez, Mercedes M., "Variaciones en el tema del exilio en el mundo alegórico de 'El museo de los esfuerzos inútiles'," *Monographic Review/Revista Monográfica*, vol. 4 (1988)
____ "Oneiric Riddles in Peri Rossi's *La nave de los locos*," *Romance Languages Annual*, vol. 1 (1989)
____ "Cristina Peri Rossi, *Solitario de amor*," *Journal of Interdisciplinary Literary Studies*, vol. 2/1 (1990)
San Román, Gustavo, "Sexual Politics in Cristina Peri Rossi," *Journal of Hispanic Research*, vol. 2/3 (Summer 1994)
Schmidt, Cynthia A., "A Satiric Perspective on the Experience of Exile in the Short Fiction of Cristina Peri Rossi," *The Americas Review*, vol. 18/3–4 (1990)

Interviews
Hughes, Psiche, "Interview with Cristina Peri Rossi," in *Unheard Words*, London: Allison and Busby, 1985
San Román, Gustavo, "Entrevista a Cristina Peri Rossi," *Revista Iberoamericana*, vol. 58/160–61 (July–December 1992)

Peru

19th- and 20th-Century Prose and Poetry

Political emancipation from Spain left Peru's social structure intact. Reflecting that continuity, Neoclassicism remained the dominant literary mode in the years after Independence and the leading intellectual figure of the age was Felipe Pardo y Aliaga, a member of the country's conservative upper echelons. Distrustful of popular democracy and an advocate of orderly progress directed by an enlightened elite, Pardo was an accomplished and versatile writer who conceived literature as a vehicle for instructing the public. He is best known as a civic poet, the bulk of his output consisting of satirical poems ridiculing the social, political and cultural state of the country. As a dramatist, he sought to raise the standard of the local theatre by adapting Spanish models to the Peruvian scene, his best play being *Frutos de la educación*, 1830 [Fruits of Education], a comedy of manners in the tradition of Moratín. He was also responsible for introducing the costumbrist sketch to Peru in his short-lived journal *El espejo de mi tierra*, 1840 [The Mirror of My Country], using it as a medium for satirising the disorder of the new Republic and the failure of the upper classes to provide effective leadership.

Very soon, however, it was Lima's emergent middle classes who increasingly dominated the literary scene. Manuel Ascensio Segura created a national theatre of quality with a corpus of thirteen plays, the best of which are *El Sargento Canuto*, 1839 [Sergeant Canuto], *La saya y manto*, 1841 [The Skirt and Shawl], *Ña Catita*, 1845 [Mistress Catita] and *Las tres viudas*, 1862 [The Three Widows]. Though he saw himself as a moralist and social critic, Segura's talent was above all that of a perceptive observer of the social scene and his plays are memorable mainly for their lively and entertaining depiction of Limeñan customs and types and for dialogues which capture the flavour of popular speech. Likewise, in the 1840s and 1850s, Segura, Ramón Rojas y Cañas and Manuel Atanasio Fuentes used the costumbrist sketch to portray the virtues and defects of the capital's middle classes and to give expression to their aspirations and grievances. In a similar fashion, from 1872 onwards, Ricardo Palma's *Tradiciones peruanas* [Peruvian Traditions] were to focus mainly on Lima's days of colonial splendour and make use of chatty historical anecdotes to undermine the mythology of the dominant elite and to enhance the middle classes' image of themselves. Segura, the costumbrists and Palma thus fostered a vision of Peru which identified the nation with Lima and its middle classes. The only work to challenge that vision was the country's first novel, Narciso Aréstegui's *El Padre Horán*, 1848 [Father Horán], which depicts the social and economic backwardness of the Cuzco region and indicts the Republican regime for its failure to improve the quality of life in the provinces.

In the 1850s there emerged a group of young writers who sought to incorporate national literature into the Western mainstream by introducing Romanticism to Peru, but that early attempt at modernisation proved a failure, since for the most part their work was derivative and mediocre. The only exceptions were the novelist Luis Benjamín Cisneros and the poet Carlos Augusto Salaverry. Cisneros combines a Romantic glorification of love with a somewhat insipid social criticism in *Julia* (1861) and *Edgardo* (1864). Salaverry's reputation rests mainly on the love poems of *Cartas a un ángel* [Letters to an Angel], published in journals from 1858 onwards.

A major turning-point in the country's history was the humiliating disaster of the War of the Pacific (1879–83), which provoked a crisis of national morale and prompted intellectuals to embark on an agonised reappraisal of every aspect of Peruvian life. In a series of speeches and essays reprinted in *Páginas libres*, 1894 [Free Pages], Manuel González Prada attributed Peru's sickness to the Spanish colonial legacy and advocated a radical modernisation which would destroy the power of the oligarchy, break Lima's stranglehold on the country and incorporate the mestizo and Indian masses into national society. To that end he called for a literature which, breaking with the traditionalism of the past, would adopt a forward-looking spirit and develop new forms of expression to confront the realities of the modern age. As a poet he himself contributed to that project, for he was one of the main precursors of the *modernista* movement and enriched and revitalised poetic expression by experimenting with new forms and metres.

The new and more radical spirit championed by González Prada was to manifest itself in the costumbrist sketch and the novel. The former underwent an evolution with Albelardo Gamarra, who, by extending its scope beyond the capital to portray customs and scenes of virtually every region of the country and by using it as a vehicle to speak out on behalf of the oppressed, asserted a new nationalism which embraced the whole of Peru and all of its people. The novel, meanwhile, became a more vigorous medium of social criticism in the hands of two female writers of the realist school. Clorinda Matto de Turner's *Aves sin nido*, 1889 (*Birds without a Nest*) addresses the social problems of the Andean highlands and protests against the oppression and exploitation of the Indian masses, while Mercedes Cabello de Carbonera's *Blanca Sol* (1889) echoes González Prada's denunciations of the moral corruption of Lima's high society.

Unfortunately, most Peruvian writing of the 19th century was artistically flawed and if Ricardo Palma stands out as the leading figure, it is precisely because he set a standard of literary professionalism which none of his compatriots were able to match. However, the advent of *Modernismo* brought a greater aesthetic awareness and significantly raised the level of literary craftsmanship. Among the best prose works is Enrique A. Carrillo's *Cartas de una turista*, 1905 [Letters from a Tourist], a novel which gently derides Peru's cultural backwardness and explores the gulf between the ideal world of the imagination and the prosaic world of everyday reality. *Cuentos malévolos*, 1904 [Malevolent Stories] by Clemente Palma, the first writer to cultivate the short story systematically, is marked by its cosmopolitan outlook and impregnated with the decadent spirit of the *fin de siècle*, manipulating ironic cynicism and black humour to subvert established religious and philosophical beliefs and conventional moral values. In poetry José Santos Chocano achieved international status and gave a new direction to the *modernista* movement by celebrating the awesome grandeur of the American landscape and the epic splendour of the continent's history, thereby asserting Hispanic America's pride in itself in the face of Anglo-Saxon encroachment. Subsequently, Alberto Ureta was to establish himself as a fine minor poet with a work characterised by a resigned melancholy at the fleetingness of time and a bitter-sweet nostalgia for moments of lost happiness.

Among later writers still operating within the *modernista* sensibility was José María Eguren, author of *Simbólicas*, 1911 [Symbolic Poems], *La canción de las figuras*, 1916 [Song of the Figures] and *Poesías*, 1929 [Poems]. Perhaps the only genuine representative of the Symbolist aesthetic in Spanish America, Eguren was Peru's first major poet of modern times. Turning his back on society to commit himself completely to his art, he lived poetry as an alternative life-style, elevated it to a medium for capturing the hidden magic of the world and through his consummate craftsmanship endowed his superficially simple and transparent verse with a rich suggestive power. Another important transitional figure was Abraham Valdelomar, who cultivated both poetry and fiction. The bulk of his work is still *modernista* in manner, most notably so in his reworking of Inca legends in *Los hijos del sol*, 1921 [Our Children of the Sun], where he re-creates the sumptuous magnificence of the pre-Columbian past. However, both in his poetry and in the stories of *El caballero Carmelo*, 1918 [Sir Carmelo], he initiates a movement away from the sophisticated cosmopolitanism of *Modernismo* by employing a simple, austere language to evoke the provincial world of his childhood and to celebrate the natural dignity and nobility of the humble folk of rural Peru. Ventura García Calderón's *La venganza del cóndor* (1924), translated into English as *The White Llama*, is likewise inspired by the aim of revealing to the world the unknown Peru beyond the capital, but though the stories are characterised by an impressive mastery of language and technique, their portrayal of national reality is superficial, conjuring up the image of an exotic and mysterious land of picturesque customs and colourful characters. By contrast, Enrique López Albujar's *Cuentos andinos*, 1920 [Andean Tales] ushers in a more realistic approach to the treatment of the rural world by focussing on the violence and brutality of life among the Indian peasantry, and though its depiction of indigenous culture is limited and distorted by Western preconceptions, it is the first work of fiction to portray the Indian convincingly as a human being.

The 1920s were a period of political and intellectual ferment which saw the spread of radical thought and the emergence of organised left-wing political movements. The leading intellectual figure of the age was José Carlos Mariátegui, whose *Siete ensayos de interpretación de la realidad peruana*, 1928 (*Seven Interpretative Essays on Peruvian Reality*) provides the first Marxist analysis of Peru's history. As a political thinker Mariátegui exercised an enormous influence, but he was equally important as a stimulator of intellectual activity. From 1926 to 1930 he edited *Amauta* [Inca Sage], a journal of socialist orientation aimed at promoting a deeper understanding of Peru and at widening its cultural horizons. It published poetry and fiction as well as articles on science, geography, politics, art and history, and not only included contributions from prominent foreign intellectuals but provided an outlet for young Peruvian writers, whatever their political affiliations. As such it gave a great boost to the intellectual life of the country.

One aspect of the ferment of the 1920s was the growth of a somewhat amorphous avant-garde movement. Much of the verse of the period manifests a continuing cultural dependency by merely aping the latest Western fashion, but the best poets assimilated the spirit and techniques of the international avant-garde to forge a new and personal poetic expression. Foremost among these was César Vallejo, who was subsequently to gain international recognition as one of the great figures of 20th-century literature. Others were Carlos Oquendo de Amat and, in the 1930s, Emilio Adolfo Westphalen and César Moro. The avant-garde era thus constitutes a watershed in the history of Peruvian poetry, since it saw the establishment of a modern poetic tradition.

The standard-bearer of the avant-garde was Alberto Hidalgo. Influenced by the Futurism of Marinetti but stylistically still conservative, his early books celebrate the beauty of cars, aeroplanes, motor cycles, sport and war, manifestations of a new creative spirit which is destroying the old world to build a new. Later, Hidalgo was to invent "simplism," his own variant of the avant-garde poetics, and his formal experimentation becomes more daring in *Química del espíritu*, 1923 [Chemistry of the Spirit], *Simplismo*, 1925 [Simplism] and *Descripción del cielo*, 1928 [Description of Heaven], where it is linked to a religion of the self, seen as the source of ultimate reality. Among the best examples of Futurist poetry are the "polyrythms" of the expatriate Juan Parra del Riego, which exploit modern imagery and free verse to convey the excitement and dynamism of 20th-century life. By contrast, the indigenist poet Alejandro Peralta makes use of avant-garde techniques to evoke the Andean rural world in *Ande*, 1926, and *Kollao*, 1934 [Aymara World]. However, second only to Vallejo's *Trilce* as the outstanding book of the 1920s is Oquendo's *5 metros de poemas*, 1927 (5 Metres of Poems), whose verbal jokes and visual games express a child-like delight in the exciting new world opened up by modernity.

Though often naive and undiscriminating, the avant-garde's enthusiastic response to modernity was an expression of the emergent middle sectors' hopes that Peru was on the verge of a radical transformation. Unfortunately, those hopes were to be frustrated as the country entered a decade of political repression and the poetry of the 1930s reflects the increasing marginalisation of the intellectual community. Westphalen's *Las ínsulas extrañas*, 1933 [Strange Islands] and *Abolición de la muerte*, 1935 [Abolition of Death], constituting as they do a Proustian search for lost time in which memory and the poetic imagination struggle against time and death to recuperate the happiness of lost love, are emblematic both because of the poet's withdrawal into a private space and because of his lonely resistance to the life-negating forces around him. For his part, the Surrealist Moro expressed his repudiation of the Peruvian environment by opting to spend most of his adult life in voluntary exile and to write his work in French, the major exception being *La tortuga ecuestre* [The Equestrian Turtle], written in 1938–39, where poetry is celebrated as an alternative life-style devoted to the subversion of dominant Western values and to the pursuit of a self-fulfilment denied him by a dehumanising society.

Meanwhile, 1928 saw the publication of two novels which in their different ways reflect the new spirit of the times. Martín Adán's *La casa de cartón* (*The Cardboard House*) is an avant-garde "portrait of the artist as a young man." By contrast, Enrique López Albújar's *Matalaché* is something of an anachronism, since it is a historical novel with a conventional romantic plot and is consciously traditional in form and manner. However, its modernity lies in the way it uses history, for like Mariátegui's *Siete ensayos* it reappraises the Independence period in order to question the value-systems on which post-Independence Peru has been built. In the 1930s José Diez-Canseco was likewise to go against the prevailing regionalist current. On the one hand, he may be regarded as a precursor of the urban fiction of the 1950s, since his novel *Duque*, 1934 [Duke] depicts the frivolous life-style of the capital's idle rich while some of the stories of *Estampas mulatas* [Mulatto Vignettes] (1929–40) focus on the dispossessed of the poorer districts of Lima and Callao. On the other, though his other tales are superficially regionalist in that they are set in various parts of the provinces, their mestizo protagonists share a common identity and way of life and are portrayed as representative of a national culture spanning city and countryside, highlands and coast.

For the most part, however, the fiction of the period was regionalist in character. The 1920s saw the growth of an indigenist movement to champion the cause of the downtrodden Indian population of the Andean region, but though it produced important works of non-fiction such as Luis E. Valcárcel's *Tempestad en los Andes*, 1927 [Storm in the Andes], fiction tended to limit itself to a crude social realism denouncing the oppression and exploitation of the Indian peasantry, typical examples being the stories of María Wiesse and Gamaliel Churata in the pages of *Amauta*. In a similar vein César Falcón's *Plantel de inválidos*, 1921 [Nursery of Cripples] and *El pueblo sin Dios*, 1928 [The People without God] and César Vallejo's *El tungsteno*, 1931 (*Tungsten*) analyse Andean society from a Marxist perspective and situate the Indian question within the context of the class struggle. Not all regionalist fiction was politically motivated, however, and Emilio Romero's *Balseros del Titicaca*, 1934 [Boatmen of Lake Titicaca] and Fernando Romero's *Doce relatos de la selva*, 1934 [Twelve Jungle Tales] are representative of a current which aimed primarily to promote among Peruvians a knowledge of their own country. The culmination of the regionalist/indigenist trend was to come with the emergence of Ciro Alegría and José María Arguedas in the second half of the 1930s. Alegría's first two novels, *La serpiente de oro*, 1935 (*The Golden Serpent*) and *Los perros hambrientos*, 1938 [The Starving Dogs], are sympathetic portrayals of the way of life of the rural peoples of the remote regions of northern Peru, while *El mundo es ancho y ajeno*, 1941 (*Broad and Alien is the World*), the indigenist novel *par excellence*, is a paradigmatic account of the destruction of the traditional Indian community by the expansion of the latifundia system. For his part Arguedas sought to dissociate himself from the simplifications of the indigenists and the stories of *Agua*, 1935 [Water] and the novel *Yawar fiesta*, 1941 (*Yawar Fiesta*) offer a deeper understanding of Indian culture and a more complex view of Andean social relationships. Together the two men's complementary interpretations of the Andean world laid the the foundations of a solid novelistic tradition.

Meanwhile, the theatre had gone into a long decline following the death of Segura, the only dramatists of any note being Leonidas Yerovi at the start of the century and José Chioino in the early 1920s, both of whom carried on the costumbrist tradition. However, the 1940s saw the beginnings of a revival. Percy Gibson Parra's *Esa luna que empieza*, 1946 [That Rising Moon] initiates a move away from costumbrist realism towards the poetic treatment of universal archetypes. Likewise, the majority of Juan Ríos Rey's eight plays are poetic reworkings of historical and cultural myths, the best example being *Ayar Manko* (1952). Sebastián Salazar Bondy, a leading promoter of theatrical activity, was himself the author of ten dramas as well as eleven brief one-act plays, his best works being the historical drama *Rodil* (1954), the comedy *El fabricante de deudas*, 1963 [The Debt Manufacturer] – an adaptation of Balzac's *Le Faiseur* – and the political allegory *El rabdomante*, 1965 [The Diviner]. In the wake of the 1940s revival, the 1950s and 1960s produced three highly successful works. Enrique Solari Swayne's *Collacocha* (1955), dramatises Latin America's striving to overcome underdevelopment through an epic representation of the struggle to dominate nature. Julio Ramón Ribeyro's *Vida y pasión de Santiago el pajarero*, 1958 [Life and Passion of Santiago the Birdman] adapts the story of an 18th-century visionary as an allegory of the artist in contemporary Peru. Alonso Alegría's *El cruce sobre el Niágara*, 1968 [Crossing Niagara] is an affirmative counter-text to *Waiting for Godot*, based on the career of the French tightrope-walker Blondin. More recently, the novelist Mario Vargas Llosa has turned his hand to writing for the stage with *La Señorita de Tacna*, 1981 (*The Young Lady from Tacna*) and *Kathie y el hipopótamo*, 1983 (*Kathie and the Hippopotamus*). However, Peru still suffers from a lack of a public of sufficient size to support commercial theatre except on a very modest scale, and the continuing paucity of official support means that semi-professional groups have to struggle to keep their heads above water. In such circumstances it is hardly surprising that, while Peruvian dramatists have produced some fine plays, on the whole they have failed to match the achievements of the country's poets and novelists in terms of both quantity and quality.

The 1940s and 1950s threw up a whole generation of poets of high quality who combined the avant-garde legacy of experimentation with a rehabilitation of more traditional forms to produce some strikingly original poetry. The dominant tendency of the 1940s was a so-called "pure poetry," the main exponents of which were Martín Adán, Jorge Eduardo Eielson and Javier Sologuren and, later, Leopoldo Chariarse and Francisco Bendezú. This poetics may be regarded as symptomatic of the sense of alienation experienced by many of the country's intellectuals, for the poets who practised it turned their backs on the surrounding reality to take refuge in the timeless world of literature, creating in poems of rigorous formal perfection an alternative space where life is lived at a higher level. The outstanding example is Adán's *Travesía de extramares*, 1950 [Voyage Beyond the Oceans], a collection of sonnets re-enacting the poet's pursuit of an ineffable ideal reality. "Pure poetry" was to persist into the 1970s, but long before then it had gone into crisis, for most of its practioners lost confidence in the transcendent powers of poetry and their later work, such as Adán's *La mano desasida* (*Canto a Macchu*

Picchu), 1964 [*The Hand Let Go (Song to Macchu Picchu)*], is given over to the expression of an acute existential anguish.

Meanwhile, the quashing of a brief experiment in democracy by the *coup d'état* of 1948 led to an upsurge of socially-committed verse, represented mainly by a group of poets – Gustavo Valcárcel, Alejandro Romualdo, Juan Gonzalo Rose and Manuel Scorza – who suffered exile during the Odría dictatorship. Much of this poetry tended to lapse into strident diatribe or declamatory effusions of revolutionary optimism, but Romualdo and Rose, in particular, were able to produce more effective work by developing more sophisticated forms of expression and by linking the social to their personal experience. Another poet of the period, Mario Florián, produced his best work, not in his later social verse, but in his earlier books, notably *Urpi*, 1944 [*Dove*], where he cultivates an Andean folk poetry rooted in popular oral tradition. Subsequently, the growing politicisation of Peruvian and Latin American society was to be reflected in the work of poets, such as Wáshington Delgado and Pablo Guevara, who began to publish towards the end of the 1950s. Their poetry, however, is different in character from that of their predecessors, for it bridges the somewhat artificial gap between private and social poetry by combining socio-political concerns with an expression of personal experience and by situating the poet as an individual in the context of social and historical processes.

Other poets are less easy to categorise. The poetry of Sebastián Salazar Bondy, for example, is essentially confessional, a testimony of his personal encounter with the world, celebrating the values of love, friendship and goodwill among human beings. The work of Blanca Varela, Peru's foremost female poet, is marked by a rebellious dissatisfaction with her condition as a woman and as a human being. Carlos Germán Belli, the outstanding poet of the generation of the 1950s, developed a highly original mock-classical manner which indirectly voices social criticism by giving expression to the frustrations of the country's middle classes and, in his later work, serves as a vehicle for metaphysical meditations.

In the narrative field the 1950s saw the emergence of a generation of writers – Enrique Congrains Martín, Oswaldo Reynoso, Eleodoro Vargas Vicuña, Carlos Eduardo Zavaleta and Julio Ramón Ribeyro – who sought to bring a more professional approach to literary activity and to modernise Peruvian writing by assimilating the technical developments of mainstream Western fiction. Their work was mainly urban, reflecting the impact of the industrialisation of the coast and the massive shift of population from the rural areas to the cities, particularly Lima. An important precursor was Sebastián Salazar Bondy, who pioneered modern urban fiction with the stories of *Naúfragos y sobrevivientes*, 1954 [*Castaways and Survivors*] and in his non-fictional *Lima la horrible*, 1964 [*Beastly Lima*] captured the dissident mood of the new generation. Thus, Congrains, in the stories of *Lima, hora cero*, 1954 [*Lima, Zero Hour*] and *Kikuyo*, 1955 [*Plague of Weeds*] and in the novel *No una sino muchas muertes*, 1957 [*Not One but Many Deaths*], portrays the hardships and frustrated ambitions of the new urban masses. Reynoso, in the stories of *Los inocentes*, 1961 [*The Innocents*] – later retitled *Lima en rock* [*Swinging Lima*]) – and the novels *En octubre no hay milagros*, 1965 [*No Miracles in October*] and *El escarabajo y el hombre*, 1970 [*The Beetle and Man*], depicts the drudgery and

struggles of the lower middle classes and the alienation of their adolescent offspring. Several of Ribeyro's stories and his novel *Los geniecillos dominicales*, 1965 [*The Sunday Goblins*] focus on sectors of the middle classes who find themselves socially displaced because of their inability to compete in the new society. However, the generation of the 1950s also renovated the regionalist tradition by producing a substantial body of work which adopted a new approach to the treatment of rural life. Ribeyro's novel *Crónica de San Gabriel*, 1960 [*Chronicle of San Gabriel*] explores the decline of the traditional land-owning oligarchy. Zavaleta's *La batalla*, 1954 [*The Battle*], *El Cristo Villenas*, 1955 [*Villenas the Christ*] and *Los Ingar*, 1955 [*The Ingars*] depict the backwardness of the rural world by focussing on underdevelopment at the level of the human personality. Vargas Vicuña, in the stories of *Nahuín*, 1953 [*In the Eye-View*] and *Taita Cristo*, 1963 [*Father Christ*], employs a lyrical manner reminiscent of the Mexican Juan Rulfo to convey the Andean peasantry's struggle for life in an inhospitable environment. Unfortunately, most of the generation subsequently gave up writing, but Zavaleta and Ribeyro maintained a constant literary activity and the latter, as the author of a corpus of short fiction dealing with universal as well as national themes, was eventually to become recognised as a major writer.

In their concern to introduce a more professional approach to the creation of fiction and to modernise narrative technique, the generation of the 1950s formed part of a continent-wide trend which was to culminate in the so-called Boom of the 1960s. In Peru the two main representatives of the new Spanish American narrative, José María Arguedas (in his second phase) and Mario Vargas Llosa, exemplify a continuing divide in national life and letters in that, while the former writes as spokesman for the Andean world and its culture, the latter is very much a novelist of the Western mainstream. That divide again manifests itself in the second wave of "new novelists" who emerged in the 1970s. Alfredo Bryce Echenique depicts the privileged world of the Hispanic oligarchy in *Un mundo para Julius*, 1970 (*A World for Julius*) and in his later novels deals with the experience of the Latin American intellectual in Europe. By contrast, Manuel Scorza, in a cycle of five novels initiated by *Redoble por Rancas*, 1970 (*Drums for Rancas*), renovates indigenist fiction by bringing to it a humorous magical realism akin to that pioneered by García Márquez.

In recent years Peruvian fiction has continued to be marked by experimentation and by the sophistication of its narrative technique. However, the most significant development has been the emergence of writers from lower-class backgrounds whose work seeks to give a history to the traditionally marginalised sectors of Peruvian society. Gregorio Martínez, in the stories of *Tierra de caléndula*, 1975 [*Marigold Country*] and the novels *Canto de sirena*, 1977 [*Siren Song*] and *Crónica de músicos y diablos*, 1991 [*Chronicle of Musicians and Devils*], re-creates the experience of the Negroid peasantry of the southern coastal region. Cronwell Jara's novel *Patíbulo para un caballo*, 1989 [*Scaffold for a Horse*] is a foundational myth telling the story of the migrant masses' conquest of a space in the city. Miguel Gutiérrez's *La violencia del tiempo*, 1992 [*The Violence of Time*] recounts the saga of a humble mestizo family over several generations. Paralleling changes which have been taking place in the country at large, fiction has thus undergone a process of democratisation and begun to reflect the multiracial character of Peruvian society.

Meanwhile, the 1960s constituted a second major watershed in modern Peruvian poetry. The new generation of poets adopted a poetic manner characterised by freer, more open forms, by multiple discourses and intertextual dialogues, and by a colloquial conversational tone that was often humorous and irreverent. By so doing, they reflected the spirit of an age marked by an internationalisation of culture, a liberalisation of the socio-political climate and a general relaxation of attitudes to life. Key figures in the literary history of the period were Javier Heraud and Luis Hernández, partly because of their role as precursors, but mainly because the mythology surrounding their lives turned them into folk heroes, symbols in their different ways of rebellion against an outmoded social order and life-style. However, the major poets of the new generation were Antonio Cisneros, Rodolfo Hinostroza and Marco Martos. Cisneros's poetry is characterised by a devastating irony, which he wields in *Comentarios reales*, 1964 [Royal Commentaries] and *Canto ceremonial contra un oso hormiguero*, 1968 [Ceremonial Song against an Anteater] to debunk the mythologies of the ruling establishment and voice his disconformity with the bourgeois life-style. Hinostroza, in *Consejero del lobo*, 1965 [Counsellor of the Wolf] and *Contra natura*, 1971 [Against Nature], asserts the freedom of the individual against the power of the state, identifying himself in the latter book with the youth movement which sought to create its own alternative order. Martos, in *Casa nuestra*, 1965 [Our House] and *Cuaderno de quejas y contentamientos*, 1969 [Notebook of Complaints and Contentments], cultivates a deliberately prosaic anti-poetry reminiscent of the Chilean Nicanor Parra and strives to reconcile a concern for social change with a distrust of ideologies.

The poets of the 1970s were to continue and develop the poetic manner of their predecessors, going even further in their cultivation of a colloquial language and tone and incorporating into their verse references to the paraphernalia of modern city life, in order to reflect the spirit of the new society that was evolving in contemporary Peru as a result of industrialisation, mass migration to the cities and the Velasco Revolution. Outstanding among them is Abelardo Sánchez León, whose work expresses the alienation of an individual estranged from the traditional, exclusive bourgeois world in which he grew up, and unsure of his place in the changing society around him. However, as in fiction, the main feature of the period was the emergence of writers of humble extraction, such as Enrique Verástegui and José Watanabe, who broke the middle class's traditional monopoly of literature and were, in effect, the literary expression of the emergent provincial lower sectors who were claiming a place and a voice in national society. This democratisation of poetry was to continue in the 1980s with the appearance of a whole generation of women poets, foremost among whom are Carmen Ollé, Giovanna Pollarolo, Patricia Alba and Mariela Dreyfus.

JAMES HIGGINS

Further Reading

Aldrich Jr, Earl M., *The Modern Short Story in Peru*, Madison: University of Wisconsin Press, 1966

Cabello de Carbonera, Mercedes, *La novela moderna: estudio filosófico*, Lima: Bacigalupi, 1892

Cornejo Polar, Antonio, *La novela peruana: siete estudios*, Lima: Horizonte, 1977

——— "Historia de la literatura del Perú republicano," in *Historia del Perú*, edited by Fernando Silva Santisteban, Lima: Mejía Baca, 1980

——— et al., *Literatura y sociedad en el Perú*, 2 vols, Lima: Hueso Húmero, 1981–82

Elmore, Peter, *Los muros invisibles: Lima y la modernidad en la novela del siglo XX*, Lima: Mosca Azul, 1993

Escobar, Alberto, *El imaginario nacional: Moro, Westphalen, Arguedas: una formación literaria*, Lima: Instituto de Estudios Peruanos, 1989

Espina, Eduardo, "Poesía peruana: 1970, 1980, 1990, etc.," *Revista Iberoamericana* 164–65 (July–December 1993)

Forgues, Roland, *Palabra viva*, 4 vols, Lima: Studium, 1988–91 [These 4 volumes consist of interviews with most of Peru's leading writers]

Gorriti, Juana Manuela (editor), *Veladas literarias de Lima*, Buenos Aires: Imprenta Europea, 1892

Gutiérrez, Miguel, *La generación del cincuenta*, Lima: Séptimo Ensayo, 1988

Higgins, James, *A History of Peruvian Literature*, Liverpool: Cairns, 1987

——— *Hitos de la poesía peruana: Siglo XX*, Lima: Milla Batres, 1993

——— *Myths of the Emergent: Social Mobility in Contemporary Peruvian Fiction*, Liverpool: Institute of Latin American Studies, 1994

Kristal, Efraín, *The Andes Viewed from the City: Literary and Political Discourse on the Indian in Peru 1848–1930*, New York; Peter Lang, 1987

Losada, Alejandro, *Creación y praxis. La producción literaria como praxis social en Hispanoamérica y el Perú*, Lima: Universidad de San Marcos, 1976

Mariátegui, José Carlos, *Siete ensayos de interpretación de la realidad peruana*, Lima: Amauta, 1928; as *Seven Interpretative Essays on Peruvian Reality*, translated by Marjory Urquidi, Austin: University of Texas Press, 1971 [The last essay, of over 100 pages, is a stimulating sociological and political interpretation of Peruvian literature from the colonial period up to the Indigenist movement]

Márquez, Ismael P., *La retórica de la violencia en tres novelas peruanas*, New York: Peter Lang, 1994

Ortega, Julio, *Figuración de la persona*, Madrid: Edhasa, 1971 [Includes essays on several 20th-century Peruvian poets]

——— *La cultura peruana: experiencia y conciencia*, Mexico City: Fondo de Cultura Económica, 1978

——— *Crítica de la identidad: la pregunta por el Perú en su literatura*, Mexico City: Fondo de Cultura Económica, 1988

Paoli, Roberto, *Estudios sobre literatura peruana contemporánea*, Florence: Università degli Studi di Firenze, 1985

Rodríguez Luis, Julio, *Hermenéutica y praxis del indigenismo: la novela indigenista de Clorinda Matto de Turner a José María Arguedas*, Mexico City: Fondo de Cultura Económica, 1980

Sánchez, Luis Alberto, *La literatura peruana: derrotero para una historia cultural del Perú*, 5 vols, Lima: Editorial de Ediventas, 1965

Tamayo Vargas, Augusto, *Apuntes para un estudio de la literatura peruana*, 2 vols, Lima: Librería Studium, 4th edition, 1977

Watson, María Isabel, *El cuadro de costumbres en el Perú decimonónico*, Lima: La Católica, 1979

Wise, David O., "Writing for Fewer and Fewer: Peruvian Fiction 1979–1980," *Latin American Research Review* 18 (1983)

Zavaleta, Carlos E., "Narradores peruanos: la generación de los cincuenta. Un testimonio," *Cuadernos Hispanoamericanos* 302 (1975)

Bibliographies

Foster, David William, *Peruvian Literature: a Bibliography of Secondary Sources*, Westport, Connecticut: Greenwood Press, 1981

Ricardo Piglia 1941–

Argentine prose writer

Since the publication of *Nombre falso* (*Assumed Name*) and *Respiración artificial* (*Artificial Respiration*), Ricardo Piglia has been the dominant voice among the group of Argentine writers that came of age in the 1960s, many of whom were to die or go into exile during the military dictatorship of 1976–83. Piglia (né Ricardo Emilio Piglia Renzi, hence his frequent alter ego, Emilio Renzi) is a talented literary critic and a popular teacher at the University of Buenos Aires, but most of his critical thinking has been published in his fiction, notably in the novella "Homenaje a Roberto Arlt" [Homage to Roberto Arlt] in *Nombre falso* and in the second half of *Respiración artificial*. This fusion of fiction and criticism has reminded many readers of Borges, and indeed a good part of the reflection on Argentine literature and culture in the works mentioned revolves around the place of Borges (and of Arlt) in them.

If Borges made the analytic detective story and the fantastic popular in the 1940s, so Piglia has set as one of his tasks the translation and promotion of the "hard-boiled" tradition in US fiction, from Hammett and Chandler to such recent voices as Paul Auster. He has directed several series of modern crime fiction for Editorial Sudamericana and others. Closer to home, he has been the most spirited defender of the self-consciously lowbrow fiction and journalism of Roberto Arlt. Arlt, he has argued, though a contemporary of Borges who died before the rise of Perón, is Argentina's quintessential modern writer, a writer who makes of his marginal status a uniquely powerful standpoint. In *Respiración* one of the characters argues that Arlt is the first Argentine writer to celebrate the fact that he read the European classics in bad Spanish translations; the same point is made wonderfully in "Homenaje a Roberto Arlt," which consists of the intrigue around a supposed lost story by Arlt, "Luba" (actually borrowed from Leonid Andreev, but sounding so much like Arlt that many readers have been fooled by the resemblance).

Piglia's early stories, published as *Jaulario* [Cage Collection] in Cuba and as *La invasión* [The Invasion] in a slightly different Argentine edition (both published in 1967), already reveal Piglia as a reader of North American fiction. One of the most effective stories in the collection is "Las actas del juicio" [Records of the Trial], the purported transcription of the statement made in court by the assassin of General Justo José Urquiza (1801–70); as such it is the first of Piglia's works to delve into a troubled period in Argentine history, the half-century of civil conflict that followed independence from Spain. Another of the stories in this early collection, "Mata-Hari 55," begins with a note that is an early statement of Piglia's poetics of narrative fiction:

La mayor incomodidad de esta historia es ser cierta. Se equivocan los que piensan que es más fácil contar hechos verídicos que inventar una anécdota, sus relaciones y sus leyes. La realidad, es sabido, tiene una lógica esquiva; una lógica que parece, a ratos, imposible de narrar.

[The most uncomfortable aspect of this story is that it is true. Those who think that it is easier to tell a true story than to make up an anecdote, with all of its inter-relations and laws, are wrong. Reality, we know, has a slant logic; a logic that seems, at times, impossible to narrate.]

It is important to note Piglia's sceptical approach to the narration of real events even as early as 1967; though he was already politically active at this point, his work does not subscribe to the naive realism that was much in vogue in the period, nor does he indulge in experimental fiction for its own sake, which was another tendency that was strong in the wake of Cortázar's *Rayuela* (*Hopscotch*).

The next collection, the magnificent *Nombre falso*, was published months before the military coup. In a 1994 note to a new edition of the book, Piglia recognizes the novella "Homenaje a Roberto Arlt" that comprises the second half of this breakthrough work as "lo mejor que he escrito" (the best thing I have written). What begins – in a tone reminiscent of the Borges stories that are disguised as book reviews – as a discussion of a project to gather together certain dispersed and unpublished works of Roberto Arlt gradually brings Arlt back to life in evocations of him by his friends and in his own words, and in the narrator's "total identification" with Arlt (to quote a phrase from Novalis quoted in Borges's "Pierre Menard"). The encounter with Arlt's friend Saúl Kostia and the struggle over the manuscript of a supposed Arlt story, "Luba," reveals the powerful links in Arlt's universe between fiction, forgery, invention and plagiarism. The novella ends with an appendix containing the text of "Luba," actually a slightly modified translation of a story by the Russian writer Andreev, who is mentioned several times in "Homenaje." The Andreev story does indeed sound so much like Arlt that a number of critics have taken it to be either an Arlt text or a perfect imitation of Arlt by Piglia; Piglia's point (developed at length in *Respiración artificial*) is that Arlt's fiction is self-consciously imitative of the European works he read in bad Spanish translations. Since "Luba" sounds so much like Arlt, but is actually earlier, Piglia has brilliantly proven the point that Borges made years before in his essays on Kafka and Hawthorne, that every writer creates his precursors. In this story Piglia is creating Arlt, and also creating a new Borges, a much more subversive one than the "real" Borges who at that time was alive and living in Buenos Aires.

Respiración artificial is also haunted by the odd couple of Roberto Arlt and Jorge Luis Borges, as well as by some other odd couples (Hitler and Kafka, Hitler and Descartes, Gombrowicz and Borges, etc.). The novel begins with the publication (in April 1976, weeks after the military coup) of a novel by Emilio Renzi based on the life of an uncle, Marcelo Maggi, who had vanished years before in a scandal that rocked the family. The novel reaches the uncle, who is living in Concordia, up the Paraná River toward Paraguay; the uncle and the nephew begin an exchange of letters that takes up most of the first half of the book, gradually interspersed with a series of documents relating to a project of historical research that Maggi is working on about an imaginary figure from 19th-century Argentine history, Enrique Ossorio. Ossorio, according to Maggi, was at work on an Utopian novel called *1979* at the time of his suicide in 1850. The fragments of the novel that are quoted are letters that very pointedly refer to the experience of the mid-1970s, torture, exile, disappearance. When Renzi travels to Concordia to meet his uncle, the papers are eventually turned over to him by one of the uncle's friends, after an astonishing all-night conversation about the relation between reality and fiction, Argentina and Europe, history and philosophy. The uncle never appears; though this is never stated directly, he has been "disappeared."

Respiración artificial is a difficult act to follow. Piglia's next work was *Prisión perpetua*, 1988 [Life Imprisonment], a new edition of *Nombre falso*, with the addition of two new stories, one about a North American friend the narrator had in Mar del Plata, the other about Nietzsche's sister's adventures in South America. His next major work, *La ciudad ausente* [The Absent City], is a futurist fantasy based on certain aspects of the life and works of Macedonio Fernández (1874–1952), and revolves around an imaginary museum in which the body of Macedonio's wife, Elena de Obieta, has been preserved and turned into a speaking machine. (This work has been turned into an opera by the Argentine composer Gerardo Gandini; it had its world premiere at the Teatro Colón, Buenos Aires, in October 1995).

Piglia's other works include a book of interviews, *Crítica y ficción*, 1986 [Criticism and Fiction], and a fascinating rewriting of a series of major texts from Argentine literature, *La Argentina en pedazos*, 1993 [Argentina in Pieces], in comic-book form, with introductory texts by Piglia and comics by a series of avant-garde Argentine artists in the medium. In this work Piglia delves again, as in his first work, into the relations between reality and fiction, into the construction of a social imaginary.

DANIEL BALDERSTON

Biography

Born Ricardo Emilio Piglia Renzi, in Adrogué, province of Buenos Aires, Argentina, 24 November 1941. Studied History at University of La Plata. Worked in publishing as reader, proof-reader and – in the 1970s – as director of Editorial Tiempo Contemporáneo's "Serie Negra" of hard-boiled novels. Visiting professor at Princeton University, New Jersey, and, briefly, at the University of California, Santa Cruz. Currently teaches in the Faculty of Philosophy and Letters of the University of Buenos Aires. Awards include the Boris Vian Prize for *Respiración artificial*.

Selected Works

Short Fiction

Jaulario, Havana: Casa de las Américas, 1967
La invasión, Buenos Aires: Jorge Álvarez, 1967
Cuentos morales, Buenos Aires: Espasa Calpe, 1995

Novels

Nombre falso, Mexico City: Siglo XXI, 1975; as *Assumed Name*, translated by Sergio Waisman, Pittsburgh: Latin American Literary Review Press, 1995
Respiración artificial, Buenos Aires: Pomaire, 1980; as *Artificial Respiration*, translated by Daniel Balderston, Durham, North Carolina: Duke University Press, 1994
Prisión perpetua, Buenos Aires: Sudamericana, 1988
La ciudad ausente, Buenos Aires: Sudamericana, 1992

Other Writings

Crónicas de Latinoamérica, edited by Ricardo Piglia, Buenos Aires: Jorge Álvarez, 1968
Crítica y ficción, Santa Fe, Argentina: Universidad Nacional del Litoral, 1986
Por un relato futuro: diálogo, Santa Fe, Argentina: Centro de Publicaciones, Universidad Nacional del Litoral, 1990 [Conversations with Juan José Saer]
La Argentina en pedazos, Buenos Aires: Ediciones de la Urraca, 1993

Further Reading

Balderston, Daniel, "El significado latente en *Respiración artificial* de Ricardo Piglia y *En el corazón de junio* de Luis Gusman," in *Ficción y política. La narrativa argentina durante el proceso militar*, edited by René Jara and Hernán Vidal, Buenos Aires: Alianza, 1987
Colás, Santiago, *Postmodernity in Latin America: the Argentine Paradigm*, Durham, North Carolina: Duke University Press, 1994 [Chapter on Piglia]
Grandis, Rita de, "La cita como estrategia narrativa en *Respiración artificial*," *Revista Canadiense de Estudios Hispánicos*," vol. 17/2 (Winter 1993)
Jagoe, Eva-Lynn Alicia, "The Disembodied Machine: Matter, Femininity and Nation in Piglia's *La ciudad ausente*," *Latin American Literary Review*, vol. 23 (1995)
Menton, Seymour, *Latin America's New Historical Novel*, Austin: University of Texas Press, 1993 [Comments on *Respiración artificial*]
Morello Frosch, Marta, "Significación e historia en *Respiración artificial* de Ricardo Piglia," in *Fascismo y experiencia literaria: reflexiones para una recanonización*, edited by Hernán Vidal, Minneapolis, Minnesota: Institute for the Study of Ideologies and Literature, 1985
_____ "Borges and Contemporary Argentine Writers. Continuity and Change," in *Borges and His Successors; the Borgesian Impact on Literature and the Arts*, edited by Edna Aizenberg, Columbia: University of Missouri Press, 1990
Williams, Raymond L., *The Postmodern Novel in Latin America: Politics, Culture and the Crisis of Truth*, New York: St Martin's Press, and London: Macmillan, 1995 [Material on *Respiración artificial*]

Interviews

Kaplan, Marina, "Between Arlt and Borges: an Interview with Ricardo Piglia," *New Orleans Review*, vol. 16/2 (Summer 1989)

Virgilio Piñera 1912–1979

Cuban dramatist, prose writer and poet

Eclectic, prolific and innovative, Virgilio Piñera is one of the principal figures of 20th-century Cuban literature. His first books were volumes of lyric poetry, *Las furias*, 1942 [The Furies], and *La isla en peso*, 1943 [The Corporeal Island]. In the same year he published one of his earliest theatrical works, *Electra Garrigó*. Seeking a broader cultural environment he moved to Argentina, where he worked in the Cuban embassy, and later as a translator and editor for the Argos publishing house. In the course of several significant periods of residence in Buenos Aires he formed a friendship with José Bianco, then editor of the important cultural journal *Sur*, to which Piñera contributed. In Argentina Piñera also headed the group responsible for the Spanish translation (1947) of Witold Gombrowicz's modern Polish classic, *Ferdydurke*. His complete plays appeared in 1960, though some of his best work was still to come. *Dos viejos pánicos* [Two Old Panics] was awarded the 1968 Casa de las Américas Prize, in the period before he was ostracized by a crudely anti-bourgeois cultural establishment in the 1970s. Piñera's first and best novel, the astonishing *La carne de René*, 1952 (*René's Flesh*) was followed by two others in the 1960s: *Pequeñas maniobras*, 1963 [Small Manoeuvres] and *Presiones y diamantes*, 1967 [Pressures and Diamonds].

Of Piñera's three novels, *La carne de René* is undoubtedly the best, for its originality and black humour. Bizarre forces vie for possession of René's flesh, erotically, physically and symbolically. The novel is an allegorical satire on human materialism using a grotesque eroticism. In the end René accepts the futility of seeking spiritual freedom, and becomes resigned to his destiny: "... y cada día que pasaba, más y más se convencía de su carnalidad, de su absoluta impotencia para dejar de ser carne." (... with every passing day he grew ever more convinced of his carnal state, of his total inability to give up being flesh). *Pequeñas maniobras* is the first-person narrative of Sebastián, an individual obsessed with avoiding all social contact, human warmth, personal or political commitment, in fact anything that might complicate or compromise his existence of acquiescent defeat. His inclination to flight and evasion, however, leads to a series of episodic adventures. Sebastián lives in various nondescript lodgings, almost marries but inevitably flees at the last moment, and moves aimlessly through society. Always on the move, always in retreat, he takes various jobs, as book salesman, street photographer and odd-job man in a society for spiritual mediums. Sebastián is a weakling, an existential fugitive of unheroic proportions. The novel includes hints of political commentary, though a less revolutionary model hero than Sebastián would be hard to imagine. *Presiones y diamantes* is almost science fiction, a rather slight socio-political fantasy that describes the disintegration of "normal" values in a large modern city.

Piñera's short fiction is informed by the literature of the Absurd, in which strange, often grotesque situations are developed to provide a metaphor for the predicament of useless existence, and the futility of man's endeavours to transcend his limitations. His characters often transform a mundane situation into an absurd obsession, and simple problems are answered with the most drastic and grotesquely hyperbolic remedies. In "La carne," 1944 [Flesh] the citizens of a town suffering famine survive by consuming their own flesh; in "Unión indestructible," 1962 [Indestructible Union], a married couple remedy the lost physicality of their love by immersing themselves in a barrel of tar, and after a few hours in the hot noonday sun can hope to be united forever. In "La montaña," 1957 [The Mountain] a man's sole purpose in life is to remove a mountain – by devouring it. With the voice of rational reason left out, the languid grotesques of these stories can proceed with excesses that become the norm.

To date Piñera has been most widely regarded for his theatre, and is Cuba's principal exponent of the Theatre of the Absurd. Although this is primarily a European genre, it has often been pointed out that certain early works, such as *Falsa alarma* [False Alarm], with its sense of the ridiculous and the irrational, precede the better-known works of Ionesco. A late work is *Dos viejos pánicos* which is a good example of Piñera's absurdist theatre. Tota and Tabo are an old couple who behave like children, crying, squabbling and leaping from one subject to another. Each has a personal obsession. Tabo collects cuttings of young people in order to burn them, and in this symbolic destruction of youth hopes to ward off his own old age. Tota is tormented by thoughts of the lover she might have married, if not for Tabo. The obsession with old age leads to a greater anguish, the fear of Fear itself. They try to kill a personified Fear, but it escapes and returns to torment them. In aspects of its stage presentation and characterization, the play suggests the influence, without derivativeness, of Samuel Beckett's *Endgame*.

In art and life, Piñera was a rebel: in relative poverty for much of his life, anti-bookish to the point of possessing hardly any books, yet well-versed in French literature, and living a life dedicated to and redeemed by literature. Long out of favour with the Cuban authorities ("Casa de las Américas" reported his death with a cursory obituary), Piñera's obscurity was one that he himself seems to have promoted. Studies of his work often declare that he is little-known, but this perspective altered in the 1980s, and is set to change further in the 1990s, as Piñera receives increasing attention as a considerable, if not a major writer.

FRANK McQUADE

Biography

Born in Cárdenas, Matanzas, Cuba, 4 August 1912 (some sources give 1910). Family moved to Camagüey in 1925. Attended the University of Havana c.1932–37: his studies were interrupted during the dictatorship of Gerardo Machado; resumed studies in 1938, for a further two years. Founding editor of *Poeta*, 1941 (two issues only). Lived in Buenos Aires from 1946 to 1958. Worked as a clerk in the Cuban Consulate, and as a translator for the publishing house Argos. Co-editor, with José Rodríguez Feo, of the literary journal *Ciclón*, 1958. After the Cuban Revolution in 1959, he contributed to numerous journals and magazines, including *Casa de* las *Américas* and *Lunes de Revolución*. Director of the publishing company Ediciones R., 1960–64. Arrested for homosexual activity in 1961 and imprisoned briefly. Allowed to continue his work as a translator in the Instituto Cubano del Libro, but isolated from all other cultural activities. Thereafter, like Lezama Lima, fell out of favour with the authorities, with the result that his last years were of misery and poverty. Awarded the Casa de las Américas Prize for Theatre, 1968 for *Dos viejos pánicos*. Died in Havana, 18 October 1979.

Selected Works

Novels
La carne de René, Buenos Aires: Siglo XXI, 1952; as *René's Flesh*, translated by Mark Schafer, Boston: Eridanos Press, 1988
Pequeñas maniobras, Havana: UNEAC, 1963
Presiones y diamantes, Havana: Unión, 1967

Short Fiction
Cuentos fríos, Buenos Aires: Losada, 1956; as *Cold Tales*, translated by Mark Schafer, Hygiene: Colorado, Eridanos Press, 1988
El que vino a salvarme, Buenos Aires: Sudamericana, 1970
Muecas para escribientes, Havana: Letras Cubanas, 1987

Plays
Aire frío, Havana: Pagran, 1959; as *Cold Air*, translated and adapted by María Irene Fornes, New York: Theatre Communications Group, 1985
Dos viejos pánicos, Havana: Casa de las Américas, 1968
Una caja de zapatos vacía, edited by Luis F. González-Cruz, Barcelona: Universal, 1986

Poetry
Las furias, Havana: Espuela de Plata, 1942
La isla en peso, Havana: Espuela de Plata, 1943
Poesía y prosa, Havana: Serafín García, 1944
La vida entera, Havana: Ediciones R., 1960

Compilations and Anthologies
Teatro completo, Havana: Ediciones R., 1960
Teatro de la crueldad, Havana: Instituto del Libro, 1967
El teatro y su doble, Havana: Instituto del Libro, 1969
Teatro inconcluso, Havana: UNEAC, 1990

Further Reading

Aguilú de Murphy, Raquel, *Los textos dramáticos de Virgilio Piñera y el teatro del absurdo*, Madrid: Pliegos, 1989
García Chichester, Ana, "Superando el caos: estado actual de la crítica sobre la narrativa de Virgilio Piñera," *Revista Interamericana de Bibliografía*, vol. 43/1 (1992)
____ "Virgilio Piñera," in *Latin American Gay Literature: a Biographical and Critical Sourcebook*, edited by David William Foster, Westport, Connecticut: Greenwood Press, 1994
González-Cruz, Luis F., "Virgilio Piñera," in *Dictionary of 20th Century Cuban Literature*, edited by Julio A. Martínez, Westport, Connecticut: Greenwood Press, 1990
McQuade, Frank, "Making Sense out of Non-Sense: Virgilio Piñera and the Short Story of the Absurd," in *After Cervantes*, edited by John Macklin, Leeds: Iberian Papers, 1993
Quiroga, José, "Fleshing out Virgilio Piñera from the Cuban Closet," in *¿Entiendes? Queer Readings, Hispanic Writings*, edited by Emilie Bergmann and Paul Julian Smith, Durham, North Carolina: Duke University Press, 1995
Torres, Carmen L., *La cuentística de Virgilio Piñera: estrategias humorísticas*, Madrid: Pliegos, 1989

Nélida Piñón 1935–

Brazilian prose writer

Together with writers of the stature of Clarice Lispector and Lygia Fagundes Telles, Nélida Piñón has transcended the boundaries of her Brazilian literary culture. She is also one of the four women (up to the mid-1990s) to have been accorded the distinction of membership of the Brazilian Academy of Letters, to which she was admitted in 1989. Piñón has published some twenty works that include novels and short stories, most translated into several Western languages. She is an active traveller, who is called to participate in international symposia, sharing the limelight with the most prestigious Latin American intellectuals.

Piñón is viewed as a vanguard writer in Brazil; she has been breaking down traditional literary barriers in Portuguese narrative discourse through her practice in experimental writing. Her ethical and aesthetic concerns reflect her interest and participation in the theoretical debate about language and the unconscious. She believes writing involves denouncing realities that have not been disseminated, so that the act of reading is turned on its head and becomes an act of subversion. She responds hesitantly when asked whether she identifies herself as a feminist and/or is concerned with feminist writing. However, she has also expressed radical ideas about language: "We're just starting to impregnate language, but haven't done enough yet to have changed it. Just a "feminine sensibility" won't give us an identity."

Her first novel *Guia-mapa de Gabriel Arcanjo*, 1961 [Guide Map of Gabriel Arcanjo] as well as her first collection of short stories, *Tempo das frutas*, 1966 [Brief Fruit] are experimental in their search for an appropriate medium of female expression to counterbalance what she considers has been the fate of Brazilian women writers. In an interview entitled "The Contamination of Language" (1982), Piñón observes that she was not supposed to write or to have ideas of her own which deserved to be recorded. So she was ashamed of anything she might write. Thus, she acted as her own censor and was terribly afraid of opening her own mind, of knowing more than she was supposed to know, of saying more than she could say." Piñón's experience reflects the complexity of women's engagement in the task of creating a language and space in which women can express themselves.

In her fiction, Piñón carefully argues the case for supporting women's right to self-expression. One instance is *A casa da paixão*, 1972 [The House of Passion], where she constructs a defence for women to express their own sexuality, something that entails defying the cultural code from which she writes. In *A força do destino*, 1977 [The Force of Destiny] she draws on the well-known play by the Spanish Duque de Rivas, *Don Alvaro, o la fuerza del sino*, 1835 [Don Alvaro, or the Force of Destiny] to thematize the creative writing process. Her most acclaimed novel to date is *A república dos sonhos*, 1984 (*The Republic of Dreams*) successfully translated not only into English, but also into French and Spanish. It narrates a double story of the history of Brazil from the Getulio Vargas period (1930–45) to 1983, the end of a long period of military rule, with a family saga about Madruga, an immigrant from Galicia in northwest Spain. It is told from the perspective of the main character's wife as she lies dying. The title alludes to the hopes raised in the heart and mind of impoverished immigrants as they settle in Brazil. This novel contributed to establish Piñón as a gifted writer of historical fiction, a genre mostly cultivated by male writers in Brazil. The narrative device Piñón uses has suggested to critics a link between this work and William Faulkner's *As I Lay Dying*.

She considers the novel the genre that allows her the most suitable space for an extended reflection on societal concerns through the depiction of characters with a natural human dimension, as they struggle with the opposite forces of good and evil.

Her most recent novel is *A doce canção de Caetana*, 1987 (*Caetana's Sweet Song*). This is a complex allegorical work whose characters – a wealthy cattle baron, Polidoro Alves, and a decadent opera singer, Caetana Toledo – embark on an exploration of their passions and aspirations, like becoming Maria Callas for one day. Caetana fulfils her dream as a simulacrum: she cannot sing but will mime to Callas as Violetta. This novel, where the *mise-en-abyme* is displayed masterfully, can be interpreted as a symbolic representation of Brazilian society interrogated in the process of writing its own story. Although Piñón's literary production will continue for some time to come, her contribution to Brazilian-Portuguese literary language has already been acknowledged. She has stated that writing in Brazilian-Portuguese is to reveal Brazil in its inner make-up, an idea to which she has herself subscribed quite successfully.

MAGDALENA GARCÍA PINTO

Biography

Born in Rio de Janeiro, Brazil, 3 May 1936, of Galician parents. Attended a German secondary school; Faculty of Philosophy of the Pontifícia Universidade Católica, Rio de Janeiro. Taught at the Federal University of Rio de Janeiro, Columbia University, New York, Johns Hopkins University, Baltimore. Professor at University of Miami. Former vice-president, Brazilian Union of Writers. Awarded the Castelão Medal and the Galícia Medal. Elected to Ordem do Cruzeiro do Sul, and Lazo de Dama de Isabel La Católica. Member of the Brazilian Academy since 1989.

Selected Works

Novels

Guia-mapa de Gabriel Arcanjo, Rio de Janeiro: GRD, 1961
Madeira feita cruz, Rio de Janeiro: GRD, 1963
Fundador, Rio de Janeiro: José Álvaro, 1969
A casa da paixão, Rio de Janeiro: Mário de Andrade, 1972
Tebas do meu coração, Rio de Janeiro: José Olympio, 1974
A força do destino, Rio de Janeiro: Record, 1977
A república dos sonhos, Rio de Janeiro: Francisco Alves, 1984; as *The Republic of Dreams*, translated by Helen Lane, New York: Knopf, 1989; London: Picador, 1994
A doce canção de Caetana, Rio de Janeiro: Guanabara, 1987; as *Caetana's Sweet Song*, translated by Helen Lane, New York: Knopf, 1992

Short Fiction

Tempo das frutas, Rio de Janeiro: José Álvaro, 1966
Sala de armas, Rio de Janeiro: Sabiá, 1973
O calor das coisas, Rio de Janeiro: Nova Fronteira, 1980

Further Reading

Costa, Horácio, "A margem de *A república dos sonhos* de Nélida Piñón," *Luso-Brazilian Review*, vol. 24/1 (1987)
González-Tosar, Luis, "Nélida Piñón ou a paixon de contar," *Revista Galega de Cultura*, vol. 28/105 (1990)
McNab, Gregory, "Abordando a história em *A república dos sonhos*," *Brasil/Brazil: Revista de Literatura Brasileira* 1 (1988)
Nunes, Maria Luíza, "*A força do destino* by Nélida Piñón," *Revista Iberoamericana* 108–09 (January–December 1979)
Pontiero, Giovanni, "Note on the Fiction of Nélida Piñón," *Review*, vol. 76/19 (1976)
Spielmann, Ellen, "Um romance como espaço auto-reflexão literaria, Nélida Piñón: *A força do destino*," *Revista de Critica Literaria Latinoamericana*, vol. 15/30 (1989)
Vargas Llosa, Mario, "Presentación de un libro de Nélida Piñón," *Revista de Cultura Brasileña* 48 (January 1979)

Sergio Pitol 1933–

Mexican prose writer

Sergio Pitol, one of the most interesting Mexican writers to emerge in the period following Juan Rulfo and Carlos Fuentes, began to obtain international recognition when he was awarded the Premio Herralde de Novela in Barcelona in late 1984 for *El desfile del amor* [Love's Parade]. Here, this novel will be considered, along with *Domar a la divina garza*, 1988 [Taming the Divine Heron], which was published four years later, and *La vida conyugal*, 1991 [Married Life], a series of novels which their author has characterized as a parodic triptych. But it should be noted that Pitol was originally known in Mexico as a short story writer; his collection, *Vals de Mefisto* [The Waltz of Mephistopholes] was awarded the Villaurrutia prize for the best book of stories published in Mexico in 1982.

El desfile del amor – at one level a detective mystery – is an example of storytelling in which an event is presented from different perspectives. Miguel del Solar, the linking protagonist, is a Mexican historian on leave from an academic post in England. The setting is Mexico City in 1973, but what concerns Miguel took place in 1942 when Mexico joined the Allies and declared war on the Axis powers; a Mexico, then, which – not long after the advent of Sinarquismo and the nationalization of oil – was host to European refugees: Trotsky, Spanish Republicans, Jews, German Communists and – often in the guise of businessmen – Nazis. In the Minerva apartment block in which Miguel was then living (a building considered eccentric both architecturally and because of its inhabitants) a young, recently arrived Austrian is murdered during a party given by Delfina Uribe to tie in with the opening of a new Escobedo exhibition at her fashionable gallery. Miguel's investigations lead to a series of meetings; with Eduviges, an anti-regime aunt-in-law; with Emma Werfel, the hagiographic daughter of an émigrée Jewish writer assaulted during the same party; and several with Delfina, "una figura pública desde su juventud" (a public figure since her youth): three striking examples from Pitol's favourite regiment of extravagant female monsters. They – together with Balmoran, an unbalanced bookseller, and Escobedo – advance and withhold information and opinion about the murder and about the involvement therein of Eduviges's brother, Arnulfo Briones (himself a subsequent victim) and his bodyguard-secretary, the sinister Martínez. After his final meeting with Delfina, Miguel is convinced he commands all the facts about the Minerva mystery, but "su mirada no lograba penetrar un velo" (he was unable to see through a veil), reinforcing his earlier reference to Tirso de Molina's *La huerta de Juan Fernández* [Juan Fernandez's Garden] and Dickens's *Our Mutual Friend*, "donde nadie era quien decía ser" (where no one was whom he was said to be).

Domar a la divina garza is a short novel whose setting is contemporary Mexico, but whose action is mainly located in Istanbul twenty-five years earlier. Triggered by a reference to the Blue Mosque, Dante C. de la Estrella – a slightly mad, middle-aged lawyer – embarks on a meandering account of his meeting with Marietta Karepetiz, "una de las más grandes farsantes de la historia" (one of history's greatest humbugs),

the widow of an archaeologist whose work included a study of a mass open-air, quasi religious shitting ceremony during the Mexican Revolution. Her graphic account of their field trip – and Dante's ignominious and messy departure from Istanbul – form the book's dénouement. Dante's story is told so obliquely that his listeners complain that "Nadie sabía ya de qué hablaba" (nobody knew any longer what he was talking about), but his implacable – and scatological – discourse holds them (and the reader) in thrall. It is an often amusing and in some ways "novel" novel, skilfully employing language – obsessional, vituperative garrulity – to depict the self-deluded, duped Dante and his loathed/loved tormentor, Marietta. Both Marietta (reminders of Hilda Tablet and Tía Julia) and Dante (echoes of Vargas Llosa's scriptwriter, the narrator in Nabokov's *Pale Fire* and the Ancient Mariner) are worthy additions to the tribe of literary monsters. Undoubtedly a *tour de force*, it is an extremely "literary" book; its modish, irrelevant opening chapter could be taken as a "homage" to Calvino, and Gogol plays an integral part in the plot.

La vida conyugal has as its protagonist Jacqueline Cascorro (her own alternative to the hated María Magdalena she was christened), who is married to a generous but increasingly unfaithful husband, Nicolás Lobato. At first she unhappily accepts her lot, then "Todo cambió en un instante, cuando al quebrar con sus manos una pata de cangrejo y oir descorchar a sus espaldas una botella de champaña . . . convirtiéndola . . . en una mujer de muy malas ideas" (Everything changed in a flash when, while she was cracking a crab's claw in her fingers, she heard at her back the uncorking of a champagne bottle . . . transforming her . . . into a woman with very wicked ideas). She begins to fall madly in love with a series of disparate lovers (in the process heightening her conjugal ardour) and, misrepresenting her husband as a rich, mediocre brute, she persuades them to murder him so that they can elope with his money. But, like Buñuel's *La vida criminal de Archibaldo de la Cruz* (*The Criminal Life of Archibaldo de la Cruz*), this is a story of murder most fouled up. Her last affair – and last murder plot – with a depressive Italian art historian coincides with the collapse of Lobato's business affairs; he flirts and the professor and Jacqueline are accused of his murder. Years later, he returns incognito to Veracruz and, after a while Jacqueline learns of this and moves back into his life – still with murderous thoughts. A coda shows us an elderly Nicolás wheeling Jacqueline in a chair. The protagonist is another example of Pitol's extravagant characters, this time in the context of a parodic *novela rosa* (romantic novel).

Pitol might be called the most international of Mexican novelists, little concerned with either magic realism or Indian problems. This hint of a more Old World exoticism seems to suggest that, paradoxically, he might be better in tune with a Mexico that has recently become financially allied to the US and Canada than many of his more typically "Mexican" contemporaries. But he is aware of criticism: he lets another of his monstrous women – Billie Upward in *Juegos florales*, 1982 [Floral Games] – advise the narrator that "tenía que escribir sobre temas más mexicanos" (he should write about more Mexican subjects). And, writing an autobiographical essay almost twenty years earlier in Warsaw, Pitol had talked of trying to create a personal world, adding "Mi método de trabajo no me permite casi la menor invención. Tengo que conocer a los personajes, haber hablado con ellos para poder recrearlos" (My way of working barely allows me the slightest invention. I have to know the characters, to have spoken with them in order to be able to recreate them). Pitol's magic is in the recreation: he offers us bizarre but believable characters, whose contradictory visions and versions of their own and other people's pasts are comic, horrific and highly suspect.

ANTHONY EDKINS

Biography
Born in Puebla, Mexico, 18 March 1933. Studied law at the Universidad Nacional Autónoma de México (UNAM), Mexico City, 1950–55; also studied in Arts Faculty of that university. Taught at UNAM; University of Veracruz, Xalapa, 1966–77, and at University of Bristol, England, 1971–72. From 1960 worked also for Ministry of Foreign Relations and was cultural attaché in France, Poland, Hungary and USSR , 1975–80. Head of cultural affairs in Ministry of Foreign Relations, 1981. Head of International Affairs at the National Institute of Fine Arts, 1982; ambassador to Czechoslovakia, 1982–87. Has also worked for publishing houses, including Oasis, 1955–60, and Tusquets, 1969–70. Contributed to many leading cultural journals; editor of La Palabra y el Hombre. Literary translator from Polish and English. Awarded the Xavier Villaurrutia Prize, 1982; Herralde Prize for the Novel (Barcelona), 1984; Grand Prize of the European Cultural Association (Poland), 1987.

Selected Works

Novels
No hay tal lugar, Mexico City: Era, 1967
El tañido de una flauta, Mexico City: Era, 1972

Nocturno de Bujara, Mexico City: Siglo XXI, 1981
Cementerio de tordos, Mexico City: Océano, 1982
Juegos florales, Mexico City: Siglo XXI, 1982
El desfile del amor, Barcelona: Anagrama, 1984
Domar a la divina garza, Barcelona: Anagrama, 1988
La casa de la tribu, Mexico City: Fondo de Cultura Económica, 1989
Cuerpo presente, Mexico City: Era, 1990
La vida conyugal, Mexico City: Era, 1991
El relato veneciano de Billie Upward, Caracas: Monte Ávila, 1992

Short Fiction
Infierno de todos, Xalapa, Mexico: Universidad Veracruzana, 1965
Los climas, Mexico City: Joaquín Mortiz, 1966
Del encuentro nupcial, Barcelona: Tusquets, 1970
Vals de Mefisto, Barcelona: Anagrama, 1984

Other Writings
Sergio Pitol, prologue by Emmanuel Carballo, Mexico City: Empresas Editoriales, 1967 [In the series "Nuevos escritores mexicanos del siglo XX presentados por si mismos"]
De Jane Austen a Virginia Woolf: seis novelistas en sus textos, Mexico City: Secretaría de Educación, 1975
Juan Soriano: el perpetuo rebelde, Mexico City: Era, 1993

Compilations and Anthologies
Asimetría: antología personal, Mexico City: UNAM, 1980

Further Reading
Costa, Olga, Sergio Pitol, Guanajuato, Mexico: Gobierno del Estado de Guanajuato, 1983
Kristal, Efraín, "El rostro y la máscara: entrevista con Sergio Pitol," Revista Iberoamericana 141 (1987)
Rest, Monika von, "'Cuerpo presente': cuento existencialista de Sergio Pitol," Cuadernos Americanos 209 (1976)

Special Issues of Journals
Texto Crítico, Veracruz, 21 (1981) [Includes articles by Russell M. Cluff, Carlos Monsiváis and Juan García Ponce]

Alejandra Pizarnik 1936–1972

Argentine poet and prose writer

Alejandra Pizarnik is now one of the most acclaimed poets of her country, yet she achieved notoriety before fame as the result of her suicide in 1972. Pizarnik felt herself to be the perpetual outsider, possibly due in part to her belonging to a first generation of Argentine Jews who had emigrated from Eastern Europe. The feeling of not belonging became the dominant motif in her poetry. Her poetic style was greatly influenced by her study of painting, which added a very visual component. Pizarnik's poetry also shows the influence of the Surrealist poets, and her perception of the poetic was that it transcended the act of writing itself and became a permanent component of life.

Pizarnik's literary production is generally considered to consist of two facets. First the public persona that is evident in the texts published during her lifetime and, second, the private realm that became evident to her readers after her death when another edition of poetry was published as well as fragments from her diaries. In addition to her poetry, she published La condesa sangrienta [The Bloody Countess], which touches on both the author's public and private domains, and remains a text that has been difficult to classify.

Pizarnik's first book of poetry, La tierra más ajena [The Most Alien Land] is one that reveals much about the young poet and her influences. Her poetry at the time was very typical of that of the first half of the 20th century and focused on elements from daily life and the enumeration often common to Surrealist poetry.

La última inocencia [The Last Innocence] and *Las aventuras perdidas* [The Lost Adventures] both contain many examples of her personal motifs of death and night. The idea that poetry is an escape from the quotidian perils of civilization is prevalent in *La última inocencia*. Death in the text is both frightening and seductive. In *Las aventuras perdidas* childhood is seen as the only time of true innocence and happiness.

While Pizarnik lived in France, she produced three editions of poetry; *Árbol de Diana* [Diana's Tree], *Los trabajos y las noches* [Labours and Nights], and *Extracción de la piedra de locura* [Extraction of the Stone of Madness]. It was during this time that the poet became obsessed with the figure of Erzébet Báthory, a 15th-century Hungarian countess who was the subject of a book by the Surrealist Valentine Penrose. Pizarnik decided to write a book (*La condesa sangrienta*) concerning the enigmatic countess, and the text itself is probably one of the strangest in Argentine literature. It was first published in the Mexican journal *Diálogos* in 1965 and finally in book form in 1971.

Pizarnik's fascination with the countess has left many critics perplexed. Bárthory was infamous for torturing over 600 young women in sexual rituals that were associated with her desire for eternal youth. The gruesome ceremonies form the foundation of Pizarnik's text, vignettes concerning the various torture techniques of the countess. Pizarnik does not condemn the noblewoman's actions, but rather simply recognizes that society's concept of "civilized" versus "uncivilized" behaviour is arbitrary and that the countess's actions may be understood as the result of her simply wielding too much power.

In the first three sections of *La condesa sangrienta*, Pizarnik writes about the particular torture instruments used, such as "La virgen del hierro" [The Iron Virgin], "Muerte por agua" [Death by Water] and "La jaula mortal" [The Lethal Cage]. All three of the particular tools allow the countess to fulfil her sexual and sadistic fantasies. The descriptions are provided in the present tense and with much attention to detail. For example, the countess's habit of wearing white (suggesting innocence and virginity) is mentioned as well as the clothing's transformation as the blood begins to soak the fabric during the torture session. The descriptions are highly lyrical, almost poetic. In the fourth vignette, Pizarnik begins to deviate from mere description to provide commentary on the motivations of the countess. In "El espejo de la malancolía" [The Mirror of Melancholy] Pizarnik makes reference to the Countess's possible lesbian persona. Throughout the text, there is an odd conjugation of positive and negative elements that provide rather jolting contrasts. There is also a voyeuristic dimension to the text, where the countess is portrayed as the ultimate voyeur, observing, contemplating the scene and inviting the reader to do the same. The final passage of the text is a meditation on the ramifications of the possession of unlimited power. *La condesa sangrienta* emerges as a disturbingly beautiful depiction of sexuality and death. It is a highly enigmatic work, and the one which has received most critical attention.

Pizarnik's last collection of poems, *El infierno musical* [The Musical Hell], was published in 1971. In addition to poetry, Pizarnik also wrote many reviews, short stories, poems, and a theatrical piece entitled *Los poseídos entre lilas* [The Possessed among Lilacs]. The final writings of the poet were compiled in *Textos de sombra y últimos poemas* [Texts of Shadow and Last Poems] by Olga Orozco and Ana Becciú in 1982. As Daniel Altamiranda contends, the fact that these are poems that Pizarnik had decided not to publish renders their publication problematic. One must take into account that these texts may not have been considered finished by the poet or at least ready to be submitted for publication, in which case it would seem unfair to subject them to the same sort of rigorous analysis that her other poetry has received. None the less, there are some thematic issues raised in the poetry that are interesting to comment on such as lesbian rape presented in "Violario."

Pizarnik continues to be one of the most discussed Argentine poets of the last thirty years and her death, if in fact it did not initiate her rise in popularity, at least contributed to making her an almost mythical figure in the realm of Argentine letters.

MELISSA A. LOCKHART

Biography

Born Flora Alejandra Pizarnik in Avellaneda, Buenos Aires, Argentina, 16 April 1936. Descended from East European immigrants. Studied in Faculty of Arts at the University of Buenos Aires and also painting with Juan Battle Planas. Lived in Paris, 1960–64. Studied French literature at the Sorbonne and translated a number of French works into Spanish. Returned to Buenos Aires and worked for *Cuadernos* (1964–68). Awarded the Buenos Aires First Prize for Poetry in 1966 and received a Guggenheim Fellowship, 1969. Two years later, in 1971, she received a Fulbright Award. Suffered recurring bouts of depression, and during a weekend leave from a psychiatric clinic in Buenos Aires, she took her life with an overdose of seconal. Died on 26 September 1972.

Selected Works

Mixed Genre
La condesa sangrienta, Buenos Aires: López Crespo, 1971

Poetry
La tierra más ajena, Buenos Aires: Botella al Mar, 1955
Árbol de Diana, Buenos Aires: Sur, 1962
Los trabajos y la noches, Buenos Aires: Sudamericana, 1965
Extracción de la piedra de locura, Buenos Aires: Sudamericana, 1968
Nombres y figuras, Barcelona: La Esquina, 1969
El infierno musical, Buenos Aires: Siglo XXI, 1971
Los pequeños cantos, Caracas: Árbol de Fuego, 1971
El deseo de la palabra, Barcelona: Seix Barral, 1975
La última inocencia y Las aventuras perdidas, Buenos Aires: Botella al Mar, 1976
Poemas, Buenos Aires: Centro Editor de América Latina, 1982

Compilations and Anthologies
Textos de sombra y últimos poemas, edited by Olga Orozco and Ana Becciú, Buenos Aires: Sudamericana, 1982
Obras completas. Poesía completa y prosa selecta, Buenos Aires: Corregidor, 1993

Further Reading
Altamiranda, Daniel, "Alejandra Pizarnik," in *Latin American Writers on Gay and Lesbian Themes*, edited by David William Foster, Westport, Connecticut: Greenwood Press, 1994

Bassnett, Susan, "Speaking With Many Voices: the Poems of Alejandra Pizarnik," in *Knives and Angels: Women Writers in Latin America*, edited by Bassnett, London: Zed Books, 1990

DiAntonio, Robert E., "On Seeing Things Darkly in the Poetry of Alejandra Pizarnik: Confessional Poetics or Aesthetic Metaphor?" *Confluencia* 2 (1987)

Foster, David William, *Gay and Lesbian Themes in Latin American Writing*, Austin: University of Texas Press, 1991

____ "Of Power and Virgins: Alejandra Pizarnik's *La condesa sangrienta*," in *Violence in Argentine Literature: Cultural Responses to Tyranny*, Columbia: University of Missouri Press, 1995

Goldberg, Florinda F., *Alejandra Pizarnik: "Este espacio que somos,"* Gaithersburg, Maryland: Hispamérica, 1994

Piña, Cristina, *La palabra como destino. Un acercamiento a la poesía de Alejandra Pizarnik*, Buenos Aires: Botella al Mar, 1981

____ *Alejandra Pizarnik*, Buenos Aires: Planeta, 1991

Running, Thorpe, "The Poetry of Alejandra Pizarnik," *Chasqui*, vol. 14/2–3 (1985)

Plural

See Journals

Poma de Ayala, Felipe Guaman

See Guaman Poma de Ayala

Punto de Vista

See Journals

Elena Poniatowska 1933–

Mexican prose writer

Elena Poniatowska has produced two of the most commented on icons of testimonial writing in Latin American literature: *Hasta no verte, Jesús mío* (*Until We Meet Again*), 1969, and *La noche de Tlatelolco: testimonios de historia oral*, 1971 (*Massacre in Mexico*). In both of these texts, which could not be more different from each other, she has used her journalistic training and instincts to the utmost. Yet she has been careful to avoid the common pitfall of like writers who tend to confuse journalism with literature. Poniatowska pioneered "new journalism" in Mexico, together with Carlos Monsiváis; but her literary works are significantly more complex than her journalistic pieces. In her literary creation, Poniatowska daringly explores the margins between fiction and the testimonial, documentary, and autobiographic types of writing; rather hybrid and experimental texts are her trademark.

In 1962, Poniatowska briefly assisted the anthropologist Oscar Lewis, one of the founders of testimonial writing, in editing one of his works focusing on the "culture of poverty." Soon afterwards, she put the lesson into practice when she got acquainted with the folksy and feisty Josefina Bórquez (1900–88), who became the Jesusa in *Hasta no verte, Jesús mío* (in Mexico, the bar call "Bottoms up!"). However, half a decade would pass before the text would be ready for print. Poniatowska avoided another pitfall of testimonial writing, besides the mentioned journalistic slant, namely the temptation of a quick score. First, she took her time to know the subject well and to break the natural barriers between two strangers, magnified by the difference in their social upbringing. In the process, Josefina ceased to be a "subject"; the professional relation between the two women became a life-long friendship and even a kind of a surrogate mother-daughter relationship. Secondly, Poniatowska put a lot of thought and creative effort into the elaboration of the log of interviews into a meaningful whole. *Hasta no verte* is a work of love and art, and it shows.

Josefina became Jesusa in a playful allusion to her conversion to a "spiritualist" sect; the title then plays with her new name and also touches on one period of her life dominated by alcohol. This game of literarization and the layers of fictionalization turn raw testimony into a testimonial novel. Poniatowska does not assert artistic freedom for freedom's sake; she uses it to free Jesusa from the superfluous and repetitive elements, in order to bring forward her essentials with greater force and artistic impact. Paradoxically, the fictionalization does not cut into the authentic voice of Jesusa. It amplifies rather her "representativity," though not in the sense the orthodox Marxist model of representativeness would have it. *Hasta no verte* falls back rather on the Spanish picaresque tradition. What sets Poniatowska's work apart from so-called "testimonial writing" is, then, not so much the artistic elaboration as the fact that she shuns prefabricated allegorical and political metanarratives. While the strict theoreticians of the testimonial genre (such as Barnet or Randall) might doubt her political "usefulness," Poniatowska realized that the image of a "strong woman," breaking every traditional stereotype, as seen against the backdrop of half a century of Mexican history, did not need any additional explanations and dissertations on womanhood, patriarchy and class struggle. Poniatowska's brand of implicit yet unequivocal feminism and political stance makes for an even stronger work of art.

The testimonies of oral history, *La noche de Tlatelolco*, rely more heavily on the journalistic work. Poniatowska showed a lot of character just by taking up the story, and she was to defy the powerful Mexican establishment several times more over this issue. In the wake of Olympic Games, the Mexican Government decided to stop the months-long student protest movement and teach the protesters a lesson; on 2 October 1968, the peaceful manifestation on Tlatelolco square ended in a massacre of students, women and children, participants as well as bystanders. The Government engaged in a massive cover-up; detentions, tortures and imprisonments followed. Poniatowska set out to provide a testimony of the student movement and the fateful evening when the unthinkable happened there, where spectators from all over the world gathered for the other spectacle.

A number of unorthodox features of *La noche* strike the reader. First, Poniatowska does not present a casebook of complete interviews and printed materials, but mixes them up in a fragmentary, polyphonic, and dialogic flow of markedly heterogeneous voices. The first part follows the course of the student movement and its consequences after the massacre; the second part concentrates on what happened at Tlatelolco. Secondly, Poniatowska surprises by the variety of testimonies she presents; as if following the Paris May (when students and workers challenged the authority of the French government), they range from slogans, graffiti, impressive one-liners, and personal accounts, to the satire, the carnivalesque and the absurd. Poniatowska does not hesitate to show the political naivete, shortcomings, and even the absurdities of the movement. Thirdly, Poniatowska not only includes samples of the protest literature generated by Tlatelolco in her testimony, but she pointedly incorporates the protest literature of other times (the conquest, Martí, Rulfo), highlighting the continuity of like phenomena throughout Mexican and Latin American history. Once again, Poniatowska manages to turn testimony into a first-rate work of art, without diminishing its factual value.

The experimental technique of the collage of heterogeneous elements, similar to Cortázar's *Rayuela* (*Hopscotch*), produces a strikingly voluble narrative flow, where points of view and counterpoints clash in hidden and open polemics. This dialogic technique, combined with the image of the student movement as seen from the street (avoiding conspicuously the high profile leaders), blunts to a great degree the movement's ideological thrust and widens the gap between the people's testimony and the Government's perspective. Although Poniatowska strives to efface herself from her narrative, *La noche* leaves no doubt about her allegiance and the firm hand with which she selects and arranges the information. When the book was awarded the prestigious Xavier Villaurrutia Prize, Poniatowska refused to accept this elegant cover-up in the name of the dead students. *La noche* has become one of the most widely-read books in Mexico; frequently, other writers have appropriated parts of it as a token of the Tlatelolco reality in their own texts.

In the novella *Querido Diego, te abraza Quiela*, 1978 (*Dear Diego*), Poniatowska has widened the margin for fiction and has further fictionalized one chapter of the already "fabulous life" of the Mexican painter Diego Rivera. Poniatowska relies especially on Bertram Wolfe's biography and, beginning with fragments of a letter from Angelina Beloff (Rivera's Russian wife) reprinted there, she "reconstructs" Angelina's (unanswered) correspondence to Diego after his return to Mexico in 1921. It is interesting to see how the unreliable aspects of Wolfe's biography add another layer of fiction to fiction. Poniatowska plays on the edge of reality and fiction, producing a powerful story of love, desire and abandonment. Or is it an indictment of the Latin male culture?

In the 1980s, Poniatowska returned to journalism. *Fuerte es el silencio*, 1980 [Strong is the Silence], is another defiant volume of political investigative reporting, uncomfortable for any "institutional revolutionary party." The testimony on the 1985 earthquake that wreaked havoc on Mexico City, *Nada, nadie: las voces del temblor*, 1988 (*Nothing, Nobody: the Voices of the Mexico City Earthquake*), was worked out in Poniatowska's writers' workshop, but could not match the impact of *La noche*.

Poniatowska's novel *La "Flor de Lís,"* 1988 [The "Flor de Lis"], is a slightly fictionalized autobiography. As such it is an important document about the human formation of this extraordinary writer, who from the heights of international elites has reached so deep into the Mexico's soul and has shown so much courage in face of the owerwhelming powers-that-be. The novel *Tinísima*, 1992, is Poniatowska's most ambitious literary work of the last decade. This half-documentary and half-fictional biographic novel about the Italian-American photographer and international revolutionary Tina Modotti evokes with compassion the "heroic years" of Mexican and international communism between the 1920s and the 1940s. *Tinísima* is a metaphor of so many human beings trapped in the treacherous historical and ideological torrents of our times.

EMIL VOLEK

Biography

Born in Paris, 19 May 1933. Family returned to Mexico in 1942. Attended the Liceo de México for one year; Convent of the Sacred Heart's Eden Hall, Torresdale, Pennsylvania, for two years; Manhattanville College, Bronx, New York. Married Guillermo Haro (died in 1988); two sons and one daughter. Journalist for *Excelsior*, 1954–55, and *Novedades*, Mexico City, since 1955. Member of editorial board of the feminist journal, *Fem*. Co-founder, Editorial Siglo XXI, Cineteca Nacional (Mexican film archive). Awards include the Centro de Escritores Fellowship, 1957; Mazatlán Prize, 1970; Xavier Villaurrutia Prize, 1970 (refused); *Revista Siempre* Prize, 1973; National Journalism Prize, 1979.

Selected Works

Novels

Hasta no verte, Jesús mío, Mexico City: Era, 1969; as *Until We Meet Again*, translated by Magda Bogin, New York: Pantheon, 1987

Querido Diego, te abraza Quiela, Mexico City: Era, 1978; as *Dear Diego*, translated by Katherine Silver, New York: Pantheon, 1986
La "Flor de Lís," Mexico City: Era, 1988
Tinísima, Mexico City: Era, 1992; as *Tinísima*, translated by Katherine Silver, New York: Farrar Straus and Giroux, 1996

Short Fiction

Lilus Kikus, Mexico City: Los Presentes, 1954
Los cuentos de Lilus Kikus, Xalapa, Mexico: Universidad Veracruzana, 1967
De noche vienes, Mexico City: Grijalbo, 1979

Testimonial and Other Writings

Palabras cruzadas: crónicas, Mexico City: Era, 1961
Todo empezó el domingo, Mexico City: Fondo de Cultura Económica, 1963
México visto a ojo de pájaro, Mexico City: Colibrí/SEP, 1968
La noche de Tlatelolco: testimonios de historia oral, Mexico City: Era, 1971; as *Massacre in Mexico*, translated by Helen Lane, New York: Viking Press, 1975
La vendedora de nubes, Mexico City: Colibrí, 1979
Gaby Brimmer, in collaboration with Gaby Brimmer, Mexico City: Grijalbo, 1979
Fuerte es el silencio, Mexico City: Era, 1980
La casa en la tierra, photographs by Mariana Yampolsky, Mexico City: INI-Fonapas, 1980
Domingo siete, Mexico City: Océano, 1982
El último guajolote, Mexico City: Fondo de Cultura Económica, 1982
¡Ay vida, no me mereces!: Carlos Fuentes, Rosario Castellanos, Juan Rulfo, la literatura de la Onda, Mexico City: Joaquín Mortiz, 1985
La raíz y el camino, illustrations by Mariana Yampolsky, Mexico City: Fondo de Cultura Económica, 1985
Estancias del olvido, photographs by Marian Yampolsky, Mexico City: INI-Centro Hidalguense de Investigaciones Históricas, 1986
Serena y alta figura, Mexico City: Océano, 1986
Tlacotalpan, photographs by Marian Yampolsky, Mexico City: Fondo de Cultura Económica, 1987
Hablando en plata, in collaboration with David Maawad, Mexico City: Centro Hidalguense de Investigaciones Históricas, 1987
México sin retoque, in collaboration with Héctor García, Mexico City: UNAM, 1987
Nada, nadie: las voces del temblor, Mexico City: Era, 1988; as *Nothing, Nobody: the Voices of the Mexico City Earthquake*, translated by Aurora Camacho de Schmidt and Arthur Schmidt, Philadelphia: Temple University Press, 1995
Juchitán de las mujeres, in collaboration with Graciela Iturbide, Mexico City: Toledo, 1989
Compañeras de México, Riverside: University of California, 1990
Todo México, 2 vols, Mexico City: Diana, 1990–93
Manuel Álvarez Bravo: el artista, su obra, sus tiempos, Mexico City: Banco Nacional de México, 1991
Frida Kahlo: la cámara seducida, photographs by Ansel Adams, Mexico City: La Vaca Independiente, 1992; as *Frida Kahlo: the Camera Seduced*, San Francisco Chronicle Books, and London: Chatto and Windus, 1992
Luz y luna: las lunitas, photographs by Graciela Iturbide, Mexico City: Era, 1994

Further Reading

Chevigny, Bell Gale, "The Transformation of Privilege in the Work of Elena Poniatowska," in *Latin American Literary Review*, vol. 13/26 (1985)
Jörgensen, Beth E., *The Writing of Elena Poniatowska: Engaging Dialogues*, Austin: University of Texas Press, 1994
Poniatowska, Elena, "*Hasta no verte, Jesús mío*," *Vuelta* 24 (1978)

____ "La muerte de Jesusa Palancares," in *La historia en la literatura iberoamericana*, edited by Raquel Chang-Rodríguez and Gabriella de Beer, Hanover, New Hampshire: Ediciones del Norte, 1989

Scott, Nina M., "The Fragmented Narrative Voice of Elena Poniatowska, *Discurso Literario*, vol. 7/2 (1990)

Starčević, Elizabeth D., "Breaking the Silence: Elena Poniatowska: Writer in Transition," in *Literatures in Transition: the Many Voices of the Caribbean Area: a Symposium*, edited by Rose S. Minc, Gaithersburg, Maryland: Hispamérica, 1982

Steele, Cynthia, "La creatividad y el deseo en *Querido Diego, te abraza Quiela*, de Elena Poniatowska," *Hispamérica* 41 (1985)

____ "Testimonio y autor/idad en *Hasta no verte, Jesús mío*, de Elena Poniatowska," in *Politics, Gender, and the Mexican Novel, 1968–1988*, Austin: University of Texas Press, 1992

Interviews

García Pinto, Magdalena, *Women Writer of Latin America: Intimate Histories*, Austin: University of Texas Press, 1991 [See chapter 7]

Hasta no verte Jesús mío

Testimonial text by Elena Poniatowska

Hasta no verte Jesús mío (1969) had to wait until the 1980s before receiving critical attention outside of Mexico. The increasing recognition of the work appears to be due to recent developments in feminist criticism in the field of Latin American literature and to a growing interest in more testimonial forms of literature based on oral histories of marginalised members of society. The text takes the form of a first-person narrative and is based on a series of interviews Elena Poniatowska conducted with a poor Mexican woman, Josefina Bórquez (1900–87), who at the time was working as a washerwoman in Mexico City. Poniatowska was attracted by Bórquez's outspokenness and her deviance from the standards expected of Mexican women. However, the text has been seen as much novel as *testimonio*, and despite its oral quality, its reliance on a real informant and its deep roots in the material reality on which testimonies depend, it is clear that *Hasta no verte, Jesús mío* has undergone much authorial mediation. Josefina Bórquez is transformed into a literary character, Jesusa Palancares, and novelistic strategies are used, such as the organisation of events in the protagonist's life into chapters which follow a broadly chronological time sequence and focus on key episodes. In a number of interviews Poniatowska has said that she has edited and embroidered her interviewee's words as well as inventing parts of the narrative.

As much has been written in the critical literature on this work about the processes of production and the extent of fictionalisation as on the content of the narrative. The debates raise some fascinating questions as to the relationship between fiction and reality, and the ethics of attempting to give voice to a less privileged Other, while altering that voice and finally claiming some form of authorship over it. While these critical debates shed much light on the relationship between fiction and "testimonio," and ask many thought-provoking questions, they do not address the reasons behind the power or the success of the novel, as they are issues which only emerge once the reader engages with the critical literature. The reader who approaches the text blindly need never know that the protagonist has any form of relationship with a non-literary "real" woman. Another strand of critical work has, thus, paid less attention to the relationship between privileged writer and marginalised interviewee, preferring to examine Jesusa as a character, a picaresque literary creation.

The major reason behind the appeal of the text is the fact that Jesusa is such a successful literary figure, whose use of vernacular Mexican Spanish makes her entirely believable. The question as to her literal existence for the reader who approaches the text as a work of fiction is not of great consequence as she expresses social, economic and poetic truths, and her words provide highly entertaining reading material. The first person narrator jumps out from the text, grabs the reader and demands attention. She has total conviction in her beliefs which are often contradictory and idiosyncratic. Jesusa Palancares makes a dramatic entrance onto the stage of characters in Latin American literature: her language has a freshness and a vitality absent in more traditional "literary" texts and her narrative, packed with anecdotes of a life full of adventure, has a fast-moving, oral quality which makes for entertaining reading.

Jesusa takes her listener through the key events and experiences of her life: from her early memories of her mother's death and her childhood with her father and her brothers and sister; her troubled relationships with a series of stepmothers; her adventures while following her father, and later her violent husband in the Mexican Revolution as a young woman, through to her experiences in Mexico City in a variety of jobs and often make do homes, and her involvement with the Spiritist Church. She provides a full commentary on all these experiences, revealing belief systems stemming from popular wisdom, popular prejudices and church dogma. The result is a rich often contradictory and always interesting word stream.

Jesusa Palancares is, then, a dynamic woman who refuses any easy attempts at categorisation. Not only does she, as Joel Hancock observed in an article of 1983, "deviate radically from the commonly portrayed stereotypes of women," she also defies the traditional representations of Mexican women. She is neither virgin (Guadalupe), nor whore, temptress, traitor, or *la Chingada* (Malinche), that is, the passive, raped victim. Most importantly, she does not depend on men for her identity, and after a brief and disastrous marriage remains single and self-sufficient. She is a curious mixture of both rebel and conformist: while she frequently challenges the official discourses of the Revolution, the institutionalisation of the Revolution, the Catholic Church and many conventions of gender relations and gender roles, at the same time she is steeped in the popular discourses of her culture. Thus, while she clearly takes pride in her rebelliousness against male attempts to dominate and use violence against her, she feels that this rebellion makes her evil; likewise she expresses prejudices against women, blaming them for men's need to exercise their power. She also shows that she has internalised racist notions of identity and looks down on her sister as she "salió más indita que yo" (turned out more of an Indian than me).

Jesusa is neither symbol nor metaphor nor archetype: she does not represent her gender or her class. Rather, she actively engages with her various labels, Mexican, woman, poor, and with the social and historical circumstances of her life, and finds her own strategies to survive both materially and emotionally. Thus, over her life she takes a range of jobs, from servant, to factory worker, to waitress, always moving on when she feels she is being over-exploited or when she feels her freedom is being curtailed. She has a number of close relationships with men, women and children and picks herself up with a greater armoury of defences when others let her down. Even *La Obra Espiritual*, the Spiritist Church, which she turns to for a dependable belief system and in order to have a sense of self worth, is abandoned when she feels she is not respected by other church members with lesser powers than hers, although she retains her beliefs which are all she has to help make sense of her reality. Jesusa Palancares is, then, an extraordinary woman. She refuses the expected roles of passive victim and fights those who try to place her within that role, on a number of occasions physically beating up men who attempt to coerce her into submission. Proud, fiery, confrontational and contradictory, she has the status of a great literary figure.

Despite the fact that Jesusa cannot be taken as representative of either her gender or her class, the texts provides many insights into conditions of life in Mexican society for poor, working class women. The hardships she faces and many of the circumstances in which she finds herself serve to convert the text into a valuable social document. These aspects provide the testimonial elements of the text for, relying on experience, Jesusa bears witness and exposes the failings of revolutionary and post-revolutionary Mexico. The reader learns about the poor conditions of employment for illiterate women with no alternative income, the abuses committed by middle and upper-class women against their servants, the violence committed by men against women, and the complete lack of any state support for all, even for those who, like Jesusa, are widows of fighters in the Revolution.

Jesusa's story offers a contradiction to official state discourses which claimed that the urban proletariat would become valued citizens in the new post-revolutionary Mexico. Jesusa's much quoted words when assessing her own place in her society, instantly negate years of state rhetoric:

Al fin de cuentas, yo no tengo patria . . . No me siento mexicana ni reconozco a los mexicanos. Aquí no existe más que pura conveniencia y puro interés. Si yo tuviera dinero y bienes, sería mexicana, pero como soy peor que la basura, pues no soy nada . . .

[When all's said and done I've got no country . . . I don't feel Mexican and I don't recognise the Mexicans. Here, there's nothing more than greed and self-interest. If I had money and possessions I'd be Mexican, but as I'm worse than garbage, I'm nothing at all . . .]

Elena Poniatowska effectively challenges dominant discourses by transmitting the voice of a woman whom most readers of Latin American literature would have no access to. The text provides an example of how literature can produce counter discourses and illustrate the value of those who are normally rendered invisible by a nation which is often deeply uncomfortable with its own people.

DEBORAH A. SHAW

Editions

First edition: *Hasta no verte, Jesús mío*, Mexico City: Era, 1969
Translation: *Until We Meet Again*, by Magda Bogin, New York: Pantheon, 1987

Further Reading

Friedman, Edward H., "The Marginated Narrator: *Hasta no verte, Jesús mío* and the Eloquence of Repression," in his *The Antiheroine's Voice: Narrative Discourse and Transformations of the Picaresque*, Columbia: University of Missouri Press, 1987

Kerr, Lucille, "Gestures of Authorship: Lying to Tell the Truth in Elena Poniatowska's *Hasta no verte, Jesús mío*," in her *Reclaiming the Author: Figures and Fictions from Spanish America*, Durham, North Carolina: Duke University Press, 1992

Kushigian, Julia A., "Transgresión de la autobiografía y el Bildungsroman en *Hasta no verte, Jesús mío*," *Revista Iberoamericana*, vol. 53/140 (July–September 1987)

Popular Culture

Brazil

In Brazil, popular culture takes many forms and may be divided into two areas: that which has its roots in the folklore of the country and often in the rural areas, versus that which is primarily the product of technology, disseminated through the mass media and generally originating in urban areas. The manifestations of popular culture that form part of the first category are *cordel* literature, poetic duels, forms of dance,

music and religious expression. In the second category one finds such elements as the ever popular soap operas, films, and sports. That is not to say that the two forms do not mingle on occasion, in fact they often have. However, this essay will be dedicated primarily to the cultural expressions of Brazilian folklore.

Cordel literature (stories on a string) refers to the popular poetry written primarily in the northeast of the country and sold on the streets, in marketplaces and town squares. The literature began to be written in the late 1800s and reached its peak in the 1940s, 1950s and 1960s. The poetry is extremely picturesque and provides a sort of running commentary on Brazilian life and customs. In the past, before television and radio, the *cordel* served also as a way for the many members of the population to receive news. It continues to serve as a forum for the views of the masses, generally the poor who comprise a very large percentage of the country's population.

The term *cordel* refers to the cord on which the early poets would hang their compositions in order to sell them. More recently, however, the poets carry their wares in a suitcase and set up shop in a busy town center, often in a market. The various pamphlets, each containing a separate poem, are spread out on the suitcase which rests on a stand. The poets will then recite their verses, but sometimes stop at the climax of the story as an incentive for their listeners to buy the poem. The mark of an excellent *cordel* poem is that which remains a crowd-pleaser in spite of the many times the listeners may have heard or read it.

The poems themselves would be printed on coarse paper and would normally carry on the front an illustration of the topic. This illustration has become a popular art form in its own right, the *xilogravura* or design created by a woodcut. *Xilogravuras* have begun to be sold and collected apart from the *cordel* and artists of this kind have also become widely known.

Cordel poetry retains many oral characteristics. It was originally composed primarily in the country's northeast, an area of seven states where roughly between a quarter to a third of the country's population resides. However, as the result of an extreme drought in the northeast at the turn of the century there was a massive migration to the urban areas of the south. The building of the capital of Brasília in the late 1950s led to yet another migration towards that region. Thus, *cordel* literature may now be found in all the above mentioned areas.

The topics covered in the *cordel* range from Brazilianized renderings of the most standard of fairy tales to commentaries on the socio-political situation of the day. The themes revolve around the plight of the poor, the bandit heroes of the backlands, local religious figures, and fables. The poems generally are didactic in nature, emphasizing the need for bravery or sound ethical decisions in life.

Although the literature of the *cordel* is one born of humble origins it has exerted an influence on many other more mainstream cultural manifestations such as established literature, theater and film. Many authors, for example, Jorge Amado, have used themes from the *cordel* in their novels. In a quest to portray an authentic national identity, cinematographers have often incorporated *cordel*-related themes into their films. Glauber Rocha's *Deus e o diabo na terra do sol* [God and the Devil in the Land of the Sun] and *Antônio das mortes* [Anthony of the Deaths] are examples of this appropriation.

There are many other forms of popular culture in Brazil such as the poetic duel, which is still practiced in the northeast. The duel is normally practiced in a public place, often a bar or a square, and the two poets take turns to insult and challenge one another using complex rhyme and rhythm schemes. The winner of the duel is the poet who has demonstrated the greatest mental agility as well as a command of the rigid rules of meter necessary for the immediate composition of verse.

Popular music is an area of culture that seems to straddle the boundary between rural cultural manifestations and those that have been produced and disseminated through the mass media. Popular music in Brazil reflects the country's diverse heritage; its indigenous, black and Portuguese traditions. Probably the most famous of the genres that have evolved is *samba*, a dance and music form most often associated with the internationally known celebration of *carnaval* or Mardi Gras. An outgrowth of classical samba is the *bossa nova*, an urban musical genre that became popular throughout the world in the early 1960s.

One final aspect of Brazilian popular culture to be discussed is that of the African-Brazilian religions, often seen to be versions of popular Catholicism. African-Brazilian religions are a combination of African, Catholic, and indigenous components. These practices date from the early 1700s and generally involved the adoration of black saints. While the adoration of these figures was initially something imposed by the slave-owners as a step towards conditioning the slaves into subservience, it became a vehicle for their solidarity and an outlet for their concerns about social justice. Candomblé and Umbanda have been the groups most studied by researchers. Umbanda, in particular, emphasizes the spirits of the dead and their ability to take possession of a living being. It is estimated that some twenty to thirty per cent of all Brazilians are involved in some sort of religious practice of African origin, and yet most would also consider themselves to be Catholics and, as the result of syncretic practices, see no discrepancy between the two.

MELISSA A. LOCKHART

Further Reading

Alvarenga, Oneyda, *Música popular brasileira*, 2nd edition, São Paulo: Duas Cidades, 1982

Bastide, Roger, *The African Religions of Brazil: toward a Sociology of the Interpenetration of Civilizations*, translated by Helen Sebba, Baltimore: Johns Hopkins University Press, 1978

Bruneau, Thomas, *The Church in Brazil, the Politics of Religion*, Austin: University of Texas Press, 1982

Curran, Mark J., *Jorge Amado e a literatura de cordel*, Salvador de Bahia: Fundação Cultural do Estado da Bahia-Fundação Casa de Rui Barbosa, 1981

_____ *A presença de Rodolfo Coelho Cavalcante na moderna literatura de cordel*, Rio de Janeiro: Nova Fronteira-Fundação Casa de Rui Barbosa, 1987

De Kadt, Emanuel, "Religion, the Church and Social Change in Brazil," in *The Politics of Conformity in Latin America*, edited by Claudio Veliz, London: Oxford University Press, 1967

Hinds Jr, Harold E. and Charles M. Tatum (editors), *Handbook of Latin American Popular Culture*, Westport, Connecticut: Greenwood Press, 1985

Proença, Manuel Cavalcanti (editor), *Antologia: literatura popular em verso*, Belo Horizonte: Itatiaia; São Paulo: Editora Universidade de São Paulo; Rio de Janeiro: Fundação Rui Barbosa, 1986

Slater, Candace, *Stories on a String: the Brazilian Literature of the Cordel*, Berkeley, University of California Press, 1982

Young, Augustus (editor), *Lampion and His Bandits: the Literature of Cordel in Brazil*, London: Menard Press, 1995

Spanish America

Popular culture is a process whereby the historic experience is shaped in the collective memory. Popular culture and its written counterpart in literature are derived principally from two sources: first, traditional elements which have been handed down from generation to generation and still have the power to excite the imagination of the contemporary society, and second, new elements which are constantly being invented and introduced in the daily lives of the masses. The massive production of *criollista* (creolist) texts in Argentina between the late 19th and early 20th centuries served a public, either in transition between the country and the city, or who had recently entered Argentina as immigrants. Popular urban *criollista* literature with its narratives of traditional rural types like the gaucho offered an identity and a way of negotiating the transition. Of all the rich traditions in Latin American rural popular culture, one of the most important is the poetry written by the peasantry, paradoxically defined as "oral literature." Related to it, yet constituting a different genre of its own, is the poetry of the *cantadores* (traveling singers). Both forms stem from a common European medieval and, to a lesser extent, Indian and African oral tradition which goes back to a multiplicity of sources: popular stories, myths and legends, medieval romances, and Iberian picaresque narrative. Such poetic forms contain epic, satirical, burlesque and fantastic elements, moral counsel, religious teachings and abundant critical commentary on everyday life and on historical and current events. The literary form that evolved into the *payadas* of the Argentine and Uruguayan gauchesque literature of the 19th and 20th centuries has its roots in this oral-based literature. Popular protest poetry and songs, such as those of the *gaucho* and pseudo-*gaucho* literature of the River Plate countries, for example, are still kept alive not only in print but also in oral performance by the working-class rural *payador* or folk-singer; or the *corridos* of the Mexican Revolution and post-revolutionary Mexico (such as the lament for Zapata's death, whose haunting melody was used as the theme-music for Kazan's *Viva Zapata*); or the *décimas* of Panama, whose rural poets use the form for social criticism in the sense that they "not only lay wounds bare but cauterize the source of the infection" (in the words of Zárates, who collected a large body of Panamanian oral poetry in the 1960s). The presence of such a living tradition of oral protest poetry means that the modern poet can address a wide public and be understood. Even quite complex intellectual statements can be conveyed, since the sentiments and moods and rhetoric are on the whole well-known and have lost little of their emotive power at the "popular" level. Popular poetry reelaborates its material, exalts it poetically, and allows the profound voice of an entire society to be heard in the poet's own voice.

Argentina's José Hernández (1834–86) wrote the most popular of the gaucho poems, *Martín Fierro*, considered by many to be the greatest and perhaps the only true epic poem produced in the Spanish-speaking republics. It is a popular poem in which the poet puts his song at the service of an oral tradition. The impulse is individual; the source is popular. In the work there is the famous *payada*, with a black. A *payada* involved a performance of traveling singers, usually two poets, who engaged in a dialogue, sometimes in a duel – a *desafío* –

of poetic improvisation, often to the accompaniment of a guitar. A good poet-singer (*cantador* or *payador*) masters various forms of poetic improvisation, characterized by definite patterns of rhyme and meter. The hero of the poem, Martín Fierro is a *payador*, the legendary gaucho balladeer or singer (Argentine popular poet), who is proud of his inventiveness as he recounts the story of his life in the verse form of *décimas*. The second part of the poem, the *Vuelta* (*The Return*), published in 1878 culminates with this *payada* or song contest between Martín Fierro and the *moreno*, brother of the black he had slain in the first part, the *Ida* (*The Departure*). The *payada* was a typical rural musical form in which gauchesque poetry had its roots. The genre is a combination of very old folklore (consisting of music, and epic, lyrical and even dramatic poetry of the Argentine countryside) and imported European elements (verse, rhyme, and stanzaic structure). In its early stages, up to around 1917, the tango dance form retained a connection with the rural musical and song forms of the Argentine *payada* and *milonga*. In this display of the skill of the gaucho poet, the two men reaffirm the suffering and the struggles of man and place them in a cosmic setting. The form of the contest – the unanswerable questions – is an example of the riddle-song found in most archaic cultures, a "knocking on the door of the Unknowable" as Huizinga calls it in *Homo Ludens*, which was also a ritualistic way of defeating the opponent.

The gaucho served as a vehicle for the construction of a genuinely "popular" national consciousness. Gauchos were a nomadic group of mestizos who lived off the herds of wild cattle on the immense grassy plains of Argentina's pampas. These representatives of the subaltern classes were used in gauchesque literature of the late 19th and early 20th centuries as a "popular" voice, purportedly that of "the people." Due to the voice of the gaucho, in consonance with the voice of the fatherland, the people became, tautologically, the voice of the nation/state, effacing the differences between dominant and dominated. The gaucho's voice is deployed by the gauchesque writers to introduce concepts such as liberty and *patria* (pride in one's country) – the universals of the European Enlightenment. This literary genre made use in written texts of the oral form of the gaucho song. In it, the patriotic gaucho was held up against the bad, anti-social gaucho. The most famous books in this tradition are Hernández's *Martín Fierro* and Ricardo Güiraldes's *Don Segundo Sombra*, 1926. The strophe of *Martín Fierro*, keeping within the metrics of Hispanic Romanticism, avoided classical rigor without displaying traditional currents: octosyllabic verses organized in sextets, with the initial verse free of rhyme. Further, the poem carried the traits of the "Romantic school": literature as an expression of society; local color; nationalism; sympathy for the people; the exotic theme of Indian customs; the exiled and doleful hero as the victim of society; Fierro's noble friendship with Cruz; the novelistic episodes of violent contrasts as in the death of Vizcacha, the fight between the Indian and Fierro in the presence of a woman, the child whose throat is cut, and the happy meetings of Fierro with his children and those of Cruz. The genre is built within the semantic opposition between the gaucho as "vagrant" (*vago* or *delincuente*) and the gaucho as "patriot" or national hero, terms which dramatize the process of nation formation. The gauchesque is one strand in the making of a popular urban culture. Its popularity is evident both in rural and urban settings.

In keeping with its roots in oral tradition, *Martín Fierro* and other works of the genre were read aloud to groups of peasants in the non-standard language of the gaucho in the local *pulpería* (a cross between a bar and a general store), as earlier gauchesque poetry was read. While it is unusual for the writings of any thinker to have an immediate impact on an uneducated public, Hernández's work had such a reception. It went into the repertory of literature transmitted through performance. Indeed, the popularity of a literary form can best be demonstrated by the degree to which a mass audience becomes *actively* involved with its dissemination and/or development. It was only after the rapid expansion of Buenos Aires, making it the first modern city in Spanish America, that the popularity of the gauchesque genre waned. Some 268 *centros criollos* (Creole centers), many named after the regions from which their members had originated, had been set up from the 1890s by rural immigrants as meeting places where traditional rural music was performed. The *baqueano* (guide) is one of four gaucho types which Domingo Faustino Sarmiento (author of *Facundo*) displays as essential to the foundation of a genuine "national literature." The others are the *rastreador* (pathfinder), the singer or *payador* (composer of oral poetry) – the gaucho prototype for the minstrel – and the *gaucho malo* or "bad gaucho." The period in which this genre flourished ran, approximately, from 1880 to 1910, as the loss of links with the old style of peasant life and the increasing social weight of the working class contributed to its decline.

As its name indicates, gauchesque poetry stood at one remove from the oral poetry that was part of gaucho culture. Its authors were educated men who, to argue their views on society, made fictional gauchos their spokesmen. It was a form apart from the extemporaneous, abstractly philosophical verse of gaucho tradition, with its typical debate format and legendary practitioners (e.g., Gabino Ezeiza, (1858–1916).

The *décima* verse form used in such *payadas* of gauchesque literature has contributed to its popularity. It is a metric combination of ten octosyllabic verses which usually have the following rhyming pattern: first verse rhyming with the fourth and fifth verses; the second verse with the third; the sixth with the seventh; and the last verse rhyming with the eighth and the ninth verses. After the fourth verse there is usually a pause in the form of a period or semi-colon, not permitted after the fifth verse (rhyming pattern: abbaaccddc). The *décima* is also referred to as the *espinela* after its founder, Vicente Espinel, the Spanish poet. The form was also used extensively in the song-text poetry of the Chilean Violeta Parra and in numerous verses of other contemporary poets, such as Xavier Villaurrutia (*Décima muerte* [Tenth Death, 1947]). Like the ballad form in Spain, the *décima* is used by learned as well as popular poets.

Elena De Costa

Further Reading

Bohlman, Philip V., *The Study of Folk Music in the Modern World*, Bloomington: Indiana University Press, 1988 [Studies the dialectics of the oral and written traditions in the epic recounting or making of collective history]

Carril, Bonifacio del, *El gaucho a través de la iconografía*, Buenos Aires: Emecé, 1979

Decotte, Alex and Maximilien Bruggmann, *Gauchos*, Buenos Aires: Librerías ABC, 1978

Escabi, Pedro C. and Elsa M. Escabi, *La décima: vista parcial del folklore (estudio etnográfico de la cultura popular de Puerto Rico)*, Río Piedras, Puerto Rico: Editorial Universitaria, 1976

López Lemus, Virgilio, *La décima. Panorama breve de la décima cubana*, Havana: Academia, 1996

Ludmer, Josefina, *El género gauchesco. Un tratado sobre la patria*, Buenos Aires: Sudamericana, 1988 [Analysis of 19th- and early 20th-century gauchesque literature; a powerful critique of Argentine populism]

Olivera de Bonfil, Alicia, *La literatura cristera*, Mexico City: Instituto Nacional de Antropología e Historia, 1970 [Chapters on *corridos* and popular poetry]

Paredes, Américo, *The Undying Love of "El Indio" Cordova: Décimas and Oral History in a Border Family*, Stanford, California: Stanford Center for Chicano Research, 1986 [Mexican-American poetry]

Prieto, Adolfo, *El discurso criollista en la formación de la Argentina moderna*, Buenos Aires: Sudamericana, 1988

Rahier, Jean, *La décima: poesía oral negra del Ecuador*, Quito: Ediciones Abya-Yala: Centro Cultural Afro-ecuatoriano, 1985–87

Rowe, William and Vivian Schelling, *Memory and Modernity: Popular Culture in Latin America*, London and New York: Verso, 1993 [Traces the main anthropological, sociological and political debates about the nature of popular culture (including oral poetry and popular drama) in Latin America]

Santa Cruz, Nicomedes, *La décima en el Perú*, Lima: Instituto de Estudios Peruanos, 1982

Sarlo, Beatriz, *Una modernidad periférica: Buenos Aires 1920 y 1930*, Buenos Aires: Nueva Visión, 1988 [Chapter 2 contains a discussion of the use of rural voices and imagery]

Slatta, Richard W., *Gauchos and the Vanishing Frontier*, Lincoln: University of Nebraska Press, 1983

Steiner, Wendy (editor), *The Sign in Music and Literature*, Austin: University of Texas Press, 1981 [See, in particular, the chapter on "Typography, Rhymes, and Linguistic Structures in Poetry," by Nicolas Ruwet, and the chapter entitled "Toward a Semiotics of Music," by Henry Orlov]

Subero, Efraín, *La décima popular en Venezuela*, Caracas: Universidad Católica Andrés Bello, Centro de Investigaciones Literarias, Instituto Humanístico de Investigación, 1977

Pornography

Pornographic literature has always provoked critical debate. Conservative and religious groups oppose it, as do politically correct feminists, and the principles enunciated by these two groups can be summarized in three statements: pornography is the theory and rape is the practice; pornography is itself violence against women; pornography is incitement to sexual hatred (Dworkin and McKinnon). However, there is a Marxist approach which considers pornography as a resistance discourse whose proponents negate the debated distinction between pornography and eroticism (according to which the latter is "redeemed" by entering the superior category of art). Instead, they argue that both discourses are part of a revolutionary process whose goal would be to unmask the normative cultural categories of gender and sex.

Etymologically, the word pornography derives from the Greek coinage *pornographos*, which means someone who writes stories about whores (*pornai*) depicted when they pursue daily activities such as shopping, gossiping, or teaching their daughters about men and money. Following the origin of this term, pornography is used to refer to the production of genitally-based material which describes both foreplay and the sexual act itself in such a way as to provoke arousal in the reader.

The influence of Spanish Catholic tradition did not allow a production on pornography in Latin American countries until the 19th century with the emergence of capitalism and the influence of other European literatures, showing an integration of these countries in the project of modernity. Many of the major figures in Latin American writing have dedicated texts to pornography, although most of these have been produced in the second half of the 20th century. Authors like José María Vargas Vila (Colombia), Alejandra Pizarnik, Alicia Steimberg and Enrique Medina (Argentina), Reinaldo Arenas and Mayra Montero (Cuba), Rubén Monasterios (Venezuela), Cristina Peri Rossi (Uruguay), María Luisa Mendoza (Mexico), have examples of pornography within their literary production.

One of the first Latin American authors to show an interest in pornography in his texts is José Mario Vargas Vila. In the last years of 19th century he wrote polemical novels centered on sexuality that were censored for their perversion; misogynous texts like the trilogy *El alma de los lirios* [The Soul of Lilies] or the novel *Ibis*, where the female body is depicted as the source of lust. Female writers grew interested in male sexual fantasies and were to adapt this tradition to their own ends. Thus in the 1950s, Alejandra Pizarnik devotes a part of her surrealistic work to parody high eroticism as shown in her essay "El textículo de la cuestión" [The Texticle of the Question].

As David Foster explains in *Bodies and Biases*, in Argentina pornography has been censored as bad writing: Enrique Medina's fiction is a case in point; or it has been published abroad, like the new texts by Diana Raznovich and Alicia Steimberg; or, as in the case of the work of Griselda Gambaro, has been considered as pornography for the well-to-do. However, in Venezuela a form of writing has developed which is openly defined as pornography. Rubén Monasterios, a journalist exponent of this phenomenon, parodies sexuality while

he shows his abilities as a writer of narrative in *Encanto de la mujer madura y otros relatos obscenos* [Charm of the Mature Woman and Other Obscene Stories]. Contemporary Venezuelan writers also write short stories, as in *Eróticos, erotómanos y otras especies* [Eroticist, Erotomaniacs and Other Species] all focused on the genital organs and on the commercialization of human sexuality.

In spite of the radical feminist critique of pornography as the source of objectification of women, there are contemporary women writers all over Latin America dedicating part of their production to pornography. The cause is the emergence in these countries of neoliberal market forces. The Mexican María Luisa Mendoza author of *De ausencia* [Of Absence] shows the intimacy of a female character who surrenders to her body's pleasures. Also important is the lesbian production by Sara Levi Calderón and Rosa María Roffiel (Mexico) who are developing a non-phallic sexuality for women. In Brazil, women like Cassandra Ríos and Adelaide Carrara concentrate on mass-consumer porn and use high writerly Portuguese to describe the obscenity of human experience in their novels. Another contemporary Brazilian author, Hilda Hilst, has also dedicated her creative efforts to writing pornographic narratives.

ANA MARÍA BRENES-GARCÍA

Further Reading

Critical Studies (general)
Califia, Pat, *Sensuous Magic*, New York: Masquerade Books, 1993
Dworkin, Andrea and C.A. Mackinnon, *Pornography and Civil Rights: a New Day for Women's Equality*, Minneapolis: Organizing Against Pornography, 1988
Feder Kittay, Eve, "Pornography and the Erotics of Domination," in *Beyond Domination: New Perspectives on Women and Philosophy*, edited by Carol C. Gould, Totowa, New Jersey: Rowman and Allanheld, 1984
Gubar, Susan and Joan Hoff (editors), *For Adult Users Only; the Dilemma of Violent Pornography*, Bloomington: Indiana University Press, 1989
Hunt, Lynn (editor), *The Invention of Pornography. Obscenity and the Origins of Modernity, 1500–1800*, New York: Zone Books, 1993
Marcuse, Herbert, *Eros and Civilization: a Philosophical Enquiry into Freud*, Boston: Beacon Press, 1955; London: Routledge and Kegan Paul, 1956
Soble, Alan, *Pornography, Marxism, Feminism, and the Future of Sexuality*, New Haven, Connecticut: Yale University Press, 1986

Critical Studies (concerning Latin America)
Booker, M. Keith, *Mario Vargas Llosa among the Postmodernists*, Gainesville: University Presses of Florida, 1994 [Chapter 7 is on *Elogio de la madrasta / In Praise of the Stepmother*]
Foster, David William, *Gay and Lesbian Themes in Latin American Writing*, Austin: University of Texas Press, 1991
_____ "Pornography and the Feminine Erotic: Griselda Gambaro's *Lo impenetrable*," *Monographic Review/Revista Monográfica* 7 (1991)
_____ "Some Proposals for the Study of Latin American Gay Culture," in his *Cultural Diversity in Latin American Literature*, Alburquerque: University of New Mexico Press, 1994

Foster, David William and Roberto Reis (editors), *Bodies and Biases: the Representation of Sexualities in Hispanic Cultures and Literatures*, Minneapolis: University of Minnesota Press, 1995

Fiction

Calderón, Sara-Levi, *Dos mujeres*, Mexico City: Diana, 1991
Coutinho, Edilberto (editor), *O erotismo no conto brasileiro: antología*, Río de Janeiro: Civilização Brasileira, 1980
Denser, Márcia (editor), *O prazer é todo meu; contos eróticos femininos*, 2nd edition, Rio de Janeiro: Record, 1984
Fernández Olmos, Margarite and Lizabeth Paravasini-Gebert (editors), *El placer de la palabra: literatura erótica femenina de América Latina; antología crítica*, Mexico City: Planeta, 1991
Gambaro, Griselda, *Lo impenetrable*, Buenos Aires: Torres Agüero, 1984; as *The Impenetrable Madam X*, translated by Evelyn Picon Garfield, Detroit: Wayne State University Press, 1991
Hilst, Hilda (Brazil), *Contos d'escárnio: textos grotescos*, São Paulo: Ediçoes Siciliano, 1990

____ *Cartas de un sedutor*, São Paulo: Editora Paulicéia, 1991
Jaramillo Levi, Enrique (editor), *El cuento erótico en México*, Mexico City: Diana, 1975
Lovera De-Sola, R.J. (editor), *Eróticos, erotómanos y otras especies*, Caracas: Alfadil Ediciones, 1983
Mendoza, María Luisa, *De ausencia*, Mexico City: Joaquín Mortiz, 1974
Monasterios, Rubén, *Encanto de la mujer madura y otros relatos obscenos*, Caracas: Línea Editores, 1987
Montero, Mayra, *La última noche que pasé contigo*, Barcelona: Tusquets, 1991
Parra, Marco Antonio de, *Cuerpos prohibidos*, Santiago de Chile: Planeta Chilena, 1991
Peri Rossi, Cristina, *Fantasías eróticas*, Madrid: Edición Temas de Hoy, 1991
Steimberg, Alicia, *El árbol del placer*, Buenos Aires: Emecé, 1986
Vargas Vila, José María, *Obras completas*, Buenos Aires: Biblioteca Nueva, 1946

Positivism

Positivist philosophy, which was deeply rooted in Latin American thought, had a major impact in the literary production of the 19th century. Positivism's early exponent was Saint-Simon (1760–1825), who by 1817 had published his *Encyclopaedia of Positive Ideas*, a philosophy of liberal politics, which heralded the supremacy of science. Auguste Comte (1798–1857), a disciple of Saint-Simon, was responsible for clearly and systematically outlining the importance of positivist philosophy in a body of work published between 1830 and 1842 entitled *Cours de philosophie positive*. Comte explained that the term "positive" meant a "special manner of philosophizing that consists of envisaging the theories in any order of ideas as having for their object the coordination of observed facts." This way of reasoning could be applied to all subjects, although Comte did not explain what he meant by "facts."

Comte developed his philosophy by means of the law of three stages. Accordingly, the first stage in the evolution of knowledge was of theological origin; in it the world had been explained according to the will of anthropomorphic gods. In the second, metaphysical abstraction had been the leading philosophy which attempted to comprehend the human condition. Finally in the third stage of development, the human mind had evolved to the positivist level, in which the world was explained in terms of scientific facts. Positivist philosophy, thus, proclaimed the necessity for empirical evidence in all areas, based on the general belief that sociology (considered at the time as the most advanced science) required the study of physical sciences (biology in particular) as a model of research. It was the duty of positivist philosophers to create a synthesis of scientific knowledge with the purpose of *reorganizing* society. Comte insisted that "mental and moral change was logically and chronologically prior to social and political change," meaning that the positivist philosopher "was to become, not a king, but a priest, a member of the 'spiritual power' . . . a priesthood, serving not some theological fiction, but Humanity itself."

Expeditions during the 19th century by Alexander von Humboldt and others, had left behind a scientific discourse whose method of direct observation and imitation of flora and fauna was adopted by Latin American writers of fiction and of non-fiction. For the Latin American writers of this period, many of whom were statesmen committed to the process of creating free post-colonial nations, the conflict between narrative (that is to say fiction) and history (science) did not exist. This lack of epistemological distinction between science and art or narrative and fact had been a long-standing practice, since one of the most salient aspects of the historical discourse of the colonies had been the distortion of observed facts. In the 1800s, following the ideological guidelines espoused by Positivism, the Latin American novel reflected the positivist philosopher's preoccupation with empirical evidence. This can be observed in the exploration of national identities and in the emphasis on historiography that characterize the novels of this period.

In particular, positivist thought was a key factor behind the production of the so-called "foundational novels," which were part of the general effort to create national identities. Historically and socially inspired, the theme of many of these novels was the romance (following Chateaubriand's model) between people of different ethnic origin. The idealized marrying of individuals from different sectors of society was meant to represent the possible solution for nations plagued by social, economic and ethnic disparity. The need to reconcile these diverse groups was perceived as absolutely necessary in order to achieve a national identity, and it is this unity of vision that brings together many novels of the period that would otherwise seem to have little in common. Novels like *Aves sin nido*, 1889 (*Birds without a Nest*) by the Peruvian writer Clorinda Matto de Turner, *María* (1867) by the Colombian Jorge Isaacs, *Cumandá* (1879) by the Ecuadorian by Juan León Mera, *Martín Rivas* (1862) by the Chilean writer Alberto Blest Gana or *Enriquillo, leyenda histórica dominicana*, 1882 (*The Cross and the Sword*) by the Dominican writer Manuel de Jesús Galván, have many similar elements. Particularly in plot and language the coherence of the novels comes, according to Doris Sommer, "from their common need to reconcile and amalgamate national constituencies, and from the strategy to cast the previously unreconciled parties, races, classes, or regions, as lovers who are 'naturally' attracted and right for one another." The idealization of poor, marginal and exploited sectors of society (of indigenous or African origin), reveals the reformist spirit of 19th-century writers and their commitment to the use of literature as a tool for the promotion of change. The anti-slavery novel, for example *Cecilia Valdés* (1882) and *Sab* (1841), by the Cuban writers Cirilo Villaverde and Gertrudis Gómez de Avellaneda respectively, also viewed the restructuring of political organization as the only practical and fair solution to the problems created by racial and social disparity.

Positivism remained strong and vital in the literature of Latin America until avant-garde forms, techniques, images and language asserted their influence. These new approaches were first seen in the poetry of the early 20th century starting with César Vallejo, and then toward the end of the decade of the 1920s in the work of fiction writers such as Roberto Arlt and Macedonio Fernández.

ANA GARCÍA CHICHESTER

See also entries on The Historical Novel, Science

Further Reading

Brushwood, John S., *Genteel Barbarism: Experiments in the Analysis of Nineteenth-Century Spanish-American Novels*, Lincoln: University of Nebraska Press, 1981 [A discussion of several novels of the period, which emphasizes what these novels perceived as a grave conflict in the creation of national identities, that is the dichotomy between the Europeanized urban areas, and the more "savage" conditions in rural sectors]

Comte, Auguste, *A General View of Positivism*, translated by J.H. Bridges, New York: Robert Speller and Sons, 1957

González Echevarría, Roberto, "Redescubrimiento del mundo perdido: el *Facundo* de Sarmiento," *Revista Iberoamericana*, vol. 54/143 (1988) [This study of Domingo Faustino Sarmiento's *Facundo* explores the impact of scientific reports written by 18th-century European explorers and explains the influence of this kind of travel literature on 19th-century fiction and non-fiction]

Sommer, Doris, "Irresistible Romance: the Foundational Fictions of Latin America," in *Nation and Narration*, edited by Homi K. Bhaba, London: Routledge, 1990 [An excellent essay which explains the impact of positivist thought in some of the novels of the 1800s]

Standley, Arline Reilein, *Auguste Comte*, Boston: Twayne, 1981 [A good introduction to the study of Comte and of his aesthetics, which also contains a very useful and complete chronology]

Abel Posse 1936–

Argentine prose writer

Abel Posse, a career diplomat and the author of ten novels and a critical reading guide to the best 101 works of world literature, *Biblioteca esencial*, 1991 [The Essential Library], is primarily identified with the new Latin American historical novel. Posse started to gain more critical attention and a wider reading public after he received the prestigious Rómulo Gallegos prize in 1987 for his novel *Los perros del paraíso*, 1983 (*The Dogs of Paradise*). This novel is part of the Columbus trilogy which includes *Daimón*, 1978 (*Daimon*) and *El largo atardecer del caminante*, 1992 [The Long Twilight of the Traveler]. Like many Argentine writers, Posse made the obligatory peregrination to Europe in the 1960s where, among other things, he studied in Paris and met writers such as Julio Cortázar, Mario Trejo, Jean-Paul Sartre and Pablo Neruda. Because of his experience in Europe, or perhaps in spite of it, Posse not only maintained a highly independent stance with respect to the continent, but he was also able to develop his dual vision of the Old and the New Worlds. This binary vision

plays a fundamental role in his Columbus trilogy. Posse's first novel, *Los bogavantes*, 1970 [The Crew], deals with the lives of Latin Americans residing in Paris during the tumultuous 1960s, and his second novel, *La boca del tigre*, 1971 [In the Mouth of the Tiger], chronicles the life of Latin Americans in another exotic setting, the Soviet Union. These novels are works of crisis in which Posse explores a reality foreign to his vision, which centers on Latin America, and they are written in a language and a voice which he still had not made his own.

A long developmental phase followed during which Posse came into contact with Latin American reality when he lived in Peru and met José María Arguedas. While Posse did not publish anything between 1971 and 1978, his contact with Peruvian reality opened up a world to him which required a new language and perspective. Posse's independence with respect to politics and ideologies and his complete adherence to literature enabled him to forge a new language and to consolidate his dual vision. Unlike some Argentine writers who traveled to Europe but who remained attached to their national reality, Posse not only eluded that trap but was able to integrate all the ostensibly disparate elements of his multinational experience into a unified vision.

The novel which marks the turning point in his writing is *Daimón*, the first novel of the Columbus trilogy. Significantly, Posse starts the trilogy with the bizarre and fantastic expedition of the demented conquistador, Lope de Aguirre, and not with Columbus's discovery of America, which is the subject of the second novel in the trilogy, *Los perros del paraíso*. Aguirre's expedition (1558–61), his rebellion against Spain's administrative empire and his attempt to create a new empire, were already historically anachronistic since his aim was to restore the medieval values of the warrior and the vassal at a time when the conquistadors were no longer needed. In *Daimón* Posse resuscitates Lope de Aguirre and his followers so that they can not only recreate their expedition but also travel across the centuries to bear witness to the Spanish colonial enterprise in Latin America. Although the three novels contain a strong historiographic subtext, Posse goes beyond official history to give the reader a metahistorical vision in which he foregrounds language and form as the true heroes of these works. Not only is official history undermined by its link to Tarot cards but past and present are blended within the framework of circular time, and Lope de Aguirre's peregrination across the centuries demonstrates the failure of the colonial enterprise and demythifies the mythic discourse of the discovery and conquest of America which is contained in the shipboard log of Christopher Columbus. In other words, *Daimón* subverts the scriptural edifice on which the whole colonial enterprise was erected *before* the reader confronts the mythic discourse of Christopher Columbus in the second novel. The other major innovation in *Daimón* is the creation of a baroque language which coincides with the eminently postmodern landscape of Latin America with its diverse cultures, races, languages and spatialized time zones which range from the prehistoric to the futuristic. Posse achieves his aim of creating a work in which his vision arises from language and not from ideas.

In *Los perros del paraíso* Posse inverts Europe and America so that Europe is illogical and irrational while the Incas and the Aztecs, in a series of anachronistic meetings, logically discuss the invasion of the Old World by using hot-air balloons. Posse subverts the canonical figure of Christopher Columbus who not only undermines the mythic discourse of the discovery and conquest of America, but also aspires to the Edenic world of Being in direct opposition to the Western obsession with the Paradise of Doing. Posse creates a Spain and Europe hovering between life and death, awaiting the seismic sexual union between Ferdinand and Isabel which will sweep away the medieval world and create a new order. Temporal and historical anachronisms abound in this novel and at one point Posse fuses all the voyages of Columbus so that they become a paradigm of all such ventures. Posse's metahistorical vision of America allows him to fuse past and present so that Ferdinand and Isabel's regime bears a striking resemblance to that of Eva and Juan Perón. Posse continues his subversion of official history, and his baroque language and the dialogic approach to the novel are foregrounded as much as the characters and story. In a final inversion Columbus is

transformed into the first integral mestizo before the erotic conquest of America begins.

The last novel of the Columbus trilogy, *El largo atardecer del caminante*, replaces the anachronistic, spatio-temporal leaps across history with the intimate story of Alvar Núñez Cabeza de Vaca's incredible journey on foot across North America (1528–1536). The highly personal tone of the narrator's voice creates a world in which Western man is an alien presence, a universe in which the foundations of the colonial enterprise are brought into serious question. Indeed, Cabeza de Vaca's intimate account constitutes the discourse of failure, the recognition that the Western world never understood the pulsating and vibrant reality of the Other, and not, New World.

As Posse's previous novels show, he criticizes the official history of Latin America as well as those Argentine writers who believe that they must talk only about Argentina in their works, while ignoring that fact that they live in a historical, telluric and human organicity which is Latin America. Each step that Posse's Cabeza de Vaca takes in the novel is one more footfall in the discourse of failure. History in this novel spirals inward toward the intimate center of this narrative voice which seeks to close the door on this enterprise.

Posse has also written four other novels which deal more directly with Argentina and especially Buenos Aires. In *Momento de morir*, 1979 [Time to Die], Medardo Rabagliati, a lawyer in Buenos Aires, becomes progressively more embroiled in the violence and death which reigns in the streets of the city as contending political groups of all political stripes struggle for power. The novel demonstrates that politics and ideological struggles are never far from Posse's fiction. In *Los demonios ocultos*, 1987 [The Hidden Demons], he explores the post-war world of Nazism. Lorca, the son of a German who has disappeared, is a journalist who becomes obsessed with locating his father. His investigation leads him to discover a Nazism which still proposes the creation of the master race. Posse's novel also investigates Argentina's link with the dark forces of Nazism which have played such a prominent role in the country's history. In *La Reina del Plata*, 1988 [The Queen of the Plata], Posse fuses the past and present in his circular temporality. In this past-present Buenos Aires, Posse revives old myths of Argentina and infuses them with new life. This novel demonstrates how Posse constantly transcends the narrow boundaries of Argentine reality in order to recontextualize and revitalize cherished national myths such as the tango, Yrigoyen and Evita. In *El viajero de Agartha*, 1989 [The Traveler of Agartha], Walter Werner, a German archeologist, abandons everything to undertake a special mission to Agartha, the so-called City of the Powers. The strange journey turns into an initiatory voyage towards the esoteric universe of the pagan mythologies on which Nazism has founded its theology of violence.

While the awarding of the Rómulo Gallegos prize in 1987 and a number of others have brought Abel Posse more recognition, his work still has not received the full critical attention that it deserves. Part of this may be due to his independent stance in relation to literary movements and his rejection of identification with any particular political ideology. While Posse works on the margins of the literary mainstream, his dynamic evolution as a writer never ceases to break new ground. Posse continuously combines and recombines the elements of his multifaceted, transnational experience which coincides closely with Latin America's pre-eminent status as a postmodern universe. Posse describes himself as a thief (*ladrón*) of many writers. Nevertheless, in his case, robbery yields a high return which can only enrich the possibilities of Latin American literature.

ROBERT L. SIMS

See also entry on The Historical Novel

Biography

Born in Córdoba, Argentina in 1936, but spent childhood in Buenos Aires. Moved to Paris in 1959. Has travelled widely as result of working as a diplomat. Publication of first novel delayed because of censorship in Franco's Spain. Recipient of the following major prizes in Argentina: Triennial National Prize, 1969–71; the Argentine National Prize for Literature. Also awarded the Rómulo Gallegos Prize (Venezuela), 1987 for *Los perros del paraíso*.

Selected Works

Novels

Los bogavantes, Buenos Aires: Brújula, 1970
La boca del tigre, Buenos Aires: Emecé, 1971
Daimón, Barcelona: Argos, 1978; as *Daimon*, translated by Sarah

Arvio, New York; Atheneum, 1992
Momento de morir, Buenos Aires: Emecé, 1979
Los perros del paraíso, Barcelona: Argos, 1983; as *The Dogs of Paradise*, translated by Margaret Sayers Peden, New York: Atheneum, 1989
Los demonios ocultos, Buenos Aires: Emecé, 1987
La Reina del Plata, Buenos Aires: Emecé, 1988
El viajero de Agartha, Buenos Aires: Emecé, 1989
El largo atardecer del caminante, Buenos Aires: Emecé, 1992
La pasión según Eva, Buenos Aires: Emecé, 1994

Other Writings

Biblioteca esencial: 101 libros fundamentales de la literatura mundial con un anexo sobre literatura argentina y rioplatense, Buenos Aires: Emecé, 1991

Further Reading

Sims, Robert L., "*Los perros del paraíso* de Abel Posse: hipertextualidad, intertextualidad, carnavalización y descubrimiento del Nuevo Mundo," *Signo y Pensamiento* 21 (1992)
Sklodowska, Elzbieta, *La parodia en la nueva novela hispanoamericana (1960–1985)*, Amsterdam and Philadelphia: Benjamins, 1991 [Section on *Los perros del paraíso* in chapter 2]
Williams, Raymond L. (editor), *The Novel in the Americas*, Niwot: University Press of Colorado, 1992 [Includes contribution on Abel Posse]

The Post-Boom

The Post-Boom may be summarized as a movement in Spanish American fiction, beginning in the 1970s, partly as a reaction against the Boom. It is a much less homogeneous and hence less easily defined movement than the Boom itself, while in addition the break with the previous movement is much less clearly visible than the shift which took place during the 1950s at the beginning of the Boom. A few Boom writers, including Vargas Llosa, Donoso and even García Márquez himself, have recognized that a change has been taking place and have adjusted some aspects of their work accordingly, so that a line of separation is hard to draw. Secondly, since about 1975, when the Post-Boom is thought to have begun to take shape, no major writer has appeared who enjoys the same stature as the great figures of the preceding generation. On the other hand, the movement has seen the triumphant emergence of a galaxy of women writers, Isabel Allende (Chile), Luisa Valenzuela (Argentina), Elena Poniatowska (Mexico), Cristina Peri Rossi (Uruguay) and Rosario Ferré (Puerto Rico) prominent among them, and this may well be seen in the end as its single most important feature. The Post-Boom novelists tend to react against two aspects of the Boom: its cosmopolitan, universalist tendency on the one hand, and its emphasis on experimentalism as a means of questioning reality on the other. Hence major features of the Post-Boom are a more specific emphasis on Latin America and a move towards re-establishing

the so-called "mimetic contract" between writer and reader. However, the extent to which this is aimed at or realized, varies considerably as we move from "ultra-realistic" "testimonial" (eye-witness) writing at one end of the Post-Boom spectrum to high fantasy and on-going narrative experimentalism at the other. Less variable is the intention to bring fiction back to a closer relationship with the here and now and with the history of Spanish America. The rise and fall of the military regimes in Chile, Uruguay and Argentina, together with the struggles in Central America and not least the run-up to the fifth centenary of the Discovery focused attention anew on the past and present of the continent.

Some writers in the Boom period, like Mario Benedetti in Uruguay and David Viñas in Argentina remained more or less faithful to old-styled realism during much of their creative cycles and were never members of the movement. They represent a certain continuity between the self-conscious neo-realism of some areas of the Post-Boom and the old tradition. But the real transition came with the early novels of Manuel Puig, which were clearly referential to the Argentina of the time and in addition popularized what was to become an important characteristic of the Post-Boom: its incorporation of "pop," "youth" and "mass" culture-elements into the new pattern of fiction. Among the first writers to practice this incorporation were Gustavo Sainz and José Agustín in Mexico and Antonio

Skármeta in Chile. The latter's *Soñé que la nieve ardía*, 1975 (*I Dreamt the Snow was Burning*), whose hero is an aspiring professional soccer player living among young political activists in Santiago under Allende, is one of the inaugural novels of the Post-Boom.

Its greatest success so far has been Isabel Allende's *La casa de los espíritus*, 1982 (*The House of the Spirits*), in which the shift from fantasy to political commitment can be observed taking place. Her subsequent easy-to-read, plot-centred novels, with their strong heroines, clear ideological stance and generally happy endings illustrate some central Post-Boom characteristics. These also include: humour and greater optimism, non-intellectual protagonists, often of working-class background, support for the oppressed and marginalized and two others especially which seem to put Allende in the middle of the Post-Boom mainstream: strong love-interest and melodrama. It is difficult to find in Boom fiction works in which love plays an important, life-enhancing role. But a major feature of the Post-Boom is its rehabilitation of the emotions. Melodrama, we know, depends on its appeal to a moral consensus in the audience or readership. Its reappearance in Allende and elsewhere in the Post-Boom is in significant contrast to the Boom's tendency to question accepted values. Finally we should notice the voicing in the Post-Boom of formerly silenced or marginalized viewpoints, especially those of women, young people and members of the real working class, but also Jews, homosexuals and ethnic minorities.

Two of the most significant Post-Boom experiences were those of exile and of living in the shadow of the fifth centenary of the Discovery. Exile, according to Allende, caused writers to become more consciously aware of their common Latin Americanness than of their individual nationalities, and re-focused their attention on the continent and its problems, of which they had felt the effects at first hand. The imminence of the Discovery celebrations, on the other hand, brought a greater awareness of history and was a factor in the rise of the New Historical Novel, perhaps the most important form of writing in the Post-Boom. It also raises one of the most difficult problems connected with the movement. How is it possible to appear to observe and report reality (in this case historical reality) confidently and unambiguously, when the Boom writers had expended so much talent and energy questioning both the notion that reality is easy to understand and the presumption that there is a simple relationship between words we use to describe it and what they purport to describe? The dilemma has produced two kinds of writing. Both belong to the Post-Boom to the extent that they are concerned specifically with Spanish America. But whereas one presents the past of Spanish America as if it were relatively intelligible and capable of yielding lessons for the present, the other presents all historical interpretation as fiction, parodying the traditional historical novel, as in *Los perros del paraíso*, 1983 (*The Dogs of Paradise*), by Abel Posse (Argentina). What this illustrates is that most Post-Boom novelists are more conscious of the status of their work as fiction than was the case before the

Boom. However, under the impact of events, some have elected to break with the "splintered mirror effect" of many Boom novels, in which the reader had to reassemble the picture of reality and was always conscious of its fragmentary and potentially unreliable nature. Recognizing that it is difficult to reflect and to interpret what is happening in Latin America if, at the same time, one continually undermines the notions of chronology, cause and effect and referentiality, these authors have perforce moved towards greater reader-friendliness. At the same time, and as part of the same process, they have tried to replace the disturbing metaphors underlying much of the fiction of the Boom, with a more reassuring vision of reality. It may be noted in passing that, to the extent that this return to referentiality and reassurance is actually part of the Post-Boom's mainstream (and opinions differ), it is not easy to relate the movement to Postmodernism, though exception might be made for parts of the new historical novel and the new detective novel in Spanish America.

Who, finally, are the representative writers (that is, principally novelists) of the Post-Boom? Skármeta mentions Ariel Dorfman, José Agustín, Gustavo Sainz and Jorge Aguilar Mora, Luis Rafael Sánchez, Manuel Puig and Eduardo Gudiño Kieffer, Reinaldo Arenas and Miguel Barnet, Oscar Collazos and Sergio Ramírez. Ricardo Piglia mentions his fellow Argentines Juan José Saer and Puig, Skármeta, Dorfman, Rafael Humberto Moreno-Durán, Agustín, Sainz and José Emilio Pacheco. Mempo Giardinelli and Abel Posse should be added to these names, together with the women writers already mentioned, Allende, Valenzuela, Poniatowska, Peri Rossi, Ferré and Ana Lydia Vega, among others.

The challenge to the Post-Boom writers seems to be to move on from the Boom, incorporating more direct referentiality and social comment in their fiction, without ignoring the Boom's legacy of sophisticated writing. The search, that is, is for a new balance between observation and imagination.

DONALD L. SHAW

Further Reading

Gutiérrez Mouat, Ricardo, "La narrativa latinoamericana del post-boom," *Revista Interamericana de Bibliografía*, 38 (1988)

Lindstrom, Naomi, "The Postboom: New Voices and Belated Discoveries, 1968–1990," in her *Twentieth-Century Spanish American Fiction*, Austin: University of Texas Press, 1994

Martin, Gerald, "After the Boom," in his *Journeys through the Labyrinth: Latin American Fiction in the Twentieth Century*, London and New York: Verso, 1989

Rama, Ángel, *Más allá del boom: literatura y mercado*, Mexico City: Marcha 1981

Shaw, Donald L., "Towards a Description of the Post-Boom," *Bulletin of Hispanic Studies*, vol. 66 (1988)

Swanson, Philip, "After the Boom," in his *Landmarks in Modern Latin American Fiction*, London: Routledge, 1990

____ *The New Novel in Latin America. Politics and Popular Culture after the Boom*, Manchester: Manchester University Press, 1995

Postmodern Writing

In Latin America, the discussion of Postmodernism in literature and culture was introduced relatively recently, gaining in prominence towards the end of the 1980s. At first sight, Postmodernism must have looked like a strictly Anglo-American affair, and the very term was confusing. In the Anglo-American context, "Modernism" is used as a period concept covering the span from about the 1910s to the 1950s; Postmodernism therefore, emerging in the turbulent 1960s, tends to be rather a break with than a continuation of modernist aesthetics. In the Hispanic context, *postmodernismo* (1905–20) is a generational concept referring to a kind of prolongation of the initially more cosmopolitan end-of-the-century *Modernismo* (1890–1905) – the Hispanic literary counterpart to Art Nouveau. The attempt made by Juan Ramón Jiménez, during his exile in the US, to expand *Modernismo* somewhat in the Anglo-American sense to cover the 1890s through 1950s (the span of his own poetic production), did not prevail, in spite of some good reasons he might have, because the image of tradition-breaking was captured by the much more radical avant-garde currents of the 1920s. Recently, Fredric Jameson has revived Ramón Jiménez's claims. In the Brazilian context, *Modernismo* is correlated with the explosion and proliferation of the international avant-garde movements in the 1920s, but its duration is expanded somewhat loosely up to at least the 1960s.

Since the 1960s, social studies have tinkered with other concepts, such as "postindustrial society," referring to the momentous social and technological changes precipitated by World War II. Outside of the Anglo-American cultural context, the discussion of Postmodernism was increasingly related to this emerging new, postmodern, "information age" and social paradigm (though certainly not "paradise," Utopian or other). In correlation to this, "Modernism" was inflated to stand surreptitiously for "modern art" at large, from the Enlightenment to the 1950s (the aesthetic and political conservatism of mainstream Anglo-American Modernism *vis-à-vis* the avant-gardes made the new quixotic mission of that term somewhat more plausible).

The confusion created by this leap from the arts and literature into apocalyptic history (the "end of modernity") was further complicated in international discussions, responsive by necessity to local contexts and sensibilities. Yet precisely these dynamics and the ensuing shift in the meaning of the pivotal concepts enhanced their tantalizing powers and their potential for meaning, something perhaps crucial for contemporary cultural developments. Without this linkage, Postmodernism could be just a short-lived fashion and, indeed, as some wishful undertakers have come to suggest, already dead (strangely enough, this "death" was pegged to 1989, the time when precisely the modern Utopian model crumbled under the Berlin Wall).

The curiosity of Latin American literary critics was aroused when the lists of "postmodernist" writers included more and more of the prominent Latin Americans; some European theoreticians of Postmodernism (such as D. W. Fokkema) went as far as to declare that the movement actually originated in Latin America – specifically with Borges. (Of course, Borges would have something to say about the fabrication of precursors.) Marxist-oriented critics, pointing out that Latin America had not experienced full modernity yet, questioned the relevance of Postmodernism in those circumstances. Since the late 1980s, a fully-fledged discussion about the possible merits of Postmodernism in Latin America has developed.

In which ways might it be profitable to apply the concepts of Postmodernism or postmodern writing to Latin American literature? Latin American postmodern writing, if any, is part of the emerging postmodern condition worldwide and also within the specific cultural, political and social contexts of the individual countries. Therefore, it has not been productive to draw a time-line, e.g., starting from the 1960s, when the unequivocal signs of new cultural forms emerge (mass media, urban popular culture, rock music and other forms of international culture, including commodification of countercultural phenomena); nor from the 1970s, when the transformation becomes massive; nor from the 1980s, because, by then, the "new" is already several decades old. Nor is it very productive, following Ihab Hassan's lead, to compile a list of rhetorical devices, because they all seem to come from one shelf, namely the avant-garde (though not necessarily from Anglo-American Modernism). In Postmodernism, the avant-garde deconstructive devices have crossed over from poetry into narrative, criticism (already present in Russian Formalism), and philosophy. It would not be productive either to identify Postmodernism with some short-lived fashions, such as *la Onda* writing in Mexico which explored, from the Boom aesthetics, the leisure culture of emerging middle-class adolescents and other paraphernalia of the 1960s. A similar aesthetic double-standard is to be found in the so-called *novela del lenguaje* (language novel) of the 1960s and 1970s: in this novel centered on language, the postmodern exploration of different strata of popular cultures (in Cabrera Infante, Sarduy, Puig or Sánchez) is coupled with a relentless attack on the illusion of representation through language that comes from the avant-garde. By contrast, the *testimonio* is founded, and founders, on the illusion of representation and representativity; its search for "unofficial history" and for the empowering of the voice and the culture of the underprivileged have been seriously undercut by *testimonio's* overt, still modern, political underpinnings.

It would be equally misleading to identify Postmodernism or postmodern writing with the Post-Boom, because this awkward, ill-defined concept cannot be taken as equivalent to either. Post-Boom refers to the narrative written in Spanish America after the fireworks of the totalizing, allegorical and experimental novels of the 1960s; but when the attempt is made to go beyond chronology and grasp more exactly the Post-Boom aesthetics, the concept disintegrates. For example, such important Post-Boom novels as Reinaldo Arenas's *El mundo alucinante*, 1969 (*Hallucinations*, also published as *The Ill-Fated Peregrinations of Fray Servando*); Ricardo Piglia's *Respiración artificial*, 1980 (*Artificial Respiration*); Isabel Allende's *La casa de los espíritus*, 1982 (*The House of the Spirits*); Laura Esquivel's *Como agua para chocolate*, 1989 (*Like Water for Chocolate*); or Jesús Díaz's *Las palabras perdidas*, 1992 [Lost Words], are all as representative and totalizing, in their own way, as the best Boom novels of Fuentes, Vargas Llosa and García Márquez. The uneasiness these postmodern novels provoke in some readers may be actually due to the fact that these works require a new art of reading, which a part of the elite audience educated on the master-allegories of the 1960s still cannot muster. The resulting fuzziness of the Post-Boom aesthetics sometimes allows that typical Boom authors, such as Severo Sarduy, writing directly within the French *nouveau roman* tradition, are paraded as prime examples of Post-Boom; yet indeed aspects of Sarduy's writing may be perceived as postmodern (such as his playing with elements of popular culture and with scriptural and gay transvestism). Further, if we identify Boom narrative or authors with "modernist" writing, and Post-Boom with "postmodernist" writing, we have to exclude from the postmodern realm precisely the authors who figure prominently on the "postmodernist" lists of the non-Latin American critics (Borges, Cortázar, García Márquez, Fuentes, Vargas Llosa, among others). Could all these critics be wrong? Are they reading "out of context"? Is reading from another context necessarily all wrong? Asking these questions does not excuse those US comparatists who impose Anglo-American patterns on Latin American writing.

Finally, these and other exercises in sweeping generalizations fail to explain some striking differences in how postmodern problematics have been received in individual Latin American countries. For example, while Brazil and Mexico jumped on the postmodern bandwagon almost effortlessly; in Argentina it encountered some vocal resistance from the male literati (although, to the contrary, it was assumed programmatically by writers with exile experience, such as Mempo Giardinelli, who lived in Mexico, and Néstor Perlongher, who actually lived in Brazil); in addition, women writers seem much less inhibited in this context. In Cuba, we sense an overwhelming desire to be (and act as if they were) "already" postmodern.

Since Latin American mainstream societies have engaged in the ever accelerating yet ever elusive "modernization," heterogeneous Latin American cultures both share the condition and, at the same time, are the beneficiaries of the crisis of the modern Western Utopian rationalism which has been driving modernization. Due to the crisis of Eurocentrism and of "modern" values, accelerated by decolonization, Latin America ceased to be "put down" a priori to a position of inferiority. Instead of searching for an identity, as if it were some "lost father" or other "origin," this might be indeed the propitious time for Latin America to forge a unique cultural identity and reinvent "from scratch," from the marvelous amalgam of the premodern, modern, antimodern and now also postmodern building blocks, and, of course, all-time forgeries. *Lo real maravilloso* (Carpentier's poetics of Latin American reality); *realismo mágico* (understood as an aesthetics of artistic creation and as a re-vision of Latin American realities); Borges's hybrid fictions, featuring a quilt made from the most distant cultures and from patches of absurd "logical gradations" (the dead-serious modernist reading mistook his knack for pastiche, his Dada-humor and sly satire for "philosophy"); or Paz's early postmodern soul-searching in *El laberinto de la soledad* (*The Labyrinth of Solitude*) and his continuous denunciation of the

crisis of modern values, have all started this process. But the novels of magical realism, to take one example, also show a double-bind: in these works, the forces of Western modernity end up defeated symbolically by Latin American premodernity; yet "the Others" have to keep playing the role of "Indians" for Western audiences. Hence, it is apparent that the equality bestowed on Latin America has been limited to culture, aesthetics and intellectual tourism. If the world does not self-destruct, it would seem that only modernization, so vilified by Latin American intellectual elites (from *Ariel* to the "good revolutionaries"), has any chance of bringing full equality. In the meantime, the prophecized "continent of the future" lies amidst ecological disaster, aggravated by population explosion and uncontrolled urbanization and deforestation. The apocalyptic parable about the end of time, *La leyenda de los soles*, 1993 [The Legend of the Suns], by Homero Aridjis, seems to be an appropriate closure and the latest reincarnation of magical realism at the end of the 20th century.

Large migrations have also produced new cultural, political and economic phenomena: the indigenous population has swamped creole or Europeanized cities, and Latin Americans at large have established numerous "beachheads" in the North or in some other former metropolis. While academic criticism spins out serial narratives about "Third World," "dependency," and other typical modern intellectual constructs, the illiterate and barefoot migrants, undocumented "aliens," and forced exiles have effected a sort of "reverse conquest" of significant bits of the "empire" and have changed it, as well as their original countries, in the process. Today, the strength of Puerto Rican literature could not be understood without its close ties to New York. Puerto Rican culture has gone a long way from the curse put on the exile in René Marqués's *La carreta*, 1951 (*The Oxcart*), to the current "love affair" with "our" New York. Mexican literature has only begun to feel the influence and to recognize the importance of border and *chicano* literature and culture. Miami and Cuba are still two hostile territories of one Cuban body and soul. These symbiotic relationships with the "significant other" have added to the already rich cultural diversification going on within. For example, contemporary Mexico shows an important revival of regional cultural centers; ever stronger writing by women; and an emergence of diverse marginal cultures (indigenous, Jewish, gay/lesbian).

Our relating Latin American Postmodernism to the process of emerging post-modernity permits us to bring into focus, and to re-evaluate, the various ideological and artistic contradictions concealed in Latin American literature since the 1940s and fruitfully to reread some recent classics from the perspective that can illuminate their "flip side," showing their "reverse" as equally authentic, if not more, as the side played to exhaustion by the earlier modernist readings. Latin American postmodern writing bears witness to this new process of transition.

EMIL VOLEK

See also entries on Chicano Literature, Cuban Writing in the United States, The Post-Boom, Puerto Rican Writing in the United States

Further Reading

Octavio Paz and his journal *Vuelta* (1976–) have pioneered the debate in Mexico and Latin America. Many useful articles have appeared in special issues of journals, such as *Vuelta* 127 (1987); *Casa del Tiempo* (Mexico), vol. 8/81 (1989); *Revista de Crítica Literaria Latinoamericana* 29 (1989); *Nuevo Texto Crítico* 6–7 (1990–91); *Politeia*, Colombia, 11 (1992); *Boundary 2*, vol. 20/3 (1993). Jaime Alazraki has explored the postmodern re-reading of Borges and Cortázar.

Alazraki, Jaime, "Borges: Entre la modernidad y la postmodernidad," in *Hacia Cortázar: aproximaciones a su obra*, Barcelona: Anthropos, 1994

Beverley, John, José Miguel Oviedo and Michael Aronna (editors), *The Postmodernism Debate in Latin America*, Durham, North Carolina: Duke University Press, 1995

Booker, M. Keith, *Vargas Llosa among the Postmodernists*, Gainesville: Univerdsity Presses of Florida, 1994

Chamberlain, Bobby J., "Pósmodenidade e a ficção brasileira dos anos 70 e 80," *Revista Iberoamericana* 164–65 (July–December 1993)

Ferman, Claudia, *Política y posmodernidad. Hacia una lectura de la antimodernidad en Latinoamérica*, Coral Gables, Florida: Iberian Studies, 1993; 2nd edition, Buenos Aires: Almagesto, 1994

Giardinelli, Mempo, "Variaciones sobre la posmodernidad," *Puro Cuento* 23 (1990)

Volek, Emil, *Literatura hispanoamericana entre la modernidad y la postmodernidad*, Bogotá: Unalcol, 1994

Williams, Raymond L., *The Postmodern Novel in Latin America: Politics, Culture and the Crisis of Truth*, New York: St Martin's Press, and London: Macmillan, 1995

Special Issues of Journals

"Modernidad y posmodernidad en América Latina," *Nuevo Texto Crítico*, vol. 3/6 (1990) and vol. 4/7 (1991)

Jean Price-Mars 1876–1968

Haitian anthropologist and man of ideas

The first occupation of Haiti by the US, between 1915 and 1934, was to have unforeseeable repercussions on the cultural life of the country. From the time independence was gained from France in 1804, the history of the first black republic had been marked by intense racial antagonism between black and mulattoes, and extreme socioeconomic division. The presence of the Americans, on whom all Haitians were able to focus their deepest resentments, provided the catalyst for the awakening of a nationalist movement that manifested itself partly, but most importantly, in a legitimized interest in the country's African heritage. A dedicated anthropologist, Jean Price-Mars remains particularly noted for a series of essays gathered during this period in a volume entitled *Ainsi parla l'Oncle* (*So Spoke the Uncle*), where he proclaimed the importance of the Haitian folklore, ethnicity and religion that had been imported from Africa, granting these cultural elements a prestige which was quite astonishing at the time, even in a world where imperialism was already in decline. Along with two of his contemporaries, Dr Arthur C. Holly and Dr J.C. Dorsainville, Price-Mars helped shape the minds of the generation of writers and intellectuals responsible in part for the present situation in Haiti.

Price-Mars dedicated his whole life's work to bridging the many rifts that have always been part of Haitian society; fortunately, he was endowed with a remarkable ability to conciliate outwardly conflicting differences. This talent was already present in childhood, when he moved easily between the austere Protestantism of his father and the fervent Catholicism of his maternal grandmother. He undertook medical studies and at the same time he actively participated in the literary circles of Port-au-Prince; when he continued to study medicine in Paris, he became involved at the same time in the burning social issues of the times. He discovered anthropology and returned to Haiti to pursue a multifaceted career as historian, ethnologist, teacher, politician and diplomat. In a feat of impartiality, he managed never to alienate himself from one side or the other of a given issue: at the same time as he was describing the current affairs of his country, he actively promoted a reassessment of Haitian history from a non-European point of view; however great his concern for the masses of illiterate Haitians, he never dissociated himself from the privileged elite minority to which he belonged by birth; he was proud of his African origins, yet he revered Haiti's cultural ties with France until his death. As late as 1966, in his speech of acceptance of the first Prix des Caraïbes awarded by the AEFMOM (Association des Écrivains d'Expression Française de la Mer et de l'Outre-Mer), he referred to "la France immortelle, la France qui est en même temps la beauté et la lumière du monde . . ." (France, immortal, both beauty and light of the world).

The work thus recognized by France was manifold; in his capacity of President of the Societé d'Histoire et de Géographie d'Haïti, Price-Mars wrote prolifically, in many genres including book reviews, testimonies for friends and colleagues, articles and essays. Consistent with his interest in genealogy and family backgrounds, he wrote noteworthy essays on the founders of his country, including "Le Sentiment de la valeur personelle chez Henry Christophe en fonction de son rôle de chef," 1934 [The Sentiment of Personal Valour in Henry Christophe, the Leader] and "J. J. Dessalines, les origines, le milieu physique, le milieu humain," 1938 [Dessalines: His Origins, His Physical and Human Environment]. His critical works focused on the literary and historical writings of various authors including Jacques Roumain, Max Coiscou and Fernando Ortiz. He founded the Institut d'Ethnologie de Port-au-Prince at the same time as becoming active in the political life of his country. President of the Société Africaine de Culture, he was a distinguished speaker and gave many lectures that were influential on the running of his country. His many interests did not divert him, however, from his main work as historian and ethnologist; his two main concerns throughout his life were the relations between Haiti and her neighbours (with many articles written on the dealings between Haiti, the Dominican Republic, Cuba and the United States) and the African side of the racial and cultural origins of the Haitian people. It is this latter aspect of his work that gave rise to his best-known volume, *Ainsi parla l'Oncle*, a compilation of essays that was a direct reaction to his encounter with Gustave Lebon whose work *Lois psychologiques de l'évolution des peuples* [The Psychological Laws Governing the Evolution of Peoples] concluded that the outcome of racial mixture can only be a retarded or deficient species of humanity.

In a series of eight essays, Price-Mars draws attention to the Haitian peasantry with particular reference to its language, religion, African origins and mores. Haitians could no longer be considered as mere descendants of slaves to a superior white race, but as inheritors of a timeless cultural wealth handed down, through the generations, directly from Africa. The Creole language and the oral traditions of Haitians were now seen as indispensable tools in the passing on of this heritage. Voodoo was no longer a religion of primitive people, but rather a religion in its early stages, expressing animism and dynamism rather than fetishism. Price-Mars's pursuit of the authentic, left itself open to various interpretations: "At its most benign," says J. Michael Dash in his article "Blazing Mirrors: the Crisis of the Haitian Intellectual," "the cult of authenticity meant the honouring of artistic intuition and a rediscovery of the expressiveness of Creole. At its most extreme, it meant the celebration of cannibalism, black magic, sensual abandon and dictatorship." However factual Price-Mars's reasoning, he nevertheless tends to consider the African race and culture superior to all others; the reason for this may not be personal but, instead, the result of his approach to the subject: the science of anthropology being the product of European thinking, it may have been inevitable that the researcher would produce a conclusion that one race is superior to another. But his earnest enquiry and his exalting of a people who were despised the world over earned him one of his lesser-known accolades, that of precursor to the *Négritude* movement; affectionately referring to him as "l'Oncle" during a speech made in 1956 on the occasion of Price-Mars's eightieth birthday, Léopold Sédar Senghor acknowledged him as follows: "L'Oncle légitimait les raisons de ma quête, confirmait ce que j'avais pressenti. Car, me montrant les trésors de la Négritude qu'il avait découverts sur et dans la terre haïtienne, il m'apprenait à découvrir les mêmes valeurs, mais vierges et plus fortes, sur et dans la terre africaine." (Our Uncle validated the reasons for my research, confirming my suspicions. Indeed, by showing me the treasures of Négritude he has discovered about, and in, the land of Haiti, he taught me to discover the same values in Africa, although as yet untouched and more powerful).

Recognition of the wealth of the African contribution to the Haitian ethos was an essential step in defining national identity in Haiti. Although the deeper content of Price-Mars's teaching and beliefs failed to solve the problems of his country to any extent, these have nevertheless a universal application; in a world where cultural and racial mixing is becoming the norm, this final observation from Price-Mars, the reconciler of dualities, sums up an important lesson for all people regardless of race, culture and religion: "Acceptez donc le patrimoine ancestral comme un bloc. Faites-en le tour, pesez-le, examinez-le avec intelligence et circonspection, et vous verrez comme dans un mirroir brisé qu'il reflète l'image réduite de l'humanité toute entière." (Take your ancestral heritage as a whole. Look it over, weigh it up, study it with intelligence and care, and you will notice that, like a cracked mirror, it reflects a miniaturized image of all humanity).

CHRISTINE A.F. ROBINSON

See also entry on Fernando Ortiz

Biography

Born in Haiti, 1876. Studied medicine in Port-au-Prince and in Paris, 1895–1900. Chargé d'Affaires in Washington, DC, 1903–10. This experience made him acutely aware of racism and as a result he devoted the rest of his life to the study of African civilizations and Haitian folklore. Died in 1968.

Selected Works

La Vocation de l'élite, Port-au-Prince: Imprimerie E. Chenet, 1919
Ainsi parla l'Oncle. Essais d'éthnographie, Port-au-Prince: Imprimerie de Compiegne, 1928; as *So Spoke the Uncle*, translated with an introduction by Magdaline W. Shannon, Washington, DC: Three Continents Press, 1983
Une Étape de l'évolution haïtienne, Port-au-Prince: Imprimerie "La Presse," 1929(?)
Formation ethnique, folk-lore et culture du peuple haïtien, Port-au-Prince: V. Valcin Imprimeur, 1939
La République d'Haïti et la république Dominicaine: les aspects divers d'un problème d'histoire, de géographie et d'éthnologie. . ., Port-au-Prince: n.p., 1953
De Sainte Domingue à Haïti: essai sur la culture, les arts et la littérature, Paris: Présence Africaine, 1959
Silhouette de nègres et de négrophiles, Paris: Présence Africaine, 1960
De la Préhistoire d'Afrique à l'histoire d'Haïti, Port-au-Prince: Imprimerie de l'Etat, 1962

Further Reading

Depestre, René, "Jean Price Mars et le mythe de l'Orphée noir," in *Pour la Révolution, pour la poésie*, Montréal: Léméac, 1975
_____ "La Négritude de Jean Price Mars," in *Bonjour et adieu a la négritude*, Paris: Laffont, 1980
Duvalier, François, *Éléments d'une doctrine*, Port-au-Prince: Presses Nationales d'Haïti, 1968
Fouchard, Jean and Emmanuel C. Paul (editors), *Témoignages sur la vie et l'oeuvre de Jean Price-Mars*, Port-au-Prince: Imprimerie de l'État, 1956
Nicholls, David, *From Dessalines to Duvalier: Race, Colour and National Independence in Haiti*, London: Macmillan, 1988

Prison Writing

Since institutional violence is such an accepted part of Latin American experience, its appearance in the continent's literature seems predominantly documentary from the time of Independence. One manifestation of this experience is prison writing, which includes works such as Hernán Valdés's *Tejas Verdes* (1974) in which he relates his experiences in a concentration camp run by the Chilean secret police. His testimony forms part of an extensive bibliography of fictional and documentary literature that treats the violence of repressive Latin American societies. These materials focus on the use of torture, secret police, extra-legal death squads and clandestine jails as institutionalized means of social and political control. From Eduardo Pavlovsky's drama on professional torturers, *El señor Galíndez* (1973) novels on official torture like Manuel Puig's *El beso de la mujer araña*, 1976 (*Kiss of the Spider Woman*) and Carlos Martínez Moreno's *El color que el infierno nos escondiera*, 1981 (*El infierno*), to the personal testimony by Jacobo Timerman, *Preso sin nombre, celda sin número*, 1981 (*Prisoner without a Name, Cell without a Number*), there is a constellation of works in which it is difficult to distinguish between the fictional and the documentary.

Writers employ various forms of narrative to describe prison life: the memoir or the diary; episodic accounts rather than tightly structured narratives; a series of soliloquies and digressions, etc. The characters most often represent symbolic and ethical imperatives as well as aesthetic and psychological ones, as protagonists frequently muse on the meaning of moral guilt and responsibility. The subject matter of such polemical and provocative narratives, whether they be in a specific or unspecified time and place, includes descriptions of the unjust incarceration of political prisoners. Quite often these are based on eyewitness accounts and, as Ariel Dorfman asserts in *Hacia la liberación del lector latinoamericano* (*Some Write to the Future*), such prison testimonials have mainly a threefold function: "to *accuse* the executioners, to *record* the sufferings and the epics, to *inspire* the other combatants in the middle of retreat. A fourth function (not always of primary concern) is to carry out a rational analysis of the problems and the reversals that are being suffered today." Since much of this literature is born of urgency – the need to denounce atrocities through personal accounts as opposed to "official" versions – prison writing becomes a chronicle of protest and subversion in many instances. Prison narratives are an integral part of the resistance itself, since they not only recount strategies of resistance, but are themselves one such strategy. And, most significantly, the literary recording of prison life transgresses the silence willed by the authorities, as well as being a valuable source of sociohistorical information. From a literary perspective, prison narratives constitute a productive interfacing of a narrative explicitly framed by an author or author/protagonist but attributable to historically "real" individuals.

In contrast to narrative prison writings, plays which emerge from the concentration camps usually are the work of internees who are novice writers. But, not unlike their narrative counterparts, these short (usually one act) dramatic productions result from the desire *to communicate* a particular message about a lived experience. The act of writing or, in many instances, re-enacting a memorized performance text uncommitted to paper during internment is a continuation of the act of resistance and of survival. It is still resistance, but now in words: what the prisoners lived through together, shared, and were able to reconstruct and then perform in front of their peers *during* their detention as a collective enterprise from conception to performance, is also a means of communicating with the outside world. It is an act of catharsis at the same time that it is a demonstration of political denunciation and personal defiance in the face of repression. Among the prison dramas written by the Chilean Oscar Castro, former member of the theatre group El Aleph, were *La guerra* [The War], *Sálvese quien pueda* [Run for Your Life], *La noche suspendida* [The Interrupted Night], *Casimiro Peñafleta, preso político* [Casimiro Peñafleta, Political Prisoner] and *Vida, pasión y muerte de Casimiro Peñafleta* [Life, Passion and Death of Casimiro Peñafleta]. In these politicized theatre sketches, the performances took the form of *happenings* due to the total involvement of the camp. And, it was humor and irony, innuendos and double meanings that became strategies subtly to poke fun at prison guards while, at the same time "entertaining" them with the performance text. In effect, their tormentors become accomplices in their own denunciation in these spontaneously performed works. Humor and irony, popular stories and anecdotes are incorporated into these dramatic vignettes of prison life, and, among the prisoners themselves who have become writers-directors-actors of their own lived scripts, a sense of collectivity grows strong and speaks through a thousand cracks of the prison or concentration camp walls. It is community theatre *within* a small closed community that we see here, an expression as much of the desire to keep one's sanity by re-creating personal experiences in pseudo-fictional form as a collective whole as it is the need to scorn one's oppressors before their very eyes without suffering reprisals for doing so. In contemporary Latin American theatre, particularly in countries like Argentina, Cuba, Mexico and Brazil there is a tradition of using public spectacle for sociohistorical information. What links documentary prison writing – whether narrative or dramatic – to the intricacies of fiction in Latin America is its association with the long-standing literary tradition of the region, that is, the close relationship between writing and reality, between literary discourse and fact, between detached author and involved participant. Given the essential value of the sociopolitical commentary and recreation of lived reality Latin Americans have learned to expect from their fellow artists, it is not surprising that prison writing has emerged in the service of sociopolitical awareness and as a testimonial of personal human endurance and triumph in the face of physical violence and psychological assault. Prison writing and political detention, the struggle against torture and the opposition to censorship are at once social and political movements. The counterdiscourse of political detainees constitutes a threatening culture, a challenge to both the secrecy requirement of torture and the disciplinary sanctions that read these incarcerated textual interventions out of the curriculum.

ELENA DE COSTA

Further Reading

Narratives and Drama

Benedetti, Mario, *Pedro y el capitán*, Mexico City: Nueva Imagen, 1979; as "Peter and the Captain," translated by Freda Beberfall, *Modern International Drama*, vol. 19/1

Boal, Augusto, *Torquemada*, in *Teatro latinoamericano de agitación*, Havana: Casa de las Américas, 1972

Cabieses, Manuel, *Chile: 11808 horas en campos de concentración*, prologue by Argenis Martínez, Rocinante, Caracas: 1975

Carrasco, Rolando, *Prigué*, prologue by Luis Corvalán, Moscow: Nóvosti, 1977

Cayetano Carpio, Salvador, *Secuestro y capucha*, Quito, Ecuador: Conejo, 1982

Díaz, Nidia, *Nunca estuve sola*, San Salvador: UCA Editores, 1988

Gambaro, Griselda, *El campo*, Buenos Aires: Ediciones Insurrexit, 1967; as *The Camp*, translated by William I. Oliver in *Voices of Change in the Spanish American Theatre*, Austin: University of Texas Press, 1971

Guadalupe Martínez, Ana, *Las cárceles clandestinas de El Salvador*, Sinaloa, Mexico: Universidad Autónoma de Sinaloa, 1980

Polari de Alverga, Alex, *Camarim de prisioneiro*, São Paulo: Global, 1980

Puig, Manuel, *El beso de la mujer araña*, Barcelona: Seix Barral, 1976; as *Kiss of the Spider Woman*, translated by Thomas Colchie, New York: Knopf, 1979; London: Arena, 1984

Quijada Cerda, Aníbal, *Cerco de púas*, Havana: Casa de las Américas, 1977

Rojas, Rodrigo, *Jamás de rodillas (Acusación de un prisionero de la junta fascista de Chile)*, prologue by Volodia Teitelboim, Moscow: Nóvosti, 1974

Timerman, Jacobo, *Preso sin nombre, celda sin número*, New York: Random Editores, 1981; as *Prisoner without a Name, Cell without a Number*, translated by Toby Talbot, New York: Knopf, 1981

Valdés, Hernán, *Tejas Verdes. Diario de un campo de concentración en Chile* Barcelona: Ariel, 1974; as *Tejas Verdes. Diary of a Concentration Camp in Chile*, translated by Jo Labanyi, London: Gollancz, 1975

Critical Studies

Bunster-Burotto, Ximena, "Surviving beyond Fear: Women and Torture in Latin America," in *Women and Change in Latin America*, edited by June Nash and Helen Safa, South Hadley, Massachusetts: Bergin and Garvey, 1985

Camps, Ramón Juan Alberto, *El poder en la sombra*, Buenos Aires: ROCA Producciones S.R.L., 1983 [First published as *Caso Timerman*, Buenos Aires: Tribuna Abierta, 1982]

Correa, Luisa Rodríguez, "El arte en la cárcel," *La Hira*, Montevideo (19 September 1984)

Dorfman, Ariel, "El teatro en los campos de concentración," an interview with Oscar Castro, *Araucaria de Chile 6* (1979)

Harlow, Barbara, "Cárceles clandestinas: El Salvador," in *Women, Writing, and Political Detention*, Hanover, New Hampshire: University Press of New England, 1992

Ianni, Octavio, *Imperialismo y cultura de la violencia en América Latina*, Mexico City: Siglo XXI, 1970

Partnoy, Alicia, *The Little School: Tales of Disappearance and Survival in Argentina*, translated by the author with Lois Athey and Sandra Braunstein, Pittsburgh: Cleis Press, 1986; London: Virago, 1988

Prizes

There are countless literary prizes available to writers from Latin America; it seems as if almost every nation, every province, every town has its awards for one genre or another. So numerous are the prizes offered that they tend sometimes to lose significance. This entry therefore only highlights some of the most important in the 20th century.

The Nobel, best known and most valuable of the international literary prizes, first awarded in 1901 and open to writers in any language, has been won to date by five Spanish American writers: Chilean poets Gabriela Mistral (1945) and Pablo Neruda (1971), Guatemalan novelist Miguel Ángel Asturias (1967), Colombian novelist Gabriel García Márquez (1982), and Mexican poet and prose writer Octavio Paz (1990). Others, including Brazilian authors, have been in the running; perhaps the most often mentioned is Borges, some observers having claimed that politics explain the failure of nominees such as him.

In addition to prizes open to international competition by writers in any tongue, there are others available only to writers in Spanish or Portuguese; many such prizes are offered in the Iberian peninsula. The most prestigious for writers in Spanish is the "Premio Miguel de Cervantes," which was established in 1967 by the Spanish Ministry of Culture; recipients receive a substantial sum of money from the hands of the King of Spain, in a ceremony held at Alcalá de Henares (where Cervantes once studied); this prize has been won by Carpentier, Borges, Onetti, Paz, Sábato, Fuentes, Roa Bastos, Bioy Casares, Enrique Larreta, Dulce María Loynaz and Mario Vargas Llosa. Another "royal" prize from Spain is the Premio Príncipe de Asturias de las Letras; Uslar Pietri, for example, has won this award. A third such prize is the "Reina Sofía" for poetry, first awarded in 1992, and to a Chilean: Gonzalo Rojas.

The "Premio Biblioteca Breve" was the most important of a number of awards offered by publishing houses, in this case Seix Barral; many of the writers of the Boom were helped to prominence by this annual award, and during the years when it was being made (from the late 1950s to the early 1970s) Seix Barral acquired something of a reputation for publishing what was new and significant. The "Premio Biblioteca Breve" recognised specific unpublished novels; among Spanish American winners were Vargas Llosa (for *La ciudad y los perros* [*The Time of the Hero*]), Cabrera Infante (for *Tres tristes tigres* [*Three Trapped Tigers*]), and Fuentes (for *Cambio de piel* [*A Change of Skin*]).

In Spanish America itself, the Rómulo Gallegos prize, named after the Venezuelan novelist and president (in 1947), stands out; its value is some $10,000. Several of the most successful novelists of the 20th century have received this award: the first winner was Vargas Llosa for his *La casa verde*, 1967 (*The Green House*), and García Márquez won it five years later (for *Cien años de soledad* [*One Hundred Years of Solitude*]), and then Fuentes (*Terra Nostra*); other winners have been del Paso (*Palinuro de México* [*Palinuro of Mexico*]), Posse (*Los perros del paraíso* [*The Dogs of Paradise*]), Mejía Vallejo (*La casa de dos palmas* [*The House with Two Palms*]), Uslar Pietri (*La visita en el tiempo* [*The Recurring Visit*]), and Giardinelli (*El santo oficio de la memoria* [*The Holy Office of Memory*]).

The Casa de las Américas prizes were launched in Cuba in 1959, shortly after Castro came to power. They are awarded for various categories of writing in addition to the traditional genres (for example, for children's literature and for testimonial fiction), and for writing from different geographical or linguistic communities of Latin America, including Brazil, Caribbean Creole, and indigenous languages. In addition to giving recognition to writers, these awards have helped to keep Cuba on the cultural stage; while they are not of great monetary value, they are numerous: some 450 awards have been made during the period up to 1995. Many prominent Latin American writers have won, or have served as members of juries; however, the disaffection of some famous writers with the aftermath of the Revolution has reduced participation.

In Brazil, the national government offers National Cultural Awards through the Ministry of Education and Culture in literature, the visual arts, film and folklore. In the case of local government, the most prestigious prize is the Paraná State Short Story Prize, offered for an unpublished collection. Winning it has launched the career of several distinguished writers, among them: Dalton Trevisan, Rubem Fonseca and Lydia Fagundes Telles. The Brazilian Academy of Letters offers several prizes, of which the most important is the annual Machado de Assis Prize, awarded to authors for their complete works. Other prizes include the Odorico Mendes for translation into Portuguese, and the Monteiro Lobato Prize for Children's Literature. Finally, there is the Camões Prize, established in 1989 with the support of both the Portuguese and Brazilian governments. Brazilian writers who have won it are João Cabral de Melo Neto and Rachel de Queiroz.

PETER STANDISH

Further Reading

To date, very little has been written on this subject in relation to Latin America, even though the various political agendas involved would make this a fascinating subject

Stern, Irwin (editor-in-chief), "Prizes," in his *Dictionary of Brazilian Literature*, Westport, Connecticut: Greenwood Press, 1988
"The Nobel Prize in Literature, 1967–1987," special issue of *World Literature Today*, Norman, Oklahoma (Spring 1988)

Protest Literature

In Latin America, the Catholic Church has been one of the pillars of the established order for centuries. However, its authority began to be undermined from within during the 1960s. This was when Christian base communities, inspired by Vatican II – grounded in "liberation theology" – began to nurture dissent by challenging the legitimacy of established structures and laying foundations for new forms of leadership and solidarities. In so doing, they have encouraged a plethora of subaltern texts, both written and orally produced as performance texts in marginalized communities throughout Latin America, particularly in slum areas on the outskirts of large cities (the Chilean *poblaciones* or *villas miserias* and *campamentos* or squatter settlements, for example) in South America, and in remote rural regions inhabited mainly by illiterate and semi-literate peasants in Central America.

Pre-conquest peasant-based beliefs, which are perpetuated and reinforced through rituals, contribute to a continued collective identity and, as is often the case, form the basis of the literature of resistance that has emerged in recent years. Protest literature has the potential for being a liberating discourse, which challenges its public to transform their world through emancipatory action, as opposed to mythical literary texts whose transformative potential is limited by ideology. Writers began to depict previously marginalized worlds, visions and voices. They used their art as a medium for political consciousness-raising as they explored the changing representations of shifting sociopolitical and historical power relationships. Novelists, dramatists and poets began to approach issues that are a key to an understanding of Latin America and its cultural images – among them, colonialism, institutionalized violence, revolution, identity and self-definition, and socioeconomic centrality versus marginality – with a variety of strikingly powerful and innovative artistic techniques. This was a literarily defined movement as opposed to simple agitprop or political pamphleteering devoid of stylistic concerns and focused on a single ideology. The writers involved in protest literature prefer to address a thinking public, an audience that will enter into a dialectical exchange with one another, prompted by the literary work, in order to explore solutions to the issues raised in the literary text. The insistence on the "here-and-now" of historical reality and its conditions of possibility underwrites much of the project of protest or resistance literature as emphasis is placed, to a large extent, on the political as the power to change the world.

Latin American writers, with few exceptions, confess to an engagement with reality that is *entrañable* or visceral, and it would seem that the vitality of their writing is connected to the urgency with which they perceive and experience that reality – the interaction between self and circumstance. Since the 19th century, the writer in Latin America has not only addressed the most vital concerns of his society (social reality) but has also traditionally wielded enormous influence as a man of letters, as witness, social conscience, and as a voice of protest whenever necessary. Indeed, in the 1970s in authoritarian countries many writers were imprisoned, tortured and "disappeared" not to mention forced into exile for their denunciation of sociopolitical injustices. Whatever the form of discourse – prose, poetry, theatre – or rhetorical devices, the writer's vocation in Latin America has consistently entailed a moral imperative to speak out on issues of national concern – or when that is not feasible, to encode political dissent into his discourse through "creative" approaches to bypass censorship.

One direct form of protest writing is the Socialist Realist novel which provided the reader with information on the sufferings and alienation of Chilean coal-miners (see the entry on Baldomero Lillo), Indian mine-laborers, and on the exploitation of the marginalized in general. With the appearance of works such as Oscar Lewis's *Los hijos de Sánchez* (*Children of Sánchez*), sociological information was diverted into documentary and non-fictional channels (case histories, for example). Of course, social protest writing and documentary realism have demonstrated a more decisive, critical, self-reflective and, at times, propagandistic function in countries which have undergone a revolution (i.e., Mexico, Nicaragua and Cuba) or countries which have experienced social unrest and political restructuring, such as the military dictatorships of Chile, Argentina, Uruguay and Brazil in the 1970s. Contemporary prose writers in these countries have tended to write on political themes, notably novels of political oppression, a major concern of protest literature in the latter half of the 20th century.

[]Spanish American poetry today is full of protest, and one need only look at the shanty towns on the outskirts of any major city to comprehend the reasons for its popularity. The contrasts between poverty and wealth in the vast majority of Latin American countries is so blatant that the poets of social protest must bear witness to the situations they observe by writing *poesía testimonial* (testimonial or "witnessing" poetry). The situations described usually relate to some kind of social injustice (so this poetry is also *poesía social*), and since the poets are generally not only deeply involved in the society that they portray but committed to a line of action, what they produce is essentially *poesía comprometida* (engaged poetry). And, since there is discontent with the social scene depicted, most of this poetry is likely to be *poesía de protesta* as well. Protest can take many forms, however, some of which involve an attempt to alter the situation by violent or undemocratic means. A poet's work, in this instance, may therefore be categorized as *revolucionaria*, *insurreccionista*, *guerrillera or subversiva* (revolutionary, insurrectionist, guerrilla, or subversive). The role of poetry in the liberation struggle itself has been a crucial one, both as a force for mobilizing a collective response to occupation and domination and as a repository for popular memory and consciousness. Often this poetry written in the context of national liberation organizations and resistance movements remains singularly unavailable to the literary institutions for two reasons: its limited production and dissemination in print, and the fact that it does not conform to conventional and canonical criteria adhered to by poets in the North. The roots of Latin American protest poetry lie in the songs and poetry of the various Independence movements. Although the ideologies have changed over the years, many of the issues remain at the core of social ills: tyranny, exploitation, brutality, atrocities and injustices of all sorts. The language of praise of heroism, nobility, self-sacrifice, and physical and moral courage of the victimized in society is pitted against the denunciation of their oppressors. The epic epithets, the turns of phrase, the stock similes and heightening allusions to heroic precedent also largely are a return to that earlier period of engaged poetry, with many modern additions gaining currency in part because they are entering an accepted system for referring to events which move both audience and poet – one which would not only be at the service of a cause but also, effectively, accessible to the mass audience it was meant to reach.

The idea of exposure, to *desenmascarar* (unmask) the realities that lie hidden beneath the façade of a democratic Latin America is the first and foremost task of writers of protest literature. But more than exposure, they see their role as educating both themselves and their audience to the subaltern Other, consisting of the marginalized segments of society who until this point had been both invisible and voiceless. The author of protest literature seeks to create a dialogue among all socioeconomic sectors of society, a public debate that ultimately leads to steps to resolve the problems inherent in the country's social and political institutions. The concept is a radical one in that literature aspires to create "public cultures of dissent." Mainstream bourgeois literature of the high culture gradually has begun to adapt itself to a more widespread audience, to gain a wider appeal, especially through popular theatre and poetry. As a result, self-representations of subordinated groups (such as the Chicano theatre presentations of Luis Valdez's El Teatro Campesino) have gained in popularity as did the "forgotten" or erased histories, texts, memories, experiences, and community narratives of other marginalized groups in the society.

ELENA DE COSTA

See also entries on Augusto Boal, Ernesto Cardenal, Roque Dalton, Guerrilla Poetry, Jorge Icaza, Pablo Neruda

Further Reading

Creative Works

Alegría, Claribel and Darwin J. Flakoll (editors and translators), *On the Front Line: Guerrilla Poems of El Salvador*, Willimantic, Connecticut: Curbstone Press, 1989
Carballido, Emilio, *El día que se soltaron los leones. Teatro*, Mexico City: Fondo de Cultura Económica, 1960; as *The Day They Let the Lions Loose*, translated by William I. Oliver, in *Voices of Change in the Spanish American Theatre*, Austin: University of Texas Press, 1971

Dorfman, Ariel, *Viudas*, Mexico City: Siglo XXI, 1981; as *Widows*, translated by Stephen Kessler, New York: Pantheon, 1983

Márquez, Robert (editor), *Latin American Revolutionary Poetry / Poesía revolucionaria latinoamericana*, New York: Monthly Review Press, 1974 [bilingual anthology]

Traba, Marta, *Conversación al sur*, Mexico City: Siglo XXI, 1981; as *Mothers and Shadows*, translated by Jo Labanyi, London: Readers International, 1986

Wolff, Egon, *Flores de papel*, Havana: Casa de las Américas, 1970; as *Paper Flowers*, translated by Margaret Sayers Peden, Columbia: University of Missouri Press, 1971

Critical Studies

Allende, Isabel, *et al.*, *Paths of Resistance: the Art and Craft of the Political Novel*, Boston: Houghton Mifflin, 1989

Beverley, John and Marc Zimmerman, *Literature and Politics in the Central American Revolutions*, Austin: University of Texas Press, 1990

Boal, Augusto, *Técnicas latinoamericanas de teatro popular: una revolución copérnica al revés*, Buenos Aires: Corregidor, 1975

Collazos, Oscar, *et al.*, *Literatura en la revolución y revolución en la literatura*, Mexico City: Siglo XXI, 1971

De Costa, Elena, *Collaborative Latin American Popular Theatre from Theory to Form, from Text to Stage*, New York: Peter Lang, 1992

Dorfman, Ariel, *Hacia la liberación del lector latinoamericano*, Hanover, New Hampshire: Ediciones del Norte, 1984; as *Some Write to the Future*, translated by the author and George R. Shivers, Durham, North Carolina: Duke University Press, 1991

Gonzalez, Mike and David Treece, *The Gathering of Voices: the Twentieth-Century Poetry of Latin America*, London and New York: Verso, 1992

Ortega, Julio, *The Poetics of Change: the New Spanish American Narrative*, translated by Galen D. Greaser, Austin: University of Texas Press, 1984

Pring Mill, Robert, "Both in Sorrow and in Anger: Spanish American Protest Poetry," *Cambridge Review* 91 (20 February 1970)

____ "The Scope of Spanish American Committed Poetry," in *Homenaje a Rodolfo Grossman*, Frankfurt: Peter Lang, 1977

Poética de la población marginal. Fundamentos materialistas para una historiografía estética, Minneapolis, Minnesota: Prisma Institute, 1987

Puerto Rico

19th- and 20th-Century Prose and Poetry

The first three centuries of Spanish colonial rule were characterized by the production of historical texts – chronicles, accounts, letters, memoirs; e.g., Fray Íñigo Abbad's *Historia geográfica, civil, y política de la Isla de San Juan Bautista de Puerto Rico*, 1788 [Geographic, Civil and Political History of the Island of San Juan Bautista de Puerto Rico] – which later Puerto Rican writers will explore in search of their cultural roots.

The word, devoid of utilitarian contingency and elevated to an artistic means of personal and collective expression, is also present in the form of a rich oral tradition. This popular tradition, a popular muse with Hispanic roots – the African-American contribution, as Efraín Barradas explains in *Para entendernos: Inventario poético puertorriqueño* [To Understand Ourselves: a Puerto Rican Poetic Inventory], downplayed by Hispanophiles, is also an essential part of this popular tradition. Its principal forms of expression are found in the *copla* (four-line stanza), the *décima* (ten-line stanza) its preferred vehicle, the hexasyllabic *aguinaldos* and *villancicos* (Christmas carols) and the folkloric short story with Juan Bobo, whose "bobería" is more apparent than real, as protagonist.

The first "criollo" name of note is that of María Babiana Benítez (1783(?)–1873) Puerto Rico's first female poet. Her "La ninfa de Puerto Rico a la Justicia," 1832 [The Nymph of Puerto Rico to Justice] reflects the influence of Spanish Neoclassical and particularly Spanish Golden Age poets, and introduces some of the major themes and attitudes of the island's poetry: the Edenic vision of Puerto Rico, cultural Hispanophilia and political commitment.

For others, Puerto Rican literature begins with the publication of *Aguinaldo puertorriqueño* [Puerto Rican Carol] of 1843. It is a collective endeavor consisting of verse and prose pieces composed by a group of young writers who wished to produce an entirely *indígena* (indigenous) work that would rise above the *vulgares coplas de Navidad* (coarse Christmas coplas). That is to say, this *Primer aguinaldo* [First Carol] was written by a group of aspiring literati who wanted to become the voice of an incipient bourgeoisie that, understandably, rejected the popular. Direct descendants of the *Primer aguinaldo* are the *Album puertorriqueño* [Puerto Rican Album] published in Barcelona in 1844 by a group of Puerto Rican university students, which included Manuel Alonso (1822–89) and Santiago Vidarte (1828–48), as well as the *Cancionero de Borinquen* [Songbook of Borinquen] published by the same group in 1846, and the second *Aguinaldo puertorriqueño* which appeared in San Juan also in 1846. These works belong to a first Romantic period. They signal the beginning of a *criollista* attitude from which soon would arise a truly national literature.

In 1849, while still a student in Barcelona, Manuel Alonso published the first edition of *El Gíbaro* [The Gíbaro] the first Puerto Rican classic. This compilation of twenty-one *escenas* (scenes), eight in verse and thirteen in prose, eclectic with respect to genre – includes Esproncedian poems (Espronceda was a major Spanish Romantic), a sonnet, short stories with supernatural elements, descriptive *romances* (ballads), scenes of local color, essays in literary criticism – transcends the trivial anecdote and the picturesque detail in order to define what is Puerto Rican. Colonial society was evolving and Manuel Alonso was aware that the rural world he had captured in *El Gíbaro* was disappearing; he wished to leave a written record of it, but as spokesman for the liberal ideals of a rising bourgeoisie he did not bemoan its disappearance. This attitude sets him apart from the costumbrists of the first decades of the 20th century, who, after the shattering events of 1898 sought spiritual strength and support in the past.

Full blown Romanticism – as was the case in Spain – was a late arrival in Puerto Rico, and then, due to the stifling colonial censorship, was deprived of its revolutionary thrust. It coexisted with Neoclassicism, and actually gave way to its reincidence after the death of the two leading Romantic figures, Alejandro Tapia y Rivera (1826–82) and José Gautier Benítez (1851–80). Romanticism, particularly in the prose genres has been characterized as "escapist," inclined toward exotic themes, settings and characters. Yet this superficial exoticism veils multiple allusions to Puerto Rican reality of the time, and Romanticism's affinity for bygone epochs results in works that recreate the island's indigenous past.

Alejandro Tapia y Rivera was Puerto Rico's first great man of letters. He was the creator of Puerto Rican theater, the island's first novelist, a serious historian and a fine poet. He is best known for his plays, among them *Bernardo de Palissy o El heroísmo del trabajo* [Bernardo de Palissy or the Heroism of Work], staged in 1857, considered the best of his dramas, and *La cuarterona* [The Quadroon Woman], published in 1867, which dealt with the subject of racial prejudice, his only play with a contemporary Caribbean setting. Tapia published, in Madrid in 1878, a long epic-philosophical poem, "La Sataniada" [The Sataniade], dedicated to Lucifer, in which Tapia attempts to summarize his vision of the world. He is Puerto Rico's most noted Romantic novelist. In 1848 he wrote *El heliotropo* [The Heliotrope], a short romantically impassioned narrative and in 1862 produced as part of a collection of diverse works entitled *El bardo de Guamaní* [The Bard of Guamaní], the *leyenda* (legend), *La palma del cacique* [The Cacique's Palm], which recreates the conflicts between Indians and Spaniards during the conquest of the island. *El bardo de Guamaní* also includes Tapia's first novel *La antigua sirena* [The Ancient Siren], set in medieval Venice. *La leyenda de los veinte años*, 1874 [The Legend of the Twenty Years], a narration of conflictive love, displays genuine emotion for the Puerto Rican landscape. The novel *Cofresí* (1876), is a work which relies on invention and does not contribute any historical facts to the biography of the protagonist, the Puerto Rican pirate of the same name. In 1872 Tapia published one of his best novels, *Póstumo el transmigrado* [Póstumo the Transmigrated] on the transmigration of souls. Its sequel, *Póstumo el envirginado*, 1882 [Póstumo the Envirgined] is a novelized argument in favor of women's rights. Finally, in 1880, he published two short novels of spiritually refined love, *Enardo y Rosael* [On the Banks of the Rhine], which again takes up the theme of the transmigration of souls, and *A orillas del Rhin* [On the Banks of the Rhine].

The first important lyric poet in the history of Puerto Rican literature is José Gautier Benítez. His two major themes are love and country. Patriotic emotion inspired his most original

and lasting work, the poems "Ausencia," [Absence], "Regreso" [Return] and "Canto a Puerto Rico [Song to Puerto Rico]. In his representation of nature as voluptuous and gentle, Gautier Benítez sings to the Edenic landscape of Borinquen, a major theme of Puerto Rico's lyric poets, as for instance in Santiago Vidarte's "Insomnio" [Insomnia].

As stated earlier, the deaths of Tapia and Gautier Benítez marked the beginning of a period in which a Neoclassical reaction coexists with Romanticism and pre-*Modernismo*. José Gualberto Padilla (1829–96), popularly known as "El Caribe," was the so-called "capitán del antirromanticismo" (captain of anti-Romanticism) due to his fondness for Spanish Golden Age poetry, his devotion to satire and his view that art has a social or pedagogical function. He is best remembered for his unfinished "Canto a Puerto Rico" [Song for Puerto Rico], the first attempt to synthesize the material, historical and spiritual essence of his homeland.

Puerto Rico's most distinguished 19th-century lyric poet is Lola Rodríguez de Tío (1843–1924). The Romanticism of her three works, *Mis cantares*, 1876 [My Songs], *Claros y nieblas*, 1885 [Bright Intervals and Mist], and *Mi libro de Cuba*, 1893 [My Book on Cuba] – is tempered by her imitation of Spanish Golden Age poets and her use of the traditional *copla*. The resulting simplicity of some of her octosyllabic quatrains makes her a precursor of José Martí's *Versos sencillos* [Simple Verses], although she never identified herself with the new *modernista* sensibility, finding her most enduring inspiration precisely in the popular poetry that the new sensibility rejected in favor of more cosmopolitan and aristocratic refinements.

Francisco Gonzalo Marín (Pachín) was a 19th-century soldier-poet. Pachín Marín's commitment to the independence of his homeland, whether in a tone of exalted romanticism, or as in his later poems in *Romances*, 1892 [Ballads], closer to Martí's *Versos sencillos*, is his main theme.

A third literary current coexisted with Neoclassicism and Romanticism – the "criollismo" initiated by Manuel Alonso in 1849 with *El Gíbaro*. *Criollismo* (Creolism) encompassed all varieties of realism in Puerto Rican letters, including Costumbrism, Naturalism and the new Social Realism that characterized the "Generación del 30" [Generation of the 1930s] in the 20th century. The most representative author of this costumbrist version of Realism of the end of the century was Manuel Fernández Juncos (1846–1928). His "cuadros de costumbres," published in newspapers, were later compiled in the following volumes: *Tipos y caracteres*, 1882 [Types and Characters], *Costumbres y tradiciones*, 1883 [Customs and Traditions], *Cuentos y narraciones*, 1907 [Stories and Narrations] and *La última hornada*, 1928 [The Last Batch].

Before continuing with the "Generation of 1898," a brief allusion should be made to the greatest figure in Puerto Rico's cultural history: Eugenio María de Hostos. Hostos wrote on politics, pedagogy, sociology, philosophy, morals, law, economics, history, literary criticism, biography; he practiced all literary forms, especially the treatise and the essay. The one work we need mention here is his novel *Peregrinación de Bayoán*, 1863 [The Pilgrimage of Bayoán] written in the form of a diary. Bayoán is basically a Romantic work which criticizes the evils of the Spanish colonial regime in the Caribbean, and proposes a confederation, symbolized by the names of its characters: Bayoán (Puerto Rico), Darién (Cuba) and Guarionex (Santo Domingo).

It is entirely appropriate as José Luis González proposes in *Literatura y sociedad en Puerto Rico* to speak of a "Generation of 1898" not only in regards to Spain, but also in reference to Puerto Rican literature. For both countries the Spanish–American War had disastrous consequences. For Spain it marked the culmination of a process of decadence, for Puerto Rico it meant that its protracted struggle for liberty was thwarted precisely when a resolution was in sight. In literary terms the effect was similar in Spain and Puerto Rico: a rejection of the purely aesthetic proposals of *Modernismo*. Pure literary concerns were set aside in order to ponder the more pressing question of what was to become of Puerto Rico politically. "Modernismo" in Puerto Rico is principally "Americanist" or militant. Another phenomenon of capital importance in the intellectual life of the country and which will persist well into the future is the spiritual return to Spain as a defensive reaction against the denaturalizing policies of the new colonial regime.

Among the narrators the major figure of this generation was Manuel Zeno Gandía (1855–1930). Although he is often classified as a Naturalist writer and imitator of Zola, in fact it is only *La charca*, 1894 [The Mud Pool], the second in a series of four novels subtitled *Crónicas de un mundo enfermo* [Chronicles of a Sick World], that is markedly naturalistic à la Zola. In fact, Zeno Gandía's novels are closer to the Realism of Stendhal and Flaubert, and of Pardo Bazán and Galdós, and the Naturalism present in the first novel of the series *Garduña* – published in 1896, but written in 1890 – and *La charca* is totally absent from the last two novels *El negocio*, 1922 [The Business] and *Redentores*, 1925 [Redeemers]. Zeno Gandía exposes the illnesses of the society of his time believing, as did Zola, in the redeeming purpose of art. During the long hiatus between *Garduña* and the last two novels, Zeno Gandía dedicated himself to the struggle for Puerto Rican independence. Disillusioned, he decided to continue his *Crónicas*. *Redentores* [Redeemers] is a bitter denunciation of the political situation of the island under United States sovereignty.

Among the poets José de Diego (1866–1918) best exemplifies this position. De Diego does not reproach *Modernismo* its formal and linguistic innovations, many of which he employed brilliantly in his own work, but rather, that in its early escapism, it led poets away from their patriotic sentiments and ideals. His third book, *Cantos de rebeldía*, 1916 [Songs of Rebellion] crystallizes his aesthetic and political ideals. All complementary themes in his work – Hispanism, Latinism, etc. – derive from one central motif, achieving Puerto Rican independence.

The other outstanding *modernista* poet was Luis Lloréns Torres (1876(?)–1944). As its editor, his name is linked to *La Revista de las Antillas* (1913–14), a publication that encouraged and promoted the *modernista* poets. Lloréns Torres is a *modernista* of the second movement, that is, of the Americanist variant. For this reason his models are Santos Chocano, Darío and, above all, Whitman. He brings together the Creolism of Alonso, the patriotic lyricism of Gautier Benítez and the defensive Hispanophilia of De Diego. On the one hand, Lloréns Torres is remembered for the soaring eloquence, reminiscent of Whitman, of his "Canción de las Antillas" [Song of the Antilles], and on the other, for his masterful use of the *décima*.

It was also Lloréns Torres who attempted to transcend *Modernismo* in Puerto Rico with two *-isms* which he put forward in *Sonetos sinfónicos*, 1914 [Symphonic Sonnets]: *pancalismo* (todo-belleza) [all beauty] and *panedismo* (todo-verso) [all verse], under the sign of Whitman and Darío, respectively.

The first post-war attempt at a literary movement was *diepalismo* – this name combines the first syllable of the last names of its initiators, J.I. de Diego Padró (1899–1974) and Luis Palés Matos (1898–1959). Begun in 1921, its innovation was to replace logic with phonetic value, utilizing onomatopoeia as the only basis for its new poetry. Although it lacked followers, Palés Matos continued cultivating the onomatopoeia in his *negrista* poems. Palés Matos is best remembered as initiator of this Caribbean movement with *Tuntún de pasa y grifería* (1937). A better fate awaited the *Noísta* group let by Evaristo Ribera Chevremont (1896–1976), who, on his return from Spain in 1924, began to disseminate the new aesthetic theories current in Europe. In addition, as was the case with many other avant-garde poets, given the patriotic fervor created by Pedro Albizu Campos (1891–1965) and his Partido Nacionalista Puertorriqueño during the decade of the 1930s, Rivera Chevremont combined formal experimentation with thematic nationalism. The successor to *noísmo* was *atalayismo* (1929–c.36), which gathered strength during the 1930s, again combining formal innovations with political commitment, as for example in the work of Clemente Soto Vélez. *Atalayismo* produced some notable works: Graciani Miranda Archilla's *Responsos a mis poemas naúfragos*, 1930 [Responses to My Castaway Poems], Fernando González Alberty's *Grito*, 1931 [Scream] and Luis Hernández Aquino's *Niebla lírica*, 1931 [Lyrical Fog]. Hernández Aquino (1907–88), author of *Isla para la angustia*, 1943 [An Island for Anguish] – and Samuel Lugo (1905–85), are key figures in the next movement, *integralismo*, which parts company with the other expressions of the avant-garde, in that it is a movement affirming Puerto Rican and Hispanic values in the face of the hegemony achieved by the cultural presence of the United States. *Trascendentalismo*, with its most representative poet, Félix Franco Oppenheimer (1912–), opposed the materialistic euphoria enjoyed by those in favor of the Estado Libre Asociado [Commonwealth], by striking a religious note, in an attempt to elevate man to a more spiritual plane.

Three poets who belonged to this period, but who transcended any particular movement are Julia de Burgos (1914–53), Juan Antonio Corretjer (1908–85) and Francisco Matos Paoli (b. 1915). Julia de Burgos's work is a bridge that links the late vanguard of the 1930s with the existentialist anguish of the 1950s. In the final analysis, the strength of her poetry is that it is deeply personal: the principal theme of the poetry of Julia de Burgos is Julia de Burgos. All other themes – nature, death, country – are subordinated to the poet's ego. Her poetry prefigures the strong feminine and feminist current that began in the 1960s, as well as the literature of the Puerto Rican immigrants in New York. The poetry of Juan Antonio Corretjer also spans several decades. Beginning with the Neocreolist affirmation of "Regresemos a la montaña," 1929 [Let's Return to the Mountain] his work can be characterized as an attempt to reconstruct a lost Edenic world. It is this creation of a mythical image of Puerto Rico, that makes Corretjer the national poet of Puerto Rico. Francisco Matos Paoli also defies classification in terms of generation or literary movement. He practiced a hermetic or pure poetry, which nevertheless shares with Puerto Rican literature one central theme: political commitment.

Zeno Gandía's successor is Enrique A. Laguerre (b. 1906) the most important novelist of the Generation of the 1930s. This group of writers formed the first literary movement to come together as a conscious expression of the national will. The members of this generation clearly perceived the threat posed to Puerto Rican cultural integrity by the cultural influence of the United States and concurred on the need to look for the authentically autochthonous, to delve into the past in order to find the living roots of what is truly Puerto Rican, to denounce debasing influences in order to plan a future course of action for the country. The Generation of the Thirties is dominated by essayists, the most influential being Antonio S. Pedreira (1898–1939) and Tomás Blanco (b. 1900), whose *Insularismo*, 1934 [Insularism] and *Prontuario histórico de Puerto Rico*, 1935 [Historical Handbook of Puerto Rico], respectively, were the first attempts to articulate Puerto Rico's historical conscience. Its literary activity centers on the Department of Hispanic Studies of the University of Puerto Rico, founded in 1927, and is given momentum by *Índice* (1929–31) the history, literature, arts and sciences monthly journal founded by Pedreira and others.

The death of Zeno Gandía in 1930 left a void in terms of the novel which is filled by Laguerre. Olga Casanova in *La novela puertorriqueña contemporánea* divides Laguerre's novels in two groupings. The first includes *La llamarada*, 1935 [The Blaze], *Solar Montoya*, 1941 [Montoya Plantation], *La resaca*, 1949 [The Undertow] and to a certain degree *Los dedos de la mano*, 1951 [The Fingers of the Hand]. The second is composed of *El 30 de febrero*, 1943 [The 30th of February], *La ceiba en el tiesto*, 1956 [The Ceiba Tree in the Flowerpot], *El laberinto*, 1959 [The Labyrinth], *Cauce sin río*, 1962 [Riverbed without a River], *El fuego y su aire*, 1970 [The Fire and Its Air], and *Los amos benévolos*, 1976 [The Benevolent Masters]. More recently Laguerre has published *Infiernos privados*, 1986 [Private Hells], *Por boca de los caracoles*, 1990 [Through the Mouth of Sea Shells], and *Los gemelos*, 1992 [The Twins]. The first grouping is characterized by the telluric theme, the rural setting and the *jíbaro* (Puerto Rican peasant) and his vicissitudes. In the second, responding to Puerto Rico's industrialization and urbanization and rapidly growing urban middle class, the city is the dominant setting. The first novels clearly show the influence of the Spanish American regionalist novel, whereas by the time of *El laberinto* Laguerre begins to utilize some of the narrative techniques used by Faulkner, Hemingway and Joyce, and *El fuego y su aire* and *Los amos benévolos* are in line with the formal experimentation of the Boom.

In contrast with the Generation of the 1930s, the "Generación del 50" (Generation of the 1950s) is best represented not by essayists, but by fiction writers. It includes Abelardo Díaz Alfaro (b. 1919), René Marqués (1919–79), José Luis González (b. 1926), Pedro Juan Soto (b. 1928) and Emilio Díaz Valcárcel (b. 1929). José Luis González may very well be the central figure of the group. Not only is he considered as the initiator of this generation by all of its members who acknowledge their debt to him for having been the first to publish innovative stories – *En la sombra*, 1943 [In the Shadow] appeared when he was only seventeen, followed by *Cinco cuentos de sangre*, 1945 [Five Blood Stories] and *El hombre en la calle*, 1948 [The Man in the Street] . The narrative of José Luis González possesses most of the characteristics that René Marqués in the prologue to his *Cuentos puertorriqueños de hoy*, 1958 [Present Day Puerto Rican Stories] points to as typical of the Generation of the 1950s: First, as with the Generation of the Thirties, the writers of this generation affirm "lo puertorriqueño," but they go beyond the emphasis on the local in order to adopt a more "universal" posture. Social and political concerns are present, but these writers are more interested in Man's psychological and metaphysical problems. Certain new themes are incorporated into Puerto Rican literature: sex, solitude, death, incommunication, etc. Second, costumbrism and descriptions of nature disappear or play an insignificant role. We are now dealing with the life of the urban dweller, and also with the lives of Puerto Ricans who live abroad: New York, Korea, Spain, etc. Third, these writers attempt an objective approach to contemporary problems – alienation, rootlessness, the search for identity. Finally, they are concerned with formal and stylistic innovations inspired by the aesthetic and literary tendencies in France, England and especially in the United States – Faulkner, Hemingway, Steinbeck, Dos Passos. These very same foreign writers are also influential in the rest of Spanish America, and therefore, there is a resulting affinity between Puerto Rican and Spanish American authors. The combination of formal innovations, a preoccupation with man's existential problems, and political commitment and social concerns – the protagonists of the works are often a reflection of the author who acts as a witness of the times – places Puerto Rican literature, and particularly narrative, within the literary current which will be designated as the Boom.

The next generation of Puerto Rican writers, the "Generación del 70" (Generation of the 1970s), is strong in terms of the narrative, but also in terms of the historical essay. A new wave of historians attempts to complete and reassess the historical record: Guillermo A. Baralt, *Esclavos rebeldes*, 1982 [Rebellious Slaves], Fernando Picó, *Libertad y servidumbre en el Puerto Rico del siglo XIX*, 1979 [Liberty and Servitude in 19th-Century Puerto Rico] and *Amargo café*, 1981 [Bitter Coffee], Ángel Quintero Rivera, *Conflictos de clases y política en Puerto Rico*, 1977 [Class Conflicts and Politics in Puerto Rico], to mention just a few. This concern with reevaluating history, already present in the Boom, has resurfaced in Post-Boom narrative as a mini-boom of the historical novel, to which Puerto Rico has made its own contribution in three novels by Edgardo Rodríguez Juliá, *La renuncia del héroe Baltasar* [The Resignation of Hero Baltasar], *La noche oscura del Niño Avilés*, 1981 [The Dark Night of Niño Avilés] and *El camino de Yyaloide* [The Yyaloide Road], which describe 18th-century society on the island as demographically and culturally African-Caribbean. Perhaps the volume of essays *El país de cuatro pisos*, 1980 [The Country of Four Floors] by José Luis González best exemplifies this reevaluation of history and culture. González demonstrates how the dominant class has perpetrated a hoax by imposing its culture, the product of the patrician lifestyles of the coffee "hacendados," as the totality of Puerto Rican culture – the *danza* as the typical musical and dance form, the *jíbaro* and the telluric as the main themes in literature. This generation of writers revindicates the African-Caribbean and the popular as the predominant components of the island's culture, whether in the novels of Luis Rafael Sánchez – *La guaracha del Macho Camacho*, 1976 (*Macho Camacho's Beat*), *La importancia de llamarse Daniel Santos*, 1988 [The Importance of Being Called Daniel Santos] – or in the chronicles of Edgardo Rodríguez Juliá – *Las tribulaciones de Jonás*, 1981 [The Tribulations of Jonás], *El entierro de Cortijo*, 1983 [Cortijo's Funeral], *Una noche con Iris Chacón*, 1986 [A Night with Iris Chacón], *Puertorriqueños*, 1988 [Puerto Ricans], *El cruce de la Bahía de Guánica*, 1989 [The Crossing of Guánica Bay] – or in the short stories of José Antonio Ramos, for instance in his character Papo Impala. On the other hand, Juan G. Gelpí in *Literatura y paternalismo en Puerto Rico* sees Luis Rafael Sánchez and Edgardo Rodríguez Juliá as transitional figures inasmuch as they continue the magisterial inflection, the paternalistic discourse of Pedreira and Marqués. Gelpí sees the short stories of Edgardo Sanabria Santaliz – *El día que el hombre pisó la luna*, 1984 [The Day Man Stepped on the Moon] – and the novel *Felices días, tío Sergio*, 1986 [Happy Days, Uncle Sergio] by Magali García Ramis as works of "aprendizaje" (apprenticeship) in which the paternal figure is dead, absent or is replaced as in the case of Ramis's novel, by a homosexual. For Gelpí the three writers who best exemplify the break with the paternalistic canon are: Manuel Ramos Otero, *El cuento de la Mujer de Mar*, 1979 [The Story of the Woman of the Sea] with its themes of exile in New York and homosexuality – Rosario Ferré (b. 1942), *Papeles de Pandora*, 1976 (*The Youngest Doll*), with its representation of feminine eroticism and its repression by patriarchal discourse – Ana Lydia Vega (b. 1946), *Vírgenes y mártires*, 1981 [Virgins and Martyrs], co-authored with Carmen Lugo Filippi, and *Encancaranublado y otros cuentos de naufragio*, 1982 [Encancaranublado and Other Castaway Stories] – whose writing on day-to-day ironies and humorous incidents break with the linguistic puritanism, seriousness and pessimism of the paternalistic canon.

Since the 1960s poetry has assumed new forms of representation and attempted renovation based on a political and ideological act of faith. The poets of the 1960s came together around two magazines *Guajana* (1962–78) and *Mester* (1967–70). *Guajana*, founded by university students and edited by Vicente Rodríguez Nietzsche (b. 1942) is the more important of the two. Under the influence of the Cuban Revolution, these politicized poets saw their poetry as a weapon to be used for the liberation of their people. Literature must start by reinforcing the national culture as a pre-requisite for the liquidation of colonialism. On the one hand, these poets saw their "realist" poetry as breaking with the "pure" poetry of their immediate predecessors. On the other hand, *Guajana* dedicated issues to those poets who preceded them in the struggle, such as Luis Lloréns Torres, Luis Palés Matos and Julia de Burgos. Ultimately, though, much of the poetry which appeared in *Guajana* fell outside the political ideology of the publication. The poets of *Mester* agree essentially with the position of the poets of *Guajana*: the idea of culture as the foundation of the national. Some of the major poetic figures of this decade are:

Andrés Castro Ríos (b. 1942), Marina Arzola (1939–76), Marcos Rodríguez Frese (b. 1941), Juan Saez Burgos (b. 1943) and Ángela María Dávila (b. 1944).

The 1970s were also characterized by the influence of two literary magazines, *Ventana* (1972–77) [Window] – founded by José Luis Vega (b. 1948) and other young poets – which appeared regularly for a year and a half, and after that only irregularly, and *Zona de carga y descarga*, (1972–75) [Loading and Unloading Zone]. The editors of *Ventana*, in contrast to those of *Guajana* and *Mester*, defended the view that ideology ought not to occupy the entire focus of the poetic work, and that instead a balance should prevail between historical necessity and creative freedom. In contrast to *Guajana*, *Mester* and *Ventana*, which concentrated on poetry, *Zona* placed equal emphasis on other genres, and also represented an opening to new currents in literary criticism, and a modernization of a critical apparatus still too closely linked to Hispanism. *Zona* also included works by writers from other Spanish American countries such as Vargas Llosa, Donoso, Lezama Lima and Sarduy, who served as models for liberation and transformation while expanding the island's literary frontiers. In essence, *Zona*, like *Ventana*, rejected the type of literature whose political commitment lead to a neglect of form and an impoverishment of content, advancing the view that Puerto Rican reality in all its complexity can best be explored through the personal dimensions of poetic imagination. Nevertheless, the poets of the 1970s and 1980s show elements of continuity with the social symbols of Puerto Rico's literary tradition. Some of the most important poets of the period are Edwin Reyes (b. 1944), Iván Silén (b. 1944) – *Los poemas de Filí-Melé*, 1976 [The Poems of Filí-Melé] – Rosario Ferré – *Fábulas de la garza desangrada*, 1982 [Fables of the Bleeding Heron], where Ferré destroys myths that keep in place the social and cultural obligations which nullify women as true human beings – Olga Nolla and Luz Ivonne Ochart. The 1980s saw the publication of the poetry of José Luis Vega, Jorge A. Morales, Aurea María Sotomayor, Vanessa Droz and Manuel Ramos Otero. Among these writers poetry achieves a radical liberation, imposing itself on the basis of authenticity, as a discourse of imagination and desire. In poetry the general movement over these last three decades has been towards the personal and the intimate without rejecting the political paradigms and the struggle for social justice.

BENJAMÍN TORRES CABALLERO

See also entries on Rosario Ferré, René Marqués, Puerto Rican Writing in the United States, Luis Rafael Sánchez, Ana Lydia Vega

Further Reading

Casanova, Olga, *La novela puertorriqueña contemporánea. Los albores de un decir (Hasta 1975)*, San Juan, Puerto Rico: Instituto de Cultura Puertorriqueña, 1986

Gelpí, Juan G., *Literatura y paternalismo en Puerto Rico*, Río Piedras: Editorial de la Universidad de Puerto Rico, 1993

González, José Emilio, *La poesía contemporánea de Puerto Rico (1930–1960)*, San Juan, Puerto Rico: Instituto de Cultura Puertorriqueña, 1972

González, José Luis, *Literatura y sociedad en Puerto Rico (De los cronistas de Indias a la generación del 98)*, Mexico City: Fondo de Cultura Económica, 1976

_____ *El país de cuatro pisos y otros ensayos*, 7th edition, Río Piedras, Puerto Rico: Huracán, 1989

González, Rubén, *Crónica de tres décadas. Poesía puertorriqueña actual – de los sesenta a los ochenta*, Río Piedras: Editorial de la Universidad de Puerto Rico, 1989

González Pérez, Aníbal, "Apuntes sobre literatura y esclavitud en el Puerto Rico del siglo XIX," in *Contextos: literatura y sociedad latinoamericanas del siglo XIX*, edited by Evelyn Picon Garfield and Ivan Schulman, Urbana: University of Illinois Press, 1991

Hernández Aquino, Luis, *Nuestra aventura literaria (Los ismos en la poesía puertorriqueña) 1913–1948*, Río Piedras: Editorial de la Universidad de Puerto Rico, 1964

_____ *El modernismo en Puerto Rico (prosa y poesía)*, Río Piedras, Puerto Rico: La Torre, 1967

Marqués, René, *El puertorriqueño dócil y otros ensayos*, San Juan, Puerto Rico: Antillana, 1977

Ortega, Julio, *Reapropiaciones: cultura y nueva escritura en Puerto Rico*, Río Piedras: Editorial de la Universidad de Puerto Rico, 1991

Pedreira, Antonio S., *Insularismo*, Río Piedras, Puerto Rico: Edil, 1973 [Seminal essay on Puerto Rican national identity]

Rivera Nieves, Irma, *El tema de la mujer en el pensamiento social de "Hostos,"* San Juan: Universidad de Puerto Rico, 1992

Rodríguez Juliá, Edgardo, *Puertorriqueños: álbum de la sagrada familia puertorriqueña a partir de 1898*, Madrid: Playor, 1988

Zavala, Iris M. and Rafael Rodríguez (editors), *The Intellectual Roots of Independence: an Anthology of Puerto Rican Political Essays*, New York: Monthly Review Press, 1980

Anthologies

Acevedo, Ramón Luis (editor), *Del silencio al estallido: narrativa femenina puertorriqueña*, Río Piedras, Puerto Rico: Cultural, 1991

Barradas, Efraín (editor), *Apalabramiento. Diez cuentistas puertorriqueños de hoy*, Hanover, New Hampshire: Ediciones del Norte, 1983

_____ *Para entendernos: inventario poético puertorriqueño. Siglos XIX y XX*, San Juan: Insitituto de Cultura Puertorriqueña, 1992

Marqués, René (editor), *Cuentos puertorriqueños de hoy*, San Juan: Club del Libro de Puerto Rico, 1959

Marzán, Julio (editor), *Inventing a Word. An Anthology of Twentieth-Century Puerto Rican Poetry*, New York: Columbia University Press, 1980

Bibliographies and Dictionaries

Foster, David William, *Puerto Rican Literature: a Bibliography of Secondary Sources*, Westport, Connecticut: Greenwood Press, 1982

Rivera de Álvarez, Josefina, *Diccionario de literatura puertorriqueña*, 2nd revised edition, 2 vols, San Juan, Puerto Rico: Instituto de Cultura Puertorriqueña, 1967

Special Issues of Journals

Revista Iberoamericana, vol. 59/162–63 (January–June 1993)

Puerto Rican Writing in the United States

While the first major corpus of texts by Puerto Ricans in the United States took shape in the 1960s with what is known as Nuyorican literature (writing by Puerto Ricans living in New York City), it should be noted that the first Puerto Ricans to write about the mainland experience were those who arrived in the 19th century as political exiles of Spanish colonial rule. However, Jesús Colón and Bernardo Vega are generally considered the earliest Nuyorican writers in that they did not visit the mainland as members of the exile community to reside in New York temporarily; they arrived in the opening decades of the 20th century with the large wave of immigrants that followed US colonial intervention and remained for most of their lives employed in the cigar industry and as journalists, participating in labor movements and local politics. Thus, both were involved in the everyday life of their community and their works comprise a committed documentation of the growth of that community.

Although published in 1977, Vega's autobiographical *Memorias de Bernardo Vega* [Memoirs of Bernardo Vega] was written in the 1940s and attests to the experience of the immigrant population between the first and second world wars. Vega contributed to newspapers and ran his own weekly, *Gráfico* [Graphic] from 1927 until 1931. Colón's articles appeared in organs such as *El Nuevo Mundo* [The New World], *Pueblos Hispanos* [Hispanic Communities], *Liberación*

[Liberation] and *The Daily Worker*. His *Memories of a Puerto Rican in New York* (1961), includes pieces from "As I see it from here," his column in *The Daily Worker*. These pieces are important in terms of their expression of a transethnic solidarity with the racially oppressed and the working classes. A second volume of Colón's essays, *The Way It Was and Other Writings*, was published in 1993.

By 1950, one third of the population of Puerto Rico had relocated to places as far afield as New York City and Hawaii. In addition to heavy industrialization which drained resources and caused environmental damage, the island endured other negative by-products of US colonialism ranging from cultural subjugation and assimilation to the imposition of the English language and the enforced sterilization of sectors of its female population. Such traumatic factors have indelibly marked the history both of Puerto Rico and its migrant population in the US. The literary production of the diaspora is inextricably linked to the experience of colonization as well as to the intensified experience of discrimination and poverty which accompanies the minority experience in the US. After World War II, the principal factor to impact the US Puerto Rican community and its cultural production was the boom in migration of workers to the mainland coinciding with the period of Operation Bootstrap. This large scale influx radically altered the identity of the existing Puerto Rican community, much as the Mariel generation was to do in the case of US Cubans. While the preceding wave of emigrants of the early 20th century consisted, predominantly, of artisans and laborers, the late 1940s and 1950s saw the arrival of what was largely an unskilled rural underclass.

Not surprisingly, the boom in migration became a central theme in the national literature of Puerto Rico. René Marqués's drama *La carreta*, 1963 (*The Oxcart*) and Pedro Juan Soto's novel *Spiks* (1954) are arguably the best examples of this tendency and derive from the authors' direct experience of the New York community. In addition to the thematization of the diaspora in narrative and drama, works by island poets such as Julia de Burgos, Clemente Soto Vélez and Juan Antonio Corretjer drew on a first-hand experience of life in New York in the 1940s. Although island writers had direct knowledge of the migrant life, their works constitute a literature *about* the US Puerto Rican community, not a literature produced *by* the latter. Texts by authors such as Soto and Marqués may be characterized by their reductionist representation of the immigrant experience and by a failure to recreate the linguistic singularity of the urban community. A sense of unfamiliarity and distance arises especially from their use of a standard Spanish which does not reflect the emergent US Puerto Rican biliguality and interlinguality. Yet, since the US Puerto Rican experience had hitherto been rendered, for the most part only in autobiographical and journalistic writings, the island authors are important in that they provide the first accomplished literary treatments of that mainland experience.

In further contrast with island writings of the 1950s about life in New York, one of the first works to offer a more faithful representation of the city community is Guillermo Cotto-Thorner's *Trópico en Manhattan* (1960). The significance of this novel lies in its reproduction of the interlingual and neologistic texture of spoken language which the author explains in a glossary entitled "Neorkismos". In this way, he displays both a familiarity with US Puerto Rican language and a recognition of the importance of the latter as a vital aspect of the cultural identity of the community. Indeed, Cotto-Thorner's portrayal of the New York Puerto Ricans occupies a transitional position in that it prefigures the kind of writing which boomed at the end of 1960s, when Nuyorican literature proper first emerged as an identifiable body of literary works.

The narrative of the late 1960s and early 1970s followed in the tradition of the autobiographical mode favored by the early writers of the New York experience such as Colón and Vega. Among the first novels are *Island in Harlem* (1966) by Manuel Manrique, *Run Baby Run* (1968) by Nicky Cruz, *Frankie Cristo* (1972) by Humberto Cintrón, *Carlito's Way* (1975) by Edwin Torres and *Nobody's Hero* (1976) by Lefty Barreto. Set largely in the ghetto, these works deal with the issue of identity in the context of their characters' involvement in street gangs. *Island in Harlem* is noteworthy for its focus on racial differences within the Puerto Rican community in terms of the conflict between its black protagonist and his white rival. Of the early novels, the most accomplished work, one also dealing with the experience of a dark-skinned Puerto Rican, is Piri Thomas's *Down These Mean Streets* (1967). In the latter, the narrator recounts his early life in Harlem and an involvement with gangs, violence and drugs leading to eventual imprisonment. Thomas's account is continued in subsequent works,

Savior, Savior, Hold My Hand (1972) and *Seven Long Times* (1975).

Through the 1980s and 1990s, with works such as *Family Instalments: Memories of Growing Up Hispanic* (1982) by Edward Rivera and *Eldorado in East Harlem* (1992) by Victor Rodríguez, US Puerto Rican narrative is characterizable primarily by its representation of barrio life and by its concern for issues of ethnic identity and community. Especially notable in US Puerto Rican narrative has been the contribution of women authors. One of the leading prose writers is Nicolasa Mohr who, in works such as *Nilda* (1973), *El Bronx Remembered* (1975), *In Nueva York* (1977) and *Rituals of Survival* (1985), explores the woman's experience within the Nuyorican community. While Mohr provides a significant feminist perspective on the latter, Georgia-based Judith Ortiz Cofer treats a different context of the Puerto Rican experience. In *Silent Dancing* (1990) she documents a childhood divided between Puerto Rico and New Jersey, while her first novel, *The Line of the Sun* (1989), focuses more exclusively on the Puerto Rican community in New Jersey. Another outstanding contribution to the corpus of prose by US Puerto Rican women writers is the recent work by Esmeralda Santiago, *When I Was Puerto Rican* (1992).

Like narrative, US Puerto Rican poetry derives primarily from the localized context of New York yet, unlike narrative, it is a genre linked with the period of political protest in the 1960s. Given its possibilities as a performative genre, poetry provided a means for the communication of socio-political concerns during the protest period. Within that politicized climate, those figures who were to become the major poets of the 1970s and 1980s, such as Miguel Algarín and Pedro Pietri, were involved in activism for the improvement of the situation of US Puerto Ricans. In the late 1960s, the alliance of a political agenda with cultural production is concretized by the opening of Algarín's Nuyorican Poet's Café and *El Taller Boricua* [The Boricua Workshop]. Both comprised spaces in which political discussion was fomented and poetry conceived and performed in such a way that the two were inseparable. The coexistence of the ideological and the aesthetic, and its embodiment in a performative medium, is a salient characteristic of the works of some of today's better known poets such as Tato Laviera, Algarín and Pietri. Pietri's *Puerto Rican Obituary* (1973) was among the first collections to be published and treats the everyday struggle of the urban, ethnic community. The collectively-oriented writing of the streets pioneered by Pietri marks a common practice in poetry of the 1970s and is exemplified in the works of others such as Dadi Piñero, Jack Agueros, José Antonio Figueroa, Jesus Papoleto Menéndez and Felipe Luciano.

In addition to their thematization of the situation of the ethnic community and their articulation of the urban context, respective works by Algarín and Laviera such as *Mongo Affair* (1979) and *La carreta Made a U-Turn*, 1979 [The Oxcart Made a U-Turn] merit attention in terms of their incorporation of African-Caribbean rhythm so as to enhance their performative quality. Moreover, in collections such as Algarín's *Mongo Affair* and Miguel Piñero's *La Bodega Sold Dreams* (1980), while the focus is the Nuyorican community, both poets express the transethnic solidarity shown by Jesús Colón. Their notion of community derives from the barrio yet exceeds the confines of the latter as alliances are forged across ethnic and racial boundaries. In works such as *Body Bee Calling from the Twenty First Century* (1982), Algarín moves away from the collective, objective focus of his earlier poetry but continues to explore issues of identity and community through a subjective and abstract meditation on his own corporeality. That introspective tone which departs from the collectivist sensibility of the early poetry is characteristic of the work of one of the most renowned US Puerto Rican poets, Victor Hernández Cruz. While other poets of the late 1960s and early 1970s were largely ignored by mainstream presses, Hernández Cruz published his second volume *Snaps* in 1968 with Random House and, in collections such as *Mainland* (1973), *Tropicalization* (1976) and *By Lingual Wholes* (1982), he has continued to produce highly subjective and sophisticated poetry. Yet, Hernández Cruz's work stands alongside that of his contemporaries as a vital contribution to the US Puerto Rican tradition and finds resonance with the latter specifically in terms of his use of rhythm and interlinguality.

Recent poetry by women constitutes another strand in a diverse US Puerto Rican tradition. Foremost among women poets are Sandra María Esteves, Aurora Levins-Morales and Rosario Morales. The collaborative work of the latter two, *Getting Home Alive* (1986), articulates a communal sense of identity and solidarity given by a textual linkage of varied ethnic, racial and socio-economic contexts in the spirit of Jesús Colón. Their work depicts a community derived from an assemblage of associated differences underlain by a pan-American, pan-Latina and pan-ethnic feminism. Similarly, in *Yerba Buena* (1980) and *Bluestown Mockingbird Mambo* (1990), Sandra María Esteves explores the problematics of self-representation in the contexts of ethnicity and gender. Especially significant is Esteves's poem "A Julia y a mí" [To Julia and Me] which establishes a connection with island poet Julia de Burgos and stresses the importance of the latter for contemporary US Puerto Rican writers. The tendency towards the articulation of a pan-Latino consciousness in US Puerto Rican poetry is also seen in the work of Martín Espada. In *Trumpets from the Islands of Their Eviction* (1987) and *Rebellion is the Circle of a Lover's Hands* (1990), Espada foregrounds a concern for the situation of US Latinos. Evidence of his solidarity and of his desire to be accessible to Spanish speakers is the publication of a bilingual edition of the latter work.

Interestingly, much of the poetry by US Puerto Ricans written in Spanish does not emphasize a commitment to the plight of working-class Puerto Ricans, nor does it engage so directly in questions concerned with the collective. Works such as *Después del suicidio*, 1970 [After the Suicide] by Iván Silén, *Una puertorriqueña en Penna*, 1974 [A Puerto Rican Woman in Pennsylvania] by Luz María Umpierre and, more recently, *La voz de mujer que llevo adentro*, 1990 [The Woman's Voice which I Carry Within] by Alfredo Villanueva Collado, rarely address the urban context of the Puerto Rican experience or the issues of identity, discrimination and oppression which have traditionally accompanied that experience. Like Hernández

Cruz, these writers opt for a more subjective focus which, nevertheless, serves in turn to enrich and diversify the US Puerto Rican tradition of which they undoubtedly form a part.

WILSON NEATE

Further Reading

Critical Studies

Aparicio, Frances, "La vida es un Spanglish disparatero: Bilingualism in Nuyorican Poetry," in *European Perspectives on Hispanic Literature of the United States*, edited by Genevieve Fabre, Houston: Arte Público Press, 1988

Cortez, Felix, Ángel Falcón and Juan Flores, "The Cultural Expression of Puerto Ricans in New York City: a Theoretical Perspective and Critical Review," *Latin American Perspectives*, vol. 3/3 (1976)

Espada, Martín, "Documentaries and Declamadores: Puerto Rican Poetry in the United States," in *A Gift of Tongues: Critical Challenges in Contemporary American Poetry*, edited by Marie Harris and Kathleen Aguero, Athens: University of Georgia Press, 1987

Flores, Juan, *Divided Borders: Essays on Puerto Rican Identity*, Houston: Arte Público Press, 1993

Gordils, Yanis, "Island and Continental Puerto Rican Literature: Cross Cultural and Intertextual Considerations," *ADE Bulletin* 91 (Winter 1988)

Miller, John, "The Emigrant and the City: Four Puerto Rican Writers," *Revista Chicano-Riqueña*, vol. 6/1 (1977)

Mohr, Eugene, *The Nuyorican Experience: Literature of the Puerto Rican Minority*, Westport, Connecticut: Greenwood Press, 1982

Bibliographies and Anthologies

Acosta Belén, Edna, "The Literature of the Puerto Rican Migration in the United States: an Annotated Bibliography," *ADE Bulletin* 91 (Winter 1988)

Algarín, Miguel and Miguel Piñero, *Nuyorican Poetry: an Anthology of Puerto Rican Words and Feelings*, New York: Morrow, 1975

Babín, María Teresa and Stan Steiner (editors), *Borinquén. An Anthology of Puerto Rican Literature*, New York: Knopf, 1974

Barradas, Efraín and Rafael Rodríguez (editors), *Herejes y mitificadores: muestra de poesía puertorriqueña en los Estados Unidos*, Río Piedras, Puerto Rico: Huracán, 1980

Matilla, Alfred and Iván Silén (editors), *The Puerto Rican Poets*, New York: Bantam, 1972

Marzán, Julio (editor), *Inventing a Word. An Anthology of Twentieth-Century Puerto Rican Poetry*, New York: Columbia University Press, 1980

Poetry and Narrative

Algarín, Miguel, *On Call*, Houston: Arte Público Press, 1985

Labarthe, Pedro Juan, *Son of Two Nations: the Private Life of a Columbia Student*, New York: Carranza, 1931

Fernández, Carole, *Sleep of the Innocents*, Houston: Arte Público Press, 1990

Figueroa, José Ángel, *East One Hundredth Street*, Detroit: Broadside, 1973

Laviera, Tato, *AmeRícan*, Houston: Arte Público Press, 1985

Meléndez, Jesús Papoleto, *Street Poetry and Other Poems*, New York: Barlenmir, 1972

Rivera, Oswald, *Fire and Rain*, New York: Four Walls Eight Windows, 1990

Manuel Puig 1932–1990

Argentine prose writer and dramatist

Manuel Puig's unexpected death at the age of fifty-seven prevented him from enjoying the late explosion of popularity inspired by the success of the musical version of his best-known novel, *El beso de la mujer araña*, 1976 (*Kiss of the Spider Woman*). A hostile off-Broadway reception to this new venture had greatly distressed him during the final weeks of his life and he would almost certainly have been surprised by later events. The "massacre," as he called it, was but one of many disappointments in a professional life that had started with a period of critical silence, probably the result of the disconcerting cinematic references in his novels, which was followed first by expressions of incomprehension and then by a wave of animosity, to say nothing of a series of devastating setbacks.

Although he did not live to bask in the recognition that he has received posthumously, albeit indirectly, he did at least witness an improvement in critical understanding of his work. It had always proved difficult to classify him and this seemed to provoke a certain distrust in his readers with regard to the quality and importance of his writings; some even saw him as a fellow-traveller of the leading players in the Latin American Boom. Since there are no stylistic or ideological bases for this view, it may have been because he was thirty-five when his first novel, *La traición de Rita Hayworth*, 1968 (*Betrayed by Rita Hayworth*), was published, too old to fit comfortably into a "junior Boom" or a "petit Boom"; and, of course, it was far too soon for the more respectable-sounding Post-Boom, to which he clearly belongs. Indeed, hindsight gives us the confidence to assert that Puig was always a postmodern writer, different, even alienated, from the great cultural-commercial narrative flowering of the 1960s.

With his avowed aversion to jargon and literary pretension, Puig himself affected an attitude of indifference towards questions of categorization; none the less, he was in fact hyper-sensitive to reader reception and most disturbed by what he judged misreadings of his texts. He never, as was often claimed, condemned the *cursilería*, or pretentious vulgarity, of some of his fictional creations, admitting instead that he found it sympathetic and touching. He was happiest with those critics who saw him as dedicated to the cause of human happiness, querying invented sources of social and interpersonal injustice, non-dogmatic, open-minded and committed to an even-handed vision of culture.

Even-handedness and open-mindedness are close neighbours of ambivalence, and in an eminently postmodern manner, he had always been a stranger to certainty. This is evident in his novels, not only in his desire for impossible reconciliations between mutually-incompatible alternatives, but also in his vision of the constitution of art and culture. His inclusion of references to the cinema, and the mass media in general, together with his faithful reproduction of the speech patterns of the lower-middle class of the River Plate area, were originally censured by critics who claimed that there was an insurmountable distance between what he was doing and "literature." But those who later came to his defence were not immune from misconceptions either; they placed undue emphasis on the author's passion for tangos and boleros and Hollywood melodramas and ignored his carefully-calculated references to highbrow and middlebrow cultural areas.

In the late 1980s, critics at last began to appreciate the import of his dismissal of the "great divide" between mass culture and "serious" art. He was not pitting one against the other but valuing both as indicators of human truths. It was also realized that his concern for the socially marginal, particularly women and homosexuals, was not a plea for rigid feminism or for homosexual orthodoxy. Finally, it became clear, even to those who had earlier insisted on seeing him as an enthusiastic advocate of social Utopias, that his ideology and tastes were full of contradictions and conflict and that his world-view was basically pessimistic, in spite of the heart-warming optimism he often expressed in interviews. His texts are celebrations of the deeply-moving flexibility of the human mind as it seeks to defend itself against the intolerable constitutional rigours of life, few of which could be eliminated by increased social justice.

Perhaps the most touching example of this is found in *Sangre de amor corrrespondido*, 1982 (*Blood of Requited Love*), one of Puig's least appreciated texts. In a monologue which is frequently interrupted by challenging denials of everything he affirms, an uneducated, unloved, destitute Brazilian labourer re-writes his own history, eventually settling for a swaggering, macho version of it which bears little resemblance to the facts. But he survives.

To classify Puig's writings as lighthearted and "camp," as some have done, is to ignore the fact that so few Puig characters do in fact survive. It is undeniable that humour sometimes is a by-product of the non-distanced irony employed by the author as he deals with his less sophisticated creations, but he does not mock them and the strong vein of naturalistic determinism in the novels tends to preclude the possibility of a happy ending. Toto, the child-protagonist of the Bildungsroman that is *La traición de Rita Hayworth* does reach adulthood, but by this time he is disappointed, even cynical; Gladys, in *The Buenos Aires Affair* (1973), resists the temptation to kill herself but takes a sleeping-pill in order to withdraw from life; like Ana, in *Pubis angelical* (1979) – another survivor – she can no longer depend on her consolatory romantic convictions. Prospects for both these women are bleak. All Puig's other protagonists die: some, like Nené in *Boquitas pintadas*, 1969 (*Heartbreak Tango*), and Ramírez in *Maldición eterna a quien lea estas páginas*, 1980 (*Eternal Curse on the Reader of These Pages*), are completely disillusioned.

It is worth noting, however, the postmodern paradox that in general Puig's characters survive by means of hope and faith; this is true, too, in the theatrical works that he wrote in the 1980s. He is only too conscious that things will turn out badly, aware of the presence of death threatening beauty and love and enthusiasm and desire but he is determined to underline human courage, however misguided, in the face of the ineluctable.

The way he himself coped with disappointment and setbacks is proof of the survival instinct that moved him so much when he observed it in others. His early childhood in a culturally sterile town in the pampas, his difficult relationship with his father, unsatisfying periods at school, then university in Buenos Aires, and the horrors of military service strengthened a desire for the exotic which was already manifest in his love of the cinema. He set out on his travels, but did little more than wash dishes in restaurants in Italy, England and Sweden, his self-esteem dwindling. No-one was interested in his early attempts at writing, either in Europe or in Argentina, to which he returned in 1960. A year later, he won a scholarship to work at the Cinecittà but soon discovered that film-making was not to his taste, least of all when it was permeated by the intellectual Neorealist movement of the day. He was by then thirty and jobless, and he resolved to try his hand at writing another film script. This became *La traición de Rita Hayworth*, which he finished in the United States, where he had gone to live in 1963. Even now his life was not easy. Two publishing contracts were cancelled because of censorship problems and when, at last, *La traición* appeared it was not well received. However, Gallimard then brought out the French translation of *Boquitas pintadas* and *Le Monde* judged this one of the best books of the year; people began to look at its predecessor with new eyes.

Persecution in Argentina at the hands of the supporters of Juan Domingo Perón and his widow, "Isabelita," who succeeded to the presidency of the country on her husband's death in 1974, together with his avowed distaste for current Argentine society and, perhaps, his ever-present escapist exoticism spurred Puig to move on: to Mexico, to New York, and then to Brazil. It was in 1989 that he made his final move: back to Mexico, where he died.

In the meantime, thanks to the personal intervention of Isabelita Perón, he had received no royalties for the film of *Boquitas pintadas*, many of his later books had been harshly criticized (*The Buenos Aires Affair* was proscribed both in Argentina and in Spain), and he had suffered lack of recognition for his film scripts, some of which were changed without his permission; no-one was interested in his early work, and in his home country there actually seemed to be a vendetta against him – when *El beso de la mujer araña* finally appeared there, it was ignored. His theatrical ventures were not all that successful either, with the exception of *Misterio del ramo de rosas*, 1987 (*Mystery of the Rose Bouquet*), but this had to be withdrawn when the London theatre in which it was being presented was destroyed by fire. The film version of *El beso de la mujer araña* was indeed an international hit, but it was not to Puig's liking. And then came the disastrous reception of the first version of the musical.

Even so, at the end of his life, however depressing the setbacks he had endured, he was fundamentally optimistic, still moved and excited by everything. In spite of his fundamental clearsightedness, he never gave up. Like his favourite creations, he too loved and hoped, even if he did not believe.

PAMELA BACARISSE

Biography

Born in General Villegas, Province of Buenos Aires, Argentina, 28 December 1932. Moved to Buenos Aires, 1946. Attended US boarding school in the capital from 1946; studied architecture in 1950, then philosophy, from 1951, at the University of Buenos Aires; received scholarship to study film directing, with Vittorio De Sica, and screenwriting with Cesare Zavattini at the Centro Sperimentale di Cinematografia, Rome, 1956. Travelled throughout Europe, 1956–63, and worked at a variety of jobs, including: translator and teacher of English and Spanish, London and Rome, 1956–57, dishwasher and language tutor, London and Stockholm, 1958–59, assistant film director and translator of subtitles, Rome, Paris and Buenos Aires, 1957–61; clerk for Air France, New York, 1963–67. Returned to Buenos Aires, 1967. Visiting lecturer, Columbia University, New York; lived in Brazil, 1973–75, New York, 1976–80, and based in New York and Rio de Janeiro, 1980–89; settled in Cuernavaca, Mexico, 1989. Awarded the Curzio Malaparte Prize (Italy), 1966; San Sebastian Festival Jury Prize, 1978. Died in Cuernavaca, 22 July 1990.

Selected Works

Novels

La traición de Rita Hayworth, Buenos Aires: Jorge Álvarez, 1968; as *Betrayed by Rita Hayworth*, translated by Suzanne Jill Levine, New York: Dutton, 1971; London: Arena, 1984

Boquitas pintadas, Buenos Aires: Sudamericana, 1969; as *Heartbreak Tango: a Serial*, translated by Suzanne Jill Levine, New York: Dutton, 1973; London: Arena, 1987

The Buenos Aires Affair (original title), Buenos Aires: Sudamericana, 1973; as *The Buenos Aires Affair*, translated by Suzanne Jill Levine, New York: Dutton, 1976; London: Faber and Faber, 1989

El beso de la mujer araña, Barcelona: Seix Barral, 1976; as *Kiss of the Spider Woman*, translated by Thomas Colchie, New York: Knopf, 1979; London: Arena, 1984

Pubis angelical, Barcelona: Seix Barral, 1979; as *Pubis angelical*, translated by Elena Brunet, New York: Random House, 1986; London: Faber and Faber, 1987

Maldición eterna a quien lea estas páginas, Barcelonal: Seix Barra1, 1980; as *Eternal Curse on the Reader of These Pages*, translated by the author, New York: Random House, 1982; London: Arena, 1985

Sangre de amor correspondido, Barcelona: Seix Barral, 1982; as *Blood of Requited Love*, translated by Jan L. Grayson, New York: Random House, 1984; London: Faber and Faber, 1989

Cae la noche tropical, Barcelona: Seix Barral, 1988; as *Tropical Night Falling*, translated by Suzanne Jill Levine, New York: Simon and Schuster, 1991; London: Faber and Faber, 1992

Plays

Bajo un manto de estrellas, with *El beso de la mujer araña*, Barcelona: Seix Barral, 1983; as *Under a Mantle of Stars*, translated by Ronald Christ, New York: Lumen, 1985; revised translation, 1993

El beso de la mujer araña, from his novel, with *Bajo un manto de estrellas*, Barcelona: Seix Barral, 1983; as *Kiss of the Spider Woman*, translated by Michael Feingold, in *Drama Contemporary: Latin America*, edited by George W. Woodyard and Marion Peter Holt, 1986; also translated by Allan Baker, Oxford: Amber Lane Press, 1987

La cara del villano; Recuerdo de Tijuana, Barcelona: Seix Barral, 1985 [screenplays]

Misterio del ramo de rosas, Barcelona: Seix Barral, 1987; as *Mystery of the Rose Bouquet*, translated by Allan Baker, London: Faber and Faber, 1988

Further Reading

Alter, Robert, "Mimesis and the Motive for Fiction," *Tri-Quarterly* 42 (1978)

Bacarisse, Pamela, "The Projection of Peronism in the Novels of Manuel Puig," in *The Historical Novel in Latin America: a Symposium*, edited by Daniel Balderston, Gaithersburg, Maryland: Ediciones Hispamérica and the Roger Thayer Stone Center for Latin American Studies, Tulane University, 1986

____ *The Necessary Dream. A Study of the Novels of Manuel Puig*, Cardiff: University of Wales Press, and Totowa, New Jersey: Barnes and Noble, 1988

____ "Superior Men and Inferior Reality: Manuel Puig's *Pubis angelical*," *Bulletin of Hispanic Studies*, vol. 66/1 (1989)

____ "*Boquitas pintadas*," *Landmarks in Contemporary Latin American Fiction*, edited by Philip Swanson, London: Routledge, 1990

____ "Manuel Puig's *sentimiento trágico de la vida*," *World Literature Today* (Autumn 1991)

____ *Impossible Choices: the Implications of the Cultural References in the Novels of Manuel Puig*, Calgary, Alberta: University of Calgary Press, and Cardiff: University of Wales Press, 1993

Borinsky, Alicia, *Ver/ser visto (Notas para una analítica poética)*, Barcelona: Antoni Bosch, 1978

Echavarren, Roberto and Enrique Giordano, *Montaje y alteridad del sujeto*, Santiago de Chile: Instituto Profesional del Pacífico, 1986

Kerr, Lucille, *Suspended Fictions. Reading Novels by Manuel Puig*, Urbana: University of Illinois Press, 1987

MacAdam, Alfred, "Things as They Are," in his *Modern Latin American Narratives: the Dreams of Reason*, Chicago: University of Chicago Press, 1977

Merrim, Stephanie, "For a New (Psychological) Novel in the Works of Manuel Puig," *Novel: a Forum on Fiction*, vol. 17/2 (1984)

Muñoz, Elías Miguel, *El discurso utópico de la sexualidad en Manuel Puig*, Madrid: Pliegos, 1987

Rodríguez Monegal, Emir, "El folletín rescatado," *Revista de la Universidad de México*, vol. 27/2 (1972)

Smith, Paul Julian, *Representing the Other: "Race," Text and Gender in Spanish American Narrative*, Oxford: Clarendon Press, 1992 [Chapter 5 contains a section on *Boquitas pintadas*]

Wyers Weber, Frances, "Manuel Puig at the Movies," *Hispanic Review*, vol. 49/2 (1981)

Interviews

Bacarisse, Pamela, "An Interview with Manuel Puig," *Carnal Knowledge. Essays on the Flesh, Sex and Sexuality in Hispanic Letters and Film*, edited by Bacarisse, Pittsburgh: Ediciones Tres Ríos, 1993

Corbatta, Jorgelina, "Encuentros con Manuel Puig," *Revista Iberoamericana* (April–September 1983)

Roche, Armando Almada, *Buenos Aires, cuán será el día que me quieras: conversaciones con Manuel Puig*, Buenos Aires: Vinciguerra, 1992

Sosnowski, Saúl, "Manuel Puig. Entrevista," *Hispamérica*, vol. 3 (May 1973)

Special Issues of Journals

World Literature Today (Autumn 1991)

El beso de la mujer araña

Novel by Manuel Puig

It appears to be a cliché – albeit an implausible one, given the success of *El beso de la mujer araña* in its various metamorphoses – to complain of the difficulty involved in choosing one single text by Manuel Puig for detailed consideration. Even so,

it is an unsatisfying and unsatisfactory exercise, and for more than one reason. First, Puig was far less of a one-book writer than were many of his contemporaries or immediate predecessors: in the twenty years between *La traición de Rita Hayworth*, 1968 (*Betrayed by Rita Hayworth*), and *Cae la noche tropical*, 1988 (*Tropical Night Falling*), he published six other novels and at least five, possibly all, of these are worthy of equal attention. Then there is the indisputable fact that one Puig novel does not really provide complete access to his cosmovision, which is gradually illuminated (even if not completely clarified) by the repetition of favourite themes and preoccupations and by the accumulation of intertextual cultural references that reappear and inter-relate in the different works. Finally, the relationship between the original text and the film, the musical, and even to an extent the stage version (which Puig himself wrote) of *El beso de la mujer araña*, is an uncomfortable one, and idiosyncratic directorial emphases and the need for reduction and elimination have served to blur the original multifaceted character of the novel. Indeed, those who come to the word from the image or the action or the music come contaminated by extraneous interpretations and assemblage, and even those whose first experience was with the written text cannot entirely escape this contamination.

Nevertheless, it has to be conceded that of all Puig's novels it is *El beso de la mujer araña* which has truly captured the public imagination, possibly because this story of two Argentine men imprisoned for what is most distinctive about them (political activism in the case of Valentín, and in that of Molina a sexual orientation which has led to a charge of corruption of minors), is all things to all (wo)men. It has a suspenseful plot, with the shocking revelation halfway through that Molina is being rewarded for (theoretically) betraying Valentín, and it also includes a string of self-contained mini-narratives in the form of the film plots recounted by Molina to pass the time and to project his own condition and ideology; each of these shamelessly tugs at the heartstrings while cross-referring to the main narrative and to the other recounted films. In the end, it is the originally unappealing Molina who wins the reader's sympathy as he falls hopelessly in love with the heterosexual Valentín; when he is released from prison, he manages to avoid betraying his cellmate, and it is Valentín's companions in the armed political struggle who kill him. He dies not for the cause, but for love.

The novel has been classified as a plea for homosexual emancipation; a protest against political oppression; the vindication of the mass media; a search for identity; an exercise in the death-defying utilization of narrative; a demythifying picture of Buenos Aires; an elaboration on the psychosexual theories of the 1960s; a treatise on bisexuality; a celebration of pop culture – or a postmodern affirmation that mass culture and high art serve the same purpose; an investigation into "seeing" and the gulf between aesthetics and ethics; even as a defence of women. Perhaps the most important view of all is that of an emotion-starved public which has judged it the story of devoted, hopeless love, albeit in an original, not to say irregular, context.

It is certainly all of these; no one interpretation automatically invalidates the others. Indeed, the trap associated with adapting a novel for a largely visual medium lies in the need to select, eliminate and reduce, resulting in arbitrary points of focus. For example, if a film-maker wishes – as Babenco did in his 1984 movie – to underline the element of political oppression, he will change the *hortus conclusus* setting of a windowless prison cell, with all that it connotes, and give the public a view of the horrors taking place within the range of vision of the prisoners. Even the author himself, when adapting the book for the theatre, was obliged to select only one of Molina's narratives, thereby suppressing the important web of cross-references that exists between this and all the others. It could be suggested that ideally *El beso de la mujer araña* should be read and not seen (or heard), and that it should be read as a postmodern novel, with all the insecurity and discomfort and uncertainty and sense of confusion that such a reading will inevitably produce. There is no point in seeking answers, least of all sociopolitical answers; it is difficult enough to construct a comprehensible question.

Nevertheless, there are certain clearcut narrative, symbolic and thematic points that should probably not be overlooked. How, as an example of the first category, can the reader approach the character of Molina without being aware of the futility – or, rather, impossibility – of his making meaningful vital choices? Though he is indisputably a simulacrum of a conventional pre-feminist woman, a position which might conceivably merit censure, virtually all his other circumstances have been determined for him: his love of men (though he is not, he claims, a homosexual but a woman in a man's body); his overwhelming desire for romantic, monogamous love (at odds with his inevitable life-style); the uncomfortable Freudian division of his loyalties between his ailing mother and his cellmate; his impossible dream of being married to an exclusively heterosexual man; his exceptional need for beauty in a dirty and ugly world.

The symbolism of the film plots is equally significant: Molina identifies with the girl in the first, an adaptation of *Cat People* (1942), who turns into a wild animal when sexually aroused, and with the heroine of the second (invented) plot, *Destino* (Fate), who was born near the frontier between two warring countries and supports the "wrong" side for love, and for the love of beauty. Then there is the misleading appearance of the female protagonist of Molina's version of *The Enchanted Cottage* (1945), with her inner beauty, virtue and culture visible only to the blind or one blinded by the magic of love, and the *cabaretera* (night-club singer) of the Mexican story, whose selfless motives and fidelity are misjudged by all, and who loses the man she loves. There are countless more examples of symbolic protagonists and images which connote familiar problems.

Then, although one book does not furnish enough evidence to make an exhaustive list of Puig's favourite themes, *El beso de la mujer araña* indubitably highlights many of these, from cosmic injustice to social exploitation, from the need for blind faith to the essential nature of love, which solves nothing and cannot ensure a happy ending but which will make life seem to be worth living.

Ultimately, perhaps, the success of all the versions of this text can be attributed to Puig's humanitarian, non-judgmental vision of his fellow men and women as creatures who do not merit the apparently predestined suffering which is their lot and who bravely and absurdly refuse to accept that what they see around them is all there is.

PAMELA BACARISSE

Editions

First edition: *El beso de la mujer araña*, Barcelona: Seix Barral, 1976
Translation: *Kiss of the Spider Woman*, by Thomas Colchie, New York: Knopf, 1979; London: Arena, 1984

Further Reading

Pellón, Gustavo, "Manuel Puig's Contradictory Strategies: Kitsch Paradigms versus Paradigmatic Structure in *El beso de la mujer araña* and *Pubis angelical*," *Symposium*, vol. 37/ 3 (1983)
Swanson, Philip, "Sailing Away on a Boat to Nowhere: *El beso de la mujer araña* and *Kiss of the Spider Woman*, from Novel to Film," in *Essays on Hispanic Themes in Honour of Edward C. Riley*, edited by Swanson and Jennifer Lowe, Edinburgh: University of Edinburgh, 1989
Yúdice, George, "*El beso de la mujer araña y Pubis angelical*: entre el placer y el saber," in *Literature and Popular Culture. A Symposium*, edited by Rose S. Minc, Gaithersburg, Maryland: Hispamérica and Montclair State College, 1981

Q

Quechua Literature

The origins of Quechua literature date back to the age of carving petroglyphs on the craggy rock outcroppings, in the weaving of the tunics on the back strap looms, and the striking of slabs of granite from the rock quarries. Indeed, these manifestations of culture are "read" as texts when Andean scholars pause to consider the knowledge and belief systems of the Quechua peoples. Much of what is considered as literature of the Quechuas is dependent on the efforts of archeologists, anthropologists, ethnohistorians and folklorists who assemble the corpus we commonly label as Quechua literature.

While Quechua peoples lacked the tradition of alphabetic writing, the Andean peoples did possess an elaborate record-keeping device which allows us access to their cultural artifacts. An intricate set of strings and knots based on a decimal system, in the care of a specialist trained in interpretation, is the archive of the historical accounts, the literature, and the material facts of Inca civilization as it spread to the reaches of present day Ecuador, Bolivia, Chile and Argentina. Although the *kipu* is preserved in museum collections around the world, unfortunately, much of the knowledge it contained is irretrievable. With the death of *kipu* specialists in the aftermath of the Spanish invasion, what is salvaged from the colonial period is dependent on the efforts of religious and secular intellectuals who encouraged the writing down in European script the lore of the conquered Andean peoples.

Four well-known texts of Quechua literature all date from the turn of the 17th century. These few indigenous oriented texts share a common theme in describing the accommodation and resistance of indigenous peoples to Spanish rule, as well as narrating the rich cultural traditions of the Andean region. Only one manuscript, the myths of Huarochiri, is written primarily in Quechua with marginal annotations inserted in Spanish by the priest Francisco de Ávila. The thirty-one chapters and two supplements tell a narrative of a remote past, the mythic cycle of Paria caca, the invasions of Huarochiri territory by their neighbors, the Incas, and the missionary activities of the Spanish. The recent English translation of the manuscript includes an introductory essay and explanatory notes by Frank Salomon, which serve to outline the narrative strategies in the text along with descriptions of Quechua esthetics. Salomon notes that the text is a compendium of the oral and the literate traditions; the prose contains numerous markers of recorded spontaneous speech in Quechua as well as framing devices (chapters, for example) common to European books. As a result of his field work in Peru, Alejandro Ortiz Rescaniere has interwoven recent versions and supplements to the Huarochiri tales in *Huarochiri, 400 años después*, 1980 [Huarochiri, 400 Years Later].

We can glean from the three other indigenous colonial texts (written in Spanish) reference to the Quechua literary tradition. Garcilaso de la Vega, the son of a Spanish soldier and an Incan noblewoman, gives us examples of Quechua lyric in addition to his commentary on the training and duties of intellectuals in the empire. His *Comentarios reales*, 1609 (*Royal Commentaries of the Incas*) describes the governing of the Empire, ritual ceremonies, agriculture and the belief system existent before the moment of conquest and the changes wrought after the invasion by Europeans. Joan Santacruz Pachacuti Yamqui Sallqamaygua, in his *Relación de Antigüedades deste Reyno del Pirú*, 1613 [Account of the Antiquities of the Kingdom of Peru] includes many examples of ritualized Quechua speech, imploring the deities to grant the people bountiful crops, good health, and freedom from the ravages of adverse climactic events. Felipe Guaman Poma de Ayala likewise preserves many of the ceremonial verses common to planting, harvest, and occasions of state and provides valuable insights through his black and white line drawings. His transcriptions of the songs in his *Nueva Corónica y Buen Gobierno*, 1612 (*Letter to a King*) attest to the importance of Quechua lyric, which was often recited accompanied by the high-pitched bleat of a sacrificial llama. Diego de Castro Titu Cusi Yupanqui's *Relación de la conquista del Perú*, 1570 [Account of the Conquest of Peru], although written entirely in Spanish, nevertheless provides us with an indigenous perspective on the ravages of conquest, its aftermath, and the natives' reaction to the European system of writing.

Other documents written by Spanish missionaries and government officials also provide examples of Quechua literature from the colonial period. Cristóbal de Molina includes a sampling of Quechua ritual verse (similar to those verses found in Santacruz Pachacuti) in his writing. Recent archival research carried out by Pierre Duviols documents additional examples of sacred prayers from the testimony of Quechua speakers who were accused of the practice of idolatry (17th century).

The Quechua drama *Ollantay* survives in several manuscripts (possibly dating from the 18th century) and in various translations since the 19th century. The tale of the warrior hero Ollantay who falls in love with an Incan *accla* (chosen woman) is more than a simple romantic narrative. The Inca Pachacuti's refusal to allow Ollantay to marry Cusi Ccóyllur brings the elaborate political organization of Incan territory into high relief in the play, as the hero rebels against royal power that emanates from Cuzco. In fashioning this drama about rebellion, we glimpse the dissatisfaction of the peoples conquered by the Incan troops and forced to serve in campaigns to conquer others. However, the play serves to reinforce the power of the rulers from Cuzco for Ollantay is later appointed to high office by Pachacuti's son, Cusi Ccóyllur is released from prison, and the two are permitted to reunite, along with a daughter sheltered in a convent during their long separation.

The memory of Atahualpa, the Incan ruler executed by the Spanish invader Francisco Pizarro, is promulgated in Quechua drama and poetry, with recourse to an elegiac tone. *Tragedia del fin de Atawallpa* [The Tragedy of the Death of Atawallpa], transcribed in 1871, contains three acts in which Atahualpa's dream about the Spanish is interpreted, the mystery of European writing is commented upon and, finally, the Spaniards come before the Inca in his palace whereupon Pizarro plunges his sword into the Incan ruler. The final scene in this drama depicts Pizarro doubly cursed by Spanish king and the native peoples of the Andes, leading to his death at the close of the play. Such just retribution is not found in two other well-known poems: "*Apu Inka Atawallpaman*" [For the Inca Atahualpa] and "*Atawallpa wañuy*" [The Death of Atahualpa]. Both versions lament the cruel circumstances of the ruler's demise and convey despair at what the future may hold for the conquered peoples. A version of the drama of conquest is still colorfully performed in Oruru, Bolivia, every year where Atahualpa's death occupies central stage. In addition, in the collected myths about Inkarrí, a composite Atahualpa figure, a millennial subtext is revealed; Inkarrí, beheaded by the Spanish, will return to lead his people out of poverty and subjugation when his buried head and his buried body grow back together again to form one whole piece.

For José María Arguedas this tragic, cosmic anguish is frequently expressed in Quechua poetry and prose after the death of Atahualpa:

Creemos que con estos versos se inicia claramente el período de la desolación en la literatura quechua. El hombre peruano antiguo se despide del universo creado por sus manos e ingresa bruscamente en la servidumbre aún no concluída . . .

[We believe that from the time of these poems a time of "desolation" is expressed in Quechua literature. The ancient Peruvians saw the last of a universe created by their own hands and entered very abruptly into a servitude that has no end . . .]

Many of the anthologies of Quechua verse compiled by Lira, Farfán, Escobar, Mera, Arguedas and the Montoyas give evidence of this theme, along with profound feelings of amorous attraction, planting and harvest songs, and songs about everyday objects and occurrences. Certainly, the *Autobiografía*, 1977 [Autobiography] of Gregorio Condori Mamani explains poignantly his isolation at being raised an orphan and the solace he sought in the Quechua oral tradition to create a sense of place for himself. In fact, the hardships of incarceration or military boot camp are alleviated by the tales and songs of Quechua-speaking companions.

A similar expression of isolation colors the poetry of Juan Wallparimachi Mayta, an orphan, who writes of absence of his beloved and of maternal attention. In another context, he is remembered as the author of the translation to Quechua of a proclamation of independence in February of 1811. In recent years, Quechua speakers – along with other indigenous communities – have published outspoken declarations of their rights and proclamations of their cultural heritage. With increasing fervor, and increasingly sophisticated access to national media, indigenous communities are determining both who they are and what they represent as defined by their own criteria, not by categories imposed upon them by others. Literary production, such as the poems by Ariruma Kowii, mirror this self-conscious reflection and the vigorous promotion of indigenous values.

REGINA HARRISON

Further Reading

Boone, Elizabeth and Walter D. Mignolo (editors), *Writing without Words: Alternative Literacies in Mesoamerica and the Andes*, Durham, North Carolina: Duke University Press, 1994

Harrison, Regina, *Signs, Songs and Memory in the Andes: Translating Quechua Language and Culture*, Austin: University of Texas Press, 1989

Ossio, Juan M. (editor), *Ideología mesiánica del mundo andino*, Lima: Ignacio Prado Pastor, 1973

Rachel de Queiroz 1910–

Brazilian prose writer, literary translator and dramatist

Rachel de Queiroz's literary production situates her among the classic writers of Brazilian literature. This is meant in the sense of language and verbal brilliance; in the sense, also, of her humanity and warm vision of the everyday life of humble people. A pioneer of the so-called "Novel of the northeast" (together with José Américo de Almeida, José Lins do Rego and Jorge Amado) she also explores the popular imagination, and is able, with the creativity of an outstanding storyteller, to value the treasure trove to be found in the oral tradition. Her first novel *O quinze*, 1930 [The Year Nineteen Fifteen], was published when she was only twenty years old. It is a work set against a social backdrop and is realistic in its portrayal of a people's struggle against poverty and drought, reflecting the social fermentation of the age. With this portrayal she established a cycle, that of the novel of the northeast, which examines the life and the land of that region in fiction.

In *O quinze*, whose title refers to a year of severe drought, one of the most dramatic periods of a region in the Brazilian interior is described using sombre panels, linked to the lives of the characters. It can be seen as a document that treats the fictional material in an objective manner. Devoid of sentimentality, it portrays the clash of lives, and the pathetic encounters and separations.

There followed other novels, a wide journalistic output (collected in various volumes of chronicles), plays, children's literature and innumerable translations – especially of Charlotte Brontë's works – a particular favourite of hers.

The conflicts of life determine the characteristics that will remain in her later works: characteristics such as: directness of language; succinct episodes; and concise descriptions. This regional variant of Realism surpasses the "novel of manners" because it brings to life the social material and passes judgement on it, without being sensationalist or aggressive. One person's drama becomes everybody's everyday story. Among the characters in her novels – and in her plays – the female ones are of special interest. In *O quinze*, the dialogue and settings betray the dramatic elements. Though a theatrical scene might be able to cover or reveal more adequately certain situations, the thematic constants cannot surpass the novel's power of expression. She created paradigmatic female types: the strong and the submissive; the legendary Dona Brites; and the no less legendary Maria Bonita. They were created with lucidity, and with a capacity to observe the subtle nuances of a woman's behaviour. Queiroz gives impetus to fiction as life and humanity, and integrates herself in the regional dramas. The intensity of these dramas is increased because she is present, participating in them, and infusing them with passion. Psychological inquiry makes her face drought, the *cangaceiro* (the bandit) and fanaticism.

Having reached literary maturity, new possibilities unfold in later novels, such as *João Miguel*, 1932 [John Michael]. The novel is like an extension of *O quinze*, in another space: a common man, his crime and his woman. But it still remains in the saga of the northeast, with a character that could have played a part in the earlier novel.

In *Caminho de pedras*, 1937 [Stony Road] the social preoccupations, whose exponent is a female character, Noemí, are presented through revolutionary fervour. In her path towards the moment of liberation and consciousness she confronts, with firmness and resolution, the many difficulties that she encounters. The novel is structured to achieve a balance between context and individual behaviour, intimate impulses (the passionate relationship between Roberto and Noemí) and social impulses (the revolutionary cause). The novel is one of compromise, but its critique of politics (of the authoritarian government that allows social misery) does not reduce the quality of the fiction of a writer capable of structuring novelistic elements with sensitivity.

The rural drama of a drought finds its complement in the drama of urban poverty. Provincial bourgeois society closes the cycle in *As três Marias*, 1939 (*The Three Marias*). It is shaped by personal experience and narrated in the first person, which gives the novel an autobiographical feel: because of its reconstruction through memory and the protagonist's longing to communicate, full of questions and doubts. The novel addresses the problem of the emancipation of women, prisoners of traditional social structures, and addresses, too, their fight to demolish prejudice. Queiroz abandons the political novel in favour of psychological inquiry of an intimate nature. The female characters to be found at the convent school, lend themselves to social inquiry. In *Dora, Doralina* (1975), the narrator surpasses herself in terms of characterisation, creating a gallery of unforgettable characters. Objective information is transfigured by the range of images.

In *Memorial de Maria Moura*, 1992 [Maria Moura's Memorial], there is a permeation of history and fiction summoned up by memory. Action and introspection alternate in an intricate combination. The changes in point of view of the characters/narrators express the intimacy of each of them. Besides the protagonist who lends her name to the title of the novel, *Memorial de Maria Moura* is narrated by other characters such as Beato Romano (Father José Maria, also on the run from the police). The narrative voice does not comment on the action, and the exposition of social problems (a characteristic of Queiroz's works) instead comes about through the circumstances of a narration that reports and informs. One story penetrates another and complements it. Ironically, the novel is dedicated to "Her Majesty Elizabeth I, Queen of England (1558–1603), for her inspiration." The queen, Elizabeth I, celibate like Maria Moura, armed ships and men in order to attack the galleons that transported gold to Europe from the New World. Maria Moura plans crimes and hold-ups but has a code of honour. She crosses frontiers and creates her own history, becoming a symbol of liberty and of courage. The female character wants to dispense with frontiers and transcend space: Maria Moura by right of conquest through power and force; Marialva, through her ingenuous dreams.

Secrets cross one another in the various strands of the novel: that of Maria Moura's confession to the ex-priest, and his own secret which follows; the cubicle wherein are locked mysteries and treasures, and the trunk that holds "the things rescued from the fire." Desire, frustrated and oppressed by the law, pulsates in the work, and the spaces (such as the confessional) are profaned by transgressions. There are traces in the writing of the linguistic effort involved, since the novel has been created using almost solely the lexicon of the age.

With Queiroz, women's literary language entered the sphere of social themes. She was the first female Brazilian novelist to inscribe herself on an equal plane with her male counterparts, and was the first woman member of the Brazilian Academy of Literature. From the regionalist novel (which consisted of a critical and anti-exotic outlook) to the urban novel, she is characterized by her power of reconstruction of the age, and the power of synthesis. Political engagement and penetrating analysis of behaviour are brought together in a humane manner.

Queiroz also saw the value of the *crônica* or newspaper feature as a vehicle for literary expression. She fused power of observation with direct language, and objective perception with the capacity to bear witness.

BELLA JOZEF

translated by Luis González Fernández

Biography
Born in Fortaleza, Ceará, Brazil, 17 November 1910. Attended the Colégio da Imaculada Conceição, Fortaleza, 1921–25; completed training as a primary school teacher at the age of 15. Teacher from 1925 to 1930. From 1927, contributor, and later editor of *O Ceará*; from 1930 weekly newspaper and magazine columnist for various publications including *Última Hora*, *Jornal do Comércio*, *Folha Carioca* and *A Cigarra*. Member of the Brazilian Communist Party from 1931 to 1933, expelled. Imprisoned, briefly, as a Leftist intellectual by Getúlios Vargas's government, 1937. Translator of Russian and English literary works for the publishers José Olympio, Rio de Janeiro, from the early 1940s. Brazilian delegate to the United Nations General Assembly and its Human Rights Commission, 1966. Recipient of numerous literary awards including: Graça Aranha Foundation Prize, 1931; Felipe d'Oliviera Society Prize, 1939 for *As três Marias*; *O Estado de São Paulo* Saci Prize, 1953; Brazilian Academy Machado de Assis Prize, 1957; National Book Institute Theatre Prize, 1959; Paulo Brito Prize, 1959. First Woman Member of the Brazilian Academy of Letters, 1977.

Selected Works

Novels
O quinze, Fortaleza, Brazil: Estabelecimento Gráfico Urânia, 1930
João Miguel, Rio de Janeiro: Schmidt, 1932
Caminho de pedras, Rio de Janeiro: José Olympio, 1937
As três Marias, Rio de Janeiro: José Olympio, 1939; as *The Three Marias*, translated by Fred P. Ellison, Austin: University of Texas Press, 1963
Dora, Doralina, Rio de Janeiro: José Olympio, 1975; as *Dora Doralina*, translated by Dorothy Scott Loos, New York: Avon, 1984
Memorial de Maria Moura, São Paulo: Siciliano, 1992

Journalism (*crônicas*)
A donzela e a moura Torta, Rio de Janeiro: José Olympio, 1948
100 crônicas escolhidas, Rio de Janeiro: José Olympio, 1958
O brasileiro perplexo, Rio de Janeiro: Editora do Autor, 1963
O caçador de tatu, Rio de Janeiro: José Olympio, 1967
"As meninhas" e outras crônicas, Rio de Janeiro: José Olympio, 1976
O jogador de sinuca e mais historinhas, Rio de Janeiro: José Olympio, 1980

Plays
Lampião: drama em 5 quadros, Rio de Janeiro: José Olympio, 1953
A beata Maria do Egito: peça em 3 atos e 4 quadros, Rio de Janeiro: José Olympio, 1958

Compilations and Anthologies
Obra reunida, Rio de Janeiro: José Olympio, 1989

Further Reading
Almeida, José Mauricio Gomes, "O regionalismo nordestino de 30," in *A tradição regionalista no romance brasileiro*, Rio de Janeiro: Achiami, 1981
Bruno, Haroldo, *Rachel de Queiroz: crítica, biografia, bibliografia, depoimento, seleção de textos, iconografia*, Rio de Janeiro: Cátedra, and Brasilia: Instituto Nacional do Livro, 1977
Courteau, Joanna, "The Problematic Heroine in the Novels of Rachel de Queiroz," *Luso-Brazilian Review*, vol. 22/2 (1985)
____ *Dora, Doralina*: the Sexual Configuration of Discourse," *Chasqui*, vol. 20/1 (1991)
Ellison, Fred P., "Rachel de Queiroz," in his *Brazil's New Novel: Four Northeastern Masters*, Berkeley: University of California Press, 1954
Filho, Adonias, "Rachel de Queiroz," in his *O romance brasileiro de 30*, Rio de Janeiro: Bloch, 1969
Portella, Eduardo (editor), *O romance de 30 no nordeste*, Fortaleza, Brazil: Universidade Federal do Ceará, 1983

Horacio Quiroga 1878–1937

Uruguayan short story writer

Horacio Quiroga is a serious contender for the symbolic title "father of the Latin American Short Story." Among the first to advance a theory (however sketchy) of the short story form, he was probably the first to cultivate it to the exclusion of other literary modes (his poetry, like that of Cervantes, largely being both forgotten and forgettable). He not only crafted some of the most classic short narratives of the Spanish language, but established it as a literary genre of value, not as the short-winded sibling of the novel, but on its own merits. Influenced by Poe (whose commentary on Hawthorne's *Twice-Told Tales* is clearly visible in Quiroga's ideas), Quiroga also served as a model for more recent narrators, such as Julio Cortázar. Hence he serves both as a figure of historical dimensions in the development of literature in Spanish America, and as a writer of high value and standards on his own.

Both the biography and the short fiction of Horacio Quiroga are characterized by tragedy, violence and inevitable fatalism as man confronts two all-powerful antagonists: nature and his own existential fate. Quiroga's own death, by suicide, followed those of his father, stepfather and wife (the latter dying after a full week of suffering) and the accidental shooting, by the young Quiroga himself, of a close friend. In his tales death is just as pervasive, protean and arbitrary, serving finally to portray human life as a pre-ordained struggle that, however valiant, affirms inglorious destiny and the futility of individual action. In Quiroga, hope is foolish illusion, a lie to which we cling even knowing full well the awful and mortal truth it hides.

Quiroga is usually, and appropriately, classified as a regionalist or creolist writer, for he sets his tales in specific locales, typically the jungle of the Paraná River region, where Uruguay and Argentina blur together, where people live isolated from the adornments and comforts of civilization. (A few tales enter the realm of the sociopolitical, such as "Los Mensú" [The Contract Laborers]). As in other writers of this group – Rómulo Gallegos, Ricardo Güiraldes, José Eustasio Rivera – the untamable hostility of the jungle is man's most visible foe, the one whose action brings his brief life to a sudden end by the diseases, snakebites or accidents which affirm what he knew all along: that he simply cannot win, regardless of what it is he was striving for when struck down. Neither economic success, personal recognition, freedom from oppression nor even love itself can survive in Quiroga's representation of nature.

These themes, generally recognized by Quiroga's readers and critics, are valid, and can readily be observed in his most famous stories, many of which are available in English and in multiple anthologies of Spanish American literature. Yet there are aspects of Quiroga's works that are too often overlooked, since the overwhelming violence of life seems to drown out other messages he has for us, in some of which his characters themselves bear part of the blame for their tragic ends. In other words, man is always a victim of life; but he is also, at times, a victim of his own nature and failings, and even of his own aspirations, since these predispose him to vulnerabilities he might avoid if he could but take refuge in stoicism and ironic rejection of existence.

In "El hombre" [The Man], the nameless protagonist slips while crossing a fence he had built around his banana patch, an action he had taken in the selfsame way every day: but this day, for no identifiable cause, he is to die. Nothing is different: he has done nothing unusual, is aware of no great crimes; all about him is just as always while his life drains into the soil his own work had softened. The futility of his life and the absurdity of its end are sad enough. Yet a final blow comes, for the last thing he sees is his own horse, awaiting the man's final breath to begin eating the very plants which had symbolized his owner's life.

Similarly, "El hombre muerto" [The Dead Man] steps on an unseen snake, an event equally lacking cause-and-effect relationship as that of "El hombre." And like the first protagonist, this man finds disillusionment: whereas the first one sees his life's work about to be destroyed along with himself, the Dead Man begins to feel better only as he draws his last breath. Hope, as we said, is illusion, as we readers, like his characters, know very well. Yet Quiroga's skill and our own refusal or inability to recognize such a harsh and unrelenting view leads us, and them, to hope in vain. This man was "dead" – doomed, along with his life's labor – from the first. And yet again, the father of "El hijo" [The Son] sees his only child, whom he had thought dead of a gunshot while hunting, finally return: but in the last scene the narrator reveals that the "son" is but a hallucination of the man's mind, unable to cope with the death that has in fact been real all along.

These tales exemplify the all-powerful and soulless cruelty of nature and inhuman fate. Yet, as was mentioned earlier, Quiroga wrote tales with another dimension, which are also much better antecedents of the short story of the latter part of the 20th century in their use of ambiguity, dualities and psychological penetration. These stories merge with the others to give us a full view of Quiroga, who was – perhaps without fully knowing it – something of an existentialist before his time: life is a dead-end, but the individual contributes to the specifics of his demise. Two examples of such narratives may suffice.

"El almohadón de plumas" [The Feather Pillow] presents, in its grotesque ending, a parasitic creature, which has slowly and nightly drained a young bride of blood from its hiding place in her feather pillow. Hostile, arbitrary nature once again? Only in part, for a closer reading of the tale finds ample reason to realize that there exists a parallel between the creature and the new husband, whose coldness, distance and inability or unwillingness to meet his wife's inner needs suck her spirit dry. (María Luisa Bombal's "El árbol" [The Tree] has close parallels). Indeed, the creature can be seen as symbolic only of this psychological "parasitism," as having no physical existence, although the story works best by giving both readings full credence. This interpretive openness – are both true? only one? and if only one reading is "true," which? – typifies more recent Latin American writing, and in technique and theme is a worthy precedent for Cortázar, Borges and others.

"La gallina degollada" (translated both as "The Decapitated Chicken" and "Justice," the latter title involving a liberty on the translator's part) is a classic of gore, horror and dual retribution: the arbitrary, blind "retribution" of existential hostility – a couple's sons, deeply longed for to sanctify their marriage, suffer a fever of no particular origin and become physically repulsive and mentally retarded – and another, "caused," if there ever is true causality in Quiroga, by their failure to respond positively to their tragedy. Instead, they abandon their sons, the daily visual reminder of their failing marriage, personal flaws and impotent fury at life and each other. Their neglect is partially responsible for the final scene, where, imitating a maid's preparation of a chicken for a meal, the sons behead their younger sister, the only normal offspring of the ill-fated couple. This couple, and the husband in "El almmohadón de pluma," are in a sense innocent; yet all suffer the horrors of a fate beyond their powers either to forsee or to forestall, and in which they must share some of the blame.

Quiroga is a master in the use of narrative focus and point of view; of symbolism – the coffin-like canyons of "A la deriva" [Drifting], for instance; and of the subtle use of narrative versus chronological time. His prose is more often stark than beautiful, for stark are his themes, but his blending of the *mot juste*, use of narrative structures which allow no irrelevant distractions and skillfully facilitate their themes' full impact, and his creative use of symbolism and simple unilinear action make him a widely-read and still-influential master of the short story. These characteristics, expressive of his chosen themes, give us a writer who concentrates on the tragic in metaphysical terms, that which has no adequate explanation. He always reminds us of our limitations, vulnerabilities and frailties, and that fate may – however we may hope or struggle against it – overwhelm our human condition.

PAUL W. BORGESON, JR

Biography

Born in Salto, Uruguay, 31 December 1878. Father died in a hunting accident a few months later. Family moved to Córdoba, Argentina, c.1878 and returned to Salto in 1883; moved to Montevideo in 1891. Attended the University of Montevideo, briefly. Began to publish in local magazines from 1897. Founding editor of *Revista de Salto*, 1899–90. Visited Paris, returning to Montevideo in July 1900. Accidentally shot and killed a friend, 1902 and left for Buenos Aires. Taught Spanish at the British School, Buenos Aires, 1903. Offical photographer on an expedition to Misiones in northeast Argentina, led by the poet Leopoldo Lugones. In 1904, settled in Chaco province in the north of the Argentine and planted cotton, 1904, but the venture failed and he abandoned the project a year later. Taught at the Escuela Normal, Buenos Aires, 1906–11; fell in love with a pupil, Ana María Cires, whom he married in 1909; one daughter and one son. Moved to San Ignacio, Misiones, on the river Paraná, where he assumed post of registrar. Ana María died a lingering death, having taken poison, 1915. Returned to Buenos Aires and settled there with his children, 1916. Worked in the Uruguyan consolate, Buenos Aires, 1917–25; returned to Misiones, 1925. Married María Elena Bravo, a friend of his daughter, in 1927. Appointed Uruguay's honorary consul in San Ignacio, 1935. Diagnosed as having cancer and committed suicide, 19 February 1937.

Selected Works

Short Fiction
Los arrecifes de coral, Montevideo: El Siglo Ilustrado, 1901 [prose and verse]
El crimen del otro, Buenos Aires: Emilio Spinelli, 1904
Cuentos de amor, de locura y de muerte, Buenos Aires: Sociedad Cooperativa Editora, Imprenta Mercatali, 1917
Cuentos de la selva para niños, Buenos Aires: Sociedad Cooperativa Editora "Buenos Aires," 1918
El salvaje, Buenos Aires: Sociedad Cooperativa Editora "Buenos Aires," 1920
Anaconda, Buenos Aires: Agencia General de Librería y Publicaciones, 1921
El desierto, Buenos Aires: Babel, 1924
"La gallina degollada" y otros cuentos, Buenos Aires: Babel, 1925
Los desterrados, Buenos Aires: Babel, 1926
Suelo natal, Buenos Aires: F. Crespillo, 1931
Más allá, Buenos Aires: Lautaro, 1935

Novels
Historia de un amor turbio, Buenos Aires: Arnaldo Moen y Hermano, 1908
Pasado amor, Buenos Aires: Babel, 1929

Play
Las sacrificadas, Buenos Aires: Sociedad Cooperativa Editora "Buenos Aires," 1920

Translations
South American Jungle Tales, translated by Arthur Livingston, New York: Diffield, 1922; London: Methuen, 1923
The Decapitated Chicken and Other Stories, translated by Margaret Sayers Peden, Austin: University of Texas Press, 1976
The Exiles and Other Stories, translated and edited by J. David Danielson and Elsa K. Gambarini, Austin: University of Texas Press, 1987

Compilations and Anthologies
Obras inéditas y desconocidas, edited by Ángel Rama, 8 vols, Montevideo: Arca, 1967–73 [Volume 7, *Sobre literatura*, contains the following important articles: "La crisis del cuento nacional" and "La retórica del cuento"]
Cuentos completas, 2 vols, Montevideo: Ediciones de la Plaza, 1978
Novelas completas, Montevideo: Ediciones del Atlántico, 1979

Further Reading

Alazraki, Jaime, "Un tema y tres cuentos de Horacio Quiroga," *Cuadernos Americanos*, vol. 173/6 (1970)
_____ "Relectura de Horacio Quiroga," in *El cuento hispanoamericano ante la crítica*, edited by Enrique Pupo-Walker, Madrid: Castalia, 1973
Amorim, Enrique, *El Quiroga que yo conocí*, Montevideo: Arca, 1983
Barrenechea, Ana María and Emma Susana Speratti Piñero, "Realismo e imaginación en la obra de Horacio Quiroga," in their *La literatura fantástica en Argentina*, Mexico City: Imprensa Universitaria, 1957
Beardsell, Peter R., *Quiroga. Cuentos de amor de locura y de muerte*, London: Grant and Cutler, 1986
Bratosevich, Nicolás A.S., *El estilo de Horacio Quiroga en sus cuentos*, Madrid: Gredos, 1973
Espinosa, Enrique, *Trayectoria de Horacio Quiroga*, Buenos Aires: Babel, 1980
Flores, Ángel (editor), *Aproximaciones a Horacio Quiroga*, Caracas: Monte Ávila, 1976

Jitrik, Noé, *Horacio Quiroga: una obra de experiencia y riesgo*, Montevideo: Arca, 1967

Martínez Morales, José Luis, *Horacio Quiroga: teoría y práctica del cuento*, Xalapa, Mexico: Universidad Veracruzana, 1982

Martul Tobío, Luis and Kathleen N. March, "Ejes conceptuales del pensamiento de Horacio Quiroga," *Cuadernos Hispano-americanos* 443 (May 1987)

Montenegro, Ernesto, *et al.*, "Focus on Horacio Quiroga," *Review* 19 (1976)

Mora, Gabriela, "Horacio Quiroga y Julio Cortázar: dos teóricos del cuento," *Revista Canadiense de Estudios Hispánicos*, vol. 11/3 (Spring 1987)

Odber de Baubeta, Patricia Anne, "'The Dead Man' and 'The Decapitated Chicken' by Horacio Quiroga," in *Reference Guide to Short Fiction*, edited by Noelle Watson, Detroit and London: St James Press, 1994

Paoli, Roberto, "El perfecto cuentista: comentario a tres textos de Horacio Quiroga," *Revista Iberoamericana*, vol. 58/160–61 (July–December 1992)

Pearson, Lon, "Horacio Quiroga's Obsessions with Abnormal Psychology and Medicine as Reflected in 'La gallina degollada,'" *Literature and Psychology*, Providence, Rhode Island, vol. 32/2 (1988)

Rodríguez Monegal, Emir, *Genio y figura de Horacio Quiroga*, Buenos Aires: Editorial Universitaria, 1967

____ *El desterrado: vida y obra de Horacio Quiroga*, Buenos Aires: Losada, 1968

Soumerou, Raul Victor, "Intrusos en el trópico: a propósito de *Anaconda* de Horacio Quiroga," *Cahiers d'Études Romanes*, Paris, 12 (1987)

Teodoresco, P.G., "El camino de la ideología sociopolítica de Horacio Quiroga," *Ideologies and Literature*, vol. 3/12 (March–May 1980)

Selection of Short Stories

By Horacio Quiroga

Horacio Quiroga wrote more than 200 short stories. These cover a wide range of themes and situations, and draw on numerous traditions and models, some listed in his *Decálogo del perfecto cuentista* [Ten Commandments for the Perfect Short Story Writer], others mentioned in his letters and critical writings. His literary relationship with Edgar Allan Poe has been well documented and, in literature as in life, Quiroga is most typically associated with the frontier experience, writing in a similar vein to Jack London. His profoundly ironic view of his fellow men extends to their reading practices as well as their behaviour. Hence, in "La miel silvestre" [Wild Honey], the narrator begins by ridiculing the boyish fantasies that arise from readings of Jules Verne and other tales of adventure, but then introduces a grimmer, more threatening tone with such evocative comments as "límites imprevistos" (unforeseen limits), clearly a euphemism for death. We see Quiroga constructing a personality, setting up a "fall-guy," someone doomed to disaster. Gabriel is not of the stuff of heroes. A chubby, pink-faced accountant who likes milky tea and sweet pastries, he wants to experience adventure, but is reluctant to muddy his new hiking boots. Gabriel decides to go hunting. The narrative is almost reminiscent of certain children's fairy tales, with danger, possibly death lying in wait in the woods. On the first day of his adventure, Gabriel does not venture into the woods, but on the second – with the usual Quirogian foreshadowing – he walks for about a league, then falls asleep, almost getting himself eaten by ants. On the third day, prolonging tension for the reader, Gabriel goes into the bush with his machete, eats wild honey and suffering from paralysis, is eaten alive by ants. Far from a detailed description of the horrors about to take place, there is understatement and factual comment, the same technique applied so effectively in "El almohadón de plumas" [The Feather Pillow]. The real horror derives from his chilling comparison of the fully conscious Gabriel with a terrified child. One of the words most frequently used by Quiroga is "inexorable," and this in fact describes much of the contents of his narrative, a relentless march towards death. A tragic conclusion is inevitable, all that remains to be seen is how the calamity unfolds, with foreshadowing achieved through the careful selection of vocabulary to describe significant choices and their consequences.

Much in the same vein is "El hijo" [The Son]. A third-person, omniscient narrative, this story is almost identical in tone and technique to "El hombre muerto" [The Dead Man]. We find the same accumulations and repetitions, the intensifying adverbs and the triple structure of adverbs, adjectives or nouns placed together, and the Quirogian technique of contrast, the burning heat of the midday sun set alongside the coldness of death. Quiroga toys with his readers, setting up certain emotions in the reader, because of the child's youth and innocence, the father's devotion and impotence. All the father's hopes, his love and his whole life are centred on the child. Fully aware of the dangers, his own limitations, he has done his best to teach his son not to take risks but this, we know, is not enough. From the very outset, the child's death is a foregone conclusion: as soon as the father warns him to take care, we suspect that something awful is about to happen to this child setting off with his shotgun and cartridges. This emphasis on the shotgun and the father's complacency can only reinforce our suspicion. Following the father's stream of consciousness, there is a growing awareness that all is not well. The father's hallucinations, treated as fantasy sequences, are indicative of the man's state of health and mind, but they also foreshadow the child's death. Just when he relaxes, a shot rings out. When the boy does not return, first he makes excuses for him, then begins to experience growing anxiety. As in other short stories, Nature can only be held at bay, never completely overcome, and the greatest irony of all is that the very tools that men use to tame Nature eventually become the instruments of Nature's revenge: the machete, the gun, but especially barbed wire, to represent an encroaching "civilization" which Quiroga held in contempt. There is, of course, further irony in the fact that the father's premonitory hallucination comes true. Just as he had seen in his vision, the boy is hanging upside down from a post, his legs tangled in barbed wire. There are different ways of interpreting this dénouement: Nature is fighting back, man is being punished for his complacency. However, when we consider the phrase "su hijo bien amado" (his dearly beloved son) in conjunction with the strong visual image of the child hanging on a post in a virtual crucifixion scene, there appear to be strong biblical resonances. But since this sacrifice has been made in vain, not as part of a redemptive process, perhaps Quiroga is suggesting that the Christian message is essentially void of significance, an aspect which might be explored in reading his other stories.

Quiroga has often been compared with Kipling, whose works he read in French translation, principally because of points of contact between the *Just So Stories* and the *Cuentos de la selva (South American Jungle Tales)*. Apart from Quiroga's own reference to Kipling in "La retórica del cuento" [The Rhetoric of the Short Story], there are similar animal protagonists as well as common storytelling devices. Compare, for example: "Now this is the next tale, and it tells how the Camel got his big hump," and "Aquí se cuenta la historia de un tigre que se crió y educó entre los hombres, y que se llamaba Juan Darién" (Here is told the tale of a tiger who was raised and educated among men and whose name was Juan Darién). Arguably, Quiroga mixes the ingredients of what might be an inocuous children's tale to produce a much darker depiction of human nature. The tiger motif is particularly strong in "Juan Darién," a story which has much in common with *The Jungle Book* and *The Second Jungle Book*, set in a far-off land, with the odd allusion to Bengal. However, the whole story appears more ambiguous than *The Jungle Book*. While there is genuine compassion for the tiger-child, just what is the moral lesson? Certainly that human beings are often less compassionate and more brutal than the animals to whom they claim superiority. Although motherhood is treated as almost sacred, both stories focus on cruelty and rejection: Mowgli is turned out of the pack and has to leave the jungle, only to come up against the hostility of ignorant and superstitious villagers. For his part, Juan Darién is cast out by the human beings, tortured, and after a last visit to his foster mother's grave, returns to the wild jungle.

"El espectro" [The Spectre] demonstrates familiarity with novels and films about the far West. It is hardly surprising that Quiroga should be attracted by this genre, given his own background. The American West and Kipling's India are much closer to his own experiences than, say, early 20th-century Europe. In this tale, the narrator's ideals of masculine behav-iour seem to match Quiroga's own preoccupations. The fantasy element occurs when what happens on screen affects the way the other characters live, prefiguring the plot of Woody Allen's *The Purple Rose of Cairo*, as Pablo Rocca has pointed out. The actor Duncan Wyoming dies, and leaves his widow Enid to be cared for, but not "consoled" by his best friend, the screenwriter Grant. The couple watch Wyoming's film over and over again, but as they grow closer, the dead husband becomes increasingly jealous, and finally steps out of the screen to seek his revenge. Grant shoots at him, but the bullet penetrates his own temple. Enid dies three days later. In the afterlife, they are inseparable, and spend all their time at film premières, waiting to see Wyoming's last film, and thus return to life through the channel that Wyoming has opened up.

Quiroga the craftsman is equally at home with a third- or first-person narrative and it would be interesting to establish which is used for what purposes. We can distinguish Gothic horror, animal tales, the wilderness narratives and fantasy, and there is another category, which overlaps with those previously mentioned, his *grim* fairytales. Uniformity of style and consistency in his narrative technique may lead readers to underestimate his versatility of theme and setting, yet there can be no doubt that he is perfectly at home with more than one setting, the main difference being that when he writes about the jungle, there is much more detail, presumably because the natural world is as much a character in his narrative as the human beings or animals.

PATRICIA ANNE ODBER DE BAUBETA

Anthologies and Compilations

Todos los cuentos, Colección Archivos, Asociación Archivos de la Literatura Latinoamericana, del Caribe y Africana del Siglo XX, in collaboration with UNESCO and the Fondo de Cultura de España, 1993 [Scholarly edition coordinated by Jorge Lafforgue and Napoleón Baccino Ponce de León, with articles by, among others, Milagros Ezquerro, Jorge Lafforgue, Dario Puccini and Beatriz Sarlo]

R

Graciliano Ramos 1892–1953

Brazilian prose writer

Considered the most expressive name in the second moment of Brazilian Modernism, Graciliano Ramos departs from other northeastern writers of the 1930s, since while sharing their main concern with the regional reality, he also proceeds with the experimentation that characterized the generation of 1922. Accordingly, for each of his narratives Graciliano contrives different aesthetic solutions, hence the unique style of works such as *São Bernardo* and *Vidas secas* (*Barren Lives*). It is true, however, that Ramos neglected the grammatical liberty introduced by the first Modernists, opting instead for traditional syntax. Thus he is considered an experimental writer, but a "*classical* experimentalist."

So, if in *Caetés* the reader comfortably faces a narrative that as a whole does not break new ground, that is definitely not the case with the two novels (among the most important written by this "classical experimentalist") that followed his debut. In the first of the two, *São Bernardo*, Ramos focuses on the rural reality of the farm São Bernardo, whose proprietor Paulo Honório is given the narration; in the second, *Angústia* (*Anguish*), the writer turns to urban reality, giving the narration this time to a lesser civil servant.

Despite the common factor – the narration in the first person – the narrative strategy in *São Bernardo* is organized differently from *Caetés* and *Angústia* in that its narrator is introduced to us during the very act of composing the novel. This disposition allows the discussion of literary creation, ever present in Graciliano's works, to be intensified to the point of primary importance. Similarly, the direct, objective, "dry" style for which the writer was renowned finds here one of its moments of maximum expression, in this case documenting in a concrete way the awkwardness of a pragmatic and ill-read man like Paulo Honório in the role of writer. In fact, the style of Paulo Honório, consisting of short, brisk sentences, bears witness to his personality whose most remarkable features are rudeness and pragmatism. When a man like this turns to literature he is certainly not motivated by aesthetic reasons, and as a matter of fact Paulo Honório resorts to it with a well-defined goal. He needs to confess, relieve his conscience, and since he has no friends, being too proud and not believing in religious consolation, he then opts for the symbology of the confessional novel. Throughout the pages that he writes a picture takes shape: a man that, having conquered his place in the sun the hard way, assimilated on his trajectory all the selfishness and brutality of a competitive system, being at last aware of it all: "Creio que nem sempre fui egoísta e brutal. A profissão é que me deu qualidades tão ruins. É a desconfiança que me aponta inimigos em toda parte! A desconfiança é também conseqüência da profissão" (I don't believe I have always been egoistic and brutal. It is this profession that has given these vicious characteristics. And that terrible distrust of mine that discovers enemies everywhere! This distrust is another consequence of my profession). Paulo Honório, who became the owner of the São Bernardo farm, gradually lost his humane values, being able to see the world only in terms of profit. He thus ceased to be a person and ended up representing the farm itself. In order to have an heir he marries Madalena, an idealistic teacher whom he is to destroy with his attitude of proprietor extended to human beings. Madalena commits suicide, victim of Paulo Honório's violence; he then realizes that he had destroyed the only being he ever loved.

The solitude of Paulo Honório is followed by the *Angústia* of Luís da Silva who, between two worlds with which he cannot identify – the rural world of his parents and grandparents and the urban one he finds himself in – appears to the reader to be continually falling apart until he eventually commits a crime. He murders his rival, a successful graduate who took his lover from him. In this way he hopes to solve his existential dilemma, his anguish as the last member of a disintegrating rural family whose members had come to the city to try their luck, but found only constant misery, persistent economic and social inferiority. This fragmentary narrative (more than in *São Bernardo* we observe here an extraordinary interplay between past and present) concretely documents such degradation, whose major evidence is the insignificance of the very name Luís da Silva. It contrasts significantly with the complex surnames of his grandfather (Trajano Pereira de Aquino Cavalcante e Silva) or even the father (Camilo Pereira da Silva). This continuous degradation culminates in the delirium of Luís da Silva that in a single paragraph covers the last eleven pages of the novel.

One should note that the experimentalism of Graciliano Ramos is less of an end in itself than a means employed by the author to intensify a reality the better to narrate it. *Vidas secas* and the works that followed are no exception and confirm the rule. That is actually the moment when Graciliano turns to the biographic reports of *Infância* (*Childhood*), *Viagem* [*Voyage*] and *Memórias do cárcere* [*Jail Prison Memoirs*]. In the last of these he narrates the vicissitudes of his political imprisonment during 1936–37.

In the context of Brazilian literature Graciliano Ramos stands out as one of the most provocative names, having significantly contributed to its coming of age in all senses, but especially with respect to the aesthetic representation of social problems.

TERESINHA V. ZIMBRÃO DA SILVA

Biography
Born in Quebrângulo, Alagoas, Brazil, 27 October 1892. Family moved when he was two to Buíque, Pernambuco where his father bought a cattle ranch. Years of severe drought caused his father to resume former occupation as a shopkeeper. Distressing childhood according to his own account in *Infância* (1945) of a brutal father and neurotic mother. Began to read avidly from the age of ten. Studied in Viçosa and Maceió, Alagoas, but dropped out of high school and helped father run his store. Travelled to Rio de Janeiro, 1914, and worked there as a journalist. Returned after some months to become his father's partner. Married Augusta de Barros and bought his father's store. Successful in business. Learnt several European languages and translated from the English and the French (Camus's *La Peste* in the case of the latter). Store became intellectual centre of Palmeira dos Índios. Organized private school for children. Agreed to stand as mayor, 1928, and won election. Married Heloísa Medeiros in 1933 (his first wife had died). Served as director of State Printing Office (1930–33) and director of Public Instruction in Alagoas (1933–36). Second novel, *São Bernardo*, placed him at once among Brazil's most distinguished writers. In 1936, after Getúlio Vargas assumed presidency, dismissed from post without explanation, arrested and sent to Rio where he remained in jail without a trial for a year. Released in January 1937, again without explanation. Health undermined by this experience. Spent wretched period in Rio until he obtained an editorial position on a newspaper and, in Kafkaesque way, appointed federal inspector of schools by the very same government that had imprisoned him arbitrarily. Joined the Communist Party in 1945. Elected president of Brazilian Writers' Association and visited countries of the Soviet bloc in this capacity, 1952. Upon his return fell gravely ill and died after an operation on 20 March 1953.

Selected Works

Novels
Caetés, Rio de Janeiro: Schmidt, 1933
São Bernardo, Rio de Janeiro: Ariel, 1934; as *São Bernardo*, translated by Robert Scott-Buccleuch, London: Peter Owen, 1975
Angústia, Rio de Janeiro: José Olympio, 1936; as *Anguish*, translated by Lewis C. Kaplin, New York: Knopf, 1972

Vidas secas, Rio de Janeiro: José Olympio, 1938; as *Barren Lives*, translated by Ralph E. Dimmick, Austin: University of Texas Press, 1961
Brandão entre o mar e o amor, in collaboration with Jorge Amado, José Lins do Rego, Aníbal Machado and Rachel de Queiroz, São Paulo: Martins, 1942

Short Fiction
Dois dedos, Rio de Janeiro: Acadêmica, 1945
Histórias incompletas, Pôrto Alegre: Globo, 1946
Insônia, Rio de Janeiro: José Olympio, 1947
Histórias verdadeiras, Rio de Janeiro: Vitória, 1951

Children's Fiction
A terra dos meninos pelados, Pôrto Alegre: Globo, 1939
Histórias de Alexandre, Rio de Janeiro: Leitura, 1944

Other Writings
Infância, Rio de Janeiro: José Olympio, 1945; as *Childhood*, translated by Celso de Oliveira, London: Peter Owen, 1979
Memórias do cárcere, 4 vols, Rio de Janeiro: José Olympio, 1953; as *Jail Prison Memoirs*, translated by Thomas Colchie, New York: Evans, 1974
Viagem, Rio de Janeiro: José Olympio, 1954 [On travels in Czechoslovakia and the USSR]
Linhas tortas, São Paulo: Martins, 1962
Viventes das Alagoas, São Paulo: Martins, 1962
Cartas, Rio de Janeiro: Record, 1981 [correspondence]

Compilations and Anthologies
Obras completas, 10 vols, São Paulo: Martins, 1961

Further Reading
Graciliano Ramos's work has benefited in the main from structuralist readings that have been applied to Brazilian literature since the 1960s.

Bosi, Alfredo, "Graciliano Ramos," in his *História concisa da literatura brasileira*, São Paulo: Cultrix, 1970
Bosi, Alfredo, José Carlos Garbuglio and Valentin Facioli (contributing editors), *Graciliano Ramos*, São Paulo: Ática, 1987 [A comprehensive introduction to Ramos's work with the participation of other scholars, including Antônio Cândido]
Brasil, Assis, *Graciliano Ramos*, Rio de Janeiro: Simões, 1969
Brayner, Sônia and Afrânio Coutinho (editors), *Graciliano Ramos*, Rio de Janeiro: Civilização Brasileira, 1978
Cândido, Antônio, *Ficção e confissão: ensaio sobre a obra de Graciliano Ramos*, Rio de Janeiro: José Olympio, 1956
Lima, Valdemar de Souza, *Graciliano Ramos em Palmeira dos Índios*, Rio de Janeiro: Civilização Brasileira, 1980
Malard, Letícia, *Ensaio de literatura brasileira: ideologia e realidade em Graciliano Ramos*, Belo Horizonte, Brazil: Itatiaia, 1976
Mazzara, Richard A., *Graciliano Ramos*, New York: Twayne, 1974
Oliveira, Celso Lemos de, *Understanding Graciliano Ramos*, Columbia: University of South Carolina Press, 1988
Puccinelli, Lamberto, *Graciliano Ramos: relações entre ficção e realidade*, São Paulo: Quíron, 1975
Zilberman, Regina, "*São Bernardo*" e o processo de comunicação, Pôrto Alegre: Movimento, 1975

Regionalism

Brazil

The term *regionalista* (regionalist) denotes a literary work that focuses on a certain region and on its features (geography, nature), as well as on the kind of social and historical background that has that region as a frame. Most regionalist works also deal with the human beings who inhabit the region in question (peasants, miners, backlanders), bringing regionalism very close to a fiction which is most of the times Realist/ Neorealist in its general outlines.

A significant portion of Brazilian literature is fuelled by nationalism. At least since the 18th century we find literary works that aim to explore the uniqueness of the Brazilian character, seeking to outline a national identity for the country. From this standpoint, to portray the tropical milieu was a way of searching for Brazilianness. For this reason, we may say that regionalism has played an extremely important role in Brazilian literature, especially during the second half of the 19th century (Romanticism, in particular) and during the first half of the 20th century (the Modernist novel of the 1930s). Although regionalist features are present throughout the history of Brazilian literature, within the limits of an encyclopedia article it is best to concentrate on the second of these crucial moments.

Traditionally, in Brazil's literary historiography, in the 19th century the novels that portray the interior (i.e., not urban novels) are known as "sertanistas" (related to the *sertão* or backlands). We may call regionalist *Inocência*, 1872 (*Innocence*) by Visconde de Taunay (1843–99) and O *garimpeiro*, 1872 [The Prospector]) by Bernardo Guimarães (1825–84), among other works of the period. This kind of literature continues through the works of Inglês de Sousa (1853–1918) writing under the pseudonym Luís Dolzani, Afonso Arinos (1868–1916), Afrânio Peixoto (1876–1947) and Valdomiro Silveira (1873–1941), until the 1930s, when literary historiography explicitly called *regionalistas* authors like José Américo de Almeida (1887–1980), José Lins do Rego (1901–57), Jorge Amado (1912–), Graciliano Ramos (1892–1953) and Rachel de Queiroz (1910–). Although the term is generally used to allude to the writers whose work focuses primarily on the northeast, the truth is that it could easily be applied to the works of writers from other regions, like João Simões Lopes Neto (1865]–1916) or Érico Veríssimo (1905–75), from the south. This is one of the concepts that was incorporated into literary criticism, but that ended up by losing its original critical insight.

Luiz Costa Lima once wrote that Brazilian fiction obeys the primacy of observation (primado da observação). According to Lima, Brazilian literature does not often create a ficionality; it is nurtured instead by a mimesis that attempts to capture "realistically" Brazilian reality. In other words, Brazilian literary texts are not constructed with the awareness of being symbolic representations, made up by means of verbal signs. This observation could probably be endorsed by tying it to the obsession with nationalism that was mentioned before. Lacking a glorious historical past (Brazil was a former colony of Portugal), writers, in order to foreground the national character, must turn to Brazilian nature. Most Brazilian literature since Independence in 1822, following the Imperial state, engaged in the project of nation-building; as the tropical scenario is different from the European one, to pinpoint the "natureza americana" (American nature, as the Romantic Alencar used to call the Brazilian landscape) was to stress Brazilianness. In the last decades of the 19th century, with the exhaustion of Indianism, it is safe to say that *sertanista* novels fulfilled this ideological role.

In the 1930s, the novel in particular and literature in general engage with social problems. In the overall account of the novel of the period, writing in 1988 Antônio Cândido observed that this kind of fiction was "neonaturalistic in character, taking advantage of the linguistic liberation undertaken by the 1922 Modernists (reality was a decisive element in this kind of novel). It attempted to show, in a direct manner, what Brazilian society was like, to identify men's problems and anguishes, with an acute sense of context, that is, a dominant concern in regard to the setting, the society, the behaviour of the people. For this reason, the majority of the period's novelists gave the impression that language was something that should be subordinated to theme. And theme moved to the forefront with its power of protest, accusation and revelation, as happens in narratives with a social tendency, as was common at that time, in Brazil and elsewhere." Cândido's observation, although it is brief, touches on some of the main features of the *regionalista* novel: the social commitment, the portrayal of reality, the intention to capture a social and human landscape as well as of being a form or protest against the social order, with literary language becoming secondary.

However, one must bring into the discussion some other aspects that will give more complexity to Cândido's words. Brazil was experiencing a transition from a rural, traditional society into an urban and industrialized one. The hegemony of the landowners in power was now being shared by the new bourgeois sectors; the old ruling class – mainly composed of sugar plantation owners from the northeast and of the Paraíba valley coffee barons – was experiencing decadence at least since the turn of the century. In most cases, the novel of the 1930s will picture the social fabric from the perspective of the old patriarchal and seigniorial society now in decline, nostalgically lamenting that the "good old times" are gone. Instead of focusing on the changes that were taking place in Brazilian society then, this fiction leant towards the past. Ideologically speaking, this has been a way of providing a sort of genealogy to the new composition of the ruling classes, since an alliance between the rural landlords and the bourgeois sectors will characterize the Old Republic (1889–1930).

The paradigmatic example here would be José Lins do Rego's sugar cane cycle, a kind of Proustian *recherche* or search into the colonel's times. Graciliano Ramos's works are more critical of the beginning of capitalism in Brazil, but it would be more appropriate to understand his fiction as one traversed by contradictions, divided between a traditional and a capitalistic order.

ROBERTO REIS

Further Reading

Almeida, José Maurício Gomes de, *A tradição regionalista no romance brasileiro, 1875–1945*, Rio de Janeiro: Achiamé, 1981

Cândido, Antônio, "No começo era de fato o verbo," introduction to *A paixão segundo GH* by Clarice Lispector, Florianópolis: Editora da UFSC, 1988

Dacanal, José Hildebrando, *O romance de 30*, Pôrto Alegre, Brazil: Mercado Aberto, 1982

Lima, Luiz Costa, *O controle do imaginário*, São Paulo: Brasiliense, 1984

Reis, Roberto, *A permanência do círculo – hierarquia no romance brasileiro*, Niterói/Brasília: EDUFF/INL, 1987

Spanish America

In Spanish American literature the term "regionalism" overlaps with several other labels such as *criollismo, mundonovismo, posmodernismo*, the novel of the land, and autochthonous writing. Literary works falling under any of these categories generally present the land, people and/or customs of a particular locality as the common denominator that provides the region depicted with its identity. The use of distinctly American themes, language (popular speech, dialect, regional vocabulary), and folklore, and the insertion of social commentary and protest, are some of the most pervasive characteristics of this literature. Authors of regional narratives place special emphasis on rural settings and often portray the physical environment as a telluric force exercising control over the characters. In the so-called novel of the land, for example, nature can even assume the role of protagonist.

Elements of regionalism have been a part of Spanish American writing since its beginnings. Regional motifs can be found in every genre – from the gaucho plays of Florencio Sánchez and the essays of José Vasconcelos to African-Caribbean poetry – but regionalism as an artistic tendency has had its greatest impact in prose fiction. The heyday of the regional narrative extended roughly from 1915 to 1945 and its influence continued to be felt in the 1950s in the narratives of Juan Rulfo, Miguel Ángel Asturias and João Guimarães Rosa.

Regional novels comprised the first group of Spanish American works routinely translated into English and other European languages. Appealing to a much wider audience than the works of the Spanish American *modernistas*, these novels helped usher Spanish American literature into the international literary arena. Regional writers abandoned the pure aestheticism and infatuation with the foreign that characterized the early phase of *Modernismo* in order to concentrate on traditional themes and subject matter closer to home. Collectively, their works do not easily fall into a single style distinctive of a period, such as Realism; instead, they cover a range of techniques from the Romantic to the vanguard.

During the 19th century, Spanish American authors seemed obsessed with imitating foreign models. Following the Spanish-American War and the outbreak of World War I, imitation was no longer the rule as intellectuals from Mexico to Argentina came to the realization that the United States and Europe had ceased to serve as viable cultural models. The hemispheric celebrations around 1910 of the centennial of Spanish American independence seemed an appropriate occasion for each country to re-examine its national spirit, values and identity. Writers began to consider autochthonous American elements as suitable source material for their works. They found artistic inspiration in the physical environment and landscape, the indigenous populations, local traditions, linguistic peculiarities, and the various social, political and economic realities of their region or homeland. Regionalism and nationalism, especially cultural nationalism, became closely intertwined. America with its picturesque diversity and folkways captured the imagination of foreign audiences; at the same time, it appealed to the national pride of readers at home. To some, these works underscored Spanish America's inherent spirituality as defined by Rodó in *Ariel*. As an affirmation of cultural identity, many authors utilized regional vocabulary in their writings. A regional novel of this period, for example, would often feature a glossary as an appendix to the text so as to make the work intelligible to native speakers of Spanish in other countries.

The traditional conflicts around which literature revolves such as societal clashes (man versus society), psychological turmoil within a character (man versus himself), and the struggle against the environment (man versus nature) have all found their way into regional works. Social protest, an element conspicuously absent from the *modernista* aesthetic, came to the forefront in the *posmodernista* era. Stimulated by an emerging social consciousness, writers championed the indigenous underclass and exposed injustices as they sought to forge or re-define a national identity.

The regionalist tendency eventually spread to every Spanish American country. One of the earliest manifestations of literary regionalism during the period of its ascendency was the novel of the Mexican Revolution, epitomized by Mariano Azuela's *Los de abajo* (*The Underdogs*), published in 1915. The three most widely heralded works in the regionalist vein appeared in the 1920s. In Colombia José Eustasio Rivera documented the exploitation of rubber workers in *La vorágine*, 1924 (*The Vortex*), a novel of the jungle notable for its author's use of poetic descriptions rather than photographic realism. In *Don Segundo Sombra* (1926), Ricardo Güiraldes offered a nostalgic evocation of Argentina's national symbol, the gaucho. And in Venezuela, Rómulo Gallegos's *Doña Bárbara* (1929), a novel of the plains that re-enacts the confrontation between civilization and barbarism, came to be considered by many as the country's national book. Another leading regional writer, the Uruguayan Horacio Quiroga, devoted himself almost exclusively to the short story. Nature plays an influential role in many of his tales of violence and madness, especially those set in the harsh tropical environment of Misiones Province in the northeastern portion of Argentina.

Indigenist works, with their concern for the plight of the Indian population, a people marginalized by society and victimized by prejudice and exploitation, provide yet another variation on regional subject matter. In the Andean countries the portrayal of indigenous characters has evolved from the type found in 19th-century *indianista* works – the romanticized noble savage living in harmony with nature – to the brutally realistic creations drawn from the *indigenista* perspective. The Ecuadorian writer Jorge Icaza reflects the social and political concerns characteristic of the latter viewpoint in his famous novel *Huasipungo*, 1934 (*The Villagers*). One of the most important developments in Ecuadorian literature was the formation of the Group of Guayaquil, a trio of young writers

(Demetrio Aguilera Malta, Joaquín Gallegos Lara and Enrique Gil Gilbert), who employed crude language and dialect in creating a more realistic, documentary narrative. Their short story collection *Los que se van*, 1930 [Those Who Leave] charted the course for much of the socially-committed literature of succeeding decades.

Regionalism continued strong in the 1940s. In Costa Rica, Carlos Luis Fallas developed the theme of anti-imperialism in his novel *Mamita Yunai* (1941), and in Chile Eduardo Barrios, a master of the urban psychological novel, made a noteworthy contribution to rural fiction with *Gran señor y rajadiablos*, 1948 [Great Lord and Hell-raiser].

Regional writing, whether its sub-category is the novel of the Mexican Revolution, the novel of the land, gaucho literature, or the indigenist narrative, focuses on the readily observable external reality of a particular region. As a result of the literary rediscovery of America that occurred during the first half of the 20th century, external reality came to be considered one of the determining factors in the definition of national and personal identity. The regionalists pursued a two-fold agenda – one aesthetic and the other sociopolitical – as they explored the literary possibilities of autochthonous themes, characters, and language. Their incorporation of telluric, geographic, racial and linguistic factors created a sense of place and produced a self-conscious literature acutely aware of its self-defining features. The best of these works transcend their provincial limitations in order to address human values, aspirations and sentiments on a universal scale.

MELVIN S. ARRINGTON, JR

See also entries on Mariano Azuela and *Los de abajo*, Eduardo Barrios, José de la Cuadra, Rómulo Gallegos and *Doña Bárbara*, João Guimãraes Rosa, Ricardo Güiraldes, Jorge Icaza, Indianism, Indigenism, Horacio Quiroga, José Eustasio Rivera, Juan Rulfo

Further Reading

Alonso, Carlos J., *The Spanish American Regional Novel: Modernity and Autochthony*, Cambridge and New York: Cambridge University Press, 1990

Carpentier, Alejo, "Problématica de la actual novela latinoamericana," in *Tientos y diferencias*, Mexico City: UNAM, 1964

Fitz, Earl E., "Regionalism as a Shaping Force," in his *Rediscovering the New World: Inter-American Literature in a Comparative Context*, Iowa City: University of Iowa Press, 1991

Franco, Jean, *The Modern Culture of Latin America: Society and the Artist*, London: Pall Mall Press, and New York: Praeger, 1967 [Chapters 2–4 are relevant]

Hernández de Norman, Isabel, *La novela criolla en las Antillas*, New York: Plus Ultra, 1977

Latcham, Ricardo, *El criollismo*, Santiago de Chile: Editorial Universitaria, 1956

León Hazera, Lydia, *La novela de la selva hispanoamericana. Nacimiento, desarrollo y transformación. Estudio estilístico*, Bogotá: Publicaciones del Instituto Caro y Cuervo, 1971

Sommer, Doris (editor), *The Places of History: Regionalism Revisited in Latin America*, Durham, North Carolina: Duke University Press, 1996

Vargas Llosa, Mario, "Primitives and Creators," *Times Literary Supplement* (4 November 1968)

José Lins do Rego 1901–1957

Brazilian prose writer

This scion of a wealthy sugar plantation family in Brazil's northeastern state of Paraíba stands among the four giants of regionalist fiction of his region. Along with Rachel de Queiroz of Ceará, Graciliano Ramos of Alagoas, and Jorge Amado of Bahia, José Lins do Rego defines the most characteristic literary and cultural expression of 20th-century Brazil, whose influence begins in the late 1920s and extends to the present time (1997).

Lins do Rego's university studies at the Law School of Recife (Pernambuco) brought him into contact with the sociologist Gilberto Freyre, then involved in the inauguration of a cultural revival based on the revalidation of "Region and Tradition." In part inspired by the São Paulo Modernists of 1922 and in part reacting against a perceived over-emphasis on urban modernity and the cosmopolitan ascendancy of southern Brazil, the new generation of northeastern scholars convened its first northeastern regionalist congress in 1926 and made public its manifesto in that year. Freyre would serve for decades as the guiding light of the movement from his vantage point as sociologist, while Jorge de Lima would prove to be its most illustrious poet and Lins do Rego its most prolific writer of documentary fiction.

The best and most typical of Lins do Rego's novels are based on his own memories of childhood and adolescence on the sugar plantation, interspersed with the sometimes tragic drama of the passage of backland bandit/vigilante bands. A half dozen novels composed from 1932 to 1936, and a further one in 1943 form what is commonly called his "Sugar Cane Cycle," with the same nucleus of characters of several generations reappearing in four or more of the works. These novels are: *Menino de engenho* (1932), *Doidinho* (1933), *Bangüê*, 1934 (all three of which have been translated under the general title, *Plantation Boy*); *O moleque Ricardo*, 1935 [Richard the Street Kid], *Usina*, 1936 [The Sugar Mill], and, although connected somewhat less directly to the home plantation, *Fogo morto*, 1943 [Dead Fire]. Carlos de Melo, the author's fictional persona, is the protagonist of all but two novels of the series: he is a young boy bereft of mother and raised by grandparents and aunts on the plantation of the patriarch-grandfather, Zé Paulino (the persona of Lins do Rego's own grandfather), in *Menino de engenho*, the maladjusted boarding school student in *Doidinho*, the newly graduated lawyer attempting to administer the semi-mechanized home plantation in *Bangüê*, and the failed administrator watching his plantation pass into the hands of a larger and more mechanized corporate entity in *Usina*. While these novels trace the childhood, adolescent education, and adult career of a wealthy white plantation boy, *O moleque Ricardo* and part of *Usina* accompany Carlos de Melo's black playmate Ricardo on his unflagging effort to succeed in life outside the plantation environment; he goes to work in the city of Recife, joins a strike action by local laborers, is imprisoned and sentenced to a term in the national penitentiary, is subsequently released, returns to his home plantation to assume a responsible position, and ultimately dies attempting to defend the property against marauders.

Couched in a direct, accessible prose style worthy of the best in journalistic writing, the novels of the "Sugar Cane Cycle" integrate personal memoirs of the author's own life, his observations of the broad spectrum of plantation living and administration in his native region, the experiences of others employed in the larger economic sphere of the more urban northeastern region, and a good measure of imagination to recreate a way of life already on the wane at the time of writing. There is an elegiac quality about Lins do Rego's fiction, a penetrating melancholy of the inevitable as tradition and technical progress confront each other and individual lives are caught in the machinery of micro and macro economics. Generations come and go, either adapting to change or being pushed aside by it; man's inhumanity to man is vividly portrayed at every turn, be it in the exploitation of wife, employee (frequently an ex-slave), or the weaker member of a socioeconomic unit. Yet the author has no "axe to grind" nor political program to advocate, unlike some other members of his generation; his perspective is at once personal and sociological, and his characters are typical of countless others of their time and status in regional society. The picturesque quality of *Menino de engenho* in its vivid youthful recreation of the sights, aromas, tastes and feel of traditional plantation life, is balanced by the lurking fear always present in the narrator-protagonist's (sub)conscious, and the cycle continues the natural evolution of the qualities present in its initial volume.

Fogo morto, perhaps Lins do Rego's finest work, is related to the nucleus of the "Sugar Cane Cycle" in that it deals with a similar process of inevitable change and decadence, though in the context of a neighboring plantation belonging to friends of the Melo family. The novel also incorporates the marked presence and activity of *cangaceiros* (backland bandits), showing its kinship with another pair of Rego novels sometimes called the "Cangaço (Outlaw) Cycle": *Pedra Bonita* (1938) and *Cangaceiros* (1953). *Fogo morto* is a violent work in which those who own their own land are no less prey to the conflict between government military forces and backland bandits than are those who till the lands of others; all are equally victimized, and the question of who is more or less to blame for the situation becomes a moot one in the face of the generalized agony. Three of the author's most outstanding characters dominate the three segments of this novel; they are the decadent plantation owner Lula, the angry saddlemaker José Amaro, and the quixotic old Vitorino.

The two novels mentioned above, which form the sequential "Cangaço Cycle," trace the life of parents and sons of a rural family caught in the atavistic net of collective guilt borne by generations of descendants of messianic cult followers from the mid-19th century. Pawns of traditional factional hatred and of the harsh natural conditions under which they live, younger family members face two "obvious" choices in so far as vocation is concerned: cultivate vengeance by joining a roving group of *cangaceiros* or devote themselves to the religious cult forming around the latest messianic figure in the region. Lins do Rego synthesizes in this pair of novels the complex human dynamic leading to both types of violent societal aberration without placing unilateral blame on any institution or group.

The eight novels that comprise the "Sugar Cane" and "Outlaw" cycles constitute the lion's share of Lins do Rego's fictional production and together comprise a broad sociological spectrum of rural life in the dry northeastern region of Brazil in the early decades of the 20th century. However, there are four other novels by him that explore facets of human awareness and behavior which, without forming a cohesive group or "cycle," are somewhat alike in privileging psychological introspection, more urban or cosmopolitan (generally coastal) environments, and an individualistic sensibility and erotic lyricism. These novels are: *Pureza*, 1937; *Riacho doce*, 1939 [Sweetwater Creek]; *Agua-mãe*, 1941 [Mother Liquor]; and *Eurídice*, 1947. *Pureza* traces psychological processes in an isolated human environment, while *Eurídice* accompanies the anguish of passion, infidelity, and interpersonal stress against a background of urban politics of the Vargas period. *Agua-mãe* is a coastal novel set in the saline-processing area near Cabo Frio, with the backdrop of the inherent mysteries of night, the sea, and intergenerational incomprehension spanning three families. *Riacho doce* presents the drama of a young Swedish business couple assigned to Brazil by a petroleum corporation, as the wife attempts to adapt to the "new" culture that envelops them with its folklore and societal expectations. Female characters play an increasingly important role in these four novels, though Lins do Rego is clearly experimenting with a lyrical style of writing and a delicate probing of sensibility with which he is less comfortable than the more sociological backland context and documentary, journalistic style of the best of his fiction.

Among the best-known of Lins do Rego's non-fictional prose works are his autobiography, *Meus verdes anos*, 1956 [My Tender Years], and the book-length essay *Presença do nordeste na literatura brasileira*, 1957 [Presence of the Northeast in Brazilian Literature]. His essays are of a piece with his regionalist fiction, conveying the same commitment to his land and people and the same fundamental sadness about the nature of things. His novels exercised a profound influence on Portuguese fiction writers of the World War II period, several of whom followed in his footsteps in the novelistic recreation of their own socio-geographic subregions.

MARY L. DANIEL

See also entries on Jorge Amado, Gilberto Freyre, Rachel de Queiroz, Graciliano Ramos, Regionalism: Brazil

Biography

Born in Paraíba State, Brazil, 3 June 1901. Grew up on a sugar plantation surrounded by former slaves and their children. Educated privately in Itabaiana, Paraíba (now João Pessoa); attended law school, Recife, 1919. Founded the Regionalist Movement with Gilberto Freyre, José Américo de Almeida, Olívio Montenegro, among others. Wrote literary reviews, political articles for newspapers and journals in Paraíba and Recife. Moved to Rio de Janeiro in 1935. Member of the Brazilian Academy of Letters, 1955. Died in Rio de Janeiro, 12 September 1957.

Selected Works

Novels

Menino de engenho, Rio de Janeiro: Adeusen, 1932; as *Plantation Boy*, translated by Emmi Baum, New York: Knopf, 1966
Doidinho, Rio de Janeiro: Ariel, 1933 [Translation included in *Plantation Boy*, New York: Knopf, 1966]
Bangüê, Rio de Janeiro: José Olympio, 1934 [Translation included in *Plantation Boy*, New York: Knopf, 1966]
O moleque Ricardo, Rio de Janeiro: José Olympio, 1935
Usina, Rio de Janeiro: José Olympio, 1936
Pureza, Rio de Janeiro: José Olympio, 1937; as *Pureza: a Brazilian Novel*, translated by Lucie Marion, London: Hutchinson, 1948
Pedra Bonita, Rio de Janeiro: José Olympio, 1938
Riacho doce, Rio de Janeiro: José Olympio, 1939
Agua-mãe, Rio de Janeiro: José Olympio, 1941
Fogo morto, Rio de Janeiro: José Olympio, 1943
Eurídice, Rio de Janeiro: José Olympio, 1947
Cangaceiros, Rio de Janeiro: José Olympio, 1953

Other Writings

Histórias da Velha Totônia, Rio de Janeiro: José Olympio, 1936 [children's fiction]
Gordos e magros, Rio de Janeiro: Casa do Estudante do Brasil, 1942 [essays]
Poesia e vida, Rio de Janeiro: Universal, 1945 [essays]
Homens, seres e coisas, Rio de Janeiro: Ministério da Educação e Saúde, 1952 [essays]
A casa e o homem, Rio de Janeiro: Organização Simões, 1954 [essays]
Meus verdes anos, Rio de Janeiro: José Olympio, 1956 [memoirs]
Presença do nordeste na literatura brasileira, Rio de Janeiro: Ministério da Educação e Saúde, 1957
O vulcão e a fonte, Rio de Janeiro: Cruzeiro, 1958

Compilations and Anthologies

Obras, 11 vols, Rio de Janeiro: José Olympio, 1947
Romances reunidos e ilustrados de José Lins do Rego, 5 vols, Rio de Janeiro, José Olympio, 1960–61
Romances reunidos e ilustrados de José Lins do Rego, 12 vols, Rio de Janeiro and Brasília: n.p., 1980

Further Reading

Coutinho, Eduardo F., *O romance do açúcar: José Lins do Rego, vida e obra*, Rio de Janeiro and Brasília: José Olympio, 1970
Coutinho, Eduardo F. and Angela Bezerra de Castro (editors), *José Lins do Rego*, Rio de Janeiro: Civilização Brasileira, 1991 [An excellent collection of essays]
Sobreira, Ivan Bichara, *O romance de José Lins do Rego*, João Pessoa, Brazil: Editorial Universitária, 1971

Resistance Literature in Spanish America

Through the centuries, Latin Americans have been inventing and redefining subversive strategies that allow them to form their own everyday culture of resistance. For example, during and after the Spanish conquest and massacre of the indigenous inhabitants of the New World, the local resistance to the foreign invader was transmitted through oral tradition and through a reinterpretation of the ancient myths (i.e., *Inkarri*, *Taki Onkoy* in Peru). This type of resistance preserved both the ancient tradition and the social memory of the Quechuan and other Native Peruvian cultures.

During the early 17th century, two works *Nueva Corónica y Buen Gobierno* (*Letter to a King*) and *Relación de Antigüedades deste Reyno del Piru* [Account of the Antiquities of the Kingdom of Peru] were written by Felipe Guaman Poma de Ayala and Joan de Santacruz Pachacuti Yamqui Sallqamaygua, respectively. These works are generally considered the first written discourses which counteract the culture of the Spanish invader. In *Nueva Corónica* (1612), Guaman Poma subversively criticizes the rule of the Spanish viceroyalty in Peru and informs the reader about the Incan culture.

Comentarios reales de los Incas (*Royal Commentaries of the Incas*) is the written testimony of a bilingual mestizo who lived in both the Quechuan and the Spanish cultures. In *Comentarios*, Garcilaso de la Vega describes the splendor of the Incan Empire. This book is doubly subversive: published for the first time in Spain in 1609 and written in the language of the invader; it reterritorialized the hegemonic and colonialist Spanish center.

In the 18th century there were other written expressions of resistance. The appearance, clandestine circulation and publication of autobiographies, letters and diaries by Latin Americans during this century provide evidence of an insurgent spirit, not only that of the creoles, but also that of the mestizos, the indigenous people, and the slaves fighting against tyrannical Spanish rule in the colonies. Discontent gave birth to the organization of the first armed independence movements and gave voice to resistance movements that tried to free the continent. After independence, however, resistance swelled again against the unequal social order imposed on the new republics by the new dominant creole class. The creole class had managed to reproduce the same repressive colonial system of the Spanish invader. One text that cleverly documents the situation of the slaves in the colonies is *Autobiografía de un esclavo* [Autobiography of a Slave] written by a Cuban slave, Juan Francisco Manzano (1797–1854). The most relevant literary aspect of this text is the constant simulation of an oral discourse, one that emphasizes its testimonial function.

For the 19th-century *modernista* writer, resistance was aimed at the Spanish literary canon and the economic power of imperialist nations. This writer subversively started the quest for an autonomous Latin American identity. The significance of *Modernismo* for the Latin American cultural production of the 19th century cannot be denied. As a cultural and literary movement, *Modernismo* rapidly contributed to the international circulation and acceptance of Latin American literary texts. *Modernismo*'s cultural agenda has recently been revised and reformulated; the traditional formal criteria by which literary critics have defined and analyzed the literary works produced by the *modernista* writers have changed. Some outstanding literary devices of resistance employed by the *modernista* works are the transformation of textual forms, changes in the traditional topics and characters represented in literary works, and the process of rewriting master texts. Nevertheless, *modernistas* in their works still showed a marked cultural dependence on Europe. During the 19th century, the ideology of the dominant class in Latin American reproduced mainstream Western aesthetic values and the Western concept of a uniform national culture. By doing so, it excluded and repressed all other subaltern groups and ancient cultures.

The *modernista* writer with one of the most revolutionary projects was the Cuban poet and essayist José Martí (1853–95). Martí warned the new emergent republics against the economic power and imperialist intervention of the United States. *Ismaelillo* [Little Ishmael], *Flores del destierro* [Flowers of Exile] and *En las entrañas del monstruo* (*Inside the Monster: Writings on the United States and American Imperialism*) are some of his most subversive texts. Martí's revolutionary vision also led him to publish a magazine devoted to children's literature called *La Edad de Oro* [The Golden Age]. Rubén Darío (1867–1916), another *modernista*, also denounced the menace of the American imperialism in the poem, "Roosevelt," and in the chronicle "Cake-Walk: el baile de moda" [Cake-Walk: The New Dance], published in 1903 in *La Revista Moderna de México* [The Modern Magazine of Mexico], an important *modernista* magazine edited by Jesús E. Valenzuela and Amado Nervo.

In the 19th century, women writers began to resist actively the oppression of the Latin American patriarchal societies. There was a strong Pan-American sisterhood among these women writers which permitted them to read and exchange ideas through their works. Women writers such as Gertrudis Gómez de Avellaneda (1814–73) Juana Manuela Gorriti (1818–92), Clorinda Matto de Turner (1852–1909) and Mercedes Cabello de Carbonera (1845–1909) denounced the hypocrisy of the dominant class and institutions of the Latin American countries. Gorriti organized literary evenings in La Paz, Lima, Santiago de Chile and Buenos Aires, where writers of both sexes read their works, discussed literary topics and analysed the political situation of their countries. These women writers reformulated the woman's role in the new republics,

criticized the corruption of their governments, as well as, the corruption of the social and religious institutions, and restored the value of the ancient cultures, collecting, and publishing native and regional oral literature. Some of the most representative resistance works that challenged the 19th century Latin American patriarchal and totalitarian societies are novels such as *Aves sin nido* (*Birds without a Nest*), *Índole* [Human Nature] and *Herencia* [Heritage] by Matto de Turner and *El conspirador: autobiografía de un hombre público* [The Conspirator: Autobiography of a Public Man] by Cabello de Carbonera. The book that best illustrates the sisterhood among these women writers and their commitment to participate in a joint effort to integrate their native and national cultures, as well as, to subvert the literary canon of the period is *Cocina ecléctica* [Eclectic Cuisine] – a book of recipes. The repertoire of writers included in this anthology of recipes can assist the critic to start studying the cultural contribution of each of these women.

A range of strategies of resistance were deployed in the early 20th century. The Latin American writer resists the discourse of the metropolis and overcomes cultural isolation, by contributing to a Pan-American exchange of ideas through the publication of different magazines and journals which promoted avant-garde literature or (the case of *Amauta* in Peru) radical politics. The most well-known magazines of this period are *Contemporáneos* (Mexico), *Revista de Avance* (Cuba), *Los Nuevos* (Colombia), *Martín Fierro* (Argentina), and *Las Moradas* (Peru). In these magazines Latin American intellectuals discussed and redefined the sociohistorical role of the artist and the writer as subjects of historical transformation. As a result, the essay is the most representative type of resistance text written during the beginning of the 20th century. During the mid-20th century, several Latin American intellectuals and writers participated in the promotion of the European – mainly French – avant-garde movements. Two historical events clearly influenced these intellectuals: the Russian Revolution and the Spanish Civil War. Most Latin American writers supported the Republican party in Spain; some even fought on the Republican front. A unique example of resistance poetry written in the battle site is *España aparta de mí este cáliz* (*Spain, Take This Cup from Me*) by César Vallejo.

In the last three decades, aside from the production of literary discourses of resistance, several Latin American writers, critics and thinkers have also written analytic works about the Latin American culture of resistance. In the last three decades, journals such as *Revista de Literatura Chilena en el Exilio* [Journal of Chilean Literature in Exile] and *Index on Censorship* incorporate theoretical and analytic texts about the Latin American culture of resistance in their publications. Working in a different medium, the *arpilleras* of Chile, Bolivia and Peru, subvert official history by using their hands to weave and sew their social memory into colorful tapestries for which the material used is sackcloth.

Is there any common topic within the extensive corpus of resistance literature that can link all Latin American works of this kind? There is a metaphor that helps intersect and relate all the oral and written discourses of resistance in Latin American: the *body divided*, the "*body in pain*." Pablo Neruda in his *Confieso que he vivido* (*Memoirs*) states "that there is an old theme, a "body divided" that recurs in the folk poetry of all the countries". This metaphor expresses the disintegration of entire communities and cultures in Latin America as a result of violent armed and cultural repressions: Native cultures repressed, rural families forced to migrate to the overcrowded urban centers, entire families in exile, individuals still missing, books burned, etc. The function then, of oral and written resistance literatures, has been the reintegration of the Latin American *body divided* by means of discourses that preserve the representation of the oppressed in the social memory, educate the new generations about the transformation of the social order, and that seize the territory of the repressive culture through the voices which historically never would have been heard.

FANNY D. ARANGO-RAMOS

Further Reading

Barrios de Chungara, Domitila, *La mujer y la organización*, La Paz: Unitas, 1980

Benedetti, Mario, *El escritor latinoamericano y la revolución posible,* Buenos Aires: Alfa, 1974

Cardenal, Ernesto, *El evangelio en Solentiname*, 2 vols, Salamanca: Sígueme, 1976–78; as *The Gospel in Solentiname*, translated by Donald Walsh, New York: Orbis Books, 1978–82

Cortázar, Julio, *Textos políticos*, Barcelona: Plaza y Janés, 1985

Dalton, Roque, *Poetry and Militancy in Latin America*, translated by James Scully, Willimantic, Connecticut: Curbstone Press, 1981

Díaz, José Pedro and Germán Wettstein, *Exilio-Inxilio: dos enfoques*, Montevideo: Instituto Testimonios de las Comarcas del Mundo, 1989

Dorfman, Ariel, *Reader's nuestro que estás en la tierra*, Mexico City: Nueva Imagen, 1980; as *The Empire's Old Clothes: What the Lone Ranger, Babar and other Innocent Heroes Do to Our Minds*, New York: Pantheon, and London: Pluto Press, 1983

___ *Hacia la liberación del lector latinoamericano*, Hanover, New Hampshire: Ediciones del Norte, 1984; as *Some Write to the Future*, translated by the author and George R. Shivers, Durham, North Carolina: Duke University Press, 1991

Galeano, Eduardo, *Las venas abiertas de América Latina*, Montevideo: Universidad de la República, 1971; as *The Open Veins of Latin* America, translated by Cedric Belfrage, New York: Monthly Review Press, 1973

Mariátegui, José Carlos, *Siete ensayos de interpretación de la realidad peruana*, Lima: Amauta, 1928; as *Seven Interpretative Essays on Peruvian Reality*, translated by Marjory Urquidi, Austin: University of Texas Press, 1971

Molloy, Sylvia, *At Face Value: Autobiographical Writing in Spanish America*, Cambridge and New York: Cambridge University Press, 1991

Primer coloquio sobre literatura chilena (de la resistencia y el exilio), Mexico City: UNAM, 1980

Rama, Ángel, *Literatura y clase social*, Mexico City: Folios, 1983

Vallejo, César, *Literatura y arte*, Buenos Aires: Mediodía, 1966

Verani, Hugo J. (editor), *Las vanguardias literarias en América Latina (manifiestos, proclamas y otros escritos)*, 2nd edition, Mexico City: Fondo de Cultura Económica, 1990

La Revue du Monde Noir

See Journals

Alfonso Reyes 1889–1959

Mexican prose writer, scholar, poet and literary translator

If one had to select Latin America's greatest man of letters, Alfonso Reyes would surely be one of the most impressive contenders for the title. Reyes's staggeringly prolific output spans many disciplines and styles, and his influence as a writer, as a scholar and as a cultural figure has been as profound as it would no doubt be long-lasting. His work has received a great deal of critical attention, although the often academic nature of his writing has meant that, especially outside Mexico, none of his works has ever received the sort of widespread popularity accorded to some of his more flamboyant colleagues and admirers.

The defining moment for Alfonso Reyes came in the period around or immediately after the Mexican Revolution. In conjunction with Pedro Henríquez Ureña, he founded the Ateneo de la Juventud (Atheneum of Youth), a group which later went on to enjoy a considerable literary and philosophical reputation. The Ateneo opposed the Positivist, technocratic intellectual mood prevalent during the Porfirian dictatorship of the late 19th century, and replaced the scientific rhetoric with a humanistic regard for aesthetics and classical scholarship. Reyes helped to develop a new discourse of the human spirit, the likes of which had been totally rejected under the scientific rationalism of the old order. Throughout his adult life, Reyes represented the possibility of humanist erudition in Mexico, his sheer presence exerting an influence over his peers and his successors as irresistible as that of any one of his most outstanding works.

Reyes's written *oeuvre* is so vast and so varied that it is difficult to reduce to one clear set of definitive statements, but all his works share certain important features. As a classical scholar of considerable talent, Reyes developed an attitude towards writing in which erudition, discipline and precision are keystones in the art of literary production. The style of his work has been commented on many times. Although Reyes deals with complex and sophisticated issues, his lucidity of expression communicates vast amounts of information with a barely perceptible stylistic ease. The work falls into several key categories: literary criticism; works on a classical theme; poetry; philosophical essays; and fictional narrative.

Reyes's devotion to "universal" literature and literary forms is tenacious in the face of national calls to make a literature that was specifically Mexican. It would be easy to dismiss Reyes's stance as depoliticised in comparison with some of his colleagues who took up Mexicanist or indigenist positions in the 1930s and 1940s. But it is important to remember that the position adopted by Reyes and the Ateneo was itself politically charged in the light of the scientific obsessions of the previous regime. Throughout his career, Reyes remained true to an aesthetic ideal. *Cuestiones estéticas*, 1911 [Questions of Aesthetics] is an early and highly influential text which upholds aesthetic value as an intangible absolute towards which it is a duty to strive. In a sense it could be argued that Reyes's tremendous influence bequeathed to Mexico an international canon with which it had previously had little contact. It was Reyes who championed not only the classics, but the literature of Spain, especially the canonical plays of the Golden Age. It was Reyes who wrote persuasively of the delights of Chesterton and Oscar Wilde and who translated Chekhov and Jules Romains. Each of Reyes's critical essays is a *tour de force*, not only of observation but also of construction and style.

However, it is the influence of the Greek and Roman classics on Reyes that is crucial. Something of the 19th-century European tradition of classical philology lives on in his writing. There is a three-fold involvement with the classics in his work: classical criticism, translation and classically-oriented invention. Reyes's body of classical criticism ranges from Socrates to the Hellenistic philosophers; from Homer and Virgil to the essence of Greek tragedy. The essays which make up this corpus mark out a specific case for the relevance of this sort of scholarship in post-revolutionary Mexico. Rigorous and astute, they argue passionately for the importance of the classical canon. Didactic tracts on ancient rhetoric or literary criticism such as "La crítica en la edad ateniense" and "La antigua retórica," 1941 [Criticism in the Age of Athens and Ancient Rhetoric] are persuasive testaments to Reyes's unswerving belief in the centrality of that canon within Western civilization. Together, these essays constitute a particular version of classical literature, in which "universal" ethical and spiritual values are subjected to a thorough and profound examination.

These beliefs led Reyes to disseminate classical literature by translating some of the greatest texts, notably the *Iliad* (*La Ilíada*, published in 1951). Lucid and professional, this trans-

lation typically manages to convey something of the flavour of the original while drawing on a Mexican poetic idiom that breathes a rhythmic contemporary life into the Homeric epic.

The task of the translator, a communicator bridging chasms of language, culture and time, can in many ways be said to dominate Reyes's output. The classics not only inspired him to take up scholarship but also to invent, or reinvent, metaphors, poetry and narrative on the basis of the classical tradition. The challenge to articulate Mexican reality from that basis is repeated again and again in his work. In "Discurso por Virgilio" (1933) for instance, Virgil's *Georgics* are reworked in an evocative discussion of government wine-growing policies. In addition, the classical training of Reyes's mind makes his a singular voice in Mexico's political and cultural struggle to reappropriate its ancient heritage. In *Visión de Anáhuac*, 1917 [Vision of Anáhuac], a poetic treatment of the conquistadors' vision of Mexico's ancient capital, Mexico itself provides the opportunity for a new sort of classical scholarship, in which pre-Colombian civilization offers scope for precise insights on the nature of the relationship between the ancient and the modern.

Reyes's most famous literary invention, however, is the dazzling *Ifigenia cruel*, 1924 [Cruel Iphigenia]. Based on a detailed reading of the versions of the myth of Iphigenia at Tauris, this piece reads like a Greek tragedy in Castilian and is written in a poetic language seldom surpassed in Latin American literature. The premise is that Iphigenia, seized away from Aulis just before sacrifice, arrives at Tauris to find herself a revered priestess, but, in contrast to the canonical version, Reyes's heroine has lost her memory, and the drama resides in her attempt to know herself and break the cycle of violence that afflicts her family. The poem's treatment of memory has been variously interpreted as a commentary on Mexico's struggle with the past and its identity, or as a poetic treatment of "universal" themes of human self-knowledge, or as a personal tract on Reyes's own position – his family were intimately involved with the dictatorship he opposed. The truth is that this strange and haunting piece itself articulates the impossible dilemma of the universal versus the particular; the responsibility towards one's peers versus the responsibility towards oneself; the need for personal understanding versus the need to understand broader social and political historical realities.

Ifigenia cruel is a poetic masterpiece. The ability of Reyes's work at its best to maintain an even-handed, aporetic approach to ethical questions, while creating a linguistic landscape as precise as it is rich in allusions, marks the best of his poetic output. Even early efforts, such as those collected in *Pausa*, 1924 [Pause] which owe much to *modernista* movements of the early years of the 20th century, display great originality as well as great learning. Throughout his career, Reyes produced volumes of verse which at best play with and rejuvenate forms and genres of poetic discourse, tackling the sonnet, the elegy, the romance, the epic and the lyric with as much fervour as his treatment of tragedy. Even less successful examples, which can seem so dry and academic that they work as little more than scholastic exercises in literary approximation, are always brilliantly executed.

If Reyes's poetry can sometimes disappoint, as an essayist, his talent seems to have been endlessly consistent. On literature, on aesthetics, on ethics, on history, Reyes is always clear, precise and economical in his use of language. A mordant wit is never far from the more polemic pieces, such as *Lo mexicano y lo universal*, 1932 [Mexicaness and Universality]; a restrained and measured stateliness graces the pages of his most evocative criticism, such as *Capítulos de literatura española*, 1939 [Chapters on Spanish Literature]. Above all, however, Reyes's great gift is rigour. The logical exposition which had previously been the preserve of the Mexican technocrats finds itself transported onto Reyes's humanist endeavour. The arguments are sound, the logic seamless and penetrating, and the overall effect is of a discourse that is supremely compelling. It is scarcely surprising that Reyes has become the paradigm of the Latin American essayist.

Throughout the 1920s, 1930s and 1940s, Reyes prioritized the application of a rigorous intelligence to major philosophical themes. There are essays on morality, historiography, the history of language and literary theory. Apart from the unmistakable trace of European humanism, there are references to Hegel, Fichte, Nietzsche and Croce. What emerges is not so much an original thinker, who could be called a philosopher in his own right, but a tremendously wise and attentive reader whose ability to synthesise material both ancient and modern in succinct arguments sheds light on major debates. What also emerges is a pervasive ethics characterised by a notion of respect for the self and for others, and a plea for moderation which may seem unremarkable, but is extraordinary in its consistency and in the calm and uncomplicated authority of the voice which articulates it.

Reyes also reflected on the nature of the Americas and on Mexico's cultural mix. In "Posición de América," 1942 [The Position of America] for example, Reyes sets out his own vision of the fusion of European and native American traditions in a text which, although it rejects some of the more ecstatic claims of other American commentators on similar themes, is quietly visionary. Despite the clear desire to take part in the feast of Western civilization, Reyes remains aware of his Mexican roots and of the dynamics of the relationship between the Old World and the New.

The very reasonableness which makes Reyes such a compelling essayist also makes him a solid but unremarkable writer of narrative fiction, that type of literature which has been most successfully exported by Latin America. His stories have all the rigour and allusiveness one would expect, but have never reached a large audience. The most telling comparison is with Jorge Luis Borges, with whom Reyes shared a friendship and an occasional correspondence. Reyes's stories display the same learning and sophistication as those of Borges, but somehow lack that twist of the bizarre imagination which have elevated the Argentine writer to international stardom. Perhaps this accounts for the fact that Reyes is little known outside Mexico. This is a pity. For all his faults, the world has produced few men of letters so complete as Alfonso Reyes.

MAURICE BIRIOTTI

Biography

Born in Monterrey, Mexico, 17 May 1889. Father, General Bernardo Reyes, was governor of the state of Nuevo Léon. Settled in Mexico City, 1906, and took part in a movement of cultural renewal and educational reform. This culminated in the foundation, with Antonio Caso, José Vasconcelos and Pedro Henríquez Ureña

(a distinguished scholar from the Dominican Republic) of the Ateneo de la Juventud (Atheneum of Youth). Inaugurated the chair of Spanish Language and Literature at Universidad Nacional Autónoma de México (UNAM), Mexico City, 1912. After the death of his father in 1913, accepted appointment as second secretary of the Mexican legation in France. This was the beginning of a long career in the diplomatic service which was to keep him abroad for many years. Following the German invasion of Paris in 1914, moved to Madrid where he earned his living as a literary translator and editor of the cultural section of the newspaper *El Sol*. In the 1920s and 1930s he occupied several important diplomatic posts, including those of ambassador to Argentina and Brazil. Returned to Mexico in 1939. Appointed director of the Colegio de Mexico, a cultural research centre that welcomed exiled scholars (such as those fleeing Franco's Spain), and fostered research in the humanities. Also helped establish the Colegio Nacional (1945) which offered regular series of lectures in the arts and the sciences open to the general public. Elected director of the Mexican Academy of the Language in 1957. Recipient: National Prize for Literature, 1945, but the Nobel Prize eluded him despite lobbying on his behalf. Died as a result of heart attack, 27 December 1959.

Selected Works

Poetry
Huellas, Mexico City: Botas, 1922
Ifigenia cruel, Madrid: Calleja, 1924
Romances del Río de Enero, Maastricht, Holland: Halcyon, 1933
A la memoria de Ricardo Güiraldes, Rio de Janeiro: n.p., 1934
Minuta, Maastricht, Holland: Halcyon, 1935
Cantata en la tumba de Federico García Lorca, Buenos Aires: n.p., 1937
La crítica en la edad ateniense, Mexico City: El Colegio de México, 1941
Pasado inmediato y otros ensayos, Mexico City: El Colegio de México, 1941
La antigua retórica, Mexico City: Fondo de Cultura Económica, 1942
La experiencia literaria, Buenos Aires: Losada, 1942
Los siete sobre Deva, Mexico City: Tezontle, 1942
Última Tule, Mexico City: Editorial Universitaria, 1942
El deslinde, Mexico City: El Colegio de México, 1944
Tentativas y orientaciones, Mexico City: Nuevo Mundo, 1944
Capítulos de literatura española (II), Mexico City: La Casa de España, 1945
Por mayo era, por mayo . . ., Mexico City: Cultura, 1946
Cortesía, Mexico City: Cultura, 1948
Grata compañía, Mexico City: Tezontle, 1948
Letras de la Nueva España, Mexico City: Fondo de Cultura Económica, 1948
Junta de sombras, Mexico City: El Colegio Nacional, 1949
Homero en Cuernavaca, Mexico City: Bajo el signo "Ábside," 1949

Novels
El plano oblicuo, Madrid: Europa, 1920
El testimonio de Juan Peña, Rio de Janeiro: Sur, 1930
Verdad y mentira, Madrid: Aguilar, 1950
Quince presencias, Madrid: Obregón, 1955

Other Writings
Cuestiones estéticas, Paris: Ollendorf, 1911
Cartones de Madrid, Mexico City: Cultura, 1917
El suicida, Madrid: García y Saez, 1917
Visión de Anáhuac, San José, Costa Rica: El Convivio, 1917
Retratos reales e imaginarios, Mexico City: Lectura Selecta, 1920
El cazador: ensayos y divagaciones (1911–1920), Madrid: Biblioteca Nueva, 1921

Simpatías y diferencias, 5 vols, Madrid: Teodoro, 1921–26
Calendario, Madrid: Imprenta Ciudad Lineal, 1924
Cuestiones gongorinas, Madrid: Espasa Calpe, 1927
Horas de Burgos, Rio de Janeiro: Villas Boas, 1932
La caída, Rio de Janeiro: Villas Boas, 1933
Las vísperas de España, Buenos Aires: Sur, 1937
Mallarmé entre nosotros, Buenos Aires: Destiempo, 1938
Capítulos de literatura española, Mexico City: La Casa de España en Mexico, 1939
Norte y sur, Mexico City: Leyenda, 1944 [essays]
Ancorajes , Mexico City: Tezontle, 1951
Memorias de cocina y bodega, Mexico City: Tezontle, 1953
Trayectoria de Goethe, Mexico City: Fondo de Cultura Económica, 1954
Parentalia, Mexico City: Los Presentes, 1954 [memoirs]
Las burlas veras, 2 vols, Mexico City: Tezontle, 1957–59
Albores, Mexico City: El Cerro de la Silla, 1960 [memoirs]
A campo traviesa, Mexico City: El Cerro de la Silla, 1960
Al yunque (1944–1958), Mexico City: Tezontle, 1960
Oración del nueve de febrero, Mexico City: Era, 1963 [memoirs]
Anecdotario, Mexico City: Era, 1968 [memoirs]
Diario (1911–1930), Guanajuato, Mexico: Universidad de Guanajuato, 1969 [memoirs]
Vida y ficción, edited by Ernesto Mejía Sánchez, Mexico City: Fondo de Cultura Económica, 1970
Monterrey (Correo literario de Alfonso Reyes), Rio de Janeiro and Buenos Aires, *Revistas Literarias Mexicanas (Antena, Monterrey, Examen, Número)*, Mexico City, 1980 [facsimile edition]

Correspondence

Correspondance (1923–52), edited by Paulette Patout, Paris: Klincksieck, 1972 [Correspondence in French between Reyes and Valery Larbaud]
Epistolario Alfonso Reyes–José M. Chacón, edited by Zenaida Gutiérrez-Vega, Madrid: Fundación Universitaria Española, 1976
Cartas echadas: correspondencia 1927–1959, edited by Héctor Perea, Mexico City: Fondo de Cultura Económica, 1976 [Correspondence between Reyes and Victoria Ocampo]
Epistolario íntimo, 1906–1946, 3 vols, edited by Juan Jacobo de Lara, Santo Domingo, Dominian Republic: UNPHU, 1981–83 [Correspondence between Reyes and Pedro Henríquez Ureña]

Compilations and Anthologies

Obras completas, 25 vols, Mexico City: Fondo de Cultura Económica, 1955–91
Antología de Alfonso Reyes, edited by José Luis Martínez, Mexico City: Fondo de Cultura Económica, 1965
Antología personal, edited by Ernesto Mejía Sánchez, Mexico City: Fondo de Cultura Económica, 1983

Translations

The Position of America, and Other Essays, translated by Harriet de Onís, New York: Knopf, 1950
Mexico in a Nutshell, and Other Essays, translated by Charles Ramsdell, Berkeley: University of California Press, 1964

Further Reading

Alonso, Amado, "Alfonso Reyes," in his *Materia y forma en poesía*, Madrid: Gredos, 1955
Cuspinera, Margarita Vera (editor), *Alfonso Reyes: homenaje de la Facultad de Filosofía y Letras*, Mexico City: Fondo de Cultura Económica, 1981
Earle, Peter G., "Alfonso Reyes," in *Historia del ensayo hispanoamericano*, edited by Earle and Robert G. Mead, Mexico City: Andrea, 1973
Ellison, Fred P., "Alfonso Reyes, Brazil and the Story of a Passion," *Los Ensayistas* 18–19 (1985)
Homenaje de El Colegio Nacional a Alfonso Reyes, Mexico City: Fondo de Cultura Económica, 1965
Olguín, Manuel, *Alfonso Reyes: ensayista; vida y pensamiento*, Mexico City: n.p., 1956
Patout, Paulette, *Alfonso Reyes et la France*, Paris: Klincksieck, 1978
Reyes, Alicia, *Genio y figura de Alfonso Reyes*, Buenos Aires: Eudeba, 1976
Robb, James Willis, *Estudios sobre Alfonso Reyes*, Bogotá: El Dorado, 1976
_____ *Por los caminos de Alfonso Reyes*, Mexico City: INBA, 1981
Villaurrutia, Xavier, "Alfonso Reyes: un hombre de caminos," in *Obras*, 2nd edition, Mexico City: Fondo de Cultura Económica, 1966

João Ubaldo Ribeiro 1941–

Brazilian prose writer

João Ubaldo Ribeiro's first short stories appeared in literary supplements at the end of the 1950s. His first full-length work, *Setembro não tem sentido*, 1968 [September Makes No Sense], waited five years for publication and tells of the frustrations of a group of intellectuals. With its prophetic air, alluding to the imposition of a military regime in the near future, it is "the charge of the light brigade of tradition." Even at this early stage, Ubaldo Ribeiro's work had already begun to question the myth of Brazilian national identity.

However, it was *Sargento Getúlio*, 1971 (*Sergeant Getúlio*), which established Ubaldo Ribeiro as one of Brazil's major writers of contemporary fiction. The protagonist embodies the tragic human condition of the people of northeastern Brazil, living by conflicting values and overcome by isolation and the struggle for survival. Orality predominates in the timeless narrative of two men united by hate and violence. The figure of the sergeant has been equated with the author's father, but in reality is an amalgamation of various personalities.

Vencecavalo e outro povo, 1974 [Vencecavalo and the Other Village] – described by the author as a fairy tale – is a parable which incorporates both tragic and comic elements in an attempt to show the fragility of those in power who turn against the community. Vencecavalo is a rebellious, picaresque hero.

Vila Real, 1979 [Royal Town], is a novel which Ubaldo Ribeiro prefers to call epic, using colloquial language in written form. It also employs the archaic structures used in the northeast of Brazil and is intended to contribute to the creation of a classic model of the region. The main character, Argemiro, is a man from the country who finds himself at the head of a resistance movement, struggling to retake the land where he lives and works following eviction by a mining company. The character is reminiscent of Antônio Conselheiro, from Canudos, who appears in both *Os sertões* (*Rebellion in the Backlands*) by Euclides da Cunha and Mario Vargas Llosa's *La guerra del fin del mundo* (*The War of the End of the World*). There is little action. The narrator employs an epic-poetic form, underlining the medieval traits of the *sertão*. Biblical influences can also be found in the depiction of religious inspiration. Elements such as the "desafio" (*payada* or *gaucho* folksong) come from the "literatura de cordel" (popular "literature on a string").

Ubaldo Ribeiro's most ambitious work to date is *Viva o povo brasileiro*, 1984 (*An Invincible Memory*). Dedicated to his childhood friend, film director Glauber Rocha, the novel covers three centuries, using the technique of *mise en abîme* to move between them. The narrative does not follow the action chronologically: it begins in 1823 in Puerta de las Ballenas on the island of Itaparica (Bahia), moves backwards to 1627 and comes forward again to 1977. It is the living history of Brazil, a denouncement of oppression which accords little importance to the official version of history, celebrated dates or heroic acts, depicting the evolution of a people in fresco form. The novel privileges lesser events and the dramas of unimportant lives by using cross sections. Ubaldo Ribeiro constructs with minute detail a historical canvas, covering the Wars of Independence, when a heroic lieutenant confronts Portuguese fire, to the 1970s, with a fierce and corrupt dictatorship. He incorporates the fantastic by parodying the Battle of Tuiuti in the Paraguayan War, when the *orixás* (gods of the "candomblé") enter the fray like the gods of the Iliad.

The narrator depicts "the everyday heroes." The main characters are the Brazilian people themselves. The narrative captures dozens of characters, souls flying above Itaparica, a world of barons, slaves (before and after abolition), native Indians, industrialists, soldiers and workers. Each section contains an individual story, like that of the *caboclo* (backwoodsman), Capiroba, who has had the notion of sin instilled in him by the missionaries but who prefers to eat the tender flesh of the Dutch. The stories are not unconnected. Common factors are the resistance of Itaparica and elements of the bourgeoisie of São Paulo, primitive society and its destruction, the first attempts at emancipation, the rise and fall of a rural pseudo-aristocracy and part of the landowning elite, the affirmation of a nascent mercantile bourgeoisie and the constant oppression of the Brazilian people. A pretentious relationship is developed between the real, objective world and an imaginary world of exaggeration and grotesque distortion.

The text is agile, fluent and ironic using harmonious language. Without limiting himself to the relatively unsophisticated documentalism of "literature of truth" and the naturalist theories of the 1970s, Ubaldo Ribeiro deconstructs romantic discourse while simultaneously incorporating a political element in his text instead of merely describing it. The narrator often makes use of parody of certain Brazilian authors such as José de Alencar and João Guimarães Rosa. Without intending to produce a violent literature, the author was concerned with producing works related to his roots, independent and uncolonised; in the author's own words, texts "engaged with the affirmation of Brazilian identity." In similar vein to Mário de Andrade's character Macunaíma, he satirises false heroism.

In the work metaphorically entitled *O sorriso do lagarto*, 1989 (*The Lizard's Smile*), adultery, abuse of power and urban violence are combined with the questioning of human nature and the inability of people to change the course of their lives. Using both humour and eroticism, the text deals with the transitory nature of life. A biologist, Juan Pedroso, goes through life terrorised by the stare of a lizard with two tails. Events take place on the island of Itaparica, where the biologist, his lover, a priest, a doctor and a corrupt politician are the main characters. Through science, the narrator explores the debate surrounding the dichotomy of Good versus Evil, popular versus erudite and preconceived notions of truth.

The work of João Ubaldo Ribeiro, rooted in the popular culture of Brazil, can be considered a portrait of his people and his time.

BELLA JOZEF

translated by Carol Tully

See also entries on José de Alencar, Mário de Andrade, João Guimarães Rosa, Popular Culture: Brazil, Regionalism: Brazil

Biography

Born on the Island of Itaparica, All Saints Bay, Bahia, Brazil, 23 January 1941. Attended the Federal University of Bahia, 1959–62, received LL.B in 1962; University of Southern California, Los Angeles, 1964–65, MS in public administration, 1965. Married three times: 1) Maria Beatriz Gordilho Moreira Caldas (divorced); 2) Mônica Maria Roters (divorced), two daughters; 3) Berenice de Carvalho Batella, one son and one daughter. Professor of political science at the Federal University of Bahia, and the Catholic University of Salvador, Bahia. Editor-in-Chief of the newspaper *Tribuna da Bahia*, Salvador, Bahia; served as journalist or editor for numerous other newspapers. Participated in the International Writers Program, University of Iowa, Iowa City. Awarded the State of Rio de Janeiro Golfinho de Ouro [Golden Dolphin] Prize; Brazilian Book Chamber Jabuti [Tortoise] Prize (twice); São Paulo Association of Art Critics Award; Brazilian National Foundation for Literature for Young People Award; Gulbenkian Foundation Scholarship (Portugal). Commander, Order of Merit of Portugal.

Selected Works

Novels

Setembro não tem sentido, Rio de Janeiro: José Álvaro, 1968

Sargento Getúlio, Rio de Janeiro: Artenova, 1971; as *Sergeant Getúlio*, translated by the author, Boston: Houghton Mifflin, 1978; London: André Deutsch, 1980

Vila Real, Rio de Janeiro: Nova Fronteira, 1979

Viva o povo brasileiro, Rio de Janeiro: Nova Fronteira, 1984; as *An Invincible Memory*, translated by the author, New York: Harper and Row, and London: Faber and Faber, 1989

O sorriso do lagarto, Rio de Janeiro: Nova Fronteira, 1989; as *The Lizard's Smile*, translated by Clifford Landers, New York: Atheneum, 1994; London: André Deutsch, 1995

A vingança de Charles Tiburone, Rio de Janeiro: Nova Fronteira, 1990

Other Writings
Vencevalo e outro povo, Rio de Janeiro: Artenova, 1974 [short fiction]
Política: quem manda, porque manda, como manda, Rio de Janeiro: Nova Fronteira, 1983 [political essay]
Vida e paixão de Pandonar, o terrível, Rio de Janeiro: Nova Fronteira, 1983 [children's fiction]

Further Reading
DiAntonio, Robert, "Chthonian Visions and Mythic Redemption in João Ubaldo Ribeiro's *Sergeant Getúlio*," *Modern Fiction Studies*, vol. 32/3 (1986)

Rocha, Glauber, prologue to *Setembro não tem sentido*, Rio de Janeiro: José Álvaro, 1969
Valente, Luiz Fernando, "Fiction as History: the Case of João Ubaldo Ribeiro," *Latin American Research Review*, vol. 28/1 (1993)
_____ "Sátira e anti-história em João Ubaldo Ribeiro," in *La historia en la literatura iberoamericana*, edited by Gabriella de Beer and Raquel Chang-Rodríguez, Hanover, New Hampshire: Ediciones del Norte, 1989

Interviews
Price, Greg, *Latin America. The Writer's Journey*, London: Hamish Hamilton, 1990

José Eustasio Rivera 1888–1928

Colombian novelist and poet

The literary legacy of José Eustasio Rivera consists of *Tierra de promisión* [The Promised Land], a collection of fifty-five sonnets that blend *modernista* aestheticism with autochthonous thematic content, and *La vorágine* (*The Vortex*), a novel considered one of the landmarks of Spanish American regionalism. The national and international recognition garnered by these two works place him at the forefront of Colombian literature of the first half of the 20th century.

Rivera was a member of the patriotic, civic-minded "Generación del Centenario" (Centennial Generation), a group of Colombian writers who took their name from the celebration of the first hundred years of national independence. *Tierra de promisión* constitutes a poetic expression of his national pride. In three sections the volume offers a panoramic literary canvas of the country's colorful rural landscapes – the jungle, the mountains and the plains. The sonnets evoke nature's idyllic beauty and convey Rivera's emotional response to his surroundings. The physical environment at once influences and reflects his mood. For example, when darkness falls and the swallow's melancholy song fills the air – "la tarde se nubló de pena" (the evening clouded over with grief) – the poet shares nature's sorrow: "mi alma también atardeció" (my soul also grew dark). Rivera's poetry contains numerous vestiges of Spanish American *Modernismo*, as is illustrated by his depiction of creatures of the animal world as precious stones and art objects: a fish becomes "un estuche de carne guarnecido de plata" (a silver-plated jewel box of flesh); a snake appears as a "rica diadema" (rich diadem) and a "pálida gema" (pale gem); a black beetle is a "vagabunda joya" (wandering jewel).

La vorágine has inspired heated debate among critics ever since its publication in 1924. They have argued over the merits of its aesthetic features as opposed to its value as a document of social protest. They have also been unable to agree on the artistic tendency or movement to which Rivera belongs. The labels applied to him and his works cover the gamut from Romantic, Parnassian, Realist, Naturalist, and *modernista* to post-*modernista*. Of these, the last seems most appropriate, at least in terms of literary chronology. *La vorágine* can be read as a documentary exposé of the crimes committed against the *caucheros* (rubber workers) and also as a poetic description of man's encounter with the treacherous beauty of the tropical landscape.

Much of the disagreement among critics centers on the semi-autobiographical protagonist, Arturo Cova, who, like Rivera, is a poet. To some, Cova is ill-conceived and unconvincing, an impulsive, melodramatic figure lacking in appeal to modern readers. Others see him as a multi-faceted, introspective individual whose delicate psyche suffers from the maddening effects of the jungle's enchantment. Cova and his companion Alicia, a young woman he has victimized, flee the city in order to avoid a scandal. Cova's travels, his flight from Bogotá to the plains and his pursuit of Alicia into the jungle, signify an archetypal journey or quest. The couple's sojourn on the plains aquaints them with the violence and picturesque qualities of rural life. The inclusion of *costumbrista* scenes evoking local customs, such as the cock fight, is typical of regional works of this period. Rivera also interrupts the main narrative with an interpolated story, another characteristic common to the novel of the 1920s. The haunting legend of the jungle spirit Mapiripana provides an etiological explanation for the origin of the rivers and streams. More importantly, however, her conquest of the missionary metaphorically signals the triumph of nature over human adversaries and foreshadows Cova's ultimate destiny.

Rivera's works reflect popular and literary impressions of Amazonia. The depictions of the jungle in both *Tierra de promisión* and *La vorágine* incorporate stereotypical notions regarding the inherent exoticism of the tropics. In the former work, written before he had seen the rain forest, the poet was limited to creating scenes and descriptions based on popular tradition and his imagination. In writing the novel, however, he drew on an additional source – the people he met and the sights he witnessed in his travels in the jungle region. As a result, the novel is more linguistically diverse, alternating poetic descriptions (some of the identical imagery used in the sonnets) with popular speech and a rich vocabulary of regional expressions.

In the eyes of most critics, Rivera's two major works present antithetical views of Colombia's natural environment with *Tierra de promisión* showcasing the scenic beauty of the jungle and plains and *La vorágine* capturing the violent and inhospitable aspects of those terrains. In spite of this apparent dichotomy, his lyrics and narrative have several features in common. In both Rivera employs a tripartite structure, depicts the beauty and violence of the life-death cycle, develops the *modernista* theme of the pursuit of an unattainable ideal, and couches his descriptions in an impressionistic, poetic language. He privileges landscape, making it the prime subject of his sonnets and endowing it with the attributes of a character in the novel. In *Tierra de promisión* and *La vorágine* Rivera's attitude toward the environment seems to be one of ambivalence. Although he spent most of his life in the city, he felt a deep kinship with the rural regions of Colombia. The savage paradise he created was a product of his literary imagination and personal experiences. Given the antithetical aspect of this imaginary precinct, it is not surprising that he responded to it with alternating feelings of attraction and repulsion.

In *La vorágine* Rivera perverts the natural order of things by means of personification and dehumanization. In the words of the rubber gatherer Clemente Silva, the trees are all "perverse, aggressive, or hypnotic." Once an incision is made, a liquid stream of sap begins to flow like "tragic tears" and "white blood." When Silva becomes lost deep in the jungle without supplies, he wanders "animalizado por la floresta . . . masticando tallos, cáscaras, hongos, como bestia herbívora" (brutalized by the forest . . . chewing on plant stems, peels, mushrooms, like a herbivore). Suffering from the paralyzing effects of beriberi, Arturo Cova finds parallels between his condition and that of the trees: his swollen legs resemble the roots of certain palm trees and his blood is like "warm sap."

If, in *Tierra de promisión*, Rivera's intentions were purely aesthetic, in *La vorágine*, he broadened his scope to include a social dimension (denunciation of injustices) as well as an artistic one (poetic descriptions of nature). His chief image in the novel, that of a devouring vortex, signifies an omnipresent menace, whether it manifests itself as *tambochas* (army ants) marching across the jungle floor consuming everything in their path, as piranhas stripping the flesh from the body of Cova's adversary, Barrera, or as an anthropomorphic jungle enticing, then disorienting its victims and eventually devouring them. The most memorable appearance of the vortex occurs in the novel's famous last line where the reader learns the fate of Cova and his party: "Los devoró la selva" (The jungle swallowed them up).

Although Rivera's sonnets have been all but ignored by present-day scholars, his novel continues to inspire critical commentary, including postmodern readings. In *The Spanish American Regional Novel*, Carlos J. Alonso views Cova's battle against hostile nature as a metaphor for the poet's struggle with language in the act of literary creation. In a similar vein,

Raymond Leslie Williams interprets the novel as a dramatization of the process of writing and Cova as "a patently literary character creating a self-consciously "literary" text – an explicitly arranged writing." These recent assessments of *La vorágine* attest to its lasting significance and its centrality to any discussion of the concept of literature and the creative process in Latin America.

MELVIN S. ARRINGTON, JR

Biography

Born in Neiva, Colombia in 1888. First son in family of four boys and seven girls. Father was a modest farmer. Attended boarding school in Neiva at the age of seven, but left the following year and worked on the family farm. From then, in and out of school for several years. At the age of eighteen won government scholarship and entered teacher's training college in Bogota, run by La Salle brothers. On leaving worked as inspector of small schools, but critical of teaching methods and officialdom. Accepted bureaucratic position in governor's office. Enrolled in Law Faculty of National University. In September 1922 appointed secretary of the Boundary Commission which was attempting to sort out boundary disputes with Venezuela. Spent ten months in the jungle of the Orinoco region. On his return given seat by Conservative Party in the House of Representatives: resigned after three months. *La vorágine* appeared in 1924. Its exposure of slavery in the rubber fields of Colombia, Brazil and Venezuela provoked international interest. Travelled to New York to work on a revised version of his novel and to oversee its translation into English, 1928. Died there unexpectedly on 1 December 1928. Cause of death unknown because there was no autopsy.

Selected Works

Oda a España. El Tropical, Ibagüé, Colombia, 1910 [poetry]
Tierra de promisión, Bogotá: Casa Arboleda y Valencia, 1921 [poetry]
La vorágine, Bogotá: Tamayo y Cía, 1924; as *The Vortex*, translated by Earle K. James, New York: Putnam, 1935

Further Reading

Alonso, Carlos J., *The Spanish American Regional Novel: Modernity and Autochthony*, Cambridge and New York: Cambridge University Press, 1990 [Chapter 5 is on *La vorágine*]
Ford, Richard, "El marco narrativo de *La vorágine*," *Revista Iberoamericana*, vol. 42/96–97 (1976)
Franco, Jean, "Image and Experience in *La vorágine*," *Bulletin of Hispanic Studies* 41 (1964)
Gutiérrez Girardot, Rafael, "*La vorágine* de José Eustasio Rivera: su significación permanente para las letras de lengua española, *Casa de las Américas*, Havana, vol. 34/194 (January–March 1994)
Menton, Seymour, "*La vorágine*: Circling the Triangle," *Hispania* 59 (1976)
Molloy, Sylvia, "Contagio narrativo y gesticulación retórica en *La vorágine*," *Revista Iberoamericana* 141 (1987)
Neale-Silva, Eduardo, *Horizonte humano: vida de José Eustasio Rivera*, Mexico City: Fondo de Cultura Económica, 1960
Ordóñez, Montserrat (editor), "*La vorágine*": textos críticos, Bogotá: Alianza, 1987
Quiroga, Horacio, "La selva de José Eustasio Rivera," in "*La vorágine*": textos críticos, edited by Montserrat Ordóñez, Bogotá: Alianza, 1987
Sommer, Doris, *Foundational Fictions: the National Romances of Latin America*, Berkeley, University of California Press, 1991 [Chapter 9 is on *Doña Bárbara* and *La vorágine*]
Walker, John, *Rivera: La vorágine*, London: Grant and Cutler, 1988

Augusto Roa Bastos 1917–

Paraguayan prose writer, poet and dramatist

Widely regarded as one of Latin America's greatest living authors of fiction, winner of the Cervantes prize and other honors, Augusto Roa Bastos is almost certainly the best-known writer ever to come out of Paraguay. Unfortunately, Paraguay has historically exported some of its greatest literary figures by deporting or exiling them, and it is to this ironic circumstance that Roa Bastos's international reputation is due in part. Beginning with the Paraguayan Civil War of 1947, Roa Bastos's four decades of exile have exposed him to fellow writers and a vast readership he may never have known had he remained in his country. To say this, of course, is not to deny the personal tragedy of Roa Bastos's exile nor is it to undervalue his lifelong commitment to Paraguay. Raised in Iturbe, a small town in the Paraguayan interior, Roa Bastos has remained very much the native son. Much of his fiction is set in and around Iturbe, and the author's involvement with Paraguayan affairs, including politics, has never been seriously interrupted. Hence, when the fall of the Stroessner dictatorship in 1989 finally enabled Roa Bastos to return freely, he did so not as a stranger, but as a venerated elder statesman. Since then he has increased his activities in Paraguay while maintaining his long-time residence in Toulouse, France.

Roa Bastos began his literary career as a poet. Along with Josefina Pla, Hérib Campos Cervera and others, he contributed to the renewal of Paraguayan poetry in the 1940s, publishing *El ruiseñor de la aurora y otros poemas* [The Nightingale of Dawn and Other Poems] in 1942. Another book of verse, *El naranjal ardiente* [The Burning Orange Grove], did not appear till 1960, years after its contents – including Roa Bastos's only writings in Guaraní – were composed. Roa Bastos never felt at home in his poetic vocation, however, and his efforts since the early 1950s have been almost entirely in the genre of prose fiction. Translated into a variety of languages, awarded prizes, even made into film, Roa Bastos's fiction has truly assumed a place in the world literary pantheon. At times his narratives – and particularly his short stories – resemble those of the best Latin American regionalist writers, Mexico's Juan Rulfo for example, or Peru's José María Arguedas, in that they record the pulsations of a particular human community. But like Rulfo and Arguedas, Roa Bastos understood the universality of the particular. He understood that universality in art need not be achieved at the expense of a regional loyalty, and that what is common to all may well be found in what is specific to a few. Hence the global appeal of these stories about the lost and the powerless in the nether places of South America's least understood country. Roa Bastos's success has been precisely this: to create broadly human works of art from the regional and national tragedy of Paraguay and the profound circumstance of his own exile.

In 1953 Roa Bastos published his first book of short stories, *El trueno entre las hojas* [Thunder among the Leaves], in which the characters' suffering assumes the dimensions of ancient tragedy. Like many of Roa Bastos's other narratives, these early stories draw their thematic material from the Paraguayan context of economic instability and political repression, especially as these problems affect the rural poor. As his fiction matured, however, Roa Bastos appears to have realized that these themes, however important, are merely accidents on the surface of something at once vaster, deeper and more personal, something developed in the macrocosm of history and lived out in the microcosm of the individual. Hence many of the later stories, and even more so the novels, incorporate the historical motif of dictatorship and the personal one of exile. Story collections published while Stroessner was in power (1954–89) include, among others, *El baldío* [Vacant Ground], *Madera quemada* [Burnt Wood], *Moriencia* [The Experience of Dying], *Cuerpo presente* [Lying in State], *Antología personal* [Personal Anthology], and *Contar un cuento y otros relatos* [To Tell a Tale and Other Stories].

Roa Bastos's first novel, *Hijo de hombre* (*Son of Man*), appeared in 1960 after winning the Losada International Novel Competition of 1959, and in 1990 the author re-published it in an altered version. *Hijo de hombre* is in many ways *the* Paraguayan epic, embracing as it does much of the nation's history, from Dr Gaspar Rodríguez de Francia's dictatorship (1814–40) to the period immediately following the 1932–35 Chaco War with Bolivia. What unites *Hijo de hombre* despite the relative autonomy of its chapters is a series of thematic dichotomies – freedom/oppression, justice/injustice, heroism/betrayal, and so forth – woven into the lives of the principal characters: Miguel Vera, Gaspar Mora, Casiano and Nati Jara, and Cristóbal (Kiritó) Jara. In terms of structure, the novel generally alternates between the heroic suffering of Mora and the Jaras, and the morally ambiguous recollections of the indecisive intellectual Vera. By theme and structure, therefore, it is tempting to consign this novel to the Manichaean "good versus evil" tradition of Latin American fiction. Such an interpretation, however, fails to account for the complexities of a work of art in which none of the main characters is a mere puppet in the service of Good or of Evil. In its affirmation of a spiritualized popular struggle, *Hijo de hombre* may be said to anticipate the "theology of liberation" of ensuing decades, but it does so in a deeper way than merely positing the triumph of the downtrodden. For Roa Bastos, as for the best of the liberation theologians, human beings are sophisticated creatures in whom the fragile spark of redemption must be nurtured if it is not to be snuffed out. This nurturing takes place in solidarity with one's fellow strugglers, and its process is a continuum along which Roa Bastos's protagonists are never static, never frozen in Manichaen postures of absolute virtue or vice.

Similar affirmations may be made concerning Roa Bastos's masterpiece *Yo el Supremo* (*I the Supreme*), except that here the focus is on a character in whom one would suppose the redemptive spark to be completely extinguished, Paraguay's notorious dictator Dr Francia. Unlike Carpentier's *El recurso del método* (*Reasons of State*) and García Márquez's *El otoño del patriarca* (*The Autumn of the Patriarch*), which present composites of various dictators, Roa Bastos's novel purports to be primarily a "dictation" by this singular historical figure, a testament which he, Roa Bastos, has merely "compiled" for posterity. By thus seeming to allow the dictator to speak for himself, Roa Bastos rescues him from the oversimplifying memory of his victims. This is not to say that Roa Bastos's dictator is a revisionist version who "wasn't so bad after all." Roa Bastos's Francia is all that we had been taught, yet also much more: profoundly evil, yet also profoundly idealistic, profoundly pitiful, profoundly moving, in short, profoundly human.

Roa Bastos's later novels – *Vigilia del Almirante*, [Vigil of the Admiral], *El Fiscal*, [The Prosecutor] and *Contravida* [Counterlife] – continue his tradition of a searching humanism made potent by bold narrative experimentation. While the first two of these parallel *Yo el Supremo* in their narrative treatment of major historical figures (Christopher Columbus and the Paraguayan leader, Solano López, respectively), *Contravida* undertakes a sort of reprise of Roa Bastos's fictional world, deconstructing and reconstructing many of the characters, settings, and themes found in his previous works. The most important feature of these novels, however, may well be the extrinsic fact that all were published in the post-Stroessner period. The relationship between Paraguay's exiled writers and those who remained in the country has been a matter of controversy among some Paraguayans, particularly now that the exiles are free to return. Roa Bastos has inevitably – and unwillingly – been drawn into this dichotomy, but his vitality as a writer even after his return from exile is proof of the ultimate hollowness of such divisions. For most readers, Augusto Roa Bastos has earned a place above the fray, having made of his own and his country's resilience an emblem to which all human beings can aspire.

TRACY K. LEWIS AND TERESA MÉNDEZ-FAITH

Biography

Born in Asunción, Paraguay, 13 June 1917. Fluent in Spanish and Guaraní, spent much of his childhood in the town of Iturbe, where his father worked on a sugar plantation. Later attended military school in Asunción, and fought as a teenager in the Chaco War against Bolivia, 1932–35. Worked in a bank in Asunción and later editorial staff member for *El País*. Near the end of World War II, travelled in England and France. With the 1947 Civil War in Paraguay, began his exile from the country. Resident in Buenos Aires and, after 1975, in Toulouse, France, working variously as a writer and Professor of Guaraní and Spanish American studies at the University of Toulouse. Visited Paraguay sporadically during this period; in 1982 was arrested again and ejected from the country. Since the end of the dictatorship in 1989, has returned freely while maintaining French residence. Recipient of the following awards: Premio de Letras del Memorial de América Latina (Brazil), 1988; Miguel de Cervantes Prize, 1989; Condecoración de la Orden Nacional del Mérito (Paraguay), 1990. Paraguayan signatory to Morelia Declaration, 1991, calling for global ecological reform and indigenous rights.

Selected Works

Novels

Hijo de hombre, Buenos Aires: Losada, 1960; as *Son of Man*, translated by Rachel Caffyn, London: Gollancz, 1965; New York: Monthly Review Press, 1988
Yo el Supremo, Buenos Aires: Siglo XXI, 1974; as *I the Supreme*, translated by Helen Lane, New York: Knopf, 1986; London: Faber and Faber, 1987

Vigilia del Almirante, Asunción, Paraguay: RP Ediciones, 1992
El Fiscal, Buenos Aires: Sudamericana, 1993
Contravida, Asunción, Paraguay: El Lector, 1994

Short Fiction

El trueno entre las hojas, Buenos Aires: Losada, 1953
El baldío, Buenos Aires: Losada, 1966
Los pies sobre el agua, Buenos Aires: CEDAL, 1967
Madera quemada, Santiago de Chile: Editorial Universitaria, 1967
Moriencia, Caracas: Monte Ávila, 1969
Cuerpo presente y otros textos, Buenos Aires: CEDAL, 1971
El pollito de fuego, Buenos Aires: Ediciones de La Flor, 1974
Los juegos, 2 vols, Buenos Aires: Ediciones de La Flor, 1979; as *Los juegos de Carolina y Gaspar*, Mexico: CIDCLI, 1994 [for children]
Contar un cuento y otros relatos, edited by Ana Becciú, Buenos Aires: Kapelusz, 1984

Poetry

El ruiseñor de la aurora y otros poemas, Asunción, Paraguay: Imprenta Nacional, 1942
El naranjal ardiente, nocturno paraguayo, Asunción, Paraguay: Diálogo, 1960

Screenplays

Shunko (1960), *Alias Gardelito* (1963), *El Señor Presidente* (1966), *Don Segundo Sombra* (1968), *Yo el Supremo* (1991)

Other Writings

Cándido López, Parma, Italy: F. M. Ricci, 1976
Imagen y perspectivas de la narrativa latinoamericana actual, Mexico City: UNAM, 1979
Lucha hasta el alba, Asunción: Arte Nuevo, 1979
Rafael Barrett y la realidad paraguaya a comienzos del siglo, Stockholm: Instituto de Estudios Latinoamericanos, 1981
El tiranosaurio del Paraguay da sus últimas boqueadas, Buenos Aires: Frente Paraguayo, 1986
Carta abierta a mi pueblo, Buenos Aires: Frente Paraguayo, 1986
El texto cautivo: el escritor y su obra, Alcalá de Henares, Spain: Fundación Colegio del Rey, 1990
Mis reflexiones sobre el guión cinematográfico y el guión de "Hijo de hombre," Asunción: RP Ediciones, 1993

Compilations and Anthologies

Antología personal, Mexico City: Nueva Imagen, 1980
Escritos políticos de Augusto Roa Bastos, edited by Marta Teresa Casteros, Buenos Aires: Instituto de Estudios de Literatura Latinoamericana, 1984
Augusto Roa Bastos: antología narrativa y poética, edited by Paco Tovar, Barcelona: Ánthropos, 1991

Further Reading

Aldana, Adolfo L., *La cuentística de Augusto Roa Bastos*, Montevideo: Géminis, 1975
Bareiro Saguier, Rubén, "Estratos de la lengua guaraní en la escritura de Augusto Roa Bastos," *Estudios Paraguayos*, vol. 10/2 (1982)
Burgos, Fernando (editor), *Las voces del karaí: estudios sobre Augusto Roa Bastos*, Madrid: Edelsa, 1988
Foster, David William, *The Myth of Paraguay in the Fiction of Roa Bastos*, Chapel Hill: University of North Carolina, 1969
―― *Augusto Roa Bastos*, Boston: Twayne, 1978
Lewis, Tracy K., *Roa Bastos: precursor del post-boom*, Mexico City: Katún, 1983

_____ "*El naranjal ardiente* de Augusto Roa Bastos: cifra textual de la biculturalidad paraguaya," in *Primer simposio internacional sobre estudios latinoamericanos*, Asunción, Paraguay: IDIAL, 1989

Méndez-Faith, Teresa. *Paraguay: novela y exilio*, Somerville, New Jersey: SLUSA, 1985

Sosnowski, Saúl (editor), *Augusto Roa Bastos y la producción cultural americana*, Buenos Aires: Ediciones de La Flor, 1986

Yo el Supremo

Novel by Augusto Roa Bastos

Since its publication in 1974, *Yo el Supremo* has assumed the status of "masterpiece" in the public eye. If taken to mean the sole climax of Roa Bastos's distinguished career, the term is probably inappropriate, but as a tribute to the quality of this novel it is certainly correct. *Yo el Supremo* is commonly considered part of two trilogies: first, the triad of Latin American "dictator narratives," of which the other two are Carpentier's *El recurso del método*, 1974 (*Reasons of State*) and García Márquez's *El otoño del patriarca*, 1975 (*The Autumn of the Patriarch*), and second, Roa Bastos's own "Paraguayan trilogy," of which the others are *Hijo de hombre*, 1960 (*Son of Man*) and *El Fiscal*, 1993 [The Prosecutor]. *Yo el Supremo*, in other words, has a deliberate place in both the broad, horizontal spectrum of contemporary Latin American letters and the deep, vertical, downward and inward probing of the best Paraguayan writing.

To consider *Yo el Supremo* within these trilogies only enhances qualities which it displays perfectly well on its own. Good as the other novels are, one need not read them for clues to the universality and profound personal vision of *Yo el Supremo*. The novel's central character is a historical figure, the dictator Dr José Gaspar Rodríguez de Francia, who ruled Paraguay from 1814 to 1840. To reveal his protagonist's story, Roa hit upon an ingenious and deceptively simple device: he allows the *dictator* to *dictate*. That is to say, the bulk of the text is precisely Dr Francia's "dictation" to his secretary Patiño, a vast panoply of musings, reminiscences, facts and exhortations of which Roa Bastos declares himself merely the "compiler." Unrestricted to conventional "this-worldly" chronologies, the novel's action is situated posthumously and prefaced by a proclamation in the dictator's handwriting, announcing the dismemberment of his body. Thus placed at the beginning of the novel, the proclamation has the vital function of unraveling the "dictation" which follows. Hence the reader is treated to the building and un-building of an immense, detailed panorama of Paraguayan history from colonial times to the present, a parade of figures and forces from almost two centuries of national and international evolution. Culled from various sources which the "compiler" cites in a "Final Note" at the end, this multitude of information flows together in a complex reconstruction of Francia's life and legacy. Posterity's judgment has been hard on Francia, but not unanimous, and it is this ambiguity which resonates so vibrantly in Roa Bastos's narrative. By relegating himself to the status of "compiler" Roa Bastos subverts the traditional idea of the author as creator of his work, and by ceding the narrative function to the dictator, he diversifies and humanizes a man whom history is tempted to remember with one-dimensional horror. Killer, monster, sadist: these images are not invalidated by the text, but they are complemented and contextualized by other images as the dictator's own words confront documents and legends that have emerged concerning him in the course of history. Dr Francia is at once culprit and judge, tyrant and defender of his tyranny, perpetrator and justifier of policies which at least punished the corrupt and kept at bay those outside forces which would have ground Paraguay to dust. Roa Bastos's Francia thus stands in sharp contrast to the lesser satraps of later days, especially Stroessner, whose murderous policies had no higher purpose than personal enrichment and the perpetuation of power.

Traditional scholarship would insist upon some discussion of the "themes" woven into *Yo el Supremo*, and indeed, one can undertake to produce a catalogue of these: liberty and repression, the moral costs of national independence, the personal hell of the tyrant, and so forth. One quickly discovers, however, that the array of these "messages" is almost innumerable, and that their individual content is probably less important than the discourse which encourages their expression. Putting it another way, we may say that discourse *is* content in *Yo el Supremo*, not in the sense of Marshall McLuhan's famous dictum, but in the way Roa Bastos's language embodies a vision of human interaction. In posing questions rather than solutions, in eschewing the unitary and embracing the pluralistic, in juxtaposing dictation and dissent, in gravitating always *away* from the entrenched and coercive Word-that-went-before and *toward* alternative emerging discourse, in humanizing the tyrant, Roa Bastos's language encodes freedom. As Carlos Pacheco states in his introduction to the novel (Caracas, 1986), Roa Bastos relativizes *el Supremo*, placing the latter's authoritarian voice in the company of other, contrary, voices. The dictator's discourse vies with competing discourses, not only from political opponents and subsequent generations, but from within his own soul. This relativization, however, is not to be confused with moral relativism. As Pacheco indicates – and his echoes of Bakhtin here are quite deliberate – Roa Bastos's well-defined position is precisely this facilitation of the multiple positions of one's fellow human beings, this rejection of partisan monoliths, this profoundly democratic commitment to the complexity of life.

At its most superficial level, *Yo el Supremo* is "about" the historical figure Francia, but by installing himself in the dictator's psyche, Augusto Roa Bastos gives us a narrative that is "within" Francia and as such, "about" the world as he sees it. And that world includes the reader. *Yo el Supremo* reverses the normal perspective of historical fiction, which contemplates the deeds of "real" heroes and villains from the safe haven of the ether around them, as if these protagonists were pure surface, empty sheaths of skin responding solely to surrounding stimuli. Roa Bastos's Francia is surface substantiated by mind, heart and will; it is *he* who contemplates and defines his surroundings, and ultimately he who contemplates the ether in which the reader sits. The novel is about Dr Francia; but also *through* Francia, it is about us.

TRACY K. LEWIS AND TERESA MÉNDEZ-FAITH

Editions

First edition: *Yo el Supremo*, Buenos Aires: Siglo XXI, 1974
Critical edition: edited with an introduction by Carlos F. Pacheco, Caracas: Biblioteca Ayacucho, 1986
Translation: *I the Supreme*, by Helen Lane, New York: Knopf, 1986; London: Faber and Faber, 1987

Further Reading

Aceves, R., *et al.*, *Acercamientos críticos a "Yo el Supremo" de Augusto Roa Bastos*, Guadalajara, Mexico: Universidad de Guadalajara, 1990
Dellepiane, Ángela B., "Tres novelas de la dictadura: *El recurso del método, El otoño del patriarca, Yo el Supremo*," *Cara* 29 (1977)

Foster, David William, "Augusto Roa Bastos' *I the Supreme*: the Image of a Dictator," *Latin American Literary Review* 7 (1975)
Seminario sobre "Yo el Supremo" de Augusto Roa Bastos, Poitiers, France: Centre de Recherches Latino-Americaines de l'Université de Poitiers, 1976
Textos sobre el texto: segundo seminario sobre "Yo el Supremo" de Augusto Roa Bastos, Poitiers, France: Centre de Recherches Latino-Americaines de l'Université de Poitiers, 1980
Weldt-Basson, Helene Carol, *Augusto Roa Bastos's "I the Supreme": a Dialogic Perspective*, Columbia: University of Missouri Press, 1993

José Enrique Rodó 1871–1917

Uruguayan essayist

The foremost figure in *modernista* essay writing in Spanish, José Enrique Rodó's influence can be judged from two angles: his literary criticism and his philosophy of art and morality. Just as his own prose is characterised by Apollonian balance in ideas and style, he rejected the decadent versions of *Modernismo* prevalent in Spanish at the time. His attitude in this respect is expounded in his 1899 essay on Darío, his first work to have international repercussion, where he hails the Nicaraguan as the first professional poet in Latin America. "Nada sino el arte" (Nothing but art), Rodó approvingly finds in the best Darío. Rodó's typical even-handed stance shows in this essay. On the one hand, he defends Darío from critics that request more life in his poetry by praising his individuality. On the other hand, as well as criticising some specific poems, Rodó attacks Darío's more frivolous followers for their "pecado de profanación" (sin of profanation) in depriving spiritual things of their innocence. The essay closes with a piece of advice to the poet on his imminent visit to Spain: may he take with him encouragement for the flowering of the common language and renewed vigour to the uncertain youth of Spain. In fact, this is the very task Rodó set himself in his most influential work, *Ariel*, a short essay where he exhorts the youth of Latin America not to pursue only materialistic goals to the detriment of their spiritual development.

Rodó's role of mentor to the young is evident throughout his work, although much of it was written in his twenties and thirties. Whilst *Ariel* is Rodó's most explicit message to young Latin Americans, his most ambitious work is *Motivos de Proteo*, 1909 (*The Motives of Proteus*), where he focuses on the evolution of the personality. Inspired by the figure of Proteus, Rodó produced a work which is difficult to classify: a book of wisdom made up of 158 short chapters that can stand on their own as expanded aphorisms. The book opens with the statement that "Reformarse es vivir . . ." (Life is constant renewal . . .), and sets out to explore the tools of conscious transformation, the unconscious forces that affect the personality, the notions of vocation and genius and its lesser alternatives (such as dilettantism), the value of travelling and the positive roles of love, hope and willpower.

The reader is told that although the human self is constant changing, we should not be merely victims of change but instead strive to be its agents through self-knowledge, conviction and awareness of circumstances around us. We must not lose the curiosity of childhood and fall into personal stagnancy. We must learn to live with change not drastically but gradually: in Rodó's own image, personal growth should follow not a straight line but a curve; we must also be ready to cope with the unexpected. These several points are made clear in chapter 7: "Rítmica y lenta evolución de ordinario; reacción esforzada si es preciso; cambio consciente y ordenado, siempre" (Evolution following a regular pace as the ordinary pattern; forceful reaction if necessary; conscious and directed change, always). As the book's title indicates, the self for Rodó is far from a simple or unified entity, and therefore there are sections on inner contradictions and on the fears that individuals encounter within themselves. There are, indeed, advantages to inner complexity: unlike the dilettante, the ascetic or the stoic, for whom it may inspire pleasing curiosity, craving for a static essence or passive surrendering to circumstances, Rodó proposes that from our multifacetic nature we draw inspiration for constant renewal and evolution: individual "variación espontánea" (spontaneous variation) thus parallels the evolutionary processes in nature and society, and the "perenne reacción de los contrarios" (perennial reaction of opposites) is the stuff from which original thought arises.

Rodó's text aims to represent development, the preface speaking of a book in perpetual becoming, an open book. This is evident also in the language used, rich in similes and metaphors from nature and traditional trades (e.g., action follows from self-discovery like he who builds a home with stones from his own quarry, or forges a sword from his own iron mine, extensive classical and modern references, and the periodic inclusion of parables that have assumed a semi-independent existence since the book was first published. One of the most famous and beautifully written is "Los seis peregrinos" [The Six Pilgrims], where four individuals abandon the journey out of doubts over their commitment, whilst the two who finally arrive at their destination represent on the one hand, the undesirable somnambulistic fervour of the fanatic and on the other, the equilibrium of the person who, whilst aware of the best of worldly experience, guides his life according to a higher goal.

The underlying philosophy in Rodó's work is humanist and idealist in the sense that it aims to address issues that affect individuals regardless of their specific circumstances. The fact that he does not engage in the details of actual social contexts has led to criticism from different quarters, which one of Rodó's most sensitive and incisive critics, the Uruguayan Carlos Real de Azúa (whose rambling and rich style might owe something to Rodó's influence), has summarised with flair in his article on "El problema de la valoración de Rodó" [The Problem of Evaluating Rodó]. The main areas of attack are social and religious. The exponents of the latter criticise the absence of an appetite for the Absolute in Rodó's protean philosophy. Those who take a social or political stance denounce the bourgeois origins of Rodó's ideas, dismiss his liberalism as supportive of the status quo and question his dislike of mass mediocrity and his doctrine of inner freedom; they also point to the lack of specific references in his work to the burning issues of Latin America, considering Rodó's European and urban sources of little relevance to the experience of the greatest section of Latin American society and in particular its Amerindian population. What is common in the social critiques is an unwillingness to engage with Rodó's ideas at the level he intended them to be understood. It is evident, however, that his ideas are not incompatible with practical or political concerns. In fact, not only did Rodó write on social and historical matters (see, for instance, his essays on Bolívar or Montalvo and his study on labour in Uruguay), but he also produced several important papers during his time as a member of parliament. It is also worthy of mention to an English-speaking reader that he was a fundamental source of inspiration to the Labour politician Aneurin Bevan for whom, according to his biographer Michael Foot, "next to Marx, and in a few respects superseding Marx, Rodó had the most powerful effect on his intellectual outlook."

Rodó's propensity to search in European sources is understandable for a man of his time and nationality. Uruguay lacks an Amerindian culture and its population has been drawn from European immigrants (Rodó's father was from Barcelona). As Real de Azua's brilliant prologue to the Ayacucho edition (1976) shows, Motivos de Proteo can be related to the situation of Uruguay at the time of writing, when Rodó felt the effects of cultural asphyxia. He had planned to publish his major work in Barcelona during a journey that only materialised several years later when he became the European correspondent for a Buenos Aires newspaper. He was to die in Europe, nine months after leaving Montevideo. Three years later his remains were repatriated and buried with full state honours before a massive crowd. A sign of his national importance was the spontaneous decision by students in Montevideo to interrupt and call off a demonstration on hearing the news

of his death. Rodó's conciliatory manner – often reflected in his periodic style – could also be seen as a response to rather turbulent times in Uruguayan politics, which only ended in 1904 with the last caudillo rebellion. It may be, furthermore, that the enduring respect for Rodó in Uruguayan official circles and his inclusion in school syllabuses has contributed to the country's tradition of political partnership and common sense during the bulk of this century.

GUSTAVO SAN ROMÁN

Biography

Born in Montevideo, Uruguay, 15 July 1871. Educated by tutors at home, then at private and state schools. Co-founder, with Víctor Pérez Petit, and Carlos and Daniel Martínez Virgil, of *Revista Nacional de Literatura y Ciencias Sociales*, which ran 1895–97. Wrote for several newspapers throughout adult life. Professor of Literature, University of Montevideo, 1898–1902. Elected to the House of Representatives. Director of National Library; 1902–05 and 1908–14. Deputy for Montevideo; 1912 corresponding member, Royal Academy of the Spanish Language. Travelled to Europe as correspondent for *La Nación* of Buenos Aires, 1916: visited Portugal, Spain and Italy. Died in Palermo, 1 May 1917.

Selected Works

La vida nueva, 3 vols, Montevideo: Dornaleche y Reyes, 1897–1900
    I. "El que vendrá" and "La novela nueva," Montevideo: Dornaleche y Reyes, 1897
    II. *Rubén Darío*, Montevideo: Dornaleche y Reyes, 1899
    III. *Ariel*, Montevideo: Dornaleche y Reyes, 1900; as *Ariel*, translated by Margaret Sayers Peden, Austin: University of Texas Press, 1988·
Liberalismo y Jacobinismo, Montevideo: El Siglo Ilustrado, 1906
Motivos de Proteo, Montevideo: J.M. Serrano, 1909; as *The Motives of Proteus*, translated by Ángel Flores with an introduction by Havelock Ellis, London: Allen and Unwin, 1929
El mirador de Próspero, Montevideo: J.M. Serrano, 1913
El camino de Paros, Valencia: Editorial Cervantes, 1919

Compilations and Anthologies

Obras completas, 7 vols, Valencia: Editorial Cervantes, 1917–27
Obras completas, edited by Emir Rodríguez Monega1, Madrid: Aguilar, 1957; augmented 2nd edition, 1967 [excellent introduction, prologue and bibliography]

Further Reading

An early 20th-century thinker, such as Rodó, has fallen out of fashion, something which is reflected in the publication dates of several of the critical studies listed below. These, however, help to place him in his historical context and shed light on how the history of ideas has developed in Spanish America.

Albarrán Puente, Glicerio, *El pensamiento de José Enrique Rodó*, Madrid: Cultura Hispánica, 1953
Barbagelata, Hugo D., *Rodó y sus críticos*, Paris: Agencia General de Librerías, 1920 [Contains articles by Leopoldo Alas, Darío and Unamuno]
Ette, Ottmar, "Así habló Próspero; Nietzsche, Rodó y la modernidad filosófica de Ariel," *Cuadernos Hispanoamericanos* 528 (June 1994)
Foot, Michael, *Aneurin Bevan*, 2 vols, London: Macgibbon and Kee, 1962–73; New York: Atheneum, 1963–74
Henríquez Ureña, Max, *Rodó y Rubén Darío*, Havana: Sociedad Educativa Cuba Contemporánea, 1918
Meyer-Minnemann, Klaus, *La novela hispanoamericana del "fin de siècle,"* Mexico City: Fondo de Cultura Económica, 1991 [Chapter three has a section on Rodó's *nueva novela*]

Real de Azúa, Carlos, "El problema de la valoración de Rodó," in his *Historia visible e historia esotérica*, Montevideo: Arca, 1975
—— Prologue to *Ariel* and *Motivos de Proteo*, Caracas: Biblioteca Ayacucho, 1976
Rivera Rodas, Oscar, "El discurso crítico, autoritario y narcisista," *Revista de Crítica Literaria Latinoamericana*, Lima, vol. 15/30 (1989)
Silva Cencio, Jorge A., *Rodó y la legislación social*, Montevideo: Marcha, 1972
Van Delden, Maarten, "The Banquets of Civilization: the Idea of Ancient Greece in Rodó, Reyes and Fuentes," *Annals of Scholarship: an International Quarterly in the Humanities and Social Sciences*, Detroit, vol. 7/3 (1990)
Zaldumbide, Gonzalo, *José Enrique Rodó*, New York and Paris: Bailly Baillière, 1918

Ariel

Essay by José Enrique Rodó

The essay takes the form of a farewell speech by an old schoolmaster. The teacher, called Prospero by his pupils, sets out to advise his class, paradigmatic of the youth of America to whom the book is dedicated, on the virtues of idealism. He does so under the gaze of a statue of Ariel which decorates his study. After an introduction which establishes the symbolic value of Ariel and Caliban in *The Tempest*, as the forces of reason and instinct respectively, the text is divided into six parts. Part one deals with the renovating role of youth, whose energy is needed to build the future of the continent, in particular at the current time when cynicism and despair appear to hold sway. Prospero warns that although nature has endowed youth with enthusiasm, it still requires ideals to realize its full potential. Part two expounds on the need for each individual to develop his personality in all its potential and across the full range of abilities, stressing that disinterested concerns must not be discarded for the benefit of narrow specialization. This section contains the famous story of the "hospitable King" who, though generally immersed in the life of state, retires periodically to a private chamber to meditate. The tale is an allegory of the well-rounded individual, who must find room for the pursuance of *otium*, that is, of creative idleness. Part three posits the awareness of beauty as the guiding principle behind education. Aesthetics and ethics are equally worthy forms of disinterested pursuit and the prevalence of one over the other implies an imbalance, as in frivolous art or stern asceticism. Part four is concerned with the utilitarian attitude, and discusses the then current view that democracy implies mediocrity; Prospero's stance typifies Rodó's tendency to reconcile contradictory positions by accepting the benefits of each. Democracy should combine egalitarian Christian values with Hellenic respect for hierarchy, and Prospero envisages that democracy, like science, is bound to improve through education and knowledge. The ideal state is one where all are given the same opportunity so that the best can reach positions of leadership. Part five, which became the most influential, focuses on the United States, where utilitarian goals seemed to Prospero to dominate to the detriment of distinterested moral and artistic excellence. After a complimentary review of the attributes of North American society, Prospero expresses concern over a growing Latin American *nordomanía* (a fixation with "the North") which risks overlooking the subcontinent's own roots in the Latin tradition. He is particularly critical of the United States' apparent contempt for European civilization. Part six concentrates on Latin America. Prospero notes that already in the subcontinent there are great cities that could lose sight of cultural development, and exhorts his audience, as the forgers of the future, to follow the inspiration of Ariel, symbol of constant human self-improvement, "idealidad y orden en la vida, noble inspiración en el pensamiento, desinterés en moral, buen gusto en arte, heroísmo en la acción, delicadeza en las costumbres" (idealism and order in life, noble inspiration in thought, selflessness in morality, good taste in art, heroism in action, delicacy in habits).

The ideas which inspired Rodó were dominant at the time in the West, his main influences being French (Renan, Taine, Montaigne, Fouillée), English and American (Macaulay, Carlyle, Emerson), as well as the classics. (In his critical edition of *Ariel*, Gordon Brotherston presents a succint and scholarly review of Rodó's sources). But Rodó tended to pick and mix from these sources and to criticize them if need be, as in the case of Renan's oligarchical theories, which he rejected as reactionary. It is also relevant to stress the historical context within which *Ariel* was written: in the wake of the war of 1898 when the US defeated Spain and won control over her last colonies in the continent. But although the book's criticism of the "Colossus of the North" carries a largely implicit rejection of that country's growing hegemony over its Latin neighbours, sight should not be lost of Rodó's mainly philosophical enterprise. His idealism is best understood as representative of a contemporary response to the excesses of positivism and its corollary, utilitarianism.

Ariel has been the target of much praise as well as much criticism. The book and his author spawned a movement of Latin American intellectuals known as *arielismo* which included, at some point in their careers, such figures as Pedro Henríquez Ureña and Alfonso Reyes. In Uruguay in 1917, a students' seminar christened itself *Ariel* and published a review to spread the message of the book from 1919 to 1931. It is worthy of note that the first president of *Ariel* was Carlos Quijano, who was to found *Marcha* (1939–74), an influential weekly renowned for its cultural section and for its increasingly *americanista* stance. Quijano, a political scientist proud of his *arielista* beginnings and the undisputed *maestro* of a whole generation of Uruguayan intellectuals, set himself the task of combining high standards of morality with a shrewd analysis of the social reality of Uruguay and Latin America.

A summary of the critical views on Rodó up to the mid-1960s is provided in the previous essay; two more recent attacks are worthy of mention. The first is Roberto Fernández Retamar's powerful *Calibán* (1971). Written from both a Marxist and a Third World perspective, which sees Prospero as European invader and Caliban as enslaved Amerindian, this essay overturns the allegory of Rodó's work: "Our symbol then is not Ariel, as Rodó thought, but rather Caliban." Retamar's stance is based on the notion of *mestizaje*, a concept which was closer to his own experience (and that of the sources he quotes, Martí, Bolívar, Vasconcelos and others from the northern part of Latin America) than to the Uruguayan Rodó. But otherwise the text is fairly respectful of its predecessor.

Preferring to read *Ariel* at a political rather than philosophical level, the critic sees its most enduring value as a "launching pad" for later and more politically aware perceptions of the United States. He also grants that *Ariel* "exalts democracy, moral values, and emulation," and calls his own essay a homage to "the great Uruguayan whose centenary is being celebrated this year." In a postscript, "*Calibán* Revisited" (1986), the author gives the context to his essay: a time of tension between the revolutionary leaders in Cuba, and the "ivory tower [Latin American] intellectuals" living in Europe. There were two main reasons for the tension; the first was the writers' support or indifference towards *Mundo Nuevo*, the review edited by Emir Rodríguez Monegal and reputedly funded by the CIA. (Monegal's second edition of Rodó's complete works is contemporary with *Mundo Nuevo*). The second reason was the dispute over the "Padilla case," which led some Latin American writers in Europe to write two letters criticising Fidel Castro. *Calibán* is thus perhaps best seen as a response to what Rodó could symbolise to a supporter of Cuba in the context of 1971, namely a distancing by Latin American intellectuals from the social realities of their continent. A more recent and much more negative critique is Roberto González Echevarría's chapter on *Ariel* in his 1985 book, *The Voice of the Masters*, written in Yale deconstructionist vein. The main charge, pursued by a range of associations in the chapter, concerns the "violence" implicit in the generic form of *Ariel*, which, it is argued, though apparently a dialogue is in effect a lecture and thus a discourse of authority. The problem with this reading is that it allocates a malice of intention to *Ariel* which seems unnecessary. Rodó was quite open about *Ariel* being a work of "propaganda" (his word) for the future of Latin America, and its didactic intention, reinforced by the choice of a classroom for the setting, is quite explicit in the essay itself. (As for Echevarría's charges of paternalism on the part of Prospero, the reader is directed to chapter 77 of Rodó's *Motivos de Proteo*, on the position of the master).

It would seem as if the future of this slim volume will continue to waver between attempts to apply its contents to contemporary preoccupations and to rescue the author's intentions and context. A sign, presumably, of its status as a seminal text.

GUSTAVO SAN ROMÁN

See also entries on Caliban, *Une Tempête* (Aimé Césaire), Civilization and Barbarism

Editions

First edition: *La vida nueva*, III: *Ariel*, Montevideo: Dornaleche y Reyes, 1900

Critical editions: edited with an introduction by Gordon Brotherston, Cambridge: Cambridge University Press, 1967; there is a later edition, with a prologue by Carlos Real de Azua and a chronology by Ángel Rama, Caracas: Biblioteca Ayacucho, 1976. This volume includes *Motivos de Proteo*.

Translation: *Ariel*, by Margaret Sayers Peden, Austin: University of Texas Press, 1988 [Foreword by James W. Symington; prologue by Carlos Fuentes; glossary of names; annotated bibliography]

Further Reading

Fernández Retamar, Roberto, *Caliban and Other Essays*, translated by Edward Baker; foreword by Fredric Jameson, Minneapolis: University of Minnesota Press, 1989

González Echevarría, Roberto, "The case of the Speaking Statue: *Ariel* and the Magisterial Rhethoric of the Latin American Essay," in his *The Voice of the Masters: Writing and Authority in Modern Latin American Literature*, Austin: University of Texas Press, 1985

Gonzalo Rojas 1917–

Chilean poet

In one of Latin America's "republic of poets," namely, Chile, Gonzalo Rojas received little attention before the late 1970s. Then, with *Oscuro* [Darkness] in 1977 and subsequent volumes, he has been acknowledged by many critics in both his own country and Hispanic American as the most important living Chilean poet.

His relatively inconspicous status up to the age of sixty (he had published just two books of verse before *Oscuro*) is partly explainable, of course by his late start in publishing. Before 1977 he had an important, if informal, role as the poet's poet; through both personal contact and a close reading, many younger aspirants to lyrical perfection were influenced by his restless incursions into the unknown. It can also be noted that a late start in learning to read – at the age of eight in Rojas's case – is not necessarily an obstacle to a writer's development and proficiency.

As a person Rojas is unassuming, disarmingly natural, and also totally confident. In poetry his motivation is constant; the depth and breadth of his vision, close to infinite. In a revealing recollection, "De donde viene uno," 1988 [Where One Comes From], he declares: "And my view of the world? My perspectives are mainly three: numinous in the context of the holy; the erotic and all the dialects of love; and that of the immediate witness of immediate life (even though it is claimed that no one testifies in favor of witness) included in that are the actions of the political witness, but without affiliation. Probably one should resort to silence. But no. Not yet. At least not yet. I'm undergoing a rebirth in the best sense, a re-childhood, a spontaneity I can hardly explain. It's as if I allowed language to speak through me. It resembles carelessness, yet its a maximum awareness. I'm letting the waters speak, and rise, and express themselves."

Thus, this poet strives to write on the basis of that trinity of perspectives: the spirit (lo numinoso), sexuality understood as inseparable from love, and as a privileged witness of immediate, remote and recondite things. Like Walt Whitman and Pablo Neruda before him, he considers all material and every object and circumstances to have poetic potential: for example, a squashed butterfly as the image of ultimate victimization, a search – of cosmic as well as of comic porportions – for a female hair, a black cat as a metaphor of infinite dangers, Greek deities in sporadic rebirth, a mirror that doesn't reflect, the implicit threats of a helicopter, a 14th-century archpriest on a bicycle and, over and over, a buzzing sound (el zumbido). To his ear this sound is many things: a symbol of origins, the underside of language, fear, exhilaration, a message from unkown sources and, especially, the fundamental music of poetry. In the testimony quoted above ("De done viene uno") he recalls that when he began to write at an early age "verses buzzed in my ears, and I set about transcribing them, right away, almost as I do now."

A distinctive feature of the leading Chilean poets of the 20th century, including Gabriela Mistral, Vicente Huidobro (his claims of having established the trend he called Creacionismo not withstanding), Neruda, Pablo de Rokha, Nicanor Parra and Rojas himself, is their extreme individuality. That is, they did not initiate movements, fashions or schools comparable to English Romanticism, Hispanic American Modernismo, or French Surrealism. Rather, they exercised the five experimental senses and registered their discoveries in a kind of expansive, continuous autobiography. Such is the case with Rojas's poem "Carbón" [Coal], an intense recollection of his father, the persevering miner exploited by his employers and embittered by misfortune, who is about to return home late at night. In the context of his creative independence it should be noted that after a brief courtship in 1938 with a trendy and quasi-Surrealist group in Chile organized and named Mandrágora by Braulio Arenas, Enrique Gómez-Correa and Jorge Cáceres, Gonzalo Rojas withdrew from it, describing its members as "lacking the genius" and originality of Europe's best poets of the times.

Thus, varied influences rather than any current fashion strongly affected him; his favorite creators were also his heroes – those who apparently "lived" their poetry rather than writing it as a separatist ritual – and ranged from Mistral, Huidobro and Neruda in his own land to Quevedo, Whitman, Lautréamont and Vallejo elsewhere. That broad congeniality served him well in his discovery of magical mysteries.

His individuality aside, Rojas often stresses the deeper requirement of an intimate relationship between poet and listener ("Not for the reader: for the listener" is the dedication to his second largest collection – 177 poems – Del relámpago [From the Lightning]. Thus, rather than a precarious development from juvenile simplicity to complex maturity as

in the case with many poets, Gonzalo Rojas has given us a perennial, continuous work that reflects and reconsiders and interrogates the universe at every turn.

PETER G. EARLE

Biography

Born in Chile, 1917. Member of Chilean Generation of 1938. Father a miner. Studied in the Faculty of Arts, University of Santiago. Taught miners of the Atacama desert region to read, early 1940s. Teacher in Venezuela, 1975–79. Professor at Brigham Young University, Provo, Utah, in late 1980s. Recipient of the following awards: National Prize for Literature, 1992; Reina Sofía Prize for Poetry, 1992.

Selected Works

Poetry
La miseria del hombre, Valparaíso: Romas, 1948
Contra la muerte, Santiago de Chile: Editorial Universitaria, 1964
Oscuro, Caracas: Monte Ávila, 1977
Transtierro, Madrid: Taranto, 1979
Del relámpago, Mexico City: Fondo de Cultura Económica, 1981; augmented 2nd edition, 1984
Críptico y otros poemas, Iztapalapa: Universidad Autónoma Metropolitana, Unidad Iztapalapa, 1984
El alumbrado, Santiago de Chile: Ganymedes, 1986
El alumbrado y otros poemas, Madrid: Cátedra, 1987
Antología personal, Mexico City: Premiá Editora, 1988
Materia de testamento, Madrid: Hiperión, 1988
Antología de aire, Santiago de Chile: Fondo de Cultura Económica, 1991
Las hermosas: poesías de amor, Madrid: Hiperión, 1991

Essays and Testimonial Works
"Darío y más Darío, in Rubén Darío, 1867–1967, Concepción, Chile: Ediciones de la Revista Atenea, 1967
"La palabra," in Antología de la poesía chilena, edited by Alfonso Calderón, Santiago de Chile: Editorial Universitaria, 1970
"Poesía y resistencia: viento del pueblo," in Casa de las Américas, vol. 14/83 (March–April 1974)
"Testimonio sobre Pablo de Rokha," Revista Iberoamericana 106–07 (January–June 1979)
"Recado del errante," in Gabriela Mistral, edited by Miella Servodidio and Marcelo Coddou, Xalapa, Mexico: Universidad Veracruzana, 1980
"De done viene uno," introduction to his Materia de testamento, Madrid: Hiperión, 1988

Translation
Schizotext and Other Poems, translated by Russell M. Cluff and L. Howard Quackenbush, New York: Peter Lang, 1988

Compilations and Anthologies
Cinco visiones: selección de poemas, Salamanca: Ediciones Universidad de Salamanca, 1992

Further Reading
Coddou, Marcelo, Poética de la poesía activa, Madrid: Lar, 1984
———— Nuevos estudios sobre la poesía de Gonzalo Rojas, Santiago de Chile: Sinfronteras, 1986
Giordano, Enrique (editor), Poesía y poética de Gonzalo Rojas, Santiago de Chile, Instituto Profesional del Pacífico, 1987

May, Hilda R., *La poesía de Gonzalo Rojas*, Madrid: Hiperión, 1991

Rojas, Nelson, *Estudios sobre la poesía de Gonzalo Rojas*, Madrid: Playor, 1984

Sefamí, Jacobo, *El espejo trizado: la poesía de Gonzalo Rojas*, Mexico City: UNAM, 1992

Interviews

Benedetti, Mario, "Gonzalo Rojas y su poesía activa," in his *Los poetas comunicantes*, Montevideo: Marcha, 1972

Peña, Juan Andrés, *Conversaciones con la poesía chilena*, Santiago de Chile: Pehuén, 1990 [Chapter 3 is a comprehensive interview with Gonzalo Rojas]

Manuel Rojas 1896–1973

Chilean prose writer

Manuel Rojas was born in Argentina and certain dualities of his formative years led to a constant movement, during a third of his life, between Buenos Aires and turn-of-the-century Santiago de Chile; the latter being at that time much less metropolitan than the Argentine capital. These are continuous shifts that begin to define the wandering nature both of his own self and that of his characters, with the panorama of the high Andes becoming fixed, insistently, as the focal point of his vision. He spent time also in Rosario and in Mendoza, the latter, a town on the eastern slopes of the Andes. It is in the former that he took to reading, in that domestic way that he was to recall in *Hijo de ladrón*, 1951 (*Born Guilty*), swapping serialized stories for peaches; in Mendoza he made his earliest contacts with anarchists. There he worked as a navvy on the trans-Andean Railway, then under construction; he helped to bring in the grape harvest and did several other jobs that brought him into close contact with plain, enthusiastic folk who communicated new ideas to him, sometimes extravagant convictions, but an indisputable faith in human destiny. It was his apprenticeship in life, as he was to repeat in nearly all his stories, with their pressing demands: pangs of hunger, biting cold, all of which led him to make an impassioned plea for the bare essentials which human beings must have to live with dignity.

Rojas's production may be divided into two main periods, separated by a lengthy authorial silence. 1924, the year in which he probably settled in Chile (or 1926 when he published his first collection of short stories, *Hombres del sur* [Men of the South]), marks the beginning of a literary period which culminates very precisely in 1938, when the Popular Front saw victory at the polls. This is the year when Rojas published his significant collection of essays, *De la poesía a la revolución* [From Poetry to Revolution], which brings together essays he had conceived over a period of ten years (the earliest dates from 1930). They consist of an examination of the changes Rojas perceives in world narrative, of the *criollismo* that had marked Chilean literature of the previous decades; *De la poesía a la revolución* is also a rigorous self-criticism of Rojas's first period as a writer, that characterized by *Hombres del sur* and *El delincuente*, 1929 [The Delinquent]. It follows that between 1938 and 1951 Rojas published nothing in book form (his contributions to the journal, *Babel*, are of another order and

El bonete maulino, 1943 [The Bonnet from the Maule River] is largely a collection of earlier stories). This silence that lasted for over a decade was the gestation period of his most influential novel, *Hijo de ladrón*, which gave him a continental readership and made him the outstanding Chilean narrative writer of the first half of the 20th century.

Both in his major novels and in his last work, *La oscura vida radiante* [A Life of Darkness and Light], Rojas's literary world remained firmly in the 1920s, or in the years immediately preceding them. It is on that threshold or annunciatory evening that *Lanchas en la bahía*, 1932 [Boats in the Bay], his most typical story of the early period takes place, and also his massive later novels: *Hijo de ladrón, Mejor que el vino*, 1958 [Better Than Wine] and *Sombras contra el muro*, 1964 [Shadows on the Wall]. Almost the last lines of the 1932 story contain the saying "A freir monos en Guayaquil" or, "take a running jump at yourself,"(something that is remembered and repeated in the 1964 novel). Effectively, these "shadows on the wall" are echoes and prolongations of earlier lives that are now shown – on what wall? We do not know whether on the Wailing Wall or that of Jericho, as is suggested to readers, in tense contradiction, until the end of this notable text.

The years before 1920 are charged with anarchist preaching. The IWW (Industrial Workers of the World), as from 1914 at least, gave some measure of organization to anarchist circles, which functioned in a chaotic way. The shadow of that unfortunate youth, Efraín Plaza Olmedo, passes through *Sombras contra el muro*. He belonged to anarchist legends of the period, and there is a detailed account of his misfortunes by Carlos Vicuña Fuentes in his classic testimonial, *La tiranía en Chile* [The Tyranny in Chile]. *Sombras contra el muro* also contains several references to that breviary of the anarcho-individualists, Max Stirner's *The Ego and its Property*. Stirner was one of the thinkers criticized by Marx and Engels in *The German Ideology* and who, according to many accounts, made a considerable impact on Chilean literature of the period.

This evidence makes it possible to correct the existential or existentialist character often attributed to Rojas's fiction. This alleged Existentialism in Rojas's work is nothing other than the specific form taken by his anarchism, the particular tone in which anarchist experiences – via Stirner, appear in his production. The characters that people Rojas's world, who have something of the worker, something of the drifter, and are nearly always criminally inclined, are what allows a gradual transformation of anarchism as a social ideal, in a particular subjective posture of separation, tension and hostility towards society. The narratives pass through accumulated layers of characters, from those with craft-based jobs, to those made redundant and, then, tramps until reaching specific forms of the lumpen in the occupation and activity of thieves.

Thus, in principle, *Hijo de ladrón* is revealed to us as a theological metaphor in which the thieves of Mount Calvary dwell with two others, the name of one being none other than Christian. The religious substratum of anarchism flowers here, inasmuch as it is the lay sedimentation of evangelical conduct. Not "son of God," but "son of a thief": in this ascendancy – hounded and on the fringes of society – Aniceto Hevia, the main hero of Rojas's cycle of novels, founds his most humbled nobility, in the midst of the monotonous and wretched landscape of the lives of his fellow beings. In the 1960s Rojas was to write an important travel book about a journey to Israel, *Viaje al país de los profetas*, 1969 [Journey to the Land of the Prophets], and in this way Stirner and the Bible come together to offer a Utopian international gospel which Rojas, as a skilled narrator, modulates in accordance with experiences of the period and the local conditions of the trans-Andean region.

JAIME CONCHA

translated by Verity Smith

Biography

Born in Buenos Aires, Argentina, 8 January 1896. Family moved to Santiago de Chile, 1899. From 1900 to 1922 travelled continually from the Chilean to the Argentine side of the Andes working at a variety of jobs and learning various skills. Clashed with authorities owing to his support of anarchism. Wrote for anarchist newspapers such as *La Batalla* (Chile) and *La Protesta* (Buenos Aires), from 1915. Actor and prompter in the Teatro de Alejandro Flores, 1919–20; on tour in Argentina and Uruguay with Teatro de Mario-Padín, 1921–22. Won second prize in a two short story contests organised by Buenos Aires publications in 1922 and 1923. Continued to work in a range of jobs. Married María Eugenia Baeza in 1928 (died in 1936); three children. In the early 1930s he began to run the printing press of the University of Chile. Contributed to the newspaper *La Últimas Noticias*, 1933–41. President of the Society of Chilean Writers, 1937. Married Valeria López Edwards in 1941 (separated in 1962). Director of the Anales de la Universidad de Chile (Annals of the University of Chile),

1951. Taught at several universities in the United States from 1959 to 1963. Married Hortensia Dittborn in 1963. On his return to Chile he contributed to the literary journal *Ercilla* and hosted the TV programme, "Jurado Literario" (Literary Jury). Travelled abroad, 1966–67. Awarded Chilean National Prize for Literature, 1957. Died 11 March 1973.

Selected Works

Short Fiction

Hombres del sur, Santiago de Chile: Nascimento, 1926
El delincuente, Santiago de Chile: Imprenta Universitaria, 1929
Lanchas en la bahía, Santiago de Chile: Zig-Zag, 1932 [novella]
Travesía, Santiago de Chile: Nascimento, 1934
El bonete maulino, Santiago de Chile: Cruz del Sur, 1943

Novels

La ciudad de los Césares, Santiago de Chile: Ercilla, 1936
Hijo de ladrón, Santiago de Chile: Nascimento, 1951; as *Born Guilty*, translated by Frank Gaynor, New York: Library Publishers; 1955; London: Gollancz, 1956
Mejor que el vino, Santiago de Chile: Zig-Zag, 1958
Punta de rieles, Santiago de Chile: Zig-Zag, 1960
Sombras contra el muro, Santiago de Chile: Zig-Zag, 1964
La oscura vida radiante, Buenos Aires: Sudamericana, 1971

Other Writings

De la poesía a la revolución, Santiago de Chile: Ercilla, 1938 [articles and essays]
Viaje al país de los profetas, Buenos Aires: Ediciones Zlotopioro, 1969

Anthologies and Compilations

Antología de cuentos, Santiago de Chile: Zig-Zag, 1957

Further Reading

Fleak, Kenneth, *The Chilean Short Story: Writers from the Generation of 1950*, New York: Peter Lang, 1989 [Chapter 2 is on "Trends in the Early 20th Century," and has a section on Manuel Rojas]
Goic, Cedomil, *La novela chilena. Los mitos degradados*, Santiago de Chile: Editorial Universitaria, 1968
Silva Castro, Raúl, *Historia crítica de la novela chilena*, Madrid: Ediciones Cultura Hispánica,1960

Bibliographies

Lagunas, Jorge-Román, "Bibliografía de y sobre Manuel Rojas," *Revista de Literatura Chilena* 27–28 (1986)

Romanticism

In Western culture, Romanticism was the first aesthetic response to both the French and the Industrial Revolutions. In Spanish America and Brazil it acquired a character of its own. Here Romanticism coincided with the realisation of political independence which, in the majority of countries, took place during the first quarter of the 19th century and continued up to the end of the century. Romanticism evolved in stages and involved various generations.

In Brazil, the decision to move the court to Rio de Janeiro (1808), with the beginning of extensive urban planning, and the declaration of political independence (1822) provided the framework for the development of historical autonomy. Between 1820 and 1870, the social structure was altered through changes in the economic system, and wide ranging educational reforms were carried out. The abolition of slavery (though not until the 1880s in Cuba and Brazil) meant that the American republics led the way for the United States and Great Britain. Romanticism signalled the birth of the modern concept of literature. It was not a short lived phenomenon but instead an approach to life, the impact of which continues to be felt in the most original literature of the present day. With subtleties and traits which differ from those of the European school, it was the first literary movement to emerge in the history of the fledgling republics, without signalling a complete break with Neoclassical ideals.

The Spanish American nations and Brazil owe their literary independence to Romanticism. Through it they achieved freedom of thought and expression and began the process of national consolidation. As Samuel Putman puts it, "The relationship between art and society was never so intimate." Art interacted closely with society and in the Spanish American nations writers were, above all, men of action, dedicated to reform as a form of public service. No other period can claim such wide socio-political influence. Romanticism in Spanish American and Brazilian literature sought to follow European rhythms, marking itself out as the first theory of literature with an ideological conscience, whilst at the same time insisting on giving its aesthetic a national content. It blossomed in Brazil and Argentina before the other American nations due to the close links with Europe enjoyed by these countries. In those countries with a low standard of colonial literature, like the Río de la Plata, Romanticism triumphed vigorously. In Peru, Colombia and Mexico it was more conservative in tone and Spanish models more numerous. Despite the success still enjoyed then by some authors (Espronceda, Larra, Zorrilla), the Spanish model weakened or disappeared.

On the whole, Romantic output in Brazil conformed more to bourgeois conventions, with a moralistic aim more akin to Tennyson or Longfellow than to Byron, Keats or Nerval. The Romantic rejection of contemporary reality and industrialisation is coupled with many more progressive traits. The break with Spanish tradition was made possible by the growing relations of France and Great Britain with the American nations which were indebted to French and British doctrines for their liberty. This relationship was also aided by the personal contact of American writers with Europe. The first Argentine Romantic, Esteban Echeverría, was living in Paris when Victor Hugo's *Hernani* was premièred (1830) and he found in Romanticism an aesthetic revolution which paved the way for self-expression for every national or regional group. Echeverría published his first Romantic manifesto, *Elvira, o la novia del Plata*, 1832 [Elvira, or The Bride of the River Plate], in the same year as the Duque de Rivas's *El moro expósito* [The Moorish Foundling]. He introduced the anti-aristocratic orientation of French Romanticism, a factor which also came to the fore with the Mexican insurgents of 1820. Byron served as a model for Romanticism in the River Plate and Brazil, where Domingos José Gonçalves de Magalhães introduced Romanticism with *Suspiros poéticos e saüdades*, 1836 [Poetic Sighs and Yearnings], which celebrates history through the lives of its heroes.

Romanticism made certain genres its own and gathered others of a typically local character. It reworked traditional forms, giving them a new dimension. The European canons were reelaborated with great originality and new myths were discovered. The new aesthetic embraced poetry, drama and fiction in particular. The mainstay was poetry, seen as a weapon in the struggle for freedom (with a particular preference being shown for anonymous popular poetry). However, the genres in vogue which had most success were the theatre and the novel. Urban Romantic fiction, a projection of the bourgeoisie, depicted, in general, a stable image of the world. The vitality of Romanticism was embodied in the theatre, the centre of incipient worldliness. Spanish America gave the mother country two of its best Romantic dramatists: Ventura de la Vega (1807–65) and Gertrudis Gómez de Avellaneda (1814–73). On the Brazilian stage of the period, already blessed with established companies, melodrama reached its peak. The historical novel provoked controversy in America but took root as part of the Romantic spirit. The popularisation of culture fostered a revived interest in historical knowledge. The success of the new aesthetic stemmed from characteristics individual to Romanticism and the period surrounding the foundation of the Spanish American nations. The Romantics questioned history in an attempt to affirm their nationality. Memory acquired a psycho-social role through the cult of Historicism. In Mexico, a school of writers emerged in the wake of *El fistol del diablo*, 1845 [The Devil's Tiepin] by Manuel Payno, which excels in its description of customs. Typical American elements emerged in scenes of local colour and traditions. This fusion of local colour and history helped to define the national profile and supercede the tendency to imitate European models. The *feuilleton* (serial novel), also came to the fore through the periodical press and was a favourite with Brazilian readers. Journalistic activity played an important role, not only in its capacity as a new mode of cultural expression, but because it voiced the desires of the collective, as well as providing a vehicle for the creation of public opinion. It fostered both writing as a profession and the formation of a reading public. There are three distinguishable trends in Spanish American and Brazilian Romanticism. The first emphasizes landscape and has socio-historical ramifications. The second concentrates on indigenous issues and seeks the perfect Indian. The third is nationalist in tone and is based on the essential characteristics of the movement such as local colour. The theme of black slavery impassioned the writers of the West Indies in particular. So-called "Black Literature" still exists today. The Cuban writer Gertrudis Gómez de Avellaneda, who lived most of her life in Spain, where she achieved notable success, wrote the novel *Sab* (1841) in which the slave sacrifices his fortune and his life for the love of his mistress. Inspired by a historical topic, Avellaneda wrote *Guatimozín* (1846), which deals with an episode from the Conquest of Mexico and the life of Hernán Cortés.

The emerging peoples of Spanish America and Brazil were swept away by a lyricism inspired by Nature and the theme of impossible love. Von Humboldt's journey through Spanish America provided the facts for a new vision of nature. The geographical dimension became an issue in the definition of identity. Enthused by the spirit of naturalist investigation, Europe went in search of paradise lost. Landscape should be described in terms of the spirit, from a subjective viewpoint. The feeling for Nature was integral to the work of art and a refuge from all ills. The Romantics saw Nature as the reflection of man, discovering also an aesthetic dimension to the concept of homeland. True emotive resonance could be found in the contemplation of Nature in two respects: firstly, as a projection of emotion, and secondly, linked to the desire to capture local colour (*costumbrismo*). Chateaubriand's discovery of the poetry of the great forests during his trip to North America inspired the discovery of native landscape in Spanish American literature. However, the phenomena of American nature must have had different significance for Chateaubriand than for the Cuban José María Heredia (1803–39), with his melancholy and subjective reflections on nature in the poem "En el teocali de Cholula" [In the Aztec Temple of Cholula]. The most significant Romantic novel, *María* (1867), by the Colombian Jorge Isaacs, employs the vision of nature offered by Chateaubriand and Bernardin de Saint-Pierre. The confrontation of Man and Nature results in the mythification of the peasant hero, the gaucho or plainsman of Venezuela. The gaucho poets are linked to a popular and spontaneous trend in poetry.

Whereas the Europeans turned to the Middle Ages as the period of the birth of nations, in Spanish America and Brazil the creation of a past was combined with the problem of national identity. The regression to medieval Europe with its troubadours and crusades was replaced in Spanish America by the memory of an indigenous heritage. The modelling of a national hero was seen as a priority by many writers. The idealisation of the Indian further developed the cliché of the "noble savage," already present in Columbus's letters. The break with classical mythology in favour of indigenous folklore was inspired by European Romantics such as Victor Hugo, Musset and Ferdinand Denis, who lived in Brazil. However, in many cases, Romanticism viewed the Indian as a picturesque element about to disappear or one persecuted by the cruelty of the so-called superior race (cf. *Tabaré*, by Zorrilla de San Martín). The principal symbol of the homeland was the Indian, who, in Europe, exemplified natural man. With Romanticism, the Indian became an aesthetic object, a literary hero and a mytho-historical ancestor, related to the restoration of the myth of childhood and, because he represented the Middle Ages, a necessary factor in the search for national origins. The most interesting novels of this period were written in Brazil. Of

particular note is Joaquim Manuel de Macedo, who describes scenes of daily life and José de Alencar who wrote historical novels and also some dealing with indigenous themes. *Iracema* (*Iracema, the Honey-Lips, a Legend of Brazil*) by Alencar, is an anagram of America, symbolising the indigenous civilisation which surrenders to the white conqueror and dies in the process. Alencar highlights the need for the adaptation of foreign ways to the Brazilian atmosphere, defending native motifs, themes and, above all, the indigenous as an expression of nationality. The foremost historical novel dealing with an Indian theme is *Enriquillo*, 1882 (*The Cross and the Sword*) by the Dominican, Manuel de Jesús Galván (1834–1910). The novel tells of Enriquillo's revolt and eventual pardon by Charles V of Spain and is based on original documents. The aesthetic aspect of the novel is sacrificed in favour of historical accuracy. The Indian is no longer a decorative figure and acquires heroic proportions with dialogues of dramatic quality. Brazilian Romanticism reaches its peak with Antônio Gonçalves Dias who gave the myth of the indigenous past poetic form.

Socio-political themes were inspired by the events of the Paraguayan War and the abolitionist campaign. Like its French model, the imagination in Romanticism replaces the conservative tone of Indian oriented themes, a development which can be seen in the mythical dedication of origin through prophecy and clairvoyance in the work of the eloquent poet, Antônio de Castro Alves (1847–71). Nationalist sentiment, one of the Utopias of Romanticism, which attempts to find an *American* mode of expression, is a consequence of the special situation of the fledgling nations. It is a motif which does not echo European works. The romantic period highlights the traits which are destined to define the national literatures but it does not disconnect them from the past. Having achieved political liberty, the goal became spiritual freedom. In many cases, the angst of political freedom led to exile and death, be it real or imaginary. In relation to the language of Romanticism, characterised by the emphasis on emotion and imprecision of thought, there emerged the first attempts to establish an "American language." The main innovations were incorporated into the dictionary and vocabulary of the continent and served to give literary status to American types. After Romanticism, the national literary language no longer accorded with that of the mother country. By giving life to new forms of expression and thought, Spanish American and Brazilian Romanticism accelerated the development of a native literature, relevant to social reality. It prepared the way for the radical departures of modern times, beginning a cycle of autonomy and maturity.

BELLA JOZEF

translated by Carol Tully

Further Reading

Brushwood, John S., *Genteel Barbarism: Experiments in the Analysis of Nineteenth-Century Spanish-American Novels*, Lincoln: University of Nebraska Press, 1981

Castagnaro, R. Anthony, *The Early Spanish American Novel*, New York: Las Américas, 1971

Goic, Cedomil, *Historia y crítica de la literatura hispanoamericana*, vol. 2, *Del romanticismo al modernismo*, Barcelona: Editorial Crítica, 1990

Jozef, Bella, *Historia de la literatura hispanoamericana*, 2nd edition, Rio de Janeiro: Francisco Alves, 1982 [Chapter 4 is on Romanticism]

Nikolayevna Kuteischikova, Vera, "El Romanticismo y el problema de la conciencia nacional en la literatura latinoamericana en el siglo XIX," in *Literatura y sociedad latinoamericanas del siglo XIX*, edited by Evelyn Picon Garfield and Ivan Schulman, Urbana: University of Illinois Press, 1991

Paz, Octavio, *Los hijos del limo: del romanticismo a la vanguardia*, Barcelona: Seix Barral, 1974; as *Children of the Mire: Modern Poetry from Romanticism to the Avant Garde*, translated by Rachel Phillips, Cambridge, Massachusetts: Harvard University Press, 1974

Sommer, Doris, *Foundational Fictions: the National Romances of Latin America*, Berkeley: University of California Press, 1991 [Chapters on *Amalia*, *Sab*, *María*, *O Guaraní*, etc.]

Yáñez, Mirta, *La narrativa del romanticismo en Latinoamérica*, Havana: Letras Cubanas, 1989

Sílvio Romero 1851–1914

Brazilian critic

Sílvio Romero produced a quite astonishing number of studies of Brazilian literature, culture, and society during his long and distinguished career. The most important and influential of his works, however, is the *História da literatura brasileira* [History of Brazilian Literature], first published in 1888. While it can be argued that the major figures of nationalistic Romanticism, Antônio Gonçalves Dias and José de Alencar in particular, had created the fact of an independent Brazilian literature, the idea of Brazilian literature – its character, is origins, its relationship to the nation itself – remains in large measure the product of Sílvio Romero's *História*. To one degree or another, everything that has been written about the literature of Brazil since 1888 is a reaction to – and, in many cases, an on-going argument with – Romero's conception of the nation and its literary tradition.

Romero was a disciple of the philosopher, jurist, and Germanist Tobias Barreto (1839–89), with whom he studied at the Faculty of Law in Recife and whom he considered the greatest intellectual and writer Brazil had produced. Through Barreto, Romero came into contact with contemporary European literature, philosophy and science. These readings led Romero and Barreto's other disciples to reject the individualism, emotionalism and idealism of Brazilian Romanticism and to see science as the salvation of humanity, of Brazil, and, even, of Brazilian literature. Barreto, Romero, and other members of what Romero always called, somewhat pompously, the "School of Recife," tried their hands at producing anti-Romantic "scientific poetry," but these attempts largely failed as literary works.

Scientificism, however, remained the central focus of Romero's thought; in his *Da crítica e sua exata definição* [On Criticism and Its Exact Definition], published in 1909, Romero defined criticism as "alguma coisa que se pode aplicar, não diretamente aos fenômenos ou fatos quaisquer da natureza ou da sociedade, porque esta é a função da ciência, sim às vistas, teorias, doutrinas, interpretações que de tais fatos deram os que deles se ocuparam" (something that cannot be applied directly to the phenomena or facts of nature or of society, which is, rather, the proper function of science, it can be applied to the views, theories, doctrines, or interpretations developed by those who dealt with those facts or phenomena). Criticism, therefore, while not quite a science, was a method of synthesis applied to literature; the goal of literary expression, in Romero's view, was not simply or even primarily the creation of works of art but, rather, the representation of natural and social phenomena. As this emphasis on content rather than form suggests, Romero's greatest strength was the collection of large numbers of facts and details about literary history, and there is no question that his wide-ranging and generally precise scholarship revolutionized our knowledge of colonial Brazilian literature. And because Romero's anti-Romantic definition of literature stressed the collective rather than the individual, the second task of the critic was to organize and to classify the facts he had collected, creating a linear framework of what he called "currents" and "schools" to which all Brazilian writers could be assigned. The broad outlines of Romero's chronology still form the basis of most Brazilian literary historiographies dealing with the period from 1500 to about the middle of the 19th century. His view of writers of his own time, however, was severely warped, both by his own concept of what literature should be and by his personal enthusiasms and antipathies. As a result, many of Romero's judgments in this area are just plain wrong-headed. The most obvious examples are his glorification of Tobias Barreto and his insistence that Machado de Assis was, at best, a minor talent.

Underlying Romero's vision of Brazilian literature as the product of a series of collective movements was his belief that the nation's culture as a whole was the expression of a far vaster collective, the inhabitants of Brazil and their unique national character. One purpose of his *História*, then, was to define that national character, a task which Romero had set for himself as early as 1870, and which remained a central preoccupation in all of his writings. The fundamental and irreconcilable contradictions in Romero's view of Brazil's national character are very evident today; at least some of his contemporaries recognized them as well, and Romero's less pompous and self-assured texts provide some evidence that he was aware of their existence. As Antônio Cândido has pointed out, these contradictions were not simply personal idiosyncrasies on Romero's part, but reflected the intense ambivalence of the society in which he lived; some of that ambivalence survives even today.

At the most basic level, Romero was forever torn between emotion and what he defined as science. He had grown up on a plantation in Sergipe, and his intense memories of the songs and stories he had heard as a child led Romero to break with Tobias Barreto, who believed that popular culture was unworthy of scientific attention, and to begin his study of national character by collecting numerous examples what we would now call folklore. Once the task of collection was complete, however, Romero clearly could not make the connections that today seem so obvious; popular culture and literary culture are not linked in any coherent way, and the collective folk traditions of African, Amerindian and European populations in Brazil are described as almost entirely separate from each other. Romero went farther than any of his predecessors in accepting the idea that slavery and the African presence had played central roles in the creation of Brazil's society, culture, and economy; it is typical of Romero that he roots this acceptance in nostalgic recollections of the slave women who helped raise him. Even more important, Romero admits the existence of widespread miscegenation thoughout Brazilian history and society – not just Amerindian-European miscegenation, which Romantic writers like Gonçalves Dias and Alencar had endeavored to use as a metaphor for the creation of a uniquely Brazilian identity in the distant colonial past, but the on-going and far more problematic African-European miscegenation. Romero's *História*, after all, was published in 1888 – the year of Abolition. But while Romero is prepared to argue the centrality of those of African descent in Brazilian culture, and even to imply that the prototypical Brazilian is in fact the product of miscegenation, his readings in European science and pseudo-science and the influence of Tobias Barreto – a mulatto who spent his whole life negating his origins – conspired to undermine this radically modern and inclusive vision of Brazilian society. Romero's life experiences and his observation of the society in which he lived pushed him towards a positive view of those of African descent and their impact on Brazil; Barreto, Social Darwinism, and Haeckel's theories of race all pushed Romero to deny the validity of the African contribution and, in fact, to question the basic viability of a society built upon miscegenation. Romero thus simultaneously accepted and rejected miscegenation, praised the vital diversity of Brazil and feared that its inherently inferior non-European roots would forever condemn the nation to ignorance and poverty. Once again, Romero convinced himself, science was the only solution – and, once again, what Romero viewed as science turned out to be wrong: he declared that the "inferior" racial groups in Brazil were dying out as part of natural, Darwinian process, and that by sometime around 1940 the nation's population would be entirely European. Some future historian of Brazilian literature, Romero seems to have believed, would look on his own *História* as essentially archaeological in nature, describing the characteristics and the enduring influence on the creation of what he called "the Brazilian soul" of racial groups long since extinct.

DAVID T. HABERLY

Biography

Born Sílvio Vasconcelos da Silveira Ramos Romero, in the town of Lagarto, province of Sergipe, Brazil, 21 April 1851. Lived with his parents on their plantation until he was five, then stayed in parents home in Lagarto until he was twelve. Father a merchant. Studied in the Ateneu Fluminense, Rio de Janeiro, 1863–67. In 1868 he began to study law at Recife. The following year he published the booklet "A poesia contemporânea e a sua Intuição Naturalista." Became a government administrator in Estância, in the province of Sergipe, but resigned in order to enter politics; elected provincial deputy, 1875. Married Clorinda Diamantina Correia de Araújo in the same year. Left Recife in 1876 to become the municipal judge in charge of orphans in Parati, an old town in the state of Rio de Janeiro. Moved to Rio de Janeiro, 1879. Wife died in 1884, at the age of twenty-five. Worked as a teacher and as a journalist. Staff writer for the newspaper *Diário de Notícias*, 1891. In 1897 he became a founding member of the Brazilian Academy of Letters. Served as a federal deputy, 1900–02. Died 17 July 1914.

Selected Works

A literatura brasileira e a crítica moderna, Rio de Janeiro: Imprensa Industrial, 1880
Cantos populares do Brasil, Lisbon: Nova Livraria Internacional, 1883
Contos populares do Brasil, Lisbon: Nova Livraria Internacional, 1885
Estudos de literatura contemporânea, Rio de Janeiro: Laemmert, 1885
História da literatura brasileira, 2 vols, Rio de Janeiro: Garnier, 1888; modern editions of this work are based on the revised 3rd edition, Rio de Janeiro: José Olympio, 1943
Ensaios de sociologia e literatura, Rio de Janeiro: Garnier, 1901

Compilations and Anthologies

Sílvio Romero: teoria, crítica e história literária, edited by Antônio Cândido, Rio de Janeiro: Livros Técnicos e Científicos Editora, 1978

Further Reading

These are the major studies of Romero's theory and practice of criticism. The most useful is that by Antônio Cândido, the only 20th-century Brazilian critic whose scope and influence are comparable to those of Romero.

Cândido, Antônio, *O método crítico de Sílvio Romero*, São Paulo: Editora da Universidade de São Paulo, 1988
Moraes Filho, Evaristo de, *Medo à utopia: o pensamento social de Tobias Barreto e Sílvio Romero*, Rio de Janeiro: Nova Fronteira, 1985
Rabello, Sylvio, *Itinerário de Sílvio Romero*, Rio de Janeiro: Civilização Brasileira, 2nd edition, 1967
Souza, João Mendonça de, *Sílvio Romero, o crítico e o polemista*, Rio de Janeiro: Emebê, 1976

Rosa, João Guimarães

See Guimarães Rosa

Jacques Roumain 1907–1944

Haitian poet and prose writer

Jacques Roumain's literary production is inseparable from his political engagement and from the historical events which fashioned his life. One of Haiti's most important writers, Roumain helped to create a cultural awareness in black Haitian literature and to reorient political thought, through his poetry and fiction as well as through his journalism and speeches.

When in 1927 Roumain, the son of well-to-do landowners, returned to his native island after several years of studying and travelling in Europe, he was deeply disturbed by the social and political conditions in his country, including its occupation by the US military (1915–34). Roumain saw Haiti as a static society divided between a feudal peasant class and an exploitative mulatto Establishment. The country's hierarchical structure reproduced the social stratification of colonialism. If a black middle-class was slowly emerging, its obsessive search for black authenticity, the "noiriste" movement, created racial myths and tensions, while the mulattoes were still viewing France as their intellectual province.

By 1928, Roumain became actively involved in the Nationalist struggle against the American occupation and set out to free Haiti from all foreign domination in every aspect of life. Participating in student strikes and writing numerous articles against the American presence, he was imprisoned on several occasions. But in 1931, when it became apparent that the new Nationalist governement of Sténio Vincent would not improve conditions for the proletariat, Roumain turned to communism. Distressed by his people's hunger, ignorance, and disease, Roumain saw their state as irremediably hopeless. He therefore joined clandestine activities aimed at creating a Haitian Communist Party. But, accused of being an anarchist, he was imprisoned in the National Penitentiary in January 1933. While in jail, he was able to continue his political activities through writing letters and essays to the press. Released from prison in 1936, he chose to leave the increasingly dictatorial government of Haiti for Belgium and finally Paris, where he pursued his training in ethnology, particularly exploring the African origins of the Haitian people. During his exile, he also travelled extensively in Martinique, Cuba, Mexico and the United States, where he studied poverty and political oppression. When in 1941 he finally returned to Haiti, he – along with Alfred Métraux, Jean Price-Mars and others, founded an ethnological research center, the "Bureau d'Ethnologie." As first director of the Bureau, he published a number of ethnological studies and, at the same time, devoted considerable efforts to disseminate and popularize ethnology. During that period, he supported again the intellectual and material progress of the peasants. But, at the end of 1942, Roumain was sent by the new regime of Elie Lescot to Mexico as Haiti's chargé d'affaires. A year later, he fell sick and returned to die in Port-au-Prince in August 1944.

Roumain's literary production reflects the major political and philosophical currents in his life. The publication of Jean Price-Mars' *Ainsi parla l'oncle*, 1928 (*So Spoke the Uncle*) which emphasizes the relationships of folklore to literature, represented for Roumain an essential step toward achieving authentic Haitian values and cultural forms. Helping to create the "indigenist" movement, Roumain supported the "Haitianization" of literature, replacing French imitation with a representation of Haiti's own racial perspectives, sensibility and subject matters. Roumain also called attention to the South American and Harlem Renaissance authors who shared similar cultural and political experiences with Haiti.

With other intellectuals, Roumain founded the short-lived *Revue Indigène*, 1927 [Indigenous Review] and later *La Trouée 559* [The Break Through] where he published his first, rather lyrical poems despite the indigenous claim of the founders. But by 1931, Roumain's literary writings began to reflect his political and cultural preoccupations. *La Proie et l'ombre* [The Prey and the Shadow], a collection of short stories, depicts the aimlessness of bourgeois existence through several heroes, lucid enough to realize that they live in a void. All the stories of this first fictional work evoke the alienation of the privileged intellectuals unable to reach the Creole-speaking blacks. And in *Les Fantoches* [The Puppets], a series of scenes rather than a fully developed novel, the author casts the antithesis between two extreme classes of Haitian society, the bourgeois and the peasant, and reveals the fundamental corruption of Haitian politics.

With *La Montagne ensorcelée*, 1931 [The Bewitched Mountain], prefaced by Price-Mars, Roumain published his first significant literary work – a "peasant" novel, i.e., a narrative built around folk culture and reflecting his socialist leanings. The story is about a rural community which, beset by calamities, finds a scapegoat in an old woman suspected of sorcery. In their misery and despair, the peasants seek to gain control of their condition through superstitious beliefs. Through the constant shift in points of view – from neutral literary description to peasant narrative reflecting folk mentality and speech – the author guides the readers to perceive the life of the village and its inhabitants on several levels of reality. This narrative technique will contribute to the great literary achievement of Roumain's last novel, *Gouverneurs de la rosée*, 1944 (*Masters of the Dew*). Meanwhile, Roumain continued writing poetry and published in *Haïti-Journal* four poems evoking the problem of race and the universal black experience.

During 1932–34, Roumain conceived the idea of writing a "cycle" of novels, alternately dealing with urban middle-class society and Haitian peasant life. During his incarceration (1934 to 1936), he worked on an urban novel, "Le Champ du potier" that remained incomplete at his death.

He began his second peasant novel, *Gouverneurs de la rosée*, during the first year of his exile in Belgium, finishing it eight years later. In 1944, the book appeared posthumously in Port-au-Prince and in Paris, enjoying an immediate success. Haitian in its setting, the story of *Gouverneurs de la rosée* conveys a universal meaning. It is the portrayal of humanity's eternal struggle against the natural elements and against its own destructive tendencies.

When after fifteen years of Cuban plantation work, Manuel returns to his Haitian mountain village, he is confronted with the terrible droughts that have left his people hungry and split into two enemy camps. Thanks to his courage and determination and Annaïse's love, Manuel finds a spring which, he hopes, will reconcile the villagers in a cooperative effort to direct the water through the fields and gardens of the village. Having learned in Cuba the value of worker solidarity, he attempts to convey that value to the disheartened peasants. Manuel falls victim to one man's envy and jealousy, but his death will finally bind the village together in its recovered prosperity. Through its bilingual narrative, a mixture of classic French and Creole rendering the reality of the land, *Gouverneurs de la rosée* is one of the best illustrations of an indigenist aesthetic. Its stress on Voodoo as the African heritage of the Haitian people reveals Price-Mars's influence. Further, the focus on economic life and the need to return to work on the land, as well as the imperative to fight political corruption, illustrate the thematic elements Roumain brought to Caribbean literature.

The courage and great achievement of Jacques Roumain, the writer, lie in his relentless criticism of the Haitian elite, and of the several oppressive regimes that attempted to eliminate him. In so doing, Roumain initiates a literary tradition with a consistent political mission.

MARIE-AGNÈS SOURIEAU

Biography

Born in Port-au-Prince, Haiti, 4 June 1907. Attended the Saint Louis de Gonzague secondary school, Port-au-Prince. Finished his secondary education in Berne and Zurich, Switzerland. Travelled in Germany, France and the United Kingdom. Briefly studied agronomy in Madrid but returned to Port-au-Prince in 1927. Co-founder of the *Revue Indigène* (1927) where he published his own short stories and poems together with his own translations into French. Appointed head of division in Ministry of Interior, 1931. Resigned and became political activist. Imprisoned in 1933 and again in 1934, after founding the Communist Party of Haiti. Sentenced by military tribunal to three years of penal servitude. This broke his health. On being released in 1936, travelled to Belgium and then to Paris where he studied Human Paleonthology at the Sorbonne. Moved to the United States in 1939 where he continued his studies at Columbia University, New York. Later, travelled to Martinique and Havana. In latter he worked with the mulatto poet, Nicolás Guillén. Able to return to Haiti in 1941. Appointed Chargé d'Affaires to Mexico in 1943. Ill health obliged him to return home in 1944. Died in Port-au-Prince, 18 August 1944.

Selected Works

Novels and Short Fiction

La Proie et l'ombre, Port-au-Prince: La Presse, 1930
Les Fantoches, Port-au-Prince, Imprimerie de l'État, 1931
La Montagne ensorcelée, Port-au-Prince: Chassaing, 1931
Gouverneurs de la rosée, Port-au-Prince: Imprimerie de l'État, 1944; as *Masters of the Dew*, translated by Langston Hughes and Mercer Cook, New York: Reynal and Hitchcock, 1947
Bois d'ébène, Port-au-Prince: Deschamps, 1945; as *Ebony Wood / Bois d'ébène*, translated by Sydney Shapiro, New York: Interworld Press, 1972

Translations

When the Tom-Tom Beats: Selected Prose and Poems, translated by Joanne Fungaroli and Ronald Sauer, Washington, DC: Azul, 1995

Further Reading

Cobb, Martha, *Harlem, Haiti and Havana: a Comparative Critical Study of Langston Hughes, Jacques Roumain, Nicolás Guillén*, Washington, DC: Three Continents Press, 1979
Conturie, Christiane, *Comprendre "Gouverneurs de la rosée" de Jacques Roumain*, Issy-les-Molineaux, France: Classiques Africains, 1980
Dorsinville, Roger, *Jacques Roumain*, Paris: Présence Africaine, 1981
Makouta-Mboukou, Jean Pierre, *Une Lecture de "Gouverneurs de la rosée,"* Abidjan: Nouvelles Editions Africaines, 1987
Prat, Michel, *Gouverneurs de la rosée, Jacques Roumain: analyse critique*, Paris: Hatier, 1986

Juan Rulfo 1918–1986

Mexican prose writer

While a small group of friends always admired Juan Rulfo's writings, as they read the manuscripts of the short stories later collected in *El llano en llamas*, 1953 (*The Burning Plain*) and his novel *Pedro Páramo* (1955), Rulfo's great international renown came as a surprise, because it was based on only two slim books. Perhaps the surprise was greater for Rulfo, who did not publish any other novel or collection of short stories for more than twenty-five years after the appearance of *El llano en llamas*. Critics have called this time lapse, "Rulfo's silence," and the paradox is that his renown increased steadily in inverse proportion to his literary productivity, at the same time that readers anxiously expected new works from him. Rulfo's silence is worth considering since it has a correlative in his own prose, which tends to seek the conciseness of poetry, to avoid explicitness, and to manage language as precisely as a poet would do. Implosion rather than explosion would be a key concept to understand his literary system, how he tried to write, and finally his idea of literature. A very private person, introspective and shy but at the same time humorous and witty when he felt comfortable in the presence of other people, Rulfo brought to literature these same personal qualities. And he also brought hidden aspects of his own life to his writings. One of his most read and admired short stories, "¡Diles que no me maten!" (Tell Them Not to Kill Me!) has a close relationship to a family tragedy: the killing of his father, when Juan Rulfo was still a child. It would not be surprising, then, that one of the main themes in his work is the search for the father. And that is the starting point of *Pedro Páramo*, when Juan Preciado relates: "Vine a Comala porque me dijeron que vivía aquí mi padre, un tal Pedro Paramo." (I came to Comala because I was told that my father, a certain Pedro Páramo, lived here). The theme of the presence/absence of the father is fundamental not only in these two examples but throughout his work.

Rulfo came to Mexican narrative when the literary tradition of the "Novel of the Mexican Revolution" was still hegemonic, and when Mexico itself could not yet take some distance from the most belligerent and violent period in its history, the Mexican Revolution. This social and political movement started in 1910 as an uprising against Porfirio Díaz, the Dictator for more than three decades, and it did not stop even after institutional accords named a new President, because in 1926 another uprising disturbed the fragile political equilibrium. This second uprising had religious motivations, it was called the "rebellion of the Cristeros" (self-designated followers of Christ the King) and had a strong impact on Rulfo's imagination. This can be seen in the title story of *El llano en llamas*, in "La noche que lo dejaron solo"(The Night They Left Him Alone), "El hombre" (The Man) and others, together with important passages of the novel, *Pedro Páramo*. The impact of the Cristero rebellion, as well as autobiographical incidents, helped Rulfo shape his narrative world introducing violence in a peculiar way: sudden and stripped from any ethical consideration.

The tradition of the Mexican Revolution in the novel is important not only from a historical point of view, but mainly because Rulfo renewed this tradition in terms of both form and style. While almost every novelist of the time was representing the strong influence of French Naturalism in literature, Rulfo developed his writing in a novel fashion and helped transform Mexican narrative in a radical way. As a very disorganized and spontaneous reader, he brought to Mexican literature the distant influences of Nordic writers such as Selma Lagerlöf, C.M. Ramuz (*Derborance*), Sillampaa, Bjornson, Hauptmann, and the first Hamsun. His influences also included the gothic element discovered in love stories such as *Wuthering Heights* by Emily Brontë, and all these stimuli contributed to Rulfo's own gothicism. Rulfo put his literary universe on the borders of the fantastic, creating an almost surrealistic, moonlike space. The town of Comala is "un lugar sobre las brasas" (a place on burning embers). In *Pedro Páramo*, Juan Preciado arrives in Comala searching for his father, but he encounters only what seem to be ghosts, murmurs, cries emerging from the walls, until he discovers that everybody is already dead: the reader discovers that the story of Pedro Páramo is being told by a dead man, Juan Preciado, from a deep tomb. It has a complex combination of reality and dream, hope and fear, love and hate, which are never separated. This made his narrative most surprising, original and admired. There are some short stories, such as "Luvina", in which the characters wonder where they are: "¿En qué país estamos, Agripina? . . . ¿Qué país es éste, Agripina?" (What country are we in, Agripina? . . . What sort of country is this, Agripina?), such is the dreamlike atmosphere the narrative creates.

Rulfo started writing the novel *Pedro Páramo* in August 1953, while a Fellow of the Centro Mexicano de Escritores. He intended to call this novel *Los desiertos de la Tierra* [The Deserts of the Earth]. When he finished it the following year, it bore the title *Los murmullos* [The Murmurs] but between January and March 1954, a fragment of it was published in a magazine, announcing the forthcoming novel as *Una estrella junto a la luna* [A Star Near the Moon]. All these titles refer to different aspects of the novel: the spectacular isolated landscape, the ghosts and their murmurs, the love story between Pedro Páramo and Susana San Juan. Finally, the book appeared under the title *Pedro Páramo*, the name of one of the main characters, because the same publishing house had recently published *Los falsos rumores* [The False Rumours], by Gastón García Cantú, and the publishers wanted to avoid any confusion. During the following forty years, *Pedro Páramo* would become the best known of all Mexican novels, and it brought its author well deserved recognition.

There has been a "mythic" reading of Rulfo's work, mostly by other writers, like Octavio Paz and Carlos Fuentes, who see universal themes in Rulfo's work, and even classical ones. Juan Preciado, in his search for his father, would then be a modern version of Telemachus searching for Ulysses. But there is also a more historical reading of Rulfo's stories, considering his strong views on social and political issues, and how they were expressed in his literature. In this sense, we can read his novel and short stories as a deconstruction of political power, and also as an unavoidable critique of the economic and social reforms brought about by the new bourgeoisie which benefited from the Revolution. With great irony, "Nos han dado la tierra" (They Gave Us the Land) comments on the agrarian reform that gave the most unproductive lands to the poorest; "El día del derrumbe" (The Day of the Quake) mocks political discourse and political authorities; and *Pedro Páramo* is one of the most powerful portraits of the "cacique" (the local political boss) to have emerged from Mexican literature.

JORGE RUFFINELLI

Biography

Born in Apulco, near Sayula, Mexico, 16 May 1918. In childhood experienced the Cristero rebellion, a rural backlash to the Mexican Revolution in the state of Jalisco. Father murdered during the revolt and his mother died of a heart attack in 1927. Attended the Luis Silva school for orphans, Guadalajara, 1928–1932; seminary and secondary school, Guadalajara, 1932–c.34; studied law at the Universidad Nacional Autónoma de México (UNAM) Mexico City, 1934–35: forced to give up studies because of financial pressures. Worked for the government immigration department in Mexico City, Tampico, Guadalajara and Veracruz, 1935–46. Co-founder, with Juan José Arreola and Antonio Alatorre, of the literary review, *Pan*, 1944. Married Clara Aparicio in 1947, one daughter and three sons. Worked for Goodrich-Euzkadi rubber company, 1947–54; staff member of the publishing section of the Papaloapan Commission for land development, Veracruz, 1955–56. Wrote screenplays, Mexico City, c.1956–59; worked in television, Guadalajara, 1959–62; staff member, from 1962, then director of the editorial department until 1986, Instituto Nacional Indigenista (National Institute for Indigenous Studies), Mexico City. Adviser, and Fellow, Centro Mexicano de Escritores. Elected member of the Mexican Academy of Letters, 1980. Awarded the National Literature Prize, 1970; Príncipe de Asturias Prize (Spain), 1983. Died in Mexico City, 7 January 1986.

Selected Works

El llano en llamas, Mexico City: Fondo de Cultura Económica, 1953; as *The Burning Plain and Other Stories*, translated by George D. Schade, Austin: University of Texas Press, 1967 [short fiction]

Pedro Páramo, Mexico City: Fondo de Cultura Económica, 1955; as *Pedro Páramo: a Novel of Mexico*, translated by Lysander Kemp, New York: Grove Press, and London: Calder, 1959; also translated by Margaret Sayers Peden, London: Serpent's Tail, 1994

El gallo de oro y otros textos para cine, edited by Jorge Ayala Blanca, Mexico City: Era, 1980 [film scripts]

Inframundo, El México de Juan Rulfo, Mexico City: INBA, 1980; as *Inframundo: the Mexico of Juan Rulfo*, translated by Frank Janney, Hanover, New Hampshire: Ediciones del Norte, 1983 [Articles on Rulfo followed by a large selection of black and white photographs of rural Mexico taken by Rulfo]

Compilations and Anthologies

Toda la obra, edited by Claude Fell, Madrid: Archivos, 1991 [The most comprehensive and best-documented compilation of Rulfo's works, it includes 16 studies by leading specialists]

Los cuadernos de Juan Rulfo, edited by Clara Aparicio de Rulfo, Mexico City: Era, 1994

Further Reading

Fares, Gustavo C., *Juan Rulfo: la lengua, el tiempo y el espacio*, Buenos Aires: Almagesto, 1994

González Boixo, José Carlos, *Claves narrativas de Juan Rulfo*, León: Universidad de León, 1980; revised edition, 1984

Jiménez de Baez, Yvette, *Juan Rulfo, del páramo a la esperanza*, Mexico City: Fondo de Cultura Económica, 1990

La narrativa de Juan Rulfo. Interpretaciones críticas, Mexico City: Secretaría de Educación Pública, 1974

Leal, Luis, *Juan Rulfo*, Boston: Twayne, 1983

López Mena, Sergio, *Los caminos de la creación en Juan Rulfo*, Mexico City: UNAM, 1993

Lorente-Murphy, Silvia, *Juan Rulfo: realidad y mito de la revolución mexicana*, Madrid: Pliegos, 1988

Portal, Magda, *Rulfo: dinámica de la violencia*, Madrid: Ediciones Cultura Hispánica, 1984

Recopilación de textos sobre Juan Rulfo, Havana: Casa de las Américas, 1969

Rodríguez Alcalá, Hugo, *El arte de Juan Rulfo*, Mexico City: INBA, 1965

Ruffinelli, Jorge, *El lugar de Rulfo y otros ensayos*, Xalapa, Mexico: Universidad Veracruzana, 1980

Special Issues of Journals
Inti 13–14 (1981)
Cuadernos Hispanoamericanos 421–23 (1985)
Revista Iberoamericana 150 (1990)

Pedro Páramo

Novel by Juan Rulfo

In *Pedro Páramo* (1955), the souls of Rulfo's dead countrymen cannot rest in peace. Anything can awake them and make them relive their squalid lives; yet nothing can ever break their solitude, in life or in death. Their search for origin is in vain: the only thing they find is paradise turned into arid heath (Mexican *páramo*), love into madness, life into deathwish, history into myth and exhaustion. Land, life, and even death are poisoned by anger. Rulfo has magnificently tied together the different threads from his stories in *El llano en llamas*, 1953 (*The Burning Plain*), and mixed them together in this bleak carnival, this anguished parable of modern Mexico. Through this striking yet familiar dance of death, Rulfo exorcises Mexico's violent past and present, leaving it symbolically buried, together with his own literature, under a heap of stones which epitomizes Mexico's malevolent patriarchs. Who could go on writing after this unforgiving reading of the Mexican "labyrinth of solitude"?

Pedro Páramo takes place in Rulfo's native Jalisco, using this rural backdrop to symbolically represent half a century of Mexican history, from the dictatorship of Porfirio Díaz, through the Revolution, to the aftermath of the Cristero uprising in 1926–29. Behind the deceptively simple façade of his characters and their rustic discourse, hides a stunning virtuosity of narrative techniques turning the apparent chaos of narrative fragments, points of view, upside-down chronology, and causal logic into an artistic structure executed with clockwork precision. What makes the novel unique is its masterful blend of the stark vision and modern experimental techniques with Mexican folklore and traditional culture. The traditional rural culture that had emerged from the colonial baroque syncretism becomes in the hands of Rulfo a phantasmagoric, almost surrealistic vehicle for mythic unreality, black humor, social satire and the absurd. *Pedro Páramo* has become a part of the Mexican national myth and is one of Mexico's founding fictions.

In all his writing, Rulfo works with the greatest economy of means. This places special emphasis on each single element of the narrative. No wonder Rulfo continued to tinker with the text – sometimes augmenting, sometimes reducing the supposed chaos – in all major editions published during his lifetime (1955, 1959, 1964, 1981). The textual segmentation, that fluctuates from one edition to another, has produced confusion among the critics. In each edition, the textual sequence is broken into different narrative fragments, yet remaining always plausible. In the last edition, Rulfo strengthened the graphic marks and established seventy segments, ranging from a couple of lines up to eight pages in length. This textual flux, similar to that of a mobile, brings into question the concept of the text itself.

The textual fluctuations are only one among the whole string of voluble characteristics present in the world of the novel, where elements like life and death, the before and after, cause without effect and effect without cause, affirmation and denial, do not exclude one another but coexist, tied together by a thread of folklore and the presence of the absurd. A change or vacillation in the microcontext that would normally stand out in a different type of work, is absorbed in this case and is perfectly naturalized by the macrocontext. Does it matter, in this topsy-turvy world, if one dream is positive in one edition and negative in another? If a skeleton is male or female? If Susana's father and the spiritual Father blend into the same ghostly figure?

Rulfo's characters are imprisoned within themselves as if in tombs. Their dialogues are monologues most of the time, or uncooperative responses, that produce silence, reserve, and all kinds of absurd situations. Communication advances through miscommunication and is as phantasmagoric as its participants. The beginning of the novel serves as a paradigm for this plunge into each character's labyrinth of solitude.

The critical reception of *Pedro Páramo* was as absurd as the work itself and attests to the radical changes that the literary code has undergone since that time. In the 1950s, viewed from the perspective of ageing Realism, *Pedro Páramo* appeared to be too chaotic (especially in its first half); and it was rumored, maliciously, that the editors had to help Rulfo organize his masterpiece. After the Boom of experimentalism in the 1960s, the novel seemed actually too well organized (especially in its second half), qualifying only as a forerunner of the new novel. However, a close reading of Rulfo's work shows that the textual and semantic mobile created by this unpretentious country fellow outmatches many textbook experiments of the smooth urban yuppies.

Readers can identify relatively easily the nuclear narratives of *Pedro Páramo*, although these elements must be pieced together from the polyphony of "parallel memories" of the dead. We can establish the following sequence of events: 1. Pedro Páramo's early adolescence and his love for Susana; 2. the beginning of Pedro Páramo's local tyranny; 3. the fast life of Miguel Páramo; 4. the return of Susana at the start of the Mexican Revolution; 5. the death of Comala following Susana's demise and Pedro Páramo's assassination; 6. Juan Preciado's search for a father; and 7. the timelessness of death and the reawakening of the dead.

The novel begins with Juan Preciado's search for his father (6) and ends with Pedro Páramo's murder, sometime before, by one of his other sons (5). This narrative framework, highlighting the father-son relationship, acts as a catalyst of meaning for what transpires in between.

The difficult part comes when the reader attempts to relate the nuclear narratives of the text to the historical chronology. A number of dates can be established with some precision, others only approximately, because the text plays at "hide and seek" with the reader. The reader-detective must continually weigh historical references and allusions, and must pay special attention to the Catholic religious cycle and its rituals. The parody of Catholic ritual symbolism is omnipresent throughout the novel. In some instances, Rulfo's original manuscripts can help understand the apparent disorder: it appears that, at the last minute, the writer "reassigned" some segments, consolidated them around the figure of Miguel Páramo, and thus added more confusion to what he had already created. As a result, Rulfo produced an aporia: Miguel's death, which coincides with the appearance of Halley's comet (May 1910), was shifted along with the comet and all related events to the end of October, thus leaving Eduviges in the air (she was alive in May, but was already dead by October). Yet what does a little more absurdity mean in *Pedro Páramo*?

It is interesting to reflect on the extent to which the historical background can be reconstructed. It seems that Rulfo, who had up to a point carefully established the historical, chronological and geographic supporting structures, started to dismantle them with a vengeance. In this sense, *Pedro Páramo* becomes a postrealist novel, where Realism and its conventions are but a pretext for their subversion and parody.

Another way to look at the novel and organize its structure is through "latent content." Following the principles of mythic analysis expounded by Claude Lévi-Strauss, we can broach two cycles of semantic oppositions that underlie the text of *Pedro Páramo*. The first cycle can be formulated as follows: 1. the overrating versus 2. the underrating of blood relations (the parent-child relationship); 3. exaggerated love versus 4. exaggerated hate (the lovers, husbands and wives, masters and servants relations). The second cycle is: 1. paradise versus 2. *páramo* (myth, recent history, and prophecy of future abandonment); 3. Porfirio Díaz's dictatorship versus 4. the Revolution (modern Mexican history). In the first (individual) cycle, the excesses destroy life. In the second (social) cycle, socialized violence poisons paradise; modern Mexican history could not break with Mexico's destructive past; modern Mexico is dominated by the curse and the myth of exhaustion.

A myth normally offers some mediation between opposites and some solution to the problems presented; *Pedro Páramo* does not. The novel ends with the destruction of patriarchy, but there is no solution to the absurd melodrama, no breath of air, no room for life. In comparison with Rulfo's cosmic pessimism, the absurd *endgames* in Beckett have something almost comic about them; at least Beckett's characters somehow manage, precariously, to go on living.

Critics have recognized from the start that behind the father-son relation lurks the Oedipus myth. This observation has "opened the floodgates" for archetypal criticism and has produced numerous simplified allegorical readings of the novel, based on everything imaginable, from ancient and Aztec myths to those of psychoanalysis. Yet the mythical layer of the novel relies more on Mexican realities than on the Oedipus myth. Some of these realities include the patriarchal system, social violence, the stoic resignation of the oppressed, the degradation of woman (the *chingada*), the deification of the mother, the absence of the father, the "mistress on the side" (*casa chica* or love nest), incest and sexual abuse. All these elements continue to characterize Mexican rural culture and live on under the mask of "modern" Mexico.

EMIL VOLEK

Editions

First edition: *Pedro Páramo*, Mexico City: Fondo de Cultura Económica, 1955

Critical edition: in *Juan Rulfo: toda la obra*, edited by Claude Fell, Madrid: Archivos, 1991 [Includes also several articles on this work]

Translation: *Pedro Paramo: a Novel of Mexico*, by Lysander Kemp, New York: Grove Press, and London: Calder, 1959

Further Reading

Freeman, George Ronald, *Paradise and Fall in Rulfo's "Pedro Páramo." Archetype and Structural Unity*, Morelos, Mexico: CIDOC, 1970 [An example of archetypal criticism]

Munguía Cárdenas, Federico, *Antecedentes y datos biográficos de Juan Rulfo*, Guadalajara: Unidad Editorial, 1987

Sommers, Joseph (editor), *La narrativa de Juan Rulfo*, Mexico City: Sep/Setentas, 1974

Volek, Emil, "*Pedro Páramo* de Juan Rulfo: una obra aleatoria en busca de su texto y del género literario," *Revista Iberoamericana* 150 (1990); from another angle, in his *Literatura hispano-americana entre la modernidad y la postmodernidad*, Cuadernos de Trabajo Nr. 9, Bogotá: Facultad de Ciencias Humanas, Universidad Nacional de Colombia, 1994

S

Ernesto Sábato 1911–

Argentine prose writer

Early in his first collection of essays, *Uno y el universo*, 1945 [One and the Universe], Ernesto Sábato remarks that "Las obras sucesivas de un escritor son como las ciudades que se construyen sobre las ruinas de las anteriores" (The successive works of any writer are like cities, each built on the ruins of its predecessors). His own work demonstrates this principle time and time again: the essays frequently take up themes – and often large portions of text – from earlier essays, while the novels not only review characters and episodes, *Sobre héroes y tumbas* (*On Heroes and Tombs*) from *El túnel* (*The Tunnel*) and *Abaddón, el exterminador* (*The Angel of Darkness*) from both of those, but also incorporate material found in the essays. Indeed, in many ways *Abaddón, el exterminador* represents a summing-up of Sábato's life's work and the processes which brought it into being, though, as usual in his novels and philosophical essays, he avoids direct comment on the political affairs of the day.

Politically, Sábato has had most to say in two separate phases: first, under Aramburu in 1956, his self-defence, *El caso Sábato* [The Sábato Affair], and his review of Peronism, *El otro rostro del peronismo* [The Other Face of Peronism]; and then in 1984 the report, *Nunca más* [Never Again], prepared by a committee of investigation chaired by him, on the atrocities and disappearances under the military dictatorship of the 1970s. Sábato's leaning towards the Left in these documents, though not uncritical, is as unapologetic as elsewhere in his writings.

The philosophical and literary essays (which have been considerably modified in successive editions) pursue a number of common themes. One constant concern is the development of science and the scientific method, and the search for rational explanations of observed phenomena, all too often hindered by metaphysicians and theologians. Sábato's survey of the development of western European thought since the pre-Socratics virtually ignores both medieval neo-Aristotelianism and Renaissance neo-Platonism, condemning the former for its dogmatism and the latter for its mysticism, but he is equally quick to condemn any kind of facile or unthinking pragmatism. At the same time, in his view, post-Enlightenment science has become too theoretical, too abstract, expressed in mathe-matical language beyond the comprehension of ordinary people, who therefore stand in awe or fear of scientists, yet are compelled to trust them.

The human element is a powerful factor for Sábato, whether the threat be ultimate nuclear darkness or some other techno-logical disaster; the image of the human being presented in *Hombres y engranajes* [Men and Gears] as no more than a cog in the grinding wheels of the universal machine is remi-niscent of Chaplin in *Modern Times*. He declares that over the past four hundred years humanity has been subjected to the tyrannies of rationalism and enlightened despotism, or Romanticism and revolution, and materialism in all its mani-festations, before being faced in mid-20th century by forms of totalitarianism, both communist and fascist. Though these concerns are prominent in *Abaddón, el exterminador*, the three novels are devoted primarily to probing the psychological pres-sures exerted on individual characters in specific situations. These characters, as Sábato has stated on several occasions, frequently represent the author himself, or more accurately, aspects of his personality, making the fictions exercises in self-exploration.

Sábato's first novel, *El túnel*, came out between *Uno y el universo* and *Hombres y engranajes*. The protagonist-narrator, Juan Pablo Castel, writes from an asylum for the criminally insane, where he is detained for the murder of María Iribarne, and his narrative tells the story of their brief relationship. He had observed her reaction to one work in the one-man exhi-bition of his paintings and, believing that she could help him to discover its meaning, sought her out. The relationship which follows their eventual chance meeting is bedevilled by his jeal-ously possessive reaction to her insistence on maintaining both her marriage and her close friendship or affair with a distant cousin, Hunter. Finally, after obtaining what he believes to be clear evidence of her infidelity, he destroys the painting and stabs María to death. Castel leads an intensely lonely life, governed by an obsession with rationality; the painting, enti-tled "Maternidad" (Motherhood), contained an inset panel, depicting a woman looking out to sea, which Castel sensed was a key to his unconscious, hitherto sternly controlled in his carefully structured art. As Sábato recalls in *Heterodoxia*

[Heterodoxy], according to Jung we all bear in our unconscious self the image of the opposite sex, and in men that expression of the feminine, the *anima*, is the source of art in all its forms. María Iribarne's apparent grasp of the painting's meaning offered him the possibility of balancing the conscious and unconscious aspects of his personality, but her inability or unwillingness to devote herself exclusively to his quest for self-knowledge drives him to despair. Castel's insane jealousy leads him to destroy for ever his only chance of achieving psychological wholeness, and killing María Iribarne, the key to his inspiration, ends his artistic career.

Sábato continued his self-exploration through fiction in *Sobre héroes y tumbas*, a much longer and more complex novel than *El túnel*. While *Sobre héroes y tumbas* provides as background an account of some episodes from Argentina's violent 19th-century history and sketches of society and culture in mid-20th century, the main story concerns the brief affair between Martín and Alejandra, which is hindered by her incestuous relationship with Fernando Vidal Olmos, her father, and ends when she kills Fernando and commits suicide by setting fire to her room in the Olmos family house. Martín left Buenos Aires soon afterwards for a new life in Patagonia. Most of this story is told by Martín to Bruno, who had also had an interest in Alejandra and, some thirty years earlier, in her mother, Georgina; at that time his rival was the same Fernando Vidal Olmos, Georgina's cousin. Fernando's own "Informe sobre ciegos" (Report on the Blind) reveals his obsessive personality and state of mind just before he goes to his death. Bruno therefore knows Alejandra directly, learns details of her affair with Martín and Martín's own life in discussions with him in 1955 and on his return from the south a few years later, and complements his own knowledge of Fernando through the "Informe sobre ciegos." Fernando's travel abroad, including contacts with Surrealist artists in Paris, and his insisting (like Castel) on reason, suggest aspects of Sábato's own experience; like Bruno, Fernando is also close to Sábato in age. Fernando can be seen as representing the "shadow," the dark side of the writer's personality, while the *anima* manifests herself as, in turn, Fernando's mother Ana María, his cousin Georgina and his daughter Alejandra. Martín serves as catalyst to Bruno's analysis, the fiction through which Sábato plumbs his own psyche.

Sábato's next major work was *El escritor y sus fantasmas* [The Writer and His Ghosts]. The first two parts, omitted in later editions, offered commentary on his two novels, developed from the answers to the questions most frequently put to him, and an essay on the forms and concerns of the contemporary novel. The more substantial third part reverts to the pattern of *Uno y el universo*, ranging from epigrams to extended essays on writers and themes. Here Sábato rejects the limitations imposed by a single, objective point of view, and by a realism which excludes fantasy or dreams, and argues for the *novela total*, the "total novel," which attempts to incorporate all possible aspects of events and their psychological consequences for the people/characters involved.

Much of this is re-stated and put into effect in *Abaddón, el exterminador*, in which Bruno again serves as focus, witnessing events and hearing Sabato's own accounts of his experiences. (The unaccented "Sabato" is the form adopted in this novel). One strand in the novel deals with political repression and its most powerful tool, torture. Marcelo, the principal victim, is the son of old friends of Sabato and involved in revolutionary politics; Sabato discusses with Marcelo and other young people the role of literature in the revolutionary struggle. The Martín-Alejandra-Fernando triangle of *Sobre héroes y tumbas* is replaced by Sabato-Agustina-Nacho, but this element is given less attention than in the earlier novel. Sabato explores the dark side of his psyche, personified as R., a second self, and expressed in sexual activity, frequently associated with blindness. After writing *El túnel*, he had been asked about Allende's blindness by a mysterious Dr Schneider, who does not reappear until after the publication of *Sobre héroes y tumbas*, when he asked about the "Informe sobre ciegos," leading Sabato to investigate Schneider's background, in which he finds connections with Nazi Germany. Schneider represents evil, a recurring theme in the novel, linked with occult practices and apocalyptic visions, for daring to reveal which Sabato is subjected to unbearable psychological pressure. It is left to Bruno to find a tombstone bearing Sabato's name in the cemetery where Bruno's (i.e. Sabato's) father was buried twenty years earlier. The inscription ends with the single word "paz" (peace), suggesting that Sabato's struggle for self-understanding has been successful, though again at the cost of losing the sources of inspiration which lie on the dark side of the psyche.

RON KEIGHTLEY

Biography

Born in Rojas, Province of Buenos Aires, Argentina, 24 June 1911. Attended the Colegio Nacional, 1924–28; School of Physical Sciences, National University of La Plata, 1929–37, PhD in physics 1937; Joliot-Curie Laboratory, Paris, 1938; Massachusetts Institute of Technology, Cambridge, 1939. Married Matilde Kuminsky-Richter in 1934; two sons. Professor of theoretical physics, National University of La Plata, 1940–45: forced to resign by the Perón government. Contributed to the literary journal *Sur*. Worked for UNESCO, Paris, 1947: resigned after two months. Editor of the newspaper, *Mundo Argentino*, 1955: resigned because of restrictions on freedom of speech. Director of cultural relations, Ministry of Foreign Relations and Culture, 1958–59: resigned. Invited to speak at various universities including, Paris, Rome and Madrid, 1962; visited Puerto Rico and the United States, 1963. Chair, National Commission of the Disappeared, 1983. Recipient of numerous awards including: Argentine Association for the Progress of Science Fellowship, 1937; Buenos Aires Municipal Prize, 1945; Institute of Foreign Relations Prize (West Germany), 1973; Consagración Nacional Prize, 1974; Argentine Society of Writers Prize of Honour, 1974; Prix du Meilleur Livre Étranger (France), 1977; Gran Cruz al Mérito Civil (Spain), 1979; Gabriela Mistral Prize, 1984; Miguel de Cervantes Prize, 1985; Jerusalem Prize, 1989.

Selected Works

Novels

El túnel, Buenos Aires: Sur, 1948; as *The Outsider*, translated by Harriet de Onís, New York: Knopf, 1950; as *The Tunnel*, translated by Margaret Sayers Peden, New York: Ballantine, and London: Jonathan Cape, 1988

Sobre héroes y tumbas, Buenos Aires: Fabril, 1961; as *On Heroes and Tombs*, translated by Helen Lane, Boston: Godine, 1981; London: Jonathan Cape, 1982

Abaddón, el exterminador, Buenos Aires: Sudamericana, 1974; as *The Angel of Darkness*, translated by Andrew Hurley, New York: Ballantine, 1991; London, Jonathan Cape, 1992

Essays and Other Writings

Uno y el universo, Buenos Aires: Sudamericana, 1945

Hombres y engranajes: reflexiones sobre el dinero, la razón y el derrumbe de nuestro tiempo, Buenos Aires: Emecé, 1951

Heterodoxia, Buenos Aires: Emecé, 1953

El otro rostro del peronismo: carta abierta a Mario Amadeo, 2nd edition, Buenos Aires: López, 1956

El caso Sábato: torturas y libertad de prensa – carta abierta al General Aramburu, Buenos Aires: privately printed, 1956

Tango: discusión y clave, Buenos Aires: Losada, 1963

El escritor y sus fantasmas, Madrid: Aguilar, 1963

Pedro Henríquez Ureña, Buenos Aires: Ediciones Culturales Argentinas, 1967

Tres aproximaciones a la literatura de nuestro tiempo: Robbe-Grillet, Borges, Sartre, Santiago de Chile: Editorial Universitaria, 1968

La convulsión política y social de nuestro tiempo, Buenos Aires: Edicom, 1969

Itinerario, Buenos Aires: Sur, 1969

La cultura en la encrucijada nacional, Buenos Aires: Ediciones de Crisis, 1973

Diálogos, in collaboration with Jorge Luís Borges, Buenos Aires: Emecé, 1976

Los libros y su misión en la liberación e integración de la América Latina, Buenos Aires: Embajada de Venezuela, 1978

Apologías y rechazos, Barcelona: Seix Barral, 1979

Cuatro hombres de pueblo, illustrated by Antonio Berni, Buenos Aires: La Ciudad, 1979

La robotización del hombre y otras páginas de ficción y reflexión, Buenos Aires: Centro Editor del América Latina, 1981

L'Écrivain et la catastrophe, Paris, Seuil, 1986; augmented edition, as *The Writer in the Catastrophe of Our Time*, translated by Asa Zatz, Tulsa, Oklahoma: Council Oak Books, 1990

Compilations and Anthologies

Obras de ficción, Buenos Aires: Losada, 1966

Obras: ensayos, Buenos Aires: Losada, 1970

Narrativa completa, Barcelona: Seix Barral, 1982

Páginas de Ernesto Sábato, Buenos Aires: Celtia, 1983

Lo mejor de Ernesto Sábato, Barcelona: Seix Barral, 1989

Further Reading

Callan, Richard J., "Sábato's Fiction: a Jungian Interpretation," *Bulletin of Hispanic Studies*, vol. 51 (1974)

Dellepiane, Ángela B., *Ernesto Sábato. El hombre y su obra. (Ensayo de interpretación y análisis literario)*, New York: Las Américas, 1968

Giacoman, Helmy F., *Homenaje a Ernesto Sábato. Variaciones interpretativas en torno a su obra*, New York: Anaya/Las Américas, 1973

Martínez, Z. Nelly, *Ernesto Sábato*, Buenos Aires: Sudamericana, 1974

Oberhelman, Harley Dean, *Ernesto Sábato*, Boston: Twayne, 1970

Urbina, Nicasio, *La significación del género. Estudio semiótico de las novelas y ensayos de Ernesto Sábato*, Miami: Universal, 1992

Wainerman, Luis, *Sábato y el misterio de los ciegos*, Buenos Aires: Losada, 1971

Bibliographies

Urbina, Nicasio, "Bibliografía crítica completa de Ernesto Sábato," *Revista de Crítica Literaria Latinoamericana*, vol. 14/27 (1988) [includes thematic index]

Interviews

Entre la letra y la sangre: conversaciones con Carlos Catania, Barcelona: Seix Barral, 1989

Special Issues of Journals

Cuadernos Hispanoamericanos, vol. 131/391–93 (1983)

Anthropos, Revista de Documentación Científica de la Cultura, Barcelona, 55–56 (1985)

Revista Iberoamericana, vol. 58/158 (1992)

Abaddón, el exterminador

Novel by Ernesto Sábato

Sábato's third novel carries still further the investigation of his own psyche, first essayed in *El túnel* (*The Tunnel*) and then expanded in *Sobre héroes y tumbas* (*On Heroes and Tombs*). In the first novel the author remained wholly invisible behind the narrator, Juan Pablo Castel, and in the second Bruno serves as focus, gathering and reflecting on material drawn from various sources, but in *Abaddón, el exterminador*, Sábato himself (using the unaccented Sabato as his name) plays a role as one character among others. The complexities of *Sobre héroes y tumbas* are greatly increased, though at bottom the problem remains the same, along lines predictable from *El escritor y sus fantasmas* [The Writer and His Ghosts].

The initial challenge, presented in three short chapters, is for Bruno Bassan to make a novel, in Sabato's manner, but without his collaboration, out of three disparate and apparently unconnected events: an alcoholic's vision of a great dragon in the night sky, Marcelo Carranza's death under torture at the hands of security police and Nacho Izaguirre's surveillance of his sister Agustina. As the novel progresses, the reader learns that both Marcelo and Nacho were known to Sabato, while *el loco* Barragán's apocalyptic vision reflects Sabato's own.

As in *Sobre héroes y tumbas*, Bruno receives and comments on confidences made to him, now including those by Sabato himself, and from time to time he witnesses actions or discussions of importance for the development of the argument. Other characters, such as Quique or Carlucho, provide vital social background and commentary, but Sabato himself, as writer, philosopher, politically engaged person or simple human being remains at the heart of the novel. Scattered over more than a hundred sections of varying length is an account of Sabato's psychological development, though not in chronological order. Reconstructed from the evidence presented, Sabato's sexual experience begins with a pubertal infatuation with Maria Etchebarne, his schoolteacher, which ends abruptly when he finds her blinded by acid thrown in her face. In 1927, at the age of sixteen, he encounters María de la Soledad, of mysterious parentage and seemingly ageless, though of his own age – the characteristic of the *anima*. Following her through dark passages leading from a house in the Calle de Arcos, he finds himself in a room beneath the Church of the Immaculate Conception in Belgrano and there, under the direction of the enigmatic R., receives his sexual initiation with her; Soledad's genitalia take the form of a single eye, recalling the eye which Fernando was forced to penetrate in the "Informe sobre ciegos." This episode is withheld until near the end of the novel, where it becomes an explanation of all that has subsequently transpired in Sabato's life as narrated so far; R. has by then already been established as Sabato's dark side or

Jungian shadow. While Sabato was working as a physicist in Paris in 1938, R. had manifested himself, causing the separation of Sabato from his wife M. (Matilde, in real life) and their young son. Sabato had also undergone there an extracorporeal experience in which one self had followed a woman with eyes like María Etchebarne's to her apartment, where he found her with her hands covering her face, while another self had been engaged in routine activities. One of Sabato's last actions in the novel is to revisit the house in the Calle de Arcos, now near-ruined, and follow the tunnel; what he finds there is not disclosed, but when he emerges and returns to his home, he finds his other self seated at his desk, weeping.

R. does not return until about 1972, when his purpose is to urge a reluctant Sabato to renew his writing on the Sect, using a new set of characters, however closely they may follow the pattern of *Sobre héroes y tumbas*. Thus Sabato becomes involved with Agustina, the sister of Nacho, whom Sabato has known since he was a small boy in Carlucho's kiosk some ten years earlier. The relationship with Agustina is not given prominence, but her behaviour clearly resembles Alejandra's, with Sabato as an elderly Martín. Agustina and Nacho are tormented by their incestuous relationship, made worse by his jealousy of both Sabato and Pérez Nassif, her employer; the pattern resembles the Alejandra-Fernando-Molinari triangle of *Sobre héroes y tumbas*, though with ages and dispositions redistributed. Nacho's observation of Agustina with Pérez Nassif at the end of the novel is one of the three items presented for Bruno's consideration.

Sabato's friendship with the Carranza family and their circle provide a means of surveying Argentine social, cultural and political life. Marcelo Carranza, the son of the house, is engaged in subversive activities and has given shelter to a former comrade of Che Guevara, whose death is recounted at some length, with corroboration and/or contrasting material drawn from military documents. Sabato's contribution to the cause takes the form of discussing the role of literature in the service of revolution in seminars and in private conversation. Marcelo's detention and interrogation under torture bring about his death, the second of the three starting-points; his body is disposed of in a weighted sack tipped into the river.

The callous treatment of Marcelo's corpse and the brutality of his torture, foreshadowed in the novel by the written statement of a social worker who had survived, is merely an extreme expression of the sick society documented in Nacho's collection of newspaper cuttings. These range from letters to the editor on the twists in the plot of soap operas, and other similar trivia, to murder, pollution of the environment, Vietnam atrocities and Hiroshima. Others offer a response: Helder Camara attacks torture, Linus Pauling condemns nuclear testing. Similar matters are raised in dialogue throughout the novel, creating an atmosphere of pervasive evil. Sabato himself was forced by R. in 1938 to admit to blinding sparrows as a schoolboy in Rojas – an act attributed to Fernando in *Sobre héroes y tumbas* – though he insists that it was done under the dominating influence of R. In the same year he came into contact with Molinelli, whose interest in alchemy and the occult have led him to the conclusion that science is leading the world into danger in the pursuit of power; this was one of Sabato's motives for abandoning nuclear physics.

The European political crises of 1938 are not mentioned, but the development of Nazism became a cause for concern to Sabato some ten years later, when he met the mysterious Schneider, who asked him about the significance of Allende's blindness in *El túnel*. His suspicions were again aroused in 1962 when Schneider reappeared and asked about Fernando and the "Informe sobre Ciegos" in *Sobre héroes y tumbas*, leading Sabato to investigate Schneider's background and possible connections with Nazi Germany and its ideology. In 1972, when Sabato's need to write is growing, the possibility that Schneider may have reappeared alarms him. Among other extremist ideas which worry Sabato come the doctrines of Dr Alberto J. Gandulfo, according to whom Satan won the great battle in the heavens and in the guise of Jehovah has ruled the world ever since, inflicting sadistic punishment and promoting evil at every opportunity. Sabato concurs, regretting that the message is devalued by the messenger, and adding that there have always been those ready to denounce the deception, reveal the truth, and proclaim the Sect of the Blind as Satan's active agents; Hiroshima and Vietnam were the work of Satan, as no truly good, all-powerful God could permit such evil. The dragon spread across the heavens seen by the drunken Barragán, the third of Bruno's starting-points, announces the imminence of the final battle – Armageddon, though Sabato avoids the word. There is no vision of what may follow the great destruction.

Evil on a cosmic scale dominates human life at all levels; nations seek to destroy nations, societies are torn apart by warring factions, relationships crumble as partners fight for dominance. To all these things Sabato bears witness as a character subject to the same forces as those around him in this fiction. From within his role of character he advocates exploration of the individual psyche as a path to understanding human society as a whole – Dostoevsky and Kafka have far more to offer to the revolutionary cause than has Soviet social realism. It is here that Bruno has a role to play in the fiction. In *Sobre héroes y tumbas* Bruno was in possession of certain facts from the past, observed a few actions in the present and received Martín's testimony. In *Abaddón, el exterminador*, Bruno observes some of the action and receives in confidence Sabato's own accounts of events, with no distinction between the experiences of the fictional character and those of the author of the novel. Bruno, like R., is of Sabato's age; the death of Bruno's father in the fictional Capitán Olmos recreates the death of Ernesto Sabato's father in Rojas. Like the character, Bruno has problems with writing, amounting to acute writer's block. The writer's public self is represented by Sabato/S., holding strong opinions on politics and literature, as befits an active mind, but the inner Sabato is seen in Sabato/R., subject to powers operating in the subconscious. Sight, scientific observation and reason are the enemies of the powers of darkness, capable of revealing their agents and their works. The imagery of blindness and blinding is associated with the dark side of the psyche, the shadow, and with evil, but also with the (pro)creative sexual act, here linked specifically with one manifestation of the *anima*, Soledad, the quest for whom in the return to the Calle de Arcos ends in failure, signalled in the weeping of the other self.

RON KEIGHTLEY

Editions

First edition: *Abaddón, el exterminador*, Buenos Aires: Sudamericana, 1974

Translation: *The Angel of Darkness*, by Andrew Hurley, New York: Ballantine, 1991; London: Jonathan Cape, 1992

Further Reading

Bacarisse, Salvador, "*Abaddón, el exterminador*: Sábato's Gnostic Eschatology," in *Contemporary Latin American Fiction*, edited by Bacarisse, Edinburgh: Scottish Academic Press, 1980

Barrera López, Trinidad, *La estructura de "Abaddón, el exterminador*," Seville: Escuela de Estudios Hispano-Americanos, 1982

Montenegro, Nivia, "The Structural and Thematic Elements in *Abaddón, el exterminador* (Abbadon the Exterminator)," *Latin American Literary Review*, vol. 12 (1978)

Montiel, Luis, "Ernesto Sábato: ojos para lo sagrado," *Revista Iberoamericana*, vol. 53/141 (1987)

Roberts, Gemma, *Análisis existencial de "Abaddón, el exterminador" de Ernesto Sábato*, Boulder, Colorado: Society of Spanish and Spanish-American Studies, 1990

El túnel

Novel by Ernesto Sábato

Like Albert Camus's *L'Étranger*, 1942 (*The Outsider*) and Camilo José Cela's *La familia de Pascual Duarte*, 1942 (*Pascual Duarte's Family*), *El túnel* takes the form of the confession of a condemned murderer, but with important differences: Meursault first tells a plain tale of the circumstances in which he killed another man and then reports how it is refashioned by opposing advocates in court; Pascual, though showing some concern about the conditions under which he writes, offers an ostensibly artless account of his life of violence up to the killing of his mother, revealing more of himself than he calculates in the process; Juan Pablo Castel takes for granted the notoriety of his crime, and constantly interrupts his story to digress on minor details or to analyse minutely his thought processes, both at the time of writing and throughout the period during which his victim, María Iribarne, dominated his life.

The story as Castel tells it is simple. In the Argentine spring of 1946, an exhibition of his paintings includes a work entitled "Maternidad" (Motherhood) which contains an inset panel, set upper left, a *ventanita* or small window through which can be seen a woman gazing out to sea. One visitor, later revealed as María Iribarne, spends some time contemplating this picture, causing Castel to believe that she has understood it. Some agonising months of searching for her pass before a chance encounter enables him to ask her about the painting. His clumsiness spoils their first brief exchange, but her hurried and apologetic declaration when she catches up with him restores his hope. He now knows how to find her again, and soon afterwards he waylays her and initiates a dialogue on the meaning of the painting. Before their next meeting, María contrives his encounter with her blind husband, Allende, while she is away at Hunter's ranch. While the simple message Allende hands to him excites Castel's passion, the very existence of Allende, together with Hunter's reputation, and

María's devious actions, arouse in him powerful feelings of jealousy. A letter from María commenting on "Maternidad" in terms of her own experience gives him new hope, and they embark upon a sexual relationship, constantly overshadowed by his obsessive jealousy. His constant probing leads eventually to her walking out. Temporarily reconciled through letters, Castel visits Hunter's ranch, achieving a brief happiness there when María re-enacts the *ventanita* scene of "Maternidad," but with Castel inserted. Overcome with new doubts and suspicion, Castel leaves the following morning. Further attempts to see María come to nothing. Finally, driven by despair, and after destroying "Maternidad," Castel goes back to the ranch, and spies on María and Hunter until he is convinced they are lovers. Forcing his way into the house, he kills María, repeatedly stabbing her in the belly. On returning to Buenos Aires, he tells Allende what he has done, only to be told he is a fool. In the short final chapter, Castel contemplates his situation in an asylum for the criminally insane.

All other characters can only be known through what Castel chooses to report of them, which in practice is very little; more than half of the narrative is concerned with Castel's own thoughts, feelings and actions, and his analyses of situations. Outside the long central episode at Hunter's ranch, there are reports of only half-a-dozen face-to-face dialogues between Castel and María, and a handful of communications by telephone. From these data one can construct a rough account of María Iribarne's past and present: a relationship in adolescence with a certain Juan (with resemblances to Alejandra and Marcos in *Sobre héroes y tumbas*), virtually ignored by Castel; a more recent affair with a man named Richard; marriage to Allende; and the suspected liaison with Hunter which Castel believes he has confirmed during his vigil on the night of her death. In her words, both spoken and written, as reported by Castel, María shows herself fully aware of the danger she represents, but he misreads her attempts to discourage him.

Juan Pablo Castel's failure to comprehend María Iribarne's behaviour arises from his deeply flawed, egocentric worldview. He applies what he believes to be rigorous logical reasoning to events and circumstances without recognising the possibility that human fallibility could apply to himself, and that his premises may be false. When pure chance brings about the desired outcome of his "reasoning," in the form of the first encounter with María Iribarne, he is at a loss to know what to say to her. His "deductions" regarding her behaviour are purely intuitive, as when he accuses her of smiling at him in the darkness, or based on false logic, as when he believes that she only simulates pleasure in lovemaking because he detects in a prostitute a reaction which he finds similar María's. These difficulties in establishing a true relationship are a product of Juan Pablo Castel's fundamentally introspective solitude. We are informed from time to time of his aversion to critics, to art galleries, etc., but he particularly hates, or fears, societies, clubs or any other sort of group with some common interest. He prefers to remain aloof, setting his own norms and conditions.

The inset *ventanita* in "Maternidad" came to Castel unbidden and is out of keeping with his usual excessively formal, architectural style. He was instinctively drawn to María when he first saw her studying "Maternidad;" she appeared to empathise with the *ventanita*, and he swiftly concludes that she alone can provide the explanations he seeks; she seems ageless, already known to him, though she warns him that she will cause him much suffering. In short, María exhibits the characteristics of a Jungian *anima*. Once he has witnessed her reaction, he paints inspired by her, in a new, passionate style, quite distinct from his former manner. Feelings and emotions hitherto constrained or repressed break out on his canvases; what once were monuments and temples are now shattered ruins, as his passions erupt. Recognition of the *anima* has opened the way to the unconscious, the shadow or dark side of his psyche, but when María betrays his trust, through her relationship with Hunter, he is still not ready to achieve a new equilibrium and pass from the matriarchal stage to maturity by accepting her other archetypal characteristics. The *ventanita* is therefore the first thing he destroys, before destroying María Iribarne herself; the desperate appeal for understanding has failed. In the final chapter he tells us that he continues to paint, sure that his work is beyond the comprehension of the medical officers of the asylum. He himself has destroyed the only person capable of understanding his work, the bridge between external reality and the dark world of the creative forces within him.

As narrator, Castel declares that he will be satisfied if even one reader understands him. Through painting he had gained just such an audience, but the resulting strain on his psyche proved too great to bear. María Iribarne's human failings,

aspects of behaviour which remain alien to Castel, do not provide the control over the unconscious he needs and so he relapses into his inner world, still unable to communicate through his art.

RON KEIGHTLEY

Editions

First edition: *El túnel*, Buenos Aires: Sur, 1948
Critical editions: *El túnel*, edited by Ángel Leiva, Madrid: Cátedra, 1976; *El túnel*, edited by Peter Standish, London: Harrap, 1980 [introduction and notes in English]
Translation: *The Tunnel*, by Margaret Sayers Peden, New York: Ballantine, and London: Jonathan Cape, 1988

Further Reading

Baker, Armand, "Psychic Integration and the Search for Meaning in Sábato's *El túnel*," *Hispanic Journal*, vol. 5/2 (1984)
González-del-Valle, Luis T. and Catherine Nickel, "Contemporary Poets to the Rescue: the Enigmatic Narrator in Sabato's *El túnel*," *Rocky Mountain Review*, vol. 40/1–2 (1986)
Köhler, R., "Aproximación a *El túnel* de Ernesto Sábato," *Ibero* 2 (1969)
Nelson, William, "Sábato's *El túnel* and the Existential Novel," *Modern Fiction Studies*, vol. 32/3 (1986)
Urbina, Nicasio, "Código narrativo en *El túnel* de Sábato: implicaciones semióticas," *Semiosis: Seminario de Semiótica, Teoría, Análisis* 21 (1988)

Juan José Saer 1937–

Argentine prose writer and poet

In Juan José Saer's 1983 novel *El entenado* (*The Witness*), the narrator, a Spanish cabin boy, who has been cast ashore on the banks of a great South American river, reports that the local Indians hold that a certain stretch of beach on the shore of that river is the centre of the universe. Elsewhere in the book he reports their using a word for that place, Colastiné. Saer is here revealing in condensed form the secret heart of his fictional universe, centred on Colastiné, a suburb where Saer once lived in the city of Santa Fe (in Santa Fe province in the littoral region of Argentina), the setting of most of his fiction. Unlike Faulkner or Onetti, who stake exclusive claims to a territory that is theirs by virtue of their having invented it (however closely based on places they knew), Saer's claim to Santa Fe results from the intensity with which his characters live in the place. Reading Saer's work one hears the cabin boy's words echo in the dialogue that animates a twenty-one block walk through Santa Fe in *Glosa*, 1986 [Gloss]; in the flooding of the riverbank in "A medio borrar" [Half-Erased], from the short story collection *La mayor*, 1976 [Dis/Misproportions]; in the Italian's discovery of the Argentine plains in *La ocasión*, 1988 (*The Event*), even in the ritualistic barbecue scenes in

El limonero real, 1974 [The Royal Lemon Tree]. A work of an unusual degree of coherence and cohesiveness, Saer's novels and stories often use the same characters (Tomatis, Wenceslao, el Ladeado, el Gato and others) and almost always the same setting.

Critics often cite Borges as the strongest influence on Saer; although Borges is clearly one of Saer's literary heroes, the latter's fidelity to place and to a group of fictional characters is much more reminiscent of Faulkner or Onetti than it is of Borges. Perhaps it would be more accurate to say that Borges saves Saer from his early regionalism, and allows his later work to have a metafictional dimension that it might not have had otherwise. Nevertheless, it was in the early "regionalist" works that Saer invented the characters who people most of his later fiction, so his relation to the perennial debates about regionalism and universalism is unusually complicated.

Some of Saer's work is strongly (some would say tendentiously or heavily) marked by the objectivist tradition of the French new novel, notably in *El limonero real* and *Nadie, nada, nunca*, 1980 (*Nobody, Nothing, Never*). Some of his other late fiction almost includes the telling of stories, though in most cases the telling of the story turns out ultimately to be the revelation that there is no story to tell. Thus, in *El entenado*, to give an example of a novel that comes close to having a plot, the narration of events halts about halfway through the book, ceding to a philosophical meditation on the meaning of the life of the now-destroyed Indian tribe. This meditation is defined as an exercise in failure: the cabin boy, now grown old, realizes that when he was among the Indians he failed to understand what he saw around him, and that those who might have been his informants are now all dead. His task becomes, then, a more urgent work of memory and analysis, precisely because his testimony is unique, though faulty.

Saer moved to France in 1968 and his literature is only obliquely related to the literature of political commitment and denunciation of the military dictatorships of the late 1960s and (better known outside Argentina) of 1976–83. In his essay on the River Plate, *El río sin orillas*, 1991 [The River without Banks], he discusses Perón and the military dictators at some length, but far more interesting are the tantalizing patterns of reference in his fiction. *El entenado*, for instance, anticipates the plethora of works on the "discovery of the New World" or the "Encounter" that appeared around 1992; Saer's novel is a sorrowful and angry text about genocide, and yet its urgency has to do with more recent genocide. David Viñas writes in *Indios, ejército y fronteras*, 1982 [Indians, Army and Frontiers], that the Indians killed in the "Conquest of the Desert" were "the disappeared of 1879," and Saer's novel quietly recalls the more recent genocide with such details as the bodies floating in the river. Similarly, much of the power of *Glosa* derives from the ironic contrast between the innocent intellectualism of the two main characters, who do not know what the reader knows, that they are to be swallowed up in the catastrophies of the 1970s in Argentina.

Little of Saer's work is available yet in English, the exceptions being *El entenado*, *Nadie, nada, nunca* and *La ocasión*. Widely considered the greatest of the living writers in Argentina, Saer deserves our attention. A master stylist, Saer reflects on memory and language in terms as profound as any of our contemporaries. The narrator of *El entenado*, for instance, writes at the beginning of his account: "Lo desconocido es una abstracción; lo conocido, un desierto; pero lo conocido a medias, lo vislumbrado, es el lugar perfecto para hacer ondular deseo y alucinación" (The unknown is an abstraction, the known, a desert; but the half-known, what is only glimpsed, is the perfect place for the movements of desire and hallucination), words that are echoed at the close of the same novel when the narrator states: "sabemos únicamente lo que condesciende a mostrarse" (we only know what condescends to reveal itself). Saer's work seduces the imagination with glimpses into what cannot be fully revealed or fully known.

DANIEL BALDERSTON

Biography

Born in Serodino, in the province of Santa Fe, Argentina, 28 June 1937. Parents were Syrian immigrants. Moved to the city of Santa Fe in 1949. Studied philosophy and law. Teacher at the Santa Fe Cinematographic Institute, Colastiné Norte, 1962, where he also wrote scripts for some short films. Settled in Paris in 1968. Taught literature at the University of Haute Bretagne, Rennes, and later at Besançon. Currently lives in Paris. Awarded Nadal Prize, 1987 for *La ocasión*.

Selected Works

Short Fiction
En la zona, 1957–1960, Santa Fe, Argentina: Castellví, 1960
Palo y hueso, Buenos Aires: Camarga Junior, 1965
Unidad de lugar, Buenos Aires: Galerna, 1967
Cicatrices, Buenos Aires: Sudamericana, 1969
La mayor, Barcelona: Planeta, 1976

Novels
Responso, Buenos Aires: Jorge Álvarez, 1964
La vuelta completa, Rosario: Biblioteca Popular Constancio C. Vigil, 1966
El limonero real, Buenos Aires: Planeta, 1974
Nadie, nada, nunca, Mexico City: Siglo XXI, 1980; as *Nobody, Nothing, Never*, translated by Helen Lane, London and New York: Serpent's Tail, 1993
El entenado, Mexico City: Folios, 1983; as *The Witness*, translated by Margaret Jull Costa, London and New York: Serpent's Tail, 1990
Glosa, Buenos Aires: Alianza, 1986
La ocasión, Barcelona: Destino, 1988; as *The Event*, translated by Helen Lane, London and New York: Serpent's Tail, 1995
Lo imborrable, Buenos Aires: Alianza, 1993
La pesquisa, Buenos Aires: Seix Barral, 1994

Poetry
El arte de narrar (poemas 1960–1975), Caracas: Fundarte, 1977

Other Writings
Juan José Saer por Juan José Saer, Buenos Aires: Celtia, 1986 [Includes a variety of writings by Saer himself, together with an extensive essay on his work by María Teresa Gramuglio]
Una literatura sin atributos, Santa Fe, Argentina: Universidad Nacional del Litoral, 1986
Por un relato futuro: diálogo, Santa Fe, Argentina: Centro de Publicaciones, Universidad Nacional del Litoral, 1990 [Conversation with the Argentine author, Ricardo Piglia]
El río sin orillas: tratado imaginario, Madrid: Alianza, 1991

Compilations and Anthologies
Narraciones, 2 vols, Buenos Aires: Centro Editor de América Latina, 1983

Further Reading

Corbatta, Jorgelina, "*En la zona*: germen de la praxis poética de Juan José Saer," *Revista Iberoamericana* 155–56 (1991)
Jitrik, Noé, "Entre el corte y la continuidad. Hacia una escritura crítica," *Revista Iberoamericana* 102–03 (January–June 1978)
Prieto, Adolfo, "Los años sesenta," *Revista Iberoamericana* 125 (October–December 1983)
Rama, Ángel, "Los contestatarios del poder," prologue to the anthology *Novísimos narradores hispanoamericanos en Marcha*, Mexico City: Marcha, 1981
Solotorevsky, Myrna, *La relación mundo-escritura en textos de Reinaldo Arenas, Juan José Saer y Juan Carlos Martínez*, Gaithersburg, Maryland: Hispamérica, 1993 [Chapter on Saer]
Stern, Mirta, "Juan José Saer: construcción y teoría de la ficción narrativa," *Hispamérica*, vol. 13/37 (1984)

Interviews
"Juan José Saer: Interviewed by Claudio Canaparo," *Journal of Latin American Cultural Studies*, vol. 4/1 (1995)

Gustavo Sainz 1940–

Mexican novelist

Along with José Agustín, Gustavo Sainz is considered a founder of the Mexican narrative movement known as *la Onda* (New Wave) whose principal themes highlight the problems of the urban middle-class in Mexico City. Sainz's first novel, *Gazapo*, 1965, tells the story of a young man, Menelao, who has great difficulty in separating himself economically and emotionally from his family. The story also recounts Menelao's relationship with his girlfriend Gisela, revealed in the narrative through an erotic discourse. Using the lives of Menelao and Gisela the author portrays the urban environment of young people and the many problems they encounter in Mexico City. Structurally, Sainz employs the tape recorder as a narrative device. In this way he alters the reader's sense of time and space in order to present the story from different points of view.

Obsesivos días circulares, 1969 [Obsessive Circular Days] focuses on two characters. Terencio, the principal narrator, works as a night watchman in a private high school. The school is owned by a gangster, Papá la Oca. The novel is characterized by political overtones since it also narrates the crimes and killings associated with Papá la Oca. This work is divided into four parts. The first centers on the life of a professional assassin employed by Papá la Oca, Sarro, and his lover, Yin. The second part describes Terencio's vacations in Acapulco where he unexpectedly encounters his ex-wife Leticia. In this section the reader is informed of this previous relationship through Terencio's narration of his sexual fantasies and desires for his wife. The third part focuses on a voyeuristic character, La Cripta, who also works for Terencio's boss. This section ends and the fourth part begins when Terencio leaves for Acapulco to perform a secret mission ordered by Papá la Oca. Convinced that Papá la Ocá wants to kill him, Terencio mitigates his fear of dying by reconstructing the ending of classic Mexican novels he has read, such as Carlos Fuentes's *La región más transparente* (*Where the Air is Clear*) and Juan Rulfo's *Pedro Páramo*.

Sainz's third novel, *La princesa del Palacio de Hierro*, 1974 (*The Princess of the Iron Palace*), narrates the life of an anonymous, lower-middle-class woman who works at the Iron Palace, a Mexican department store. This nameless character typifies the Mexican middle class and the economic problems that it confronted in the 1960s and 1970s. A principal theme treated in the novel is the cultural dichotomy between different generations. Here, the older generation is identified by nationalistic icons (Agustín Lara) while the younger is associated with elements of urban culture (the use of drugs, the sexual revolution). The novel is distinguished by Sainz's use of popular language which symbolizes this new, urban and young middle class. The setting of the novel, Mexico City, is presented as a destructive, sometimes deadly, labyrinth. These cultural conflicts and social themes symbolize the economic and social contractions of the Mexican capital, a city undergoing a process of modernization and unable to meet the demands of its growing population.

Compadre Lobo, 1977 [Godfather Lobo] recounts the life of Lobo, a young man who aspires to be a painter. A typical Bildungsroman, the protagonist/narrator takes the reader through the different stages of his life as he struggles to achieve artistic and literary recognition. The action of the story primarily takes place at night and the setting is a recreation of the working-class neighborhoods in which the protagonist was raised. Lobo's use of popular language contrasts sharply with the official cultural discourse which dominates in his artistic world. The manner in which Sainz ends this novel marks an important moment in his narrative. It is the first time in which he uses a contemporary historical event, the silent protest of 1968 pre-dating the Tlatelolco massacre, to contextualize his narrative. It is significant since literary critics had characterized his narrative as a-historical.

The change towards a historical narrative is confirmed with *Fantasmas aztecas*, 1982 [Aztec Phantoms]. The setting and the action of the novel center on the excavation of the Templo Mayor in Mexico City. As the narrator/novelist rides around the city in a taxi, he guides the reader on an historical journey through Mexican history. He does this in order to present an interpretation of his generation and times as a symbolic reenactment of Aztec society and age. The narrative structure recreates this chronological and cultural juxtaposition by intertwining the past, present and future.

In *Paseo en trapecio*, 1985 [Trapezoid Ride], the nameless protagonist and narrator travels from New Mexico to Mexico City. On his arrival in his native city he experiences ambivalent feelings which oscillate between antagonism and nostalgia, inhospitality and melancholy, hatred and love. The protagonist's emotions are an expression of his psychological and physical displacement which affects his sense of identity. This emptiness and displacement represents both a psychological vacuum as well as the physically-exiled status of the narrator. Two other motifs are important in this novel. First, Sainz portrays the city as an allegorical circus in order to criticize Mexican socio-political and cultural institutions. Second, the novel eulogizes Mexican intellectuals who are important to Sainz's literary generation, figures such as Agustín Yánez, José Revueltas and Parménedis García Saldaña.

The novel *Muchacho en llamas*, 1988 [A Young Man in Flames] is set in Mexico City during the early 1960s and narrates a creative period in the life of Sofocles, a young writer. While the protagonist reflects on the creative process itself, transforming the novel into a metatext, he also engages the reader in the actual writing of his first piece of fiction. Sofocles's novel is the story of his adventures during approximately a year's span in Mexico City. Thus, his narrative is a Bildungsroman which also provides a cultural testimony of the early years of an important decade in Mexican history. In this way the protagonist's milieu supplies a palimpsest-like mosaic filled with historical and cultural references which infuse both the young man's novel and *Muchacho en llamas*. The autobiographical relationship between the protagonist and Sainz is very important.

The publication of *A la salud de la serpiente*, 1991 [A Toast to the Serpent's Health] marks an important moment in the evolution of Sainz's fiction. Although *Compadre Lobo* used a student-led political protest as a chronological reference to mark the novel's end, another, the 1968 Tlatelolco massacre, now serves as the principal theme of this historical narrative. Two stories are told. The first is the autobiography of a young intellectual participating in the University of Iowa International Writer's Workshop. The writer experiences this significant event in Mexican history only at a distance and through letters sent by friends living in Mexico, Latin America and Europe. The second story is a more general "new" chronicle which tells of the massacre, an event of primary significance in understanding that particularly turbulent time as well as contemporary Mexican socio-political and cultural realities.

Retablo de inmoderaciones y heresiarcas, 1992 [Altarpiece of Immoderations and Heresies] is a Neobaroque narrative which novelistically and typographically recreates a Baroque *retablo*. Set in colonial Mexico, the novella narrates the struggles of a young man, accused of being a heretic, who is incarcerated by the Inquisition. This masterful narrative incorporates a number of discourses: poetic and historical, inquisitorial and religious, mystic and erotic. The novella examines the literary and cultural heritage of New Spain and begins with three epigraphs that foreground its socio-political theme: creole ideology, identity and consciousness. Sainz's work scrutinizes the contradictions of the colonial system: the demands of creoles for representation in their government; the existence of two different economic and educational systems; the depiction of corruption in the Church; and the identification of a new *mestizaje*.

SALVADOR C. FERNÁNDEZ

Biography
Born in Mexico City, 13 July 1940. Attended the Universidad Nacional Autónoma de México (UNAM), and the Colegio de México. Editor of *El Calendario de Ramón López Velarde*, the supplement *La Semana de Bellas Artes*, *Siete* magazine. Contributor to numerous newspapers and scriptwriter for radio and television. Attended the International Writing Program, University of Iowa, Iowa City, 1968. Director of the literature section, Instituto Nacional de Bellas Artes, Mexico City. Professor of modern and classical languages, University of New Mexico, Albuquerque, 1981–90; Visiting Professor at the University of Northern Illinois, Dekalb and Washington University, St Louis; Professor, Indiana University, Bloomington. Awarded the Xavier Villaurrutia Prize, 1974 for *La princesa del Palacio de Hierro*; Guggenheim Fellowship, 1976; Tinker Fellowship, 1980.

Selected Works

Novels
Gazapo, Mexico City: Joaquín Mortiz, 1965; as *Gazapo*, translated by Hardie St Martin, New York: Farrar Straus and Giroux, 1968

Obsesivos días circulares, Mexico City: Joaquín Mortiz, 1969
La princesa del Palacio de Hierro, Mexico City: Joaquín Mortiz, 1974; as *The Princess of the Iron Palace*, translated by Andrew Hurley, New York: Grove Press, 1987
Compadre Lobo, Mexico City: Grijalbo, 1977
Fantasmas aztecas: un pre-texto, Mexico City: Grijalbo, 1982
Paseo en trapecio, Mexico City: Edivisión, 1985
Muchacho en llamas, Mexico City: Grijalbo, 1988
A la salud de la serpiente, Mexico City: Grijalbo, 1991
Retablo de inmoderaciones y heresiarcas, Mexico City: Joaquín Mortiz, 1992
La muchacha que tenía la culpa de todo, Monterrey: Castillo, 1995
Salto de tigre blanco, Mexico City: Joaquín Mortiz, 1996

Other Writings
Gustavo Sainz, Mexico City: Empresas, 1966 [autobiography]

Compilations and Anthologies
Ojalá te mueras y otras novelas clandestinas mexicanas, Barcelona: Océano, 1982

Further Reading
Brushwood, John S., "Sobre el referente y la transformación narrativa de las novelas de Carlos Fuentes y Gustavo Sainz," *Revista Iberoamericana*, vol. 47/116–17 (1981)
Cortínez, Veronica, "La conquista de una tradición: *Gazapo* como oposición y analogía de *Las buenas conciencias*," *Confluencia*, vol. 7/1 (1991)
DiAntonio, Robert, "The Actualization of Reader Consciousness in Gustavo Sainz's *La princesa del Palacio de Hierro*," *Confluencia*, vol. 4/1 (1988)
Domínguez Colavita, Federica, "*Gazapo* de Gustavo Sainz: tema y estructura," *Revista/Review Interamericana*, vol 10/2 (1980)
Filer, Malva E., "La ciudad y el tiempo mexicano en la obra de Gustavo Sainz," *Hispámerica*, vol. 13/39 (1984)
Hancock, Joel, "Gustavo Sainz's *Compadre Lobo*: a dissection of the Creative Impulse," *Revista Canadiense de Estudios Hispánicos*, vol. 7/2 (1983)
____ "Re-Defining Autobiography: Gustavo Sainz's *A la salud de la serpiente*," *Revista de Estudios Hispánicos*, vol. 29/1 (January 1995)
Jones, Julie, "The Dynamics of the City: Gustavo Sainz's *La princesa de Palacio de Hierro*," *Chasqui*, vol. 12/1 (1982)
Muller, Inke, "*Obsesivos días circulares* de Gustavo Sainz: análisis de la situación narrativa," *Literatura Mexicana*, vol. 2/2 (1991)
Ruffinelli, Jorge, "*Compadre Lobo* de Gustavo Sainz: un ejercicio de autobiografía," *Hispamérica*, vol. 10/29 (1981)
Sefamí, Jacobo, "Vertiginosidad del fuego: *Muchacho en llamas* de Gustavo Sainz," *Revista Canadiense de Estudios Hispánicos*, vol. 15/1 (1990)
Williams, Raymond L., "The Reader and the Recent Novels of Gustavo Sainz," *Hispania*, vol. 65/3 (1982)

Salarrué 1899–1975

Salvadorean prose writer, poet and painter

The work of Salvador Salazar Arrué, who published under the name of Salarrué, is exceptional in the context of a regional literature that historically has been ignored by the more cosmopolitan centers of culture in Latin America. He is one of the few Central American writers who has been recognized to the extent of being mentioned in many of the classic histories of Latin American literature as well as being included in numerous anthologies of the Latin American short story. His acknowledged mastery of the short story is indeed justified. What stands to be corrected, however, is the almost exclusive identification of Salarrué with his collection of stories about Salvadorean campesinos, *Cuentos de barro* [Clay Stories]. While these stories do figure significantly in the development of *costumbrismo* in Central America, and are justifiably praised for their realistic and compassionate portrayal of the indigenous population of El Salvador, they are only one of the many literary accomplishments of this highly original and prolific Salvadorean writer and artist.

It would be impossible to describe or deeply comprehend the work of Salarrué without reference to theosophy, an eclectic system of belief that strives for a synthesis, through reason and intuition, of the essential truths of religion, science and philosophy, with an ethics of universal brotherhood and social responsibility. Among the esoteric principles of theosophy are the belief in astral spheres within which one moves by desire and will, and the essential unity of all life. Salarrué, like many other writers, educators and politicians of Central America during the late 19th and early 20th centuries, was drawn to this vision of a universe guided by the dynamic interplay of the seemingly contradictory and opposing forces of masculine and feminine, yin and yang, light and dark, good and evil. He remained faithful throughout his life to his quest for an ever more profound comprehension of the nature of the universe. This spiritual quest permeates his entire *oeuvre*, both his writing and his painting, at times explicitly, at times as an implicit world view.

In his first published work, a short novel based on the legend of the Black Christ, he delves into a theme that continued to intrigue him until the end of his long and productive life in 1975: the nature of good and evil. In *El cristo negro*, 1926 [The Black Christ] he reverses the expected manifestations of good and evil to lead the reader to question accepted notions of goodness and saintliness. In later collections of short stories he returns to this theme, positing evil as an attribute of God, the infant Jesus as the Devil, saints as sinners, and sinners as saints.

As a young man, Salarrué was awarded a scholarship in 1916 by the Salvadorean government to study art at the Corcoran School of Art in Washington, DC. When he returned to El Salvador, he combined his interest in multiple spheres of consciousness with his penchant for fantasy and his unique brand of experimentation with the creative potential of language to produce his second major work, *O' Yarkandal* (1929), a collection of stories that defy classification, but that resemble legends, fairy tales, creation myths and archetypal dream scenes. He illustrated the book with paintings that reproduce visually this "remoto imperio" (remote empire) where one encounters cities of winged men, islands adrift in unknown seas, strange perfumes and gardens perenially in bloom, whose first man and woman were born from the egg of a bird known as Alm-a (soul). *O' Yarkandal* is a book of pure creation for which Salarrué has invented even a language, bilsac, the fabrication of which he describes in the prologue as having been a euphonic and euphoric experience. His sensual, almost tactile delight in language is another of the characteristics of Salarrué's prose that makes it identifiable and memorable.

After experimenting with the invention of language in *O' Yarkandal*, he published *Cuentos de barro* in 1933, which is considered by many critics to be his best work. Salarrué was born in Sonsonate, a region of El Salvador with a strong indigenous presence. In *Cuentos de barro* he recreates with great compassion the rural indigenous world he loved. While these stories are part of the at once beloved and maligned tradition of costumbrist literature so popular in Central America at the turn of the century, they do not, as is often the case with this genre, paint an innocent picture of rural simplicity, but rather face clearly the reality of a people long oppressed by a system that does not favor their class or ethnicity. Which is not to say that they are framed in a political ideology, but that Salarrué does not turn from evil or injustice, whether in the *patrón* (boss), the campesino, or himself, choosing rather to accept it and mold it into narrative. He has been praised in Central America not only for his mastery of the short story, but also for his humanity. Salvadorean writer Manlio Argueta described him, in his poem entitled "Salarrué," as "Maestro de la ternura / en un país de guerra" (Teacher of tenderness / in a country of war). Besides his ability to deal tenderly with his characters, even in their violence and vengeance, what makes these stories so appealing is the obvious love of the author for the real language spoken by the people of a specific ethnicity in a specific geographic space. The non-Salvadorean reader must make reference to the glossary invariably included in Salarrué's books to appreciate the vernacular used in all his rural stories. Besides *Cuentos de barro*, these appear primarily in *Trasmallo*, 1954 [Net] and *La espada y otras narraciones*, 1960 [The Sword and Other Narratives].

Salarrué's delight in language combines in a unique way with his sense of fantasy and humor in *Cuentos de cipotes* [Kids' Stories], stories not for children, he explains in the prologue, but by children, more specifically, by the child in him. They are the stories children tell each other or tell adults, although adults never listen. They are small stories that speak like kids, full of mispronunciations, malapropisms, riddles, rhymes and invented language. They are silly, ingenuous, wise and candid. The first edition was illustrated by his wife, Zelié Lardé, considered to be El Salvador's first "primitive" artist, while the second edition was illustrated by his daughter, Maya, who followed artistically in her mother's footsteps. Like everything he wrote, these stories are influenced by his fascination with the essential unity of all planes of existence, in this case the child that lives in the adult and the maturity of the child, the wisdom of nonsense, and the foolishness of being serious.

Finally, there are the stories some critics have called his cosmopolitan ones, but that might also be described as urban-esoteric. Besides the time he spent studying art in Washington, Salarrué also lived in New York and Washington in the early 1950s when he served as cultural attaché at the Salvadorean Embassy. These places and the kinds of people he met there appear in tales that explore such phenomena as astral travel, reincarnation, and, again, the nature of good and evil. Sophisticated settings form the background for esoteric mind games in a world of international travel, archeological digs and elegant mansions on Riverside Drive.

Salarrué was a bohemian, an eccentric, an artist and a theosophist. A Central American writer who sometimes went to cocktail parties with ambassadors and sometimes was so poor he traded his paintings for art supplies. He was a tall man with fair skin and green eyes who was once described as resembling a sleepwalker who went through life with his eyes open, but in some other world. For all his eccentricity, he was an active and important figure in Salvadorean and Central American art and literature. Critics tend to address either his telluric, socially realistic stories, such as those of *Cuentos de barro*, or his fantastic, imaginative narratives, such *O' Yarkandal*. Sergio Ramírez, for example, in the prologue to *El ángel del espejo y otros relatos*, 1977 [The Angel of the Mirror and Other Tales], acknowledges the importance of both of these tendencies, but sees them as separate spheres that are never integrated. Ramón Luis Acevedo, on the other hand, suggests in his essay "Lo fantástico y lo maravilloso en O' Yarkandal de Salarrué," that these two worlds are perhaps not so separate as they may appear. But the nature of Salarrué's vision has not yet been adequately described. His body of work is diverse and original. From numerous points in the universe he begins his stories, stories that inevitably end up in the same place: face to face with the mystery. A serious, full-length study of the man and his work is yet to be written. Given the range of his interests and the esoteric nature of many of his pursuits, it will be a difficult but worthwhile task.

JANET N. GOLD

Biography

Born Salvador Salazar Arrué in Sonsonate, El Salvador, 22 October 1899. Mother schoolteacher. Parents separated before child was born. Attended primary school in San Salvador. At the age of ten he published his first writings in the newspaper, *Diario de Salvador*. Secondary education at Instituto Nacional. Tutored in painting by a Russian artist. Received small grant from Salvadorean government and in 1917 started to study at Corcoran Academy in Washington, DC. Returned to El Salvador, 1919. Worked as writer and illustrator for the literary journals, *Espiral* and *Germinal*. In these

he published his first regional stories accompanied by his own illustrations. Married Zelié Lardé, 1922, a primitivist painter from family of writers and intellectuals, in 1922; three daughters. Acquired interest in theosophy and esoteric literature. In 1928 began to publish in *Patria* [Homeland], a newspaper founded by his friend the essayist Alberto Masferrer. Later became its director and editor-in-chief. Published also in the newspaper, *Queremos* [We Want] and the literary journal, *Cactus*. After the publication of *Cuentos de barro* in 1933 he met Gabriela Mistral who facilitated a Chilean edition of this collection of short stories. Appointed officer in charge of cultural affairs in the US, 1946. Returned to El Salvador in 1951. General director of fine arts, 1962–64: resigned owing to inadequate government funding. Together with the poet Claudio Lars, received the highest honour accorded by the Salvadorean Academy of the Language, 1969. Died in El Salvador, November 1975.

Selected Works

Novels

El cristo negro, San Salvador: Biblioteca Nacional, 1926
El señor de la burbuja, San Salvador: n.p, 1927; 3rd edition, San Salvador: Ministerio de Educación, 1977
La sed de Sling Bader, San Salvador: Ministerio de Educación, 1971
Catleya Luna, San Salvador: Ministerio de Educación, 1974

Short Fiction

O'Yarkandal, Cuscatlan, El Salvador: Tipografía Patria, 1929
Remontando el Uluán, San Salvador: Agua y Arena, 1932
Cuentos de barro, San Salvador: La Montaña, 1933
Eso y más, Santa Ana, El Salvador: Editorial Ir, 1940
Cuentos de cipotes, 2 vols, San Salvador: Nosotros, 1945; augmented edition, 1961
Trasmallo, San Salvador: Ministerio de Cultura, 1954
La espada y otras narraciones, San Salvador: Ministerio de Cultura, 1960

Poetry

Mundo nomasito, San Salvador: Editorial Universitaria de El Salvador, 1975

Compilations and Anthologies

Cuentos, with a prologue by Roque Dalton, Havana: Casa de las Américas, 1968
Obras escogidas, edited by Hugo Lindo, 2 vols, San Salvador: Editorial Universitaria de El Salvador, 1969–70
Salarrué: "El ángel del espejo" y otros relatos, edited by Sergio Ramírez, Caracas: Biblioteca Ayacucho, 1977

Further Reading

Acevedo, Ramón Luis, " Salarrué, novelista o la esencial paradoja de la existencia," in his *La novela centroamericana*, Río Piedras, Puerto Rico: Editorial Universitaria, 1982
Lindo, Hugo, prologue to *Obras escogidas*, San Salvador: Editorial Universitaria de El Salvador, 1969
Ramírez, Sergio, prologue to *Salarrué: "El ángel del espejo" y otros relatos*, Caracas: Biblioteca Ayacucho, 1977

Sebastián Salazar Bondy 1924–1964

Peruvian dramatist, poet and prose writer

In "Testamento ológrafo" [Holograph Testament], a poem written shortly before his death, Sebastián Salazar Bondy sardonically bequeaths a last image of himself: that of a man wasted away by illness, gazing sadly at the city of Lima, whose enervating atmosphere reduces hopes and dreams to frustration, and looking back on a life of frantic activity which has seen his ambitions only partially realised. That poem is a remarkably honest and accurate self-assessment, for though Salazar packed a great deal into his tragically short life, his achievements fell somewhat short of his goals. As the author of plays, poems, short stories and essays, he left behind him an estimable body of work, but he never succeeded in establishing himself as a major writer. In part, this was because he was continually experimenting with different genres and manners in search of the form of self-expression which best suited him, only to end up spreading himself too thinly. However, as "Testamento ológrafo" implies, it is also partly attributable to the limitations of the Peruvian cultural scene, which led him to divert much of his energy in other directions. Confronted with the difficulties facing a creative artist in an underdeveloped Third World country, Salazar campaigned to foster an environment in which artistic activity could flourish. He was a tireless promoter of the arts – writing book reviews, giving public lectures, editing anthologies, organising exhibitions, collaborating in the creation of journals and competitions and offering encouragement and help to aspiring young writers. Above all, he was at the forefront of a movement to develop a vigorous modern theatre: he was the country's leading theatre critic in the 1950s. In 1951 he was responsible for reorganising the Ministry of Education's theatrical division, he was the inspiration behind the founding of the Club de Teatro company in 1953 and he was directly involved in theatrical productions as director and artistic adviser. Predictably perhaps, his endeavours failed to produce a major transformation of the Peruvian cultural environment, but they did have the effect of encouraging creativity and the fact that writers such as Mario Vargas Llosa have acknowledged their debt to him is confirmation that modern Peruvian literature would have been considerably poorer without his example and inspiration.

As a consequence of this dispersal of his energies, Salazar's writing is uneven in quality and though it includes some fine work, its value lies mainly in its contribution to the creation of a modern cultural tradition, which he himself regarded as a national priority. Above all, his output of ten full-length dramas and eleven brief one-act plays was central to the revitalisation of the Peruvian theatre which began in the late 1940s. His career as a dramatist was marked by continual experimentation as he sought, with varying success, to reconcile the concepts of theatre as entertainment and as a vehicle for social criticism. Thus, his first play, *Amor, gran laberinto* [Love, the Great Labyrinth], is a political allegorical farce, with grotesque, puppet-like figures in the style of Valle-Inclán. Subsequently, he went on to cultivate a realistic type of theatre in the shape of social and historical dramas, the best of which,

Rodil (1952), focuses on the eponymous leader of Spain's last stand against the forces of independence as a symbol of the intransigent defence of conservative tradition. Later, he staged a series of satirical-costumbrist comedies on the model of the French popular theatre, the most successful being *El fabricante de deudas*, 1964 [The Debt Manufacturer], which adapts Balzac's *Le Faiseur* [The Schemer] to the Limeñan scene to satirise the capitalist financial system. His last play, *El rabdomante*, 1965 [The Diviner] reverts to political allegory to explore the role of the artist in the revolutionary process.

Salazar was also a fine poet and occupies an honorable place among the generation who emerged in the 1940s and 1950s to produce one of the richest national poetries in Latin America. His is a confessional poetry written in a simple conversational style which found its best expression in the posthumously published *El tacto de la araña* [The Spider's Touch]. Unashamedly sentimental in character, his verse expresses his strong emotional attachment to the people and places who make up his world, and celebrates the values of love, friendship, goodwill among human beings. Its dominant tone is perhaps one of melancholy, born of his awareness of the precariousness of all things human and of social injustice, which he felt personally as an offence against life and a blight on the country he loved. Despite that, his poetry communicates a tremendous love of life and a commitment to living it to the full with all its imperfections.

Salazar ranks, too, as one of the pioneers of modern urban fiction in that the stories of *Náufragos y sobrevivientes*, 1954 [Castaways and Survivors] portray the drab and precarious existence of Lima's lower-middle classes. However, the prose work for which he is most likely to be remembered is the essay *Lima la horrible*, 1964 [Beastly Lima], a personal diagnosis of Peruvian society in the dissident tradition of Manuel González Prada and José Carlos Mariátegui and similar in manner to Octavio Paz's interpretation of the Mexican national character in *El laberinto de la soledad*, 1950 (*The Labyrinth of Solitude*). Here Salazar argues that coastal Peru remains marked by the legacy of Spanish colonialism, not only in the persistence of antiquated social structures and class divisions, but in a conformist mentality conditioned by a Hispanic mythology, which has been manipulated by the ruling elite and which it is necessary to debunk in order to build a modern democratic Peru. *Lima la horrible* is probably Salazar's most important work, for it encapsulates the spirit of much modern Peruvian writing and formulates the ideology underpinning it.

JAMES HIGGINS

Biography

Born in Lima, Peru, 4 November, 1924. Attended Colegio Alemán, transferred to Colegio San Agustín de Lima because of a financial crisis (father's business went bankrupt in 1933); studied literature at Universidad de San Marcos, 1940–46. Taught at a high school, briefly; worked in the Biblioteca Nacional. Lived in Buenos Aires, 1947–52 where he wrote for the newspaper *La Nación*. Returned to Lima, contributed to *La Prensa*, 1951–56. Travelled to Paris on a

French government scholarship and studied at the National Conservatory of Dramatic Arts. Awarded the Premio Nacional de Teatro, 1952 for *Rodil* and in 1965 (posthumously) for *El rabdomante*. Died on 4 July 1964.

Selected Works

Poetry
Voz desde la vigilia, Lima: Hermes, 1944
Máscara del que duerme, Buenos Aires: Botella al Mar, 1949
Confidencia en alta voz, Lima: Vida y Palabra, 1960
Vida de Ximena, Lima: La Rama Florida, 1960
Conducta sentimental, Bogotá: Celza, 1963
El tacto de la araña / Sombras como cosas sólidas, Lima: Francisco Moncloa, 1966

Short Fiction
Náufragos y sobrevivientes, Lima: Club del Libro Peruano, 1954
Pobre gente de París, Lima: Mejía Baca, 1958
Diós en el cafetín, Lima: Populibros Peruanos, 1964
Alférez Arce, teniente Arce, capitán Arce ..., Lima: Casa de la Cultura del Perú, 1969 [Unfinished novel]

Plays
Amor, gran laberinto, in *Teatro peruano contemporáneo*, Lima: Huascarán, 1948
Rodil, Lima: Perendena, 1952
No hay isla féliz, Lima: Club de Teatro, 1954
El fabricante de deudas, Lima: Nuevo Mundo, 1964

Other Writings
Antología general de la poesía peruana, Lima: Librería Internacional de Perú, 1957
Lima la horrible, Mexico City: Era, 1964
Poesía quechua, with a translation and notes by Salazar Bondy, Mexico City: UNAM, 1964
Ollantay y cantos y narraciones quechuas, Lima: Peisa, 1974 [Translations into Castilian by José María Arguedas, César Miró and Salazar Bondy]

Compilations and Anthologies
After the death of Salazar Bondy there was a project to compile his complete works in six volumes under the title *Obras de Sebastián Salazar Bondy*. The first three volumes appeared in 1967, published in Lima by Francisco Moncloa: I. *Comedias y juguetes*; II. *Piezas dramáticas*; III. *Poema Todo esto es mi país*, Mexico City: Fondo de Cultura Económica, 1987

Further Reading
Alfaro-Alexander, Ana María, *Hacia la modernización de la narrativa peruana*, New York: Peter Lang, 1992
Caballero, Juan, *El teatro de Sebastián Salazar Bondy*, Lima: García Ribeyro, 1975
Natella, Arthur A., *The New Theatre of Peru*, New York: Senda Nueva de Ediciones, 1982
Solorguren, Javier, *Tres poetas, tres obras. Belli – Delgado – Salazar Bondy*, Lima: Instituto Raúl Porras Barrenechea, 1969
Vargas Llosa, Mario, "Sebastián Salazar Bondy y la vocación del escritor en el Perú," *Contra viento y marea (1962–1982)*, Barcelona: Seix Barral, 1983

Luis Rafael Sánchez 1936–

Puerto Rican prose writer and dramatist

Luis Rafael Sánchez first won international critical acclaim with the publication of *La guaracha del Macho Camacho*, 1976 (*Macho Camacho's Beat*). However, this and his only other novel, *La importancia de llamarse Daniel Santos*, 1988 [The Importance of Being Daniel Santos], form only part of a long and successful career as a short story writer, playwright, and essayist.

In Puerto Rico, Sánchez was first recognized as a writer of short fiction, whilst his coming of age as a writer is well illustrated by the trajectory of his short story career. His first stories, from the end of the 1950s, such as "El trapito" [Beloved Rag], "Destierro" [Exile], and "Espuelas" [Spurs], generally follow the literary model set by the established writers of his youth. The work of most of these, writers such as René Marqués and Abelardo Díaz Alfaro, is characterized by an idealization of Puerto Rico's Spanish heritage, harsh criticism of modern city life as opposed to a harmonious, traditional rural life, political didacticism, the portrayal of heroic sacrifice and a refined, literary Spanish.

With the publication of his only collection of short stories, *En cuerpo de camisa*, 1966 [Shirt Sleeves Unbuttoned], Sánchez extensively challenged his literary forefathers. Spanish culture succumbs to the threatening seduction of African-Antillean culture ("Aleluya negra" [Black Aleluya]), the modern city is no longer tragically threatening but is treated parodically ("Que sabe a paraíso" [The Taste of Paradise], "Etc."), whilst the paradise lost of rural life becomes an intolerant hell for the homosexual mulatto and classless pariah who is the protagonist of "¡Jum!" [Huh!]. Didacticism is replaced by irony and satire, heroic sacrifice by the marginalized anti-hero(ine)'s negotiation with mainstream culture. Meanwhile, formal Spanish is replaced by a coarsely humorous urban Puerto Rican vernacular galvanized as a baroque literary style through a recuperation of the grotesque identified with Quevedo and Valle-Inclán. This ground-breaking collection was the foundation for Sánchez's most mature work, which developed the features that characterize *En cuerpo de camisa*.

Almost simultaneously with his recognition as a short story writer, Sánchez initiated his career as a playwright. His first play, the prize-winning *La espera*, 1959 [Waiting], is indeed based on a short story of the same name published by Sánchez in 1957 and involves the unrequited love between a solitary woman, who eventually dies of pneumonia, and the unnamed man who daily passes outside her window. Both the play and short story poignantly examine time's existential and ultimately tragic dimensions.

Sánchez's work as a playwright ranges over several forms. *Cuento de Cucarachita Viudita*, 1959 [Tale of Doñita Widowbug] is adapted from a popular folktale into children's theatre, whilst *Los ángeles se han fatigado*, 1960 [The Angels Have Grown Weary], *La hiel nuestra de cada día*, 1961 [Give Us This Day Our Daily Bile], and *... O casi el alma*, 1964 [Soul by a String] are, respectively, a monologue and two naturalist works, all examining existentialist crises of identity occasioned by disillusionment and religious faith. *La pasión según Antígona Pérez*, 1968 [The Passion According to Antígona Pérez] combines classically tragic political drama – involving the martyrdom of a female dissident under an imaginary Latin American dictatorship – with Brechtian elements. However, it is the development of forms first explored in *Farsa del amor compradito*, 1960 [Farce of True Love's Bargain], and renovated much later in *Parábola del Andarín*, 1979 [Parable of the Long Distance Walker], which has culminated in his finest play to date, *Quíntuples*, 1985 [Quintuplets].

In *Farsa del amor compradito*, Sánchez deploys the absurdist possibilities of commedia dell'arte, Pirandello, Valle-Inclán's *esperpento*, and again Brecht's distancing devices, to produce a playful farce, whose burlesque form is undone in *Quíntuples*. The leading characters of *Quíntuples*, like those of *Parábola*, are the members of a show business troupe, whose exhaustion of their stereotypical roles in pleasurable performance questions the very terms of their subjectivity, thus opening the way to unforeseen socio-political and national configurations exceeding those offered by a colonial history.

In his many essays, mostly published in Puerto Rican or Spanish newspapers and magazines, Sánchez foregrounds the cultural and political context for his other writing. As in all his work, Puerto Rico's colonial status and national identity are central concerns. He attacks what he considers the undermining of language and vital institutions under colonialism ("La generación o sea," 1972 [The You Know Generation]), the tawdry bourgeois values that accompany colonialism ("El debut en Viena," 1975 [Debut in Vienna]), as well as speaking up against racism ("La gente de color: cariños y prejuicios," 1972 [People of Colour: Affection and Prejudice]). Moreover, he has written compassionately about the prejudice faced by Puerto Ricans in North America ("La guagua aérea," 1983 [The Flying Bus]), the ties that bind them to the island, and the international invisibility of Puerto Ricans ("Puertorriqueño he nacido," 1991 [Puerto Rican by Birth]).

Sánchez has also written essays concerning literature, music and cinema. In these, he often discusses artists and writers who have helped shape his own work, such as Fellini ("Cine de nuestro tiempo: *La Dolce Vita*," 1961 [Cinema of Our Time: *La Dolce Vita*]), James Baldwin ("De James Baldwin. Un ensayo profético," 1963 [About James Baldwin. A Prophetic Essay]), and the Puerto Rican writer, Abelardo Díaz Alfaro ("Los lujos de la memoria," 1991 [The Luxuries of Memory]). Moreover, the Spanish language, humour, places and events that define him as a Puerto Rican ("El cuarteto nuevayorkés,"

1993 [New York Quartet]), Latin American and Caribbean ("Las señas del Caribe," 1993 [The Marks of the Caribbean]), are also discussed.

Sánchez's recent *La guagua aérea* (1994), is a collection of essays that arguably excludes his more polemical work, but that provides a broad sample of his various interests as an essayist. The title essay, a revised version of his 1983 essay of the same name, formed the basis for a locally highly successful but disappointing 1993 Puerto Rican film production of, again, the same name. The movie redirected Sánchez's critically comic reflection on the Puerto Rican diaspora into a complacently mainstream vehicle of light entertainment.

Though Sánchez has only written two novels, they, along with *Quíntuples*, constitute the pinnacle of his work. As in his short stories and plays, the novels portray aspects of a resilient Puerto Rican popular culture whose daily survival is made possible by a reworking of the terms of its dependence. Such appropriation and dependency is further complicated by race, class and sexual considerations, so that popular culture is revealed as a network of negotiated or conflicting power relations.

In Sánchez's earliest short stories ("El trapito" [The Little Rag]), frustrated national aspirations can only be expressed through tragically symbolic acts of violence. Hope for the fulfilment of national aspirations is obscured by the fatalistic tone of these stories, which only provide cathartic tragedy or stubbornly irrational resistance ("Espuelas" [Spurs]). As Sánchez's work matures, there are stories of ingenious survival under colonialism by means of subterfuge ("Aleluya negra") or the violent assertion of a degraded communality ("¡Jum!"). However, neither course of action is able to liberate the colonial subject from a national dependence that is consolidated by incorporating disputes according to its own rules. At these earlier stages, Sánchez seems to consider the colonial delimitation of a differentiated subaltern as the major obstacle to any post-colonial project beyond Free Associated Statehood. The "Associated Freedom" of the island's relationship with the United States highlights the long-standing containment by colonialism of the emancipatory possibilities of subaltern hybridity, appropriation, and discontent. But, though there might seem to be a need for a strategic essentialism, in the face of a constitutionally preempted hybridity and violence, this is not the route Sánchez chooses to take in his two novels.

If in 1966, when *En cuerpo de camisa* was published, Sánchez presented the unruliness of recalcitrance as being incorporated by colonialism, in the novels, even between the novels, there is an increasing optimism inherent in Sánchez's broadening perspectives. In *La guaracha del Macho Camacho*, popular culture provides a space where the subaltern colonial subject may defend communality against impersonal capitalist colonialism. Meanwhile, twelve years later, in *La importancia de llamarse Daniel Santos*, Puerto Rican colonial dependency is viewed in the broader context of Latin Americans' subjection to a Third-World status. Nevertheless, if the lot of most Latin Americans is subordination, the latter is resisted in a popular culture that affirms a differentiated Latin American communality which unites multiple aspirations in a shared identity embodied by the figure of the popular hero. Thus, the legend of the bolero singer Daniel Santos locally supersedes, at the level of daily microhistories, the restrictions of dominant colonialist, capitalist and class ideologies. Consequently, particular situations in social, sexual, class, geographical and race hierarchies are highlighted as specifically defensible, even offensive, points from which to mount a concerted resistance.

If Sánchez's developing preoccupations in the two novels and his most recent play, *Quíntuples*, are increasingly invested in the assertiveness of popular culture, then the latter provides not only a site of resistance but also the foundations for unprecedented individual, national, and pan-American identities.

JOHN PERIVOLARIS

See also entry on Guillermo Cabrera Infante

Biography

Born in Humacao, Puerto Rico, 17 November 1936, into a working-class family. Family moved to San Juan, 1948. Actor for Puerto Rican radio in his late teens; also acted in the theatre. Studied at Humanities Faculty of the University of Puerto Rico, 1956. Scholarship to Columbia University, New York, 1959. Master's degree from New York University, 1963. PhD from University of Madrid, 1967. Lecturer in Hispanic Literature, University of Puerto Rico, 1969. Awarded Guggenheim Fellowship in 1985, which allowed him to start writing *La importancia de llamarse Daniel Santos*. In the 1990s spends half the year teaching at the City University of New York (CUNY) and the rest of the time travelling and writing.

Selected Works

Novels and Short Fiction

En cuerpo de camisa, San Juan, Puerto Rico: Lugar, 1966
La guaracha del Macho Camacho, Buenos Aires: Ediciones de La Flor, 1976; as *Macho Camacho's Beat*, translated by Gregory Rabassa, New York: Pantheon, 1980
La importancia de llamarse Daniel Santos, Hanover, New Hampshire: Ediciones del Norte, 1988

Plays

Los ángeles se han fatigado, La farsa del amor compradito, San Juan, Puerto Rico: Lugar, 1960
. . . O casi el alma (Auto de fe en tres actos), in *Teatro puertorriqueño* (Séptimo festival), San Juan, Puerto Rico: Instituto de Cultura Puertorriqueña, 1965
La pasión según Antígona Pérez (crónica americana en dos actos), Hato Rey, Puerto Rico: Lugar, 1968
Farsa del amor compradito. La hiel nuestra de cada día. Los ángeles se han fatigado, Río Piedras, Puerto Rico: Editorial Antillana, 1976
Quíntuples, Hanover, New Hampshire: Ediciones del Norte, 1985

Essay

La guagua aérea, Río Piedras, Puerto Rico: Editorial Cultural, 1994

Further Reading

Alvarado, Ana D., María Milagros López and Wanda E. Ramos, "Celebrating Life and the Rearticulation of Mytho-Misogyny: Women Unearthing the "*Machosaurus*," *Sargasso*, San Juan, 6 (1989) [on *Daniel Santos*]
Barradas, Efraín, *Para leer en puertorriqueño: acercamiento a la obra de Luis Rafael Sánchez*, Río Piedras, Puerto Rico: Cultural, 1981 [The best introduction to the writer's work]
Cachán, Manuel, "*En cuerpo de camisa* de Luis Rafael Sánchez: la antiliteratura del otro puertorriqueño," *Revista Iberoamericana* 59 (January–June 1993)
Colón Zayas, Eliseo, "La problemática del ser puertorriqueño en los cuentos de Luis Rafael Sánchez," *Pensamiento Crítico*, San Juan, Puerto Rico, vol. 4/26 (October–November 1981)
Fernández Olmos, Margarite, "Luis Rafael Sánchez and Rosario Ferré: Sexual Politics and Contemporary Puerto Rican Narrative, *Hispania* 70 (March 1987)
Gelpí, Juan G., "La cuentística antipatriarcal de Luis Rafael Sánchez," *Hispamérica*, vol. 15/43 (1986)
González, José Luis, "Plebeyismo y arte en el Puerto Rico de hoy," in his *El país de cuatro pisos y otros ensayos*, Río Piedras, Puerto Rico: Huracán, 1980
González Echevarría, Roberto, "La vida es una cosa *phenomenal*: *La guaracha del Macho Camacho* y la estética de la novela actual," in his *Isla a su vuelo fugitiva*, Madrid: Porrúa Turanzas, 1983
Lugo-Ortiz, Agnes I., "Community at Its Limits: Orality, Law, Silence and the Homosexual Body in Luis Rafael Sánchez's '¡Jum!,'" in *¿Entiendes?: Queer Readings, Hispanic Writings*, edited by Emilie Bergmann and Paul Julian Smith, Durham, North Carolina: Duke University Press, 1995
Ortega, Julio, "Teoría y práctica del discurso popular (Luis Rafael Sánchez y la nueva escritura puertorriqueña)," in his *Reapropiaciones: cultura y nueva escritura en Puerto Rico*, Río Piedras: Universidad de Puerto Rico, 1991
Perivolaris, John, "¡El cuento no es el cuento! ¡El cuento es quien lo cuenta!: Terms of Subjectivity in Luis Rafael Sánchez's *Quíntuples* (1985)," *Journal of Hispanic Research*, London, 3 (1994–95)
Vázquez Arce, Carmen, *Por la vereda tropical: notas sobre la cuentística de Luis Rafael Sánchez*, Buenos Aires: Ediciones de La Flor, 1994 [Exhaustive study of the short stories which pays due attention to tone and humour. Includes comprehensive bibliography]
Zamora, Lois Parkinson, "Cliches and Defamiliarization in the Fiction of Manuel Puig and Luis Rafal Sánchez," *The Journal of Aesthetics and Art Criticism*, 41 (1983)

Bibliographies

Hernández Vargas, Nélida and Daisy Caraballo Abréu (editors), *Luis Rafael Sánchez: crítica y bibliografía*, Río Piedras: Universidad de Puerto Rico, 1985

La guaracha del Macho Camacho

Novel by Luis Rafael Sánchez

Luis Rafael Sánchez's novelistic debut presents the interrelated lives of a corrupt Puerto Rican senator, Vicente Reinosa, his repressed upper-class wife, Graciela Alcántara, his working-class mulatto mistress, La China Hereje (The Heretical Chinawoman), and his wastrel son, Benny. Narrative development is minimal, since the action is centred on a massive San Juan traffic jam, from which the narration constantly digresses by means of flashbacks, fantasy, daydreams, as well as cross-cutting between episodes and characters.

If the growth of Puerto Rican cities marks the shift from an agrarian to an industrial economy, then the traffic jam that constitutes the central motif of *La guaracha* is perhaps a metaphor for Puerto Rico's stagnation under capitalist North American colonialism. In this situation, the incapacity of official politics to conceive a postcolonial project that might fulfil Puerto Rican national aspirations is countered by the immediate agency of everyday life. Immediacy is afforded by the physical terms of the human body as the centre of popular communal life and is best exemplified by the *guaracha* (a popular form of Caribbean music) of the title. The song, "La vida es una cosa fenomenal" (Life is a Phenomenal Thing), not only provides the mass media with a vehicle capable of taking the country by storm but also provides its listeners with a much desired "dogma nacional de salvación" (national dogma of salvation).

Commodification does not limit itself to the promotion and broadcasting of hit songs but pervades all levels of Puerto Rican life, stimulates a consumerist attitude to the world, and propels personal relationships. Identity itself is modelled according to the consumption of images of media and show business stars. For instance, Graciela takes Jacqueline Onassis and Elizabeth Taylor as her role models whilst La China Hereje models herself on the Puerto Rican cabaret queen, Iris Chacón, so that the former's middlebrow tastes situate her as middle class, whilst the latter's distinctly lowbrow role model identifies her unmistakably as lower class.

If human and social relationships are commodified under a system of North American colonialism, then the latter's process of modernization transforms the natural environment into an urban dystopia, the "desamparada isla de cemento nombrada Puerto Rico" (defenceless island of concrete named Puerto Rico"). However, the transformations undergone by modern Puerto Rico perhaps are never definitive.

Though the song, "La vida es una cosa fenomenal," disguises the less than ideal conditions of everyday life in the Puerto Rican colony through the escapism of its infantile lyrics: "las trompetas hablan de cálidos encuentros de una piel con la otra, las trompetas hablan de ondulaciones lentas y espasmódicas" (the trumpets speak of the hot encounter of one skin with another, the trumpets speak of slow, spasmodic undulations). Thus, despite its packaging and apparent message, popular music clears a space for the inscription of the body, pleasure, and personal relationships in the capitalist mass media. Moreover, the undulating slowness of the rhythm suggests the implied dancer's, or lover's, control as a subject, rather than passive consumer. Meanwhile, the spasmodic nature of the suggested and suggestive dance points to the dancer's powerful potential for spontaneous violence motivated by the daily physical discomfort of Puerto Rico as a "cuerpo de desconcierto" (restless body) which depends, as a colony, on an imported economic and political system whose First World aspirations it cannot or never should fulfil. But if the trumpets above have a political sound throughout, this dimension consists of intimate pleasure reclaimed in everyday life. Hence, the immediate context of a bus passenger's despair, arising from the disparity between the dream of capitalist progress and the feeling that "el país no funciona" (the country is out of order), is not provided by established political processes, which are discredited by being represented by Vicente and other political figures satirized in the book. Instead, alienation from official channels of action leads those who do not form part of the privileged, car-owning, elites of the country, the other travellers on the same bus, to stake out their own space in a spontaneous outbreak of dancing and singing to the piped-in *guaracha* that subsumes despair in Puerto Rican popular culture's movable feast.

The communality of the bus scene may be contrasted to La China Hereje's seclusion in the flat where she acts as Vicente's sexual servant. This contrast perhaps highlights cogently the island's uneven development, as well as the incomplete alienation of daily life, where pockets of communality resist the commerce of individuals as consumers or commodities. On the one hand, therefore, La China individually seeks self-fulfilment through identifying with the fetishized images she consumes of Iris Chacón. On the other hand, the community of bus-riding Puerto Ricans is not taken in. While on board the traffic-jammed bus, a passenger who is well aware of the limits of progress asserts that "el país no funciona" (the country is out of order), the ensuing rush-hour scene of unrushed singing and dancing represents wilfully unproductive freedom from the constraints of labour. Thus, the failure of capitalist colonialism to incorporate fully Puerto Ricans is demonstrated.

In the culturally segregated world of *La guaracha del Macho Camacho*, communal pleasure is the prerogative of underprivilege. Though benefitting from the material advantages of being a privileged elite, the class to which Vicente and his family belong is excluded from the "permanente fiesteo" (permanent partying) of popular culture. Vicente is plagued by the *guaracha* that has taken the country by storm and starts humming it contritely and without pleasure, isolated in his car. Meanwhile, Benny's fantasies concerning his Ferrari excite him to masturbation, which is described in its unattractive "fofa desnudez" (limp nakedness) as a counterpart to the juxtaposed episode of La China Hereje's enjoyable childhood memory of her masturbation of three cousins. Moreover, Graciela's preoccupation with the lifestyles of the rich and famous only leads her to jealousy and an attack of hysteria, a counterpart to La China Hereje's pleasurable identification with Iris Chacón. Significantly, the *guaracha*'s accompaniment of Graciela's hysterical attack contrasts with La China's previous enjoyment of the music Graciela considers an "himno orillero, himno repulsivo, himno populachero" (a deadbeat hymn, a repulsive hymn, a hymn of the mob").

In *La guaracha*, a defence of the communal takes place within the context of the colonial marketplace, threateningly represented by the impersonal modernity of the city. On the other hand, twelve years later, in *La importancia de llamarse Daniel Santos*, 1988 [The Importance of Being Called Daniel Santos] popular culture aggressively, even offensively, asserts a multiple but unified Latin American identity, made possible by Latin Americans' personal identification with the figure of the popular hero. Thus, the legendary bolero singer, Daniel Santos, becomes the exemplary focus of a differentiated, international Latin American culture, and Sánchez's work enters a new phase of optimism.

JOHN PERIVOLARIS

Editions

First edition: *La guaracha del Macho Camacho*, Buenos Aires: Ediciones de La Flor, 1976

Translation: *Macho Camacho's Beat*, by Gregory Rabassa, New York: Pantheon, 1980

Further Reading

Gelpí, Juan G., *Literatura y paternalismo en Puerto Rico*, San Juan: Editorial de la Universidad de Puerto Rico, 1993 [Includes brilliant account of *La guaracha* in relation to major Puerto Rican debates on culture]

Schlau, Stacey, "Mass Media Images of the *puertorriqueña* in *La guaracha del Macho Camacho*, in *Modern Latin American Fiction*, edited by Harold Bloom, New York: Chelsea House, 1990

Severo Sarduy 1937–1993

Cuban prose writer and poet

Although his poetry, short stories and art reviews received early recognition in Havana's established cultural circles in the 1950s, it was the novels and essays written during his Parisian exile that brought Severo Sarduy to the attention of the Western world's literary community. His decision to live in France was an intellectual, aesthetic affirmation. Unlike the other Cuban writers who went into exile during the first years after the Cuban Revolution, Sarduy disengaged himself from any public denouncement of his country's political situation. Also, the exploration of erotic themes and sexually explicit language in his work, frequently in a setting of gay and transvestite entertainment, could have been regarded as decadent in post-revolutionary Cuba.

As an adolescent, Sarduy's poetry had appeared in *Ciclón*, an iconoclastic journal founded by Virgilio Piñera and José (Pepe) Rodríguez Feo in January 1955. But it was his incisive art criticism in *Lunes de Revolución* [Monday in the Revolution] that won him a fellowship to study at the École du Louvre in 1959. He left Cuba at the onset of the Revolution, enroling at the Sorbonne after the fellowship period had ended. While he was there, Sarduy joined the Structuralist *Tel-Quel* group formed by Roland Barthes, Philippe Sollers, Claude Lévi-Strauss and others. His first novel, *Gestos*, 1963 [Gestures], was immediately translated into French, Danish, Italian, German and Polish. It was an experimental work, influenced by the action painting movement, which he transferred to the text as "action writing." Through a fast-paced sequence of fragmented events, images and voices in the streets, *Gestos* captured the frenzied rhythm of Batista's last days, under the threat of terrorism and sabotage.

Many elements of the mature novelist are already present in *Gestos*. Sarduy's parody of popular culture and mass-media, influenced by American fads subliminally incorporated into Cuban society in the 1950s, as well as his preoccupation with language, identity and sense of national destiny, reappeared in many forms in his fiction. In *De dónde son los cantantes*, 1967 (*From Cuba with a Song*) Sarduy's search for a definition of nationality enters an ontological dimension, perhaps as a result of his physical separation from the island's geographical reality. Divided into three different stories, a complex symbolic and linguistic network connects the segments. By dealing separately with each of Cuba's ethnic groups – the Spanish, the Chinese, the African – and their respective contributions to the nation's history, he addresses the theme of syncretism as something already accomplished, not as a dilemma.

Sarduy's reputation as a writer became fully established in 1972, after receiving the Medicis International Award, one of France's highest literary honours, for his novel *Cobra*. As in his previous work, Sarduy continued to challenge conventional syntax and linear thought in *Cobra*. He again describes a world inhabited by irreverent, paradoxical characters in constant transformation, driven by erotic forces and verbal exuberance. The theme of metamorphosis as a metaphor for Cuban identity was originally introduced as a pictorial statement by artist Wifredo Lam, thus establishing the transgressive nature of Island culture. But in *Cobra* the changes are projected onto a cosmogenic level. Scientific discourse is incorporated into the text through epigraphs at the beginning of each chapter. They deal with the Big Bang theory, the binary star system or the gravitational phenomena of a red shift, suggesting the metaphoric conception of the characters. It is also an allusion to the myths of modern man – how he has replaced old religious beliefs with scientific "facts."

In *Maitreya*, 1978 and in *Colibrí*, 1984 [Hummingbird] sexual changes appear as the product of displacement. Identities are never found in the long, circular voyages of the characters, who move through untamed expanses of land (sometimes the East, sometimes Latin America) and through the extravagances of their linguistic expression. They are novels of exile; an exile the author seeks to dramatize by disassembling and mythifying it.

Sarduy published a total of eight novels, the last two – *Cocuyo*, 1990 [The Glow Worm] and *Los pájaros en la playa*, 1993 [The Birds on the Beach] – being the most autobiographical. He also left several books of poetry. Most are costly, limited editions difficult to obtain, illustrated by artists such as Ehrhardt, Leonor Fini, Kuhn Weber and Ramón Alejandro. *Epitafios*, published posthumously, deals with the knowledge of his tragic illness and his death from AIDS.

The dialogical scope of Sarduy's aesthetic vision took an early direction in the years he collaborated with the leading French intellectuals and theoreticians of *Tel-Quel* (1965–72). He was, for a while, the only Latin American writer capable of understanding Lacan, Barthes and Lévi-Strauss. His first collection of essays, *Escrito sobre un cuerpo*, 1969 (*Written on a Body*), is considered an authoritative and lucid application of structuralism in Spanish. In *Barroco*, 1974 [Baroque], Sarduy explains his theories on the historical relation between literary and scientific discourses. It remains as one of his most remarkable contributions to Latin American literary thought.

LOURDES GIL

Biography

Born in Camagüey, Cuba, 25 February 1937. Attended the Instituto de Segunda Enseñanza de Camagüey; Faculty of Medicine, University of Havana, 1956–58; fellowship at the École du Louvre to study Art History, 1959–60; École Pratique des Hautes Études at the Sorbonne. Contributed to the journal *Lunes de Revolución*, 1959 and in the same year left Cuba to study in Paris. Lived in Paris for the rest of his life; became a French citizen in 1967. Director of the Latin American collection at the publishing house Editions du Seuil, 1969–90, and of the Latin American division at the publishing company Gallimard, 1990–93. Received the Medicis International Award, 1972 for *Cobra*; Paul Gilson and Italia Awards for radio and television, 1983. Died in 1993.

Selected Works

Novels

Gestos, Barcelona: Seix Barral, 1963
De dónde son los cantantes, Mexico City: Joaquín Mortiz, 1967; as *From Cuba with a Song*, translated by Suzanne Jill Levine, in *Triple Cross: Three Short Novels*, New York: Dutton, 1972; reprinted as a separate volume, Los Angeles: Sun and Moon Press, 1994
Cobra, Buenos Aires: Sudamericana, 1972; as *Cobra*, translated by Suzanne Jill Levine, New York: Dutton, 1975
Maitreya, Barcelona: Seix Barral, 1978; as *Maitreya*, translated by Suzanne Jill Levine, Hanover, New Hampshire: Ediciones del Norte, 1986
Colibrí, Barcelona: Argos Vergara, 1984
El Cristo de la rue Jacob, Barcelona: Mall, 1987; as *Christ on the Rue Jacob*, translated by Suzanne Jill Levine and Carol Maier, San Francisco: Mercury House, 1995
Cocuyo, Barcelona: Tusquets, 1990
Los pájaros en la playa, Barcelona: Tusquets, 1993

Plays

La playa, Paris: Cahiers Renauld-Barrault, 1965
Para la voz (includes *La playa*, *La caída*, *Relato*, *Los matadores de hormigas*), Madrid, Fundamentos, 1978; as *For Voice* (includes *The Beach*, *Fall*, *Re-Cite*, *The Ant-Killers*), translated by Philip Barnard, Pittsburgh: Latin American Literary Review Press, 1985

Poetry

Flamenco, Stuttgart: Manus-Presse, 1969
Mood Indigo, Stuttgart: Manus-Presse, 1969
Merveilles de la nature, Paris: Pauvet, 1971
Overdose, Las Palma, Mallorca: Inventorios Provicionales, 1972
Big Bang, para situar en órbita cinco máquinas, pour situer en orbite cinq machines de Ramón Alejandro, Montpellier: Fata Morgana, 1973; Barcelona: Tusquets, 1974
Daiquirí, Santa Cruz, Tenerife: n.p., 1980
Un testigo fugaz y disfrazado, Barcelona: Mall, 1985

Essays

Escrito sobre un cuerpo: ensayos de crítica, Buenos Aires: Sudamericana, 1969; as *Written on a Body*, translated by Carol Maier, New York: Lumen, 1989
Barroco, Buenos Aires: Sudamericana, 1974
La Doublure, Paris: Flammarion, 1981
La simulación, Caracas: Monte Ávila, 1982
Micro-ópera de Benet Rossell, in collaboration with Annemieke van de Pas, Barcelona: Ambit, 1984
Nueva inestabilidad, Mexico City: Vuelta, 1987
Ensayos generales sobre el Barroco, Mexico City: Fondo de Cultura Económica, 1987
Jean Cortot, Paris: Maeght, 1992
Epitafios, Imitación, Aforismos, Miami: Universal, 1994

Further Reading

Bush, Andrew, "Literature, History, and Literary History: a Cuban Family Romance," *Latin American Literary Review*, vol. 8/16 (1980)
Cabanillas, Francisco, *Escrito sobre Severo: una relectura de Severo Sarduy*, Miami: Universal, 1995
González Echevarría, Roberto, *La ruta de Severo Sarduy*, Hanover: New Hampshire: Ediciones del Norte, 1987
Guerrero, Gustavo, *La estrategia neobarroca: estudio sobre el resurgimiento de la poética barroca en la obra narrativa de Severo Sarduy*, Barcelona: Mall, 1987
Kushigian, Julia, *Orientalism in the Hispanic Literary Tradition: in Dialogue with Borges, Paz, Sarduy*, Albuquerque: University of New Mexico Press, 1991
MacAdam, Alfred, "Severo Sarduy: Vital Signs," in his *Modern Latin American Narratives: the Dreams of Reason*, Chicago: University of Chicago Press, 1977
Méndez Ródenas, Adriana, *Severo Sarduy: el neobarroco de la transgresión*, Mexico City: UNAM, 1983
Montero, Oscar, *The Name Game: Writing/Fading Writer in "De dónde son los cantates,"* Chapel Hill: University of North Carolina Press, 1988
Pellón, Gustavo "Severo Sarduy's Strategy of Irony: Paradigmatic Indecision in *Cobra* and *Maitreya*," *Latin American Literary Review*, vol. 11/23 (1983)
Pérez, Rolando, *Severo Sarduy and the Religion of the Text*, Lanham, Maryland: University Press of America, 1988
Prieto, René, "The Ambivalent Fiction of Severo Sarduy," *Symposium* 1 (1985)
Sanchez-Boudy, José, *La temática novelística de Severo Sarduy: "De dónde son los cantantes,"* Miami: Universal, 1985
Santí, Enrico Mario, "Textual Politics: Severo Sarduy," *Latin American Literary Review*, vol. 8/16 (1980)

Bibliographies

González Echevarría, Roberto, "Para una bibliografía de y sobre Severo Sarduy (1955–1971)," *Revista Iberoamericana*, vol. 38 (1972)

Special Issues of Journals

Review (Winter 1974)

Domingo Faustino Sarmiento 1811–1888

Argentine politician, educator, man of letters

Champion of the principles of the European Enlightenment in Latin America, and exemplary model of a protean Romantic spirit, Domingo Faustino Sarmiento's career and achievements highlight many of the tensions and paradoxes between Eurocentric ideals and the problems facing the new and fledgling republics in the Americas in the 19th century. Characterized, not without reason, with such grand epithets as author of a nation, the design and magnitude of his vision of Argentina was so expansive that some of its consequences are detectable today. He is, undoubtedly, the most famous of 19th-century Argentine liberal intellectuals: educator, journalist, polemicist and politician (president of his country), with historians focusing attention primarily on his economic policies, strategies for the progressive democratization of his country, and his vision of a modern society through education. All these aspects of his life's work and personality are to be felt in his most famous literary work, *Civilización y barbarie. La vida de Juan Facundo Quiroga* (*Life in the Argentine Republic in the Days of the Tyrants*).

In politics, Sarmiento was a lifelong opponent of *caudillismo* (rule by a strong man); inevitably his great adversary was Juan Manuel Rosas, the "federal" dictator and opponent of central government in Buenos Aires. Sarmiento, on the other hand, was an "unitario," advocating the necessity in Argentina for a strong, unified form of constitution if progress was to be achieved. In 1829, the year Rosas came to power, Sarmiento fought with the "unitarios" against Rosas, and in his periods of exile in Chile he carried on an indefatigable campaign against him, in the Chilean press and in *Facundo*.

Facundo is a polemical work, attacking what Sarmiento considered to be the baneful influence of the gaucho's values on Argentine political and cultural life. His main message in the first part of the book is that although the nature of the terrain makes Argentina an obvious unity, the nature of gaucho society militates against this unity. In the first chapter he begins with a description of the land and shows how the vast pampas, drained by rivers which finish in the River Plate estuary, make Argentina "una e indivisible" (one and indivisible). However, the natural unity of the Republic is not that of Rosas, which is based on brute force and terror, or as Sarmiento puts it, "la unidad en la barbarie y en la esclavitud" (unity in barbarism and slavery). It is "la unidad en la civilización y en la libertad" (unity in civilization and freedom). Life on the pampas is presented as a type of non-society, with the gaucho living an isolated and nomadic life. There are no centres of population, no towns where social customs and laws can be built up. Government is impossible, and so of course is education. The education of the gaucho, Sarmiento tells us, revolves entirely around horses; his equestrian skills lead him to scorn the town-dweller, and the habit of defying and overcoming nature (capturing a horse, killing a bull or a jaguar), engenders in him an intense sense of individualism. The whole first section of the book is enlivened by anecdotes concerning the feats of the gauchos. This is particularly true of the second chapter, which deals with various gaucho types: the *rastreador* (tracker),

baquiano (guide), *gaucho malo* (a gaucho who has gone to the bad), and the *payador* (singer), whose skills Sarmiento relates with obvious relish, whilst attempting to demonstrate how the individualism of these types is of its nature barbaric and inimical to progress and civilization.

Sarmiento's attitude is ostensibly to attack the gaucho, Facundo Quiroga (one of Rosas's Federalist caudillo leaders, assassinated in Córdoba in 1835) and Rosas; in short, "barbarie." Yet, as the work progresses his secret admiration for the gaucho becomes ever more apparent. The individualism of the gaucho, so harmful to society, is none the less admirable in itself. The very brutality of Facundo exerts a certain fascination over this liberal advocate of civilized values, and Sarmiento even goes so far as to remark that egoism and brutality are at the heart of all great characters of history. When *Facundo* was written, Romanticism was at its height in Spain. The great, titanic individual that Facundo Quiroga embodies could hardly fail to attract a representative intellectual writing in the 1840s: they are as much Romantic heroes as Espronceda's "El pirata" or Rivas's "Don Alvaro." Thus Sarmiento's own enthusiasm undermines his ideological polarity "civilización-barbarie," and the ambivalent presentation of the gaucho as both villain and hero is one of the fascinations of this early example of "literatura gauchesca."

Viajes por Europa, Africa y América [Journeys through Europe, Africa and the United States] is a travel commentary in epistolary form, a richly costumbrist account told with spirited Romantic energy, and is perhaps most interesting for revealing the extent of Sarmiento's use of the United States as a model for his utopian vision of Argentina. Even more idealistic (and scorned as far-fetched by Sarmiento's contemporaries) were the programs developed in his political treatise "Argirópolis," 1850 [City of Silver], advocating a federal system unifying Argentina, Paraguay and Uruguay. *Recuerdos de provincia* [Memoirs of Provincial Life] is a set of memoirs evoking Sarmiento's childhood and youth, not unlike his early autobiography *Mi defensa* (1843), but more mature in tone and of superior literary quality. Its purpose is partly to clear his good name in the face of slurs perpetrated against him by Rosas and his agents. This leads, however, to a propaganda exercise of his own, as he polishes and prepares his past for the great political role he is to play in the future.

Sarmiento provides the modern scholar with an inroad for the discussion of historical and critical discourses in the Americas. His seminal influence in the formation of modern Argentina, at the crux of politics and letters offers space for a rethinking of the categories of meaning used to isolate literature from history. He embodies the duality of man of letters and visionary politician, even if his vision was unrealistically Utopian and has in many ways gone unfulfilled.

FRANK McQUADE

See also entries on Caliban, Caudillismo and Dictatorship, Civilization and Barbarism

Biography

Born in San Juan, Argentina, 15 February 1811, fifth child and only son of six surviving offspring. Learned to read at the age of four. Attended the Escuela de la Patria, San Juan, 1816–25. Strongest formative influence in his childhood was his uncle, José de Oro, a priest who assisted in his education. Grew up in rough, dangerous frontier environment in which the local *caudillos* (regional chieftains) fought one another for control of provinces in the Argentine interior. Sarmiento supported the Unitarians (anti-Federalist, anti-Spanish and anti-*caudillo*). Forced into exile in Chile in 1831. Able to return to San Juán in 1836 where he opened the Colegio de Santa Rosa de América, a school for young ladies, 1839. Founded the newspaper *El Zonda*: forced to close after six issues. Imprisoned for conspiracy, released and sent into exile once more. Travelled in United States, Europe and north Africa, inspecting educational systems, 1845–48. The United States impressed him most; has been said that he analyzed it "at the high point of its possibilities." Married Benita Martínez Pastoriza shortly after his return to Chile in 1848; separated from her at end of 1862. Governor of the province of San Juan 1862–64; ambassador to the United States 1865–68; President of the Republic of Argentina 1868–74. Died in Asunción, Paraguay, 11 September 1888.

Selected Works

Sarmiento's Complete Works (*Obras*, Santiago de Chile/Buenos Aires: F. Lajouane, 1885–1903) run to 52 volumes. Principal works include:

Mi defensa, Santiago de Chile: n.p., 1843
Civilización y barbarie. La vida de Juan Facundo Quiroga, Santiago de Chile: n.p., 1845; as *Life in the Argentine Republic in the Days of the Tyrants, or Civilization and Barbarism*, translated, with an extensive introduction, by Mrs Horace Mann, New York: Hurd and Houghton, 1868
Viajes por Europa, Africa y América, Santiago de Chile: J. Belin, 1849–51; the United States component as *Travels in the United States in 1847*, translated, with an introduction by Michael Aaron Rockland, Princeton, New Jersey: Princeton University Press, 1970
Recuerdos de provincia, Santiago de Chile: n.p., 1850
Vida de Abrán Lincoln, New York: Appleton, 1866
Conflictos y armonías de las razas en América, 2 vols, Buenos Aires: n.p., 1883

Further Reading

Anderson Imbert, Enrique, *Genio y figura de Sarmiento*, Buenos Aires: Editorial Universitaria, 1967
Bunkley, Allison Williams, *The Life of Sarmiento*, Princeton, New Jersey: Princeton University Press, 1952
Criscenti, Joseph T. (editor), *Sarmiento and His Argentina*, Boulder, Colorado: Lynne Rienner, 1993
Earle, Peter G., "Sarmiento," in *Prophet in the Wilderness: the Works of Ezequiel Martínez Estrada*, Austin: University of Texas Press, 1971
Halperín Donghi, Tulio, Iván Jaksi, Gwen Kirkpatrick and Francine Masiello (editors), *Sarmiento: Author of a Nation*, Berkeley: University of California Press, 1994
Jitrik, Noé, *Muerte y resurrección de Facundo*, Buenos Aires: Centro Editor de América Latina, 1968
Katra, William H., *Domingo F. Sarmiento: Public Writer (between 1839 and 1852)*, Tempe: Arizona State University, 1985
Martínez Estrada, Ezequiel, *Sarmiento*, Buenos Aires: Argos, 1946
Ocampo, Victoria, "Sarmiento," *Sur*, vol. 8/47 (1938)
Salomon, Noël, *Realidad, ideología y literatura en el "Facundo" de D.F. Sarmiento*, Amsterdam: Rodopi, 1984

Special Issues of Journals

Revista Iberoamericana, vol. 54/143 (April–June 1988)
Filología, vol. 23/2 (1988)
Cuadernos Americanos, vol. 3/13 (1989)
Río de la Plata: Culturas 8 and 9 (1989)

Simone Schwarz-Bart 1938–

Guadeloupean novelist

Simone Schwarz-Bart's novels belong to the growing body of Caribbean fiction by black women writers who are reclaiming their personal stories by rewriting the histories of their peoples. Through this process of coming to narrative mastery Schwarz-Bart attempts to retrieve repressed origins and to establish a personal and collective identity. Her voice especially expresses and interprets the predicament of the Antillean woman and the reality in which she dwells – a reality anchored in the Guadeloupean soil – from the point of view of the female author, as well as of her mostly female characters. Indeed, Schwarz-Bart's women characters are so decisive in the remaking of Antillean history that they tend to become national epic heroines. Despite their failures, they challenge and subvert their condition, recalling their heritage to those who have chosen conspicuously to silence it. As several critics have observed, Simone Schwarz-Bart has become a variation of the traditional "griot," a storyteller of the legendary Antillean past which acquires a universal dimension in the present. Indeed, through the characters' fundamental human suffering they are able to create an authentic art of living and a pattern for Antillean resistance.

Schwarz-Bart's first two novels – co-authored by her husband, the French novelist André Schwarz-Bart – relate to her subsequent individual texts. The couple's original joint goal was to reconstruct the history of Guadeloupe in a cycle of historical novels, which they never completed. In *Un Plat de porc aux bananes vertes*, 1967 [A Dish of Pork with Green Bananas] the non-linear narrative alternates between past and present, Paris and Martinique, Creole and French, reality and fantasy. This technique allows the reader to perceive the female protagonist's inner life, which mirrors her painful memories and her feelings of shame and guilt. Her traumatic past symbolizes the master's version of the Antillean people as a fallen, cursed race who deserve their sufferings. The heroine's destructive view of herself prevents her from overcoming her alienation from a past represented by the archetypal figure of her grandmother, mentally enslaved forever.

The second collaborative novel, *La Mulâtresse Solitude*, 1972 (*A Woman Named Solitude*) recreates the poignant story of a maroon girl in Guadeloupe. This fictional biography explores the legendary, but also historical, character of Solitude –Simone Schwarz-Bart's slave ancestor – and reinterprets the colonial bi-cultural, bi-colored Antillean society at the time of emancipation. Solitude is a pivotal figure for the Guadeloupean writer since she represents the tenacious desire to be black – to reclaim her African origin – in a white-dominated world. Offspring of the slave ship rape by a white sailor of her West African mother, Solitude is a mulatto, who cannot belong to the prevailing black community even though it is exploited and despised. Moreover, her subservient attitude and her vulnerability reflect her impotence against the white male-dominated world. Totally displaced within the violent social conflict which overwhelms her, Solitude loses her sanity before being executed for her crimes.

In contrast, Télumée Miracle, the heroine of *Pluie et vent sur Télumée Miracle*, 1972 (*The Bridge of Beyond*), symbolizes the triumph of ordinary life over annihilation and self-destruction. Télumée tells the poignant story of a poor, aged black peasant woman who has shaped her own destiny and reached inner peace. Her reminiscences are part of the history of her own people, an exploration of everyday experience told from the perspective of her chosen grandmother, whose ancestral wisdom makes her a repository of the collective memory. The female point of view is crucial since Télumée's foremothers are extraordinary mythical heroines. Their resilience and enduring love in the face of the most terrible hardships symbolize the island's survival and greatness. In this magnificent and rich novel, Schwarz-Bart is not so much concerned with the socio-political situation of a people as with their psyche. The writer strives to correct the "official" version of history, the colonizer's distortions and silences, in order to establish an alternative view of her people's destiny. Schwarz-Bart's writing technique contributes to this re-vision. Through Télumée's Creole voice, the text functions as a vehicle of orality. The dialectical tension between the written and oral discourse allows the author to convey the specificity of traditional oral communication with its African origin and transferral to Guadeloupe.

In a different register and seven years later, Schwarz-Bart published *Ti Jean L'Horizon*, 1979 (*Between Two Worlds*), the story of the adventures of a Guadeloupean folk hero, Ti Jean, who journeys to other continents and even to other worlds, in search of his roots. The narrative, which focuses for the first time on a male character, explores the hero's Antillean quest for his and his people's rightful place in the world. Through an extremely complex series of adventures which deconstruct the traditional myths associated with Antillean identity and which lead the reader along a difficult path filled with constantly shifting spaces and time limits, Ti Jean finally assumes the destiny of his island. With great irony, Schwarz-Bart proceeds to demystify the magical yearnings that have prevented the Antilleans from defining their true identity. The myth of return to Africa and of the power of the dead over the living, as well as the reverence for "Mother France," and the lure of macho heroism are all shattered. Through his numerous ordeals, Ti Jean acquires the necessary knowledge, the true "connaissance," that gains him access to wisdom: one's identity is to be found at home. Guadeloupe provides the space for self-realization.

Ton Beau capitaine (*Your Handsome Captain*), a short play evoking the misery of an Haitian immigrant worker forced to exile in Guadeloupe, was published in 1987. Schwarz-Bart's extensive use of music, song, dance and cassette tapes successfully convey the inarticulate eloquence of the illiterate husband and wife who, in their longing for each other, try to express their feelings. This play lacks the literary achievement of the previous novels, but it nevertheless succeeds in exposing the island's remarkable socio-cultural diversity which often translates into racial tensions. It is also a testimony to the tragedy of the destitute and exploited Haitian people.

Simone Schwarz-Bart's fiction articulates the power of love and hope and the possibility of plenitude against silence, madness and destruction. With her beautifully crafted narrative, the Antilles find a true liberating voice and discover a regenerating landscape.

MARIE-AGNÈS SOURIEAU

Biography

Born Simone Bruman on 8 January 1938. Place of birth uncertain: in an interview published in *Elle* magazine (1973), Schwarz-Bart gave her place of birth as Charente-Maritime in France, adding that she did not visit Guadeloupe until she was three years old. Her mother, she said, was a governess and her father was in the army in her early childhood. Subsequently, she has given Pointe-à-Pitre, the capital of Guadeloupe, as her place of birth, possibly as a response to the criticism that her portrayal of the Caribbean is too exotic to be the work of an insider. Educated at Pointe-à-Pitre and Dakar. Left Guadeloupe in 1958 to study in France. Married the author André Schwarz-Bart in 1960; later collaborated with him on works of fiction. Two sons, Jacques and Bernard. Settled in Guadeloupe with her husband in 1978. Owner of an antiques shop in Pointe-à-Pitre.

Selected Works

Un Plat de porc aux bananes vertes, in collaboration with André Schwarz-Bart, Paris: Seuil, 1967
La Mulâtresse Solitude, in collaboration with André Schwarz-Bart, Paris: Seuil, 1972; as *A Woman Named Solitude*, translated by Ralph Manheim, New York: Atheneum, and London: Secker and Warburg, 1973
Pluie et vent sur Télumée Miracle, Paris: Seuil, 1972; as *The Bridge of Beyond*, translated by Barbara Bray, New York: Atheneum, 1974; London: Heinemann Educational Books, 1982
Ti Jean L'Horizon, Paris: Points, 1979; as *Between Two Worlds*, translated by Barbara Bray, New York: Harper and Row, 1981
Ton Beau capitaine, Paris: Seuil, 1987; as *Your Handsome Captain*, translated by Jessica Harris, in *Plays by Women: an International Anthology*, edited by Françoise Kourilsky and Catherine Temerson, New York: Ubu Repertory Theatre Publications, 1989 [play]

Further Reading

Bouchard, Monique, *Une Lecture de "Pluie et vent sur Télumée Miracle" de Simone Schwarz-Bart*, Fort-de-France: Presses Universitaires Créoles, and Paris: L'Harmattan, 1990

Okpanachi, Sunday, *La Misère et l'aliénation dans l'oeuvre de Simone Schwarz-Bart*, Bordeaux: Rones, n.d.

Rodríguez, Ileana, *House/Garden/Nation: Space, Gender and Ethnicity in Post-Colonial Latin American Literatures by Women*, translated by Rodríguez and Robert Carr, Durham, North Carolina: Duke University Press, 1994 [Chapter 5 is on Schwarz-Bart]

Shelton, Marie-Denise, "Women Writers of the French-Speaking Caribbean," in *Caribbean Women Writers. Essays from the First International Conference*, edited by Selwyn R. Cudjoe, Wellesley, Massachusetts: Calaloux, 1990

Toureh, Fanta, *L'Imaginaire dans l'oeuvre de Simone Schwarz-Bart. Approche d'une mythologie antillaise*, Paris: L'Harmattan, 1986

Science in Spanish American literature

Latin American narrative has long been mediated by scientific discourse, first that of the natural sciences, later that of the human sciences, and soon, it would appear, that of the communicational sciences.

The central trope of the mediation of Latin American narrative by the natural sciences is the nature metaphor, exemplified in Andrés Bello's *Silvas americanas*. Bello's description of American flora sets the tone for the many Romantic writers of the 19th century. The nature metaphor exalts the natural world and at the same time links Latin American culture with the uniqueness and wonder of the flora, fauna and physical geography of the New World. The greatness of Latin American nature was projected onto Latin American civilization and culture. This move, an extension of the Romantic notion of organic form, is illustrated in José Martí's "Nuestra América" (Our America). Martí, it should be noted in passing, also reviewed physics books for the *New York Sun*.

The discourse of evolutionary 19th-century European science mediates the construction of the Latin American nature metaphor. A major influence in Latin American narrative of this period was the scientific traveler and travelogue, names such as Alexander von Humboldt, Charles-Marie de la Condamine and Charles Darwin. In both narrative and travelogue, the uniqueness of the New World is reported and then interpreted by a scientific observer whose objective "method" qualifies him to read nature and so reveal its truth. The influence of the scientific travelogue can be seen in such works as Domingo Faustino Sarmiento's *Facundo* (*Life in the Argentine Republic in the Days of the Tyrants*), Anselmo Suárez y Romero's *Francisco*, and Euclides da Cunha's *Os sertões* (*Rebellion in the Backlands*).

With the end of World War I, and the concomitant devaluation of Positivism and general "decline of the West," natural science lost its privileged position as master discourse. European civilization was no longer seen as the logical *telos* of evolution. An anthropology that recognized multiple cultures seemed to offer the possibility of a new beginning, a new way of reconstituting a fragmented world. In the New World this often meant vindicating the Indian legacy or *indigenismo*. The Museo de Antropología in Lima, the Instituto Nacional de Antropología in Mexico and the Sociedad de Folklore Cubano (whose first president was Fernando Ortiz) were all established in this period. Also, primarily through the work of Bronislaw Malinowski and Margaret Mead, ethnography emerged as a science in its own right. Marcel Griaule's expedition and Claude Lévi-Strauss's travels in Latin America were soon to happen. These and other circumstances led to the privileging of anthropological discourse.

An anthropological bent has been present in Latin American literature since its inception. It begins with Columbus who, in 1494, left Fray Ramón Pané in Hispaniola to live with the *Taínos*, learn their language, customs and religion, and record his findings. Pané's *Relación acerca de las antigüedades de los indios*, 1498 [Account of the Antiquities of the Indians], along with other early documents such as Álvar Núñez Cabeza de Vaca's *Naufragios* [Shipwrecks] establish an anthropological model, before the emergence of that discipline, that has been significant in Latin American texts until the present. But it is only after 1920 that anthropology's scientific discourse about culture becomes the dominant mediation in Latin American narrative. The object of scientific discourse changes from nature to language and myth, and this is reflected in Latin American narrative. A few key names serve to illustrate the extent of this change: Miguel Ángel Asturias (*Leyendas de Guatemala* [Legends of Guatemala]), Alejo Carpentier (*¡Écué-yamba-O!* [Praise the Lord!] and *Los pasos perdidos* (*The Lost Steps*), with its close parallels to *Tristes tropiques* [Sad Tropics]), and Lydia Cabrera (*El monte* [The Mountain]), also a student of Fernando Ortiz, studied ethnology in Paris in the 1930s. Severo Sarduy (*De dónde son los cantantes*, in English as *From Cuba with a Song*) was a student of Roger Bastide, and José María Arguedas (*Los ríos profundos*, translated as *Deep Rivers*) was an anthropologist, as was Miguel Barnet (*Biografía de un cimarrón*, in English, *Autobiography of a Runaway Slave*).

After 1950, as Latin America attempted once more to liberate itself from hegemonic influences, usually North American interests, the "objectivity" of anthropology and ethnography came to be questioned. The literary nature of anthropological discourse was brought to light. This crisis in anthropology has given rise to a critical metadiscourse seen in the work of anthropologists such as Clifford Geertz and James Clifford. In Latin American narrative, there appears a concomitant critique of the authoritative discourse of anthropology, for example Mario Vargas Llosa's *El hablador* (*The Storyteller*), while authors such as Augusto Roa Bastos (*Yo el Supremo*, in

English, *I the Supreme*) go so far as to point out the literary nature of the metadiscourse of anthropology.

The crisis of conscience in anthropology and ethnography created a metadiscourse in the second half of the 20th century within the social sciences and within Latin American narrative – *Rayuela* (*Hopscotch*); *Yo el supremo*. In a similar way, the environmental crisis of the final decades of the 20th century has produced a metadiscourse within the natural sciences and within the novel.

In the second half of the 20th century, the naturalist discourse of science gives way to the cybernetic paradigm. This new informational/communicational/cybernetic discourse has produced a new type of social text, a new reality or "hyper-reality" as Jean Baudrillard would have it, and a new narrative metadiscourse. Fernando Contreras Castro's *Única mirando al mar*, 1993[Unica Gazing at the Sea] is a quintessential example of this new metadiscourse. In *Única*, Contreras Castro turns the ethnographic gaze of science upon itself to show us the mediation of the new scientific metaphor – the cybernetic society – in the construction of the late 20th-century Latin American consumer society. In the "communicational" novel the question of identity –the traditional Latin American binaries of city/country, civilization/barbarism, European/indigenous, etc. – is elided in a disposable consumer culture in which the media "code" constitutes all identities through the very act of consumption.

Another important movement in the second half of the 20th century among Latin America poets has been the science-poetry movement, with names such as Ernesto Cardenal (*Cántico cósmico*) and Rafael Catalá (*Cienciapoesía* and the journal *Ometeca*). This movement aims to reconcile the differences between the humanities and the sciences by revealing the scientific mediation of literature, and the humanistic mediation of science. These newer developments foreground the mediation of techno-science in the new Latin American reality in which the operative term in culture is no longer "multi" but media. As Latin America becomes more integrated into the global information age, we can expect the mediation of the communicational sciences to play an ever more prominent role in Latin American literature.

JERRY HOEG

See also entries on José María Arguedas, Carlos Germán Belli, Lydia Cabrera, *Cántico cósmico* (Ernesto Cardenal), Fernando Ortiz, Science Fiction, Travel Writing

Further Reading

Welch and Figueras give an overview of 19th-century scientific travel in Latin America. James Clifford explains the history of anthropology and ethnography. González Echevarría combines these two currents, adds Latin American literature and comes up with a fascinating book to which I am indebted for my brief account here. (To date, this would seem to be the only definitive work on literature and science in Latin America.) Cardenal and Catalá offer the finest in science-poetry. Also, the first half of Catalá's book is an excellent essay in which he lays the theoretical groundwork for dissecting the mediation of the discourse of science. The journal *Ometeca* focuses on literature and science in Hispanic cultures; volume 2, number 2 (1991) treats Ernesto Cardenal.

Arancibia, Juana Alcira (editor), *Encuentro de la literatura con la ciencia y el arte*, Buenos Aires: O Cruxavaes, 1990
Cardenal, Ernesto, *Cántico cósmico*, Managua: Nueva Nicaragua, 1989; as *Cosmic Canticle*, translated by John Lyon, Willimantic: Connecticut: Curbstone Press, 1993
Catalá, Rafael, *Cienciapoesía*, Minneapolis: Prisma, 1986
___ "Para una teoría latinoamericana de las relaciones de la ciencia con la literatura: La cienciapoesía," *Revista Filosofía*, vol. 28/ 67–68 (1990)
Clifford, James, *The Predicament of Culture: Twentieth-Century Ethnography, Literature, and Art*, Cambridge, Massachusetts: Harvard University Press, 1988
Contreras Castro, Fernando, *Única mirando al mar*, San José, Costa Rica: ABC, 1993
González Echevarría, Roberto, *Myth and Archive: a Theory of Latin American Narrative*, Cambridge and New York: Cambridge University Press, 1990
Lapidot, Ema, *Borges and Artificial Intelligence. An Analysis in the Style of Pierre Menard*, New York: Peter Lang, 1991
Welch, Thomas L. and Miriam Figueras (editors), *Travel Accounts and Descriptions of Latin America and the Caribbean, 1800–1920: a Selective Bibliography*, Washington, DC: Organization of American States, 1982

Science Fiction

Science fiction in the popular sense of the term is not normally associated with Latin American literary production, since this genre is often thought to flourish only in the most technologically advanced societies. Therefore, critics who examine the production of science fiction in Latin America from this angle, claim that there is little of it. Yet in the second half of the 20th century, the development a different kind of science fiction has emerged in Latin America and Europe, one that is more "literary," dealing not only with the physical sciences but also with politics, economics, psychology, anthropology and ethics. The stories that deal with the future and follow this trend take on political or economic changes in society as their subject leaving technology in the background. They use allegory and satire, they create Utopias or dystopias that reflect the hidden anxieties and fears of the particular historical moment. It is this new way of conceiving science fiction – one that is not limited to telling stories of sophisticated spaceships and green Martians – that launched an explosion of the genre in Latin America from the 1960s and allows it to be alive and well today.

Edgar Allan Poe and Jules Verne are seen as the major influences on 19th-century Latin American science fiction, which explains its general gothic atmosphere on the one hand, and its recurrent theme of scientific progress on the other. Most of the early Latin American science fiction stories, though, are tinted by Christian morality and want to show the danger of scientific research. The Argentine Eduardo Ladislao Holmberg is seen as one of the first writers of the genre after the publication of his novel *Viaje maravilloso del señor Nic-Nac*, 1875 [The Wonderful Journey of Mr Nic-Nac]. Other authors of the same period who also reflected the new scientific ideas in some of their less-known writings are Horacio Quiroga, Amado Nervo, Leopoldo Lugones and Rubén Darío. The first half of the 20th century also witnessed the occasional example of speculative fiction by prominent writers such as Macedonio Fernández, Santiago Dabove and Francisco L. Urquizo. Understandably, scientific experiments to obtain world peace was one of the most popular subjects of the genre during this time. From the 1930s on, the Argentines Jorge Luis Borges, Adolfo Bioy Casares and Roberto Arlt produced some of the best-known fiction associated with this genre in Latin America. Stories such as Borges's *El Aleph* (*The Aleph*) mix science and metaphysics, and Bioy Casares's *La invención de Morel* (*The Invention of Morel and Other Stories*) is considered a classic: a man taking refuge on an apparently deserted island meets a series of people who turn out to be holograms, three-dimensional reflections created by Morel's invention, a machine that is activated by the tides. Some critics would classify this story, and Latin American science fiction in general, as belonging to the realm of the fantastic, their reasoning for this assertion being that their main forms of expression have been moral allegories and parables. These critics like to contrast Latin American production with that of the Anglo-Saxon countries by pointing out that while the latter enjoys detailed descriptions of wonderful machines, the former prefer to deal with the consequences those machines would have on human beings. That contrast, however, seems to be too crude in the light of

a vast production of contemporary "Anglo-Saxon" science fiction that not only deals with outer space but, also, with psychological of social issues.

Anglo-Saxon science fiction has undoubtedly influenced its Latin American counterpart, especially from the 1950s when works by writers such as Ray Bradbury, Arthur C. Clarke and Isaac Asimov became available in translation. The Argentine Sergio Gaut admits that influence by declaring in *Plural* (1985) that the Latin American writers who read Anglo-Saxon science fiction in their formative years had already lost their "purity" when they first started writing their own. The 1960s witnessed a veritable explosion of the genre in Latin America, both in terms of the production of texts by authors who dedicate all their efforts to the genre and the creation of specialized magazines. A list of representative writers would prove to be too long, but some key names from this period are the Chilean Hugo Correa, the Brazilian Jerónimo Monteiros, the Cubans Miguel Collazo, Manuel Herrera and Ángel Arango, the Mexican Carlos Olvera, and the Argentines Angélica Gorodischer, Eduardo Goligorsky and Alberto Vanasco. During this period we find the first critical analyses dedicated to the study of Latin American science fiction in the light of its value and function. Thus, we find studies by critics such as Pablo Capanna, Mario Langer and Eduardo Goligorsky.

Today the genre enjoys great popularity among its faithful readers, if not a warm reception from academic literary critics, who still consider science fiction, unfairly so, to be a genre of inferior quality. Most of the authors of the genre today do not write mainstream literature, but dedicate all their efforts instead to the production of speculative fiction. Among these professional authors we should note: the Cuban Daína Chaviano, the Venezuelan Luis Britto García, the Peruvian José B. Adolph, the Uruguayan Mario Levrero, the Mexican Mauricio-José Schwarz, and, as already mentioned, Angélica Gorodischer from Argentina. The major centers of production in the 1990s are Argentina and Cuba. Argentine science fiction is strongly influenced by psychoanalysis, which reflects the importance given to this discipline in Buenos Aires as capital of the country open to ideas from abroad. The Cuban penchant for science fiction might be explained by the freedom from political censorship that results from the extrapolation of social problems to imaginary worlds that appear not to have any relation to the real one.

The bulk of Latin American science fiction has a base in the Social Sciences, although it deals with a wide variety of themes. Bernard Goorden, in his key article reprinted in *Plural* (1985), has identified several themes that occur in 20th-century Latin American science fiction that he considers to be original. Goorden theorizes that a continent whose population is the result of a great mixture of races produces science fiction with a strong preference for the theme of the alien, the symbolic representative of a different race. Since this genre is by no means limited to the written word, mention should be made of Elíseo Subiela's successful movie *Hombre mirando al sudeste* [Man Facing Southeast], as an example of that motif. Other classic science fiction themes, such as time travel and the end of the world, are exploited in an original way by Latin

American writers, yet others, such as the mad scientist, are more or less ignored by them. In any case, science fiction production in Latin America expresses Latin American conceptualizations of the future, and thus at the same time reflects Latin American conceptualizations of the present.

YOLANDA MOLINA GAVILÁN

Further Reading

General

Acosta, Oscar, *et al.*, *Primera antología de la ciencia ficción latinoamericana*, Buenos Aires: Rodolfo Alonso, 1970

Capanna, Pablo, *Sentido de la ciencia ficción*, Buenos Aires: Columba, 1966

"Coloquio a distancia: preguntas de *Plural* a relevantes autores de ciencia ficción latinoamericana," *Plural*, Mexico City, 163 (1985)

Goorden, Bernard and A. E. Van Vogt (editors), *Lo mejor de la ciencia ficción latinoamericana*, Buenos Aires: Hispamérica, 1988

Argentina

Gandolfo, Elvio E. (editor), "La ciencia ficción argentina," in *Los universos vislumbrados. Antología de la ciencia ficción argentina*, edited by Jorge A. Sánchez, Buenos Aires: Andrómeda, 1978

Gorodischer, Angélica, *Trafalgar*, Buenos Aires: El Cid, 1979

Planells, Antonio, "La literatura de anticipación y su presencia en Argentina," *Revista Iberoamericana de Bibliografía*, vol. 40/1 (1990)

Souto, Marcial (editor), *Ciencia ficción en la Argentina*, Buenos Aires: Eudeba, 1985

Vanasco, Alberto and Eduardo Goligorsky, *Adiós al mañana*, Buenos Aires: Minotauro, 1967

Vásquez, María Esther, "Angélica Gorodischer: una escritora latinoamericana de ciencia ficción," *Revista Iberoamericana*, vol. 49/123–24 (1983)

Cuba

Arango, Ángel, *Robotomaquia*, Havana: Unión, 1967

___ *Transparencia*, Havana: Unión, 1982

Chaviano, Daína, *Amoroso planeta*, Havana: Letras Cubanas, 1983

Hurtado, Oscar (editor), *Cuentos cubanos de lo fantástico y lo extraordinario*, Havana: UNEAC, 1968

Mexico

Larson, Ross, *Fantasy and Imagination in the Mexican Narrative*, Tempe: Center for Latin American Studies, Arizona State University, 1977 [Chapter on science fiction in Mexico]

Olvera, Carlos, *Mejicanos en el espacio*, Mexico City: Diógenes, 1968

Manuel Scorza 1928–1983

Peruvian prose writer and poet

Manuel Scorza's first book of poetry, *Las imprecaciones* [Curses] was published in Mexico in 1955. One of the stories surrounding the spelling of his last name, which was Escorza, is that this book contained a typographic error. It has also been pointed out that the writer had already used the better-known spelling as early as 1952. These poems, like earlier ones of solidarity with Bolivian miners, show social commitment and a desire to speak for the voiceless or marginalized. He returned to Peru in 1956 and, with other writers, set up the publishing house Populibros Peruanos, which gained international attention before going bankrupt, thereby seriously affecting Scorza's financial situation.

In 1959 the peasant leaders of the Department of Pasco organized resistance manoeuvres with resulting government oppression. Scorza joined the Movimiento Comunal de Perú (Peruvian Communal Organization) became its general secretary, and denounced the government's actions in the media. Soon after he visited Cerro de Pasco and began reporting on the events he witnessed.

While he continued to write poetry during this period – *Los adioses*, 1959 [The Farewells], *Desengaños del mago*, 1961 [The Magician's Disenchantments] and *Requiem para un gentilhombre*, 1962 [Requiem for a Gentleman], clearly, these are experiences which will be given fictive form in his cycle of novels. President Fernando Belaúnde Terry also assigned him the editorship of an anthology of modern Peruvian poetry in 1963. The volume contained the work of the Generation of the 1950s, with its writing in the tone of political combat.

After his second marriage, Scorza left Peru once more so he could write the series of works for which he has become best known, although another volume of poetry, *El vals de los reptiles* [The Waltz of the Reptiles] was to appear in 1970. From Paris, where he resided from 1968 until 1978, Scorza composed the lyrical yet stark story of the peasant resistance in Pasco, titled *La guerra silenciosa* [The Silent War]. It consists of five books, described as novels or (by the author himself), as *cantares* (ballads). These are: *Redoble por Rancas*, 1970 (*Drums for Rancas*); *Historia de Garabombo, el invisible*, 1972 (*Garabombo the Invisible*); *El Cantar de Agapito Robles*, 1977 [The Ballad of Agapito Robles]; *El jinete insomne*, 1978 [The Sleepless Rider]; and *La tumba del relámpago*, 1979 [Requiem for a Lightning Bolt].

For Scorza, exile became necessary in order to write but, by his own admission, it was extremely painful. He was never far from Peruvian politics, however, and was asked by the communities about which he had written to run for election for the Constituent Assembly. He did become a candidate for the FOCEP (Frente Obrero, Campesino, Estudiantil y Popular), but withdrew in protest against government intimidatory practices. He later became secretary, then vice-president, of the FOCEP (Popular Front of Workers, Students and Peasants).

The return to Paris in 1984 after several years residence in Peru may have been the result of frustration with the Peruvian political situation. Scorza was working on *El verdadero descubrimiento de Europa* [The True Discovery of Europe], but it was left unfinished. A trilogy was also in progress, and was to be titled *Fuego y cenizas* [Fire and Ashes]. Its first volume, *La danza inmóvil* [The Motionless Dance], appeared in 1983 and is a love story set in Paris. The second volume was to be *Los pétalos de la quimera* [The Chimera's Petals].

For Scorza, literature was a forum for the judging of injustices past and present, a space where history could be reviewed and, in some cases, heard for the first time. His own writing was a constant protest against conditions suffered by the indigenous majority in Peru. Whether classified as *indigenista* or *neoindigenista* – terms with which the author himself did not agree – or as magical realism, the five works of the *Guerra silenciosa* cycle began with the belief that the Spanish Conquest had initiated a period in which time stood still, or more accurately, had ceased to exist, in the political and cultural sense, for the Indians. The Quechuas of the Andean highlands were excluded from history and thus silenced, their world very real yet minimized, distorted or destroyed by European elements. Except for the Quechua language, all the Andean world, from the inhabitants to the flora and fauna to the events that have been and are taking place there, is combined in the Silent War to portray a reality whose severity becomes absurd when described by Scorza. Characters metamorphosize, time ceases to exist, everything is exaggerated, and political conditions become literary farces. The almost surreal images and characters of the first book progress, however, toward the nearly total demythification and deliberate "textualization" or writing of a more accurate account, in the fifth book. Time is a vital element in Manual Scorza's concept of Peru as nation and culture, for its serves multiple purposes, including that of contrasting the European and Indian cosmovisions, the nature and goals of official (written) history, the clash between words and deeds. Space, or place, is the other key coordinate for defining national identity, and once again points up the discrepancies in the conceptualization of reality that coexist within the national boundaries. Humour in the form of satire, parody, and irony, is another of Scorza's techniques which expresses criticism of injustices past and present. At no point, however, is the real Peru far from the narrative. The author himself also closely shadows the narrator's voice and literally figures as an anonymous witness on occasion. The entire cycle is an intense counterplay of oblivion versus memory, individual versus community, objective versus subjective, tradition and myth versus modernization and empirical documentation.

Whether one considers Manual Scorza to be an *indigenista* or *neoindigenista* writer, this literary modality still must be part of the cultural context out of which his work came. His work is one of profound social protest and provides a major renovation of the techniques by which the highland region had been represented in Peruvian fiction, at a time when such an effort was much needed. The intertextuality with other works, periods, genres and styles gave new life to the litera-ture dealing with Indians, so masterfully produced by Scorza's fellow countryman José María Arguedas, whose spiritual offspring Scorza considered himself to be. Ironically, while dealing less directly with historical reality, his novels perhaps bring the experience of himself and the marginalized peasants closer to readers of all origins.

KATHLEEN N. MARCH

Biography

Born in Lima, Peru, 9 September 1928. Developed severe asthma at an early age and the family left Lima for Acoria, Huancavelica (his mother's village), where parents set up a bakery. Educated at a private school run by the Salesian Brothers; Colegio Militar Leoncio Prada, Lima (same school as Mario Vargas Llosa); Universidad Nacional de San Marcos, Lima. While at university became active in struggle against President Manuel Prado (1939–45). In late teens travelled to Chile and Argentina. From 1948 organized student protest against General Manuel Odría (1948–56). Arrested and imprisoned for one year. Exiled from Peru. Lived in Argentina, Chile and Brazil, working as perfume vendor, bookseller, proofreader and lecturer, then settled in Mexico. Studied at Universidad Nacional Autónoma de México (UNAM). Entered poetry competition at UNAM under different names, awarded first three prizes. Became involved in Bolivian miners' politics after publishing "Cantos a los mineros." Returned to Peru in 1956 where he lived for 11 years. Married Lydia Hyle in 1956; one daughter and one son. In late 1950s set up the co-operative publishing house, Populibres Peruanos, with other writers, which eventually went bankrupt. Involved in peasant uprisings at Pasco in 1959. Secretary general, Movimiento Comunal del Perú. Arrested and exiled from Cerro de Pasco. Married Cecilia Hare in 1966. Left Peru in 1967 and settled in Paris for ten years. Returned to Peru, 1978. Stood as candidate for FOCEP (Frente Obrero Campesino, Estudiantil y Popular) but withdrew candidacy. Vice-president, FOCEP, 1980. Returned to Paris, 1983. Awarded the National Prize for Literature. Died in a plane crash in Spain, 27 November 1983. Three other Spanish American literary figures – Ángel Rama, his wife Marta Traba and the Mexican writer Jorge Ibargüengoitia – died in the same accident.

Selected Works

Novels

La guerra silenciosa/The Silent War series:
    Redoble por Rancas, Barcelona: Planeta, 1970; as *Drums for Rancas*, translated by Edith Grossman, New York: Harper, and London: Secker and Warburg, 1977
    Historia de Garabombo, el invisible, Barcelona: Planeta, 1972; as *Garabombo the Invisible*, translated by Anna-Marie Aldaz, New York: Peter Lang, 1994
    Cantar de Agapito Robles, Caracas: Monte Ávila, 1977
    El jinete insomne, Caracas: Monte Ávila, 1978
    La tumba del relámpago, Madrid: Siglo XXI, 1979
La danza inmóvil, Barcelona: Plaza y Janés, 1983

Poetry

Las imprecaciones, Mexico City: Viento del Pueblo, 1955
Hidalgo, Mexico City: Instituto Nacional Indigenista, 1956
Los adioses, Lima: Festivales del Libro, 1959
Desengaños del mago, Lima: Festivales del Libro, 1961
Réquiem para un gentilhombre, Lima: Santiago Velarde, 1962

Compilations and Anthologies

El vals de los reptiles, Mexico City: UNAM, 1970 [poetry and essays]

Poesía, Lima: Secretaría de Educación y Cultura, 1986
Obra poética, Lima: PEISA, 1990
Obras completas, 6 vols, Mexico City: Siglo XXI, 1990–91

Further Reading
Aldaz, Anna-Marie, *The Past of the Future: the Novelistic Cycle of Manuel Scorza*, New York: Peter Lang, 1990

Forgues, Roland, *La estrategia mítica de Manuel Scorza*, Lima: Centro de Estudios para el Desarrollo y la Participación, 1991
Meyer, Doris (editor), *Lives on the Line: the Testimony of Contemporary Latin American Authors*, Berkeley: University of California Press, 1988

José Asunción Silva 1865–1896

Colombian poet and prose writer

José Asunción Silva is often classified as a "precursor" of the Modernist movement in Spanish America, in part for chronological reasons: the year of his death, 1896, is the same as that of the older Manuel Gutiérrez Nájera, for instance and occurs after the deaths of José Martí and Julián del Casal. It also predates Rubén Darío's *Cantos de vida y esperanza*, 1905 [Songs of Life and Hope], a work which many critics view as the finest poetic expression of the movement. Yet, a careful reading of Silva's works reveals him (along with his Cuban contemporary del Casal) to be a full member of Darío's Modernism, and indeed among its most outstanding poets.

Another, more surreptitious reason for Silva's anomalous categorization on the edges of Modernism, is the discomfort some literary scholars feel at the heavy doses of sentiment – especially in the form of bitter sarcasm and parody – more neatly associated with the previous Romantic movement. Yet a rectification of Silva's place in the Hispanic literary panorama brings a more judicious realization that the movement does not at all "transcend" sentiment by eliminating it, as some would have it, but by coupling it with the artistic and intellectual balances Modernism successfully brought to the frequent excesses of Romanticism. Hence – and this is no novel observation – Modernism is less a reaction against Romanticism than an incorporation of its finest contributions into early 20th-century art: a strongly conceived artistic perception, the intense struggle of the poet with society, nature, fate and self.

The relative paucity of Silva's *oeuvre* remains one of the gaps in Spanish American poetry, just as the richness and beauty of what he did produce in his short life are one of its lasting monuments, both because he died, by his own hand, still a young man (at least in chronology), and because a good portion of what he himself considered his best work was lost in a shipwreck. While we cannot, of course, evaluate a writer on the basis of his lost poems, what Silva left behind, although poorly organized and still subject to dispute as to its definitive versions, is sufficiently varied, original and masterful to place him among Spanish American's best poets of all times.

Silva's art in many ways laments the passage of time not only in a generic, philosophical way, such as in "Día de difuntos" [Day of the Dead], but in specific historical context:

the death of the old ways – tradition, stability, coherence – and profound doubts about the changes the 20th century was already producing in Latin America and of which Silva was in fact an early victim. A few decades earlier Silva would have been the beneficiary of a socio-economic system granting him immediate and all but unassailable recognition and privilege. Yet the onslaught of unfettered early 20th-century capitalism turned the family business into both an unwanted responsibility for the young Silva on the death of his father, and a confirmation for him that Jorge Manrique (the famous 15th-century Spanish poet) was right: "todo tiempo passado fue mejor" (all past times were better). The conflict between an idealized world, associated with childhood and past times, and the signs of the bad new days to come is a recurring theme in Silva's verse, and in his only novel, *De sobremesa* [Table Talk].

"Los maderos de San Juan" [The San Juan Lumberyard] exemplifies Silva's disillusionment and the feeling of powerlessness to affect the passage of time for the better. In this lovely lament, a grandmother rocks her grandson on her knee while singing a traditional children's song, partly made up nonsense words which merely establish a rhythm imitative of the regularity of the lumberyard's saws: "triqui triqui triqui tran / los maderos de San Juan." Alternating with the direct presentation of this scene are the reflections of another voice, relating the grandmother's nostalgic feelings for her own girlhood and the losses and pains that time has brought her. The voice tells us that such will assuredly be the boy's fate as well, as it is, in Silva's view, for all: he will remember this same scene, longing for his own innocence and her love, after his grandmother's death. This poem could simply be a moving portrayal of the "tempus fugit" theme, but there is another, quite subtle note introduced by the poet's intervention: where earlier he said that the woman's knees are firm and hard and that "ambos agitados ... están" (both are excited), this time her knees are "tired," and he says "ambos *conmovidos* ... están" (both are *moved*). That is to say that the boy in his innocence has somehow perceived, and hence already begun to share, his elder's sadness: he has, then, already begun to experience the very loss and disenchantment with life that she feels during the very act of trying to protect him from them.

The lovely sadness of "Los maderos de San Juan," the pain of love lost ("Nocturno," his most famous poem, and "Poeta, di paso" [Poet, Speak Softly]), the absurd inevitability of death itself ("Muertos" [The Dead] and "La Calavera" [The Skull]) and the solitude of the artist ("La respuesta de la tierra" [The Earth's Reply]) typify one Silvan attitude and the one most often associated with him. Yet the revelation of painful truths produces in other poems a quite different tonality, and we have a different Silva, one highly ironic and often sarcastically bitter toward life, fate and his times, expressed most forcefully in decadentist parody (present in Darío, but much less typical in him than in Silva). Thus he excoriates the noble-sounding ideal of the French Revolution – "Egalité" – by suggesting that the only way that a common man (to whom he applies the homely name "Juan Lanas") and a member of the aristocratic elite – the Emperor of China – are equal is when "the human beast" trembles in the "sexual spasm" of orgasm: then we see that, indeed, "both are the same animal." In other words, what binds the human species together is its vulgarity, base urges and carnal crassness. Similarly, "Madrigal" portrays a young woman's innocent beauty ("tu tez rosada y pura, tus formas gráciles" [your pink and pure face, the grace of your form]) in exquisitely refined detail, only to be trampled: for "todo eso está, y a gritos, pidiendo un hombre" (all that is shouting out, asking for a man).

In this same parodic vein, Silva strikes out at medicine as empty, since what we really need is a cure for life, as in "Psychotherapy" and "Capsules." Philosophy is just as vain and impotent as medicine, for he tells the studious man that "cuando llegues en postrera hora / a la última morada, / sentirás una angustia matadora / de no haber hecho nada" (when, in your last hour, you come to your final home, you will feel the killing anguish of having done: nothing). Socio-economic change produces only a mass of materialistic Sancho Panzas (the image of the robber barons of the time), nihilism and mindless violence ["Futura"]. Thus he portrays, in "Lazarus," a man miraculously returned to life, facing the world anew, only to return sobbing to his burial ground, envying the dead.

It is, at times, difficult to conjoin into one body of work tonalities and expressive modes so seemingly disparate; but Silva's work is consistently characterized by the powerful sentiments spoken of above, expressed with the most effective stylistic control, rhythmic skill and inventive use of language, as in his famous parody of the most derivative and mushy-penned followers of Darío, "Sinfonía color de fresas con leche" [Symphony in Strawberries and Milk]. Silva's is, finally, the poetic legacy of a man whose aspirations, as in Darío, Martí

and del Casal, could never be satisfied by life and its (and his own) inevitable imperfections: he thus writes from the very heart of the Modernist movement itself, to remind us of its messages to our own "Postmodern" times.

PAUL W. BORGESON, JR

Biography

Born in Bogotá, Colombia, 26 November 1865. Educated at various private schools; left school in 1881 to work in his father's import store. First poems published in 1884. Father ruined by civil war that broke out in 1885. Visited Europe in 1885 and returned to Colombia in 1889. Father died in 1887 and José Asunción's sister, Elvira, in 1891. Appointed Secretary of the Colombian Legation in Caracas, 1894. On his return journey to Colombia in 1895, the boat on which he was travelling sank off the Colombian coast, and a number of his manuscripts were lost. Resigned from diplomatic corps. Suffered acute depression. Committed suicide, 24 May 1896.

Selected Works

De sobremesa, Bogotá: Cromos, 1925
El libro de versos, 1883–1896, Bogotá: Cromos, 1928
El libro de versos, facsimile edition, Bogotá: Horizonte, 1945
Intimidades, edited by Hector H. Orjuela, Bogotá: Instituto Caro y Cuervo, 1977

Compilations and Anthologies

Poesías. Edición definitiva, prologue by Miguel de Unamuno and notes by Baldomero Sanín Cano, Paris: Michaud, 1923
Obras completas, 2 vols, Buenos Aires: Plus Ultra, 2nd edition, 1968
Obras completas de José Asunción Silva, Medellín, Colombia: Editorial Bedout, 1970
Obra completa, edited by Hector H. Orjuela, Nanterre, France: Centre de Recherches Latino-Américaines, 1990

Further Reading

Camacho Guizado, Eduardo, *La poesía de José Asunción Silva*, Bogotá: Ediciones Universidad de Los Andes, 1968
Ingwersen, Sonya A., *Light and Longing: Silva and Darío. Modernism and Religious Heterody*, New York: Peter Lang, 1986
Loveluck, Juan, "*De sobremesa*: novela desconocida del Modernismo," *Revista Iberoamericana*, vol. 31/59 (1965)
Osiek, Betty T., *José Asunción Silva*, Boston: Twayne, 1978
Picon Garfield, Evelyn, "*De sobremesa*: el diario íntimo y la mujer prerrafaelita," in *Nuevos asedios al modernismo*, edited by Ivan Schulman, Madrid: Taurus, 1987
Villanueva Collado, Alfredo, "Arte, ciencia y la creación de estructuras narrativas por José Asunción Silva," in *Encuentro de la literatura con la ciencia y el arte*, edited by Juana Alcira Arancibia, Buenos Aires: O Cruxavaes, and Westminster, California: Instituto Literario y Cultural Hispánico, 1990

Silva, Bernardo Guimarães de

See Guimarães

Antonio Skármeta 1940–

Chilean prose writer

A university-trained teacher and critic of Spanish American literature, with a masters degree from New York's Columbia University (1966), Antonio Skármeta is not only an accomplished novelist, short-story writer and film-maker, but is also a highly articulate commentator on his generation's outlook and practice of fiction. His articles and interviews are of major importance for the understanding of many aspects of the Post-Boom. Born in Antofagasta in northern Chile of Yugoslavian immigrant origin, he is one of the relatively few Chilean writers who do not spring from the middle and upper classes and his work marks a break with the genteel tradition in Chilean fiction. After 1966 he taught at the University of Santiago, translated works by Melville, Scott Fitzgerald, Kerouac, Mailer and others, and achieved prominence by winning the Casa de las Américas Prize with his second collection of short stories *Desnudo en el tejado*, 1969 [Naked on the Roof]. In 1975 came the publication of his first novel *Soñé que la nieve ardía* (*I Dreamt the Snow was Burning*) completed in exile after he had been forced to leave Chile by the military coup against the Allende government, which he had supported, two years earlier. He was to spend thirteen years in exile, chiefly in West Berlin where he taught in the Academy of Cinema and Television. He wrote successful radio plays and made a number of films with the Director Peter Lillienthal, as well as publishing four more novels, including his best so far, *Ardiente paciencia*, 1985 (*Burning Patience*), also filmed.

In Skármeta's early short stories the intellectual and existential preoccupations frequently present in Boom writing still re-emerge sporadically. But they tend to be offset by the instinctive vitality of the young protagonists, whose appearance along with their zest, youth-culture, pop music and enjoyment of sport, is often seen as part of the shift towards the Post-Boom. There is a return of confidence, indicated by the title of Skármeta's first collection of stories, *El entusiasmo*, 1967 [Enthusiasm]. Here and later, brief experiences of loving sexuality, as in "La Cenicienta en San Francisco" [Cinderella in San Francisco], create epiphanic moments of affirmation of life, of yea-saying. They overcome, not just personal loneliness, but existential solitude. Chaos and absurdity give way to a sense of reconciliation with an uncontaminated world. "Otherness" is conquered; inner understanding and mutual reassurance are established. In *Desnudo en el tejado* Skármeta's approach to reality is tempered by elements of fantasy, but notable stories, such as "Basketball" still deal with adolescent or post-adolescent rites of passage in which life's hostility is disarmed.

The rise and fall of the Allende government in Chile radicalized Skármeta's political stance and strongly influenced all his subsequent writing up to and including *Ardiente paciencia*. *Tiro libre*, 1973 [Fire at Will], his third collection of stories, marks the ideological shift, with some tales, such as "El cigarrillo" [The Cigarette] which are now overtly political. *Soñé que la nieve ardía* centres on a group of young people living under the Allende administration and the evolution of one of them, Arturo, who aspires to be a professional football player. The chain of events concerning him chronicles his reluctant move towards greater Left Wing commitment. The novel is dominated by two symbols: soccer, with its high rewards and star-system, standing for selfish individualism, and Arturo's virginity, which represents his political and social immaturity. He fails as a professional player, but is finally sexually initiated by Susana, a working-class girl. Because of its political theme, its young, semi-proletarian characters and the way it reaches out towards a new balance between "observed" and "created" reality, *Soñé . . .* is one of the inaugural novels of the Post-Boom. *No pasó nada*, 1985 [Nothing Happened], is Skármeta's contribution to recent exile fiction, an important genre in the Post-Boom. The young protagonist, Lucho, undergoes experiences in West Berlin, where he lives in exile with his parents, which illustrate the values of Chileanness. These, it is implicit in the novel, will survive political repression at home and be needed in the new post-Pinochet Chile. The difficulty for Skármeta was to transcend the usual limitations of exile writing: nostalgia, resentment and partisan attitudes. He overcomes them by dealing sensitively with the universal problems of adolescence, especially Lucho's growing awareness of the other sex. A teenage affair leads to a fight with an older German boy which takes on the quality of a rite of passage to adulthood. It is followed by a symbolic reconciliation and the triumph of positive values of friendship and solidarity as Lucho's antagonist learns to support the Chilean exile movement.

La insurrección, 1982 (*The Insurrection*), is set in provincial Nicaragua during the Sandinista uprising and depicts the fall of the Somoza regime in the city of León. It is as close as Skármeta ever comes to a fully committed, revolutionary novel. Few others proclaim faith in individual and collective insurrectionary effort as boldly as *La insurrección*. It is to be contrasted with, for example, Vargas Llosa's *Historia de Mayta*, 1984 (*The Real History of Alejandro Mayta*), which attempts to undermine such writings. Centred on a collective protagonist, the humble Menor family, the novel develops slowly towards its climax, the neighbourhood's attack on the local barracks, which is sprayed with petrol from a pipe passed through their houses and set on fire. The reader is brought gradually to understand and share the motives which drive the people from passivity to open rebellion against gross military oppression. Even more noteworthy than in *Soñé que la nieve ardía* is the active participation of women in the political struggle, which has allowed Skármeta to claim justifiably that he is a feminist writer, another factor linking him to the Post-Boom, in which feminist and other minority voices are clearly heard. By contrast, *Ardiente paciencia* returns to Chile and to the rise and fall of Allende. The novel is pre-eminently a love story, in which a Nobel prizewinner, the poet Pablo Neruda, figures prominently as a protective father-figure for a couple of young working-class lovers. Their idyll runs parallel to the life of the Allende government. It begins in the run-up to Allende's election and is consummated on the night of his victory. A second climax of love-making, this time collective, comes when Neruda wins the Nobel Prize. But when the poet returns to Chile to die and Allende's government is overthrown, the hero, Mario, a young postman, is arrested and "disappeared." The novel, which begins happily, ends in bitterness. Nevertheless, because of its earlier lightheartedness and superb portraits of Neruda and his young protegés, surrounded by their delightful and amusing friends and neighbours, this is Skármeta's most entertaining and brilliantly written novel to date, a major contribution to modern Spanish American fiction.

Match Ball (1989) is set in Europe and marks a new direction in Skármeta's writing. The central character, Papst, is an archetypal figure of the masculine middle-class crisis. A married, wealthy, expatriate physician in his early fifties, working in West Berlin, where he has a lucrative practice, he falls madly in love with an enigmatic, adolescent tennis-star, Sophie Mass, destroying his marriage and his career, as well as plunging into folly and crime, while pursuing her and trying to hold off a younger rival. The theme is the rejection of hollow and unsatisfying middle-class values and the search for an impossible renewal of youth, love and sexuality. It illustrates the return to neo-romanticism characteristic of one of the main currents of writing in the Post-Boom. But underlying it is the universal fear of growing old and slipping into comfortable conformity. *Match Ball* is the story of the last hurrah of a man of the hippie era in a period which has been taken over by yuppies. His confession is the swan-song of a generation. Despite his unforgivable behaviour to his wife, refusal to heed warnings and utter lack of self control, Papst manages to distance himself at times from his plight and retains just enough droll self-awareness to keep our minimal interest and respect. Sophie, on the other hand, is utterly different from earlier female characters in Skármeta's work and her motivation for leading Papst on is far from clear. She seems to be both seeking a father-figure and rejecting male domination. She remains puzzlingly imperturbable in the face of the nightmare she unleashes on her two lovers.

Up to *Match Ball* what matters in Skármeta is his return to a more reader-friendly manner of writing than that of the Boom writers, with strong emphasis on love-interest and on the here and now of Spanish America. These are all promi-

nent characteristics of the Post-Boom of which he is one of the most representative writers.

DONALD L. SHAW

Biography

Born in Antofagasta, Chile, 7 November 1940. Attended the University of Chile, Santiago; Columbia University, New York, MA, 1966. Married Cecilia Boisier in 1964 (divorced); two sons; married Nora Preperski. Professor of contemporary Latin American literature, University of Chile, early 1970s; left Chile after military coup in 1973. Professor of screenwriting, Academy of Cinema and Television, West Berlin, 1978–81; since 1981 freelance writer and filmmaker. Returned to Chile in 1989 and is a popular TV personality; runs workshops for young writers. The novel *Ardiente paciencia* was adapted for film (as *Il postino*), directed by Michael Radford, 1994. Awarded the Casa de las Américas Prize, 1969 for *Desnudo en el tejado*; Daniel Belmar Prize, 1969; Biarritz Film Festival Prize, 1983; Huelva Film Festival Prize, 1983; Guggenheim Fellowship, 1986.

Selected Works

Short Fiction

El entusiasmo, Santiago de Chile: Zig-Zag, 1967
Desnudo en el tejado, Buenos Aires: Sudamericana, 1969
Tiro libre, Buenos Aires: Siglo XXI, 1973
El ciclista de San Cristóbal, Santiago de Chile: Quimantú, 1973
Novios y solitarios, Buenos Aires: Losada, 1975
No pasó nada y otros relatos, Santiago de Chile: Pehuén, 1985
La Cenicienta en San Francisco y otros cuentos, Santiago de Chile: Andrés Bello, 1990

Novels

Soñé que la nieve ardía, Barcelona: Planeta, 1975; as *I Dreamt the Snow was Burning*, translated by Malcolm Coad, London and New York: Readers International, 1985
Chileno!, translated by Hortense Carpentier, New York: Morrow, 1979
La insurrección, Hanover, New Hampshire: Ediciones del Norte, 1982; as *The Insurrection*, translated by Paul Sharp, Ediciones del Norte, 1983
Ardiente paciencia, Buenos Aires: Sudamericana, and Hanover, New Hampshire: Ediciones del Norte, 1985; as *Burning Patience*, translated by Katherine Silver, New York: Pantheon, 1987; London: Methuen, 1988
Match Ball, Buenos Aires: Sudamericana, 1989 [in Spanish]

Screenplay: *Ardiente paciencia*, 1983

Translations

Watch Where the Wolf is Going, translated by Donald L. Schmidt and Federico Cordovez, London: Readers International, 1991 [Selection of short stories]

Further Reading

Bumas, Ethan Shaskan, "Metaphor's Exile: the Poets and Postmen of Antonio Skármeta," *Latin American Literary Review*, vol. 21/41 (1993)
Lemaitre, Monique J., *Skármeta: una narrativa de la liberación*, Santiago de Chile: Pehuén, 1991
Lira, Constanza, *Skármeta: la inteligencia de los sentidos*, Santiago de Chile: Dante, 1985

Shaw, Donald L., " 'La Cenicienta en San Francisco' by Antonio Skármeta," *Revista de Estudios Hispánicos*, vol. 21/2 (1987)
____ "The Structure of Antonio Skármeta's *Soñé que la nieve ardía*," *The Americas Review*, vol. 18/3–4 (1990)
____ "Fictional Technique in Skármeta's *La insurrección*," *Antípodas*, vol. 3 (1991)
____ *Antonio Skármeta and the Post Boom*, Hanover, New Hampshire: Ediciones del Norte, 1994
Silva Cáceres, Raúl, *et al.*, *Del cuerpo a las palabras: la narrativa de Antonio Skármeta*, Madrid: Literatura Americana Reunida, 1983
Tittler, Jonathan, "Toward a Revolutionary Writing: Antonio Skármeta's *La insurrección*," *Literature and Revolution*, edited by David Bevan, Amsterdam: Rodopi, 1989

Ardiente paciencia

Novel by Antonio Skármeta

Skármeta's most popular novel, *Ardiente paciencia* (*Burning Patience*), was first a play and then a successful movie, which the author himself directed. (More recently the novel has also inspired a moving Italian version, *Il postino* [The Postman]). The action takes place in and around the town of Isla Negra, on the Chilean coast, between 1969 and 1973. Its creation was owed to two circumstances: Chile's political trauma and Pablo Neruda's prominence on the national scene during these years. The protagonist of this tragicomedy, Mario Jiménez, is a likeable seventeen-year-old youth of modest means who accepts employment as a postman, mainly because his only client is Chile's most famous bard, Pablo Neruda. In order to strike up a friendship with Neruda, Mario buys a copy of his *Odas elementales* (*The Elemental Odes*), asks the author to autograph it, and, through their subsequent conversations, comes to realize the power of the metaphor. Another reason for Mario's friendship with Neruda is Beatriz González, a comely barmaid whose affection, with the aid of Neruda's verses, Mario gradually succeeds in winning. But, just when he begins to anticipate an idyllic future with Beatriz (he fully intends to marry her), he "came up against one of Chile's more terrifying institutions: the mother-in-law."

Rosa de González, Beatriz's mother, is a blunt-spoken, worldly-wise widow determined to protect her daughter from the wiles of male predators such as Mario Jiménez; she also recognizes Neruda's love poems when Beatriz repeats them to her as Mario's own creations. Then, in a hilarious conversation between Rosa and Neruda (with Mario concealed behind a curtain), Rosa hurls accusations of plagiarism against the youth, "a seducer of minors," and threatens to cause him bodily injury if Neruda does not keep him away from her daughter. Being a practical woman, however, she eventually agrees to the couple's marriage, after seeing that "the floodgates had already been flung open."

Subsequent events include Salvador Allende's election (September 1970), his appointment of Neruda as ambassador to France, Neruda's winning the Nobel Prize, and the military coup against Allende (September 11, 1973). The novel ends tragically with the ailing Neruda's return from Paris to Isla Negra, his death a few days after the coup, and Mario's arrest and disappearance.

Much of the novel's humor derives from its overall ironic tone and, in particular, from its ironic treatment of the four major characters, all of whom are presented by an detached, but not unsympathetic, narrator. Thus the mature Neruda, whose past love affairs are legend, contrasts sharply with Mario, the callow youth obsessed with the opposite sex and about to experience the rite of passage to manhood. On the other hand, Rosa de González's cynical attitude toward men, coupled with her intense alarm over the effects of Neruda's love poems, differs just as sharply from her daughter's innocence and gullibility.

Another source of humor is Skármeta's use of hyperbole, reminiscent of García Márquez, especially in the love scenes between Mario and Beatriz: " despegó el orgasmo de Beatriz hacia la noche sideral con una candencia que. . . le inspiró las siguientes palabras al cura párroco en su desvelo de la torre: 'magnificat, stabat, pange lingua, dies irae, benedictus, kyrie eleison, angelica.'" (Beatriz released her orgasm into the starry night with such a cadence that it . . . inspired the parish priest doing vigil in the tower to utter these words: 'magnificat, stabat, pange lingua, dies irae, benedictus, kyrie eleison, angelica'). Also reminiscent of García Márquez are the occasional dashes of absurd humor: "Cuando al mínimo Jiménez le debutaron los dientes, consta en los barrotes de la jaula que intentó aserrucharlos con sus lechosos caninos. Las encías coronadas de astillas introdujeron a otro personaje en la hostería y en el exangüe presupuesto de Mario: el dentista." (When baby Jiménez began to teethe, he took to sawing off the bars of his cage with his new molars, an activity that filled his gums with splinters and added a new claimant to Mario's rapidly declining resources: the dentist).

In another comic scene, Neruda and Mario become victims of irony when, confident that the revered poet will smooth the way for Mario's romance with Beatriz, they play the Beatles' recording of "Mr Postman" and dance joyfully about the room while waiting for the widow González's arrival to speak with Neruda. But after her departure and Mario's reappearance from behind the curtain, Neruda massages his ear, rolls his eyes, and exclaims: " . . . now I know what a boxer feels like when he has been knocked out in the first round."

Humor is tempered by poignancy, however, when Neruda's nostalgic letter from Paris asks Mario to send him a tape recording of the sounds of the sea and when Mario writes his "Ode to the Snow Over Neruda in Paris," a beautiful poem filled with metaphors conveying how much Neruda is missed by his friends at home. Recorded on tape, Mario's poem is followed by the cries of Pablo Neftalí Jiménez González, Neruda's godson. Another memorable moment is Neruda's Nobel Prize speech in Stockholm, shown on television in Chile, in which his quotation from a poem by Rimbaud reveals the origin of the book's title: "Only with burning patience shall we conquer the splendid city that will give light, justice, and dignity to all men."

Additional political elements deftly woven into the narrative texture include Neruda's brief presidential candidacy for the socialist Partido Unidad Popular and, after Allende's election, the many problems plaguing his regime: food shortages, trucker strikes, bombings by right-wingers, and street protests by middle-class women pounding on pots and pans. But far more dramatic are the brutal military coup and its aftermath:

the telegrams from foreign governments offering Neruda asylum and Mario's emotional meeting with the poet moments before he is taken to the hospital to die.

Skármeta wrote *Ardiente paciencia* in Germany, where he spent many years in exile after the military coup in his homeland. His novel pays homage not only to Chile's greatest poet, but also to the Allende supporters who, like Mario Jiménez, remained in Chile and suffered the consequences. But what emerges as perhaps the most important theme of this tragicomedy is the power of language, more specifically the power of poetry, to motivate human behavior. Thus, as mentioned above, Neruda's verses ignite amorous passion in Beatriz and fear in Rosa (whose comments are ironically sprinkled with refrains), but additional evidence of this theme is the elaborate precautions taken by the government at Neruda's funeral in order to prevent a violent protest by the poet's hordes of ardent admirers. And, in the final lines of the novel, we are told that military officials have, out of fear no doubt, confiscated the issues of *La Quinta Rueda* [The Fifth Wheel], a poetry journal to which Mario has submitted one of his poems. Skármeta himself has commented on his homage to language in his work, that is, on his efforts to capture a mixture of the cultured and popular prose used by Chileans. The oxymoron of Skármeta's title, moreover, poetically condenses the repressed yearnings of a freedom-loving nation caught in the grip of a brutal dictatorship.

GEORGE R. MCMURRAY

Editions

First edition: *Ardiente paciencia*, Buenos Aires: Sudamericana, and Hanover, New Hampshire: Ediciones del Norte, 1985
Translation: *Burning Patience*, by Kathleen Silver, New York: Pantheon, 1987; London: Methuen, 1988

Further Reading

The bibliography on *Ardiente paciencia* is surprisingly small. Possibly the best remarks on this novel are by the author himself in Mario Blanc's interview listed below.

Bannura-Spriga, M.G., "El juego y el deseo en la obra de Antonio Skármeta," *Inti: Revista de Literatura Hispánica* 24–25 (Fall–Spring 1986–87)
Blanc, Mario, "Antonio Skármeta: cuentos y novelas," *Chasqui*, vol. 13/2 (November 1989)
Cortínez, V., "Polifonía: Isabel Allende y Antonio Skármeta, *Plaza: Revista de Literatura*, nos 14–15 (Spring–Fall 1988)
Filer, Malva E., "*Ardiente paciencia*," *World Literature Today* 60 (1986)
McMurray, George R., "Antonio Skármeta," in *Encyclopedia of World Literature in the Twentieth Century*, edited by Steven R. Serafin and Walter D. Glanze, vol. 5, New York: Continuum, 1993

Carlos Solórzano 1922–

Guatemalan/Mexican playwright

Though Guatemalan by birth, Carlos Solórzano's life and career have been so closely intertwined with Mexico, where he has lived since 1939, that some critics have taken recently to listing him as Guatemalan/Mexican. This great-grandson of a former president of Guatemala has combined a literary career with an academic one, having established the program "Carrera de Arte Dramático" at the Universidad Nacional Autónoma de México (UNAM) where he has taught for many years. Solórzano has also contributed to journals and newspapers in Europe, Puerto Rico, Latin America and the United States.

Widely acknowledged as both a scholar and critic of theater in Latin America, Solórzano's published works include, in addition to his newspaper and journal articles, (a selection of which were published by the UNAM), two novels, two works about Latin American theater, three theater anthologies, and eleven plays. Despite his incursions into other literary genres, Solórzano's paramount contribution to Spanish American letters lies in his drama. Though not as extensive as the work of many of his peers, his plays, however, challenge readers to

rethink their position on those questions which have troubled human beings through the ages, and to do so from a universal rather than from a regional perspective. His insistence on this viewpoint aroused some criticism in Mexico, initially over the choice of his *Los fantoches* [The Puppets] to represent Mexico in the United Nations Theater Festival in Paris in 1963. None the less, the author defended his choice, pointing out that he had not ignored what is essentially Mexican in this play, (and by extension all his theater), but had incorporated it as a point of departure in his writing.

Solórzano's creative writing, and in particular his writing for the theater, reveals the influence of several major European authors, an impact the dramatist freely acknowledges. While one cannot necessarily specify the precise effect on Solórzano of the different artists who fell within his purview, four names stand out: Ghelderode, Camus, Artaud and Unamuno. From a philosophical perspective, the last of these is quite important. Early on the Basque philosopher/author had captured the attention of the young Guatemalan writer to the degree that the Spaniard's works became the topic of Solórzano's master's thesis as well as his doctoral dissertation. Unamuno's impact on Solórzano is both substantive and pervasive. Fundamental in the philosophy of both men is the word "agitar" (to shake), symbolic of the reluctance of either one to accept a theory simply because someone postulates it. As Rivas remarked in his study on Solórzano, "Agitar para Solórzano implica conmover, hacer pensar al espectador." (To agitate for Solórzano implies to move, to make the spectator think). Both authors struggle with the concept of death which they perceive as the ultimate insult to mankind. Both, while acknowledging the existence of a creator, have considerable difficulty with the institutionalized church and what they perceive as its rigidness and insensitivity.

Less ideological is the effect of the above mentioned dramatists on Solórzano's theater. He knew both Camus and the Belgian playwright Ghelderode. To the former he attributed the inspiration for his play, *Doña Beatriz*. With the latter he shared many themes, chief among them the issue of good and evil and the related question of culpability. Though he had never met Artaud and knew him only through his plays, both writers have in common a poetic and religious dimension to their respective dramatic writings.

While one may consider Solórzano's plays from various points of view, even grouping them according to thematic focus, certain traits inform all of his dramas. Principal among these is the issue of the reason for man's being. Characters often refer to "the sin of having been born." Whether they be the tormented puppets of *Los fantoches*, the harassed heroine of *El sueño del ángel* [The Angel's Dream], or the bedeviled Beatriz of *Las manos de Dios* [The Hands of God], they rail against fate as they question in vain the rationale of their existence. In more than half of his plays the author's anticlerical bias figures significantly. Also customary in his theater is a preoccupation with good and evil, not in the conventional moral sense but rather in relation to the right of people to exercise their free will. In an interview with Esteban Rivas, Solórzano stated his position quite clearly when he said, "Pecar es optar . . . y ser dueño de su propia conciencia, de optar es el mejor bien del hombre." (To sin is to choose . . . and to be master of one's own conscience; to choose is man's greatest good). A review of the casts of Solórzano's plays reveals that the majority of his characters have no proper names. This technique explains the withdrawn nature and lack of communication typical of many of the characters in his dramas, which, in turn, underscores their existential aloneness.

Solórzano's is an urbane theater which reflects not only the diversity of his intellectual and artistic experience, but also his practical training in architecture and work as a theater director. Through it runs his constant preoccupation with the relationship of man with the world in which he finds himself. In an interview with Teresa Méndez-Faith which appeared in the Fall 1984 issue of *Latin American Theatre Review* he acknowledged this when he said:

Pues hay un tema que sí me preocupa, que me preocupó siempre . . . es que yo encuentro que, en general, hemos nacido en un mundo hóstil y que a nosotros, los pobladores del siglo XX nos cuesta mucho trabajo reconciliarnos con él.

[Well, there is a theme which concerns me, which always has . . . the fact is that I find that, in general, we were born into a hostile world and that it costs us, the inhabitants of the 20th century a great deal of work to reconcile ourselves to it.]

FRANCESCA COLECCHIA

Biography

Born in San Marcos, Guatemala, 1 May 1922. Moved to Mexico in 1939, where he has since made his home. Attended the Universidad Nacional Autónoma de México (UNAM), Mexico City, degree in architecture, 1944, and PhD in literature, 1948. Married Beatrice Caso in 1946; one son (deceased) and two daughters. Received Rockefeller Foundation grant in 1948, to study drama at the Sorbonne, Paris, 1948–50. Founder and director of the Teatro Universitario Profesional, 1950–60 and Teatro Estudiantil Universitario, 1950–52. Visiting professor at several American universities including, Southern California, Kansas, Arizona, and Colombia. Has also served as correspondent for *Rendez-vous du Théâtre* and *Primer Acto* as well as drama critic for *Siempre*. Former director of the Museo Nacional de Teatro. Currently, Latin America area editor for the *Enciclopedia Mundial del Teatro Contemporáneo*. Professor at UNAM, since the mid-1990s. Awarded the Premio Universidad, Universidad Nacional Autónoma, 1989; Miguel Ángel Asturias National Literature Prize (Guatemala), 1989.

Selected Works

Plays

La muerte hizo la luz, in *Revista de Guatemala*, vol. 3 (October–December 1951) [one-act play]
Doña Beatriz, Mexico City: Helio, 1954
El hechicero, Mexico City: Cultura, 1955
Las manos de Dios, Mexico City: Costa-Amic, 1957
Los fantoches, *Cruce de vías* and *El crucificado*, in *Tres Actos*, Mexico City: El Unicornio, 1959 [one-act play]
El sueño del ángel, in *Tercera antología de obras en un acto*, Mexico City: Colección Teatro Mexicano, 1960 [one-act play]
El zapato, in *Crononauta 2* (1966) [one-act play]
Mea culpa, in *Teatro de Carlos Solórzano*, Mexico City: UNAM, 1992 [one-act play]

Novels

Los falsos demonios, Mexico City: Joaquín Mortiz, 1966
Las celdas, Mexico City: Joaquín Mortiz, 1971

Other Writings

Espejo de novelas, Mexico City: UNAM, 1945
Teatro latinoamericano del siglo XX, Buenos Aires: Nueva Visión, 1961; revised edition, New York: Macmillan, 1963
Teatro guatemalteco contemporáneo, Madrid: Aguilar, 1964 [anthology]
El teatro hispanoamericano contemporáneo, 2 vols, Mexico City: Fondo de Cultura Económica, 1964 [anthology]
El teatro latinoamericano en el siglo XX, Mexico City: Pormaca, 1964
Teatro breve hispanoamericano contemporáneo, Madrid: Aguilar, 1969 [anthology]
Testimonios teatrales de Méjico, Mexico City: UNAM, 1973

Compilations and Anthologies

Teatro, San José, Costa Rica, EDUCA, 1972 [Contains *Los fantoches*, *El crucificado*, *Las manos de Dios*, *El sueño del ángel*]

Teatro breve, Mexico City: Joaquín Mortiz, 1977 [Contains *El zapato, cruce de vías, El sueño del ángel, Mea culpa, El crucificado, Los fantoches*]

Translations

Crossroads and Other Plays, translated by Francesca Colecchia, Rutherford, New Jersey: Fairleigh Dickinson University Press, and London: Associated University Presses, 1993

Further Reading

Feliciano, Wilma, "Myth and Theatricality in Three Plays by Carlos Solórzano," *Latin American Theatre Review*, vol. 25/1 (1991)

Higuero, Francisco Javier, "Incomunicación múltiple en el teatro breve de Solórzano," *Latin American Theatre Review*, vol. 26/1 (Fall 1992)

Martínez-Rivas, Esteban, *Carlos Solórzano y el teatro mexicano*, Mexico City: Impresos Anahuac, 1970

Ostergaard, Anne-Grethe, "Semiología de la destrucción y autodestrucción en el teatro de Carlos Solórzano," *Revista Canadiense de Estudios Hispánicos*, vol. 7/1 (Autumn 1982)

Rosenberg, John R., "The Ritual of Solórzano's *Los manos de Dios*," *Latin American Theatre Review*, vol. 17/2 (1984)

Osvaldo Soriano 1943–

Argentine prose writer

Osvaldo Soriano's first novel *Triste, solitario y final* [Sad, Lonely and Final] was published in 1973. It was intended to be not only a tribute to Stan Laurel and Oliver Hardy but also to the detective novel genre *à la* Raymond Chandler, demonstrably so since the first edition was dedicated to these three figures. In fact, the novel is quite obviously the result of a passionate interest in Chandler and a melancholy vignette of the most celebrated characters of the early years of Hollywood. As well as Laurel and Hardy, there are Chaplin, Philip Marlowe himself (Chandler wrote Hollywood scripts), Buster Keaton, John Wayne, Jerry Lewis, etc. Behind the tribute there is a vague criticism, mostly nostalgic although at times quite bitter, of Chaplin's film *Modern Times* and a nod and a wink at the "anti-imperialist" (i.e., anti-US) criticism which dominated intellectual and literary circles in those days. This criticism is personified in the novel by Soriano himself who appears, in the third person, as a minor character.

His second novel, *No habrá más penas ni olvidos* (*A Funny Dirty Little War*), was finished by mid-1975. This was just after the death of Perón and, because of the exploits of the Triple A, the State's repressive apparatus during that period, it was difficult to publish anything in Argentina. This was particularly true of a book like this one which dealt in allegorical terms with the political factions vying for control of the Peronist movement. The novel is set in a small provincial town called (not without a certain sarcasm) Colonia Vela. (The literal meaning is Vigil Colony. Vela has the following meanings: state of being awake; a nuisance; a funeral wake; facing the music; a candle. It is not clear which meaning(s) Soriano has in mind].

In fact the novel sets out to be a sort of pocket history of the Peronist movement, seen through the hopes, fears and failures of archetypal figures in Argentine society, as the title itself, a line from a Carlos Gardel tango, suggests. The novel did not appear until 1982 when it was published in Spain. *No habrá más penas ni olvido* is perhaps Soriano's best-known book abroad because the Argentine director, Hector Oliveira, adapted it for film, under the same title. Its commercial success, especially in Argentina, was due to the fact that the script, which is not entirely faithful to the novel, touched a particularly salient topic at that moment in Argentine history: the idea of looking back at the immediate past, at the question of recovering memory connected with what happened during the military dictatorship from 1976 to 1983.

In exile, first in Belgium then in Paris, Soriano began writing *Cuarteles de invierno* (*Winter Quarters*). It is a short novel, and bearing in mind the characters and background, it can be seen as the continuation in a different form of *No habrá más penas ni olvido*. Characters such as a boxer past his peak, a disillusioned ex-Communist in an authoritarian society, a middle-class family seen through its everyday life (poverty, above all) populate this novel. It is also set in the imaginary town of Colonia Vela, to some extent an allegory of Argentina not only under the 1976–83 military dictatorship but under the series of dictatorship which dominated Argentina in the previous fifty years.

Soriano's next books, *A sus plantas rendido un león*, 1987 [A Lion Cowering at Its Feet] and *Una sombra ya pronto serás*, 1990 (*Shadows*) are more widely known in Europe and the US than his previous work. They belong to the period after Soriano's return to Argentina, and they deal with what was to become a constant theme in his work: failed but somehow curious characters, sordid stories with a certain irony, arid desolate environments that somehow recall the Patagonian landscapes which Soriano knew as a child in Cipolletti. So, obscure failures can be affectionate and full of vitality at the same time; sordid, poor environments can become material paradises – unexpected as well as decadent – a mixture of humour and melancholy. The titles of these novels are also indicative of their subject matter: "A sus plantas rendido un león" (a conquered lion at their feet) is a line from the Argentine national anthem and "Una sombra ya pronto serás"

(You'll soon be a shade) is a verse from the famous tango "Caminito" (Narrow Path).

After his return from exile in 1983, the political allusions in Soriano's writing slowly changed, notably in his recent work *El ojo de la patria*, 1992 [The Eye of the Fatherland], to a more interesting and solid analysis of Argentine society. A certain scepticism about everyday events and characters motivates Soriano's narrators; at the same time it is a lucid ironical view, full of a humour both bitter and disdainful. This evolution of sorts comes to fruition in *El ojo de la patria*, in which countless cultural and historical stereotypes are introduced into the plot to give caustic social significance through oblique and unexpected double meanings.

As well as being a novelist, Soriano has had a long career as a journalist for various publications in Argentina and abroad. He has written about football, politics, aspects of Argentine society and literature. *Artistas, locos y criminales* [Artists, Madmen and Criminals] is a collection of articles that Soriano wrote for *La Opinión* in Buenos Aires between 1972 and 1974, which were published in 1983. Similarly, *Rebeldes, soñadores y fugitivos* [Rebels, Dreamers and Fugitives] published in 1987, is a compilation of articles which originally appeared in various newspapers and journals.

As part of a generation decimated by political repression, Osvaldo Soriano is one of the few Argentine writers (another example would be Horacio Vásquez Rial) who, after political and journalistic experiences, has developed creatively in more literary directions without abandoning a critical view of society.

CLAUDIO CANAPARO

translated by Ann Wright

Biography

Born in Mar del Plata (a large seaside resort on the coast of the province of Buenos Aires), Argentina, in 1943. Full-time journalist; contributed to *La Opinión* and *Panorama*. Went into exile after the military coup of 1976. Lived in Brussels and then took up residence in Paris. Returned to Argentina briefly in 1983 and settled there in 1984. (The film version of his novel *No habrá más pena ni olvido* was made in 1983 and later won the Silver Bear prize at the Berlin Film Festival.) Took up journalism again and writes regularly for the Buenos Aires newspaper, *Página/12*.

Selected Works

Novels

Triste, solitario y final, Buenos Aires: Corregidor, 1973
No habrá más penas ni olvido, Barcelona: Bruguera, 1982; as *A Funny Dirty Little War*, translated by Nick Caistor, London and New York: Readers International, 1986
Cuarteles de invierno, Barcelona: Bruguera, 1982, as *Winter Quarters*, translated by Nick Caistor, London and New York: Readers International, 1989
A sus plantas rendido un león, Buenos Aires: Sudamericana, 1987
Una sombra ya pronto serás, Buenos Aires: Sudamericana, 1990, as *Shadows*, translated by Alfred MacAdam, New York: Knopf, 1993
El ojo de la patria, Buenos Aires: Sudamericana, 1992

Other Writings

Artistas, locos y criminales, Buenos Aires: Bruguera, 1983 [articles]
Rebeldes, soñadores y fugitivos, Buenos Aires: Editora/12, 1987

Further Reading

Barr, Lois Baer, "*Cuarteles de invierno*: the Reign of the Unrighteous," *Revista de Estudios Hispánicos*, vol. 19/3 (October 1985)
Catelli, Nora, "Desde el vértigo hacia el abismo," *Quimera: Revista de Literatura*, no. 19 (May 1982)
Cornia, Mathieu S., "La realidad tragicómica de Osvaldo Soriano," *Chasqui*, vol. 17/1 (May 1988)
Gandolfo, Elvio E., "Osvaldo Soriano: cómo contar la historia," in *Los héroes difíciles: la literatura policial en la Argentina y en Italia*, edited by Giuseppe Petronio, et al., Buenos Aires: Corregidor, 1991
Ingaramo, Elías, *Turbios purgatorios*, Rosario, Argentina: Ideacción, 1992
Morán, Carlos Roberto, "La obra de Osvaldo Soriano," *Revista Nacional de Cultura*, (October 1984)
Rama, Ángel, *La novela en América Latina, 1920–1980*, Bogotá: Procultura / Instituto Colombiano de Cultura, 1982
Soumerou, Raul, "Crónica de la derrota con honra: tres novelas de Osvaldo Soriano: *Triste, solitario y final*, *No habrá más penas ni olvido*, *Cuarteles de invierno*," *Cahiers d'Études Romanes*, Paris (1990)

Interviews

Giacomino, Marta, "Espacios de soledad," *Quimera: Revista de Literatura* (May 1989)

Sousândrade 1833–1902

Brazilian poet

Chronologically a member of the second generation of Brazilian Romantic poets, Sousândrade diverges radically from his contemporaries in both themes and style. He is generally considered a precursor of 20th-century Imagism and Modernism, "born thirty years too soon," more akin to Ezra Pound than to his own generation and possessing a marked awareness of international affairs and a grasp of intercontinental cultural affinities.

After completing his university studies in letters and mining engineering at the Sorbonne, Sousândrade served as a teacher of Greek in his native state of Maranhão, in northern Brazil, and also engaged in farming. He subsequently traveled widely throughout Amazónia, the Andean region, Central America, and Europe, and resided for several years in New York City before returning to Brazil; this substantial foreign experience laid the groundwork for his most famous poetic work, the thirteen-canto narrative *Guesa errante* [Wandering Inca] (begun in the late 1850s and published in segments between 1874 and 1877).

Guesa errante is inspired indirectly by Byron's *Childe Harold's Pilgrimage* as regards its overarching geographical structure and travel theme. It is more closely related in spirit, however, to native Andrean myths of cyclical sacrifice, "rebirth," and the magical *guesa*; Sousândrade identifies himself with the *guesa* as the semi-mythical creature flies from continent to continent, absorbing and reacting to the cultural phenomena observed in each and incorporating bits of local and national folklore and news (in the respective original languages) in a massive poem couched in quasi-limerick verse form. This epic travelogue may, in its multicultural focus and high-spirited tone, be considered a precursor of Mário de Andrade's 1928 novel about "the hero without character," *Macunaíma* (*Macunaima*), whose protagonist travels magically to all regions of Brazil and expresses himself in an idiolect combining baroque, Amerindian, immigrant and standard Brazilian Portuguese characteristics. Canto 10 of the *Guesa errante*, subtitled "O Inferno de Wall Street" [The Wall Street Inferno], recreates the ambience of the New York Stock Exchange, with intercalated newspaper headlines, street vendor calls, references to US political scandals and religious and abolitionist rhetoric of the 1860s, and contextual echoes of Platonic philosophy and European literatures. Other cantos of this "formless epic" are set in the Andean and Amazonian regions of South America (cantos 1–3), the province (later state) of Maranhão, Brazil (cantos 4–5), the urban elegance of Rio de Janeiro (canto 6), western Europe (canto 7), northwestern Africa (fragmentary canto 7), Maranhão (canto 8), the Antilles, Central America, and Gulf of Mexico (canto 9), the Pacific Ocean, Colombia, Venezuela, and Peru (canto 11), an oceanic voyage around Cape Horn to Argentina, thence back to the Andes (canto 12), and finally Maranhão, Brazil

(canto 13). Sousândrade's attempt to capture, to evaluate and to compile into one gigantic poetic work the contemporary reality of three continents in the third quarter of the 19th century failed to achieve a wide reading public due to its deviance from normative Romantic patterns. Only seventy-five years later would it be "rediscovered" by analysts of Brazilian Modernism and Concretism and proclaimed to be a truly revolutionary work of literature.

Two other smaller poetic works by Sousândrade correspond more closely to the typical Romantic paradigm, though both are set in decassylabic blank verse. These are *Harpas selvagens*, 1857 [Savage Harps], his first published collection, and *Novo Éden*, 1893 [New Eden], composed in homage to the Brazilian Republic (declared in 1889) by this ardent Republican. In both volumes, the influence of classical Greek literature and mythology is apparent, and the poetic phrase possesses an elegance and "liquid" flow not present in the *Guesa errante*.

Mary L. Daniel

Biography

Born Joaquim de Sousa Andrade in São Luís, state of Maranhão, Brazil in 1833. Studied literature and mining engineering at the Sorbonne, Paris. Travelled widely throughout Latin America, Europe and the United States. Visited England where he attacked Queen Victoria in the press; left hurriedly and returned home where it is said that he sold the bricks of his house to stay alive. Lived in New York City where he published the first volume of his *Obras poéticas* (1874). Returned to town of Maranhão and taught Greek at a secondary school. Died in poverty and neglect at his home, the ironically named Quinta da Vitória, in 1902.

Selected Works

Harpas selvagens, Rio de Janeiro: Laemmert, 1857
Guesa errante, New York: n.p., 1874–77; critical edition, São Luís, Maranhão: Edições Sioge, 1979
Novo Éden, Maranhão: João d'Aguiar Almeida, 1893

Compilations and Anthologies

Poesia, Rio de Janeiro: AGIR, 1966
Sousândrade: ineditos, edited by Frederick G. Williams and Jomar Moraes, São Luís, Maranhão: Departamento de Cultura do Estado, 1970
Sousândrade: prosa, edited by Frederick G. Williams and Jomar Moraes, São Luís, Maranhão: Ediçoes Sioge, 1978

Further Reading

Campos, Augusto and Haroldo de, *Re/Visão de Sousândrade*, São Paulo: Edições Invenção, 1964 [Includes critical texts, an anthology, glossary and bibliography]
Lobo, Luiza, *Épica e modernidade em Sousândrade*, São Paulo: Presença/EDUSP, 1986
Williams, Frederick G., *Sousândrade: vida e obra*, São Luís, Maranhão: Edições Sioge, 1976

Alfonsina Storni 1892–1938

Argentine poet

Alfonsina Storni was born in Switzerland in 1892, her parents, of Italian-Swiss origin moved back to Argentina when she was four years old and her father, an alcoholic, died in 1906. She never married, and in the struggle to support herself and her son, born in 1912, she took on a number of jobs, but concentrated when she could on teaching, journalism and poetry. She is well-known as a Latin American woman poet, but the irony that undercuts the romantic voice in her work has not been widely appreciated; it may stem from her lack of the financial or educational advantages commonly found in women who succeed in a male-dominated literary world. These difficulties perhaps accentuated her tendency to view sexual relationships with the critical as well as romantic gaze revealed in her recurrently ironical portrayal of masculinity and in the conversational poems to her mother, "Bien pudiera ser" [It May Be] and "Palabras a mi madre" [To My Mother].

Her work can be divided into three stages; the first, from *La inquietud del rosal*, 1916 [The Rosetree's Fears], to *Ocre*, 1925 [Ochre], displays a Romantic heritage mixed with *modernista* influences. In the second, Storni did not publish poetry, but wrote conference papers, articles and plays, including the unsuccessful *El amo del mundo*, 1927 [Master of the World]. She made two trips to Europe and met members of the Spanish avant-garde. The influence of the Generation of 1927, particularly of Gerardo Diego and Federico García Lorca, can be seen in the return to verse which marks the third and final stage of her work. *Mundo de siete pozos* [World of Seven Wells] was published in 1934 and *Mascarilla y trébol* [Death Mask and Clover], posthumously in 1938. Storni had been treated for breast cancer in 1935, and three years later, to avoid further surgical intervention, she drowned herself off the coast at Mar del Plata on 25 October.

Storni came to regret the Romanticism of *La inquietud del rosal* and would have chosen to exclude it from subsequent anthologies. One poem, however, "La loba" [She-Wolf] is worth noting as an introduction to a recurrent theme in her work – alienation, after the birth of her illegitimate son, from the traditionally passive feminine role: the she-wolf, or outcast, confronts, but does not threaten, the vulnerable flock who have remained dependent on their male shepherd.

In 1918, *El dulce daño* [Sweet Pain], traces an erotic interlude, playing with the clichés of romantic love in "Transfusión" [Transfusion] but culminating in the rejection of the lover in "Viaje finido" [Journey's End]. A new development then begins with "Tú me quieres blanca" [You Love Me White], which has been widely appreciated for its charming and witty dismantling of the poetic imagery of romantic love. In *Irremediablemente*, 1919 [Incurably], two opposing sections mark a dichotomy of passion which describes the contradictions of the female role, the first controlled and humble, the second overlaid with bitterness and anger. The harmonious visions of "Paz" [Peace], "Tarde fresca" [Cool Afternoon], "Miedo divino" [Divine Fear] and of traditional sex roles in "El hombre sereno" [Serene Man] are offset by poems such as "Hombre pequeñito" [Little Man] which mocks the male lover

and the tradition of the *carcel de amor* (prison of love). Poems written to a mute interlocutor explore a pain often related to the subordinate female position. In "Bien pudiera ser" [It Might Well Be], she deals, in passionate and violent imagery, with women's inherited legacy of silence, which can be challenged or disrupted through writing.

Her reputation was made in 1920 by the award of the "Primer Premio Municipal" of Buenos Aires to *Languidez* [Languor]. Death is a recurrent motif and subtle variations in the sense of human impotence are revealed in "Carta lírica a otra mujer" [Lyrical Letter to Another Woman] and "Borrada" [Erased]. *Ocre* (1925), the final collection in this first stage of her work, shows Storni's increasing maturity. Often in sonnet form, it continues her exploration of the relationship between the sexes. Love may be a death-force, men, in "Olvido" [Oblivion], are unattainable and cold, and the ideal lover is a dream, "El engaño" [Delusion] which enslaves women to the romantic fantasies of the poem "Inútil soy" [I Am Worthless]. But this collection is also lightened by an ironic glimpse of the sex roles in poems such as "Divertidas estancias a Don Juan" [Comic Lines to Don Juan], "El tímido amante" [Timid Lover] and the light-hearted "Epitafio a mi tumba" [Epitaph on My Grave] which shows a mature, if disenchanted, love of life.

Storni spent three years with a travelling theatre company and sang in bars, although her unwillingness to admit to the latter shows her fear of compromising her social position. She also taught in drama academies and wrote a number of farces and successful plays for children. *El amo del mundo* was a failure, despite her bid to appeal to a wider audience by changing the original title, *Dos mujeres* (Two Women) to "Master of the World." It ridicules the moral double standards of men, while showing how they too are victims of the sexual stereotyping that confines women.

After a break of almost ten years and two journeys to Europe, Storni returned to poetry. The last two collections show a new sense of personal freedom, revealed in a more dispassionate view of the the external world. *Mundo de siete pozos* is influenced by a Spanish avant-garde movement, *ultra-ísmo*, and tends to abandon the theme of love to concentrate on visual detail. Many critics have pointed out the relationship between the prevalence of sea imagery in her work and her chosen death, and here "Yo en el fondo del mar" [At the Bottom of the Sea], and "Luna de marzo sobre el mar" [March Moon over the Sea] are not so much romantic projections as impressionistic visions of an external world. However a number of poems, such as "Canción de la mujer astuta" [The Smart Woman's Song], return with apparent inevitability to the "biological binding" of the female voice.

Mascarilla y trébol contains fifty-two unrhymed sonnets. Storni considered them her most successful work. She describes how they were written rapidly, in a trance-like state, overshadowed by the encroaching threat of death. The mask of the title has been interpreted as a death mask and the clover as the grass growing over graves; the recurrent themes are of disintegration, regeneration and salvation through writing.

It opens with the powerful and disturbing "A Eros" [To Eros] which marks a reassessment and rejection of the romanticism of the earlier work. The disenchanted voice dissects her sadistic god of love and throws him back, now a useless collection of rags, into the waves. "Regreso a mis pájaros" [Return to My Birds] and "Ya estoy de nuevo" [I Am Back] explore return and reparation, and "El sueño" [The Dream], is no longer a romantic fantasy, but a disturbing prelude to death.

It is not the fear of death but the acceptance of its release which prevails, and the measured tone and gentle irony of the poem "Voy a dormir" [I Am Going to Sleep] might stand as an epitaph to Storni's life and work. This calm leave-taking concludes in an aside, dismissing that silent male other who has dominated the work, since the poet has at last been released from the self-consciously female body that has confined both her life and her writing.

JO EVANS

Biography

Born in Sala Capriasca, a small village in an Italian canton of Switzerland, 29 May 1892. Family had emigrated earlier to Argentina and returned in 1896, settling in the city of San Juan. Family lost their fortune in the national slump of 1903. Joined José Tallavi's theatre company in 1907 and toured Argentina for a year. Obtained primary school teacher's diploma in 1910; started teaching in Rosario, a city in the interior, 1911. Illegitimate son, Alejandro Alfonso, born in 1912. Moved to Buenos Aires in same year. Accepted in time by intellectual community and made friends with fellow-writer Horacio Quiroga. Earned her living through a wide range of jobs including as a drug store cashier and journalist. Held several teaching posts including one at the Labardén Children's Theatre. Awarded the Buenos Aires Municipal Prize in 1920, for *Languidez*. Underwent surgery for cancer of the breast in 1935 and drowned herself on 25 October 1938 owing to a recurrence of cancer.

Selected Works

Poetry

La inquietud del rosal, Buenos Aires: La Facultad, 1916
El dulce daño, Buenos Aires: Sociedad Cooperativa Editorial Limitada, 1918
Irremediablemente, Buenos Aires: Sociedad Cooperativa Editorial Limitada, 1919
Languidez, Buenos Aires: Sociedad Cooperativa Editorial Limitada, 1920
Poesías, Buenos Aires: Ediciones Selectas América, 1923
Ocre, Buenos Aires: Babel, 1925
Poemas de amor, Buenos Aires: Nosotros, 1926 [prose poems]
Mundo de siete pozos, Buenos Aires: Tor, 1934
Mascarilla y trébol. Círculos imantados, Buenos Aires: El Ateneo, 1938

Plays

El amo del mundo, in *Bambalinas*, Buenos Aires, vol. 9/470 (16 April 1927)
Dos farsas pirotécnicas, Buenos Aires: Cooperativa Editorial Buenos Aires, 1932

Compilations and Anthologies

Teatro infantil, Buenos Aires: Ramón J. Roggero, 1950
Obra poética completa, Buenos Aires: Meridión, 1964

Translations

Selected Poems, edited by Marion Freeman, translated by Mary Crow, Jim Normington and Kay Short, Fredonia, New York: White Pine Press, 1987

Further Reading

Andreola, Carlos Alberto, *Alfonsina Storni: inédita*, Buenos Aires: Cabant, 1974
Delgado, Josefina, *Alfonsina Storni. Una biografía*, Buenos Aires: Planeta, 1990
Evans, Jo, "White Women, Idealization and Death in Two Poems by Alfonsina Storni," *Journal of Hispanic Research*, vol. 2/1 (Autumn 1993)
Fishburn, Evelyn, "Alfonsina Storni: a Feminist Reading of Her Poetry," in *Feminist Readings on Spanish and Latin-American Literature*, edited by L.P. Condé and S.M. Hart, Lampeter, Wales: Edwin Mellen Press, 1991
Gómez Paz, Julieta, *Leyendo a Alfonsina Storni*, Buenos Aires: Losada, 1966
Koch, Dolores E., "Delmira, Alfonsina, Juana y Gabriela," *Revista Iberoamericana* 132–33 (July–December 1985) [Special number devoted to Spanish American women writers]
Nalé Roxlo, Conrado and Mabel Mármol, *Genio y figura de Alfonsina Storni*, Buenos Aires: Eudeba, 1964
Percas, Helena, *La poesía femenina argentina 1810–1950*, Madrid: Cultura Hispánica, 1958
Phillips, Rachel, *Alfonsina Storni: from Poetess to Poet*, London: Támesis, 1975
Rojas, Margarita, *et al.*, *Las poetas del buen humor*, Caracas: Monte Ávila, 1991
Vitier, Cintio, "La poesía de Alfonsina Storni," *Revista Nacional de Cultura*, Caracas, vol. 13 (1939)

Sur

See Journals

Surrealism

There is no doubt that Surrealism was the most influential of the inter-war avant-garde movements in Europe. The first Surrealist manifesto of 1924, written by André Breton, and signed by a group of poets and painters, grew out of the nihilism of the Parisian Dada movement in the aftermath of World War I. Against this Dada despair, Surrealism's Utopian programme was based on Freud's recent discoveries of the unconscious, dream-work, libido and repression, and a Rimbaudian revolutionary call to change life. Surrealism's leader, the poet André Breton, based all his theoretical writings on the subversive notions of automatic writing (anybody could be a poet; inspiration comes after writing as quickly as possible and not changing what emerges), and objective chance (a sudden encounter between desire and empiric reality that reveals the true or sur-reality). Both tenets suggest that the ego (common sense, rationality, the social self) had to be by-passed in order to find real inspiration, and integration with life. The aim was to catch "the real functioning of thought." At the level of writing Breton defined Surrealist poetics as "les mots font l'amour" (words make love) with the sense that an authentic language lay waiting in the unconscious to be revealed on paper and release the poet from the snare of contradictions and inauthenticity which entraps everybody.

Behind this revolutionary call to break into a more fulfilling reality (super-reality), there was also a Surrealist group politics which had an in-group of creative individuals continuously defining themselves against their enemies (the bourgeoisie). This group energy manifested itself in games, shock tactics, manifestos, magazines, rallies, etc. In this sense Breton was seen as a tyrannical "pope" excommunicating dissidents (like Antonin Artaud) while defending the purity of his Surrealist territory. The history of Surrealism as defined by Maurice Nadeau is a narrative of this in-group's activities. This version is concerned with French poets, mainly located in Paris. The cosmopolitan nature of the Surrealist group was made up by the painters, not limited by language, with many coming from Spain (Dalí, Domínguez, etc.) and Latin America (Matta, Lam, etc.).

From the 1924 Surrealist manifesto to Breton's death in 1966 only a few Latin American writers actively participated in this inner circle of Parisian writers, and only because they either changed their language to French, as did the Peruvian poet César Moro who later brought his Surrealist poetics to Mexico with the International Surrealist Exhibition in 1940, and then Peru, or were immediately translated in the Surrealist magazines as was the Mexican poet Octavio Paz, a brilliant expositor of Breton's thought (see Jason Wilson, 1979). The French language, as much as literary or political or ethical factors, kept most Latin Americans on the fringes of the main, ever-changing Surrealist group lead by Breton. If Surrealism is defined along Bretonian lines, then the movement did not involve Latin American culture. But this orthodox Bretonian view is not the real story of Surrealism.

For many Latin American writers Surrealism offered an exciting theory of the imagination, and a poetics that promised plenty. As something in the air Surrealism is crucial in evaluating Latin American culture from the 1930s to the 1970s. The main difference between Parisian orthodoxy and how Latin Americans adopted Surrealism is that for the latter, Surrealism was mainly an individual's response, not a group's, and that it remained literary rather than a praxis altering action, and defining a political stance. Many Latin American writers picked out bits and pieces of the Surrealist adventure as a personal response to the problematics of writing and being a good writer. A good example is the way the Mexican poet Xavier Villaurrutia, associated with the Contemporáneos group, developed Surrealist insights without ever calling himself a Surrealist.

However, there were attempts in Latin America to found Surrealist cells. In Argentina the poet and critic Aldo Pellegrini claimed to have launched the first Surrealist magazine as early as 1928, but it was not until the Peronist 1960s that a group of poets and painters, gathered round the magazine *A Partir de Cero* [Starting from Zero] edited by Enrique Molina from 1952 to 1956, could be said to have any literary importance. There was also a group in Chile lead by Braulio Arenas associated with the magazine *La Mandrágora* (1938–1943). These nuclei of mimetic Surrealist activities have been studied and anthologised by Stefan Baciu.

Surrealism had a further function in Latin American poetry in that many writers defined themselves against Surrealism's baroque facilities where automatic writing led to a rhetorical abuse of dark tropes. The list of those who reacted against Surrealism constitutes one of the main strands of the Latin American poetic tradition and includes the César Vallejo of the late 1920s onwards, the Neruda of the late 1930s on, Ernesto Cardenal, Nicanor Parra and the later politicised testimonial poets from Juan Gelman to Roque Dalton. From the distance of Latin America, Surrealism's free rein to sloppy writing, divorced from Breton's acute poetics, was perceived negatively as another aspect of slavish European imitation.

Although André Breton denounced the prose of fictional realism, Surrealism had a surprisingly liberating effect on Latin American narrative. First there were writers who participated in the café-life of Paris on the fringes of the Surrealist activities like Miguel Ángel Asturias, Ernesto Sábato and Alejo Carpentier who adapted elements of the Surrealist adventure in their fiction. Austurias explored the otherness of the Mayan mind derived from Surrealism's fascination with anthropology; Sábato explored the catacombs of the mind, and evil, following his friendship with Oscar Domínguez; Carpentier developed his theory of Latin America's uniqueness – "lo real maravilloso" (the marvellous in the real) – from the Surrealism's evaluation of le merveilleux in everyday life. Julio Cortázar is possibly the closest of the Boom writers to the Surrealist spirit in his novel *Rayuela*, 1963 (*Hopscotch*), grounded in chance play and erotics, and linked to a Surrealist tradition of dissidence that includes Rimbaud, Jarry, Artaud and Crevel.

Surrealism in this general sense spread to Latin America so completely that a proper grasp of Latin American culture from the 1930s to the 1970s cannot be had without recourse to Surrealist poetics. If Surrealism is defined in a narrow Parisian way then its only great exponent in Latin America is Octavio

Paz. But if it is conceived as in the air, then Surrealism helped form the continent's main writers of the time, especially in opposition to the dogmatic and exclusive Bretonian orthodoxy, and would include key works by Huidobro, Neruda, Parra, Vallejo, Asturias, Fuentes, Sábato, Cortázar, Donoso and others.

JASON WILSON

See also entries on César Moro, Paris

Further Reading

Baciu, Stefan, *Antología de la poesía surrealista latinoamericana*, Mexico City: Joaquín Mortiz, 1974

____ *Surrealismo latinoamericano: preguntas y respuestas*, Valparaíso, Chile: Universidad de Valparaíso, 1979

Benedetti, Mario, *Los poetas comunicantes*, Montevideo: Marcha, 1969

Maturo, Graciela, *Proyecciones del surrealismo en la literatura argentina*, Buenos Aires: Ediciones Culturales Argentinas, 1967

Nadeau, Maurice, *The History of Surrealism*, translated by Richard Howard, New York: Macmillan, 1965; London: Jonathan Cape, 1968

Schnieder, Luis Mario, *México y el surrealismo (1925–1950)*, Mexico City: Arte y Libros, 1978

Wilson, Jason, *Octavio Paz: a Study of His Poetics*, Cambridge: Cambridge University Press, 1979

T

José Juan Tablada 1871–1945

Mexican prose writer, poet, art critic and literary translator

It has been said that to understand a man, one must understand his times. This expression is very appropriate for anyone truly interested in the work of José Juan Tablada, a writer who witnessed both the rise and fall of the Porfirio Díaz regime. Like many of the writers who lived through the *belle époque* and the Mexican Revolution, Tablada was influenced both positively and negatively by the political and cultural circumstances of his lifetime. Porfirio Díaz's subsidization of the press, his modernization of Mexico, and his interest in 19th-century French culture and thought should not be overlooked, therefore, when one tries to explain the often contradictory nature of Tablada's work. It should not come as a surprise, then, that at one point in his career Tablada is capable of writing epic poetry linking Porfirio Díaz to Juárez and a number of other illustrious warrior-saviors – Cuahtémoc, Morelos, Hidalgo, Zaragosa – and is also able to blast Madero in his theatrical comedy *Madero-Chantecler, tragi-comedia zoológico política* [Madero-Chantecler: a Tragi-comedy of the Political Zoo], accusing Madero of being both a drunkard and a megalomaniac. While at another point, in his journalistic pieces, Tablada can turn around and wield a justifiable blow against US imperialism and the cultural trade offs that were being made in Mexico. Although critics have traditionally excused Tablada's "excesses" and overlooked the merit of his prose work, even for instance, his art criticism (Tablada's articles in *International Studio*, *Survey Graphic* and *Shadowland* open our eyes to the work of painters like Diego Rivera), most will agree that Tablada achieved significant success in his poetry by experimenting with *modernista* language and by maintaining an iconoclast posture. This poetry itself is also permeated by the same intellectual and cultural environment of his generation, and an appreciation of its true originality can only be made when one begins to understand and link Tablada's work with his period.

Tablada's *decandentista* period, the work he produced in conjunction with his participation in *La Revista Moderna*, 1898–1904 [The Modern Magazine], reflects the spirit that had led him early in his career to seek rehabilitation from a morphine addiction (1897). From the beginning of his poetic career, Tablada had immersed himself in the romantic rebellious spirit of French poets like: Baudelaire, Jean Moréas, Pierre Louÿs, Victor Hugo, José María Heredia and Théodore de Banville. Not only had Tablada translated the work of these and other French authors, but he resolutely believed that their poetic sense of rebellion should be reaffirmed, relived and rewritten from within Mexico. Through *decadentismo*, Tablada sought to define a darker side of *Modernismo*; he wanted to transform the exotic "escapes" that characterized Rubén Darío's poetry. Like his friend and collaborator Leopoldo Lugones, Tablada developed a vocabulary of exotic images that were more "sinfully" erotic. He aimed to dethrone Venus and he constantly reached for that supersensitive state of poetry which would allow him to "cut through life's cruelty." One consequence of Tablada's pursuit is an increased emphasis on the metaphor in poetic construction and a heightened familiarity with French poetry, something one can find in the work of contemporary poets like Octavio Paz.

The first edition of *El florilegio* [The Floral Wreath] contains most of Tablada's *decadentista* work. Three poems from this book are worth mentioning, because they help establish his iconoclastic use of metaphor and his particular interest in erotic exoticism. In the love poem, "Onix" [Onyx], Tablada juxtaposes a sad poet-lover with the symbolic embodiment of both a priest and a warrior-lover. Like the priest the poet-lover awaits a coming – a metaphor for the dark and obscure epoch of squashed passions. He pleads to be cleansed, to burn again in the fires of real pure love (exemplified by the priest), or be reduced to ashes. In "Laos Deu," Tablada recounts a poet's journey from darkness to light, from one side of faithfulness to the other – a journey of purification. Rescued from the darkness of his dreams filled with succubi, the awareness of having lived like a night owl, and the sensation of having crawled like an insect, the poet recalls the "dark mass" of his past. The poet himself still "bleeds from his penitence" and still seems intoxicated by the pleasures of the other world. In "Misa Negra" (Black Mass), Tablada expresses a poet's wish to set aside the fiery words of previous poets in order to express more appropriately his love for a woman. Unlike other poets, the poet of "Misa Negra" prefers a poetic vocabulary that includes the smell of prayer (reverent incense of desire), the chapel (the woman's skirt as an altar), and penitence itself (the refuge and consolation that a woman's body provides). These three poems share not only Tablada's awareness that ancient religions evolved from and revolved around sexual experience, but they also share the same striking opposition: erotic versus religious poetry. This union of opposites had to have been a very ironic slap-in-the-face for Mexican moralists who condoned both the Díaz regime's institutionalized control of prostitution and promoted chaste Catholic weddings. What is more important in terms of Tablada's work, is the new and exotic poetic territory that was formed, something that reminds one of Baudelaire's "ugly beauty."

This same type of dynamic opposition and Tablada's interest in love continue to motivate the poet in the poems that he later would add to *El florilegio* before its second printing. Tablada reveals the same exotic eroticism in poems like "En el viejo parque" [In the Old Park]. In this case, Tablada expresses the desire that a poet should be free to release Pan from his prison of unfulfilled emotions, to lead him through every Ovidian pleasure, and to protect him from the perils of such a trip. Throughout the new edition of *El florilegio*, Tablada seeks to demonstrate that the exotic places of "poetry past" have already been realized in the modern world and what remains for a modern poet is to invent new exotic places. For instance, instead of writing about Japan itself, a poet should reach beyond the obvious exoticism of this foreign land. In "Noche de opium," Tablada chooses to depict a saddened, moonstruck and beautiful Japanese princess who has decided to escape her lovesickness via an opium-induced dream.

In *Al sol y bajo la luna* [In the Sun and Under the Moon] Tablada begins to demonstrate the brevity and conciseness that will characterize most of his later poetry. The dense vocabulary and complexity of verses in *El florilegio* will be exchanged for brevity both in sequence and pattern. As Tablada states in *Un día . . . poemas sintéticos* [One Day . . . Synthetic Poems], contemporary man needs contemporary poetry, something straightforward and ironic. This change in style, however, did not dampen Tablada's experimental and iconoclastic nature, nor diminish the importance of his interest in French culture.

Although many poets and critics recognize Tablada's influence over his contemporaries, especially his experimentation with haiku, few realize that many of the poems of *Li-Po y otros poemas ideográficos* [Li Po and Other Ideographic Poems], his most renown book of haiku, are actually translations of English translations of the original Chinese poet's work. The true originality of Tablada's work lies in his selection of Li Po's poetry (Li Po is one of the most outstanding Chinese poets, particularly in terms of Romantic poetry) and the graphic manner in which Tablada transcribes his translations (The poem, "Un pájaro que trina" [A Trilling Bird], for instance, is in itself a drawing of a bird singing.). Like the French writers Judith Goncourt and Pierre Loti, who first incorporated Chinese and Japanese culture into their writing, Tablada found inspiration in the ideographic nature of the oriental text. "Día nublado" [Cloudy Day], for instance, is a poem written to be read from left to right and "Impresión de La Habana" [Impression of Havana] reads like a hypermedia text. One looks at the graphic icon of a window formed by four sentences and then reads the sentences to discover the poet's impressions as he looks from within the window to that beyond.

Of course, not all of Tablada's poetry is transgressive, nor should it all be linked to his early interests in French culture. In *Un día . . . poemas sintéticos* and in *El jarro de flores* [A Flower Vase] Tablada reverts back to his youth and his interest in nature, entomology, botany, etc. In these books of haiku, Tablada records his impressions of plants, animals and wildlife – something more consistent with the poetry of his Japanese poet and friend Asataro Okada. This same nostalgic interest in the world that surrounds him also allows Tablada to rediscover Mexico, as he returns from exile. (During the Mexican Revolution, Tablada was forced to live in Paris). In the book of poems, *La feria* [The Fair], Tablada continued to write this more simple and nostalgic poetry. In this book he celebrates not only the small fish-shaped soap bar of his youth, but in poems like "El figón" [The Diner] he depicts his country by recourse to stock cultural symbols:, the *ajonjolí* (sesame seed), the nopal, the chili and the Aztec.

As Tablada approached maturity, his poetry became self-reflexive as he relived through his writing the experiences and memories of his youth. *Intersecciones* [Intersections] and his prose work *La feria de la vida* [Life's Fair] best represent this last period of work. Again, Tablada can wander from his youthful infatuation with a prostitute named Antoñica to a perceptive criticism of journalism as it was produced at the turn of the century. Nevertheless, this more mature poetry cannot escape the influence of the *belle époque* nor the Modernity that the Díaz regime forced upon Mexico. Tablada's ironic and quick wit produce in this case barbed appraisals of Mexico's history and culture, instead of the exotic metaphors of Tablada's *decadentista* poetry.

Indeed, one finds it difficult to appraise Tablada's poetic accomplishment without first considering the cultural matrix from which it sprang. This matrix has a way of changing the order of one's appreciation of Tablada's experimentation. By beginning to understand the *belle époque* and the Mexican Revolution, one begins to define more clearly the directions of Tablada's iconoclasm. Tablada's poetics enabled him to fuse the European and Oriental poetic traditions with Mexican literary tradition and to generate an interest within Latin America as a whole for poetry with more graphic and metaphoric reduction, amplification, and purity. In a sense Tablada's poetry as well as his other writing has been overlooked.

WILLIAM P. KEETH

Biography

Born in Mexico City, 3 April 1871. During his youth, he lived with his family, which included five sisters, in an upper-class neighborhood in Tacubaya. Received primary and secondary education essentially in French; attended the private school, Institución Kathain and later the Colegio de Grosso. Forced by his parents to enter the Colegio Militar (military academy) in the Chapultepec Castle. After abandoning military school, worked as an accountant for the Central Railway, where his writing talents were discovered. A friend in the accounting department arranged an interview for him with Rafael Reyes Spíndola, editor of *El Universal*. As Tablada's career as a journalist matured, he contributed poetry and articles to numerous publications including: *La Patria Ilustrada* (1888), *El Universal* (1889–94), *El Partido Liberal* (1890), *El Siglo XIX* (1892–1893), *El País* (1893), *Revista Azul* (1894), *Diario del Hogar* (1894–1903), *El Mundo* (1896),

Revista de Revistas (1896), La Revista Moderna (1898–1904) and El Mundo Ilustrado (1902–1904). Married Justo Sierra Méndez's niece, Evangelina Sierra (later divorced). Lived in Paris, 1911–12. Editor-in-chief of El Imparcial, 1912–13. House raided during the early stages of the Mexican Revolution as a result of his political writings. Forced into exile and lived in Texas and then New York. Married Nina Cabrera in 1918. Returned to Mexico, briefly. Held diplomatic posts in Colombia and Ecuador: resigned in 1920. Returned to New York. Editor of Mexican Art and Life, New York. Travelled to Mexico in 1936, once more returned to New York. Published extensively on art and politics and translated many French, Portuguese and Japanese texts into Spanish. Died of a heart attack in New York City, 2 August 1945.

Selected Works

Poetry

El florilegio (poemas) 1891–1897, Mexico City: Tipografía de Ignacio Escalante, 1899
Al sol y bajo la luna, Paris: Librería de la viuda de Charles Bouret, 1918
Un día . . . poemas sintéticos, Caracas: Imprenta Bolívar, 1919
Li-Po y otros poemas ideográficos, Caracas: Imprenta Bolívar, 1920
El jarro de flores: disociaciones líricas, New York: "Escritores Sindicados," 1922
La feria (poemas mexicanos), New York: Mayans Impresor, 1928

Novel

La resurrección de los ídolos, Mexico City: El Universal Ilustrado, 1924

Play

Madero-Chantecler, tragi-comedia zoológico política de rigurosa actualidad en tres actos y en verso, Mexico City: Compañía Aserradora de Maderos, 1910

Other Writings

Tiros al blanco (actualidades políticas), Mexico City: n.p., 1909
La defensa social / Historia de la campaña de la División del Norte, Mexico City: Imprimería del Gobierno Federal, 1913

Los días y las noches de París, Paris: Librería de la viuda de Charles Bouret, 1918
En el país del sol, New York: Appleton, 1919
Historia del arte en México, Mexico City: Compañía Nacional Editora "Aguilas," 1927
La feria de la vida (memorias), Mexico City: Botas, 1937
Del humorismo a la carcajada, Mexico City: Editorial Mexicana, 1944

Compilations and Anthologies

Los mejores poemas, edited by Hector Valdés, with a prologue by José María González de Mendoza; Mexico City: UNAM, 1971
Obras, edited by Hector Valdés, 2 vols, Mexico City: UNAM, 1971–81 [Contains poetry, political satire, articles on Paris]
Sátira política, edited by Jorge Ruedas de la Serna and Esperanza Lara Velázquez, Mexico City: UNAM, 1981

Further Reading

Baciu, Stefan, Antología de la poesía surrealista latinoamericana, Mexico City: Joaquín Mortiz, 1974 [Among the precursors are José Juan Tablada and the Peruvian poet José María Eguren]
Los cuatro poetas; Gutiérrez Nájera, Urbina, Icaza, Tablada, with a preliminary note by Antonio Acevedo Escobedo, Mexico City: Ediciones de la Secretaría de Educación Pública, 1944
García de Aldridge, Adriana, "Las fuentes chinas de José Juan Tablada," Bulletin of Hispanic Studies, vol. 60/2 (1983)
Hernández Palacios, Esther, " 'Misa Negra' o el sacrilegio inacabado del modernismo," La Palabra y el Hombre 77 (1991)
Lara Velázquez, Esperanza, La iniciación poética de José Juan Tablada, Mexico City: UNAM, 1988
Mariscal Acosta, Amanda, La poesía de José Juan Tablada, Mexico City: Impresora Económica, 1949
Mendieta Alatorre, Ángeles, Tablada y la gran época de la transformación cultural, Mexico City: Secretaría de Educación Pública, 1966
Paz, Octavio, "Estela de José Juan Tablada," in Las peras del olmo, Mexico City: Editorial Universitaria, 1957
Tanabe, Atsuko, El japonismo de José Juan Tablada, Mexico City: UNAM, 1981

Néstor Taboada Terán 1929–

Bolivian prose writer

Néstor Taboada Terán might be described as a constructive iconoclast: he has always been prepared to defy the stifling orthodoxy which he sees as a great malaise in Bolivia. He has likened this approach to breaking windows: however, his is a literature of provocation rather than of vandalism, and the value of his work has been recognised with several literary prizes in Bolivia and Argentina.

Taboada's non-conformist nature was evident by his early twenties, and by the beginning of the 1970s he had already been under scrutiny by a succession of military governments, most notably that of Hugo Banzer who ordered his arrest in

1972. Taboada was exiled to Argentina after six months' solitary confinement, and spent around eight years as an exile in Buenos Aires.

Taboada's political convictions had an early influence both on the style and the subject matter of his work: his first novel El precio del estaño, 1960 [The Price of Tin] was criticised for its doctrinaire view of class struggle typical of the Bolivian mining novel, but broke with the genre in its rehabilitation of the tin baron Simón Patiño – hitherto a figure of revulsion due as much to his mixed blood, according to Taboada, as to any abuse of workers. This kind of false demonisation, whether on racial, dynastic or political grounds, has always been among the targets of his fiction.

Marxist affiliations alllowed the young Taboada to travel, which resulted in writing such as *Cuba, paloma de vuelo popular*, 1964 [Cuba, Dove of Popular Flight], *Chile con el corazón a la izquierda*, 1971 [Chile with Its Heart on the Left], and the anthology *Ecuador en el cuento*, 1976 [Ecuador in Its Stories]. This list evinces a clear identification with Latin American rather than simply Bolivian problems; the latter are aired in novels which relate national to continental realities. This is the case with his second novel, *El signo escalonado*, 1975 [The Stepped Symbol]: the title refers to indigenous motifs as well as the Nazi swastika's appearance during the 1930s, when the novel is set. The novel presents an unusual approach to the Chaco War (see the entry on Bolivia), considering its causes rather than its outcome.

It is generally thought that Taboada's best novel is *Manchay Puytu, el amor que quiso ocultar Dios* [Manchay Puytu, the Love that God Sought to Hide], published in Argentina in 1977. This is based on a tale, dating from colonial times and based in the then silver-boom city of Potosí, which is used as a symbolic melting-pot. Indeed, miscegenation in ethnic and cultural terms is central to the novel and its underlying project: a vision of a multicultural Bolivia which has resolved its internal and external problems. Indigenous storytelling and European Enlightenment ideas vie with the reactionary nature of Spanish isolationism, typified by the Inquisition, as an Indian priest attempts to resolve the dilemma inherent in his situation. Padre Antonio is indigenous but serves foreign masters. This makes him a pariah, a condition well understood by the author during this period of persecution.

Several collections of short stories show a similar concern with the question of *mestizaje*, or cultural integration. The best-known of these, *Indios en rebelión*, 1968 [Rebelling Indians], deals with the indigenous population's problems in coping with new-found responsibilities and liberties after the 1952 Revolution.

Taboada's earlier revolutionary tendencies have been modified to a general anti-imperialist commitment evident in recent work such as *Requerimiento al rey de España*, 1992 [Requirement made of the King of Spain] which, in describing a visit to the Andes by Pope John Paul II, turns the discourse of colonialist enterprise on its head. The three most recent novels confirm his self-description as a historian writing fiction. *Manchay Puytu* is in fact the first in a trilogy of Andean historical novels. It is followed by *Angelina Yupanki, marquesa de la conquista*, 1992 [Angelina Yupanki, Marchioness of the conquest] which takes a historical figure from the conquest as a bridge between Indian and Spanish worlds comparable to La Malinche in Mexico. *Ollantay, la guerra de los dioses*, 1994 [Ollantay, War of the Gods], which reworks a Quechua-language drama depicting Inca history, is the third. Taboada's latest project depicts an imaginary relationship between Queen Victoria and Mariano Melgarejo, a 19th-century Bolivian president generally seen as a colourful tyrant. This era, according to legend, saw the British monarch erase Bolivia from the map. Taboada, who has been heavily criticised for addressing such material, seeks to identify and satirise the conditions which gave rise to the myth. This, and the rehabilitation of Melgarejo contained in the novel, make the work typical of the most

respected living writer (and most feared polemicist) in Bolivia.

Taboada has not been concerned solely with breaking images: he has been a revisionist, addressing again points already covered by previous generations of writers. He has taken themes from Bolivian history and regenerated them and has also written historical works, such as *La revolución degollada* [The Throttled Revolution] and *Colombia*, both published in 1974. This aspect of his work shows a preoccupation with forging a new identity not only for his own country but for Latin America as a whole. It is a question of acknowledging what is already there; Taboada was born in La Paz in 1929, and consequently belongs to a generation which spent its childhood in the shadow of the Chaco War of 1932–35. This conflict broke the mould of Bolivian political life, and created the atmosphere of discontent which was to result in the 1952 Revolution. As for many of his contemporaries, it meant personal loss: when Taboada was three years old, his father died in the Chaco. As José Ortega has stated, the war also created a new challenge for the Bolivian writer: "La preocupación del novelista boliviano ... desde el despertar social que trajo la Guerra del Chaco es – y continúa siendo – la erradicación de las estructuras socio-político-económicas de origen tradicional y oligárquico con el fin de realizar la progresiva incorporación del indio a la comunidad boliviana." (The Bolivian novelist's concern, as from the social awakening provoked by the Chaco War, is – and continues to be – the eradication of the socio-economic and political structures of traditional and oligarchic origin, so as to reinsert the Indian, bit by bit, into the Bolivian community).

As a response to this challenge, Taboada Terán has attempted to synthesise the political and historical processes of his country in a literature which makes use of microcosm, a continual movement outward from within: "Mi objetivo como escritor del País Secreto fue siempre llegar a la literatura desde adentro para obtener carta de legitimidad, si se quiere poderes sobrenaturales para decidir el destino de mis personajes." (My objective as a writer from the Secret Country has always been to reach literature from inside so as to achieve legitimacy; if you will, so as to obtain supernatural powers to determine the destiny of my characters).

This has entailed speculation, too, on the destiny of his country. In this he has to take into account Bolivia's ethnic diversity. Taboada is a *mestizo* born in La Paz. His mother, however, is from Cochabamba. This gives him a dual heritage, since the two cities have different indigenous languages, Aymara and Quechua respectively. With these languages as well as Spanish, Taboada is well-equipped to understand and observe the most populous areas of Bolivia. The geographical span of his writing does not, however, extend to the eastern and northern lowlands, which include the important city of Santa Cruz. Taboada has been criticised for this omission of the largest part of Bolivian territory. However, La Paz and Cochabamba constitute the main axis around which the country's political and economic life has developed until recently.

Knowledge of two Indian languages has meant access to a wealth of indigenous stories and beliefs, which have been much used in Taboada's fiction. His mother was influential in this, and an important source of material: "Mi madre fue una importante cultora de la literatura oral. En mi niñez escuché de sus labios varios relatos y uno de ellos fue la leyenda del *Manchay Puytu*. Cuarenta años después la llevaría a la novela." (My mother was an important practitioner of oral literature. In my childhood I heard her tell many stories and one of them was the legend of *Manchay Puytu*. Forty years later I would transfer it to my novel).

Taboada's work is notoriously difficult to categorise, since it embraces a gamut of other disciplines, including history and ethnography. His main preoccupations are with the re-examination of Bolivian reality through key moments in the country's history, and he has described himself as a historian who works in fiction.

Among the autobiographical traits to be found in Taboada's novels is the condition of exile which accompanies a passion for travel. Many of his characters are travellers, and all the novels feature protagonists who are deeply influenced by some form of journey. The love of travel appears to be the paternal contribution to his character; his father is described as "Andariego como gitano, sastre de obra fina, raza blanca y apellidos de prosapia chuquisaqueña" (As much of a wanderer as a gypsy, a fine tailor, a white man of Chuquisaca ancestry).

Taboada's work can be seen as inheriting something of the tradition of Andean polemical literature unique to that region and reflecting as much white pro-indianist opinion as indigenist grievances themselves. His career aim is to give the fullest possible picture of Bolivian reality: "Tengo el ambicioso plan de llegar a una decena de novelas de corte testimonial sobre mi País Secreto" (My ambition plan is to write a dozen testimonial novels about my Secret Country). This term "país secreto" is used to convey Bolivia's isolation from the world at large and, because of its inaccessibility, provides an accurate image despite the country's long history of exploitation by British and US interests.

KEITH J. RICHARDS

Biography

Born in La Paz, Bolivia in 1929. Grew up with a knowledge of Quechua and Aymara languages, which has given him access to a storehouse of Indian stories and beliefs. Father died at the beginning of the Chaco War (1932–35). Involved in revolutionary Marxist politics and thus under suspicion by the authorities. Imprisoned in 1972; spent six months in solitary confinement. Settled in Argentina with his family. Returned to Bolivia alone after eight years. Cultural director in universities of Oruro and Cochabamba. Founder and editor of the journals *Cultura Boliviana* and *Letras Bolivianas*. Regular contributor to the Jesuit-run newspaper, *Presencia*, La Paz. Recipient of several national literary awards and, in 1978, the Faja de Honor (Sash of Honor) of the Argentine Writers' Association for *Manchay Puytu*.

Selected Works

Short Fiction

Claroscuro, La Paz: Editorial e Imprenta Artística, 1948
Germen, La Paz: Editorial e Imprenta Artística, 1950
Mientras se oficia el escarnio, La Paz: Colección Popular, 1968
Indios en rebelión: hechos de la revolución boliviana, La Paz and Cochabamba: Editorial Los Amigos del Libro, 1968
El tinku de laimes y jucumanis, Santiago de Chile: Colección "Ahora," 1970
Sweet and Sexy, Cochabamba: Cuadernos de Vientos Nuevos, 1977

Novels

El precio del estaño: una tragedia boliviana, La Paz: Librería Juventud, 1960
El signo escalonado, Buenos Aires: Ediciones del Sol, 1975
Manchay Puytu, el amor que quiso ocultar Dios, Buenos Aires: Sudamericana, 1977
Angelina Yupanki, marquesa de la conquista, Barcelona: Apóstrofe, 1992
Ollantay, la guerra de los dioses, Buenos Aires: Quetzal, 1994

Other Writings

Cuba, paloma de vuelo popular (crónica de viaje), Oruro, Bolivia: Editorial Universitaria, 1964
Chile con el corazón a la izquierda, Oruro, Bolivia: Editorial Universitaria, 1971
Colombia: Jorge Eliecer Gaitán, Buenos Aires: Centro Editor de América Latina, 1974
La revolución degollada, Buenos Aires: Centro Editor de América Latina, 1974
Bolivia en el cuento: antología de ayer y de hoy, Buenos Aires: Convergencia, 1976
Los frutos del árbol de la libertad, Cochabamba, Bolivia: Instituto de Formación y Capacitación, 1983
La difícil aurora, Cochabamba, Bolivia: Instituto de Formación y Capacitación, 1984
Requerimiento al rey de España, La Paz: Ediciones Casa de la Cultura, 1992

Further Reading

Fisbach, Erich, "Deseo, transgresiones y represiones sexuales en *Manchay Puytu, el amor que quiso ocultar Dios* del boliviano Néstor Taboada Terán," *Journal of Hispanic Research*, vol. 1/1 (Autumn 1992)
García Pabón, Leonardo, "Deseo, muerte e historia en *Manchay Puytu*," in *El paseo de los sentidos. Estudios de literatura contemporánea boliviana*, edited by García Pabón and Wilma Torrico, La Paz: Instituto Boliviano de la Cultura, 1983
Richards, Keith J., "Sexuality and Death: Cultural Synthesis and the Grotesque in Néstor Taboada Terán's *Manchay Puytu, el amor que quiso ocultar Dios*," *Journal of Hispanic Research*, London, 3 (1994–95)
Taboada Terán, Néstor (editor), *Oficio del coraje*, Cochabamba, Bolivia: Editorial Los Amigos del Libro, 1981
Vallejo de Bolívar, Gaby, "La dimensión mágica-mítica en *El signo escalonado*," in his *En busca de los nuestros*, Cochabamba, Bolivia: Editorial Los Amigos de Libro, 1987

Lygia Fagundes Telles 1923–

Brazilian prose writer

Lygia Fagundes Telles rose to prominence as a woman writer in Brazil, a country in which previously unquestioned truths, and the very possibility of truth, become problematic. This is an axiom which applies to the state of flux at all levels of social interaction, be it within the discources of gender, race or class, or in the realm of the individual psyche. For these reasons, fragmentation, instability and change are of the essence in her writing, as is the case also with some of her contemporaries: Clarice Lispector, Carlos Drummond de Andrade and Rachel de Queiroz, to name but a few.

Of the many aspects one might choose to highlight in her prose fiction, the themes of metamorphosis, and of the struggle for power, stand out as constants in both her long and short narratives. They are present in her novels – *Ciranda de pedra* (*The Marble Dance*), *As meninas* (*The Girl in the Photograph*) – and in her short fiction: *Seminário dos ratos* (*Tigrela and Other Stories*), *Antes do baile verde*. Metamorphosis is seen here as a phenomenon to be considered not only in its natural forms (the life changes between birth and death) but also (and more pertinently in a consideration of this author's work) in its "unnatural" or fantastic dimensions, usually in the context of a variety of power struggles. It is unnatural metamorphosis, of a fantastic or fairy-tale kind, that Fagundes Telles most often deploys as her central trope to produce an effect of horror in most of her writing, above all in her short stories.

But change, whether feared or desired – or both, as is often the case throughout this author's work – can also become synonymous with revolution. Social revolution foreseen here as coming about usually through violent upheaval, lies at the heart of the deceptively fantastic universe created by Fagundes Telles. Attempts at radical change frequently originate in the margins, and target the corruption and obsolescence seen to be inherent in the status quo. This applies equally to realist plots and to those more easily classifiable as works of magical realism. The process of metamorphosis is always insinuated in a variety of power struggles which, however fantastically disguised, derive from the clear concerns of everyday reality. Although, as already indicated, sometimes the change feared is simply that associated with the natural life cycles, more often the process of change involves a tension: between the unchanged self and the threatening transforming Other; between the unchanged self and a threatening changing world; or between the uncontrollably changing self and the environment inducing that involuntary change in the disempowered self.

These changes always point implicitly or explicitly to a political undercurrent of issues of class and gender. Elsewhere, these are endorsed by the author's occasional statements supporting social justice and women's rights. An unequal distribution of wealth, class divisions, poverty and sexual inequality, are key preoccupations in a body of narrative fiction clearly concerned with the need for *positive* change in a country and in a period perceived as transitional.

However, a perceived need is not always underpinned by a belief in the likelihood of its fulfilment. The intellectual heritage of Fagundes Telles can be traced back to such precursors of pessimism as Machado de Assis, whose work she invokes in her own literary production. In the foreground is the panorama of a 20th-century Brazil, torn by political dissent and unstable regimes, which eliminates the possibility of radical change and leads to the presentation of a more sombre vision of meta-morphosis-as-decay. Works such as *As meninas* or *Seminário dos ratos* provide a glimpse into a world of *Realpolitik* in which change signifies destruction.

Of the various recurring themes previously highlighted, sexual politics and the gender power struggle inform Fagundes Telles's writing more insistently even than class or national politics. It is in this context that the potentially violent implications of the trope of metamorphosis are most fully explored. The author offers a vision of a patriarchal society in which women are largely disempowered. She creates female characters who turn themselves from victims into aggressors. The nature of this transformation, traceable back as far as *Ciranda de pedra* (1954), reappears throughout her work, in short stories such as "Confissão de Leontina" [Leontina's Confession] and "Herbarium" [Herbarium], each of which witnesses a disempowered young girl transformed through a hard experience of abuse (or disabuse of former beliefs), into a metaphorical or actual monster, castrater or destroyer of the male Other. The male figures are representative of oppressive patriarchal forces ultimately undone by the vengeful impulse of the rebellious female.

Metamorphosis, whether with or without the magical, fantastic, or horror elements, becomes the nihilistic response to disillusion at both individual and collective levels. In a universe of fictions in which hope of attaining a better world is inevitably disappointed, metamorphosis is the means whereby Fagundes Telles's characters overcome near-destruc-tion. They are newly self-invented she-devils engaged in puni-tive missions, which often culminate in "triumphant" murder "sem remorso, quer mesmo?" (without remorse, would you believe it?) Anger, and the refusal to offer facile, happy endings, are the characteristics that situate Lygia Fagundes Telles in an already vast corpus of women's writing. Its trademark is a gaze defined by the "hunger, rebellion and rage" typical of earlier 19th-century gothic and near-gothic writing, as a response to social circumstances too little changed at the beginning of the 20th century.

MARIA MANUEL LISBOA

Biography

Born in São Paulo, Brazil, 19 April 1923; daughter of a district chief of police/public prosecutor. Educated at various schools. Studied law at the University of São Paulo. Married twice: Gofredo da Silva Telles (divorced 1961); Paulo Emílio Salles Gomes (died 1977). Recipient of numerous awards including: Instituto Nacional do Livro Prize, 1958 for *Histórias do desencontro*; Guimarães Rosa Prize, 1972; Brazilian Academy of Letters Award, 1973; Pedro Nava Award, 1989. Member of Brazilian Academy of Letters.

Selected Works

Short Fiction
Praia viva, São Paulo: Martins, 1944
O cacto vermelho, Rio de Janeiro: Mérito, 1949
Histórias do desencontro, Rio de Janeiro: José Olympio, 1958
Histórias escolhidas, São Paulo: Boa Leitura, 1961
A confissão de Leontina, Sá de Bandeira, Brazil: Angola, 1964
O jardim selvagem, São Paulo: Martins, 1965
Antes do baile verde, Rio de Janeiro: Bloch, 1970; revised and
     augmented edition, Rio de Janeiro: José Olympio, 1971
Seminário dos ratos, Rio de Janeiro: Nova Fronteira, 1977; as
     Tigrela and Other Stories, translated by Margaret A. Neves, New
     York: Avon, 1986
Filhos pródigos, São Paulo: Livraria Cultura, 1978
A disciplina do amor: fragmentos, Rio de Janeiro: Nova Fronteira,
     1980
Mistérios: ficções, Rio de Janeiro: Nova Fronteira, 1981
10 contos escolhidos, Brasília: Horizonte, 1984
Venha ver o pôr-do-sol & outros contos, São Paulo: Ática, 1988
As horas nuas, Rio de Janeiro: Nova Fronteira, 1989

Novels
Porão e sobrado, São Paulo: n.p., 1938
Ciranda de pedra, Rio de Janeiro: Nova Fronteira, 1954; as *The Marble
     Dance*, translated by Margaret A. Neves, New York: Avon, 1986
Verão no aquário, São Paulo: Martins, 1963
As meninas, Rio de Janeiro: José Olympio, 1973; as *The Girl in the
     Photograph*, translated by Margaret A. Neves, New York: Avon,
     1982
Capitu, São Paulo: Siciliano, 1993

Compilations and Anthologies
Seleta, edited by Nelly Novaes Coelho, Rio de Janeiro: José
     Olympio, 1971
*Lygia Fagundes Telles: seleção de textos, notas, estudos biográfico,
     histórico e crítico, exercícios*, edited by Leonardo Monteiro, São
     Paulo: Abril Educação, 1980

Os melhores contos, edited by Eduardo Portella, São Paulo: Global,
     1984

Further Reading
Very little has been written specifically on Lygia Fagundes Telles.
The works by Eliade and by Todorov listed below are general
studies on the fantastic, an important aspect of her work.

Ataíde, Vicente, "A narrativa de Lygia Fagundes Telles," in his
     A narrativa de ficção, São Paulo: McGraw Hill, 1974
Coronado, Guillermo de la Cruz, "O ódio caímico em Lygia e
     Unamuno," in *Letras de Hoje*, Pôrto Alegre, Brazil: PUCRS (11),
     1973
Costigan, Lucia Helena, "Literatura e ditadura: aspectos da ficção
     brasileira pós 64 em alguns dos escritos de Lygia Fagundes
     Telles e de Nélida Piñón," *Hispanic Journal*, vol. 13/1(Spring
     1992)
Eliade, Mircea, *Mito e realidade*, São Paulo: Perspectiva, 1972
Lucas, Fabio, "A ficção giratória de Lygia Fagundes Telles,"
     Travessia, Florianópolis, 20 (1990)
Pinto, Cristina Ferreira, "A decadência da família brasileira ou a
     descentralização do pai," in her *O bildungsroman femenino:
     quatro exemplos brasileiros*, São Paulo: Perspectiva, 1990
Silva, Antônio Manuel dos Santos, "Existência e coisificação nos
     contos de Lygia Fagundes Telles," *Revista de Letras*, São Paulo,
     26–27 (1986–87)
Silva, Vera Maria Tietzmann da, *A metamorfose nos contos de
     Lygia Fagundes Telles*, Rio de Janeiro: Presença, 1985
____ *A ficção intertextual de Lygia Fagundes Telles*, Goiânia:
     Cegraf/UFG, 1992
Todorov, Tzvetan, *Introduction à la littérature fantastique*, Paris:
     Seuil, 1970
Tolman, Jon M., "New Fiction: Lygia Fagundes Telles," *Review* 30
     (September–December 1981)

Interviews
Price, Greg, *Latin America. The Writer's Journey*, London: Hamish
     Hamilton, 1990

Testimonial Writing

During the 1960s, Latin America was going through a period
of massive social change and upheaval. The Cuban Revolution
of 1959 brought new vigor to a sclerotic Marxism with its
youthful recklessness, and it appeared poised to harness the
ferment to effect radical change overnight. The Revolution
sought for a suitable literary genre that would best express
those times of renewal, passion and expectation. In this respect,
the novel failed miserably (the plight of Carpentier in
producing the announced "novel of the revolution" was symptomatic). Something more agile was needed; poetry alone was
not enough. A testimony of things to come was called for. In
1970 this genre was anointed by the new prize instituted by
the Cuban Casa de las Américas. The splendors and the misery

of the *testimonio*, its pretence and inner contradictions as well
as its recent extinction, could not be understood without this
umbilical cord to the Revolution.

This new testimonial writing emerges as a hybrid enterprise
carving its space out of documentary writing, autobiographical report, eye-witness literature, the literature of resistance
and protest, and the New Testament. Strangely enough, the
sense of an ending and of an impending new era is of
paramount importance for the very foundations of this testimony. The embrace of "apocalypse now" separates the *testimonio* from its closest forerunners: the nonfiction novel
(Truman Capote, Norman Mailer), the new journalism, the
ethnic cultural narratives (Ricardo Pozas) and the social or

anthropological documents on the "culture of poverty" (popularized by Carolina Maria de Jesús and Oscar Lewis).

The foundational value of Miguel Barnet's *Biografía de un cimarrón*, 1966 (*The Autobiography of a Runaway Slave*), needs to be recognized. Barnet manages to accomplish a real *tour de force* in combining, in the case of a former runaway slave, *lo real maravilloso* (Carpentier's "marvelous in the real") with the appropriate political perspective. The *Biografía* testifies to the fact that, within the span of one life, Cuba has come from slavery to socialist revolution. The allegorical, figural interpretation (in the sense of Erich Auerbach) of the Cuban Revolution as the climaxing *telos* of modern Cuban history is thus unmistakably established. Yet the very interest of Barnet's narrative lies rather in his recovery of a specific Cuban and Caribbean cultural history, and the biography of the former slave is actually cut off at the beginning of this century. The emphasis on cultural anthropology, which turns the narrative into an encyclopedia of cultural history, characterizes some other better-known testimonial works, such as Elena Poniatowska's *Hasta no verte, Jesús mío*, 1969 (*Until We Meet Again*); or Elizabeth Burgos Debray's *Me llamo Rigoberta Menchú*, 1983 (*I, Rigoberta Menchú*). *Rigoberta Menchú* shares the contradictions of Barnet's *Biografía*: both narratives are framed by the apocalyptic fervor of their times, by what appears to be the last gasp of Western Utopian modernity; yet, as narratives, they are interesting through their rescue of a Latin American premodern cultural heritage, something that has become a postmodern task. In Poniatowska, the Utopian moment is also somewhat present, through aspects of the Mexican student movement of 1968, in her collage of testimonial voices and documents in *La noche de Tlatelolco*, 1971 (*Massacre in Mexico*).

The new testimonial writing aspired to be the record of living history. Its mission was, more specifically, to challenge "official," bourgeois history, to fill the voids in the record, to seek the other side of the coin, and generally to empower the voice of the underprivileged and the repressed. The audible voice of the witness-situated testimonial writing *vis-à-vis* documentary or nonfiction literature at large. Yet the muses assisting at the birth of the genre had stipulated that it should not be just any voice fitting this large category of the under-represented: this voice had to be representative of the ongoing social struggles from the revolutionary (sometimes directly Marxist) point of view. The orthodox theoreticians of the *testimonio*, Barnet and Margaret Randall, are refreshingly clear about this. Therefore, special witnesses and special biographies were privileged. An "enemy" could still be used, provided that he could testify about the worthiness of the revolutionary cause; thus Abelardo Cuadra's testimony about Sandino and about the young Fidel Castro, in *Hombre del Caribe*, 1977 [Man of the Caribbean]. In *testimonio* the "other" is meant to be "us."

This overriding clause of partisan "representativity" undercuts the specific mission of testimony. Testimonial writing, thus defined, aimed at a predetermined allegorical and political level of meaning and "usefulness." The subversive powers of testimony were castrated in the official socialist *testimonio*. A genre based apparently on a contract with truth and reality produced a stream of exemplary parables of ritual social experience. It is not surprising then to find that the Lacanian imaginary of these allegories throve on models coming from Stalinist Socialist Realism, invented in the Soviet Union in the 1930s for an analogous purpose. Among the better known testimonies, is Omar Cabezas's *La montaña es algo más que una inmensa estepa verde*, 1982 (*Fire from the Mountain*); yet even this frame-up is humanized by the most convincing description of how corporal functions are negotiated by an urbanite in the jungle.

The problems of *testimonio* start with the selection and presentation of the protagonists: Rigoberta Menchú, Domitila, or Huillca are all radical left-wing political activists or labor union leaders. Yet they are presented as ordinary people. The subtitles and translations tend to stress this aspect: "an Indian woman in Guatemala," "a woman of the Bolivian mines," "a Peruvian peasant speaks." In the introduction to *Biografía de un cimarrón* (not included in the English version), Barnet tells how he selected the protagonist for this work. He learned from the Cuban press about two interesting subjects, each over one hundred years old: a black woman – former slave, *santera* (practitioner of the African cult known as *santería*), and spiritualist – and a black man, also a former slave, but with no particular interest in cults. The latter had been a runaway and later took part in the Cuban War of Independence. After this he was involved in a brothel brawl aptly described on the back cover of the Spanish edition as "a battle against the North Americans." Barnet says that he "dismissed the old woman" right away for the figure more representative from his point of view, Esteban Montejo. With this logic, the feisty woman protagonist of Elena Poniatowska's *Hasta no verte, Jesús mío* would never make it into such a *testimonio*. This type of selection process reaches the level of farce in Barnet's *La vida real*, 1986 [Real Life]. To write this testimony, Barnet contacted members of the Caribbean old-timers' Leftist hangout in New York, the Julio Antonio Mella Club, found a Cuban who had immigrated to the US in the early 1950s, never returned to Cuba, yet remained Cuban and a romantic revolutionary in his heart. This "real life" story was meant to paste over the flood of the Cuban refugees from the then recent Mariel and the ever deepening moral crisis of the Revolution. Barnet wrote his well-intentioned allegorical potboiler while living in the US on a Guggenheim fellowship in the early 1980s.

A special problem is posed by the many intellectuals who have given testimony, in their own voice, to the upheavals, dramas, and tragedies of the 1960s to 1980s: the Salvadorean Roque Dalton, in his strangely prophetic autobiographical novel *¡Pobrecito poeta que era yo!*, 1976 [What a Dud Poet I Was!]; the Chileans Jorge Edwards, in *Persona non grata*, 1973 (later editions are less self-censored), and Hernán Valdés, in *Tejas Verdes: diario de un campo de concentración*, 1974 (*Tejas Verdes: a Concentration Camp Diary*) the Guatemalan Mario Payeras; the Nicaraguan Omar Cabezas; or the Cubans Carlos Franqui, in *Retrato de familia con Fidel*, 1981 (*Family Portrait with Fidel*), Armando Valladares, in *Contra toda esperanza*, 1985 (*Against All Hope*) or, in a marginal sense, Reinaldo Arenas in *Antes que anochezca*, 1992 (*Before Night Falls*), among others. All of them have been changed, some crushed, by their experience. Only Dalton, Valdés, Payeras and Cabezas enter the canon, because all are accepted revolutionary intellectuals (or were: Dalton was executed by his comrades in arms allegedly "for treason;" Payeras expressed more critical points of view in his later work). Edwards would not fit in with his *Persona non grata*, detailing his experience as Allende's envoy to Cuba, but might come close with his Chilean post-coup non-fiction novels. The Cuban dissidents would have no chance whatsoever in spite of the ample representativity of what they have to say. It would appear that the *testimonio* and the channels of its propagation not only create and privilege yet another official history, but also help repress inconvenient eye-witness accounts.

There are more problems with the Latin American *testimonio*, such as the memory and the self-censorship of the interviewee; the invasiveness of the interview-technique, in spite of the pretended self-effacement of the interviewer; and the editing process, producing a narrative from a log of interviews and dialogues. Literarization is only another additional layer mediating between the authentic word, and world, of the Other and the domesticated end-result. Therefore, the difference between testimony and testimonial novel is much less important than the political and allegorical strictures imposed on the genre as constitutive fiction at its official birth.

Although the pre-selected witnesses appear to speak in the first-person, who is actually in control of their words? Who is the author? The legal lability of the situation is exposed in translations which upgrade the characters to "authors" and reclassify the authors of the Spanish originals as "editors," "collaborators," or "co-authors." The author of the *biography* of a runaway slave becomes the editor of an *autobiography* supposedly authored by the illiterate Esteban Montejo. The point here is not so much that "characters" and "authors" appear to be reversible legal and literary fictions, but the fact that, while the scruples of the Anglo-Saxon law return to the interviewed parties authority and liability, the witnesses might have lost their authentic voices whatever their personal legal or literary status might be. Not even the Nobel Prize for Peace awarded, in 1992, to the protagonist of *Me llamo Rigoberta Menchú* can change this situation.

EMIL VOLEK

See also entries on Autobiography, Miguel Barnet, Roque Dalton, Jorge Edwards, Prison Writing

Further Reading

The best introduction to the problems and criticism is Sklodowska's middle-of-the-road book; many sharper insights have appeared recently in various "second thoughts" on the *testimonio*. The political-allegorical strictures of the genre are espoused by its orthodox theorists, Barnet and Randall.

Barnet, Miguel, "The Documentary Novel," *Cuban Studies*, vol. 11/1 (1981)
____ *La fuente viva*, Havana: Letras Cubanas, 1983
____ "La novela testimonial: alquimia de la memoria," *Criticarte*, Caracas 6 (1987)
Beverley, John, "Through all Things Modern: Second Thoughts on Testimonio," in his *Against Literature*, Minneapolis: University of Minnesota Press, 1993
____ "El testimonio en la encrucijada," *Revista Iberoamericana* 164–65 (1993)
Randall, Margaret, "¿Qué es, y cómo se hace un testimonio?" *Revista de Crítica Literaria Latinoamericana* 36 (1992)
Sklodowska, Elzbieta, *Testimonio hispanoamericano: historia, teoría, poética*, New York: Peter Lang, 1992
____ "Spanish American Testimonial Novel – Some Afterthoughts," *New Novel Review*, vol.1/2 (1994)
Volek, Emil, "Las modalidades del Testimonio y *Hasta no verte, Jesús mío* de Elena Poniatowska," in *Literatura mexicana/ Mexican Literature*, edited by José Miguel Oviedo, Philadelphia: University of Pennsylvania, 1993
____ "Hecho/documento/ficción: Testimonio, crónicas, el contexto como autor y otras trampas de la fe," in *Actas de la Asociación Internacional de Hispanistas, Irvine 1992*, vol. 4, edited by Juan Villegas, Irvine: University of California, 1994

Theatre in Latin America

Theatre in Brazil from 1822

A key conflict has shaped the existence of the theatre in Brazil from its inception to the present – an attraction to, and repulsion of national elements in both its written and performed versions. The many gestures toward popular culture and the equally forceful movement away from it have taken diverse forms and guises throughout the history of the dramatic arts in Brazil. Examples of this conflict are found from the outset, in the theatre of Father José de Anchieta (1534–97), which presents an almost schizophrenic split between the outdoor staging of simple, direct works performed mostly in Tupi for the native masses who were to be converted to Catholicism, and the writing of elaborate Latin pieces to be performed indoors for the students and teachers at the Jesuit *colégios*.

The conflict reappears in full force at the very inception of Romanticism in the theatre of Brazil, in the figures of Domingos José Gonçalves de Magalhães (1811–82), João Caetano dos Santos (1808–63), and Luís Carlos Martins Pena (1815–48). Magalhães and João Caetano are usually credited with starting Brazil's Romantic theatre, their vastly different life experiences notwithstanding, when Caetano staged and performed the title role in Magalhães's *Antônio José ou o poeta e a inquisição* [António José, or the Poet and the Inquisition], which opened in 1838, a truly remarkable year in the history of Brazilian theatre, as it also witnessed the premiere (also staged by João Caetano's company) of Brazil's first *comédia de costumes* (comedy of manners), *O juiz de paz da roça* (*A Rural Justice of the Peace*), a key development in the trend favoring the national element in Brazilian theatre. The play launched at the peak of his artistic power the career of Martins Pena, Brazil's most accomplished creator of comedies of manners, and the nation's first author to write solely for the theatre.

Romanticism in Brazil is often characterized as a struggle between the need for the arts to reflect the nation's defining elements and the continued strong pull of European influences. The basic conflict recurs in the theatrical careers of poet Antônio Gonçalves Dias (1823–64) and novelist José de Alencar (1829–77), both ultimately unable to harmonize the two currents in their dramatic endeavors, although the latter's attempts at abolitionist theatre (as in *Mãe* [Mother], premiered 1860) include elements of a more popular theatre. Nor did other 19th-century manifestations such as thesis plays and *teatro de casaca* (or "tailcoat plays," as Realist theatre was known in Brazil), succeed in resolving the conflict, although its leading practitioners, Joaquim Manuel de Macedo (1820–82) and José Joaquim da França Júnior (1838–90), did for the most part succeed in presenting a convincing picture of national identity, as in Macedo's *O primo da Califórnia* ([The Cousin from California], premiered 1855) and França Júnior's *Como se fazia um deputado* ([How Representatives Were Elected], premiered 1882).

While it is essentially true that the extended influence and enormous popularity of such long drawn out 19th-century forms as the comedy of manners and its offshoot, the revue or *teatro de revista* (whose best-known practitioner is the prolific Artur Azevedo, 1855–1908, author of the beloved *A capital federal* [The Nation's Capital], premiered 1897), deferred by several decades the coming of modernity to the stages of Brazil, it must be made clear that it was precisely those practitioners of the light theatre who kept alive the national element in the first two or three decades of this century.

Although two generations of theatre critics perpetuated the wrong notion that Brazilian Modernism generally ignored the theatre, recent studies have demonstrated that a number of the artists associated with the movement had a strong interest in the theatre and did in fact participate in the theatrical scene of their day, whether writing plays, organizing theatre groups, designing and painting sets, or directing productions. While the theatre of Oswald de Andrade (1890–1954) has deserved intense critical scrutiny since the revolutionary staging of his *O rei da vela* ([The Candle Baron], published 1937) by Teatro Oficina in 1967, the contributions of other Modernists – such as Eugênia and Álvaro Moreyra, Renato Viana, Flávio de Carvalho, Antônio de Alcântara Machado and Mário de Andrade, all profoundly aware of the need to enlist the theatre in their struggle for the expression of a national identity in Brazilian art – remain largely unexplored.

Modernismo's strong nationalist streak and anti-elitist, people-oriented rhetoric paved the way for the regionalist trend that pervaded the Brazilian theatre in the 1950s and 1960s. Championed by authors such as Jorge Andrade (1922–84), Alfredo Dias Gomes (b. 1922), Ariano Suassuna (b. 1927),

João Cabral de Melo Neto (b. 1920), Hermilo Borba Filho (1917–76), Rachel de Queiroz (b. 1910), and others – all members of an elite (intellectual, economic, often both) who felt the urgency to integrate the several pairs of opposing facets (national/imported, popular/elitist, traditional/avant-garde, etc) – Regionalist theatre (or, at least, its most representative works) succeeded on the thematic level while failing to take significant risks with regard to form and/or staging. Among the most successful of these plays are revisited forms with a new, social message, be it *autos* (such as Suassuna's *Auto da compadecida* [The Rogue's Trial], premiered 1956, and Cabral de Melo Neto's *Morte e vida severina* [Death and Life of a Common Man], premiered 1965) or tragedies (such as Dias Gomes's *O pagador de promessas* (*Payment as Promised*) and Jorge Andrade's *Pedreira das almas* [Quarry of Souls], both of which were first produced in 1960).

Such formal risks were mostly the domain of innovative theatre groups that had begun to appear in the 1940s. The ongoing conflict between the two tendencies under consideration is well illustrated by a comparison between such popular-oriented groups as Teatro de Arena de São Paulo or Recife's Teatro Popular do Nordeste, and on the other hand, the clearly elitist Teatro Brasileiro de Comédia (TBC) and the smaller companies it spawned, or were formed upon its demise. A related issue is the role of foreign producers (such as Franco Zampari) and directors (Adolfo Celi, Luciano Salce, Ruggero Jacobbi, Gianni Ratto, Maurice Vaneau, Eugênio Kusnet and especially, Zbigniew Ziembinsky) in shaping modern Brazilian theatre. The towering figure of Ziembinsky (1908–78) – who did eventually join the TBC but is more readily associated with the Rio de Janeiro-based group, Os Comediantes, which he directed in 1943 in the ground-breaking staging of Nelson Rodrigues's *Vestido de noiva* (*The Wedding Dress*) that is generally seen as the beginning of Brazil's modern theatre – provides the student of the ample conflicts that inform the theatre of Brazil with yet another facet of such paradoxes and antagonisms. Here we have a foreign-born and foreign-trained director and actor revolutionizing the Brazilian theatre by introducing to its stages long-overdue contributions from Expressionism, Jungian psychology, dramatic representations of myth, innovative uses of sound, lighting and stage division – but doing so upon the solid textual structure provided by Nelson Rodrigues's vision and artistry.

Equally important and closely related to these fundamental oppositions are the cases of Black theatre groups (such as the Teatro Experimental do Negro, directed by Abdias do Nascimento (b. 1914)) and student theatre groups (the theatre arm of CPC-UNE, and several university ensembles), both with profound political implications for their contemporaries of the 1940s, 1950s, and early 1960s, as well as for their followers and students in subsequent decades.

During the military regime of 1964–85, especially in the late 1960s and early 1970s, the period when repression was most intense, the equation assumes a new feature, as the popular element – as appropriated by members of the intellectual elite – is identified with those who were actively resisting the dictatorship. This is most obvious in plays such as *Se correr o bicho pega, se ficar o bicho come* ([If You Run the Beast Will Catch You, if You Don't It Will Eat You] first performed in 1966) and other works by Oduvaldo Viana Filho (Vianinha;

1936–74). The musical element takes center stage in productions of groups such as Opinião and in the historical plays of Arena, *Arena conta Zumbi* ([Arena Tells the Story of Zumbi], premiered 1965) and *Arena conta Tiradentes* ([Arena Tells the Story of Tiradentes] premiered 1967), both co-authored by the group's co-directors, Augusto Boal (b. 1931) and Gianfrancesco Guarnieri (b. 1934). Music is also central to another historical allegory of the resistance theatre of the 1960s and 1970s, Chico Buarque (b. 1944) and Ruy Guerra's *Calabar, o elogio da traição* [Calabar, in Praise of Treason], published in 1973 but banned from the stage until 1979). Elements of the Absurd tradition are also incorporated into the Brazilian theatre of protest, as is evident in such plays as Leilah Assunção's *Fala baixo senão eu grito* [Speak Softly or I'll Scream], premiered in 1969 and Roberto Athayde's *Apareceu a Margarida* (*Miss Margarida's Way*), premiered in 1973, as well as in the discovery and productions of the heretofore never-staged plays of the 19th-century genius, Joaquim José de Campos Leão (Qorpo-Santo, 1829–83). A number of plays of the period and of subsequent years as well, depict the experiences of those whom the oppressor has determined to be "marginal:" the unemployed or underemployed, prostitutes, pimps, thieves, drug addicts, street children, homosexuals. Foremost among playwrights of this line is Plínio Marcos (b. 1935), the author of two of the most important plays of the period, *Dois perdidos numa noite suja*, 1966 [Two Lost in a Filthy Night] and *Navalha na carne*, 1967 [Razor in the Flesh]. Following the gradual abolition of censorship and the return to a more democratic regime in the late 1970s and early 1980s, previously banned plays could finally be staged, foremost among them Vianinha's *Rasga coração*, 1979 [Heart Rending] and João Ribeiro Chaves Neto's *Patética*, 1980 [Pathétique].

The 1980s and first half of the 1990s saw a number of trends and developments: the preeminence of the stage director, or *encenador*, with Antunes Filho (b. 1929), Gerald Thomas (b. 1954), Bia Lessa (b. 1958) and Geraldo Villella (b. 1960) as the most salient names; a shift away from political commitment and social protest, and toward a more intense interest in examining the individual experience, often returning to childhood and adolescence in search of answers and solace, traits eminently noticeable in the plays of Naum Alves de Souza and Maria Adelaide Amaral (both born in 1942); the widely accepted recognition of Nelson Rodrigues as the most important playwright in the history of Brazilian theatre, made possible by a series of stagings of Nelson's plays done by Antunes and Grupo Macunaíma in the early and mid-1980s (*Nelson Rodrigues: o eterno retorno* [Nelson Rodrigues: the Eternal Return] and *Nelson 2 Rodrigues*); stage adaptations of texts from other genres or of plays from other periods and/or theatre traditions (for example, Pessoal do Victor's dramatic version of Marcelo Rubens Paiva's autobiography, *Feliz ano velho* [Happy Old Year] in 1983; *Augusto Matraga*, Macunaíma's 1986 stage rendition of the last short story in Guimarães Rosa's *Sagarana* [1946]; Ornitorrinco's stagings of Molière's *Le Malade imaginaire* and Shakespeare's *A Midsummer Night's Dream* in 1989–1991; and Bia Lessa's 1994 version of Robert Musil's novel *O homem sem qualidades* [*Der Mann ohne Eigenschaften; The Man without Qualities*]); the emergence of the inimitable work of Denise

Stoklos (b. 1950), whose approach shares a good deal with performance art and can be traced to the most essential aspects of the theatre, hence Stoklos's characterization of her art as Teatro Essencial; and finally, the continued success of major international theatre festivals in São Paulo, Belo Horizonte, Curitiba and Londrina.

Even the briefest of introductions to Brazilian theatre must take into account the longstanding opposition between a theatre centered (geographically as well as intellectually) on the Rio de Janeiro-São Paulo area, and the theatre located in other, traditionally "peripherical" states (regionalist theatre's gestures and advances notwithstanding). The passage of time and the enormous penetration of television have not fundamentally changed such state of affairs, with the most prestigious groups, such as present-day Grupo Macunaíma (directed by Antunes Filho), Teatro do Ornitorrinco (directed by Cacá Rosset), Companhia da Opera Seca (directed by Gerald Thomas), Boi Voador (directed by Ulysses Cruz), and Uzyna Uzona (directed by José Celso Martínez Correa, former leader of Grupo Oficina), all located in São Paulo. A related issue is, whether these groups are indeed the most outstanding ones, or are they the groups that happen to be singled out by most critics, who in turn, happen to be based in the Rio de Janeiro-São Paulo area. This state of affairs excludes (or at least, marginalizes) a number of prominent groups located in other parts of the country, as for example, Londrina's Grupo Delta, Pôrto Alegre's Cem Modos and Tear, Belo Horizonte's Galpão and Giramundo, and Acre's Poronga. Worthy of special attention, as a successful reconciler of a number of these oppositions and antagonisms, is Grupo União e Olho Vivo, led by a veteran of the struggle for popular theatre in Brazil, César Vieira (Edibal Almeida Piveta, b. 1931).

Although not known for cradling theorists of the theatre, Brazil has produced at least one major name – Augusto Boal. In spite of a penchant for controversy and his many years away from Brazil, Boal has written seminal theoretical pieces – *Teatro do oprimido e outras poéticas políticas*, 1974 (*Theater of the Oppressed*); *Técnicas latinoamericanas de teatro popular*, 1975 – that continue to be of central importance to the issues addressed above. Other names worthy of note are either more traditional critics (Décio de Almeida Prado, Sábato Magaldi and Yan Michalski) or younger, university-trained critics who have been active in more recent years, such as Edélcio Mostaço, Mariângela Alves de Lima and Alberto Guzik.

A consideration of the split between popular theatre and bourgeois theatre in the theatre of Brazil should include authoritarianism and the role of the State, in various forms and degrees of intervention, be it through the Serviço Nacional de Teatro (or any of the other names the organ has had through the years), through subsidies (for building theatres and other spaces; for tickets to Projeto Mambembão and others), awards, overt or indirect censorship, the closing down of theatres, the arrest and torture of actors and directors, and so forth. The issue of authoritarianism, so deeply interwoven with Brazilian culture and politics, also encompasses the composition of a theatrical canon. Diverse as its shapers have been throughout its history, the canon or body of works chosen to typify the theatre of Brazil is remarkable for its consistent exclusion of large groups that ought to have been *represented* but were marginalized by virtue of their slight economic and political strengths, which in turn, must be explained by the repression they have been subjected to since colonial times.

Finally, a word about representation: italicizing the verb in the previous paragraph is deliberate. Normally a rather loaded term, "representation" takes on additional urgency in theatre criticism. Issues of race, class, gender and sexual orientation acquire additional relevance when we deal with the performing arts. In the context of dependency (whether economic, political, cultural, etc), "representation" begs to be more carefully thought out. In the case of the theatre of Brazil, one point that must be questioned is who is or has been representing whom, and on what grounds. The legitimation or denunciation of the canon that has resulted from such representations must be the ultimate goal of any serious study of the history of the theatre in Brazil.

Severino J. Albuquerque

Theatre in Colombia, Cuba, Mexico and Peru

Colombia

In 19th-century Colombia, the earliest expressions of this genre include the politically focused, neoclassically inspired plays of José Fernández Madrid (1788–1830) and Luis Vargas Tejada (1802–29). These dramatists were concerned not so much with the plight of the downtrodden, as with disseminating an image of the native American as a "noble savage." By these means they sought to press their case for an end to colonial rule. Such plays were undramatic and didactic in nature, yet they skillfully exploited the view of the Spaniards as colonial oppressors and the Catholic Church as their handmaiden.

The two most important initiators of Colombia's modern theatre are Antonio Álvarez Lleras (1892–1956) and Luis Enrique Osorio (1896–1966). Influenced by Ibsen and the Spanish playwright Jacinto Benavente, Álvarez Lleras produced realistic thesis dramas, aimed at social reform, while Osorio wrote plays of more direct social protest influenced by dramatists such as Shaw, Pirandello and O'Neill. It was not until the contemporary period that the more popularly oriented theatre began to flourish. In particular, the work done by the Nuevo Teatro and it drama theorist, Enrique Buenaventura, helped to create a more socially engaged theatre which utilized dance, song and satire. Despite inevitable differences in stylistic and thematic concerns, Colombian popular theatre shares with Spanish Golden Age tragedy the notion, expounded by Lope de Vega, for example, of *enseñar entreteniendo*, that is, both to entertain and to teach a moral and often, a political lesson that could easily be grasped by the audience. It was during these formative years of the late 1960s that the Colombian theatre began the violent and dogmatic process of breaking away from a dependent cultural tradition. This was essential in order to create a thematics and stylistics that could represent not only the continent, but the cultural and political specificity of Colombia. The flavor of this experimental theatrical movement is most clearly displayed within the context of festivals and workshops (*talleres*), theatre collectives, university groups and the popular theatre movement.

The role of Enrique Buenaventura, Santiago García and Carlos José Reyes in developing the New Popular Theatre is significant, since each dramatist not only contributed to Colombia's national dramaturgy and to restructuring its means of production, but each one also helped to lay the basis for Latin American dramatic theory. Enrique Buenaventura, a leading playwright in Colombia, and one of Latin America's best directors and theoreticians, pioneered this new theatrical form in the 1950s. He brought to this task first-hand knowledge of three of the most dynamic exponents of Brechtian theatre: the Berliner Ensemble, Giorgio Strehler's Piccolo Teatro di Milano, and Jean Vilar's T.N.P., in France. By democratizing both the production and consumption of Colombian drama through the incorporation of oral tradition and popular culture in their dramatic and performance texts, Enrique Buenaventura in Cali (Teatro Experimental de Cali or TEC) and Santiago García in Bogotá (La Candelaria), have been able to combine social commitment with artistic integrity. Colombian dramatists experiment continuously with dramatic form, accepting European as well as Latin American dramatic trends while seeking an original expression capable of communicating their unique regional reality. The undeclared civil war known as *la Violencia* (The Violence) that plagued Colombia between 1948 and 1965, is the subject of Buenaventura's one-act plays collected in *Papeles del infierno*, 1968 [Documents from Hell]. The same period is explored in García's *Guadalupe, años sin cuenta*, 1975 [Guadalupe, Uncounted Years], a collective production based on exhaustive historical research of primarily by means of oral history.

Carlos José Reyes is also concerned with *la Violencia* and its sociopolitical consequences in such plays as *Bandidos* [Bandits] or *Farsa de una guerra de nunca acabar*, 1962 [Farce about a Never-ending War] and *Soldados*, 1967 [Soldiers] each of which contains sketches of the brutality of *la Violencia* both among the common people and within the armed forces.

Collective creation in Colombian theatre underscores the contemporary dramatists' need to create in accordance with the needs of their time and people. The in-depth research undertaken among the people for themes and forms of dramatic expression which, ultimately to emerge from them; the involvement of the public, actors and dramatists in the creative process from the preliminary research into the subject matter through the final staging of the play; and the elaborate reworkings of previous texts based on public feedback. This theory of drama seeks to assist in bringing about basic structural changes in Colombian society, and it leaves behind both regional tradition and the writing culture that was the exclusive domain of a ruling elite.

Cuba

The use of theatre for political ends is a constant in the trajectory of Cuban drama from colonial times to the end of the 20th century. However, a different kind of theatre began around 1936, one which espoused a cosmopolitan conception of art directed to a minority audience. The socially-oriented dramatists writing at the same time tended strongly toward a simplistic propaganda theatre with a direct sociopolitical message rather than an open-ended, consciousness-raising dénouement.

From the late 19th century until roughly 1930, the politically expressive *sainete* (farce), the local variant of the Spanish *género chico* (consisting of short comedies and operettas) was the dominant fare for theatre-goers in Havana. Such works depicted urban slums within the context of a series of confrontations or melodramatic scenes played by character types speaking (or singing) in urban discourse with a musical background. Even as crude commercial theatre, these *sainetes* served as vehicles for expressions of political resentment.

In the early 1960s José Triana (see separate entry) and Antón Arrufat revitalized the tragic form and combined strong political content, dramatic metaphor and creative theatrical structures to produce an internationally recognized theatre. Triana's *Medea en el espejo*, 1960 [Medea in the Mirror], *Parque de la fraternidad*, 1962 [Fraternity Park], *La muerte del ñeque*, 1963 [The Death of Enterprise] and *La noche de los asesinos*, 1965 (*The Criminals*), and Arrufat's *Los siete contra Tebas* [The Seven Against Thebes] as metaphoric commentaries on Cuban society, led to major political and artistic polemics within Cuba. Whether the plays were intended to be counter-revolutionary by their authors or not, they were interpreted as such, and this was a critical factor leading to a tightening of censorship and an increasing sovietization of literature. Another dramatist who suffered in this period was Virgilio Piñera (see separate entry), by far the most outstanding Cuban playwright of the 20th century, and one who had a considerable impact on Arrufat.

The formation of contemporary Cuban theatre owes much also to the work and influence of popular theatrical groups and the proliferation of festivals (the first of these took place in Havana in 1961), specialized journals, and the emergence of a number of organizations dedicated to stimulating theatrical production and research. Cuba's Teatro Cueva, founded as early as the 1930s, sought to reach the populace with experimental pieces which did not conform to the narrow demands of commercial theatre (the aforementioned *sainete*), but attempted rather to produce a national theatre concerned with the broader issues of socioeconomic conditions in a broad spectrum of Latin American countries. It is due to such a broad-based vision combined with the desire for experimentation of form that the theatre of sociopolitical overtones of such dramatists as Triana and Arrufat was given fertile ground in which to develop. A further expression of independent theatre's desire to reach the populace, rather than to be confined to major urban centers, was the surge of theatre collectives in the 1960s, such as the Teatro Escambray, a sociodidactic theatre with a focus on the immediacy of both clarifying and resolving a current social problem. Founded in 1968 by Sergio Corrieri, the Grupo Teatro Escambray calls on the public to act as an assembly of commentators at the close of each theatrical piece, much in the manner of the Brazilian Augusto Boal's forum theatre. An open discussion among all parties – audience members and theatre practitioners – is used as a means of resolving conflict and bringing about immediate change. Indeed, in tandem with its sociopolitical goals, the Castro regime sought to elevate the cultural experience of the Cuban people through theatre and promoted the shift of theatrical activity from the capital to the provinces by traveling Brígadas del Teatro (Teatrova, Teatro La Yaya, Teatro de Acero, among others).

Cuban revolutionary theatre uses drama as a vehicle for doctinal principles and the exaltation of "patriotic" denunciation, public confession of errors, and the absolute dedication to production. This socialized form of Cuban theatre is known as the Teatro Nuevo (the New Theatre). It focuses on the return of Cuban theatre to the people through some form of collective creation and the staging of particular issues or problems of immediate interest or concern to the communities within which these drama companies work. In more recent years, however, with the waning of enthusiasm for collective theatre for both historical and political reasons, there has been something of a resurgence of an author-centered theatre, the psychological portrayal of individualized characters, and the predominance of written texts over collectively debated performance-texts with multiple versions. And in these plays there is a re-examination of identity, the Cuban living in his country and the exiled Cuban, generational conflicts, and a more unbiased self-introspection of the country and its people. As a step out of the domain of collective creations, Alberto Pedro Torrientes's *Week-end en Bahía* examines the conflicts that emerge between the Cuban who has remained in his native land and the self-exiled Cuban who has chosen to emigrate to the United States. Although an authorial bias is present in this dramatic piece, respect for both political choices is maintained in Torrientes's work. With the institutionalization of the Cuban Revolution completely integrated into the sociopolitical and economic fabric of Cuban society and its longevity assured, at least until the death of Fidel Castro, there is currently a mandate from the public to develop alternate modes of theatrical expression in order to demonstrate diverse perspectives rather than to re-enforce a single point of view. Emerging artists in Cuba articulated a new set of expectations: that they be allowed to make theatre for themselves without government intervention or influence. This has resulted in Havana's reorganization of its cultural policy since 1989 and, just as Lezama Lima is a cult figure among young poets, so the absurdist plays of Virgilio Piñera have entered the Cuban canon.

Mexico

Mexican literature, strictly speaking, was born with the Independence movement just after the turn of the 19th century. But Mexican literature, the theatre in particular, is as old as the earliest civilized inhabitants of Meso-America. Historically, theatre in Mexico has been a powerful force for social change from pre-Columbian times, and it has frequently combined religious and political concerns with performance practice to create a style of drama unique to the region. From the earliest contacts between Cortés and the Aztecs through the Spanish-influenced colonial theatre to the politically charged contemporary drama, Mexican theatre has been used as a vehicle of religious conversion and cultural coercion, political propaganda and satire, as well as social denunciation and reform. Early Mexican drama comprised only occasional pieces (productions without dialogue or written in crude language for the purpose of evangelizing the Indians) and secular comedies presented as interludes at religious festivals.

Since its independence from Spain, Mexico has become one of the major theatrical centers in Latin America, giving rise to a number of experimental groups on the popular theatre front, the government-sponsored Instituto Nacional de Bellas Artes (INBA) and its subdivision, the Escuela de Arte Dramático founded in 1947, as well as hosting countless theatre festivals for amateur and avant-garde groups. But the creative spirit of aesthetic and sociopolitical revolution, incorporating such major European trends as existentialism, the theatre of the absurd, and the theatre of cruelty and of ritual did not become the hallmark of Mexican theatre until the mid-20th century. Indeed, one critic, Antonio Magaña Esquivel in his *Medio siglo de teatro mexicano* [Half a Century of Mexican Theatre], goes as far as to state that prior to 1928, "Mexican theatre could not find its place and aspiring dramatists had nowhere to go." For their part, Ruth Lamb and Antonio Magaña Esquivel, in their *Breve historia del teatro mexicano* [Brief History of the Mexican Theatre], note that the early years of the 20th century even saw a decline from previous years. It was apparent that during the 19th century Mexican theatre did not have an artistic or cultural function and popular theatrical representations were often "subliterary" comedies of political satire. However, in the period 1928–43 a new consciousness emerged which led to the establishment of theatrical groups and a renewed interest in so-called serious drama. These groups emphasized trends and techniques of the contemporary European and American stages, bringing Mexican theatre into the mainstream of world drama. The Grupo de los Siete, 1923 (Group of Seven), for example, set Pirandello, Chekhov, O'Neill, and others as their models. Later groups such as Villaurrutia's Grupo de Ulises (1928) and the Teatro Orientación (Orientation Theatre, 1932–34 and 1938–39) also followed European and US trends. And it was from the government-sponsored Teatro de Orientación that several talented dramatists emerged, including the group's founder Celestino Gorostiza (1904–67) and Xavier Villarrutia (1903–50) who made a considerable contribution to the new Mexican theatre. Under the direction of Salvador Novo (1904–74), the Theatre section of INBA fostered the development of theatre research and production, providing financial support as well as professional stimulation for dramatists, actors, and directors.

The prolific playwright Emilio Carballido (b. 1925) was the outstanding product of the Novo-inspired revival, blending the Mexican circumstance with an appeal that transcended the personal. In spite of the major contributions of such dramatists and, later, that of the documentary theatre of Vicente Leñero, Mexican theatre did not gain popular acceptance and critical viability until the early 1950s. Although Mexican theatre suffered several significant declines in the mid-1920s and the mid-1940s, a new generation of dramatists stimulated theatrical production, first in 1928 and then in 1947, and once again in 1967. It was in the late 1960s that several young writers, still laboring in university *talleres* or workshops (primarily those of Emilio Carballido), began to write and then to publish and stage plays on university magazines and theatres. At the same time or shortly thereafter, other classes and workshops were organized under the direction of Luisa Josefina Hernández, Hugo Argüelles, Héctor Azar and Vicente Leñero, to name only the most well-known. It was the beginning of a "new generation" of dramatists. The first wave of such plays (1967–73) was, in great part, drama of social protest written from the perspective of a youthful generation and reflective of a generation gap as part of their dramatic conflict. Subsequently, plays showed greater thematic depth and progressively more conscious use of formal elements, becaming also more "popular" in focus. The "Nueva Dramaturgia" series sponsored by the Universidad Nacional Autónoma de México (UNAM) was created exclusively for the young playwrights, producing quality works on a variety of themes, which were staged not only in the capital but also throughout Mexico and even abroad. In contrast to the commercially successful realistic, traditional dramas of social commentary rather than social protest about interpersonal relationships of the 1950s and early 1960s (plays by Luis G. Basurto, Wilberto Cantón, Jorge Ibargüengoitia, Sergio Magaña and Rafael Solana), these new works were more socially conscious and more technically innovative (Emilio Carballido, Luisa Josefina Hernández, Vicente Leñero, Hugo Argüelles, Héctor Azar, Maruxa Vilalta, Carlos Fuentes, Sabina Berman, Tomás Espinosa, Oscar Liera, Víctor Hugo Rascón Banda, Oscar Villegas, Jesús González Dávila and Carlos Olmos). Many of these playwrights demonstrate a shift in thematic focus away from the problems of the generation gap and toward an examination of Mexico's history, culture, folklore and society, the question of what comprises reality, and they include criticism of the power structure.

While in most of Latin America theatre groups and *creación colectiva* were of some importance during the 1960s and 1970s, Mexico has no groups of comparable stature to Colombia's La Candelaria and TEC (Teatro Experimental de Cali), Chile's ICTUS, and Argentina's Teatro Abierto, since collective theatre has not made any significant inroads into new Mexican drama, perhaps because its theatre companies have experimented rather less with alternative forms of creating and staging plays. In contrast to the pattern of institutional violence, political instability, censorship, and exile prevalent in other Latin American countries, Mexico's Nueva Dramaturgia movement has responded to relative political stability and the promises that emerged from the Mexican Revolution: a looking toward the past for an understanding of the present. But in consonance with other Latin American countries during the 1960s and 1970s, Mexican theatre was rich in experimental, independent, or fringe theatre groups that performed in the street, in city squares, in schools, on rooftops, or wherever else that was available to them. This marginal theatre included *teatro al aire libre* (open-air theatre), *teatro de la sierra* (theatre of the mountains), *teatro regional* (regional theatre), *teatro participativo* (participatory theatre), *teatro estudiantil* (student theatre), *el tercer teatro* (the third theatre), *teatro de la calle* or *carpas* (street or tent theatre) and *teatro independiente* (independent theatre), all of which played a peripheral role to the dominant theatrical culture.

Contemporary Mexican theatre of the post-1968 era clearly testifies to the distance that Mexican dramatic expression has traveled from its uncertain origins in the pre-Hispanic legacy, in its Spanish colonial heritage, and in its modern independence and revolutionary movements. Authors like Elena Garro and Luisa Josefina Hernández have contributed to the survival of a Mexican theatrical tradition and have helped keep Mexico abreast of recent trends. For example, the development of Hernández as a playwright, coincides closely with the evolution of Mexican drama generally, from psychological realism to theatre of cruelty and impact drama, from farce, comedy, tragicomedy to a theatre of commitment. From *La paz ficticia*, 1960 [The Fictive Peace] through *La historia de un anillo*, 1961 [The Story of a Wedding Band] to *La fiesta del mulato*, 1966 (*The Mulatto's Orgy*) and *Quetzalcoatl* (1968), Luisa Josefina Hernández's nonrealistic theatre challenges the primacy of form over content as it examines certain incidents in Mexican history that can be made to reveal insights into basic Mexican traits and mentalities.

Peru

Theatrical representation played an important role in lending pomp and ceremony to the religious ritual that sustained the power of the Inca empire. Drama is at the core of official celebrations in which drama, oratory, actors, music and dance came together to provide an allegory of state theology and to communicate the heroic deeds of Inca warriors. When the Incan empire was in decline, another dramatic form arose – the dramatization of comedy, fables and sarcastic poetry – as a means of criticizing both their human enemies and their own gods. Much indigenous literary expression in the form of drama and spectacle was lost, except in isolated rural areas, during the colonial period.

Modern Peruvian theatre began to flourish after World War II. Its resurgence is related to the publication of a trilogy of award-winning plays, Percy Gibson Parra's *Esa luna que empieza*, 1946 [That Rising Moon], Juan Ríos's *Don Quijote* (1946), and Sebastián Salazar Bondy's *Amor, gran laberinto*, 1948 [Love, the Great Labyrinth]. With the founding of the Dirección Nacional de Teatro (National Theatre Office) in 1946, theatrical groups were formed and literary competitions were established with the subsequent production of plays that were universal, psychological and poetic. Since the 1950s Peruvian dramatic production has been dominated by group theatre and university-sponsored theatre. But it is a tribute to Salazar Bondy (see separate entry) that Peruvian theatrical expression moved away from folklore and foreign archetypes. Founder of the Club de Teatro (The Theatre Club) in 1953, Salazar Bondy contributed a series of works dedicated to Peruvian reality later in his life dealing with social marginalization, lack of communication, loss of freedom, and human suffering through Brechtian modes of dramatization in *No hay isla feliz*, 1954 [There is No Happy Island], *El fabricante de deudas*, 1964 [The Debt Manufacturer] and *El Rabdomante*, 1965 [The Diviner]. There are many theatre groups that use Andean perspectives on reality in the form of music, the oral tradition, legend, and myth to highlight present-day social conflict and raise consciousness.

But it was Eugenio Barba's theatre group, Odin Teatret (Odin Theatre) which is credited with transforming Peruvian theatre with its production at the 1978 Ayacucho theatre competition. This initiated a movement known as El Teatro del Cuerpo (The Theatre of the Body). Thereafter, collective theatre proliferated with Yego Teatro Ensamble, Ayllu (Communal Theatre), Cocolido, Mesa de Teatro, the renowned Cuatrotablas (Four Planks) and Yuyachkani, from which many of the aforementioned groups sprang as splinter groups. Both the highly successful groups of Cuatrotablas and Yuyachkani present a vanguard theatre combined with the 1960s technique of collective theatre's careful investigation of local realities, placing socioeconomic problems in relief for analysis and the open-ended questioning of participatory audiences, often set within a festival-like atmosphere incorporating song, dance and musical accompaniment as a hallmark of its popular roots. The prolific theatre production within Peru during the 1970s and 1980s, in particular, reflects its overriding commitment since colonial times to capture the essence of Andean traditions and culture and thus establish some semblance of national identity. This is based on the integration of the *sierra* (highlands) into a national project, the creation of social awareness and cultural identity despite the multicolored, paradoxically static yet mobile environment from which it sprang. In recent years several theatrical organizations have been formed in Peru: Federación Nacional de Teatro Peruano (National Federation of Peruvian Theatre, 1971), Federación Nacional de Teatro Popular del Perú (National Federation of Popular Theatre of Peru, 1972), Teatro Nacional Popular (National Popular Theatre, 1972), Asociación Nacional de Escritores y Artistas (National Association of Writers and Artists, 1983), Centro Peruano de Autores Teatrales (Center for Peruvian Dramatists, 1983) and Movimiento de Teatro Independiente (The Movement for Independent Theatre, 1985), which sponsors the literary journal *Colectivo* (Confluence) begun in 1987. Due to the existence of such groups, both experimental and popular theatre have been promoted throughout the country, especially at the grassroots level. The New Theatre in Peru initiated in the 1970s and early 1980s presents a diverse array of themes and dramatic approaches ranging from the theatre of the absurd and black humor of the marginalized in urban settings in Juan Rivera Saavedra's dramas, the plays of social and class conflict in the works of Grégor Díaz and Hernando Cortés, Jorge Acuña's mime theatre, to Víctor Zavala's popular theatre of national acclaim. Finally, Mario Vargas Llosa adds a more cosmopolitan dimension to his dramas, *La señorita de Tacna*, 1981 (*The Young Lady from Tacna*) and *Kathie y el hipopótamo*, 1983 (*Kathy and the Hippopotamus*) by cultivating a self-conscious literature that reflects on the author's creative struggle with his work of art.

ELENA DE COSTA

The Theatre of the Southern Cone – Argentina, Chile and Uruguay

It is the attempt to forge an environment in which theatre could flourish that presents itself as a constant in the history of the theatre of Argentina, Uruguay and Chile, the countries of the Southern Cone. The articulation of this goal can be summarized in three broad categories: the creation of an informed audience through the translation and production of international theatre; the promotion of national authors; the creation of schools where theatre professionals would be formed. These were already present in the aims of the Sociedad del Buen Gusto Teatral (Society for Good Taste in the Theatre), founded in Buenos Aires in 1817, which sought to shake off European influence and to foster national output. This impulse is shared in Chile where the Generation of 1842, through Andrés Bello in particular, was fundamental in actively promoting Romantic theatre. And it is the Romantic, combining love, politics and tragedy, that opens the way for the treatment of national issues in Esteban Echeverría (1805–51), and Luis Ambrosio Morante (1755–1837) in the River Plate, and Salvador Sanfuentes (1817–60) and Eusebio Lillio (1826–1910) in Chile.

An indication of the success of the creation of a theatre environment, despite the instability and dictatorships of the 19th century, is to be found in the vitality of the theatre of the River Plate at the turn of the 20th century. Largely, this is due to the growth of sophisticated audiences: in the Teatro Colón, Buenos Aires could boast one of the most modern theatres in the world, and Montevideo had the impressive Teatro Solís. The audiences knew the best theatre from Europe, and were aware of the latest international theatre, the key dramatists, directors and actors. And although the period is largely characterised by a dependence on and adherence to European drama, the fact that the early years of the 20th century are regarded as something of a Golden Age is testimony to the fact that the foundations for national theatres had been laid.

In Chile it is *costumbrismo* (sketches of local customs) that follows from Romanticism and becomes the dominant theatrical form. 1858 saw *El jefe de familia* [The Head of the Household] by Alberto Blest Gana (1830–1920) and *La beata* [The Pious Woman] by Daniel Barros Grez (1834–1907), both local comedies of manners, and regarded as the first Chilean dramas. *El tribunal de honor* [The Court of Honour] by Daniel Caldera (1855–96) was based on local scandal, and brought local themes into the theatre. And, developing from costumbrism, the Realist works of Antonio Acevedo Hernández (1886–1962) are linked to the growing workers' movement. Armando Moock (1894–1936), chronicled the everyday drama of the petite bourgeoisie, tackling problems of modernity and incipient feminism. The culmination of costumbrist drama was, surely, the production in 1928 of *La viuda de Apablanza* [The Widow of Apablanza] by Germán Luco Cruchaga (1894–1936), a lament for the betrayal of old values.

There is general critical agreement that one of the key moments in the theatre of the River Plate is that of the production by the travelling circus family, the Podestá Brothers of Uruguay, of the gaucho pantomime *Juan Moreira* (1884). Dramatized from the already popular serialized novel by Eduardo Gutiérrez, *Juan Moreira* was based on a gaucho forced to deal with a changing social order, in which he feels increasingly marginalized and victimized. Performed at first as a pantomime, it was scripted in 1886, initiated gaucho drama, and later entered the established theatres of Buenos Aires, where it would inevitably wither. The gaucho drama saw its natural end when Martiniano Leguizamón (1858–1935) in *Calandria*, 1896 [Songbird] sought to turn the gaucho into a creole, to make him part of the new social order.

It was this new social order that provided the backdrop for Uruguay's Florencio Sánchez (1875–1910), who has been called Latin America's first dramatist. His early work proved him to be an acute and accurate observer of local life and customs, as well as a dedicated creator of "dramas de tesis," plays that developed a specific argument and declaration of point of view, sometimes of a solution. These plays are based

largely in the rural areas, constantly evoking a disappearing world, where the old and the new values sit uncomfortably alongside one another, a vision that culminates in the bleak *Barranca abajo*, 1905 [Downhill Struggle].

The other form that shaped the development of theatre the turn of the century was the Spanish *sainete*. Commercial in design and popular in appeal, the *sainete* was largely costumbrist in nature and relied on popular caricatures and social satire. The *sainete criollo*, reliant on tragicomedy, and using the language of the marginalized communities was a reflection of the lives of recent immigrants, mostly from Italy, who struggled in the miserable conditions of the *conventillos*, or tenement blocks. If the *sainete criollo* seemed to look to use the hopeless struggles of the recent immigrants as entertainment, then the *grotesco criollo*, descended from the Italian grotesque, and which emerged with Armando Discépolo (1884–1936) and Francesco T. Defillipis Novoa (1889–1930), explored their anguished sense of dislocation and disenchantment, the incapacity to find a way out of the marginalized position they inhabited. In plays such as Discépolo's *Stefano* (1928), and Defillipis Novoa's *He visto a Dios*, 1930 [I Have Seen God], the dynamics of the old and the new, the internal and the external, laughter and tragedy do battle, often erupting in verbal or physical violence, the ineffectual response of those imprisoned in the New World, in which they have invested all their dreams. If gaucho theatre is the beginning of a portrayal of national reality in drama, then the *grotesco criollo* is a form that gave expression in theatre to specific experiences of the new Latin American, and in so doing created a voice that would have resonances throughout the 20th century.

With these dramatists, as well as poetic innovators like Juan Guzmán Cruchaga (1896–1979) in Chile, the first years of the 20th century did indeed look promising. But this period is followed by the comparative poverty of the following years, until the creation of the first independent theatre in 1930, the Teatro del Pueblo (The People's Theatre) under the direction of Leonidas Barletta, part of a movement towards independent theatres that was evidenced throughout Latin America. It was independent theatre, that is, theatre that is not commercial in nature, and that does not depend on subsidies, that provided a revitalization of the art, by establishing a type of manifesto for theatre production and practice. Between then and the 1960s the independent theatres – groups such as Juan B. Justo (1933), Teatro la Máscara (1937), Teatro El Galpón (1949) in Uruguay under the direction of Atahualpa del Cioppo, and the Teatro Popular Ictus (1955) in Chile – became the backbone of theatre.

In Chile the creation of university theatres gave the impulse needed in a theatre that was deemed to have stagnated and allowed commercial concerns to take over. By the late 1930s, however, a new generation was propelling intellectual change, largely from within the universities. In 1941, the Teatro Experimental de la Universidad de Chile, and in 1943, the Teatro de Ensayo de la Universidad Católica were founded. Again the aims of these groups are enlightening. The Teatro Experimental de la Universidad de Chile stated these as the diffusion of classical and modern theatre, the formation of theatre schools, the dissemination of theatre beyond social elites, and the introduction of a professional attitude to theatre.

What, in many ways, is the rearticulation of the intellectual and artistic aims of the new nation states in the 19th century takes on its own shape and dynamic in the 20th. So we see the new theatre groups seeking to expand their audiences through touring, through schools accessible to as many as possible and through the forms of creation adopted. The key new form was collective creation, the dominant form of the highly politicized and radicalized 1960s. It relied on group dynamic, on the elaboration of the text through workshops, improvisation, investigation, and would often include open discussion with the audience.

What came to be known as the new Latin American theatre was the breeding ground for the dramatists and directors who have shaped the theatre of the second half of the 20th century, in some cases to the present day. A substantial group of dramatists emerged from the university theatres in Chile. Luis Alberto Heiremans (1928–1964) was a poetic dramatist of stylized realism, with such plays as *El abanderado*, 1962 [The Outlaw]. Sergio Vodanovic occupied himself with the middle classes, with social justice, struggles in *Deja que los perros ladren*, 1959 [Let the Dogs Bark] and *Viña: tres comedias en traje de baño*, 1964 [Viña del Mar: Three Comedies in a Bathing Suit] and *Nos tomamos la universidad*, 1971 [We Took the University]. Egon Wolff gave Chile such enduring plays as *Los invasores*, 1963 [The Invaders], *Flores de papel*, 1970 [Paper Flowers], later adding *La balsa de la Medusa*, 1984 [The Raft of the Medusa] to complete a trilogy about the political upheavals and complacencies of the middle classes. Jorge Díaz was the first Chilean dramatist to explore the theatre of the absurd with *El cepillo de dientes*, 1961 [The Toothbrush]. Later, in *Topografía de un desnudo*, 1966 [Topography of a Naked Man] he joined writers such as Isidora Aguirre (b. 1919) whose *Población Esperanza*, 1959 [Shanty Town Called Hope] and *Los papeleros*, 1963 [The Paper Gatherers] enter into a social and politically committed arena of theatre, and whose musical comedy *La pérgola de las flores*, 1960 [The Flower Market] must be classed as one of the great Latin American hits.

In Argentina Samuel Eichelbaum was active in the independent movement. Conrado Nalé-Roxlo was in the vanguard of theatre expression exploring a theatre of the imagination in a conscious attempt to fight the boundaries of the predominant natural realism, in *La cola de la sirena*, 1941 [The Mermaid's Tail], *Una viuda difícil*, 1944 [A Difficult Widow].

1957 saw the first Festival de Teatro Libre, opened with a performance of Agustín Cuzzani's (1924–87) great success, *El centroforward murió al amanecer* [The Centre Forward Died at Dawn] by the Teatro la Máscara. The same year saw *Tres historias para ser contadas* [Three Stories to Be Told] by Osvaldo Dragún (b. 1929) – an early work of an author who has long united experimentation in form with social commitment. And in the 1960s a number of dramatists whose world can be said to rooted in the tradition of the grotesque emerged. Roberto Cossa's grotesque vision would come into its own in the 1970s with plays like *La nona*, 1977 [The Grandmother]. Griselda Gambaro (b. 1928) wrote about undercurrents of the manipulation of power in, for example, *El campo*, 1967 (The Camp), as did Eduardo Pavlovsky in *El señor Galíndez* (1973).

At the core of the new theatre movement in Uruguay was Atahualpa del Cioppo, instrumental in bringing to the public both international drama and the work of new Uruguyan writers. Juan Carlos Patrón's (1905–79) *Procesado 1040*, 1957 [Accused Number 1040] was one of the biggest successes of Uruguayan theatre, and dealt with the lack of defenses of the ordinary man in the face of the state machine. Andrés Castillo, founder of the Teatro Universitario, is the author of *No somos nada*, 1966 [We Are Nothing], a work of social denunciation using the grotesque. Two playwrights active in the 1950s and 1960s were committed to critical appraisal of their society as well as to innovation in terms of the means of expression of the social imagination. They were Carlos Maggi (b. 1922) with such plays as *La biblioteca*, 1959 [The Library], and Mauricio Rosencof (b. 1933) with, for example, *Los caballos*, 1967 [The Horses]. Both fell silent with the military rule in the 1970s, Rosencof was imprisoned from 1972–85, and Maggi was silent throughout the dictatorship.

It is in the 1970s, when the three countries fell under military rule, that the term Southern Cone acquires a cultural and social coherence. The impact of the dictatorships is notorious: theatres were closed, individuals were captured and tortured, groups went into exile, and different levels of censorship were at work. The initial years saw the disintegration and disarticulation of the independent theatres, and a general disorientation in terms of finding theatre languages to express the new reality. The voices that emerged were defined by a response to the need to occupy a space of opposition, and similar themes run through the period: the arbitrary use of power, the diminishing social space, marginalization, fragmentation of social structures.

In Chile, Ictus opened the way for effective comment on the regime with *Pedro, Juan y Diego*, 1976 [Peter, John and Diego], and the group Taller de Investigación Teatral followed with *Tres Marías y una Rosa*, 1979 [Three Maries and One Rose]. New voices to emerge are those of Marco Antonio de la Parra (b. 1952), who created scenic worlds of the cruelly absurdist limbo in which people lived, and Juan Radrigón (b. 1937), who explored the world of extreme and powerless marginality. In Argentina Griselda Gambaro focused on the grotesque mechanics of authoriatarianism in plays such as *La malasangre*, 1982 [Bitter Blood] and *Del sol naciente*, 1984 [Of the Rising Sun], as did Eduardo Pavlovsky's *El Señor Lafargue* (1983). The project of the group Teatro Abierto '81 became an intellectual *cause célèbre*, and laid the foundation for a series of original plays by writers such as Roberto Cossa. And in Uruguay similar themes inform Mercedes Rein and Jorge Curi's *El herrero y la muerte*, 1981 [The Blacksmith and Death], Carlos Manuel Varela's *Alfonso y Clotilde*, Alberto Paredes's *Decir adiós*, 1979 [To Say Goodbye], Pedro Orgambide's *Prohibido Gardel*, 1978 [Gardel is Forbidden], and Jacobo Langsner's popular *Esperando la carroza*, 1974 [Waiting for the Carriage], a "grotesque in two acts."

There are two elements that characterize this theatre, and that pave the way for present day trends. One is that it follows almost without exception the ethos and aesthetics of the independent theatres. And the second is that there had been created in all three countries an encoded theatre language which was nevertheless absolutely transparent to the initiated audience, creating a real complicity within the theatre space. By the 1980s these elements are perceived to be restrictive, and an impulse for change, a search for a new language, new forms of creation and a certain distancing from this complicity from the audience began to become manifest. The work of Andrés Pérez, Alfredo Castro and Mauricio Celedón in Chile, of groups like Los Macocos and Los Melli in Argentina, and Alvaro Ahunchaín and Luis Vidal in Uruguay are all testimony to these trends. Following reports in the *Latin American Theatre Review* (1992), three main identifying features can be noted tentatively. First, that there are few new dramatists, texts are elaborated collectively; second, there is a tendency towards an incorporation of other forms into the theatre; and third, there has been a move towards a more intimate, less discursive and naturalist style. Looking on from the outside, the sense is of a rearticulation of the creation of the theatre environment, and also of a theatre that is ready to enter the world stage, but now not to borrow as in the 19th century, but to offer a real resilience and identity.

CATHERINE BOYLE

Contemporary Chicano Theatre

The work of Luis Valdez with El Teatro Campesino (The Peasant Theatre) in the 1960s is generally accepted not only as the foundation for contemporary Chicano drama but also as one of the most important and influential contributions to contemporary Chicano literature as a whole. Like much agit-prop theatre of the period, Valdez's *actos* (acts) blended Brechtian method with direct socio-political criticism, popular humor, the use of stereotypes, slapstick and satire. The first *actos* of the mid-1960s treated issues related to labor problems and were performed *by* field workers *for* field workers with a view to raising consciousness and encouraging support for the United Farmworkers Union (UFW).

A significant aspect of Valdez's early work, which has a bearing on subsequent literature, is that his characters spoke the popular, interlingual blend of English and Spanish employed by many Chicanos. None the less, by 1967 Valdez had dissociated himself from the UFW and his productions became more professional and began to break new ground thematically and stylistically. His pieces started to explore the diversity of the Chicano experience in other contexts such as education, the city and Vietnam and increasingly incorporated pre-Columbian and mythical themes in such a way as to create a contrast with the realism of his earlier work.

Just as much of the poetry of the Movement period is characterized by its concern for the socio-cultural and historical reality of the Chicano community, albeit expressed in highly individual and diverse ways, theatre follows a similar trajectory. While Luis Valdez continued to employ drama as a didactic vehicle, his thematic foci broadened and culminated in a form of ritualistic theatre called "mitos" (myths) which blended pre-Columbian and Christian beliefs in an attempt to address and to shape *Chicanismo* (Chicano identity) at a spiritual level. Another group that emerged in the early 1970s to rival El Teatro Campesino and to pursue the realist approach, increasingly being discarded by Valdez, was the Santa Barbara Teatro de la Esperanza (Theatre of Hope).

Under the direction of Jorge Huerta, Esperanza offered a collectively oriented, documentary theatre influenced by Brechtian ideas. The latter characteristics are exemplified in their most accomplished work *Guadalupe* (first performed in 1974) which dramatized contemporary events concerning a case of educational discrimination.

Compared with poetry and narrative, there has been significantly less dramatic output by Chicanos over the last two decades. Luis Valdez has remained a constant presence and, although his theatre has become progressively more crafted and complex, it still displays elements present in his early *actos* and *mitos*. A case in point is his award-winning *Zoot Suit* (1977), which later became a successful film. Another enduring figure since the mid-1970s has been Carlos Morton who has written a number of plays notable for their varied stylistic character and their thematic breadth. His works include socio-documentary pieces on contemporary events (*The Many Deaths of Danny Rosales*, 1974 and *The Savior*, 1986), recontextualized versions of works from other traditions (*Johnny Tenorio*, 1983 and *The Miser of Mexico*, 1989) and satirical reworkings of Christian myth (*El Jardín*, 1974 [The Garden] and *Pancho Diablo*, 1989).

Like other genres, Chicano drama of the 1980s attested to an ongoing accommodation of previously repressed voices. Although Estela Portillo's 1971 play *The Day of the Swallows* treated a lesbian character ostracized by her community, it was not until the 1980s that Chicanos and Chicanas began again to approach issues of sexuality openly in drama. Two of the more significant works in this respect were Edgar Pomba's *Reunion* (1981), the first Chicano play to bring male homosexuality to the stage, and Cherríe Moraga's *Giving Up the Ghost* (1985) which deals with lesbian sexuality. In the same way that Moraga's play is formally innovative, breaking with traditional theatrical conventions and syntax, the work of Denise Chávez also borders more on the realm of performance than that of conventional theatre. Particularly noteworthy is Chávez's *Novena narrativas y ofrendas Nuevomexicanas*, 1987 [Narrative Novena and New Mexican Offerings] which comprises nine monologues by women representative of diverse Chicana experiences.

In the context of performance, nevertheless, perhaps the most important contribution has been the collective work of *teatropoesía* [theatre-poetry] by San Francisco area Chicanas, *Tongues of Fire*, a hybrid assemblage of pieces drawn from different genres which comprises an articulation of a complex, plural Chicana subject. Just as there is no singular author of the work, no unitary characters are developed by means of a traditional, linear narrative; rather the participation of the multiple performers of the pieces serves to explore the range of Chicana experiences and identities as well as the possibilities of linking the multiple aspects of the latter.

WILSON NEATE

Further Reading

Brazil
Aguiar, Flávio, *Os homens precários: inovação e convenção na dramaturgia de Qorpo-Santo*, Pôrto Alegre, Brazil: A Nação / Instituto Estadual do Livro, 1975

Arêas, Vilma Sant'Anna, *Na tapera de Santa Cruz: uma leitura de Martins Pena*, São Paulo: Martins Fontes, 1987

Arrabal, José and Mariângela Alves de Lima, *Teatro: o seu demônio é beato. O nacional e o popular na cultura brasileira*, São Paulo: Brasiliense, 1983

Bader, Wolfgang (editor), *Brecht no Brasil: experiências e influências*, Rio de Janeiro: Edições Paz e Terra, 1987

Castro, Ruy, *O anjo pornográfico: a vida de Nelson Rodrigues*, São Paulo: Companhia das Letras, 1992

Clark, Fred M., *Impermanent Structures: Semiotic Readings of Nelson Rodrigues' "Vestido de noiva," "Album de família," and "Anjo Negro,"* Chapel Hill: Department of Romance Languages, University of North Carolina, 1991

Clark, Fred M. and Ana Lúcia Gazolla de García, *Twentieth-Century Brazilian Theatre: Essays*, Chapel Hill, North Carolina: Hispanófila, and Valencia: Albatros, 1978

Damasceno, Leslie H., *Espaço cultural e convenções teatrais na obra de Oduvaldo Vianna Filho*, translated from the unpublished dissertation by Iná Camargo Costa, Campinas: UNICAMP, 1994

Dória, Gustavo A., *Moderno teatro brasileiro: crônica de suas raízes*, Rio de Janeiro: Serviço Nacional de Teatro, 1975

George, David, *Teatro e antropofagia*, translated by Eduardo Brandão, São Paulo: Global, 1985

_____ *Grupo Macunaíma: carnavalização e mito*, São Paulo: Perspectiva / Editora da Universidade de São Paulo, 1990

_____ *The Modern Brazilian Stage*, Austin: University of Texas Press, 1992

Guinsburg, Jacó, *Diálogos sobre teatro*, edited by Armando Sérgio da Silva, São Paulo: Editora da Universidade de São Paulo, 1992

Guzik, Alberto, *TBC: Crônica de um sonho. O teatro brasileiro de comédia, 1948–1964*, São Paulo: Perspectiva, 1986

Khéde, Sônia Salomão, *Censores de pincenê e gravata: dois momentos da censura teatral no Brasil*, Rio de Janeiro: Codecri, 1981

Kuhner, Maria Helena, *Teatro popular: uma experiência*, Rio de Janeiro: Francisco Alves, 1975

Leite, Luiza Barreto, *A mulher no teatro brasileiro*, Rio de Janeiro: Espetáculo, 1965

Lins, Ronaldo Lima, *O teatro de Nelson Rodrigues: uma realidade em agonia*, Rio de Janeiro: Francisco Alves, 1979

Magaldi, Sábato, *Panorama do teatro brasileiro*, São Paulo: DIFEL, 1962

_____ *Um palco brasileiro: o Arena de São Paulo*, São Paulo: Editora Brasiliense, 1984

_____ *Nelson Rodrigues: dramaturgia e encenações*, São Paulo: Perspectiva / Editora da Universidade de São Paulo, 1987

Martins, Antônio, *Artur Azevedo, a palavra e o riso*, São Paulo: Perspectiva, and Rio de Janeiro: Editora da UFRJ, 1988

Mendes, Miriam Garcia, *A personagem negra no teatro brasileiro entre 1838 e 1888*, São Paulo: Ática, 1982

Michalski, Yan, *O teatro sob pressão: uma fonte de resistência*, Rio de Janeiro: Jorge Zahar, 1985

Mostaço, Edelcio, *Teatro e política: Arena, Oficina, Opinião*, São Paulo: Proposta, 1982

Peixoto, Fernando, *Teatro Oficina, 1958–1982: trajetória de uma rebeldia cultural*, São Paulo: Brasiliense, 1982

Prado, Décio de Almeida, *A presentação do teatro brasileiro moderno: crítica teatral 1947–1955*, São Paulo: Martins, 1956

_____ *Teatro em progresso: crítica teatral, 1955–1964*, São Paulo: Martins, 1964

_____ *João Caetano: o ator, o empresário, o repertório*, São Paulo: Perspectiva, 1972

_____ *Exercício findo: crítica teatral, 1964–1968*, São Paulo: Perspectiva, 1987

_____ *O teatro brasileiro moderno, 1930–1980*, São Paulo: Perspectiva / Editora da Universidade de São Paulo, 1988

Rosenfeld, Anatol, *O mito e o herói no moderno teatro brasileiro*, São Paulo: Perspectiva, 1982

Ruiz, Roberto, *O teatro de revista no Brasil: das origens à primeira guerra mundial*, Rio de Janeiro: INACEN, 1988

Silva, Armando Sérgio da, *Oficina: do teatro ao te-ato*, São Paulo: Perspectiva, 1981

Süssekind, Flora, *As Revistas de Ano e a invenção do Rio de Janeiro*, Rio de Janeiro: Nova Fronteira, 1986

Teatro Experimental do Negro: testemunhos, Rio de Janeiro: Edições GRD, 1966

Veneziano, Neyde, *O teatro de revista no Brasil: dramaturgia e convenções*, Campinas: UNICAMP, 1991

Windmüller, Kathe, *"O Judeu" no teatro romântico brasileiro: uma revisão da tragédia de Gonçalves de Magalhães*, São Paulo: Centro de Estudos Judaicos, Universidade de São Paulo, 1984

General Studies on Theatre in Spanish America or Ibero America

Albuquerque, Severino J., *Violent Acts: a Study of Contemporary Latin American Theatre*, Detroit: Wayne State University Press, 1991

Boal, Augusto, *Teatro del oprimido y otras poéticas políticas*, Buenos Aires: Ediciones de La Flor, 1974; as *Theater of the Oppressed*, translated by Charles A. and Maria-Odilia Leal McBride, New York: Urizen Books, and London: Pluto Press, 1979

_____ *Técnicas latinoamericanas de teatro popular*, Buenos Aires: Corregidor, 1975

Dauster, Frank N., *Historia del teatro hispanoamericano: siglos IX y XX*, revised 2nd edition, Mexico City: Andrea, 1973

De Costa, Elena, *Collaborative Latin American Popular Theater: from Theory to Form, from Text to Stage*, New York: Peter Lang, 1992

Eidelberg, Nora, *Teatro experimental hispanoamericano, 1960–1980; la realidad social como manipulación*, Minneapolis: Institute for the Study of Ideologies and Literature, 1985

Jones, Willis Knapp, *Behind Spanish American Footlights*, Austin: University of Texas Press, 1966

Latin American Theatre Review, vol. 25/2 (1992) [special number to mark the journal's 25th anniversary]

Luzuriaga, Gerardo, *Introducción a las teorías latinoamericanas del teatro*, Puebla, Mexico: Universidad Autónoma de Puebla, 1990

Lyday, Leon F. and George W. Woodyard (editors), *Dramatists in Revolt: the New Latin American Theater*, Austin: University of Texas Press, 1976

Martin, Randy, *Socialist Ensembles: Theater and State in Cuba and Nicaragua*, Minneapolis: University of Minnesota Press, 1994

Monleón, José, *América Latina: teatro y revolución*, Caracas: Ateneo de Caracas, 1978

Pianca, Marina, *El teatro de Nuestra América: un proyecto continental (1959–1989)*, Minneapolis: Institute for the Study of Ideologies and Literature, 1990

Rizk, Beatriz, *El nuevo teatro latinoamericano: Una lectura histórica*, Minneapolis: Prisma Institute, 1987

Rojo, Grínor, *Los orígenes del teatro hispanoamericano contemporáneo*, Santiago de Chile: Ediciones Universitarias de Valparaíso, 1972

Roster, Peter and Mario Rojas (editors), *De la colonia a la postmodernidad: teoría teatral y crítica sobre teatro latinoamericano*, Buenos Aires: Galerna, 1992

Solórzano, Carlos, *El teatro latinoamericano en el siglo XX*, Mexico City: Pormaca, 1964

Taylor, Diana, *Theatre of Crisis: Drama and Politics in Latin America*, Lexington: University Press of Kentucky, 1991

Taylor, Diana and Juan Villegas (editors), *Negotiating Performance: Gender, Sexuality and Theatricality in Latin/o America*, Durham, North Carolina: Duke University Press, 1995

Versényi, Adam, *Theatre in Latin America*, Cambridge and New York: Cambridge University Press, 1993 [Despite title, does not cover Brazil]

Weiss, Judith A., *et al.*, *Latin American Popular Theatre*, Albuquerque: University of New Mexico Press, 1993

Studies on the Theatre in Individual Spanish American Countries

Argentina

Giordano, Enrique, *La teatralización de la obra dramática: de Florencio Sánchez a Roberto Arlt*, Mexico City: Premiá, 1982

Marial, José, *Teatro y país. (Desde 1810 a Teatro Abierto)*, Buenos Aires: Agon, 1983

Pellettieri, Osvaldo, *Cien años de teatro argentino (1886–1990): del "Moreira" a Teatro Abierto*, 2nd edition, Buenos Aires: Galerna, 1994

Tschudi, Lilian, *Teatro argentino actual (1960–1972)*, Buenos Aires: García Cambeiro, 1974

Chile

Boyle, Catherine, *Chilean Theater, 1973–1985: Marginality, Power, Selfhood*, Rutherford, New Jersey: Fairleigh Dickinson University Press, 1992

Fernández, Teodosio, *El teatro chileno contemporáneo (1941–1973)*, Madrid: Playor, 1982

Rojo, Grínor, *Muerte y resurección del teatro chileno, 1973–1983*, Madrid: Michay, 1985

Colombia

Buenaventura, Enrique, *EL ARTE NUEVO de hacer Comedias y el NUEVO TEATRO*, Cali, Colombia: TEC Publications, no.5, n.d.

González Cajiao, Fernando, *Historia del teatro en Colombia*, Bogotá: Instituto Colombiano de Cultura, 1986

Reyes, Carlos José and Maida Watson Espener (editors), *Materiales para una historia del teatro en Colombia*, Bogotá: Instituto Colombiano de Cultura, 1978

Cuba

Colón, Edwin Teurbe and José Antonio González, *Historia del teatro en La Habana*, Santa Clara, Cuba: Letras Cubanas, 1980 [Definitive work on the history of Cuban theatre]

Leal, Rine (editor), *Teatro Escambray*, Havana: Letras Cubanas, 1978

Leal, Rine, *Breve historia del teatro cubano*, Havana: Letras Cubanas, 1980

Montes Huidobro, Matías, *Persona, vida y máscara en el teatro cubano*, Miami: Universal, 1973

Ecuador

Descalzi, Ricardo, *Historia crítica del teatro ecuatoriano*, Quito: Casa de la Cultura Ecuatoriana, 1968

Mexico

Argudín, Yolanda, *Historia del teatro en México: desde los rituales prehispánicos hasta el arte dramático de nuestros días*, Mexico City: Panorama Editorial, 1985

Del-Río, Marcela, *Perfil del teatro de la Revolución Mexicana*, New York: Peter Lang, 1993

Foster, David William, *Estudios sobre teatro mexicano contemporáneo: semiología de la competencia teatral*, New York: Peter Lang, 1984

Frischmann, Donald H., *El nuevo teatro popular en México*, Mexico City: Instituto Nacional de Bellas Artes, 1990

Usigli, Rodolfo, *México en el teatro*, Mexico City: Imprenta Mundial, 1932; as *Mexico in the Theater*, translated by Wilder P. Scott, University, Mississsippi: Romance Monographs, 1976

Paraguay

Pla, Josefina, *Cuatro siglos de teatro en el Paraguay: el teatro paraguayo desde sus orígenes hasta hoy (1544–1988)*, 3 vols, Asunción, Paraguay: Universidad Católica Nuestra Señora de la Asunción, 1990

Peru

Joffré, Susana, *Teatro peruano – el teatro universitario*, Lima: Minerva, Colección Teatro de los Grillos, 1982

Mariátegui, José Carlos, *Nuestro teatro y su actual período de surgimiento*, Lima: Teatro de la Universidad de San Marcos, 1969

Natella, Arthur F., *The New Drama of Peru*, Montclair: Senda Nueva de Ediciones, 1982

Anthologies of Brazilian and Spanish American Plays (including some in English translation)

Casas, Myrna (editor), *Teatro de la vanguardia: Contemporary Spanish American Theatre*, Lexington, Massachusetts: D.C. Heath, 1975

Colecchia, Francesca and Julio Matas, *Selected Latin American One-Act Plays*, Pittsburgh: University of Pittsburgh Press, 1973

Dauster, Frank N., Leon Lyday and George W. Woodyard (editors), *Nueve dramaturgos hispanoamericanos* vols 1–3, Ottawa: Girol Books, 1979

Quackenbush, L. Howard (editor), *Teatro del absurdo hispanoamericano*, Mexico City: Patria, 1987

Ripoll, Carlos and Andrés Valespino, *Teatro hispanoamericano. Antología crítica*, 2 vols, New York: Anaya, 1972–73

Contemporary Chicano Theatre

Anthologies

Garza, Roberto J. (editor), *Contemporary Chicano Theater*, Notre Dame: University of Notre Dame Press, 1976

Huerta, Jorge (editor), *Necessary Theater: Six Plays about the Chicano Experience*, Houston: Arte Público Press, 1989

Kanellos, Nicolas and Jorge Huerta (editors), *Nuevos Pasos: Chicano and Puerto Rican Drama*, Houston: Arte Público Press, 1989

Critical Studies

Broyles González, Yolanda (editor), *El Teatro Campesino: Theater in the Chicano Movement*, Austin: University of Texas Press, 1994

Bruce-Novoa, Juan, "Revolutionizing the Popular Image: Essay on Chicano Theatre," *Latin American Literary Review*, vol. 5/10 (1977)

Huerta, Jorge, "Chicano Agit-Prop: The Early *Actos* of El Teatro Campesino," *Latin American Theatre Review* 11 (1977)

____ *Chicano Theater: Themes and Forms*, Ypsilanti, Michigan: Bilingual Press, 1982

Kanellos, Nicolas (editor), *Mexican American Theater: Then and Now*, Houston: Arte Público Press, 1983
——— *Mexican American Theater: Legacy and Reality*, Houston: Arte Público Press, 1987
Yarbro-Bejarano, Yvonne, "From 'acto' to 'mito': a Critical Reappraisal of the Teatro Campesino," in *Modern Chicano Writers*, edited by Joseph Sommers and Tomás Ybarra-Frausto, Englewood Cliffs, New Jersey: Prentice-Hill, 1979

——— "*Teatropoesía* by Chicanas in the Bay Area: *Tongues of Fire*," in *Mexican American Theater Then and Now*, edited by Nicolas Kanellos, Houston: Arte Público Press, 1983
——— "Cherríe Moraga's *Giving Up the Ghost* and the Representation of Female Desire," *Third Woman*, vol. 3/1 (1986)
——— "The Female Subject in Chicano Theatre: Sexuality, 'Race' and Class," *Theatre Journal* 38 (1986)

Transculturation

Coined in the 1940s by the Cuban anthropologist and theorist of African-Cuban movements, Fernando Ortiz (1881–1969), the term is used as a refinement of, and in contrast to the Anglo-American sociological term, "acculturation," which describes a process of assimilation and absorption of minority cultures by dominant ones. Transculturation seeks to describe cultural transformation in terms of a synthesis of systems which produces new and differentiated cultural hybrids. The interaction of values of European colonialism and the New World provides the principal environment for this form of cultural encounter.

The attempts of a "dominant" culture to circumscribe the characteristics of another society in its own terms or its own image is discernible as far back as the earliest Spanish and Portuguese chronicles, such as those of Columbus and Pero Vaz de Caminha. These explorers draw upon European referents in order to chart and represent the New World, thereby re-inventing it in terms of their own perceptions. In the 20th century the interaction of fusing cultures is explored with anguish in the work of the Peruvian novelist José María Arguedas, as he traces the confrontation between Andean, Quechua culture and the 20th-century forces of modernization. Transculturation may also be seen in the complex shifting of racial and social interrelationships in the United States today, with both the integration and the sense of conscious differentiation of the Chicano. The mixing of cultures at the " borders" where they find each other is part of the writings of, for example, the Chicana Gloria Anzaldúa.

The late Uruguayan critic Ángel Rama was chiefly responsible for the introduction of the term into literary studies in the 1970s. Rama examined the phenomenon of transculturation, both for dispossessed peoples and for the writer and intellectual, in both the sense of "culture shock" and in the discovery of the cultural diversity traditionally obscured by the belief that the (South American) continent is a homogeneous unit. Transculturation also has implications for a post-colonial unpacking of cultural power relations. In her study of 18th- and 19th-century travel writing, Mary Louise Pratt examines the German explorer and naturalist Alexander von Humboldt's legacy in the Americas, as his vision of South America is taken up by political figures such as Bolívar, or writers, such as Alejo Carpentier – principally in *Los pasos perdidos* (*The Lost Steps*) and *Tientos y diferencias* [Gropings and Differences]. She demonstrates how the process can be appraised from the opposite direction, as Humboldt's Romantic vision is itself revealed to be a transcultural product. A Euro-American view, in this sense, can be seen to have been constructed as much from the outside in as from the inside out.

Transculturation is a process which takes place in the "contact zone" between the peripheral and the dominant metropolitan culture, but involves not only superimpositions of aspects of the dominant culture, but also mechanisms of selection and absorption. The fusion of two or more interacting cultures, for example in the case of Cuba – an archetypal colonial crossroads – has been described in terms of "grafts and transplants," of synthesis and transformation, and not simply of dominance and imposition by a "superior" culture. The spread and adaptation of theories of transculturation for contemporary literary and historical study, therefore, propose a de-emphasis on binarisms and straightforward oppositions in social, political and sexual power relations, and a new focus on what Diana Taylor calls "long term reciprocities;" for, rather than being a resistance theory, such as feminism, which may abolish itself in achieving a new assertion of sexual power hegemony, transculturation is a theory of processes, emphasising the vitality of minority structures in the face of assumptions of colonial subordination or cultural indebtedness.

FRANK McQUADE

See also entry on Fernando Ortiz

Further Reading

Pratt, Mary Louise, *Imperial Eyes: Travel Writing and Transculturation*, London and New York: Routledge, 1992
Rama, Ángel, *Trasculturación narrativa en América Latina*, Mexico City: Siglo XXI, 1982
Taylor, Diana, "Transculturating Transculturation," in *Performing Arts Journal*, vol. 38 (1991)

Translation

Brazil

Translation has always been of paramount importance to Brazil, a country on the outer edge of Western civilization. In the 1990s, 80% of all the printed material in Brazil, from user manuals to literary works, including every conceivable genre, are translations.

Prior to the arrival of Europeans, the population of the sub-continent that was to become the Brazilian nation consisted of semi-nomadic Indian tribes – variously estimated by scholars to have numbered between one and five million individuals – who spoke between two and three thousand different languages which have now been divided by researchers into 102 language groups and three large families: Tupy, Macro-Ge and Arawak. There is evidence that such human groups were in contact, and it may be safely assumed that such contact included oral translations, since Indian languages completely lacked writing systems.

The arrival of Europeans brought an even greater linguistic variety to the sub-continent. The first document produced by this arrival bears evidence of the first translation act in Brazil. This is the letter written by Pero Vaz de Caminha, the scribe of the Portuguese fleet commanded by Admiral Pedro Álvares Cabral (1467–c.1520) that reached Brazil on 21 April 1500. Caminha's letter of 1 May 1500 reports the finding of new lands to the Portuguese king, Dom Manuel I (1415–1512), and describes how Europeans and natives interacted by means of gestures.

The letter also describes how a few men were left behind, to live with the Indians, and learn their language. Throughout early colonial times this situation often repeated itself. Either convicted deportees deliberately left behind by their captains, or adventurers shipwrecked on the shores of Brazil, many Europeans learned Indian languages and became interpreters and were known as "línguas" (literally "tongues"). The services of such professionals were used when colonizers' raiding parties were sent inland to capture and enslave Indians or to search for gold and precious stones.

When Jesuit priests went to Brazil to attempt to convert the Indians in 1549, they found that the languages spoken by the Indians living along the coast of Brazil bore such similarity that a *lingua franca* had developed, called *Abanheenga*. Perceiving the usefulness of a *lingua franca* for their missionary purposes, the Jesuits produced a simplified version of this language, which they called *Nheengatu*, or "beautiful language," and gave it a written form.

Father José de Anchieta (c.1533–97), who has been beatified by the Catholic Church and is known as "The Apostle of Brazil," wrote the *Arte da gramática na língua mais usada na costa do Brasil* [Art of the Grammar of the Most Used Language on the Coast of Brazil]. Soon, other religious texts were translated into *Nheengatu*, such as the *Catechism* and the *Summary of Christian Doctrine*.

Nheengatu, also known as *língua geral* (general language), was taught at the Jesuit colleges, so that it eventually became widespread in colonized Brazil, being used not only as a means of communication between Indians and Europeans, but also among Brazilians, that is, Europeans who had become established in Brazil and their often mixed-race offspring. *Nheengatu* was used even in the administrative and legal affairs of the colony, with the result that "línguas," or interpreters remained in full demand by the administration.

Even Africans, brought to Brazil as slaves to work in the fields and mines when it was realized that the Indians were unable to adapt to forced labour, learned *Nheengatu*. Although the Africans too developed their own *linguae francae*, a form of Yoruba in the north and northeast, and Congoese in the south, the colonizers' system of separating Africans of the same language (Yoruba, Kimbundu, Hausa and others) and of separating families upon arrival in Brazil prevented any African language from having the same impact as *Nheengatu*.

The dominance of *Nheengatu* came to an end, however, when, in 1759, the Marquis of Pombal (1721–82), virtual dictator of Portugal and its colonies between 1750 and 1777, who feared the growing power of the Jesuits, expelled them from Portugal and Brazil, forbade the use of *Nheengatu* in Brazil, and closed all the Jesuit colleges.

From this point onwards, the hegemony of Portuguese was ensured, aided by several factors. Foreign invasions were consistently fended off; borders with Spanish American nations were agreed upon either peacefully or by military action; and the Indians were either absorbed into the general, Portuguese-speaking population by miscegenation, decimated by European diseases to which they had no immunity or by the severity of forced labour, or pushed into the recesses of the sub-continent by those who wanted their lands. There are today 150,000 Indians in Brazil, living in reserves, of which 30% are native speakers of Portuguese.

The need of translations therefore became one of communication mainly with foreign nations and individuals. Already in 1850, legislation was passed that regulated the profession of sworn translator. Sworn translators are those who translate official documents; and they are much needed by the import-export business, among others.

The publication of translated works, however, came late to Brazil. All manufacture was forbidden in the colony by the Portuguese Crown, which of course included the printing business. The importation of books into Brazil suffered the same heavy censorship that was applied to the book trade in Portugal. It was not until the Portuguese Royal family, fleeing Napoleon's troops, came to Brazil in 1808 that a legally operating printing house was established in Brazil, the *Impressão Régia* (Royal Press) founded by the Prince Regent Dom João (later Dom João VI; 1767–1826).

The first work published by *Impressão Régia* was a translation of Leonhard Euler's (1707–1783) *Elements of Algebra*. Many academic and scientific works were published in rapid succession, perhaps in an attempt to quench the country's thirst for knowledge. The first literary translation published by *Impressão Régia* was of Alexander Pope's *Essay on Criticism*, translated and annotated by Fernando José de Portugal, the Marquis of Aguiar (1752–1817). During this period, however, most of the translations were from French, or from other languages via French or Spanish, which is known as "indirect translation."

Impressão Régia enjoyed the monopoly over the printing industry until 1822, when Brazil became independent. From that moment on, it became possible for a Brazilian printing industry to develop. This development, however, was slowed down by the lack of machinery and raw materials in Brazil, a consequence of the ban on industries during colonial times. As a result, post-colonial Brazilian writers such as José de Alencar (1829–1877) and Machado de Assis (1839–1908) had their works published in Europe by such publishing houses as Livraria Garnier and Livraria Bertrand in Paris. In this way, the business of publishing Brazilian works flourished in Europe.

During the early stages of the publishing industry in Brazil, most translated works were reprints of translations already published in Portugal. It was not until the publishing business achieved a certain degree of development that Brazilian translations became predominant. The work of Brazilian writers Monteiro Lobato (1882–1948) and Érico Veríssimo (1905–75) as translators and editors greatly contributed towards this.

By the 1970s, publishing had become fully established in Brazil, with the country having become an exporter of paper pulp. The number of published translations grew, and the major language of translation turned from French into English, as a result of Brazil having fallen under the sphere of influence of the United States.

Although the influence of foreign writers on Brazilian ones may be attributed to translations, as Onédia Barboza has discussed in *Byron no Brasil: traduções*, 1974 [Byron in Brazil: Translations], it is equally valid to point out that Brazilian intellectuals have normally been able to read in a foreign language, chiefly French and Spanish, and later English. It is in fact Brazil's major writers that have been its translators, such as: Manuel Bandeira, Cecília Meireles, José Lins do Rego, Carlos Drummond de Andrade, Rachel de Queiroz, Lúcio Cardoso and Clarice Lispector.

A major contribution to the evolution of translation in Brazil was made by Hungarian-born Paulo Rónai (1907–73), author of the first Brazilian work on the subject, *Escola de tradutores*, 1952 [School of Translators], followed by *Homens contra Babel*, 1964 [Men against Babel] and *A tradução vivida*, 1976 [Translation Experienced]. Rónai, working with Aurélio Buarque de Hollanda Ferreira (1910–) translated and edited the collection *Mar de histórias*, 1945 (*A Sea of Stories*) and later the collection of classics from all over the world called "Nobel Library." The work on the translation of these selections was a veritable proving ground for translators new to the task.

At present a Brazilian theory of translation is being developed. Known as the "cannibalist" theory of translation, its principles have become known outside the frontiers of Brazil. The authors of this theory are the Campos brothers, Haroldo and Augusto, Concrete poets who have translated authors such as Pound, e.e. cummings, Joyce, Mallarmé, Mayakovsky, Valéry, Poe, and Lewis Carroll, among others. Their views of translation are derived from the works of Walter Benjamin, Roman Jakobson and Ezra Pound. The main source of inspiration for them, however, has been the idea of "cannibalism" expounded by the Brazilian Modernist Movement of 1922, chiefly the *Manifesto canibalista* [Cannibalist Manifesto] by Oswald de Andrade. According to Andrade's theory, a colonized people devours what the colonizers offer them, but spits out what is noxious to them; what they keep they make wholly theirs by altering it to suit their own needs.

HELOISA GONÇALVES BARBOSA

Further Reading

No Brazilian work to date deals specifically with the history of translation. A few pointers may be found in Paes, José Paulo, *Tradução, a ponte necessária: aspectos e problemas da arte de traduzir*, São Paulo: Ática, 1990. Additional works used in this compilation are listed below.

Anchieta, José de, *Arte gramática da língua mais usada na costa do Brasil*, São Paulo: Edições Loyola, 1990 [facsimile of the 1595 edition]

Andrade, Oswald de, *Do pau-brasil à antropofagia e às utopias: manifestos, teses de concursos e ensaios*, Rio de Janeiro: Civilização Brasileira, 1970

Campos, Augusto de and Haroldo de Campos (editors and translators), *Panorama do Finnegan's Wake*, São Paulo: Perspectiva, 1970

Campos, Augusto de, *Verso, reverso, controverso*, São Paulo: Perspectiva, 1978

____ *O anticrítico*, Lisbon: Ática, 1960; São Paulo: Companhia das Letras, 1986

Campos, Haroldo de, "A poética da tradução," in his *A arte no horizonte do provável*, São Paulo: Perspectiva, 1969

____ "Da tradução como criação e como crítica," in his *Metalinguagem*, 3rd edition, São Paulo: Cultrix, 1976

____ *A operação do texto*, São Paulo: Perspectiva, 1976

Coulthard, Malcolm and C.R. Caldas-Coulthard (editors), *Tradução: teoria e prática*, Florianópolis, Brazil: UFSC, 1991

Hallewell, Laurence, *Books in Brazil: a History of the Publishing Trade*, Metuchen, New Jersey: Scarecrow Press, 1982

Houaiss, Antônio, *O português no Brasil*, Rio de Janeiro: Unibrade-Centro de Cultura, 1985

Martins, Wilson, *História da inteligência brasileira*, 7 vols, São Paulo: Cultrix, 1976–79

Pagano, Adriana Silvina, "Literatura e tradução literária: alguns pontos de interrelação," *Anuario Brasileño de Estudios Hispánicos*, vol. 4 (1994)

Portinho, Waldívia and Waltensir Dutra, "Paulo Rónai, tradutor e mestre de tradutores," *Tradterm* 1 (1994)

Rónai, Paulo, *Babel e antibabel*, São Paulo: Perspectiva, 1970

____ *A tradução vivida*, 2nd revised and augmented edition, Rio de Janeiro: Nova Fronteira, 1981

____ *Escola de tradutores*, 5th revised and augmented edition, Rio de Janeiro: Nova Fronteira, 1987

Sodré, Nélson Werneck, *A história da imprensa no Brasil*, Rio de Janeiro: Civilização Brasileira, 1966

Spanish America

Due to the explosive appearance of Hispanic American literature on the international literary scene beginning in the 1960s, its spectacular presence today in English translation is wondrous. The growing body of diverse texts in translation – especially in fiction and poetry – attests to an expanding interest in the Hispanic world by English readers. In part, the transition of the world toward a postmodern global village supports attention of cross-cultural interests and exoticism. It is experienced through the food, the sensual music, the romantic climes, and the colorful, primitive beauty of Hispanic America as it continues to lure technology-driven, fast-paced, urban, First World reader/tourists into its mysterious, multicultural web. The power of this exoticism can be appreciated by the overwhelming success of Laura Esquivel's best seller, *Como agua para chocolate*, 1989, translated in 1992 as *Like Water for Chocolate*. The other aspects involving translation – historical, professional, commercial and technical – also provide useful insights into the nature of this volcanic eruption of translated literature from Hispanic America.

Early interest in Hispanic American literature in the English-speaking world is due largely to the translations by Harriet de Onís of Social Realist novels, chronicles, essays and short stories. Her, perhaps, over-prolific output as a literary translator includes the following texts: Martín Luis Guzmán's *El águila y la serpiente*, 1928 (*The Eagle and the Serpent*), Ciro Alegría's *El mundo es ancho y ajeno*, 1941 (*Broad and Alien is the World*) and a selection from Ricardo Palma's *Tradiciones peruanas*, published in 1945 under the title *The Knights of the Cape and 37 Other Selections from the Tradiciones peruanas*, Alfonso Reyes's *The Position of America, and Other Essays*, 1950. De Onís also translated outstanding Brazilian works such as *Grandes sertãos: veredas*, 1956 (*The Devil to Pay in the Backlands*, 1963) by João Guimarães Rosa. Within a generation or two, other female translators – Edith Grossman, Helen Lane, Margaret Sayers Peden and Suzanne Jill Levine – would pick up the gauntlet to become internationally famous for their translations of Hispanic American fiction. In fact, Levine has gone one step further by writing a book on translation, *The Subversive Scribe: Translating Latin American Fiction* (1991), focusing primarily on her translations of Cuban writer Guillermo Cabrera Infante's fiction, especially *Tres tristes tigres*, 1965 (*Three Trapped Tigers*, 1971).

The so-called Boom period of fiction in the 1960s signified literary experimentation and creativity, giving international notoriety to Hispanic American writers, as in the case of Jorge Luis Borges, who was awarded the Fomentor Prize with Samuel Beckett in 1961. The multitude of translations that followed the Boom period is due mainly to the early work of Gregory Rabassa, who undertook to translate the most challenging writers such as Gabriel García Márquez, Mario Vargas Llosa, José Lezama Lima and Julio Cortázar. The impact of two of his translations, *Hopscotch* (1966) by Julio Cortázar, and *One Hundred Years of Solitude* (1970) by Gabriel García Márquez, has been considerable; in fact, Margaret Sayers Peden, whose translations include Carlos Fuentes's *The Hydra Head* (1978), *Terra Nostra* (1976), and *Distant Relations* (1982), believes that *Hopscotch*, "must surely be considered one of the breakthrough publications in Latin American literature in the English-speaking world, setting the stage for many works to follow," as she observes in the *Handbook of Latin American Studies*. North American novelist John Barth and critic Larry McCaffery agree; and Johnny Payne, in his landmark study, *Conquest of the New Word: Experimental Fiction and Translation in the Americas* (1993), confirms their statements: "*One Hundred Years of Solitude*, the New Word, the "single work," looms large as a continent, invigorating all post-1960s fictional innovation."

In a quieter way, the discovery through translations of major Hispanic American avant-garde poets – César Vallejo, Vicente Huidobro, Pablo Neruda – occurred during the 1960s. In an effort to move away from European influences and redefine notions of self and identity in their poetry, North American poets increasingly looked abroad. Robert Bly, as poet, critic and translator, spearheaded an effort to introduce Surrealism into North American poetry through Spanish and Spanish American poets. Bly welcomed Hispanic American poetry as the most relevant contemporary poetry because of its particular surrealist impulse that draws on the poet's inner life as well as on the outside world. Bly stated in an article of 1958 that "if we look abroad, we see some astonishing landscapes: the Spanish tradition, for instance, of great delicacy, which grasps modern life as a lion grabs a dog, and wraps it in heavy countless images, and holds it firm in a terrifically dense texture, in which there is Pablo Neruda, a great poet ten times over, as well as García Lorca and César Vallejo." Bly, along with the poet James Wright, produced the first English translation of the Peruvian poet César Vallejo in 1962, *Twenty Poems of César Vallejo*. They collectively produced *Neruda and Vallejo: Selected Poems* in 1972. John Felstiner's fascinating book, *Translating Neruda: the Way to Macchu Picchu* (1980), discusses Neruda's reception in the United States and evauates English translations (including Bly's) of the poet's works, listing thirty-six, including his own renditions, from 1934 to 1976 (five in the 1930s and 1940s, five in the 1950s, eight in the 1960s, and eighteen in the 1970s). Interestingly, other important North American poets, among them W.S. Merwin, Denise Levertov, William Carlos Williams, Mark Strand and Langston Hughes have translated and continue to translate poetry by Neruda, Vallejo, Octavio Paz and Nicolás Guillén.

The importance of their poetry and the call for new translations has led to a plethora of new and edited volumes. An important literary press that promotes Hispanic American literature in translation, Latin American Literary Review Press, published a bilingual edition of Vallejo's first book of poetry, *Los heraldos negros* (*The Black Heralds*), in 1990. In that same year, Margaret Sayers Peden translated *Selected Odes of Pablo Neruda*. Neruda's *Canto General* was translated by Jack Schmitt in 1991 and includes a critical introduction by Roberto González Echevarría. Octavio Paz's epic poem, *Sunstone*, first published in 1957, was translated by his longtime translator, Eliot Weinberger, in 1991.

With this growing body of translated works of fiction and poetry, a certain pattern has emerged with a handful of Hispanic authors dominating the panorama of literary translation in recent times. In his essay ,"Hispanic Fiction in Translation: Some Considerations Regarding Recent Literary History," in *Language at the Crossroads* (1988), Michael Scott Doyle points out that the pattern may be due to an "imbalanced historical appreciation of Hispanic fiction by the American reader. Translators and publishers can provide historical corrective to this imbalance by making available in the future a greater representation of contemporary Hispanic novelists and short story writers." Here Scott Doyle reveals that out of a list of 190 writers represented by 140 titles in translation in the United States, Spain accounts for 18% (35 titles); Argentina, 25% (25 titles); Mexico, 15%; Cuba, 11%; Peru, 8.5%; Colombia, 7%; Chile, 5%; Ecuador and Guatemala, less than 3% each; Nicaragua, Puerto Rico, and Uruguay, just over 1% each; El Salvador, less than 1%; and seven countries – Bolivia, Costa Rica, the Dominican

Republic, Honduras, Panama, Paraguay and Venezuela were not represented in English. Nine authors – Jorge Luis Borges, Alejo Carpentier, Julio Cortázar, José Donoso, Carlos Fuentes, Gabriel García Márquez, Juan Goytisolo, Manuel Puig and Mario Vargas Llosa – account for 77 of the 140 titles in English. Nine from a list of 190 writers, 4.7% of the total constitute 55% of the translations into English in the United States. In the world of book reviews of translations, Margaret Sayers Peden has noted that the number of reviews between 1965 and 1988 of Mario Vargas Llosa's works, form an inverted pyramid, from one in 1965 to seventy-six in 1987–88: "Vargas Llosa *exploded* in English-language consciousness in 1986; prior to that year, forty-nine reviews appeared in the sources I consulted; forty-three reviews were published in 1986 alone."

Doyle concludes his study saying that what was once too little of a good thing, contemporary Hispanic American fiction, has turned into too much of too little, the over representation of a select few. While today the numbers and players may have changed the aforementioned statistics somewhat, there is growing concern as to the possible effects of such skewed figures; in fact, Johnny Payne's book probes the deeper structures of this phenomenon: "The dissemination of Latin American fiction in translation none the less has produced many positive results in terms of bringing a modicum of world attention . . . to Latin American literature. Likewise, my project here has not been to present the Boom as nothing more than a calculated instance of economic opportunism but rather to suggest how a body of literature, selectively produced and disseminated in conjunction with certain cultural crises and the economic demands of consumer culture, becomes subject to extremely limited possibilities of interpretation within that culture."

Payne's exciting study is indicative of the level at which writers, translators, critics and reviewers are beginning to examine the world of literary translation in the 1990s. There has been a profusion of works in translation, including new critical editions of older, "classical" works, i.e., *The Underdogs*, by Mariano Azuela, first published in serial form in an El Paso newspaper in 1916, and now considered the most representative novel of the Mexican Revolution. By the 1960s it had become one of the best-known and most translated works of Spanish American literature. In 1979, Stanley L. Robe produced a translation of the original El Paso version. Other English translations appeared in 1930, 1963 and 1979, which were based presumably on an enlarged Mexican edition of 1920. The latest (1992) critical edition by Frederick H. Fornoff includes an introduction by Seymour Menton, the translation itself, a glossary and a section of "Background and Criticism." Evelio Echevarría has said that this latest edition "offers plenty of material for the historian and the professor of international literature. But the book can also be enjoyed at a simpler level. It is essentially a compelling tale of human conflicts, grippingly told."

One important factor contributing to the explosion of post-Boom translations of Hispanic American literature in recent times in the United States is greater translation of women writers, whose works have hit the best-seller lists and been made into movies (*Like Water for Chocolate* by Laura Esquivel, and *The House of the Spirits* by Isabel Allende).

Another factor is the expanding publication of anthologies in translation, especially poetry and short stories; for instance, Nora Erro-Peralta's *Beyond the Border: a New Age in Latin American Women's Fiction* (1991), Celia Correas de Zapata's *Short Stories by Latin American Women: the Magic and the Real* (1990), Ilan Stavan's *Tropical Synagogues: Short Stories by Jewish-American Writers* (1994), Thomas Colchie's *A Hammock beneath the Mangoes: Stories from Latin America* (1991), Carmen Esteves's *Green Cane and Juicy Flotsam: Short Stories by Caribbean Women* (1991) and Barbara Paschke's *Clamor of Innocence: Central American Short Stories* (1988). Another significant factor concerns the publishers. Besides the mainstream New York publishers who continue to publish the canonized Boom writers, it is important to point out the role of university presses and, amazingly, small presses, have played in expanding the corpus. The long-established Pan American Series at the University of Texas Press is considered a cornerstone of published translations of Spanish American literature. The University of Nebraska Press has created the Latin American Women Writers series. Other universities – University of California, Los Angeles and Wayne State University – publish translations in their Latin American Literature and Culture series. A formidable, growing press that has made a significant contribution is the Latin American Literary Review. Finally, examples of the efforts being made by small presses include City Lights Press (San Francisco), Curbstone Press (Willimantic, Connecticut), and White Pine Press (Fredonia, New York), the last of which in 1987 initiated its Secret Weavers Series, in response to the neglect suffered by Latin American women as writers and citizens in a marginalized position in Latin American society. According to its editor, Chilean author and Wellesley College Professor Marjorie Agosín, the series presents "for the first time in English the most powerful and striking voices of 20th-century Latin American women writers, both contemporary writers and their mentors, weaving a landscape of ritual magic and imagination."

Critical studies concerning diverse issues facing the translator of Latin American literature are also beginning to surface. For some time now, the journal *Translation Review* (University of Texas, Dallas) has been providing articles focusing on problems of reviewing translations of Hispanic American literature, fidelity in the translation of titles, and the need to consider new translations of earlier works. One important compilation of critical studies, *Translating Latin America: Culture as Text*, produced from a 1990 conference sponsored by the Center for Research in Translation, State University of New York at Binghamton, delves into serious issues confronting the translator, such as: new modes of transculturation, bilingualism, and code-switching (English-Spanish), especially with the increase in Latin American and Chicano writers in the United States working in two languages, that is, an interlanguage; a growing body of testimonial narrative, a hybrid genre that incorporates diverse forms of discourses in the texts; the translated new novel as a text for studying and teaching of historical themes: authority and subordination, gender relationships, military-civilian relations, the city and the countryside, contemporary politics, history and the search for identity, and possible futures; "translational imperialism," according to Clayton Eshelman, in which a First World translator works on a Third World writer, that is, the translator as colonizer; translating race and culture, in which terms tainted by their racist history would call into question their usage; the limitations of American (unlike British) English that lacks, except for the South, the types of dialects that can be represented typographically; and the study of actual differences between the original and the translation, resulting from certain shifts, displacements, additions, omissions, puns, jokes, clichés, rhymes, or expletives. And always looming on the horizon is the outright bad translation, not because the translator does not understand the language, but because he or she does not know the culture. In order to interpret a literary text successfully, critics must first understand the originating culture of that text; similarly, translators often must translate an entire culture in order to translate a single literary text better. In that way, serious problems could be avoided, as outlined in a recent review of a translation of recent Mexican short stories by Debra Castillo: "[Her] ... translation is flawed by her literal renderings of too many large words and by awkward phrases ... Ponderous phrases, common in Mexican literature, are particular and peculiar to that culture. In English, they are embarrassing. Take license, translators!" Translation may be totally impossible, but it's absolutely necessary.

DICK GERDES

Further Reading

General

Bassnett, Susan and André Lefevere (editors), *Translation, History, Culture: a Sourcebook*, London and New York: Routledge, 1992

Graham, Joseph F. (editor), *Difference in Translation*, Ithaca, New York: Cornell University Press, 1985

Rabassa, Gregory, "Translation: the Recreative Art," *Humanities* 2 (December 1982)

Sur, "Problemas de la traducción," special issue dedicated to translation (Buenos Aires, January–December 1976)

Literary Translation in Relation to Latin America

Aparicio, Frances R., *Versiones, interpretaciones y creaciones*, Gaithersburg, Maryland: Hispámerica, 1991 [Has historical dimension and also considers "translation" from painting to the written word]

Borges, Jorge Luis, "Los traductores de las *1001 Noches*," in his *Historia de la eternidad*, augmented edition, Buenos Aires: Emecé, 1953

Levine, Suzanne Jill, *The Subversive Scribe: Translating Latin American Fiction*, St Paul, Minnesota: Graywolf Press, 1991 [Does not cover translation from Portuguese]

Mead, Jr, Robert G., "After the Boom: the Fate of Latin American Literature in English Translation," *Américas*, vol. 30/4 (April 1978)

Meyer, Doris (editor), *Rereading the Spanish American Essay: Translations of 19th and 20th Century Women's Essays*, Austin: University of Texas Press, 1995

Payne, Johnny, *Conquest of the New Word: Experimental Fiction and Translation in the Americas*, Austin: University of Texas Press, 1993

Scott Doyle, Michael, "Hispanic Fiction in Translation: Some Considerations Regarding Recent Literary History," in *Languages at Crossroads: Proceedings of the 29th Annual Conference of the American Translators' Association*, edited by Deanna Lindberg Hammond, Medford, New Jersey: Learned Information, 1988

Shaw, Bradley A., *Latin American Literature in English Translation: an Annotated Bibliography*, New York: New York University Press, 1976

Wilson, Jason, *An A to Z of Modern Latin American Literature in English Translation*, London: Institute of Latin American Studies, 1989

Literary Translation in Relation to Specific Authors and Countries

Enkvist, Inger, *On Translating Mario Vargas Llosa: the Novels of Mario Vargas Llosa in English, French and Swedish Translation*, Madrid: Vox Hispánica, 1993

Felstiner, John, *Translating Neruda: the Way to Macchu Picchu*, Stanford, California: Stanford University Press, 1980

Hernández, Orlando José, "This Uncanny Tricky Business: Translation and Ideology in Puerto Rican Literature," in *Images and Identities: the Puerto Rican in Two World Contexts*, edited by Asela Rodríguez de Laguna, Oxford: Transaction Books, 1987

Pagano, Adriana Silvina, "Literary Translation in Argentina," *Revista de Estudos Germânicos* (1991–92)

Sayers Peden, Margaret, "Mario Vargas Llosa in English Translation: a Survey of Translator Reception," *Ideas '92*, vol. 2/1 (1992)

Travel Literature

It is only recently with Paul Fussell's *Abroad* (1980), that travel writing began to be taken seriously, and studied at universities. But what constitutes travel literature is still being defined. A genre approach reveals the travel book to be an eclectic and refreshing hybrid of memoir, essay and autobiography in the realist mode, dealing with a verifiable place, and with an identifiable narrator. The genre approach does not decide quality, but does make the apparently simple travel narrative more complex by exploring the many narrative devices (dialogue, plot, characterization, etc.) employed. A further approach would be to explore the travel book within a self-referential tradition of travel writing, this being the one adopted by both James Buzard and Stephen Greenblatt, where problems of writing and invention and realism are encoded in the narratives themselves. A third approach to travel literature would be to see it as an expression of ideology, and part of the centre-periphery debate, this being the angle explored by Edward Said and Mary Louise Pratt. Here the traveller is a representative of impersonal historical forces, and travel literature a sub-theme of the discourse of imperialism. A fourth approach would look into the problematics of recording and remembering, looking at diaries, different versions, the illusion of realism, attempts at creating visual images, and how brute experience is transferred into words.

In complex ways Latin America is the creation of foreigners writing about the New World, from the earliest chroniclers like Bernal Díaz, to scientific travellers like Alexander von Humboldt and Charles Darwin, to later literary explorers such as D.H. Lawrence and Graham Greene. These texts are aimed at those back home, and hope to dissipate ignorance and awaken envy, though poor travel books confirm prejudice and stereotype. The version of Latin America that this tradition of foreigners gives depends on many factors from length of stay to familiarity with local culture, but the aim is to offer a vision of a different place in terms of a rhetoric of cultural shock. Fiction can carry this informative task just as efficiently and travelogues often overlap with narrative, and sometimes vie with narrative as in the case of Lawrence or Greene on Mexico. Many realist novels are read as "news from somewhere" and seek to instruct.

Indeed, much of Latin American literature can be seen as a parallel attempt to those travelogues written by foreigners, but with the intention to inform native readers about ignored parts of their own continent, especially given the Latin American cultural fascination with Europe and abroad, and the frequent hostility between neighbouring countries. The realist tradition of narrative in Latin America that opens with Horacio Quiroga, and is often called "regionalist," functions rhetorically as travel writing creating verifiable images of hinterlands (Gallegos, Rivera, Azuela etc.). Later writers like Rulfo or Carpentier establish their verisimilitude from implicit travel books, a point examined by González Echevarría in his study *Myth and Archive* (1990). García Márquez's Macondo is a metaphor of this unexplored, off-the-tourist-route Latin America, often ignored by urban Latin Americans themselves. But it is Alejo Carpentier's *Los pasos perdidos*, 1953 (*The Lost Steps*), that mimics a trip up the Orinoco in the wake of Raleigh and Humboldt to establish itself as the seminal fusion of travel book and novel exploring Latin America's hidden uniqueness.

There is not a strong tradition of Latin American empirical observation or of Latin American travel writing, and even less on travelling within the Latin American continent. Sarmiento is a good example of a writer capable of creating a hybrid text based on travel literature and including biography, geography, essay and diatribe. This applies to *Facundo*, 1845 (*Life in the Argentine Republic in the Days of the Tyrants*), but his actual travel writing only explored the United States and Europe. For a native tradition of verifiable observations the reader has to turn away from the few like Vasconcelos who have written explicit travelogues, and read poets like Neruda or Cardenal or fiction writers like Quiroga, Rivera or García Márquez, to match the kind of observations made by the great foreign travellers in Latin America.

JASON WILSON

Further Reading

Bassnett, Susan, *Comparative Literature: a Critical Introduction*, Oxford: Blackwell, 1993 [Chapter 5 is on the politics of travellers' tales]

Buzard, James, *The Beaten Track: European Tourism, Literature, and the Ways to "Culture," 1800–1918*, Oxford and New York: Oxford University Press, 1993

Fussell, Paul, *Abroad: British Literary Traveling Between the Wars*, Oxford and New York: Oxford University Press, 1980

González Echevarría, Roberto, *Myth and Archive: a Theory of Latin American Narrative*, Cambridge and New York: Cambridge University Press, 1990

Greenblatt, Stephen, *Marvelous Possessions: the Wonder of the New World*, Oxford: Oxford University Press, and Chicago: University of Chicago Press, 1991

Karsen, Sonja, "Latin America through French, German and Austrian Eyes," in her *Ensayos de literatura e historia iberoamericana*, New York: Peter Lang, 1988

Pfeiffer, Erna, *Exiliadas, emigrantes, viajeras*, Frankfurt: Vervuert Verlag, 1995

Porter, Dennis, *Haunted Journeys: Desire and Transgression in European Travel Writing*, Princeton, New Jersey: Princeton University Press, 1991

Pratt, Mary Louise, *Imperial Eyes: Travel Writing and Transculturation*, London and New York: Routledge, 1992

Said, Edward, *Culture and Imperialism*, New York: Knopf, 1993; London: Vintage, 1994

Walker, John, "A Little Corner of the World: British Travel Writers in the Argentine: an Overview," *Revista Interamericana de Bibliografía*, vol. 44/2 (1994)

Wilson, Jason, *Traveller's Literary Companion to South and Central America*, Brighton: In Print, 1993

Dalton Trevisan 1925–

Brazilian short story writer

Recognized critically as Brazil's most outstanding contemporary short story writer, Dalton Trevisan none the less provokes debate in view of his repetitive dramatization of seemingly trivial themes of populist behavior, all taking place in his hometown of Curitiba in the southern state of Paraná. His stories incessantly depict lower-middle and working-class mores as well as marginalized taboo figures such as prostitutes and homosexuals who belie the chaste codes of a provincial society colonized by standards of appearance. He is considered something of a literary taboo by some critics, and his deliberate repetition of the same figures, situations and circumstances across all collections has been misunderstood. Moreover, from an elitist position, Trevisan's scabrous and dark repetitive tales may be falsely misconstrued as the exploitation of the shallow thematics of cheap sex and domestic violence. However, in the more than twenty collections since his first in 1959, *Novelas nada exemplares* [Far from Exemplary Tales], Trevisan has been acknowledged over the years as an innovator in Brazilian fiction because his stories and vignettes not only evoke the popular as a sustained subject matter for literature, but also explore and introduce new formulations of the story genre. With his juxtaposition of clipped tales, novellas, aphorisms, reflections, poems and dialogue tableaux in the same collection, Trevisan blurs the parameters of the short story genre. Thus, in form as well as in content, his novellas are not exemplary in terms of conventional story narrative. This formal and thematic irreverence is demonstrated in his aesthetic experimentation with calculated ellipsis, minimalist dialogue, scant description, and brief – even one sentence – dramas, categorized specifically by the author as haiku, tales that identify trenchantly with the cultural behavior and widespread hardships of Brazil's popular classes. This identification was evidenced early in Trevisan's career after publishing his first stories in *Joaquim*, the 1946 literary magazine that motivated a young generation of Curitiban writers, frustrated by provincial isolation, toward new visions and expressive approaches that would connect them with the outside world. During the same period, Trevisan began to edit and publish his tales in the typographical form of popular chapbooks known in Brazil as the *literatura de cordel*, printed and performed by modern working-class troubadors. Trevisan's recent republication of some of these as *ministórias* in the colloquially driven *Ah, É?* (1994) point to his unbroken link to Brazil's oral tradition.

Critical studies on Trevisan have alluded to his use of populist themes but few have developed his connection to Brazil's popular oral tradition. Addressing Trevisan's type of populist scenarios, performed by anti-heroes of lost illusions, as the expression of a modern picaresque, Wilson Martins also interprets Trevisan's insistence on the popular as descendant of Brazil's 19th-century Manuel Antônio de Almeida and his realistic treatment of common types. However, Trevisan's approach differs in his popular voicing because he expresses these in an unadorned prose that reproduces the clipped banalities and colorful idioms of uncultured Johns and Marys who reappear pervasively in collection after collection. Here,

popular voices are not manipulated by the God-shots of Naturalist omniscience. Instead, Trevisan's mastery of popular voicing emerges in his use of visceral dialogue and other narrative techniques of immediacy such as first-person and interior monologue. In addition, Trevisan's stories intensify popular cultural voicing beyond the patrimonialist vision found in the politics of official culture, often promoting the popular as exotic folklore. His prose neither succumbs to the self-exoticism frequently attributed to Latin American nationalist fiction, nor does it portray paternalistically a picturesque or epic panorama of the folk and their lore. Employing the persona and orality of the popular, Trevisan restages everyday modes of living and survival to call attention to an often unforgotten aspect of Brazilian society. In doing so, he imparts the ubiquitous presence of working-class values, depravaties and fantasies, revolving around the themes of sex and death where social and psychological vampires in the form of machista-minded men stalk women who in some cases learn to fight back, albeit, never escaping unscathed from these encounters. By creating mock-melodramatic situations that become comic via an unobtrusive irony, Trevisan's disturbingly stark treatment above all allows the different but familiar characters to speak for themselves. This comedic and ironic stance undoes the sameness implied in mass and elite cultures' frequently melodramatic or stereotypical image of the popular classes because Trevisan shows the myriad of differences, diversifications and contradictions within similar situations. In perfecting this type of voicing via a stylistic reworking of former tales, Trevisan also evokes the variations-on-a-theme technique, a basic rule of universal composition expressed in the form of variation as practiced by the *cordel* composers and singers. In cultivating identification through repetition, Trevisan is able to refine the different nuances of language and behavior that make his voices come alive.

With an original style highlighting the mythology of an urban cosmos that harbors rapists, adultresses, cuckolds and murders, reminding the reader of the lurid tabloids of popular rags, Trevisan uses prototypes whose linguistic banalites and contemporary slang pique the reader's curiosity and, ironically, the recognition of a covert and taboo form of existence that pulsates secretively behind closed doors. The images of blood-red passion and violence manifested in each story collection, where social and moral codes are deconstructed, paint the pervasive harm that people inflict on each other, thereby implying the treacherous ways a socially-rooted authoritarian system infiltrates the souls of individuals and turns them into warring instruments of individual violence. Trevisan's allusions to the insidious tyranny in the recesses of a closeted Curitiba signal his evocation of a hypocritical and repressed world where the treatment of women may serve as a disturbing reminder of other forms of societal repression. For example, the use of the sexually explicit is central to Trevisan's social and political views of power and subjugation. He thus appropriates erotica to unmask the oppressive components in society. In this vein, the actions of his subjugated female characters striking back aggressively can be seen as an attempt to revolt against patriarchy. This pattern of behavior is most evident in his 1988 collection *Pão e sangue* [Bread and Blood]. Here, in the context of social satire, Trevisan's unobtrusive critical eye strives to expose socio-religious cultural myths and codes that are transgressed by his characters, perhaps suggesting that certain patriarchal and ecclesiastical norms may no longer serve as valid ethics.

Canonized as Brazil's foremost contemporary writer after having won in 1968 the much coveted State of Curitiba national prize for the best short story writer, Trevisan has been prolific and steady in his publications. While all of his collections maintain similar themes, it was his 1974 collection, *O pássaro de cinco asas* [The Bird with Five Wings], that witnessed the beginning of a change in the story genre with the inclusion of a few haiku pieces. Ever since, Trevisan appears to be aiming for the perfect haiku, while at the same time producing non-haiku narratives. Readily apparent in such collections as *Essas malditas mulheres*, 1982 [Those Damned Women] and *Pão e sangue* among others, this combination is also reproduced in his most recent publication, *Dinorá: novos mistérios*, 1994 [Dinorá: New Mysteries], a collection that contains poems and even a novella-like story along with intertextual responses to the Bible and to certain novels by Machado de Assis. Although Trevisan experimented in 1985 with an actual novella, *A polaquinha*, depicting the sordidness of a lower-middle class girl's descent into prostitution, his voice continually returns to the short form as the vehicle for his sardonic picture of a debased human comedy. Seen by some critics as a stylistic minimalist, Trevisan nevertheless creates a vast world of strife, passion and violence in characters who travel repeatedly upon a *via crucis* of belief, want and affliction. His gallery of Joãos and Marias presents a Brazilian everyman and everywoman from the lower classes who seek solace from an urbanized world of injustice and adversity. With his original vision and postmodernist art, Trevisan "bridges the gap" by awakening an often elitist and complacent reading public to a daring view of the popular.

Translated into many languages, including English, Spanish, German, Dutch and Polish, Trevisan's stories and dialogues served as the script for Joaquim Pedro de Andrade's 1975 film, *A guerra conjugal* [Conjugal War]. Owing to the growing acceptance and validation of Trevisan's special brand of narrative, it is expected that more translations will be forthcoming, especially if one bears in mind that the one and only story collection in English translation was published more than twenty years ago.

NELSON H. VIEIRA

Biography

Born in Curitiba, Brazil, 14 January 1925. Has chosen to spend his life in his native Curitiba where he worked in the family's ceramic factory after abandoning the study of law. In 1945 began to write police reports and to review films for Curitiban newspapers. Travelled to Europe in 1950. Married in 1953. Founded the literary journal *Joaquim*, 1946 in which he published his early short stories; in the 1950s, published stories in cheap newsprint editions at his own expense. Recipient of the following important awards: Brazilian Book Chamber; Pen Club of Brazil; National Short Story Competition. Trevisan shuns publicity and for this reason remains a somewhat mysterious figure.

Selected Works

Novelas nada exemplares, Rio de Janeiro: José Olympio, 1959
Cemiterio de elefantes: contos, Rio de Janeiro: Civilização Brasileira, 1962
O vampiro de Curitiba, Rio de Janeiro: Civilização Brasileira, 1965; as *The Vampire of Curitiba and other Stories*, translated by Gregory Rabassa, New York: Knopf, 1972
Desastres do amor: contos, Rio de Janeiro: Civilização Brasileira, 1968
A guerra conjugal, Rio de Janeiro: Civilização Brasileira, 1969
O rei da terra: contos, Rio de Janeiro: Civilização Brasileira, 1972
O pássaro de cinco asas: contos, Rio de Janeiro: Civilização Brasileira, 1974
A faca no coração, Rio de Janeiro: Civilização Brasileira, 1975
Abismo de rosas: contos, Rio de Janeiro: Civilização Brasileira, 1976
A trombeta do anjo vingador, Rio de Janeiro: Codecri, 1977
Crimes de paixão, Rio de Janeiro: Record, 1978
Virgem louca, loucos beijos, Rio de Janeiro: Record, 1979
Lincha tarado, Rio de Janeiro: Record, 1980
Chrorinho brejeiro: contos, Rio de Janeiro: Record, 1981
Essas malditas mulheres, Rio de Janeiro: Record, 1982
Meu querido assassino, Rio de Janeiro: Record, 1983
Contos eróticos, Rio de Janeiro: Record, 1984
A polaquinha, Rio de Janeiro: Record, 1985
Pão e sangue, Rio de Janeiro: Record, 1988
Em busca de Curitiba perdida, Rio de Janeiro: Record, 1992
Ah, É?, Rio de Janeiro: Record, 1994
Dinorá: novos mistérios, Rio de Janeiro: Record, 1994

Further Reading

Gomes, Álvaro Cardoso and Carlos Alberto Vechi (editors), *Dalton Trevisan: seleção de textos, notas, estudo biográfico, histórico e crítico e exercícios*, São Paulo: Abril Educação, 1981
Ledford-Miller, Linda, "Shoes for Little Peter: Narrative Technique in Trevisan's Not-At-All Exemplary Novella, *Pedrinho*," *Brasil-Brazil: a Journal of Brazilian Literature*, Brown University, Rhode Island, vol. 3/4 (1990)
_____ "The Perverse Passions of Dalton Trevisan," in *Literature and the Bible*, edited by David Bevan, Amsterdam: Rodopi, 1994
Vieira, Nelson H., "João e Maria: Dalton Trevisan's Eponymous Heroes," *Hispania* (March 1986)

José Triana 1931–

Cuban dramatist and poet

José Triana's literary career is inextricably connected to the cause of Cuban liberation. Raised in Bayamo, the cradle of the Cuban War of Independence of 1868, by a father who was both a fervent defender of the Republic during the Spanish Civil War and an avid promoter of local culture, including theater, Triana came early on to see an easy affinity between revolution and theater. For political reasons, among them having participated in the 26th of July Movement, Triana found himself obliged to move to Spain in 1955. There, in exile, he wrote *El Mayor General hablará de Teogonía*, 1960 [The Major General Will Speak on Theogony]. This first play is ostensibly written against the tyranny of the 1920s, but is in reality directed against the Cuban dictator Batista, who had assumed office for the second time in 1952. The double time frame, which emphasizes the unchanging nature of tyranny in two distinct decades, is an early indication of what is to become a recurrent theme in Triana's dramatic production: the form or the structure of power is not affected by changes in the ideological contents.

The next three plays, *Medea en el espejo*, 1960 [Medea in the Mirror], *El parque de la Fraternidad*, 1962 [Fraternity Park] and *La muerte del Ñeque*, 1964 [The Death of Enterprise] underscore the need to establish a new sociopolitical structure in order to escape the vicious circle of revolution and repression. In these three pieces, Triana seeks to demonstrate the need for a new way of ordering human relationships. Triana parodies the "official" history in an effort to give voice to the marginalized elements of Cuban society that constitute the Island's "unofficial" history.

La muerte del Ñeque illustrates Triana's dramatic trajectory. Though the action in the play takes place in the 1950s, and can be read as an indictment of political corruption under Batista, it is also a warning of things to come after the Cuban Revolution, as corruption had indeed begun by late 1963 and early 1964. Triana's point, soon to be proven by the Castro government, is that the same corruption and repression that was present under Batista would inevitably resurface after Castro came to power. For Triana, as long as power is conceived of in terms of struggle, repression must inevitably accompany this struggle. Only a new order, a new structure, can change the process.

From this line of thought, then, emerged Triana's best-known play, *La noche de los asesinos* (*The Criminals*) (written in 1964, produced in 1966 and winner of the Casa de las Américas Prize in 1965). A central feature in *La noche* is the constant interchange of roles among the three characters, Cuca, Lalo and Beba. The three siblings take turns playing the roles of Father, Mother, Neighbor, Police, Judge, Prosecutor and Witness in an ongoing "play within a play," a continuing *projet* whose subject matter – never realized – is the murder of their parents. The play is a critique of the revolutionary process. No matter what role each character assumes, they can find no escape from the cyclical violence of the struggle for power. Violence always leads to reciprocal violence. The roles available to them are predetermined by the competitive, spectral coding that mediates relations of power. The house in which the children perform their play within a play serves as a metaphor of the national/family structure which constrains the repertoire of possible roles within Cuba's system of socio-political communication and exchange. The children argue over changing the names of the rooms – the living room is to be called the kitchen and vice versa – but fail to see that the structure of the house is not affected by changing the names of the rooms (ideologies). They still remain trapped within the structure of the house. The repetitive oscillation through time between dominator and dominated that first appeared in *El Mayor General* is highlighted in *La noche*. Though the names and ideologies may change – Castro for Batista or Ortega for Somoza – the violent and repressive nature of the struggle for power remains the same through time. Revolutionary "progress" is illusory. In fact, the claim of each new revolution to create a "new" reality is shown to be a fiction, a myth. So long as the nature of the struggle for power remains constant, the only changes are in the identities of the individuals who fill the role of victimizer and victim. As the play demonstrates, the role of "victim" is a necessary one, for the children define themselves in opposition to their parents, who represent authority. The children cast the blame for their misery onto each other and onto their parents, while the parents, in their turn, do the same. Lalo justifies his own violent acts as a response to the violence perpetrated on him by his parents, claiming his parents initiated the violence. His parents punctuate the sequence of events in the opposite manner, and so blame Lalo for introducing the violence. In the "trial" that takes place in the play, the parents take turns blaming each other for initiating the violence in their (the parents') relationship. Within the structure of the struggle for power, a symmetrical oscillation is established. No matter how the parties to the conflict punctuate their relations, as long as they accept the frame imposed by the violent nature of the power struggle they are doomed to an eternal repetition, to an oscillation ad infinitum. Thus the ritualized repetitive element of murder, or ritual sacrifice, highlighted in the play is part and parcel of the nature of the struggle for power. The revolution brings change only in terms of defining who shall be the sacrificial victim, and as Triana demonstrates, this definition is a direct function of power: those without power are defined as "victim" by those with the power to do so.

Thus, another aspect of Triana's work deals with those defined as sacrificial victim and their relation to the official version of history. Triana's professional and personal life is illustrative of the changing winds of power. When *La noche* was first performed it was hailed as a cultural achievement of the Cuban Revolution. It was not long, however, before it became obvious that what had at first appeared to be a critique of the Batista regime could be applied with equal facility to the Castro government. Triana's support among the Cuban cultural elite soon eroded and he was forced first into internal exile, forbidden to write or publish, and later, in 1980, was again exiled from Cuba. The same people that had at first supported him now abandoned him and finally drove him once more from his homeland. After *La noche*, we may note a new dimension in Triana's theatrical production. Whereas in the earlier plays he had dealt with the social groups that inhabited the margins of Cuban society – blacks, mulattos, the impoverished – in an attempt to show that these groups too were worthy of a tragic dimension, that their lives had passion and meaning, in the plays that follow *La noche* Triana deals with the problems of racism, sexism, honor, hypocrisy and repression in a manner that includes and indicts the middle and upper classes. *Palabras comunes*, a reworking of *Diálogo para mujeres*, 1979 [Dialogue for Women], is the story of a white, middle-class Cuban family during the transition from Spanish to North American rule, from 1894 to 1914. As is so often the case in Triana's plays, the work simultaneously refers to the Cuba of the 1980s. The play points out the sexual and racial hierarchy of power relations – white male at the top and black female at the bottom – that permits the exploitation of those defined as beneath one in this hierarchy. The concept of *honra* (honor) is the motor that drives the sexual and racial economy. The female characters in the play produce and reproduce, across the generations, the Oedipal pattern of sexual repression and inhibition that constrains their social communication and exchange. To contest these relations of power is to be marked as "other" or sacrificial victim, a fate which befalls Victoria in the play. *Honra* is the social equivalent of the political structure that constrains the revolutionary struggle for power. Both structures, and they overlap and are intertwined, generate an endless cycle of repression and violence, an eternal repetition of the same process. Though the names of the players may change from context to context, the rules of the game appear immune to change. Thus the allegorical structure of the house in *La noche* – nation, family, government – and the allegorical words that constrain our social selves – *honra*, be it family honor, a woman's honor, or personal honor – both represent those shared structures, our social and political norms or rules, that define and limit our sociopolitical communication, both in word and in deed. What Triana seeks to manifest through his theater is the need to contest the structures that trap us in a narrow range of actions, in a repetitive series of endless oscillations between what only appear to be choices, but are in reality two sides of the same coin, the same endless cycle of violence and repression, of honor, hypocrisy and revenge. Both *honra* and revolution require an "other," a sacrificial victim. And when that victim gains power, be s/he man or woman, black or white, capitalist or Marxist, the only alternative available under the present structuring of power is to continue the cycle. Triana points out the ultimate futility, and human cost, of seeking change within a sociopolitical structure that essentially permits only two options in its repertoire of social roles: victim or victimizer, master or slave. Triana shows the fruitlessness of contesting relations of power from within the structure that informs these relations and the need to evolve beyond a system trapped in endless cycles of reciprocal violence.

JERRY HOEG

Biography

Born in Camagüey, Cuba, 4 January 1931. Attended the Escuela Bautista in Bayamo to 1950; Instituto de Manzanillo, Oriente, received degree in 1952; studied philosophy at University of Santiago de Cuba, 1952–54; University of Madrid, 1955–57. From 1956 to 1957 he studied theatre under José Franco at the Sociedad de Bellas Artes in Madrid. Member of the troupe Grupo Didi, 1956–57, and scenic artist with Teatro Ensayo in 1958. From 1958 to 1959 he travelled to France, Belgium, Italy and England and returned to Cuba at the time of the Revolution. Worked for the Cuban telecommunications company. Editor, Editorial Nacional de Cuba and the Instituto Cubano del Libro, 1963–80. Visiting Professor of drama and literature attached to the Ministry of Education in 1964 and 1967. Throughout the 1960s he contributed to numerous Cuban literary journals including *Lunes de Revolución* and *Casa de las Américas*, and the French periodicals *Lettres Nouvelles* and *Cahiers Renaud-Barrault*. Married Chantal Dumaine in 1968. Left Cuba in 1980 because of increasing government restrictions on his writing and moved to Paris. Visiting Professor at Dartmouth College, New Hampshire, 1981–82. Awarded the Casa de las Américas Prize, 1965 for *La noche de los asesinos* and Gallo del La Habana in 1966.

Selected Works

Plays

El parque de la Fraternidad, Havana: UNEAC, 1962 [Includes *Medea en el espejo* and *El Mayor General hablará de Teogonía*]
La muerte del Ñeque, Havana: Ediciones R., 1964
La noche de los asesinos, Havana: Casa de las Américas, 1965; as *The Criminals*, in *The Modern Stage in Latin America: Six Plays*, edited by George Woodyard, New York: Dutton, 1971
Palabras comunes, in *Tramoya. Cuaderno de Teatro de la Universidad Veracruzana*, 1987
Ceremonial de guerra, Honoloulu: Editorial Persona, 1990

Poetry

De la madera de los sueños, Madrid: Gráficos Bachende, 1958
Coloquio de sombras, in *Cuadernos Hispanoamericanos* 374 (1981)
Aproximaciones, Málaga: Plaza de la Marina, 1989
Cuaderno de familia, Málaga: Dador / Quinto Centenario, 1990

Compilations and Anthologies

Teatro, Madrid: Verbum, 1991 [Contains *Medea en el espejo*, *La noche de los asesinos*, *Palabras comunes*]

Further Reading

Álvarez-Borland, Isabel and David George, "*La noche de los asesinos*: Text, Staging and Audience," *Latin American Theatre Review*, vol. 20/1 (1986)
Campa, Ramón de la, *José Triana: ritualización de la sociedad cubana*, Madrid: Cátedra, 1979
Fernández-Fernández, Ramiro, "José Triana habla de su teatro," *Románica* 15 (1978–79)
Hoeg, Jerry, "Coding, Context, and Punctuation in Triana's *La noche de los asesinos*," *Gestos* 15 (1993)
Lolo, Eduardo, *Las trampas del tiempo y sus memorias*, Miami: Hallmark, 1991
March, Anne, "Genet, Triana, Kopit: Ritual as Dance Macabre," *Modern Drama*, vol. 15/4 (1973)
Nigro, Kirsten, "*La noche de los asesinos*: Playscript and stage enactment," *Latin American Theatre Review*, vol. 11/1 (1977)

Nigro, Kirsten (editor), *Palabras más que comunes: ensayos sobre el teatro de José Triana*, Boulder: Colorado: Society of Spanish and Spanish-American Studies, 1994

Ortega, Julio, "*La noche de los asesinos*," *Cuadernos Americanos* 164 (1969)

Taylor, Diana, "Framing the Revolution: Triana's *La noche de los asesinos* and *Ceremonial de Guerra*," *Latin American Theatre Review*, vol. 24/1 (1980)

Taylor, Diana (editor), *En busca de una imagen: ensayos críticos sobre Griselda Gambaro y José Triana*, Ottawa: Girol, 1989

Zalacaín, Daniel, *Teatro absurdista hispanoamericano*, Valencia: Albatros/Hispanófila, 1985

Tropiques

See Journals

U

Ubaldo Ribeiro, João

See Ribeiro

Uruguay

19th- and 20th-Century Prose and Poetry

The Uruguayan literary canon is a pedagogical apparatus, a monument to and of the National Imaginary, and the crystallization of a social struggle for cultural hegemony. With this in mind, and considering that any synthesis is also a system of exclusions, some key moments in Uruguayan cultural history will be mapped-out, mostly through canonical literary texts.

The foundations of Uruguayan literature can be traced to Francisco Acuña de Figueroa (1790–1862) and Bartolomé Hidalgo (1788–1822). Although both are canonized as Neoclassicists, they paradigmatically represent the main fractures that inform 19th-century literature until the advent of *Modernismo*. Acuña de Figueroa is the foremost Neoclassic poet in the La Plata area. Author of the national anthem, among many other celebratory, commissioned works, Acuña has been considered a mediocre lyric and heroic poet, but an extraordinary satirist. His burlesque poetry includes epigrams, chronicles of bull-fighting and parodic epic poems full of political and literary allusions. One of the canon's untouchables due to his shifting, opportunistic politics, Acuña has lately been re-evaluated as a distant forerunner of concrete and visual poetry. The recent re-publication of his licentious *Nomenclatura y apología del carajo* [Nomenclature and Apology of the Prick] and the religiously ambiguous game-prayer "La *Salve* multiforme" [The Multiform *Salve*] are cases in point.

While Acuña represents the erudite colonial and urban *letrado* (man of letters), Hidalgo, a mulatto fully immersed in the revolution for independence, is the founder of gauchesque poetry. The gauchos, seminomadic, landless rural peons, became, because of their skilful riding and cattle herding, the main source of manpower in the Wars of Independence. Hidalgo's genius was to appropriate the gaucho's oral culture and to transform it into a literary genre. He invented a gauchesque language, hybrid literary forms (the *cielitos* [song and dance] and dialogues), and a new mode of production which combined urban printing techniques with rural singing performance. Gauchesque poetry and theatre, which should not be confused with gaucho culture, are, by far, the most original cultural apparatus in 19th-century Latin America. Both Acuña's and Hidalgo's productions exemplify the early fracture between two publics, two markets, two opposing cultures, a contradiction usually referred to as one between the elitist and the popular, the city and the countryside, the traditional and the new, or, as Domingo Faustino Sarmiento put it, between "civilization and barbarism." This contradiction traverses the history of the entire region, and its axis is gauchesque literature, the intermediary between the *letrado*'s organizational projects and the gaucho's social needs. Originally attracted to the revolutionary camp by Hidalgo's *cielitos*, the gauchos were later drafted by the armies of opposing political parties during countless civil wars. Thus arises a second, truly propagandistic gauchesque production. It coincides with the exile of the Romantics of the Young Argentine movement to Montevideo, where they united with their Uruguayans counterpart around the periodical *El Iniciador* [The Initiator], and is best represented by Hilario Ascasubi (1807–75) and Estanislao del Campo (1834–80), both Argentines by birth. Their literary production, both gauchesque and *letrado*, during the Great War (1836–51) however, pertains to a pre-national culture of this region, independent of state boundaries. Antonio Lussich's *Los tres gauchos orientales* [The Three Oriental Gauchos] and José Hernández's *El gaucho Martín Fierro* (*The Gaucho Martín Fierro*), two key texts published in 1872, deal with more specifically national issues. The combined impact of economic modernization and the civil wars culminates in the gauchos' virtual extinction by the end of the 19th century. This situation empowers the transformation of gauchesque poetry into *criollismo*, a "tamed gauchesque poetry," and an elegy to the vanishing gaucho, symbolically elevated to a national ideomyth at the very time of his real social decimation. Creole writers, such as Alcides de María (1858–1908) and Orosmán Moratorio (1852–98), led by Elías Regules (1860–1929), the founder of traditionalism, spread this Neoromantic, nationalistic creed from journals such as *El Fogón* ([The Camp Fire] 1895–1913), as resistance to the tremendous impact of massive immigration, technological modernization, and economic adaptation to international capitalism.

Neoromanticism, associated with the creation of a national historiography by Francisco Bauzá (1849–99), Isidoro de María (1815–1906) and Carlos María Ramírez (1848–98), pervaded other foundational discourses, necessary corollaries to the institutionalization of the modern state, which included paramount educational reform by the positivist philosopher José Pedro Varela (1845–79). Juan Zorrilla de San Martín (1855–1931) – the Poet of the Fatherland – invented a Carlylean national mythology in *La leyenda patria*, 1879 [Legend of the Fatherland] and *Tabaré* (1888). These long, epic poems – oratorical rhetoric in verse – established the nation's foundational ideomyths in the extinct Charruan warriors and defeated caudillos, who automatically became the very pillars of the Uruguayan national imaginary. Fusing Walter Scott's Romanticism with Realist aesthetics, Eduardo Acevedo Díaz's (1851–1924) historical novels and gaucho romances founded a national narrative obsessed with the remnants of an ideologically unresolved past.

With the turn of the century, the literary and cultural climate changed gear. The NeoRomantics, torn between Positivist pragmatism and spiritualist idealism in their efforts to forge a National Imaginary, gave way to a new generation, born in the complex ideological flux of modernity, who initiated a creative, cultural explosion. Several aesthetic trends and contradictory philosophical schools converge in the amorphous generation of 1900. Canonical *modernista* poetry, characterized by its aestheticism, cosmopolitanism, exoticism and apparent escapism, is to be found in the figures of Julio Herrera y Reissig (1875–1910), Roberto de las Carreras (1873–1964), María Eugenia Vaz Ferreira (1875–1924) and Delmira Agustini (1886–1914). All of them, however, produced an excessive *Modernismo*: Agustini's overt sexuality pushed patriarchy to its limits, de las Carreras's dandyism scandalized social decorum, Herrera's hyperbolic and metaphoric gunfire deconstructed the very premises of *modernista* aesthetics. Because these *modernistas* were denied the traditional role of *letrados*, as members of a class in the process of extinction and due to their reluctance to professionalize in capitalist terms, their self-marginalization led them to capture the inner contradictions of peripheric modernity, and consequently to produce the most ferociously ambiguous response to it. Another sort

of ambiguity pervades the naturalistic, creole short-stories by Javier de Viana (1868–1926), and the more ambitious production of Carlos Reyles (1868–1926), a rich land-owner like Viana, who applied in his *modernista-criollista* novels and essays a conservative theory fusing Nietzsche, Marx and Social Darwinism, in order to demonstrate the natural superiority and national necessity of his class. Reyles developed his "ideology of strength" in direct response to the politics of José Batlle y Ordóñez (1856–1929) who, from a base of urban, lower-middle classes, blue-collar workers and immigrants, transformed the Uruguayan state into the most socially oriented democracy in the Americas. This democratic revolution made possible the consolidation of a new imaginary of the Model Republic, based on cosmopolitan insularism: Uruguay became an oddity, an almost European enclave on Latin American soil. Horacio Quiroga (1878–1937), another prominent member of the 1900 Generation, also reacted against the inevitability of mass society, though in a very tangential and complex way. He exiled himself to the Argentine jungles of Misiones, where, isolated from modern affairs, he cultivated a primitive self-image and perfected his metaphysically exotic short stories, which he published in Argentine magazines, thus becoming a truly modern professional writer.

Prominent in the climate of Batlle's Model Republic was the "social question," promoted by two of the main ideological discourses of modernity, anarchism and socialism. Although most of the *modernistas* adhered to some sort of libertarianism, there were a few decided activists. Ángel Falco (b. 1885) and Álvaro Armando Vasseur (1878–1969) projected the progressive cosmopolitanism of the city through their poetic rhetoric of barricade, a quasi-mystical defense of the down-trodden, and a proletarian internationalism diluted by a certain aristocratic intellectualism. Eventually, most of the anarchist poets would be co-opted by Batllism, while Emilio Frugoni (1880–1969) would become the upmost symbol of socialist politics. But it was theatre, the only truly popular media of the time, which allowed for the expression of anarchist and socialist ideas. It was in fact, an international theatre, covering a common market in both Argentina and Uruguay and was the most original mode of cultural production, following the gauchesque. This theatre arose from the mimes performed in itinerant creole circuses and was developed by the binational Podestá family. It combined drama, music and dance, fused creolist *payadas* (improvised song versification) with the Neoromantic *folletín* (serialized novels), and adapted European minor genres to allow for the symbolic representation of conflicting cultures and ideologies. Florencio Sánchez (1875–1910) and later, Ernesto Herrera (1889–1917) are the major representatives of a myriad of dramatists who portrayed in hundreds of plays the conflicts brought about by modernization, as expressed through such themes as the vanishing gaucho, struggling immigrants, class conflicts, ethnic differences, pre-capitalist and capitalist generations. Despite its general critique of traditional values, this theatre conveys the most radical analysis of the impact of peripheric modernization on the city and the countryside.

The most internationally renowned essayist of the generation of 1900 is José Enrique Rodó (1872–1917), whose early *Ariel* (1900) catapulted him to continental acclaim. Written in reaction to the Spanish-American War and the US seizure of

Cuba and Puerto Rico, *Ariel* provided young Hispanic American intellectuals with a compensatory ideology for resisting US expansionism in a symbolic way. Arielism became a trademark of Hispanic American spiritual superiority and inner sovereignty as opposed to the materialist ideology espoused by US capitalism. Despite his cultural anti-imperialism, Rodó despised mass society, and opposed Batlle's democratic project, in another dubious reaction to peripheric modernity that goes well beyond Uruguayan borders and continues to infuse Latin American thought even now.

Once the most radical excesses of *Modernismo* began to recede, the divergent strands of *criollismo*, internationalism, aestheticism, exoticism and theatrical realism converged in a modern nationalist revival, sparked by the various European vanguardisms. This movement, which embraces all forms of art, is best exemplified in painting, and in particular by Pedro Figari's (1882–1950) multi-faceted production, including early theorization in *Arte, estética, ideal*, 1912 [Art, Aesthetics, Ideal], a partially failed, pedagogical institutionalization of "industrial art," modeled after the Arts and Crafts School, and his own painting, best described as universal nativism. Figari accomplished the bucolic representation of local people and landscapes, with an ironic twist that harmonized the nostalgic recovery of popular traditions with a cosmological Utopia well-embedded in his post-impressionist palette. It is symptomatic that his Nativism coincided with the consolidation of a modern, urban society, and explains the reproduction of the rural landscape from an already urban and cosmopolitan point of view. This is equally true of Eduardo Fabini's musical impressionism (1882–1950), the poetry of Fernán Silva Valdés (1887–1975), Pedro Leandro Ipuche (1889–1976) and José Alonso y Trelles (who wrote under the pseudonym El Viejo Pancho, 1857–1924), the chronicles by Justino Zavala Muniz (1898–1968), the rural short stories by Francisco Espínola (1901–73) and Juan José Morosoli (1899–1957), the popular legends by Serafín J. García (1908–85), and the somber novels by Enrique Amorim (1900–60). Although universal nativism seems to extend to most of the artistic and literary production of the 1920s, a strictly urban and cosmopolitan literature, as exemplified by Alberto Zum Felde's literary criticism (1889–1976), begins to establish itself with increasing prominence. Theatrical production, directly linked to urban audiences since Sánchez's founding years, tended in this direction. José Pedro Bellán (1889–1930) dealt with women's emancipation in a patriarchal society in both his novels and his theatre. This heated political issue concludes, under Carlos Vaz Ferreira's humanist pragmatism (1873–1958), with one of the most advanced legal corpus in the Americas. Juan Parra del Riego (1894–1925), a Peruvian by birth, celebrated popular culture in his experimental, polirhythmic poetry on soccer, just as Alfredo Mario Ferreiro (1899–1959) paid tribute to any and all modern artifacts in his ultimately nostalgic Futurism. This absurdist, humoristic and sometimes fantastic literature led to Felisberto Hernández's (1902–64) overcharged atmospheres and Kafkian translation of Uruguayan intrahistory. Despite its apparent Utopianism, exemplified in the universal constructivism of José Torres García's art (1874–1949) and the jubilant optimism of the poetry of Juana de Ibarbourou (1895–1979), this literature was already mined with a certain melancholic skepticism. It heralded the open criticism of the

generation of 1945, another promotion loosely organized around several periodicals, among them Carlos Quijano's *Marcha* (1939–74). The hypercriticism of the generation of 1945, traced duly back to the philosophy of Vaz Ferreira, must be interpreted as an intellectual reaction to the first signs of the economic, social, political and imaginary crises of the Model Republic. This explains the fact that while previous production was eminently literary, literature from the 1950s on will be inextricably bound to social, historical and political discourses. Indeed, some of the best writers are anthropologists (Daniel Vidart), historians (Alberto Methol Ferré and José Pedro Barrán), philosophers (Arturo Ardao and Juan Luis Segundo), literary critics (Emir Rodríguez Monegal and Ángel Rama), or all of the above (Carlos Real de Azúa). The crisis of the Model Republic led to a complete revision of Uruguayan nationhood. Many embraced some sort of revolutionary politics; others fell prey to a profoundly existential nihilism. Both cases are paradigmatically represented by Mario Benedetti and Juan Carlos Onetti, respectively. Benedetti's novels, short stories and journalistic articles portrayed Montevidean everyday life so candidly that all his books, coinciding with an editorial boom, became instant best-sellers. The middle classes identified with Benedetti's ironically irascible rendition of Uruguayan hegemonic culture, and helped to challenge society's self-image at the time of its crisis. Onetti, a master novelist, represents a full-fledged indictment of Uruguayan culture as well, and perhaps its more exact interpretation. In all of his novels Onetti develops a sordid and tangoesque world of alienated, perversely sexist and solitary characters who reflect the bankruptcy of the "Switzerland of America." Like many other writers and intellectuals, Onetti was forced into exile in 1975 by the military dictatorship. His refusal to return from Spain after neodemocratic restoration in 1985, and his wish not to be buried on Uruguayan soil, must be read as his ultimate statement. But Onetti's harshness toward Uruguayan culture is not exceptional. The ethical inquiry in Carlos Martínez Moreno's novels or the oppressive depiction of marginal experiences in Armonía Somers, is paralleled in the poetry of Humberto Megget (1926–61), Ida Vitale (b. 1928), Idea Vilariño (b. 1920), Líber Falco (1906–55) and Sarandy Cabrera (b. 1923). The founding in 1942 of the *Comedia Nacional*, through the united efforts of writer and politician Zavala Muniz, author-impresario Ángel Curotto and the Spanish-born actress Margarita Xirgu, began a second theatrical Golden Age, which extended, in the 1950s and 1960s, into the full-fledged production of an independent theatre movement. Numerous troupes stage plays by Andrés Castillo, Antonio Larreta, Carlos Maggi and Mauricio Rosencof, who explore and dissect social and cultural disintegration through the combination of absurdist and expressionist comedy and carnivalesque, grotesque tragedy.

By the end of the 1960s, Uruguay had entered into a definitive social and political crisis. Economic debacle, institutional instability, trade-unionist defiance, urban guerrilla warfare, and military repression shaped the climate of violent confrontation that forged literary responses to a now unstable universe. The poetry of Hugo Achúgar, Jorge Arbeleche, Nancy Bacelo, Washington Benavides, Marosa di Giorgio, Circe Maia and Walter Ortiz y Ayala, and narratives by Anderssen Banchero, Gley Eyherabide, Híber Conteris, Sylvia Lago, Mario Levrero,

Cristina Peri Rossi and Teresa Porzecanski, all share a political urgency manifested in an allegorical leap of the imagination. Their sense of urgency can probably be best exemplified by Eduardo Galeano's best-seller *Las venas abiertas de América Latina*, 1971 (*The Open Veins of Latin America*), in which his nervously journalistic style contrasts sharply with an ambitious scope.

The military coup of 1973 marked the beginning of the end. Neofascist repression forced most of the intelligentsia into exile, thus breaking Uruguayan cultural production in two: a culture of exile, which, cut loose from its moorings, drifted between a nostalgic longing for the no longer viable Model Republic, and its own enrichment through marginality in other hegemonic environments. The counterculture of *in*xile, a culture of endurance due to repressive military politics under neofascism, was forced to resort to non-canonical artistic and literary means. This climate nurtured a highly coded poetry that added the new voices of Rafael Courtoisie, Alfredo Fressia, Ibero Gutiérrez, Alicia Migdal and Eduardo Milán. The "popular song" movement, the main vehicle of cultural resistance, became the cauldron for a renaissance of several subcultural genres such as carnival's *murga* and African-Uruguayan *candombe*, as well as rural folk music and several trends of fusion rock. Some of the best poetry was produced to be sung, in exile by Alfredo Zitarrosa or Jaime Roos, or in inxile, by Leo Masliah, Horacio Buscaglia, Fernando Cabrera, and *murga* bands such as *La soberana* and *Falta y resto*.

After the restoration of neodemocracy in 1985, the counterculture of inxile gave way to a proliferation of subcultures, on a fragmented scene characterized by intense confrontation, aesthetic diversity, and the emergence of new cultural practices and artistic discourses. The testimonial literature by Fernando Butazzoni, Eleuterio Fernández Huidobro, Ernesto González Bermejo and Rosencof, and the narrative inquiry into the colonial and indigenous past by Alejandro Paternain, Tomás de Mattos and Napoleón Baccino Ponce de León, as well as the plays of Milton Schinca and Alberto Restuccia, contribute to a new questioning of national identity. The popular subcultures, suppressed until now, have created a place for themselves. Popular song is no longer enough to convey the creativity of the youngest poets, who resort to graffiti, underground magazines, performances and presses devoted exclusively to production on the edge of hegemonic culture.

The liminal post-vanguardist poetry by Cecilia Álvarez, Héctor Bardanca, Lalo Barrubia, Luis Bravo, Silvia Guerra, or Gustavo Wojciechowski, complements narratives by Pablo Casacuberta, Mario Delgado Aparaín, Leo Masliah, Elbio Rodríguez Barilari and Gabriel Vieira, who all seek, through the hybridization of genres and styles, to translate the perplexity of a culture at the postnational crossroads. They produce, alongside other liminoid discourses such as graffiti, rock or carnival, the most profound demystification of hegemonic Uruguayan culture ever witnessed. Paradoxically, they prove, as well, its inner vitality in the postmodern transnational arena.

ABRIL TRIGO

Further Reading

Achúgar, Hugo, *Poesía y sociedad (Uruguay 1880–1911)*, Montevideo: Arca, 1985

Benedetti, Mario, *Literatura uruguaya siglo XX*, 2nd edition, Montevideo: Alfa, 1969

Kantaris, Elia Geoffrey, *The Subversive Psyche. Contemporary Women's Narrative from Argentina and Uruguay*, Oxford: Clarendon Press, 1996

Moraña, Mabel, *Memorias de la generación fantasma*, Montevideo: Montesexto, 1988

Olivera-Williams, María Rosa, "La literatura uruguaya del Proceso: exilio/ insilio; continuismo/ invención," *Nuevo Texto Crítico* 3 (1988)

Oreggioni, Alberto (editor), *Diccionario de literatura uruguaya*, 3 vols, Montevideo: Arca, 1987–91

Rama, Ángel (editor), *Cien años de raros: antología y prólogo*, Montevideo: Arca, 1966

Rama, Ángel, *La generación crítica (1939–1969)*, Montevideo: Arca, 1971

Rela, Walter, *Historia del teatro uruguayo 1808–1968*, Montevideo: Ediciones Banda Oriental, 1969

Sosnowski, Saúl (editor), *Represión, exilio y democracia: la cultura uruguaya*, College Park: University of Maryland, and Montevideo: Ediciones Banda Oriental, 1987

Trigo, Abril, *Caudillo, estado nación. Literatura, historia e ideología en el Uruguay*, Gaithersburg, Maryland: Hispamérica, 1990

Zum Felde, Alberto, *Proceso intelectual del Uruguay*, 3 vols, Montevideo: Ediciones del Nuevo Mundo, 3rd edition, 1967

Special Issues of Journals

Revista Iberoamericana, vol. 58/160–61 (July–December 1992)
Afro-Hispanic Review, vol. 12/2 (Fall 1993) [Contains several articles on African-Uruguayan writers]

Rodolfo Usigli 1905–1979

Mexican dramatist

Nearly forty plays, created over a period of as many years and ranging from one-act farces to a full-length historical drama in verse, constitute the dramatic work of Rodolfo Usigli. Few have been translated, many of them are still unperformed and many remained unpublished until the collected edition in two volumes (1963–66), which regrettably did not include the Shavian prefaces Usigli wrote for some of the plays – they were reprinted in a third volume (1979). Fortunately, Usigli's detailed stage directions make the action of his plays easy to visualise, compensating in some measure for the lack of performances.

Usigli's comedies and dramas of family life typically present cases of marital infidelity, clashes between generations, and secrets from the past which threaten the present. In *El niño y la niebla*, 1936 [The Child and the Mist], Marta attempts to turn Daniel, the son of her loveless marriage to Guillermo Estrada, against his father, and through hypnopaedic suggestion she persuades the boy, a sleepwalker, that he must kill Guillermo. Daniel wakes up as he is about to shoot, goes out and kills himself. Marta refuses to leave Guillermo for her lover Mauricio, fearing that any other child of hers would inherit her family's madness, which she has now recognised in Daniel. Mental instability also plays a part in *Jano es una muchacha*, 1952 [Janus is a Girl]; Marina, schoolgirl daughter of Víctor Iglesias, has unknowingly repeated her dead mother Arcelia's fascination with a brothel, which Víctor is forced to admit that he owns; Arcelia's experiences there were the result of her sense of guilt after being raped. Víctor further confesses that his real love, which he has suppressed for years, is for Arcelia's sister Eulalia; horrified and disgusted, Eulalia kills him. The secret concealed from Carlos Torres-Mendoza in *La familia cena en casa*, 1942 [The Family Dines at Home] concerns his dead father's conduct; Carlos believes his friend Enrique's accusation that his malpractice and swindling had created the family fortune. His mother Matilde sets matters right by revealing that her husband had in fact secretly helped Enrique's father to avoid loss of all his assets and later supported Enrique's family when his mother's gambling had threatened ruin. The farewell tour by Verónica in *La función de despedida*, 1949 [Farewell Performance], begins in her home town, where she stays in a guest-house run by Manuel, the childhood sweetheart whom she had left behind when she set out on her stage career. Verónica's recognition of Manuel comes late, but in time to prevent him from repeating the errors of the past by frustrating his own children's ambitions.

Excessive respect for appearances and the concealment of true motives, which provide so much of the material for the plays on social themes, were easily carried over into Usigli's political satires, a subgenre he cultivated throughout his career. His first explorations of the field produced the *Tres comedias impolíticas*, 1933–35 [Three Impolitic Comedies], in the first of which, *Noche de estío* [A Night in High Summer], during what proves to be an abortive communist coup, the General/President makes a spirited defence of the Mexican Revolution and the benefits it has brought, and of his own

exercise of power, to two of his ministers and four members of the younger generation of varied views, but once the danger has passed his chief concern is to ensure that what has transpired remains secret. The second play, *El Presidente y el ideal* [The President and the Ideal], presents, in a series of sketches set in a school, a university, a newspaper office, an army mess, a peasant community, a café and a meeting of mothers of schoolchildren, the comic effects of the introduction of President Ávalos's doctrinaire socialist program. The politicians declare that Ávalos must soon fall, but when they and the military meet at the residence of "el Jefe" (the General of *Noche de estío*) to confront the president, it is Ávalos who emerges triumphant, while the former leader is expelled – just as Calles was by President Cárdenas following the Mexican presidential election of 1934. Such specific reference to contemporary politics is avoided in the third play of the set, *Estado de secreto* [State of Secrecy], which portrays the corrupt dealings of a minister of sufficient guile and influence as to be able to deceive the president over a murder committed by one of his aides and eventually to achieve the president's resignation. The minister of *La última puerta*, 1934–36 [The Last Door], is never seen, and indeed his very existence is doubted by those who attend his office daily; when they mount an assault on his office, he resigns. Inadequate cultural policies and corrupt administration are also a main issue in *La exposición*, 1955–59 [The Exhibition], though much of the play concerns art, artists and their critics in modern Mexico, where by that time Usigli himself had held various influential official positions.

One other play falls within this category, though it is not set in Mexico but in "Indolandia," the southern neighbour of powerful "Demolandia;" *Un día de éstos*, 1953 (*One of These Days*), deals with the fortuitous accession to the presidency of a senior official, following the assassination of the country's political leaders. Gómez Urbina's principal tasks as president are to investigate the assassinations and prepare for new elections; his efficiency enables him to discover the truth, but as a former president is involved, he needs to gain the people's support for administering justice. This he does by provoking Demolandia, expelling the ambassador on the grounds of unwarranted interference in Indolandian affairs, and blackmailing former presidents into paying off the national debt from the fortunes they built up during their terms in office. An attempted assassination fails, but brings on a fatal heart attack, whereupon the politicians immediately break into a squabble over the succession. The fantasy world of Indolandia and Demolandia may not offer any realistic solution to Mexican problems, but the play includes acute observations on contemporary geopolitics, with Maoist China, Argentina and Britain also appearing under transparent aliases.

Gómez Urbina in some ways recalls César Rubio, the central character of *El gesticulador*, 1938 (*The Great Gesture*, or *Another Caesar*), and Usigli's most complex creation. César, a historian who taught the Mexican Revolution in Mexico City, moves north to his home town in search of a better living, against the wishes of his children. His opportunity comes through exploiting his knowledge of a leading figure of the Revolution who shared his name and birthplace to impress Bolton, a young US historian. When Bolton publicises his "discovery" of the legendary César Rubio, César is caught up in local politics, becoming the official PRI candidate for the provincial governorship. His knowledge of his namesake and of the Revolution makes his success certain, causing his rival, who had killed the other Rubio in 1916, to have him assassinated. Like Gómez Urbina, César emerges from obscurity to demonstrate real ability to formulate policy, but he is not given the chance to put his ideas to the test. His tragic flaw is the self-delusion which leads him to adopt another man's identity, in the belief that his policies will benefit Mexico. As in his other political plays, Usigli points clearly to popular disillusionment with the results of the revolutionary struggle, not least because of the corruption which bedevils the higher echelons of the ruling party. The Revolution itself in 1915–17, seen from the sidelines of a working-class suburb of Mexico City, is presented in *Las madres*, 1949–60 [Mothers], a loosely-structured pageant of a society at war, torn apart by factions, where fathers are mostly away at the front, replaced as role models by brutal soldiery.

Usigli's preoccupation with Mexico's identity underlies his three major historical plays. The earliest, *Corona de sombra*, 1943 (*Crown of Shadows*), deals with the brief reign of the Emperor Maximilian, seen in flashback during a conversation in 1927 between a Mexican historian and Maximilian's widow Charlotte. The scenes from the past show Maximilian as convinced of the necessity to draw all Mexicans into the political process, against the advice of *criollo* aristocrats and European military commanders. In the historian's view Maximilian achieved true independence for Mexico, though failing personally. An earlier opportunity to establish Mexican independence presented itself to Cortés, who in *Corona de fuego*, 1943 (*Crown of Fire*), is seen contemplating an alliance with Cuauhtémoc, eventually rejected in favour of the benefit to be gained from loyalty and obedience to Charles V of Spain. The circumstances of the miracle at Tepeyácatl in 1531, which created the conditions for the cult of Our Lady of Guadalupe, are the subject of *Corona de luz*, 1963 (*Crown of Light*): for Fray Juan de Zumárraga, bishop of Mexico, the true miracle lies in the acceptance of the event by the Indian population as a miracle of their own, not alien but Mexican.

RON KEIGHTLEY

Biography

Born in Mexico City, 17 November 1905. Both parents were recent immigrants to Mexico. Father died when Rodolfo was a baby; Polish mother a beneficial influence in his formative years. She raised four children during the decade of the Mexican Revolution and, despite a tough life, taught her children Polish, German and French. Usigli struggled against both physical handicaps (poor eyesight and hearing) and poverty. Unable to complete secondary education, but attended adult evening courses for two years (1923–25). By 1933 he was working at the Universidad Nacional Autónoma de México (UNAM) and held an administrative post in the Ministry of Education. Recieved a Rockefeller scholarship to study drama at Yale University, New Haven, Connecticut, 1935–36. Joined diplomatic service and spent period 1944–46 in France. Able to meet George Bernard Shaw whom he had venerated for many years. *El gesticulador* premiered in Mexico City in 1947 and was a success. Travelled abroad again in 1956 and held diplomatic posts in Lebanon (1957–60) and Norway (1960–72). Returned to Mexico in early 1970s. Last years were of loneliness and bitterness because his dramaturgy had been superseded by that of a younger generation. Died in Mexico City, 8 June 1979.

Selected Works

Plays
Teatro completo de Rodolfo Usigli, Mexico City: Fondo de Cultura Económica, 3 vols, 1963–79 [A full list of these plays is given in the bibliography of Peter R. Beardsell's study on Usigli (see below)]

Essays
México en el teatro, Mexico City: Imprenta Mundial, 1932; as *Mexico in the Theater*, translated by Wilder P. Scott, University, Mississippi: Romance Monographs, 1976
Anatomía del teatro, Mexico City: Gráficas Menhir, 1967
Conversaciones y encuentros de Rodolfo Usigli, Mexico City: Novaro, 1974

Novel
Ensayo de un crimen, Mexico City: América, 1944

Poetry
Conversación desesperada, poemas, Mexico City: Caudernos de México Nuevo, 1938

Further Reading

Beardsell, Peter R., *A Theatre for Cannibals. Rodolfo Usigli and the Mexican Stage*, Rutherford, New Jersey: Fairleigh Dickinson University Press, and London: Associated University Presses, 1992
Compton, Timothy G. "Máscaras mexicanas' in Rodolfo Usigli's *Jano es una muchacha*," *Latin American Theatre Review*, vol. 25/1 (1991)
Donahue, Francis, "Toward a Mexican National Theatre," *Revista Iberoamericana*, vol. 19/3–4 (1989)
Foster, David William, "*El gesticulador*: El Gran Teatro de México," in his *Estudios sobre teatro méxicano contemporáneo: semiología de la competencia teatral*, New York: Peter Lang, 1984
Layera, Ramón, "Mecanismos de fabulación y mitificación de la historia en las 'Comedias impolíticas' y las *Coronas* de Rodolfo Usigli," *Latin American Theatre Review*, vol. 18/2 (1985)
Moraña, Mabel, "Historicismo y legitimación del poder en *El gesticulador* y *Corona de sombra*," *Revista Iberoamericana*, vol. 55/148–49 (1989)

Arturo Uslar Pietri 1906–

Venezuelan prose writer

Arturo Uslar Pietri is certainly one of the most renowned writers of contemporary Venezuelan literature. The depth of his culture, the breadth of his interests and the range of his publications are impressive: for almost seven decades (since the 1920s) he has been making frequent contributions in the following fields: poetry, short stories, journalistic articles, novels, plays, and essays are part of his voluminous work.

Uslar's vocation for public service explains the form and orientation of the major part of his essayistic work. Very few of his essays are of a lyrical or speculative nature. Most of them, before being collected in books, have appeared in "Pizarrón" [Blackboard], a weekly syndicated column that he has been publishing with very few interruptions, since 1947. Uslar's special talent is to present even the most complicated subject in a clear and understandable way. His goal has been to reach not just an intellectual elite, but the largest possible audience. Many of his articles deal with current events he interprets with characteristic lucidity and synthetic power. He frequently resorts to catchy phrases and symbols to convey his ideas. In July 1936 in an article appearing in a Caracas newspaper he coined the phrase "Sembrar el petróleo" (Sowing Our Oil). With remarkable insight he warned of a future catastrophe if the economic benefits derived from oil were not used to improve Venezuela's agricultural output and create new industries that would free the country from its dependence on that product. Years later, in De una a otra Venezuela, 1950 [From One Venezuela to Another], he identified as Venezuela's defining historical plight, the battle against the Minotaur of Oil, a monster devouring the vital substance of his country. The exorbitant and foolish squandering by Venezuelans of the profits from petroleum is the "festín de Baltasar" (Belshazzar's feast). The message of future doom, he said, was already visible, just as it was to the biblical king in the midst of his orgy.

In many of his essays Uslar searches for the identity of Venezuelans and Latin Americans. In Letras y hombres de Venezuela, 1948 [Men and Literature in Venezuela], he identified important traits in the collective soul from which Venezuelan literature stems: a passion for equality, a messianic cult and the psychology of the mestizo. In other essays Uslar expands his search to find the true source of Latin American uniqueness. Some of his observations had previously appeared in the writings of José Vasconcelos, Alfonso Reyes and Germán Arciniegas. But Uslar's original contributions to the subject are also important. In Las Nubes, 1951 [The Clouds], mestizaje is described as the essential feature of Latin American identity. For Uslar, though, the racial aspect is not as important or significant as the cultural one. He believes that many 19th-century thinkers erred in seeing the mixing of races as an undesirable trait of inferiority: "They forgot that Europe was a veritable racial hodge-podge and that the mixing of races . . . was far from being the sole cause or only form of cultural mestizaje." This latter characteristic, according to Uslar, may be seen, for example, in Latin American art and literature, where the linear succession of schools and epochs which characterizes Europe, is replaced by a simultaneous coexistence of old and new tendencies. In Godos, insurgentes y visionarios, 1986 [Conservatives, Insurgents and Visionaries], Uslar invites Latin Americans to accept all the elements of their past and cast aside the prejudices that have prevented them from fully understanding their heritage, or the representative nature of the many caudillos (strong men) that have dominated their history.

This deep desire to understand the past may explain why, to this date, Uslar has written mostly historical novels. Uslar sees history not only as an explanation of the past, but also as "an opportunity for creating the future." Rather than being interested in the linear history of events and people, he has focused on "that process of making and unmaking, more suitable for the novelist than the historian" (Del hacer y deshacer [About Doing and Undoing]). Uslar's seven novels, published between 1931 and 1990, cover an ample historical panorama. The most successful of them and one that has received the greatest critical acclaim is Las lanzas coloradas, 1931 (The Red Lances). The most important episodes in this novel take place at the beginning of 1814, a period characterized by furious battles between the royalist Boves and the generals in the rebel camp. The reduced historical space allows a more dramatic and poetic presentation of the plot. Before deciding to write this novel, Uslar had thought of preparing a movie script. Many critics have pointed out the cinematographic qualities of this work. Uslar's focus changes alternatively between the two main characters. This parallelistic technique is also used with respect to Boves and Bolívar, whose arrivals are announced by powerful and rhythmic leitmotifs.

The language has the most varied nuances, from the colorful deformations in the fables told by the African slaves, to the graphic description of the gory battles where blood itself has a life of its own. Uslar illuminates a tragic period of Venezuelan history and present the conflict as a veritable civil war where class and racial hatred play a significant role. Las lanzas coloradas gives an epic flavor to its battle scenes and spins a story that keeps its readers enthralled. The novelist integrates successfully the lyrical, dramatic and epic elements in his work, without the unnecessary interference of the narrator, or the excessive details of other historical novels.

Uslar's subsequent novels did not attain the critical success enjoyed by Las lanzas coloradas. Critics noted the traditional format and lack of experimentation in these works. Uslar's conservative formal approach may be explained by his desire to give more depth and prominence to the periods and events related to his protagonists. Furthermore, he was not willing to enhance artistic creativity at the expense of historical truthfulness. In his last two novels, La isla de Róbinson, 1981 [Robinson's Island], and La visita en el tiempo, 1990 [The Recurring Visit], non-traditional techniques are added. In the former, two different streams of time illuminate Simón Rodríguez's personality, ideas, triumphs and failures. In the latter, mythopoetic elements associated with Hamlet, Calderón's Segismundo and Don Juan are developed and woven around the figure of Don John of Austria, the winner at the battle of Lepanto. These novels represent a modest but significant attempt by Uslar to satisfy some of his critics' objections, without resorting to the falsification evidenced in some popular historical novels written by other Latin American writers.

Uslar's short stories have received greater critical acclaim than his novels. He has shown in that genre the desire to revise constantly and to renew his themes, emphases, techniques and narrative approaches. Uslar's first collection of short stories, *Barrabás y otros relatos*, 1928 [Barabbas and Other Stories], had a great impact on Venezuelan letters. Most critics consider this book a landmark that signals the beginning of the modern short story in Venezuela. Before *Barrabás*, the dominant approach had been *criollismo*, with its often plastic and superficial native landscape and excessive description of "typical" garments and dialect. *Barrabás* does not completely exclude the native scenery (six of its sixteen stories have regional settings), but it generally avoids stereotypical language or the usual small town setting of *costumbrista* stories. The influence of avant-garde movements in *Barrabás* may be detected in its metaphorical images and in the use of oneiric or subconscious states. The cosmopolitan element is present in several stories. One of them, which provides the name to the collection, depicts Barabbas as a passive human being involved involuntarily in a trascendental event.

In his second collection, *Red*, 1936 [The Net], Uslar effectively introduces magical realism in Latin American letters. A few years later, he would define this orientation as the "treatment of man as a mystery in the midst of realistic data" and also as "a poetic discovery or denial of reality" (*Letras y hombres*). In magical realism, there is an unusual fact or circumstance whose logic or satisfactory explanation is withheld by the writer. More than one third of the stories in *Red* can be ascribed to magic realism. On the other hand, almost all the stories in the book have native settings. The avant-garde images so prevalent in *Barrabás* are practically absent. Literary techniques are much more varied and include the use of counterpoint, superposition of time levels, unattributed dialogs, personification and alliteration.

In *Treinta hombres y sus sombras*, 1949 [Thirty Men and Their Shadows], Uslar again changes his approach. He continues to present *criollo* scenarios, but does away with metaphoric recourses while using the simplest or most direct descriptive techniques. Uslar realizes a deeper immersion into his country's rural environment and its culture by incorporating a modest amount of dialectal words and expressions, and a greater representation of collective psychology and folkloric elements related to the oral tradition of Indians and other rural communities.

In his last two collections of short stories, Uslar changes course again. This time, magic realism and rural settings lose importance to urban environments and political and metaphysical themes. In *Pasos y pasajeros*, 1966 [Sketches of Travellers], he uses more often than before the first-person narrative voice in order to attain a more intimate approach to his characters. In *Los ganadores*, 1980 [The Winners], the apocalyptical theme acquires significant relevance.

Arturo Uslar's many talents and versatility have inspired admiration in many fellow Latin Americans. He has been called "a tropical Goethe" and the most intelligent Venezuelan of his generation. Jorge Luis Borges once said, in order to describe his many achievements, that there were many men in that single name.

In spite of these tributes, Uslar's recognition has not been as widespread as that achieved by the Boom writers. It is possible that his centrist and moderate positions on political and economic matters have contributed, outside Venezuela and Spain, to the lesser appreciation of his work, a preterition that stands in contrast with the greater appeal enjoyed by other Latin American writers on the left side of the political spectrum. Uslar's important contribution to the historical novel (besides *Las lanzas coloradas*) may one day receive its due when less subjective evaluative criteria prevail. Regardless of his lack of success outside the essay and the short story, Uslar's extraordinary versatility and profound intuition makes him stand out, like Unamuno in his time, as a towering figure in the public life of his country. Arturo Uslar has gained recognition, not only for his literary achievements but also for having served, since the 1930s, as a committed thinker trying to bring awareness, understanding and resolution to the most pressing and intricate problems of his time.

JORGE MARBÁN

Biography

Born in Caracas, Venezuela, 16 May 1906; son of General Arturo Uslar and of Helena Pietri. Preparatory education in private schools. Enrolled at Central University of Venezuela, 1923; PhD in political science, 1929. Entered diplomatic corps and sent to Paris where he shared an apartment for a time with Miguel Ángel Asturias and Alejo Carpentier. Returned to Venezuela in 1934 and began career as university teacher. Appointed Minister of Education, 1939, of Finance, 1941, and of the Interior, 1942. Legitimate government overthrown by coup in 1945. Went into exile and lived in Canada and the United States. Taught Spanish American literature at Columbia University, New York, 1947. Returned to Venezuela in 1950 and earned his living by teaching and journalism. Elected as independent senator in National Congress for Caracas, 1959. Unsuccessful candidate for presidency in 1963. Secretary General of an opposition party of the Right, the Frente Nacional Democrático. Served as senator, 1964–69. Awarded the Rómulo Gallegos Prize in 1990 for *La visita en el tiempo*.

Selected Works

Short Fiction
Barrabás y otros relatos, Caracas: Vargas, 1928
Red, Caracas: Elite, 1936
Treinta hombres y sus sombras, Buenos Aires: Losada, 1949
Pasos y pasajeros, Madrid: Taurus, 1966
El prójimo y otros cuentos, Barcelona: Bruguera, 1978
Los ganadores, Barcelona: Seix Barral, 1980

Novels
Las lanzas coloradas, Madrid: Zeus, 1931; as *The Red Lances*, translated by Harriet de Onís, New York: Knopf, 1963
El camino de El Dorado, Buenos Aires: Losada, 1947
El laberinto de fortuna: un retrato en la geografía, Buenos Aires: Losada, 1962
El laberinto de fortuna: estación de máscaras, Buenos Aires: Losada, 1964
Oficio de difuntos, Barcelona: Seix Barral, 1976
La isla de Róbinson, Barcelona: Seix Barral, 1981
La visita en el tiempo, Madrid: Mondadori, 1990

Plays

Teatro, Caracas and Madrid: EDIME, 1958 [Includes *El día de Antero Albán*, *La Tebaida*, *El dios invisible* and *La fuga de Miranda*]

Chúo Gil y las tejedoras, Caracas: Vargas, 1960

Essays

Letras y hombres de Venezuela, Mexico City: Fondo de Cultura Económica, 1948

De una y otra Venezuela, Caracas: Mesa Redonda, 1950

Las nubes, Caracas: Ministerio de Educación, 1951

Tierra venezolana, Caracas: EDIME, 1953

Breve historia de la novela hispanoamericana, Caracas: EDIME, 1954

El otoño en Europa, Caracas: Mesa Redonda, 1954

Valores humanos, Caracas: EDIME, 1955

La ciudad de nadie; El otoño en Europa; Un turista en el Cercano Oriente, Buenos Aires: Losada, 1960

Del hacer y deshacer de Venezuela, Caracas: Ateneo, 1962

En busca del nuevo mundo, Mexico City: Fondo de Cultura Económica, 1969

El globo de colores, Caracas: Monte Ávila, 1975

Fantasmas de dos mundos, Barcelona: Seix Barral, 1979

Bolívar hoy, Caracas: Monte Ávila, 1983

Godos, insurgentes y visionarios, Barcelona: Seix Barral, 1986

Los venezolanos y el petróleo, Caracas: Banco de Venezuela, 1990

La creación del Nuevo Mundo, Madrid: Mapfre, 1991

Anthologies and Compilations

Obras selectas, Caracas: EDIME, 1967

Cuarenta ensayos, edited by Efrain Subero, Caracas: Monte Ávila, 1990

Cuarenta cuentos, edited by Efrain Subero, Caracas: Monte Ávila, 1990

Cuentos de la realidad mágica, Madrid: Mondadori, 1992

Further Reading

There are very few studies on Arturo Uslar Pietri in English. In Spanish, Domingo Miliani is considered to be the most important critic of his narrative work. Uslar's conservative positions have elicited a few negative appraisals from Marxist critics such as Mario Sczichman and Manuel Caballero. The bibliography by the Fundación Polar and Alexis Márquez's intertextual analysis of Uslar's historical novels are among the most important recent contributions to the understanding and critical appraisal of his work.

Barrientos, Juan José, "Aguirre y la rebelión de los Marañones," *Cuadernos Americanos*, nueva época 2 (March–April 1948)

Beaupied, Aida M. and Luz María Umpierre, "*Écriture* de ambigüedad en 'La lluvia' de Arturo Uslar Pietri," *Hispanic Journal*, vol. 3/2 (Spring 1982)

Caballero, Manuel, "Uslar Pietri, Garmendia: Two Nations," *Cultura Universitaria* vol. 1 (1966)

Cluff, Russell M., "El realismo mágico en los cuentos de Uslar Pietri," *Cuadernos Americanos* 294 (January–February 1976)

Curraño de Dobsky, Inés, "*Las lanzas coloradas*: una mitificación de la historia," *Revista de Literatura Hispanoamericana*, Maracaibo, vol. 2 (January–June 1972)

Eskenazi, Margarita, *Uslar Pietri: muchos hombres en un solo nombre*, Caracas: Caralex, 1988

Fabbiani Ruiz, José, "De *Barrabás* a *Treinta hombres y sus sombras*," in *Cuentos y cuentistas*, Caracas: Cruz del Sur, 1951

Fundación Polar, *Contribución a la Biblio-hemerografía de Arturo Uslar Pietri*, Caracas: Ex-Libris, 1989

Garmendia, Salvador, prologue to *Moscas, árboles y hombres*, Barcelona: Planeta, 1972

Hamilton, Carlos D., "Arturo Uslar Pietri, novelista contemporáneo," *Cuadernos Americanos* 242 (1982)

Marbán, Jorge, "La génesis de la violencia americana en tres novelas históricas de Uslar Pietri," *Explicación de Textos Literarios*, vol. 10/1 (1981)

_____ "El tema político en la cuentística de Arturo Uslar Pietri," *Crítica Hispánica*, vol. 12/1–2 (1990)

_____ "*La visita en el tiempo* de Arturo Uslar Pietri: estructuras míticas en una novela histórica," *Explicación de textos literarios*, vol. 22/1 (1993)

Márquez Rodríguez, Alexis, *Historia y ficción en la novela venezolana*, Caracas: Monte Ávila, 1991

Miliani, Domingo, "La sociedad venezolana en una novela de Arturo Uslar Pietri. Aproximación al análisis de *Las lanzas coloradas*," *Thesaurus*, vol. 23/2 (1968)

_____ *Arturo Uslar Pietri: renovador del cuento venezolano*, Caracas: Monte Ávila, 1969

_____ "Arturo Uslar Pietri. La lucha con el minotauro," *Revista Iberoamericana* vol., 60/166–67 (January–June 1994)

Oropeza, José Napoleón, *Para forjar un rostro: notas sobre la novelística venezolana actual*, Valencia, Venezuela: Vadell, 1984

Peña, Alfredo, *Conversaciones con Arturo Uslar Pietri*, Caracas: Ateneo, 1978

Polanco Alcántara, Tomás (editor), *El valor humano de Arturo Uslar Pietri*, Caracas: Ediciones de la Academia Nacional de la Historia, 1984

Sczichman, Mario, *Uslar. Cultura y dependencia*, Caracas: Vadell y Hermanos, 1975

Vivas Maldonado, José Luis, *La cuentística de Arturo Uslar Pietri*, Caracas: Ediciones de la Universidad Central, 1963

V

Luisa Valenzuela 1938–

Argentine prose writer

The most marked characteristic of Luisa Valenzuela's fiction is a pushing against censorship of all kinds. She said, in an unpublished interview of 1984: "Yo creo que las cosas hay que decirlas. Que lo que se tiene que evitar son las barreras de la autocensura, o peor que la autocensura, las barreras de esa censura interna que te impide decir ciertas verdades, y que te impide decir así, lo que en el fondo uno está queriendo decir, sin saberlo." (I believe that things must be said. That what must be avoided are the barriers of self-censorship, or worse than self-censorship, the barriers of that internal censorship which prevents you from saying that which deep down you really want to say without realising it). This striving for a kind of freedom takes the form of writing which often plays with language, with shifting narrators, with perceptions of the unconscious, and reveals tremendous humour.

Her first novel, *Hay que sonreír*, 1966 (*Clara*) shows interestingly feminist leanings. It describes with sympathy and humour the events in the life of a naive young prostitute whose main ambition is to "use her head." The novel plays on the paradigm of the "good woman / whore," as the girl is "saved" by a series of men, all of whom exploit and silence her in different ways. There is an ironic twist towards the end in an episode in which she is at last permitted to "use her head," but rather than using it as she had imagined, for thought, she is allowed to use it only as an object, an Aztec flower in a side-show. Ultimately, in a further twist, in what becomes an almost inevitable, logical step, her throat is cut, thus severing the recalcitrant head. It is a theatrical enactment of the archetypal Greek image which equates woman with matter and the body and man with the mind or the head. Any attempt at disrupting this state of affairs leads to a revelation of the difficulties surrounding women's access to thought and to language.

This was followed by a collection of short stories, *Los heréticos*, 1967 [The Heretics], which again has a playful quality, and whose subject matter is encapsulated in its title, and then in 1972 by what is without a doubt her most radical novel, *El gato eficaz*, 1972 [The Effective Cat].

It is virtually impossible to provide any meaningful synopsis of this novel since it has virtually no plot or stabilising elements. It is, however, a very richly textured work, a *tour de force* which plays with masks, one of Valenzuela's obsessions, and with supple, shifting narrators to create a work which can be seen ultimately to deconstuct the notion of binary oppositions: black/white, life/death, and most fruitfully, masculine/feminine. The novel constantly emphasises the cultural nature of rigid notions of femininity, and pleads at its end for a rebirth, a need for greater openness and fluidity in our views of identity and gender difference.

The horrendous political violence in Argentina, which began in the mid 1970s, was to have a profound effect on Valenzuela's work. As she said in an interview given to Magdalena García Pinto: "There comes a time when you can't break away from it, when the horror becomes so great that silencing it is worse." While the playfulness, humour and fragmentation continue, the focus is now on the fear, violence and disappearances which had become an overwhelming reality.

Aquí pasan cosas raras, 1975 (*Strange Things Happen Here*), is a series of short stories, charged with a mordant humour, which with great humanity point out the pain, the tragedy and often also the absurdity of this terrible political situation, and it is reflected to a greater or lesser degree in all of Valenzuela's subsequent work, even, it could be said, in a novel that would appear to be distanced in both time and space, the later *Novela negra con argentinos*, 1990 (*Black Novel with Argentines*). This work, which has some of the characteristics of a thriller, is set in New York, among Argentine exiles, but the paranoia apparent in their lives and the difficulties that they encounter conjure up almost a mirror image of the psychological mindset and violence which had existed in their homeland.

Probably the most interesting novel to have emerged from this period is one which deals overtly with the political situation, *Cola de lagartija*, 1983 (*The Lizard's Tail*). The key players in this work are a wizard; a thinly-disguised López Rega, Argentina's Minister of Welfare during Perón's last government and that of his third wife, Isabel; and others representing Perón himself, his second wife, Evita, long dead, but still a potent myth in Argentine culture and the military rulers. On the other side are the Argentine people, particularly those opposed to the terror, symbolised by a writer by the name of Luisa Valenzuela. But while these references to historical fact are crucial to an understanding of the novel it is far from being a historical or even realist text, rather it works within the realms of myth, of metaphor, of the unconscious and of the materiality of language. The wizard plots his dreams of omnipotence to the point where he actually implodes, and in the meantime the counterforce, Luisa Valenzuela, works constantly seeking increasingly inventive tactics to bring about his downfall. Ultimately by becoming ever more fluid, even to the extent of rewriting language, she is the one who survives to tell the tale, while his rigidity and arrogance are self-defeating.

So it is that even in this unusual novel which is so specific in terms of its setting and of the situation it portrays, Valenzuela's major themes return. For it is by means of a language outside of normally accepted discourse, beyond the tentacles of censorship, that freedom is achieved, and this struggle is particularly relevant for women who must get beyond the limitations imposed on them and search for what she describes in "Mis brujas favoritas" (My Favourite Witches) as "un lenguaje femenino en absoluto emparentado con aquellas azucaradas palabras con las que hemos sido recubiertas a lo largo de siglos" (a feminine language which has absolutely nothing to do with those sickly-sweet words we have been coated with over the centuries).

LINDA CRAIG

Biography

Born in Buenos Aires, Argentina, 26 November 1938. Attended Belgrano Girls' School; Colegio Nacional Vicente López, Buenos Aires; University of Buenos Aires, BA. Married Théodore Marjak in 1958 (divorced); one daughter. Lived in Paris, 1958–61; assistant editor of Sunday supplement, La Nación, Buenos Aires, 1964–69; freelance journalist in the United States, Europe and Mexico, 1970–73, and Buenos Aires, 1973–79; writer-in-residence, Columbia University, New York, 1980–83; Visiting Professor, New York University, 1984–89; Fellow, New York Institute for the Humanities. Lived in New York, Buenos Aires and Tepoztlán, Mexico, 1978–89. Recipient of several awards including Fondo Nacional de las Artes Award, 1966 and 1973; Instituto Nacional de Cinematografía Award, 1973; Fulbright Fellowship, 1969–70; Guggenheim Fellowship, 1983.

Selected Works

Novels

Hay que sonreír, Buenos Aires: Américalee, 1966; translated as Clara, in Clara: Thirteen Short Stories and a Novel, 1976
El gato eficaz, Mexico City: Joaquín Mortiz, 1972
Cola de lagartija, Buenos Aires: Bruguera, 1983; as The Lizard's Tail, translated by Gregory Rabassa, New York: Farrar Straus and Giroux, 1983; London: Serpent's Tail, 1987
Realidad nacional desde la cama, Buenos Aires: Sudamericana, 1990; as Bedside Manners, translated by Margaret Jull Costa, New York: High Risk Books, and London: Serpent's Tail, 1995 [novella]
Novela negra con argentinos, Hanover, New Hampshire: Ediciones del Norte, 1990; as Black Novel with Argentines, translated by Tony Talbot, New York: Simon and Schuster, 1992

Short Fiction

Los heréticos, Buenos Aires: Paidós, 1967
Aquí pasan cosas raras, Buenos Aires: Ediciones de La Flor, 1975; translated as Strange Things Happen Here: Twenty-Six Short Stories and a Novel, 1979

Como en la guerra, Buenos Aires: Sudamericana, 1977; translated as He Who Searches, in Strange Things Happen Here: Twenty-Six Short Stories and a Novel, 1979
Libro que no muerde, Mexico City: UNAM, 1980
Cambio de armas, Hanover, New Hampshire: Ediciones del Norte, 1982; as Other Weapons, translated by Deborah Bonner, Hanover, New Hampshire: Ediciones del Norte, 1985
Donde viven las águilas, Buenos Aires: Celtia, 1983; translated as Up Among the Eagles, in Open Door, 1988
Blame, New York: Simon and Schuster, 1992
Simetrías, Buenos Aires: Sudamericana, 1993

Anthologies in Translation

Clara: Thirteen Short Stories and a Novel, translated by Hortense Carpentier and Jorge Castello, New York: Harcourt Brace, 1976 [Includes the novel Hay que sonreír and the stories from Los heréticos]
Strange Things Happen Here: Twenty-Six Stories and a Novel, translated by Helen Lane, New York: Harcourt Brace, 1979 [Includes the novel He Who Searches and the stories from Aquí pasan cosas raras]
Open Door, translated by Hortense Carpentier, et al., San Francisco, California: North Point Press, 1988; London: Serpent's Tail, 1992 [Includes the novel Up Among the Eagles]
The Censors, translated by Hortense Carpentier, et al., Willimantic, Connecticut: Curbstone Press, 1988 [Includes Clara; Strange Things Happen Here and Open Door]

Other Writings

"Mis brujas favoritas," in Theory and Practice of Feminist Literary Criticism, edited by Gabriela Mora and Karten Van Hooft, Ypsilanti, Michigan: Bilingual Press, 1982
"The Other Face of the Phallus," in Reinventing the Americas, edited by Bell Gale Chevigny and Gari Laguardia, Cambridge: Cambridge University Press, 1986
"So-Called Latin American Writing," in Critical Theory, Cultural Politics and Latin American Narrative, edited by Steven M. Bell, Albert H. Le May and Leonard Orr, Notre Dame, Indiana: University of Notre Dame Press, 1993

Further Reading

Castillo, Debra A., "Appropriating the Master's Weapons: Luisa Valenzuela," in her Talking Back: Toward a Latin American Feminist Criticism, Ithaca, New York: Cornell University Press, 1992
Cordones-Cook, Juanamaría, Poética de transgresión en la novelística de Luisa Valenzuela, New York: Peter Lang, 1991
Craig, Linda, "Women and Language: Luisa Valenzuela's El gato eficaz," in Feminist Readings on Spanish and Spanish American Literature, edited by L.P. Condé and S.M. Hart, Lampeter, Wales: Edwin Mellen Press, 1991
Díaz, Gwendolyn, "De Hegel a Lacan: el discurso del deseo en Cambio de armas de Luisa Valenzuela," Revista Iberoamericana, vol. 59/164–65 (July–December 1993)
Guest, Victoria, Reweaving the Violated Marriage: Strategies for Confronting the Discourse of Political Terror in Luisa Valenzuela's "The Lizard's Tail," Stanford, California: Stanford University Press, 1990
Hart, Stephen M., White Ink: Essays on Twentieth Century Feminine Fiction in Spain and Latin America, London: Támesis, 1993 [Chapter 5 has section on El gato eficaz]
Magnarelli, Sharon, Reflections/Refractions: Reading Luisa Valenzuela, New York: Peter Lang, 1988 [At time of publication the most comprehensive critical work on Valenzuela]
Martínez, Nelly Z., El silencio que habla: aproximación a la obra de Luisa Valenzuela, Buenos Aires: Coregidor, 1994

Pye, Geralyn, "Political Football: Sports, Power and Machismo in Luisa Valenzuela's *The Lizard's Tail*," *Studies in Latin American Popular Culture* 13 (1994)

Rubio, Patricia, "La fragmentación: principio ordenador en la ficción de Luisa Valenzuela," in *Canción de Marcela: mujer y cultura en el mundo hispano*, edited by David Valjalo, Madrid: Orígenes, 1989

Interviews

García Pinto, Magdalena, *Women Writers of Latin America: Intimate Histories*, Austin: University of Texas Press, 1991

Special Issues of Journals

Review of Contemporary Fiction: Luisa Valenzuela Number, vol. 6/3 (Fall 1986)

César Vallejo 1892–1938

Peruvian poet and prose writer

César Vallejo vies with the Chilean poet, Pablo Neruda, for the coveted honor of best Spanish American poet of the 20th century, yet the semantic difficulty of his poetry has often meant that he is not as well-known outside the Spanish-speaking world as he deserves to be. Author of a novel, short fiction, two dramas, a collection of essays on Marxism and literary theory, two books on Soviet Russia, and over two hundred newspaper articles, Vallejo is now mainly remembered for his poetry. Anyone who reads his biography – a string of unhappy love affairs, imprisonment on trumped-up charges, inability to find stable employment either in Peru or in Europe, recurring bouts of debilitating illness, expulsion from France, marriage to a domineering and sometimes cruel wife – will not be surprised to find that he had little luck when it came to publishing his work. The majority of his work – and, in particular, his poetry – was published posthumously. His first collection of poems, *Los heraldos negros*, 1918 (*The Black Heralds*) – they actually came out a year later – was published in Lima; epigonically Romantic, they nevertheless hinted at what was to come later. *Trilce* (1922), again published in Lima, is a collection of avant-garde poems, heavily influenced by the new literary works Vallejo was reading at the time in magazines from Europe. From the time Vallejo moved to Paris in 1923 until his death in 1938, however, he published no new poetic works (*Trilce* was re-issued as a friendly gesture by some Spanish friends during his exile in Madrid, after being expelled for political reasons from France in the early 1930s). Were a number of poetic works not discovered among his posthumous papers by his widow, Georgette de Vallejo, we might never have been the wiser, and Vallejo would have been remembered as a good poet of the minor league. His widow, in 1939, published a collection of her late husband's poems (by now she was beginning to assert ownership rights in a way that offended some of Vallejo's artistic contemporaries such as the Spanish poet, Juan Larrea) which she named *Poemas humanos*, and which included a collection of poems entitled "Poemas en prosa" and another collection entitled "España, aparta de mí este cáliz" (*Spain, Take This Cup from Me*). The wisdom of this title was questioned by some, notably by Juan Larrea; more important than the title, however, is the question as to

how many of these poems Vallejo would have published as they were, and how many he would have submitted to further revision. The latter is likely, since Vallejo was an extremely meticulous and language-conscious poet, and the poems which now appear in *Poemas humanos* are of uneven quality. The question as to when the poems were written is also a much-debated one; the poems collected under the title "Poemas en prosa" can be identified as having being written in the mid to late 1920s, given their allusion to contemporary events; the poems collected as "España, aparta de mí este cáliz" were clearly written in response to the Spanish Civil War as it unfolded before Vallejo's horrified eyes (war broke out in July 1936, Vallejo died in April 1938, and the conflict ended in May 1939). (In a curious twist of fate, a collection of poems entitled *España, aparta de mí este cáliz*, was uncovered in 1981 in the Montserrat Monastery; a member of the religious order there who had a soft spot for poetry – of whatever political persuasion – had concealed a number of them, which were hot off the press in Barcelona, knowing that Franco's troops would destroy them if they came across them). The poems entitled *Poemas humanos* present more of a problem but, by analysing their allusions to historical events, it is possible to deduce that they were written over a period of time from the late 1920s to the mid-1930s, and typed up over a period of about six months preceding Vallejo's death.

Vallejo's work is best understood if split into five main stages which are: 1915–18 *Modernismo*; 1919–26 the avant-garde; 1927–31 Marxism (Trotskyism gradually transformed into Stalinism); 1932–35 political disillusionment; 1936–38 Christian Marxism. Representative of the first phase are his collection of poems, *Los heraldos negros*, which shows clear signs of Vallejo's literary apprenticeship in *Modernismo*, but also hints at a new poetic voice, one which eschews the Graeco-Roman world of mythology in favour of a mythology of the quotidian, and uses Christian symbology in incongruous, disorientating contexts. Some poems openly question God's role in the universe, some demonstrate the stirrings of an Amerindian consciousness, and others hint at the growth of social concern for the have-nots of the world. Poems such as "A mi hermano Miguel" [To My Brother Michael] show

Vallejo's skill in the use of colloquial language and everyday situations, tied to his ability to conjure up the world of the child, that would become the hallmark of his poetry. Some of these concerns would continue in his later collection of poems, *Trilce* – published not coincidentally it would seem in the same year as Joyce's *Ulysses* — such as the poems dedicated to his immediate family, and those which conjure up the lost magic of childhood. But there is also a palpable change in poetic diction and subject-matter. Some of the poems talk about the sexual act in a way that is remarkably explicit given the time they were published. Most of the poems demonstrate Vallejo's willingness to expand the resources of the Spanish language in order to create a new vision: neologism, provincialism, archaism, typographical innovation, letter spacing, caligrammatics, slang and legalese all find their way into his poetic armoury. Vallejo had certainly learned many of these techniques through his reading of avant-garde poetry from France, and to some extent Spain in magazines such as *Cervantes* and *Cosmópolis*, but the results were much more original. A typical poem of this phase is *Trilce* XIX (see essay, below).

His *Poemas en prosa* were written approximately between 1923 and 1927 when Vallejo was already installed in Paris, and are mainly vignettes of his everyday life. *Poemas humanos*, written probably, as mentioned above over an extended period from the later 1920s to the mid-1930s, show evidence of Vallejo's growing political commitment over those years; Vallejo was a frequent visitor to the bookstore of *L'Humanité*, the communist newspaper, he read Marxist and Leninist theory, and his poetry reflects this shift towards the political sphere. About one half of the poems of *Poemas humanos* take the collective realm as their point of departure; some of these express enthusiasm for the collective ethos of communism, some express dismay at the exploitation and pain experienced by the proletariat, while others express disillusionment with politics and politicians. The other half of the poems have a personal focus and typically show us the poet bemoaning his fate. One of the best poems of this period is "Los desgraciados" [Wretched Beings] which uses Christian imagery to focus on the exploitation of the proletariat.

España, aparta de mí este cáliz, published in 1939 and written during the first two years of the Spanish Civil War (1936–38), is a paean to the Republican militiamen who were fighting against Franco's trained military troops; it expresses a political faith in the Republican cause through the motif of Christian resurrection, a rather unusual choice given the proletarian and often anti-clerical bias of the Republicans, and especially the communists who supported the Republican war effort. Some of the best poems of *España, aparta de mí este cáliz* focus on a war hero; poem III, for example, describes the life and death of a railwayman, Pedro Rojas, and expresses the continuing force of the ideal for which he died by having him resurrected in the final stanza. Likewise, "Masa" (Mass), perhaps Vallejo's most famous poem, focuses on a moment on the battlefield when a dead Republican militiaman is miraculously brought back to life through the collective love of mankind.

Perhaps most significant about Vallejo's work is the way it straddles the First and the Third Worlds; Vallejo lived roughly two-thirds of his life in the Third World (Peru: 1892–1923), and one-third in the First World (France: 1923–38: excluding short sojourns in Spain in 1930–32 and the Soviet Union in 1928, 1929, and 1931). Since his poetic juvenilia (*Los heraldos negros* and *Trilce*) were influenced by iconoclastic literary movement of First-World provenance (*Modernismo* and the avant-garde), this would tend to make Vallejo a Third-World writer dependent, like his nation's economy, on the First World. But his years in Europe, and especially his reading of Marxist philosophy, changed the framework of that dependency. The mystique of Paris, the City of Light, so visible from the colonial periphery of Peru disappeared as Vallejo approached the source of its power, and this pilgrimage eventually led to a harsh critique of imperialist politics. From the articles he wrote during the late 1920s it is clear that Vallejo saw Marxism as providing a clear answer to the question as to why the developed world was as it was and the underdeveloped world as it was, since it revealed the exploitation of the Other (whether as proletariat or prime-matter nation) which underlies capitalism. Vallejo, in effect, thereby reversed the process – so common in anthropology – whereby the knowledge of the Native Informant is "stolen," technologized and circulated as First World scholarship; Paris became the Native Informant, and cultural counterexploitation was able to take place. What is more, Vallejo's conversion to Marxism while in Europe provided him with an intellectual "non-Western" home within the intellectual climate of Paris and, in the process, sketched out the blueprint of a cultural path that later generations of Latin American intellectuals would follow.

STEPHEN M. HART

Biography

Born in Santiago de Chuco, Peru, 16 March 1892. Attended a secondary school in Huamachuco, 1905–08; Trujillo University, 1910–11, but left to find employment, resumed formal studies, 1913–17, BA, 1915. Worked in his father's notary office, in mine offices, as a tutor, and in an estate accounts office. Teacher at Centro Escolar de Varones and Colegio Nacional de San Juan while at Trujillo University. Moved to Lima in 1918 and taught at Colegio Barrós, 1918–19, and another school, 1920. Visited his home town, Santiago de Chuco, in 1918 and became unintentionally involved in a political riot. Fled to Trujillo but arrested and imprisoned there for three and a half months. Teacher at Colegio Guadalupe, 1921–23. Moved to Paris in 1923 and thereafter lived in Europe. Secretary, Iberoamerican press agency, 1925; contributed to the magazines *Mundial* and *Variedades*, Lima. Co-founder, with Juan Larrea, *Favorables-París-Poema*: closed after two issues, 1926. Travelled to the Soviet Union, 1928. Married Georgette Phillipart, and the couple travelled through Eastern Europe and the Soviet Union. Member of the Spanish Communist Party, 1930; expelled from France because of his political activity and moved to Madrid. Translator for the publishing house Cenit. Returned to Paris, clandestinely in 1932 and lived in extreme poverty; made two further trips to Spain, 1934 and 1937. Died in Paris of tuberculosis, 15 April 1938.

Selected Works

Poetry

Los heraldos negros, Lima: Souza Ferreya, 1919; as *The Black Heralds*, translated by Richard Schaaf and Kathleen Ross, Pittsburgh: Latin American Literary Review Press, 1990; also translated by Barry Fogden, Lewes, Sussex: Allardyce Barnett, 1995

Trilce, Lima: Talleres Tipográficos de la Penitenciaría,1922; as
  Trilce, translated by Rebecca Seiferle, Riverdale-on-Hudson, New
  York: Sheep Meadow Press, 1992
Poemas humanos, edited by Georgette Vallejo, Paris: Presses
  Modernes, 1939; as *Human Poems*, translated by Clayton
  Eshleman, New York: Grove Press, 1969
España, aparta de mí este cáliz, Mexico City: Seneca, 1939; as
  Spain, Take This Cup from Me, translated by Clayton Eshleman
  and José Rubia Barcia, New York: Grove Press, 1974

Short Fiction
Escalas melografiadas, Lima: Talleres Tipográficos de la
  Penitenciaría, 1923
Fabla salvaje, Lima: Colegio La Novela Peruana, 1923

Novel
El tungsteno, Madrid: Cenit, 1931; as *Tungsten*, translated by
  Robert Mezey, Syracuse, New York: Syracuse University Press,
  1988

Compilations and Anthologies
Novelas y cuentos completos, Lima: Francisco Moncloa, 1967; 2nd
  edition, 1970
Obra poética completa, edited by Georgette Vallejo, Lima: Francisco
  Moncloa, 1968
César Vallejo: an Anthology of His Poetry, edited by James Higgins,
  Oxford: Pergamon Press, 1970 [in Spanish]
Obras completas, 3 vols, Lima: Mosca Azul, 1973–74
Poesía completa, edited by Juan Larrea, Barcelona: Seix Barral,
  1978
Desde Europa: crónicas y artículos 1923–1938, edited by Jorge
  Puccinelli, 2nd edition, Lima: Ediciones Fuente de Cultura
  Peruana, 1987
Obra poética, edited by Américo Ferrari, Madrid: CSIC, 1988

Anthologies in Translation
Twenty Poems, translated by Robert Bly, James Wright and John
  Knoepfle, Madison, Minnesota: Sixties Press, 1962 [bilingual
  edition]
Neruda and Vallejo: Selected Poems, translated by Robert Bly, James
  Wright and John Knoepfle, Boston: Beacon Press, 1971 [bilingual
  edition]
Selected Poems, edited and translated by Gordon Brotherston and
  Ed Dorn, Harmondsworth: Penguin, 1976 [bilingual edition]
The Complete Posthumous Poetry, translated by Clayton Eshleman
  and José Rubia Barcia, Berkeley: University of California Press,
  1978 [bilingual edition]
César Vallejo: a Selection of His Poetry, translated by James
  Higgins, Liverpool: Cairns, 1987 [bilingual edition]

Other Writings
Rusia en 1931: reflexiones al pie del Kremlin, Madrid: Ulises,
  1931
El romanticismo en la poesía castellana, Lima: Baca y Villanueva,
  1954
Rusia ante el segundo plan quinquenal, Lima: Editorial Gráfica
  Labour, 1965
Literatura y arte, Buenos Aires: Mediodía, 1966
Cartas a Pablo Abril, Buenos Aires: Alonso, 1971

Further Reading
Adamson, Joseph, *Wounded Fiction: Modern Poetry and
  Deconstruction*, New York: Garland, 1988
Costa, Juan Francisco, *Estudio crítico y antología de César Vallejo*,
  Montevideo: Signos, 1990
Delgado, W. (editor), *Visión del Perú. Homenaje a César Vallejo*,
  Lima: Milla Batres, 1969
Ferrari, Américo, *El universo poético de César Vallejo: ensayo*,
  Caracas: Monte Ávila, 1972
Flores, Ángel (editor), *Aproximaciones a César Vallejo*, 2 vols, New
  York: Las Américas, 1971
Franco, Jean, *César Vallejo: the Dialectics of Poetry and Silence*,
  Cambridge and New York: Cambridge University Press, 1976
Hart, Stephen M., *Religión, política y ciencia en la obra de César
  Vallejo*, London: Támesis, 1987
Higgins, James, *César Vallejo en su poesía*, Lima: Seglusa, 1989
Lambie, George, *El pensamiento político de César Vallejo y la
  guerra civil española*, Lima: Milla Batres, 1993
Larrea, Juan, *César Vallejo y el surrealismo*, Madrid: Corazón,
  1976
____ *Al amor de Vallejo*, Valencia: Pre-Textos, 1982
Ortega, Julio (editor), *César Vallejo*, Madrid: Taurus, 1975
____ *La teoría poética de César Vallejo*, Providence, Rhode Island:
  Del Sol, 1986
Paredes Carbonell, Juan, *César Vallejo: tipología del discurso
  poético*, Trujillo: SEA, 1990
Paz Varia, Miguel, *Vallejo: formas ancestrales en su poesía*, Lima:
  Marimba, 1989
Sobrevilla, David, *César Vallejo: poeta nacional y universal*, Lima:
  Amaru, 1994
Soto, C., *César Vallejo: poeta cristiano y metafísico*, Lima: Mejía
  Baca, 1969
Vegas García, Irene, *Trilce: estructura de un nuevo lenguaje*, Lima:
  Pontificia Universidad Católica del Perú, 1982

Bibliographies
Rela, Walter, *César Vallejo: cronología anotada 1892–1938*,
  Montevideo: El Galeón, 1992

Trilce XIX

Poem by César Vallejo

The poem chosen for analysis, *Trilce* XIX, is representative of
the early work of César Vallejo, and is a superb example of
Spanish American avant-garde poetry of the 1920s. It reads as
follows:

> A trastear, Hélpide dulce, escampas,
> cómo quedamos de tan quedarnos.
> Hoy vienes apenas me he levantado.
> El establo está divinamente meado
> y excrementido por la vaca inocente
> y el inocente asno y el gallo inocente.
>
> Penetra en la maría ecuménica.
> Oh sangabriel, haz que conciba el alma,
> el sin luz amor, el sin cielo,
> lo más piedra, lo más nada,
> hasta la ilusión monarca.
>
> ¡Quemaremos todas las naves!
> ¡Quemaremos la última esencia!
> Mas si se ha de sufrir de mito a mito,
> y a hablarme llegas masticando hielo,
> mastiquemos brasas,
> ya no hay dónde bajar,
> ya no hay dónde subir.
>
> Se ha puesto el gallo incierto, hombre.

[By strumming, sweet Helipede, you uncloud / how we remain in what is left to us. // Today you come as soon as I have risen / The stable is being divinely urinated and defecated by the innocent cow / and the innocent ass and the innocent cock // Penetrate the ecumenical mary / Oh saintgabriel, face what the soul conceives / the lightless love, the skyless / the stoniest, the most nothing / up to the monarchical illusion // We will burn every nave! / We will burn the ultimate essence! // But if we must suffer from myth to myth / and to talk to me you come chewing ice, / let's chew living coals, / now there's nowhere to fall, / now there's nowhere to rise. // The cock itself has doubted, man.]

This poem was written when Vallejo was in prison in 1921, and it describes a mind clutching at straws, trying to make sense of his life after the recent death of his mother, a failed relationship and a bad career move. The poem opens with the poet's description of a half-vision of the Greek god of Hope, Hélpide, although this apparition seems distant and deceptive given that the poet still finds himself trapped on earth (l. 2). In stanza 2, the poet berates Hope for coming to visit him when he has only just got up, and this introduces a note of trivialization which runs its course through the rest of the poem. The remainder of stanza 2 then turns to another type of Hope, the birth of Christ, although since he refers to the stable having excrement and urine in it, we are at the furthest remove from the naive pietism of the Christmas card. Stanza 3 opens with another scene which is likely to be the growth of the Christian Church; here Hope is described as "penetrating" the "Ecumenical Mary" (a metonym for the Church), but, again, since Vallejo refers to Hope creating a number of things which are hardly positive ("love without light . . . until the monarchical illusion"), we again see that the poet is being ironic. In stanza 4, the poet describes the paths traced out as similar to two great events of history; the first when, in Veracruz in 1519, Cortes burned his boats and forced his men to accompany him in their seemingly foolhardy mission to conquer the Aztec empire, and the second involving the medieval experiment of alchemy in which metals were melted down in order to discover their quintessence and turn them into gold. By stanza 6, the poet advises Hope to take a more realistic stance. "If you are always bringing me different newer versions of Hope," he seems to be saying, "at least bring me one which will stay put if you chew it over." Hence the reason for the at first odd reference to "masticating" ice and masticating cinders. Cinders will stay in your mouth, while ice (like the illusion of an ill-founded hope) will soon melt and disappear. Given this impossible situation, as the poem concludes, there seems to be no way out, either up (to heaven) or down (to hell) (ll. 17–18). The last line of the poem is supremely ironic; given the above, even the cockerel which was meant to crow three times during the night preceding the Crucifixion when Peter, according to the synoptic gospels, was betraying Christ, has forgotten his lines. But now we have a sense of the overall meaning of the poem, it is important to remember that its semantic power derives not from its idea but from the way in which it has been expressed.

What follows is a reading which emphasizes the rhetorical dimension of the poem and, for the sake of convenience, four aspects of the poem, crucial for any close textual analysis, will be examined separately: melopoeia, phanopoeia, third-person knowledge, and literary allusiveness. For ease of comprehension a poetry map is appended (p. 825) which shows how these four elements fit together.

With regard to the melopoeia/signifier level of *Trilce* XIX, it is clear that the poem has no fixed metric scheme (indeed it seems to be almost a failed sonnet), but it does have rhymes such as "levantado-meado" (ll. 3–4), "hielo-cielo" (l. 9, l. 15) and assonant rhymes such as "alma-nada" (l. 8, l. 10) and "hielo-incierto" (l. 15, l. 19); thus the deliberate disruption of the rhyme scheme gives a sense of fragmentation which suits the mood of the poem. *Trilce* XIX has some examples of Joycean word-play, such as "excrementido" which fuses together "mentido" and "excrementado" and introduces the notion that the holiness of the Nativity is belied by animal excrement, as well as "sangabriel," a porte-manteau word in which the Archangel Gabriel has been demoted twice, once from archangel to saint and once through loss of his capital letter; playing with upper- and lower-case letters was a very common feature of Vallejo's verse of this period and derived from the avant-garde, mainly French, poets he was reading at the time. Thus, Vallejo is exploring the melopoeic level of language in order to create new meanings; he is starting from the signifier and engendering the signified rather than vice-versa.

With regard to the phanopoeic qualities of the poem, *Trilce* XIX demonstrates sensitivity to the visual arrangement of words; in particular the use of the blank space in l. 11 suggests emptiness and visually reinforces the meaning of "nada" of the previous line. The favoured rhetorical figure, clearly ahead of the others, is the metaphor. Metaphor is be understood, given its etymology ("meta," change + "pherein," to bear) as the description of two ideas or objects as if identical; unlike the metonym or the synecdoche, the metaphor is not based on customary associations, but instead provides access to a new vision. A good example is the "hielo/brasas" contrast in stanza 5, which suggests a distinction between the competing philosophies of idealism and materialism (a very common struggle, indeed, within the Romantic mind, and one whose power was not lost on Vallejo). The contrast posited in the metaphor is "hielo" = idealism just as "brasas" = materialism; chewing on "cinders" is a strikingly graphic way of describing the pain involved in ruminating on the material limitations of human existence.

Unlike the metaphor, the metonym involves the substitution of one thing for another, and perhaps the best way to grasp the difference between metaphor and metonym is to see the latter, following its etymology ("meta" change + "onoma," name) in terms of substitution of a name, and as possessing a more prosaic quality; in this context we may recall that the celebrated Formalist, Roman Jakobson, saw metonymy as the favourite device of prose (and the metaphor as the best trope for poetry). (In a novel, for example, we could see the array of characters as metonymic substitutions for the people that the novelist knew in real life; thus Vetusta is a metonymic substitution for Oviedo in Clarín's classic 19th-century novel, *La Regenta*). In Vallejo's poem we have one clear example of metonymy: "Hélpide" is a metonym for hope (= the Greek word for hope, here personalized), although Vallejo, as with

Saint Gabriel, has deliberately mis-spelt it ("Elpide" is the customary transcription). There are also some synecdoches in Vallejo's poem. The synecdoche, as its etymology suggests ("sun" with + "dekhesthai" to take), means the substitution of a part for the whole, and it can be a very effective device in poetry. The American poet, Robert Frost, for example, was fond of calling himself a "Synecdochist" because he believed that it is the nature of poetry "to have intimations of something more than itself" and much the same might be said of Vallejo's verse. A good example in Vallejo's poem is "la maría ecuménica" to signify the Church, since the Virgin Mary is part of the Church.

With regard to third-person knowledge, *Trilce* XIX clearly expresses a great deal of metaphysical uncertainty about the truth value of the Incarnation. With regard to religion, the poem has many references to the synoptic gospels, some of which have already been touched on, such as the Archangel Gabriel, the Nativity scene, and Peter's denial of Christ. Most of these events are treated ironically, as already noted; but it is important to underline that this is not a poem expressing indifference to spiritual matters such as one might find in the work of a Matthew Arnold; Vallejo's poem expresses an anguished uncertainty about Christian doctrine, and particularly the Immaculate Conception, and the possibility that it has led to an illusory belief in a spiritual kingdom ("hasta la ilusión monarca"). With regard to mythology, the central idea of the poem is that mankind has been shunted from one belief system to another without rhyme or reason ("sufrir de mito a mito"). There is a crucial reference to Greek culture in the form of the Greek god of Hope, as already noted. In suggesting that the Greek god of Hope was reincarnated in the form of Christ (ll. 1–6), the poem alludes to a very common intellectual pattern of the Renaissance, namely, the demonstration that the Classical world was a necessary prelude to the Christian world; Vallejo, here, however, is invoking the idea, only to dismiss it as inconsequential.

In terms of literary allusiveness, we should note immediately that *Trilce* XIX is written in the avant-garde style of the poems which Vallejo was reading in magazines such as *Cosmópolis* and *Cervantes* which arrived in Lima from Europe in the first

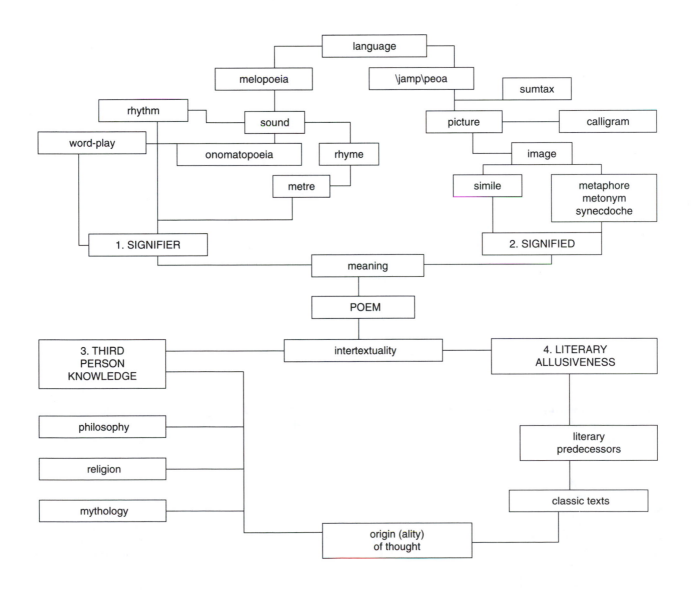

two decades of the century and revolutionized the artistic ambiance of the time. In *Trilce* Vallejo explored typographic lay-out on the page, switch-coding letter cases (namely the untraditional use of capital and lower-case letters), as in "sangabriel" discussed above.

When looking at Vallejo's poem from these four vantage points (melopoeia, phanopoeia, third-person knowledge and literary allusiveness), we arrive at a clearer sense of how the poem demonstrates imaginative and intellectual power. The main idea of the poem is its questioning of the truth value of the master narratives of Western civilization (Greek and Christian culture), and its use of irony to make that point. Vallejo reinforces his sense of metaphysical anguish by disrupting the system of language; in a world in which metaphysical uncertainties are subverted, *Trilce* XIX argues, language itself is not immune from destabilization.

STEPHEN M. HART

See also entry on Avant-Garde

Editions
First edition: *Trilce*, Lima: Talleres Tipográficos de la Penitenciaría, 1922
Critical editions: in *Obra poética*, edited by Ricardo González Vigil, vol. 1, Lima: Banco del Crédito del Perú, 1991; edited by Julio Ortega, Madrid: Cátedra, 1991
Translations: There are three different translations of the whole of *Trilce*. Of these, the one used in the article is that by Rebecca Seiferle, in a bilingual edition, as *Trilce*, Riverdale-on-Hudson, New York: Sheep Meadow Press, 1992. Also highly recommended is that by Clayton Eshleman, New York: Marsilio, 1992

Further Reading
McGuirk, Bernard, "Undoing the Romantic Discourse: a Case-Study in Post-Structuralist Analysis. Vallejo's *Trilce* I," *Romance Studies* 5 (1984)
Neale-Silva, Eduardo, *César Vallejo en su fase trílcica*, Madison: University of Wisconsin Press, 1975
Saldívar, D., "Develando a *Trilce*," *Cuadernos Americanos* 247 (1983)

Blanca Varela 1926–

Peruvian poet

Blanca Varela published her first volume of poetry, *Ese puerto existe* [That Port Exists], in 1959, a decade and a half after her Peruvian contemporaries had begun making their public appearance. She is, however, linked with the poets Javier Sologuren, Jorge Eduardo Eielson, Sebastián Salazar Bondy, and the painter Fernando de Szyszlo through friendships, aesthetic affinities and common intellectual interests, which can be appreciated in her collaboration with them in the editing of the journal *Amaru* (1967–71), founded and directed by the poet Emilio Adolfo Westphalen.

Since its beginnings, Varela's poetry has generally been confined to a small circle of select readers, which has expanded recently. The limited distribution and analysis of her works is due, in part, to the fact that her literary production consists of relatively few texts; to the long silences between the publication of each work – five books during a period of more than thirty-five years; the limited contact with academia; and a wary attitude towards literary competitions, public appearances and readings. In the last decade, her poetry has been recognized and distributed throughout the continent thanks to the publication in Mexico of *Canto villano* [Plain Song], a collection containing almost all her works dating up to 1986. At the time of publication, her most recent book had appeared in 1994.

As with the rest of her contemporaries, Varela took part in the study of the cultural situation of 20th-century Peru, and became familiar with post-war European culture at first hand. While she was married to Fernando de Szyszlo, they lived in Europe and the United States for several years before returning to Peru.

At first glance, one perceives a strong, almost unbearable, emotional intensity in Varela's poetic language. With regard to this, in an interview she gave in 1978, she stated: "I think that poetry resides not in the quantity but in the intensity. It's like working at very high temperatures that don't permit one to remain there for long periods of time. The poet works in very delicate zones of the conscious." Critics such as José Miguel Oviedo and Roberto Paoli have recognized in the emotions presented in Varela's poetry a Surrealist "morality of passion" and a "parasurrealist climate," respectively.

Her poems accumulate surprising images, possessing great associative possibilities, and dealing with oneiric or illusory atmospheres, as in "Puerto Supe" [Port Supe]: "cielo, sombra veloz / nubes do espanto, oscuro torbellino de alas" (sky, fleeting shadow / clouds of fear, dark whirlwind of wings), or in "Historias de Oriente" [Stories of the Orient]: "Cierta mañana Cosme abrió los ojos y vio a su perro envuelto en una nube azul. / Con un alfiler lo persiguió varios meses" (One morning, Cosme opened his eyes and saw his dog wrapped in a blue cloud. / With a pin he chased him for several months).

Varela achieves this emotional force in part through the careful use of metaphors of apparent sentimentality that, placed side by side, do not flow subtly one into the other but rather create frictions of diverse qualities. The play of emotions is transported from an atmosphere of collective illusion to an atmosphere where the intimate is coldly observed. Her metaphors force the cohabitation of a melodramatic rhetoric and a corporeal vocabulary whose rawness dangerously approaches scatology. Varela suggests scenarios where everyday relationships, emotional routines, commonplace topics within families, are illusions hidden behind unconscious expectations: tranquil love, a stable economy, one's own home, an attractive body, permanent happiness. This can be seen in the poem "Vals del 'Ángelus'" [Waltz of the "Angelus"]: "Ve lo que has hecho di mí, la madre que devora a sus crías, la que se traga sus lágrimas y engorda, la que debe abortar en cada luna, la que sangra todos los días del año". (Look what you have made of me, the mother that devours her offspring, the one that swallows her tears and grows fat, the one that must abort with each moon, the one that bleeds every day of the year), also in "Secreto de familia" [Family Secret]: "la piel del hombre se quema con el sueño / arde desaparece la piel humana / sólo la roja pulpa del can es limpia / la verdadera luz habita su legaña / tú eres el perro / tú eres el desollado can de cada noche / sueña contigo misma y basta" (The skin of man is burned by the dream / the human skin burns disappears / only the red pulp of the dog is clean / the true light inhabits the secretion of its eyes / you are the dog / you are the skinned cur of each night / dream about yourself and that's all), or in "Último poema de junio" [Last Poem of June]: "Pienso en esa flor que se enciende en mi cuerpo. La hermosa, la violenta flor del ridículo. Pétalo de carne y hueso. ¿Pétalos? ¿Flores? Peciosismo bienvestido, muertodehambre, vaderretro. (I think about that flower that ignites inside my body. The beautiful, violent flower of the ridiculous. Petal of flesh and bone. Petals? Flowers? Well-dressed exquisiteness, pitiful, vade-retro).

With her poetry, Varela disturbs the collective dream constructed around one's possible capacity for uncalculated or unconscious love. Her critics also find a strong presence of dissatisfaction, scepticism, rudeness, bareness, humour, irony, helplessness and self pity, that are refined and strengthened throughout her literary production.

The collective dream of domestic stability evoked by Varela is a way of linking the routine with the fragile reaffirmation of identity that the individual finds in intimacy. According to Cristina Graves, this option arises from the female condition of the writer: "Because the house, the home, represents the illusion *par excellence* of stability and security, and women, in particular, assume the responsibility for maintaining the appearance of 'normality' despite their capacity to 'turn the page,' to see the other side of things. Women will dream of life day after day in their 'paradise' of appearances in order not to destroy the illusion of security, of eternity."

Varela also disturbs this "paradise" with constant references to animals. Among her fauna, insects and pets abound as in "Lady's Journal": "el ratón te contempla extasiado / la araña no se atreve a descender ni un milímetro más a la tierra / el café es un espectro azul sobre la hornilla" (the mouse contemplates you in ecstasy, the spider does not dare descend one more millimetre towards the earth / the coffee is a blue ghost over the burner) and in "Secreto de familia" [Family Secret]: "es un sueño estás sola / no hay otro / la luz no existe / tú eres el perro tú eres la flor que ladra / afila dulcements tu lengua / tu dulce negra lengua de cuatro patas" (it is a dream you are alone / there is no-one else / the light does not exist / you are the dog you are the flower that barks / gently sharpen your tongue / your sweet black four-legged tongue). In addition to the animal dimension there is a constant, calculated, sometimes subtle, sometimes shocking, treatment of the body,

as in "Camino a Babel" [Pathway to Babel]: "ayúdame mantra purísima / divinidad del esófago y el píloro. // si golpeas infinitas veces tu cabeza / contra lo imposible / eres lo imposible" (help me purest mantra / divinity of the oesophagus and the pylorus. / If you bang your head infinite times / against the impossible / you are the impossible).

The theme of identity, as for example in "Identikit" and "Curriculum vitae," is a constant in her poetry, often drawing freely from a masculine lyric self, generally assumed in a rigorous and harsh tone that reminds the reader how illusory gender identification can be. Another important constant is the theme of maternity, that appears in poems such as "Antes del día [Before the Day], "Madonna," "Jutbol" [Soccer]. In these and other poems, Varela tends to treat love with a high level of ambivalence, the object of love seems to undergo a metamorphosis and the feelings toward the lover or the spouse are extended to include the forbidden figures of mother and child, as in "Casa de cuervos" [House of Crows]: "ego te absolvo de mí / laberinto hijo mío" (ego I absolve you of myself / labyrinth son of mine). In other poems, this ambivalence includes geographic space, the big city or native scenery (the city of Lima and the Peruvian coast).

The power of Varela's poetry and the freedom with which it has transgressed certain tacit limits of our collective perception, among them those corresponding to the realm of patriarchy and masculine insecurity, has made her work one of the most important points of reference in discussions regarding gender and literature written by Peruvian women in the second half of the 20th century.

LUIS REBAZA-SORALUZ

Biography

Born in Lima, Peru, 1926. Married Fernando de Syzlo (separated); has children. Lived in the United States and Paris for many years. Director of the Peruvian branch of the Mexican publishing house, Fondo de Cultura Económica.

Selected Works

Poetry

Ese puerto existe y otros poemas, Xalapa, Mexico: Universidad Veracruzana, 1959
Luz de día, Lima: La Rama Florida, 1963
Valses y otras falsas confesiones, Lima: Instituto Nacional de Cultura, 1972
Canto villano, Lima: Arybalo, 1978
El libro de barro, Madrid: Ediciones del Tapir, 1993
Ejercicios materiales, Caracas: Fondo Editorial Pequeña Venecia, 1994

Compilations and Anthologies

Canto villano: poesía reunida, 1949–1983, Mexico City: Fondo de Cultura Económica, 1986
Camino a Babel: antología, Lima: Municipalidad de Lima Metropolitana, 1986
Poesía escogida, 1949–1991, Barcelona: Icaria, 1993

Further Reading

Escobar, Alberto, "Luz de día," *Revista Peruana de Cultura* 2 (1964)

Ferrari, Américo, "Varela: explorando los 'bordes espeluznantes,'" [*Canto villano*], *Hueso Húmero* 21 (1986)

Gazzolo, Ana M., "Blanca Varela y la batalla poética," *Cuadernos Hispanoamericanos* 466 (1989)

Graves, Cristina, "Con el ángel entre los dedos," *Hueso Húmero* 4 (1980)

Jiménez, Reynaldo, "Contra el regreso a Babel," *Oráculo* 2 (1981)

Ortega, Julio, "Blanca Varela," in his *Figuración de la persona*, Madrid: Edhasa, 1971

Oviedo, José Miguel, "Blanca Varela o la persistencia de la memoria," *Escrito al margen*, 2nd edition, Mexico City: Premiá Editora, 1987

Paoli, Roberto, "Itinerarios de renuncia, de mesura y de aventura: Abril, Moreno Jimeno, Varela, Romualdo," in his *Estudios sobre literatura peruana contemporánea*, Florence: Università degli Studi di Firenze, 1985

Paz, Octavio, "Destiempos de Blanca Varela," in his *Puertas al campo*, Mexico City: UNAM, 1966

Pollarolo, Giovanna, "Blanca reunida," [*Canto villano*], *Debate*, vol. 8/40 (1986)

Schwartz, Perla, "Blanca Varela: poesía de ausencias," [*Canto villano*], *Plural*, vol. 15/178 (1986)

Bibliography

González Vigil, Ricardo, "Blanco Varela," in *Poesía peruana. Antología general*, vol. 3, *De Vallejo a nuestros días*, Lima: Edubanco, 1984

Mario Vargas Llosa 1936–

Peruvian prose writer and dramatist

Mario Vargas Llosa's prolific narrative work – one of the most representative and influential of the so-called Boom of the Spanish American novel in the 1960s – can be grouped into two lengthy periods (perhaps three if the tendencies and preoccupations that have begun to emerge in his work of the 1980s crystallize in future ones). The first group consists of *Los jefes*, 1959 [The Leaders], his only collection of short stories, the novella *Los cachorros*, 1967 (*The Cubs*), and the novels *La ciudad y los perros*, 1963 (*The Time of the Hero*), *La casa verde*, 1966 (*The Green House*) and *Conversación en La Catedral*, 1969 (*Conversation in The Cathedral*). The intention, subject-matter and form of these works could not be more varied, above all in the case of the novels, but they constitute a whole in terms of the complexity of the narrative project and the aesthetic vision they convey. The novels' connections with the world of *Los jefes* and *Los cachorros* should not be overlooked altogether, since they form part of the same fictive world in which violent or marginalized characters and misfits preponderate.

What the three novels show is a geometric progression in the number of stories told and the ways these interact. The basic design of *La ciudad y los perros* is binary: a microcosm (the Leoncio Prado School) and a macrocosm (the city, Lima and its outskirts); each with its own tone, rhythm and sources of conflict, the two being presented in opposition and forming a contrast. In *La casa verde* the structure has a scrupulously symmetrical arrangement, regulated by five main stories and two vast, opposed spaces (on the one hand, Piura on the northern coast of Peru; on the other, the Amazonian jungle). Between their interstices there flow minor episodes and incidents which turn the whole into a labyrinthine but rigorous design of constantly expanding times, spaces and adventures.

Conversación en La Catedral is structurally less symmetrical than the earlier novel, but its scope is even wider, having the proportions of a veritable historical saga. A striking feature of all these novels is how the various plots are interwoven, the number and range of characters and, in addition, the virtuosity of the techniques employed to represent objective reality, the moral consequences of interpersonal relations, the introspective attitude of the meditation on history, etc., in a highly dramatic way. Vargas Llosa's efforts are always directed towards being *inclusive* and *centripetal*, spurred on by the unattainable ideal of the "novela total" (total novel): creating a double of the real world, as complete as possible and governed by its own laws; better said, a fictive *rival* of the original from which it sprang. For this reason, according to the author's notion of literature, the novelist can be seen as a "deicide," a craftsman intent on denying, surpassing or completing the divine creation, adding his own imaginary constructions.

Although in *La ciudad y los perros* and *Conversación en La Catedral* there are elements associated with urban realism (which he discovered through the so-called "Generation of the 1950s" during his formative years in Lima), it must be acknowledged that in the rest of his work the author has shown a reiterated predilection for wild open spaces where adventures on a grand scale are still possible. The jungle has proved to be a favourite setting, being present in several of his novels. There is a strongly "regionalist" strand in him that can be related to the novels of that aesthetic which flourished in the 1930s. The jungle, the desert, the parched Brazilian northeast (the *sertão*) are areas that have allowed him to examine the conduct of characters who must square up to an environment, their own or otherwise, always hostile and presenting a challenge they inevitably find attractive. Owing to the absence of a set of socially valid norms, these are ideal spaces for rebels, adventurers or the dispossessed who, having nothing to lose, can dream of escaping from the pressures of the "establishment" and invent a destiny tailor-made for them. The young cadets and their cynical army instructors in *La ciudad y los perros*; the traffickers in rubber, the villanous buddies and prostitutes of *La casa verde*; the corrupt politicians, venal journalists and "Zavalita," the thwarted intellectual, of *Conversación en La Catedral*, are all very different but have a common destiny of violence, degradation and frustration.

Vargas Llosa's second creative phase begins with *Pantaleón y las visitadoras*, 1973 (*Captain Pantoja and the Special Service*), and is followed by *La tía Julia y el escribidor*, 1977 (*Aunt Julia and the Scriptwriter*), *La guerra del fin del mundo*, 1981 (*The War of the End of the World*), *Historia de Mayta*, 1984 (*The Real Life of Alejandro Mayta*), *¿Quién mató a Palomino Molero?*, 1986 (*Who Killed Palomino Molero?*), *El hablador*, 1987 (*The Storyteller*), *Elogio de la madrastra*, 1988 (*In Praise of the Stepmother*) and *Lituma en los Andes*, 1993 (*Death in the Andes*). In effect, we have here two series within the same period of production, something which may well become easier to discern in time: on the one hand there are the essentially political novels (*La guerra del fin del mundo, Historia de Mayta* and *Lituma en los Andes*); on the other, those that re-elaborate autobiographical events or concern his own novelistic theory (*Pantaleón y las visitadoras, La tía Julia y el escribidor, ¿Quién mató a Palomino Molero?*). This is a period marked by a reflective attitude, as much concerned with the fundamental questions about modern Latin American society as with the narrative art he uses to represent them. To a greater or lesser extent, both modes of this period reveal that the author has modified considerably his quest for the totalizing narrative, concentrating now on less complicated stories within more restricted spatio-temporal limits, although the contrapuntal effect which involves the parallel development of two or more stories remains fundamental to his art. In the same way, it is notorious that his (original) realist convictions have undergone a crisis: now, rather than displaying the extensive possibilities of realism, his interest lies in underlining its limitations, the inevitable treason that the language of fiction practices on the objective world and real experience.

Of his most recent production, the work which is both most significant and ambitious in scope is, without doubt, *La guerra del fin del mundo*; also the most unusual in his repertoire, since it is the only one that does not take place in Peru and whose theme is not taken directly from life. Instead it is a re-elaboration of materials taken from a book, the classic *Os sertões*, 1902 (*Rebellion in the Backlands*), by Euclides da Cunha. In the Brazilian original, da Cunha describes the extraordinary rebellion of Canudos provoked by a messianic leader, Antônio Consejero, who imperilled the stability of the new Brazilian republic until it was bloodily quelled. On this basis the author creates a vast picture, one of epic proportions, in which he freely reconstructs events from Brazilian history as a case study that permits him to reflect on questions still relevant now; religious fanaticism, the role of intellectuals and politicians, violence, tradition and social change, and so on. *Historia de Mayta* focuses political reflection on Peru itself, presenting it in the context of the country's present crisis, at the same time as it comments on the dilemma of writing a novel on those subjects and in those circumstances. *Lituma en los Andes* is the author's first excursion into the Andean world, torn apart by terrorist violence and the tensions it imposes on an archaic world ruled by mythical beliefs and customs.

Pantaleón, La tía Julia, Quién mató, and *Elogio* have a lighter touch and a farcical slant. The presence of humour in these novels is related to his new attitude towards the realism of his first period and to his desire to use fiction as a vehicle for self-reference and, at times, self-parody. This is very clear in *La tía Julia*, but also in *Historia de Mayta* and *El hablador*; increasingly, the narrator abandons the lofty objectivity of his early novels to assume a role in his own fiction, at once engendering and criticizing it. There is another type of parody in *¿Quién mató a Palomino Molero?*, which uses the stock components of the thriller but distorts them, so as to give the story the grotesque air of a police romp. This conscious exaggeration is present also in *Elogio*. Although this is the author's first erotic novel, it is most definitely not the first in which the elements of perversion and transgression in the sphere of sexuality put in an appearance. On the contrary: it has been a characteristic feature – apparent as from *La ciudad* – that he is an admirer of Bataille, Sade and licentious literature in which he sees another expression of the individual's eternal rebellion against the norms of the social world.

Vargas Llosa has accompanied this process of aesthetic renewal with the development of other interests. He underwent experiences that produced a marked readjustment of his intellectual and personal positions. His work as a critic, which began early through his journalism, produced consistent results as from the 1970s; among these are his study *Gabriel García Márquez: historia de un deicidio*, 1971 [García Márquez: the Story of a Deicide], 1971, his essay *La orgía perpetua. Flaubert y "Madame Bovary,"* 1975 (*The Perpetual Orgy*) and, since then, collections of articles on literature, culture and politics, titled *Contra viento y marea*, 1983 [Against Wind and Tide], and *Desafíos a la libertad*, 1994 [Challenges to Freedom]. But that complex process can be better appreciated in *El pez en el agua*, 1993 (*A Fish in the Water*), a remarkable book of memoirs that offers, once again in contrapuntal mode, the story of his childhood and youth together with that of his immersion, many years later, in the world of politics. *La señorita de Tacna*, 1981 (*The Young Lady from Tacna*), marks the start (or the re-start, if one takes into consideration a remote, adolescent foray into theatre) of a period of intense interest in this genre. His other plays to date are *Kathie y el hipopótamo*, 1983 (*Kathy and the Hippopotamus*), *La Chunga*, 1986 and *El loco de los balcones*, 1993 [The Madman of the Balconies].

JOSÉ MIGUEL OVIEDO

translated by Verity Smith

Biography

Born in Arequipa, Peru, 28 March 1936. Parents separated, and so brought up by mother and maternal grandparents in Cochabamba, Bolivia, 1937–45, Piura, northern Peru, 1945–46, then in Lima. Educated in Bolivia to 1945. Parents reconciled when he was about eight years old. Attended Leoncio Prado Military Academy, Lima, 1950–52; Colegio Nacional San Miguel de Piura, 1952; studied literature and law University of San Marcos, 1955–57; University of Madrid, 1957–59, PhD, 1959. Held several part-time jobs while a student, including: journalist, for *La Industria*, Piura, c.1952; co-editor of the literary journals, *Cuadernos de Conversación*, 1957 and *Literatura*, 1959. Married Julia Urquidi in 1955 (divorced 1964). Journalist for Radio Panamericana and *La Crónica*, both in

Lima. Moved to Paris in 1959 because he felt that in Peru he could not earn his living as a serious writer. Precarious existence in Paris working as Spanish teacher, journalist for Agence-France-Presse, and broadcaster for Radio Télévision Française, early 1960s. Visited Peru in 1964. Member of the editorial board, *Casa de las Américas*, Havana, 1965. Married Patricia Llosa in 1965; two sons and one daughter. Contributor to the magazine *Caretas*, Lima, 1966. Lecturer, Queen Mary College and subsequently reader at King's College, both University of London, 1966–68; Visiting Professor, University of Washington, Seattle, 1968, University of Puerto Rico, Río Piedras, 1969. Moved to Barcelona, 1970. Established permanent residence in Peru, 1975. Visiting Professor, Columbia University, New York, 1975, University of Jerusalem, 1976, Cambridge University, 1977; President, PEN Club International, 1977; Writer-in-Residence, Smithsonian Institution, Washington, DC, 1979; lectured and travelled in Japan, 1980. Visiting Professor, Florida International University, Miami, 1991, and Wissenschaftskolleg, Berlin, 1991–92. Fredemo (Democratic Front) candidate in Peruvian presidential elections, 1990. Recipient of numerous awards including: Leopoldo Alas Prize, 1959; Biblioteca Breve Prize (Spain), 1962 for *La ciudad y los perros*; Rómulo Gallegos Prize (Venezuela), 1967 for *La casa verde*; National Critics' Prize (Spain), 1967 for *La casa verde*; Peruvian National Prize, 1967 for *La casa verde*; Critics' Annual Prize for Theatre (Argentina), 1981 for *La señorita de Tacna*; Prince of Asturias Prize (Spain), 1986; Miguel de Cervantes Prize, 1994.

Selected Works

Novels

La ciudad y los perros, Barcelona: Seix Barral, 1963; as *The Time of the Hero*, translated by Lysander Kemp, New York: Grove Press, 1966; London: Jonathan Cape 1967

La casa verde, Barcelona: Seix Barral, 1966; as *The Green House*, translated by Gregory Rabassa, New York: Harper, 1968; London: Jonathan Cape, 1969

Conversación en La Catedral, Barcelona: Seix Barral, 1969; as *Conversation in The Cathedral*, translated by Gregory Rabassa, New York: Harper, 1975

Pantaleón y las visitadoras, Barcelona: Seix Barral, 1973; as *Captain Pantoja and the Special Service*, translated by Gregory Kolovakos and Ronald Christ, New York: Harper, and London: Jonathan Cape, 1978

La tía Julia y el escribidor, Barcelona: Seix Barral, 1977; as *Aunt Julia and the Scriptwriter*, translated by Helen Lane, New York: Farrar Straus and Giroux, 1982; London: Faber and Faber, 1983

La guerra del fin del mundo, Barcelona: Seix Barral, 1981; as *The War of the End of the World*, translated by Helen Lane, New York: Farrar Straus and Giroux, 1984; London: Faber and Faber, 1985

Historia de Mayta, Barcelona: Seix Barral, 1984; as *The Real Life of Alejandro Mayta*, translated by Alfred MacAdam, New York: Farrar Straus and Giroux, and London: Faber and Faber, 1986

¿Quién mató a Palomino Molero?, Barcelona: Seix Barral, 1986; as *Who Killed Palomino Molero?* translated by Alfred MacAdam, New York: Farrar Straus and Giroux, 1987; London: Faber and Faber, 1988

El hablador, Barcelona: Seix Barral, 1987; as *The Storyteller*, translated by Helen Lane, New York: Farrar Straus and Giroux, 1989; London: Faber and Faber, 1990

Elogio de la madrastra, Barcelona: Tusquets, 1988; as *In Praise of the Stepmother*, translated by Helen Lane, New York: Farrar Straus and Giroux, 1990; London: Faber and Faber, 1991

Lituma en los Andes, Barcelona: Planeta, 1993; as *Death in the Andes*, translated by Edith Grossman, New York: Farrar Straus and Giroux, and London: Faber and Faber, 1996

Short Fiction

Los jefes, Barcelona: Rocas, 1959; translated in *The Cubs and Other Stories*, 1979

Los cachorros, Barcelona: Lumen, 1967; translated in *The Cubs and Other Stories*, 1979

The Cubs and Other Stories, translated by Gregory Kolovakos and Ronald Christ, New York: Harper, 1979; London: Faber and Faber, 1991

Plays

La señorita de Tacna, Barcelona: Seix Barral, 1981; as *The Young Lady from Tacna*, translated by David Graham-Young, in *Three Plays*, 1990

Kathie y el hipopótamo, Barcelona: Seix Barral, 1983; as *Kathie and the Hippopotamus*, translated by David Graham-Young, in *Three Plays*, 1990

La Chunga, Barcelona: Seix Barral, 1986; as *La Chunga*, translated by David Graham-Young, in *Three Plays*, 1990

Three Plays, translated by David Graham-Young, London: Faber and Faber, 1990

El loco de los balcones, Barcelona: Seix Barral, 1993

Essays and Other Writings

La novela en América Latina; diálogo, in collaboration with Gabriel García Márquez, Lima: Milla Batres, 1968

La literatura en la revolución y la revolución en la literatura, in collaboration with Julio Cortázar and Oscar Collazos, Mexico City: Siglo XXI, 1970

Historia secreta de una novela, Barcelona: Tusquets, 1971

Gabriel García Márquez: historia de un deicidio, Barcelona: Seix Barral, 1971

La novela y el problema de la expresión literaria en Perú, Buenos Aires: América Nueva, 1974

La orgía perpetua: Flaubert y Madame Bovary, Madrid: Taurus 1975; as *The Perpetual Orgy: Flaubert and Madame Bovary*, translated by Helen Lane, New York: Farrar Straus and Giroux, 1986; London: Faber and Faber, 1987

José María Arguedas: entre sapos y halcones, Madrid: Cultura Hispánica del Centro Iberoamericano de Cooperacíon, 1978

La utopía arcaica, Cambridge: Cambridge University Centre for Latin American Studies, 1978

Art, Authenticity and Latin American Culture, Washington, DC: Woodrow Wilson Center, 1981(?)

Entre Sartre y Camus, Río Piedras, Puerto Rico: Huracán, 1981

Contra vientro y marea (1962–1982), 3 vols, Barcelona: Seix Barral, 1983–90

La cultura de la libertad, la libertad de la cultura, Santiago de Chile: Fundación Eduardo Frei, 1985

Diálogo sobre la novela latinoamericana, in collaboration with Gabriel García Márquez, Lima: Perú Andino, 1988

La verdad de las mentiras: ensayos sobre literatura, Barcelona: Seix Barral, 1990; as *A Writer's Reality*, Syracuse, New York: Syracuse University Press, 1990; London: Faber and Faber, 1991

Carta de batalla por Tirant lo Blanc, Barcelona: Seix Barral, 1991

El pez en el agua: memorias, Barcelona: Seix Barral, 1993; as *A Fish in the Water: Memoirs*, translated by Helen Lane, New York: Farrar Straus and Giroux, and London Faber and Faber, 1994

Desafíos a la libertad, Madrid: Aguilar, 1994

Compilations and Anthologies

Obras escogidas, Madrid: Aguilar, 1978

Making Waves, edited and translated by John King, London: Faber and Faber, 1996 [selection of newspaper articles]

Further Reading

Boland, Roy C., *Mario Vargas Llosa: Oedipus and the "Papa" State*, Madrid: Voz, 1988

Booker, M. Keith, *Vargas Llosa among the Postmodernists*, Gainesville: University Presses of Florida, 1994

Christ, Ronald, "Rhetorics of the Plot," in *Modern Latin American Fiction*, New York: Chelsea House, 1990 [Article on *Pantaleón y las visitadoras*]

Feal, Rosemary Geisdorfer, *Novel Lives: the Fictional Autobiographies of Guillermo Cabrera Infante and Mario Vargas Llosa*, Chapel Hill: University of North Carolina Press, 1986

Gerdes, Dick, *Mario Vargas Llosa*, Boston: Twayne, 1985

González, Aníbal, "Journalism and the Ethics of Writing: Borges, García Márquez, Vargas Llosa, Poniatowska," in his *Journalism and the Development of Spanish American Narrative*, Cambridge: Cambridge University Press, 1993

Magnarelli, Sharon, *The Lost Rib*, Lewisburg, Pennsylvania: Bucknell University Press, 1985 [Chapter on *La ciudad y los perros*]

Oviedo, José Miguel (editor), *Mario Vargas Llosa*, Madrid: Taurus, 1981

Oviedo, José Miguel, *Mario Vargas Llosa: la invención de una realidad*, 3rd edition, Barcelona: Seix Barral, 1982

Rivera-Rodas, Oscar, *El metateatro y la dramática de Vargas Llosa*, Amsterdam and Philadelphia: John Benjamins, 1992

Rossman, Charles and Alan Warren Friedman, *Mario Vargas Llosa: a Collection of Critical Essays*, Austin: University of Texas Press, 1978

Rowe, William, "Liberalism and Authority: the Case of Mario Vargas Llosa," in *On Edge: the Crisis of Contemporary Latin American Culture*, edited by George Yúdice, Jean Franco and Juan Flores, Minneapolis: University of Minnesota Press, 1992

Standish, Peter, *Vargas Llosa: La ciudad y los perros*, Valencia, Spain: Grant and Cutler, 1982

Williams, Raymond L., *Mario Vargas Llosa*, New York: Ungar, 1986

Interviews

Sett, Ricardo A., *Sobre la vida y la política*, Buenos Aires: Intermundo, 1989

Special Issues of Journals

World Literature Today, vol. 52/1 (1974)

Review, 14 (1975). Number dedicated to *Conversación en La Catedral*

Antípodas, vol. 1/1 (December 1988)

La casa verde

Novel by Mario Vargas Llosa

La casa verde is Vargas Llosa's second novel, and some would argue his best. Like several others, it draws heavily on his personal experiences; not long after its publication in 1966, the author explained the genesis of *La casa verde* in lectures which later were published in the form of a short book entitled *Historia secreta de una novela*, 1971 [The Secret Story of a Novel]. In that book, he tells of two formative experiences in his life which provided the basis for the novel.

The first is a year (1945) that he spent in Piura, a town near the coast in northern Peru; he was then still a young boy, and had just come back from Bolivia to live in his native country. He recalls how with his friends he would spy on a mysterious green house on the outskirts of town, a house which would come to life at night, exercising a somehow evil attraction on the boys, who dubbed its ladies "habitantas" and taunted its patrons with cries of recognition, without really understanding quite what their activities were. Another important recollection from this time is of a run-down suburb called the "Mangachería," whose people were noisy, violent and hostile to outsiders, especially to their rivals in a more prosperous suburb known as the "Gallinacera." The mature Vargas Llosa would later revisit Piura and understand the sordid details of the "casa verde." Piura came to provide one of the main settings for the novel, with activity centred on that brothel.

The other main setting is the jungle, and this is seen to have arisen from a second of the author's formative experiences: in 1957 he went on a trip into the interior with a group of anthropologists from San Marcos University, learning about the Indians he would later portray; he visited a Catholic mission, saw the dedication of the nuns but also became aware of how Indian girls were being drafted into servitude or prostitution on the coast; he heard of the activities of rubber traffickers, of how an Indian chief called Jum had been tortured for standing up to them; finally, he listened to tales of a rubber-dealer of Japanese descent who was said to have many wives and a private kingdom. These two settings and the experiences described are developed in *La casa verde*. (Vargas Llosa explains that writing was a matter of dressing things up to mask the truth, rather as if the process were akin to a striptease in reverse). The "casa verde" of the title may therefore be understood to refer both literally to the building in Piura and metaphorically to the jungle. The female protagonist who provides the major link between the two settings is an Indian girl, transported from the one to the other, to work in the brothel in Piura, where she is nicknamed "Selvática" (a name that suggests her roots in the jungle).

La casa verde is, formally at least, as complex as Vargas Llosa's first novel and it employs some of the same narrative devices. Five storylines unfold and are seen to intertwine in a narrative structure that has been said to mimic a complex river system, and indeed, is central to the novel is a story being told by a character who is travelling all the while down a river. Along with his recollections and confessions to his companion, we have the tales of other characters, told in different sections of the narrative, and in somewhat different styles.

The reader is faced with a bewildering start to the novel, whose opening pages do not take time to introduce characters in any apparently logical or cohesive way; during the opening section of the book the reader must largely guess who the participants are, which of them is talking at any given time, and what significance it all may have. The first section presents military men dealing with nuns at a jungle mission from which Indian girls escape. Only much later will the reader understand that here were presented the essential elements of the narrative, its main theme and two of its main characters.

One of Vargas Llosa's aims is to come closer to a simultaneity of events than is generally thought possible in literature; thus, for example, he may seek ways of conveying the perception of the fly on someone's nose at the same time as the perception that someone else is talking, at the same time as the perception that an observer of this is feeling hungry. In other words, he attempts to undermine the linearity inherent in language. Indeed, this may be seen as symptomatic of his narrative strategy on a grand scale: the comfortable chronology which may serve to organize events into palatably logical sequences is abandoned in favour of a jigsaw effect: pieces which do not seem immediately to fit into a pattern or to bear relation to each other, until, eventually, a full picture emerges. And, again like a jigsaw, the final picture that emerges is not absolutely precise. The rationale behind all this complication is that life itself comes in chaotic and inconvenient bits which we must piece together into patterns as best we can, while truth is not as absolute as we might perhaps prefer it to be. Mention should also be made of the extensive use of what the author calls "vasos comunicantes," by which he means a technique involving an apparent exchange between characters who exist in different times and places; for example, two characters are in conversation and one is recounting some past experience to the other when the protagonists of that past experience seem to come to life in the narrative present, addressing the listener directly. It is a technique somewhat like a cinematic flashback, and one used with great frequency and variety. This technique is particularly important as a unifying force in *La casa verde*, because it forges narrative bridges between distant settings and over a timespan of decades.

Reference has already been made to five main storylines. One involves the role of a jungle mission from which girls are taken to prosperous coastal families; from this mission comes the virginal Bonifacia, who will become Selvática once a prostitute in Piura. A second is that of Fushía, the man of Japanese parentage, who is travelling the Marañón river with an old friend and telling him his life story, on his way to die of leprosy in the jungle. A third concentrates on the brothel, founded by a stranger who is reputed to have ridden unannounced into town one day, the enigmatic Don Anselmo; the activities in the "casa verde" outrage the righteous Padre García who sees to it that it is burned to the ground, but it rises like the Phoenix from the ashes, rebuilt by Anselmo's daughter Chunga, while he becomes the resident harpist. Fourthly, there is an account of the activities of the "caucheros" (rubber dealers) in the jungle, the abuse of and rebellion by Indians, and the role in all this of the garrison. Finally, there is the story of the self-styled "Inconquistables," a group of hard-drinking and gambling youths from the Mangachería who frequent the "casa verde."

On the fringe of this last group is Sergeant Lituma; apart from Selvática, he is the only character to act in both the jungle and coastal settings, and therefore is of particular significance. Introduced in the very first words of the novel (though not identified by name) he is there in the jungle with the garrison, where Bonifacia is, while he will also have a relationship with her years later once she has been renamed Selvática and is working in her new location, Piura. (Lituma – and to a lesser degree some other characters in *La casa verde* – reappears in later works by Vargas Llosa, including the recent *Lituma en los Andes*).

There are some ninety characters in *La casa verde* and they may usefully be grouped in relation to each of the main settings. In the jungle setting, we find those in the mission, of whom Bonifacia is by far the most important; there are the Indians (in particular Jum as defender of rights and sufferer of torture); present by implication but always faceless are "the

authorities" who in fact operate from a base of ignorance in Lima; two characters stand out from among the personnel of the garrison: Lituma, for reasons already mentioned, and Delgado, a captain whose personal desire for revenge allows the assault on Jum; lastly, there are the "caucheros," who include the unscrupulous Reátegui, Fushía and his confessor-companion Aquilino, and the partner of several of them and mother of some of their children, Lalita. As to Piura, we have Anselmo, Chunga and Selvática as main characters attached to the brothel; the lower-middle class "Gallinacera" is represented by Juana Baura and Toñita (the latter having had a child, Chunga, by Anselmo); the prosperous or influential Piurans are represented by Padre García, Dr Zevallos, and the Seminario family (with which Lituma has crossed swords); finally, there are the "Inconquistables," two of whom (Lituma and Josefino) have been romantically involved with Selvática.

The formal divisions of the novel require comment because they relate closely to the dynamics of action and character development. The novel has four parts, followed by an Epilogue; each begins with an opening chapter which the author has elsewhere called an "umbral" (threshold). In addition to an "umbral," Parts 1 and 3 each contain four further chapters; parts 2 and 4 each have three. Thus a structural link exists between 1 and 3 and between 2 and 4. However, the chapters themselves are subdivided into shorter sections, numbering five in the cases of parts 1 and 2, and four in the cases of parts 3 and 4. Thus another structural link, cutting across the first, is set up between 1 and 2 on the one hand, and 3 and 4 on the other. Furthermore, the Epilogue has a total of five components if one includes the "umbral" in the count, four if one does not, thus pointing to two of the previously mentioned configurations. All of which makes for structural elegance; but more importantly, the formal links also suggest thematic ones, establishing patterns that enhance and direct the reading. A small but significant illustration is the fact that each grouping of five sections begins in the jungle and ends in Piura, hinting at the oppositions and transitions that are the very backbone of the novel, and implicit in its title.

From the foregoing it will be seen that there is a complex series of interrelationships among the characters, often involving love, parentage or violence. Insofar as it is clear, the picture that emerges by the end of the novel is not edifying: it is largely one of abuse and betrayal. The solidarity of the "Inconquistables" is a sham; it is even Selvática who maintains them with her earnings. The agents of religion, ostensibly civilizing the natives, have in fact been sending them into a life of servitude and sordidness. Economically, the Indians are victims of *criollo* greed. Selvática, clumping about awkwardly in her ill-fitting heels, is living proof, an anachronism, just like the green house flourishing in the coastal desert. It is with some irony that Anselmo's establishment is said to have brought civilization to Piura.

Not surprisingly, the early Vargas Llosa was often called a pessimist, yet he himself rejected that accusation, and other critics have talked of "environmental determinism" or fatalism. In this respect the Epilogue to the novel is worthy of attention, since unlike most, it does not simply introduce material subsequent to the main action, but takes the reader back to the beginning, and relates events that must have occured at the start of it all thus forcing the reader to reconsider what has been read. Two particular episodes in the Epilogue deserve comment: in one, Fushía dies and Nature obscures the smell and sight of his body, suggesting that we have come full circle (somewhat as in Carpentier's story *Viaje a la semilla* (*Journey Back to the Source*); in the other, Reátegui brings an Indian girl (presumably the one who will become Bonifacia/Selvática) to the jungle mission, as if really to begin the story.

The picture remains somewhat indistinct as the novel ends, the jigsaw pieces now largely in place: the truth is not absolute, the "facts" never quite clear. Love does appear to be a matter of commerce or the use of women by men (but wasn't there genuine tenderness between the disabled Toñita and Anselmo?; isn't Lalita, worn out and ugly though she is, also a survivor for whom we have a sneaking respect?). And was there ever really a first "casa verde," or was it, like the Phoenix, a myth?

Motivated by deeply felt concerns for social justice, Vargas Llosa shook his audience during his speech of acceptance on winning the prestigious Rómulo Gallegos prize in 1967; the role of the writer, he claimed, was to criticize the status quo: "La literatura es fuego" [Literature Burns]. Yet, trenchant though its socioeconomic criticisms are, *La casa verde* is not simply a piece of propaganda. It is a very carefully structured and controlled literary artefact whose roots are also aesthetic, a novel that takes some satisfaction in its own ambiguities and considerable formal elegance.

PETER STANDISH

Editions

First edition: *La casa verde*, Barcelona: Seix Barral, 1966
Translation: *The Green House*, by Gregory Rabassa, New York: Harper and Row, 1968; London: Jonathan Cape, 1969

Further Reading

Fenwick, Margaret J., *Literary Analysis: Reflections on Vargas Llosa's "The Green House,"* Minneapolis: Institute for the Study of Ideologies and Literature, 1981
Luchting, Wolfgang A., "Los mitos y lo mitizante en *La casa verde*," *Mundo Nuevo* 43 (January 1970)
Martin, Gerald, *Journeys through the Labyrinth: Latin American Fiction in the Twentieth Century*, London and New York: Verso, 1989 [Chapter 7 includes a section on *La casa verde*]

Historia de Mayta

Novel by Mario Vargas Llosa

Since the publication in 1963 of *La ciudad y los perros* (*The Time of the Hero*), Mario Vargas Llosa's literary production has been defined by his relentless study of Peruvian historical processes and society, and by his critical commentary on political and religious fanaticism, extreme conditions which predictably bring about apocalyptic consequences. His *Conversación en La Catedral* 1969 (*Conversation in The Cathedral*) is a devastating indictment of the deterioration of Peru's moral fiber, the result of years of political corruption and betrayal, social decay, and the loss of all sense of personal integrity. A controversial figure in his own country and abroad,

Vargas Llosa has consistently and overtly injected his personal, social and political ideology into his fiction, with varying degrees of success.

Historia de Mayta, 1984 (*The Real Life of Alejandro Mayta*), a novel that exhibits the structural complexities for which the Peruvian novelist is well known, examines the events of a failed, Marxist-Leninist insurrection which actually took place in the Peruvian Andes in the early 1960s. Vargas Llosa's novel reconstructs this obscure episode but places it in 1958, a year before the military victory of the Cuban Revolution. The ideological implications of this act of fiction are obvious. The emergence in Peru in 1980 of a wave of political terrorism, unprecedented by its blind violence, had shocked the country and the world. An extremist Maoist revolutionary movement operating under the name of *Sendero Luminoso* (Shining Path) had laid siege to the newly elected populist government of Fernando Belaúnde Terry, a fragile democracy trying to assert itself after twelve years of socialist military dictatorship. Ironically, it was during Belaúnde's first term as President – he was deposed by a military coup – that he had stamped on several guerrilla movements that had erupted in the wake of Fidel Castro's success. By placing the fictitious events before they had actually happened, the author sends the clear message that the orgy of violence perpetrated by *Sendero Luminoso* had its origin in the almost romantic insurrections of the 1960s, ill-fated revolutionary attempts led mostly by inexperienced intellectuals.

Written on several narrative temporal levels, the novel is a vastly modified reconstruction of the real events. Led by the flat-footed, overweight, ageing Trotskyist Alejandro Mayta, and by the self-proclaimed socialist, second lieutenant Vallejos, a ragtag band of adolescent would-be insurgents take up arms and head for the Andean highlands, but is quickly overtaken and decimated by the police. Vallejos is summarily executed, Mayta is captured, and the badly shaken boys are returned to their shocked parents. The insignificance of this farcical episode would have remained in historical obscurity had it not been for the investigation carried on by a writer – the novel's narrator and real protagonist – intent on recreating, twenty-five years later, the events of the aborted revolt with the purpose of using them as material for a novel.

During the course of his research, the novelist-narrator interviews a number of people whose testimonies serve to create a conflictive image of Mayta's personality, from his childhood as a devout boy destined for priesthood, to his alleged homosexuality and failure as a clandestine idealogue whose revolutionary doctrines did not produce any followers. In the process of creating a novel within a novel, Vargas Llosa appeals to the narrative techniques that have characterized his writing. The chronological sequence of events is distorted by the multiple intersection of texts that the reader has to reconstruct in order to have access to the whole story. The strategy of narrative fragmentation cuts across the different levels of "reality" in the fiction and allows the novelist-narrator to insert himself in the text as a protagonist who produces multiple and contradictory versions of Mayta's life. The proliferation of claims to the real life of Alejandro Mayta serves the purpose of integrating the author's ideology and of presenting his critical appraisal of social revolution in general. To this effect the novel presents an apocalyptic vision of Peru; United States Marines and Cuban troops are invading the country, with civil war, pestilence and famine posing the imminent threat of total destruction. It is in this atmosphere of social deterioration that the novelist-narrator desperately tries to finish his novel, an obsession about the act of writing that can be attributed to Vargas Llosa himself through his well-known commentaries on his art.

The multiple contradictions in the text are progressively revealed through the conversations between the novelist-narrator and those who claim that have known Mayta. The image of the well-intentioned, albeit naive revolutionary, is thoroughly demolished, and the picture that emerges is that of a man who has failed at everything that he has attempted, from his tortuous marital life to the inept implementation of his political convictions. It soon becomes evident to the reader that the multiple constructs of Mayta's life are nothing but lies, inventions by the novelist-narrator who takes advantage of an obscure character to create a fiction. This twist in the novel is a confirmation of Vargas Llosa's contention that fiction is more effective than history in the recreation of the past. The presence in the novel of "reliable" witnesses and of a chronicler who records their testimonies is the affirmation that the writing of historical fiction entails the re-reading and re-writing of an official history. The effect of this subversive act is to provide the conditions for literary imagination to confront and challenge what passes for historical truth.

ISMAEL P. MÁRQUEZ

Editions

First edition: *Historia de Mayta*, Barcelona: Seix Barral, 1984
Translation: *The Real Life of Alejandro Mayta*, by Alfred MacAdam, New York: Farrar Straus and Giroux, and London: Faber and Faber, 1986

Further Reading

Boland, Roy C., *Mario Vargas Llosa: Oedipus and the Papa State*, Madrid: Voz, 1988 [Chapter 7 is on *Historia de Mayta*]

Dunkerley, James, "Mario Vargas Llosa: Parables and Deceits," *New Left Review* 162 (March–April 1987) [A review article on the novel in its English translation]

Enkvist, Inger, "Reader Response to *Historia de Mayta* in Translation," *Antípodas*, vol. 3 (July 1991)

Souza, Raymond D., "*Historia de Mayta* y la ironía de la utopía," in his *La historia en la novela hispanoamericana moderna*, Bogotá, Colombia: Tercer Mundo, 1988

Vargas Llosa, Mario, *Mario Vargas Llosa: a Writer's Reality*, with an introduction by Myron I. Lichtblau, Syracuse, New York: Syracuse University Press, 1991 [Chapter 8 is on *Historia de Mayta*]

José Vasconcelos 1882–1959

Mexican essayist, educator and politician

Reading José Vasconcelos's *Memorias* [Memoirs] and most of his other works, and taking into account his very active participation in Mexican politics during and after the Revolution, gives one a clear impression of his strong-headedness and egocentricity. Vasconcelos was a writer of high moralistic ambition and strong temperament, Rector of the National University (1920–21) a vigorous Secretary of Public Education (1921–24), a presidential candidate himself in 1929, and a candid critic of Mexican culture and governmental practices for the rest of his life.

In *Memorias* (1936–39), particularly in the second of its four volumes *La tormenta* [The Storm], Vasconcelos repeatedly asserts his role as civic missionary, often contrasting those he considers to be morally and politically virtuous (spiritual descendants of the legendary Mayan Messiah Quetzalcóatl) like Madero and his supporters, and those he characterizes as actively and hypocritically evil (descendants of the truculent Aztec god of war Huitzilopochtli) like Victoriano Huerta and his collaborators. In his own memoirs (*El río* [The River]) Luis Cardoza y Aragón has written "his idiosyncrasy (his intellectual capacity aside) shows itself in his ability to love and hate at the same time." That "ability" permeates Vasconcelos's historical and theoretical essays as well as his autobiographical writing – for example, *La raza cósmica*, 1925 (*The Cosmic Race*), *Indología*, 1926 [Indiology], *Bolivarismo y monroísmo*, 1934 [Bolívar's Ideals versus the Monroe Doctrine], *Breve historia de México*, 1937 [A Brief History of Mexico] and *Estética*, 1933 [My Aesthetics]. Thus, his temperament was inseparable from his moral imperatives; for him, human conduct was driven by the extremes of good and bad, with little room for compromise. He lacked the measured detachment of his stylistically more refined contemporaries, Alfonso Reyes and José Ortega y Gasset, and channeled his epic wrath into the writing of his political and cultural allegations.

In *Ulises criollo* [A Creole Ulysses], and its sequel *La tormenta*, the author narrates his experiences from childhood (including an elementary school year in Eagle Pass, Texas) to the time of his appointment as Rector of the National University of Mexico in 1920. The third and fourth volumes of *Memorias*, *El desastre* [The Disaster] and *El proconsulado* [The Proconsul], are more politically detailed but less coherent than *Ulises criollo* and *La tormenta*. They embrace the author's experience as rector and re-organizer of the national university and as Secretary of Education, in which capacity he established a nationwide system of public schools and libraries, a vigorous literacy campaign, and a massive publishing program of textbooks; furthermore, he made the walls of the National Palace and several other public buildings available to the muralist painters, Diego Rivera, José Clemente Orozco, David Alfaro Siqueiros and Roberto Montenegro.

Over a decade before, Vasconcelos had been an influential member, together with Alfonso Reyes, Antonio Caso, Pedro Henríquez Ureña, Martín Luis Guzmán, Julio Torri and others, of the Ateneo de la Juventud [Athenaeum of Youth], founded in October, 1909. The group represented a cultural rebellion against the Positivist philosophy which they believed had been used and abused by Porfirio Díaz's regime as a pretext for maintaining social and economic inequality; the Ateneo's sentiments were clearly pro-revolutionary.

From that time, and at an intensified pace starting in 1921, Mexican art and literature experienced a new sense of national autonomy. Indigenous culture, which for three decades preceding the Revolution had been systematically ignored by administrators and the intellectual elite, was now enhanced and incorporated into the work of many artists and writers. *Mestizaje* (racial mixture and synthesis) was esteemed in all its ethic and esthetic potentiality; and it found eloquent expression in Vasconcelos's most frequently mentioned work, *La raza cósmica*. In this short book and its thematic sequel, *Indología*, as well as in his long and rambling *Estética*, the author concentrates on the future of Mexico and Latin America rather than their past frustrations. His synonym for the cosmic race is "the fifth race," referring to an idealized synthesis of the world's four basic ethnic groups: African, Anglo-European, Indian and Asiatic. The evolutionary result would be a eugenically pleasing people (at least to Vasconcelos; "the ugly shall not procreate," he declares bluntly) who would establish its Utopian and aesthetically pleasing capital of spiral-shaped buildings in the climatically pleasing region of the Amazonian basin. And the innate human desire for beauty would ultimately dissolve all material adversity.

That same desire permeated his personal relationships, as well as his writing; and it underlies a sensualized and irrationalistic philosophy which he applied to all reality. Accordingly the recurrent image of "Adriana," alias Elena Arizmendi, the lover who haunts the pages of *Ulises criollo* and *La tormenta*, symbolizes his Romantic quest of impossible perfections. Paradoxically, Vasconcelos the civilizer, the educator, and the political hero (who actually won the presidential election stolen from him by fraud in 1929) was not immune to deplorable prejudices (including a brief courtship with Nazi and Fascist dogma in 1940 and 1941). Privately and publicly he was a Dionysian spirit who lived and wrote as a tragic figure; he had portrayed himself as a modern Ulysses, but the adventures he experienced in his succession of exiles were notably less stimulating than those of Homer's hero. His tragedy is seen in the contrast between the ideals he articulated as an educator and civic crusader in his best works, written mostly in the decade starting in 1925, and his frustrations and largely recalcitrant opinions over the last twenty years of his life. It is in that context that his vigorous and uneven works should be read.

PETER G. EARLE

Biography

Born in Oaxaca, Mexico, 28 February 1882. Both parents were a strong formative influence. Mother well read and encouraged son to read and discuss literary works. Father was a customs inspector and thus family moved frequently along the US border. This enabled child to attend school in the US. Studied law at the National School of Jurisprudence, graduated in 1905. Married Serafina Miranda in 1909 (died), two children. Co-founder of Ateneo de la Juventud (Athenaeum of Youth), 1909; it existed as a formal body only until 1914 but played crucial part in revival of culture after deadening official policy of Positivism. From 1910 to 1930 absorbed in revolutionary and political activities. Supporter of Francisco Madero who was killed in 1913. Imprisoned by General Victoriano Huerta who assumed control on Madero's death. Appointed minister of Public Education in 1914, but left for New York the following year when his own faction was defeated. Stayed in US until assassination of Venustiano Carranza in May, 1920. Travelled in US and visited Peru. Dedicated himself to several business ventures. On returning to Mexico, headed Ministry of Public Education, 1920–24 – a vast undertaking and the most valuable service Vasconcelos rendered to his country. Resigned in order to stand for governorship of state of Oaxaca. Lost the election and alleged fraud. Went abroad in 1925, first to Europe and subsequently taught at several universities in the US (Chicago, Stanford, Berkeley). After the assassination of Álvaro Obregón (1928), before he took office as president of Mexico, Vasconcelos returned in 1929 to stand for presidency. Lost, and again alleged fraud. Returned to US and declared himself the legal Mexican head of state. Debarred from re-entering Mexico for this reason. Lived and worked abroad for ten years. Returned to Mexico in 1938. For next twenty years played active part in intellectual life of Mexico. Director of National Library, Library of Mexico and founding member of El Colegio de México. Married Esperanza Cruz in 1942, one son. Died in Mexico City, 30 June 1959.

Selected Works

Autobiography

Memorias, 2 vols, Mexico City: Fondo de Cultura Económica, 1982
    Ulises criollo, Mexico City: Botas, 1935
    La tormenta, Mexico City: Botas, 1936
    El desastre, Mexico City: Botas, 1938
    El proconsulado, Mexico City, Botas 1939

Prose Works

La raza cósmica, Barcelona: n.p., 1925; as *The Cosmic Race*, translated by Didier T. Jaen, Los Angeles: California State University, 1979
Indología: una interpretación de la cultura ibero-americana, Paris: Agencia Mundial Librería, 1926
Estética, Mexico City: Botas, 1933
Bolivarismo y monroísmo, Santiago de Chile: Ercilla, 1934
Breve historia de México, Mexico City: Botas, 1937
La flama: los de arriba en la revolución, Mexico City: Continental, 1959

Compilations and Anthologies

Páginas escogidas, edited by Antonio Castro Leal, Mexico City: Botas, 1940
Antología de José Vasconcelos, edited by Genaro Fernández MacGregor, Mexico City: Secretaría de Educación Pública, 1942; 2nd edition, Mexico City: Oasis, 1982
Discursos, 1920–1950, Mexico City: Botas, 1950
Obras completas, 4 vols, Mexico City: Libros Mexicanos Unidos, 1957–61
José Vasconcelos y la Universidad, edited by Álvaro Matute and Ángeles Ruiz, Mexico City: UNAM, 1983
Obra selecta, edited by Christopher Domínguez Michael, Caracas: Biblioteca Ayacucho, 1992

Further Reading

Bar-Lewaw Mulstock, Itzhak, *José Vasconcelos, vida y obra*, Mexico City: Clásica Selecta Editora Librera, 1966

Blanco, José Joaquín, *Se llamaba Vasconcelos: una evocación crítica*, Mexico City: Fondo de Cultura Económica, 1977

Cardoza y Aragón, Luis, *El río. Novelas de caballería*, Mexico City: Fondo de Cultura Económica, 1986

De Beer, Gabriella, *José Vasconcelos and His World*, New York: Las Américas, 1966

Fell, Claude, *José Vasconcelos. Los años del águila, 1920–1925*, Mexico City: UNAM, 1989

Giordano, Jaime, "Notas sobre Vasconcelos y el ensayo hispanoamericano del siglo veinte," *Hispanic Review*, vol. 61/3 (1973)

Haddox, John H., *Vasconcelos of Mexico, Philosopher and Prophet*, Austin: University of Texas Press, 1967

Krauze, Enrique, "Pasión y contemplación en Vasconcelos," *Vuelta* 78 and 79 (May–June 1983)

Magdaleno, Mauricio, *Las palabras perdidas*, Mexico City: Fondo de Cultura Económica, 1956

Martínez, José Luis, "La obra literaria de José Vasconcelos," in his *Literatura mexicana, siglo XX*, vol. I, Mexico City: Antigua Librería Robredo, 1949

Robles, Martha, *Entre el poder y las letras. Vasconcelos en sus memorias*, Mexico City: Fondo de Cultura Económica, 1989

Interviews

Carballo, Emmanuel, in *Protagonistas de la literatura mexicana de siglo XX*, Mexico City: Empresa Editoriales, 1986

Ana Lydia Vega 1946–

Puerto Rican prose writer

Ana Lydia Vega began to write in the 1970s, a time when prose writing flourished in Puerto Rico. Publications like *Zona de Carga y Descarga* [Loading and Unloading Zone] and *Penélope o el otro mundo* [Penelope or the Other World] were established, providing island writers with suitable outlets for their material. Vega, a professor of French language and literature at the University of Puerto Rico, is one of the island's most innovative short story writers of the second half of the 20th century. Her collections of short fiction include *Vírgenes y mártires*, 1981 [Virgins and Martyrs], *Encancaranublado y otros cuentos de naufragio*, 1982 [Encancaranublado and Other Shipwreck Stories], *Pasión de historia y otras historias de pasión*, 1987 [A Passion for History and Other Stories of Passion], and *Falsas crónicas del sur*, 1991 (*True and False Romances*). She also edited and collaborated in a collection of essays entitled *El tramo ancla: ensayos puertorriqueños de hoy*, 1988 [The Stretch of Anchor: Puerto Rican Essays of Today] and recently a number of her essays that appeared previously in the island's newspapers have been published as *Esperando a Loló y otros delirios generacionales*, 1994 [Waiting for Lolo and Other Generational Deliriums].

Vega's prose style and use of language are bold and innovative; women's rights, the plight of the exploited, and, in general, the Caribbean area together with its people and history are always at the forefront of her reflections and concerns.

The short story, "Pollito Chicken," [Chick Chicken] from the collection *Vírgenes y mártires* serves as an example of Vega's innovative style and discourse. The title of the short story refers to a children's bilingual song which, among other tools, was utilized by the American colonial government during the first half of the 20th century to transform Puerto Ricans into English speakers. Spanish-English code-switching is used in the story to indicate the main character's distorted identity and ideological confusion. Susie Bermiúdez, a young Puerto Rican woman who has lived in the United States for a decade, devalues her culture and her compatriots and wishes to become fully integrated into North American society even though it views her as inferior. Although this character always speaks in English, during a crucial moment in which her unconscious takes over, she reverts to Spanish, thus, at least at a deep level, her Puerto Rican identity is affirmed. As Diana L. Vélez states: "The ideological project of this story is that of national unity, unity between the *asimilaos* [assimilated] and the islanders, for, though she might deny it, Suzie Bermiúdez is, in the final analysis, a Puerto Rican just like the island puertorriqueños, [Puerto Ricans] who are Ana Lydia Vega's ideal readers."

Many of Vega's works are concerned with portraying women's changing role in Puerto Rican society and exploring women's relationships with men. In "Letra para salsa y tres soneos por encargo" [Letter for Salsa and Three Songs by Request], from *Vírgenes y mártires*, sex roles are reversed as the woman assumes the initiative in a male/female relationship and throws off the trappings of female victim. After several days of being treated as a sexual object and putting up with the verbal harassment of a man who seems solely dedicated to loathing in the streets, she answers his advances with a simple question: "¿Vamos?" (Shall we go?) and drives him to a motel where she proceeds to pay the bill and lead him to the hotel room. Having become her sexual object, the man is unable to perform sexually. The story includes three possible endings, entitled "Soneo I," "Soneo II," and "Soneo III." All three endings show that the woman is politically concerned and aware of her position as a member of the oppressed working class, while it is suggested, especially in "Soneo III," in which we see the man return to his usual street corner where he continues his verbal harassment of women, that Puerto Rican men are being left behind as women adapt to the new social and economic developments. Also the role of woman as writer is examined in stories like "Pasión de historia" from the collection *Pasión de historia y otras historias de pasión* and "Cuento en camino" [Travel Story] from *Falsas crónicas del sur*. In the first of the two, the main character, Carola, travels to Europe to work on a novel based on the violent murder of a Puerto Rican woman by an ex-lover. Ironically, the would-be writer ends up murdered by her own ex-lover. In the last scene of "Cuento en camino" we are faced by a young woman who tells the reader that her head is full of words and that she cannot wait to get home, sit at her desk, and take out her typewriter.

The stories collected in *Encancaranublado y otros cuentos de naufragio* are a denunciation of the exploitation and oppression suffered by the native inhabitants of the Caribbean. In the first story of the collection, "Encancaranublado," three men, one Haitian, one Dominican, and one Cuban find themselves aboard a tiny boat floating in the Caribbean sea. For them this sea becomes nothing more than a dangerous body of water that separates them from the "pursuit of happiness." Their goal is Miami, Florida and on their way there they begin to compare the economic and social situations in their three nations. Their conversation develops into a fight making all three end up in the water. Eventually an American ship picks them up and they are sent to the lower levels of the vessel accompanied by these words from the captain, "Get those niggers down there and let the Spiks [Puerto Ricans] take care of 'em." The story underscores the lack of solidarity among the people of the Caribbean and also the unjust relationships based on economic imbalance and racial discrimination which exist between the United States and the Caribbean islands. The lack of unity among the people of the Caribbean is also the subject of the story "Puerto Príncipe abajo" [Puerto Principe Down There] from *Vírgenes y mártires* which is divided into ten short sections each entitled "Diapositiva" [Slide] and each presenting a description of a Haitian scene. In this story a group of Puerto Rican tourists travel to Haiti and, as its title suggests, the group spends its time there as if "looking down" at Haitians and their society. Their condescending attitude is exhibited through, for example, racist comments such as, "Ave María, qué oscuridá, como está el prieto ahí . . ." (Holy Mary, what darkness, how many niggers . . .). Moreover, the Puerto Rican tourists pity the Haitians and view their country's poverty as a direct result of its condition as an independent nation while the text implies that Puerto Ricans should pity themselves for their own colonial status. Vega proposes in these two stories that it is the disunion among its people, negative racial attitudes, and lack of pride in things from the Caribbean that is leaving Antilleans at the mercy of more powerful nations.

Puerto Rican history becomes the focus of Vega's work in the last story of *Pasión de historia*, "Sobre tumbas y héroes (Folletín de caballería boricua)" [About Tombs and Heroes: a Puerto Rican Chivalresque Soap] and in *Falsas crónicas del sur*. The first questions the methods used by historians while the second is a collection of stories and anecdotes about the history of Puerto Rico's southern area. Some of the events that inspire the stories are well known, such as the central event, the Ponce massacre of 1937, of the story "Un domingo de Lilianne" [One of Lilliane's Sundays]. Looking at the collection as a whole, one notices that many of the stories have a female protagonist and that they are organized in chronological order covering Puerto Rico's history from 1859 to the present. The first story of the collection, "El baúl de Miss Florence: Fragmentos para un novelón romántico," [Miss Florence's Trunk: Fragments for a Romantic Trash Novel] is set during slavery and its main character is a female English tutor, Miss Florence. Vega's story represents a female version of history that rises out of the interstices allowed by official history. It is Vega's own *Falsas crónicas* that answers Miss Florence's questions, "¿Quién leerá estos labios mudos? ¿Quién desenterrará mi trunca historia de amor y le pondrá palabras?" (Who will read my silent lips? Who will unearth my truncated love story and put words to it?) as the book becomes an example of how a female narrative voice may retell the history of a Caribbean island and simultaneously inscribe women in this history.

In conclusion, Vega's work examines the changing values of Puerto Rican society and the influence of the colonial North American presence on the Island. Through an especially biting humour she examines the contradictions and distortions of traditional Puerto Rican values. Generally her characters, male and female, belong to the working class. Most importantly, Vega's language rises out of Puerto Rican popular culture and serves as a tool for social criticism.

LINDA M. RODRÍGUEZ

Biography

Born in Santurce, Puerto Rico, 6 December 1946. Attended the University of Puerto Rico; University of Provence. Professor of French and Caribbean literature, University of Puerto Rico, Río Piedras. Awarded the Casa de las Américas Prize, 1982 for *Encaranublado*; Juan Rulfo International Prize, 1984 for *Pasión de historia*; Guggenheim Fellowship, 1989.

Selected Works

Short Fiction

Vírgenes y mártires, in collaboration with Carmen Lugo Filippi, Río Piedras, Puerto Rico: Antillana, 1981

Encancaranublado y otros cuentos de naufragio, Havana: Casa de las Américas, 1982

Pasión de historia y otras historias de pasión, Buenos Aires: Ediciones de La Flor, 1987

Falsas crónicas del sur, illustrated by Walter Torres, Río Piedras: Editorial de la Universidad de Puerto Rico, 1991; as *True and False Romances: Stories and a Novella*, translated by Andrew Hurley, London: Serpent's Tail, 1994

Cuentos calientes, Mexico City: UNAM, 1992

Esperando a Lolo y otros delirios generacionales, San Juan, Puerto Rico: Editorial de la Universidad de Puerto Rico, 1994

Further Reading

Boling, Becky, "The Reproduction of Ideology in Ana Lydia Vega's "Pasión de historia" and "Caso omiso," *Letras Femeninas*, vol. 17/1-2 (1991)

Fernández Olmos, Margarite, "From a Woman's Perspective: the
Short Stories of Rosario Ferré and Ana Lydia Vega," in
Contemporary Women Authors of Latin America, Brooklyn, New
York: Brooklyn College Press, 1983

González, Anibal, "Ana Lydia Pluravega: unidad y multiplicidad
caribeñas en la obra de Ana Lydia Vega," *Revista
Iberoamericana*, vol. 56/162–63 (1993)

Vélez, Diana L., "*Pollito Chicken*: Split Subjectivity, National
Identity and the Articulation of Female Sexuality in a Narrative
by Ana Lydia Vega," *The Americas Review*, vol. 14/2 (1986)

Interview

Hernández, Elizabeth, "Women and Writing in Puerto Rico: an
Interview with Ana Lydia Vega," *Callaloo*, vol. 17/3 (1994)

Venezuela

19th- and 20th-Century Prose and Poetry

There are different ways of portraying the literature of a
country. In the following brief account the chosen method is
one that could be particularly productive for both the lay
reader and the reader acquainted with Venezuelan literature.
A contrast between this national tradition and the Spanish
American one as a whole underscores the most striking feature
of the Hispanic world: the paradoxical homogeneity of unmistakably diverse regions and cultures. Throughout its historical
development, Venezuelan literature has played different roles
in the Latin American context; sometimes it has been a leading
influence, sometimes almost a marginal provincial voice. The
following observations will try to define not only a history, but
also a set of useful elements to depict in general terms what
is unique about a particular country and its writers.

In comparison with other areas of Spanish America, such as
Central America, the Middle Andes or the Caribbean, the
poverty of the Venezuelan colonial period in the literary realm
is notorious, due to a lack of sophisticated pre-Columbian societies and also to the peripheral administrative condition of
Captaincy-General, which failed to attract a large number of
European colonists, including artists. The scarcity of memorable texts before Independence, therefore, invests the letters
of the first decades of the 19th century with a Golden Age
aura. Andrés Bello was the first Venezuelan writer who was
influential in other countries, but it is important to bear in
mind that he represents the ideals of a generation of his countrymen that decisively participated in the political reform of
all Spanish America: Simón Rodríguez, Francisco de Miranda
and Simón Bolívar, among others. One should notice that the
writings of these men emphasized what could be useful for
society in every intellectual enterprise. The most commonly
used genres are the moral epistle, the essay, the diary, the
political speech, i.e., varieties of literature close to the treatise
or oratory, left behind by later aesthetic trends, such as
Romanticism. It is arguable that modern Venezuelan literature
was born under the rule of 18th-century European
Enlightenment ideals, especially those of pragmatic involvement in creating a country. During the 19th century, nearly all
Venezuelan literature shows signs of this initial influence. In
the years that followed the separation from Spain, literature
was rarely considered an independent institution. Instead, it

was a device intended to improve communication among
intellectuals and their society; in fact, it was deliberately used
as a means of education or caveat.

The goal of freeing Latin America from European domination was a long term cultural problem as well as an immediate
political task for both Bello and Rodríguez. A poem such as
Bello's *Alocución a la poesía*, 1823 [Address to Poetry] suggests
a literary conflict between the New and the Old Worlds that
is expressed, nevertheless, in traditional European terms (the
metrical pattern of the Spanish *silva* and the use of Horatian
and Virgilian quotations) that perfectly render Bello's cautious
and moderate separatist views. On the other hand, *Sociedades
americanas en 1828* [Latin American Societies in 1828], a
long essay, with several versions written and published by
Simón Rodríguez between 1828 and 1842 in different South
American cities, is noticeably more audacious in its demand
for New World originality. This volume even attempts to create
a new way of writing by incorporating mathematical symbols
and distributing paragraphs, words, and sentences on the space
of the page in order to emphasize graphically and to analyze
certain ideas. Regardless of the revolutionary projects of Bellos
and Rodríguez, it is essential to remember that although both
were always conscious of the European roots of their thought,
their way of thinking was modern in the sense of privileging
the need for invention and cultural renewal. With these authors
as founding fathers, Venezuelan literature is linked to modernity from its very beginning and owes very little to the colony
or to the indigenous societies.

The international scope of action of the Venezuelan
liberators scattered a whole generation of reputable writers
throughout many nations. Bello published his most important
poems in England and then chose Chile as his new home;
Rodríguez, after spending many years in Europe, travelled
extensively through the Andes and finally died in Peru;
Miranda lived in Europe, fought for the independence of the
United States, participated in the French Revolution, and ended
his life as a prisoner in Spain; Bolívar went to Europe,
campaigned through the Antilles and the Andes, and died in
Colombia. Because Venezuela was deprived of its most brilliant
thinkers, ruined by a ferocious war of independence (which
reduced the national population by a third) and immediately

thereafter torn apart by decades of civil wars and political crisis, the rest of the 19th century could be described as a relatively weak era of minor authors. This was not the case in other Spanish American nations such as Argentina and Chile, which saw the beginnings of a stable and uninterrupted literary tradition in their first years of republican life. Oratorical genres and texts involved with political institutions prevailed from the 1830s to the 1880s. This fact could be interpreted as a survival of the idea of literature as a social tool, but also as the incapacity of Venezuelan society to develop a sense of literature as an autonomous institution. The familiar essay, the novel, and the short story are scarce and far from being coherent systems of aesthetic contact between authors and public. The only exception to this rule in the map of genres is the *artículo de costumbres* (the periodical essay of manners). Venezuela provided the ideal place for its full development as a collective literary form of expression, since it fulfilled the need for narratives and for the subjective reflection of both writers and readers. This explains the strength and abundance of this genre and the relative dearth of the novel or the predictable essay. Juan Manuel Cagigal, Fermín Toro, Daniel Mendoza, Nicanor Bolet Peraza and Francisco de Sales Pérez are only a few of the many authors who saw the *artículo de costumbres* as a vehicle to convey their ideas and to exhibit their fictional techniques, which were subordinated to the goal of depicting national reality, especially in its more regional and daily aspects. Daniel Mendoza, in particular, is the Spanish American writer who most eagerly tried, around the 1840s, to create a variety of *costumbrismo* closer to the New World than to the classical Spanish authors of the genre: Larra, Mesonero Romanos and Estébanez Calderón.

There exists yet another possible explanation for the absence of a solid novelistic tradition in Venezuela during the 19th century: the persistence of Neoclassicism, which did not favor such kind of literature in the Hispanic world. Other artistic movements, Romanticism and Realism, for instance, though already widely spread throughout Spanish America in the 1830s and 1840s, never enjoyed in Venezuela the continuity and vigor of Neoclassical poetics; at least, these trends were not in violent opposition in this country as they were in Argentina or Chile. Some of the most representative Venezuelan writers of the 19th century (Fermín Toro, Cecilio Acosta, José Antonio Calcaño) were ambiguously attracted by a variety of preferences. Several others dogmatically shared the conservative Neoclassical ideals which somehow accompanied the literary tastes of the Spanish Royal Academy; in fact, the Venezuelan Rafael María Baralt was the first Latin American ever to become a member of that institution in 1853. Both his style as a poet and orator and his purist views about the Spanish language were famous internationally. His celebrity was never to be matched by the efforts of his fellow countrymen who defended individualism and sentimental subjectivity and tried to follow the Romantic revolution in literature (José Antonio Maitín, Juan Vicente González).

By the end of the 19th century *costumbrismo* became more peripheral; writers of fiction and essay, increasingly prestigious. Moreover, the presence of Romantic ideas and stylistic elements finally seemed to be strengthened in the prose of Eduardo Blanco and the verses of Juan Antonio Pérez Bonalde. In the 1880s and 1890s the conflict between what was considered to be "foreign" and what was "national" deepened as an aesthetic factor. Undoubtedly, the consequence of this was the appearance of one of the most constant debates in Venezuelan literary life ever: the struggle between *cosmopolitismo* and *criollismo* (a word which in Spanish America stands for nationalism and, hence, not to be hastily associated with the English word *Creole*). The art of the Americas knows this false dichotomy under different names; in Venezuela, though, this superficial contradiction has adopted, at least until the 1980s, a more constant and violent tone among critics and writers, who have opposed *modernistas* against *criollistas* at first, then, sometimes loosely, *regionalistas* against *vanguardistas*, *intimistas* against *comprometidos* [engaged], *líricos* against *urbanos* and so on.

Spanish American *Modernismo*, José Martí and Rubén Darío being its founders and leaders, tried to reach a compromise on the dispute. Venezuelan *Modernismo*, in particular, denied the existence of contraries and instead synthesized them in a rather emphatic way. Leading magazines like *El Cojo Ilustrado* [The Cultivated Limper] (1892–1915) and *Cosmópolis* (1894–95) clearly proposed the gathering of cultural introspection and extrospection as one of their dearest goals. For example, the three directors of *Cosmópolis*, Pedro César Dominici, Pedro Emilio Coll and Luis Manuel Urbaneja Achelpohl, wrote in a wide aesthetic spectrum that ranged from the most exquisite and Parisian decadence (Dominici) to a dramatic realism that closely portrayed the people and habits of the nation in an urgent project of patriotic redemption (Urbaneja Achelpohl). Indeed, the two Venezuelan authors linked to the *modernista* movement who were to become internationally renowned and certainly memorable, Manuel Díaz Rodríguez and Rufino Blanco Fombona, are excellent models of the reconciliation of supposedly antagonistic preferences. In two of the most representative Latin American novels of the turn of the century, *Ídolos rotos*, 1901 [Broken Idols] and *Sangre patricia*, 1902 [Patrician Blood], Díaz Rodríguez showed the fictional possibilities of *Modernismo* as a drive for metaliterary validation and the acceptance of a new form of idealism, while *Peregrina*, his last novel (1920), "returns" to regional imagery, though without renouncing the previous pattern of quasi-mystical stylistic refinement. Rufino Blanco Fombona, on the other hand, in his vehement and barbaric tone, transformed from a gallant and almost decorative poet into a preacher of patriotism and political art.

A point to be underscored in Venezuelan *Modernismo*, which was the second opportunity the country had to be a leading presence in Spanish American literature, is the importance of its prose genres (essay, novel, short-story) and the general irrelevance of its poetry, the contrary of what happened in the rest of the Hispanic world. Ironically, perhaps the most attractive poet of Venezuela during the first three decades of the 20th century was José Antonio Ramos Sucre, a *posmodernista* rediscovered in the 1960s, who chose prose as a suitable vehicle for his poetry.

The first half of the 20th century is, in Venezuela, an age of dominant meditation about national problems and identity. One of the main consequences of this self-questioning was the revitalization of surviving 19th-century trends such as Realism and Naturalism in the novels of Rómulo Gallegos, who mapped the country in books that systematically depicted different environments: *Doña Bárbara* (1929) and *Cantaclaro* (1934) (the southwestern and central plains), *Canaíma* (1936) (the southeastern jungle), and so forth. Venezuela became an object to be explored and understood not only spatially, but also chronologically; the essay, the short story and the novel frequently engaged in the dramatization of historical events as in the works of Arturo Uslar Pietri, Mariano Picón-Salas, Mario Briceño Iragorry, or Isaac Pardo, while contemporary history was also dealt with in narrative and testimonial genres by authors such as José Rafael Pocaterra, Ramón Díaz Sánchez and Miguel Otero Silva. Poetry lingered on a conservative combination of folksy Romanticism and *modernista* exquisiteness as in Andrés Eloy Blanco or Aquiles Nazoa. As a result, the international avant-garde, whose influence was so powerful at the time in other Spanish American countries (Peru, Argentina, Chile), never became firmly entrenched in Venezuela. The experimental or individualistic consciousness had almost nothing to do with the didactic and provincial spirit most Venezuelan writers shared before the 1960s.

Of course, there were some exceptions. Fernando Paz Castillo and Jacinto Fombona Pachano avoided any sort of poetry of manners and sometimes reached a sincere tone of intimate meditation. Although Teresa de la Parra wrote realistic novels, as did Gallegos, the psychological depth and autonomy of her characters rejected any use of fiction as a direct political device. The same should be said of the later narratives of Enrique Bernardo Núñez, who succeeded in insinuating a mythic side of Latin American history. Also remarkable is the unique work of Julio Garmendia, one of the few Venezuelans who dared to write fantastic short stories in the 1920s and who, consequently, has only been recognized as a major author many decades later.

As already suggested, Venezuelan literature synchronized again with the rest of Spanish American literature only around the 1950s. Since this time, the skills associated with writing as a progressive political activity have been disappearing, increasingly thwarted by a concern with individual, aesthetic, metaphysical and even religious matters.

Such diversity is fully expressed in the poetry of Vicente Gerbasi, Juan Liscano and Juan Sánchez Peláez, who are certainly inspired by some surviving Romanticism, but thoroughly sublimated by the Surrealist experience. Gerbasi's sober affective world, Liscano's polyphonic blend of eroticism and paced meditation, and Sánchez Peláez's dreamlike verbal imagery are almost classic models for contemporary poets. Their efforts made possible, thereafter, in the 1960s and 1970s, the reshaping of the landscape and the human understanding of it in the lyrical creations of Ramón Palomares, Enrique Hernández D'Jesús, Luis Alberto Crespo and Eugenio Montejo. Montejo in particular has developed a complex vision of the universe in which the poetic *persona* becomes an element of a harmonious cosmos expressed in the poem by means of peacefulness and equilibrium. Other significant poets already well-known before the 1980s are Alfredo Silva Estrada, Francisco Pérez Perdomo, Juan Calzadilla, Jorge Nunes, Rafael Cadenas, Armando Romero and Julio Miranda, all of whom write with highly intellectual, even abstract overtones, brought down to earth sometimes by the expression of affection (Nunes), sometimes by looking at reality in unexpected perspectives (Miranda).

Among the latest trends in Venezuelan poetry is the combination of coloquial speech and urban or everyday topics represented in the 1980s by groups such as *Tráfico* [Traffic] and *Guaire* (named after a polluted river that runs through Caracas). This type of poetry is connected to a truly Latin American tendency whose internationally imitated canon includes Ernesto Cardenal and José Emilio Pacheco. Rafael Arráiz Lucca and Blanca Strepponi are two of the Venezuelan poets of the 1980s whose work has been evolving in the 1990s into more complex and personal patterns, far from any tribalism or simplistic avant-garde.

Contemporary Venezuelan narrators owe a great deal to *El falso cuaderno de Narciso Espejo*, 1952 [Narcissus Mirror's Apocryphal Notebook] and *La misa de Arlequín*, 1962 [Harlequin's Mass], the later novels of Guillermo Meneses, milestones in a national tradition of fictional texts about the reading and writing of fiction. With the publication of these books, narrative experiments became common among Venezuelans and the legacy of early Modernist European and North American writers was finally assimilated. Oswaldo Trejo, for instance, explores the possibilities of linguistic playfulness inspired by the literary adventures of James Joyce or Raymond Queneau; Salvador Garmendia elaborates a gloomy variety of social expressionism (named *informalismo* by critics such as Ángel Rama); fragmentary techniques and distortion in the representation of time are used by Luis Britto García, Adriano González León and Carlos Noguera; and still other authors, such as José Balza, deepen Meneses's metafictional discoveries by adding to them an overrefined style which certainly reveals an amazing persistence of *Modernismo* in Venezuelan narrative practices.

During the so-called Boom of the Latin American novel, Venezuela was certainly absent from the world stage. The reason is not to be found in the aesthetic quality of the national production, since at least the works of Meneses and Salvador Garmendia have been highly praised by international critics. Rather, the explanation seems to be related to a precise social phenomenon: the 1960s and 1970s were decades of democratic consolidation and apparent economic prosperity in Venezuela, in contrast to the rest of the region. Venezuela did not attract the world's attention and, even more significantly, was not publicized abroad by political émigrés interested in making their homeland known. In the 1990s, since the Boom is over and the country is submerged in a pitiful financial crisis, all conditions seem favorable for an international rediscovery of Venezuelan novelists. Some works of the 1980s and 1990s prove that Venezuela is ready to enter a period of mature and thoughtful use of certain technical devices that Latin American authors from the 1960s and 1970s made well-known. Intertextuality, for instance, is now a conscious means of creation. *Homo Sapiens* (1990) by Oscar Rodríguez Ortiz and *Voces al atardecer*, 1990 [Voices at Dusk] by Francisco Rivera are superbly designed junctions of quotations and allusions in which writing and reading become inseparable tasks. Rodríguez Ortiz adds an elegant raid into the realm of eroticism to the textual collage of his short novel. Rivera, on the other hand, while structuring a vast, realistic and highly complex text which takes into account all the varieties of Spanish spoken in Caracas, succeeds in depicting characters and situations that interweave convincingly and constitute moving representations of human passions along with a subtle series of meditations on the process of artistic creation. Another interesting development in the new narrative is the contribution of detective fiction to texts that exhibit their own genre theory: *Los platos del diablo*, 1985 [The Devil's Dishes] by Eduardo Liendo is perhaps the best example. Other noteworthy authors of fiction of recent years are Humberto Mata and Antonio López Ortega.

Since the 1950s, the essay, like the narrative, has acquired an international conscience in Venezuela. To the nationalistic autism of topics and oratorical expression dominated by the pedagogical and collective impulse in the 1930s, 1940s and 1950s, the new texts have opposed an aesthetic understanding of the world, in which the individual has found a place and organizes the production of knowledge. From that standpoint, the most respected and influential essayists of contemporary Venezuela are Juan Liscano, Guillermo Sucre and Francisco Rivera, whose ideas of the essay are based on the distinction of personal and artistic reasoning from other rigidly institutionalized forms of research.

MIGUEL GOMES

See also entries on Rómulo Gallegos, Miguel Otero Silva, Teresa de la Parra, Arturo Uslar Pietri

Further Reading

Karsen, Sonja, *Ensayos de literatura e historia iberoamericana*, New York: Peter Lang, 1988 [Chapter on Venezuela contains sections on Rufino Blanco Fombona and *Doña Bárbara*]

Lewis, Marvin A., *Ethnicity and Identity in Contemporary Afro-Venezuelan Literature*, Columbia: University of Missouri Press, 1992

Liscano, Juan, *Panorama de la literatura venezolana actual*, Caracas: Alfadil, 1984

Miliani, Domingo, *Tríptico venezolano*, Caracas: Fundación de Promoción Cultural de Venezuela, 1985

Picón-Salas, Mariano, *Formación y proceso de la literatura venezolana*, Caracas: Monte Ávila, 1984

Rama, Ángel, *Ensayos sobre literatura venezolana*, Caracas: Monte Ávila, 1985

Special Issues of Journals
Revista Iberoamericana 166–67 (January–June 1994)

Érico Veríssimo 1905–1975

Brazilian prose writer

Along with Jorge Amado, Érico Veríssimo became one of the most popular Brazilian writers. Their respective debuts coincided with the regional developments of the Brazilian modernist movement. The former became one of the great names from the northeast, the latter shone from the opposite extreme of the country, the southern region. Within Veríssimo's vast corpus of fiction, complemented by memoirs and travel books, two great novelistic cycles stand out: the first, providing a synchronic picture, consists of urban social novels and narrates the saga of the petty bourgeoisie in the south, contemporaneous with the author. The second, of epic dimensions, is the diachronic mosaic developed in the trilogy *O tempo e o vento* (*Time and the Wind*).

From the novel *Clarissa* (the starting point of the novelist's career) to *Saga*, in the fashion of Honoré de Balzac, Veríssimo presented a chronological history of a group of characters. So, even though initially the reader is introduced to the existential conflicts of the adolescent Clarissa and her cousin, the proud Vasco, in a small country village, the reader will re-encounter both characters transferred to the capital of the state, Pôrto Alegre, where they face the challenges of life in a big city. In *Caminhos cruzados* (*Crossroads and Destinies*), Veríssimo experiments with the technique of "counterpoint" (inspired by the English writer Aldous Huxley), which he would develop further in his later works. Through this technique different points of view (in this case the writer's and the characters') are juxtaposed. This narrative fragmentation works as a formal record of the very fragmentation of reality, and of the identity crisis of the individual in modern society. On the other hand, Veríssimo, like Huxley, fuses fiction and essay by using the narrator's voice to elaborate reflections on social politics and philosophy.

In the cycle *O tempo e o vento*, which consists of three parts (*O continente* [The Continent], *O retrato* [The Picture] and *O arquipélago* [The Archipelago]), the "counterpoint" technique is employed to juxtapose temporal levels: present time against past time. The reconstitution of the latter is organized by an explicit relationship with the former. Two hundred years in the history of two southern families are covered, the Terra Cambará and the Amaral, a saga coinciding with the very formation of Rio Grande do Sul (Brazil's most southerly state), whose heroic settlement dating back to the 18th century is here recorded. It is therefore the epic of a region, from the initial land disputes between the Portuguese and the Spaniards during the colonial period, to the separatist struggles in the early 19th century (when the "farrapos" fighting the "imperialists" attempted to secede from the rest of Brazil), to important events in the mid-20th century. However, it is also the saga of patriarchal society in this part of the American continent since the author narrates its acclimatization, its apogee, and final decadence when challenged by the new emerging social class that had already been predominant in Europe and the US for some time, i.e., the bourgeoisie. And so the historical reflections motivated by *O tempo e o vento* go beyond regional boundaries to the point of allowing an analysis of social problems in the Brazil of Veríssimo's own period, which relate also to the whole of Latin America.

In *O senhor embaixador* (*His Excellency the Ambassador*) and *O prisioneiro* [The Prisoner] Veríssimo departs, for the first time, from the context of Rio Grande do Sul, in order to write a kind of international political novel. The social engagement of the author then became explicit and was further accentuated when, with the novel *Incidente em Antares* [Incident in Antares], he returned to a Brazilian context to fictionalize the historic moment of strict censorship and political repression experienced in Brazil in the 1970s. Thus in his last novel, conceived with the techniques of magical realism, seven corpses that were not buried because of a strike promote a critique of the prevailing moral and social system.

TERESINHA V. ZIMBRÃO DA SILVA

Biography

Born in the city of Cruz Alta, Rio Grand do Sul, Brazil, 17 December 1905. Education interrupted by separation of his parents. Obliged to take on a job as clerk. Decided on a career in letters after the publication of one of his stories in a Pôrto Alegre journal. Secretary of the magazine *Revista do Globo* [World Review] and later became its editor. Translated literary texts for the publishing house, Globo. In 1941, spent three months in the United States at the invitation of Department of State. Taught at the University of California, Berkeley, 1943; lectured at a number of universities and stayed in the US until 1946. Director of the cultural division of Pan-American Union, Washington, DC, 1953–56. Travelled to Europe in 1959. Suffered a heart attack in 1961. Continued to write and travelled frequently to Europe; visited Israel in 1966. In 1972, a national celebration of his contribution to literature was held in Brazil. First Brazilian writer to live by his pen, the first to gain best-seller status and the first to attempt the modern, urban novel. Died in Pôrto Alegre, 28 November 1975.

Selected Works

Novels

Clarissa, Pôrto Alegre, Brazil: Globo, 1933
Caminhos cruzados, Pôrto Alegre, Brazil: Globo 1935; as *Crossroads and Destinies*, translated by L.C. Kaplan, London: Arco, 1956; New York: Greenwood Press, 1969
Música ao longe, São Paulo: Nacional, 1935
Olhai os lírios do campo, Pôrto Alegre, Brazil: Globo 1938; as *Consider the Lilies of the Field*, translated by Jean Neel Karnoff, New York: Macmillan, 1947
Saga, Pôrto Alegre, Brazil: Globo, 1940
O resto é silêncio, Pôrto Alegre, Brazil: Globo, 1943; as *The Rest is Silence*, translated by L.C. Kaplan, New York: Macmillan, 1946; London: Arco, 1956
O tempo e o vento: O continente, Pôrto Alegre, Brazil: Globo 1949; as *Time and the Wind*, translated by Linton Barrett, New York: Macmillan, 1951; London: Arco, 1954

O tempo e o vento: O continente; O retrato, Pôrto Alegre, Brazil: Globo, 1951
Noite, Rio de Janeiro: Globo, 1954; as *Night*, translated by Linton Barrett, New York: Macmillan, and London: Arco, 1956
O tempo e o vento: O continente; O retrato; O arquipélago, Pôrto Alegre, Brazil: Globo, 1961
O senhor embaixador, Pôrto Alegre, Brazil: Globo, 1965; as *His Excellency the Ambassador*, translated by Linton Barrett and Marie McDavid Barrett, New York: Macmillan, 1967
O prisioneiro, Pôrto Alegre, Brazil: Globo, 1967
Incidente em Antares, Pôrto Alegre, Brazil: Globo, 1971

Children's Literature

As aventuras do avião vermelho, Pôrto Alegre, Brazil: Globo, 1936
Rosemaria no castelo encantado, Pôrto Alegre, Brazil: Globo, 1936
As aventuras de Tibicuera, que são também as aventuras do Brasil, Pôrto Alegre, Brazil: Globo, 1937
Os três porquinhos pobres, Pôrto Alegre, Brazil: Globo, 1937
O urso com música na barriga, Pôrto Alegre, Brazil: Globo, 1938
Aventuras no mundo da higiene, Pôrto Alegre, Brazil: Globo, 1939
Outra vez os três porquinhos, Pôrto Alegre, Brazil: Globo, 1939
Viagem à aurora do mundo, Pôrto Alegre, Brazil: Globo, 1939
A vida do elefante Basílio, Pôrto Alegre, Brazil: Globo, 1939
A vida de Joana d'Arc, Pôrto Alegre, Brazil: Globo, 1940
Gente e bichos: histórias infantis, Pôrto Alegre, Brazil: Globo, 1956

Travel Writing

Gato preto em campo de neve, Pôrto Alegre, Brazil: Globo, 1941
A volta do gato preto, Pôrto Alegre, Brazil: Globo, 1946
México. Historia duma viagem, Pôrto Alegre, Brazil: Globo, 1957; as *Mexico*, translated by Linton Barrett, New York: Orion Press, and London: Macdonald, 1960
Israel em abril, Pôrto Alegre, Brazil: Globo, 1969

Other Writings

Fantoches, Pôrto Alegre, Brazil: Globo, 1932 [short fiction]
Brazilian Literature: an Outline, New York: Macmillan, 1945
Solo de clarineta: memórias, 2 vols, Pôrto Alegre, Brazil: Globo, 1973–76

Compilations and Anthologies

Ficção completa, 5 vols, Rio de Janeiro: Aguilar, 1966–67

Further Reading

The works of Érico Veríssimo have not received the critical acclaim they deserve, a situation that has improved only to some extent since the publication of the monograph by Flávio Loureiro Chaves.

Bosi, Alfredo, "Érico Veríssimo," in his *História concisa da literatura brasileira*, São Paulo: Cultrix, 1970
Chaves, Flávio Loureiro, *Érico Veríssimo: realismo e sociedade*, Pôrto Alegre, Brazil: Globo, 1976
Martins, Wilson, "Érico Veríssimo," in *A literatura brasileira: o Modernismo*, vol. 6, São Paulo: Cultrix, 1969
Zilberman, Regina, *A literatura no Rio Grande do Sul*, Pôrto Alegre, Brazil: Mercado Aberto, 1982

Xavier Villaurrutia 1903–1950

Mexican poet, dramatist and prose writer

There can have been few writers so devoted to the cause of literature as Xavier Villaurrutia, critic, poet, playwright and cultural commentator. A towering, enigmatic figure in the history of 20th-century Mexican literature, his importance is easier to reflect upon than to analyse in detail. The work for which he is most famous, his lyric poetry, amounts to little more than a slim volume, and yet its influence, seldom fully acknowledged, resonates throughout Latin America.

Villaurrutia was a key member of the Contemporáneos group of writers and thinkers which emerged in the 1920s and 1930s and whose participants identified themselves firmly as the inheritors of European "universal" literary and aesthetic values. Rejecting the nationalistic calls to write a politicised and specifically Mexican literature, this group found in Villaurrutia the embodiment of much that it stood for: possessed of a remarkable literary intelligence and a singular devotion to the most minute literary detail, as well as a prodigious knowledge of classical, romantic and contemporary literature, Villaurrutia stands out as one of Mexico's greatest men of letters. It is perhaps ironic that despite his painstaking devotion to the "universal" canon, his reputation has mainly flourished in Mexico, while that of some of his more overtly Mexicanist contemporaries has spread throughout the literary and critical communities of Europe and the United States.

Perhaps the best way to approach Villaurrutia's work is to examine the numerous pithy and astute pieces of literary criticism which he wrote. These essays give us first of all a sense of his literary antecedents: Rilke, Cocteau, Valéry, Nerval among European writers; Sor Juana Inés de la Cruz, Ramón López Velarde, Rafael López and Alfonso Reyes, among Mexicans. They also provide a flavour of Villaurrutia's unique literary sensibility. Rigorously subjecting itself to the task of a painstaking exegesis, his literary criticism is a masterpiece of precise observation and constitutes a philosophical treatise on the nature of reading and understanding; in particular, articulating a Titanic struggle between emotion and intellect in which for the most part the intellect emerges triumphant.

This struggle finds its echoes in Villaurrutia's most famous and important literary output, his poetry. Critics tend to agree that this can be divided into three discrete periods, each with a distinctive solution to the question of the relationship between rigour, technique and restraint on the one hand, and the need to give voice to the most effusive and intangible of human feelings on the other.

The early poetry, best represented in *Reflejos*, 1926 [Reflections], is a pyrotechnic display of brilliant effects. There is a compelling precision in the writing: no rhythm is insufficiently elaborated; each punctuation mark appears to have been located with an almost scholarly attention to detail. What the poems lack in heartfelt emotional content, they make up for in their muscular play of wit and erudition. Poetic references, classical allusions and unexpected puns abound. This is poetry about poetry itself. Words, cut adrift from the constraints of context or common meaning, acquire a deconstructive force, a logic of their own as irony gains the upper hand.

It is commonly acknowledged that Villaurrutia's best poetry was still to come. When *Nocturnos*, 1931 [Nocturnes] and, especially, *Nostalgia de la muerte*, 1938 (*Nostalgia for Death*) appeared, the youthful brilliance of the early work came into contact with the mature workings of a literary and philosophical intellect. These works maintain an extraordinary equilibrium between style and content, thinking and feeling, word and meaning. The central preoccupations are night and death, and they are worked through with dazzling insights.

Night is portrayed as that time at which experience is suspended in a kind of liminality which is both terrifying and liberating. Death, particularly in "Décima muerte," (Tenth Death) the poem which has come to epitomise Villaurrutia's talent, emerges as shaping our essential human condition, identifying a profound metaphysical loneliness. Although death was later to become a theme adopted as part of Mexico's own cultural heritage, in Villaurrutia (overtly at least) the treatment has less to do with Mexican folk attitudes than with the work of the French poets and Rilke, as well as a weighty and impressive European philosophical tradition, which includes Max Scheler and, according to some critics, Martin Heidegger. However, something of the quintessentially Catholic, Mexican nature of Villaurrutia's experience is never far from the surface.

The poetry of Villaurrutia's third period has fared less well with critics. When *Canto a la primavera*, 1948 [Song to Spring] appeared, it was clear that an important change had taken place in his literary attitudes. Here, Villaurrutia attempts to give free rein to his emotions and to achieve an exuberant homage to such traditional poetic themes as Spring, love and desire. The intellectual restraint of the earlier work gives way to a passionate poetic outburst controlled only by the metrical demands of the form. Critics have tended to dismiss this later work as unworthy of Villaurrutia's talent and good taste, but there is much here that deserves closer attention. For one thing, the technical and linguistic mastery has scarcely diminished; for another, these poems have tended to be read without a trace of wit: recognition of the irony they articulate transforms them and makes them rather more problematic than their detractors would have us believe.

While Villaurrutia's reputation rests mainly on his poetry, it is important not to ignore the significant contribution he made to theatre. Along with Rodolfo Usigli, he stands as one of the most important dramatists in Mexico's history. Writing drama took up most of Villaurrutia's creative energies, particularly in his later years and his output is both copious and influential.

The five one-act plays collected in *Autos profanos*, 1941 [Profane Sacramental Autos] represent Villaurrutia's early dramatic work. They belong to a world which is as strange as it is timeless. The characters, who can appear stiff or unrealistic, are cast as representatives of different intellectual positions in a series of animated philosophical debates which shun the conventions of realism in favour of the precise development of an argument. There is something of the Platonic dialogue in these pieces, and yet the poet's attitude to language and the delicate architectural balance of the prose rescue the plays from incurring the charge of being dry or scholastic.

Villaurrutia's early plays with their expertly-crafted plots were a great success. His later plays were also performed to great public and critical acclaim. However, they work better when read than performed. The profound religious and philosophical musings of *La hiedra*, 1941 [Ivy] or *La mujer legítima*, 1943 [The Legitimate Wife] articulate eternal enigmas of human interaction in a dramatic texture so dense with allusions and subtle ironies that the plays come alive only with the most attentive and concentrated reading.

One especially provocative example of this later work, *Invitación a la muerte*, 1944 [Invitation to Death], takes as its premise Hamlet's existential and ethical crisis, transposing it onto a young Mexican grappling with the dilemmas of modern Mexico. In this piece perhaps more than any other, it is possible to perceive in sharp focus the tension between Mexicanness and universality so fundamental to Villaurrutia's literary stance. The various aporias posited by the drama both mark out the boundaries of this dichotomy and signal Villaurrutia's rigorous and forward-looking rejection of easy philosophical answers.

Villaurrutia's output also includes criticism of film, theatre and the visual arts, as well as the prose piece, *Dama de corazones*, 1928 [Lady of Hearts] which is an innovative and unusual avant-garde attempt at a novel consisting of tortured and demanding interior monologues. This is certainly worthy of more critical attention than it has so far received, with its fine prose style and careful exposition.

As a man of letters, Villaurrutia excelled. Through its profound impact on later writers such as Octavio Paz, his poetry, criticism and drama will no doubt continue to exert a singular influence over Mexican literature for some time to come.

MAURICE BIRIOTTI

Biography

Born in Mexico City, 27 March 1903. Attended the Colegio Francés; Escuela Preparatoria Nacional; and the School of Jurisprudence. Abandoned study of law because he became financially independent. Co-founder, with Jaime Torres Bodet, of the review *La Falange* (The Phalanx), 1922. Joined civil service and was employed first in Ministry of Health and later in editorial department of Ministry of Education. Helped to found the reviews *Ulises* (1927–28) and *Contemporáneos* (1928). Founded the Teatro Ulises (1928) and, with José Gorostiza, the Teatro Orientación. Spent the academic year 1935–36 at Yale Drama School, having won a Rockefeller Foundation scholarship. In 1936 founded the drama group of the Electrician's Union and was its director until 1939. Appointed to chair at National Drama School. On the surface, at least, Villaurrutia's life was rather uneventful. This may be because of his homosexuality which, in the context of the period, made prudent the adoption of a low profile. Died of a heart attack in Mexico City, 25 December, 1950. After his death, the Xavier Villaurrutia prize was established in his honour.

Selected Works

Poetry
Reflejos, Mexico City: Cultura, 1926
Dos nocturnos, Mexico City: Barandal, 1931
Nocturnos, Mexico City: Fábula, 1931
Nocturno de los Ángeles, Mexico City: Hipocampo, 1936
Nocturno mar, Mexico City: Hipocampo, 1937
Nostalgia de la muerte, Buenos Aires: Sur, 1938; as *Nostalgia for Death*, translated by Eliot Weinberger, Port Townsend, Washington: Copper Canyon Press, 1993

Plays
Parece mentira, Mexico City: Mundial, 1934
¿En qué piensas?, Mexico City: Letras de México, 1938
Sea Ud. breve, Mexico City: Nandino, 1938
Autos profanos, Mexico City: Letras de México, 1941
La hiedra, Mexico City: Nueva Cultura, 1941
La mujer legítima, Mexico City: Loera y Chávez, 1943
Invitación a la muerte, Mexico City: Letras de México, 1944
El yerro candente, Mexico City: Letras de México, 1945
El pobre Barba Azul, Mexico City: Sociedad General de Autores de México, 1948
La tragedia de las equivocaciones, Guanajuato, Mexico: Gráficos Guanajuato, 1950
El solterón, Mexico City: Colección Teatro Mexicano, 1954

Novel
Dama de corazones, Mexico City: Ulises, 1928

Compilations and Anthologies
"*Décima muerte*" *y otros poemas no coleccionados*, Mexico City: Nueva Voz, 1941
"*Canto a la primavera*" *y otros poemas*, Mexico City: Stylo, 1948
Obras, edited by Miguel Capistrán, Alí Chumacero and Luis María Schneider, Mexico City: Fondo de Cultura Económica, 1953; revised and augmented edition, 1966
Cartas de Villaurrutia a Novo: 1935–1936, Mexico City: INBA, 1966
Antología, edited by Octavio Paz, Mexico City: Fondo de Cultura Económica, 1980

Further Reading

Cypess, Sandra Messinger, "The Influence of the French Theater in the Plays of Xavier Villaurrutia," *Latin American Theatre Review*, vol. 3/1 (1969)
Dauster, Frank N., *Xavier Villaurrutia*, New York: Twayne, 1971
Forster, Merlin H., *Fire and Ice: the Poetry of Xavier Villaurrutia*, Chapel Hill: University of North Carolina Press, 1976
Moretta, Eugene, *La poesía de Xavier Villaurrutia*, Mexico City: Fondo de Cultura Económica, 1976
_____ "Villaurrutia y Gorostiza: hacia una visión más amplia de los poetas 'Contemporáneos,'" *Cuadernos Americanos* 224 (May–June 1979)
Paz, Octavio, *Xavier Villaurrutia en persona y en obra*, Mexico City: Fondo de Cultura Económica, 1978

Cirilo Villaverde 1812–1894

Cuban prose writer

Cirilo Villaverde's long and active life spans almost the entire 19th century. Born on a sugar plantation near the town of San Diego de Núñez in Pinar de Río province, Cuba, and dying in New York where he lived in exile for decades, he led a life rich in political episodes and conspiracies as well as literary activities. Some maintain that his life was his best work, unquestionably an exaggeration when one considers his monumental novel *Cecilia Valdés* (*Cecilia Valdés, or Angel's Hill*), which offers the reader a totalizing vision of the Cuba, especially Havana, of his time.

Villaverde's formative childhood years were spent in the country on the plantation where his father held a job as medical doctor tending to the slaves, and there the boy saw with his own eyes the evils of slavery. This left an indelible impression on his mind and imagination, as he himself has recorded: "I stayed there until the age of six or seven, witnessing while I played and ran about almost all the scenes of cruelty, that on the threshold of old age, I painted in my novel *Cecilia Valdés*."

In 1837 he began his pursuit of literature, publishing his first stories and short novels in little magazines or newspapers. His earliest fictions, like *El espetón de oro*, 1838 [The Golden Sword] – considered to be the first novel published in Cuba – were of an exalted Romantic nature, full of horror and violent deaths. Another of these novels, *El ave muerte* [The Death Bird], deals with incest, a theme Villaverde develops very significantly in *Cecilia Valdés* later on. The quality of these early works, of accentuated sentimentality and artificiality, is questionable. The author himself sought to forget them, not even mentioning them when many years afterwards he gave a summary of his previous works in a prologue to *Cecilia Valdés* in 1882.

More importantly, he published an early version of *Cecilia Valdés*, first as a short story, then as a short novel in 1839, which emphasizes *costumbrista* aspects, but does not really touch on the antislavery theme omnipresent in the 1882 definitive edition. Other works Villaverde published during these years were *El penitente*, a historical novel set in 18th-century Havana with interesting descriptions of city life but which portrayed exaggeratedly idealized characters. During these years he also wrote *El guajiro* [The Cuban Peasant] in 1842, published much later in 1890, a story based on a white country peasant type from his native province, describing customs there with a certain gusto, and *Dos amores* [Two Loves], published in serial form in 1843, and as a book in 1858, a sentimental novel mixed with some strong realistic touches. Finally, Villaverde paid homage again to his native western Pinar del Río province in a compelling work, *La excursión a Vuelta Abajo* [The Excursion to Vuelta Abajo], published first in Havana newspapers in 1838–39 and 1843, much later in book form in 1891. In this volume of *costumbrista* sketches, the author paints in stark vivid strokes the human misery occasioned by slavery.

Starting in 1834, Villaverde took part in a noted literary circle in Havana headed by Domingo del Monte, a significant cultural promoter of this period. Del Monte tried to get his group to abandon Romanticism and write in a more realistic fashion. He astutely foresaw that changing the literary focus was a possible way of changing society in Cuba, especially aspects dealing with slavery. Out of this Del Monte group emerged various antislavery novels. As Ivan Schulman has pointed out, del Monte was essentially very conservative. He truly wanted to do away with the slave trade, but without violence or upheaval and – what seems unthinkable to readers of today – "finally cleanse Cuba of the African race." Villaverde did not follow many of his mentor's ideas, for he was imprisoned in 1848 because of his participation in political activity against the government. He escaped from jail and fled to Florida.

During the long years of exile spent mainly in New York, Villaverde abandoned his novel writing career and turned his attention almost wholly to political activities, seeking Cuba's separation from Spain. First he favored annexation to the United States, but when this plan fell apart, he promoted Cuba's independence. In 1855 he met another Cuban exile, Emilia Casanova, who was very active in the separatist movement. They married and she helped him in all his activities. His former enthusiasm for fiction was now focused on sociopolitical writing and journalism. He returned to Havana only twice during the years abroad, first in 1858 to 1860 when the Spaniards granted an amnesty, only later to revoke it, and for a two week visit in 1888. In 1879, after a lapse of forty years, he set about finishing his long antislavery masterpiece, *Cecilia Valdés*, which was published in New York in 1882.

Unlike many other Cuban exiles living in New York, Villaverde did not belong to the wealthy bourgeoisie. Though he produced a considerable body of minor works – journalism, *costumbrista* sketches and short novels – and fought with his pen for Cuba's freedom, today his fame rests squarely on his extraordinary novel *Cecilia Valdés*.

GEORGE D. SCHADE

Biography

Born in the region of Vuelta Abajo, Pinar del Río, Cuba, 28 October 1812. Sixth of ten children. Father worked as a medical doctor on a sugar plantation where there were over 300 slaves. In 1823 sent to Havana for schooling. Studied philosophy and law at the Seminario de San Carlos, obtaining a law degree in 1834. After practicing briefly this profession, he gave it up, exasperated by the widespread corruption he found among judges and lawyers. For a while he taught at the Colegio Real Cubano in Havana and also at La Empresa in Matanzas. Joined literary circle formed by Domingo del Monte. Delmontine circle believed in reform rather than in abolition of slavery. In the 1830s abandoned creative writing for politics. By 1847 he was a conspirator in the Club de La Habana, a group which supported independence from Spain only as a first step towards annexation by the US. Joined Narciso López in failed uprising against colonial governor in 1848. Captured and jailed, but managed to escape to Florida after a few months. Travelled to New York where he acted as secretary to Narciso López. López organized three abortive expeditions to Cuba, was captured and executed in

1851, whereupon Villaverde returned to journalism and teaching. When the first War of Cuban Independence (the Ten Years' War) broke out in 1868, Villaverde supported independence from Spain without annexation. Founded and edited magazines in New York and New Orleans. Opened school in New Jersey in 1874. Made two trips to Cuba. During the first (1858) he bought a publishing house, La Antilla, and helped to found the magazine *La Habana*. Died in New York, 20 October 1894.

Selected Works

El espetón de oro, Havana: Imprenta Oliva, 1838
Teresa. Novela original, Havana: n.p., 1839
Cecilia Valdés, o La Loma del Ángel, Havana: Imprenta Literaria, 1839; definitive version: New York: Imprenta El Espejo, 1882; as *Cecilia Valdés, or Angel's Hill*, translated by Sydney G. Gest, New York: Vantage Press, 1962
La joven de la flecha de oro, Havana: Imprenta Terán, 1841
El librito de cuentos y las conversaciones, Havana: n.p., 1847
General López, the Cuban Patriot, New York: n.p., 1851
El señor Saco con respecto a la revolución de Cuba, New York: n.p., 1852
Dos amores, Havana: n.p., 1858
La revolución de Cuba vista desde Nueva York, New York: n.p., 1869
El penitente, New York: n.p., 1889
El guajiro, Havana: n.p., 1890
La excursión a Vuelta Abajo, Havana: Imprenta "El Pilar," 1891

Further Reading

Most of the criticism on Villaverde's work is confined to *Cecilia Valdés*. The paucity of general studies and of critical material on other works by this author is reflected in the list below.

Arrufat, Antón, "Cirilo Villaverde: *Excursión a Vuelta Abajo*," *Casa de las Américas*, vol. 2/10 (1962)
Sánchez, Julio C., *La obra novelística de Cirilo Villaverde*, Madrid: Orbe Novo, 1973

Cecilia Valdés

Novel by Cirilo Villaverde

Cirilo Villaverde first published a short primitive edition of *Cecilia Valdés* in 1839. After a forty year lapse due to the vagaries of an exile's life, he was only able to finish his work and publish the definitive edition in 1882. Its full title was *Cecilia Valdés, o La Loma del Ángel: novela de costumbres cubanas* (literally; Cecilia Valdés, or Angel Hill: a Novel of Cuban Customs); the important subtitle calls attention to one of the novel's main features, the portrayal of 19th-century Cuban life and customs. Villaverde incorporated the early version, with some changes, into the 1882 edition as the beginning chapters of his monumental book. Here, it is this definitive edition that will be examined, since it constitutes the real novel.

Since its publication many have come to regard *Cecilia Valdés* as a national novel, associated with Cuba's identity and struggle for freedom. Villaverde's heroine has been immensely popular over the years with the Cuban public, renowned in a musical revue as well as in several film versions: a legendary figure. Indeed, her compatriots recognize her, though they never have read a page of the book. Alert readers interested in identification will also realize that Villaverde's initials are the same as Cecilia's: CV. Critics have been more grudging to pay homage, though many, especially the Cubans, seem full of praise for the realistic and accurate portrayal of Spanish colonial Cuba. But, well into the 20th century, eminent critics failed to recognize the novel's worth: for example, Anderson Imbert complained about "its melodramatic plot" and "crude realism without novelistic expression," an unduly harsh judgment. Raimundo Lazo, though he lauds many of the novel's virtues, still finds fault with the author's novelistic technique. Only in the last twenty-five years has *Cecilia Valdés* come to be better understood and appreciated in all its aspects. Cedomil Goic brushed aside attacks on Villaverde's "simple novelistic art," perceptively calling the novel "one of the first expressions of a narrative world presented in a complex and multicolored fashion." If we examine the work in depth, not only its vigorous antislavery protest and theme, but also its dense texture, exterior structure and interior design, we will discover that it yields up rich treasures and unexpected finds.

Typical of many voluminous 19th-century novels, *Cecilia Valdés* runs to 500 or 600 pages in many editions. It is divided into four parts with a very brief concluding epilogue. The time frame spans only nineteen years, from Cecilia's birth in 1812 to the birth of her daughter in 1831, encapsulating the incestuous love affair between the gorgeous, light-skinned mulatta Cecilia and Leonardo Gamboa, white, rich and the spoiled son of a Spanish slave trader, Don Cándido. The lovers, unbeknownst to them, have the same father, and this makes for considerable suspense, even though the reader knows from the start.

In Part I, Villaverde introduces us to the young lovers with their respective families and also devotes much space to the description of a typical mulatto party called La Cuna. In the detailed account of this colorful celebration, the author advances his plot by presenting many of the characters who attend, including Cecilia and Leonardo. In Part II, Villaverde lingers on the world of high society and the Spanish masters in Havana. Here he includes a lengthy description of a fancy ball which contrasts sharply with La Cuna. In Part III, the scene shifts to the country. Some episodes take place at the coffee plantation of Isabel Ilincheta, Leonardo's fiancée and a kindly, humanitarian young lady beloved by her slaves. The rest of the action in this part occurs at La Tinaja, an infamous sugar plantation belonging to Don Cándido Gamboa where the slaves are treated monstrously. In Part IV, the narrator takes us back to the streets of Havana, where we plunge into the underworld. Finally, we learn what happens to various characters in the succinct epilogue, which ends with an allusion to Dionisio (one of the Gamboa's town slaves) being condemned to hard labor building streets, just as the novel opened with a minute description of the Havana streets where Cecilia played as a little girl, charming everyone. The novel contains other interesting parallels, such as Leonardo's lost Swiss gold watch, which turns up at various odd times and places in the text and which augurs ill for what may happen to him in the end.

The novel unfolds, then, in its leisurely three-decker way with subplots and coincidences, long stretches of description interlarded with lively narration, often in dramatic dialogue, and we get to see past Villaverde's sometimes awkward mechanisms into what the author humanly knows: excesses of every sort – greed, stupidity, cowardice, manipulativeness, dissolute-ness, prejudice (especially racial), ambition, pride, pretension and cruelty. On one level, the author presents us with an ample portrayal of the socioeconomic and cultural worlds of early 19th-century Cuba. This vision includes all social classes and castes, starting at the top with members of the Spanish colonial government, then the military hierarchy, then the commercial world with its shopkeepers and street vendors, the educational institutions, markets, fiestas, etc. and in Part III, how life in the country differs markedly from life in the big city. Through all this multicolored reality, the reader becomes acquainted with a large number and variety of characters of different races, colors and mixes – all shades of black, white and brown – and their ways of living and working.

Besides this painting of the period on a grand scale, two other important thematic strands weave synchronically through the volume: first, a series of love stories (couples and couplings) and second, an exploration of the problem of slavery, which seems to seep into all parts of the novel, corrupting and corroding life. Most of the love affairs are adulterous and some, incestuous. Incest, particularly, represents a collapse of family values, and the author mirrors this collapse in his description of crumbling Spanish colonial palaces, a decom-position echoed even more poignantly seventy-five years later by another Cuban novelist, Alejo Carpentier, in *El acoso* (*The Chase*).

In addition to the rivalry for Leonardo between Cecilia and Isabel, another woman, doña Rosa de Sandoval, plays a key role in the amorous intrigue. Mother of Leonardo and from one of the wealthiest families in Havana, she has a domi-neering, manipulative personality, and like Cecilia, is prone to jealous rages – provoked by the past love affairs of her husband, Don Cándido. She also displays an almost unhealthy passion for her son, whom she has ruined by giving in to his every whim, even setting up a house, ironically, for Cecilia, where the two can have their trysts. Most of the other char-acters in the book tend to come across as rather more one-dimensional, typifying some element of society. Thus we have Cecilia's grandmother, Señá Josefa, who raises the girl, all self-abnegation and sacrifice; Leonardo, superficial and spineless as the idle rich young man; Nemesia, Cecilia's friend and José Dolores's sister, all intrigue and astuteness who knows how to excite Cecilia's jealousy, etc.

The stories of all the couples/lovers, mostly unmarried but in each case with one of the parties wanting to marry, are interwoven skillfully into the plot: Cecilia/Leonardo, Leonardo/Isabel, Cecilia/José Dolores, Cándido/Rosa, and Cándido/Charo (Cecilia's mother who went insane after her baby daughter was born and taken from her). In each of the above cases, the tragic outcome of their love lies in the problems engendered in this society dominated by slavery and racial mixing (in the context of a racist society). For example, at the end of the novel, José Dolores, egged on by the furious Cecilia, kills Leonardo before he can marry Isabel. The individual domestic discord repeats over and over the social disharmony at the heart of Cuban society.

Readers of *Cecilia Valdés* have always been greatly impressed by the theme of slavery rampant in the novel, and especially in recent times, outraged at the brutal way it is depicted in the volume. We know that Villaverde was attacking with reform in mind when he described the wretched living conditions of many of his black characters. Doris Sommer, struck by what she calls the "slipperiness of racial relations" in the book, maintains that "hardly anyone in *Cecilia Valdés* escapes the charge of racism, not the mulatta, nor her white lover, and certainly not the white narrator." Villaverde, who spent most of his life battling against the Spanish tyranny in Cuba and protesting vigorously at the treatment of blacks by the whites, would doubtless agree with the first part of this indictment alluding to Cecilia and Leonardo, the lovers, but would most likely be puzzled or indignant at the inclusion of the white narrator/author, i.e., himself, in this racist charge. Despite such a possible blemish, the novel holds up well. And Sommer's negative reaction lends credence to the notion of the book's multicolored variety and ambiguity, for it continues to yield fresh and contradictory readings.

GEORGE D. SCHADE

See also entries on Gertrudis Gómez de Avellaneda, *A escrava Isaura* (Bernardo Guimarães)

Editions

First edition: *Cecilia Valdés, o La Loma del Ángel*, New York: Imprenta El Espejo, 1882

Critical edition: edited with an introduction by Jean Lamore, Madrid: Cátedra, 1992 [An excellent and up-to-date assessment of the novel by this French Hispanist. Especially good on slavery, the drama of the mulattos, and Cecilia as myth and reality]

Translation: *Cecilia Valdés, or Angel's Hill*, by Sydney G. Gest, New York: Vantage Press, 1962 [An earlier translation was published in 1935]

Further Reading

Álvarez García, Imeldo (editor), *Acerca de Cirilo Villaverde*, Havana: Letras Cubanas, 1982 [The editor has gathered together in this useful volume 22 articles on the author and *Cecilia Valdés*, ranging from 19th-century contemporaries like Ramón de Palma, Manuel de la Cruz and José Martí to Jean Lamore]

Álvarez García, Imeldo, *La obra narrativa de Cirilo Villaverde: Cecilia Valdés*, Havana: Letras Cubanas, 1984

Rivas, Mercedes, *Literatura y esclavitud en la novela cubana del siglo XIX*, Seville: Escuela de Estudios Hispanoamericanos, 1990

Schulman, Ivan, "Reflections on Cuba and its Antislavery Literature," *Annals of South Eastern Conference on Latin American Studies* 7 (1976) [A thought-provoking article. Concentrates on the Del Monte circle and its influence]

David Viñas 1929–

Argentine prose writer and dramatist

David Viñas presents somewhat of a paradox in terms of literary criticism devoted to his prodigious, genre-diverse and yet highly unified corpus. In spite of having continuously published novels, plays, short stories and essays since 1955 and having been awarded numerous literary prizes, Viñas has received relatively little critical attention in comparison with other Latin American writers like Gabriel García Márquez and Mario Vargas Llosa, both of whom also incorporate their national histories into their works. Few writers have investigated their national history with as much depth and passion as Viñas. He constantly probes Argentina's history with the aim of finding a solution to what he considers the debilitating circularity of Argentine and, by extension, Latin American, history. The cyclical movement of Argentina's history constitutes the central theme and focal point of his corpus, and this repetitive movement condemns Argentina and Latin America to repeat the errors of the past. Part of the explanation for the paucity of critical attention may stem from the fact that from the publication of his first novel, *Cayó sobre su rostro*, 1955 [He Fell on His Face], Viñas has not deviated from his essential focus on investigating Argentine history, even in the face of the spectacular successes of the Latin American Boom writers. His work is a constant process of questioning and denunciation, often within a Marxist dialectical framework of thesis and antithesis. While the sociopolitical and historical focus of his literary work may have mistakenly led critics to consider his fiction less innovative and original in comparison with other Boom writers, he nevertheless shares their deep concern with the circularity of history.

Of Viñas's many works, his 1967 novel, *Los hombres de a caballo* [Men on Horseback], and *Cuerpo a cuerpo*, 1979 [Face to Face], clearly demonstrate the dynamic evolution of his writing and the depth and coherence of his vision. In Jorge G. Castañeda's far-reaching study of the Latin American Left, *Utopia Disarmed: the Latin American Left After the Cold War* (1993), he says of Argentina: "Argentina has always imported and exported revolutionaries. Argentines have mixed exile, revolution, and travel as have few others. They have also repeatedly defied all efforts of inclusion into a tidy classification of the hemisphere's leftist revolutionary or reformist currents. The Argentine armed left, in so far as it can be identified as such, has had a disproportionate – and rarely constructive – influence on the Latin American universe." This contradictory stance manifests itself in David Viñas's writing and his vision of history.

Los hombres de a caballo, one of the first texts to deal extensively with the Perón era, focuses on the military establishment, the repository of tradition. Viñas sees this institution as the embodiment of bourgeois values and the liberal ideology which no longer perpetuates itself on a national but on a continental level. The novel centers on Operation Ayacucho which takes place at the end of 1964. Ironically, the name Ayacucho that the military uses to christen their operation designed to eradicate the guerillas was also the name of the 1824 battle which marked the end of Spanish domination in Latin America.

Viñas's bifocal view of history leads him to structure his novel as a contrapuntal tension between past and present, a circular movement in which the positive aims of the 1824 Ayacucho campaign are transformed into a military operation to eradicate them.

In a more restricted sense, the novel centers on the life of a military family – the Godoys – and their participation in Argentine history. The novel's complex structure of historical mirrors-mirages opens the door to a more meditative stance on the nature of history. The novel is divided into three long segments which correspond to the preparatory stages for the military operation, the operation itself, and the return to Buenos Aires. Within each chapter Viñas has inserted sections which describe the past of Emilio's family. His father, grandfather, great-grandfather and great-great-grandfather were all military men, and Emilio's son will bear the same name as the first Godoy – José María. Metaphorically, then, the circle will be complete and Argentina will remain locked in its closed, circular history. Although Emilio starts to question this circular process, he never breaks out of the vicious circle, and his family's identity can only be defined in military terms. Viñas clearly shows that the military tradition renews itself from one generation to the next like a self-fulfilling prophecy, and that tradition is rarely questioned. In this novel, the roles and the errors of the past repeat themselves in an endless cycle. At each step Viñas questions and denounces this atrophied tradition in order to shake the foundations of the old order which continues to obstruct Argentina's development.

In 1979, Viñas published his darkest and perhaps most technically innovative novel, *Cuerpo a cuerpo*, (his original title was *Tango*), which he wrote during his exile in Spain and after his two children, Mini and Paco, and his two friends, Haroldo Conti and Rodolfo Walsh, had disappeared without a trace. The novel centers on the investigation of the journalist, Gregorio Yantorno, of the life of General Alejandro C. Mendiburu. The structure of the novel recreates the tango of Argentine history through the face to face (or face-off) of contrapuntal fragments from different historical periods which underscores the circular movement of Argentine history within a closed circuit. If Viñas structures *Cuerpo a cuerpo* like *Los hombres de a caballo*, he pushes this collage technique to the limit, superimposing different levels and epochs in a series of sixty-nine sections. Argentina's history spirals inward and, with each cycle, the process of fragmentation continues to increase. History remains indissolubly linked to the sclerotic traditions of the military establishment which adamantly rejects any idea of change or evolution.

As Yantorno penetrates layer after layer of the general's life, he discovers a series of events which not only link Argentina's past and present but also create a past-present; that is, while the novel centers on contemporary Argentina, it never loses sight of the circular movement of national history as embodied in the military establishment. Although the novel certainly bears witness to and denounces the atrocities perpetrated by the Argentine military regime during the late 1970s, it also indicts General Mendiburu and reveals the emptiness of the military establishment. As Estela Valverde points out in her book, *David Viñas: en busca de una síntesis de la historia argentina*, 1989 [David Viñas: In Search of a Synthesis of Argentine History], the journalist Yantorno is the alter ego of David Viñas, for both are determined to discover the truth and reveal the true underpinnings of Argentine history. In addition, according to Valverde, General Mendiburu is also an alter ego of Viñas, the person he could have become if he had let himself be swept up in the circular flow of Argentine history. General Mendiburu is the person who simultaneously exposes and embodies the idea of the Argentina's historical circularity, and he recognizes the lack of synthesis not only in Argentine but also in Latin American history. In this novel Viñas moves beyond the illusions of *Los hombres de a caballo*. The military establishment remains locked in its historical circularity, and the writer no longer plays an effective role in his country's destiny. The novel's structure underscores the pessimism and extreme process of fragmentation which Argentina's historical circularity has produced.

Viñas's intense focus on national history shows that it constantly oscillates between thesis and antithesis without ever reaching a creative synthesis which can produce positive change. According to Viñas, Argentines have willfully ignored their circular history which condemns them to repeat the errors of the past. In short, they lack any historical memory. Viñas also believes that only the military possesses a sense of tradition and an awareness of the past, so that it embodies the values and essence of Argentina. The military sets a dangerous precedent since it acts only out its own limited sense of identity, and this can lead to the horrors of the late 1970s in Argentina or the failed dream of omnipotence of the Falklands War in 1982. Viñas depicts a world of Manichean binary oppositions in which no synthesis is possible, in which Argentina continues to move in a closed circle leading to increasing fragmentation and disillusionment. Unlike many of the Latin American Boom writers who similarly view history as circular, Viñas remains solidly rooted within the confines of national history. Although his novels certainly extend far beyond the borders of Argentina, the circular movement of history in his works spirals inward towards an uncertain fate.

ROBERT L. SIMS

See also entry on The Historical Novel

Biography

Born in Buenos Aires, Argentina, 28 July 1929. Educated initially by "curas y militares" (priests and army officers); studied at the University of Buenos Aires; received doctorate from the University of Rosario, Argentina. Co-founder, with his brother Ismael, of the journal *Contorno*, 1953–57. Being a Marxist he suffered considerably during the military dictatorship in Argentina, 1976–83; spent period 1973–83 in exile, teaching at universities in Germany, Denmark and California. Returned to Argentina in 1984. Professor of Literature at the University of Buenos Aires, since the mid-1990s. Used the pseudonym Raquel Weinbaum when writing for the press. Also writes scripts for film and television. Recipient of the following awards: National Prize for Literature, 1962 and 1971; Casa de las Américas Prize, 1967; Argentine Critics' Prize, 1970 and 1973; National Theatre Prize, 1972.

Selected Works

Novels

Cayó sobre su rostro, Buenos Aires: Doble P: 1955
Los años despiadados, Buenos Aires: Letras Universitarias, 1956
Un dios cotidiano, Buenos Aires: Kraft, 1957
Los dueños de la tierra, Buenos Aires: Losada, 1959
Dar la cara, Buenos Aires: Jamcana, 1962
Los hombres de a caballo, Havana: Casa de las Américas, 1967
Cosas concretas, Buenos Aires: Tiempo Contemporáneo, 1969
Jauría, Buenos Aires: Granica, 1974
Cuerpo a cuerpo, Mexico City: Siglo XXI, 1979
Claudia conversa, Buenos Aires: Planeta Argentina, 1995

Short Fiction

Las malas costumbres, Buenos Aires: Jamcana, 1963

Essays

Literatura argentina y realidad política, Buenos Aires: Jorge Álvarez, 1964; revised edition, Buenos Aires: Siglo XX, 1971–75:
    1. *De Sarmiento a Cortázar*, 1971
    2. *Apogeo de la oligarquía*, 1975
    3. *La crisis de la ciudad liberal*, 1973
Laferrère: del apogeo de la oligarquía a la crisis de la ciudad liberal, Rosario, Argentina: Universidad Nacional del Litoral, 1965
En la semana trágica, Buenos Aires: Jorge Álvarez, 1966
Argentina: ejército y oligarquía, Havana: Casa de las Américas, 1967
De los montoneros a los anarquistas, Buenos Aires: C. Pérez, 1971
Grotesco, inmigración y fracaso: Armando Discépolo, Buenos Aires: Corregidor, 1973
¿Qué es el fascismo en Latinoamérica?, Barcelona: La Gaya Ciencia, 1977
México y Cortés, Madrid: Hernando, 1978
Ultramar, Madrid: Edascal, 1980
Contrapunto político en América Latina: Siglo XX, Mexico City: Instituto de Capacitación Política, 1982
Indios, ejército y frontera, Mexico City: Siglo XXI, 1982
Anarquistas en América Latina, Mexico City: Katún, 1983

Plays

Lisandro, Buenos Aires: Merlin, 1971
Dorrego, Maniobras, Túpac Amarú, Buenos Aires: Ediciones Cepe, 1974

Biography

Louis Pasteur, in collaboration with Marta Eguía, Madrid: Hernando, 1977

Further Reading

Cano, C.J., "Épica y misoginia en *Los hombres de a caballo*," *Revista Iberoamericana* 96–97 (1976)
Foster, David William, "David Viñas: lecturas descontructivas y correctivas de la historia socio-cultural argentina," *Ideologies and Literature* (Fall 1987)
Rasi, H.M., "David Viñas, novelista y crítico comprometido," *Revista Iberoamericana* 95 (1976)
Rodríguez Monegal, Emir, "David Viñas en su contorno," *Mundo Nuevo*, Paris, 18 (December 1967)
Rosa, Nicolás, "Sexo y novela," in his *Crítica y significación*, Buenos Aires: Galerna, 1970

Shaw, Donald L., *Nueva narrativa hispanoamericana*, 2nd edition, Madrid: Cátedra, 1983 [Chapter 6 has section on Viñas]

Sosnowski, Saúl, "*Los dueños de la tierra* de David Viñas: cuestionamiento e impugnación del liberalismo," Toulouse,

France, *Caravelle* 25 (1975)

Valverde, Estela, *David Viñas: en busca de una síntesis de la historia argentina*, Buenos Aires: Plus Ultra, 1989

Vuelta

See Journals

María Elena Walsh 1930–

Argentine poet, prose writer and author of children's literature

When still a teenager María Elena Walsh won acclaim from the Argentine cultural elite for her first book of poetry, *Otoño imperdonable*, 1947 [Unforgivable Autumn], whose melancholic tone, formal perfection and elegiac idealism led anthologists to include her among the Neoromantic poets of the Generation of 1940. A plaquette, *Apenas viaje* [Brief Journey], and the joint volume with Ángel Bonomini, *Baladas con Ángel* [Ballads with Angel], followed in 1948 and 1952, respectively. However, increasingly disillusioned by both poetry and politics in Argentina, and unwilling to continue the creative activity she described as "bordering on madness," Walsh left to live in Europe in 1952–56. In Paris, with poet and ethnomusicologist Leda Valladares, she formed the duo "Leda and María" and enjoyed considerable success singing traditional folklore in night-clubs and music-halls, thus acquiring the musical training she would employ so magisterially later. This was the first of the various changes in direction that would characterize her remarkably versatile public career.

Walsh has always taken pride in her Anglo-Argentine family legacy of words and play in two languages. Europe, therefore, afforded her "a reconciliation with paradise lost" that inspired the poetry for children she also set to music and adapted for stage and television. Her work both broke with the traditional paradigm of much foundational children's literature designed to "inculcar respetabilidad, historia versificada y obediencia" (inculcate respectability, patriotism and obedience), and also provided an intelligent alternative to the contemporary cultural colonization by the US embodied in the Walt Disney productions. Following the example of José Sebastián Tallon, she sought to amuse and challenge her child audience in order to encourage intellectual autonomy. Her chief sources of inspiration came from the nursery rhymes, limericks of Edward Lear, and Lewis Carroll's *Alice*, the ballads and carols of Hispanic folklore, and the ingenious wordplay of French Surrealist Robert Desnos's *Chantefleurs et Chantefables*, 1944 [Singingflowers and Singingfables]. Walsh's intention was, however, to adapt, to make "spiritual" rather than literary translations of poetic play, which readers from Argentina – and, indeed, from all Spanish America – could seize immediately. Thus, an ugly demon from Brazil lent his particularly euphonious name to her first collection of poems for children, *Tutú Marambá*, that appeared in 1960. Typically Walsh exorcised any evil connections by reassuring her young readers about the redemptive powers of the friendship of "the excellent people who live in this house of paper." These included Confite the cat, the feminist monkey Jacinta in all her silken finery, a grandmotherly but studious cow from Humahuaca, the tragic Ophelia Mouse, and, perhaps most memorable of all, the not too distant relative of Old Mother Hubbard, Doña Anémona Disparate, herself. They were joined in 1963, in *El reino del revés* [The Topsy-Turvey Kingdom], by, among others, Monoliso and his passion for the Twist, Don Enrique del Meñique, and Manuelita the tortoise who undertook an epic journey from Pehuajó to Paris. Most of these characters appeared in Walsh's shows for children that enjoyed long runs and an extended life in the recordings of her wonderfully inventive musical settings. Keeping up the momentum, in 1965, "como un bicho en la punta del lápiz [y] se ponen a correr por su cuenta en el papel" (like an insect which having fallen in the inkwell [and] then runs wildly across the page), came Walsh's collection of limericks, *Zoo loco* [The Zoo-illogical Gardens], while in the following year Walsh turned to prose, recounting tales of the magical forest of Gulubú, and delighting in the various vicissitudes of an elephant named *Dailán Kifki*. With changes in the sociopolitical climate in Argentina, however, the light-heartedness of much of the early whimsy faded as, in 1977 in *Chaucha y Palito* [Nickel and Dime], Walsh felt constrained to argue more directly in favour of social justice and greater tolerance of difference.

Until recently children's literature has rarely merited serious consideration but new studies underscore the creativity and innovative subversiveness of Walsh's topsey-turvey world of the mind at play that offers an alternative order from which to question and reinterpret perceived reality. Writing from what she ironically calls the "despised suburbs of Mount Parnassus," Walsh has exploited a richly poetic vein with verve and talent in order to create a new lore for *cebollitas* (as children are called in the popular idiom of the River Plate), that has deservedly achieved classic status.

Following the success of her shows for children, in the late 1960s Walsh turned to an adult audience, putting on a series of one woman performances of the type she had admired in the *café-concerts* of Paris. Blending together with her own considerable charisma, the professionalism of French entertainers Charles Trenet and Georges Brassens and the combination of folklore and social concerns she found in Brecht and the American protest singer Woody Guthrie, Walsh virtually metamorphosed the urban folksong. For ten years from 1968 she enthralled audiences with her quizzical look at Argentine society, shot through with nostalgia, tenderness, solidarity, and, increasingly, anger at the persistent infringement of civil liberties in that period. Two collections made available the lyrics of her songs, *Juguemos en el mundo* [Let's Play in the World] in 1970, and *Cancionero contra el mal de ojo* [A Songbook against the Evil Eye] in 1976, while recordings by Walsh herself and later, most notably, by Susana Rinaldi and the Zupay Quartet, captured the breadth of her musical eclecticism that aligned so memorably *baguala*, *zamba* and *guajira* with Bach and Ravel, or *tango* and jazz.

In 1965, with *Hecho a mano* [Made by Hand], Walsh had again "agonized a little longer" to produce a new aesthetic for poetry that would be distinctly colloquial in tone and centred on contemporary issues, without losing the technical mastery that had been her hallmark from the beginning. Particularly innovative are her eight poetic "epistles" celebrating woman as lover, subject rather than object of desire. *Hecho a mano* is a pivotal work, with obvious connections through pastiche and parody with her poetic nonsense for children, and some clear indications of the use of different registers, humour, and the decidedly feminist content of the writing that followed. If Walsh published little between 1978 and 1982, poems like "Contratango" [An Anti-*tango*], "Fiesta patria" [Civic Holiday] and "Solo de madre" [Solo for a Mother] were valiant rallying cries against the power of the patriarchy, once more epitomized in Argentina by military uniforms. These and almost all Walsh's previous poetry were collected in the anthology of 1984, *Los poemas* [Poems]. The change in 1990 to prose for her "palimpsest," *Novios de antaño* [Hearthrobs of Yesteryear], "an autobiographical fantasy" depicting life in the decade 1930–40, brought Walsh her first best-seller for adult readership.

Always an outspoken feminist, Walsh has used most imaginatively a variety of genres to combat "la horripilante misoginia y niñofobia de nuestra cultura hebreocristiana" (the horrifying misogyny and child phobia of our Judeo-Christian culture) and also to celebrate feminism as "this century's real revolution." Thus, in her writing for children Walsh has systematically avoided sexual stereotypes by foregrounding instead some new-age protagonists like the Indian medicine woman in her revisionist rendering of the British invasion of Argentina in 1806, *El diablo inglés*, 1974 [The English Devil], the aeronautical grandmother of *Bisa Vuela* (1985), or, most recently, in *La nube traicionera*, 1989 [The Treacherous Cloud], her free version of one of French novelist George Sand's tales for children, "Le nuage rose," where Luisa, "the cloud-spinner," demonstrates how the female tradition can be a positive source of strength and solidarity. Equally, in her popular songs Walsh has immortalized the army of under-valued women who are exploited in the home, in domestic service, and in underpaid teaching jobs. More subversively, writing in the late 1960s and early 1970s within the conventions of the woman's page and television soap operas, forms that most feminists refused to consider seriously, Walsh deliberately set out to undermine the passive, ultra-conservative image of the traditional female role in society.

The subversive quality of Walsh's writing was not lost on the military junta: one of her poems published in 1979 for wide diffusion in the daily press, "Complicidad de la víctima" [Complicity of the Victim], caused her name to be placed on the black list, whilst radio and television stations were advised against airing her work at this time. But Walsh returned, "like the cicada" of possibly her most famous song, "Como la cigarra," [Like the Cicada] her symbol of indomitability with which so many throughout Latin America have identified. The essays she wrote for the newspaper *El Clarín* during the worst years of the *Proceso* (the 1976–83 military dictatorship) displayed extraordinary lucidity and courage that won her respect both within Argentina and outside. These were collected in 1993, together with some earlier writings, under the title of the article that stunned readers on 17 August 1979 by the audacity of her denunciation of systematic political repression, *Desventuras en el País-Jardín-de-Infantes* [Misadventures in Kindergarten Country]. They attest the constancy of Walsh's imaginative, ethical approach to social issues in a country where censorship and acquiescence have so often been the accepted way of life.

In a long and multi-faceted career Walsh has used successfully a variety of modes of expression to reach the general public that, in turn, has responded with affection by venerating her as a familiar icon of Argentine popular culture.

K.M. SIBBALD

Biography

Born near Buenos Aires, Argentina, 1 February 1930. Father of mixed Irish and English stock; mother of Spanish descent. Father worked on the railways and was musically inclined. Studied at the National School of Fine Arts, but although she obtained a degree, was a mediocre student. Published poems in national newspapers and magazines in her mid-teens. Spent three years in the United States, then travelled to Europe with a friend and fellow-folklorist, Leda Valladares. Settled in Paris where they earned their living by performing in clubs. On returning to Argentina they toured the provinces with their folk songs. Began to write for children in 1950s and to work for children's television in 1959. Started one woman shows in 1966. Co-wrote and co-produced a film for children in 1971, "Juguemos en el mundo" [Let's Play in the World].

Selected Works

Poetry

Otoño imperdonable, Buenos Aires: privately printed, 1947; Buenos Aires: Ediciones del Bosque, 1948
Apenas viaje, Buenos Aires: El Balcón de Madera, 1948
Baladas con Ángel, published with *Argumento del enamorado* by Ángel Bonomini, Buenos Aires: Losada, 1952
Casi milagro, Montevideo: Cuadernos Julio Herrera y Reissig, 1958
Hecho a mano, Buenos Aires: Fariña, 1965
Los poemas, Buenos Aires: Sudamericana, 1984
Las canciones, Buenos Aires: Seix Barral, 1994

Children's Literature

Tutú Marambá, Buenos Aires: "author's edition," 1960; and Buenos Aires: Fariña, 1963

El reino del revés, Buenos Aires: Fariña, 1963

Zoo loco, Buenos Aires: Fariña, 1964

Cuentopos de Gulubú, Buenos Aires: Fariña, 1966

Dailán Kifki, Buenos Aires: Fariña, 1966

El diablo inglés, Buenos Aires: Estrada, 1974

Angelito, Buenos Aires: Estrada, 1974

El país de la geometría, Buenos Aires: Estrada, 1974

La sirena y el capitán, Buenos Aires: Estrada, 1974

Chaucha y Palito, Buenos Aires: Sudamericana, 1977

Bisa Vuela, Buenos Aires: Hispamérica, 1985

La nube traicionera, Buenos Aires: Sudamericana, 1989 [A free version of "Le nuage rose" by George Sand]

Other Writings

Aire libre, Buenos Aires: Estrada, 1967 [school reader]

Novios de antaño (1930–1940), Buenos Aires: Sudamericana, 1990

Desaventuras en el País-Jardín-de-Infantes, Buenos Aires: Sudamericana, 1993 [newspaper articles]

Compilations and Anthologies

Versos folklóricos para cebollitas, Buenos Aires: Fariña, 1966

Versos para cebollitas, Buenos Aires: Fariña, 1966

Versos tradicionales para cebollitas, Buenos Aires: Sudamericana, 1974

Cancionero contra el mal de ojo, Buenos Aires: Sudamericana, 1976 [song lyrics]

A la madre, Buenos Aires: Sudamericana, 1981

Further Reading

Dujovne, Alicia, *María Elena Walsh*, Madrid: Júcar, 1982 [An extended interview with the author, of mainly biographical interest]

Foster, David William, "Playful Ecphrasis: María Elena Walsh and Children's Literature in Argentina," *Mester* (1984)

Gómez Paz, Julieta, *Cuatro actitudes poéticas: Alejandra Pizarnik; Olga Orozco; Amelia Biagioni; María Elena Walsh*, Buenos Aires: Conjunta, 1977

Luraschi, Ilse Adriana and K.M. Sibbald, *María Elena Walsh o "el desafío de la limitación,"* Buenos Aires: Sudamericana, 1993 [The first authoritative study on Walsh]

Pujol, Sergio A., *"Como la cigarra." Biografía de María Elena Walsh*, Buenos Aires: Beas, 1993 [popular biography]

Emilio Adolfo Westphalen 1911–

Peruvian poet and prose writer

Prior to the 1980s, Emilio Adolfo Westphalen never published an edition of poetry larger than 200 copies and during the years from 1936 to 1979 stopped publishing poetry altogether (at certain points even stopped writing poetry). This limited distribution and misleading "period of inactivity" have helped to obscure the importance of Westphalen's contribution as a poet, writer, and critic of both literature and art. Few people realize that even during Westphalen's "period of inactivity" he had advanced, as editor, two important avant-garde magazines (*Las moradas*, 1947–49 and *Amaru*, 1967–71), worked as a professor of pre-conquest art, and toured three countries (Italy, the United States, and Mexico) as a cultural attaché or ambassador for Peru. Indeed, Westphalen is not simply an orthodox Surrealist poet of the 1930s, his work has significantly matured, and he has influenced two or three generations of Peruvian writers and artists in a multifarious way. The nature of this influence has only begun to be questioned, understood and weighed.

As a "literate" poet, Westphalen has read extensively. Nevertheless, one can still substantiate an argument that would demonstrate how Westphalen's work has been significantly influenced by the works of Eguren (*Simbólicas*), Vallejo (*Trilce*), Juan Ramón Jiménez (*Platero y yo* [Platero and I]) and several others. Westphalen has also benefited from the

catalysis of friendship. Among Westphalen's closest friends are Martín Adán, Estuardo Nuñez, Xavier Abril, José María Arguedas and César Moro. These combined influences have been instrumental in forming a poetry that, in the most general descriptive terms, seems mystical, allusive, passionate – a poetry of silences, simultaneity, and unlimited space.

Westphalen's first period, that of the 1930s, is characteristically more hermetic and much harder to understand than his later work. This initial poetry includes: *Las ínsulas extrañas* [Strange Islands], *Abolición de la muerte* [Abolition of Death], parts of "Belleza de una espada clavada en la lengua" [Beauty of a Sword Piercing One's Tongue], from the book of the same title, and *Cuál es la risa* [What is Laughter], published some forty-five years later thanks to the efforts of André Coyné. With the exception of *Cuál es la risa*, these early works have been republished along with the autobiographical essay, "Poetas en la Lima de los años treinta" [Lima Poets in the 1930s] in *Otra imagen deleznable* [Another Fragile Image]. Westphalen's interests in experimental poetry, Surrealism, and the Spanish mystics led him during this early period towards an exploration of the individual and his passion or desire. For Westphalen, this exploration occurs in a poetic reality inclusive of both conscious and subconscious elements, a poetic world where one migrates between the real and the "marvelous." Many times Westphalen's world is decentered, dispensing with the traditional corporeal "yo" (first person "I").

The poetry that Westphalen has written after 1980 (his second period of poetry) is predominantly more brief than his earlier work; it is comprised of compact imagery, contains less complicated semantic structures, and frequently is written in the prose poem form. This poetry includes: *Arriba bajo el cielo* [Above Below the Sky], *Máximas y mínimas de sapiencia pedestre* [Maxims, Maxima and Minima of Pedestrian Sapience], *Ha vuelto la Diosa Ambarina* [The Amber Goddess has Returned], and *Belleza de una espada clavada en la lengua*. The latter is an anthology of both Westphalen's early and late poetry; however, it does not include the poems in *Cuál es la risa* nor those in *Ha vuelto la Diosa Ambarina*.

The most popularly embraced poems of Westphalen's production are those that were written during his early period in *Las ínsulas extrañas* and in *Abolición de la muerte*. In the first collection of poems, Westphalen uses a poetic language constructed from archetypical images: shadow, fire, water, blood and tears. The title *Las ínsulas extrañas* alludes to the mysticism of St John of the Cross, although for Westphalen this allusion does not embody the entire mystical process of spiritual purification. Westphalen is only interested in the silent inner music that the mystic pursues and the struggle to describe this experience. The second collection, *Abolición de la muerte* is an extended allegory dedicated to the poet's pursuit of his beloved one, a young nymph, or beauty itself. In this instance, Westphalen's poetry is even more baroque and surreal. In many poems a series of descriptive images or "overlay" quickens to the point of stream-of-consciousness.

A closer examination of *Las ínsulas extrañas* reveals how Westphalen seeks to define those internal islands of thought and emotion characteristic of mysticism. He explores love, passion, and desire in both conscious and subconscious territories. The majority of these poems describe the altered emotive states of a soul in its union with and separation from the beloved. Both the beloved and the soul itself are often described as natural forms other than the corporeal body. Westphalen's poetic world often appears open-ended and evanescent.

In Westphalen's free verse, there are no signals to indicate when voices have changed; there are no tags to prioritize one particular voice or to authenticate one message, feeling, or image. Westphalen collages together both multiple points of view and images. Only repetition and isotopic cohesion preserve a fleeting poetic nucleus. Often Westphalen uses hyperbolic comparisons and semantic dissociation in order to accentuate the synesthetic nature of one's existence within nature and the desire to fuse with the beloved.

Westphalen's poetic composition reminds one of Huidobro's parachutes or even Lorca's guitar strings. Eyes can become new skies and horizons, internal and external visions; trees can represent human struggle, shoes the march of time. The poetic "yo," "Ud.," "tú" (the first person "I" and second person formal and informal "you") become malleable. Westphalen intensifies this same complicated web of baroque-like description in works such as *Abolición de la muerte*, this time with less fragmentation of subjects. One might consider *Cuál es la risa* Westphalen's most Surreal and experimental extension of this same poetic.

Despite the critical emphasis placed on Westphalen's early works, one should not overlook his more mature prose poetry. Although less hermetic, these works still reveal noteworthy skill. In fact, reading Westphalen's work chronologically backwards can help to unlock some of his early imagery. For instance, in the collection of poems "Porciones de sueño para mitigar avernos" [Pieces of Dreams to Mitigate Hells] included for the first time as part of *Belleza de una espada clavada en la lengua*, Westphalen directs our attention to those extremely emotional yet seemingly inconceivable moments when we feel as if we have died or our soul has been amputated. In *Ha vuelto la Diosa Ambarina* Westphalen pursues ineffable poetic moments. This time he demonstrates how signs, words, and gestures have no meaning in themselves, but rather serve only as "pointers." As in his earlier work, Westphalen stresses how closing one's eyes can reveal more than contemplating night itself. In *Nueva serie* [New Series], Westphalen overtly mixes social criticism with his poetic agenda. He criticizes contemporary society's devaluation of death and its role in defining life. In *Remanentes de naufragio* [Remnants of a Shipwreck] Westphalen uses one-sentence prose poems to emphasize those unreal and impossible spaces that only the poetic and philosophical imagination can conceive. And finally in *Máximas y mínimas de sapiencia pedestre* he explores many of the same common threads of his poetic imagery (fate, dreams, pain, water, sexual desire); however, this time Westphalen uses a colloquial style similar to that of a story, fairy tale, or joke.

The only works of Westphalen's late period that do not echo his earlier poetry are *Arriba bajo el cielo* and *El niño y el río* [The Boy and the River]. These collections were written separately but published together forming only one part of *Belleza de una espada clavada en la lengua*. The first group of poems is a short allegory in which a black-martin's behavior, a symbol of Rome's typical socialite, is juxtaposed against an owl's behavior – Giorgio de Chirico's intellectual curiosity and ghost-like existence. The second work, dedicated to Arguedas (most probably because of Arguedas's fond remembrances of those childhood Quechuan fables he heard) tells a fable of a child and his adventures beside and within a river. For Westphalen the river assumes mythical proportions and becomes a magical playground where a child innocently discovers the beauty and mystery of nature.

Whether one chooses to start at the beginning or wishes to read Westphalen's poetry chronologically in reverse, one will inevitably encounter this poet's labor – to congeal the allusive moment, feeling, or thought. In each period of his work, Westphalen creates a system of images that expresses these thoughts and feelings in a mutually imaginary and real world. In both his more colloquial framework or more surreal and experimental web of images, Westphalen pushes the reader beyond words, signals towards a marvelous/real space that heightens his/her synesthetic experience and echoes of mythical beginning. For Westphalen, poetry, like music, should be constructed utilizing silence; a poet must divide and break up silence – what is not said, not known, at times not seen, something dreamed, something ineffable and unexplored.

WILLIAM P. KEETH

See also entries on Martín Adán, César Moro, Surrealism, César Vallejo

Biography

Born in Lima, Peru, in 1911. Attended *Deutsche Schule* preparatory school, and studied originally to be a civil engineer. After failing a university entrance exam, he changed direction and began pursuing his real interest, literature. Thereafter, he studied in the Facultad de Letras at the National University, San Marcos, Lima. After publishing his first two books of poetry, Westphalen worked on the first Surrealist Exhibition in Lima, helped publish and edit four avant-garde magazines, and became a professor of pre-Columbian art. Later, he served as a cultural attaché in New York and in Rome. From 1971 to 1983 he again travelled as a cultural attaché in Italy, Mexico and Portugal. Currently lives in Lima, although as reported in *El Comercio* (29 December 1994), is suffering from both illness and poverty.

Selected Works

Poetry

Las ínsulas extrañas, Lima: Compañía de Impresiones y Publicidad, 1933
Abolición de la muerte, Lima: Ediciones Perú Actual, 1935
Otra imagen deleznable, Mexico City: Fondo de Cultura Económica, 1980
Arriba bajo el cielo, Lisbon: n.p., 1982
Máximas y mínimas de sapiencia pedestre, Lisbon: n.p, 1982
Ha vuelto la Diosa Ambarina, Mexico City: UNAM, 1989

Belleza de una espada clavada en la lengua, Lima: Ediciones Richay, 1986
Bajo zarpas de la quimera: poemas 1930–1988, edited by José Ángel Valente, Madrid: Alianza, 1991

Other Writings

Dos soledades, in collaboration with J.R. Ribeyro, Lima: Instituto Nacional de Cultura, 1974
"Poesía quechua y pintura abstracta," in *Szyszlo: indagación y collage de Mirlo Lauer*, Lima: Mosca Azul Editores, 1975

Further Reading

Alquie, Ferdinand, *Filosofía del surrealismo*, Barcelona: Seix Barral, 1974
Bary, Leslie, "El surrealismo en Hispanoamérica y el 'yo' de Westphalen," *Revista de Crítica Literaria Latinoamericana* 27 (1988)
Escobar, Alberto, *El imaginario nacional: Moro, Westphalen, Arguedas: una formación literaria*, Lima: IEP Ediciones, 1989
Fernández Cozman, Camilo, "*Las ínsulas extrañas*" *de Emilio Adolfo Westphalen*, Lima: Naylamp Editores, 1990
González Vigil, Ricardo, "La aventura vanguardista," in his *El Perú es todas las sangres*, Lima: Fondo Editorial de la Pontificia Universidad Católica del Perú, 1991
Higgins, James, *Hitos de la poesía peruana: siglo XX*, Lima: Milla Batres, 1993 [Section on Westphalen in chapter 2]

Women's Writing

19th Century

The first task that the student of 19th-century Spanish American women's literature must undertake is to examine the cultural conditions which allowed the entry of women into public discourse after three centuries of virtual intellectual anonymity. Apart from solitary figures such as Sor Juana Inés de la Cruz, colonial literature was largely produced by men and addressed to a male audience. In contrast, the 19th century saw the advent of the Latin American woman writer who wrote not only for a specific female readership but for the nation as a whole. This phenomenon needs to be considered in the context of a complex process of cultural modernization in which the emergence of the novel as a privileged literary genre plays a central role. The novel, in the view of the liberal intelligentsia, was to have a "civilizing" influence on a reading public in need of modern cultural paradigms, by focusing on the healing charms of the domestic order and thereby counterbalancing the violent avatars of political life taking place at the time. As the private sphere of family affections became established as a narrative focus in the novel, women came to be highly valued as special creatures who, by virtue of their "natural" purity and moral strength, were capable of contributing to the task of nation formation. A number of important novels were published under titles that suggest the mobilization of symbols that encouraged the identification of the imagined nation with a bourgeois feminine sphere, e.g., *Soledad*, 1847 [Solitude] and *Amalia*, 1851 (*Amalia: a Romance of the Argentine*) by the Argentines Bartolomé Mitre and José Mármol respectively; *Julia* (1861) by the Peruvian Luis Benjamín Cisneros; *Clemencia* (1869) by the Mexican Ignacio Manuel Altamirano; and the much celebrated *María*, 1867 (*María, a South American Romance*) by the Colombian Jorge Isaacs, among others. In most of these novels, gender distinctions were used to play with the oppositions of civilization and barbarism and colonialism and republicanism. In the case of the Argentine novels, the "true" symbolic nation was perceived as feminine and inserted within a discursive polarity that saw the urbane-spiritual-modern heroine in opposition to the materialistic-rustic-authoritarian male villain.

The above occurred at a time when Latin American societies were experiencing a profound transformation of values under the impact of their encounter with Northern European modernity. The secularization that women were undergoing – with increased access to education and the demise of colonial models of feminine conduct – contributed to making the period propitious for women's entry into public discourse. A flurry of romances, legends, essays and serialised fiction signed by women were published both in book form and in that quintessential 19th-century literary space – the periodical press. However, it is clear that women writers did not identify with the master narratives of nationalism circulating at the time, which constructed the newly founded republics as essentially Christian, white and western. Rather, deconstructing the civilization/barbarism opposition, they allied themselves with those groups that were being marginalized by the projects of modernization, particularly Indians, ex-slaves and women. The Cuban Gertrudis Gómez de Avellaneda's novel *Sab* (1841) is an abolitionist narrative published half a century before slavery was finally abolished in her native Cuba. In a later novel, the eponymous hero *Guatimozín* (1846) represents the trials and tribulations of a people in their struggle against the invading forces of Cortés. In the case of the Peruvian Clorinda Matto de Turner, her two novels of life in the Andes *Aves sin nido*, 1889 (*Birds without a Nest*), and *Índole*, 1892 [*Human Nature*], explores the viability of a mestizo as opposed to a creole national culture. The Colombian Soledad Acosta de Samper published, among a myriad of other works, the novel *Dolores* (1867), a lucid study of leprosy seen in its symbolic dimension as a disease of punishment for dissent resulting in social isolation. The Argentine Juana Manuela Gorriti gives a space in her prolific productions to the voices of persecuted gauchos, Guaraní and Quechua Indians, black slaves and their descendants, and above all, to women as the subaltern gender. Their perspectives offered an alternative version to the one circulated by official history. In *Los misterios del Plata*, 1846 [The Mysteries of the River Plate], Juana Manso de Noronha successfully interweaves a critique of political tyranny with a critique of marriage, where the notion of the domestic order as harmonious and separate from the dangers of public life is demolished. Other writers, amongst them the Argentine Mercedes Rosas de Rivera and the Peruvians Mercedes Cabello de Carbonera and Teresa González de Fanning, explored critically the few and restricted roles available to women in modern societies. In *Blanca Sol* (1889), a novel written by Cabello, the eponymous heroine commits herself to a loveless marriage in order to secure economic and social stability. The novel ends dramatically when, alone and abandoned, she enters a life of prostitution to support her children, thus illustrating the limitations of a social system that offered few options to women outside marriage.

It is possible to argue that in some countries, like Argentina and Peru, 19th-century life was dominated by a feminine belletristic presence; and that in the specific case of Peru, literary life was dominated by women. In others, the most notorious case being that of Mexico, a different process seems to have taken place in the sphere of literary production which resulted in a masculinization of literary discourse. It is hoped that as the field begins to attract critical attention from Hispanists, studies focusing on the specificity of single countries with their particular and complex social and historical interrelations will become available and will throw light on the many questions that remain unresolved.

FRANCESCA DENEGRI

See also entries on Soledad Acosta de Samper, Juana Manuela Gorriti, Clorinda Matto de Turner

20th Century

From a *fin-de-siècle* perspective, the biased notion that women were not capable of matching dominant masculine artistic quality has been rectified. Women's writing in the 20th century has been the focus of steady and growing interest from both the general public and from critics in the field of literary studies. In mapping out the literary tapestry Latin American women writers have woven during this century, it is helpful to conceptualize it as a complex and varied spectacle appearing in front of the reader. As the access of women to lettered culture increased, so they entered the textual dialogue with their male contemporaries and with women in other cultures. At first, in small numbers, with a steadier output by mid-century, women's writing has reached substantial proportions in the last quarter of the 20th century. 20th-century women writers have cultivated not only all the traditional literary genres, but have also explored new textual possibilities and have revitalized others. Creative writing amounted partly to a process of appropriation and reappropriation of some traditional strategies, partly to a substantial revision of the canon. Thematically, women writers have explored in their stories and poems charted and uncharted territories as they imagine multiple stories of women's diverse life experiences. These protagonists constitute a multifarious gallery of female characterization that signals the vitality of female literary production. Linguistically, in many cases, they have tested the limits of language in experimental writing in prose, poetry and drama. In brief, they have founded, and expanded, a cultural space of their own from which to speak, and in which to inscribe the female subject. In this regard, female writers have entered the scene of writing in earnest. The result is that they have produced an innovative body of writing that is easily identifiable within the literary production of 20th-century Latin America.

The public emergence of women writers that began during the modernization process in Latin America, a process which first exhibited particular vitality in Argentina, Brazil, Chile, Cuba, Mexico and Uruguay, was followed by a more rapid pace of modernization that included the struggle for civil rights. Involvement in various demands for equal justice with men brought about more women's involvement in Bolivia, Peru, Colombia, Venezuela, Nicaragua, El Salvador, Guatemala, Puerto Rico and the Dominican Republic. From journal writing and memoirs, poems and novels at the turn of the 19th century, to the writing of intimate and dramatic poetry, to extensive cultivation of the short story, drama, and the novel, to testimonials of abuse and oppression, women have acceded to the world of letters, and in many cases, received widespread recognition from a sceptical cultural establishment on an unprecedented scale. At the end of the 20th century, some Latin American women writers have become well-known, and, in some cases, they have overshadowed major male figures as in the case of the Chilean Isabel Allende and the Mexican Laura Esquivel. Their works has been translated and read throughout the world; they have received major awards, and have remained in the top best-sellers's lists in several countries. Both these writers share the celebrity status so cherished in the *fin-de-siècle* postmodernist cultural scene. Allende's novels have been selected and bought for scripts of elaborate Hollywood cinema productions, as in the case of *The House of the Spirits*, starring Meryl Streep and Jeremy Irons, or *Of Love and Shadows*. Similarly, the widely acclaimed Mexican production of *Like Water for Chocolate* brought a major box-office success and celebrity status to author Laura Esquivel, a film based on her first novel, *Como agua para chocolate*. The remarkable success of their first published work has brought recognition to other writers, as in the case of the Mexican Elena Garro with her memorable *Los recuerdos del porvenir* (*Recollections of Things to Come*), or, more recently, to Mexican Ángeles Mastretta with her novel *Arráncame la vida* (*Mexican Bolero*).

When Latin American women began to write, the strategy they used was the appropriation of male models, to deconstruct the overriding patriarchal production process of meaning, by which the male imaginary assigned women the all encompassing role of womb. By locating women within the symbol of cyclical fertility, personal female experience was devalued, and this in turn, entailed excluding them from the discourse of knowledge. A critique of the status of women in society has been documented in the subcontinent since the 16th century, in the writings of the Mexican nun Sor Juana Inés de la Cruz.

It is a feature of women's writing to perform the transgressive act of creating a space in the cracks and interstices of the masculine canon. Women in Latin American write to engender a parallel space for the inscription of female voices within a textual practice that attempts restitution of a devalued space and time. To this end, they have cultivated the geography of quotidian life, they have travelled the labyrinth of love as an alternative to romance, they have inscribed the stories of a long struggle for individual and collective identity, or they have documented the horrors of physical and psychological abuse, torture and oppression as gesticulations of individual and institutional revenge.

Concerned with canonical depictions of female characters and culture in male writing, women's writing has fostered a dynamic in, at least, two different directions: on the one hand, women scholars have engaged in surveying the archives to recover lost or forgotten texts about the lives of women in convents in the colonial period throughout the Latin American subcontinent, as they have recovered and published 19th-century diaries, letters, short stories, novels and poems; on the other, contemporary female writers have focused specifically on the infinite wealth of women's stories that has expanded considerably the scope of women's experience. From a reflexive perspective then, both activities achieve a positive balance in the sense of having constructed a body of literary texts that has advanced considerably our knowledge of women's lives and culture.

MAGDALENA GARCÍA PINTO

See also entry on Best-Sellers

Further Reading

In the 1970s and 1980s literary critics have centred their attention on female literary production of earlier periods. This activity has also stimulated the publication of anthologies to disseminate the work of lesser-known or new authors, as is the case of *Women's Writing in Latin America* edited by Sara Castro-Klaren, Sylvia

Molloy and Beatriz Sarlo in 1991, or *The Renewal of the Vision: Voices of Latin American Women Poets*, edited by Marjorie Agosín and Cola Franzen in 1987.

General

Agosín, Marjorie, *Silencio e imaginación: metáforas de la escritura femenina*, Mexico City: Katún, 1986
____ *Las hacedoras; mujer, imagen, escritura*, Santiago de Chile: Cuarto Propio, 1993
Agosín, Marjorie (editor), *A Dream of Light and Shadow: Portraits of Latin American Women Writers*, Albuquerque: University of New Mexico Press, 1995
Arancibia, Juana Alcira (editor), *Evaluación de la literatura femenina de hispanoamérica del siglo XX*, 2 vols, San José, Costa Rica: EDUCA, 1985–87
Davies, Catherine (editor), *Women Writers in Twentieth Century Spain and Spanish America*, Lampeter, Wales: Edwin Mellen Press, 1993
Hart, Stephen M., *White Ink. Essays on Twentieth Century Feminine Fiction in Spain and Latin America*, London: Támesis, 1993
Kantaris, Elia G., *The Subversive Psyche. Contemporary Women's Narrative from Argentina and Uruguay*, Oxford: Clarendon Press, and New York: Oxford University Press, 1996
Lindstrom, Naomi, *Women's Voice in Latin American Literature*, Washington, DC: Three Continents Press, 1989
Lindstrom, Naomi and Carmelo Virgillo (editors), *Woman as Myth and Metaphor in Latin American Literature*, Columbia: University of Missouri Press, 1985
Picon Garfield, Evelyn, *Women's Voices from Latin America: Interviews with Six Contemporary Authors*, Detroit: Wayne State University Press, 1987
Picon Garfield, Evelyn (editor), *Women's Fiction from Latin America*, Detroit: Wayne State University Press, 1988
Rodríguez, Ileana, *House/Garden/Nation: Space, Gender and Ethnicity in Post-Colonial Latin American Literatures by Women*, translated by Rodríguez and Robert Carr, Durham, North Carolina: Duke University Press, 1994
Shea, Maureen E., *Women as Outsiders: Undercurrents of Oppression in Latin American Women's Novels*, San Francisco: Austin and Winfield, 1994
Sblodowska, Elzbieta, "La escritura femenina: una contra-corriente paródica," in her *La parodia en la nueva novela hispanoamericana (1960–1985)*, Amsterdam and Philadelphia: Benjamins, 1991

Studies on Women Writers from Individual Countries in the Region

Coelho, Nelly Novaes, *A literatura feminina no Brasil contemporâneo*, São Paulo: Siciliano, 1993
Fares, Gustavo and Eliana Hermann, *Escritoras argentinas contemporáneas*, New York: Peter Lang, 1993
Flori, Mónica R., *Streams of Silver: Six Contemporary Women Writers from Argentina*, Lewisburg, Pennsylvania: Bucknell University Press, 1995
Franco, Jean, *Plotting Women. Gender and Representation in Mexico*, New York: Columbia University Press, and London: Verso, 1989
Masiello, Francine, *Between Civilization and Barbarism: Women, Nation and Literary Culture in Modern Argentina*, Lincoln: University of Nebraska Press, 1992
Percas de Ponseti, Helena, *La poesía femenina argentina 1810–1950*, Madrid: Cultura Hispánica, 1958
Quinlan, Susan Canty, *The Female Voice in Contemporary Brazilian Narrative*, New York: Peter Lang, 1991
Rojas, Ricardo, *La literatura argentina. Ensayo filosófico sobre la evolución de la cultura en el Plata*, 8 vols, 2nd edition, Buenos Aires: Librería "La Facultad, 1925 [Volume 8 contains chapter on Argentine women writers]

Saldívar, Samuel G., *Evolución del personaje femenino en la novela mexicana*, Lanham, Maryland: University Press of America, 1985

Steele, Cynthia, *Politics, Gender and the Mexican Novel 1968–1988*, Austin: University of Texas Press, 1992

Vianna, Lucía Helena (editor), *Mulher e literatura*, IV Seminário, Niteroi: Abralic, 1992

Anthologies in Translation

Agosín, Marjorie (editor), *Landscapes of a New Land: Fiction by Latin American Women*, Buffalo, New York: White Pine Press, 1989

Hopkinson, Amanda, *Lovers and Comrades: Women's Resistance Poetry from Central America*, London: Women's Press, 1989

Bibliographies

Marting, Diane E. (editor), *Women Writers of Spanish America: an Annotated Bio-Bibliographical Guide*, Westport, Connecticut: Greenwood Press, 1987

____ (editor), *Spanish American Women Writers: a Bio-Bibliographical Source Book*, Westport, Connecticut: Greenwood Press, 1990

Interviews

García Pinto, Magdalena, *Historias íntimas. Conversaciones con diez escritoras latinoamericanas*, Hanover, New Hampshire: Ediciones del Norte, 1988; as *Women Writers of Latin America: Intimate Histories*, translated by the author and Trudy Balch, Austin: University of Texas Press, 1991

Pfeiffer, Erna, *Exiliadas, emigrantes, viajeras. Encuentros con diez escritoras latinoamericanas*, Frankfurt and Madrid: Iberoamericana, 1995

Special Issues of Journals

Revista Iberoamericana, vol. 51/132–33 (1985)

"Latin American Women's Contemporary Writing and Arts," *Review: Latin American Literature and Art* 48 (Spring 1994)

Workshops

A "taller literario," or literary workshop, is a seminar, discussion group, or the like, which emphasizes an exchange of ideas and the demonstration and application of techniques, skills, etc. Literary workshops encompass a variety of genres – theatre, poetry, and prose (short fiction and testimonial writing). Perhaps one of the most significant contributions of the new social/popular movements in Latin America has been the creation of a political culture manifested in a broader concept of democracy and methods of political resistance, entailing novel forms of organization and of cultural action. A particularly striking example of popular culture as resistance and community building, expressed not only in the language of opposition but in an attempt to transform personal experiences into artistry are the literary workshops which have sprung up throughout Latin America today. Typically, literary workshops or *talleres* have taken three distinct forms in Latin America: first, creative writing sessions designed to stimulate literary talent and to complement literacy or educational programs; second, therapeutic writing sessions (usually initiated through the oral medium) designed to alleviate private pain as well as providing a record for the public archive, particularly of traumatic events, such as political torture and execution, "disappearances," destitution and other such atrocities; and third, more action-oriented writing workshops modeled after the Brazilian pedagogue Paulo Freire's concept of conscientization (an awareness of one's own oppressive situation and a demonstration of the oppressed's ability to transform this state of oppression through self and social empowerment). The community-based literary works resulting from such work-shops serve as alternative, people-controlled media that provide information, an outlet for social discontent and, in general, drastically improve interpersonal communication within the community, often leading to community building. The latter usually takes the form of theatre collectives. Such literacy- or culture-based workshops view education as a means for promoting community or "revolutionary" action, usually in the form of the renowned theatre workshops using the dramaturgical methods of Freire's fellow countryman, Augusto Boal (see separate entry). Furthermore, the concept of *talleres* has been influenced by the tenets of the Theology of Liberation whereby Christ's message of love can only be actualized in a society without exploitation, a society responsible for its own destiny. The *talleres* are thus an attempt not only to widen access to literary creation, but also to create new audiences and to develop artistic forms capable of expressing the experiences specific to the country of origin, two pre-conditions for the growth of an autonomous national artistic tradition. The participants in the *talleres* often bear witness to daily events, chronicling and commenting like the storytellers of oral poetry on acts of persecution and hardship experienced by the people.

For the *teatristas* (theatre workshop members) of Latin America to reveal reality is to denounce it. But in the context of the workshop where open discussion and debate are encouraged among the participants, a denunciation of reality signifies also an effort to reconstruct it. To call the endeavors of dramatic facilitators theatre workshops in a strictly literary or performance sense, however, is a misrepresentation of the broader scope of such organized groups. One of the main functions of this theatre of liberation, as it is often called, is to organize communities utilizing drama as a vehicle. Intricately linked to the philosophy espoused by liberation theology, theatre groups not only work to promote cultural activity in rural areas, but also help with community and even agricultural development, reforestation and more (as was the case in Alan Bolt's Nicaraguan-based community theatre movement and so-called "Bamboo" Workshops).

The theatrical production that was created from these workshops through collective cultural action encouraged the development of economic people's co-operatives. In addition, they contributed to the effective organization of strikes and political rallies, and provided the people with a range of skills. The collective method of creation and the documentary theatre, originally used as an investigative medium in connection with national or international issues of relevance, have now given way to more practical approaches to community building – in a literal sense – than the rhetoric of the previously politically-oriented theatre collectives. The overarching project of many of these workshops if to foment popular culture as a process of self-discovery, transformation and liberation through critical insights into cultural histories, traditions and recent events. Thus, the educational theatre of the *talleres* and the political theatre of the *colectivos* (collectives) complement one another in that they are both firmly rooted in popular theatre.

In 1989, the Escuela Internacional de Teatro de la América Latina (The International Theatre School of Latin America and the Caribbean) was founded. Its purpose is to allow workshops to exchange strategies and approaches to the theatre as a contribution to the continuing search for a Latin American and Caribbean identity. Supported by Cuba's prestigious Casa de las Américas (a Cuban government institution devoted to the promotion of Latin American culture, ideas, and art), the "school" (an international workshop of sorts itself) seeks "the defence and exploration of a Latin American and Caribbean identity in addition to the ideals of liberation and sovereignty for our peoples" (the school's constitution dated 28 April 1989). The *feria de talleres* (workshop fairs), which accompany these and other more local theatre workshops, generally focus on dramaturgy, popular dance, karate, music, singing, masks, movement, and debates on various artistic, cultural and social issues. Often renowned guest playwrights (such as Argentina's Osvaldo Dragún) or directors (such as Santiago García, founder and director of the theatre collective La Candelaria of Bogotá, Colombia) are invited from abroad to share their insights with the workshop members. Raw materials based on a performer's exploration of themes and images usually result in theatre facilitators, in conjunction with the *teatristas*, assembling a performance text.

Perhaps the country that is most identified with literary workshops, poetry *talleres* in particular, is Nicaragua when the Sandinistas were in power in the 1980s. Ernesto Cardenal, poet, liberation theologian and then Minister of Culture showed his organizational skills by promoting popular culture as a vehicle for a new national identity, a project that was a major part of Sandinista government policy. The government-sponsored poetry workshops invited participants, including the newly literate, to express their experience in poetry. These poems contribute to the formation of a written popular memory without documentary emphasis. Their aim is to locate

emotion precisely in time and place, in the vernacular, by using a modern open poetics rather than trying to imitate prestigious poetic forms of the past. This discourse about the collective sphere averts what is called a "culture of silence" in which there is an erasure of memory of such significant events by creating a culture of dissent and witness, of mutual affirmation through the voice of the community. The Nicaraguan poetry workshops were organized by the Ministry of Culture throughout the country as an experiment (not only in the rural sectors), but also among the army, the police force, the air force, the state secret police and Somocista prisoners. Advocating a simple poetry defined as *exteriorismo*, which concentrates on verbal economy and observed reality, Cardenal set out his own set of rules for writing poetry used in the workshops – free verse and the vernacular. One of the basic tenets of the Nicaraguan poetry workshops was the weaving of memory and everyday life, so that the war against the dictatorial regime of Somoza would be recalled not in an idealized official version but as moments of personal affectivity, as faces, names, gestures – a living "album" of personal experience. The poetry workshops were thus concerned with individual memory in the expression of poetic creativity. Imitating Brazilian *cantadores* or minstrels and the gaucho *payador*, to some degree, the organizers of such workshops took the role of the oral poets – to process and disseminate information in a rural locality – and applied it to the written text. The purpose of this oral approach was to foster the first acts of writing of a populace which had only recently acquired literacy through an intensive literacy campaign just after the Sandinista Revolution.

Here, granted lack of space, Nicaragua has been selected to illustrate the function and objectives of literary workshops in a revolutionary context. Another obvious example is Cuba where, again, after 1959 an elaborate network of *talleres* were developed as a way to make literature and the arts accessible to a wider range of people and to encourage them to write about their local history. In addition, there is a rich culture of these *talleres* in Brazil, Colombia, Chile and the Central American countries.

ELENA DE COSTA

Further Reading

Boal, Augusto, *Teatro do oprimido y otras poéticas políticas*, Buenos Aires: Ediciones de La Flor, 1974; as *Theater of the Oppressed*, translated by Charles A. and Maria-Odilia Leal McBride, New York: Urizen Books, and London: Pluto Press, 1979

Freire, Paulo, *Cultural Action for Freedom*, Cambridge, Massachusetts: Harvard Educational Review, 1970; Harmonsworth: Penguin, 1972

Johnson, Kent (editor and translator), *A Nation of Poets: Writings from the Poetry Workshops of Nicaragua*, Los Angeles: West End Press, 1985

Martin, Randy, "Country and City: Theatre in Revolution," *The Drama Review*, vol. 31/4 (Winter 1987)

Pianca, Marina, "Entrevista con César Escusa, Director del Taller de Teatro del Centro de Comunicación Popular de Villa El Salvador, Perú," in *Testimonios de teatro latinoamericano*, Buenos Aires: Grupo Editor Latinoamericano, 1991

Pring-Mill, Robert, "The Workshop Poetry of Sandinista Nicaragua," *Antilia*, vol. 1/2 (1984)

Schechner, Richard, *Between Theater and Anthropology*, Philadelphia: University of Pennsylvania Press, 1985

Y

Agustín Yáñez 1904–1980

Mexican prose writer and journalist

Agustín Yáñez is the author of one of the most seminal works of modern Mexican fiction – the novel *Al filo del agua*, 1947 (*The Edge of the Storm*). His production includes numerous novels, essays and newspaper articles. So prolific was Yáñez as a writer that only a selection of his works can be reviewed here.

Flor de juegos antiguos, 1942 [A Flowering of Old Games] consists of short stories recreating the author's infancy and early adolescence. Set in Guadalajara, they celebrate its smells, noises, colours and streets; the life of a Mexican child described through his surroundings. In his next collection of short stories, *Archipiélago de mujeres*, 1943 [Women's Archipelago] , the "state of adolescent sensibilities" as Yáñez himself calls it, is portrayed both through the landscape and the social situations he develops. *Los sentidos al aire*, 1964 [Senses into the Air] and *La ladera dorada*, 1978 (The Golden Hillside), also collections of short fiction, symbolise maturity and old age respectively. They complete this cycle in which Yáñez tried to describe in narrative form, through the perception of his characters and their milieu, what he himself called the stages of the "Mexican man."

Despite being born in Guadalajara, Agustín Yáñez was spiritually and mentally a mountain man; that is he belonged to the mountains of Jalisco, Caxcama and especially Yahualica. The essay *Yahualica* (1946) and even more so *Al filo del agua*, developed this perception of mountains, a way of linking to an oral tradition, an indigenous past and a constant presence of the geography as the contours of the land are a definitive affirmation of the meaning of the characters. *Al filo del agua* was the result of a conflict; on the one hand, the encounter/loss of Yáñez's highland roots – his past, tradition, family ties – and on the other, the political interests of the public figures, the illustrious academic and the practising Catholic. In this sense, *Al filo del agua* can be considered in some ways to be the first social novel of present-day Mexico. It is a novel in which the misery and poverty of a region, its possible causes, motives and reasons are described through the eyes of a storyteller, with his own prejudices, ideas and values. The history of the Mexican novel in this century has in *Al filo del agua* a standard-bearer whose influence has still not stopped.

Modernity, invented by 20th-century critics, and attributed to this novel, is in fact the basic element in *Al filo del agua*.

La tierra pródiga [The Prodigal Land], is a novel which uses social and geographical description; brimming with allegorical references to Yáñez's native Jalisco. The problems of the rural Mexican bourgeoisie are explored and as an outward manifestation of this idea, their land presents a socio/geographical challenge. According to Jean Franco among others, *La tierra pródiga* should also be classed as atypical.

Las tierras flacas, 1962 (*The Lean Lands*) gives an account of the vicissitudes (isolation, money problems) of small landowners on arid, barely workable, infertile land, and *Ojerosa y pintada*, 1960 [Haggard and Made-up], a portrait of the Mexican capital, complete this cycle which Yáñez himself called "the country and the people."

Las vueltas del tiempo, 1973 [The Turns of Time] with its casual, predominantly conversational style and *La creación*, 1959 [The Creation] whose theme is artistic creativity and in which well-known celebrities mingle with fictional characters, are not typical of the apparently homogeneous nature of Yáñez's other stories.

Prolific writer, teacher and essayist, civil servant and insatiable journalist, Yáñez was not, as Carlos Monsiváis put it, "a bad writer with a good book." Yáñez was not only a writer, but also a clever, wise and erudite journalist who joined the literary elite of his time. José Revueltas, who belonged to the same generation, said that he was "a bureaucrat of intelligence and a croupier of literature." Jean Franco, perhaps less critically, offers a more accurate description: "Yáñez matches perfectly the image of the bourgeois intellectuals who came after Cárdenas searching for national regeneration. They often moot the idea of writing literature suited to creating and consolidating the collective consciousness; an instrument for creating America; literature's supporting role in education; that through educating people it is possible to change society."

Informed, up-to-date and observant, Yáñez, like Octavio Paz and many other writers of his generation, was an administrator in many governments and of one single regime. Such a statement, contrary to what the actual literary establishment in Mexico might think, does not detract or add to his writings.

"Yáñez, the timid upstart," concludes Franco, "may not be to our taste but it doesn't diminish in the slightest the literary work of this shadowy novelist."

Yáñez's writings fall into a constant pattern in Mexican literature, that of the intellectual linked to the establishment. They can be considered an allegory *par excellence* of a whole intellectual class who moulded cultural life in Mexico after the Revolution; mid-way between academia and non-denominational opinion (Catholic and provincial), vacillating between government and a pretence at opposition. For Yáñez, literature was subsidiary to his work as a civil servant, journalist or man of ideas; this attitude is what defines him best. Despite his impressive literary output, he will surely be remembered more as an important figure in literary and educational institutions than as a good writer. His place, if we need to assign him one, lies in the political chronicle of Mexico's social institutions rather than in the history of the Mexican novel. To paraphrase Carlos Monsiváis, we could say that Augustín Yáñez was an acquiescent journalist who wrote an unexpected book.

CLAUDIO CANAPARO

translated by Ann Wright

Biography
Born in Guadalajara, Mexico, 4 April 1904, into family of labourers. Raised in very conservative environment. Studied law in Guadalajara and trained as a teacher of literature. Published essays and literary translations in the Guadalajara journal *Bandera de provincias*. Obtained Masters at UNAM in early 1930s and appointed Professor of Literary Theory at that university. Director of broadcasting, Bureau of Public Education, 1932–34. At this time his career turned towards politics, diplomacy and cultural affairs. Mexican representative at UNESCO; governor of state of Jalisco, 1953–59. Ambassador to Argentina and Secretary of Public Education, 1964–70. Remained in public life until his death. *Al filo del agua* (1947) became required reading in state schools. Died in Mexico City, 17 January 1980.

Selected Works

Short Fiction
Flor de juegos antiguos, Guadalajara: Universidad de Guadalajara, 1942
Archipiélago de mujeres, Mexico City: UNAM, 1943
Los sentidos al aire, Mexico City: Instituto Nacional de Bellas Artes, 1964
La ladera dorada, Mexico City: Grijalbo, 1978

Novels
Al filo del agua, Mexico City: Porrúa, 1947; as *The Edge of the Storm*, translated by Ethel Brinton, Austin: University of Texas Press, 1963
La creación, Mexico City: Fondo de Cultura Económica, 1959
Ojerosa y pintada, Mexico City: Libro-Mex Editores, 1960
La tierra pródiga, Mexico City: Fondo de Cultura Económica, 1960
Las tierras flacas, Mexico City: Joaquín Mortiz, 1962; as *The Lean Lands*, translated by Ethel Brinton, Austin: University of Texas Press, 1968
Las vueltas del tiempo, Mexico City: Joaquín Mortiz, 1973

Essays
Por tierras de Nueva Galicia, Guadalajara: Revista *Avanza*, 1928
Espejismo de Juchitán, Mexico City: UNAM, 1940
Genio y figuras de Guadalajara, Mexico City: Abside, 1942
El contenido social de la literatura iberoamericana, Mexico City: El Colegio de México , 1944
Fichas mexicanas, Mexico City: El Colegio de México, 1945
Yahualica, Mexico City: Editorial de la Cámara de Diputados, 1946
Don Justo Sierra: su vida, sus ideas y sus obras, Mexico City: UNAM, 1950
Discursos por Jalisco, Mexico City: Editorial Porrúa, 1958
Días de Bali, Mexico City: Edición del Banco del Pequeño Comercio, 1964
Santa Anna: espectro de una sociedad, Mexico City: Océano, 1982

Further Reading
Brushwood, John S., *Mexico in its Novel: a Nation's Search for Identity*, Austin: University of Texas Press, 1966
Carballo, Emmanuel, *Diecinueve protagonistas de la literatura mexicana del siglo XX*, Mexico City: Empresas Editoriales, 1965 [Lengthy section on Yáñez]
Dellepiane, Ángela B., "Releyendo *Al filo del agua*," *Cuadernos Americanos*, vol. 34/201 (1975)
Giacoman, Helmy F. (editor), *Homenaje a Agustín Yáñez: variaciones interpretativas en torno a su obra*, New York: Las Américas, 1973
Martínez, José Luis, prologue to Yáñez's *Obras escogidas*, Mexico City: Aguilar, 1968 ["Introduction" would be a more accurate term since it is over 100 pages long]
Sommers, Joseph, *After the Storm: Landmarks of the Modern Mexican Novel*, Albuquerque: University of New Mexico Press, 1968
Walker, John L., "Timelessness through Memory in the Novels of Agustín Yáñez," *Hispania*, vol. 57/3 (1974)
Young, Richard A., "Perspectivas autobiográficas en *Flor de juegos antiguos* de Agustín Yáñez," *Ábside*, vol. 40/3 (1976)
____ *Agustín Yáñez y sus cuentos*, London: Támesis, 1978

Special Issues of Journals
Mester, vol. 12/1–2 (1983)

Alicia Yánez Cossío 1929–

Ecuadorian prose writer

Although her earliest publications were poems that dealt with such themes as maternal love and social injustice, since the appearance of her first novel in 1973 (*Bruna, soroche y los tíos*) [Bruna, Altitude Sickness, Aunts and Uncles], Alicia Yánez Cossío has distinguished herself as one of Ecuador's principal novelists of the last twenty-five years. Author of five published novels and one collection of short stories, Yánez Cossío has overcome the legacy of one-book writers in Ecuador. Her continued growth and productivity as an author have contributed to creating both a standard of excellence for future writers and an awareness that an on-going narrative tradition does exist in Ecuadorian literature. Moreover, her literary achievements are especially impressive when bearing in mind that to date few women in Ecuador have been recognized as major contributors to national letters.

Yánez Cossío's success, however, has not come about without considerable sacrifice. It has long been said that to publish in Ecuador is to remain unpublished. An inadequate and inefficient publishing apparatus at both the regional and national levels has prevented most Ecuadorian writers from reaching their readers. Limited editions and poor distribution of books have practically cut off Ecuadorian writers from the international circuit. Such has been the fate of Yánez Cossío. Of course, the effects of this general malaise suffered by most Ecuadorian writers has been exacerbated in Yánez Cossío's case. Because she is a woman in a male dominated profession/society, expectations and standards have frequently been colored by prejudice and unfounded skepticism.

Despite such capricious accusations as her having imitated García Márquez's *Cien años de soledad* (*One Hundred Years of Solitude*), or the reluctance by some to read her work assiduously, Yánez Cossío has persevered. Her fiction knows no boundaries with regards to themes and narrative techniques. Corruption, social injustice, the role of women, the excesses of consumer-driven societies, and the dangers of technology are just a few of Yánez Cossío's preferred themes; irony, satire, hyperbole, caricature, and parody constitute her principal modes of expression. This thematic and technical diversity, however, does not lack coherence and unity. In each work, Yánez Cossío responds and reacts to one underlying concern – the tensions and conflicts inherent in a world that wavers between tradition and change.

Most of Yánez Cossío's work focuses on life in Ecuador's central range of the Andes where her characters find themselves torn between the forces of an oppressive colonial past and the dehumanization of modern society's infatuation with material gain. Yánez Cossío avoids simplistic dichotomies, however. The power of her novels and short stories lies in her ability to capture the complexities and contradictions that characterize the struggle to achieve a balance between the best of the old and the new. While she makes clear that continuing to live in the past threatens to asphyxiate her characters with its taboos and anacronistic conventions, she also warns her readers against blindly sacrificing traditional values for the gold and glitter of consumerism.

In *Bruna, soroche y los tíos*, a young woman rebels against a patriarchal society and becomes a kind of clarion for social change. Bruna is not only a symbol of the emergence of a new woman in search of a more meaningful lifestyle, but she also constitutes a role model for all youth who must accept the challenge of creating a new society capable of succeeding in the modern world. *Yo vendo unos ojos negros*, 1979 [I Sell Some Dark Eyes], Yánez Cossío's second novel, reiterates her deep concern over women's place in modern society and the need to overcome the taboos and traditions which continue to stifle growth and development. At the same time, she insists on the need for solidarity between women and men, particularly in their struggle to create a new socioeconomic order based on social justice and freedom. With regards to *La cofradía del mullo del vestido de la Virgen Pipona*, 1985 [The Sisterhood of the Sacred Vestments of the Plump Virgin] and *La Casa del Sano Placer*, 1989 [The House of Wholesome Pleasure], Yánez Cossío continues examining her favorite themes, but with a definite turn towards parody and satire. These later novels reveal clearly an evolution in her command of narrative technique and humor.

To conclude, Alicia Yánez Cossío is one of a number of Ecuadorian writers who await serious critical attention and adequate distribution beyond national borders. Her work to date exemplifies the major tendencies and artistic quality of much of Latin America's post-Boom fiction. Readers of contemporary narrative fiction interested in the Andean region and/or Latin American women writers will find much to enjoy in Yánez Cossío's work.

MICHAEL HANDELSMAN

Biography

Born in Quito, Ecuador, in 1929. Married the Cuban anthropologist, Luis Campos with whom she has five children, all of whom have been raised in Ecuador. In 1952, she received a scholarship to study journalism at the Institute of Hispanic Culture in Madrid, Spain. Teacher at the Cotopaxi Academy in Ecuador for many years. In 1972, her first novel, *Bruna, soroche y los tíos*, was awarded first prize in a literary competition for the novel sponsored by Guayaquil's leading newspaper, *El Universo*.

Selected Works

Novels
Bruna, soroche y los tíos, Quito: Casa de la Cultura Ecuatoriana, 1973
Yo vendo unos ojos negros, Quito: Casa de la Cultura Ecuatoriana, 1979
Más allá de las islas, Quito: Don Bosco, 1980
La cofradía del mullo del vestido de la Virgen Pipona, Quito: Planeta, 1985
La Casa del Sano Placer, Quito: Planeta, 1989

Short Fiction
El beso y otras fricciones, Bogotá: Ediciones Paulina, 1975

Poetry
Poesía, Quito: Casa de la Cultura Ecuatoriana, 1974

Further Reading
Gerdes, Dick, "An Embattled Society: Orality Versus Writing in Alicia Yánez Cossío's *La cofradía del mullo del vestido de la Virgen Pipona*," *Latin American Literary Review*, vol. 18/36 (July–December 1990)

Handelsman, Michael, "En busca de una mujer nueva: rebelión y resistencia en *Yo vendo unos ojos negros* de Alicia Yánez Cossío," *Revista Iberoamericana* 144–45 (July–December 1988)
Scott, Nina M., "Alicia Yánez Cossío: una perspectiva feminina sobre el pasado del Ecuador," *Discurso Literario*, vol. 4/2 (1987)

Z

Juan Zorrilla de San Martín 1855–1931

Uruguayan poet, essayist and orator

The national poet of Uruguay, Juan Zorrilla de San Martín is the foremost local representative of Romanticism and one of the last Romantic poets in Spanish. His most famous work, *Tabaré*, came out the same year as Rubén Darío's *Azul*, 1888 [Blue]. A committed but liberal Catholic, Zorrilla engaged in debates with the prevailing contemporary positivists, who nevertheless respected him. He wrote in different genres but with a consistency of sentiment and belief across all of his work. He began as a poet and later turned to the essay; he is also one of the greatest exponents of public oratory in modern Spanish.

His first important piece, *La leyenda patria*, 1879 [Legend of the Fatherland], already contained the programme Zorrilla was to support throughout his life: the celebration of *patria* and God. The poem was written soon after his return home from a long stay in Argentina and Chile where his parents had sent him for a Catholic education that was not easily available in a Uruguay then dominated by rationalism. The *leyenda* was Zorrilla's contribution to a (belated) poetry competition set up to inaugurate a monument celebrating Uruguay's declaration of independence from Brazil in 1825. Although the poem far exceeded the length specified by the rules, it was unanimously hailed as the winner by the crowd who gathered to listen to the author recite it in what by all accounts was an enthralling performance. Zorrilla's two main concerns are conspicuous in the poem; it begins "Es la voz de la Patria . . . Pide gloria . . . / Yo obedezco esa voz." (It is the voice of the Nation. It demands glory . . . / I obey that voice.); and it ends "¡Protege, oh Dios, la tumba de los libres! / Protege a nuestra patria independiente, / Que inclina a Ti tan sólo, / Sólo ante Ti, la coronada frente." (Protect, oh God, the grave of the free! / Protect our independent nation, / Which bows before You only, / Only before You, its crowned head).

Zorrilla's success on this occasion set him up as the nation's orator; from then on he was to express popular and official feelings at home and abroad often throughout his life. Two examples of this work are his speech in Montevideo in 1920 on the arrival from Italy of the remains of Enrique Rodó, his famous compatriot, and his oration of 1892 at La Rábida when he was chosen to represent all Latin American delegates during the celebrations of the 400th anniversary of Colón's arrival in America. Zorrilla's other main contribution to nation-building is the voluminous *La epopeya de Artigas,* 1910 [The Epic of Artigas], commissioned by the government as a source of inspiration to potential sculptors of a statue of the national hero of Uruguay, José Gervasio Artigas (1764–1850). The work is historical, and although written in a literary tone, it is a major contribution to the revisionary movement against the black legend which surrounded Artigas during the 19th century. The *epopeya* is a sort of *Facundo* in reverse; like Sarmiento, Zorrilla sees his subject as the personification of his country; but unlike his predecessor, who saw Facundo Quiroga as a despicable result of Argentina's barbaric circumstances (and who put Artigas in the same class, Sarmiento's book being one of the sources of Artigas's *Leyenda negra*), Zorrilla's subject is positive: Artigas is "el héroe autóctono" not only of Uruguay but of Spanish America as a whole. Amongst other parallels with Sarmiento's *Facundo*, Zorrilla uses geography and history to buttress his vision of the man and his country (e.g., Uruguay is different from Brazil on grounds of language, and from Argentina for its having its own natural ports and a considerable history as a detached zone of the United Provinces of the River Plate). Zorrilla's reflections on nationhood continued to occupy him until his later life, when he published one of his finest essays, *El sermón de la paz,* 1924 [The Sermon on Peace]. A further illustration of Zorrilla's close symbiosis with his country's development is the decision by the Bank of Uruguay to finance the publication of his complete works in 1929 as a homage on the fiftieth anniversary of *La leyenda patria*. Supervising the sixteen volumes of this edition was one of Zorrilla's last tasks before his death.

But the work of Zorrilla's which has achieved most renown outside the River Plate is *Tabaré,* 1888 (*Tabaré: an Indian Legend of Uruguay*). A text highly respected at home, still enjoying popular favour and forming part of school syllabuses, it is one of the great narrative poems in modern Spanish. Its plot would have appealed to both inhabitants of the River Plate and Spaniards of the time.

Tabaré tells of the ill-fated blend of Spain and the American continent in the person of the eponymous hero, a blue-eyed mestizo son of a Charrúa chief and a captive Spanish woman. Tabaré grows to be a sad and melancholy character who is confused about his identity: half pagan Indian, half Catholic Spaniard (he was baptized by his mother shortly before her death). His improbable nature, it is suggested, makes it impossible for him to survive. The plot tells how Tabaré is captured by the men of the Spanish Captain Don Gonzalo de Orgaz, who had come to the Charrúa land accompanied by his wife Doña Luz and his sister Blanca. When the latter sees Tabaré, she becomes enthralled by the peculiarity of his being a mestizo with blue eyes; the Indian for his part grows disturbed on seeing in the girl Blanca a new version of his dead mother. Although at first Tabaré does not speak to Blanca, he spends his nights awake by her tent. His noctambulist habits preoccupy Doña Luz, who persuades her husband to release the Charrúa so as to protect the girl, although Blanca herself continues to be fascinated by the Indian. During an attack on the Spanish post, the young Charrúa chief Yamandú captures Blanca with libidinous plans. When the sexual consummation is about to take place, Tabaré arrives to rescue the girl and to kill Yamandú. As he is returning with Blanca in order to hand her back to her brother, the latter mistakes the sobbing of an ambiguously enamoured Blanca who is sad at the impossibility of interracial love, and he kills Tabaré.

Until recently, criticism of *Tabaré* was mild, and whilst the poetic merits of the work were generally acknowledged, faults were found concerning its lack of realism, its epic pretensions, or the imperfections of the references to the Tupi language allocated by Zorrilla to the Charrúas. As tastes changed, and in particular as the 1992 debate over the Spanish conquest of America developed, the work invited new readings. It was always clear that *Tabaré* could be read productively as an idealized account of the beginnings of Uruguay. This was justified by two external aspects to the poem. The first was the official absence of Indians in Uruguay since shortly after the country's independence in 1830; the second factor was the overt intention of the author's work in general to contribute to the construction of a Uruguayan national identity. There has been a series of recent studies which stress this aspect. Hugo Achúgar notes that "la respuesta estético-ideológica que realizaba el patricio letrado Zorrilla, atendía a un proyecto histórico superior: la consolidación de la nacionalidad" (the aesthetic and ideological response of the educated patrician Zorrilla fitted a higher historical project: the consolidation of national identity). For her part, Doris Sommer says that Zorrilla's text expresses a contemporary revival of Catholic humanism in Spanish America. Javier García Méndez (1992) has seen *Tabaré* as a cultural buttress to the contemporary political and economic demands to make the country appealing to foreign trade. More specifically, the two last-mentioned critics see the poem as a Romantic mechanism to settle the accounts with the official extermination of the Charrúas in Uruguay, Sommer speaks of a "collective exorcism." These recent critiques are powerful, but may make Zorrilla's ideological programme for *Tabaré* sound more hermetic that it appears in the poem. Although it is clear, as these critics say, and as Zorrilla himself openly states to his wife in the poem's "Dedicatoria," that the native American had to disappear to allow for the birth of a new Hispanic and Christian nation, the poem also suggests that there is a certain price to pay for

that privilege. As it turns out, the pain of Blanca-Spain at the outcome is not negligible and her evident fascination for Tabaré has to be repressed.

GUSTAVO SAN ROMÁN

See also entries on Indianism, Juan León Mera

Biography
Born in Montevideo, Uruguay, 28 December 1855; father Spanish, from Santander; mother, Uruguayan, died two years after the child's birth. Educated mostly with Jesuits in Santa Fe, Argentina; studied law at the University of Santiago, Chile, graduated in 1877. Returned to Montevideo to work as judge, 1878. Married Elvira Blanco Sienra. Founder of the Catholic newspaper *El Bien Público*, 1879. Professor of Literature, 1880–85. Corresponding member of the Royal Academy of the Spanish language, 1885. Fled to Argentina after incurring the displeasure of President General Santos. In 1887 his wife died at Tigre, outside Buenos Aires; Zorrilla and children returned to Montevideo. Editor of revived *El Bien Público*; deputy for Montevideo until 1890. Married Concepción Blanco, his first wife's sister, in 1889 (died in 1907). From 1891–98 Plenipotentiary Minister first in Spain, where he delivered some famous speeches, and then in France, his post ceasing after new disagreement with president Juan Lindolfo Cuestas. Editor of *El Bien Público*, for another period, 1899–1904. Professor of international law, 1899–1906, and Professor of art theory, 1907–31, Univerity of Montevideo. Appointed as signatory of notes at National Bank, 1903; beginning of consistently good relations with presidents; delivered many official speeches. Died in Montevideo, 3 November 1931.

Selected Works
Notas de un himno, Santiago de Chile: La Estrella de Chile, 1877
La leyenda patria, Montevideo: La Reforma, 1879
Tabaré, Montevideo: Barreiro y Ramos, 1888; as *Tabaré; an Indian Legend of Uruguay*, translated by Walter Owen, Washington, DC: Pan American Union, 1956 [bilingual edition]
Resonancias del camino, Paris: Imprimerie Nouvelle, 1896
Huerto cerrado, Montevideo: Dornaleche y Reyes, 1900
Conferencias y discursos, Montevideo: Barreiro y Ramos, 1905
La epopeya de Artigas, 2 vols, Montevideo: Barreiro y Ramos, 1910
Detalles de la historia rioplatense, Montevideo: Claudio García, 1917
El sermón de la paz, Montevideo: El Siglo Ilustrado, 1924
El libro de Ruth, Montevideo: Arduino Hermanos, 1928

Compilations and Anthologies
Obras completas, 16 vols, Montevideo: Imprenta Nacional Colorada, 1930
Correspondencia de Zorrilla de San Martín y Unamuno, edited by Arturo Sergio Visea, Montevideo: INIAL, 1956
Obras escogidas, Madrid: Aguilar, 1967

Further Reading
Achúgar, Hugo, *Poesía y sociedad (Uruguay 1880–1911)*, Montevideo: Arca, 1985
García Méndez, Javier, "*Tabaré* o la leyenda blanca," *Brecha*, Montevideo, vol. 31/1 (1992)
Ibáñez, Roberto, "La leyenda patria y su contorno histórico," in *Homenaje al poeta Juan Zorrilla de San Martín*, Montevideo: Cámara de Senadores, 1959
Lauxar (Osvaldo Crispo Acosta), *Juan Zorrilla de San Martín*, Montevideo: La Casa del Estudiante, 1955
Pickenhayn, Jorge Oscar, *El amplio mundo de Juan Zorrilla de San Martín* Montevideo: Barreiro y Ramos, 1992
San Román, Gustavo, "Negotiating Nationhood: the Repressed Desire of the Native in *Tabaré*," *Forum for Modern Language Studies*, vol. 24/4 (1993)
Sommer, Doris, *Foundational Fictions: the National Romances of Latin America* Berkeley: University of California Press, 1991

INDEXES

TITLE INDEX

The name(s) in parentheses after the title will direct the reader to the appropriate entry, where full publication information is given. The date given is that of first publication. Revised titles and English-language translations, if different fron the original, are listed, with their appropriate dates. Titles that appear in **bold** are subjects of individual essays.

ABC de Castro Alves (Amado) 1941
A la Madre (Walsh) 1981
A la memoria de Ricardo Güiraldes (Reyes) 1934
A la orilla del mundo y primer día (Paz) 1942
A morta (O. Andrade) 1937
A partir de Manhattan (Lihn) 1979
A sus plantas rendido un león (Soriano) 1987
A través de mi espejo (Diego) 1981
Abaddón, el exterminador (Sábato) 1974
Abierta oscuridad (Gelman) 1994
Abismo de rosas (Trevisan) 1976
Abolición de la muerte (Westphalen) 1935
Abolición de la propiedad (Agustín) 1969
Aborígenes (Martínez Moreno) 1964
Abrojos (Darío) 1887
Absurdo entre cuatro paredes (Dorfman) 1968
Acerca de la escritura (Peri Rossi) 1991
Acomodador (Ferré) 1986
Acoso (Carpentier) 1956
Actos de fe en Guatemala (Asturias) 1980
Acuario (Alegría) 1955
Açúcar (Freyre) 1939
Adán (Huidobro) 1914
Adán Buenosayres (Marechal) 1948
Adelaide Ristori (Machado de Assis) 1955
Adiós a mamá (Arenas) 1995
Adiós, poeta (Edwards) 1990
Adiós Robinson (Cortázar) 1984
Adioses (Onetti) 1954
Adioses (Scorza) 1959
Adjectivo y sus arrugas (Carpentier) 1980
Adrogué (Borges) 1977
Adúltera (Martí) 1935
Adventures of a Photographer in La Plata (Bioy Casares) 1989
Adventures of Maqroll (Mutis) 1995
Adversos milagros (Bioy Casares) 1969
Aeronauta (Meireles) 1952
Afanes (Bioy Casares) 1983

Affaire d'honneur (Hibbert) 1988
África (Arlt) 1991
Africanía de la música folklórica de Cuba (F. Ortiz) 1950
Agonía de "Rasu-Ñiti," (Arguedas) 1962
Agosto (Fonseca) 1990
Agrestes (Melo Neto) 1985
Agua (Arguedas) 1935
Agua de arroz (Lihn) 1968
Agua-mãe (Rego) 1941
Agua que no has de beber (Cisneros) 1971
Agua quemada (Fuentes) 1981
Água viva (Lispector) 1973
Agua y cauce (Otero Silva) 1937
Agua y la noche (J.L. Ortiz) 1933
Agua y viento (Paz) 1959
Aguafuertes españolas (Arlt) 1936
Aguafuertes porteñas (Arlt) 1933
¿Aguila o sol? (Paz) 1951
Águila y la serpiente (Guzmán) 1928
Águilas (Mallea) 1943
Aguiluchos (Marechal) 1922
Aguja de marear (García Calderón) 1936
Ah, É? (Trevisan) 1994
Ahí viene la plaga (Agustín) 1985
Ainsi parla l'Oncle (Price-Mars) 1928
Airborn (Paz) 1981
Aire conmovido (J.L. Ortiz) 1949
Aire frío (Piñera) 1959
Aire libre (Walsh) 1967
Aires de México (Prosas) (Altamirano) 1940
Akeké y la jutíce (Barnet) 1978
Al bello aparecer de este lucero (Lihn) 1983
Al filo del agua (Yáñez) 1947
Al margen (Barrett) 1912
Al pie de la letra (Castellanos) 1959
Al sol y bajo la luna (Tablada) 1918
Al yunque (Reyes) 1960
Alabanza del bolo alimenticio (C. Belli) 1979
Álamo y el viento (J.L. Ortiz) 1947
Alba sube (J.L. Ortiz) 1937
Albanza del reino (Mutis) 1985

Albores (Reyes) 1960
Álbum de familia (Castellanos) 1971
Álbum de zoología (Pacheco) 1985
Album familiar (Alegría) 1982
Alclasán (Asturias) 1939
Além do apenas moderno (Freyre) 1973
Aleph (Borges) 1949
Alfarrá bios (Alencar) 1873
Alférez Arce, teniente Arce, capitán Arce (Salazar Bondy) 1969
Alguien que anda por ahí (Cortázar) 1977
Alguma poesia (C. Andrade) 1930
Alhajadito (Asturias) 1961
Alhos & bugalhos (Freyre) 1978
All Fires the Fire (Cortázar) 1973
All Green Shall Perish (Mallea) 1967
Alléluia pour une femme-jardin (Depestre) 1982
Alma (O. Andrade) 1917
Alma do Lazaro (Alencar) 1873
Alma matinal (Mariátegui) 1950
Alma y las colinas (J.L. Ortiz) 1956
Almacén como otro cualquiera (Diego) 1978
¡Alocución bolivarense! (Núñez) 1885
Alta traición (Pacheco) 1985
Altazor (Huidobro) 1931
Alternating Current (Paz) 1973
Alto es el sur (Asturias) 1952
Alturas de Macchu Picchu (Neruda) 1950
Alucinados (D'Halmar) 1935
Alumbrado (G. Rojas) 1986
Amalia (Mármol) 1855
Amar se aprende amando (C. Andrade) 1985
Amar, verbo intransitivo (M. Andrade) 1927
Amares (Galeano) 1993
Amarillo celeste (S. Ocampo) 1972
América es un ajiaco (F. Ortiz) 1940
América, fábula de fábulas (Asturias) 1972
América Latina para entenderte mejor (Galeano) 1990
Americanas (Machado de Assis) 1875

Doorman (Arenas) 1991
Dora, Doralina (Queiroz) 1975
Dorando la píldora (Dorfman) 1985
Dormir al sol (Bioy Casares) 1973
Dorrego (Viñas) 1974
Dos amores (Villaverde) 1858
Dos congresos (Martí) 1985
Dos crímenes (Ibargüengoitia) 1979
Dos darsas pirotécnicas (Storni) 1932
Dos fantasías memorables (Bioy Casares, Borges) 1946
Dos fundaciones de Buenos Aires (Larreta) 1933
2000 (Neruda) 1974
Dos Nocturnos (Villaurrutia) 1931
Dos retratos (Lange) 1956
Dos señores conversan (Bryce Echenique) 1990
Dos soledades (Westphalen) 1974
Dos Venecias (Ferré) 1992
Dos vidas del pobre Napoleón (Gálvez) 1954
Dos viejos pánicos (Piñera) 1968
Doscientas ballenas azules (Glantz) 1979
200 exercícios e jogos para o ator e o não-ator (Boal) 1977
Dostoevsky's Last Night (Peri Rossi) 1995
Double Flame (Paz) 1993
Doublure (Sarduy) 1981
Doubtful Strait (Cardenal) 1995
Doze noturnos de Holanda (Meireles) 1952
Draft of Shadows (Paz) 1979
Dream of Heroes (Bioy Casares) 1987
Dreamtigers (Borges) 1963
Drums for Rancas (Scorza) 1977
Du Réalisme Merveilleux des Haïtiens (Alexis) 1956
Duas aguas (Melo Neto) 1956
Dueños de la tierra (Viñas) 1959
Dulce daño (Storni) 1918
Duques de Endor (Arévalo Martínez) 1940
Dyakout 1, 2, 3 (Morisseau-Leroy) 1983

Eagle and the Serpent (Guzmán) 1930
Eagle or Sun? (Paz) 1970
Ebony Wood (Roumain) 1972
¡Ecce Pericles! (Arévalo Martínez) 1945
Ecopoemas (N. Parra) 1982
Ecos del alma (Huidobro) 1911
Écrivain et la catastrophe (Sábato) 1986
Ecuador amargo (Adoum) 1949
Ecuatorial (Huidobro) 1918
¡Écue-yamba-Ó! (Carpentier) 1933
Edad despareja (Amorim) 1938
Edades poéticas (Carrera Andrade) 1958
Edge of the Storm (Yáñez) 1963
Egberto Gismonti (Gullar) 1979
Ejercicios materiales (Varela) 1994
El que vendrá (Rodó) 1897
El que vino a salvarme (Piñera) 1970
Eldorado y las ocupaciones nocturnas (Adoum) 1961
Elegía (Ibarbourou) 1967
Elegía (Neruda) 1974
Elegía a Jacques Roumain en el cielo de Haití (Guillén) 1948

Elegía a Jesús Menéndez (Guillén) 1951
Elegía cubana (Guillén) 1952
Elegía sin nombre (Ballagas) 1936
Elegías italianas (Girri) 1957
Elemental Odes (Neruda) 1990
Elementary Odes (Neruda) 1961
Elementos de la noche (Pacheco) 1963
Elementos del desastre (Mutis) 1953
Elogio de Ameghino (Lugones) 1915
Elogio de la danza (Morejón) 1982
Elogio de la madrastra (Vargas Llosa) 1988
Elogio de la sombra (Borges) 1969
Elogio de las cosas de la tierra (Mistral) 1979
Elsinore (Elizondo) 1988
Elvira (Echeverría) 1832
Em busca de Curitiba perdida (Trevisan) 1992
Embajador de Torlania (Arévalo Martínez) 1960
Emergency Poems (N. Parra) 1972
Emisarios (Mutis) 1984
Empeños de una casa (Juana Inés de la Cruz) 1692
Empire's Old Clothes (Dorfman) 1983
Emulo lipolidón (Asturias) 1935
En Bética no bella (C. Belli) 1961
En busca del nuevo mundo (Uslar Pietri) 1969
En Cuba (Cardenal) 1972
En cuerpo de camisa (Sánchez) 1966
En el aura del sauce (J.L. Ortiz) 1970–71
En el costado de la luz (Argueta) 1968
En el mundo de los seres ficticios (Gálvez) 1961
En el mundo de los seres reales (Gálvez) 1965
En el país del sol (Tablada) 1919
En el restante tiempo terrenal (C. Belli) 1988
En el revés del cielo (Orozco) 1987
En la creciente oscuridad (Mallea) 1973
En la humedad del secreto (Dalton) 1994
En la letra (Girri) 1972
En la masmédula (Girondo) 1954
En la masvida (Girondo) 1972
En la pampa (Larreta) 1955
En la sangre (Cambaceres) 1887
En la semana trágica (Viñas) 1966
En la verbena de Madrid (García Calderón) 1920
En la zona (Saer) 1960
En las calles (Icaza) 1935
En las montañas (Jaimes Freyre) 1906
¿En qué piensas? (Villaurrutia) 1938
En un hermoso día de verano (Jaimes Freyre) 1907
En una ciudad llamada San Juan (Marqués) 1960
Encancaranublado (Vega) 1982
Encarnação (Alencar) 1875
Encounters (García Ponce) 1989
Encuentros (García Ponce) 1972
End of the Game (Cortázar) 1967
Enemigo rumor (Lezama Lima) 1941
Enemigo y la mañana (Adoum) 1952

Enemigos del alma (Mallea) 1950
Engenheiro francês no Brazil (Freyre) 1940
Enigma interior (Gálvez) 1907
Ensaios de sociologia e literatura (Romero) 1901
Ensayo de un crimen (Usigli) 1944
Ensayos quemados en Chile (Dorfman) 1974
Enseignements de l'histoire (Lhérisson) 1894
Entenado (Saer) 1983
Entrada en materia (García Ponce) 1968
Entrañas de niño (Carrasquilla) 1914
Entre crotos y sabihondos (Arlt) 1969
Entre cubanos (F. Ortiz) 1913
Entre dos tías y un tío (Mera) 1891
Entre la dicha y la tiniebla (Diego) 1986
Entre la novela y la historia (Gálvez) 1962
Entre la piedra y la flor (Paz) 1941
Entre Marx y una mujer desnuda (Adoum) 1976
Entre Sartre y Camus (Vargas Llosa) 1981
Entrevista (Giardinelli) 1986
Entry into Matter (García Ponce) 1976
Entusiasmo (Skármeta) 1967
Enumeración de la patria (S. Ocampo) 1942
Envenenada (F. Hernández) 1931
Envíos (Girri) 1967
Epigramas (Cardenal) 1961
Epílogo wagneriano (Herrera y Reissig) 1902
Episodios novelescos de la historia patria (Acosta de Samper) 1887
Epístolas y poemas (Darío) 1885
Epitafios, Imitación, Aforismos (Sarduy) 1994
Epitaph of a Small Winner (Machado de Assis) 1952
Epopeya de Artigas (Zorrilla de San Martín) 1910
Eras imaginarias (Lezama Lima) 1971
Eréndira (García Márquez) 1983
Ermitão da Glória (Alencar) 1873
Ermitão de Muquém (Guimarães) 1866
Éros dans un train chinois (Depestre) 1990
Erosiones (Glantz) 1984
Errancia sin fin (García Ponce) 1981
Esa fauna (Monterroso) 1992
Esa sangre (Azuela) 1956
Esau and Jacob (Machado de Assis) 1966
Esaú e Jacó (Machado de Assis) 1904
Escada (O. Andrade) 1921
Escalas melografiadas (Vallejo) 1923
Escándalo y soledades (Girri) 1956
Escena contemporánea (Mariátegui) 1925
Escola das facas (Melo Neto) 1980
Escolha o seu sonho (Meireles) 1964
Escrava Isaura (Guimarães) 1875
Escrava que não é Isaura (M. Andrade) 1925
Escravo nos anúncios de jornais brasileiros do século XIX (Freyre) 1963
Escrito a ciegas (Adán) 1961
Escrito en Cuba (Lihn) 1969
Escrito sobre un cuerpo (Sarduy) 1969
Escritor latinoamericano y la revolución posible (Benedetti) 1974
Escritor y sus fantasmas (Sábato) 1963

Guerra del fin del mundo (Vargas Llosa) 1981

Guerra del tiempo (Carpentier) 1958

Guerra dos Mascates (Alencar) 1873-74

Guerra gaucha (Lugones) 1905

Guerra interior (Mallea) 1963

Guerra silenciosa (Scorza) 1970-79

Guerrilla de México (Guzmán) 1915

Guesa errante (Sousândrade) 1874-77

Guía de la joven poesía ecuatoriana (Carrera Andrade) 1939

Guia de Ouro Preto (Bandeira) 1938

Guia-mapa de Gabriel Arcanjo (Piñon) 1961

Guia prático, histórico e sentimental da cidade da Recife (Freyre) 1934

Guirnalda con amores (Bioy Casares) 1959

Guirnalda del silencio (Carrera Andrade) 1926

Guitarra (Echeverría) 1842

Guitarra indócil (V. Parra) 1978

Gunther Stapenhorst (Arreola) 1946

Há uma gota de sangue em cada poema (M. Andrade) 1917

Ha vuelto la Diosa Ambarina (Westphalen) 1989

Habana para un infante difunto (Cabrera Infante) 1979

Habla el algarrobo (V. Ocampo) 1959

Hablador (Vargas Llosa) 1987

Hablando en plata (Poniatowska) 1987

Hablar de poesía (García Marruz) 1986

Hace tiempos (Carrasquilla) 1935-36

Hacedor (Borges) 1960

Hacia el sur (Gelman) 1982

Hacia la liberación del lector latinoamericano (Dorfman) 1984

Hadriana dans tous mes rêves (Depestre) 1988

Haïti chérie (Condé) 1987

Hallali (Huidobro) 1918

Hallazgo y otros cuentos del mar (Lillo) 1956

Hallucinated City (M. Andrade) 1968

Hallucinations (Arenas) 1971

Hampa afro-cubana (F. Ortiz) 1906

Han tocado a degüello (Gálvez) 1951

Hand and the Glove (Machado de Assis) 1970

Happytown (Morisseau-Leroy) 1982

Hard Rain (Dorfman) 1990

Harp and the Shadow (Carpentier) 1990

Harpas selvagens (Sousândrade) 1857

Hasta aquí (Benedetti) 1974

Hasta no verte, Jesús mío (Poniatowska) 1969

Hay que sonreír (Valenzuela) 1966

He Who Searches (Valenzuela) 1979

Heartbreak Tango (Puig) 1973

Hechicero (Solórzano) 1955

Hechizo de Tomayquichua (López Albújar) 1943

Hecho a mano (Walsh) 1965

Hechos y leyendas de nuestra América (Aguilera Malta) 1975

Hechos y relaciones (Gelman) 1980

Helena (Machado de Assis) 1876

Helicópteros (Dalton) 1980

Helicopters in the Kingdom of Peru (Cisneros) 1981

Hell Has No Limits (Donoso) 1972

Heptamerón (Marechal) 1966

Heraldos negros (Vallejo) 1919

Hérémakhonon (Condé) 1976

Herencia (Matto de Turner) 1895

Heréticos (Valenzuela) 1967

Heritage of Quincas Borba (Machado de Assis) 1954

Hermano asno (Barrios) 1922

Hermano Quiroga (Martínez Estrada) 1957

Hermosas (G. Rojas) 1991

Héroe de las mujeres (Bioy Casares) 1978

Heroic and Creative Meaning of Socialism (Mariátegui) 1995

Heroínas mexicanas (Fernández de Lizardi) 1955

Heróis e vilões no romance brasileiro (Freyre) 1979

Heterodoxia (Sábato) 1953

Hidalgo (Scorza) 1956

Hidalgo conquistador (Acosta de Samper) 1907

Hidalgos de Zamora (Acosta de Samper) 1898

Hidden Life (Dourado) 1969

Hiedra (Villaurrutia) 1941

Hiel nuestra de cada día (Sánchez) 1976

High Art (Fonseca) 1986

High Noon in Latin America (Fuentes) 1983

Highroad of Saint James (Carpentier) 1970

Hija de Jefte (Jaimes Freyre) 1889

Hijo de hombre (Roa Bastos) 1960

Hijo de la pampa (Lugones) 1916

Hijo de ladrón (M. Rojas) 1951

Hijo pródigo (Arévalo Martínez) 1956

Hijos del aire (Paz) 1981

Hijos del limo (Paz) 1974

Hills of Massabielle (Condé) 1991

Hima-Sumac (Matto de Turner) 1892

Hipogeo Secreto (Elizondo) 1968

His Excellency the Ambassador (Veríssimo) 1967

História da literatura brasileira (Romero) 1888

Historia de arrabal (Gálvez) 1922

Historia de Garabombo, el invisible (Scorza) 1972

Historia de la calle Corrientes (Marechal) 1937

Historia de la crisis mundial (Mariátegui) 1959

Historia de la edad media y de los tiempos modernos (Jaimes Freyre) 1895

Historia de la eternidad (Borges) 1936

Historia de la noche (Borges) 1977

Historia de María Griselda (Bombal) 1946

Historia de Mayta (Vargas Llosa) 1984

Historia de un amor turbio (Quiroga) 1908

Historia de una pasión argentina (Mallea) 1937

História do Brasil (Mendes) 1932

Historia General del Perú (Garcilaso de la Vega) 1617

Historia personal del "Boom," (Donoso) 1971

Historia prodigiosa (Bioy Casares) 1956

Historia secreta de una novela (Vargas Llosa) 1971

Historia universal de la infamia (Borges) 1935

Historiales (Larreta) 1921

Histórias da meia-noite (Machado de Assis) 1873

Histórias da província de Minas Gerais (Guimarães) 1872

Histórias da Velha Totônia (Rego) 1936

Histórias de Alexandre (Ramos) 1944

Historias de amor (Amorim) 1938

Historias de amor (Bioy Casares) 1972

Historias de cronopios y de famas (Cortázar) 1962

Historias desaforadas (Bioy Casares) 1986

Histórias do desencontro (Telles) 1958

Histórias e sonhos (Barreto) 1920

Historias fantásticas (Bioy Casares) 1972

Histórias incompletas (Ramos) 1946

Historias prohibidas del Pulgarcito (Dalton) 1974

Histórias sem data (Machado de Assis) 1884

Histórias verdadeiras (Ramos) 1951

History of an Argentine Passion (Mallea) 1983

Hogar sólido (Garro) 1958

Hojarasca (García Márquez) 1955

Hojas al viento (Casal) 1890

Hojas sueltas (Gutiérrez Nájera) 1912

Holandesa en América (Acosta de Samper) 1888

Holy Place (Fuentes) 1972

Holy Saturday (Martínez Estrada) 1988

Holy Smoke (Cabrera Infante) 1985

Holy Wednesday (Gálvez) 1934

Homage to the American Indians (Cardenal) 1973

Hombre de los ojos azules (Gálvez) 1928

Hombre de paja (Buitrago) 1964

Hombre planetario (Carrera Andrade) 1959

Hombre que hablaba de Octavio de Cádiz (Bryce Echenique) 1985

Hombre que lo tenía todo, todo, todo (Asturias) 1981

Hombre que parecía un caballo (Arévalo Martínez) 1915

Hombre sensible (Arlt) 1991

Hombre y sus sueños (Marqués) 1948

Hombres de a caballo (Viñas) 1967

Hombres de maíz (Asturias) 1949

Hombres del hombre (Barrios) 1950

Hombres del sur (M. Rojas) 1926

Hombres en soledad (Gálvez) 1938

Hombres en su siglo (Paz) 1984

Hombres y engranajes (Sábato) 1951

Home is the Sailor (Amado) 1964

Homem (Azevedo) 1887

Homem de branco (Filho) 1987

GENERAL INDEX

Numbers in **bold** indicate subjects with their own entries.

NOTES ON ADVISERS
AND CONTRIBUTORS

Abel, Christopher. Senior Lecturer (Associate Professor) of Latin American History, University College, London. Author of *Política, iglesia y partidos en Colombia* (1987); co-editor (with Nissa Torrents) of *José Martí, Revolutionary Democrat* (1986); *Latin American Imperialism and the State* (1991), and *Poverty, Welfare and Development in Latin America* (1993), *Health, Hygiene and Sanitation in Latin America* (1996). **Essay:** Fernando Ortiz.

Adorno, Rolena. Professor of Romance Languages, Princeton University. Author of *Guaman Poma: Writing and Resistance in Colonial Peru* (1986); co-author (with Kenneth J. Andrien) *Transatlantic Encounters: Europeans and Andeans in the Sixteenth Century* (1991). Member of the following editorial boards: *Colonial Latin American Review*, *Hispanic Issues*, *Indiana Journal of Hispanic Literatures*, *Latin American Literary Review*. **Essays:** El Inca Garcilaso de la Vega; *Comentarios reales de los Incas* (Garcilaso de la Vega).

Agosín, Marjorie. Poet, feminist, literary critic and Associate Professor of Spanish, Wellesley College. Editor of the Secret Weaver series, consisting of creative works by Latin American women, published by the White Pine Press. Recent publications include *Violeta Parra: santa de pura greda*, with Inés Dölz Blackburn (1988), *Violeta Parra o la expresión inefable* (1992), *Las hacedoras: mujer, imagen y escritura* (1993), and editor of *These Are Not Sweet Girls: Latin American Women Poets* (1994) and *A Dream of Light and Shadows: Portraits of Latin American Women Writers* (1995). **Essays:** Violeta Parra; *Las décimas* (Violeta Parra).

Albuquerque, Severino J. Associate Professor of Portuguese, University of Wisconsin. Author of *Violent Acts: a Study of Contemporary Latin American Theater* (1991); *Português para principiantes* (1993) and numerous articles in *Latin American Theater Review*, *Modern Drama*, etc. Member of the editorial board of *Luso-Brazilian Review*, *Latin American Theater Review*; member of Executive Committee of MLA's Division of Luso-Brazilian Language and Literature. **Essay:** Theatre: Brazil

Alvarez, José B. IV, Teaching associate, Arizona State University. Author of articles on Cuban film and literature of the 1980s. **Essay:** Miguel Otero Silva.

Alverio, Carmen S., Assistant Professor at Regis University, Denver, Colorado. Author of articles on Panamanian narrative in *Revista/Review Interamericana*, *Revista Nacional de Cultura* (Panamá) and *Exégesis* (Puerto Rico). Editor of the last of these in 1994. Presently working on a study of contemporary Panamanian literature. **Essay:** Panama.

Arango-Ramos, Fanny D. Teaching associate and doctoral candidate at Arizona State University. Article on Mercedes Cabello de Carbonera in *Revista Hispánica Moderna* (December 1994). **Essay:** Resistance Literature.

Armacanqui-Tipacti, Elia J. Formerly elementary school teacher and high school teacher in Peru. Now Assistant Professor at Lawrence University, Appleton, Wisconsin. Author of articles on Sor Juana Inés de la Cruz and Sor María Manuela de Santa Ana. **Essays:** Colonial Literature: Peru; Mysticism.

Armas, Emilio de. Poet and literary critic. Author of (among other volumes) *Casal* (1981), *La frente bajo el sol* (1988), *Junto al álamo de los sinsontes* (1988), *Blanco sobre blanco* (1993) and *Sólo ardiendo* (1995). Editor of *José Lezama Lima. Poesía* (1992). Editor of Editorial América, Miami. Having left Cuba, he works as a translator for *The Miami Herald*. **Essays:** Emilio Ballagas; Julián del Casal; Cuba; José Lezama Lima; José Martí.

Arrington, Melvin S. Jr. Associate Professor of Modern Languages, University of Mississippi. Journal articles on Boom writers and contributions in several dictionaries of Latin American writers published in the 1990s. Member of the editorial board of *Romance Monographs*. **Essays:** *Doña Bárbara* (Gallegos); Ricardo Jaimes Freyre; Enrique Larreta; Regionalism: Spanish America; José Eustasio Rivera.

Arrington, Teresa R. Assistant Professor of Spanish, University of Mississippi. Article on Fanny Buitrago in *Spanish American Women Writers: a Bio-Bibliographical Source Book* (1990). Has published on Spanish linguistics, foreign language teaching methodology and transformational grammar. Currently Executive Director of the Mississippi Foreign Language Association. **Essay:** Fanny Buitrago.

Bacarisse, Pamela. (1934–1996). Until her untimely death, Professor of Spanish, Latin American and Peninsular Portuguese Literature at Pittsburgh University. Author of several books on Manuel Puig (see main entry on this writer); she also edited the volume *Carnal Knowledge. Essays on the Flesh, Sex and Sexuality in Hispanic Letters and Film* (1993). Secretary-Treasurer of the Instituto Internacional de Literatura Iberoamericana; member of the editorial committee of the *Revista Iberoamericana*. **Essays:** Manuel Puig; *El beso de la mujer araña* (Puig).

Balderston, Daniel. Professor of Spanish, Tulane University. A principal research interest is Argentine literature. Editor of *The Literary Universe of Jorge Luis Borges* (1986), *The Historical Novel in Latin America: a Symposium* (1986), *The Latin American Short Story: an Annotated Guide to Anthologies and Criticism* (1992), *Out of Context: Historical Reference and the Representation of Reality in Borges* (1993). He has also translated works of fiction by Sylvia Molloy, Ricardo Piglia and Silvina Ocampo. Member of editorial board of *Hispania*. **Essays:** Silvina Ocampo; Ricardo Piglia; Juan José Saer.

Barbosa, Heloisa Gonçalves. Senior Lecturer (Associate Professor) at Federal University of Rio de Janeiro. Author of *Procedimentos técnicos da tradução: uma nova proposta* (1990). **Essay:** Translation: Brazil.

Biriotti, Maurice. Lecturer, Department of Hispanic Studies, University of Birmingham. Specialist in critical theory and Chicano studies. Has published on Juan José Arreola and popular culture. Co-editor (with Nicola Miller) *What is an Author?* (1993). **Essays:** Juan José Arreola; José Gorostiza; Alfonso Reyes; Xavier Villaurrutia.

Boland, Roy C. (Adviser). Professor of Spanish at University of La Trobe, Melbourne, Australia. Major publications include *Mario Vargas Llosa: Oedipus and the " Papa" State* (1988). Editor of the journal *Antípodas*, and co-editor (with Alun Kenwood) of the volume *War and Revolution in Hispanic Literature* (1990). He is currently editing a volume of Salvadorean short fiction. **Essays:** Manlio Argueta; El Salvador.

Boldy, Steven. Lecturer (Assistant Professor), Department of Spanish and Portuguese, University of Cambridge. Author of *The Novels of Julio Cortázar* (1980) and of a critical edition of *Agua quemada* by Carlos Fuentes (1995). He is also the author of several articles and review articles on Fuentes, and of articles on Borges, Carpentier, Isaacs and Rulfo. **Essays:** Carlos Fuentes; *Agua quemada* (Fuentes).

Borgeson, Paul W. Jr., Associate Professor of Spanish, University of Illinois. Author of *Hacia el hombre nuevo: poesía y pensamiento de Ernesto Cardenal* (1984); editor of *La lucha permanente: arte y sociedad en "La espiga amotinada"* (1994) and of *Carlos Germán Belli, Los talleres del tiempo* (1992). Has now completed a critical edition of the poetry of Carlos Germán Belli. **Essays:** Carlos Germán Belli; "En Bética no bella" (Germán Belli); Esteban Echeverría; José Hernández; *Martín Fierro* (José Hernández); Horacio Quiroga; José Asunción Silva.

Boyle, Catherine. Lecturer (Assistant Professor) in Latin American Studies, King's College, University of London. Author of *Chilean Theater, 1973–1985* (1992) and of numerous articles on Spanish American theatre. An editor of *Journal of Latin American Cultural Studies.* **Essay:** Theatre: Argentina, Chile and Uruguay.

Brandellero, Sara. MA in Brazilian literature, Universidade de Brasília (1994); article in *Cerrados* (March 1993); chapter on "A fábula" in *O imaginário nas narrativas populares.* **Essays:** *A rosa do povo* (Drummond de Andrade); Vinícius de Moraes.

Brenes-García, Ana María. Research student and teaching assistant at Arizona State University. Author of an article on Lorca and Gabriela Mistral in *Letras Peninsulares* and of one on Montserrat Roig in *Hispania.* **Essays:** Erotic and Homoerotic Writing; Juana de Ibarbourou; Land and Literature; Marianism; Pornography.

Brookshaw, David (Adviser). Senior Lecturer (Associate Professor) and Chairman of the Department of Hispanic, Portuguese and Latin American Studies, University of Bristol. Publications in book form are *Race and Color in Brazilian Literature* (1986) and *Paradise Betrayed: Brazilian Literature of the Indian* (1989). Member of the editorial board of *Journal of Afro-Latin American Studies and Literatures.* **Essays:** African-Brazilian Literature; Foundational Literature; Indianism: Brazil.

Caistor, Nick. Writer and broadcaster on Latin American affairs; senior producer, BBC World Service. Literary translator and editor of several books on Latin American politics and culture including *The Faber Anthology of Contemporary Latin*

American Short Stories (1988), *Nunca más: Report on the Disappeared in Argentina* (1986) and *Argentina: a Guide to the People, Politics and Culture* (1996). Latin American editor of *Index on Censorship.* **Essays:** Edouard Glissant; Álvaro Mutis.

Camurati, Mireya. Professor of Spanish American literature, SUNY at Buffalo. Her studies in book form include *La fábula en Hispanoamérica* (1978), *Poesía y poética de Vicente Huidobro* (1980) and *Bioy Casares y el alegre trabajo de la inteligencia* (1990). She is also the co-editor of *Philosophy and Literature in Latin America: a Critical Assessment of the Current Situation* (1989). **Essay:** Adolfo Bioy Casares.

Canaparo, Claudio. Lecturer (Assistant Professor), Department of Spanish, University of Exeter. Principal research interests are 20th century Argentine literature and literary theory, and the work of Reinaldo Arenas. **Essays:** *El juguete rabioso* and *Aguafuertes porteñas* (Arlt); Eugenio Cambaceres; Juan Gelman; "Asomos" (Gelman); Jorge Ibargüengoitia; *El astillero* (Onetti); Juan L. Ortiz; Osvaldo Soriano; Agustín Yáñez.

Chirol, Marie-Magdeleine. Assistant Professor of French, University of Missouri at Columbia. Author of articles in the *Revue de Littérature Comparée, The French Review* and other journals of language, linguistics and literature. **Essay:** Fernand Hibbert.

Colecchia, Francesca. Professor of Modern Languages and Literatures, Duquesne University, Pennsylvania. Editor of two bibliographies in book form on García Lorca (1979, 1982); co-editor (with Julio Matas) of *Selected Latin American One-Act Plays* (1973) and (with Luis F. González Cruz) *Cuban Theater in the United States* (1992); editor of *"Crossroads" and Other Plays by Carlos Solórzano* (1993). Assistant editor *Estudios* and member of the editorial board of *Duquesne Hispanic Review.* **Essays:** René Marqués; Carlos Solórzano.

Concha, Jaime. Professor of Latin American Studies, University of California at San Diego. Author of numerous monographs on Chilean poets, including those on Pablo Neruda (1972), Vicente Huidobro (1980) and Gabriela Mistral (1986). He is also the author of *La sangre y las letras* (1988). **Essays:** Marxism; Manuel Rojas.

Craig, Linda. Senior Lecturer (Associate Professor), University of East London. Contribution on Valenzuela's *El gato eficaz* in *Feminist Readings on Spanish and Latin American Literature* (1991). **Essay:** Luisa Valenzuela.

Curley, Dermot. Director of language school in London. Author of book on Salvador Elizondo, *En la isla desierta* (1986). **Essays:** Salvador Elizondo; Metafiction (with Verity Smith).

Da Silva, Teresinha V. Zimbrão. Lecturer (Assistant Professor) at Universidade Federal do Espírito Santo, Brazil. Articles on Machado de Assis in *Letras e Letras* and *Colóquio/Letras.* **Essays:** Oswald de Andrade; "Manifesto antropófago" (Andrade); *Dom Casmurro* (Machado de Assis); Modernismo: Brazil; Graciliano Ramos; Érico Veríssimo.

Daniel, Mary L., Professor of Portuguese, University of Wisconsin. Author of *João Guimarães Rosa: travessia literária* (1968) and of articles in a range of important US journals. Co-editor of *Luso-Brazilian Review* and currently associate editor of *Purdue Studies in Romance Literatures*. **Essays:** José Pereira da Graça Aranha; João Guimarães Rosa; José Lins do Rego; Sousândrade.

Davies, Catherine (Adviser). Professor of Spanish, University of Manchester. Publications in book form are *Rosalía de Castro no seu tempo* (1987) and *Contemporary Feminist Fiction in Spain* (1994). She has also edited, introduced and contributed to *Women Writers in Twentieth-Century Spain and Spanish America* (1993) and, with Anny Brooksbank-Jones, *Latin American Women's Writing: Feminist Readings in Theory and Crisis* (1996). Member of the editorial boards of *Forum for Modern Language Studies*, *Journal of Hispanic Research* and *Támesis Books*. **Essays:** Lydia Cabrera; Fina García Marruz; Nancy Morejón.

Davies, Lloyd Hughes. Lecturer (Assistant Professor), Department of Hispanic Studies, University of Wales. Article on Puig's *Boquitas pintadas* in *Iberoromania* (1995). **Essay:** *El Señor Presidente* (Asturias).

Dawes, Greg. Associate Professor, Department of Foreign Languages and Literatures, North Carolina State University. Author of *Aesthetics and Revolution: Nicaraguan Poetry 1979–1990* (1993), and of articles in *Revista de Crítica Literaria Latinoamericana*, *Postmodern Culture* and *Nuevo Texto Crítico*. **Essays:** Pablo Neruda; "Alturas de Macchu Picchu" (Neruda); Nicaragua.

De Costa, Elena. Associate Professor of Spanish and Chairman of the Department of Languages and Literatures, Carroll College, Wisconsin. Author of *Collaborative Latin American Popular Theatre: from Theory to Form, from Text to Stage* (1992). **Essays:** Autobiography; Caudillismo and Dictatorship; Jorge Edwards; Griselda Gambaro; *Sóngoro cosongo* (Guillén); Literacy Campaigns: Brazil; Mayan Literature; Náhuatl Literature; Orality; Popular Culture: Spanish America; Prison Writing; Protest Literature; Theatre: Colombia, Cuba, Mexico and Peru; Workshops.

Dedenbach-Salazar Sáenz, Sabine. Formerly Acting Director, Institute of Amerindian Studies, University of St Andrews, Scotland. Author of a considerable range of publications on the language and literature of the Quechua and Aymara peoples, and on religious discourse in colonial Peru. She is also a translator into German of the chronicles of Fray Bernardino de Sahagún (1989). **Essay:** Aymara Literature.

Denegri, Francesca. Lecturer (Assistant Professor), University College, London. Author of *El abanico y la cigarrera* (1996), a study of women's narrative in 19th-century Argentina, Bolivia and Peru. Forthcoming is an anthology of the work of Juana Manuela Gorriti. **Essays:** Manuel González Prada; Juana Manuela Gorriti; Clorinda Matto de Turner; Women's Writing: 19th Century

Dinneen, Mark. Lecturer (Assistant Professor) in Latin American Literature, University of Southampton. Author of articles on popular culture of the Brazilian northeast, and of *Listening to the People's Voice* (1996), on the work of Ariano Suassuna. **Essays:** José Américo de Almeida; Jorge Amado; Manuel Bandeira; Augusto Boal; Gilberto Freyre; *Casa grande e senzala* (Freyre).

Earle, Peter G. Emeritus Professor, University of Pennsylvania. Authority on the literary essay in Spanish America. Important publications are *Prophet in the Wilderness. The Works of Ezequiel Martínez Estrada* (1971), and, with Robert G. Mead Jr., *Historia del ensayo hispanoamericano* (1973). An editor of *Hispanic Review* and advisory editor of *Revista Hispánica Moderna*. Translator of Aguilera Malta's novel *El secuestro del general*. **Essays:** The Essay; Ezequiel Martínez Estrada; Gonzalo Rojas; José Vasconcelos.

Edkins, Anthony. A poet who also specializes in the translation of poetry. Books of poetry are *Worry Beads* (1976) and *Rock Pool* (1992). Co-editor and translator of *The Poetry of Luis Cernuda* (1971) and translator of Javier Tomeo's *The Coded Letter/Dear Monster* (1991). Teacher in Spanish Department, University College, London; reader for Penguin Books and other publishers. **Essay:** Sergio Pitol.

Evans, Jo. Lecturer (Assistant Professor), Department of Spanish, University College, London. Author of articles in *Journal of Hispanic Research*, *Bulletin of Hispanic Studies* and of *Moving Reflections: Gender, Faith and Aesthetics in the Work of Ángela Figuera Aymerich* (1996). **Essay:** Alfonsina Storni.

Febles, Jorge. Professor of Spanish, Western Michigan University. Author of *Cuentos olvidados de Alfonso Hernández Catá* (1982), and of articles in *Hispania*, *The Americas Review*, *Latin American Theatre Review* and *Revista Chilena de Literatura*. **Essays:** Eliseo Diego; *Nuestra América* (Martí); *Versos sencillos* (Martí).

Fernández, Salvador C. Assistant Professor, Occidental College, Los Angeles. Author of articles in *Hispania*, *Hispanic Journal*, *World Literature Today* and other journals. **Essay:** Gustavo Sainz.

Finnegan, Nuala. Lecturer (Assistant Professor), Department of Modern Languages, University of Strathclyde, Glasgow. PhD candidate with dissertation on Rosario Castellanos. **Essay:** Claribel Alegría.

Fishburn, Evelyn. Professor of Latin American Studies, University of North London. Author of *The Portrayal of Immigration in Nineteenth Century Argentine Fiction 1845–1902* (1981) and co-author (with Psiche Hughes) of *A Dictionary of Borges* (1990). An edition of *Latin American Short Stories by Women* is forthcoming. **Essays:** Caliban; Civilization and Barbarism.

Foster, David William (Adviser). Regent's Professor of Spanish, Arizona State University. A prolific scholar who over the years has published several important volumes on Argentine culture, and who also pioneered the production of reliable works of reference on Latin American literature. He has also undertaken a considerable amount of editorial work. A former editor of the Twayne Latin American series, he presently edits a series of reference works on Latin American literature for Garland. Other fields of interest are Mexican narrative and drama, and writing by gays in Latin America. Among his most recent publications are, as editor, *Handbook of Latin American Literature*, 2nd edition (1992), *Mexican Literature: a History* (1994) and, as author, *Gay and Lesbian Themes in Latin American Writing* (1991).

Ganderton, Denise. Senior Lecturer (Associate Professor), University of North London. Author of entries on French women writers in *Bloomsbury Guide to Women's Literature* (1992). **Essays:** Aimé Césaire; *Une Tempête* (Césaire).

García Chichester, Ana. Assistant Professor, Mary Washington College, Virginia. Author of articles on Virgilio Piñera, Cabrera Infante, Miguel Barnet and Mempo Giardinelli. Entry on Virgilio Piñera in *Latin American Gay Literature: a Biographical and Critical Sourcebook* (1994), edited by David William Foster. **Essays:** Miguel Barnet; Teresa de la Parra; *Las memorias de Mamá Blanca* (Teresa de la Parra); Positivism.

García Pinto, Magdalena. Director of Women's Studies, University of Missouri at Columbia. Author of *Historias íntimas: conversaciones con diez escritoras latinoamericanas* (1988; English version, 1991). Editor of Cátedra edition of the complete poems of Delmira Agustini (1993). Contributing editor for Handbook of Latin American Studies (1983 to present), and contributing editor for the *Encyclopedia of Latin American History and Culture* (1996). **Essays:** Avant-Garde; Antonio Cisneros; Rubén Darío; Feminism; Julio Herrera y Reissig; César Moro; Nélida Piñón; Women's Writing: 20th Century.

Gerdes, Dick. Professor of Spanish, University of New Mexico, Fulbright fellow. Specialist on literature of the Andean region; author of Twayne volume on Vargas Llosa (1985). Translator of Bryce Echenique's *Un mundo para Julius* (*A World for Julius*, 1992) and of Diamela Eltit's *El cuarto mundo* (*The Fourth World*, 1995). Associate editor of *Hispania*. **Essay:** Translation: Spanish America.

Gil, Lourdes. Cuban poet, literary critic and editor; resident in the United States. Her most recent volumes of poetry include *Blanca aldaba preludia* (1989) and *Empieza la ciudad* (1993). Guest editor of the Latin American Writers Institute (New York, 1994); co-editor of Lyra Society for the Arts, New Jersey (1987–1990). **Essays:** Cuban Writing in the United States; Severo Sarduy.

Glickman, Nora. Associate Professor, Department of Modern Languages, Queen's College, CUNY. She has a particular interest in drama and is the author of works of fiction, of which the most recent is *Mujeres-Memorias-Malogros* (1991). Also co-editor (with Robert DiAntonio) of *Tradition and Innovation: Reflections of Latin American Jewish Issues*

Writing (1993) and, with Gloria F. Waldman, of *Argentine Jewish Theatre: a Critical Anthology* (1996). **Essay:** Jewish Writing: South America.

Goic, Cedomil. Formerly Professor of Latin American Studies at Ann Arbor, University of Michigan (returned to Chile at the end of 1994). Author of *La poesía de Vicente Huidobro* (1956; reprinted 1974), and of numerous volumes on Chilean literature, from Ercilla to the present. His more recent studies are the 3-volume *Historia y crítica de la literatura hispanoamericana* (1988–91) and *Los mitos degradados: ensayos de comprensión de la literatura* (1992). **Essay:** Chile.

Gold, Janet N. Associate Professor, Department of Spanish, University of New Hampshire. Specialist in the literature of Central America and author of *Clementina Suárez: Her Life and Poetry* (1995). **Essays:** Costa Rica; Honduras; Salarrué.

Gomes, Miguel. Assistant Professor, the University of Connecticut at Storrs. Author of *El pozo de las palabras. Ensayos críticos* (1990) and of *Poéticas del ensayo venezolano del siglo XX* (1996). He also edited the volume *Estética del modernismo hispanoamericano* (1996), and an anthology of the poetry of Oswald de Andrade (1988). Author of articles published in a range of specialist journals. **Essay:** Venezuela.

Gómez Ocampo, Gilberto. Assistant Professor of Spanish, Wabash College, Indiana. Author of *Entre "María" y "La vorágine": la literatura colombiana finisecular* (1988). Assistant editor, *Revista de Estudios Colombianos*. Present research interests include 19th-century Latin American writers and intellectuals who resided in London. **Essays:** Soledad Acosta de Samper; Tomás Carrasquilla; Rafael Núñez.

Gonzalez, Mike. Senior Lecturer (Associate Professor) of Latin American Studies, University of Glasgow. Co-author, with David Treece, of *The Gathering of Voices: the Twentieth-Century Poetry of Latin America* (1992). **Essays:** America, the Invention of; Guerrilla Poetry; José Carlos Mariátegui.

Good, Carl. Doctoral candidate, University of California at Irvine. Author of articles on Sor Juana de la Cruz, and *El eterno femenino* by Rosario Castellanos. **Essay:** Nellie Campobello.

Grant, Catherine. Lecturer (Assistant Professor), University of Strathclyde, Glasgow. Articles on Rosario Castellanos, Alejandra Pizarnik, Argentine cinema of the 1980s, and on "Queer Theorrhea and What It All Might Mean for Feminists." **Essays:** Rosario Castellanos; Olga Orozco.

Guyer, Leland. Associate Professor of Spanish and Portuguese, Macalester College, Saint Paul, Minnesota. Author of book on the Portuguese writer, Fernando Pessoa (1982); translator of Ferreira Gullar's *Dirty Poem/Poema sujo* (1990), and of short fiction by Clarice Lispector and Lygia Fagundes Telles. **Essay:** Ferreira Gullar.

Haberly, David T. Professor of Portuguese, University of Virginia. Author of *Three Sad Races: Racial Identity and*

National Consciousness in Brazilian Literature (1983) and contributor to the Brazilian volume of the *Cambridge History of Latin American Literature* (1996). **Essays:** José de Alencar; Aluísio Azevedo; Olavo Bilac; Antônio de Castro Alves; Antônio Gonçalves Dias; Bernardo Guimarães; Sílvio Romero.

Handelsman, Michael. Professor of Spanish and Latin American Studies, University of Tennessee, Knoxville. His publications in book form are *El modernismo en las revistas literarias del Ecuador: 1895–1930* (1981), *Incursiones en el mundo literario del Ecuador* (1988) and three volumes on Benjamín Carrión (1986, 1989, 1992). President of the South Eastern Council of Latin American Studies (1991) and co-founder and Secretary of the Asociación de Ecuatorianistas de Norteamérica. **Essay:** Alicia Yánez Cossío.

Harrison, Regina. Professor of Latin American Literature and Quechua, University of Maryland at College Park. Author of *Signs, Songs and Memory in the Andes: Translating Quechua Language and Culture* (1989) and *"True" Confessions: Quechua and Spanish Cultural Encounters in the Viceroyalty of Peru* (1992). President of the New England Council of Latin American Studies. Awarded Singer Kovacs Book Prize of the Modern Language Association. **Essays:** Ecuador; Indianism: Spanish America; Quechua Literature.

Hart, Stephen M. (Adviser). Professor of Latin American Studies, University of Kentucky. Author of several volumes on Spanish and Spanish American literature, including *Religión, política y ciencia en la obra de César Vallejo* (1987) and *White Ink. Essays on Twentieth Century Feminine Fiction in Spain and Latin America* (1993). Associate editor *Romance Quarterly*; Associate Dean, Faculty of Arts. **Essays:** José Joaquín Fernández de Lizardi; César Vallejo; "Trilce XIX" (Vallejo).

Harvey, Sally (1946–1995). Appointed to the Prince of Asturias Chair in Spanish at University of Auckland, 1994. Co-editor of *Antípodas* and author of *Carpentier's Proustian Fiction* (1994). **Essay:** Alejo Carpentier.

Higgins, James. Professor of Spanish and Chairman of the Department of Hispanic Studies, University of Liverpool. Leading authority on Peruvian literature, particularly on 20th-century poetry. Author of a study on César Vallejo and translator of his poetry. Author of several other volumes, including *A History of Peruvian Literature* (1987) and *Hitos de la poesía peruana* (1993). **Essays:** Peru; Sebastián Salazar Bondy.

Hoeg, Jerry. Assistant Professor of Spanish, Pennsylvania State University at Fayette. Author of article on Triana's *La noche de los asesinos* (*Gestos*, 1993). **Essays:** Science; José Triana.

Hoffmann, Léon-François. Professor of French, University of Princeton, New Jersey. Author of several volumes on the literature of Haiti. Among the most recent are *Haïti: couleurs, croyances, créole* (1989); *Haïti: lettres et l'être* (1992) and *Littérature d'Haïti* (1995). He is also the author of an extensive bibliography on the literature of Haiti. **Essays:** Jacques-Stéphen Alexis; Oswald Durand; Justin Lhérisson; Félix Morisseau-Leroy.

Hood, Edward Waters. Assistant Professor of Modern Languages, University of Northern Arizona. Author of *La ficción de Gabriel García Márquez: repetición e intertextualidad* (1993). He also has an interest in contemporary Nicaraguan literature by women. **Essay:** Gioconda Belli.

Horan, Elizabeth. Associate Professor and Director of Comparative Studies in Literature, Arizona State University. Author of *Gabriel Mistral. An Artist and Her People* (1994). She has also translated and written the introduction to *Happiness* by Marjorie Agosín (1993), and contributed to the volume *Into Print: American Women and Print Culture*. **Essay:** Gabriela Mistral.

Hughes, Psiche. Teacher of Latin American Literature, City Literary Institute, London; part-time lecturer, Birkbeck College, University of London. Co-author, with Evelyn Fishburn, of *A Dictionary of Borges* (1990). Has also published articles in scholarly journals on the work of Borges, and is the translator of Cristina Peri Rossi's *The Ship of Fools* (1989). **Essays:** *El amor en los tiempos del cólera* (García Márquez); Cristina Peri Rossi.

Johnson, Julie Greer. Professor of Spanish, University of Georgia, Athens. Her publications in book form are *Women in Colonial Spanish American Literature: Literary Images* (1983), *The Book in the Americas: the Role of Books and Printing in the Development of Culture and Society in Colonial Latin America* (1988) and *Satire in Colonial Spanish America: Turning the New World Upside Down* (1993). **Essay:** Colonial Literature: New Spain.

Johnson, Peter T. (Adviser). Bibliographer for Latin America, Spain and Portugal, and Lecturer, Program in Latin American Studies, Princeton University.

Jones, Anny Brooksbank. Senior Lecturer (Associate Professor), Department of Modern Languages, Nottingham Trent University. Co-editor (with Catherine Davies) of, and contributor to *Latin American Women's Writing: Feminist Readings on Theory and Crisis* (1996). Her book, *The Women of Spain*, will appear in December 1996. She has also published many articles in scholarly journals on feminist issues in the Hispanic world. **Essay:** Feminist Literary Theory.

Jordan, Paul. Lecturer (Assistant Professor), University of Sheffield. PhD (Cambridge) with thesis on the work of Roberto Arlt. Article on Juan Goytisolo's *Juan sin tierra* in *Modern Languages Review* (1989). **Essays:** Roberto Arlt; *Rayuela* (Cortázar).

Jozef, Bella. Emeritus Professor of Spanish American Literature, Federal University, Rio de Janeiro. Fulbright Scholar and Visiting Professor at the Hebrew University of Jerusalem, the Centre for Studies on Rómulo Gallegos and the Universidad Complutense in Madrid. Her major studies include *O jogo mágico* (1980), *A máscara e o enigma* (1986) and *Historia de la literatura hispanoamericana* (Portuguese version, 1989; Spanish translation, 1991). She has been awarded several prizes and honours, both in Brazil and other countries, for her contributions to scholarship. **Essays:** Andrés Bello; Leopoldo Marechal; Rachel de Queiroz; João Ubaldo Ribeiro; Romanticism.

Katra, William H. Professor of Spanish, University of Wisconsin at Eau Claire. Publications in book form include two studies on Sarmiento (1985, 1993) and *The Argentine Generation of 1837: Echeverría, Sarmiento, Alberdi, Mitre. An Ideological Interpretation* (1996). He is also the author of *Contorno: Literary Engagement in Post-Peronist Argentina* (1986). **Essays:** Argentina: 19th Century; José Mármol; Nationalism.

Keeth, William P. Doctoral candidate and teaching assistant, Arizona State University. **Essays:** José Juan Tablada; Emilio Adolfo Westphalen.

Keightley, Ron. Formerly Professor of Spanish, Monash University, Australia (1972–1992). Author of several articles on medieval and Renaissance narrative in Spanish and Catalan, and of articles on the transmission of Boethius and Eusebius. **Essays:** Miguel Ángel Asturias; Ricardo Palma; Ernesto Sábato; *Abaddón, el exterminador* (Sábato); *El túnel* (Sábato); Rodolfo Usigli.

Kerr, Lucille. Professor of Spanish and Comparative Literature, University of Southern California, Los Angeles. Author of *Suspended Fictions: Reading Novels by Manuel Puig* (1987) and *Reclaiming the Author: Figures and Fictions from Spanish America* (1992). Articles in a wide range of important journals, including *Diacritics, Texto Crítico* and *Revista de Crítica Literaria Latinoamericana*. Presently review editor of *Latin American Literary Review* and associate editor of *Purdue Studies in Romance Literatures*. **Essays:** José Donoso; *Casa de campo* (Donoso).

King, John. Director, School of Comparative American Studies, University of Warwick. His major publications in book form are a study of the Argentine literary journal *Sur* (1985) and *Magical Reels: a History of Cinema in Latin America* (1990). He has also edited and contributed to several important volumes on Latin American Literature and film, and is an editor of the Verso series, Critical Studies in Latin American Culture. **Essays:** Journals: *Plural, Punto de Vista, Sur*; Victoria Ocampo.

Kinsella, John Myles. Associate Professor of Spanish and Portuguese, University of Southern Maine. Author of *Lo trágico y su consuelo: un estudio de la obra de Martín Adán* (1989) and of *Diálogo de conflito: a poesia de Carlos Drummond de Andrade* (1995). **Essays:** Martín Adán; Carlos Drummond de Andrade.

Lewis, Tracy K. Associate Professor of Spanish and Latin American Studies, SUNY at Oswego. Areas of specialization include Paraguayan biculturality and translations from Guaraní. He has published two Castilian translations of Guaraní writers in the Paraguayan cultural magazine, *Ñe ëngatu* (1993, 1994). **Essays:** Rafael Barrett; *Lo que son los yerbales* (Barrett); Paraguay (with Teresa Méndez-Faith);

Augusto Roa Bastos (with Teresa Méndez-Faith); *Yo el Supremo* (Roa Bastos; with Teresa Méndez-Faith).

Lindstrom, Naomi. Professor of Spanish and Portuguese, University of Texas at Austin. Areas of specialization include 20th-century Argentine literature and women's writing. Recent publications in book form are *Jorge Luis Borges: a Study of the Short Fiction* (1990), *Women's Voice in Latin American Literature* (1989), and *Twentieth-Century Spanish American Fiction* (1994). Currently Director of Publications, Institute of Latin American Studies, University of Texas, Austin. **Essay:** Cultural Dependency.

Lisboa, Maria Manuel. Lecturer (Assistant Professor), St John's College, Cambridge. Author of articles on Machado de Assis and Lygia Fagundes Telles, and of *Machado de Assis and Feminism: Re-Reading the Heart of the Companion* (1996) **Essays:** *A escrava Isaura* (Bernardo Guimarães); *A hora da estrela* (Lispector); Joaquim Maria Machado de Assis; Lygia Fagundes Telles.

Lobo, Luiza. Associate Professor of Comparative Literature, Federal University, Rio de Janeiro. Her most important publications in book form are *Épica e modernidade em Sousândrade* (1986) and *Teorias poéticas do Romantismo* (1987). She has also contributed chapters on Brazilian women's fiction to collections of essays, and is the translator into Portuguese of a critical edition of *50 poemas de Robert Burns* (1995). **Essay:** Brazil: 20th Century.

Lockhart, Darrell B. Assistant Professor, Department of Foreign Languages, North Carolina A&T State University. Editor of *Latin American Jewish Writers: a Critical Dictionary* (1996). **Essays:** Augusto D'Halmar; Ricardo Güiraldes; *Don Segundo Sombra* (Güiraldes); Leopoldo Lugones.

Lockhart, Melissa A. Assistant Professor, University of Arizona, Tucson. Articles on Brazilian playwright Nelson Rodrigues. **Essays:** Cecília Meireles; Alejandra Pizarnik; Popular Culture: Brazil.

Luis, María Begoña de. Professor of Astrophysics, Department of Physics, Universidad Nacional de Educación a Distancia, Madrid. She is the co-author of a 2-volume study on general physics (1990), and of an introduction to astrophysics (1993). An area of specialization is astronomy in the context of literature. **Essay:** *Cántico cósmico* (Cardenal).

McMurray, George R. Professor Emeritus, Colorado State University. Major publications include monographs on Gabriel García Márquez (1978) and Jorge Luis Borges (1980). More recently, he has published *Spanish American Writing since 1941: a Critical Survey* (1987). **Essays:** Mariano Azuela; *Los de abajo* (Azuela); Martín Luis Guzmán; *Ardiente paciencia* (Skármeta).

McQuade, Frank. Formerly Lecturer (Assistant Professor), University of Leeds; articles on Virgilio Piñera and Sarmiento. **Essays:** Journals: *Marcha, Mundo Nuevo, Orígenes,* and *Vuelta*; Virgilio Piñera; Domingo Faustino Sarmiento; Transculturation.

Maíz-Peña, Magdalena. Assistant Professor, Spanish Department, Davidson College, North Carolina. Author of essay in *Spanish American Women Writers: A Bio-Bibliographical Source Book*, edited by Diane E. Marting (1990), and of articles in *Revista Hispánica Moderna, Texto Crítico* and other scholarly journals. **Essays:** Diamela Eltit; Margo Glantz.

Marbán, Jorge. Professor of Spanish, College of Charleston, South Carolina. Author of comparative study on Camus and Cela (1973), and of *La Florida: cinco siglos de historia hispánica* (1979). He has also published in article form on Arturo Uslar Pietri. **Essay:** Arturo Uslar Pietri.

March, Kathleen N. Associate Professor of Spanish, University of Maine. Specialist in literary translation from Galician Portuguese and Castilian. Translator of works by Rosalía de Castro and Gioconda Belli and author of *De musa a literata: el feminismo en la narrativa de Rosalía de Castro* (1994). Translator and editor of *An anthology of Galician Short Stories: Asi vai o conto* (1991). **Essays:** Ventura García Calderón; Jorge Icaza; Enrique López Albújar; Manuel Scorza.

Márquez, Ismael P. Assistant Professor, Department of Modern Languages, University of Oklahoma. Author of *La retórica de la violencia en tres novelas peruanas* (1994) and co-editor (with César Ferreira) of *Los mundos de Alfredo Bryce Echenique: textos críticos* (1994). Advisory editor, editorial board of *The Comparatist.* **Essays:** José María Arguedas; *Los ríos profundos* (Arguedas); *Historia de Mayta* (Vargas Llosa).

Martin, Gerald (Adviser). Andrew Mellon Professor of Modern Languages and Chairman of Department of Hispanic Studies, University of Pittsburgh. Most recent major publication is *Journeys through the Labyrinth: Latin American Fiction in the Twentieth Century* (1989); has also contributed several chapters to *Cambridge History of Latin America.* Official biographer of Gabriel García Márquez. Editor, Pittsburgh University Press series of translations of Latin American literature. Member of the editorial board of *Revista iberoamericana.* **Essays:** Rafael Arévalo Martínez; Guatemala.

Martín, Mario. Assistant Professor of Spanish, Department of Literature and Languages, East Texas State University. Author of "Nineteenth Century Prose Fiction," in *Mexican Literature: a History* (1994), edited by David William Foster. **Essay:** Mexico: 19th Century.

Martínez, Pablo A. Assistant Professor of Spanish and Latin American Literature, Trinity University, Texas. He has edited and introduced *El poder del gran señor* by Iván Egüez (1992), and published articles on Spanish and Spanish American writers in specialist journals in both Ecuador and the US. **Essays:** Jorge Enrique Adoum; *Entre Marx y una mujer desnuda* (Adoum); José de la Cuadra.

Martul Tobío, Luis. Associate Professor, Department of Romance Languages, University of Santiago de Compostela, Galicia. Author of critical edition of *Sab* by Gertrudis Gómez de Avellaneda (1993), and of articles on Spanish American writers in *Cuadernos Hispanoamericanos* and *Anales de Literatura Hispanoamericana.* **Essays:** The Historical Novel; Juan León Mera.

Masoliver, Juan Antonio. Reader (Associate Professor) and head of Spanish section in Faculty of Law, Languages and Communication, at University of Westminster, London. Author of books of poetry including *En el bosque de Celia* (1995) and of fiction: *Beatriz Miami* (1991). He is also the editor of *The Origins of Desire* (1993), a collection of modern Spanish short stories. **Essay:** Augusto Monterroso.

Méndez-Faith, Teresa. Professor of Spanish and Latin American Literature, St. Anselm's College, New Hampshire. Publications in book form are *Paraguay: novela y exilio* (1985), *Con-textos literarios hispanoamericanos* (1986). She is also the editor of *Breve antología de la literatura paraguaya* (1994) and *Breve diccionario de la literatura paraguaya* (1994). **Essays:** Paraguay, with Tracy K. Lewis; Augusto Roa Bastos (with Tracy K. Lewis); *Yo el Supremo* (Roa Bastos), with Tracy K. Lewis).

Molina Gavilán, Yolanda. Teaching associate, Arizona State University. Author of scholarly articles, and translator of Rosa Montero's *La función delta* (*The Delta Function,* 1992). **Essay:** Science Fiction.

Murphy, Marie. Associate Professor of Spanish, Loyola College, Baltimore. Author of *Authorizing Fictions: José Donoso's "Casa de campo"* (1992), and of articles on Donoso and Rosario Ferré. **Essay:** Rosario Ferré.

Murray, Patricia. Senior Lecturer (Associate Professor), University of North London. Articles in *Knives and Angels: Women Writers in Latin America,* edited by Susan Bassnett (1990) and in the special issue on Wilson Harris of the *Review of Contemporary Fiction.* **Essays:** *Cien años de soledad* (García Márquez); Myth.

Neate, Wilson. Assistant Professor, Department of Foreign Languages, Central Michigan University. Author of articles on Chicano writing in *Gender, Self and Society* (1992) and *Melus* (1994). His study "Contemporary Cbicano/a Writing, Ethnicity and the Question of Community" will appear in 1997. **Essays:** Chicano Literature; Puerto Rican Writing in the United States; Theatre: Contemporary Chicano Theatre.

Negrín, María L. Teacher at University of Miami. Formerly an editor for Letras Cubanas. **Essays:** Reinaldo Arenas; Miguel de Carrión; Carlos Loveira.

Noble, Pat. Formerly subject librarian, and currently consultant, the Latin American Collection, University of London Library. Past president of SALAM and editor of the papers of their 38th annual meeting (published in 1995). Co-author (with Ann Wade) of *The Future of Latin American Research Collections in the United Kingdom* (1993), and (with Rory Miller) of *Information Technology for Latin Americanists* (1994). **Essay:** Libraries.

Oakley, R.J. Senior Lecturer (Associate Professor) in Hispanic Studies, University of Birmingham. Publications in the field of Brazilian literature include articles in *Bulletin of Hispanic Studies* (63, 1986) and *Modern Languages Review* (78, 1983). Essay: Afonso Henriques de Lima Barreto.

Odber de Baubeta, Patricia Anne. Senior Lecturer (Associate Professor) in Department of Hispanic Studies, University of Birmingham. Commissioning editor of Portuguese Plays in Translation, Edwin Mellen Press; translator of António Ferreira's *O cioso* (*The Jealous Man*); author of articles in several journals, including *Vida Hispánica* and *Portuguese Studies*. Essays: Carlos Martínez Moreno; Short Stories (Quiroga).

Ormerod, Beverley. Associate Professor, Department of French Studies, University of Western Australia. Author of *An Introduction to the French Caribbean Novel* (1985) and co-author (with Jean-Marie Volet) of *Romancières africaines d'expression française* (1994). Essay: Francophone West Indies.

Oviedo, José Miguel. Trustee Professor, University of Pennsylvania. Among his best-known studies are monographs on Ricardo Palma (1964) and Mario Vargas Llosa (1970, 1977, 1982); the collection of essays *Narradores peruanos* (1968) and many other volumes, including two on José Martí (1986, 1989). Recipient of both a Rockefeller and a Guggenheim scholarship; Visiting Professor at the University of Essex, England. Member of the editorial board of *Vuelta* (Mexico) and *Hispanic Review*. Essay: Mario Vargas Llosa.

Pagano, Adriana Silvina. Lecturer (Assistant Professor) of Translation Theory, Federal University of Minas Gerais (Brazil). Author of several articles on literary translation and translation theory, including "Blowing up Translation Theory," "Literary Translation in Argentina" and "On Film Subtitles." Essay: Literary Theory.

Pastén B., J. Agustín. Assistant Professor of Latin American Literature, University of Nebraska. Author of articles in *The Semiotic Review of Books* and *Semiotics*. Essays: Manuel Gutiérrez Nájera; Ramón López Velarde.

Pastor, Brigida. Lecturer (Assistant Professor), Department of Spanish, University of Edinburgh. Author of articles on Gertrudis Gómez de Avellaneda in *Romance Quarterly*, *Journal of the Association for Contemporary Iberian Studies* and other publications. Essay: Gertrudis Gómez de Avellaneda.

Peña, Luis H. Associate Professor and Chair of Spanish Department, Davidson College, North Carolina. Author of *La metamorfosis del deseo: una aproximación a la narrativa mexicana contemporánea* (1990), and of many articles on Mexican literature in volumes of essays and scholarly journals such as *Texto Crítico*, *Revista de Crítica Literaria Latinoamericana* and *Conjunto*. Essays: Ignacio Manuel Altamirano; Juan García Ponce.

Perivolaris, John. PhD from Cambridge University (1995) with thesis on the work of Luis Rafael Sánchez. Presently Research Fellow at University of Wales, Cardiff. Articles on Carlos Fuentes and Luis Rafael Sánchez in *Journal of Hispanic Research*. Essays: Luis Rafael Sánchez; *La guaracha del Macho Camacho* (Sánchez).

Perrone, Charles A. Associate Professor of Portuguese and Luso-Brazilian Literature and Culture, University of Florida. Author of *Masters of Contemporary Brazilian Song* (1989), *Letras e letras* (1988) and *Seven Faces: Brazilian Poetry since Modernism* (1996). Co-editor (with Richard A. Preto-Rodas and Alfred Hower) of *Cronicas brasileiras: nova fase* (1994); editor and translator of *Taxi or Poem of Love in Transit*, by Adriano Espínola (1992). Essay: Concrete Poetry.

Piñón, Nélida (Adviser). See her own entry.

Podalsky, Laura. Assistant Professor, Department of Foreign Languages, Bowling Green State University, Ohio. Articles in *Velvet Light Trap*, *Studies in Latin American Popular Culture*, and an essay in *Mediating Two Worlds: the Americas and Europe*, edited by John King, Ana Lopez and Manual Alvarado (1993). Essays: Film: Brazil; Film: Spanish America.

Rebaza-Soraluz, Luis. Lecturer (Assistant Professor), King's College, London. Poet and literary critic. In the first category, his publications include *Del reino y la frontera* (1985, 1991), *Soñó que en una plaza* (1989) and *Dos solitudes* (1990). He has also published interviews with several writers, and is the author of articles on Manuel González Prada and Vargas Llosa, among others. Essays: José María Eguren; Enrique Lihn; José Emilio Pacheco; Blanca Varela.

Reis, Roberto (1949–1994). Until his premature death, Professor of Brazilian Literature and Culture, University of Minnesota. Author of literary criticism, poetry and narrative. Published collection of short stories, *A dor da bruxa*, in 1973 and the novel, *A hora da teia*, in 1982. Editor of *A permanencia do círculo* (1987) and author of *The Pearl Necklace* (1992), a collection of essays on Brazilian literature which was awarded the Alfred Hower Prize. Past vice-president of the Brazilian Studies Association (BRASA). Former editor of *Ideologies and Literature*, and of the Brazilian section of *Revista Iberoamericana*. Essays: Autran Dourado; Adonias Filho; *Grande sertão: veredas* (Guimarães Rosa); João Cabral de Melo Neto; Regionalism: Brazil

Richards, Keith J. Lecturer (Assistant Professor), University of Leeds. Specialist in Bolivian culture. Doctoral thesis on Néstor Taboada Terán (1994); article on this author in *Journal of Hispanic Research*. Essays: Bolivia; Felipe Guaman Poma de Ayala; Néstor Taboado Terán.

Roberts, Nicole. Teaching assistant and PhD candidate, University of Birmingham. Essays: Mulatto; Négritude.

Robinson, Christine A.F. Visiting Lecturer (Assistant Professor), Department of French, King's College, London (1993–1995); member of the Institute of Linguists. Essay: Jean Price-Mars.

Robledo, Angela I. Professor in Department of Literature, National University of Colombia. Co-author (with María Mercedes Jaramillo and Flor María Rodríguez-Arenas) of *¿Y las mujeres?: ensayos sobre literatura colombiana* (1991). She is also the co-editor (with María Mercedes Jaramillo) of *Escritura y diferencia. Autoras colombianas del siglo XX* (1994) and has published a critical edition of *Jerónima Nava Y Saavedra (1669–1727): autobiografía de una monja venerable* (1994). **Essay:** Colonial Literature: New Granada.

Rodríguez, Linda M. Assistant Professor, Department of English, University of Puerto Rico. Author of articles on *Sab* by Gertrudis Gómez de Avellaneda, Aída Cartagena Portalatín's *Escalera para Electra* and one on the subject of "La novela histórica y la mujer caribeña." **Essays:** Dominican Republic; Ana Lydia Vega.

Rowe, William (Adviser). Professor of Latin American Cultural Studies and director of the Centre of Latin American Cultural Studies, King's College, University of London; an editor of the *Journal of Latin American Cultural Studies*. Publications include *Mito e ideología en la obra de José María Arguedas* (1979), *Juan Rulfo: El llano en llamas* (1987) and, with Vivian Schelling, *Memory and Modernity: Popular Culture in Latin America* (1991). His most recent publication is *Hacia una poética radical: ensayos de hermenéutica cultural* (1996). **Essays:** Gabriel García Márquez; Magical Realism.

Rubio, Patricia. Associate Professor of Spanish American Literature, Skidmore College, Saratoga Spring, New York. Compiler, with Richard Young, of the annotated bibliography *Carpentier ante la crítica* (1985); compiler of *Gabriela Mistral ante la crítica: bibliografía anotada* (1995). Author of *La fragmentación en la narrativa de Luisa Valenzuela* (1986) and of *Carmen Naranjo: escritura y política* (1994). **Essay:** Elena Garro.

Ruffinelli, Jorge. Professor in Department of Spanish and Portuguese, Stanford University, California. Editor of *Texto Crítico* (Veracruz) and *Nuevo Texto Crítico* (Stanford). Author of a considerable number of volumes on Latin American literature and cultural journals. He has published monographs on the work of Arlt, Onetti and Revueltas. Among his more recent publications in book form are *El lugar de Rulfo y otros ensayos* (1980) and *Crítica en marcha* (2nd edition, 1982). **Essays:** Enrique Amorim; Mario Benedetti; Mempo Giardinelli; Juan Carlos Onetti; Juan Rulfo.

Sabat de Rivers, Georgina. Professor of Latin American Literature, SUNY at Stony Brook. Author of *Estudios de literatura hispanoamericana: Sor Juana Inés de la Cruz y otros poetas barrocos de la Colonia* (1992) and of two studies on Sor Juana (1976, on the "Sueño," and 1982). Co-editor (with Elias L. Rivers) of *Sor Juana Inés de la Cruz. Obras selectas* (1976). She also edited a special number on Sor Juana of the *University of Dayton Review* (1983). **Essays:** Juana Inés de la Cruz; *Divino Narciso* (Juana Inés de la Cruz); *Primero sueño* (Juana Inés de la Cruz).

Salvador, Nélida. Professor of literary theory, University of Buenos Aires. Her more recent publications include *Macedonio*

Fernández: precursor de la antinovela (1986); the introductory essay to *Lírica argentina posterior a 1950* (1988); *Novela argentina del siglo XX* (1994); and *Sur: índice general (1967–1992)*, 1993. **Essays:** Argentina: 20th Century; Macedonio Fernández.

San Román, Gustavo. Lecturer (Assistant Professor), Department of Spanish, University of St. Andrews (Scotland). Articles on Horacio Quiroga, Juan Carlos Onetti and Cristina Peri Rossi. He has also published an interview with the last of these writers. **Essays:** Felisberto Hernández; José Enrique Rodó; *Ariel* (Rodó); Juan Zorilla de San Martín.

Schade, George D. Professor of Spanish, the University of Texas at Austin. Translator of works by Juan Rulfo and J.J. Arreola; author of *Costumbrismo y novela sentimental* (1979) and of *La segunda generación modernista* (1979). Has published articles on 19th- and 20th-century Spanish American fiction, travel literature and autobiography in leading US journals of literary criticism. **Essays:** Jorge Isaacs; Cirilo Villaverde; *Cecilia Valdés* (Villaverde).

Schelling, Vivian (Adviser). Lecturer (Assistant Professor) in Third World Studies, University of East London. Author of *A presença do povo na cultura brasileira: um ensaio sobre Mário de Andrade e Paulo Freire* (1990); co-author (with William Rowe) of *Memory and Modernity: Popular Culture in Latin America* (1991). **Essay:** Mário de Andrade.

Scott, Nina M. Professor of Spanish, Amherst College, Massachusetts. Co-editor of *Coded Encounters: Writing, Gender and Ethnicity in Colonial Latin America* (1994). Other publications include the translation of an introduction to Gertrudis Gómez de Avellaneda's *Sab and Autobiography* (1993), and articles on Latina writers and on Sor Juana Inés de la Cruz. Member of the Executive Board of *Latin American Research Review*. **Essays:** Conventual Writing; *Respuesta a Sor Filotea* (Juana Inés de la Cruz).

Scott, Renée. Associate Professor of Spanish, University of North Florida. She has published articles on the work of Rosario Castellanos and Isabel Allende and a book: *Javier de Viana: un narrador del Novecientos* (1986). **Essays:** Delmira Agustini; "Íntima" and "Otra estirpe" (Agustini).

Sefamí, Jacobo. Associate Professor, Department of Spanish and Portuguese, University of California at Irvine. His publications in book form are *El destierro apacible y otros ensayos* (1987), *Contemporary Spanish American Poets: a Bibliography of Primary and Secondary Sources* (1992), and *El espejo trizado: la poesía de Gonzalo Rojas* (1992). Contributing editor, on Mexican poetry, to the *Handbook of Latin American Studies*. **Essay:** Poetry (Paz).

Serna, Juan Antonio. PhD candidate, Arizona State University. **Essay:** José Agustín.

Shaw, Deborah A. Lecturer (Assistant Professor), School of Languages, University of Portsmouth. Co-author of article on *Como agua para chocolate*; author of "Gender and Class

Relations in Elena Poniatowska's *De noche vienes* (*Bulletin of Hispanic Studies*, 1995) and of "The Mexican Writer as Critical Invention" (*Latin American Crosscurrents in Gender Theory*, 1996). **Essays**: Best-Sellers: Isabel Allende; Best-Sellers: Laura Esquivel; *Hasta no verte Jesús mío* (Poniatowska).

Shaw, Donald L. (Adviser). Brown-Forman Professor of Latin American Literature, University of Virginia. Has published on both Peninsular and Spanish American writers. In the former category, he is the author of the volume *The Nineteenth Century* (1972) in the series *A Literary History of Spain*, and in the latter he has books on Carpentier (1985) Borges (1976, 1992), and Skármeta (1994). He is also the author of *Nueva narrativa hispanoamericana* (1981). **Essays**: Jorge Luis Borges; "Nueva refutación del tiempo" (Borges); "El jardín se senderos que se bifurcan" (Borges); Rómulo Gallegos; Modernismo: Spanish America; The Post-Boom; Antonio Skármeta.

Shubow, Jenny. MA, London University, with dissertation on Roque Dalton. Presently completing her PhD on Eduardo Galeano, with particular reference to *Memoria del fuego*. **Essays**: Roque Dalton; Poems (Dalton).

Sibbald, K.M. Professor of Spanish, McGill University, Canada. Publications in book form include *El hombre y la obra* (1990); co-author (with Ilse Adriana Luraschi), *María Elena Walsh o "el desafío de la limitación* (1993); co-editor (with Howard Young), *T.S. Eliot and Hispanic Modernity, 1924–1993* (1994). Presently member of the advisory board of *Hispanic Journal*. Distinguished Woman Scholar in Residence, Queen's University, Ontario (1988). **Essays**: María Luisa Bombal; Norah Lange; María Elena Walsh.

Simpson, Amelia. Teacher in Department of Romance Languages and Literatures, University of Florida. Author of *Detective Fiction from Latin America* (1990) and *Xuxa: the Mega-Marketing of Gender, Race and Modernity* (1993). She has also edited and translated *New Tales of Mystery and Crime from Latin America* (1992). **Essay**: Detective Fiction.

Sims, Robert L. Professor of Foreign Languages, Virginia Commonwealth University. Author of many articles on Spanish American literature, and of two works on García Márquez: one on the evolution of myth (1984) and a more recent one on Márquez's early journalism (1991; English version, 1992). Review editor of *Revista de estudios colombianos*, *The Comparatist* and *New Novel Review*; contributing editor for *Chasqui*. **Essays**: Colombia; Abel Posse; David Viñas.

Slick, Sam L. Professor in Department of Foreign Languages and Literatures, University of Southern Mississippi. Author of *José Revueltas* (Twayne, 1983), and an editor of *Historical Dictionary of the Spanish Empire, 1492–1975* (1992). **Essays**: Literacy Campaigns: Cuba and Nicaragua; Mestizo.

Smart, Ian Isidore. Professor of Spanish, Howard University, Washington. Author of *Central American Writers of West Indian Origin: a New Hispanic Literature* (1984) and of *Nicolás Guillén, Popular Poet of the Caribbean* (1990). He is also a literary translator, the author of a work of fiction, *Sanni*

Mannitae (1994), managing editor and co-founder of *Afro-Hispanic Review* (1982–87), and vice-president and co-founder of the Afro-Hispanic Institute (1982 to the present). **Essays**: African-American Literature: Central and South America; African-Caribbean Literature; Nicolás Guillén.

Smith, Verity. Contributing editor of this volume, for which she has also translated articles. Honorary Research Fellow, Queen Mary and Westfield College (University of London). Books on Valle-Inclán and on Carpentier's *Los pasos perdidos*; Cubanist. Member of the editorial boards of *Antípodas* (Australia) and *Journal of Hispanic Research* (London). **Essays**: Canon; *El siglo de las luces* (Carpentier); Children's Literature; "Nocturno XXXII" (Darío); Identity; Dulce María Loynaz; Metafiction (with Dermot Curley); Paris.

Solotorevksy, Myrna. Professor of Latin American Studies, Hebrew University of Jerusalem. Her major studies in book form are *José Donoso: incursiones en su producción novelesca* (1983); *Literatura – paraliteratura: Puig, Borges, Donoso, Cortázar, Vargas Llosa* (1988) and *La relación mundo-escritura en textos de Reinaldo Arenas, Juan José Saer y Juan Carlos Martínez* (1993). Editor of *Reflejos*. **Essays**: *Arturo, la estrella más brillante* (Arenas); Para-Literature.

Sourieau, Marie-Agnès. Assistant Professor, Department of Modern Languages and Literatures, Fairfield University, Connecticut. **Essays**: Maryse Condé; René Depestre; Journals: *La Revue du Monde Noir*, *Tropiques*; Jacques Roumain; Simone Schwarz-Bart.

Spindler Li, William. Writer and poet. Author of articles on Latin American culture and politics published in both learned journals and newspapers. Poetry broadcast on BBC Latin America Service. **Essays**: Jorge Carrera Andrade; "Cada objeto es un mundo" (Carrera Andrade).

Standish, Peter. Professor and Chairman of Department of Spanish, University of North Carolina. Books on *La ciudad y los perros* (1983) and *Aura*; compiler (with Rob Isbister) of *A Concordance to the Works of Jorge Luis Borges* (1992) Contributing editor (with Terry Peavler) of *Structures of Power: Essays on Twentieth-Century Spanish American Fiction* (1996). General editor of two volumes on the culture of Spanish America (1996) in the Gale series on *Twentieth Century Culture*. **Essays**: Bildungsroman; The Boom; Julio Cortázar; Indigenism; Prizes; *La casa verde* (Vargas Llosa).

Stavans, Ilan. Associate Professor of Hispanic Studies, Amherst College, Massachusetts. Author and literary critic. Publications include *Imagining Columbus: the Literary Voyage* (1993), and *Growing up Latino: Memoirs and Stories* (1993). He has also edited *Tropical Synagogues: Short Stories by Jewish Latin American Writers* (1994) and is currently editing a volume of Latin American essays for Oxford University. **Essays**: Jewish Writing: Mexico, Central American and the Spanish-Speaking Caribbean; Fernando del Paso.

Torres Cabellero, Benjamín. Associate Professor of Spanish, Western Michigan University. Author of *Gabriel García*

Márquez o la alquimia del incesto (1987) and *Literatura e ideología* (1989). He also publishes in learned journals and in the cultural supplement of the Puerto Rican newspaper *El Nuevo Día*. **Essay:** Puerto Rico.

Trigo, Abril. Associate Professor, Department of Spanish and Portuguese, Ohio State University. Author of *Caudillo, estado, nación: literatura, historia e ideología en el Uruguay* (1990). **Essay:** Uruguay.

Van Delden, Maarten. Assistant Professor of Comparative Literature, New York University. Author of many articles on Carlos Fuentes; guest editor of special issue on Latin American intellectuals for *Annals of Scholarship*. **Essay:** Essays (Paz).

Vieira, Nelson H. Professor of Luso-Brazilian Literature, Brown University, Rhode Island. Most recent publications in book form are *Brasil e Portugal; a imagem recíproca* (1991), *Construindo a imagem do judeu* (1994) and *Jewish Voices in Brazilian Literature* (1995). American editor for *Brasil/Brazil* and associate editor for *Modern Language Studies*. **Essays:** Rubem Fonseca; Dalton Trevisan.

Volek, Emil. Professor of Spanish, Arizona State University. Publications in book form include *Cuatro claves para la modernidad* (1984), *Metaestructuralismo* (1986), *Antología del Formalismo ruso y el grupo de Bajtin* (1992), *Literatura hispanoamericana entre la modernidad y la postmodernidad* (1994). **Essays:** Guillermo Cabrera Infante; *El reino de este mundo* (Carpentier); *Aura* (Fuentes); Mexico: 20th Century; *El laberinto de la soledad* (Paz); Elena Poniatowska; Postmodern Writing; *Pedro Páramo* (Rulfo); Testimonial Writing.

Waag, C. Michael. Associate Professor of Latin American Literature, Murray State University, Kentucky. Author of many articles on Ecuadorian literature which have appeared in *Perspectives on Contemporary Literature*, *Revista Ibero-americana* and other scholarly journals. **Essay:** Demetrio Aguilera Malta.

Walker, John. Professor and Chairman of Department of Spanish, Queen's University, Ontario. Author of books on Eduardo Barrios (1983), Manuel Gálvez, R.B. Cunninghame Graham (1978, 1982, 1986) and on José Eustasio Rivera's *La vorágine* (1988). He is also the author of numerous articles on travel writing in the River Plate region. **Essays:** Eduardo Barrios; Ariel Dorfman; Manuel Gálvez; Baldomero Lillo; Eduardo Mallea.

Weldt-Basson, Helene Carol. Assistant Professor of Spanish, Department of Modern Languages, Fordham University, New York. Author of articles on 20th-century Spanish American literature and of *Augusto Roa Bastos's "I the Supreme": a Dialogic Perspective* (1993). **Essays:** *La muerte de Artemio Cruz* (Fuentes); *El general en su laberinto* (García Márquez).

White, Steven F. Associate Professor of Modern Languages and Literatures, St Lawrence University, New York. Poet, translator and critic. Author of, among other volumes, *From the Country of Thunder* (poetry, 1990); *Poets of Nicaragua: 1918–1979* (poetry in translation, 1982); *Modern Nicaraguan Poetry: Dialogues with France and the United States* (criticism, 1993). Awarded Academy of American Poets Prize (1975 and 1977). **Essays:** Ernesto Cardenal; Vicente Huidobro; Murilo Mendes; Nicanor Parra.

Williamson, Edwin (Adviser). Professor of Hispanic Studies, University of Edinburgh. Author of *The Penguin History of Latin America* (1992), and of studies of García Márquez and Alejo Carpentier. He is also an established authority on Cervantes, whose publications in this field include *The Halfway-House of Fiction: "Don Quixote" and Arthurian Romance* (1984) and, as editor, *Cervantes and the Modernists: the Question of Influence* (1994). He is currently completing a major biography of Jorge Luis Borges.

Wilson, Jason (Adviser). Reader (Associate Professor) in Department of Spanish, University College, London. His research interests are wide-ranging and include poetry (particularly that of the Spanish American avant-garde) and travel writing. He is also interested in literary translation and is the author of *An A-Z of Modern Latin American Literature in English Translation* (1989). Other publications in book form are on Octavio Paz (1979 and 1986) and the *Traveller's Literary Companion to South and Central America* (1993). **Essays:** Oliverio Girondo; Alberto Girri; Surrealism; Travel Literature.

Wood, David. Lecturer (Assistant Professor), Department of Hispanic Studies, Sheffield University. Publications include an "Annotated Bibliography of Alfredo Bryce Echenique" (1994) and "Style indirect libre and Alienation in *Un mundo para Julius*" (1994). **Essays:** Alfredo Bryce Echenique; *Un mundo para Julius* (Bryce Echenique); Eduardo Galeano.

Yannuzzi, Andrea. Formerly clinical psychologist and editor of *Revista argentina de psicología* (1984–86). Presently Teaching Fellow, Department of Hispanic Languages and Literatures, Pittsburgh University. **Essay:** Clarice Lispector.

Zilberman, Regina. Professor of Theory of Literature and Brazilian Literature, at the Catholic University of Rio Grande do Sul. She has published several books on aspects of children's literature in Brazil, together with a volume on *gaúcho* literature, another on reception theory, and *A literatura no Rio Grande do Sul* (1980). Editor of *Brasil/Brazil*, Brown University, where she was a Visiting Scholar in 1986–87. **Essay:** Brazil: 19th Century.

Translators

Beswick, Jaine. MA in Language and Linguistics, with a specialization in Spanish and Portuguese phonetics, University of Manchester. Currently undertaking research for a PhD on aspects of Galician linguistics at the University of Bristol. Associate of the Institute of Linguistics.

Craig, Ian. Graduate in Spanish and English literature, Westfield College, University of London. MA in literary translation, University of Essex. Now PhD student at Queen Mary and Westfield College, researching on censorship in relation to children's fiction in translation during the early years of the Franco regime.

Glen, Jo. Graduate in Spanish literature, Westfield College, University of London. Has taught English to foreign students and Spanish language and literature at a London secondary school. Presently freelances as a translator.

González Fernández, Luis. Graduate in Spanish and English literature, Westfield College, University of London. Now writing his doctoral thesis on "Spectacle in Spanish and English Devil-Plays (1570–1650)." He also publishes short stories and *crónicas* of London life in *El mono de la tinta* (Burgos).

James, Patricia. Graduate in Spanish language and literature, Westfield College, University of London.

Smith, Verity. See under Advisers and Contributors.

Tully, Carol. PhD from London University on aspects of German and Spanish Romanticism. Translator of Thomas Oberender's play *Three Days in May*, performed at the Cheltenham Festival (1995), and of Taniana Tsouvelis's *In the Lemon Grove*, performed at the Royal Court Theatre, London (1996).

Varea, Isabel. Graduate in Spanish with Portuguese, King's College, London. Translator of audio material for Channel Four and BBC documentaries. Her translations in book form include volumes on the visual arts, gastronomy, film, music and complementary medicine.

Wright, Ann. Graduate in Iberian and Latin American Studies, University College, London. Specializes in translation of film subtitles. Also translator of many works of fiction and non-fiction. Among the most important are *The Fragrance of Guava, I Rigoberta Menchú, Che Guevara: the motorbike diaries, a journey around South America*. She has also translated *Bolero* by Ángeles Mastretta and Carlos Manuel Martínez's novel *El infierno*.